University Casebook Series

February, 1990

ACCOUNTING AND THE LAW, Fourth Edition (1978), with Problems Pamphlet (Successor to Dohr, Phillips, Thompson & Warren)

George C. Thompson, Professor, Columbia University Graduate School of Business.
Robert Whitman, Professor of Law, University of Connecticut.
Ellis L. Phillips, Jr., Member of the New York Bar.
William C. Warren, Professor of Law Emeritus, Columbia University.

ACCOUNTING FOR LAWYERS, MATERIALS ON (1980)

David R. Herwitz, Professor of Law, Harvard University.

ADMINISTRATIVE LAW, Eighth Edition (1987), with 1989 Case Supplement and 1983 Problems Supplement (Supplement edited in association with Paul R. Verkuil, Dean and Professor of Law, Tulane University)

Walter Gellhorn, University Professor Emeritus, Columbia University.
Clark Byse, Professor of Law, Harvard University.
Peter L. Strauss, Professor of Law, Columbia University.
Todd D. Rakoff, Professor of Law, Harvard University.
Roy A. Schotland, Professor of Law, Georgetown University.

ADMIRALTY, Third Edition (1987), with Statute and Rule Supplement

Jo Desha Lucas, Professor of Law, University of Chicago.

ADVOCACY, see also Lawyering Process

AGENCY, see also Enterprise Organization

AGENCY—PARTNERSHIPS, Fourth Edition (1987)

Abridgement from Conard, Knauss & Siegel's Enterprise Organization, Fourth Edition.

AGENCY AND PARTNERSHIPS (1987)

Melvin A. Eisenberg, Professor of Law, University of California, Berkeley.

ANTITRUST: FREE ENTERPRISE AND ECONOMIC ORGANIZATION, Sixth Edition (1983), with 1983 Problems in Antitrust Supplement and 1989 Case Supplement

Louis B. Schwartz, Professor of Law, University of Pennsylvania.
John J. Flynn, Professor of Law, University of Utah.
Harry First, Professor of Law, New York University.

BANKRUPTCY, Second Edition (1989)

Robert L. Jordan, Professor of Law, University of California, Los Angeles.
William D. Warren, Professor of Law, University of California, Los Angeles.

BANKRUPTCY AND DEBTOR–CREDITOR LAW, Second Edition (1988)

Theodore Eisenberg, Professor of Law, Cornell University.

BUSINESS CRIME (1990)

Harry First, Professor of Law, New York University.

BUSINESS ORGANIZATION, see also Enterprise Organization

BUSINESS PLANNING, Temporary Second Edition (1984)

David R. Herwitz, Professor of Law, Harvard University.

BUSINESS TORTS (1972)

Milton Handler, Professor of Law Emeritus, Columbia University.

CHILDREN IN THE LEGAL SYSTEM (1983) with 1988 Supplement

Walter Wadlington, Professor of Law, University of Virginia.
Charles H. Whitebread, Professor of Law, University of Southern California.
Samuel Davis, Professor of Law, University of Georgia.

CIVIL PROCEDURE, see Procedure

CIVIL RIGHTS ACTIONS (1988), with 1989 Supplement

Peter W. Low, Professor of Law, University of Virginia.
John C. Jeffries, Jr., Professor of Law, University of Virginia.

CLINIC, see also Lawyering Process

COMMERCIAL AND DEBTOR–CREDITOR LAW: SELECTED STATUTES, 1989 EDITION

COMMERCIAL LAW, Second Edition (1987)

Robert L. Jordan, Professor of Law, University of California, Los Angeles.
William D. Warren, Professor of Law, University of California, Los Angeles.

COMMERCIAL LAW, Fourth Edition (1985)

E. Allan Farnsworth, Professor of Law, Columbia University.
John Honnold, Professor of Law, University of Pennsylvania.

COMMERCIAL PAPER, Third Edition (1984)

E. Allan Farnsworth, Professor of Law, Columbia University.

COMMERCIAL PAPER, Second Edition (1987) (Reprinted from COMMERCIAL LAW, Second Edition (1987))

Robert L. Jordan, Professor of Law, University of California, Los Angeles.
William D. Warren, Professor of Law, University of California, Los Angeles.

COMMERCIAL PAPER AND BANK DEPOSITS AND COLLECTIONS (1967), with Statutory Supplement

William D. Hawkland, Professor of Law, University of Illinois.

COMMERCIAL TRANSACTIONS—Principles and Policies (1982)

Alan Schwartz, Professor of Law, University of Southern California.
Robert E. Scott, Professor of Law, University of Virginia.

COMPARATIVE LAW, Fifth Edition (1988)

Rudolf B. Schlesinger, Professor of Law, Hastings College of the Law.
Hans W. Baade, Professor of Law, University of Texas.
Mirjan P. Damaska, Professor of Law, Yale Law School.
Peter E. Herzog, Professor of Law, Syracuse University.

COMPETITIVE PROCESS, LEGAL REGULATION OF THE, Fourth Edition (1990), with 1989 Selected Statutes Supplement

Edmund W. Kitch, Professor of Law, University of Virginia.
Harvey S. Perlman, Dean of the Law School, University of Nebraska.

CONFLICT OF LAWS, Eighth Edition (1984), with 1989 Case Supplement

Willis L. M. Reese, Professor of Law, Columbia University.
Maurice Rosenberg, Professor of Law, Columbia University.

CONSTITUTIONAL LAW, Eighth Edition (1989), with 1989 Case Supplement

Edward L. Barrett, Jr., Professor of Law, University of California, Davis.
William Cohen, Professor of Law, Stanford University.
Jonathan D. Varat, Professor of Law, University of California, Los Angeles.

CONSTITUTIONAL LAW, CIVIL LIBERTY AND INDIVIDUAL RIGHTS, Second Edition (1982), with 1989 Supplement

William Cohen, Professor of Law, Stanford University.
John Kaplan, Professor of Law, Stanford University.

CONSTITUTIONAL LAW, Eleventh Edition (1985), with 1989 Supplement (Supplement edited in association with Frederick F. Schauer, Professor of Law, University of Michigan)

Gerald Gunther, Professor of Law, Stanford University.

CONSTITUTIONAL LAW, INDIVIDUAL RIGHTS IN, Fourth Edition (1986), (Reprinted from CONSTITUTIONAL LAW, Eleventh Edition), with 1989 Supplement (Supplement edited in association with Frederick F. Schauer, Professor of Law, University of Michigan)

Gerald Gunther, Professor of Law, Stanford University.

CONSUMER TRANSACTIONS (1983), with Selected Statutes and Regulations Supplement and 1987 Case Supplement

Michael M. Greenfield, Professor of Law, Washington University.

CONTRACT LAW AND ITS APPLICATION, Fourth Edition (1988)

Arthur Rosett, Professor of Law, University of California, Los Angeles.

CONTRACT LAW, STUDIES IN, Third Edition (1984)

Edward J. Murphy, Professor of Law, University of Notre Dame.
Richard E. Speidel, Professor of Law, Northwestern University.

CONTRACTS, Fifth Edition (1987)

John P. Dawson, late Professor of Law, Harvard University.
William Burnett Harvey, Professor of Law and Political Science, Boston University.
Stanley D. Henderson, Professor of Law, University of Virginia.

CONTRACTS, Fourth Edition (1988)

E. Allan Farnsworth, Professor of Law, Columbia University.
William F. Young, Professor of Law, Columbia University.

CONTRACTS, Selections on (statutory materials) (1988)

CONTRACTS, Second Edition (1978), with Statutory and Administrative Law Supplement (1978)

Ian R. Macneil, Professor of Law, Cornell University.

COPYRIGHT, PATENTS AND TRADEMARKS, see also Competitive Process; see also Selected Statutes and International Agreements

COPYRIGHT, PATENT, TRADEMARK AND RELATED STATE DOCTRINES, Second Edition (1981), with 1988 Case Supplement, 1989 Selected Statutes Supplement and 1981 Problem Supplement

Paul Goldstein, Professor of Law, Stanford University.

COPYRIGHT, Unfair Competition, and Other Topics Bearing on the Protection of Literary, Musical, and Artistic Works, Fifth Edition (1990), with 1990 Statutory Supplement

Ralph S. Brown, Jr., Professor of Law, Yale University.
Robert C. Denicola, Professor of Law, University of Nebraska.

CORPORATE ACQUISITIONS, The Law and Finance of (1986), with 1989 Supplement

Ronald J. Gilson, Professor of Law, Stanford University.

CORPORATE FINANCE, Third Edition (1987)

Victor Brudney, Professor of Law, Harvard University.
Marvin A. Chirelstein, Professor of Law, Columbia University.

CORPORATION LAW, BASIC, Third Edition (1989), with Documentary Supplement

Detlev F. Vagts, Professor of Law, Harvard University.

CORPORATIONS, see also Enterprise Organization

CORPORATIONS, Sixth Edition—Concise (1988), with Statutory Supplement (1989)

William L. Cary, late Professor of Law, Columbia University.
Melvin Aron Eisenberg, Professor of Law, University of California, Berkeley.

CORPORATIONS, Sixth Edition—Unabridged (1988), with Statutory Supplement (1989)

William L. Cary, late Professor of Law, Columbia University.
Melvin Aron Eisenberg, Professor of Law, University of California, Berkeley.

CORPORATIONS AND BUSINESS ASSOCIATIONS—STATUTES, RULES, AND FORMS (1989)

CORPORATIONS COURSE GAME PLAN (1975)

David R. Herwitz, Professor of Law, Harvard University.

CORRECTIONS, SEE SENTENCING

CREDITORS' RIGHTS, see also Debtor-Creditor Law

CRIMINAL JUSTICE ADMINISTRATION, Third Edition (1986), with 1989 Case Supplement

Frank W. Miller, Professor of Law, Washington University.
Robert O. Dawson, Professor of Law, University of Texas.
George E. Dix, Professor of Law, University of Texas.
Raymond I. Parnas, Professor of Law, University of California, Davis.

CRIMINAL LAW, Fourth Edition (1987)

Fred E. Inbau, Professor of Law Emeritus, Northwestern University.
Andre A. Moenssens, Professor of Law, University of Richmond.
James R. Thompson, Professor of Law Emeritus, Northwestern University.

CRIMINAL LAW AND APPROACHES TO THE STUDY OF LAW (1986)

John M. Brumbaugh, Professor of Law, University of Maryland.

CRIMINAL LAW, Second Edition (1986)

Peter W. Low, Professor of Law, University of Virginia.
John C. Jeffries, Jr., Professor of Law, University of Virginia.
Richard C. Bonnie, Professor of Law, University of Virginia.

CRIMINAL LAW, Fourth Edition (1986)

Lloyd L. Weinreb, Professor of Law, Harvard University.

CRIMINAL LAW AND PROCEDURE, Seventh Edition (1989)

Ronald N. Boyce, Professor of Law, University of Utah.
Rollin M. Perkins, Professor of Law Emeritus, University of California, Hastings College of the Law.

CRIMINAL PROCEDURE, Third Edition (1987), with 1989 Supplement

James B. Haddad, Professor of Law, Northwestern University.
James B. Zagel, Chief, Criminal Justice Division, Office of Attorney General of Illinois.
Gary L. Starkman, Assistant U. S. Attorney, Northern District of Illinois.
William J. Bauer, Chief Judge of the U.S. Court of Appeals, Seventh Circuit.

CRIMINAL PROCESS, Fourth Edition (1987), with 1989 Supplement

Lloyd L. Weinreb, Professor of Law, Harvard University.

DAMAGES, Second Edition (1952)

Charles T. McCormick, late Professor of Law, University of Texas.
William F. Fritz, late Professor of Law, University of Texas.

DECEDENTS' ESTATES AND TRUSTS, Seventh Edition (1988)

John Ritchie, late Professor of Law, University of Virginia.
Neill H. Alford, Jr., Professor of Law, University of Virginia.
Richard W. Effland, late Professor of Law, Arizona State University.

DISPUTE RESOLUTION, Processes of (1989)

John S. Murray, President and Executive Director of The Conflict Clinic, Inc., George Mason University.
Alan Scott Rau, Professor of Law, University of Texas.
Edward F. Sherman, Professor of Law, University of Texas.

DOMESTIC RELATIONS, see also Family Law

DOMESTIC RELATIONS, Successor Edition (1984) with 1989 Supplement

Walter Wadlington, Professor of Law, University of Virginia.

EMPLOYMENT DISCRIMINATION, Second Edition (1987), with 1989 Supplement

Joel W. Friedman, Professor of Law, Tulane University.
George M. Strickler, Professor of Law, Tulane University.

EMPLOYMENT LAW (1987), with 1987 Statutory Supplement and 1989 Case Supplement

Mark A. Rothstein, Professor of Law, University of Houston.
Andria S. Knapp, Adjunct Professor of Law, University of California, Hastings College of Law.
Lance Liebman, Professor of Law, Harvard University.

ENERGY LAW (1983) with 1986 Case Supplement

Donald N. Zillman, Professor of Law, University of Utah.
Laurence Lattman, Dean of Mines and Engineering, University of Utah.

ENTERPRISE ORGANIZATION, Fourth Edition (1987), with 1987 Corporation and Partnership Statutes, Rules and Forms Supplement

Alfred F. Conard, Professor of Law, University of Michigan.
Robert L. Knauss, Dean of the Law School, University of Houston.
Stanley Siegel, Professor of Law, University of California, Los Angeles.

ENVIRONMENTAL POLICY LAW 1985 Edition, with 1985 Problems Supplement (Supplement in association with Ronald H. Rosenberg, Professor of Law, College of William and Mary)

Thomas J. Schoenbaum, Professor of Law, University of Georgia.

EQUITY, see also Remedies

EQUITY, RESTITUTION AND DAMAGES, Second Edition (1974)

Robert Childres, late Professor of Law, Northwestern University.
William F. Johnson, Jr., Professor of Law, New York University.

ESTATE PLANNING, Second Edition (1982), with 1985 Case, Text and Documentary Supplement

David Westfall, Professor of Law, Harvard University.

ETHICS, see Legal Profession, Professional Responsibility, and Social Responsibilities

ETHICS AND PROFESSIONAL RESPONSIBILITY (1981) (Reprinted from THE LAWYERING PROCESS)

Gary Bellow, Professor of Law, Harvard University.
Bea Moulton, Legal Services Corporation.

EVIDENCE, Sixth Edition (1988 Reprint)

John Kaplan, Professor of Law, Stanford University.
Jon R. Waltz, Professor of Law, Northwestern University.

EVIDENCE, Eighth Edition (1988), with Rules, Statute and Case Supplement (1989)

Jack B. Weinstein, Chief Judge, United States District Court.
John H. Mansfield, Professor of Law, Harvard University.
Norman Abrams, Professor of Law, University of California, Los Angeles.
Margaret Berger, Professor of Law, Brooklyn Law School.

FAMILY LAW, see also Domestic Relations

FAMILY LAW Second Edition (1985), with 1988 Supplement

Judith C. Areen, Professor of Law, Georgetown University.

FAMILY LAW AND CHILDREN IN THE LEGAL SYSTEM, STATUTORY MATERIALS (1981)

Walter Wadlington, Professor of Law, University of Virginia.

FEDERAL COURTS, Eighth Edition (1988), with 1989 Supplement

Charles T. McCormick, late Professor of Law, University of Texas.
James H. Chadbourn, late Professor of Law, Harvard University.
Charles Alan Wright, Professor of Law, University of Texas, Austin.

FEDERAL COURTS AND THE FEDERAL SYSTEM, Hart and Wechsler's Third Edition (1988), with 1989 Case Supplement, and the Judicial Code and Rules of Procedure in the Federal Courts (1989)

Paul M. Bator, Professor of Law, University of Chicago.
Daniel J. Meltzer, Professor of Law, Harvard University.
Paul J. Mishkin, Professor of Law, University of California, Berkeley.
David L. Shapiro, Professor of Law, Harvard University.

FEDERAL COURTS AND THE LAW OF FEDERAL-STATE RELATIONS, Second Edition (1989), with 1989 Supplement

Peter W. Low, Professor of Law, University of Virginia.
John C. Jeffries, Jr., Professor of Law, University of Virginia.

FEDERAL PUBLIC LAND AND RESOURCES LAW, Second Edition (1987), with 1990 Case Supplement and 1984 Statutory Supplement

George C. Coggins, Professor of Law, University of Kansas.
Charles F. Wilkinson, Professor of Law, University of Oregon.

FEDERAL RULES OF CIVIL PROCEDURE and Selected Other Procedural Provisions, 1989 Edition

FEDERAL TAXATION, see Taxation

FOOD AND DRUG LAW (1980), with Statutory Supplement

Richard A. Merrill, Dean of the School of Law, University of Virginia.
Peter Barton Hutt, Esq.

FUTURE INTERESTS (1958)

Philip Mechem, late Professor of Law Emeritus, University of Pennsylvania.

FUTURE INTERESTS (1970)

Howard R. Williams, Professor of Law, Stanford University.

FUTURE INTERESTS AND ESTATE PLANNING (1961), with 1962 Supplement

W. Barton Leach, late Professor of Law, Harvard University.
James K. Logan, formerly Dean of the Law School, University of Kansas.

GOVERNMENT CONTRACTS, FEDERAL, Successor Edition (1985), with 1989 Supplement

John W. Whelan, Professor of Law, Hastings College of the Law.

GOVERNMENT REGULATION: FREE ENTERPRISE AND ECONOMIC ORGANIZATION, Sixth Edition (1985)

Louis B. Schwartz, Professor of Law, Hastings College of the Law.
John J. Flynn, Professor of Law, University of Utah.
Harry First, Professor of Law, New York University.

HEALTH CARE LAW AND POLICY (1988)

Clark C. Havighurst, Professor of Law, Duke University.

HINCKLEY, JOHN W., JR., TRIAL OF: A Case Study of the Insanity Defense (1986)

Peter W. Low, Professor of Law, University of Virginia.
John C. Jeffries, Jr., Professor of Law, University of Virginia.
Richard C. Bonnie, Professor of Law, University of Virginia.

INJUNCTIONS, Second Edition (1984)

Owen M. Fiss, Professor of Law, Yale University.
Doug Rendleman, Professor of Law, College of William and Mary.

INSTITUTIONAL INVESTORS, (1978)

David L. Ratner, Professor of Law, Cornell University.

INSURANCE, Second Edition (1985)

William F. Young, Professor of Law, Columbia University.
Eric M. Holmes, Professor of Law, University of Georgia.

INTERNATIONAL LAW, see also Transnational Legal Problems, Transnational Business Problems, and United Nations Law

INTERNATIONAL LAW IN CONTEMPORARY PERSPECTIVE (1981), with Essay Supplement

Myres S. McDougal, Professor of Law, Yale University.
W. Michael Reisman, Professor of Law, Yale University.

INTERNATIONAL LEGAL SYSTEM, Third Edition (1988), with Documentary Supplement

Joseph Modeste Sweeney, Professor of Law, University of California, Hastings.
Covey T. Oliver, Professor of Law, University of Pennsylvania.
Noyes E. Leech, Professor of Law Emeritus, University of Pennsylvania.

INTRODUCTION TO LAW, see also Legal Method, On Law in Courts, and Dynamics of American Law

INTRODUCTION TO THE STUDY OF LAW (1970)

E. Wayne Thode, late Professor of Law, University of Utah.
Leon Lebowitz, Professor of Law, University of Texas.
Lester J. Mazor, Professor of Law, University of Utah.

JUDICIAL CODE and Rules of Procedure in the Federal Courts, Students' Edition, 1989 Revision

Daniel J. Meltzer, Professor of Law, Harvard University.
David L. Shapiro, Professor of Law, Harvard University.

JURISPRUDENCE (Temporary Edition Hardbound) (1949)

Lon L. Fuller, late Professor of Law, Harvard University.

JUVENILE, see also Children

JUVENILE JUSTICE PROCESS, Third Edition (1985)

Frank W. Miller, Professor of Law, Washington University.
Robert O. Dawson, Professor of Law, University of Texas.
George E. Dix, Professor of Law, University of Texas.
Raymond I. Parnas, Professor of Law, University of California, Davis.

LABOR LAW, Tenth Edition (1986), with 1989 Case Supplement and 1986 Statutory Supplement

Archibald Cox, Professor of Law, Harvard University.
Derek C. Bok, President, Harvard University.
Robert A. Gorman, Professor of Law, University of Pennsylvania.

LABOR LAW, Second Edition (1982), with Statutory Supplement

Clyde W. Summers, Professor of Law, University of Pennsylvania.
Harry H. Wellington, Dean of the Law School, Yale University.
Alan Hyde, Professor of Law, Rutgers University.

LAND FINANCING, Third Edition (1985)

The late Norman Penney, Professor of Law, Cornell University.
Richard F. Broude, Member of the California Bar.
Roger Cunningham, Professor of Law, University of Michigan.

LAW AND MEDICINE (1980)

Walter Wadlington, Professor of Law and Professor of Legal Medicine, University of Virginia.
Jon R. Waltz, Professor of Law, Northwestern University.
Roger B. Dworkin, Professor of Law, Indiana University, and Professor of Biomedical History, University of Washington.

LAW, LANGUAGE AND ETHICS (1972)

William R. Bishin, Professor of Law, University of Southern California.
Christopher D. Stone, Professor of Law, University of Southern California.

LAW, SCIENCE AND MEDICINE (1984), with 1989 Supplement

Judith C. Areen, Professor of Law, Georgetown University.
Patricia A. King, Professor of Law, Georgetown University.
Steven P. Goldberg, Professor of Law, Georgetown University.
Alexander M. Capron, Professor of Law, University of Southern California.

LAWYERING PROCESS (1978), with Civil Problem Supplement and Criminal Problem Supplement

Gary Bellow, Professor of Law, Harvard University.
Bea Moulton, Professor of Law, Arizona State University.

LEGAL METHOD (1980)

Harry W. Jones, Professor of Law Emeritus, Columbia University.
John M. Kernochan, Professor of Law, Columbia University.
Arthur W. Murphy, Professor of Law, Columbia University.

LEGAL METHODS (1969)

Robert N. Covington, Professor of Law, Vanderbilt University.
E. Blythe Stason, late Professor of Law, Vanderbilt University.
John W. Wade, Professor of Law, Vanderbilt University.
Elliott E. Cheatham, late Professor of Law, Vanderbilt University.
Theodore A. Smedley, Professor of Law, Vanderbilt University.

LEGAL PROFESSION, THE, Responsibility and Regulation, Second Edition (1988)

Geoffrey C. Hazard, Jr., Professor of Law, Yale University.
Deborah L. Rhode, Professor of Law, Stanford University.

LEGISLATION, Fourth Edition (1982) (by Fordham)

Horace E. Read, late Vice President, Dalhousie University.
John W. MacDonald, Professor of Law Emeritus, Cornell Law School.
Jefferson B. Fordham, Professor of Law, University of Utah.
William J. Pierce, Professor of Law, University of Michigan.

LEGISLATIVE AND ADMINISTRATIVE PROCESSES, Second Edition (1981)

Hans A. Linde, Judge, Supreme Court of Oregon.
George Bunn, Professor of Law, University of Wisconsin.
Fredericka Paff, Professor of Law, University of Wisconsin.
W. Lawrence Church, Professor of Law, University of Wisconsin.

LOCAL GOVERNMENT LAW, Second Revised Edition (1986)

Jefferson B. Fordham, Professor of Law, University of Utah.

MASS MEDIA LAW, Third Edition (1987)

Marc A. Franklin, Professor of Law, Stanford University.

MUNICIPAL CORPORATIONS, see Local Government Law

NEGOTIABLE INSTRUMENTS, see Commercial Paper

NEGOTIATION (1981) (Reprinted from THE LAWYERING PROCESS)

Gary Bellow, Professor of Law, Harvard Law School.
Bea Moulton, Legal Services Corporation.

NEW YORK PRACTICE, Fourth Edition (1978)

Herbert Peterfreund, Professor of Law, New York University.
Joseph M. McLaughlin, Dean of the Law School, Fordham University.

OIL AND GAS, Fifth Edition (1987)

Howard R. Williams, Professor of Law, Stanford University.
Richard C. Maxwell, Professor of Law, University of California, Los Angeles.
Charles J. Meyers, late Dean of the Law School, Stanford University.
Stephen F. Williams, Judge of the United States Court of Appeals.

ON LAW IN COURTS (1965)

Paul J. Mishkin, Professor of Law, University of California, Berkeley.
Clarence Morris, Professor of Law Emeritus, University of Pennsylvania.

PLEADING AND PROCEDURE, see Procedure, Civil

POLICE FUNCTION, Fourth Edition (1986), with 1989 Case Supplement

Reprint of Chapters 1–10 of Miller, Dawson, Dix and Parnas's CRIMINAL JUSTICE ADMINISTRATION, Third Edition.

PREPARING AND PRESENTING THE CASE (1981) (Reprinted from THE LAWYERING PROCESS)

Gary Bellow, Professor of Law, Harvard Law School.
Bea Moulton, Legal Services Corporation.

PROCEDURE (1988), with Procedure Supplement (1989)

Robert M. Cover, late Professor of Law, Yale Law School.
Owen M. Fiss, Professor of Law, Yale Law School.
Judith Resnik, Professor of Law, University of Southern California Law Center.

PROCEDURE—CIVIL PROCEDURE, Second Edition (1974), with 1979 Supplement

The late James H. Chadbourn, Professor of Law, Harvard University.
A. Leo Levin, Professor of Law, University of Pennsylvania.
Philip Shuchman, Professor of Law, Cornell University.

PROCEDURE—CIVIL PROCEDURE, Fifth Edition (1984), with 1989 Supplement

Richard H. Field, late Professor of Law, Harvard University.
Benjamin Kaplan, Professor of Law Emeritus, Harvard University.
Kevin M. Clermont, Professor of Law, Cornell University.

PROCEDURE—CIVIL PROCEDURE, Fourth Edition (1985), with 1989 Supplement

Maurice Rosenberg, Professor of Law, Columbia University.
Hans Smit, Professor of Law, Columbia University.
Harold L. Korn, Professor of Law, Columbia University.

PROCEDURE—PLEADING AND PROCEDURE: State and Federal, Sixth Edition (1989)

David W. Louisell, late Professor of Law, University of California, Berkeley.
Geoffrey C. Hazard, Jr., Professor of Law, Yale University.
Colin C. Tait, Professor of Law, University of Connecticut.

PROCEDURE—FEDERAL RULES OF CIVIL PROCEDURE, 1989 Edition

PRODUCTS LIABILITY (1980)

Marshall S. Shapo, Professor of Law, Northwestern University.

PRODUCTS LIABILITY AND SAFETY, Second Edition, (1989), with 1989 Statutory Supplement

W. Page Keeton, Professor of Law, University of Texas.
David G. Owen, Professor of Law, University of South Carolina.
John E. Montgomery, Professor of Law, University of South Carolina.
Michael D. Green, Professor of Law, University of Iowa

PROFESSIONAL RESPONSIBILITY, Fourth Edition (1987), with 1989 Selected National Standards Supplement

Thomas D. Morgan, Dean of the Law School, Emory University.
Ronald D. Rotunda, Professor of Law, University of Illinois.

PROPERTY, Fifth Edition (1984)

John E. Cribbet, Professor of Law, University of Illinois.
Corwin W. Johnson, Professor of Law, University of Texas.

PROPERTY—PERSONAL (1953)

S. Kenneth Skolfield, late Professor of Law Emeritus, Boston University.

PROPERTY—PERSONAL, Third Edition (1954)

Everett Fraser, late Dean of the Law School Emeritus, University of Minnesota.
Third Edition by Charles W. Taintor, late Professor of Law, University of Pittsburgh.

PROPERTY—INTRODUCTION, TO REAL PROPERTY, Third Edition (1954)

Everett Fraser, late Dean of the Law School Emeritus, University of Minnesota.

PROPERTY—FUNDAMENTALS OF MODERN REAL PROPERTY, Second Edition (1982), with 1985 Supplement

Edward H. Rabin, Professor of Law, University of California, Davis.

PROPERTY, REAL (1984), with 1988 Supplement

Paul Goldstein, Professor of Law, Stanford University.

PROSECUTION AND ADJUDICATION, Third Edition (1986), with 1989 Case Supplement

Reprint of Chapters 11–26 of Miller, Dawson, Dix and Parnas's CRIMINAL JUSTICE ADMINISTRATION, Third Edition.

PSYCHIATRY AND LAW, see Mental Health, see also Hinckley, Trial of

PUBLIC REGULATION OF DANGEROUS PRODUCTS (paperback) (1980)

Marshall S. Shapo, Professor of Law, Northwestern University.

PUBLIC UTILITY LAW, see Free Enterprise, also Regulated Industries

REAL ESTATE PLANNING, Third Edition (1989), with 1989 Problem and Statutory Supplement

Norton L. Steuben, Professor of Law, University of Colorado.

REAL ESTATE TRANSACTIONS, Revised Second Edition (1988), with Statute, Form and Problem Supplement (1988)

Paul Goldstein, Professor of Law, Stanford University.

RECEIVERSHIP AND CORPORATE REORGANIZATION, see Creditors' Rights

REGULATED INDUSTRIES, Second Edition, (1976)

William K. Jones, Professor of Law, Columbia University.

REMEDIES, Second Edition (1987)

Edward D. Re, Chief Judge, U. S. Court of International Trade.

REMEDIES, (1989)

Elaine W. Shoben, Professor of Law, University of Illinois.
Wm. Murray Tabb, Professor of Law, Baylor University.

SALES, Second Edition (1986)

Marion W. Benfield, Jr., Professor of Law, University of Illinois.
William D. Hawkland, Chancellor, Louisiana State Law Center.

SALES AND SALES FINANCING, Fifth Edition (1984)

John Honnold, Professor of Law, University of Pennsylvania.

SALES LAW AND THE CONTRACTING PROCESS (1982)

Reprint of Chapters 1–10 of Schwartz and Scott's Commercial Transactions.

SECURED TRANSACTIONS IN PERSONAL PROPERTY, Second Edition (1987) (Reprinted from COMMERCIAL LAW, Second Edition (1987))

Robert L. Jordan, Professor of Law, University of California, Los Angeles.
William D. Warren, Professor of Law, University of California, Los Angeles.

SECURITIES REGULATION, Sixth Edition (1987), with 1989 Selected Statutes, Rules and Forms Supplement and 1989 Cases and Releases Supplement

Richard W. Jennings, Professor of Law, University of California, Berkeley.
Harold Marsh, Jr., Member of California Bar.

SECURITIES REGULATION, Second Edition (1988), with Statute, Rule and Form Supplement (1988)

Larry D. Soderquist, Professor of Law, Vanderbilt University.

SECURITY INTERESTS IN PERSONAL PROPERTY, Second Edition (1987)

Douglas G. Baird, Professor of Law, University of Chicago.
Thomas H. Jackson, Professor of Law, Harvard University.

SECURITY INTERESTS IN PERSONAL PROPERTY (1985) (Reprinted from Sales and Sales Financing, Fifth Edition)

John Honnold, Professor of Law, University of Pennsylvania.

SOCIAL RESPONSIBILITIES OF LAWYERS, Case Studies (1988)

Philip B. Heymann, Professor of Law, Harvard University.
Lance Liebman, Professor of Law, Harvard University.

SOCIAL SCIENCE IN LAW, Second Edition (1990)

John Monahan, Professor of Law, University of Virginia.
Laurens Walker, Professor of Law, University of Virginia.

TAXATION, FEDERAL INCOME (1989)

Stephen B. Cohen, Professor of Law, Georgetown University

TAXATION, FEDERAL INCOME, Second Edition (1988), with 1989 Supplement

Michael J. Graetz, Professor of Law, Yale University.

TAXATION, FEDERAL INCOME, Sixth Edition (1987)

James J. Freeland, Professor of Law, University of Florida.
Stephen A. Lind, Professor of Law, University of Florida and University of California, Hastings.
Richard B. Stephens, late Professor of Law Emeritus, University of Florida.

TAXATION, FEDERAL INCOME, Successor Edition (1986), with 1989 Legislative Supplement

Stanley S. Surrey, late Professor of Law, Harvard University.
Paul R. McDaniel, Professor of Law, Boston College.
Hugh J. Ault, Professor of Law, Boston College.
Stanley A. Koppelman, Professor of Law, Boston University.

TAXATION, FEDERAL INCOME, VOLUME II, Taxation of Partnerships and Corporations, Second Edition (1980), with 1989 Legislative Supplement

Stanley S. Surrey, late Professor of Law, Harvard University.
William C. Warren, Professor of Law Emeritus, Columbia University.
Paul R. McDaniel, Professor of Law, Boston College.
Hugh J. Ault, Professor of Law, Boston College.

TAXATION, FEDERAL WEALTH TRANSFER, Successor Edition (1987)

Stanley S. Surrey, late Professor of Law, Harvard University.
Paul R. McDaniel, Professor of Law, Boston College.
Harry L. Gutman, Professor of Law, University of Pennsylvania.

TAXATION, FUNDAMENTALS OF CORPORATE, Second Edition (1987), with 1989 Supplement

Stephen A. Lind, Professor of Law, University of Florida and University of California, Hastings.
Stephen Schwarz, Professor of Law, University of California, Hastings.
Daniel J. Lathrope, Professor of Law, University of California, Hastings.
Joshua Rosenberg, Professor of Law, University of San Francisco.

TAXATION, FUNDAMENTALS OF PARTNERSHIP, Second Edition (1988)

Stephen A. Lind, Professor of Law, University of Florida and University of California, Hastings.
Stephen Schwarz, Professor of Law, University of California, Hastings.
Daniel J. Lathrope, Professor of Law, University of California, Hastings.
Joshua Rosenberg, Professor of Law, University of San Francisco.

TAXATION, PROBLEMS IN THE FEDERAL INCOME TAXATION OF PARTNERSHIPS AND CORPORATIONS, Second Edition (1986)

Norton L. Steuben, Professor of Law, University of Colorado.
William J. Turnier, Professor of Law, University of North Carolina.

TAXATION, PROBLEMS IN THE FUNDAMENTALS OF FEDERAL INCOME, Second Edition (1985)

Norton L. Steuben, Professor of Law, University of Colorado.
William J. Turnier, Professor of Law, University of North Carolina.

TORT LAW AND ALTERNATIVES, Fourth Edition (1987)

Marc A. Franklin, Professor of Law, Stanford University.
Robert L. Rabin, Professor of Law, Stanford University.

TORTS, Eighth Edition (1988)

William L. Prosser, late Professor of Law, University of California, Hastings.
John W. Wade, Professor of Law, Vanderbilt University.
Victor E. Schwartz, Adjunct Professor of Law, Georgetown University.

TORTS, Third Edition (1976)

Harry Shulman, late Dean of the Law School, Yale University.
Fleming James, Jr., Professor of Law Emeritus, Yale University.
Oscar S. Gray, Professor of Law, University of Maryland.

TRADE REGULATION, Second Edition (1983), with 1987 Supplement

Milton Handler, Professor of Law Emeritus, Columbia University.
Harlan M. Blake, Professor of Law, Columbia University.
Robert Pitofsky, Professor of Law, Georgetown University.
Harvey J. Goldschmid, Professor of Law, Columbia University.

TRADE REGULATION, see Antitrust

TRANSNATIONAL BUSINESS PROBLEMS (1986)

Detlev F. Vagts, Professor of Law, Harvard University.

TRANSNATIONAL LEGAL PROBLEMS, Third Edition (1986) with Documentary Supplement

Henry J. Steiner, Professor of Law, Harvard University.
Detlev F. Vagts, Professor of Law, Harvard University.

TRIAL, see also Evidence, Making the Record, Lawyering Process and Preparing and Presenting the Case

TRUSTS, Fifth Edition (1978)

George G. Bogert, late Professor of Law Emeritus, University of Chicago.
Dallin H. Oaks, President, Brigham Young University.

TRUSTS AND SUCCESSION (Palmer's), Fourth Edition (1983)

Richard V. Wellman, Professor of Law, University of Georgia.
Lawrence W. Waggoner, Professor of Law, University of Michigan.
Olin L. Browder, Jr., Professor of Law, University of Michigan.

UNFAIR COMPETITION, see Competitive Process and Business Torts

WATER RESOURCE MANAGEMENT, Third Edition (1988)

The late Charles J. Meyers, formerly Dean, Stanford University Law School.
A. Dan Tarlock, Professor of Law, II Chicago-Kent College of Law.
James N. Corbridge, Jr., Chancellor, University of Colorado at Boulder, and Professor of Law, University of Colorado School of Law.
David H. Getches, Professor of Law, University of Colorado School of Law.

WILLS AND ADMINISTRATION, Fifth Edition (1961)

Philip Mechem, late Professor of Law, University of Pennsylvania.
Thomas E. Atkinson, late Professor of Law, New York University.

WRITING AND ANALYSIS IN THE LAW (1989)

Helene S. Shapo, Professor of Law, Northwestern University
Marilyn R. Walter, Professor of Law, Brooklyn Law School
Elizabeth Fajans, Writing Specialist, Brooklyn Law School

University Casebook Series

CONSTITUTIONAL LAW

By

GERALD GUNTHER

William Nelson Cromwell Professor of Law,
Stanford University

ELEVENTH EDITION

Mineola, New York
THE FOUNDATION PRESS, INC.
1985

COPYRIGHT © 1937, 1941, 1946, 1950, 1954, 1959, 1965, 1970, 1975, 1980 THE FOUNDATION PRESS, INC.
COPYRIGHT © 1985 By THE FOUNDATION PRESS, INC.
Printed in the United States of America

Library of Congress Cataloging in Publication Data

Gunther, Gerald, 1927–
  Constitutional law.

  (University casebook series)
  Rev. ed. of: Cases and materials on constitutional
law. 10th ed. 1980.
  Includes index.
  1. United States—Constitutional law—Cases.
I. Gunther, Gerald, 1927–   . Cases and materials
on constitutional law. II. Title. III. Series.
KF4549.G85 1985   342.73   85–13030
ISBN 0–88277–233–3 347.302

    Gunther Const.Law 11th Ed. UCB
    6th Reprint—1990

For Barbara, Daniel, Andrew

PREFACE TO THE ELEVENTH EDITION

This book is a major revision of the prior edition. The basic structure of the book is unchanged; the substantial reorganization and rewriting are reflected in the contents of the chapters. The Preface to the Ninth Edition described in detail my approach to structure and content. That preface appears in the immediately following pages.

There have been only two changes in the coverage of the individual chapters. I have eliminated the old chapter 6, on intergovermental immunities and interstate relationships, and incorporated its contents into other chapters. And I have reorganized the materials on freedom of expression in such a way that the two old chapters (old chapters 12 and 13) are replaced in this edition by three new ones (chapters 11, 12 and 13).

Within this largely unchanged chapter organization, the contents are often new. The last five years of constitutional law have been very lively and important ones, and the literature in the field has been voluminous and often stimulating. These developments, and changes in my own analyses, have required the rethinking of recurrent problems and the incorporation of new developments. The text includes much new writing designed to provide clearer, more focused analyses as well as considerable internal reorganization. In many places I have replaced strings of questions (often rhetorical ones) with more concise explanations, in the interest of providing background and promoting more probing analyses.

For example, the handling of the treatment of suspect and quasi-suspect classifications in chap. 9, on equal protection, has been changed to facilitate ultimate focus on the two most controversial problems in the area: the battle over the "purpose-impact" distinction; and the treatment of the "benign" use of race and sex classifications. Similarly, the new chapters on freedom of expression strive for a more helpful presentation. They begin (in chap. 11), as in prior editions, with the treatment of a highly protected variety of content, the "subversive speech" area; but they then move on to types of speech whose content is either much less protected or not protected at all under the First Amendment, via techniques such as "categorization." And chap. 12, the second free speech chapter, begins with a systematic overview of a range of techniques in vogue on the modern Court—including the "content-based"/"content-neutral" distinction—before turning to problems of time, place and manner regulations of the public forum. But a listing of changes in the internal organization cannot reflect the full scope of the reexamination: the contents of the analytical notes and the other new materials (especially in Part III, Individual Rights) are the best evidence of the scope of this revision.

Writing a constitutional law book of manageable size has been a challenge more formidable than ever. In fact, this book is nearly 100 pages shorter than the Tenth Edition—and far shorter than that edition plus the over 500 pages of its most recent supplement. But I cannot claim the major share of the credit for that somewhat reduced bulk: the addition of new materials and new analyses has meant an increase in the number of words; the greater compactness of the volume is attributable to modern technology—the new typography the computerization process permits.

This book includes all of the major changes to early February 1985. Subsequent developments will be reported in the usual annual supplements, beginning with one to be published in the summer of 1985. The supplements will be prepared, as they have been for the last two years, by Professor Frederick Schauer of the University of Michigan Law School.

Users of the book will no doubt continue to exercise individual judgments regarding coverage and sequence. I myself do not try to teach all of the materials in my two semesters of constitutional law each year. (In recent years, for example, I have frequently omitted chapters 6, 14 and 15, and covered only selected portions of chapters 3, 4 and 5. Moreover, over the last two years, I have experimented in the introductory course with moving from chapter 1 directly to the individual rights materials in chapters 8 and 9 before returning to the federalism materials in Part II, concluding with the problems of congressional enforcement of the post-Civil War Amendments in chap. 10.) But, as I noted in the Preface to the Ninth Edition, "I make changes in sequence each time I teach a constitutional law course."

My aim in this book continues to be to provide stimulating materials to promote serious, critical study of constitutional interpretation and decisionmaking. The structure and content of the book continue to reflect my own experiences with students and, above all, my own tastes. As I have said in the past, "I have sought to compile the kind of volume I would most enjoy using in class." *

Adequate acknowledgment of valuable suggestions and criticisms would include not only those named in earlier prefaces but also the many other teachers and students whose reactions have stimulated me to rethink and revise. As I have acknowledged in the past, I am especially grateful for two thoughtful reviews of the Ninth Edition, by Ken Karst in the Harvard Law Review and by Jack Hyman in the Stanford Law Review. To that special list, I now add Fred Schauer, who has not only prepared the recent supplements (as he will those to this edition) but also shared with me his suggestions for use in preparing this revision. Moreover, among the large number of teachers who have given me their thoughts about desirable revisions (both general and specific), Ken Karst, Henry Monaghan, George Anastaplo and David Sobelsohn warrant singling out for special thanks.

---

* In the editing of the materials, deletions are indicated by the use of brackets rather than ellipses.

But my deepest thanks at this moment must go to a group of very special people whose help and devotion in recent months were essential to the timely completion of this book: Frances Martin, whose extraordinary combination of intelligence and effectiveness make her just about the perfect secretary; Stanford law students Martin Wald and Evan Tager (who was of special help on the religion chapter) and, above all, three Stanford law students—Kate Bloch, Edgar Saenz and Michael Zeller—who were at my side throughout the preparation of this book and whose admirable energy and thoroughness were invaluable. Finally, for the retention of my sanity, I want to thank, as I did in the Preface to the Ninth Edition, the classical music stations in the San Francisco area; and, for major contributions toward that same end, I want to add my gratitude to Elaine Cattell of the Stanford Law Library staff, whose generous sharing of her collection of Dr. Who videotapes provided, nightly, a much needed 22 minutes of energizing relaxation that enabled me to survive the long post-dinner hours at my desk most evenings over many months.

GERALD GUNTHER

Stanford, California
May, 1985

PREFACE TO THE NINTH EDITION

I have enjoyed writing this casebook. I have not enjoyed such postwriting tasks as the reading of galleys. So, too, with this final step: for me, writing a preface is a chore, not a joy. I do not think that prefaces are *necessary* evils: no prefatory capsule can provide an adequate overview of contents; after months of writing (and after preparing a detailed Table of Contents), I would prefer to have readers gather what this book is all about by examining the pages that follow. Nevertheless, I have not resisted the tradition of beginning with a preface. My reasons go beyond the pressures of conformity. There is independent ground for some introductory words in the need to explain the fact that, although this is the first edition of the book to bear solely my name, it carries the designation of a Ninth Edition. Sketching the history of the book in turn prompts some comments on my approach—and affords opportunity, too, for acknowledgments of aid and stimulation received.

Evolution. This book is the successor to a series begun by Noel T. Dowling, late Harlan Fiske Stone Professor of Constitutional Law at Columbia University. Noel Dowling's first edition was published in 1937. The final one bearing only his name, the Sixth Edition, appeared in 1959. In the late fifties, Noel Dowling urged that Herbert Wechsler and I undertake the continuation of the casebook. We ultimately agreed to do so, with the understanding that we would be free to elaborate (or depart from) the Dowling model in order to reflect our own ideas. Noel Dowling, that true and fine gentleman, readily concurred.

Early in the 1960s, Herbert Wechsler and I outlined an approach for a new edition. Other commitments kept us from carrying through our plans immediately. In the fall of 1964, I agreed to prepare an updating of Noel Dowling's last edition. That task, I found, provided the opportunity for considerable rewriting as well. Thus, the 1965 edition—the Seventh Edition, Dowling and Gunther—was a partial implementation of the sketch Herbert Wechsler and I had drawn. That revision proved extensive enough to prompt Herbert Wechsler to urge me to go ahead on my own in future editions.

I completed that substantial revision with the Eighth Edition—the 1970 edition, Gunther and Dowling. When I turned to the preparation of this Ninth Edition, then, I anticipated that the task would largely be one of updating my earlier revisions. I underestimated the changes in the intervening years, in constitutional doctrine and in my own thinking—and underestimated my own compulsiveness as well. As I worked on this edition, the effort to restrict my focus to recent changes proved too confining. My teaching and writing since the last edition had led me to rethink a wide range of problems. I accordingly found it far more satisfying to rewrite.

xxiii

This edition, then, is a complete revision of the predecessors. It is, above all, a reflection of my own tastes, in organization and in analysis, as of 1975. Yet in casebook writing generally—and especially in revising a book with the history of this one—no author is an island. Although Noel Dowling and I never collaborated, his influence persists: as with earlier editions, I have tried to preserve the strengths which gained the Dowling book such wide acceptance for nearly three decades. And though Herbert Wechsler's name has never appeared as co-author in this series, his imprint remains strong—not only because of the sketch for a revision he and I prepared in the early sixties, but also, and primarily, because of the pervasive influence that friend and former Columbia colleague has had on my own thinking. Their efforts provided the base for this outlet for my own views and tastes.

Approach. My approach is best reflected in the materials which follow: as I have said, the detailed Table of Contents and the text convey my views about structure and analysis far better than anything I can say here. The book is fairly traditional in structure—but, I hope, original and stimulating in content. My aim is to promote serious, critical study of constitutional interpretation and decisionmaking. There are at least three ways of structuring a constitutional law casebook: the traditional topical organization, emphasizing doctrinal themes, functional problems, and constitutional provisions; the historical, chronological one; and the methodological, process oriented one, focusing on pervasive problems of modes of adjudication, allocations of decisionmaking authority, and sources of constitutional interpretation, from text and history to structural and contemporary values. I believe that all three perspectives are essential ones. My choice of the traditional, topical organization rests on the belief that it continues to be the best vehicle for the pursuit of all the major themes.

No casebook writer's juggling capacities are equal to the task of keeping all of those themes at the forefront at all times. My major device for pursuit of that goal has been to intersperse extensive notes throughout the topical organization. Repeatedly, I call attention to the historical context. Even more often, I examine the recurrent questions of process, methodology, and allocations of decisionmaking authority. That far more extensive textual commentary in this edition marks one of the major changes from previous ones. I have gone beyond brief, occasionally rhetorical questions to attempt clearer exposition of groundwork and fuller analysis of interrelationships. I have also sought to promote a sharper focus on the most challenging questions by providing introductory overviews to chapters of special richness and complexity—e.g., those on equal protection, freedom of expression, and congressional power to implement, and perhaps to modify, rights under the post-Civil War Amendments.

The difficulties of intertwining a range of organizing themes are matched by the problems of assuring attention to several layers of issues. Identifying doctrinal developments—where we are, where we have been, where we may be going—is a necessary but not sufficient ingredient of constitutional law materials for an informed lawyer and decisionmaker. What are legitimate sources and adequate justifications for constitutional interpretation? What is the authority and responsibility of nonjudicial organs for constitutional interpretation? What is the meaning of, and justification for, the varying modes of judicial review, the varying intensities of judicial scrutiny? Themes such as these, noted repeatedly in earlier editions, are more fully and more systematically traced in this one.

I have made some changes in the organization of the book, and more changes in relative space allocations. But the basic structure of recent editions remains intact: I begin with an examination of judicial review authority in Part I; Part II deals with problems of governmental structure; Part III turns to issues of individual rights. The major change in Part I has been the deferral of detailed consideration of jurisdictional themes in the exercise of judicial review. Consideration of "case or controversy" and related limitations on judicial authority now appears as chapter 15, the last chapter. Developments of those "jurisdictional" principles—issues such as standing and ripeness and abstention—have increasingly been influenced by the underlying substantive rights involved, and I have accordingly found it easier to deal with those problems after an examination of substantive materials.

Part II, on structure, continues to deal not only with questions of federalism, but also with problems of separation of powers. When I reintroduced a chapter on separation of powers in the last edition, some readers questioned its utility, on the ground that most of those concerns were obsolete and that there were in any event too few judicial decisions to make the problems "teachable." The events culminating in the Nixon impeachment proceedings and the War Powers Resolution of 1973 have quieted the charges of obsolescence; and, though there are more court decisions now, I have never thought that constitutional law was a subject to be pursued solely in judicial opinions. I have retained considerable emphasis on problems of federalism, though in condensed form. They are materials vital to an understanding of court roles and capacities; they provide illuminating historical perspective; and they retain sufficient practical significance to warrant contemporary study. The major deletion in Part II has been the long chapter on state taxation of interstate commerce: a fuller study of problems of state regulation of commerce seems to me to provide a more interesting and useful context for an examination of governing principles and competing considerations.

Part III, on individual rights, receives greater emphasis than ever: it now occupies about two-thirds of the book. That is an inevitable reflection of the direction and rapid pace of modern constitutional developments. When Noel Dowling wrote his Preface to his first edition in 1937, he began by saying that his principal aim was "to build a course [on] the major theme of the regulatory power of government." Preoccupation with governmental power was understandably central in a book published in the wake of the New Deal's Court-packing crisis.

Preoccupation with individual rights is similarly understandable in a book published in the wake of Warren era changes and in the midst of Burger era modifications. Equal protection was the theme of one of the shortest chapters in Dowling's first edition; it is the title of the longest chapter in this one. My two chapters on freedom of expression exceed even the equal protection analysis in length. Substantive due process developments have been reorganized to contrast more sharply the discredited use of that doctrine in an earlier era with its modern revival in the contraception and abortion decisions. And the powers of Congress under the post-Civil War Amendments, powers moribund in 1937, warrant an expanded chapter with detailed analytical notes in this edition. (That chapter, chapter 11, has been moved from Part II to Part III of the book to permit consideration of the legislative role after judicial interpretations of due process and equal protection are examined.)

Over the years, some areas once staples of constitutional law courses have developed such an identity and complexity of their own as to warrant treatment as separate disciplines. What was once the fate of administrative law, for example, has now become appropriate for the constitutional requirements of criminal procedure. Some samples of those developments are retained, for the light they throw on the general evolution of due process standards and the incorporation controversy; but full treatment of the details is left to other courses. Despite deletions such as that, this book is somewhat longer than the Eighth Edition—though considerably shorter than that edition plus the nearly 500 pages of its most recent Supplement. I believe I have kept the book to manageable size. But, as in the past, I have refused to permit editing of cases to degenerate into the gathering of skeletal segments of opinions. I have resorted to textual treatment and summaries even more frequently than before; but some of the space saved through that technique has been absorbed by the fuller descriptive and analytical notes. But the selection of materials here, and their organization, should not be viewed as an effort at dogmatic prescription of essentials. I myself do not teach all the materials each year. Moreover, I make changes in sequence each time I teach a constitutional law course. Users of the book will no doubt continue to use individual judgments as to coverage and sequence. My aim has been to provide as stimulating and full a treatment of the covered problems as space permits.

Perhaps more important than these comments about approach and coverage is the reiteration of a theme I stated in earlier editions: "Inevitably, I relied heavily upon my own experience with students and, above all, my own tastes: I have sought to compile the kind of volume I would most enjoy using in class." I expect to enjoy using this one, though its organization is probably closer to what I did the last time I taught than what I will do when I teach next. I think constitutional law is an important, serious, endlessly intriguing and constantly enjoyable subject. Conveying that sense to my students has always been my highest goal. To convey some of that sense to the users of this book is its chief purpose.

Acknowledgments. Adequate acknowledgment would include everyone I have talked with about constitutional law, and all I have read about it. A more circumscribed focus would reemphasize the debts I owe to Noel Dowling and Herbert Wechsler. In more recent years, I have benefited above all from the stimulating collegiality of Paul Brest and William Cohen. Both were engaged in casebook writing while I was at work on this edition. I have learned much from Paul Brest's brilliant, original, lucid Processes of Constitutional Decisionmaking (1975). I have benefited as well from portions of the manuscript of a book on civil liberties for undergraduates which William Cohen is preparing in collaboration with another colleague, John Kaplan. I have also been helped by valuable comments from those who have used my book at other schools: the late and much missed Alexander M. Bickel and Harry Kalven, Jr.; my recent colleagues at Harvard, John Hart Ely, Andrew L. Kaufman, and Laurence H. Tribe; and Gerhard Casper, Norman Dorsen, R. Kent Greenawalt, Kenneth L. Karst, Hans Linde, Arnold Loewy, Paul J. Mishkin, the Hon. Jon O. Newman, Michael E. Smith, and Frank R. Strong, among many others.

I am grateful, too, to the Stanford students who helped me with the chores of citechecking and proofreading. And over the years, I have been especially fortunate in having had the assistance of extraordinary secretaries. I acknowledged the great contributions of Bess Hitchcock in my earlier editions. I feared catastrophe when she retired; that prospect was averted when B Fahr came to work with me. I would praise her remarkable combination of intelligence and effectiveness even more loudly were I not afraid that a colleague would steal her. Without her—and without the classical music stations in the San Francisco area—timely completion of this book, and retention of my sanity, would have been impossible.

GERALD GUNTHER

Stanford, California
June, 1975

*

SUMMARY OF CONTENTS

PART I

THE JUDICIAL FUNCTION IN CONSTITUTIONAL CASES

PART II

THE STRUCTURE OF GOVERNMENT: NATION AND STATES IN THE FEDERAL SYSTEM

TABLE OF CONTENTS

PART I

THE JUDICIAL FUNCTION IN CONSTITUTIONAL CASES

PART II

THE STRUCTURE OF GOVERNMENT: NATION AND STATES IN THE FEDERAL SYSTEM

PART III

INDIVIDUAL RIGHTS

TABLE OF CONTENTS

TABLE OF CONTENTS

APPENDICES

TABLE OF CASES

Principal cases are in italic type. Nonprincipal cases are in roman type.
References are to pages.

CONSTITUTIONAL LAW

*

Part I

THE JUDICIAL FUNCTION IN CONSTITUTIONAL CASES

Chapter 1

THE NATURE AND SOURCES OF THE SUPREME COURT'S AUTHORITY

Introduction. Constitutional law courses and materials emphasize Supreme Court decisions. But the Supreme Court is not the only court authorized to examine constitutional claims, and courts are not the only forums for significant constitutional debates. In the cases that follow, only a very few passages of the constitutional text get extensive scrutiny: the few words about judicial power in Art. III; the allocations of legislative powers found especially in Art. I, § 8; the individual rights guarantees in the Bill of Rights and the post-Civil War Amendments. Yet many of the other provisions significantly affect the operations of constitutional government: those dealing with selection and structure of Presidency and Congress are obvious illustrations. And some provisions (that on impeachment, for instance) have given rise to major constitutional controversies that have not reached the courts.

Yet more than pedagogical tradition supports the emphasis on the Supreme Court. On those questions that do get to court, the Supreme Court's last word makes it obviously the most important judicial voice. And a remarkable range of constitutional questions *has* reached the Court: the nearly 500 volumes of reports of a Court increasingly preoccupied with constitutional questions are no doubt the richest source of constitutional law. It is traditional, too, to begin the examination of constitutional law problems with opinions from the Court presided over by Chief Justice John Marshall early in the 19th century. Thus, Part I begins with Marbury v. Madison; Part II, with McCulloch v. Maryland and Gibbons v. Ogden. Attention to Marshall Court cases is more than a ritualistic bow to historical landmarks: the reason is not simply that those cases were important in the development of judicial authority and federal power allocations; it is also that those cases of the early 1800s—much more so than many of the decisions of intervening years—are important *now*.

So it is with Marbury v. Madison, which follows. Some attention to it would be justified if it represented no more than the historical fact of the Court's first elaborate statement of its judicial review powers. But the extensive concern with Marbury here would not be warranted if it were a closed book. Instead, Marbury is very much alive: it rests on reasoning significant for the exercise of judicial power today.

To what extent, for example, is the authority asserted in Marbury simply an incidental byproduct of the ordinary judicial function in deciding lawsuits: to look to the governing law, to consider the Constitution as one relevant source of law—and, in cases of conflicting legal statements, to give priority to the Constitution and to refuse enforcement of any contravening legal statement? To what extent does the Marbury authority rest instead on a claim that the Constitution thrust a more extraordinary mission upon the Supreme Court: that

1

the Court was endowed with a roving commission to police the other branches, as the central guardian of constitutional norms and the special enforcer of constitutional restrictions? In the proper reading of Marbury, in the answers to these questions, may lie answers to many of the questions raised in this chapter (and further pursued in chap. 15): May Congress curtail the Court's constitutional business? May or must the Court intervene in all constitutional disputes? When is resort to the Court appropriate? When permissible? Who may obtain answers to constitutional questions from the Court? When? As to what questions?

Understanding the core reasoning of Marbury, then, is essential to thinking about Court power today. And appreciation of the Marbury reasoning in turn requires some attention to historical antecedents and context. The assertions of the power of judicial review, and the justifications for it, did not spring fullblown in 1803: they reflected a variety of earlier developments. And it was only because a concrete dispute had been brought to the Court that John Marshall had an opportunity to speak about judicial power. To develop these themes of intellectual and political history, as well as to explore a number of legal issues opened up by Marbury, is the purpose of the materials that follow the case.

SECTION 1. JUDICIAL REVIEW: THE BASES AND IMPLICATIONS OF MARBURY v. MADISON

MARBURY v. MADISON

1 Cranch * 137, 2 L.Ed. 60 (1803).

[William Marbury was one of those named a justice of the peace for the District of Columbia at the very close of the Federalist Administration of President John Adams, during a rash of last minute judicial appointments in March 1801 (described in the historical note which follows this case). The incoming Jefferson Administration chose to disregard those appointments for which formal commissions had not been delivered before the end of Adams' term. Marbury and some disappointed colleagues then decided to go directly to the Supreme Court, in the December Term 1801, to compel Jefferson's Secretary of State Madison to deliver their commissions. The Court did not announce a decision on this 1801 request until February 1803. Before printing the opinion, the reporter summarized the earlier proceedings. His paragraph is reprinted here both to clarify the technical posture of the case and to dramatize (by adding some proper names in brackets) the involvement of John Marshall in the underlying dispute.]

---

* 1 Cranch was the first volume devoted wholly to the reports of cases in the Supreme Court. It was not published until 1804. The 1790s cases were reported by A. J. Dallas in volumes which also covered Pennsylvania decisions. In 1816 Congress made provision for an official reporter. Henry Wheaton of New York was the first incumbent. He was succeeded in 1827 by Richard Peters, Jr., with whom he became involved in litigation, Wheaton v. Peters, 8 Pet. 591 (1834), on whether a reporter "has or can have any copyright in the written opinions delivered by this Court." Wheaton lost. In 1884 it was announced (108 U.S. vi) that it "is the custom of the Court to cite decisions reported since Wallace only by the number in the official series, as '91 U.S.,' '92 U.S.,' &c." Up to 91 U.S., the reporters, and number of volumes for each, were as follows: Dallas, 4; Cranch, 9; Wheaton, 12; Peters, 16; Howard, 24; Black, 2; Wallace, 23.

Almost all of the principal cases in this volume, and most of those discussed in the notes, are decisions of the United States Supreme Court. Accordingly, the tribunal is not named in the materials below unless it is a court other than the Supreme Court.

At the last term, viz., December term, 1801, William Marbury, Dennis Ramsay, Robert Townsend Hooe, and William Harper, by their counsel, Charles Lee, Esq., late attorney general of the United States, severally moved the court for a rule to James Madison, Secretary of State of the United States, to show cause why a mandamus should not issue commanding him to cause to be delivered to them respectively their several commissions as justices of the peace in the District of Columbia. This motion was supported by affidavits [including one by John Marshall's brother James] of the following facts: that notice of this motion had been given to Mr. Madison; that Mr. Adams, the late President of the United States, nominated the applicants to the senate for their advice and consent to be appointed justices of the peace of the District of Columbia; that the senate advised and consented to the appointments; that commissions in due form were signed by the said President appointing them justices, &c.; and that the seal of the United States was in due form affixed to the said commissions by the Secretary of State [John Marshall]; that the applicants have requested Mr. Madison to deliver them their said commissions, who has not complied with that request; and that said commissions are withheld from them. [Whereupon] a rule was laid to [show cause].

Afterwards, on the 24th of February [1803], the following opinion of the Court was delivered by the Chief Justice [MARSHALL]:

At the last term on the affidavits then read and filed with the clerk, a rule was granted in this case, requiring the Secretary of State to show cause why a mandamus should not issue, directing him to deliver to William Marbury his commission as a justice of the peace for the county of Washington, in the district of Columbia.

No cause has been shown, and the present motion is for a mandamus. The peculiar delicacy of this case, the novelty of some of its circumstances, and the real difficulty attending the points which occur in it, require a complete exposition of the principles on which the opinion to be given by the court is founded.

These principles have been, on the side of the applicant, very ably argued at the bar. In rendering the opinion of the court, there will be some departure in form, though not in substance, from the points stated in that argument.

In the order in which the court has viewed this subject, the following questions have been considered and decided:

1st. Has the applicant a right to the commission he demands?

2d. If he has a right, and that right has been violated, do the laws of this country afford him a remedy?

3d. If they do afford him a remedy, is it a mandamus issuing from this court?

The first object of inquiry is—1st. Has the applicant a right to the commission he demands?

[It is] decidedly the opinion of the court, that when a commission has been signed by the president, the appointment is made; and that the commission is complete, when the seal of the United States has been affixed to it by the [secretary of state].

Mr. Marbury, then, since his commission was signed by the president, and sealed by the secretary of state, was appointed; and as the law creating the office, gave the officer a right to hold for five years, independent of the executive, the appointment was not revocable, but vested in the officer legal rights, which are protected by the laws of his country.

To withhold his commission, therefore, is an act deemed by the court not warranted by law, but violative of a vested legal right.

This brings us to the second inquiry; which is 2dly. If he has a right, and that right has been violated, do the laws of his country afford him a remedy?

The very essence of civil liberty certainly consists in the right of every individual to claim the protection of the laws, whenever he receives an injury. One of the first duties of government is to afford that protection. [The] government of the United States has been emphatically termed a government of laws, and not of men. It will certainly cease to deserve this high appellation, if the laws furnish no remedy for the violation of a vested legal right.

If this obloquy is to be cast on the jurisprudence of our country, it must arise from the peculiar character of the case.

It behooves us then to enquire whether there be in its composition any ingredient which shall exempt it from legal investigation, or exclude the injured party from [legal redress].

Is it in the nature of the transaction? Is the act of delivering or withholding a commission to be considered as a mere political act, belonging to the executive department alone, for the performance of which entire confidence is placed by our constitution in the supreme executive; and for any misconduct respecting which, the injured individual has no remedy.

That there may be such cases is not to be questioned; but that every act of duty, to be performed in any of the great departments of government, constitutes such a case, is not to be [admitted].

It follows, then, that the question, whether the legality of an act of the head of a department be examinable in a court of justice or not, must always depend on the nature of that [act].

By the constitution of the United States, the President is invested with certain important political powers, in the exercise of which he is to use his own discretion, and is accountable only to his country in his political character, and to his own conscience. To aid him in the performance of these duties, he is authorized to appoint certain officers, who act by his authority and in conformity with his orders.

In such cases, their acts are his acts; and whatever opinion may be entertained of the manner in which executive discretion may be used, still there exists, and can exist, no power to control that discretion. The subjects are political. They respect the nation, not individual rights, and being entrusted to the executive, the decision of the executive is conclusive. The application of this remark will be perceived by adverting to the act of congress for establishing the department of foreign affairs. This officer, as his duties were prescribed by that act, is to conform precisely to the will of the President. He is the mere organ by whom that will is communicated. The acts of such an officer, as an officer, can never be examinable by the courts.

But when the legislature proceeds to impose on that officer other duties; when he is directed peremptorily to perform certain acts; when the rights of individuals are dependent on the performance of those acts; he is so far the officer of the law; is amenable to the laws for his conduct; and cannot at his discretion sport away the vested rights of others.

The conclusion from this reasoning is, that where the heads of departments are the political or confidential agents of the executive, merely to execute the will of the President, or rather to act in cases in which the executive possesses a constitutional or legal discretion, nothing can be more perfectly clear than that their acts are only politically examinable. But where a specific duty is assigned by law, and individual rights depend upon the performance of that duty, it seems equally clear, that the individual who considers himself injured, has a right to resort to the laws of his country for a [remedy].

It is, then, the opinion of the Court [that Marbury has a right to the commission; a refusal to deliver which is a plain violation of that right, for which the laws of his country afford him a remedy.

It remains to be enquired whether,

3dly. He is entitled to the remedy for which he applies. This depends on—1st. The nature of the writ applied for, and,

2dly. The power of this court.

1st. The nature of the writ.

[This] writ, if awarded, would be directed to an officer of government, and its mandate to him would be, to use the words of Blackstone, "to do a particular thing therein specified, which appertains to his office and duty and which the court has previously determined, or at least supposes, to be consonant to right and justice." Or, in the words of Lord Mansfield, the applicant, in this case, has a right to execute an office of public concern, and is kept out of possession of that right.

These circumstances certainly concur in this case.

Still, to render the mandamus a proper remedy, the officer to whom it is to be directed, must be one to whom, on legal principles, such writ may be directed; and the person applying for it must be without any other specific and legal remedy.

1st. With respect to the officer to whom it would be directed. The intimate political relation, subsisting between the president of the United States and the heads of departments, necessarily renders any legal investigation of the acts of one of those high officers peculiarly irksome, as well as delicate; and excites some hesitation with respect to the propriety of entering into such investigation. Impressions are often received without much reflection or examination, and it is not wonderful, that in such a case as this, the assertion, by an individual, of his legal claims in a court of justice, to which claims it is the duty of that court to attend, should at first view be considered by some, as an attempt to intrude into the cabinet, and to intermeddle with the prerogatives of the executive.

It is scarcely necessary for the court to disclaim all pretensions to such a jurisdiction. An extravagance, so absurd and excessive, could not have been entertained for a moment. The province of the court is, solely, to decide on the rights of individuals, not to enquire how the executive, or executive officers, perform duties in which they have a discretion. Questions, in their nature political, or which are, by the constitution and laws, submitted to the executive, can never be made in this court.

But, if this be not such a question; if so far from being an intrusion into the secrets of the cabinet, it respects a paper, which, according to law, is upon record, and to a copy of which the law gives a right, on the payment of ten cents; if it be no intermeddling with a subject, over which the executive can be considered as having exercised any control; what is there in the exalted station of the officer, which shall bar a citizen from asserting, in a court of justice, his legal rights, or shall forbid a court to listen to the claim; or to issue a mandamus, directing the performance of a duty, not depending on executive discretion, but on particular acts of congress and the general principles of law?

[Where the head of a department] is directed by law to do a certain act affecting the absolute rights of individuals, in the performance of which he is not placed under the particular direction of the President, and the performance of which, the President cannot lawfully forbid, and therefore is never presumed to have forbidden; as for example, to record a commission, or a patent for land, which has received all the legal solemnities; or to give a copy of such record; in such cases, it is not perceived on what ground the courts of the country are further excused from the duty of giving judgment, that right be done to an injured individual, than if the same services were to be performed by a person not the head of a [department].

This, then, is a plain case for a mandamus, either to deliver the commission, or a copy of it from the record; and it only remains to be enquired,

Whether it can issue from this court.

The act to establish the judicial courts of the United States authorizes the Supreme Court "to issue writs of mandamus in cases warranted by the principles and usages of law, to any courts appointed, or persons holding office, under the authority of the United States." *

The secretary of state, being a person holding an office under the authority of the United States, is precisely within the letter of the description; and if this court is not authorized to issue a writ of mandamus to such an officer, it must be because the law is unconstitutional, and therefore absolutely incapable of conferring the authority, and assigning the duties which its words purport to confer and assign.

The constitution vests the whole judicial power of the United States in one Supreme Court, and such inferior courts as congress shall, from time to time, ordain and establish. This power is expressly extended to all cases arising under the laws of the United States; and, consequently, in some form, may be exercised over the present case; because the right claimed is given by a law of the United States.

In the distribution of this power it is declared that "the Supreme Court shall have original jurisdiction in all cases affecting ambassadors, other public ministers and consuls, and those in which a state shall be a party. In all other cases, the Supreme Court shall have appellate jurisdiction."

It has been insisted, at the bar, that as the original grant of jurisdiction, to the supreme and inferior courts, is general, and the clause, assigning original jurisdiction to the Supreme Court, contains no negative or restrictive words, the power remains to the legislature, to assign original jurisdiction to that court in other cases than those specified in the article which has been recited; provided those cases belong to the judicial power of the United States.

If it had been intended to leave it in the discretion of the legislature to apportion the judicial power between the supreme and inferior courts according to the will of that body, it would certainly have been useless to have proceeded further than to have defined the judicial power, and the tribunals in which it should be vested. The subsequent part of the section is mere surplusage, is entirely without meaning, if such is to be the construction. If congress remains at liberty to give this court appellate jurisdiction, where the constitution has declared their jurisdiction shall be original; and original jurisdiction where the

---

* The full text of Section 13 of the Judiciary Act of 1789, 1 Stat. 73: *"And be it further enacted,* That the Supreme Court shall have exclusive jurisdiction of all controversies of a civil nature, where a state is a party, except between a state and its citizens; and except also between a state and citizens of other states, or aliens, in which latter case it shall have original but not exclusive jurisdiction. And shall have exclusively all such jurisdiction of suits or proceedings against ambassadors, or other public ministers, or their domestics, or domestic servants, as a court of law can have or exercise consistently with the law of nations; and original, but not exclusive jurisdiction of all suits brought by ambassadors, or other public ministers, or in which a consul, or vice consul, shall be a party. And the trial of issues of fact in the Supreme Court, in all actions at law against citizens of the United States, shall be by jury. *The Supreme Court shall also have appellate jurisdiction from the circuit courts and courts of the several states, in the cases herein after specially provided for; and shall have power to issue writs of prohibition to the district courts, when proceeding as courts of admiralty and maritime jurisdiction, and writs of mandamus, in cases warranted by the principles and usages of law, to any courts appointed, or persons holding office, under the authority of the United States."* [Emphasis in final sentence added.]

constitution has declared it shall be appellate; the distribution of jurisdiction, made in the constitution, is form without substance.

Affirmative words are often, in their operation, negative of other objects than those affirmed; and in this case, a negative or exclusive sense must be given to them or they have no operation at all.

It cannot be presumed that any clause in the constitution is intended to be without effect; and, therefore, such a construction is inadmissible, unless the words require [it].

When an instrument organizing fundamentally a judicial system, divides it into one supreme, and so many inferior courts as the legislature may ordain and establish; then enumerates its powers, and proceeds so far to distribute them, as to define the jurisdiction of the supreme court by declaring the cases in which it shall take original jurisdiction, and that in others it shall take appellate jurisdiction; the plain import of the words seems to be, that in one class of cases its jurisdiction is original, and not appellate; in the other it is appellate, and not original. If any other construction would render the clause inoperative, that is an additional reason for rejecting such other construction, and for adhering to their obvious meaning.

To enable this court, then, to issue a mandamus, it must be shown to be an exercise of appellate jurisdiction, or to be necessary to enable them to exercise appellate jurisdiction.

It has been stated at the bar that the appellate jurisdiction may be exercised in a variety of forms, and that if it be the will of the legislature that a mandamus should be used for that purpose, that will must be obeyed. This is true, yet the jurisdiction must be appellate, not original.

It is the essential criterion of appellate jurisdiction, that it revises and corrects the proceedings in a cause already instituted, and does not create that cause. Although, therefore, a mandamus may be directed to courts, yet to issue such a writ to an officer for the delivery of a paper, is in effect the same as to sustain an original action for that paper, and, therefore, seems not to belong to appellate, but to original jurisdiction. Neither is it necessary in such a case as this, to enable the court to exercise its appellate jurisdiction.

The authority, therefore, given to the Supreme Court, by the act establishing the judicial courts of the United States, to issue writs of mandamus to public officers, appears not to be warranted by the constitution; and it becomes necessary to enquire whether a jurisdiction, so conferred, can be exercised.

The question, whether an act, repugnant to the constitution, can become the law of the land, is a question deeply interesting to the United States; but, happily, not of an intricacy proportioned to its interest. It seems only necessary to recognize certain principles, supposed to have been long and well established, to decide it.

That the people have an original right to establish, for their future government, such principles as, in their opinion, shall most conduce to their own happiness, is the basis on which the whole American fabric has been erected. The exercise of this original right is a very great exertion; nor can it, nor ought it, to be frequently repeated. The principles, therefore, so established, are deemed fundamental. And as the authority from which they proceed is supreme, and can seldom act, they are designed to be permanent.

This original and supreme will organizes the government, and assigns to different departments their respective powers. It may either stop here, or establish certain limits not to be transcended by those departments.

The government of the United States is of the latter description. The powers of the legislature are defined and limited; and that those limits may not be mistaken, or forgotten, the constitution is written. To what purpose are powers limited, and to what purpose is that limitation committed to writing, if these limits may, at any time, be passed by those intended to be restrained? The distinction between a government with limited and unlimited powers is abolished, if those limits do not confine the persons on whom they are imposed, and if acts prohibited and acts allowed, are of equal obligation. It is a proposition too plain to be contested, that the constitution controls any legislative act repugnant to it; or, that the legislature may alter the constitution by an ordinary act.

Between these alternatives there is no middle ground. The constitution is either a superior, paramount law, unchangeable by ordinary means, or it is on a level with ordinary legislative acts, and, like other acts, is alterable when the legislature shall please to alter it.

If the former part of the alternative be true, then a legislative act contrary to the constitution is not law: if the latter part be true, then written constitutions are absurd attempts, on the part of the people, to limit a power in its own nature illimitable.

Certainly all those who have framed written constitutions contemplate them as forming the fundamental and paramount law of the nation, and consequently, the theory of every such government must be, that an act of the legislature, repugnant to the constitution, is void.

This theory is essentially attached to a written constitution, and is, consequently, to be considered, by this court, as one of the fundamental principles of our society. It is not therefore to be lost sight of in the further consideration of this subject.

If an act of the legislature, repugnant to the constitution, is void, does it, notwithstanding its invalidity, bind the courts, and oblige them to give it effect? Or, in other words, though it be not law, does it constitute a rule as operative as if it was a law? This would be to overthrow in fact what was established in theory; and would seem, at first view, an absurdity too gross to be insisted on. It shall, however, receive a more attentive consideration.

 It is emphatically the province and duty of the judicial department to say what the law is. Those who apply the rule to particular cases, must of necessity expound and interpret that rule. If two laws conflict with each other, the courts must decide on the operation of each.

So if a law be in opposition to the constitution; if both the law and the constitution apply to a particular case, so that the court must either decide that case conformably to the law, disregarding the constitution; or conformably to the constitution, disregarding the law; the court must determine which of these conflicting rules governs the case. This is of the very essence of judicial duty.

 If, then, the courts are to regard the constitution, and the constitution is superior to any ordinary act of the legislature, the constitution, and not such ordinary act, must govern the case to which they both apply.

Those then who controvert the principle that the constitution is to be considered, in court, as a paramount law, are reduced to the necessity of maintaining that courts must close their eyes on the constitution, and see only the law.

This doctrine would subvert the very foundation of all written constitutions. It would declare that an act which, according to the principles and theory of our government, is entirely void, is yet, in practice, completely obligatory. It would declare that if the legislature shall do what is expressly forbidden, such act, notwithstanding the express prohibition, is in reality effectual. It would be giving to the legislature a practical and real omnipotence, with the same breath which professes to restrict their powers within narrow limits. It is prescribing limits, and declaring that those limits may be passed at pleasure.

That it thus reduces to nothing what we have deemed the greatest improvement on political institutions—a written constitution—would of itself be sufficient, in America, where written constitutions have been viewed with so much reverence, for rejecting the construction. But the peculiar expressions of the constitution of the United States furnish additional arguments in favour of its rejection.

The judicial power of the United States is extended to all cases arising under the constitution.

Could it be the intention of those who gave this power, to say that in using it the constitution should not be looked into? That a case arising under the constitution should be decided without examining the instrument under which it arises?

This is too extravagant to be maintained.

In some cases, then, the constitution must be looked into by the judges. And if they can open it at all, what part of it are they forbidden to read or to obey?

There are many other parts of the constitution which serve to illustrate this subject. It is declared that "no tax or duty shall be laid on articles exported from any state." Suppose a duty on the export of cotton, of tobacco, or of flour; and a suit instituted to recover it. Ought judgment to be rendered in such a case? Ought the judges to close their eyes on the constitution, and only see the law?

The constitution declares that "no bill of attainder or ex post facto law shall be passed."

If, however, such a bill should be passed, and a person should be prosecuted under it; must the court condemn to death those victims whom the constitution endeavors to preserve?

"No person," says the constitution, "shall be convicted of treason unless on the testimony of two witnesses to the same overt act, or on confession in open court."

Here the language of the constitution is addressed especially to the courts. It prescribes, directly for them, a rule of evidence not to be departed from. If the legislature should change that rule, and declare *one* witness, or a confession *out* of court, sufficient for conviction, must the constitutional principle yield to the legislative act?

From these, and many other selections which might be made, it is apparent, that the framers of the constitution contemplated that instrument as a rule for the government of *courts,* as well as of the legislature.

Why otherwise does it direct the judges to take an oath to support it? This oath certainly applies, in an especial manner, to their conduct in their official character. How immoral to impose it on them, if they were to be used as the instruments, and the knowing instruments, for violating what they swear to support!

The oath of office, too, imposed by the legislature, is completely demonstrative of the legislative opinion on this subject. It is in these words: "I do solemnly swear that I will administer justice without respect to persons, and do equal right to the poor and to the rich; and that I will faithfully and impartially discharge all the duties incumbent on me as _____, according to the best of my abilities and understanding, agreeably to *the constitution,* and laws of the United States."

Why does a judge swear to discharge his duties agreeably to the constitution of the United States, if that constitution forms no rule for his government? If it is closed upon him, and cannot be inspected by him?

If such be the real state of things, this is worse than solemn mockery. To prescribe, or to take this oath, becomes equally a crime.

It is also not entirely unworthy of observation that in declaring what shall be the *supreme* law of the land, the *constitution* itself is first mentioned; and not the laws of the United States generally, but those only which shall be made in *pursuance* of the constitution, have that rank.

Thus, the particular phraseology of the constitution of the United States confirms and strengthens the principle, supposed to be essential to all written constitutions, that a law repugnant to the constitution is void; and that *courts,* as well as other departments, are bound by that instrument.

The rule must be discharged.

THE HISTORICAL SETTING OF THE MARBURY CASE

1. *The political environment.* a. *Judicial "reform."* The Marbury case was an early manifestation of the clashes between the Jeffersonian Republicans and the Marshall Court. John Marshall, Secretary of State in the Cabinet of lame-duck President John Adams, was nominated Chief Justice in January 1801 and took his oath of office on February 4, 1801. On February 17, the House of Representatives elected Thomas Jefferson as President. Marshall continued to act as Secretary of State through March 3, 1801, the end of Adams' term. Indeed, he may have stayed on somewhat longer: on March 4, 1801—the day Marshall as Chief Justice administered the oath of office to new President Jefferson—he agreed to comply with Jefferson's request "to perform the duties of Secretary of State until a successor be appointed."[1]

Four days before Jefferson's election, the Federalist Congress reorganized the federal judiciary. The Circuit Court Act of February 13, 1801, relieved the Justices of the Supreme Court of circuit-riding duty. In the past, Circuit Courts had been manned by District Court judges and Supreme Court Justices; the 1801 law established sixteen Circuit Court judgeships. The Jeffersonians were indignant: to them, the Circuit Court Act was the defeated Federalists' device to maintain control of one branch of the government. As expected, the new judgeships went to Federalists, for Adams hastily nominated his "midnight judges" during the last two weeks of his term. The Jeffersonians' concern went beyond patronage: the partisan enforcement of the Alien and Sedition Laws had been a major target of their attacks in the political warfare that preceded the election of 1800.

Marbury and his co-petitioners were not among the "midnight judges" named pursuant to the Circuit Court Act. Their positions had been created even later: the Organic Act of the District of Columbia was passed on February 27, 1801, less than a week before the end of Adams' term. The Act authorized the President to name justices of the peace for the District. Adams named forty-two justices on March 2, 1801, and the Senate confirmations came on March 3, Adams' last day in office. The commissions of the petitioners in the Marbury case had been signed by Adams—as well as signed and sealed by Acting Secretary of State Marshall—but they had not been delivered by the end of the day; and the new President chose to treat them as a "nullity." As John Marshall wrote two weeks later, "I should [have] sent out the commissions which had been signed & sealed but for the extreme hurry of the time."

Marshall was therefore intimately acquainted with the facts of the Marbury controversy. Yet the issue of the existence of the commissions was extensively considered in the Court hearing in the Marbury case. For example, an affidavit

---

1. Oster, The Political and Economic Doctrines of John Marshall (1914), 182.

by James Marshall—John Marshall's brother—was introduced to prove the existence of some of the commissions. (James Marshall stated that he was to deliver a number of the commissions but that, "finding he could not conveniently carry the whole," he returned "several of them" to his brother's office. 1 Cranch, at 146.) In view of his involvement in the controversy, should Marshall have disqualified himself from participation in the decision? Compare Martin v. Hunter's Lessee, p. 29 below, where Marshall did not sit because he and his brother James were interested property owners.

The Jeffersonians soon demonstrated that they would not complacently accept Federalist entrenchment in the judiciary: they made repeal of the Circuit Court Act of 1801 an early item of business in the new Congress. The 1801 Act was repealed on March 31, 1802, while the Marbury case was pending in the Supreme Court. The 1802 Act essentially reestablished the old Circuit Court system, with Supreme Court Justices and District Judges once again manning the Circuit Court benches. During these congressional debates, a few Jeffersonians for the first time questioned the Court's authority to consider the constitutionality of congressional acts. There was still another sign of the mounting hostility to the Court: Congress abolished the June and December Terms of the Supreme Court created by the 1801 Act and provided that there would be only one Term, in February. Accordingly, there was no Court session in 1802; the Court that had received Marbury's petition in December, 1801 could not reconvene until February 1803.

b. *Impeachment.* The Jeffersonians soon unsheathed a still more potent weapon. Early in 1802, the House voted to impeach Federalist District Judge John Pickering of New Hampshire, and many feared that impeachment of Supreme Court Justices would follow. The choice of Pickering as the first target was a "tragic blunder," however. Pickering, an insane drunkard, was plainly incompetent to serve as a judge, but it took some stretching to convert this into "Treason, Bribery, or other high Crimes and Misdemeanors," as required by Art. II, § 4, of the Constitution.[2] Nevertheless, the Senate voted to remove Pickering from office in March 1804.[3]

On the day after Pickering's removal, Congress moved on to bigger game: the House impeached Supreme Court Justice Samuel Chase. To the Jeffersonians, Chase was a glaring example of Federalist abuse of judicial office: he had made electioneering statements from the bench in 1800, and he had conducted several vindictive sedition and treason trials. A few months after the Marbury decision, he provided the immediate provocation for his impeachment: in May 1803, in a partisan charge to the federal grand jury in Baltimore, he criticized the Jeffersonians' repeal of the 1801 Circuit Court Act. The Senate tried Chase early in 1805. Were judges impeachable for conduct that did not constitute an indictable offense? The debate was lengthy and important: if the case against Chase succeeded, it was widely expected, John Marshall and other federal

---

2. The problem of dealing with incompetent federal judges persists. In the 1970s, there were mounting arguments that Congress should establish machinery to discipline and even remove incompetent federal judges by means short of impeachment. Supporters of such legislation argued that impeachment was too cumbersome, that a more efficient mechanism to air grievances against incompetent judges was necessary, and that disciplinary commissions had worked well in many states. Opponents argued that impeachment is the only permissible constitutional route, that more elaborate disciplinary machinery would threaten the autonomy of federal judges, and that instances of incompetence among federal judges were too rare to warrant creation of so risky a new weapon. In October 1979, the Senate adopted a proposal to establish federal disciplinary machinery. S.1873, 96th Cong., 1st Sess. However, the Senate, moved by constitutional concerns pertaining to the impeachment clause and to judicial autonomy, refused to include a removal sanction in the legislation; the most severe sanction adopted by Congress was to prevent a judge from sitting in cases. See Judicial Conduct and Disability Act of 1980, 94 Stat. 2035. (See also the materials on separation of powers, chap. 6 below.)

3. See Turner, "The Impeachment of John Pickering," 54 Am.Hist.Rev. 485 (1949).

judges would be next. But the Senate vote did not produce the constitutional majority necessary to convict Chase. The impeachment weapon was deflated— it was a "farce," "not even a scare-crow," as Jefferson reluctantly concluded. The Jefferson-Marshall dispute continued, but the Court had survived the most critical stage.[4]

2. *Were there alternative grounds of decision?* Most contemporary commentary on the Marbury decision ignored the passages on the authority of the courts to consider the constitutionality of congressional acts. Instead, Jeffersonians criticized the Court's assertion of the right to examine some executive acts. Was Marshall's opinion a reflection of a "masterful sense of strategy," as is often alleged? Was it a shrewd scheme in which the denial of mandamus avoided an immediate confrontation with the executive and provided a shield for the Court's criticism of Jefferson's behavior—and for its assertion and exercise of judicial review over statutes? See, e.g., McCloskey, The American Supreme Court (1960), 40: "The decision is a masterwork of indirection, a brilliant example of Marshall's capacity to sidestep danger while seeming to court it, to advance in one direction while his opponents are looking in another."

Some critics of Marbury insist that, given Marshall's conclusion, the Court had no business saying any more than that it lacked jurisdiction. Were the opening parts of the opinion, on remedies against executive illegality, unnecessary or inappropriate? Jefferson insisted until the end of his life that most of the opinion was "merely an *obiter* dissertation of the Chief Justice."[5] Compare the materials on avoidance of constitutional questions, chap. 15, p. 1539, below. Other critics have insisted that Marshall could and should have made those important final pages on judicial review unnecessary by resolving the preliminary issues differently. For example, more than the signing and sealing might have been held necessary to complete the appointment, or greater presidential authority regarding appointees might have been recognized. See the materials on the presidential removal power, p. 378, below. And a position that mandamus was not available against Cabinet officials was possible. Note the further developments in Kendall v. United States (1838; p. 384, below).

Moreover, the Court's interpretations of Sec. 13 and Art. III have been attacked. Marshall's underlying conception of mutually exclusive categories of original and appellate jurisdiction has not prevailed. Congress still may not add to the Court's original jurisdiction, and so the specific holding of Marbury still stands. But Congress may grant lower courts jurisdiction over cases within the constitutional description of Supreme Court original jurisdiction—and cases of that description may then come to the Supreme Court on review. For example, Sec. 13 itself recognized concurrent original jurisdiction in the lower courts, and several Supreme Court Justices on circuit had sustained lower court jurisdiction in a foreign consul case as early as 1793, United States v. Ravara, 2 Dall. 297. Years later, the Supreme Court agreed. Börs v. Preston, 111 U.S. 252 (1884). And Marshall himself, in a rare admission of error, called some of his statements about Art. III in Marbury unduly broad when he rejected Virginia's arguments against the Supreme Court's exercise of appellate jurisdiction in a case involving a state, in Cohens v. Virginia, 6 Wheat. 264 (1821), p. 37, below.[6]

---

4. See generally 1 Warren, The Supreme Court in United States History (rev. ed. 1926); III Beveridge, The Life of John Marshall (1919); Baker, John Marshall—A Life in Law (1974); and Ellis, The Jeffersonian Crisis: Courts and Politics in the Young Republic (1971).

5. Jefferson to Justice William Johnson, June 12, 1823, 1 S.Car.His. & Gen.Mag. 1, 9–10 (1900).

6. See generally Powell, Vagaries and Varieties in Constitutional Interpretation (1956), and Van Alstyne, "A Critical Guide to Marbury v. Madison," 1969 Duke L.J. 1.

A few years after Marbury, the Marshall Court also exercised the power to hold a state statute unconstitutional. In Fletcher v. Peck, 6 Cranch (1810), a case from a lower federal court, a statute of Georgia was held to be in violation of

THE LEGITIMACY OF JUDICIAL REVIEW

Introduction. Was the judicial review authority asserted in Marbury v. Madison a usurpation? That question has long sparked controversy. See, e.g., the extensive attack on judicial review in Boudin, Government by Judiciary (1932). And the debate lives. See, e.g., the elaborate defense of legitimacy in Berger, Congress v. The Supreme Court (1969). The attackers say that Marshall's opinion is question-begging and weak; that the Constitution does not explicitly authorize judicial review; that the Framers did not clearly intend to grant that extraordinary power; and that the pre-Convention theories and practices were not sufficiently clear and widespread to provide legitimation. The materials that follow reflect that ongoing debate. After a brief review of the historical roots of the authority and of the Convention debates, there are longer excerpts from two significant early statements bearing on Marshall's reasoning: the most important anticipation of that reasoning, Hamilton's No. 78 of The Federalist; and the most important judicial attack on Marbury, the Gibson dissent in a Pennsylvania case, Eakin v. Raub. Professor Herbert Wechsler's debate with Judge Learned Hand illustrates the continuing controversy regarding the constitutional justification for Marbury—a controversy that bears immediately on contemporary evaluations and exercises of the Court's power.

1. *Historical antecedents.* Though Marshall's opinion in Marbury talked about general principles and constitutional text, not historical data, efforts to justify judicial review have often provoked explorations of historical roots. Some of the searches have followed rather remote and tangential byways. For example, there has been frequent mention of Lord Coke's famous statement in Dr. Bonham's Case, at 8 Rep. 118a (C.P. 1610), that "the common law will controul acts of Parliament, [and] adjudge them to be utterly void" when the acts are "against common right and reason." But that was hardly descriptive of British practice in the seventeenth century; by the eighteenth, it was not even respectable dictum. More in point was the appellate jurisdiction of the Privy Council over colonial courts; but invalidation of legislation through that route was rare and unpopular. The practice of state courts in the years immediately following independence holds the greatest promise as a source of relevant information. But here, too, the examples are few and controversial; and there is doubt that many people at the Convention or in the early national period knew about the scattered actual or alleged examples of judicial invalidation of state legislation such as Holmes v. Walton, a New Jersey case of 1780.[1]

The spread of general ideas conducive to the acceptance of judicial review was in any event probably more important than the existence of specific precedents.[2] A pervasive theme, and one reflected in Marshall's reasoning, was

the contract clause (see chap. 8, sec. 2, below). Authority to review state court decisions was sustained in Martin v. Hunter's Lessee, p. 29 below. After Marbury, the Court did not hold another major federal law unconstitutional until the controversial and ill-fated decision in Dred Scott v. Sandford, 19 How. 393 (1857).

1. See also Berger, Congress v. The Supreme Court (1969), which finds support for judicial review in these precedents even while recognizing their spottiness: Berger insists that the argument does not "hinge upon whether there existed an established *practice* of judicial review, but rather on the Founders' *belief*" that precedents and statements like Coke's supported court enforcement of constitutional limits.

For an extensive selection of articles examining the antecedents of judicial review, see vol. 1 of Selected Essays on Constitutional Law (1938). Compare also the discussion of the antecedents in Goebel, Antecedents and Beginnings to 1801 (1 History of the Supreme Court of the United States) (1971), with Nelson, "Changing Conceptions of Judicial Review: The Evolution of Constitutional Theory in the States, 1790–1860," 120 U.Pa.L.Rev. 1166 (1972). On Goebel's conclusion that the doctrine of judicial review was "preached [during the 1780s] apparently without protest," Nelson comments that "Goebel somewhat overstates his case."

2. See generally Bailyn, The Ideological Origins of the American Revolution (1967), and

the development of written constitutions, with the assurance of limited government as a major purpose. Constitutionalism was hardly an American invention,
but Americans had an unusually extensive experience with basic documents of
government, from royal charters to state constitutions and the Articles of
Confederation. Yet the constitutional historians who justify judicial review as a
natural outgrowth of constitutionalism make an argument that is incomplete. It
is possible to have a constitution without having judicial review. There is
accordingly a large question-begging element in deriving judicial enforceability
simply from the existence of written constitutions: to say that a government
cannot exceed its constitutional powers does not demonstrate *who* is to decide
whether there is conflict with the constitution. Viewing a constitution as a
species of "law," then, becomes a vital link between constitutionalism and
judicial competence to decide constitutional issues. That link, hardly a prominent feature in the political theory of the Revolutionary era, is central in the
Marbury opinion.

As this background of ideas and practices indicates, Marshall's assertion of
judicial review authority in Marbury was no sudden innovation or single-handed
achievement. But the pre-Convention heritage hardly made the 1803 result
inevitable. Nor does that heritage clearly tell us what view of judicial authority
in constitutional interpretation was central to Marshall when he wrote Marbury.
Did he truly consider the Constitution-interpreting function of courts merely
incidental to their ordinary role? Or did he claim a *special* Constitution-enforcing
responsibility for the courts—a responsibility that would make courts the
primary enforcers of limits on government, a responsibility that would make
constitutional interpretation the primary business of the Supreme Court? Put
another way: Was the Marbury opinion merely concerned with establishing
judicial *competence* to interpret the Constitution (because courts were already in
the business of deciding legal questions, because the Constitution was a species
of law, and because Articles III and VI confirmed that the Constitution was a
variety of law that might come before the courts)? Or was Marshall chiefly
concerned with carving out for courts a role as *special*—supreme, perhaps even
exclusive—guardians of constitutional norms? The Marbury opinion does not
yield an entirely clear answer to these questions. Marbury can be read as
emphasizing a narrow, incidental role of courts in constitutional cases; but there
are also passages suggesting a broader, central role for courts. As later
materials in this book demonstrate, the debate about the proper reading of
Marbury continues to this day. And as those materials also indicate, the answers
to the questions raised in this paragraph may govern attitudes about the proper
timing, scope, and content of constitutional decisions.

2. *The Constitutional Convention.* The Constitution does not explicitly grant
the judicial review power asserted in Marbury. That silence has made the
legitimacy debate possible. Did the Framers intend to grant the power? Some
efforts to demonstrate an original understanding supporting judicial review have
relied heavily on Framers' statements not made in Philadelphia in 1787. See
Beard, The Supreme Court and the Constitution (1912). But the most
persuasive data regarding the Framers' intent are of course the Convention

Wood, The Creation of the American Republic,
1776–1787 (1969). See also Vile, Constitutionalism and the Separation of Powers (1967), Katz,
"The Origins of American Constitutional
Thought," in 3 Perspectives in American History
474 (Bailyn & Fleming, eds., 1969), and Grey,
"Origins of the Unwritten Constitution: Fundamental Law in American Revolutionary
Thought," 30 Stan.L.Rev. 843 (1978).

The influential book by Wood finds an especially hospitable climate for the development of

judicial review in the evolving theories of the
1780s, particularly the replacement of traditional
notions of legislative sovereignty by emphasis on
popular sovereignty. Note Hamilton's argument
in No. 78 of the Federalist, below, that courts
"were designed to be an intermediate body between the people and the legislature"—and the
echoes of that theme in the Marbury opinion.

debates themselves. See Farrand, The Records of the Federal Convention of 1787 (1911).

The Convention context in which the most important statements regarding judicial power were made was the discussion of the Council of Revision proposal—a proposal that Justices join with the President in the veto process. That provision was rejected, partly on grounds supporting the legitimacy of judicial review. According to Madison's Notes, Luther Martin, for example, thought "the association of the Judges with the Executive" a "dangerous innovation": "A knowledge of mankind, and of Legislative Affairs cannot be presumed to belong in a higher degree to the Judges than to the Legislature. And as to the Constitutionality of laws, that point will come before the Judges in their proper official character. In this character they have a negative on the laws. Join them with the Executive in the Revision and they will have a double negative. It is necessary that the Supreme Judiciary should have the confidence of the people. This will soon be lost, if they are employed in the task of remonstrating agst. popular measures of the Legislature." [3] An incisive brief survey of the debates concludes: "The grant of judicial power was to include the power, where necessary in the decision of cases, to disregard state or federal statutes found to be unconstitutional. Despite the curiously persisting myth of usurpation, the Convention's understanding on this point emerges from its records with singular clarity." [4] Compare the survey of the historical data on legitimacy in Leonard W. Levy's excellent introduction to a paperback volume of selected essays edited by him, Judicial Review and the Supreme Court (1967).[5]

3. *The Federalist Papers.* Support for judicial review far more explicit than anything found in the Convention debates appears in The Federalist. Hamilton, Jay and Madison wrote these newspaper essays in defense and explanation of the proposed Constitution as campaign documents in the ratification battle in New York. They have become the classic commentaries on the Constitution. The papers most directly concerned with the judiciary were five written by Alexander Hamilton, Nos. 78 through 82 of The Federalist. No. 82, for example, supports Supreme Court review of state court decisions. And the most famous, No. 78, contains some striking parallels to—as well as some provocative variations on—the Marbury v. Madison theme.

Hamilton, Federalist No. 78

[Whoever] attentively considers the different departments of power must perceive, that in a government in which they are separated from each other, the judiciary, from the nature of its functions, will always be the least dangerous to the political rights of the constitution; because it will be least in a capacity to annoy or injure them. The executive not only dispenses the honors, but holds the sword of the community. The legislature not only commands the purse, but prescribes the rules by which the duties and rights of every citizen are to be

---

3. Note also Elbridge Gerry's argument that judges should not sit on the Council of Revision because "they will have a sufficient check agst. encroachments on their own department by their exposition of the laws, which involved a power of deciding on their Constitutionality."

4. Bator, Mishkin, Shapiro & Wechsler, Hart & Wechsler's The Federal Courts and the Federal System (2d ed. 1973), 9. [This volume is cited hereinafter as Hart & Wechsler, Federal Courts (2d ed. 1973).]

For an argument that courts were only to invalidate congressional acts interfering with judicial operations—and an attack on the accuracy

of Madison's Notes—see Crosskey, Politics and the Constitution in the History of the United States (1953); for a criticism of Crosskey's "self-defense" theory, see Berger, Congress v. The Supreme Court (1969), 154–65.

5. Levy quotes Edward S. Corwin's testimony on the 1937 Court-Packing Plan: "[I]n blunt language he declared, 'The people who say the framers intended [judicial review] are talking nonsense'—to which he hastily added, 'and the people who say they did not intend it are talking nonsense.'" Levy adds: "A close textual and contextual examination of the evidence will not result in an improvement on these propositions."

regulated. The judiciary on the contrary has no influence over either the sword or the purse, no direction either of the strength or of the wealth of the society, and can take no active resolution whatever. It may truly be said to have neither Force nor Will, but merely judgment; and must ultimately depend upon the aid of the executive arm even for the efficacy of its judgments.

This simple view of the matter suggests several important consequences. It proves incontestibly that the judiciary is beyond comparison the weakest of the three departments of power; that it can never attack with success either of the other two; and that all possible care is requisite to enable it to defend itself against their attacks. [The] complete independence of the courts of justice is peculiarly essential in a limited constitution. By a limited constitution I understand one which contains certain specified exceptions to the legislative authority; such for instance as that it shall pass no bills of attainder, no ex post facto laws, and the like. Limitations of this kind can be preserved in practice no other way than through the medium of the courts of justice; whose duty it must be to declare all acts contrary to the manifest tenor of the constitution [void].

Some perplexity respecting the right of the courts to pronounce legislative acts void, because contrary to the constitution, has arisen from an imagination that the doctrine would imply a superiority of the judiciary to the legislative power. It is urged that the authority which can declare the acts of another void, must necessarily be superior to the one whose acts may be declared void. As this doctrine is of great importance in all the American constitutions, a brief discussion of the grounds on which it rests cannot be unacceptable.

There is no position which depends on clearer principles, than that every act of a delegated authority, contrary to the tenor of the commission under which it is exercised, is void. No legislative act therefore contrary to the constitution can be valid. To deny this would be to affirm that the deputy is greater than his principal; that the servant is above his master; that the representatives of the people are superior to the people themselves; that men acting by virtue of powers may do not only what their powers do not authorise, but what they forbid.

If it be said that the legislative body are themselves the constitutional judges of their own powers, and that the construction they put upon them is conclusive upon the other departments, it may be answered, that this cannot be the natural presumption, where it is not to be collected from any particular provisions in the constitution. It is not otherwise to be supposed that the constitution could intend to enable the representatives of the people to substitute their *will* to that of their constituents. It is far more rational to suppose that the courts were designed to be an intermediate body between the people and the legislature, in order, among other things, to keep the latter within the limits assigned to their authority. The interpretation of the laws is the proper and peculiar province of the courts. A constitution is in fact, and must be, regarded by the judges as a fundamental law. It therefore belongs to them to ascertain its meaning as well as the meaning of any particular act proceeding from the legislative body. If there should happen to be an irreconcilable variance between the two, that which has the superior obligation and validity ought of course to be preferred; or in other words, the constitution ought to be preferred to the statute, the intention of the people to the intention of their agents.

Nor does this conclusion by any means suppose a superiority of the judicial to the legislative power. It only supposes that the power of the people is superior to both; and that where the will of the legislature declared in its statutes, stands in opposition to that of the people declared in the constitution, the judges ought to be governed by the latter, rather than the former. They ought to regulate their decisions by the fundamental laws, rather than by those which are not fundamental. [The] independence of the judges [is] requisite to guard the constitution and the rights of individuals from the effects of those ill humours which the arts of designing men, or the influence of particular conjunctures, sometimes disseminate among the people themselves, and which, though they speedily give place to better information and more deliberate reflection, have a tendency in the meantime to occasion dangerous innovations in the government, and serious oppressions of the minor party in the [community].

4. *Justice Gibson's dissent in Eakin v. Raub, 12 S. & R. 330 (Pa.1825).* The following excerpts are from a dissent denying that the Pennsylvania Supreme Court was authorized to consider the constitutionality of acts of the state legislature. The excerpts are printed here because Gibson's opinion is a rare judicial disagreement with Marshall's reasoning in Marbury. Does Gibson succeed in casting real doubt upon Marshall's basic premises? [6]

Gibson in Eakin v. Raub

I am aware, that a right to declare all unconstitutional acts void, without distinction as to either [state or federal] constitution, is generally held as a professional dogma; but I apprehend, rather as a matter of faith than of reason. [I]t is not a little remarkable, that although the right in question has all along been claimed by the judiciary, no judge has ventured to discuss it, except Chief Justice Marshall; [and] if the argument of a jurist so distinguished for the strength of his ratiocinative powers be found inconclusive, it may fairly be set down to the weakness of the position which he attempts to [defend].

[The] constitution is said to be a law of superior obligation; and consequently, that if it were to come into collision with an act of the legislature, the latter would have to give way; this is conceded. But it is a fallacy, to suppose, that they can come into collision *before the judiciary.* [The] constitution and the *right* of the legislature to pass the act, may be in collision; but is that a legitimate subject for judicial determination? If it be, the judiciary must be a peculiar organ, to revise the proceedings of the legislature, and to correct its mistakes; and in what part of the constitution are we to look for this proud preeminence? [I]t is by no means clear, that to declare a law void, which has been enacted according to the forms prescribed in the constitution, is not a usurpation of legislative power. It is an act of sovereignty; and sovereignty and legislative power are said by Sir William *Blackstone* to be convertible terms. It is the business of the judiciary, to interpret the laws, not scan the authority of the lawgiver; and without the latter, it cannot take cognizance of a collision between a law and the constitution. So that, to affirm that the judiciary has a right to judge of the existence of such collision, is to take for granted the very thing to be proved.

[But] it has been said to be emphatically the business of the judiciary, to ascertain and pronounce what the law is; and that this necessarily involves a consideration of the constitution. It does so: but how far? If the judiciary will inquire into anything beside the form of enactment, where shall it stop? There must be some point of limitation to such an inquiry; for no one will pretend, that a judge would be justifiable in calling for the election returns, or scrutinizing the qualifications of those who composed the legislature. [I]t will not be pretended, that the legislature has not, at least, an equal right with the judiciary to put a construction on the constitution; nor that either of them is infallible;

---

6. Five years after writing this dissent, Justice Gibson was a strong contender for a seat on the United States Supreme Court, but President Andrew Jackson ultimately named Gibson's fellow-Pennsylvanian, Henry Baldwin. Twenty years after Eakin v. Raub, when Gibson had become Pennsylvania's Chief Justice, he announced that he had changed his mind, both because an intervening state constitutional convention had silently "sanctioned the pretensions of the courts" and because of his "experience of the necessity of the case." Norris v. Clymer, 2 Pa. 277 (1845).

nor that either ought to be required to surrender its judgment to the other. Suppose, then, they differ in opinion as to the constitutionality of a particular law; if the organ whose business it first is to decide on the subject, is not to have its judgment treated with respect, what shall prevent it from securing the preponderance of its opinion by the strong arm of power? [T]he soundness of any construction which would bring one organ of the government into collision with another, is to be more than suspected; for where collision occurs, it is evident, the machine is working in a way the framers of it did not intend.

[But] the judges are sworn to support the constitution, and are they not bound by it as the law of the land? [The] oath to support the constitution is not peculiar to the judges, but is taken indiscriminately by every officer of the government, and is designed rather as a test of the political principles of the man, than to bind the officer in the discharge of his duty: otherwise, it were difficult to determine, what operation it is to have in the case of a recorder of deeds, for instance, who, in the execution of his office, has nothing to do with the constitution. But granting it to relate to the official conduct of the judge, as well as every other officer, and not to his political principles, still, it must be understood in reference to supporting the constitution, *only as far as that may be involved in his official duty;* and consequently, if his official duty does not comprehend an inquiry into the authority of the legislature, neither does his oath. [But] do not the judges do a *positive* act in violation of the constitution, when they give effect to an unconstitutional law? Not if the law has been passed according to the forms established in the constitution. The fallacy of the question is, in supposing that the judiciary adopts the acts of the legislature as its own; whereas, the enactment of a law and the interpretation of it are not concurrent acts, and as the judiciary is not required to concur in the enactment, neither is it in the breach of the constitution which may be the consequence of the enactment; the fault is imputable to the legislature, and on it the responsibility exclusively rests.[7]

5. *The Hand-Wechsler debate.* For an illuminating revival of the legitimacy debate, and sharp disagreement about the basis for judicial review in the constitutional text, see Hand, The Bill of Rights (1958), 1–30, and Wechsler, "Toward Neutral Principles of Constitutional Law," in Principles, Politics, and Fundamental Law (1961), 4–10. Judge Learned Hand insisted that there was "nothing in the United States Constitution that gave courts any authority to review the decisions of Congress." He claimed that "it was a plausible—indeed to my mind an unanswerable—argument" that such an authority was inconsistent with separation of powers and asserted that "when the Constitution emerged from the Convention in September 1787, the structure of the proposed government, if one looked to the text, gave no ground for inferring that the decisions of the Supreme Court [were] to be authoritative upon the Executive and the Legislature." Judge Hand found justification for the Supreme Court's assumption of judicial review authority solely in the practical need "to prevent the defeat of the venture at hand"—to keep the government from foundering. Professor Wechsler, relying on the Art. VI Supremacy Clause and on Art. III, replied: "I believe the power of the courts is grounded in the language of the Constitution and is not a mere interpolation."

The Hand-Wechsler debate of the mid-20th century illustrates how the legitimacy issue may influence views regarding the contemporary exercise of the power. Thus, Judge Hand concluded that "since this power is not a logical deduction from the structure of the Constitution but only a practical condition

---

7. Justice Gibson was careful to limit his attack on the Marbury rationale to the issue of judicial review of the acts of a coordinate legislature. Near the end of his opinion, he emphasized that state courts have not only the power but also the duty to invalidate state laws when they conflict with "supreme" federal obligations. See the materials on Supreme Court review of state court judgments, sec. 2 below.

upon its successful operation, it need not be exercised whenever a court sees, or thinks that it sees, an invasion of the Constitution. It is always a preliminary question how importunately the occasion demands an answer." (Compare the materials on discretionary abstention, chap. 15, p. 1519, below.) Professor Wechsler objected to so broad a discretion to decline to adjudicate a constitutional objection in a case properly before a court: "For me, as for anyone who finds the judicial power anchored in the Constitution, there is no such escape from the judicial obligation; the duty cannot be attenuated in this way." (The "duty," he added, was "not that of policing or advising legislatures or executives," but rather simply "to decide the litigated case and to decide it in accordance with the law.")

The Hand-Wechsler debate illustrates, too, that evaluations of the content as well as the timing of contemporary court decisions may evolve from discussions beginning with concern over legitimacy. Since Wechsler's defense of legitimacy is so closely tied to implications of the judicial function, he insisted that Constitution-interpreting courts must above all act like courts. Accordingly, he warned against "ad hoc evaluation" as "the deepest problem of our constitutionalism" and insisted that decisions must rest on "neutral principles": "the main constituent of the judicial process is precisely that it must be genuinely principled, resting with respect to every step that is involved in reaching judgment on analysis and reasons quite transcending the immediate result that is achieved." [8] To Judge Hand, judicial review of legislative choices inevitably turned courts into "a third, legislative, chamber," adding: "For myself it would be most irksome to be ruled by a bevy of Platonic Guardians, even if I knew how to choose them, which I assuredly do not."

6. *Judicial review and democracy.* As the Hand-Wechsler debate illustrates, concern with the bases of judicial review in constitutional history and text is often closely connected with explorations of the consistency between judicial review and democratic government. Views on that issue, too, may profoundly affect exercises and evaluations of the judicial power, as is amply revealed in many of the opinions in this volume. Anxiety about the undemocratic aspects of judicial review, for example, tends to support the judicial self-restraint stance long associated with Justice Frankfurter—the reluctance to set aside the judgments of other organs of government.

Leonard W. Levy's paperback, Judicial Review and the Supreme Court (1967), includes a critical analysis of the major contending arguments regarding the propriety of judicial invalidation of legislative decisions. Classic statements viewing judicial review as undemocratic and as undercutting popular responsibility are Thayer, "The Origin and Scope of the American Doctrine of Constitutional Law," 7 Harv.L.Rev. 129 (1893), and Commager, Majority Rule and Minority Rights (1943). Important defenses of judicial intervention are Rostow, "The Democratic Character of Judicial Review," 66 Harv.L.Rev. 193 (1952), and C.L. Black, Jr., The People and the Court: Judicial Review in a Democracy (1960). For an especially provocative and sophisticated effort to justify judicial intervention while recognizing that it is countermajoritarian, see Bickel, The Least Dangerous Branch (1962). As noted, the issues in this debate are recurrent themes in judicial opinions and permeate any constitutional law course. The problems are best explored in the specific contexts of the cases below. See, e.g., the issues of judicial intervention and democratic processes raised by Justice Stone's Carolene Products footnote (p. 473 below) and by the opinions in the modern substantive due process cases (chap. 8, sec. 3, below).

8. See also Greenawalt, "The Enduring Significance of Neutral Principles," 78 Colum.L. Rev. 982 (1978).

Closely related to this debate about the propriety and scope of judicial intervention are several other themes that recur throughout this book. For example, views about the legitimacy of judicial review may influence attitudes about the appropriate sources of constitutional interpretation. To what extent must the Court confine itself to the text and history of the relevant constitutional provision? To what extent may it rely on inferences from the structures and relationships established by the basic document? See C. L. Black, Jr., Structure and Relationship in Constitutional Law (1969). To what extent is the Court authorized to implement values derived from sources outside the written document—e.g., the society's political and moral values, or the Justices' personal ones? [9] See generally, Brest, Processes of Constitutional Decisionmaking (1975), and note especially chap. 8 below. Moreover, views about the legitimacy of judicial review and its consistency with democracy may influence positions about the appropriate deference the Court owes to legislative judgments. When should a legislative judgment be accorded a strong "presumption of constitutionality" and be sustained so long as it is merely "reasonable"? When may the Court properly apply stricter scrutiny and demand that more than "mere rationality" be shown in support of a legislative judgment? These themes surface in a variety of contexts, in every chapter of Parts II and III of this book. Note, e.g., the intense controversies about appropriate standards of review in the varying interpretations of the frequently litigated due process and equal protection clauses of the 14th Amendment. And see especially the recent disputes about the proper occasions for "minimal scrutiny" and "strict scrutiny"—or some intermediate standard—in applying the equal protection clause, chap. 9 below.

9. The last in this series of questions has sparked an especially vigorous scholarly debate in recent years. Typically, that debate is now couched as a battle between "interpretivism" and "noninterpretivism"—between the view that judges can only enforce norms stated or clearly implicit in the Constitution and the position that courts can legitimately go beyond those sources. Examples of "noninterpretivist" positions include the claim that the Court has the obligation to articulate the changing content of the nation's fundamental values and that it is charged with evolving and applying the society's fundamental principles. For contemporary arguments that noninterpretive review is legitimate, see especially the work of Professors Michael J. Perry and Thomas C. Grey. For Perry, see The Constitution, the Courts, and Human Rights (1982); for Grey, see "Do We Have An Unwritten Constitution?" 27 Stan.L.Rev. 703 (1975). Perry advocates noninterpretive review as "a crucial agency" of "political-moral maturation" and as an "agency of moral evaluation and growth." Grey's open-ended version of judicial review harks back to notions of natural rights. Grey characterizes Marshall's Marbury opinion and Hamilton's Federalist No. 78 as "classic expositions" of the "interpretive mode of judicial review." Modern reiterations of the interpretive mode include Linde, "Judges, Critics and the Realist Tradition," 82 Yale L.J. 227 (1972), and Monaghan, "Of 'Liberty' and 'Property,'" 62 Corn.L.J. 405 (1977). Compare Brest, "The Misconceived Quest For The Original Understanding," 60 B.U.L.Rev. 204 (1980), and generally Brest & Levinson, Processes of Constitutional Decisionmaking (2d Ed. 1983).

The contending positions involved in the "interpretivist"-"noninterpretivist" debate surface frequently in opinions and commentaries throughout this book. It is wise to reserve judgment for now on the relative merits of the contending positions. But it may be appropriate to warn that "interpretivism" and "noninterpretivism" are not sharply distinctive positions, that behind each label lies a range of approaches rather than a single one, and that a particular view may not be easily categorizable. For example, John Hart Ely's position is sometimes viewed as "noninterpretivist" (see his "Constitutional Interpretivism: Its Allure and Impossibility," 58 Ind.L.J. 399 (1978)), but Ely's approach is by no means as open-ended as Perry's or Grey's. Instead, Ely limits himself to implications drawn from the constitutional system of representative government and rejects the most open-ended, "fundamental values" varieties of judicial review. Thus, his view can just as readily be called a variety of "interpretivism." Indeed, in his more recent efforts at self-characterization, Ely suggests that his position is either one of "broad interpretivism" or "a position that does not fall entirely into either camp." What is clear is that he stands somewhere in between "clause-bound interpretivism" and "a value-laden form of noninterpretivism." See, e.g., Ely, "Foreword: On Discovering Fundamental Values," 92 Harv. L.Rev. 5 (1978), and Ely's important 1980 book, Democracy and Distrust: A Theory of Judicial Review, at 88–89. For further discussions of the "interpretivist"-"noninterpretivist" debate, see esp. chap. 8, sec. 3, below.

7. *Judicial review abroad.* Since World War II, while Americans have continued to agonize over the justifiability of judicial review, more and more other nations have looked to courts to enforce constitutional norms. Judicial review has become especially important in Germany and Italy. Most judicial review mechanisms in civil law countries differ from the American in form: for example, creation of special Constitutional Courts has been common. But the American experience has been an important "persuasive authority" as to basic theory; and in practice there are signs of "a converging trend" in the exercise of judicial review in the American and civil law systems, as a sophisticated commentator suggests.[10]

THE AUTHORITATIVENESS OF THE COURT'S CONSTITUTIONAL INTERPRETATIONS

Introduction. To what extent are other departments of government obligated to follow judicial interpretations of the Constitution? Must, or may, the President and Congress give independent consideration to questions of constitutionality in the exercise of their official functions? Are the courts the ultimate, even the exclusive, interpreters of the Constitution, or do other organs of government share in that authority? Questions such as these raise the issue of the true scope of the power of judicial review. Is judicial review simply a byproduct of a court's duty to decide cases within its jurisdiction in accordance with law, including the Constitution; or do courts have special competence to interpret law, including the Constitution, so that they are ultimate, supreme interpreters of the Constitution? Even Marshall's reasoning in Marbury v. Madison, though leaning to the former, more modest view, is not free from ambiguity. And later developments—not only popular expectations but also Court assertions such as those in the 1958 decision in Cooper v. Aaron, note 6 below—suggest a broader binding effect for judicial interpretations.

To promote examination of these questions, notes 1 to 4 below present a series of presidential statements claiming varying degrees of autonomy vis-à-vis judicial interpretations, in a variety of contexts. Consider, with regard to each statement, whether anything in the President's position is inconsistent with Marshall's justification for judicial review in Marbury. Consider, too, whether the presidential positions are inconsistent with other possible justifications for judicial review. And consider especially whether any of the presidential statements is inconsistent with the modern Court's claims in Cooper v. Aaron (note 6 below)—claims which include the assertion that a Supreme Court interpretation of the Constitution "is the supreme law of the land." (Note also the additional comments and questions about the presidential assertions, in note 5 below.)

Recall that much of Marshall's argument in Marbury was directed against contentions that courts lacked *competence* or *authority* to consider issues of constitutionality. Can it be argued on the basis of that Marshall argument that a judicial interpretation is the *ultimate, final* one? That it is *binding* on those not parties to the litigation? That the judiciary is the *exclusive* source of constitutional interpretations? Recall Marshall's quite modest, defensive statement that the Constitution is "a rule for the government of *courts* as well as the legislature"

10. Cappelletti, "The Significance of Judicial Review of Legislation in the Contemporary World," in Ius Privatum Gentium (Festschrift for Max Rheinstein, 1969), 147. See also Cappelletti, "The 'Mighty Problem' of Judicial Review and the Contribution of Comparative Analysis," 53 S.Cal.L.Rev. 409 (1980), Symposium, "Constitutional Judicial Review of Legislation . . . ," 56 Temp.L.Q. 287 (1983), Gunther, "The Constitution of Ghana—An American's Impressions and Comparisons," 8 U.Ghana L.J. 2 (1971), and Cappelletti & Cohen, Comparative Constitutional Law: Cases and Materials (1979).

and his conclusion that "*courts,* as well as other departments, are bound by that instrument." Yet Marshall also stated: "It is emphatically the province and duty of the judicial department to say what the law is." Does that sentence support a *special* judicial competence, a *superior* role, in constitutional interpretation? Contrast Hamilton's stronger statement in No. 78 of The Federalist, above: "The interpretation of the laws is the proper and *peculiar* province of the courts." (Emphasis added.)

1. *Thomas Jefferson.* a. *Letter to Abigail Adams, Sept. 11, 1804* (8 The Writings of Thomas Jefferson (Ford ed. 1897), 310):

"You seem to think it devolved on the judges to decide on the validity of the sedition law. But nothing in the Constitution has given them a right to decide for the Executive, more than to the Executive to decide for them. Both magistracies are equally independent in the sphere of action assigned to them. The judges, believing the law constitutional, had a right to pass a sentence of fine and imprisonment; because that power was placed in their hands by the Constitution. But the Executive, believing the law to be unconstitutional, was bound to remit the execution of it; because that power has been confided to him by the Constitution. That instrument meant that its co-ordinate branches should be checks on each other. But the opinion which gives to the judges the right to decide what laws are constitutional, and what not, not only for themselves in their own sphere of action, but for the Legislature & Executive also, in their spheres, would make the judiciary a despotic branch."

b. *Letter to William C. Jarvis, Sept. 28, 1820* (10 The Writings of Thomas Jefferson (Ford ed. 1899), 160):

"You seem [to] consider the judges as the ultimate arbiters of all constitutional questions; a very dangerous doctrine indeed, and one which would place us under the despotism of an oligarchy. [The] constitution has erected no such single tribunal, knowing that to whatever hands confided, with the corruptions of time and party, its members would become despots. It has more wisely made all the departments co-equal and co-sovereign within themselves. If the legislature fails to pass laws for a census, for paying the judges and other officers of government, for establishing a militia, for naturalization as prescribed by the constitution, or if they fail to meet in congress, the judges cannot issue their mandamus to them; if the President fails to supply the place of a judge, to appoint other civil or military officers, to issue requisite commissions, the judges cannot force him. [The] judges certainly have more frequent occasion to act on constitutional questions, because the laws of *meum* and *tuum* and of criminal action, forming the great mass of the system of law, constitute their particular department."

2. *Andrew Jackson—Veto Message (on bill to recharter the Bank of the United States), July 10, 1832* (2 Messages and Papers of the Presidents (Richardson ed. 1896), 576, 581–583):

"It is maintained by the advocates of the bank that its constitutionality in all its features ought to be considered as settled by precedent and by the decision of the Supreme Court. [McCulloch v. Maryland, 4 Wheat. 316 (1819), p. 72 below.] To this conclusion I can not assent. Mere precedent is a dangerous source of authority, and should not be regarded as deciding questions of constitutional power except where the acquiescence of the people and the States can be considered as well settled. [If] the opinion of the Supreme Court covered the whole ground of this act, it ought not to control the coordinate authorities of this Government. The Congress, the Executive, and the Court must each for itself be guided by its own opinion of the Constitution. Each public officer who takes an oath to support the Constitution swears that he will support it as he understands it, and not as it is understood by others. It is as much the duty of the House of Representatives, of the Senate, and of the

President to decide upon the constitutionality of any bill or resolution which may be presented to them for passage or approval as it is of the supreme judges when it may be brought before them for judicial decision. The opinion of the judges has no more authority over Congress than the opinion of Congress has over the judges, and on that point the President is independent of both. The authority of the Supreme Court must not, therefore, be permitted to control the Congress or the Executive when acting in their legislative capacities, but to have only such influence as the force of their reasoning may deserve.

"But in the case relied upon the Supreme Court have not decided that all the features of this corporation are compatible with the Constitution. [Under] the decision of the Supreme Court [it] is the exclusive province of Congress and the President to decide whether the particular features of this act are *necessary* and *proper* in order to enable the bank to perform conveniently and efficiently the public duties assigned to it as a fiscal agent, and therefore constitutional, or *unnecessary* and *improper,* and therefore unconstitutional. Without commenting on the general principle affirmed by the Supreme Court, let us examine the details of this act in accordance with the rule of legislative action which they have laid down. It will be found that many of the powers and privileges conferred on it can not be supposed necessary for the purpose for which it is proposed to be created, and are not, therefore, means necessary to attain the end in view, and consequently not justified by the Constitution."

3. *Abraham Lincoln.* a. *Speeches during the Lincoln-Douglas Senatorial Campaign, July, October 1858.* (2 The Collected Works of Abraham Lincoln (Basler ed. 1953), 494; 3 id. 255):

[July 10, 1858:] "I have expressed heretofore, and I now repeat, my opposition to the Dred Scott Decision [Dred Scott v. Sandford, 19 How. 393 (1857)], but I should be allowed to state the nature of that opposition. [What] is fairly implied by the term Judge Douglas has used, 'resistance to the Decision?' I do not resist it. If I wanted to take Dred Scott from his master, I would be interfering with property. [But] I am doing no such thing as that, but all that I am doing is refusing to obey it as a political rule. If I were in Congress, and a vote should come up on a question whether slavery should be prohibited in a new territory, in spite of that Dred Scott decision, I would vote that it should."

[Oct. 13, 1858:] "We oppose the Dred Scott decision in a certain way. [We] do not propose that when Dred Scott has been decided to be a slave by the court, we, as a mob, will decide him to be free. We do not propose that, when any other one, or one thousand, shall be decided by that court to be slaves, we will in any violent way disturb the rights of property thus settled; but we nevertheless do oppose that decision as a political rule which shall be binding on the voter, to vote for nobody who thinks it wrong, which shall be binding on the members of Congress or the President to favor no measure that does not actually concur with the principles of that decision. [We] propose so resisting it as to have it reversed if we can, and a new judicial rule established upon this subject."

b. *First Inaugural Address, March 4, 1861* (6 Messages and Papers of the Presidents (Richardson ed. 1897), 5, 9–10):

"I do not forget the position assumed by some that constitutional questions are to be decided by the Supreme Court, nor do I deny that such decisions must be binding in any case upon the parties to a suit as to the object of that suit, while they are also entitled to very high respect and consideration in all parallel cases by all other departments of the Government. And while it is obviously possible that such decision may be erroneous in any given case, still the evil effect following it, being limited to that particular case, with the chance that it may be overruled and never become a precedent for other cases, can better be borne than could the evils of a different practice. At the same time, the candid citizen must confess that if the policy of the Government upon vital questions affecting the whole people is to be irrevocably fixed by decisions of the Supreme Court, the instant they are made in ordinary litigation between parties in personal actions, the people will have ceased to be their own rulers, having to that extent practically resigned their Government into the hands of that eminent tribunal."

4. *Franklin D. Roosevelt.* a. *Letter to Congressman Hill, July 6, 1935* (4 The Public Papers and Addresses of Franklin D. Roosevelt (1938), 297–98): [The letter was written after the Supreme Court's 1935 decision in the Schechter case (p. 123 below), the "sick chicken" case construing national regulatory powers narrowly and invalidating an important segment of New Deal emergency legislation, the National Industrial Recovery Act. President Roosevelt nevertheless urged Congress to enact a law establishing an NIRA-like regulatory scheme for the bituminous coal industry. The President's letter explained the need for the law, noted that its constitutionality depended on "whether production conditions directly affect, promote or obstruct interstate commerce," and added the passage which follows.] "Manifestly, no one is in a position to give assurance that the proposed act will withstand constitutional tests. [But] the situation is so urgent and the benefits of the legislation so evident that all doubts should be resolved in favor of the bill, leaving to the courts, in an orderly fashion, the ultimate question of constitutionality. A decision by the Supreme Court relative to this measure would be helpful as indicating, with increasing clarity, the constitutional limits within which this Government must operate. [I] hope your committee will not permit doubts as to constitutionality, however reasonable, to block the suggested legislation." [1]

b. *Proposed speech on the Gold Clause Cases, Feb. 1935* (1 F.D.R.—His Personal Letters, 1928–1945 (Elliott Roosevelt ed. 1950), 459–60): [This was a draft of a speech President Roosevelt planned to deliver in the event the Court decided against the Government on the constitutionality of abrogating "gold clauses" in federal obligations. In fact, the Court decided for the Roosevelt Administration, and the speech was not delivered. See Perry v. United States, 294 U.S. 330 (1935).] "I do not seek to enter into any controversy with the distinguished members of the Supreme Court of the United States who have participated in this [decision]. They have decided these cases in accordance with the letter of the law as they read it. But it is appropriate to quote a sentence from the First Inaugural Address of President Lincoln: [quoting the "At the same time" sentence in note 3b, above].

"[It] is the duty of the Congress and the President to protect the people of the United States to the best of their ability. It is necessary to protect them from the unintended construction of voluntary acts, as well as from intolerable burdens involuntarily imposed. To stand idly by and to permit the decision of the Supreme Court to be carried through to its logical, inescapable conclusion would so imperil the economic and political security of this nation that the legislative and executive officers of the Government must look beyond the narrow letter of contractual obligations, so that they may sustain the substance of the promise originally made in accord with the actual intention of the parties. [I] shall immediately take such steps as may be necessary, by proclamation and by message to [Congress]."

5. *The autonomy of the coordinate branches.* a. *Some comments on the presidential statements.* If constitutional interpretation were a special or exclusive judicial function, most of the quoted presidential statements would be indefensible. Yet

---

1. Congress promptly enacted the legislation urged by the President; but the Court, less than a year later, invalidated the Bituminous Coal Conservation Act of 1935, in the Carter case (p. 126 below). On the Court crisis provoked by invalidations of New Deal laws, see p. 128 below.

are not most of them consistent with the major thrust of Marshall's rationale in Marbury—the rationale that rests judicial review not on any special judicial guardianship of constitutional norms, but simply on the courts' duty to decide cases before them in accordance with the relevant law? Recall Herbert Wechsler's description of judicial duty in his "Neutral Principles" lecture, noted above: under Marbury, the duty is "not that of policing or advising Legislatures or Executives," but rather simply the duty "to decide the litigated case and to decide it in accordance with the law."

The presidential statements suggest, too, that attention to context is essential if uncritical condemnation is to be avoided whenever other branches claim some autonomy in constitutional judgments. In the Jackson bank veto situation (note 2 above), the Supreme Court had indeed spoken. But Jackson emphasized the autonomy of "the Congress or the Executive when acting in their legislative capacities": though bank recharter legislation would be constitutional under McCulloch v. Maryland, Congress or the President could refuse to enact new legislation because of constitutional doubts. Would the broader view of judicial authority in Cooper v. Aaron (note 6b below) deny that a member of Congress may (indeed, must) vote against legislation he or she believes to be unconstitutional, even though the law would be constitutional under the standards of prior Court decisions? Is there any greater difficulty as a matter of constitutional principle with the variety of legislative autonomy President Roosevelt urged upon Congressman Hill (note 4b above)?

Jefferson (note 1a) and Lincoln (note 3) were faced with prior judicial decisions that spoke with special immediacy to the problems that confronted them. Yet Jefferson was defending the exercise of the pardoning power, a power specifically vested in the President with broad discretion; he insisted simply on autonomy in his "own sphere of action." And Lincoln was careful to distinguish between direct interference with the Court decision in Dred Scott's case and acceptance of the constitutional interpretation of that case "as a political rule." All of these positions fell short of direct conflict with a court order; each recognized judicial authority to adjudicate constitutionality with respect to the case before the court and simply insisted on autonomy within the President's own "spheres of action."

Only President Roosevelt's proposed speech on the "gold clause" issue (note 4b above) contemplated direct defiance of a court order, direct contravention of the narrow, classical justification of Marbury. And serious presidential considerations of direct defiance have been very rare indeed. There is a legend that President Jackson, shortly before his veto of the bank recharter bill, said of a Supreme Court decision: "John Marshall has made his decision. Now let him enforce it." The decision was Worcester v. Georgia, 6 Pet. 515 (1832), where the Marshall Court held that Georgia had no legislative authority over Cherokee Nation lands. In fact, Jackson's support for enforcement of the decision was never put to a test: though he was no doubt unhappy about it, the litigation was abandoned before any call for presidential assistance arose. See Burke, "The Cherokee Cases: A Study in Law, Politics, and Morality," 21 Stan.L.Rev. 500 (1969). More recently, while Special Prosecutor Jaworski's effort to gain access to Watergate tapes was pending before the courts, President Nixon and his counsel hinted that the President might not comply with an order to turn over the tapes. Yet on the day in 1974 that the Supreme Court decision against the President was handed down, in United States v. Nixon (p. 388 below), President Nixon announced that he had instructed his counsel "to take whatever measures are necessary to comply with that decision in all respects."

If the Marbury rationale leaves to legislators and the President considerable autonomy even in the face of Supreme Court interpretations quite closely in point, their authority and obligation to consider constitutionality would seem even greater when they are writing on a relatively blank slate. Yet even in those situations, legislators sometimes suggest that problems of constitutionality are solely the courts' business. Is such a stance defensible under Marbury? Under Cooper v. Aaron, which follows? Under the Constitution? [2]

b. *Legitimate disagreement and improper defiance.* Is never-ending, chaotic questioning of Court interpretations inevitable if one takes a narrow view of authoritativeness? Consider the solution advanced in Wechsler, "The Courts and the Constitution," 65 Colum.L.Rev. 1001, 1008 (1965), which draws on aspects of President Lincoln's position quoted in note 3b above. Lincoln spoke of the "chance" that the ruling "may be overruled and never become a precedent for other cases." Wechsler comments: "When that chance has been exploited and has run its course, with reaffirmation rather than reversal of decision, has not the time arrived when its acceptance is demanded, without insisting on repeated litigation? The answer here, it seems to me, must be affirmative, both as the necessary implication of our constitutional tradition and to avoid the greater evils that will otherwise ensue."

Does this position permit too broad a range of challenges to Court rulings, in theory and in practice? And is such criticism acceptable only so long as it is calm and rational? Note Professor Jaffe's observation that intense criticism is especially appropriate as well as likely in the area of constitutional adjudication: "There will be and there should be popular response to the Supreme Court's decision; not just the 'informed' criticism of law professors but the deep-felt, emotion-laden, unsophisticated reaction of the laity. This is so because more than any court in the modern world the Supreme Court 'makes policy,' and is at the same time so little subject to formal democratic control. [Yet] those who urge the Court on to political innovation are outraged when its decisions arouse, as they must, resentment and political attack." Jaffe, "Impromptu Remarks," 76 Harv.L.Rev. 1111 (1963).

6. *Is the Court "the ultimate interpreter of the Constitution"?—Some modern assertions.* a. *Cooper v. Aaron: Are Court interpretations "the supreme law of the land"?* The opinion in COOPER v. AARON, 358 U.S. 1 (1958), provides the major judicial support for a view widely held by the public, that the Court is the ultimate or supreme interpreter of the Constitution. Cooper v. Aaron arose against a background of opposition by Governor Faubus and other Arkansas officials against public school desegregation in Little Rock. The state officials claimed that they were not "bound" by the Supreme Court's basic school desegregation ruling, the 1954 decision in Brown v. Board of Education, 347 U.S. 483 (p. 635 below). Arkansas was not a party in the Brown case; but a later lower court order directed desegregation by the Little Rock school board, and the state officials tried to prevent the school board from complying with that desegregation decree.[3] In that context, the Supreme Court could have limited

2. See, e.g., some of the comments during the hearings on the Civil Rights Act of 1964, noted at p. 159 below. And see generally Morgan, Congress and the Constitution (1966), and Brest, "The Conscientious Legislator's Guide to Constitutional Interpretation," 27 Stan.L.Rev. 585 (1975).

3. To recall the context of Cooper v. Aaron more precisely: The Little Rock school board, seeking to desegregate the public schools pursuant to a plan approved by the lower federal court, was blocked in its efforts by Governor Faubus' action in calling out the National Guard in September 1957. The Governor placed Little Rock's Central High School "off limits" to black students. After a trial court injunction against the Governor, the troops were withdrawn. Thereafter, black students were able to attend

school under the protection of federally-commanded troops. In February 1958, the school board sought a long postponement of the desegregation program. The U.S. District Court granted that relief, after noting the "chaos, bedlam and turmoil" and finding the situation "intolerable." The Court of Appeals reversed; and that decision was affirmed by the Supreme Court. The Supreme Court found that the school officials had acted in "entire good faith" but concluded that "the actions of the other state agencies responsible for those conditions compel us to reject the Board's legal position. [The] constitutional rights of respondents are not to be sacrificed or yielded to the violence and disorder which have followed upon the actions of the Governor and Legislature."

itself to its reminder that state officials lacked "power to nullify a federal court order." But the Court's response—signed by each of the nine Justices—went considerably beyond: instead of confining itself to implementing the Little Rock lower federal court decree, it spoke broadly about the impact of the 1954 ruling in Brown on the Arkansas officials.[4] In that dictum in Cooper, the Justices asserted:

"[W]e should answer the premise of the actions of the Governor and Legislature that they are not bound by our holding in the Brown case. It is necessary only to recall some basic constitutional propositions which are settled doctrine. Article VI of the Constitution makes the Constitution the 'supreme Law of the Land.' In 1803, Chief Justice Marshall, speaking for a unanimous Court, referring to the Constitution as 'the fundamental and paramount law of the nation,' declared in the notable case of Marbury v. Madison, that 'It is emphatically the province and duty of the judicial department to say what the law is.' This decision declared the basic principle that the federal judiciary is supreme in the exposition of the law of the Constitution, and that principle has ever since been respected by this Court and the Country as a permanent and indispensable feature of our constitutional system. It follows that the interpretation of the Fourteenth Amendment enunciated by this Court in the Brown case is the supreme law of the land, and Art. VI of the Constitution makes it of binding effect on the States 'any Thing in the Constitution or Laws of any State to the Contrary notwithstanding.' Every state legislator and executive and judicial officer is solemnly committed by oath taken pursuant to Art. VI, ¶ 3, 'to support this Constitution.'"

Was that Court view of its own powers truly a statement of "settled doctrine"? Was it merely a restatement of Marbury v. Madison—or was it a substantial expansion of the authority asserted by Chief Justice Marshall? Assuming that most of the presidential views noted above are consistent with Marbury, can they also be reconciled with Cooper v. Aaron?[5]

b. *Additional Court "restatements" of Marbury.* Since Cooper v. Aaron, the Court has found several other occasions to assert broad views of its judicial review authority. For example, in holding legislative reapportionment disputes justiciable in Baker v. Carr in 1962 (p. 1617 below), Justice Brennan's majority opinion referred in passing to the "responsibility of this Court as ultimate interpreter of the Constitution." And Chief Justice Warren relied on that comment a few years later in his majority opinion defending the Court's power to review the exclusion of Congressman Adam Clayton Powell from the House of Representatives: the Chief Justice stated in Powell v. McCormack in 1969 (p. 399 below), that "it is the responsibility of this Court to act as the ultimate interpreter of the Constitution. Marbury v. Madison."

Still more recently, the Burger Court invoked Marbury for broad and questionable inferences about judicial power in another context, in the Watergate tapes litigation, United States v. Nixon in 1974 (p. 388 below). Chief Justice Burger's opinion in the Nixon case repeatedly cited Marbury and stated

---

4. Note the suggestion of a "crucial difference" between Governor Faubus' stated opposition to the Brown decision and his efforts to block school board implementation of a desegregation plan approved by the federal court in Arkansas, in Horowitz & Karst, Law, Lawyers and Social Change (1969), 253. Are the authors persuasive in their analogy—"it is the difference between arguing with the umpire and refusing to leave the base when you are called out"?

5. Note Gunther, "The Subtle Vices of the 'Passive Virtues'—A Comment on Principle and Expediency in Judicial Review," 64 Colum.L.

Rev. 1, 25 (1964): "[Bickel, The Least Dangerous Branch (1962)] draws from Marbury v. Madison [the] notion that the Court's 'doctrines are not to be questioned,' by citizens or by other departments of government. [That] confuses Marshall's assertion of judicial authority to interpret the Constitution with judicial exclusiveness; that confuses Marbury v. Madison with statements in the Little Rock case, Cooper v. Aaron." For a defense of the Cooper v. Aaron approach, see Farber, "The Supreme Court and the Rule of Law: Cooper v. Aaron Revisited," 1983 U.Ill.L. Rev. 387.

at one point: "The President's counsel [reads] the Constitution as providing an absolute privilege of confidentiality for all presidential communications. Many decisions of this Court, however, have unequivocally reaffirmed the holding of [Marbury v. Madison] that 'it is emphatically the province and duty of the judicial department to say what the law is.'" Does that "however" make sense? Does acceptance of Marbury mean that the Constitution cannot be read to vest final authority to decide certain issues in other branches? Note the materials on "political questions," chaps. 6 and 15 below.[6]

7. *The legal consequences of judicial "invalidation."* Under the classic Marbury theory, a court confronted with an unconstitutional statute simply refuses enforcement to that law in the case before it. In civil law countries, by contrast, a court exercising judicial review issues a ruling of general invalidity binding on all, not just on the parties before it. But here, too, civil law and American law are closer in practice than in theory. Thus, it does not tell the whole story to say, as an American court once said, that a decision upon constitutionality "affects the parties only, and there is no judgment against the statute." Shephard v. Wheeling, 4 S.E. 635 (W.Va.1887). For example, some practical reach of a court ruling beyond the immediate parties is assured by the ordinary judicial adherence to stare decisis.

Yet to say that an invalidity ruling affects more than the parties is not to say that it is the same as wiping a statute off the books. It is as inaccurate to claim too broad an impact for a ruling as it is to state it too narrowly. The best-known example of overstatement is an assertion in Norton v. Shelby County, 118 U.S. 425 (1886), a statement that has required some important qualifications: "An unconstitutional act is not a law; it confers no rights; it imposes no duties; it affords no protection; it creates no office; it is [as] inoperative as though it had never been passed."

But a law held unconstitutional in an American court is by no means so wholly a nullity, as the Attorney General quite persuasively advised President Roosevelt in 1937. The Supreme Court had held the District of Columbia minimum wage law unconstitutional in 1923, in the Adkins case; but in 1937, in sustaining a similar Washington law in the West Coast Hotel Co. case, the Court formally overruled Adkins. (The cases are in chap. 8, sec. 1, below.) The Attorney General advised that the 1923 ruling had simply "suspend[ed]"

---

6. Gunther, "Judicial Hegemony and Legislative Autonomy: The Nixon Case and the Impeachment Process," 22 U.C.L.A. L.Rev. 30 (1974), suggests one possible answer to the questions: "That 'however' suggests that the Marbury passage helps answer the executive privilege contention. [But] there is nothing in Marbury v. Madison that precludes a constitutional interpretation which gives final authority to another branch.

"I do not believe that the Court intended to announce that every constitutional issue requires final adjudication on the merits by the judiciary. As in the past, there are likely to be issues in the future which the Court will find to have been 'committed by the Constitution to another branch of government.' [Baker v. Carr.] For example, I would think (and hope) that a [Senate] conviction on impeachment would be found unreviewable in the courts. Nor do I mean to suggest that the Court's result was wrong on the merits: I think checks and balances arguments make a non-absolute view of executive privilege appropriate. I simply suggest that the argument for absolute executive privilege deserved a more

focused, careful, separable answer than the Court's invocation of Marbury v. Madison provides.

"In short, I think the Court's overbroad reliance on Marbury was at the least a non sequitur and at worst dangerous nonsense. And the Judiciary Committee debate on article III [of the Articles of Impeachment against Richard M. Nixon, based on his refusal to comply with congressional subpoenas] illustrates some of the danger. [Many of the legislators] who opposed article III did so on the basis of statements echoing the misleading tenor of the objectionable parts of the Court's opinion in United States v. Nixon: somehow it was incongruous in the American scheme that Congress should decide that constitutional issue on its own; somehow it was inappropriate to have the legislature rather than the judiciary resolve this dispute between the legislative and executive branches."

[For one version of the evolution of the United States v. Nixon opinion within the Supreme Court, see Woodward & Armstrong, The Brethren: Inside the Supreme Court (1979), 287–347.]

enforcement, and that the act was valid and enforceable after the 1937 decision, explaining: "The decisions are practically in accord in holding that the courts have no power to repeal or abolish a statute, and that notwithstanding a decision holding it unconstitutional a statute continues to remain on the statute books." 39 Ops.Atty.Gen. 22 (1937).[7]

SECTION 2. SUPREME COURT AUTHORITY TO REVIEW STATE COURT JUDGMENTS: THE MARTIN v. HUNTER'S LESSEE ISSUES

MARTIN v. HUNTER'S LESSEE, 1 Wheat. 304 (1816), ranks second only to Marbury v. Madison among the important decisions of the Marshall era articulating the contours of federal judicial authority. The Martin decision defended the legitimacy of Supreme Court review of state court judgments resting on interpretations of federal law and rejected the highest Virginia court's challenge to the constitutionality of § 25 of the Judiciary Act of 1789. Sec. 25 essentially provided for Supreme Court review of final decisions of the highest state courts rejecting claims based on federal law—including federal constitutional law. (The full text of § 25—together with its broader modern counterpart, 28 U.S.C. § 1257—is printed at p. 55 below.)

In many respects, the textual and historical support for the Supreme Court authority asserted in Martin is stronger than can be mustered for Marbury v. Madison. The Court had sporadically exercised § 25 authority for years prior to the Virginia challenge in Martin. As Justice Story's opinion in Martin elaborates, some support for the authority can be drawn from the language of Articles III and VI of the Constitution. Moreover, an expectation of Supreme Court review of state court judgments runs through the Constitutional Convention debates. At the Convention, the establishment of inferior federal courts was a major source of controversy. The relevant provisions of Art. III reflect a compromise between opposing views: one insisting on the mandatory creation of lower federal courts; the other leaving initial application of federal law entirely to the state courts. The compromise left the creation and jurisdiction of lower federal courts largely to the discretion of Congress. That compromise, as well as the supremacy clause of Art. VI, contemplated that federal questions would initially arise in state as well as federal courts and assumed that Supreme Court review would insure any necessary uniformity.

---

7. The Supreme Court itself has had occasion to warn that the problem is more subtle and complex than the Norton language suggested. In Chicot County Drainage District v. Baxter State Bank, 308 U.S. 371 (1940), for example, Chief Justice Hughes stated that it is "manifest from numerous decisions that an all-inclusive statement of a principle of absolute retroactive invalidity cannot be justified." For a more recent rejection of the Norton overstatement that unconstitutional laws are wholly inoperative, see Chief Justice Burger's opinion in Lemon v. Kurtzman II, 411 U.S. 192 (1973). See generally Field, The Effect of an Unconstitutional Statute (1935).

Chief Justice Hughes in the Chicot County case stressed that "a principle of absolute retroactive invalidity" was unsupportable, while recognizing retroactivity as the normal consequence of judicial invalidation. More recently, attention has shifted from the typical rule of retroactivity to the permissibility of giving only prospective effect to rulings of unconstitutionality. That problem was raised especially by the Warren Court's rapid expansion of federal constitutional rights in criminal proceedings (see chap. 7, sec. 3, below). May the Court announce new guarantees without permitting all those already convicted to benefit from those new rights? Beginning with Linkletter v. Walker, 381 U.S. 618 (1965), the Court held that it could indeed withhold retroactive effect for its ruling under some circumstances. Determining which new rules should be limited to prospective effect—and deciding what "prospectivity" should mean—has given rise to repeated controversies since Linkletter.

Despite that strong support for the Supreme Court decision in Martin, some attention to the Martin controversy is warranted, because of contemporary as well as historical concerns. The excerpts below delineate the core of the contending positions of the Virginia judges and of Justice Story of the Supreme Court. They throw light on the question of what the fighting in the early 19th century was all about: for example, did the Virginians advocate a hopelessly unworkable, anarchical scheme of allocation of authority among state and federal courts? Beyond that, the Martin materials also introduce continuingly important themes: the existence of state as well as federal courts as interpreters of federal law; the obligation as well as authority of state courts to heed the "supreme" law; the complex interrelations between state and federal judiciaries in a system which apportions the function of interpreting federal (including constitutional) law among the judicial structures of separate, state and federal, governments.[1]

1. *The background of the Martin litigation.* The immediate provocation for the Supreme Court's decision sustaining the constitutionality of § 25 of the Judiciary Act of 1789 was the refusal by the Virginia Court of Appeals (announced in 1815) to obey the Supreme Court mandate in Fairfax's Devisee v. Hunter's Lessee, 7 Cranch 603 (1813). That Fairfax ruling in turn was the culmination of land litigation that had been instituted many years earlier, in 1791. The dispute concerned the vast land holdings of Lord Fairfax. Virginia claimed that it had properly seized the Fairfax properties prior to 1783 as lands belonging to British loyalists during the Revolution. Virginia parceled out some of the land to its own citizens; and Hunter claimed the land in issue under such a grant from the State of Virginia. Martin claimed title under a devise from Fairfax: he insisted that the Fairfax lands were protected against seizure because of the Peace Treaty of 1783 and the Jay Treaty of 1794. In short, Hunter's claim rested on a series of Virginia statutes relating to the forfeiture to the State of lands owned by British subjects; Martin's position, by contrast, was that title to the land acquired under the Fairfax will in 1781 had not vested in Virginia prior to 1783, and that it was thereafter protected by the treaty provisions.

Although Hunter had instituted his action to establish his right to the land as early as 1791, the litigation was in abeyance for almost two decades. In the interim, there were complicated negotiations—negotiations which involved John Marshall, for the future Chief Justice and his brother James had contracted for the purchase of a large part of the Fairfax estate from the Fairfax heirs.[2] It was

---

1. Additional aspects of the problem of federal-state court relations are noted below. Note especially the consideration of the "adequate state grounds" obstacle to Supreme Court review of state court decisions (including the return to the Martin litigation, at p. 57, as illustrative of that obstacle). Those "adequate state grounds" materials may usefully be pursued at this point. See also chap. 15, sec. 4B, on federal court intervention in state court proceedings. Full exploration of these problems is left to courses on federal jurisdiction. See, e.g., Hart & Wechsler, Federal Courts (2d ed. 1973); Wright, Federal Courts (4th ed. 1983).

2. Because of that involvement, John Marshall did not participate in the Supreme Court decisions in 1813 and 1816. The task of writing the opinions of the Court fell to Justice Joseph Story. Story, a Jeffersonian Republican from Massachusetts, had been appointed to the Court by President Madison in 1811. His nationalist

positions in Martin and many other cases disappointed some Jeffersonians—including Thomas Jefferson himself. But the Jeffersonian heritage included nationalist as well as localist strands; and in a state such as Massachusetts, nationalism was understandably popular with Jeffersonians. New England Federalists had increasingly turned to states' rights beliefs in opposition to a national government controlled by Jeffersonians; support for strong national institutions was accordingly an attractive ideology for Jeffersonians such as Story. The ambivalence in Jeffersonian thinking about national and state powers is illustrated by the contrasting reactions of ex-Presidents Jefferson and Madison to the controversial § 25 sustained in the Martin decision: Jefferson sided with the critics of the Martin ruling; Madison dissociated himself from them and, in strong letters over many years, defended the legitimacy and necessity of § 25 review.

not until 1810 that the Virginia Court of Appeals first ruled on the case—and decided for Hunter and the effectiveness of Virginia's seizure of the Fairfax lands. It was that decision that the Supreme Court reversed, siding with Martin in 1813. Pursuant to that 1813 decision, the Supreme Court mandate, in strong language, "instructed" and "commanded" the Virginia judges to enter judgment for Martin.

The issue of compliance with that mandate stirred considerable controversy in Virginia. It was a somewhat surprising time for states' rights agitation to reemerge in Virginia. A divided nation was at war with England; James Madison, the President from Virginia, was trying to unite the nation against vociferous states' rights criticisms from anti-war forces centered in New England; and yet the Virginia judges, with their ruling on § 25, initiated new waves of states' rights attacks that were to engulf the Marshall Court for years. The issue was argued at length before the Virginia Court of Appeals in 1814. However, no decision was announced until well after a year later, in 1815: apparently, the Virginia judges delayed publication in order to avoid encouraging the secessionist feelings mounting in New England near the close of the War of 1812.

2. *The core of the Virginia judges' position in Martin.* a. The Virginia judges produced several opinions but united in a strongly worded joint conclusion: "The Court is unanimously of opinion, that the appellate power of the Supreme Court of the United States does not extend to this court, under a sound construction of the constitution of the United States; that so much of the 25th section of the act of Congress to establish the judicial courts of the United States, as extends the appellate jurisdiction of the Supreme Court to this court, is not in pursuance of the constitution of the United States; that the writ of error in this case was improvidently allowed under the authority of that act; that the proceedings thereon in the Supreme Court were *coram non judice* in relation to this court; and that obedience to its mandate be declined by this court."[3]

The bases for the Virginia judges' joint conclusion are indicated by the following excerpts from the opinion of Judge Cabell: "[The power of the national government operates on] individuals in their individual capacity. No one presumes to contend, that the state governments can operate compulsively on the general government or any of its departments, even in cases of unquestionable encroachment on state authority. [Such] encroachment of jurisdiction could neither be prevented nor redressed by the state government, or any of its departments, *by any procedure acting on the Federal Courts.* I can perceive nothing in the constitution which gives to the Federal Courts any stronger claim to prevent or redress, *by any procedure acting on the state Courts*, an equally obvious encroachment on the Federal jurisdiction. The constitution of the United States contemplates the independence of both governments, and

---

3. The most influential member of the Virginia's highest court was no doubt Spencer Roane—a life-long Jeffersonian critic of Federalist John Marshall, an active political leader as well as eminent judge, a frequent contributor to the organ of the Richmond leadership of Virginia politics, the "Richmond Enquirer," and a vociferous and articulate critic of Marshall Court opinions beginning with the Martin case.

Only in the Martin case did Spencer Roane have the opportunity to cross swords with Marshall Court decisions in his official capacity. His objections to later decisions—McCulloch v. Maryland in 1819 (p. 72 below) and Cohens v. Virginia in 1821 (p. 37 below)—were even stronger. That opposition was expressed in pseu-

donymous essays in the "Richmond Enquirer"; and John Marshall was so stung by them that he resorted to pseudonymous newspaper responses of his own after McCulloch. See Gunther (ed.), John Marshall's Defense of McCulloch v. Maryland (1969). On Roane generally, see Note, "Judge Spencer Roane of Virginia: Champion of States' Rights—Foe of John Marshall," 66 Harv. L.Rev. 1242 (1953). And for fuller accounts of the Martin litigation, see 4 Beveridge, The Life of John Marshall (1919), 144–67; 1 Warren, The Supreme Court in United States History (rev. ed. 1926), 442–53; and 2 Crosskey, Politics and the Constitution in the History of the United States (1953), 785–814.

regards the *residuary* sovereignty of the states, as not less inviolable, than the *delegated* sovereignty of the United States. It must have been foreseen that controversies would sometimes arise as to the boundaries of the two jurisdictions. Yet the constitution has provided no umpire, has erected no tribunal by which they shall be settled. The omission proceeded, probably, from the belief, that such a tribunal would produce evils greater than those of the occasional collisions which it would be designed to remedy.

"[If] this Court should now proceed to enter a judgment in this case, according [to] instructions of the Supreme Court, the Judges of this Court, in doing so, must act either as Federal or as State Judges. But we cannot be made Federal Judges without our consent, and without commissions. Both these requisites being wanting, the act could not, therefore, be done by us, constitutionally, as Federal Judges. We must, then, in obeying this mandate, be considered still as State Judges. We are required, as State Judges to enter upon a judgment, not our own, but dictated and prescribed to us by another Court. [But], before one Court can dictate to another, the judgment it shall pronounce, it must bear, to that other, the relation of an appellate Court. The term appellate, however, necessarily includes the idea of *superiority.* But one Court cannot be correctly said to be *superior* to another, unless both of them belong to the same sovereignty. It would be a misapplication of terms to say that a Court of Virginia is *superior* to a Court of Maryland, or vice versa. The Courts of the United States, therefore, belonging to one sovereignty, cannot be appellate Courts in relation to the State Courts, which belong to a different sovereignty— and of course, their commands or instructions impose no obligation.

"[The] act of Congress now under consideration, attempts, in fact, to make the State Courts *Inferior Federal Courts.* [The] appellate jurisdiction of the Supreme Court of the United States [under Art. III of the Constitution] must have reference to the inferior Courts of the United States, and not to State Courts. [It] has been contended that the constitution contemplated only the objects of appeal, and not the tribunals from which the appeal is to be taken; and intended to give to the Supreme Court of the United States appellate jurisdiction in all the cases of federal cognizance. But this argument proves too much, and what is utterly inadmissible. It would give appellate jurisdiction, as well over the courts of England or France, as over the State courts; for, although I do not think the State Courts are *foreign* Courts in relation to the Federal Courts, yet I consider them not less *independent* than foreign Courts."

b. In considering the feasibility and justifiability of a judicial scheme such as that contemplated by the Virginia judges, note that they did *not* deny the supremacy of valid federal law under Art. VI of the Constitution, nor their obligation to give effect to superior federal law in state court adjudication. In the Martin litigation, for example, they acknowledged that alien property holdings that existed at the time of the treaties of 1783 and 1794 were protected by those superior federal guarantees. They insisted, however, that the Fairfax interests had been validly seized by the State prior to 1783. Nor did the Virginia judges deny the legitimacy of a federal judicial enforcement machinery. Paradoxically, their response to nationalist needs was to point to the congressional authority under Art. III to expand the number and jurisdiction of the lower federal courts. For example, to the argument that without the appellate jurisdiction "there will be no other mode by which congress can extend the judicial power of the United States to the cases of federal cognizance; that there will, consequently, be no uniformity of decision," Judge Cabell replied: "All the purposes of the constitution of the United States will be answered by the erection of Federal Courts, into which any party, plaintiff or defendant, concerned in a case of federal cognizance, *may* carry it for adjudication."

In short, the Virginia position, rather than totally flouting federal supremacy or advocating direct resistance to federal court orders, was a more moderate assertion of limited state judicial autonomy: to the extent judiciary legislation left federal questions to arise and make their way through the state courts, final adjudication had to be by that judicial system; if that channeling of cases proved unsatisfactory, the federal government's recourse was to route federal issues into lower federal courts at an earlier point. In that view, the only impermissible federal intervention was to tell the highest state court judges that they had interpreted federal law incorrectly: it was only Supreme Court review of final state court decisions that the Virginia judges considered an impermissible trampling upon state judicial autonomy.

3. *The core of Justice Story's opinion for the Supreme Court in Martin.* The Virginia court's challenge stirred Justice Story into an elaborate response. To attack federal judicial power was to strike at a subject particularly close to his heart. Even before Martin v. Hunter's Lessee came to the Supreme Court, Story had devoted some of his extrajudicial energies to the drafting and advocating of federal legislation which would have expanded federal jurisdiction to the maximum extent possible under the Constitution—to a point not reached even under modern judiciary legislation. (On those lobbying efforts by Story, see p. 50 below.) At the outset of his detailed examination of Art. III in Martin, Story inserted several paragraphs suggesting that its provisions were "mandatory upon the legislature." But he soon abandoned that theme [4] and rested most of his analysis on the assumption that Art. III left considerable discretion to Congress with respect to the allocation of jurisdiction to federal courts. He argued:

"But, even admitting that the language of the constitution is not mandatory, and that congress may constitutionally omit to vest the judicial power in courts of the United States, it cannot be denied that when it is vested, it may be exercised to the utmost constitutional extent.

"This leads us to the consideration of the great question, as to the nature and extent of the appellate jurisdiction of the United States. We have already seen, that appellate jurisdiction is given by the constitution to the supreme court, in all cases where it has not original jurisdiction; subject, however, to such exceptions and regulations as congress may prescribe. It is, therefore, capable of embracing every case enumerated in the constitution, which is not exclusively to be decided by way of original jurisdiction. [W]hat is there to restrain its exercise over state tribunals, in the enumerated cases? The appellate power is not limited by the terms of the third article to any particular courts. [It] is the *case,* then, and not the *court,* that gives the jurisdiction. If the judicial power extends to the case, it will be in vain to search in the letter of the constitution for any qualification as to the tribunal where it depends. It is incumbent, then, upon those who assert such a qualification, to show its existence, by necessary implication.

"[It must] be conceded that the constitution not only contemplated, but meant to provide for cases within the scope of the judicial power of the United States, which might yet depend before state tribunals. It was foreseen that in the exercise of their ordinary jurisdiction, state courts would incidentally take cognisance of cases arising under the constitution, the laws and treaties of the United States. Yet, to all these cases, the judicial power, by the very terms of the constitution, is to extend. It cannot extend by original jurisdiction if that was already rightfully and exclusively attached in the state courts, which (as has been already shown) may occur; it must, therefore, extend by appellate

4. Justice Story's dicta about the "mandatory" nature of Art. III are considered more fully below, at p. 49.

jurisdiction, or not at all. It would seem to follow that the appellate power of the United States must, in such cases, extend to state tribunals; and if in such cases, there is no reason why it should not equally attach upon all others within the purview of the constitution.

"It has been argued that such an appellate jurisdiction over state courts is inconsistent with the genius of our governments, and the spirit of the constitution. That the latter was never designed to act upon state sovereignties, but only upon the people, and that if the power exists, it will materially impair the sovereignty of the states, and the independence of their courts. We cannot yield to the force of this reasoning; it assumes principles which we cannot admit, and draws conclusions to which we do not yield our assent. It is a mistake [to believe] that the constitution was not designed to operate upon states, in their corporate capacities. It is crowded with provisions which restrain or annul the sovereignty of the states in some of the highest branches of their prerogatives. The tenth section of the first article contains a long list of disabilities and prohibitions imposed upon the states. Surely, when such essential portions of state sovereignty are taken away, or prohibited to be exercised, it cannot be correctly asserted that the constitution does not act upon the states. [When], therefore, the states are stripped of some of the highest attributes of sovereignty, [it] is certainly difficult to support the argument that the appellate power over the decisions of state courts is contrary to the genius of our institutions. The courts of the United States can, without question, revise the proceedings of the executive and legislative authorities of the states, and if they are found to be contrary to the constitution, may declare them to be of no legal validity. Surely, the exercise of the same right over judicial tribunals is not a higher or more dangerous act of sovereign power.

"Nor can such a right be deemed to impair the independence of state judges. It is assuming the very ground in controversy to assert that they possess an absolute independence of the United States. In respect to the powers granted to the United States, they are not independent; they are expressly bound to obedience, by the letter of the constitution; and if they should unintentionally transcend their authority, or misconstrue the constitution, there is no more reason for giving their judgments an absolute and irresistible force, than for giving it to the acts of the other co-ordinate departments of state sovereignty.

"The argument urged from the possibility of the abuse of the revising power, is equally unsatisfactory. It is always a doubtful course, to argue against the use or existence of a power, from the possibility of its abuse. It is still more difficult by such an argument, to ingraft upon a general power a restriction which is not to be found in the terms in which it is given. From the very nature of things, the absolute right of decision, in the last resort, must rest some-where—wherever it may be vested, it is susceptible of abuse. In all questions of jurisdiction, the inferior, or appellate court, must pronounce the final judgment; and common sense, as well as legal reasoning, has conferred it upon the latter.

"It is further argued, that no great public mischief can result from a construction which shall limit the appellate power of the United States to cases in their own courts: first, because state judges are bound by an oath to support the constitution of the United States, and must be presumed to be men of learning and integrity; and secondly, because congress must have an unquestionable right to remove all cases within the scope of the judicial power from the state courts to the courts of the United States, at any time before final judgment, though not after final judgment. As to the first reason—admitting that the judges of the state courts are, and always will be, of as much learning, integrity and wisdom, as those of the courts of the United States, (which we very cheerfully admit,) it does not aid the argument. It is manifest that the constitution has proceeded upon a theory of its own, and given or withheld powers according to the judgment of the American people, by whom it was adopted. We can only construe its powers, and cannot inquire into the policy or principles which induced the grant of them. The constitution has presumed (whether rightly or wrongly we do not inquire) that state attachments, state prejudices, state jealousies, and state interests, might sometimes obstruct, or control, or be supposed to obstruct or control, the regular administration of justice. Hence, in controversies between states; between citizens of different states; between citizens claiming grants under different states; between a state and its citizens, or foreigners, and between citizens and foreigners, it enables the parties, under the authority of congress, to have the controversies heard, tried and determined before the national tribunals. No other reason than that which has been stated can be assigned, why some, at least, of those cases should not have been left to the cognizance of the state courts. In respect to the other enumerated cases—the cases arising under the constitution, laws and treaties of the United States, cases affecting ambassadors and other public ministers, and cases of admiralty and maritime jurisdiction—reasons of a higher and more extensive nature, touching the safety, peace and sovereignty of the nation, might well justify a grant of exclusive jurisdiction.

"This is not all. A motive of another kind, perfectly compatible with the most sincere respect for state tribunals, might induce the grant of appellate power over their decisions. That motive is the importance, and even necessity of *uniformity* of decisions throughout the whole United States, upon all subjects within the purview of the constitution. Judges of equal learning and integrity, in different states, might differently interpret a statute, or a treaty of the United States, or even the constitution itself: if there were no revising authority to control these jarring and discordant judgments, and harmonize them into uniformity, the laws, the treaties and the constitution of the United States would be different in different states. [The] public mischiefs that would attend such a state of things would be truly deplorable; and it cannot be believed that they could have escaped the enlightened convention which formed the constitution. What indeed, might then have been only prophecy, has now become fact; and the appellate jurisdiction must continue to be the only adequate remedy for such evils.

"[The power of Congress] to remove suits from state courts to the national courts [forms] the second ground upon which the argument we are considering has been attempted to be sustained. This power of removal is not to be found in express terms in any part of the constitution; if it be given, it is only given by implication, as a power necessary and proper to carry into effect some express power. [I]f the right of removal from state courts exist before judgment because it is included in the appellate power, it must, for the same reason, exist after judgment. And if the appellate power by the constitution does not include cases pending in state courts, the right of removal, which is but a mode of exercising that power, cannot be applied to them. Precisely the same objections, therefore, exist as to the right of removal before judgment, as after, and both must stand or fall together. Nor, indeed, would the force of the arguments on either side materially vary, if the right of removal were an exercise of original jurisdiction. It would equally trench upon the jurisdiction and independence of state tribunals.

"On the whole, the court are of opinion, that the appellate power of the United States does extend to cases pending in the state courts; and that the 25th section of the judiciary act, which authorizes the exercise of this jurisdiction in the specified cases, by a writ of error, is supported by the letter and spirit of the constitution. We find no clause in that instrument which limits this power; and we dare not interpose a limitation where the people have not been disposed to create one.

"Strong as this conclusion stands upon the general language of the constitution, it may still derive support from other sources. It is an historical fact, that this exposition of the constitution, extending its appellate power to state courts, was, previous to its adoption, uniformly and publicly avowed by its friends, and admitted by its enemies, as the basis of their respective reasonings, both in and out of the state conventions. It is an historical fact, that at the time when the judiciary act was submitted to the deliberations of the first congress, composed as it was, not only of men of great learning and ability, but of men who had acted a principal part in framing, supporting or opposing that constitution, the same exposition was explicitly declared and admitted by the friends and by the opponents of that system. It is an historical fact, that the supreme court of the United States have, from time to time, sustained this appellate jurisdiction in a great variety of cases, brought from the tribunals of many of the most important states in the Union, and that no state tribunal has ever breathed a judicial doubt on the subject, or declined to obey the mandate of the supreme court, until the present occasion. This weight of contemporaneous exposition by all parties, this acquiescence of enlightened state courts, and these judicial decisions of the supreme court through so long a period, do, as we think, place the doctrine upon a foundation of authority which cannot be shaken, without delivering over the subject to perpetual and irremediable doubts." [5]

4. *Cohens v. Virginia: Supreme Court review of state criminal cases.* Justice Story's confident and forceful opinion in Martin v. Hunter's Lessee did not end the agitation over the justifiability of § 25 of the 1789 Judiciary Act. Instead, the Martin dispute signalled the beginning of waves of attacks on § 25. Those attacks were symptoms of more pervasive states' rights concerns in the immediate post-Martin years. They were concerns stimulated especially by a series of Marshall Court decisions striking down a variety of state actions. For example, the 1819 decision in McCulloch v. Maryland (p. 72 below), sustaining the constitutionality of the Bank of the United States and barring state taxation of the Bank as the nation was entering an economic depression, set off waves of protest—including an effort by Ohio to provoke relitigation of the McCulloch issues by seizing more than $100,000 from the vaults of the Bank branch in Chillicothe, Ohio. John Marshall's repudiation of that effort produced not only a reaffirmation of McCulloch but also important new, expansive assertions about federal judicial authority. Osborn v. Bank of the United States, 9 Wheat. 738 (1824).[6]

Sec. 25 was a common—though by no means the only—target of those states' rights attacks. Most often, hostility to § 25 manifested itself in efforts to

---

5. At the end of the opinion, Justice Story avoided the abrasive "instruct" and "command" language in the 1813 judgment in Fairfax's Devisee v. Hunter's Lessee that had provoked the confrontation with the Virginia Court of Appeals. He concluded instead: "We have not thought it incumbent on us to give any opinion upon the question, whether this court have authority to issue a writ of mandamus to the court of appeals to enforce the former judgments, as we do not think it necessarily involved in the decision of this cause. It is the opinion of the whole court, that the judgment of the court of appeals of Virginia, rendered on the mandate in this cause, be reversed."

In a separate opinion, Justice William Johnson—President Jefferson's first appointee to the Marshall Court—stated: "It will be observed in this case, that the court disavows all intention to decide on the right to issue compulsory process

to the state courts; thus leaving us, in my opinion, where the constitution and laws place us—supreme over persons and cases, as far as our judicial powers extend, but not asserting any compulsory control over the state tribunals. In this view, I acquiesce in their opinion, but not altogether in the reasoning or opinion of my brother who delivered it."

6. Note also two other decisions in the same Term as McCulloch that contributed to the mounting states' rights fervor: Dartmouth College v. Woodward, 4 Wheat. 518 (1819), finding the New Hampshire legislature's effort to modify the college charter a violation of the contract clause; and Sturges v. Crowninshield, 17 U.S. (4 Wheat.) 122 (1819), once again relying on the contract clause, to invalidate retroactive state insolvency legislation. (See chap. 8, sec. 2B, below.)

obtain congressional repeal of the provision. See note 5 below. But there was one important post-Martin occasion for the Supreme Court to address the issue once again: it came in COHENS v. VIRGINIA, 6 Wheat. 264 (1821). That case arose from the conviction of the Cohen brothers in a Norfolk court for selling District of Columbia lottery tickets in violation of Virginia laws. The Cohens claimed that, under the supremacy clause, they were immune from state laws in selling congressionally authorized lottery tickets. The Supreme Court ultimately decided against them on the merits, reading the congressional statute as conferring no such immunity. But the major issue was the jurisdictional one: did the Supreme Court have constitutional authority to review state criminal judgments? Virginia's counsel not only reiterated the arguments advanced in the Martin case, but found new ones. They emphasized that here, unlike in Martin, the State was a named party in the case, and they argued especially that the grant of original jurisdiction to the Supreme Court of cases "in which a state shall be a party" excluded the exercise of appellate jurisdiction in such cases. They claimed, too, that the Constitution did not confer federal judicial power in controversies between a State and its own citizens and that the Eleventh Amendment in any event barred review. Those arguments gave the Court the opportunity not only to reaffirm but also to extend the principles of Martin v. Hunter's Lessee.

Cohens v. Virginia at last gave John Marshall the chance to have his say on the § 25 issue officially. In Martin, in 1816, he had not sat and therefore could not join in repudiating the challenges by Spencer Roane and his Virginia colleagues. In 1819, spurred by Spencer Roane's newspaper criticisms of McCulloch, Marshall had gotten a defense of § 25 into print, but only in the course of pseudonymous essays signed by "A Friend of the Constitution." See Gunther, ed., John Marshall's Defense of McCulloch v. Maryland (1969). Now, with Cohens, it was Marshall's turn to speak officially, and Roane's to be relegated to sideline criticism in the newspapers. In Roane's most vitriolic attack, the "Algernon Sidney" essays in the "Richmond Enquirer," he explained why Cohens was a "most monstrous and unexampled decision."

Marshall's Cohens opinion rejecting the jurisdictional challenge restated the defense of the constitutionality of § 25 and answered Virginia's new contentions by concluding "that the judicial power, as originally given, extends to all cases arising under the constitution or a law of the United States, whoever may be the parties." The fact that a state was a party made no difference: review authority in the Cohens case rested not on the nature of the parties but on the nature of the questions in the case. Marshall's opinion pointed out that cases to which the jurisdiction of the federal courts may extend fall into two classes: "In the first, their jurisdiction depends on the character of the cause, whoever may be the parties. This class comprehends 'all cases in law and equity arising under this constitution, the laws of the United States, and treaties made, or which shall be made, under their authority.' This clause extends the jurisdiction of the Court to all the cases described, without making in its terms any exception whatever, and without any regard to the condition of the party. [In] the second class, the jurisdiction depends entirely on the character of the parties. In this are comprehended 'controversies between two or more States, between a State and citizens of another State,' and 'between a State and foreign States, citizens or subjects.' If these be the parties, it is entirely unimportant what may be the subject of controversy. Be it what it may, these parties have a constitutional right to come into the Courts of the Union."

Marshall's defense of Supreme Court review in Cohens took a harsher view of the reliability of state judges than Story had expressed in Martin. Marshall's statements no doubt reflected his mounting anxieties about states' rights attacks in the 1816–21 period. For example, he commented: "In many States, the judges are dependent for office and for salary on the will of the legislature. [When] we observe the importance which [the Constitution] attaches to the independence of judges, we are the less inclined to suppose that it can have intended to leave these constitutional questions to tribunals where this independence may not exist, in all cases where a State shall prosecute an individual who claims the protection of an act of Congress. [A constitution] is framed for ages to come. [Its] course cannot always be tranquil. It is exposed to storms and tempests, and its framers must be unwise statesmen indeed, if they have not provided it, as far as its nature will permit, with the means of self-preservation from the perils it may be destined to encounter. No government ought to be so defective in its organization, as not to contain within itself the means of securing the execution of its own laws against other dangers than those which occur every day."

5. *State challenges to Supreme Court authority and authoritativeness—19th century variants and 20th century emulations.* A number of states other than Virginia challenged the right of the Supreme Court to review state court decisions in the period before the Civil War—often on grounds far broader than those advanced by Virginia in the Martin and Cohens cases.[7] The courts of seven states issued challenges. And in Congress, there were several attempts to repeal § 25—the first major one in 1821, immediately after Cohens; the most serious one in 1831. The critical significance of § 25 was appreciated, for example, by John C. Calhoun, long before he emerged as the chief public spokesman for nullification (the claimed power of a state to block—at least temporarily, until the Constitution could be amended—enforcement of "unconstitutional" federal laws within the state). Months before he privately drafted the South Carolina Exposition of 1828, years before he publicly advocated nullification, Calhoun suggested that, if § 25 could be repealed, more drastic remedies (such as nullification and, years later, secession) would be unnecessary.[8]

The position of Virginia in Martin and Cohens should be distinguished from the more extreme positions denying the general authoritativeness—and occasionally the specific enforceability—of federal court decisions, on the ground of the states' right to "interpose" their own interpretations of the Constitution against federal action. These "interposition" statements ranged from the general protest of the Virginia and Kentucky Resolutions of 1798 to South Carolina's nullification in 1832 and the later secession effort. Though these more extreme contentions tended to share common premises (e.g., the compact theory of the Union) and common language (e.g., "null and void" declarations), they varied widely in operative consequences.[9]

7. See generally Warren, "Legislative and Judicial Attacks on the Supreme Court of the United States—A History of the Twenty-Fifth Section of the Judiciary Act," 47 Am.L.Rev. 1, 161 (1913).

8. See, e.g., a letter by John C. Calhoun to Senator Littleton W. Tazewell of Virginia, August 25, 1827 (in the Calhoun Papers, The Library of Congress), speculating about possible remedies for "the protection of one portion of the people against another." With the increasingly evident minority status of the South, he suggested, there was only "one effectual remedy, a veto on the part of the local interest, or, under our system, on the Part of the States." Months before he became an advocate of nullification as the form of that "veto," he wrote as well: "[This] negative would in truth exist were it not for a provision in a single act of Congress, I mean the 25th Section of the Judiciary act of 1789; the existence or nonexistence of which provision, would make an entire change in the operation of our system. If the appellate power from the State courts to the U. States court provided for by the 25th Sec. did not exist, the practical consequence would be, that each government would have a negative on the other, and thus possess the most effectual remedy, that can be conceived against encroachment. Under this view, this provision becomes one of the deepest importance, much more so, than any other in the statute books; and altho' among the oldest, it ought not to be considered too late to enquire, by what authority Congress adopted it; and how far it can be reconciled with the Sovereignty of the States, as to their reserved rights?"

9. An excellent sampling of the state resolutions appears in Ames, State Documents on Federal Relations (1906).

In examining the pre-Civil War state contentions, it is important to read the broad assertions in light of the specific remedial, operative portions of the state resolutions.   As with the presidential statements quoted in the notes following Marbury v. Madison, above, it is useful to distinguish between statements (a) denying that constitutional interpretations are *exclusively* the function of the federal courts or that federal court interpretations bind the nation, and (b) asserting that specific federal court orders may be directly disobeyed.   Compare, for example, Madison's 1800 Report on the Virginia Resolutions [denying that "the judicial authority is to be regarded as the sole expositor of the Constitution in the last resort," in the context of urging congressional repeal of the Alien and Sedition Laws], with direct state defiance of federal court authority [e.g., the South Carolina Nullification Ordinance of 1832, making punishable as contempt the taking of certain appeals to the United States Supreme Court, 1 S.C. Statutes at Large 330 (1836); the act of December 1832, carrying the Ordinance into effect, providing that anyone arrested pursuant to a federal court order enforcing the tariff shall be entitled to habeas corpus and to damages for unlawful imprisonment, id. at 372; Georgia's defiance of the mandate in Worcester v. Georgia, 6 Pet. 515 (1832); and the bill passed by the Georgia House of Representatives in 1793, stating that "any Federal Marshal, or any other person" seeking to execute the mandate in Chisholm v. Georgia, 2 Dall. 419 (1793), shall be "guilty of felony, and shall suffer death, without the benefit of clergy, by being hanged."]

For modern state "interposition" resolutions, reviving the pre-Civil War tradition, see, e.g., 1 Race Rel.L.Rep. 437–447 (1956) (1956 legislative resolutions of Alabama, Georgia, Mississippi, South Carolina, and Virginia, in the wake of Brown v. Board of Education, the School Segregation Case).   For Supreme Court replies, see Cooper v. Aaron, 358 U.S. 1 (1958), p. 26 above, and Bush v. Orleans Parish School Board, 364 U.S. 500 (1960).   In Bush, the Court, per curiam, denied motions for a stay of a three-judge District Court order enjoining the enforcement of Louisiana interposition laws directed at school desegregation.   The Court quoted from the District Court decision, 188 F.Supp. 916, 926: "The conclusion is clear that interposition is not a *constitutional* doctrine.   If taken seriously, it is illegal defiance of constitutional authority."   The Supreme Court added: "The main basis for challenging this ruling is that the State of Louisiana 'has interposed itself in the field of public education over which it has exclusive control.'   This objection is without substance, as we held, upon full consideration, in Cooper v. Aaron." [10]

6.   *Enforcement of Court mandates.*   A Supreme Court reversal of a state court judgment may not be determinative of the outcome of the case.   Ordinarily, the Supreme Court merely remands for "proceedings not inconsistent with the opinion of this Court."   Under such a mandate, the state court is free to consider any undetermined questions or even to reexamine already decided matters of state law.   If it is contended that the state court failed to follow the Supreme Court mandate, the appropriate remedy, when available, is to seek a new review of the judgment.   In cases of state recalcitrance, the Supreme Court has at times entered judgment and awarded execution, or remanded with specific directions to enter judgment.[11]

---

10. On the importance of Supreme Court review of cases challenging state laws, see, in addition to Martin and Cohens, Justice Holmes' well-known statement: "I do not think the United States would come to an end if we lost our power to declare an Act of Congress void.   I do think the Union would be imperiled if we could not make that declaration as to the laws of the several States."   Holmes, Collected Legal Papers (1920), 295.

11. See generally 28 U.S.C. §§ 2106 and 1651, and Stern & Gressman, Supreme Court Practice (5th ed., 1978).   A number of statutory provisions suggest specific remedies to overcome resistance to federal court orders.   As to the powers and duties of United States marshals in

SECTION 3. CONGRESSIONAL POWER TO CURTAIL THE JURISDICTION OF FEDERAL COURTS

EX PARTE McCARDLE

7 Wall. 506, 19 L.Ed. 264 (1869).

[Under the post-Civil War Reconstruction Acts, Congress imposed military government on a large number of former Confederate States. McCardle was a Mississippi newspaper editor in military custody on charges of publishing "incendiary and libelous articles." He brought this habeas corpus proceeding under an Act of Congress of February 5, 1867, which authorized federal courts to grant habeas corpus to anyone restrained "in violation of the Constitution" and also authorized appeals to the Supreme Court. After the Circuit Court denied McCardle's habeas petition, he appealed to the Supreme Court. After the Supreme Court sustained jurisdiction of that appeal, 6 Wall. 318 (1868), and after argument was heard on the merits, Congress passed the Act of March 27, 1868. That law stated that so much of the 1867 Act "as authorized an appeal from the judgment of the Circuit Court to the Supreme Court of the United States, or the exercise of any such jurisdiction by said Supreme Court, on appeals which have been, or may hereafter be taken, be, and the same is, hereby repealed." The historical context is described further in note 1 following the opinion dismissing the appeal.]

The Chief Justice [CHASE] delivered the opinion of the Court.

The first question necessarily is that of jurisdiction; for, if the act of March, 1868, takes away the jurisdiction defined by the act of February, 1867, it is useless, if not improper, to enter into any discussion of other questions.

It is quite true, as was argued by the counsel for the petitioner, that the appellate jurisdiction of this Court is not derived from acts of Congress. It is, strictly speaking, conferred by the Constitution. But it is conferred "with such exceptions and under such regulations as Congress shall make."

It is unnecessary to consider whether, if Congress had made no exceptions and no regulations, this court might not have exercised general appellate jurisdiction under rules prescribed by itself. For among the earliest acts of the first Congress, at its first session, was the act of September 24th, 1789, to establish the judicial courts of the United States. That act provided for the organization of this court, and prescribed regulations for the exercise of its jurisdiction.

The source of that jurisdiction, and the limitations of it by the Constitution and by statute, have been on several occasions subjects of consideration here. In the case of Durousseau v. The United States, 6 Cranch 307 (Marshall, C.J.; 1810) particularly, the whole matter was carefully examined, and the court held, that while "the appellate powers of this court are not given by the judicial act, but are given by the Constitution," they are, nevertheless, "limited and regulated by that act, and by such other acts as have been passed on the subject." The court said, further, that the judicial act was an exercise of the power given by the Constitution to Congress "of making exceptions to the appellate jurisdiction of the Supreme Court." "They have described affirmatively," said the court,

executing judgments, see, e.g., 28 U.S.C. § 672; as to the use of the contempt power in the event of "[d]isobedience or resistance," see 18 U.S.C. §§ 401, 402; as to the use of armed forces by the executive "to enforce the laws of the United States," see 10 U.S.C. §§ 332, 333. See general-ly Reference Note, "Enforcement of Court Orders—Federal Contempt Proceedings and Prevention of Obstruction," 2 Race Rel.L.Rep. 1051 (1957), and Pollitt, "Presidential Use of Troops to Execute the Laws: A Brief History," 36 N.C.L.Rev. 117 (1958).

"its jurisdiction, and this affirmative description has been understood to imply a negation of the exercise of such appellate power as is not comprehended within it."

The principle that the affirmation of appellate jurisdiction implies the negation of all such jurisdiction not affirmed having been thus established, it was an almost necessary consequence that acts of Congress, providing for the exercise of jurisdiction, should come to be spoken of as acts granting jurisdiction, and not as acts making exceptions to the constitutional grant of it.

The exception to appellate jurisdiction in the case before us, however, is not an inference from the affirmation of other appellate jurisdiction. It is made in terms. The provision of the act of 1867 affirming the appellate jurisdiction of this court in cases of habeas corpus is expressly repealed. It is hardly possible to imagine a plainer instance of positive exception.

We are not at liberty to inquire into the motives of the legislature. We can only examine into its power under the Constitution; and the power to make exceptions to the appellate jurisdiction of this court is given by express words.

What, then, is the effect of the repealing act upon the case before us? We cannot doubt as to this. Without jurisdiction the court cannot proceed at all in any cause. Jurisdiction is power to declare the law, and when it ceases to exist, the only function remaining to the court is that of announcing the fact and dismissing the cause. And this is not less clear upon authority than upon principle.

Several cases were cited by the counsel for the petitioner in support of the position that jurisdiction of this case is not affected by the repealing act. But none of them, in our judgment, afford any support to it. They are all cases of the exercise of judicial power by the legislature, or of legislative interference with courts in the exercising of continuing jurisdiction.

On the other hand, the general rule, supported by the best elementary writers, is, that "when an act of the legislature is repealed, it must be considered, except as to transactions past and closed, as if it never existed." And the effect of repealing acts upon suits under acts repealed, has been determined by the adjudications of this court. [We have] held that no judgment could be rendered in a suit after the repeal of the act under which it was brought and prosecuted. It is quite clear, therefore, that this court cannot proceed to pronounce judgment in this case, for it has no longer jurisdiction of the appeal; and judicial duty is not less fitly performed by declining ungranted jurisdiction than in exercising firmly that which the Constitution and the laws confer.

Counsel seem to have supposed, if effect be given to the repealing act in question, that the whole appellate power of the court, in cases of habeas corpus, is denied. But this is an error. The act of 1868 does not except from that jurisdiction any cases but appeals from Circuit Courts under the act of 1867. It does not affect the jurisdiction which was previously exercised.

The appeal of the petitioner in this case must be dismissed for want of jurisdiction.

THE SCOPE OF THE CONGRESSIONAL POWER

Introduction. Consider, in examining the principal case and the following notes: How far-reaching is the congressional power sustained in McCardle? Does the historical context of that case substantially weaken its force as precedent? Is it possible to state principled limits on the power of Congress to enact "Exceptions" and "Regulations" of the Supreme Court's appellate jurisdiction? Does Art. III impose significant limits? Do other provisions of the Constitution—for example, the Fifth Amendment? Do basic constitutional assumptions about judicial review impose enforceable limits on the power of Congress? Is the Court really vulnerable to serious political reprisals from Congress unless limiting principles on McCardle can be stated? Or are there significant practical restraints on the jurisdiction-limiting weapon?

1. *McCardle in historical context.* Congressional policies after the Civil War produced sharp conflicts with the other branches. President Andrew Johnson opposed the Reconstruction Acts, for example; and there were repeated efforts to test their constitutionality in the courts. The McCardle case moved to a climax at the height of the tension between Congress and President and after two efforts to elicit Court rulings had failed.

Soon after the basic provisions of reconstruction legislation had been passed over the President's veto, challenges in the courts were launched. Prospects for success seemed good if the Court reached the merits: the military government features looked vulnerable in view of a case decided by the Supreme Court just before the reconstruction laws were passed. Ex parte Milligan, 4 Wall. 2 (1867). The first attack on the reconstruction laws in the Court came when Mississippi challenged their constitutionality through an action to enjoin presidential enforcement. But in Mississippi v. Johnson, 4 Wall. 475 (1867), the Court concluded that it lacked power to issue such an order against the President. (Cf. United States v. Nixon, p. 388 below.) Georgia immediately brought a similar action against the Secretary of War. Once again the Court dismissed on jurisdictional grounds: it held in Georgia v. Stanton, 6 Wall. 50 (1868), that the suit raised nonjusticiable political questions. But then, while Congress was considering measures to curb the judicial threat to reconstruction, the Court took jurisdiction of McCardle's appeal.

With that constitutional challenge formally before the Court and with argument on the merits already concluded (but, as the official report noted, "before conference in regard to the decision proper to be made"), Congress passed the 1868 law withdrawing appellate jurisdiction. By then, impeachment proceedings against President Johnson had begun. Nevertheless, he vetoed the law. With the Court standing by and withholding action on the case before it pending the outcome of the political battle, Congress overrode the veto. Argument on the jurisdiction-curtailing law was then sought in the Court. And, as one more manifestation of the political crisis hovering over the case, that argument had to be postponed because of (as the official report put it) "the Chief Justice being detained from his place here, by his duties in the Court of Impeachment."

There was one more effort to elicit a ruling on reconstruction after the dismissal of the McCardle appeal. In Ex parte Yerger, 8 Wall. 85 (1869), the Court took jurisdiction of a proceeding by another petitioner in military detention in Mississippi. Yerger, like McCardle, had unsuccessfully sought habeas in a lower federal court. But Yerger came to the Supreme Court by a route different from McCardle's: he did not invoke the appeal provision of the 1867 Act; accordingly, the Court found, the 1868 repeal did not apply. Yet a decision on the constitutionality of the Reconstruction Acts was once again averted: before the Court could rule on the merits, Yerger was released from military custody.[1]

2. *The vitality of McCardle and the Klein case.* Congress has not given the Court cause to reexamine McCardle directly, but Justice Douglas found occasion to call it in question in a footnote to a dissent some years ago. "There is a serious question whether the McCardle case could command a majority view

---

1. For a thorough exploration of the background of McCardle, see Fairman, Reconstruction and Reunion 1864–88, Part One (6 History of the Supreme Court of the United States) (1971). See also Van Alstyne, "A Critical Guide to Ex Parte McCardle," 15 Ariz.L.Rev. 229 (1973).

today," he said in an opinion joined by Justice Black in Glidden Co. v. Zdanok, 370 U.S. 530, 605 (1962). The Glidden case, with a plurality opinion by Justice Harlan, dealt mainly with the distinction between Art. I "legislative courts" and Art. III courts. The context of Justice Douglas' remark about McCardle was as follows: "The opinion of my Brother Harlan stirs a host of problems that need not be opened. What is done will, I fear, plague us for years. First, that opinion cites with approval Ex parte McCardle, 7 Wall. 506, in which Congress withdrew jurisdiction of this Court to review a habeas corpus case that was *sub judice* and then apparently draws a distinction between that case and United States v. Klein, 13 Wall. 128 [1872], where such withdrawal was not permitted in a property claim. There is a serious question whether the McCardle case could command a majority view today. Certainly the distinction between liberty and property (which emanates from this portion of my Brother Harlan's opinion) has no vitality even in terms of the Due Process Clause."

Is that all there is to the Klein-McCardle distinction? Consider the fuller statement of Klein which follows: it suggests that the Klein-McCardle difference may not reflect simply a preference of property over liberty; instead, Klein may rest on a principle more acceptable today—a principle of continuing utility as a limit on congressional power over jurisdiction. Justice Harlan's reference to Klein came in the following passage in Glidden: "The authority [of Congress to control the jurisdiction of Art. III courts] is not, of course, unlimited. In 1870, Congress purported to withdraw jurisdiction from the Court of Claims and from this Court on appeal over cases seeking indemnification for property captured during the Civil War, so far as eligibility therefor might be predicated upon an amnesty awarded by the President, as both courts had previously held that it might. Despite Ex parte McCardle, the Court refused to apply the statute to a case in which the claimant had already been adjudged entitled to recover by the Court of Claims, calling it an unconstitutional attempt to invade the judicial province by prescribing a rule of decision in a pending case. United States v. Klein."

In the Klein controversy, earlier rulings had held that a presidential pardon satisfied the statutory requirement that a property claimant was not a supporter of the "rebellion." The new statute enacted while Klein's appeal was pending provided that a pardon was to be taken as showing quite the opposite, that the claimant *had* aided the rebellion, and went on to provide that the courts were to dismiss such claims for want of jurisdiction. The opinion holding the law unconstitutional stated that the Court would have upheld it as an exercise of the "exceptions" power if "it simply denied the right of appeal in a particular class of cases." But here the jurisdictional language was only "a means to an end": "to deny to pardons granted by the President the effect which this court had adjudged them to have." The Court concluded that dismissing the appeal would allow Congress to "prescribe rules of decision to the Judicial Department of the government in cases pending before it," and that was a violation of separation of powers principles.

Note also Hart & Wechsler, Federal Courts (2d ed. 1973), 316, viewing Klein as holding that it is "an unconstitutional invasion of the judicial function when Congress purports, not to withdraw jurisdiction completely, but to bind the Court to decide a case in accordance with a rule of law independently unconstitutional on other grounds." [2] Consider the modern Court-curbing

---

2. Note the reiteration of the Klein principle in Justice Rutledge's dissent in Yakus v. United States, 321 U.S. 414, 468 (1944): "It is one thing for Congress to withhold jurisdiction. It is entirely another to confer it and direct that it be exercised in a manner inconsistent with constitutional requirements or, what in some instances may be the same thing, without regard to them. [W]henever the judicial power is called into play it is responsible directly to the fundamental law and no other authority can intervene to force or authorize the judicial body to disregard it." See generally Young, "Congressional Regulation of Federal Courts' Jurisdiction: United States v.

proposals in note 4 below: Which are legitimate jurisdictional controls and which are efforts to dictate the outcome of a case on the merits? Which are withdrawals of whole categories of cases, and which are simply efforts to withdraw particular issues from judicial consideration in cases otherwise left to the courts for decision on the merits? If Klein is read to bar withdrawal of particular issues where that is tantamount to directing the outcome of a case, does that draw into question as well the legitimacy of congressional withdrawal of jurisdiction of an entire class of cases, when that withdrawal of jurisdiction is prompted by a desire to affect the outcome?

3. *The search for constitutional limits on congressional power over appellate jurisdiction.* Assertions of broad congressional power to make exceptions to appellate jurisdiction, as in McCardle, understandably have proved tempting to some critics of modern Supreme Court decisions—as they have to Court critics since the days of the Marshall Court. As described in note 4 below, controversial decisions of the Warren and Burger Courts—abortion, school busing, school prayer, and so forth—have prompted recurrent congressional efforts to curb the Court's jurisdiction. And these efforts have in turn spurred searches for principles to blunt that congressional weapon. How persuasive are the limiting principles articulated in recent years? For a review of the controversy, see Gunther, "Congressional Power to Curtail Federal Court Jurisdiction: An Opinionated Guide to the Ongoing Debate," 36 Stan.L.Rev. 201 (1984).

a. *"Internal" restraints: Limits on congressional power arguably inherent in Art. III itself.* In examining the arguable limits on congressional power, it is useful to distinguish between "internal" restraints—those traceable to Art. III itself—and "external" ones—those derived from constitutional provisions other than Art. III. An Art. III limit on congressional power initially articulated by Professor Henry M. Hart, Jr., has been widely resorted to by Court defenders in and out of Congress. That restraining principle argues that the "exceptions" power of Congress cannot be exercised in a way that would interfere with the "essential" or "core" functions of the Court. Hart urged that "the exceptions must not be such as will destroy the essential role of the Supreme Court in the constitutional plan." See Hart, "The Power of Congress to Limit the Jurisdiction of Federal Courts: An Exercise in Dialectic," 66 Harv.L.Rev. 1362, 1365 (1953). The leading modern advocates of such a limit are Professor Leonard Ratner [3] and the Reagan Administration's first Attorney General, William French Smith.[4]

Klein Revisited," 1981 Wis.L.Rev. 1189; Currie, "The Constitution in the Supreme Court: Civil War and Reconstruction," 51 U.Chi.L.Rev. 131 (1984).

Yakus involved a congressional effort in the Emergency Price Control Act of 1942 to restrict constitutional litigation to a single federal court. It provided that the validity of OPA regulations could be tested only in an administrative proceeding, subject to review by a specially constituted Emergency Court of Appeals and ultimately by the Supreme Court. The Yakus petitioners had not resorted to this exclusive statutory procedure and were accordingly not permitted to raise the defense of invalidity in a criminal prosecution for violation of an OPA regulation. The Supreme Court majority affirmed the convictions: "There is no constitutional requirement that that test [of the validity of a regulation] be made in one tribunal rather than in another, so long as there is an opportunity to be heard and for judicial review which satisfies the demands of due process, as is the case here."

3. E.g., "Congressional Power Over the Appellate Jurisdiction of the Supreme Court," 109 U.Pa.L.Rev. 157 (1960); "Majoritarian Constraints on Judicial Review: Congressional Control of Supreme Court Jurisdiction," 27 Vill.L. Rev. 929 (1982). Ratner would interpret the Art. III congressional power as if it read: "With such exceptions and under such regulations as Congress may make, not inconsistent with the essential functions of the Supreme Court under this Constitution." He posits two such functions: to maintain the supremacy of federal law; and to provide "ultimate resolution of inconsistent or conflicting interpretations of federal law by state and federal courts." Would § 25 of the 1789 Act have met that test? Would the present jurisdictional provisions? See the old and new statutory provisions, p. 54 below. Ratner would hold unconstitutional any effort to bar review "in every case involving a particular subject."

4. Attorney General Smith echoed the Hart-Ratner position in a letter addressed to the Chair of the Senate Judiciary Committee in response to

What *is* the "essential" or "core" role of the Court? Compare with the Hart argument and its progeny the position of Wechsler in "The Courts and the Constitution," 65 Colum.L.Rev. 1001 (1965), rejecting constitutional arguments that would prohibit any alterations of appellate jurisdiction "motivated by hostility to the decisions of the Court": "I see no basis for this view and think it antithetical to the plan of the Constitution for the courts—which was quite simply that the Congress would decide from time to time how far the federal judicial institutions should be used within the limits of the federal judicial power." [5] See also Gunther, above: "To me, the main question raised by [the "essential functions"] kind of argument is whether it confuses the familiar with the necessary, the desirable with the constitutionally mandated. [U]ltimately I cast my lot with [those] who find quite unpersuasive the case for [these] internal restraints." [6]

b. *"External" restraints: Restraints drawn from constitutional sources other than Art. III.* Even if Art. III cannot be persuasively read to curtail congressional power over appellate jurisdiction, other limitations in the Constitution, as in the Bill of Rights, apply. For example, Congress could not bar Supreme Court review by excluding certain litigants on the basis of race or political beliefs. Indeed, recent efforts to articulate constitutional limits on congressional power increasingly tend to rely on such "external" restraints rather than Art. III itself. That trend is an understandable response to modern Court doctrine: the Fifth Amendment's due process limit on Congress [7] is now read to incorporate the Fourteenth Amendment's equal protection guarantee as well, and the expansive interpretations of due process and equal protection by the Warren and Burger Courts (see chaps. 8 and 9 below) have beckoned searchers for constitutional limits on congressional legislation regarding jurisdiction. Note the review of recent "external" restraints arguments in Gunther, above: "It is widely agreed that legislation singling out particular classes of *litigants* on the basis of their race or other 'suspect' classifications, or injuring them in the exercise of fundamental federal rights, triggers a strict scrutiny inquiry and is in effect presumably invalid, justifiable only after a frequently impossible demonstration that the legislation serves a compelling governmental interest and utilizes the least burdensome means to achieve that interest. Hence, the argument goes, singling

inquiries about the constitutionality of that portion of the Helms Bill (see note 4 below) that would withdraw the Court's appellate jurisdiction over cases relating to "voluntary" school prayers. The Attorney General argued that Congress may not constitutionally make "'exceptions' to Supreme Court jurisdiction which would intrude upon the core functions of the Supreme Court as an independent and equal branch in our system of separation of powers" and that "Congress can limit the Supreme Court's appellate jurisdiction only up to the point where it impairs the Court's core functions in the constitutional scheme." Letter from Attorney General Smith to Senator Strom Thurmond, May 6, 1982, in 128 Cong. Rec. S4727–4730.

5. Recall also Chief Justice Chase's comment in McCardle: "We are not at liberty to inquire into the motives of the legislature." Why not? The Court's inhibitions about inquiring into legislative motives are examined more fully in later portions of this book. See, e.g., p. 219 below.

6. See also, e.g. Constitutional Restraints Upon the Judiciary: Hearings Before the Subcomm.

on the Constitution of the Senate Comm. on the Judiciary, 97th Cong., 1st Sess. (1981) (esp. the statement by Professor William Van Alstyne); Bator, "Congressional Power Over the Federal Courts," 27 Vill.L.Rev. 1032 (1982), and Redish, "Congressional Power to Regulate Supreme Court Appellate Jurisdiction Under the Exceptions Clause: An Internal and External Examination," 27 Vill.L.Rev. 900 (1982).

To determine congressional power on the basis of the "constitutional plan" and the "essential" functions of the Supreme Court invites return to basic issues of Marbury v. Madison and judicial review. Thus, the Wechsler argument includes a reminder that federal courts do not pass on constitutional questions because of any "special function vested in them to enforce the Constitution or police the other agencies of government."

7. For discussion of a traditional due process limit on congressional power, see Battaglia v. General Motors Corp., 169 F.2d 254, 257 (2d Cir.1948), discussed in the Hart article noted above.

out classes of *issues* for primary or exclusive adjudication in state rather than federal courts is similarly vulnerable to constitutional challenge.[8]

"[The] central question raised by such invocations of the equal protection-strict scrutiny lines of cases is whether they can properly be read to condemn jurisdiction-channelling laws by Congress—laws which prescribe primary reliance on state courts for some subjects of federal question litigation and allow access to federal courts for others. [This] is not a frivolous argument; but I do not think it is in the end persuasive. Rather, it strikes me as ultimately circular and question-begging. The central problem [is] that it too readily expands the reasons for the obvious flaw in laws which distinguish among *litigants* on the basis of race or other forbidden criteria and extends the constitutional attack to jurisdictional statutes which differentiate on the basis of *subject matter.* The basic difficulty is that there simply is no principle requiring all classes of federal question litigation to be handled in the same way. If one pays adequate heed to the Art. III compromise giving Congress the power to make decisions about appropriate channelling of federal issues as between federal and state courts, assigning some classes of cases to the state courts does not 'discriminate against' or 'burden' or 'prejudice' the rights involved in those cases."[9]

    c. *Practical considerations.* There are practical limitations on congressional resort to the power to curb federal court jurisdiction. If access to the Supreme Court were barred, for example, decision would be left to lower courts, with inconsistent results and a threat to the uniformity need articulated by Justice Story in Martin v. Hunter's Lessee. Moreover, the unpopular Supreme Court decisions that prompted the congressional response would remain on the books. Indeed, it can be argued that the congressional power over appellate jurisdiction ultimately is a source of strength rather than weakness for the Court. Thus, Hart and Wechsler suggest [Federal Courts (2d ed. 1973) at 363] that it may be "politically healthy" that "the limits of congressional power have never been completely clarified": "In some circumstances, may not attempts to restrict jurisdiction be an appropriate and important way for the political branches to register disagreement with the [Court]? And is it not enormously significant in this regard that, ever since McCardle, such 'attempts' have, in the main, been just that, that Congress has not significantly cut back the Supreme Court's jurisdiction in a 'vindictive' manner despite the enormous unpopularity from time to time of some of its rulings?"[10]

---

8. See, e.g., Tribe, "Jurisdictional Gerrymandering: Zoning Disfavored Rights Out of the Federal Courts," 16 Harv.C.R.–C.L.L.Rev. 129 (1981). Tribe relies especially on a 1969 decision, Hunter v. Erickson, p. 632 below.

9. Note also Gunther's elaborations: "The underlying assumption that relegation of a federal claim to the state court invariably produces less vigorous enforcement of the federal right [is] itself suspect." After emphasizing the original understanding underlying Art. III and the fact that many state courts today give more vigorous enforcement to some federal rights than the Supreme Court does, Gunther adds: "Does my position not overlook the obvious [anti-federal courts] motivation of the members of Congress who introduce these jurisdiction-stripping proposals?" He insists that there are "fatal flaws" in the argument that such allegedly improper "motivation" should prompt the Court to strike down the jurisdictional curbs. He identifies the deepest problem with such arguments as "whether there truly is an unconstitutional motive when Congress redraws jurisdictional lines in part because it dislikes certain federal court decisions. Assertions that such a motive is unconstitutional in any judicially enforceable sense rest, once again, on circular, question-begging reasoning. [In] short, the issue goes back to whether or not one reads Art. III, as I would, to grant a very broad discretion to Congress in assigning federal question litigation to state or federal courts. In my view, the basic structure of Art. III provides precisely that power. [Congressional] implementation of [its] disaffection would, after all, simply rely on [the] originally contemplated role of state courts as enforcers of federal rights. [Moreover], disaffection-based jurisdictional statutes have been sustained in the past [with respect to lower federal courts]." See the notes beginning at p. 49 below. Note also the discussion of potential congressional power under Sec. 5 of the Fourteenth Amendment, considered in chap. 10 below.

10. Note also Professor Charles L. Black's argument that the existence of congressional power over federal court jurisdiction (and the traditional forbearance of Congress in using it) is

4. *Congressional control of appellate jurisdiction: Modern efforts.* a. *The Roberts defense.* During the Warren and Burger years, the congressional interest in appellate jurisdiction usually stemmed from proposals for piecemeal withdrawals. Ironically, not long before, there had been serious attention to suggestions to *deprive* Congress of that weapon. Former Justice Owen J. Roberts, for example, proposed a constitutional amendment to assure the Court's appellate jurisdiction in all constitutional cases. "Now is the Time: Fortifying the Supreme Court's Independence," 35 A.B.A.J. 1 (1949). Senator John Marshall Butler of Maryland, with the support of several bar associations, introduced such an amendment in 1953. S.J.Res. 44, 83d Cong., 1st Sess. The Senate approved, but the House tabled.

b. *The Jenner-Butler attack.* Within a few years, Congress became more concerned with curtailing jurisdiction than with safeguarding it. See, e.g., Senator Jenner's bill—provoked by several Warren Court decisions—eliminating appellate jurisdiction in cases involving, for example, the federal employees' security program, state subversive legislation, and state bar admissions. S. 2646, 85th Cong., 1st Sess. (1957). The rapid shift in political winds was symbolized by Senator John Marshall Butler: a sponsor of the pro-Court amendment in 1953, he now joined with Senator Jenner to sponsor a revised version of the Jenner proposal. The Jenner-Butler bill [S. 3386, 85th Cong., 2d Sess. (1958)] would have included the following provision, prompted by the 1957 decisions in Konigsberg and Schware (p. 1367 below): "[The] Supreme Court shall have no jurisdiction to review, either by appeal, writ of certiorari, or otherwise, any case where there is drawn into question the validity of any law, rule, or regulation of any State, or of any board of bar examiners, or similar body, or of any action or proceeding taken pursuant to any such law, rule, or regulation pertaining to the admission of persons to the practice of law within such State." Was that Jenner-Butler provision constitutional? [11]

c. *The 1968 crime control bill and some questions.* The Senate Judiciary Committee's version of the 1968 crime control bill—provoked by decisions such as Miranda v. Arizona, 384 U.S. 436 (1966)—included a provision which stated that neither the Supreme Court nor any other Art. III court "shall have jurisdiction to review or to reverse, vacate, modify, or disturb in any way, a ruling of any trial court of any State in any criminal prosecution admitting in evidence as voluntarily made an admission or confession of any accused." That Report contained an elaborate defense of congressional power over jurisdiction, but all anti-Miranda provisions couched in jurisdictional terms were eliminated on the floor of the Senate prior to passage of the Omnibus Crime Control and Safe Streets Act of 1968. Do the 1950s and 1960s proposals raise constitutional questions? Under McCardle? Under Klein? Under Marbury v. Madison?

"the rock on which rests the legitimacy of the judicial work in a democracy." Black, "The Presidency and Congress," 32 Wash.&Lee L.Rev. 841 (1975), and Black, Decision According to Law (1981). For a partial agreement with Black, see Perry, The Constitution, the Courts, and Human Rights (1982).

11. The Jenner-Butler bill was narrowly defeated. For the political struggle, see Murphy, Congress and the Court (1962), and Hearings on S. 2646, 85th Cong., Limitation of the Appellate Jurisdiction of the Supreme Court (1957–58). See generally Elliott, "Court-Curbing Proposals in Congress," 33 Notre Dame Law. 597 (1958).

Another provision in the Jenner-Butler omnibus proposal—in reaction to such cases as Watkins (1957, p. 1405 below)—would have amended 2 U.S.C. § 192, the congressional contempt statute. That law states that anyone "who having been summoned as a witness" by any congressional committee and who wilfully "refuses to answer any question pertinent to the question under inquiry" shall be guilty of a misdemeanor. The Jenner-Butler bill would have added: "Provided, That for the purposes of this section any question shall be deemed pertinent unless timely objection is made thereto on the ground that such question lacks pertinency, or when such objection is made, if such question is ruled pertinent by the body conducting the hearing." Note that the basic provision made "pertinency" an element of the statutory crime, and that the Jenner-Butler bill would have deprived the courts of power to adjudicate that element. Would that Jenner-Butler provision have been subject to constitutional attack under Klein?

d. *Anti-busing legislation.* Note the range of restraints on the courts in the anti-busing proposals that followed in the wake of the 1971 Swann decision on school desegregation remedies. The proposals and their fate are noted below, p. 719. Are they supportable as exercises of Art. III power? Or does their validity turn on the scope of the substantive power of Congress over desegregation remedies, under § 5 of the Fourteenth Amendment (see chap. 10, sec. 4, below)?

e. *The Helms Amendments and other recent efforts to curb appellate jurisdiction.* The most recent wave of efforts to curb the Court's appellate jurisdiction crested in the early 1980s. Senator Jesse Helms of North Carolina was frequently at the center of those efforts, and one of his proposals, a bill to curb federal court jurisdiction in cases involving "voluntary" school prayers, received the most continuous attention in Congress. The Helms effort began in 1979. The Helms Amendment to S. 210, 96th Cong., 1st Sess., would have removed jurisdiction over such cases from all federal courts—lower ones as well as the Supreme Court.[12] Senator Kennedy attacked that proposal on the Senate floor as an evisceration of the principle of Martin v. Hunter's Lessee. Senator Helms responded by referring to "the acknowledged power of Congress to make exceptions and prescribe regulations to the appellate power." Was Senator Kennedy's reliance on Martin persuasive? Was the Helms amendment consistent with McCardle and Klein? Marbury? Is Congress overstepping its bounds if its jurisdictional curbs bar access to *all* federal courts, not just the Supreme Court? (On the last question, see the next group of notes.)

In the 97th Congress, which convened in 1981, proposals to curb the Court's appellate jurisdiction in specified categories of cases went well beyond the school prayer issue targeted by Senator Helms and attracted more attention than they had in years. During 1981 and 1982, some 30 jurisdiction-stripping bills were introduced in Congress, with some eliciting extensive committee hearings.[13] The proposals would have eliminated the Court's appellate jurisdiction in a number of controversial areas, including busing and abortion as well as school prayers. All those proposals failed. The major one, a renewed Helms Amendment on school prayers, was blocked as a result of a successful filibuster. Although the school prayer proposals were reintroduced in the 98th Congress, in 1983–84, the momentum behind the efforts had waned considerably, largely because many opponents to the challenged Court ruling had shifted their energies to an attempt to amend the Constitution to permit voluntary school prayers. See chap. 14 below. However, immediately after the school prayer constitutional amendment failed on March 20, 1984, Senator Helms stated on the Senate floor: "There is more than one way to skin a cat, and there is more than one way for Congress to provide a check on arrogant Supreme Court Justices who routinely distort the Constitution to suit their own notions of public policy." 130 Cong.Rec. S2901. Apparently, then, Senator Helms intends to continue to pursue enactment of his jurisdiction-stripping proposal.

---

12. The Amendment would have added two new sections to 28 U.S.C.:

"§ 1259. Notwithstanding the provisions of section 1253, 1254, and 1257 of this chapter, the Supreme Court shall not have jurisdiction to review, by appeal, writ of certiorari, or otherwise, any case arising out of any State statute [which] relates to voluntary prayers in public schools and public buildings.

"§ 1364. Notwithstanding any other provision of law, the district courts shall not have jurisdiction of any case or question which the Supreme Court does not have jurisdiction to

review under Section 1259." [For the 1962 school prayer decision challenged by this proposal, see p. 1487 below.]

13. See the collection of proposals in Baucus & Kay, "The Court Stripping Bills: Their Impact on the Constitution, the Courts, and Congress," 27 Vill.L.Rev. 988 (1982). The most comprehensive hearings are printed in Constitutional Restraints upon the Judiciary: Hearings Before the Subcomm. on the Constitution of the Senate Comm. on the Judiciary, 97th Cong., 1st Sess. (1981).

CONGRESS AND THE LOWER FEDERAL COURTS

1. *Justice Story's position.*   Most of Justice Story's opinion in Martin v. Hunter's Lessee, p. 29 above, rested on the assumption that Art. III was "not mandatory, and that congress may constitutionally omit to vest the judicial power in courts of the United States." But before he reached that central portion of his opinion, Justice Story wrote several paragraphs of quite a different tenor, suggesting that the Judiciary Article of the Constitution was indeed to be "mandatory upon the legislature." Some have viewed Story's "mandatory" passages as meaning that Congress *must* establish lower federal courts with the fullest possible jurisdiction—something Congress has never done. Others have read the passages to mean that Congress must at least vest the fullest possible appellate jurisdiction in the Supreme Court in the absence of comprehensive lower federal court jurisdiction—again, something Congress has never done. (Think, for example, of cases between citizens of different states arising in the state courts: they are cases within the federal judicial power, but they have never been reviewable in the Supreme Court.)

In Martin v. Hunter's Lessee, Justice Story's "mandatory" passages stated: "The language of [Art. III] throughout is manifestly designed to be mandatory upon the legislature. Its obligatory force is so imperative, that congress could not, without a violation of its duty, have refused to carry it into operation. The judicial power of the United States *shall be vested* (not may be vested) in one supreme court, and in such inferior courts as congress may, from time to time, ordain and establish. [If], then, it is a duty of congress to vest the judicial power of the United States, it is a duty to vest the *whole judicial power.* The language, if imperative as to one part, is imperative as to all. If it were otherwise, this anomaly would exist, that congress might successively refuse to vest the jurisdiction in any one class of cases enumerated in the constitution, and thereby defeat the jurisdiction as to all; for the constitution has not singled out any class on which congress are bound to act in preference to others.

"The next consideration is as to the courts in which the judicial power shall be vested. It is manifest that a supreme court must be established: but whether it be equally obligatory to establish inferior courts, is a question of some difficulty. If congress may lawfully omit to establish inferior courts, it might follow, that in some of the enumerated cases the judicial power could nowhere exist. The supreme court can have original jurisdiction in two classes of cases only. [Congress] cannot vest any portion of the judicial power of the United States, except in courts ordained and established by itself; and if in any of the cases enumerated in the constitution, the state courts did not then possess jurisdiction, the appellate jurisdiction of the supreme court (admitting that it could act on state courts) could not reach those cases, and, consequently, the injunction of the constitution, that the judicial power *"shall be vested,"* would be disobeyed. It would seem, therefore, to follow, that congress are bound to create some inferior courts, in which to vest all that jurisdiction which, under the constitution, is *exclusively* vested in the United States, and of which the supreme court cannot take original cognizance. They might establish one or more inferior courts; they might parcel out the jurisdiction among such courts, from time to time, at their own pleasure. But the whole judicial power of the United States should be, at all times, vested either in an original or appellate form, in some courts created under its authority."

Were those Story remarks intended to be legally binding on Congress? Or were they merely a moral appeal to Congress? The latter explanation seems more consistent with Story's contemporaneous actions. In other cases, for example, he dismissed cases not within the jurisdictional statutes, on the ground that the lower court "has no jurisdiction which is not given by some statute."

White v. Fenner, 29 Fed.Cas. 1015, No. 17,547 (Cir.Ct.R.I.1818). Perhaps even more significant are his activities as legislative lobbyist at the time of Martin. Story, who had seen state challenges to federal authority at close range in his New England circuit duties during the War of 1812, was particularly anxious to make use of the relative harmony at the end of the War to solidify national institutions. Over a period of years, he wrote letters to associates influential in Congress urging legislation and frequently enclosing drafts.[1] One of his favorite projects was a comprehensive judicial code. In submitting one of his drafts, he made it clear that he did not think that Article III automatically created lower courts with full jurisdiction: "The object of this section is to give to the Circuit Court *original* jurisdiction of all cases intended by the Constitution to be confided to the judicial power of the United States, where that jurisdiction has not been already delegated by law. If it was proper in the Constitution to provide for such a jurisdiction, it is wholly irreconcilable with the sound policy or interests of the Government to suffer it to slumber. [It] is truly surprising and mortifying to know how little effective power now exists in this department. [I will] illustrate my positions by a reference to a single class of cases. No Court of the United States has any general delegation of authority 'in all cases in law and equity arising under the Constitution [etc.].' The consequence is, that in thousands of instances arising under the laws of the United States, the parties are utterly without remedy, or with a very inadequate remedy."

The general "federal question" jurisdiction Story desired in 1816 was not in fact vested in the lower federal courts until 1875. Apparently, then, Story's dicta in Martin were an appeal to Congress—an appeal that failed. Moreover, the view that the creation and jurisdiction of lower federal courts was largely left to Congress [2] is supported by the debates at the Constitutional Convention. And the Convention compromise was reflected in the Judiciary Act of 1789 as well, creating some lower federal courts with some, but not nearly all, of the potential federal jurisdiction described in Art. III.

2. *Congressional control of lower federal court jurisdiction: Arguable modern limitations?* a. *Barring access to lower courts.* The Constitution and recurrent statements in Court opinions [3] suggest a broad congressional authority over lower federal court jurisdiction. Are there nevertheless limits inherent in Art. III on what Congress may do? For example, is there an "essential" role for lower federal courts analogous to that argued for Supreme Court appellate jurisdiction? Few arguments of that nature have been voiced. But note

---

1. In December 1815, for example, Story asked the aid of the new Reporter, Henry Wheaton, in "vindicating the necessity of establishing other great national institutions: the extension of the jurisdiction of the courts of the U.S. over *the whole* extent contemplated in the Constitution; the appointment of national notaries public & national justices of the peace; national port wardens & pilots for all the ports of the U.S.; a national bank; & a national bankrupt law." 1 The Life and Letters of Joseph Story (W.W. Story ed. 1851), 271.

2. Among the most explicit decisions sustaining that view is Sheldon v. Sill, 8 How. 441 (1850), upholding the assignee clause of the 1789 Judiciary Act against a claim that the statute could not bar lower court jurisdiction of a case within the description of cases in Art. III.

3. Note, e.g., Justice Stewart's majority opinion in Allen v. McCurry, 449 U.S. 90 (1980), rejecting the lower courts' reliance on an alleged "generally framed principle that every person

asserting a federal right is entitled to one unencumbered opportunity to litigate that right in a federal district court." He commented that "the authority for this principle is difficult to discern. It cannot lie in the Constitution, which makes no such guarantee, but leaves the scope of the jurisdiction of the federal district courts to the wisdom of Congress." He added: "The only other conceivable basis for [such a principle] is hardly a legal basis at all, but rather a general distrust of the capacity of the state courts to render correct decisions on constitutional issues." He repudiated that contention by relying on earlier decisions that had reaffirmed "the constitutional obligation of the state courts to uphold federal law" and had expressed "confidence in their ability to do so." See also Palmore v. United States, 411 U.S. 389 (1973) ("[Under Art. III], if inferior federal courts were created, [Congress was not] required to invest them with all the jurisdiction it was authorized to bestow.")

Eisenberg, "Congressional Authority to Restrict Lower Federal Court Jurisdiction," 83 Yale L.J. 498 (1974), concluding: "It can now be asserted that the [existence of lower federal courts] in some form is constitutionally required." [4] Contrast Bator, "Congressional Power Over the Jurisdiction of the Federal Courts," 27 Vill.L.Rev. 1030 (1982): "If the Congress decides that a certain category of case arising under a federal law should be litigated in a state court, subject to Supreme Court review, neither the letter nor the spirit of the Constitution has been violated. What has happened is that Congress has taken up one of the precise options which the Constitutional Framers specifically envisaged."

Can it at least be argued that Congress may not impose limits on lower federal courts when it is motivated by hostility to unpopular decisions? Recall, e.g., the Helms Amendment noted above, which included jurisdictional curbs directed at the lower federal courts as well as the Supreme Court. Note that the Supreme Court had no difficulty in sustaining the Norris-LaGuardia Act of 1932, depriving federal courts of "jurisdiction" to issue injunctions in labor disputes—a jurisdictional curb largely motivated by congressional hostility to excessive intervention by federal courts in labor disputes. Lauf v. E.G. Shinner & Co., 303 U.S. 323 (1938). (The "external restraints" arguments considered earlier with respect to appellate jurisdiction are applicable to curbs on lower court jurisdiction as well.)

  b. *Barring access to all federal courts.* Even if constitutional restraints on congressional power are not persuasive with respect to curbs on Supreme Court or lower court jurisdiction, can a stronger case be made for restraints when Congress seeks to block jurisdiction of *all* federal courts—the Supreme Court as well as the lower courts—in a specified class of cases? Some of the modern jurisdiction-stripping proposals, such as the Helms Amendment, take just such a form. Professor Lawrence Sager has argued that Art. III requires that there must be *some* federal judicial forum for the enforcement of federal constitutional rights—either an "inferior" court or the Supreme Court.[5] Sager relies primarily on an "inherent" limitation: the guarantee of federal judicial independence in Art. III (the tenure and salary provisions governing federal judges). He notes that many state judges are not afforded such protections and argues that some Art. III forum is constitutionally mandated for the enforcement of federal constitutional rights. Compare Professor Martin Redish's reply that Sager "effectively adopts a 'floating' essential functions thesis." See Redish, "Constitutional Limitations on Congressional Power to Control Federal Jurisdiction: A Reaction to Professor Sager," 77 Nw.U.L.Rev. 143 (1982). Redish argues that the tenure and salary provisions relied on by Sager were simply designed "to preserve the integrity of the federal courts when they actually were used," not to assure that federal courts must be used.[6]

---

  4. Eisenberg relied on the "need" for lower federal courts to enforce "innovative" Supreme Court decisions in areas such as desegregation and reapportionment, and on the impossibility, given the modern Court's workload, of Supreme Court review of all state court cases involving federal issues.

  5. Sager, "Foreword: Constitutional Limitations on Congress' Authority to Regulate the Jurisdiction of the Federal Courts," 95 Harv.L. Rev. 17 (1981).

  6. See generally Gunther, "Congressional Power to Curtail Federal Jurisdiction: An Opinionated Guide to the Ongoing Debate," 36 Stan. L.Rev. 201 (1984).

  Since restrictions on federal courts ordinarily leave state courts as available forums, curtailments of federal jurisdiction do not typically require confrontation of the difficult and unsettled problem of access to *some* judicial forum. Is there, for example, a general due process right of access to a court to review adverse administrative determinations? That is a question which the Supreme Court "studiously has avoided," as Justice Douglas stated in his dissent in Ortwein v. Schwab, 410 U.S. 656 (1973) (chap. 9 below). However, it is widely assumed that under some circumstances due process does require access to a court. See, e.g., Justice Brandeis' concurrence in St. Joseph Stock Yards Co. v. United States, 298 U.S. 38 (1936), and generally Hart & Wechs-

3. *Modern proposals to curtail lower federal court jurisdiction.* a. *The proposed "Human Life Statute."* In 1981, Senator Helms and Congressman Hyde introduced their "Human Rights Statute" directed at the 1973 abortion decision, Roe v. Wade (p. 517 below). The bill's aim was to authorize broader state control of abortions. Sec. 1 of the bill (considered in chap. 10 below) invoked the asserted congressional power to modify the Fourteenth Amendment by stating a finding that there is "a significant likelihood that actual human life exists from conception." In addition to that substantive provision, the Helms-Hyde bill also included a jurisdictional section, Sec. 2, designed to curtail lower federal court jurisdiction in abortion cases.[7] The Helms-Hyde bill was approved by a Senate subcommittee in 1981, but further congressional action was sidetracked when some foes of abortion expressed constitutional doubts about the bill and pressed (unsuccessfully) for constitutional amendments directed at Roe v. Wade.[8] Would Sec. 2 of the Helms-Hyde proposal be constitutional?

b. *Anti-busing proposals.* In March 1982, the Senate adopted a proposal by Senator Johnston of Louisiana to curb busing—the Neighborhood School Act of 1982 (further discussed at p. 719 below). The proposal would have allowed federal judges to order busing only in narrowly confined circumstances. The proposal relied in part on congressional power regarding lower federal court jurisdiction under Art. III.

Although further action on the proposal was blocked in the House, consider the opposing views voiced on the legitimacy of the proposal under Art. III, § 1. Attorney General William French Smith, who had taken a very narrow view of congressional power to curb Supreme Court jurisdiction (see p. 44 above), endorsed the constitutionality of the Art. III-based anti-busing provisions. In a letter to the Chair of the House Judiciary Committee on May 6, 1982, he concluded that "Congress may, within constraints imposed by provisions of the Constitution other than Article III, limit the jurisdiction or remedial authority of the inferior federal courts." He noted that the proposal related "only to one aspect of the remedial power of the inferior federal courts—not unlike the Norris-LaGuardia Act." He argued that the bill had only a "limited effect on the courts' remedial power" and that "a necessary inference" from the Framers' decision to leave the creation of lower federal courts to the discretion of Congress was "that, once created, the scope of the courts' jurisdiction was also discretionary." Nor did he find any Fifth Amendment limitations applicable, since the provisions "neither create a racial classification nor evidence a discriminatory purpose." [9] Senator Thomas Eagleton took issue with much of the Attorney General's position. He argued that the practical and legal *adequacy* of the remaining remedies was crucial to the constitutional validity of the restrictions on court-ordered busing. He insisted that, in those cases where busing was the only practical remedy, barring that remedy "would be invalid either as an impermissible congressional interference with the essentials of the

---

ler, Federal Courts (2d ed. 1973), and Jaffe, Judicial Control of Administrative Action (1965). [The problems of curtailment of all judicial review and of constitutional rights of access to courts are pursued more fully in courses in federal jurisdiction and administrative law.]

7. Sec. 2 stated: "Notwithstanding any other provision of law, no inferior federal court ordained and established by Congress under article III of the Constitution of the United States shall have jurisdiction to issue any restraining order, temporary or permanent injunction, or declaratory judgment in any case involving or arising from any state law or municipal ordinance that (1)

protects the rights of human persons between conception and birth, or (2) prohibits, limits, or regulates (a) the performance of abortions, or (b) the provision at public expense of funds, facilities, personnel, or other assistance for the performance of abortions."

8. The Helms-Hyde proposal was reintroduced in the 98th Congress in 1983 as S. 26.

9. The Attorney General also suggested that the provision might be justified under Sec. 5 of the Fourteenth Amendment, as noted in chap. 10 below. Compare the Court's subsequent decision on *state* efforts to restrict busing, p. 720 below.

independent judicial function or as a violation of the provisions of the Constitution outside of the Article III power (e.g., Due Process)." [10]

SECTION 4.   THE MODERN FRAMEWORK OF JUDICIAL REVIEW: SUPREME COURT JURISDICTION AND PRACTICE

Introduction. What are the contemporary jurisdictional and procedural groundrules that govern the exercise of Supreme Court authority? How does the Court conduct its business? The purpose of this section is to give an overview of the main features and problems of the modern framework. Art. III of the Constitution provides the foundation. But on the few words of that Article has been built a complex superstructure, of congressional statutes and Supreme Court Rules and practices.

Art. III, § 1, for example, provides for "one supreme Court." But it is for Congress to set the size of the Court. The number of Justices has been set at nine since 1869. But earlier in the 19th century, the number fluctuated quite frequently: at the time of Marbury v. Madison, for example, it was six; and at the time of Martin v. Hunter's Lessee, it was seven. Most of the increases in the early years came because the number of federal judicial circuits grew with the expansion of the country, and sitting on circuit was a major part of a Supreme Court Justice's duties until well into the 19th century. But the congressional power over size is also a potential source of political checks on the Court. President Franklin D. Roosevelt's proposed Court-curbing weapon in 1937 was to expand the size of the Court. (See the materials on the Court-packing Plan, p. 128 below.) Even such relatively routine legislation as that setting the time at which the Court shall convene can be made to serve political ends: recall the Jeffersonian legislation which caused the decision in Marbury to be postponed until 1803, as noted at p. 11. Under present law (28 U.S.C. § 2), the Court is directed to convene for "a term of court commencing on the first Monday in October of each year." Because of that provision, a typical session—from the fall to the following summer—is referred to as the "October Term."

The more complex Art. III ingredients of the judicial framework are the provisions of Art. III, § 2, stating that the Judicial Power shall extend to certain specified "Cases" and "Controversies." What constitutes a "case" or "controversy" suitable for federal judicial resolution is a complex and much-litigated question; some of its ramifications are explored in chap. 15. After listing those categories of "Cases" and "Controversies" within the federal judicial power, Art. III, § 2, proceeds to address the Supreme Court's jurisdiction specifically: "In all Cases affecting Ambassadors, other public Ministers and Consuls, and those in which a State shall be a Party, the supreme Court shall have original Jurisdiction. In all the other Cases before mentioned, the supreme Court shall

---

10. Senator Eagleton argued that "hobbling the judiciary by denying it the remedy necessary to vindicate a constitutional right may well be the same as nullifying the constitutional right itself." Eagleton, "Amending the Constitution by the Back Door: A Battle Won . . . But Will We Survive the War?" 39 J.Mo.Bar 113 (1983). See also the Tribe and Sager articles noted earlier.

In 1983, S. 139, a bill "to provide for civil rights in public schools," was introduced in Con-gress (and approved by a Senate subcommittee in March 1984). Relying in part on congressional power under Art. III, § 1, the bill would bar any lower federal court from ordering the assignment or transportation to any school, or the exclusion therefrom, of any student on the basis of race, color, or national origin. Would that proposal be constitutional under Attorney General Smith's analysis? Under Senator Eagleton's?

have appellate Jurisdiction, both as to Law and Fact, with such Exceptions, and under such Regulations as the Congress shall make." Some of the problems inherent in those words have already surfaced, in cases such as Marbury, Martin, and McCardle. What concerns us now is the fleshing out of those jurisdictional categories. The original jurisdiction need not detain us: it is rarely invoked; and it is even more rarely the source of significant constitutional interpretations.[1] The present contours of the Court's appellate jurisdiction—the avenues to review in the Supreme Court from lower federal and state courts—are the major concerns of the materials that follow. After sketching the outlines of contemporary jurisdictional provisions—and some of their problems—the materials look at the Supreme Court's Rules and its practices governing the exercise of review. The section concludes with an examination of the contemporary concern about the Supreme Court's growing workload and the major and controversial proposals engendered by that concern—proposals for substantial changes in the way the Supreme Court conducts its business.

APPELLATE JURISDICTION: THE STATUTES

1. *Review of state court judgments.* a. *The appeal and certiorari provisions and the proposed elimination of obligatory review.* For most of the 20th century, review of state court proceedings has been governed by § 1257 of Title 28 of the U.S. Code:

"Final judgments or decrees rendered by the highest court of a State in which a decision could be had, may be reviewed by the Supreme Court as follows:

"(1) By appeal, where is drawn in question the validity of a treaty or statute of the United States and the decision is against its validity.

"(2) By appeal, where is drawn in question the validity of a statute of any state on the ground of its being repugnant to the Constitution, treaties or laws of the United States, and the decision is in favor of its validity.

"(3) By writ of certiorari, where the validity of a treaty or statute of the United States is drawn in question or where the validity of a State statute is drawn in question on the ground of its being repugnant to the Constitution, treaties or laws of the United States, or where any title, right, privilege or immunity is specially set up or claimed under the Constitution, treaties or statutes of, or commission held or authority exercised under, the United States."

This statutory scheme was designed to distinguish between obligatory, mandatory review (review by "appeal") and discretionary review (review by "certiorari"). Though that distinction does not emerge on the face of the law, the clear congressional purpose was to delineate two different review routes to the Supreme Court from state courts: review as a matter of the appellant's right, in "appeals"; review if the Court chose to exercise its discretion, in "certiorari" situations. The "appeal"-"certiorari" distinction came under mounting attack beginning in the late 1970s. The critics of the "appeal" provision, concerned about the Court's mounting workload, urged that the Court be given full discretion to determine what cases it would decide on the merits. In 1979, the Senate approved a bill to repeal most of the Court's obligatory jurisdiction, retaining mandatory appeals only in those cases which must be heard by three-judge District Courts. (See p. 62 below.)[1] Despite widespread agreement that

1. For a rare example, see South Carolina v. Katzenbach, p. 933 below. See generally 28 U.S.C. § 1251 and Hart and Wechsler, Federal Courts (2d ed. 1973), chap. 3.

1. The Supreme Court Jurisdiction Act of 1979 (S. 450, 96th Cong., 1st Sess.), introduced by Senator DeConcini, would have deleted from 28 U.S.C. § 1257 all references to appeals from

this reform is desirable, its enactment by Congress has so far been blocked by parliamentary obstacles; but adoption is probable in the near future.

All nine Justices supported the virtual elimination of obligatory review when the issue was before Congress in the late 1970s. In a letter, they stated that "the Court is required to devote time and other finite resources to deciding on the merits cases which do not, in Chief Justice Taft's words, 'involve principles, the application of which are of wide public importance or governmental interest, and which should be authoritatively declared by the final court.' To the extent that we are obligated by statute to devote our energies to these less important cases we cannot devote our time and attention to the more important issues and cases constantly pressing for resolution in increasing volume." Even though the proposal is no doubt constitutional, is it wise? [2] Can a plausible argument be made that at least a portion of the Court's appellate jurisdiction should remain obligatory? Which portion? [3]

  b. *Assuring supremacy and uniformity.* Note the similarities and differences between the modern jurisdictional statute, 28 U.S.C. § 1257, and its earliest antecedent, § 25 of the Judiciary Act of 1789, considered in Martin v. Hunter's Lessee, p. 29 above.[4] Note that under § 25 (and indeed well into the 20th century), Supreme Court review was available only if the state court *denied* federal claims—e.g., by sustaining a state statute against federal objections or by setting aside a federal law. Jurisdiction was broadened in 1914, when Supreme Court review was for the first time extended to cases in which the state court had *sustained* rather than rejected the federal claim. Thus, assurance of greater uniformity in interpretation of federal law, rather than mere assurance of federal supremacy, did not become a major goal of the review statute until the 20th century.

Is the uniformity need adequately met today? Not even the 1914 extension, now reflected in 28 U.S.C. § 1257(3), provided for the correction of *all* errors in state court interpretations of federal law. The decision which provoked the 1914 change illustrates the point. In Ives v. South Buffalo Ry. Co., 201 N.Y. 271, 94 N.E. 431 (1911), the state court had held New York's workmen's

state court judgements, leaving certiorari—see § 1257(3)—as the only route for review. Similarly the bill would have eliminated appeals from *federal* Courts of Appeals by deleting subsection (2) of 28 U.S.C. § 1254 (p. 62 below).

  2. In initially introducing the bill in 1978, Senator DeConcini stated: "It is [my] view, and the view of many others, that there is little justification for the obligatory appellate jurisdiction. Certainly there are categories of cases which annually produce questions of such magnitude that it is important that the Supreme Court review them. But such questions regularly appear on its certiorari docket as well. [Under my proposal] the Court would be able to concentrate all of its decisional time on cases which it regards as significant." He noted that "obligatory cases are forming an increasingly larger percentage of all cases decided on the merits. In 1942 they comprised 28 percent of all cases decided on the merits. By 1976 that figure had climbed to 47 percent."

  3. Note Senator DeConcini's comment when he reintroduced his bill in 1979: "[E]ven if the idea of having an obligatory jurisdiction were sound, there is no practical way of describing, in legislation, the kinds of cases that should fall within it."

  4. The text of § 25: "That a final judgment or decree in any suit, in the highest court of law or equity of a State in which a decision in the suit could be had, where is drawn in question the validity of a treaty or statute of, or an authority exercised under the United States, and the decision is against their validity; or where is drawn in question the validity of a statute of, or an authority exercised under any State, on the ground of their being repugnant to the constitution, treaties or laws of the United States, and the decision is in favour of such their validity, or where is drawn in question the construction of any clause of the constitution, or of a treaty, or statute of, or commission held under the United States, and the decision is against the title, right, privilege or exemption specially set up or claimed by either party, under such clause of the said constitution, treaty, statute or commission, may be re-examined and reversed or affirmed in the Supreme Court of the United States upon a writ of error. [But] no other error shall be assigned or regarded as a ground of reversal in any such case as aforesaid, than such as appears on the face of the record, and immediately respects the before mentioned questions of validity or construction of the said constitution, treaties, statutes, commissions, or authorities in dispute."

compensation law unconstitutional under the due process clauses of the state as well as the federal constitution. The New York court's interpretation of the federal due process clause was thought to be more restrictive than the Supreme Court's position, yet no review was possible under the old jurisdictional statute. But, ironically, not even the 1914 expansion would have permitted review in the Ives case—because of the "adequate state grounds" barrier to Supreme Court review, considered in note 2 below.

c. *The appeal-certiorari distinction.* Under § 25 and its 19th century revisions, Supreme Court review was obligatory: all state cases within the statute could be taken to the Supreme Court as a matter of right, by writ of error. The 1914 expansion introduced review at the discretion of the Supreme Court in certain cases; and that method was expanded by the Judges' Bill of 1925, which produced 28 U.S.C. § 1257(3), the present certiorari provision.[5] Determination of whether appeal or certiorari was the appropriate review route lay to a considerable extent within the discretion of counsel in framing the federal objection in the state court. That control by litigants rested largely on the interpretation of a predecessor to 28 U.S.C. § 1257 in Dahnke-Walker Milling Co. v. Bondurant, 257 U.S. 282 (1921).[6]

2. *The "adequate and independent state grounds" barrier to Supreme Court review of state court decisions.* The Court has long held that it lacks power to review state court decisions that rest on "adequate and independent state grounds." Efforts to obtain review of such decisions are dismissed for lack of jurisdiction. Thus, where a state court has addressed both state and federal questions in deciding a case, its decision is not reviewable if the state ground alone is sufficient to support its judgment. In such a situation, an error in the state court's interpretation of federal law would not affect the result in the case. Determining whether a state court's reliance on a state law ground bars Supreme Court review is a frequently encountered and complex problem. State grounds of decision may be substantive or procedural: a state court ruling may rest on a mixture of state and federal substantive grounds; or a state court may fail to reach a federal issue because of an allegedly dispositive state procedural barrier. In either situation, assessing the "adequacy" and "independence" of the state ground may be difficult. The intricacies of these problems are pursued in federal jurisdiction courses.[7] But the theoretical underpinnings and a few of the practical consequences of the substantive and procedural branches of the "adequate and independent state grounds" barrier are worth noting here.

a. *Theoretical underpinnings.* Justice Jackson, in Herb v. Pitcairn, 324 U.S. 117 (1945), summarized the adequate state grounds rule and its theoretical bases as follows: "This Court [has always] adhered to the principle that it will not review judgments of state courts that rest on adequate and independent state grounds. [The reason] is found in the partitioning of power between the state and federal judicial systems and in the limitations of our own jurisdiction. Our

---

5. On the practice in appeal and certiorari cases, and the extent to which discretionary elements play a role in the disposition of appeals, see the next group of notes and sec. 4A of chap. 15, p. 1590 below.

6. Dahnke-Walker stated that obligatory review is available not only where a state law is sustained against a federal challenge "on its face"—i.e., in all its possible applications—but even where the law's constitutionality is challenged only with respect to its application to a particular set of facts. The Court stated that the latter type of challenge could be viewed as a proper appeal under 28 U.S.C. § 1257(2), even though it would have been reviewable only by

certiorari, under § 1257(3), if the challenge had been one simply asserting a "title, right, privilege or immunity" arising under federal law. Justice Brandeis' dissent in Dahnke-Walker predicted, with substantial accuracy: "If jurisdiction upon writ of error [what is now known as an "appeal"] can be obtained by the mere claim in words that a state statute is invalid, if so construed as to 'apply' to a given state of facts, the right to a review will depend, in large classes of cases, not upon the nature of the constitutional question involved, but upon the skill of counsel."

7. See generally Hart & Wechsler, Federal Courts (2d ed. 1973), chap. 5, and Wright, Federal Courts (4th ed. 1983), chap. 12.

only power over state judgments is to correct them to the extent that they incorrectly adjudge federal rights. And our power is to correct wrong judgments, not to revise opinions. We are not permitted to render an advisory opinion, and if the same judgment would be rendered by the state court after we corrected its views of federal laws, our review could amount to nothing more than an advisory opinion." Justice Jackson found the rule a constitutional mandate, in view of the Art. III preclusion of advisory opinions by federal courts (see chap. 15). Others have suggested that, whether or not the rule is constitutionally required, it is mandated by the jurisdictional statutes.[8]

    b. *State substantive law: Modern changes (Michigan v. Long).* In constitutional litigation, the most common example of an independent and adequate state substantive ground is a state court ruling that a state law violates both the federal constitution and an identical or similar provision in the state constitution.[9] In principle, it is clear that even though the state court opinion may include an elaborate discussion of the meaning of the federal guarantee—an interpretation that may be wrong—the Supreme Court will not review if the state judges rest their decision on their own constitutional provision as well. In such a situation, correction of the state court's interpretation would not change the outcome of the case; Court correction of the state court's error would accordingly be an unpermitted advisory opinion, even though the erroneous state court ruling would constitute a nonuniform interpretation of federal law.

    Interrelated developments in recent years have made applications of the adequate state grounds principle controversial. These developments are products of the Burger Court's occasional proclivity to cut back on federal constitutional guarantees announced by the Warren Court, especially in the area of

8. See, e.g., Justice Brennan's comment in Fay v. Noia, 372 U.S. 391 (1963), stating that it was unnecessary to decide "whether the adequate state ground rule is constitutionally compelled or merely a matter of the construction of the statutes defining this Court's appellate review," since "the present statute governing our review of state court decisions, 28 U.S.C. § 1257, limited as it is to '*judgments or decrees* rendered by the highest court of a State in which a decision could be had' (emphasis supplied), provides ample statutory warrant" for the rule.

9. The problem of adequate and independent state grounds may also surface in the context of federal issues that are nonconstitutional. For an early manifestation of the complexities of interrelated state and federal substantive grounds in such a nonconstitutional setting, recall Martin v. Hunter's Lessee, p. 29 above. In deciding the merits of that litigation, the Virginia judges had not denied that federal treaties protected lands held by aliens as of 1783; they insisted instead that as a matter of Virginia law the Fairfax lands had been seized by the State prior to 1783. Moreover, most of the Virginia judges stated that their judgment for Hunter was independently supportable on the basis of a legislatively approved Compromise adopted while the litigation was in abeyance in the 1790s. Justice Story, in examining those asserted state grounds of decision in 1816, found neither acceptable. He rejected the relevance of the Act of Compromise because it was not pleaded on the face of the record and therefore was not properly before the Supreme Court under the terms of § 25 of the Judiciary Act of 1789. And the state court's

view as to who owned the lands in 1783 was not found controlling by Justice Story because of his concern about potential evasion of federal guarantees. In a sweeping statement, he argued: "How, indeed, can it be possible to decide whether a [land] title be within the protection of a treaty, until it is ascertained what that title is, and whether it have a legal validity?" He added: "If the court below should decide, that the title was bad, and therefore not protected by the treaty, must not this court have a power to decide the title to be good, and, therefore, protected by the treaty?"

    Under modern practice, the Martin case would not be reviewable in the Supreme Court. The Court would take note of the existence of the Act of Compromise. The state property ruling would give more difficulty: the modern Supreme Court would not disregard it as readily and totally as Story did; its concern about state evasion of federal guarantees by disingenuous statements of state law would prompt only limited reexamination of the state property ruling, not a wholesale displacement.

    Similar problems occasionally surface in constitutional litigation, especially with regard to the protection of "property" under the due process clauses and the protection of "contracts" under the contracts clause. Determining what is "property" and what is a "contract" for purposes of the federal guarantees rests initially on an inquiry into state law, although a state is not free to manipulate those concepts in order to evade federal protections.

criminal defendants' rights. One resultant development was that a number of state courts began to invalidate state laws in opinions which, while primarily discussing the federal constitution (although arguably out of line with narrower Burger Court rulings), were nevertheless allegedly immune from Court review because of an additional, brief statement by the state court that a similar state constitutional provision had also been violated as well.[10] While that pattern was developing, some Justices of the Supreme Court were probably increasingly frustrated by the existence of such "erroneous" yet unreviewable federal constitutional rulings in the state court reports.

These developments may well have helped prompt the Court's 1983 decision in MICHIGAN v. LONG, 463 U.S. 1032. That decision purports not to disturb the traditional view that an independent and adequate state ground bars Supreme Court jurisdiction. But the ruling does a virtual about-face regarding the working guidelines for determining the reviewability of state court decisions in situations where the state court opinion is not absolutely clear about the bases on which it rests. The traditional presumption was that the Court lacked jurisdiction unless its authority to review was clear on the face of the state court opinion. When faced with uncertainty, the Court in the past occasionally remanded such cases to the state court for clarification. But more commonly, the Court would deny jurisdiction where there was uncertainty. Under the new approach, by contrast, the Court will no longer remand for clarification or dismiss for lack of jurisdiction, but will instead treat as reviewable any state ruling that is less than crystal-clear. However, the state court can still preclude Supreme Court review if it clearly states that it was relying on an independent state ground.

In Michigan v. Long, the state court had held that Long's search and seizure rights had been violated. The Michigan court's opinion discussed primarily Fourth Amendment principles as elaborated by the Supreme Court. However, the state court opinion also made two references to the search and seizure guarantee in the Michigan Constitution. Most important was a statement at the conclusion of its opinion, for it was the kind of statement that in recent years had been recurrently invoked by state courts as a way of barring Court review: "We hold, therefore, that the deputies' search of the vehicle was proscribed by the Fourth Amendment to the United States Constitution, *and* art. 1 § 11 of the

---

10. Should such traditionally unreviewable state court ventures into federal constitutional law be praised as creative, or criticized as irresponsible? For an admiring evaluation, see Karst, "Serrano v. Priest: A State Court's Responsibilities and Opportunities in the Development of Federal Constitutional Law," 60 Calif.L. Rev. 720 (1972). See generally Brennan, "State Constitutions and the Protection of Individual Rights," 90 Harv.L.Rev. 489 (1977), and Howard, "State Courts and Constitutional Rights in the Day of the Burger Court," 60 Va.L.Rev. 873 (1976). For an especially principled examination of state court interpretations of *state* constitutional provisions, see Linde, "First Things First: Rediscovering the States' Bills of Rights," 9 U.Balt.L.Rev. 379 (1980). See also Collins, "Reliance on State Constitutions—Away From a Reactionary Approach," 9 Hastings Const.L.Q. 1 (1981), criticizing those for whom a "state bill of rights is little more than a handy grab bag filled with a bevy of clauses that may be exploited in order to circumvent disfavored United States Supreme Court decisions" and objecting to the growing trend to employ "state constitutions in a selective and simply reactionary manner in order to obtain a desired objective." Collins advocates a "moving away from a reactionary or instrumentalist approach" and a move toward "a principled or doctrinal basis [for] reliance on state constitutions."

Quite often, nonreviewable statements about federal law by state courts have had considerable impact on other courts. See, e.g., Serrano v. Priest, 5 Cal.3d 584, 487 P.2d 1241 (1971), sustaining a challenge to interdistrict inequalities in school financing in an opinion discussing federal law at length yet immune from Court review— immune because of the perception of the adequate state grounds barrier at that time as well as because the ruling was probably not "final" for jurisdictional purposes. In Serrano, the California Supreme Court's extensive discussion of federal law was followed by several other state and federal courts before the Supreme Court took a different view of the federal equal protection clause in the Rodriguez case in 1973, p. 789 below.

Michigan Constitution.'' (Emphasis added.) Nevertheless, Justice O'CONNOR'S majority opinion asserted jurisdiction and reversed on the merits.

Justice O'Connor insisted that there was need to "reexamine" the application of the adequate state grounds principle because "we have thus far not developed a satisfying and consistent approach for resolving [the] vexing issue [of determining] whether various forms of references to state law constitute adequate and independent state grounds." She stated the new approach as follows: "If the state court decision indicates clearly and expressly that it is alternatively based on bona fide separate, adequate, and independent grounds, we, of course, will not undertake to review the decision. [Our] requirement of a 'plain statement' that a decision rests upon adequate and independent state grounds does not in any way authorize the rendering of advisory opinions. Rather, in determining, as we must, whether we have jurisdiction to review a case that is alleged to rest on adequate and independent state grounds, we merely assume that there are no such grounds when it is not clear from the opinion itself that the state court relied upon an adequate and independent state ground and when it fairly appears that the state court rested its decision primarily on federal law." Applying that standard here, she stated: "Our review of the decision below [leaves] us unconvinced that it rests upon an independent state ground. Apart from its two citations to the state constitution, the court below relied *exclusively* on its understanding of [federal] cases. [The] references to the state constitution in no way indicate that the decision below rested on grounds in any way *independent* from the state court's interpretation of federal law. Even if we accept that the Michigan constitution has been interpreted to provide independent protection for certain rights also secured under the Fourth Amendment, it fairly appears in this case the Michigan Supreme Court rested its decision primarily on federal law. [It] appears to us that the state court 'felt compelled by what it understood to be federal constitutional considerations to construe [its] own law in the manner it did.' "

The heart of Justice O'Connor's reasoning was as follows: "Respect for the independence of state courts, as well as avoidance of rendering advisory opinions, have been the cornerstones of this Court's refusal to decide cases where there is an adequate and independent state ground. It is precisely because of this respect for state courts, and this desire to avoid advisory opinions, that we do not wish to continue to decide issues of state law that go beyond the opinion that we review, or to require state courts to reconsider cases to clarify the grounds of their decision. Accordingly, when, as in this case, a state court decision fairly appears to rest primarily on federal law, or to be interwoven with the federal law, and when the adequacy and independence of any possible state law ground is not clear from the face of the opinion, we will accept as the most reasonable explanation that the state court decided the case the way it did because it believed that federal law required it to do so. If a state court chooses merely to rely on federal precedents as it would on the precedents of all other jurisdictions, then it need only make clear by a plain statement in its judgment or opinion that the federal cases are being used only for the purpose of guidance, and do not themselves compel the result that the court has reached. In this way, both justice and judicial administration will be greatly improved. [We] believe that such an approach will provide state judges with a clearer opportunity to develop state jurisprudence unimpeded by federal interference, and yet will preserve the integrity of federal law." She also noted that "outright dismissal of cases [that are unclear about their state grounds bases] is clearly not a panacea because it cannot be doubted that there is an important need for uniformity in federal law, and that this need goes unsatisfied when we fail to review an opinion that rests primarily upon federal grounds and where the *independence* of an alleged state ground is not apparent from the four corners of the opinion."

Justice STEVENS' dissent took sharp issue with the majority's approach: "The state law ground is clearly adequate to support the judgment, but the question whether it is independent of the [state court's] understanding of federal law is more difficult. Four possible ways of resolving that question present themselves: (1) asking [the state court] directly, (2) attempting to infer from all possible sources of state law what the [state court] meant, (3) presuming that adequate state grounds are independent unless it clearly appears otherwise, or (4) presuming that adequate state grounds are *not* independent unless it clearly appears otherwise. This Court has, on different occasions, employed each of the first three approaches; never until today has it even hinted at the fourth. [The Court] rejects the first approach as inefficient and unduly burdensome for state courts, and rejects the second approach as an inappropriate expenditure of our resources. [Although] I find both of those decisions defensible in themselves, I cannot accept the Court's decision to choose the fourth approach over the third—to presume that adequate state grounds are intended to be dependent on federal law unless the record plainly shows otherwise.

"If we reject the intermediate approaches, we are left with a choice between two presumptions: one in favor of our taking jurisdiction, and one against it. Historically, the latter presumption has always prevailed.[11] [Since approaches (1) and (2)] are now to be rejected, however, I would think that stare decisis would call for a return to historical principle. Instead, the Court seems to conclude that because some precedents ought to be rejected, we must overrule them all." He stated that, even if he agreed that the Court was free to assert "presumptive jurisdiction over the decisions of sovereign states," he would not agree that an "expansive attitude makes good sense." He insisted that respect for state courts, avoidance of advisory opinions, and the interest in managing scarce federal judicial resources all counseled "against the exercise of federal jurisdiction." He insisted, too, that "a policy of judicial restraint—one that allows other decisional bodies to have the last word in legal interpretation until it is truly necessary for this Court to intervene—enables this Court to makes its most effective contribution to our federal [system]."

Justice Stevens insisted that a case such as Long's "hardly compels a departure from tradition." He noted that cases such as this did not involve deprivation of federal rights. "Rather, they are cases in which a state court has upheld a citizen's assertion of a right, finding the citizen to be protected under both federal and state law. The complaining party is an officer of the state itself, who asks us to rule that the state court interpreted federal rights too broadly and 'overprotected' the citizen. Such cases should not be of inherent concern to this Court. [Michigan] simply provided greater protection to one of its citizens than some other State might provide or, indeed, than this Court might require throughout the country." He added: "I believe that in reviewing the decisions of state courts, the primary role of this Court is to make sure that persons who seek to *vindicate* federal rights have been fairly heard."[12] The

11. Quoting from an earlier case, Justice Stevens stated: "Where the judgment of the state court rests on two grounds, one involving a federal question and the other not, or if it does not appear upon which of two grounds the judgment was based, and the ground independent of a federal question is sufficient in itself to sustain it, this Court will not take jurisdiction."

12. A similar approach was advocated by several commentators in the years immediately

preceding Michigan v. Long. See, e.g., Sager, "Fair Measure: The Legal Status of Under-enforced Constitutional Norms," 91 Harv.L.Rev. 1212, 1248 (1978) (arguing that the Court should at times decline to set aside state court decisions "based upon a broader reading of the pertinent federal constitutional norm than that which the Court would itself adopt"); Tribe, American Constitutional Law (1978), 32 (suggesting that a state court may give a federal constitutional

majority had offered "only one reason" for asserting jurisdiction over cases such as this: the "need for uniformity in federal law." Justice Stevens responded: "Of course, the supposed need to 'review an opinion' clashes directly with our oft-repeated reminder that 'our power is to correct wrong judgments, not to revise opinions.' Herb v. Pitcairn. The clash is not merely one of form: the 'need for uniformity in federal law' is truly an ungovernable engine. That same need is no less present when it is perfectly clear that a state ground is both independent and adequate. In fact it is equally present if a state prosecutor announces that he believes a certain policy of nonenforcement is commanded by federal law. Yet we have never claimed jurisdiction to correct such errors, no matter how egregious they may be. [We] do not sit to expound our understanding of the Constitution to interested listeners in the legal community; we sit to resolve disputes. If it is not apparent that our views would affect the outcome of a particular case, we cannot presume to interfere." [13]

     c.   *State procedural law.*   As noted earlier, an allegedly adequate and independent state ground may be procedural rather than substantive. The typical state procedural ground case differs from the state substantive ground situation. In the substantive ground model, the state court discusses federal as well as state issues; the problem on Supreme Court review is to assess the importance and independence of the state ground in the state-federal mix. In the usual procedural ground case, by contrast, the state court does not get to the federal claim at all. Rather, the state decision relies solely on the state law and holds that noncompliance with a state procedural requirement precludes adjudication of the federal issue. Suppose, for example, a state criminal defendant objects to introduction of evidence on the ground that it was illegally seized, or to a confession on the ground that it was coerced. Suppose, moreover, the state court refuses to rule on the merits of those objections on the ground that they were not raised in accordance with state procedural groundrules—e.g., "with fair precision" or "in due time." May the Supreme Court on review nevertheless get to the federal objection? Or is the state procedural ground "adequate" to support the conviction? Should the Supreme Court decide the federal issue despite a state court ruling that it was not properly raised?

     That problem arises from the fact that state courts have from the beginning been a significant initial forum for the adjudication of federal claims. And from the beginning, a state's control of its own judicial machinery has carried considerable autonomy in prescribing the processes for the raising of all claims (federal as well as state) in the state courts. Ordinarily, then, compliance with state procedural requirements as to the time and manner of raising and preserving federal questions is necessary in order to invoke Court review. Yet deference to state procedures has never been total: precluding all Court review upon a state court's mere recital of a state procedural ground would endanger vindication of federal rights. What, then, are the governing considerations in determining whether the asserted state procedural ground is "adequate" to

guarantee a broader reading than the Supreme Court would).

     13.   In a closing passage, Justice Stevens stated that he was "thoroughly baffled by the Court's suggestion that it must stretch its jurisdiction" in order to show respect for the independence of state courts. He asked: "Would we show respect for the Republic of Finland by convening a special sitting for the sole purpose of declaring that its decision to release an American citizen was based upon a misunderstanding of American law?"

Justice BLACKMUN concurred in the judgment but refused to join the majority's jurisdictional approach: "Although I agree with the Court that uniformity in federal criminal law is desirable, I see little efficiency and an increased danger of advisory opinions in the Court's new approach." Justice BRENNAN's dissent, joined by Justice MARSHALL, dealt almost entirely with the merits of the search and seizure issue. His sole comment on reviewability came in a passing footnote: "I agree that the Court has jurisdiction to decide this case." (For a useful comment on Michigan v. Long, see Collins, "Plain Statements: The Supreme Court's New Requirement," 70 A.B.A.J. 92 (March 1984).)

preclude review? The Court has often said that a state court's refusal to decide a federal question must rest on "fair" and "substantial" grounds.

This is not the place to explore in depth what is necessary to establish "unfairness" or "insubstantiality." But a statement from Justice Clark's dissent in Williams v. Georgia, 349 U.S. 375, 399 (1955), usefully summarizes the typical avenues of Supreme Court inquiry: "A purported state ground is not independent and adequate in two instances. *First,* where the circumstances give rise to an inference that the state court is guilty of an evasion—an interpretation of state law with the specific intent to deprive a litigant of a federal right. [A footnote at this point added: "This charge upon the integrity of a State Supreme Court is so serious that this Court has restricted such findings to cases where the state court decision lacked 'fair support' in the state law."] *Second,* where the state law, honestly applied though it may be, and even dictated by the precedents, throws such obstacles in the way of enforcement of federal rights that it must be struck down as unreasonably interfering with the vindication of such rights." For a somewhat greater Court willingness to reexamine procedural grounds, see Henry v. Mississippi, 379 U.S. 443 (1965), where the majority—in examining an asserted state ground of "waiver"—suggested that state procedural grounds are subject to broader Court reexamination than state substantive grounds.[14]

3. *Review of judgments of federal courts.* The most commonly invoked basis for review of federal court decisions is 28 U.S.C. § 1254, which provides for Supreme Court review of cases in the Courts of Appeals. Its most important provisions authorize review as follows:

"(1) By writ of certiorari granted upon the petition of any party to any civil or criminal case, before or after rendition of judgment or decree;

"(2) By appeal by a party relying on a State statute held by a court of appeals to be invalid as repugnant to the Constitution, treaties or laws of the United States, but such appeal shall preclude review by writ of certiorari at the instance of such appellant, and the review on appeal shall be restricted to the Federal questions presented."[15]

APPELLATE JURISDICTION: SUPREME COURT RULES, PRACTICES, PROBLEMS

1. *Appeal.* a. Though the cases within the certiorari jurisdiction have long outnumbered those on appeal, the several hundred efforts a year to invoke the appeal jurisdiction have traditionally comprised an important portion of the

14. Justice Brennan's majority opinion in Henry stated "that a litigant's procedural defaults in state proceedings do not prevent vindication of his federal rights unless the State's insistence on compliance with its procedural rule serves a legitimate state interest. In every case we must inquire whether the enforcement of a procedural forfeiture serves such a state interest. If it does not, the state procedural rule ought not be permitted to bar vindication of important federal rights."

On the impact of Henry, see Wright, Federal Courts (4th ed. 1983), 751 (criticizing the Henry approach as confusing the adequate state ground problem and suggesting that it has not proved "a significant break with the past"). See generally Hill, "The Inadequate State Ground," 65 Colum. L.Rev. 943 (1965), and Sandalow, "Henry v. Mississippi and the Adequate State Ground:

Proposals for a Revised Doctrine," 1965 Sup.Ct. Rev. 187.

15. During recent decades, obligatory review of Courts of Appeals decisions was rare: there was little occasion for Courts of Appeals to hold state statutes unconstitutional [see § 1254(2) above] because actions to enjoin state laws had to be brought before three-judge district courts under 28 U.S.C. § 2281; and three-judge court decisions were directly appealable to the Supreme Court. But that pattern was changed in the late 1970s, when congressional action sharply curtailed the availability of three-judge courts. Note especially the repeal of 28 U.S.C. § 2281 in 1976. These changes made Courts of Appeals decisions falling within § 1254(2) more likely; but, as noted earlier (p. 54), recently proposed legislative changes would eliminate most bases for obligatory Supreme Court review.

Court's workload. The appeal route is theoretically obligatory, but the Court does not afford oral argument and disposition with full opinion in every case allegedly within the appeal jurisdiction. Instead, the Court uses a screening mechanism: an appeal is initiated by filing a "jurisdictional statement." Its contents are prescribed by Rule 15 of the Supreme Court.[1] The jurisdictional statement is required to demonstrate not only why the case falls within the appeal provisions of the jurisdictional statutes, but also "why the questions presented are so substantial as to require plenary consideration, with briefs on the merits and oral argument, for their resolution." See Rule 15(e) and (h). Most appeals are handled solely on the basis of that jurisdictional statement and the response to it. Thus, even in cases satisfying the technical requirements of the jurisdictional statute, the Court may decide to dispose of the case summarily, for want of "substantiality." In cases from state courts, the Supreme Court denotes such dispositions by "dismissing" the appeal; in cases from lower federal courts, the judgment below is summarily "affirmed." When the Court's examination of the jurisdictional statement persuades it that plenary consideration is warranted, the Court enters an order to "note probable jurisdiction." As a matter of Court practice, the votes of four Justices are sufficient to grant a full hearing to an appeal.

b. Are summary dispositions on "insubstantiality" grounds votes on the merits? They certainly are as a matter of theory: as Justice Brennan commented in Ohio ex rel. Eaton v. Price, 360 U.S. 246 (1959): "Votes to affirm summarily, and to dismiss for want of a substantial federal question, it hardly needs comment, are votes on the merits of a case." Yet the Court has increasingly resorted to summary dispositions of appeals even when the questions presented hardly seem frivolous. Over the years, "insubstantiality" dispositions of appeals have come to be viewed as less weighty precedents than cases decided with opinion after argument. (See chap. 15 below.) Nevertheless, even summary "insubstantiality" dispositions of appeals can properly be cited as rulings on the merits—unlike denials of certiorari.

c. Under the statutory framework distinguishing appeals as of right from certiorari review within the Court's discretion, the Court seemingly has no escape from saying something on the merits in a case meeting all of the technical requirements of the appeal jurisdiction. Nevertheless, there have been some cases of that variety in which the Court has refused to exercise jurisdiction and has declined to decide on the merits. Can that practice be defended? May discretionary ingredients appropriate on certiorari properly enter the judgment on whether to entertain an appeal? That problem—of duty and discretion regarding adjudication—recurs throughout chap. 15.[2]

2. *Certiorari.* a. The Court's discretionary jurisdiction—the route by which review is sought in most cases—is invoked by filing a petition for writ of certiorari. Supreme Court Rule 21 prescribes the contents of the petition. The major purpose of the petition is to demonstrate that the case is "certworthy"— that it is of sufficient general significance, and not simply of importance to the parties in the case, to warrant review. The votes of four Justices are needed for a grant of review on certiorari. The Court's Rule 17 is an attempt to state in general terms the "Considerations Governing Review on Certiorari." Rule 17(1) provides: "A review on writ of certiorari is not a matter of right, but of judicial discretion, and will be granted only where there are special and important reasons therefor. The following, while neither controlling nor fully

---

1. The Supreme Court Rules as revised in 1980 are printed at 445 U.S. 985. See generally Stern & Gressman, Supreme Court Practice (5th ed., 1978).

2. See the material on discretionary dismissals of appeals, including the Naim litigation, at p. 1592 below. That material can usefully be pursued at this point.

measuring the Court's discretion, indicate the character of reasons that will be considered.

"(a) When a federal court of appeals has rendered a decision in conflict with the decision of another federal court of appeals on the same matter; or has decided a federal question in a way in conflict with a state court of last resort; or has so far departed from the accepted and usual course of judicial proceedings, or so far sanctioned such a departure by a lower court, as to call for an exercise of this Court's power of supervision.

"(b) When a state court of last resort has decided a federal question in a way in conflict with the decision of another state court of last resort or of a federal court of appeals.

"(c) When a state court or a federal court of appeals has decided an important question of federal law which has not been, but should be, settled by this Court, or has decided a federal question in a way in conflict with applicable decisions of this Court."

Over the years, as the number of certiorari petitions has increased and the consequent Court workload has grown, Justices have repeatedly urged lawyers to use greater self-restraint in filing petitions. An early, typical exhortation came in a speech by Chief Justice Vinson to the ABA in 1949 (69 S.Ct. v). He complained that "too many" of the certiorari petitions "reveal a serious misconception on the part of counsel concerning the role of the Supreme Court in our federal system." He added: "Lawyers might be well-advised, in preparing petitions for certiorari, to spend a little less time discussing the merits [and] a little more time demonstrating why it is important that the Court should hear them." Despite that plea, the number of petitions increased in most of the recent years. Some observers have argued that admonitions from the bench cannot curb the flow so long as other actions by the Court encourage filings—actions such as unpredictable grants of certiorari as well as changes in substantive doctrine stimulating litigation in new areas. Others have suggested that the Court could help by providing guidelines more specific than those in Rule 17 or by giving reasons when it denies a certiorari petition. (For arguments against the latter route, see the comments in the next paragraph.) Most recent examinations of the certiorari workload assume that, if any relief is needed, it will require structural changes by Congress rather than actions by the Justices. (See the notes on proposals to reduce the Court's workload, following this section.) [3]

b. Unlike the summary disposition of an appeal for "insubstantiality," a denial of a petition for certiorari is not a decision on the merits. Justice Frankfurter explained the significance that should be (and usually is) given a denial of certiorari in a separate opinion in Maryland v. Baltimore Radio Show, 338 U.S. 912 (1950): "[A] denial simply means that fewer than four members of the Court deemed it desirable to review a decision of the lower court as a matter 'of sound judicial discretion.' [A] variety of considerations underlie denials of the writ, and as to the same petition different reasons may lead different Justices to the same result. This is especially true of petitions for review on writ of certiorari to a State court. Narrowly technical reasons may lead to denials. Review may be sought too late; the judgment of the lower court may not be final; it may not be the judgment of a State court of last resort; the decision may be supportable as a matter of State law, not subject to

---

3. Recently, however, the Justices have taken a few steps toward invoking self-help for reducing the size of the Court's dockets. Thus, in an effort to discourage frivolous litigation, the Court, in an unprecedented action, awarded $500 to the respondents in Tatum v. Regents of Nebraska-Lincoln, 462 U.S. —— (1983), as "appro- priate damages" pursuant to Supreme Court Rule 49.2 for filing a "frivolous" petition for certiorari. See also In re Brose, 462 U.S. —— (1983), one of a number of modern cases in which Chief Justice Burger has protested against frivolous appeals.

review by this Court, even though the State court also passed on issues of federal law. A decision may satisfy all these technical requirements and yet may commend itself for review to fewer than four members of the Court. Pertinent considerations of judicial policy here come into play. A case may raise an important question but the record may be cloudy. It may be desirable to have different aspects of an issue further illumined by the lower courts. Wise adjudication has its own time for ripening.

"Since there are these conflicting and, to the uninformed, even confusing reasons for denying petitions for certiorari, it has been suggested from time to time that the Court indicate its reasons for denial. Practical considerations preclude. [If] the Court is to do its work it would not be feasible to give reasons, however brief, for refusing to take these cases. The time that would be required is prohibitive, apart from the fact as already indicated that different reasons not infrequently move different members of the Court in concluding that a particular case at a particular time makes review undesirable. [Accordingly], this Court has rigorously insisted that [a] denial carries with it no implication whatever regarding the Court's views on the merits of a case which it has declined to review. The Court has said this again and again; again and again the admonition has to be repeated." [Though the Court still does not give reasons for denial of certiorari, there has been a growing tendency for Justices to note their dissents from denials and occasionally to give their reasons in separate opinions.] [4]

c. The Court's growing workload—largely attributable to the increase of certiorari petitions—is indicated by the statistics summarizing the business of the October 1983 Term: 4162 cases finally disposed of, with 163 opinions of the Court; review granted in 194 cases. See "The Supreme Court, 1983 Term," 98 Harv.L.Rev. 307 (1984), and generally Hart, "Foreword: The Time Charts of the Justices," 73 Harv.L.Rev. 84 (1959). In recent decades, there has been a striking increase in the annual number of cases: compare, with the 4162 cases disposed of in the 1983 Term, 3,943 in the 1978 Term, 3,117 in the 1968 Term, 1,763 in the 1958 Term, and 1,426 in the 1948 Term. However, after a generation of fairly steady increases, the caseload has remained relatively constant in recent years. The number of cases disposed of with full opinion has not varied significantly over the years: e.g., the Court resolved 154 cases with written opinions in the 1948 term.

Statistics such as these—growth in the size of the Dockets in recent decades, decline in the percentage of cases reviewed—have helped inspire recent recommendations on the workload such as those considered in the next note. But these sheer numbers, like most statistics, can be somewhat misleading. Though the burden is no doubt heavy, the figures should not be read to suggest that the Court discusses every petition at its weekly conferences. Copies of each petition do indeed go to the chambers of each Justice. But most Justices use the

---

4. See generally Linzer, "The Meaning of Certiorari Denials," 79 Colum.L.Rev. 1227 (1979).

In recent decades, there have been sporadic controversies—on and off the Court—regarding Supreme Court practice in handling certiorari cases. Among the areas of dispute: (a) grants of certiorari in employees' injury actions under federal statutes, on the issue of the adequacy of the evidence, see Note, "Supreme Court Certiorari Policy in Cases Arising Under the FELA," 69 Harv.L.Rev. 1441 (1956); (b) the obligation of a Justice to vote on the merits after certiorari has been granted, see Leiman, "The Rule of Four,"

57 Colum.L.Rev. 975 (1957); (c) the dismissal of certiorari as "improvidently granted" after argument on the merits, see Rice v. Sioux City Cemetery, 349 U.S. 70 (1955), and the revival of that controversy in Burrell v. McCray, 426 U.S. 471 (1976), and New York v. Uplinger, 467 U.S. ___ (1984); (d) the summary disposition of cases on the merits, in brief per curiam memoranda, see Note, "Supreme Court Per Curiam Practice: A Critique," 69 Harv.L.Rev. 707 (1956). See also Justice Stevens' lecture, "The Life-Span of a Judge-Made Rule," 58 N.Y.U.L.Rev. 1 (1983), for the arguments for and against the abolition of the Rule of Four.

assistance of their law clerks to prepare brief summaries of petitions.[5] In recent years, several Justices have asked their law clerks to participate in a pooled effort for summarizing petitions.[6] Moreover, the Court has an internal procedure to avoid discussion of the large percentage of certiorari petitions that are clearly not "certworthy": before the conference, the Chief Justice prepares a "dead list"; unless one of the other Justices requests that a case on that list be discussed, review is automatically denied. In short, 4000 cases on the Docket do not mean 4000 fungible cases requiring equal periods of time. Many indeed do require considerable attention, from the Justices and their clerks; many more—depending on the views and experience of each Justice—can be evaluated very quickly indeed. But with all of these qualifications, the workload for each Justice remains considerable. Evaluation of the magnitude of the problem has divided the Justices and observers; and those divisions have surfaced in the debates on the modern reform proposals summarized in the materials that follow.

PROPOSALS TO REDUCE THE SUPREME COURT'S WORKLOAD

Since the early 1970s, concern over the pressures of the Court's workload have generated a range of proposals for changes in the federal court structure. Those proposed changes—typically in the form of creating a new layer of appellate courts between the Courts of Appeals and the Supreme Court— produced widespread controversy on and off the Court but no major legislation from Congress in the 1970s. In the early 1980s, Congress considered only more modest proposals, and there was no assurance that even these would be enacted. A review of the modern proposals and some of the criticisms they generated provides an overview of some contemporary problems pertaining to the Court's conduct of its business.

1. *The Freund Committee Report, 1972.* The central and most controversial proposal by a committee headed by Professor Paul A. Freund was the creation of a National Court of Appeals to reduce the certiorari workload of the Court.[1] The Freund Committee's central proposal urged the establishment of a new court whose primary function would be to take over the bulk of the Supreme Court's certiorari-screening function. The new National Court of Appeals would be composed of seven judges drawn on a rotating basis from the federal courts of appeals. All review requests from the existing Courts of Appeals would go initially to that new court instead of the Supreme Court. The new court would have the final authority to deny review of the "majority" of cases and would finally decide cases of "true conflict between circuits." Every year,

---

5. On the often exaggerated role of the law clerks, see Wilkinson, Serving Justice—A Supreme Court Clerk's View (1974). For another view of the clerks' role—and the willingness of some clerks during the 1969–1976 period to breach the confidentiality of the clerk-Justice relationship—see Woodward and Armstrong, The Brethren (1979).

6. See Alsup, "A Policy Assessment of the National Court of Appeals," 25 Hast.L.J. 1313 (1974). For recent thorough examinations of the Court's modes of doing business, see two articles by Arthur D. Hellman, "The Supreme Court, the National Law, and the Selection of Cases for the Plenary Docket," 44 U.Pitt.L.Rev. 521 (1983), and "Error Correction, Lawmaking, and the Supreme Court's Exercise of Discretionary Re-

view," 44 U.Pitt.L.Rev. 795 (1983). Note also Gunther, "The Highest Court, the Toughest Issues," 6 Stan.Mag. 34 (1978).

1. See Federal Judicial Center, Report of the Study Group on the Caseload of the Supreme Court (1972). To the Committee, the statistics of the Court's workload—"both in absolute terms and the mounting trend"—indicated "that the conditions essential for the performance of the Court's mission do not exist." Was the trend truly a "mounting" one? That was certainly a fair statement when the Freund Committee Report was written. But that trend did not continue after the Freund Committee Report was issued, as the statistics in the preceding note illustrate.

it would be expected to certify about 400 cases to the Supreme Court, and the Supreme Court would then select a limited number of those for full hearing on the merits. The Freund Committee insisted that its proposal was "worth adopting" even though it involved some "loss of control" by the Supreme Court over its docket. The debate spurred by that Report[2] soon helped generate alternate proposals.

2. *The Hruska Commission Report, 1975.* In 1975, the Commission on Revision of the Federal Court Appellate System (chaired by Senator Hruska) recommended the creation of a quite different kind of National Court of Appeals.[3] The Hruska Commission's National Court of Appeals of seven judges would not take any of the certiorari-screening function from the Supreme Court. Instead, it would receive cases in two ways: (1) by reference from the existing Courts of Appeals when a prompt national precedent seemed desirable; and (2) by referrals from the Supreme Court in cases warranting a resolution with national effect but not significant enough for immediate decision on the merits by the Court. A bill to implement the Hruska Commission's proposal provoked considerable criticism in congressional committee hearings in 1976. Congress took no action on the proposal.

3. *Reform proposals since the late 1970s.* Beginning in the late 1970s, after the lack of congressional action on the earlier reform proposals, several Justices, in extrajudicial as well as judicial statements, urged reforms; but other Justices insisted that no structural changes were needed. For example, Justice White, joined by Justice Blackmun, took the occasion of a denial of certiorari to write an opinion calling for congressional attention to the Court's workload problems. Justice White's dissent in Brown Transport Corp. v. Atcon Inc., 439 U.S. 1014 (1978), noted that plenary consideration had been denied in many review-worthy cases in recent years and commented that "we are now extending plenary review to as many cases as we can adequately consider, decide and explain by full opinion." He concluded: "There is not doubt that those concerned with the coherence of the federal law must carefully consider the various alternatives available to assure that the appellate system has the capacity to function in the manner contemplated by the Constitution. As [the Freund

---

2. See, e.g., Bickel (a member of the Freund Committee), The Caseload of the Supreme Court, and What, If Anything, To Do About It (Amer. Enterprise Inst.1973); C. Black, "The National Court of Appeals: An Unwise Proposal," 83 Yale L.J. 883 (1974); Symposium, "Should the Appellate Jurisdiction of the United States Supreme Court Be Changed?" 27 Rutgers L.Rev. 878 (1974); Casper and Posner, "A Study of the Supreme Court's Caseload," 3 J. Legal Studies 339 (1974); and Griswold, "The Supreme Court's Case Load," 1973 U.Ill.L.F. 615.

3. See Commission on Revision of the Federal Court Appellate Court System, Structure and Internal Procedures: Recommendations for Change (1975).

Still another alternative surfaced between the time of the Freund Committee report in 1972 and the Hruska Commission's report in 1975. That recommendation was to create a national division of the U.S. Court of Appeals. In order to avoid the criticism directed at congressional delegation of the Supreme Court's screening function to a new body, this scheme would have the Supreme Court itself delegate the power to

decide certain classes of cases to the new tribunal, with a limited Supreme Court opportunity to reexamine the decisions below. See Hufstedler, "Courtship and Other Legal Arts," 60 A.B.A.J. 545 (1974).

This proposal, like that of the Freund Committee, encountered vigorous criticism. See especially the late Chief Justice Warren's evaluation, "Let's Not Weaken the Supreme Court," 60 A.B. A.J. 77 (1974). After referring to the Freund Committee proposal as "an unnecessary and unwarranted disruption of the Supreme Court's exercise of its own vested jurisdiction," Chief Justice Warren argued that the ABA-endorsed suggestion was "even more ill-advised and irrelevant with respect to the workload problems of the Supreme Court." Moreover, he perceived constitutional problems: "[T]here is a serious question whether Congress has the constitutional power, once it has vested certain appellate jurisdiction in the Supreme Court, [to] authorize a delegation of any part of that jurisdiction to an inferior court." Is there substance to that constitutional concern?

Committee and the Hruska Commission] have already noted, there is grave doubt that this function is being adequately performed.[4]

Despite the criticisms of the reform proposals and the continued inaction in Congress, several Justices continued to plead for structural change in the early 1980s. Chief Justice Burger spoke out most often. In 1983, he began advocating that Congress create a temporary, experimental panel—in effect, a temporary National Court of Appeals, to be set up for a five-year period. The panel would be composed of existing federal judges serving on rotation for a year or less, with the authority to decide "all intercircuit conflicts and possibly, in addition, a defined category of statutory interpretation cases."[5]

Transitional Note. This chapter has sketched only the framework of constitutional adjudication; it does not explore the additional "jurisdictional" and "procedural" ramifications essential to a full comprehension of the process of constitutional adjudication. Those added materials seem at times to be esoteric technicalities; but the rules about when the Court will speak, and as to what issues, go to the heart of the Court's place in the constitutional scheme. Those ramifications can usefully be considered at this point; but they are postponed in this edition to the last chapter, chap. 15. They are placed at the end of the book for two related reasons: first, further exploration of the Supreme Court review process at this point would unduly postpone consideration of the substantive content of governmental powers and individual rights; second, the Court's delineation of "jurisdictional" and "procedural" groundrules is often affected by the substantive doctrines at stake, so that examination of such issues as standing and ripeness can better take place after an examination of the substantive developments. The following chapters, accordingly, turn to those substantive problems; at the end, in chap. 15, the book returns to the

---

4. In a separate opinion, Chief Justice Burger praised Justice White's statement as "sound" and "an important service." He recalled that he as well as Justices White, Blackmun, Powell and Rehnquist had submitted letters to the Hruska Commission generally agreeing "on the need for some relief" for the Court. Note, however, a separate memorandum by Justice Brennan, which countered with the reminder that he had advised the Hruska Commission that he "remains completely unpersuaded [that] there is any need for a new National Court."

In the spring of 1979, a new, more modest proposal directed at the workload problem surfaced in Congress. Senator Kennedy introduced a bill to transfer appeals in certain specialized areas to new appellate courts in order to eliminate conflicts between the circuits in tax, patent, trademark and similar areas of law. Some of Senator Kennedy's aims were achieved with the passage of the Federal Courts Improvement Act of 1982, 96 Stat. 25. That law established a new federal appellate court, the Court of Appeals for the Federal Circuit. This thirteenth circuit court is the result of a merger of the former Court of Customs and Patent Appeals and the appellate functions of the former Court of Claims.

5. As originally proposed by the Chief Justice, the judges would have been drawn from a pool made up of two judges from each Court of Appeals, from which 7 or 9 would be drawn for limited periods of actual service. Burger, "Annual Report on the State of the Judiciary," 69

A.B.A.J. 442 (1983). The Chief Justice also asked Congress to create a tripartite commission to study the workload problems, evaluate the effectiveness of the new temporary panel, and recommend either the continuation of the intercircuit appeals panel or adoption of one of the other proposed structural reforms suggested in recent years. Although legislation was quickly introduced in Congress to implement these proposals, criticism was soon voiced and Congress did not act. Some of the strongest opposition to the proposed intercircuit tribunal came from judges of the Courts of Appeals. Thus, Chief Judge Feinberg of the Second Circuit called "the need for additional capacity to resolve conflict among the circuits" "exaggerated" and Chief Judge Lay of the Eighth Circuit argued that there is utility in percolation of law in certain areas prior to final resolution. See 15 The Third Branch No. 11 (1983). By June 1983, the Chief Justice indicated that he was prepared to modify his proposal by having only one Court of Appeals judge designated from each circuit to create the pool. See 15 The Third Branch No. 6 (1983). (For a strong criticism of the Chief Justice's proposal, see Hellman, "Caseload, Conflicts and Decisional Capacity: Does the Supreme Court Need Help?" 67 Judicature 28 (1983). For a survey of reform proposals, see Note, "Of High Designs: A Compendium of Proposals to Reduce the Workload of the Supreme Court," 97 Harv.L.Rev. 307 (1983).)

groundrules governing the exercise of Court authority,[6] the theme opened up by this chapter.

6. See also the preliminary consideration of "political questions" and justiciability in chap. 6, at p. 397 below.

Part II

THE STRUCTURE OF GOVERNMENT: NATION AND STATES IN THE FEDERAL SYSTEM

Introduction. Stronger government was necessary, but government must not become too powerful: these were dominant concerns to the Framers, and the Constitution reflects their effort to accommodate these needs and risks. That document granted greater powers to the central government to cure some of the weaknesses under the Articles of Confederation; yet the Constitution also assured restraints on governmental power. To the drafters of 1787, protection against excessive concentrations of power lay less in explicit limits such as the "shall nots" of the Bill of Rights than in diffusions of power among a variety of governmental units. Thus, the Constitution allocated powers among nation and states: a federal division of powers was achieved by specifying (most notably in Art. I, § 8) those powers Congress might exercise and by emphasizing (in the Tenth Amendment) that undelegated powers were "reserved to the States respectively, or to the people." Moreover, the less-than-total powers given to the national government were diffused among three separate branches, separately delineated in the first three Articles of the Constitution.

Part II of this book deals with these grants and dispersals of power. These chapters explore not only the governmental actions these grants justify but also the limits these grants imply. How can the scope of national authority be articulated with an adequate regard for the interest in local autonomy? That is the focus of chapters 2 through 4: they examine the extent and limits of authority when national power seeks to reach arguably local affairs. (See also chapter 10, exploring the scope of congressional power under the post-Civil War Amendments.) Chapter 5 focuses on the states rather than on national authority—and especially on the limits on state power imposed by national governmental concerns, particularly as reflected in the grant to Congress of the power to regulate interstate commerce. And chapter 6, finally, turns from the nation-state dimension to examine the restraints imposed by the separation of powers within the national government—by the distribution of national powers among executive, legislative, and judicial branches.

Chapter 2

NATIONAL POWERS AND LOCAL ACTIVITIES: ORIGINS AND RECURRENT THEMES

Introduction: Federalism—Antiquarian Relic? Contemporary Value? Federalism is the major concern of Part II of this book. The first three chapters of Part II, on the scope of the powers granted to Congress by the Constitutional Convention, include the most controversial impacts of federalism on American history. Again and again in these pages, legislation enacted with great popular support is held unconstitutional by the Supreme Court, particularly in the early decades of this century. And in a larger number of instances, states' rights arguments— some principled, some disingenuous—have defeated or delayed action by Congress. The materials that follow focus on federalism-related limits on national power: limits developed in the interest of curtailing national intrusion into local affairs, as distinguished from restraints stemming from individual rights guarantees (considered in Part III of this book).

The controversial impacts of federalism-related limits suggest questions relevant to much of what follows: What were the historical justifications for American federalism? How successfully has the Supreme Court applied those values to changing circumstances? These questions in turn raise even more basic ones: Does federalism retain substantial value in the 20th century, or is it an obsolete obstruction to be dismissed with minimal lip service? And should the Supreme Court be the predominant custodian of federalism? Are significant Court-imposed limits on congressional power unnecessary because local interests are adequately safeguarded by the political processes? Even if judicial checks on Congress are inappropriate, is the Court nevertheless compelled to act as the interventionist umpire of the federal system vis-à-vis the states, by blocking state impingements on national interests?[1]

The appropriate role of the Court in the evolution of federalism is an issue apparent on the face of many of the materials that follow. Related, equally pervasive questions typically lurk beneath the surface: What are the values, historical and contemporary, of federalism? Can it still be said that federalism increases liberty, encourages diversity, promotes creative experimentation and responsive self-government? Or is it a legalistic obstruction, a harmful brake on governmental responses to pressing social issues, a shield for selfish vested interests? Is federalism a theme that constitutional law must grapple with simply because it is *there*, in the Constitution? In confronting federalism issues, should the Court seek primarily to minimize the obstacles that the complexities of the federal structure put in the way of meeting modern needs? Or does federalism embody more appealing values that deserve some of the imaginative enthusiasm with which modern constitutional law embraces the promotion of such values as equality and freedom of speech?

"[D]iversity, pluralism, experimentation, protection from arbitrary majoritarianism and over-centralization, and a greater degree of citizen participation"—so

---

1. Note Justice Holmes' famous remark: "I do not think the United States would come to an end if we lost our power to declare an Act of Congress void. I do think the Union would be imperiled if we could not make that declaration as to the laws of the several States." Holmes, Collected Legal Papers (1920), 295.

71

a modern report articulating the values inherent in American federalism put it.[2] Yet, as that report illustrates, those values will not be adequately realized unless the federal system can respond more effectively to such pressing modern problems as "[t]he malaise of our metropolitan areas." The report urges "aggressive and imaginative" structural and fiscal assistance so that states—with boundaries reflecting history rather than current functional needs—may help cure the "illness" of "the problem of making metropolitan areas governable." Note that the United States has not been the only country to resort to federalism for the purpose of governing large geographical areas with diverse local needs. The federal model has also provided a mechanism for governments of other nations, as well as for international cooperation.[3] The frictions and accommodations during nearly two centuries of American experience—the concerns of the materials that follow—deserve consideration not only for their own sake but also for the light they shed on federalism's capacity to adapt to future needs, here and elsewhere.

McCULLOCH v. MARYLAND

4 Wheat. 316, 4 L.Ed. 579 (1819).

[Congress chartered the Second Bank of the United States in 1816. The Bank soon established branches in many states. Its branch in Baltimore quickly became the most active of all. In April 1818, the Maryland legislature adopted "An Act to impose a Tax on all Banks or Branches thereof in the State of Maryland, not chartered by the Legislature." The law provided that any banks operating in Maryland "without authority from the State" could issue bank notes only on stamped paper, furnished by the State upon payment of a fee varying with the denomination of each note; but any bank subject to that requirement could "relieve itself" from it "by paying annually, in advance, [the] sum of fifteen thousand dollars." The statute also provided for penalties for violators: for example, the president, cashier and all other officers of the bank were to "forfeit" five hundred dollars "for each and every offense." The penalties were enforceable by indictment or by "action of debt, in the County Court," "one half to the informer, and the other half to the use of the State."

[This action for the statutory penalty was brought in the County Court of Baltimore County by one John James, suing for himself and the State, against James McCulloch, the Cashier of the Baltimore branch of the Bank of the United States. It was admitted that the Bank was doing business without authority from the State and that McCulloch had issued bank notes without complying with the Maryland law. The case was decided against McCulloch on the basis of an agreed statement of facts, and the decision was affirmed by the Maryland Court of Appeals. From there, the case was taken by writ of error to the Supreme Court.[1] For the historical context of the dispute, see the materials following the Court's opinion.]

2. Advisory Commission on Intergovernmental Relations, Urban America and the Federal System (1969), 105.

3. See generally Wheare, Federal Government (4th ed. 1963); Macmahon (ed.), Federalism: Mature and Emergent (1955); Friedrich, Trends of Federalism in Theory and Practice (1968); and Davis, The Federal Principle: A Journey Through Time in Quest of a Meaning (1978).

1. Court Reporter Henry Wheaton noted that "[t]his case involving a constitutional question of great importance; and the sovereign rights of the United States and the State of Maryland; and the Government of the United States having directed their Attorney General to appear for the plaintiff in error, the Court dispensed with its general rule, permitting only two counsel to argue for each party." Six counsel (United States Attorney General William Wirt, Daniel Webster and William Pinkney for the Bank; State Attorney General Luther Martin, Joseph Hopkinson and Walter Jones for Maryland) argued the case over a period of nine days. The opinion was delivered only three days after the arguments had been concluded.

Mr. Chief Justice MARSHALL delivered the opinion of the Court.

In the case now to be determined, the defendant, a sovereign state, denies the obligation of a law enacted by the legislature of the Union, and the plaintiff, on his part, contests the validity of an act which has been passed by the legislature of that state. The constitution of our country, in its most interesting and vital parts, is to be considered; the conflicting powers of the government of the Union and of its members, as marked in that constitution, are to be discussed; and an opinion given, which may essentially influence the great operations of the government. No tribunal can approach such a question without a deep sense of its importance, and of the awful responsibility involved in its decision. But it must be decided peacefully, or remain a source of hostile legislation, perhaps of hostility of a still more serious nature; and if it is to be so decided, by this tribunal alone can the decision be made. On the Supreme Court of the United States has the constitution of our country devolved this important duty.

The first question made in the cause is, has Congress power to incorporate a bank? It has been truly said that this can scarcely be considered as an open question, entirely unprejudiced by the former proceedings of the nation respecting it. The principle now contested was introduced at a very early period of our history, has been recognised by many successive legislatures, and has been acted upon by the judicial department, in cases of peculiar delicacy, as a law of undoubted obligation. [The] power now contested was exercised by the first Congress elected under the present constitution. The bill for incorporating the bank of the United States did not steal upon an unsuspecting legislature, and pass unobserved. Its principle was completely understood, and was opposed with equal zeal and ability. After being resisted, first in the fair and open field of debate, and afterwards in the executive cabinet, with as much persevering talent as any measure has ever experienced, and being supported by arguments which convinced minds as pure and as intelligent as this country can boast, it became a law. The original act was permitted to expire; but a short experience of the embarrassments to which the refusal to revive it exposed the government, convinced those who were most prejudiced against the measure of its necessity, and induced the passage of the present law. It would require no ordinary share of intrepidity to assert that a measure adopted under these circumstances was a bold and plain usurpation, to which the constitution gave no countenance. These observations belong to the cause; but they are not made under the impression that, were the question entirely new, the law would be found irreconcilable with the constitution.

In discussing this question, the counsel for the State of Maryland have deemed it of some importance, in the construction of the constitution, to consider that instrument not as emanating from the people, but as the act of sovereign and independent states. The powers of the general government, it has been said, are delegated by the states, who alone are truly sovereign; and must be exercised in subordination to the states, who alone possess supreme dominion.

It would be difficult to sustain this proposition. The Convention which framed the constitution was indeed elected by the state legislatures. But the instrument, when it came from their hands, was a mere proposal, without obligation, or pretensions to it. It was reported to the then existing Congress of the United States, with a request that it might "be submitted to a convention of delegates, chosen in each State by the people thereof, under the recommendation of its legislature, for their assent and ratification." This mode of proceeding was adopted; and by the convention, by Congress, and by the state legislatures, the instrument was submitted to the people. They acted upon it in the only manner in which they can act safely, effectively, and wisely, on such a subject, by assembling in convention. It is true, they assembled in their several states—and where else should they have assembled? No political dreamer was ever wild enough to think of breaking down the lines which separate the states, and of compounding the American people into one common mass. Of consequence, when they act, they act in their states. But the measures they adopt do not, on that account, cease to be the measures of the people themselves, or become the measures of the state governments.

From these conventions the constitution derives its whole authority. The government proceeds directly from the people; is "ordained and established" in the name of the people; and is declared to be ordained, "in order to form a more perfect union, establish justice, ensure domestic tranquility, and secure the blessings of liberty to themselves and to their posterity." The assent of the states, in their sovereign capacity, is implied in calling a convention, and thus submitting that instrument to the people. But the people were at perfect liberty to accept or reject it; and their act was final. It required not the affirmance, and could not be negatived, by the state governments. The constitution, when thus adopted, was of complete obligation, and bound the State sovereignties.

[The] government of the Union, then (whatever may be the influence of this fact on the case), is, emphatically, and truly, a government of the people. In form and in substance it emanates from them. Its powers are granted by them, and are to be exercised directly on them, and for their benefit.

This government is acknowledged by all to be one of enumerated powers. The principle, that it can exercise only the powers granted to it, [is] now universally admitted. But the question respecting the extent of the powers actually granted, is perpetually arising, and will probably continue to arise, as long as our system shall exist. [Nonetheless, if] any one proposition could command the universal assent of mankind, we might expect it would be this— that the government of the Union, though limited in its powers, is supreme within its sphere of action.

[Among] the enumerated powers, we do not find that of establishing a bank or creating a corporation. But there is no phrase in the instrument which, like the articles of confederation, excludes incidental or implied powers; and which requires that everything granted shall be expressly and minutely described. [The Articles of Confederation had provided that each state "retains" every power not "expressly delegated."] Even the 10th amendment, which was framed for the purpose of quieting the excessive jealousies which had been excited, omits the word "expressly," and declares only that the powers "not delegated to the United States, nor prohibited to the States, are reserved to the States or to the people"; thus leaving the question, whether the particular power which may become the subject of contest has been delegated to the one government, or prohibited to the other, to depend on a fair construction of the whole instrument. The men who drew and adopted this amendment had experienced the embarrassments resulting from the insertion of this word in the articles of confederation, and probably omitted it to avoid those embarrassments. A constitution, to contain an accurate detail of all the subdivisions of which its great powers will admit, and of all the means by which they may be carried into execution, would partake of the prolixity of a legal code, and could scarcely be embraced by the human mind. It would probably never be understood by the public. Its nature, therefore, requires, that only its great outlines should be marked, its important objects designated, and the minor ingredients which compose those objects be deduced from the nature of the objects themselves. That this idea was entertained by the framers of the American constitution, is not only to be inferred from the nature of the instrument, but from the language. Why else were some of the limitations, found in the ninth section of the 1st article, introduced? It is also, in some degree, warranted by their having omitted to use any restrictive term which might prevent its receiving a fair and just interpretation. In considering this question, then, we must never forget that it is *a constitution* we are expounding.

Although, among the enumerated powers of government, we do not find the word "bank," or "incorporation," we find the great powers to lay and collect taxes; to borrow money; to regulate commerce; to declare and conduct a war; and to raise and support armies and navies. The sword and the purse, all the external relations, and no inconsiderable portion of the industry of the nation, are entrusted to its government. It can never be pretended that these vast powers draw after them others of inferior importance, merely because they are inferior. [But] it may with great reason be contended, that a government, entrusted with such ample powers, on the due execution of which the happiness and prosperity of the nation so vitally depends, must also be entrusted with ample means for their execution. The power being given, it is the interest of the nation to facilitate its execution. It can never be their interest, and cannot be presumed to have been their intention, to clog and embarrass its execution by withholding the most appropriate means. Throughout this vast republic, from the St. Croix to the Gulph of Mexico, from the Atlantic to the Pacific, revenue is to be collected and expended, armies are to be marched and supported. The exigencies of the nation may require that the treasure raised in the north should be transported to the south, that raised in the east conveyed to the west, or that this order should be reversed. Is that construction of the constitution to be preferred which would render these operations difficult, hazardous, and expensive? Can we adopt that construction (unless the words imperiously require it) which would impute to the framers of that instrument, when granting these powers for the public good, the intention of impeding their exercise by withholding a choice of means? If, indeed, such be the mandate of the constitution, we have only to obey; but that instrument does not profess to enumerate the means by which the powers it confers may be executed; nor does it prohibit the creation of a corporation, if the existence of such a being be essential to the beneficial exercise of those powers. It is, then, the subject of fair inquiry, how far such means may be employed.

[The] government which has a right to do an act, and has imposed on it the duty of performing that act, must, according to the dictates of reason, be allowed to select the means; and those who contend that it may not select any appropriate means, that one particular mode of effecting the object is excepted, take upon themselves the burden of establishing that exception. [The] power of creating a corporation, though appertaining to sovereignty, is not, like the power of making war, or levying taxes, or of regulating commerce, a great substantive and independent power, which cannot be implied as incidental to other powers, or used as a means of executing them. It is never the end for which other powers are exercised, but a means by which other objects are accomplished. [The] power of creating a corporation is never used for its own sake, but for the purpose of effecting something else. No sufficient reason is, therefore, perceived, why it may not pass as incidental to those powers which are expressly given, if it be a direct mode of executing them.

But the constitution of the United States has not left the right of Congress to employ the necessary means, for the execution of the powers conferred on the government, to general reasoning. To its enumeration of powers is added that of making "all laws which shall be necessary and proper for carrying into execution the foregoing powers, and all other powers vested by this constitution, in the government of the United States, or in any department thereof." The counsel for the State of Maryland have urged various arguments, to prove that this clause, though in terms a grant of power, is not so in effect; but is really restrictive of the general right, which might otherwise be implied, of selecting means for executing the enumerated powers.

[The] argument on which most reliance is placed, is drawn from the peculiar language of this clause. Congress is not empowered by it to make all laws, which may have relation to the powers conferred on the government, but such only as may be *"necessary and proper"* for carrying them into execution. The word *"necessary"* is considered as controlling the whole sentence, and as limiting the right to pass laws for the execution of the granted powers, to such as are indispensable, and without which the power would be nugatory. That it excludes the choice of means, and leaves to Congress, in each case, that only which is most direct and simple.

Is it true, that this is the sense in which the word "necessary" is always used? Does it always import an absolute physical necessity, so strong, that one thing, to which another may be termed necessary, cannot exist without that other? We think it does not. If reference be had to its use, in the common affairs of the world, or in approved authors, we find that it frequently imports no more than that one thing is convenient, or useful, or essential to another. To employ the means necessary to an end, is generally understood as employing any means calculated to produce the end, and not as being confined to those single means, without which the end would be entirely unattainable. [It] is essential to just construction, that many words which import something excessive should be understood in a more mitigated sense—in that sense which common usage justifies. The word "necessary" is of this description. It has not a fixed character peculiar to itself. It admits of all degrees of comparison. [A] thing may be necessary, very necessary, absolutely or indispensably necessary. To no mind would the same idea be conveyed by these several phrases. This comment on the word is well illustrated by the passage cited at the bar, from the 10th section of the 1st article of the constitution. It is, we think, impossible to compare the sentence which prohibits a state from laying "imposts, or duties on imports or exports, except what may be *absolutely* necessary for executing its inspection laws," with that which authorizes Congress "to make all laws which shall be necessary and proper for carrying into execution" the powers of the general government, without feeling a conviction that the convention understood itself to change materially the meaning of the word "necessary," by prefixing the word "absolutely." This word, then, like others, is used in various senses; and, in its construction, the subject, the context, the intention of the person using them, are all to be taken into view.

Let this be done in the case under consideration. The subject is the execution of those great powers on which the welfare of a nation essentially depends. It must have been the intention of those who gave these powers, to insure, as far as human prudence could insure, their beneficial execution. This could not be done by confining the choice of means to such narrow limits as not to leave it in the power of Congress to adopt any which might be appropriate, and which were conducive to the end. This provision is made in a constitution intended to endure for ages to come, and, consequently, to be adapted to the various *crises* of human affairs. To have prescribed the means by which government should, in all future time, execute its powers, would have been to change, entirely, the character of the instrument, and give it the properties of a legal code. It would have been an unwise attempt to provide, by immutable rules, for exigencies which, if foreseen at all, must have been seen dimly, and which can be best provided for as they occur. To have declared that the best means shall not be used, but those alone without which the power given would be nugatory, would have been to deprive the legislature of the capacity to avail itself of experience, to exercise its reason, and to accommodate its legislation to circumstances. If we apply this principle of construction to any of the powers of the government, we shall find it so pernicious in its operation that we shall be compelled to discard it.

[Take], for example, the power "to establish post offices and post roads." This power is executed by the single act of making the establishment. But, from this has been inferred the power and duty of carrying the mail along the post road, from one post office to another. And, from this implied power, has again been inferred the right to punish those who steal letters from the post office, or rob the mail. It may be said, with some plausibility, that the right to carry the mail, and to punish those who rob it, is not indispensably necessary to the establishment of a post office and post road. This right is indeed essential to the beneficial exercise of the power, but not indispensably necessary to its existence. So, of the punishment of the crimes of stealing or falsifying a record or process of a Court of the United States, or of perjury in such Court. To punish these offences is certainly conducive to the due administration of justice. But courts may exist, and may decide the causes brought before them, though such crimes escape punishment.

[If a] limited construction of the word "necessary" must be abandoned in order to punish, whence is derived the rule which would reinstate it, when the government would carry its powers into execution by means not vindictive in their nature? If the word "necessary" means "needful," "requisite," "essential," "conducive to," in order to let in the power of punishment for the infraction of law; why is it not equally comprehensive when required to authorize the use of means which facilitate the execution of the powers of government without the infliction of punishment?

In ascertaining the sense in which the word "necessary" is used in this clause of the constitution, we may derive some aid from that with which it is associated. Congress shall have power "to make all laws which shall be necessary and *proper* to carry into execution" the powers of the government. If the word "necessary" was used in that strict and rigorous sense for which the counsel for the State of Maryland contend, it would be an extraordinary departure from the usual course of the human mind, as exhibited in composition, to add a word, the only possible effect of which is to qualify that strict and rigorous meaning; to present to the mind the idea of some choice of means of legislation not straitened and compressed within the narrow limits for which gentlemen contend.

But the argument which most conclusively demonstrates the error of the construction contended for by the counsel for the State of Maryland, is founded on the intention of the Convention, as manifested in the whole clause. To waste time and argument in proving that, without it, Congress might carry its powers into execution, would be not much less idle than to hold a lighted taper to the sun. As little can it be required to prove, that in the absence of this clause, Congress would have some choice of means. That it might employ those which, in its judgment, would most advantageously effect the object to be accomplished. That any means adapted to the end, any means which tended directly to the execution of the constitutional powers of the government, were in themselves constitutional. This clause, as construed by the State of Maryland, would abridge, and almost annihilate this useful and necessary right of the legislature to select its means. That this could not be intended, is, we should think, had it not been already controverted, too apparent for controversy. We think so for the following reasons: 1st. The clause is placed among the powers of Congress, not among the limitations on those powers. 2nd. Its terms purport to enlarge, not to diminish the powers vested in the government. It purports to be an additional power, not a restriction on those already granted. No reason has been, or can be assigned for thus concealing an intention to narrow the discretion of the national legislature under words which purport to enlarge it.

[The] result of the most careful and attentive consideration bestowed upon this clause is, that if it does not enlarge, it cannot be construed to restrain the powers of Congress, or to impair the right of the legislature to exercise its best judgment in the selection of measures to carry into execution the constitutional powers of the government. If no other motive for its insertion can be suggested, a sufficient one is found in the desire to remove all doubts respecting the right to legislate on that vast mass of incidental powers which must be involved in the constitution, if that instrument be not a splendid bauble.

We admit, as all must admit, that the powers of the government are limited, and that its limits are not to be transcended. But we think the sound construction of the constitution must allow to the national legislature that discretion, with respect to the means by which the powers it confers are to be carried into execution, which will enable that body to perform the high duties assigned to it, in the manner most beneficial to the people. Let the end be legitimate, let it be within the scope of the constitution, and all means which are appropriate, which are plainly adapted to that end, which are not prohibited, but consist with the letter and spirit of the constitution, are constitutional.

[If] a corporation may be employed indiscriminately with other means to carry into execution the powers of the government, no particular reason can be assigned for excluding the use of a bank, if required for its fiscal operations. To use one, must be within the discretion of Congress, if it be an appropriate mode of executing the powers of government. That it is a convenient, a useful, and essential instrument in the prosecution of its fiscal operations, is not now a subject of controversy. All those who have been concerned in the administration of our finances, have concurred in representing its importance and necessity; and so strongly have they been felt, that statesmen of the first class, whose previous opinions against it had been confirmed by every circumstance which can fix the human judgment, have yielded those opinions to the exigencies of the nation. [But], were its necessity less apparent, none can deny its being an appropriate measure; and if it is, the degree of its necessity, as has been very justly observed, is to be discussed in another place. Should Congress, in the execution of its powers, adopt measures which are prohibited by the constitution; or should Congress, under the pretext of executing its powers, pass laws for the accomplishment of objects not entrusted to the government; it would become the painful duty of this tribunal, should a case requiring such a decision come before it, to say that such an act was not the law of the land. But where the law is not prohibited, and is really calculated to effect any of the objects entrusted to the government, to undertake here to inquire into the degree of its necessity, would be to pass the line which circumscribes the judicial department, and to tread on legislative ground. This court disclaims all pretensions to such a power.

After this declaration, it can scarcely be necessary to say that the existence of state banks can have no possible influence on the question. No trace is to be found in the constitution of an intention to create a dependence of the government of the Union on those of the states, for the execution of the great powers assigned to it. Its means are adequate to its ends; and on those means alone was it expected to rely for the accomplishment of its ends. To impose on it the necessity of resorting to means which it cannot control, which another government may furnish or withhold, would render its course precarious, the result of its measures uncertain, and create a dependence on other governments, which might disappoint its most important designs, and is incompatible with the language of the constitution. But were it otherwise, the choice of means implies a right to choose a national bank in preference to state banks, and Congress alone can make the election.

After the most deliberate consideration, it is the unanimous and decided opinion of this Court, that the act to incorporate the Bank of the United States is a law made in pursuance of the constitution, and is a part of the supreme law of the land. The branches, proceeding from the same stock, and being conducive to the complete accomplishment of the object, are equally constitutional. It would have been unwise to locate them in the charter, and it would be unnecessarily inconvenient to employ the legislative power in making those subordinate arrangements. [It] being the opinion of the Court, that the act incorporating the bank is constitutional; and that the power of establishing a branch in the State of Maryland might be properly exercised by the bank itself, we proceed to inquire—

2. Whether the State of Maryland may, without violating the constitution, tax that branch?

That the power of taxation is one of vital importance; that it is retained by the states; that it is not abridged by the grant of a similar power to the government of the Union; that it is to be concurrently exercised by the two governments: are truths which have never been denied. But, such is the paramount character of the constitution, that its capacity to withdraw any subject from the action of even this power, is admitted. The states are expressly forbidden to lay any duties on imports or exports, except what may be absolutely necessary for executing their inspection laws. If the obligation of this prohibition must be conceded, [the] same paramount character would seem to restrain, as it certainly may restrain, a state from such other exercise of this power, as is in its nature incompatible with, and repugnant to, the constitutional laws of the Union. [On] this ground the counsel for the bank place its claim to be exempted from the power of a State to tax its operations. There is no express provision for the case, but the claim has been sustained on a principle which so entirely pervades the constitution, is so intermixed with the materials which compose it, so interwoven with its web, so blended with its texture, as to be incapable of being separated from it, without rending it into shreds. This great principle is, that the constitution and the laws made in pursuance thereof are supreme; that they control the constitution and laws of the respective States, and cannot be controlled by them.

[The] argument on the part of the State of Maryland is, not that the states may directly resist a law of Congress, but that they may exercise their acknowledged powers upon it, and that the constitution leaves them this right in the confidence that they will not abuse it. Before we proceed to examine this argument, and to subject it to the test of the constitution, we must be permitted to bestow a few considerations on the nature and extent of this original right of taxation, which is acknowledged to remain with the states. It is admitted that the power of taxing the people and their property is essential to the very existence of government, and may be legitimately exercised on the objects to which it is applicable, to the utmost extent to which the government may choose to carry it. The only security against the abuse of this power, is found in the structure of the government itself. In imposing a tax the legislature acts upon its constituents. This is in general a sufficient security against erroneous and oppressive taxation. [But] the means employed by the government of the Union have no such security, nor is the right of a state to tax them sustained by the same theory. Those means are not given by the people of a particular state, [but] by the people of all the states. They are given by all, for the benefit of all—and upon theory, should be subjected to that government only which belongs to all.

It may be objected to this definition, that the power of taxation is not confined to the people and property of a State. It may be exercised upon every object brought within its jurisdiction. This is true. But to what source do we trace this right? It is obvious, that it is an incident of sovereignty, and is co-extensive with that to which it is an incident. [The] sovereignty of a State extends to everything which exists by its own authority, or is introduced by its permission; but does it extend to those means which are employed by Congress to carry into execution powers conferred on that body by the people of the United States? We think it demonstrable that it does not. Those powers are not given by the people of a single State. They are given by the people of the United States, to a government whose laws, made in pursuance of the constitution, are declared to be supreme. Consequently, the people of a single State cannot confer a sovereignty which will extend over them.

If we measure the power of taxation residing in a State, by the extent of sovereignty which the people of a single State possess, and can confer on its government, we have an intelligible standard. [We] have a principle which is safe for the states, and safe for the Union. We are relieved, as we ought to be, from clashing sovereignty; from interfering powers; from a repugnancy between a right in one government to pull down what there is an acknowledged right in another to build up; from the incompatibility of a right in one government to destroy what there is a right in another to preserve. We are not driven to the perplexing inquiry, so unfit for the judicial department, what degree of taxation is the legitimate use, and what degree may amount to the abuse of the power. The attempt to use it on the means employed by the government of the Union, in pursuance of the constitution, is itself an abuse, because it is the usurpation of a power which the people of a single State cannot give. We find, then, on just theory, a total failure of this original right to tax the means employed by the government of the Union, for the execution of its powers. The right never existed, and the question whether it has been surrendered, cannot arise.

But, waiving this theory for the present, let us resume the inquiry, whether this power can be exercised by the respective states, consistently with a fair construction of the constitution? That the power to tax involves the power to destroy; that the power to destroy may defeat and render useless the power to create; that there is a plain repugnance, in conferring on one government a power to control the constitutional measures of another, which other, with respect to those very measures, is declared to be supreme over that which exerts the control, are propositions not to be denied. But all inconsistencies are to be reconciled by the magic of the word CONFIDENCE. Taxation, it is said, does not necessarily and unavoidably destroy. To carry it to the excess of destruction would be an abuse, to presume which, would banish that confidence which is essential to all government.

But is this a case of confidence? Would the people of any one state trust those of another with a power to control the most insignificant operations of their state government? We know they would not. Why, then, should we suppose that the people of any one state should be willing to trust those of another with a power to control the operations of a government to which they have confided their most important and most valuable interests? In the legislature of the Union alone, are all represented. The legislature of the Union alone, therefore, can be trusted by the people with the power of controlling measures which concern all, in the confidence that it will not be abused. This, then, is not a case of confidence, and we must consider it as it really is.

If we apply the principle for which the State of Maryland contends, to the constitution generally, we shall find it capable of changing totally the character of that instrument. We shall find it capable of arresting all the measures of the government, and of prostrating it at the foot of the states. [If] the states may tax one instrument, employed by the government in the execution of its powers, they may tax any and every other instrument. They may tax the mail; they may tax the mint; they may tax patent rights; they may tax the papers of the custom-house; they may tax judicial process; they may tax all the means employed by the government, to an excess which would defeat all the ends of government. This was not intended by the American people. They did not design to make their government dependent on the states. [The] question is, in truth, a question of supremacy; and if the right of the States to tax the means employed by the general government be conceded, the declaration that the constitution, and the laws made in pursuance thereof, shall be the supreme law of the land, is empty and unmeaning declamation.

[It] has also been insisted, that, as the power of taxation in the general and state governments is acknowledged to be concurrent, every argument which would sustain the right of the general government to tax banks chartered by the states, will equally sustain the right of the states to tax banks chartered by the general government. But the two cases are not on the same reason. The people of all the states have created the general government, and have conferred upon it the general power of taxation. The people of all the states, and the states themselves, are represented in Congress, and, by their representatives, exercise this power. When they tax the chartered institutions of the states, they tax their constituents; and these taxes must be uniform. But, when a state taxes the operations of the government of the United States, it acts upon institutions created, not by their own constituents, but by people over whom they claim no control. It acts upon the measures of a government created by others as well as themselves, for the benefit of others in common with themselves. The difference is that which always exists, and always must exist, between the action of the whole on a part, and the action of a part on the whole—between the laws of a government declared to be supreme, and those of a government which, when in opposition to those laws, is not supreme. But if the full application of this argument could be admitted, it might bring into question the right of Congress to tax the State banks, and could not prove the right of the States to tax the Bank of the United States.

[We conclude] that the states have no power, by taxation or otherwise, to retard, impede, burden, or in any manner control, the operations of the constitutional laws enacted by Congress to carry into execution the powers vested in the general government. This is, we think, the unavoidable consequence of that supremacy which the constitution has declared. We are unanimously of opinion, that the law passed by the legislature of Maryland, imposing a tax on the Bank of the United States, is unconstitutional and void.

This opinion does not deprive the states of any resources which they originally possessed. It does not extend to a tax paid by the real property of the bank, in common with the other real property within the state, nor to a tax imposed on the interest which the citizens of Maryland may hold in this institution, in common with other property of the same description throughout the state. But this is a tax on the operations of the bank, and is, consequently, a tax on the operation of an instrument employed by the government of the Union to carry its powers into execution. Such a tax must be unconstitutional.

[Reversed.]

IMPLIED NATIONAL POWERS AND THE NECESSARY AND PROPER CLAUSE—THE HISTORICAL CONTEXT

Introduction. The nation was 30 years old when the Bank case came to the Supreme Court. The issues presented were not novel ones in 1819: both the specific question of the constitutionality of the Bank and the general one regarding the scope of national powers had been repeatedly debated since the beginning. These notes focus on the highlights of the contentions before 1819 and during the following decade. The McCulloch decision, important as it is, was no more the end than the beginning of the debate. The scope of the national legislature's authority to reach local affairs is a characteristic, never-ending problem of our federal system. It continues to breed conflicts and to generate searches for new accommodations; and the next two chapters will trace these conflicts and accommodations from Marshall's day to ours.

1. *The allocation of powers in the Articles of Confederation and the Constitution.* a. *The Confederation.* The American federal structure allocates powers between nation and states by enumerating the powers delegated to the national government and acknowledging the retention by the states of the remainder. That allocation technique did not originate at the 1787 Constitutional Convention. The Articles of Confederation followed a similar scheme. What the Convention contributed was an expansion of enumerated national powers to remedy perceived weaknesses under the Articles. Thus, the most important enumeration of congressional powers in the Constitution, Art. I, § 8, had a counterpart quite similar in form if not in scope in one of the Articles of Confederation, Art. IX.[1]

Art. II of the Articles emphasized the limited nature of the delegation of powers to the central government by stating that each state retained "every Power, Jurisdiction and right, which is not by this confederation expressly delegated to the United States." That provision has its counterpart in the Tenth Amendment of the Constitution, which omits the adverb "expressly" in assuring that the "powers not delegated to the United States" nor prohibited to the States "are reserved to the States respectively, or to the people." [Recall Marshall's reference in the McCulloch opinion to that change.] The move from the Articles to the Constitution was not, then, one from a central government of no powers to one with all powers; rather, it was a shift from one with fewer powers to one with more powers (and with improved machinery to enforce those powers, through a separate national executive and judiciary).[2] And the Tenth Amendment was designed to allay fears that were an understandable concomitant of greater powers, fears frequently expressed in the ratification debates: the fears of an excessively powerful, excessively centralized national

---

1. Art. IX provided: "The United States in Congress assembled, shall have the sole and exclusive right and power of determining on peace and war—[of] sending and receiving ambassadors—entering into treaties and alliances, provided that no treaty of commerce shall be made whereby the legislative power of the respective States shall be restrained from imposing such imposts and duties on foreigners, as their own people are subjected to, or from prohibiting the exportation or importation of any species of goods or commodities whatsoever—[of] granting letters of marque and reprisal in times of peace—appointing courts for the trial of piracies and felonies committed on the high seas and establishing courts for receiving and determining finally appeals in all cases of captures.

"[The] United States in Congress assembled shall also have the sole and exclusive right and

power of regulating the alloy and value of coin struck by their own authority, or by that of the respective States—fixing the standard of weights and measures throughout the United States—regulating the trade and managing all affairs with the Indians, not members of any of the States, provided that the legislative right of any State within its own limits be not infringed or violated—establishing or regulating post-offices from one State to another, throughout all the [United States]—making rules for the government and regulation of [the] land and naval forces, and directing their [operations]."

2. See Gunther, "Toward 'A More Perfect Union': Framing and Implementing the Distinctive Nation-Building Elements of the Constitution," in Aspects of American Liberty—Philosophical, Historical, and Political (Corner ed., 1977).

government.[3] Note the differences between the congressional power grants in the two documents. The most important new specifications were the grants of the powers to levy taxes and to regulate interstate and foreign commerce. It was the lack of those powers (the Confederation's funds, for example, came from the states, who had the sole power to impose taxes) that had been widely blamed for the failures of the Articles.

b. *The Constitutional Convention.* Consensus that the new Constitution should strengthen national powers did not inevitably mean that a more ample enumeration of powers would be the chosen technique. Rather than building on the enumeration format of the Articles, a simpler, more general, more inclusive statement of congressional powers was conceivable. That, indeed, was the approach the Convention adopted initially. Is it significant in determining the breadth of the granted powers that the specification route was ultimately followed in Art. I? At the Convention, the Virginia plan proposed "[t]hat the National Legislature ought to be empowered to enjoy the Legislative Rights vested in Congress by the Confederation; and moreover to legislate in all cases, to which the separate States are incompetent, or in which the harmony of the United States may be interrupted by exercise of individual legislation." And the Convention delegates, indeed, twice voted for formulations in similarly general terms.[4] The ultimate scheme of Art. I, § 8—specifying the granted powers and ending with the Necessary and Proper Clause in paragraph 18— originated in the Convention's Committee of Detail.

There was virtually no discussion of the Necessary and Proper Clause at the Convention. Many of the fears of a powerful central government during the ratification debates focused on that Clause, however. Defenders of the Constitution—e.g., Hamilton and Madison—insisted that the Clause was "harmless" and that objections to it were a "pretext." As Madison explained in Federalist No. 44: "Had the Constitution been silent on this head, there can be no doubt that all the particular powers requisite as means of executing the general powers would have resulted to the government, by unavoidable implication." Note the similarity to McCulloch.

2. *The Jefferson-Hamilton debate on the Bank in 1791.* With the establishment of the new government, agreement among the supporters of the new Constitution on general formulations soon gave way to conflicts on applications. The best known dispute in Washington's Administration warrants special attention: it was characteristic of the emerging conflicts between broad and narrow constructionists; and it focused on the very issue that ultimately came to the Court in McCulloch—and provided some of the ideological legacy that found its way into Marshall's opinion.

In December 1790, Alexander Hamilton, Washington's Secretary of the Treasury, sent to the House of Representatives a lengthy Report urging the incorporation of a national bank. He listed as among its principal advantages "[t]he augmentation of the active or productive capital," a greater "facility as to the government in obtaining pecuniary aids, especially in sudden emergencies," and the "facilitating of the payment of taxes." Less than two months later, Congress enacted a law creating the First Bank of the United States—a law much like the one passed in 1816 and sustained in McCulloch. While the bill was on Washington's desk, the President requested opinions on its constitutionality from Attorney General Edmund Randolph, Secretary of State Thomas Jefferson, and Alexander Hamilton. Randolph's first response stated that the measure was unconstitutional. Jefferson's answer agreed with Randolph's re-

---

3. See generally Storing & Dry, What the Anti-Federalists Were *For* (1981), as well as Storing's seven-volume collection, The Complete Anti-Federalist (1981).

4. See 1 Farrand, The Records of the Federal Convention of 1787 (1911), 47, 53; 2 id., 21.

sult, but Hamilton insisted that his project was constitutional. The President followed his Treasury Secretary's advice. Excerpts from the Jefferson and Hamilton opinions follow.

Jefferson:

I consider the foundation of the Constitution as laid on [the Tenth Amendment]. [To] take a single step beyond the boundaries thus specially drawn around the powers of Congress, is to take possession of a boundless field of power, no longer susceptible of any definition. The incorporation of a bank, and the powers assumed by this bill, have not, in my opinion, been delegated to the United States, by the Constitution.

I. They are not among the powers specially [enumerated].

II. Nor are they within either of the general phrases, which are the two following:—

1. To lay taxes to provide for the general welfare of the United States, that is to say, "to lay taxes for *the purpose* of providing for the general welfare." For the laying of taxes is the *power,* and the general welfare the *purpose* for which the power is to be exercised. They are not to lay taxes *ad libitum for any purpose they please;* but only *to pay the debts or provide for the welfare of the Union.* In like manner, they are not *to do anything they please* to provide for the general welfare, but only to *lay taxes* for that purpose. To consider the latter phrase, not as describing the purpose of the first, but as giving a distinct and independent power to do any act they please, which might be for the good of the Union, would render all the preceding and subsequent enumerations of power completely useless. It would reduce the whole instrument to a single phrase, that of instituting a Congress with power to do whatever would be for the good of the United States; and, as they would be the sole judges of the good or evil, it would be also a power to do whatever evil they please. [On the taxing and spending powers, see chap. 4, below.]

[It] is known that the very power now proposed *as a means* was rejected as *an end* by the Convention. [A] proposition was made to them to authorize Congress to open canals, and an amendatory one to empower them to incorporate. But the whole was rejected, and one of the reasons for rejection urged in debate was, that then they would have a power to erect a bank, which would render the great cities, where there were prejudices and jealousies on the subject, adverse to the reception of the Constitution.

2. The second general phrase is, "to make all laws *necessary* and proper for carrying into execution the enumerated powers." But they can all be carried into execution without a bank. A bank therefore is not *necessary,* and consequently not authorized by this phrase. It has been urged that a bank will give great facility or convenience in the collection of taxes. Suppose this were true: yet the Constitution allows only the means which are *"necessary."* [If] such a latitude of construction be allowed to this phrase as to give any non-enumerated power, it will go to every one, for there is not one which ingenuity may not torture into a *convenience* in some instance *or other,* to *some one* of so long a list of enumerated powers. It would swallow up all the delegated powers. [Therefore] it was that the Constitution restrained them to the *necessary* means, that is to say, to those means without which the grant of power would be nugatory. [Can] it be thought that the Constitution intended that for a shade or two of *convenience,* more or less, Congress should be authorized to break down the most ancient and fundamental laws of the several States; such as those against Mortmain, the laws of Alienage, the rules of descent, the acts of distribution, the laws of escheat and forfeiture, the laws of monopoly? Nothing but a necessity invincible by any other means, can justify such a prostitution of [laws].

Hamilton:

[It] is unquestionably incident to *sovereign power* to erect corporations, and consequently to *that* of the United States, in *relation* to the *objects* intrusted to the management of the government. The difference is this: where the authority of the government is general, it can create corporations in *all cases;* where it is confined to certain branches of legislation, it can create corporations *only* in those cases. [It] is conceded that *implied powers* are to be considered as delegated equally with *express ones.* Then it follows, that as a power of erecting a corporation may as well be *implied* as any other thing, it may as well be employed as an *instrument* or *means* of carrying into execution any of the specified powers, as any other *instrument* or *means* whatever. The only question must be [whether] the means to be employed, or, in this instance, the corporation to be erected, has a natural relation to any of the acknowledged objects or lawful ends of the government. Thus a corporation may not be erected by Congress for superintending the police of the city of Philadelphia, because they are not authorized to *regulate* the *police* of that city. But one may be erected in relation to the collection of taxes, or to the trade with foreign countries, or to the trade between the States; [because] it is the province of the Federal Government to *regulate* those objects, and because it is incident to a general *sovereign* or *legislative* power to *regulate* a thing, to employ all the means which relate to its regulation to the best and greatest advantage.

[The] Secretary of State maintains, that no means are to be considered *necessary* but those without which the grant of the power would be *nugatory.* Nay, so far does he go in his restrictive interpretation of the *word,* as even to make the case of *necessity* which shall warrant the constitutional exercise of the power to depend on *casual* and *temporary* circumstances; an idea which alone refutes the construction. The *expediency* of exercising a particular power, at a particular time, must, indeed, depend on circumstances; but the constitutional right of exercising it must be uniform and invariable, the same today as tomorrow. All the arguments, therefore, against the constitutionality of the bill derived from the accidental existence of certain State banks—institutions which happen to exist today [may] disappear tomorrow—must not only be rejected as fallacious, but must be viewed as demonstrative that there is a *radical* source of error in the reasoning.

It is certain, that neither the grammatical nor popular sense of the term ["necessary"] requires that construction. According to both, *necessary* often means no more than *needful, requisite, incidental, useful* or *conducive to.* It is a common mode of expression to say, that it is *necessary* for a government or a person to do this or that thing, when nothing more is intended or understood, than that the interests of the government or person require, or will be promoted by, the doing of this or that thing. [The] whole turn of the clause containing ["necessary"] indicates, that it was the intent of the Convention, by that clause, to give a liberal latitude to the exercise of the specified powers. [To] understand the word as the Secretary of State does, would be to depart from its obvious and popular sense, and to give it a restrictive operation, an idea never before entertained. It would be to give it the same force as if the word *absolutely* or *indispensably* had been prefixed to it.

Such a construction would beget endless uncertainty and embarrassment. The cases must be palpable and extreme, in which it could be pronounced, with certainty, that a measure was absolutely necessary, or one, without which the exercise of a given power would be nugatory. There are few measures of any government which would stand so severe a test. To insist upon it, would be to make the criterion of the exercise of any implied power, a *case of extreme necessity;* which is rather a rule to justify the overleaping of the bounds of constitutional authority, than to govern the ordinary exercise of it. [The] *degree* in which a measure is necessary can never be a *test* of the legal right to adopt it; that must be a matter of opinion, and can only be a *test* of expediency. The *relation* between the *measure* and the *end;* between the *nature* of the *means* employed towards the execution of a power, and the object of that power, must be the criterion of constitutionality, not the more or less of *necessity* or *utility.* [This] restrictive interpretation of the word *necessary* is also contrary to this sound maxim of construction; namely, that the powers contained in a constitution of government [ought] to be construed liberally in advancement of the public good. [The] means by which national exigencies are to be provided for, national inconveniences obviated, national prosperity promoted, are of such infinite variety, extent, and complexity, that there must of necessity be great latitude of discretion in the selection and application of those means. Hence, consequently, the necessity and propriety of exercising the authorities intrusted to a government on principles of liberal construction.

[But] while on the one hand the construction of the Secretary of State is deemed inadmissible, it will not be contended, on the other, that the clause in question gives any *new* or *independent* power. But it gives an explicit sanction to the doctrine of *implied powers,* and is equivalent to an admission of the proposition that the government, as to its *specified powers* and *objects,* has plenary and sovereign authority, in some cases paramount to the States; in others, co-ordinate with it. [The] criterion is the *end,* to which the measure relates as a *means.* If the *end* be clearly comprehended within any of the specified powers, and if the measure have an obvious relation to that *end,* and is not forbidden by any particular provision of the Constitution, it may safely be deemed to come within the compass of the national authority. There is also this further criterion, which may materially assist the decision: Does the proposed measure abridge a pre-existing right of any State or of any individual? If it does not, there is a strong presumption in favor of its constitutionality, and slighter relations to any declared object of the Constitution may be permitted to turn the scale.

Another argument made use of by the Secretary of State is, the rejection of a proposition by the Convention to empower Congress to make corporations, either generally, or for some special purpose. [W]hatever may have been the nature of the proposition, or the reasons for rejecting it, it includes nothing in respect to the real merits of the question. [If] a power to erect a corporation in any case be deducible, by fair inference, from the whole or any part of the numerous provisions of the Constitution of the United States, arguments drawn from extrinsic circumstances, regarding the intention of the Convention, must be rejected. [It] remains to show the relation of such an institution to one or more of the specified powers of the government. Accordingly it is affirmed that it has a relation, more or less direct, to the power of collecting taxes, to that of borrowing money, to that of regulating trade between the States, and to those of raising and maintaining fleets and armies. To the two former the relation may be said to be immediate; and in the last place it will be argued, that it is clearly within the provision which authorizes the making of all *needful rules and regulations* concerning the *property* of the [United States].

3. *Broad and narrow construction: The Jeffersonian positions and the 1805 Marshall reply.* The fear of "consolidation" of powers in the national government did not end with the 1791 Bank controversy. Indeed, strict construction of congressional authority became a central plank in the opposition platform of the Jeffersonian Republicans later in the decade. In 1798, when Jefferson drafted the Kentucky Resolutions and Madison those of Virginia, their protests against the Federalists' Alien and Sedition Acts were not simply defenses of First Amendment freedoms. The Resolutions also reflected an insistence on states' rights. Madison protested against the tendency of "the Federal Government to

enlarge its powers by forced constructions" (Virginia Resolutions). Jefferson protested against the "construction applied by the general government" to such provisions as the Necessary and Proper Clause and asserted that "words meant by [the Constitution] to be subsidiary [ought] not to be so construed as themselves to give unlimited powers" (Kentucky Resolutions).

After the Republicans assumed power in 1801, the responsibilities of their offices induced Jefferson and Madison to depart from consistent adherence to the strict construction position. At times, it was left to a few orthodox Republicans such as John Randolph and John Taylor of Caroline and Spencer Roane to defend the traditional Jeffersonian creed. Yet, from a number of sources—and for a variety of motives, from philosophical conviction to temporary self-interest—the opposing positions on national powers were kept alive to and beyond the year McCulloch was decided.

The purity of Jefferson's constitutional principles was more apparent in the years before and after his presidential terms than while he was in office. President Jefferson found it possible, for example, to overcome his constitutional scruples regarding the purchase of Louisiana: though at first he thought it "important, in the present case, to set an example against broad construction," he ultimately dropped his plan to seek a constitutional amendment to ratify his actions: "[If] our friends shall think differently, certainly I shall acquiesce with satisfaction; confiding, that the good sense of our country will correct the evil of construction when it shall produce ill effects." [5] Compare Jefferson's colorful articulation of strict constructionists' fears when he commented, just before he was elected President, on a bill to grant a federal charter to a mining company: "Congress are authorized to defend the nation. Ships are necessary for defence; copper is necessary for ships; mines, necessary for copper; a company necessary to work the mines; and who can doubt this reasoning who has ever played at 'This is the House that Jack Built'? Under such a process of filiation of necessities the sweeping clause makes clean work." (Note the recurrent manifestations of "House That Jack Built" arguments in the cases in the next chapter.)

While Jefferson was in the White House, supporters of national legislation continued to maintain that congressional powers should be broadly construed. And an early opinion by Chief Justice Marshall gave support to that position, in the Fisher case, a case anticipating the more elaborate discussion in McCulloch.[6]

4. *National powers after the War of 1812.* The controversy over the scope of congressional powers intensified in the years immediately before the McCulloch decision. Before and during the War, New England Federalists hostile to the Republican Administrations began to embrace strict construction theories. By the end of the War, the Federalist Party was in its death throes. But proposals for ambitious congressional programs now came from a new generation of Republicans, especially in the short period of nationalistic optimism that followed the end of the War of 1812. (Recall the broad-scale national action advocated by Justice Story at the time of Martin v. Hunter's Lessee, as noted at p. 50 above.)

5. See 8 The Writings of Thomas Jefferson (Ford ed.), 248, 262; and generally Levy, Jefferson and Civil Liberties—The Darker Side (1963).

6. In sustaining a law giving priority, in insolvency cases, to debts owing to the United States, Marshall said: "In construing [the Necessary and Proper Clause] it would be incorrect and would produce endless difficulties, if the opinion should be maintained that no law was authorised which was not indispensably necessary to give effect to a specified power. Where various systems might be adopted for that purpose, it might be said with respect to each, that it was not necessary, because the end might be obtained by other means. Congress must possess the choice of means, and must be empowered to use any means which are in fact conducive to the exercise of a power granted by the constitution." United States v. Fisher, 2 Cranch 358, 396 (1805).

The drive to charter the Second Bank of the United States was only a small part of that wave of nationalism. In 1816, for example, John C. Calhoun was still more than a decade away from his role as chief theoretician of the Nullifiers; in 1816, Calhoun was the legislative leader who successfully steered the Bank bill through the House, supported the tariff, and proposed a national system of roads and canals. So with Henry Clay: as Speaker of the House early in 1817, he praised Calhoun's roads and canals bill and defended his American System—particularly those "most worthy" subjects, "Internal Improvements and Domestic Manufacturers."[7] Yet these nationalistic proposals stirred opposition—in Congress, where Daniel Webster was among the critics for a while, in the White House, and in the country at large. Moreover, the opposition arguments were frequently couched in constitutional terms. President Madison, for example, vetoed Calhoun's bill establishing an internal improvements fund from the bonus paid to the United States under the Bank charter. He found "insuperable difficulty [in] reconciling the bill with the Constitution," for authority for the congressional action was not "among the enumerated powers" and did not fall "by any just interpretation" within the Necessary and Proper Clause. (Compare the Butler case, p. 202 below.)

McCulloch, then, was not an abstract or novel exercise in constitutional interpretation. The scope of congressional powers had been a continuous and controversial issue in American debates from the start. McCulloch added a weighty ingredient to the debate—but the debate continued. President Monroe, for example, vetoed the Cumberland Road Bill in 1822—though the Justices, unofficially (and despite the barrier to advisory opinions), did not agree with his position.[8] With President John Quincy Adams' election in 1825, a strong supporter of broad congressional powers came into office at last. Adams' proposals included not only internal improvements but also national action in aid of education and science. But by now Congress was reluctant, and the Adams Administration faced increasingly hostile constitutional and political criticism.

Much of the constitutional criticism in the 1820s came from the state legislatures. The resolutions adopted illustrate both the pervasiveness of the criticism and the challenges to McCulloch inherent in the attacks. See generally Ames, State Documents on Federal Relations (1906). Late in 1825, for example, the South Carolina legislature—still years away from Nullification but increasingly discontented with national actions—asked a special committee to report on "the decisions of the federal judiciary and the acts of Congress contravening the letter and spirit of the Constitution." There was little doubt about the prime judicial target: as a similar committee reported two years later "with great pain," the "reasoning of the Court in the case of McCulloch" was "founded on a misconstruction" of the Constitution. That was the premise that underlay the action of the South Carolina legislature in December 1825, when it adopted the special committee's recommended Resolutions attacking a range of assertions of power in Congress.[9]

7. On Calhoun, see 1 The Papers of John C. Calhoun (Meriwether ed. 1959). On Clay, see especially 2 The Papers of Henry Clay (Hopkins ed. 1961), 308.

8. See letter of Justice William Johnson (purporting to report on behalf of his "Brother Judges" as well) to President James Monroe in 1822, ending with the suggestion that "it would not be unproductive of good, if the Secretary of State were to have the opinion of this Court on the Bank question, printed and dispersed through the Union." See 1 Warren, The Supreme Court in United States History (rev. ed. 1926), 597.

9. The South Carolina Resolutions stated:

"1. *Resolved,* That Congress does not possess the power, under the constitution, to adopt a general system of internal improvement as a national measure.

"2. *Resolved,* That a right to impose and collect taxes, does not authorize Congress to lay a tax for any other purposes than such as are necessarily embraced in the specific grants of power, and those necessarily implied therein.

"3. *Resolved,* That Congress ought not to exercise a power granted for particular objects, to

The impact of McCulloch v. Maryland extended far beyond the immediate issues of the case and far beyond its own day—not only to South Carolina in the 1820s, but also to the recurrent disputes about the scope of congressional power since. But it is not enough to view McCulloch in its larger setting; a word about the immediate context accordingly follows.

5. *The Bank controversy: Politics and economics.* The expiration of the charter of the First Bank of the United States in 1811 coincided with—and to some extent contributed to—increasing national fiscal difficulties. Financial problems were aggravated during the War of 1812, and demands for a new national bank proliferated. By the end of the War, even President Madison—who, in his 1800 Report on his Virginia Resolutions, had echoed Jefferson's argument that the first Bank was unconstitutional—began to urge consideration of a successor institution: in his Annual Message of December 1815, he advised Congress that "the probable operation of a national bank will merit consideration."

The Republicans in Congress did not need that reminder. They had approved a new bank charter almost a year earlier, but the President had vetoed it in January 1815. But the Veto Message demonstrated that the Administration's constitutional position had shifted: while disapproving the details of the bill, President Madison had "waive[d]" the question of congressional power to incorporate a bank, "as being precluded in my judgment by repeated recognitions under varied circumstances of the validity of such an institution in acts of the legislative, executive, and judicial branches of the Government." In 1816, Congress established a Second Bank acceptable to Madison; and Marshall's 1819 opinion sustaining its constitutionality took pains to remind the nation of Madison's "waiver."

The Bank got off to a flourishing start. In 1817 and for most of 1818, few questions about constitutionality were raised: the country was in a postwar economic boom, trade was active, prices were rising. And the Bank, which could have exercised some of the regulatory functions of a modern central bank by controlling credit expansion, chose instead to be "liberal" and to encourage the speculative boom. The harsh morning-after was not far off, however: by the fall of 1818, a financial panic and depression shook the economy. The Bank, short of specie reserves, called in its excessive loans—and the debtors (state banks as well as private individuals) reacted with understandable anger toward the central "monied power," the "monster" Bank. In October 1818, a congressional investigation of the Bank began, and there was considerable support for repeal of its charter. The January 1819 report of the investigating committee found that the Bank had indeed suffered from loose management under its first president, William Jones. But the charter-repeal move failed in February 1819; instead, Jones resigned and was succeeded by the far more competent Langdon Cheves.

When the McCulloch case came before the Court, then, the Bank was at the center of the most heated issue of the congressional session. Moreover, by early 1819, the Baltimore branch of the Bank—one of 18 branches in existence at the time—was the most controversial of the Bank's operations, for reasons going quite beyond Maryland's tax. As cashier, James McCulloch was no minor functionary: in the Bank's structure, the branch cashiers were the chief local agents of the national management. And during the congressional investigation, McCulloch was the Bank's main legislative lobbyist in Washington. He

effect other objects, the right to effect which has never been conceded.

"4. *Resolved,* That it is an unconstitutional exercise of power, on the part of Congress, to tax the citizens of one State to make roads and canals for the citizens of another State.

"5. *Resolved,* That it is an unconstitutional exercise of power, on the part of Congress, to lay duties to protect domestic manufacturers." 1 Statutes at Large of South Carolina (1836), 229, 231.

was even more busy at home: the Baltimore branch was the most active of all, and McCulloch and his cohorts were systematically looting the Bank by instigating unsecured loans and by sanctioning unreported overdrafts. Reports of Baltimore misconduct were circulating in Washington by late 1818; by the time the case was argued in March 1819, there were rumors that McCulloch was heavily implicated. But there were also indignant denials of the rumors. Official charges of McCulloch's misconduct did not come until a month after the Court decision; and in May, he was removed from office. Criminal proceedings against McCulloch and his associates were brought by Maryland and continued for several years. But Maryland had no embezzlement statute as yet, and the difficult effort to obtain a common law conspiracy conviction failed.

Thus, the banner of national power in the McCulloch case was carried by a most unsavory figure, a scoundrel whose schemes cost the Bank more than a million dollars. But the Bank controversy litigated in the McCulloch case was not merely a Baltimore matter. The hard times, and the antipathy of state banks under pressure from the Bank of the United States, produced anti-Bank measures in a number of states—some antedating the Maryland tax law. Indiana and Illinois flatly prohibited banks not chartered by the state. Tennessee, Georgia, North Carolina, Kentucky and Ohio—like Maryland—imposed taxes on "foreign" bank operations, taxes that were typically even more burdensome than Maryland's. Similar efforts in several other state legislatures failed by narrow margins. The Court's decision did not silence all of the attacks: in the face of the McCulloch decision in March 1819, Ohio in September chose to collect its $50,000 per branch tax by force. Ohio agents seized more than $100,000 from the vaults of the Bank's Chillicothe branch, in order to stimulate a relitigation of the McCulloch issues. The Ohio leaders insisted that the issues had not been adequately and fully aired in the Maryland litigation. It took another Court decision—Osborn v. Bank of the United States, 9 Wheat. 738 (1824)—to settle the Ohio dispute, reaffirm McCulloch, and validate the Bank's statutory authority to sue in the federal courts. By that time the Bank's difficulties had eased: it was managed more competently—by Cheves' successor, Nicholas Biddle—and the nation had recovered from the depression. Not until the Jackson Administration did the Bank face another severe attack. And the Jackson challenge was fatal: the McCulloch decision was not an adequate shield against President Jackson's veto of the 1832 Bank recharter, and the Bank went out of existence in 1836.[10]

6. *The Bank controversy: The constitutional contentions and John Marshall's pseudonymous defense.* By contrast with the often bitter and sometimes bizarre political controversies that engulfed the Bank, the constitutional submissions in the McCulloch case were calm and largely predictable. True, the arguments of the Bank's lawyers—Attorney General Wirt, William Pinkney and Daniel Webster—are reflected in the Marshall opinion. But counsels' arguments were primarily conduits for constitutional contentions that had become routine in debates during the preceding three decades. Though Daniel Webster's reputation was substantially enhanced by his Court arguments in 1819, it was William Pinkney who was the major orator in the McCulloch case. And neither Webster nor Pinkney considered the McCulloch argument the chief challenge of the 1819 Term: they were preoccupied with other cases, especially their possible encounter if the Dartmouth College Case (p. 488 below) were to be reargued. As Pinkney wrote Webster in December 1818, a preargument "interchange of Ideas" among co-counsel for the Bank seemed unnecessary,

---

10. For additional background on the Bank controversy, see Catterall, The Second Bank of the United States (1902), and Hammond, Banks and Politics in America—From the Revolution to the Civil War (1957).

since the argument probably would involve "little else than the threadbare topics connected with the constitutionality of the establishment of the Bank."

The constitutional arguments were not novel, and the pro-Bank holding was no surprise. But to the far-sighted, the case signified more than the immediate result. For John Marshall and his Virginia states' rights critics, especially, what was truly at stake was McCulloch's impact on national programs other than the Bank and, above all, on the general scope of national powers. General principles of constitutional interpretation really did matter the most in the long run. And general principles were central in a fierce ideological newspaper debate that ensued—with Spencer Roane of Virginia as the chief pseudonymous critic in the Richmond Enquirer, and John Marshall himself, for the only time in his career, as chief pseudonymous newspaper defender of the Court.

Within weeks of the McCulloch decision, the Richmond Enquirer, the press organ of Virginia states' rights leaders, began publishing elaborate attacks. Marshall saw in them a revival of the feared strict constructionist principles of 1798: if they prevailed, "the constitution would be converted into the old confederation." The Chief Justice, afraid that no one else would make an adequate defense, took to the newspapers himself. In April 1819, he wrote two essays for a Philadelphia paper. But then Judge Spencer Roane—the chief participant in the defiant state court decision that was reversed in Martin v. Hunter's Lessee and a leading Virginia politician as well as ideologue—sharply attacked McCulloch in a series of essays signed "Hampden." Marshall, his letters disclose, found himself "more stimulated on this subject than on any other because I believe the design to be to injure the Judges & impair the constitution." Anxious and intense, he hastily wrote 9 elaborate essays that were published in the Alexandria Gazette over the pseudonym "A Friend of the Constitution." [11]

The Bank aspects of the case were hardly mentioned in this newspaper battle, either by the attackers or by Marshall. As Marshall realized, it was doctrine, not result, that troubled the Virginians: they would have preferred "an obsequious, silent opinion without reasons"; it was "our heretical reasoning" that was "pronounced most damnable." And it was that reasoning that concerned Marshall most: he defended it against charges that it legitimated unlimited congressional powers; he denied that McCulloch endorsed consolidation; he insisted that the decision struck a moderate balance between excessively broad and unduly narrow conceptions of national powers. (His elaborations are considered further in the next group of notes.)

7. *The national bank—A "private" or "public" institution?* Note that Marshall in McCulloch said very little about the organization and operations of the Bank. Should he have said more? Recall also that the Bank's success was considerably greater during its prosperous first year than in the depression months immediately preceding the decision. Could the 1819 circumstances have been relied on to challenge the constitutionality of the Bank, if the 1816 context provided substantial basis for the congressional judgment to charter the Bank? (See also the further questions about Marshall's opinion in the next group of notes.)

The Bank was manifestly not a purely governmental operation—not like a mint or an army fort. As early as 1790, Hamilton had argued, in proposing a national bank: "To attach full confidence to an institution of this nature, it appears to be an essential ingredient in its structure, that it shall be under a *private* not a *public* direction—under the guidance of *individual interest,* not of *public policy."* Any suspicion that the nationally chartered bank was "too much influenced by *public necessity,"* he asserted, would "be a canker that would

---

11. For these essays (unearthed in the 1960s) and their background, see Gunther (ed.), John   Marshall's Defense of McCulloch v. Maryland (1969).

continually corrode the vitals of the credit of the bank." He added: "The keen, steady, and, as it were, magnetic sense of their own interest as proprietors, in the directors of a bank, pointing invariably to its true pole—the prosperity of the institution,—is the only security that can always be relied upon for a careful and prudent administration" and for "permanent confidence" in the bank.[12] Obviously, Hamilton and, later, the proponents of the Second Bank expected substantial governmental benefits from a congressionally chartered bank, as a source of loans, as a depository and fiscal agent, and as a stabilizer of currency. But these benefits were to be byproducts of the bank's operations as a largely private, profit-making, commercial institution. The charter of the Second Bank accordingly provided that 80% of the stock ownership and of the directors were to be private. Walter Jones and Joseph Hopkinson mentioned the "private" nature of the Bank in the course of their argument in McCulloch, though mainly on the question of the Bank's immunity from state taxation rather than of its constitutionality under Art. I. Were the "private" features relevant, on either question? Should Marshall have discussed them? Compare Plous and Baker, "McCulloch v. Maryland: Right Principle, Wrong Case," 9 Stan.L.Rev. 710 (1957).

CONGRESSIONAL POWER, THE JUDICIAL FUNCTION, AND POLITICAL RESTRAINTS

1. *Restraints on congressional power: Some general questions about judicially-imposed limitations.* Consider, in examining the McCulloch opinion and the cases in the next two chapters, what principled limits courts can and should impose to guard against excessive intrusion of national authority into local affairs. Are courts capable of articulating effective federalism-related limits (as distinguished from limits designed to protect individual rights, considered in Part III below)? Or is the imposition of restraints best left largely or wholly to the political process, in view of the representation of local interest in the national government? (See the Wechsler argument in note 3 below.) Did Marshall's McCulloch opinion legitimate an unlimited congressional discretion? In intent? In language? In effect?[1]

a. *Necessary and proper means to achieve enumerated ends: Judicial scrutiny of means-ends relationships.* One way in which Marshall in McCulloch tried to suggest judicially enforceable limits on congressional powers was to articulate criteria to determine whether the means chosen by Congress were adequately related to legitimate ends. Marshall spoke of means "which tended directly to the execution" of delegated powers, means which were "appropriate" and "plainly adapted" to achieving legitimate ends. Ever since McCulloch, the Supreme Court has been engaged in efforts, often unsuccessful, to put teeth into those limits. Implementing the "means"-"ends" requirement has raised a host of puzzling subsidiary questions. For example, how attenuated a chain of inferences put forth by defenders of congressional legislation will suffice to justify a law as a "necessary and proper" means to effectuate a granted power? (Recall the "House That Jack Built," slippery slope argument that Jefferson feared.) Must the proffered "means"-"ends" justification be one that was in fact considered by the enacting Congress, or may it be supplied subsequent to enactment, by counsel's argument or by the Justices' speculations about the justifications the legislature *might* have relied upon? Does the required "reason-

---

12. See Hamilton's Report to the House on a National Bank, Dec. 13, 1790.

1. It bears emphasizing that general, preliminary questions such as these—here and elsewhere in this book—are not designed to elicit immedi-

ate answers. Instead, they are intended to serve as guideposts in examining the materials that follow, and they are included for the purpose of calling attention to recurrent problems in the judicial enforcement of constitutional norms.

able relation"—or "plausible relation"—nexus between means and ends turn on standards of logic? Of empiric observation? Is the required nexus "uniform and invariable, the same today as tomorrow," or does it depend on "circumstances" "at a particular time"? (Recall Hamilton's argument, noted above.) What "time": Date of enactment? Date of adjudication? [2]

Marshall wrote his pseudonymous "Friend of the Constitution" essays of 1819 to counter Roane's charges that McCulloch gave "a *general* letter of attorney to the future legislators of the union," that in fact "the court had granted to congress unlimited powers under the pretext of a discretion in selecting means." Marshall insisted that the required means-ends relationship *was* a judicially enforceable one, and some of his essays tried to elaborate the requirement. For example, "neither a feigned convenience nor a strict necessity; but a reasonable convenience, and a qualified necessity," had to be shown to demonstrate that means were constitutional; means must have "a plain relation to the end," they must be "direct, natural and appropriate." McCulloch, he insisted, denied "the unlimited power of congress to adopt any means whatever." [3] (But to what "ends" *was* the Bank an appropriate "means"? Should Marshall have explored the actual structure and operation of the Bank more fully? Or was he justified in largely deferring to Congress (and to history) on the issue of the appropriateness of the Bank?)

Despite Marshall's insistence that the means-ends inquiry represented a significant judicial restraint on Congress, it can be argued that Roane was right after all about the effective scope of congressional discretion after McCulloch, given the broad exercises of national power sustained by the Court in the cases that follow. More than 150 years later, it is possible to claim that Roane was in the end right about the "consolidating" effect of McCulloch, if not about Marshall's purpose. Was that because Marshall did not seriously look for limits? Because the McCulloch limits were inadequate? Could better limits have been stated? [4]

b. *"Pretext": Judicial inquiry into congressional purposes and abuses of power.* In articulating limits on congressional choices, Marshall spoke not only of the required means-ends relationships, but also of inquiry into congressional purposes. Can courts effectively assure legislative good faith in exercising powers? Can and should courts scrutinize the nature and purity of legislative motives? [5] Marshall asserted in McCulloch—and emphatically reiterated in his newspaper replies to Roane—that the Court would invalidate laws "for the accomplishment of objects, not entrusted to the government," laws enacted "under the pretext"

---

2. The problem of judicial scrutiny of means-ends relationships arises not only in the context of federalism limits on congressional power. It recurs throughout this volume, and may well be the most frequently invoked technique in the judicial review of the validity of federal and state legislation. See, e.g., the discussion of a "means-oriented" scrutiny under the due process clause in chap. 8 and under the equal protection clause in chap. 9. See also Gunther, "The Supreme Court, 1971 Term: Foreword: [A] Model for a Newer Equal Protection," 86 Harv.L.Rev. 1 (1972), and Flemming v. Nestor, p. 215 below.

3. See Gunther (ed.), John Marshall's Defense of McCulloch v. Maryland (1969).

4. Consider Gunther (ed.), above, at 20: "The degree of centralization that has taken place [since McCulloch] may well have come about in the face of Marshall's intent rather than in accord with his expectations. That centraliza-

tion may be the inevitable consequence of economic and social changes. And this development may suggest the impossibility of articulating general constitutional standards capable of limiting those centralizing forces, particularly through judicial action. But to say this is very different from saying that Marshall knew he was engaging in a hopeless task."

5. What *are* the institutional and practical difficulties inhibiting such inquiries? That problem will recur in later materials in this volume. See, e.g., chaps. 4 and 7, below. See generally, Ely, "Legislative and Administrative Motivation in Constitutional Law," 79 Yale L.J. 1205 (1970), Brest, "Palmer v. Thompson: An Approach to the Problem of Unconstitutional Legislative Motive," 1971 Sup.Ct.Rev. 95, and Symposium, "Legislative Motivation," 15 San Diego L.Rev. 925 (1978).

of exercising granted powers.[6] Is the "pretext" limitation really capable of judicial enforcement? Does it require a judicial determination of the "true" object of the law—of congressional purposes and motives? Are otherwise constitutional laws invalidated by impermissible "pretext" statements by Congress? More basically, should the Art. I, § 8, powers of Congress be read as specifying the permissible *aims* (or ends or purposes) of legislation, or simply the permissible, objectively determinable *areas* of national regulation? Does the commerce clause, for example, authorize legislative control for any purpose so long as the *field* regulated is that of "interstate commerce"? (Such a view would authorize Congress to seek "morality," "police" objectives—e.g., to legislate against prostitution or for racial justice or against rioters—so long as the sanction of the law took hold on some commerce-connected activity.) Or must the regulation be enacted with a primarily commercial purpose? Or must the evil being regulated at least have commercial dimensions? [For further pursuit of these problems in the context of the commerce power, see Hammer v. Dagenhart, Darby, and related materials in chap. 3.]

2. *Some additional questions on the Marshall opinion in McCulloch.* a. How useful is Marshall's emphasis on the theme that "it is *a constitution* we are expounding"?[7] Is that more than a truism? Was anyone denying that? Does the emphasis on *constitutional* interpretation aid in the delineation of implied powers? Is a broad construction of national powers an inevitable consequence of interpreting *"a constitution"?* Could not Spencer Roane and other states' righters have argued that their views, too, had in mind *"a constitution"*—that the Constitution as they interpreted it was no less *"a constitution"* because it provided for tighter controls on national power and greater protection of state authority in a federal scheme of divided sovereignty?

b. How significant was the Necessary and Proper Clause to Marshall's result? Is it fair to say that he had established his conclusion—that the Constitution legitimated implied powers—even before he came to the consideration of that Clause in Art. I, § 8, cl. 18? How persuasive is Marshall's textual and contextual reading of the Necessary and Proper Clause once he reaches it? More broadly, consider the sources of Marshall's interpretation: to some extent he relies on text; to some extent, on history. McCulloch also includes considerable emphasis on "inference from the structures and relationships created by the constitution." See C.L. Black, Jr., Structure and Relationship in Constitutional Law (1969). Note the way Marshall relies heavily upon considerations of structure and relationship, not only to justify his views on congressional powers but also to defend his position on the Bank's immunity from state taxation. Professor Black's book advocates a greater emphasis on structural interpretation, as against often "manipulative" textual exegesis. Inferences from structures and relationships are often defensible; but are they more immune from the risk of manipulation than resort to other sources of constitutional interpretation?[8]

6. See, e.g., Gunther (ed.), above, at 187; see also Marshall's newspaper statement at 173: "It is not pretended that this right of selection [of means] may be fraudulently used to the destruction of the fair land marks of the constitution. Congress certainly may not, under the pretext of collecting taxes, or of guaranteeing to each state a republican form of government, alter the law of descents; but if the means have a plain relation to the end—if they be direct, natural and appropriate," they are constitutional.

7. Justice Frankfurter once called this statement "the single most important utterance in the literature of constitutional law—most important because most comprehensive and comprehending." Frankfurter, "John Marshall and the Judicial Function," 69 Harv.L.Rev. 217 (1955).

8. Note that the Necessary and Proper Clause, by its own terms, is *not* limited to implementing the allocations of power in Art. I, § 8. Rather, it applies as well to "all other Powers vested by this Constitution in the Government of the United States." See, e.g., the reliance on McCulloch in interpreting the scope of congressional enforcement powers under the post-Civil War Amendments, in chap. 10 below.

c. What, in Marshall's view, was the source of the Bank's immunity from the state tax: Text? History? Structures and relationships? [9] The nationalist value preferences of a portion of early 19th century society? Marshall's personal nationalist views? Should Marshall have considered more fully, on the question of state taxing power, the practical operations of the Bank, including its largely private ownership? Should he have considered a narrower rule more responsive to Maryland's discriminatory tax—a tax not applicable to all banks but only to those not chartered by the State? How far-reaching are Marshall's implications as to governmental immunity? How can his principles justify what he suggests in the last paragraph of his opinion: a valid tax on the Bank's real property, or on Maryland citizens' holdings of Bank stock? (See also the additional materials on intergovernmental tax immunities at p. 333 below.)

3. *Restraints on congressional power: The Political Safeguards of Federalism.* a. *Wechsler.* Consider, in examining the Court's efforts to formulate limiting principles in the cases that follow, whether the need for judicial efforts to safeguard federalism values is minimal in view of the representation of local interests in the political structure of the national government. Do these "political safeguards" operate with equal effectiveness with regard to all kinds of congressional action? As effectively in cases of morals regulation as in cases of economic regulation? As effectively when the spending power is invoked (see chap. 4, sec. 2) as with proposals for direct regulation of local affairs? These questions are raised by the following excerpts from Wechsler, "The Political Safeguards of Federalism—The Role of the States in the Composition and Selection of the National Government," in Principles, Politics, and Fundamental Law (1961), 49–82: [10]

"Our constitution makers established a central government authorized to act directly upon individuals through its own agencies—and thus they formed a nation capable of function and of growth. To serve the ends of federalism they employed three main devices: (1) They preserved the states as separate sources of authority and organs of administration—a point on which they hardly had a choice. (2) They gave the states a role of great importance in the composition and selection of the central government. (3) They undertook to formulate a distribution of authority between the nation and the states, in terms which gave some scope at least to legal processes for its enforcement.

"Scholarship [has] given most attention to the last of these enumerated mechanisms perhaps because it has been fascinated by the Supreme Court and its interpretations of the power distribution clauses of the Constitution. The continuous existence of the states as governmental entities and their strategic role in the selection of the Congress and the President are so immutable a feature of the system that their importance tends to be ignored. Of the framers' mechanisms, however, they have had and have today the larger influence upon the working balance of our federalism. The actual extent of central intervention in the governance of our affairs is determined far less by the formal power distribution than by the sheer existence of the states and their political power to influence the action of the national authority.

9. See Black, Structure and Relationship in Constitutional Law (1969), 15: "Marshall's reasoning on this branch of the case is, as I read it, essentially structural. It has to do in great part with what he conceives to be the warranted relational proprieties between the national government and the government of the states, with the structural corollaries of national supremacy—and, at one point, of the mode of formation of the Union. [In] this, perhaps the greatest of our constitutional cases, judgment is reached not fundamentally on the basis of that kind of textual exegesis which we tend to regard as normal, but on the basis of reasoning from the total structure which the text has created."

10. The excerpts are reprinted here with the permission of the publisher, © copyright 1961 by the President and Fellows of Harvard College. The substance of the essay also appears in 54 Colum.L.Rev. 543 (1954), and in Selected Essays on Constitutional Law 1938–62 (1963), 185.

"[National action has] always been regarded as exceptional in our polity, an intrusion to be justified by some necessity, the special rather than the ordinary case. This point of view cuts even deeper than the concept of the central government as one of granted, limited authority, articulated in the tenth amendment. National power may be quite unquestioned in a given situation; those who would advocate its exercise must none the less answer the preliminary question why the matter should not be left to the states. Even when Congress acts, its tendency has been to frame enactments on an ad hoc basis to accomplish limited objectives, supplanting state-created norms only so far as may be necessary for the purpose. Indeed, with all the centralizing growth throughout the years, federal law is still a largely interstitial product, rarely occupying any field completely, building normally upon legal relationships established by the states. As Henry Hart and I have put it elsewhere: 'Congress [acts] against the background of the total *corpus juris* of the states in much the way that a state legislature acts against the background of the common law, assumed to govern unless changed by legislation.' As a state legislature views the common law as something to be left alone unless a need for change has been established, so Congress has traditionally viewed the governance of matters by the states. [The] tradition plainly serves the values of our federalism in so far as it maintains a burden of persuasion on those favoring national intervention.

"If I have drawn too much significance from the mere fact of the existence of the states, the error surely will be rectified by pointing also to their crucial role in the selection and the composition of the national authority. More is involved here than that aspect of the compromise between the larger and the smaller states that yielded their equality of status in the Senate. Representatives no less than Senators are allotted by the Constitution to the states, although their number varies with state population as determined by the census. Though the House was meant to be the 'grand depository of the democratic principle of the government,' as distinguished from the Senate's function as the forum of the states, the people to be represented with due deference to their respective numbers were *the people of the states.* And with the President, as with Congress, the crucial instrument of the selection—whether through electors, or, in the event of failure of majority, by the House voting as state units—is again the states. The consequence, of course, is that the states are the strategic yardsticks for the measurement of interest and opinion, the special centers of political activity, the separate geographical determinants of national as well as local politics. [But see the modern, "one person-one vote" reapportionment decisions, p. 1615 below.]

"[To] the extent that federalist values have real significance they must give rise to local sensitivity to central intervention; to the extent that such a local sensitivity exists, it cannot fail to find reflection in the Congress. Indeed, the problem of the Congress is and always has been to attune itself to national opinion and produce majorities for action called for by the voice of the entire nation. It is remarkable that it should function thus as well as it does, given its intrinsic sensitivity to any insular opinion that is dominant in a substantial number of the states. [The] President must be [the] main repository of 'national spirit' in the central government. But both the mode of his selection and the future of his party require that he also be responsive to local values that have large support within the states. And since his programs must, in any case, achieve support in Congress [he] must surmount the greater local sensitivity of Congress before anything is done.

"If this analysis is correct, the national political process in the United States—and especially the role of the states in the composition and selection of the central government—is intrinsically well adapted to retarding or restraining new intrusions by the center on the domain of the states. Far from a national authority that is expansionist by nature, the inherent tendency in our system is precisely the reverse, necessitating the widest support before intrusive measures of importance can receive significant consideration, reacting readily to opposition grounded in resistance within the states. Nor is this tendency effectively denied by pointing to the size or scope of the existing national establishment. However useful it may be to explore possible contractions in specific areas, such evidence points mainly to the magnitude of unavoidable responsibility under the circumstances of our time.

"It is in light of this inherent tendency, reflected most importantly in Congress, that the governmental power distribution clauses of the Constitution gain their largest meaning as an instrument for the protection of the states. Those clauses, as is well known, have served far more to qualify or stop intrusive legislative measures in the Congress than to invalidate enacted legislation in the Supreme Court. [This] does not differ from the expectation of the framers quite as markedly as might be thought. For the containment of the national authority Madison did not emphasize the function of the Court; he pointed to the composition of the Congress and to the political [processes].

"The prime function envisaged for judicial review—in relation to federalism—was the maintenance of national supremacy against nullification or usurpation by the individual states, the national government having no part in their composition or their councils. This is made clear by the fact that reliance on the courts was substituted, apparently on Jefferson's suggestion, for the earlier proposal to give Congress a veto of state enactments deemed to trespass on the national domain. And except for the brief interlude that ended with the crisis of the thirties, it is mainly in the realm of such policing of the states that the Supreme Court has in fact participated in determining the balances of federalism.[11] This is not to say that the Court can decline to measure national enactments by the Constitution when it is called upon to face the question in the course of ordinary litigation; the supremacy clause governs there as well. It is rather to say that the Court is on weakest ground when it opposes its interpretation of the Constitution to that of Congress in the interest of the states, whose representatives control the legislative process and, by hypothesis, have broadly acquiesced in sanctioning the challenged Act of Congress."

b. *Choper.* Two decades after the publication of the Wechsler position, Dean Jesse H. Choper relied on somewhat similar premises to support a more extreme conclusion. In Judicial Review and the National Political Process (1980), Choper argues that the Court should "abstain from deciding constitutional questions of national power versus states' rights," largely in order "to ease the commendable and crucial task of judicial review in cases of individual constitutional liberties."[12] Like Wechsler, Choper claims that "[n]umerous structural aspects of the national political system serve to assure that states' rights

---

11. "Of the great controversies with respect to national power before the Civil War, only the Bank and slavery within the territories were carried to the Court and its participation with respect to slavery was probably its greatest failure. The question of internal improvements, for example, which raised the most acute problem of constitutional construction, was fought out politically and in Congress. After the War only the Civil Rights Cases and income tax decisions were important in setting limits on national power— until the Child Labor Case and the New Deal decisions. The recasting of constitutional positions since the crisis acknowledges much broader power in the Congress—as against the states— than it is likely soon or ever to employ." [Footnote by Professor Wechsler. Compare National

League of Cities and its progeny, in chap. 3, sec. 7, below.]

[The Wechsler views were initially set forth in 1954 and published in book form in 1961. Do the expansive invocations of congressional power in the years since then undermine any part of the Wechsler thesis? In recent decades, congressional exercises of its powers have grown considerably in frequency and scope, as the next two chapters illustrate. Can it still be said as confidently as Wechsler was able to say that "the national political process [is] intrinsically well adapted to retarding or restraining new intrusions by the center on the domain of the states"?]

12. Toward that same end, Choper also argues that the Court should "abstain from decid-

will not be trampled, and the lesson of practice is that they have not been." In arguing that "constitutional questions that concern the scope of national power vis-a-vis the states" should be held "nonjusticiable," Choper claims that federalism issues, unlike individual liberties ones, are issues of "practicality" rather than "issues of principle." Moreover, he finds a greater likelihood of "fair resolution [of federalism issues] within the national political chambers." Accordingly, "the thoroughly effective voice of the states in the national lawmaking system allows the Court to forgo review of that class of issues."

Choper claims that his approach would promote the Court's institutional strength in defending individual liberties by removing from the judicial arena a group of decisions that sometimes "result in a hostile public attitude toward the Court." He insists, too, that judicial review is unnecessary even in situations of "Congress and the President joining forces and ignoring clear constitutional mandate," for in such cases "it is probably futile to rely on the Court to right the matter." In any event, "as a general matter, Congresses and Presidents have been extremely solicitous of the sovereign prerogatives of the states." Thus, although Choper concedes that federalism values are clearly expressed in the Constitution, he concludes that, in order to "conserve the Court's precious capital for those cases in which it is really needed," the Court should "explicitly hold that it will not pass on constitutional questions concerning the reach of national authority versus states' rights," in part to "shield it from hostile public and official reactions."

Note that Choper's proposal goes well beyond Wechsler's. Wechsler had stated: "This is not to say that the Court can decline to measure national enactments by the Constitution when it is called upon to face the question in the course of ordinary litigation; the supremacy clause governs there as well." May the Court nevertheless decline to reach the merits in such cases, as Choper urges? [13] Even if Court refusal to adjudicate can be reconciled with the principles of Marbury and the Supremacy Clause, are Choper's policy arguments persuasive? For example, would the Court's defense of individual liberties, which Choper would make the Court's virtually exclusive function, be tolerable to the public if the Court declined jurisdiction over most or all other constitutional issues? Recall the questions at the beginning of the Wechsler excerpt. Do the political safeguards on which Choper, like Wechsler, relies so heavily operate with equal effectiveness with regard to all kinds of congressional action? As effectively in cases of morals regulation as in cases of economic regulation? Questions such as these are pursued in the next chapter.[14]

ing ultimate issues of constitutional authority between Congress and the President." See chap. 6 below.

13. Compare the materials on "Discretion to Decline the Exercise of Jurisdiction" in chap. 15, sec. 4, below.

14. As the materials that follow show, the modern Court has quite consistently adhered to a generous reading of the congressional power to select means in federalistic contexts. Contrast a group of cases that involved individual rights limits rather than federalistic restraints on national power: there, a majority of the Court adopted a surprisingly narrow reading of the Necessary and Proper Clause. The cases involved the extension of court martial jurisdiction over civilians associated with the armed forces. See Reid v. Covert, 354 U.S. 1 (1957), and Kinsella v. United States ex rel. Singleton, 361 U.S. 234 (1960). In Kinsella, the majority opinion, after quoting states' rights writings of James Madison, asserted that the Necessary and Proper Clause "is not itself a grant of power." In a dissent in a later case not involving individual rights concerns, Justice Douglas sought to apply that narrow reading to invalidate a national law challenged solely on federalistic grounds. United States v. Oregon, 366 U.S. 643 (1961). [For an argument that the Court would have been better advised to rest its decisions in the court martial cases on restrictions stemming from specific individual rights guarantees rather than on interpretations of Art. I (and on resulting unusual, narrow readings of the Necessary and Proper Clause), see Gunther, Cases and Materials on Constitutional Law (9th ed. 1975), 118–26.]

Chapter 3

THE COMMERCE POWER

Introduction. The poor condition of American commerce and the proliferating trade rivalries among the states were the immediate provocations for the calling of the Constitutional Convention. One of the new Constitution's major innovations was a response to those concerns: Congress was granted the power "To Regulate Commerce with foreign Nations, and among the Several States." That grant was to suppress the "interfering and unneighbourly regulations of some States"—regulations which, "if not restrained by a national controul," would prove to be ever more "serious sources of animosity and discord." (Hamilton's No. 22 of The Federalist.) The national commerce power, it was hoped, would put an end to hostile state restrictions, retaliatory trade regulations, protective tariffs on imports from other states.

That congressional power, designed to promote a national market and curb Balkanization of the economy, has been a subject of extensive and continuous consideration by the Court since Marshall's day. The commerce power has had a two-fold impact: as a restraint on state action (considered in chap. 5), and as a source of national authority (the concern of this chapter). In the hundreds of cases in which *state* regulations and taxes have been challenged under the commerce clause, free trade—a value clearly rooted in the history of the clause—is the national interest that claims protection. In the cases in which the clause is invoked to justify *congressional* regulation, the nexus with historical purposes is often more tenuous. But the modern pressures for national action on a widening range of problems have prompted increasingly intense searches for constitutional justifications among the enumerated powers. And in these searches, the commerce clause has proved to be a frequently attractive and often hospitable base for the assertion of regulatory authority.

This chapter examines in some detail the Court's efforts to articulate the scope and limits of the commerce power. That examination is worthwhile not only for its own sake—for the sake of tracing the contours of congressional authority—but also for its institutional aspects, for the light it sheds on the Court's general capacity to develop enforceable limits on governmental powers. Many of the doctrines in these cases have proved ineffective as restraints; some have been explicitly abandoned by the Court. After nearly 200 years of government under the Constitution, there are very few judicially enforced checks on the commerce power. In examining the contemporary constitutional terrain, consider: Did the limits unsuccessfully articulated by past courts fail because they were unjustifiable in content? Because they were applied inconsistently and with result-oriented biases? What principled limits were possible? What limits remain? Does the history of commerce clause litigation suggest that judicially-developed doctrines limiting government tend to be facades for the personal preferences of the judges? Are restraints designed to protect individual rights likely to be more principled and effective in the long run than the federalism-related limits considered here?

These problems underlie the recurrent questions of commerce power doctrine which surface throughout this chapter. Often, Congress has sought to deal with problems far removed from the evils that gave rise to the commerce clause. Should the purpose of Congress determine the legitimacy of resort to the commerce power? Can a standard of constitutionality distinguish between "commercial" or "economic" legislation on the one hand and "moral," "police" regulation on the other? Between local affairs remote from commerce and intrastate activities with a sufficiently close connection to interstate commerce? Even if adequate judicially enforceable limits are beyond the Court's capacity (or proper institutional role), do the text and structure of the Constitution nevertheless establish federalistic restraints which a legislator should heed in considering proposals for national action? [1]

SECTION 1. THE MARSHALL COURT'S GROUNDWORK

GIBBONS v. OGDEN

6 Wheat. 1, 6 L.Ed. 23 (1824).

[The New York legislature granted to Robert Livingston and Robert Fulton the exclusive right to operate steamboats in New York waters. By assignment from Livingston and Fulton, Aaron Ogden acquired monopoly rights to operate steamboats between New York and New Jersey. Thomas Gibbons, a former partner of Ogden, began operating two steamboats between New York and Elizabethtown, New Jersey, in violation of Ogden's monopoly. Gibbons' boats were enrolled and licensed as "vessels employed in the coasting trade" under a federal law of 1793 (1 Stat. 305). Ogden obtained an injunction from the New York Court of Chancery ordering Gibbons to stop operating his ferries in New York waters. 4 Johns.Ch. 150 (1819). The highest New York court affirmed. 17 Johns. 488 (1820). Only a part of Chief Justice Marshall's opinion sustaining Gibbons' appeal is printed here—that portion discussing the national commerce power. The rest of the Marshall opinion—the part dealing with the validity of the New York monopoly under the Constitution and the federal law—appears at p. 232 below, with other materials on commerce clause and Supremacy Clause restraints on state power.]

Mr. Chief Justice MARSHALL [delivered the opinion of the Court].

The appellant contends that this decree is erroneous, because the laws which purport to give the exclusive privilege it sustains, are repugnant to the constitution and laws of the United States.

They are said to be repugnant—1st. To that clause in the constitution which authorizes congress to regulate commerce.

[The Constitution] contains an enumeration of powers expressly granted by the people to their government. It has been said, that these powers ought to be construed strictly. But why ought they to be so construed? Is there one sentence in the constitution which gives countenance to this rule? [What] do

---

1. This chapter singles out the commerce power to explore federalistic limits on national regulation because congressional resort to that power has been the most prolific source of litigation. But the general problem of localist restraints on national power is not confined to commerce power issues. There is some doctrinal, and an even closer historical, connection between the commerce cases in this chapter and the taxing and spending power materials in the next. On the doctrinal relationship, compare, e.g., the problem of abuses of power—invoking a delegated power as a "pretext" to achieve ulterior ends—in the Child Labor Case, Hammer v. Dagenhart (p. 117 of this chapter), with the Child Labor Tax Case (p. 193 of the next chapter). On the historical relationship, compare the Court's efforts to curb exercises of the commerce power in the early decades of this century with similar efforts to restrain congressional uses of other Art. I, § 8, powers: e.g., the 1936 decision in the Carter case (p. 126 of this chapter) parallels the 1936 decision in a spending power case, United States v. Butler (p. 202 of the next chapter). These and other doctrinal and historical interrelations are developed in several notes below.

gentlemen mean, by a strict construction? If they contend only against that enlarged construction, which would extend words beyond their natural and obvious import, we might question the application of the term, but should not controvert the principle. If they contend for that narrow construction which, in support of some theory not to be found in the constitution, would deny to the government those powers which the words of the grant, as usually understood, import, and which are consistent with the general views and objects of the instrument—for that narrow construction, which would cripple the government, and render it unequal to the objects for which it is declared to be instituted, and to which the powers given, as fairly understood, render it competent—then we cannot perceive the propriety of this strict construction, nor adopt it as the rule by which the constitution is to be expounded. [If], from the imperfection of human language, there should be serious doubts respecting the extent of any given power, it is a well settled rule, that the objects for which it was given, especially when those objects are expressed in the instrument itself, should have great influence in the construction.

[The] words are, "congress shall have power to regulate commerce with foreign nations, and among the several states, and with the Indian tribes." The subject to be regulated is commerce; and [to] ascertain the extent of the power, it becomes necessary to settle the meaning of the word. The counsel for the appellee would limit it to traffic, to buying and selling, or the interchange of commodities, and do not admit that it comprehends navigation. This would restrict a general term, applicable to many objects, to one of its significations. Commerce, undoubtedly, is traffic, but it is something more—it is intercourse. It describes the commercial intercourse between nations, and parts of nations, in all its branches, and is regulated by prescribing rules for carrying on that intercourse. [All] America understands, and has uniformly understood, the word "commerce" to comprehend navigation. It was so understood, and must have been so understood, when the constitution was framed. The power over commerce, including navigation, was one of the primary objects for which the people of America adopted their government, and must have been contemplated in forming it.

[To] what commerce does this power extend? The constitution informs us, to commerce "with foreign nations, and among the several states, and with the Indian tribes." It has [been] universally admitted that these words comprehend every species of commercial intercourse between the United States and foreign nations. No sort of trade can be carried on between this country and any other, to which this power does not extend. [The] subject to which the power is next applied, is to commerce "among the several states." The word "among" means intermingled with. A thing which is among others, is intermingled with them. Commerce among the states, cannot stop at the external boundary line of each state, but may be introduced into the interior.

It is not intended to say that these words comprehend that commerce which is completely internal, which is carried on between man and man in a state, or between different parts of the same state, and which does not extend to or affect other states. Such a power would be inconvenient, and is certainly unnecessary. Comprehensive as the word "among" is, it may very properly be restricted to that commerce which concerns more states than one. The phrase is not one which would probably have been selected to indicate the completely interior traffic of a state, because it is not an apt phrase for that purpose; and the enumeration of the particular classes of commerce to which the power was to be extended, would not have been made, had the intention been to extend the power to every description. The enumeration presupposes something not enumerated; and that something, if we regard the language or the subject of the sentence, must be the exclusively internal commerce of a state. The genius and character of the whole government seem to be, that its action is to be applied to all the external concerns of the nation, and to those internal concerns which affect the states generally; but not to those which are completely within a particular state, which do not affect other states, and with which it is not necessary to interfere, for the purpose of executing some of the general powers of the government. The completely internal commerce of a state, then, may be considered as reserved for the state itself.

But in regulating commerce with foreign nations, the power of congress does not stop at the jurisdictional lines of the several states. It would be a very useless power, if it could not pass those lines. The commerce of the United States with foreign nations, is that of the whole United States; every district has a right to participate in it. The deep streams which penetrate our country in every direction, pass through the interior of almost every state in the Union, and furnish the means of exercising this right. If congress has the power to regulate it, that power must be exercised whenever the subject exists. If it exists within the states, if a foreign voyage may commence or terminate at a port within a state, then the power of congress may be exercised within a state.

[This] principle is, if possible, still more clear, when applied to commerce "among the several states." They either join each other, in which case they are separated by a mathematical line, or they are remote from each other, in which case other states lie between them. What is commerce "among" them; and how is it to be conducted? Can a trading expedition between two adjoining states, commence and terminate outside of each? And if the trading intercourse be between two states remote from each other, must it not commence in one, terminate in the other, and probably pass through a third? Commerce among the states must, of necessity, be commerce with the states. In the regulation of trade with the Indian tribes, the action of the law, especially when the constitution was made, was chiefly within a state. The power of congress, then, whatever it may be, must be exercised within the territorial jurisdiction of the several states.

[We] are now arrived at the inquiry—What is this power? It is the power to regulate; that is, to prescribe the rule by which commerce is to be governed. This power, like all others vested in congress, is complete in itself, may be exercised to its utmost extent, and acknowledges no limitations, other than are prescribed in the constitution. These are expressed in plain terms, and do not affect the questions which arise in this case. If, as has always been understood, the sovereignty of congress, though limited to specified objects, is plenary as to those objects, the power over commerce with foreign nations, and among the several states, is vested in congress as absolutely as it would be in a single government, having in its constitution the same restrictions on the exercise of the power as are found in the constitution of the United States. The wisdom and the discretion of congress, their identity with the people, and the influence which their constituents possess at elections, are, in this, as in many other instances, as that, for example, of declaring war, the sole restraints on which they have relied, to secure them from its abuse. They are the restraints on which the people must often rely solely, in all representative governments.

The power of congress, then, comprehends navigation, within the limits of every state in the Union; so far as that navigation may be, in any manner, connected with "commerce with foreign nations, or among the several States, or with the Indian tribes." It may, of consequence, pass the jurisdictional line of New York, and act upon the very waters to which the prohibition now under consideration applies.

[Powerful] and ingenious minds, taking, as postulates, that the powers expressly granted to the government of the Union, are to be contracted, by construction, into the narrowest possible compass, and that the original powers of the states are retained, if any possible construction will retain them, may, by a course of well digested, but refined and metaphysical reasoning, founded on these premises, explain away the constitution of our country, and leave it, a magnificent structure, indeed, to look at, but totally unfit for use. They may so entangle and perplex the understanding, as to obscure principles, which were before thought quite plain, and induce doubts where, if the mind were to pursue its own course, none would be perceived. In such a case, it is peculiarly necessary to recur to safe and fundamental [principles]. [Additional excerpts from Chief Justice Marshall's opinion invalidating the New York monopoly grant, and from Justice Johnson's concurrence appear in chap. 5, at p. 232 below.]

THE MARSHALL COURT'S LEGACY AND MODERN PROBLEMS

1. *Gibbons v. Ogden: A doctrine for all needs?* Gibbons v. Ogden, like McCulloch, is frequently and prominently cited in modern decisions sustaining very expansive exercises of congressional powers. Is that modern reliance on Marshall justifiable? Consider Wickard v. Filburn, 317 U.S. 111 (1942) (p. 135 below), one of the most important discussions of the commerce power. Justice Jackson's opinion for the Court in Wickard stated: "At the beginning Chief Justice Marshall described the federal commerce power with a breadth never yet exceeded. Gibbons v. Ogden. He made emphatic the embracing and penetrating nature of this power by warning that effective restraints on its exercise must proceed from political rather than from judicial processes." Is that a fair statement? Does Gibbons abandon all judicial restraints? After McCulloch, Marshall vehemently denied Spencer Roane's charge that his principles gave Congress unlimited authority. Did Gibbons give Congress the carte blanche denied by McCulloch? What judicial limits did Marshall assert? Even if Justice Jackson in 1942 overstated the holding of Gibbons, do the modern commerce power decisions in effect validate the Jackson dictum in Wickard? [1]

2. *Early commerce power legislation.* During the first century under our Constitution, most of the Court's discussions of the scope of the commerce power arose—as in Gibbons v. Ogden—in cases dealing with limits on state action affecting interstate commerce. And in most of those cases (unlike Gibbons), Congress had not exercised its power at all. Rather, the commerce clause came into play only because state laws were challenged as infringing on the freedom of interstate commerce allegedly guaranteed by Art. I, § 8, even though Congress' authority under that clause was unexercised and "dormant." (Those limits on state regulation are developed in chap. 5, sec. 1, below.) Nevertheless, the concepts of interstate commerce developed in those state regulation cases served as a source of limits on national action when Congress turned to major uses of the commerce power in later years. See, e.g., the Knight case, p. 106 below.

Large-scale regulatory action by Congress did not begin until the Interstate Commerce Act of 1887 and the Sherman Anti-Trust Act of 1890. Challenges to those statutes—examined in the next section—initiated the major modern confrontations between the Court and congressional authority over commerce. But there were occasional exercises of the national commerce power even before 1887. For example, Congress enacted laws to improve water and land

---

1. In light of this final question, it may be useful to turn now to Wickard as a vantage point from which to survey the developments in commerce power doctrine between the early 19th century and the mid-20th.

transportation.[2] And there was also some commerce legislation of a "police" character, as in United States v. Marigold, 9 How. 560 (1850) (prohibiting the importation of counterfeit money). But the most troublesome problems about the reach of the national power did not emerge until Congress turned to weightier legislative efforts. The rapid 19th century developments in industrialization, transportation and communication produced national economic problems and demands for congressional regulation. Control of railroad rates and of restraints on competition were the early congressional responses to these demands and yielded the Knight and Shreveport cases below.

3. *Emerging doctrinal difficulties: Regulation of national economic problems vs. regulation of "police" problems.* a. *The central problem of sec. 2: Regulating intrastate activities because of their relationship to interstate commerce.* It was in cases such as Shreveport and Knight that the Court tried to state the extent to which Congress may regulate local activities because of their relationship with interstate commerce. The doctrinal problems of those cases foreshadow the difficulties encountered in subsequent efforts at national economic regulation—especially the New Deal attempts considered in the cases from Schechter to Wickard, secs. 4 and 5 below. How far, and with what justification, may Congress reach intrastate activities related to national economic concerns? Can the local production of goods be regulated because it "affects" interstate commerce? Or is the production of goods not reachable by the commerce power, because production neither is commerce nor has a "direct" effect on commerce? These problems are the focus of sec. 2 below.

b. *The central problem of sec. 3: "Police" regulations—morality, crime and the commerce power.* Efforts to deal with the emerging problems of the national economy were not the only examples of expanded congressional resort to the commerce power starting with the closing years of the 19th century. In a contemporaneous development, Congress also manifested an increased interest in problems of morality and criminality—gambling, prostitution, theft. Those congressional "police" regulations came to the Court contemporaneously with the new national economic regulations. Did the Court handle those two types of laws differently? Should they have been handled differently? Are laws directed at police problems less justifiable invocations of the commerce power than regulations of economic problems? Is it useful, or possible, to distinguish national legislation dealing with police problems—directed ultimately at "bad" local activities—from laws concerned with national economic problems? Is it constitutionally significant that police legislation typically relied, as the regulatory technique, on prohibition of interstate transportation rather than direct control of local activities? (See, e.g., the Lottery Case and Hammer v. Dagenhart, below.) Did these police regulations invoke the commerce power as a "pretext"? Should the Court consider the ulterior purpose of legislation, if the law's immediate sanction falls on the movement of commerce across state lines? Problems such as these are the concern of sec. 3 below.

The distinctions suggested in the preceding two paragraphs, even if valid, may be more difficult to apply than to state. What if economic and "police" objectives both underlie legislation? Can a distinction between economic and "police" purposes be applied, for example, to regulations of working conditions and to restrictions on racial discrimination (see secs. 5 and 6 below)? Can and should the Court make such a distinction on the basis of the primary purposes of

---

2. See, e.g., Roberts v. Northern Pacific Railway Co., 158 U.S. 1 (1894) (creation of a corporation for the purpose of building railroads); Luxton v. North River Bridge Co., 153 U.S. 525 (1894) (creation of a corporation with authority to construct a bridge); California v. Central Pacific Railway Co., 127 U.S. 1 (1888) (charter-ing of interstate carrier). See also The Daniel Ball, 10 Wall. 557 (1871) (federal inspection law for steam vessels applied to river steamers built to operate solely within the boundaries of one state; Court noted that ship carried goods in interstate commerce and accordingly was "an instrumentality of that commerce").

the legislators? Even if the Court, for institutional reasons, finds it impossible to curb questionable invocations of the power, should a legislator be troubled by attempts to use the commerce clause for social or moral—predominantly noneconomic—objectives? Questions such as these should be borne in mind in examining the ensuing sections.

_____

SECTION 2. THE BEGINNINGS OF MODERN ECONOMIC REGULATION: JUSTIFYING NATIONAL REGULATION OF LOCAL ACTIVITIES ON THE BASIS OF THEIR RELATIONSHIP TO INTERSTATE COMMERCE

_____

Introduction—The requisite "local"-"interstate" connection: Knight and Shreveport as sources of contending approaches. The two earliest examples of major modern regulatory legislation—the Sherman Anti-Trust Act of 1890 and the Interstate Commerce Act of 1887—produced important Court efforts to formulate commerce clause doctrine. The Sherman Act came before the Court in 1895, in the Sugar Trust case, United States v. E.C. Knight Co. (1895). The most important early Court encounter with the Interstate Commerce Act came two decades later, in the Shreveport Rate case (1914). The doctrinal approaches of these cases cast significant, and somewhat contradictory, shadows over subsequent litigation. Thus, when New Deal laws came before the Court in the 1930s, the differing progeny of the Knight and Shreveport cases offered the Justices a choice of standards. Until 1936, the Court drew on the Knight heritage and invalidated major national laws; beginning with 1937, the Shreveport approach, more receptive to expansive congressional uses of the commerce power, became central.

The Knight and Shreveport cases presented similar problems. In a sense, the Court struggled with the "means"-"ends" theme addressed by Marshall in McCulloch. Typically, the Government argued that local activities could be reached as a "means" of implementing the "end" of regulating interstate commerce. What were the standards to be applied when Congress sought to invoke the commerce power to reach arguably "local" economic activities? What constituted an adequate connection between the "local" and the "interstate"? Was the required relationship one of logical nexus or of practical impact? The Knight case symbolizes the former; the Shreveport case, the latter. Knight suggested that the local activity was not reachable unless it had a "direct" rather than an "indirect" effect on interstate commerce: an attempt to monopolize sugar refining, though of significant interstate economic consequences, was not controllable through federal legislation because the relationship between "manufacturing" and "commerce" was "indirect." In the Shreveport case, by contrast, "local" railroad rates were reachable because of their practical, economic impact on interstate transportation.

The next group of notes deals with the Knight case and its immediate consequences for antitrust enforcement. That group is followed by notes focusing on the Shreveport case and related problems. The logical nexus, "direct"-"indirect" emphasis of Knight, it turned out, did not prove a significant barrier to application of the antitrust laws. But it did leave a legacy of doctrine capable of being invoked in other contexts; and that legacy proved decisive in the early New Deal cases. When the Court struck down national economic regulations in the 1930s, the "direct"-"indirect" distinction of Knight proved fatal to congressional efforts, in cases such as Carter (p. 126 below). But then, quite suddenly, in the wake of Franklin Delano Roosevelt's Court-packing plan of 1937, the Court became more receptive to national economic regulation.

And the Shreveport heritage was invoked to provide support for that new constitutional direction: an emphasis on the substantial economic effect of the local activity on interstate commerce played a central role in such cases as Wickard (p. 135 below).

THE KNIGHT CASE, THE LOGICAL NEXUS STANDARD, AND ANTITRUST ENFORCEMENT

1. *The Knight approach and its sources.* In the Sugar Trust Case, UNITED STATES v. E.C. KNIGHT CO., 156 U.S. 1 (1895), the Supreme Court affirmed the dismissal of a Government civil action to set aside, under the Sherman Anti-Trust Act, the acquisition by the American Sugar Refining Company of the stock of four other sugar refineries.[1] The Government alleged that the acquired companies had produced about 33% of all sugar refined in the United States, and that American's acquisition gave it control of 98% of the nation's sugar refining capacity. The Court's decision rested on statutory construction; but that interpretation was premised on confining constitutional doctrines, especially the view that Congress could not under the commerce clause reach a monopoly in "manufacture."

Chief Justice FULLER's majority opinion indicated that, even conceding "the existence of a monopoly in manufacture," the monopoly could not be "directly suppressed here." He stated: "Doubtless the power to control the manufacture of a given thing involves in a certain sense the control of its disposition, but this is a secondary and not the primary sense; and although the exercise of that power may result in bringing the operation of commerce into play, it does not control it, and affects it only incidentally and indirectly. Commerce succeeds to manufacture, and is not a part of it." Monopolies might sometimes be regulated under the commerce power, but only when "the transaction is itself a monopoly of commerce."

In elaborating the distinction between "manufacture" and "commerce," Chief Justice Fuller relied heavily on decisions which had not involved congressional exercises of commerce power at all but rather questions of state authority in the face of the "dormant" commerce clause. What weight should have been given to those opinions stemming from a state rather than a national regulatory context? He relied particularly on Kidd v. Pearson, 128 U.S. 1 (1888), sustaining an Iowa prohibition of the manufacture of intoxicating liquors intended for export to other states. Chief Justice Fuller quoted from the Court's opinion in Kidd: "No distinction is more popular to the common mind, or more clearly expressed in economic and political literature, than that between manufacture and commerce. Manufacture is transformation—the fashioning of raw materials into a change of form for use. The functions of commerce are different. The buying and selling and the transportation incidental thereto constitute commerce. [If] it be held that [regulation of commerce] includes the regulation of all such manufactures as are intended to be the subject of commercial transactions in the future, it is impossible to deny that it would also include all productive industries that contemplate the same thing. The result would be that Congress would be invested, to the exclusion of the States, with the power to regulate, not only manufactures, but also agriculture, horticulture, stock raising, domestic fisheries, mining—in short every branch of human industry. For is there one of them that does not contemplate, more or less clearly, an interstate or foreign market? [The] power being vested in Congress

---

1. Sec. 1 of the Sherman Act prohibited any contract, combination or conspiracy "in restraint of trade or commerce among the several states." Sec. 2 provided penalties for any person "who shall monopolize, or combine or conspire [to] monopolize any part of the trade or commerce among the several states."

and denied to the States, it would follow as an inevitable result that the duty would devolve on Congress to regulate all of these delicate, multiform and vital interests—interests which in their nature are and must be local."

That approach of the Kidd case governed Chief Justice Fuller's Knight analysis and led him to insist that the nexus between the local and the interstate was a qualitative one of logical relationships, rather than an empiric one of economic impacts. As he put it: "Contracts, combinations, or conspiracies to control domestic enterprise in manufacture, agriculture, mining, production in all its forms, or to raise or lower prices or wages, might unquestionably tend to restrain external as well as domestic trade, but the restraint would be an indirect result, however inevitable and whatever its extent, and such result would not necessarily determine the object of the contract, combination, or conspiracy." He added: "Slight reflection will show that if the national power extends to all contracts and combinations in manufacture, agriculture, mining, and other productive industries, whose ultimate result may affect external commerce, comparatively little of business operations and affairs would be left for state control." [2] Those standards barred the suit against the Sugar Trust: the challenged actions "related exclusively to the acquisition of the Philadelphia refineries" and "bore no direct relation to commerce between the States." Chief Justice Fuller added: "The object was manifestly private gain in the manufacture of the commodity, but not through the control of interstate or foreign commerce." To be sure, the sugar business was a national one; "but this was no more than to say that trade and commerce served manufacture to fulfil its function." In short, a monopoly of "the manufacture" could not be treated by the Court as an attempt "to monopolize commerce, even though, in order to dispose of the product, the instrumentality of commerce was necessarily invoked." The first Justice Harlan submitted a strong dissent.

2. *The limited impact of Knight on antitrust enforcement.* Though the Knight approach was to prove a major obstacle to national economic regulation in the 1930s (see sec. 4 below), it did not paralyze antitrust enforcement. In a number of cases soon after Knight, the Court perceived a range of constitutional justifications for applying the Sherman and Clayton Acts. Thus, in Addyston Pipe & Steel Co. v. United States, 175 U.S. 211 (1899), the Court sustained an action against six companies manufacturing iron pipe who had made agreements in restraint of competition. The Court found that the aim of the agreement was not only to restrain manufacturing but also "to directly and by means of such combination increase the prices." This was held to be a "direct restraint upon interstate commerce." And in Northern Securities Co. v. United States, 193 U.S. 197 (1904), the 5 to 4 decision sustained an action to set aside the control acquired by Northern over two companies operating parallel railroad lines. Justice Holmes urged in dissent that the statute be construed in such a way as "not to raise grave doubts" about its constitutionality. Recalling the "indirect effect" language of Knight, he added: "Commerce depends upon population, but Congress could not, on that ground, undertake to regulate marriage and divorce. If the act before us is to be carried out according to what seems to be the logic of the argument for the Government, which I do not believe that it will be, I can see no part of the conduct of life with which on similar principles

2. Passages such as this reflect the much-criticized concept of "dual federalism" characteristic of Court opinions of the pre-1937 era—the notion that the powers reserved to the states operated as an independent limitation on the scope of national powers, that state and national legislative domains were mutually exclusive areas. When Justice Stone remarked in Darby in 1941 (p. 138 below) that the Tenth Amendment is "but a truism that all is retained which has not been surrendered," the statement was widely hailed as a reminder of the death of "dual federalism" after 1937. See Corwin, "The Passing of Dual Federalism," 36 Va.L.Rev. 1 (1950). But should the abandonment of rigid, mutually exclusive categories of state and federal competence carry with it abandonment of all concern with federalistic, structural limits on the exercise of national powers? See secs. 5 to 7 below.

Congress might not interfere." Could marriage and divorce be regulated under the theory of Justice Holmes' dissent in Hammer v. Dagenhart, p. 117 below (a dissent that became the majority view a generation later)?[3]

More recently, the Court has said that "Congress wanted to go to the utmost extent of its Constitutional power in restraining trust and monopoly agreements." United States v. South-Eastern Underwriters Association, 322 U.S. 533, 558 (1944) (holding the business of insurance to be covered by the antitrust laws despite older rulings stating that insurance was not commerce). Nevertheless, some modern decisions find businesses outside antitrust coverage as a matter of statutory construction, though within the reach of the commerce power.[4]

THE SHREVEPORT RATE CASE AND THE ORIGINS OF THE "SUBSTANTIAL ECONOMIC EFFECTS" APPROACH

Introduction. Even while the Knight approach and its emphasis on the "direct"-"indirect" distinction remained on the books, the Court began to develop a quite different analysis of the nexus necessary to justify regulation of "local" matters under the commerce power. The railroad context was the most prolific source of this alternate approach—an alternative emphasizing the practical, quantitative rather than the logical, qualitative relationship between the "local" and the "interstate." Most of the early congressional attempts to regulate the railroad industry withstood constitutional attack: the Court repeatedly sustained the laws under the commerce power because of the physical or economic effects of the intrastate activities regulated on interstate commerce. The Shreveport case (note 1 below) is the best example of this approach; and the analyses of Shreveport and other railroad cases (note 2 below) were to provide useful constitutional underpinnings for the Court's increasingly benign attitude toward national economic regulation since 1937 (sec. 5 below).

But the Shreveport view was not the only route toward expanded national regulatory power opened by the cases of the early 20th century. There was also

---

3. Application of the Sherman Act to labor activities began with Loewe v. Lawlor, 208 U.S. 274 (1908). That case involved an attempt to organize workers on hats through a boycott of hat manufacturers' products shipped in commerce. Despite the attempt, in the Clayton Act of 1914, to prevent application of the antitrust laws to organizing activities by labor, some boycotts and strikes continued to be held illegal, as in Duplex Printing Press Co. v. Deering, 254 U.S. 443 (1921). In response, the Norris-LaGuardia Act of 1931 restricted federal injunctions in labor disputes.

It has been suggested that the Court's principles in these labor antitrust cases "were strikingly deficient in neutrality," especially in contrast with some of the cases—see sec. 4 below—in which Congress sought to aid labor. Wechsler, Principles, Politics & Fundamental Law (1961), 32. Were these Court principles also non-neutral in comparison with those relied on in antitrust suits against business activities?

4. The best-known example is professional baseball. In Toolsen v. New York Yankees, 346 U.S. 356 (1953), the Court found reserve clauses in players' contracts outside the antitrust laws. The Court pointed to a decision in 1922 in which

Justice Holmes had stated for the Court that "personal effort, not related to production, is not a subject of commerce." Federal Baseball Club v. National League, 259 U.S. 200. In Toolsen, the Court stated: "The business [has] been left for thirty years to develop, on the understanding that it was not subject to existing antitrust [laws]. Without reexamination of the underlying issues, the judgments below are affirmed on the authority of Federal Baseball Club, [so] far as that decision determines that Congress had no intention of including the business of baseball within the scope of the federal antitrust laws." The Court has adhered to Federal Baseball and Toolsen: in a 5 to 3 decision in Flood v. Kuhn, 407 U.S. 258 (1972), Justice Blackmun's majority opinion, while recognizing that the exemption of baseball from the antitrust laws was "an anomaly" and "an aberration," refused "to overturn those cases judicially when Congress, by its positive inaction, has allowed those decisions to stand for so long." Other professional sports, however, have been held subject to the antitrust laws. See United States v. International Boxing Club, 348 U.S. 236 (1955), and Radovich v. National Football League, 352 U.S. 445 (1957).

an occasional willingness to reach arguably "local" matters by viewing them as being "in" interstate commerce: in those cases, considered in note 3 below, the rationale for reaching intrastate activities was not the practical effect of the "local" on the "interstate," but rather the argument that seemingly local matters could be viewed as part of a continuous "stream" or "current" of commerce. That "current of commerce" approach shared with the Shreveport analysis the characteristic of emphasizing practical, economic relationships rather than qualitative, logical ones.

1.   *The Shreveport Rate case.*   In HOUSTON E. & W. TEXAS RY. CO. v. UNITED STATES (THE SHREVEPORT RATE CASE), 234 U.S. 342 (1914), Justice HUGHES' majority opinion sustained congressional authority to reach intrastate rail rates discriminating against interstate railroad traffic.   The Interstate Commerce Commission, after setting rates for transportation of goods between Shreveport, Louisiana, and points within Texas, ordered several railroads to end their practice of setting rates for hauls between points within Texas which were proportionately less than the rates for transportation from Texas points to Shreveport, Louisiana.   For example, the rate to carry wagons from Marshall in East Texas to Dallas, a distance of 147.7 miles, was 36.8 cents; the rate from Marshall to Shreveport, Louisiana, only 42 miles away, was 56 cents. (Shreveport competed with Texas cities such as Dallas for shipments from East Texas.)   The ICC found that this rate structure "unjustly discriminated in favor of traffic within the state of Texas, and against similar traffic between Louisiana and Texas," and ordered the railroads to end the discrimination.   In challenging that ICC order, the railroads argued that "Congress is impotent to control the intrastate charges of an interstate carrier."

Justice Hughes rejected that challenge.   He insisted that congressional authority, "extending to these interstate carriers as instruments of interstate commerce, necessarily embraces the right to control their operations in all matters having such a close and substantial relation to interstate traffic that the control is essential or appropriate to the security of that traffic, to the efficiency of the interstate service, and to the maintenance of conditions under which interstate commerce may be conducted upon fair terms and without molestation or hindrance.   As it is competent for Congress to legislate to these ends, unquestionably it may seek their attainment by requiring that the agencies of interstate commerce shall not be used in such manner as to cripple, retard, or destroy it.   The fact that carriers are instruments of intrastate commerce, as well as of interstate commerce, does not derogate from the complete and paramount authority of Congress over the latter, or preclude the Federal power from being exerted to prevent the intrastate operations of such carriers from being made a means of injury to that which has been confided to Federal care.   Whenever the interstate and intrastate transactions of carriers are so related that the government of the one involves the control of the other, it is Congress, and not the State, that is entitled to prescribe the final and dominant rule, for otherwise Congress would be denied the exercise of its constitutional authority and the State, and not the Nation, would be supreme within the national field."

Justice Hughes found support in earlier decisions authorizing congressional control of some intrastate activities in the interest of the physical safety of interstate railroad operations.   (See also note 2 below.)   He summarized one of those decisions as follows: "[In] the Second Employers' Liability Cases [223 U.S. 1 (1912)], it was insisted that while Congress had the authority to regulate the liability of a carrier for injuries sustained by one employee through the negligence of another, where all were engaged in interstate commerce, that power did not embrace instances where the negligent employee was engaged in intrastate commerce.   The court said that this was a mistaken theory, as the causal negligence when operating injuriously upon an employee engaged in interstate commerce, had the same effect with respect to that commerce as if the negligent employee were also engaged therein." In relating these decisions dealing with the physical impacts of local activities to the Shreveport problem of economic impacts, Justice Hughes explained: "While these decisions sustaining the Federal power relate to measures adopted in the interest of the safety of persons and property, they illustrate the principle that Congress in the exercise of its paramount power may prevent the common instrumentalities of interstate and intrastate commercial intercourse from being used in their intrastate operations to the injury of interstate commerce. This is not to say that Congress possesses the authority to regulate the internal commerce of a State, as such, but that it does possess the power to foster and protect interstate commerce, and to take all measures necessary or appropriate to that end, although intrastate transactions of interstate carriers may thereby be controlled." Justice Hughes accordingly concluded: "It is for Congress to supply the needed correction where the relation between intrastate and interstate rates presents the evil to be corrected, and this it may do completely, by reason of its control over the interstate carrier in all matters having such a close and substantial relation to interstate commerce that it is necessary or appropriate to exercise the control for the effective government of that commerce." (Justices Lurton and Pitney noted their dissents.)

2. *Other examples of local railroad matters with an adequate impact on interstate commerce.* The Shreveport case was only one of a series justifying the regulation of local rate structures because of the economic burdens imposed by the intrastate situation on interstate activities. See, e.g., Railroad Commission of Wisconsin v. Chicago, Burlington & Quincy Railroad, 257 U.S. 563 (1922), where the Court sustained an ICC order requiring a blanket increase in all intrastate rates, even though state law prescribed a lower maximum. In upholding such economic regulations, the Court drew on earlier decisions sustaining national regulation of local matters where the local activity imposed a *physical* rather than an economic burden on interstate transportation. Safety regulations understandably were the easiest to sustain under this rationale, for they presented the most readily observable manifestations of local activities burdening interstate commerce: the obstruction to interstate movement caused by local accidents was a visible, physical one. See, in addition to the safety law decisions noted in the Shreveport excerpts, the approach in SOUTHERN RAILWAY CO. v. UNITED STATES, 222 U.S. 20 (1911). That case involved the Federal Safety Appliance Act. The Court sustained a penalty judgment imposed for operating railroad cars equipped with defective couplers. Three of the cars were used in moving intrastate traffic. The Act covered all cars "used on any railroad engaged in interstate commerce"; the Court found that this provision was satisfied because the intrastate cars were used "on a railroad which is a highway of interstate commerce" and the law did not require that the cars be used "in moving interstate traffic." The application of the statute to intrastate vehicles was found constitutional, "not because Congress possesses any power to regulate intrastate commerce as such, but because its power to regulate interstate commerce [may] be exerted to secure the safety of the persons and property transported therein and of those who are employed in such transportation no matter what may be the source of the dangers which threaten it." The Court emphasized "practical considerations" that "are of common knowledge," including the fact that "the absence of appropriate safety appliances from any part of any train is a menace not only to that train, but to others." [1]

---

1. Note the reliance on a similar rationale in sustaining national regulation of labor relations (to avert obstructions of commerce threatened by strikes) in the Jones & Laughlin case, p. 131 below.

3. *The "current of commerce" theory.* a. *The Swift case.* While the Court's emphasis on "practical considerations" was providing one type of rationale for demonstrating the impact of the local on the interstate (as in Southern Railway), several other decisions were sketching an alternate basis for arguing that an intrastate activity should be reachable under the commerce power. The "current of commerce" rationale suggested that some local activities were controllable not because of their effects on commerce, but because they could themselves be viewed as "in" commerce or as an integral part of the "current of commerce." Justice Holmes' opinion in Swift & Co. v. United States, 196 U.S. 375 (1905), provided the impetus. In sustaining a Sherman Act injunction against price fixing by meat dealers, Justice Holmes used the following language: "When cattle are sent for sale from a place in one State, with the expectation that they will end their transit, after purchase, in another, and when in effect they do so, with only the interruption necessary to find a purchaser at the stockyard, and when this is a typical, constantly recurring course, the current thus existing is a current of commerce among the States, and the purchase of the cattle is a part and incident of such commerce." He commented: "[C]ommerce among the States is not a technical legal conception, but a practical one, drawn from the course of business."

b. *The congressional reliance.* Congress successfully drew on this "current of commerce" concept in drafting subsequent regulation of stockyard practices. The Packers and Stockyards Act of 1921 was aimed primarily at preventing "unfair, discriminatory, or deceptive practices" by meat packers in interstate commerce. One of the provisions of the Act stated that a "transaction in respect to any article shall be considered to be in commerce if such article is part of that current of commerce usual in the livestock and meat packing industries, whereby livestock [and its products] are sent from one State with the expectation that they will end their transit, after purchase, in [another]. Articles normally in such current of commerce shall not be considered out of such current through resort being had to any means or device intended to remove transactions in respect thereto from the provisions of this Act."

c. *Stafford v. Wallace.* Commission men and dealers in stockyards, subject to Secretary of Agriculture regulation of their charges and practices under the 1921 Act, challenged its constitutionality. The Court rejected the attack in STAFFORD v. WALLACE, 258 U.S. 495 (1922). Chief Justice TAFT's majority opinion contained the following passages: "The stockyards are not a place of rest or final destination. [The] stockyards are but a throat through which the current flows, and the transactions which occur therein are only incident to this current from the West to the East, and from one State to another. Such transactions can not be separated from the movement to which they contribute and necessarily take on its character. The commission men are essential in making the sales without which the flow of the current would be obstructed, and this, whether they are made to packers or dealers. The dealers are essential to the sales to the stock farmers and feeders. The sales are not in this aspect merely local transactions. They create a local change of title, it is true, but they do not stop the flow; they merely change the private interests in the subject of the current, not interfering with, but, on the contrary, being indispensable to its continuity. The origin of the livestock is in the West, its ultimate destination known to, and intended by, all engaged in the business is in the Middle West and East either as meat products or stock for feeding and fattening. This is the definite and well-understood course of business. The stockyards and the sales are necessary factors in the middle of this current [of commerce].

"The reasonable fear by Congress that such acts, usually lawful and affecting only intrastate commerce when considered alone, will probably and more or less constantly be used in conspiracies against interstate commerce or constitute a direct and undue burden on it, expressed in this remedial legislation, serves the same purpose as the intent charged in the Swift indictment to bring acts of a similar character into the current of interstate commerce for federal restraint. Whatever amounts to more or less constant practice, and threatens to obstruct or unduly to burden the freedom of interstate commerce is within the regulatory power of Congress under the commerce clause, and it is primarily for Congress to consider and decide the fact of the danger and meet it. This court will certainly not substitute its judgment for that of Congress in such a matter unless the relation of the subject to interstate commerce and its effect upon it are clearly non-existent." [2]

SECTION 3.   NATIONAL "POLICE" REGULATION: PROHIBITION OF INTERSTATE COMMERCE AS A TOOL

Introduction.   In the cases in the preceding section, the Court confronted congressional efforts to impose direct regulations on local activities—regulations allegedly justified by the nexus between the local activity and interstate commerce.   When that technique of regulation was used, the Court pursued a wavering course, from the restrictive interpretation of Knight to the more generous one of Shreveport.   Yet in the same era, the Court rendered a series of decisions—reviewed in the first part of this section—consistently receptive to congressional regulation.   The cases which follow differ from those in sec. 2 in two respects.   First, the objective of the legislation seemed to be primarily moral, as with efforts to control gambling and prostitution; the aim was typically quite far removed from the economic concerns that had prompted the commerce clause.   Second, the technique of regulation differed: the congressional sanction was typically imposed at the state line, though the "harm" sought to be alleviated was primarily local; the form of regulation was to prohibit certain kinds of interstate movements.   That commerce-prohibiting technique gave the Court far less trouble than when Congress sought to impose sanctions directly upon intrastate activity.   But when legislators sought to apply the technique to a problem with significant economic as well as moral dimensions, that of child labor, the Court called a halt, at least for a generation.   In examining the materials in this section, consider whether there was any justification for the differing Court responses to the problems and techniques in the materials that follow and those considered in sec. 2.   Which variety of legislation was closer to the original purposes of the commerce clause?   Which technique of regulation was more susceptible to effective judicial scrutiny?

CHAMPION v. AMES [THE LOTTERY CASE]

188 U.S. 321, 23 S.Ct. 321, 47 L.Ed. 492 (1903).

[Appellant was indicted for shipping a box of Paraguayan lottery tickets from Texas to California in violation of the Federal Lottery Act of 1895.   The law prohibited importing, mailing, or interstate transportation of lottery tickets. Appellant challenged the constitutionality of the Act by seeking release on habeas corpus.   The Circuit Court dismissed the writ.]

Mr. Justice HARLAN delivered the opinion of the Court.

2. Does Chief Justice Taft's last paragraph rest on a different justification than the "current of commerce" approach of his first?   Is there a significant difference between the "effect on commerce" and the "current of commerce" rationales?   Note the attempt to rely on these justifications in later commerce clause cases, considered in secs. 4 and 5 below.

[We] are of opinion that lottery tickets are subjects of traffic and therefore are subjects of commerce, and the regulation of the carriage of such tickets from State to State, at least by independent carriers, is a regulation of commerce among the several States. But it is said [that] the authority given Congress was not to *prohibit,* but only to *regulate.* [Are] we prepared to say that a provision which is, in effect, a *prohibition* of the carriage of such articles from State to State is not a fit or appropriate mode for the *regulation* of that particular kind of commerce? If lottery traffic, *carried on through interstate commerce,* is a matter of which Congress may take cognizance and over which its power may be exerted, can it be possible that it must tolerate the traffic, and simply regulate the manner in which it may be carried on? Or may not Congress, for the protection of the people of all the States, and under the power to regulate interstate commerce, devise such means within the scope of the Constitution, and not prohibited by it, as will drive that traffic out of commerce among the States?

In determining whether regulation may not under some circumstances properly take the form or have the effect of prohibition, the nature of the interstate traffic which [the Act sought] to suppress cannot be overlooked. When enacting that statute Congress no doubt shared the views upon the subject of lotteries heretofore expressed by this court. In Phalen v. Virginia [8 How. 163 (1850) (state regulation)], the Court observed that the suppression of nuisances injurious to public health or morality is among the most important duties of Government. [If] a State, when considering legislation for the suppression of lotteries within its own limits, may properly take into view the evils that inhere in the raising of money, in that mode, why may not Congress, invested with the power to regulate commerce among the several States, provide that such commerce shall not be polluted by the carrying of lottery tickets from one State to another? In this connection it must not be forgotten that the power of Congress to regulate commerce among the States is plenary, is complete in itself, and is subject to no limitations except such as may be found in the Constitution. [What clause] can be cited which [countenances] the suggestion that one may, of right, carry [from] one State to another that which will harm the public morals?

[Congress] does not assume to interfere with traffic or commerce in lottery tickets carried on exclusively within the limits of any State, but has in view only commerce of that kind among the several States. It has not assumed to interfere with the completely internal affairs of any State, and has only legislated in respect of a matter which concerns the people of the United States. As a State may, for the purpose of guarding the morals of its own people, forbid all sales of lottery tickets within its limits, so Congress, for the purpose of guarding the people of the United States against the "widespread pestilence of lotteries" and to protect the commerce which concerns all the States, may prohibit the carrying of lottery tickets from one State to another. In legislating upon the subject of the traffic in lottery tickets, as carried on through interstate commerce, Congress only supplemented the action of those States—perhaps all of them—which, for the protection of the public morals, prohibit the drawing of lotteries, as well as the sale or circulation of lottery tickets, within their respective limits. It said, in effect, that it would not permit the declared policy of the States, which sought to protect their people against the mischiefs of the lottery business, to be overthrown or disregarded by the agency of interstate commerce. We should hesitate long before adjudging that an evil of such appalling character, carried on through interstate commerce, cannot be met and crushed by the only power competent to that end.

[It] is said, however, that if, in order to suppress lotteries carried on through interstate commerce, Congress may exclude lottery tickets from such commerce, that principle leads necessarily to the conclusion that Congress may arbitrarily exclude from commerce among the States any article, commodity or thing, of whatever kind or nature, or however useful or valuable, which it may choose, no matter with what motive. [It] will be time enough to consider the constitutionality of such legislation when we must do so. The present case does not require the court to declare the full extent of the power that Congress may exercise. [It] would not be difficult to imagine legislation that [would be] hostile to the objects for the accomplishment of which Congress was invested with the general power to regulate commerce among the several States. But [the] possible abuse of a power is not an argument against its existence. If what is done by Congress is manifestly in excess of the powers granted to it, then upon the courts will rest the duty of adjudging that its action is neither legal nor binding upon the people. But if what Congress does is within the limits of its power, and is simply unwise or injurious, the remedy is that suggested by Chief Justice Marshall in [Gibbons]. [The Court quoted the "wisdom [and] discretion of Congress" passage from Gibbons. Cf. note 1 after Gibbons, p. 113 above.]

Affirmed.

Mr. Chief Justice FULLER, with whom concur Mr. Justice BREWER, Mr. Justice SHIRAS and Mr. Justice PECKHAM, dissenting.

[That] the purpose of Congress in this enactment was the suppression of lotteries cannot reasonably be denied. That purpose is avowed in the title of the act, and is its natural and reasonable effect, and by that its validity must be tested. [D]oubtless an act prohibiting the carriage of lottery matter would be necessary and proper to the execution of a power to suppress lotteries; but that power belongs to the States and not to Congress. To hold that Congress has general police power would be to hold that it may accomplish objects not entrusted to the General Government, and to defeat the operation of the 10th Amendment. But apart from the question of *bona fides,* this act cannot be brought within the power to regulate commerce among the several States, unless lottery tickets are articles of commerce, and, therefore, when carried across state lines, of interstate commerce; or unless the power to regulate interstate commerce includes the absolute and exclusive power to prohibit the transportation of any thing or anybody from one State to another. [Is] the carriage of lottery tickets from one State to another commercial intercourse? [The dissent concluded that it was not "commercial intercourse."]

If a lottery ticket is not an article of commerce, how can it become so when placed in an envelope or box or other covering, and transported by an express company? [That] is to transform a non-commercial article into a commercial one simply because it is transported. I cannot conceive that any such result can properly follow. It would be to say that everything is an article of commerce the moment it is taken to be transported from place to place, and of interstate commerce if from State to State. [An] invitation to dine, or to take a drive, or a note of introduction, all become articles of commerce under the ruling in this case, by being deposited with an express company for transportation. [The] necessary consequence is to take from the States all jurisdiction over the subject so far as interstate communication is concerned. It is a long step in the direction of wiping out all traces of state lines, and the creation of a centralized Government. [It] will not do to say [that] state laws have been found to be ineffective for the suppression of lotteries, and therefore Congress should interfere. The scope of the commerce clause of the Constitution cannot be enlarged because of present views of [public interest]. [At this point, the dissent quoted Marshall's "pretext" statement in McCulloch, at p. 78 above.]

The power to prohibit the transportation of diseased animals and infected goods over railroads or on steamboats is an entirely different thing, for they would be in themselves injurious to the transaction of interstate commerce, and, moreover, are essentially commercial in their nature. And the exclusion of diseased persons rests on different ground, for nobody would pretend that persons could be kept off the trains because they were going from one State to another to engage in the lottery business. However enticing that business may be, we do not understand these pieces of paper themselves can communicate bad principles by contact. [I] regard this decision as inconsistent with the views of the framers of the Constitution, and of Marshall, its great expounder. Our form of government may remain notwithstanding legislation or decision, but, as long ago observed, it is with governments, as with religions, the form may survive the substance of the [faith].

SUCCESSFUL EARLY USES OF THE COMMERCE-PROHIBITING POWER

1. *The ghost of Marshall.* Note the competing uses of Marshall statements in the Harlan and Fuller opinions. Was the "wisdom [and] discretion of Congress" quotation from Gibbons v. Ogden, used by Harlan, apposite to the problem of the principal case? Did that make it unnecessary to consider the "pretext" statement in McCulloch v. Maryland, quoted by Fuller? Would it have been possible to sustain the statute on the assumption that its true "object" was the control of a local "harm"—intrastate lottery-promoting activities? On the theory that gambling "affected" or "burdened" commerce? On the basis of the "current of commerce" theory? Should the Court have insisted on an adequate justification for reaching intrastate activities? Was the failure to require such a justification (and the acceptance of the rationale that this was merely a regulation of interstate commerce) fatal to the development of commerce power doctrine of sufficient integrity? Note the questions following the Child Labor Case at p. 120 below, and compare the later uses of the commerce-prohibiting power, sec. 5 below.

2. *The impact on Congress.* Early-twentieth century reformers seeking a constitutional basis for broader federal "police" measures quickly seized on the encouragement provided by the majority position in the Lottery Case. In 1906, for example, Senator Albert J. Beveridge successfully proposed a Meat Inspection Amendment to an appropriations bill. The Amendment, backed by President Theodore Roosevelt and by popular support generated by such exposés as Upton Sinclair's "The Jungle," became law: it prohibited interstate shipment of meats that had not been federally inspected. In the same session, Congress enacted the Pure Food and Drugs Act. Later that year, Senator Beveridge suggested a law excluding from commerce goods produced by child labor. He was confident that the Lottery Case "absolutely settled" the constitutionality of his proposal. But passage of a child labor law was still a decade away—and the Court found the 1916 Child Labor Act unconstitutional after all, in Hammer v. Dagenhart, the next principal case.[1]

3. *Exclusion of "harmful" goods.* The Lottery Case precedent was, however, adequate to sustain a wide variety of early-twentieth century laws excluding objects deemed harmful from interstate commerce. Decisions sustaining the Pure Food and Drugs Act and the Mann (White Slave) Act were especially important in building the hopes that were crushed by Hammer v. Dagenhart.[2]

a. *Impure foods.* In HIPOLITE EGG CO. v. UNITED STATES, 220 U.S. 45 (1911), a shipment of adulterated preserved eggs had been confiscated under the Pure Food and Drugs Act of 1906. The action was challenged on

1. See Braeman, "Albert J. Beveridge and the First National Child Labor Bill," 60 Indiana Magazine of History 1 (1964), and Braeman, "The Square Deal in Action: A Case Study in the Growth of the 'National Police Power,' " in Braeman, Bremner and Walter, Change and Continuity in Twentieth Century America (1964), 35–80.

2. See Cushman, "The National Police Power Under the Commerce Clause of the Constitution," 3 Minn.L.Rev. 289, 381 (1919).

the ground that "the shipment had passed out of interstate commerce before the seizure of the eggs." A unanimous Court rejected the attack. Justice McKENNA emphasized that the case involved "illicit articles—articles which the law seeks to keep out of commerce, because they are debased by adulteration." There could therefore be no insistence that "the articles must be apprehended [before] they have become a part of the general mass of property of the State." He insisted: "The question here is whether articles which are outlaws of commerce may be seized wherever found. [Can] they escape the consequences of their illegal transportation by being mingled at the place of destination with other property? To give them such immunity would defeat, in many cases, the provision for their confiscation, and their confiscation or destruction is the especial concern of the law. The power to do so is certainly appropriate to the right to bar them from interstate commerce, and completes its purpose, which is not to prevent merely the physical movement of adulterated articles, but the use of them, or rather to prevent trade in them between the States by denying to them the facilities of interstate commerce. And appropriate means to that end, which we have seen is legitimate, are the seizure and condemnation of the articles at their point of destination. [McCulloch]."

How far-reaching is that application of McCulloch? Does it justify a direct ban on producing adulterated goods as a "means appropriate to the right to bar them from interstate commerce"? Only if the goods are intended for interstate shipment? Does it justify national marriage and divorce standards as an "appropriate means" to implement a ban on interstate movement of persons married or divorced in violation of national standards? Only if the persons getting married or divorced intend to travel interstate? Does it offer a bootstrap technique for reaching local affairs via the prohibition route: in order to regulate a local matter, simply prohibit interstate movements connected with it and then reach the local matter as an incidental means to implement the interstate prohibition? Note the elaboration of this justification of local control as an incident of interstate commerce prohibition in Darby, p. 138 below.

b. *The Mann Act.* The Mann Act, prohibiting the transportation of women in interstate commerce for immoral purposes, was upheld in HOKE v. UNITED STATES, 227 U.S. 308 (1913). Again, Justice McKENNA wrote for a unanimous Court. He cited, in addition to the Lottery Case, United States v. Popper, 98 Fed. 423 (N.D.Cal.1899), involving an 1897 law prohibiting the "carrying of obscene literature and articles designed for indecent and immoral use from one State to another." The opinion in Hoke contained one of the broadest early statements of the commerce-prohibiting power: "[T]he powers reserved to the States and those conferred on the Nation are adapted to be exercised, whether independently or concurrently to promote the general welfare, material and moral. This is the effect of the decisions, and surely if the facility of interstate transportation can be taken away from the demoralization of lotteries, the debasement of obscene literature, the contagion of diseased cattle or persons, the impurity of food and drugs, the like facility can be taken away from the systematic enticement to and the enslavement in prostitution and debauchery of women, and, more insistently, of girls. [The] principle established by the cases is the simple one, when rid of confusing and distracting considerations, that Congress has power over transportation 'among the several States'; that the power is complete in itself, and that Congress, as an incident to it, may adopt not only means necessary but convenient to its exercise, and the means may have the quality of police regulations."[3]

---

3. Justice McKENNA dissented, however, when the Court, in a 5 to 3 decision, found the Mann Act applicable to activities not constituting "commercialized vice." CAMINETTI v. UNITED STATES, 242 U.S. 470 (1917). Justice DAY wrote for the majority. The dissent ar-

HAMMER v. DAGENHART [THE CHILD LABOR CASE]

247 U.S. 251, 38 S.Ct. 529, 62 L.Ed. 1101 (1918).

[The District Court had enjoined, on constitutional grounds, the enforcement of a congressional law of 1916 excluding from interstate commerce the products of child labor.]

Mr. Justice DAY delivered the opinion of the Court.

[Is] it within the authority of Congress in regulating commerce among the states to prohibit the transportation in interstate commerce of manufactured goods, the product of a factory in which, within thirty days prior to their removal therefrom, children under the age of fourteen have been employed, or children between the ages of fourteen and sixteen years have been employed or permitted to work more than eight hours in any day, or more than six days in any week, or after the hour of 7 o'clock p.m., or before the hour of 6 o'clock a.m.?

[The commerce power] is one to control the means by which commerce is carried on, which is directly the contrary of the assumed right to forbid commerce from moving and thus destroying it as to particular commodities. But it is insisted that adjudged cases in this court establish the doctrine that the power to regulate given to Congress incidentally includes the authority to prohibit the movement of ordinary commodities. [The] cases demonstrate the contrary. They rest upon the character of the particular subjects dealt with and the fact that the scope of governmental authority, state or national, possessed over them is such that the authority to prohibit is as to them but the exertion of the power to regulate. [After discussing such decisions as the Lottery Case, Hipolite and Hoke (see the preceding notes), the Court continued:]

In each of these instances the use of interstate transportation was necessary to the accomplishment of harmful results. In other words, although the power over interstate transportation was to regulate, that could only be accomplished by prohibiting the use of the facilities of interstate commerce to effect the evil intended. This element is wanting in the present case. [The] act in its effect does not regulate transportation among the states, but aims to standardize the ages at which children may be employed in mining and manufacturing within the states. The goods shipped are of themselves harmless. The act permits them to be freely shipped after thirty days from the time of their removal from the factory. When offered for shipment, and before transportation begins, the labor of their production is over, and the mere fact that they were intended for interstate commerce transportation does not make their production subject to federal control. [Over] interstate transportation, or its incidents, the regulatory power of Congress is ample, but the production of articles, intended for interstate commerce, is a matter of local regulation. [If] it were otherwise, all manufacture intended for interstate shipment would be brought under federal control to the practical exclusion of the authority of the States. [Kidd v. Pearson.]

gued that "everybody knows that there is a difference between the occasional immoralities of men and women and that systematized and mercenary immorality epitomized in the statute's graphic phrase 'White-slave traffic.' And it was such immorality that was in the legislative mind and not the other. The other is occasional, not habitual—inconspicuous—does not offensively obtrude upon public notice. Interstate commerce is not its instrument as it is of the other, nor is prostitution its object or its end. It may, indeed, in instances, find a convenience in crossing state lines, but this is its accident, not its aid."

Could this objection to the interpretation of the Act be the basis of a valid constitutional objection? One year after Caminetti, the Court held the Child Labor Law unconstitutional, in the case that follows. Note that Justice Day once again wrote the majority opinion—and that Justice McKenna was once again with the dissenters.

It is further contended that the authority of Congress may be exerted to control interstate commerce in the shipment of child-made goods because of the effect of the circulation of such goods in other States where the evil of this class of labor has been recognized by local legislation, and the right to thus employ child labor has been more rigorously restrained than in the State of production. In other words, that the unfair competition, thus engendered, may be controlled by closing the channels of interstate commerce to manufacturers in those States where the local laws do not meet what Congress deems to be the more just standard of other States.

There is no power vested in Congress to require the States to exercise their police power so as to prevent possible unfair competition. Many causes may coöperate to give one State, by reason of local laws or conditions, an economic advantage over others. The Commerce Clause was not intended to give to Congress a general authority to equalize such conditions. In some of the States laws have been passed fixing minimum wages for women, in others the local law regulates the hours of labor of women in various employments. Business done in such States may be at an economic disadvantage when compared with States which have no such regulations; surely, this fact does not give Congress the power to deny transportation in interstate commerce to those who carry on business where the hours of labor and the rate of compensation for women have not been fixed by a standard in use in other States and approved by Congress. [The] grant of power to Congress over the subject of interstate commerce was to enable it to regulate such commerce, and not to give it authority to control the States in their exercise of the police power over local trade and manufacture. [That] there should be limitations upon the right to employ children in mines and factories in the interest of their own and the public welfare, all will admit. [I]t may be desirable that such laws be uniform, but our Federal Government is one of enumerated powers [McCulloch]. The maintenance of the authority of the States over matters purely local is as essential to the preservation of our institutions as is the conservation of the supremacy of the federal power in all matters entrusted to the Nation.

[We] have neither authority nor disposition to question the motives of Congress in enacting this legislation. [T]he necessary effect of this act is, by means of a prohibition against the movement in interstate commerce of ordinary commercial commodities, to regulate the hours of labor of children in factories and mines within the States, a purely state authority. Thus the act in a two-fold sense is repugnant to the Constitution. It not only transcends the authority delegated to Congress over commerce but also exerts a power as to a purely local matter to which the federal authority does not extend. The far reaching result of upholding the act cannot be more plainly indicated than by pointing out that if Congress can thus regulate matters entrusted to local authority by prohibition of the movement of commodities in interstate commerce, all freedom of commerce will be at an end, and the power of the States over local matters may be eliminated, and thus our system of government be practically destroyed.

[Affirmed.]

Mr. Justice HOLMES, dissenting.[1]

The single question in this case is whether Congress has power to prohibit the shipment in interstate or foreign commerce [of the products specified in the statute]. The objection urged against the power is that the States have exclusive control over their methods of production and that Congress cannot meddle with them, and taking the proposition in the sense of direct intermeddling I agree to it and suppose that no one denies it. But if an act is within the powers

1. Justices McKenna, Brandeis, and Clarke joined Justice Holmes' dissent.

specifically conferred upon Congress, it seems to me that it is not made any less constitutional because of the indirect effects that it may have, however obvious it may be that it will have those effects.

[The] first step in my argument is to make plain what no one is likely to dispute—that the statute in question is within the power expressly given to Congress if considered only as to its immediate effects and that if invalid it is so only upon some collateral ground. The statute confines itself to prohibiting the carriage of certain goods in interstate or foreign commerce. Congress is given power to regulate such commerce in unqualified terms. It would not be argued today that the power to regulate does not include the power to prohibit. Regulation means the prohibition of something, and when interstate commerce is the matter to be regulated I cannot doubt that the regulation may prohibit any part of such commerce that Congress sees fit to forbid. [The] question then is narrowed to whether the exercise of its otherwise constitutional power by Congress can be pronounced unconstitutional because of its possible reaction upon the conduct of the States in a matter upon which I have admitted that they are free from direct control. [I] should have thought that the most conspicuous decisions of this Court had made it clear that the power to regulate commerce and other constitutional powers could not be cut down or qualified by the fact that it might interfere with the carrying out of the domestic policy of any State.

The manufacture of oleomargarine is as much a matter of state regulation as the manufacture of cotton cloth. Congress levied a tax upon the compound when colored so as to resemble butter that was so great as obviously to prohibit the manufacture and sale. In a very elaborate discussion the present Chief Justice excluded any inquiry into the purpose of an act which apart from that purpose was within the power of Congress. McCray v. United States, 195 U.S. 27. [See p. 195 below] [And] to come to cases upon interstate commerce, notwithstanding [the Knight case], the Sherman Act has been made an instrument for the breaking up of combinations in restraint of trade and monopolies, using the power to regulate commerce as a foothold, but not proceeding because that commerce was the end actually in mind. The objection that the control of the States over production was interfered with was urged again and again but always in vain. The [Pure Food and Drugs Act] applies not merely to articles that the changing opinions of the time condemn as intrinsically harmful but to others innocent in themselves, simply on the ground that the order for them was induced by a preliminary fraud. Weeks v. United States, 245 U.S. 618. It does not matter whether the supposed evil precedes or follows the transportation. It is enough that in the opinion of Congress the transportation encourages the evil. I may add that in the cases on the so-called White Slave Act it was established that the means adopted by Congress as convenient to the exercise of its power might have the character of police regulations.

[The] notion that prohibition is any less prohibition when applied to things now thought evil I do not understand. But if there is any matter upon which civilized countries have agreed—far more unanimously than they have with regard to intoxicants and some other matters over which this country is now emotionally aroused—it is the evil of premature and excessive child labor. I should have thought that if we were to introduce our own moral conceptions where in my opinion they do not belong, this was preëminently a case for upholding the exercise of all its powers by the United States. But I had thought that the propriety of the exercise of a power admitted to exist in some cases was for the consideration of Congress alone and that this Court always had disavowed the right to intrude its judgment upon questions of policy or morals. It is not for this Court to pronounce when prohibition is necessary to regulation if it ever may be necessary—to say that it is permissible as against strong drink but not as against the product of ruined lives.

The act does not meddle with anything belonging to the States. They may regulate their internal affairs and their domestic commerce as they like. But when they seek to send their products across the state line they are no longer within their rights. If there were no Constitution and no Congress their power to cross the line would depend upon their neighbors. Under the Constitution such commerce belongs not to the States but to Congress to regulate. It may carry out its views of public policy whatever indirect effect they may have upon the activities of the States. Instead of being encountered by a prohibitive tariff at their boundaries the State encounters the public policy of the United States which it is for Congress to express. The public policy of the United States is shaped with a view to the benefit of the nation as a whole. If, as has been the case within the memory of men still living, a State should take a different view of the propriety of sustaining a lottery from that which generally prevails, I cannot believe that the fact would require a different decision from that reached in Champion v. Ames. Yet in that case it would be said with quite as much force as in this that Congress was attempting to intermeddle with the State's domestic affairs. The national welfare as understood by Congress may require a different attitude within its sphere from that of some self-seeking State. It seems to me entirely constitutional for Congress to enforce its understanding by all the means at its command.

PROBLEMS AND CONSEQUENCES OF THE CHILD LABOR CASE

1. *Effective limits on the commerce power and the Holmes dissent.* a. Justice Day's distinction of earlier cases involving the commerce-prohibiting power has been widely criticized as unpersuasive. But it may also be argued that the Holmes dissent (which the Court adopted as a majority position a generation later) was needlessly broad. The point of the questions that follow is to suggest that a view of the commerce power was possible that would have sustained the Child Labor Law without embracing so far-reaching a view of congressional power.

For example, should Justice Holmes have paid greater attention to the "unfair competition" effects of interstate shipment of the goods? Are the evils produced by child labor-made goods more closely related to "commercial" concerns than the evils involved in the Mann Act decisions and Lottery Case? Is it possible to argue that the Child Labor Act was more "economic," "commercial" in purpose than most of the "police" regulations sustained in the cases between the Lottery Case and Hammer?

Recall that, in his Northern Securities dissent (p. 107 above), Justice Holmes could see "no part of the conduct of life with which on similar principles Congress might not interfere," if the "logic of the argument for the Government" were accepted. Is this criticism also appropriate for the "logic of the argument" of the Holmes dissent in Hammer? Was Justice Holmes simply ceasing to argue restrictions on the commerce-prohibiting power because the majority had abandoned the opportunity to adhere to principled limitations in the cases beginning with the Lottery Case? Was it necessary to ignore the "collateral" effects of the law and to limit judicial vision to the "immediate effects" of the statute in order to justify the Child Labor Law? Would it not have been possible to concede that the law in effect regulated local production for interstate commerce, and yet sustain it because the activities regulated "affected" commerce? Note that Holmes' dissent suggests that the states "are free from direct control" regarding child labor. If that is so, is his position not an endorsement of the "pretext" usage of power condemned by Marshall in McCulloch.[1]

b. Holmes' "hands-off" policy ultimately prevailed in 1941, in Darby (p. 138 below), when the Court explicitly overruled Hammer v. Dagenhart. If the Holmesian position is justifiable in view of institutional limitations on the Court—e.g., the difficulties of identifying congressional "purposes" and "pretext" abuses of power—does it follow that a legislator is wholly free to vote for commerce power regulations with primarily moral rather than commercial objectives? Even when judicial unwillingness to invalidate is predictable, is not a legislator nevertheless compelled—given the lawmaker's constitutional oath— to examine his or her purposes in supporting legislation and to determine whether those purposes are consistent with the constitutional allocations of power?[2]

2. *Later efforts to curb child labor.* After the Hammer decision, Congress sought to regulate child labor through the taxing power. That law was invalidated in the Child Labor Tax Case in 1922 (p. 193 below). Justice Holmes was with the majority there. After the unsuccessful legislative efforts, Congress submitted to the states a proposed constitutional amendment authorizing national child labor laws. The amendment was never ratified; but the need for ratification largely disappeared in view of the Court's decision in 1941, in Darby (p. 138 below).

SECTION 4. THE COURT THREATENS THE NEW DEAL

Introduction. President Franklin D. Roosevelt took office in 1933 in the midst of a grave economic crisis and with a call for "action, and action now." Symptoms of the Great Depression were everywhere: sharp drops in employment, production, income; widespread business failures and home mortgage foreclosures. The response was swift: an unprecedented flow of far-reaching measures came from Congress—torrentially during the dramatic "First Hundred Days," with more deliberate speed thereafter.

Many New Deal measures were based on the commerce power, for the "problems were economic, and the Commerce Clause was the enumerated power most directly concerned with business and economic, or commercial matters." And the regulatory justification typically invoked to reach those economic problems was the "affecting commerce" one considered in sec. 2 above. The commerce-prohibiting technique appeared blocked by the Child Labor Case (see sec. 3); and prohibitions of interstate movements seemed in any event an awkward approach to the New Deal's problems. Practically as well as legally, then, efforts to regulate intrastate affairs based upon their relationship to interstate commerce seemed the far more attractive approach. Cases such as the Shreveport decision were encouraging; yet cases like Knight looked the other way. Would the New Deal measures survive judicial scrutiny?

1. The majority's position in Hammer did not wholly bar the use of the commerce-prohibiting technique in other areas of regulation. See, e.g., Brooks v. United States, 267 U.S. 432 (1925) (sustaining the constitutionality of the National Motor Vehicle Theft Act of 1919). For use of the commerce-prohibiting device in later years, see the notes after Darby, p. 138 below.

2. Justice Holmes himself did perceive such a difference between the judge's and the legislator's duties on constitutional questions. In a letter of April 3, 1919, Holmes wrote to then District Judge Learned Hand, on problems such as those presented by the Child Labor Case: "In my opinion Congress may have what ulterior motives they please if the act passed in the immediate aspect is within its powers—though personally, were I a legislator I might think it dishonest to use powers in that way." [The letter is printed in Gunther, "Learned Hand and the Origins of Modern First Amendment Doctrine: Some Fragments of History," 27 Stan.L.Rev. 719 (1975).]

There could be no certainty, for "there was ample authority in the Supreme Court opinions looking both ways." [1] Stern, "The Commerce Clause and the National Economy, 1933–1946," 59 Harv.L.Rev. 645, 646 (1946).

The first signs from the Court were encouraging. Early in 1934, 5 to 4 decisions sustained state laws in the face of attacks that were clearly substantial under prior interpretations of the contract and due process clauses. [2] A few months later, however, in the first Court test of a major New Deal law, the National Industrial Recovery Act of 1933 was wounded, though the reach of the commerce power was not discussed: in the "hot oil" case, the petroleum code under the NIRA was invalidated on the ground of excessive delegation of legislative power to the executive. Panama Refining Co. v. Ryan, 293 U.S. 388 (1935). But an important early New Deal measure—a 1933 Joint Resolution declaring "gold clauses" in private contracts to be "against public policy"—was sustained, Norman v. Baltimore & Ohio Railroad Co., 294 U.S. 240 (1935), though the Government won only a narrow victory in its attempt to avoid payment under gold clauses in public obligations, Perry v. United States, 294 U.S. 330 (1935).

There was still no ruling on major New Deal regulation under the commerce clause, however. That did not come until later in 1935. In the first test, the Court invalidated a measure not central to the New Deal program, the Railroad Retirement Act of 1934. RAILROAD RETIREMENT BOARD v. ALTON RAILROAD CO., 295 U.S. 330 (1935). That decision was an especially gloomy omen because, as noted in sec. 2, Congress had long regulated railroad matters and had seldom encountered constitutional obstacles. Nevertheless, the 5 to 4 decision in Alton invalidated a law establishing a compulsory retirement and pension plan for all carriers subject to the Interstate Commerce Act. Justice ROBERTS' majority opinion concluded that the law was "not in purpose or effect a regulation of interstate commerce within the meaning of the Constitution." He rejected the argument that pensions were "related to efficiency of transportation." If "the fostering of a contented mind on the part of an employee" were accepted as "in any just sense a regulation of interstate transportation," he insisted, "obviously there is no limit to the field of so-called regulation." Was it not "apparent," he asked, that such regulations "are really and essentially related solely to the social welfare of the worker, and therefore remote from any regulation of commerce as such?" [3]

The Alton decision proved to be an accurate omen of doom. Attempts to justify more important New Deal laws under the commerce power failed soon after: three weeks after Alton, the Government lost the Schechter case challenging the National Industrial Recovery Act—a decision that seemed a return to "the horse-and-buggy age" to President Roosevelt. In the following year, the commerce clause basis once again failed when the Bituminous Coal Conserva-

1. Stern, "The Commerce Clause and the National Economy, 1933–1946," 59 Harv.L.Rev. 645, 646 (1946).

2. Home Building & Loan Association v. Blaisdell, 290 U.S. 398 (1934) (mortgage moratorium law); Nebbia v. New York, 291 U.S. 502 (1934) (milk price regulation)—both considered in chap. 8 below.

3. Justice Roberts recognized that the Court had long sustained railroad legislation such as the Safety Appliance Act, the Employers' Liability Act, and hours-of-service laws. Those, he insisted, were distinguishable because they had "a direct and intimate connection with the actual operation of the railroads." He conceded, too, that Congress probably could enact a compulsory workmen's compensation law for railroad workers. But that variety of legislation was supposedly distinguishable because the pension law sought "to attach to the relation of employer and employee a new incident, without reference to any existing obligation or legal liability, solely in the interest of the employee, with no regard to the conduct of the business, or its safety or efficiency, but purely for social ends." Chief Justice Hughes' dissent, joined by Justices Brandeis, Stone and Cardozo, insisted that it was "clear that the morale of railroad employees has an important bearing on the efficiency of the transportation service, and that a reasonable pension plan by its assurance of security is an appropriate means to that end."

tion Act of 1935 was held unconstitutional in the Carter case. And the New Deal's failures were not limited to commerce power cases: in the same year, for example, an effort to resort to the spending power as justification for national regulation of agricultural production was rejected by the Court, in the Butler case (p. 202 below).

The Schechter and Carter cases follow. Consider whether the majority positions were consistent with earlier commerce clause rulings. Can any of the decisions be justified as "principled"—as a decision that rests on "reasons that in their generality and their neutrality transcend any immediate result that is involved"? [4] Or were those decisions simply willful fiats by a Supreme Court majority hostile to reform, as many New Deal critics of the Court charged?

THE SCHECHTER CASE AND ITS AFTERMATH

1. *The decision.* The most dramatic and most controversial New Deal effort to combat the Depression and revive the economy was the enactment of the National Industrial Recovery Act of 1933. The NIRA authorized the President—ordinarily upon application by trade associations—to promulgate "codes of fair competition for the trade or industry." Several hundred codes were soon adopted. The typical code contained provisions regarding unfair trade practices, minimum wages and prices, maximum hours and collective bargaining. Violation of any code provision "in any transaction in or affecting interstate commerce" was made punishable as a misdemeanor.

The Act was held unconstitutional in the "sick chicken" case, SCHECHTER POULTRY CORP. v. UNITED STATES, 295 U.S. 495 (1935). By then, the regime of the NIRA was near an end in any event; the Roosevelt Administration's fears about Schechter, and the President's "horse-and-buggy age" comment on it, reflected concerns about the fate of more permanent New Deal innovations. The NIRA scheme had worked well at the outset, with widespread public support. But by the time Schechter came to the Court, the regulatory structure was disintegrating in the face of waning enthusiasm, administrative difficulties, and lower court injunctions. The Supreme Court test of the Act was not sought by the Government: the record in the Schechter case contained few data to show the nexus between the slaughterer and the interstate poultry market; and application of the law to a relatively small segment of the national economy—a wholesale poultry market in Brooklyn—was hardly an ideal context to seek validation of the law. But after the Second Circuit invalidated the application of the wage and hour requirements to Schechter— though sustaining Schechter's convictions on most charges of code violation— the Government decided not to oppose Supreme Court review. The Court granted certiorari on April 15, 1935, only two months before the Act was to expire. And the decision came on May 27, 1935, just before the Act would have died of its own force.[1]

The Schechter case stemmed from convictions for violating the wage, hour, and trade practice provisions of the "Code of Fair Competition for the Live Poultry Industry of the Metropolitan [New York City] Area." Ninety-six percent of the poultry marketed in New York came from other states; but Schechter sold only to local poultry dealers. Poultry was ordinarily purchased from commission men in New York City, trucked to Schechter's Brooklyn

---

4. Wechsler, "Toward Neutral Principles of Constitutional Law," 73 Harv.L.Rev. 1, 19 (1959).

1. On the Government's litigation strategy regarding the NIRA and the Schechter case, see

Stern, "The Commerce Clause and the National Economy, 1933–1946," 59 Harv.L.Rev. 645 (1946).

slaughterhouses, and sold there to retailers. Schechter's challenge had two prongs: first, that the Act unconstitutionally delegated legislative power [see p. 366 below]; second, that the application of the Act to intrastate activities exceeded the commerce power. The Court agreed with both grounds and held that the wages and hours of Schechter's employees were not subject to federal control.

The Government's defense of the Act tried to rely on two strains in prior doctrine (see sec. 2 above): the "stream of commerce" rationale of Swift and Stafford v. Wallace; and the "affecting commerce" legacy of Shreveport. Chief Justice HUGHES' opinion for the Court rejected both analogies. These were not "transactions *in* interstate commerce," he insisted: the interstate transactions regarding poultry ended when the shipments reached the Brooklyn slaughterhouses; neither the slaughtering nor the sale by Schechter were "transactions in interstate commerce." Schechter's activities, in short, were not "in a 'current' or 'flow' of interstate commerce." Moreover, the Chief Justice refused to find that Schechter's transactions "directly *affect*' interstate commerce." In applying the "affecting commerce" rationale, he insisted, "there is a necessary and well-established distinction between direct and indirect effects." He elaborated: "Direct effects are illustrated by the railroad cases we have cited, as, e.g., the effect of failure to use prescribed safety appliances on railroads which are the highways of both interstate and intrastate commerce, injury to an employee engaged in interstate transportation by the negligence of an employee engaged in an intrastate movement, the fixing of rates for intrastate transportation which unjustly discriminate against interstate commerce. But where the effect of intrastate transactions upon interstate commerce is merely indirect, such transactions remain within the domain of state power. If the commerce clause were construed to reach all enterprises and transactions which could be said to have an indirect effect upon interstate commerce, the federal authority would embrace practically all the activities of the people and the authority of the State over its domestic concerns would exist only by sufferance of the federal government."

Applying those principles to Schechter's operations, Chief Justice Hughes insisted that the hours and wages of Schechter employees "have no direct relation to interstate commerce." He rejected the Government argument "that hours and wages affect prices; that slaughterhouse men sell at a small margin above operating costs; that labor represents 50 to 60 per cent. of these costs; that a slaughterhouse operator paying lower wages or reducing his costs by exacting long hours of work, translates his saving into lower prices; that this results in demands for a cheaper grade of goods; and that the cutting of prices brings about a demoralization of the price structure." That argument, the Chief Justice found, "proves too much": "If the federal government may determine the wages and hours of employees in the internal commerce of a State, because of their relation to cost and prices and their indirect effect upon interstate commerce, it would seem that a similar control might be exerted over other elements of cost, also affecting prices, such as the number of employees, rent, advertising, methods of doing business, etc. All the processes of production and distribution that enter into costs could likewise be controlled. If the cost of doing an intrastate business is in itself the permitted object of federal control, the extent of the regulation of cost would be a question of discretion and not of power."

Finally, Chief Justice Hughes rejected an even broader argument "based upon the serious economic situation which led to the passage of the Recovery Act,—the fall in prices, the decline in wages and employment, and the curtailment of the market for commodities." He found no constitutional justification in "the great importance of maintaining wage distributions which would provide the necessary stimulus in starting 'the cumulative forces making for expanding commercial activity.' " To that argument[2] he replied: "Without in any way disparaging this motive, it is enough to say that the recuperative efforts of the federal government must be made in a manner consistent with the authority granted by the Constitution." In a similar vein, he had said at the outset of his opinion: "Extraordinary conditions do not create or enlarge constitutional power."

Justice CARDOZO, joined by Justice Stone, submitted a brief concurring opinion—a particularly notable one because they were among the Justices who typically dissented from other decisions invalidating New Deal legislation. Justice Cardozo agreed with Chief Justice Hughes on both grounds: not only was there "unlawful delegation"—"This is delegation running riot"—; there was also the "far-reaching and incurable" commerce power objection. On the latter, he elaborated: "There is a view of causation that would obliterate the distinction between what is national and what is local in the activities of commerce. Motion at the outer rim is communicated perceptibly, though minutely, to recording instruments at the center. A society such as ours 'is an elastic medium which transmits all tremors throughout its territory; the only question is of their size.' Per Learned Hand, J., in the court below. The law is not indifferent to considerations of degree. Activities local in their immediacy do not become interstate and national because of distant repercussions. What is near and what is distant may at times be uncertain. [There] is no penumbra of uncertainty obscuring judgment here. To find immediacy or directness here is to find it almost everywhere. If centripetal forces are to be isolated to the exclusion of the forces that oppose and counteract them, there will be an end to our federal system."

2. *The aftermath.* In a press conference soon after Schechter, President Roosevelt articulated the Administration's concerns about the decision. According to him, the case raised "the big issue in the country": "Does this decision mean that the United States Government has no control over any national economic problem?" He added that the decision "—if you accept the obiter dicta and all the phraseology of it—seems to be squarely on the side of restoring to the States forty-eight different controls over national economic problems. [In] some ways it may be the best thing that has happened to the country for a long time that such a decision has come from the Supreme Court, because it clarifies the issue."[3]

But the Schechter language was not necessarily fatal to the New Deal cause. As to doctrine, the "very weakness of the Schechter case, from the Government's viewpoint, was its saving grace." The Court had not yet passed on congressional power "to control trade practices or labor relations [in] any major

---

2. Note a similar argument paraphrased in the Stern article, footnote 1 above, emphasizing "that depressed business conditions had catastrophically affected all commerce" and "that a possible remedy was to increase the purchasing power of all wage earners through wage and hour regulation, thereby increasing the demand for products to be shipped in commerce." Such an argument, Stern notes, would apply to all workers, "irrespective of whether they themselves were in activities related to interstate activities." Wage and hour regulation of employees such as Schechter's would thus be "a reasonable means of improving the nation's business and the commerce—interstate or intrastate—of which that business consisted. The argument treats the whole national economy as inseparable into interstate and intrastate segments, insofar as the fluc-

tuations of the business cycle are concerned." Stern notes that Government counsel realized in 1935 that such an argument had "little chance of success in the judicial climate of the period."

Was that argument a more plausible one factually than the "demoralization of the price structure" theme pressed by the Government and rejected by Chief Justice Hughes? Would a better record or a more substantial economic argument have persuaded the Court? Or would the "direct"-"indirect" distinction have proved an immovable obstacle? Note the continued invocation of that distinction in Carter, the next principal case.

3. 4 The Public Papers and Addresses of Franklin D. Roosevelt (1938), 212, 218–19.

industry, such as petroleum, lumber, coal or steel." In future litigation, "the case—and perhaps its language—could clearly be distinguished, when and if such regulation was attempted." [4]

The attempt to move the New Deal forward despite the Schechter language was made immediately. For example, the right of collective bargaining, recognized in the NIRA, was guaranteed in a more permanent statute: the National Labor Relations Act (Wagner Act) became law on July 5, 1935. And President Roosevelt quickly urged Congress to enact a law establishing an NIRA-like regulatory scheme for the bituminous coal industry. While that bill was pending in a House subcommittee, President Roosevelt wrote his controversial letter to Congressman Hill—the letter ending with the statement: "I hope your committee will not permit doubts as to constitutionality, however reasonable, to block the suggested legislation." (Recall the excerpts at p. 24 above.) The bill became law soon after; and a court challenge was filed the next day. That test case produced the Carter decision, which follows.

CARTER v. CARTER COAL CO.

298 U.S. 238, 56 S.Ct. 855, 80 L.Ed. 1160 (1936).

[Among the objectives of the Bituminous Coal Conservation Act of 1935 was the regulation of maximum hours and minimum wages in coal mines. Producers were to comply with a national bituminous coal code. The minimum wage and maximum hour provisions of the code, binding on all code members, were negotiated by a specified percentage of producers' and workers' representatives. The sanction imposed to make the provisions effective was, in effect, to levy a tax of 13.5% on all producers who did not accept the code. Carter brought a stockholder's suit against his company to enjoin it from paying the tax and complying with the code. The lower court sustained the Act. The following passages from Justice Sutherland's majority opinion explain why the Act could not be sustained under the commerce clause.[1]]

Mr. Justice SUTHERLAND [delivered the opinion of the Court].

Certain recitals contained in the act plainly suggest that its makers were of the opinion that its constitutionality could be sustained under some general federal power, thought to exist, apart from the specific grants of the Constitution. [The recitals] are to the effect that the distribution of bituminous coal is of national interest, affecting the health and comfort of the people and the general welfare of the nation.[2] [The] proposition, often advanced and as often discredited, that the power of the federal government inherently extends to purposes affecting the nation as a whole with which the states severally [cannot] adequately deal, and the related notion that Congress, entirely apart from those powers delegated by the Constitution, may enact laws to promote the general

---

4. Stern, footnote 1 above, 59 Harv.L.Rev. at 662.

1. The Government conceded, in light of the Child Labor Tax Case (p. 193 below), that the Act could not be sustained under the taxing power: the "tax" was a "penalty"; to be valid, it had to be justified under the commerce power.

In addition to the wage, hour and other labor provisions, the code also provided for minimum and maximum prices for sales of bituminous coal. However, the majority opinion spoke mainly of the labor provisions of the code. The price provisions were found inseparable from the labor provisions; hence the entire Act fell without

separate consideration of the constitutionality of the price regulations under the commerce power. (Another, much briefer, portion of the majority opinion concluded that the labor provisions also constituted an unconstitutional delegation of legislative power to private persons.) By contrast, Justice Cardozo's dissent (below) found the price provisions constitutional under the commerce power and argued that the suit was premature with respect to the labor provisions. (See also Chief Justice Hughes' opinion, below.)

2. The recitals of the Act also stated that it was justified because the production and distribution of coal "directly affect interstate commerce."

welfare, have always definitely [been] rejected by this court. [The] general purposes which the act recites [are] beyond the power of Congress except so far, and only so far, as they may be realized by an exercise of some specific power granted by the Constitution. [W]e find no grant of power which authorizes Congress to legislate in respect of these general purposes unless it be found in the commerce clause—and this we now [consider].

[T]he effect of the labor provisions of the [act] primarily falls upon production and not upon commerce. [P]roduction is a purely local activity. It follows that none of these essential antecedents of production constitutes a transaction in or forms any part of interstate commerce. [Schechter.] Everything which moves in interstate commerce has had a local origin. Without local production somewhere, interstate commerce, as now carried on, would practically disappear. Nevertheless, the local character of mining, of manufacturing and of crop growing is a fact, and remains a fact, whatever may be done with the products. [That] the production of every commodity intended for interstate sale and transportation has some effect upon interstate commerce may [be] freely granted; and we are brought to the final and decisive inquiry, whether here that effect is direct, as the "preamble" recites, or indirect. The distinction is not formal, but substantial in the highest degree, as we pointed out in [Schechter].

Whether the effect of a given activity or condition is direct or indirect is not always easy to determine. The word "direct" implies that the activity or condition invoked or blamed shall operate proximately—not mediately, remotely, or collaterally—to produce the effect. It connotes the absence of an efficient intervening agency or condition. And the extent of the effect bears no logical relation to its character. The distinction between a direct and an indirect effect turns, not upon the magnitude of either the cause or the effect, but entirely upon the manner in which the effect has been brought about. If the production by one man of a single ton of coal intended for interstate sale and shipment, and actually so sold and shipped, affects interstate commerce indirectly, the effect does not become direct by multiplying the tonnage, or increasing the number of men employed, or adding to the expense or complexities of the business, or by all combined. It is quite true that rules of law are sometimes qualified by considerations of degree, as the government argues. But the matter of degree has no bearing upon the question here, since that question is not—What is the *extent* of the local activity or condition, or the *extent* of the effect produced upon interstate commerce? but—What is the *relation* between the activity or condition and the effect?

Much stress is put upon the evils which come from the struggle between employers and employees over the matter of wages, working conditions, the right of collective bargaining, etc., and the resulting strikes, curtailment and irregularity of production and effect on prices; and it is insisted that interstate commerce is *greatly* affected thereby. But, in addition to what has just been said, the conclusive answer is that the evils are all local evils over which the federal government has no legislative control. [Such] effect as they may have upon commerce, however extensive it may be, is secondary and indirect. An increase in the greatness of the effect adds to its importance. It does not alter its character. [A] reading of the entire opinion [in Schechter] makes clear, what we now declare, that the want of power on the part of the federal government is the same whether the wages, hours of service, and working conditions, and the bargaining about them, are related to production before interstate commerce has begun, or to sale and distribution after it has [ended].[3]

---

3. In a separate opinion, Chief Justice HUGHES agreed that the labor provisions were invalid, but thought the price provisions were constitutional and separable from the invalid labor ones. In finding the labor provisions constitutionally flawed, he conceded that the com-

Mr. Justice CARDOZO [dissenting].[4]

[I] am satisfied that the Act is within the power of the central government in so far as it provides for minimum and maximum prices. [Whether] it is valid also in other provisions that have been considered and condemned in the opinion of the court, I do not find it necessary to determine [now]. Regulation of prices being an exercise of the commerce power in respect of interstate transactions, the question remains whether it comes within that power as applied to intrastate sales where interstate prices are directly or intimately affected. Mining and agriculture and manufacture are not interstate commerce considered by themselves, yet their relation to that commerce may be such that for the protection of the one there is need to regulate the other. [Schechter.] Sometimes it is said that the relation must be "direct" to bring that power into play. In many circumstances such a description will be sufficiently precise to meet the needs of the occasion. But a great principle of constitutional law is not susceptible of comprehensive statement in an adjective. The underlying thought is merely this, that "the law is not indifferent to considerations of degree." [Schechter, concurring opinion.] It cannot be indifferent to them without an expansion of the commerce clause that would absorb or imperil the reserved powers of the states. At times, as in the case cited, the waves of causation will have radiated so far that their undulatory motion, if discernible at all, will be too faint or obscure, too broken by cross-currents, to be heeded by the law. In such circumstances the holding is not directed at prices or wages considered in the abstract, but at prices or wages in particular conditions. The relation may be tenuous or the opposite according to the facts. Always the setting of the facts is to be viewed if one would know the closeness of the tie. Perhaps, if one group of adjectives is to be chosen in preference to another, "intimate" and "remote" will be found to be as good as any. At all events, "direct" and "indirect," even if accepted as sufficient, must not be read too narrowly. [A] survey of the cases shows that the words have been interpreted with suppleness of adaptation and flexibility of meaning. The power is as broad as the need that evokes it.

[What the railroad cases] really mean is that the causal relation in such circumstances is so close and intimate and obvious as to permit it to be called direct without subjecting the word to an unfair or excessive strain. There is a like immediacy here. Within rulings the most orthodox, the prices for intrastate sales of coal have so inescapable a relation to those for interstate sales that a system of regulation for transactions of the one class is necessary to give adequate protection to the system of regulation adopted for the other. The argument is strongly pressed [that] this may not be true in all communities or in exceptional conditions. If so, the operators unlawfully affected may show that the Act to that extent is invalid as to [them].

THE COURT–PACKING PLAN

1. *The background and fate of the plan.* The foregoing decisions persuaded the Roosevelt Administration that strong measures were needed to save the New Deal. Several major New Deal laws had already been held unconstitutional; others—the National Labor Relations Act and the Social Security Act among them—might well meet a similar fate. The Carter decision confirmed

merce power "embraces the power to protect [commerce] from injury, whatever may be the source of the dangers which threaten it," but insisted that "Congress may not use this protective authority as a pretext for the exertion of power to regulate activities and relations within the States which affect interstate commerce only indirectly."

4. Justices Brandeis and Stone joined Justice Cardozo's dissent.

the worst anticipations generated by Schechter. And there were others as well.[1] As a result of that course of decisions, conviction hardened within the Administration that something had to be done about the Court. But President Roosevelt did not make Court reform an issue in the 1936 election. Rather, he waited until February 1937 to propose changes, giving reasons that seemed disingenuous to many. A month later, in a radio address, he challenged the Court more directly and defended his plan more forthrightly. But the content of the plan, and its original method of presentation, provoked widespread opposition—including that of a number of New Deal supporters. After extensive hearings, the Senate Judiciary Committee rejected the proposal in June 1937. While the controversy was raging, the Court handed down a number of decisions sustaining regulatory statutes, and Justice Van Devanter retired. The final Senate debate was almost anti-climactic: proposed amendments by the proponents failed to save the heart of the plan, and in late July it was in effect killed. The following excerpts are from documents in Sen.Rep.No. 711, 75th Cong., 1st Sess. (1937) (Reorganization of the Federal Judiciary—Adverse Report of the Committee on the Judiciary).

a. *The Proposed Bill:* When any judge of a court of the United States, appointed to hold his office during good behavior, has heretofore or hereafter attained the age of seventy years and has held a commission or commissions as judge of any such court or courts at least ten years, continuously or otherwise, and within six months thereaftei has neither resigned nor retired, the President, for each such judge who has not so resigned or retired, shall nominate, and by and with the advice and consent of the Senate, shall appoint one additional judge to the court to which the former is commissioned. [No judge shall] be so appointed if such appointment would result in (1) more than fifteen members of the Supreme Court of the United States. [Six Justices were over seventy in 1937: Butler (71), Hughes (75), Sutherland (75), McReynolds (75), Van Devanter (78), and Brandeis (81).]

b. *The President's Message to Congress, Feb. 5, 1937:* [It is] one of the definite duties of the Congress constantly to maintain the effective functioning of the Federal judiciary. [A]t the present time the Supreme Court is laboring under a heavy burden. [P]art of the problem of obtaining a sufficient number of judges to dispose of cases is the capacity of the judges themselves. This brings forward the question of aged or infirm judges—a subject of delicacy and yet one which requires frank discussion. [Modern] complexities call also for a constant infusion of new blood in the courts, just as it is needed in executive functions of the Government and in private business. [I], therefore, earnestly recommend that the necessity of an increase in the number of judges be supplied by legislation providing for the appointment of additional judges in all Federal courts, without exception, where there are incumbent judges of retirement age who do not choose to retire or to resign.

c. *Letter of Chief Justice Charles Evans Hughes to Senator Burton K. Wheeler, March 21, 1937:* In response to your inquiries, I have the honor to present the following statement with respect to the work of the Supreme Court: 1. The Supreme Court is fully abreast of its work. [7.] An increase in the number of Justices of the Supreme Court, apart from any question of policy, which I do not discuss, would not promote the efficiency of the Court. It is believed that it would impair that efficiency so long as the Court acts as a unit. There would be more judges to hear, more judges to confer, more judges to discuss, more judges to be convinced and to decide. The present number of Justices is thought to be large enough so far as the prompt, adequate, and efficient conduct of [our work] is concerned.

d. *Radio Address by President Roosevelt, March 9, 1937:* I want to talk with you very simply about the need for present action in this crisis—the need to meet the unanswered challenge of one-third of a nation ill-nourished, ill-clad, ill-housed. [When] the Congress has sought to stabilize national agriculture, to improve the conditions of labor, to safeguard business against unfair competition, to protect our national resources, and in many other ways to serve our clearly national needs, the majority of the Court has been assuming the power to pass on the wisdom of these acts of the

---

1. Thus, the Agricultural Adjustment Act, sought to be justified under the spending power, was held unconstitutional in the Butler case in 1936 (p. 202 below). And in a decision a few weeks after Carter, the divided Court confirmed that federalism barriers were not the only obsta- cles economic regulations would encounter: in the Morehead v. New York ex rel. Tipaldo decision in 1936 (p. 465 below), the Court invalidated a state law establishing minimum wages for women as a violation of the due process clause of the 14th Amendment.

Congress—and to approve or disapprove the public policy written into these laws. This is not only my accusation, it is the accusation of most distinguished Justices of the present Supreme Court. [See especially Justice Stone's vigorous dissent in the Butler case in 1936, p. 202 below.]

[We] have, therefore, reached the point as a Nation where we must take action to save the Constitution from the Court and the Court from itself. We must find a way to take an appeal from the Supreme Court to the Constitution itself. We want a Supreme Court which will do justice under the Constitution—not over it. [My] plan has two chief purposes: By bringing into the judicial system a steady and continuing stream of new and younger blood, I hope, first, to make the administration of all Federal justice speedier and therefore less costly; secondly, to bring to the decision of social and economic problems younger men who have had personal experience and contact with modern facts and circumstances under which average men have to live and work. This plan will save our National Constitution from hardening of the judicial arteries. We cannot rely on an amendment as the immediate or only answer to our present difficulties. [An] amendment like the rest of the Constitution is what the Justices say it is rather than what its framers or you might hope it is.

e. *Conclusion of Adverse Report of Senate Judiciary Committee, June 14, 1937:* We recommend the rejection of this bill as a needless, futile, and utterly dangerous abandonment of constitutional principle. [Under] the form of the Constitution it seeks to do that which is unconstitutional. [I]ts practical operation would be to make the Constitution what the executive or legislative branches of the Government choose to say it is—an interpretation to be changed with each change of administration. It is a measure which should be so emphatically rejected that its parallel will never again be presented to the free representatives of the free people of America.

2. *The impact of the plan.* Two years after his Court-packing plan was rejected, President Roosevelt claimed that he had lost the battle but won the war. Do the decisions since 1937 support that assertion? The Jones & Laughlin case, which follows, was decided on April 12, 1937, while the debate was still raging. Observe, in examining the commerce power cases in sec. 5, the fate of the "direct"-"indirect" standard of the Knight-Schechter-Carter line of cases. Could any of the cases since 1937 have been decided the same way if that standard had prevailed? As interpreted by the majority in the pre-1937 cases? As interpreted by Justice Cardozo in Schechter and Carter? Note the reliance on the Shreveport legacy of "practical effects" in the post-1937 cases. Note also that, in several major decisions, the majority proved itself willing to go further than the Government's narrower, more hesitant arguments. And note the fuller economic record submitted by the Government in the cases that follow: contrast, e.g., the economic data in Jones & Laughlin with those in Schechter.[2]

---

2. The commerce power decisions were not the only indications of a changing judicial response. Two weeks before Jones & Laughlin, for example, the Court overruled prior decisions invalidating minimum wage laws as violative of due process. West Coast Hotel Co. v. Parrish, p. 465 below. West Coast Hotel, in particular, provoked the charge that Justice Roberts had changed his position in the face of the Roosevelt challenge—the "switch in time" that supposedly "saved the Nine." But, as a memorandum left by the Justice demonstrates, the Court voted in West Coast Hotel weeks before the judicial reorganization plan was announced. See Frankfurter, "Mr. Justice Roberts," 104 U.Pa.L.Rev. 311 (1955). Compare Justice Roberts' votes in Alton, Schechter and Carter, above, with those in the commerce clause decisions which follow; and compare his position in United States v. Butler with that in Steward Machine Co. v. Davis (pp.

202 and 208 below). Note the changes in Court personnel from 1937 through 1941: President Roosevelt made seven appointments—Justices Black, Reed, Frankfurter, Douglas, Murphy, Byrnes and Jackson.

The background and consequences of the Court-packing plan are discussed in Jackson, The Struggle for Judicial Supremacy (1941). For the political aspects of the controversy, see the useful contemporary account in Alsop and Catledge, The 168 Days (1938); the colorful modern review in Baker, Back to Back—The Duel Between FDR and the Supreme Court (1967); and the astute retrospective analysis in Chapter 15, "Court Packing: The Miscalculated Risk," Burns, Roosevelt: The Lion and the Fox (1956). See also Leuchtenburg, "The Origins of Franklin D. Roosevelt's 'Court-Packing Plan,'" 1966 Sup. Ct.Rev. 347.

SECTION 5. THE COMMERCE POWER SINCE 1937— CONSTITUTIONAL REVOLUTION OR CONTINUITY?

NLRB v. JONES & LAUGHLIN STEEL CORP.

301 U.S. 1, 57 S.Ct. 615, 81 L.Ed. 893 (1937).

[This was the major case testing the constitutionality of the National Labor Relations Act of 1935. Unlike Schechter, this test arose in a context desired by the Government: labor practices in a large industry. In a proceeding initiated by a union, the NLRB found that the company had engaged in "unfair labor practices" by discriminatory discharges of employees for union activity. The Board ordered the company to end discrimination and coercion. When the company failed to comply, the NLRB sought judicial enforcement of its order, but the Court of Appeals denied the Board's petition on the ground that "the order lay beyond the range of federal power."]

Mr. Chief Justice HUGHES delivered the opinion of the Court.

[The NLRB] has found: The corporation [is] engaged in the business of manufacturing iron and steel in plants situated in Pittsburgh and nearby Aliquippa, Pennsylvania. It manufactures and distributes a widely diversified line of steel and pig iron, being the fourth largest producer of steel in the United States. With its subsidiaries—nineteen in number—it is a completely integrated enterprise, owning and operating ore, coal and limestone properties, lake and river transportation facilities and terminal railroads located at its manufacturing plants. It owns or controls mines in Michigan and Minnesota. It operates four ore steamships on the Great Lakes. It owns coal mines in Pennsylvania. It operates towboats and steam barges used in carrying coal to its factories. [It owns two railroads that connect its plants to major lines.] Much of its product is shipped to its warehouses in Chicago, Detroit, Cincinnati and Memphis,—to the last two places by means of its own barges and transportation equipment. In Long Island City, New York, and in New Orleans it operates structural steel fabricating shops in connection with the warehousing of semi-finished materials sent from its works. Through one of its wholly-owned subsidiaries it owns, leases and operates stores, warehouses and yards for the distribution of equipment and supplies for drilling and operating oil and gas wells and for pipe lines, refineries and pumping stations. It has sales offices in twenty cities in the United States and a wholly-owned subsidiary which is devoted exclusively to distributing its product in Canada. Approximately 75 per cent. of its product is shipped out of Pennsylvania.

Summarizing these operations, the Labor Board concluded that the works in Pittsburgh and Aliquippa "might be likened to the heart of a self-contained, highly integrated body. They draw in the raw materials from Michigan, Minnesota, West Virginia, Pennsylvania in part through arteries and by means controlled by the respondent; they transform the materials and then pump them out to all parts of the nation through the vast mechanism which the respondent has elaborated." To carry on the activities of the entire steel industry, 33,000 men mine ore, 44,000 men mine coal, 4,000 men quarry limestone, 16,000 men manufacture coke, 343,000 men manufacture steel, and 83,000 men transport its product. Respondent has about 10,000 employees in its Aliquippa plant, which is located in a community of about [30,000 people].

First. The scope of the Act.—The Act is challenged in its entirety as an attempt to regulate all industry, thus invading the reserved powers of the States over their local concerns. It is asserted [that] the Act is not a true regulation [of] commerce or of matters which directly affect it but on the contrary has the fundamental object of placing under the compulsory supervision of the federal government all industrial labor relations within the nation. [We] think it clear that the National Labor Relations Act may be construed so as to operate within the sphere of constitutional authority. The jurisdiction conferred upon the Board, and invoked in this instance, is found in § 10(a), which [provides]: "The Board is empowered [to] prevent any person from engaging in any unfair labor [practice] affecting commerce." The critical words of this provision, prescribing the limits of the Board's authority in dealing with the labor practices, are "affecting commerce." [There] can be no question that the [commerce] contemplated by the Act [is] interstate and foreign commerce in the constitutional sense. The Act also defines the term "affecting commerce" (§ 2(7)): "The term 'affecting commerce' means in commerce, or burdening or obstructing commerce or the free flow of commerce, or having led or tending to lead to a labor dispute burdening or obstructing commerce or the free flow of commerce."

[The] grant of authority to the Board does not purport to extend to the relationship between all industrial employees and [employers] regardless of effects upon interstate or foreign commerce. It purports to reach only what may be deemed to burden or obstruct that commerce and, thus qualified, it must be construed as contemplating the exercise of control within constitutional bounds. It is a familiar principle that acts which directly burden or obstruct interstate or foreign commerce, or its free flow, are within the reach of the congressional power. Acts having that effect are not rendered immune because they grow out of labor disputes. [It] is the effect upon commerce, not the source of the injury, which is the criterion. [Whether] or not particular action does affect commerce in such a close and intimate fashion as to be subject to federal control [is] left by the statute to be determined as individual cases arise. We are thus to inquire whether in the instant case the constitutional boundary has been [passed].

Third. The application of the Act to employees engaged in production.—The principle involved.—Respondent says that whatever may be said of employees engaged in interstate commerce, the industrial relations and activities in the manufacturing department of respondent's enterprise are not subject to federal regulation. The argument rests upon the proposition that manufacturing in itself is not commerce. [Kidd v. Pearson; Schechter; Carter.] The Government distinguishes these cases, [urging] that these activities constitute a "stream" or "flow" of commerce, of which the Aliquippa manufacturing plant is the focal point, and that industrial strife at that point would cripple the entire movement. Reference is made to [Stafford v. Wallace]. [Respondent] contends that the instant case presents material distinctions. The raw materials which are brought to the plant are delayed for long periods and, after being subjected to manufacturing processes, "are changed substantially as to character, utility and value." The finished products which emerge "are to a large extent manufactured without reference to pre-existing orders and contracts and are entirely different from the raw materials which enter at the other end."

[We] do not find it necessary to determine whether these features of defendant's business dispose of the asserted analogy to the "stream of commerce" cases. The instances in which that metaphor has been used are but particular, and not exclusive, illustrations of the protective power which the Government invokes in support of the present Act. The congressional authority to protect interstate commerce from burdens and obstructions is not limited to transactions which can be deemed to be an essential part of a "flow" of interstate or foreign commerce. Burdens and obstructions may be due to injurious action springing from other sources. The fundamental principle is that the power to regulate commerce is the power to enact "all appropriate legislation" for "its protection and advancement"; to adopt measures "to promote its growth and insure its safety"; "to foster, protect, control and restrain." That power is plenary and may be exerted to protect interstate commerce "no matter what the source of the dangers which threaten it." Although activities may be intrastate in character when separately considered, if they have such a close and substantial relation to interstate commerce that their control is essential or appropriate to protect that commerce from burdens and obstructions, Congress cannot be denied the power to exercise that control. [Schechter.] Undoubtedly the scope of this power must be considered in the light of our dual system of government and may not be extended so as to embrace effects upon interstate commerce so indirect and remote that to embrace them, in view of our complex society, would effectually obliterate the distinction between what is national and what is local and create a completely centralized government. Id. The question is necessarily one of degree. [That] intrastate activities, by reason of close and intimate relation to interstate commerce, may fall within federal control is demonstrated in the case of carriers who are engaged in both interstate and intrastate transportation. [The] close and intimate effect which brings the subject within the reach of federal power may be due to activities in relation to productive industry although the industry when separately viewed is local. [T]he fact that the employees here concerned were engaged in production is not determinative. The question remains as to the effect upon interstate commerce of the labor practice involved. [In Schechter], we found that the effect there was so remote as to be beyond the federal power. [In Carter], the Court was of the opinion that the provisions of the statute relating to production were invalid upon several grounds. [These] cases are not controlling here.

Fourth. Effects of the unfair labor practice in respondent's enterprise.—Giving full weight to respondent's contention with respect to a break in the complete continuity of the "stream of commerce" by reason of respondent's manufacturing operations, the fact remains that the stoppage of those operations by industrial strife would have a most serious effect upon interstate commerce. In view of respondent's far-flung activities, it is idle to say that the effect would be indirect or remote. It is obvious that it would be immediate and might be catastrophic. We are asked to shut our eyes to the plainest facts of our national life and to deal with the question of direct and indirect effects in an intellectual vacuum. Because there may be but indirect and remote effects upon interstate commerce in connection with a host of local enterprises throughout the country, it does not follow that other industrial activities do not have such a close and intimate relation to interstate commerce as to make the presence of industrial strife a matter of the most urgent national concern. When industries organize themselves on a national scale, making their relation to interstate commerce the dominant factor in their activities, how can it be maintained that their industrial labor relations constitute a forbidden field into which Congress may not enter when it is necessary to protect interstate commerce from the paralyzing consequences of industrial war? We have often said that interstate commerce itself is a practical conception. It is equally true that interferences with that commerce must be appraised by a judgment that does not ignore actual experience.

Experience has abundantly demonstrated that the recognition of the right of employees to self-organization and to have representatives of their own choosing for the purpose of collective bargaining is often an essential condition of industrial peace. Refusal to confer and negotiate has been one of the most prolific causes of strife. This is such an outstanding fact in the history of labor disturbances that it is a proper subject of judicial notice and requires no citation of [instances].[1]

---

1. The Court also found that the means used by the Act did not violate the due process clause of the Fifth Amendment.

Reversed.

Mr. Justice McREYNOLDS [dissented].[2]

Any effect on interstate commerce by the discharge of employees shown here, would be indirect and remote in the highest degree, as consideration of the facts will show. In [Jones & Laughlin] ten men out of ten thousand were discharged; in the other cases only a few. The immediate effect in the factory may be to create discontent among all those employed and a strike may follow, which, in turn, may result in reducing production, which ultimately may reduce the volume of goods moving in interstate commerce. By this chain of indirect and progressively remote events we finally reach the evil with which it is said the legislation under consideration undertakes to deal. A more remote and indirect interference with interstate commerce or a more definite invasion of the powers reserved to the states is difficult, if not impossible, to imagine.

It is gravely stated that experience teaches that if an employer discourages membership in "any organization of any kind" "in which employees participate, and which exists for the purpose in whole or in part of dealing with employers concerning grievances, labor disputes, wages, [etc.]," discontent may follow and this in turn may lead to a strike, and as the outcome of the strike there may be a block in the stream of interstate commerce. Therefore Congress may inhibit the discharge! Whatever effect any cause of discontent may ultimately have upon commerce is far too indirect to justify Congressional regulation. Almost anything—marriage, birth, death—may in some fashion affect [commerce].

Transitional Note. Jones & Laughlin gave new life to the "affecting commerce" rationale—the rationale justifying national regulation of intrastate activities because of their practical effect on interstate commerce. Five years later, in Wickard v. Filburn (1942), the Court elaborated and expanded that rationale. Wickard is printed immediately below, to permit tracing the development of that "affecting commerce" doctrinal strand at this point. But in between Jones & Laughlin and Wickard, the Court made another major contribution to an expansive reading of the commerce power, in United States v. Darby in 1941. Consideration of Darby is postponed until after Wickard, because Darby deals with the "commerce-prohibiting" device as well as the "affecting commerce" technique of regulation; printing Darby after Wickard accordingly aids separate focus on the modern aspects of the commerce-prohibiting problems first encountered in the Lottery Case and in Hammer v. Dagenhart, sec. 3 above.[3]

---

2. The dissent in this 5 to 4 decision was joined by Justices Van Devanter, Sutherland and Butler.

Justice McReynolds' dissent was also applicable to two companion cases: NLRB v. Fruehauf Trailer Co., 301 U.S. 49 (1937), involving the largest trailer manufacturer in the nation, with sales offices in 12 states; and NLRB v. Friedman-Harry Marks Clothing Co., 301 U.S. 58 (1937), involving a Virginia clothing manufacturer. In the latter case, the majority emphasized that over 99 percent of the raw materials came from other states and that over 80 percent of the products were sold to other states. The dissent pointed out that the company produced "less than one-half of one per cent of the men's clothing produced in the United States and employs 800 of the 150,000 workmen engaged therein."

3. The decisions sustaining national power in Wickard and Darby, unlike that in Jones & Laughlin, were unanimous. There were rapid changes in the composition of the Court after Jones & Laughlin: by the time of the Darby decision, all of the four dissenters in Jones & Laughlin had left. Justice McReynolds was the last to go: he retired just a few days before Darby was announced.

WICKARD v. FILBURN

317 U.S. 111, 63 S.Ct. 82, 87 L.Ed. 122 (1942).

[Filburn, a farmer in Ohio, sued Wickard, the Secretary of Agriculture, to enjoin enforcement of a marketing penalty imposed under the Agricultural Adjustment Act of 1938, as amended, "upon that part of his 1941 wheat crop which was available for market in excess of the market quota established for his farm." Filburn attacked the marketing quota provisions of the Act as, inter alia, beyond the commerce power. The lower court enjoined enforcement on other grounds, and Secretary Wickard appealed.]

Mr. Justice JACKSON delivered the opinion of the Court.

[The] appellee for many years past has owned and operated a small farm in [Ohio]. It has been his practice to raise a small acreage of [wheat]; to sell a portion of the crop; to feed part to poultry and livestock on the farm, some of which is sold; to use some in making flour for home consumption; and to keep the rest for the following seeding. The intended disposition of the crop here involved has not been expressly stated. In July of 1940, pursuant to the Agricultural Adjustment Act of 1938, as then amended, there was established for the appellee's 1941 crop a wheat acreage allotment of 11.1 acres and a normal yield of 20.1 bushels of wheat an acre. [He] sowed, however, 23 acres, and harvested from his 11.9 acres of excess acreage 239 bushels, which under the [Act] constituted farm marketing excess, subject to a penalty of 49 cents a bushel, or $117.11 in all. The appellee has not paid the penalty and he has not postponed or avoided it by storing the excess under regulations of the Secretary of Agriculture, or by delivering it up to the Secretary. [The] general scheme of the [Act] as related to wheat is to control the volume moving in interstate and foreign commerce in order to avoid surpluses and shortages and the consequent abnormally low or high wheat prices and obstructions to commerce.

[It] is urged that under the Commerce [Clause], Congress does not possess the power it has in this instance sought to exercise. The question would merit little consideration since our decision in [United States v. Darby], except for the fact that this Act extends federal regulation to production not intended in any part for commerce but wholly for consumption on the farm. [Under the Act], marketing quotas not only embrace all that may be sold without penalty but also what may be consumed on the premises. [The] sum of this is that the Federal Government fixes a quota including all that the farmer may harvest for sale or for his own farm needs, and declares that wheat produced on excess acreage may neither be disposed of nor used except upon payment of the penalty, or except it is stored as required by the [Act].

Appellee says that this is a regulation of production and consumption of wheat. Such activities are, he urges, beyond the reach of Congressional power under the Commerce Clause, since they are local in character, and their effects upon interstate commerce are at most "indirect." In answer the Government argues that the statute regulates neither production nor consumption, but only marketing; and, in the alternative, that if the Act does go beyond the regulation of marketing it is sustainable as a "necessary and proper" implementation of the power of Congress over interstate commerce. The Government's concern lest the Act be held to be a regulation of production or consumption, rather than of marketing, is attributable to a few dicta and decisions of this Court which might be understood to lay it down that activities such as "production," "manufacturing," and "mining" are strictly "local" and, except in special circumstances which are not present here, cannot be regulated under the commerce power because their effects upon interstate commerce are, as matter of law, only "indirect." Even today, when this power has been held to have great latitude, there is no decision of this Court that such activities may be regulated where no part of the product is intended for interstate commerce or intermingled with the subjects thereof. We believe that a review of the course of decision under the Commerce Clause will make plain, however, that questions of the power of Congress are not to be decided by reference to any formula which would give controlling force to nomenclature such as "production" and "indirect" and foreclose consideration of the actual effects of the activity in question upon interstate commerce.

At the beginning Chief Justice Marshall described the federal commerce power with a breadth never yet exceeded. [Gibbons v. Ogden.] He made emphatic the embracing and penetrating nature of this power by warning that effective restraints on its exercise must proceed from political rather than from judicial processes. [Recall the comment on this passage at p. 103 above. Justice Jackson proceeded to review commerce power decisions since Gibbons. He noted that cases such as Knight had established a "line of restrictive authority," but that "other cases" had "called forth broader interpretations of the Commerce Clause destined to supersede the earlier ones, and to bring about a return to the principles first enunciated [in] Gibbons v. Ogden." He commented: "In some cases sustaining the exercise of federal power over intrastate matters the term 'direct' was used for the purpose of stating, rather than of reaching, a result; in others it was treated as synonymous with 'substantial' or 'material'; and in others it was not used at all. Of late its use has been abandoned in cases dealing with questions of federal power under the Commerce Clause." After quoting from the Shreveport Rate Case, Justice Jackson continued:]

The Court's recognition of the relevance of the economic effects in the application of the Commerce Clause, exemplified by this statement, has made the mechanical application of legal formulas no longer feasible. Once an economic measure of the reach of the power granted to Congress in the Commerce Clause is accepted, questions of federal power cannot be decided simply by finding the activity in questions to be "production" nor can consideration of its economic effects be foreclosed by calling them "indirect." [Whether] the subject of the regulation in question was "production," "consumption," or "marketing" is, therefore, not material for purposes of deciding the question of federal power before us. That an activity is of local character may help in a doubtful case to determine whether Congress intended to reach it. [But] even if appellee's activity be local and though it may not be regarded as commerce, it may still, whatever its nature, be reached by Congress if it exerts a substantial economic effect on interstate commerce, and this irrespective of whether such effect is what might at some earlier time have been defined as "direct" or "indirect."

[The] parties have stipulated a summary of the economics of the wheat industry. Commerce among the states in wheat is large and important. Although wheat is raised in every state but one, production in most states is not equal to consumption. [The] wheat industry has been a problem industry for some years. Largely as a result of increased foreign production and import restrictions, annual exports of wheat and flour from the United States during the ten-year period ending in 1940 averaged less than 10 per cent of total production, while during the 1920's they averaged more than 25 per cent. The decline in the export trade has left a large surplus in production which, in connection with an abnormally large supply of wheat and other grains in recent years, caused congestion in a number of markets; tied up railroad cars; and caused elevators in some instances to turn away grains, and railroads to institute embargoes to prevent further congestion. [In] the absence of regulation the price of wheat in the United States would be much affected by world conditions.

During 1941, producers who cooperated with the Agricultural Adjustment program received an average price on the farm of about $1.16 a bushel, as compared with the world market price of 40 cents a bushel.

[The] effect of consumption of homegrown wheat on interstate commerce is due to the fact that it constitutes the most variable factor in the disappearance of the wheat crop. Consumption on the farm where grown appears to vary in an amount greater than 20 per cent of average production. The total amount of wheat consumed as food varies but relatively little, and use as seed is relatively constant. The maintenance by government regulation of a price for wheat undoubtedly can be accomplished as effectively by sustaining or increasing the demand as by limiting the supply. The effect of the statute before us is to restrict the amount which may be produced for market and the extent as well to which one may forestall resort to the market by producing to meet his own needs. That appellee's own contribution to the demand for wheat may be trivial by itself is not enough to remove him from the scope of federal regulation where, as here, his contribution, taken together with that of many others similarly situated, is far from trivial.

It is well established by decisions of this Court that the power to regulate commerce includes the power to regulate the prices at which commodities in that commerce are dealt in and practices affecting such prices. One of the primary purposes of the Act in question was to increase the market price of wheat, and to that end to limit the volume thereof that could affect the market. It can hardly be denied that a factor of such volume and variability as home-consumed wheat would have a substantial influence on price and market conditions. This may arise because being in marketable condition such [home-grown] wheat overhangs the market and, if induced by rising prices, tends to flow into the market and check price increases. But if we assume that it is never marketed, it supplies a need of the man who grew it which would otherwise be reflected by purchases in the open market. Home-grown wheat in this sense competes with wheat in commerce. The stimulation of commerce is a use of the regulatory function quite as definitely as prohibitions or restrictions thereon. This record leaves us in no doubt that Congress may properly have considered that wheat consumed on the farm where grown, if wholly outside the scheme of regulation, would have a substantial effect in defeating and obstructing its purpose to stimulate trade therein at increased [prices].[1]

Reversed.

THE COMMERCE POWER, THE NATIONAL MARKET, AND THE SCOPE OF THE WICKARD RATIONALE

1. *The scope of the Wickard rationale.* Was the "national market" theory essential to sustain the sanction imposed in Wickard v. Filburn? Could Congress have imposed a limit on farm production directly, without the superstructure of the market control scheme, by simply invoking the "affecting commerce" argument?

Justice Jackson in Wickard still required a showing of "substantial economic effect on interstate commerce." But is any real substance left to the notion of substantiality if that requirement is satisfied whenever the activity regulated, "taken together with that of many others similarly situated, is far from trivial"? Does that aggregation approach leave any local activities so minimal as to be unreachable? Is the scope of Wickard limited by Justice Jackson's emphasis on

---

1. The Court also rejected the claim that the Act was "a deprivation of property without due process of law contrary to the Fifth Amendment, both because of its regulatory effect on the appellee and because of its alleged retroactive effect."

the economic magnitude of the wheat production problem? Is aggregation allowable only when the resultant economic problem is of truly substantial dimensions? Is the scope of Wickard limited by the fact that Congress was dealing with a genuine economic problem? Or is the aggregation theory also usable for national "police" regulations? (Cf. the Perez case, p. 148 below.) Note Justice Rutledge's broad statement in Mandeville Island Farms v. American Crystal Sugar Co., 334 U.S. 219, 236 (1948): "Congress' power to keep the interstate market free of goods produced under conditions inimical to the general welfare [Darby, below], may be exercised in individual cases without showing any specific effect upon interstate commerce"; "it is enough that the individual activity when multiplied into a general practice is subject to federal control [Wickard], or that it contains a threat to the interstate economy that requires preventive regulation." But, as later notes elaborate, there may be reason for caution to avoid reading too much into such broad dicta. Compare, for example, Justice Harlan's comment in Maryland v. Wirtz in 1968 (p. 155 below), suggesting that Wickard did *not* mean "that Congress may use a relatively trivial impact on commerce as an excuse for broad general regulation of state or private activities." [1]

2. *Invocations of the market concept.* The concept of a national market in goods proved a useful source of constitutional justifications for congressional regulation of activities "in" or "affecting" commerce in a number of modern cases, both before Wickard and since. As an example, consider Mulford v. Smith: After the Court invalidated the Agricultural Adjustment Act of 1933 in Butler in 1936 (p. 202 below) as an unconstitutional regulation of "local" production, Congress enacted the Agricultural Adjustment Act of 1938. The marketing quota provisions of the Act were sustained as a regulation of a channel of commerce. Mulford v. Smith, 307 U.S. 38 (1939). Penalties imposed by the Act were payments to the government of one-half the market price of all tobacco sold above the marketing quota, the fine to be paid by warehousemen and deducted by them from the purchase price paid to the farmer. The Court—three years after Butler—emphasized that the Act did not purport to control production, noted that the Act regulated commerce "at the throat where tobacco enters the stream of commerce,—the marketing warehouse," and concluded: "Any rule, such as that embodied in the Act, which is intended [to] prevent the flow of commerce from working harm to the people of the nation, is within the competence of Congress." [2]

UNITED STATES v. DARBY

312 U.S. 100, 61 S.Ct. 451, 85 L.Ed. 609 (1941).

[Darby, a Georgia lumber manufacturer, challenged an indictment charging him with violating the Fair Labor Standards Act of 1938. The District Court quashed the indictment, holding that the Act was unconstitutional because it

1. The problems of limits, if any, on the contemporary scope of the commerce power are pursued in later notes in this chapter.

2. Note also the use of the marketing concept in the upholding of congressional efforts to fix prices of goods and services in transactions in or affecting commerce in United States v. Rock Royal Co-operative, 307 U.S. 533 (1939) (milk); Sunshine Coal & Anthracite Co. v. Adkins, 310 U.S. 381 (1940) (coal); and FPC v. Natural Gas Pipeline Co., 315 U.S. 575 (1942) (natural gas).

And note United States v. Wrightwood Dairy Co., 315 U.S. 110 (1942), justifying federal price regulation of milk produced and sold intrastate on the basis of "marketing" and "affecting commerce" theories and explaining that "the marketing of a local product in competition of a like commodity moving interstate may so interfere with interstate commerce or its regulation as to afford a basis for Congressional regulation of intrastate activity."

sought to regulate hours and wages of employees in local manufacturing activities.]

Mr. Justice STONE delivered the opinion of the Court.

[The] two principal questions [in] this case are, *first*, whether Congress has constitutional power to prohibit the shipment in interstate commerce of lumber manufactured by employees whose wages are less than a prescribed minimum or whose weekly hours of labor at that wage are greater than a prescribed maximum, and, *second*, whether it has power to prohibit the employment of workmen in the production of goods "for interstate commerce" at other than prescribed wages and hours.

[The Act] set up a comprehensive legislative scheme for preventing the shipment in interstate commerce of certain products and commodities produced in the United States under labor conditions as respects wages and hours which fail to conform to standards set up by the Act. Its purpose, as we judicially know from the declaration of policy in § 2(a) of the Act, and the reports of Congressional committees proposing the legislation, [is] to exclude from interstate commerce goods produced for the commerce and to prevent their production for interstate commerce, under conditions detrimental to the maintenance of the minimum standards of living necessary for health and general well-being; and to prevent the use of interstate commerce as the means of competition in the distribution of goods so produced, and as the means of spreading and perpetuating such substandard labor conditions among the workers of the several [states]. Section 15(a)(1) makes unlawful the shipment in interstate commerce of any goods "in the production of which any employee was employed in violation of [secs. 6 and 7]," which provide [that] during the first year of operation of the Act a minimum wage of 25 cents per hour shall be paid [and] that the maximum hours of employment for employees [without] increased compensation for overtime, shall be forty-five hours a week. § 15(a)(2) makes it unlawful to violate [the] minimum wage and maximum hour requirements [for] employees engaged in production of goods for commerce. [The] indictment charges that appellee is engaged [in] the business of acquiring raw materials, which he manufactures into finished lumber with the intent, when manufactured, to ship it in interstate commerce to customers outside the state, and that he does in fact so ship a large part of the lumber so [produced].

The prohibition of shipment of the proscribed goods in interstate commerce. § 15(a)(1) prohibits, and the indictment charges, the shipment in interstate commerce, of goods produced for interstate commerce by employees whose wages and hours of employment do not conform to the requirements of the Act. [T]he only question arising under the commerce clause with respect to such shipments is whether Congress has the constitutional power to prohibit them.

While manufacture is not of itself interstate commerce the shipment of manufactured goods interstate is such commerce and the prohibition of such shipment by Congress is indubitably a regulation of the commerce. The power to regulate commerce is the power "to prescribe the rule by which commerce is governed." Gibbons v. Ogden. It extends not only to those regulations which aid, foster and protect the commerce, but embraces those which prohibit it. It is conceded that the power of Congress to prohibit transportation in interstate commerce includes noxious articles, stolen articles, kidnapped persons, and articles such as intoxicating liquor or convict made goods, traffic in which is forbidden or restricted by the laws of the state of destination. [But] it is said that the present prohibition falls within the scope of none of these categories; that while the prohibition is nominally a regulation of the commerce its motive or purpose is regulation of wages and hours of persons engaged in manufacture, the control of which has been reserved to the states and upon which Georgia and some of the states of destination have placed no restriction; that the effect of the present statute is not to exclude the prescribed articles from interstate commerce in aid of state regulation as in Kentucky Whip & Collar,[1] but instead, under the guise of a regulation of interstate commerce, it undertakes to regulate wages and hours within the state contrary to the policy of the state which has elected to leave them unregulated.

The power of Congress over interstate commerce [can] neither be enlarged nor diminished by the exercise or non-exercise of state power. Congress, following its own conception of public policy concerning the restrictions which may appropriately be imposed on interstate commerce, is free to exclude from the commerce articles whose use in the states for which they are destined it may conceive to be injurious to the public health, morals or welfare, even though the state has not sought to regulate their use. Such regulation is not a forbidden invasion of state power merely because either its motive or its consequence is to restrict the use of articles of commerce within the states of destination. [It] is no objection to the assertion of the power to regulate interstate commerce that its exercise is attended by the same incidents which attend the exercise of the police power of the states.

[The] motive and purpose of the present regulation is plainly to make effective the Congressional conception of public policy that interstate commerce should not be made the instrument of competition in the distribution of goods produced under substandard labor conditions, which competition is injurious to the commerce and to the states from and to which the commerce flows. The motive and purpose of a regulation of interstate commerce are matters for the legislative judgment upon the exercise of which the Constitution places no restriction and over which the courts are given no control. "The judicial cannot prescribe to the legislative department of the government limitations upon the exercise of its acknowledged power."[2] Whatever their motive and purpose, regulations of commerce which do not infringe some constitutional prohibition are within the plenary power conferred on Congress by the Commerce Clause. Subject only to that limitation, presently to be considered, we conclude that the prohibition of the shipment interstate of goods produced under the forbidden substandard labor conditions is within the constitutional authority of Congress.

[T]hese principles of constitutional interpretation have been so long and repeatedly recognized by this Court as applicable to the Commerce Clause, that there would be little occasion for repeating them now were it not for the decision of this Court twenty-two years ago in Hammer v. Dagenhart. In that case it was held by a bare majority of the Court over the powerful and now classic dissent of Mr. Justice Holmes [that] Congress was without power to exclude the products of child labor from interstate commerce. The reasoning and conclusion of the Court's opinion there cannot be reconciled with the conclusion which we have reached, that the power of Congress under the Commerce Clause is plenary to exclude any article from interstate commerce subject only to the specific prohibitions of the Constitution. Hammer v. Dagenhart has not been followed. The distinction on which the decision was rested that Congressional power to prohibit interstate commerce is limited to articles which in themselves have some harmful or deleterious property—a distinction which was novel when made and unsupported by any provision of the Constitution—has long since been abandoned. [The] thesis of the opinion

---

1. In Kentucky Whip & Collar Co. v. Illinois Central Railroad Co., 299 U.S. 334 (1937), the Court sustained the Ashurst-Summers Act, which made it unlawful to transport convict-made goods into any state where the receipt, sale or possession of such goods violated state law.

2. In support of the last two sentences, the Court cited a number of cases involving the taxing power (and rejecting claims that Congress had abused its power to tax by seeking regulatory objectives through taxation): McCray v. United States, Sonzinsky v. United States, and Veazie Bank v. Fenno. These taxing power cases are considered in chap. 4, sec. 1, below.

that the motive of the prohibition or its effect to control in some measure the use or production within the states of the article thus excluded from the commerce can operate to deprive the regulation of its constitutional authority has long since ceased to have force. [The] conclusion is inescapable that Hammer v. Dagenhart was a departure from the principles which have prevailed in the interpretation of the Commerce Clause both before and since the decision and that such vitality, as a precedent, as it then had has long since been exhausted. It should be and now is overruled.

Validity of the wage and hour requirements. Section 15(a)(2) and §§ 6 and 7 require employers to conform to the wage and hour provisions with respect to all employees engaged in the production of goods for interstate commerce. As appellees' employees are not alleged to be "engaged in interstate commerce" the validity of the prohibition turns on the question whether the employment, under other than the prescribed labor standards, of employees engaged in the production of goods for interstate commerce is so related to the commerce and so affects it as to be within the reach of the power of Congress to regulate it.

[The] power of Congress to regulate interstate commerce extends to the regulation through legislative action of activities intrastate which have a substantial effect on the commerce or the exercise of the Congressional power over it. [In] such legislation Congress has sometimes left it to the courts to determine whether the intrastate activities have the prohibited effect on the commerce, as in the Sherman Act. It has sometimes left it to an administrative board or agency to determine whether the activities sought to be regulated or prohibited have such effect, as in the case [of] the National Labor Relations Act. [And] sometimes Congress itself has said that a particular activity affects the commerce, as it did in the present Act, the Safety Appliance Act and the Railway Labor Act. In passing on the validity of legislation of the class last mentioned the only function of courts is to determine whether the particular activity regulated or prohibited is within the reach of the federal power.

Congress, having by the present Act adopted the policy of excluding from interstate commerce all goods produced for the commerce which do not conform to the specified labor standards, it may choose the means reasonably adapted to the attainment of the permitted end, even though they involve control of intrastate activities. Such legislation has often been sustained with respect to powers, other than the commerce power, [when] the means chosen, although not themselves within the granted power, were nevertheless deemed appropriate aids to the accomplishment of some purpose within an admitted power of the national government. [A] familiar like exercise of power is the regulation of intrastate transactions which are so commingled with or related to interstate commerce that all must be regulated if the interstate commerce is to be effectively controlled. Shreveport Case. Similarly Congress may require inspection and preventive treatment of all cattle in a disease infected area in order to prevent shipment in interstate commerce of some of the cattle without the treatment. It may prohibit the removal, at destination, of labels required by the Pure Food & Drugs Act to be affixed to articles transported in interstate commerce. McDermott v. Wisconsin [below].

[We] think also that § 15(a)(2), now under consideration, is sustainable independently of § 15(a)(1), which prohibits shipment or transportation of the proscribed goods. As we have said the evils aimed at by the Act are the spread of substandard labor conditions through the use of the facilities of interstate commerce for competition by the goods so produced with those produced under the prescribed or better labor conditions; and the consequent dislocation of the commerce itself caused by the impairment or destruction of local businesses by competition made effective through interstate commerce. The Act is thus directed at the suppression of a method or kind of competition in interstate commerce which it has in effect condemned as "unfair," as the Clayton Act has condemned other "unfair methods of competition" made effective through interstate commerce.

[The] means adopted by § 15(a)(2) for the protection of interstate commerce by the suppression of the production of the condemned goods for interstate commerce is so related to the commerce and so affects it as to be within the reach of the commerce power. Congress, to attain its objective in the suppression of nationwide competition in interstate commerce by goods produced under substandard labor conditions, has made no distinction as to the volume or amount of shipments in the commerce or of production for commerce by any particular shipper or producer. It recognized that in present day industry, competition by a small part may affect the whole and that the total effect of the competition of many small producers may be great. [So] far as [Carter] is inconsistent with this conclusion, its doctrine is limited in principle by the decisions under the Sherman Act and the National Labor Relations Act, which [we] follow.

[Our] conclusion is unaffected by the Tenth Amendment which [states] but a truism that all is retained which has not been surrendered.[3] There is nothing in the history of its adoption to suggest that it was more than declaratory of the relationship between the national and state governments as it had been established by the Constitution before the amendment or that its purpose was other than to allay fears that the new national government might seek to exercise powers not granted, and that the states might not be able to exercise fully their [reserved powers].[4]

Reversed.

THE COMMERCE–PROHIBITING TECHNIQUE AS A MODERN REGULATORY TOOL: THE IMPLICATIONS OF DARBY

1. *The search for limits.* a. *Imposing the prohibition sanction at the state border.* Do the "prohibition of shipment" aspects of Darby leave any "local" private sector activities outside of congressional power—at least so long as the commerce-prohibiting technique is used? Consider again the questions raised earlier, after Hammer v. Dagenhart in sec. 3. Now, Hammer v. Dagenhart is overruled. Now, with Darby, the Court disavows all control over the "motive and purpose" of such regulation—citing only taxing power cases as authority.

3. In the generation after the Darby decision, this "truism" passage was widely quoted in Court opinions endorsing broad exercises of congressional power. Many commentators assumed that the Court was unlikely ever to strike down another law of Congress on the ground that it exceeded the commerce power. But a footnote in Justice Marshall's majority opinion in Fry v. United States, 421 U.S. 542 (1975), served warning that the reports of the death of federalistic limitations might be premature. Though sustaining the application of temporary federal wage controls to state employees in a narrow opinion, Justice Marshall commented: "While the Tenth Amendment has been characterized as a 'truism,' stating merely that 'all is retained which has not been surrendered,' United States v. Darby, it is not without significance. The Amendment expressly declares the constitutional policy that Congress may not exercise power in a fashion that impairs the States' integrity or their ability to function effectively in a federal system." A year later, that observation blossomed into a prevailing opinion, in National League of Cities v. Usery in 1976, where the Court (with Justice Marshall among the dissenters) held a federal law unconstitutional on federalistic grounds for the first time in 40 years. National League of Cities is printed in sec. 7 of this chapter, at p. 170 below, and its impact and implications are explored in that section. (The decision invalidated the application of the Fair Labor Standards Act, the same law as that involved in Darby, to certain state employees. Compare the 1985 decision in Garcia, noted at p. 169 below.)

4. The Court also rejected the contention that the minimum wage and maximum hours provisions violated the due process clause of the Fifth Amendment.

Was such a broad disavowal of judicial scrutiny necessary or justified? Consider, in examining cases in sec. 1 of the next chapter, involving the taxing power as a regulatory device, whether the Court has in fact disavowed all "motive and purpose" control in the tax area. Does the disavowal in Darby signify a final rejection of the "pretext" limitation in McCulloch, where Marshall stated that the Court would invalidate laws "for the accomplishment of objects not entrusted to the government"? Does Darby signify the end of judicial concern for the "spirit" of the Constitution—the implications of the federal structure—which Marshall referred to in McCulloch? Would and should the Court sustain, as commerce power-supported legislation, prohibitions of interstate movement of persons not educated, or married, in accordance with national standards? Could Congress at least prohibit interstate shipment of goods by such persons? What "objects" are "entrusted" to Congress by the commerce clause? Should the Court restrict Congress to "commercial," "economic" objects? Did the opportunity to impose such a limit pass with the line of decisions that began with the Lottery Case?

What explains the Court's failure to impose effective restraints on the "commerce-prohibiting" technique? The earlier Court's doctrinal chaos and inconsistency as to scrutiny of congressional purposes (compare the Lottery Case with Hammer v. Dagenhart)—the inconsistency that prompted the Holmes dissent in Hammer v. Dagenhart? Modern perceptions of interrelationships within the economy? Felt institutional constraints, reflecting the Court's concern about its competence to ascertain congressional purposes and motives? Do any of these possible sources of the Court's retreat justify inattention to federalistic restraints by a member of Congress voting on proposed legislation?

b. *The commerce-prohibiting technique as the basis for direct sanctions on intrastate activities: The superbootstrap suggestion of Darby.* The preceding comments on Darby and its antecedents suggest that judicial noninterference is at its greatest when Congress prohibits the crossing of state lines. Recall, however, that when Congress has sought to impose sanctions directly on the intrastate activity, justifications have typically relied on the "affecting commerce" rationale, as the series of cases culminating in Wickard v. Filburn indicated. But there are passages in Darby suggesting that resort to the "affecting commerce" rationale may no longer be necessary to justify sanctions directed at activities within a state. Those passages, read most broadly, suggest that Darby offers an end run around the "affecting commerce" rationale.

Consider the portion of the opinion beginning with the heading: "Validity of the wage and hour requirements." These "requirements" were applicable directly to employees engaged in the production of goods for interstate commerce. Yet the first rationale Justice Stone offers for the constitutionality of the requirements does not speak about impact of the local activity on interstate commerce. Rather, the "end" which is invoked in this passage to justify the local "means" is the relationship of the local sanction to the *ban* on interstate shipments (not the relationship between the local sanction and a national commercial problem). Does that mean that regulation of local activities can now be justified *without* any showing of the impact of the local activity on commerce—simply by having the regulatory scheme include a ban on interstate shipments, and then justifying the regulation as a means to effectuate that "commerce-prohibiting" sanction?

This passage in Darby seems to support just such an approach. To examine the passage in somewhat more detail: It sustains the wage and hour regulations of production activities as "means reasonably adapted to the attainment of the permitted end" of "excluding from interstate commerce all goods produced" under non-conforming standards. It is only *after* offering this justification that the Court also finds the production regulations "sustainable independently," because of the "effect of" the intrastate activities on interstate commerce itself—the more typical Wickard, "affecting commerce" rationale. If the first of the Court's alternative rationales were taken at face value, all discussion of "affecting commerce" or "stream of commerce" justifications would become unnecessary. If it were taken at face value, Congress could presumably regulate any intrastate activity through a two-step bootstrap device, without ever having to justify the relationship of the regulated local activity to a national economic problem. All Congress need do if that branch of the Darby analysis is taken seriously is (1) prohibit interstate movement of goods or persons connected with that activity (aware that, under the first part of Darby, prohibition sanctions are essentially self-validating and do not require any independent nexus to national commercial problems), and (2) directly regulate the intrastate activity itself, as a "means reasonably adapted to the attainment of the permitted end" of interstate prohibition. Would general acceptance of this technique constitute a judicial confession of the bankruptcy of commerce power doctrine? Are the "political safeguards of federalism" adequate protection against abuses of such a power, even in areas of regulation without major economic dimensions? These questions rest, as noted, on a literal reading of the Darby Court's first ground for sustaining the production regulations. But perhaps such a reading is unwarranted. After all, it was merely an alternative holding: the Court did go on to justify the production regulations in the traditional "affecting commerce" manner. And there may be political inhibitions in Congress against excessive invocation of the "prohibition" technique.[1]

2. *Control of acts performed after the interstate movement ends: The Sullivan case.* UNITED STATES v. SULLIVAN, 332 U.S. 689 (1948), ranks with Darby among the broadest modern statements of the reach of the commerce-prohibiting technique. Darby dealt with activities preceding interstate shipment; Sullivan sustained federal regulation applied to activities long after the interstate shipment had ended. And the reasoning in Sullivan, even more so than some passages in Darby, may be unduly cavalier and broad—and unduly insensitive to federalistic limitations.

a. *The extent of the reach.* In Sullivan, Justice BLACK's opinion for the Court sustained a conviction for violating the Federal Food, Drug and Cosmetic Act of 1938. Sullivan was a retail druggist in Columbus, Ga., who had bought a properly labeled 1000-tablet bottle of sulfathiazole from an Atlanta, Ga., wholesaler. The bottle had been shipped to the Atlanta wholesaler by a Chicago supplier six months earlier. Three months after the purchase by the Columbus druggist, he made two retail sales of 12 tablets each. He removed the tablets from the bottle and placed them in pill boxes marked "sulfathiazole." The pill boxes did not have directions for use or warnings of danger. Section 301(k) of the Act prohibits misbranding a drug "if such act is done while such article is held for sale after shipment in interstate commerce and results in such article being misbranded." Sullivan was charged with misbranding because of his omission of the directions and warnings on the pill boxes.

The Court of Appeals reversed respondent's conviction by concluding that Section 301(k) should be "held to apply only to the holding for the first sale by

---

1. In examining the remaining materials in this chapter, consider whether the concerns voiced in this note are justified. Consider, too, Herbert Wechsler's comment: "One of the speculations that I must confess I find intriguing is upon the question whether there are any neutral principles that might have been employed to mark the limits of the commerce power [in] terms more circumscribed than the virtual abandonment of limits in the principle that has pre-vailed." Wechsler, "Toward Neutral Principles of Constitutional Law," 73 Harv.L.Rev. 1, 23–24 (1959). In reflecting on the contents of this section, consider what limits might have been articulated—and what limits exist. Do any of the materials in the rest of this chapter suggest limits on the broadest implications of Darby? Is there need to fashion greater limits? Are greater limits possible?

the importer after interstate shipment": the court feared that a broader reading "would result in far-reaching inroads upon customary control by local authorities of traditionally local activities." The Supreme Court reversed. Justice Black was able to dispose of the constitutional objection in one paragraph:[2] "It is contended that the Act as we have construed it is beyond any authority granted Congress by the Constitution. [A] similar challenge was made against the Pure Food and Drugs Act of 1906, and rejected, in McDermott v. Wisconsin, 228 U.S. 115 [1913]. That Act did not contain § 301(k), but it did prohibit misbranding and authorized seizure of misbranded articles after they were shipped from one State to another, so long as they remained 'unsold.' The authority of Congress to make this requirement was upheld as a proper exercise of its powers under the commerce clause. There are two variants between the circumstances of [McDermott] and this [case]. In the McDermott case the labels involved were on the original containers; here the labels are required to be put on other than the original containers—the boxes to which the tablets were transferred. Also, in [McDermott] the possessor of the labeled cans held for sale had himself received them by way of an interstate sale and shipment; here, while the petitioner had received the sulfathiazole by way of an intrastate sale and shipment, he bought it from a wholesaler who had received it as the direct consignee of an interstate shipment. These variants are not sufficient [to] detract from the applicability of the McDermott holding to the present decision. In both cases alike the question relates to the constitutional power of Congress under the commerce clause to regulate the branding of articles that have completed an interstate shipment and are being held for future sales in purely local or intrastate commerce. The reasons given for the McDermott holding therefore are equally applicable and persuasive here. And many cases decided since the McDermott decision lend support to the validity of § 301(k). See, e.g., [Wickard; Darby]."[3]

  b. *The adequacy of the justification.* What is the constitutional basis for this application of the Act? Use of "means reasonably adapted" to "implementing" the commerce-prohibiting provisions, as in Darby's alternative rationale? (Section 301(c) forbids the "introduction [into] interstate commerce" of misbranded drugs.) Control of local activities "affecting" commerce, as in Wickard? Control of activities "in" commerce? Does the Court's opinion provide an adequate explanation? Do the citations of Darby and Wickard? Does the citation of McDermott?[4]

2. Before reaching the constitutional issue, Justice Black made some comments on the interpretation of the statute which may bear on his curt dismissal of the commerce clause challenge. He justified a broad reading of "misbranding" because "the chief purpose of forbidding the destruction of the label is to keep it intact for the information and protection of the consumer. That purpose would be frustrated when the pills the consumer buys are not labeled as required, whether the label has been torn from the original container or the pills have been transferred from it to a non-labeled one." He found that the application of the "literal language" of § 301(k) to Sullivan was "thoroughly consistent with the general purposes of the Act. For the Act as a whole was designed primarily to protect consumers from dangerous products." The aim was "to ensure federal protection until the very moment the article is passed into the hands of the consumer by way of an intrastate transaction."

3. Justice Rutledge concurred; Justice Frankfurter, joined by Justices Reed and Jack-

son, dissented on the construction of the Act, without mentioning the constitutional issue.

4. In McDermott, a grocer possessing cans labeled "corn syrup," as required by federal law, was convicted under a Wisconsin law requiring that such cans carry only a "glucose" label. The Court, in reversing the state conviction, stated that "Congress may determine for itself the character of the means necessary to make its purpose effectual in preventing the shipment in interstate commerce of articles of a harmful character, and to this end may provide the means of inspection, examination and seizure necessary. [The] real opportunity for Government inspection may only arise when, as in the present case, the goods as packed have been removed from the outside box in which they were shipped and remain, as the act provides, 'unsold.'" Note that in McDermott, the retailer had received the goods from a wholesaler in another state; and that the holding of the case was to reverse his conviction under a state law found to conflict with a federal act— under the supremacy clause and preemption prin-

3. *Limitless power to regulate economic problems?—The Public Utility Holding Company Act cases.* Although the commerce-prohibiting technique validated in the Darby case has been a particularly favored one for reaching "moral" problems ever since the days of the Lottery Case, it is of course available to deal with matters of genuinely substantial economic significance as well. A series of constitutional challenges to the Public Utility Holding Company Act of 1935 illustrates that usage and raises additional issues as well. In this series of cases, the "affecting commerce" approach occasionally surfaces as an added support for the congressional prohibition of commerce, as indeed it was resorted to as an alternative explanation in Darby itself. Perhaps more surprisingly, the Court's justifications in this series of cases are unusually detailed—more detailed than one might expect if the commerce-prohibiting technique were a virtually self-validating device. In examining these cases, then, consider: To what extent do the decisions rest on commerce-prohibiting techniques of the Lottery Case-Darby variety? To what extent are they independently justified, or justifiable, on "in" commerce or "affecting" commerce grounds? Do these decisions demonstrate that no doctrinal limits on the modern commerce power exist when it is invoked to meet national economic needs?

In Electric Bond & Share Co. v. SEC, 303 U.S. 419 (1938), the Court, with only Justice McReynolds dissenting, sustained provisions compelling registration of holding companies and prohibiting the use of the instrumentalities of commerce (and of the mails) by unregistered companies: "When Congress lays down a valid rule to govern those engaged in transactions in interstate commerce, Congress may deny to those who violate the rule the right to engage in such transactions. [The Lottery Case]." Contrast the fuller explanation in North American Co. v. SEC, 327 U.S. 686 (1946), where the Court unanimously sustained a provision authorizing the SEC to require each holding company engaged in commerce to limit its operations to a single integrated public utility system. Justice Murphy wrote: "he ownership of securities of operating companies [has] a real and substantial relation to the interstate activities of holding companies. [The] broad commerce clause does not operate so as to render the nation powerless to defend itself against economic forces that Congress decrees inimical or destructive to the national economy. Rather it is an affirmative power commensurate with the national needs. It is sufficient to reiterate the well-settled principle that Congress may impose relevant conditions and requirements on those who use the channels of interstate commerce in order that those channels will not become the means of promoting or spreading evil, whether of a physical, moral or economic nature. *This power permits Congress to attack an evil directly at its source, provided that the evil bears a substantial relationship to interstate commerce.* [The] fact that an evil may involve a corporation's financial practices, its business structure or its security portfolio does not detract from the power of Congress under the commerce clause to promulgate rules in order to destroy that evil. Once it is established that the evil concerns or affects commerce in more states than one, Congress may act. [Congress in the Act] was concerned with the economic evils resulting from uncoordinated and unintegrated public utility holding company systems [and] had power under the commerce clause to attempt to remove those evils by ordering the holding companies to divest themselves of the securities that made such evils possible." [Emphasis added.][5]

ciples considered in chap. 5 below. Given those distinguishing circumstances, did Justice Black give undue weight to the McDermott language?

5. Was that stated justification surprisingly detailed, given the Darby rationale? Could the corporate structure be controlled simply as an

implementation of the conditional ban on the use of commerce facilities? Note the italicized sentence. Does that suggest a greater limitation on congressional power than that indicated by the alternative justifications given in Darby?

The opinions in these Public Utility Holding Act cases are favorite sources for broad phrases to support assertions that the modern commerce power is virtually limitless.[6] Yet the limits may be somewhat more substantial than the broad phrases suggest, if the passages are read with a grain of salt and in context. If the commerce power is truly limitless, what explains the extensive Court justifications for uses of the power? Cases disposing of constitutional qualms as curtly as Sullivan are rare. Note that even the generous language in the North American case repeatedly speaks of "*economic* evils" and states that the evil regulated must have a substantial relationship to commerce (not simply that the person or activity reached must have some nexus with commerce, whether or not the evil regulated relates to that nexus).[7]

The problem of reading broad dicta as to the reach of the commerce power with an eye to their particular contexts is not confined to cases focusing on the commerce-prohibiting technique. The widely held view that the modern commerce power is virtually limitless draws support from "affecting commerce" as well as "commerce-prohibiting" cases. Again, some caution against inferring too much from broad judicial statements may be warranted. For example, Wickard, an "affecting commerce" case, is a favorite citation to support assertions of de facto unlimited commerce power. Yet the broad statements in that case, it should be recalled, appear in an opinion articulating at length the factual and theoretical underpinnings for the justification relied on there. And note Justice Harlan's comment in a majority opinion a generation after Wickard, in Maryland v. Wirtz, 392 U.S. 183 (1968), stating: "Neither here nor in Wickard has the Court declared that Congress may use a relatively trivial impact on commerce as an excuse for broad general regulation of state or private activities."[8]

THE COMMERCE POWER AND CRIME: SOME MODERN PROBLEMS

Introduction. Expansion of federal criminal jurisdiction raises some of the most sensitive problems of potential congressional impingement upon the values

6. In addition to the passages quoted above, note American Power & Light Co. v. SEC, 329 U.S. 90 (1946), involving the "death sentence" provision of the Act. Justice Murphy once again wrote for the Court. His opinion included the following passage: "[Congress] has undoubted power under the commerce clause to impose relevant conditions and requirements on those who use the channels of interstate commerce so that those channels will not be conduits for promoting or perpetuating economic evils. [To] deny that Congress has power to eliminate evils connected with pyramided holding company systems [is] to deny that Congress can effectively deal with problems concerning the welfare of the national economy. [The] federal commerce power is as broad as the economic needs of the nation."

7. Consider, as an example of this problem, the issue suggested by Katzenbach v. McClung, p. 165 below: May racial discrimination at a restaurant be prohibited simply because the restaurant has some nexus with commerce (e.g., because it serves mustard produced out-of-state)? Or does the commerce clause require that it is *racial discrimination* (the evil regulated), not simply *any* aspect of the restaurant's operations, that

must have a relationship to interstate commerce? Contrast the statements of Attorney General Kennedy and Assistant Attorney General Marshall in the Senate hearings on the 1964 Civil Rights Act, p. 159 below.

8. Consider also the Five Gambling Devices case, p. 152 below. It is a statutory interpretation case, to be sure. Yet if all the earlier dicta were to be taken at face value, should not the Justices have accepted the Government's view of the reach of the law without difficulty? Do the Justices' opinions suggest lingering constitutional limits on the commerce power? Or is it more realistic to say that any commerce power law able to muster a majority in Congress will be found constitutional by the Court? Note the statement by Justice Jackson (the author of Wickard) in his Gambling Devices opinion: "While general statements, out of these different contexts, might bear upon the subject one way or another, it is apparent that the precise question tendered to us now is not settled by any prior decision." And note his reliance on "the implications and limitations of our federal system" and his sensitivity to "affairs considered normally reserved to the states" when he turned to the statutory interpretation problem.

of federalism. Criminal laws are among the clearest examples of federal regulation of "traditionally local" concerns. Moreover, the substantial economic dimensions of the "evils" regulated are often far less evident in federal criminal legislation than, for example, in the regulatory laws of the New Deal era. The risks of abuse of national power in national criminal statutes were evident as early as the measures directed at gambling and prostitution at the beginning of the century. And the risks persist in the mounting modern resort to the commerce power as the basis for new federal criminal laws, relying both on the "commerce-prohibiting" and "affecting commerce" techniques.

This group of notes examines some of the modern uses of the power. Do they raise serious constitutional problems? Do they risk violating the "spirit" of the Constitution Marshall spoke of in the McCulloch case? Are the modern uses likely to encounter difficulties in the Court? Even if they pass muster in the Court, should members of Congress be troubled by these reliances on the commerce power? If the broad dicta of Darby and Wickard are taken at face value, few if any uses of the commerce power should give any real difficulty to the Court. And there is some evidence that the modern Court's "hands-off" attitude carries over to commerce power-based criminal laws. Yet there are occasional countersignals as well: in the context of statutory interpretation, at least, the Justices sometimes voice misgivings about the expansion of federal criminal jurisdiction.

PEREZ v. UNITED STATES

402 U.S. 146, 91 S.Ct. 1357, 28 L.Ed.2d 686 (1971).

Mr. Justice DOUGLAS delivered the opinion of the Court.

The question in this case is whether Title II of the Consumer Credit Protection Act, as construed and applied to [Perez], is a permissible exercise by Congress of its powers under the Commerce Clause. [Perez] is one of the species commonly known as "loan sharks" which Congress found are in large part under the control of "organized crime."[1] "Extortionate credit transactions" are defined as those characterized by the use or threat of the use of "violence or other criminal means" in enforcement. There was ample evidence showing petitioner was a "loan shark" who used the threat of violence as a method of collection. He loaned money to one Miranda, owner of a new butcher shop, making a $1,000 advance to be repaid in installments of $105 per week for 14 weeks. Perez demanded repayments and regularly increased his demands. Miranda, pressed by the rising demands, sold his butcher shop. Negotiations went on, Miranda finally saying he could only pay $25 a week. [Perez] said that was not enough, that Miranda should steal or sell drugs if necessary to get the money to pay the loan, and that if he went to jail it would be better than going to a hospital with a broken back or [legs]. [Perez was convicted under Title II of the Act.]

---

1. [The Act] contains the following findings by Congress:

"(1) Organized crime is interstate and international in character. Its activities involve many billions of dollars each year. It is directly responsible for murders, willful injuries to person and property, corruption of officials, and terrorization of countless citizens. A substantial part of the income of organized crime is generated by extortionate credit transactions.

"(2) Extortionate credit transactions are characterized by the use, or the express or implicit threat of the use, of violence or other criminal means to cause harm to person, reputation, or property as a means of enforcing [repayment].

"(3) Extortionate credit transactions are carried on to a substantial extent in interstate and foreign commerce and through the means and instrumentalities of such commerce. Even where extortionate credit transactions are purely intrastate in character, they nevertheless directly affect interstate and foreign commerce." [Footnote by Justice Douglas.]

The constitutional question [under the commerce clause] is a substantial one.

Two "loan shark" amendments to the bill that became this Act were proposed in the House. [There] were objections [to these amendments] on constitutional grounds [during the congressional debates]. Congressman Eckhardt of Texas said:

"Should it become law, the amendment would take a long stride by the Federal Government toward occupying the field of general criminal law and toward exercising a general Federal police power; and it would permit prosecution in Federal as well as State courts of a typically State offense. [I] believe that Alexander Hamilton, though a federalist, would be astonished that such a deep entrenchment on the rights of the States in performing their most fundamental function should come from the more conservative quarter of the House."

Senator Proxmire presented to the Senate the Conference Report approving essentially [a] "loan shark" provision suggested in the House, saying:

"Once again these provisions raised serious questions of Federal-State responsibilities. Nonetheless, because of the importance of the problem, the Senate conferees agreed to the House provision. Organized crime operates on a national scale. One of the principal sources of revenue of organized crime comes from loan sharking. If we are to win the battle against organized crime we must strike at [its] source of revenue and give the Justice Department additional tools to deal with the problem. The problem simply cannot be solved by the States alone. We must bring into play the full resources of the Federal Government."

The Commerce Clause reaches, in the main, three categories of problems. First, the use of channels of interstate or foreign commerce which Congress deems are being misused, as, for example, the shipment of stolen goods or of persons who have been kidnaped. Second, protection of the instrumentalities of interstate commerce, as, for example, the destruction of an aircraft, or persons or things in commerce, as, for example, thefts from interstate shipments. Third, those activities affecting commerce. It is with this last category that we are here concerned.

[After quoting from Gibbons v. Ogden, Justice Douglas continued:] Decisions which followed departed from that view; but by the time of [Darby] and the broader view of [Wickard], the Commerce Clause announced by Chief Justice Marshall had been restored. [In Darby], *a class of activities* was held properly regulated by Congress without proof that the particular intrastate activity against which a sanction was laid had an effect on commerce. [Perez] is clearly *a member of the class* which engages in "extortionate credit transactions" as defined by Congress.

It was the "class of activities" test which we employed in [Heart of Atlanta Motel, p. 164 below] to sustain an Act of Congress requiring hotel or motel accommodations for Negro guests. [In] a companion case, Katzenbach v. McClung [p. 165 below], we ruled on the constitutionality of the restaurant provision of the same Civil Rights Act which regulated the restaurant "if [it] serves or offers to serve interstate travelers or a substantial portion of the food which it serves [has] moved in commerce." Apart from the effect on the flow of food in commerce to restaurants, we spoke of the restrictive effect of the exclusion of Negroes from restaurants on interstate travel by Negroes. [In] emphasis of our position that it was the *class of activities* regulated that was the measure, we acknowledged that Congress appropriately considered the "total incidence" of the practice on commerce. Where the *class of activities* is regulated and that *class* is within the reach of federal power, the courts have no power "to excise, as trivial, individual instances" of the class. Maryland v. Wirtz [p. 155 below].

Extortionate credit transactions, though purely intrastate, may in the judgment of Congress affect interstate commerce. [The] findings of Congress are quite adequate on that ground. [The] essence of all [the congressional] reports and hearings was summarized and embodied in formal congressional findings. They supplied Congress with the knowledge that the loan shark racket provides organized crime with its second most lucrative source of revenue, exacts millions from the pockets of people, coerces its victims into the commission of crimes against property, and causes the takeover by racketeers of legitimate businesses.

We have mentioned in detail the economic, financial, and social setting of the problem as revealed to Congress. We do so not to infer that Congress need make particularized findings in order to legislate. We relate the history of the Act in detail to answer the impassioned plea of [Perez] that all that is involved in loan sharking is a traditionally local activity. It appears, instead, that loan sharking in its national setting is one way organized interstate crime holds its guns to the heads of the poor and the rich alike and syphons funds from numerous localities to finance its national operations.

Affirmed.

Mr. Justice STEWART, dissenting.

Congress surely has power under the Commerce Clause to enact criminal laws to protect the instrumentalities of interstate commerce, to prohibit the misuse of the channels or facilities of interstate commerce, and to prohibit or regulate those intrastate activities that have a demonstrably substantial effect on interstate commerce. But under the statute before us a man can be convicted without any proof of interstate movement, of the use of the facilities of interstate commerce, or of facts showing that his conduct affected interstate commerce. I think the Framers of the Constitution never intended that the National Government might define as a crime and prosecute such wholly local activity through the enactment of federal criminal laws.

In order to sustain this law we would, in my view, have to be able at the least to say that Congress could rationally have concluded that loan sharking is an activity with interstate attributes that distinguish it in some substantial respect from other local crime. But it is not enough to say that loan sharking is a national problem, for all crime is a national problem. It is not enough to say that some loan sharking has interstate characteristics, for any crime may have an interstate setting. And the circumstance that loan sharking has an adverse impact on interstate business is not a distinguishing attribute, for interstate business suffers from almost all criminal activity, be it shoplifting or violence in the streets. Because I am unable to discern any rational distinction between loan sharking and other local crime, I cannot escape the conclusion that this statute was beyond the power of Congress to enact. The definition and prosecution of local, intrastate crime are reserved to the States under the Ninth and Tenth Amendments.

CONSTITUTIONAL AND STATUTORY PROBLEMS OF MODERN CRIMINAL LEGISLATION

1. *The implications of Perez.* Is the majority's statement of the commerce power justification in Perez adequate? Consider the comment on Perez by Robert L. Stern, formerly of the Solicitor General's Office and a participant in many Government efforts to apply the commerce power to national economic problems since the 1930s: "Even a lawyer who fought for a realistic interpretation which would recognize that in commercial matters the United States was one nation finds himself surprised at where we are now—and at how readily the recent expansion is accepted. [The] ease with which the public and the

judiciary now swallow the federal regulation of what were once deemed exclusively local matters undoubtedly reflects the general integration of the nation, in disregard of state lines." Stern, "The Commerce Clause Revisited— The Federalization of Intrastate Crime," 15 Ariz.L.Rev. 271 (1973). Note also Stern's suggestion that the "key to [Perez] may be found in the difficulty of proving in each individual case that the loan shark had an interstate connection even when it existed." Stern quotes (as had the Court in Perez) from Westfall v. United States, 274 U.S. 256, 259 (1927): "[W]hen it is necessary in order to prevent an evil to make the law embrace more than the precise thing to be prevented it may do so." Is that remark by Justice Holmes adequate to overcome federalism objections and to authorize all-embracing national regulation of even the local elements of a problem whenever it is "difficult" to prove the interstate elements?

How far-reaching is the Perez rationale?[1] Stern asks: "Can Congress forbid the possession or transfer of all pills, or all white pills, because of the difficulty of distinguishing dangerous pills from others and because some might move interstate?" If that question is answered in the affirmative, does the answer rest on another limitless "bootstrap" principle, subject only to the practical restraint that "Congress is unlikely to interject the federal government into local transactions without good reason"? Recall the "superbootstrap" technique which served as an alternative ground in Darby. Do the materials in the notes that follow suggest that the Court may yet require more of Congress than the conclusory findings in the loan shark statute?[2]

2. *Modern legislation.* Interest in commerce power-based criminal laws received fresh impetus with the widely publicized war on crime that commenced during the 1960s and that continues in the 1980s. Although the modern crime laws occasionally rely on the "affecting commerce" rationale (as in the Perez case), the "commerce-prohibiting" technique continues to be the favorite approach.[3] Consider, for example, the following section of 18 U.S.C., one of several anti-crime provisions enacted in response to Kennedy Administration proposals in 1961. Does it raise substantial constitutional difficulties?[4]

§ 1952. *"Interstate and foreign travel or transportation in aid of racketeering enterprises.*

"(a) Whoever travels in interstate or foreign commerce or uses any facility in interstate or foreign commerce, including the mail, with intent to—

1. Stern draws from Perez the principle that "Congress may regulate local acts which in themselves have no interstate nexus or effect if as a practical matter it is difficult to distinguish such transactions from others which may have some relation to interstate commerce." (Stern describes Perez as "the first case" upholding federal regulation "of a well-defined but possibly overinclusive class of substantive criminal activity on the grounds that in order to exercise effectively the commerce power over an interstate evil, individual acts unconnected with that evil must also be reached.")

2. Note the comment in 49 Tex.L.Rev. 568, 573 (1971): "[W]hile Congress 'finds and declares' that purely intrastate extortionate extensions of credit affect interstate commerce, it fails to specify *how* interstate commerce is affected by those transactions."

3. Use of the "commerce-prohibiting" technique, though somewhat curtailed by the Child Labor Case, never came to a complete halt after its early validation in the Lottery Case. Though early uses of the technique were primarily concerned with harm in the state of destination, harms in the state of origin of the interstate movement have also been included within the sweep of the general technique of using the commerce-prohibiting method for police power objectives. Recall, e.g., the ban on interstate transportation of stolen motor vehicles, sustained in Brooks v. United States in 1925, and the limited ban on shipping convict-made goods, sustained in the Kentucky Whip & Collar case in 1937, as noted above. See also, e.g., the Federal Kidnapping Act, Gooch v. United States, 297 U.S. 124 (1936).

4. Note that the 1960s laws such as this typically included the jurisdictional bases within the definition of the crime. In the more recent efforts to codify the federal criminal laws—efforts that began in the 1970s—that traditional approach has been abandoned. Instead, each substantive section in the modern proposals is typically accompanied by a separate "jurisdictional" provision. Is that abandonment of the traditional approach insensitive to the limited nature of national powers?

"(1) distribute the proceeds of any unlawful activity; or

"(2) commit any crime of violence to further any unlawful activity; or

"(3) otherwise promote, manage, establish, carry on, or facilitate the promotion, management, establishment or carrying on, of any unlawful activity, and thereafter performs or attempts to perform any of the acts specified in subparagraphs (1), (2), and (3), shall be fined not more than $10,000 or imprisoned for not more than five years, or both.

"(b) ['Unlawful activity'] means (1) any business enterprise involving gambling, liquor on which the Federal excise tax has not been paid, narcotics, or prostitution offenses in violation of the laws of the State in which they are committed or of the United States, or (2) extortion, bribery, or arson in violation of the laws of the State in which committed or of the [United States]." [5]

3. *The "implications of the federal system" as a restraint on statutory interpretation.* Though Congress has used the commerce power extensively for criminal legislation and though the Court has been willing to sustain congressional action reaching local activity where congressional purposes are evident (as in Perez), the Court has repeatedly rejected federal prosecutors' efforts to read less clear statutes as reaching deeply into traditionally local domains. Should the federalistic concerns voiced by the Court in these statutory interpretation contexts find their way into constitutional interpretation as well? Should those concerns inhibit legislators faced with new proposals for federal criminal legislation?

a. *The Five Gambling Devices case.* UNITED STATES v. FIVE GAMBLING DEVICES, 346 U.S. 441 (1953), involved the interpretation of the "incidental registration and reporting provisions" of a 1951 statute prohibiting shipment of gambling machines in interstate commerce. The information-eliciting provisions of the law were applicable to "every manufacturer and dealer in gambling devices"; they were not expressly limited to persons with some nexus to interstate commerce. The case involved three companion proceedings: two criminal indictments, and one libel to forfeit several gambling machines seized by the FBI in a country club in Tennessee. The Government argued that the statute should be applied according to its literal terms, without any requirement that the particular activities be shown to have any relationship to interstate commerce. As to constitutional justification, the Government argued that, "to make effective the prohibition of transportation in interstate commerce, Congress may constitutionally require reporting of all intrastate transactions." In a 5 to 4 decision, the Court affirmed the dismissals of all the proceedings on statutory grounds.

The case is of special interest because all of the Justices who commented on the commerce power issue found the hovering constitutional problems substantial. The most intriguing opinion is that in support of the majority result by Justice JACKSON, joined by Justices Frankfurter and Minton. Under a broad reading of the "super-bootstrap" analysis in the Darby case, the Government's "regulate-the-local-activity-as-a-means-of-implementing-the-interstate-prohibition" argument should have been persuasive. And Justice Jackson, the writer of Wickard, had been identified with very broad statements about the commerce power. Against that background, the constitutional doubts in this case are especially notable.

On the constitutional issue, Justice Jackson commented: "We do not intimate any ultimate answer to the appellees' constitutional questions other than to observe that they cannot be dismissed as frivolous, nor as unimportant to the

---

5. The format of the Kennedy Administration's anti-racketeering law apparently inspired the pattern of the anti-riot amendments in the Civil Rights Act of 1968. Thus, the 1968 law, 18 U.S.C. § 2101, after opening with a phrase virtually identical to that in § 1952, prohibited travel or use of interstate commerce facilities to "incite a riot" and related activities. Contrast another provision of the 1968 Civil Rights Act (the "Civil Obedience Act"), which, in criminalizing activities risking "civil disorders," reflected greater reliance on the "affecting commerce" rather than the "commerce-prohibiting" technique. See 18 U.S.C. § 231.

nature of our federation. No precedent of this Court sustains the power of Congress to enact legislation penalizing failure to report information concerning acts not shown to be in, or mingled with, or found to affect commerce." What about the alternative, "super-bootstrap" theory of Darby? Justice Jackson's caveat may be applicable to that theory as well as to other broad dicta: "While general statements, out of these different contexts, might bear upon the subject one way or another, it is apparent that the precise question tendered to us now is not settled by any prior decision."

Rather than resolving the constitutional question, Justice Jackson construed the statute narrowly to avoid problems of constitutionality. And in his statutory interpretation, federalism concerns again played a role: "We do not question that literal language of this Act is capable of the broad, unlimited construction urged by the Government. [But] we must assume that the implications and limitations of our federal system constitute a major premise of all congressional legislation, though not repeatedly recited therein. Against the background of our tradition and system of government, we cannot say that the lower courts, which have held as a matter of statutory construction that this Act does not reach purely intrastate matters, have not made a permissible interpretation. We find in the text no unmistakable intention of Congress to raise the constitutional questions implicit in the Government's effort to apply the Act in its most extreme impact upon affairs considered normally reserved to the states." [6]

b. *The Gambling Devices approach in the 1970s.* Several decisions in the early 1970s adhered to the Five Gambling Devices approach of rejecting, because of federalism considerations, broad Government interpretations of new criminal statutes. But more recently, the Court has seemed more ready to accept interpretations applying statutes in borderline areas.

For example, in United States v. Bass, 404 U.S. 336 (1971), Justice Marshall's majority opinion reversed a conviction for possession of firearms in violation of a provision of the Omnibus Crime Control and Safe Streets Act of 1968, which applies to any person convicted of a felony "who receives, possesses, or transports in interstate commerce or affecting commerce [any] firearm." There had been no showing that defendant's firearms were commerce-related. The prosecution claimed that the commerce limitations in the law applied only to "transports" and that possession and receipt were punishable without showing a connection with commerce. The Court disagreed: "Because its sanctions are criminal, and because, under the Government's broader reading, the statute would mark a major inroad into a domain traditionally left to the States, we refuse to adopt the broad reading in the absence of a clearer direction

---

6. Justice Jackson noted, too, that supporters of the bill had emphasized that the law was not intended to displace state law enforcement. Yet "here it was the [FBI] which entered a country club and seized slot machines not shown ever to have had any connection with interstate commerce. [If] this is not substituting federal for state enforcement, it is difficult to know how it could be accomplished. [These] cases, if sustained, would substantially take unto the Federal Government the entire pursuit of the gambling device."

Justice CLARK, joined by Chief Justice Warren and Justices Reed and Burton, dissented; but even Justice Clark recognized that the constitutional issue was not a trivial one. He thought the information-eliciting requirements justifiable as "reasonably necessary, appropriate and probably essential means for enforcing the ban on interstate transportation of gambling devices."

But he conceded that his conclusion was "not inevitably dictated by prior decisions of the Court." He noted, too, that the information requirements as to local transactions were "certainly not a mere ruse designed to invade areas of control reserved to the states," but were "naturally and reasonably adapted to the effective exercise of" the commerce power. Moreover, he emphasized that Congress had not "sought to *regulate* local activity": in such a case, "its power would no doubt be less clear." He thought the distinction between obtaining information and "regulating" a "substantial" one. [Has the distinction become less "substantial" since 1953? Recall the sustaining of a "regulatory" criminal law in Perez in 1971.] Justice BLACK, joined by Justice Douglas, concurred in the result because of the vagueness of the reporting provisions, without reaching the commerce power issue.

from Congress. [U]nless Congress conveys its purpose clearly, it will not be deemed to have significantly changed the federal-state balance." [7]

Several years later, however, the majority adopted a broad construction of a federal criminal law in the face of federalistic concerns, in Scarborough v. United States, 431 U.S. 563 (1977). That case involved the very provision regarding possession of firearms that had been at issue in Bass. In Bass, the Government had made no effort at all to demonstrate a connection with commerce. In Scarborough, the Government did make a minimal effort to demonstrate a commerce nexus, and it proved enough to satisfy the Court. The Government showed only that the firearms had once moved in commerce; it did not attempt to show that the defendant had obtained them after his felony conviction. But that showing, the Court found, was "sufficient to satisfy the statutorily required nexus between the possession of the firearms by a convicted felon and commerce." The Court did recognize that the strict statutory construction approach of Bass mandated "caution where the federal-state balance is implicated." But it found no occasion to invoke that principle here, because the statute's meaning seemed clear rather than ambiguous.

MODERN USES OF THE "AFFECTING COMMERCE" RATIONALE: A FURTHER LOOK AT PRACTICAL AND THEORETICAL LIMITS

Introduction. The preceding groups of notes focused primarily on contemporary problems regarding invocations of the "commerce-prohibiting" technique, in noneconomic contexts. This final group of notes returns to the "affecting commerce" approach of the line of cases culminating in Wickard v. Filburn,[1] and to regulations with primarily economic rather than "police" objectives. When these techniques and subjects of regulation are involved, what, if any, limits to the reach of the modern commerce power can be identified? The first note calls attention to restraints in congressional exercises of power. The second note provides some illustrative examples of recent congressional uses of the power and asks whether any approaches the constitutional boundaries. The concluding materials return once more to the problem of judicially imposable limitations: e.g., can preferred "affecting commerce" rationales be rejected as resting on too insubstantial a nexus between the local and the interstate?[2]

1. *Statutory reach short of constitutional limits.* As the scope of the commerce power has expanded, the actual range of national control has increasingly come to turn on congressional choices rather than constitutional limits. But the fact that Congress chooses not to go as far as the Constitution permits does not make constitutional doctrines irrelevant. Thus, as the Five Gambling Devices case illustrated, constitutional limits affect statutory interpretation. Moreover, just as Congress has not in fact entered all areas of potential control, it frequently does not go to the constitutional limit in the areas actually regulated. Accordingly, the statutory coverage formula often raises the central issue in drafting and interpreting modern commerce clause regulations. Compare, for example, the broad "affecting commerce" formula in the National Labor Relations Act (in Jones & Laughlin) with the narrower scope of the Fair Labor Standards Act (in Darby) as to employees engaged "in the production of goods for commerce."

---

7. For other cases following the Bass approach, see Rewis v. United States, 401 U.S. 808 (1971), and United States v. Enmons, 410 U.S. 396 (1973).

1. Recall, however, that the "affecting commerce" approach surfaced even in the context of

modern federal criminal legislation—e.g., in Perez.

2. Many of the questions raised throughout this chapter recur in a particularized context in the next section, on the public accommodations provisions of the Civil Rights Act of 1964.

2. *Modern legislation using the "affecting commerce" technique.*   Do the following provisions in 21 U.S.C. press "affecting commerce" justifications too far, in view of the scope of the commerce power in cases such as Wickard?

a. *Drugs.*

§ 360 [Added in 1962]. *"Registration of drug producers. . . .*

"(b) On or before December 31 of each year every person who owns or operates any establishment in any State engaged in the manufacture, preparation, propagation, compounding, or processing of a drug or drugs shall register with the Secretary his name, places of business and all such establishments." [3]

b. *Oleomargarine.*

§ 347 [added in 1950]. *"Intrastate sales of colored oleomargarine—Law governing.*

"(a) Colored oleomargarine or colored margarine which is sold in the same State or Territory in which it is produced shall be subject in the same manner and to the same extent to the provisions of this chapter as if it had been introduced in interstate commerce. . . .

"(c) No person shall possess in a form ready for serving colored oleomargarine or colored margarine at a public eating place unless a notice that oleomargarine or margarine is served is displayed prominently and conspicuously in such place and in such manner as to render it likely to be read and understood by the ordinary individual being served in such eating place or is printed or is otherwise set forth on the menu in type or lettering not smaller than that normally used to designate the serving of other food items. . . .

§ 347a. *"Congressional declaration of policy regarding oleomargarine sales.*

"The Congress finds and declares that the sale, or the serving in public eating places, of colored oleomargarine or colored margarine without clear identification as such or which is otherwise adulterated or misbranded within the meaning of this chapter depresses the market in interstate commerce for butter and for oleomargarine or margarine clearly identified and neither adulterated nor misbranded, and constitutes a burden on interstate commerce in such articles. Such burden exists, irrespective of whether such oleomargarine or margarine originates from an interstate source or from the State in which it is sold."

c. *The significance of congressional findings.*   What is the significance of congressional findings, such as those in the preceding laws?   Are they significant in congressional consideration?   In constitutional litigation?   Are they useful in Court adjudication?   Necessary?   Determinative? [4]

3. *Potential limits on the commerce power: "Trivial" economic impacts?   State autonomy?*   Coverage of the Fair Labor Standards Act was extended by two amendments in the 1960s.   Constitutional challenges to these 1961 and 1966 amendments first came to the Court in MARYLAND v. WIRTZ, 392 U.S. 183 (1968).   The Court sustained both amendments.   The case cast important light on the contemporary availability of both the "trivial impacts" and the "state autonomy" defenses to applications of commerce clause regulations.[5]   Maryland v. Wirtz continues to be good law with respect to the existence and application

---

3. Public Law 87–781, which included 21 U.S.C. § 360, stated: "The Congress hereby finds and declares that in order to make regulation of interstate commerce in drugs effective, it is necessary to provide for registration and inspection of all establishments in which drugs are manufactured, prepared, [or] processed; that the products of all such establishments are likely to enter the channels of interstate commerce and directly affect such commerce; and that the regulation of interstate commerce in drugs without provision for registration and inspection of establishments that may be engaged only in intrastate commerce in such drugs would discriminate against and depress interstate commerce in such drugs, and adversely burden, obstruct, and affect such interstate commerce."

4. Recall the passage in Perez (p. 148 above), where Justice Douglas stated, in a tenor quite characteristic of the modern Court, that he was not inferring "that Congress need make particularized findings in order to legislate," yet nevertheless related "the history of the Act in detail" in resolving the constitutional issue. (Note also the discussion and disposition of the problem raised by the legislative record in the consideration of the public accommodations provisions of the Civil Rights Act of 1964, in the next section.)

5. Note also, as another potential limit, the occasional advocacy of special judicial scrutiny when Congress seeks to regulate a "historically local" field. Recall that Hamilton suggested such a limit as early as 1791 (p. 85 above). Similar arguments have surfaced recurrently

of the "trivial impacts" defense. But the decision's rejection of the "state autonomy" defense did not stand up: eight years later, in National League of Cities (p. 170 below), that aspect of the Wirtz case was overruled.

a. *"Trivial impacts."* The 1961 amendment considered in Wirtz dealt with a major traditional concern of the FLSA, employees in *private* industry. Prior to the amendment, coverage was limited to employees "engaged in commerce or in the production of goods for commerce." The 1961 extension included every employee who "is employed in an enterprise engaged in commerce or in the production of goods for commerce." In effect, that amendment extended protection "to the fellow employees of any employee who would have been protected by the original Act." Justice HARLAN's majority opinion found this "enterprise concept" constitutionally justified on alternative grounds: either under the original "unfair competition" theory of Darby or on the Jones & Laughlin "labor dispute" theory. In the course of his opinion, Justice Harlan asserted continuing limits on "affecting commerce" theories by stating: "We uphold the enterprise concept on the explicit premise that an 'enterprise' is a set of operations whose activities in commerce would all be expected to be affected by the wages and hours of any group of employees, which is what Congress obviously intended. So defined, the term is quite cognizant of limitations on the commerce power. Neither here nor in Wickard has the Court declared that Congress may use a relatively trivial impact on commerce as an excuse for broad general regulation of state or private activities. The Court has said only that where a general regulatory statute bears a substantial relation to commerce, the de minimis character of individual instances arising under that statute is of no consequence." [6]

b. *State autonomy.* A different variety of limitation was suggested in response to the 1966 amendment to the FLSA, which applied the Act to employees of *state*-operated schools and hospitals. The Wirtz majority upheld that application against charges of interference with the autonomy of the operations of state government. Justice HARLAN's majority opinion found the argument that the Act interfered with "sovereign state functions" untenable. Justice DOUGLAS' dissent, joined by Justice Stewart, thought the majority's position "unexceptionable" as "an exercise in semantics" if "congressional federalism is the standard," but insisted that "what is done here is nonetheless such a serious invasion of state sovereignty protected by the Tenth Amendment that it is in my belief not consistent with our constitutional federalism." In 1974, Congress amended the Fair Labor Standards Act once again, this time removing almost all of the remaining special exemptions of employees of state governmental units. Once again, the statute was challenged on state autonomy grounds. This time the challenge succeeded: the state autonomy theme voiced by Justice Douglas' dissent in Wirtz prevailed; the state employees' aspect of Wirtz was overruled; and, for the first time in four decades, a law of Congress based on the commerce clause was held unconstitutional on federalistic grounds.

since. Note, e.g., Justice Douglas' dissent, joined by Justice Whittaker, in United States v. Oregon, 366 U.S. 643 (1961), where the majority sustained a law providing for the vesting in the United States of the property of an intestate veteran. Justice Douglas commented: "[W]hen the Federal Government enters a field as historically local as the administration of decedents' estates, some clear relation of the asserted power to one of the delegated powers should be shown. At times the exercise of delegated power reaches deep into local problems. Wickard v. Filburn. But there is no semblance of likeness here. The need of the Government to enter upon the administration of veterans' estates [is] no crucial

phase of the ability of the United States to care for ex-service men and women or to manage federal fiscal affairs. Today's decision does not square with our conception of federalism. [I] do not see how a scheme for administration of decedents' estates of the kind we have here can possibly be necessary and proper to any power delegated to Congress."

6. Note also Justice Rehnquist's comment in his concurrence in Hodel (p. 177 below): "[T]here *are* constitutional limits on the [commerce power]. [E.g., our] cases have consistently held that the regulated activity must have a *substantial* effect on interstate commerce."

This 1976 decision, National League of Cities v. Usery, is printed in sec. 7 below, and the current dimensions of the state autonomy barrier as announced in the 1976 ruling and elaborated in several later decisions are explored there. Before turning to that section, consider the modern limits on congressional regulation of the *private* sector in the late-20th century context of efforts to curb racial discrimination in public accommodations, examined in the next section.

SECTION 6. THE COMMERCE POWER AND RACIAL DISCRIMINATION: THE CIVIL RIGHTS ACT OF 1964

Introduction. This section pursues the question raised in the preceding materials by examining the use of the commerce power in a particular context: the controversial invocation of the power for the purpose of banning racial discrimination in public accommodations. The focus here is on congressional consideration and judicial scrutiny of Title II of the Civil Rights Act of 1964. Excerpts from the hearings and the text of the statute precede the Court decisions on its constitutionality and scope. The legislative deliberations illustrate some of the problems of selecting appropriate constitutional bases and drafting adequate statutory coverage formulas. In examining the hearings, consider especially the legislators' independent obligations to consider constitutionality as well as policy in their lawmaking roles. These excerpts remind that constitutional discussions are not an exclusive judicial function in our system of government. And the Court decisions sustaining the legislation raise anew the problems of acceptable rationales and potential limits in the exercise of the power to regulate interstate commerce.

This section also serves as a preview of constitutional problems in congressional civil rights legislation—a subject pursued more fully in later chapters. Congressional action to protect civil rights has been sporadic. After a period of intensive activity during Reconstruction, from 1866 to 1875, Congress was virtually silent for over three-quarters of a century. A revival of legislative productivity began with the Civil Rights Act of 1957. Most federal civil rights laws have been based on the post-Civil War Amendments. (Congressional authority under those Amendments is the focus of chap. 10.) But, as the 1964 Act illustrates, Art. I, § 8, may also provide authority for legislation to protect civil rights. The title of the Act [1] reflects not only the wide-ranging content of the law but also the varied sources of power invoked: there is reference not only to the commerce but also to the spending power in Art. I, § 8; there is also reference to legislative power under the 14th and 15th Amendments. But it is the portion of the legislation based on the commerce power that is the special concern here.

---

1. The 1964 legislation is entitled: "An Act to enforce the constitutional right to vote, to confer jurisdiction upon the district courts of the United States to provide injunctive relief against discrimination in public accommodations, to au- thorize the Attorney General to institute suits to protect constitutional rights in public facilities and public education, [to] prevent discrimination in federally assisted programs, [and] for other purposes." Pub.L. 88–352, 78 Stat. 241.

A. THE COVERAGE OF THE STATUTE

TITLE II—INJUNCTIVE RELIEF AGAINST DISCRIMINATION IN PLACES OF PUBLIC ACCOMMODATION [2]

Sec. 201. (a) All persons shall be entitled to the full and equal enjoyment of the goods, services, facilities, privileges, advantages, and accommodations of any place of public accommodation, as defined in this section, without discrimination or segregation on the ground of race, color, religion, or national origin.

(b) Each of the following establishments which serves the public is a place of public accommodation within the meaning of this title if its operations affect commerce, or if discrimination or segregation by it is supported by State action:

(1) any inn, hotel, motel, or other establishment which provides lodging to transient guests, other than an establishment located within a building which contains not more than five rooms for rent or hire and which is actually occupied by the proprietor of such establishment as his residence;

(2) any restaurant, cafeteria, lunchroom, lunch counter, soda fountain, or other facility principally engaged in selling food for consumption on the [premises]; or any gasoline station;

(3) any motion picture house, theater, concert hall, sports arena, stadium or other place of exhibition or entertainment; and

(4) any establishment (A)(i) which is physically located within the premises of any establishment otherwise covered by this subsection, or (ii) within the premises of which is physically located any such covered establishment, and (B) which holds itself out as serving patrons of such covered establishment.

(c) The operations of an establishment affect commerce within the meaning of this title if (1) it is one of the establishments described in paragraph (1) of subsection (b); (2) in the case of an establishment described in paragraph (2) of subsection (b), it serves or offers to serve interstate travelers or a substantial portion of the food which it serves, or gasoline or other products which it sells, has moved in commerce; (3) in the case of an establishment described in paragraph (3) of subsection (b), it customarily presents films, performances, athletic teams, exhibitions, or other sources of entertainment which move in commerce; and (4) in the case of an establishment described in paragraph (4) of subsection (b), it is physically located within the premises of, or there is physically located within its premises, an establishment the operations of which affect commerce within the meaning of this [subsection].

(d) Discrimination or segregation by an establishment is supported by State action within the meaning of this title if such discrimination or segregation (1) is carried on under color of any law, statute, ordinance, or regulation; or (2) is carried on under color of any custom or usage required or enforced by officials of the State or political subdivision thereof; or (3) is required by action of the State or political subdivision thereof. [See chap. 10, below.]

(e) The provisions of this title shall not apply to a private club or other establishment not in fact open to the public, except to the extent that the facilities of such establishment are made available to the customers or patrons of an establishment within the scope of subsection (b).

Sec. 202. All persons shall be entitled to be free, at any establishment or place, from discrimination or segregation of any kind on the ground of race, color, religion, or national origin, if such discrimination or segregation is or purports to be required by any law, statute, ordinance, regulation, rule, or order of a State or any agency or political subdivision thereof.

Sec. 203. No person shall (a) withhold, deny, or attempt to withhold or deny, or deprive or attempt to deprive, any person of any right or privilege secured by section 201 or 202, or (b) intimidate, threaten, or coerce, or attempt to intimidate, threaten, or coerce any person with the purpose of interfering with any right or privilege secured by section 201 or 202, or (c) punish or attempt to punish any person for exercising or attempting to exercise any right or privilege secured by section 201 or 202. [Sec. 204 provides for private civil relief; Sec. 205, for civil actions by the Attorney General in certain cases.]

---

2. The text printed here follows the numbering in Pub.L. 88–352, 78 Stat. 241. See also the renumbered version, 42 U.S.C. §§ 2000a–2000a–6.

B. THE CONGRESSIONAL DELIBERATIONS

Introduction. Consideration of the proposals that became the 1964 Act produced extensive hearings before several committees, and lengthy debates on the floor of both houses of Congress. Constitutional issues were discussed exhaustively. The selections that follow are from hearings in the early stages of the process, before the Senate Commerce Committee in July and August 1963.[3] The Committee had before it the Kennedy Administration's proposal on discrimination in public accommodations. Before the Administration bill was submitted to Congress in late June, it was widely reported that it would rely solely on the commerce clause.[4] Examine the coverage provisions of Title II in light of the concerns expressed during the hearings. Note the reluctance of some Senators to utilize the commerce clause rather than the Fourteenth Amendment. Was there basis for that reluctance in the Constitution or in the Court's decisions? Should a Senator be concerned even if the Court's decisions left the matter doubtful—or should that issue be left to the Court? Suppose a legislator has no doubts that a commerce clause-based law would be sustained by the courts. May the legislator nevertheless claim that it is the lawmaker's right, or duty, to consider questions of constitutional "propriety" in casting his vote?[5]

Note that the bill as enacted omitted the recital of findings. Were Senator Monroney's statements about the importance of findings justified? Was there merit in Senator Magnuson's position on the respective roles of Congress and Court in determining the reach of the commerce clause? Note the significant differences regarding the scope of the commerce power between the views of Attorney General Kennedy and of Assistant Attorney General Marshall. Whose view was more justifiable on the basis of the materials in this chapter?

THE SENATE COMMITTEE HEARINGS, 1963

MR. [ROBERT F.] KENNEDY [ATTORNEY GENERAL]. [We] base this on the commerce clause which I think makes it clearly constitutional. In my personal judgment, basing it on the 14th amendment would also be constitutional. [I] think that there is argument about the 14th amendment basis—going back to the 1883 Supreme Court decision [Civil Rights Cases, 109 U.S. 3, p. 860 below], and the fact that this is not State action—that therefore Congress would not have the right under the 14th amendment to pass any legislation dealing with it. [Senator], I think that there is an injustice that needs to be remedied. We have to find the tools with which to remedy that injustice. [There] cannot be any legitimate question about the commerce clause. That is clearly constitutional. We need to obtain a remedy. The commerce clause will obtain a remedy and there won't be a problem about the [constitutionality].

SENATOR MONRONEY [DEM., OKLA.]. [Mr.] Attorney General, I think most of the members of this committee are sincerely in agreement with your strong plea for the elimination of discrimination. I think most of them would like to have legislation that could achieve this end instantly and totally. But many of us are worried about the use

---

3. Hearings Before the Senate Committee on Commerce on S. 1732, 88th Cong., 1st Sess., parts 1 and 2.

4. As introduced, the bill included references to the Fourteenth Amendment as well, but the commerce power focus predominated: for example, the proposed title was "Interstate Public Accommodations Act"; the introductory series of findings dealt almost entirely with commerce; the commerce emphases, and the afterthought nature of the Fourteenth Amendment reliance, were highlighted by the final "finding" that the "burdens on and obstructions to commerce which are described above can best be removed by invoking the powers of Congress under the Fourteenth Amendment and the commerce clause of the Constitution"; and the coverage

provisions were entirely in commerce terms. (Section 201(d) of the Act, on discrimination "supported by State action," was added subsequently, during the congressional consideration of the bill.) Note the Gunther comments made at the time when the proposal rested solely on the commerce power, printed below, after the excerpts from the hearings.

5. See generally Morgan, Congress and the Constitution (1966), and Brest, "The Conscientious Legislator's Guide to Constitutional Interpretation," 27 Stan.L.Rev. 585 (1975). (For further examination of the constitutional difficulties in the Fourteenth Amendment approach—and the relevance of the Thirteenth Amendment—see chap. 10 below.)

the interstate commerce clause will have on matters which have been for more than 170 years thought to be within the realm of local control under our dual system of State and Federal Government. [Is] the test whether the line of business has a substantial effect on interstate commerce? Lodgings are covered, if they are public, and transients are served. Does that mean that all lodging houses under your theory of the effect on interstate commerce would be under Federal regulation, regardless of whether the transients that were using the lodgings were intrastate or interstate?

MR. KENNEDY. That is correct. If it is a lodging, a motel, that opens its doors to the general public, invites the general public, then it would be [covered].

SENATOR MONRONEY. [If] we pass this bill, even though the end we seek is good, I wonder how far we are stretching the [Constitution].

MR. KENNEDY. The point I would make, Senator, is that we are not going beyond any principle of the use of the commerce clause that has not already been clearly established, which has been passed in this Congress, and which has been ruled on by the courts. We are not stretching the [commerce clause].

SENATOR MONRONEY. I grant you that I can see ample evidence under all the historic interpretations of the interstate commerce clause that the Hilton hotel chain is in interstate commerce, that your national food stores are in interstate commerce, that your variety stores which have lunch counters are in interstate commerce. [I] think Congress does have the right to regulate those businesses under the commerce clause, because they operate in many States. But I find it rather difficult to stretch the clause to cover an eating place simply because some of its meat moves from one State into another; or because the vegetables they serve come from Florida; or the oranges come from [California].

MR. KENNEDY. What I am saying is that there is precedent for passing this kind of legislation. With these precedents and with the great need that exists, the legislation should be as inclusive as possible, as long as it doesn't affect a personal or social [relationship].

SENATOR MONRONEY. I strongly doubt that we can stretch the Interstate Commerce Clause that far. [Under] your summary of the court's actions, there would hardly be any field of business [that] is exempt from Federal [regulation].

MR. KENNEDY. No, I didn't say that, Senator. That is not my [point].

SENATOR MONRONEY. I am trying to get it straight. I am not trying to misinterpret you. If the court decisions and all the precedents that you have mentioned [mean] that a business, no matter how intrastate in its nature, comes under the interstate commerce clause, then we can legislate for other businesses in other fields in addition to the discrimination legislation that is asked for here.

MR. KENNEDY. If the establishment is covered by the commerce clause, then you can regulate; that is [correct].[6]

THE CHAIRMAN [SENATOR MAGNUSON, DEM., WASH.]. I think we ought to get this in perspective. Congress doesn't determine what is under the interstate commerce clause. The Constitution and court decisions determine that. [We] are talking about how far you want to go [in] a particular field with a bill. [Whether] a business is in interstate commerce or not is a question of the interpretation of the Constitution and of the courts' rules in these [matters].

SENATOR THURMOND [DEM. (later REP.), S.C.]. [Isn't] it true that all of the acts of Congress based on the commerce clause which you have mentioned [were] primarily designed to regulate economic affairs of life and that the basic purpose of this bill is to regulate moral and social affairs?

MR. KENNEDY. Well, Senator, let me say this: I think that the discrimination that is taking place at the present time is having a very adverse effect on our economy. So I think that it is quite clear that under the commerce clause even if it was just on that aspect and even if you get away from the moral aspect—I think it is quite clear that this kind of discrimination has an adverse effect on the economy. I think all you have to do is look at some of the southern communities at the present time and the difficult time that they are having.

6. Compare the testimony by Assistant Attorney General Marshall, below, and the following paragraph in a memorandum on the constitutionality of Title II subsequently submitted by the Justice Department and printed in an appendix to the Hearings (part II, at p. 1296):

"Of course, there are limits on congressional power under the Commerce Clause. It may be conceded that Congress does not hold the power to regulate all of a man's conduct solely because he has relationship with interstate commerce. What is required is that there be a relationship between interstate commerce and the evil to be regulated. Over the course of the years, various tests have been established for determining whether this relationship exists. The proposed legislation clearly meets these tests."

SENATOR THURMOND. And you would base this bill on the economic features rather than the social and moral aspect?

MR. KENNEDY. I think the other is an extremely important aspect of it that we should keep in [mind].

SENATOR THURMOND. Now how could the denial of services to an individual [who] has no intention of leaving that State be a burden on interstate commerce?

MR. KENNEDY. Because we are talking about a cumulative situation here, Senator. It is not just an individual. If this was just an individual situation and there was one restaurant or one motel or one hotel, we wouldn't all be sitting here today. What this is is a general practice, and a practice that has existed for many, many, many years. What we are trying to do is to get at that general practice. The cumulative effect of a number of establishments which take in transients, and some of which would be interstate, some of which would be intrastate—the cumulative effect of all these has a major effect on interstate commerce. That is the theory, and it is a theory that has been borne out in a number of decisions. And I suppose the best known is [Wickard], where the man just ran his own wheat [farm].

SENATOR THURMOND. What does "substantial" [mean]?

MR. KENNEDY. I don't think you can have any mathematical precision and a cutoff line. There has been a good deal of legislation that has been passed by Congress [where] you have expressions such as this. What is "interstate commerce"? Even if you didn't have "substantial," Senator, how would you be able to define it? You can't define, with mathematical precision, "interstate commerce." [But] I think you could work it out in the individual [case].

SENATOR THURMOND. I am just trying to find out what, so a fellow would know, for instance, if he got three-fourths of his business from interstate travelers, would he be covered by this bill?

MR. KENNEDY. I would think he [would].

SENATOR THURMOND. And only 30 percent was interstate; [covered]?

MR. KENNEDY. [It] probably would. But I think it would depend somewhat where the [business] was established and perhaps a number of other [factors].

SENATOR THURMOND. Twenty percent?

MR. KENNEDY. Again, I think it would depend on other factors.

SENATOR THURMOND. What other factors?

MR. KENNEDY. Was he near an airport, Senator? I don't know.

SENATOR THURMOND. What difference does it make whether he is near an airport or 10 miles from the airport if 20 percent of his business came from out of State? Would he have to serve them?

MR. KENNEDY. I think these other factors play a role in it, Senator—whether an establishment deals with those in interstate commerce. That would be a factor you would have to take into consideration. I would say that perhaps it very well might be covered. But I think that [he] wouldn't have any problem if he wouldn't [discriminate].

SENATOR MONRONEY. I would like to ask the Attorney General for the purpose of the record to give us the effect in law, if any, of [the "Findings"]. This is the ordinary preamble of the bill, is it not; and would not have any effect before the courts in determining the scope of the law? [The] Court, whatever it decided on the scope of the interstate commerce clause, [would] base its decision on the other sections of the bill, and this is merely, I guess, what the Court would call obiter dicta.

MR. KENNEDY. That is [correct].

THE CHAIRMAN [MAGNUSON]. When you use the commerce clause for a social objective there is plenty of precedent for that, too. We did that in the Mann Act; we did that in the Pinball Act, and the gambling regulations for social reasons. [It] is a matter of public policy. The commerce clause is there. We can't stretch it, restrict it, or do anything with it. It is there. The Constitution will not change unless we have a constitutional [amendment].

SENATOR COOPER [REP., KY.]. I do not suppose that anyone would seriously contend that the administration is proposing legislation [because] it has suddenly determined [that] segregation is a burden on interstate commerce. We are considering legislation because we believe [that] all citizens have an equal right to have access to goods, services, and facilities which are held out to be available for public use and patronage. If there is a right to the equal use of accommodations held out to the public, it is [a] constitutional right under the 14th amendment. It has nothing to do with whether a business is in interstate commerce or whether discrimination against individuals places a burden on commerce. It does not depend upon the commerce clause and cannot be limited by that clause, in my [opinion]. If we are going to deal with this question of the use of public accommodations, I think it imperative that Congress should enact legislation which would meet it fully and squarely as a right under the 14th amendment, and not indirectly and partially as the administration's approach would do. Rights under the Constitution apply to all citizens, and the integrity and dignity of the individual should not be placed on lesser grounds such as the [commerce clause].

MR. [BURKE] MARSHALL [ASSISTANT ATTORNEY GENERAL, CIVIL RIGHTS DIVISION]. [Let] me dispel at the outset a possible misconception concerning the scope of [the bill]. We do not propose to regulate the businesses covered merely because they are engaged in some phase of interstate commerce. Discrimination by the establishments covered in the bill should be prohibited because it is that discrimination itself which adversely affects interstate commerce. Section 2 of the bill describes in detail the effect of racial discrimination on national commerce. Discrimination burdens Negro interstate travelers and thereby inhibits interstate travel. It artificially restricts the market available for interstate goods and services. It leads to the withholding of patronage by potential customers for such goods and services. It inhibits the holding of conventions and meetings in segregated cities. It interferes with businesses that wish to obtain the services of persons who do not choose to subject themselves to segregation and discrimination. And it restricts business enterprises in their choice of location for offices and plants, thus preventing the most effective allocation of national resources. Clearly, all of these are burdens on interstate commerce and they may therefore be dealt with by the [Congress].

SENATOR PASTORE [DEM., R.I.]. [I] believe in this bill, because I believe in the dignity of man, not because it impedes our [commerce]. Now, it might well be that I can effect the same remedy through the commerce clause. But I like to feel that what we are talking about is a moral issue, an issue that involves the morality of this great country of ours. And that morality, it seems to me, comes under the 14th amendment, where we speak about immunities and where we speak about equal protection of the law. I would like to feel that the [Court] is given another chance to review it, not under the commerce clause, but under the 14th amendment. [Do] you see anything wrong in that?

MR. MARSHALL. Senator, I think it would be a mistake to rely solely on the 14th amendment. This [bill] relies on the 14th amendment, and also relies on the commerce clause. I think it is plainly constitutional. I think if it relied solely on the 14th amendment, it might not be held constitutional. I think it would be a disservice to pass a bill that was later thrown out by the [Court].

SENATOR PASTORE. I am not being critical of you. I am merely stating my own position. I am saying we are being a little too careful, cagey, and cautious, in debating this question of the 14th amendment. I realize you should bring all of the tools at your disposal and that is what you are [doing].

THE CHAIRMAN [MAGNUSON]. [What] is in interstate commerce? As a matter of public policy, we may all come to the conclusion you wouldn't want to put this under that authority. But there is no use of us here belaboring the point of what the interstate commerce clause includes, how far it may or may not extend, because it is written.

MR. JAMES J. KILPATRICK [JOURNALIST]. [S]ir, this is your primary obligation before it ever hits that court, to make that judgment, to bring to bear on it all the thought, power, energy, and intellect that you can to make the primary decision as to whether it is or is not [constitutional].

MR. [BRUCE] BROMLEY [N.Y. ATTORNEY; FORMER JUDGE, N.Y. COURT OF APPEALS]. [I] concede that Congress does not hold the power to regulate all of a man's conduct solely because he has at some time in the past imported goods in interstate commerce. And I not only concede, I assert there must be some connection between interstate commerce and the evil to be [regulated].

SENATOR MONRONEY. [I] am still troubled on the interstate commerce clause. There are no restrictions on what we can rule to be in interstate commerce. [Is] there any cutoff place—not just on bias, but on regulation, on policing powers of industry, corporate and otherwise—that the Federal Government would have? I always presumed [that] there were certain definite limits beyond which we couldn't go in controlling matters which were intrastate in nature.

MR. BROMLEY. My dear Senator, I think there are plainly limits. Let's just take a very simple one. You can't apply this law to a little barber shop whose activities have no substantial effect on interstate commerce. And you can't apply it in any area [unless] you are dealing with some activity which is either in the stream of commerce or has a substantial effect [upon] commerce. I don't see, sir, why that worries you in the slightest.

———

SOME COMMENTS FROM THE SIDELINES

a.   *Gunther.*   Consider the following excerpts from a letter by the author of this book to the Department of Justice, dated June 5, 1963—several weeks before the Senate hearings printed above, and two weeks before the submission of the Administration bill to Congress, while the Administration's reported proposals still rested solely on the commerce power. Was there substance to the concerns expressed? Were all bases for concern removed by the testimony ultimately presented to Congress, as reflected in the Supreme Court opinions in Heart of Atlanta and McClung, below?

"I was happy to note that the Administration has put off for a few days the submission of its new civil rights proposals to Congress. I hope that the additional time will permit the Justice Department to reexamine its reported decision to rely exclusively on the commerce clause. [My] basic difficulties with the proposal in light of our constitutional structure may be briefly stated. If a federal ban on discrimination in such businesses as stores and restaurants is to be enacted, it should rest on the obviously most relevant source of national power, the Fourteenth Amendment, rather than the tenuously related commerce clause. The proposed end run by way of the commerce clause seems to me [ill-advised].

"Let me elaborate somewhat: I know of course that the commerce power is a temptingly broad one. But surely responsible statutory drafting should have a firmer basis than, for example, some of the loose talk in recent newspaper articles about the widely accepted, unrestricted availability of the commerce clause to achieve social ends. Some qualifications seem in order. Thus, most of the obviously 'social' laws, as with lottery and prostitution legislation, have their immediate impact on the interstate movement and rest on the power to prohibit that movement. Most 'social' laws are not directly aimed at intrastate affairs, are not attempts to regulate internal activities as such. Where immediate regulations of intrastate conduct have been imposed, a demonstrable economic effect on interstate commerce [has] normally been required. That kind of showing has been made, for example, with regard to the control of 'local' affairs in the labor relations and agricultural production fields. The commerce clause 'hook' has been put to some rather strained uses in the past, I know; but the substantive content of the commerce clause would have to be drained beyond any point yet reached to justify the simplistic argument that all intrastate activity may be subjected to any kind of national regulation merely because some formal crossing of an interstate boundary once took place, without regard to the relationship between the aim of the regulation and interstate trade. The aim of the proposed anti-discrimination legislation, I take it, is quite unrelated to any concern with national commerce in any substantive sense.

"It would, I think, pervert the meaning and purpose of the commerce clause to invoke it as the basis for this legislation. And the strained use now suggested for the commerce power cannot even be justified by the argument that a national problem exists in an area to which the Constitution does not address itself. The Fourteenth Amendment, after all, [specifically] focuses on the problem of racial discrimination; and the fifth section of the Amendment as well as the Necessary and Proper Clause speak to congressional power to enforce it. [I] would much prefer to see the Government channel its resources of ingenuity and advocacy into the development of a viable interpretation of the Fourteenth Amendment, the provision with a natural linkage to the race problem. That would seem to me a considerably less demeaning task than the construction of an artificial commerce facade; and it would carry the incidental benefit of giving the Department the opportunity to aid the Supreme Court in the fashioning of a more adequate rationale for the modern scope of the Fourteenth Amendment than is now apparent in this much criticized area of constitutional [law]."

b.   *Wechsler.*   Compare a passage from a July 18, 1963, letter by Professor Herbert Wechsler to the Chairman of the Senate Commerce Committee:

"I should add that I see nothing fictive in the proposition that the practices to which the measure is directed may occur in or affect 'the commerce that concerns more States than one' or, even more plainly, may occur, as the Taft-Hartley Act requires, in an industry which affects such commerce. There are, in fact, effects upon such matters as the free movement of individuals and goods across State lines, the level of demand for products of the national market and the freedom of enterprises engaged in interstate commerce to abandon the restrictions that some of their local competitors may impose.

To legislate within the area of such effects on commerce seems to me to fall within the great tradition of the Congress in the exercise of this explicit power."

C. THE COURT DECISIONS

HEART OF ATLANTA MOTEL v. UNITED STATES

379 U.S. 241, 85 S.Ct. 348, 13 L.Ed.2d 258 (1964).

Mr. Justice CLARK delivered the opinion of the Court.

This is a declaratory judgment [action] attacking the constitutionality of Title II of the Civil Rights Act of 1964. [Appellant owns] and operates the Heart of Atlanta Motel which has 216 rooms available to transient guests. The motel is located on Courtland Street, two blocks from downtown Peachtree Street. It is readily accessible to interstate highways 75 and 85 and state highways 23 and 41. Appellant solicits patronage from outside [Georgia] through various national advertising [media]; it maintains over 50 billboards and highway signs within [Georgia]; it accepts convention trade from outside Georgia and approximately 75% of its registered guests are from out of State. Prior to passage of the Act the motel had followed a practice of refusing to rent rooms to Negroes, and it alleged that it intended to continue to do so. [The District Court sustained the Act.] The sole question [is] the constitutionality of [the Act] as applied to these facts.

The Senate Commerce Committee made it quite clear that the fundamental object of Title II was to vindicate "the deprivation of personal dignity that surely accompanies denials of equal access to public establishments." At the same time, however, it noted that such an objective has been and could be readily achieved "by congressional action based on the commerce power of the Constitution." Our study of the legislative record, made in the light of prior cases, has brought us to the conclusion that Congress possessed ample power in this regard, and we have therefore not considered the [Fourteenth Amendment] grounds relied upon.

[While] the Act as adopted carried no congressional findings the record of its passage through each house is replete with evidence of the burdens that discrimination by race or color places upon interstate commerce. [This] testimony included the fact that our people have become increasingly mobile with millions of all races traveling from State to State; that Negroes in particular have been the subject of discrimination in transient accommodations, having to travel great distances to secure the same; that often they have been unable to obtain accommodations and have had to call upon friends to put them up overnight; [and] that these conditions had become so acute as to require the listing of available lodging for Negroes in a special guidebook which was itself "dramatic testimony of the difficulties" Negroes encounter in travel. [We] shall not burden this opinion with further details since the voluminous testimony presents overwhelming evidence that discrimination by hotels and motels impedes interstate travel [both in impairing "the Negro traveler's pleasure and convenience" and in "discouraging travel on the part of a substantial portion of the Negro community"].

[The] determinative test of the exercise of power by the Congress under the Commerce Clause is simply whether the activity sought to be regulated is "commerce which concerns more States than one" and has a real and substantial relation to the national interest. [The] same interest in protecting interstate commerce which led Congress to deal with segregation in interstate carriers and the white slave traffic has prompted it to extend the exercise of its power to gambling; to criminal enterprises; to deceptive practices in the sale of products; to fraudulent security transactions; to misbranding of drugs; to wages and hours; to members of labor unions; to crop control; to discrimination against shippers; to the protection of small business from injurious price cutting; to resale price maintenance; to professional football; and to racial discrimination by owners and managers of terminal restaurants. That Congress was legislating against moral wrongs in many of these areas rendered its enactments no less valid. In framing [Title II] Congress was also dealing with what it considered a moral problem. But that fact does not detract from the overwhelming evidence of the disruptive effect that racial discrimination has had on commercial intercourse. It was this burden which empowered Congress to enact appropriate legislation, and given this basis for the exercise of its power, Congress was not restricted by the fact that the particular obstruction to interstate commerce with which it was dealing was also deemed a moral and social wrong.

It is said that the operation of the motel here is of a purely local character. But, assuming this to be true, "if it is interstate commerce that feels the pinch, it does not matter how local the operation that applies the squeeze." [Thus] the power of Congress to promote interstate commerce also includes the power to regulate the local incidents thereof, including local activities in both the States of origin and destination, which might have a substantial and harmful effect upon that commerce. One need only examine the evidence which we have discussed above to see that Congress may—as it has—prohibit racial discrimination by motels serving travelers, however "local" their operations may appear.

[We], therefore, conclude that the action of the Congress in the adoption of the Act as applied here to a motel which concededly serves interstate travelers is within the power granted it by the Commerce Clause of the Constitution, as interpreted by this Court for 140 [years].

Affirmed.[1]

KATZENBACH v. McCLUNG

379 U.S. 294, 85 S.Ct. 377, 13 L.Ed.2d 290 (1964).

Mr. Justice CLARK delivered the opinion of the Court.

This case was argued with [Heart of Atlanta Motel]. This complaint for injunctive relief [attacks] the constitutionality of the [Civil Rights Act of 1964] as applied to a restaurant. [A]n injunction was issued restraining appellants from enforcing the Act against the restaurant. [We reverse.]

Ollie's Barbecue is a family-owned restaurant in Birmingham, Alabama, specializing in barbecued meats and homemade pies, with a seating capacity of 220 customers. It is located on a state highway 11 blocks from an interstate one and a somewhat greater distance from railroad and bus stations. The restaurant caters to a family and white-collar trade with a take-out service for Negroes. It employs 36 persons, two-thirds of whom are Negroes. In the 12 months preceding the passage of the Act, the restaurant purchased locally approximately $150,000 worth of food, $69,683 or 46% of which was meat that it bought from a local supplier who had procured it from outside the State. The District Court expressly found that a substantial portion of the food served in the restaurant had moved in interstate commerce. The restaurant has refused to serve Negroes in its dining accommodations since its original opening in 1927,

---

1. Excerpts from the concurring opinions of Justices Black, Douglas and Goldberg—applicable to this case and to McClung, which follows— appear below, after the majority opinion in Mc-Clung.

and since July 2, 1964, it has been operating in violation of the Act. The court below concluded that if it were required to serve Negroes it would lose [substantial business].[1]

Sections 201(b)(2) and (c) place any "[restaurant] principally engaged in selling food for consumption on the premises" under the Act "if [it] serves or offers to serve interstate travelers or a substantial portion of the food which it serves [has] moved in commerce." Ollie's Barbecue admits that it is covered by these provisions of the Act. The Government makes no contention that the discrimination at the restaurant was supported by the State of Alabama. There is no claim that interstate travelers frequent the restaurant. The sole question, therefore, narrows down to whether Title II, as applied to a restaurant receiving about $70,000 worth of food which has moved in commerce, is a valid exercise of the power of Congress. The Government has contended that Congress had ample basis upon which to find that racial discrimination at restaurants which receive from out of state a substantial portion of the food served does, in fact, impose commercial burdens of national magnitude upon interstate commerce. The appellees' major argument is directed to this premise. They urge that no such basis existed.

[As] we noted in Heart of Atlanta Motel both Houses of Congress conducted prolonged hearings on the Act. [W]hile no formal findings were made, which of course is not necessary, it is well that we make mention of the testimony at these hearings the better to understand the problem before Congress and determine whether the Act is a reasonable and appropriate means toward its solution. The record is replete with testimony of the burdens placed on interstate commerce by racial discrimination in restaurants. A comparison of per capita spending by Negroes in restaurants, theaters, and like establishments indicated less spending, after discounting income differences, in areas where discrimination is widely practiced. This condition, which was especially aggravated in the South, was attributed in the testimony of the Under Secretary of Commerce to racial segregation. [This] diminutive spending springing from a refusal to serve Negroes and their total loss as customers has, regardless of the absence of direct evidence, a close connection to interstate commerce. The fewer customers a restaurant enjoys the less food it sells and consequently the less it buys. [In] addition, the Attorney General testified that this type of discrimination imposed "an artificial restriction on the market" and interfered with the flow of merchandise. [In] addition, there were many references to discriminatory situations causing wide unrest and having a depressant effect on general business conditions in the respective communities.

[Moreover] there was an impressive array of testimony that discrimination in restaurants had a direct and highly restrictive effect upon interstate travel by Negroes. This resulted, it was said, because discriminatory practices prevent Negroes from buying prepared food served on the premises while on a trip, except in isolated and unkempt restaurants and under most unsatisfactory and often unpleasant conditions. This obviously discourages travel and obstructs interstate commerce for one can hardly travel without eating. Likewise, it was said that discrimination deterred professional, as well as skilled, people from moving into areas where such practices occurred and thereby caused industry to be reluctant to establish there.

[We] believe that this testimony afforded ample basis for the conclusion that established restaurants in such areas sold less interstate goods because of the

---

1. As summarized by Justice Clark, the District Court had concluded that Congress "had legislated a conclusive presumption that a restaurant affects interstate commerce [if it] offers to serve interstate travelers or if a substantial portion of the food which it serves has moved in commerce. This, the [lower] court held, it could not do because there was no demonstrable connection between food purchased in interstate commerce and sold in a restaurant and the conclusion of Congress that discrimination in the restaurant would affect that commerce."

discrimination, that interstate travel was obstructed directly by it, that business in general suffered and that many new businesses refrained from establishing there as a result of it. Hence the District Court was in error in concluding that there was no connection between discrimination and the movement of interstate commerce. The court's conclusion that such a connection is outside "common experience" flies in the face of stubborn fact.

It goes without saying that, viewed in isolation, the volume of food purchased by Ollie's Barbecue from sources supplied from out of state was insignificant when compared with the total foodstuffs moving in commerce. But, as our late Brother Jackson said [in] Wickard: [quoting Justice Jackson's "aggregation" passage]. [We] noted in Heart of Atlanta that a number of witnesses attested to the fact that racial discrimination was not merely a state or regional problem but was one of nationwide scope. Against this background, we must conclude that while the focus of the legislation was on the individual restaurant's relation to interstate commerce, Congress appropriately considered the importance of that connection with the knowledge that the discrimination was but "representative of many others throughout the country, the total incidence of which if left unchecked may well become far-reaching in its harm to commerce." With this situation spreading as the record shows, Congress was not required to await the total dislocation of commerce. [Much] is said about a restaurant being local but "even if appellee's activity be local and though it may not be regarded as commerce, it may still, whatever its nature, be reached by Congress if it exerts a substantial economic effect on interstate commerce." [Wickard.]

The appellees contend that Congress has arbitrarily created a conclusive presumption that all restaurants meeting the criteria set out in the Act "affect commerce." Stated another way, they object to the omission of a provision for a case-by-case determination—judicial or administrative—that racial discrimination in a particular restaurant affects commerce. But Congress' action in framing this Act was not unprecedented. [Here, as in Darby], Congress has determined for itself that refusals of service to Negroes have imposed burdens both upon the interstate flow of food and upon the movement of products generally. Of course, the mere fact that Congress has said when particular activity shall be deemed to affect commerce does not preclude further examination by this Court. But where we find that the legislators, in light of the facts and testimony before them, have a rational basis for finding a chosen regulatory scheme necessary to the protection of commerce, our investigation is at an end. The only remaining question—one answered in the affirmative by the court below—is whether the particular restaurant either serves or offers to serve interstate travelers or serves food a substantial portion of which has moved in interstate commerce. The appellees urge that Congress, in passing the Fair Labor Standards Act and the National Labor Relations Act, made specific findings which were embodied in those statutes. Here, of course, Congress has included no formal findings. But their absence is not fatal to the validity of the statute, [for] the evidence presented at the hearings fully indicated the nature and effect of the burdens on commerce which Congress meant to alleviate.

Confronted as we are with the facts laid before Congress, we must conclude that it had a rational basis for finding that racial discrimination in restaurants had a direct and adverse effect on the free flow of interstate commerce. [We think] that Congress acted well within its power to protect and foster commerce in extending the coverage of Title II only to those restaurants offering to serve interstate travelers or serving food, a substantial portion of which has moved in interstate commerce. The absence of direct evidence connecting discriminatory restaurant service with the flow of interstate food, a factor on which the appellees place much reliance, is not, given the evidence as to the effect of such practices on other aspects of commerce, a crucial matter. [The Act], as here applied, we find to be plainly appropriate in the resolution of what the Congress found to be a national commercial problem of the [first magnitude].

Reversed.[2]

Mr. Justice DOUGLAS, concurring.

[Though] I join the Court's opinions, I am somewhat reluctant here, as I was in Edwards v. California, 314 U.S. 160, 177 [p. 315 below], to rest solely on the Commerce Clause. My reluctance is not due to any conviction that Congress lacks power to regulate commerce in the interests of human rights. It is rather my belief that the right of people to be free of state action that discriminates against them because of race, like the "right to persons to move freely from State to State," "occupies a more protected position in our constitutional system than does the movement of cattle, fruit, steel and coal across state lines." [The] result reached by the Court is for me much more obvious as a protective measure under the Fourteenth Amendment than under the Commerce Clause. For the former deals with the constitutional status of the individual not with the impact on commerce of local activities or vice versa. [A] decision based on the Fourteenth Amendment would have a more settling effect, making unnecessary litigation over whether a particular restaurant or inn

---

2. Does the application of Title II to Ollie's Barbecue rest on persuasive commerce power justifications? Does the statutory coverage formula adequately mesh with the constitutional rationale? Does McClung persuasively link restaurant discrimination with the interstate flow of food? Is it more persuasive in linking restaurant discrimination with obstruction of interstate travel? Were more persuasive commerce power rationales available? Recall the comments after Perez (p. 148 above): Could the McClung decision be justified on the ground that regulation of intrastate discrimination is necessary because of the difficulty of distinguishing discrimination which affects interstate commerce from that which does not? Would that rationale be inconsistent with proper federalistic restraints? Could Congress have relied on the "superbootstrap" commerce-prohibiting technique—e.g., by prohibiting the shipment of interstate goods to racially discriminatory restaurants, and then banning local restaurant discrimination as a means to implement that interstate prohibition? Recall the comments after Darby, p. 138 above.

In a concurring opinion in McClung, Justice BLACK stated that not "every remote, possible, speculative effect on commerce" should be accepted "as an adequate constitutional ground to uproot and throw into the discard all our traditional distinctions between what is purely local [and] what affects the national interest." He insisted, moreover, that "some isolated and remote lunchroom which sells only to local people and buys almost all its supplies in the locality may possibly be beyond the reach of the [commerce] power of Congress." But here, "we do not consider the effect on interstate commerce of only one isolated, individual, local event, without regard to the fact that this single local event when added to many others of a similar nature may impose a burden on interstate commerce by reducing its volume or distorting its flow." Relying on the "aggregation" theory of Wickard, he

found the application of the Act valid under the commerce power and therefore found it unnecessary to consider whether it was also "constitutionally supportable under section 5 of the Fourteenth Amendment."

But five years later, in Daniel v. Paul, 395 U.S. 298 (1969), Justice Black was the sole dissenter when the Court upheld the Act as applied to the Lake Nixon Club near Little Rock, Arkansas. The club was a "232-acre amusement area with swimming, boating, sun bathing, picnicking, miniature golf, dancing facilities and a snack bar." Justice Brennan's majority opinion found the snack bar to be a covered public accommodation under §§ 201(a)(2) and 201(c)(2). That status automatically brought the entire establishment within the Act, under §§ 201(b)(4) and 201(c)(4). The snack bar, he found, was covered under either criterion of § 201(c)(2): it offered "to serve interstate travelers"; and "a substantial portion of the food served [there had] moved in interstate commerce."

Justice Black's dissent stated that he would have agreed with the result if the 1964 Act had been based on § 5 of the Fourteenth Amendment. But, since Congress had "tied the Act and limited its protection" to the commerce power, a finding was required that the Club's operation "affect commerce" within the meaning of § 201(c); and to him, the lower courts' fact findings did not support application of the Act here. He objected to extending coverage of the Act to "this country people's recreation center, lying in what may be, so far as we know, a little 'sleepy hollow' between Arkansas hills miles away from any interstate highway. This would be stretching the Commerce Clause so as to give the Federal Government complete control over every little remote country place of recreation in every nook and cranny of every precinct and county in every one of the 50 States. This goes too far for me."

is within the commerce definitions of the Act or whether a particular customer is an interstate traveler. [While] I agree with the Court that Congress in fashioning the present Act used the Commerce Clause to regulate racial segregation, it also used (and properly so) some of its power under § 5 of the Fourteenth Amendment. [Our] decision should be based on the Fourteenth Amendment, thereby putting an end to all obstructionist strategies and allowing every person—whatever his race, creed, or color—to patronize all places of public accommodation without discrimination whether he travels interstate or intrastate.[3]

SECTION 7. STATE AUTONOMY AS A LIMIT ON THE COMMERCE POWER: THE IMPACT AND FATE OF NATIONAL LEAGUE OF CITIES

Introduction. With the National League of Cities decision in 1976 (which follows), the state autonomy barrier to congressional regulation seemed to gain new vitality. But the approach that produced the first holding in 40 years that a federal law exceeded congressional powers did not prevail in a series of cases in the early 1980s. The four dissenters in National League of Cities were in the majority in all of the cases of the early 1980s. And the holding in National League of Cities itself may prove to be short-lived: at the end of its 1983–84 Term, the Court ordered reargument in a case—GARCIA v. SAN ANTONIO METRO. TRANSIT AUTH.—with a specific request to the parties to address the issue of whether "the principles of the Tenth Amendment as set forth in [National League of Cities] should be reconsidered."[1] Nevertheless, attention to National League of Cities and its progeny is warranted here, both to examine the merits of the contending positions in this series of cases and to consider the persuasiveness and judicial enforceability of the recurrent state autonomy theme in commerce power litigation.[2]

---

3. In a separate concurrence, Justice GOLDBERG joined the Court's opinions in both cases but added that he "would underscore" that the primary purpose of the 1964 Act was "the vindication of human dignity and not mere economics." He added that Congress "clearly had authority under both § 5 of the Fourteenth Amendment and the Commerce Clause" to enact the law.

1. The Garcia case challenged the application of the Fair Labor Standards Act to a public transit authority. In late February 1985, shortly after the cutoff date for this edition, the Court handed down Garcia. Justice Blackmun's majority opinion in the 5 to 4 decision announced that National League of Cities "is overruled." Chief Justice Burger and Justices Powell, Rehnquist, and O'Connor dissented.

The opinions in Garcia will appear in the 1985 Supplement. Any subsequent elaborations and modifications of Garcia will appear in subsequent Supplements to this edition. That Garcia and its overruling of a less-than-a-decade-old case may itself prove not to be a wholly stable precedent, especially in view of expected personnel changes on the Court, is hinted at in the dissenting opinions of Justices Rehnquist and O'Connor in Garcia. Thus, Justice Rehnquist commented: "I do not think it incumbent on those of us in dissent to spell out further the fine points of a principle that will, I am confident, in time again command the support of a majority of this Court." In any event, whether or not Garcia survives unaltered in the near future, the materials in this section on National League of Cities and its elaborations continue to warrant examination, both because of the problems of federalism they address and because of the background they provide for a study of the justifiability of the Garcia ruling.

2. This series of cases, all arising under the commerce clause, also cast added light on the modern scope of the "affecting commerce" rationale. In each case, the Court found that the requirements of that rationale were satisfied; but some of the Justices nevertheless went on to insist that structural implications of the federal system reflected in the Tenth Amendment and in notions of state autonomy barred application of the federal law.

NATIONAL LEAGUE OF CITIES v. USERY

426 U.S. 833, 96 S.Ct. 2465, 49 L.Ed.2d 245 (1976).

[The original Fair Labor Standards Act of 1938, upheld in Darby, specifically excluded the states from its coverage. In 1974, however, in the culmination of a series of broadening amendments, Congress extended the Act to cover employees of state and local governments. The District Court sustained the validity of the 1974 amendments, even though it thought the state autonomy challenge "substantial," stating that it felt "obliged to apply the Wirtz opinion (p. 155 above) as it stands."]

Mr. Justice REHNQUIST delivered the opinion of the Court.

[The congressional commerce power] over areas of private endeavor [has] been held to be limited only by the requirement that "the means chosen by [Congress] must be reasonably adapted to the end permitted by the Constitution." Appellants in no way challenge these decisions establishing the breadth of authority granted Congress. [Their] contention, on the contrary, is that when Congress seeks to regulate directly the activities of States as public employers, it transgresses an affirmative limitation on the exercise of its power akin to other commerce power affirmative limitations contained in the Constitution. Congressional enactments which may be fully within the grant of legislative authority contained in the Commerce Clause may nonetheless be invalid because found to offend against [the Sixth and Fifth Amendments]. Appellants' essential contention is that the 1974 amendments to the Act, while undoubtedly within the scope of the Commerce Clause, encounter a similar constitutional barrier because they are to be applied directly to the States and subdivisions of States as employers.

This Court has never doubted that there are limits upon the power of Congress to override state sovereignty, even when exercising its otherwise plenary powers to tax or to regulate commerce. [In] Wirtz, for example, the Court took care to assure the appellants that it had "ample power to [prevent] 'the utter destruction of the State as a sovereign political entity,'" which they feared. [In Fry v. United States, 421 U.S. 542 (1975)],[1] the Court recognized that an express declaration of this limitation is found in the Tenth Amendment: "While the Tenth Amendment has been characterized as a 'truism,' stating merely that 'all is retained which has not been surrendered,' United States v. Darby, it is not without significance. The Amendment expressly declares the constitutional policy that Congress may not exercise power in a fashion that impairs the States' integrity or their ability to function effectively in a federal system."

[These recent expressions] trace back to earlier decisions of this Court recognizing the essential role of the States in our federal system of government. [The Government] argues that the cases in which this Court has upheld sweeping exercises of authority by Congress, even though those exercises preempted state regulation of the private sector, have already curtailed the sovereignty of the States quite as much as the [1974 amendments]. We do not agree. It is one thing to recognize the authority of Congress to enact laws regulating individual businesses necessarily subject to the dual sovereignty of the government of the Nation and of the State in which they reside. It is quite another to uphold a similar exercise of congressional authority directed not to

---

1. The Fry case, decided a year before National League of Cities, was the first modern signal of a growing sensitivity on the Court to federalistic limits. Although the Court sustained the application of temporary federal wage controls to state employees, Justice Marshall's ma-jority opinion was a narrow one. He emphasized that the federal action was an emergency measure of limited scope and that it did not appreciably intrude upon state sovereignty. Fry is discussed further in the opinions in this case.

private citizens, but to the States as States. We have repeatedly recognized that there are attributes of sovereignty attaching to every state government which may not be impaired by Congress, not because Congress may lack an affirmative grant of legislative authority to reach the matter, but because the Constitution prohibits it from exercising the authority in that manner. In Coyle v. Smith, 221 U.S. 559 (1911), the Court gave this example of such an attribute: "The power to locate its own seat of government and to determine when and how it shall be changed from one place to another, and to appropriate its own public funds for that purpose, are essentially and peculiarly state [powers]."

One undoubted attribute of state sovereignty is the States' power to determine the wages which shall be paid to those whom they employ in order to carry out their governmental functions, what hours those persons will work, and what compensation will be provided where these employees may be called upon to work overtime. The question we must resolve in this case, then, is whether these determinations are "functions essential to separate and independent existence" [Coyle] so that Congress may not abrogate the States' otherwise plenary authority to make them.

In their complaint appellants advanced estimates of substantial costs which will be imposed upon them by the 1974 amendments. Since the District Court dismissed their complaint, we take its well-pleaded allegations as true, although it appears from appellee's submissions [that] resolution of the factual disputes as to the effect of the amendments is not critical to our disposition of the case. Judged solely in terms of increased costs in dollars, these allegations show a significant impact on the functioning of the governmental bodies involved. [California, for example,] which must devote significant portions of its budget to fire suppression endeavors, estimated that application of the Act to its employment practices will necessitate an increase in its budget of between $8 million and $16 million.

Increased costs are not, of course, the only adverse effects which compliance with the Act will visit upon state and local governments, and in turn upon the citizens who depend upon those governments. [F]or example, California asserted that it could not comply with the overtime costs (approximately $750,000 per year) which the Act required to be paid to California Highway Patrol cadets during their academy training program. California reported that it had thus been forced to reduce its academy training program from 2,080 hours to only 960 hours, a compromise undoubtedly of substantial importance to those whose safety and welfare may depend upon the preparedness of the [California Highway Patrol].

Quite apart from the substantial costs imposed upon the States and their political subdivisions, the Act displaces state policies regarding the manner in which they will structure delivery of those governmental services which their citizens require. The Act, speaking directly to the States *qua* States, requires that they shall pay all but an extremely limited minority of their employees the minimum wage rates currently chosen by Congress. It may well be that as a matter of economic policy it would be desirable that States, just as private employers, comply with these minimum wage requirements. But it cannot be gainsaid that the federal requirement directly supplants the considered policy choices of the States' elected officials and administrators as to how they wish to structure pay scales in state employment. The State might wish to employ persons with little or no training, or those who wish to work on a casual basis, or those who for some other reason do not possess minimum employment requirements, and pay them less than the federally prescribed minimum wage. It may wish to offer part time or summer employment to teenagers at a figure less than the minimum wage, and if unable to do so may decline to offer such employment at all. But the Act would forbid such choices by the States. The only "discretion" left to them under the Act is either to attempt to increase their revenue to meet the additional financial burden imposed upon them by paying congressionally prescribed wages to their existing complement of employees, or to reduce that complement to a number which can be paid the federal minimum wage without increasing revenue.

This dilemma presented by the minimum wage restrictions may seem not immediately different from that faced by private employers, who have long been covered by the Act and who must find ways to increase their gross income if they are to pay higher wages while maintaining current earnings. The difference, however, is that a State is not merely a factor in the "shifting economic arrangements" of the private sector of the economy, but is itself a coordinate element in the system established by the framers for governing our federal union.

The degree to which the FLSA amendments would interfere with traditional aspects of state sovereignty can be seen even more clearly upon examining the overtime requirements of the Act. The general effect of these provisions is to require the States to pay their employees at premium rates whenever their work exceeds a specified number of hours in a given period. The asserted reason for these provisions is to provide a financial disincentive upon using employees beyond the work period deemed appropriate by Congress. [We] do not doubt that this may be a salutary result, and that it has a sufficiently rational relationship to commerce to validate the application of the overtime provisions to private employers. But, like the minimum wage provisions, the vice of the Act as sought to be applied here is that it directly penalizes the States for choosing to hire governmental employees on terms different from those which Congress has sought to impose. This congressionally imposed displacement of state decisions may substantially restructure traditional ways in which the local governments have arranged their affairs. [The] requirement imposing premium rates upon any employment in excess of what Congress has decided is appropriate for a governmental employee's workweek, for example, appears likely to have the effect of coercing the States to structure work periods in some employment areas, such as police and fire protection, in a manner substantially different from practices which have long been commonly accepted among local governments of this Nation.

[Our] examination of the effect of the [1974 amendments] satisfies us that both the minimum wage and the maximum hour provisions will impermissibly interfere with the integral governmental functions of these bodies. We do not think that particularized assessments of actual impact are crucial, [because the application of the amendments will] significantly alter or displace the States' abilities to structure employer-employee relationships in such areas as fire prevention, police protection, sanitation, public health, and parks and recreation. [I]t is functions such as these which governments are created to provide, services such as these which the States have traditionally afforded their citizens. If Congress may withdraw from the States the authority to make those fundamental employment decisions upon which their systems for performance of these functions must rest, we think there would be little left of the States' "separate and independent existence." [Coyle].[2] Thus, [the] dispositive factor is that

---

2. Can the preceding few sentences (or Justice Rehnquist's opinion generally) be read as supporting an interpretation of National League of Cities that emphasizes the claims of individuals against government rather than the state-federal balance? That is the suggestion in Tribe, American Constitutional Law (1978), 313. Tribe argues that the opinion may be read "to suggest the existence of protected expectations—of rights—to basic government services." He claims that congressional legislation that "endangers the provision of certain vital services, unlike similar legislation directed only at private parties or at government services usually provided only privately, is constitutionally problematic not because it strikes an unacceptable balance between national and state interests as such, but because it hinders and may even foreclose attempts by

Congress has attempted to exercise its Commerce Clause authority to prescribe minimum wages and maximum hours to be paid by the States in their capacities as sovereign governments. In so doing, Congress has sought to wield its power in a fashion that would impair the States' "ability to function effectively within a federal system." [Fry.] This exercise of congressional authority does not comport with the federal system of government embodied in the Constitution. We hold that insofar as the challenged amendments operate to directly displace the States' freedom to structure integral operations in areas of traditional governmental functions, they are not within the authority granted Congress by Art. I, § 8, cl. 3.[3]

One final matter requires our attention. Appellee has vigorously urged that we cannot, consistently with the Court's decisions in Wirtz and Fry, rule against him here.

[We] think our holding today quite consistent with Fry. The enactment at issue there [the Economic Stabilization Act of 1970, temporarily freezing the wages of state and local government employees,] was occasioned by an extremely serious problem which endangered the well-being of all the component parts of our federal system and which only collective action by the National Government might forestall. The means selected were carefully drafted so as not to interfere with the States' freedom beyond a very limited, specific period of time. The effect of the across-the-board freeze authorized by that Act, moreover, displaced no state choices as to how governmental operations should be structured nor did it force the States to remake such choices themselves. Instead, it merely required that the wage scales and employment relationships which the States themselves had chosen be maintained during the period of the emergency. Finally, the Economic Stabilization Act operated to reduce the pressures upon state budgets rather than increase them. These factors distinguish the statute in Fry from the provisions at issue here. The limits imposed upon the commerce power when Congress seeks to apply it to the States are not so inflexible as to preclude temporary enactments tailored to combat a national emergency.

[With] respect to the Court's decision in Wirtz, we reach a different conclusion. [There] are undoubtedly factual distinctions between the two situations, but in view of the conclusions expressed earlier in this opinion we do not believe the reasoning in Wirtz may any longer be regarded as authoritative. Wirtz relied heavily on the Court's decision in United States v. California, 297 U.S. 175 (1936). The opinion quotes the following language from that case: " '[We] look to the activities to which the states have traditionally engaged as marking the boundary of the restriction upon the federal taxing power. But there is no such limitation upon the plenary power to regulate commerce. The State can no more deny the power if its exercise has been authorized by Congress than can an individual.' " But we have reaffirmed today that the States as States stand on a quite different footing than an individual or a

states or localities to meet their citizens' legitimate expectations of basic government services." See also Tribe, "Unravelling National League of Cities: The New Federalism and Affirmative Rights to Essential Government Services," 90 Harv.L.Rev. 1065 (1977), and Michelman, "States' Rights and States' Roles: The Permutations of 'Sovereignty' in National League of Cities v. Usery," 86 Yale L.J. 1165 (1977). (For other claims of affirmative constitutional rights to essential governmental services, resting on the equal protection clause rather than on interpretations of National League of Cities, see chap. 9, sec. 4, below.)

3. We express no view as to whether different results might obtain if Congress seeks to affect integral operations of state governments by exercising authority granted it under other sections of the Constitution such as the Spending Power, Art. I, § 8, cl. 1, or § 5 of the Fourteenth Amendment. [Footnote by Justice Rehnquist.] [In a virtually contemporaneous opinion, Justice Rehnquist sustained the power of Congress to reach the states under § 5 of the Fourteenth Amendment. Fitzpatrick v. Bitzer, 427 U.S. 445 (1976)].

corporation when challenging the exercise of Congress' power to regulate commerce. We think the dicta[4] from United States v. California simply wrong.[5] Congress may not exercise that power so as to force directly upon the States its choices as to how essential decisions regarding the conduct of integral governmental functions are to be made. We agree that such assertions of power, if unchecked, would indeed, as Mr. Justice Douglas cautioned in his dissent in Wirtz, allow "the National Government [to] devour the essentials of state sovereignty," and would therefore transgress the bounds of the authority granted Congress under the Commerce Clause. While there are obvious differences between the schools and hospitals involved in Wirtz and the fire and police departments affected here, each provides an integral portion of those governmental services which the States and their political subdivisions have traditionally afforded their citizens. We are therefore persuaded that Wirtz must be overruled.

Reversed and remanded.

Mr. Justice BLACKMUN, concurring.

[Although] I am not untroubled by certain possible implications of the Court's opinion—some of them suggested by the dissents—I do not read the opinion so despairingly as does my Brother Brennan. In my view, the result with respect to the statute under challenge here is necessarily correct. I may misinterpret the Court's opinion, but it seems to me that it adopts a balancing approach, and does not outlaw federal power in areas such as environmental protection, where the federal interest is demonstrably greater and where state facility compliance with imposed federal standards would be essential. With this understanding [of] the Court's opinion, I join it.

Mr. Justice BRENNAN, with whom Mr. Justice WHITE and Mr. Justice MARSHALL join, dissenting.

[It must] be surprising that my Brethren should choose this Bicentennial year of our independence to repudiate principles governing judicial interpretation of our Constitution settled since the time of Chief Justice John Marshall, discarding his postulate that the Constitution contemplates that restraints upon exercise by Congress of its plenary commerce power lie in the political process and not in the judicial process. [Gibbons v. Ogden; see also Wickard.] My Brethren do not successfully obscure today's patent usurpation of the role reserved for the political process by their purported discovery in the Constitution of a restraint derived from sovereignty of the States on Congress' exercise of the commerce power. [There is] no restraint based on state sovereignty requiring or permitting judicial enforcement anywhere expressed in the Constitution; our decisions over the last century and a half have explicitly rejected the existence of any such restraint on the commerce power.

[My] Brethren thus have today manufactured an abstraction without substance, founded neither in the words of the Constitution nor on precedent. An abstraction having such profoundly pernicious consequences is not made less so by characterizing the 1974 amendments as legislation directed against the

---

4. The holding of United States v. California, as opposed to the language quoted in the text, is quite consistent with our holding today. There California's activity to which the congressional command was directed was not in an area that the States have regarded as integral parts of their governmental activities. It was, on the contrary, the operation of a railroad engaged in "common carriage by rail in [commerce]." [Footnote by Justice Rehnquist.]

5. The dissent leaves no doubt from its discussion that in its view Congress may under its commerce power deal with the States as States just as it might deal with private individuals. We venture to say that it is this conclusion, rather than the one we reach, which is in the words of the dissent a "startling restructuring of our federal [system]." Even the [Government], defending the 1974 amendments in this Court, does not take so extreme a position. [Footnote by Justice Rehnquist.]

"States *qua* States." [M]y Brethren make no claim that the 1974 amendments are not regulations of "commerce"; rather they overrule Wirtz in disagreement with historic principles that United States v. California reaffirmed. [My] Brethren are also repudiating the long line of our precedents holding that a judicial finding that Congress has not unreasonably regulated a subject matter of "commerce" brings to an end the judicial role. "Let the end be legitimate [etc.]." McCulloch v. Maryland.

The reliance of my Brethren upon the Tenth Amendment as "an express declaration of [a state sovereignty] limitation"[1] not only suggests that they overrule governing decisions of this Court that address this question but must astound scholars of the Constitution. For not only early decisions, Gibbons v. Ogden, McCulloch v. Maryland, and Martin v. Hunter's Lessee, hold that nothing in the Tenth Amendment constitutes a limitation on congressional exercise of powers delegated by the Constitution to Congress. Rather, as the Tenth Amendment's significance was more recently summarized: "The amendment states but a truism that all is retained which has not been surrendered." [Darby.] Today's repudiation of [an] unbroken line of precedents that firmly reject my Brethren's ill-conceived abstraction can only be regarded as a transparent cover for invalidating a congressional judgment with which they disagree. The only analysis even remotely resembling that adopted today is found in a line of opinions dealing with the Commerce Clause and the Tenth Amendment that ultimately provoked a constitutional crisis for the Court in the 1930's. E.g., Carter; Butler; Hammer v. Dagenhart. [Today], the Fair Labor Standards Act is invalidated in its application to all state employees "in [any areas] that the States have regarded as integral parts of their governmental activities." This standard is a meaningless limitation on the Court's state sovereignty doctrine. [I] cannot recall another instance in the Court's history when the reasoning of so many decisions covering so long a span of time has been discarded roughshod. [Today's decision is] an ipse dixit reflecting nothing but displeasure with a congressional judgment. [Certainly] the paradigm of sovereign action—action *qua* State—is in the enactment and enforcement of state laws. Is it possible that my Brethren are signaling abandonment of the heretofore unchallenged principle that Congress "can, if it chooses, entirely displace the States to the full extent of the far-reaching Commerce Clause"? [T]he ouster of state laws obviously curtails or prohibits the States' prerogatives to make policy choices respecting subjects clearly of greater significance to the "State *qua* State" than the minimum wage paid to state employees.

[My] Brethren do more than turn aside longstanding constitutional jurisprudence that emphatically rejects today's conclusion. More alarming is the startling restructuring of our federal system, and the role they create therein for the federal judiciary. This Court is simply not at liberty to erect a mirror of its own conception of a desirable governmental structure. If the 1974 amendments have any "vice," my Brother Stevens is surely right that it represents "merely [a] policy issue which has been firmly resolved by the branches of government having power to decide such questions." [It] is unacceptable that the judicial process should be thought superior to the political process in this area. Under the Constitution the judiciary has no role to play beyond finding that Congress has not made an unreasonable legislative judgment respecting

1. The Court relies on Fry v. United States, but I cannot subscribe to reading Fry as departing, without analysis, from a principle that has remained unquestioned for over 150 years. [Fry] did not say that there is a limit in the Tenth Amendment on the exercise of a delegated power, but instead said that "Congress may not exercise power in a fashion [that]." The only import of the footnote in Fry, then, is that Congress may not invade state sovereignty by exercising powers not delegated to it by the Constitution; since the wage ceilings at issue in Fry were clearly within the commerce power, we found no "drastic invasion of State [sovereignty]." [Footnote by Justice Brennan].

what is "commerce." My Brother Blackmun suggests that controlling judicial supervision of the relationship between the States and our National Government by use of a balancing approach diminishes the ominous implications of today's decision. Such an approach, however, is a thinly veiled rationalization for judicial supervision of a policy judgment that our system of government reserves to Congress.

Judicial restraint in this area merely recognizes that the political branches of our Government are structured to protect the interests of the States, as well as the Nation as a whole, and that the States are fully able to protect their own interests in the premises. [Judicial] redistribution of powers granted the National Government by the terms of the Constitution violates the fundamental tenet of our federalism that the extent of federal intervention into the State's affairs in the exercise of delegated powers shall be determined by the States' exercise of political power through their representatives in Congress. See Wechsler, [the "political safeguards" essay quoted at p. 95 above]. [Any] realistic assessment of our federal political system, dominated as it is by representatives of the people *elected from the States,* yields the conclusion that it is highly unlikely that those representatives will ever be motivated to disregard totally the concerns of these States. [My] Brethren's disregard for precedents recognizing these long-settled constitutional principles is painfully obvious in their cavalier treatment of [Wirtz]. [The] best I can make of it is that the 1966 FLSA amendments are struck down and Wirtz is overruled on the basis of the conceptually unworkable essential function test; and that the test is unworkable is demonstrated by my Brethren's inability to articulate any meaningful distinctions among state-operated railroads, state-operated schools and hospitals, and state-operated police and fire departments. We are left then with a catastrophic judicial body blow at Congress' power under the Commerce Clause. Even if Congress may nevertheless accomplish its objectives—for example by conditioning grants of federal funds upon compliance with federal minimum wage and overtime standards, cf. Oklahoma v. Civil Service Comm'n, 330 U.S. 127, 144 (1947) [p. 213 below]—there is an ominous portent of disruption of our constitutional structure implicit in today's mischievous decision. I dissent.

Mr. Justice STEVENS, dissenting.

The Court holds that the Federal Government may not interfere with a sovereign state's inherent right to pay a substandard wage to the janitor at the state capitol. The principle on which the holding rests is difficult to perceive. The Federal Government may, I believe, require the State to act impartially when it hires or fires the janitor, to withhold taxes from his pay check, to observe safety regulations when he is performing his job, to forbid him from burning too much soft coal in the capitol furnace, from dumping untreated refuse in an adjacent waterway, from overloading a state-owned garbage truck or from driving either the truck or the governor's limousine over 55 miles an hour. Even though these and many other activities of the capitol janitor are activities of the state *qua* state, I have no doubt that they are subject to federal regulation.

[As] far as the complexities of adjusting police and fire departments to this sort of federal control are concerned, I presume that appropriate tailormade regulations would soon solve their most pressing problems. After all, the interests adversely affected by this legislation are not without political power. [T]here is no dissent from the proposition that the Federal Government's power over the labor market is adequate to embrace these employees. Since I am unable to identify a limitation on that federal power that would not also invalidate federal regulation of state activities that I consider unquestionably permissible, I am persuaded that this statute is [valid].

THE MEANING AND VITALITY OF NATIONAL
LEAGUE OF CITIES

Introduction. After announcing National League of Cities in 1976, the Court did not again turn to the issues it raised until 1981, in the Hodel case below. Since 1981, the Court has had repeated occasion to explore and restate the state autonomy limit.[1] All of the laws challenged in the early 1980s were sustained; and in almost all of these cases, the prevailing opinions were written by Justices other than those who had joined in Justice Rehnquist's plurality opinion in National League of Cities.

1. *Some questions about National League of Cities.* Does Justice Rehnquist's approach make sense either in terms of constitutional values or policy reasons? Can the language and structure of the Constitution be read persuasively to guarantee the existence of states as separate political entities? Did the FLSA's application to states truly threaten any such constitutional interest? Did Justice Rehnquist state an adequately clear and judicially enforceable standard? Was the three-part "restatement" of the National League of Cities standard in Hodel (note 2 below) a preferable standard (and an accurate restatement)? Was Justice Brennan's vehement dissent persuasive in insisting that Justice Rehnquist's approach was a repudiation of principles "settled since the time of Chief Justice John Marshall"? Did any case in this chapter before National League of Cities involve federal sanctions imposed directly upon the states, rather than federal regulation of entities in the private sector? Does it make any sense, in terms of principle or practice, to impose, as Justice Rehnquist does, limits on federal regulation of "States *qua* States," given the Court's broad validation of congressional regulation of the private sector in the modern cases? Does the "balancing" approach advocated in Justice Blackmun's concurrence make sense? (Note that Justice Blackmun was with the majority in all of the early 1980s cases, noted below, rejecting state autonomy challenges to federal laws.)[2]

2. *Hodel.* HODEL v. VIRGINIA SURFACE MIN. & RECL. ASS'N, 452 U.S. 264 (1981), was probably the easiest of the 1980s cases, for it involved a federal regulatory scheme directed at the private sector rather than at the states themselves. Nevertheless, it provided occasion for the Court to restate the

---

1. EPA v. Brown, 431 U.S. 99 (1977), was an early opportunity to explore the implications of National League of Cities, but the Court managed to dispose of the case without reaching the merits. Arguably, EPA v. Brown presented the Court with more difficult issues than any raised in the 1980s series of cases. (But see FERC v. Mississippi, p. 180 below.) In the EPA group of cases, state officials had challenged the Environmental Protection Agency's authority to issue regulations *compelling* state enforcement of federal standards in situations where the state had failed to adopt a voluntary implementation plan. Under the EPA regulations, states were apparently required, for example, to adopt and fund inspection and maintenance programs for automobiles, and failure to adopt such programs would apparently have authorized enforcement sanctions by the EPA directly against the states. The lower courts had struck down the EPA regulations on statutory grounds, but had also noted that serious constitutional questions would be raised if the Act were read in accordance with the Government's view. Instead of deciding the merits, the Court vacated the judgments and remanded the cases "for consideration of moot-

ness." (In its Supreme Court brief, the Government had conceded "the necessity of removing from the regulations all requirements that the States submit legally adopted regulations," and that concession provided the occasion for the remand.) See generally Salmon, "The Federalist Principle: The Interaction of the Commerce Clause and the Tenth Amendment in the Clean Air Act," 2 Colum.J.Env.L. 290 (1976).

2. What are the implications of National League of Cities for the possibility of raising state autonomy barriers to national action under powers other than the commerce clause? Note footnote 3 to Justice Rehnquist's opinion. The implications of state autonomy concerns for the validity of congressional conditions on spending programs are pursued in the discussion of Oklahoma v. United States Civil Service Commission in chap. 4, p. 213 below. On the relevance of state autonomy concerns to congressional powers under the post-Civil War Amendments, see footnote 3 to Justice Rehnquist's opinion and Justice Brennan's majority opinion in EEOC v. Wyoming, p. 187 below.

National League of Cities approach as a three-part test, a test frequently reiterated in the later cases.[3] Hodel rejected pre-enforcement facial challenges, based on the commerce clause and the Tenth Amendment, to the Surface Mining Control and Reclamation Act of 1977, a law which imposed significant limits on private mining operations.[4] Justice MARSHALL's opinion for the Court, after finding local mining activities well within the commerce power, also rejected the claim that standards for surface coal mining on "steep slopes" violated state autonomy by interfering with the states' "traditional governmental function" of regulating land use and by impairing the states' ability to make "essential decisions."

On the basic commerce power issue, Justice Marshall rejected the argument that "land *as such*" was outside the scope of the commerce power. He stated that courts "must defer to a congressional finding that a regulated activity affects interstate commerce, if there is any rational basis for such a finding. [Heart of Atlanta; McClung.]" (Compare Justice Rehnquist's concurrence, below.) Here, the legislative record provided "ample support" for the congressional findings that the regulated activity "affects interstate commerce." In turning to the Tenth Amendment objections to the "steep-slope" provisions, Justice Marshall restated the National League of Cities criteria in a manner much relied on in the subsequent cases: "[In] order to succeed, a claim that congressional commerce power legislation is invalid under the reasoning of National League of Cities must satisfy *each* of three requirements. First, there must be a showing that the challenged statute regulates the 'States as States.' Second, the federal regulation must address matters that are indisputably 'attributes of state sovereignty.' And third, it must be apparent that the States' compliance with the federal law would directly impair their ability 'to structure integral operations in areas of traditional governmental functions.' "[5] Here, he found, the Tenth Amendment challenge failed "because the first of the three requirements is not satisfied."

Justice Marshall emphasized that the challenged provisions governed only "the activities of coal mine operators who are private individuals and businesses. Moreover, the States are not compelled to enforce the steep-slope standards, to expend any state funds, or to participate in the federal regulatory program in any manner whatsoever. If a State does not wish to submit a proposed permanent program that complies with the [Act], the full regulatory burden will be borne by the Federal Government. Thus, there can be no suggestion that the Act commandeers the legislative processes of the States by directly compelling them to enact and enforce a federal regulatory program. [Justice Marshall noted, with a cf. reference, EPA v. Brown (footnote 1 above) and related cases. Compare FERC v. Mississippi, p. 180 below.] The most that can be said is that the [Act] establishes a program of cooperative federalism that allows the States, within limits established by federal minimum standards, to enact and administer their own regulatory programs." Justice Marshall also rejected the argument that "the threat of federal usurpation of their regulatory roles coerces the States [or that] the Act directly regulates the States as States because it establishes mandatory minimum federal standards." He pointed out that that challenge

3. A companion case, Hodel v. Indiana, 452 U.S. 314 (1981), reached the same conclusion on both the commerce power and Tenth Amendment issues.

4. For example, the Act required "steep-slope" operators to reclaim the mined area by returning the site to its "approximate original contour."

5. In a footnote at this point, Justice Marshall added: "Demonstrating that these three requirements are met does not, however, guarantee that a Tenth Amendment challenge [will] succeed. There are situations in which the nature of the federal interest advanced may be such that it justifies state submission." He cited, inter alia, Justice Blackmun's concurrence in National League of Cities.

rested on the assumption "that the Tenth Amendment limits congressional power to pre-empt or displace state regulation of private activities affecting interstate commerce. This assumption is incorrect." Although congressional preemptive laws "obviously curtail or prohibit the States' prerogatives to make legislative choices," the "Supremacy Clause [see chap. 5] permits no other result." [6]

In an opinion concurring only in the judgment, Justice REHNQUIST expressed concern about the possible implications of the Court's language regarding the scope of congressional power to regulate the *private* sector. His fear was directed at the Court's assertion that "regulation will be upheld if Congress had a rational basis for finding that the regulated activity affects interstate commerce." He added: "In my view, the Court misstates the test. [It] has long been established that the commerce power does not reach activity which merely 'affects' interstate commerce. There must instead be a showing that regulated activity has a *substantial* effect on that commerce." He cited cases through Wickard and added quotations from Wirtz and Heart of Atlanta. He added, however: "Though I believe the Court errs in its statement of the 'test,' it may be that I read too much into the Court's choice of language." Thus, he noted that Justice Marshall had mentioned at one point that "Congress did have a rational basis for concluding that surface coal mining has substantial effects on interstate commerce." [7]

3. *United Transportation Union.* The Court was once again unanimous in its holding when it rejected a state autonomy challenge to the application of the Railway Labor Act to the state-owned Long Island Railroad, owned by New York since 1966, in UNITED TRANSPORTATION UNION v. LONG ISLAND RAILROAD CO., 455 U.S. 678 (1982). Drawing on the three-pronged test articulated in Hodel, Chief Justice BURGER focused on the third part and concluded that there was no interference with "traditional [state]

---

6. Justice Marshall added: "Congress could constitutionally have enacted a statute prohibiting any state regulation of surface coal mining. We fail to see why the [Act] should become constitutionally suspect simply because Congress chose to allow the States a regulatory role. [Nothing] in National League of Cities suggests that the Tenth Amendment shields the States from pre-emptive federal regulation of *private* activities affecting interstate commerce."

7. In more general passages, Justice Rehnquist thought it "illuminating" to note "that one of the greatest 'fictions' of our federal system is that the Congress exercises only those powers delegated to it. [The] manner in which this Court has construed the Commerce Clause amply illustrates the extent of this fiction. Although it is clear that the people, through the States, *delegated* authority to Congress to [regulate commerce], one could easily get the sense from this Court's opinions that the federal system exists only at the sufferance of Congress." But he added some caveats. Although under the Court's interpretations, Congress' commerce power was "broad indeed," "there *are* constitutional limits on the [commerce power]. [It] would be a mistake to conclude that Congress' power [is] unlimited. Some activities may be so private or local in nature that they simply may not be *in* commerce. Nor is it sufficient that the person or activity reached have *some* nexus with interstate commerce. Our cases have consistent-

ly held that the regulated activity must have a *substantial* effect on interstate commerce. [Moreover], Congress' findings of substantial effect] must be supported by a 'rational basis' and are reviewable by the courts." He added that, "[i]n many ways," the Court's language in Hodel was "consistent with that approach," since it "exhaustively" analyzed "Congress' articulated justifications for the exercise of its power" and concluded that "Congress' detailed factual findings [were] sufficient to justify the exercise of that power." Though Congress had "stretched its authority to the 'nth degree,' our prior precedents compel me to agree with the Court's conclusion. [It] is my uncertainty as to whether the Court intends to broaden, by some of its language, [the "substantial economic effect" test] that leads me to concur only in the [judgment]."

In a concurring notation, Chief Justice BURGER stated that he agreed with Justice Rehnquist's view that "we often seem to forget" the "*substantial*" effect" doctrine but added that he joined Justice Marshall's opinion because it "acknowledges and reaffirms that doctrine." In another concurrence, Justice POWELL stated that the decisions "over many years" made clear that the Act was within the commerce power, even though it mandated "an extraordinarily intrusive program of federal regulation and control of land use and land reclamation, activities normally left to state and local governments."

functions." [8]   Operation of railroads, he stated, had "traditionally been a function of private industry, not state or local governments." The modern phenomenon of state acquisitions of formerly private railroads did not "alter the historical reality that the operation of railroads is not among the functions *traditionally* performed by state and local governments." The Chief Justice claimed that his emphasis on the "traditional" "was not meant to impose a static historical view of state functions"; instead, the "traditional" criterion was designed to further the central inquiry "into whether the federal regulation affects basic state prerogatives in such a way as would be likely to hamper the state government's ability to fulfill its role in the Union and endanger its 'separate and independent existence.'" [9]   (The unanimity in the Court's post-National League of Cities holdings came to an end in the next principal case, a case that presented more substantial state autonomy challenges.)

FERC v. MISSISSIPPI

456 U.S. 742, 102 S.Ct. 2126, 72 L.Ed.2d 532 (1982).

Justice BLACKMUN delivered the opinion of the Court.

[This case rejected a constitutional challenge to Titles I and III, and § 210 of Title II, of the Public Utility Regulatory Policies Act of 1978 (PURPA). The Act, designed to combat a nationwide energy crisis, sought to encourage conservation of oil and natural gas by utilities in order to lessen the nation's dependence on foreign oil. Titles I and II, concerned with electric and gas utilities respectively, directed state utility commissions to "consider" the adoption of specific federal "rate design" and regulatory standards. Despite the extent and detail of the federal standards, no state agency was *required* to follow standards. However, the Act required state agencies to adopt certain procedures in proceedings held to consider the adoption of federal standards. Section 210 of Title II sought to encourage the development of cogeneration and small power production facilities in order to reduce the demand for traditional fossil fuels. In order to remove perceived financial burdens discouraging such development, the Act authorized the Federal Energy Regulatory Commission (FERC) to exempt those facilities from certain state regulations that imposed burdens on the development. FERC was also directed to promulgate rules to facilitate sales of electricity to and purchases of electricity from the favored cogeneration and small power production facilities.

[The lower court found PURPA beyond the commerce power (citing the Carter case) and held also, on the basis of National League of Cities, that the Act "trenches on state sovereignty" and constituted "a direct intrusion on integral and traditional functions" of Mississippi. Relying on Hodel, Justice Blackmun readily found the commerce clause objection "without merit." He emphasized the "clear and specific" findings by Congress that "the regulated activities have an immediate effect on interstate commerce" and noted that these

---

8. Despite his reliance on the three-pronged test, the Chief Justice suggested that a balancing analysis could be superimposed on those criteria. He stated that, even if the Hodel requirements were met, the federal law might still be constitutional because the "federal interest may still be so great as to 'justif[y] state submission.'" Recall footnote 5 above and note the discussion of the balancing analysis in EEOC v. Wyoming, below.

9. Was the Chief Justice's explanation of his allegedly fluid notion of the "traditional" persuasive? Chief Justice Burger stated: "Just as the

Federal Government cannot usurp traditional state functions, there is no justification for a rule which would allow the states, *by acquiring functions previously performed by the private sector,* to erode federal authority in areas [such as railroads] traditionally subject to federal statutory regulation." (Emphasis added.) He added: "[In] addition, a state acquiring a railroad does so knowing that the railroad is subject to this longstanding and comprehensive scheme of federal regulation."

findings had "a rational basis" amply supported by the legislative history. He then turned to the state autonomy issue:]

IV. [The] Tenth Amendment issue [is] somewhat novel. [National League of Cities] presented a problem the Court often confronts: the extent to which state sovereignty shields the States from generally applicable federal regulation. In PURPA, in contrast, the Federal Government attempts to use state regulatory machinery to advance federal goals. To an extent, this presents an issue of first impression. PURPA, for all its complexity, contains essentially three requirements: (1) § 210 has the States enforce standards promulgated by FERC; (2) Titles I and III direct the States to consider specified ratemaking standards; and (3) those Titles impose certain procedures on state commissions. We consider these three requirements in turn:

A. Section 210. On its face, this appears to be the most intrusive of PURPA's provisions. The question of its constitutionality, however, is the easiest to resolve. Insofar as § 210 authorizes FERC to exempt qualified power facilities from "State laws and regulations," it does nothing more than pre-empt conflicting state enactments in the traditional way. Clearly, Congress can pre-empt the States completely in the regulation of retail sales by electricity and gas utilities and in the regulation of transactions between such utilities and cogenerators. The propriety of this type of regulation—so long as it is a valid exercise of the commerce power—was made clear in National League of Cities, and was reaffirmed in [Hodel]: [the] Federal Government may displace state regulation even though this serves to "curtail or prohibit the States' prerogatives to make legislative choices respecting subjects the States may consider important."

Section 210's requirement that "each State regulatory authority shall, after notice and opportunity for public hearing, *implement* such rule [for] each electric utility for which it has ratemaking authority" (emphasis added) is more troublesome. The statute's substantive provisions require electricity utilities to purchase electricity from, and to sell it to, qualifying cogenerator and small power production facilities. Yet FERC has declared that state commissions may implement this by, among other things, "an undertaking to resolve disputes between qualifying facilities and electric utilities arising under [PURPA]." In essence, then, the statute and the implementing regulations simply require the Mississippi authorities to adjudicate disputes arising under the statute. Dispute resolution of this kind is the very type of activity customarily engaged in by the Mississippi Public Service Commission.

Testa v. Katt, 330 U.S. 386 (1947), is instructive and controlling on this point. There, the Emergency Price Control Act [of 1942] created a treble-damages remedy, and gave jurisdiction over claims under the Act to state as well as federal courts. The courts of Rhode Island refused to entertain such claims, although they heard analogous state causes of action. This Court upheld the federal program. It observed that state courts have a unique role in enforcing the body of federal law, and that the Rhode Island courts had "jurisdiction adequate and appropriate under established local law to adjudicate this action." Thus the state courts were directed to heed the constitutional command that "the policy of the federal Act is the prevailing policy in every state," " 'and should be respected accordingly in the courts of the State.' " So it is here. The Mississippi Commission has jurisdiction to entertain claims analogous to those granted by PURPA, and it can satisfy § 210's requirements simply by opening its doors to claimants. That the Commission has administrative as well as judicial duties is of no significance. Any other conclusion would allow the States to disregard both the pre-eminent position held by federal law throughout the Nation [and] the congressional determination that the federal rights granted by PURPA can appropriately be enforced through state adjudicatory machinery. Such an approach, Testa emphasized, "flies in the face of the fact that the States of the Union constitute a nation" and "disregards the purpose and effect of Article VI of the Constitution."

B. Mandatory Consideration of Standards. We acknowledge that "the authority to make [fundamental] decisions" is perhaps the quintessential attribute of sovereignty. See National League of Cities. Indeed, having the power to make decisions and to set policy is what gives the State its sovereign nature. [It] would follow that the ability of a state legislative (or, as here, administrative) body [to] consider and promulgate regulations of its choosing must be central to a State's role in the federal system. Indeed, the nineteenth century view, expressed in a well known slavery case, was that Congress "has no power to impose upon a State officer, as such, any duty whatever, and compel him to perform it." Kentucky v. Dennison, 24 How. 66 (1861). Recent cases, however, demonstrate that this rigid and isolated statement from Kentucky v. Dennison—which suggests that the States and the Federal Government in all circumstances must be viewed as coequal sovereigns—is not representative of the law today.[1] While this Court never has sanctioned explicitly a federal command to the States to promulgate and enforce laws and regulations, cf. EPA v. Brown, there are instances where the Court has upheld federal statutory structures that in effect directed state decision-makers to take or to refrain from taking certain actions. [E.g., Fry.] [And] certainly Testa v. Katt reveals that the Federal Government has some power to enlist a branch of state government—there the judiciary—to further federal ends.[2] In doing so, Testa clearly cut back on both the quoted language and the analysis of the Dennison case of the preceding century.

Whatever all this may forebode for the future, or for the scope of federal authority in the event of a crisis of national proportions, it plainly is not necessary for the Court in this case to make a definitive choice between competing views of federal power to compel state regulatory activity. Titles I and III of PURPA require only *consideration* of federal standards. And if a State has no utilities commission, or simply stops regulating in the field, it need not even entertain the federal proposals. [T]he commerce power permits Congress to pre-empt the States entirely in the regulation of private utilities. In a sense, then, this case is only one step beyond [Hodel]. [Similarly here], Congress could have pre-empted the field, at least insofar as private rather than state activity is concerned; PURPA should not be invalid simply because, out of deference to state authority, Congress adopted a less intrusive scheme and allowed the States to continue regulating in the area on the condition that they *consider* the suggested federal standards.[3] While the condition here is affirmative in nature—that is, it directs the States to entertain proposals—nothing in this Court's cases suggests that the nature of the condition makes it a constitutionally improper one. There is nothing in PURPA "directly compelling" the States to enact a legislative program. In short, because the two challenged Titles simply condition continued state involvement in a pre-emptible area on the consideration of federal proposals, they do not threaten the States' "separate and independent existence," and do not impair the ability of the States "to

1. Justice O'Connor reviews the constitutional history at some length, ultimately deriving the proposition that the Framers intended to deny the Federal Government the authority to exercise "military or legislative power over state governments," *instead* "allow[ing] Congress to pass laws directly affecting individuals." If Justice O'Connor means this rhetorical assertion to be taken literally, it is demonstrably incorrect. See, e.g., [Transportation Union; Fry]. [Footnote by Justice Blackmun.]

2. [Justice O'Connor] finds each of these cases inapposite. Yet the purported distinctions are little more than exercises [in the art of ipse dixit]. [Footnote by Justice Blackmun.]

3. [Justice O'Connor's] response to this is peculiar. Certainly, it is a curious type of federalism that encourages Congress to pre-empt a field entirely, when its preference is to let the States retain the primary regulatory role. [Footnote by Justice Blackmun.]

function effectively in a federal system." To the contrary, they offer the States a vehicle for remaining active in an area of overriding concern.

We recognize, of course, that the choice put to the States—that of either abandoning regulation of the field altogether or considering the federal standards—may be a difficult one. And that is particularly true when Congress, as is the case here, has failed to provide an alternative regulatory mechanism to police the area in the event of state default. Yet in other contexts the Court has recognized that valid federal enactments may have an effect on state policy—and may, indeed, be designed to induce state action in areas that otherwise would be beyond Congress' regulatory authority. Thus in Oklahoma v. Civil Service Comm'n [1947; p. 213 below], the Court upheld Congress' power to attach conditions to grants-in-aid received by the States, although the condition under attack involved an activity that "the United States is not concerned with, and has no power to regulate." [Thus] it cannot be constitutionally determinative that the federal regulation is likely to move the States to act in a given way, or even to "coerc[e] the States" into assuming a regulatory [role]. Equally as important, it has always been the law that state legislative and judicial decisionmakers must give preclusive effect to federal enactments concerning nongovernmental activity, no matter what the strength of the competing local interests. [It] may be unlikely that the States will or easily can abandon regulation of public utilities to avoid PURPA's requirements. But this does not change the constitutional analysis: as in [Hodel], "[t]he most that can be said is that the [Act] establishes a program of cooperative federalism that allows the States, within limits established by federal minimum standards, to enact and administer their own regulatory programs, structured to meet their own particular needs." [4] In short, Titles I and III do not involve the compelled exercise of Mississippi's sovereign powers. And, equally important, they do not set a mandatory agenda to be considered in all events by state legislative or administrative decisionmakers. As we read them, Titles I and III simply establish requirements for continued state activity in an otherwise pre-emptible [field]. [5]

C. The Procedural Requirements. Titles I and III also require state commissions to follow certain notice and comment procedures when acting on the proposed federal standards. In a way, these appear more intrusive than the

---

4. [Justice O'Connor] suggests that our analysis is an "absurdity" and variously accuses us of "conscript[ing]" state utility commissions into the national bureaucratic army," of transforming state legislative bodies into "field offices of the national bureaucracy," of approving the "dismemberment of state government," of making state agencies "bureaucratic puppets of the Federal Government," and—most colorfully—of permitting "Congress to kidnap state utility commissions." While these rhetorical devices make for absorbing reading, they unfortunately are substituted for useful constitutional analysis. For while Justice O'Connor articulates a view of state sovereignty that is almost mystical, she entirely fails to address our central point.

[The] partial dissent fails to identify precisely what is "absurd" about [PURPA's] scheme. [Though Justice O'Connor finds [Hodel] inapposite, [the] parallel is striking. [While] it is true that PURPA conditions continued state regulatory activity on the performance of certain affirmative tasks, the partial dissent nowhere explains why—so long as the field is pre-emptible—the nature of the condition is relevant. And while PURPA's requirements in practice may be more intrusive and more difficult for the States to

avoid than was the legislation at issue in [Hodel], Justice O'Connor herself acknowledges that an "evaluation of intrusiveness [is] simply irrelevant to the constitutional inquiry." [Footnote by Justice Blackmun.]

5. Justice O'Connor's partial dissent accuses us of undervaluing National League of Cities, and maintains that our analysis permits Congress to "dictate the agendas and meeting places of state legislatures." These apocalyptic observations, while striking, are overstated and patently inaccurate. We hold only that Congress may impose conditions on the State's regulation of private conduct in a pre-emptible area. This does not foreclose a Tenth Amendment challenge to federal interference with the State's ability "to structure employer-employee relationships" while providing "those governmental services which [its] citizens require," as was the case in National League of Cities. It does not suggest that the Federal Government may impose conditions on state activities in fields that are not pre-emptible, or that are solely of intrastate concern. And it does not purport to authorize the imposition of general affirmative obligations on the States. [Footnote by Justice Blackmun.]

"consideration" provisions; while the latter are essentially hortatory, the procedural provisions obviously are prescriptive. [We] uphold the procedural requirements under the same analysis employed above in connection with the "consideration" provisions. If Congress can require a state administrative body to consider proposed regulations as a condition to its continued involvement in a pre-emptible field—and we hold today that it can—there is nothing unconstitutional about Congress' requiring certain procedural minima as that body goes about undertaking its tasks. The procedural requirements obviously do not compel the exercise of the State's sovereign powers, and do not purport to set standards to be followed in all areas of the state commission's endeavors.

[Reversed.]

Justice POWELL, concurring in part and dissenting in part.

[The Act] imposes unprecedented burdens on the States. As Justice O'Connor ably demonstrates, it intrusively requires them to make a place on their administrative agenda for consideration and potential adoption of federally proposed "standards." The statute does not simply ask States to consider quasi-legislative matters that Congress believes they would do well to adopt. It also prescribes administrative and judicial procedures that States must follow in deciding whether to adopt the proposed standards. At least to this extent, I think the PURPA violates the Tenth Amendment. [Under the Court's] "threat of preemption" reasoning, Congress—one supposes—could reduce the States to federal provinces. But [the] Commerce Clause and the Tenth Amendment embody distinct limitations on federal power. That Congress has satisfied the one demonstrates nothing as to whether Congress has satisfied the other.

"The general rule, bottomed deeply in belief in the importance of state control of state judicial procedure, is that federal law takes state courts as it finds them." Hart, The Relations Between State and Federal Law, 54 Colum.L.Rev. 489, 508 (1954). I believe the same principle must apply to other organs of state government. It may be true that the procedural provisions of the PURPA that prompt this dissent may not effect dramatic changes in the laws and procedures of some States. But I know of no other attempt by the Federal Government to supplant state-prescribed procedures that in part define the nature of their administrative agencies. If Congress may do this, presumably it has the power to pre-empt state-court rules of civil procedure and judicial review in classes of cases found to affect commerce. This would be the type of gradual encroachment hypothesized by Professor Tribe: "Of course, no one expects Congress to obliterate the states, at least in one fell swoop. If there is any danger, it lies in the tyranny of small decisions—in the prospect that Congress will nibble away at state sovereignty, bit by bit, until someday essentially nothing is left but a gutted shell." [Despite] the appeal—and indeed wisdom—of Justice O'Connor's evocation of the principles of federalism, I believe precedents of this Court support the constitutionality of the substantive provisions of this Act. Accordingly, to the extent the procedural provisions may be separable, I would affirm in part and reverse in part.

Justice O'CONNOR, with whom the Chief Justice [BURGER] and Justice REHNQUIST join, concurring in the judgment in part and dissenting in part.

I agree with the Court that the Commerce Clause supported Congress' enactment of [PURPA]. I disagree, however, with much of the Court's Tenth Amendment analysis. Titles I and III of PURPA conscript state utility commissions into the national bureaucratic army. This result is contrary to the principles of National League of Cities, antithetical to the values of federalism, and inconsistent with our constitutional history.

[I. The] Court's conclusion [rests] upon a fundamental misunderstanding of the role that state governments play in our federalist system. State legislative and administrative bodies are not field offices of the national bureaucracy. Nor are they think tanks to which Congress may assign problems for extended study. Instead, each State is sovereign within its own domain, governing its citizens and providing for their [general welfare]. [Application of the principles of the cases from National League of Cities to Hodel] to the present case reveals the Tenth Amendment defects in Titles I and III. Plainly those titles regulate the "States as States." While the statute's ultimate aim may be the regulation of private utility companies, PURPA addresses its commands solely to the States. Instead of requesting private utility companies to adopt [PURPA] standards, Congress directed state agencies to appraise the appropriateness of those standards. [I] find it equally clear that Titles I and III address "attribute[s] of state sovereignty." [The] power to make decisions and set policy [embraces] more than the ultimate authority to enact laws; it also includes the power to decide which proposals are most worthy of consideration, the order in which they should be taken up, and the precise form in which they should be debated. PURPA intrudes upon all of these functions. [If] Congress routinely required the state legislatures to debate bills drafted by congressional committees, it could hardly be questioned that the practice would affect an attribute of state sovereignty. PURPA, which sets the agendas of agencies exercising delegated legislative power in a specific field, has a similarly intrusive effect. Finally, PURPA directly impairs the States' ability to "structure integral operations in areas of traditional governmental functions." Utility regulation is a traditional function of state government, and the regulatory commission is the most integral part of that function. By taxing the limited resources of these commissions, and decreasing their ability to address local regulatory ills, PURPA directly impairs the power of state utility commissions to discharge their traditional functions efficiently and effectively.

The Court sidesteps this analysis, suggesting that the States may escape PURPA simply by ceasing regulation of public utilities. [The] Court's "choice" is an absurdity, for if its analysis is sound, the Constitution no longer limits federal regulation of state governments. Under the Court's analysis, for example, [National League of Cities] would have been wrongly decided, because the States could have avoided the [FLSA] by "choosing" to fire all employees subject to that Act and to close those branches of state government. Similarly, Congress could dictate the agendas and meeting places of state legislatures, because unwilling States would remain free to abolish their legislative bodies. I do not agree that this dismemberment of state government is the correct solution to a Tenth Amendment challenge.

The choice put to the States by [the] statute upheld in [Hodel] is quite different from the decision PURPA mandates. [The] Surface Mining Act does not force States to choose between performing tasks set by Congress and abandoning all mining or land use regulation. That statute is "a program of cooperative federalism" because it allows the States to choose either to work with Congress in pursuit of federal surface mining goals or to devote their legislative resources to other mining and land use problems. By contrast, there is nothing "cooperative" about a federal program that compels state agencies either to function as bureaucratic puppets of the Federal Government or to abandon regulation of an entire field traditionally reserved to state authority. Yet this is the "choice" the Court today forces upon the States. The Court defends its novel decision to permit federal conscription of state legislative power by citing [a few] cases upholding statutes that "in effect directed state decision makers to take or to refrain from taking certain actions." Testa v. Katt is the most suggestive of these decisions. [Application] of Testa to legislative power, however, vastly expands the scope of that decision. Because trial courts of general jurisdiction do not choose the cases that they hear, the requirement that they evenhandedly adjudicate state and federal claims falling within their jurisdiction does not infringe any sovereign authority to set an agenda. [But] the power to choose subjects for legislation is a fundamental attribute of legislative power, and interference with this power unavoidably undermines state sovereignty. Accordingly, the existence of a congressional authority to "enlist [the state] judiciary [to] further federal ends" does not imply an equivalent power to impress state legislative bodies into federal service. The Court, finally, reasons that because Congress could have preempted the entire field of intrastate utility regulation, the Constitution should not forbid PURPA's "less intrusive scheme." The Court's evaluation of intrusiveness, however, is simply irrelevant to the constitutional inquiry. The Constitution permits Congress to govern only through certain channels. If the Tenth Amendment principles articulated in [National League of Cities and Hodel] foreclose PURPA's approach, it is no answer to argue that Congress could have reached the same destination by a different route. This Court's task is to enforce constitutional limits on congressional power, not to decide whether alternative courses would better serve state and federal interests.

I do not believe, moreover, that Titles I and III of PURPA are less intrusive than pre-emption.[1] When Congress preempts a field, it precludes only state legislation that conflicts with the national approach. The States usually retain the power to complement congressional legislation, either by regulating details unsupervised by Congress or by imposing requirements that go beyond the national threshold. Most importantly, after Congress pre-empts a field, the States may simply devote their resources elsewhere. This country does not lack for problems demanding legislative attention. PURPA, however, drains the inventive energy of state governmental bodies by requiring them to weigh its detailed standards, enter written findings, and defend their determinations in state court. While engaged in these congressionally mandated tasks, state utility commissions are less able to pursue local proposals for conserving gas and electric power. The States might well prefer that Congress simply impose the standards described in PURPA; this, at least, would leave them free to exercise their power in other areas.

Federal pre-emption is less intrusive than PURPA's approach for a second reason. [Congressional] compulsion of state agencies, unlike preemption, blurs the lines of political accountability and leaves [local] citizens feeling that their representatives are no longer responsive to local needs. [In] addition to promoting experimentation, federalism enhances the opportunity of all citizens to participate in representative government. [Citizens], however, cannot learn

1. In 1975, then Attorney General Edward H. Levi responded to a similar argument that the "greater" power of preemption includes the "lesser" power of demanding affirmative action from state governments. Attorney General Levi remarked that "it is an insidious point to say that there is more federalism by compelling a State instrumentality to work for the Federal Government." In a similar vein, he warned against "lov[ing] the States to their demise." [Footnote by Justice O'Connor.]

[Attorney General Levi's comments came in the course of announcing the Justice Department's opposition to a proposed federal no-fault insurance law that would have compelled the states to enact and implement state no-fault laws through state regulatory agencies. The Justice Department expressed constitutional doubts concerning "the authority of Congress to employ a regulatory scheme that requires the States to devote their funds and personnel, and to create agencies and facilities to administer a Federal law, regardless of local feeling." For an endorsement of the Justice Department's position, see Kaden, "Politics, Money, and State Sovereignty: The Judicial Role," 79 Colum.L.Rev. 847 (1979). See also Dorsen, "The National No-Fault Motor Vehicle Insurance Act: A Problem in Federalism," 49 N.Y.U.L.Rev. 45 (1974). Kaden's article, written before the 1980s weakening of National League of Cities, suggested: "Only when a federal program coopts the state's political processes by interfering with legislative and executive discretion in a significant way should the courts have to intervene. Such an effect can not be determined solely by fiscal impact; [the] effect on organizational structure and the allocation of nonfiscal resources are other important criteria. [It] may in fact be possible to define more precisely the area of constitutional protection by distinguishing between federal directives that order existing state agencies to apply federal regulatory standards, and those that oblige the states to create new regulatory mechanisms."]

the lessons of self-government if their local efforts are devoted to reviewing proposals formulated by a far-away national legislature. If we want to preserve the ability of citizens to learn democratic processes through participation in local government, citizens must retain the power to govern, not merely administer, their local problems. Finally, our federal system provides a salutary check on governmental power. [Today], the Court disregards this warning and permits Congress to kidnap state utility commissions into the national regulatory family. Whatever the merits of our national energy legislation, I am not ready to surrender this state legislative power to the [FERC].

II. [The] Court's result, moreover, is at odds with our constitutional history, which demonstrates that the Framers consciously rejected a system in which the national legislature would employ state legislative power to achieve national ends. The principal defect of the Articles of Confederation [was] that the new National Government lacked the power to compel individual action. Instead, the central government had to rely upon the cooperation of state legislatures to achieve national goals. [The] Constitution cured this defect by permitting [direct enforcement of federal law by] the National Government [against] the individual citizen. [At] the same time that the [Framers] fashioned this principle, they rejected two proposals that would have given the National Legislature power to supervise directly state governments. [The] Framers substituted judicial review of state laws for congressional control of state legislatures. [The] National Government received the power to enact its own laws and to enforce those laws over conflicting state legislation. The States retained the power to govern as sovereigns in fields that Congress cannot or will not pre-empt. This product of the Constitutional Convention, I believe, is fundamentally inconsistent with a system in which either Congress or a state legislature harnesses the legislative powers of the other [sovereign].

EEOC v. WYOMING, 460 U.S. 226 (1983): Less than a year after the FERC case, the Court, again dividing 5 to 4, once again rejected a state autonomy defense, this time in a setting closest yet to National League of Cities itself. And this time, one of the members of the majority, Justice Stevens, urged "prompt rejection" of National League of Cities. The EEOC case challenged the 1974 extension of the federal Age Discrimination in Employment Act (ADEA) to state and local governments. The Act bars employment discrimination on the basis of age except "where age is a bona fide occupational qualification." [1] Justice BRENNAN's majority opinion concluded that "the degree of federal intrusion in this case is sufficiently less serious than it was in National League of Cities so as to make it unnecessary for us to override Congress's express choice to extend its regulatory authority to the States." He reviewed National League of Cities and emphasized that its state immunity principle "is a functional doctrine [whose] ultimate purpose is not to create a sacred province of state autonomy, but to ensure that the unique benefits of a federal system [not] be lost through undue federal interference in certain core state functions." He then turned to the three-part test of Hodel (as supplemented by Justice Blackmun's balancing standard). Justice Brennan explained: "The first requirement—that the challenged federal statute regulate the 'States as States'—is plainly met in this case." [2] The second requirement—that the

1. The case arose out of the involuntary retirement of a Wyoming game warden at age 55. ADEA barred retirement at so early an age. The U.S. Equal Employment Opportunity Commission (EEOC) upheld the warden's complaint and filed suit against the State. The lower court dismissed the suit on the basis of the Tenth Amendment. The Court reversed.

2. "It is worth emphasizing, however, that it is precisely this prong of [the] test that marks it as a specialized immunity doctrine rather than a broad limitation on federal authority. '[A]

federal statute address an 'undoubted attribute of state sovereignty'—poses significantly more difficulties.[3] We need not definitively resolve this issue, however, nor do we have any occasion to reach the final balancing step of the inquiry, [for] we are convinced that, even if Wyoming's decision to impose forced retirement on its game wardens does involve the exercise of an attribute of state sovereignty, the [Act] does not 'directly impair' the State's ability to 'structure integral operations in areas of traditional governmental functions.' "

Justice Brennan explained that conclusion as follows: "The management of state parks is clearly a traditional state function. [But] the purpose of the [National League of Cities doctrine] was to protect States from federal intrusions that might threaten their 'separate and independent existence.' " Decision of that issue, he insisted, must depend "on considerations of degree." And here, as noted, he found the degree of federal intrusion sufficiently less serious than in National League of Cities. Here, the only claimed state interest in its retirement policies was in assuring the physical preparedness of game wardens to perform their duties. But the federal law did not bar the State from dismissing those found to be unfit. All the Act required was that the state achieve its goals "in a more individualized and careful manner"; it did not require the State to abandon its fitness concern completely. Moreover, Wyoming could continue its age 55 policy if it could demonstrate that age is a "bona fide occupational qualification" for game wardens. Thus, in contrast to National League of Cities, "even the State's discretion to achieve its goals *in the way it thinks best* is not being overriden entirely, but is merely being tested against a reasonable federal standard."

In concluding his elaborate effort to distinguish National League of Cities, Justice Brennan also noted that here, unlike the 1976 case, there was no showing of a "potential impact of the [federal scheme] on the States' ability to structure operations and set priorities over a wide range of decisions." [4] In this case, nothing "portends anything like the same wide-ranging and profound threat to the structure of the state governance." For example, "we cannot conclude from the nature of the [Act] that it would have either a direct or an obvious negative effect on state finances. [Moreover], whatever broader social and economic purposes could be imagined for this [state retirement law] would not, we are convinced, bring with them either the breadth or the importance of the state policies identified in

wealth of precedent attests to congressional authority to displace or pre-empt state laws regulating *private* activity affecting interstate commerce when these laws conflict with federal law. [Although] such congressional enactments obviously [curtail] the States' prerogatives to make legislative choices, [the] Supremacy Clause permits no other result.' [Hodel.]" [Footnote by Justice Brennan.]

3. In a footnote at this point, Justice Brennan, after stating that it was "somewhat unclear" precisely what National League of Cities meant by an " 'undoubted attribute' of state sovereignty," added: "A State's employment relationship with its workers can, under certain circumstances, be one vehicle for the exercise of its core sovereign functions." He noted that in National League of Cities, the power to determine wages was tied "to the exercise of the States' public welfare interest in providing jobs to persons who would otherwise be unemployed. Moreover, some employment decisions are so clearly connected to the execution of underlying sovereign choices that they must be assimilated into them for purposes of the Tenth Amendment [as with the relationship between government workers' hours and 'the unimpeded exercise of the State's role as provider of emergency services']. But we are not to be understood to suggest that every state employment decision aimed simply at advancing a generalized interest in efficient management—even the efficient management of traditional state functions—should be considered to be an exercise of an 'undoubted attribute of state sovereignty.' "

4. "We do not mean to suggest that such consequential effects could be enough, by themselves, to invalidate a federal statute." [Footnote by Justice Brennan.]

National League of Cities." [5]　Accordingly, the extension of the Act was valid under the commerce power.[6]

Justice STEVENS, while joining Justice Brennan's opinion, added a concurrence "about the larger perspective in which I view the underlying issues." Central to that larger perspective was his discussion of the commerce clause, which he described as the "Framers' response to the central problem that gave rise to the Constitution itself." [7]　He noted the "universal agreement on the proposition that Congress has ample power to regulate the terms and conditions of employment throughout the economy" and continued: "Congress may not, of course, transcend specific limitations on its exercise of the commerce power that are imposed by other provisions of the Constitution.　But there is no limitation in the text of the Constitution that is even arguably applicable [here]. The only basis for questioning the [Act] is the pure judicial fiat found in this Court's opinion in [National League of Cities].　Neither the Tenth Amendment, nor any other provision of the Constitution, affords any support for that judicially constructed limitation.　[In] my opinion, that decision must be placed in the same category as [Knight, Hammer v. Dagenhart, and Carter]—cases whose subsequent rejection is now universally regarded as proper.　I think it so plain that National League of Cities not only was incorrectly decided, but also is inconsistent with the central purpose of the Constitution itself, that it is not entitled to the deference that the doctrine of stare decisis ordinarily commands for this Court's precedents.　Notwithstanding my respect for that doctrine, I believe that the law would be well served by a prompt rejection of National League of Cities' modern embodiment of the spirit of the Articles of Confederation." [8]

The major dissent was by Chief Justice BURGER, joined by Justices Powell, Rehnquist, and O'Connor.　The Chief Justice concluded: "The Court decides today that Congress may dictate to the [states] detailed standards governing the selection of state employees.　[Although] the opinion reads the Constitution to allow Congress to usurp this fundamental state function, [I] fail to see where it

5. "Even if the minimal character of the federal intrusion in this case did not lead us to hold that the [Act] survives the third prong of the Hodel inquiry, it might still, when measured against the well-defined federal interest in the legislation, require us to find that the nature of that interest 'justifies state submission.'　We note, incidentally, that the strength of the federal interest underlying the Act is not negated by the fact that the federal government happens to impose mandatory retirement on a small class of its own workers.　Once Congress has asserted a federal interest, and once it has asserted the strength of that interest, we have no warrant for reading into the ebbs and flows of political decisionmaking a conclusion that Congress was insincere in that declaration, and must from that point on evaluate the sufficiency of the federal interest as a matter of law rather than of psychological analysis."　[Footnote by Justice Brennan.]

6. In view of that holding, Justice Brennan found it unnecessary to decide whether the Act was also sustainable under the congressional power in § 5 of the Fourteenth Amendment. But he did specifically reaffirm that, "when properly exercising its power under § 5, Congress is not limited by the same Tenth Amendment constraints that circumscribe the exercise of its Commerce Clause powers [Rome v. United States

(1980); p. 937 below]."　Moreover, Justice Brennan disagreed with the lower court's view that the § 5 power could not come into play unless Congress "expressly articulated its intent to legislate under § 5," as it had not done here.　Justice Brennan replied that, while it was necessary that courts must be "able to discern some legislative purpose or factual predicate that supports the exercise of [§ 5] power," that did not mean that Congress "need anywhere recite the words 'Section 5' or 'Fourteenth Amendment' or 'equal protection,'" for "[t]he constitutionality of action taken by Congress does not depend on recitals of the power which it undertakes to exercise" (quoting Woods v. Miller (1948; p. 222 below).　[Additional § 5 aspects of the EEOC case are noted below, in chap. 10, sec. 4, at p. 970.]

7. Note Justice Powell's disagreement with that emphasis, in his separate dissent below.

8. Justice Stevens' opinion ended as follows: "In exercising its power to regulate the national market for the services of individuals, [may] Congress regulate both the public sector and the private sector of that market, or must it confine its regulation to the private sector?　If the power is to be adequate to enable the National Government to perform its central mission, that question can have only one answer."

grants to the National Government the power to impose such strictures on the states either expressly or by implication. The reserved powers of the states and Justice Brandeis' classic conception of the states as laboratories [9] are turned on their heads when national rather than state governments assert the authority to make decisions on the age standard of state law enforcement officers. [Nothing] in the Constitution permits Congress to force the states into a Procrustean national mold that takes no account of local needs and conditions."

In discussing the commerce power issue, the Chief Justice began with the three prongs of the Hodel test. He found the first prong clearly satisfied. With respect to the second, whether the Act addressed matters that are "attributes of state sovereignty," he found Wyoming's goal of assuring the physical preparedness of its game wardens "surely an attribute of sovereignty, for parks and recreation services were identified in National League of Cities as traditional state activities protected by the Tenth Amendment. Even more important, it is the essence of state powers to choose—subject only to *constitutional* limits—who is to be part of the state government." He gave the most extensive attention to the third prong—"that the federal intrusion must impair the ability of the state to structure integral operations." In finding such an impairment, he emphasized that the Act "can give rise to increased employment costs caused by forced employment of older individuals" and noted such "severe" noneconomic hardships as barring the hiring of those "physically best able to do the job" and impeding promotion opportunities.[10]

Justice POWELL, joined by Justice O'Connor, submitted an additional opinion in order "to record a personal dissent from Justice Stevens' novel view of our Nation's history." He strongly disagreed with Justice Stevens' emphasis on the centrality of the commerce clause in the Constitution: "[One] can be reasonably sure that few of the Founding Fathers thought that trade barriers among the States were 'the central problem,' or that their elimination was the 'central mission' of the Constitutional Convention. Creating a National Government within a federal system was far more central than any 18th century concern for interstate commerce." He accordingly wrote separately to "place the Commerce Clause in proper historical perspective, and further to suggest that even today federalism is not, as Justice Stevens appears to believe, utterly subservient to that Clause." He noted that the position of the commerce clause in the list of delegated Congressional powers "hardly suggests that it was the 'central' concern of the [framers]" and added: "One would never know from the concurring opinion that the Constitution formed a federal system, comprising of a National Government with delegated powers and state governments that retain a significant measure of sovereign authority." He found it "impossi-

---

9. New State Ice Co. v. Liebmann, 285 U.S. 262, 311 (1932) (Brandeis, J., dissenting).

10. The Chief Justice also noted that Congress, even while barring mandatory early retirement of state employees, had written numerous "enclaves" of exceptions into the Act for several groups of federal employees. Nor was the Chief Justice persuaded that the application of the federal law could be justified under Justice Blackmun's balancing test in National League of Cities. He concluded that the "largely theoretical benefits to the Federal Government" did not "outweigh the very real danger that a fire may burn out of control because the firefighters are not physically able to cope; or that a criminal may escape because a law enforcement officer's reflexes are too slow; [or] that an officer may be injured or killed for want of capacity to defend himself. These factors may not be real to Con-

gress but it is not Congress' responsibility to prevent them; they are nonetheless real to the states. I would hold that Commerce Clause powers are wholly insufficient to bar the states from dealing with or preventing these dangers in a rational manner. Wyoming's solution is plainly a rational means." [The Chief Justice summarized the constitutional interests asserted by the Federal Government as "preventing unnecessary demands on the social security system and other maintenance programs," "protecting employees from arbitrary discrimination," and "eliminating unnecessary burdens on the free flow of commerce."] Chief Justice Burger also found that the Act could not be sustained under § 5 of the Fourteenth Amendment. That aspect of his opinion is pursued further in chap. 10, sec. 4, below, at p. 970.

ble" to believe that the Constitution would have been proposed or ratified "if it had been understood that the Commerce Clause embodied the National Government's 'central mission,' a mission to be accomplished even at the expense of regulating the personnel practices of state and local governments." [11]   Justice Powell concluded that Justice Stevens' opinion "recognizes no limitation on the ability of Congress to override state sovereignty in exercising its powers under the Commerce Clause. His opinion does not mention explicitly either federalism or state sovereignty. [Under] this view it is not easy to think of any state function—however sovereign—that could not be pre-empted." [12]

11. Justice Powell also discussed the Tenth Amendment, the aspect of the Bill of Rights which "explicitly recognizes the retained power of the States. [This] limitation was, of course, implicit in the Constitution as originally ratified. [Furthermore], the inherent federal nature of the system is clear from the structure of the National Government itself. [It] was also clear from the contemporary debates that the Founding Fathers intended the Constitution to establish a federal system."

12. Justice Brennan's narrow reading of National League of Cities and Justice Stevens' exhortation that it be rejected outright contributed to the backdrop of the Court action in the Garcia case in 1985. As noted at p. 169 above, Garcia overruled National League of Cities.

Chapter 4

OTHER NATIONAL POWERS IN THE 1787
CONSTITUTION

Scope Note. Because of the central role of the commerce power as a source of national authority to regulate local activities, that power was the focus of the preceding chapter. This chapter turns more briefly to several other national powers granted by the Constitutional Convention—powers which have also had significant regulatory impacts on the allocation of authority within the federal system. The taxing and spending powers are of special interest because of their close functional and doctrinal ties to the commerce power. The Constitutional Convention delegated the taxing and spending powers in the opening clause of Art. I, § 8: "The Congress shall have power To lay and collect Taxes, Duties, Imposts, and Excises, to pay the Debts and provide for the common Defence and general Welfare of the United States." The manner in which taxes are imposed and the way in which revenues are spent have significant regulatory impacts. As with the commerce power, the taxing and spending powers have been invoked to regulate "police" as well as economic problems. Not surprisingly, regulations through taxing and spending have been resorted to in periods, as in the early 20th century, when the need for legislation seemed great and direct regulation through the commerce power was under constitutional clouds. To what extent are the limits pertaining to taxing and spending regulations similar to, and to what extent are they different from, those considered in connection with the commerce power? Those are the primary themes of secs. 1 and 2. Sec. 3 briefly considers two other sources of national authority that are significant to the federal scheme, though even less frequently litigated:[1] it deals with national powers relating to war and foreign relations (especially through treaties).[2]

SECTION 1. THE TAXING POWER

Introduction. To what extent may the congressional taxing power be used as a means of national regulation of arguably local affairs?[1] The materials in this

---

1. For a summary of additional national powers in the 1787 Constitution (which are not examined in detail in this volume), see footnote 1 at the beginning of sec. 3 below, at p. 221.

2. For a comprehensive view of national powers with significant impact on the federal system, one other important basis for congressional action should be noted. That additional source lies not in the 1787 document but in the post-Civil War changes. The 13th, 14th, and 15th Amendments all specify that Congress may "enforce this article by appropriate legislation." That authority long lay dormant because of congressional inaction and restrictive judicial interpretations. But modern congressional efforts and new Court approaches have dramatized the

vast impact of those Amendments on the federal system. The effect of the post-Civil War Amendments on congressional authority is examined in chap. 10 below. (Consideration is postponed to chap. 10 because those issues are best examined after exploring the *judicial* interpretations of the self-executing impacts of those Amendments, in the absence of implementing legislation by Congress.)

1. This section does not deal with national taxation that is clearly for revenue purposes, but the power of Congress to tax for those purposes should of course be borne in mind. The Court has said that the power "is given in the Constitution, with only one exception and only two qualifications. Congress cannot tax exports, and it

section examine the Court's handling of that problem, and they are offered primarily for critical comparison with the preceding commerce power cases. A number of relationships between the two lines of cases has already been noted. For example, tax cases were relied on in the Hammer v. Dagenhart dissent and in Darby; and Congress has repeatedly invoked one of the powers when the other proved to be an inadequate basis for national regulation, as in the child labor area.

Consider, in examining these cases, the similarities and the differences in the development of limits on the commerce and taxing powers. Do the differences in doctrine reflect differences in the nature of the problems? Has the Court been more successful in curbing "abuses" of the taxing power than of the commerce power? Is it easier to detect an invocation of the power to tax as a "pretext"? In short, compare the search for "motive" and "purpose" in tax cases with that in commerce cases. And consider whether it is important to distinguish taxes whose regulatory impact depends on the immediate deterrent effect on the taxed activity from those whose regulatory impact stems from collateral reporting provisions of the tax law.

CHILD LABOR TAX CASE
[BAILEY v. DREXEL FURNITURE CO.]

259 U.S. 20, 42 S.Ct. 449, 66 L.Ed. 817 (1922).

[A few months after the Court had held regulation of child labor through the commerce power unconstitutional in Hammer v. Dagenhart (p. 117 above), Congress enacted the Child Labor Tax Law of 1919. That law imposed a federal excise tax of 10% of annual net profits on every employer of child labor in the covered businesses. The coverage provisions were essentially identical to those in the act invalidated in Hammer v. Dagenhart, except for the interstate commerce feature. After paying a tax of over $6000, the Company successfully brought a refund suit in the District Court.]

Mr. Chief Justice TAFT delivered the opinion of the Court.

[The] law is attacked on the ground that it is a regulation of the employment of child labor in the States—an exclusively state function under the Federal Constitution and within the reservations of the Tenth Amendment. It is defended on the ground that it is a mere excise tax levied by the Congress of the United States under its broad power of taxation conferred by § 8, Article I, of the Federal Constitution. We must construe the law and interpret the intent and meaning of Congress from the language of the act. [Does] this law impose a tax with only that incidental restraint and regulation which a tax must inevitably involve? Or does it regulate by the use of the so-called tax as a penalty? If a tax, it is clearly an excise. If it were an excise on a commodity or other thing of value we might not be permitted under previous decisions of this court to infer solely from its heavy burden that the act intends a prohibition instead of a tax. But this act is more. It provides a heavy exaction for a departure from a detailed and specified course of conduct in business. The course of business is that employers shall employ in mines and quarries, children of an age greater than 16 years; in mills and factories, children of an age greater than 14 years, and shall prevent children of less than 16 years in mills and factories from working more than 8 hours a day or 6 days in a week. If an

must impose direct taxes by the rule of apportionment, and indirect taxes by the rule of uniformity. Thus limited, and thus only, it reaches every subject, and may be exercised at discre-

tion." License Tax Cases, 5 Wall. 462, 471 (1867). For a rare modern interpretation of the uniformity requirement, see United States v. Ptasynski, 462 U.S. 74 (1983).

employer departs from its prescribed course of business, he is to pay the government one-tenth of his entire net income in the business for a full year. The amount is not to be proportioned in any degree to the extent or frequency of the departures, but is to be paid by the employer in full measure whether he employs five hundred children for a year, or employs only one for a day. Moreover, if he does not know the child is within the named age limit, he is not to pay; that is to say, it is only where he knowingly departs from the prescribed course that payment is to be exacted. Scienter is associated with penalties, not with taxes. The employer's factory is to be subject to inspection at any time not only by the taxing officers of the Treasury, the Department normally charged with the collection of taxes, but also by the Secretary of Labor and his subordinates whose normal function is the advancement and protection of the welfare of the workers. In the light of these features of the act, a court must be blind not to see that the so-called tax is imposed to stop the employment of children within the age limits prescribed. Its prohibitory and regulatory effect and purpose are palpable. All others can see and understand this. How can we properly shut our minds to it?

[Out of] a proper respect for the acts of a coordinate branch of the Government, this court has gone far to sustain taxing acts as such, even though there has been ground for suspecting from the weight of the tax it was intended to destroy its subject. But [here], the presumption of validity cannot prevail, because the proof of the contrary is found on the very face of the provisions. Grant the validity of this law, and all that Congress would need to do, hereafter, in seeking to take over to its control any one of the great number of subjects of public interest, jurisdiction of which the States have never parted with, and which are reserved to them by the Tenth Amendment, would be to enact a detailed measure of complete regulation of the subject and enforce it by a so-called tax upon departures from it. To give such magic to the word "tax" would be to break down all constitutional limitation of the powers of Congress and completely wipe out the sovereignty of the States.

The difference between a tax and a penalty is sometimes difficult to define and yet the consequences of the distinction in the required method of their collection often are important. Where the sovereign enacting the law has power to impose both tax and penalty the difference between revenue production and mere regulation may be immaterial, but not so when one sovereign can impose a tax only, and the power of regulation rests in another. Taxes are occasionally imposed in the discretion of the legislature on proper subjects with the primary motive of obtaining revenue from them and with the incidental motive of discouraging them by making their continuance onerous. They do not lose their character as taxes because of the incidental motive. But there comes a time in the extension of the penalizing features of the so-called tax when it loses its character as such and becomes a mere penalty with the characteristics of regulation and punishment. Such is the case [here]. Although Congress [does not] expressly declare that the employment within the mentioned ages is illegal, it does exhibit its intent practically to achieve [this] result by adopting the criteria of wrongdoing and imposing its principal consequence on those who transgress its standard. The case before us can not be distinguished from that of Hammer v. Dagenhart. [This] case requires as did the Dagenhart Case the application of the principle announced by Chief Justice Marshall in [McCulloch], in a much quoted passage [—the "pretext" passage].

But it is pressed upon us that this court has gone so far in sustaining taxing measures the effect or tendency of which was to accomplish purposes not directly within congressional power that we are bound by authority to maintain this law. The first of these is Veazie Bank v. Fenno, 8 Wall. 533 [1869]. In that case, the validity of a law which increased a tax on the circulating notes of persons and state banks from one per centum to ten per centum was in question. [The] second objection was stated by the court: "It is insisted, however, that the tax [is] so excessive as to indicate a purpose on the part of Congress to destroy the franchise of the bank, and is, therefore, beyond the constitutional power of Congress." To this the court answered: "The first answer to this is that the judicial cannot prescribe to the legislative departments of the government limitations upon the exercise of its acknowledged powers. The power to tax may be exercised oppressively upon persons, but the responsibility of the legislature is not to the courts, but to the [people]." It will be observed that the sole objection to the tax there was its excessive character. Nothing else appeared on the face of the act. It was an increase of a tax admittedly legal to a higher rate and that was all. There were no elaborate specifications on the face of the act, as here, indicating the purpose to regulate matters of state concern and jurisdiction through an exaction so applied as to give it the qualities of a penalty for violation of law rather than a tax. [But] more than this, what was charged to be the object of the excessive tax was within the congressional authority, as appears from the second answer which the court gave to the objection. After having pointed out the legitimate means taken by Congress to secure a national medium or currency, the court said: "Having thus, in the exercise of undisputed constitutional powers, undertaken to provide a currency for the whole country, it cannot be questioned that Congress may, constitutionally, secure the benefit of it to the people by appropriate legislation. To this end, [Congress] may restrain, by suitable enactments, the circulation as money of any notes not issued under its own authority."

[The] next case is that of McCray v. United States, 195 U.S. 27 [1904]. That, like [Veazie], was the increase of an excise tax upon a subject properly taxable in which the taxpayers claimed that the tax had become invalid because the increase was excessive. It was a tax on oleomargarine, a substitute for butter. The tax on the white oleomargarine was one-quarter of a cent a pound, and on the yellow oleomargarine [was] ten cents per pound. This court [upheld the tax, applying] the same principle as that applied in [Veazie] Bank Case. It was that Congress, in selecting its subjects for taxation, might impose the burden where and as it would and that a motive disclosed in its selection to discourage sale or manufacture of an article by a higher tax than on some other did not invalidate the tax. In neither of these cases did the law objected to show on its face as does the law before us the detailed specifications of a regulation of a state concern and business with a heavy exaction to promote the efficacy of such [regulation].

[Finally], United States v. Doremus, 249 U.S. 86 [1919], involved the validity of the Narcotic Drug Act, which imposed a special tax on the manufacture, importation and sale or gift of opium or coca leaves or their compounds or derivatives. It required every person subject to the special tax to register with the Collector of Internal Revenue his name and place of business and forbade him to sell except upon the written order of the person to whom the sale was made on a form prescribed by the Commissioner of Internal Revenue. [The] validity of a special tax in the nature of an excise tax on the manufacture, importation and sale of such drugs was, of course, unquestioned. The provisions for subjecting the sale and distribution of the drugs to official supervision and inspection were held to have a reasonable relation to the enforcement of the tax and were therefore held valid.[1] The court said that the act could not be

---

1. The "special tax" at the time of the Doremus case was $1 per year. Compare the later decision in Nigro v. United States, 276 U.S. 332 (1928), where the Court noted that the Narcotic Drug Act had been amended to produce substantial revenue from the tax and added: "If there was doubt of the character of this act as an alleged subterfuge, it has been removed by the change whereby what was a nominal tax before was made a substantial one."

declared invalid just because another motive than taxation, not shown on the face of the act, might have contributed to its passage. This case does not militate against the conclusion we have reached in respect of the law now before us. The court, there, made manifest its view that the provisions of the so-called taxing act must be naturally and reasonably adapted to the collection of the tax and not solely to the achievement of some other purpose plainly within state power.

For the reasons given, we must hold the Child Labor Tax Law invalid. [Affirmed.] [2]

THE USE OF THE TAXING POWER FOR REGULATORY PURPOSES

1. *The prior decisions.* The important regulatory tax cases before the Child Labor Tax Case—Veazie, McCray, and Doremus—are described in Chief Justice Taft's opinion. Are the prior decisions distinguishable, or did the principal case manifest a significant shift in approach? Note that the relationship of the principal case to those earlier tax decisions is similar to that of Hammer v. Dagenhart to the earlier commerce-prohibiting cases (e.g., the Lottery Case and the cases sustaining the Mann Act and the Pure Food and Drug Act).

2. *Early 20th century commerce and tax cases: Parallels and contrasts.* a. Note that Justice Holmes was in the majority in the Child Labor Tax Case—just four years after his dissent in Hammer v. Dagenhart. In the principal case, he joined in looking beyond the congressional label to invalidate because of forbidden purpose; in his dissent in Hammer v. Dagenhart, he had insisted that the Court could *not* look to purposes and obvious collateral effects and must sustain a law using the commerce-prohibiting technique. Are Holmes' positions in the two cases reconcilable? Moreover, in Hammer v. Dagenhart, Holmes had relied on McCray, the oleomargarine tax case, to show that judicial inquiry into congressional purpose was improper. And the McCray tax decision of 1904, in turn, had relied on the commerce power Lottery Case of 1903 in rejecting the notion "that the judiciary may restrain the exercise of lawful power on the assumption that a wrongful purpose or motive has caused the power to be exerted." At the time of Hammer v. Dagenhart in 1918, in short, Holmes was opposing judicial invalidation because of improper purpose in tax (McCray) as well as commerce (Lottery, Child Labor) cases. By 1922, in the principal case, had Holmes abandoned that position? In commerce as well as in tax cases? Because he was in the minority in Hammer? Only in tax cases? Only in some tax cases— because bad purpose was clearer in the principal case than in McCray? Compare Justice Frankfurter's "purpose" position in Kahriger, below, and note the additional questions on tax-commerce parallels and contrasts after Kahriger.

b. Shortly after the Narcotics Act decision in Doremus in 1919, Justice Holmes wrote to Judge Learned Hand: "As to the [Drug Act case], *(between ourselves)* I am tickled at every case of that sort as they seem to me to confirm the ground of my dissent in the Child Labor case last term. Hammer v. Dagenhart. Also, I think the drug act cases rightly decided. In my opinion Congress may have what ulterior motives they please if the act passed in the immediate aspect is within their powers—though personally, were I a legislator I might think it dishonest to use powers in that way." [1] Are Justice Holmes' positions in Doremus and the Child Labor Tax Case reconcilable? Are the cases distinguishable because the economic sanction in the child labor situation (10% of net

---

2. Only Justice Clarke dissented.

1. Oliver Wendell Holmes to Learned Hand, April 3, 1919, quoted in Gunther, "Learned Hand and the Origins of Modern First Amendment Doctrine," 27 Stan.L.Rev. 719 (1975).

profits for noncompliance) was more substantial than that in the narcotics situation ($1 a year at the time of Doremus)? Which way should that distinction cut? Which scheme was more justifiable as a regulatory device incidental to a revenue raising measure? [2]

c. Hill v. Wallace, 259 U.S. 44 (1922), decided on the same day as—and with reliance on—the Child Labor Tax Case, again illustrates alternate uses of the taxing and commerce powers. In Hill, the Court invalidated the Future Trading Act, under which a tax of 20 cents was imposed on every bushel of grain involved in a contract or sale for future delivery—except sales on boards of trade certified as meeting the detailed regulatory requirements of the federal law. The Hill decision was urged upon the Court to show the invalidity of a subsequent commerce power-based regulation of boards of trade, the 1922 Grain Future Trading Act. But that Act was sustained in Chicago Board of Trade v. Olsen, 262 U.S. 1 (1923).[3]

3. *From the Child Labor Tax Case to Kahriger.* In United States v. Constantine, 296 U.S. 287 (1935), defendant was convicted of conducting the business of retail dealer in malt liquor contrary to the laws of Alabama without having paid a special excise tax of $1000 imposed by Congress. He had paid the normal tax of $25 for conducting the business, and the question presented was "whether the exaction of $1000 in addition, by reason solely of his violation of state law, is a tax or penalty." Justice Roberts' opinion for the Court concluded that "the indicia which the section exhibits of an intent to prohibit and to punish violations of state law as such are too strong to be disregarded, remove all semblance of a revenue act and stamp the sum it exacts as a penalty. In this view the statute is a clear invasion of the police power, inherent in the [states]. Reference was made in the argument to decisions [holding] that where the power to tax is conceded the motive for the execution may not be questioned. [They] are not authority where, as [here], under the guise of a taxing act the purpose is to usurp the police powers of the state." [4] But Sonzinsky v. United States, 300 U.S. 506 (1937), sustained the National Firearms Act of 1934, which imposed a $200 annual license tax on dealers in firearms. Noting that the tax "is productive of some revenue," the Court said "we are not free to speculate as to the motives which moved Congress to impose it, or as to the extent to which it may operate to restrict the activities taxed. As it is not attended by an offensive regulation, and since it operates as a tax, it is within the national taxing power." [5]

---

2. Note generally Cushman, "Social and Economic Control Through Federal Taxation," 18 Minn.L.Rev. 759 (1934), concluding "that we have at present two available judicial techniques for dealing with the validity of national police regulations under the taxing power": the criterion of "objective constitutionality," or "judicial obtuseness," which permits the Court to sustain a regulatory tax; and the "penalty" theory, which invalidates the statute because it "imposes a penalty, rather than levies a tax."

3. For similar successive invocations of the fiscal and commerce powers, compare United States v. Butler, p. 202 below, with Mulford v. Smith, p. 138 above (agricultural production and marketing).

4. Justice Cardozo, joined by Justices Brandeis and Stone, dissented: "Thus the process of psychoanalysis has spread to unaccustomed fields."

5. See also United States v. Sanchez, 340 U.S. 42 (1950), which upheld the Marihuana Tax Act of 1937. The Act placed a tax ($100 per ounce) on the transfer of marijuana to an unregistered person. The statute contained no regulations other than the registration provisions and had as its primary objective the restriction of the traffic to accepted industrial and medicinal channels, with only a secondary objective of raising revenue. The tax was sustained as "a legitimate exercise of the taxing power despite its collateral regulatory purpose and effect."

UNITED STATES v. KAHRIGER

345 U.S. 22, 73 S.Ct. 510, 97 L.Ed. 754 (1953).

Mr. Justice REED delivered the opinion of the Court.

The issue raised by this appeal is the constitutionality of the occupational tax provisions of the Revenue Act of 1951, which levy a tax on persons engaged in the business of accepting wagers, and require such persons to register with the Collector of Internal Revenue.[1] [An attack on the tax scheme as violating the self-incrimination privilege of the Fifth Amendment was rejected by the majority. That aspect of Kahriger was overruled fifteen years later, in the Marchetti case, noted below. The passages from the opinion printed here focus on the other ground of the constitutional challenge: the claim that Congress, "under the pretense of exercising its power to tax, has attempted to penalize illegal intrastate gambling through the regulatory features of the Act" and "has thus infringed the police power which is reserved to the states."[2]]

[Appellee] would have us say that, because there is legislative history[3] indicating a congressional motive to suppress wagering, this tax is not a proper exercise of such taxing power. [But an] intent to curtail and hinder, as well as tax, was also manifest in the series of cases beginning with [Veazie], and in each of them the tax was [upheld]. It is conceded that a federal excise tax does not cease to be valid merely because it discourages or deters the activities taxed. Nor is the tax invalid because the revenue obtained is negligible. Appellee, however, argues that the sole purpose of the statute is to penalize only illegal gambling in the states through the guise of a tax measure. As with the above excise taxes which we have held to be valid, the instant tax has a regulatory effect. But regardless of its regulatory effect, the wagering tax produces

1. In a footnote, Justice Reed quoted the provisions of the Act imposing on covered persons an annual excise tax of 10% on all wagers, a special tax of fifty dollars per year, and a requirement that name, residence, place of business, and name and residence of each employee, be registered with the Collector of Internal Revenue.

Justice Reed did not quote a number of other provisions of the law, including one requiring the Collector to "place and keep conspicuously in his office, for public inspection, an alphabetical list of the names" of all taxpayers under these provisions, and to furnish certified copies of those lists "upon application of any prosecuting officer of any State, county, or municipality."

Should Justice Reed have quoted those provisions as well? Is there a significant difference between (a) regulatory effects challenged because of the direct impact of the tax in deterring the taxed activity, and (b) regulatory effects challenged because of the impact of collateral enforcement features of the tax (such as registration), as in Doremus, above, and arguably in Kahriger as well? See also footnote 3 below and note 2 following this case.

2. The District Court had sustained that claim on the authority of United States v. Constantine, 296 U.S. 287 (1935), note 3 preceding this case. Justice Reed disagreed, noting that Sonzinsky v. United States (also in note 3) had

explained Constantine as turning on the fact that the subject of the tax was "described or treated as criminal by the taxing statute." Here, by contrast, the wagering tax "applies to all persons engaged in the business of receiving wagers, regardless of whether such activity violates state law."

3. There are suggestions in the debates that Congress sought to hinder, if not prevent, the type of gambling taxed. See 97 Cong.Rec. 6892:

"Mr. Hoffman of Michigan. Then I will renew my observation that it might if properly construed be considered an additional penalty on the illegal activities.

"Mr. Cooper. Certainly, and we might indulge the hope that the imposition of this type of tax would eliminate that kind of activity." 97 Cong.Rec. 12236: "If the local official does not want to enforce the law and no one catches him winking at the law, he may keep on winking at it, but when the Federal Government identifies a law violator, and the local newspaper gets hold of it, and the local church organizations get hold of it, and the people who do want the law enforced get hold of it, they say, 'Mr. Sheriff, what about it? We understand that there is a place down here licensed to sell liquor.' He says, 'Is that so? I will put him out of business.'" [Footnote by Justice Reed.]

revenue. As such it surpasses both the narcotics and firearms taxes which we have found valid.[4]

It is axiomatic that the power of Congress to tax is extensive and sometimes falls with crushing effect on businesses deemed unessential or inimical to the public welfare, or where, as in dealing with narcotics, the collection of the tax also is difficult. [The] difficulty of saying when the power to lay uniform taxes is curtailed, because its use brings a result beyond the direct legislative power of Congress, has given rise to diverse decisions. In that area of abstract ideas, a final definition of the line between state and federal power has baffled judges and legislators. While the Court has never questioned the ["pretext"] statement of Mr. Chief Justice Marshall in [McCulloch], the application of the rule has brought varying holdings on constitutionality. Where federal legislation has rested on other congressional powers, such as [the] Commerce Clause, this Court has generally sustained the statutes, despite their effect on matters ordinarily considered state concern. [Where] Congress has employed the taxing clause a greater variation in the decisions has resulted. The division in this Court has been more acute. Without any specific differentiation between the power to tax and other federal powers, the indirect results from the exercise of the power to tax have raised more doubts. [It] is hard to understand why the power to tax should raise more doubts because of indirect effects than other federal powers. Unless there are [penalty] provisions extraneous to any tax need, courts are without authority to limit the exercise of the taxing power. All the provisions of this excise are adapted to the collection of a valid tax. Nor do we find the registration requirements of the wagering tax offensive. All that is required is the filing of names, addresses, and places of business. This is quite general in tax returns. Such data are directly and intimately related to the collection of the tax and are "obviously supportable as in aid of a revenue purpose." [Sonzinsky.] The registration provisions make the tax simpler to [collect].

Reversed.

Mr. Justice JACKSON, concurring.

I concur in the judgment and opinion of the Court, but with such doubt that if the minority agreed upon an opinion which did not impair legitimate use of the taxing power I probably would join it. But we deal here with important and contrasting values in our scheme of government, and it is important that neither be allowed to destroy the other. [Of course], all taxation has a tendency, proportioned to its burdensomeness, to discourage the activity taxed. One cannot formulate a revenue-raising plan that would not have economic and social consequences. [But] here is a purported tax law which requires no reports and lays no tax except on specified gamblers whose calling in most states is illegal. It requires this group to step forward and identify themselves, not because they, like others, have income, but because of its source. This is difficult to regard as a rational or good-faith revenue measure, despite the deference that is due Congress. On the contrary, it seems to be a plan to tax out of existence the professional gambler whom it has been found impossible to prosecute out of existence.

[The] United States has a system of taxation by confession. That a people so numerous, scattered and individualistic annually assesses itself with a tax liability, often in highly burdensome amounts, is a reassuring sign of the stability and

---

4. One of the indicia which appellee offers to support his contention that the wagering tax is not a proper revenue measure is that the tax amount collected under it was $4,371,869, as compared with an expected amount of $400,000,000 a year. The figure of $4,371,869, however, is relatively large when it is compared with the $3,501 collected under the tax on adulterated and processed or renovated butter and filled cheese, the $914,910 collected under the tax on narcotics, including marihuana and special taxes, and the $28,911 collected under the tax on firearms, transfer and occupational taxes. [Footnote by Justice Reed.]

vitality of our system of self-government. [It] will be a sad day for the revenues if the good will of the people toward their taxing system is frittered away in efforts to accomplish by taxation moral reforms that cannot be accomplished by direct legislation.   But the evil that can come from this statute will probably soon make itself manifest to Congress.   The evil of a judicial decision impairing the legitimate taxing power by extreme constitutional interpretations might not be transient.   Even though this statute approaches the fair limits of constitutionality, I join the decision of the Court.

Mr. Justice FRANKFURTER, dissenting.

[When] oblique use is made of the taxing power as to matters which substantively are not within the powers delegated to Congress, the Court cannot shut its eyes to what is obviously, because designedly, an attempt to control conduct which the Constitution left to the responsibility of the States, merely because Congress wrapped the legislation in the verbal cellophane of a revenue measure.   Concededly the constitutional questions presented by such legislation are difficult.   On the one hand, courts should scrupulously abstain from hobbling congressional choice of policies, particularly when the vast reach of the taxing power is concerned.   On the other hand, to allow what otherwise is excluded from congressional authority to be brought within it by casting legislation in the form of a revenue measure could, as so significantly expounded in the Child Labor Tax Case, offer an easy way for the legislative imagination to control "any one of the great number of subjects of public interest, jurisdiction of which the States have never parted with."   I say "significantly" because Mr. Justice Holmes and two of the Justices who had joined his dissent in [Hammer v. Dagenhart] agreed with the opinion in the Child Labor Tax Case.

[What] is relevant to judgment here is that, even if the history of this legislation as it went through Congress did not give one the libretto to the song, the context of the circumstances which brought forth this enactment—sensationally exploited disclosures regarding gambling in big cities and small, the relation of this gambling to corrupt politics, the impatient public response to these disclosures, the feeling of ineptitude or paralysis on the part of local law-enforcing agencies—emphatically supports what was revealed on the floor of Congress, namely, that what was formally a means of raising revenue for the Federal Government was essentially an effort to check if not to stamp out professional gambling.

A nominal taxing measure must be found an inadmissible intrusion into a domain of legislation reserved for the States not merely when Congress requires that such a measure is to be enforced through a detailed scheme of administration beyond the obvious fiscal needs, as in the Child Labor Tax Case.   That is one ground for holding that Congress was constitutionally disrespectful of what is reserved to the States.   Another basis for deeming such a formal revenue measure inadmissible is presented by this case.   In addition to the fact that Congress was concerned with activity beyond the authority of the Federal Government, the enforcing provision of this enactment is designed for the systematic confession of crimes with a view to prosecution for such crimes under State law.   [The] motive of congressional legislation is not for our scrutiny, provided only that the ulterior purpose is not expressed in ways which negative what the revenue words on their face express and which do not seek enforcement of the formal revenue purpose through means that offend those standards of decency in our civilization against which due process is a [barrier].[5]

---

5. Justice Frankfurter appended a brief notation to his opinion: "Mr. Justice DOUGLAS, while not joining in the entire opinion, agrees with the views expressed herein that this tax is an attempt by the Congress to control conduct which the Constitution has left to the responsibil-

THE TAXING AND COMMERCE POWERS: MODERN PARALLELS AND CONTRASTS

1. *Divergent paths.* Does Kahriger suggest more substantial modern limits on regulatory taxes than on commerce power-based legislation? Does it suggest greater judicial scrutiny of congressional action than the Court was willing to undertake in Darby and Wickard? Recall the questions in note 2 after the Child Labor Tax Case. With respect to judicial inquiry into the purposes and collateral effects of the commerce-prohibiting technique, the majority view in Hammer v. Dagenhart was overruled in Darby. Has there been a parallel development regarding the taxing power? Is the majority approach in the Child Labor Tax Case (1922) more respectable today than the discredited Hammer v. Dagenhart (1918) position? Note that Justice Stone's opinion in Darby relied on McCray and Veazie Bank (the early taxing power cases discussed in the Child Labor Tax Case) in support of his refusal to inquire into the motive and purpose of commerce regulation; and Stone's opinion was for a unanimous Court. In the commerce area, in short, the modern Court has apparently abandoned all "pretext" control. Yet as to taxing, in Kahriger, there are several dissents on that abuse of power issue from members of the post-1937 Court. Is the difference explainable?

2. *Judicial competence to ascertain primary congressional purposes.* Justice Reed in Kahriger thought it "hard to understand why the power to tax should raise more doubts because of indirect effects than other federal powers." What *is* the explanation of the difference? Is it because "ordinary," revenue-raising taxes are less likely to have "indirect effects" than "ordinary" commerce regulations? But see Justice Jackson's concurrence: "One cannot formulate a revenue-raising plan that would not have economic and social consequences." Is it because the federal scheme conveys clearer implications about the primary purpose of tax than of commerce legislation? Because it implies more clearly that taxes must have a primary revenue-raising objective, and that Congress may only pursue other objectives so long as they are ancillary to revenue-raising? But is there no historical guidance about the proper primary purpose of commerce regulations? And if some Justices are willing to distinguish between primary and ancillary

ity of the States." Another dissent—by Justice BLACK, joined by Justice Douglas—relied solely on the self-incrimination provision of the Fifth Amendment.

The Fifth Amendment aspect of Kahriger was overruled 15 years later, in Marchetti v. United States, 390 U.S. 39 (1968). Justice Harlan's majority opinion repeatedly referred to the statutory provision printed in footnote 1 to the Kahriger case, but not mentioned by Justice Reed in Kahriger. But a year after the Marchetti case, the Court rejected a constitutional challenge based on it and directed at the statutory prohibitions on selling narcotic drugs and marijuana without the written order forms required by law. Minor v. United States (and Buie v. United States), 396 U.S. 87 (1969). Though the majority spoke only of the Fifth Amendment claim, Justice Douglas' dissent, joined by Justice Black, reached the federalism problem as well. In urging the reversal of Minor's conviction for selling heroin without an order form, Justice Douglas noted: "The Federal Government does not have plenary power to define and punish criminal acts." Moreover, Justice Douglas was not per-

suaded by a suggestion that "a statute imposing a flat ban on sales of heroin might be sustainable under the Commerce Clause": "We are concerned in this case with what the Congress did, not with what it might have done or might yet do in the future. It is clear that what Congress did [was] to enact a taxing measure." The majority limited its response to that federalism objection to a footnote: "[Even viewing the provision] as little more than a flat ban on certain sales, it is sustainable under the powers granted Congress in Art. I, § 8," citing cases such as United States v. Sullivan and Darby.

Should congressional authority be tested in terms of the powers it *purports* to exercise? Or should the Court use its own imaginativeness to search for sources of power that *might* justify a statute? Compare Justice Douglas' majority opinion in Woods, a 1948 war power case at p. 222 below: "The question of the constitutionality of action taken by Congress does not depend on recitals of the power which it undertakes to exercise." Recall the discussion of this issue in a number of the cases in the preceding chapter.

objectives with respect to the taxing power, why are they unwilling—or view themselves as incompetent—to do so with respect to the commerce power?

Was the wagering tax a variety of tax that "discourages or deters the activities taxed" because of the impact of the taxing sanction? Or did the regulatory impact stem from the collateral reporting features, as in Doremus? Should Justice Reed have focused on those features rather than the "regulatory effect" of the tax itself? Or are the "abuse of power" problems raised by those two varieties of regulatory impacts essentially similar? Are the kinds of data Justice Frankfurter relies on to identify "ulterior purpose" in Kahriger the kinds the Court *should* rely on? In taxing cases? In commerce power cases as well?

SECTION 2. THE SPENDING POWER

Introduction. The national spending power is probably the most important of all Art. I, § 8 powers in its impact on the actual functioning of the federal system. Whether in the context of payments to individuals for particular purposes (as with old age support under Social Security) or of conditional grants to states (as with education or welfare) or of direct financing of federal entrepreneurial operations (as with the TVA), national decisions about spending involve pervasive policy choices and have significant regulatory consequences. Yet litigation about the scope of the power has been rare, for restrictive doctrines regarding standing to sue have traditionally barred taxpayer challenges to federal spending programs. (See chap. 15.) But the constitutional questions are no less real for the sparsity of judicial decisions. From the beginning, spending proposals have provoked disputes: at the time of McCulloch, for example, the constitutionality of federal spending for roads and canals was a subject of lively debate. And the scope of the spending power has been a recurrent source of controversy ever since. What *are* the legitimate purposes of national spending? What is the proper role of courts in assessing legitimacy when justiciability principles permit decisions on the merits? What conditions may Congress impose on spending programs? What is constitutionally required with respect to the relationship between the condition, the particular program, and the "general welfare"? To what extent may Congress "coerce" state or individual behavior when it resorts to the carrot of federal funds rather than the stick of civil and criminal sanctions? These are the questions for major attention in examining the materials in this section.

UNITED STATES v. BUTLER

297 U.S. 1, 56 S.Ct. 312, 80 L.Ed. 477 (1936).

Mr. Justice ROBERTS delivered the opinion of the Court.

[This decision invalidated one of the major New Deal measures, the Agricultural Adjustment Act of 1933. The Act sought to raise farm prices by curtailing agricultural production. It authorized the Secretary of Agriculture to make contracts with farmers to reduce their productive acreage in exchange for benefit payments. The payments were to be made out of funds payable by the processor: a processing tax was imposed "upon the first domestic processing" of the particular commodity. A processing tax on cotton was imposed upon the Hoosac Mills Corporation. Butler and his coreceivers for the company successfully attacked the tax, claiming that it was an integral part of an unconstitutional program to control agricultural production.] [1]

The Government asserts that even if the respondents may question the propriety of the appropriation embodied in the statute their attack must fail because Article I, § 8 of the Constitution authorizes the contemplated expenditure of the funds raised by the tax. This contention presents the great and the controlling question in the case. [There] should be no misunderstanding as to the function of this court in such a case. It is sometimes said that the court assumes a power to overrule or control the action of the people's representatives. This is a misconception. [When] an act of Congress is appropriately challenged in the courts as not conforming to the constitutional mandate the judicial branch of the Government has only one duty,—to lay the article of the Constitution which is invoked beside the statute which is challenged and to decide whether the latter squares with the former. [This] court neither approves nor condemns any legislative policy. Its delicate and difficult office is to ascertain and declare whether the legislation is in accordance with, or in contravention of, the provisions of the Constitution; and, having done that, its duty ends. [After noting that the Government had not sought to justify the Act on the basis of the commerce power, Justice Roberts continued:]

The clause thought to authorize the [Act] confers upon the Congress power "to lay and collect Taxes, Duties, Imposts and Excises, to pay the Debts and provide for the common Defence and general Welfare of the United States." [It] is not contended that this provision grants power to regulate agricultural production upon the theory that such legislation would promote the general welfare. The Government concedes that the phrase "to provide for the general welfare" qualifies the power "to lay and collect taxes." The view that the clause grants power to provide for the general welfare, independently of the taxing power, has never been authoritatively accepted. Mr. Justice Story points out that if it were adopted "it is obvious that under color of the generality of the words, to 'provide for the common defence and general welfare,' the government of the United States is in reality, a government of general and unlimited powers, notwithstanding the subsequent enumeration of specific powers." The true construction undoubtedly is that the only thing granted is the power to tax for the purpose of providing funds for payment of the nation's debts and making provision for the general welfare. Nevertheless, the Government asserts that warrant is found in this clause for the adoption of the [Act]. The argument is that Congress may appropriate and authorize the spending of moneys for the "general welfare"; that the phrase should be liberally construed to cover anything conducive to national welfare; that decision as to what will promote such welfare rests with Congress alone, and the courts may not review its determination; and finally that the appropriation under attack was in fact for the general welfare of the United States.

[Since] the foundation of the Nation, sharp differences of opinion have persisted as to the true interpretation of the phrase. Madison asserted it amounted to no more than a reference to the other powers enumerated in the subsequent clauses of the same section; that, as the United States is a govern-

---

1. Before turning to the merits, the Court rejected the Government's challenge to Butler's standing to sue. The Government had claimed that under cases such as Frothingham v. Mellon (p. 1543 below), taxpayers could not question federal spending programs. But the Court found that barrier inapplicable. It found that this was not merely a taxpayers' suit "to restrain the expenditure of the public monies." Rather, the taxpayers here "resist the exaction as a step in an authorized plan." The taxing and spending as-pects of a statute imposing an earmarked tax could not be separated: "The whole revenue from the levy is appropriated in aid of crop control; none of it is made available for general governmental use." The Court accordingly found "that the act is one regulating agricultural production; that the tax is a mere incident of such regulation; and that the respondents have standing to challenge the legality of the exaction."

ment of limited and enumerated powers, the grant of power to tax and spend for the general national welfare must be confined to the enumerated legislative fields committed to the Congress. In this view the phrase is mere tautology, for taxation and appropriation are or may be necessary incidents of the exercise of any of the enumerated legislative powers. Hamilton, on the other hand, maintained the clause confers a power separate and distinct from those later enumerated, is not restricted in meaning by the grant of them, and Congress consequently has a substantive power to tax and to appropriate, limited only by the requirement that it shall be exercised to provide for the general welfare of the United States. Each contention has had the support of those whose views are entitled to weight. This court has noticed the question, but has never found it necessary to decide which is the true construction. Mr. Justice Story, in his Commentaries, espouses the Hamiltonian position. We shall not review the writings of public men and commentators or discuss the legislative practice. Study of all these leads us to conclude that the reading advocated by Mr. Justice Story is the correct one. While, therefore, the power to tax is not unlimited, its confines are set in the clause which confers it, and not in those of § 8 which bestow and define the legislative powers of the Congress. It results that the power of Congress to authorize expenditure of public moneys for public purposes is not limited by the direct grants of legislative power found in the Constitution.

[We] are not now required to ascertain the scope of the phrase "general welfare of the United States" or to determine whether an appropriation in aid of agriculture falls within it. Wholly apart from that question, another principle embedded in our Constitution prohibits the enforcement of the [Act]. The Act invades the reserved rights of the states. It is a statutory plan to regulate and control agricultural production, a matter beyond the powers delegated to the federal government. The tax, the appropriation of the funds raised, and the direction for their disbursement, are but parts of the plan. They are but means to an unconstitutional end. [It] is an established principle that the attainment of a prohibited end may not be accomplished under the pretext of the exertion of powers which are granted [quoting Marshall's "pretext" statement in McCulloch].

[If] the taxing power may not be used as the instrument to enforce a regulation of matters of state concern with respect to which the Congress has no authority to interfere [e.g., Child Labor Tax Case], may it, as in the present case, be employed to raise the money necessary to purchase a compliance which the Congress is powerless to command? The Government asserts that whatever might be said against the validity of the plan if compulsory, it is constitutionally sound because the end is accomplished by voluntary co-operation. There are two sufficient answers to the contention. The regulation is not in fact voluntary. The farmer, of course, may refuse to comply, but the price of such refusal is the loss of benefits. The amount offered is intended to be sufficient to exert pressure on him to agree to the proposed regulation. The power to confer or withhold unlimited benefits is the power to coerce or destroy. If the cotton grower elects not to accept the benefits, he will receive less for his crops. [The] result may well be financial ruin. [This] is coercion by economic pressure. The asserted power of choice is illusory.

[But] if the plan were one for purely voluntary co-operation it would stand no better so far as federal power is concerned. At best, it is a scheme for purchasing with federal funds submission to federal regulation of a subject reserved to the states. It is said that Congress has the undoubted right to appropriate money to executive officers for expenditure under contracts between the government and individuals. [But] appropriations and expenditures under contracts for proper governmental purposes cannot justify contracts which are not within federal power. And contracts for the reduction of acreage and the control of production are outside the range of that power. An appropriation to be expended by the United States under contracts calling for violation of a state law clearly would offend the Constitution. Is a statute less objectionable which authorizes expenditure of federal moneys to induce action in a field in which the United States has no power to intermeddle? The Congress cannot invade state jurisdiction to compel individual action; no more can it purchase such action.

[We] are not here concerned with a conditional appropriation of money, nor with a provision that if certain conditions are not complied with the appropriation shall no longer be available. By the [Act] the amount of the tax is appropriated to be expended only in payment under contracts whereby the parties bind themselves to regulation by the Federal Government. There is an obvious difference between a statute stating the conditions upon which moneys shall be expended and one effective only upon assumption of a contractual obligation to submit to a regulation which otherwise could not be enforced. Many examples pointing the distinction might be cited. We are referred to appropriations in aid of education, and it is said that no one has doubted the power of Congress to stipulate the sort of education for which money shall be expended. But an appropriation to an educational institution which by its terms is to become available only if the beneficiary enters into a contract to teach doctrines subversive of the Constitution is clearly bad. An affirmance of the authority of Congress so to condition the expenditure of an appropriation would tend to nullify all constitutional limitations upon legislative power.

[Congress] has no power to enforce its commands on the farmer to the ends sought by the [Act]. It must follow that it may not indirectly accomplish those ends by taxing and spending to purchase compliance. The Constitution and the entire plan of our government negative any such use of the power to tax and to spend as the act undertakes to authorize. It does not help to declare that local conditions throughout the nation have created a situation of national concern; for this is but to say that whenever there is a widespread similarity of local conditions, Congress may ignore constitutional limitations upon its own powers and usurp those reserved to the states. [If the Act is] a proper exercise of the federal taxing power, evidently the regulation of all industry throughout the United States may be accomplished by similar exercises of the same power. [The] sole premise [of the Government's argument] is that, though the makers of the Constitution, in erecting the federal government, intended sedulously to limit [its powers], they nevertheless by a single clause gave power to the Congress to tear down the barriers, to invade the states' jurisdiction, and to become a parliament of the whole people, subject to no restrictions save such as are self-imposed. The argument when seen in its true character and in the light of its inevitable results must be [rejected].

Affirmed.

Mr. Justice STONE, dissenting.[1]

The power of courts to declare a statute unconstitutional is subject to two guiding principles of decision which ought never to be absent from judicial consciousness. One is that courts are concerned only with the power to enact statutes, not with their wisdom. The other is that while unconstitutional exercise of power by the executive and legislative branches of the government is

---

1. The opening and closing paragraphs in this dissent—a dissent joined by Justices Brandeis and Cardozo—are of special historical interest: it was passages like these that President Roosevelt relied on in his attacks on the Court at the time of the Court-packing plan. See, e.g., his radio address of March 9, 1937, quoted at p. 129 above: "[T]he Court has been assuming the power to pass on the wisdom of these acts of the Congress. [That] is not only my accusation. It is the accusation of most distinguished Justices of the present Supreme Court."

subject to judicial restraint, the only check upon our own exercise of power is our own sense of self-restraint. For the removal of unwise laws from the statute books appeal lies not to the courts but to the ballot and to the processes of democratic government.

[As] the present depressed state of agriculture is nation wide in its extent and effects, there is no basis for saying that the expenditure of public money in aid of farmers is not within the specifically granted power of Congress to levy taxes to "provide for [the] general welfare." The opinion of the Court does not declare otherwise. [Of] the assertion that the payments to farmers are coercive, it is enough to say that no such contention is pressed by the taxpayer, and no such consequences were to be anticipated or appear to have resulted from the administration of the act. The suggestion of coercion finds no support in the record or in any data showing the actual operation of the act. Threat of loss, not hope of gain, is the essence of economic coercion.

[It] is upon the contention that state power is infringed by purchased regulation of agricultural production that chief reliance is placed. [The] Constitution requires that public funds shall be spent for a defined purpose, the promotion of the general welfare. Their expenditure usually involves payment on terms which will insure use by the selected recipients within the limits of the constitutional purpose. Expenditures would fail of their purpose and thus lose their constitutional sanction if the terms of payment were not such that by their influence on the action of the recipients the permitted end would be attained. The power of Congress to spend is inseparable from persuasion to action over which Congress has no legislative control. Congress may not command that the science of agriculture be taught in state universities. But if it would aid the teaching of that science by grants to state institutions, it is appropriate, if not necessary, that the grant be on the condition, incorporated in the Morrill Act, that it be used for the intended purpose. Similarly it would seem to be compliance with the Constitution, not violation of it, for the government to take and the university to give a contract that the grant would be so used. It makes no difference that there is a promise to do an act which the condition is calculated to induce. Condition and promise are alike valid since both are in furtherance of the national purpose for which the money is appropriated. [It] is a contradiction in terms to say that there is power to spend for the national welfare, while rejecting any power to impose conditions reasonably adapted to the attainment of the end which alone would justify the expenditure.

The limitation now sanctioned must lead to absurd consequences. The government may give seeds to farmers, but may not condition the gift upon their being planted in places where they are most needed or even planted at all. The government may give money to the unemployed, but may not ask that those who get it shall give labor in return, or even use it to support their families. [It] may support rural schools, [but] may not condition its grant by the requirement that certain standards be maintained. [Do] all its activities collapse because, in order to effect the permissible purpose, in myriad ways the money is paid out upon terms and conditions which influence action of the recipients within the states, which Congress cannot command? The answer would seem plain. If the expenditure is for a national public purpose, that purpose will not be thwarted because payment is on condition which will advance that purpose. The action which Congress induces by payments of money to promote the general welfare, but which it does not command or coerce, is but an incident to a specifically granted power, but a permissible means to a legitimate end. If appropriation in aid of a program of curtailment of agricultural production is constitutional, and it is not denied that it is, payment to farmers on condition that they reduce their crop acreage is constitutional. It is not any the less so because the farmer at his own option promises to fulfill the condition.

That the governmental power of the purse is a great one is not now for the first time announced. [The] suggestion that it must now be curtailed by judicial fiat because it may be abused by unwise use hardly rises to the dignity of argument. So may judicial power be abused. [The] power to tax and spend is not without constitutional restraints. One restriction is that the purpose must be truly national. Another is that it may not be used to coerce action left to state control. Another is the conscience and patriotism of Congress and the Executive. [A] tortured construction of the Constitution is not to be justified by recourse to extreme examples of reckless congressional spending which might occur if courts could not prevent—expenditures which, even if they could be thought to effect any national purpose, would be possible only by action of a legislature lost to all sense of public responsibility. Such suppositions are addressed to the mind accustomed to believe that it is the business of courts to sit in judgment on the wisdom of legislative action. Courts are not the only agency of government that must be assumed to have capacity to govern. Congress and the courts both unhappily may falter or be mistaken in the performance of their constitutional duty. But interpretation of our great charter of government which proceeds on any assumption that the responsibility for the preservation of our institutions is the exclusive concern of any one of the three branches of government, or that it alone can save them from destruction is far more likely, in the long run, "to obliterate the constituent members" of "an indestructible union of indestructible states" than the frank recognition that language, even of a constitution, may mean what it says: that the power to tax and spend includes the power to relieve a nationwide economic maladjustment by conditional gifts of money.

CONDITIONAL SPENDING AND THE BUTLER CASE

1. *The majority opinion.* Was the Butler majority's endorsement of the Hamilton-Story position on the spending power consistent with the result? Did the majority in effect adopt the Madison position after all? If the power to spend for the "general Welfare" is not limited by the other grants of power in Art. I, § 8, why was it unconstitutional to spend for the purpose of reducing agricultural production, even though that production was not (in 1936) directly reachable under the other powers? If, as the majority apparently concedes, "conditional appropriation of money," including to education, is permissible, why is conditional spending to aid farmers unconstitutional? Was the problem of agricultural production less "general" than that of education? Could the Government have given money to farmers who voluntarily cut agricultural production, with provisions that grants would not be renewed if productive acreage were not reduced? What constitutional difference should it make that the Act involved contractual arrangements? What were the permissible purposes of—and permissible conditions on—spending after Butler? Can the result in Butler be reconciled with the 1937 Social Security cases, which follow?

2. *The dissent.* Was Justice Stone persuasive in asserting in his dissent: "Threat of loss, not hope of gain, is the essence of economic coercion"? What restrictions on the spending power would the dissenters recognize? Justice Stone states that "the purpose must be truly national." Is the Court competent to identify "non-national" purposes in the face of a judgment by the national legislature that a spending program serves the national interest? Justice Stone also asserts that the spending power "may not be used to coerce action left to state control." Does he not effectively sanction economic coercion of farmers? Would there nevertheless be a barrier in Justice Stone's view if the national

program sought to compel state governments rather than individuals to take affirmative action? [1] What constitutional standards must conditions on spending meet under Justice Stone's view? Is it enough that the conditions are relevant to the general welfare? Is there a more focused requirement that the condition be related to the purpose of the particular spending program? [2]

THE 1937 SOCIAL SECURITY CASES

After the Butler case, New Dealers feared that the Social Security Act of 1935 was in danger of judicial invalidation. But in companion cases in 1937, during the Court-packing controversy, the Court sustained the unemployment compensation and old age benefits schemes of the Social Security Act. The first of these cases, Steward Machine, probably raised the more difficult issue, for it involved a federal taxing structure designed to induce states to adopt laws complying with federal standards (and accordingly encountered a state coercion-state autonomy claim). The second case, Helvering v. Davis, did not try to enlist state legislatures but instead involved merely an exclusively federal spending scheme. It accordingly raised anew questions of the scope of the direct federal spending power. Were these decisions consistent with Butler? What restraints on national power under Art. I, § 8, cl. 1 remained after these decisions?

1. The 5 to 4 decision in STEWARD MACHINE CO. v. DAVIS, 301 U.S. 548 (1937), sustained the unemployment compensation provisions of the Social Security Act. Title IX of the Act imposed a payroll tax on employers of eight or more. Unlike the tax in the Butler case, this tax was not earmarked but went into general funds. But a credit provision in the tax sought to promote the enactment of state laws that complied with federal standards. Under the scheme an employer was entitled to a credit of up to 90% of the federal tax for any contributions to a state unemployment fund certified by a federal agency as meeting the requirements of the Act. As described by the Court, some of the federal requirements were "designed to give assurance that the state unemployment compensation law shall be one in substance as well as name." Others were "designed to give assurance that the contributions shall be protected against loss after payment to the state." Among the latter was a provision requiring that state funds be paid over immediately to the Secretary of the Treasury to the credit of the "Unemployment Trust Fund," to be managed by the Secretary, with payments made to state authorities upon proper requisitions. The company sought a refund of taxes paid under Title IX.

Justice CARDOZO's majority opinion concluded that the scheme was "not void as involving the coercion of the States in contravention of the Tenth Amendment or of restrictions implicit in our federal form of government." He insisted that it had not been shown that "the tax and the credit in combination are weapons of coercion, destroying or impairing the autonomy of the states." He explained: "To draw the line intelligently between duress and inducement there is no need to remind ourselves of facts as to the problem of unemployment that are now matters of common knowledge. [During] the years 1929 to

---

1. Recall the modern state autonomy cases in sec. 7 of the previous chapter, and compare the Steward Machine case, which follows.

2. Note Justice Stone's comment: "If the expenditure is for a national public purpose, that purpose will not be thwarted because payment is on condition which will advance that purpose." Note also his earlier reference to "conditions reasonably adapted to the attainment of the end which alone would justify the expenditure." What "purpose," what "end," did Justice Stone have in mind? Merely a relationship to the general welfare? Or a relationship to the purpose of the particular spending program? What criteria for judicial scrutiny of conditional spending remained after the 1937 Social Security cases, which follow? After Flemming v. Nestor, the 1960 decision at p. 215 below?

1936, when the country was passing through a cyclical depression, the number of the unemployed mounted to unprecedented heights. Often the average was more than 10 million; at times a peak was attained of 16 million or more. Disaster to the breadwinner meant disaster to dependents. Accordingly the roll of the unemployed, itself formidable enough, was only a partial roll of the destitute or needy. The fact developed quickly that the states were unable to give the requisite relief. The problem had become national in area and dimensions. There was need of help from the nation if the people were not to starve. It is too late today for the argument to be heard with tolerance that in a crisis so extreme the use of the moneys of the nation to relieve the unemployed and their dependents is a use for any purpose narrower than the promotion of the general welfare. Cf. [Butler].

"In the presence of this urgent need for some remedial expedient, the question is to be answered whether the expedient adopted has overlept the bounds of power. The assailants of the statute say that its dominant end and aim is to drive the state legislatures under the whip of economic pressure into the enactment of unemployment compensation laws at the bidding of the central government. Supporters of the statute say that its operation is not constraint, but the creation of a larger freedom, the states and the nation joining in a cooperative endeavor to avert a common evil. Before Congress acted, unemployment compensation insurance was still, for the most part, a project and no more. Wisconsin was the pioneer. Her statute was adopted in 1931. At times bills for such insurance were introduced elsewhere, but they [usually] did not reach the stage of law. [Many states] held back through alarm lest, in laying such a toll upon their industries, they would place themselves in a position of economic disadvantage as compared with neighbors or competitors. [Two] consequences ensued. One was that the freedom of a state to contribute its fair share to the solution of a national problem was paralyzed by fear. The other was that in so far as there was failure by the states to contribute relief according to the measure of their capacity, a disproportionate burden, and a mountainous one, was laid upon the resources of the Government of the nation.

"The [Act] is an attempt to find a method by which all these public agencies may work together to a common end. Every dollar of the new taxes will continue in all likelihood to be used and needed by the nation as long as states are unwilling, whether through timidity or for other motives, to do what can be done at home. At least the inference is permissible that Congress so believed, though retaining undiminished freedom to spend the money as it pleased. On the other hand fulfillment of the home duty will be lightened and encouraged by crediting the taxpayer upon his account with the Treasury of the nation to the extent that his contributions under the laws of the locality have simplified or diminished the problem of relief and the probable demand upon the resources of the fisc. Duplicated taxes, or burdens that approach them, are recognized hardships that government, state or national, may properly avoid. [If] Congress believed that the general welfare would be better promoted by relief through local units than by the system then in vogue, the cooperating localities ought not in all fairness to pay a second time.

"Who then is coerced through the operation of this statute? Not the taxpayer. He pays in fulfillment of the mandate of the local legislature. Not the state. Even now [Alabama] does not offer a suggestion that in passing the unemployment law she was affected by duress. [The] difficulty with petitioner's contention is that it confuses motive with coercion. [E]very rebate from a tax when conditioned upon conduct is in some measure a temptation. But to hold that motive or temptation is equivalent to coercion is to plunge the law in endless difficulties. The outcome of such a doctrine is the acceptance of a philosophical determinism by which choice becomes impossible. Till now the law has been guided by a robust common sense which assumes the freedom of the will as a working hypothesis in the solution of its problems. The wisdom of the hypothesis has illustration in this case. We cannot say that [Alabama] was acting, not of her unfettered will, but under the strain of a persuasion equivalent to undue influence, when she chose to have relief administered under laws of her own making, by agents of her own selection, instead of under federal laws, administered by federal officers, with all the ensuing evils, at least to many minds, of federal patronage and power. There would be a strange irony, indeed, if her choice were now to be annulled on the basis of an assumed duress in the enactment of a statute which her courts have accepted as a true expression of her will.

"[In] ruling as we do, we leave many questions open. We do not say that a tax is valid, when imposed by act of Congress, if it is laid upon the condition that a state may escape its operation through the adoption of a statute unrelated in subject matter to activities fairly within the scope of national policy and power. No such question is before us. In the tender of this credit Congress does not intrude upon fields foreign to its function. The purpose of its intervention, as we have shown, is to safeguard its own treasury and as an incident to that protection to place the states upon a footing of equal opportunity. Drains upon its own resources are to be checked; obstructions to the freedom of the states are to be leveled. It is one thing to impose a tax dependent upon the conduct of the taxpayers, or of the state in which they live, where the conduct to be stimulated or discouraged is unrelated to the fiscal need subserved by the tax in its normal operation, or to any other end legitimately national. The Child Labor Tax Case and Hill v. Wallace, were decided in the belief that the statutes there condemned were exposed to that reproach. It is quite another thing to say that a tax will be abated upon the doing of an act that will satisfy the fiscal need, the tax and the alternative being approximate equivalents. In such circumstances, if in no others, inducement or persuasion does not go beyond the bounds of power. We do not fix the outermost line. Enough for present purposes that wherever the line may be, this statute is within it. Definition more precise must abide the wisdom of the future.

"The statute does not call for a surrender by the states of powers essential to their quasi-sovereign existence. [A] credit to taxpayers for payments made to a state under a state unemployment law will be manifestly futile in the absence of some assurance that the law leading to the credit is in truth what it professes to be. An unemployment law framed in such a way that the unemployed who look to it will be deprived of reasonable protection is one in name and nothing more. What is basic and essential may be assured by suitable conditions. The terms embodied in these sections are directed to that end. A wide range of judgment is given to the several states as to the particular type of statute to be spread upon their books. [What] they may not do, if they would earn the credit, is to depart from those standards which in the judgment of Congress are to be ranked as fundamental." [1]

---

1. Justice Cardozo found the Butler decision distinguishable: "None of [the objections there] is applicable to the situation here developed. (a) The proceeds of the tax in controversy are not earmarked for a special group. (b) The unemployment compensation law which is a condition of the credit has had the approval of the state and could not be a law without it. (c) The condition is not linked to an irrevocable agreement, for the state at its pleasure may repeal its [law], terminate the credit, and place itself where it was before the credit was accepted. (d) The condition is not directed to the attainment of an unlawful end, but to an end, the relief of unemployment, for which nation and state may lawfully cooperate."

Justices McReynolds, Sutherland, Van Devanter and Butler dissented. In another 5 to 4 decision on the same day, the Court sustained the Unemployment Compensation Law enacted by Alabama to fit into the scheme of the federal Act. Carmichael v. Southern Coal & Coke Co., 301 U.S. 495 (1937).

2. In a companion case to Steward Machine, HELVERING v. DAVIS, 301 U.S. 619 (1937), Justice CARDOZO again wrote for the majority, with only Justices McReynolds and Butler dissenting. Helvering v. Davis upheld the old age benefits provisions in Titles VIII and II of the Social Security Act of 1935. Those provisions established an entirely federal program: they laid special taxes on covered employers and employees and provided for the payment of federal old age benefits. Justice Cardozo's opinion rejected the Tenth Amendment challenge by relying on the endorsement of the Hamilton-Story position on the spending power in Butler. He noted that "difficulties" remain even when a broad view of the power to spend is accepted: "The line must still be drawn between one welfare and another, between particular and general. Where this shall be placed cannot be known through a formula in advance of the event. There is a middle ground or certainly a penumbra in which discretion is at large. The discretion, however, is not confided to the courts. The discretion belongs to Congress, unless the choice is clearly wrong, a display of arbitrary power, not an exercise of judgment."

Here, it was clear, "Congress did not improvise a judgment when it was found that the award of old age benefits would be conducive to the general welfare." Justice Cardozo explained: "The problem is plainly national in area and dimensions. Moreover, laws of the separate states cannot deal with it effectively. Congress, at least, had a basis for that belief. [Apart] from the failure of resources, states and local governments are at times reluctant to increase so heavily the burden of taxation to be borne by their residents for fear of placing themselves in a position of economic disadvantage. [We] have seen this in our study of the problem of unemployment compensation. [Steward Machine.] A system of old age pensions has special dangers of its own, if put in force in one state and rejected in another. The existence of such a system is a bait to the needy and dependent elsewhere, encouraging them to migrate and seek a haven of repose. Only a power that is national can serve the interests of all." He concluded: "When money is spent to promote the general welfare, the concept of welfare or the opposite is shaped by Congress, not the states. So the concept be not arbitrary, the locality must yield." [2]

FEDERAL GRANTS TO STATES AND INDIVIDUALS: SOME MODERN PRACTICES AND PROBLEMS

1. *The practical dimensions of federal grants to states.* The traditional and pervasive nature of federal spending programs was recognized in the Butler opinions. Federal policy guidance (and control) via the spending power, especially through conditional grants-in-aid to state and local governments, goes back to the 19th century. The size and range of the programs have increased considerably over the years, and detailed federal conditions have proliferated.[1]

2. In later cases, the Court has repeatedly endorsed a broad congressional discretion regarding the scope of the spending power. See, in addition to United States v. Gerlach Live Stock Co., 339 U.S. 725 (1950), Buckley v. Valeo, 424 U.S. 1 (1976) (chap. 13 below). In rejecting a claim that the provisions for public financing of presidential election campaigns in the Federal Election Campaign Act exceeded the spending power, the Court in Buckley replied that the contention "erroneously treats the General Welfare Clause as a limitation upon congressional power. It is rather a grant of power the scope of which is quite expansive, particularly in view of the enlargement of power by the Necessary and Proper Clause. [McCulloch.] Congress has power to regulate Presidential elections and primaries; and public financing of Presidential elections as a means to reform the electoral process was clearly a choice within the granted power. It is for Congress to decide which expenditures will promote the general welfare."

1. For a discussion of early practices, see Elazar, The American Partnership: Intergovernmental Co-operation in the Nineteenth Century United States (1962). For a survey and commentary on mid-20th century dimensions, see two 1955 publications by the Commission on Intergovernmental Relations: Twenty-Five

During the 1960s, there was growing opposition to narrow categorical grants-in-aid and widespread advocacy of broader, less restricted block grants to states and local governments.[2] The drive for "no strings money" instead of "strings money" finally bore fruit in the 1970s: in October, 1972, President Nixon signed a major general revenue sharing law, the State and Local Fiscal Assistance Act of 1972. But the battle between advocates of block grants and categorical grants continues.[3]

2. *The constitutional problems of federal grants to states: State autonomy as a limit?* Recall that in Steward Machine, the 1937 unemployment compensation case, Justice Cardozo asked whether the Social Security Act involved "the coercion of the States in contravention of the Tenth Amendment or of restrictions implicit in our federal form of government." He found no constitutional violation then. But in the years since, federal conditions on assistance to states have multiplied.[4] When, if ever, do such conditions run counter to "restrictions implicit in our federal form of government"? When do conditions become so pervasive, when do they impinge so much on the structure and operations of state governments, as to warrant judicial constraint? So far, the Court has shown little receptivity to challenges to federal spending conditions on state autonomy grounds. Is greater receptivity warranted? Are the modern concerns about state autonomy limits on the commerce power, voiced in National League of Cities, p. 170 above, also applicable to the spending power?[5] Justice

Grant-in-Aid Programs, and A Report to the President.

2. See, e.g., Advisory Commission on Intergovernmental Relations, Tenth Annual Report (1969), 6: "Unless state and local governments are permitted 'free,' albeit limited, access to the prime power source—the Federal Income Tax—their positions within our federal system are bound to deteriorate."

3. See generally Stolz, Revenue Sharing: Legal and Policy Analysis (1974), and "Symposium: The New Federalism and the Cities," 52 J1.Urban Law 55 (1974).

See also the criticism of conditioned federal grants to states by Robert Cover in "Federalism and Administrative Structure," 92 Yale L.J. 1342 (1983): "By debilitating, if not disarming, the alternative sources of political power in our federal structure, 'cooperative federalism' undermines the only viable restraint on the congressional exercise of enumerated powers: the political process. Thus, cooperative ventures should be considered of dubious constitutionality. 'Combative federalism,' under which federal programs are exclusively federal, presents a desirable alternative. [To] protect the feedback mechanism that permits states to react to federal actions, the federal government ought to do more itself; it ought to provide funds directly, and be responsible for the administration of the programs it funds. Only the ensuing combat, prompted by the reactions of the states, can guarantee an effective political check on the exercise of national power." Compare the critical comments on Cover in Rose-Ackerman, "Cooperative Federalism and Co-optation," 92 Yale L.J. 1344 (1983), arguing that "Cover's concerns are misplaced."

4. For a recent example, note the enactment of a federal law in 1984 that would deny some federal highway funds to states that refuse to

raise their drinking age to 21. President Reagan, frequently an advocate of state autonomy, said in signing the law: "The problem is bigger than the individual states." According to a press report, "[a]lthough it passed with overwhelming support on Capitol Hill, even some of those supporting the measure said privately that it was coercive." See The New York Times, July 18, 1984. The law requires the withholding of 5% of federal highway construction funds from states that do not enact a minimum drinking age of 21 by October 1, 1986. If the state still has not enacted such a law by October 1, 1987, 10% of the federal funds will be withheld. The amounts withheld would be returned once a state raised its drinking age.

5. Kaden, "Politics, Money, and State Sovereignty: The Judicial Role," 79 Colum.L.Rev. 847 (1979), writing in the period between National League of Cities in 1976 and the 1980s cases diluting the state autonomy concern, argued that state autonomy limits *should* be applicable to the spending power. Kaden's article, which included an extensive review of modern examples of restrictions on states through the spending power, suggested as a judicially enforceable limit the following: "[To] oblige the Congress to explore all alternatives and select the means of achieving its purpose in the manner least restrictive of state sovereignty interests would invite an excessive level of judicial interference. [However], when the federal law goes further and obliges the state to structure a new agency composed according to federal mandate, [the] extent of interference with the political choices made by state officials justifies the imposition of a greater burden on the Congress than is provided by a simple test of rational relationship. In these circumstances, when the condition is of the type that would exceed the congressional power under the commerce clause because of its interference with state

Rehnquist left that question open in National League of Cities. But five years later, he stated in dictum in Pennhurst State School v. Halderman, 451 U.S. 1 (1981): "There are limits on the power of Congress to impose conditions on the States pursuant to its spending power [e.g., Steward Machine; Fullilove v. Klutznick (p. 769 below); see National League of Cities]. Even the [plaintiffs] recognize the 'constitutional difficulties' with imposing affirmative obligations on the States pursuant to the spending power. That issue, however, is not now before us." [6] Would a heightened state autonomy concern require a modification of the standards applied in the Oklahoma case, which follows?

a.   Three decades before the National League of Cities case, the Court gave short shrift to a state's claim that federal highway funds could not be conditioned on the state's compliance with a provision of the Hatch Act. The challenged provision states that no state official primarily employed in activities "financed in whole or in part" by federal funds shall "take any active part" in political activities. In OKLAHOMA v. CIVIL SERVICE COMM'N, 330 U.S. 127 (1947), the federal agency ordered the removal of a State Highway Commissioner who was also the state chairman of the Democratic Party. Failure by the state to comply with the federal requirement risked a federal order cutting off highway grants "in an amount equal to two years compensation" of the Commissioner.

Justice REED's majority opinion rejected Oklahoma's challenge to the removal order: "While the United States is not concerned with, and has no power to regulate, local political activities as such of state officials, it does have power to fix the terms upon which its money allotments to states shall be disbursed. [The] end sought by Congress through the Hatch Act is better

autonomy, the Court may properly oblige Congress to demonstrate that the requirement is related to the achievement of an important governmental objective. This level of justification has been used, for example, in [sex discrimination cases, chap. 9 below]. [This] may provide a reasonable formula for protecting the states' political processes against the coopting effects of certain types of grant conditions without unduly interfering with the basic capacity of the national political process to distribute authority in the federal system."

6. Other statements in Pennhurst suggested a somewhat different view of the nature of federal spending programs than that followed since Steward Machine. Pennhurst at least suggested that the modern Court may be growing more reluctant to interpret federal-state grant programs as including conditions imposing affirmative obligations on the states. The case involved a 1974 law providing funds to participating states to aid them in programs for the care and treatment of the mentally retarded. The act included a "bill of rights" provision for mentally retarded persons. Justice Rehnquist's majority opinion held that this provision "simply does not create substantive rights." In the course of reaching this conclusion, he described the nature of the spending power as follows: "[Our] cases have long recognized that Congress may fix the terms on which it shall disburse federal money to the States. Unlike legislation enacted under [§ 5 of the Fourteenth Amendment], however, legislation enacted pursuant to the spending power is

much in the nature of a contract: in return for federal funds, the States agree to comply with federally imposed conditions. The legitimacy of Congress' power to legislate under the spending power thus rests on whether the State voluntarily and knowingly accepts the terms of the 'contract.' [See, e.g., Steward Machine.] There can, of course, be no knowing acceptance if a State is unaware of the conditions or is unable to ascertain what is expected of it. Accordingly, if Congress intends to impose a condition on the grant of federal moneys, it must do so unambiguously. By insisting that Congress speak with a clear voice, we enable the States to exercise their choice knowingly, cognizant of the consequences of their participation." He concluded that the "bill of rights" provision did "no more than express a congressional preference for certain kinds of treatment" and did not impose affirmative obligations on the states. He criticized the lower court for failing to recognize the "well-settled distinction between congressional 'encouragement' of state programs and the imposition of binding obligations on the States." Justice White, joined by Justices Brennan and Marshall, submitted a partial dissent. He insisted that the provision at issue "was intended by Congress to establish requirements which participating States had to meet." And in a footnote replying to the majority's "contract" approach to grants-in-aid, he commented: "None of the cases cited by the Court suggest, much less hold, that Congress is required to condition its grant of funds with contract-like exactitude."

public service by requiring those who administer funds for national needs to abstain from active political partisanship. So even though the action taken by Congress does have effect upon certain activities within the state, it has never been thought that such effect made the federal act invalid. [Oklahoma] adopted the 'simple expedient' of not yielding to what she urges is federal coercion. [The] offer of benefits to a state by the United States dependent upon cooperation by the state with federal plans, assumedly for the general welfare, is not unusual. [E.g., Steward Machine.]" [7]

   b. Would the Oklahoma challenge loom larger if it had been advanced after National League of Cities? Consider the comment in Kaden (footnote 5, above): "[The] Steward-Oklahoma test for evaluating conditions [on federal spending programs] has generally led lower federal courts mechanically to reject challenges [on] the theory that the availability of a nominal option of 'not yielding' means that the statute induces but does not coerce participation. [In cases] involving state challenges to some of the elaborate conditions to federal aid imposed in the food stamp and medicaid programs, the Rehabilitation Act, the Urban Mass Transit Act, the Health Planning Act, and the Highway Beautification Act, this has been the uniform result. [The] Oklahoma standard [may] have had some plausibility at a time when federal aid amounted to a small fraction of all state and local government spending, and most federal funds were distributed for specific projects. But given the drastic increases in the amounts of federal funds and the formula-based entitlements in aid programs enacted since 1960, it is unrealistic for anything to depend on the state's nominal right not to participate. Nor does the requirement that the condition be rationally related to the purpose of the grant program afford significant protection for state sovereignty. [Virtually] any condition, no matter how intrusive, is likely to pass." [8] Did the Oklahoma challenge deserve a fuller answer from the Court even in 1947? Note Professor (later Justice) Linde's criticism and suggestion in "Justice Douglas on Freedom in the Welfare State," 39 Wash.L.Rev. 4 (1964): "[P]robably no one can say today how much state and local tax revenue—the lifeblood of local autonomy—is committed to programs the standards for which are set and controlled under federal law. Yet there must be limits on such conditions if the political values of federalism are to be preserved despite this fiscal centralization. [Justice] Reed's easy generalizations about conditioned federal spending prove too much. Even the liberal dissenters in 1936 had found the power to spend not beyond constitutional limitations: 'it may not be used to coerce action left to state control.' [U.S. v. Butler.] If Congress chose to forbid any state officer who spends federal grants to take part in a political campaign, could Oklahoma not choose to have an elected highway commission? [State officers] increasingly administer programs aided by federal funds; may Congress constitutionally decide which may be elected, which others politically appointed, and which must be in a nonpartisan career status? Surely a line may be perceived between such conditions and conditions that go to the substance of the federally supported project, for instance that it fit a national plan, or be soundly engineered, or meet prescribed standards of hours, wages, or nondiscrimination in employment, or be fairly and honestly administered." Is there merit in Linde's criticism? Is it clear that "a line may be perceived" between conditions which impinge unduly on state autonomy and "conditions that go to the substance of the federally supported project"? [9]

7. Justices Black and Rutledge dissented without opinion. (On the rejection of First Amendment challenges to federal and state prohibitions of political activities by public employees, see chap. 13, sec. 4, below.)

8. For Kaden's suggestions on greater judicial scrutiny, see footnote 5 above.

9. Does the recent development of federal revenue sharing, with its "unrestricted" block grants, assure a greater concern for the state interest in its "organizational form and structure"? Not necessarily: though revenue sharing involves fewer "substantive" conditions on federal grants, there have been proposals for greater

3. *Federal grants to individuals: Constitutional restraints on "substantive" conditions?* In his dissent in the Butler case, Justice Stone suggested that conditions in federal spending programs must be "reasonably adapted to the attainment of the end which alone would justify the expenditure." Is that a continuing (and significant) requirement for federal conditioned spending programs, even after the 1937 Social Security cases? Consider Flemming v. Nestor, which follows, where the Court in 1960 divided about the constitutionality of conditions in the Social Security Act. True, the limiting considerations urged in that case did not stem from the nature of the federal system. Rather, they were based on individual rights concerns. But the due process objection considered by the Court has a close similarity to a theme in Justice Stone's opinion in Butler: a requirement that the condition be "reasonably adapted" to the end can be viewed either as a derivation from the Necessary and Proper Clause of Art. I, § 8, or as an aspect of the "reasonableness" requirement of due process.[10] Thus, Justice Harlan's due process discussion in Flemming asked whether the conditions were "relevant" to the purposes of the Social Security system. Consideration of the due process objection in Flemming, then, is an appropriate conclusion to this general examination of potential judicial constraints on legislative selection of conditions in spending programs. Moreover, Flemming offers an opportunity to pursue the problem of judicial scrutiny of legislative motivation, as developed in the notes following the case.[11]

FLEMMING v. NESTOR

363 U.S. 603, 80 S.Ct. 1367, 4 L.Ed.2d 1435 (1960).

Mr. Justice HARLAN delivered the opinion of the Court.

From a decision [holding] § 202(n) of the Social Security Act unconstitutional, the Secretary of [HEW] takes this direct appeal. [Sec. 202(n)] provides for the termination of old-age, survivor, and disability insurance benefits payable [to] an alien individual who, after September 1, 1954, is deported under § 241(a) of the Immigration and Nationality Act on any one of certain grounds specified in § 202(n). Appellee, an alien, immigrated to this country from Bulgaria in 1913, and became eligible for old-age benefits in November 1955. In July 1956 he was deported pursuant to [the] Immigration and Nationality Act for having been a member of the Communist Party from 1933 to 1939.

"procedural" safeguards to assure local participation in the spending of the federal funds. See, e.g., Stolz, "Revenue Sharing—New American Revolution or Trojan Horse?" 58 Minn.L.Rev. 1 (1973), an extensive commentary on the State and Local Fiscal Assistance Act of 1972. Stolz urges: "The single most important aspect in determining the program's future will be the participation of local citizens in the decision making process. [A] 'New American revolution' of democratic participation in the local decision making process will be required. [A] requirement of information disclosure and participation at the local level is not inconsistent with the 'no-strings' rhetoric." Does that suggest a concern diametrically opposed to Linde's: a view that federal conditions regarding local governmental processes are less rather than more objectionable than "conditions that go to the substance of the federally supported project"? Does that make

sense in terms of the constitutional values of federalism?

10. Note the modern decisions imposing equal protection "rationality" restraints on conditions in spending programs, as noted in chap. 9 below.

11. Flemming v. Nestor also raises the question of whether the congressional discretion in selecting means is narrower when the limiting considerations stem from individual rights guarantees rather than from federalism concerns, as in McCulloch. In Flemming, a variety of individual rights guarantees (including due process) were urged as restraints on congressional legislation. Consider the varying attitudes, in the several opinions, about the appropriate intensity of judicial scrutiny; and contrast those positions with the degree of scrutiny in cases involving only federalistic limitations.

This being one of the benefit-termination deportation grounds specified in § 202(n), appellee's benefits were terminated soon thereafter.

[We] think that the District Court erred in holding that § 202(n) deprived appellee of an "accrued property right" [in violation of the due process clause of the Fifth Amendment]. Appellee's right to Social Security benefits cannot properly be considered to have been of that order. [To] engraft upon the Social Security system a concept of "accrued property rights" would deprive it of the flexibility and boldness in adjustment to ever-changing conditions which it demands. [This] is not to say, however, that Congress may exercise its power to modify the statutory scheme free of all constitutional restraint. The interest of a covered employee under the Act is of sufficient substance to fall within the protection from arbitrary governmental action afforded by the Due Process Clause. In judging the permissibility of the cut-off provisions of § 202(n) from this standpoint, it is not within our authority to determine whether the Congressional judgment expressed in that section is sound or equitable, or whether it comports well or ill with the purposes of the Act. [Helvering v. Davis.] Particularly when we deal with a withholding of a noncontractual benefit under a social welfare program such as this, we must recognize that the Due Process Clause can be thought to interpose a bar only if the statute manifests a patently arbitrary classification, utterly lacking in rational justification.

Such is not the case here. The fact of a beneficiary's residence abroad—in the case of a deportee, a presumably permanent residence—can be of obvious relevance to the question of eligibility. One benefit which may be thought to accrue to the economy from the Social Security system is the increased over-all national purchasing power resulting from taxation of productive elements of the economy to provide payments to the retired and disabled, who might otherwise be destitute or nearly so, and who would generally spend a comparatively large percentage of their benefit payments. This advantage would be lost as to payments made to one residing abroad. For these purposes, it is, of course, constitutionally irrelevant whether this reasoning in fact underlay the legislative decision, as it is irrelevant that the section does not extend to all to whom the postulated rationale might in logic apply. See [Steward Machine.] Nor, apart from this, can it be deemed irrational for Congress to have concluded that the public purse should not be utilized to contribute to the support of those deported on the grounds specified in the statute. We need go no further to find support for our conclusion that this provision of the Act cannot be condemned as so lacking in rational justification as to offend due process.

The remaining, and most insistently pressed, constitutional objections rest upon Art. I, § 9, cl. 3, and Art. III, § 2, cl. 3, of the Constitution, and the Sixth Amendment. It is said that the termination of appellee's benefits amounts to punishing him without a judicial trial; [that] the termination of benefits constitutes the imposition of punishment by legislative act, rendering § 202(n) a bill of attainder;[1] [and] that the punishment exacted is imposed for past conduct not unlawful when engaged in, thereby violating the constitutional prohibition on ex post facto laws. Essential to the success of each of these contentions is the validity of characterizing as "punishment" in the constitutional sense the termination of benefits under § 202(n). In determining whether legislation which bases a disqualification on the happening of a certain past event imposes a punishment, the Court has sought to discern the objects on which the enactment in question was focused. Where the source of legislative concern can be thought to be the activity or status from which the individual is barred, the disqualification is not punishment even though it may bear harshly

---

1. The bill of attainder restraint is explored further in chap. 13 below.

upon one affected. The contrary is the case where the statute in question is evidently aimed at the person or class of persons disqualified.

[Turning] to the particular statutory provision before us, appellee cannot successfully contend that the language and structure of § 202(n), or the nature of the deprivation, requires us to recognize a punitive design. Here the sanction is the mere denial of a noncontractual governmental benefit. No affirmative disability or restraint is imposed, and certainly nothing approaching the "infamous punishment" of imprisonment. [Moreover,] it cannot be said [that] the disqualification of certain deportees from receipt of Social Security benefits while they are not lawfully in this country bears no rational connection to the purposes of the legislation of which it is a part, and must without more therefore be taken as evidencing a Congressional desire to punish. Appellee argues, however, that the history and scope of § 202(n) prove that no such postulated purpose can be thought to have motivated the legislature, and that they persuasively show that a punitive purpose in fact lay behind the statute. We do not agree.

We observe initially that only the clearest proof could suffice to establish the unconstitutionality of a statute on such a ground. Judicial inquiries into Congressional motives are at best a hazardous matter, and when that inquiry seeks to go behind objective manifestations it becomes a dubious affair indeed. Moreover, the presumption of constitutionality with which this enactment, like any other, comes to us forbids us lightly to choose that reading of the statute's setting which will invalidate it over that which will save it. [Section 202(n)] was enacted as a small part of an extensive revision of the Social Security program. [The House Committee Report states] that the termination of benefits would apply to those persons who were "deported from the United States because of illegal entry, conviction of a crime, or subversive activity." It was evidently the thought that such was the scope of the statute resulting from its application to deportation under the 14 named paragraphs of § 241(a) of the Immigration and Nationality [Act].[2]

Appellee argues that this history demonstrates that Congress was not concerned with the *fact* of a beneficiary's deportation—which it is claimed alone would justify this legislation as being pursuant to a policy relevant to regulation of the Social Security system—but that it sought to reach certain *grounds* for deportation, thus evidencing a punitive intent. It is impossible to find in this meagre history the unmistakable evidence of punitive intent which, under principles already discussed, is required before a Congressional enactment of this kind may be struck down. [Moreover], the grounds for deportation referred to in the Committee Report embrace the great majority of those deported, as is evident from an examination of the four omitted grounds, summarized in the margin.[3] Inferences drawn from the omission of those grounds cannot establish, to the degree of certainty required, that Congressional concern was wholly with the acts leading to deportation, and not with the fact of deportation.[4] [The] same answer must be made to arguments drawn from the

2. Paragraphs (1), (2) and (10) of § 241(a) relate to unlawful entry, or entry not complying with certain conditions; paragraphs (6) and (7) apply to "subversive" and related activities; the remainder of the included paragraphs are concerned with convictions of designated crimes, or the commission of acts related to them, such as narcotics addiction or prostitution. [Footnote by Justice Harlan.]

3. They are: (1) persons institutionalized at public expense within five years after entry because of "mental disease, defect, or deficiency" not shown to have arisen subsequent to admis-

sion (§ 241(a)(3)); (2) persons becoming a public charge within five years after entry from causes not shown to have arisen subsequent to admission (§ 241(a)(8)); (3) persons admitted as non-immigrants [who] fail to maintain, or comply with the conditions of, such status (§ 241(a)(9)); (4) persons knowingly and for gain inducing or aiding, prior to or within five years after entry, any other alien to enter or attempt to enter unlawfully (§ 241(a)(13)). [Footnote by Justice Harlan.]

4. Were we to engage in speculation, it would not be difficult to conjecture that Congress may

failure of Congress to apply § 202(n) to beneficiaries voluntarily residing abroad. [Congress] may have failed to consider such persons; or it may have thought their number too slight, or the permanence of their voluntary residence abroad too uncertain, to warrant application of the statute to them, with its attendant administrative problems of supervision and enforcement. Again, we cannot with confidence reject all those alternatives which imaginativeness can bring to mind, save that one which might require the invalidation of the statute.

Reversed.

Mr. Justice BRENNAN, with whom The Chief Justice [WARREN] and Mr. Justice DOUGLAS join, dissenting.

[The Court] escapes the common-sense conclusion that Congress has imposed punishment by finding the requisite rational nexus to a granted power in the supposed furtherance of the Social Security program "enacted pursuant to Congress' power to 'spend money in aid of the "general welfare." ' " I do not understand the Court to deny that but for that connection, § 202(n) would impose [unconstitutional punishment]. The [Court] rejects the inference that the statute is "aimed at the person or class of persons disqualified" by relying upon the presumption of constitutionality. This presumption might be a basis for sustaining the statute if in fact there were two opposing inferences which could reasonably be drawn from the legislation, one that it imposes punishment and the other that it is purposed to further the administration of the Social Security program. The Court, however, does not limit the presumption to that use. Rather the presumption becomes a complete substitute for any supportable finding of a rational connection of § 202(n) with the Social Security program.

[It] seems to me that the statute itself shows that the sole legislative concern was with "the person or class of persons disqualified." Congress did not disqualify for benefits all beneficiaries residing abroad or even all dependents residing abroad who are aliens. [Sec. 202(n) includes] persons who were deported "because of unlawful entry, conviction of a crime, or subversive activity." The section, in addition, covers those deported for such socially condemned acts as narcotic addiction or prostitution. The common element of the 14 grounds is that the alien has been guilty of some blameworthy conduct. In other words Congress worked its will only on aliens deported for conduct displeasing to the lawmakers. This is plainly demonstrated by the remaining four grounds of deportation, those which do not result in the cancellation of benefits. Two of those four grounds cover persons who become public charges within five years after entry for reasons which predated the entry. A third ground covers the alien who fails to maintain his nonimmigrant status. The fourth ground reaches the alien who, prior to or within five years after entry, aids other aliens to enter the country illegally. [This] appraisal of the distinctions drawn by Congress [impels] the conclusion, beyond peradventure, that the distinctions can be understood only if the purpose of Congress was to strike at "the person or class of persons disqualified." The Court inveighs against invalidating a statute on "implication and vague conjecture." Rather I think the Court has strained to sustain the statute on "implication and vague conjecture," in holding that the congressional concern was "the activity or status from which the individual is barred." Today's decision sanctions the use of the spending power not to further the legitimate objectives of the Social Security program but to inflict hurt upon those who by their conduct have incurred the displeasure of [Congress].[5]

---

have been led to exclude these four grounds of deportation out of compassionate or *de minimis* considerations. [Footnote by Justice Harlan.]

5. Justices BLACK and DOUGLAS also submitted dissents. See generally O'Neil, "Un-

constitutional Conditions: Welfare Benefits with Strings Attached," 54 Calif.L.Rev. 443 (1966).

THE SCOPE OF JUDICIAL INQUIRY: PURPOSE, MOTIVE, AND RATIONALITY

1. *The scope of inquiry in Flemming v. Nestor.* Is Justice Harlan's scrutiny of conditions-purposes (means-ends) relationships consistent with the standards regarding permissible conditions on governmental spending programs as discussed in the spending power cases of the 1930s? The limitations urged in Flemming do not stem from considerations of state autonomy. Should that alter the scope of congressional discretion as to conditions? If the due process limitation discussed in Justice Harlan's opinion is viewed as identical with the rational relationship standard under the Necessary and Proper Clause, is it accurate to say that neither Justice Harlan nor Justice Brennan applies a standard of judicial scrutiny of congressional choices regarding means that is identical with the standard of McCulloch and its progeny? Is it accurate to say that Justice Harlan is even more deferential to congressional means-ends judgments than the Art. I-federalism cases? And that Justice Brennan is more skeptical of legislative choices than most earlier cases were? Is either deviation from the norm of the federalism context (toward greater judicial deference to or greater scrutiny of Congress) justifiable?

2. *The congressional objectives: Legislative actuality or judicial imaginativeness?* Why is it "constitutionally irrelevant whether this reasoning in fact underlay the legislative decision," as Justice Harlan maintains? Must the Court sustain legislation if it can *imagine* a rational argument for the condition, whether or not that argument was *in fact* considered by Congress? Note the close of the majority opinion: "Again, we [cannot] reject all those alternatives which imaginativeness can bring to mind." Do considerations of propriety or feasibility inhibit the Court from demanding an affirmative showing that the legislative deliberations—rather than the Court's (or counsel's) "imaginativeness"—supply the basis for a finding of rationality? Do these considerations bar the Court from considering evidence in the legislative history that improper grounds *were* relied on by Congress, even if rational grounds *could* have been given by a hypothetical legislature? Recall the earlier national power cases: To what extent was the need to reach local matters as a means of regulating interstate commerce, for example, justified by arguments in fact considered by Congress, rather than by imaginative afterthoughts by counsel and Court?[1]

3. *Purpose, motive, and the draft card burning case.* Note the discussion of "purpose" and "motive" in Justice Harlan's opinion in Flemming. Does the Court disavow all inquiry into these issues, as it did in Darby, for example? Is it enough that a rational legislator *might* have had a legitimate purpose? Or is the Court willing to consider the "purpose" manifested in the legislative history? Is it possible to examine "purpose" without improper psychological inquiries into legislative "motive"? Is the dissent's view of purpose based on inferences from the face of the statute, inferences from the effects of the statute, evidence drawn from the record of legislative deliberation, or guesses as to hidden motives of legislators? Would, and should, clear-cut statements in the legislative record evidencing an aim to punish affect the majority's analysis in Flemming?

1. The problems raised by these questions are recurrent ones in judicial review. Note especially the extensive attention to these issues in chaps. 8 and 9 below, in connection with review under the "minimum rationality" model of scrutiny of legislative action drawn from the due process and equal protection guarantees. Should courts test laws on the basis of purposes a hypothetical reasonable legislator *might* have had, or should courts assess "reasonableness" in terms of purposes *articulated* or actually considered by the legislature? Should courts hypothesize possible means-ends relationships, or should they demand a showing of how the chosen means contribute to the achievement of the legislative objectives? See the fuller exploration in the later chapters and in Gunther, "Foreword: [A] Model for a Newer Equal Protection," 86 Harv.L.Rev. 1 (1972) (considered in chap. 9).

For a characteristic statement of judicial inhibitions about inquiries into legislative purpose and motive, see United States v. O'Brien, 391 U.S. 367 (1968). There, the Court rejected a number of constitutional challenges to a conviction under a 1965 amendment to the draft law which prohibited knowing destruction or mutilation of draft cards. One of the claims was that the amendment was unconstitutional because the "purpose" of Congress was "to suppress freedom of speech." The Court rejected that argument "because under settled principles the purpose of Congress [is] not a basis for declaring this legislation unconstitutional." [2] Chief Justice Warren's majority opinion elaborated as follows:

"Inquiries into congressional motives or purposes are a hazardous matter. When the issue is simply the interpretation of legislation, the Court will look to statements by legislators for guidance as to the purpose of the legislature,[3] because the benefit to sound decision-making in this circumstance is thought sufficient to risk the possibility of misreading Congress' purpose. It is entirely a different matter when we are asked to void a statute that is, under well-settled criteria, constitutional on its face, on the basis of what fewer than a handful of Congressmen said about it. What motivates one legislator to make a speech about a statute is not necessarily what motivates scores of others to enact it, and the stakes are sufficiently high for us to eschew guesswork. We decline to void essentially on the ground that it is unwise [to void] legislation which Congress had the undoubted power to enact and which could be reenacted in its exact form if the same or another legislator made a 'wiser' speech about it."

Was this passage adequate as a description of judicial practice? Was it persuasive as a statement of the proper scope of judicial scrutiny? What inhibits the Court in examining motivation in this case (and in cases such as Darby)? Is it the *difficulty* of ascertaining legislative motivation? Is it the *futility* of doing so—the sense that judicial invalidation on motivation grounds would not bar the legislature from reenacting a statute with the same operative effect, but without the previously fatal indicia of improper motivation? Is it the sense of *institutional* restraint—the awkwardness of having the judiciary tell the legislators that they acted for improper reasons? Is greater Court examination of actual legislative purposes and motives desirable? Should the answers depend on the particular constitutional provision invoked?[4]

SECTION 3. WAR, FOREIGN AFFAIRS, AND FEDERALISM

Scope Note. The commerce, taxing, and spending powers considered in the preceding materials are by far the most important national powers with an impact on federalism concerns, but they are by no means the only ones. The

2. The Court's rejection of additional First Amendment claims is considered in chap. 12 below, at p. 1170.

3. "The Court may make the same assumption in a very limited and well-defined class of cases where the very nature of the constitutional question requires an inquiry into legislative purpose. The principal class of cases is readily apparent—those in which statutes have been challenged as bills of attainder. [T]he inquiry into whether the challenged statute contains the necessary element of punishment has on occasion led the Court to examine the legislative motive in enacting the statute. [We] face no such inquiry in this case." [Footnote by Chief Justice Warren.]

4. Note the reemergence of these problems in a variety of contexts in later chapters—e.g., the controversy about appropriate judicial inquiry into motive and purpose in Palmer v. Thompson (1971; p. 690 below). Note also the Court's emphasis on purpose rather than effect in delineating the requirements for demonstrating racial discrimination under the equal protection clause, in Washington v. Davis (1976) and its progeny (p. 693 below).

limited purpose of this section is to examine briefly what federalistic constraints may exist on two other potentially broad sources of authority: the war power; and the national government's powers to make treaties and deal with foreign affairs. These powers more frequently risk impingement on constitutional concerns other than state autonomy: both the war power and the foreign affairs power often generate controversies involving separation of powers and individual rights issues. Consideration of the powers in the context of those countervailing interests is postponed to later chapters (see, e.g., chap. 6, on separation of powers); here, the limited sampling of additional national powers focuses on their impacts on federalism. It should be borne in mind that, like all powers of the national government, the powers considered here typically benefit from the broad construction of discretion in the choice of means first articulated in McCulloch v. Maryland.[1]

---

1. *Other congressional powers.* As the text of the Necessary and Proper Clause shows, the Clause grants Congress not only the authority to implement the powers enumerated in Art. I, but also the authority to enforce "all other Powers" granted to the national government.

Among the Art. I, § 8 powers not considered in detail here is the power to "coin money" and "regulate the Value thereof," see, e.g., one of the "gold clause" cases, Norman v. Baltimore & Ohio Railroad Co., 294 U.S. 240 (1935). Note also the power over copyrights and patents, see Mazer v. Stein, 347 U.S. 201 (1954). See also the postal power in Art. I, § 8—though it more frequently gives rise to individual rights rather than federalism concerns. See, e.g., Rowan v. Post Office Department (1970; p. 1211 below).

For an example of a source of national power outside of Art. I, see Art. III, § 2: the federal judicial power over cases in admiralty and maritime jurisdiction was early construed as a source of legislative power as well. See Note, "From Judicial Grant to Legislative Power: The Admiralty Clause in the Nineteenth Century," 67 Harv.L.Rev. 1214 (1954). Note also the power to dispose of, and make regulations pertaining to, federal property, in Art. IV, § 3. See, e.g., Kleppe v. New Mexico, 426 U.S. 529 (1976).

The constitutional amendment process. Article V, on amending the Constitution, also contains important, though rarely discussed, powers of Congress that may have an important impact on the federal-state balance. Art. V specifies two methods for initiating the amendment process: Congress, by a two-thirds vote, may propose amendments for ratification by three-fourths of the states; or two-thirds of the states may apply to Congress for the calling of a constitutional convention "for proposing Amendments." The first, congressionally-initiated method is the traditionally used one, and it may produce significant shifts in the allocation of power between nation and states, as with the post-Civil War

Amendments. Congressional action relating to that amendment route can be controversial. Note, e.g., the congressional decision in 1978 to extend the period for ratification of the proposed Equal Rights Amendment until 1982, and to refuse permission to states to rescind prior votes for ratification.

There is even greater potential for controversy in the untried second, state-initiated amendment route. For example, by the summer of 1984, 32 states had applied for a constitutional convention to add a balanced budget amendment to the Constitution. There is no doubt that Congress is under a duty to call such a convention when 34 valid state applications are at hand. But in most other respects, the convention route is clouded by uncertainty. The most widely debated question has been whether Congress may limit the scope of deliberations at a convention (e.g., to the balanced budget issue), or whether a convention is entitled to set its own agenda. For the view that Congress can limit the convention agenda in accordance with the purpose reflected in the state applications, see, e.g., ABA Special Constitutional Convention Study Comm., Amendment of the Constitution by the Convention Method under Article V (1974), and Van Alstyne, "Does Article V Restrict the States to Calling Unlimited Conventions Only?" 1978 Duke L.J. 1295 (1979). For arguments that Congress cannot effectively limit the scope of the convention, see, e.g., Black, "Amending the Constitution," 82 Yale L.J. 189 (1972), Dellinger, "The Recurring Question of the 'Limited' Constitutional Convention," 88 Yale L.J. 1623 (1979), and Gunther, "The Convention Method of Amending the United States Constitution," 14 Ga.L.Rev. 1 (1979). In August 1984, the Senate Judiciary Committee approved a bill to set procedures for (and impose limits on) constitutional conventions. See Constitutional Convention Procedures Act of 1984, Sen.Rep. No. 98–594, 98th Cong., 2d Sess.

A. THE WAR POWER

WOODS v. MILLER CO.

333 U.S. 138, 68 S.Ct. 421, 92 L.Ed. 596 (1948).

Mr. Justice DOUGLAS delivered the opinion of the Court.

The case is here on a direct appeal [from] a judgment of the District Court holding unconstitutional Title II of the Housing and Rent Act of 1947. The District Court was of the view that the authority of Congress to regulate rents by virtue of the war power ended with the Presidential Proclamation terminating hostilities on December 31, 1946,[1] since that proclamation inaugurated "peace-in-fact" though it did not mark termination of the war. It also concluded that, even if the war power continues, Congress did not act under it because it did not say [so].

[The] war power sustains this legislation. The Court said in Hamilton v. Kentucky Distilleries Co., 251 U.S. 146, 161 [1919], that the war power includes the power "to remedy the evils which have arisen from its rise and progress" and continues for the duration of that emergency. Whatever may be the consequences when war is officially terminated, the war power does not necessarily end with the cessation of hostilities. [In Hamilton] and Ruppert v. Caffey, 251 U.S. 264 [1920], prohibition laws which were enacted after the Armistice in World War I were sustained as exercises of the war power because they conserved manpower and increased efficiency of production in the critical days during the period of demobilization, and helped to husband the supply of grains and cereals depleted by the war effort. [The] constitutional validity of the present legislation follows a fortiori from those cases. The legislative history of the present Act makes abundantly clear that there has not yet been eliminated the deficit in housing which in considerable measure was caused by the heavy demobilization of veterans and by the cessation or reduction in residential construction during the period of hostilities due to the allocation of building materials to military projects. Since the war effort contributed heavily to that deficit, Congress has the power even after the cessation of hostilities to act to control the forces that a short supply of the needed article created. If that were not true, the Necessary and Proper Clause would be drastically limited in its application to the several war powers.

[We] recognize the force of the argument that the effects of war under modern conditions may be felt in the economy for years and years, and that if the war power can be used in days of peace to treat all the wounds which war inflicts on our society, it may not only swallow up all other powers of Congress but largely obliterate the Ninth and the Tenth Amendments as well. There are no such implications in today's decision. We deal here with the consequences of a housing deficit greatly intensified during the period of hostilities. [Any] power, of course, can be abused. But we cannot assume that Congress is not alert to its constitutional responsibilities. [The] question of the constitutionality of action taken by Congress does not depend on recitals of the power which it undertakes to exercise. Here it is plain from the legislative history that Congress was invoking its war power to cope with a current condition of which the war was a direct and immediate [cause].

Reversed.

---

1. That proclamation recognized that "a state of war still exists." On July 25, 1947, [the] President issued a statement in which he declared that "The emergencies declared by the President on September 8, 1939, and May 27, 1941, and the state of war continue to exist, however, and it is not possible at this time to provide for terminating all war and emergency powers." [Footnote by Justice Douglas.]

Mr. Justice JACKSON, concurring.

I agree with the result in this case, but the arguments that have been addressed to us lead me to utter more explicit misgivings about war powers than the Court has done. The Government asserts no constitutional basis for this legislation other than this vague, undefined and undefinable "war power." No one will question that this power is the most dangerous one to free government in the whole catalogue of powers. It usually is invoked in haste and excitement when calm legislative consideration of constitutional limitation is difficult. It is executed in a time of patriotic fervor that makes moderation unpopular. And, worst of all, it is interpreted by judges under the influence of the same passions and pressures. Always, as in this case, the Government urges hasty decision to forestall some emergency or serve some purpose and pleads that paralysis will result if its claims to power are denied or their confirmation delayed.

Particularly when the war power is invoked to do things to the liberties of people, or to their property or economy that only indirectly affect conduct of the war and do not relate to the management of the war itself, the constitutional basis should be scrutinized with care.

I think we can hardly deny that the war power is as valid a ground for federal rent control now as it has been at any time. We still are technically in a state of war. I would not be willing to hold that war powers may be indefinitely prolonged merely by keeping legally alive a state of war that had in fact ended. I cannot accept the argument that war powers last as long as the effects and consequences of war, for if so they are permanent—as permanent as the war debts. But I find no reason to conclude that we could find fairly that the present state of war is merely technical. We have armies abroad exercising our war power and have made no peace terms with our allies, not to mention our principal enemies. I think the conclusion that the war power has been applicable during the lifetime of this legislation is unavoidable.[2]

DOMESTIC REGULATION THROUGH THE WAR POWER

As Woods illustrates, the war power is available for national regulation of a wide range of problems, of the "police" as well as the economic variety. Note, for example, the rationale for sustaining the post-World War I prohibition law as described in Woods. Was there adequate judicial scrutiny in the Hamilton and Ruppert cases in 1919–20? Or are those decisions additional illustrations of the early 20th century Court's insensitivity to federalism values when Congress moved against such "evils" as immorality and crime? (Recall the Court's endorsement of the commerce-prohibiting power in cases beginning with the Lottery Case, p. 112 above.) Compare the Court's statement in the 1919 decision in Hamilton v. Kentucky Distilleries Co., sustaining the post-World War I prohibition law (enacted prior to the adoption of the 18th Amendment): after recognizing that the national government "lacks the police power," the Court insisted "that when the United States exerts any of the powers conferred upon it by the Constitution, no valid objection can be based upon the fact that such exercise may be attended by the same incidents which attend the exercise by a State of its police power, or that it may tend to

---

2. Another concurring opinion, by Justice Frankfurter, is omitted.

Justice Jackson's stance of noting misgivings, often in concurring opinions, was one he took in a variety of contexts. Recall, for example, his doubts about the taxing power in the Kahriger case, p. 198 above, and about the commerce power in the Five Gambling Devices case, p. 152 above. There are similar examples in later chapters: e.g., on the war power and individual rights, in Korematsu v. United States, p. 624 below, and on equal protection restraints on economic regulation, in Railway Express Agency v. New York, p. 597 below.

accomplish a similar purpose." Are there judicially enforceable limits on war power-based regulation, either of the economic or the "police" variety?

———

B.   TREATIES, FOREIGN AFFAIRS, AND FEDERALISM

———

Introduction. Are federalistic constraints relevant when the national government engages in the conduct of foreign relations? To what extent does the national government's authority over foreign affairs authorize national regulation of an otherwise local area? These are the central concerns of this section; other constitutional problems pertaining to international affairs are left to later chapters.[1] Most of the materials in this section involve domestic regulatory consequences of national action resting on the treaty power. The final note considers whether there is a foreign affairs power of Congress independent of authority derived from treaties—and what the source of that power is. The central question in this section, then, is: To what extent may a treaty authorize national regulation of local affairs not reachable under other grants of power?

———

MISSOURI v. HOLLAND

252 U.S. 416, 40 S.Ct. 382, 64 L.Ed. 641 (1920).

Mr. Justice HOLMES delivered the opinion of the court.

This is a bill in equity brought by the State of Missouri to prevent a game warden of the United States from attempting to enforce the [1918] Migratory Bird Treaty Act [on the ground] that the statute is an unconstitutional interference with the rights reserved to the States by the Tenth Amendment. [The District Court held the Act unconstitutional.] On December 8, 1916, a treaty between the United States and Great Britain was proclaimed by the President. It recited that many species of birds in their annual migrations traversed certain parts of the United States and of Canada, that they were of great value as a source of food and in destroying insects injurious to vegetation, but were in danger of extermination through lack of adequate protection. It therefore provided for specified closed seasons and protection in other forms, and agreed that the two powers would take or propose to their law making bodies the necessary measures for carrying the treaty out. The [Act] prohibited the killing, capturing or selling any of the migratory birds included in the terms of the treaty except as permitted by [federal] regulations compatible with those terms. [It] is unnecessary to go into any details, because [the] question raised is the general one whether the treaty and statute are void as an interference with the rights reserved to the States.

To answer this question it is not enough to refer to the Tenth Amendment [because] by Article II, § 2, the power to make treaties is delegated expressly, and by Article VI treaties made under the authority of the United States, [are] declared the supreme law of the land. If the treaty is valid there can be no dispute about the validity of the statute under Article I, § 8, as a necessary and proper means to execute the powers of the Government. [It] is said that a treaty cannot be valid if it infringes the Constitution, that there are limits, therefore, to the treaty-making power, and that one such limit is that what an act of Congress could not do unaided, in derogation of the powers reserved to the

———

1. See, e.g., chap. 6, on separation of powers, for the problems of executive-legislative relations pertaining to the conduct of foreign relations.

States, a treaty cannot do. [The fact that an] earlier act of Congress that attempted by itself and not in pursuance of a treaty to regulate the killing of migratory birds within the States had been held bad [in two lower court decisions] cannot be accepted as a test of the treaty power. Acts of Congress are the supreme law of the land only when made in pursuance of the Constitution, while treaties are declared to be so when made under the authority of the United States. It is open to question whether the authority of the United States means more than the formal acts prescribed to make the convention. We do not mean to imply that there are no qualifications to the treaty-making power; but they must be ascertained in a different way. It is obvious that there may be matters of the sharpest exigency for the national well being that an act of Congress could not deal with but that a treaty followed by such an act could, and it is not lightly to be assumed that, in matters requiring national action, "a power which must belong to and somewhere reside in every civilized government" is not to be found. [We] are not yet discussing the particular case before us but only are considering the validity of the test proposed. With regard to that we may add that when we are dealing with words that also are a constituent act, like the [Constitution], we must realize that they have called into life a being the development of which could not have been foreseen completely by the most gifted of its begetters. It was enough for them to realize or to hope that they had created an organism; it has taken a century and has cost their successors much sweat and blood to prove that they created a nation. The case before us must be considered in the light of our whole experience and not merely in that of what was said a hundred years ago. The treaty in question does not contravene any prohibitory words to be found in the Constitution. The only question is whether it is forbidden by some invisible radiation from the general terms of the Tenth Amendment. We must consider what this country has become in deciding what that Amendment has reserved.

The State [founds] its claim of exclusive authority upon an assertion of title to migratory birds, an assertion that is embodied in statute. No doubt it is true that as between a State and its inhabitants the State may regulate the killing and sale of such birds, but it does not follow that its authority is exclusive of paramount powers. [As] most of the laws of the United States are carried out within the States and as many of them deal with matters which in the silence of such laws the State might regulate, such general grounds are not enough to support Missouri's claim. Valid treaties of course "are as binding within the territorial limits of the States as they are elsewhere throughout the dominion of the United States." No doubt the great body of private relations usually fall within the control of the State, but a treaty may override its power. [Here] a national interest of very nearly the first magnitude is involved. It can be protected only by national action in concert with that of another power. The subject matter is only transitorily within the State and has no permanent habitat therein. But for the treaty and the statute there soon might be no birds for any powers to deal with. We see nothing in the Constitution that compels the Government to sit by while a food supply is cut off and the protectors of our forests and our crops are destroyed. It is not sufficient to rely upon the States. The reliance is vain, and were it otherwise, the question is whether the United States is forbidden to act. We are of opinion that the treaty and statute must be [upheld].

Decree affirmed.[1]

---

1. Justices VAN DEVANTER and PITNEY dissented.

THE SCOPE AND LIMITS OF THE TREATY POWER

1. *The supremacy of treaties over state law.* As Missouri v. Holland reminds, a treaty made by the President with the required concurrence of two-thirds of the Senate is, under the Supremacy Clause of Art. VI, § 2, part of "the supreme Law of the Land" which takes precedence over contrary state laws. Even before the days of the Marshall Court, the Court began to implement the principle that a valid treaty overrides a state law on matters otherwise within state control. For example, in Ware v. Hylton, 3 Dall. 199 (1796), a treaty was held to have overridden a Virginia confiscation law.[2] Similarly, in Hauenstein v. Lynham, 100 U.S. 483 (1880), a Virginia law providing for the escheat to the state of real estate of aliens dying intestate had to give way to a treaty, with the Court quoting from a treatise stating that "all questions which may arise between us and other powers, be the subject-matter what it may, fall within the treaty-making power."

2. *Limits on the treaty power?—The subject-matter of treaties.* Are there any judicially enforceable limits on the permissible subject-matter of a treaty? Whenever Art. I powers prove insufficient to reach a local problem, may the national government overcome that obstacle simply by making a treaty with a cooperating foreign government? Are there any traditionally local questions that cannot be "properly the subject of negotiation with a foreign country"? Does not the fact that a treaty exists, that a treaty about a particular matter *has* been negotiated, demonstrate that the matter *is* a proper subject for negotiation? Can the courts scrutinize the good faith of President and Senate in entering into treaties? [3]

3. *The Bricker Amendment controversy.* In the early 1950s, widely voiced concerns that the treaty power was the Achilles heel of the Constitution—that any and all constitutional limitations could be overridden via the international agreement route—spurred efforts to amend the Constitution. Justice Holmes' broad statements in Missouri v. Holland proved popular and frequently quoted sources for those anxious to demonstrate the substantiality of the threat to constitutional restrictions. Moreover, the fears that generated popular support for the Bricker Amendment were fed by occasional arguments made in American courts that relied on United Nations provisions.[4]

---

2. Recall also the conflict between state confiscations and federal treaties that culminated in Martin v. Hunter's Lessee in 1816, p. 29 above.

3. The "properly the subject of negotiation" phrase comes from DeGeofroy v. Riggs, 133 U.S. 258 (1890). Justice Field stated: "The treaty power [is] unlimited except by those restraints which are found in [the Constitution] against the action of the government or of its departments, and those arising from the nature of the government itself and of that of the States. It would not be contended that it extends so far as to authorize what the Constitution forbids, or a change in the character of the government or in that of one of the States, or a cession of any portion of the territory of the latter, without its consent. But with these exceptions, it is not perceived that there is any limit to the questions which can be adjusted touching any matter which is properly the subject of negotiation with a foreign country." Compare comment b to ALI, Restatement (Second) Foreign Relations Law of the United States § 117 (1965): "An international agreement of the United States must relate to the external concerns of the nation as distinguished from matters of a purely internal nature." Are these statements effective limits on the treaty power? If not, are there others? (Note that, in terms of domestic effect, congressional legislation is on a par with treaties, so that a later act of Congress supersedes a prior treaty. See the Chinese Exclusion Case, 130 U.S. 581 (1889): "[The] last expression of the sovereign will must control.") Fear about a potentially unlimited treaty power spawned the Bricker Amendment controversy of the 1950s, considered in the next note.

4. The concern was that the UN Charter or resolutions by UN agencies (e.g., the Draft Covenant on Civil and Political Rights) might undercut American constitutional guarantees. For example, Art. 55 of the UN Charter states that the UN shall promote "universal respect for, and observance of, human rights and fundamental freedoms without distinction as to race, sex, language, or religion." In Sei Fujii v. State, 217 P.2d 481 (1950), a California District Court of Appeal held an alien land law invalid on the ground that the UN Charter was self-executing. The California Supreme Court, however, rested

Those anxieties produced Senator Bricker's constitutional amendment proposal. The version recommended by the Senate Judiciary Committee in 1953 included the statement, as Sec. 1: "A provision of a treaty which conflicts with this Constitution shall not be of any force or effect." And Sec. 2 added: "A treaty shall become effective as internal law in the United States only through legislation which would be valid in the absence of treaty." That second section in particular was directed against the doctrine of enlargement of congressional powers through treaties, as in Missouri v. Holland, as well as against the principle that treaties can be self-executing, as has been true since Ware v. Hylton, note 1 above. After extensive debates in the Senate in 1954, various modifications were offered. A substitute by Senator George of Georgia attracted a majority vote of 60 to 31 in February 1954—just short of the required two-thirds. The George substitute included the statement: "A provision of a treaty or other international agreement which conflicts with this Constitution shall not be of any force or effect." Similar proposals during the next three years also failed.

4. *The reassurance of Reid v. Covert.* While the Bricker Amendment debate was still alive, the Supreme Court handed down REID v. COVERT, 354 U.S. 1 (1957); and Justice BLACK's plurality opinion contained a passage directly responsive to some of the concerns voiced by the supporters of the Bricker Amendment. Did it give adequate reassurance on all of their concerns? Reid v. Covert dealt mainly with congressional power under Art. I, § 8, to provide for military jurisdiction over civilian dependents of American servicemen overseas. But in a passage relevant to the Bricker issue, the Court also rejected an argument that the law might be independently supportable because of the existence of an international agreement. Executive agreements [5] had been entered into with other countries permitting American military courts to exercise exclusive jurisdiction over offenses by American servicemen or their dependents overseas. The Government argued that the challenged statute could be sustained "as legislation which is necessary and proper to carry out the United States' obligations under the international agreements." Justice Black replied:

"The obvious and decisive answer to this, of course, is that no agreement with a foreign nation can confer power on the Congress, or on any other branch of Government, which is free from the restraints of the Constitution." He found nothing in the history or language of the Supremacy Clause, Art. VI, § 2, "which intimates that treaties and laws enacted pursuant to them do not have to comply with the provisions of the Constitution." Rather, he thought it "clear that the reason treaties were not limited to those made in 'pursuance' of the Constitution [see the text of Art. VI] was so that agreements made by the United States under the Articles of Confederation [would] remain in effect." He added: "It would be manifestly contrary to the objectives of those who created the Constitution, as well as those who were responsible for the Bill of Rights—let alone alien to our entire constitutional history and tradition—to construe Article VI as permitting the United States to exercise power under an international agreement without observing constitutional prohibitions." Moreover, he found nothing contrary in Missouri v. Holland. Justice Black explained: "There the Court carefully noted that the treaty involved was not inconsistent with any specific provision of the Constitution." Noting that Missouri v. Holland had been solely concerned with the Tenth Amendment, he added: "To the extent that the United States can validly make treaties, the people and the States have delegated their power to the National Government

its affirmance of the result on the 14th Amendment, 242 P.2d 617 (1952), after finding that the UN Charter provision was "not self-executing."

5. On the distinction between executive agreements and treaties, see chap. 6 below, at p. 367.

and the Tenth Amendment is no barrier." Justice Black's comments contributed greatly to putting to rest the concerns that treaties might be the basis for
domestic action affecting individual rights beyond the limits governing other
national powers.

———

THE FOREIGN AFFAIRS POWER OF CONGRESS: NATURE AND SOURCES

The national government's treaty power is explicitly granted in the Constitution. Is there also a foreign affairs power of Congress independent of authority
to implement validly adopted treaties? Where in the Constitution is it found?
Is it an inference from granted power? Or does it derive from extraconstitutional sources, as the Court has sometimes suggested? Is the notion of
extraconstitutional sources of power consistent with the premises of constitutional government?

a. That there is a power in Congress to regulate foreign affairs has been
repeatedly recognized by the Court. The source of the power remains unclear,
however. For a modern statement of the power, see Perez v. Brownell, 356
U.S. 44, 57 (1958), sustaining a statutory provision regarding loss of citizenship: "Although there is in the Constitution no specific grant to Congress of
power to enact legislation for the effective regulation of foreign affairs, there
can be no doubt of the existence of this power in the law-making organ of the
Nation. See, [e.g., United States v. Curtiss-Wright Export Corp., 299 U.S.
304, 318]. The States that joined together to form a single Nation and to
create, through the Constitution, a Federal Government to conduct the affairs of
that Nation must be held to have granted that Government the powers
indispensable to its functioning effectively in the company of sovereign nations.
The Government must be able not only to deal affirmatively with foreign
nations, as it does through the maintenance of diplomatic relations with them
and the protection of American citizens sojourning within their territories. It
must also be able to reduce to a minimum the frictions that are unavoidable in a
world of sovereigns sensitive in matters touching their dignity and interests." [1]

b. In the Curtiss-Wright passage cited in Perez, Justice Sutherland's majority opinion had discussed, in 1936, the supposedly "fundamental" differences
"between the powers of the federal government in respect to foreign or
external affairs and those in respect of domestic or internal affairs." He insisted
that the "two classes of power are different, both in respect of their origin and
their nature. The broad statement that the federal government can exercise no
powers except those specifically enumerated in the Constitution, and such
implied powers as are necessary and proper to carry into effect the enumerated
powers, is categorically true only in respect of our internal affairs. In that field,
the primary purpose of the Constitution was to carve from the general mass of
legislative powers *then possessed by the states* such portions as it was thought
desirable to vest in the federal government, leaving those not included in the
enumeration still in the states. [That] this doctrine applies only to powers
which the states had, is self-evident. And since the states severally never
possessed international powers, such powers could not have been carved from
the mass of state powers but obviously were transmitted to the United States
from some other source." His review of history led him to conclude that "the
investment of the federal government with the powers of external sovereignty
did not depend upon the affirmative grants of the Constitution. The powers to
declare and wage war, to conclude peace, to make treaties, to maintain

———

1. The provision sustained in Perez v. Brown-   253 (1967), but the Perez passage quoted in text
ell was invalidated in Afroyim v. Rusk, 387 U.S.   was not challenged in Afroyim.

diplomatic relations with other sovereignties, if they had never been mentioned in the Constitution, would have vested in the federal government as necessary concomitants of nationality." Justice Sutherland's Curtiss-Wright dictum is questionable historically [2] and certainly represents an approach to national powers notably different from that applied to other powers since the days of McCulloch. Nevertheless, as Perez illustrates, it represents a pervasive thread in Court discussions of foreign affairs matters.[3]

c. How extensive is the congressional power "to enact legislation for the effective regulation of foreign affairs"? Is it limited to matters that are generally the subject matter of foreign relations? Can the Court reexamine the good faith of—or factual basis for—a congressional assertion that a problem *is* a foreign affairs concern? Is this congressional power subject to any greater federalistic limits than the Geofroy v. Riggs "properly the subject of negotiation" criterion regarding treaties? [4]

d. The national concern with foreign affairs is a powerful one, even though its bases are not fully spelled out in the Constitution. It supports not only congressional action; its mere existence, though unexercised, may preclude state action as well. (Compare the impact of the unexercised, "dormant" commerce power on state action, chap. 5 below.) The impact of the national power as a restraint on state authority is illustrated by Zschernig v. Miller, 389 U.S. 429 (1968), where the Court barred application of a state alien inheritance law because it intruded "into the field of foreign affairs which the Constitution entrusts to the President and the Congress."

2. See Lofgren, "United States v. Curtiss-Wright Corporation: An Historical Reassessment," 83 Yale L.J. 1 (1973).

3. See generally Henkin, Foreign Affairs and the Constitution (1972). (The Curtiss-Wright case is considered further in chap. 6, at p. 363, below).

4. See generally Henkin, "The Treaty Makers and the Law Makers: The Law of the Land and Foreign Relations," 107 U.Pa.L.Rev. 903 (1959).

Chapter 5

STATE REGULATION AND THE NATIONAL ECONOMY: CONSTITUTIONAL LIMITS AND CONGRESSIONAL ORDERING

Scope Note. In accordance with the plan sketched at the outset of Part II, the focus now shifts to the impact of the federal system's division of powers on the scope of *state* authority. Chapters 2, 3, and 4 examined the scope of *national* powers as limited by localist concerns; this chapter completes the examination of the major constitutional aspects of federalism, with special emphasis on the limits on *state* powers that flow from national concerns. Once again, the pervasive questions are the sources and adequacy of constitutional limitations: Do the constraints arise from text? From history? From inferences based on the structure of the Constitution? From society's values—or those of the Justices? Once again, the recurrent problem is the adequacy of the articulations and implementations of constitutional values. On what basis, and to what extent, do the grants of enumerated powers to the national government, and the exercises of those powers, curtail state authority? This chapter explores those problems mainly in the context of the commerce power; but similar restrictions on state authority arise in connection with other national powers as well.[1]

The commerce barrier to state action arises in two, frequently overlapping, situations. In the first, Congress has been wholly silent: it has taken no action, express or implied, indicating its own policy on a given subject matter. In that situation, the objection to state authority rests entirely on the "dormant" commerce clause of Art. I, § 8—on the unexercised commerce power itself, and on the free trade value it symbolizes. In the second situation, Congress *has* exercised the commerce power, *has* indicated its policy, and the challenge to state action rests on valid, "supreme" national legislation which compels inconsistent state action to give way—by virtue not only of the exercise of the commerce power under Art. I, § 8, but also because of the effect of the supremacy clause in Art. VI. These materials are designed to focus attention on the appropriate roles of Court and Congress in furthering commerce clause values; on the source and scope of commerce power-based barriers to state action; and on the extent of congressional authority to overturn Court-discovered obstacles to state action.[2]

---

1. See, e.g., as to bankruptcy, Sturges v. Crowinshield, 4 Wheat. 122 (1819), and Perez v. Campbell, 402 U.S. 637 (1971); as to foreign affairs, Zschernig v. Miller, 389 U.S. 429 (1968); as to copyright, Goldstein v. California, 412 U.S. 546 (1973); as to patents, Kewanee Oil Co. v. Bicron Corp., 416 U.S. 470 (1974).

2. In recent years, the Court has revitalized another constitutional barrier to state action with purposes that somewhat overlap those of the commerce clause: the privileges and immunities clause of Art. IV, § 2, which guarantees to the "Citizens of each State [all] Privileges and Immunities of Citizens in the several States." Like the commerce clause, the Art. IV provision can be seen as directed against state legislation that discriminates against out-of-state economic interests or that erects a protectionist barrier against out-of-state competition. Decisions on the Art. IV provision accordingly are considered in this chapter (sec. 1C(6)), together with related commerce clause developments. [Note also that the equal protection guarantee of the Fourteenth Amendment can be invoked as a tool against economic protectionism, as in Zobel v. Williams (1982; p. 842 below).] This chapter concludes (in sec. 3) with a brief survey of other interstate obligations in Art. IV, and with further materials

SECTION 1. STATE REGULATION AND THE DORMANT COMMERCE CLAUSE

Introduction. 1. *The vision and the achievement.* In the cases in this section, state legislation is challenged on the basis of the dormant, unexercised commerce power. In these cases, Congress has not acted; instead, the Court has taken it upon itself to implement the values of the grant of power to Congress in the commerce clause by restricting state impingements on interstate commerce. What is the justification for the Court's assumption of that task? How effectively has the Court performed it? Has its performance matched its aspirations?

The Court has not always been articulate, nor the Justices always in agreement, about the governing values in the hundreds of cases in which state laws have been challenged as contravening the commerce clause. But the aspirations that have guided the Court surface occasionally in the opinions. Few Justices have stated them more eloquently than Justice Jackson. H.P. Hood & Sons v. DuMond (1949; p. 289 below) provided the occasion for one of his most notable statements about the free trade goals of the commerce clause. The passages below offer useful introductory comments on the Court's aims in commerce clause litigation. In examining the materials that follow, consider how well the Court's decisions do (and can) "give reality" to Justice Jackson's articulation of the "vision of the Founders." Justice Jackson said in Hood:

"The Commerce Clause is one of the most prolific sources of national power and an equally prolific source of conflict with legislation of the state. While the Constitution vests in Congress the power to regulate commerce among the states, it does not say what the states may or may not do in the absence of congressional action. [Perhaps] even more than by interpretation of its written word, this Court has advanced the solidarity and prosperity of this Nation by the meaning it has given to these great silences of the Constitution. [The] principle that our economic unit is the Nation, which alone has the gamut of powers necessary to control of the economy, including the vital power of erecting customs barriers against foreign competition, has as its corollary that the states are not separable economic units. [The] material success that has come to inhabitants of the states which make up this federal free trade unit has been the most impressive in the history of commerce, but the established interdependence of the states only emphasizes the necessity of protecting interstate movement of goods against local burdens. [The] distinction between the power of the State to shelter its people from menaces to their health or safety and from fraud, even when those dangers emanate from interstate commerce, and its lack of power to retard, burden or constrict the flow of such commerce for their economic advantage, is one deeply rooted in both our history and our law. [This] Court consistently has rebuffed attempts of states to advance their own commercial interests by curtailing the movement of articles of commerce, either into or out of the state, while generally supporting their right to impose even burdensome regulations in the interest of local health and safety. [Our] system, fostered by the Commerce Clause, is that every farmer and every craftsman shall be encouraged to produce by the certainty that he will have free access to every market in the Nation, that no home embargoes will withhold his exports, and no foreign state will by customs duties or regulations exclude them. Likewise, every consumer may look to the free competition from every producing area in the Nation to protect him from exploitation by any. Such was the vision of the Founders; such has been the doctrine of this Court which has given it [reality]."

on the intergovernmental immunities problem
raised in McCulloch, p. 72 above.

2. *The source of the vision.* What are the sources of the values articulated in Hood? How can the Court justify expending so much of its energy for more than 150 years on implementing values such as these? It is not a task explicitly given to the Court by the Constitution. The Constitution does indeed, as in Art. I, § 10, impose limitations on the states—e.g., with respect to imposing duties on imports or exports. But there is no broad textual limit on state impingements on interstate commerce, nor any explicit barrier to state protectionism or discrimination against trade. For such limitations, the Court has drawn not on any overt restraints, but rather on the grant of power to Congress to regulate interstate commerce. Into that affirmative grant the Court has read self-executing limits on state legislation when Congress has not acted. To justify these implications from the commerce clause, the Court has relied largely on history and on inferences from the federal structure. The additional passages from Justice Jackson's opinion in Hood which follow reflect some of these sources of the Court's vision. Do these sources justify the limits on state power announced in the cases below? Are the limits adequately responsive to the articulated historical concerns? Justice Jackson summarized the history as follows:

"When victory relieved the Colonies from the pressure for solidarity that war had exerted, a drift toward anarchy and commercial warfare between states began. '[Each] State would legislate according to its estimate of its own interests, the importance of its own products, and the local advantages or disadvantages of its position in a political or commercial view.' This came 'to threaten at once the peace and safety of the Union.' The sole purpose for which Virginia initiated the movement which ultimately produced the Constitution was 'to take into consideration the trade of the United States; to examine the relative situations and trade of the said States; to consider how far a uniform system in their commercial regulations may be necessary to their common interest and their permanent harmony' and for that purpose the General Assembly of Virginia in January of 1786 named commissioners and proposed their meeting with those from other states. The desire of the Forefathers to federalize regulation of foreign and interstate commerce stands in sharp contrast to their jealous preservation of the state's power over its internal affairs. No other federal power was so universally assumed to be necessary, no other state power was so readily relinquished. [As Madison] indicated, 'want of a general power over Commerce led to an exercise of this power separately, by the States, wch [sic] not only proved abortive, but engendered rival, conflicting and angry regulations.' The necessity of centralized regulation of commerce among the states was so obvious and so fully recognized that the few words of the Commerce Clause were little illuminated by debate."

A. EARLY DEVELOPMENTS

GIBBONS v. OGDEN

9 Wheat. 1, 6 L.Ed. 23 (1824).

[In the first part of his opinion in this case challenging New York's steamboat monopoly grant, Chief Justice MARSHALL considered the reach of the congressional commerce power into local affairs. (See chap. 3, p. 100, above.) In the portion printed here, Marshall discussed the impact of the commerce clause, and of national legislation based upon it, on state authority.]

[I]t has been urged, with great earnestness, that although the power of congress to regulate commerce with foreign nations, and among the several states, be co-extensive with the subject itself, and have no other limits than are prescribed in the constitution, yet the states may severally exercise the same power, within their respective jurisdictions. In support of this argument, it is said, that they possessed it as an inseparable attribute of sovereignty, before the formation of the constitution, and still retain it, except so far as they have surrendered it by that instrument; that this principle results from the nature of the government, and is secured by the tenth amendment; that an affirmative grant of power is not exclusive, unless in its own nature it be such that the continued exercise of it by the former possessor is inconsistent with the grant, and that this is not of that description. The appellant, conceding these postulates, except the last, contends that full power to regulate a particular subject, implies the whole power, and leaves no residuum; that a grant of the whole is incompatible with the existence of a right in another to any part of it.

[The] grant of the power to lay and collect taxes is, like the power to regulate commerce, made in general terms, and has never been understood to interfere with the exercise of the same power by the states; and hence has been drawn an argument which has been applied to the question under consideration. But the two grants are not, it is conceived, similar in their terms or their nature. Although many of the powers formerly exercised by the states, are transferred to the government of the Union, yet the state governments remain, and constitute a most important part of our system. The power of taxation is indispensable to their existence, and is a power which, in its own nature, is capable of residing in, and being exercised by, different authorities at the same time. [When] each government exercises the power of taxation, neither is exercising the power of the other. But, when a state proceeds to regulate [interstate or foreign] commerce, it is exercising the very power that is granted to congress, and is doing the very thing which congress is authorized to do. There is no analogy, then, between the power of taxation and the power of regulating commerce.

[But] the inspection laws are said to be regulations of commerce, and are certainly recognised in the constitution, as being passed in the exercise of a power remaining with the states. That inspection laws may have a remote and considerable influence on commerce, will not be denied; but that a power to regulate commerce is the source from which the right to pass them is derived, cannot be admitted. The object of inspection laws, is to improve the quality of articles produced by the labour of a country; to fit them for exportation; or, it may be, for domestic use. They act upon the subject, before it becomes an article of [commerce], and prepare it for that purpose. They form a portion of that immense mass of legislation, which embraces every thing within the territory of a state, not surrendered to the general government; all which can be most advantageously exercised by the states themselves. Inspection laws, quarantine laws, health laws of every description, as well as laws for regulating the internal commerce of a state, and those which respect turnpike roads, ferries, &c., are component parts of this mass.

No direct general power over these objects is granted to congress; and, consequently, they remain subject to state legislation. If the legislative power of the Union can reach them, it must be for national purposes; it must be where the power is expressly given for a special purpose, or is clearly incidental to some power which is expressly given. It is obvious, that the government of the Union, in the exercise of its express powers, that, for example, of regulating [interstate commerce], may use means that may also be employed by a state, in the exercise of its acknowledged powers; that, for example, of regulating commerce within the state. [If] a state, in passing laws on subjects acknowledged to be within its control, and with a view to those subjects, shall adopt a measure of the same character with one which congress may adopt, it does not derive its authority from the particular power which has been granted, but from some other, which remains with the state, and may be executed by the same means. All experience shows, that the same measures, or measures scarcely distinguishable from each other, may flow from distinct powers; but this does not prove that the powers themselves are identical. Although the means used in their execution may sometimes approach each other so nearly as to be confounded, there are other situations in which they are sufficiently distinct, to establish their individuality. In our complex system, presenting the rare and difficult scheme of one general government, whose action extends over the whole, but which possesses only certain enumerated powers; and of numerous state governments, which retain and exercise all powers not delegated to the Union, contests respecting power must arise. Were it even otherwise, the measures taken by the respective governments to execute their acknowledged powers, would often be of the same description, and might, sometimes, interfere. This, however, does not prove that the one is exercising, or has a right to exercise, the powers of the other.

[It] has been contended by counsel for the appellant, that, as the word "to regulate" implies in its nature, full power over the thing to be regulated, it excludes, necessarily, the action of all others that would perform the same operation on the same thing. That regulation is designed for the entire result, applying in those parts which remain as they were, as well as to those which are altered. It produces a uniform whole, which is as much disturbed and deranged by changing what the regulating power designs to leave untouched, as that on which it has operated. There is great force in this argument, and the court is not satisfied that it has been refuted.

Since, however, in exercising the power of regulating their own purely internal affairs, whether of trading or police, the states may sometimes enact laws, the validity of which depends on their interfering with, and being contrary to, an act of congress passed in pursuance of the constitution, the court will enter upon the inquiry, whether the laws of New York [have], in their application to this case, come into collision with an act of congress, and deprived a citizen of a right to which that act entitles him. Should this collision exist, it will be immaterial, whether those laws were passed in virtue of a concurrent power "to regulate commerce with foreign nations and among the several states," or, in virtue of a power to regulate their domestic trade and police. In one case and the other, the acts of New York must yield to the law of congress; and the decision sustaining the privilege they confer, against a right given by a law of the Union, must be erroneous.

[Chief Justice Marshall found the New York steamboat monopoly grant to be in conflict with the federal laws licensing those engaged in the coastal trade. Accordingly, the state law was invalid under the supremacy clause of Art. VI of the Constitution. He thus disagreed with Chancellor Kent's view in the state court that the coasting license was merely intended to immunize American ships from the burdens imposed on foreign shipping.[1] The Supreme Court decree accordingly reversed the decision below. As a result, Gibbons, the federal

---

1. Note the veiled criticism of John Marshall's interpretation of the federal licensing law by Justice Thurgood Marshall, a century and a half later. In Douglas v. Seacoast Products, Inc., 431 U.S. 265 (1977), the 20th century Justice Marshall stated: "Although it is true that the Court's view in Gibbons of [congressional intent] is considered incorrect by commentators, its provisions have been repeatedly reenacted in substantially the same form. We can safely assume that Congress was aware of the holding, as well as the criticism, of [Gibbons]. We have no doubt that Congress has ratified the statutory interpretation of Gibbons and its progeny."

licensee, prevailed, and the injunction proceeding brought by Ogden, the holder of the New York monopoly, was dismissed.][2]

Reversed.[3]

WILLSON v. BLACK BIRD CREEK MARSH CO.

2 Pet. 245, 7 L.Ed. 412 (1829).

[The Company was authorized by a Delaware law to build a dam in Black Bird Creek—which flowed into the Delaware River—and also to "bank" the adjoining "marsh and low ground." The dam obstructed navigation of the creek. Willson and others were owners of a sloop licensed under the federal navigation laws. The sloop "broke and injured" the Company's dam in order to pass through the creek. The Company successfully sued for damages; the state courts rejected Willson's defense that the law authorizing the dam violated the commerce clause.

[William Wirt—who, with Daniel Webster, had argued against New York's power to establish the steamboat monopoly in Gibbons—was counsel for the Company. He described the creek as "one of those sluggish reptile streams, that do not run but creep, and which, wherever it passes, spreads its venom, and destroys the health of all those who inhabit its marshes." (Wirt wrote poetry and novels as an avocation.) He argued: "[C]an it be asserted, that a law authorizing the erection of a dam, and the formation of banks which will draw off the pestilence, and give to those who have before suffered from disease, health and vigour, is unconstitutional? The power given by the constitution to congress to regulate commerce, may not be exercised to prevent such measures; and there has been no legislation by congress under the constitution, with which the proceedings of the defendants under the law of Delaware have interfered."]

Mr. Chief Justice MARSHALL delivered the opinion of the Court.[1]

The act of assembly by which the plaintiffs were authorized to construct their dam, shows plainly that this is one of those many creeks, passing through a deep level marsh adjoining the Delaware, up which the tide flows for some distance. The value of the property on its banks must be enhanced by excluding the water from the marsh, and the health of the inhabitants probably improved. Measures calculated to produce these objects, provided they do not come into collision with the powers of the general government, are undoubtedly within those which are reserved to the states. But the measure authorized by this act stops a

---

2. See generally Baxter, The Steamboat Monopoly (1972). The supremacy clause-preemption principle relied on for the holding in Gibbons is explored further below, in sec. 2A of this chapter.

3. Justice JOHNSON—a Jeffersonian Republican from South Carolina and President Jefferson's first appointee to the Court, see Morgan, Justice William Johnson: The First Dissenter (1954)—submitted a concurring opinion which was more nationalistic than Marshall's. Justice Johnson, instead of joining Marshall's reliance on the federal licensing law, rested instead on the ground suggested but not embraced by Marshall: the exclusiveness of the national commerce power. Note, however, that for Johnson, as for Marshall, denial of a state power to regulate commerce did not mean total state inability to enact laws with some *effect* on commerce. For Johnson, as for Marshall, the "purpose" of the

state legislation was a critical criterion in distinguishing between permissible and impermissible state laws. After stating that the federal commerce power "must be exclusive," he added: "It is no objection to the existence of distinct, substantive powers, that, in their application, they bear upon the same subject. [E.g., the same goods imported may be the subject of commercial regulation, yet also of state health regulation, because the goods may be "the vehicle of disease."] [The] different purposes [of the federal and state laws] mark the distinction between the powers brought into action. [Wherever] the powers of the respective governments are frankly exercised, with a distinct view to the ends of such powers, they may act upon the same object, or use the same means, and yet the powers be kept perfectly distinct."

1. The opinion printed here is essentially the full text of Marshall's explanation.

navigable creek, and must be supposed to abridge the rights of those who have been accustomed to use it.

[The] counsel for the plaintiffs in error insist that it comes in conflict with the power of the United States "to regulate commerce with foreign nations and among the several states." If congress had passed any act which bore upon the case; any act in execution of the power to regulate commerce, the object of which was to control state legislation over those small navigable creeks into which the tide flows, and which abound throughout the lower country of the middle and southern states; we should feel not much difficulty in saying that a state law coming in conflict with such act would be void. But congress has passed no such act. The repugnancy of the law of Delaware to the constitution is placed entirely on its repugnancy to the power to regulate commerce with foreign nations and among the several states; a power which has not been so exercised as to affect the question. We do not think that the act empowering the [Company] to place a dam across the creek, can, under all the circumstances of the case, be considered as repugnant to the power to regulate commerce in its dormant state, or as being in conflict with any law passed on the subject.

[Affirmed.]

THE MARSHALL COURT DECISIONS AND THE TANEY COURT GROPINGS BEFORE COOLEY

1. *The Marshall legacy: "Exclusive" commerce power or "tentative idea"?* Gibbons v. Ogden and the Black Bird case were Marshall's only opportunities to write about the impact of the commerce clause on state regulatory authority. It is sometimes said that Marshall viewed the commerce power as exclusive. Is that borne out by his opinions? To be sure, Marshall in Gibbons did note the "great force" in the argument for exclusiveness and said that he was "not satisfied that it has been refuted." But he rested ultimately on the supremacy clause; and his suggestion of a possibly exclusive national commerce power coexisted with a recognition of state power to enact legislation which might affect commerce—"[i]nspection laws, quarantine laws, health laws of every description." The "objects" of legislation were apparently significant to him, as they were to Justice Johnson. Given Marshall's inclination toward that limited variety of "exclusiveness" in Gibbons, how is his brief opinion in Black Bird explainable? Was it a retreat from exclusiveness? Was it based on the notion that the Delaware law was a "health" law rather than a "commercial" regulation? Was it an unarticulated move toward a variety of "balancing" of state and national interests—a sustaining of the state law because the need for it was great and the burden it imposed on interstate commerce was small? [1]

Marshall's approach has occasionally been deprecated as absorption in "abstract criteria." Consider, in examining the subsequent developments, whether the early Taney Court decisions, the Cooley case (p. 238 below), and such modern cases as Southern Pacific (p. 248 below) substituted improved, more "realistic" standards for Marshall's "abstract criteria." In Gibbons, Marshall emphasized the purpose of state regulation in distinguishing permissible "po-

---

1. Consider the soundness of Professor Felix Frankfurter's observation, before he was appointed to the Court: "Had it been given to Marshall to sharpen his coordinate ideas of the exclusive federal commerce power and the reserved state police power through the refining process of litigation, a fruitful analysis might well have eventuated. But employed by minds less sophisticated, less sensitive to the exigencies of government, Marshall's tentative ideas were turned into obscuring formulas whereby issues were confused and evaded." Frankfurter, The Commerce Clause Under Marshall, Taney and Waite (1937), 31. The Taney Court's early attempts to formulate criteria, reviewed in the next note, provide some illustrations supporting Frankfurter's view that Marshall's "tentative ideas" *were* turned into "obscuring formulas."

lice" regulations from impermissible "commerce" regulations. Note that, despite the apparent rejection of "purpose" inquiries in Cooley, a "purpose" emphasis reemerged in the post-Cooley cases.

2. *The early Taney Court's search.* For a decade and a half after John Marshall's death in 1835—during the first half of the tenure of Marshall's successor, Roger Brooke Taney—the Court groped for formulations with little clarity or agreement. Some of the Justices sought to follow what they perceived to be Marshall's guidance: state regulations of "commerce" were prohibited, but "police" regulations were constitutional. Chief Justice Taney himself took a position at the polar extreme from the exclusiveness of the commerce power. To Taney, *no* implied prohibitions from the dormant commerce clause were acceptable: state regulations of commerce were valid "unless they come in conflict with a law of Congress." (See his opinion in the License Cases, note 2b.) With the Cooley decision in 1851, a new majority approach evolved at last. Before turning to the Cooley case, consider the following sampling of the search for standards in the years preceding Cooley.

a. *The Miln case.* In Mayor of the City of New York v. Miln, 11 Pet. 102 (1837), the Court sustained a New York statute requiring the master of a vessel arriving in the port of New York from any point out of the state to report the names, residences, etc., of the passengers. The Court found the law to be "not a regulation of commerce, but of police," and accordingly found it unnecessary to examine the question whether the power to regulate commerce "be or be not exclusive of the States." Justice Story delivered a dissenting opinion in which he insisted on the exclusiveness of the commerce power and held the state law unconstitutional, adding: "In this opinion I have the consolation to know that I had the entire concurrence, upon the same grounds, of that great constitutional jurist, the late Mr. Chief Justice Marshall. Having heard the former arguments, his deliberate opinion was, that the act of New York was unconstitutional." [2]

b. *The License Cases,* 5 How. 504 (1847), sustained state laws requiring licenses for the sale of intoxicating liquors. In rejecting challenges by sellers who had brought liquor from outside the state, the Court was unanimous in result, but could not agree on a majority view; instead, the Justices produced six opinions. Chief Justice Taney stated: "It is well known that upon this subject a difference of opinion has existed, and still exists, among the members of this court. But with every respect for the opinion of my brethren with whom I do not agree, it appears to me to be very clear, that the mere grant of power to the general government cannot [be] construed to be an absolute prohibition to the exercise of any power over the same subject by the States. The controlling and supreme power over commerce with foreign nations and the several States is undoubtedly conferred upon Congress. Yet, in my judgment, the State may nevertheless, for the safety or convenience of trade, or for the protection of the health of its citizens, make regulations of commerce for its own ports and harbours, and for its own territory; and such regulations are valid unless they come in conflict with a law of Congress."

---

2. See also the sharply divided Taney Court's decision in the Passenger Cases, 7 How. 283 (1849), invalidating two other state laws: a New York statute imposing on the masters of ships coming from foreign or other state ports a tax for each passenger, the revenue to be used to defray the costs of examination of passengers for contagious diseases and to maintain a hospital for the treatment of those found to be diseased; and a similar Massachusetts tax applicable to aliens, with the further requirement that the master should post a bond in the amount of $1000 for each alien likely to become a public charge. Five Justices concurred in the result and four (including Chief Justice Taney) dissented. There was no opinion by the Court, but a series of individual opinions. (Compare Edwards v. California (1941; p. 315 below), invalidating a 20th century effort to exclude out-of-state indigents.)

COOLEY v. BOARD OF WARDENS OF THE PORT OF PHILADELPHIA

12 How. 299, 13 L.Ed. 996 (1851).

[A Pennsylvania law of 1803 required ships entering or leaving the port of Philadelphia to engage a local pilot to guide them through the harbor. For failure to comply, the law imposed a penalty of half the pilotage fee, payable to the Board for a fund for superannuated pilots and their dependents. The state courts held Cooley liable for the penalty, as consignee of two ships engaged in the coastal trade that had left the port without a local pilot. In addition to the 1803 Pennsylvania law, the case involved a 1789 congressional statute which provided that "all pilots in the bays, inlets, rivers, harbors, and ports in the United States shall continue to be regulated in conformity with the existing laws of the states, respectively, wherein such pilots may be, or with such laws as the states may respectively hereafter enact for the purpose, until further legislative provision shall be made by Congress."]

Mr. Justice CURTIS delivered the opinion of the Court.

[Regulations of pilots do] constitute regulations of navigation, and consequently of commerce, within the just meaning of [the commerce clause]. [It] becomes necessary, therefore, to consider whether this law of Pennsylvania, being a regulation of commerce, is valid [in view of the grant of the commerce power to Congress]. If the law of Pennsylvania, now in question, had been in existence at the date of this act of Congress, we might hold it to have been adopted by Congress, and thus made a law of the United States, and so valid. [But] the law on which these actions were founded was not enacted till 1803. What effect then can be attributed to so much of the act of 1789, as declares, that pilots shall continue to be regulated in conformity, "with such laws as the States may respectively hereafter enact for the purpose, until further legislative provision shall be made by Congress"?

If the States were divested of the power to legislate on this subject by the grant of the commercial power to Congress, it is plain this act could not confer upon them power thus to legislate. If the Constitution excluded the States from making any law regulating commerce, certainly Congress cannot regrant, or in any manner reconvey to the States that power. And yet this act of 1789 gives its sanction only to laws enacted by the States. This necessarily implies a constitutional power [in the States] to legislate. [Holding] these views we are brought directly and unavoidably to the consideration of the question, whether the grant of the commercial power to Congress, did per se deprive the States of all power to regulate pilots. This question has never been decided by this court, nor, in our judgment, has any case depending upon all the considerations which must govern this one, come before this court.

[The] diversities of opinion, [which] have existed on this subject, have arisen from the different views taken of the nature of this power. But when the nature of a power like this is spoken of, when it is said that the nature of the power requires that it should be exercised exclusively by Congress, it must be intended to refer to the subjects of that power, and to say they are of such a nature as to require exclusive legislation by Congress. Now the power to regulate commerce, embraces a vast field, containing not only many, but exceedingly various subjects, quite unlike in their nature; some imperatively demanding a single uniform rule, operating equally on the commerce of the United States in every port; and some, like the subject now in question, as imperatively demanding that diversity, which alone can meet the local necessities of navigation.

Either absolutely to affirm, or deny that the nature of this power requires exclusive legislation by Congress, is to lose sight of the nature of the subjects of this power, and to assert concerning all of them, what is really applicable but to a part. Whatever subjects of this power are in their nature national, or admit only of one uniform system, or plan of regulation, may justly be said to be of such a nature as to require exclusive legislation by Congress. That this cannot be affirmed of laws for the regulation of pilots and pilotage is plain. The act of 1789 contains a clear and authoritative declaration by the first Congress, that the nature of this subject is such, that until Congress should find it necessary to exert its power, it should be left to the legislation of the States; that it is local and not national; that it is likely to be the best provided for, not by one system, or plan of regulations, but by as many as the legislative discretion of the several States should deem applicable to the local peculiarities of the ports within their limits.

Viewed in this light, so much of this act of 1789 as declares that pilots shall continue to be regulated "by such laws as the States may respectively hereafter enact for that purpose," instead of being held to be inoperative, as an attempt to confer on the States a power to legislate, of which the Constitution had deprived them, is allowed an appropriate and important signification. It manifests the understanding of Congress, at the outset of the government, that the nature of this subject is not such as to require its exclusive legislation. The practice of the States, and of the national government, has been in conformity with this declaration, from the origin of the national government to this time; and the nature of the subject when examined, is such as to leave no doubt of the superior fitness and propriety, not to say the absolute necessity, of different systems of regulation, drawn from local knowledge and experience, and conformed to local wants. How then can we say, that by the mere grant of power to regulate commerce, the States are deprived of all the power to legislate on this subject, because from the nature of the power the legislation of Congress must be exclusive?

[It] is the opinion of a majority of the court that the mere grant to Congress of the power to regulate commerce, did not deprive the States of power to regulate pilots, and that although Congress has legislated on this subject, its legislation manifests an intention, with a single exception, not to regulate this subject, but to leave its regulation to the several states. To these precise questions, which are all we are called on to decide, this opinion must be understood to be confined. It does not extend to the question what other subjects, under the commercial power, are within the exclusive control of Congress, or may be regulated by the States in absence of all congressional legislation; nor to the general question, how far any regulation on a subject by Congress may be deemed to operate as an exclusion of all legislation by the States upon the same [subject].

Affirmed.[1]

---

1. Justices McLEAN and WAYNE dissented; Justice DANIEL concurred on other grounds.

For an examination of a modern variety of pilotage law, see Ray v. Atlantic Richfield Co., 435 U.S. 151 (1978). The Court relied on the supremacy clause in finding that a local pilotage requirement had been preempted by federal law. However, a local provision requiring tug escorts was not found preempted by federal law and survived commerce clause scrutiny as well, in partial reliance on Cooley. The majority commented: "Similar in its nature to a local pilotage requirement, a requirement that a vessel take on a tug escort when entering a particular body of water is not the type of regulation that demands a uniform national rule. [Cooley.]"

THE MEANING OF COOLEY

1. *The doctrine (and problems) of Cooley.* Cooley steered a middle course between the polar positions that had clashed in the earlier Taney Court cases. It rejected the view that the congressional commerce power was exclusive and that the states therefore lacked *all* power to regulate commerce. But it also rejected the view that the commerce clause, in the absence of national legislation, imposed *no* limits on the states at all. Cooley recognized *some* concurrent state regulatory power over commerce and adopted a position that has sometimes been called one of selective exclusiveness. But what *was* that middle course?

Cooley identified as the determinative factor the "subject" of regulation; it appeared to abandon the "purpose" inquiry. According to Cooley, some subjects are "of such a nature" as to require "a single uniform rule" by Congress; others are local, "imperatively demanding that diversity which alone can meet the local necessities." But Cooley left unanswered questions about how the "subjects" were to be identified and distinguished. For example, what was the "subject" found to be "local and not national" in Cooley itself? All pilotage regulation? Pilotage regulation with a certain purpose? (Presumably, the Cooley Court assumed that the pilotage rule was directed at the safety of local harbor traffic. Could it have been argued that an additional purpose was to assure the economic support of local pilots? Would the Cooley formula have permitted such an argument to be taken into account?) Pilotage regulation with a certain effect? Pilotage regulation recognized by Congress to be "local"? And once a subject is recognized as "local" under the Cooley doctrine, does every variety of state regulation become permissible? Or are there still limitations? For example, may a state give preference to local businesses when it regulates a "local" subject? Nor do these questions exhaust the uncertainties left in the wake of Cooley. For example, Cooley does not clarify the proper level of generalization when a "national subject"-"local subject" distinction is invoked. Thus, does Cooley require that an entire field—e.g., the field of railroad regulation—be categorized as either "local" or "national"? Or may some state regulations of railroads be permissible while others are invalid? Questions such as these were left to be explored in the decades to come.

2. *The effect of congressional consent.* The Cooley Court gave only a limited effect to the congressional law of 1789 authorizing state pilotage laws. Justice Curtis did find one "appropriate and important signification" for it: he viewed it simply as guidance to the Court in determining whether pilotage was a "local" or "national" subject. But the Court emphatically refused to consider the congressional declaration as binding: "If the Constitution excluded the States from making any law regulating commerce, certainly Congress cannot regrant or in any manner reconvey to the States that power." To the Cooley Court, commerce clause restrictions—like any other "constitutional" restrictions (but cf. Katzenbach v. Morgan, p. 946 below)—were untouchable by Congress: once the Court found a constitutional barrier, Congress could not remove it. That aspect of Cooley has been undercut by later developments. After a tortuous course of decisions, the Cooley decision was modified to authorize Congress to consent to state regulations of commerce even though those regulations would otherwise be barred by the dormant commerce power.[1]

3. *The role of the Court in the absence of congressional action.* Although later decisions significantly recast the meaning of Cooley, at least one of its aspects has retained majority support: the scope of state power over commerce is not to be determined either by giving the dormant commerce clause a wholly preclusive effect or by giving it no effect at all. Rather, the continuously dominant

---

1. See especially Prudential Insurance Co. v. Benjamin (1946; p. 329 below). The justifica- tions for congressional authority to grant such "consent" are explored in sec. 2B below.

position since Cooley has been that the commerce clause by its own force bars some, but not all, state regulation.   Taney's initial position, that Congress should be the sole protector of interstate trade from excessive state regulations and that the Court should play no role in the absence of congressional action, has never attracted majority support.   In examining the materials that follow, consider whether the Court's continuing expenditure of efforts to protect interstate commerce from excessive state burdens is justified.   Ordinarily, a legislature is more competent than a court to devise flexible and comprehensive solutions.   Moreover, the Constitution does not explicitly bar excessive state regulations, and the typical asserters of commerce clause claims in the courts are by no means impotent in the political process.   Nevertheless, for more than a century, most Justices have voted to strike down some state regulations rather than leaving the issue solely to Congress.   Does the Court's assumption of a major role in this area make sense in terms of history, structure, policy and effectiveness? [2]

4.   *The modern meaning of Cooley.*   A fair number of modern cases cite Cooley as the authoritative (though obviously somewhat obscure) guide.   (E.g., Southern Pacific in 1945, p. 248 below.)   But it is clear that the modern Court engages in a far more complex process for distinguishing between permissible and impermissible state regulations than that suggested by the Cooley formula. Often, the invocation of the "local"-"national" distinction of Cooley constitutes a conclusory label for judgments resting on considerations going far beyond the Cooley Court's emphasis on the "subject" of the regulation.   For example, the "purpose" inquiry rejected by Cooley forms an important ingredient of modern judicial techniques.   (See especially the cases searching for protectionist and discriminatory purposes, in sec. 1C.)   Moreover, even in cases where the modern Court does not focus on questionable or forbidden purposes, the Justices have moved toward a "balancing" of state and national interests, even while citing Cooley.   Thus, Southern Pacific (p. 248 below), which crystallized the modern "balancing" approach at least in transportation cases, can be viewed as an amalgam of the Cooley "effect" emphasis with the pre-Cooley "purpose" concern, even while paying continued lip service to Cooley.[3]

---

2.   Even some of the modern Justices who initially urged a very limited judicial role ultimately came around to the majority position. Justices Black and Douglas, for example, argued early in their judicial careers that the implicit ban of the commerce clause should extend no further than to ban discriminatory state laws.   But in later years, both voted to invalidate state laws because they cast an excessive, although not clearly discriminatory, burden on commerce. Compare, e.g., Justice Douglas' dissent in the Southern Pacific case in 1945 (p. 248 below) with his majority position in Bibb in 1959 (p. 253 below).

Although there is a wide consensus on the modern Court that the judicial role in safeguarding commerce from state regulations ought to go beyond that urged by Taney, the appropriate extent of that role continues in dispute.   For example, there is recurrent debate between those who argue that the Court should engage, in a wide range of cases, in the "balancing" of state and national interests (developed primarily in the transportation area, see sec. 2B below), and those who urge that the Court's primary if not exclusive task should be to identify and invalidate protectionist and discriminatory state laws—laws

that give an undue preference to in-state economic interests over out-of-state competitors (see sec. 2C below).   For modern comments urging a sharply reduced reliance on the dormant commerce clause, see, e.g., Eule, "Laying the Dormant Commerce Clause to Rest," 91 Yale L.J. 425 (1982), and Tushnet, "Rethinking the Dormant Commerce Clause," 1979 Wis.L.Rev. 125.

3.   A good example of the way Cooley is typically used in modern cases is California v. Zook, 336 U.S. 725 (1949).   There the Court stated: "Certain first principles are no longer in doubt.   [When] Congress has not specifically acted we have accepted the Cooley case's broad delineation of the areas of state and national power over interstate commerce.   [Absent] congressional action, the familiar test is that of uniformity versus locality: if a case falls within an area in commerce thought to demand a uniform national rule, state action is struck down. If the activity is one of predominantly local interest, state action is sustained.   *More accurately,* the question is whether the state interest is outweighed by a national interest in the unhampered operation of interstate commerce." (Emphasis added.)   That "more accurate" restatement of Cooley is a reflection of the modern

B. STATE REGULATION OF TRANSPORTATION [1]

THE SEARCH FOR STANDARDS AFTER COOLEY

Introduction. The Cooley test continued to be cited in the increasing number of state regulation cases that came to the Court at the end of the 19th century and in the early decades of the 20th. In the late 19th century, the growth of a nationwide railroad system spurred demands for more extensive legislative controls. But invocations of Cooley seemed increasingly mechanical, obscuring underlying Court concerns with often unarticulated factors—the weight of the state interests, the possibility of protectionist motives, and the extent of burdens on interstate commerce. For a while, the Justices tried to distinguish between permissible "indirect" regulations of commerce and invalid "direct" ones. But that distinction, too, encountered increasing criticism as being too mechanical and conclusory. The inadequacy of the prevailing doctrines, from Cooley to its supplementation or supplanting by "direct"-"indirect" talk,[2] paved the way for the more candid, more complex, but also overtly more subjective "balancing" approach of such modern cases as Southern Pacific (p. 248 below).

1. *Difficulties in applying Cooley.* The early railroad regulation cases frequently cited Cooley, but it was difficult to square the course of the decisions with any simplistic application of the "national"-"local" distinction. For example, the Court held unconstitutional an early state ban on freight rate discrimination by railroads in Wabash, St. Louis & P. Ry. Co. v. Illinois, 118 U.S. 557 (1886), insisting that regulations of interstate shipments were of a "national," not "local," character. Indeed, the Court suggested in Wabash that all interstate railroad regulations were prohibited because interstate transportation would be unduly burdened if each of the through-states "can fix its own rules for prices, for modes of transit, for times and modes of delivery, and all other incidents of transportation to which the word 'regulation' can be applied."[3] But, whatever the Cooley "subject" in Wabash was, it was not all that broad: the Court soon made it clear that the Wabash ruling did not cover *all* incidents of transportation "to which the word 'regulation' can be applied." Just two years after Wabash, for example, the Court sustained a state examination requirement applied to engineers on interstate trains. Smith v. Alabama, 124 U.S. 465 (1888).

2. *The rise and decline of the "direct"-"indirect" distinction.* Smith v. Alabama, above, justified the state regulation of railroad engineers on the ground that the law rested on safety considerations and that its impact on commerce was merely

---

"balancing" approach crystallized four years before Zook, in Southern Pacific, below.

1. Beginning a fuller examination of the post-Cooley developments with a group of cases typically involving transportation facilities is not intended to suggest that the principles in this group of cases are or should necessarily be different from those governing the cases involving largely interstate trade problems, considered in sec. 1C. Rather, the aim is to begin with cases where the evident state interest is not typically protectionism but, instead, clearly legitimate state concerns such as safety. Even in the latter situation, Court invalidations of state laws have been quite common, as the cases illustrate. By contrast, the cases in the next section, sec. 1C, typically raise the fact or suspicion of more questionable state interests such as protection of in-state interests

and discrimination against out-of-state competitors.

2. See generally Stern, "The Problems of Yesteryear—Commerce and Due Process," 4 Vand.L.Rev. 446 (1951), commenting that such labels as "direct" and "indirect" made it "difficult, if not impossible," to tell "whether these expressions merely constituted different methods of stating the Cooley doctrine, or whether the Court was applying different tests."

3. A few months after Wabash (but probably not as a direct consequence of the decision), earlier pressures on Congress bore fruit and the Interstate Commerce Act of 1887 was adopted— a law that nationalized regulations of rates affecting interstate railroads, but did not purport to bar state regulation of most other "incidents of transportation."

"indirect," not "direct." [4]   This "direct"-"indirect" distinction became a frequently invoked one.   It was often a mechanical and obscuring distinction, as critics claimed; but even in the era of those labels, many cases engaged in a more subtle investigation akin to modern "balancing" and repeatedly considered empirical data regarding the extent of the burden on commerce.

A good example is the litigation involving a Georgia safety law that came before the Court twice early in this century.   The Georgia blowpost law required railroads to erect posts 400 yards from railroad crossings and directed locomotive engineers to blow their train whistles when passing the posts and to "simultaneously" check their speed "so as to stop in time should any person [be] crossing" the tracks.   Plaintiffs suing for injuries in crossing accidents relied on noncompliance with the law in claiming negligence; railroad defendants insisted that the law violated the commerce clause.   In Southern Railway Co. v. King, 217 U.S. 524 (1910), the Court sustained the law.   There, the pleadings had alleged that the state law imposed a "direct burden" on interstate traffic.   But in affirming a judgment against the railroad, the Court emphasized that the pleadings "set forth no facts which would make the operation of the statute unconstitutional." [5]   A few years later, with more factually oriented pleadings, a challenge to the application of the Georgia law succeeded, in Seaboard Air Line Ry. v. Blackwell, 244 U.S. 310 (1917).   In the 1917 case, the railroad's pleading alleged that along the 123 miles from Atlanta to the South Carolina border, there were 124 grade crossings; that compliance with the law would require "practically a full stop at each of the road crossings"; that each stop would take from three to five minutes; and that compliance by the train involved in the accident would have lengthened the duration of the trip from a 4½ hours run into one of more than 10½ hours.   The state courts held that any burden on commerce was "indirect"; the Court reversed, finding the case distinguishable from Southern Railway because the facts missing there were alleged here and the railroad's allegations accordingly compelled "the conclusion that the statute is a direct burden" on commerce.   Like reliance on Cooley, then, invocations of "direct"-"indirect" distinctions could not always obscure the fact that more particularized analyses underlay the results.

3. *Justice Stone's attack on the "direct"-"indirect" distinction.*   Justice (later Chief Justice) Harlan Fiske Stone, who joined the Court in 1926, soon took the lead in urging more useful and realistic criteria.   In Di SANTO v. PENNSYLVANIA, 273 U.S. 34 (1927), Justice STONE (joined by Justices Holmes and Brandeis) submitted an important dissent in a case holding unconstitutional, on "direct burden" grounds, a state law imposing a license fee of $50 on travel agents selling steamship tickets for foreign travel.   The license was granted only on proof of good character and fitness and was revokable for misbehavior.   The majority found the law to be a "direct burden" on commerce and insisted that the "purpose" of a "direct" regulation was irrelevant.   In his dissenting challenge to the "direct"-"indirect" distinction, Justice Stone insisted that that approach was "too mechanical, too uncertain in its application, and too remote from actualities, to be of value."   He added: "[We] are doing little more than using labels to describe a result rather than any trustworthy formula by which it is reached.   [It] seems clear that those interferences [with commerce that are] not deemed forbidden are to be sustained, not because the effect on commerce is nominally indirect, but because a consideration of all the facts and circumstances, such as the nature of the regulation, its function, the character of the

---

4.   Many other "safety" laws were similarly sustained.   A number are reviewed (and distinguished) in Southern Pacific, p. 248 below.

5.   The Court added: "[For all that appears] the crossing [may] have been so located and of such dangerous character as to make the slacken-

ing of trains at that point necessary to the safety of those using the public highway, and a statute making such requirement only a reasonable police regulation, and not an unlawful attempt to regulate or hinder interstate commerce."

business involved and the actual effect on the flow of commerce, lead to the conclusion that the regulation concerns interests peculiarly local and does not infringe the national interest in maintaining the freedom of commerce across state lines." [6]

4. *The licensing cases.* Inquiries into the "purpose" of state regulations and the interests the state sought to further seemed to be irrelevant in the usual formulations of both the Cooley standard and the "direct"-"indirect" distinction. Yet, as Justice Stone argued, judicial perceptions of the law's purpose often seemed in fact determinative. That observation is illustrated by two cases involving state denials of certificates of convenience and necessity to applicants seeking to use the highways as interstate motor carriers. BUCK v. KUYKEN-DALL, 267 U.S. 307 (1925); BRADLEY v. PUBLIC UTILITIES COMM'N, 289 U.S. 92 (1933). The license denial was set aside in Buck and sustained in Bradley; in each case, Justice BRANDEIS wrote for the Court.[7]

Buck, a Washingtonian, wanted to operate an "auto stage line," to carry passengers and freight between Portland and Seattle. He was denied a certificate by Washington on the ground that the territory was "already being adequately served by other carriers." In reversing, Justice Brandeis said: "It may be assumed [that] appropriate state regulations adopted primarily to promote safety upon the highways and conservation in their use are not obnoxious to the Commerce Clause, where the indirect burden imposed upon interstate commerce is not unreasonable. [The] provision here in question is of a different character. Its primary purpose is not regulation with a view to safety or to conservation of the highways, but the prohibition of competition. It determines not the manner of use, but the persons by whom the highways may be used. It prohibits such use to some persons while permitting it to others for the same purpose and in the same manner. Moreover it determines whether the prohibition shall be applied by resort, through state officials, to a test which is peculiarly within the province of federal action—the existence of adequate facilities for conducting interstate commerce." But in the Bradley case, eight years after Buck, the Court sustained Ohio's denial of a certificate to operate between Cleveland, Ohio, and Flint, Michigan. The stated reason for denial was that the highway to be used was "so badly congested by established motor vehicle operations, that the addition of the applicant's proposed service would create and maintain an excessive and undue hazard to the safety and security of the traveling public, and the property upon such highway." Justice Brandeis distinguished Buck by noting that there "safety was doubtless promoted when the certificate was denied," but "promotion of safety was merely an incident of the denial [designed] to prevent competition." Here, by contrast, "the purpose of the denial was to promote safety; and the test employed was congestion of the highway. The effect of the denial upon interstate commerce was merely an incident. [The] Commerce Clause is not violated by denial of the certificate, [if] upon adequate evidence denial is deemed necessary to promote public safety." [8]

---

6. The Di Santo decision was overruled in California v. Thompson, 313 U.S. 109 (1941), but Justice Stone's "actualities"-oriented, balancing approach did not gain full majority support until 1946, in Southern Pacific, below. Nevertheless, "direct"-"indirect" terminology continues to surface in occasional modern cases. See e.g., Justice Stewart's formulation in the Pike case in 1970, in the passage quoted at p. 245 below.

7. Note that Justice Brandeis, who had joined Justice Stone's dissent in Di Santo, nevertheless used "direct"-"indirect" terminology in these cases, as he did throughout his career.

8. Since Buck and Bradley, the licensing of interstate motor carriers has become largely federalized as a result of congressional regulation, especially the Motor Carrier Act of 1935, an amendment to the Interstate Commerce Act.

THE MODERN BALANCING APPROACH

Introduction. In the cases that follow, the modern Court developed a balancing technique for analyzing commerce clause objections to state regulations, weighing the strength of state interests against the burdens on interstate commerce. Most of these cases arose in the context of regulations of transportation facilities; and the most recent cases concern the regulation of interstate truckers. Congressional laws of the 1980s have mooted the precise issues in most of these cases by prescribing federal standards.[1] Continued attention to these cases is nevertheless warranted, not only for transportation issues that are not yet governed by federal law but also, and more importantly, for their bearing on commerce clause adjudication in areas outside transportation.

1. *The impact of modern federal legislation.* The federal laws of the 1980s prescribe uniform weight and width requirements as well as maximum length requirements for the trucks using the Interstate Highway System and other "qualifying" Federal-aid highways. For the first time, trailer lengths are federally regulated. Under the laws, states must modify their laws to comply with the federal standards, and both injunctive relief and withholding of federal funds are available as remedies against non-complying states.[2]

2. *The relevance of balancing outside the transportation area.* The Court's struggles with the evolution and contents of the balancing technique in the transportation cases that follow raise the question of the appropriateness of balancing in the interstate trade cases in sec. 2C below. While many of the sec. 2C cases focus on the identification of state protectionism and discrimination, the balancing approach surfaces in many of them as well. Even in those cases where the Court does not engage in balancing, questions remain whether the Court's narrower preoccupation is too limited and whether additional, balancing inquiries would also be appropriate.

For an important example of the role of balancing even in modern trade rather than transportation cases, note the much cited statement in Justice STEWART's majority opinion in PIKE v. BRUCE CHURCH, INC., 397 U.S. 137 (1970).[3] In "rephrasing" the "general rule" in commerce clause cases, Justice Stewart stated for a unanimous Court: "Where the statute regulates evenhandedly to effectuate a legitimate local public interest, and its effects on interstate commerce are only incidental, it will be upheld unless the burden imposed on such commerce is clearly excessive in relation to the putative local benefits. If a legitimate local purpose is found, then the question becomes one of degree. And the extent of the burden that will be tolerated will of course depend on the nature of the local interest involved, and on whether it could be promoted as well with a lesser impact on interstate activities. Occasionally the Court has candidly undertaken a balancing approach in resolving these issues [Southern Pacific, below], but more frequently it has spoken in terms of 'direct' and 'indirect' effects and burdens."

---

1. See the Surface Transportation Assistance Act of 1982 (Pub.L. 97–424, 96 Stat. 2097) and the Department of Transportation Appropriations Act, 1983 (Pub.L. 97–369, 96 Stat. 1765).

2. In the legislative history accompanying the new federal uniform weight requirements, Congress indicated that the existence of differing weight laws in the states imposed an "undue burden on interstate commerce." In examining the cases that follow, consider whether this congressional determination should be read to suggest that *all* state highway regulations should receive close judicial scrutiny. Or should a different inference for judicial action be drawn from this congressional action: Does this evidence of congressional willingness to deal with the problem of state burdens on interstate commerce in the highway area indicate that Congress is fully able to protect its own prerogatives and the interests of interstate commerce *without* the active assistance of the courts?

3. Pike (more fully considered at p. 297 below) invalidated an Arizona requirement requiring that local cantaloupes be crated within the state, in order to enhance the reputation of Arizona cantaloupes.

SOUTH CAROLINA STATE HIGHWAY DEPARTMENT v. BARN-
WELL BROS., 303 U.S. 177 (1938): The evolution of balancing on the
modern Court got off to an unpromising start in the Barnwell case in 1938.
Justice Stone, who had advocated a variety of balancing as early as his DiSanto
dissent eleven years earlier, instead applied a very deferential standard of review
in sustaining a state highway regulation in Barnwell. But just 8 years later, in
the 1946 decision in Southern Pacific (the next principal case), Stone, now
Chief Justice, wrote one of the major modern balancing opinions in invalidating
a state railroad regulation. The tension between the deferential scrutiny of
1938 and the stricter scrutiny of 1946 preoccupied the Court in a series of post-
Southern Pacific trucking cases—cases which, as the materials that follow will
illustrate, moved ever closer to exercising as rigorous a review in highway cases
as in the Southern Pacific railroad case.

The Barnwell case was a challenge to a 1933 South Carolina law prohibiting
the use on state highways of trucks exceeding a width of 90 inches or a gross
weight of 20,000 pounds. The District Court, while finding that the state
restrictions passed muster under the Fourteenth Amendment as applied to
intrastate trucks, assumed that the commerce clause imposed a "more exacting"
standard before state regulations could be applied to interstate traffic. After
weighing conflicting evidence, the District Court found that interstate trucking
had become a national industry; that from 85 to 90% of interstate motor trucks
were 96 inches wide with a gross weight of more than ten tons; that only four
other states prescribed a gross weight as low as South Carolina's 20,000 pounds;
and that several nationwide bodies had recommended less restrictive weight and
width limitations. After identifying the substantial burdens on commerce, the
District Court held that the law was an unreasonable means of preserving
highways, because wheel or axle weight rather than gross weight were more
relevant factors in preserving concrete highways, and because the width limitation bore no reasonable relation to highway safety, especially in view of the fact
that all other states permitted a width of 96 rather than 90 inches. In reversing
the District Court ruling, Justice STONE stated:

"While the constitutional grant to Congress of power to regulate interstate
commerce has been held to operate of its own force to curtail state power in
some measure,[1] it did not forestall all state action affecting interstate commerce.
Ever since [Black Bird and Cooley], it has been recognized that there are
matters of local concern, the regulation of which unavoidably involves some
regulation of interstate commerce but which, because of their local character
and their number and diversity, may never be fully dealt with by Congress.
Notwithstanding the commerce clause, such regulation in the absence of Congressional action has for the most part been left to the [states]. The commerce
clause, by its own force, prohibits discrimination against interstate commerce,
whatever its form or method, and the decisions of this Court have recognized
that there is scope for its like operation when state legislation nominally of local
concern is in point of fact aimed at interstate commerce, or by its necessary
operation is a means of gaining a local benefit by throwing the attendant
burdens on those without the state. [It] was to end these practices that the

---

1. State regulations affecting interstate commerce, whose purpose or effect is to gain for
those within the state an advantage at the expense of those without, or to burden those out of
the state without any corresponding advantage to
those within, have been thought to impinge upon
the constitutional prohibition even though Congress has not [acted].

Underlying the stated rule has been the
thought, often expressed in judicial opinion, that

when the regulation is of such a character that its
burden falls principally upon those without the
state, legislative action is not likely to be subjected to those political restraints which are normally exerted on legislation where it affects adversely
some interests within the [state]. [Footnote by
Justice Stone. Compare his famous Carolene
Products footnote in the same year, printed and
discussed at 473 below.]

commerce clause was adopted. [The] commerce clause has also been thought to set its own limitation upon state control of interstate rail carriers so as to preclude the subordination of the efficiency and convenience of interstate traffic to local service requirements.

"But the present case affords no occasion for saying that the bare possession of power by Congress to regulate the interstate traffic forces the states to conform to standards which Congress might, but has not adopted, or curtails their power to take measures to insure the safety and conservation of their highways which may be applied to like traffic moving intrastate. Few subjects of state regulation are so peculiarly of local concern as is the use of state highways. There are few, local regulation of which is so inseparable from a substantial effect on interstate commerce. Unlike the railroads, local highways are built, owned and maintained by the state or its municipal subdivisions. The state has a primary and immediate concern in their safe and economical administration. The present regulations, or any others of like purpose, if they are to accomplish their end, must be applied alike to interstate and intrastate traffic, both moving in large volume over the highways. The fact that they affect alike shippers in interstate and intrastate commerce in large number within as well as without the state is a safeguard against their abuse. [With] respect to the extent and nature of the local interests to be protected and the unavoidable effect upon interstate and intrastate commerce alike, regulations of the use of the highways are akin to local regulation of rivers, harbors, piers and docks, quarantine regulations, and game laws, which, Congress not acting, have been sustained even though they materially interfere with interstate commerce. [This] Court has often sustained the exercise of [state power over state highways] although it has burdened or impeded interstate commerce. [So] long as the state action does not discriminate, the burden is one which the Constitution permits because it is an inseparable incident of the exercise of a legislative authority, which, under the Constitution, has been left to the states.

"Congress, in the exercise of its plenary power to regulate interstate commerce, may determine whether the burdens imposed on it by state regulation, otherwise permissible, are too great, and may, by legislation designed to secure uniformity or in other respects to protect the national interest in the commerce, curtail to some extent the state's regulatory power. But that is a legislative, not a judicial function. [In] the absence of such legislation the judicial function, under the commerce clause as well as the Fourteenth Amendment, stops with the inquiry whether the state Legislature in adopting regulations such as the present has acted within its province, and whether the means of regulation chosen are reasonably adapted to the end sought.

"Here the first inquiry has already been resolved by our decisions that a state may impose non-discriminatory restrictions with respect to the character of motor vehicles moving in interstate commerce as a safety measure and as a means of securing the economical use of its highways. In resolving the second, courts do not sit as Legislatures, either state or national. [When] the action of a Legislature is within the scope of its power, fairly debatable questions as to its reasonableness, wisdom and propriety are not for the determination of courts, but for the legislative body. [It] is not any the less a legislative power committed to the states because it affects interstate commerce, and courts are not any the more entitled, because interstate commerce is affected, to substitute their own for the legislative judgment. [Since] the adoption of one weight or width regulation, rather than another, is a legislative not a judicial choice, its constitutionality is not to be determined by weighing in the judicial scales the merits of the legislative choice and rejecting it if the weight of evidence presented in court appears to favor a different standard. Being a legislative judgment it is presumed to be supported by facts known to the legislature unless facts judicially known or proved preclude that possibility. Hence, in reviewing the present determination we examine the record, not to see whether the findings of the court below are supported by evidence, but to ascertain upon the whole record whether it is possible to say that the legislative choice is without rational basis. [Not] only does the record fail to exclude that possibility, but it shows affirmatively that there is adequate support for the legislative judgment." [2]

SOUTHERN PACIFIC CO. v. ARIZONA

325 U.S. 761, 65 S.Ct. 1515, 89 L.Ed. 1915 (1945).

[The Arizona Train Limit Law of 1912 prohibited operating railroad trains of more than 14 passenger or 70 freight cars. In 1940, the State sued the Company to recover the statutory penalties for violating the law. After an extended trial, the trial court found the law to be an unconstitutional burden on commerce. The Arizona Supreme Court reversed, concluding that a state law enacted in the exercise of the police power, with some reasonable relation to health and safety, could not be overturned despite its adverse affect on interstate commerce. The U.S. Supreme Court reversed. After rejecting a contention that Congress, by authorizing the ICC to regulate train lengths, had superseded state power, the Court turned to the commerce clause challenge.]

Mr. Chief Justice STONE delivered the opinion of the Court.

[Although] the commerce clause conferred on the national government power to regulate commerce, its possession of the power does not exclude all state power of regulation. [But] ever since [Gibbons v. Ogden], the states have not been deemed to have authority to impede substantially the free flow of commerce from state to state, or to regulate those phases of the national commerce which, because of the need of national uniformity, demand that their regulation, if any, be prescribed by a single authority.[1] [Cooley.] Whether or not this long-recognized distribution of power between the national and the state governments is predicated upon the implications of the commerce clause itself, [or] upon the presumed intention of Congress, where Congress has not spoken, Dowling, Interstate Commerce and State Power, 27 Va.Law Rev. 1, the result is the same. In the application of these principles some enactments may be found to be plainly within and others plainly without state power. But between these extremes lies the infinite variety of cases, in which regulation of local matters may also operate as a regulation of commerce, in which reconciliation of the conflicting claims of state and national power is to be attained only by some appraisal and accommodation of the competing demands of the state and national interests involved. [For] a hundred years it has been accepted constitutional doctrine that the commerce clause, without the aid of Congressional legislation, [affords] some protection from state legislation inimical to the national commerce, and that in such cases, where Congress has not acted, this Court, and not the state legislature, is under the commerce clause the final arbiter of the competing demands of state and national interests. [Cooley.]

Congress has undoubted power to redefine the distribution of power over interstate commerce. It may either permit the states to regulate the commerce in a manner which would otherwise not be permissible, [or] exclude state regulation even of matters of peculiarly local concern which nevertheless affect

---

2. Justices CARDOZO and REED did not participate in this decision.

1. In applying this rule the Court has often recognized that to the extent that the burden of state regulation falls on interests outside the state, it is unlikely to be alleviated by the operation of those political restraints normally exerted when interests within the state are [affected]. [Footnote by Chief Justice Stone.]

interstate commerce.[2] But in general Congress has left it to the courts to formulate the rules thus interpreting the commerce clause in its application, doubtless because it has appreciated the destructive consequences to the commerce of the nation if their protection were withdrawn, and has been aware that in their application state laws will not be invalidated without the support of relevant factual material which will "afford a sure basis" for an informed judgment. Meanwhile, Congress has accommodated its legislation, as have the states, to these rules as an established feature of our constitutional [system].

Hence the matters for ultimate determination here are the nature and extent of the burden which the state regulation of interstate trains, adopted as a safety measure, imposes on interstate commerce, and whether the relative weights of the state and national interests involved are such as to make inapplicable the rule, generally observed, that the free flow of interstate commerce and its freedom from local restraints in matters requiring uniformity of regulation are interests safeguarded by the commerce clause from state interference. [The] findings show that the operation of long trains [is] standard practice over the main lines of the railroads of the United States, and that, if the length of trains is to be regulated at all, national uniformity in the regulation adopted, such as only Congress can prescribe, is practically indispensable to the operation of an efficient and economical national railway [system].

[The] unchallenged findings leave no doubt that the Arizona Train Limit Law imposes a serious burden on the interstate commerce conducted by [appellant]. Enforcement of the law in Arizona, while train lengths remain unregulated or are regulated by varying standards in other states, must inevitably result in an impairment of uniformity of efficient railroad operation because the railroads are subjected to regulation which is not uniform in its application. Compliance with a state statute limiting train lengths requires interstate trains of a length lawful in other states to be broken up and reconstituted as they enter each state according as it may impose varying limitations upon train lengths. The alternative is for the carrier to conform to the lowest train limit restriction of any of the states through which its trains pass, whose laws thus control the carriers' operations both within and without the regulating state.[3] [If] one state may regulate train lengths, so may all the others, and they need not prescribe the same maximum limitation. The practical effect of such regulation is to control train operations beyond the boundaries of the state exacting it because of the necessity of breaking up and reassembling long trains at the nearest terminal points before entering and after leaving the regulating state. The serious impediment to the free flow of commerce by the local regulation of train lengths and the practical necessity that such regulation, if any, must be prescribed by a single body having a nation-wide authority are apparent.

The trial court found that the Arizona law had no reasonable relation to safety, and made train operation more dangerous. [This] conclusion was rested on facts found which indicate that such increased danger of accident and personal injury as may result from the greater length of trains is more than offset by the increase in the number of accidents resulting from the larger number of trains when train lengths are reduced. In considering the effect of

2. On the congressional authority to "redefine the distribution of power over interstate commerce," see sec. 2B of this chapter.

3. Chief Justice Stone noted that nearly 95% of rail traffic in Arizona was interstate. The state law required appellant to haul over 30% more trains in Arizona. The financial impact of the added cost of train operations was about $1,000,000 a year. Moreover, reduction in train lengths caused delays because of the need to break up and remake long trains. He noted, too, that Arizona was the only state with a 14 passenger car limit, and one of only two states with a 70 freight car limit. He commented, moreover, that it was frequently not feasible to reassemble trains near the Arizona border, "with the result that the Arizona limitation governs the flow of traffic as far east as El Paso, Texas," and as far west as Los Angeles.

the statute as a safety measure, therefore, the factor of controlling significance for present purposes is not whether there is basis for the conclusion of the Arizona Supreme Court that the increase in length of trains beyond the statutory maximum has an adverse effect upon safety of operation. The decisive question is whether in the circumstances the total effect of the law as a safety measure in reducing accidents and casualties is so slight or problematical as not to outweigh the national interest in keeping interstate commerce free from interferences which seriously impede it and subject it to local regulation which does not have a uniform effect on the interstate train journey which it interrupts.[4]

[We] think, as the trial court found, that the Arizona Train Limit Law, viewed as a safety measure, affords at most slight and dubious advantage, if any, over unregulated train lengths, because it results in an increase in the number of trains and train operations and the consequent increase in train accidents of a character generally more severe than those due to slack action. Its undoubted effect on the commerce is the regulation, without securing uniformity, of the length of trains operated in interstate commerce, which lack is itself a primary cause of preventing the free flow of commerce by delaying it and by substantially increasing its cost and impairing its efficiency. In these respects the case differs from those where a state, by regulatory measures affecting the commerce, has removed or reduced safety hazards without substantial interference with the interstate movement of trains. Such are measures abolishing the car stove; requiring locomotives to be supplied with electric headlights; providing for full train crews; and for the equipment of freight trains with cabooses. The principle that, without controlling Congressional action, a state may not regulate interstate commerce so as substantially to affect its flow or deprive it of needed uniformity in its regulation is not to be avoided by "simply invoking the convenient apologetics of the police power." [Here] we conclude that the state does go too far. Its regulation of train lengths, admittedly obstructive to interstate train operation, and having a seriously adverse effect on transportation efficiency and economy, passes beyond what is plainly essential for safety since it does not appear that it will lessen rather than increase the danger of accident. Its attempted regulation of the operation of interstate trains cannot establish nation-wide control such as is essential to the maintenance of an efficient transportation system, which Congress alone can prescribe.

[Appellees] especially rely on the full train crew cases, [e.g., Missouri Pacific Railway Co. v. Norwood, 283 U.S. 249], and also on [Barnwell], as supporting the state's authority to regulate the length of interstate trains. While the full train crew laws undoubtedly placed an added financial burden on the railroads in order to serve a local interest, they did not obstruct interstate transportation or seriously impede it. They had no effects outside the state beyond those of picking up and setting down the extra employees at the state boundaries; they involved no wasted use of facilities or serious impairment of transportation efficiency, which are among the factors of controlling weight here. [Barnwell involved state regulation of] highways, a legislative field over which the state has a far more extensive control than over interstate railroads. [There], we were at pains to point out that there are few subjects of state regulation affecting interstate commerce which are so peculiarly of local concern as is the use of the

---

4. In engaging in this inquiry, Chief Justice Stone stated: "The principal source of danger of accident from increased length of trains is the resulting increase of 'slack action' of the train. Slack action is the amount of free movement of one car before it transmits its motion to an adjoining coupled car. [On] comparison of the number of slack action accidents in Arizona with those in Nevada, where the length of trains is now unregulated, the trial court found that with substantially the same amount of traffic in each state the number of accidents was relatively the same in long as in short train operations. [Reduction] of the length of trains also tends to increase the number of accidents because of the increase in the number of trains. [The] record lends support to the trial court's conclusion that the train length limitation increased rather than diminished the number of accidents."

state's highways.   Unlike the railroads, local highways are built, owned and maintained by the [state].   [The] fact that [state safety regulations] affect alike shippers in interstate and intrastate commerce in great numbers, within as well as without the state, is a safeguard against regulatory abuses.   The contrast between the present regulation and the full train crew laws in point of their effects on the commerce, and the like contrast with the highway safety regulations, in point of the nature of the subject of regulation and the state's interest in it, illustrate and emphasize the considerations which enter into a determination of the relative weights of state and national interests where state regulation affecting interstate commerce is attempted.   Here examination of all the relevant factors makes it plain that the state interest is outweighed by the interest of the nation in an adequate economical and efficient railway transportation service, which must prevail.

Reversed.[5]

Mr. Justice BLACK, dissenting.

[In] the state court a rather extraordinary "trial" took place.   [Before] the state trial court finally determined that the dangers found by the legislature in 1912 no longer existed, it heard evidence over a period of 5½ months which appears in about 3,000 pages of the printed record before us.   It then adopted findings of fact submitted to it by the railroad, which cover 148 printed pages, and conclusions of law which cover 5 pages.   [This] new pattern of trial procedure makes it necessary for a judge to hear all the evidence offered as to why a legislature passed a law and to make findings of fact as to the validity of those reasons.   If under today's ruling a court does make findings as to a danger contrary to the findings of the legislature, and the evidence heard "lends support" to those findings, a court can then invalidate the law.   In this respect, the Arizona County Court acted, and this Court today is acting, as a "super-legislature."   Even if this method of invalidating legislative acts is a correct one, I still think that the "findings" of the state court do not authorize today's decision.   [When] we finally get down to the gist of what the Court today actually decides, it is this: [that] running shorter trains would increase the cost of railroad operations.   [This] record in its entirety leaves me with no doubt whatever that many employees have been seriously injured and killed in the past, and that many more are likely to be so in the future, because of "slack movement" in trains.   [It] may be that offsetting dangers are possible in the operation of short trains.   The balancing of these probabilities, however, is not in my judgment a matter for judicial determination, but one which calls for legislative [consideration].

Mr. Justice DOUGLAS, dissenting.

I have expressed my doubts whether the courts should intervene in situations like the present and strike down state legislation on the grounds that it burdens interstate commerce.   McCarroll v. Dixie Greyhound Lines, 309 U.S. 176 [1940].   My view has been that the courts should intervene only where the state legislation discriminated against interstate commerce or was out of harmony with laws which Congress had enacted.   It seems to me particularly appropriate that that course be followed here.   For Congress has given the [ICC] broad powers of regulation over interstate carriers.   [W]e are dealing here with state legislation in the field of safety where the propriety of local regulation has long been recognized.   Whether the question arises under the Commerce Clause or the Fourteenth Amendment, [the] legislation is entitled to a presumption of [validity].

---

5. Justice RUTLEDGE concurred only in the result.

SOUTHERN PACIFIC AND ITS AFTERMATH

1. *The contrast between Southern Pacific and Barnwell.* Clearly, Southern Pacific reflected greater judicial scrutiny than Barnwell had.[1] Were Chief Justice Stone's reasons for distinguishing Barnwell in Southern Pacific persuasive: the "peculiarly local" nature of highways; the local ownership of highways? Apparently, that distinction has become less persuasive in the years since 1945. In the post-Southern Pacific trucking cases that follow, the extent of judicial scrutiny has moved steadily closer to Southern Pacific and away from Barnwell. What explains the changes in scrutiny? Arguably, the Court has been influenced by the changes in the relative degree of state and federal financing of highways after 1938. Similarly, the growth in importance of the trucking industry since 1938, and the changes in the relative economic conditions of the trucking and railroad industries in more recent decades, may have had an impact. What is clear from the cases from Bibb (1959) to Kassel (1981), below, is that the Court has displayed a steadily growing interest in safeguarding interstate trucking from excessive state burdens.

2. *The changing criteria of judicial scrutiny.* Consider the ingredients of Stone's Southern Pacific approach, so strikingly different from that in Barnwell. Early in his opinion, Stone used language akin to that in Cooley. But he then went on to engage in a lengthy balancing process. Thus, Southern Pacific is another example of actual judicial scrutiny involving a good deal more than that suggested by the Cooley formulation.

The evolution of Chief Justice Stone's position between Barnwell and Southern Pacific may have been influenced by an article by Professor Noel T. Dowling, an article (cited by Stone) that appeared between the two decisions, "Interstate Commerce and State Power," 27 Va.L.Rev. 1 (1940).[2] Dowling (who was to become the Harlan Fiske Stone Professor of Law at Columbia) articulated an approach in 1940 that was very close to Stone's Southern Pacific balancing analysis in 1945. Dowling criticized the "direct"-"indirect" test as "far from satisfying"—as indeed Stone had done as early as his DiSanto dissent in 1927. But Dowling drew another doctrine from the cases: that, in the absence of congressional consent, "a Congressional negative will be presumed" where state regulation produces an "unreasonable interference" with commerce. Adoption of that "unreasonable interference" standard, he explained, would "involve an avowal that the Court is deliberately balancing national and local interests and making a choice as to which of the two *should* prevail." That, he conceded, would involve "a policy judgment." He emphasized, moreover, that "the test of reasonableness in interstate commerce cases" was "not the same" as in due process cases: "In a sense, a state law must take the hurdle of due process before it comes to the interstate barrier."

The evolution from Barnwell to Southern Pacific does indeed reflect such an intensification of judicial scrutiny, from the "mere reasonableness" of a due process, police power standard, to the balancing approach of determining "unreasonable" burdens under the commerce clause. And, as the trucking

---

1. Note the dates of the decisions. Barnwell came in 1938, shortly after the Court-packing controversy, shortly after the Court's retreat from judicial intervention in a number of areas. By the time of Southern Pacific in 1945, the Court's "hands off" attitude in national power and due process cases had gained strength. Yet there were already omens of a greater—though selective—judicial readiness to intervene. Note also Justice Stone's "double standards" footnote in the Carolene Products case (p. 473 below)—a footnote in 1938 (the year of Barnwell) sug-

gesting a political process rationale for identifying those areas warranting special judicial scrutiny. In short, Southern Pacific indicates that state regulation of commerce had become an "interventionist" rather than a "hands-off" area for Stone by 1945. Why not in 1938, at the time of Barnwell?

2. See also a Dowling article after Southern Pacific, "Interstate Commerce and State Power— Revised Version," 47 Colum.L.Rev. 547 (1947).

cases that follow indicate, the more intensive commerce clause scrutiny applied in the railroad context in Southern Pacific has to a growing extent been carried over to highway regulations. Is the greater judicial scrutiny of the balancing variety justified in commerce clause cases? [3]

3. *State full crew laws after Southern Pacific.* In invalidating the train length law in Southern Pacific, Chief Justice Stone explicitly distinguished cases such as Norwood (1931), which had sustained state full train crew laws. Yet there was considerable doubt whether full crew laws could survive the stricter judicial scrutiny authorized by Southern Pacific. Nevertheless, a renewed challenge to the Arkansas full train crew laws proved unsuccessful. In BROTHERHOOD OF LOCOMOTIVE FIREMEN & ENGINEMEN v. CHICAGO R. I. & P. R. CO., 393 U.S. 129 (1968), the lower court, relying in part on the Southern Pacific approach, had held full crew laws unconstitutional, finding that they had "no substantial effect on safety" and placed "substantial financial burdens" on the carriers. The Court reversed. Justice BLACK's majority opinion concluded that the lower court had "indulged in a legislative judgment wholly beyond its limited authority" under the commerce clause. Disputes about the laws, he commented, "will continue to be worked out in the legislatures and in various forms of collective bargaining."

BIBB v. NAVAJO FREIGHT LINES, INC., 359 U.S. 520 (1959): The Bibb case was the Court's first indication that, even in trucking cases, the Justices might be willing to exercise greater scrutiny than that in Barnwell and that some version of the intensified review of Southern Pacific might be appropriate even in highway cases. Notably, Justice Douglas wrote for the majority in Bibb, even though he had been one of those who had earlier opposed any significant judicial role in commerce clause cases going beyond the safeguarding against discrimination. Bibb held invalid an Illinois law requiring the use of contour mudguards on trucks and trailers operating on Illinois highways. That requirement conflicted with an Arkansas rule requiring straight mudguards and forbidding contoured ones. Moreover, at least 45 states authorized the use of straight mudguards.

Justice DOUGLAS' opinion began by echoing the tenor of (and citing) Barnwell: "The power of the State to regulate the use of its highways is broad and pervasive. [Safety] measures carry a strong presumption of validity. [If] there are alternative ways of solving a problem, we do not sit to determine which of them is best suited to achieve a valid state objective. Policy decisions are for the state legislature, absent federal entry into the field." But he quickly moved on to indicate that Barnwell did not wholly reflect the present commerce clause limit on state safety regulations of highways: "Unless we can conclude on the whole record that 'the total effect of the law as a safety measure in reducing accidents and casualties is so slight or problematical as not to outweigh the national interest in keeping interstate commerce free from interferences which seriously impede it' [Southern Pacific], we must uphold the statute." Justice Douglas proceeded to examine the evidence regarding the "substantial" cost of equipping interstate trucks with contour mudguards and the relative safety

---

3. Contrast Chief Justice Stone's endorsement of balancing in Southern Pacific with his objections to quasi-legislative judgments in Barnwell—and with Justice Black's objections to elaborate trials on the benefits and burdens of state laws in his Southern Pacific dissent. This contrast once again raises the issue of the appropriate judicial role and competence in commerce clause cases. Are courts institutionally equipped to undertake balancing inquiries? Are such inquiries worthwhile investments of the courts' energies? Is balancing the appropriate approach not only in transportation cases but also in *all* situations involving allegations of excessive burdens on interstate commerce? (The problems of judicial "balancing" are not limited to the commerce clause areas considered in this chapter. Compare the role of—and controversy about—judicial balancing in the individual rights chapters in Part III of this book.)

advantages of contour mudguards over the conventional or straight mudguards. He concluded that examination by stating: "If we had here only a question whether the cost of adjusting an interstate operation to these new local safety [regulations] unduly burdened interstate commerce, we would have to sustain the law. [The] same result would obtain if we had to resolve the much discussed issues of safety presented in this case." But he proceeded to assert: "This case presents a different issue. [Here, unlike earlier cases, the equipment prescribed by Illinois] would conflict with the standards of another State, making it necessary, say, for an interstate carrier to shift its cargo to differently designed vehicles once another state line was reached. We had a related problem in [Southern Pacific]." Given the conflicting Arkansas requirement, "if a trailer is to be operated in both [Illinois and Arkansas], mudguards would have to be interchanged, causing a significant delay in an operation where prompt movement may be of the essence." Moreover, the Illinois law seriously interfered with the "interline" operations of motor carriers—"the interchanging of trailers between an originating carrier and another carrier when the latter serves an area not served by the former." Justice Douglas noted: "These 'interline' operations provide a speedy through-service for the shipper." Since the challenging truckers' mileage in Illinois was only a small part of their national movements, he was persuaded that there was a "rather massive showing of burden on interstate commerce."

The State countered with a claim that contour mudguards were a reasonable exercise of the police power (because they prevented the throwing of debris into the windshields of passing cars and trailing vehicles) and argued that a federal court was "precluded from weighing the relative merits of the contour mudguard against any other kind of mudguard and must sustain the validity of the statute notwithstanding the extent of the burden it imposes on commerce." Understandably, the State placed its major reliance on Barnwell. Justice Douglas conceded that there was "language in [Barnwell] which read in isolation from such later decisions as [Southern Pacific], would suggest that no showing of burden on interstate commerce is sufficient to invalidate local safety regulations in the absence of some element of discrimination against interstate commerce." But he proceeded:

"The various exercises by the States of their police power stand [on] an equal footing. All are entitled to the same presumption of validity when challenged under the Due Process Clause of the Fourteenth Amendment. [Similarly] the various state regulatory statutes are of equal dignity when measured against the Commerce Clause. Local regulations which would pass muster under the Due Process Clause might nonetheless fail to survive other challenges to constitutionality that bring the Supremacy Clause into play. Like any local law that conflicts with federal regulatory measures, [state] regulations that run afoul of the policy of free trade reflected in the Commerce Clause must also bow. This is one of those cases—few in number—where local safety measures that are nondiscriminatory place an unconstitutional burden on interstate commerce. [A] State which insists on a design out of line with the requirements of almost all the other States may sometimes place a great burden of delay and inconvenience [on] interstate motor carriers. [Such] a new safety device [may] be so compelling that the innovating State need not be the one to give way. But the present showing—balanced against the clear burden on commerce—is far too inconclusive to make this mudguard meet that test. [The] heavy burden which the Illinois mudguard law places on the interstate movement of trucks and trailers seems to us to pass the permissible limits even for safety regulations." [1]

1. Justice HARLAN, joined by Justice Stewart, concurred in the judgment, stating: "The opinion of the Court clearly demonstrates the heavy burden, in terms of cost and interference

RAYMOND MOTOR TRANSPORTATION, INC. v. RICE, 434 U.S. 429 (1978): Nearly 20 years after Bibb, the Raymond decision expanded Bibb's slight inroad into Barnwell-type judicial deference to state highway regulations. Raymond invalidated Wisconsin regulations which generally barred from its highways trucks longer than 55 feet. Double-trailer units, which have come into increasing use in recent years, are normally 65 feet long. The impact of the Wisconsin requirement was closer to Arizona's in Southern Pacific than to Illinois' in Bibb: trucks complying with Wisconsin's shorter length requirement would not have been barred from the highways of any other state. Nevertheless, the Raymond Court invalidated the Wisconsin regulations, finding that Wisconsin had offered virtually no evidence to support its safety measure. Moreover, the Court noted an additional factor undermining the strength of the safety justification: exemptions in the Wisconsin regulations seemed to be protectionist in nature, benefiting primarily Wisconsin industries. (This concern with possible protectionism is characteristic of a large number of modern cases, as the materials in sec. 1C repeatedly illustrate.) Three years after Raymond, in Kassel, the next principal case, a more sharply divided Court invalidated an Iowa truck length requirement similar to Wisconsin's in Raymond. The Raymond case is discussed in Kassel, and the two major themes of Raymond—balancing and safeguarding against protectionism—are further elaborated there. (Note that the Kassel invalidation occurred even though Iowa in that case, unlike Wisconsin in Raymond, *had* submitted significant evidence in defense of its safety regulation.) [1]

KASSEL v. CONSOLIDATED FREIGHTWAYS CORP.

450 U.S. 662, 101 S.Ct. 1309, 67 L.Ed.2d 580 (1981).

Justice POWELL announced the judgment of the Court and delivered an opinion in which Justice WHITE, Justice BLACKMUN, and Justice STEVENS joined.

with 'interlining,' which the [Illinois law] imposes on interstate commerce. In view of the [lower court findings] that the contour mudflap 'possesses no advantages' in terms of safety over the conventional flap permitted in all other States, and indeed creates certain safety hazards, this heavy burden cannot be justified on the theory that the Illinois statute is a necessary, appropriate, or helpful local safety measure."

After Bibb, could the Cooley principle have been invoked to argue that *all* state mudguard regulations were unconstitutional—i.e., that if Illinois' mudguard requirement was invalid, that must be because mudguards are a subject requiring "uniform" rather than "diverse" regulation under Cooley? If that argument were accepted, Arkansas' straight mudguard requirement would have fallen as a result of Bibb. But, given the Court's reasoning in Bibb as amplified in later cases, it is probably more plausible to argue that Arkansas' requirement would have fallen only if it had been shown to be both burdensome on commerce and no more effective than that of Illinois. In short, the modern Court is not likely to invalidate a state law merely because it creates a *risk* of multiple inconsistent burdens, because other states *might* enact conflicting laws in the same area. Rather, as in Bibb, the Court is

likely to insist on a showing that *actual* inconsistent burdens exist. Contrast the earlier attitude, in Southern Pacific: "If one state may regulate train lengths, so may all the others."

1. The prevailing opinion in Raymond was written by Justice POWELL, who noted that Wisconsin had "virtually defaulted in its defense of the regulations as a safety measure." Moreover, exemptions in the regulations favoring Wisconsin industries "weaken the presumption in favor of the validity of the general limit, because they undermine the assumption that the State's own political processes will act as a check on local regulations that unduly burden interstate commerce." He concluded that the regulations were invalid "because they place a substantial burden on interstate commerce [and] cannot be said to make more than the most speculative contribution to highway safety. [Wisconsin] has failed to make even a colorable showing that its regulations contribute to highway safety." Justice BLACKMUN's concurrence, joined by Chief Justice Burger and Justices Brennan and Rehnquist, joined Justice Powell's opinion but emphasized the "narrow scope" of the decision and the "illusory nature of the safety interests in this case." (Justice STEVENS did not participate in the case.)

The question is whether an Iowa statute that prohibits the use of certain large trucks within the State unconstitutionally burdens interstate commerce.

I. * [Consolidated Freightways] is one of the largest common carriers in the country. [Among] other routes, Consolidated carries commodities through Iowa on Interstate 80, the principal east-west route linking New York, Chicago, and the West Coast, and on Interstate 35, a major north-south route. Consolidated mainly uses two kinds of trucks. One consists of a three-axle tractor pulling a 40-foot two-axle trailer. This unit, commonly called a single, or "semi," is 55 feet in length overall. Such trucks have long been used on the Nation's highways. Consolidated also uses a two-axle tractor pulling a single-axle trailer which, in turn, pulls a single-axle dolly and a second single-axle trailer. This combination, known as a double, or twin, is 65 feet long overall. Many trucking companies, including Consolidated, increasingly prefer to use doubles to ship certain kinds of commodities. Doubles have larger capacities, and the trailers can be detached and routed separately if necessary. Consolidated would like to use 65-foot doubles on many of its trips through Iowa.

[Iowa], however, by statute restricts the length of vehicles that may use its highways. Unlike all other States in the West and Midwest, Iowa generally prohibits the use of 65-foot doubles within its borders. Instead, most truck combinations are restricted to 55 feet in length. Doubles, mobile homes, trucks carrying vehicles such as tractors and other farm equipment, and singles hauling livestock, are permitted to be as long as 60 feet. Notwithstanding these restrictions, Iowa's statute permits cities abutting the state line by local ordinance to adopt the length limitations of the adjoining State.[1]

Because of Iowa's statutory scheme, Consolidated cannot use its 65-foot doubles to move commodities through the State. Instead, the company must do one of four things: (i) use 55-foot singles, (ii) use 60-foot doubles; (iii) detach the trailers of a 65-foot double and shuttle each through the State separately; or (iv) divert 65-foot doubles around Iowa. Dissatisfied with these options, Consolidated filed this suit in the District Court averring that Iowa's statutory scheme unconstitutionally burdens interstate commerce. Iowa defended the law as a reasonable safety measure enacted pursuant to its police power. The State asserted that 65-foot doubles are more dangerous than 55-foot singles and, in any event, that the law promotes safety and reduces road wear within the State by diverting much truck traffic to other States. In a 14-day trial, both sides adduced evidence on safety, and on the burden on interstate commerce imposed by Iowa's law. On the question of safety, the District Court found that the "evidence clearly establishes that the twin is as safe as the semi." [It] applied the standard we enunciated in [Raymond] and concluded that the state law impermissibly burdened interstate commerce: "[The] *total effect* of the law as a safety measure in reducing accidents and casualties is so slight and problematical that it does not outweigh the national interest in keeping interstate commerce free from interferences that seriously impede it." [The] Court of Appeals agreed. [We] affirm.

II. [A] state's power to regulate commerce is never greater than in matters traditionally of local concern. For example, regulations that touch upon safety—especially highway safety—are those that "the Court has been most reluctant

---

1. Justice Powell also noted two other relevant Iowa exemptions. First, an Iowa truck manufacturer could obtain a permit to ship trucks as long as 70 feet. Second, permits were available to move oversized mobile homes if the unit was to be moved from a point within Iowa or delivered to an Iowa resident. In commenting on the second exemption, Justice Powell stated: "The parochial restrictions in the mobile home provision were enacted after Governor Ray vetoed a bill that would have permitted the interstate shipment of all mobile homes through Iowa. Governor Ray commented, in his [1972] veto message: 'This bill [would] make Iowa a bridge state as these oversized units are moved into Iowa after being manufactured in another state and sold in a third. None of the activity would be of particular economic benefit to Iowa.'"

to invalidate.'' Raymond. Indeed, ''if safety justifications are not illusory, the court will not second guess legislative judgment about their importance in comparison with related burdens on interstate commerce.'' Raymond (Blackmun, J., concurring). Those who would challenge such bona fide safety regulations must overcome a ''strong presumption of validity.'' [Bibb.] But the incantation of a purpose to promote the public health or safety does not insulate a state law from Commerce Clause attack. Regulations designed for that salutary purpose nevertheless may further the purpose so marginally, and interfere with commerce so substantially, as to be invalid under the Commerce Clause. In [Raymond], we declined to ''accept the State's contention that the inquiry under the Commerce Clause is ended without a weighing of the asserted safety purpose against the degree of interference with interstate commerce.'' This ''weighing'' by a court requires—and indeed the constitutionality of the state regulation depends on—''a sensitive consideration of the weight and nature of the state regulatory concern in light of the extent of the burden imposed on the course of interstate commerce.'' Id.; accord, [Pike; Bibb; Southern Pacific].

III.   Applying these general principles, we conclude that the Iowa truck-length limitations unconstitutionally burden interstate commerce. [This] case is Raymond revisited.   Here, as in Raymond, the State failed to present any persuasive evidence that 65-foot doubles are less safe than 55-foot singles. Moreover, Iowa's law is now out of step with the laws of all other midwestern and western States.   Iowa thus substantially burdens the interstate flow of goods by truck.   In the absence of congressional action to set uniform standards, some burdens associated with state safety regulations must be tolerated.   But where, as here, the State's safety interest has been found to be illusory, and its regulations impair significantly the federal interest in efficient and safe interstate transportation, the state law cannot be harmonized with the Commerce Clause.

A.   Iowa made a more serious effort to support the safety rationale of its law than did Wisconsin in Raymond, but its effort was no more persuasive.   As noted above, the District Court found that the ''evidence clearly establishes that the twin is as safe as the semi.''   The record supports this finding.   The trial focused on a comparison of the performance of the two kinds of trucks in various safety categories.   [The] District Court found [that] the 65-foot double was at least the equal of the 55-foot single in the ability to brake, turn, and maneuver.   The double, because of its axle placement, produces less splash and spray in wet weather.   And, because of its articulation in the middle, the double is less susceptible to dangerous ''off-tracking,''[2] and to wind.

None of these findings is seriously disputed by Iowa.   Indeed, the State points to only three ways in which the 55-foot single is even arguably superior: singles take less time to be passed and to clear intersections; they may back up for longer distances; and they are somewhat less likely to jackknife.   The first two of these characteristics are of limited relevance on modern interstate highways.   As the District Court found, the negligible difference in the time required to pass, and to cross intersections, is insignificant on 4-lane divided highways because passing does not require crossing into oncoming traffic lanes [Raymond] and interstates have few, if any, intersections.   The concern over backing capability also is insignificant because it seldom is necessary to back up on an interstate.   In any event, no evidence suggested any difference in backing capability between the 60-foot doubles that Iowa permits and the 65-foot doubles that it bans.   Similarly, although doubles tend to jackknife somewhat more than singles, 65-foot doubles actually are less likely to jackknife than 60-foot doubles.   Statistical studies supported the view that 65-foot doubles are at

---

2. ''Off-tracking'' refers to the extent to which the rear wheels of a truck deviate from the path of the front wheels while turning. [Footnote by Justice Powell.]

least as safe overall as 55-foot singles and 60-foot doubles. [In sum], although Iowa introduced more evidence on the question of safety than did Wisconsin in Raymond, the record as a whole was not more favorable to the State.[3]

B. Consolidated, meanwhile, demonstrated that Iowa's law substantially burdens interstate commerce. Trucking companies that wish to continue to use 65-foot doubles must route them around Iowa or detach the trailers of the doubles and ship them through separately. Alternatively, trucking companies must use the smaller 55-foot singles or 60-foot doubles permitted under Iowa law. Each of these options engenders inefficiency and added expense. The record shows that Iowa's law added about $12.6 million each year to the costs of trucking companies. Consolidated alone incurred about $2 million per year in increased costs. In addition to increasing the costs of the trucking companies (and, indirectly, of the service to consumers), Iowa's law may aggravate, rather than ameliorate, the problem of highway accidents. Fifty-five foot singles carry less freight than 65-foot doubles. Either more small trucks must be used to carry the same quantity of goods through Iowa, or the same number of larger trucks must drive longer distances to bypass Iowa. In either case, [the] restriction requires more highway miles to be driven to transport the same quantity of goods. Other things being equal, accidents are proportional to distance traveled. Thus, if 65-foot doubles are as safe as 55-foot singles, Iowa's law tends to *increase* the number of accidents, and to shift the incidence of them from Iowa to other States.

IV. Perhaps recognizing the weakness of the evidence supporting its safety argument, and the substantial burden on commerce that its regulations create, Iowa urges the Court simply to "defer" to the safety judgment of the State. It argues that the length of trucks is generally, although perhaps imprecisely, related to safety. The task of drawing a line is one that Iowa contends should be left to its legislature. The Court normally does accord "special deference" to state highway safety regulations. [Raymond.] [Less] deference to the legislative judgment is due, however, where the local regulation bears disproportionately on out-of-state residents and businesses. Such a disproportionate burden is apparent here. Iowa's scheme, although generally banning large doubles from the State, nevertheless has several exemptions that secure to Iowans many of the benefits of large trucks while shunting to neighboring States many of the costs associated with their use.

At the time of trial there were two particularly significant exemptions. First, singles hauling livestock or farm vehicles were permitted to be as long as 60 feet. [T]his provision undoubtedly was helpful to local interests. Cf. Raymond (exemption in Wisconsin for milk shippers). Second, cities abutting other States were permitted to enact local ordinances adopting the larger length limitation of the neighboring State. This exemption offered the benefits of longer trucks to individuals and businesses in important border cities without burdening Iowa's highways with interstate through traffic. Cf. Raymond (exemption in Wisconsin for shipments from local plants). The origin of the "border cities exemption" also suggests that Iowa's statute may not have been designed to ban dangerous trucks, but rather to discourage interstate truck traffic. In 1974, the legislature

---

3. In suggesting that Iowa's law actually promotes safety, the dissenting opinion ignores the findings of the courts below and relies on largely discredited statistical evidence. The dissent implies that a statistical study identified doubles as more dangerous than singles. At trial, however, the author of that study—Iowa's own statistician—conceded that his calculations were statistically biased, and therefore "not very meaningful."

The dissenting opinion also suggests that its conclusions are bolstered by the fact that the American Association of State Highway and Transportation Officials (AASHTO) recommends that States limit truck lengths. The dissent fails to point out, however, that AASHTO specifically recommends that States permit 65-foot doubles. [Footnote by Justice Powell.]

passed a bill that would have permitted 65-foot doubles in the State. Governor Ray vetoed the bill. He said: "I find sympathy with those who are doing business in our state and whose enterprises could gain from increased cargo carrying ability by trucks. However, with this bill, the Legislature has pursued a course that would benefit only a few Iowa-based companies while providing a great advantage for out-of-state trucking firms and competitors at the expense of our Iowa citizens."[4] After the veto, the "border cities exemption" was immediately enacted and signed by the Governor.

It is thus far from clear that Iowa was motivated primarily by a judgment that 65-foot doubles are less safe than 55-foot singles. Rather, Iowa seems to have hoped to limit the use of its highways by deflecting some through traffic.[5] In the [lower courts], the State explicitly attempted to justify the law by its claimed interest in keeping trucks out of Iowa. The Court of Appeals correctly concluded that a State cannot constitutionally promote its own parochial interests by requiring safe vehicles to detour around it.

V. In sum, the statutory exemptions, their history, and the arguments Iowa has advanced in support of its law in this litigation, all suggest that the deference traditionally accorded a State's safety judgment is not warranted. The controlling factors thus are the findings of the District Court, accepted by the Court of Appeals, with respect to the relative safety of the types of trucks at issue, and the substantiality of the burden on interstate commerce. Because Iowa has imposed this burden without any significant countervailing safety interest[6] its statute violates the [Commerce Clause].[7]

Affirmed.

Justice BRENNAN, with whom Justice MARSHALL joins, concurring in the judgment.

Iowa's truck length regulation challenged in this case is nearly identical to the Wisconsin regulation struck down in [Raymond]. In my view the same Commerce Clause restrictions that dictated that holding also require invalidation of Iowa's regulation insofar as it prohibits 65-foot doubles. The reasoning bringing me to that conclusion does not require, however, that I engage in the debate between my Brothers Powell and Rehnquist over what the District Court record shows on the question whether 65-foot doubles are more dangerous than shorter trucks. With all respect, my Brothers ask and answer the wrong question. For me, analysis of Commerce Clause challenges to state regulations must take into account three principles: (1) The courts are not empowered to second-guess the empirical judgments of lawmakers concerning the utility of

---

4. [E]xceptions also are available to benefit Iowa truck makers and Iowa mobile home manufacturers or purchasers. Although these exemptions are not directly relevant to the controversy over the safety of 65-foot doubles, they do contribute to the pattern of parochialism apparent in Iowa's statute. [Footnote by Justice Powell.]

5. The dissenting opinion insists that we defer to Iowa's truck-length limitations because they represent the collective judgment of the Iowa legislature. This position is curious because, as noted above, the Iowa legislature approved a bill legalizing 65-foot doubles. The bill was vetoed by the Governor, primarily for parochial rather than legitimate safety reasons. The dissenting opinion is at a loss to explain the Governor's interest in deflecting interstate truck traffic around Iowa. [Footnote by Justice Powell.]

6. [The District Court] found that the statute did not discriminate against such commerce.

Because the record fully supports the decision below with respect to the burden on interstate commerce, we need not consider whether the statute also operated to discriminate against that commerce. The latter theory was neither briefed nor argued in this Court. [Footnote by Justice Powell.]

7. Justice Rehnquist in dissent states that, as he reads the various opinions in this case, "only four Justices invalidate Iowa's law on the basis of the analysis in Raymond." It should be emphasized that Raymond, the analysis of which was derived from the Court's opinion in [Pike], was joined by each of the eight Justices who participated. Today, Justice Brennan finds it unnecessary to reach the Raymond analysis because he finds the Iowa statute to be flawed for a threshold reason. [Footnote by Justice Powell.]

legislation. (2) The burdens imposed on commerce must be balanced against the local benefits actually sought to be achieved by the State's lawmakers, and not against those suggested after the fact by counsel. (3) Protectionist legislation is unconstitutional under the Commerce Clause, even if the burdens and benefits are related to safety rather than economics.

I. [The Powell and Rehnquist opinions are both] predicated upon the supposition that the constitutionality of a state regulation is determined by the factual record created by the State's lawyers in trial court. But that supposition cannot be correct, for it would make the constitutionality of state laws and regulations depend on the vagaries of litigation rather than on the judgments made by the State's lawmakers. In considering a Commerce Clause challenge to a state regulation, the judicial task is to balance the burden imposed on commerce against the local benefits sought to be achieved by the State's *lawmakers*. In determining those benefits, a court should focus ultimately on the regulatory purposes identified by the lawmakers and on the evidence before or available to them that might have supported their judgment. See generally Clover Leaf Creamery [1981; p. 285 below]. Since the court must confine its analysis to the purposes the lawmakers had for maintaining the regulation, the only relevant evidence concerns whether the lawmakers could rationally have believed that the challenged regulation would foster those purposes. It is not the function of the court to decide whether *in fact* the regulation promotes its intended purpose, so long as an examination of the evidence before or available to the lawmaker indicates that the regulation is not wholly irrational in light of its purposes.[1]

II. My Brothers Powell and Rehnquist make the mistake of disregarding the intention of Iowa's lawmakers and assuming that resolution of the case must hinge upon the argument offered by Iowa's attorneys: that 65-foot doubles are more dangerous than shorter trucks. They then [reach] opposite conclusions as to whether the evidence adequately supports that empirical judgment. I repeat: my Brothers Powell and Rehnquist have asked and answered the wrong question. For although Iowa's lawyers in this litigation have defended the truck length regulation on the basis of the safety advantages of 55-foot singles and 60-foot doubles over 65-foot doubles, Iowa's actual rationale for maintaining the regulation had nothing to do with these purported differences. Rather, Iowa sought to discourage interstate truck traffic on Iowa's highways. Thus, the safety advantages and disadvantages of the types and lengths of trucks involved in this case are irrelevant to the decision.[2]

---

1. Moreover, I would emphasize that in the field of safety—and perhaps in other fields where the decisions of State lawmakers are deserving of a heightened degree of deference—the role of the courts is not to balance asserted burdens against intended benefits as it is in other fields. Compare Raymond (Blackmun, J., concurring) (safety regulation) with [Pike] (regulation intended "to protect and enhance the reputation of growers within the State"). In the field of safety, once the court has established that the intended safety benefit is not illusory, insubstantial, or nonexistent, it must defer to the State's lawmakers on the appropriate balance to be struck against other interests. I therefore disagree with my Brother Powell when he asserts that the degree of interference with interstate commerce may in the first instance be "weighed" against the State's safety [interests]. [Footnote by Justice Brennan.]

2. My Brother Rehnquist claims that the "argument" that a Court should defer to the actual purposes of the lawmakers rather than to the post hoc justifications of counsel "has been consistently rejected by the Court in other [contexts]." The extent to which we may rely upon post hoc justifications of counsel depends on the circumstances surrounding passage of the legislation. Where there is no evidence bearing on the actual purpose for a legislative classification, our analysis necessarily focuses on the suggestions of counsel. Even then, "marginally more demanding scrutiny" is appropriate to "test the plausibility of the tendered purpose." Schweiker v. Wilson [1981; p. — below] (Powell, J., dissenting). But where the lawmakers' purposes in enacting a statute are explicitly set forth, or are clearly discernible from the legislative history, this Court should not take—and, with the possible exception of United States Railroad Retirement Board v. Fritz [1980; p. 610 below] (Brennan, J., dissenting), has not taken—the extraordinary step of disregarding the *actual* purpose in favor of some "imaginary basis or purpose." McGinnis v. Royster [p. 606 below]. The principle of separa-

Although the Court has stated that "[i]n no field [has] deference to state regulation been greater than that of highway safety," it has declined to go so far as to presume that size restrictions are inherently tied to public safety. [Raymond.] The Court has emphasized that the "strong presumption of validity" of size restrictions "cannot justify a court in closing its eyes to uncontroverted evidence of record," ibid—here the obvious fact that the safety characteristics of 65-foot doubles did not provide the motivation for either legislators or Governor in maintaining the regulation.

III.   Though my Brother Powell recognizes that the State's actual purpose in maintaining the truck length regulation was "to limit the use of its highways by deflecting some through traffic," he fails to recognize that this purpose, being *protectionist* in nature, is *impermissible* under the Commerce Clause.[3]   The Governor admitted that he blocked legislative efforts to raise the length of trucks because the change "would benefit only a few Iowa-based companies while providing a great advantage for out-of-state trucking firms and competitors at the expense of our Iowa citizens." Appellant [Kassel], Director of the Iowa Department of Transportation, while admitting that the greater 65-foot length standard would be *safer* overall, defended the more restrictive regulations because of their benefits *within Iowa*. [Iowa] may not shunt off its fair share of the burden of maintaining interstate truck routes, nor may it create increased hazards on the highways of neighboring States in order to decrease the hazards on Iowa highways.   Such an attempt has all the hallmarks of the "[simple] protectionism" this Court has condemned in the economic area.   Philadelphia v. New Jersey [1978; p. 266 below.]   Just as a State's attempt to avoid interstate competition in economic goods may damage the prosperity of the Nation as a whole, so Iowa's attempt to deflect interstate truck traffic has been found to make the Nation's highways as a whole more hazardous.   That attempt should therefore be subject to "a virtually per se rule of invalidity."   Ibid.   This Court's heightened deference to the judgments of state lawmakers in the field of safety is largely attributable to a judicial disinclination to weigh the interests of safety against other societal interests, such as the economic interest in the free flow of commerce.   Here, the decision of Iowa's lawmakers to promote *Iowa's* safety and other interests at the direct expense of the safety and other interests of neighboring States merits no such deference.   No special judicial acuity is demanded to perceive that this sort of parochial legislation violates the Commerce Clause.   [Baldwin v. Seelig (1935); p. 279 below.]

Justice REHNQUIST, with whom The Chief Justice [BURGER] and Justice STEWART join, dissenting.

tion of powers requires, after all, that we defer to the elected lawmakers' judgment as to the appropriate means to accomplish an end, not that we defer to the arguments of lawyers.

If, as here, the only purpose ever articulated by the State's lawmakers for maintaining a regulation is illegitimate, I consider it contrary to precedent as well as to sound principles of constitutional adjudication for the courts to base their analysis on purposes never conceived by the lawmakers. This is especially true where, as the dissent's strained analysis of the relative safety of 65-foot doubles to shorter trucks amply demonstrates, the post hoc justifications are implausible as well as imaginary. I would emphasize that, although my Brother Powell's plurality opinion does not give as much weight to the illegitimacy of Iowa's actual purpose as I do, both that opinion and this concurrence have found the

actual motivation of the Iowa lawmakers in maintaining the truck length regulation highly relevant to, if not dispositive of, the case. [Footnote by Justice Brennan. The cases relied on by Justice Brennan in this footnote are equal protection, not commerce clause, cases. The Court's division about the relevance of "actual purpose" recurs frequently in modern equal protection cases, especially those reviewing economic regulations under the "rationality" standard commonly applied in equal protection (as well as due process) cases. The debate on that issue is more fully considered below, in chap. 8, sec. 1, and chap. 9, sec. 1.]

3.   It is not enough to conclude, as my Brother Powell does, that "the deference traditionally accorded a State's safety judgment is not warranted." [Footnote by Justice Brennan.]

The result in this case suggests, to paraphrase Justice Jackson, that the only state truck length limit "that is valid is one which this court has not been able to get its hands on." [Although] the plurality and concurring opinions strike down Iowa's law by different routes, I believe the analysis in both opinions oversteps our "limited authority to review state legislation under the commerce clause" and seriously intrudes upon the fundamental right of the States to pass laws to secure the safety of their [citizens].

I.   It is necessary to elaborate somewhat on the facts as presented in the plurality opinion to appreciate fully what the Court does today. Iowa's action in limiting the length of trucks which may travel on its highways is in no sense unusual. Every [state] regulates the length of vehicles permitted to use the public roads. Nor is Iowa a renegade in having length limits which operate to exclude the 65-foot doubles favored by Consolidated. These trucks are prohibited in other areas of the country as well, some 17 States and the District of Columbia, including all of New England and most of the Southeast. [In short], the persistent effort in the plurality opinion to paint Iowa as an oddity standing alone to block commerce carried in 65-foot doubles is simply not supported [by the facts].

II.   [Justice Rehnquist next turned to "the appropriate analysis to be applied."] [The] Court very recently reaffirmed the long-standing view that "in no field [has] deference to state regulation been greater than that of highway safety." [Raymond.] [Those] challenging a highway safety regulation must overcome a "strong presumption of validity." [Bibb.] A determination that a state law is a rational safety measure does not end the Commerce Clause inquiry. A "sensitive consideration" of the safety purpose in relation to the burden on commerce is required. [Raymond.] When engaging in such a consideration the Court does not directly compare safety benefits to commerce costs and strike down the legislation if the latter can be said in some vague sense to "outweigh" the former. Such an approach would make an empty gesture of the strong presumption of validity accorded state safety measures, particularly those governing highways. It would also arrogate to this Court functions of forming public policy, functions which, in the absence of congressional action, were left by the [Framers] to state legislatures. These admonitions are peculiarly apt when, as here, the question involves the difficult comparison of financial losses and "the loss of lives and limbs of workers and people using the highways." The purpose of the "sensitive consideration" referred to above is rather to determine if the asserted safety justification, although rational, is merely a pretext for discrimination against interstate commerce. We will conclude that it is if the safety benefits from the regulation are demonstrably trivial while the burden on commerce is great. [The] nature of the inquiry is perhaps best illustrated by examining those cases in which state safety laws have been struck down on Commerce Clause grounds. [Southern Pacific; Bibb.] [The cases] demonstrate that the safety benefits of a state law must be slight indeed before it will be struck down under the dormant Commerce Clause.

III.   There can be no doubt that the challenged statute is a valid highway safety regulation and thus entitled to the strongest presumption of validity against Commerce Clause challenges. [There] can also be no question that the particular limit chosen by Iowa [is] rationally related to Iowa's safety objective. [Iowa] adduced evidence supporting the relation between vehicle length and highway safety. The evidence indicated that longer vehicles take greater time to pass, thereby increasing the risks of accidents, particularly during the inclement weather not uncommon in Iowa. Longer trucks are more likely to clog intersections, and although there are no intersections on the Interstate Highways, the order below went beyond the highways themselves and the concerns about greater length at intersections would arise "at every trip origin, every trip destination, every intermediate stop for picking up trailers, reconfiguring loads, change of drivers, eating, refueling—every intermediate stop would generate this type of situation." [Iowa also] introduced evidence that doubles are more likely than singles to jackknife or upset. [Additional summaries of evidence omitted.] In sum, there was sufficient evidence presented at trial to support the legislative determination that length is related to safety, and nothing in Consolidated's evidence undermines this conclusion.

The District Court approached the case as if the question were whether Consolidated's 65-foot trucks were as safe as others permitted on Iowa highways. [The] question, however, is whether the Iowa Legislature has acted rationally in regulating vehicle lengths and whether the safety benefits from this regulation are more than slight or problematical. [See, e.g., Barnwell.] The answering of the relevant question is not appreciably advanced by comparing trucks slightly over the length limit with those at the length limit. It is emphatically not our task to balance any incremental safety benefits from prohibiting 65-foot doubles as opposed to 60-foot doubles against the burden on interstate commerce. Lines drawn for safety purposes will rarely pass muster if the question is whether a slight increment can be permitted without sacrificing safety. The question is rather whether it can be said that the benefits flowing to Iowa from a rational truck length limitation are "slight or problematical." See Bibb. The particular line chosen by Iowa—60 feet—is relevant only to the question whether the limit is a rational one. Once a court determines that it is, it considers the overall safety benefits *from the regulation* against burdens on interstate commerce, and not any marginal benefits from the scheme the State established as opposed to that the plaintiffs desire. See [Southern Pacific; Barnwell]. The difficulties with the contrary approach are patent. While it may be clear that there are substantial safety benefits from a 55-foot truck as compared to a 105-foot truck, these benefits may not be discernible in 5-foot jumps. Appellee's approach would permit what could not be accomplished in one lawsuit to be done in ten separate suits, each challenging an additional five feet. Any direct balancing of marginal safety benefits against burdens on commerce would make the burdens on commerce the sole significant factor, and make likely the odd result that similar state laws enacted for identical safety reasons might violate the Commerce Clause in one part of the country but not [another].

It must be emphasized that there is nothing in the laws of nature which makes 65-foot doubles an obvious norm. Consolidated operates 65-foot doubles on many of its routes simply because that is the largest size permitted in many States through which Consolidated travels. Doubles can and do come in smaller sizes. [Striking] down Iowa's law because Consolidated has made a voluntary business decision to employ 65-foot doubles, a decision based on the actions of other state legislatures, would essentially be compelling Iowa to yield to the policy choices of neighboring States. Under our Constitutional scheme, however, there is only one legislative body which can pre-empt the rational policy determination of the Iowa Legislature and that is Congress. Forcing Iowa to yield to the policy choices of neighboring States perverts the primary purpose of the Commerce Clause, that of vesting power to regulate interstate commerce in Congress, where all the States are [represented].[1]

[The] plurality [claims] that "[t]his case is Raymond revisited."[2] Raymond, however, does not control this case. [The] Raymond court repeatedly stressed

---

1. The extent to which the assertion of a violation of the Commerce Clause is simply an effort to compel Iowa to yield to the decisions of its neighbors is clearest if one asks whether Iowa's law would violate the Commerce Clause if the 17 States which currently prohibit Consolidated's 65-foot doubles were not in the East and Southeast but rather surrounded Iowa. [Footnote by Justice Rehnquist.]

2. [My] Brother Brennan votes to strike down Iowa's law not because the safety benefits

that the State "made no effort to contradict [evidence] of comparative safety with evidence of its own," that the trucking companies' evidence was "uncontroverted," and that the State "virtually defaulted in its defense of the regulations as a safety measure." By contrast, [Iowa] has adduced evidence sufficient to support its safety claim and has rebutted much of the evidence submitted by Consolidated. Furthermore, the exception to the Wisconsin prohibition which the Court specifically noted in Raymond finds no parallel in this case. [E.g.,] the exception in Raymond permitted oversized vehicles to travel from plant to plant in Wisconsin or between a Wisconsin plant and the border. [T]his discriminated on its face between Wisconsin industries and the industries of other States. The border cities exception to the Iowa length limit does not. Iowa shippers in cities with border city ordinances may use longer vehicles in interstate commerce, but interstate shippers coming into such cities may do so as well. Cities without border city ordinances may neither export nor import on oversized [vehicles].

My Brother Brennan argues that the Court should consider only *the* purpose the Iowa legislators *actually* sought to achieve by the length limit, and not the purposes advanced by Iowa's lawyers in defense of the statute. This argument calls to mind what was said of the Roman Legions: that they may have lost battles, but they never lost a war, since they never let a war end until they had won it. The argument has been consistently rejected by the Court in other [i.e., equal protection] contexts, and Justice Brennan can cite no authority for the proposition that possible legislative purposes suggested by a state's lawyers should not be considered in Commerce Clause cases. The problems with a view such as that advanced in the concurring opinion are apparent. To name just a few, it assumes that individual legislators are motivated by one discernible "actual" purpose, and ignores the fact that different legislators may vote for a single piece of legislation for widely different reasons. How, for example, would a court adhering to the views expressed in the concurring opinion approach a statute, the legislative history of which indicated that 10 votes were based on safety considerations, 10 votes were based on protectionism, and the statute passed by a vote of 40–20? What would the *actual* purpose of the *legislature* have been in that [case]? [3]

[The] effort in both the plurality and concurring opinions to portray the legislation involved here as protectionist is in error. Whenever a State enacts more stringent safety measures than its neighbors, in an area which affects commerce, the safety law will have the incidental effect of deflecting interstate commerce to the neighboring States. Indeed, the safety and protectionist motives cannot be separated: The whole purpose of safety regulation of vehicles is to *protect* the State from unsafe vehicles. If a neighboring State chooses *not* to protect its citizens from the danger discerned by the enacting State, that is its business, but the enacting State should not be penalized when the vehicles it considers unsafe travel through the neighboring State. The other States with

of Iowa's law are illusory—indeed, he specifically declines to consider the safety benefits—but because he views it as protectionist in nature. As I read the various opinions in this case, therefore, only four Justices invalidate Iowa's law on the basis of the analysis in Raymond. [Footnote by Justice Rehnquist.]

3. [Although] both my Brother Brennan and I have cited cases from the equal protection area, it is not clear that the analysis of legislative purpose in that area is the same as in the present context. It may be more reasonable to suppose that proffered purposes of a statute, whether advanced by a legislature or post hoc by lawyers, cloak impermissible aims in Commerce Clause cases than in equal protection cases. Statutes generally favor one group at the expense of another, and the equal protection clause was not designed to proscribe this in the way that the Commerce Clause was designed to prevent local barriers to interstate commerce. Thus even if my Brother Brennan's arguments were supportable in Commerce Clause cases, that analysis would not carry over of its own force into the realm of equal protection generally. But even in the Commerce Clause area, his arguments are [unpersuasive]. [Footnote by Justice Rehnquist.]

truck length limits that exclude Consolidated's 65-foot doubles would not at all be paranoid in assuming that they might be next on Consolidated's "hit list." The true problem with today's decision is that it gives no guidance whatsoever to these States as to whether their laws are valid or how to defend them. For that matter, the decision gives no guidance to Consolidated or other trucking firms either. Perhaps, after all is said and done, the Court today neither says nor does very much at all. We know only that Iowa's law is invalid and that the jurisprudence of the "negative side" of the Commerce Clause remains hopelessly confused.[4]

C. DISCRIMINATION, PROTECTIONISM, AND EXCESSIVE BURDENS: BARRIERS TO THE INTERSTATE FLOW OF GOODS AND RESOURCES

1. SOME BASIC THEMES

Introduction. The major aim of this subsection is to promote critical examination of some recurrent themes in commerce clause decisions: the antipathy to state "discrimination" against out-of-state interests, and the blocking of state "protectionism" that gives undue advantages to local interests over out-of-state competitors. The hostility to discrimination and protectionism has its roots in the historical purposes of the commerce clause. Recall Justice Jackson's statement in Hood, quoted at the beginning of this chapter (p. 231), where he asserted that the Court "consistently has rebuffed attempts of states to advance their own commercial interests by curtailing the movement of articles of commerce, either into or out of the state, while generally supporting their right to impose even burdensome regulations in the interest of local health and safety." Recall, too, Justice Jackson's statement of the governing ideal: "Free access" by producers to every market in the nation; no "home embargoes" against exports; no foreign state exclusion of imports. Justice Jackson insisted, too, that "every consumer may look to the free competition from every producing area in the Nation."

But stating that "vision of the Founders" is easier than implementing it. Problems of implementation are best illustrated by the cases in this section— cases mostly dealing with interstate trade. Explicit concerns with discriminatory purposes and protectionist effects have been rare in the preceding transportation cases; they are often prominent in the cases that follow. In the railroad and trucking cases, the Court typically assumed the state's good faith in asserting legitimate health or safety concerns. The Court's safeguarding of commerce came mainly via the Southern Pacific "balancing" analysis, an analysis that explicitly focused only on the relative strength of the state's legitimate interests and the extent of the burden on the interstate movement. As the Pike formulation (p. 245) illustrates, a similar balancing formula has at times been applied in the trade area as well. But even in the transportation cases, a search for forbidden "economic" purposes—especially for state endeavors to give a competitive advantage to local economic interests—occasionally surfaced. Recall especially Kassel (p. 255), with the differing emphases given by Justices Powell and Brennan to the relevance of the exemptions in Iowa's truck length law and of the Governor's veto message. In the cases that follow, suspicion of

---

4. As noted at p. 245 above, congressional action subsequent to the Kassel decision has mooted the specific issue in the case by authorizing the use of 65-foot long double trailer trucks.

the state's good faith in asserting legitimate local interests and search for discriminatory or protectionist purposes and effects are far more common.

Condemnation of state "discrimination" against interstate commerce has evoked a widespread consensus on the Court over the years. But "discrimination" can be a chameleon-like term. The opening cases in this subsection introduce the range of usages of terms such as "discrimination" and "protectionism." In the first case, Philadelphia v. New Jersey, discriminatory means are evident on the face of the state law and the Court finds it unnecessary to resolve the debate about the true purpose of the law, in view of those forbidden means. But evidence of discrimination is seldom so obvious. More commonly, the Court is suspicious about the real, arguably forbidden purpose of laws articulating facially valid, legitimate concerns. And, increasingly, the Court emphasizes the "discriminatory effect" of the law, either to add strength to its inference of forbidden purposes or as an independent ground for invalidation. See, e.g., Hunt and Dean Milk (both in these opening materials, at pp. 272 and 271).[1]

PHILADELPHIA v. NEW JERSEY

437 U.S. 617, 98 S.Ct. 2531, 57 L.Ed.2d 475 (1978).

Justice STEWART delivered the opinion of the Court.

[The Court held unconstitutional a 1973 New Jersey law which prohibited the importation of most "solid or liquid waste which originated or was collected outside the territorial limits of this State."[1] The ban was challenged by operators of private landfills in New Jersey and by several cities in other states that had agreements with those operators for waste disposal. A state trial judge declared the law unconstitutional because it discriminated against interstate commerce. The highest state court reversed, holding that the law advanced vital health and environmental objectives with no economic discrimination against, and with little burden upon, interstate commerce. In holding the law unconstitutional, Justice Stewart's majority opinion found that it had not been preempted by federal legislation and rejected suggestions that interstate movement of waste was not "commerce" within the commerce clause. Turning to the central issues, he proceeded as follows:]

Although the Constitution gives Congress the power to regulate commerce among the States, many subjects of potential federal regulation under that power inevitably escape congressional attention "because of their local character and their number and diversity." [Barnwell.] In the absence of federal legislation, these subjects are open to control by the States so long as they act within the restraints imposed by the Commerce Clause itself. See [Raymond]. The bounds of these restraints appear nowhere in the words of the Commerce Clause, but have emerged gradually in the decisions of this Court giving effect

---

1. The range of meanings of the "discrimination" label also raises problems in areas outside of the commerce clause. Similar but not wholly identical problems are presented especially by the equal protection provision of the Fourteenth Amendment, the provision whose major thrust is to bar "discrimination" against racial and other traditionally disadvantaged minorities. In the equal protection cases, too, problems arise regarding discrimination "on the face" of the law, the search for undisclosed discriminatory purpose and intent, and the role of data regarding discriminatory "effect" in demonstrating unconstitutional discrimination. These problems are pur-

sued at length in chap. 9. The structure of the introductory materials in this sec. 1C(1) of this chapter somewhat resembles the organization regarding the types of invalid discrimination under equal protection in chap. 9, below.

1. The law explicitly barred the import of out-of-state waste "except garbage to be fed to swine" unless the state environmental commissioner determined that importation could be permitted "without endangering the public health, safety and welfare." The commissioner's regulations made only four narrow exceptions to the ban.

to its basic purpose.   That broad purpose was well expressed by Mr. Justice Jackson in his opinion for the Court in [Hood].[2]

The opinions of the Court through the years have reflected an alertness to the evils of "economic isolation" and protectionism, while at the same time recognizing that incidental burdens on interstate commerce may be unavoidable when a State legislates to safeguard the health and safety of its people.   Thus, where simple economic protectionism is effected by state legislation, a virtually per se rule of invalidity has been erected.   See, e.g., [Hood, p. 289 below; Toomer v. Witsell, p. 309 below; Baldwin v. Seelig, p. 279 below; Buck, p. 244 above].   The clearest example of such legislation is a law that overtly blocks the flow of interstate commerce at a State's borders.   Cf. Welton v. Missouri.[3]   But where other legislative objectives are credibly advanced and there is no patent discrimination against interstate trade, the Court has adopted a much more flexible approach, the general contours of which were outlined in [Pike].   [Justice Stewart quoted his Pike formulation, p. 245 above.]   See also [e.g., Raymond (p. 245 above); Hunt (which follows)].   The crucial inquiry, therefore, must be directed to determining whether [the law] is basically a protectionist measure, or whether it can fairly be viewed as a law directed to legitimate local concerns, with effects upon interstate commerce that are only incidental.

[Justice Stewart noted the contending positions of the state and the challengers regarding the actual purpose of the law, but found it unnecessary to resolve the conflict.   The highest state court had concluded that the law was "designed to protect, not the State's economy, but its environment."   The challengers claimed that the law, "while outwardly cloaked 'in the currently fashionable garb of environmental protection,' [is] actually no more than a legislative effort to suppress competition and stabilize the cost of solid waste disposal for New Jersey residents."   In response, the state denied that the law "was motivated by financial concerns or economic protectionism," insisting that the "complaint is not that New Jersey has forged an economic preference for its own commercial interests, but rather that it has denied a small group of its entrepreneurs [i.e., its private landfill operators] an economic opportunity to traffic in waste in order to protect the health, safety and welfare of the citizenry at large."   Justice Stewart stated:]

This dispute about ultimate legislative purpose need not be resolved, because its resolution would not be relevant to the constitutional issue to be decided in this case.   Contrary to the evident assumption of the [state] and the parties, the evil of protectionism can reside in legislative means as well as legislative ends.   Thus, it does not matter whether the ultimate aim of [the law] is to reduce the waste disposal costs of New Jersey residents or to save remaining open lands from pollution, for we assume New Jersey has every right to protect its residents' pocketbooks as well as their environment.   And it may be assumed as well that New Jersey may pursue those ends by slowing the flow of *all* waste into the State's remaining landfills, even though interstate commerce may incidentally be affected.   But whatever New Jersey's ultimate purpose, it may not be accomplished by discriminating against articles of commerce coming

2.   Recall the passages from Hood quoted at the beginning of this chapter.   Justice Stewart also used a passage from Justice Jackson's opinion in Hood quoting Baldwin v. Seelig (1935; p. 279 below), a quotation stating that "what is ultimate is the principle that one state in its dealings with another may not place itself in a position of economic isolation."

3.   Welton v. Missouri, 91 U.S. 275 (1876), is one of the earliest and most widely cited condemnations of state laws discriminatory on the face of the statute.   Welton invalidated a Missouri license requirement for peddlers (itinerant sellers).   The law applied only to peddlers of merchandise "not the growth, produce, or manufacture of the State"; peddlers of Missouri goods did not need a license.   Justice Field stated for the Court that the "very object" of the commerce clause was to protect "against discriminating State legislation."

from outside the State unless there is some reason, apart from their origin, to treat them differently. Both on its face and in its plain effect, [the law] violates this principle of nondiscrimination.

The Court has consistently found parochial legislation of this kind to be constitutionally invalid, whether the ultimate aim of the legislation was to assure a steady supply of milk by erecting barriers to allegedly ruinous outside competition [Baldwin v. Seelig]; or to create jobs by keeping industry within the State [e.g., Foster-Fountain Packing (1928; p. 279 below)]; or to preserve the State's financial resources from depletion by fencing out indigent immigrants, Edwards v. California [1941; p. 315 below.] In each of these cases, a presumably legitimate goal was sought to be achieved by the illegitimate means of isolating the State from the national economy. Also relevant here are the Court's decisions holding that a State may not accord its own inhabitants a preferred right of access over consumers in other States to natural resources located within its borders. [E.g.,] Pennsylvania v. West Virginia [1923; p. 294 below]. These cases stand for the basic principle that a "State is without power to prevent privately owned articles of trade from being shipped and sold in interstate commerce on the ground that they are required to satisfy local demands or because they are needed by the people of the State." [4] [Foster-Fountain.]

The New Jersey law at issue in this case falls squarely within the area that the Commerce Clause puts off limits to state regulation. On its face, it imposes on out-of-state commercial interests the full burden of conserving the State's remaining landfill space. It is true that in our previous cases the scarce natural resource was itself the article of commerce, whereas here the scarce resource and the article of commerce are distinct. But that difference is without consequence. In both instances, the State has overtly moved to slow or freeze the flow of commerce for protectionist reasons. It does not matter that the State has shut the article of commerce inside the State in one case and outside the State in the other. What is crucial is the attempt by one State to isolate itself from a problem common to many by erecting a barrier against the movement of interstate trade.

The appellees argue that not all laws which facially discriminate against out-of-state commerce are forbidden protectionist regulations. In particular, they point to quarantine laws, which this Court has repeatedly upheld even though they appear to single out interstate commerce for special treatment. In the appellees' view, [this law] is analogous to such health-protective measures, since it reduces the exposure of New Jersey residents to the allegedly harmful effects of landfill sites. It is true that certain quarantine laws have not been considered forbidden protectionist measures, even though they were directed against out-of-state commerce. But those quarantine laws banned the importation of articles such as diseased livestock that required destruction as soon as possible because their very movement risked contagion and other evils. Those laws thus did not discriminate against interstate commerce as such, but simply prevented traffic in noxious articles, whatever their origin.

The New Jersey statute is not such a quarantine law. There has been no claim here that the very movement of waste into or through New Jersey endangers health, or that waste must be disposed of as soon and as close to its point of generation as possible. The harms caused by waste are said to arise after its disposal in landfill sites, and at that point, as New Jersey concedes, there

4. We express no opinion about New Jersey's power, consistent with the Commerce Clause, to restrict to state residents access to state-owned resources, compare [e.g.] Toomer v. Witsell; or New Jersey's power to spend state funds solely on behalf of state residents and businesses, compare Hughes v. Alexandria Scrap Corp. [1976; p. 299 below]. Also compare [Barnwell] with [Southern Pacific]. [Footnote by Justice Stewart.]

is no basis to distinguish out-of-state waste from domestic waste. If one is inherently harmful, so is the other. Yet New Jersey has banned the former while leaving its landfill sites open to the latter. The New Jersey law blocks the importation of waste in an obvious effort to saddle those outside the State with the entire burden of slowing the flow of refuse into New Jersey's remaining landfill sites. That legislative effort is clearly impermissible under the [commerce clause]. Today, cities in Pennsylvania and New York find it expedient or necessary to send their waste into New Jersey for disposal, and New Jersey claims the right to close its borders to such traffic. Tomorrow, cities in New Jersey may find it expedient or necessary to send their waste into Pennsylvania or New York for disposal, and those States might then claim the right to close their borders. The Commerce Clause will protect New Jersey in the future, just as it protects her neighbors now, from efforts by one State to isolate itself in the stream of interstate commerce from a problem shared by all.

[Reversed.]

Mr. Justice REHNQUIST, with whom The Chief Justice [BURGER] joins, dissenting.

[Sanitary] landfills have replaced incineration as the principal method of disposing of solid waste. [In 1973, New Jersey] legislatively recognized the unfortunate fact that landfills also present extremely serious health and safety problems. First, in New Jersey, "virtually all sanitary landfills can be expected to produce leachate, a noxious and highly polluted liquid which is seldom visible and frequently pollutes [ground] and surface waters." The natural decomposition process which occurs in landfills also produces large quantities of methane and thereby presents a significant explosion hazard. Landfills can also generate "health hazards caused by rodents, fires and scavenger birds" and, "needless to say, do not help New Jersey's aesthetic appearance nor New Jersey's noise or water or air pollution problems." [For] the moment, [appellees] must continue to use sanitary landfills to dispose of New Jersey's own solid waste despite the critical environmental problems thereby created.

The question presented in this case is whether New Jersey must also continue to receive and dispose of solid waste from neighboring States, even though these will inexorably increase the health problems discussed above. The Court answers this question in the affirmative. New Jersey must either prohibit *all* landfill operations, leaving itself to cast about for a presently nonexistent solution to the serious problem of disposing of the waste generated within its own borders, or it must accept waste from every portion of the United States, thereby multiplying the health and safety problems which would result if it dealt only with such wastes generated within the State. [Our] precedents establish that the Commerce Clause does not present appellees with such a Hobson's [choice].

In my opinion, [the cases sustaining quarantine laws] are dispositive of the present one. Under them, New Jersey may require germ-infected rags or diseased meat to be disposed of as best as possible within the State, but at the same time prohibit the *importation* of such items for disposal at the facilities that are set up within New Jersey for disposal of such material generated *within* the State. The physical fact of life that New Jersey must somehow dispose of its own noxious items does not mean that it must serve as a depository for those of every other State. Similarly, New Jersey should be free under our past precedents to prohibit the importation of solid waste because of the health and safety problems that such waste poses to its citizens. The fact that New Jersey continues to, and indeed must continue to, dispose of its own solid waste does not mean that New Jersey may not prohibit the importation of even more solid waste into the State. I simply see no way to distinguish solid waste, on the record of this case, from germ-infected rags, diseased meat, and other noxious items.

[According] to the Court, the New Jersey law is distinguishable from [quarantine] laws, and invalid, because the concern of New Jersey is not with the *movement* of solid waste but with the present inability to safely *dispose* of it once it reaches its destination. But I think it far from clear that the State's law has as limited a focus as the Court imputes to it: Solid waste which is a health hazard when it reaches its destination may in all likelihood be an equally great health hazard in transit. Even if the Court is correct in its characterization of New Jersey's concerns, I do not see why a State may ban the importation of items whose movement risks contagion, but cannot ban the importation of items which, although they may be transported into the State without undue hazard, will then simply pile up in an ever increasing danger to the public's health and safety. The Commerce Clause was not drawn with a view to having the validity of state laws turn on such pointless distinctions.

[The] Court implies that the challenged laws must be invalidated because New Jersey has left its landfills open to domestic waste. But, as the Court notes, this Court has repeatedly upheld quarantine laws "even though they appear to single out interstate commerce for special treatment." The fact that New Jersey has left its landfill sites open for domestic waste does not, of course, mean that solid waste is not innately harmful. Nor does it mean that New Jersey prohibits importation of solid waste for reasons other than the health and safety of its population. New Jersey must out of sheer necessity treat and dispose of its solid waste in some fashion, just as it must treat New Jersey cattle suffering from hoof-and-mouth disease. It does not follow that New Jersey must, under the Commerce Clause, accept solid waste or diseased cattle from outside its borders and thereby exacerbate its problems. [Because] I find no basis for distinguishing the [health] laws under challenge here from our past cases upholding state laws that prohibit the importation of items that could endanger the population of the State, I dissent.

DEAN MILK CO. v. MADISON

340 U.S. 349, 71 S.Ct. 295, 95 L.Ed. 329 (1951).

Mr. Justice CLARK delivered the opinion of the Court.

[A Madison, Wis., ordinance barred the sale of pasteurized milk unless it had been processed and bottled at an approved pasteurization plant within a radius of five miles from the central square of Madison. Within that five-mile area were five processing plants, only three of which did business in Madison. Within the county in which Madison is located were 5,600 dairy farms. Justice Clark stated that the total raw milk production of these farms was more than ten times the requirements of Madison. Madison officials inspected the plants and farms every 30 days. Dean Milk, which challenged the ordinance, was based in Illinois, bought its milk from farms in northern Illinois and southern Wisconsin, and pasteurized it at its two Illinois plants, 65 and 85 miles from Madison. Dean Milk was denied a license to sell its products in Madison solely because its plants were more than five miles away. Dean Milk's farms and plants were licensed and inspected by Chicago public health authorities, and its milk was labeled "Grade A" under a Chicago ordinance which had adopted rating standards recommended by the U.S. Public Health Service. The Chicago ordinance, like that of Madison, was patterned on the Model Milk Ordinance of the U.S. Public Health Service. Justice Clark noted, however, that "Madison contends and we assume that in some particulars its ordinance is more rigorous than that of Chicago." The highest state court rejected the commerce clause attack. Justice Clark concluded that "the ordinance imposes an undue burden on interstate commerce." He explained:]

[There can be no] objection to the avowed purpose of this enactment. We assume that difficulties in sanitary regulation of milk and milk products originating in remote areas may present a situation in which "it appears that the matter is one which may appropriately be regulated in the interest of the safety, health and well-being of local communities." [But] this regulation, like the provision invalidated in Baldwin v. Seelig [p. 279 below], in practical effect excludes from distribution in Madison wholesome milk produced and pasteurized in Illinois. [In] thus erecting an economic barrier protecting a major local industry against competition from without the State, Madison plainly discriminates against interstate commerce.[1] This it cannot do, even in the exercise of its unquestioned power to protect the health and safety of its people, if reasonable nondiscriminatory alternatives, adequate to conserve legitimate local interests, are available. Cf. Baldwin v. Seelig; Minnesota v. Barber [p. 277 below]. A different view, that the ordinance is valid simply because it professes to be a health measure, would mean that the Commerce Clause of itself imposes no limitations on state action other than those laid down by the Due Process Clause, save for the rare instance where a state artlessly discloses an avowed purpose to discriminate against interstate goods. Our issue then is whether the discrimination inherent in the Madison ordinance can be justified in view of the character of the local interests and the available methods of protecting them.

[It] appears that reasonable and adequate alternatives are available. If [Madison] prefers to rely upon its own officials for inspection of distant milk sources, such inspection is readily open to it without hardship for it could charge the actual and reasonable cost of such inspection to the importing producers and processors. Moreover, appellee Health Commissioner of Madison testified that as proponent of the local milk ordinance he had submitted the provisions here in controversy and an alternative proposal based on § 11 of the Model Milk Ordinance recommended by the [U.S.] Public Health Service. The model provision imposes no geographical limitation on location of milk sources and processing plants but excludes from the municipality milk not produced and pasteurized conformably to standards as high as those enforced by the receiving city. In implementing such an ordinance, the importing city obtains milk ratings based on uniform standards and established by health authorities in the jurisdiction where production and processing occur. The receiving city may determine the extent of enforcement of sanitary standards in the exporting area by verifying the accuracy of safety ratings of specific plants or of the milkshed in the distant jurisdiction through the [U.S.] Public Health Service. The Commissioner testified that Madison consumers "would be safeguarded adequately" under either proposal and that he had expressed no preference. [The Commissioner and a state official] agreed that a local health officer would be justified in relying upon the evaluation by the Public Health Service of enforcement conditions in remote producing areas.

To permit Madison to adopt a regulation not essential for the protection of local health interests and placing a discriminatory burden on interstate commerce would invite a multiplication of preferential trade areas destructive of the very purpose of the Commerce Clause. Under the circumstances here presented, the regulation must yield to the principle that "one state in its dealings with another may not place itself in a position of economic isolation." Baldwin v. Seelig.

[Reversed.]

1. It is immaterial that Wisconsin milk from outside the Madison area is subjected to the same proscription as that moving in interstate [commerce]. [Footnote by Justice Clark.]

Mr. Justice BLACK, with whom Mr. Justice DOUGLAS and Mr. Justice MINTON concur, dissenting.

[I] disagree with the Court's premises, reasoning, and judgment. (1) This ordinance does not exclude wholesome milk coming from Illinois or anywhere else. It does require that all milk sold in Madison must be pasteurized within five miles of the center of the city. But there was no finding in the state courts [that Dean] is unable to have its milk pasteurized within the defined geographical [area]. (2) Characterization of [the law] as a "discriminatory burden" on interstate commerce is merely a statement of the Court's result, which I think incorrect. [B]oth state courts below found that [the law] represents a good-faith attempt to safeguard public health by making adequate sanitation inspections possible. While we are not bound by these findings, I do not understand the Court to overturn them. Therefore, the fact that [the law], like all health regulations, imposes some burden on trade, does not mean that it "discriminates" against interstate commerce. (3) This health regulation should not be invalidated merely because the Court believes that alternative milk-inspection methods might insure the cleanliness and healthfulness of Dean's Illinois milk. [I have found no case] in which a bona fide health law was struck down on the ground that some other method of safeguarding health would be as good as, or better than, the one the Court was called on to review. [If], however, the principle announced today is to be followed, the Court should not strike down local health regulations unless satisfied beyond a reasonable doubt that the substitutes it proposes would not lower health standards. I do not think that the Court can so satisfy itself on the basis of its judicial knowledge. And the evidence in the record leads me to the conclusion that the substitute health measures suggested by the Court do not insure milk as safe as the Madison ordinance requires. [From] what this record shows, and from what it fails to show, I do not think that either of the alternatives suggested by the Court would assure the people of Madison as pure a supply of milk as they receive under their own ordinance. On this record I would uphold the Madison law. At the very least, however, I would not invalidate it without giving the parties a chance to present evidence and get findings on the ultimate issues the Court thinks crucial—namely, the relative merits of the Madison ordinance and the alternatives suggested by the Court today.

HUNT v. WASHINGTON APPLE ADVERTISING COMM'N

432 U.S. 333, 97 S.Ct. 2434, 53 L.Ed.2d 383 (1977).

Mr. Chief Justice BURGER delivered the opinion of the Court.

In 1973, North Carolina enacted a statute which required, inter alia, all closed containers of apples sold, offered for sale, or shipped into the State to bear "no grade other than the applicable U.S. grade or standard." In an action brought by the Washington State Apple Advertising Commission, a three-judge Federal District Court invalidated the statute insofar as it prohibited the display of Washington State apple grades on the ground that it unconstitutionally discriminated against [interstate commerce]. Washington State is the Nation's largest producer of apples, its crops accounting for approximately 30% of all apples grown domestically and nearly half of all apples shipped in closed containers in interstate commerce. [Because] of the importance of the apple industry to the State, its legislature has undertaken to protect and enhance the reputation of Washington apples by establishing a stringent, mandatory inspection program [which] requires all apples shipped in interstate commerce to be tested under strict quality standards and graded accordingly. In all cases, the

Washington State grades [are] the equivalent of, or superior to, the comparable grades and standards adopted by the [U.S. Dept. of] Agriculture (USDA).

[In] 1972, the North Carolina Board of Agriculture adopted an administrative regulation, unique in the 50 States, which in effect required all closed containers of apples shipped into or sold in the State to display either the applicable USDA grade or a notice indicating no classification. State grades were expressly prohibited. In addition to its obvious consequence—prohibiting the display of Washington State apple grades on containers of apples shipped into North Carolina—the regulation presented the Washington apple industry with a marketing problem of potentially nationwide significance. Washington apple growers annually ship in commerce approximately 40 million closed containers of apples, nearly 500,000 of which eventually find their way into North Carolina, stamped with the applicable Washington State variety and grade. [Compliance] with North Carolina's unique regulation would have required Washington growers to obliterate the printed labels on containers shipped to North Carolina, thus giving their product a damaged appearance. Alternatively, they could have changed their marketing practices to accommodate the needs of the North Carolina market, i.e., repack apples to be shipped to North Carolina in containers bearing only the USDA grade, and/or store the estimated portion of the harvest destined for that market in such special containers. As a last resort, they could discontinue the use of the preprinted containers entirely. None of these costly and less efficient options was very attractive to the industry. Moreover, in the event a number of other States followed North Carolina's lead, the resultant inability to display the Washington grades could force the Washington growers to abandon the State's expensive inspection and grading system which their customers had come to know and rely on over the 60-odd years of its existence. With these problems confronting the industry, the [Commission] petitioned the North Carolina Board of Agriculture to amend its regulation to permit the display of state grades. [No] relief was granted. Indeed, North Carolina hardened its position shortly thereafter by enacting the regulation into law. [Nonetheless], the Commission once again requested an exemption. [This] request, too, was denied.

Unsuccessful in its attempts to secure administrative relief, the Commission instituted this action challenging the constitutionality of the statute. [The] District Court found that the North Carolina statute, while neutral on its face, actually discriminated against Washington State growers and dealers in favor of their local counterparts [and] concluded that this discrimination [was] not justified by the asserted local interest—the elimination of deception and confusion from the marketplace—arguably furthered by the [statute].

We [turn] to the appellants' claim that the District Court erred in holding that the North Carolina statute violated the Commerce Clause. [Appellants] maintain that [the] burdens on the interstate sale of Washington apples were far outweighed by the local benefits flowing from what they contend was a valid exercise of North Carolina's [police powers]. Prior to the statute's enactment, appellants point out, apples from 13 different States were shipped into North Carolina for sale. Seven of those States, including [Washington], had their own grading systems which, while differing in their standards, used similar descriptive labels (e.g., fancy, extra fancy, etc.). This multiplicity of inconsistent state grades [posed] dangers of deception and confusion not only in the North Carolina market, but in the Nation as a whole. The North Carolina statute, appellants claim, was enacted to eliminate this source of deception and confusion. [Moreover], it is contended that North Carolina sought to accomplish this goal of uniformity in an evenhanded manner as evidenced by the fact that its statute applies to all apples sold in closed containers in the State without regard to their point of origin.

[As] the appellants properly point out, not every exercise of state authority imposing some burden on the free flow of commerce is invalid, [especially] when the State acts to protect its citizenry in matters pertaining to the sale of foodstuffs. By the same token, however, a finding that state legislation furthers matters of legitimate local concern, even in the health and consumer protection areas, does not end the inquiry. [Dean Milk.] Rather, when such state legislation comes into conflict with the Commerce Clause's overriding requirement of a national "common market," we are confronted with the task of effecting an accommodation of the competing national and local interests. [E.g., Pike.] We turn to that task.

As the District Court correctly found, the challenged statute has the practical effect of not only burdening interstate sales of Washington apples, but also discriminating against them. This discrimination takes various forms. The first, and most obvious, is the statute's consequence of raising the costs of doing business in the North Carolina market for Washington apple growers and dealers, while leaving those of their North Carolina counterparts unaffected. [This] disparate effect results from the fact that North Carolina apple producers, unlike their Washington competitors, were not forced to alter their marketing practices in order to comply with the statute. They were still free to market their wares under the USDA grade or none at all as they had done prior to the statute's enactment. Obviously, the increased costs imposed by the statute would tend to shield the local apple industry from the competition of Washington apple growers and dealers who are already at a competitive disadvantage because of their great distance from the North Carolina market. Second, the statute has the effect of stripping away from the Washington apple industry the competitive and economic advantages it has earned for itself through its expensive inspection and grading system. The record demonstrates that the Washington apple-grading system has gained nationwide acceptance in the apple trade. [The record] contains numerous affidavits [stating a] preference [for] apples graded under the Washington, as opposed to the USDA, system because of the former's greater consistency, its emphasis on color, and its supporting mandatory inspections. Once again, the statute had no similar impact on the North Carolina apple industry and thus operated to its benefit.

Third, by prohibiting Washington growers and dealers from marketing apples under their State's grades, the statute has a leveling effect which insidiously operates to the advantage of local apple producers. [With] free market forces at work, Washington sellers would normally enjoy a distinct market advantage vis-à-vis local producers in those categories where the Washington grade is superior. However, because of the statute's operation, Washington apples which would otherwise qualify for and be sold under the superior Washington grades will now have to be marketed under their inferior USDA counterparts. Such "downgrading" offers the North Carolina apple industry the very sort of protection against competing out-of-state products that the Commerce Clause was designed to prohibit. At worst, it will have the effect of an embargo against those Washington apples in the superior grades as Washington dealers withhold them from the North Carolina market. At best, it will deprive Washington sellers of the market premium that such apples would otherwise command.

Despite the statute's facial neutrality, the Commission suggests that its discriminatory impact on interstate commerce was not an unintended byproduct, and there are some indications in the record to that effect. The most glaring is the response of the North Carolina Agriculture Commissioner to the Commission's request for an exemption following the statute's passage in which he indicated that before he could support such an exemption, he would "want to have the sentiment from our apple producers *since they were mainly responsible for this legislation being passed."* [Moreover], we find it somewhat suspect that North Carolina singled out only closed containers of apples, the very means by which apples are transported in commerce, to effectuate the statute's ostensible consumer protection purpose when apples are not generally sold at retail in their shipping containers. However, we need not ascribe an economic protection motive to the North Carolina Legislature to resolve this case; we conclude that the challenged statute cannot stand insofar as it prohibits the display of Washington State grades even if enacted for the declared purpose of protecting consumers from deception and fraud in the marketplace.

When discrimination against commerce of the type we have found is demonstrated, the burden falls on the State to justify it both in terms of the local benefits flowing from the statute and the unavailability of nondiscriminatory alternatives adequate to preserve the local interests at stake. [Dean Milk.] North Carolina has failed to sustain that burden on both scores. [The] States unquestionably possess a substantial interest in protecting their citizens from confusion and deception in the marketing of foodstuffs, but the challenged statute does remarkably little to further that laudable goal at least with respect to Washington apples and grades. The statute [permits] the marketing of closed containers of apples under *no* grades at all. Such a result can hardly be thought to eliminate the problems of deception and confusion created by the multiplicity of differing state grades; indeed, it magnifies them by depriving purchasers of all information concerning the quality of the contents of closed apple containers. Moreover, although the statute is ostensibly a consumer protection measure, it directs its primary efforts, not at the consuming public at large, but at apple wholesalers and brokers who are the principal purchasers of closed containers of apples. And those individuals are presumably the most knowledgeable individuals in this area. Since the statute does nothing at all to purify the flow of information at the retail level, it does little to protect consumers against the problems it was designed to eliminate. Finally, we note that any potential for confusion and deception created by the Washington grades was not of the type that led to the statute's enactment. Since Washington grades are in all cases equal or superior to their USDA counterparts, they could only "deceive" or "confuse" a consumer to his benefit, hardly a harmful result.

In addition, it appears that nondiscriminatory alternatives to the outright ban of Washington State grades are readily available. For example, North Carolina could effectuate its goal by permitting out-of-state growers to utilize state grades only if they also marked their shipments with the applicable USDA label. In that case, the USDA grade would serve as a benchmark against which the consumer could evaluate the quality of the various state grades. If this alternative was for some reason inadequate to eradicate problems caused by state grades inferior to those adopted by the USDA, North Carolina might consider banning those state grades which, unlike Washington's, could not be demonstrated to be equal or superior to the corresponding USDA categories. Concededly, even in this latter instance, some potential for "confusion" might persist. However, it is the type of "confusion" that the national interest in the free flow of goods between the States demands be tolerated.

[Affirmed.] *

---

* Hunt was an 8 to 0 decision. Justice REHNQUIST did not participate in the case.

THE MEANINGS OF "DISCRIMINATION": FACIAL INVALIDITY, PURPOSE INQUIRIES, AND BALANCING TECHNIQUES

1. *"Discrimination."* All three preceding cases (three cases that are frequently cited by the modern Court) repeatedly invoke the term "discrimination." But, as these cases illustrate, "discrimination" is not a self-defining term. The most wide-ranging consensus about the term is in its application to explicitly protectionist provisions. That is the sense in which Philadelphia v. New Jersey uses the term. The explicit ban on most out-of-state waste in New Jersey's law convinced the majority that the state had resorted to forbidden means—means forbidden by a virtual per se rule banning facial discrimination. As Justice Stewart said: "Whatever New Jersey's ultimate purpose, it may not be accomplished by discriminating against articles of commerce coming from outside the State unless there is some reason, apart from their origin, to treat them differently." New Jersey's law violated this basic "principle of nondiscrimination," both "on its face and in its plain effect." Justice Stewart found only very limited exceptions to the principle that "all laws which facially discriminate against out-of-state commerce are forbidden protectionist regulations": "certain quarantine laws" are permissible, but New Jersey's law was "not such a quarantine law." [1]

But facial discriminations are rare. The regulations in Dean Milk and Hunt were invalidated even though they were *not* facially discriminatory. What laws beyond the explicitly discriminatory warrant the "discrimination" label? One possible view is that the label should be reserved for those situations where a discriminatory *purpose* can be demonstrated. (Purposeful discrimination is often hidden rather than overt, so that proof of a forbidden purpose may include data beyond the face of the law and may rely on inferences from the effects of a state rule.) Another, even broader use of "discrimination" includes within the forbidden category regulations whose "effect" is to favor local interests and disadvantage out-of-state ones. The "effect" and "purpose" concepts are considered in the next two notes.[2]

2. *"Discriminatory effect."* Both Dean Milk and Hunt rested primarily on findings that the fatal flaw of the challenged regulations was their "discriminatory effect." In Dean Milk, the Court did not charge that the Madison ordinance was enacted in bad faith and indeed emphasized that its "avowed purpose" was a legitimate one. Similarly in Hunt, the Court invalidated the law without feeling compelled to "ascribe an economic protection motive to the North Carolina Legislature." When the Court uses the "discrimination" label simply to describe effects rather than to attribute purposes, is it doing anything that could not be done as well, and perhaps more clearly, by balancing legitimate local justifications such as health against the burdens on commerce (with the anti-competitive aspects of the burden playing a role in the analysis)? Note that Dean Milk in its "alternatives" inquiry (which is also invoked in Hunt) really states something of a balancing formula. (See note 4 below.) Note, too, that the Pike "balancing" formulation (p. 245 above) is frequently mentioned in cases which also talk about "discrimination in effect."

1. Note that the "out-of-state commercial interests" burdened by the New Jersey law were not primarily business interests (the out-of-state interests typically involved in the cases in this section), but rather the interests of out-of-state cities seeking to dispose of their waste. Should the commerce clause be read to protect extrastate governmental rather than commercial interests?

2. The problems of the often amorphous invocations of "discrimination" labels are pursued not only in these introductory notes but also in a number of additional contexts in the rest of this section. Note especially the comments on Baldwin v. Seelig, a frequently invoked symbol of the Court's battle against discrimination and protectionism, in the notes at p. 281 below.

Consider more fully the use of "discrimination" in Dean Milk. The majority asserts that "Madison plainly discriminates against interstate commerce," yet immediately adds (in footnote 1) that it is "immaterial" that intrastate milk from outside the Madison area was subject to the same prohibition as that moving in interstate commerce. Should it be relevant that a local regulation burdens some intrastate as well as out-of-state producers? Arguably, the impact on intrastate businesses assures political safeguards against risks of abuse against interstate commerce. Yet there may be the counterargument that at least some burdens on intrastate interests in addition to interstate ones should be considered "immaterial" because otherwise protectionist lawmakers might escape condemnation simply by making some of their rules applicable to some intrastate businesses as well.[3]

3. *"Purpose": Motivational analysis and the identification of forbidden purposes.* Improper "purpose" in the sense of illegitimately motivated or intentional discriminatory action is one of the most common uses of "discrimination" in general usage. Yet none of the preceding cases openly ascribed improper purposes or motivations to the lawmakers whose enactments were invalidated under the commerce clause. In Philadelphia v. New Jersey, the majority found it unnecessary to characterize New Jersey's purpose because of the discriminatory means used by New Jersey. In Dean Milk, the majority did not charge that the Madison ordinance was enacted in bad faith. But Dean Milk did mention that milk production is a "major local industry" in the Madison area and struck down the ordinance because it could not survive the scrutiny appropriate to regulations with a discriminatory effect. And in Hunt, the Court found it unnecessary to ascribe a protectionist motive to the legislature, even though Chief Justice Burger found "some indications in the record" that the "discriminatory impact on interstate commerce was not an unintended byproduct" of the law. (Recall also the speculation about purpose in Justice Powell's opinion in Kassel, p. 255 above. Only Justice Brennan's concurrence there was willing to rest on an express finding of discriminatory purpose: he concluded that Iowa's purpose in enacting the short truck length limit, "being *protectionist* in nature, is *impermissible* under the Commerce Clause.")

What makes the Court so reluctant to ascribe improper purposes and motivations to challenged laws in commerce clause cases? The Court traditionally has been reluctant to do so in cases involving legislation enacted by the coordinate branch, Congress. (Recall the commerce and taxing power cases in chaps. 3 and 4 above, and especially the comments on the O'Brien case, p. 220 above.) But in areas outside that of commerce clause restraints on states (especially in equal protection cases, see chap. 9, sec. 2, below), the Court has been far more ready to find "purposeful discrimination" in cases involving the acts of state and local legislatures than in cases involving Congress. And in some of the cases in the former group, data regarding the effects of the challenged action provide important bases for inferring illegitimate purposes.

---

3. Note also Minnesota v. Barber, 136 U.S. 313 (1890), relied on in Dean Milk. Barber invalidated a Minnesota law forbidding the sale of meat unless there had been an inspection by a local official within 24 hours of the animal's slaughter. The Court held that the law could not be applied to meat from animals slaughtered in Illinois: "[The] enactment of a similar statute by each one of the states [would] result in the destruction of commerce among the several States"; the "obvious and necessary" result of the law was to create discrimination against the products and businesses of other states. Compare Mintz v. Baldwin, 289 U.S. 346 (1933), upholding a New York law prohibiting the importation of cattle unless they were from herds certified as being free from Bang's disease. Should Mintz have been decided differently had the Court known that Bang's disease was "widespread" in New York and that "no steps were being taken to see that the incoming cattle were placed in clean herds"? See Freund, "Review and Federalism," in Supreme Court and Supreme Law (Cahn ed., 1954), 86, 99.

Should the Court be more willing to engage in open purpose and motivation inquiries when state regulations of commerce are challenged? [4]

4. *Judicial inquiry into "reasonable nondiscriminatory alternatives."* Dean Milk is the most frequently cited case for introducing judicial inquiry into "reasonable nondiscriminatory alternatives," at least in "discriminatory effect" cases. But the concept of judicial examination of alternative means of regulation was suggested even earlier,[5] and it has frequently been reiterated since, even in formulations of general balancing standards.[6] Is judicial inquiry into less burdensome alternative methods of regulation appropriate? Feasible? When a "rationality" standard of scrutiny prevails, courts do *not* speculate about alternatives; they sustain the legislative choice if it is *a* reasonable method of promoting the state interest. (See, e.g., the modern economic regulation-due process cases in chap. 8, sec. 1, and recall the congressional choice of means under McCulloch.) Yet the Court has developed a more intensive scrutiny, including consideration of "alternatives," in order to protect commerce clause values. Consider whether that concern with alternatives is criticizable as a frequently haphazard, uninformed judicial intrusion into legislative spheres. (Recall Justice Black's dissent in Dean Milk.) Whatever its merits, inquiry into available alternatives has become a common ingredient in commerce clause cases. The concern with alternatives may be especially understandable in view of the development of commerce clause doctrine: even without explicit reference to available alternatives, balancing inquiries by their nature engage in quite elaborate quasi-legislative evaluations.[7]

---

2. STATE BARRIERS TO INCOMING TRADE: HINDERING ACCESS OF OUT–OF–STATE COMPETITORS TO LOCAL MARKETS

Introduction. One of the most frequent invocations of the commerce clause has been to challenge state regulations that allegedly insulate in-state businesses

4. A more explicit focus by the Court on "purpose" might also aid the Court in articulating more clearly which state policies that hamper interstate commerce are permissible under the commerce clause, and which are not. Given the ambiguous content of "discrimination" labels, the concept furnishes only vague guidance beyond facial discriminations of the Pennsylvania v. New Jersey variety. On the other hand, frequent resort to the balancing technique of the Pike or Southern Pacific varieties can be criticized as being too amorphous, open-ended, ad hoc and subjective. A more systematic effort to identify forbidden state policies thus might clarify the operative principles in the commerce clause area.

In a sense, identification of forbidden policies is implicit in many of the cases, though often inadequately aired. The cases that follow should be scrutinized for the light they may throw on such underlying principles. In reading them, try to identify what the forbidden aims *are:* E.g., protecting in-state economic interests against out-of-state competition? Preferring in-state users over out-of-staters in regulating access to scarce local resources? Demanding that in-state businesses perform certain production operations in the home state, in order to contribute to the state's economic development? Examples of such policies appear in the cases that follow.

5. Recall, e.g., the statement in Southern Pacific (p. 248 above) that the Arizona train length law went beyond "what is plainly essential for safety."

6. Recall the Pike balancing formula (p. 245 above), stating that the permissibility of burdens on commerce turns in part on whether the "local interest [could] be promoted as well with a lesser impact on interstate activities."

7. As with the problems of "discrimination," aspects of "alternative means" analyses resurface in other contexts in later chapters. A decade after Dean Milk, for example, the Court began to apply scrutiny of "alternatives" in cases in which the allegedly burdened constitutional value was not free trade but the First Amendment. See, e.g., the reliance on the Dean Milk approach in the First Amendment context in Shelton v. Tucker (1960; chap. 13 below). Today, inquiry about the existence of less burdensome alternative means has become a common part of the Court's "strict scrutiny" of claimed impingements upon a range of fundamental personal interests—interests not only under the First Amendment but also under the "new equal protection" and "substantive due process" concepts in modern Fourteenth Amendment cases, as the materials in Part III illustrate.

from out-of-state competition.   Hunt, above, illustrates the role of the commerce clause in that context.   But not every state law that hampers out-of-state sellers is invalid.   The difficult task is to determine how much state regulation with an impact on commerce is too much.[1]   With this subsection, we begin an examination of some of the difficulties in the application of the basic themes in the preceding introductory cases.

"HOSTILE" ECONOMIC BARRIERS—AND "CATCHWORDS AND LABELS"

1. *Justice Cardozo's Baldwin v. Seelig opinion.*   As the introductory cases illustrate, Baldwin v. Seelig is one of the most frequently quoted rulings in the modern cases.   It contains one of the Court's strongest and broadest statements against economic isolationism.   In examining the case, consider whether its statement was too broad, in principle or on the facts, and whether its theme can be reconciled with an equally broad statement two years later, in Silas Mason (note 2 below).   BALDWIN v. G.A.F. SEELIG, INC., 294 U.S. 511 (1935), dealt with the impact on interstate trade of a state effort, prompted by the Depression of the 1930s, to stabilize milk prices.   The New York Milk Control Act of 1933 set the minimum prices to be paid to milk producers by New York dealers.   A year before Baldwin, the Court had recognized that the law did not violate due process limits on the state's police power so far as its wholly intrastate impact was concerned.   (Nebbia v. New York, p. 462 below.)   But Baldwin held that the commerce clause barred the application of the law to out-of-state milk producers.   Seelig, a New York milk dealer, bought milk in Vermont at prices lower than the New York minimum.   The law prohibited New York sales of out-of-state milk if the milk had been purchased below the price for similar purchases within New York.   The State refused to license Seelig to sell milk in New York unless there was an agreement to conform to the state's price regulation regarding the sale of imported milk.   The Court unanimously held unconstitutional that application of the law.

Justice CARDOZO stated that New York's regulation "set a barrier to traffic between one state and another as effective as if customs duties, equal to the price differential, had been laid upon the [goods].   Nice distinctions have been made at times between direct and indirect burdens.   They are irrelevant when the avowed purpose of the obstruction, as well as its necessary tendency, is to suppress or mitigate the consequences of competition between the states.   Such an obstruction is direct by the very terms of the hypothesis.   We are reminded in the opinion below that a chief occasion of the commerce clause was 'the mutual jealousies and aggressions of the States, taking form in customs barriers and other economic retaliation.'   [If] New York, in order to promote the economic welfare of her farmers, may guard them against competition with the cheaper prices of Vermont, the door has been opened to rivalries and reprisals that were meant to be averted by subjecting commerce between the states to the power of the nation."

The Court rejected the argument that the Act was justified by the state's aim to assure "a regular and adequate supply of pure and wholesome milk."   Supply is jeopardized, New York claimed, when farmers cannot earn a living income: "the economic motive is secondary and subordinate;   the state intervenes to

---

1.   See Powell, Vagaries and Varieties in Constitutional Interpretation (1956), 178, recalling that, "after my students had searched in vain for a formula, I suggested that one might safely say that the states may regulate commerce some, but not too much."   That was a variant of an earlier quip by Professor Thomas Reed Powell in his mock Restatement of Constitutional Law, stating in effect that Congress may regulate commerce, that the states may also regulate commerce but not too much, and that how much was too much was beyond the scope of his Restatement.

make its inhabitants healthy, and not to make them rich." Justice Cardozo replied that this argument could not justify the Act as a valid "police" measure with only "incidental" impact on commerce: "This would be to eat up the rule under the guise of an exception. Economic welfare is always related to health. Let such an exception be admitted, and all that a state will have to do in times of stress and strain is to say that its farmers and merchants and workmen must be protected against competition from without, lest they go upon the poor relief lists or perish altogether. To give entrance to that excuse would be to invite a speedy end of our national solidarity. The Constitution was framed under the dominion of a political philosophy less parochial in range. It was framed upon the theory that the peoples of the several states must sink or swim together, and that in the long run prosperity and salvation are in union and not division. [The] line of division between direct and indirect restraints of commerce involves in its marking a reference to considerations of degree. Even so, the borderland is wide between the restraints upheld as incidental and those attempted here. Subject to the paramount power of the Congress, a state may [e.g.] regulate the importation of unhealthy swine or cattle [e.g., Mintz v. Baldwin] or decayed or noxious foods. [It] may give protection to travelers against the dangers of overcrowded highways. [None] of these statutes—inspection laws, game laws, laws intended to curb fraud or exterminate disease—approaches in drastic quality the statute here in controversy which would neutralize the economic consequences of free trade among the states." Justice Cardozo added: "What is ultimate is the principle that one state in its dealings with another may not place itself in a position of economic isolation. Formulas and catchwords are subordinate to this overmastering requirement. [The] police power [may] not be used by the state of destination with the aim and effect of establishing an economic barrier against competition with the products of another [state]. Restrictions so contrived are an unreasonable clog on the mobility of commerce. They set up what is the equivalent of a rampart of customs duties designed to neutralize advantages belonging to the place of origin. They are thus hostile in conception as well as burdensome in result." [2]

2. *Justice Cardozo's Silas Mason opinion.* Compare, with Justice Cardozo's broad-gauged condemnation of New York's economic barrier in Baldwin v. Seelig, his rejection of a similar attack, on a tax barrier, in HENNEFORD v. SILAS MASON CO., 300 U.S. 577 (1937). That decision upheld a Washington use tax on goods bought in other states. Washington law placed a 2% tax on retail sales within Washington; another section imposed a "compensating tax" on the price of goods (including transportation costs) for the "privilege of using" in Washington goods bought at retail out of the state. (The use tax was inapplicable to any article which had already been subjected to a sales or use tax of at least 2%; for articles previously taxed at less than 2% there was a prorated exemption from the use tax.) The point of that scheme was clear to the Court: as Justice CARDOZO put it in his opinion for a unanimous Court, local retail sellers "will be helped to compete upon terms of equality with retail dealers in other states who are exempt from a sales tax"; local buyers will "no longer [be] tempted to place their orders in other states" to escape the local sales tax.

Nevertheless, this was not a forbidden economic barrier to Justice Cardozo: "Equality is the theme that runs through all sections of the statute. [When] the

2. Justice Cardozo also rejected the argument that the economic security for farmers sought by the law was justified not only as a means of assuring to consumers a steady supply of a basic food but also as a way to assure high quality dairy products (because underpaid farmers would be "tempted to save the expense of sanitary precautions"). In disposing of that asserted health objective, Justice Cardozo stated that the "evils springing from uncared for cattle must be remedied by measures of repression more direct and certain than the creation of a parity of prices between New York and other states. [Whatever] relation there may be between earnings and sanitation is too remote and indirect to justify obstructions to the normal flow of commerce. [One] state may not put pressure of that sort upon others to reform their economic standards."

account is made up, the stranger from afar is subject to no greater burdens as a consequence of ownership than the dweller within the gates. [In] each situation the burden borne by the owner is balanced by an equal burden where the sale is strictly local." Nor were the reasons for the use tax fatal. The challengers attacked it as "equivalent to a protective tariff." Justice Cardozo was not impressed: "[M]otives alone will seldom, if ever, invalidate a tax that apart from its motives would be recognized as [lawful]. Least of all will they be permitted to accomplish that result when equality and not preference is the end to be achieved. Catch words and labels, such as the words 'protective tariff,' are subject to the dangers that lurk in metaphors and symbols, and must be watched with circumspection lest they put us off our guard. [A] tax upon use [unlike a tariff] is not a clog on the process of importation at all." Justice Cardozo insisted, moreover, that Baldwin v. Seelig was distinguishable. That case, he stated "is far apart from this one. [New York] was attempting to project its legislation within the borders of another state by regulating the price to be paid in that state for milk acquired there. She said in effect to farmers in Vermont: your milk cannot be sold by dealers to whom you ship it in New York unless you sell it to them in Vermont at a price determined here. What Washington is saying to sellers beyond her borders is something very different. In substance what she says is this: You may ship your goods in such amounts and at such prices as you please, but the goods when used in Washington after the transit is completed, will share an equal burden with goods that have been purchased here."

3. *An adequate difference between Baldwin's "hostile" economic barrier and Silas Mason's benign "equalization"?* Are Baldwin and Silas Mason truly reconcilable, as Justice Cardozo claimed? His characterization of the Baldwin law as a "hostile" "customs barrier" may have been unduly harsh, while his characterization of the Silas Mason tax as an "equality measure" may have been unduly benign. Arguably, he too was "put off guard" by the "catchwords" he warned against in both cases. But the cases may be more reconcilable in result than in reasoning. Both cases involved some "extraterritorial" impacts of the state laws: in Baldwin, the New York distributor subject to New York's law was to be discouraged from buying from Vermont farmers; similarly, the Washington tax discouraged buying from out-of-state sellers. A more persuasive distinction may lie in the fact that Washington's use tax cancelled *only one* advantage the out-of-state seller had (because he was not subject to a sales tax) while New York's scheme cancelled *all* the advantages the Vermont producer had because of lower costs of production—taxes as well as all other costs. Washington's plan, in short, still permitted some price competition; New York's did not. But is the free trade ideal so eloquently described by Justice Cardozo in Baldwin adequately achieved by a finding that at least *some* price competition remains in the consumer market? Arguably, the Court would have been clearer if it had identified as truly forbidden a state purpose of eliminating *all* price competition, or if it had resorted to an avowed balancing analysis. In any event, the distinction between the cases may be narrower than Justice Cardozo's broad "hostile" "customs barrier" and "equality" characterizations suggest.

ADDITIONAL CASES ON BARRIERS TO INCOMING TRADE

1. As Hunt (p. 272 above) illustrates, the modern Court remains vigilant against economic protectionism. In doing so, it often draws on the theme of Baldwin v. Seelig and the approach of Dean Milk. But, as the following sampling of cases illustrates, that type of challenge is by no means universally successful. Indeed, the survival of the Dean Milk analysis was put in temporary doubt only a few months after Dean Milk, in BREARD v. ALEXANDRIA, 341

U.S. 622 (1951). There, the majority sustained the application of a "Green River type of ordinance" [1]—an Alexandria, La., ordinance prohibiting door-to-door solicitation of orders to sell goods except by consent of the occupants. Breard, a Texan, led a crew of salespersons who solicited subscriptions for national magazines on behalf of a Pennsylvania corporation. Justice REED's majority opinion rejected all constitutional objections to the ordinance—under the First Amendment as well as under the commerce clause.[2] He rejected Breard's claim that the "practical operation of the ordinance" imposed "an undue and discriminatory burden" on commerce. Breard argued that Dean Milk demonstrated that "this Court will not permit local interests to protect themselves against out-of-state competition by curtailing interstate business." But Justice Reed was not persuaded: "It was partly because the regulation [in Dean Milk] discriminated against interstate commerce that it was struck down. [Nor] does the clause as to alternatives [in Dean Milk] apply to the Alexandria ordinance. Interstate commerce itself knocks on the local door. It is only by regulating that knock that the interests of the home may be protected by public as distinct from private action." [3]

Despite Breard (which may have rested on the unusually strong local interest in protecting the privacy and repose of residents), Dean Milk has retained considerable vitality. For example, a unanimous Court relied on its principles in striking down a Mississippi milk regulation in A. & P. TEA CO., INC. v. COTTRELL, 424 U.S. 366 (1976). The state regulation provided that milk from another state could be sold in Mississippi only if the other state accepted Mississippi milk on a reciprocal basis. A. & P. challenged that regulation after it was refused a permit to sell milk in its Mississippi stores that was processed in its Louisiana plant. Even though A. & P.'s Louisiana milk satisfied Mississippi's quality criteria, it could not obtain the permit because Louisiana had not signed a reciprocity agreement with Mississippi. Justice BRENNAN relied on the balancing standard of Pike (p. 245 above) and rejected the lower court's effort to distinguish Dean Milk. In his view, the lower court had given inadequate weight to "the interference effected by the [reciprocity clause] upon the national interest in freedom for the national commerce" and had attached too much weight to the state interests served. He noted that, although the Mississippi requirement was not as "absolute and universal" a bar as that in Dean Milk, "the practical effect" was similar.

2. Another effort to rely on Dean Milk, and on Hunt as well, failed in EXXON CORP. v. GOVERNOR OF MARYLAND, 437 U.S. 117 (1978). That 7 to 1 decision sustained a law prohibiting producers or refiners of petroleum products from operating retail service stations in Maryland. (No gasoline is produced or refined in the state.) Maryland acted in response to evidence that stations operated by producers and refiners (about 5% of Maryland's service stations) had received preferential treatment during the 1973 petroleum shortage. The challengers claimed that the law discriminated against and imposed an undue burden on interstate commerce. Justice STEVENS' majority opinion rejected both claims.

---

1. The Green River type of ordinance derives its label from the town of Green River, Wyo., which, as the Court explained, "undertook in 1931 to remedy by ordinance the irritating incidents of house-to-house canvassing for sales."

2. The First Amendment objections to bans on solicitors are examined in later chapters.

3. Chief Justice VINSON's dissent, joined by Justice Douglas, insisted that the Dean Milk principles *were* applicable: "Lack of discrimination on its face has not heretofore been regarded as sufficient to sustain an ordinance without inquiry into its practical effects upon interstate commerce. E.g., [Dean Milk; Minnesota v. Barber]. [I] think it plain that a 'blanket prohibition' upon appellant's solicitation discriminates against and unduly burdens interstate commerce in favoring local retail merchants. 'Whether or not it was so intended, those are its necessary effects.'" (In another dissent, Justices Black and Douglas objected to the ordinance on First Amendment grounds.)

On the former claim, Justice Stevens stated: "Plainly, the [law] does not discriminate against interstate goods, nor does it favor local producers and refiners. Since Maryland's entire gasoline supply flows in interstate commerce and since there are no local producers or refiners, such claims of disparate treatment between interstate and local commerce would be meritless. Appellants, however, focus on the retail market, arguing that the effect of the statute is to protect in-state independent dealers from out-of-state competition. [They] rely on the fact that [the] divestiture requirements [fall] solely on interstate companies. But this fact does not lead, either logically or as a practical matter, to a conclusion that the State is discriminating against interstate commerce at the retail level. [There] are several major interstate marketers of petroleum that own and operate their own retail gasoline stations. [E.g., Sears, Roebuck.] These interstate dealers, who compete directly with the Maryland independent dealers, are not affected by the Act because they do not refine or produce gasoline. In fact, the Act creates no barriers whatsoever against interstate independent dealers; it does not prohibit the flow of interstate goods, place added costs upon them, or distinguish between in-state and out-of-state companies in the retail market. The absence of any of these factors fully distinguishes this case from those in which a State has been found to have discriminated against interstate commerce. See, e.g., [Hunt; Dean Milk]. For instance, the Court in Hunt noted that the challenged state statute raised the cost of doing business for out-of-state dealers, and, in various other ways, favored the in-state dealer in the local market. No comparable claim can be made here. While the refiners will no longer enjoy their same status in the Maryland market, in-state independent dealers will have no competitive advantage over out-of-state dealers. The fact that the burden of a state regulation falls on some interstate companies does not, by itself, establish a claim of discrimination against interstate commerce." [4]

Turning to the claim that the law "impermissibly *burdens* interstate commerce," Justice Stevens found it no more persuasive, even though some refiners might be driven from the Maryland market: "[Even if that happens], there is no reason to assume that their share of the entire supply will not be promptly replaced by other interstate refiners. The source of the consumers' supply may switch from company-operated stations to independent dealers, but interstate commerce is not subjected to an impermissible burden simply because an otherwise valid regulation causes some business to shift from one interstate supplier to another." The challengers also claimed that the law interfered with "the natural functioning of the interstate market" and would "surely change the market structure by weakening the independent refiners." [5] Justice Stevens

4. "If the effect of a state regulation is to cause local goods to constitute a larger share, and goods with an out-of-state source to constitute a smaller share, of the total sales in the market—as in Hunt and Dean Milk—the regulation may have a discriminatory effect on interstate commerce. But the Maryland statute has no impact on the relative proportions of local and out-of-state goods sold in Maryland and, indeed, no demonstrable effect whatsoever on the interstate flow of goods. The sales by independent retailers are just as much a part of the flow of [commerce] as the sales made by the refiner-operated stations." [Footnote by Justice Stevens.]

5. For an earlier rejection of a challenge resting largely on the impact of a state law in changing the market structure of an industry, see the upholding of the Oregon Bottle Law in

American Can Co. v. Oregon Liquor Control Commission, 15 Or.App. 618, 517 P.2d 691 (1973). The 1971 Oregon law in effect sought to ban the use of nonreturnable bottles and to substitute, by using a refund system, the use of returnable containers. The out-of-state challengers claimed that "non-returnable containers are essential to the existence of national and regional [beverage] markets." An Oregon appellate court rejected that claim, claiming that the only commerce clause restraint on state laws outside the transportation area was "protectionist state action" that "discriminates against interstate commerce." Was that an accurate statement of the proper standard? Compare Note, "State Environmental Protection Legislation and the Commerce Clause," 87 Harv.L.Rev. 1762 (1974), arguing that the state court erred in failing to apply a balancing analysis, but concluding that the law

replied: "We [cannot] accept appellants' underlying notion that the Commerce Clause protects the particular structure or methods of operation in a retail market. See [Breard]. [The] Clause protects the interstate market, not particular interstate firms, from prohibitive or burdensome regulations. It may be true that the consuming public will be injured by the loss of the high-volume, low-priced stations operated by the independent refiners, but again that argument relates to the wisdom of the statute, not to its burden on commerce." [6]

Justice BLACKMUN was the sole dissenter. (Justice Powell did not participate.) The dissent insisted that the Maryland law was discriminatory in effect and that the majority's distinction of Hunt and Dean Milk was unpersuasive. Consider whether Justice Blackmun's argument was plausible. He claimed that the state scheme constituted "impermissible discrimination against interstate commerce in *retail* gasoline marketing," noting that the effect of the divestiture provision was "to protect in-state retail service station dealers from the competition of the out-of-state businesses." [7] Given that discriminatory impact, "the burden falls upon the State to justify the distinction with legitimate state interests that cannot be vindicated with more evenhanded regulation." Here, Maryland had failed to carry this burden. Maryland's "laudable goal [cannot] be accepted without further analysis, just as the Court could not accept the mere assertion of a public health justification in Dean Milk. Here 'the State ignores the second half of its responsibility'; it does not even attempt to demonstrate why competition cannot be preserved without banning the out-of-state interests from the retail market." [8]

Justice Blackmun was unpersuaded by the claim that this case was distinguishable from Hunt in view of the absence of discrimination against nonintegrated, out-of-state retailers: "The Court did not strike down the provision [in Hunt] because it discriminated against the marketing techniques of *all* out-of-state growers. The provision imposed no discrimination on growers from States that employed only the [USDA] grading system. Despite this lack of universal discrimination, the Court [invalidated the law] because it discriminated against a single segment of out-of-state marketers of apples. [In] this regard, the [Maryland law is] identical to, not distinguishable from, the North Carolina statute in Hunt. Here, the discrimination has been imposed against a segment of the out-of-state retailers of gasoline, namely, those who also refine or produce petroleum. [To] accept [the majority's argument that] discrimination must be universal to offend the Commerce Clause naively will foster protectionist discrimination against interstate commerce. In the future, states will be able to insulate in-state interests from competition by identifying the most potent segments of out-of-state business, banning them, and permitting less effective out-of-state actors to remain. [It] is true that merely demonstrating a burden on some out-of-state actors does not prove unconstitutional discrimination. But

probably should have survived balancing scrutiny. See also the Clover Leaf Creamery case, which follows, and recall the invalidation of another environmental law in Philadelphia v. New Jersey, p. 266 above.

6. Justice Stevens also rejected the suggestion that "because the economic market for petroleum products is nationwide, no State has the power to regulate the retail marketing of gas." He replied that the Court had only rarely held that the commerce clause "itself pre-empts an entire field from state regulation, and then only when a lack of national uniformity would impede the flow of interstate goods. [E.g., Cooley.]" Here, the real fear was not of differing state regulations, but rather that other states would also adopt divesti-

ture provisions. That problem was "not one of national uniformity."

7. Justice Blackmun noted that, of the stations insulated from out-of-state competition, more than 99% were operated by local business interests, and that of the businesses wholly excluded from participating in the state's retail gasoline market, "95% were out-of-state firms, operating 98% of the stations in the class."

8. For example, Maryland could control unfair pricing or allocation practices through less discriminatory legislation by controlling the evils stemming from short-term leases through controls of "the leasing of all service stations, not just those owned by the out-of-state integrated producers and refiners."

when the burden is significant, when it falls on the most numerous and effective group of out-of-state competitors, when a similar burden does not fall on the class of protected in-state businessmen, and when the State cannot justify the resulting disparity by showing that its legislative interests cannot be vindicated by more evenhanded regulation, unconstitutional discrimination exists." [9]

3. *The current state of the law.* The preceding modern cases, together with the principal case that follows, reflect the Court's current grapplings with commerce clause challenges to state laws barring out-of-state competitors from local markets. Consider the adequacy of the analyses reflected in the modern decisions. Do they coherently and consistently apply the lessons of the introductory cases (Philadelphia v. New Jersey, Dean Milk, and Hunt) as well as the Pike formula quoted at p. 245 above? Have the concepts of "discrimination" been adequately clarified, and have they proved useful? Has the Court adequately identified which state preferential policies warrant condemnation under the commerce clause? Note that in the final principal case, which follows, the Court examines both a "discrimination" claim and the application of the Pike formula. That variety of dual examination has surfaced repeatedly in modern cases. Consider whether a merger of discrimination and balancing analyses might be preferable; and consider too whether discrimination analyses should be merged *into* balancing standards, as one factor in appropriate balancing. Consider, moreover, whether such a merger would encourage or inhibit clearer identifications of impermissible state policies under the commerce clause.

MINNESOTA v. CLOVER LEAF CREAMERY CO.

449 U.S. 456, 101 S.Ct. 715, 66 L.Ed.2d 659 (1981).

Justice BRENNAN delivered the opinion of the Court.

In 1977, the Minnesota Legislature enacted a statute banning the retail sale of milk in plastic nonreturnable, nonrefillable containers, but permitting such sale in other nonreturnable, nonrefillable containers, such as paperboard milk cartons. Respondents contend that the statute violates the Equal Protection and Commerce Clauses of the Constitution.

I.   The purpose of the Minnesota statute is set out as § 1: "The legislature finds that the use of nonreturnable, nonrefillable containers for the packaging of milk and other milk products presents a solid waste management problem for the state, promotes energy waste, and depletes natural resources. The legislature therefore [determines] that the use of nonreturnable, nonrefillable containers for packaging milk and other milk products should be discouraged and that the use of returnable and reusable packaging for these products is preferred and should be encouraged." Section 2 of the Act forbids the retail sale of milk and fluid milk products, other than sour cream, cottage cheese, and yogurt, in nonreturnable, nonrefillable rigid or semirigid containers composed at least 50% of plastic. [The state trial court held the law unconstitutional. The federal grounds it relied on were based on the due process and equal protection clauses of the Fourteenth Amendment as well as the commerce clause. After

---

9. The state court in Exxon had attempted to distinguish Dean Milk on the ground that "the wholesale flow of petroleum products into the State was not restricted." In rejecting that contention, Justice Blackmun reemphasized that the discrimination here "exists with regard to retailing. The fact that gasoline will continue to flow into the State does not permit the State to deny out-of-state firms the opportunity to retail it once it arrives." He insisted that the burden on the flow of out-of-state products had been no greater in Dean Milk than here and concluded by accusing the majority of failing to heed Justice Cardozo's admonition in Baldwin v. Seelig that "the peoples of the several states must sink or swim together." (Recall that the same Baldwin passage was cited by the *majority* just a few weeks later, in invalidating a state ban on out-of-state waste in Philadelphia v. New Jersey, p. 266 above.)

holding extensive evidentiary hearings, the court concluded that the law "will not succeed in effecting the Legislature's published policy goals" and that, contrary to the statement of purpose in § 1, the "actual basis" for the Act "was to promote the economic interests of certain segments of the local dairy and pulpwood industries at the expense of the economic interests of other segments of the dairy industry and the plastics industry." The Supreme Court of Minnesota affirmed the lower court on the federal equal protection and due process grounds without reaching the commerce clause issue. The highest state court found that the purpose of the act "was to promote the state interests of encouraging the reuse and recycling of materials and reducing the amount and type of material entering the solid waste stream," but concluded that the "evidence conclusively demonstrates that the discrimination against plastic nonrefillables is not rationally related to the Act's objectives." The Court reversed.]

II. [Justice Brennan first considered the equal protection challenge. He found the "rational basis" test applicable and concluded that the legislative distinction between plastic and nonplastic nonreturnable milk containers was "rationally related to achievement of the statutory purposes." That aspect of the case is considered further in chap. 9, sec. 1, at p. 606 below.]

III. The [state] District Court also held that the Minnesota statute is unconstitutional under the Commerce Clause because it imposes an unreasonable burden on interstate commerce.[1] [When] legislating in areas of legitimate local concern, such as environmental protection and resource conservation, States are nonetheless limited by the Commerce Clause. See [e.g., Hunt; Southern Pacific]. If a state law purporting to promote environmental purposes is in reality "simple economic protectionism," we have applied a "virtually per se rule of invalidity." Philadelphia v. New Jersey.[2] Even if a statute regulates "evenhandedly," and imposes only "incidental" burdens on interstate com-

---

1. The Minnesota Supreme Court did not reach the Commerce Clause issue. The parties and amici have fully briefed and argued the question, and because of the obvious factual connection between the rationality analysis under the Equal Protection Clause and the balancing of interests under the Commerce Clause, we will reach and decide the question. [Footnote by Justice Brennan.]

2. A court may find that a state law constitutes "economic protectionism" on proof either of discriminatory effect, see Philadelphia v. New Jersey, or of discriminatory purpose, see [Hunt]. Respondents advance a "discriminatory purpose" argument, relying on a finding by the District Court that the Act's "actual basis was to promote the economic interests of certain segments of the local dairy and pulpwood industries at the expense of the economic interests of other segments of the dairy industry and the plastics industry." We have already considered and rejected this argument in the equal protection context and do so in this context as well. [Footnote by Justice Brennan. Are Justice Brennan's characterizations of Philadelphia v. New Jersey and Hunt persuasive? Did the former case truly turn on "discriminatory effect"? Did the latter case truly turn on "discriminatory purpose"?]

[Justice Brennan's disposition of the "discriminatory purpose" argument rested simply on a reference to its rejection in the equal protection context, as the last sentence in his footnote shows. His only discussion in the equal protection context came in an earlier footnote. That footnote stated: "Respondents, citing the District Court's Finding of Fact, [also] assert that the actual purpose for the Act was illegitimate: to 'isolate from interstate competition the interests of certain segments of the local dairy and pulpwood industries.' We accept the contrary holding of the Minnesota Supreme Court that the articulated purpose of the Act is its actual purpose. In equal protection analysis, this Court will assume that the objectives articulated by the legislature are actual purposes of the statute, unless an examination of the circumstances forces us to conclude that they 'could not have been a goal of the legislation.' Here, a review of the legislative history supports the Minnesota Supreme Court's conclusion that the principal purposes of the Act were to promote conservation and ease solid waste disposal problems. The contrary evidence cited by respondents [is] easily understood, in context, as economic defense of an Act genuinely proposed for environmental reasons. We will not invalidate a state statute under the Equal Protection Clause merely because some legislators sought to obtain votes for the measure on the basis of its beneficial side effects on state industry." Compare this reliance on equal protection standards of scrutiny in a commerce clause context with Justice Powell's comment in footnote 1 of his partial dissent, below.]

merce, the courts must nevertheless strike it down if "the burden imposed on such commerce is clearly excessive in relation to the putative local benefits." [Pike]. Moreover, "the extent of the burden that will be tolerated will of course depend on the nature of the local interest involved, and on whether it could be promoted as well with a lesser impact on interstate activities." Ibid.

Minnesota's statute does not effect "simple protectionism," but "regulates evenhandedly" by prohibiting all milk retailers from selling their products in plastic, nonreturnable milk containers, without regard to whether the milk, the containers, or the sellers are from outside the State. This statute is therefore unlike statutes discriminating against interstate commerce, which we have consistently struck down. [E.g., Hunt.] Since the statute does not discriminate between interstate and intrastate commerce, the controlling question is whether the incidental burden imposed on interstate commerce by the Minnesota Act is "clearly excessive in relation to the putative local benefits." [Pike]. We conclude that it is not. The burden imposed on interstate commerce by the statute is relatively minor. Milk products may continue to move freely across the Minnesota border, and since most dairies package their products in more than one type of containers, the inconvenience of having to conform to different packaging requirements in Minnesota and the surrounding States should be slight. Within Minnesota, business will presumably shift from manufacturers of plastic nonreturnable containers to producers of paperboard cartons, refillable bottles, and plastic pouches, but there is no reason to suspect that the gainers will be Minnesota firms, or the losers out-of-state firms. Indeed, two of the three dairies, the sole milk retailer, and the sole milk container producer challenging the statute in this litigation are Minnesota firms.[3]

Pulpwood producers are the only Minnesota industry likely to benefit significantly from the Act at the expense of out-of-state firms. Respondents point out that plastic resin, the raw material used for making plastic nonreturnable milk jugs, is produced entirely by non-Minnesota firms, while pulpwood, used for making paperboard, is a major Minnesota product. Nevertheless, it is clear that respondents exaggerate the degree of burden on out-of-state interests, both because plastics will continue to be used in the production of plastic pouches, plastic returnable bottles, and paperboard itself, and because out-of-state pulpwood producers will presumably absorb some of the business generated by the Act.

Even granting that the out-of-state plastics industry is burdened relatively more heavily than the Minnesota pulpwood industry, we find that this burden is not "clearly excessive" in light of the substantial state interest in promoting conservation of energy and other natural resources and easing solid waste disposal problems, which we have already reviewed in the context of equal protection analysis. We find these local benefits ample to support Minnesota's decision under the Commerce Clause. Moreover, we find that no approach with "a lesser impact on interstate activities" [Pike] is available. Respondents have suggested several alternative statutory schemes, but these alternatives are either more burdensome on commerce than the Act (as, for example, banning all nonreturnables) or less likely to be effective (as, for example, providing incentives for recycling).

In [Exxon], we upheld a Maryland statute barring producers and refiners of petroleum products—all of which were out-of-state businesses—from retailing

---

3. [The] existence of major in-state interests adversely affected by the Act is a powerful safeguard against legislative abuse. [Barnwell.] [Footnote by Justice Brennan.] [The challengers included not merely in-state interests, but also a non-Minnesota company that manufactured equipment for producing plastic nonreturnable milk jugs, a non-Minnesota dairy that sold milk products in Minnesota in plastic nonreturnable milk jugs, a non-Minnesota manufacturer of polyethyline resin that sold such resin in many states, including Minnesota, and a plastics industry trade association.]

gasoline in the State. We stressed that the Commerce Clause "protects the interstate market, not particular interstate firms, from prohibitive or burdensome regulations." A nondiscriminatory regulation serving substantial state purposes is not invalid simply because it causes some business to shift from a predominantly out-of-state industry to a predominantly in-state industry. Only if the burden on interstate commerce clearly outweighs the State's legitimate purposes does such a regulation violate the Commerce Clause.

[Reversed.] [4]

Justice POWELL, concurring in part and dissenting in part.

[Justice Powell agreed that the law survived the equal protection challenge, but argued that the commerce clause issue should not be reached and should instead be remanded for consideration by the Supreme Court of Minnesota. After quoting the trial court's findings about the statute's actual discriminatory purpose, he proceeded:] These findings were highly relevant to the question whether the statute discriminated against interstate commerce. See Philadelphia v. New Jersey. [Indeed], the trial court's findings normally would require us to conclude that the Minnesota Legislature was engaging [in] discrimination, as they were not rejected by the Minnesota Supreme Court. That court simply invalidated the statute on equal protection grounds, and had no reason to consider the claim of discrimination against interstate commerce. The Minnesota Supreme Court did accept the *avowed* legislative purpose of the statute. [The] Court today reads [this] as an implied rejection of the trial court's specific [discrimination] finding. [In] my view, however, the Minnesota Supreme Court was merely assuming that the statute was intended to promote its stated purposes. It was entirely appropriate for that court to accept, for purposes of equal protection analysis, the purpose expressed in the statute. When the court did so, however, there is no reason to conclude that it intended to express or imply any view on any issue it did not consider. In drawing its conclusions, the court included no discussion whatever of the Commerce Clause issue and, certainly, no rejection of the trial court's express and repeated findings concerning the legislature's actual purpose.[1]

I conclude therefore that this Court has no basis for *inferring* a rejection of the quite specific factfindings by the trial court. The Court's [commerce clause] decision today [is] flatly contrary to the only relevant specific findings of fact. Although we are not *barred* from reaching the Commerce Clause issue, in doing so we also act without the benefit of a decision by the highest court of Minnesota on the question. In these circumstances, it is both unnecessary, and in my opinion inappropriate, for this Court to decide the Commerce Clause issue. [I] would remand the case with instructions to consider specifically whether the statute discriminated impermissibly against interstate commerce.[2]

---

4. Justice REHNQUIST did not participate in the case.

1. Commerce Clause analysis differs from analysis under the "rational basis" test. Under the Commerce Clause, a court is empowered to disregard a legislature's statement of purpose if it considers it a pretext. See [Dean Milk] ("A different view, that the ordinance is valid simply because it professes to be a health measure, would mean that the Commerce Clause of itself imposes no limitations on state action other than those laid down by the Due Process Clause, save for the rare instance where a state artlessly discloses an avowed purpose to discriminate against interstate goods"). [Footnote by Justice Powell.]

2. A dissent by Justice STEVENS rested primarily on an unusual argument that federal review of the case should have been confined to a determination of whether the state courts had articulated the proper federal equal protection standard (which, in his view, they had). He contended that regulation of the relationship between the state courts and the state legislature was beyond federal judicial authority: in his view, the Court lacked power to assert that "it is not the function of a *state court* to substitute its evaluation of legislative facts for that of a state legislature." But Justice Stevens also agreed with Justice Powell that the majority should not have reached the commerce clause issue. More-

3. LIMITING ACCESS OF OUT–OF–STATERS TO LOCAL PRODUCTS AND RESOURCES

Introduction. In the preceding section, state restrictions were attacked as efforts to hamper out-of-state *sellers* from reaching the local market. The cases in this subsection involve state barriers hampering foreign *buyers* seeking access to local products and resources. In the cases below the challenged state is typically charged with engaging in hoarding. As before, the state laws are attacked as discriminatory or protectionist or unduly burdensome; as before, the attackers typically claim that the state is pursuing impermissible "economic" purposes. The most continuously litigated areas here are state efforts to give preferential access to local interests in the use of a state's natural resources. The pervasive question is the extent to which a state may impose embargoes or other restraints on outgoing trade.

H.P. HOOD & SONS v. Du MOND

336 U.S. 525, 69 S.Ct. 657, 93 L.Ed. 865 (1949).

Mr. Justice JACKSON delivered the opinion of the Court.

[Hood was a Boston milk distributor. The Boston area obtained 90% of its milk supply from outside of Massachusetts. Hood had long obtained milk from New York producers and had maintained three receiving depots there. Hood sought a New York license to establish a fourth depot, a few miles away from two of its existing depots. The N.Y. Commissioner of Agriculture and Markets denied a license for the depot on the basis of a state law stating that licenses for new plants could not be issued unless the Commissioner was satisfied that "issuance of the license will not tend to a destructive competition in a market already adequately served, and that the issuance of the license is in the public interest." The state courts rejected Hood's commerce clause challenge to the license denial.]

This case concerns the power of [New York] to deny additional facilities to acquire and ship milk in interstate commerce where the grounds of denial are that such limitation upon interstate business will protect and advance local economic interests. The Commissioner found that Hood, if licensed at Greenwich, would permit its present suppliers, at their option, to deliver at the new plant rather than the old ones and for a substantial number this would mean shorter hauls and savings in delivery costs. The new plant also would attract twenty to thirty producers, some of whose milk Hood anticipates will or may be diverted from other buyers. Other large milk distributors have plants within the general area and dealers serving Troy obtain milk in the locality. He found that Troy was inadequately supplied during the preceding short season.

[The] present controversy begins where the Eisenberg decision [1] left off. New York's regulations, designed to assure producers a fair price and a

over, for reasons related to the major basis of his dissent, he urged that the Court should have respected the highest state court's fact findings. He argued that the Minnesota Supreme Court's equal protection conclusion, that the law was not rationally related to legitimate state interests, undercut the majority's commerce clause premise that the law promoted ample "local benefits."

   1. Milk Control Board v. Eisenberg Farm Products Co., 306 U.S. 346 (1939), sustained the application of a Pennsylvania minimum price regulation to a New York milk dealer who bought milk from Pennsylvania producers for shipment out of state. The Company operated a milk receiving plant in Pennsylvania where the milk it bought from Pennsylvania farmers was cooled for less than 24 hours; then all of it was shipped to New York. Pennsylvania law set the minimum price to be paid by dealers to milk producers and required dealers to obtain a license. Claiming that the Pennsylvania Milk Control Act of 1935 was similar to the New York law involved in Baldwin v. Seelig (p. 279 above), Eisenberg argued that application of the

responsible purchaser, and consumers a sanitary and modernly equipped handler, are not challenged here but have been complied with. It is only additional restrictions, imposed for the avowed purpose and with the practical effect of curtailing the volume of interstate commerce to aid local economic interests, that are in question here, and no such measures were attempted or such ends sought to be served in the Act before the Court in the Eisenberg case. Our decision in a milk litigation most relevant to the present controversy deals with the converse of the present situation. [Justice Jackson quoted from Baldwin v. Seelig.]

This distinction between the power of the State to shelter its people from menaces to their health or safety and from fraud, even when those dangers emanate from interstate commerce, and its lack of power to retard, burden or constrict the flow of such commerce for their economic advantage, is one deeply rooted in both our history and our law. [Justice Jackson's statements on commerce clause history and interpretation are quoted at the beginning of this chapter.] [Baldwin v. Seelig] is an explicit, impressive, recent and unanimous condemnation by this Court of economic restraints on interstate commerce for local economic advantage, but it does not stand alone. This Court consistently has rebuffed attempts of states to advance their own commercial interests by curtailing the movement of articles of commerce, either into or out of the state, while generally supporting their right to impose even burdensome regulations in the interest of local health and safety. As most states serve their own interests best by sending their produce to market, the cases in which this Court has been obliged to deal with prohibitions or limitations by states upon exports of articles of commerce are not numerous. [The Court reviewed a number of decisions in which states had not been permitted to bar the export of local

Act was similarly unconstitutional. The state courts agreed with Eisenberg, but the Court reversed.

Justice Roberts' majority opinion explained: "The purpose of the [law] obviously is to reach a domestic situation in the interests of the welfare of the producers and consumers of milk in Pennsylvania." To evaluate the commerce clause challenge, he noted, required "weighing the nature of [Eisenberg's] activities, and the propriety of local regulation of them." In rejecting the challenge, he emphasized that the activity affected was "essentially local in Pennsylvania": "If dealers conducting receiving stations in [Pennsylvania] were free to ignore the requirements of the statute on the ground that all or a part of the milk they purchase is destined to another state the uniform operation of the statute locally would be crippled and might be impracticable. Only a small fraction of the milk produced by farmers in Pennsylvania is shipped out of the Commonwealth. There is, therefore, a comparatively large field remotely affecting and wholly unrelated to interstate commerce within which the statute operates." Accordingly, the impact on commerce was only "incidental" and not unconstitutional. Justice Roberts insisted that Baldwin v. Seelig was distinguishable because that decision "condemned an enactment aimed solely at interstate commerce attempting to affect and regulate the price to be paid for milk in a sister state, and we indicated that the attempt amounted in effect to a tariff barrier set up against milk imported into the enacting state."

Was that a fair characterization of Baldwin? Was Baldwin truly distinguishable? Could the Baldwin regulation have been defended as necessary to protect the integrity of New York's concededly valid intrastate price control scheme?

Note also the rejection of a commerce clause challenge to another law designed to promote a local economic concern, in Parker v. Brown, 317 U.S. 341 (1943). There, Chief Justice Stone's opinion sustained a California raisin marketing scheme compelling each producer to put most of its raisin crop under the marketing control of a program committee, for the purpose of eliminating price competition among producers. Chief Justice Stone's opinion sustaining that scheme conceded that there was a "substantial effect" on commerce since 95% of the raisins were marketed interstate. Nevertheless, noting that the raisin marketing problem was "local in character" and one "urgently demanding state action for the economic protection of those engaged in one of its important industries," he sustained the scheme after balancing the local and national interests. He stressed that the program sought to prevent "the demoralization of the industry" and "was not aimed at nor did it discriminate against interstate commerce." (It may be significant that, although Congress had not explicitly authorized such state schemes, the Court noted that "Congress, by its agricultural legislation, has recognized the distressed condition of much [of] agricultural production" and that *federal* price stabilization programs had similar effects on commerce.)

resources for the benefit of local consumers—e.g., Pennsylvania v. West Virginia, Foster-Fountain Packing, and Toomer v. Witsell, all noted below.]

[The] principle that our economic unit is the Nation, which alone has the gamut of powers necessary to control of the economy, including the vital power of erecting customs barriers against foreign competition, has as its corollary that the states are not separable economic units. [In Baldwin v. Seelig, the Court] but followed the principle that the state may not use its admitted powers to protect the health and safety of its people as a basis for suppressing competition. [Buck v. Kuykendall, p. 244 above.] [This] Court has not only recognized this disability of the state to isolate its own economy as a basis for striking down parochial legislative policies designed to do so, but it has recognized the incapacity of the state to protect its own inhabitants from competition as a reason for sustaining particular exercises of the commerce power of Congress to reach matters in which states were so disabled. Cf. [Steward Machine Co., p. 208 above].

The material success that has come to inhabitants of the states which make up this federal free trade unit has been the most impressive in the history of commerce, but the established interdependence of the states only emphasizes the necessity of protecting interstate movement of goods against local burdens and repressions. We need only consider the consequences if each of the few states that produce copper, lead, high-grade iron ore, timber, cotton, oil or gas should decree that industries located in that state shall have priority. What fantastic rivalries and dislocations and reprisals would ensue if such practices were begun! Or suppose that the field of discrimination and retaliation be industry. May Michigan provide that automobiles cannot be taken out of that State until local dealers' demands are fully met? Would she not have every argument in the favor of such a statute that can be offered in support of New York's limiting sales of milk for out-of-state shipment to protect the economic interests of her competing dealers and local consumers? Could Ohio then pounce upon the rubber-tire industry, on which she has a substantial grip, to retaliate for Michigan's auto monopoly? [At this point, Justice Jackson made the statement reprinted at the end of the Hood excerpts printed at the beginning of this chapter at p. 231 above, ending with: "Such was the vision of the Founders; such has been the doctrine of this Court which has given it reality."]

The State, however, insists that denial of the license for a new plant does not restrict or obstruct interstate commerce, because petitioner has been licensed at its other plants without condition or limitation as to the quantities it may purchase. [In] the face of affirmative findings that the proposed plant would increase petitioner's supply, we can hardly be asked to assume that denial of the license will not deny petitioner access to such added supplies. While the state power is applied in this case to limit expansion by a handler of milk who already has been allowed some purchasing facilities, the argument for doing so, if sustained, would be equally effective to exclude an entirely new foreign handler from coming into the State to purchase. [Since] the statute as applied violates the Commerce Clause and is not authorized by federal legislation pursuant to that Clause, it cannot stand.

[Reversed and remanded.]

Mr. Justice BLACK [joined by Justice MURPHY] dissenting.

Had a dealer supplying New York customers applied for a license to operate a new plant, the commissioner would have been compelled under the Act to protect petitioner's plants supplying Boston consumers in the same manner that this order would have protected New York consumers. [T]he Court cannot attribute to the commissioner an invidious purpose to [discriminate]. The language of this state Act is not discriminatory, the legislative history shows it was not so intended, and the commissioner has not administered it with a hostile eye. The Act must stand or fall on this basis notwithstanding the overtones of the Court's opinion. If petitioner [is] to be placed above and beyond this law, it must be done solely on this Court's new constitutional formula which bars a state from protecting itself against local destructive competitive practices so far as they are indulged in by dealers who ship their milk into other states. [The] Cooley balancing-of-interests principle [is] today supplanted by the philosophy of the Duckworth concurring opinion.[1] For the New York statute is killed by a mere automatic application of a new mechanistic formula. [The] basic question here is not the greatness of the commerce clause concept, but whether all local phases of interstate business are to be judicially immunized from state laws against destructive competitive business practices such as those prohibited by New York's law. [While] I have doubt about the wisdom of this New York law, I do not conceive it to be the function of this Court to revise that state's economic [judgments].

Mr. Justice FRANKFURTER, with whom Mr. Justice RUTLEDGE joins, dissenting.

If the Court's opinion has meaning beyond deciding this case in isolation, its effect is to hold that no matter how important to the internal economy of a State may be the prevention of destructive competition, and no matter how unimportant the interstate commerce affected, a State cannot as a means of preventing such competition deny an applicant access to a market within the State if that applicant happens to intend the out-of-state shipment of the product that he buys. I feel constrained to dissent because I cannot agree in treating what is essentially a problem of striking a balance between competing interests as an exercise in absolutes. Nor does it seem to me that such a problem should be disposed of on a record from which we cannot tell what weights to put in which side of the scales.

[The] Court's opinion deems the decision in [Baldwin v. Seelig] as most relevant to the present controversy. But it is the essential teaching of that case that "considerations of degree" determine the line of decision between what a State may and what a State may not regulate. [Guarding] against out-of-state competition is a very different thing from curbing competition from whatever source. A tariff barrier between States, moreover, presupposes a purpose to prefer those who are within the barrier; where no such preference appears there can be no justification for reprisals and there is consequently little probability of them. In the determination that an extension of petitioner's license would tend to destructive competition, the fact that petitioner intended the out-of-state shipment of what it bought was, so far as the records tell us, wholly irrelevant; under the circumstances, any other applicant, no matter where he meant to send his milk, would presumably also have been refused a license. [As] matters now stand, [it] is impossible to say whether or not the restriction of competition among dealers in milk does in fact contribute to their economic well-being and, through them, to that of the entire industry. And if we assume that some contribution is made, we cannot guess how much. [E.g., why] when the State has fixed a minimum price for producers, does it take steps to keep competing dealers from increasing the price by bidding against each other for the existing supply? [How] much of a strain would be put on the price structure maintained by the State by a holding that it cannot regulate the

1. Justice Black's reference was to the concurring opinion by Justice Jackson in Duckworth v. Arkansas, 314 U.S. 390 (1941). The case sustained a statute requiring a permit for the transportation of intoxicating liquor through the State. Justice Jackson agreed with the result on the basis of the Twenty-first Amendment but argued that, absent that provision, the law would have been invalid. In his view, the inertia of government made it unlikely that Congress, hardpressed with more urgent matters, would correct minor obstructions of interstate commerce: "The practical result is that in default of action by us, [the states] will go on suffocating and retarding and Balkanizing American commerce, trade and industry."

competition of dealers buying for an out-of-state market? [We] should, I submit, have answers at least to some of these questions before we can say either how seriously interstate commerce is burdened by New York's licensing power or how necessary to New York is that power. [My] conclusion [is] that the case should be [remanded].

———

ECONOMIC PURPOSES, PER SE RULES, AND BALANCING

Was Justice Jackson persuasive in characterizing the Hood restraint as forbidden economic discrimination? Does Hood reject a balancing approach in favor of a per se rule when the state interest is economic rather than health or safety? Arguably, Hood can be read as indicating that balancing continues, but that economic objectives tend to tip the scale against the state regulation. Arguably, the major flaw in Hood was the reason given by the state for denying Hood's license (and the fact that the applicant whose license was denied happened to be from out of state). Arguably, the licensing scheme in its application created too much of a risk of economic protectionism.[1] Viewing the facts in Hood together with the decisions in Eisenberg and Parker (footnote 1 to Hood), the Hood ruling can perhaps be interpreted more narrowly than some of Justice Jackson's broad statements suggest: perhaps it stands for no more than that out-of-staters cannot be subjected to laws excluding new competitors in order to protect existing businesses. But Hood raises a broader problem as well. To what extent can a state prefer domestic needs in curtailing the export of local products? Justice Jackson emphasized the commerce clause thrust against "home embargoes." The scope of that anti-embargo principle has troubled the Court in a large number of contexts, both before Hood and since. State control of its natural resources has been an especially litigated subject. An examination of natural resources cases follows.

———

STATE RESTRAINTS ON EXPORTS OF ITS NATURAL RESOURCES

1. *The mounting hostility to state embargoes on local resources.* A number of early cases sustained state preferences for local users of natural resources. Often, those cases rested on notions of state property interests. More recently, however, the Court has barred most state efforts to give preference to local interests. The Hood case itself is a strong statement of the anti-embargo principle; and Philadelphia v. New Jersey (p. 266 above) has already provided

---

1. Consider also the light shed on Hood in a case decided a year later, Cities Service Gas Co. v. Peerless Oil & Gas Co., 340 U.S. 179 (1950). There, the Court rejected a commerce clause attack on a state regulation of natural gas prices designed to conserve an important local resource. An Oklahoma agency fixed a minimum wellhead price on all natural gas taken from a field, requiring a pipeline company to pay more than the prevailing rates. Most of the gas from the field was destined for consumers outside of Oklahoma. Justice Clark's opinion emphasized Oklahoma's justifiable concern with "preventing rapid and uneconomic dissipation of one of its chief natural resources" by inferior uses of the gas at bargain rates. Citing Eisenberg and Parker, he stated that, "in a field of this complexity with such diverse interests involved, we cannot say that there is a clear national interest so harmed that the state price-fixing orders here employed" are barred by the commerce clause. He distinguished Hood by saying: "The vice in the regulation invalidated [there] was solely that it denied facilities to a company in interstate commerce on the articulated ground that such facilities would divert milk supplies needed by local consumers; in other words, the regulation discriminated against interstate commerce. There is no such problem here. The price regulation applies to all gas taken from the field, whether destined for interstate or intrastate consumers." Was that a persuasive distinction? Or was it in effect a narrowing of Hood? (Justice Jackson silently joined Justice Clark's Cities Service opinion.)

an example of the modern Court's unwillingness to tolerate reserving a local resource for local needs. How comprehensive is the anti-embargo principle? [1]

In the early cases the Court often endorsed local preferences in broad terms. For example, Geer v. Connecticut, 161 U.S. 519 (1896), upheld a law that prevented the killing of certain game birds for the purpose of shipment out of the state, even though intrastate commerce in game birds was permitted. The Court emphasized property rights: the birds were collectively owned by the people of the state. More recently, Geer was overruled in light of later decisions, in Hughes v. Oklahoma (1979; note 2 below). Hudson County Water Co. v. McCarter, 209 U.S. 349 (1908), sustained a law prohibiting the transportation of water from the state's rivers and lakes to any other state. The Court noted that the state, as "guardian of the public welfare," had a strong interest in maintaining local rivers "substantially undiminished." Can the water case survive later developments any more than the game bird case did? Cf. the Sporhase case, p. 296 below.

But even in earlier decades, some local barriers were invalidated. Thus, in Pennsylvania v. West Virginia, 262 U.S. 553 (1923), West Virginia had required that all local needs for natural gas be met before any gas could be exported. The majority found that requirement a "prohibited interference" with interstate commerce. But in a dissent Justice Holmes insisted that he could "see nothing in the commerce clause to prevent a State from giving a preference to its inhabitants in the enjoyment of its natural advantages." In the modern cases, the most common theme has been that of Pennsylvania v. West Virginia (relied on in Hood). Sometimes, the privileges and immunities clause of Art. IV, a clause invoked with increasing frequency as a reinforcement of the commerce clause's anti-embargo principle, has played a central role. That was the case, for example, in Toomer v. Witsell (1948; p. 309 below), invalidating South Carolina's discriminatory license fee on nonresidents trawling for shrimp in its waters.[2] (The scope of the Art. IV provision is explored in a separate subsection below, sec. 1C(6), at p. 307.) Moreover, the state has been able to escape commerce clause restraints in modern cases when it acts as a "market participant" rather than a "market regulator." The scope of the increasingly important "market participant" exception is pursued in sec. 1C(5) below.[3]

2. HUGHES v. OKLAHOMA, 441 U.S. 322 (1979), overruled Geer v. Connecticut and held invalid under the commerce clause an Oklahoma law forbidding any person to "transport or ship minnows for sale outside the state which were seined or procured within the waters of this state." Hughes was a Texan engaged in the commercial minnow business who was charged with violating the law for transporting from Oklahoma to Texas a load of natural minnows purchased from an Oklahoma minnow dealer. After holding that the Geer exception should be overruled, Justice BRENNAN's majority opinion found that the statute could not survive scrutiny under modern commerce clause standards.

Justice Brennan found that the Geer approach had been undermined by subsequent decisions. Geer had rested on the view that a state had the power, as representative of its citizens who "owned" in common all wild animals within the state, to "control not only the *taking* of game, but the *ownership* of game that

---

1. See generally Hellerstein, "Hughes v. Oklahoma: The Court, the Commerce Clause, and State Control of Natural Resources," 1979 Sup. Ct.Rev. 51.

2. See also the Hicklin (1978) and Camden (1984) cases, pp. 308 and 311 below, invalidating, on the basis of Art. IV, provisions preferring residents over nonresidents for certain jobs. But see the White case (p. 305 below), sustaining

such a preference against a commerce clause challenge. And note the Baldwin case (1978; p. 310 below), rejecting an Art. IV challenge to an elk-hunting license scheme imposing substantially higher fees on nonresidents than on residents.

3. See, e.g., Reeves, Inc. v. Stake (1980; p. 299 below) permitting a state to confine to its residents the sale of cement produced in state-owned plants.

had been lawfully reduced to possession." The Geer "ownership" approach had been diluted and rejected in later natural resources cases—e.g., Pennsylvania v. West Virginia and Toomer v. Witsell. This case was the first "on all fours with Geer." And that made it appropriate to say: "We now conclude that challenges under the Commerce Clause to state regulations of wild animals should be considered according to the same general rule applied to state regulations of other natural resources, and therefore expressly overrule Geer. We thus bring our analytical framework into conformity with practical realities. [At] the same time, the general rule we adopt [makes] ample allowance for preserving [the] legitimate state concerns for conservation and protection of wild animals underlying the 19th century legal fiction of state ownership."

After reciting the balancing standards of Pike and Hunt, Justice Brennan stated that the Oklahoma law "on its face discriminates against interstate commerce. [E.g., Philadelphia v. New Jersey.] [Such] facial discrimination by itself may be a fatal defect, regardless of the State's purpose, because 'the evil of protectionism can reside in legislative means as well as legislative ends.' At a minimum such facial discrimination invokes the strictest scrutiny of any purported legitimate local purpose and of the absence of nondiscriminatory alternatives." Here, that scrutiny was fatal. While the state interest in conservation was legitimate, the scope of that interest was "narrower under this analysis than it was under Geer": "The fiction of state ownership may no longer be used to force those outside the State to bear the full costs of 'conserving' the wild animals within its borders when equally effective nondiscriminatory conservation measures are available." And here, Oklahoma had not only failed to resort to the least discriminatory alternative, but had indeed chosen to express its legitimate interest "in the way that most overtly discriminates against interstate commerce."[4] Overruling Geer did not mean that the states were powerless to conserve wildlife within their borders. But "States may promote this legitimate purpose only in ways consistent with the basic principle that 'our economic unit is the Nation' [Hood], and that when a wild animal 'becomes an article of commerce, [its] use cannot be limited to the citizens of one State to the exclusion of citizens of another State' [Geer; Field, J., dissenting]."

Justice REHNQUIST, joined by Chief Justice Burger, dissented, arguing that the ownership language of cases such as Geer was "simply a shorthand way of describing a State's substantial interest in preserving and regulating the exploitation of [natural resources] within its boundaries for the benefit of its citizens. [The] range of regulations that a State may adopt under these circumstances is extremely broad, particularly where, as here, the burden on interstate commerce is, at most, minimal." He emphasized that there was no showing here that "requiring appellant to purchase his minnows from hatcheries [not subject to the statute] instead of from persons licensed to seine minnows from the State's waters in any way increases appellant's costs of doing business." Moreover, hatchery minnows and naturally seined minnows apparently were fungible. Hence, any minimal burden on petitioner was "more than outweighed by Oklahoma's substantial interest in conserving and regulating exploitation of its natural minnow population."

3. NEW ENGLAND POWER CO. v. NEW HAMPSHIRE, 455 U.S. 331 (1982), is a particularly strong and succinct modern statement, by a unanimous Court, condemning state restrictions on the export of natural resources. For

---

4. Justice Brennan explained: "The State places no limits on the number of minnows that can be taken by licensed minnow dealers; nor does it limit in any way how these minnows may be disposed of within the State. Yet it forbids the transportation of any commercially significant number of natural minnows out of the State for sale. [The law] is certainly not a 'last ditch' attempt at conservation after nondiscriminatory alternatives have proved unfeasible. It is rather a choice of the most discriminatory means even though nondiscriminatory alternatives would seem likely to fulfill the State's purported legitimate local purpose more effectively."

many years, the Company had exported most of the hydroelectric energy generated at its federally licensed power stations on the Connecticut River in New Hampshire. In 1980, a New Hampshire agency withdrew the Company's authority to export the locally generated power. The agency acted pursuant to a state law banning the exportation of energy whenever the agency determined that the energy "is reasonably required for use within this state and that the public good requires that it be delivered for such use." Chief Justice BURGER's rejection of the commerce clause challenge was brief:

"Our cases consistently have held that the Commerce Clause [precludes] a state from mandating that its residents be given a preferred right of access, over out-of-state consumers, to natural resources located within its borders or to the products derived therefrom. E.g., [Hughes; Philadelphia v. New Jersey]." [5] After quoting from Philadelphia v. New Jersey, he continued: "[The order challenged here] is precisely the sort of protectionist regulation that the Commerce Clause declares off-limits to the states. The [state agency] has made clear that its order is designed to gain an economic advantage for New Hampshire citizens at the expense of [the Company's] customers in neighboring states. Moreover, it cannot be disputed that [the agency's] 'exportation ban' places direct and substantial burdens on transactions in interstate commerce. Such state-imposed burdens cannot be squared with the Commerce Clause when they serve only to advance 'simple economic protectionism.' Philadelphia v. New Jersey." [6]

---

5. The Chief Justice added in a footnote: "We find no merit in New Hampshire's attempt to distinguish these cases on the ground that it 'owns' the Connecticut River. [Whatever] the extent of the State's proprietary interest in the river, the pre-eminent authority to regulate the flow of navigable waters resides with the Federal Government, which has licensed [the Company] to operate [the] hydroelectric plants. New Hampshire's purported 'ownership' [therefore] provides no justification for restricting or conditioning the use of these federally licensed units. Moreover, New Hampshire has done more than regulate use of the resource it assertedly owns; it has restricted the sale of electric energy, a product entirely distinct from the river waters used to produce it. This product is manufactured by a private corporation using privately owned facilities. Thus, New Hampshire's reliance on Reeves, Inc. v. Stake [p. 299 below]—holding that a state may confine to its residents the sale of products it *produces*—is misplaced."

6. The major issue in the case turned on New Hampshire's unsuccessful claim that Congress, in the Federal Power Act, had expressly consented to the export restriction.

Note also the reiteration of the Court's skepticism about state export controls on natural resources a few months after the New Hampshire case, in Sporhase v. Nebraska, 458 U.S. 941 (1982). That case involved a state restriction on the export of ground water. Because of the traditional recognition of the predominance of state law in the delineation of water rights, advocates of state restraints in the interest of "conservation" had long maintained that the regulation of water resources enjoyed a special, broad immunity from commerce clause restrictions on export bans. But the Court's 7 to 2 decision,

while acknowledging some state authority to restrict export of water, refused to accept the State's broadest immunity claims. Accordingly, the Court held unconstitutional a portion of a statutory restriction on the withdrawal of ground water from any well within Nebraska intended for use in an adjoining state. Justice Stevens' majority opinion rejected, inter alia, the state court's reliance on such cases as Geer and Hudson County Water which had rested on the "fiction" of state ownership of its water. With respect to the state's claim that water "property" was entitled to special exemptions from commerce clause scrutiny, Justice Stevens stated: "Although [the State's] greater ownership interest may not be irrelevant to Commerce Clause analysis, it does not absolutely remove [the State's rules about] ground water from such scrutiny. For [the State's] argument is still based on the legal fiction of State ownership." Applying the Pike balancing formula, and invoking Hood, he found that some of the State's restrictions constituted an "explicit barrier to commerce." Justice Rehnquist, joined by Justice O'Connor, dissented. He conceded that a state could not discriminate even when it regulated a resource such as water. [He gave as an example of forbidden discrimination the Hughes case.] But here the state restriction was permissible: there was no discrimination or even any burden on interstate commerce because Nebraska had recognized only a limited right to use ground water and there could be no "commerce" of an article that "cannot be reduced to possession under state law and in which the State recognizes only a usufructuary right. [The State] grants landowners only a right to *use groundwater on the land from which it has been extracted.*"

4.   REQUIRING BUSINESS OPERATIONS TO BE PERFORMED IN THE HOME STATE [1]

Introduction.   As this group of cases illustrates, the Court has been consistently skeptical of claimed state interests that require the processing of a state's products in the exporting state before they may be shipped out-of-state.   The situation in these cases is the converse of those presented in cases such as Minnesota v. Barber (1890; p. 277 above) and Dean Milk (1951; p. 270 above), where regulations required that some processing activities be performed in the importing state on goods that came from out-of-state.

1.   FOSTER–FOUNTAIN PACKING CO. v. HAYDEL, 278 U.S. 1 (1928), was an early case (decided during the era of Geer v. Connecticut) invalidating a home state processing requirement.   It involved a Louisiana law banning the shipment of shrimp out of the state until hulls and heads (supposedly needed for fertilizer) had been removed. (Fertilizer or chicken feed made from shrimp hulls or heads could, however, be shipped out of the state.)   In striking down the law, Justice BUTLER's majority opinion distinguished Geer and stated: "As the representative of its people, the State might have retained the shrimp for consumption and use therein.   But, in direct opposition to conservation for intrastate use, this [law] permits all parts of the shrimp to be shipped and sold outside the State.   The purpose is not to retain the shrimp for the use of the people of Louisiana; it is to favor the canning of the meat and the manufacture of bran in Louisiana by withholding raw or unshelled shrimp from the Biloxi [Mississippi] plants.   But by permitting its shrimp to be taken and all the products thereof to be shipped and sold in interstate commerce, the State necessarily releases its hold.   [Clearly] such authorization [put] an end to the trust upon which the State is deemed to own or control the shrimp for the benefit of its people.   [The] practical operation and effect of the provisions complained of will be directly to obstruct and burden interstate commerce. [Pennsylvania v. West Virginia.]"

2.   PIKE v. BRUCE CHURCH, INC., 397 U.S. 137 (1970), has already been noted repeatedly because of its widely cited balancing formulation printed at p. 245 above.   That case involved a modern home state processing requirement.   Church was an Arizona grower of high quality cantaloupes.   Instead of packing them in Arizona, it transported them to nearby California facilities; when packed in California, they were not identified as Arizona-grown.   Arizona prohibited Church from shipping uncrated cantaloupes from the company's Arizona ranch.   Compliance with the requirement that the cantaloupes be packed in Arizona would have required a capital outlay of $200,000 to pack Church's $700,000 cantaloupe crop.

Although the law was initially passed to protect the reputation of Arizona growers by preventing the shipment of inferior produce, the state interest relied on here was "to promote and preserve the reputation of Arizona growers by prohibiting deceptive packaging."   In invalidating the requirement, Justice STEWART's opinion for a unanimous Court, after stating the balancing formula quoted earlier, noted that this law was not one to promote safety or to protect consumers from unfit goods.   Rather, its "purpose and design are simply to protect and enhance the reputation of growers within the State.   These are surely legitimate state interests.   [But] application of the Act [to Church] has a far different impact, and quite a different purpose.   [Arizona] is not complaining because the company is putting the good name of Arizona on an inferior or deceptively packaged product, but because it is not putting that name

---

1.   See the Pike case, note 2 below, stating that "the Court has viewed with particular suspicion state statutes requiring business operations to be performed in the home State that could more efficiently be performed elsewhere."

on a product that is superior and well packaged. [Although] it is not easy to see why the other growers of Arizona are entitled to benefit at the company's expense from the fact that it produces superior crops, we may assume that the asserted state interest is a legitimate one. But the State's tenuous interest in having the company's cantaloupes identified as originating in Arizona cannot constitutionally justify the requirement that the company build and operate an unneeded $200,000 packing plant in the State. The nature of that burden is, constitutionally, more significant than its extent. For the Court has viewed with particular suspicion state statutes requiring business operations to be performed in the home State that could more efficiently be performed elsewhere. Even where the State is pursuing a clearly legitimate local interest, this particular burden on commerce has been declared to be virtually per se illegal. [E.g., Foster-Fountain.]" [2]

3. *Excessive barriers to business entry.* The Pike balancing formula and the concerns with parochialism reflected in these cases have also surfaced in modern decisions involving limits on business entry. A good example is Lewis v. BT Investment Managers, Inc., 447 U.S. 27 (1980). There, Justice Blackmun's opinion for a unanimous Court struck down a Florida law prohibiting ownership of local investment advisory businesses by out-of-state banks, bank holding companies and trust companies. (The law barred only some, not all, out-of-state investment advisors.) Justice Blackmun noted that the law "prevents competition in local markets by out-of-state firms with the kinds of resources and business interests that make them likely to attempt de novo entry" and found the law " 'parochial' in the sense that it overtly prevents foreign enterprises from competing in local markets." He found it unnecessary to decide whether the law was "per se invalid, for we are convinced that the disparate treatment of out-of-state bank holding companies cannot be justified as an incidental burden necessitated by legitimate local concerns." He invoked "the general principle that the Commerce Clause prohibits a State from using its regulatory power to protect its own citizens from outside competition. See [e.g., Hood]." Justice Blackmun, who had dissented in Exxon, p. 282 above, found the majority ruling there distinguishable here.[3]

---

5. THE "MARKET PARTICIPANT" EXCEPTION TO COMMERCE CLAUSE RESTRAINTS

Introduction. In a series of recent cases, a divided Court has carved out a significant exception from the usual commerce clause scrutiny: the Court's usual concern about detecting parochialism has been found inappropriate when the state operates not as a "regulator" of the free market but rather as a "market participant." The impact of that exception has been felt particularly in situations where the state itself produces goods for commerce or where it engages in a program of subsidies or other economic incentives to aid in-state businesses. In examining the cases in which this exception has been developed, consider whether it makes sense as a general concept. Is there good reason to leave the

2. Note also the modern cases preventing states from preferring their own employees over nonresidents—e.g., Toomer v. Witsell, Hicklin v. Orbeck, and the Camden case, all decided under the privileges and immunities clause of Art. IV and noted in sec. 1C(6) below.

3. Note also Edgar v. MITE Corp., 457 U.S. 624 (1982), where a sharply divided Court held unconstitutional the interstate commerce impacts of the Illinois Business Take-Over Act, designed to regulate tender offers made to target compa-

nies that had certain specified business contacts with Illinois. The only ground on which the majority was able to agree was the Pike balancing formula: the majority concluded that the Act imposed "a substantial burden on interstate commerce which outweighs its putative local benefits." (Note that in this case the Pike balancing formula was applied in a context which, unlike many of its other applications, did *not* involve a state law with any protectionist purpose or effect.)

states alone in these situations where the Court does not apply the usual commerce clause restraints? Also consider whether, even if the basic concept is justifiable, the Court's applications are persuasive. Consider especially whether there is an adequate difference between the decisions prohibiting state hoarding of its natural resources (sec. 1C(3) above) and a case such as Reeves, the next principal case, which permitted South Dakota to hoard the cement it produced at its state-owned plants. Because of the growing vigor of (and controversy about) the market participant exception, a look at all of the major cases in which the Court has discussed it is warranted.[1]

The market participant exception was launched, in an unusual context, in HUGHES v. ALEXANDRIA SCRAP CORP., 426 U.S. 794 (1976). That case involved what was in effect a state subsidy scheme, a scheme under which Maryland acted as a buyer of goods in commerce in a plan to rid the state of abandoned automobiles. The terms of the bounty scheme strongly favored in-state processors. The law was challenged by a Virginia processor because the system discouraged suppliers from taking hulks outside the state for processing. Justice POWELL's majority opinion found that the Maryland scheme was not "the kind of action with which the Commerce Clause is concerned." Unlike such prior cases as Pike, Hood, and Foster-Fountain, on which the challengers relied, "Maryland has not sought to prohibit the flow of hulks or to regulate the conditions under which it may occur. Instead, it has entered into the market itself to bid up their price [as] a purchaser, in effect, of a potential article of interstate commerce [and has restricted] its trade to its own citizens or businesses within the State." He insisted, too, that "nothing in the purposes animating the Commerce Clause prohibits a State [from] participating in the market and exercising the right to favor its own citizens over others." The Alexandria Scrap decision is discussed further in the cases that follow.[2]

REEVES, INC. v. STAKE

447 U.S. 429, 100 S.Ct. 2271, 65 L.Ed.2d 244 (1980).

Mr. Justice BLACKMUN delivered the opinion of the Court.

1. See generally Anson & Schenkkan, "Federalism, the Dormant Commerce Clause, and State-Owned Resources," 59 Tex.L.Rev. 71 (1980), and Wells & Hellerstein, "The Governmental-Proprietary Distinction in Constitutional Law," 66 Va.L.Rev. 1073, 1121–41 (1980). Cf. Varat, "State 'Citizenship' and Interstate Equality," 48 U.Chi.L.Rev. 487 (1981).

2. Justice STEVENS joined Justice Powell's opinion, but emphasized in a concurrence that it was "important to differentiate between commerce which flourishes in a free market and commerce which owes its existence to a state subsidy program. Our cases finding that a state regulation constitutes an impermissible burden on interstate commerce all dealt with restrictions that adversely affected the operation of a free market. This case is unique because the commerce which Maryland has 'burdened' is commerce which would not exist if Maryland had not decided to subsidize a portion of the automobile scrap-processing business. [A] failure to create that commerce would have been unobjectionable because the Commerce Clause surely does not impose on the States any obligation to subsidize

out-of-state business. Nor, in my judgment, does that Clause inhibit a State's power to experiment with different methods of encouraging local industry. Whether the encouragement takes the form of a cash subsidy, a tax credit, or a special privilege intended to attract investment capital, it should not be characterized as a 'burden' on commerce." A dissent by Justice BRENNAN, joined by Justices White and Marshall, insisted that the Court had too summarily rejected the applicability of the standard line of commerce clause cases (e.g., Pike, Hood, and Dean Milk) and concluded that the case should be remanded for development of a fuller factual record.

The Alexandria Scrap case was decided on the same day as National League of Cities, the state autonomy case printed at p. 170 above. Indeed, Justice Brennan's dissent in Alexandria Scrap suggested that National League of Cities was "the motivating rationale behind this holding." Were the principles of National League of Cities persuasively applicable to this case? (Note also the references to National League of Cities in Reeves, the next principal case.)

The issue in this case is whether, consistent with the Commerce Clause, [South Dakota], in a time of shortage, may confine the sale of the cement it produces solely to its residents.

I. In 1919, South Dakota undertook plans to build a cement plant. The project, a product of the State's then prevailing Progressive political movement, was initiated in response to recent regional cement shortages that "interfered with and delayed both public and private [enterprises]." The plant [soon] produced more cement than South Dakotans could use. Over the years, buyers in no less than nine nearby States purchased cement from the State's plant. Between 1970 and 1977, some 40% of the plant's output went outside the State. The plant's list of out-of-state cement buyers included petitioner Reeves, Inc. Reeves is a ready-mix concrete distributor [in Wyoming]. From [1958 to 1978], Reeves purchased about 95% of its cement from the South Dakota plant. [In] turn, Reeves has supplied three northwestern Wyoming counties with more than half their ready-mix concrete [needs].

As the 1978 construction season approached, difficulties at the plant slowed production. Meanwhile, a booming construction industry spurred demand for cement both regionally and nationally. The plant found itself unable to meet all orders. Faced with the same type of "serious cement shortage" that inspired the plant's construction, the [State Cement] Commission "reaffirmed its policy of supplying all South Dakota customers first and to honor all contract commitments, with the remaining volume allocated on a first come, first served basis." [1] Reeves, which had no pre-existing long-term supply contract, was hit hard and quickly by this development. [In 1978, the plant stopped fulfilling Reeves' orders.] Unable to find another supplier, Reeves was forced to cut production by 76% in mid-July. [Reeves challenged the plant's preference policy in federal court. The District Court found the policy to be unconstitutional "hoarding." The Court of Appeals reversed, relying on Alexandria Scrap. On certiorari the Court remanded for further consideration in light of Hughes v. Oklahoma, p. 294 above. On remand the Court of Appeals distinguished Hughes and adhered to its prior decision.] [2] We granted [certiorari] to consider once again the impact of the Commerce Clause on state proprietary activity.

II. [After reviewing Alexandria Scrap, Justice Blackmun continued:] The basic distinction drawn in Alexandria Scrap between States as market participants and States as market regulators makes good sense and sound law. As that case explains, the Commerce Clause responds principally to state taxes and regulatory measures impeding free private trade in the national marketplace. There is no indication of a constitutional plan to limit the ability of the States themselves to operate freely in the free market. The precedents comport with this distinction. [3]

---

1. It is not clear when the State initiated its policy preferring South Dakota customers. The record, however, shows that the policy was in place at least by 1974. [Footnote by Justice Blackmun.]

2. We now agree with the Court of Appeals that Hughes v. Oklahoma does not bear on [the] analysis here. That case involved a State's attempt "to prevent privately owned articles of trade from being shipped and sold in interstate commerce." Thus, it involved precisely the type of activity distinguished by the Court in Alexandria Scrap. [Footnote by Justice Blackmun.]

3. Alexandria Scrap does not stand alone. In American Yearbook Co. v. Askew, 339 F.Supp. 719 (M.D.Fla.1972), a three-judge District Court upheld a Florida statute requiring the State to obtain needed printing services from in-state shops. It reasoned that "state proprietary functions" are exempt from Commerce Clause scrutiny. This Court affirmed summarily. 409 U.S. 904 (1972). Numerous [other] courts have rebuffed Commerce Clause challenges directed at similar preferences that exist in "a substantial majority of the [states]." [Footnote by Justice Blackmun.]

Restraint in this area is also counseled by considerations of state sovereignty,[4] the role of each State " 'as guardian and trustee for its people,' " and "the long recognized right of trader or manufacturer, engaged in an entirely private business, freely to exercise his own independent discretion as to parties with whom he will deal." [5] Moreover, state proprietary activities may be, and often are, burdened with the same restrictions imposed on private market participants. Evenhandedness suggests that, when acting as proprietors, States should similarly share existing freedoms from federal constraints, including the inherent limits of the Commerce Clause.   Finally, as this case illustrates, the competing considerations in cases involving state proprietary action often will be subtle, complex, politically charged, and difficult to assess under traditional Commerce Clause analysis.   Given these factors, Alexandria Scrap wisely recognizes that, as a rule, the adjustment of interests in this context is a task better suited for Congress than this Court.

III.   South Dakota, as a seller of cement, unquestionably fits the "market participant" label more comfortably than a State acting to subsidize local scrap processors.   Thus, the general rule of Alexandria Scrap plainly applies here. Petitioner argues, however, that the exemption for marketplace participation necessarily admits of exceptions.   While conceding that possibility, we perceive in this case no sufficient reason to depart from the general rule.

A.   In finding a Commerce Clause violation, the District Court emphasized "that the Commission [made] an election to become part of the interstate commerce system."   The gist of this reasoning [is] that one good turn deserves another.   Having long exploited the interstate market, South Dakota should not be permitted to withdraw from it when a shortage arises.   This argument is not persuasive.   It is somewhat self-serving to say that South Dakota has "exploited" the interstate market.   An equally fair characterization is that neighboring States long have benefited from South Dakota's foresight and industry.   [Our] rejection of [this] market-exploitation theory fundamentally refocuses analysis.   It means that to reverse we would have to void a South Dakota "residents only" policy even if it had been enforced from the plant's very first days.   Such a holding, however, would interfere significantly with a State's ability to structure relations exclusively with its own citizens.   It would also threaten the future fashioning of effective and creative programs for solving local problems and distributing government largesse.   A healthy regard for federalism and good government renders us reluctant to risk these [results].

B.   Undaunted by these considerations, petitioner advances four more arguments for reversal: First, petitioner protests that South Dakota's preference for its residents responds solely to the "non-governmental objectiv[e]" of

---

4. [Considerations] of sovereignty independently dictate that marketplace actions involving "integral operations in areas of traditional governmental functions"—such as the employment of certain state workers—may not be subject even to congressional regulation pursuant to the commerce power. [National League of Cities].   It follows easily that the intrinsic limits of the Commerce Clause do not prohibit state marketplace conduct that falls within this sphere.   Even where "integral operations" are not implicated, States may fairly claim some measure of a sovereign interest in retaining freedom to decide how, with whom, and for whose benefit to [deal]. [Footnote by Justice Blackmun.]

5.   When a State buys or sells, it has the attributes of both a political entity and a private business.   Nonetheless, the dissent would dismiss altogether the "private business" element of such activity and focus solely on the State's political character.   The Court, however, heretofore has recognized that "*[l]ike private individuals and businesses,* the Government enjoys the unrestricted power to produce its own supplies, to determine those with whom it will deal, and to fix the terms and conditions upon which it will make needed purchases."   Perkins v. Lukens Steel Co., 310 U.S. 113, 127 (1940) (emphasis added).   While acknowledging that there may be limits on this sweepingly phrased principle, we cannot ignore the similarities of private businesses and public entities when they function in the marketplace. [Footnote by Justice Blackmun.]

protectionism. Therefore, petitioner argues, the policy is per se invalid. See Philadelphia v. New Jersey. We find the label "protectionism" of little help in this context. The State's refusal to sell to buyers other than South Dakotans is "protectionist" only in the sense that it limits benefits generated by a state program to those who fund the state treasury and whom the State was created to serve. Petitioner's argument apparently also would characterize as "protectionist" rules restricting to state residents the enjoyment of state educational institutions, energy generated by a state-run plant, police and fire protection, and agricultural improvement and business development programs. Such policies, while perhaps "protectionist" in a loose sense, reflect the essential and patently unobjectionable purpose of state government—to serve the citizens of the State.

Second, petitioner echoes the District Court's warning: "If a state in this union, were allowed to hoard its commodities or resources for the use of their own residents only, a drastic situation [of retaliatory embargoes of, e.g., coal and timber] might [evolve]." This argument, although rooted in the core purpose of the Commerce Clause, does not fit the present facts. Cement is not a natural resource, like coal, timber, wild game, or minerals. It is the end product of a complex process whereby a costly physical plant and human labor act on raw materials. South Dakota has not sought to limit access to the State's limestone or other materials used to make cement. Nor has it restricted the ability of private firms or sister States to set up plants within its borders. Moreover, petitioner has not suggested that South Dakota possesses unique access to the materials needed to produce cement. Whatever limits might exist on a State's ability to invoke the Alexandria Scrap exemption to hoard resources which by happenstance are found there, those limits do not apply here.

Third, it is suggested that the South Dakota program is infirm because it places South Dakota suppliers of ready-mix concrete at a competitive advantage in the out-of-state market; Wyoming suppliers, such as petitioner, have little chance against South Dakota suppliers who can purchase cement from the State's plant and freely sell beyond South Dakota's borders. The force of this argument is seriously diminished, if not eliminated, by several considerations. The argument necessarily implies that the South Dakota scheme would be unobjectionable if sales in other States were totally barred. It therefore proves too much, for it would tolerate even a greater measure of protectionism and stifling of interstate commerce than the challenged system allows. [The] competitive plight of out-of-state ready-mix suppliers cannot be laid solely at the feet of South Dakota. It is attributable as well to their own States' not providing or attracting alternative sources of supply and to the suppliers' own failure to guard against shortages by executing long-term supply contracts with the South Dakota plant.

In its last argument, petitioner urges that, had South Dakota not acted, free market forces would have generated an appropriate level of supply at free market prices for all buyers in the region. Having replaced free market forces, South Dakota should be forced to replicate how the free market would have operated under prevailing conditions. This argument appears to us to be simplistic and speculative. The very reason South Dakota built its plant was because the free market had failed adequately to supply the region with cement. There is no indication, and no way to know, that private industry would have moved into petitioner's market area, and would have ensured a supply of cement to petitioner either prior to or during the 1978 construction season. Indeed, it is quite possible that petitioner would never have existed—far less operated successfully for 20 years—had it not been for South Dakota cement.

C. We conclude, then, that the arguments for invalidating South Dakota's resident-preference program are weak at best. Whatever residual force inheres in them is more than offset by countervailing considerations of policy and fairness. Reversal would discourage similar state projects, even though this project demonstrably has served the needs of state residents and has helped the entire region for more than a half century. Reversal also would rob South Dakota of the intended benefit of its foresight, risk, and industry. Under these circumstances, there is no reason to depart from the general rule of Alexandria Scrap.

[Affirmed.]

Mr. Justice POWELL, with whom Mr. Justice BRENNAN, Mr. Justice WHITE, and Mr. Justice STEVENS join, dissenting.

The South Dakota Cement Commission has ordered that in times of shortage the state cement plant must turn away out-of-state customers until all orders from South Dakotans are filled. This policy represents precisely the kind of economic protectionism that the Commerce Clause was intended to prevent.[1] The Court, however, finds no violation of the Commerce Clause, solely because the State produces the cement. I agree with the Court that [South Dakota] may provide cement for its public needs without violating the Commerce Clause. But I cannot agree that [it] may withhold its cement from interstate commerce in order to benefit private citizens and businesses within the State.

I. The need to ensure unrestricted trade among the States created a major impetus for the drafting of the Constitution. [The] Commerce Clause has proved an effective weapon against protectionism. The Court has used it to strike down limitations on access to local goods, be they animal, Hughes v. Oklahoma; vegetable, [Pike]; or mineral, Pennsylvania v. West Virginia. [This] case presents a novel constitutional question. The Commerce Clause would bar legislation imposing on private parties the type of restraint on commerce adopted by South Dakota. See [Pennsylvania v. West Virginia].[2] Conversely, a private business constitutionally could adopt a marketing policy that excluded customers who come from another State. This case falls between those polar situations. [The] question is whether the Commission's policy should be treated like state regulation of private parties or like the marketing policy of a private business.

The application of the Commerce Clause to this case should turn on the nature of the governmental activity involved. If a public enterprise undertakes an "integral operatio[n] in areas of traditional governmental functions" [National League of Cities], the Commerce Clause is not directly relevant. If, however,

1. By "protectionism," I refer to state policies designed to protect private economic interests within the State from the forces of the interstate market. I would exclude from this term policies relating to traditional governmental functions, such as education, and subsidy programs like the one at issue in [Alexandria Scrap]. [Footnote by Justice Powell.]

2. The Court attempts to distinguish prior decisions that address the Commerce Clause limitations on a State's regulation of natural resource exploitation. The Court contends that cement production, unlike the activities involved in those cases, "is the end product of a complex process whereby a costly physical plant and human labor act on raw materials." The Court's distinction fails in two respects. First, the principles articulated in the natural resources cases also have been applied in decisions involving agricultural production, notably milk processing. E.g., Hood; [Pike]. More fundamentally, the Court's definition of cement production describes all so-

phisticated economic activity, including the exploitation of natural resources. The extraction of natural gas, for example, could hardly occur except through a "complex process whereby a costly physical plant and human labor act on raw materials."

The Court also suggests that the Commerce Clause has no application to this case because South Dakota does not "posses[s] unique access to the materials needed to produce cement." But in its regional market, South Dakota has unique access to *cement*. A cutoff in cement sales has the same economic impact as a refusal to sell resources like natural gas. Customers can seek other sources of supply, or find a substitute product, or do without. Regardless of the nature of the product the State hoards, the consumer has been denied the guarantee of the Commerce Clause that he "may look [to] free competition from every producing area in the Nation to protect him from exploitation by any." [Hood.] [Footnote by Justice Powell.]

the State enters the private market and operates a commercial enterprise for the advantage of its private citizens, it may not evade the constitutional policy against economic Balkanization. This distinction derives from the power of governments to supply their own needs and from the purpose of the Commerce Clause itself, which is designed to protect "the natural functioning of the interstate market," [Alexandria Scrap]. In procuring goods and services for the operation of government, a State may act without regard to the private marketplace and remove itself from the reach of the Commerce Clause. But when a State itself becomes a participant in the private market for other purposes, the Constitution forbids actions that would impede the flow of interstate commerce. These categories recognize no more than the "constitutional line between the State as government and the State as trader."

The Court holds that South Dakota, like a private business, should not be governed by the Commerce Clause when it enters the private market. But precisely because South Dakota is a State, it cannot be presumed to behave like an enterprise " 'engaged in an entirely private business.' " A State frequently will respond to market conditions on the basis of political rather than economic concerns. To use the Court's terms, a State may attempt to act as a "market regulator" rather than a "market participant." In that situation, it is a pretense to equate the State with a private economic actor. State action burdening interstate trade is no less state action because it is accomplished by a public agency authorized to participate in the private market.

II. The threshold issue is whether South Dakota has undertaken integral government operations in an area of traditional governmental functions, or whether it has participated in the marketplace as a private firm. If the latter characterization applies, we also must determine whether the State Commission's marketing policy burdens the flow of interstate trade. This analysis highlights the differences between the state action here and that before the Court in [Alexandria Scrap].

[Unlike] the market subsidies at issue in Alexandria Scrap, the marketing policy of the South Dakota Cement Commission has cut off interstate trade.[3] The State can raise such a bar when it enters the market to supply its own needs. In order to ensure an adequate supply of cement for public uses, the State can withhold from interstate commerce the cement needed for public projects. The State, however, has no parallel justification for favoring private, in-state customers over out-of-state customers. [The] effect on interstate trade is the same as if the state legislature had imposed the policy on private cement producers. The Commerce Clause prohibits this severe restraint on commerce.

III. I share the Court's desire to preserve state sovereignty. But the Commerce Clause long has been recognized as a limitation on that sovereignty, consciously designed to maintain a national market and defeat economic provincialism. The Court today approves protectionist state policies. In the absence of contrary congressional action, those policies now can be implemented as long as the State itself directly participates in the market.[4] By enforcing the Commerce Clause in this case, the Court would work no unfairness on the people of South Dakota. They still could reserve cement for public projects

3. One distinction between a private and a governmental function is whether the activity is supported with general tax funds, as was the case for the reprocessing program in Alexandria Scrap, or whether it is financed by the revenues it generates. In this case, South Dakota's cement plant has supported itself for many years. There is thus no need to consider the question whether a state-subsidized business could confine its sales to local residents. [Footnote by Justice Powell.]

4. Since the Court's decision contains no limiting principles, a State will be able to manufacture any commercial product and withhold it from citizens of other States. This prerogative could extend, for example, to pharmaceutical goods, food products, or even synthetic or processed energy sources. [Footnote by Justice Powell.]

and share in whatever return the plant generated. They could not, however, use the power of the State to furnish themselves with cement forbidden to the people of neighboring States. The creation of a free national economy was a major goal of the States when they resolved to unite under the Federal Constitution. The decision today cannot be reconciled with that purpose.

WHAT LIMITS TO THE MARKET PARTICIPANT EXCEPTION?

1. WHITE v. MASS. COUNCIL OF CONSTR. EMPLOYERS, 460 U.S. 204 (1983), applied the Alexandria Scrap-Reeves market participant exception to sustain a Boston requirement that at least 50% of the workforce on all construction projects funded wholly by the city must be Boston residents.[1] In invalidating the requirement, the highest state court had emphasized its significant impact on commerce and the fact that it was more sweeping than necessary to achieve its objectives. In reversing, Justice REHNQUIST stated: "While relevant if the Commerce Clause imposes restraints on the city's activity, [the state court's] characterization is of no help in deciding whether those restraints apply." He added: "If the city is a market participant, then the Commerce Clause establishes no barrier to conditions such as these which the city demands for its participation." He concluded: "Insofar as the city expended only its own funds in entering into construction contracts for public projects, it was a market participant and entitled to be treated as such under the rule of [Alexandria Scrap]."

Justice BLACKMUN's dissent with respect to the city-funded projects, joined by Justice White, emphasized that the city's action imposed restrictions on private firms and therefore did not fall within the market participant exception.[2] He stated: "Boston's executive order goes much further [than Alexandria Scrap or Reeves]. The city has not attempted merely to choose the 'parties with whom [it] will deal.' Instead, it has imposed as a condition of obtaining a public construction contract the requirement that *private firms* hire only Boston residents for 50% of specified jobs. Thus, the order directly restricts the ability of private employers to hire nonresidents, and thereby curtails nonresidents' access to jobs with private employers. I had thought it well established that, under the Commerce Clause, States and localities cannot impose restrictions granting their own residents either the exclusive right, or a priority, to private sector economic opportunities. See [e.g., Hood; cf. Hicklin v. Orbeck (1978), p. 311 below]. Such restrictions are not immune from attack under the

1. The challenged executive order by the Mayor of Boston was in fact broader than that: it applied to all construction projects "funded in whole or in part by City funds, or funds which, in accordance with a federal grant or otherwise, the City expends or administers, and to which the City is a signatory to the construction contract." The Court sustained the application of the 50% requirement to projects funded in part by federal grants, for reasons noted in the next footnote.

As noted below, Justice Blackmun wrote the dissent in White, objecting to the application of the market participant exception to wholly city-funded projects and distinguishing Reeves. (Note that it was Justice Blackmun who had written the broad opinion in Reeves—and that it had been Justice Powell, the author of Alexandria Scrap, who wrote the dissent from its application in Reeves.) Contrast the decision in this case, *rejecting* a commerce clause attack, with the Camden case, p. 308 below, *sustaining* an Art. IV attack on a similar employment preference.

2. With respect to the applicability of the requirement to projects funded in part by the federal government, Justice Blackmun concluded that federal regulations "affirmatively permit" the type of parochial favoritism expressed in the order; and commerce clause restraints on states are not applicable to congressionally authorized action. On the issue of federally funded programs, the Court was accordingly unanimous. Justice Blackmun noted that "Congress unquestionably has the power to authorize state or local discrimination against interstate commerce that otherwise would violate the dormant aspect of the Commerce Clause." He cited Prudential Insurance Co. v. Benjamin, the 1946 decision discussed in sec. 2B below, at p. 329.

Commerce Clause solely because a city has imposed them as conditions to its contracts with private employers. [The] simple unilateral refusals to deal that the Court encountered in Reeves and Alexandria Scrap were relatively pure examples of a seller's or purchaser's simply choosing its bargaining partners, 'long recognized' as the right of traders in our free enterprise system. The executive order in this case, in notable contrast, by its terms is a direct attempt to govern private economic relationships. The power to dictate to another those with whom *he* may deal is viewed with suspicion and closely limited in the context of purely private economic relations. When exercised by government, such a power is the essence of regulation." [3] He accordingly concluded that the order was a "protectionist measure" subject to the rule of "virtually per se invalidity established by many of this Court's cases. See, e.g., Philadelphia v. New Jersey."

2. SOUTH–CENTRAL TIMBER DEVELOPMENT, INC. v. WUN-NICKE, 467 U.S. —— (1984), was the first Court ruling to *reject* a state defense under the market participant exception. The case struck down an Alaska law limiting the sale of timber from state lands to those who would at least partially process the timber within Alaska before shipping it out of the state. Justice WHITE's plurality opinion found the market participant exception inapplicable and invalidated the requirement on traditional commerce clause grounds.[1] On the market participant exception, Justice White reiterated the general rule of the preceding cases ("if a State is acting as a market participant, rather than as a market regulator, the dormant Commerce Clause places no limitation on its activities"), stated that the "precise contours of the market-participant doctrine have yet to be established," and found all of the earlier cases distinguishable. Unlike Alexandria Scrap, Alaska sought to impose "conditions downstream in the timber-processing market." And although Reeves indicated that there were no commerce power restraints on the state's "power to choose the terms on which it will sell," that case "did not—and did not purport to—sanction the imposition of any terms that the State might desire." This Alaska case involved three elements not present in Reeves: "foreign commerce, a natural resource, and restrictions on resale." And although the White case had upheld a requirement that reached beyond "the boundary of formal privity of contract" (see footnote 2 to White, above), that did not mean *all* conditions imposed on the buyer under the contract of sale were permissible: "That privity of contract is not always the outer boundary of permissible state activity does not necessarily mean that the Commerce Clause has no application within the boundary of formal privity. The market-participant [doctrine] is not carte blanche to impose any conditions that the State has the economic power to dictate, and does not

---

3. Justice Rehnquist's majority opinion responded to this argument as follows: "We agree with Justice Blackmun that there are some limits on a state or local government's ability to impose restrictions that reach beyond the immediate parties with which the government transacts business. Cf. Hicklin v. Orbeck. We find it unnecessary in this case to define those limits with precision, except to say that we think the Commerce Clause does not require the city to stop at the boundary of formal privity of contract. In this case, the Mayor's executive order covers a discrete, identifiable class of economic activity in which the city is a major participant. Everyone affected by the order is, in a substantial if informal sense, 'working for the city.' Wherever the limits of the market participation exception may lie, we conclude that the executive order in this case falls well within the scope of Alexandria

Scrap and Reeves." (But see Justice White's subsequent opinion in the South-Central Timber Development case, which follows.)

1. Only six Justices participated in the ruling on the commerce clause issue. Justice White was joined by Justices Brennan, Blackmun and Stevens. Justice Rehnquist, joined by Justice O'Connor, dissented. Justice Marshall did not participate. And Justice Powell, joined by Chief Justice Burger, concurred in a notation limited to the only issue the Court of Appeals had reached: whether Congress had implicitly authorized the Alaska scheme. Disagreeing with the lower court, Justice Powell joined only that part of Justice White's opinion finding no such authorization. He urged that the commerce clause issue be remanded to the lower court.

validate any requirement merely because the State imposes it upon someone with whom it is in contractual privity."

Justice White summarized his position as follows: "The limit of the market-participant doctrine must be that it allows a State to impose burdens on commerce within the market in which it is a participant, but allows it to go no further. The State may not impose conditions, whether by statute, regulation, or contract, that have a substantial regulatory effect outside of that particular market. Unless the 'market' is relatively narrowly defined, the doctrine has the potential of swallowing up the rule that States may not impose substantial burdens on interstate commerce even if they act with the permissible state purpose of fostering local industry." And here the relevant market was the sale of timber as such and did not include processing: "Although the State may be a participant in the timber market, it is using its leverage in that market to exert a regulatory effect in the processing market, in which it is not a participant." [2]

Justice REHNQUIST's dissent, joined by Justice O'Connor, insisted that the market participant exception *was* applicable: "The contractual term at issue here no more transforms Alaska's sale of timber into 'regulation' of the processing industry than the resident-hiring preference imposed by [Boston in White] constituted regulation of the construction industry. Alaska is merely paying the buyer of the timber indirectly, by means of a reduced price, to hire Alaska residents to process the timber. Under existing precedent, the State could accomplish that same result in any number of ways. For example, the State could choose to sell its timber only to those companies that maintain active primary-processing plants in Alaska. [Reeves.] Or the State could directly subsidize the primary-processing industry within the State. [Alexandria Scrap.] The State could even pay to have the logs processed and then enter the market only to sell processed logs. It seems to me unduly formalistic to conclude that the one path chosen by the State as best suited to promote its concerns is the path forbidden it by the Commerce Clause." [3]

---

6. THE ROLE OF THE PRIVILEGES AND IMMUNITIES CLAUSE OF ART. IV

Introduction. The function of the privileges and immunities clause of Art. IV—the first paragraph of § 2 of Art. IV—overlaps those of several other provisions of the Constitution. For example, like the commerce clause, Art. IV, § 2 serves as a restraint on state efforts to bar out-of-staters from access to local resources. As the Court has recognized, there is a "mutually reinforcing

2. Having found the market participant exception inapplicable, Justice White found it easy to invalidate the state restriction on traditional commerce clause principles. After quoting from Pike, he concluded: "Because of the protectionist nature of Alaska's local-processing requirement and the burden on commerce resulting therefrom, we conclude that it falls within the rule of virtual per se invalidity of laws that 'bloc[k] the flow of interstate commerce at a State's borders.' Philadelphia v. New Jersey." The fact that the challenger was engaged in foreign rather than interstate commerce added strength to that conclusion: "It is a well-accepted rule that state restrictions burdening foreign commerce are subjected to a more rigorous and searching scrutiny."

3. Responding to this, Justice White's plurality opinion argued that Justice Rehnquist's posi-

tion "would validate [any] contractual condition that the State had the economic power to impose, without regard to the relationship of the subject matter of the contract and the condition imposed. If that were the law, it would have been irrelevant that the employees in [White] were in effect 'working for the city.' If the only question were whether the condition is imposed by contract, a residency requirement could have been imposed with respect to the work force on all projects of any employer doing business with the city." A separate notation by Justice BRENNAN, who joined Justice White's opinion, stated: "In my view, Justice White's treatment of the market-participant doctrine and the response of Justice Rehnquist point up the inherent weakness of the doctrine. See [Alexandria Scrap, Brennan, J., dissenting]."

relationship between the Privileges and Immunities Clause of Art. IV, § 2, and the Commerce Clause—a relationship that stems [in part from] their shared vision of federalism."[1] And modern Justices have increasingly drawn on the Art. IV provision in a number of contexts.[2] But the close relationship between Art. IV, § 2 and the commerce clause does not mean that they are wholly synonymous in impact. As the next principal case illustrates, a state policy may survive commerce clause scrutiny and yet succumb to Art. IV, § 2.[3]

The injunction that the "Citizens of each State shall be entitled to all Privileges and Immunities of Citizens in the several States" was a briefer version of (but had the same purpose as) a similar provision in the Articles of Confederation. In the first significant judicial interpretation of the clause, Justice Bushrod Washington, after describing the scope of the clause in language encompassing a broad range of "fundamental rights," nevertheless sustained the challenged law.[4] The opinions in the Camden case (and the footnotes to those opinions), below, illustrate the contemporary dimensions of Art. IV, § 2.[5] Consider especially the extent to which Art. IV and the commerce clause overlap and the extent to which these two limits on state power in the federal system do and should differ in their scope.

UNITED BLDG. & CONSTR. TRADES v. CAMDEN

465 U.S. 208, 104 S.Ct. 1020, 79 L.Ed.2d 249 (1984).

Justice REHNQUIST delivered the opinion of the Court.

A municipal ordinance of [Camden, N.J.] requires that at least 40% of the employees of contractors and subcontractors working on city construction projects be Camden residents.[1] Appellant, the United Building and Construc-

---

1. Hicklin v. Orbeck, 437 U.S. 518 (1978) (noted further below).

2. The commerce clause is not the only provision to which Art. IV is closely related. The thrust of Art. IV (barring discrimination by one state against citizens of another state) also overlaps with a function of another anti-discrimination provision, the equal protection clause of the Fourteenth Amendment. Note especially Justice O'Connor's concurrence in Zobel v. Williams (1982; chap. 9, p. 842, below). There, the majority relied entirely on equal protection in invalidating an Alaska scheme for distributing income from its natural resources to residents on the basis of length of residence in the state. Justice O'Connor, however, insisted that equal protection standards were satisfied but that the scheme ran afoul of Art. IV, § 2. (The Fourteenth Amendment also contains its own privileges and immunities clause. That provision bars state infringements on the privileges of *national* rather than state citizenship. So far, the Court's interpretations have made it the least significant of the provisions in § 1 of the Fourteenth Amendment. See chap. 7, at p. 417 below.)

3. The Camden case, which follows, invalidated a city preference for Camden, N.J., residents for work on city construction projects. The decision rests on Art. IV, § 2. In contrast, an essentially identical preference, adopted by Boston, survived commerce clause scrutiny in the White case, p. 305 above, on the basis of the market participant exception. Does the differ-

ence in result make sense, in view of the fact that both clauses stem in part from "their shared vision of federalism"?

4. Corfield v. Coryell, 4 Wash.C.C. 371, 6 F.Cas. 546 (C.C.E.D.Pa.1823). For excerpts from Corfield, and for an important reliance on Justice Washington's discussion of "fundamental rights" under Art. IV in interpreting the Fourteenth Amendment, see the Slaughter-House Cases (1873; p. 410 below). Justice Washington's "fundamental rights" emphasis has also reemerged in modern Art. IV cases, as the next principal case (and the cases it discusses) illustrates.

5. See generally Varat, "State 'Citizenship' and Interstate Equality," 48 U.Chi.L.Rev. 487 (1981), and Simson, "Discrimination Against Nonresidents and the Privileges and Immunities Clause of Article IV," 128 U.Pa.L.Rev. 379 (1979). See also Ely, "Choice of Law and the State's Interest in Protecting Its Own," 23 Wm. & Mary L.Rev. 173 (1981).

1. The ordinance was adopted in 1980 pursuant to a statewide affirmative action plan for public work programs. The local residents preference that was added to the ordinance provided, as amended: "The developer/contractor, in hiring for jobs, shall make every effort to employ persons residing within the City of Camden but, in no event, shall less than forty percent (40%) of the entire labor force be residents of the City of Camden." The contractor was also obliged to

tion Trades Council of Camden and Vicinity (the Council), challenges that ordinance as a violation of the Privileges and Immunities Clause [of Art. IV]. The Supreme Court of New Jersey rejected [that] attack on the ground that the ordinance discriminates on the basis of *municipal,* not state, residency. The court "decline[d] to apply the Privileges and Immunities Clause in the context of a municipal ordinance that has identical effects upon out-of-state citizens and New Jersey citizens not residing in the locality."[2] We conclude that the challenged ordinance is properly subject to the strictures of the Clause. We therefore reverse the [judgment] and remand the case for a determination of the validity of the ordinance under the appropriate constitutional standard.

[We] first address the argument [that] the Clause does not even apply to a *municipal* ordinance such as this. Two separate contentions are advanced in support of this position: first, that the Clause only applies to laws passed by a *State* and, second, that the Clause only applies to laws that discriminate on the basis of *state* citizenship. The first argument can be quickly rejected. The fact that the ordinance in question is a municipal, rather than a state, law does not somehow place it outside the scope of the [Clause]. [It] is as true of the Privileges and Immunities Clause as of the Equal Protection Clause that what would be unconstitutional if done directly by the State can no more readily be accomplished by a city deriving its authority from the State. Thus, even if the ordinance had been adopted solely by Camden, and not pursuant to a state program or with state approval, the hiring preference would still have to comport with the [Clause].

The second argument merits more consideration. The New Jersey Supreme Court concluded that the Privileges and Immunities Clause does not apply to an ordinance that discriminates solely on the basis of *municipal* residency. The Clause is phrased in terms of *state* [citizenship]. "The primary purpose of this clause like the clauses between which it is located—those relating to full faith and credit and to interstate extradition of fugitives from justice—was to help fuse into one Nation a collection of independent, sovereign States. It was designed to insure to a citizen of State A who ventures into State B the same privileges which the citizens of State B enjoy. For protection of such equality the citizen of State A was not to be restricted to the uncertain remedies afforded by diplomatic processes and official retaliation." Toomer v. Witsell.[3] Municipal residency classifications, it is argued, simply do not give rise to the same concerns.

We cannot accept this argument. We have never read the Clause so literally as to apply it only to distinctions based on state citizenship. [Despite] some initial uncertainty, it is now established that the terms "citizen" and "resident" are "essentially interchangeable" for purposes of analysis of most cases under the [clause]. A person who is not residing in a given State is ipso facto not residing in a city within that State. Thus, whether the exercise of a privilege is

ensure that any subcontractors working on such projects adhered to the same requirement.

2. The New Jersey Supreme Court had also rejected a commerce clause challenge to the hiring plan, relying on the market participant exception to the commerce clause. Subsequently, the Court decided the Boston preference case, White (p. 305 above). As a result of that decision, the appellant abandoned its commerce clause challenge. (Justice Rehnquist noted that White had "specifically declined to pass on the merits of a privileges and immunities challenge to the [Boston] mayor's executive order because the court below did not reach the issue.")

3. Toomer v. Witsell, 334 U.S. 385 (1948), relied on Art. IV to invalidate South Carolina's discriminatory license fee on residents trawling for shrimp in its waters. Note the similarity to the commerce clause cases in sec. 1C(4) hampering out-of-staters' access to local resources. Note also Douglas v. Seacoast Products, Inc., 431 U.S. 265 (1977), invalidating a Virginia law limiting access by nonresidents to fish in the state's waters but relying on a supremacy clause-preemption ground rather than on Art. IV or the commerce clause.

conditioned on state residency or on municipal residency, he will just as surely be excluded.

Given the Camden ordinance, an out-of-state citizen who ventures into New Jersey will not enjoy the same privileges as the New Jersey citizen residing in Camden. It is true that New Jersey citizens not residing in Camden will be affected by the ordinance as well as out-of-state citizens. And it is true that the disadvantaged New Jersey residents have no claim under the Privileges and Immunities Clause. But New Jersey residents at least have a chance to remedy at the polls any discrimination against them. Out-of-state citizens have no similar opportunity, and they must "not be restricted to the uncertain remedies afforded by diplomatic processes and official retaliation." [4] We conclude that Camden's ordinance is not immune from constitutional review at the behest of out-of-state residents merely because some in-state residents are similarly disadvantaged. Cf. [Zobel v. Williams (O'Connor, J., concurring), p. 842 below].

Application of the [Clause] to a particular instance of discrimination against out-of-state residents entails a two-step inquiry. As an initial matter, the court must decide whether the ordinance burdens one of those privileges and immunities protected by the Clause. [Baldwin].[5] Not all forms of discrimination against citizens of other States are constitutionally suspect. "Some distinctions between residents and nonresidents merely reflect the fact that this is a Nation composed of individual States, and are permitted; other distinctions are prohibited because they hinder the formation, the purpose, or the development of a single Union of those States. Only with respect to those 'privileges' and 'immunities' bearing upon the vitality of the Nation as a single entity must the State treat all citizens, resident and nonresident, equally." Ibid. As a threshold matter, then, we must determine whether an out-of-state resident's interest in employment on public works contracts in another State is sufficiently "fundamental" to the promotion of interstate harmony so as to "fall within the purview of the [Clause]." Id.

Certainly, the pursuit of a common calling is one of the most fundamental of those privileges protected by the Clause. Many, if not most, of our cases expounding the [Clause] have dealt with this basic and essential activity. See, e.g., [Hicklin v. Orbeck (1978), footnote 7 below; Toomer]. Public employ-

---

4. The dissent suggests that New Jersey citizens not residing in Camden will adequately protect the interests of out-of-state residents and that the scope of the [Clause] should be measured in light of this political reality. What the dissent fails to appreciate is that the Camden ordinance at issue in this case was adopted pursuant to a comprehensive, state-wide program applicable in all New Jersey cities. The Camden resident-preference ordinance has already received state sanction and approval, and every New Jersey city is free to adopt a similar protectionist measure. Some have already done so. Thus, it is hard to see how New Jersey residents living outside Camden will protect the interests of out-of-state citizens.

More fundamentally, the dissent's proposed blanket exemption for all classifications that are less than state-wide would provide States with a simple means for evading the strictures of the [Clause]. Suppose, for example, that California wanted to guarantee that all employees of contractors and subcontractors working on construction projects funded in whole or in part by state funds are state residents. Under the dissent's analysis, the California legislature need merely divide the State in half, providing one resident-hiring preference for Northern Californians on all such projects taking place in Northern California, and one for Southern Californians on all projects taking place in Southern California. State residents generally would benefit from the law at the expense of out-of-state residents; yet, the law would be immune from scrutiny under the Clause simply because it was not phrased in terms of *state* citizenship or residency. Such a formalistic construction would effectively write the Clause out of the Constitution. [Footnote by Justice Rehnquist.]

5. Baldwin v. Montana Fish and Game Comm'n, 436 U.S. 371 (1978), rejected an Art. IV attack on a Montana elk-hunting license scheme imposing substantially higher fees on nonresidents than on residents. The majority opinion by Justice Blackmun (the dissenter in the Camden case) insisted that the precedents could best be understood in terms of the "fundamental rights" approach of Corfield v. Coryell (above) and concluded that, "[w]hatever rights or activities may be 'fundamental' " under Art. IV, "elk hunting by nonresidents in Montana is not one of them."

ment, however, is qualitatively different from employment in the private sector; it is a subspecies of the broader opportunity to pursue a common calling. We have held that there is no fundamental right to government employment for purposes of the Equal Protection Clause. Massachusetts v. Murgia [1976; p. 608 below]. Cf. McCarthy v. Philadelphia Civil Service Comm'n, 424 U.S. 645 (1976) (per curiam) (rejecting equal protection challenge to municipal residency requirement for municipal workers).[6] And in White [p. 305 above] we held that for purposes of the Commerce Clause everyone employed on a city public works project is, "in a substantial if informal sense, 'working for the city.' "

It can certainly be argued that for purposes of the Privileges and Immunities Clause everyone affected by the Camden ordinance is also "working for the city" and, therefore, has no grounds for complaint when the city favors its own residents. But we decline to transfer mechanically into this context an analysis fashioned to fit the Commerce Clause. Our decision in White turned on a distinction between the city acting as a market participant and the city acting as a market regulator. The question whether employees of contractors and subcontractors on public works projects were or were not, in some sense, working for the city was crucial to that analysis. [But] the distinction between market participant and market regulator relied upon in White to dispose of the Commerce Clause challenge is not dispositive in this context. The two Clauses have different aims and set different standards for state conduct.

The Commerce Clause acts as an implied restraint upon state regulatory powers. Such powers must give way before the superior authority of Congress to legislate on (or leave unregulated) matters involving interstate commerce. When the State acts solely as a market participant, no conflict between state *regulation* and federal regulatory authority can arise. [White; Reeves; Alexandria Scrap.] The Privileges and Immunities Clause, on the other hand, imposes a direct restraint on state action in the interests of interstate harmony. Hicklin v. Orbeck.[7] This concern with comity cuts across the market regulator-market participant distinction that is crucial under the Commerce Clause. It is discrimination against out-of-state residents on matters of fundamental concern which triggers the Clause, not regulation affecting interstate commerce. Thus, the fact that Camden is merely setting conditions on its expenditures for goods and services in the marketplace does not preclude the possibility that those conditions violate the Privileges and Immunities Clause. [Much] the same analysis [as in Hicklin] is appropriate to a city's efforts to bias private employment decisions in favor of its residents on construction projects funded with public monies. The fact that Camden is expending its own funds or funds it administers in accordance with the terms of a grant is certainly a factor—perhaps the crucial factor—to be considered in evaluating whether the statute's discrimina-

---

6. Could the requirement in McCarthy withstand an Art. IV challenge in light of the decision in the Camden case?

7. Hicklin v. Orbeck, 437 U.S. 518 (1978), was a unanimous decision a few weeks after Baldwin; it invalidated an Alaska law requiring that residents be preferred over nonresidents in certain jobs. The "Alaska Hire" law was "an attempt to force virtually all businesses that benefit in some way from the economic ripple effect of Alaska's decision to develop its oil and gas resources to bias their employment practices in favor of the State's residents." Justice Brennan's opinion stated that Alaska had not demonstrated "that nonresidents were 'a peculiar source of the evil' [the law] was enacted to remedy, namely Alaska's 'uniquely high unemployment.' " He

accordingly concluded that Alaska's discrimination against nonresidents did not "bear a substantial relationship to the particular 'evil' they [were] said to present." (Justice Brennan's opinion found additional support for the result in commerce clause cases pertaining to a state's control over its natural resources.)

In a footnote to his opinion in the Camden case, Justice Rehnquist commented: "Under the dissent's formalistic approach, the 'Alaska Hire' statute in Hicklin would have been exempt from any challenge under the [Clause] if the Alaska legislature had simply excluded from the hiring preference the residents of one remote county. Yet the discriminatory effect on out-of-state residents, with which, after all, the Clause is concerned, would have been the same."

tion violates the [Clause]. But it does not remove the Camden ordinance completely from the purview of the Clause.

In sum, Camden may, without fear of violating the Commerce Clause, pressure private employers engaged in public works projects funded in whole or in part by the city to hire city residents. But that same exercise of power to bias the employment decisions of [contractors] against out-of-state residents may be called to account under the Privileges and Immunities Clause. A determination of whether a privilege is "fundamental" for purposes of that Clause does not depend on whether the employees of private contractors and subcontractors engaged in public works projects can or cannot be said to be "working for the city." The opportunity to seek employment with such private employers is "sufficiently basic to the livelihood of the Nation" [Baldwin] as to fall within the purview of the [Clause] even though the contractors and subcontractors are themselves engaged in projects funded in whole or part by the city.

The conclusion that Camden's ordinance discriminates against a protected privilege does not, of course, end the inquiry. We have stressed in prior cases that "[l]ike many other constitutional provisions, the privileges and immunities clause is not an absolute." [Toomer.] It does not preclude discrimination against citizens of other States where there is a "substantial reason" for the difference in treatment. "[T]he inquiry in each case must be concerned with whether such reasons do exist and whether the degree of discrimination bears a close relation to them." Id. As part of any justification offered for the discriminatory law, nonresidents must somehow be shown to "constitute a peculiar source of the evil at which the statute is aimed." Id.

[Camden] contends that its ordinance is necessary to counteract grave economic and social ills. Spiralling unemployment, a sharp decline in population, and a dramatic reduction in the number of businesses located in the city have eroded property values and depleted the city's tax base. The resident hiring preference is designed, the city contends, to increase the number of employed persons living in Camden and to arrest the "middle class flight" currently plaguing the city. The city also argues that all nonCamden residents employed on city public works projects, whether they reside in New Jersey or Pennsylvania, constitute a "source of the evil at which the statute is aimed." That is, they "live off" Camden without "living in" Camden. Camden contends that the scope of the discrimination practiced in the ordinance, with its municipal residency requirement, is carefully tailored to alleviate this evil without unreasonably harming nonresidents, who still have access to 60% of the available positions.

Every inquiry under the Privileges and Immunities Clause "must [be] conducted with due regard for the principle that the states should have considerable leeway in analyzing local evils and in prescribing appropriate cures." [Toomer.] This caution is particularly appropriate when a government body is merely setting conditions on the expenditure of funds it controls. The Alaska Hire statute at issue in Hicklin v. Orbeck swept within its strictures not only contractors and subcontractors dealing directly with the State's oil and gas; it also covered suppliers who provided goods and services to those contractors and subcontractors. We invalidated the Act as "an attempt to force virtually all businesses that benefit in some way from the economic ripple effect of Alaska's decision to develop its oil and gas resources to bias their employment practices in favor of the State's residents." No similar "ripple effect" appears to infect the Camden ordinance. It is limited in scope to employees working directly on city public works projects. Nonetheless, we find it impossible to evaluate Camden's justification on the record as it now stands. No trial has ever been held in the case. No findings of fact have been made. The Supreme Court of New Jersey certified the case for direct appeal after the brief administrative proceedings that led to approval of the ordinance by the State Treasurer. It would not be appropriate for this Court either to make factual determinations as an initial matter or to take judicial notice of Camden's decay. We, therefore, deem it wise to remand the case to the [New Jersey Supreme Court].

[Reversed and remanded.]

Justice BLACKMUN, dissenting.

For over a century the underlying meaning of the Privileges and Immunities Clause [has] been regarded as settled: at least absent some substantial noninvidious justification, a State may not discriminate between its own residents and residents of other States on the basis of state citizenship. Today, however, the Court casually extends the scope of the Clause by holding that it applies to laws that discriminate *among* state residents on the basis of *municipal* residence, simply because discrimination on the basis of municipal residence disadvantages citizens of other States "ipso facto." This novel interpretation arrives accompanied by little practical justification and no historical or textual support whatsoever. Because I believe that the [Clause] was not intended to apply to the kind of municipal discrimination presented by this case, I would affirm the judgment [below].

I. The historical underpinnings of the [Clause] are not in serious dispute. The Clause was derived from the fourth Article of Confederation [1] and was designed to carry forward that provision's prescription of interstate comity. Both the text of the Clause and the historical record confirm that the Framers meant to foreclose any one State from denying citizens of other States the same "privileges and immunities" accorded its own citizens. [While] the Framers thus conceived of the [Clause] as an instrument for frustrating discrimination based on state citizenship, there is no evidence of any sort that they were concerned by intrastate discrimination based on municipal residence. The most obvious reason for this is also the most simple one: by the time the Constitution was enacted, such discrimination was rarely practiced and even more rarely successful. [In] light of the historical context in which the [Clause] was adopted, it hardly is surprising that none of this Court's intervening decisions has suggested that the Clause applies to discrimination on the basis of municipal residence. To the contrary, while the Court never has addressed the question directly, it repeatedly has proceeded on the assumption that the "Privileges and Immunities of Citizens" to which the Clause refers are entitlements held equally by all citizens of a State.

I am somewhat at a loss to understand how the Court's decision today can be reconciled with its reasoning in [Zobel, p. 842 below].[2] The Alaska statute at issue in Zobel fell outside the scope of the Privileges and Immunities Clause for the elementary reason that it did not discriminate between state residents and nonresidents on the basis of state residence; rather, it discriminated *among* state residents in a way that disadvantaged nonresidents as well but did not thereby implicate the underlying concerns of the Privileges and Immunities Clause.

1. "The better to secure and perpetuate mutual friendship and intercourse among the people of the different States in this Union, the free inhabitants of each of these States, paupers, vagabonds and fugitives from justice excepted, shall be entitled to all privileges and immunities of free citizens in the several States; and the people of each State shall have free ingress and regress to and from any other State, and shall enjoy therein all the privileges of trade and commerce, subject to the same duties, impositions and restrictions as the inhabitants thereof [respectively.]." Articles of Confederation, Art. IV (1777). [Footnote by Justice Blackmun.]

2. Justice O'Connor, who concurred in the judgment in Zobel, wrote separately to express the contrary view that the [Clause] applied to the Alaska statute even though the statute arguably "discriminates among classes of residents, rather than between residents and nonresidents." The Court's apparent reliance on Justice O'Connor's concurrence and its failure to note the position of the Court in Zobel are one measure of the inconsistency between today's decision and [Zobel]. [Footnote by Justice Blackmun.]

The Camden ordinance presently before the Court occupies precisely the same position. The Court's decision clashes with other Privileges and Immunities Clause precedents as well. The Court recognizes, as it must, that the [Clause] does not afford state residents any protection against their own State's laws. When this settled rule is combined with the Court's newly-fashioned rule concerning municipal discrimination, however, it has the perverse effect of vesting non-New Jersey residents with constitutional privileges that are not enjoyed by most New Jersey residents themselves. This result is directly contrary to the Court's longstanding position that the [Clause] does not give nonresidents "higher and greater privileges than are enjoyed by the citizens of the state itself." When judicial alchemy transmutes gold into lead in this fashion, it is time for the Court to re-examine its reasoning.

Finally, the Court fails to attend to the functional considerations that underlie the [Clause]. The Clause has been a necessary limitation on state autonomy not simply because of the self-interest of individual States, but because state parochialism is likely to go unchecked by state political processes when those who are disadvantaged are by definition disenfranchised as well. The Clause remedies this breakdown in the representative process by requiring state residents to bear the same burdens that they choose to place on nonresidents; "by constitutionally tying the fate of outsiders to the fate of those possessing political power, the framers insured that their interests would be well looked after." J. Ely, Democracy and Distrust 83 (1980). As a practical matter, therefore, the scope of the Clause may be measured by asking whether failure to link the interests of those who are disadvantaged with the interests of those who are preferred will consign the former group to "the uncertain remedies afforded by diplomatic processes and official retaliation." [Toomer.]

Contrary to the Court's tacit assumption, discrimination on the basis of municipal residence is substantially different in this regard from discrimination on the basis of state citizenship. The distinction is simple but fundamental: discrimination on the basis of municipal residence penalizes persons within the State's political community as well as those without. The Court itself points out that while New Jersey citizens who reside outside Camden are not protected by the [Clause], they may resort to the State's political processes to protect themselves. What the Court fails to appreciate is that this avenue of relief for New Jersey residents works to protect residents of other States as well; disadvantaged state residents who turn to the state legislature to displace ordinances like Camden's further the interests of nonresidents as well as their own.[3] Nor is this mechanism for relief merely a theoretical one: in the past decade, several States [have] repealed or forbidden protectionist ordinances like the one at issue here. The Court [has] applied the [Clause] without regards for the political ills [that] it was designed to cure.[4]

3. The Court suggests that reliance on the state political process is misplaced because the Camden ordinance itself "was adopted pursuant to a state-wide program applicable in all New Jersey cities" and has received "state sanction and approval." [The] Court's observation reduces to the pedestrian point that the Camden ordinance has been adopted by the city and has yet to be displaced by the state legislature. That fact says nothing at all about the likelihood that the ordinance will be repealed in the future, of course, particularly should it develop on remand that interested parties like appellant ultimately must seek political rather than judicial vindication. [Footnote by Justice Blackmun.]

4. Rather than respond directly to these considerations, the Court finds it easier to take issue with what it characterizes as "the dissent's proposed blanket exemption" from the [Clause] "for all classifications that are less than state-wide." The Court's refusal to accept such an exemption is understandable; what is curious is why the Court attributes the exemption to this dissent. [I] am no less prepared than the Court has been in the past to apply the [Clause] when the classification at issue is practically equivalent to those explicitly identified by the Clause. If the Alaska legislature were to try to rehabilitate the "Alaska Hire" statute invalidated in Hicklin, by excluding "the residents of one remote county" from the hiring preference, for example, the classification would come within the ambit of the Clause because it would bear the same sort of practical relationship to a classification based on state

It still might be possible to redeem the Court's decision if it were compelled by the language of the [Clause]. The Court itself, however, concedes that its interpretation of the Clause does not attach readily to a constitutional provision phrased solely in terms of state citizenship. [Whenever] this Court has departed from the literal language of the Clause in the past, it has remained faithful to the underlying purposes of the Clause. [I] believe that the Court's decision today does not satisfy that requirement.[5]

A RIGHT OF PERSONAL MOBILITY: WHAT CONSTITUTIONAL SOURCES?

The Court has long—and with increasing frequency in recent years—recognized a constitutionally protected individual interest in migrating from state to state. But the Justices have been clearer about the existence of a protected right to interstate mobility than about the constitutional sources of the right.[1] Calling attention to the interest in personal mobility is appropriate at this point because both the commerce clause and the privileges and immunities clause of Art. IV have been among the constitutional provisions the Court has drawn upon in addressing restraints on personal mobility.

The best known commerce clause case is EDWARDS v. CALIFORNIA, 314 U.S. 160 (1941), where the Court invalidated a law making it a misdemeanor to bring into California "any indigent person who is not a resident of the State, knowing him to be an indigent person." The so-called "anti-Okie law" became especially controversial during the Great Depression. California argued, as the Court put it, "that the huge influx of migrants into California in recent years has resulted in problems of health, morals, and especially finance, the proportions of

citizenship as do classifications based on state residence. The Court fails to explain why a classification that benefits all state residents *other* than the residents of a single locality stands in the same position, in terms of the practical considerations underlying the Clause, as a classification that benefits *only* the residents of one locality.

The Court raises the alternative prospect that a State might evade the [Clause] by dividing itself in half and granting the residents in each half of the State employment preferences over residents in the other half of the State. The Clause exists to protect against those classifications that a State's political process cannot be relied on to prevent, however, not those that it can, and there is no reason to believe that state residents will be willing to forgo access to employment in one half of a State merely to obtain privileged access to jobs in the other half. The fact that no State has attempted anything resembling the Court's proposed maneuver in the two centuries since the adoption of the Clause, despite the fact that none of this Court's precedents has foreclosed the option, strongly suggests that state political processes can be trusted to prevent this kind of Balkanization. The Court cannot justify deforming the Constitution's response to real problems by invoking imaginary and unrealistic ones. [Footnote by Justice Blackmun.]

5. I argued without success last Term [that] ordinances like Camden's violate the dormant Commerce Clause. [White.] Although the Privileges and Immunities Clause and the Commerce Clause embody closely related principles of interstate relations, I agree with the Court that in certain circumstances the two Clauses "set different standards for state conduct." This is one such circumstance; the Commerce Clause entails a substantive policy of unimpeded interstate commerce that is impermissibly undermined by local protectionism even when intrastate commerce is penalized as well. See [Dean Milk]. [Footnote by Justice Blackmun.]

1. See Ely, Democracy and Distrust (1980), 177, stating: "The Constitution makes no mention of any [right to travel from state to state]. By now we know that cannot be determinative, but we are entitled to some sort of explanation of why the right is appropriately attributable. In recent years the Court has been almost smug in its refusal to provide one." A "right to travel" terminology has been especially widely used in equal protection cases, particularly ones scrutinizing durational residency requirements regarding voting, receipt of welfare benefits, and access to divorce courts. Cases such as those are considered in chap. 9 below. A good illustration of the stance that evoked Ely's criticism is the majority's statement in Shapiro v. Thompson (1969; welfare benefits; p. 832 below): "We have no occasion to ascribe the source of this right to travel interstate to a particular constitutional provision." (The "right to travel" language in equal protection cases can be better understood as a reference to the right to migrate from one state to another and settle there.)

which are staggering." [2]   The Court was unanimous in striking down the law, but the Justices differed about the proper reasoning.   Justice BYRNES' majority opinion relied solely on the commerce clause.   He reiterated the commerce clause "prohibition against attempts on the part of any single State to isolate itself from difficulties common to all of them by restraining the transportation of persons and property across its borders."   He added: "It is frequently the case that a State might gain a momentary respite from the pressure of events by the simple expedient of shutting its gates to the outside world.   But, in the words of Mr. Justice Cardozo: 'The Constitution was framed [upon] the theory that the peoples of the several States must sink or swim together, and that in the long run prosperity and salvation are in Union and not division.'   Baldwin v. Seelig. It is difficult to conceive of a statute more squarely in conflict with this theory than the [one] challenged here.   [The] burden upon interstate commerce is intended and immediate; it is the plain and sole function of the statute. Moreover, the indigent nonresidents who are the real victims of the statute are deprived of the opportunity to exert political pressure upon the California legislature in order to obtain a change in policy.   [Barnwell.]"   In addition, invoking the Cooley approach, he stated that "the social phenomenon of large-scale interstate migration is [certainly] a matter of national concern [and] does not admit of diverse treatment by the several States."   He concluded: "We think this statute must fail under any known test of the validity of State interference with interstate commerce."

Justice DOUGLAS' concurrence, joined by Justices Black and Murphy, found the commerce clause ground inappropriate here: "I am of the opinion that the right of persons to move freely from State to State occupies a more protected position in our constitutional system than does the movement of cattle, fruit, steel and coal across state lines." [3]   He insisted that the right was a "fundamental" one, an "incident of *national* citizenship protected by the privileges and immunities clause of the Fourteenth Amendment against state interference." [4]   (Another concurrence, by Justice JACKSON, also relied on the Fourteenth Amendment provision and also thought the commerce clause inappropriate: "[The] migrations of a human being [do] not fit easily into my notions as to what is commerce.")   But Justice Douglas also noted that "there are expressions in the cases that this right of free movement of persons is an incident of *state* citizenship protected against discriminatory state action by Art. IV, § 2 of the Constitution."   For example, Justice Bushrod Washington's discussion in Corfield v. Coryell (p. 308 above) of "fundamental" rights protected by Art. IV gave as one illustration the "right of a citizen of one State to pass through, or to reside in any other state, for the purposes of trade, agriculture, professional pursuits, or otherwise."   Moreover, protection of interstate mobility in effect underlies a number of the modern Art. IV decisions reviewed in the preceding principal case.   Still other cases have drawn the protection of interstate mobility from even more general sources, especially inferences drawn from the structure of the Constitution.   See, e.g., Justice

---

2. Counsel for California had stated to the Court: "A social problem in the South and Southwest for over half a century, the 'poor white' tenants and share croppers, following reduction of cotton planting, droughts and adverse conditions for small-scale farming, swarmed into California. [The "ordinary routine" of the indigent newcomers allegedly had been to go on relief as soon as possible.] Naturally, when these people can live on relief in California better than they can by working in Mississippi, Arkansas, Texas or Oklahoma, they will continue to come to this State."   Cf. Steinbeck, The Grapes of Wrath (1939). (Earl Warren, as Attorney General of California, signed the State's brief in Edwards.)

3. Recall the dispute about the proper constitutional ground for the public accommodations provisions of the 1964 Civil Rights Act, in chap. 3 above.

4. That Fourteenth Amendment provision has so far been invoked only very rarely by the Court.   Indeed, Justice Jackson's concurrence in Edwards recalled that the Court had called it an " 'almost forgotten' clause."   See the additional discussion of the clause in chap. 7 below, at p. 417.

Stewart's majority opinion in United States v. Guest (1966; federal civil rights violence law; p. 905 below): "Although the Articles of Confederation provided that 'the people of each State shall have free ingress and regress to and from any other State,' [5] that right finds no explicit mention in the Constitution. The reason, it has been suggested, is that a right so elementary was conceived from the beginning to be a necessary concomitant of the stronger Union the Constitution created. In any event, freedom to travel throughout the United States has long been recognized as a basic right under the Constitution." [6]

SECTION 2. CONGRESSIONAL ORDERING OF FEDERAL–STATE RELATIONSHIPS

Scope Note. Most of the materials in sec. 1 emphasized limits on state regulatory power derived from the commerce clause itself. But in many cases the commerce clause is not entirely "dormant"; with increasing frequency, objections based on the *exercise* of the congressional power are joined with those resting on the constitutional *grant* of the power. That, indeed, was so as early as Gibbons v. Ogden; it is even more common in the context of proliferating national legislation of the 20th century. This section briefly examines the impact of congressional exercises of power.

The major concern is with two types of congressional action: (1) laws allegedly imposing new limits on state authority (sec. 2A); and (2) laws allegedly removing preexisting barriers to state regulation (sec. 2B). Much of the material deals with national laws pertaining to commerce, but congressional action is of course significant with regard to a wide range of other delegated powers as well, as the next principal case illustrates. This section highlights what has been a pervasive but somewhat obscured phenomenon in the earlier materials: that the Court in fact operates as an important yet only a limited partner of Congress in articulating federalism limits on state power; that Congress often plays a decisive role in determining the relations between state and federal power; and that the interrelationships between state and federal law present subtle and complex problems for Congress and Court.

A. PREEMPTION OF STATE AUTHORITY

Introduction. When Congress exercises a granted power, the federal law may supersede state laws and preempt state authority, because of the operation of the supremacy clause of Art. VI. In those cases, it is ultimately Art. VI, not the commerce clause or some other grant of delegated power, that overrides the state law. When a valid federal statute explicitly bars certain types of state action, there are no difficulties. But problems arise when the federal legislation

---

5. But note that the Articles' counterpart to the Art. IV privileges and immunities clause contained a specific exception for "paupers, vagabonds and fugitives from justice."

6. See also Crandall v. Nevada, 6 Wall. 35 (1867), which invalidated a tax on passengers leaving the state via common carriers and emphasized the citizen's basic "right to come to the seat of [the national] government." That decision, which has since been read as implying a right to move freely throughout the nation, presumably rested on structural inferences, since it

was rendered before the ratification of the Fourteenth Amendment and did not rest on any specific provision of the original Constitution. Crandall is discussed in the Slaughter-House Cases (p. 410 below), where the majority gave it as an example of a right of *national* citizenship protected by the privileges and immunities clause of the Fourteenth Amendment. (On the "liberty" to travel abroad—rather than interstate—that is protected by the due process clauses, see, e.g., Aptheker v. Secretary of State (1964), p. 1034 below.)

does not clearly disclose its intended impact on state laws. In those situations, the claim is nevertheless often made that congressional action "preempts" state authority regarding the same subject matter. The Court's preemption rulings often turn on a determination of congressional intent in the setting of the particular text, history and purposes of the federal legislation involved. This section does not deal with the details of the differing statutory contexts in which preemption problems arise. Instead, these materials attempt to identify some recurrent themes (and to examine some widely used formulas) in cases that seek to determine whether congressional action has preempted state authority. The principal case that follows provides an illustration of the modern Court's approach to preemption issues in a controversial context. The notes following that case pursue some general themes in preemption litigation, with a special effort to identify considerations operative in preemption cases that closely resemble factors that were significant in the dormant commerce clause cases considered in sec. 1.[1]

PACIFIC GAS & ELEC. CO. v. STATE ENERGY COMM'N

461 U.S. 190, 103 S.Ct. 1713, 75 L.Ed.2d 752 (1983).

Justice WHITE delivered the opinion of the Court.

[This decision sustained a California law dealing with the problem of finding a long-term solution for disposing of nuclear wastes. Sec. 25524.2 of the law, adopted in 1976, imposes a moratorium on the certification of nuclear energy plants until the State Energy Resources Conservation & Development Commission "finds that there has been developed and that the United States through its authorized agency has approved and there exists a demonstrated technology or means for the disposal of high-level nuclear waste." "Disposal" is defined as a "method for the permanent and terminal disposition" of such waste. P.G.&E. sought a declaratory judgment that this provision was preempted by the federal Atomic Energy Act of 1954 as amended and therefore invalid under the supremacy clause. The District Court granted that relief, but the Court of Appeals reversed. The Supreme Court agreed with the Court of Appeals' result.[*]]

The turning of swords into plowshares has symbolized the transformation of atomic power into a source of energy in American society. To facilitate this development the federal government relaxed its monopoly over fissionable

---

1. In considering the preemption cases, as in the entire area of congressional ordering, it is useful to bear in mind an observation in Hart & Wechsler, The Federal Courts and the Federal System (2d ed. 1973), 470: "Federal law is generally interstitial in its nature. It rarely occupies a legal field completely. [Federal] legislation, on the whole, has been conceived and drafted on an ad hoc basis to accomplish limited objectives. It builds upon legal relationships established by the states, altering or supplanting them only so far as necessary for the special purpose. Congress acts, in short, against the background of the total corpus juris of the states in much the way that a state legislature acts against the background of the common law, assumed to govern unless changed by legislation."

* The District Court had also found another provision of the state law invalid because it was "preempted by and in conflict with the Atomic Energy Act." That provision, § 25524.1(b), dealt with the interim storage of spent fuel and provided that, before additional nuclear plants could be built, the Energy Commission had to determine on a case-by-case basis that there would be "adequate capacity" for storage of a plant's spent fuel rods "at the time such nuclear facility requires [such] storage." Both the intermediate appellate court and the Court found that provision not ripe for adjudication. Justice White agreed with the Court of Appeals' conclusion that "we cannot know whether the Energy Commission will ever find a nuclear plant's storage capacity to be inadequate." Justice White added that, "because we hold today that § 25524.2 is not preempted by federal law, there is little likelihood that industry behavior would be uniquely affected by whatever uncertainty surrounds the interim storage provisions. In these circumstances, a court should not stretch to reach an early, and perhaps premature, decision respecting § 25524.1(b)."

materials and nuclear technology, and in its place, erected a complex scheme to promote the civilian development of nuclear energy, while seeking to safeguard the public and the environment from the unpredictable risks of a new technology. Early on, it was decided that the states would continue their traditional role in the regulation of electricity production. The interrelationship of federal and state authority in the nuclear energy field has not been simple. [This] case emerges from the intersection of the federal government's efforts to ensure that nuclear power is safe with the exercise of the historic state authority over the generation and sale of electricity.

[A] nuclear reactor must be periodically refueled and the "spent fuel" removed. This spent fuel is intensely radioactive and must be carefully stored. The general practice is to store the fuel in a water-filled pool at the reactor site. For many years, it was assumed that this fuel would be reprocessed; accordingly, the storage pools were designed as short-term holding facilities with limited storage capacities. As expectations for reprocessing remained unfulfilled, the spent fuel accumulated in the storage pools, creating the risk that nuclear reactors would have to be shutdown. This could occur if there were insufficient room in the pool to store spent fuel and also if there were not enough space to hold the entire fuel core when certain inspections or emergencies required unloading of the reactor. In recent years, the problem has taken on special urgency. [Government] studies indicate that a number of reactors could be forced to shut down in the near future due to the inability to store spent fuel.

There is a second dimension to the problem. Even with water-pools adequate to store safely all the spent fuel produced during the working lifetime of the reactor, permanent disposal is needed because the wastes will remain radioactive for thousands of years. [Problems] of how and where to store nuclear wastes [have] engendered considerable scientific, political, and public debate. There are both safety and economic aspects to the nuclear waste issue: first, if not properly stored, nuclear wastes might leak and endanger both the environment and human health; second, the lack of a long-term disposal option increases the risk that the insufficiency of interim storage space for spent fuel will lead to reactor-shutdowns, rendering nuclear energy an unpredictable and uneconomical adventure. The California [laws] at issue here are responses to these [concerns].

It is well-established that within Constitutional limits Congress may preempt state authority by so stating in express terms. Absent explicit preemptive language, Congress' intent to supersede state law altogether may be found from a "scheme of federal regulation so pervasive as to make reasonable the inference that Congress left no room to supplement it," "because the Act of Congress may touch a field in which the federal interest is so dominant that the federal system will be assumed to preclude enforcement of state laws on the same subject," or because "the object sought to be obtained by the federal law and the character of obligations imposed by it may reveal the same purpose." Fidelity Federal Savings & Loan Ass'n v. de la Cuesta, 458 U.S. 141 (1982); [Rice; p. 325 below]. Even where Congress has not entirely displaced state regulation in a specific area, state law is preempted to the extent that it actually conflicts with federal law. Such a conflict arises when "compliance with both federal and state regulations is a physical impossibility" [Florida Lime; p. 326 below], or where state law "stands as an obstacle to the accomplishment and execution of the full purposes and objectives of Congress." Hines v. Davidowitz [p. 325 below].

Petitioners [present] three major lines of argument as to why § 25524.2 is preempted. First, they submit that the statute—because it regulates construction of nuclear plants and because it is allegedly predicated on safety concerns— ignores the division between federal and state authority created by the Atomic

Energy Act, and falls within the field that the federal government has preserved for its own exclusive control. Second, the statute, and the judgments that underlie it, conflict with decisions concerning the nuclear waste disposal issue made by Congress and the [federal] Nuclear Regulatory Commission. Third, the California statute frustrates the federal goal of developing nuclear technology as a source of energy. We consider each of these contentions in turn.

A. Even a brief perusal of the Atomic Energy Act reveals that, despite its comprehensiveness, it does not at any point expressly require the States to construct or authorize nuclear power plants or prohibit the States from deciding, as an absolute or conditional matter, not to permit the construction of any further reactors. Instead, petitioners argue that the Act is intended to preserve the federal government as the sole regulator of all matters nuclear, and that § 25524.2 falls within the scope of this impliedly preempted field. But as we view the issue, Congress, in passing the 1954 Act and in subsequently amending it, intended that the federal government should regulate the radiological safety aspects involved in the construction and operation of a nuclear plant, but that the States retain their traditional responsibility in the field of regulating electrical utilities for determining questions of need, reliability, cost and other related state concerns. Need for new power facilities, their economic feasibility, and rates and services, are areas that have been characteristically governed by the States. [Thus], "Congress legislated here in a field which the States have traditionally occupied [so] we start with the assumption that the historic police powers of the States were not to be superseded by the Federal Act unless that was the clear and manifest purpose of Congress." [Rice.]

The Atomic Energy Act must be read, however, against another background. [Until 1954] the use, control and ownership of nuclear technology remained a federal monopoly. The Atomic Energy Act of 1954 grew out of Congress' determination that the national interest would be best served if the Government encouraged the private sector to become involved in the development of atomic energy for peaceful purposes under a program of federal regulation and licensing. The Act implemented this policy decision by providing for licensing of private construction, ownership, and operation of commercial nuclear power reactors. The AEC, however, was given exclusive jurisdiction to license the transfer, delivery, receipt, acquisition, possession and use of nuclear materials. Upon these subjects, no role was left for the states.

The Commission, however, was not given authority over the generation of electricity itself, or over the economic question whether a particular plant should be built. [The] Nuclear Regulatory Commission (NRC), which now exercises the AEC's regulatory authority, does not purport to exercise its authority based on economic considerations, [and] utility financial qualifications are only of concern to the NRC if related to the public health and safety. It is almost inconceivable that Congress would have left a regulatory vacuum; the only reasonable inference is that Congress intended the states to continue to make these judgments. Any doubt that ratemaking and plant-need questions were to remain in state hands was removed by § 271, which provided: "Nothing in this chapter shall be construed to affect the authority or regulations of any Federal, State or local agency with respect to the generation, sale, or transmission of electric power produced through the use of nuclear facilities licensed by the [Commission]." [This] regulatory structure [remained] unchanged, for our purposes, until 1965, when the following proviso was added to § 271: "*Provided,* that this section shall not be deemed to confer upon any Federal, State or local agency any authority to regulate, control, or restrict any activities of the Commission." [This] account indicates that from the passage of the Atomic Energy Act in 1954 [to] the present day, Congress has preserved the dual regulation of nuclear-powered electricity generation: the federal government maintains complete control of the safety and "nuclear" aspects of energy generation; the states exercise their traditional authority over the need for additional generating capacity, the type of generating facilities to be licensed, land use, ratemaking, and the like.

The above is not particularly controversial. But deciding how § 25524.2 is to be construed and classified is a more difficult proposition. At the outset, we emphasize that the statute does not seek to regulate the construction or operation of a nuclear powerplant. It would clearly be impermissible for California to attempt to do so, for such regulation, even if enacted out of non-safety concerns, would nevertheless directly conflict with the NRC's exclusive authority over plant construction and operation. Respondents appear to concede as much. Respondents do broadly argue, however, that although safety regulation of nuclear plants by states is forbidden, a state may completely prohibit new construction until its safety concerns are satisfied by the federal government. We reject this line of reasoning. State safety regulation is not preempted only when it conflicts with federal law. Rather, the federal government has occupied the entire field of nuclear safety concerns, except the limited powers expressly ceded to the states. When the federal government completely occupies a given field or an identifiable portion of it, as it has done here, the test of preemption is whether "the matter on which the state asserts the right to act is in any way regulated by the federal government." [Rice.] A state moratorium on nuclear construction grounded in safety concerns falls squarely within the prohibited field. Moreover, a state judgment that nuclear power is not safe enough to be further developed would conflict directly with the countervailing judgment of the NRC that nuclear construction may proceed notwithstanding extant uncertainties as to waste disposal. A state prohibition on nuclear construction for safety reasons would also be in the teeth of the Atomic Energy Act's objective to insure that nuclear technology be safe enough for widespread development and use—and would be preempted for that reason.

That being the case, it is necessary to determine whether there is a nonsafety rationale for § 25524.2. [The California Assembly Committee which proposed the bill] reported that the waste disposal problem was "largely economic or the result of poor planning, *not* safety related." The Committee explained that the lack of a federally approved method of waste disposal created a "clog" in the nuclear fuel cycle. Storage space was limited while more nuclear wastes were continuously produced. Without a permanent means of disposal, the nuclear waste problem could become critical leading to unpredictably high costs to contain the problem or, worse, shutdowns in reactors. "Waste disposal *safety*," the [Committee] notes, "is not directly addressed by the bills, which ask only that a method [of waste disposal] be chosen and accepted by the federal government." [Although specific] indicia of California's intent in enacting § 25524.2 are subject to varying interpretation, [we] should not become embroiled in attempting to ascertain California's true motive. First, inquiry into legislative motive is often an unsatisfactory venture. United States v. O'Brien [p. 220 above]. [Second], it would be particularly pointless for us to engage in such inquiry here when it is clear that the states have been allowed to retain authority over the need for electrical generating facilities easily sufficient to permit a state so inclined to halt the construction of new nuclear plants by refusing on economic grounds to issue certificates of public convenience in individual proceedings. In these circumstances, it should be up to Congress to determine whether a state has misused the authority left in its hands. Therefore, we accept California's avowed economic purpose as the rationale for enacting § 25524.2. Accordingly, the statute lies outside the occupied field of nuclear safety regulation.

B. Petitioners' second major argument concerns federal regulation aimed at the nuclear waste disposal problem itself. It is contended that § 25524.2 conflicts with federal regulation of nuclear waste disposal, with the NRC's decision that it is permissible to continue to license reactors, notwithstanding uncertainty surrounding the waste disposal problem, and with Congress' recent passage of legislation directed at that problem.

[The NRC has promulgated extensive and detailed regulations concerning the operation of nuclear facilities and the handling of nuclear materials. The regulations specify design and control requirements for fuel storage and handling of radioactive waste, both at the reactor site and away from the reactor. But no federal agency has yet licensed any permanent disposal facilities, and there is continued authorization of storage of spent fuel at reactor sites in pools of water. In 1977, the NRC refused to halt reactor licensing until a method of permanent disposal was certified.] The NRC concluded that, given the progress toward the development of disposal facilities and the availability of interim storage, it could continue to license new reactors. The NRC's imprimatur, however, indicates only that it is safe to proceed with such plants, not that it is economically wise to do so. Because the NRC order does not and could not compel a utility to develop a nuclear plant, compliance with both it and § 25524.2 are possible. Moreover, because the NRC's regulations are aimed at insuring that plants are safe, not necessarily that they are economical, § 25524.2 does not interfere with the objective of the federal regulation. Nor has California sought through § 25524.2 to impose its own standards on nuclear waste disposal. The statute accepts that it is the federal responsibility to develop and license such technology. As there is no attempt on California's part to enter this field, one which is occupied by the federal government, we do not find § 25524.2 preempted any more by the NRC's obligations in the waste disposal field than by its licensing power over the plants [themselves].[1]

C. Finally, it is strongly contended that § 25524.2 frustrates the Atomic Energy Act's purpose to develop the commercial use of nuclear power. It is well established that state law is preempted if it "stands as an obstacle to the accomplishment of the full purposes and objectives of Congress." [E.g., Hines; Florida Lime]. There is little doubt that a primary purpose of the Atomic Energy Act was, and continues to be, the promotion of nuclear power. [It] is true, of course, that Congress has sought to simultaneously promote the development of alternative energy sources, but we do not view these steps as an indication that Congress has retreated from its oft-expressed commitment to further development of nuclear power for electricity generation. The Court of Appeals is right, however, that the promotion of nuclear power is not to be accomplished "at all costs." The elaborate licensing and safety provisions and the continued preservation of state regulation in traditional areas belie that. Moreover, Congress has allowed the States to determine—as a matter of economics—whether a nuclear plant vis-a-vis a fossil fuel plant should be built.

---

1. Justice White also considered the impact of the Nuclear Waste Policy Act of 1982, "a new piece [added] to the regulatory puzzle." The Act provides for "a multi-faceted attack on the problem." For example, it authorizes repositories for disposal of waste, expansion of interim storage, and research and development. Moreover, it provides a scheme for financing. Justice White stated that while the new law "may convince state authorities that there is now a sufficient federal commitment to fuel storage and waste disposal that licensing of nuclear reactors may resume, and, indeed, this seems to be one of the purposes of the Act, it does not appear that Congress intended to make that decision for the states through this legislation." Thus, the Senate adopted an amendment designed to preempt state regulation in cases such as this. The Senate language was omitted in the House, in part to avoid affecting this pending case. Justice White concluded: "While we are correctly reluctant to draw inferences from the failure of Congress to act, it would, in this case, appear improper for us to give a reading to the Act that Congress considered and rejected. Moreover, it is certainly possible to interpret the Act as directed at solving the nuclear waste disposal problem for existing reactors without necessarily encouraging or requiring that future plant construction be undertaken."

The decision of California to exercise that authority does not, in itself, constitute a basis for preemption. Therefore, while the argument of petitioners and the United States has considerable force, the legal reality remains that Congress has left sufficient authority in the states to allow the development of nuclear power to be slowed or even stopped for economic reasons. Given this statutory scheme, it is for Congress to rethink the division of regulatory authority in light of its possible exercise by the states to undercut a federal objective. The courts should not assume the role which our system assigns to Congress.

[Affirmed.]

Justice BLACKMUN, with whom Justice STEVENS joins, concurring in part and concurring in the judgment.

I join the Court's opinion, except to the extent it suggests that a State may not prohibit the construction of nuclear power plants if the State is motivated by concerns about the safety of such plants. Since the Court finds that California was not so motivated, this suggestion is unnecessary to the Court's holding. More important, I believe the Court's dictum is wrong in several respects.

I. [First], Congress has occupied not the broad field of "nuclear safety concerns," but only the narrower area of how a nuclear plant should be constructed and operated to protect against radiation hazards. States traditionally have possessed the authority to choose which technologies to rely on in meeting their energy needs. Nothing in the Atomic Energy Act limits this authority, or intimates that a State, in exercising this authority, may not consider the features that distinguish nuclear plants from other power sources. On the contrary, § 271 of the Act indicates that States may continue, with respect to nuclear power, to exercise their traditional police power over the manner in which they meet their energy needs. There is, in short, no evidence that Congress had a "clear and manifest purpose" [Rice] to force States to be blind to whatever special dangers are posed by nuclear [plants].

II. The Court's second basis for suggesting that States may not prohibit the construction of nuclear plants on safety grounds is that such a prohibition would conflict with the NRC's judgment that construction of nuclear plants may safely proceed. A flat ban for safety reasons, however, would not make "compliance with both federal and state regulations [a] physical impossibility." [Florida Lime.] The NRC has expressed its judgment that it is safe to proceed with construction and operation of nuclear plants, but neither the NRC nor Congress has mandated that States do so.

III. A state regulation also conflicts with federal law if it "stands as an obstacle to the accomplishment and execution of the full purposes and objectives of Congress." [Hines.] The Court suggests that a safety-motivated state ban on nuclear plants would be pre-empted under this standard as well. But Congress has merely encouraged the development of nuclear technology so as to make another source of energy available to the States; Congress has not forced the States to accept this particular source. A ban on nuclear plant construction for safety reasons thus does not conflict with Congress' objectives or purposes. [In sum], Congress simply has made the nuclear option available, and a State may decline that option for any reason. Rather than rest on the elusive test of legislative motive, therefore, I would conclude that the decision whether to build nuclear plants remains with the States. In my view, a ban on construction of nuclear power plants would be valid even if its authors were motivated by fear of a core meltdown or other nuclear catastrophe.[1]

---

1. A year after the principal case, a closely related issue came before the Court in Silkwood v. Kerr-McGee Corp., 464 U.S. 238 (1984). The majority in the 5 to 4 ruling in Silkwood reiterat-ed the position of the principal case regarding total federal preemption of the field of nuclear energy safety but nevertheless upheld a state court ruling, based on state law, that punitive

TRENDS IN PREEMPTION CASES: THE IMPACT OF COMMERCE CLAUSE DOCTRINES IN ASCERTAINING CONGRESSIONAL PURPOSES

Introduction. Although the federal legislation at issue in the principal case did not rest on the commerce power, commerce clause-based congressional action frequently gives rise to preemption issues. This group of notes deals with several allegedly preemptive laws resting on the commerce power. The notes explore some general statements and some underlying themes in the cases. General preemption formulations of decades-old cases (note 1 below) recur in the modern cases, including the principal case. And the sampling of preemption cases in the commerce area (note 2) calls attention to the possible influence of doctrines familiar from state regulation of commerce cases in determining whether Congress has preempted state authority. In considering that theme, note the following statement from a thoughtful student comment of a generation ago, in Note, "Pre-emption as a Preferential Ground: A New Canon of Construction," 12 Stan.L.Rev. 208 (1959): "The [Court] appears to use essentially the same reasoning process in a case nominally hinging on pre-emption as it has in past cases in which the question was whether the state law regulated or burdened interstate commerce. [The] Court has adopted the same weighing of interests approach in pre-emption cases that it uses to determine whether a state law unjustifiably burdens interstate commerce. In a number of situations the Court has invalidated statutes on the pre-emption ground when it appeared that the state laws sought to favor local economic interests at the expense of the interstate market. On the other hand, when the Court has been satisfied that valid local interests, such as those in safety or in the reputable operation of local business, outweigh the restrictive effect on interstate com-

damages could be awarded for harm caused by the escape of plutonium from a federally-licensed nuclear facility. The majority held that the ruling regarding preemption of safety concerns in the P.G.&E. case did *not* extend as far as preempting the state tort remedy. Finding this form of state safety concern permissible, the Court acknowledged the seeming inconsistency with P.G.&E. but placed the blame at the feet of Congress: "[As] we understand what was done over the years in the legislation concerning nuclear energy, Congress intended to stand by both concepts and to tolerate whatever tension there was between them. We can do no less. It may be that the award of damages based on [state law] is regulatory in the sense that a nuclear plant will be threatened with damages liability if it does not conform to state standards, but that regulatory consequence was something that Congress was quite willing to accept." The punitive damages award was not based on violation of federal safety requirements, nor had Congress provided any tort remedy for nuclear damage accidents. Justice White, the author of the P.G.&E. opinion, also wrote the majority opinion in Silkwood.

A dissent by Justice Powell, joined by Chief Justice Burger and Justice Blackmun, argued at length that the ruling was inconsistent with that in P.G.&E., concluding: "The Court's decision, in effect, authorized lay juries and judges in each of the states to make regulatory judgments as to whether a federally licensed nuclear facility is

being operated safely. [This] authority is approved [even though the NRC] found no relevant violation of its stringent safety requirements worthy of punishment. [It] is not reasonable to infer that Congress intended to allow juries of lay persons [to] impose unfocused penalties solely for the purpose of punishment and some undefined deterrence. These purposes wisely have been left within the regulatory authority and discretion of the NRC." In another dissent, Justice Blackmun, joined by Justice Marshall, emphasized the "incompatibility" between this case and P.G.&E. and "the fact that the Court is by no means compelled to reach the result it espouses today." He conceded that compensatory damages were permissible, as a complement to the federal standards and because they were "an implicit part of the federal regulatory scheme," but argued that state punitive damages were preempted. [Consider whether it is possible to explain the decision in Silkwood in light of P.G.&E. Can the Silkwood ruling be understood on the basis of factors beyond the Court's preoccupation with the details of the statutory scheme? Does it perhaps rest on quasi-constitutional considerations regarding the weight of the state interest, considerations akin to those recurrently aired in the commerce clause balancing cases in sec. 1? If so, what unusually strong interests would explain Silkwood? The traditional state control of its own system of tort liability and damages for harms occurring within the state?]

merce, the Court has rejected the pre-emption argument and allowed state regulation to stand."

1. *The typical formulas: The Rice and Hines cases.* In many modern cases, including P.G.&E., the Court has pointed to preemption standards articulated in two decisions of the 1940s, RICE v. SANTA FE ELEVATOR CORP., 331 U.S. 218 (1947), and HINES v. DAVIDOWITZ, 312 U.S. 52 (1941). In Rice,[1] Justice DOUGLAS' majority opinion stated: "The question in each case is what the purpose of Congress was. Congress legislated here in a field which the States have traditionally occupied. So we start with the assumption that the historic police powers of the States were not to be superseded by the Federal Act unless that was the clear and manifest purpose of Congress. Such a purpose may be evidenced in several ways. The scheme of federal regulation may be so pervasive as to make reasonable the inference that Congress left no room for the States to supplement it. Or the Act of Congress may touch a field in which the federal interest is so dominant that the federal system will be assumed to preclude enforcement of state laws on the same subject. [Or] the object sought to be obtained by the federal law and the character of obligations imposed by it may reveal the same purpose. Or the state policy may produce a result inconsistent with the objective of the federal statute." In Hines,[2] Justice BLACK's majority opinion stated: "[Where] the federal government, in the exercise of its superior authority in this field, has enacted a complete scheme of regulation and has therein provided a standard for the registration of aliens, states cannot, inconsistently with the purpose of Congress, conflict or interfere with, curtail or complement, the federal law, or enforce additional or auxiliary regulations. There is not—and from the very nature of the problem there cannot be—any rigid formula or rule which can be used as a universal pattern to determine the meaning and purpose of every act of Congress. This Court, in considering the validity of state laws in the light [of] federal laws touching the same subject, has made use of the following expressions: conflicting; contrary to; occupying the field; repugnance; difference; irreconcilability; inconsistency; violation; curtailment; and interference. But none of these expressions provides an infallible constitutional test or an exclusive constitutional yardstick. In the final analysis, there can be no one crystal clear distinctly marked formula. Our primary function is to determine whether, under the circumstances of [this] case, Pennsylvania's law stands as an obstacle to the accomplishment and execution of the full purposes and objectives of Congress."

Examine carefully the several criteria listed by Justice Douglas in the Rice case. Note the parallels to the criteria used in some of the cases in sec. 1, above, where state laws were challenged as conflicting with the dormant commerce power itself rather than with its exercise by Congress—with the constitutional grant of power to Congress rather than with its implementation in federal legislation. Note especially the similarity between Justice Douglas' second criterion in Rice and the Cooley standard. Consider the extent to which these formulations support the Stanford Law Review comment noted above. And consider especially the support for that evaluation in the cases in the next note.

1. The Rice case dealt with the impact of the United States Warehouse Act on the power of states over warehousing practices. Rice operated federally licensed public warehouses for the storage of grain in Illinois.

2. Hines barred enforcement of Pennsylvania's Alien Registration Act of 1939 because of the federal Alien Registration Act of 1940. Much of the opinion dealt with the broad nation-al power over immigration and aliens rather than its specific exercise. But even in this traditionally federal area, not all state regulation is barred. Thus, Hines was distinguished in DeCana v. Bica, 424 U.S. 351 (1976), sustaining a California law which prohibited the knowing employment of aliens not entitled to lawful residence in the United States if such employment would have an adverse effect on lawful resident workers.

2. *The Campbell and Florida Lime cases.* a. In CAMPBELL v. HUSSEY, 368 U.S. 297 (1961), the Court found provisions of the Georgia Tobacco Identification Act barred by the 1935 Federal Tobacco Inspection Act. The Georgia law required that tobacco of a certain type—defined in accordance with federal standards—be marked with a white identifying tag when received in warehouses for sale. Justice DOUGLAS' plurality opinion rejected the argument that the Georgia requirement was valid because it "merely supplements the federal regulation": "We do not have here the question whether Georgia's law conflicts with the federal law. Rather we have the question of preemption. [Congress], in legislating concerning the types of tobacco sold at auction, preempted the field." Under the federal program, "complementary state regulation is as fatal as state regulations which conflict with the federal scheme." Justice BLACK's dissent, joined by Justices Frankfurter and Harlan, insisted that "the Court's opinion presents not so much as one fact which indicates that Congress actually intended [to] preclude the States from passing laws which require only that warehousemen place a label on each lot of tobacco offered for sale truthfully showing its official federal type. [Instead], the Court proceeds from the bare fact of congressional legislation to the conclusion of federal pre-emption by application of a mechanistic formula which operates independently of congressional intent." [1]

b.   Campbell v. Hussey was distinguished in FLORIDA LIME AND AVO-CADO GROWERS, INC. v. PAUL, 373 U.S. 132 (1963), involving avocados certified as mature under the federal regulations but containing less than the minimum California oil content. Justice BRENNAN's majority opinion concluded that "there is neither such actual conflict between the two schemes of regulation that both cannot stand in the same area, nor evidence of a congressional design to pre-empt the field." He noted that there was no "physical impossibility" of complying with both standards and that the "maturity of avocados seems to be an inherently unlikely candidate for exclusive federal regulation. [Federal] regulation by means of minimum standards [of] agricultural commodities, however comprehensive *for those purposes* [of marketing] that regulation may be, does not of itself import displacement of state control over the distribution and retail sale of those commodities in the interests of the *consumers* of the commodities within the State." Nor could the Court find "an unambiguous congressional mandate" to exclude state regulation. The federal law here involved, unlike that in Campbell v. Hussey, concerned "minimum" rather than "uniform" standards. The statutory scheme was "one of maturity regulations drafted and administered locally by the growers' own representatives, and designed to do no more than promote orderly competition among the South Florida growers." (The Court did not pass on commerce clause objections because of an inadequate trial record and remanded the case.) [2]

---

1. Compare with Campbell v. Hussey the 1977 decision in Hunt (the Washington Apples case), p. 272 above. Note that in Campbell, the white tags were required for a type of tobacco principally grown in Georgia. Other types, including those grown by nearby Carolina growers, were to be labeled with blue tags. The lower court had noted: "Both the purpose and effect of the Georgia enactment were to make a distinction at the markets, by the color tags, between tobacco grown in Georgia and that grown elsewhere. The effect was to create a wide disparity of price between the two groups of tobacco, the Carolina growers receiving a much lower amount." Did the effort to promote locally grown tobacco—and the use of white tags, to emphasize the availability of the higher quality

tobacco—warrant mention by the majority as relevant to its preemption ruling?

2. Ten years after the Supreme Court's decision in the avocado case, a federal district court held the California law unconstitutional, finding that the "application of the California statute to Florida avocados discriminates against Florida avocados and unreasonably burdens interstate marketing of Florida avocados in violation of the Commerce Clause" by "imposing a standard which is irrational as applied to Florida avocados." The lower court found: "Since 1925, and intensifying in more recent years, the California 8 percent oil content requirement has been maintained and applied against Florida-grown avocados, as the result of pressure from the California avocado industry, for the purpose, inter alia, of

Justice WHITE's dissent, joined by Justices Black, Douglas and Clark, concluded that the supremacy clause barred the application of California's "inconsistent and conflicting" legislation. The dissenters saw the federal scheme as a "comprehensive regulatory program" and insisted that California's interest was identical to the federal one. "There is no health interest here. The question is [a] purely economic one. [Despite] the repeated suggestions to this effect in the Court's opinion, there is no indication that the state regulatory scheme has any purpose other than protecting the good will of the avocado industry—such as protecting health or preventing deception of the public—unless as a purely incidental byproduct."

c. Consider to what extent these modern decisions rest more on considerations like those articulated in the dormant commerce clause cases, sec. 1 above, than on detailed examination of congressional scheme and purpose. Note, e.g., the emphasis in the Florida Lime dissent on the state interest: "no health interest"; "a purely economic one." Do differing perceptions about the true state purpose, a central factor in commerce clause cases, explain the division on the Court in the Florida Lime preemption case? [3]

3. *The impact of unexercised federal authority.* A recurrent issue in preemption cases is the meaning to be attributed to the federal authorities' failure to exercise power to regulate a particular area. Should such unexercised authority be taken to leave regulation to the states, or to bar state regulation as an expression of a federal intent to bar *any* regulation? The Court has sometimes, but not always, relied on the existence of unexercised federal administrative authority to justify a preemption finding. Compare Napier v. Atlantic Coast Line, 272 U.S. 605 (1926) (railroad safety equipment), and Castle v. Hayes Freight Lines, 348 U.S. 61 (1954) (suspension of right to use highways for violation of state truck weight limits), with Southern Pacific, p. 248 above (railroads) and Bibb, p. 253 above (trucks). The first pair of cases produced preemption findings in part on the basis of unexercised ICC authority; the second pair did not. For a recent statement viewing the existence of unexercised authority as indicating a congressional determination that such authority should not be exercised by anyone, see Arkansas Electric Corp. v. Arkansas Public Service Comm'n, 461 U.S. 375 (1983): "[A] federal decision to forgo regulation in a given area may imply an authoritative federal determination that the area is best left *un*regulated, and in that event would have as much preemptive force as a decision *to* regulate."

B. CONSENT TO STATE LAWS

Introduction. May Congress, instead of precluding state action through preemption, validate state laws that, in the absence of such federal consent, would violate the dormant commerce clause? In the Cooley case, the Court indicated that Congress could not validate laws which were "unconstitutional" under the commerce clause; yet a century later, it seemed clear to Justice Stone in the Southern Pacific case that the "undoubted" congressional "power to redefine the distribution of power over interstate commerce" included the

---

excluding competition from Florida avocados in California markets." J.R. Brooks & Son v. Reagan (N.D.Cal.1973). The case is discussed in Deutsch, "Precedent and Adjudication," 83 Yale L.J. 1553 (1974).

3. In recent years, the Florida Lime case has frequently joined the 1940s decisions (note 1 above) among the standard citations for prevailing preemption formulas. See, e.g., in addition

to the principal case, Chicago & N.W. Transportation Co. v. Kalo Brick & Tile, 450 U.S. 311 (1981): "Pre-emption of state law by federal statute [is] not favored 'in the absence of persuasive reasons—either that the nature of the regulated subject matter permits no other conclusion, or that the Congress has unmistakably so ordained.' [Florida Lime.]"

authority "to permit the states to regulate the commerce in a manner which would otherwise not be permissible." What is the justification for that congressional authority? What is its scope? The examples of congressional "consent" in this section explore these problems.[1]

1. *The Wilson Act and the Rahrer case.* a. In LEISY v. HARDIN, 135 U.S. 100 (1890), the Court invalidated an Iowa law prohibiting the sale of intoxicating liquors as applied to beer brewed in Illinois and offered for sale in the "original package" in Iowa. Chief Justice Fuller, after reviewing the Cooley doctrine, tied it to congressional intent and stated that "inasmuch as interstate commerce [is] national in its character, and must be governed by a uniform system, so long as Congress does not pass any law to regulate it, or allowing the States so to do, it thereby indicates its will that such commerce shall be free and untrammeled." He insisted that Peirce v. New Hampshire (one of the License Cases, p. 237 above), "in so far as it rests on the view that the law of New Hampshire was valid because Congress had made no regulation on the subject, must be regarded as having been distinctly overthrown by numerous cases." Accordingly, he concluded that Leisy "had the right to import this beer into that State, [and] had the right to sell it, by which act alone it would become mingled in the common mass of property within the State. Up to that point of time, we hold that, *in the absence of congressional permission to do so,* the State had no power to interfere by seizure." [Emphasis added.]

b. In August, 1890, only a few months after the decision in Leisy v. Hardin, Congress passed the Wilson Act which provided that all intoxicating liquors "transported into any state or territory, or remaining therein, for use, consumption, sale, or storage therein, shall upon arrival in such state or territory be subject to the operation and effect of the laws of such state or territory enacted in the exercise of its police powers, to the same extent and in the same manner as though [such] liquors had been produced in such state or territory, and shall not be exempt therefrom by reason of being introduced therein in original packages or otherwise." Soon after, the Court held that by virtue of this Act a state may apply its prohibition laws to sales of intoxicating liquors in the original packages. IN RE RAHRER, 140 U.S. 545 (1891). According to Rahrer, "Congress has not attempted to delegate the power to regulate commerce, or to exercise any power reserved to the States, or to grant a power not possessed by the States, or to adopt state laws. [It] imparted no power to the State not then possessed, but allowed imported property to fall at once upon arrival within the local jurisdiction." The Court added: "No reason is perceived why, if Congress chooses to provide that certain designated subjects of interstate commerce shall be governed by a rule which divests them of that character at an earlier period of time than would otherwise be the case, it is not within its competency to do so."

2. *The Webb-Kenyon Act.* In 1913, Congress passed the Webb-Kenyon Act, an "Act divesting intoxicating liquors of their interstate character in certain cases"—a reliance on the "divesting" language of Rahrer, above. The law prohibited the shipment of liquor into a state if the liquor was to be "in any manner used in violation of any law of such State." In an action to compel a railroad to accept a consignment of liquor for shipment to West Virginia, the defendant argued that such shipment was illegal under the Webb-Kenyon Act because West Virginia law barred shipment of liquor into the State. The plaintiff countered that the federal law was unconstitutional. Clark Distilling Co. v. Western Maryland R. Co., 242 U.S. 311 (1917), upheld the federal law,

1. On the problems of congressional "consent," see generally Bikle, "The Silence of Congress," 41 Harv.L.Rev. 200 (1927); Dowling, "Interstate Commerce and State Power," 27 Va. L.Rev. 1 (1940), and "Interstate Commerce and State Power—Revised Version," 47 Colum.L. Rev. 547 (1947).

finding that the Act was "but a larger degree of exertion of the identical power which was brought into play in the [Wilson Act]." [2]

3. *The McCarran Act and the Prudential case.* a. In 1944, the Supreme Court found that the Sherman Anti-Trust Act of 1890 applied to the insurance business, even though the Court had held in 1868 that insurance was not commerce. United States v. South-Eastern Underwriters Ass'n, 322 U.S. 533 (1944). The Court concluded that "a nationwide business" such as insurance "is not deprived of its interstate character merely because it is built [upon] contracts which are local in nature." In response, Congress enacted the McCarran Act of 1945, 59 Stat. 33, which not only deferred and limited the applicability of antitrust laws to the business, but also sought to assure continued state authority over insurance. The Act contained a declaration "that the continued regulation and taxation by the several States of the business of insurance is in the public interest, and that silence on the part of the Congress shall not be construed to impose any barrier to the regulation or taxation of such business by the several States." And sec. 2 of the law provided: "(a) The business of insurance [shall] be subject to the laws of the several States which relate to the regulation or taxation of such business. (b) No Act of Congress shall be construed to invalidate, impair, or supersede any law enacted by any State for the purpose of regulating the business of insurance, or which imposes a fee or tax upon such business, unless such Act specifically relates to the business of insurance."

b. In PRUDENTIAL INSURANCE CO. v. BENJAMIN, 328 U.S. 408 (1946), the Company, a New Jersey corporation, objected to the continued collection of a long-standing tax of 3% of the premiums received from all business done in South Carolina. No similar tax was required of South Carolina corporations. The Court assumed that the tax was "discriminatory" and hence invalid under commerce clause decisions. Nevertheless, the Court held that the McCarran Act validated the tax. Justice RUTLEDGE disagreed with the Company's contention that "Congress' declaration of policy adds nothing to the validity of what the states have done within the area covered by the declaration." To accept that claim "would ignore the very basis on which [the] Clark Distilling case [has] set the pattern of the law for governing situations like that now presented." He stated:

"Not yet has this Court held such a disclaimer [of a commerce clause prohibition] invalid. [On] the contrary, in each instance it has given effect to the congressional judgment contradicting its own previous one. It is true that rationalizations have differed concerning those decisions. [But] the results have been lasting and are at least as important, for the direction given to the process of accommodating federal and state authority, as the reasons stated for reaching

2. The substance and much of the language of the Webb-Kenyon Act was written into the Twenty-first Amendment, which also repealed the Eighteenth. Does the broad recognition of state power over liquor in the Twenty-first Amendment make commerce clause concerns wholly inapplicable in that area? Justice Brandeis once so suggested for a unanimous Court: "Since that amendment, the right of a State to prohibit or regulate the importation of intoxicating liquor is not limited by the commerce clause." Finch Co. v. McKittrick, 305 U.S. 395 (1939). In more recent decades, however, the Court has made it clear that the Amendment does *not* bar all commerce clause challenges and does *not* leave absolute control of liquor traffic to the states. See, e.g., Hostetter v. Idlewild Bon Voyage Liquor Corp., 377 U.S. 324 (1964), hold-

ing that New York could not prohibit the sale of tax-free liquor to departing international airline passengers for delivery upon arrival at foreign destinations. See also Bacchus Imports, Ltd. v. Dias, 469 U.S. —— (1984), barring Hawaii's discriminatory excise tax on wholesale liquor sales despite the existence of the Twenty-first Amendment. In order to encourage development of the Hawaiian liquor industry, the state had exempted a locally produced brandy and fruit wine from the tax. The majority concluded that the Amendment was not intended "to empower States to favor local liquor industries by erecting barriers to competition." Three dissenters insisted that the Amendment made permissible what would otherwise be a violation of the commerce clause.

them. [Apart from the] function of defining the outer boundary of its power, whenever Congress' judgment has been uttered affirmatively to contradict the Court's previously expressed view that specific action taken by the states in Congress' silence was forbidden by the commerce clause, this body has accommodated its previous judgment to Congress' expressed approval. Some part of this readjustment may be explained in ways acceptable on any theory of the commerce clause and the relations of Congress and the courts toward its functioning. Such explanations, however, hardly go to the root of the matter. For the fact remains that, in these instances, the sustaining of Congress' overriding action has involved something beyond correction of erroneous factual judgment in deference to Congress' presumably better-informed view of the facts, and also beyond giving due deference to its conception of the scope of its powers, when it repudiates, just as when its silence is thought to support, the inference that it has forbidden state action."

"[W]e would be going very far to rule that South Carolina no longer may collect her tax. To do so would flout the expressly declared policies of both Congress and the state. Moreover it would establish a ruling never heretofore made and in doing this would depart from the whole trend of decision in a great variety of situations most analogous to the one now presented. [The] power of Congress over commerce exercised entirely without reference to coordinated action of the states is not restricted, except as the Constitution expressly provides, by any limitation which forbids it to discriminate against interstate commerce and in favor of local trade. [This] broad authority Congress may exercise alone, subject to those limitations, or in conjunction with coordinated action by the states, in which case limitations imposed for the preservation of their powers become inoperative and only those designed to forbid action altogether by any power or combination of powers in our governmental system remain effective. Here both Congress and South Carolina have acted, and in complete co-ordination, to sustain the tax. It is therefore reinforced by the exercise of all the power of government residing in our scheme. Clear and gross must be the evil which would nullify such an exertion, one which could arise only by exceeding beyond cavil some explicit and compelling limitation imposed by a constitutional [provision] designed and intended to outlaw the action taken entirely from our constitutional framework."

c. Justice Rutledge's conclusion regarding very broad congressional "consent" power is clearer than his reasoning. Congress can "consent" to any variety of state legislation impinging on commerce: in the exercise of the national commerce power, it can permit state laws the Court would otherwise consider "unconstitutional" under the dormant commerce clause. To the Cooley Court, congressional "consent" authority was questionable; to Justice Rutledge a century later, the authority was clear. Why? What explanations *do* go "to the root of the matter," in Justice Rutledge's phrase? What "something beyond" justifies congressional authority today?

After examining the Rutledge opinion, Noel Dowling confessed that "I was still not sure that my vision had caught the 'something beyond.'" Dowling, "Interstate Commerce and State Power—Revised Version," 47 Colum.L.Rev. 547 (1947). In his earlier "State Power" article, 27 Va.L.Rev. 1 (1940), Dowling had suggested rationalizing congressional "consent" by viewing commerce clause restraints as resting on implied congressional policy: "[I]n the absence of affirmative consent a Congressional negative will be presumed [against] state action [unreasonably interfering with interstate commerce], the presumption being rebuttable at the pleasure of Congress." Is that explanation preferable to Justice Rutledge's effort to explain the "consent" power?[3] Does

3. My colleague William Cohen finds Justice Rutledge's explanation clearer and more persua-   sive than Noel Dowling did. After examining the line of cases culminating in Prudential Insur-

this congressional power to consent to otherwise "unconstitutional" state laws support arguments for a similar congressional power to modify constitutional restraints on state authority *outside* the commerce area? Does congressional power under § 5 of the Fourteenth Amendment, for example, authorize Congress to validate state laws otherwise unconstitutional under the due process and equal protection clauses of § 1 of that Amendment? [4]

4. *Other devices for congressional ordering of federal-state relationships.* Congressional consent and preemption are two examples of a wide range of techniques Congress may employ in the ordering of the complex relations between nation and state. Additional examples illustrating the devices Congress may employ include: the congressional role in determining the scope of intergovernmental immunities, p. 333 below; federal incorporation or adoption of state law— either expressly (as in the Federal Tort Claims Act or in the Federal Assimilative Crimes Act, see United States v. Sharpnack, 355 U.S. 286 (1958)) or by implication, as in many areas of tax, copyright and bankruptcy law; and state administration of federal law, as in the unemployment compensation scheme of the Social Security Act, p. 208 above, or in the varied exercises of the federal spending power through conditional grants-in-aid to the states, chap. 4, sec. 2, or in the utilization of state courts and agencies for federal law enforcement (recall the discussion in FERC v. Mississippi, p. 180 above). See generally Hart, "The Relations Between State and Federal Law," 54 Colum.L.Rev. 489 (1954).

SECTION 3. SOME OTHER ASPECTS OF FEDERALISM: A BRIEF SURVEY

Scope Note. Beginning with chap. 2, this book has explored, at some length, the major constitutional issues of the federal system. As a final section of these federalism materials, the following pages look briefly at some additional constitutional dimensions of federalism—dimensions that cannot feasibly be explored at length here. This section will begin with a brief review of commerce clause restraints on state taxation, move on to problems of intergovernmental tax and regulatory immunities, and conclude with a final look at constitutional provisions pertaining to interstate relations. Although full exploration of these issues is beyond the scope of this book, a brief review helps provide a fuller picture of the roles of nation and state in our federalistic Constitution.

A. STATE TAXATION AND FREE TRADE

Sec. 1 of this chapter examined at length the problems of state regulations challenged under the commerce clause. But regulation is not the only variety of state legislative activity subject to commerce clause restraints. A similarly prolific source of litigation has been state taxation challenged as impinging upon

---

ance, Cohen discerned "a rather bright line for determining when congressional consent to otherwise unconstitutional state laws will be effective." In his view, "Congress can validly consent to state laws when [the] constitutional limitation on state power is not matched by a similar or identical limitation on federal power." See Cohen, "Congressional Power to Define State Power to Regulate Commerce," in 2 Courts and Free Markets (Sandalow & Stein, eds., 1982), 523, and

Cohen, "Congressional Power to Validate Unconstitutional State Laws: A Forgotten Solution to an Old Enigma," 35 Stan.L.Rev. 387 (1983).

4. That Fourteenth Amendment problem has become a widely debated one in the wake of such decisions as Katzenbach v. Morgan (1966; p. 946 below); it will be explored in chap. 10, sec. 4, of this book.

interstate commerce. States need tax revenues, and the Court has recognized that state tax bases would be unjustifiably curtailed if *all* interstate business were immunized from tax obligations: "Even interstate business must pay its way, by bearing its share of local tax burdens." Yet, with respect to taxes as with regulations, the commerce clause "by its own force" creates "an area of trade free from interference by the State." States may not impose discriminatory or unduly burdensome taxes, for the Court has feared that, without commerce clause restraints, interstate business would be subject to the risk of multiple taxation, with most or all of its property or income being subjected to the tax scheme of each state in which it does business. From the beginning, the Court has sought to draw lines distinguishing between the permissible and the impermissible state tax. As in the regulatory area, it has sought to accommodate legitimate local needs and the interest in a national economy. The decisions are numerous, difficult to organize, and even more difficult to comprehend in their totality. As the Court itself has said, in an understatement: "The decisions have been 'not always [clear], consistent or reconcilable.'"[1]

The cases have been what Justices have called a "tangled underbrush" and a "quagmire" because in the area of state taxation the variables are even more numerous and complex and the tools of analysis even more uncertain than in the field of state regulation of commerce. Types of taxes and types of taxed activities vary widely. The most commonly litigated taxes have been property taxes, sales and use taxes, net and gross receipts taxes, and license and franchise taxes. The typical subjects of taxation have been interstate transportation and interstate sales, and various segments thereof. Moreover, far more than in the state regulatory area, the Court has had great difficulty in assessing the validity of particular tax schemes: in the search for legitimate interests, the need for revenue can always be set forth.

The special complexity of state tax problems has prompted some Justices to voice perceptions of judicial incompetence. Advocacy of a substantial Court withdrawal from the tax area has been more common than in the regulatory area. A well-known statement appeared in a 1940 dissent by Justice Black: "Spasmodic and unrelated instances of litigation cannot afford an adequate basis for the creation of integrated national rules. [The problem raised by the challenged tax should accordingly be left] for consideration of Congress in a nation-wide survey of the constantly increasing barriers to trade among the States."[2] Yet, assuming that Congress *is* more competent to solve the problem, what should the Court do in the absence of congressional guidance: let the challenged tax stand, or invalidate it? The characteristic majority stance has been to exercise some continued commerce clause scrutiny even while urging legislative assistance. But congressional responses have been sparse and narrow of range. In the 1960s, after extensive studies, a House committee did recommend a comprehensive legislative solution. But the proposed Interstate Taxation Act failed to pass after extensive hearings revealed widespread opposition, especially from state tax authorities adversely affected by particular recommendations. Accordingly, the problems of judicially enforced restraints on state taxes in the interest of the national economy continue to be of considerable importance. Although many of the old barriers to state taxes have been discarded, state taxes continue to generate about as much litigation for the modern Court as state regulations.[3] However, pursuit of the intricacies of state taxation in a book on the basics of constitutional law would require more time

---

1. Northwestern States Portland Cement Co. v. Minnesota, 358 U.S. 450 (1959).

2. Justice Black dissenting (joined by Justices Frankfurter and Douglas) in McCarroll v. Dixie Greyhound Lines, 309 U.S. 176 (1940).

3. For recent examples of Court decisions on state taxation, see Westinghouse Electric Corp. v. Tully, 466 U.S. — (1984), and Armco, Inc. v. Hardesty, 468 U.S. — (1984).

and space than the undertaking warrants. Detailed consideration of commerce clause limits on state taxes is accordingly not attempted here.[4]

B. INTERGOVERNMENTAL TAX IMMUNITIES

As McCulloch v. Maryland (p. 72 above) has already illustrated, one of the constitutional principles that governs relations between state and nation is that neither may destroy the autonomy of the other. In McCulloch itself, John Marshall struck down Maryland's tax on the operations of a federal instrumentality, the Bank of the United States. For over a century after McCulloch, constitutional tax immunities expanded in a number of directions. Marshall in McCulloch had indicated that his views of federal immunity from state taxation did not imply a reciprocal immunity of state operations from federal taxes. Nevertheless, the post-Civil War Court held that state activities did enjoy a reciprocal immunity from federal taxation. Collector v. Day, 11 Wall. 113 (1871). Moreover, the Court steadily expanded the circle of immunities, from the primary immunity of the government itself to the derivative immunity of third persons—employees, lessees, patentees—in some ways related to governmental activities. In the late 1930s, that circle began to contract. For example, Helvering v. Gerhardt, 304 U.S. 405 (1938), and Graves v. New York ex rel. O'Keefe, 306 U.S. 466 (1939), held that the salaries of the employees of one government are not immune from income taxes imposed by the other. In recent years, intergovernmental tax immunities have continued to wane, although the Court continues to enforce a few constitutional tax immunities, as when states impose property taxes directly on federal property.[1]

Increasingly, however, the modern scope of federal immunities turns on congressional statements recognizing or waiving immunities. Thus, when the specific McCulloch issue resurfaced in the Court a century and a half later, in First Agric. Bank v. State Tax Comm'n, 392 U.S. 339 (1968), the Court emphasized the dimensions of the *statutory* grant of immunity. Justice Thurgood Marshall's dissent, joined by Justices Harlan and Stewart, argued that, in light of the "present functions and role of national banks," they should not be considered "constitutionally immune from nondiscriminatory state taxation." He suggested that McCulloch and other "hoary cases" could "and perhaps should" be read as banning only discriminatory taxes. That would "require a re-evaluation of the validity of the doctrine of intergovernmental tax immunities—a doctrine which does not rest upon any specific provisions of the Constitution, but rather upon this Court's concepts of federalism." Since Congress is able to provide statutory immunities, "there is little reason for this Court to cling to the view that the Constitution itself makes federal instrumentalities immune from state taxation in the absence of authorizing legislation." For an effort to articulate "a narrow approach to governmental tax immunity" for the 1980s, see United States v. New Mexico, 455 U.S. 720 (1982). There Justice Blackmun stated the basic principles as follows: "The one constant [is] simple enough to express: a State may not, consistent with the Supremacy Clause, lay a tax 'directly upon the United States.' [But] the limits on the immunity doctrine are [as] significant as the rule itself. [What] the Court's cases leave room for, then,

---

4. For fuller analyses of the field, see, e.g., chap. 9 of Gunther & Dowling, Constitutional Law (8th ed., 1970); Hellerstein, "State Taxation and the Supreme Court: Toward a More Unified Approach to Constitutional Adjudication?" 75 Mich.L.Rev. 1426 (1977); and Hunter, "Federalism and State Taxation of Multistate Enterprises," 32 Emory L.J. 89 (1983).

1. See Rohr Aircraft Corp. v. San Diego County, 362 U.S. 628 (1960). For an extensive modern review of "the development of the constitutional doctrine of state immunity from federal taxation"—and an opinion reading that doctrine quite narrowly—see Massachusetts v. United States, 435 U.S. 444 (1978).

is the conclusion that tax immunity is appropriate in only one circumstance: when the levy falls on the United States itself, or on an agency or instrumentality so closely connected to the Government that the two cannot realistically be viewed as separate entities. [This] view, we believe, comports with the principal purpose of the immunity doctrine, that of forestalling 'clashing sovereignty' [McCulloch], by preventing the States from laying demands directly on the Federal Government." But even under this "narrow approach," the Court continues to scrutinize closely those taxes alleged to discriminate against the federal government. See, e.g., Memphis Bank & Trust Co. v. Garner, 459 U.S. 392 (1983).[2]

C. INTERGOVERNMENTAL REGULATORY IMMUNITIES

As with intergovernmental tax immunities, intergovernmental regulatory immunities have already surfaced in the earlier materials. Structural considerations reinforced by the Tenth Amendment give some protection against federal laws enacted under the Art. I powers of Congress that threaten to undermine state autonomy. The dimensions of that state autonomy limit have divided the Court in a number of cases over the last decade. The developments, beginning with National League of Cities in 1976, are explored in chap. 3 at p. 170 above. To what extent is there a correlative immunity of federal operations from state regulation? The immunity principle of McCulloch v. Maryland applies here as well. The leading case is Johnson v. Maryland, 254 U.S. 51 (1920), relying on McCulloch in reversing the conviction of a post office employee for driving a truck without a state license. Justice Holmes' opinion for the Court concluded: "It seems to us that the immunity of the instruments of the United States from state control in the performance of their duties extends to a requirement that they desist from performance until they satisfy a state officer upon examination that they are competent for a necessary part of them and pay a fee for permission to go on." But he left the scope of the immunity somewhat unclear: "Of course an employee of the United States does not secure a general immunity from state law while acting in the course of his employment. [It] very well may be that, when the United States has not spoken, the subjection to local law would extend to general rules that might affect incidentally the mode of carrying out the employment—as, for instance, a [statute] regulating the mode of turning at the corners of streets." The federal immunity from state regulation may at times be claimed by those in a close relationship with the government; and the scope of the immunity, as in the state tax area, turns largely on congressional policy. See, for example, Miller v. Arkansas, 352 U.S. 187 (1956), barring application of a state licensing scheme to a federal contractor because of a "conflict" between the state requirement and federal regulations designed to ensure the reliability of contractors.[1] As in the state tax area, moreover, the Court is particularly alert to state regulations based on hostility to federal law. For example, in North Dakota v. United States, 460 U.S. 300 (1983), several state laws were evidently enacted to slow down or control federal acquisition of easements pursuant to the Migratory Bird Conservation Act. Applying a standard of whether the state laws were "hostile to federal interests," Justice Blackmun's opinion found that standard met here.[2]

---

2. For a fuller treatment of this group of problems, see chap. 6, sec. 1, of Gunther, Constitutional Law (10th ed., 1980).

1. See also Hancock v. Train, 426 U.S. 167 (1976).

2. For a fuller review of these problems, see sec. 1 of chap. 6 of Gunther, Constitutional Law (10th ed., 1980).

D. INTERSTATE RELATIONSHIPS

A number of constitutional provisions impose interstate obligations or facilitate interstate relationships. The major constitutional source of interstate obligations, Art. IV, § 2, contains two important restraints: the interstate privileges and immunities clause (explored above, in sec. 1C(6) of this chapter), and the obligation regarding rendition of fugitives from justice.[1] The rendition clause of Art. IV, § 2, speaks in mandatory terms: a fugitive from justice "shall [be] delivered up" on "Demand of the executive Authority of the State from which he fled." But that duty is not enforceable against a governor. In Kentucky v. Dennison, 24 How. 66 (1861), Chief Justice Taney stated that "the words, 'it shall be the duty,' [were] not used as mandatory and compulsory, but as declaratory of the moral duty [which the Constitution created]." Congress has enacted legislation to deal with interstate fugitives from justice.[2] Moreover, many states have adopted the Uniform Law to Secure the Attendance of Witnesses from Within or Without a State in Criminal Proceedings. In New York v. O'Neill, 359 U.S. 1 (1959), the Court sustained the Act as adopted by Florida.

The major device for interstate collaboration recognized in the Constitution is the interstate compact. Art. I, § 10 states that no state "shall, without the Consent of the Congress, [enter into] any Agreement or Compact with another State." Interstate compacts have been used to deal with a wide variety of interstate and regional problems, including boundaries, natural resources regulation and allocation, flood control, transportation, taxation, and crime control. Congress has at times encouraged compacts by giving advance consent, as with crime and flood control. But not all interstate agreements require congressional consent. Virginia v. Tennessee, 148 U.S. 503 (1893), stated that the compact clause is directed at the formation of any combination "which may tend to increase [the] political influence of the contracting States" so as to "impair the supremacy of the United States," and that there are "many matters upon which different States may agree that can in no respect concern the United States." The application of these criteria divided the Court in U.S. Steel Corp. v. Multistate Tax Commission, 434 U.S. 452 (1978), finding that the Multistate Tax Compact drafted in 1966 was not invalid for lack of congressional consent.[3]

1. The most litigated provision of Art. IV is the full faith and credit clause in § 1. Full faith and credit problems are examined in conflicts of laws courses and are not pursued here.

2. See the Fugitive Felon and Witness Act of 1934, 18 U.S.C. § 1073.

3. See Engdahl, "Characterization of Interstate Arrangements: When Is a Compact Not a Compact?" 64 Mich.L.Rev. 63 (1965). See also, on Court interpretation of interstate compacts, West Virginia ex rel. Dyer v. Sims, 341 U.S. 22 (1951). See generally Zimmermann & Wendell, The Interstate Compact Since 1925 (1951); Ridgeway, Interstate Compacts: A Question of Federalism (1971); and sec. 2 of chap. 6 in Gunther, Constitutional Law (10th ed., 1980).

Chapter 6

SEPARATION OF POWERS:
THE PRESIDENT, CONGRESS, AND THE COURT

Introduction. This final chapter of Part II, like the four preceding ones, deals with problems of structure and relationships among units of government. The preceding chapters focused on allocations of power between nation and states. This chapter turns to the allocation of power among the three branches of the national government. The Framers limited power by diffusing authority on a horizontal as well as a vertical plane. Chapters 2 through 5 examined the vertical dimension, the division of powers between national and state governments; this chapter samples problems of the horizontal plane, the separation of powers among President, Congress, and Court.

The makers of the Constitution, influenced not only by their own experiences but also by theorists such as Montesquieu, consciously provided for allocation of national authority among the executive, legislative, and judicial branches. That separation is symbolized by the discrete treatment of each branch, in Articles I, II, and III of the Constitution. But, as an examination of the constitutional provisions reveals, separation was not intended to be airtight. Repeatedly, powers are intermixed, as with the participation of the President in the legislative process through the veto power. And repeatedly, restraints by one branch upon another are authorized, as with the impeachment power. Beyond the explicit restraints and overlaps, moreover, lie boundary lines indistinct in the original document and further blurred by historical practice. Those areas of uncertainty have left ample room for competitions among the branches—conflicts most often resolved by tests of political strength. Those conflict-producing ambiguities may themselves have contributed to furthering the Framers' purpose of combating excessive concentration of power; but they also yield an area of constitutional law with special disappointments for those yearning for clear lines. In the area of separation of powers, far more so than with problems of federalism and individual rights, judicial resolutions have been relatively sparse and political accommodations have predominated. As Justice Jackson commented in his concurring opinion in the Steel Seizure Case, which follows: "A century and a half of partisan debate and scholarly speculation yields no net result but only supplies more or less apt quotations from respected sources on each side of any question." Yet sparsity of Court decisions does not make separation of powers any less important and challenging an area of constitutional interpretation. The raw materials for study here, more than in other areas, lie in executive documents and legislative assertions as well as in Court opinions. But as in other areas, text and history and inferences from structure and relationships warrant searches for appropriate guidelines.

The sampling of separation of powers problems here begins with some examples of competition between President and Congress over the authority to make policy governing national affairs. To what extent does the constitutional grant of executive powers authorize the President to fashion policy in the absence of, or in the face of, congressional decisionmaking? In what manner may Congress impose restraints on executive discretion? Sec. 1A examines the boundaries between executive powers and legislative authority in the domestic sphere; Sec. 1B considers the boundaries with regard to external affairs, with particular emphasis on conflicts regarding the making of foreign policy and the use of military force. Sec. 2 turns to problems concerning the autonomy of each of the branches vis-á-vis interferences by the others. To what extent does the separation of powers protect each branch against intervention in its internal processes? To what degree are the legislative and executive branches amenable to judicial process? To what extent does the Constitution grant final, nonreviewable authority to decide some constitutional issues to organs of government other than the courts? Sec. 2 includes an examination of the Watergate Tapes litigation culminating in the 1974 decision in United States v. Nixon as a case study presenting several of the interrelated problems in this section: the amenability of the President to judicial process; the claimed finality of his judgment regarding the scope of executive privilege; and the contents of a judicially delineated executive privilege for confidential communications.

SECTION 1. THE AUTHORITY TO MAKE NATIONAL POLICY: THE CONFLICT BETWEEN LEGISLATIVE POWERS AND EXECUTIVE AUTHORITY

A. DOMESTIC AFFAIRS

Presidential leadership and congressional lawmaking. Because the President is the elected official with a national constituency and the party leader, the actual influence of the Presidency on national policy is obviously great. What of the President's constitutional authority to devise and implement policy to deal with domestic problems in the private sector? Does the Chief Executive have residual emergency power to regulate private conduct? Do the specified executive powers in Art. II or the inherent powers of the Presidency authorize the President to act when Congress has been silent? Are there any circumstances in which the President's powers take precedence even over conflicting congressional directives? Or is the President limited to the specific tasks assigned by Art. II and to the execution of laws Congress enacts? The executive power to make "law" has evoked frequent and intense battles, most commonly over abstractions, with Presidents as well as commentators on opposing sides. But the operative and most helpful answers may lie less in embracive absolutes than in discriminating distinctions and practical adjustments: compare, for example, the broad assertions of Justice Black with the more detailed analysis of Justice Jackson in the Steel Seizure Case in 1952, and contrast Chief Justice Burger's majority opinion with Justice White's dissent in Chadha, the legislative veto case in 1983. Both decisions appear as principal cases, below.

YOUNGSTOWN SHEET & TUBE CO. v. SAWYER
[THE STEEL SEIZURE CASE]

343 U.S. 579, 72 S.Ct. 863, 96 L.Ed. 1153 (1952).

Mr. Justice BLACK delivered the opinion of the Court.

[We] are asked to decide whether [President Truman] was acting within his constitutional power when he issued an order directing the Secretary of Commerce [Sawyer] to take possession of and operate most of the Nation's steel mills. The mill owners argue that the President's order amounts to lawmaking, a legislative function which the Constitution has expressly confided to the

Congress and not to the President. The Government's position is that the order was made on findings of the President that his action was necessary to avert a national catastrophe which would inevitably result from a stoppage of steel production, and that in meeting this grave emergency the President was acting within the aggregate of his constitutional powers as the Nation's Chief Executive and the Commander in Chief of the [Armed Forces]. The issue emerges here from the following series of events:

In the latter part of 1951 [during the Korean War], a dispute arose between the steel companies and their employees over terms and conditions [for] new collective bargaining agreements. [Efforts to settle the dispute—including reference to the Federal Wage Stabilization Board—failed.] On April 4, 1952, the [Steelworkers'] Union gave notice of a nation-wide strike called to begin [on] April 9. The indispensability of steel as a component of substantially all weapons and other war materials led the President to believe that the proposed work stoppage would immediately jeopardize our national defense and that governmental seizure of the steel mills was necessary in order to assure the continued availability of steel. Reciting these considerations for his action, the President, a few hours before the strike was to begin, issued Executive Order 10340 [directing] the Secretary of Commerce to take possession of most of the steel mills and keep them running. The Secretary immediately issued his own possessory orders, calling upon the presidents of the various seized companies to serve as operating managers for the United States. [The] next morning the President sent a message to Congress reporting his [action]. Congress has taken no action. Obeying the Secretary's orders under protest, the companies brought proceedings against him in the District Court, [which] on April 30 issued a preliminary injunction restraining the Secretary from "continuing the seizure and possession of the plants [and] from acting under the purported authority of Executive Order No. 10340." [1] On the same day the Court of Appeals stayed the District Court's injunction. Deeming it best that the issues raised be promptly decided by this Court, we granted certiorari on May 3 and set the cause for argument on May 12. [This decision was announced soon after, on June 2, 1952.]

The President's power, if any, to issue the order must stem either from an act of Congress or from the Constitution itself. There is no statute that expressly authorizes the President to take possession of property as he did here. Nor is there any act of Congress to which our attention has been directed from which such a power can fairly be implied. [There] are two statutes which do authorize the President to take both personal and real property under certain conditions, [the Selective Service Act of 1948 and the Defense Production Act of 1950]. However, the Government admits that these conditions were not met and that the President's order was not rooted in either of the statutes. The Government refers to the seizure provisions of one of these statutes [the 1950 Act] as "much too cumbersome, involved, and time-consuming for the crisis which was at hand." Moreover, the use of the seizure technique to solve labor disputes in order to prevent work stoppages was not only unauthorized by any congressional enactment; prior to this controversy, Congress had refused to

---

1. In addition to defending President Truman's authority on the merits, the Government made a procedural argument: it claimed that injunctive relief should be denied because the steel companies had not shown "that their available legal remedies were inadequate or that their injuries from seizure would be irreparable." The Government argued that, if the seizure were ultimately held unlawful, the companies could recover compensation in the Court of Claims for unlawful taking. Justice Black, however, found no reason for delay in reaching the constitutionality of the seizure. Not only was there doubt about the right to sue in the Court of Claims for seizures of this sort, but the seizures "were bound to result in many present and future damages of such nature as to be difficult, if not incapable, of measurement." For an argument that the barriers to equitable relief were more substantial than the Court's summary disposition suggested, see Freund, "Foreword: The Year of the Steel Case," 66 Harv.L.Rev. 89 (1952).

adopt that method of settling labor disputes. When the Taft-Hartley Act was under consideration in 1947, Congress rejected an amendment which would have authorized such governmental seizures in cases of emergency. [Instead], the plan sought to bring about settlements by use of the customary devices of mediation, conciliation, investigations by boards of inquiry, and public reports. In some instances temporary injunctions were authorized to provide cooling-off periods. All this failing, unions were left free to strike [and the President was then required to report to Congress on the emergency].

It is clear that if the President had authority to issue the order he did, it must be found in some provision of the Constitution. And it is not claimed that express constitutional language grants this [power]. The contention is that presidential power should be implied from the aggregate of his powers under the Constitution. Particular reliance is placed on provisions in Article II which say that "The executive Power shall be vested in a President"; that "he shall take Care that the Laws be faithfully executed"; and that he "shall be Commander in Chief of the [Army and Navy]."

The order cannot properly be sustained as an exercise of the President's military power as Commander in Chief of the Armed Forces. The Government attempts to do so by citing [cases] upholding broad powers in military commanders engaged in day-to-day fighting in a theater of war. Such cases need not concern us here. Even though "theater of war" be an expanding concept, we cannot with faithfulness to our constitutional system hold that the [Commander in Chief] has the ultimate power as such to take possession of private property in order to keep labor disputes from stopping production. This is a job for the Nation's lawmakers, not for its military authorities. Nor can the seizure order be sustained because of the several constitutional provisions that grant executive power to the President. In the framework of our Constitution, the President's power to see that the laws are faithfully executed refutes the idea that he is to be a lawmaker. The Constitution limits his functions in the lawmaking process to the recommending of laws he thinks wise and the vetoing of laws he thinks bad. And the Constitution is neither silent nor equivocal about who shall make laws which the President is to execute [quoting Art. I, § 1, and Art. I, § 8, cl. 18].

The President's order does not direct that a congressional policy be executed in a manner prescribed by Congress—it directs that a presidential policy be executed in a manner prescribed by the President. The preamble of the order itself, like that of many statutes, sets out reasons why the President believes certain policies should be adopted, proclaims these policies as rules of conduct to be followed, and again, like a statute, authorizes a government official to promulgate additional [regulations] consistent with the policy proclaimed and needed to carry that policy into execution. The power of Congress to adopt such public policies as those proclaimed by the order is beyond question. It can authorize the taking of private property for public use. It can make laws [e.g.] regulating the relationships between employers and [employees]. The Constitution does not subject this lawmaking power of Congress to presidential or military supervision or control.

It is said that other Presidents without congressional authority have taken possession of private business enterprises in order to settle labor disputes. But even if this be true, Congress has not thereby lost its exclusive constitutional authority to make laws necessary and proper to carry out the powers vested by the Constitution "in the Government of the United States, or any Department or Officer thereof." The Founders of this Nation entrusted the lawmaking power to the Congress alone in both good and bad times. It would do no good to recall the historical events, the fears of power and the hopes for freedom that lay behind their choice.   Such a review would but confirm our holding that this seizure order cannot stand.

Affirmed.[2]

Mr. Justice FRANKFURTER [concurring].

Although the considerations relevant to the legal enforcement of the principle of separation of powers seem to me more complicated and flexible than may appear from what Mr. Justice Black has written, I join his opinion because I thoroughly agree with the application of the principle to the circumstances of this [case].   The issue before us can be met, and therefore should be, without attempting to define the President's powers comprehensively.   I shall not attempt to delineate what belongs to him by virtue of his office beyond the power even of Congress to contract; what authority belongs to him until Congress acts; what kind of problems may be dealt with either by the Congress or by the President or by both; what power must be exercised by the Congress and cannot be delegated to the [President].

It cannot be contended that the President would have had power to issue this order had Congress explicitly negated such authority in formal legislation. [In view of the Taft-Hartley Act of 1947], Congress has expressed its will to withhold this power from the President as though it had said so in so many words.   [In effect], Congress said to the President, "You may not seize.   Please report to us and ask for seizure power if you think it is needed in a specific situation."   [The] content of the three authorities of government is not to be derived from an abstract analysis.   The areas are partly interacting, not wholly disjointed.   The Constitution is a framework for government.   Therefore the way the framework has consistently operated fairly establishes that it has operated according to its true nature.   Deeply embedded traditional ways of conducting government cannot supplant the Constitution or legislation, but they give meaning to the words of a text or supply them.   It is an inadmissibly narrow conception of American constitutional law to confine it to the words of the Constitution and to disregard the gloss which life has written upon them. In short, a systematic, unbroken, executive practice, long pursued to the knowledge of the Congress and never before questioned, engaged in by Presidents who have also sworn to uphold the Constitution, making as it were such exercise of power part of the structure of our government, may be treated as a gloss on "executive Power" vested in the [President].   [Justice Frankfurter added an elaborate historical appendix to his opinion.]   [But the] list of executive assertions of the power of seizure in circumstances comparable to the present reduces to three in the six-month period from June to December of 1941.   [These] three isolated instances do not add up, either in number, scope, duration or contemporaneous legal justification, to the kind of executive construction of the Constitution [necessary to justify the action here].   Nor do they come to us sanctioned by long-continued acquiescence of Congress giving decisive weight to a construction by the Executive of its [powers].

Mr. Justice JACKSON, concurring in the judgment and opinion of the Court.

[A] judge, like an executive advisor, may be surprised at the poverty of really useful and unambiguous authority applicable to concrete problems of executive power as they actually present themselves.   Just what our forefathers did envision, or would have envisioned had they foreseen modern conditions, must be divined from materials almost as enigmatic as the dreams Joseph was called upon to interpret for Pharaoh.   A century and a half of partisan debate and scholarly speculation yields no net result but only supplies more or less apt

---

2. The decision was 6 to 3.   Although all but one of the concurring Justices—Justice Clark— joined the opinion as well as the judgment an- nounced by Justice Black, the separate opinions included important variations on Justice Black's theme.

quotations from respected resources on each side of any question. They largely cancel each other. And court decisions are indecisive because of the judicial practice of dealing with the largest questions in the most narrow way. The actual art of governing under our Constitution does not and cannot conform to judicial definitions of the power of any of its branches based on isolated clauses or even single Articles torn from context. While the Constitution diffuses power the better to secure liberty, it also contemplates that practice will integrate the dispersed powers into a workable government. It enjoins upon its branches separateness but interdependence, autonomy but reciprocity. Presidential powers are not fixed but fluctuate, depending upon their disjunction or conjunction with those of Congress. We may well begin by a somewhat over-simplified grouping of practical situations in which a President may doubt, or others may challenge, his powers, and by distinguishing roughly the legal consequences of this factor of relativity.

1. When the President acts pursuant to an express or implied authorization of Congress, his authority is at its maximum, for it includes all that he possesses in his own right plus all that Congress can delegate.[1] In these circumstances, and in these only, may he be said (for what it may be worth) to personify the federal sovereignty. If his act is held unconstitutional under these circumstances, it usually means that the Federal Government as an undivided whole lacks power. A seizure executed by the President pursuant to an Act of Congress would be supported by the strongest of presumptions and the widest latitude of judicial interpretation, and the burden of persuasion would rest heavily upon any who might attack it.

2. When the President acts in absence of either a congressional grant or denial of authority, he can only rely upon his own independent powers, but there is a zone of twilight in which he and Congress may have concurrent authority, or in which its distribution is uncertain. Therefore, congressional inertia, indifference or quiescence may sometimes, at least as a practical matter, enable, if not invite, measures on independent presidential responsibility. In this area, any actual test of power is likely to depend on the imperatives of events and contemporary imponderables rather than on abstract theories of law.

3. When the President takes measures incompatible with the expressed or implied will of Congress, his power is at its lowest ebb, for then he can rely only upon his own constitutional powers minus any constitutional powers of Congress over the matter. Courts can sustain exclusive presidential control in such a case only by disabling the Congress from acting upon the subject. Presidential claim to a power at once so conclusive and preclusive must be scrutinized with caution, for what is at stake is the equilibrium established by our constitutional system.

Into which of these classifications does this executive seizure of the steel industry fit? It is eliminated from the first by admission, for it is conceded that no congressional authorization exists for this seizure. [Can] it then be defended under flexible tests available to the second category? It seems clearly eliminated from that class because Congress has not left seizure of private property an

---

1. It is in this class of cases that we find the broadest recent statements of presidential power, including those relied on here. [Curtiss-Wright (1936; p. 363 below)] involved, not the question of the President's power to act without congressional authority, but the question of his right to act under and in accord with an Act of Congress. The constitutionality of the Act under which the President had proceeded was assailed on the ground that it delegated legislative powers to the President. Much of the Court's opinion is [dic-tum]. That case does not solve the present controversy. It recognized internal and external affairs as being in separate categories, and held that the strict limitation upon congressional delegations of power to the President over internal affairs does not apply with respect to delegations of power in external affairs. It was intimated that the President might act in external affairs without congressional authority, but not that he might act contrary to an [Act of Congress]. [Footnote by Justice Jackson.]

open field but has covered it by three statutory policies inconsistent with this seizure. [This] leaves the current seizure to be justified only by the severe tests under the third grouping, where it can be supported only by any remainder of executive power after subtraction of such powers as Congress may have over the subject. In short, we can sustain the President only by holding that seizure of such strike-bound industries is within his domain and beyond control by [Congress].

[History does not leave] it open to question, at least in the courts, that the executive branch [possesses] only delegated powers. [But] because the President does not enjoy unmentioned powers does not mean that the mentioned ones should be narrowed by a niggardly construction. [I give] to the enumerated powers the scope and elasticity afforded by what seem to be reasonable, practical implications instead of the rigidity dictated by a doctrinaire textualism. The Solicitor General seeks the power of seizure in three clauses of the Executive Article, the first reading, "The executive Power shall be vested in a [President]." [I] cannot accept the view that this clause is a grant in bulk of all conceivable executive power but regard it as an allocation to the presidential office of the generic powers thereafter stated. The clause on which the Government next relies is that "The President shall be Commander in Chief of the Army and Navy of the United States." [T]his loose appellation is sometimes advanced as support for any presidential action, internal or external, involving use of force, the idea being that it vests power to do anything, anywhere, that can be done with an army or navy. That seems to be the logic of an argument tendered at our bar—that the President having, on his own responsibility, sent American troops abroad derives from that act "affirmative power" to seize the means of producing a supply of steel for them. [No] doctrine that the Court could promulgate would seem to me more sinister and alarming than that a President whose conduct of foreign affairs is so largely uncontrolled, and often even is unknown, can vastly enlarge his mastery over the internal affairs of the country by his own commitment of the Nation's armed forces to some foreign venture. I do not, however, find it necessary or appropriate to consider the legal status of the Korean enterprise to discountenance argument based on it.

[The] Constitution expressly places in Congress power "to raise and *support* Armies" and "to *provide* and *maintain* a Navy." (Emphasis supplied.) This certainly lays upon Congress primary responsibility for supplying the armed forces. Congress alone controls the raising of revenues and their appropriation and may determine in what manner and by what means they shall be spent for military and naval procurement. I suppose no one would doubt that Congress can take over war supply as a Government [enterprise]. That military powers of the Commander in Chief were not to supersede representative government of internal affairs seems obvious from the Constitution and from elementary American history. [I] should indulge the widest latitude of interpretation to sustain his exclusive function to command the instruments of national force, at least when turned against the outside world for the security of our society. But, when it is turned inward, not because of rebellion but because of a lawful economic struggle between industry and labor, it should have no such [indulgence]. The third clause in which the Solicitor General finds seizure powers is that "he shall take Care that the Laws be faithfully executed." That authority must be matched against [the due process clause of the Fifth Amendment]. One [clause] gives a governmental authority that reaches so far as there is law, the other gives a private right that authority shall go no farther. These signify about all there is of the principle that ours is a government of laws, not of men, and that we submit ourselves to rulers only if under rules.

The Solicitor General lastly grounds support of the seizure upon nebulous, inherent powers never expressly granted but said to have accrued to the office from the customs and claims of preceding administrations. The plea is for a resulting power to deal with a crisis or an emergency according to the necessities of the case, the unarticulated assumption being that necessity knows no law. Loose and irresponsible use of adjectives colors all nonlegal and much legal discussion of presidential powers. "Inherent" powers, "implied" powers, "incidental" powers, "plenary" powers, "war" powers and "emergency" powers are used, often interchangeably and without fixed or ascertainable meanings. The vagueness and generality of the clauses that set forth presidential powers afford a plausible basis for pressures within and without an administration for presidential action beyond that supported by those whose responsibility it is to defend his actions in court. The claim of inherent and unrestricted presidential powers has long been a persuasive dialectical weapon in political controversy. While it is not surprising that counsel should grasp support from such unadjudicated claims of power, a judge cannot accept self-serving press statements of the attorney for one of the interested parties as authority in answering a constitutional question, even if the advocate was himself.[2] But prudence has counseled that actual reliance on such nebulous claims stop short of provoking a judicial [test].

In view of the ease, expedition and safety with which Congress can grant and has granted large emergency powers, certainly ample to embrace this crisis, I am quite unimpressed with the argument that we should affirm possession of them without statute. Such power either has no beginning or it has no end. If it exists, it need submit to no legal restraint. I am not alarmed that it would plunge us straightway into dictatorship, but it is at least a step in that wrong direction. As to whether there is imperative necessity for such powers, it is relevant to note the gap that exists between the President's paper powers and his real powers. The Constitution does not disclose the measure of the actual controls wielded by the modern presidential [office]. Vast accretions of federal power, eroded from that reserved by the States, have magnified the scope of presidential [activity].

Executive power has the advantage of concentration in a single head in whose choice the whole Nation has a part, making him the focus of public hopes and expectations. No other personality in public life can begin to compete with him in access to the public mind through modern methods of communications. By his prestige as head of state and his influence upon public opinion he exerts a leverage upon those who are supposed to check and balance his power which often cancels their effectiveness. Moreover, rise of the party system has made a significant extraconstitutional supplement to real executive power. [I] cannot be brought to believe that this country will suffer if the Court refuses further to aggrandize the presidential office, already so potent and so relatively immune from judicial review, at the expense of Congress. But I have no illusion that any decision by this Court can keep power in the hands of Congress if it is not wise and timely in meeting its problems. A crisis that challenges the President equally, or perhaps primarily, challenges Congress. If not good law, there was wordly wisdom in the maxim attributed to Napoleon that "The tools belong to the man who can use them." We may say that power to legislate for emergencies belongs in the hands of Congress, but only Congress itself can prevent power from slipping through its [fingers]. With all its defects, delays and inconveniences, men have discovered no technique for long preserving free government except that the Executive be under the law, and that the law be

2. Justice Jackson, named to the Court by President Franklin D. Roosevelt, was the U.S. Attorney General when he was nominated.

made by parliamentary deliberations. Such institutions may be destined to pass away. But it is the duty of the Court to be last, not first, to give them up.[3]

Mr. Chief Justice VINSON, with whom Mr. Justice REED and Mr. Justice MINTON join, dissenting.

[Chief Justice Vinson's dissent, the longest of the opinions, began with a review of "our responsibilities in the world community" in the post-World War II period and with a summary of the "large body of implementing legislation" by Congress to aid "our self-preservation through mutual security."] [If] the President has any power under the Constitution to meet a critical situation in the absence of express statutory authorization, there is no basis whatever for criticizing the exercise of such power in this [case]. We are not called upon today to expand the Constitution to meet a new situation. For, in this case, we need only look to history and time-honored principles of constitutional law—principles that have been applied consistently by all branches of the Government throughout our history. It is those who assert the invalidity of the Executive Order who seek to amend the Constitution in this case. A review of executive action demonstrates that our Presidents have on many occasions exhibited the leadership contemplated by the Framers when they made the President Commander in Chief, and imposed upon him the trust to "take Care that the Laws be faithfully executed." With or without explicit statutory authorization, Presidents have at such times dealt with national emergencies by acting promptly and resolutely to enforce legislative programs, at least to save those programs until Congress could act. Congress and the courts have responded to such executive initiative with consistent approval. [Chief Justice Vinson undertook a lengthy examination of historical episodes from George Washington to Franklin D. Roosevelt, including:]

Beginning with the Bank Holiday Proclamation and continuing through World War II, executive leadership and initiative were characteristic of President Franklin D. Roosevelt's administration. [Six] months before Pearl Harbor, a dispute at a single aviation plant at Inglewood, California, interrupted a segment of the production of military [aircraft]. President Roosevelt ordered the seizure of the plant "pursuant to the powers vested in [him] by the Constitution and laws of the United States, as President [and] Commander in [Chief]." The Attorney General [Jackson] vigorously proclaimed that the President had the moral duty to keep this Nation's defense effort a "going concern." [Before and after Pearl Harbor], industrial concerns were seized to avert interruption of needed production. During the same period, the President directed seizure of the Nation's coal mines to remove an obstruction to the effective prosecution of the war. [At] the time of the seizure of the coal mines [a] bill to provide a statutory basis for seizures [was] before Congress. As stated by its sponsor, the purpose of the bill was not to augment Presidential power, but to "let the country know that the Congress is squarely behind the President." [This] is but a cursory summary of executive leadership. But it

---

3. Each of the other Justices in the majority also wrote separate opinions. Justice Douglas' was a broad one; Justices Burton and Clark wrote narrowly. Justice DOUGLAS concluded that the presidential seizure was legislative in nature; that it constituted "taking" in the constitutional sense, requiring just compensation under the Fifth Amendment; that the President has no power to raise revenues; and that the "branch of government that has the power to pay compensation for a seizure is the only one able to authorize a seizure." Justice BURTON concluded that President Truman's order "invaded the jurisdiction of Congress" because Congress had "pre-scribed for the President specific procedures, exclusive of seizure, for his use in meeting the present type of emergency." Justice CLARK, the only Justice in the majority who did not join Justice Black's opinion, similarly emphasized that Congress had prescribed methods to be followed by the President for emergencies such as this. He added, however, "that in the absence of such action by Congress, the President's independent power to act depends upon the gravity of the situation confronting the nation." [Justice Clark, like Justice Jackson, had been U.S. Attorney General, in the Truman Administration.]

amply demonstrates that Presidents have taken prompt action to enforce the laws and protect the country whether or not Congress happened to provide in advance for the particular method of execution. [T]he fact that Congress and the courts have consistently recognized and given their support to such executive action indicates that such a power of seizure has been accepted throughout our [history].

Much of the argument in this case has been directed at straw men. We do not now have before us the case of a President acting solely on the basis of his own notions of the public welfare. Nor is there any question of unlimited executive power in this case. The President himself closed the door to any such claim when he sent his Message to Congress stating his purpose to abide by any action of Congress, whether approving or disapproving his seizure action. Here, the President immediately made sure that Congress was fully informed of the temporary action he had taken only to preserve the legislative programs from destruction until Congress could act. The absence of a specific statute authorizing seizure of the steel mills as a mode of executing the laws—both the military procurement program and the anti-inflation program—has not until today been thought to prevent the President from executing the laws. [Here], there is no statute prohibiting the action taken by the [President]. Executive inaction in [this] situation, courting national disaster, is foreign to the concept of energy and initiative in the Executive as created by the Founding Fathers. [The] broad executive power granted by Article II to an officer on duty 365 days a year cannot, it is said, be invoked to avert disaster. Instead, the President must confine himself to sending a message to Congress recommending action. Under this messenger-boy concept of the Office, the President cannot even act to preserve legislative programs from destruction so that Congress will have something left to [act upon].

THE STEEL SEIZURE CASE AND THE JACKSON ANALYSIS

1. *Dicta and holding.* Does Justice Black recognize *any* "emergency powers" of the President? Does the majority of the Court? Is Justice Black's opinion unduly broad? [1] Is the problem "more complicated," as Justice Frankfurter suggests? What holding does the majority truly agree upon? Does it go beyond the third category described by Justice Jackson? Does the case stand for any principle other than that the President may not establish domestic policy "incompatible with the expressed or implied will of Congress"? Do the broader statements in Justice Black's opinion suggest that the Court was unwise to speak about the merits? [2]

1. Arguably, Justice Black's broad statements were in part provoked by the broad arguments of the Government. Note, e.g., the arguments at the District Court hearing, printed in Westin, The Anatomy of a Constitutional Law Case (1958), 56–65. Consider the exchange between District Judge Pine and Assistant Attorney General Baldridge: "*The Court:* So [the Constitution] limited the powers of the Congress and limited the powers of the judiciary, but did not limit the powers of the Executive. Is that what you say? *Mr. Baldridge:* That is the way we read Article II of the Constitution. *The Court:* I see." A few days after the argument, President Truman issued a statement: "The powers of the President are derived from the Constitution, and they are limited, of course, by the provisions of the Constitution." For President Truman's sub-

sequent reflections, see Truman, II Memoirs: Years of Trial and Hope (1956), 475–78, concluding: "Whatever the six justices of the Supreme Court meant by their differing opinions, [the President] must always act in a national emergency."

2. For a sampling of the extensive commentary provoked by the case, see the contrasting views in Kauper, "The Steel Seizure Case: Congress, the President, and the Supreme Court," 51 Mich.L.Rev. 141 (1952), and Corwin, "The Steel Seizure Case: A Judicial Brick Without Straw," 53 Colum.L.Rev. 53 (1953). For a careful historical study, see Marcus, Truman and the Steel Seizure Case: The Limits of Presidential Power (1977).

2. *The Jackson distinctions and their applicability.* a. *Domestic affairs.* Does Justice Jackson's distinction among three types of situations provide a useful general framework for the analysis of presidential power problems? To what extent do the other opinions accept that framework? To what extent do the various opinions accept Justice Frankfurter's view that unquestioned and continuous "executive practice" "may be treated as a gloss on 'Executive power'" granted by Art. II? How persuasive should such "practice" be in constitutional interpretation?

Justice Jackson's first category—presidential action pursuant to congressional authority—refers to the most common variety of executive action. Justice Jackson's second category—presidential action in the context of congressional silence—presents greater difficulty. Justice Jackson suggests "a zone of twilight" in which President and Congress "may have concurrent authority." Congressional authority in that zone typically stems from Art. I, § 8, powers.[3] But what is the source of executive power in that twilight zone? What are the "flexible tests" appropriate for that twilight zone? Is it in any event a presidential authority subject to being overriden by congressional action? Are there any situations in the domestic sphere that fall within Justice Jackson's third category: a presidential power to act even in the face of contrary congressional directions? Are any such powers granted by Art. II? Note, e.g., the controversy over the power to impound funds, below.[4]

b. *External affairs.* Can and should Justice Jackson's tripartite distinction be applied outside the domestic sphere? Are there more explicit constitutional grants of autonomous presidential authority as to external affairs? See the materials in sec. 1B below. Note especially the controversy over the War Powers Resolution of 1973, a congressional effort to delineate guidelines for the use of armed forces in hostilities. Is that Resolution an exercise of congressional authority in Justice Jackson's second category—a congressional effort to speak where there long had been congressional silence in "a zone of twilight"? Or is it an exercise of congressional power in Justice Jackson's third category that does not improperly tread upon autonomous executive power?

INS v. CHADHA

462 U.S. 919, 103 S.Ct. 2764, 77 L.Ed.2d 317 (1983).

Chief Justice BURGER delivered the opinion of the Court.

3. Note that the congressional power under the necessary and proper clause, Art. I, § 8, cl. 18, is not limited to implementation of powers specifically granted to Congress. Instead, it enables Congress to make all laws "necessary and proper for carrying into Execution the foregoing Powers, and *all other Powers* vested by this Constitution in the Government of the United States, or in any Department or Officer thereof." (Emphasis added.) Should this congressional implementation power be read as giving priority to congressional resolutions of conflicts between the legislative and executive branches in the "zone of twilight"? See generally Van Alstyne, "The Role of Congress in Determining Incidental Powers of the President and of the Federal Courts: A Comment on the Horizontal Effect of The Sweeping Clause," 40 Law & Contemp.Probs. 102 (1976).

4. Of all the opinions in the Steel Seizure Case, Justice Jackson's has been the mostly widely relied on in judicial decisions and academic commentary. For an example of an analysis akin to that of Justice Jackson, note several of the concurring opinions in the Pentagon Papers case (1971; p. 388 below). Note also Justice Rehnquist's prevailing opinion in the Iranian assets case, Dames & Moore v. Regan (1981; p. 368 below). Justice Rehnquist, in the course of reaching his "narrow" conclusions there, repeatedly spoke approvingly of Justice Jackson's tripartite analysis. (Justice Rehnquist was once a law clerk to Justice Jackson.) However, in a critical passage of the opinion, he emphasized instead Justice Frankfurter's concurrence in the Steel Seizure Case—the emphasis in the Frankfurter opinion on treating a "systematic, unbroken, executive practice" as a "gloss" on the President's "Executive Power." See generally Chemerinsky, "Controlling Inherent Presidential Power: Providing a Framework for Judicial Review," 56 S.Cal.L.Rev. 863 (1983).

[These consolidated cases present] a challenge to the constitutionality of the provision in § 244(c)(2) of the Immigration and Nationality Act, 8 U.S.C. § 1254(c)(2), authorizing one House of Congress, by resolution, to invalidate the decision of the Executive Branch, pursuant to authority delegated by Congress to the Attorney General of the United States, to allow a particular deportable alien to remain in the United States.

I. Chadha is an East Indian who was born in Kenya and holds a British passport. He was lawfully admitted to the United States in 1966 on a nonimmigrant student visa. His visa expired on June 30, 1972. On October 11, 1973, the District Director of the Immigration and Naturalization Service [INS] ordered Chadha to show cause why he should not be deported for having "remained in the United States for a longer time than permitted." Pursuant to § 242(b) of the [Act], a deportation hearing was held before an immigration judge on January 11, 1974. Chadha conceded that he was deportable for overstaying his visa and the hearing was adjourned to enable him to file an application for suspension of deportation under § 244(a)(1) of the Act.

[After] Chadha submitted his application for suspension of deportation, the deportation hearing was resumed on February 7, 1974. [The] immigration judge found that Chadha met the requirements of § 244(a)(1): he had resided continuously in the United States for over seven years, was of good moral character, and would suffer "extreme hardship" if deported. Pursuant to § 244(c)(1) of the Act, the immigration judge suspended Chadha's deportation and a report of the suspension was transmitted to Congress.[1] [Once] the Attorney General's recommendation for suspension of Chadha's deportation was conveyed to Congress, Congress had the power under § 244(c)(2) of the Act to veto the Attorney General's determination that Chadha should not be deported. Section 244(c)(2) provides: "(2) In the case of an alien specified in paragraph (1) of subsection (a) of this subsection—if during the session of the Congress at which a case is reported, or prior to the close of the session of the Congress next following the session at which a case is reported, either the Senate or the House of Representatives passes a resolution stating in substance that it does not favor the suspension of such deportation, the Attorney General shall thereupon deport such alien or authorize the alien's voluntary departure at his own expense under the order of deportation in the manner provided by law. If, within the time above specified, neither the Senate nor the House of Representatives shall pass such a resolution, the Attorney General shall cancel deportation proceedings."

The June 25, 1974 order of the immigration judge suspending Chadha's deportation remained outstanding as a valid order for a year and a half. For reasons not disclosed by the record, Congress did not exercise the veto authority reserved to it under § 244(c)(2) until the first session of the 94th Congress. This was the final session in which Congress, pursuant to § 244(c)(2), could act to veto the Attorney General's [determination]. The session ended on December 19, 1975. [On] December 12, 1975, Representative Eilberg [chairman of a House subcommittee] introduced a resolution opposing "the granting of permanent residence in the United States to [six] aliens," including Chadha. [The] resolution had not been printed and was not made available to other Members of the House prior to or at the time it was voted on. So far as the record before us shows, the House consideration of the resolution was based on Representative Eilberg's statement from the floor that "[i]t was the feeling of

---

1. Section 244(c)(1) provided: "Upon application by any alien who is found by the Attorney General to meet the requirements of subsection (a) of this section the Attorney General may in his discretion suspend deportation of such alien. If the deportation of any alien is suspended under the provisions of this subsection, a complete and detailed statement of the facts and pertinent provisions of law in the case shall be reported to Congress with the reasons for such suspension. Such reports shall be submitted on the first day of each calendar month in which Congress is in session."

the committee, after reviewing 340 cases, that the aliens contained in the resolution [Chadha and five others] did not meet these statutory requirements, particularly as it relates to hardship; and it is the opinion of the committee that their deportation should not be suspended." The resolution was passed without debate or recorded vote. Since the House action was pursuant to § 244(c)(2), the resolution was not treated as an Article I legislative act; it was not submitted to the Senate or presented to the President for his action.

After the House veto of the Attorney General's decision to allow Chadha to remain in the United States, the immigration judge reopened the deportation proceedings to implement the House order deporting Chadha. Chadha moved to terminate the proceedings on the ground that § 244(c)(2) is unconstitutional. The immigration judge held that he had no authority to rule on the constitutional validity of § 244(c)(2). On November 8, 1976, Chadha was ordered deported pursuant to the House action. [The Board of Immigration Appeals dismissed Chadha's appeal, on the same ground as that given by the immigration judge.] [Chadha] filed a petition for review of the deportation order in the [U.S. Court of Appeals for the Ninth Circuit]. The [INS joined Chadha before the Court of Appeals] in arguing that § 244(c)(2) is unconstitutional. [The] Court of Appeals invited both the Senate and the [House] to file briefs amici curiae. [The Court of Appeals held that the House was without constitutional authority to order Chadha's deportation.] [The] essence of its holding was that § 244(c)(2) violates the constitutional doctrine of separation of powers. [We] now affirm.

II. Before we address the important question of the constitutionality of the one-House veto provision of § 244(c)(2), we first consider several challenges to the authority of this Court to resolve the issue raised. [The Court determined that it had appellate jurisdiction, that the one-house veto provision was severable from the remainder of § 244,[2] that Chadha had standing to challenge the constitutionality of the one-house veto, that nothing other than a decision on constitutionality was likely to give Chadha his desired relief, that the Court of Appeals had proper jurisdiction of the case before it, and that a case or controversy existed.]

G. *Political Question.* It is also argued that this case presents a nonjusticiable political question.[3] [It] is argued that Congress' Article I power "To establish a uniform Rule of Naturalization," combined with the Necessary and Proper Clause, grants it unreviewable authority over the regulation of aliens. The plenary authority of Congress over aliens under Art. I, § 8, cl. 4 is not open to question, but what is challenged here is whether Congress has chosen a constitutionally permissible means of implementing that power. [A] brief review of those factors which may indicate the presence of a nonjusticiable political question satisfies us that our assertion of jurisdiction over this case does no violence to the political question doctrine.[4] [Congress] apparently directs its

---

2. On the severability issue, the Chief Justice rejected the argument by Congress that, if the provision for the one-house veto were found unconstitutional, all of § 244 must fall. In that event, the Attorney General would have no authority to suspend Chadha's deportation and Chadha would be deported. The Chief Justice noted the "unambiguous" language of the severability provision in the Act. This created a presumption of severability that was "supported by the legislative history." He added: "Although it may be that Congress was reluctant to delegate final authority over cancellation of deportations, such reluctance is not sufficient to overcome the [presumption]." He concluded: "Plainly, Congress' desire to retain a veto in this

area cannot be considered in isolation but must be viewed in the context of Congress' irritation with the burden of private immigration bills. [There] is insufficient evidence that Congress would have continued to subject itself to the onerous burdens of private bills had it known that § 244(c)(2) would be held unconstitutional." [Compare Justice Rehnquist's dissent on this issue.]

3. See the additional materials on the political questions barrier in § 2C of this chapter and in chap. 15 below.

4. Here, the Chief Justice quoted the standards for identifying nonjusticiable political ques-

assertion of nonjusticiability to [the existence of a textually demonstrable constitutional commitment of the issue to a coordinate political department], asserting that Chadha's claim is "an assault on the legislative authority to enact [§ 244(c)(2)]." But if this turns the question into a political question virtually every challenge to the constitutionality of a statute would be a political question. Chadha indeed argues that one House of Congress cannot constitutionally veto the Attorney General's decision to allow him to remain in this country. No policy underlying the political question doctrine suggests that Congress or the Executive, or both acting in concert and in compliance with Art. I, can decide the constitutionality of a statute; that is a decision for the courts.[5] [It] is correct that this controversy may, in a sense, be termed "political." But the presence of constitutional issues with significant political overtones does not automatically invoke the political question doctrine. Resolution of litigation challenging the constitutional authority of one of the three branches cannot be evaded by courts because the issues have political implications in the sense urged by Congress. Marbury v. Madison was also a "political" case, involving as it did claims under a judicial commission alleged to have been duly signed by the President but not delivered. But "courts cannot reject as 'no law suit' a bona fide controversy as to whether some action denominated 'political' exceeds constitutional authority." [Baker v. Carr.]

III. A. We turn now to the question whether action of one House of Congress under § 244(c)(2) violates strictures of the Constitution. [The] fact that a given law or procedure is efficient, convenient, and useful in facilitating functions of government, standing alone, will not save it if it is contrary to the Constitution. Convenience and efficiency are not the primary objectives—or the hallmarks—of democratic government and our inquiry is sharpened rather than blunted by the fact that Congressional veto provisions are appearing with increasing frequency in statutes which delegate authority to executive and independent agencies.[6] [Justice White] undertakes to make a case for the proposition that the one-House veto is a useful "political invention," and we need not challenge that assertion. We can even concede this utilitarian argument although the long range political wisdom of this "invention" is arguable. [But] policy arguments supporting even useful "political inventions" are subject to the demands of the Constitution which defines powers and, with respect to this subject, sets out just how those powers are to be exercised. Explicit and unambiguous provisions of the Constitution prescribe and define the respective functions of the Congress and of the Executive in the legislative process. Since the precise terms of those familiar provisions are critical to the

tions, as set forth in Baker v. Carr (1962) and quoted at p. 397 in § 2C of this chapter.

5. The suggestion is made that § 244(c)(2) is somehow immunized from constitutional scrutiny because the Act containing [it] was passed by Congress and approved by the President. Marbury v. Madison resolved that question. The assent of the Executive to a bill which contains a provision contrary to the Constitution does not shield it from judicial review. In any event, eleven Presidents, from Mr. Wilson through Mr. Reagan, who have been presented with this issue have gone on record at some point to challenge Congressional vetoes as unconstitutional. [Furthermore], it is not uncommon for Presidents to approve legislation containing parts which are objectionable on constitutional grounds. For example, after President Roosevelt signed the Lend-Lease Act of 1941, Attorney General Jackson released a memorandum explaining the Presi-

dent's view that the provision allowing the Act's authorization to be terminated by concurrent resolution was unconstitutional. Jackson, A Presidential Legal Opinion, 66 Harv.L.Rev. 353 (1953). [Footnote by the Chief Justice.]

6. At this point, the Chief Justice quoted the following passage from Abourezk, "The Congressional Veto: A Contemporary Response to Executive Encroachment on Legislative Prerogatives," 52 Ind.L.Rev. 323, 324 (1977): "Since 1932, when the first veto provision was enacted into law, 295 congressional veto-type procedures have been inserted in 196 different statutes as follows: from 1932 to 1939, five statutes were affected; from 1940–49, nineteen statutes; between 1950–59, thirty-four statutes; and from 1960–69, forty-nine. From the year 1970 through 1975, at least one hundred sixty-three such provisions were included in eighty-nine laws."

resolution of this case, we set them out verbatim.[7] [These] provisions of Art. I are integral parts of the constitutional design for the separation of powers. [We] find that the purposes underlying the Presentment Clauses, Art. I, § 7, cls. 2, 3, and the bicameral requirement of Art. I, § 1 and § 7, cl. 2, guide our resolution of the important question presented in this case. The very structure of the articles delegating and separating powers under Arts. I, II, and III exemplify the concept of separation of powers and we now turn to Art. I.

B. *The Presentment Clauses.* The records of the Constitutional Convention reveal that the requirement that all legislation be presented to the President before becoming law was uniformly accepted by the Framers. Presentment to the President and the Presidential veto were considered so imperative that the draftsmen took special pains to assure that these requirements could not be circumvented. During the final debate on Art. I, § 7, cl. 2, James Madison expressed concern that it might easily be evaded by the simple expedient of calling a proposed law a "resolution" or "vote" rather than a "bill." As a consequence, Art. I, § 7, cl. 3 was added. [The] decision to provide the President with a limited and qualified power to nullify proposed legislation by veto was based on the profound conviction of the Framers that the powers conferred on Congress were the powers to be most carefully circumscribed. It is beyond doubt that lawmaking was a power to be shared by both Houses and the President. [The] President's role in the lawmaking process also reflects the Framers' careful efforts to check whatever propensity a particular Congress might have to enact oppressive, improvident, or ill-considered [measures].

C. *Bicameralism.* The bicameral requirement of Art. I, §§ 1, 7 was of scarcely less concern to the Framers than was the Presidential veto and indeed the two concepts are interdependent. By providing that no law could take effect without the concurrence of the prescribed majority of the Members of both Houses, the Framers reemphasized their belief, already remarked upon in connection with the Presentment Clauses, that legislation should not be enacted unless it has been carefully and fully considered by the Nation's elected officials. [After quoting from James Wilson, Alexander Hamilton, and Joseph Story, the Chief Justice continued:] We see therefore that the Framers were acutely conscious that the bicameral requirement and the Presentment Clauses would serve essential constitutional functions. The President's participation in the legislative process was to protect the Executive Branch from Congress and to protect the whole people from improvident laws. The division of the Congress into two distinctive bodies assures that the legislative power would be exercised only after opportunity for full study and debate in separate settings. The President's unilateral veto power, in turn, was limited by the power of two thirds of both Houses of Congress to overrule a veto thereby precluding final arbitrary action of one person. It emerges clearly that the prescription for legislative action in Art. I, §§ 1, 7 represents the Framers' decision that the legislative power of the Federal government be exercised in accord with a single, finely wrought and exhaustively considered, procedure.

7. The Chief Justice quoted the following provisions of Art. I: "All legislative Powers herein granted shall be vested in a Congress of the United States, which shall consist of a Senate *and* a House of Representatives." Art. I, § 1.

"Every Bill which shall have passed the House of Representatives *and* the Senate, *shall,* before it become a Law, be presented to the [President]." Art. I, § 7, cl. 2.

"*Every* Order, Resolution, or Vote to which the Concurrence of the Senate and House of Representatives may be necessary (except on a question of Adjournment) *shall be* presented to the President of the United States; and before the Same shall take Effect, *shall be* approved by him, or being disapproved by him, *shall be* re-passed by two thirds of the Senate and House of Representatives, according to the Rules and Limitations prescribed in the Case of a Bill." Art. I, § 7, cl. 3. [Emphases by the Chief Justice.]

IV.　[We must establish whether] the challenged action under § 244(c)(2) is of the kind to which the procedural requirements of Art. I, § 7 apply. Not every action taken by either House is subject to the bicameralism and presentment requirements of Art. I. Whether actions taken by either House are, in law and fact, an exercise of legislative power depends not on their form but upon "whether they contain matter which is properly to be regarded as legislative in its character and effect." [The quotation was from a Senate Report of 1897.] Examination of the action taken here by one House pursuant to § 244(c)(2) reveals that it was essentially legislative in purpose and effect. In purporting to exercise power defined in Art. I, § 8, cl. 4 to "establish an uniform Rule of Naturalization," the House took action that had the purpose and effect of altering the legal rights, duties and relations of persons, including the Attorney General, Executive Branch officials and Chadha, all outside the legislative branch. Section 244(c)(2) purports to authorize one House of Congress to require the Attorney General to deport an individual alien whose deportation otherwise would be cancelled under § 244. The one-House veto operated in this case to overrule the Attorney General and mandate Chadha's deportation; absent the House action, Chadha would remain in the United States. Congress has *acted* and its action has altered Chadha's status.

The legislative character of the one-House veto in this case is confirmed by the character of the Congressional action it supplants. Neither the House of Representatives nor the Senate contends that, absent the veto provision in § 244(c)(2), either of them, or both of them acting together, could effectively require the Attorney General to deport an alien once the Attorney General, in the exercise of legislatively delegated authority,[8] had determined the alien should remain in the United States. Without the challenged provision in § 244(c)(2), this could have been achieved, if at all, only by legislation requiring deportation.[9] Similarly, a veto by one House of Congress under § 244(c)(2) cannot be justified as an attempt at amending the standards set out in § 244(a)(1), or as a repeal of § 244 as applied to Chadha. Amendment and repeal of statutes, no less than enactment, must conform with Art. I.

The nature of the decision implemented by the one-House veto in this case further manifests its legislative character. After long experience with the clumsy, time consuming private bill procedure, Congress made a deliberate

8. Congress protests that affirming the Court of Appeals in this case will sanction "lawmaking by the Attorney General. [Why] is the Attorney General exempt from submitting his proposed changes in the law to the full bicameral process?" To be sure, some administrative agency action—rule making, for example—may resemble "lawmaking." [Clearly], however, "[i]n the framework of our Constitution, the President's power to see that the laws are faithfully executed refutes the idea that he is to be a lawmaker." [Steel Seizure Case.] When the Attorney General performs his duties pursuant to § 244, he does not exercise "legislative" power. The bicameral process is not necessary as a check on the Executive's administration of the laws because his administrative activity cannot reach beyond the limits of the statute that created [it]. The constitutionality of the Attorney General's execution of the authority delegated to him by § 244 involves only a question of delegation doctrine [see p. 365 below]. The courts [can] enforce adherence to statutory standards. It is clear, therefore, that the Attorney General acts in his presumptively Art. II capacity when he administers the [Act].

Executive action under legislatively delegated authority that might resemble 'legislative' action in some respects is not subject to the approval of both Houses of Congress and the President for the reason that the Constitution does not so require. That kind of Executive action is always subject to check by the terms of the legislation that authorized it; and if that authority is exceeded it is open to judicial review as well as the power of Congress to modify or revoke the authority entirely. A one-House veto is clearly legislative in both character and effect and is not so checked; the need for the check provided by Art. I, §§ 1, 7 is therefore clear. Congress' authority to delegate portions of its power to administrative agencies provides no support for the argument that Congress can constitutionally control administration of the laws by way of a Congressional veto. [Footnote by the Chief Justice.]

9. We express no opinion as to whether such legislation would violate any constitutional provision. [Footnote by the Chief Justice.]

choice to delegate to the Executive Branch [the] authority to allow deportable aliens to remain in this country in certain specified circumstances. It is not disputed that this choice to delegate authority is precisely the kind of decision that can be implemented only in accordance with the procedures set out in Art. I. Disagreement with the Attorney General's decision on Chadha's deportation—that is, Congress' decision to deport Chadha—no less than Congress' original choice to delegate to the Attorney General the authority to make that decision, involves determinations of policy that Congress can implement in only one way: bicameral passage followed by presentment to the President. Congress must abide by its delegation of authority until that delegation is legislatively altered or revoked.[10]

Finally, we see that when the Framers intended to authorize either House of Congress to act alone and outside of its prescribed bicameral legislative role, they narrowly and precisely defined the procedure for such action. There are but four provisions in the Constitution, explicit and unambiguous, by which one House may act alone with the unreviewable force of law, not subject to the President's veto: (a) The House of Representatives alone was given the power to initiate impeachments. Art. I, § 2, cl. 6; (b) The Senate alone was given the power to conduct trials following impeachment on charges initiated by the House and to convict following trial. Art. I, § 3, cl. 5; (c) The Senate alone was given final unreviewable power to approve or to disapprove presidential appointments. Art. II, § 2, cl. 2; (d) The Senate alone was given unreviewable power to ratify treaties negotiated by the President. Art. II, § 2, cl. 2. Clearly, when the Draftsmen sought to confer special powers on one House, independent of the other House, or of the President, they did so in explicit, unambiguous terms.[11] These carefully defined exceptions from presentment and bicameralism underscore the difference between the legislative functions of Congress and other unilateral but important and binding one-House acts provided for in the Constitution. These exceptions are narrow, explicit, and separately justified; none of them authorize the action challenged here. On the contrary, they provide further support for the conclusion that Congressional authority is not to be implied and for the conclusion that the veto provided for in § 244(c)(2) is not authorized by the constitutional design of the powers of the Legislative Branch.

Since it is clear that the action by the House under § 244(c)(2) was not within any of the express constitutional exceptions authorizing one House to act alone, and equally clear that it was an exercise of legislative power, that action was subject to the standards prescribed in Article I.[12] The bicameral require-

---

10. This does not mean that Congress is required to capitulate to "the accretion of policy control by forces outside its chambers." Javits and Klein, Congressional Oversight and the Legislative Veto: A Constitutional Analysis, 52 N.Y.U.L.Rev. 455, 462 (1977). The Constitution provides Congress with abundant means to oversee and control its administrative creatures. Beyond the obvious fact that Congress ultimately controls administrative agencies in the legislation that creates them, other means of control, such as durational limits on authorizations and formal reporting requirements, lie well within Congress' constitutional power. See [e.g.] Kaiser, Congressional Action to Overturn Agency Rules: Alternatives to the "Legislative Veto," 32 Ad.L.Rev. 667 (1980). [Footnote by the Chief Justice.]

11. An exception from the Presentment Clauses was ratified in Hollingsworth v. Virginia, 3 Dall. 378 (1798). There the Court held presidential approval was unnecessary for a proposed constitutional amendment which had passed both Houses of Congress by the requisite two-thirds [majority]. [Footnote by the Chief Justice.]

12. Justice Powell's position is that the one-House veto in this case is a *judicial* act and therefore unconstitutional as beyond the authority vested in Congress by the Constitution. We agree that there is a sense in which one-House action pursuant to § 244(c)(2) has a judicial cast, since it purports to "review" Executive action. [To] be sure, it is normally up to courts to decide whether an agency has complied with its statutory mandate. But the attempted analogy between judicial action and the one-House veto is less than perfect. Federal courts do not enjoy a roving mandate to correct alleged excesses of administrative agencies; we are limited by Art. III [and] no justiciable case or controversy was presented by the Attorney General's decision to

ment, the Presentment Clauses, the President's veto, and Congress' power to override a veto were intended to erect enduring checks on each Branch and to protect the people from the improvident exercise of power by mandating certain prescribed steps. To preserve those checks, and maintain the separation of powers, the carefully defined limits on the power of each Branch must not be eroded. To accomplish what has been attempted by one House of Congress in this case requires action in conformity with the express procedures of the Constitution's prescription for legislative action: passage by a majority of both Houses and presentment to the President.

The veto authorized by § 244(c)(2) doubtless has been in many respects a convenient shortcut; the "sharing" with the Executive by Congress of its authority over aliens in this manner is, on its face, an appealing compromise. In purely practical terms, it is obviously easier for action to be taken by one House without submission to the President; but it is crystal clear [that] the Framers ranked other values higher than efficiency. [There] is unmistakable expression of a determination that legislation by the national Congress be a step-by-step, deliberate and deliberative process. The choices we discern as having been made in the Constitutional Convention impose burdens on governmental processes that often seem clumsy, inefficient, even unworkable, but those hard choices were consciously made by men who had lived under a form of government that permitted arbitrary governmental acts to go unchecked. There is no support in the Constitution or decisions of this Court for the proposition that the cumbersomeness and delays often encountered in complying with explicit Constitutional standards may be avoided, either by the Congress or by the President. [Steel Seizure Case.] With all the obvious flaws of delay, untidiness, and potential for abuse, we have not yet found a better way to preserve freedom than by making the exercise of power subject to the carefully crafted restraints spelled out in the [Constitution].

[Affirmed.]

Justice POWELL, concurring in the judgment.

The Court's [decision] apparently will invalidate every use of the legislative veto. The breadth of this holding gives one pause. Congress has included the veto in literally hundreds of statutes, dating back to the 1930s. Congress clearly views this procedure as essential to controlling the delegation of power to administrative agencies.[1] One reasonably may disagree with Congress' assessment of the veto's utility, but the respect due its judgment as a coordinate branch of Government cautions that our holding should be no more extensive than necessary to decide this case. In my view, the case may be decided on a narrower ground. When Congress finds that a particular person does not satisfy the statutory criteria for permanent residence in this country it has assumed a judicial function in violation of the principle of separation of powers. Accordingly, I concur in the judgment.

I. A. The Framers perceived that "[t]he accumulation of all powers legislative, executive and judiciary in the same hands, whether of one, a few or

---

allow Chadha to remain in this country. We are aware of no decision, and Justice Powell has cited none, where a federal court has reviewed a decision of the Attorney General suspending deportation [pursuant to § 244(a)(1)]. This is not surprising, given that no party to such action has either the motivation or the right to appeal from it. [Thus], Justice Powell's statement that the one-House veto in this case is "clearly adjudicatory" simply is not supported by his accompanying assertion that the House has "assumed a function ordinarily entrusted to the federal courts." We are satisfied that the one-House veto is legislative in purpose and effect and subject to the procedures set out in Art. I. [Footnote by the Chief Justice.]

1. [Whether a legislative veto] complies with the Presentment Clauses may well turn on the particular context in which it is exercised, and I would be hesitant to conclude that every veto is unconstitutional on the basis of the unusual example presented by this litigation. [Footnote by Justice Powell.]

many, and whether hereditary, self appointed, or elective, may justly be pronounced the very definition of tyranny." The Federalist No. 47 (J. Madison). Theirs was not a baseless fear. [One] abuse that was prevalent during the Confederation was the exercise of judicial power by the state legislatures. The Framers were well acquainted with the danger of subjecting the determination of the rights of one person to the "tyranny of shifting majorities." [2] [It] was to prevent the recurrence of such abuses that the Framers vested the executive, legislative, and judicial powers in separate branches. Their concern that a legislature should not be able unilaterally to impose a substantial deprivation on one person was expressed not only in this general allocation of power, but also in more specific provisions, such as the Bill of Attainder Clause, Art. I, § 9, cl. 3. [This] Clause, and the separation of powers doctrine generally, reflect the Framer's concern that trial by a legislature lacks the safeguards necessary to prevent the abuse of power.

B. The Constitution does not establish three branches with precisely defined boundaries. [See Justice Jackson's concurrence in the Steel Seizure Case.] [But] where one branch has impaired or sought to assume a power central to another branch, the Court has not hesitated to enforce the doctrine. Functionally, the doctrine may be violated in two ways. One branch may interfere impermissibly with the other's performance of its constitutionally assigned function. See [e.g.] United States v. Nixon [1974; p. 388 below]. Alternatively, the doctrine may be violated when one branch assumes a function that more properly is entrusted to another. See [Steel Seizure Case]. This case presents the latter situation.

II. [On] its face, the House's action appears clearly adjudicatory.[3] The House did not enact a general rule; rather it made its own determination that six specific persons did not comply with certain statutory criteria. It thus undertook the type of decision that traditionally has been left to other branches. Even if the House did not make a de novo determination, but simply reviewed the [INS's] findings, it still assumed a function ordinarily entrusted to the federal courts.[4] [The] impropriety of the House's assumption of this function is confirmed by the fact that its action raises the very danger the Framers sought to avoid—the exercise of unchecked power. In deciding whether Chadha deserves to be deported, Congress is not subject to any internal constraints that prevent it from arbitrarily depriving him of the right to remain in this country. Unlike the judiciary or an administrative agency, Congress is not bound by established

---

2. Justice Powell took the "tyranny of shifting majorities" phrase that he used repeatedly from an article by former Attorney General Levi, "Some Aspects of Separation of Powers," 76 Colum.L.Rev. 371 (1976). Levi, speaking about the abuses by legislators during the Confederation era, had stated: "The supremacy of legislatures came to be recognized as the supremacy of faction and the tyranny of shifting majorities."

3. [In] determining whether one branch unconstitutionally has assumed a power central to another branch, the traditional characterization of the assumed power as legislative, executive, or judicial may provide some guidance. But reasonable minds may disagree over the character of an act and the more helpful inquiry, in my view, is whether the act in question raises the dangers the Framers sought to avoid. [Footnote by Justice Powell.]

4. The Court reasons in response to this argument that the one-house veto exercised in this case was not judicial in nature because the deci-

sion of the [INS] did not present a justiciable issue that could have been reviewed by a court on appeal. The Court notes that since the administrative agency decided the case in favor of Chadha, there was no aggrieved party who could appeal. Reliance by the Court on this fact misses the point. Even if review of the particular decision to suspend deportation is not committed to the courts, the [House] assumed a function that generally is entrusted to an impartial tribunal. In my view, the legislative branch in effect acted as an appellate court by overruling the [INS's] application of established law to Chadha. And unlike a court or an administrative agency, it did not provide Chadha with the right to counsel or a hearing before acting. Although the parallel is not entirely complete, the effect on Chadha's personal rights would not have been different in principle had he been acquitted of a federal crime and thereafter found by one House of Congress to have been guilty. [Footnote by Justice Powell.]

substantive rules. Nor is it subject to the procedural safeguards, such as the right to counsel and a hearing before an impartial tribunal, that are present when a court or an agency adjudicates individual rights. The only effective constraint on Congress' power is political, but Congress is most accountable politically when it prescribes rules of general applicability. When it decides rights of specific persons, those rights are subject to "the tyranny of a shifting majority." [In] my view, when Congress undertook to apply its rules to Chadha, it exceeded the scope of its constitutionally prescribed authority. I would not reach the broader question whether legislative vetoes are invalid under the Presentment Clauses.

Justice WHITE, dissenting.

Today the Court not only invalidates § 244(c)(2) of the [Act], but also sounds the death knell for nearly 200 other statutory provisions in which Congress has reserved a "legislative veto." For this reason, the Court's decision is of surpassing importance. And it is for this reason that the Court would have been well-advised to decide the case, if possible, on the narrower grounds of separation of powers, leaving for full consideration the constitutionality of other congressional review statutes operating on such varied matters as war powers and agency rulemaking, some of which concern the independent regulatory agencies. The prominence of the legislative veto mechanism in our contemporary political system and its importance to Congress can hardly be overstated. It has become a central means by which Congress secures the accountability of executive and independent agencies. Without the legislative veto, Congress is faced with a Hobson's choice: either to refrain from delegating the necessary authority, leaving itself with a hopeless task of writing laws with the requisite specificity to cover endless special circumstances across the entire policy landscape, or in the alternative, to abdicate its lawmaking function to the executive branch and independent agencies. To choose the former leaves major national problems unresolved; to opt for the latter risks unaccountable policymaking by those not elected to fill that role. Accordingly, over the past five decades, the legislative veto has been placed in nearly 200 statutes.[1] The device is known in every field of governmental concern: reorganization, budgets, foreign affairs, war powers, and regulation of trade, safety, energy, the environment and the economy.

I. The legislative veto developed initially in response to the problems of reorganizing the sprawling government structure created in response to the Depression. [Over] the quarter century following World War II, Presidents continued to accept legislative vetoes by one or both Houses as constitutional, while regularly denouncing provisions by which Congressional committees reviewed Executive activity.[2] The legislative veto balanced delegations of statutory authority in new areas of governmental involvement: the space program, international agreements on nuclear energy, tariff arrangements, and adjustment of federal pay rates. During the 1970's the legislative veto was important in resolving a series of major constitutional disputes between the President and Congress over claims of the President to broad impoundment, war, and national emergency powers. The key provision of the War Powers Resolution authorizes the termination by concurrent resolution of the use of armed forces in hostilities. [See p. 371 below.] A similar measure resolved the problem posed by Presidential claims of inherent power to impound

---

1. An extensive compilation in an appendix to Justice White's dissent described 56 current statutes containing one-house and two-house legislative veto provisions, grouped into six broad categories: foreign affairs and national security; budget; international trade; energy; rulemaking; and miscellaneous.

2. Presidential objections to the [legislative] veto, until the veto by President Nixon of the War Powers Resolution, principally concerned bills authorizing committee [vetoes]. [Footnote by Justice White.]

appropriations. [See p. 361 below.] [Although] the War Powers Resolution was enacted over President Nixon's veto, the Impoundment Control Act was enacted with the President's approval. These statutes were followed by others resolving similar [problems].

Even this brief review [demonstrates] that the legislative veto is more than "efficient, convenient, and useful." It is an important if not indispensable political invention that allows the President and Congress to resolve major constitutional and policy differences, assures the accountability of independent regulatory agencies, and preserves Congress' control over lawmaking. Perhaps there are other means of accommodation and accountability, but the increasing reliance of Congress upon the legislative veto suggests that the alternatives to which Congress must now turn are not entirely satisfactory.[3] [The] history of the legislative veto also makes clear that it has not been a sword with which Congress has struck out to aggrandize itself at the expense of the other branches—the concerns of Madison and Hamilton. Rather, the veto has been a means of defense, a reservation of ultimate authority necessary if Congress is to fulfill its designated role [as] the nation's lawmaker. [The] Executive has [often] agreed to legislative review as the price for a broad delegation of authority. To be sure, the President may have preferred unrestricted power, but that could be precisely why Congress thought it essential to retain a check on the exercise of delegated authority.

II.   For all these reasons, the apparent sweep of the Court's decision today is regrettable. The Court's Article I analysis appears to invalidate all legislative vetoes irrespective of form or subject. Because the legislative veto is commonly found as a check upon rulemaking by administrative agencies and upon broad-based policy decisions of the Executive Branch, it is particularly unfortunate that the Court reaches its decision in a case involving the exercise of a veto over deportation decisions regarding particular individuals. Courts should always be wary of striking statutes as unconstitutional; to strike an entire class of statutes based on consideration of a somewhat atypical and more-readily indictable exemplar of the class is irresponsible. [If] the legislative veto were as plainly unconstitutional as the Court strives to suggest, its broad ruling today would be more comprehensible. But, the constitutionality of the legislative veto is anything but clearcut. The issue divides scholars, courts, attorneys general, and the two other branches of the National Government. If the veto devices so flagrantly disregarded the requirements of Article I as the Court today suggests, I find it incomprehensible that Congress, whose members are bound by oath to uphold the Constitution, would have placed these mechanisms in nearly 200 separate laws over a period of 50 years.

The reality of the situation is that the constitutional question posed today is one of immense difficulty over which the executive and legislative branches—as well as scholars and judges—have understandably disagreed. That disagreement stems from the silence of the Constitution on the precise question: The Constitution does not directly authorize or prohibit the legislative veto. Thus, our task should be to determine whether the legislative veto is consistent with the purposes of Art. I and the principles of Separation of [Powers].[4] We should

---

3. While Congress could write certain statutes with greater specificity, it is unlikely that this is a realistic or even desirable substitute for the legislative veto. "Political volatility and the controversy of many issues would prevent Congress from reaching agreement on many major problems if specificity were required in their enactments." Fuchs, Administrative Agencies and the Energy Problem, 47 Ind.L.J. 606, 608 (1972). [Oversight] hearings and congressional investigations have their purpose, but unless Congress is to be rendered a think tank or debating society, they are no substitute for the exercise of actual authority. [Finally], the passage of corrective legislation after agency regulations take effect or Executive Branch officials have acted entail the drawbacks endemic to a retroactive [response]. [Footnote by Justice White.]

4. I limit my concern here to those legislative vetoes which require either one or both Houses of Congress to pass resolutions of approval or

not find the lack of a specific constitutional authorization for the legislative veto surprising, and I would not infer disapproval of the mechanism from its absence. From the summer of 1787 to the present the government of the United States has become an endeavor far beyond the contemplation of the Framers. Only within the last half century has the complexity and size of the Federal Government's responsibilities grown so greatly that the Congress must rely on the legislative veto as the most effective if not the only means to insure their role as the nation's lawmakers. But the wisdom of the Framers was to anticipate that the nation would grow and new problems of governance would require different solutions. Accordingly, our Federal Government was intentionally chartered with the flexibility to respond to contemporary needs without losing sight of fundamental democratic principles. This was the spirit in which Justice Jackson penned his influential concurrence in the [Steel Seizure Case]. This is the perspective from which we should approach the novel constitutional questions presented by the legislative veto. In my view, neither [Art. I nor] the doctrine of separation of powers is violated by this mechanism by which our elected representatives preserve their voice in the governance of the nation.

III. [The] power to exercise a legislative veto is not the power to write new law without bicameral approval or presidential consideration. The veto must be authorized by statute and may only negative what an Executive department or independent agency has proposed. On its face, the legislative veto no more allows one House of Congress to make law than does the presidential veto confer such power upon the President. Accordingly, the Court properly recognizes that it "must establish that the challenged action under § 244(c)(2) is of the kind to which the procedural requirements of Art. I, § 7 apply" and admits that "not every action taken by either House is subject to the bicameralism and presentation requirements of Art. I."

A. The terms of the Presentment Clauses suggest only that bills and their equivalent are subject to the requirements of bicameral passage and presentment to the President. [The] historical background of the Presentation Clause itself [reveals] only that the Framers were concerned with limiting the methods for enacting new legislation. [There] is no record that the Convention contemplated, let alone intended, that these Article I requirements would someday be invoked to restrain the scope of Congressional authority pursuant to duly-enacted law. When the Convention did turn its attention to the scope of Congress' lawmaking power, the Framers were expansive. [McCulloch.]

B. The Court heeded this counsel in approving the modern administrative state. The Court's holding today that all legislative-type action must be enacted through the lawmaking process ignores that legislative authority is routinely delegated to the Executive branch, to the independent regulatory agencies, and to private individuals and groups. [This] Court's decisions sanctioning such delegations make clear that Article I does not require all action with the effect of legislation to be passed as a law. Theoretically, agencies and officials were asked only to "fill up the details," and the rule was that "Congress cannot delegate any part of its legislative power except under a limitation of a prescribed standard." [In] practice, however, restrictions on the scope of the power that could be delegated diminished and all but disappeared. [See p. 365 below.] [The] wisdom and the constitutionality of these broad delegations are matters that still have not been put to rest. But for present purposes, [the] cases establish that by virtue of congressional delegation, legislative power can be exercised by independent agencies and Executive departments without the

disapproval, and leave aside the questions arising from the exercise of such powers by committees of Congress. [Footnote by Justice White.] [In another footnote, Justice White stated that he agreed with Justice Rehnquist that Congress did not intend the one-House veto provision challenged here to be severable.]

passage of new legislation. For some time, the sheer amount of law—the substantive rules, that regulate private conduct and direct the operation of government—made by the agencies has far outnumbered the lawmaking engaged in by Congress through the traditional process. There is no question but that agency rulemaking is lawmaking in any functional or realistic sense of the term. [These] regulations bind courts and officers of the federal government, may preempt state law, and grant rights to and impose obligations on the public. In sum, they have the force of law.

If Congress may delegate lawmaking power to independent and executive agencies, it is most difficult to understand Article I as forbidding Congress from also reserving a check on legislative power for itself. Absent the veto, the agencies receiving delegations of legislative or quasi-legislative power may issue regulations having the force of law without bicameral approval and without the President's signature. It is thus not apparent why the reservation of a veto over the exercise of that legislative power must be subject to a more exacting test. In both cases, it is enough that the initial statutory authorizations comply with the Article I requirements. [Under] the Court's analysis, the Executive Branch and the independent agencies may make rules with the effect of law while Congress, in whom the Framers confided the legislative power, may not exercise a veto which precludes such rules from having operative force. If the effective functioning of a complex modern government requires the delegation of vast authority which, by virtue of its breadth, is legislative or "quasi-legislative" in character, I cannot accept that Article I—which is, after all, the source of the non-delegation doctrine—should forbid Congress from qualifying that grant with a legislative veto.[5]

C.   The Court also takes no account of perhaps the most relevant consideration: However resolutions of disapproval under § 244(c)(2) are formally characterized, in reality, a departure from the status quo occurs only upon the concurrence of opinion among the House, Senate, and President. Reservations of legislative authority to be exercised by Congress should be upheld if the exercise of such reserved authority is consistent with the distribution of and limits upon legislative power that Article I provides.

1.   [The] history of the Immigration Act makes clear that § 244(c)(2) did not alter the division of actual authority between Congress and the Executive. At all times, whether through private bills, or through affirmative concurrent resolutions, or through the present one-House veto, a permanent change in a deportable alien's status could be accomplished only with the agreement of the Attorney General, the House, and the Senate.

2.   The central concern of the presentation and bicameralism requirements of Article I is that when a departure from the legal status quo is undertaken, it is done with the approval of the President and both Houses of Congress—or, in the event of a presidential veto, a two-thirds majority in both Houses. This interest is fully satisfied by the operation of § 244(c)(2). The President's approval is found in the Attorney General's action in recommending to Congress that the deportation order for a given alien be suspended. The House

---

5.   The Court's other reasons for holding the legislative veto subject to the presentment and bicameral passage requirements require but brief discussion. [For example, the Court] argues that "the legislative character of the challenged action of one House is confirmed by the fact that when the Framers intended to authorize either [House] to act alone and outside of its prescribed bicameral legislative role, they narrowly and precisely defined the procedure for such action." [The] short answer is that all of these carefully defined exceptions to the presentment and bicameralism strictures do not involve action of the Congress pursuant to a duly-enacted statute. Indeed, for the most part these powers—those of impeachment, review of appointments, and treaty ratification—are not legislative powers at all. The fact that it was essential for the Constitution to stipulate that Congress has the power to impeach and try the President hardly demonstrates a limit upon Congress' authority to reserve itself a legislative veto, through statutes, over subjects within its lawmaking authority. [Footnote by Justice White.]

and the Senate indicate their approval of the Executive's action by not passing a resolution of disapproval within the statutory period.   Thus, a change in the legal status quo—the deportability of the alien—is consummated only with the approval of each of the three relevant actors.   The disagreement of any one of the three maintains the alien's pre-existing status: the Executive may choose not to recommend suspension; the House and Senate may each veto the recommendation.   The effect on the rights and obligations of the affected individuals and upon the legislative system is precisely the same as if a private bill were introduced but failed to receive the necessary [approval].

IV.   The Court of Appeals struck § 244(c)(2) as violative of the constitutional principle of separation of powers.   It is true that the purpose of separating the authority of government is to prevent unnecessary and dangerous concentration of power in one branch.   [But] the history of the separation of powers doctrine is also a history of accommodation and practicality.   Apprehensions of an overly powerful branch have not led to undue prophylactic measures that handicap the effective working of the national government as a whole.   The Constitution does not contemplate total separation of the three branches of Government.   [Our] decisions reflect this judgment.   As already noted, the Court, recognizing that modern government must address a formidable agenda of complex policy issues, countenanced the delegation of extensive legislative authority to executive and independent agencies.   The separation of powers doctrine has heretofore led to the invalidation of government action only when the challenged action violated some express provision in the Constitution. [E.g., Buckley v. Valeo (1976; p. 378 below); Myers v. United States (1926; p. 379 below); United States v. Klein (1871; p. 43 above).]   Because we must have a workable efficient government, this is as it should [be].   Section 244(c) (2) survives [the] test [of prior decisions].

[The] Court believes that the legislative veto we consider today is best characterized as an exercise of legislative or quasi-legislative authority.   Under this characterization, the practice does not, even on the surface, constitute an infringement of executive or judicial prerogative.   [Nor] does § 244 infringe on the judicial power, as Justice Powell would hold.   Section 244 makes clear that Congress has reserved its own judgment as part of the statutory process. Congressional action does not substitute for judicial review of the Attorney General's decisions.   [The] courts have not been given the authority to review whether an alien should be given permanent [status].   Moreover, there is no constitutional obligation to provide any judicial review whatever for failure to suspend deportation.   [I] do not suggest that all legislative vetoes are necessarily consistent with separation of powers principles.   A legislative check on an inherently executive function, for example that of initiating prosecutions, poses an entirely different question.   But the legislative veto device here—and in many other settings—is far from an instance of legislative tyranny over the Executive.   It is a necessary check on the unavoidably expanding power of the agencies, both executive and independent, as they engage in exercising authority delegated by Congress.

V.   I regret that I am in disagreement with my colleagues on the fundamental questions that this case presents.   But even more I regret the destructive scope of the Court's holding.   It reflects a profoundly different conception of the Constitution than that held by the Courts which sanctioned the modern administrative state.   Today's decision strikes down in one fell swoop provisions in more laws enacted by Congress than the Court has cumulatively invalidated in its history.   I fear it will now be more difficult "to insure that the fundamental policy decisions in our society will be made not by an appointed official but by the body immediately responsible to the people," Arizona v. California, 373 U.S. 546, 626 (1963) (Harlan, J., dissenting).   I must dissent.

Justice REHNQUIST, with whom Justice WHITE joins, dissenting.

[Because] I believe that Congress did not intend the one-House veto provision of § 244(c)(2) to be severable, I dissent. [By] severing § 244(c)(2), the Court permits suspension of deportation in a class of cases where Congress never stated that suspension was appropriate. I do not believe we should expand the statute in this way without some clear indication that Congress intended such an expansion. [The] Court finds that the legislative history of § 244 shows that Congress intended § 244(c)(2) to be severable because Congress wanted to relieve itself of the burden of private bills. But the history elucidated by the Court shows that Congress was unwilling to give the Executive Branch permission to suspend deportation on its own. [Congress] has never indicated that it would be willing to permit suspensions of deportation unless it could retain some sort of veto. It is doubtless true that Congress has the power to provide for suspensions of deportation without a one-House veto. But the Court has failed to identify any evidence that Congress intended to exercise that power. On the contrary, Congress' continued insistence on retaining control of the suspension process indicates that it has never been disposed to give the Executive Branch a free [hand].[1]

CHADHA AND THE LEGISLATIVE VETO CONTROVERSY

The Chadha ruling was the Court's first full encounter with the political and academic debates that had raged for years about the constitutionality of legislative vetoes.[1] Chadha attempts to resolve most of the controversy in sweeping terms. Does it try to decide too much? Arguably, Chief Justice Burger's opinion is in the tradition of Justice Black's in the Steel Seizure Case; arguably, Justice White's dissent echoes more faithfully the more discriminating approach of Justice Jackson in the Steel Seizure Case. Consider the persuasiveness of the various opinions in Chadha. What questions remain open after Chadha? Clearly, severability problems in many other statutes containing legislative veto provisions remain to be adjudicated.[2] Consider, too, whether Chadha leaves open the possibility of arguments that legislative veto provisions are still permissible in contexts where congressional power may be especially strong, as with the appropriation of funds and the waging of war. For example, can the

---

1. Two weeks after the decision in Chadha, the Court affirmed without opinion two rulings of the Court of Appeals for the District of Columbia Circuit. These rulings had struck down not only the one-house veto provision in the Natural Gas Policy Act of 1978 but also the two-house veto in the Federal Trade Commission Improvements Act of 1980. See, e.g., Process Gas Consumers Group v. Consumers Energy Council, 463 U.S. — (1983). The Court also denied certiorari to review several other decisions that had struck down two-house veto provisions. Did Chadha leave room for distinguishing two-house vetoes from one-house ones? Should they have been distinguished? See generally Strauss, "Was There a Baby in the Bathwater? A Comment on the Supreme Court's Legislative Veto Decision," 1983 Duke L.J. 789. Despite Chadha, Congress has continued to enact legislative veto provisions in a number of statutes. Congress has apparently assumed that fear of budgetary retaliation would assure that the executive branch would honor the provisions. Simultaneously, Congress has had before it a range of

regulatory reform laws to provide new congressional restraints other than the legislative veto, as well as constitutional amendments to authorize legislative vetoes. See Cong.Quart. Weekly Report, Oct. 29, 1983, and The New York Times, Dec. 21, 1983.

1. For some samples of that controversy, see, e.g. (in addition to pp. 399–401 of Gunther, Constitutional Law, 10th ed., 1980, and the articles cited in Chadha itself), Bruff & Gellhorn, "Congressional Control of Administrative Regulation: A Study of Legislative Vetoes," 90 Harv. L.Rev. 1369 (1977); Schwartz, "The Legislative Veto and the Constitution—A Reexamination," 46 Geo.Wash.L.Rev. 351 (1978); and Dixon, "The Congressional Veto and Separation of Powers: The Executive on a Leash?" 56 N.C.L.Rev. 423 (1978).

2. Recall the contending positions regarding severability in Chadha, in footnote 2 of the Chief Justice's opinion and in Justice Rehnquist's dissent.

legislative veto provisions in the Impounding Control Act of 1974 (p. 362 below) and the War Powers Resolution of 1973 (p. 371 below) survive constitutional challenge after Chadha? If all or most legislative vetoes are barred by Chadha, what alternative techniques are left to Congress for controlling executive and administrative implementations of federal laws? [3]

THE IMPOUNDMENT CONTROVERSY

Introduction. Does the President have inherent constitutional power to refuse to spend funds appropriated by Congress—even when Congress *mandates* such spending? A claimed executive authority to impound was one of the executive-legislative conflicts which reached new levels of intensity and scope in the 1970s. The "power of the purse" is traditionally associated with Congress and is reflected in several provisions of Art. I. Yet Presidents have repeatedly refused to spend money appropriated by Congress. Most of those refusals rested on express or implied grants of executive discretion in the legislation. Exercise of executive power in that situation readily falls within the first of Justice Jackson's three categories in the Steel Seizure case. In 1973, in the face of mounting congressional criticism and court challenges to executive impoundment, President Nixon turned to constitutional justifications, asserting an inherent discretion to impound even in the face of a mandatory spending directive from Congress. He claimed that there was an "absolutely clear" "constitutional right" of the President to "impound" funds when the spending "would mean either increasing prices or increasing taxes for all the people." That position moved the central issue in the impoundment controversy from Justice Jackson's first category to his third category.[1]

1. *The Impounding Control Act of 1974.* Increasingly broad executive claims were matched by increasingly insistent proposals for congressional countermeasures. Efforts initiated by Senator Ervin culminated in the enactment of the Congressional Budget and Impounding Control Act of 1974, 88 Stat. 297. That Act—like the War Powers Resolution of 1973, p. 371 below—represents congressional action of an unusual and especially important nature. Instead of congressional directives regarding substantive governmental policies, it delineates structures and processes. It is legislation that can be viewed as quasi-constitutional in nature, for it seeks to clarify and define basic relationships among the branches of government.

3. A footnote to Chief Justice Burger's opinion in Chadha provided a reminder that Congress could, for example, resort to a "report and wait" provision. Such a provision was approved by the Court as early as Sibbach v. Wilson, 312 U.S. 1 (1941). The statute involved in Sibbach provided that the Federal Rules of Civil Procedure "shall not take effect until they shall have been reported to Congress by the Attorney General at the beginning of a regular session thereof and after the close of such session." As the Chief Justice noted in Chadha: "The statute did *not* provide that Congress could unilaterally veto the Federal Rules. Rather, it gave Congress the opportunity to review the Rules before they became effective and to pass legislation barring their effectiveness if the Rules were found objectionable."

1. In the only modern Court case on the impoundment issue, the executive branch raised only a statutory claim that the President was authorized to impound funds. The Court unanimously rejected that claim in Train v. New York, 420 U.S. 35 (1975). However, several federal trial courts considered (and rejected) presidential claims to impound based on inherent constitutional powers. See, e.g., Local 2677 v. Phillips, 358 F.Supp. 60 (D.D.C.1973).

For a sampling of the extensive literature produced by the controversy, see, e.g., Abascal & Kramer, "Presidential Impoundment Part I: Historical Genesis and Constitutional Framework," 62 Geo.L.J. 1549 (1974); Abascal & Kramer, "Presidential Impoundment Part II: Judicial and Legislative Responses," 63 Geo.L.J. 149 (1974); and Mikva & Hertz, "Impoundment of Funds—The Courts, The Congress and The President: A Constitutional Triangle," 69 Nw. U.L.Rev. 335 (1974).

The 1974 Act attempts to impose substantial restraints on presidential authority to impound, requiring legislative approval of executive decisions to reduce or end programs for which funds are authorized. The Act distinguishes between two types of impoundments. Where the President proposes simply to *defer* the expenditure of appropriated funds, the initiative to curb falls on Congress: either house may disapprove the deferral by adopting a simple resolution. Under the Act, presidential deferral proposals take effect unless "either House of Congress passes an impoundment resolution disapproving such proposed deferral." But for proposed presidential impoundments to *terminate* a particular spending authority, or to withhold funds beyond the end of the fiscal year, the executive action is permissible only with the affirmative concurrence of both houses of Congress. In such instances the presidential recommendations do not take effect unless, within 45 days after transmittal of the President's proposal, "the Congress has completed action on a rescission bill rescinding all or part of the amount proposed to be rescinded." To enable Congress to exercise these controls, the Act requires the President to report all proposed impoundment actions.[2]

2. *Constitutional problems?* Do the impoundment control provisions of the 1974 Act raise any constitutional problems? As applied to domestic spending programs? As applied to foreign programs—cf. sec. 1B below? Can any plausible constitutional arguments be made that executive discretion to impound is an inherent power untouchable by Congress? Does the congressional spending power in Art. I, § 8, resolve any conflicts in favor of the legislative branch, in situations in Justice Jackson's third category? Can the legislative veto aspects of the 1974 Act be justified in the wake of the Chadha case, above?

B. FOREIGN AFFAIRS AND USE OF ARMED FORCES

Introduction. Are the limits on presidential policy-making authority in the domestic sphere, considered in sec. 1A, substantially attenuated when the context is foreign affairs and the use of armed forces? Is the inherent executive power that was restrained in the Steel Seizure Case available to the President when the action is external rather than domestic? What are the President's powers as Chief Executive and "Commander in Chief"? Curtiss-Wright, which follows, contains broad statements about the special responsibility of the President in foreign relations. Does that special role include any constitutional authority other than the specific functions allocated in Art. II? These questions, suggested by Curtiss-Wright, introduce the problems of executive-legislative competition in the materials that follow. For example, does the President have autonomous authority to make foreign policy via executive agreements and thereby bypass the treaty route in which the Senate participates? Concern about executive agreements was one of the fears that fueled the Bricker Amendment campaign in the 1950s (recall chap. 4, sec. 3, above). A decade later, warnings of risks of congressional subservience to the President came from different

---

2. The 1974 Act also includes affirmative measures to increase the capability of Congress to make comprehensive judgments on budget matters. These measures were designed to counter the Nixon Administration's claim that Congress was institutionally incapable of making such comprehensive judgments. Thus, the Act established new budget committees to prepare tentative recommendations, to be adopted as concurrent resolutions in May. A Congressional Budget Office was created. Each September, after congressional committees have completed action on spending bills, Congress is to take another overall look at the budget and is authorized to pass a second concurrent resolution adjusting the targets established earlier. Critics of congressional handling of budget matters maintain that the Act has not achieved its objectives and that congressional attention to budget issues continues haphazard.

sources: many of those who deprecated the anxieties of Bricker Amendment proponents demanded, in the context of the Vietnam controversy, that Congress assert greater control.

The Vietnam debate also attracted special attention to the President's authority regarding the use of armed forces. Art. II designates the President as "Commander in Chief." Art. I grants Congress the authority to "declare War." To what extent do these powers conflict? How can they be accommodated? To what extent may military forces be used without a formal declaration of war? To what extent must and can Congress participate in the decisionmaking process? Constitutional questions such as these have seldom come to the courts. Growing congressional concern with these issues culminated in 1973 in the enactment of several measures to curtail presidential authority to commit American combat forces. Most importantly, the War Powers Resolution of 1973 sought to delineate more explicit guidelines for presidential action and to assure greater participation by Congress. That Resolution was objected to by President Nixon on constitutional grounds. The materials in this section are in part designed to provide background for consideration of whether the efforts to restrain presidential authority in the War Powers Resolution (p. 371 below) raise questions of unconstitutional interference with Art. II powers.

UNITED STATES v. CURTISS–WRIGHT EXPORT CORP.

299 U.S. 304, 57 S.Ct. 216, 81 L.Ed. 255 (1936).

[A Joint Resolution of Congress in 1934 authorized the President to prohibit the sale of arms and munitions to countries engaged in armed conflict in the Chaco. President Roosevelt immediately proclaimed such an embargo. Curtiss-Wright was indicted for conspiracy to sell arms to Bolivia (one of the countries involved in the Chaco dispute) and challenged the Joint Resolution as an unconstitutional delegation of legislative power to the President. The lower court sustained that challenge.]

Mr. Justice SUTHERLAND delivered [the opinion of the Court].

Whether, if the Joint Resolution had related solely to internal affairs, it would be open to the challenge that it constituted an unlawful delegation of legislative power to the Executive, we find it unnecessary to determine. The whole aim of the resolution is to affect a situation entirely external to the United States, and falling within the category of foreign affairs. [A]ssuming (but not deciding) that the challenged delegation, if it were confined to internal affairs, would be invalid, may it nevertheless be sustained on the ground that its exclusive aim is to afford a remedy for a hurtful condition within foreign territory? [The Court first considered the differences between national powers regarding external and domestic affairs, "both in respect of their origin and their nature." Excerpts from those passages, asserting that national foreign affairs powers "did not depend upon the affirmative grants of the Constitution," are printed at p. 228 above. The Court then turned to the special role of the President in the conduct of foreign affairs:]

Not only, as we have shown, is the federal power over external affairs in origin and essential character different from that over internal affairs, but participation in the exercise of the power is significantly limited. In this vast external realm, with its important, complicated, delicate and manifold problems, the President alone has the power to speak or listen as a representative of the nation. He *makes* treaties with the advice and consent of the Senate; but he alone negotiates. [It] is important to bear in mind that we are here dealing not alone with an authority vested in the President by an exertion of legislative power, but with such an authority plus the very delicate, plenary and exclusive power of the President as the sole organ of the federal government in the field of international relations—a power which does not require as a basis for its exercise an act of Congress, but which, of course, like every other governmental power, must be exercised in subordination to the applicable provisions of the Constitution. It is quite apparent that if, in the maintenance of our international relations, embarrassment [is] to be avoided and success for our aims achieved, congressional legislation which is to be made effective through negotiation and inquiry within the international field must often accord to the President a degree of discretion and freedom from statutory restriction which would not be admissible were domestic affairs alone involved. Moreover, he, not Congress, has the better opportunity of knowing the conditions which prevail in foreign countries, and especially is this true in time of war. He has his confidential sources of information. He has his agents in the form of diplomatic, consular and other officials. Secrecy in respect of information gathered by them may be highly necessary, and the premature disclosure of it productive of harmful [results].

When the President is to be authorized by legislation to act in respect of a matter intended to affect a situation in foreign territory, the legislator properly bears in mind the important consideration that the form of the President's action—or, indeed, whether he shall act at all—may well depend, among other things, upon the nature of the confidential information which he has or may thereafter receive, or upon the effect which his action may have upon our foreign relations. This consideration [discloses] the unwisdom of requiring Congress in this field of governmental power to lay down narrowly definite standards by which the President is to be [governed].

Reversed.[1]

SOME PROBLEMS SUGGESTED BY CURTISS–WRIGHT

1. *The special presidential role in foreign affairs.* As already noted in chap. 4, sec. 3, the national government's power over foreign affairs, while widely recognized as broad, is largely based on historical and structural inferences rather than explicit constitutional delegations. And the contours of that national power remain uncertain in a number of respects, for adjudications are sparse and assertions and practices in political contexts are numerous and at times inconsistent. The Curtiss-Wright case has already been noted at p. 228 for its broad readings of *national* foreign affairs authority. Some of Justice Sutherland's broad statements on that problem have been questioned. Is there also reason to question some of the Curtiss-Wright assertions about *presidential* authority?

Even if a broad national authority over foreign affairs exists, uncertainty remains about the allocation of powers between President and Congress in the exercise of that authority. Did Curtiss-Wright contain excessively broad dicta regarding the presidential predominance in external relations? Recall footnote 1 in Justice Jackson's opinion in the Steel Seizure case, noting that Curtiss-Wright did not involve a question of presidential power to act in a twilight zone, without congressional authority (Justice Jackson's second category), "but the question of his right to act under and in accord with an Act of Congress"; and that, though Curtiss-Wright "intimated that the President might act in external affairs without Congressional authority," it did not state "that he might act contrary to an Act of Congress" (Justice Jackson's third category). What may the President do in the face of congressional efforts to control executive

------

1. Justice McREYNOLDS dissented without opinion.

actions? What external affairs powers does the President have in the absence of congressional action? [2]

2. *Presidential authority to abrogate treaties.* May the President terminate a treaty without the participation of Congress? That question reached the Court in GOLDWATER v. CARTER, 444 U.S. 996 (1979), but the Court refused to decide the merits. The case arose in the following circumstances: In December 1978, President Carter announced that the United States would recognize the People's Republic of China as the sole government of that country and would simultaneously withdraw recognition of the Republic of China (Taiwan). A week later, the State Department notified the Taiwan government that the Mutual Defense Treaty of 1955 with the Republic of China would terminate on January 1, 1980, in accordance with a provision of the treaty that permitted either party to terminate it on one year's notice. Senator Goldwater, joined by other Senators, brought suit to enjoin the President from terminating the treaty without a two-thirds vote of the Senate. (The Constitution requires a two-thirds vote of the Senate to ratify a treaty, but is silent about termination; the plaintiffs claimed that a similar vote was necessary to end a treaty.) The lower courts reached the merits (with the Court of Appeals sustaining the President's authority to terminate), but the Supreme Court, without hearing argument, ordered that the Senators' complaint be dismissed. However, the Justices could not agree on the reasons why the Goldwater suit was inappropriate for judicial resolution.[3]

Only one of the Justices in the Goldwater case reached the merits. Justice BRENNAN stated that he would affirm the judgment of the Court of Appeals "insofar as it rests upon the President's well-established authority to recognize, and withdraw recognition from, foreign governments." Disagreeing with the view of some of his colleagues that the case presented a nonjusticiable "political question," he urged a "narrow" answer on the merits: "Abrogation of the defense treaty with Taiwan was a necessary incident to Executive recognition of the Peking government, because the defense treaty was predicated upon the now-abandoned view that the Taiwan government was the only legitimate political authority in China. Our cases firmly establish that the Constitution remits to the President alone the power to recognize, and withdraw recognition from, foreign regimes. That mandate being clear, our judicial inquiry into the treaty rupture can go no further." [4]

3. *Delegation of legislative powers to the executive.* In its most immediate aspect, Curtiss-Wright was a case about delegation of legislative powers. Delegation problems involve no conflicts between President and Congress but, if anything, excessive harmony: the charge is not that Congress has usurped presidential powers, but rather that Congress has sought to give to the executive too much of its own legislative power. Curtiss-Wright holds that limits on delegation of

2. Among the most frequently mentioned "exclusive" presidential powers (in addition to claims derived from the Curtiss-Wright opinion) are the authority to recognize foreign governments and to act as Commander-in-Chief of the armed forces. See the materials on executive agreements and on control of the armed forces, below. See generally Henkin, Foreign Affairs and the Constitution (1972).

3. The divided majority's reasons are further examined in the final chapter below, at p. 1612. Four Justices (Justice Rehnquist, joined by Chief Justice Burger and Justices Stewart and Stevens) insisted that the case presented a nonjusticiable "political question." Justice Powell concurred in the result, but insisted that the political question barrier was inapplicable here. The other Justices

in the majority did not explicitly address the justiciability issue.

4. Justice Brennan cited United States v. Pink (p. 368 below, involving an executive agreement incidental to the President's recognition authority) as one of his precedents. Compare Judge MacKinnon's opinion dissenting from the Court of Appeals en banc decision sustaining presidential authority to terminate treaties: "[Whatever] expansion the Curtiss-Wright decision occasioned in the President's power in foreign affairs, that expansion has its limitations. The decision cannot be read to trample upon the history of treaty terminations, which is based on the original understanding that termination would be a power shared by the branches."

powers are less restrictive in the foreign affairs field than in the domestic area. What are those limits? How valid is the distinction between the two spheres?

a. *Domestic sphere.* In the domestic area, the Court had imposed substantial restraints on delegation of legislative powers in the years immediately preceding Curtiss-Wright. Recall the Schechter case (1935; p. 123 above), one of the controversial early New Deal cases, in which the Court unanimously invalidated the provision of the National Industrial Recovery Act which authorized the President to approve "codes of fair competition." (Justice Cardozo in Schechter commented: "This is delegation running riot.") See also Panama Ref. Co. v. Ryan, 293 U.S. 388 (1935), the "hot oil" case, striking down another provision of the NIRA as excessive delegation. But in subsequent cases of domestic economic regulation, the Court did not find the delegation barrier a substantial one. See, e.g., Yakus v. United States, 321 U.S. 414 (1944).

In recent years, however, approving references to Schechter's delegation point have occasionally surfaced in the opinions, to the surprise of some observers. In National Cable Television Ass'n v. United States, 415 U.S. 336 (1974), Justice Douglas' majority opinion construed the fee-setting authority of federal agencies narrowly to avoid constitutional problems of delegation. Justice Marshall's dissent, joined by Justice Brennan, thought the alleged constitutional problems "nonexistent": "The notion that the Constitution narrowly confines the power of Congress to delegate authority to administrative agencies, which was briefly in vogue in the 1930's, has been virtually abandoned by the Court for all practical purposes, at least in the absence of a delegation creating 'the danger of overbroad, unauthorized, and arbitrary application of criminal sanctions in the area of [constitutionally] protected freedoms.' This doctrine is surely as moribund as the substantive due process approach of the same era—for which the Court is fond of writing an obituary [see chap. 8 below]—if not more so. It is hardly surprising that, until today's decision, the Court has not relied upon [Schechter] almost since the day it was decided."

Nevertheless, there have been further attempts to revitalize the delegation analysis. Justice Rehnquist has urged that the delegation doctrine is a basis for invalidation of some modern congressional grants of authority to administrative agencies. See especially American Textile Mfrs. Inst. v. Donovan, 452 U.S. 490 (1981), which involved interpretation of the Occupational Safety and Health Act of 1970. The Act authorizes the Administrator (OSHA) to promulgate mandatory federal standards governing health and safety in the workplace. The most controversial provision, § 6(b)(5), states that OSHA "shall set the standard which most adequately assures, *to the extent feasible,* [that] no employee will suffer material impairment of health or functional capacity even if such employee has regular exposure to the hazard dealt with by such standard for the period of his working life." (Emphasis added.) The central issue in the case was OSHA's right or duty to engage in cost-benefit analysis before promulgating standards. Justice Rehnquist's dissent, joined by Chief Justice Burger, argued that § 6(b)(5) "unconstitutionally delegated to the Executive Branch the authority to make the 'hard policy choices' properly the task of the legislature." [5] He insisted that the Act exceeded Congress' power "to delegate legislative authority to nonelected officials." In his view, inclusion of the phrase "to the extent feasible" "rendered what had been a clear, if somewhat unrealistic, statute into one so vague and precatory as to be an unconstitutional delegation." He elaborated: "The words 'to the extent feasible' were used to mask a fundamental policy disagreement in Congress. [I] do

---

5. Justice Rehnquist relied heavily on his concurring opinion in Industrial Union Department v. American Petroleum Institute, 448 U.S. 607 (1980). [The Industrial Union case involved the "benzene standard," a safeguard against cancer. The American Textile case dealt with the "cotton dust standard," a safeguard against "brown lung" disease.]

not mean to suggest that Congress, in enacting a statute, must resolve all ambiguities or must 'fill in all of the blanks.' Even the neophyte student of government realizes that legislation is the art of compromise. [But the typical compromise] is a far cry from this case, where Congress simply abdicated its responsibility for the making of a fundamental and most difficult policy [choice]."

b. *Foreign sphere.* Does the Schechter doctrine have even less vitality in the foreign affairs sphere? Contrast with Curtiss-Wright the decision in Kent v. Dulles, 357 U.S. 116 (1958), reading a passport control statute narrowly to avoid constitutional problems and denying to the Secretary of State the authority to withhold passports on the basis of beliefs and associations. The opinion emphasized the right-to-travel aspect of "liberty" as the major lurking constitutional problem. But it also contained a passage stating that, if the "right to exit" is to be regulated, "it must be pursuant to the lawmaking functions of the Congress. [Steel Seizure Case.] And if that power is delegated, standards must be adequate to pass scrutiny by the accepted test. See Panama Refining Co. v. Ryan." Was that 1958 citation of Panama Refining, the domestic regulation "hot oil" case of 1935 (and the failure to cite Curtiss-Wright in a foreign travel case), surprising? [6]

THE PRESIDENT, CONGRESS, AND EXECUTIVE AGREEMENTS

Introduction. Over the years, the executive branch has frequently resorted to executive agreements rather than treaties in its foreign relations activities. Concerns have recurrently been voiced that the executive agreements route may unduly intrude upon the Senate's role by bypassing treaty-making. Fears have also been voiced that executive agreements may be on a par with treaties and may thus be able to supersede prior legislation. To a large extent, the magnitude of those risks turns on when such agreements are constitutionally justified. Are they supportable simply on the basis of an inherent presidential authority? To what extent can executive agreements be justified as incidental to specified Art. II powers? Must all executive agreements be made in pursuance of a statute? And may Congress bar or overturn executive agreements? The following materials sample that range of problems raised by the executive agreements device.

1. *The Belmont Case.* In UNITED STATES v. BELMONT, 301 U.S. 324 (1937), the Court sustained the validity of an executive agreement and held that it took precedence over conflicting state policy. Justice Sutherland, who had written Curtiss-Wright a year earlier, wrote for the majority in Belmont. The agreement arose out of the American diplomatic recognition of the Soviet Union in 1933. At the same time as President Roosevelt recognized the Soviet Union, an exchange of diplomatic correspondence between the President and Maxim Litvinov effected an assignment to the United States of all Soviet claims against Americans who held funds of Russian companies seized after the Revolution. The Belmont suit was brought by the United States in reliance upon that assignment, to recover funds deposited by a Russian corporation with a private New York banker. The lower courts dismissed the action on the ground that implementing the U.S.S.R.'s confiscation would violate the public

---

6. But note the modern Court's citation of Curtiss-Wright in Regan v. Wald, 468 U.S. ___ (1984), holding that presidential restrictions on travel to Cuba had been authorized by Congress. Compare the implicit reliance on quasi-delegation principles in Hampton v. Mow Sun Wong (exclusion of aliens from federal employment; 1976; p. 676 below). But note the Court's receptiveness to broad delegation of authority to the President with regard to oil imports, in FEA v. Algonquin SNG, Inc., 426 U.S. 548 (1976).

policy of New York. Justice SUTHERLAND's majority opinion emphasized that the recognition, the establishment of diplomatic relations, and the assignment "were all parts of one transaction, resulting in an international compact between the two governments." He had no doubt that the negotiations and the agreements "were within the competence of the President": "in respect of what was done here, the Executive had authority to speak as the sole organ." And the assignment and agreements, unlike treaties, did not require the Senate's participation. He noted that "an international compact, as this was, is not always a treaty which requires the participation of the Senate. There are many such compacts, of which a protocol, a modus vivendi, a postal convention, and agreements like that now under consideration are illustrations." And the supremacy clause's required that contrary state policies must give way.[1]

2. *Sources of authority for executive agreements.* Does Belmont, against the background of Curtiss-Wright, support a broad autonomous presidential authority to enter into executive agreements? Or is it important to distinguish among sources for particular agreements? Is it useful to invoke the three-pronged analysis of Justice Jackson's opinion in the Steel Seizure Case? Many executive agreements fall within his first category: they are adopted pursuant to statutory authority, as in the Trade Agreements Act, authorizing modification of tariffs through presidential agreements. The Litvinov agreement involved in Belmont, by contrast, rested on the specifically delegated presidential authority regarding diplomatic recognition, in Art. II, § 3. As to such agreements, it is arguable that Congress possesses no authority to interfere with executive power. Could Congress enact guidelines for the negotiation of executive agreements under the necessary and proper clause? Is there a broader inherent executive power such as that suggested in Curtiss-Wright which may justify executive agreements? Even in the face of contrary congressional directives? Note that in the Belmont case, the argued limits on executive agreements stemmed from conflicting policies of the state, not from inconsistent policies of Congress. On conflicts between federal legislation and executive agreements, see United States v. Capps, 204 F.2d 655 (1953), where the Fourth Circuit held that an agreement with Canada regarding the importation of potatoes was invalid because it conflicted with a prior law enacted by Congress under its power over foreign commerce. The Supreme Court affirmed that judgment without reaching the important issue of the validity of the executive agreement. 348 U.S. 296 (1955). The Court of Appeals decision in Capps suggests need for care in reading the broad approval of executive agreements in cases such as Belmont.

Note the modern Court endorsement of presidential action pursuant to an executive agreement in the Iranian assets case, DAMES & MOORE v. REGAN, 453 U.S. 654 (1981). The case involved President Carter's January 1981 Executive Agreement with Iran, an agreement negotiated in order to obtain the release of American hostages in Iran. Executive orders issued pursuant to the Agreement provided, inter alia, for "nullification" of prejudgment attachments of Iranian assets and for "suspension" of all claims pending in American courts that could be presented to a new Iran-United States Claims Tribunal for binding arbitration. The Government defended its actions by relying in part on inherent executive powers under Art. II. But Justice REHNQUIST's validation of the executive actions did not endorse so broad a claim. Instead, the Court found the presidential implementation of the Agreement supported either by specific congressional authorization or by implied congressional consent and acquiescence. With respect to the latter, Justice Rehnquist emphasized that

---

1. Note also the reappearance of the Litvinov Assignment before the Court in United States v. Pink, 315 U.S. 203 (1942). Justice Douglas' opinion for the Court stated that the President "has the power to determine the policy [to] govern the question of recognition" and that such "international compacts and agreements as the Litvinov Assignment have a similar dignity" as treaties under the Supremacy Clause.

"Congress has acquiesced in [the] longstanding practice of claims settlement by executive agreement." He defended that assertion in several ways. At one point, he invoked prior cases such as United States v. Pink, and argued that those cases "recognized that the President does have some measure of power to enter into executive agreements without obtaining the advice and consent of the Senate." He conceded that Pink had rested on the President's recognition power. But he also quoted from a broader ruling by Judge Learned Hand, Ozanic v. United States, 188 F.2d 228 (2d Cir.1951): "The constitutional power of the President extends to the settlement of mutual claims between a foreign government and the United States, at least when it is an incident to the recognition of that government; and it would be unreasonable to circumscribe it to such controversies. The continued mutual amity between this nation and other powers again and again depends upon a satisfactory compromise of mutual claims: the necessary power to make such compromises has existed from the earliest times and been exercised by the foreign offices of all civilized nations." [2]

In the course of his opinion, Justice Rehnquist referred repeatedly to the Jackson and Frankfurter opinions in the Steel Seizure Case. He found Justice Jackson's tripartite approach "analytically useful," but added that "executive action in any particular instance falls, not neatly in one of three pigeon holes, but rather at some point along a spectrum running from explicit congressional authorization to explicit congressional prohibition. This is particularly true as respects cases such as the one before us, involving responses to international crises the nature of which Congress can hardly have been expected to anticipate in any detail." And in examining the President's authority to suspend claims, Justice Rehnquist relied ultimately on Justice Frankfurter's opinion in the Steel Seizure Case. He stated: "Past practice does not, by itself, create power, but 'long-continued practice, known to and acquiesced in by Congress, would raise a presumption that the [action has been] taken in pursuance of its consent.' [Such a] practice is present here and such a presumption is also appropriate. In light of the fact that Congress may be considered to have consented to the President's action in suspending claims, we cannot say that action exceeded the President's powers." Justice Rehnquist emphasized the "narrowness" of the decision and noted that this was not a situation "in which Congress has in some way resisted the exercise of Presidential authority." See generally "Symposium: Dames & Moore v. Regan," 29 U.C.L.A.L.Rev. 977 (1982).

3. *Executive agreements as alternatives to treaties.* To what extent may the Senate's role in international relations be curtailed by using executive agreements rather than treaties? [3] One purpose of the Bricker Amendment proposals (p. 226 above) was to block the executive agreement bypass. For example, sec. 2 of the version that failed narrowly in 1954 stated: "An international agreement other than a treaty shall become effective as internal law in the United States only by an act of Congress." To what extent could such a result be achieved by legislation? Compare § 8(a)(2) of the War Powers Resolution of 1973, p. 371 below, a congressional effort to curb the impact of treaties on the use of American military forces. [4]

---

2. Note that the Executive Agreement in the Iranian Assets Case was *not* negotiated in connection with the recognition of a foreign government; but note also that the Court, rather than resting on inherent executive power under Art. II, relied primarily on congressional authorization or acquiescence.

3. See generally Mathews, "The Constitutional Power of the President to Conclude Interna-

tional Agreements," 64 Yale L.J. 345 (1955), and Henkin, Foreign Affairs and the Constitution (1972).

4. On the inability of executive agreements and treaties to override nonfederalistic constitutional guarantees, recall Reid v. Covert, p. 227 above.

THE PRESIDENT, CONGRESS, AND THE USE
OF ARMED FORCES

Introduction. The mounting controversy in the late 1960s about American military involvement in Southeast Asia produced unprecedented debate and action regarding the competing spheres of authority of President and Congress in the commitment of military force overseas. Increasingly, the White House claimed autonomous authority under the constitutional powers of the President, especially as Commander in Chief. Increasingly, Congress sought to interpose its judgment, relying especially on its powers to "declare War" and to "raise and support Armies." The materials in these notes sample some of the historical and legal data relevant to an analysis of the constitutional debate during and after the American engagement in Vietnam. These materials are intended to throw light on two pervasive problems: Was there legal justification for the use of military forces in Vietnam without a formal declaration of war? Does Congress have power to enact guidelines for the use of armed forces in overseas hostilities short of a declaration of war?

Two documents are printed at the outset to symbolize those problems and to help focus consideration of the materials which follow. The first document, a dissent from a denial of certiorari, airs some of the questions about the legality of American military involvement in Southeast Asia. The second document raises questions about the respective authorities of Congress and President to determine policy for any future use of armed forces in foreign hostilities. It is the War Powers Resolution of 1973, a joint resolution enacted by Congress after President Nixon had vetoed it on constitutional grounds. These documents focus on problems to be examined in considering the materials which follow: Was there adequate constitutional basis for the use of American troops in Vietnam? Is Congress acting within its constitutional powers, or is it intruding into exclusive executive authority, in its effort to assure greater legislative participation in decisionmaking about the use of armed forces?[1]

1. *The constitutionality of the Vietnam conflict: Justice Stewart's dissent.* The questions Justice Stewart raises below came in one of a considerable number of cases in which unsuccessful efforts were made to bring the constitutional controversy over Vietnam to the Supreme Court.[2] Justice Stewart's dissent came in MORA v. McNAMARA, 389 U.S. 934 (1967). Mora was a challenge by army draftees who had been ordered to a West Coast base for transport to Vietnam. They brought suit to prevent the carrying out of the orders and to obtain a declaratory judgment that American military activities in Vietnam were "illegal." The lower federal courts dismissed their action. Justice STEWART's dissent from the denial of certiorari, joined by Justice Douglas, stated:

"There exist in this case questions of great [magnitude]. I. Is the present United States military activity in Vietnam a 'war' within the meaning of [Art. I, § 8, cl. 11] of the Constitution? II. If so, may the Executive constitutionally order the petitioners to participate in that military activity, when no war has been declared by the Congress? III. Of what relevance to Question II are the

---

1. Although the Vietnam dispute is history, the problems raised by these materials are of continuing significance. Consider, for example, the relevance of the War Powers Resolution of 1973 to subsequent uses of military force by the executive branch, from post-1973 involvements in Southeast Asia to 1980s actions in Grenada, Lebanon and Central America. Some of the post-1973 controversies are noted below.

2. There were recurrent dissents from the Court's denials of review, especially by Justice Douglas. In addition to the case noted in the

text see, e.g., McArthur v. Clifford, 393 U.S. 1002 (1968), Massachusetts v. Laird, 400 U.S. 886 (1970), and DaCosta v. Laird, 405 U.S. 979 (1972). A recurrent barrier to gaining access to courts was that of justiciability—the contention that the claims presented "political questions" not for the courts. The justiciability issues are considered further below. Most lower courts found most issues nonjusticiable; some found challenges partly justiciable but typically rejected attacks on the war on the merits. See, e.g., Orlando v. Laird, 443 F.2d 1039 (2d Cir.1971).

present treaty obligations of the United States?   IV. Of what relevance to Question II is the Joint Congressional ('Tonkin Gulf') Resolution of [August 10, 1964]?" [3]   These are large and deeply troubling questions.   Whether the Court would ultimately reach them depends, of course, upon the resolution of serious preliminary issues of justiciability.   We cannot make these problems go away simply by refusing to hear the case of three obscure Army privates.   I intimate not even tentative views upon any of these matters, but I think the Court should squarely face them by granting certiorari."

2. *The War Powers Resolution of 1973.*   [Consider the constitutional problems about allocation of authority between President and Congress raised by the following joint resolution adopted in 1973:] [4]

SHORT TITLE

Section 1.   This joint resolution may be cited as the "War Powers Resolution."

PURPOSE AND POLICY

Sec. 2.   (a) It is the purpose of this joint resolution to fulfill the intent of the framers of the Constitution of the United States and insure that the collective judgment of both the Congress and the President will apply to the introduction of United States Armed Forces into hostilities, or into situations where imminent involvement in hostilities is clearly indicated by the circumstances, and to the continued use of such forces in hostilities or in such situations.

(b) Under article I, section 8, of the Constitution, it is specifically provided that the Congress shall have the power to make all laws necessary and proper for carrying into execution, not only its own powers but also all other powers vested by the Constitution in the Government of the United States, or in any department or officer thereof.

(c) The constitutional powers of the President as Commander-in-Chief to introduce United States Armed Forces into hostilities, or into situations where imminent involvement in hostilities is clearly indicated by the circumstances, are exercised only pursuant to (1) a declaration of war, (2) specific statutory authorization, or (3) a national emergency created by attack upon the United States, its territories or possessions, or its armed forces.

CONSULTATION

Sec. 3.   The President in every possible instance shall consult with Congress before introducing United States Armed Forces into hostilities or into situations where imminent involvement in hostilities is clearly indicated by the circumstances, and after every such introduction shall consult regularly with the Congress until United States Armed Forces are no longer engaged in hostilities or have been removed from such situations.

REPORTING

Sec. 4.   (a) In the absence of a declaration of war, in any case in which United States Armed Forces are introduced—

(1) into hostilities or into situations where imminent involvement in hostilities is clearly indicated by the circumstances;

3. Some of these questions are further explored below.

4. 87 Stat. 555, Public Law 93–148, 93d Cong. (H.J.Res. 542, adopted over a veto by President Nixon on Nov. 7, 1973). The Resolution—like the Impounding Control Act of 1974, p. 361 above—is an unusual, quasi-constitutional variety of congressional action, delineating not substantive policy but processes and relationships.

Some of the questions raised by the Resolution are pursued below.   Note the books by two Senators who played an active role in efforts to curb presidential powers, Javits, Who Makes War? (1973), and Eagleton, War and Presidential Power (1974).   And, among the voluminous writing on the problems raised by this group of notes, see especially Henkin, Foreign Affairs and the Constitution (1972); Note, "Congress, The President, and the Power to Commit Forces to Combat," 81 Harv.L.Rev. 1771 (1968); Van Alstyne, "Congress, the President, and the Power to Declare War," 121 U.Pa.L.Rev. 1 (1972); Dept. of State, "The Legality of [U.S.] Participation in the Defense of Vietnam," 75 Yale L.J. 1088 (1966); and Franck & Weisband, Foreign Policy by Congress (1979).

(2) into the territory, airspace or waters of a foreign nation, while equipped for combat, except for deployments which relate solely to supply, replacement, repair, or training of such forces; or

(3) in numbers which substantially enlarge United States Armed Forces equipped for combat already located in a foreign nation;

the President shall submit within 48 hours to the Speaker of the House of Representatives and to the President pro tempore of the Senate a report, in writing, setting forth—

(A) the circumstances necessitating the introduction of United States Armed Forces;

(B) the constitutional and legislative authority under which such introduction took place; and

(C) the estimated scope and duration of the hostilities or [involvement].

CONGRESSIONAL ACTION

Sec. 5. [(b)] Within sixty calendar days after a report is submitted or is required to be submitted pursuant to section 4(a)(1), whichever is earlier, the President shall terminate any use of United States Armed Forces with respect to which such report was submitted (or required to be submitted), unless the Congress (1) has declared war or has enacted a specific authorization for such use of United States Armed Forces, (2) has extended by law such sixty-day period, or (3) is physically unable to meet as a result of an armed attack upon the United States. Such sixty-day period shall be extended for not more than an additional thirty days if the President determines and certifies to the Congress in writing that unavoidable military necessity respecting the safety of United States Armed Forces requires the continued use of such armed forces in the course of bringing about a prompt removal of such forces.

(c) Notwithstanding subsection (b), at any time that United States Armed Forces are engaged in hostilities outside the territory of the United States, its possessions and territories without a declaration of war or specific statutory authorization, such forces shall be removed by the President if the Congress so directs by concurrent [resolution].

INTERPRETATION OF JOINT RESOLUTION

Sec. 8. (a) Authority to introduce United States Armed Forces into hostilities or into situations wherein involvement in hostilities is clearly indicated by the circumstances shall not be inferred—

(1) from any provision of law (whether or not in effect before the date of the enactment of this joint resolution), including any provision contained in any appropriation Act, unless such provision specifically authorizes the introduction of United States Armed Forces into hostilities or into such situations and states that it is intended to constitute specific statutory authorization within the meaning of this joint resolution; or

(2) from any treaty heretofore or hereafter ratified unless such treaty is implemented by legislation specifically authorizing the introduction of United States Armed Forces into hostilities or into such situations and stating that it is intended to constitute specific statutory authorization within the meaning of this joint [resolution].

(d) Nothing in this joint resolution—

(1) is intended to alter the constitutional authority of the Congress or of the President, or the provisions of existing treaties; or

(2) shall be construed as granting any authority to the President with respect to the introduction of United States Armed Forces into hostilities or into situations wherein involvement in hostilities is clearly indicated by the circumstances which authority he would not have had in the absence of this joint [resolution].

THE PRIZE CASES

1. *The opinions.* A rare, and limited, Court consideration of presidential powers to commit armed forces came during the Civil War. In the PRIZE CASES, 2 Black 635 (1863), ships carrying goods to the Confederate States were seized by Union ships, pursuant to President Lincoln's April 1861 order declaring a blockade of Southern ports. The Court sustained most of the seizures challenged in these cases in a 5 to 4 decision, even though there had been no congressional declaration of war. Justice GRIER's majority opinion, in

considering "whether, at the time this blockade was instituted, a state of war existed which would justify a resort to these means of subduing the hostile force," included the following passages:

"By the Constitution, Congress alone has the power to declare a national or foreign war. It cannot declare war against a State, or any number of States, by virtue of any clause in the Constitution. The Constitution confers on the President the whole Executive power. He is bound to take care that the laws be faithfully executed. He is Commander-in-chief of the Army and Navy of the United States. [He] has no power to initiate or declare a war either against a foreign nation or a domestic State. But by the Acts of Congress of February 28th, 1795, and 3d of March, 1807, he is authorized to call out the militia and use the military and naval forces of the United States in case of invasion by foreign nations, and to suppress insurrection against the government of a State or of the United States.

"If a war be made by invasion of a foreign nation, the President is not only authorized but bound to resist force, by force. He does not initiate the war, but is bound to accept the challenge without waiting for any special legislative authority. And whether the hostile party be a foreign invader, or States organized in rebellion, it is none the less a war, although the declaration of it be *'unilateral.'* [The] President was bound to meet [the Civil War] in the shape it presented itself, without waiting for Congress to baptize it with a name. [Whether] the President in fulfilling his duties, as Commander-in-chief, in suppressing an insurrection, has met with such armed hostile resistance, and a civil war of such alarming proportions as will compel him to accord to them the character of belligerents, is a question to be decided *by him,* and this Court must be governed by the decisions and acts of the political department of the Government to which this power was [entrusted].

"If it were necessary to the technical existence of a war, that it should have a legislative sanction, we find it in almost every act passed at the extraordinary session of the Legislature of 1861, which was wholly employed in enacting laws to enable the Government to prosecute the war with vigor and efficiency. And finally, in 1861, we find Congress [passing] an act 'approving, legalizing, and making valid all the acts, proclamations, and orders of the President, &c., as if they had been *issued and done under the previous express authority* and direction of the Congress of the United States.' [Without] admitting that such an act was necessary under the circumstances, it is plain that if the President had in any manner assumed powers which it was necessary should have the authority or sanction of Congress, [this] ratification has operated to perfectly cure the defect. [W]e are of the opinion that the President had a right, *jure belli,* to institute a blockade of ports in possession of the States in rebellion, which neutrals are bound to regard."

Justice NELSON's dissent, joined by Chief Justice Taney and Justices Catron and Clifford, included the following passages: "[Before an] insurrection against the established Government can be dealt with on the footing of a civil war, [it] must be recognized or declared by the war-making power of the Government. [There] is no difference in this respect between a civil or a public [war]. The Acts of 1795 and 1807 did not, and could not, under the Constitution, confer on the President the power of declaring war against a State of this Union, or of deciding that war existed, and upon that ground authorize the capture and confiscation of the property of every citizen of the State whenever it was found on the waters. The laws of war, whether the war be civil or *inter gentes,* as we have seen, convert every citizen of the hostile State into a public enemy, and treat him accordingly, whatever may have been his previous conduct. This great power over the business and property of the citizen is reserved to the legislative department by the express words of the Constitution. It cannot be delegated or surrendered to the Executive. Congress alone can determine whether war exists or should be declared; and until they have acted, no citizen of the State can be punished in his person or property, unless he has committed some offense against a law of Congress passed before the act was committed, which made it a crime and defined the punishment. The penalty of confiscation for the acts of others with which he had no concern cannot lawfully be inflicted." [Congressional ratification of the seizures was found ineffective as an ex post facto law.]

2. *The bearing of the Prize Cases on modern problems.* What light do the opinions in the Prize Cases throw on the constitutionality of the Vietnam conflict and on the constitutionality of the War Powers Resolution of 1973? As to the former question, Justice Douglas' dissents from denials of certiorari in cases challenging the Vietnam involvement referred several times to the Prize Cases. For example, in dissenting in McArthur v. Clifford, 393 U.S. 1002 (1968), he commented that the Prize Cases involved "an internal insurrection which would perhaps be analogous here if the Vietnamese were invading the United States": "Would [the decision] have been the same if Lincoln had had an expeditionary force fighting a 'war' overseas?" Does the majority position in the Prize Cases cast constitutional doubt on some of the restrictions on executive authority in the War Powers Resolution of 1973? Note that the Resolution recognizes presidential Commander-in-Chief authority to react to national emergencies caused by threatened attacks, a power acknowledged by the Framers and in the Prize Cases. Is the description of national emergencies in the Resolution sufficiently broad to encompass traditionally recognized executive powers? [1] Is the time limitation on executive authority in the War Powers Resolution a valid restraint on presidential emergency powers to

---

1. The Senate version of the Resolution, rejected in conference in 1973, included among situations where presidential use of armed forces was permitted a reference to the necessity to protect and evacuate American citizens and nationals abroad whose lives are threatened. Does the omission of that situation in the enacted version limit presidential authority? Does the President have authority to use force in a situation such as that of the American hostages in Iran in 1979–1980? After the Carter Administration's ill-fated effort in April 1980 to rescue the American hostages held in Iran, the Administration argued that the rescue was not subject to the Resolution because it constituted a humanitarian effort. In light of the terms and history of the Resolution, was that a persuasive legal argument? This problem of presidential authority had engendered controversy during the prior Administration as well. For example, President Ford used armed forces to evacuate Americans and South Vietnamese from Saigon at the end of April 1975. Earlier in that month, the President had asked for congressional "clarification" to use military force. Though most legislators took the view that the President had inherent authority to evacuate endangered Americans (despite the silence in the Resolution), there was considerable doubt about the evacuation of foreign nationals.

Until 1980, then, the War Powers Resolution appeared to have little inhibitory effect on presidential action; but it is noteworthy that the typical uses of force by the executive involved

"rescue" missions. In the early 1980s, by contrast, the purposes of the uses of military force typically were less focused, more open-ended, and hence more likely to involve the nation in the kinds of longer-term hostilities toward which the Resolution was directed. The major uses of military personnel in the early 1980s involved Central America (Nicaragua, El Salvador, and Honduras), Lebanon, and Grenada. (Only the last of these was claimed to be a "rescue" undertaking.) Although the executive branch and Congress continue to disagree about the applicability of the War Powers Resolution, it is arguable that the hovering effect of the Resolution caused the executive to limit engagements, as with the extent of the El Salvador involvement and the duration of the Grenada occupation, in order to avoid a conflict with the congressional Resolution. In the case of Lebanon, an agreement was reached between the two branches with the Resolution very much in the forefront of discussions. Even though the Reagan Administration continued to question the constitutionality of aspects of the Resolution and urged major modifications of it, Congress' more assertive stance may have led the executive branch to take the need for congressional participation somewhat more seriously in the 1980s than was true in the late 1970s. For a careful review of experiences under the Resolution, see Note, "The Future of the War Powers Resolution," 36 Stan.L. Rev. —— (1984).

respond to attacks? [For further consideration of constitutional problems raised by the Resolution, see p. 376 below.]

CONGRESSIONAL EFFORTS TO LIMIT THE PRESIDENT'S USE OF THE ARMED FORCES

1. *Modern congressional concern before the War Powers Resolution of 1973.* a. *The Fulbright Committee.* The growing Vietnam controversy of the late 1960s prompted the modern congressional concern with presidential use of armed forces. The major early forum for the constitutional debates was the Senate Committee on Foreign Relations under the chairmanship of Senator J. William Fulbright. As part of the Committee's search for better methods of reasserting congressional participation, the Committee in 1967 produced a Report, "National Commitments." The Report contained an extensive review of constitutional groundrules and historical developments in the expanding role of the executive branch. The Committee examined what it perceived as the 20th century expansion of executive power, noting: "The trend initiated by Theodore Roosevelt, Taft and Wilson, and accelerated by Franklin Roosevelt, continued at a rapid rate under Presidents Truman, Eisenhower, Kennedy, and Johnson, bringing the country to the point at which the real power to commit the country to war is now in the hands of the President. [The] last four Presidents [have] all asserted unrestricted executive authority to commit the armed forces without the consent of Congress, and Congress, for the most part, has acquiesced in the transfer of its war power to the [Executive]. Claims to unlimited executive authority over the use of armed force are made on grounds of both legitimacy and necessity. The committee finds both sets of contentions unsound [and] rejects the contention that the war powers as spelled out in the Constitution are obsolete and strongly recommends that the Congress reassert its constitutional authority over the use of the armed forces. [All] that is required is the restoration of constitutional procedures which have been permitted to atrophy. [The] committee does not believe that formal declarations of war are the only available means by which Congress can authorize the President to initiate limited or general hostilities. Joint resolutions such as those pertaining to Formosa, the Middle East, and the Gulf of Tonkin [1964] are a proper method of granting authority, provided that they are precise as to what is to be done and for what period of time, and provided that they do in fact *grant authority* and not merely express approval of undefined action to be taken by the President." [1]

In the late 1960s, a law review comment concluded: "[Any] attempt to brand particular conflicts as constitutional or unconstitutional is likely to be of little consequence. The constitutional analysis is better viewed as yielding a working directive to the executive and legislative branches that the commitment of country to war be accomplished only through the closest collaboration possible, rather than an automatic formula for condemning or approving particular presidential action. The question should be: what concrete steps should the two branches take to assure that the policies behind the constitutional

---

1. For the full text of the Report, see Sen. Rep. No. 797, 90th Cong., 1st Sess. (1967). (For excerpts, see Gunther, Constitutional Law (10th ed. 1980), 417–22.) The Fulbright Committee's version of historical practice and developments has not gone unchallenged. For a different emphasis, see Sofaer, "The Presidency, War, and Foreign Affairs: Practice Under the Framers," 40 Law & Contemp.Probs. 12 (1976), arguing that the early national practice included considerable executive initiative and warning against attributing "the evils produced by our recent Presidents and Congresses to the violation of imagined norms allegedly established by the leaders of our constitutional period." See also Sofaer, War, Foreign Affairs and Constitutional Power: The Origins (1976), and Henkin, Foreign Affairs and the Constitution (1972).

scheme are served?" [2] Was that the proper question? Were the progressively more "concrete steps" by Congress to delineate the boundaries of constitutional power and practice (traced below) appropriate, useful, and constitutional?

b. *Congressional policy statements and funds cut-offs.* In the wake of the Fulbright Committee's deliberations, the Senate in June 1969 adopted a "sense of the Senate" resolution stating that "a national commitment by the United States results only from affirmative action taken by the executive and legislative branches [by] means of a treaty, statute, or concurrent resolution of both Houses of Congress, specifically providing for such commitment." Did that statement mark a change in constitutional doctrine? Were the problems resolvable via congressional policy statements? Congressional efforts to control military activities in Southeast Asia soon turned to the appropriations route. After a series of unsuccessful attempts, the efforts finally bore fruit in 1973—after the Vietnam cease-fire had been negotiated. The strongest language was in the Case-Church Amendment, adopted in June 1973, stating that no appropriations, past or future, could be used to finance the "involvement" of American forces in Indochina "unless specifically authorized" by Congress. In the same month, Congress took final action on an amendment cutting off all funds for American combat activities in Cambodia and Laos, in response to ongoing American bombing in Cambodia. After President Nixon successfully vetoed that provision, he signed a "compromise" in July 1973, with a funds cut-off provision carrying an August effective date. The President agreed to seek congressional authorization for any military action in Indochina after that date.

2. *Congressional guidelines: Constitutional problems in the War Powers Resolution of 1973?* Recurrent efforts to use the guidelines technique to limit presidential war-making powers culminated in the adoption of the War Powers Resolution of 1973, printed above. Does the Resolution present constitutional problems? The Resolution was enacted after a veto by President Nixon. In his October, 1973, veto message, the President insisted that the Resolution was not only "dangerous to the best interests of our nation" but also "unconstitutional." He especially objected to two provisions which "would attempt to take away, by a mere legislative act, authorities which the President has properly exercised under the Constitution for almost 200 years." He singled out § 5(b), requiring the president to withdraw American forces from foreign hostilities within 60 or 90 days unless Congress grants authorization, and § 5(c), requiring immediate withdrawal of forces if Congress so directs by concurrent resolution—a resolution not subject to presidential veto. President Nixon stated: "I believe that both these provisions are unconstitutional. The only way in which the constitutional powers of a branch of the Government can be altered is by amending the Constitution—and any attempt to make such alterations by legislation alone is clearly without force." The President explained that he was "particularly disturbed by the fact that certain of the President's constitutional powers as Commander-in-Chief of the Armed Forces would terminate automatically" after 60 days without "overt congressional action." In effect, the President added, "the Congress is here attempting to increase its policy-making role through a provision which requires it to take absolutely no action at all. In my view, the proper way for the Congress to make known its will [is] through a positive action. [O]ne cannot become a responsible partner unless one is prepared to take responsible action." [3] Can the legislative veto aspects of the

---

2. Note, "Congress, the President, and the Power to Commit Forces to Combat," 81 Harv. L.Rev. 1771 (1968).

3. Note one respect in which the Resolution arguably is weaker than earlier proposals: The Resolution relegated the description of the exclusive circumstances under which the President can introduce American forces into hostilities without a declaration of war to a section entitled "Purpose and Policy"; Senator Eagleton and others who criticized the Resolution as too weak argued that the "Purpose and Policy" section has no statutory effect. Critics of the measure also urged that, rather than imposing a restraint on

War Powers Resolution survive constitutional scrutiny in light of the Chadha case, p. 346 above? Is it arguable that the delegated congressional powers regarding war and the use of armed forces make for an especially strong case to justify legislative veto participation by Congress? [4]

In addition to the constitutional questions raised in the President's veto message, does the Resolution present other constitutional difficulties? Note that the Resolution does not limit the use of armed forces to formal declarations of war; it also includes "specific statutory authorization," though it excludes mere congressional appropriations. Are the congressional "authorizations" recognized by the 1973 Resolution constitutionally adequate alternatives for formal declarations of war? Recall also the questions about the scope of "national emergency" under § 2 of the Resolution and about the time limits, in light of the traditional recognition of presidential power to repel attacks. (See the questions after the Prize Cases, p. 374 above). Note also the traditional recognition of presidential authority to use armed forces to protect the lives and property of Americans abroad. The statement of circumstances under which the President may use force in § 2(c) of the 1973 Resolution does not include any such authority. Does that improperly curtail constitutional powers of the President? Finally, can a measure such as the War Powers Resolution, designed to provide a legal framework for the resolution of executive-legislative conflicts in this area, adequately deal with the varying circumstances arising in foreign relations? Or must resolution of conflicts between the branches inevitably turn upon the political processes of negotiation and accommodation? It is arguable that, even though the political processes must play a large role, the War Powers Resolution can at least help to create an atmosphere that will facilitate the operation of those political processes.[5]

SECTION 2. THE INTEGRITY AND AUTONOMY OF THE THREE BRANCHES: INTERFERENCES WITH THE INTERNAL AFFAIRS OF ANOTHER BRANCH; COMMITMENT OF CONSTITUTIONAL ISSUES FOR FINAL DECISIONS BY NONJUDICIAL BRANCHES

Introduction. The preceding section considered problems of competition between President and Congress in making policy for the domestic and foreign spheres. This section samples a range of problems pertaining to the autonomy the executive and legislative branches may claim in efforts to ward off interferences by each other and by the judiciary. To what extent may Congress control the appointment and removal of executive personnel? To what extent may it intrude into the internal processes of the executive branch? To what extent are the President and members of Congress amenable to judicial process? To what extent are constitutional issues committed for final decision to Congress or the President rather than to the Court?

the President, the Resolution actually licenses the President to engage in brief military actions, since Congress is unlikely, once American forces are engaged, to terminate such actions before the 60 or 90 day periods expire.

4. See generally Comment, "Congressional Control of Presidential War-Making Under the War Powers Act: The Status of a Legislative Veto After Chadha," 132 U.Pa.L.Rev. 1217

(1984). See also Note, "The Future of the War Powers Resolution," 36 Stan.L.Rev. —— (1984). Cf. Glennon, "The War Powers Resolution: Sad Record, Dismal Promise," 17 Loy.L.A.L.Rev. 657 (1984).

5. Recall the brief review of experience with the War Powers Resolution in the early 1980s, at p. 374 above, and see the Stanford Law Review Note cited in the preceding footnote.

The sampling of these interrelated issues of executive and legislative autonomy and judicial authority begins with an examination of the control of executive personnel. When may Congress restrain the President's power to appoint and remove subordinates? On what grounds may Congress exercise its power to impeach and remove the President? Attention then turns to problems of amenability to the judicial process. The central focus of the section is the Watergate Tapes litigation culminating in the decision in United States v. Nixon in 1974. That case raises several questions: Can the President be brought to court? What are the contours of executive privilege? Who has the authority to determine those contours? A study of that litigation accordingly draws together several of the strands in this section: amenability to judicial process; scope of executive privilege; authority to delineate that scope. And the last of these issues offers an opportunity for an exploration of one of the ingredients of the "political questions" concept: what issues *are* constitutionally committed for final decisions to branches other than the courts?

A. CONGRESS AND THE CONTROL OF EXECUTIVE PERSONNEL AND PROCESSES: PRESIDENTIAL POWER TO REMOVE SUBORDINATES; IMPEACHING THE PRESIDENT

1. *Congress and the President's power to appoint "Officers of the United States."* Art. II, § 2, cl. 2, the Appointments Clause, reinforces separation of powers principles by providing that the President "shall nominate, and by and with the Advice and Consent of the Senate, shall appoint [Ambassadors], Judges of the Supreme Court, and all other Officers of the United States, whose appointments are not herein otherwise provided for, and which shall be established by Law: but the Congress may by Law vest the Appointment of such inferior Officers, as they think proper, in the President alone, in the Courts of Law, or in the Heads of Departments." In BUCKLEY v. VALEO, 424 U.S. 1 (1976), the Court's per curiam opinion relied on the Appointments Clause in holding unconstitutional, for most purposes, the composition of the Federal Election Commission [FEC] established by the Federal Election Campaign Act. Under the law, a majority of the FEC members was appointed by the President pro tempore of the Senate and the Speaker of the House. The FEC was given "direct and wide-ranging" enforcement power such as instituting civil actions against violations of the Act as well as "extensive rulemaking and adjudicative powers" such as formulating general policies regarding the administration of the law. The Court held that such powers could be exercised only by "Officers of the United States" appointed in accordance with the Appointments Clause and "therefore cannot be exercised by [the FEC] as presently constituted." According to the Court, an agency with a majority of congressionally named personnel could only exercise those powers that Congress might delegate to one of its own committees—e.g., investigatory and informative powers; since only "Officers" appointed in the constitutionally prescribed manner could undertake executive or quasi-judicial tasks, the FEC could not exercise such functions. (Congress, soon after the Buckley decision, cured the constitutional flaw by reconstituting the FEC with a membership consisting entirely of presidential appointees.)

The Buckley opinion insisted that "any appointee exercising significant authority pursuant to the laws of the United States is an Officer of the United States, and must, therefore, be appointed in the manner prescribed by [the Appointments Clause]." Although Congress could vest appointment of "inferior Officers" in "Courts of Law" or "Heads of Departments" instead of the

President, providing for the appointment of most FEC members by congressional officials was impermissible, since they could not be considered "Heads of Departments." The Court rejected the argument that, because of "the extraordinary authority reposed in Congress to regulate elections, this case stands on a different footing than if Congress had exercised its legislative authority in another field." The defenders of the FEC structure also argued that "Congress had good reason for not vesting in a Commission composed wholly of Presidential appointees the authority to administer the Act, since the administration of the Act would undoubtedly have a bearing on any incumbent President's campaign for reelection." To that argument, the Court responded that "such fears, however rational, do not by themselves warrant a distortion of the Framers' work." Finally, the Court rejected the claim "that Congress may provide for this manner of appointment under the Necessary and Proper Clause of Art. I." Again, "the Appointments Clause by clear implication prohibits it from doing so."

2. *Congress and the President's power to remove subordinates.* The only explicit constitutional reference to the removal of executive personnel is in the impeachment provisions, considered below. But from the outset, a power to remove subordinate executive officials by routes other than impeachment has been assumed. Is that power solely in the President? Or may Congress limit presidential removal authority? The first modern judicial answer was a broad endorsement of executive autonomy, but subsequent decisions have found considerable room for congressional participation.[1]

In Myers v. United States, 272 U.S. 52 (1926), the Court held unconstitutional a legislative provision that certain groups of postmasters could not be removed by the President without the consent of the Senate. Chief Justice Taft's opinion for the Court rested on an expansive reading of executive powers under Art. II and found the statute an unconstitutional restriction on the President's control over executive personnel. The Chief Justice found that it was a "reasonable implication" from the President's power to execute the laws that "he should select those who were to act for him under his direction in the execution of the laws." And it was an additional plausible implication that "as his selection of administrative officers is essential to the execution of the laws by him, so must be his power of removing those for whom he can not continue to be responsible." Less than a decade after Myers, however, the Court curtailed some of its implications and distinguished the decision in holding that the President could not remove a member of an independent regulatory agency in defiance of restrictions in the statutory framework. Humphrey's Executor v. United States, 295 U.S. 602 (1935). Justice Sutherland's opinion for the Court found that the Federal Trade Commission Act specified the causes for removal of Commissioners and held that, in view of the functions of the agency, Congress could limit the President's power of removal. The Court found the Myers principle limited to "purely executive officers." The FTC, by contrast, "cannot in any proper sense be characterized as an arm or an eye of the executive": under the statute, its duties were to be "free from executive control." Rather, it acted "in part quasi-legislatively and in part quasi-judicially." The Myers rule, then, stands simply for "the unrestrictable power of the President to remove purely executive officers." More recently, the Court applied the Humphrey's rather than the Myers rule in Wiener v. United States, 357 U.S. 349 (1958), involving the removal of a member of the War Claims Commission. The statute establishing that Commission, unlike the one in Humphrey's Executor, was silent on removal and did not specify permissible grounds to remove. But the Court emphasized that the Commission's function

---

1. See generally Corwin, The President: Office and Powers (4th ed. 1957).

was of an "intrinsic judicial character" and held the removal illegal. As to officers who were not purely executive, power to remove existed "only if Congress may fairly be said to have conferred it." The Court noted: "This sharp differentiation derives from the difference in functions between those who are part of the Executive establishment and those whose tasks require absolute freedom from Executive interference." [2]

3. *Congressional power over presidential papers.* In NIXON v. ADMINISTRATOR OF GENERAL SERVICES, 433 U.S. 425 (1977), the Court rejected a range of on-the-face constitutional challenges to the Presidential Recordings and Materials Preservation Act of 1974, adopted by Congress to assure governmental custody of documents and tape recordings accumulated during the tenure of former President Nixon. The law was enacted four months after Nixon resigned amidst the threat of impeachment. (See the next note.) It directed the Administrator of General Services, an executive official, to take custody of the Nixon materials and to promulgate regulations for their screening by archivists for the purpose of returning to Nixon those that are personal and private in nature. Moreover, the Administrator was directed to prepare regulations governing public access to those materials that were to remain in the custody of the Government. Nixon challenged the law on several grounds, including a claimed violation of separation of powers principles. [3] The Court sustained the Act by a 7 to 2 division. Justice Brennan wrote the majority opinion; Chief Justice Burger and Justice Rehnquist submitted dissents. The Court found that problems of public access were not ripe for decision, since governing regulations had not yet become effective. Thus, only the archivists' custody and screening provisions were properly before the Court. The Justices in the majority—in several concurring opinions as well as in Justice Brennan's majority opinion—tried to emphasize the narrowness of the decision, stressing the uniqueness of the Nixon resignation and its aftermath. The dissenters, by contrast, saw the decision as a threat to presidential power generally and warned about its potential impact on the functioning of the executive branch.

Nixon made a number of "separate but interrelated" arguments with respect to executive autonomy, all designed to demonstrate that the "Act encroaches upon the Presidential prerogative to control internal operations of the Presidential office." In repudiating the challenge, Justice BRENNAN insisted that Nixon's view of separation of powers was "inconsistent with the origins of that doctrine, recent decisions of the Court, and the contemporary realities of our political system." He noted that the Court had rejected the view that "the Constitution contemplates a complete division of authority between the three branches"; instead, it had adopted a "more pragmatic, flexible approach." The

2. For another area in which presidential powers and congressional legislation may produce conflicts, consider the President's power to grant reprieves and pardons, Art. II, § 2. Recall United States v. Klein (1871; p. —— above). The Court has repeatedly stated in dictum that the presidential pardon power is not subject to legislative control. See, e.g., Ex parte Garland, 4 Wall. 333 (1866). However, the presidential pardoning power "has never been held to take from Congress the power to pass acts of general amnesty." See Brown v. Walker, 161 U.S. 591, 601 (1896). For a modern reiteration of the breadth of the presidential pardoning power, see Schick v. Reed, 419 U.S. 256 (1974), a 6 to 3 decision rejecting a constitutional attack by one who had been sentenced to death by a court-martial and whose sentence had been commuted by the President to life imprisonment subject to the condition

that he would not thereafter be eligible for parole. Chief Justice Burger's majority opinion found the condition within presidential power. Note the statement in the opinion that "the power flows from the Constitution alone, not from any legislative enactments, and [it] cannot be modified, abridged, or diminished by the Congress." The Court stated that the President may attach "any condition which does not otherwise offend the Constitution."

3. In addition to Nixon's general separation of powers challenge, the majority also rejected Nixon's claims based on presidential privilege doctrines (see United States v. Nixon, p. 388 below), privacy interests, First Amendment associational rights, and the Bill of Attainder Clause of the Constitution.

touchstone for determining whether separation of powers principles had been violated was whether one branch's action vis-à-vis another constituted undue "disruption." He explained that the "disruption" inquiry "focuses on the extent to which [the Act] prevents the executive branch from accomplishing its constitutionally assigned functions." [See United States v. Nixon, p. 388 below.] Justice Brennan concluded that there was nothing "unduly disruptive of the Executive Branch" here. Chief Justice BURGER's dissent put forth three reasons for finding a violation of separation of powers principles. First, the Act constituted congressional coercion of the President "in matters relating to the operation and conduct of his office." Second, it was "an exercise of executive—not legislative—power by the Legislative Branch"—i.e., the exclusive presidential power "to control files, records and papers of the office." Third, the Act worked "a sweeping modification of the constitutional privilege and historical practice of confidentiality of every Chief Executive since 1789." [4]

4. *Impeaching the President.* The proceedings of the House Judiciary Committee during the spring and summer of 1974 provoked the most intense national attention to problems of impeachment in more than a century. The most important constitutional problem aired in the debates culminating in the Committee approval of three Articles of Impeachment against President Nixon pertained to the scope of impeachable offenses.[5] In the course of those debates, seldom examined provisions of the constitutional text—especially Art. II, § 4, and Art. I, §§ 2 and 3—were pored over, and relevant historical precedents and policy considerations were probed. American experience with the impeachment weapon has been sparse: Andrew Johnson is the only President who was impeached, escaping conviction and removal by the Senate by only one vote; most impeachments voted by the House involved federal judges; the Senate has voted to convict in only four instances, all involving judges.

Art. II, § 4, states: "The President, Vice President and all civil Officers of the United States, shall be removed from Office on Impeachment for, and Conviction of, Treason, Bribery, or other high Crimes and Misdemeanors." What is the scope of the phrase "other high Crimes and Misdemeanors"? What presidential misconduct is properly the subject of impeachment proceedings? Must the conduct constitute a criminal offense? If the scope of impeachable offenses is not coextensive with criminality, what acceptable criteria can be stated? What criminal behavior may not be impeachable? What noncriminal conduct may be impeachable? The modern debate about impeachable offenses focused on two contending views: President Nixon's counsel claimed that "other high Crimes and Misdemeanors" is limited to serious acts which would be indictable as criminal offenses; the staff of the Judiciary Committee insisted that the scope of impeachable offenses and of criminality are not synonymous, and that the impeachment route may reach serious abuses of office or breaches of trust not constituting criminal acts. The main support for the President's position came from the terminology used in the Constitution, though the text is not unambiguous. The main reliance of the defenders of the broader position was on history—both English historical background and the evidence as to the intent of the Framers. Moreover, both sides marshalled policy arguments on their behalf.

---

4. Several of the Justices supporting the majority result also submitted separate statements emphasizing the narrowness of the decision, in view of the special justifications for and limited objectives of the legislation. Justice REHNQUIST submitted a separate dissent.

5. This note is limited to that problem. A range of other constitutional problems were brought to the fore during the consideration of the Nixon impeachment—e.g., whether judgments of conviction in the Senate after votes of impeachment in the House are judicially reviewable, and the extent to which a President may assert claims of executive privilege in the course of impeachment inquiries. Those questions are considered below.

Thus, Presidential counsel James D. St. Clair argued: "Those who seek to broaden the impeachment power invite the use of power 'as a means of crushing political adversaries or ejecting them from office.' The acceptance of such an invitation would be destructive to our system of government and to the fundamental principle of separation of powers. The Framers never intended that the impeachment clause serve to dominate or destroy the executive branch of the government." Constitutional text and history, they concluded, required as a basis for impeachment not merely "a criminal offense, but one of a very serious nature committed in one's governmental capacity." [6] By contrast, the view of the legal staff of the impeachment inquiry argued that criminality should not be the central issue: treason and bribery are specifically named not because they are crimes but because "they are constitutional wrongs that subvert the structure of government, or undermine the integrity of office and even the Constitution itself, and thus are 'high' offenses in the sense that word was used in English impeachments." The impeachment staff insisted that, in the English practice and in several of the American impeachments, the emphasis was not on criminality but on "the significant effects of the conduct—undermining the integrity of office, disregard of constitutional duties and oath of office, arrogation of power, abuse of the governmental process, adverse impact on the system of government. Clearly, these effects can be brought about in ways not anticipated by the criminal law." [7]

The three Articles of Impeachment adopted by the House Judiciary Committee in late July 1974 followed the approach of the impeachment inquiry staff. The more general articles, Articles I and II, dealt with the Watergate cover-up and related abuses of power.[8] Art. I focused on the Watergate cover-up and concluded that, "[in] all of this, Richard M. Nixon has acted in a manner contrary to his trust as President and subversive of constitutional government." Art. II charged, with a similar conclusion, that Nixon had "repeatedly engaged in conduct violating the constitutional rights of citizens, impairing the due and proper administration of justice and the conduct of lawful inquiries, or contravening the laws governing agencies of the executive branch and the purposes of these agencies." Among the specific acts alleged in this Article was the attempt to obtain confidential information in income tax returns, misusing the FBI to obtain information and using it for purposes unrelated to national security or other lawful purposes, and maintaining a secret investigative unit within the office of the President. Consider whether the charges in these Articles reflected appropriate criteria of impeachable offenses.[9]

---

6. St. Clair et al., Summary of an Analysis of the Constitutional Standard for Presidential Impeachment (released February 28, 1974).

7. Staff Report, Constitutional Grounds for Presidential Impeachment (released February 22, 1974). See also, in general agreement with the impeachment inquiry's staff, the thoughtful study by the Committee on Legislation of the Association of the Bar of the City of New York, The Law of Presidential Impeachment (1974). See also Berger, "Impeachment: The Constitutional Problems" (1973); Black, "Impeachment: A Handbook" (1974); and the airing of these issues in the historic public deliberations of the House Judiciary Committee in the summer of 1974, and

in the Committee's final report, Report on the Impeachment of Richard M. Nixon, H.R.Rep. No. 1035, 93d Cong., 2d Sess.

8. Art. III, on defiance of House subpoenas, is noted at p. 395 below, with other problems of executive privilege.

9. All three Articles were adopted by the House Committee. However, further proceedings on the Articles—including a vote by the full House and a trial in the Senate—were abandoned when President Nixon resigned on August 9, 1974, after the release of the Watergate tapes in the wake of the Court's decision in United States v. Nixon, p. 388 below.

B. AMENABILITY TO JUDICIAL PROCESS: LEGISLATIVE AND EXECUTIVE IMMUNITIES

1. *Legislative immunity and the Speech or Debate Clause.* Art. I, § 6, states that Senators and Representatives "shall not be questioned in any other Place" for "any Speech or Debate in either House." In recent years, the Court has had repeated occasion to construe (and divide about) the scope of that immunity of national legislators. Note, for example, Powell v. McCormack (1969; p. 399 below), where, on the basis of that Clause, an action challenging a Congressman's exclusion from the House was dismissed against those defendants who were members of Congress; but the Clause did not preclude the Court's review of the merits of the challenged congressional action "since congressional employees were also sued." A more extensive consideration of the Clause came in United States v. Brewster, 408 U.S. 501 (1972), a 6 to 3 decision holding that the Clause did not bar prosecution of a former Senator for accepting a bribe relating to his actions on postage rate legislation. Chief Justice Burger's majority opinion concluded that the Clause did not protect all conduct "*relating* to the legislative process"; it only "protects against inquiry into acts which occur in the regular course of the legislative process and the motivation for those acts." Here, he explained, the prosecution could succeed simply by showing acceptance of the bribe, without getting into the question whether the illegal promise was performed.[1] The Court has also had several occasions to consider the role of the Clause in suits against legislators for invasions of private interests in reputation and privacy. In Doe v. McMillan, 412 U.S. 306 (1973), parents of students sought relief for alleged invasion of privacy in the dissemination of a congressional committee report on the D.C. school system. The 6 to 3 decision found the Clause to be only a partial barrier to suit. According to Justice White's majority opinion, the Clause provides absolute immunity from suit for introducing the allegedly injurious material at committee hearings and for voting for publication of the committee report. But there is no absolute immunity for those who, "with authorization from Congress, distribute materials which allegedly infringe on the rights of individuals": distributing such materials is actionable despite congressional authorization when the dissemination of information is "beyond the reasonable requirements of the legislative function." The dissenters insisted that the ruling contravened not only the Clause but also general principles of separation of powers. Similarly, in Hutchinson v. Proxmire, 443 U.S. 111 (1979) (further noted in chap. 13 below), the Court held that Senator Proxmire could not claim immunity under the Clause from a defamation suit based on statements made in press releases and newsletters. Chief Justice Burger's majority opinion emphasized that such publicity was not "essential to the deliberations of the Senate," that the Clause applied only to "legislative activities," and that it therefore did not "grant immunity for defamatory statements scattered far and wide by mail,

---

1. Justices Brennan, White and Douglas dissented in Brewster. But later that Term, Justice White spoke for the majority in the 5 to 4 decision in Gravel v. United States, 408 U.S. 606 (1972), a case growing out of a grand jury investigation into the disclosure of the Pentagon Papers. The Court held that a Senator could invoke the protection of the Clause to block questioning of his assistant, but that the immunity covered only legislative acts and did not bar investigation of alleged arrangements for private publication of the Pentagon Papers. Justices Douglas and Brennan, the other dissenters in Brewster, were also in the minority in the Gravel

case. [Gravel was distinguished in Harlow v. Fitzgerald (1982; p. 387 below), where the Court refused to grant White House aides the same "derivative" absolute immunity to which legislators' aides are entitled under Gravel.]

For further consideration of the type of problem raised in the Brewster case, see United States v. Helstoski, 442 U.S. 477 (1979), dealing with the restrictions the Clause places on the admissibility of evidence in a trial on charges that a former Congressman had, while a legislator, accepted money in return for promising to introduce private bills.

press, and the electronic media." Justice Brennan's dissent insisted that "public criticism by legislators of unnecessary governmental expenditures, whatever its form, is a legislative act shielded by the Speech or Debate Clause."

2. *Executive immunity.* a. *Judicial process.* Unlike legislators, executive officials are not granted any express immunity in the Constitution. And the Court long ago rejected any inference from separation of power principles that executive officers are wholly immune from court orders. Indeed, Thomas Jefferson's irritation about Marbury v. Madison stemmed largely from John Marshall's assertion that courts *could* issue mandamus against Cabinet members in proper cases. And Cabinet members have repeatedly been defendants before courts, as in the Steel Seizure Case. However, the development of judicial remedies against executive action has been a slow one. The Marbury v. Madison dicta about mandamus to compel performance of ministerial acts bore fruit in Kendall v. United States, 12 Pet. 524 (1838). But that holding did not assure easy access to courts. The difficulties of asserting claims against the United States and its officials have stemmed particularly from uncertainties in the law of remedies and from the occasional availability of the defense of sovereign immunity.[2]

b. *Criminal liability.* Can an executive immunity from *criminal* prosecution nevertheless be implied from the existence of the impeachment provisions? The last clause in Art. I, § 3, states that "the Party convicted" in an impeachment proceeding "shall nevertheless be liable and subject to Indictment, Trial, Judgment, and Punishment, according to Law." Does that mean that an official must be removed and convicted through the impeachment route before he can be tried criminally? Vice President Agnew raised that contention prior to his resignation, in response to grand jury proceedings against him. The Justice Department's response was that only the President, not the Vice President, was immune from criminal prosecution while in office. Was the Justice Department's distinction between the President and the Vice President persuasive? There are some statements in the Convention Debates and in the Federalist Papers reflecting an assumption that impeachment and removal of the President would precede any criminal trial. See, e.g., Hamilton's Federalist Nos. 65 and 69. But the major argument made on behalf of presidential immunity from criminal prosecution rested on inferences from the unique and important nature of the office.[3]

3. *Presidential immunity.* a. *Amenability to judicial process.* The President's unique position raises special problems of amenability to judicial process, even though the President, like other executive officials, cannot rely on an explicit grant of immunity in the Constitution. While the courts have reviewed presidential actions through the device of suits against Cabinet members since the Kendall case, above, suits naming the President as a defendant have been extremely rare. Recall Mississippi v. [President Andrew] Johnson (1867; p. 42 above). There, the Court refused to enjoin President Johnson from executing the Reconstruction Acts, and used language which suggested that the President was ordinarily not reachable directly by judicial process. The Court emphasized enforcement problems. Attorney General Stanbery had made additional arguments, emotionally and forcefully, in his jurisdictional plea in Mississippi v. Johnson. To issue an order against the President, he suggested, implied the power to enforce the order; and even if the physical power existed,

---

2. See generally "Developments in the Law—Remedies Against the United States and Its Officials," 70 Harv.L.Rev. 827 (1957), and Monaghan, "Marbury and the Administrative State," 83 Colum.L.Rev. 1 (1983). (See also the materials on the Watergate Tapes litigation, which follow.)

3. Compare Bickel, "The Constitutional Tangle," The New Republic (Oct. 6, 1973), with Berger, "The President, Congress, and the Courts," 83 Yale L.J. 1111 (1974).

punishing a President for contempt would in effect remove him from office—and would accordingly usurp the impeachment route. The claim that the President is not amenable to judicial process was renewed in the course of the Watergate Tapes litigation. Mississippi v. Johnson, as well as the implications of the Burr trial and its subpoena to Thomas Jefferson, were repeatedly aired in the Nixon case arguments. Presidential Counsel St. Clair, for example, recalled the Johnson case and the Stanbery argument in his presentation to the Supreme Court. The issue was considered at some length in the lower court proceedings in the Watergate Tapes litigation. The Supreme Court's result in United States v. Nixon is clear: a court order directed to the President did issue. But did the court adequately consider the separable issue of amenability? That problem is considered with other aspects of United States v. Nixon, the next principal case.

   b. *Absolute presidential immunity from civil liability.* The 5 to 4 decision in NIXON v. FITZGERALD, 457 U.S. 731 (1982), held that "the President is absolutely [rather than qualifiedly] immune from civil damages liability for his official acts"—at least "in the absence of explicit affirmative action by Congress." [1] The case arose out of the following circumstances: Fitzgerald, a widely publicized "whistle blower" of the late 1960s, lost his position as a management analyst with the Department of the Air Force in 1970. He had attained national prominence because of his testimony before a congressional subcommittee during which he exposed substantial cost overruns in the development of a military transport plane. His testimony embarrassed and angered Defense Department officials and he lost his job. Fitzgerald's federal court action charged violation of his First Amendment and statutory rights; he named as defendants former President Nixon as well as other Nixon Administration officials. [2]

   Justice POWELL's majority opinion concluded that Nixon, "as a former President, [is] entitled to absolute immunity from damages liability predicated on his official acts. We consider this immunity a functionally mandated incident of the President's unique office, rooted in the constitutional tradition of the separation of powers and supported by our history." In elaborating the reasons for that immunity, Justice Powell emphasized the President's "unique position in the constitutional scheme." He distinguished earlier decisions granting only qualified immunity to persons holding other executive positions: "The President's unique status under the Constitution distinguishes [him]." He elaborated: "Because of the singular importance of the President's duties, diversion of his energies by concern with private lawsuits would raise unique risks to the effective functioning of government. As is the case with prosecutors and judges—for whom absolute immunity now is established—a President must concern himself with matters likely to 'arouse the most intense feelings.' [In] view of the visibility of his office and the effect of his actions on countless people, the President would be an easily identifiable target for suits for civil

1. Could Congress change the absolute immunity established by this case? Justice Powell's majority opinion left that question open. Contrast Chief Justice BURGER'S position: although he joined Justice Powell's opinion, he argued in his concurrence that the presidential immunity was mandated by the constitutional separation of powers and insisted: "[T]he Court's holding, in my view, effectively resolves [the congressional power] issue; once it is established that the Constitution confers absolute immunity, as the Court holds today, legislative action cannot alter that result. Nothing in the Court's opinion is to be read as suggesting that a Constitutional holding of this Court can be legislatively overruled or modified. Marbury v. Madison." Justice WHITE, while dissenting from the majority's holding, in effect agreed with the Chief Justice on the issue of congressional power to alter the immunity: "We are never told [how] or why Congressional action could make a difference. It is not apparent that any of the propositions relied upon by the majority to immunize the President would not apply equally to such a statutory cause of action; nor does the majority indicate what new principles would operate to undercut those propositions."

2. Regarding the defendants other than the President, see Harlow v. Fitzgerald (a companion case to Nixon v. Fitzgerald), noted below.

damages. Cognizance of this personal vulnerability frequently could distract a President from his public duties, to the detriment not only of the President and his office but also the [Nation]." Justice Powell conceded that "separation of powers doctrine does not bar every exercise of jurisdiction over the President. [See, e.g., United States v. Nixon, below.] But our cases also have established that a court, before exercising jurisdiction, must balance the constitutional weight of the interest to be served against the dangers of intrusion on the authority and functions of the Executive Branch. When judicial action is needed to serve broad public interests—as when the Court acts, not in deroga-tion of the separation of powers, but to maintain their proper balance, cf. [The Steel Seizure Case], or to vindicate the public interest in an ongoing criminal prosecution, see United States v. Nixon—the exercise of jurisdiction has been held warranted. In the case of this merely private suit for damages based on a President's official acts, we hold it is not." [3]

In a passage of his opinion that roused the special wrath of the dissenters, Justice Powell refused to follow the analysis typically applied in delineating the scope of the absolute immunity of other officials. The usual, "functional" approach limits absolute immunity to specified duties of the office, as Justice Powell conceded: "In defining the scope of an official's absolute privilege, this Court has recognized that the sphere of protected action must be related closely to the immunity's justifying purposes. Frequently our decisions have held that an official's absolute immunity should extend only to acts in performance of particular functions of his office." But he went on to insist that that approach was inappropriate with regard to the President: "In view of the special nature of the President's constitutional office and functions, we think it appropriate to recognize absolute Presidential immunity from damages liability for acts within the 'outer perimeter' of his official responsibility." He explained: "[T]he President has discretionary responsibilities in a broad variety of areas, many of them highly sensitive. In many cases it would be difficult to determine which of the President's innumerable 'functions' encompassed a particular action. In this case, for example, [Fitzgerald] argues that he was dismissed in retaliation for his testimony to Congress—a violation of [federal statutes]. The Air Force, however, has claimed that the underlying reorganization [which cost Fitzgerald his job] was undertaken to promote efficiency. Assuming that [Nixon] ordered the reorganization in which [Fitzgerald] lost his job, an inquiry into the President's motives could not be avoided under the kind of 'functional' theory asserted both by [Fitzgerald] and the dissent. Inquiries of this kind could be highly intrusive." Nor would Justice Powell accept the argument that Nixon would have acted "outside the outer perimeter of his duties" if he ordered Fitzgerald's discharge: "Adoption of this construction thus would deprive absolute immunity of its intended effect."

Justice Powell added: "A rule of absolute immunity for the President will not leave the nation without sufficient protection against misconduct on the part of the chief executive. There remains the constitutional remedy of impeach-ment. In addition, there are formal and informal checks on Presidential action that do not apply with equal force to other executive officials. The President is subjected to constant scrutiny by the press. Vigilant oversight by Congress also may serve to deter Presidential abuses of office, as well as to make credible the threat of impeachment. Other incentives to avoid misconduct may include a desire to earn re-election, the need to maintain prestige as an element of

3. "The Court has recognized before that there is a lesser public interest in actions for civil damages than, for example, in criminal prosecu-tions. [Contrary] to the suggestion of Justice White's dissent, it is not true that our jurispru-dence ordinarily supplies a remedy in civil dam-ages for every legal wrong. The dissent's objec-tions on this ground would weigh equally against absolute immunity for any official. Yet the dis-sent makes no attack on the absolute immunity recognized for judges and [prosecutors]." [Foot-note by Justice Powell.]

Presidential influence, and a President's traditional concern for his historical stature. The existence of alternative remedies and deterrents establishes that absolute immunity will not place the President 'above the law.' "

Justice WHITE, joined by Justices Brennan, Marshall and Blackmun, submitted a long and vehement dissent. He especially objected to the majority's failure to follow the usual approach in other absolute immunity cases. Citing Butz v. Economou, 438 U.S. 478 (1978), he noted that the Court had held that, "although public officials perform certain functions that entitle them to absolute immunity, the immunity attaches to particular functions—not to particular offices." In his view, that approach should apply to the President as well: "Attaching absolute immunity to the office of the President, rather than to particular activities that the President might perform, places the President above the law. It is a reversion to the old notion that the King can do no wrong." He charged that the majority's abandonment of "basic principles" tracing back to Marbury v. Madison rested on a judgment that had "few, if any, indicia of a judicial decision; it is almost wholly a policy choice, a choice that is without substantial support and that in all events is ambiguous in its reach and import," and "very poor policy" to boot. He insisted, moreover, that the majority's "generalized absolute immunity" could not be sustained "when examined in the traditional manner and in light of the traditional judicial sources." Justice White summarized the appropriate "functional" immunity approach he would apply as follows: "The scope of immunity is determined by function, not office. [Whatever] may be true of the necessity of [a] broad immunity in certain areas of executive responsibility,[1] the only question that must be answered here is whether the dismissal of employees falls within a constitutionally assigned executive function, the performance of which would be substantially impaired by the possibility of a private action for damages. I believe it does not." [2]

THE WATERGATE TAPES LITIGATION: AMENABILITY TO JUDICIAL PROCESS; EXECUTIVE AUTONOMY; THE SCOPE OF EXECUTIVE PRIVILEGE

Introduction. The Supreme Court's decision in United States v. Nixon follows. The Court's decision bears on some of the issues already considered and raises additional ones. Examination of the various strands of the Nixon case is postponed to the notes following the case. But at the outset, it may be useful to note that there are indeed several issues intertwined in the litigation, and that the issues may be more separable than the Court's treatment suggests. The Nixon decision stemmed from an effort by Special Prosecutor Jaworski to obtain access to tape recordings and other documents pertaining to presidential

---

1. For example, "instances in which the President participates in prosecutorial decisions."

2. In a companion ruling, the Court refused to extend the absolute presidential immunity to the President's senior aides. Harlow v. Fitzgerald, 457 U.S. 800 (1982). The petitioners, Harlow and Butterfield, were Nixon aides charged with participating in the same conspiracy as that alleged in Nixon v. Fitzgerald. Rejecting a blanket absolute immunity claim, Justice Powell noted: "For executive officials in general, [our] cases make plain that qualified immunity represents the norm." He rejected the argument that presidential aides were entitled to a "derivative" absolute immunity by analogy to the rationale of Gravel v. United States (p. 383 above), regarding aides to members of Congress.

Granting the "derivative" immunity could not be reconciled with the "functional" approach used in most prior immunity cases. Moreover, the broad immunity could not be justified on the basis of the "special functions" of White House aides: "For aides entrusted with discretionary authority in such sensitive areas as national security or foreign policy, absolute immunity might well be [justified]. But a 'special functions' rationale does not warrant a blanket recognition of absolute immunity for all Presidential aides in the performance of all their duties." (Several Justices submitted separate statements in Harlow, but only Chief Justice Burger refused to join Justice Powell's opinion. He argued that the Gravel approach to legislators' aides should be applied to presidential aides as well.)

conversations and allegedly necessary to press criminal proceedings against several defendants other than the President for conspiracy to obstruct justice and other charges. President Nixon raised several defenses, not always clearly distinguished in the Court's opinion. The constitutional defenses pertaining to separation of powers involved at least three different strands. First, there was the claim introduced in the preceding group of notes, that the President was not amenable to judicial process and that impeachment and removal were preconditions to judicial proceedings. Second, there was the argument that, even if he were subject to court orders, the scope of executive privilege was a constitutional issue committed to the executive branch for final decision under the constitutional scheme. That was an argument, in short, that "executive privilege" was one of those constitutional issues not justiciable, one to be finally decided by a branch of the government other than the courts. (See the further discussion of that aspect of the "political questions" doctrine at p. 396 below.) Third, there was the argument on the merits of the executive privilege issue: even if the President was amenable to judicial process and even if the scope of executive privilege was an issue to which courts could speak, the Court should find the subpoenaed tapes within the appropriate scope of executive privilege, in view of the need for confidentiality in the executive branch. Did the Court adequately distinguish among, and adequately respond to, each of these contentions: (1) presidential immunity; (2) presidential autonomy and finality; (3) the scope of executive privilege?

UNITED STATES v. NIXON

418 U.S. 683, 94 S.Ct. 3090, 41 L.Ed.2d 1039 (1974).

Mr. Chief Justice BURGER delivered the opinion of the Court.

This litigation presents for review the denial of a motion, filed [on] behalf of the [President] in the case of United States v. Mitchell et al., to quash a third-party subpoena duces tecum issued by the [District Court] pursuant to Fed.R. Crim.Proc. 17(c). The subpoena directed the President to produce certain tape recordings and documents relating to his conversations with aides and advisers. The court rejected the President's claims of absolute executive privilege, of lack of jurisdiction, and of failure to satisfy the requirements of [Rule 17(c)].

[The case arose from a federal grand jury indictment on March 1, 1974, of seven associates of President Nixon [1] for conspiracy to obstruct justice and other offenses relating to the Watergate burglary. The President was named as an unindicted coconspirator. On April 18, 1974, the District Court, upon motion of the Special Prosecutor, issued a subpoena duces tecum to the President requiring him to produce, before the September 8 trial date, certain tapes and documents relating to precisely identified meetings between the President and others. On April 30, the President released edited transcripts of 43 conversations, including portions of 20 conversations subject to subpoena in the present case. On May 1, the President's counsel filed a "special appearance" and moved to quash the subpoena. This motion was accompanied by a formal claim of executive privilege. On May 20, the District Court denied the motion and ordered the "President or any [subordinate] with custody or control" of the subpoenaed items to deliver them to the court, together with tape copies of those parts of the subpoenaed recordings for which transcripts had been released

---

1. The seven defendants were John N. Mitchell, H.R. Haldeman, John D. Ehrlichman, Charles W. Colson, Robert C. Mardian, Kenneth W. Parkinson, and Gordon Strachan. Each of the defendants had occupied a position of responsibility either on the White House staff or with the Committee for the Re-election of the President. Colson entered a guilty plea on another charge and was dropped as a defendant.

on April 30. The President appealed to the Court of Appeals, but, before a decision in that court, the Supreme Court granted certiorari before judgment.[2] Before turning to the major issues in the case, the Court held that (1) the District Court order was an appealable order and that the case was properly "in" the Court of Appeals when the Supreme Court granted certiorari; (2) the Special Prosecutor's subpoena duces tecum satisfied the requirements of Fed.R. Crim.Proc. 17(c)—i.e., the requisite relevancy, admissibility, and specificity were shown; and (3) that the case was not a nonjusticiable intrabranch dispute (between the President and the Special Prosecutor, who acted pursuant to authority delegated by the President). The Chief Justice then turned to the central portion of its opinion, entitled "The Claim of Privilege," and proceeded as follows:]

A. [W]e turn to the claim that the subpoena should be quashed because it demands "confidential conversations between a President and his close advisors that it would be inconsistent with the public interest to produce." The first contention is a broad claim that the separation of powers doctrine precludes judicial review of a President's claim of privilege. The second contention is that if he does not prevail on the claim of absolute privilege, the court should hold as a matter of constitutional law that the privilege prevails over the subpoena duces tecum. In the performance of assigned constitutional duties each branch of the Government must initially interpret the Constitution, and the interpretation of its powers by any branch is due great respect from the others. The President's counsel [reads] the Constitution as providing an absolute privilege of confidentiality for all Presidential communications. Many decisions of this Court, however, have unequivocally reaffirmed the holding of [Marbury v. Madison] that "it is emphatically the province and duty of the judicial department to say what the law is." [Recall the comments on this passage in chap. 1, at p. 27 above.]

No holding of the Court has defined the scope of judicial power specifically relating to the enforcement of a subpoena for confidential Presidential communications for use in a criminal prosecution, but other exercises of powers by the Executive Branch and the Legislative Branch have been found invalid as in conflict with the Constitution. [Powell v. McCormack, p. 399 below; Steel Seizure Case.] In a series of cases, the Court interpreted the explicit immunity conferred by express provisions of the Constitution on Members of the House and Senate by the Speech or Debate Clause. [See p. 383 above.] Since this Court has consistently exercised the power to construe and delineate claims arising under express powers, it must follow that the Court has authority to interpret claims with respect to powers alleged to derive from enumerated powers. [Notwithstanding] the deference each branch must accord the others, the "judicial Power of the United States" vested in the federal courts by [Art. III] can no more be shared with the Executive Branch than the Chief Executive, for example, can share with the Judiciary the veto power, or the Congress share with the Judiciary the power to override a Presidential veto. Any other conclusion would be contrary to the basic concept of separation of powers and the checks and balances that flow from the scheme of a tripartite government. We therefore reaffirm that it is the province and the duty of this Court "to say what the law is" with respect to the claim of privilege presented in this case. [Marbury v. Madison.]

2. The Court granted certiorari on May 31, heard argument on July 8, and decided the case on July 24, 1974, while the House Judiciary Committee was considering the Articles of Impeachment noted at p. —— above. For a criticism of the Court's decision to bypass full consideration in the Court of Appeals and to grant extraordinarily speedy review in the case—a criticism noting the effect of the Court's timing judgment in aborting completion of the impeachment process—see Gunther, "Judicial Hegemony and Legislative Autonomy: The Nixon Case and the Impeachment Process," 22 U.C.L.A.L.Rev. 30 (1974).

B. In support of his claim of absolute privilege, the President's counsel urges two [grounds]. The first [is] the valid need for protection of communications between high Government officials and those who advise and assist them in the performance of their manifold duties; the importance of this confidentiality is too plain to require further discussion. Human experience teaches that those who expect public dissemination of their remarks may well temper candor with a concern for appearances and for their own interests to the detriment of the decision-making process. Whatever the nature of the privilege of confidentiality of Presidential communications in the exercise of Art. II powers, the privilege can be said to derive from the supremacy of each branch within its own assigned area of constitutional duties. Certain powers and privileges flow from the nature of enumerated powers;[3] the protection of the confidentiality of Presidential communications has similar constitutional underpinnings. The second ground asserted [to support] the claim of absolute privilege rests on the doctrine of separation of powers. Here it is argued that the independence of the Executive Branch within its own sphere insulates a President from a judicial subpoena in an ongoing criminal prosecution, and thereby protects confidential Presidential communications. However, neither the doctrine of separation of powers, nor the need for confidentiality of high level communications, without more, can sustain an absolute, unqualified Presidential privilege of immunity from judicial process under all circumstances. The President's need for complete candor and objectivity from advisers calls for great deference from the courts. However, when the privilege depends solely on the broad, undifferentiated claim of public interest in the confidentiality of such conversations, a confrontation with other values arises. Absent a claim of need to protect military, diplomatic, or sensitive national security secrets, we find it difficult to accept the argument that even the very important interest in confidentiality of Presidential communications is significantly diminished by production of such material for in camera inspection with all the protection that a district court will be obliged to provide.

The impediment that an absolute, unqualified privilege would place in the way of the primary constitutional duty of the Judicial Branch to do justice in criminal prosecutions would plainly conflict with the function of the courts under Art. III. In designing the structure of our Government and dividing and allocating the sovereign power among three co-equal branches, the [Framers] sought to provide a comprehensive system, but the separate powers were not intended to operate with absolute independence. [To] read the Art. II powers of the President as providing an absolute privilege as against a subpoena essential to enforcement of criminal statutes on no more than a generalized claim of the public interest in confidentiality of non-military and nondiplomatic discussions would upset the constitutional balance of "a workable government" and gravely impair the role of the courts under Art. III.

C. Since we conclude that the legitimate needs of the judicial process may outweigh Presidential privilege, it is necessary to resolve those competing interests in a manner that preserves the essential functions of each branch. The right and indeed the duty to resolve that question does not free the judiciary from according high respect to the representations made on behalf of the

---

3. The Special Prosecutor argues that there is no provision in the Constitution for a presidential privilege as to his communications corresponding to the privilege of Members of Congress under the Speech or Debate Clause. But the silence of the Constitution on this score is not dispositive. "The rule of constitutional interpretation announced in McCulloch v. Maryland, that that which was reasonably appropriate and relevant to the exercise of a granted power was to be consid-

ered as accompanying the grant, has been so universally applied that it suffices merely to state it." Marshall v. Gordon, 243 U.S. 521, 537 (1917). [Footnote by the Chief Justice.] [Does this statement mean that incidental powers of the President can be inferred from the Constitution? Recall that McCulloch and the necessary and proper clause refer to powers of Congress, not to the powers of the President.]

President. The expectation of a President to the confidentiality of his conversations and correspondence, like the claim of confidentiality of judicial deliberations, for example, has all the values to which we accord deference for the privacy of all citizens and added to those values the necessity for protection of the public interest in candid, objective, and even blunt or harsh opinions in Presidential decision-making. A President and those who assist him must be free to explore alternatives in the process of shaping policies and making decisions and to do so in a way many would be unwilling to express except privately. These are the considerations justifying a presumptive privilege for Presidential communications. The privilege is fundamental to the operation of government and inextricably rooted in the separation of powers under the [Constitution].

But this presumptive privilege must be considered in light of our historic commitment to the rule of law. This is nowhere more profoundly manifest than in our view that "the twofold aim [of criminal justice] is that guilt shall not escape or innocence suffer." We have elected to employ an adversary system of criminal justice in which the parties contest all issues before a court of law. The need to develop all relevant facts in the adversary system is both fundamental and comprehensive. The ends of criminal justice would be defeated if judgments were to be founded on a partial or speculative presentation of the facts. The very integrity of the judicial system and public confidence in the system depend on full disclosure of all the facts, within the framework of the rules of evidence. To ensure that justice is done, it is imperative to the function of courts that compulsory process be available for the production of evidence needed either by the prosecution or by the defense.

Only recently the Court restated the ancient proposition of law, albeit in the context of a grand jury inquiry rather than a trial, "that 'the public [has] a right to every man's evidence,' except for those persons protected by a constitutional, common law, or statutory privilege," Branzburg v. Hayes [p. 1431 below]. The privileges referred to by the Court are designed to protect weighty and legitimate competing interests [e.g., self-incrimination, attorney, and priest privileges] [and] are not lightly created nor expansively construed, for they are in derogation of the search for truth. In this case the President challenges a subpoena served on him as a third party requiring the production of materials for use in a criminal prosecution; he does so on the claim that he has a privilege against disclosure of confidential communications. He does not place his claim of privilege on the ground they are military or diplomatic secrets. As to these areas of Art. II duties the courts have traditionally shown the utmost deference to presidential responsibilities. [No] case of the Court, however, has extended this high degree of deference to a President's generalized interest in confidentiality. Nowhere in the Constitution [is] there any explicit reference to a privilege of confidentiality, yet to the extent this interest relates to the effective discharge of a President's powers, it is constitutionally based. The right to the production of all evidence at a criminal trial similarly has constitutional dimensions. [It] is the manifest duty of the courts to vindicate [the Sixth and Fifth Amendment] guarantees and to accomplish that it is essential that all relevant and admissible evidence be produced.

In this case we must weigh the importance of the general privilege of confidentiality of Presidential communications in performance of his responsibilities against the inroads of such a privilege on the fair administration of criminal justice.[4] The interest in preserving confidentiality is weighty indeed and

---

4. We are not here concerned with the balance between the President's generalized interest in confidentiality and the need for relevant evidence in civil litigation, nor with that between the confidentiality interest and congressional demands for information, nor with the President's interest in preserving state secrets. We address only the conflict between the President's assertion of a generalized privilege of confidentiality against the constitutional need for relevant evi-

entitled to great respect. However, we cannot conclude that advisers will be moved to temper the candor of their remarks by the infrequent occasions of disclosure because of the possibility that such conversations will be called for in the context of a criminal prosecution. On the other hand, the allowance of the privilege to withhold evidence that is demonstrably relevant in a criminal trial would cut deeply into the guarantee of due process of law and gravely impair the basic function of the courts. A President's acknowledged need for confidentiality in the communications of his office is general in nature, whereas the constitutional need for production of relevant evidence in a criminal proceeding is specific and central to the fair adjudication of a particular criminal [case]. Without access to specific facts a criminal prosecution may be totally frustrated. The President's broad interest in confidentiality of communications will not be vitiated by disclosure of a limited number of conversations preliminarily shown to have some bearing on the pending [trials]. We conclude that when the ground for asserting privilege as to subpoenaed materials sought for use in a criminal trial is based only on the generalized interest in confidentiality, it cannot prevail over the fundamental demands of due process of law in the fair administration of criminal justice. The generalized assertion of privilege must yield to the demonstrated, specific need for evidence in a pending criminal trial.

D. If a President concludes that compliance with a subpoena would be injurious to the public interest he may properly, as was done here, invoke a claim of privilege on the return of the subpoena. Upon receiving a claim of privilege from the Chief Executive, it became the further duty of the District Court to treat the subpoenaed material as presumptively privileged and to require the Special Prosecutor to demonstrate that the Presidential material was "essential to the justice of the [pending criminal] case." [5] [We] affirm the order of the District Court that subpoenaed materials be transmitted to that court. We now turn to the important question of the District Court's responsibilities in conducting the in camera examination of Presidential materials or communications delivered under the compulsion of the subpoena duces tecum.

E. [The Court proceeded to offer guidelines to the District Court in implementing the decision.] Statements that meet the test of admissibility and relevance must be isolated; all other material must be excised. [The] District Court has a very heavy responsibility to see to it that Presidential conversations, which are either not relevant or not admissible, are accorded that high degree of respect due the [President]. Mr. Chief Justice Marshall sitting as a trial judge in [Burr] was extraordinarily careful to point out that: "[I]n no case of this kind would a Court be required to proceed against the president as against an ordinary individual." Marshall's statement cannot be read to mean in any sense that a President is above the law, but relates to the singularly unique role under Art. II of a President's communications and activities, related to the performance of duties under that Article. Moreover, a President's communications and activities encompass a vastly wider range of sensitive material than would be true of any "ordinary individual." It is therefore necessary in the public interest to afford Presidential confidentiality the greatest protection consistent with the fair administration of justice. The need for confidentiality even as to idle conversations with associates in which casual reference might be made concerning political leaders within the country or foreign statesmen is too obvious to call for further treatment. We have no doubt that the District Judge

dence in criminal trials. [Footnote by the Chief Justice.]

5. Here and elsewhere in the opinion, Chief Justice Burger cited and quoted from the Aaron Burr treason trial in the early 19th century (in which John Marshall, sitting on the Circuit Court, had issued a subpoena to President Thomas Jefferson). See United States v. Burr, 25 Fed.Cas. 187 (No. 14,694) (1807).

will at all times accord to Presidential records that high degree of deference suggested in [Burr].

Affirmed.[6]

A transitional note. Recall the distinction, in the notes introducing United States v. Nixon, among three varieties of problems presented by that case: the amenability of the President to judicial process; the arguable constitutional autonomy of the executive branch to make final decisions about executive privilege; and the scope of executive privilege. Further examination of those three strands of the Nixon problem is the purpose of the remaining materials in this chapter. After a brief reexamination of the amenability problem, the last of the strands—the scope of executive privilege—will be examined before turning to the second of the themes, the autonomy problem. The autonomy issue is postponed to the end of this group of notes to permit further pursuit of a broader problem: the "commitment to other branches" aspect of the political questions concept.

PRESIDENTIAL AMENABILITY TO JUDICIAL PROCESS AFTER THE NIXON CASE

In result, United States v. Nixon clearly answered the unresolved question as to whether the President is wholly immune from judicial process. But did the Court adequately justify that aspect of its result? Did it adequately respond to the doubts that had been voiced by the post-Civil War Court in Mississippi v. Johnson, doubts noted above? And does the Nixon opinion, holding the President subject to a subpoena for evidence needed in a criminal case, throw light on the problem of the amenability of a President to criminal prosecution?

The amenability of President Nixon to the Special Prosecutor's subpoena was confronted more squarely in the earlier rounds of the Watergate Tapes litigation. Judge Sirica ruled in 1973 that the President was not immune from compulsory process when he granted Special Prosecutor Cox's demand for materials sought by the grand jury investigating Watergate matters.[1] The District Judge found the separation of powers argument against issuance of compulsory court process an "unpersuasive" contention that "overlooks history." He added: "It is true that [Mississippi v. Johnson] left open the question whether the President can be required by court process to perform a purely ministerial act, but to persist in the opinion, after 1952, that he cannot would seem to exalt the form of the Youngstown [Steel Seizure] case over its

---

6. Justice REHNQUIST did not participate.

Before the decision in the case, the President and his representatives had left it unclear whether Nixon would obey an adverse Court decision. In the oral argument before the Court, for example, Presidential Counsel St. Clair had emphasized that the President "has his obligations under the Constitution." But eight hours after the Court decision was announced, President Nixon's office issued a statement reporting that he would comply. Among the 64 tape recordings covered by the decision was a particularly damaging one of conversations on June 23, 1972, six days after the Watergate burglary. On August 5, President Nixon released transcripts of those conversations. On August 8, President Nixon announced that he would resign on the next day. (After his resignation, Nixon returned to his residence in San Clemente, California. In 1980, he moved to New York City, into the house that had, for decades, been Judge Learned Hand's home. Nixon later sold that house.)

Among the many comments on the Nixon case, in the legal literature, see especially the articles in "Symposium: United States v. Nixon." 22 U.C.L.A.L.Rev. 1 (1974), Freund, "Foreword: On Presidential Privilege," 88 Harv. L.Rev. 13 (1974), and Cox, "Presidential Privilege," 122 U.Pa.L.Rev. 1383 (1974). For the alleged "inside story" of the evolution of the opinion in the Nixon case, see Woodward & Armstrong, The Brethren (1979).

1. In re Grand Jury Subpoena Duces Tecum Issued to Richard M. Nixon, 360 F.Supp. 1 (D.D.C.1973).

substance. Though the Court's order there went to the Secretary of Commerce, it was the direct order of President Truman that was reversed."

The Court of Appeals 5 to 2 decision sustained Judge Sirica's approach.[2] The majority insisted that the President was "legally" bound by an order enforcing a subpoena even though a court might lack physical power to enforce its judgment. (Compare the discussion in Powell v. McCormack, p. 399 below.) The per curiam opinion contended that, "to find the President immune from judicial process, we must read out of Burr and [Steel Seizure] [their] underlying principles." The majority proceeded to reject every argument for executive immunity: "Lacking textual support, counsel for the President nonetheless would have us infer immunity from the President's political mandate, or from his vulnerability to impeachment, or from his broad discretionary powers. These are invitations to refashion the Constitution, and we reject [them]. That the Impeachment Clause may qualify the court's power to sanction non-compliance with judicial orders is immaterial. Whatever the qualifications, they were equally present in [the Steel Seizure Case]. The legality of judicial orders should not be confused with the legal consequences of their breach; for the courts in this country always assume that their orders will be obeyed, especially when addressed to responsible government officials." [3] In the second round of the Watergate Tapes litigation—the subpoena culminating in United States v. Nixon—Judge Sirica relied simply on his position in the 1973 case. Should the Court have addressed the amenability issue more fully? Were the lower courts' references to the Steel Seizure Case and the Burr trial persuasive? Were the Court's repeated citations of Marbury v. Madison helpful on the amenability issue?

THE PROPER SCOPE OF EXECUTIVE PRIVILEGE

1. *Executive privilege and the Nixon case.* Assuming that the judiciary was the proper department to define the scope of executive privilege—the question that is postponed to the next group of notes—did the Court give the right answer in the Nixon case? What were the arguments supporting such a privilege? What were the Court's reasons for rejecting "an absolute, unqualified, presidential privilege" stemming from "the very important interest in confidentiality of presidential communications" pertaining to "nonmilitary and nondiplomatic discussions"? What considerations outweigh the qualified confidentiality privilege which the Court does recognize? Note the Court's footnote 4, as to the potential competing considerations not reached in this case. What about claims of privilege based on the "need to protect military, diplomatic, or sensitive national security secrets"? Are they to be scrutinized by balancing as well? Or are they absolute privileges rather than qualified ones? [1]

The confidentiality privilege recognized in the Nixon case is found to rest on a constitutional basis. If the privilege is constitutionally based, to what extent may Congress legislate guidelines about the scope of the privilege? Note the comment in Justice White's majority opinion in EPA v. Mink, 410 U.S. 73 (1973), construing the executive secrecy exemption in the Freedom of Informa-

---

2. Nixon v. Sirica, 487 F.2d 700 (D.C.Cir. 1973).

3. Compare the comment in Judge Wilkey's dissenting opinion in the Court of Appeals: "[If] the court has no physical power to enforce its subpoena should the President refuse to comply, [then] what purpose is served by determining whether the President is 'immune' from process? It can hardly be questioned that in any direct confrontation between the Judiciary and the Ex-

ecutive, the latter must prevail. Therefore, the 'issue' of whether the President is amenable to court process is an illusory [one]."

1. Recall also the reasons given in Nixon v. Fitzgerald (p. 385 above) for granting the President an absolute immunity from civil liability. Were some of the reasons for that immunity relevant to determining the scope of executive privilege?

tion Act of 1966, 5 U.S.C. § 552. Justice White commented: "Congress could certainly have provided that the Executive Branch adopt new procedures or it could have established its own procedures—subject only to whatever limitations the Executive privilege may be held to impose upon such congressional ordering." What are those "limitations"? [2]

2. *Congressional inquiries and executive privilege.* There have been frequent conflicts between legislative demands for information and executive officials' refusals to comply, on instructions from the President, on grounds of interference with confidential deliberations.[3] Is the broad congressional power to investigate—see p. 1404 below—entitled to less weight in the balancing process than the interest in the "fair administration of criminal justice," the interest that outweighed the privilege claimed in the Nixon case? Note the footnote in the Nixon case stating that the Court was not passing on the balance "between the confidentiality interest and congressional demands for information." That issue arose repeatedly in the course of the Watergate investigation by Senator Ervin's Senate Select Committee. In the fall of 1973, at about the time that Special Prosecutor Cox proved successful in obtaining access to some tapes to aid in the grand jury investigation, in the Nixon v. Sirica litigation, the Senate Select Committee was unable to enforce its subpoena for tapes in the courts. The District Court rejected the Committee's claim after application of the balancing criteria first elaborated in Nixon v. Sirica. It concluded that the Committee's need to know did not outweigh the interest in executive confidentiality.[4]

3. *Executive privilege and impeachment inquiries.* Do the needs of an impeachment inquiry or trial present stronger claims for outweighing executive confidentiality needs than the needs of an ordinary congressional committee? In the late spring and early summer of 1974, President Nixon repeatedly refused to honor subpoenas issued by the House Judiciary Committee; and that refusal led to Article III of the Impeachment Articles. Earlier Presidents, in invoking executive privilege against ordinary congressional inquiries, had recognized the special strength of congressional demands in the course of an impeachment proceeding. President Nixon's growing resistance to House Committee demands culminated in a letter to Chairman Rodino on June 10, 1974. President Nixon wrote: "The Committee asserts that it should be the sole judge of presidential confidentiality. I cannot accept such a doctrine. [What] is commonly referred to now as 'executive privilege' is part and parcel of the basic doctrine of separation of powers. [If] the institution of an impeachment inquiry against a President were permitted to override all restraints of separation of powers, [this] would be an open invitation to future Congresses to use an impeachment inquiry, however frivolously, as a device to assert their own supremacy over the executive, and to reduce executive confidentiality to a nullity." The President accordingly continued to refuse to comply with impeachment inquiry subpoenas. It was that refusal that produced the final Article of the charges adopted by the Committee.[5] That Article was adopted by a

2. Recall the debate among the Justices about the congressional power to modify the absolute presidential immunity from civil liability established in Nixon v. Fitzgerald, p. 385 above.

3. See generally Dorsen & Shattuck, "Executive Privilege, the Congress and the Courts," 35 Ohio St.L.J. 1 (1974), and Berger, Executive Privilege: A Constitutional Myth (1974).

4. See Senate Select Committee on Presidential Campaign Activities v. Nixon, 370 F.Supp. 521 (D.D.C.1974). By the time that case was decided on the merits, the Special Prosecutor had already obtained the material involved, and there was special risk that publication by the Commit-

tee might prejudice impending criminal trials. What should be the result when a committee seeks such information in the absence of the risk of prejudicial trial publicity?

5. The third Article of Impeachment—which concluded, like the first two Articles noted earlier, that Nixon had acted "in a manner contrary to his trust as President and subversive of constitutional government"—charged that the President had "willfully disobeyed" a series of "duly authorized subpoenas" issued by the Impeachment Committee and had thus "interposed the powers of the Presidency against the lawful subpoenas of the House of Representatives, thereby

smaller majority of the Committee than the first two Articles. Several of the Committee members who voted against Article III did so on the basis of perceived implications of United States v. Nixon. See, e.g., the statement by Congressman Railsback: "You have two contesting political, separate but co-equal branches. What could be more natural but than to ask the third branch, which has been the traditional arbiter in disputes, to arbitrate this dispute?" In elaborating that statement, he emphasized the Court's assertion, in United States v. Nixon, that it was the "ultimate interpreter of the Constitution," and the Court's repeated quotations from Marbury v. Madison in that case. Did Article III state an impeachable offense? Did United States v. Nixon and its invocations of Marbury v. Madison make Article III an improper impeachment charge? Did the Court use overbroad language about its special role in resolving constitutional disputes? [6]

C. WHO DECIDES? EXECUTIVE AND LEGISLATIVE AUTONOMY: THE "COMMITMENT TO OTHER BRANCHES" STRAND OF THE POLITICAL QUESTION DOCTRINE

Introduction. United States v. Nixon focuses primarily on the substantive content of executive privilege. But was that a constitutional issue the *courts* should resolve? In United States v. Nixon, the question of substantive content and authority to decide were closely connected; and the Court's treatment of the case may have made the issues overlap even more than necessary. But analytically they are separate problems. It was possible to argue that the content and application of executive privilege doctrine should be viewed as one of those constitutional issues committed to another branch for final decision: that it was a nonjusticiable issue in the sense that the executive rather than the courts should have the final authority to decide it. The Court has long recognized that the Constitution does contain such nonjusticiable issues. This group of notes will examine that aspect of justiciability, first in the context of the Nixon case and then more generally.

1. *Executive autonomy, justiciability, and the Nixon case.* Did the Court adequately distinguish the issue of autonomy and substantive content of executive privilege in its handling of the Nixon case? Should the executive privilege for confidential communications have been viewed as an issue committed for final decision to the executive branch because of the implications of the Constitution? Did the Court jump too quickly from its view that the President was amenable to judicial process to a conclusion that it was for the *courts* to decide the content of executive privilege? [1] The Court in the Nixon case

---

assuming to himself functions and judgments necessary to the exercise of the sole power of impeachment vested by the Constitution in the House of Representatives."

6. For a defense of Article III of the Impeachment Articles, a criticism of the Court for overbroad statements casting a shadow over the congressional debate on that Article, and the view that "the House Committee was wise in deciding by a large margin in May to avoid going to court to enforce its subpoenas," see Gunther, "Judicial Hegemony and Legislative Autonomy: The Nixon Case and the Impeachment Process," 22 U.C.L.A.L.Rev. 30 (1974). For a criticism of Article III, see Van Alstyne, "The Third Im-

peachment Article: Congressional Bootstrapping," 60 A.B.A.J. 1199 (1974).

1. Note the comment in Gunther, "Judicial Hegemony and Legislative Autonomy: The Nixon Case and the Impeachment Process," 22 UCLA L.Rev. 30 (1974), arguing that "it was possible to decide against President Nixon's claim" as to amenability "and yet support his argument as to autonomy": "it was possible to say that in subpoena efforts incident to a criminal case there is no presidential immunity from judicial process and yet conclude that the President, as a matter of constitutional interpretation of Article II powers, had absolute discretion to determine the scope of executive privilege. Mar-

repeatedly relied on John Marshall's statements in Marbury v. Madison. But do those statements answer the executive autonomy-finality claim in a case such as Nixon? Recall the comments about the ambiguity of the Marshall statements, at p. 21 above. If they are taken to imply that the courts have a special guardianship role in constitutional interpretation, then it can indeed be argued that the Court must have the final say as to all constitutional problems. But more commonly, Marbury v. Madison is taken to mean a good deal less than that: it is taken to mean only that courts have authority to adjudicate constitutional issues when those are relevant in cases properly within their jurisdiction. This does leave it to the courts to determine their jurisdiction; but it does not preclude a constitutional interpretation which finds some issues committed to final decision by another branch. If the Marbury statement were taken at its broadest, there could be no such issues. But over most of its history, the Court *has* recognized that some issues are nonjusticiable because they are committed to other branches for final decision. The rest of these notes consider that ingredient of the political question doctrine. Do Court approaches such as those in United States v. Nixon and in Powell v. McCormack, below, cast doubt on the continued vitality of that strand of the political questions doctrine?

2. *Questions nonjusticiable because they are "committed by the Constitution to another branch of government."* The arguments for executive autonomy as to executive privilege illustrate one strand of the political question doctrine. That aspect of United States v. Nixon makes a preliminary exploration of that strand appropriate here.[2] The concept that some constitutional issues are nonjusticiable or "political" is well established; but inquiry into what the ingredients of that concept are has produced considerable uncertainty and controversy. The ingredient examined here is the most solid and confined one—and, in some commentators' views, the only legitimate one: that the *Constitution* commits the final determination of some constitutional questions to agencies other than courts. But the Court's political questions decisions cannot all be explained on that constitutional "commitment" ground. Some decisions on political question nonjusticiability emphasize the nature of the question and its aptness for judicial resolution in view of judicial competence. That strand of the political questions doctrine finds some issues nonjusticiable because they cannot be resolved by judicially manageable standards, or on the basis of data available to the courts. Still another, even more openended, strand of the concept suggests that the political question notion is essentially a problem of judicial discretion, of prudential judgments that some issues ought not to be decided by the courts because they are too controversial or could produce enforcement problems or other institutional difficulties. Those last two strands—judicially unmanageable standards and data, and prudential considerations—are more fully explored in the last chapter. The first, most clearly "constitutional interpretation" strand of political question doctrine is considered in these notes.

Consider one of the best known modern statements about the ingredients of political question nonjusticiability, in BAKER v. CARR (1962; p. 1617 below). There, the divided Court held that equal protection challenges to legislative

bury v. Madison is an especially relevant source in deciding the first issue. It is far more tenuously related to the second. Respectable arguments after all have been made, and not only by President Nixon's counsel, that absolute executive immunity [and an absolute executive privilege] is a legitimate constitutional inference. The opinion in United States v. Nixon tended to merge and blur those separate issues. And the linchpin in intertwining them was the excessive use of Marbury v. Madison." After noting that the Nixon ruling relied heavily on Marbury in responding to the President's claim, the Gunther comment argues that "there is nothing in [Marbury] that precludes a constitutional interpretation which gives final authority to another branch." (See also the additional excerpts from this article in chap. 1, at p. 28 above.)

2. Additional inquiry into the problem—especially into the other strands of the political question doctrine—appears in the final chapter of this book, at p. 1608 below.

districting schemes were justiciable and not "political." Though fuller consideration of reapportionment controversies is postponed to the last chapter, consider Baker v. Carr here for the light it throws on the various, intertwined strands of the political question concept. Justice BRENNAN's majority opinion stated: "It is apparent that several formulations which vary slightly according to the settings in which the questions arise may describe a political question, although each has one or more elements which identifies it as essentially a function of the separation of powers. Prominent on the surface of any case held to involve a political question is found a textually demonstrable constitutional commitment of the issue to a coordinate political department; or a lack of judicially discoverable and manageable standards for resolving it; or the impossibility of deciding without an initial policy determination of a kind clearly for nonjudicial discretion; or the impossibility of a court's undertaking independent resolution without expressing lack of the respect due coordinate branches of government; or an unusual need for unquestioning adherence to a political decision already made; or the potentiality of embarrassment from multifarious pronouncements by various departments on one question."

To what extent are Justice Brennan's grounds all "essentially a function of the separation of powers"? To what extent are they considerations of prudence? Of concern with "manageable standards"? In the rest of this chapter, the emphasis is on the first of his ingredients: "a textually demonstrable constitutional commitment of the issue to a coordinate political department." Herbert Wechsler has argued that that is the only legitimate ingredient of the political questions concept. He recognizes that the line between political and justiciable questions "is thin, indeed," but he adds that "it is thinner than it needs to be or ought to be": "I submit that in [political question cases], the only proper judgment that may lead to an abstention from decision is that the Constitution has committed the determination of the issue to another agency of government than the courts. Difficult as it may be to make that judgment wisely, whatever factors may be rightly weighed in situations where the answer is not clear, what is involved is in itself an act of constitutional interpretation, to be made and judged by standards that should govern the interpretive process generally. That, I submit, is *toto caelo* different from a broad discretion to abstain or intervene."[3] Contrast Alexander Bickel's view: "[O]nly by means of a play on words can the broad discretion that the courts have in fact exercised be turned into an act of constitutional interpretation. The political-question doctrine simply resists being domesticated in this fashion. There is something different about it, in kind, not in degree, from the general 'interpretive process'; something greatly more flexible, something of prudence, not construction and not principle."[4] But whatever the outer limits of the political questions doctrine, can some decisions of nonjusticiability be justified on the "commitment to other branches" ground of constitutional interpretation? Does United States v. Nixon adequately explain why the issue of executive privilege is *not* such an issue, for final decision by the executive? Consider the Court's fuller discussion of such a "constitutional commitment" claim a few years before the Nixon case, in a suit calling upon the Court to reexamine a congressional rather than a presidential nonjusticiability claim, in Powell v. McCormack, which follows.[5]

---

3. Wechsler, "Toward Neutral Principles of Constitutional Law," 73 Harv.L.Rev. 1, 7, 9.

4. Bickel, "Foreword: The Passive Virtues," 75 Harv.L.Rev. 40, 46.

5. The notes after the Powell case examine additional aspects of the "commitment to other branches" strand of the political question doctrine.

POWELL v. McCORMACK

395 U.S. 486, 89 S.Ct. 1944, 23 L.Ed.2d 491 (1969).

Mr. Chief Justice WARREN delivered [the opinion of the Court].

[Petitioner Adam Clayton Powell, Jr., was elected to the 90th Congress to represent a portion of the Harlem area of New York City. Although he met the age, citizenship, and residence requirements of Art. I, § 2, cl. 2, a House resolution prevented him from taking his seat. The House decision to bar Powell came after a House Select Committee had reported that Powell "had asserted an unwarranted privilege and immunity from the processes of the courts of New York; that he had wrongfully diverted House funds for the use of others and of himself; and that he had made false reports on expenditures of foreign currency" to a House committee. Among the relief sought by Powell was a declaratory judgment that the House refusal to seat him was unconstitutional. He also sought to enjoin the Sergeant at Arms of the House from refusing to pay his salary. The lower courts denied relief.

[Early in its opinion, the Court concluded that the case had not become moot even though Powell had been elected to and seated by the 91st Congress, since his "claim for back salary remains viable." The Court next found that the Speech or Debate Clause required dismissal of the action against members of Congress but did not bar proceeding against the congressional employees. The Court then rejected the argument that the challenged House action should be regarded as an expulsion rather than an exclusion of Powell. (Art. I, § 5, grants the House authority to expel a member "with the concurrence of two thirds." Exclusion requires only a majority vote. The vote excluding Powell was 307 to 116, larger than two-thirds. The respondents claimed that the House may expel a member for any reason whatsoever. The Court, however, treated the resolution as an exclusion, stating that it expressed "no view on what limitations may exist on Congress's power to expel or otherwise punish a member once he has been seated.")

[After finding that the case was clearly one "arising under" the Constitution and that the Court accordingly had subject matter jurisdiction, Chief Justice Warren turned to the problem of justiciability. He focused on the question "whether the structure of the Federal Government renders the issue presented a 'political question'—that is, a question which is not justiciable in federal court because of the separation of powers provided by the Constitution." In rejecting that claim, the Chief Justice stated:]

Political Question Doctrine. 1. Textually Demonstrable Constitutional Commitment. [It] is well established that the federal courts will not adjudicate political questions. In Baker v. Carr, we noted that political questions are not justiciable primarily because of the [separation of powers]. [The Court quoted the political questions criteria of Baker v. Carr printed at p. 397 above.] In order to determine whether there has been a textual commitment to a co-ordinate department of the Government, we must interpret the Constitution. In other words, we must first determine what power the Constitution confers upon the House through Art. I, § 5 ["Each House shall be the Judge of [the] Qualifications of its own Members"], before we can determine to what extent, if any, the exercise of that power is subject to judicial review. Respondents maintain that the House has broad power under § 5, and, they argue, the House may determine which are the qualifications necessary for membership. On the other hand, petitioners allege that the Constitution provides that an elected representative may be denied his seat only if the House finds he does not meet one of the standing qualifications expressly prescribed by the Constitution [i.e., the age, citizenship, and residence requirements of Art. I, § 2].

If examination of § 5 disclosed that the Constitution gives the House judicially unreviewable power to set qualifications for membership and to judge whether prospective members meet those qualifications, further review of the House determination might well be barred by the political question doctrine. On the other hand, if the Constitution gives the House power to judge only whether elected members possess the three standing qualifications set forth in the Constitution, further consideration would be necessary to determine whether any of the other formulations of the political question doctrine are "inextricable from the case at bar." [1] Baker v. Carr. In other words, whether there is a "textually demonstrable constitutional commitment of the issue to a coordinate political department" [and] what is the scope of such commitment are questions we must resolve for the first time in this [case].

In order to determine the scope of any "textual commitment" under Art. I, § 5, we necessarily must determine the meaning of the phrase to "be the Judge of the Qualifications of its own Members." Petitioners argue that the records of the debates during the Constitutional Convention; available commentary from the post-Convention, pre-ratification period; and early congressional applications of Art. I, § 5, support their construction of the section. Respondents insist, however, that a careful examination of the pre-Convention practices of the English Parliament and American colonial assemblies demonstrates that by 1787, a legislature's power to judge the qualifications of its members was generally understood to encompass exclusion or expulsion on the ground that an individual's character or past conduct rendered him unfit to serve. When the Constitution and the debates over its adoption are thus viewed in historical perspective, argue respondents, it becomes clear that the "qualifications" expressly set forth in the Constitution were not meant to limit the long-recognized legislative power to exclude or expel at will, but merely to establish "standing incapacities," which could be altered only by a constitutional amendment. Our examination of the relevant historical materials leads us to the conclusion that petitioners are correct and that the Constitution leaves the House without authority to *exclude* any person, duly elected by his constituents, who meets all the requirements for membership expressly prescribed in the Constitution. [The review of the history is omitted.]

Had the intent of the Framers emerged from these materials with less clarity, we would nevertheless have been compelled to resolve any ambiguity in favor of a narrow construction of the scope of Congress' power to exclude members-elect. A fundamental principle of our representative democracy is, in Hamilton's words, "that the people should choose whom they please to govern them." As Madison pointed out at the Convention, this principle is undermined as much by limiting whom the people can select as by limiting the franchise itself. In apparent agreement with this basic philosophy, the Convention adopted his suggestion limiting the power to expel. To allow essentially that same power to be exercised under the guise of judging qualifications would be to ignore Madison's warning [against] "vesting an improper & dangerous power in the Legislature." Moreover, it would effectively nullify the Convention's decision to require a two-third vote for expulsion. Unquestionably, Congress has an interest in preserving its institutional integrity, but in most cases that interest can be sufficiently safeguarded by the exercise of its power to punish its members for disorderly behavior and, in extreme cases, to expel a member with the concurrence of [two-thirds].

---

1. Consistent with this interpretation, federal courts might still be barred by the political question doctrine from reviewing the House's factual determination that a member did not meet one of the standing qualifications. This is an issue not presented in this case and we express no view as to its resolution. [Footnote by Chief Justice Warren.]

For these reasons, we have concluded that Art. I, § 5, is at most a "textually demonstrable commitment" to Congress to judge only the qualifications expressly set forth in the Constitution. Therefore, the "textual commitment" formulation of the political question doctrine does not bar federal courts from adjudicating petitioners' claims.

2. Other Considerations. Respondents' alternate contention is that the case presents a political question because judicial resolution of petitioners' claim would produce a "potentially embarrassing confrontation between coordinate branches" of the Federal Government. But, as our interpretation of Art. I, § 5, discloses, a determination of petitioner Powell's right to sit would require no more than an interpretation of the Constitution. Such a determination falls within the traditional role accorded courts to interpret the law, and does not involve a "lack of respect due [a] coordinate [branch] of government," nor does it involve an "initial policy determination of a kind clearly for nonjudicial discretion." Baker v. Carr. Our system of government requires that federal courts on occasion interpret the Constitution in a manner at variance with the construction given the document by another branch. The alleged conflict [2] that such an adjudication may cause cannot justify the courts' avoiding their constitutional [responsibility]. Nor are any of the other formulations of a political question "inextricable from the case at bar." Petitioners seek a determination that the House was without power to exclude Powell from the 90th Congress, which, we have seen, requires an interpretation of the Constitution—a determination for which clearly there are "judicially manageable standards." Finally, a judicial resolution of petitioners' claim will not result in "multifarious pronouncements by various departments on one question." For, as we noted in Baker v. Carr, it is the responsibility of this Court to act as the ultimate interpreter of the Constitution. Marbury v. Madison. Thus, we conclude that petitioners' claim is not barred by the political question doctrine, and [we] hold that the case is justiciable. [W]e hold that [the] House was without power to exclude [Powell] from its [membership].

Reversed and remanded.[3]

COMMITMENT OF CONSTITUTIONAL ISSUES TO OTHER BRANCHES AFTER POWELL

1. *The impact of the Powell and Nixon cases on the "commitment" strand of the political questions concept.* Given the approach of the Powell case, do any constitutional questions remain which the Court is likely to find committed to other branches for final decision? Writing several years before Powell, Herbert Wechsler's discussion of the political questions doctrine (p. 398 above) had given two examples of issues in which the commitment to other branches was "explicit" in the Constitution: convictions after impeachment, in Art. I, § 3 (Senate's "sole Power to try"); and the seating or expulsion of members of Congress in view of Art. I, § 5. The Powell decision on exclusions from Congress obviously undercuts a portion of Wechsler's statement. Is that because, on a proper reading of the Constitution, the commitment of the exclusion issue to the House is simply not as clear as Wechsler thought? Or is it because the Court's approach makes it difficult to conceive of any issue the

2. In fact, the Court has noted that it is an "inadmissible suggestion" that action might be taken in disregard of a judicial determination. McPherson v. Blacker, 146 U.S. 1, 24 (1892). [Footnote by Chief Justice Warren.]

3. A concurring opinion by Justice DOUGLAS included the statement: "If this were an

expulsion case I would think that no justiciable controversy would be presented, the vote of the House being two-thirds or more." Justice STEWART dissented, on grounds of mootness.

Court will find committed to another branch? What *was* determinative in the Court's reading of the constitutional provisions? Note the Court's statement that "it is the responsibility of this Court to act as the ultimate interpreter of the Constitution." The Court cites Marbury v. Madison for that position. Does that Court's view of its own powers rest on a fair reading of Marbury? Does that reading govern the result not only in Powell but in Nixon and in most if not all other cases of arguable commitments of constitutional issues to other branches?[1] Note the criticism in Sandalow, "Comments on Powell v. McCormack," 17 U.C.L.A.L.Rev. 172 (1969), arguing that the Court confused the questions of jurisdiction to decide and of the merits. He suggests that the source of the confusion was the Court's assumption about its role as "the ultimate interpreter of the Constitution." He adds: "On that premise, it is but a short step to the conclusion that the Court is obligated to intervene when another branch of government acts in a manner prohibited by the Constitution." If Powell is correct, he comments, "it is difficult to see [why the Court] may not similarly review expulsions from the Congress or the removal of judges or other officers upon conviction after impeachment." Is that a persuasive criticism? Compare Justice Douglas' suggestion in Powell that an expulsion decision would not be reviewable, and note the Court's footnote 1 in Powell, suggesting that "the House's factual determination that a member did not meet one of the standing qualifications" might be nonreviewable. How do those issues differ from the ones the Court did examine in Powell and Nixon?

2. *Judicial review and impeachment.* Does the approach of the Powell case throw significant doubt on the widespread assumption that Senate convictions after impeachment are not reviewable? Or does at least that Wechsler example of "explicit" commitments to another branch retain vitality?[2] If the Nixon impeachment process had continued and a conviction in the Senate had resulted, could judicial review have been sought on the ground that the Articles of Impeachment did not charge "high Crimes and Misdemeanors" and hence were not within the constitutional scope of impeachable offenses? The majority of commentators who addressed that issue during the impeachment proceedings against President Nixon concluded that convictions after impeachment are not reviewable. They relied primarily on the constitutional language and on historical understandings. Those who asserted that impeachment issues are reviewable relied primarily on the implications of Powell v. McCormack. Reexamine the data relied on in the Powell case: can a plausible case for the reviewability of impeachment issues be developed on the basis of that approach?[3]

1. For modern recognitions of commitments of constitutional issues to other branches, see Roudebush v. Hartke, 405 U.S. 15 (1972) (Art. I, § 5, commits to the Senate the final decision of which candidate "received more lawful votes" in an election for a Senate seat), and Gilligan v. Morgan, 413 U.S. 1 (1973) (Art. I, § 8, cl. 16, commits to Congress the authority to provide for "organizing, arming and disciplining the Militia"—now the National Guard).

2. For contrasting views on reviewability of convictions in impeachment proceedings, compare Berger, Impeachment: The Constitutional Problems (1973), with Black, Impeachment: A Handbook (1974).

3. See generally Committee on Federal Legislation of the Bar Association of the City of New York, The Law of Presidential Impeachment (1974). (A large majority of the Committee argued against reviewability.)

Part III

INDIVIDUAL RIGHTS

Scope Note. Part III focuses on the Constitution's protections of individual freedoms. Like most of Part II, this Part explores limitations on governmental power. In the preceding chapters, the argued limits stemmed from the allocations of power among governmental units—the division of powers between nation and states, and the separation of powers among the three branches of the national government. In the remaining chapters, the sources of the argued limits are the constitutional guarantees of individual rights. As with the earlier materials, the concern here goes well beyond the delineation of the past and present contours of constitutional doctrines. It extends to the recurrent problems regarding the process of constitutional interpretation. How can one give content to the constitutional guarantees? Are there legitimate sources of interpretation beyond text and history and structural inferences? Interpreting the relatively "specific" guarantees such as the First Amendment protections of freedom of speech and of religion is difficult enough. But the challenge is especially acute when the task is that of pouring content into the vague assurances of due process and equal protection in the 14th Amendment. Are those broad phrases appropriate vessels for judicial infusion of values drawn from sources other than constitutional text, history and structure? Do those phrases irresistibly tempt judges to read contemporary social, moral, and personal values into constitutional law?

In order to examine both the development of doctrine and the nature of the interpretive process, chap. 7, which follows, begins with a sketch of the constitutional framework and an initial venture into the problems of interpretation in a relatively uncomplicated context—the nationalizing impact on state criminal procedures of the 14th Amendment's due process guarantees. It contrasts the scope of constitutional guarantees in the original Constitution and in the post-Civil War Amendments; and it begins the exploration of the judicial function in the delineation of individual rights. A review of the "incorporation" controversy provides the vehicle for that initial exploration. Did the 14th Amendment's due process clause make the Bill of Rights—originally adopted as limits addressed solely to the federal government—applicable to the states as well? Or does the due process clause assign to the Court the more open-ended task of ascertaining what is "fundamental" to fair procedure? Are the Justices limited to enforcement of rights specified in the Constitution, or does that document authorize a broader Court function?

The tension reflected in the "incorporation" controversy echoes throughout the remaining materials. It emerges most controversially in chap. 8, on "substantive due process." The procedures by which personal rights and duties are delineated are the most obvious concerns of the due process provision; and the Court's preoccupation with criminal procedure problems in chap. 7 is accordingly a readily understandable impact of the due process clause. But the Court has not limited itself to a consideration of the *methods* of governmental action; since the late 19th century, the Court has found in due process constitutional restraints on the *content* of governmental action as well. The Court of an earlier generation found in substantive due process special protection of economic and property rights, and the rise and decline of that emphasis is traced in sec. 1 of chap. 8. The modern Court, even while repudiating that thrust of substantive due process, has elaborated a variation of its own: a constitutional protection of individual rights that are not explicit in the basic document—especially the personal rights of privacy and autonomy. That development is the focus of sec. 3 of chap. 8.

Chap. 9 turns to the developments in the interpretation of the equal protection clause of the 14th Amendment—developments occasionally parallel to those under the due process clause. From an initial concern with racial discrimination and a limited early impact on the means of governmental regulation, that clause came to have a far broader sweep during the Warren era. The "new" equal protection found constitutional safeguards for a variety of "fundamental interests," as in the area of voting. That value-laden process of equal protection interpretation bears considerable resemblance to the substantive due process mode noted above; indeed, some have referred to it as "substantive equal protection." Chap. 10 turns to two problems of 14th Amendment reach that have been most commonly raised in equal protection contexts: the applicability of the 14th Amendment's guarantees to "private" rather than "state" action; and the authority of Congress, under the enforcement power granted by § 5 of the Amendment, to enact its own interpretations of the scope of 14th Amendment guarantees, interpretations differing from the Court's delineation of the self-executing first section of the Amendment.[1]

Chaps. 11, 12, and 13 examine the guarantees of freedom of expression in the First Amendment, made applicable to the states as a result of interpretations of the 14th Amendment. The First Amendment's free speech guarantee is far more specific and explicit than the constitutional "rights" and "interests" that have emerged in the interpretations of substantive due process and the "new" equal protection. Nevertheless, the First Amendment has left ample room for controversy about the proper analysis and scope of its guarantees, as those chapters will illustrate. Chap. 14 turns to another controversial aspect of First Amendment interpretation, the religion clauses, which purport to assure the "free exercise" of religion and to safeguard against the "establishment" of religion. Chap. 15 returns to "procedural" and "jurisdictional" problems of judicial review in operation—a theme first taken up in Part I and explored further in that last chapter because the substantive contents of constitutional rights often affect the Court's dispositions of justiciability issues.

1. Somewhat similar problems about congressional powers are raised by the other post-Civil War Amendments as well, since each of those Amendments, the 13th and 15th as well as the 14th, concludes with a section granting power to Congress to "enforce" the Amendment "by appropriate legislation."

Chapter 7

THE BILL OF RIGHTS AND THE STATES:
SOME PROCEDURAL CONTENTS
OF DUE PROCESS

Introduction. The major theme of this chapter is the way in which the 14th Amendment's due process clause has been read to make applicable to state criminal proceedings virtually all of the procedural requirements that govern federal criminal law enforcement as a result of the Bill of Rights. That process of "incorporating" Bill of Rights guarantees into the 14th Amendment illustrates two larger themes. First, it provides a reminder of the federalism aspects of individual rights concerns. State constitutions typically contain bills of rights of their own; but the concern here is with the restraints imposed on the states by the *federal* Constitution. Those restraints were very few prior to the Civil War. The post-Civil War Amendments signified a major escalation in the national concern with the protection of individual rights from state governmental action. It was the 14th Amendment's due process clause that became the major vehicle for that nationalization of individual rights; and that Amendment looks to implementation of the new guarantees through the mechanism of a *national* Supreme Court and Congress. Federalism and individual rights concerns are frequently intertwined in the process of interpreting the scope of those new guarantees.

Second, this exploration of the *procedures* that due process requires of the states introduces the larger problems of the appropriate ingredients of due process interpretation.* It is easier to find a procedural content in the due process clause than to derive substantive due process doctrines from it; but even the procedural due process materials reflect the tensions that permeate all due process litigation—the tensions between "objective" standards and judicial subjectivity; between the specific and the vague; between the fixed and the flexible; between historical meaning and contemporary values; between ingredients readily traceable to constitutional text and structure and those resting ultimately on extraconstitutional values. To set the backdrop for the nationalizing impact of the post-Civil War Amendments, this chapter begins with a brief sketch of the pre-Civil War situation (sec. 1) and reviews the Court's earliest interpretation of the Amendments (sec. 2) before turning to the details of the "incorporation" dispute (sec. 3).

---

* The examination of procedural due process in this chapter is largely limited to the procedures constitutionally required in the administration of *criminal* law.

Procedural due process also plays a large role in delineating the process required in *civil* litigation and in administrative law. The discussion of the modern contours of procedural due process in the civil and administrative contexts is postponed until the final section of the next chapter, p. 566 below. The reason for that postponement is that the non-criminal procedural due process cases are of greatest interest in this book for the light they cast on the Court's interpretations of the "liberty" and "property" protected by the due process clauses of the Fifth and 14th Amendments.

SECTION 1. THE PRE–CIVIL WAR SITUATION

The 1787 document. There were relatively few references to individual rights in the original Constitution: its major concern was with governmental structures.[1] The most litigated limitation on state power protective of individual rights was the contracts clause. See p. 487 below. Moreover, prohibitions of state bills of attainder and ex post facto laws were coupled with the contract clause in Art. I, § 10; and Art. IV, § 4, announced that the "Citizens of each State shall be entitled to all Privileges and Immunities of Citizens in the several States." (See p. 307 above.) Nor was there a significantly broader spectrum of individual rights restrictions on the national government. Art. I, § 9, stated that the "privilege of the Writ of Habeas Corpus" could not be "suspended" and, paralleling restrictions on states, prohibited ex post facto laws and bills of attainder. And Art. III defined treason narrowly and assured jury trials in criminal cases.

The Bill of Rights. The ratification debates soon revealed that there was widespread demand for additional constitutional protection of individual—as well as states'—rights. In response to these pressures, Madison introduced proposals for constitutional amendments at the first session of Congress, and the first ten amendments were ratified in 1791. In the Barron case, which follows, the Marshall Court held that the Bill of Rights restricted only the national government and did not limit state authority. There was relatively little occasion for Court interpretation of the Bill of Rights before the Civil War—in part because federal criminal decisions were not ordinarily reviewable by the Supreme Court during those years.[2]

BARRON v. THE MAYOR AND CITY COUNCIL OF BALTIMORE

7 Pet. 243, 8 L.Ed. 672 (1833).

[Barron sued the City for ruining the use of his wharf in Baltimore harbor. He claimed that the City had diverted the flow of streams in the course of street construction work; that this diversion had deposited "large masses of sand and earth" near the wharf; and that the water had become too shallow for most vessels. The trial court awarded Barron $45,000, but the state appellate court reversed. Barron claimed that the state's action violated the guarantee (in the last phrase of the Fifth Amendment) that private property shall not be "taken for public use, without just compensation." The Court decided the issue of the applicability of the Fifth Amendment to state action in a jurisdictional context: under the jurisdictional statute, it could not review the case unless a federal right was involved; since in the Court's view, the Fifth Amendment did not limit state power, there was no jurisdiction. The Court rejected Barron's argument that the Fifth Amendment provision, "being in favour of the liberty of

---

1. Although the explicit guarantees of individual rights were sparse, the basic document's concerns with diffusion of power—the concerns of Part II of this book—do of course have an impact on personal autonomy, often indirectly and sometimes directly. Recall, e.g., the argument that a personal right to interstate mobility can be derived from the commerce clause, p. 315 above.

2. There was, however, widespread extrajudicial debate about the First Amendment, particularly during the controversy over the Alien and Sedition Acts of 1798. That debate proved of considerable importance in later litigation regarding freedom of expression. See p. 975 below.

the citizen, ought to be so construed as to restrain the legislative power of a state, as well as that of the United States."]

Mr. Chief Justice MARSHALL delivered the opinion of the Court.

[The question is], we think, of great importance, but not of much difficulty. The constitution was ordained and established by the people of the United States for themselves, for their own government, and not for the government of the individual states. Each state established a constitution for itself, and, in that constitution, provided such limitations and restrictions on the powers of its particular government as its judgment dictated. The people of the United States framed such a government for the United States as they supposed best adapted to their situation, and best calculated to promote their interests. The powers they conferred on this government were to be exercised by itself; and the limitations on power, if expressed in general terms, are naturally, and, we think, necessarily applicable to the government created by the instrument. They are limitations of power, granted in the instrument itself; not of distinct governments, framed by different persons and for different purposes. [If] these propositions be correct, the fifth amendment must be understood as restraining the power of the general government, not as applicable to the [states].

The ninth section [of Art. I] having enumerated, in the nature of a bill of rights, the limitations intended to be imposed on the powers of the general government, the tenth proceeds to enumerate those which were to operate on the state legislatures. These restrictions are brought together in the same section, and are by express words applied to the states. "No state shall enter into any treaty," &c. Perceiving that in a constitution framed by the people of the United States for the government of all, no limitation of the action of government on the people would apply to the state government, unless expressed in terms; the restrictions contained in the tenth section are in direct words so applied to the [states]. If the original constitution, in the ninth and tenth sections of the first article, draws this plain and marked line of discrimination between the limitations it imposes on the powers of the general government, and on those of the states; if in every inhibition intended to act on state power, words are employed which directly express that intent; some strong reason must be assigned for departing from this safe and judicious course in framing the amendments, before that departure can be assumed. We search in vain for that [reason]. Had the framers of these amendments intended them to be limitations on the powers of the state governments, they would have imitated the framers of the original constitution, and have expressed that intention. Had congress engaged in the extraordinary occupation of improving the constitutions of the several states by affording the people additional protection from the exercise of power by their own governments in matters which concerned themselves alone, they would have declared this purpose in plain and intelligible language.

But it is universally understood, it is a part of the history of the day, that the great revolution which established the constitution of the United States, was not effected without immense opposition. Serious fears were extensively entertained that those powers which the patriot statesmen, who then watched over the interests of our country, deemed essential to union, and to the attainment of those invaluable objects for which union was sought, might be exercised in a manner dangerous to liberty. In almost every convention by which the constitution was adopted, amendments to guard against the abuse of power were recommended. These amendments demanded security against the apprehended encroachments of the general government—not against those of the local governments. In compliance with a sentiment thus generally expressed, to quiet fears thus extensively entertained, amendments were proposed by the required majority in congress, and adopted by the states. These amendments contain no expression indicating an intention to apply them to the state governments. This court cannot so apply them. We are of opinion that the [just compensation] provision in the fifth amendment [is] intended solely as a limitation on the exercise of power by the government of the United States, and is not applicable to the legislation of the states. We are therefore of opinion that there is no repugnancy between the [state's action] and the constitution of the United States. This court, therefore, has no jurisdiction of the cause; and it is dismissed.

THE MARSHALL COURT'S POSITION

The Marshall Court's position that the Bill of Rights guarantees applied only to the national government and not to the states seemed a self-evident proposition to the Justices in 1833. Marshall described the question as "not of much difficulty"; indeed, counsel for the Baltimore officials—including soon-to-become Chief Justice Roger Brooke Taney—were "stopped by the Court" before they could complete their oral argument. But was the question all that easy? Note that a different inference might be drawn from the text of the Bill of Rights: the First Amendment explicitly inhibits "Congress" (but has been read to apply to the entire national government); the Seventh Amendment is explicitly addressed to "any Court of the United States"; all of the other Bill of Rights provisions speak in general terms. And a few courts, before Barron, thought those provisions generally applicable.[1] Yet Marshall—ordinarily not averse to nationalistic interpretations—refused to find the amendments applicable to the states; and his position prevailed. Note the bases of Marshall's reasoning, including his reliance on the structure of the Constitution and on "the history of the day."

SECTION 2. THE PURPOSE AND IMPACT OF THE POST–CIVIL WAR AMENDMENTS

Before the Civil War, as Barron v. Baltimore illustrates, the Constitution afforded individuals very limited protection against state action. The 13th, 14th and 15th Amendments, adopted soon after the Civil War, dramatically changed that picture. With the hindsight of more than a century, it is clear that those Amendments, and particularly the 14th, have spawned national protection of a wide range of individual rights, procedural and substantive. But that far-reaching impact was not immediately apparent. The immediate provocation for the Amendments was the Civil War concern with problems of slavery and emancipation. And the Court's first interpretation of the Amendments, in the Slaughter-House Cases below, rejected the effort to give the Amendments a content going beyond the problems which prompted them. Justice Miller's majority opinion, like Marshall's in Barron, relied strongly on historical memory: paralleling Marshall's reference to "the history of the day," Miller spoke of the history "fresh within the memory of us all"—the "history of the times" which showed the "one pervading purpose" of the Amendments to be "the freedom of the slave race, the security and firm establishment of that freedom,

---

1. See 2 Crosskey, Politics and the Constitution in the History of the United States (1953), 1049–82.

and the protection of the newly-made freeman and citizen from the oppressions of those who had formerly exercised unlimited dominion over him." To Miller and his colleagues in the majority, the Amendments were not to be given a reading which "radically changes the whole theory of the relations of the State and Federal governments to each other and of both these governments to the people"; they were not to be read to "constitute this court a perpetual censor upon all legislation of the States, on the civil rights of their own citizens." But Miller's position did not endure. Within a generation, the essence of the position of the dissenters prevailed, and a vast expansion of national power resulted.

The Slaughter-House Cases were immediately concerned with an effort to read substantive rather than procedural content into the Amendments: the effort was to use the Amendments as a weapon in support of free enterprise and against state monopoly legislation. The ultimate vindication of the dissenting position in the Slaughter-House Cases appears in the next chapter, in the materials tracing the rise of substantive due process. But the Slaughter-House Cases warrant attention here as well, for the decision implicitly speaks to the issue of the applicability to the states of the procedural guarantees of the Bill of Rights. The Slaughter-House majority's narrow reading of the Amendments meant temporary defeat for any claim that the Amendments amounted to a de facto overturning of Barron v. Baltimore. That narrow reading of the Amendments, tying them closely to the immediate historical background, meant that, for the time being, the procedural guarantees of the Bill of Rights would not be nationally enforceable safeguards in state criminal proceedings. It would be left to later generations and their broader readings of the Amendments to realize the full nationalizing potential of the post-Civil War changes. One realization came through the growth of substantive due process, traced in the next chapter. The other came in the selective (but by now virtually total) incorporation of Bill of Rights guarantees into the 14th, traced in sec. 3 of this chapter.

The Slaughter-House Cases also provide a useful, nearly contemporaneous perception of the historical background of the post-Civil War Amendments. As Justice Miller develops more fully, the 13th Amendment in 1865, gave constitutional sanction to President Lincoln's wartime Emancipation Proclamation. But that anti-slavery amendment did not end the problems of ex-slaves: their rights continued to be severely limited by the "black codes" of several states. Congress accordingly adopted the Civil Rights Act of 1866—over President Andrew Johnson's veto, based on constitutional grounds—and immediately set the amendment process in motion to assure the constitutional validity of that law. The 14th Amendment was ratified in 1868.[1] The 14th Amendment used even more sweeping, general terms than the Act it was designed to sustain: the Amendment's language was not limited to the problems of race, color, or previous condition of servitude. The last of the post-Civil War Amendments came two years later, in 1870; and that 15th Amendment did speak explicitly about racial discrimination, in voting. For generations, delineation of the scope of the Amendments was left almost entirely to the Court. But each of the three post-Civil War Amendments ended with a section authorizing Congress to enact legislation to enforce its provisions. Those congressional enforcement provisions, too, contained a vast nationalizing potential—a potential not realized until the abandonment of restrictive judicial interpretations and the revival of legislative interest in the 1960s, as the materials in chap. 10 demonstrate.

---

1. For the provisions of the post-Civil War Civil Rights Acts and their interrelationships with the Amendments and with modern civil rights laws, see chap. 10 below.

SLAUGHTER–HOUSE CASES

16 Wall. 36, 21 L.Ed. 394 (1873).

[A Louisiana law of 1869 chartered a corporation—the Crescent City Live-Stock Landing and Slaughter-House Company—and granted to it a 25-year monopoly "to maintain slaughterhouses, landings for cattle and stockyards" in three parishes. The parishes covered an area of 1154 square miles with a population of over 200,000, including the city of New Orleans. The law also prescribed the rates to be charged at the company's facilities. Butchers not included in the monopoly claimed that the law deprived them of their right "to exercise their trade" and challenged it under the 13th and 14th Amendments. The highest state court sustained the law.]

Mr. Justice MILLER delivered the opinion of the Court.

[The] regulation of the place and manner of conducting the slaughtering of animals [is] among the most necessary and frequent exercises of [the police] power. [The 1869 law] is aptly framed to remove from the more densely populated part of the city, the noxious slaughter-houses, and large and offensive collections of animals necessarily incident to [them], and to locate them where the convenience, health, and comfort of the people require they shall be located. [The] means adopted by the act for this purpose are appropriate, are stringent, and effectual. But it is said that in creating a corporation for this purpose, and conferring upon it exclusive privileges—privileges which it is said constitute a monopoly—the legislature has exceeded its power. [The only arguable constraints are those arising from the Federal Constitution. The challengers claim that the law created an "involuntary servitude" in violation of the 13th Amendment, and that it violated the 14th Amendment by abridging the "privileges and immunities" of citizens of the United States, denying the challengers "the equal protection of the laws," and depriving them "of their property without due process of law."] This Court is thus called upon for the first time to give construction to these [Amendments].

The most cursory glance at [the three post-Civil War Amendments] discloses a unity of purpose, when taken in connection with the history of the times, which cannot fail to have an important bearing on any question of doubt concerning their true meaning. Nor can such doubts, when any reasonably exist, be safely and rationally solved without a reference to that [history]. Fortunately that history is fresh within the memory of us all, and its leading features, as they bear upon the matter before us, free from doubt. [Undoubtedly] the overshadowing and efficient cause [of "the war of the rebellion"] was African slavery. In that struggle slavery, as a legalized social relation, perished. It perished as a necessity of the bitterness and force of the conflict. [Lincoln's Emancipation Proclamation] expressed an accomplished fact as to a large portion of the insurrectionary districts, when he declared slavery abolished in them all. But the war being over, those who had succeeded in re-establishing the authority of the Federal government were not content to permit this great act of emancipation to rest on the actual results of the contest or the proclamation of the Executive, both of which might have been questioned in after times, and they determined to place this main and most valuable result in the Constitution of the restored Union as one of its fundamental articles. Hence the [13th Amendment].

To withdraw the mind from the contemplation of this grand yet simple declaration of the personal freedom of all the human race within the jurisdiction of this government—a declaration designed to establish the freedom of four millions of slaves—and with a microscopic search endeavor to find in it a reference to servitudes, which may have been attached to property in certain localities, requires an effort, to say the least of it. That a personal servitude was meant is proved by the use of the word "involuntary," which can only apply to human beings. [The] word servitude is of larger meaning than slavery, as the latter is popularly understood in this country, and the obvious purpose was to forbid all shades and conditions of African slavery. It was very well understood that in the form of apprenticeship for long terms, as it had been practiced in the West India Islands, on the abolition of slavery by the English government, or by reducing the slaves to the condition of serfs attached to the plantation, the purpose of the article might have been evaded, if only the word slavery had been used. [And] it is all that we deem necessary to say [about the 13th Amendment].[1]

The process of restoring to their proper relations with the Federal government and with the other States those which had sided with the [rebellion] developed the fact that, notwithstanding the formal recognition by those States of the abolition of slavery, the condition of the slave race would, without further protection of the Federal government, be almost as bad as it was before. Among the first acts of legislation adopted by several of the States [were] laws which imposed upon the colored race onerous disabilities and burdens, and curtailed their rights in the pursuit of life, liberty, and property to such an extent that their freedom was of little value, while they had lost the protection which they had received from their former owners from motives both of interest and humanity. They were in some States forbidden to appear in the towns in any other character than menial servants. They were required to reside on and cultivate the soil without the right to purchase or own it. They were excluded from many occupations of gain, and were not permitted to give testimony in the courts in any case where a white man was a party. It was said that their lives were at the mercy of bad men, either because the laws for their protection were insufficient or were not enforced. These circumstances, whatever of falsehood or misconception may have been mingled with their presentation, forced upon the statesmen who had conducted the Federal government in safety through the crisis of the rebellion, and who supposed that by [the 13th Amendment] they had secured the result of their labors, the conviction that something more was necessary in the way of constitutional protection to the unfortunate race who had suffered so much. They accordingly [proposed the 14th Amendment].

[A] few years' experience satisfied the thoughtful men who had been the authors of the other two amendments that, notwithstanding the restraints of those articles on the States, and the laws passed under the additional powers granted to Congress, these were inadequate for the protection of life, liberty, and property, without which freedom to the slave was no boon. They were in all those States denied the right of suffrage. The laws were administered by the white man alone. It was urged that a race of men distinctively marked as was the negro, living in the midst of another and dominant race, could never be fully secured in their person and the property without the right of suffrage. Hence [the 15th Amendment].

---

1. The scope of the 13th Amendment—especially as a source of congressional power "rationally to determine what are the badges and the incidents of slavery" and to enact laws limiting private as well as state action—is examined in Jones v. Alfred H. Mayer Co. (1968; p. 924 below).

For a Court encounter with an application of the 13th Amendment to a problem other than racial discrimination, see Bailey v. Alabama, 219 U.S. 219 (1911), invalidating state laws which sought to compel "service of labor" under con-

tracts "by making it a crime to refuse or fail to perform it." But the Amendment does not ban all compulsory service—e.g., by military draftees, Selective Service Draft Law Cases, 245 U.S. 366 (1918). See generally tenBroek, "Thirteenth [Amendment]—Consummation to Abolition and Key to the Fourteenth Amendment," 39 Calif.L. Rev. 171 (1951), and on the enforcement of federal antipeonage laws, Shapiro, "Involuntary Servitude: The Need for a More Flexible Approach," 19 Rutgers L.Rev. 65 (1964).

We repeat, then, in the light of this recapitulation of events, almost too recent to be called history, but which are familiar to us all; and on the most casual examination of the language of these amendments, no one can fail to be impressed with the one pervading purpose found in them all, lying at the foundation of each, and without which none of them would have been even suggested; we mean the freedom of the slave race, the security and firm establishment of that freedom, and the protection of the newly-made freeman and citizen from the oppressions of those who had formerly exercised unlimited dominion over him. It is true that only the fifteenth amendment, in terms, mentions the negro by speaking of his color and his slavery. But it is just as true that each of the other articles was addressed to the grievances of that race, and designed to remedy them as the fifteenth. We do not say that no one else but the negro can share in this protection. Both the language and spirit of these articles are to have their fair and just weight in any question of construction. Undoubtedly while negro slavery alone was in the mind of the Congress which proposed the thirteenth article, it forbids any other kind of slavery, now or hereafter. If Mexican peonage or the Chinese coolie labor system shall develop slavery of the Mexican or Chinese race within our territory, this amendment may safely be trusted to make it void. And so if other rights are assailed by the States which properly and necessarily fall within the protection of these articles, that protection will apply, though the party interested may not be of African descent. But what we do say [is] that in any fair and just construction of any section or phrase of these amendments, it is necessary to look to the purpose which [was] the pervading spirit of them all, the evil which they were designed [to remedy].

The first section of the [14th Amendment], to which our attention is more specially invited, opens with a definition of citizenship. [I]t overturns the Dred Scott decision by making *all persons* born within the United States and subject to its jurisdiction citizens of the United States. That its main purpose was to establish the citizenship of the negro can admit [of no doubt]. The next observation is more important in view of the arguments of counsel in the present case. It is, that the distinction between citizenship of the United States and citizenship of a State is clearly recognized and established. Not only may a man be a citizen of the United States without being a citizen of a State, but an important element is necessary to convert the former into the latter. He must reside within the State to make him a citizen of it, but it is only necessary that he should be born or naturalized in the United States to be a citizen of the Union. It is quite clear, then, that there is a citizenship of the United States, and a citizenship of a State, which are distinct from each other, and which depend upon different characteristics or circumstances in the individual.

We think this distinction and its explicit recognition in this amendment of great weight in this argument, because the next paragraph of this same section, which is the one mainly relied on by the plaintiffs in error, speaks only of privileges and immunities of citizens of the United States, and does not speak of those of citizens of the several States. The argument, however, in favor of the plaintiffs rests wholly on the assumption that the citizenship is the same, and the privileges and immunities guaranteed by the clause are the same. The language is, "No State shall make or enforce any law which shall abridge the privileges or immunities of citizens of *the United States*." It is a little remarkable, if this clause was intended as a protection to the citizen of a State against the legislative power of his own State, that the word citizen of the State should be left out when it is so carefully used, and used in contradistinction to citizens of the United States, in the very sentence which precedes it. It is too clear for argument that the change in phraseology was adopted understandingly and with purpose. Of the privileges and immunities of the citizen of the United States, and of the privileges and immunities of the citizen of the State, and what they respectively are, we will presently consider; but we wish to state here that it is only the former which are placed by this clause under the protection of the Federal Constitution, and that the latter, whatever they may be, are not intended to have any additional protection by this paragraph of the [amendment].

In the Constitution, [Art. IV, § 2 (see p. 307 above) states]: "The citizens of each State shall be entitled to all the privileges and immunities of citizens of the several States." [W]e are not without judicial construction of this clause of the Constitution. The first and the leading case on the subject is that of Corfield v. Coryell, decided by Mr. Justice Washington in the Circuit Court [in] 1823. "The inquiry," he says, "is, what are the privileges and immunities of citizens of the several States? We feel no hesitation in confining these expressions to those privileges and immunities which are *fundamental*, which belong of right to the citizens of all free governments, and which have at all times been enjoyed by citizens of the several States which compose this Union, from the time of their becoming free, independent, and sovereign. What these fundamental principles are, it would be more tedious than difficult to enumerate. They may all, however, be comprehended under the following general heads: protection by the government, with the right to acquire and possess property of every kind, and to pursue and obtain happiness and safety, subject, nevertheless, to such restraints as the government may prescribe for the general good of the whole." [This] description, when taken to include others not named, but which are of the same general character, embraces nearly every civil right for the establishment and protection of which organized government is instituted. They are, in the language of Judge Washington, those rights which are fundamental. [T]hey have always been held to be the class of rights which the State governments were created to establish and secure. [Art. IV] did not create those rights, which it called privileges and immunities of citizens of the States. It threw around them in that clause no security for the citizen of the State in which they were claimed or exercised. Nor did it profess to control the power of the State governments over the rights of its own citizens. Its sole purpose was to declare to the several States, that whatever those rights, as you grant or establish them to your own citizens, or as you limit or qualify, or impose restrictions on their exercise, the same, neither more nor less, shall be the measure of the rights of citizens of other States within your jurisdiction.

[U]p to the adoption of the recent amendments, no claim or pretence was set up that those rights depended on the Federal government for their existence or protection, beyond the very few express limitations which the Federal Constitution imposed upon the [States]. But with the exception of these and a few other restrictions, the entire domain of the privileges and immunities of citizens of the [States] lay within the constitutional and legislative power of the States, and without that of the Federal government. Was it the purpose of the fourteenth amendment, by the simple declaration that no State should make or enforce any law which shall abridge the privileges and immunities of *citizens of the United States,* to transfer the security and protection of all the civil rights which we have mentioned, from the States to the Federal government? And where it is declared that Congress shall have the power to enforce that article, was it intended to bring within the power of Congress the entire domain of civil rights heretofore belonging exclusively to the States?

All this and more must follow, if the proposition of the plaintiffs in error be sound. For not only are these rights subject to the control of Congress whenever in its discretion any of them are supposed to be abridged by State legislation, but that body may also pass laws in advance, limiting and restricting the exercise of legislative power by the States, in their most ordinary and usual functions, as in its judgment it may think proper on all such subjects. And still further, such a construction followed by a reversal of the judgments of the Supreme Court of Louisiana in these cases, would constitute this court a perpetual censor upon all legislation of the States, on the civil rights of their own citizens, with authority to nullify such as it did not approve as consistent with those rights, as they existed at the time of the adoption of this amendment. The argument we admit is not always the most conclusive which is drawn from the consequences urged against the adoption of a particular construction of an instrument. But when, as in the case before us, these consequences are so serious, so far-reaching and pervading, so great a departure from the structure and spirit of our institutions; when the effect is to fetter and degrade the State governments by subjecting them to the control of Congress, in the exercise of powers heretofore universally conceded to them of the most ordinary and fundamental character; when in fact it radically changes the whole theory of the relations of the State and Federal governments to each other and of both these governments to the people; the argument has a force that is irresistible, in the absence of language which expresses such a purpose too clearly to admit of doubt. We are convinced that no such results were intended by the Congress which proposed these amendments, nor by the legislatures of the States which ratified them.

Having shown that the privileges and immunities relied on in the argument are those which belong to citizens of the States as such, and that they are left to the State governments for security and protection, and not by this article placed under the special care of the Federal government, we may hold ourselves excused from defining the privileges and immunities of citizens of the United States which no State can abridge, until some case involving those privileges may make it necessary to do so. But lest it should be said that no such privileges and immunities are to be found if those we have been considering are excluded, we venture to suggest some which owe their existence to the Federal government, its National character, its Constitution, or its laws. One of these is well described in the case of Crandall v. Nevada [6 Wall. 36 (1868) (p. 317 above)]. It is said to be the right of the citizen of this great country, protected by implied guarantees of its Constitution, "to come to the seat of government to assert any claim he may have upon that government, to transact any business he may have with it, to seek its protection, to share its offices, to engage in administering its functions. He has the right of free access to its seaports, through which all operations of foreign commerce are conducted, to the subtreasuries, land offices, and courts of justice in the several States." Another privilege of a citizen of the United States is to demand the care and protection of the Federal government over his life, liberty, and property when on the high seas or within the jurisdiction of a foreign government. [The] right to peaceably assemble and petition for redress of grievances, the privilege of the writ of habeas corpus, are rights of the citizen guaranteed by the Federal Constitution. The right to use the navigable waters of the United States, however they may penetrate the territory of the several States, all rights secured to our citizens by treaties with foreign nations, are dependent upon citizenship of the United States, and not citizenship of a State. [To] these may be added the rights secured by the thirteenth and fifteenth articles of amendment, and by the other clause of the fourteenth, next to be considered. [But] it is useless to pursue this branch of the inquiry, since we are of opinion that the rights claimed by these plaintiffs in error, if they have any existence, are not privileges and immunities of citizens of the United States within the meaning of the [clause under consideration].

The argument has not been much pressed in these cases that the defendant's charter deprives the plaintiffs of their property without due process of law, or that it denies to them the equal protection of the law. The first of these paragraphs has been in the Constitution since the adoption of the fifth amendment, as a restraint upon the Federal power. It is also to be found in some form of expression in the constitutions of nearly all the States, as a restraint upon the power of the States. [We] are not without judicial interpretation, therefore, both State and National, of the meaning of this clause. And it is sufficient to say that under no construction of that provision that we have ever seen, or any that we deem admissible, can the restraint imposed by [Louisiana] upon the exercise of their trade by the butchers of New Orleans be held to be a deprivation of property within the meaning of that provision.

"Nor shall any State deny to any person within its jurisdiction the equal protection of the laws." In the light of the history of these amendments, and the pervading purpose of them, [it] is not difficult to give a meaning to this clause. The existence of laws in the States where the newly emancipated negroes resided, which discriminated with gross injustice and hardship against them as a class, was the evil to be remedied by this clause, and by it such laws are forbidden. If, however, the States did not conform their laws to its requirements, then by the fifth section of the [Amendment] Congress was authorized to enforce it by suitable legislation. We doubt very much whether any action of a State not directed by way of discrimination against the negroes as a class, or on account of their race, will ever be held to come within the purview of this provision. It is so clearly a provision for that race and that emergency, that a strong case would be necessary for its application to any [other]. Unquestionably [the "late civil war"] added largely to the number of those who believe in the necessity of a strong National government. But, however pervading this sentiment, and however it may have contributed to the adoption of the amendments we have been considering, we do not see in those amendments any purpose to destroy the main features of the general system. Under the pressure of all the excited feeling growing out of the war, our statesmen have still believed that the existence of the States with powers for domestic and local government, including the regulation of civil rights—the rights of person and of property—was essential to the perfect working of our complex form of government, though they have thought proper to impose additional limitations on the States, and to confer additional power on that of the [Nation].

[Affirmed.]

Mr. Justice FIELD [joined by Chief Justice CHASE and Justices SWAYNE and BRADLEY], dissenting:

[The] question presented [is] one of the gravest [importance]. It is nothing less than the question whether the recent [Amendments] protect the citizens of the United States against the deprivation of their common rights by State legislation. In my judgment the fourteenth amendment does afford such [protection]. The amendment does not attempt to confer any new privileges or immunities upon citizens, or to enumerate or define those already existing. It assumes that there are such privileges and immunities which belong of right to citizens as such, and ordains that they shall not be abridged by State legislation. If this inhibition has no reference to privileges and immunities of this character, but only refers, as held by [the majority], to such privileges and immunities as were before its adoption specifically designated in the Constitution or necessarily implied as belonging to citizens of the United States, it was a vain and idle enactment, which accomplished [nothing]. With privileges and immunities thus designated or implied no State could ever have interfered by its laws, and no new constitutional provision was required to inhibit such interference. [But] if the amendment refers to the natural and inalienable rights which belong to all citizens, the inhibition has a profound [significance].

The terms, privileges and immunities, are not new in the amendment; they were in the Constitution before the amendment was adopted. [Justice Field, as had Justice Miller, quoted Justice Bushrod Washington's elaboration of Art. IV, § 2, in Corfield v. Coryell.] The privileges and immunities designated are those *which of right belong to the citizens of all free governments.* Clearly among these must be placed the right to pursue a lawful employment in a lawful manner, without other restraint than such as equally affects all persons. In the discussions in Congress upon the passage of the Civil Rights Act [of 1866] repeated reference was made to this language of Mr. Justice Washington. [What Art. IV, § 2] did for the protection of the citizens of one State against hostile and discriminating legislation of other States, the fourteenth amendment does for the protection of every citizen of the United States against hostile and discriminating legislation against him in favor of others, whether they reside in the same or in different States. If under the fourth article of the Constitution equality of privileges and immunities is secured between citizens of different States, under the fourteenth amendment the same equality is secured between citizens of the [United States].

This equality of right, with exemption from all disparaging and partial enactments, in the lawful pursuits of life, throughout the whole country, is the distinguishing privilege of citizens of the United States. To them, everywhere, all pursuits, all professions, all avocations are open without other restrictions than such as are imposed equally upon all others of the same age, sex, and condition. The State may prescribe such regulations for every pursuit and calling of life as will promote the public health, secure the good order and advance the general prosperity of society, but when once prescribed, the pursuit or calling must be free to be followed by every citizen who is within the conditions designated, and will conform to the regulations. This is the fundamental idea upon which our institutions rest, and unless adhered to in the legislation of the country our government will be a republic only in name. The fourteenth amendment, in my judgment, makes it essential to the validity of the legislation of every State that this equality of right should be respected. [I]t is to me a matter of profound regret that [the] validity [of the Louisiana law] is recognized by a majority of this court, for by it the right of free labor, one of the most sacred and imprescriptible rights of man, is violated.[1] [Grants] of exclusive privileges [are] opposed to the whole theory of free government, and it requires no aid from any bill of rights to render them void. That only is a free government, in the American sense of the term, under which the inalienable right of every citizen to pursue his happiness is unrestrained, except by just, equal, and impartial laws.[2]

Mr. Justice BRADLEY, also dissenting:

[In] my judgment, it was the intention of the people of this country in adopting [the 14th] amendment to provide National security against violation by the States of the fundamental rights of the citizen. [Any] law which

---

1. "The property which every man has in his own labor," says Adam Smith, "as it is the original foundation of all other property, so it is the most sacred and invoidable. The patrimony of the poor man lies in the strength and dexterity of his own hands; and to hinder him from employing this strength and dexterity in what manner he thinks proper, without injury to his neighbor, is a plain violation of this most sacred property. It is a manifest encroachment upon the just liberty both of the workman and of those who might be disposed to employ him. As it hinders the one from working at what he thinks proper, so it hinders the others from employing whom they think proper." (Smith's Wealth of Nations, b. 1, ch. 10, part 2.) [Footnote by Justice Field.]

2. "Civil liberty, the great end of all human society and government, is that state in which each individual has the power to pursue his own happiness according to his own views of his interest, and the dictates of his conscience, unrestrained, except by equal, just, and impartial laws." (1 Sharswood's Blackstone, 127, note 8.) [Footnote by Justice Field.]

establishes a sheer monopoly, depriving a large class of citizens of the privilege of pursuing a lawful employment, does abridge the privileges of those citizens. [In] my view, a law which prohibits a large class of citizens from adopting a lawful employment, or from following a lawful employment previously adopted, does deprive them of liberty as well as property, without due process of law. Their right of choice is a portion of their liberty; their occupation is their property. Such a law also deprives those citizens of the equal protection of the laws, contrary to the last clause of the section. [It] is futile to argue that none but persons of the African race are intended to be benefited by this amendment. They may have been the primary cause of the amendment, but its language is general, embracing all citizens, and I think it was purposely so [expressed].

But great fears are expressed that this construction of the amendment will lead to enactments by Congress interfering with the internal affairs of the [States]; or else, that it will lead the Federal courts to draw to their cognizance the supervision of State tribunals on every subject of judicial inquiry. [In] my judgment no such practical inconveniences would arise. Very little, if any, legislation on the part of Congress would be required to carry the amendment into effect. Like the prohibition against passing a law impairing the obligation of a contract, it would execute itself. [Even] if the business of the National courts should be increased, Congress could easily supply the remedy by increasing their number and efficiency. The great question is, What is the true construction of the amendment? When once we find that, we shall find the means of giving it effect. The argument from inconvenience ought not to have a very controlling influence in questions of this sort. The National will and National interest are of far greater [importance].[3]

THE AFTERMATH OF THE SLAUGHTER–HOUSE CASES: PRIVILEGES AND IMMUNITIES; DUE PROCESS

1. *Privileges and immunities of national citizenship.* The framers of the 14th Amendment had great difficulty in articulating a specific content for its broad phrases—"due process," "equal protection," "privileges and immunities." In no part of the congressional debates on the Amendment is there greater evidence of vagueness and inconsistencies than in the discussions of "privileges and immunities."[1] The Court has not been able to be much more concrete since. There have been only sporadic attempts to give the clause a more expansive scope than that found by Justice Miller in 1873. His majority position in the Slaughter-House Cases has so far prevailed: the clause is limited to a few rights of national (as distinct from state) citizenship.[2] Even though the language of the clause speaks to substantive matters more explicitly than do the

---

3. Justice SWAYNE also submitted a dissent.

1. Note a contemporary recollection that the clause "came from [Congressman] Bingham of Ohio. Its euphony and indefiniteness of meaning were a charm to him." See Fairman, "Does the Fourteenth Amendment Incorporate the Bill of Rights? The Original Understanding," 2 Stan.L. Rev. 5 (1949). Compare Graham, "Our 'Declaratory' Fourteenth Amendment," 7 Stan.L.Rev. 3 (1954). Note Justice Black's comments on Professor Fairman and on Congressman Bingham in Duncan v. Louisiana, p. 430 below.

2. The privileges and immunities clause has been relied on only once for a majority invalidation of a state law, in Colgate v. Harvey, 296 U.S. 404 (1935), striking down a Vermont tax

provision. But that interpretation of the clause was short-lived: Colgate was overruled in Madden v. Kentucky, 309 U.S. 83 (1940), where the Court reiterated Justice Miller's position. For examples of reliances on the clause by individual Justices, see Edwards v. California (1941; p. 315 above; concurring opinion of Justice Douglas joined by Justices Black and Murphy—"[t]he right to move freely from State to State"); Hague v. CIO (1939; p. 1197 below) (concurring opinion by Justice Roberts, joined by Justice Black— right to assemble and "discuss national legislation"). Note also Justice Black's partial reliance on the clause in explaining his "incorporationist" position—e.g., in his dissent in Duncan v. Louisiana, p. 430 below.

companion clauses in the first section of the 14th Amendment, the development of privileges and immunities has been overshadowed by expanding views of due process and equal protection, as the remaining materials in this volume illustrate.

For an early 20th century effort to catalogue national privileges and immunities, see Twining v. New Jersey, 211 U.S. 78 (1908), which lists the right to travel from state to state, to petition Congress, to vote for national offices, to enter the public lands, the right to be "protected against violence while in the lawful custody of a United States marshal," and "the right to inform the United States authorities of violation of its laws." Consider this list, and recall also Justice Miller's potpourri of rights "which owe their existence to the Federal government, its National character, its Constitution, or its laws." Was the privileges and immunities clause necessary to give constitutional protection to any of these? Were they not already protected, by the structural limitations implied under the McCulloch approach? And did not Congress accordingly have power to safeguard all of them even without the 14th Amendment? [3]

What explains the Court's reluctance to give a broader content to the 14th Amendment's privileges and immunities clause? Arguably, a striving for the broad reading rejected in the Slaughter-House Cases became no longer necessary when later Courts read the due process and equal protection clauses expansively. Perhaps the Court was reluctant to expand the privileges and immunities clause because it is limited to the "citizen," while the due process and equal protection clauses apply to any "person" (and "persons" include corporations). It is nevertheless possible that the moribund privileges and immunities clause may yet be revived, as a last resort shelter for expansive judicial interpretations when the elastic capacities of due process and equal protection come to be perceived as exhausted. Note the "prognosis" based on "the existent and potential needs that the privileges or immunities clause may be able to meet"—a "prognosis" by a critic of many of the Warren Court's expansions of equal protection and due process, Professor Philip B. Kurland, in "The Privileges or Immunities Clause: 'Its Hour Come Round at Last'?" 1972 Wash.U.L.Q. 405: "With government in control of so many essentials of our life, where in the Constitution can we turn for haven against the impositions of 1984? [I]f the legislative and executive discretion is to be limited by the Constitution on such matters as public education, public welfare, and public housing; police, fire, and sanitation; ecology; [and], most importantly, with reference to the right of privacy, I expect it will come as an attempt to define the privileges or immunities of American citizenship." See also Ely, Democracy and Distrust (1980), arguing that "the most plausible interpretation of the [Clause] is the one suggested by its language—that it was a delegation to future constitutional decision-makers to protect certain rights that the document neither lists, at least not exhaustively, nor even in any specific way gives directions for finding." [4]

3. The power of Congress to enforce individual rights stemming from sources other than the 14th Amendment is pursued in chap. 10, sec. 3, especially in connection with United States v. Guest (1966; p. 905 below).

4. Note also the efforts by some commentators to find justifications for broad readings in still another neglected provision of the 14th Amendment—the first sentence, conferring citizenship. For example, Professor Charles L. Black, Jr. has argued that the citizenship conferral could serve as an alternative basis for modern Court expansions of due process and equal protection, especially in the race area. Black, Structure and Relationship in Constitutional Law (1969). Note, moreover, Professor Kenneth L. Karst's imaginative argument that the "substantive core" of the 14th Amendment is "a principle of equal citizenship, which presumptively guarantees to each individual a right to be treated by the organized society as a respected, responsible, and participating member." Karst, "Foreword: Equal Citizenship under the Fourteenth Amendment," 91 Harv.L.Rev. 1 (1977).

2. *Due process.* Though the efforts to turn the privileges and immunities clause into a significant instrument for protection of individual rights have failed so far, many of the arguments of the dissenters in the Slaughter-House Cases have found their way into majority opinions through the channels of the due process and equal protection clauses. Thus, the insistence of dissenting Justice Bradley that the due process clause imposed substantive limits on state economic regulation was echoed by other dissenters for the next generation. By the end of the 19th century, a majority of the Court embraced substantive due process; and in the first three decades of the 20th century, the Court applied that doctrine frequently. Since the mid-1930s, the Court has repudiated most substantive limits on state regulation of economic affairs. Yet a substantive due process approach has reemerged more recently, on behalf of personal rights such as privacy, as discussed in the next chapter. Moreover, a range of fundamental interests have found protection in the modern emergence of the "new" equal protection.[5]

Among the broad positions implicitly rejected by the Slaughter-House Cases was the position that all the Bill of Rights guarantees were made applicable to the states by the post-Civil War constitutional changes.[6] What criminal procedure protections *were* made available in state cases as a result of the 14th Amendment's due process clause? The majority's narrow reading in the Slaughter-House Cases did not mark the end of the development of procedural due process any more than it signified a permanent halt to the evolution of substantive guarantees. But the course of development of procedural rights has differed from that respecting substantive ones. Wholesale incorporation of Bill of Rights guarantees into the 14th Amendment continues to be rejected by the Court; but the modern Court's technique of "selective incorporation" has achieved virtually the same result—nearly all of the procedural protections in the first eight Amendments now apply to the states in the same way in which they restrict federal criminal proceedings. The next section traces that development.

SECTION 3.   THE MEANING OF DUE PROCESS: CRIMINAL PROCEDURE AND THE "INCORPORATION" CONTROVERSY

Introduction. On its face, the due *process* clause most obviously governs problems of procedure. But what are the aspects of criminal procedure that the due process guarantee of the 14th Amendment requires the states to provide?[1] That issue has provoked heated debates on the Court; and pursuit of that question provides a useful introductory vehicle for exploring the difficulties of

---

5. These developments are traced in chaps. 8 and 9, below.

6. Compare Ely, Democracy and Distrust (1980), 196–97, questioning this sentence in the text and arguing that "a close reading of the various opinions [suggests] at least the possibility that all nine justices meant to take exactly that position!" In Ely's view, all nine Justices "appear" to have endorsed, "with varying degrees of clarity," the proposition that "whatever else it did, the Privileges or Immunities Clause at least applied to the states the constitutionally stated prohibitions that had previously applied only to the federal government."

1. This section's emphasis on criminal procedure is not intended as an exhaustive survey of all constitutional aspects of the criminal process; that task is left to other courses. The purpose of this section is simply to illustrate recurrent controversies about giving content to the procedural aspects of 14th Amendment due process. (Moreover, as noted earlier, problems of procedural due process outside the criminal context are postponed until the last section of the next chapter, p. 566 below.)

defining the meaning of due process. The Court's battles over issues of state criminal procedure have taken place in the larger arena of the "incorporation" controversy: Did the 14th Amendment "incorporate" or "absorb" all of the Bill of Rights guarantees and make them applicable to the states? For decades after the Slaughter-House Cases, the Court was very reluctant to impose federal constitutional requirements on state procedures; but it clothed that reluctance in formulas which proved ultimately expansive after all.

The traditional Court position was that only "fundamental" matters—rights essential to "fundamental principles of liberty and justice," rights "essential to a fair trial"—were constitutionally required in state proceedings. Those broad formulations, which have their origins in late 19th century cases, have been most articulately elaborated in the 20th century by Justices Cardozo, Frankfurter, Harlan and Powell. Beginning in the 1940s, however, a forceful counterposition began to be voiced, especially by Justice Black. He insisted that the 14th Amendment *did* incorporate the "specific" guarantees of the Bill of Rights; he objected to the vague, "natural law" formulations of the majority that spoke in terms of "fundamentals." That battle over the meaning and historical intent of due process is traced in the series of decisions beginning with Palko and Adamson below. Are at least some of the guarantees of the Bill of Rights applicable to the states as a result of the 14th Amendment? If so, do those guarantees limit the states in precisely the same way that they restrain the national government?

As the concluding cases in this chapter (beginning with Duncan) illustrate, the outcome of the incorporation battle is fairly well settled: as to doctrine, the majority has adhered to the "fundamental rights" approach and has refused to accept Justice Black's wholesale incorporation notion; in practice, most of the procedural guarantees of the Bill of Rights *have* been incorporated into the 14th Amendment, and the incorporated guarantees apply to the states in precisely the same way that they restrain the national government. Nevertheless, that battle is worth examining, especially for the light it throws on due process methodology. The controversy over procedural due process echoes as well as anticipates some of the continuing concerns about the judicial subjectivity long associated with substantive due process. What are the guidelines available to the Court in giving content to due process? Consider first the potential guidance available from text, early interpretations, and English history.

1. *Due process and procedure before the Civil War.* The procedural aspects of due process were not a wholly blank slate when the clause was put into the 14th Amendment. The Court had already had occasion to speak about the history and scope of due process in the course of interpreting the due process clause of the Fifth Amendment. The best known statement was that by Justice Curtis in the course of considering the constitutionality of a distress warrant procedure in Murray's Lessee v. Hoboken Land & Improvement Co., 59 U.S. 272 (1856): "The words, 'due process of law,' were undoubtedly intended to convey the same meaning as the words, 'by the law of the land,' in Magna Charta. [The] constitution contains no description of those processes which it was intended to allow or forbid. It does not even declare what principles are to be applied to ascertain whether it be due process. [The clause] is a restraint on the legislative as well as on the executive and judicial powers of the government. [To] what principles, then, are we to resort to ascertain whether this process, enacted by congress, is due process? To this the answer must be twofold. We must examine the constitution itself, to see whether this process be in conflict with any of its provisions. If not found to be so, we must look to those settled usages and modes of proceeding existing in the common and statute law of England, before the emigration of our ancestors, and which are shown not to have been unsuited to their civil and political condition by having been acted on

by them after the settlement of this country. [T]hough 'due process of law' generally implies and includes actor, reus, judex, regular allegations, opportunity to answer and a trial according to some settled course of judicial proceedings, [this] is not universally true." As Justice Curtis' last sentence indicates, concepts of notice and hearing have been at the core of due process from the beginning; and adaptation of those concepts to varied circumstances has contributed greatly to the flexibility of procedural due process. (See, e.g., Powell v. Alabama, note 2 below.) But Justice Curtis' major emphasis is not on flexibility but on a more confining, static reference, to English history. That history has indeed proved useful, but the Court has not limited itself to that source.

2. *The inadequacy of English history.* English history has been decisive in some cases,[2] but that history may at times be silent; and even where it speaks, the Court has not felt compelled to listen. A good example is Powell v. Alabama, 287 U.S. 45 (1932), where the Court for the first time found a limited right to counsel essential to due process in some criminal cases, despite the lack of a corresponding guarantee in the English practice of the late 18th century. In England, a full right to representation by counsel in felony cases was not granted until 1836, almost 50 years after the adoption of the U.S. Constitution. But that did not stop the Court from requiring the appointment of counsel in a capital case such as Powell. The Court relied on the "unanimous accord" in the American states regarding appointment of counsel in capital cases: it was that American practice that lent "convincing support to the conclusion we have reached as to the fundamental nature of that right." And in deriving that right, the Court reached back to the core meaning of due process articulated by Justice Curtis in note 1 above: the Powell Court emphasized that "notice and hearing" were "basic elements of the constitutional requirement of due process of law"; and the concept of a "hearing," in turn, was the basis for inferences as to legal representation: "The right to be heard would be, in many cases, of little avail if it did not comprehend the right to be heard by counsel."

Thus, the Court has not attempted to tie American lawmakers to the English tradition. For example, Hurtado v. California, 110 U.S. 516 (1884), sustained a California statute which permitted criminal proceedings to be instituted by information rather than by grand jury indictment. In explaining that conclusion, the Court used a phrase—"principles of liberty and justice"—characteristic of the flexible, open-ended majority view during much of the 20th century incorporation controversy, traced below. The Hurtado opinion stated: "There is nothing in Magna Charta [that] ought to exclude the best ideas of all systems and of every age. [Any] legal proceeding enforced by public authority, whether sanctioned by age and custom, or newly devised in the discretion of the legislative power, in furtherance of the general public good, which regards and [preserves] principles of liberty and justice, must be held to be due process of law." Not the details of English practice, but "principles of liberty and justice," became the dominant ingredients of due process. As used in cases such as Hurtado, that broad formula tended to minimize federal intervention in state criminal procedures. That, too, was the thrust of later variations on the Hurtado theme in cases such as Palko and Adamson. But, as the more recent cases show, references to vague standards such as "fundamental justice" also provided the Court with the bases for an increasing nationalization of standards of state criminal procedure.

---

2. See, e.g., Ownbey v. Morgan, 256 U.S. 94 (1921), where the Court sustained the validity of a Delaware statute under which, in foreign attachment proceedings, special bail was required of defendant as a condition of being heard on the merits. The statute in question had been modeled on the Custom of London and had been on the statute books of Delaware from early colonial days.

A. THE PALKO–ADAMSON DISPUTE: DO THE BILL OF RIGHTS GUARANTEES APPLY TO STATE CRIMINAL PROCEEDINGS?

THE BATTLE BETWEEN "SELECTIVE" AND "TOTAL" INCORPORATION

Introduction. Did the 14th Amendment in effect "incorporate" the provisions of the Bill of Rights and make them fully applicable to the states? The majority of the Court has never accepted that view. Instead, the dominant position has been that the due process clause merely requires "fundamental fairness" in state criminal proceedings. But for decades the majority has recognized that the "fundamental fairness" criterion may afford the defendant in the state criminal process a range of rights that correspond to some of the individual guarantees in the Bill of Rights. As the Court recognized as early as 1908, in Twining v. New Jersey, 211 U.S. 78: "It is possible that some of the personal rights safeguarded by the first eight Amendments against National action may also be safeguarded against state action, because a denial of them would be a denial of due process of law. If this is so, it is not because those rights are enumerated in the first eight Amendments, but because they are of such a nature that they are included in the conception of due process." That "selective" incorporation position was eloquently expounded by Justice Cardozo in Palko in 1937 (note 1 below) and was reiterated by Justice Frankfurter in Adamson in 1947 (note 2 below). But in a strong dissent in Adamson, Justice Black insisted on a different view: he argued that the 14th Amendment, rather than signifying vague notions of "fundamental fairness," meant that *all* of the individual guarantees in the Bill of Rights applied to the states. In theory, "selective" incorporation continues to be the majority view. In result, virtually all of Justice Black's ends have been achieved: the Court *has* found almost all of the Bill of Rights guarantees pertaining to the criminal process applicable to the states; but the Court has achieved that result by finding the Bill of Rights guarantees "fundamental" one by one, rather than by incorporating them in one fell swoop, as Justice Black would have done.[1]

Two themes predominate in the Palko-Adamson debate between the Cardozo-Frankfurter position and that of Black. One concerns questions of federalism; the other, problems of "objective" standards and judicial subjectivity. Cardozo and Frankfurter defended their refusal to incorporate all of the Bill of Rights into the 14th Amendment by arguing that such a position would unduly nationalize state criminal processes and would unduly limit state autonomy in the enforcement of criminal law. Black's recurrent rejoinder was that the majority's "fundamental fairness"-"essence of a scheme of ordered liberty" approach was too vague and open-ended and left too much room for subjective views. Black insisted that his "total" incorporation view would curb excessive judicial discretion by relying on the allegedly clearer standards of the "specific" guarantees of the Bill of Rights.

1. The range of rights "selectively" incorporated is reflected in Duncan v. Louisiana (1968; p. 430 below). However, as Duncan also indicates, the content of the Court's "selective" incorporation approach has changed since the days of Palko and Adamson. Instead of asking whether a particular guarantee is "implicit in the concept of ordered liberty," the modern Court asks whether the guarantee found in the Bill of Rights is "fundamental to the American scheme of justice" or "fundamental in the context of the criminal processes maintained by the American states." See the Duncan majority's footnote [11], p. 431 below.

1. *"Selective" incorporation: Cardozo in Palko.* In **PALKO v. CONNECTICUT**, 302 U.S. 319 (1937), Justice CARDOZO provided the best known articulation of the "selective" incorporation approach dominant on the Court for most of the 20th century. Connecticut permitted the State to take appeals in criminal cases. Palko's second degree murder conviction had been set aside by the highest state court on an appeal taken by the State. On retrial, he was convicted of first degree murder. He claimed that such a retrial in the federal courts would have violated the Fifth Amendment's double jeopardy guarantee, and insisted that "whatever is forbidden by the Fifth Amendment is forbidden by the Fourteenth also." Moreover, he argued more broadly that whatever would be "a violation of the original bill of rights [if] done by the federal government is now equally unlawful by force of the 14th Amendment if done by a state." Justice Cardozo replied: "There is no such general rule." He noted that the Court had refused to apply some Bill of Rights guarantees to the states (e.g., the grand jury indictment requirement and the protection against self-incrimination) even though other limits—such as free speech and aspects of the right to counsel—had been imposed on the states via the 14th Amendment. Explaining the criteria which determined which Bill of Rights safeguards were applicable to the states and which were not, Justice Cardozo stated:

"The line of division may seem to be wavering and broken if there is a hasty catalogue of the cases on the one side and the other. Reflection and analysis will induce a different view. There emerges the perception of a rationalizing principle which gives to discrete instances a proper order and coherence. The right to trial by jury and the immunity from prosecution except as the result of an indictment may have value and importance. Even so, they are not of the very essence of a scheme of ordered liberty. To abolish them is not to violate a 'principle of justice so rooted in the traditions and conscience of our people as to be ranked as fundamental.' Snyder v. Massachusetts, [291 U.S. 97 (1934)]. Few would be so narrow or provincial as to maintain that a fair and enlightened system of justice would be impossible without them. What is true of jury trials and indictments is true also [of] the immunity from compulsory self-incrimination. This too might be lost, and justice still be [done].

"We reach a different plane of social and moral values when we pass to [those guarantees of the Bill of Rights] brought within the [14th Amendment] by a process of absorption. These in their origin were effective against the federal government alone. If the [14th Amendment] has absorbed them, the process of absorption has had its source in the belief that neither liberty nor justice would exist if they were sacrificed. This is true, for illustration, of freedom of thought, and speech. Of that freedom one may say that it is the matrix, the indispensable condition, of nearly every other form of [freedom]. Fundamental too in the concept of due process, and so in that of liberty, is the thought that condemnation shall be rendered only after trial. [The] hearing, moreover, must be a real one, not a sham or a pretense. Moore v. Dempsey, 261 U.S. 86 [1923]. For that reason, ignorant defendants in a capital case were held to have been condemned unlawfully when in truth, though not in form, they were refused the aid of counsel. [Powell v. Alabama, above.] The decision did not turn upon the fact that the benefit of counsel would have been guaranteed to the defendants by [the] Sixth Amendment if they had been prosecuted in a federal court. The decision turned upon the fact that in the particular situation laid before us in the evidence the benefit of counsel was essential to the substance of a hearing.

"Our survey of the cases serves, we think, to justify the statement that the dividing line between them, if not unfaltering throughout its course, has been true for the most part to a unifying principle. On which side of the line the case made out by the appellant has appropriate location must be the next inquiry and the final one. Is that kind of double jeopardy to which the statute has subjected him a hardship so acute and shocking that our polity will not endure it? Does it violate those 'fundamental principles of liberty and justice which lie at the base of all our civil and political institutions'? Hebert v. Louisiana [272 U.S. 312 (1926)]. The answer surely must be 'no.' What the answer would have to be if the state were permitted after a trial free from error to try the accused over again or to bring another case against him, we have no occasion to consider. [The] state is not attempting to wear the accused out by a multitude of cases with accumulated trials. It asks no more than this, that the case against him shall go on until there shall be a trial free from the corrosion of substantial legal error. [This] is not cruelty at all, nor even vexation in any immoderate [degree]." [1]

2. *"Total" incorporation: Black's argument in Adamson, and Frankfurter's response.* Ten years after Palko, the majority adhered to Justice Cardozo's approach and rejected a strong challenge by Justice Black. In ADAMSON v. CALIFORNIA, 332 U.S. 46 (1947), Adamson claimed that his murder conviction violated the 14th Amendment because, in accordance with state law, the prosecution had been permitted to comment on his failure to take the stand at his trial. Justice Reed's majority opinion assumed that such a comment would violate the 5th Amendment's self-incrimination privilege in a federal proceeding. He conceded, moreover, that the 14th Amendment's due process clause guaranteed a right to a "fair trial." But, under Palko, not all Bill of Rights guarantees were protected by the 14th Amendment, and he found no ground to make the self-incrimination privilege applicable to the states in its "full scope under the 5th Amendment."

Justice BLACK's dissent, joined by Justice Douglas, contains the most famous exposition of the "total" incorporation position. He insisted that full incorporation of all Bill of Rights guarantees was the "original purpose" of the 14th Amendment and accordingly concluded that "the full protection of the Fifth Amendment's proscription against compelled testimony must be afforded" in the Adamson case. He explained: "This decision reasserts a constitutional theory spelled out in [Twining], that this Court is endowed by the Constitution with boundless power under 'natural law' periodically to expand and contract constitutional standards to conform to the Court's conception of what at a particular time constitutes 'civilized decency' and 'fundamental liberty and justice.' [I] would not reaffirm [Twining]. I think that decision and the 'natural law' theory of the Constitution upon which it relies degrade the constitutional safeguards of the Bill of Rights and simultaneously appropriate for this Court a broad power which we are not authorized by the Constitution to exercise. My reasons for believing that [Twining] should not be revitalized can best be understood by reference to the constitutional, judicial and general history that preceded and followed the [case].

"I am attaching to this dissent an appendix which contains a résumé, by no means complete, of the Amendment's history.[2] In my judgment that history

1. In Benton v. Maryland, 395 U.S. 784 (1969), the Court held that the Fifth Amendment's double jeopardy guarantee "should apply to the States through the Fourteenth." The Court added: "Insofar as it is inconsistent with this holding, Palko v. Connecticut is overruled."

2. The appendix is omitted. For an historical examination disagreeing with Justice Black's position, see Fairman, "Does the Fourteenth Amendment Incorporate the Bill of Rights? The Original Understanding," 2 Stan.L.Rev. 5 (1949). Justice Black reviewed the historical dispute and

replied to Fairman in the 1968 decision in Duncan (p. 430 below). Searches in the origins of the 14th Amendment have been inconclusive. Compare Fairman's criticism of the Black position with Crosskey, "Charles Fairman, 'Legislative History,' and the Constitutional Limitations on State Authority," 22 U.Chi.L.Rev. 1 (1954).

The implications of the "incorporation" controversy have engendered an even wider range of commentary than the historical debate. See, e.g., Schaefer, "Federalism and State Criminal Procedures," 70 Harv.L.Rev. 1 (1956); Henkin, " 'Se-

conclusively demonstrates that the language of the first section of the Fourteenth Amendment, taken as a whole, was thought by those responsible for its submission to the people, and by those who opposed its submission, sufficiently explicit to guarantee that thereafter no state could deprive its citizens of the privileges and protections of the Bill of Rights. Whether this Court ever will, or whether it now should, in the light of past decisions, give full effect to what the Amendment was intended to accomplish is not necessarily essential to a decision here. However that may be, our prior decisions, including Twining, do not prevent our carrying out that purpose, at least to the extent of making applicable to the states, not a mere part, as the Court has, but the full protection of the Fifth Amendment's provision against compelling evidence from an accused to convict him of crime. And I further contend that the 'natural law' formula which the Court uses to reach its conclusion in this case should be abandoned as an incongruous excrescence on our Constitution. [I] fear to see the consequences of the Court's practice of substituting its own concepts of decency and fundamental justice for the language of the Bill of Rights as its point of departure in interpreting and enforcing that Bill of Rights. If the choice must be between the selective process of the Palko decision applying some of the Bill of Rights to the States, or the Twining rule applying none of them, I would choose the Palko selective process. But rather than accept either of these choices, I would follow what I believe was the original purpose of the Fourteenth Amendment—to extend to all the people of the nation the complete protection of the [Bill of Rights].

"It is an illusory apprehension that literal application of some or all of the provisions of the Bill of Rights to the States would unwisely increase the sum total of the powers of this Court to invalidate state legislation. [It] must be conceded, of course, that the natural-law-due-process formula, which the Court today reaffirms, has been interpreted to limit substantially this Court's power to prevent state violations of the individual civil liberties guaranteed by the Bill of Rights. But this formula also has been used in the past, and can be used in the future, to license this Court in considering regulatory legislation, to roam at large in the broad expanses of policy and morals and to trespass, all too freely, on the legislative domain of the States as well as the Federal Government. [See chap. 8, sec. 1, below.] Since [Marbury], the practice has been firmly established [that] courts can strike down legislative enactments which violate the Constitution. This process, of course, involves interpretation, and since words can have many meanings, interpretation obviously may result in contraction or extension of the original purpose of a constitutional provision thereby affecting policy. But to pass upon the constitutionality of statutes by looking to the particular standards enumerated in the Bill of Rights and other parts of the Constitution is one thing; to invalidate statutes because of application of 'natural law' deemed to be above and undefined by the Constitution is another. 'In the one instance, courts proceeding within clearly marked constitutional boundaries seek to execute policies written into the Constitution; in the other, they roam at will in the limitless area of their own beliefs as to reasonableness and actually select policies, a responsibility which the Constitution entrusts to the legislative representatives of the people.' "[3]

lective Incorporation' in the 14th Amendment," 73 Yale L.J. 74 (1963); and Friendly, "The Bill of Rights as a Code of Criminal Procedure," 53 Calif.L.Rev. 929 (1965).

3. In a separate dissent, Justice MURPHY, joined by Justice Rutledge, announced something of a "having your cake and eating it too" position. He agreed with Justice Black that "the specific guarantees of the Bill of Rights should be carried over intact into the first section of the [14th] Amendment," but added: "I am not prepared to say that the latter is entirely and necessarily limited by the Bill of Rights. Occasions may arise where a proceeding falls so far short of conforming to fundamental standards of procedure as to warrant constitutional condemnation in terms of a lack of due process despite the absence of a specific provision in the Bill of Rights."

In a concurring opinion, Justice FRANKFURTER mounted an extensive attack on Justice Black's "total" incorporation position. He insisted that the 14th Amendment's due process clause has "independent potency" and an "independent function": it "neither comprehends the specific provisions by which the founders deemed it appropriate to restrict the federal government nor is it confined to them." Rejecting the view that the 14th Amendment is "a shorthand summary of the first eight amendments," he argued that to draw support for Adamson's claim "out of 'due process' in its protection of ultimate decency in a civilized society is to suggest that the Due Process Clause fastened fetters of unreason upon the States." He elaborated: "To suggest that it is inconsistent with a truly free society to begin prosecutions without an indictment, to try petty civil cases without the paraphernalia of a common law jury, [or] to take into consideration that one who has full opportunity to make a defense remains silent, is, in de Tocqueville's phrase, to confound the familiar with the necessary. [It] would be extraordinarily strange for a Constitution to convey such specific commands in such a roundabout and inexplicit way [as the phrase 'due process of law']." He added:

"Those reading the English language with the meaning which it ordinarily conveys, those conversant with the political and legal history of the concept of due process, those sensitive to the relations of the States to the central government as well as the relation of some of the provisions of the Bill of Rights to the process of justice, would hardly recognize the [14th Amendment] as a cover for the various explicit provisions of the first [eight]. [At] the time of the ratification of the Fourteenth Amendment the constitutions of nearly half of the ratifying States did not have the rigorous requirements of the Fifth Amendment for instituting criminal proceedings through a grand jury. It could hardly have occurred to these States that by ratifying the Amendment they uprooted their established methods for prosecuting crime and fastened upon themselves a new prosecutorial system. Indeed, the suggestion that the Fourteenth Amendment incorporates the first eight Amendments as such is not unambiguously urged. [There] is suggested merely a selective incorporation of the first eight Amendments into the [14th] Amendment. Some are in and some are out, but we are left in the dark as to which are in and which are out. Nor are we given the calculus for determining which go in and which stay out. If the basis of selection is merely that those provisions of the first eight Amendments are incorporated which commend themselves to individual justices as indispensable to the dignity and happiness of a free man, we are thrown back to a merely subjective test. [In] the history of thought 'natural law' has a much longer and much better founded meaning and justification than such subjective selection of the first eight Amendments for incorporation into the [14th]. If all that is meant is that due process contains within itself certain minimal standards which are 'of the very essence of a scheme of ordered liberty' [Palko], putting upon this Court the duty of applying these standards from time to time, then we have merely arrived at the insight which our predecessors long ago expressed. [It] ought not to require argument to reject the notion that due process of law meant one thing in the Fifth Amendment and another in the [14th].

"A construction which gives to due process no independent function but turns it into a summary of the specific provisions of the Bill of Rights [would] deprive the States of opportunity for reforms in legal process designed for extending the area of freedom. It would assume that no other abuses would

For an example of such a situation (relying on due process as a reservoir for added limits on state proceedings when no relevant "specific" provision in the Bill of Rights is available), see In re Winship, 397 U.S. 358 (1970), holding that "proof beyond a reasonable doubt is among the 'essentials of due process and fair treatment.' " Justice Black, consistent with his view in Adamson, dissented, emphasizing that "nowhere in the [Constitution] is there any statement that conviction of crime requires proof of guilt beyond a reasonable doubt."

reveal themselves in the course of time than those which had become manifest in 1791. Such a view not only disregards the historic meaning of 'due process.' It leads inevitably to a warped construction of specific provisions of the Bill of Rights to bring within their scope conduct clearly condemned by due process but not easily fitting into the pigeon-holes of the specific [provisions]. And so, [the issue in a case such as this] is not whether an infraction of one of the specific provisions of the first eight Amendments is disclosed by the record. The relevant question is whether the criminal proceedings which resulted in conviction deprived the accused of the due process of [law]. Judicial review of that [guaranty] inescapably imposes upon this Court an exercise of judgment upon the whole course of the proceedings in order to ascertain whether they offend those canons of decency and fairness which express the notions of justice of English-speaking peoples even toward those charged with the most heinous offenses. These standards of justice are not authoritatively formulated anywhere as though they were prescriptions in a pharmacopoeia. But neither does the application of the Due Process Clause imply that judges are wholly at large. The judicial judgment in applying the [Clause] must move within the limits of accepted notions of justice and is not to be based upon the idiosyncrasies of a merely personal judgment. The fact that judges among themselves may differ whether in a particular case a trial offends accepted notions of justice is not disproof that general rather than idiosyncratic standards are applied. An important safeguard against such merely individual judgment is an alert deference to the judgment of the State court under review."[4]

3. *Examining the Black-Frankfurter debate: "Specific" rights; vague guarantees; impersonal, predictable standards. a. Due process methodology in search of impersonal standards.* Justice Frankfurter's flexible due process approach in Adamson—a position echoing that of Justice Cardozo in Palko and in turn echoed by Justices Harlan and Powell in later cases—asserts that due process interpretation "is not based on the idiosyncrasies of merely personal judgment" and insists that judges "may not draw on our merely private notions." Yet could that approach be truly impersonal? What external criteria were available to give content to procedural due process? As Justice Black commented a few years after Adamson, if "canons of decency and fairness which express the notions of justice of English-speaking peoples" are to govern, "one may well ask what avenues of investigation are open to discover 'canons' of conduct so universally favored that this Court should write them into the Constitution."[5]

4. In Malloy v. Hogan, 378 U.S. 1 (1964), the Court held that the Fifth Amendment's privilege against self-incrimination *was* applicable to the states under the 14th: "Decisions of the Court since Twining and Adamson have departed from the contrary view expressed in those cases." A year later, the Court overruled the specific holding in Adamson and found unconstitutional the California rule permitting comment on the defendant's failure to testify. Griffin v. California, 380 U.S. 609 (1965).

5. Justice Black's comment came in Rochin v. California, 342 U.S. 165 (1952), one of several occasions on which Justices Frankfurter and Black renewed and elaborated their Adamson debate. Justice Frankfurter stated: "[To] practice the requisite detachment and to achieve sufficient objectivity [demands] of judges the habit of self-discipline and self-criticism, incertitude that one's own views are incontestable, and alert tolerance towards views not shared. [The] Due Process Clause may be indefinite and vague, but the mode [of] ascertainment is not self-willed. In

each case 'due process of law' requires an evaluation based on a disinterested inquiry pursued in the spirit of science, on a balanced order of facts exactly and fairly stated, on the detached consideration of conflicting claims, on a judgment not ad hoc and episodic but duly mindful of reconciling the needs both of continuity and change in a progressive society." Justice Black retorted by attacking the "nebulous standards" stated by the majority: "[I] long ago concluded that the accordion-like qualities of the ['evanescent standards of the majority's philosophy'] must inevitably imperil all the individual liberties safeguards specifically enumerated in the Bill of Rights."

For the context of the Rochin decision—in an era in which Court rulings on police behavior allegedly "shocking the conscience" were particularly unpredictable—see Note, "The Wolf-Rochin-Irvine Sequence, Fourth Amendment Violations, and 'Conduct that Shocks the Conscience,'" in Gunther, Constitutional Law (9th ed., 1975), 518.

What *were* the appropriate sources for giving content to the Palko-Adamson approach? Note the comments on a careful analysis of that approach by Sanford Kadish.[6] Kadish traces the two main routes by which the majority in the post-Adamson years sought "to eliminate the purely personal preference from flexible due process decision making": the first was "a respectful deference to the judgment of the state court or the act of the legislature under review"; the second was to rely on four types of external evidence of judgments already made by others: "the opinions of the progenitors and architects of American institutions"; "the implicit opinions of the policy-making organs of state governments"; "the explicit opinions of other American courts that have evaluated the fundamentality of a given mode of procedure"; and "the opinions of other countries in the Anglo-Saxon tradition." Kadish views due process as ultimately "more a moral command than a strictly jural precept," but suggests that there are "possibilities of reason and pragmatic inquiry" in such morally-centered due process decisionmaking. He also explores the primary values underlying procedural due process decisions: "insuring the reliability of the guilt-determining process," and "insuring respect for the dignity of the individual."

b. *Avoiding subjectivity: The problems of Justice Black's approach.* In Justice Black's view, the Palko-Adamson technique could not avoid judicial subjectivity. Did Justice Black's position avoid that difficulty any more effectively? Does incorporation of a "specific" Bill of Rights provision significantly curtail the range of judicial judgment? How specific are those guarantees? Contrast the guarantee of jury trial in civil cases involving more than $20 with the considerably more open-ended dimensions of the protection against "unreasonable" searches and seizures and the assurance of "the Assistance of Counsel." There have been recurrent disputes, for example, about whether the exclusionary rule is part of the Fourth Amendment guarantees, whether compulsory blood samples violate the Fifth Amendment's self-incrimination provision, and whether the Sixth Amendment right to counsel extends to pre-trial proceedings. Does emphasis on "specific" Bill of Rights guarantees breed warped constructions of the specific rights in order "to bring within their scope conduct clearly condemned by due process but not easily fitting into the pigeon-holes of the specific provisions," as Justice Frankfurter argued in Adamson? May that emphasis on "specifics" also have a restrictive rather than an expansive impact: may it breed a dilution of Bill of Rights guarantees in order to escape from the incorporationist "strait-jacket," as Justice Harlan was to charge?[7]

c. *Federalism and the Palko-Adamson approach.* Consciousness of federalism concerns and respect for state policy-makers permeate the majority positions of the Palko-Adamson tradition. There are elements in that tradition, however, that contravene state interests. The unpredictability of the flexible due process approach is arguably more harmful to state autonomy concerns than a more rigid—possibly more interventionist, yet also more certain—due process interpretation. In the right to counsel area, even Justice Harlan, an adherent of the Cardozo-Frankfurter position, ultimately came to support fixed rather than flexible rules. Powell v. Alabama in 1932 had required appointment of counsel

---

6. Kadish, "Methodology and Criteria in Due Process Adjudication—A Survey and Criticism," 66 Yale L.J. 319 (1957).

7. See, e.g., the Black-Harlan debate in Duncan, p. 430 below. The degree to which "vague" standards akin to due process can continue to plague the Court even when "specific" guarantees are incorporated is dramatically illustrated by the interpretations of the Eighth Amendment's prohibition of "cruel and unusual punishments." Note especially the first Death Penalty Case, Furman v. Georgia, 408 U.S. 238 (1972). Though in form the nine opinions in that case focused on the "specific" Eighth Amendment provision, the issues considered were very similar to those encountered in giving content to the "vague contours" of due process. Indeed, several of the opinions in Furman explicitly recognized the kinship between the Palko-Adamson due process approach and Eighth Amendment analysis.

in capital cases; but for years it was the Court's position in non-capital cases that appointment of counsel was required only if lack of counsel produced unfairness in a particular case—the "special circumstances" rule of Betts v. Brady, 316 U.S. 455 (1942). In the two decades of experience under that rule, many state convictions were reversed by applying that case-by-case approach. Finally, in Gideon v. Wainwright, 372 U.S. 335 (1963), Betts was overruled and a flat requirement of counsel in *all* felony cases was substituted. In a concurring opinion in Gideon, Justice Harlan commented that, in application, "the Betts v. Brady rule is no longer a reality," for the Court for years had found "special circumstances" justifying reversal for lack of counsel in virtually every case decided by it on the merits. He added: "This evolution, however, appears not to have been fully recognized by many state courts. [To] continue a rule which is honored by this Court only with lip service is not a healthy thing and in the long run will do disservice to the federal system." [8]

d. *The reign and modifications of the Palko-Adamson approach.* For a decade and a half after Adamson, the Court persisted in its efforts to apply the flexible due process analysis articulated in Palko and Adamson. Beginning in the early 1960s, however, the Warren Court—without ever formally abandoning the "fundamental fairness" standard—began to look more and more to the Bill of Rights for guidance and began to apply more and more of those guarantees to the states via the 14th Amendment. In effect, that development has made all of the criminal procedure guarantees of the Bill of Rights, except for the grand jury indictment provision of the Fifth Amendment, applicable to the states. Moreover, perceived essentials of fairness have been found in due process even though they are not specified in the Bill of Rights—as with the holding that proof beyond a reasonable doubt is a constitutional requirement in criminal cases. [9]

Duncan, the 1968 decision that follows, reviews the rapid expansion of the list of incorporated guarantees in the 1960s and illustrates the modern Court's manner of applying the modified incorporation approach. Under Palko-Adamson, the Court looked at the facts in the case before it and asked whether the challenged state action violated the "fair trial," "fundamental fairness" requirement implicit in due process; and, sometimes, the claim found essential to a fair trial corresponded to aspects of a right specified in the Bill of Rights. In the modern modification of that approach, as illustrated by Duncan, the Court proceeds on a more wholesale basis: typically, it looks to the facts in the case before it simply to ascertain whether they raise issues of the sort covered by the Bill of Rights; having identified the relevant Bill of Rights provision, the Court pays little further attention to the facts in the case and asks instead whether the relevant Bill of Rights guarantee is essential to "fundamental fairness" and should be made applicable to the states. [10] The Duncan approach raises problems of its own. The most pervasive one has been the question of the *contours* of a Bill of Rights guarantee incorporated into the 14th Amendment and made applicable to the states. When a Bill of Rights guarantee is incorporated into the 14th, does it apply to the states in precisely the same manner as it applies to the federal criminal process? Is every detail of the "incorporated" Bill of Rights provisions applicable "jot-for-jot" to the states? That problem is pursued in the notes after Duncan.

---

8. See Israel, "Gideon v. Wainwright: The 'Art' of Overruling," 1963 Sup.Ct.Rev. 211.

9. See In re Winship (1970; p. 426 above).

10. For another shift in approach in the modern "selective" incorporation era, see footnote [11] in Duncan.

B. THE MODERN APPROACH AND ITS PROBLEMS

DUNCAN v. LOUISIANA

391 U.S. 145, 88 S.Ct. 1444, 20 L.Ed.2d 491 (1968).

Mr. Justice WHITE delivered the opinion of the Court.

Appellant, Gary Duncan, was convicted of simple battery, [a misdemeanor] punishable by a maximum of two years' imprisonment and a $300 fine. Appellant sought trial by jury, but because the Louisiana Constitution grants jury trials only in cases in which capital punishment or imprisonment at hard labor may be imposed, the trial judge denied the request. Appellant was convicted and sentenced to serve 60 days in the parish prison and pay a fine of $150. Appellant [alleges] that the Sixth and [14th Amendments] secure the right to jury trial in state criminal prosecutions where a sentence as long as two years may be [imposed].

[In] resolving conflicting claims concerning the meaning of this spacious language [of due process], the Court has looked increasingly to the Bill of Rights for guidance; many of the rights guaranteed by the first eight Amendments to the Constitution have been held to be protected against state action by the Due Process Clause of the [14th] Amendment. That clause now protects the right to compensation for property taken by the State; [1] the rights of speech, press, and religion covered by the First Amendment; [2] the Fourth Amendment rights to be free from unreasonable searches and seizures and to have excluded from criminal trials any evidence illegally seized; [3] the right guaranteed by the Fifth Amendment to be free of compelled self-incrimination; [4] and the Sixth Amendment rights to counsel, [5] to a speedy [6] and public [7] trial, to confrontation of opposing witnesses, [8] and to compulsory process for obtaining witnesses. [9]

The test for determining whether a right extended by the Fifth and Sixth Amendments with respect to federal criminal proceedings is also protected against state action by the [14th Amendment] has been phrased in a variety of ways in the opinions of this Court. The question has been asked whether a right is among those " 'fundamental principles of liberty and justice which lie at the base of all our civil and political institutions,' " Powell v. Alabama; [10] whether it is "basic in our system of jurisprudence," In re Oliver; and whether it is "a fundamental right, essential to a fair trial," Gideon v. Wainwright; Malloy v. Hogan; Pointer v. Texas [380 U.S. 400, 403 (1965)]. [The majority opinions in Gideon and Pointer were written by Justice Black. Justice Brennan wrote Malloy.] The claim before us is that the right to trial by jury guaranteed by the Sixth Amendment meets these tests. The position of Louisiana, on the other hand, is that the Constitution imposes upon the States no duty to give a jury trial in any criminal case, regardless of the seriousness of the crime or the size of the punishment which may be imposed. Because we

1. Chicago, Burlington & Quincy Railway Co. v. Chicago, 166 U.S. 226 (1897). [All non-bracketed materials in the numbered footnotes to this opinion are by Justice White.]

2. See, e.g., Fiske v. Kansas, 274 U.S. 380 (1927).

3. See Mapp v. Ohio, 367 U.S. 643 (1961). [On the current vitality of Mapp, see footnote 2 to the post-Duncan notes, below.]

4. Malloy v. Hogan, 378 U.S. 1 (1964).

5. Gideon v. Wainwright, 372 U.S. 335 (1963).

6. Klopfer v. North Carolina, 386 U.S. 213 (1967).

7. In re Oliver, 333 U.S. 257 (1948).

8. Pointer v. Texas, 380 U.S. 400 (1965).

9. Washington v. Texas, 388 U.S. 14 (1967).

10. Quoting from Hebert v. Louisiana, 272 U.S. 312, 316 (1926).

believe that trial by jury in criminal cases is fundamental to the American scheme of justice, we hold that the [14th] Amendment guarantees a right of jury trial in all criminal cases which—were they to be tried in a federal court— would come within the Sixth Amendment's guarantee.[11] Since we consider the appeal before us to be such a case, we hold that the Constitution was violated when appellant's demand for jury trial was refused.

The history of trial by jury in criminal cases has been frequently told. [That history] is impressive support for considering the right to jury trial in criminal cases to be fundamental to our system of justice. [Jury] trial continues to receive strong support. The laws of every State guarantee a right to jury trial in serious criminal [cases]. We are aware of prior cases in this Court in which the prevailing opinion contains statements contrary to our holding today that the right to jury trial in serious criminal cases is a fundamental right and hence must be recognized by the States as part of their obligation to extend due process of law to all persons within their jurisdiction. [None] of these cases, however, dealt with a State which had purported to dispense entirely with a jury trial in serious criminal cases. [We] reject the prior dicta regarding jury trial in criminal cases. The guarantees of jury trial in the Federal and State Constitutions reflect a profound judgment about the way in which law should be enforced and justice administered. A right to jury trial is granted to criminal defendants in order to prevent oppression by the Government. [The] deep commitment of the Nation to the right of jury trial in serious criminal cases as a defense against arbitrary law enforcement qualifies for protection under the Due Process Clause of the [14th] Amendment, and must therefore be respected by the States.

Of course jury trial has "its weaknesses and the potential for misuse." We are aware of the long debate, especially in this century, [as] to the wisdom of

---

11. In one sense recent cases applying provisions of the first eight Amendments to the States represent a new approach to the "incorporation" debate. Earlier the Court can be seen as having asked, when inquiring into whether some particular procedural safeguard was required of a State, if a civilized system could be imagined that would not accord the particular protection. [Palko.] The recent cases, on the other hand, have proceeded upon the valid assumption that state criminal processes are not imaginary and theoretical schemes but actual systems bearing virtually every characteristic of the common-law system that has been developing contemporaneously in England and in this country. The question thus is whether given this kind of system a particular procedure is fundamental—whether, that is, a procedure is necessary to an Anglo-American regime of ordered liberty. It is this sort of inquiry that can justify the conclusions that state courts must exclude evidence seized in violation of the Fourth Amendment, Mapp v. Ohio; that state prosecutors may not comment on a defendant's failure to testify, Griffin v. California; and that criminal punishment may not be imposed for the status of narcotics addiction, Robinson v. California [370 U.S. 660 (1962)]. Of immediate relevance for this case are the Court's holdings that the States must comply with certain provisions of the Sixth Amendment, specifically that the States may not refuse a speedy trial, confrontation of witnesses, and the assistance, at state expense if necessary,

of counsel. See cases cited in nn. [5–9], above. Of each of these determinations that a constitutional provision originally written to bind the Federal Government should bind the States as well it might be said that the limitation in question is not necessarily fundamental to fairness in every criminal system that might be imagined but is fundamental in the context of the criminal processes maintained by the American States.

When the inquiry is approached in this way the question whether the States can impose criminal punishment without granting a jury trial appears quite different from the way it appeared in the older cases opining that States might abolish jury trial. See, e.g., Maxwell v. Dow, 176 U.S. 581 (1900). A criminal process which was fair and equitable but used no juries is easy to imagine. It would make use of alternative guarantees and protections which would serve the purposes that the jury serves in the English and American systems. Yet no American State has undertaken to construct such a system. Instead, every American State, including Louisiana, uses the jury extensively, and imposes very serious punishments only after a trial at which the defendant has a right to a jury's verdict. In every State, including Louisiana, the structure and style of the criminal process—the supporting framework and the subsidiary procedures—are of the sort that naturally complement jury trial, and have developed in connection with and in reliance upon jury trial.

permitting untrained laymen to determine the facts in civil and criminal proceedings. [Most] of the controversy has centered on the jury in civil cases. [Louisiana] urges that holding that the [14th] Amendment assures a right to jury trial will cast doubt on the integrity of every trial conducted without a jury. Plainly, this is not the import of our holding. Our conclusion is that in the American States, as in the federal judicial system, a general grant of jury trial for serious offenses is a fundamental right, essential for preventing miscarriages of justice and for assuring that fair trials are provided for all defendants. We would not assert, however, that every criminal trial—or any particular trial— held before a judge alone is unfair or that a defendant may never be as fairly treated by a judge as he would be by a jury. Thus we hold no constitutional doubts about the practices, common in both federal and state courts, of accepting waivers of jury trial and prosecuting petty crimes without extending a right to [jury trial].[12]

Louisiana's final contention is that even if it must grant jury trials in serious criminal cases, the conviction before us [is] constitutional because here the petitioner was tried for simple battery and was sentenced to only 60 days in the parish prison. We are not persuaded. It is doubtless true that there is a category of petty crimes or offenses which is not subject to the Sixth Amendment [and] should not be subject to the [14th Amendment]. Crimes carrying possible penalties up to six months do not require a jury trial if they otherwise qualify as petty offenses. [But here, the state] has made simple battery a criminal offense punishable by imprisonment for two years and a fine. The question [is] whether a crime carrying such a penalty is an offense which Louisiana may insist on trying without a jury. We think [not].

Reversed and remanded.*

12. Louisiana also asserts that if due process is deemed to include the right to jury trial, States will be obligated to comply with all past interpretations of the Sixth Amendment, an amendment which in its inception was designed to control only the federal courts and which throughout its history has operated in this limited environment where uniformity is a more obvious and immediate consideration. In particular, Louisiana objects to application of the decisions of this Court interpreting the Sixth Amendment as guaranteeing a 12-man jury in serious criminal cases, Thompson v. Utah, 170 U.S. 343 (1898); as requiring a unanimous verdict before guilt can be found, Maxwell v. Dow, 176 U.S. 581, 586 (1900); and as barring procedures by which crimes subject to the Sixth Amendment jury trial provision are tried in the first instance without a jury but at the first appellate stage by de novo trial with a jury, Callan v. Wilson, 127 U.S. 540, 557 (1888). It seems very unlikely to us that our decision today will require widespread changes in state criminal processes. First, our decisions interpreting the Sixth Amendment are always subject to reconsideration, a fact amply demonstrated by the instant decision. In addition, most of the States have provisions for jury trials equal in breadth to the Sixth Amendment, if that amendment is construed, as it has been, to permit the trial of petty crimes and offenses without a [jury]. [For the Court's post-Duncan struggles with the problems raised in this footnote, see the notes following this case.]

* *Incorporation since Duncan.* The process of incorporation has continued since Duncan. In Benton v. Maryland, 395 U.S. 784 (1969), the majority held "that the double jeopardy prohibition of the Fifth Amendment represents a fundamental ideal in our constitutional heritage, and that it should apply to the [States]." As a result of the selective incorporation technique illustrated by Duncan, all of the criminal process guarantees of the Bill of Rights are now applicable to the states, with the exception of the grand jury indictment provision of the Fifth Amendment and, arguably, the "excessive bail" provision of the Eighth Amendment (but see Schilb v. Kuebel, 404 U.S. 357 (1971)). Moreover, incorporation is not the sole source of 14th Amendment restraints on state procedures. Recall In re Winship (1970; p. 426 above).

Incorporation and the retroactivity problem. Traditionally, newly announced doctrines have been given fully retroactive effect by American courts, with the new standard applicable to all cases pending in the judicial system. But amidst the pressure to expand the list of incorporated rights in the 1960s, that traditional retroactivity principle was perceived as a substantial brake on the incorporation of new constitutional rights into the due process clause. Given the availability of collateral challenges to convictions via habeas corpus, the concern was that a rapid pace in incorporating new Bill of Rights guarantees would flood the federal courts and open the prison gates by permitting reliance on the newly recognized rights by prisoners whose convictions had long become final for direct review purposes. Those pragmatic considerations no doubt played a role in inducing the Court to develop major

Mr. Justice BLACK, with whom Mr. Justice DOUGLAS joins, concurring.

[I agree with the holding] for reasons given by the Court. I also agree because of reasons given in my dissent in [Adamson]. I am very happy to support this selective process through which our Court has since the Adamson case held most of the specific Bill of Rights' protections applicable to the States to the same extent they are applicable to the [Federal Government]. All of these holdings making Bill of Rights' provisions applicable as such to the States mark, of course, a departure from the Twining doctrine. [The] dissent in this case, however, makes a spirited and forceful defense of that now discredited doctrine. My Brother Harlan's objections to my Adamson dissent history, like that of most of the objectors, relies most heavily on a criticism written by Professor Charles Fairman and published in the Stanford Law Review. 2 Stan. L.Rev. 5 (1949). I have read and studied this article extensively, including the historical references, but am compelled to add that in my view it has completely failed to refute the inferences and arguments that I suggested in my Adamson [dissent].

[The dissent also] states that "the great words of the four clauses of the first section of the Fourteenth Amendment would have been an exceedingly peculiar way to say that 'The rights heretofore guaranteed against federal intrusion by the first eight Amendments are henceforth guaranteed against state intrusion as well.'" In response to this I can say only that the words "No State shall make or enforce any law which shall abridge the privileges or immunities of citizens of the United States" seem to me an eminently reasonable way of expressing the idea that henceforth the Bill of Rights shall apply to the States.[1] What more precious "privilege" of American citizenship could there be than that privilege to claim the protections of our great Bill of Rights? I suggest that any reading of "privileges or immunities of citizens of the United States" which excludes the Bill of Rights' safeguards renders the words of this section of the [14th] Amendment meaningless. [If] anything, it is "exceedingly peculiar" to read the [14th] Amendment differently from the way I do.

While I do not wish at this time to discuss at length my disagreement with Brother Harlan's forthright and frank restatement of the now discredited Twining doctrine, I do want to point out what appears to me to be the basic difference between us. [D]ue process, according to my Brother Harlan, is to be a phrase with no permanent meaning, but one which is found to shift from time to time in accordance with judges' predilections and understandings of what is best for the country. [It] is impossible for me to believe that such unconfined power is given to judges in our Constitution that is a written one in order to limit governmental power. Another tenet of the Twining doctrine as restated by my Brother Harlan is that "due process of law requires only fundamental fairness." But the "fundamental fairness" test is one on a par with that of shocking the conscience of the Court. Each of such tests depends entirely on the particular judge's idea of ethics and morals instead of requiring

exceptions to the normal retroactivity rule in the midst of the rapid expansion of selective incorporation during the 1960s. The legitimacy of those exceptions, and the appropriate contours of permissible prospectivity, have produced sharp divisions on and off the Court. See, e.g., Linkletter v. Walker, 381 U.S. 618 (1965), Stovall v. Denno, 388 U.S. 293 (1967), and Payton v. New York, 445 U.S. 573 (1980). Do the Court's frequent denials of retroactivity expose it to the charge of acting more like a legislative than a judicial body? Are the differing treatments of defendants under the varying cut-off rules arbitrary and discriminatory? (Justices Black and Douglas so

argued in dissent in several of the Linkletter line of cases.) See generally Mishkin, "Foreword: The High Court, The Great Writ, and the Due Process of Time and Law," 79 Harv.L.Rev. 56 (1965), and Beytagh, "Ten Years of Non-Retroactivity: A Critique and a Proposal," 61 Va.L. Rev. 1557 (1975).

1. My view has been and is that the Fourteenth Amendment, *as a whole*, makes the Bill of Rights applicable to the States. This would certainly include the language of the Privileges and Immunities Clause, as well as the Due Process Clause. [Footnote by Justice Black.]

him to depend on the boundaries fixed by the written words of the Constitution. [I] am not bothered by the argument that applying the Bill of Rights to the States [may] prevent States from trying novel social and economic experiments. I have never believed that under the guise of federalism the States should be able to experiment with the protections afforded [by] the [Bill of Rights]. I believe as strongly as ever that the [14th] Amendment was intended to make the Bill of Rights applicable to the States. I have been willing to support the selective incorporation doctrine, however, as an alternative, although perhaps less historically supportable than complete incorporation. The selective incorporation process, if used properly, does limit the [Court in the 14th Amendment] field to specific Bill of Rights' protections only and keeps judges from roaming at will in their own notions of what policies outside the Bill of Rights are desirable and what are not. And, most importantly for me, the selective incorporation process has the virtue of having already worked to make most of the Bill of Rights' protections applicable to the States.

Mr. Justice FORTAS, concurring.

[A]lthough I agree with the decision of the Court, I cannot agree with the implication that the tail must go with the hide: that when we hold, influenced by the Sixth Amendment, that "due process" requires that the States accord the right of jury trial for all but petty offenses, we automatically import all of the ancillary rules which have been or may hereafter be developed incidental to the right to jury trial in the federal courts. I see no reason whatever, for example, to assume that our decision today should require us to impose federal requirements such as unanimous verdicts or a jury of 12 upon the States. We may well conclude that these and other features of federal jury practice are by no means fundamental [and] that they are not obligatory on the States. [There] is no reason whatever for us [to be] bound slavishly to follow not only the Sixth Amendment but all of its bag and baggage. To take this course [would] be not only unnecessary but mischievous because it would inflict a serious blow upon the principle of [federalism].

Mr. Justice HARLAN, whom Mr. Justice STEWART joins, dissenting.

[The] Due Process Clause of the [14th] Amendment requires that [state] procedures be fundamentally fair in all respects. It does not, in my view, impose or encourage nationwide uniformity for its own sake; it does not command adherence to forms that happen to be old; and it does not impose on the States the rules that may be in force in the federal courts except where such rules are also found to be essential to basic fairness. The Court's approach to this case is an uneasy and illogical compromise among the views of various Justices on how the Due Process Clause should be interpreted. The Court does not say that those who framed the [14th] Amendment intended to make the Sixth Amendment applicable to the States. And the Court concedes that it finds nothing unfair about the procedure by which the present appellant was tried. Nevertheless, the Court reverses his conviction: it holds, for some reason not apparent to me, that the Due Process Clause incorporates the particular clause of the Sixth Amendment that requires trial by jury in federal criminal cases—including, as I read its opinion, the sometimes trivial accompanying baggage of judicial interpretation in federal contexts. I have raised my voice many times before against the Court's continuing undiscriminating insistence upon fastening on the States federal notions of criminal justice, and I must do so again in this instance. With all respect, the Court's approach and its reading of history are altogether topsy-turvy.

[The] first section of the [14th] Amendment was meant neither to incorporate, nor to be limited to, the specific guarantees of the first eight Amendments. The overwhelming historical evidence marshalled by Professor Fairman demonstrates, to me conclusively, that the Congressmen and state legislators who wrote, debated, and ratified the [14th] Amendment did not think they were "incorporating" the Bill of Rights. [N]either history, nor sense, supports using the [14th] Amendment to put the States in a constitutional straitjacket with respect to their own development in the administration of criminal or civil law. Although [I] fundamentally disagree with the total incorporation view of the [14th] Amendment, it seems to me that such a position does at least have the virtue, lacking in the Court's selective incorporation approach, of internal consistency: we look to the Bill of Rights, word for word, clause for clause, precedent for precedent because, it is said, the men who wrote the Amendment wanted it that way. [Apart] from the approach taken by the absolute incorporationists, I can see only one method of analysis that has any internal logic. That is to start with the words "liberty" and "due process of law" and attempt to define them in a way that accords with American traditions and our system of government. This approach, involving a much more discriminating process of adjudication than does "incorporation," is, albeit difficult, the one that was followed throughout the 19th and most of the present century. It entails a "gradual process of judicial inclusion and exclusion," seeking, with due recognition of constitutional tolerance for state experimentation and disparity, to ascertain those "immutable principles [of] free government which no member of the Union may disregard." Due process was not restricted to rules fixed in the past. [Nor] did it impose nationwide uniformity in details. The relationship of the Bill of Rights to this "gradual process" seems to me to be twofold. In the first place it has long been clear that the Due Process Clause imposes some restrictions on state action that parallel Bill of Rights restrictions on federal action. Second, and more important than this accidental overlap, is the fact that the Bill of Rights is evidence, at various points, of the content Americans find in the term "liberty" and of American standards of [fundamental fairness].

Today's Court still remains unwilling to accept the total incorporationists' view of the history of the [14th] Amendment. [The] Court is also, apparently, unwilling to face the task of determining whether denial of trial by jury in the situation before us, or in other situations, is fundamentally unfair. Consequently, the Court has compromised on the ease of the incorporationist position, without its internal logic. It has simply assumed that the question before us is whether the Jury Trial Clause of the Sixth Amendment should be incorporated into the Fourteenth, jot-for-jot and case-for-case, or ignored. Then the Court merely declares that the clause in question is "in" rather than "out." The Court has justified neither its starting place nor its conclusion. If the problem is to discover and articulate the rules of fundamental fairness in criminal proceedings, there is no reason to assume that the whole body of rules developed in this Court constituting Sixth Amendment jury trial must be regarded as a unit. The requirement of trial by jury in federal criminal cases has given rise to numerous subsidiary questions respecting the exact scope and content of the right. It surely cannot be that every answer the Court has given, or will give, to such a question is attributable to the Founders; or even that every rule announced carries equal conviction of this Court; still less can it be that every such subprinciple is equally fundamental to ordered liberty. Examples abound. I should suppose it obviously fundamental to fairness that a "jury" means an "impartial jury." I should think it equally obvious that the rule, imposed long ago in the federal courts, that "jury" means "jury of exactly twelve," is not fundamental to anything: there is no significance except to mystics in the number 12. Again, trial by jury has been held to require a unanimous verdict of jurors in the federal courts, although unanimity has not been found essential to liberty in Britain, where the requirement has been [abandoned].

Even if I could agree that the question before us is whether Sixth Amendment jury trial is totally "in" or totally "out," I can find in the Court's opinion no real reasons for concluding that it should be "in." The basis for differentiating among clauses in the Bill of Rights cannot be that only some clauses are in the Bill of Rights, or that only some are old and much praised, or that only some have played an important role in the development of federal law. These things are true of all. The Court says that some clauses are more "fundamental" than others, but it turns out to be using this word in a sense that would have astonished Mr. Justice Cardozo and which, in addition, is of no help. The word does not mean "analytically critical to procedural fairness" for no real analysis of the role of the jury in making procedures fair is even attempted. Instead, the word turns out to mean "old," "much praised," and "found in the Bill of Rights." The definition of "fundamental" thus turns out to be circular. [The] argument that jury trial is not a requisite of due process is quite simple. [If] due process of law requires only fundamental fairness, then the inquiry in each case must be whether a state trial process was a fair one. The Court has held, properly I think, that in an adversary process it is a requisite of fairness, for which there is no adequate substitute, that a criminal defendant be afforded a right to counsel and to cross-examine opposing witnesses. But it simply has not been demonstrated, nor, I think, can it be demonstrated, that trial by jury is the only fair means of resolving issues of fact. The jury is of course not without virtues. [The] jury system can also be said to have some inherent defects. [That] trial by jury is not the only fair way of adjudicating criminal guilt is well attested by the fact that it is not the prevailing way, either in England or in this country. In the United States, [two] experts have estimated that, of all prosecutions for crimes triable to a jury, 75% are settled by guilty plea and 40% of the remainder are tried to the court.[1] [I] see no reason why this Court should reverse the conviction of appellant, absent any suggestion that his particular trial was in fact unfair, or compel [Louisiana] to afford jury trial in an as yet unbounded category of cases that can, without unfairness, be tried to a court. [The] Court has chosen to impose upon every State one means of trying criminal cases; it is a good means, but it is not the only fair means, and it is not demonstrably better than the alternatives States might [devise].[2]

PROBLEMS OF THE MODERN APPROACH: THE CONTOURS OF "INCORPORATED" RIGHTS

1. *Incorporating Bill of Rights guarantees "jot-for-jot."* By the end of the 1960s, it was clear that virtually all Bill of Rights guarantees pertaining to criminal proceedings were incorporated in the 14th Amendment and thus applicable to the states. But the embracive scope of modern "selective" incorporation has not solved all of the problems debated during the incorporation debate of the earlier decades. In the Palko-Adamson era, advocates of the total incorporation of "specific" Bill of Rights guarantees had urged that technique as a cure for the vices of unpredictability and judicial subjectivity. During the heyday of the unmodified Palko-Adamson regime, there was indeed ample ground for the charges of uncertainty and subjectivity. Under the Cardozo-Frankfurter approach, a finding that a right reflected in one of the Bill of Rights provisions was essential to "fundamental fairness" did not mean that

---

1. Kalven & Zeisel, [The American Jury (1966)], at 12–32. [Footnote by Justice Harlan.]

2. For the final round in the long battle in which Justice Black advocated his views of incorporation in the face of criticisms from Justice Frankfurter and, later, Justice Harlan, see the separate opinions of Justices Black and Harlan in In re Winship (1970; p. 426 above).

all of the detailed interpretations of the relevant Bill of Rights provision were applicable to the states. The treatment of the Fourth Amendment's guarantee against unreasonable searches and seizures illustrates the resulting difficulties. In 1949, in Wolf v. Colorado, 338 U.S. 25, Justice Frankfurter's opinion for the Court held that the "core" of the Fourth Amendment guarantee was an ingredient of due process, but went on to find that the exclusionary rule applied in federal courts (barring the use of evidence obtained in violation of the Fourth Amendment) was not constitutionally required of the states.[1] After more than a decade of controversy and confusion in the aftermath of Wolf, the Court changed its mind. In Mapp v. Ohio, 367 U.S. 643 (1961), Justice Clark's majority opinion found the exclusionary rule to be "an essential part of the right to privacy" recognized in Wolf: henceforth, states could no longer admit evidence obtained in violation of Fourth Amendment standards.[2] Incorporation thereafter meant not merely incorporating the "core" of the Bill of Rights guarantee, but applying to the states every detail of the contours of the guarantee as delineated in judicial interpretations of the relevant provision.

From the beginning of that new era of applying the Bill of Rights provisions to the states to exactly the same extent as they applied to the federal government, some Justices objected. The objections were essentially those voiced by Justices Harlan and Fortas in Duncan, claiming that "bag and baggage," "jot-for-jot and case-for-case" incorporation would impose needlessly detailed, rigid constraints on the states. Moreover, as Justice Frankfurter had warned as long ago as Adamson, incorporation of specific Bill of Rights guarantees risked a "warped construction"—and possible dilution—of those provisions. The post-Duncan cases that follow illustrate those problems. Duncan for the first time found the Sixth Amendment jury trial provision applicable to the states. As Justice Harlan's dissent noted, that Bill of Rights guarantee had in the past, in its applications to federal proceedings, apparently mandated a 12-person, unanimous jury verdict for federal criminal convictions. But in the aftermath of Duncan, the Court found that the Sixth Amendment did *not* require 12-person, unanimous juries after all—in federal *or* state courts. In examining the post-Duncan decisions, consider whether the modern incorporation approach affords adequate defenses against the charges of subjectivity and unpredictability so long levied against the earlier Palko-Adamson technique. How predictable and coherent are the interpretations of the "specific" rights now incorporated into the 14th Amendment? Have the recent decisions vindicated the warnings that

1. As Justice Frankfurter said in Wolf, the "security of one's privacy against arbitrary intrusion by the police—which is at the core of the Fourth Amendment—is basic to a free society"; but the problem of remedies for violations of that right was susceptible to "varying solutions."

2. The full survival of the Mapp ruling is in doubt. As early as United States v. Calandra, 414 U.S. 338 (1974), the Court concluded that the exclusionary rule is "a judicially created remedy designed to safeguard Fourth Amendment rights generally through its deterrent effect, rather than a personal constitutional right of the party aggrieved." The vitality and scope of the exclusionary rule remain under attack. See, e.g., Illinois v. Gates, 462 U.S. 213 (1983) (exclusionary rule is "an issue separate from the question whether Fourth Amendment rights of the party seeking to invoke the rule were violated by police conduct"). Most recently, and most significantly, the Court has rejected the view that "the exclusionary rule is a necessary corollary of the Fourth Amendment," and has as a consequence taken on the task of "weighing the costs and benefits of preventing the use in the prosecution's case-in-chief of inherently trustworthy tangible evidence obtained in reliance on a search warrant issued by a detached and neutral magistrate that ultimately is found to be defective." The result was adoption of a "good-faith exception to the Fourth Amendment exclusionary rule," refusing to apply "the extreme sanction of exclusion" in cases in which the police conduct was "objectively reasonable" rather than "dishonest or reckless in preparing their affidavit." United States v. Leon, 468 U.S. —— (1984). Is it self-evident that the Court has the authority to fashion *any* remedial rules admittedly not *required* by the Constitution? Does the answer to this question vary with whether state or federal power is at issue? On these issues, see generally Monaghan, "Foreword: Constitutional Common Law," 89 Harv. L.Rev. 1 (1975).

incorporation of "specific" rights would produce distortion and dilution of those rights? What values are promoted by applying the incorporated guarantees to the states in exactly the same way in which they apply to the federal government? What goals are furthered, and what costs are incurred, by making all interpretations of specific guarantees applicable to the states, "bag and baggage," "jot-for-jot"?

2. *The jury trial guarantee after Duncan: Dilution of federal rights as an escape from the incorporationist "straitjacket"?* a. *The Williams case.* In WILLIAMS v. FLORIDA, 399 U.S. 78 (1970), the petitioner seeking reversal of a robbery conviction claimed that he should have been tried by a 12-person jury rather than the six-person panel provided by Florida law in all but capital cases. Justice WHITE's majority opinion concluded, however, that "the twelve-man panel is not a necessary ingredient of 'trial by jury.'" Though earlier interpretations of the Sixth Amendment had "assumed" the 12-person panel to be constitutionally necessary, Justice White explained, "that particular feature of the jury system appears to have been a historical accident, unrelated to the great purposes which gave rise to the jury in the first place." He conceded that a 12-person jury might well have been "the usual expectation" of the Framers, but argued that the constitutionally required features of a jury turned on "other than purely historical considerations": "The relevant inquiry [must] be the function that the particular feature performs and its relation to the purposes of the jury trial." Justice White found a critical purpose of a jury to be "the interposition between the accused and his accuser of the common sense judgment of a group of laymen"; and that did not require any particular number on the jury. Moreover, "neither currently available evidence nor theory suggests that the twelve-man jury is necessarily more advantageous to the defendant than a jury composed of fewer members."

In an extensive opinion concurring in the result, Justice HARLAN reiterated his adherence to the Palko-Adamson approach, restated his opposition to Duncan, and objected to the majority's "dilution" of Sixth Amendment guarantees: "The necessary consequence of this decision is that twelve-member juries are not constitutionally required in *federal* criminal trials either. [The] decision evinces, I think, a recognition that the 'incorporationist' view [of due process] must be tempered to allow the States more elbow room in ordering their own criminal systems. With that much I agree. But to accomplish this by diluting constitutional protections within the federal system itself is something to which I cannot possibly subscribe. Tempering the rigor of Duncan should be done forthrightly, by facing up to the fact that at least in this area the 'incorporation' doctrine does not fit well with our federal structure." He claimed: "I consider that before today it would have been unthinkable to suggest that the Sixth Amendment's right to a trial by jury is satisfied by a jury of six, or less, [or] by less than a unanimous verdict. [The] Court's elaboration of what is required provides no standard and vexes the meaning of the right to a jury trial in federal courts, as well as state courts, by uncertainty. Can it be doubted that a unanimous jury of 12 provides a greater safeguard than a majority vote of six?" He added: "These decisions demonstrate that the difference between a [Palko] 'due process' approach [and] 'selective incorporation' is not an abstract [one]. The 'backlash' in Williams exposes the malaise, for there the Court dilutes a federal guarantee in order to reconcile the logic of 'incorporation,' the 'jot-for-jot and case-for-case' application of the federal right to the States, with the reality of federalism. Can one doubt that had Congress tried to undermine the common-law right to trial by jury before Duncan came on the books the history today recited would have barred such action? Can we expect repeat performances when this Court is called upon to give definition and meaning to other federal guarantees that have been 'incorporated'?" [3]

b. *The Apodaca case.* Another issue left open by Duncan—the question whether a *unanimous* jury verdict is required in state courts after the incorporation of the Sixth Amendment—came before the Court in APODACA v. OREGON, 406 U.S. 404 (1972). As in Williams, the Court ruled that what had formerly been thought to be an ingredient of the Sixth Amendment guarantee was not constitutionally required after all and accordingly sustained the constitutionality of a state nonunanimous jury verdict. This time, however, the division on the Court was particularly sharp and unusual. The nonunanimous jury verdict was approved though eight of the Justices adhered to the Duncan position that each element of the Sixth Amendment jury trial guarantee is fully applicable to the states via the 14th, and even though five of the Justices read the Sixth Amendment as requiring unanimous jury verdicts. The result nevertheless sustaining the nonunanimous verdict was made possible by the decisive concurring position of Justice Powell. Following in the footsteps of Justice Harlan's argument in Duncan and Williams, Justice Powell found that the Sixth Amendment required the traditional jury unanimity in federal trials, but did not think that all of the elements of the federal guarantee should be imposed on the states as a requirement of due process.

The Oregon system sustained in Apodaca requires the vote of at least ten out of twelve jurors for conviction in noncapital cases. Justice WHITE's plurality opinion, joined by Chief Justice Burger and Justices Blackmun and Rehnquist, adhered to the Williams approach: unanimity was not constitutionally required because it "does not materially contribute to" the central function "served by the jury in contemporary society"—to interpose "the common sense judgment of a group of laymen" between accused and accuser.[4]

Justice POWELL's opinion explaining his decisive vote for the result rejected the plurality's "major premise" that "the concept of jury trial, as applicable to the States under the [14th] Amendment, must be identical in every detail to the concept required in federal courts by the Sixth Amendment." In federal proceedings, he explained, he would require unanimity, "not because unanimity is necessarily fundamental to the function performed by the jury, but because that result is mandated by history." But as to state proceedings, due process simply required that states adhere to "what is fundamental in jury trial"; and the Oregon system adequately respected the fundamentals. To impose upon the state every detail of incorporated federal guarantees would derogate basic principles of federalism and would deprive the states of "freedom to experiment with adjudicatory processes different from the federal model." Moreover,

---

3. Justice STEWART joined most of Justice Harlan's objections to the "mechanistic 'incorporation' approach." Justice MARSHALL's dissent stated that he was "convinced that the requirement of 12 should be applied to the States." In contrast, a separate opinion by Justice BLACK, joined by Justice Douglas, supported the majority view on jury size and disagreed with some of Justice Harlan's assertions: "Today's decision is in no way attributable to any desire to dilute the Sixth Amendment in order more easily to apply it to the States, but follows solely as a necessary consequence of our duty to reexamine prior decisions to reach the correct constitutional meaning in each case." He claimed that, had the question been presented to the Court in a federal case before Duncan,

"this Court would still, in my view, have reached the result announced today."

Eight years after Williams had found a six-person criminal jury permissible, the Court found that six was the minimum constitutional size and held that a five-member jury in serious criminal cases was unconstitutional. Ballew v. Georgia, 435 U.S. 223 (1978). [A separate opinion by Justice Powell in Ballew, joined by Chief Justice Burger and Justice Rehnquist, echoed the anti-"jot-for-jot" incorporation argument of Justice Harlan in Williams.]

4. Justices DOUGLAS, BRENNAN, STEWART, and MARSHALL each submitted a dissenting opinion.

under the prevailing approach, the Court ended up, here as in Williams, with "the dilution of federal rights which were, until these decisions, never seriously questioned." [5]

5. In Burch v. Louisiana, 441 U.S. 130 (1979), the Court confronted a problem it described as lying at "the intersection of our decisions concerning jury size and unanimity"—i.e., Williams and Apodaca. The Court held that "conviction by a nonunanimous six-member jury in a state criminal trial for a nonpetty offense deprives an accused of his constitutional right to trial by jury." Setting aside a conviction obtained by a 5 to 1 jury vote, Justice Rehnquist found the issue a "close" one and commented: "[H]aving already departed from the strictly historical requirements of jury trial, it is inevitable that lines must be drawn somewhere if the substance of a jury trial right is to be preserved." (He relied in part on the opposition to five-member juries voiced in the Ballew case in the preceding footnote.)

Chapter 8

SUBSTANTIVE DUE PROCESS: RISE, DECLINE, REVIVAL

Introduction. In no part of constitutional law has the search for legitimate ingredients of constitutional interpretation been more difficult and more controversial than in the turbulent history of substantive due process. To what extent does the due process clause concern itself not simply with the methods of governmental action but also with its substance? To what extent does the due process clause authorize the Court to articulate fundamental values—values not explicitly designated for special protection by the Constitution, yet values which government may not impinge upon without meeting an unusually high standard of justification? That the due process clause *can* serve as a springboard for judicial articulation of "fundamentals" has already been demonstrated in the preceding materials on the Palko-Adamson incorporation controversy. But that course of decisions led the Court to search merely for the fundamentals of *procedure*—typically, the essentials of a fair trial. In its first interpretation of the 14th Amendment, in the Slaughter-House Cases, the majority rejected any notion of *substantive* due process. But the dissenters' plea for the protection of fundamental values prevailed by the end of the 19th century.

The 1905 decision in Lochner v. New York (p. 448), striking down New York's maximum hours law for bakers, symbolizes the rise of substantive due process as a protection of economic and property rights. For three decades thereafter, the Court engaged in "Lochnerizing"—scrutinizing economic regulation with care and frequently striking down economic regulations. In the mid-1930s, judicial intervention in economic legislation began a gradual decline. Today, the use of substantive due process to give special protection to economic and property rights is discredited. Yet in recent years, substantive due process has flourished once again, as a haven for fundamental values other than economic ones; and that development is illustrated by modern decisions protecting autonomy and privacy by striking down laws banning abortions and the use of contraceptives.

These substantive due process cases, old and new, raise common issues: Are these decisions, from Lochner v. New York to Griswold v. Connecticut (p. 503) and Roe v. Wade (p. 517) and beyond, justifiable as interpretations of the Constitution? Are the fundamental values identified in such cases plausible extrapolations from constitutional text, history, or structure? Or are they ultimately extraconstitutional, noninterpretive judicial infusions? What fundamental values, if any, *may* the Court properly impose? Are there basic values—moral, social, or economic—that truly reflect a national consensus? Even if there are such values, does the existence of a consensus justify reading them into the Constitution? Do the Court's fundamental value adjudications in fact rest on an adequately widespread consensus? Or do they reflect values shared by only a segment of the society? Or do they ultimately reflect nothing more than the beliefs of a majority of Justices at a particular time? Are fundamental value adjudications unacceptable if the Court cannot demonstrate an adequate link to constitutional text, history, or structure? Is it possible to state a principled, disciplined "fundamental values" approach that safeguards adequately against merely subjective judicial lawmaking?

441

There is reason to examine the early 20th century cases of the Lochner era even though substantive due process does not impose serious restraints on economic regulation today. The economic regulation cases bear directly on the judicial function in the protection of those individual liberties that receive greater attention from the modern Court. Are the abortion and contraception decisions essentially modern examples of Lochnerizing, or are those recent judicial interventions more justifiable than the earlier ones? The resemblances between Lochner and Roe and Griswold are most evident, but there are additional linkages between the Lochner era and modern Court developments. For example, the source of the Court's interventions in the Lochner era was most commonly the "liberty" protected by the due process clauses: "liberty of contract" and its role as a constitutional support for a laissez faire economy were major preoccupations of the Justices of the Lochner years; and the term "liberty" is also the major textual basis of the Court's active enforcement of personal rights today—not only "fundamental" rights not explicitly listed in the Constitution (such as privacy), but also the "specific" First Amendment guarantees of freedom of speech, press and religion long "incorporated" into the 14th Amendment. Is there justification for the sharp decline in judicial protection of some varieties of "liberty" and the dramatic rise in judicial intervention on behalf of other kinds of "liberty"? That problem of a "double standard" pervades the rest of this book, but it is raised with special force by the contrast between the old and new varieties of substantive due process in secs. 1 and 3 of this chapter.

The Court's encounters with substantive due process in the economic sphere in sec. 1, then, not only influenced its responses to the personal rights claims considered in sec. 3 and later chapters, but also provide essential background for a critical assessment of the modern responses. Substantive due process is the major vehicle for the protection of economic interests examined in sec. 1, but it has not been the only vehicle. Sec. 1A notes some historical antecedents of economic due process developments, some early efforts to find constitutional safeguards for fundamental values. And sec. 2 surveys two themes tangential to the development of substantive due process as a protection of economic and property rights: the role of the contracts clause; and the protection of property against "taking" without just compensation.

SECTION 1. SUBSTANTIVE DUE PROCESS AND ECONOMIC REGULATION: THE RISE AND DECLINE OF JUDICIAL INTERVENTION

A. ANTECEDENTS

Introduction. Substantive due process as a protection of fundamental economic rights did not receive wholehearted support from a Supreme Court majority until the end of the 19th century. But arguments that property and economic rights were basic had long been in the air: the notion that there *were* fundamental rights, and that they were entitled to judicial protection, had considerable earlier support. Some of that support was voiced by the dissenters in the Slaughter-House Cases (p. 410 above). And the fundamental values those dissenters sought to enshrine in the post-Civil War Amendments were values in turn rooted in the thinking of earlier generations: the legacy of Blackstone and Magna Charta—as well as Adam Smith—is explicit in those dissents. As Justice Bradley noted, Blackstone had emphasized property, together with personal security and liberty, as one of the three basic rights of individuals. So, too, had John Locke's social compact philosophy. There was, then, a respectable natural law tradition which, drawing on English antecedents, viewed a written constitution not as the initial source but as a reaffirmation of a social compact preserving preexisting fundamental rights—rights entitled to protection whether or not they were explicitly stated in the basic document.[1]

1. *Calder v. Bull.* Some of those natural law ideas surfaced sporadically in early Court opinions: during the pre-Marshall years, some Justices were tempted to read the Constitution as a whole as a guarantor of fundamental rights—rights that stemmed from the social compact and did not need any explicit textual support. The prime example is Justice CHASE's opinion in 1798, in CALDER v. BULL, 3 Dall. 386. There, the Court rejected an attack on a Connecticut legislative act setting aside a probate court decree that had refused to approve a will. The legislation required a new hearing; and at that second hearing, the will was approved. The challenge to the law came from the heirs who would have taken the property if the will had been ineffective. The Court rejected their claim that the ex post facto clause barred the Connecticut act: that clause was construed as being limited to criminal legislation. But more important for present purposes is the willingness of some Justices to entertain arguments on natural law grounds. Calder v. Bull was handed down in the years before John Marshall persuaded his colleagues to abandon seriatim opinions. And of the several opinions, Justice Chase's dicta most elaborately announced an early inclination to invalidate legislation quite apart from specific constitutional limitations. Justice Chase stated (with the emphases—but not the typeface that makes s's look like f's—as they appear in the original Reports):

"I cannot subscribe to the *omnipotence* of a *State Legislature,* or that it is *absolute* and *without controul;* although its authority should not be *expressly* restrained by the *Constitution,* or *fundamental law,* of the State. The people of the *United States* erected their Constitutions, or forms of governments, to establish justice, to promote the general welfare, to secure the blessings of liberty; and to protect their *persons* and *property* from violence. The purposes for which men enter into society will determine the *nature* and *terms* of the *social* compact; and as *they* are the foundation of the *legislative* power, *they* will decide what are the *proper* objects of it: The *nature,* and *ends* of *legislative* power will limit the *exercise* of it. This *fundamental* principle flows from the very nature of our free *Republican* governments, that no man should be compelled to do what the laws do *not* require; *nor to refrain from acts which the laws permit.* There are acts which the *Federal,* or *State,* Legislature cannot do, *without exceeding their authority.* There are certain *vital* principles in our *free Republican governments,* which will determine and over-rule an *apparent and flagrant* abuse of *legislative* power; as to authorize *manifest injustice by positive law;* or to take away that security for *personal liberty,* or *private property,* for the protection whereof the government was established. An ACT of the Legislature (for I cannot call it a *law*) contrary to the *great first principles* of the *social compact,* cannot be considered a *rightful exercise* of *legislative authority.* The obligation of a law in governments established on *express compact, and on republican principles,* must be determined by the *nature* of the *power,* on which it is founded. A few instances will suffice to explain what I mean. A law that punished a citizen for an *innocent* action, or, in other words, for an act, which, when done, was in violation of no *existing* law; a law that destroys, or impairs, the *lawful private* contracts of citizens; a law that makes a man *a Judge in*

---

1. See generally Corwin, "The Basic Doctrine of American Constitutional Law," 12 Mich.L. Rev. 247 (1914); Corwin, "The 'Higher Law' Background of American Constitutional Law," 42 Harv.L.Rev. 149, 365 (1928–29); Corwin, Liberty Against Government (1948). See also Grey, "Do We Have an Unwritten Constitution?" 27 Stan.L.Rev. 703 (1975), and Grey, "Origins of the Unwritten [Constitution]," 30 Stan.L.Rev. 843 (1978). (Recall the note on the "interpretivist"-"noninterpretivist" debate, p. 20 above, and see footnote 3 below.)

his own cause; or a law that takes *property* from A. and gives it to B. It is against all reason and justice, for a people to entrust a Legislature with SUCH powers; and, therefore, it cannot be presumed that they have done it. The *genius,* the *nature,* and the *spirit,* of our State Governments, amount to a prohibition of *such acts of legislation;* and the *general principles of law and reason* forbid them. The Legislature [cannot] change *innocence* into *guilt;* [or] violate the right of an *antecedent lawful private contract;* or the *right of private property.* To maintain that our Federal, or State, Legislature possesses *such powers,* if they had not been *expressly* restrained; would, in my opinion, be a *political heresy,* altogether inadmissible in our *free* republican governments."[2]

Justice IREDELL's dicta challenged Justice Chase's natural law-social compact-vested rights approach. He stated: "[S]ome speculative jurists have held, that a legislative act against natural justice must, in itself, be void; but I cannot think that, under [a constitutional scheme allocating powers without explicit limitations], any Court of Justice would possess a power to declare it so. Sir *William Blackstone,* having put the strong case of an act of Parliament, which should authorize a man to try his own cause, explicitly adds, that even in that case, 'there is no court that has power to defeat the intent of the Legislature.' In order, therefore, to guard against so great an evil, it has been the policy of all the *American* states, which have, individually, framed their state constitutions since the revolution, and of the people of the *United States,* when they framed the Federal Constitution, to define with precision the objects of the legislative power, and to restrain its exercise within marked and settled boundaries. If any act of Congress, or of the Legislature of a state, violates those constitutional provisions, it is unquestionably [void]. If, on the other hand, the Legislature of the Union, or the Legislature of any member of the Union, shall pass a law, within the general scope of their constitutional power, the Court cannot pronounce it to be void, merely because it is, in their judgment, contrary to the principles of natural justice. The ideas of natural justice are regulated by no fixed standard: the ablest and the purest men have differed upon the subject; and all that the Court could properly say, in such an event, would be, that the Legislature (possessed of an equal right of opinion) had passed an act which, in the opinion of the judges, was inconsistent with the abstract principles of natural justice."

2. *The early Marshall Court.* In the early years of the Marshall Court, there were occasional echoes of Chase's natural law-vested rights approach. For example, in Fletcher v. Peck, 6 Cranch 87 (1810), Marshall flirted with such a notion as an alternative ground for invalidating a Georgia effort to revoke a land grant. He thought the result justified "either by general principles which are common to our free institutions, or by the particular provisions of the constitution of the United States." Justice Johnson's concurrence went even further in that direction. He repudiated any reliance on the contracts clause of the Constitution; instead, he relied on "general principle, on the reason and nature of things." But passages such as these vanished from the opinions in the later Marshall Court years. Instead, the Court linked all of its protections of economic rights to specific constitutional provisions—most often, the contracts clause. (See sec. 2B, p. 487.) In short, Justice Iredell's insistence that only explicit constitutional limits on legislative power were judicially enforceable ultimately prevailed, at least in form. Marshall's rationale for judicial authority in Marbury v. Madison helped assure that Iredell's position, not Chase's, would emerge as the dominant one: a justification for judicial review that relied so heavily on the implications of a written constitution probably found it more

---

2. Justice Chase concluded that legislative powers had not been exceeded by the Connecticut act (because the initial invalidation of the will had not created any "vested" property rights in the heirs).

congenial to justify any invalidations on the basis of explicit constitutional restraints. Nevertheless, notions of natural law and vested rights remained useful and influential, not as an adequate formal basis for invalidation, but as a source of values for giving content to the explicit guarantees such as the contract clause—and, later, substantive due process.

3. *Due process before the Civil War.* Though most pre-Civil War discussion of due process clauses in state constitutions and in the Fifth Amendment spoke of the more obvious procedural implications of due process—recall the Murray's Lessee case, p. 420 above—there were some intimations that due process might also impose substantive restraints on legislation. Thus, in the controversial Dred Scott decision [Dred Scott v. Sandford, 19 How. 393 (1857)], Chief Justice Taney's opinion—explaining why Congress could not bar slavery from the territories and why the Missouri Compromise was therefore unconstitutional—commented, without elaboration, that "An Act of Congress which deprives a citizen of the United States of his liberty or property, merely because he came himself or brought his property into a particular Territory of the United States, and who had committed no offense against the laws, could hardly be dignified with the name of due process of law." [3]

4. *Pressures toward substantive due process in the generation after the Slaughter-House Cases.* The Slaughter-House Cases in 1873 (p. 410 above)—which should be reexamined at this point—temporarily blocked the utilization of the 14th Amendment as a substantive restraint on state legislation. In 1873, a bare majority resisted the dissenters' arguments; but a generation later, a new majority embraced substantive due process, including its novel "liberty of contract" argument. It was not a sudden change: a variety of pressures, on and off the Court, contributed to the gradual conversion of due process into a more interventionist tool. For one, lawyers kept pressing the Court to restrain economic regulation despite the rebuff of the Slaughter-House Cases. As Justice Miller noted five years later, "the docket of this court is crowded with cases in which we are asked to hold that state courts and state legislatures have deprived their own citizens of life, liberty, or property without due process of law. There is here abundant evidence that there exists some strange misconception of the scope of this provision as found in the 14th Amendment. In fact, it

---

3. On the state level, the best-known pre-Civil War suggestion of a substantive ingredient in due process came in Wynehamer v. People, 13 N.Y. 378 (1856), invalidating a liquor prohibition law. As the most prolific student of due process wrote, Wynehamer read due process to "prohibit, regardless of the matter of procedure, a certain kind or degree of exertion of legislative power altogether": due process, rather than merely protecting the "mode of procedure," was made to reach "the substantive content of legislation." Corwin, Liberty Against Government (1948). See also Corwin, "The Doctrine of Due Process of Law Before the Civil War," 24 Harv.L.Rev. 366, 460 (1911). [Other substantive due process arguments before the Civil War came from anti-slavery lawyers, who argued that slavery was a deprivation of liberty without a proper basis in law (such as conviction for crime). But the influence of this type of argument on 14th Amendment developments has been discounted because it was identified almost totally with abolitionists and played no significant role in court decisions or widely accepted legal commentary.]

The usual modern position, then, is that substantive due process had very little pre-Civil War basis. See, e.g., Ely, Democracy and Distrust (1980), 18: "[We] apparently need periodic reminding that 'substantive due process' is a contradiction in terms—sort of like 'green pastel redness.'" But research in progress by another colleague, Thomas Grey, into the "prehistory" of substantive due process, challenges that traditional position. Grey concedes that the "liberty"-emphasizing aspect of substantive due process—as with the "liberty of contract" of Lochner—is indeed a late-19th century invention. But he does insist that, in the decades preceding the adoption of the 14th Amendment, an increasing number of state courts read state due process clauses as affording substantive protection to property from arbitrary legislative interferences. He sees those state court decisions as propounding a variety of vested rights theories and protections against "takings" somewhat akin to Justice Chase's dicta in Calder v. Bull. Grey claims, for example, that nearly a third of the states in the Union in 1868 had clearly construed state due process clauses to give substantive protection to property rights. (Grey's research is directed toward a book on the theme of our unwritten constitution, developing a position first propounded in his articles cited in footnote 1 above.)

would seem, from the character of many of the cases before us, and the arguments made in them, that the clause under consideration is looked upon as a means of bringing to the test of the decision of this court the abstract opinions of every unsuccessful litigant in a State court of the justice of the decision against him, and of the merits of the legislation on which such a decision may be founded." Davidson v. New Orleans, 96 U.S. 97 (1877).[4]

The lawyers' arguments that seemed a "misconception" of due process to Justice Miller reflected deeper social developments and ideological movements.[5] The growth of industrialization and corporate power in the post-Civil War years stirred popular demands and legislative responses. The new regulatory laws, opponents argued, contravened not only the economic laissez faire theories of Adam Smith but also the social views of 19th century writers such as Herbert Spencer. In his Lochner dissent, Justice Holmes was to insist that the 14th Amendment "does not enact Mr. Herbert Spencer's Social Statics." But Spencer's emphasis on the survival of the fittest in his 1850 volume, and the echoes of Social Darwinism in the writings of American defenders of economic inequalities and governmental hands-off policies, found their way into legal treatises and briefs. And, increasingly, there were responsive listeners on the bench. As Justice Brewer stated in dissent in Budd v. New York, 143 U.S. 517 (1892): "The paternal theory of government is to me odious. The utmost possible liberty to the individual, and the fullest possible protection to him and his property, is both the limitation and duty of government."[6] Soon, the seeds of substantive due process began to be visible in majority opinions.

a. *Rate regulation and the Munn case.* A leading case of the 1870s, for example, is commonly viewed as a symbol of judicial deference to legislative judgments; yet, at the same time, it suggested potential limits on legislative power. In MUNN v. ILLINOIS, 94 U.S. 113 (1877), the Court rejected an attack on a state law regulating the rates of grain elevators. Chief Justice WAITE's majority opinion emphasized that the police power included regulation of individual use of property "when such regulation becomes necessary for the public good." He relied in part on 17th century English writings to conclude that private property may be regulated when it is "affected with a public interest" and that property becomes "clothed with a public interest when used in a manner to make it of public consequence, and affect the community at large." The business owners regulated here easily fell within that category: they had a near monopoly on grain storage; regulation of their rates was similar to traditional price regulation of utilities and monopolies. The majority refused

4. Even Justice Miller, in the years between his majority opinion in Slaughter-House and his continued rejection of substantive due process in Davidson, proved not wholly immune to fundamental values arguments via other routes. For example, in 1875 he wrote for the Court in holding invalid an ordinance authorizing the issuance of municipal bonds for the benefit of private enterprise. Without tying his analysis to any particular constitutional provision, Justice Miller echoed Chase's sentiments in Calder v. Bull by writing in a well-known passage that there are "rights in every free government beyond the control of the State. [There] are limitations on such power which grow out of the essential nature of all free governments. Implied reservations of individual rights, without which the social compact could not exist, and which are respected by all governments entitled to the name." Loan Association v. Topeka, 20 Wall. 655 (1874). (Arguably, Justice Miller was able to avoid pointing to any particular constitutional

provision because the case reached the Court on diversity grounds.)

5. See generally Paul, Conservative Crisis and the Rule of Law: Attitudes of Bar and Bench 1887–1896 (1960), and Twiss, Lawyers and the Constitution: How Laissez Faire Came to the Supreme Court (1942). The lawyers' advocacy of substantive due process frequently relied on an influential treatise published in the same year the 14th Amendment was adopted, Cooley, Constitutional Limitation (1868).

6. Substantive due process flourished in some state courts before it found majority support in the Supreme Court. The leading late 19th century case was In the Matter of Jacobs, 98 N.Y. 98 (1885), holding unconstitutional a law prohibiting the manufacture of cigars in tenement houses. To the state court, the public health justification was unpersuasive, and the law interfered not only with "the profitable and free use" of property but also with "personal liberty."

to scrutinize the reasonableness of the rates: since there was power to regulate, the legislative right to establish maximum rates was implied. Chief Justice Waite added: "We know that this is a power which may be abused; but that is no argument against its existence. For protection against abuses by legislatures the people must resort to the polls." Yet the Chief Justice prefaced that passage with a statement which could later be relied on to justify judicial control of rate regulation: "Undoubtedly, in mere private contracts, relating to matters in which the public has no interest, what is reasonable must be ascertained judicially." [7]

Chief Justice Waite took a similar noninterventionist stance in The Railroad Commission Cases, 116 U.S. 307 (1886), sustaining state regulation of railroad rates. But, again, the deference to legislative judgments was joined with a passage which left the door open for greater judicial control in the future. He warned that "it is not to be inferred that this power [of] regulation [is] without limit. This power to regulate is not a power to destroy. Under pretence of regulating fares and freights, the State cannot require a railroad corporation to carry persons or property without reward; neither can it do that which in law amounts to a taking of private property for public use without just compensation, or without due process of law." [8] In the same year, in Santa Clara County v. Southern Pac. Railroad, 118 U.S. 394 (1886), the Court held, without discussion, that corporations were "persons" within the meaning of the 14th Amendment.[9] The early resistance to judicial intervention was weakening; dicta even in noninterventionist cases were leaving the door slightly ajar; and soon it swung wide open.

b. *Mugler v. Kansas.* Before long, substantive due process review ranging well beyond rate regulation and encompassing a wide variety of police power exercises was fully launched. MUGLER v. KANSAS, 123 U.S. 623 (1887), signaled the impending receptivity of the Court. Mugler sustained a law prohibiting intoxicating beverages, but the Court announced that it was prepared to examine the substantive reasonableness of state legislation. The first Justice HARLAN spoke for a Court whose composition had changed almost totally since the Slaughter-House Cases. He stated that not "every statute enacted ostensibly for the promotion" of "the public morals, the public health, or the public safety" would be accepted "as a legitimate exertion of the police powers of the State." The courts would not be "misled by mere pretences"; they were obligated "to look at the substance of things." Accordingly, if a purported exercise of the police powers "has no real or substantial relation to those objects, or is a palpable invasion of rights secured by the fundamental law,

---

7. Justice Field dissented in Munn, as he had in the Slaughter-House Cases. Note the reexamination of the Munn legacy and its legacy in Nebbia (1934; p. 462 below).

8. In the further development of judicial control of rate making, Chicago, M. & St. P. Ry. Co. v. Minnesota, 134 U.S. 418 (1890), was a significant turning point. That decision invalidated a state law authorizing administrative rate making without providing for judicial review. The immediate vice of the statute was the lack of adequate procedural protection for the railroads—the lack of judicial review. But the majority explanation suggested Court concern with substance as well as procedure: reasonableness of rates was found to be "eminently a question for judicial investigation"; depriving the railroad of the power to charge reasonable rates by administrative order would be, "in substance and effect,"

a deprivation of property without due process of law. (Justice Bradley's dissent viewed the decision as a virtual overruling of Munn v. Illinois.) By the end of the decade, the Court was wholeheartedly in the business of scrutinizing the reasonableness of rates. Smyth v. Ames, 169 U.S. 466 (1898), provided the governing rate-making formulas for decades. For a review of rate regulation developments after the 1890s (and the repudiation of the reign of Smyth v. Ames) see FPC v. Hope Natural Gas Co., 320 U.S. 591 (1944).

9. See Graham, "The 'Conspiracy Theory' of the Fourteenth Amendment," 47 Yale L.J. 371 and 48 Yale L.J. 171 (1938). Justices Black and Douglas objected to this interpretation. See the dissents in Connecticut General Life Ins. Co. v. Johnson, 303 U.S. 77 (1938), and Wheeling Steel Corp. v. Glander, 337 U.S. 562 (1949).

it is the duty of the courts to so adjudge." And facts "within the knowledge of all" would be relied on in making that determination.

c. *The Allgeyer case and liberty of contract.* Ten years later, in ALLGEYER v. LOUISIANA, 165 U.S. 578 (1897), the slow movement to substantive due process was completed: the Court for the first time invalidated a state law on substantive due process grounds. Allgeyer involved a Louisiana law that prohibited obtaining insurance on Louisiana property "from any marine insurance company which has not complied in all respects" with Louisiana law. Allgeyer was convicted for mailing a letter advising an insurance company in New York of the shipment of goods, in accordance with a marine policy. The company was not licensed to do business in Louisiana. The Supreme Court reversed, holding the statute in violation of the 14th Amendment "in that it deprives the defendants of their liberty without due process of law." Justice PECKHAM's opinion contained an extensive discussion of state power over foreign corporations and emphasized that the insurance contract was made outside Louisiana. But it was the Court's articulation of the liberty of contract that gave the case its special significance in the development of substantive due process: "The liberty mentioned in that amendment means not only the right of the citizen to be free from the mere physical restraint of his person, as by incarceration, but the term is deemed to embrace the right of the citizen to be free in the enjoyment of all his faculties; to be free to use them in all lawful ways; to live and work where he will; to earn his livelihood by any lawful calling; to pursue any livelihood or avocation, and for that purpose to enter into all contracts which may be proper, necessary and essential to his carrying out to a successful conclusion the purposes above mentioned."

Soon after the turn of the century, the expansive conception of "liberty" in Allgeyer bore fruit in more controversial contexts, exemplified by the Lochner case, which follows. When the modern Court looks back to the discredited "Allgeyer-Lochner-Adair-Coppage constitutional doctrine" (the phrase is from the Lincoln Federal Labor Union case in 1949, p. 468 below), the Allgeyer reference is not to its specific insurance setting but to its significance in opening the door to substitution of the Justices' notions of public policy and fundamental values for legislative choices regarding economic and social regulation, as assertedly took place in Lochner. Is that what happened in Lochner and its progeny? Has that due process philosophy been wholly rejected by the modern Court?

B. THE LOCHNER ERA: JUDICIAL INTERVENTION AND ECONOMIC REGULATION

LOCHNER v. NEW YORK

198 U.S. 45, 25 S.Ct. 539, 49 L.Ed. 937 (1905).

Mr. Justice PECKHAM [delivered] the opinion of the court.

[A New York law prohibited the employment of bakery employees for more than 10 hours a day or 60 hours a week. Lochner was convicted and fined for permitting an employee to work in his Utica, N.Y., bakery for more than 60 hours in one week.]

[The] employé may desire to earn the extra money, which would arise from his working more than the prescribed time, but this statute forbids the employer from permitting the employé to earn it. The statute necessarily interferes with the right of contract between the employer and [employés]. The general right to make a contract in relation to his business is part of the liberty of the individual protected by the 14th Amendment. [Allgeyer.] The right to purchase or to sell labor is part of the liberty protected by this amendment, unless there are circumstances which exclude the right. There are, however, [state police] powers [relating] to the safety, health, morals and general welfare of the public. [When] the [state legislature], in the assumed exercise of its police powers, has passed an act which seriously limits the right to labor or the right of contract in regard to their means of livelihood between persons who are sui juris (both employer and employé), it becomes of great importance to determine which shall prevail—the right of the individual to labor for such time as he may choose, or the right of the State to prevent the individual from laboring [beyond] a certain time prescribed by the State.

This court has recognized the existence and upheld the exercise of the police powers of the States in many cases which might fairly be considered as border ones, and it [has] been guided by rules of a very liberal nature, the application of which has resulted, in numerous instances, in upholding the validity of state statutes thus assailed. Among the later cases where the state law has been upheld by this court is that of Holden v. Hardy.[1] [I]t was held that the kind of employment, mining, smelting, etc., and the character of the employés in such kinds of labor, were such as to make it reasonable and proper for the State to interfere to prevent the employés from being constrained by the rules laid down by the proprietors in regard to labor. [There] is nothing in Holden v. Hardy which covers the case now before [us].

It must, of course, be conceded that there is a limit to the valid exercise of the [police power]. Otherwise the 14th Amendment would have no efficacy and the legislatures of the States would have unbounded power, and it would be enough to say that any piece of legislation was enacted to conserve the morals, the health or the safety of the [people]. The claim of the police power would be a mere [pretext]. In every case that comes before this court, therefore, [the] question necessarily arises: Is this a fair, reasonable and appropriate exercise of the [police power], or is it an unreasonable, unnecessary and arbitrary interference with the right of the individual to his personal liberty or to enter into those contracts in relation to labor which may seem to him appropriate or necessary for the support of himself and his family? Of course the liberty of contract relating to labor includes both parties to it. The one has as much right to purchase as the other to sell labor. This is not a question of substituting the judgment of the court for that of the legislature. If the act be within the power of the State it is valid, although the judgment of the court might be totally opposed to the enactment of such a law. But the question would still remain: Is it within the police power of the State? and that question must be answered by the court.

The question whether this act is valid as a labor law, pure and simple, may be dismissed in a few words. There is no reasonable ground for interfering with the liberty of person or the right of free contract, by determining the hours of labor, in the occupation of a baker. There is no contention that bakers as a class are not equal in intelligence and capacity to men in other trades or manual occupations, or that they are not able to assert their rights and care for themselves without the protecting arm of the State, interfering with their independence of judgment and of action. They are in no sense wards of the State. Viewed in the light of a purely labor law, with no reference whatever to the question of health, we think that a law like the one before us involves neither the safety, the morals nor the welfare of the public, and that the interest

---

1. Holden v. Hardy, 169 U.S. 366 (1898), sustained a Utah law limiting the employment of workers in underground mines to eight hours a day. The case was decided in the period between Allgeyer and Lochner.

of the public is not in the slightest degree affected by such an act. The law must be upheld, if at all, as a law pertaining to the health of the individual engaged in the occupation of a baker. [Clean] and wholesome bread does not depend upon whether the baker works but ten hours per day or only sixty hours a week. The limitation of the hours of labor does not come within the police power on that ground. [The] mere assertion that the subject relates though but in a remote degree to the public health does not necessarily render the enactment valid. The act must have a more direct relation, as a means to an end, and the end itself must be appropriate and legitimate, before an act can be held to be valid which interferes with the general right of an individual to be free in his person and in his power to contract in relation to his own [labor].

We think the limit of the police power has been reached and passed in this case. There is, in our judgment, no reasonable foundation for holding this to be necessary or appropriate as a health law to safeguard the public health or the health of the individuals who are following the trade of a baker. If this statute be valid, [there] would seem to be no length to which legislation of this nature might not go. [We] think that there can be no fair doubt that the trade of a baker, in and of itself, is not an unhealthy one to that degree which would authorize the legislature to interfere with the right to labor, and with the right of free contract on the part of the individual, either as employer or employé. In looking through statistics regarding all trades and occupations, it may be true that the trade of a baker does not appear to be as healthy as some other trades, and is also vastly more healthy than still others. To the common understanding the trade of a baker has never been regarded as an unhealthy one. [It] might be safely affirmed that almost all occupations more or less affect the health. There must be more than the mere fact of the possible existence of some small amount of unhealthiness to warrant legislative interference with liberty. It is unfortunately true that labor, even in any department, may possibly carry with it the seeds of unhealthiness. But are we all, on that account, at the mercy of legislative majorities?

[It] is also urged [that] it is to the interest of the State that its population should be strong and robust, and therefore any legislation which may be said to tend to make people healthy must be valid as health laws, enacted under the police power. If this be a valid argument and a justification for this kind of legislation, it follows that the protection of the Federal Constitution from undue interference with liberty of person and freedom of contract is visionary, wherever the law is sought to be justified as a valid exercise of the police power. Scarcely any law but might find shelter under such [assumptions]. Not only the hours of employés, but the hours of employers, could be regulated, and doctors, lawyers, scientists, all professional men, as well as athletes and artisans, could be forbidden to fatigue their brains and bodies by prolonged hours of exercise, lest the fighting strength of the State be impaired. We mention these extreme cases because the contention is extreme. We do not believe in the soundness of the views which uphold this law. On the contrary, we think that such a law as this, although passed in the assumed exercise of the police power, and as relating to the public health, or the health of the employés named, is not within that power, and is invalid. The act is not, within any fair meaning of the term, a health law, but is an illegal interference with the rights of individuals, both employers and employés, to make contracts regarding labor upon such terms as they may think best, or which they may agree upon with the other parties to such contracts. Statutes of the nature of that under review, limiting the hours in which grown and intelligent men may labor to earn their living, are mere meddlesome interferences with the rights of the individual, and they are not saved from condemnation by the claim that they are passed in the exercise of the police power and upon the subject of the health of the individual whose rights are interfered with, unless there be some fair ground, reasonable in and of itself, to say that there is material danger to the public health or to the health of the employés, if the hours of labor are not curtailed. [All that the State] could properly do has been done by it with regard to the conduct of bakeries, as provided for in the other sections of the act, [which] provide for the inspection of the premises where the bakery is carried on, with regard to furnishing proper wash-rooms and water-closets, [also] with regard to providing proper drainage, plumbing and painting [and] for other things of that [nature].

It was further urged [that] restricting the hours of labor in the case of bakers was valid because it tended to cleanliness on the part of the workers, as a man was more apt to be cleanly when not overworked, and if cleanly then his "output" was also more likely to be so. In our judgment it is not possible in fact to discover the connection between the number of hours a baker may work in the bakery and the healthful quality of the bread made by the workman. The connection, if any exists, is too shadowy and thin to build any argument for the interference of the legislature. If the man works ten hours a day it is all right, but if ten and a half or eleven his health is in danger and his bread may be unhealthful, and, therefore, he shall not be permitted to do it. This, we think, is unreasonable and entirely arbitrary. When assertions such as we have adverted to become necessary in order to give, if possible, a plausible foundation for the contention that the law is a "health law," it gives rise to at least a suspicion that there was some other motive dominating the legislature than the purpose to subserve the public health or welfare. This interference on the part of the legislatures of the several States with the ordinary trades and occupations of the people seems to be on the increase. [It] is impossible for us to shut our eyes to the fact that many of the laws of this character, while passed under what is claimed to be the police power for the purpose of protecting the public health or welfare, are, in reality, passed from other motives. We are justified in saying so when, from the character of the law and the subject upon which it legislates, it is apparent that the public health or welfare bears but the most remote relation to the law. The purpose of a statute must be determined from the natural and legal effect of the language employed; and whether it is or is not repugnant to the Constitution [must] be determined from the natural effect of such statutes when put into operation, and not from their proclaimed purpose.

[It] is manifest to us that the [law here] has no such direct relation to and no such substantial effect upon the health of the employé as to justify us in regarding the section as really a health law. It seems to us that the real object and purpose were simply to regulate the hours of labor between the master and his employés (all being men, sui juris), in a private business, not dangerous in any degree to morals or in any real and substantial degree, to the health of the employés. Under such circumstances the freedom of master and employé to contract with each other in relation to their [employment] cannot be prohibited or interfered with, without violating the Federal Constitution.

[Reversed].

Mr. Justice HARLAN, with whom Mr. Justice WHITE and Mr. Justice DAY concurred, [dissenting].

[There] is a liberty of contract which cannot be violated, [but] is subject to [reasonable police regulations]. It is plain that this statute was enacted in order to protect the physical well-being of those who work in [bakery] establishments. It may be that the statute had its origin in part, in the belief that employers and employés in such establishments were not upon an equal footing, and that the necessities of the latter often compelled them to submit to such exactions as unduly taxed their strength. Be this as it may, the statute must be taken as expressing the belief of the people of New York that, as a general rule, and in the case of the average man, labor in excess of sixty hours during a week in such establishments may endanger the health of those who thus labor. Whether or not this be wise legislation, it is not the province of the court to inquire. [The] courts are not concerned with the wisdom or policy of legislation. So that in determining the question of power to interfere with liberty of contract, the court may inquire whether the means devised by the State are germane to an end which may be lawfully accomplished and have a real or substantial relation to the protection of health, as involved in the daily work of the persons, male and female, engaged in [bakery] establishments. But when this inquiry is entered upon I find it impossible, in view of common experience, to say that there is here no real or substantial relation between the means employed by the State and the ends sought to be accomplished by its legislation. [Still] less can I say that the statute is, beyond question, a plain, palpable invasion of rights secured by the fundamental [law].

Professor Hirt in his treatise on the "Diseases of the Workers" has said: "The labor of the bakers is among the hardest and most laborious imaginable, because it has to be performed under conditions injurious to the health of those engaged in it. It is hard, very hard work, not only because it requires a great deal of physical exertion in an overheated workshop and during unreasonably long hours, but more so because of the erratic demands of the public, compelling the baker to perform the greater part of his work at [night]." Another writer says: "The constant inhaling of flour dust causes inflammation of the lungs and of the bronchial tubes. The eyes also suffer through this [dust]. The long hours of toil to which all bakers are subjected produce rheumatism, cramps and swollen legs. [Nearly] all bakers are pale-faced and of more delicate health than the workers of other crafts, which is chiefly due to their hard work and their irregular and unnatural mode of living. [The] average age of a baker is below that of other workmen; they seldom live over their fiftieth year." [Additional data are omitted.]

We judicially know that the question of the number of hours during which a workman should continuously labor has been, for a long period, and is yet, a subject of serious consideration among civilized peoples, and by those having special knowledge of the laws of health. [We] also judicially know that the number of hours that should constitute a day's labor in particular occupations involving the physical strength and safety of workmen has been the subject of enactments by Congress and by nearly all of the States. Many, if not most, of those enactments fix eight hours as the proper basis of a day's labor. I do not stop to consider whether any particular view of this economic question presents the sounder theory. [It] is enough for the determination of this case, and it is enough for this court to know, that the question is one about which there is room for debate and for an honest difference of opinion. There are many reasons of a weighty, substantial character, based upon the experience of mankind, in support of the theory that, all things considered, more than ten hours' steady work each day, from week to week, in a bakery or confectionery establishment, may endanger the health, and shorten the lives of the workmen, thereby diminishing their physical and mental capacity to serve the State, and to provide for those dependent upon them. If such reasons exist that ought to be the end of this case, for the State is not amenable to the judiciary, in respect of its legislative enactments, unless such enactments are plainly, palpably, beyond all question, inconsistent with the [Constitution]. A decision that the New York statute is void under the 14th Amendment will, in my opinion, involve consequences of a far-reaching and mischievous character; for such a decision would seriously cripple the inherent power of the States to care for the lives, health and well-being of their [citizens].

Mr. Justice HOLMES, dissenting.

[This] case is decided upon an economic theory which a large part of the country does not entertain. If it were a question whether I agreed with that theory, I should desire to study it further and long before making up my mind. But I do not conceive that to be my duty, because I strongly believe that my agreement or disagreement has nothing to do with the right of a majority to embody their opinions in law. It is settled by various decisions of this court that [state laws] may regulate life in many ways which we as legislators might think as injudicious or if you like as tyrannical as this, and which equally with this interfere with the liberty to contract. Sunday laws and usury laws are ancient examples. A more modern one is the prohibition of lotteries. The liberty of the citizen to do as he likes so long as he does not interfere with the liberty of others to do the same, which has been a shibboleth for some well-known writers, is interfered with by school laws, by the Post Office, by every state or municipal institution which takes his money for purposes thought desirable, whether he likes it or not. The 14th Amendment does not enact Mr. Herbert Spencer's Social Statics. The other day we sustained the Massachusetts vaccination law. Jacobson v. Massachusetts, 197 U.S. 11 [1905]. United States and state statutes and decisions cutting down the liberty to contract by way of combination are familiar to this court. [The] decision sustaining an eight hour law for miners is still recent. Some of these laws embody convictions or prejudices which judges are likely to share. Some may not. But a constitution is not intended to embody a particular economic theory, whether of paternalism and the organic relation of the citizen to the State or of laissez faire. It is made for people of fundamentally differing views, and the accident of our finding certain opinions natural and familiar or novel and even shocking ought not to conclude our judgment upon the question whether statutes embodying them conflict with the [Constitution].

General propositions do not decide concrete cases. The decision will depend on a judgment or intuition more subtle than any articulate major premise. But I think that the proposition just stated, if it is accepted, will carry us far toward the end. Every opinion tends to become a law. I think that the word liberty in the 14th Amendment is perverted when it is held to prevent the natural outcome of a dominant opinion, unless it can be said that a rational and fair man necessarily would admit that the statute proposed would infringe fundamental principles as they have been understood by the traditions of our people and our law. It does not need research to show that no such sweeping condemnation can be passed upon the statute before us. A reasonable man might think it a proper measure on the score of health. Men whom I certainly could not pronounce unreasonable would uphold it as a first instalment of a general regulation of the hours of work. Whether in the latter aspect it would be open to the charge of inequality I think it unnecessary to discuss.

THE DISCREDITED PERIOD OF JUDICIAL INTERVENTION: WHAT WAS WRONG WITH LOCHNER?

Introduction. From the Lochner decision in 1905 to the mid-1930s, the Court invalidated a considerable number of laws on substantive due process grounds.[1] Regulations of prices, labor relations (including wages and hours), and conditions for entry into business were especially vulnerable. Typically, as in Lochner, the invalidations provoked dissents, most often by Holmes and, later, Brandeis, Stone and Cardozo.[2] But even during the Lochner era, while nearly 200 regulations were struck down, most challenged laws withstood

---

1. For a comprehensive summary of the decisions of the period, see The Constitution of the United States (Gov't Printing Office, 1972 ed.). See also Wright, The Growth of American Constitutional Law (1942).

2. Among the many critics not on the Court was Learned Hand. See Hand, "Due Process of Law and the Eight-Hour Day," 21 Harv.L.Rev. 495 (1908). Moreover, the Lochner era decisions became political issues well before the New Deal

attack. Thus, the Court sustained a maximum hours law for women only three years after Lochner, in Muller v. Oregon, below; and it upheld a 10-hour day for factory workers in Bunting v. Oregon in 1917, below. Yet the extent of judicial intervention during the Lochner era was clearly substantial; and the modern Court has repeatedly insisted that it has turned its back on the evils of the Lochner philosophy. What *were* those evils? The giving of substantive content to due process? The expansive view of "liberty" and "property" to include values not specifically stated in the Constitution? The selection of the "wrong" fundamental values for special judicial protection? The failure to state adequate general standards? The failure to apply the standards with adequate consistency? The failure to apply the standards with adequate receptiveness to factual data? Excessive preoccupation with the permissibility of legislative ends? Excessive preoccupation with the "reasonableness" of legislative means—the extent to which the means contributed to the achievement of permissible ends?

Examining the cases of the Lochner era in light of questions such as these is of more than historical interest. Rejection of the Lochner heritage is a common starting point for modern Justices: reaction against the excessive intervention of the "Old Men" of the pre-1937 Court strongly influenced the judicial philosophies of their successors. Yet the modern Court has *not* drawn from Lochner the lesson that *all* judicial intervention via substantive due process is improper. Rather, it has withdrawn from careful scrutiny in most economic areas but has increased intervention regarding a range of noneconomic personal interests. Identifying the evils of the Lochner era is especially relevant, then, to determine (a) whether the modern Court's interventions avoid those evils, and (b) whether those evils warranted as substantial a withdrawal from the economic area as has taken place.

1. *Lochner and the language of the 14th Amendment.* a. *"Liberty" and economic rights.* Did the basic vice of Lochner lie in its expansive reading of "liberty"? Justice Peckham read "liberty" broadly to include freedom of contract. Some critics identify that as the basic flaw of the Lochner philosophy: they claim liberty at common law meant only freedom from physical restraint, and that it should have meant no more in the due process clause.[3] But even if that view of common law is correct, should that control the limits of "liberty" under the Constitution?

Rather than its generous reading of "liberty," is the Lochner philosophy more properly criticizable for its selection of some aspects of liberty for *special* protection? Simply reading liberty broadly need not be an interventionist doctrine: if a "mere rationality" standard is used—if legislative restraints on liberty are permissible so long as reasonable persons might think that the restraints plausibly promote broadly conceived legislative objectives—an expansive reading of liberty does not produce frequent judicial invalidations. It is only when the "liberty" allegedly infringed is thought to be "fundamental," deserving of special protection, and thus imposing on the state especially high burdens of justification for the infringement, that due process turns into an interventionist tool. As sec. 1C shows, retreat from interventionism in the economic area on the modern Court has typically not taken place via a shrinking

---

attacks of the mid-1930s—e.g., in the third party campaigns of Teddy Roosevelt in 1912 (in which Learned Hand participated) and in the Robert LaFollette campaign in 1924.

Substantive due process was far and away the most important judicial tool, but it was not the only basis for restraints on economic regulation during this period. On the role of the 14th Amendment's equal protection clause as a source of limits on economic regulation—a role which

paralleled but was less significant than that of substantive due process—see chap. 9, sec. 1, below. Recall also the restrictive interpretations of national regulatory powers considered in earlier chapters; and note the continued reliances on the contracts clause even after the advent of substantive due process, sec. 2B below.

3. See, e.g., Warren, "The New 'Liberty' under the Fourteenth Amendment," 39 Harv.L. Rev. 431 (1926).

of "liberty"; instead, it has taken the form of an extremely deferential "minimum rationality" standard in testing whether alleged infringements of economic liberties are justifiable.

b. *"Liberty" and noneconomic rights.* Note, too, that it is the reading of "liberty" beyond the narrowest common law confines that has made possible the protection of a wide range of noneconomic interests under the 14th Amendment. Not only economic regulations fell victim to substantive due process attacks in the three decades beginning with Lochner. That period also saw the early development of 14th Amendment protections of civil liberties and of the rights of the accused. The Allgeyer-Lochner philosophy formed the basis for absorbing rights such as those in the First Amendment into the 14th Amendment's concept of liberty, as chap. 11 shows. Justice Brandeis' eloquent defense of free speech in Whitney v. California (1927; p. 1007 below), included a reluctant acceptance of the triumph of substantive due process—a triumph that supported the speech protection he advocated there.[4]

Moreover, the Allgeyer-Lochner view that liberty should not be limited to its narrowest reading helped justify intervention on behalf of personal, noneconomic rights other than those that had counterparts in the First Amendment. Note, for example, the noneconomic personal liberties recognized in Meyer v. Nebraska (1923; p. 502 below), reversing a conviction of a parochial school teacher under a law prohibiting teaching "in any language other than" English. Justice McReynolds' majority opinion, squarely within the Lochner tradition, contained a broad reading of liberty that has attained renewed significance in the modern revival of substantive due process on behalf of noneconomic fundamental rights such as privacy. He stated that "liberty" denotes "not merely freedom from bodily restraint but also the right of the individual to contract, to engage in any of the common occupations of life, to acquire useful knowledge, to marry, to establish a home and bring up children, to worship God according to the dictates of his own conscience, and generally to enjoy those privileges long recognized at common law as essential to the orderly pursuit of happiness by free men."[5]

c. *"Property" and "due process".* Does criticism of the broad readings of "property" and "due process" get any closer to the roots of the Court's difficulties in the Lochner era than the questioning of the expansive view of "liberty"? A good many of the cases of the Lochner era involved restrictions on the use of property even under the narrowest reading of that term. But the Court's penchant for broad interpretations extended to "property" as well: the much-invoked right to contract, for example, was not traced solely to "liberty," as in Lochner, but was also viewed as a derivation from notions of "property." See, e.g., Coppage v. Kansas (1915; p. 459 below). The strongest textual criticism of the Court's substantive due process developments, however, focuses not on "liberty" or "property" but on the phrase "due process": How does a legitimate method of interpretation draw from a phrase with procedural connotations a basis for scrutiny of the substance of legislation? What, if any, "process" is the Court concerned with in substantive due process cases?

4. Justice Brandeis stated: "Despite arguments to the contrary which had seemed to me persuasive, it is settled that the due process clause of the 14th Amendment applies to matters of substantive law as well as to matters of procedure."

Indeed, Charles Warren's article cited above—attacking the reading of "liberty" beyond common law confines—had as its main target Gitlow v. New York (1925; p. 1002 below), where the Court for the first time assumed that the First Amendment freedoms of speech and press were "among the fundamental personal rights and liberties" protected by the 14th Amendment.

5. See also Pierce v. Society of Sisters (1925; p. 502 below), another broad reading of "liberty" to include noneconomic rights. Note the reliance on Meyer and Pierce in the 1965 decision on the Connecticut birth control law, Griswold v. Connecticut, p. 503 below; and Justice Black's rejection of those cases, as products of the Lochner philosophy, in his dissent in Griswold.

2. *Lochner and legislative ends.* Justice Peckham's opinion in Lochner did not consider liberty of contract an absolute. He, and all the other Justices, recognized that liberty of contract is subject to reasonable restraints under the police power. But what governmental objectives *are* legitimately within the police power? Does the real vice of the Lochner philosophy lie in its unduly narrow conception of those objectives? Justice Peckham recognized that "health" is a legitimate end of the police power, and most of his opinion considered whether New York's regulation could be justified as a health law— as a law to promote the health of bakers or of the consuming public. With respect to health, he was not satisfied that the means adequately promoted that legitimate state end. But there was another arguable end of the law—one that received short shrift from Justice Peckham. That justification stressed the unequal bargaining position of bakery workers and argued that a state may, under its police powers, redress perceived economic inequalities. That is what Justice Peckham called "a labor law, pure and simple"; and to him, a "purely labor law" was not within the objectives contemplated by the police power: "There is no contention that bakers as a class are not equal in intelligence and capacity to men in other trades or manual occupations. [They] are in no sense wards of the State."[6] That refusal of the Court to accept the redressing of inequalities as a legitimate ingredient of the police power lay at the base of many of the Lochner era invalidations. Coppage v. Kansas (1915; p. 459 below) makes the point very clearly: in striking down a law designed to protect labor organizing efforts, the majority stated that the police power may not be invoked to remove "those inequalities that are but the normal and inevitable result" of the exercise of rights of contract and property. Justice Holmes' dissent in Coppage, as in Lochner, was squarely directed at that narrow view of legislative ends: the police power, he insisted in Coppage, may be used "to establish the equality of position between the parties in which liberty of contract begins." And, as he said in the Lochner dissent, a constitution "is not intended to embody a particular economic theory, whether of paternalism and the organic relation of the citizen to the State or of laissez faire."[7]

It is difficult to perceive a basis for the Lochner majority's view of impermissible ends other than an improper reading of a particular economic philosophy into the Constitution. Is there a more persuasive basis for the modern Court's new assertions of impermissible ends? Or do the modern cases, analogously to Lochner, simply read a particular social philosophy into the Constitution? (See the notes following the abortion case, Roe v. Wade, at p. 517 below.) Even if the Lochner Court's view of impermissible ends is justifiable, were the applications of that position defensible? Can Lochner be squared with the cases involving miners and working women?

3. *Lochner and means-ends relationships.* a. *Minimum rationality.* The Lochner majority's objection to the New York law goes not merely to ends but also to means. Viewed as a "labor law," a law designed to protect bakery workers in an unequal bargaining position, the Lochner majority rejected the legitimacy of the legislative end out of hand. But the majority conceded the validity of health objectives. In its scrutiny of the legislation as a health law, the Court

6. Mine workers and women, by contrast, *were* among those perceived by the Lochner era Court to be "unequal" and hence, presumably, legitimate "wards." See Holden v. Hardy, above, and Muller v. Oregon, below.

7. Consider the comment in Gunther, "Foreword: In Search of Evolving Doctrine on a Changing Court: A Model for a Newer Equal Protection," 86 Harv.L.Rev. 1, 42 (1972): "[T]he primary evil of the discredited [Lochner] doctrine was the dogmatic judicial intervention regarding ends, not means. Although the Court of the early twentieth century would occasionally [permit] protective legislation designed to redress inequality, the majority's devotion to liberty of contract typically led it to deny the legitimacy of paternalistic legislation. Such laws were 'disturbing of equality of right'; most 'inequalities of fortune' were 'legitimate' consequences of the economic system, beyond the legislature's reach. Justice Holmes' classic dissents properly identified the dominant evil of that approach."

purported to be concerned only with the means invoked to promote a legitimate objective. Justice Peckham conceded that a valid health law *could* restrict liberty of contract: his test was that there must be "some fair ground, reasonable in and of itself, to say that there is material danger to [health]." Why was that test not satisfied in Lochner?

Justice Harlan's dissent, unlike that of Justice Holmes, was directed at the means rather than the ends analysis in the majority opinion.[8] Did the majority's articulated standard as to means-ends relationships differ from Justice Harlan's insistence that there be a "real or substantial relation between the means employed by the State and the end sought to be accomplished by its legislation"? Was the difference between the majority and Justice Harlan one in application rather than in statement of the rule? Note Justice Harlan's recital of data regarding the health of bakers. Did the majority disagree with those data? Note Justice Harlan's statement that it is enough that "the question is one about which there is room for debate and for an honest difference of opinion." Did the majority demand more than that? Note the majority's statement that the bakers' trade "is not an unhealthy one to that degree which would authorize the legislature to interfere." Arguably, the majority in effect imposed a greater burden of justification on the defenders of the law than "minimum rationality"; apparently, it demanded more than a showing that reasonable persons might think that the means would promote the end. If so, the majority in fact applied a stricter scrutiny than its own articulated standard suggested.

b. *Stricter scrutiny.* Is it defensible to impose a burden of justification higher than the minimum scrutiny of the "mere rationality" standard? Usually, a higher standard of justification is appropriate only when particularly cherished constitutional rights are threatened. The Lochner majority's approach apparently rested on an implicit assumption that liberty of contract *was* a fundamental value warranting special judicial protection. If so, that may constitute one of the genuine "evils" of Lochner: not the recognition that liberty of contract can be viewed as an aspect of "liberty," but rather that it is such a fundamental aspect of liberty that "mere reasonableness" in means-ends relationships will not justify restraints. In other words, it may be one of the "evils" that the Lochner Court paid only lip service to a reasonableness standard and applied stricter scrutiny of the means in fact. When such stricter scrutiny is applied, does it inevitably rest on a value judgment: not only a judgment selecting some values for special judicial protection, but also implementing that protection by "balancing" the competing public and private interests?

Court insistence on scrutiny stricter than "mere rationality" has become a commonplace modern technique in areas other than economic regulation. One way of stating a pervasive problem in the exercise of judicial review is to ask what—in constitutional text, history, structure or justifiable value choices— legitimates judicial applications of stricter scrutiny requirements in some contexts. The Court frequently exercises greater than minimal scrutiny and "balances" when it examines state regulations of commerce.[9] Higher standards of justification and stricter degrees of scrutiny also surface in later materials: e.g., with respect to the "fundamental right" of privacy, sec. 3 below, and "fundamental" First Amendment rights, chaps. 11 to 13 below.[10] Arguably, it was a major "evil" of Lochner that the majority imposed a scrutiny stricter than "mere rationality" without adequately justifying that special protection of liberty of

---

8. Would Justice Harlan have disagreed with the majority on the illegitimacy of the "labor law" end? Apparently not, to judge by his majority opinion three years later, in Adair v. United States (1908; p. 460 below).

9. Recall, for example, the Southern Pacific and Dean Milk cases in chap. 5 above.

10. Note also the strict scrutiny exercised when "fundamental interests" are impinged, under the doctrine of the "new equal protection," chap. 9 below.

contract. Why, if at all, was that special scrutiny less justified than some of the currently accepted areas of stricter scrutiny?

If the de facto stricter scrutiny of Lochner is rejected as an evil of that discredited era, does it follow that even "mere rationality" scrutiny of means— means scrutiny according to the standard stated but not followed by Justice Peckham, or that stated and followed by Justice Harlan—should be abandoned? Did the Warren Court abandon even "mere rationality" scrutiny of means in the economic area? See sec. 1C below. Is abandonment of means scrutiny in the economic area a justifiable response to the evils of Lochner? The conferral of an especially high value on liberty of contract without adequate justifications for that cherished status permeated the Lochner era, both in the narrow conception of legislative goals and the stricter scrutiny applied to legislative means. But concern with means may not be as questionable a judicial intervention as a narrow view of police power objectives. Hence, repudiation of the "evils" of the Lochner philosophy may not warrant judicial withdrawal from means scrutiny as well as from ends scrutiny. Can a genuine means scrutiny with "bite" avoid the problems of adjudication based on extraconstitutional values? [11] Arguably, the Court is better equipped to scrutinize means than ends. If the Court were to exercise greater means scrutiny, it would have to address a number of unsettled problems, including those pertaining to the relevant data for determining whether the requisite means-ends relationship exists. For example, the Court might restrict itself to data considered by the legislature or subject to judicial notice, or it might also examine data put forth by the litigants. Problems such as these are considered further below.

JUDICIAL SCRUTINY OF ECONOMIC REGULATIONS DURING THE LOCHNER ERA—SOME EXAMPLES

1. *Maximum hours—Muller, and Bunting.* MULLER v. OREGON, 208 U.S. 412 (1908), sustained an Oregon law that provided that "no female" shall be employed in any factory or laundry "more than ten hours during any one day." The conviction of Muller, a laundry operator, was affirmed by the Court, "without questioning in any respect the decision" in Lochner. Justice BREWER's opinion emphasized that the liberty of contract "is not absolute," that it was obvious that "woman's physical structure" placed her "at a disadvantage in the struggle for subsistence," and that, "as healthy mothers are essential to vigorous offspring, the physical well-being of woman becomes an object of public interest." Moreover, "woman has always been dependent upon man." Legislation to protect women "seems necessary to secure a real equality of right"; and such protective legislation is valid, "even when like legislation is not necessary for men and could not be sustained." The "inherent difference

---

11. These questions are pursued briefly in sec. 1C and more fully in the next chapter, on equal protection. Note the advocacy of a "rational means" scrutiny "with bite" in the context of equal protection in the 1972 Gunther article cited in footnote 7. That means-focused inquiry would have the Court "assess the means in terms of legislative purposes that have substantial basis in actuality, not merely in conjecture," and "would have the Justices gauge the reasonableness of questionable means on the basis of materials that are offered to the Court, rather than resorting to rationalizations created by perfunctory judicial hypothesizing." Though that article speaks of the equal protection context, the means-oriented analysis is relevant to due process as well. As the Gunther article notes: "In principle, the means-focused inquiry is as legitimate an ingredient of due process as of equal protection. [A] narrower due process inquiry focusing on *means* and deferring to legislative ends might have been far less subject to the risks of legislative paralysis through dogmatically imposed judicial values. But preoccupation with the ghost of the old due process produced a judicial overreaction and continues to cast a shadow on due process scrutiny of means as well as ends. [Evolution of greater means-oriented scrutiny] is likely to fare better along the equal protection route than on the haunted paths of due process."

between the two sexes" justified "a difference in legislation" and "upholds that which is designed to compensate for some of the burdens which rest upon her." [1] Nine years later, in BUNTING v. OREGON, 243 U.S. 426 (1917), a divided Court sustained a law establishing a maximum 10-hour day for factory workers, but permitting up to three hours a day overtime at a time-and-a-half rate. The conviction was for not paying the overtime rate. Although the Court did not mention Lochner, the ruling in effect overturned its specific holding. But the Lochner philosophy survived for another two decades.

2. *"Yellow dog" contracts, Coppage, and Adair.* a. The modern Court has referred to the discredited line of cases of the Lochner era as "the Allgeyer-Lochner-Adair-Coppage constitutional doctrine." The first two cases are noted above. Coppage and Adair involved laws protecting the right to organize unions. In COPPAGE v. KANSAS, 236 U.S. 1 (1915), Coppage had been convicted under a Kansas law directed against "yellow dog" contracts: it prohibited employers from requiring that employees agree as a condition of employment "not to join or become or remain a member of any labor organization." The Court, in an opinion by Justice PITNEY, held that the law violated due process: "Included in the right of personal liberty and the right of private property [is] the right to make contracts. [An] interference with this liberty so serious as that now under consideration, and so disturbing of equality of right, must be deemed to be arbitrary, unless it be supportable as a reasonable exercise of the police power of the State. [Conceding] the full right of the individual to join the union, he has no inherent right to do this and still remain in the employ of one who is unwilling to employ a union man, any more than the same individual has a right to join the union without the consent of that organization. [I]t is said by the [state court] to be a matter of common knowledge that 'employés, as a rule, are not financially able to be as independent in making contracts for the sale of their labor as are employers in making contracts of purchase thereof.' No doubt, wherever the right of private property exists, there must and will be inequalities of fortune; and thus it naturally happens that parties negotiating about a contract are not equally unhampered by circumstances. [But it] is from the nature of things impossible to uphold freedom of contract and the right of private property without at the

---

1. Compare the modern sex discrimination materials, in chap. 9 below.

The Muller case was also the first major one to resort to a fact-filled brief that has come to be known as a "Brandeis brief," submitted by the defenders of the legislation. At the outset of its opinion, the Court noted: "In patent cases counsel are apt to open the argument with a discussion of the state of the art. It may not be amiss, in the present case, before examining the constitutional question, to notice the course of legislation, as well as expressions of opinion from other than judicial sources. In the brief filed by Mr. Louis D. Brandeis for the defendant in error is a very copious collection of all these matters. [The] legislation and opinions referred [to] may not be, technically speaking, authorities, [yet] they are significant of a widespread belief that woman's physical structure, and the functions she performs in consequence thereof, justify special legislation. [Constitutional] questions, it is true, are not settled by even a consensus of present public opinion. [At] the same time, when a question of fact is debated and debatable, and the extent to which a special constitutional limitation goes is affected by the truth in respect to that fact, a widespread and long continued

belief concerning it is worthy of consideration. We take judicial cognizance of all matters of general knowledge." (Louis Brandeis, with the assistance of Felix Frankfurter, prepared a similar brief in litigation which led to the 1917 decision in Bunting, noted in the text. Brandeis was named to the Court before Bunting was decided; he did not participate in the decision.)

Is the "Brandeis brief" technique as useful in attacking legislation as in sustaining it? See Freund, On Understanding the Supreme Court (1949), 86–91, and Karst, "Legislative Facts in Constitutional Litigation," 1960 Sup.Ct.Rev. 75. On the utility of the "Brandeis brief" and the presentation of "constitutional facts," see also Biklé, "Judicial Determination of Questions of Fact Affecting the Constitutional Validity of Legislative Action," 38 Harv.L.Rev. 6 (1924). For more recent comments on the problem, see Alfange, "The Relevance of Legislative Facts in Constitutional Law," 114 U.Pa.L.Rev. 637 (1966), Shaman, "Constitutional Fact: The Perception of Reality by the Supreme Court," 35 U.Fla.L.Rev. 236 (1983), and Bryden, "Brandeis's Facts," 1 Constitutional Commentary 281 (1984).

same time recognizing as legitimate those inequalities of fortune that are the necessary result of the exercise of those rights. [The] 14th Amendment recognizes 'liberty' and 'property' as co-existent human rights, and debars the States from any unwarranted interference with either. [And] since a State may not strike them down directly it is clear that it may not do so indirectly, as by declaring in effect that the public good requires the removal of those inequalities that are but the normal and inevitable result of their exercise, and then invoking the police power in order to remove the inequalities, without other object in view." Justice HOLMES stated in dissent: "In present conditions a workman not unnaturally may believe that only by belonging to a union can he secure a contract that shall be fair to him. [If] that belief, whether right or wrong, may be held by a reasonable man, it seems to me that it may be enforced by law in order to establish the equality of position between the parties in which liberty of contract begins. Whether in the long run it is wise for the workingmen to enact legislation of this sort is not my concern, but I am strongly of opinion that there is nothing in the [Constitution] to prevent it." Justice DAY, joined by Justice Hughes, also dissented.

b. The Court in Coppage relied on ADAIR v. UNITED STATES, 208 U.S. 161 (1908), which had held unconstitutional, under the due process clause of the Fifth Amendment, a federal law against "yellow dog" contracts on interstate railroads. The opinion in Adair was written by Justice HARLAN, one of the dissenters in Lochner. Justice Harlan stated that the "right of a person to sell his labor upon such terms as he deems proper [is] the same as the right of the purchaser of labor to prescribe the conditions. [T]he employer and the employé have equality of right, and any legislation that disturbs that equality is an arbitrary interference with the liberty of contract." [2]

3. *Minimum wages and the Adkins case.* Though Bunting in 1917 had sustained regulation of *hours*—including a requirement of overtime wages—(and though Muller in 1908 had sustained regulation of women's working hours), the Court held in 1923 that a District of Columbia law prescribing minimum *wages* for women violated due process. ADKINS v. CHILDREN'S HOSPITAL, 261 U.S. 525 (1923). Justice SUTHERLAND emphasized that freedom of contract was "the general rule, and restraint the exception." Since Muller, he noted, the 19th Amendment had been adopted, and the civil inferiority of women was almost at a "vanishing point." Hence, the liberty of contract could not be subjected to greater restriction in the case of women than of men. The chief objection was that the law compelled payment of wages without regard to the employment contract, the business involved, or the work done; this was "a naked, arbitrary exercise" of legislative power. Justice HOLMES stated in dissent: "I confess that I do not understand the principle on which the power to fix a minimum for the wages of women can be denied by those who admit the power to fix a maximum for their hours of work. [The] bargain is equally affected whichever half you regulate. [It] will need more than the 19th Amendment to convince me that there are no differences between men and women, or that legislation cannot take those differences into account." [3]

2. What about the "disturbing of equality" in Muller v. Oregon (note 1 above), decided in the same year as Adair? Compare the Adkins case in 1923, which follows. (Justices HOLMES and McKENNA dissented in Adair.)

3. Chief Justice TAFT and Justice SANFORD also dissented. Justice BRANDEIS did not participate.

Was the 19th Amendment sufficient to explain the difference between Muller and Adkins? Or was regulation of hours more acceptable than regulation of wages because (despite the Lochner result) control of the hours worked could be seen as promoting health, a legitimate legislative end, while control of wages looked more like redressing inequalities in bargaining power in the market, a generally impermissible objective? Does that laissez faire attitude toward "equalizing" legislation even more clearly explain the majority's hostility to price regulations, in the next note? (The Adkins decision was adhered to in the Morehead case in 1936, but overruled in West Coast Hotel in 1937. See p. 465 below.)

4. *Price regulations.* The Court of the Lochner era imposed a variety of restraints on laws that interfered with the free market by controlling prices. The noninterventionist decision of the 1870s, Munn v. Illinois (p. 446 above), was read narrowly: the rate regulation authority there recognized, it was emphasized, was limited to business "affected with a public interest." Thus, public utility rate regulations were permitted, but the Court reviewed the substantive reasonableness of the rates. And in the areas of the economy not deemed to be "affected with a public interest," price regulations were barred altogether. The Court stated the general rule applied during this period to price (as well as wage) regulations as follows: "[A] state legislature is without constitutional power to fix prices at which commodities may be sold, services rendered, or property used, unless the business or property involved is 'affected with a public interest.'" Williams v. Standard Oil Co., 278 U.S. 235 (1929).[4] Compare the more generous attitude toward price regulation in Nebbia (1934; p. 462 below).

5. *Restrictions on business entry and other economic regulations.* a. *Business entry.* In a number of cases, the Court invalidated restraints on competition that curtailed entry into a particular line of business. For example, in NEW STATE ICE CO. v. LIEBMANN, 285 U.S. 262 (1932), the Court invalidated an Oklahoma law which treated the manufacture of ice like a public utility, requiring a certificate of convenience and necessity as a prerequisite to entry into the business. Under the scheme, a state agency had to find that existing facilities were not "sufficient to meet the public needs" before issuing new certificates. See also ADAMS v. TANNER, 244 U.S. 590 (1917), striking down a law prohibiting employment agencies from collecting fees from workers. The majority called that law an "arbitrary and oppressive" ban on a "useful business." Justice BRANDEIS submitted extensive, data-laden dissents in both cases to demonstrate why reasonable legislators might think the restraints necessary. Note, moreover, Liggett Co. v. Baldridge, 278 U.S. 105 (1928), invalidating a law barring corporate ownership of pharmacies unless all stockholders were pharmacists. Decisions such as these have been undermined if not explicitly overruled by the developments since the 1930s.[5]

b. *Scrutiny of means.* During the Lochner era, the Court did recognize the validity of the state interest in curtailing business practices that might defraud consumers or injure their health. When statutes of that variety were invalidated, the Court criticized the means rather than the ends of the legislation. A good example is WEAVER v. PALMER BROS. CO., 270 U.S. 402 (1926). There, the majority invalidated a total prohibition of the use, in the manufacture of bedding materials such as mattresses and quilts, of shoddy (cut up or torn up fabrics). Other secondhand materials could be used so long as they were sterilized and the finished product carried a label showing the materials used. The Court found the absolute prohibition of shoddy "purely arbitrary": protection of health and against consumer deception did not justify so drastic a remedy. As to health, the Court emphasized that the parties had agreed that "shoddy may be rendered harmless by disinfection or sterilization," even where the shoddy had been made from "filthy rags." As to public deception, the

---

4. The Williams case involved gasoline prices; see also Tyson & Brother v. Banton, 273 U.S. 418 (1927) (resale price of theatre tickets); Ribnik v. McBride, 277 U.S. 350 (1928) (employment agency fees). [The Tyson decision was explicitly overruled (in a per curiam decision) in Gold v. DiCarlo, 380 U.S. 520 (1965). Ribnik had been overruled earlier, in Olsen v. Nebraska (1941; p. 468 below).]

5. See sec. 1C below and, e.g., North Dakota Bd. of Pharmacy v. Snyder's Drug Stores, 414

U.S. 156 (1973), reversing a state court decision relying on Liggett in invalidating a similar law. Justice Douglas stated for a unanimous Court that Liggett "belongs to that vintage of decisions which exalted substantive due process by striking down state legislation which a majority of the Court deemed unwise. [The] Liggett case, being a derelict in the stream of the law, is hereby overruled."

Court noted the tagging and inspection requirements applicable to other bedding and stated: "Obviously, these regulations or others that are adequate may be effectively applied to shoddy-filled articles." Justice Holmes' dissent, joined by Justices Brandeis and Stone, argued that the lawmakers "may have been of opinion" that "the actual practice of filling comfortables with unsterilized shoddy gathered from filthy floors was wide spread"—an opinion "we must assume to be true." Moreover, it was impossible "to distinguish the innocent from the infected [final] product in any practicable way." Thus, the total ban was justifiable for health reasons, for the legislature might have "regarded the danger as very great and inspection and tagging as inadequate remedies." [6]

Would a means-oriented inquiry be appropriate in Weaver under the principles of the more recent decisions, below? Would there be any scrutiny of the means in fact by the modern Court, in view of the summary manner in which the Warren Court applied those principles? Should there be? The degree of scrutiny exercised by the majority in Weaver seems more intense than that justified by the "mere reasonableness" standard. Instead, it is similar to the "less restrictive alternatives" analysis of the Dean Milk case, chap. 5, p. 270 above? [7] Is concern with alternatives appropriate when there is no claim of impingement on a specially cherished constitutional value? If the majority's scrutiny was too strict for a "mere reasonableness" standard, was Justice Holmes' too deferential? Arguably, the Court should not be content with speculating about the opinions legislators *might* have had regarding the contributions of means to ends. Arguably, there should be a requirement that the defenders of the law present data to the Court—data which explain the way in which the means contribute to the achievement of the ends. [8]

C. THE MODERN ERA: THE DECLINE—AND DISAPPEARANCE?—OF JUDICIAL SCRUTINY OF ECONOMIC REGULATION

NEBBIA v. NEW YORK

291 U.S. 502, 54 S.Ct. 505, 78 L.Ed. 940 (1934).

Mr. Justice ROBERTS delivered the opinion of the Court.

The Legislature of New York established [in 1933] a Milk Control Board with power [to] "fix minimum and maximum [retail] prices to be charged [by] stores to consumers for consumption off the premises where sold." The Board

---

6. See also Jay Burns Baking Co. v. Bryan, 264 U.S. 504 (1924), invalidating a law requiring standardized weights for loaves of bread. The majority noted that the law in effect made it impossible to sell bread without wrappers, even though there was "a strong demand by consumers" for unwrapped bread. (Sale of unwrapped bread was not feasible under the law because of the difficulty of controlling evaporation from unwrapped bread.) The majority found the restrictions "essentially unreasonable and arbitrary," because they were "not necessary for the protection of purchasers against imposition and fraud by short weights" and "not calculated to effectuate that purpose." The problem of "short weights," the Court noted, "readily could have been dealt with in a direct and effective way."

Justice Brandeis' dissent, joined by Justice Holmes, contained another extensive summary of data, largely based on judicial notice, to show the reasonableness of the legislation—particularly to show why "legislators, bent only on preventing short weights, prohibit, also, excessive weights." He insisted that the majority's views of the reasonableness and necessity of the legislation was "an exercise of the powers of a super-legislature."

7. Cf. Struve, "The Less-Restrictive-Alternative Principle and Economic Due Process," 80 Harv.L.Rev. 1463 (1967).

8. The problem of demonstrating adequate means-ends relationships is pursued further below.

fixed nine cents as the price to be charged by a store for a quart of milk. Nebbia, the proprietor of a grocery store in Rochester, sold two quarts and a five cent loaf of bread for eighteen cents; and was convicted for violating the Board's order. [The] question for decision is whether the [Constitution] prohibits a state from so fixing the selling price of milk. We first inquire as to the occasion for the legislation and its history.

During 1932 the prices received by farmers for milk were much below the cost of production. [The] situation of the families of dairy producers had become desperate and called for state aid similar to that afforded the unemployed, if conditions should not improve. [The Court summarized the conclusions reached after an extensive study by a legislative committee:] Milk is an essential item of diet. Failure of producers to receive a reasonable return [threatens] a relaxation of vigilance against contamination. The production and distribution of milk is a paramount industry of the state, and largely affects the health and prosperity of its people. [The] fluid milk industry is affected by factors of [price] instability peculiar to itself which call for special methods of control. [The] legislature adopted [this law] as a method of correcting the evils, which the report of the committee showed could not be expected to right themselves through the ordinary play of the forces of supply and demand, owing to the peculiar and uncontrollable factors affecting the industry. [The Court then turned to the due process objection:]

Under our form of government the use of property and the making of contracts are normally matters of private and not a public concern. The general rule is that both shall be free of governmental interference. But neither property rights nor contract rights are absolute; for government cannot exist if the citizen may at will use his property to the detriment of his fellows, or exercise his freedom of contract to work them harm. Equally fundamental with the private right is that of the public to regulate it in the common interest. [The] guaranty of due process [demands] only that the law shall not be unreasonable, arbitrary or capricious, and that the means selected shall have a real and substantial relation to the object sought to be attained. It results that a regulation valid for one sort of business, or in given circumstances, may be invalid for another sort, or for the same business under other circumstances, because the reasonableness of each regulation depends upon the relevant facts. [The Court reviewed cases sustaining regulations against due process attacks—including laws "concerning sales of goods, and incidentally affecting prices."]

[But] we are told that because the law essays to control prices it denies due process. Notwithstanding the admitted power to correct existing economic ills by appropriate regulation of business, [Nebbia] urges that the direct fixation of prices is a type of regulation absolutely forbidden. [The] argument runs that the public control of rates or prices is per se unreasonable and unconstitutional, save as applied to business affected with a public interest; that a business so affected is [one] such as is commonly called a public utility; or a business in its nature a monopoly. The milk industry, it is said, possesses none of these [characteristics]. [The Court acknowledged that the dairy industry was not, "in the accepted sense of the phrase, a public utility," nor a "monopoly."] But if, as must be conceded, the industry is subject to regulation in the public interest, what constitutional principle bars the state from correcting existing maladjustments by legislation touching prices? We think there is no such principle. The due process clause makes no mention of sales or of prices any more than it speaks of business or contracts or buildings or other incidents of property. The thought seems nevertheless to have persisted that there is something peculiarly sacrosanct about the price one may charge for what he makes or sells, and that, however able to regulate other elements of manufacture or trade, with incidental effect upon price, the state is incapable of directly controlling the price itself.

This view was negatived many years ago. Munn v. Illinois. [Appellant claims that this Court there] limited permissible [price regulation] to businesses affected with a public interest [—primarily, public utilities or monopolies]. But this is a misconception. [The Court in Munn stated:] "Property does become clothed with a public interest when used in a manner to make it of public consequence, and affect the community at large." Thus understood, "affected with a public interest" is the equivalent of "subject to the exercise of the police power" and it is plain that nothing more was intended by the expression. [It] is clear that there is no closed class or category of businesses affected with a public interest, and the function of courts in the application of the Fifth and 14th Amendments is to determine in each case whether circumstances vindicate the challenged regulation as a reasonable exertion of governmental authority or condemn it as arbitrary or discriminatory. The phrase "affected with a public interest" can, in the nature of things, mean no more than that an industry, for adequate reason, is subject to control for the public good. [There] can be no doubt that upon proper occasion and by appropriate measures the state may regulate a business in any of its aspects, including the prices to be charged for the products or commodities it sells.

So far as the requirement of due process is concerned, [a] state is free to adopt whatever economic policy may reasonably be deemed to promote public welfare, and to enforce that policy by legislation adapted to its purpose. The courts are without authority either to declare such policy, or, when it is declared by the legislature, to override it. If the laws passed are seen to have a reasonable relation to a proper legislative purpose, and are neither arbitrary nor discriminatory, the requirements of due process are [satisfied]. And it is equally clear that if the legislative policy be to curb unrestrained and harmful competition by measures which are not arbitrary or discriminatory it does not lie with the courts to determine that the rule is unwise. With the wisdom of the policy adopted, with the adequacy or practicability of the law enacted to forward it, the courts are both incompetent and unauthorized to deal. [Price] control, like any other form of regulation, is unconstitutional only if arbitrary, discriminatory, or demonstrably irrelevant to the policy the legislature is free to adopt, and hence an unnecessary and unwarranted interference with individual liberty. Tested by these considerations we find no basis [for] condemning the provisions of the Agriculture and Markets Law here drawn into question.[1]

[Affirmed.]

Separate opinion of Mr. Justice McREYNOLDS [dissenting].

[Regulation] to prevent recognized evils in business has long been upheld as permissible legislative action. But fixation of the price at which "A," engaged in an ordinary business, may sell, in order to enable "B," a producer, to improve his condition, has not been regarded as within legislative power. This is not regulation, but management, control, dictation—it amounts to the deprivation of the fundamental right which one has to conduct his own affairs honestly and along customary lines. This Court has declared that [a] State may not by legislative fiat convert a private business into a public utility. [Plainly], I think, this Court must have regard to the wisdom of the enactment. At least, we must inquire concerning its purpose and decide whether the means proposed have reasonable relation to something within legislative power—whether the end is legitimate, and the means appropriate. [Here], we find direct interference with guaranteed rights defended upon the ground that the purpose was to promote the public welfare by increasing milk prices at the farm. [The court below has not] attempted to indicate how higher charges at stores to impoverished customers when the output is excessive and sale prices of producers are

    1. Recall the upholding of a commerce clause   year after Nebbia, in Baldwin v. Seelig, chap. 5,
challenge to an application of the same law a   at p. 279.

unrestrained, can possibly increase receipts at the farm. The Legislative Committee pointed out as the obvious cause of decreased consumption notwithstanding low prices, the consumers' reduced buying power. Higher store prices will not enlarge this power; nor will they decrease production. [It] is not true as stated that "the State seeks to protect the producer by fixing a minimum price for his milk." She carefully refrained from doing this; but did undertake to fix the price after the milk had passed to other owners. Assuming that the views and facts reported by the Legislative Committee are correct, it appears to me wholly unreasonable to expect this legislation to accomplish the proposed end—increase of prices at the farm. [Not] only does the statute interfere arbitrarily with the rights of the little grocer to conduct his business according to standards long accepted; [it] takes away the liberty of twelve million consumers to buy a necessity of life in an [open market].[2]

WEST COAST HOTEL CO. v. PARRISH, 300 U.S. 379 (1937): This 5 to 4 decision overruled Adkins (p. 460 above) and sustained a state minimum wage law for women. Chief Justice HUGHES' majority opinion included the following passages: "[T]he violation [of due process] alleged by those attacking minimum wage regulation for women is deprivation of freedom of contract. What is this freedom? The Constitution does not speak of freedom of contract. It speaks of liberty and prohibits the deprivation of liberty without due process of law. In prohibiting that deprivation the Constitution does not recognize an absolute and uncontrollable liberty. [Liberty] under the Constitution [is] necessarily subject to the restraints of due process, and regulation which is reasonable in relation to its subject and is adopted in the interests of the community is due process. [We] think that [the Adkins decision] was a departure from the true application of the principles governing the regulation by the State of the relation of employer and employed. [What] can be closer to the public interest than the health of women and their protection from unscrupulous and overreaching employers? [The] legislature [was] clearly entitled to consider that [women] are in the class receiving the least pay, that their bargaining power is relatively weak, and that they are the ready victims of those who would take advantage of their necessitous circumstances. The legislature was entitled to adopt measures to reduce the evils of the 'sweating system,' the exploiting of workers at wages so low as to be insufficient to meet the bare cost of living, thus making their very helplessness the occasion of a most injurious competition. The legislature had the right to consider that its minimum wage requirements would be an important aid in carrying out its policy of protection. The adoption of similar requirements by many States evidences a deep-seated conviction both as to the presence of the evil and as to the means adapted to check it. Legislative response to that conviction cannot be regarded as arbitrary or capricious, and that is all we have to [decide].

"There is an additional and compelling consideration which recent economic experience has brought into a strong light. The exploitation of a class of workers who are in an unequal position with respect to bargaining power and are thus relatively defenceless against the denial of a living wage is not only detrimental to their health and well being but casts a direct burden for their support upon the community. What these workers lose in wages the taxpayers are called upon to pay. The bare cost of living must be met. We may take judicial notice of the unparalleled demands for relief which arose during the recent period of depression. [The] community is not bound to provide what is

---

2. Justices Van Devanter, Sutherland and Butler joined the dissenting opinion.

See also Sunshine Coal Co. v. Adkins, 310 U.S. 381 (1940), rejecting, inter alia, a Fifth Amendment challenge to the price-fixing provisions of the Bituminous Coal Act of 1937: "Price control is one of the means available [for] the protection and promotion of the welfare of the economy."

in effect a subsidy for unconscionable employers. The community may direct its law-making power to correct the abuse which springs from their selfish disregard of the public interest. [Adkins is] overruled." [Justice SUTHERLAND's dissent, joined by Justices Van Devanter, McReynolds and Butler, insisted that "the meaning of the Constitution does not change with the ebb and flow of economic events" and that the law had not "the slightest relation to the capacity or earning power of the employee, to the number of hours which constitute the day's work, the character of the place where the work is to be done, or the circumstances [of] the employment." Quoting Adkins, he stated that the law compelled the employer to pay irrespective "of the ability of his business to sustain the burden. [To] the extent that the sum fixed exceeds the fair value of the services rendered, it amounts to a compulsory exaction from the employer for the support of a partially indigent person [and] therefore [arbitrarily] shifts to his shoulders a burden which, if it belongs to anybody, belongs to society as a whole."]

———

THE IMPACT OF NEBBIA AND WEST COAST HOTEL

1. *The standards of the mid-1930s.* The Nebbia and West Coast decisions obviously marked a significant shift from the Lochner era: they curtailed judicial intervention in economic regulation. But how far did they reduce judicial intervention? Do the decisions that follow simply apply the Nebbia and West Coast Hotel approaches? Or do they carry the rejection of the Lochner philosophy even further, to an even greater "hands off" position? Nebbia and West Coast Hotel obviously mark a sharp retreat from the Lochner era's restrictive attitude toward permissible legislative ends. Price control is no longer limited to the narrow category of businesses "affected with a public interest"; wage control for women is authorized with an explicit endorsement not only of the health objective but also the objective of redressing "unequal position with respect to bargaining power." Is there a similarly great retreat with respect to scrutiny of means-ends relationships? Note that Nebbia insists that the means must have "a real and substantial relation to the object sought to be attained." And note that both majority opinions contain elaborate explanations of the background and rationales for the laws sustained. Compare the curt statements (or assumptions) about legislative justifications in the later decisions, below. Were the relations between means and ends so evident there that no fuller explanation was warranted?

2. *The political context of Nebbia and West Coast Hotel.* Note that Nebbia's deference to the legislature came in 1934, just before the Court rendered its major decisions striking down a variety of New Deal laws as exceeding national powers, in Schechter in 1935 and Carter and Butler in 1936. (See chaps. 3 and 4 above.) The course of relaxation of due process restraints was not smooth: Court critics thought that due process restraints were hardening when—two years after Nebbia—the Court adhered to the Adkins decision in Morehead v. New York ex rel. Tipaldo, 298 U.S. 587 (1936), invalidating New York's minimum wage law for women. A few months after Morehead, President Roosevelt announced his Court-packing Plan; and while that controversy was raging, West Coast Hotel came down. Justice Roberts was with the majority in each case. Some viewed Justice Roberts' votes as "the switch in time that saved the Nine" from the Court-packing Plan that failed in the Senate soon after. But recall Justice Roberts' own explanation of his votes in Morehead and West Coast Hotel, in a memorandum left with Justice Frankfurter and noted at p. 130

above.[1] It is nevertheless clear that constitutional doctrine changed significantly during that period. But arguing that the shift was a response to the Court-packing Plan is easiest with respect to national powers doctrines; with respect to due process, West Coast Hotel is certainly of a deferential piece with the pre-Court-packing decision in Nebbia (written by Justice Roberts).

THE MODERN ERA: REDUCED JUDICIAL SCRUTINY OR ABDICATION?

Nebbia suggested a continuing, though reduced, judicial role in scrutinizing the means employed in economic regulations—both in its announced standard that "the means selected shall have a real and substantial relation to the object sought to be attained" and in its examination of the background of the legislation. Have the due process decisions since the mid-1930s shrunk the judicial role beyond that? Have they, in formulation or in exercise, eliminated it altogether?

1. *Economic regulation and the Carolene Products case.* In 1938, in UNITED STATES v. CAROLENE PRODUCTS CO., 304 U.S. 144, the Court rejected a due process challenge to a federal prohibition of the interstate shipment of "filled milk"—skimmed milk mixed with non-milk fats. Justice STONE's majority opinion stated: "We may assume for present purposes [that] a statute would deny due process which precluded the disproof in judicial proceedings of all facts which would show [that] a statute depriving the suitor of life, liberty, or property had a rational basis." Here, the congressional declarations that filled milk was injurious to health and a fraud upon the public did not bar such "disproof"; but challenging the "rational basis" of economic legislation, he made clear, would be a difficult task. The legislative findings, like reports of legislative committees, were simply aids to "informed judicial review," "by revealing the rationale of the legislation." But they were not essential: "Even in the absence of such aids, the existence of facts supporting the legislative judgment is to be presumed, for regulatory legislation affecting ordinary commercial transactions is not to be pronounced unconstitutional unless in the light of the facts made known or generally assumed it is of such a character as to preclude the assumption that it rests upon some rational basis within the knowledge and experience of the legislators."[1] He added:

"Where the existence of a rational basis for legislation whose constitutionality is attacked depends upon facts beyond the sphere of judicial notice, such facts may properly be made the subject of judicial inquiry, and the constitutionality of a statute predicated upon the existence of a particular state of facts may be

---

1. Justice Roberts' memorandum made it clear that the Court's conference vote in West Coast Hotel came weeks *before* the Court-packing Plan was announced; he was not responding directly to that threat. Moreover, he claimed that his Morehead vote to adhere to Adkins rested on the fact that the Court in Morehead, unlike West Coast Hotel, was not explicitly asked to overrule Adkins. Chief Justice Hughes gave a similar explanation in his majority opinion in West Coast Hotel: he stated that the Morehead decision rested on the fact that the Court "considered that the only question before it was whether the Adkins case was distinguishable and that reconsideration of that decision had not been sought." He went on to say in West Coast Hotel: "We think that the question which was not deemed to be open in the Morehead case is open and is necessarily presented here"; and the overruling of Adkins followed.

1. At this point, Justice Stone added his famous footnote 4, suggesting that there may be a stronger case for judicial intervention in regulation of matters other than "commercial transactions." That footnote 4 has been widely relied on to explain the Court's growing interventionism regarding "legislation which [restricts] political processes," even while it has retreated from review of economic regulation. The footnote is printed at p. 473 below; and the question whether that Carolene Products footnote adequately justifies the "double standard" of judicial review recurs frequently throughout the next few chapters.

challenged by showing to the court that those facts have ceased to exist. Similarly we recognize that the constitutionality of a statute, valid on its face, may be assailed by proof of facts tending to show that the statute as applied to a particular article is without support in reason because the article, although within the prohibited class, is so different from others of the class as to be without the reason for the prohibition, though the effect of such proof depends on the relevant circumstances of each case, as for example the administrative difficulty of excluding the article from the regulated class. But by their very nature such inquiries, where the legislative judgment is drawn in question, must be restricted to the issue whether any state of facts either known or which could reasonably be assumed, affords support for it. Here the demurrer challenges the validity of the statute on its face and it is evident from all the considerations presented to Congress, and those of which we may take judicial notice, that the question is at least debatable whether commerce in filled milk should be left unregulated, or in some measure restricted, or wholly prohibited."

2. *Total withdrawal from review?* Carolene Products indicated some continued willingness to consider the "rational basis" of economic legislation. In the cases in this note, the Court rejected due process attacks even more summarily. Do these "hands off" decisions indicate an even greater withdrawal from judicial scrutiny than that suggested by the standards of the 1930s decisions? Or are these cases explainable on the ground that their central concerns were the legitimacy of legislative objectives, not the reasonableness of the means?

a. *Olsen v. Nebraska.* An early example of the extreme "hands off" attitude was OLSEN v. NEBRASKA, 313 U.S. 236 (1941), where the state courts had held unconstitutional a law fixing maximum employment agency fees, in reliance on the 1928 decision in Ribnik (p. 461 above). The Court unanimously reversed, in an opinion by Justice DOUGLAS: "We are not concerned [with] the wisdom, need, or appropriateness of the legislation. [There] is no necessity for the state to demonstrate before us that evils persist despite the competition which attends the bargaining in this field. In final analysis, the only restraints which respondents have suggested for the invalidation of this legislation are those notions of public policy embedded in earlier decisions of this Court but which, as Mr. Justice Holmes long admonished, should not be read into the Constitution. [Since] they do not find expression in the Constitution, we cannot give them continuing validity as standards by which the constitutionality of the economic and social programs of the states is to be determined."

b. *The Lincoln Federal Labor Union case.* In LINCOLN FEDERAL LABOR UNION v. NORTHWESTERN IRON & METAL CO., 335 U.S. 525 (1949), the Court was again unanimous in sustaining state "right to work" laws requiring that employment decisions not be based on union membership. Justice BLACK's opinion recalled the Lochner era, when the Adair and Coppage decisions had struck down pro-union laws banning "yellow-dog contracts," and emphasized the change in doctrine since then. The "Allgeyer-Lochner-Adair-Coppage constitutional doctrine" had been repudiated; ever since Nebbia, the Court had "steadily rejected the due process philosophy enunciated in the Adair-Coppage line of cases." He added: "In doing so it has consciously returned closer and closer to the earlier constitutional principle that states have power to legislate against what are found to be injurious practices in their internal commercial and business affairs, so long as their laws do not run afoul of some specific federal constitutional prohibition, or of some valid federal law." He concluded: "Just as we have held that the due process clause erects no obstacle to block legislative protection of union members, we now hold that legislative protection can be afforded non-union workers."

c. *Ferguson v. Skrupa.* A more recent example of broad deference to legislative judgments is FERGUSON v. SKRUPA, 372 U.S. 726 (1963), sustaining a Kansas law prohibiting anyone from engaging "in the business of debt adjusting" except as an incident to "the lawful practice of law." Justice BLACK's opinion concluded that Kansas "was free to decide for itself that legislation was needed to deal with the business of debt adjusting." He reiterated that the Court had abandoned "the use of the 'vague contours' of the Due Process Clause to nullify laws which a majority of the Court believed to be economically unwise." And he added: "Unquestionably, there are arguments showing that the business of debt adjusting has social utility, but such arguments are properly addressed to the legislature, not to us. We refuse to sit as a 'super legislature to weigh the wisdom of legislation.' [Whether] the legislature takes for its textbook Adam Smith, Herbert Spencer, Lord Keynes or some other is no concern of ours." [2]

Justice HARLAN concurred in a brief separate notation, "on the ground that this state measure bears a rational relation to a constitutionally permissible objective. See [Lee Optical, below]." What is the significance of Justice Harlan's separate notation? Does his "rational relation" standard indicate greater judicial scrutiny than Justice Black's approach? Recall Justice Black's statement in the Lincoln case rejecting any judicial intervention in "commercial and business" regulation so long as state laws "do not run afoul of some specific federal constitutional prohibition." Does that suggest the total inapplicability of due process? Has the majority of the Court committed itself to so complete a withdrawal from review? Or does Lee Optical, cited by Justice Harlan, suggest that some judicial scrutiny remains? Does the variety of scrutiny exercised in Lee Optical have any teeth in fact, or is it the functional equivalent of total withdrawal, with only lip service to a judicially enforceable "rational relation" standard as to scrutiny of means? Is the "rational relation" approach of Lee Optical more deferential than the "real and substantial relation" requirement of Nebbia? Is Justice Black correct in suggesting that there is no constitutional basis for requiring more of legislatures than compliance with specific constitutional prohibitions? [3] Or can the due process clause properly be read to impose a judicially enforceable requirement that legislatures show a "real and substantial" relationship between means and ends even in the economic area?

d. *The Day-Brite case.* DAY–BRITE LIGHTING, INC. v. MISSOURI, 342 U.S. 421 (1952), is an especially striking example of the Court's readiness to dismiss due process attacks, even in unusual areas of regulation. The Court sustained a law requiring employers to give their employees four hours off from work with full pay in order to vote. The law, first enacted in the late 19th century, was assertedly designed "to end the coercion of employees by employers in the exercise of the franchise." Curtly disposing of the challenge, Justice DOUGLAS' majority opinion stated: "The liberty of contract argument pressed on us is reminiscent of the philosophy of [Lochner, Coppage, and Adkins] and others of that vintage. [We] do not sit as a super-legislature. [The] state legislatures may within extremely broad limits control practices in the business-labor field." He analogized the law to the minimum wage provision upheld in West Coast Hotel and added: "The only semblance of substance in the constitutional objection [is] that the employer must pay wages for a period in

2. Note the list of economists mentioned by Justice Black in Ferguson v. Skrupa. Suppose the legislature instead took for its textbook Karl Marx? It may be worthwhile to consider at this point the eminent domain case of Hawaii Housing Authority v. Midkiff (1984; p. 486 below), where the Court sustained condemnation and redistribution of private property in order to solve a local problem of concentrated land ownership. What if the legislature, affording the "just compensation" required for condemnations by the Constitution, sought instead to promote much broader, Marxist purposes through condemnation and redistribution of property? Would the Ferguson v. Skrupa (and Midkiff) deference to legislative judgments prevail? Would there be any principled constitutional reasons to invalidate such judgments?

3. See Linde, "Without ['Due Process']," 49 Ore.L.Rev. 125 (1970), and Linde, "Due Process of Lawmaking," 55 Nebr.L.Rev. 197 (1976).

which the employee performs no services. [Most] regulations of business necessarily impose financial burdens on the enterprise. [They] are part of the costs of our civilization. Extreme cases are conjured up where an employer is required to pay wages for a period that has no relation to [a] legitimate end. [The] present law has no such infirmity. It is designed [to] remove a practical obstacle to getting out the vote. The public welfare is a broad and inclusive concept. [The] judgment of the legislature that time out for voting should cost the employee nothing may be a debatable one. [But our recent cases] leave debatable issues as respects business, economic, and social affairs to legislative decision. We would strike down this law only if we returned to the philosophy of the Lochner, Coppage, and Adkins cases."

Was no greater scrutiny possible and justified without returning to the evils of the Lochner era? Was there no middle ground between "Lochnerizing" and the very great deference of Day-Brite? Unlike most modern economic due process and equal protection cases, Day-Brite did evoke troubled responses from two of the Justices. Justice FRANKFURTER concurred only in the result. And Justice JACKSON dissented, stating: "To sustain this statute by resort to the analogy of minimum wage laws seems so farfetched and unconvincing as to demonstrate its weakness rather than its strength." A law such as this "stands in a class by itself and should not be uncritically commended as a mere regulation of 'practices' in the business-labor field. [There] must be some limit to the power to shift the whole voting burden from the voter to someone else who happens to stand in some economic relationship to him. [Does] the success of an enticement to vote justify putting its cost on some other citizen?" [4]

WILLIAMSON v. LEE OPTICAL CO.

348 U.S. 483, 75 S.Ct. 461, 99 L.Ed. 563 (1955).

Mr. Justice DOUGLAS delivered the opinion of the Court.

[The] District Court held unconstitutional [several sections of an Oklahoma law of 1953]. First, it held invalid under the Due Process Clause [the] portions of § 2 which make it unlawful for any person not a licensed optometrist or ophthalmologist to fit lenses to a face or to duplicate or replace into frames lenses or other optical appliances, except upon written prescriptive authority of an Oklahoma licensed ophthalmologist or optometrist. An ophthalmologist is a duly licensed physician who specializes in the care of the eyes. An optometrist examines eyes for refractive error, recognizes (but does not treat) diseases of the eye, and fills prescriptions for eyeglasses. The optician is an artisan qualified to grind lenses, fill prescriptions, and fit frames. The effect of § 2 is to forbid the optician from fitting or duplicating lenses without a prescription from an ophthalmologist or optometrist. In practical effect, it means that no optician can fit old glasses into new frames or supply a lens, whether it be a new lens or one to duplicate a lost or broken lens, without a prescription. The [District Court] rebelled at the notion that a State could require a prescription [to] "take old lenses and place them in new frames and then fit the completed spectacles to the *face* of the eyeglass wearer." [The] court found that through mechanical devices and ordinary skills the optician could take a broken lens or a fragment thereof, measure its power, and reduce it to prescriptive terms. The court held that "Although [the legislature] was dealing with a matter of public interest, the

---

4. Day-Brite, like most modern challenges to economic regulation, involved equal protection as well as due process claims. In the equal protection area, the withdrawal from scrutiny of economic regulations has generally (but not wholly) paralleled that under due process. The equal protection developments—including questions about the possibility of greater means scrutiny—are pursued in sec. 1 of the next chapter.

particular means chosen are neither reasonably necessary nor reasonably related to the end sought to be achieved.''

[The] Oklahoma law may exact a needless, wasteful requirement in many cases. But it is for the legislature, not the courts, to balance the advantages and disadvantages of the new requirement. It appears that in many cases the optician can easily supply the new frames or new lenses without reference to the old written prescription. It also appears that many written prescriptions contain no directive data in regard to fitting spectacles to the face. But in some cases the directions contained in the prescription are essential, if the glasses are to be fitted so as to correct the particular defects of vision or alleviate the eye condition. The legislature might have concluded that the frequency of occasions when a prescription is necessary was sufficient to justify this regulation of the fitting of eyeglasses. Likewise, when it is necessary to duplicate a lens, a written prescription may or may not be necessary. But the legislature might have concluded that one was needed often enough to require one in every case. Or the legislature may have concluded that eye examinations were so critical, not only for correction of vision but also for detection of latent ailments or diseases, that every change in frames and every duplication of a lens should be accompanied by a prescription from a medical expert. To be sure, the present law does not require a new examination of the eyes every time the frames are changed or the lenses duplicated. For if the old prescription is on file with the optician, he can go ahead and make the new fitting or duplicate the lenses. But the law need not be in every respect logically consistent with its aims to be constitutional. It is enough that there is an evil at hand for correction, and that it might be thought that the particular legislative measure was a rational way to correct it. The day is gone when this Court uses the Due Process Clause [to] strike down state laws, regulatory of business and industrial conditions, because they may be unwise, improvident, or out of harmony with a particular school of [thought].[1]

Third, the District Court held [that] portion of § 3 which makes it unlawful ''to solicit the sale [of] frames, mountings, [or] any other optical appliances'' [violative of due process]. [R]egulation of the advertising of eyeglass frames was said to intrude ''into a mercantile field only casually related to the visual care of the public'' and restrict ''an activity which in no way can detrimentally affect the people.'' [An] eyeglass frame, considered in isolation, is only a piece of merchandise. But an eyeglass frame is not used in isolation; [it] is used with lenses; and lenses, pertaining as they do to the human eye, enter the field of health. Therefore, the legislature might conclude that to regulate one effectively it would have to regulate the other. Or it might conclude that both the sellers of frames and the sellers of lenses were in a business where advertising should be limited or even abolished in the public interest. [The] advertiser of frames may be using his ads to bring in customers who will buy lenses. If the advertisement of lenses is to be abolished or controlled, the advertising of frames must come under the same restraints; or so the legislature might think. We see no constitutional reason why a State may not treat all who deal with the human eye as members of a profession who should use no merchandising methods for obtaining [customers].[2]

[Reversed.]

---

1. Another section of the law, subjecting opticians to the regulatory scheme but exempting all sellers of ready-to-wear glasses, was held violative of equal protection by the lower court. The Court's rejection of that equal protection attack (and additional comments on the deferen-tial review stance of Lee Optical) are printed in chap. 9, at p. 600 below.

2. Two decades after Lee Optical, the Court began to include ''commercial speech''—i.e., most advertising—within the protection of the First Amendment. Critics have claimed that the

THE "HANDS OFF" APPROACH TO ECONOMIC LEGISLATION: EXCESSIVE WITHDRAWAL? JUSTIFIABLE DOUBLE STANDARD?

Introduction. The modern Court has turned away due process challenges to economic regulation with a broad "hands off" approach. No such law has been invalidated on substantive due process grounds since 1937.[1] Indeed, opinions from the Court are rare, for most appeals raising substantive due process challenges are dismissed for want of a substantial federal question; and argument is ordinarily heard only when a lower court has struck down a law. Only on a few occasions have some Justices expressed doubts about the Court's stance of extreme deference to economic regulation. This Court withdrawal from serious scrutiny raises two basic questions. First, has the Court gone too far in its withdrawal? Would it be possible, and justifiable, to exercise a level of review which would have more content than the modern "hands off" attitude and yet avoid the vices of the Lochner era? Second, is the substantial withdrawal from review in the economic area reconcilable with the modern Court's considerable intensity of review when non-economic interests are affected? Is there justification for such a double standard, for a two-tier level of scrutiny, strict in some areas, minimal or virtually nonexistent in others? And the two problems are related: Even if some "double standard" is justifiable, is the wide gap between levels of review justifiable? Or should the two levels of review draw closer together?

1. *The possibility of more substantial scrutiny of economic regulation.* Are the summary dispositions of the Court in many modern due process cases consistent with the Court's own articulated requirements? Can the theoretically still operative Nebbia standard—"that the means selected shall have a real and substantial relation to the object sought to be attained"—be translated into genuine practice? Recall the suggestions about more intense means-oriented scrutiny, p. 458 above: Can the minimal rationality standard be applied with greater "bite"? By a reduced willingness of the Court to hypothesize legislative objectives—by testing the reasonableness of the means in terms of purposes put forth by the defenders of the law, rather than the Court's attribution of purposes a legislature *might* have had? And by requiring the defenders of the law to come forth with some data to show how the means promote the legislative purposes? Can such means scrutiny avoid the dangers of judicial value infusions of the Lochner era?[2]

"commercial speech" cases represent a resurrection of the Lochner philosophy. The cases, and critical comments about them, appear at p. 1128 below.

1. The Court's response to equal protection challenges before the 1970s was very similar. Only one law was struck down on equal protection grounds during the post-1930s generation, Morey v. Doud, 354 U.S. 457 (1957); and that decision was overruled in New Orleans v. Dukes (1976; p. 607 below). Equal protection, like economic due process, typically meant "minimal scrutiny in theory and virtually none in fact." Gunther, "[A] Model for a Newer Equal Protection," 86 Harv.L.Rev. 1, 8 (1972). (The signs of somewhat greater scrutiny under equal protection since the early 1970s are examined in sec. 1 of the next chapter.)

However, some state courts, applying state constitutional provisions similar to due process and equal protection, continued throughout this period to scrutinize legislation with greater care

and to invalidate laws more frequently. See Hetherington, "State Economic Regulation and Substantive Due Process of Law," 53 Nw.U.L. Rev. 13, 226 (1958), and Paulsen, "The Persistence of Substantive Due Process in the States," 34 Minn.L.Rev. 91 (1950); cf. Struve, "The Less-Restrictive-Alternative Principle and Economic Due Process," 80 Harv.L.Rev. 1463 (1967).

2. The possibility of more genuine means scrutiny is further explored below, in the context of equal protection, in chap. 9, sec. 1. Note preliminarily the comment in McCloskey, "Economic Due Process and the Supreme Court: An Exhumation and Reburial," 1962 Sup.Ct.Rev. 34: "Why did the Court move all the way from the inflexible negativism of the old majority to the all-out tolerance of the new? Why did it not establish a halfway house between the extremes, retaining a measure of control over economic legislation but exercising that control with discrimination and self-restraint?" McCloskey sug-

2. *The new interventionism: The Carolene Products footnote.* Is the withdrawal from review of economic regulations consistent with the increased scrutiny that has marked the Court's activities in other areas? That the Court would not abandon interventionism across the board when it turned its back on Lochner was suggested in a famous footnote by Justice Stone in the Carolene Products case in 1938. While describing in the text of his opinion some guidelines for the deferential "some rational basis" review of economic legislation challenged under due process (p. 467 above),[3] Justice STONE added a footnote 4 [UNITED STATES v. CAROLENE PRODUCTS CO., 304 U.S. 144 (1938)]:

"There may be narrower scope for operation of the presumption of constitutionality when legislation appears on its face to be within a specific prohibition of the Constitution, such as those of the first ten Amendments, which are deemed equally specific when held to be embraced within the 14th. See Stromberg v. California, 283 U.S. 359, 369–370; Lovell v. Griffin, 303 U.S. 444, 452.

"It is unnecessary to consider now whether legislation which restricts those political processes which can ordinarily be expected to bring about repeal of undesirable legislation, is to be subjected to more exacting judicial scrutiny under the general prohibitions of the 14th Amendment than are most other types of legislation. On restrictions upon the right to vote, see Nixon v. Herndon, 273 U.S. 536; Nixon v. Condon, 286 U.S. 73; on restraints upon the dissemination of information, see Near v. Minnesota, 283 U.S. 697, 713–714, 718–720, 722; Grosjean v. American Press Co., 297 U.S. 233; Lovell v. Griffin, supra; on interferences with political organizations, see Stromberg v. California, supra, 369; Fiske v. Kansas, 274 U.S. 380; Whitney v. California, 274 U.S. 357, 373–378; Herndon v. Lowry, 301 U.S. 242; and see Holmes, J., in Gitlow v. New York, 268 U.S. 652, 673; as to prohibition of peaceable assembly, see De Jonge v. Oregon, 299 U.S. 353, 365.

"Nor need we enquire whether similar considerations enter into the review of statutes directed at particular religious, Pierce v. Society of Sisters, 268 U.S. 510, or national, Meyer v. Nebraska, 262 U.S. 390; Bartels v. Iowa, 262 U.S. 404; Farrington v. Tokushige, 273 U.S. 284, or racial minorities, Nixon v. Herndon, supra; Nixon v. Condon, supra; whether prejudice against discrete and insular minorities may be a special condition, which tends seriously to curtail the operation of those political processes ordinarily to be relied upon to protect minorities, and which may call for a correspondingly more searching judicial inquiry. Compare McCulloch v. Maryland, 4 Wheat. 316, 428; South Carolina v. Barnwell Bros., 303 U.S. 177, 184, n. 2, and cases cited." [4]

gested as one explanation that the "intransigence" of the majority of the Lochner era "tended to discredit the whole concept of judicial supervision"—that "extremism had bred extremism": that excessive intervention in the Lochner years bred the arguably excessive modern abdication. Would an intensified means scrutiny represent such a halfway house? And may the time now be ripe to move in that direction, under the banner of equal protection if not due process? Note McCloskey's suggested "halfway house": the Court would "not strike down an arguably rational law, but it would require some showing by the State that there was a basis for believing it to be rational and would consider evidence to the contrary presented by the affected business. Laws like those involved in [Lee Optical might] be invalidated, or at any rate more sharply queried." In 1962 McCloskey did not expect such a change to come about. Is there greater basis to

anticipate such a change today? See chap. 9 below.

3. Recall that in the same year Justice Stone also wrote the Barnwell Bros. opinion, suggesting a virtually complete withdrawal from review of state regulations challenged under the commerce clause (p. 246 above); but his opinion in the Southern Pacific case a few years later (p. 248) made clear that a more intense, "balancing" mode of review was appropriate in implementing the dormant commerce clause barrier. Recall also the variations on the political process theme (so prominent in the Carolene Products footnote) in those commerce clause opinions by Justice Stone.

4. Most of the cited cases are considered in the chapters that follow.

Justice Stone's "political process" rationale in the Carolene Products case footnote is echoed in

The "double standard" suggested by that footnote—an interventionist stance in some areas, a deferential one in others—has had a pervasive influence. As a justification for the varieties of scrutiny by the modern Court at levels higher than minimal rationality, the footnote raises a number of difficulties. (See, e.g., sec. 3, p. 527 below.) But there can be no doubt that the modern Court has been characterized by a notable activism on behalf of fundamental rights and interests outside the economic sphere. In addition to the selective incorporation of Bill of Rights guarantees of criminal procedure noted in the preceding chapter, the use of the 14th Amendment has burgeoned with respect to First Amendment rights, discrimination against racial and other minorities, fundamental rights such as privacy and autonomy, and fundamental interests such as voting, all explored below. Should, and can, judicial scrutiny in the economic due process sphere remain as deferential as in the modern cases, given the sharp intensification of review in so many other areas?

3. *Property and economic rights and the contrast with fundamental personal liberties.* Can the different standards of review be justified because of an inherent difference in the "fundamentalness" of economic rights and other personal rights? Can they be justified because of differences in judicial competence regarding economic and noneconomic rights? In the modern due process cases, the Court repeatedly states its determination to keep hands off the economic sphere. That is a recurrent theme: for example, in refusing to extend the strict scrutiny of the "new" equal protection to state welfare programs, Justice Stewart stated in Dandridge v. Williams (1970; p. 850 below) that nonintervention was appropriate in "the area of economic and social welfare" and commented that "the intractable economic, social, and even philosophical problems presented by public welfare assistance programs are not the business of this Court." But are the "social, and even philosophical" problems truly less intractable in the modern areas of intervention? Does protection of property and economic interest have less textual and historical basis than protection of other interests? Compare the recent repudiation (in another prevailing opinion) of the frequent modern efforts to explain the "double standard" of judicial intervention in terms of an allegedly sharp difference between property and noneconomic rights. Justice Stewart stated in Lynch v. Household Finance Corp., 405 U.S. 538 (1972): "[T]he dichotomy between personal liberties and property rights is a false one. Property does not have rights. People have rights. The right to enjoy property without unlawful deprivation, no less than the right to speak or the right to travel, is, in truth, a 'personal' right, whether the 'property' in question be a welfare check, a home or a savings account. In fact, a fundamental interdependence exists between the personal right to liberty and the personal right in property. Neither could have meaning without the other. That rights in property are basic civil rights has long been recognized. J. Locke, Of Civil Government; J. Adams, A Defence of the Constitutions of the Government of the United States of America; 1 W. Blackstone Commentaries * 138–140." [5]

4. *Economic rights and the contrast with First Amendment liberties.* In the area of First Amendment liberties, the modern Court has imposed very substantial restraints on state action.[6] Is the distinction between "economic" and "civil

much of the modern literature seeking to justify the Court's interventionism in selected areas. For an especially influential variant on the "political process" theme, see Ely, Democracy and Distrust (1980), repeatedly noted elsewhere in this book. See also, generally, Lusky, "Footnote Redux: A Carolene Products Reminiscence," 82 Colum.L.Rev. 1093 (1982). (Professor Lusky, who was Justice Stone's law clerk when Carolene Products was written, commented on both the background of the footnote and some of the voluminous literature it has generated.)

5. Justice Stewart's opinion in the 4 to 3 decision in Lynch was joined by Justices Douglas, Brennan and Marshall, viewed at the time as the most "liberal," interventionist Justices.

6. On First Amendment developments, see chaps. 11 to 13, especially the return to the double standard problem at p. 974 below.

liberties" cases sufficiently clear to justify the vast differences in the levels of judicial scrutiny? Is the "liberty" of the individual who is denied a master electrician's license under a guild-type state law all that different from the kind of "liberty" protected in the free speech cases? [7]

5. *The contrast with non-"specific," noneconomic fundamental rights and interests.* Is the Court's "hands-off" stance in the economic regulation cases made substantially more untenable by the modern protection of a range of fundamental values no more explicit in the Constitution than such economic rights as freedom of contract? If fundamental values other than those explicitly safeguarded in the Bill of Rights can claim substantive due process protection, can the Court justify in principle its summary rejection of economic claims? During the 1960s, the Court's "new" equal protection exercised strict scrutiny under the equal protection clause when a variety of "fundamental interests" were affected—fundamental interests such as voting and the fair administration of justice. Do those developments signify a breakdown of the economic-personal rights double standard in the equal protection area?

But the questions raised by the virtual demise of economic due process scrutiny are most acute when contrasted with the recent invigorations of the due process clause itself. In the cases in sec. 3 below, fundamental rights of "privacy" and "autonomy" are enforced in such contexts as contraception and abortion. Does the "privacy" of Griswold v. Connecticut and Roe v. Wade, for example, have any better textual or historical basis than economic rights? Do the Griswold and Roe decisions have any greater justification than Lochner? Does the revival of substantive due process in those cases cast added doubt on the virtual abandonment of scrutiny in the economic area? Even if the Court may enforce extraconstitutional values, is the present hierarchy justifiable? Perhaps economic liberties should rank lower than speech and privacy on such a scale. But should they rank so low as to justify the decline of judicial scrutiny to the level manifested in the modern economic due process cases?

6. *Transitional note.* The comparison between the Lochner era and the modern revival of substantive due process is pursued in sec. 3 below. (See especially the Lochner-Roe comparison at p. 526.) Those materials can usefully be considered at this point. But before turning to them, the next section completes the coverage of constitutional protections of economic rights with a review of (a) the "taking-regulation" distinction in due process adjudication, and (b) the role of the contracts clause.

SECTION 2. OTHER CONSTITUTIONAL SAFEGUARDS OF ECONOMIC RIGHTS: THE "TAKING–REGULATION" DISTINCTION; THE CONTRACTS CLAUSE

A. EMINENT DOMAIN AND THE "TAKING–REGULATION" DISTINCTION

Introduction. Among the earliest "specific" Bill of Rights guarantees absorbed into the 14th Amendment's due process guarantee was the Fifth Amendment's command that private property shall not "be taken for public use,

---

7. See, e.g., chap. 3, "The Right to Make a Living," in Gellhorn, Individual Freedom and Governmental Restraints (1956), 105–151, on "the significant interference with the traditional freedom to work" by "the occupational license." See generally Reich, "The New 'Property,'" 73 Yale L.J. 733 (1964). Compare also the Court's growing solicitude for procedural protections of property rights in right to hearing cases, sec. 4 below.

without just compensation." [1]   State and federal resorts to the power of eminent domain are common, and a prolific source of constitutional litigation: when government seeks to "take" private land for a new schoolhouse or a park or an airport or an urban redevelopment project, the property is "taken" through condemnation, and the owner is entitled to "just compensation." The specialized bodies of doctrine as to the meaning of "just compensation" and "public use" are largely beyond the scope of this book.[2] But one area of condemnation law touches so closely on economic due process that it warrants some mention here, though its details, too, are left to other courses. Suppose government, rather than condemning property and formally transferring title to itself, merely "regulates" its use and substantially diminishes its value? Can such governmental action give rise to an obligation to afford the property owner "just compensation" for his loss? The answer is clear: it can. What has been unclear and remains perplexing is the question of when. Justice Holmes, in the Pennsylvania Coal case, which follows, stated the "general rule": "[W]hile property may be regulated to a certain extent, if regulation goes too far it will be recognized as a taking." Government need *not* compensate the property owner for losses that are incidental consequences of valid regulation; it *must* compensate when regulation is tantamount to taking. When does governmental action give rise to a duty to compensate? When may government impose property losses without paying compensation, through "the petty larceny of the police power"?[3]

Consider what criteria can be articulated to distinguish between compensable and noncompensable impositions of property losses by government. The two cases that follow are decisions of the 1920s, but they serve to raise the problem. Can the Court do better than Justice Holmes' effort in Pennsylvania Coal? With the modern Court's expansive reading of the police power and its retreat from careful scrutiny of economic regulations, successful "taking" challenges to regulatory schemes are rare. Nevertheless, the Court continues to recognize the possibility of compensation in some circumstances, and the taking-regulation problem is addressed in some of the modern cases in a less summary manner than in the economic due process decisions. Consider, in examining these materials, what criteria might serve to draw the taking-regulation distinction: The magnitude of the harm to the private interest? The manner of imposing the harm? The degree to which the imposition interferes with legitimate private expectations? The nature and the magnitude of the public interest? Or must decision turn inevitably on a balancing of public need and private burden?[4]

---

1. See Chicago, B. & Q. R. R. Co. v. Chicago, 166 U.S. 226 (1897), (just compensation), and Missouri Pac. Ry. v. Nebraska, 164 U.S. 403 (1896) (property may not be taken for "private" rather than "public" use).

2. Note, however, the comment on "public use," at p. 485 below.

3. The phrase is Justice Holmes', from a draft opinion he prepared in a case, Jackman v. Rosenbaum Co., 260 U.S. 22 (1922), decided shortly before Pennsylvania Coal. He deleted the phrase in the final version: "my brethren, as usual and as I expected, corrected my taste. [It] is done—our effort is to please." Holmes to Laski, October 22, 1922, 1 Holmes-Laski Letters (Howe ed. 1953), 457.

4. For a valiant modern effort to articulate a general approach, see Michelman, "Property, Utility, and Fairness: Comments on the Ethical Foundations of 'Just Compensation' Law," 80 Harv.L.Rev. 1165 (1967). See also Sax, "Takings and the Police Power," 74 Yale L.J. 36 (1964), Sax, "Takings, Private Property and Public Rights," 81 Yale L.J. 149 (1971), Berger, "A Policy Analysis of the Taking Problem," 49 N.Y. U.L.Rev. 165 (1974), Dunham, "[Thirty] Years of Supreme Court Expropriation Law," 1962 Sup.Ct.Rev. 63, Ackerman, Private Property and the Constitution (1977), and Humbach, "A Unifying Theory for the Just-Compensation Cases: Takings, Regulation and Public Use," 34 Rutgers L.Rev. 243 (1982).

PENNSYLVANIA COAL CO. v. MAHON

260 U.S. 393, 43 S.Ct. 158, 67 L.Ed. 322 (1922).

Mr. Justice HOLMES delivered the opinion of the court.

This is a bill in equity [to] prevent the Pennsylvania Coal Company from mining under [the plaintiffs'] property in such way as to remove the supports and cause a subsidence of the surface and of their house. [The plaintiffs claim under] a deed executed by the Coal Company in 1878 [which] conveys the surface, but in express terms reserves the right to remove all the coal under the same, and the grantee takes the premises with the risk, and waives all claim for damages that may arise from mining out the coal. But the plaintiffs say that whatever may have been the Coal Company's rights, they were taken away by an Act of Pennsylvania [of 1921] commonly known there as the Kohler Act. [The highest state court] held that the statute was a legitimate exercise of the police power. [The 1921 law] forbids the mining of anthracite coal in such way as to cause the subsidence of, among other things, any structure used as a human habitation, with certain exceptions. [As] applied to this case the statute is admitted to destroy previously existing rights of property and contract. The question is whether the police power can be stretched so far.

Government hardly could go on if to some extent values incident to property could not be diminished without paying for every such change in the general law. As long recognized, some values are enjoyed under an implied limitation and must yield to the police power. But obviously the implied limitation must have its limits, or the contract and due process clauses are gone. One fact for consideration in determining such limits is the extent of the diminution. When it reaches a certain magnitude, in most if not in all cases there must be an exercise of eminent domain and compensation to sustain the act. So the question depends upon the particular facts. [This] is the case of a single private house. No doubt there is a public interest even in this. [But] usually in ordinary private affairs the public interest does not warrant much of this kind of interference. A source of damage to such a house is not a public nuisance even if similar damage is inflicted on others in different places. The damage is not common or public. [The law] is not justified as a protection of personal safety. That could be provided for by notice. Indeed the very foundation of this bill is that the defendant gave timely notice of its intent to mine under the house. On the other hand the extent of the taking is great. It purports to abolish what is recognized in Pennsylvania as [a "very valuable" estate in land]. If we were called upon to deal with the plaintiffs' position alone, we should think it clear that the statute does not disclose a public interest sufficient to warrant so extensive a destruction of the defendant's constitutionally protected rights.

But the case has been treated as one in which the general validity of the act should be discussed. [It] is our opinion that the act cannot be sustained as an exercise of the police power, so far as it affects the mining of coal under streets or cities in places where the right to mine such coal has been reserved. [What] makes the right to mine coal valuable is that it can be exercised with profit. To make it commercially impracticable to mine certain coal has very nearly the same effect for constitutional purposes as appropriating or destroying it. This we think that we are warranted in assuming that the statute does. It is true that [Plymouth Coal Co. v. Pennsylvania, 232 U.S. 531 [(1914), held that the legislature could] require a pillar of coal to be left along the line of adjoining property, that with the pillar on the other side of the line would be a barrier sufficient for the safety of the employees of either mine in case the other should be abandoned and allowed to fill with water. But that was a requirement for the safety of employees invited into the mine, and secured an average reciprocity of advantage that has been recognized as a justification of various laws.

The rights of the public in a street purchased or laid out by eminent domain are those that it has paid for. If in any case its representatives have been so short sighted as to acquire only surface rights without the right of support, we see no more authority for supplying the latter without compensation than there was for taking the right of way in the first place and refusing to pay for it because the public wanted it very much. The protection of private property in the Fifth Amendment presupposes that it is wanted for public use, but provides that it shall not be taken for such use without compensation. A similar assumption is made [under the 14th Amendment]. When this seemingly absolute protection is found to be qualified by the police power, the natural tendency of human nature is to extend the qualification more and more until at last private property disappears. But that cannot be accomplished in this way under the [Constitution]. The general rule at least is, that while property may be regulated to a certain extent, if regulation goes too far it will be recognized as a taking. It may be doubted how far exceptional cases, like the blowing up of a house to stop a conflagration, go—and if they go beyond the general rule, whether they do not stand as much upon tradition as upon principle. In general it is not plain that a man's misfortunes or necessities will justify his shifting the damages to his neighbor's shoulders. [We] are in danger of forgetting that a strong public desire to improve the public condition is not enough to warrant achieving the desire by a shorter cut than the constitutional way of paying for the change. [It] is a question of degree. [But this goes beyond] any of the cases decided by this [Court]. We assume, of course, that the statute was passed upon the conviction that an exigency existed that would warrant it, and we assumed that an exigency exists that would warrant the exercise of eminent domain. But the question at bottom is upon whom the loss of the changes desired should fall. So far as private persons or communities have seen fit to take the risk of acquiring only surface rights, we cannot see that the fact that their risk has become a danger warrants the giving to them greater rights than they bought.

[Reversed.]

Mr. Justice BRANDEIS, dissenting.

[Every] restriction upon the use of property imposed in the exercise of the police power deprives the owner of some right theretofore enjoyed, and is, in that sense, an abridgment by the State of rights in property without making compensation. But a restriction imposed to protect the public health, safety or morals from dangers threatened is not a taking. The restriction here in question is merely the prohibition of a noxious use. The property so restricted remains in the possession of its owner. The State does not appropriate it or make any use of it. The State merely prevents the owner from making a use which interferes with paramount rights of the [public]. The restriction upon the use of this property can not, of course, be lawfully imposed, unless its purpose is to protect the public. But the purpose of a restriction does not cease to be public, because incidentally some private persons may thereby receive gratuitously valuable special benefits. Thus, owners of low buildings may obtain, through statutory restrictions upon the height of neighboring structures, benefits equivalent to an easement of light and air. [Furthermore], a restriction, though imposed for a public purpose, will not be lawful, unless the restriction is an appropriate means to the public end. But to keep coal in place is surely an appropriate means of preventing subsidence of the surface; and ordinarily it is the only available means. Restriction upon use does not become inappropriate as a means, merely because it deprives the owner of the only use to which the property can then be profitably put. The liquor and the oleomargarine cases settled that. Nor is a restriction imposed through exercise of the police power inappropriate as a means, merely because the same end might be effected through exercise of the power of eminent domain, or otherwise at public expense. Every restriction upon the height of buildings might be secured through acquiring by eminent domain the right of each owner to build above the limiting height; but it is settled that the state need not resort to that power. If by mining anthracite coal the owner would necessarily unloose poisonous gases, I suppose no one would doubt the power of the state to prevent the mining, without buying his coal fields. And why may not the state, likewise, without paying compensation, prohibit one from digging so deep or excavating so near the surface, as to expose the community to like dangers? In the latter case, as in the former, carrying on the business would be a public nuisance.

It is said that one fact for consideration in determining whether the limits of the police power have been exceeded is the extent of the resulting diminution in value, and that here the restriction destroys existing rights of property and contract. But values are relative. If we are to consider the value of the coal kept in place by the restriction, we should compare it with the value of all other parts of the land. [The law was] obviously enacted for a public purpose; and it seems, likewise, clear that mere notice of intention to mine would [not] secure the public safety. Yet it is said that [the law] cannot be sustained as an exercise of the police power where the right to mine such coal has been reserved. The conclusion seems to rest upon the assumption that in order to justify such exercise of the police power there must be "an average reciprocity of advantage" as between the owner of the property restricted and the rest of the community; and that here such reciprocity is absent. Reciprocity of advantage is an important consideration, and may even be essential, where the State's power is exercised for the purpose of conferring benefits upon the property of a neighborhood, as in drainage projects [or] upon adjoining owners, as by party wall provisions. But where the police power is exercised, not to confer benefits upon property owners but to protect the public from detriment and danger, there is in my opinion, no room for considering reciprocity of advantage. There was no reciprocal advantage to the owner prohibited [by a number of prior decisions] from using his oil tanks, his brickyard, his livery stable, his billiard hall, his oleomargarine factory, [or] his brewery; unless it be the advantage of living and doing business in a civilized community. That reciprocal advantage is given by the act to the coal operators.

———

MILLER v. SCHOENE, 276 U.S. 272 (1928): A Virginia law provided for the destruction as a public nuisance of all ornamental red cedar trees that were or might be the source of a communicable plant disease known as cedar rust and that were growing within a prescribed radius of any apple orchard. Under the law, owners of the cedars were paid only the cost of removing their trees; they were not compensated for loss of the value of the standing cedars or the decrease in the value of their land caused by the destruction of the trees. The state courts upheld the state entomologist's order that a large number of cedars be cut down to protect nearby apple orchards. In affirming that decision and concluding that the cedars could be destroyed without paying full compensation to their owners, Justice STONE's opinion for the unanimous Court stated:

"[Cedar rust] is an infectious plant disease in the form of a fungoid organism which is destructive of the fruit and foliage of the apple, but without effect on the value of the cedar. [The] only practicable method of controlling the disease and protecting apple trees [is] the destruction of all red cedar trees, subject to the infection, located within two miles of apple orchards. The red cedar, aside from its ornamental use, has occasional use and value as lumber. It is indigenous to Virginia, is not cultivated or dealt in commercially on any substantial scale, and its value throughout the state is shown to be small as compared with that of the apple orchards of the state. Apple growing is one of the principal agricultural pursuits in Virginia. The apple is used there and exported in large quantities. Many millions of dollars are invested in the orchards, which furnish employment for a large portion of the population. [On] the evidence we may accept the conclusion of the [state court] that the state was under the necessity of making a choice between the preservation of one class of property and that of the other wherever both existed in dangerous proximity. It would have been none the less a choice if, instead of enacting the present statute, the state, by doing nothing, had permitted serious injury to the apple orchards within its borders to go on unchecked. When forced to such a choice the state does not exceed its constitutional powers by deciding upon the destruction of one class of property in order to save another which, in the judgment of the legislature, is of greater value to the public. It will not do to say that the case is merely one of a conflict of two private interests and that the misfortune of apple growers may not be shifted to cedar owners by ordering the destruction of their property; for it is obvious that there may be, and that here there is, a preponderant public concern in the preservation of the one interest over the other. [And] where the public interest is involved preferment of that interest over the property interest of the individual, to the extent even of its destruction, is one of the distinguishing characteristics of every exercise of the police power which affects property. [Where], as here, the choice is unavoidable, we cannot say that its exercise, controlled by considerations of social policy which are not unreasonable, involves any denial of due process."

THE "TAKING–REGULATION" DISTINCTION AND THE MODERN COURT

1. *Zoning and other regulations of the environment.* When can zoning laws be challenged as being compensable "takings"? Even during the heyday of economic due process, a divided Court sustained a general zoning ordinance as a valid "police regulation," in Euclid v. Ambler Realty Co., 272 U.S. 365 (1926). But the Euclid Court emphasized that it was not passing on specific applications of zoning ordinances; and two years later, in Nectow v. Cambridge, 277 U.S. 183 (1928), a particular application of a zoning law was invalidated.[1] Property owners' challenges to zoning and other environmental laws have produced much litigation in state and lower federal courts, but few come to the modern Court. One modern example is GOLDBLATT v. HEMPSTEAD, 369 U.S. 590 (1962), where, after a state court had blocked an effort to deal with a local problem via zoning, the town resorted to a "safety regulation"—and prevailed in the Court. Goldblatt owned a sand and gravel pit in a suburban area; the town had expanded rapidly. In the last of a series of local regulations of excavations, the town banned some types of mining and imposed a duty to refill some pits. Goldblatt claimed that the latest ordinance was "not regulatory" but rather amounted to confiscation of property without compensation. Justice CLARK's opinion for the Court conceded that the regulation "completely prohibits a beneficial use to which the property has previously been devoted," but nevertheless found it justified as a "reasonable," noncompensable exercise of the police power. It is noteworthy, however, that Justice Clark's discussion of "reasonableness" was more extensive than is typical in the modern economic due process cases. Moreover, he cited the Penn-

---

1. For an extremely rare invocation of the deferential standard of Euclid and Nectow to invalidate a zoning ordinance, see Justice Ste- vens' concurring opinion in Moore v. East Cleveland (1977; p. 551 below).

sylvania Coal case and recognized "that governmental action in the form of regulation cannot be so onerous as to constitute a taking." He added: "There is no set formula to determine where regulation ends and taking begins. Although a comparison of values before and after is relevant, [it] is by no means conclusive. [How] far regulation may go before it becomes a taking we need not now decide, for there is no evidence in the present record which even remotely suggests that prohibition of further mining will reduce the value of the lot in question."

The Court also rejected an on-the-face attack on a zoning ordinance in AGINS v. TIBURON, 447 U.S. 255 (1980). After appellants had acquired five acres of unimproved land in Tiburon (a scenic suburb of San Francisco) for residential development, the city adopted zoning changes which placed the land in a zone in which appellants could only build between one and five single-family residences on their tract. Justice POWELL's opinion concluded that "the zoning ordinance on its face does not take the appellants' property without just compensation." Relying on the Euclid approach, he found that the ordinance "substantially advance[d] legitimate governmental goals": the regulations were designed to protect residents "from the ill-effects of urbanization"; they benefitted "the appellants as well as the public by serving the city's interest in assuring careful and orderly development of residential property"; and, in assessing the fairness of the regulation, "these benefits must be considered along with any diminution in market value that the appellants might suffer." Most important, the regulations, though limiting development, "neither prevent the best use of appellants' land nor extinguish a fundamental attribute of ownership."[2]

The more difficult issue left open in Agins—whether a state "must provide a monetary remedy to a landowner whose property allegedly has been 'taken' by a regulatory ordinance"—came to the Court in SAN DIEGO GAS & ELECTRIC CO. v. SAN DIEGO, 450 U.S. 621 (1981).[3] The majority found that it lacked jurisdiction to review, because of the lack of a final judgment below. But the four dissenters (Justice Brennan, joined by Justices Stewart, Marshall and Powell) did reach the merits; and their position probably was in fact the majority one, since Justice Rehnquist, who agreed with the jurisdictional dismissal, stated that if he had reached the merits, he "would have little difficulty in agreeing with much of what is said in the dissenting opinion of Justice Brennan." Justice BRENNAN concluded: "The constitutional rule I propose requires that, once a court finds that a police power regulation has effected a 'taking,' the government entity must pay just compensation for the period commencing on the date the regulation first effected the 'taking,' and ending on the date the government entity chooses to rescind [the] regulation." He argued that the mere invalidation of a regulatory statute which constituted a taking "would fall far short of fulfilling the fundamental purpose of the Just Compensation Clause. That guarantee was designed to bar the government

2. The Agins Court did not reach the most controversial issue raised by the challengers. They had sought not only a declaration that the zoning was unconstitutional but also a damage award for inverse condemnation. (Inverse condemnation, the Court noted, is "a shorthand description of the manner in which a landowner recovers just compensation for taking of his property when condemnation proceedings have not been instituted [by the government].") The California Supreme Court held that a challenger to a zoning ordinance may not "sue in inverse condemnation and thereby transmute an excessive use of the police power into a lawful taking for which compensation in eminent domain must be paid"; the sole remedies for such a taking under California law were mandamus and declaratory judgment. That issue was reached by several of the Justices a year later, in the San Diego case noted in the next paragraph of the text.

3. The case involved a challenge to an ordinance rezoning much of plaintiff's property from industrial use to open-space land. The challenger argued that the rezoning constituted a taking and claimed a right to compensation. The case accordingly raised the issue not reached in Agins, whether the state could limit the remedies for "inverse condemnation"—a regulatory taking—to mandamus and declaratory judgments and refuse money damages.

from forcing some individuals to bear burdens which, in all fairness, should be borne by the public as a whole. [It] is only fair that the public bear the cost of benefits received. [The] payment of just compensation serves to place the landowner in the same position monetarily as he would have occupied if his property had not been taken." However, he rejected the claim that the city must formally condemn the property and pay full market value: "[Nothing] in the Just Compensation Clause empowers a court to order a government entity to condemn the property and pay its full fair market value, where the 'taking' already effected is temporary and reversible and the government wants to halt the 'taking.'" In short, Justice Brennan insisted that "inverse condemnation" through regulation *could* constitute a "taking" and that invalidation of the regulation was *not* a sufficient remedy without payment of monetary compensation.

2. *Historic landmarks protection and the "taking-regulation" distinction.* In its most careful look at the "taking-regulation" distinction in years, the divided Court held in PENN CENTRAL TRANSPORTATION CO. v. NEW YORK CITY, 438 U.S. 104 (1978), that the constitutional bounds of permissible regulation had not been exceeded. Under New York City's Landmarks Preservation Law, Grand Central Terminal was designated as a "landmark." The law requires the owner of a designated landmark to keep the building's exterior "in good repair" and to obtain approval from a commission before making exterior alterations. A request for approval to build a multistory office building atop Grand Central Terminal was denied by the commission because, in its view, the office tower would impair the aesthetic quality of the Terminal's "flamboyant Beaux Arts facade." The owner of the Terminal brought suit claiming that the application of the law constituted a "taking." The 6 to 3 decision rejected that claim.

Justice BRENNAN's majority opinion concluded that a city may, as part of a comprehensive historic landmarks preservation program, "place restrictions on the development of individual historic landmarks [without] effecting a 'taking.'" Though the majority undertook an extensive canvass of the "taking-regulation" precedents, it conceded once again that the application of the legal standards involved "essentially ad hoc factual inquiries" and acknowledged that the Court had been "unable to develop any 'set formula' for determining when 'justice and fairness' require that economic injuries caused by public action be compensated by the Government, rather than remain disproportionately concentrated on a few persons." Justice Brennan surveyed "several factors" that had been identified as having "particular significance." He noted that zoning laws were "classic" examples of ordinarily permissible impairments of real property interests for the sake of "the health, safety, morals or general welfare." Pennsylvania Coal, on the other hand, served as a warning that a law "that substantially furthers important public policies may so frustrate distinct investment-backed expectations as to amount to a 'taking.'" He found landmarks regulation more akin to the zoning precedents than to Pennsylvania Coal. He conceded that, unlike zoning laws and historic district legislation, "landmark laws apply only to selected parcels." But he insisted that "landmark laws are not like discriminatory, or 'reverse spot,' zoning: that is, a land use decision which arbitrarily singles out a particular parcel for different, less favorable treatment than the neighboring ones. In contrast to discriminatory zoning, [the law here] embodies a comprehensive plan to preserve structures of historic or aesthetic interest wherever they may be found in the city, [and] over 400 landmarks [have] been designated pursuant to this plan." Moreover, the interference with the owner's property was not so great as to fall within the Pennsylvania Coal principle. He emphasized that the owner's use of the air space had not been wholly banned and that the owner had exaggerated the economic effect of the law, since development rights on the restricted parcel were transferable to other nearby parcels. He concluded: "The restrictions imposed are substantially related to the promotion of the general welfare and not only permit reasonable beneficial use of the landmark site but afford [the owner] opportunities further to enhance not only the Terminal site proper but also other properties."

Justice REHNQUIST's dissent, joined by Chief Justice Burger and Justice Stevens, insisted that the severe impact of the law was not justified by either of the two exceptions to the normal rule that "destruction of property" constitutes a compensable taking. The permissible prohibition of "noxious uses"—of nuisances in the sense of Miller v. Schoene and Goldblatt—was not applicable here, since the forbidden use of the Terminal was not "dangerous to the safety, health or welfare of others." [3]   In Justice Rehnquist's view, a second exception to the compensation rule did not apply either: "Even where the government prohibits a noninjurious use, the Court has ruled that a taking does not take place if the prohibition applies over a broad cross section of land and thereby 'secure[s]' an average reciprocity of advantage.' Pennsylvania Coal. It is for this reason that zoning does not constitute a 'taking.' While zoning at times reduces *individual* property values, the burden is shared relatively evenly and it is reasonable to conclude that on the whole an individual who is harmed by one aspect of the zoning will be benefited by another. Here, however, a multimillion dollar loss has been imposed on [the owner]; it is uniquely felt and is not offset by any benefits flowing from the preservation of some 500 other 'Landmarks' in New York. [The city has] imposed a substantial cost on less than one-tenth of one percent of the buildings in New York for the general benefit of all its people. It is exactly this imposition of general costs on a few individuals at which the 'taking' protection is directed. [A] taking does not become a noncompensable exercise of police power simply because the government in its grace allows the owner to make some 'reasonable' use of his property." [4]

3. *"Taking" problems in the 1980s.* Several decisions of the 1980s indicate that the modern Court is prepared to take the Takings Clause quite seriously. Continuing the tendency that began with Penn Central in 1978, the Court in the Loretto and Monsanto rulings of the 1980s found that compensable takings *had* occurred.[5]

a. *A per se rule (rather than balancing) for "permanent physical occupations."* The 6 to 3 decision in LORETTO v. TELEPROMPTER MANHATTAN CATV CORP., 458 U.S. 419 (1982), held that, when the government authorizes a "permanent physical occupation" (albeit a "minor" one) of an owner's property, there "is a taking without regard to the public interests that [the government action] may serve." The majority rejected as inappropriate here the balancing analysis typical in modern taking cases. The Court's newly articulated per se rule led it to invalidate a New York law which provided that a

---

3. Justice Brennan, who relied on Miller and Goldblatt in part, insisted that those cases could not be distinguished on the ground that they involved "noxious" uses of land: "These cases are better understood as resting [on] the ground that the restrictions were reasonably related to the implementation of a policy—not unlike historic preservation—expected to produce a widespread public benefit and applicable to all similarly situated property."

4. For other confrontations with the "taking" problem by the post-Lochner era Court, note, e.g., the decisions sustaining compensation for "takings" by low-flying airplanes and rejecting arguments that the injuries were "merely inciden-

tal" consequences of authorized air navigation, United States v. Causby, 328 U.S. 256 (1946), and Griggs v. Allegheny County, 369 U.S. 84 (1962); and see also a series of cases holding losses from wars and riots noncompensable: United States v. Caltex, 344 U.S. 149 (1952); United States v. Central Eureka Mining Co., 357 U.S. 155 (1958); and National Board of YMCA v. United States, 395 U.S. 85 (1969).

5. Note also that Justice Brennan, the author of the majority opinion in Penn Central (which had found no compensable taking), was the Justice who took the lead in arguing for compensation for "inverse condemnations" in the San Diego case in 1981, above.

landlord must permit a cable television company to install its cable facilities upon a landlord's rental property.[6] (The highest New York court, applying the balancing analysis often used in modern cases to determine whether a regulation is a taking, had found no taking here. The Court disagreed both with the approach and the result.)

In defending the majority's per se rule, applicable to all "permanent physical occupations," Justice MARSHALL stated: "Our constitutional history confirms the rule, recent cases do not question it, and the purposes of the Takings Clause compels its retention." He insisted that the decisions confirmed a distinction "between a permanent physical occupation, a physical invasion short of an occupation, and a regulation that merely restricts the use of property." Even Penn Central and its balancing approach did not "repudiate the rule that a permanent physical occupation is a governmental action of such a unique character that it is a taking without regard to other factors that a court might ordinarily examine." Accordingly, "when the 'character of the governmental action' [Penn Central] is a permanent physical occupation of property, our cases uniformly have found a taking to the extent of the occupation, without regard to whether the action achieves an important public benefit or has only minimal economic impact on the owner." This rule was supported not only by tradition but by the policies of the Takings Clause. Justice Marshall asserted that "constitutional protection for the rights of private property cannot be made to depend on the size of the area permanently occupied," although "a court should consider the *extent* of the occupation as one relevant factor in determining the compensation due." He rejected the effort to defend the law as "simply a permissible regulation of the use of real property" and he insisted that the per se rule was not an undue interference with "the government's power to adjust landlord-tenant relationships." He added that a "property owner entertains an historically-rooted expectation of compensation, and the character of the invasion is qualitatively more intrusive than perhaps any other category of property regulation." He noted, however, that the ruling did not call into question a state's "broad power to impose appropriate restrictions upon an owner's *use* of his property."[7]

b. *Takings of intangible property.* In RUCKELSHAUS v. MONSANTO CO., 467 U.S. ___ (1984), the Court dealt with the application of the Takings Clause to intangible property. At issue were trade secrets of Monsanto, which had been disclosed to the Environmental Protection Agency pursuant to the registration, reporting, and regulation requirements of the Federal Insecticide,

---

6. Under the state law, which became effective in 1973, the landlord was not entitled to demand payment from the cable television beyond a "reasonable amount" set by a state commission. The state commission ruled that a one-time $1 payment was the normal fee to which a landlord was entitled. Before the law became effective, the Company typically obtained authorization from property owners along the cable's route, compensating the landlords at the standard rate of 5% of the gross revenues that the Company realized from the particular property.

The dissent claimed that the taking was only of about one-eighth of a cubic foot of space. The majority conceded that the invasion here was a "minor" intrusion on the property, but thought the "displaced volume" of the cables and related equipment was "in excess of 1½ cubic feet" and added: "In any event, these facts are not critical: whether the installation is a taking does not depend on whether the volume of space that it occupies is bigger than a bread box."

7. In dissenting, Justice BLACKMUN, joined by Justices Brennan and White, condemned the decision as unduly formalistic. In his view, "history teaches that takings claims are properly evaluated under a multifactor balancing test." He asserted, moreover, that the Court had not demonstrated how the law impaired private rights "in a manner *qualitatively* different from other garden-variety landlord-tenant legislation." He added: "[This] Court long ago recognized that new social circumstances can justify legislative modification of a property owner's common-law rights, without compensation, if the legislative action serves sufficiently important public interests. [But] today's decision [represents] an archaic judicial response to a modern social problem." [The state court had upheld the law after finding that it served legitimate police power purposes: "eliminating landlord fees and conditions that inhibit the development of [cable television], which has important educational and community benefits."]

Fungicide, and Rodenticide Act. Under the regulatory scheme, Monsanto could receive permission to market certain pesticides only if it disclosed its formulae and methods to the EPA, which would then make that information generally available. Monsanto claimed that this procedure amounted to a taking because the trade secrets involved were treated as its property under the relevant state law. Justice BLACKMUN'S majority opinion agreed, holding that trade secrets are sufficiently similar to more tangible forms of property to qualify as property for purposes of the Takings Clause: [8] "[T]o the extent that Monsanto has an interest in its health, safety, and environmental data cognizable as a trade-secret property right under [state] law, that property right is protected by the [Takings Clause]."

Establishing that trade secrets were property did not, of course, end the inquiry. The Court went on to say that, in general, the disclosure of information such as that involved here would be considered a taking only if the owner of the information had a "reasonable, investment-backed expectation" that the information would be kept confidential. For most of the relevant time period here, the Court found no such expectation of confidentiality: "Thus, as long as Monsanto is aware of the conditions under which the data are submitted, and the conditions are rationally related to a legitimate governmental interest, a voluntary submission of data by an applicant in exchange for the economic advantages of a registration can hardly be called a taking." But with respect to the 1972–78 period, the Court held that the version of the statute then in force did create such a reasonable expectation of confidentiality, because during those years the statute explicitly provided for protecting trade secrets from disclosure. As to this period, therefore, the Court held that a taking had taken place, that it was for a legitimate public use, and that it was therefore permissible provided that compensation was made.[9]

A NOTE ON "PUBLIC USE"

The just compensation provision refers to property "taken for *public use.*" The modern Court, in a development paralleling the decline of economic due process scrutiny, tends to be extremely deferential toward legislative determinations of what constitutes public use.[1] The characteristic Court tenor is illustrated by Berman v. Parker, 348 U.S. 26 (1954). There, Justice Douglas' opinion for a unanimous Court stated: "The role of the judiciary in determining whether [the eminent domain power] is being exercised for a public purpose is an extremely narrow one."[2] The "extremely narrow" judicial role on public

8. Justice Blackmun stated: "Although this Court never has squarely addressed the question whether a person can have a property interest in a trade secret, which is admittedly intangible, the Court has found other kinds of intangible interests to be property for purposes of the [Clause]."

9. The case was remanded for appropriate compensation proceedings under the Tucker Act, 28 U.S.C. § 1491.

1. Recall the similarly deferential stance regarding what constitutes the "Welfare of the United States" when Congress exercises its power to tax and spend for that purpose, as noted in chap. 4, at p. 211, above.

2. Berman was a challenge to a District of Columbia law authorizing the taking of private property for the purpose of redeveloping blighted areas. After condemnation, the government could lease or sell that property to private developers, who were required to conform to redevelopment plans adopted by a D.C. agency. In the course of sustaining that scheme, Justice Douglas made a much quoted statement about the breadth of governmental power: "The concept of the public welfare is broad and inclusive. The values it represents are spiritual as well as physical, aesthetic as well as monetary. It is within the power of the legislature to determine that the community should be beautiful as well as healthy, spacious as well as clean, well-balanced as well as carefully patrolled. [If] those who govern the District of Columbia decide that the Nation's Capital should be beautiful as well as sanitary, there is nothing in the Fifth Amendment that stands in the way. [The] rights of these property owners are satisfied when they receive that just compensation which the Fifth Amendment exacts as the price of the taking." (In the course of his opinion, Justice Douglas

use issues was more recently demonstrated in the Court's unanimous decision in HAWAII HOUSING AUTHORITY v. MIDKIFF, 467 U.S. ___ (1984). The decision upheld Hawaii's use of eminent domain to solve the problem of concentrated land ownership, a problem traceable to Hawaii's early feudal land tenure system. In the 1960s, the legislature found that 72 private landowners owned 47% of the State's land and the state and federal governments 49%, leaving only 4% for other private owners. Moreover, on Oahu, the most urbanized island, 22 landowners owned 72.5% of the fee simple titles. The legislature concluded that "concentrated land ownership was responsible for skewing the State's residential fee simple market, inflating land prices, and injuring the public tranquility and welfare." The Hawaii Land Reform Act of 1967, designed to compel the large landowners to break up their estates, created a mechanism for condemning residential tracts and for transfering ownership of the condemned fees simple to existing lessees. Justice O'CONNOR rejected the claim that the purpose of the Hawaii scheme was redistribution for private rather than public benefit. After reviewing Berman, she noted that the "public use" requirement was "coterminous with the scope of a sovereign's police powers." She added: "[Where] the exercise of the eminent domain power is rationally related to a conceivable public purpose, the Court has never held a compensated taking to be proscribed by the Public Use Clause. On this basis, we have no trouble concluding that the Hawaii Act is constitutional. [The] people of Hawaii have attempted [to] reduce the perceived social and economic evils of a land oligopoly traceable to their monarchs. [Regulating] oligopoly and the evils associated with it is a classic exercise of a State's police powers. [We cannot] condemn as irrational the Act's approach to correcting the land oligopoly problem. [When] the legislature's purpose is legitimate and its means are not irrational, our cases make clear that empirical debates over the wisdom of takings—no less than debates over the wisdom of other kinds of socioeconomic legislation—are not to be carried out in the federal courts. [This] is a rational exercise of the eminent domain power. [The] mere fact that property taken outright by eminent domain is transferred in the first instance to private beneficiaries does not condemn that taking as having only a private purpose. [Government] does not itself have to use property to legitimate the takings; it is only the taking's purpose, and not its mechanics, that must pass scrutiny under the Public Use Clause. [No] purely private taking is involved in this case." [3]

As the modern cases illustrate, the "public use" limitation in a broad sense relates closely to issues of economic due process. What is a public rather than a private use is often a function of both economic theory and political philosophy, akin to the questions raised in "ends" inquiries under economic due process. A narrow view of the role of the state, a la Lochner, would logically carry with it a narrow view of the contours of permissible public use. Under such a narrow view, even compensated takings would be significantly constrained by the public

repeatedly cited modern economic due process cases such as those in sec. 1C above.)

3. A month later, Midkiff was relied on in the Monsanto case (above) to find that the trade secrets disclosure provision challenged there resulted in a taking for a "public use." In Monsanto, Justice Blackmun reiterated that the judicial role "in second-guessing the legislature's judgment of what constitutes a public use is extremely narrow," citing Midkiff and Berman. [Debate over the scope of "public use" has also been central in the protracted litigation in the California courts challenging Oakland's effort to "take" the Oakland Raiders' National Football League franchise in order to abort the team's move to Los Angeles. (The author is an Oakland Raiders fan, but not a Los Angeles Raiders fan—just as he was a Brooklyn Dodgers baseball fan and, proudly, did not become a supporter of the Los Angeles Dodgers. Neither Al Davis nor Walter O'Malley has escaped his scorn. Nevertheless, some of his best friends live in Los Angeles.)]

use limitation. By contrast, a broad view, akin to that of the Holmes dissent in Lochner, would eschew using a particular conception of public use as a way of utilizing the Constitution to enforce a particular economic or political theory. The recent cases suggest that the modern Court is almost as disinclined to second-guess "public use" determinations as to curtail police power ends in due process inquiries. Would a different result have been likely in Midkiff if Hawaii's professed purpose had rested on a perception that concentrated ownership was simply unjust? Or that private ownership of property was tantamount to theft? In short, is there anything in the constitutional restrictions on eminent domain, any more than in modern economic due process, to bar a socialistic or other Marxist governmental policy?

B.　THE CONTRACTS CLAUSE

Introduction. During the first century of government under the Constitution, the prohibition of any state "Law impairing the Obligation of Contracts," Art. I, § 10, was the major restraint on state economic regulation. Since the late 19th century, when the Court began to develop substantive due process restraints on economic regulation, the contracts clause has played a less prominent role in constitutional litigation. And as economic due process restrictions waned beginning in the 1930s, contract clause barriers diminished as well. Until the 1970s, indeed, the widespread modern view was that interpretations of the contracts and due process clauses had merged to such an extent that the "results might be the same if the contract clause were dropped out of the Constitution, and the challenged statutes all judged as reasonable or unreasonable deprivations of property" under due process.[1] Yet the contracts clause deserves separate attention. It *was,* after all, the major textual basis for judicial protection of "fundamental" economic rights, not only in the pre-Civil War era but throughout the entire 19th century and into the 20th. It *is,* unlike some of the fundamental values of the Lochner era, an explicit constitutional guarantee. And, most importantly, since the late 1970s the Court has demonstrated that the contracts clause has a bite greater than that of due process. In short, the contracts clause has an importance of its own, in contemporary as well as historical terms. The opening note reviews the developments in the 19th century. The principal case that follows, the Blaisdell case, came in 1934, the same year as Nebbia (p. 462 above), and suggested a loosening of contracts clause restraints paralleling those regarding due process. The section concludes with the most recent cases—demonstrations that the contracts clause retains greater force than economic due process in some contexts.

THE CONTRACTS CLAUSE IN THE 19TH CENTURY

The major purpose of the contracts clause was to restrain state laws affecting private contracts. It was aimed mainly at debtor relief laws—e.g., laws postponing payments of debts and laws authorizing payments in installments or in commodities. Yet the Court first interpreted the contracts clause in cases involving public grants rather than private contracts. Fletcher v. Peck, 6 Cranch

------

1. Hale, "The Supreme Court and the Contract Clause: III," 57 Harv.L.Rev. 852, 890 (1944).

87 (1810); [2] New Jersey v. Wilson, 7 Cranch 164 (1812); [3] Dartmouth College v. Woodward, 4 Wheat. 518 (1819). [4] As Marshall said in Dartmouth College: "It is more than possible that the preservation of rights of this description was not particularly in the view of the framers of the Constitution. [It] is probable that interferences of more frequent recurrence, [of] which the mischief was more extensive, constituted the great motive for imposing this restriction on the State legislatures." But that was no reason for limiting the scope of the clause; and the fact that the case involved a state charter rather than a private contract made no difference. [5] A few weeks after Dartmouth College, the Marshall Court applied the contracts clause to a law closer to the "mischief" which supplied the Framers with the "great motive for imposing this restriction on the State legislatures": in Sturges v. Crowninshield, 4 Wheat. 122 (1819), the Court held unconstitutional a New York insolvency law discharging debtors of their obligations upon surrender of their property. [6]

Historians have probably exaggerated the impact of the early contracts clause decisions on American economic and legal developments. The cases did indeed restrict; but they did *not* compel legislative paralysis, they were *not* the keystone of American corporate development, they did *not* establish an inflexible safe-guard for all vested rights. [7] The lack of statutory restrictions on corporations in the 19th century, for example, was probably more attributable to the legislators' unwillingness to enact them than to any constitutionally imposed incapacities. Indeed, in Dartmouth College itself, Justice Story's concurring opinion had pointed out what state political leaders already knew well: "If the legislature mean to claim such an authority [to alter or amend corporate charters], it must be reserved in the grant. The charter of Dartmouth College contains no such reservation." A later Court noted that "many a [state] inserted, either in its statutes or in its constitutions, a provision that charters thenceforth granted should be subject to alteration, amendment or repeal at the pleasure of the legislature." [8] But many states gave special corporate privileges and failed to include adequate reservations of amending powers in corporate charters even after the Dartmouth decision. In short, the protected position of corporations later in the 19th century was due less to any shield supplied by the Court than to legislative unwillingness to impose restraints—an unwillingness reflecting the laissez faire philosophy of the day.

Moreover, from the beginning the Court's interpretations assured that, even in the absence of a reserved power to amend grants, the contracts clause would

2. In 1795, several companies had obtained a huge grant of land from the Georgia legislature. There were charges of bribery, and a new legislature annulled the grant. The grantees had in the meanwhile sold their lands to investors. The Court held the 1796 law invalid: according to Marshall, the law was barred "either by general principles which are common to our free institutions, or by the particular provisions" of the Constitution. On the background of the controversy, see Magrath, Yazoo: Law and Politics in the New Republic (1966).

3. The Court invalidated a New Jersey law of 1804 repealing a tax exemption which the colonial legislature had granted for certain lands in 1758.

4. The Court struck down New Hampshire's effort to "pack" the College Board of Trustees by increasing its size, since that law violated the 1769 royal charter of the College that had given the trustees the right to fill all vacancies on the Board.

5. For a succinct analysis of this much-discussed case, see Baxter, Daniel Webster & the Supreme Court (1966).

6. See also Green v. Biddle, 8 Wheat. (1823), invalidating Kentucky's Occupying Claimants Law, designed to make it more difficult for landowners to eject those who in good faith had settled and made improvements on Western lands.

7. For an extreme example of the recurrent hyperbole in comments on the early cases, see Sir Henry Maine's statement that the contracts clause "is the bulwark of American individualism against democratic impatience and socialistic fantasy." Popular Government (1885), 247–48.

8. Looker v. Maynard, 179 U.S. 46 (1900), sustaining a stockholders' cumulative voting statute enacted pursuant to a reserved power clause in the Michigan constitution. The Court said that such a clause gave "at least" the power to make "any alteration [which] will not defeat or substantially impair the object of the grant."

not be an inflexible barrier to public regulation.   Only a few of the bases for sustaining state regulatory authority can be noted here.[9]   Thus, just a few years after Dartmouth College, a divided Court stated that the contracts clause did not prohibit *all* state insolvency laws: Ogden v. Saunders, 12 Wheat. 213 (1827), held that such laws could be validly applied to contracts made *after* the law was enacted; the earlier decision in Sturges, the Court made clear, applied only to retroactive insolvency laws.   Moreover, the Court soon elaborated on a distinction stated in Sturges and other early cases: that the constitutional ban on the impairment of contracts "obligations" did not prohibit legislative changes in "remedies."   "Without impairing the obligation of the contract, the remedy may certainly be modified as the wisdom of the nation shall direct," the Court had said in Sturges.   And in Bronson v. Kinzie, 1 How. 311 (1843), the Court stated that the permissible scope of remedial changes depended on their "reasonableness," provided "no substantial right" was impaired.[10]   The early Court safeguarded against excessively broad interpretations of publicly granted privileges as well.   In Dartmouth College, the Court had to strain somewhat to find in the royal charter an implied inviolability of the trustees' rights.   In later years, the Court tended to be less charitable in construing the grantees' privileges.   In Providence Bank v. Billings, 4 Pet. 514 (1830), for example, Marshall refused to read an implied immunity from taxation into a bank's charter.   Taney, Marshall's successor, quickly developed the Providence Bank approach, in the better-known Charles River Bridge Case in 1837.[11]   There, the company's charter to operate a toll bridge did not prevent the state from authorizing the construction of a competing, free bridge: "[Any] ambiguity in the terms of the contract, must operate against the adventurers, and in favour of the public."   Moreover, the states were not left entirely powerless even where the interpretation of granted privileges uncovered a corporate immunity.   Certain powers of the state were held to be inalienable.   No legislative assurance that the power of eminent domain would not be exercised could prevent subsequent action taking corporate property upon the payment of just compensation.[12]   So, still more important, with at least some exercises of the police power: a Mississippi grant of a charter to operate a lottery did not bar the enforcement of a later law prohibiting lotteries.[13]   As a later Court put it broadly: "It is settled that neither the 'contract' clause nor the 'due process' clause has the effect of overriding the power of the State to establish all regulations that are reasonably necessary to secure the health, safety, good order, comfort, or general welfare of the community; that this power can neither be abdicated nor bargained away, and is inalienable even by express grant; and that all contract and property rights are held subject to its fair exercise."[14]   And so with private contracts: "[P]arties by entering into contracts may not estop the legislature from enacting laws intended for the public

---

9.   See generally Hale, "The Supreme Court and the Contract Clause," 57 Harv.L.Rev. 512, 621, 852 (1944), and Wright, The Contract Clause of the Constitution (1938).

10.   Justice Cardozo was guilty of something of an understatement when he said that the "dividing line" between remedy and obligation "is at times obscure."   Worthen Co. v. Kavanaugh, 295 U.S. 56 (1935).   Yet the permissibility of remedial changes provided some flexibility: it authorized extensions of time, for example—so long as extensions were not "so piled up as to make the remedy a shadow," as Cardozo put it.

11.   Charles River Bridge v. Warren Bridge, 11 Pet. 420 (1837).   See Kutler, Privilege and Creative Destruction: The Charles River Bridge Case (1971).

12.   See, e.g., West River Bridge Co. v. Dix, 6 How. 507 (1848).

13.   Stone v. Mississippi, 101 U.S. 814 (1880).   Chief Justice Waite stated: "All agree that the legislature cannot bargain away the police power. [No] legislature can bargain away the public health or the public morals."   But, he added, "we have held [that the contract clause] protected a corporation in its charter exemptions from taxation."   (For modern litigation on 19th century state grants of tax exemptions to railroads, see, e.g., Georgia Railroad & Banking Co. v. Redwine, 342 U.S. 299 (1952).)

14.   Atlantic Coast Line R. Co. v. Goldsboro, 232 U.S. 548 (1914).

good." [15] In the late 19th century, the Court used broad language of that sort primarily in cases involving prohibitions of matters widely regarded as "evil"— e.g., lotteries and intoxicating beverages.[16] Would the Court also sustain legislation provoked by 20th century economic crises—the modern versions of the debtor relief laws that had motivated the adoption of the contracts clause in 1787? The materials that follow focus on the interpretations of the clause in contemporary contexts.

HOME BUILDING & LOAN ASS'N v. BLAISDELL

290 U.S. 398, 54 S.Ct. 231, 78 L.Ed. 413 (1934).

[The Minnesota Mortgage Moratorium Law of 1933, enacted during the Depression, authorized relief against mortgage foreclosures and execution sales of real property. Local courts were permitted to extend the period of redemption from foreclosure sales "for such additional time as the court may deem just and equitable," but not beyond May 1, 1935. Extensions were to be conditioned upon an order requiring the mortgagor to "pay all or a reasonable part" of the fair income or rental value of the property toward the payment of taxes, insurance, interest and principal. No action for a deficiency judgment could be brought during such a court-extended period of redemption. The Blaisdells obtained a court order under the Act extending the period of redemption from a mortgage foreclosure sale, on condition that they pay the Association $40 per month. The highest state court sustained the law as an "emergency" measure.]

Mr. Chief Justice HUGHES delivered the opinion of the Court.

[In] determining whether the provision for this temporary and conditional relief exceeds the power of the State by reason of the [contract clause], we must consider the relation of emergency to constitutional power, the historical setting of the contract clause, the development of the jurisprudence of this Court in the construction of that clause, and the principles of construction which we may consider to be established. Emergency does not create power. Emergency does not increase granted power [or] diminish the restrictions imposed upon power [granted]. While emergency does not create power, emergency may furnish the occasion for the exercise of power. [The] constitutional question presented in the light of an emergency is whether the power possessed embraces the particular exercise of it in response to particular conditions. [T]he reasons which led to the adoption of [the contract clause have] frequently been described. The widespread distress following the revolutionary period, and the plight of debtors, had called forth in the States an ignoble array of legislative schemes for the defeat of creditors and the invasion of contractual obligations. Legislative interferences had been so numerous and extreme that the confidence essential to prosperous trade had been undermined and the utter destruction of credit was threatened. [It] was necessary to interpose the restraining power of a central authority in order to secure the foundations even of "private faith." But full recognition of the occasion and general purposes of the clause does not suffice to fix its precise scope. [To] ascertain the scope of the constitutional prohibition we examine the course of judicial decisions in its application. These put it beyond question that the prohibition is not an absolute one and is not to

----

15. Manigault v. Springs, 199 U.S. 473 (1905).

16. See, e.g., Stone v. Mississippi, above; Beer Co. v. Massachusetts, 97 U.S. 25 (1878). During that era, Court invalidation of state laws impairing corporate charter privileges reached its highest frequency. Between 1865 and 1888, there were 49 cases in which state laws were held invalid under the contracts clause—and 36 of these involved public grants rather than contracts between private parties. The Constitution of the United States of America (Gov't Printing Off., 1972 ed.).

be read with literal exactness like a mathematical formula. [The] inescapable problems of construction have been: What is a contract? What are the obligations of contracts? What constitutes impairment of these obligations? What residuum of power is there still in the States [to] protect the vital interests of the [community]?

Not only is the [contract clause] qualified by the measure of control which the State retains over remedial processes [see above], but the State also continues to possess authority to safeguard the vital interests of its people. [The] reservation of essential attributes of sovereign power [is] read into contracts as a postulate of the legal order. The policy of protecting contracts against impairment presupposes the maintenance of a government by virtue of which contractual relations are [worth while]. This principle of harmonizing the constitutional prohibition with the necessary residuum of state power has had progressive recognition in the decisions of this Court. [The] protective power of the State, its police power, may be exercised [in] directly preventing the immediate and literal enforcement of contractual obligations by a temporary and conditional restraint, where vital public interests would otherwise suffer. Undoubtedly, whatever is reserved of state power must be consistent with the fair intent of the constitutional limitation of that power. The reserved power cannot be construed so as to destroy the limitation, nor is the limitation to be construed to destroy the reserved power in its essential aspects. They must be construed in harmony with each other. This principle precludes a construction which would permit the State to adopt as its policy the repudiation of debts or the destruction of contracts or the denial of means to enforce them. But it does not follow that conditions may not arise in which a temporary restraint of enforcement may be consistent with the spirit and purpose of the constitutional [provision]. If state power exists to give temporary relief from the enforcement of contracts in the presence of disasters due to physical causes such as fire, flood, or earthquake, that power cannot be said to be nonexistent when the urgent public need demanding such relief is produced [by] economic causes. [It] is manifest from [our] decisions that there has been a growing appreciation of public needs and of the necessity of finding ground for a rational compromise between individual rights and public welfare. [The] question is no longer merely that of one party to a contract as against another, but of the use of reasonable means to safeguard the economic structure upon which the good of all depends.

It is no answer to say that this public need was not apprehended a century ago, or to insist that what the provision of the Constitution meant to the vision of that day it must mean to the vision of our time. If by the statement that what the Constitution meant at the time of its adoption it means today, it is intended to say that the great clauses of the Constitution must be confined to the interpretation which the framers, with the conditions and outlook of their time, would have placed upon them, the statement carries its own refutation. It was to guard against such a narrow conception that Chief Justice Marshall uttered the memorable warning—"We must never forget, that it is *a constitution* we are expounding" [McCulloch]. [When] we consider the contract clause and the decisions which have expounded it, [we] find no warrant for the conclusion that the clause has been warped by these decisions from its proper significance or that the founders of our government would have interpreted the clause differently had they had occasion to assume that responsibility in the conditions of the later day. [With] a growing recognition of public needs and the relation of individual right to public security, the Court has sought to prevent the perversion of the clause through its use as an instrument to throttle the capacity of the States to protect their fundamental [interests].

Applying the criteria established by our decisions, we conclude [inter alia]: The conditions upon which the period of redemption is extended do not appear to be unreasonable. [The] integrity of the mortgage indebtedness is not impaired; interest continues to run; the validity of the sale and the right of a mortgagee-purchaser to title or to obtain a deficiency judgment, if the mortgagor fails to redeem within the extended period, are maintained; and the conditions of redemption, if redemption there be, stand as they were under the prior law. If it be determined, as it must be, that the contract clause is not an absolute [restriction] of the State's protective power, this legislation is clearly so reasonable as to be within the legislative competency. [The] legislation is temporary in operation. It is limited to the exigency which called it forth. [T]he operation of the statute itself could not validly outlast the emergency or be so extended as virtually to destroy the contracts. We are of the opinion that the Minnesota statute as here applied does not violate the [contract clause].

Judgment affirmed.

Mr. Justice SUTHERLAND, dissenting.*

If it be possible by resort to the testimony of history to put any question of constitutional intent beyond the domain of uncertainty, the [history reviewed earlier in the dissent] leaves no reasonable ground upon which to base a denial that the [contract clause] was meant to foreclose state action impairing the obligation of contracts *primarily and especially* in respect of such action aimed at giving relief to debtors *in time of emergency.* [A] statute which materially delays enforcement of the mortgagee's contractual right of ownership and possession does not modify the remedy merely; it destroys, for the period of delay, *all* remedy so far as the enforcement of that right is concerned. The phrase "obligation of a contract" in the constitutional sense imports a legal duty to perform the specified obligation of *that* contract, not to substitute and perform, against the will of one of the parties, a different [obligation]. And a state [has] no more power to accomplish such a substitution than has one of the parties to the contract against the will of the other. [If] it could, the efficacy of the constitutional restriction would, in large measure, be made to [disappear].

CONTRACTS CLAUSE CASES BETWEEN BLAISDELL AND THE LATE 1970s

Although most cases in the four decades after Blaisdell rejected contracts clause attacks on state laws, Blaisdell did not assure the validity of all state measures. Soon after Blaisdell, for example, Worthen Co. v. Thomas, 292 U.S. 426 (1934), struck down an Arkansas law exempting most payments under life insurance policies from garnishment. Chief Justice Hughes emphasized the breadth of the exemption, noting that the relief was "neither temporary nor conditional": there was "no limitation as to time, amount, circumstances, or need."[1] Nevertheless, by the late 1960s, the restraints imposed by the contracts clause appeared minor. EL PASO v. SIMMONS, 379 U.S. 497 (1965), symbolized the Warren Court's reluctance to invalidate. The 8 to 1 decision upheld a Texas effort to wipe out the rights of purchasers of certain public lands to reinstate their interests in the lands by payment of delinquent interest.[2] Although Justice WHITE's majority opinion conceded that the Texas curtailment of reinstatement rights modified the State's contractual obligation,

---

* Justices Van Devanter, McReynolds and Butler joined the dissent.

1. See also Worthen Co. v. Kavanaugh, 295 U.S. 56 (1935), and Wood v. Lovett, 313 U.S. 362 (1941).

2. The public lands involved had been sold under a 1910 law designed to encourage settlement of the public domain—a law which, while providing for the forfeiture of the lands for non-payment of interest, also permitted the purchaser or his assigns to reinstate title indefinitely on

not merely the remedy, he found it justified because of the public interest. He insisted that "not every modification of a contractual promise" violates the contracts clause. He emphasized the importance of the State's purposes: "to restore confidence in the stability and integrity of land titles"; "to enable the State to protect and administer its property in a businesslike manner"; to respond to "the imbroglio over land titles in Texas." The unlimited reinstatement rights had spawned "opportunity for speculation." Moreover, the right to reinstate "was not the central undertaking of the seller nor the primary consideration for the buyer's undertaking," since after initial forfeiture, the buyer had only a "defeasible right to reinstatement" that could be cut off by the State by transferring the forfeited lands to third parties. Texas had acted in the face of "developments, hardly to be expected or foreseen, [that] operated to confer considerable advantages on the purchaser and his successors and a costly and difficult burden on the State. [Laws] which restrict a party to those gains reasonably to be expected from the contract are not subject to attack under the Contract Clause, notwithstanding that they technically alter an obligation of a contract." [3]

HOW FAR HAS THE MODERN COURT REVITALIZED THE CONTRACTS CLAUSE?

1. *State obligations.* In 1977, for the first time in nearly 40 years, the Court invalidated a state law as violating the contracts clause, in UNITED STATES TRUST CO. v. NEW JERSEY, 431 U.S. 1. The prevailing opinion in the 4 to 3 decision was by Justice Blackmun.[1] He suggested that a law impairing a state's *own* obligations was entitled to less deference than legislation interfering with *private* contracts. Implementing that approach, he formulated a standard of review approaching "strict scrutiny": he insisted that a law impairing a *state* obligation must be "reasonable and necessary to serve an important public purpose" in order to pass muster under the contracts clause.[2] The dissenters sharply attacked that departure from the deferential stance typical of modern contracts clause decisions and protested against the Court's revived intrusion into "economic and policy matters."

The suit was directed against the 1974 repeal of a statutory covenant made by New Jersey and New York in 1962—a covenant that had limited the ability of The Port Authority of New York and New Jersey to subsidize rail passenger

payment of delinquent interest, so long as no rights of third parties had intervened. In the ensuing decades, oil and gas discoveries made the lands far more valuable. In 1941, Texas amended the 1910 law to limit the reinstatement rights to five years. In 1947, some lands originally sold in 1910 were forfeited to Texas; in 1952, Simmons purchased the buyers' rights and tendered the delinquent interest in order to reinstate title. Simmons' reinstatement application was denied because the five-year period had expired.

3. Justice BLACK's dissent insisted that Blaisdell was clearly distinguishable because it had emphasized changes in remedies, not obligations. The unlimited reinstatement right, he insisted, was "one of the greatest [selling arguments] Texas had to promote purchase of its great surfeit of lands." Accusing the majority of using a "due process 'reasonableness' formula," he added: "With its deprecatory view of the

equities on the side of [the] claimants and its remarkable sympathy for the State, the Court through its balancing process states the case in a way inevitably destined to bypass the Contract Clause and let Texas break its solemn obligation. [I think there is] a constitutional way for Texas to do this": "compensating the holders of contractual rights for the interests it wants to destroy." [In Justice Black's view, the state interest as delineated by the majority "boiled down to the fact that Texas' contracts, perhaps very wisely made a long time ago, turned out when land soared in value, and particularly after oil was discovered, to be costly to the State."]

1. Justices Stewart and Powell did not participate. (They were both in the majority a year later in Allied Structural Steel, note 2 below.)

2. Cf. the formulation of the "intermediate" level of scrutiny in modern sex discrimination cases, as in Craig v. Boren (1976; p. 647 below).

transportation from revenues and reserves.[3] The covenant was designed in part to assure bondholders that bond revenues would not be used to any great extent to finance the predictably unprofitable rail operations. The New Jersey courts rejected the contracts clause challenge,[4] finding the 1974 repeal justified as "a reasonable exercise [of] police power." The Court reversed. Justice BLACK-MUN insisted that modern interpretations of the contracts clause had not drained that provision of all force. He claimed that neither Blaisdell nor El Paso "indicated that the Contract Clause was without meaning in modern constitutional jurisprudence, or that its limitation on state power was illusory. Whether or not the protection of contract rights comports with current views of wise public policy, the Contract Clause remains a part of our written Constitution."

Justice Blackmun had little difficulty finding that the 1974 repeal had "the effect of impairing a contractual obligation." But "a finding that there has been a technical impairment is merely a preliminary step in resolving the more difficult question whether that impairment is [unconstitutional]." And that problem required reconciliation of "the strictures of the Contract Clause with the 'essential attributes of sovereign power' necessarily reserved by the States." Yet that police power is not unlimited, he made clear. And in assessing the scope of state power, he repeatedly emphasized, a state was entitled to more deference when it interfered with private contractual obligations, as in Blaisdell, than when it sought to modify its own covenants, as here. In assessing a claim that a state had impaired its own contractual obligations, the initial question is whether the allegedly impaired contract was a valid one, for a state may not surrender "an essential attribute of its sovereignty." But the 1962 covenant could not be viewed as void ab initio: the States had "promised that revenues and reserves securing the bonds would not be depleted by the Port Authority's operation of deficit-producing passenger railroads beyond the level of 'permitted deficits.' Such a promise is purely financial and thus not necessarily a compromise of the States' reserved powers." Hence, the ultimate question was whether the States' 1974 repeal could stand.

It was in pursuing that question that Justice Blackmun set forth a standard of review more intensive than that customary in prior contracts clause cases. Where a state interference with *private* contracts is challenged, "courts properly defer to legislative judgment as to the necessity and reasonableness of a particular measure," as is "customary in reviewing economic and social regulation." (Cf. note 2 below.) But greater judicial scrutiny was warranted when a state was charged with impairing its *own* obligations: "As with laws impairing the obligations of private contracts, an impairment [of state obligations] may be constitutional if it is reasonable and necessary to serve an important public purpose. In applying this standard, however, complete deference to a legislative assessment of reasonableness and necessity is not appropriate because the State's self-interest is at stake. [If] a State could reduce its financial obligations whenever it wanted to spend the money for what it regarded as an important public purpose, the Contract Clause would provide no protection at all." Applying that "dual standard"—with heightened scrutiny for a state's impairment of its own obligations—Justice Blackmun rejected the state courts' view that the police power justified state repudiations so long as they fell short of "total destruction of the prior obligation." He accordingly proceeded to

3. The Port Authority was established by a bistate compact between New York and New Jersey; its activities (including the provision of transportation facilities) were largely financed by bonds sold to the public.

4. This suit was brought to challenge New Jersey's repeal of the 1962 covenant. (The Com-pany sued as both a trustee for and a holder of Port Authority bonds.) The New York legislature enacted a concurrent repeal of the covenant, and a separate suit was brought to challenge New York's action.

engage in an independent analysis of the "reasonableness" and "necessity" of the repeal in this case.

Justice Blackmun conceded the importance of "mass transportation, energy conservation, and environmental protection" as legislative goals. But he rejected New Jersey's contention that "these goals are so important that any harm to bondholders from repeal of the 1962 covenant is greatly outweighed by the public benefit": "We do not accept this invitation to engage in a utilitarian comparison of public benefit and private loss. Contrary to Mr. Justice Black's fear expressed in sole dissent in [El Paso], the Court has not 'balanced away' the limitation on state action imposed by the Contract Clause. Thus a State cannot refuse to meet its legitimate financial obligations simply because it would prefer to spend the money to promote the [public good]." And here, the repeal was neither "reasonable" nor "necessary." The States argued that the 1974 repeal was justified by "the States' plan for encouraging users of private automobiles to shift to public transportation" by raising bridge and tunnel tolls and using the extra revenue from those tolls to subsidize improved commuter rail service. Repeal of the 1962 covenant was supposedly necessary to implement that plan "because the new mass transit facilities could not possibly be self-supporting and the covenant's 'permitted deficits' level had already been exceeded." But that argument proved unpersuasive: "We reject this justification because the repeal was neither necessary to achievement of the plan nor reasonable in light of the circumstances."[5] Justice Blackmun rejected the claim that "choosing among these alternatives is a matter for legislative discretion," replying that "a State is not completely free to consider impairing the obligations of its own contracts on a par with other policy alternatives. Similarly, a State is not free to impose a drastic impairment when an evident and more moderate course would serve its purpose equally well." Nor was he satisfied that repeal of the covenant "was reasonable in light of the surrounding circumstances." He insisted that the situation in El Paso was quite different, with regard to "reasonableness" as well as "necessity." El Paso involved an old statute with "effects that were unforeseen and unintended by the legislature when originally adopted." Here, by contrast, the prime motivation for the repeal, "the need for mass transportation in the New York metropolitan area," was not founded on any "new development": the concerns about environmental protection and energy conservation "were not unknown in 1962, and the subsequent changes were of degree and not of kind." Accordingly, "we cannot conclude that the repeal was reasonable in the light of changed circumstances."[6]

Justice BRENNAN's strongly worded dissent, joined by Justices White and Marshall, insisted that the decision rejected the "previous understanding" "that lawful exercises of a State's police power stand paramount to private rights held under contract" and "remolds the Contract Clause into a potent instrument for overseeing important policy determinations of the state legislature. At the same time, by creating a constitutional safe haven for property rights embodied in a contract, the decision substantially distorts modern constitutional jurisprudence governing regulation of private economic interests. I might understand, though I could not accept, this revival of the [Clause] were it in accordance with some

5. Justice Blackmun questioned the "necessity" on two levels. First, he suggested that "a less drastic modification" of the covenant, rather than outright repeal, might have permitted much of the contemplated plan. Second, "without modifying the covenant at all," "the States could have adopted alternative means of achieving their twin goals of discouraging automobile use and improving mass transit." (In a footnote, he suggested the possibility of discouraging automobile use through taxes on gasoline and parking, and using those tax revenues to subsidize mass transit.)

6. In a brief concurring notation, Chief Justice BURGER stated that, to avoid contracts clause invalidation, a state must demonstrate "that the impairment was essential to the achievement of an important state purpose" and must also show "that it did not know and could not have known the impact of the contract on that state interest at the time that the contract was made."

coherent and constructive view of public policy. But elevation of the Clause to the status of regulator of the municipal bond market at the heavy price of frustration of sound legislative policymaking is as demonstrably unwise as it is unnecessary." He accused the Court of "dust[ing] off" the clause and "fundamentally misconceiv[ing]" its nature. Extending the clause to cover governmental as well as private contracts was itself an extension of the Framers' purpose, he recalled. Later decisions had sought to interpret the clause in situations such as this "consistently with the demands of our governing processes." For a century, he insisted, the "central principle" had been to accord "unusual deference to the lawmaking authority of state and local governments." But this decision "regrettably departs from the virtually unbroken line of our cases that remained true to the principle that all private rights of property, even if acquired through contract with the State, are subordinated to reasonable exercises of the States' lawmaking powers in the areas of health, environmental protection, and transportation."

The Court's approach, Justice Brennan claimed, imposed "severe substantive restraints on New Jersey's attempt to free itself from a contractual provision that it deems inconsistent with the broader interests of its citizens." He agreed that the contracts clause barred states "from disadvantaging their creditors without reasonable justification or in a spirit of oppression," but New Jersey had claimed "no such prerogatives" here. The Court's "reasonable and necessary" standard of review, he objected, "stands the Contract Clause completely on its head and both formulates and strictly applies a novel standard for reviewing a State's attempt to relieve its citizens from unduly harsh contracts entered into by earlier legislators." He added: "Not only is this apparently spontaneous formulation virtually assured of frustrating the understanding of court and litigant alike,[7] but it is wholly out of step with the modern attempts of this Court to define the reach of the [Clause] when a State's own contractual obligations are placed in issue." Moreover, there was no justification for the Court's "multi-headed view of the scope of the Clause," applying "different standards for reviewing governmental interference with public and private contractual obligations."[8]

In his closing passages, Justice Brennan expressed the hope that this invalidation would "prove a rare phenomenon, turning on the Court's particularized appraisal of the facts before it." Yet he found "reason for broader concern." He noted that "other constitutional doctrines are akin to the Contract Clause in directing their protections to the property interests of private parties"—e.g., the Fifth Amendment. In economic due process adjudication, the Court had abandoned the Lochner view of "liberty of contract." But, he added: "If today's case signals return to substantive constitutional review of States' policies, and a new resolve to protect property owners whose interest or circumstances may happen to appeal to Members of this Court, then more than the citizens of New Jersey and New York will be the losers." He added that he was not suggesting that states "should blithely proceed down the path of repudiating their obligations, financial or otherwise." But their need for "credibility in the credit market" was likely to be a substantial safeguard against that. And "in the final analysis, there is no reason to doubt that appellant's financial welfare is

---

7. In criticizing the allegedly confusing "reasonable and necessary" standard, he noted that it "represents a most unusual hybrid which manages to merge the two polar extremes of judicial intervention into one synthesis. Plainly, courts are apt to face considerable confusion in wielding such a schizophrenic new instrument."

8. On the facts, Justice Brennan argued that the 1974 repeal of the 1962 covenant was justified in part because the passage of the years had "conclusively demonstrated" that the covenant

barrier to the development of rapid transit "squarely conflicts with the legitimate needs of the New York metropolitan community." To speak of alternative measures, he claimed, was to focus on "peripheral matters"; and in any event, none of the majority's suggested alternatives met the states' needs. Moreover, the suggested alternatives intruded "deeply into complex and localized policy matters that are for the States' legislatures and not the judiciary to resolve."

being adequately policed by the political processes and the bond marketplace itself." He concluded: "[T]his Court should have learned long ago that the Constitution—be it through the Contract or Due Process Clause—can actively intrude into such economic and policy matters only if my Brethren are prepared to bear enormous institutional and social costs. [I] consider the potential dangers of such judicial interference to be intolerable."

2. *Private obligations.* The Court continued the process of reinvigorating the contract clause in ALLIED STRUCTURAL STEEL CO. v. SPANNAUS, 438 U.S. 234 (1978), a decision criticized by the dissent as "greatly expand[ing] the reach of the Clause." Unlike United States Trust a year earlier, the 1978 case involved the application of the clause to private rather than state obligations. The 5 to 3 decision [9] invalidated the application of Minnesota's Private Pension Benefits Protection Act.[10] Justice STEWART's majority opinion held that the Act's imposition of a new obligation on the employer violated the clause. He found the impact of the law both "substantial" and "severe," emphasizing that the law retroactively modified the payment obligations assumed by the Company under its voluntarily established pension plan, and that the element of reliance was vital, since the state had intervened in a previously unregulated area. Moreover, the law had an extremely narrow focus.

Justice Stewart conceded that the contracts clause had "receded into comparative desuetude" with the rise of due process jurisprudence. But, he insisted, "the Contract Clause [is] not a dead letter." And he added: "If the [Clause] is to retain any meaning at all, [it] must be understood to impose *some* limits upon the power of a State to abridge existing contractual relationships, even in the exercise of its otherwise legitimate police power." He commented that "the severity of the impairment measures the height of the hurdle the state legislation must clear. Minimal alteration of contractual obligations may end the inquiry at its first stage. Severe impairment, on the other hand, will push the inquiry to a careful examination of the nature and purpose of the state legislation. [Here, the Company] had no reason to anticipate that its employees' pension rights could become vested except in accordance with the terms of the plan. It relied heavily, and reasonably, on this legitimate contractual expectation in calculating its annual contributions to the pension fund." The law nullified "express terms of the company's contractual obligations and impose[d] a completely unexpected liability in potentially disabling amounts." He added: "[This] law simply does not possess the attributes of those state laws that in the past have survived [challenge]. The law was not even purportedly enacted to deal with a broad, generalized economic or social problem. Cf. [Blaisdell]." Moreover, the law was not "enacted to protect a broad societal interest rather than a narrow class," nor "to deal with a situation remotely approaching the broad and desperate emergency economic conditions of the early 1930's." In addition, it did not "operate in an area already subject to state regulation. [It] did not effect simply a temporary alteration of the contractual relationships of those within its coverage, but worked a severe, permanent, and immediate change in those relationships—irrevocably and retroactively. Cf. [United States Trust]. And its narrow aim was levelled not at every Minnesota employer, not even at every Minnesota employer who left the State, but only at those who had in the past been sufficiently enlightened as voluntarily to agree to establish pension plans for their employees."

---

9. Justice Blackmun did not participate.

10. Under the Act, employers who had established an employee pension plan and who terminated the plan or closed a Minnesota office were required to pay a "pension funding charge" if their pension funds were insufficient to finance full pensions for all employees who had worked at least 10 years. When the Company closed its Minnesota office in 1975, it was subjected to a charge of about $185,000 because some discharged workers, who had no vested rights under the pension plan, had been employed for more than 10 years.

Justice BRENNAN's dissent, joined by Justices White and Marshall, insisted that the clause was applicable only to laws which "diminished or nullified" private contractual obligations. Here, the law, "like all positive social legislation," simply imposed "new, additional obligations on a particular class of persons." [11] The only relevant constitutional limitation in the case was due process, and that guarantee had not been violated. The dissent argued that the state law served the important purpose of remedying "a serious problem arising from the operation of private pension plans" by providing "terminated employees with the equivalent of benefits reasonably to be expected under the plan." For Justice Brennan, enlarging the employer's obligations raised no contracts clause issue: the majority, he insisted, had acted on the "mistaken" premise that the clause protects "all contract based expectations from unjustifiable interference" and had "distort[ed]" the meaning of the clause by interpreting the ban against "impairing" obligations as "including laws which create new duties."

The Court's broad reading of the clause, Justice Brennan argued, created "anomalies" and threatened "to undermine the jurisprudence of property rights developed over the last 40 years." After noting the due process and "taking" provisions, he stated: "Decisions over the past 50 years have developed a coherent, unified interpretation of all the constitutional provisions that may protect economic expectations and these decisions have recognized a broad latitude in States to effect even severe interference with existing economic values when reasonably necessary to promote the general welfare. At the same time the prohibition of the Contract Clause [has] been limited in application to state laws that [dilute], with utter indifference to the legitimate interests of the beneficiary of a contract duty, the existing contract obligation." He added: "Today's conversion of the [Clause] into a limitation on the power of States to enact laws that impose duties additional to obligations assumed under private contracts must inevitably produce results difficult to square with any rational conception of a constitutional order. Under the Court's opinion, any law that may be characterized as 'superimposing' new obligations on those provided for by contract is to be regarded as creating 'sudden, substantial, and unanticipated burdens' and then to be subjected to the most exacting scrutiny. The validity of such a law will turn upon whether judges see it as a law that deals with a generalized social problem, whether it is temporary (as few will be) or permanent, whether it operates in an area previously subject to regulation, and, finally, whether its duties apply to a broad class of persons. The necessary consequence of the extreme malleability of these rather vague criteria is to vest judges with broad subjective discretion to protect property interests that happen to appeal to them. [There] is nothing sacrosanct about expectations rooted in contract that justify according them a constitutional immunity denied other property rights." In his view, the "only explanation for the Court's decision is that it subjectively values the interests of employers to pension plan more highly than it does the legitimate expectation interests of employees." [12]

3. *The 1983 decisions: A partial return to greater deference?* Although both of the 1978 decisions noted above had suggested stricter scrutiny, two 1983 decisions unanimously rejected contracts clause attacks on alleged state impairments of private contracts. In both cases, the Court's tone was a good deal more deferential than it had been in 1978. The first decision was ENERGY RESERVES GROUP v. KANSAS POWER & LIGHT CO., 459 U.S. 400

---

11. The majority opinion branded that a "novel construction" of the clause, "wholly contrary" to the precedents: "The narrow view that the Clause forbids only state laws that diminish the duties of a contractual obligor and not laws that increase them [has been] expressly repudiated. Moreover, in any bilateral contract the dimi-

nution of duties on one side effectively increases the duties on the other."

12. On United States Trust and Allied Steel, see generally Note, "A Process-Oriented Approach to the Contract Clause," 89 Yale L.J. 1623 (1980), and Note, "Rediscovering the Contract Clause," 97 Harv.L.Rev. 1414 (1984).

(1983). Kansas Power & Light (KPL) was a party to a 1975 contract with Energy Reserves Group (ERG), pursuant to which ERG supplied natural gas to KPL at a price that was set in the contract, but which, according to the contract, could be raised to match any governmentally fixed price that exceeded the contract price. When Congress passed the Natural Gas Policy Act of 1978, Kansas responded by enacting the Kansas Natural Gas Price Protection Act, which in effect precluded ERG from using the price escalator clause in the contract to the full extent of the 1978 federal increase. ERG claimed that the 1975 contract allowed it to take advantage of subsequent changes in governmental price ceilings and that the Kansas limitation therefore violated the contracts clause by limiting a price increase that otherwise would have been permissible under the contract.

In rejecting that challenge for a unanimous Court, Justice BLACKMUN announced a three-step inquiry derived from the Court's recent decisions. The first step was " 'whether the state law has, in fact, operated as a substantial impairment of a contractual relationship.' " [13] If there was such a "substantial impairment," then, as a second step, "the State, in justification, must have a significant and legitimate public purpose behind the regulation [United States Trust], such as the remedying of a broad and general social or economic problem. [Allied Steel.]" [14] The final step, "[o]nce a legitimate public purpose has been identified," is to determine "whether the adjustment of 'the rights and responsibilities of contracting parties [is based] upon reasonable conditions and [is] of a character appropriate to the public purpose justifying [the legislation's] adoption.' [United States Trust.] Unless the State itself is a contracting party,[15] '[a]s is customary in reviewing economic and social regulation, [courts] properly defer to a legislative judgment as to the necessity and reasonableness of a particular measure.' [Id.]"

On the first step of the inquiry, Justice Blackmun focused on the extent of state and federal regulation of the national gas industry and noted that both ERG and the contract itself acknowledged the regulated industry context. Because ERG knew at the time of the contracting that it was subject to both state and federal regulation of prices, a change in those very regulations would not constitute the "substantial impairment" required to trigger the contracts clause. "In short, ERG's reasonable expectations have not been impaired by the Kansas Act. See [El Paso]." Despite that conclusion, Justice Blackmun undertook the final two steps of the inquiry as well. He concluded that, even if there was an impairment, it was justified by Kansas' "significant and legitimate" interest in protecting consumers from the escalation of natural gas prices. On this step, he concluded that there "can be little doubt about the legitimate public purpose behind the Act." On the third step, he concluded that Kansas had chosen appropriate, reasonable means to achieve its purpose, "particularly

---

13. Justice Blackmun's phrase was from Allied Steel. He also cited United States Trust and added: "The severity of the impairment is said to increase the level of [scrutiny]. [Allied Steel.] Total destruction of contractual expectations is not necessary for a finding of substantial impairment. [United States Trust.] On the other hand, state regulation that restricts a party to gains it reasonably expected from the contract does not necessarily constitute a substantial impairment. [Id., citing El Paso.] In determining the extent of the impairment, we are to consider whether the industry the complaining party has entered has been regulated in the past. [Allied Steel.]"

14. Justice Blackmun added: "Furthermore, since Blaisdell, the Court has indicated that the

public purpose need not be addressed to an emergency or temporary situation. [United States Trust.] One legitimate state interest is the elimination of unforeseen windfall profits. [Id.] The requirement of a legitimate public purpose guarantees that the State is exercising its police power, rather than providing a benefit to special interests."

15. Justice Blackmun noted: "In almost every case, the Court has held a governmental unit to its contractual obligations when it enters financial or other markets. [In] the present case, of course, the stricter standard of [United States Trust] does not apply because Kansas has not altered its own contractual obligations."

in light of the deference to which the Kansas Legislature's judgment is entitled." [16]

A few months later, in EXXON CORP. v. EAGERTON, 462 U.S. 176 (1983), the Court was once again quite deferential in rejecting a contracts clause challenge. Moreover, Justice MARSHALL, for the unanimous Court, found it unnecessary to engage in any part of the three-step inquiry of the Energy Reserves Case. He emphasized that the alleged impairment of contractual obligations was merely the incidental by-product of "a generally applicable rule of conduct." At issue was an increase in the Alabama severance tax for oil and gas extracted from Alabama wells, coupled with a prohibition on passing through the increase from producers to purchasers. The producers challenged a ban on the pass-through under the contracts clause, on the ground that the prohibition would prevent the producers from taking advantage of provisions in existing contracts specifically allowing them to pass severance tax increases through to the purchasers. Rejecting that attack, Justice Marshall drew a sharp distinction between laws specifically directed at contractual obligations and those, like the one here, that merely had the underlying *effect* of impairing contractual rights: "This Court has long recognized that a statute does not violate the [Clause] simply because it has the effect of restricting, or even barring altogether, the performance of duties created by contracts entered into prior to its enactment. See [Allied Steel]. [Like] the laws upheld in [prior] cases [such as those barring the sale of beer and prohibiting lotteries], the pass-through prohibition did not prescribe a rule limited in effect to contractual obligations or remedies, but instead imposed a generally applicable rule of conduct designed to advance 'a broad societal interest.' [Allied Steel.] The prohibition applied to all oil and gas producers, regardless of whether they happened to be parties to sale contracts that contained [a pass-through provision]. The effect of the pass-through prohibition on existing contracts that did contain such a provision was incidental to its main effect of shielding consumers from the burden of the tax increase." Because the pass-through prohibition imposed a generally applicable rule of conduct, "it is sharply distinguishable from the measures struck down in [United States Trust and Allied Steel]," both of which involved laws whose "sole effect" was to alter contractual duties.

RETROACTIVITY AND REGULATORY LAWS

Retroactivity is a pervasive concern in the preceding cases: the extent to which reasonable private expectations are defeated by governmental action is the focus of many of the opinions. That is so not only with respect to the contracts clause, which on its face purports to safeguard prior contractual arrangements, but also in such "taking" opinions as Pennsylvania Coal. But the contracts clause applies only to state, not federal, action; and retroactive legislation may affect private rights other than those based on a "contract." Moreover, despite occasional arguments to the contrary, the ex post facto clauses have long been held to apply only to criminal, not civil, legislation. Is there any other, more general, constitutional safeguard against retroactive legislation? Some additional restraint on retroactivity has been found in due process, particularly in challenges to federal legislation. But, like the contracts clause and "taking" barriers, the due process limit may not help if there is a sufficiently overriding public interest.[1]

---

16. Justice POWELL's concurrence, joined by Chief Justice Burger and Justice Rehnquist, agreed that the threshold requirement of substantial impairment had not been satisfied, thought this conclusion "dispositive," and stated that "it is unnecessary for the Court" to address the other issues in the three-step analysis.

1. See generally Hochman, "The Supreme Court and the Constitutionality of Retroactive Legislation," 73 Harv.L.Rev. 692 (1960); Slaw-

With respect to federal legislation, the due process retroactivity barrier (like the contracts clause restraint on states) has been found greater when the government seeks to modify its own contractual obligations than when it regulates private contracts. For an example of the first situation, see Lynch v. United States, 292 U.S. 571 (1934), where the Court held that Congress could not cancel government war risk life insurance policies, as it had attempted to do in 1933 because of the economic crisis of the Depression. Justice Brandeis stated that rights against the federal government "arising out of contract with it are protected by the Fifth Amendment" and that the government could not annul them unless "the action taken falls within the federal police power or some other paramount power."[2] For an example of a retroactive change in United States obligations within "paramount" national powers, see Lichter v. United States, 334 U.S. 742 (1948) (renegotiation and recapture of excess profits on government contracts).[3]

SECTION 3. THE REVIVAL OF SUBSTANTIVE DUE PROCESS, FOR NONECONOMIC RIGHTS: PRIVACY; AUTONOMY; FAMILY RELATIONS

Introduction. We now return to the theme of sec. 1, substantive due process. The question here, as there, is whether due process authorizes the Court to resort to noninterpretive modes of constitutional adjudication: to pour into the due process clause fundamental values not traceable to constitutional text or history or structure. The modern cases below contain frequent assertions that the approach symbolized by Lochner is discredited. But is it? This section focuses on modern decisions that critics have characterized as indistinguishable from the Lochner philosophy. The modern trend began with Griswold in 1965, striking down ban on the use of contraceptives, and Roe v. Wade in 1973, invalidating most abortion laws. Do Griswold, Roe, and their progeny constitute "Lochnerizing," or are they distinguishable? Do they suggest that "Lochnerizing" is justifiable after all? Before turning to the decisions, a brief historical reminder is appropriate. Griswold and Roe were not sudden revivals of substantive due process: in one sense, they built on an aspect of the Lochner tradition that never wholly died. True, the aspect of Lochner that curtailed

son, "Constitutional and Legislative Considerations in Retroactive Lawmaking," 48 Calif.L. Rev. 216 (1960); Munzer, "A Theory of Retroactive Legislation," 61 Tex.L.Rev. 425 (1982). Hochman identifies three major factors in retroactivity cases: "the nature and strength of the public interest served"; "the extent to which the statute modifies or abrogates the asserted pre-enactment right"; and "the nature of the right which the statute alters."

2. See also Perry v. United States, 294 U.S. 330 (1935), the "gold clause" case dealing with the government's *own* obligations on its bonds; contrast, Norman v. Baltimore & Ohio Railroad Co., 294 U.S. 240 (1935), another "gold clause" case, recognizing a wider power to affect *private* obligations.

3. Cf. FHA v. Darlington, 358 U.S. 84 (1958) (a 5 to 4 decision sustaining a 1954 "clarifying" amendment restricting use of housing constructed under FHA-insured mortgage issued in 1949); and note Flemming v. Nestor, on termination of social security benefits, p. 215 above. See also Battaglia v. General Motors, 169 F.2d 254 (2d Cir.), cert. denied 335 U.S. 887 (1948), sustaining the Portal-to-Portal Pay Act of 1947, which had relieved employers of overtime pay liability created by an unanticipated Court interpretation. On the very limited bases for challenging retroactive federal tax legislation on due process grounds, see United States v. Darusmont, 449 U.S. 292 (1981). Note also the Court's deferential approach in Pension Benefit Guaranty Corp. v. R.A. Gray & Co., 468 U.S. __ (1984), commenting that "retroactive legislation does have to meet a burden not faced by legislation that has only future effects" but noting also that "the strong deference accorded legislation in the field of national economic policy is no less applicable when that legislation is applied retroactively." (On due process challenges to retroactive *state* legislation, see, e.g., Chase Securities Corp. v. Donaldson, 325 U.S. 304 (1945).)

economic regulation has clearly waned since the 1930s. But the Lochner era's protection of "fundamental values" was not wholly limited to economic rights: to the Court of that era, there was no sharp distinction between economic and noneconomic, "personal" liberties; some of the Lochner era decisions did protect personal rights; and the modern Court has no qualms about citing those decisions.

MEYER v. NEBRASKA, 262 U.S. 390 (1923), is the outstanding example. Its broad reading of "liberty" came from the pen of Justice McREYNOLDS, supposedly one of the most opinionated and reactionary of the "Old Men" of the majority that provoked the Court-packing crisis of the 1930s; and that "libertarian" Meyer decision came over the dissent of Justice Holmes. In Meyer, the Court reversed the conviction of a teacher for teaching German and thus violating a state law prohibiting the teaching of foreign languages to young children. Recall Justice McReynolds' broad view of "liberty" (noted at p. 455 above), a view encompassing the personal as well as the economic: "Without doubt, it denotes not merely freedom from bodily restraint but also the right of the individual to contract, to engage in any of the common occupations of life, to acquire useful knowledge, to marry, establish a home and bring up children, to worship God according to the dictates of his own conscience, and generally to enjoy those privileges long recognized at common law as essential to the orderly pursuit of happiness by free men." Justice McReynolds found that the Nebraska law "materially" interfered "with the calling of modern language teachers, with the opportunities of pupils to acquire knowledge, and with the power of parents to control the education of their own." A legislative interest "to foster a homogeneous people with American ideals" was understandable, particularly in view of the "[u]nfortunate experiences during the late war." But now it was a "time of peace and domestic tranquility," and there was accordingly "no adequate justification" for the restraints on liberty. He concluded: "No emergency has arisen which renders knowledge by a child of some language other than English so clearly harmful as to justify its inhibition with a consequent infringement of rights long freely enjoyed. [T]he statute as applied [is] without reasonable relation to any end within the competency of the State."

Justice McREYNOLDS wrote in a similar vein for a unanimous Court two years later, in PIERCE v. SOCIETY OF SISTERS, 268 U.S. 510 (1925), sustaining a challenge by parochial and private schools to an Oregon law requiring children to attend public schools. Again, he found "no peculiar circumstances or present emergencies which demand extraordinary measures relative to primary education." Under the Meyer view of fundamental rights, the law interfered "with the liberty of parents and guardians to direct the upbringing and education of children under their control." There was no "general power of the State to standardize its children by forcing them to accept instruction from public teachers only. The child is not the mere creature of the State; those who nurture him and direct his destiny have the right, coupled with the high duty, to recognize and prepare him for additional obligations." In the years before Griswold, the Warren Court, too, occasionally protected aspects of liberty even though they were not explicitly designated in the Constitution. For example, Aptheker v. Secretary of State (1964; p. 1034 below) invalidated a provision denying passports to Communist Party members because it "too broadly and indiscriminately restricts the right to travel and thereby abridges the liberty guaranteed by the Fifth Amendment." [1]

1. The Aptheker Court relied on a dictum six years earlier, in Kent v. Dulles, 357 U.S. 116 (1958): "The right is a part of the 'liberty' of which the citizen cannot be deprived without due process of law under the Fifth Amendment."

Compare the later reference to the Fifth Amendment right to travel in Regan v. Wald, 467 U.S. ___ (1984), upholding restrictions on travel to Cuba.

In light of modern First Amendment doctrine, those cases may be explainable on the bases of freedom of speech, association, and religion, though they did not rest on them explicitly.[2] But another decision only a few years after the supposed withdrawal from the Lochner philosophy is not readily explainable by reference to specific constitutional guarantees. SKINNER v. OKLAHOMA, 316 U.S. 535 (1942), was a forerunner of the special protection of some "fundamental interests" under the "new" equal protection, traced in the next chapter. It was an equal protection case in form, but it rested on a view akin to substantive due process. Justice DOUGLAS' opinion invalidated Oklahoma's Habitual Criminal Sterilization Act, providing for compulsory sterilization after a third conviction for a felony involving "moral turpitude," but excluding such felonies as embezzlement. Although state classifications of crimes would not ordinarily be overturned, Justice Douglas explained, that usual deference to state police power legislation was not warranted here: "We are dealing here with legislation which involves one of the basic civil rights of man. Marriage and procreation are fundamental to the very existence and survival of the race. [There] is no redemption for the individual whom the law touches. Any experiment which the State conducts is to his irreparable injury. He is forever deprived of a basic liberty. We mention these matters not to reexamine the scope of the police power of the States. We advert to them merely in emphasis of our view that *strict scrutiny* of the classification which a State makes in a sterilization law is essential, lest unwittingly, or otherwise, invidious discriminations are made against groups or types of individuals in violation of the constitutional guaranty of just and equal laws. [Sterilization] of those who have thrice committed grand larceny, with immunity for those who are embezzlers, is a clear, pointed, unmistakable discrimination."[3]

But the 1942 reference in Skinner to "fundamental," "basic" liberties was extraordinary: that decision, mixing due process and equal protection considerations, was virtually the only one in that period between the demise of Lochner and Griswold to exercise special scrutiny in favor of a "fundamental liberty" not tied to a specific constitutional guarantee. In short, between the Lochner era and Griswold, the methodology of substantive due process review on behalf of judicially defined, extraconstitutional, noninterpretive "fundamental values" was, if not wholly discarded, largely dormant. With Griswold and Roe, below, it regained greater vitality than it had had in more than a generation.

GRISWOLD v. CONNECTICUT

381 U.S. 479, 85 S.Ct. 1678, 14 L.Ed.2d 510 (1965).

Mr. Justice DOUGLAS delivered the opinion of the Court.

Appellant Griswold is Executive Director of the Planned Parenthood League of Connecticut. Appellant Buxton is a licensed physician and a professor at the

---

2. Justice Douglas so explained some of them in Griswold, below: he viewed Meyer and Pierce as enforcing "peripheral rights" stemming from the First Amendment.

3. [Emphasis added.] Compare Buck v. Bell, 274 U.S. 200 (1927), sustaining a state law for the sterilization of institutionalized mental defectives. Justice Holmes—in a much criticized opinion, though characteristic of his stance on substantive due process—rejected the due process claims summarily, saying that "three generations of imbeciles are enough." For a powerful criticism of the Holmes stance in this case (and in others), see Rogat, "The Judge as Spectator," 31 U.Chi.L.Rev. 213 (1964). For a criticism of the Skinner Court for relying on a narrow equal protection rather than a broad due process ground and thus failing to help "the thousands of institutional inmates [subject] to sterilization" at the time, see Foote, "The Proper Role of the [Supreme Court] in Civil Liberties Cases," 10 Wayne L.Rev. 457 (1964). For a recent description of the background of the eugenics movement (and of Buck v. Bell), see Kevles, "Annals of Eugenics: A Secular Faith (Parts I–IV)," The New Yorker (Oct. 8, 15, 22, and 29, 1984).

Yale Medical School who served as Medical Director for the League at its Center in New Haven—a center open and operating [in November, 1961], when appellants were arrested. They gave information, instruction, and medical advice to *married persons* as to the means of preventing conception. [Fees] were usually charged, although some couples were serviced free. [The] constitutionality [of two Connecticut provisions] is involved. [One] provides: "Any person who uses any drug, medicinal article or instrument for the purpose of preventing conception shall be fined not less than fifty dollars or imprisoned not less than sixty days nor more than one year or [both]." [The other] provides: "Any person who assists, abets, counsels, causes, hires or commands another to commit any offense may be prosecuted and punished as if he were the principal offender." The appellants were found guilty as accessories and fined $100 each, against the claim that the accessory statute as so applied violated the 14th Amendment. [The state appellate courts affirmed.] [1]

[We] are met with a wide range of questions that implicate the Due Process Clause of the 14th Amendment. Overtones of some arguments suggest that [Lochner] should be our guide. But we decline that invitation as we did in [the West Coast Hotel, Olsen v. Nebraska, Lincoln Union, and Lee Optical cases, all in sec. 1C above]. We do not sit as a super-legislature to determine the wisdom, need, and propriety of laws that touch economic problems, business affairs, or social conditions. This law, however, operates directly on an intimate relation of husband and wife and their physician's role in one aspect of that relation. The association of people is not mentioned in the Constitution nor in the Bill of Rights. The right to educate a child in a school of the parents' choice—whether public or private or parochial—is also not mentioned. Nor is the right to study any particular subject or any foreign language. Yet the First Amendment has been construed to include certain of those rights. By [Pierce v. Society of Sisters], the right to educate one's children as one chooses is made applicable to the States. [By Meyer v. Nebraska], the same dignity is given the right to study the German language in a private school. In other words, the State may not, consistently with the spirit of the First Amendment, contract the spectrum of available knowledge. The right of freedom of speech and press includes not only the right to utter or to print, but the right to distribute, the right to receive, the right to read [and] freedom of inquiry, freedom of thought, and freedom to [teach]. Without those peripheral rights the specific rights would be less secure. And so we reaffirm the principle of the Pierce and the Meyer cases. In NAACP v. Alabama [1958; p. 1350 below], we protected the "freedom to associate and privacy in one's association," noting that freedom of association was a peripheral First Amendment right. Disclosure of membership lists of a constitutionally valid association, we held, was invalid. In other words, the First Amendment has a penumbra where privacy is protected from governmental intrusion. In like context, we have protected forms of "association" that are not political in the customary sense but pertain to the social, legal, and economic benefit of the members [NAACP v. Button (1963; p. 1353 below)]. [The right of association], while it is not expressly included in the First Amendment, [is] necessary in making the express guarantees fully meaningful.

The foregoing cases suggest that specific guarantees in the Bill of Rights have penumbras, formed by emanations from those guarantees that help give them life and substance. See Poe v. Ullman (dissenting opinion) [1961; printed with Justice Harlan's concurrence in this case]. Various guarantees create zones of privacy. The right of association contained in the penumbra of

---

1. Earlier efforts to test the constitutionality of the Connecticut contraception law had been turned away by the majority of the Court on justiciability grounds. See Tileston v. Ullman (1943; p. 1577 below) and Poe v. Ullman (1961; p. 1588 below). On the Griswold Court's holding that "appellants have standing to raise the rights of the married people with whom they had a professional relationship," see chap. 15, p. 1575 below.

the First Amendment is one, as we have seen. The Third Amendment in its prohibition against the quartering of soldiers "in any house" in time of peace without the consent of the owner is another facet of that privacy. The Fourth Amendment explicitly affirms the "right of the people to be secure in their persons, houses, papers, and effects against unreasonable searches and seizures." The Fifth Amendment in its Self-Incrimination Clause enables the citizen to create a zone of privacy which government may not force him to surrender to his detriment. The Ninth Amendment provides: "The enumeration in the Constitution, of certain rights, shall not be construed to deny or disparage others retained by the people." The Fourth and Fifth Amendments were described in Boyd v. United States, 116 U.S. 616 [1886], as protection against all governmental invasions "of the sanctity of a man's home and the privacies of life." We recently referred in [Mapp v. Ohio (1961; p. 437 above)] to the Fourth Amendment as creating a "right to privacy, no less important than any other right carefully and particularly reserved to the people." We have had many controversies over these penumbral rights of "privacy and repose." [E.g., PUC v. Pollak (1952; p. 1211 below).] These cases bear witness that the right of privacy which presses for recognition here is a legitimate one.

The present case, then, concerns a relationship lying within the zone of privacy created by several fundamental constitutional guarantees. And it concerns a law which, in forbidding the *use* of contraceptives rather than regulating their manufacture or sale, seeks to achieve its goals by means having a maximum destructive impact upon that relationship. Such a law cannot stand in light of the familiar principle [that] a "governmental purpose to control or prevent activities constitutionally subject to state regulation may not be achieved by means which sweep unnecessarily broadly and thereby invade the area of protected freedoms." NAACP v. Alabama. Would we allow the police to search the sacred precincts of marital bedrooms for telltale signs of the use of contraceptives? The very idea is repulsive to the notions of privacy surrounding the marriage relationship. We deal with a right of privacy older than the [Bill of Rights]. Marriage is a coming together for better or for worse, hopefully enduring, and intimate to the degree of being sacred. The association promotes a way of life, not causes; a harmony in living, not political faiths; a bilateral loyalty, not commercial or social projects. Yet it is an association for as noble a purpose as any involved in our prior decisions.

Reversed.

Mr. Justice GOLDBERG, whom The Chief Justice [WARREN] and Mr. Justice BRENNAN join, concurring [in the Court's opinion].

[Although] I have not accepted the view that "due process" as used in the 14th Amendment incorporates all of the first eight Amendments, I do agree that the concept of liberty protects those personal rights that are fundamental, and is not confined to the specific terms of the Bill of Rights. My conclusion [that liberty] embraces the right of marital privacy though that right is not mentioned explicitly in the Constitution is supported both by numerous decisions [and] by the language and history of the Ninth Amendment, [which] reveal that the Framers [believed] that there are additional fundamental rights, protected from governmental infringement, which exist alongside those fundamental rights specifically mentioned in the first [eight] amendments.

The Ninth Amendment reads, "The enumeration in the Constitution, of certain rights, shall not be construed to deny or disparage others retained by the people." [It] was proffered to quiet expressed fears that a bill of specifically enumerated rights could not be sufficiently broad to cover all essential rights and that the specific mention of certain rights would be interpreted as a denial that others were protected. [This] Court has had little occasion to interpret the

Ninth Amendment,[1] [but to] hold that a right so basic and fundamental and so deep-rooted in our society as the right of privacy in marriage may be infringed because that right is not guaranteed in so many words by the first eight amendments [is] to ignore the Ninth Amendment and to give it no effect whatsoever. [I] do not mean to imply that the Ninth Amendment is applied against the States by the 14th [nor] that the Ninth Amendment constitutes an independent source of rights protected from infringement by either the States or Federal Government. Rather, the Ninth Amendment shows a belief of the Constitution's authors that fundamental rights exist that are not expressly enumerated in the first eight amendments and an intent that the list of rights included there not be exhaustive. [This] Court has held [that] the Fifth and 14th Amendments protect certain fundamental personal liberties. [The] Ninth Amendment simply shows the intent of the Constitution's authors that other fundamental personal rights should not be denied such protection or disparaged in any other way simply because they are not specifically listed in the [first eight amendments]. I do not see how this broadens the authority of the Court; rather it serves to support what this Court has been doing in protecting fundamental rights. [While] the Ninth Amendment [originally] concerned restrictions upon *federal* power, the subsequently enacted 14th Amendment prohibits the States as well from abridging fundamental personal liberties. [In] sum, the Ninth Amendment simply lends strong support to the view that the "liberty" protected by the Fifth and [14th] Amendments [is] not restricted to rights specifically mentioned in the first eight amendments.

In determining which rights are fundamental, judges are not left at large to decide cases in light of their personal and private notions. Rather, they must look to the "traditions and [collective] conscience of our people" to determine whether a principle is "so rooted [there] as to be ranked as fundamental." [The] entire fabric of the Constitution and the purposes that clearly underlie its specific guarantees demonstrate that the rights to marital privacy and to marry and raise a family are of similar order and magnitude as the fundamental rights specifically protected. [The] logic of the dissents would sanction federal or state legislation that seems to me even more plainly unconstitutional than the statute before us. Surely the Government, absent a showing of a compelling subordinating state interest, could not decree that all husbands and wives must be sterilized after two children have been born to them. [If] upon a showing of a slender basis of rationality, a law outlawing voluntary birth control by married persons is valid, then, by the same reasoning, a law requiring compulsory birth control also would seem to be valid. In my view, however, both types of law would unjustifiably intrude upon rights of marital privacy which are constitutionally protected.

In a long series of cases this Court has held that where fundamental personal liberties are involved, they may not be abridged by the States simply on a showing that a regulatory statute has some rational relationship to the effectuation of a proper state purpose. "Where there is a significant encroachment upon personal liberty, the State may prevail only upon showing a subordinating interest which is compelling" [Bates v. Little Rock (1960; p. 1352)]. The law must be shown "necessary, and not merely rationally related, to the accomplish-

---

1. This Amendment has been referred to as "The Forgotten Ninth Amendment," in a book with that title by Bennet B. Patterson (1955). Other commentary on the Ninth Amendment includes Redlich, "Are There Certain [Rights] Retained by the People?" 37 N.Y.U.L.Rev. 787 (1962), and Kelsey, "The Ninth Amendment of the Federal Constitution," 11 Ind.L.J. 309 (1936). As far as I am aware, until today this Court has referred to the Ninth Amendment only in United Public Workers v. Mitchell, 330 U.S. 75, 94–95; Tennessee Electric Power Co. v. TVA, 306 U.S. 118, 143–144; and Ashwander v. TVA, 297 U.S. 288, 330–331. See also Calder v. Bull, 3 Dall. 386, 388; Loan Assn. v. Topeka, 20 Wall. 655, 662–663. . . . . [Footnote by Justice Goldberg.]

ment of a permissible state policy." [McLaughlin v. Florida (1964; p. 627).] The State, at most, argues that there is some rational relation between this statute and what is admittedly a legitimate subject of state concern—the discouraging of extra-marital relations. It says that preventing the use of birth-control devices by married persons helps prevent the indulgence by some in such extra-marital relations. The rationality of this justification is dubious, particularly in light of the admitted widespread availability to all persons [in] Connecticut, unmarried as well as married, of birth-control devices for the prevention of disease, as distinguished from the prevention of conception. But, in any event, it is clear that the state interest in safeguarding marital fidelity can be served by a more discriminately tailored statute, which does not, like the present one, sweep unnecessarily broadly, reaching far beyond the evil sought to be dealt with and intruding upon the privacy of all married couples. [Connecticut] does have statutes [which] prohibit adultery and fornication. These statutes demonstrate that means for achieving the same basic purpose of protecting marital fidelity are available to Connecticut without the need to "invade the area of protected freedoms." [Finally], it should be said of the Court's holding today that it in no way interferes with a State's proper regulation of sexual promiscuity or [misconduct]. In sum, I believe that the right of privacy in the marital relation is fundamental and basic—a personal right "retained by the people" within the meaning of the [Ninth Amendment].

Mr. Justice HARLAN, concurring in the judgment.

[I] find myself unable to join the Court's opinion. The reason is that it seems to me to evince an approach to this case very much like that taken by my Brothers Black and Stewart in dissent, namely: the Due Process Clause of the 14th Amendment does not touch this Connecticut statute unless the enactment is found to violate some right assured by the letter or penumbra of the Bill of Rights. [In] my view, the proper constitutional inquiry in this case is whether this Connecticut statute infringes the Due Process Clause of the 14th Amendment because the enactment violates basic values "implicit in the concept of ordered liberty," [Palko]. For reasons stated at length in my dissenting opinion in Poe v. Ullman [see the excerpts below], I believe that it does. While the relevant inquiry may be aided by resort to one or more of the provisions of the Bill of Rights, it is not dependent on them or any of their radiations. The Due Process Clause of the 14th Amendment stands, in my opinion, on its own bottom. [While] I could not more heartily agree that judicial "self restraint" is an indispensable ingredient of sound constitutional adjudication, I do submit that the formula suggested for achieving it is more hollow than real. "Specific" provisions of the Constitution, no less than "due process," lend themselves as readily to "personal" interpretations by judges whose constitutional outlook is simply to keep the Constitution in supposed "tune with the times." [Judicial self-restraint will be achieved] only by continual insistence upon respect for the teachings of history, solid recognition of the basic values that underlie our society, and wise application of the great roles that the doctrines of federalism and separation of powers have played [in] preserving American freedoms. Adherence to these principles will not, of course, obviate all constitutional differences of opinion among judges, nor should it. Their continued recognition will, however, go farther toward keeping most judges from roaming at large in the constitutional field than will the interpolation into the Constitution of an artificial and largely illusory restriction on the content of the Due Process Clause.

[Justice Harlan relied on his dissent in POE v. ULLMAN, 367 U.S. 497 (1961), where he had elaborated his due process approach and had found the application of the Connecticut law unconstitutional. The Poe majority had failed to reach the merits: it had managed to dismiss the appeal on justiciability grounds. (See p. 1588 below.) Excerpts from Justice HARLAN's dissent in Poe follow:]

[I] believe that a statute making it a criminal offense for *married couples* to use contraceptives is an intolerable and unjustifiable invasion of privacy in the conduct of the most intimate concerns of an individual's personal life. [I] feel it desirable at the outset to state the framework of Constitutional principles in which I think the issue must be [judged]. It is not the particular enumeration of rights in the first eight Amendments which spells out the reach of 14th Amendment due process, but rather, as was suggested in another context long before the adoption of that Amendment, those concepts which are considered to embrace those rights "which [are] *fundamental;* which belong [to] the citizens of all free governments" [Corfield v. Coryell], for "the purposes [of securing] which men enter into society" [Calder v. Bull]. [Through] the course of this Court's decisions, [due process] has represented the balance which our Nation, built upon postulates of respect for the liberty of the individual, has struck between that liberty and the demands of organized society. [The] balance of which I speak is the balance struck by this country, having regard to what history teaches are the traditions from which it developed as well as the traditions from which it broke. That tradition is a living thing. A decision of this Court which radically departs from it could not long survive, while a decision which builds on what has survived is likely to be sound. No formula could serve as a substitute, in this area, for judgment and restraint. [The] full scope of the liberty guaranteed by the Due Process Clause cannot be found in or limited by the precise terms of the specific guarantees elsewhere provided in the Constitution. This "liberty" is not a series of isolated points pricked out in terms of [such specific guarantees as speech and religion]. It is a rational continuum which, broadly speaking, includes a freedom from all substantial arbitrary impositions and purposeless restraints, see [e.g., Allgeyer; Nebbia], and which also recognizes [that] certain interests require particularly careful scrutiny of the state needs asserted to justify their abridgment. Cf. [e.g., Skinner].

It is argued by appellants that the judgment implicit in this statute—that the use of contraceptives by married couples is immoral—is an irrational one, that in effect it subjects them in a very important matter to the arbitrary whim of the legislature, and that it does so for no good purpose. [Yet] the very inclusion of the category of morality among state concerns indicates that society is not limited in its objects only to the physical well-being of the community, but has traditionally concerned itself with the moral soundness of its people as well. Indeed to attempt a line between public behavior and that which is purely consensual or solitary would be to withdraw from community concern a range of subjects with which every society in civilized times has found it necessary to deal. The laws regarding marriage which provide both when the sexual powers may be used and the legal and societal context in which children are born and brought up, as well as laws forbidding adultery, fornication and homosexual practices which express the negative of the proposition, confining sexuality to lawful marriage, form a pattern so deeply pressed into the substance of our social life that any Constitutional doctrine in this area must build upon that basis. It is in this area of sexual morality, which contains many proscriptions of consensual behavior having little or no direct impact on others, that [Connecticut] has expressed its moral judgment that all use of contraceptives is improper. [Certainly], Connecticut's judgment is no more demonstrably correct or incorrect than are the varieties of judgment, expressed in law, on marriage and divorce, on adult consensual homosexuality, abortion, and sterilization, or euthanasia and suicide. If we had a case before us which required us to decide simply, and in abstraction, whether the moral judgment implicit in the application of the present statute to married couples was a sound one, the very controversial nature of these questions would, I think, require us to hesitate long before concluding that the Constitution precluded Connecticut from choosing as it has among these various views.[1] [But we] are not presented simply with this moral judgment to be passed on as an abstract proposition. The secular state is not an examiner of consciences: it must operate in the realm of behavior, of overt actions, and where it does so operate, not only the underlying, moral purpose of its operations, but also the *choice of means* becomes relevant to any Constitutional judgment on what is [done].

Precisely what is involved here is this: the State is asserting the right to enforce its moral judgment by intruding upon the most intimate details of the marital relation with the full power of the criminal law. Potentially, this could allow the deployment of all the incidental machinery of the criminal law, arrests, searches and seizures; inevitably, it must mean at the very least the lodging of criminal charges, a public trial, and testimony as to the corpus delicti. Nor could any imaginable elaboration of presumptions, testimonial privileges, or other safeguards alleviate the necessity for testimony as to the mode and manner of the married couples' sexual relations, or at least the opportunity for the accused to make denial of the charges. In sum, the statute allows the State to enquire into, prove and punish married people for the private use of their marital intimacy.

The statute must pass a more rigorous Constitutional test than that going merely to the plausibility of its underlying rationale. This enactment involves what, by common understanding throughout the English-speaking world, must be granted to be a most fundamental aspect of "liberty," the privacy of the home in its most basic sense, and it is this which requires that the statute be subjected to "strict scrutiny." That aspect of liberty which embraces the concept of the privacy of the home receives explicit Constitutional protection at two places only [—the Third and Fourth Amendments]. [It] is clear, of course, that [this] statute does not invade the privacy of the home in the usual sense, since the invasion involved [here] doubtless usually would [be] accomplished without any physical intrusion whatever into the home. What the statute undertakes to do, however, is to create a crime which is grossly offensive to this privacy, while the Constitution refers only to methods of ferreting out substantive [wrongs]. But such an analysis forecloses any claim to Constitutional protection against this form of deprivation of privacy, only if due process in this respect is limited to what is explicitly provided in the Constitution, divorced from the rational purposes, historical roots, and subsequent developments of the relevant provisions. [If] the physical curtilage of the home is protected, it is surely as a result of solicitude to protect the privacies of the life within. Certainly the safeguarding of the home does not follow merely from the sanctity of property rights. The home derives its pre-eminence as the seat of family life. And the integrity of that life is something so fundamental that it has been found to draw to its protection the principles of more than one explicitly granted Constitutional right. [See, e.g., Meyer; Pierce.] Of [the] whole "private realm of family life" it is difficult to imagine what is more private or more intimate than a husband and wife's [marital relations].

Of course, [there] are countervailing considerations. [I]t would be an absurdity to suggest either that offenses may not be committed in the bosom of the family or that the home can be made a sanctuary for crime. The right of privacy [is] not an absolute. Thus, I would not suggest that adultery, homosexuality, fornication and incest are immune from criminal enquiry, however privately practiced. [But] not to discriminate between what is involved in this case and either the traditional offenses against good morals or crimes which,

---

1. This passage is discussed in the notes following Roe v. Wade, the next principal case.

though they may be committed anywhere, happen to have been committed or concealed in the home, would entirely misconceive the argument that is being made. Adultery, homosexuality and the like are sexual intimacies which the State forbids altogether, but the intimacy of husband and wife is necessarily an essential and accepted feature of the institution of marriage, an institution which the State not only must allow, but which always it has fostered and protected. It is one thing when the State exerts its power either to forbid extra-marital sexuality altogether, or to say who may marry, but it is quite another when, having acknowledged a marriage and the intimacies inherent in it, it undertakes to regulate by means of the criminal law the details of that intimacy. In sum, [the] intrusion of the whole machinery of the criminal law into the very heart of marital privacy, requiring husband and wife to render account before a criminal tribunal of their uses of that intimacy, is surely a very different thing indeed from punishing those who establish intimacies which the law has always forbidden and which can have no claim to social protection.

[Since the law] marks an abridgment of important fundamental liberties, [it] will not do to urge in justification [simply] that the statute is rationally related to the effectuation of a proper state purpose. A closer scrutiny and stronger justification than that are required. Though the State has argued the Constitutional permissibility of the moral judgment underlying this statute, [its arguments do not] even remotely [suggest] a justification for the obnoxiously intrusive means it has chosen to effectuate that policy. [But] conclusive, in my view, is the utter novelty of this enactment. [No State] has made the *use* of contraceptives a crime. [Though] undoubtedly the States [should] be allowed broad scope in experimenting, [I] must agree with [Justice Jackson's concurrence in Skinner] that "There are limits to the extent to which a legislatively represented majority may [conduct] experiments at the expense of the dignity and personality" of the individual. In this instance these limits are, in my view, reached and [passed].

Mr. Justice WHITE, concurring in the judgment.

[This] is not the first time this Court has had occasion to articulate that [liberty] includes the right "to marry, establish a home and bring up children" [Meyer] and "the liberty [to] direct the upbringing and education of children" [Pierce], and that these are among "the basic civil rights of man." [Skinner.] These decisions affirm that there is a "realm of family life which the state cannot enter" without substantial justification. Prince v. Massachusetts, 321 U.S. 158 [1944]. Surely the right invoked in this case, to be free of regulation of the intimacies of the marriage relationship, "come[s] to this Court with a momentum for respect lacking when appeal is made to liberties which derive merely from shifting economic arrangements." Kovacs v. Cooper [1949; Frankfurter, J.; p. 980 below]. The Connecticut [law] deals rather substantially with this relationship. [A] statute with these effects bears a substantial burden of justification when attacked under the 14th Amendment. [An] examination of the justification offered, however, cannot be avoided by saying that the Connecticut anti-use statute invades a protected area of privacy and association or that it demeans the marriage relationship. The nature of the right invaded is pertinent, to be sure, for statutes regulating sensitive areas of liberty [do] require "strict scrutiny" and "must be viewed in light of less drastic means for achieving the same basic purpose." [But] such statutes, if reasonably necessary for the effectuation of a legitimate and substantial state interest, and not arbitrary or capricious in application, are not [invalid].

There is no serious contention that Connecticut thinks the use of artificial or external methods of contraception immoral or unwise in itself, or that the anti-use statute is founded upon any policy of promoting population expansion. Rather, the statute is said to serve the State's policy against all forms of promiscuous or illicit sexual relationships, be they premarital or extramarital, concededly a permissible and legitimate legislative goal. Without taking issue with the premise that the fear of conception operates as a deterrent to such relationships in addition to the criminal proscriptions Connecticut has against such conduct, I wholly fail to see how the ban on the use of contraceptives by married couples in any way reinforces the State's ban on illicit sexual relationships. [It] is purely fanciful to believe that the broad proscription on use facilitates discovery of use by persons engaging in a prohibited relationship or for some other reason makes such use more unlikely and thus can be supported by any sort of administrative consideration. Perhaps the theory is that the flat ban on use prevents married people from possessing contraceptives and without the ready availability of such devices for use in the marital relationship, there will be no or less temptation to use them in extramarital ones. This reasoning rests on the premises that married people will comply with the anti-use ban in regard to their marital relationship, notwithstanding total nonenforcement in this context and apparent nonenforcibility, but will not comply with criminal statutes prohibiting extramarital affairs and the anti-use statute in respect to illicit sexual relationships, a premise whose validity has not been demonstrated and whose intrinsic validity is not very evident. At most the broad ban is of marginal utility to the declared objective. A statute limiting its prohibition on use to persons engaging in the prohibited relationship would serve the end posited by Connecticut in the same way, and with the same effectiveness, or ineffectiveness, as the broad anti-use statute under attack in this case. I find nothing in this record justifying the sweeping scope of this statute, with its telling effect on the freedoms of [married persons].

Mr. Justice BLACK [joined by Justice STEWART] dissenting.

[The] law is every bit as offensive to me as it is to my Brethren [who], reciting reasons why it is offensive to them, hold it unconstitutional. [But] I cannot [join] their conclusion that the evil qualities they see in the law make it unconstitutional. [The] Court talks about a constitutional ["right of privacy"]. There are, of course, guarantees in certain specific constitutional provisions which are designed in part to protect privacy at certain times and places with respect to certain activities. Such, for example, is the [Fourth Amendment]. But I think it belittles that Amendment to talk about it as though it protects nothing but "privacy." One of the most effective ways of diluting or expanding a constitutionally guaranteed right is to substitute for the crucial word or words of a constitutional guarantee another word or words, more or less flexible and more or less restricted in meaning. This fact is well illustrated by the use of the term "right of privacy" as a comprehensive substitute for the [Fourth Amendment]. "Privacy" is a broad, abstract and ambiguous concept which can easily be shrunken in meaning but which can [also] easily be interpreted as a constitutional ban against many things other than searches and seizures. [I] get nowhere in this case by talk about a constitutional "right of privacy" as an emanation from one or more constitutional provisions.[1] I like my privacy as well as the next one, but I am nevertheless compelled to admit that government has a right to invade it unless prohibited by some specific constitutional [provision].

This brings me to the arguments made by my Brothers Harlan, White and Goldberg. [I] discuss the due process and Ninth Amendment arguments together because on analysis they turn out to be the same thing—merely using

---

1. The phrase "right to privacy" appears first to have gained currency from an article written by Messrs. Warren and (later Mr. Justice) Brandeis in 1890 which urged that States should give some form of tort relief to persons whose private affairs were exploited by others. The Right to Privacy, 4 Harv.L.Rev. 193. [Now, this Court exalts] a phrase which Warren and Brandeis used in discussing grounds for [common law] tort relief, to the level of a constitutional [rule]. [Footnote by Justice Black.]

different words to claim [the] power to invalidate any legislative act which the judges find irrational, unreasonable or offensive. [If the due process] formulas based on "natural justice" [are] to prevail, they require judges to determine what is or is not constitutional on the basis of their own appraisal of what laws are unwise or unnecessary.[2] The power to make such decisions is of course that of a legislative body. [I] do not believe that we are granted power [to] measure constitutionality by our belief that the legislation is arbitrary, capricious or unreasonable, or accomplishes no justifiable purpose, or is offensive to our own notions of "civilized standards of conduct." [Of] the cases on which my Brothers White and Goldberg rely so heavily, undoubtedly the reasoning of two of them supports their result here—as would that of a number of others which they do not bother to name, e.g., [Lochner, Coppage and Adkins]. The two they do cite and quote from, [Meyer] and [Pierce], were both decided in opinions by Mr. Justice McReynolds which elaborated the same natural law due process philosophy found in [Lochner]. [The] reasoning stated in Meyer and Pierce was the same natural law due process philosophy which many later opinions repudiated, and which I cannot [accept].

My Brother Goldberg has adopted the recent discovery that the Ninth Amendment as well as the Due Process Clause can be used by this Court as authority to strike down all state legislation which this Court thinks violates "fundamental principles of liberty and justice," or is contrary to the "traditions and collective conscience of our people." He also states, without proof satisfactory to me, that in making decisions on this basis judges will not consider "their personal and private notions." One may ask how they can avoid considering them. [The Framers did not give this Court] veto powers over [lawmaking]. Nor does anything in the history of the Amendment offer any support for such a shocking doctrine. [That] Amendment was passed [to] assure the people that the [Constitution] was intended to limit the Federal Government to the powers granted expressly or by necessary implication. [This] fact is perhaps responsible for the peculiar phenomenon that for a period of a century and a half no serious suggestion was ever made that the Ninth Amendment, enacted to protect state powers against federal invasion, could be used as a weapon of federal power to prevent state legislatures from passing laws they consider appropriate to govern [local affairs].

I realize that many good and able men have eloquently spoken and written, sometimes in rhapsodical strains, about the duty of this Court to keep the Constitution in tune with the times. [I] reject that philosophy. The Constitution makers knew the need for change and provided for it [through the amendment process]. [The] Due Process Clause with an "arbitrary and capricious" or "shocking to the conscience" formula was liberally used by this Court to strike down economic legislation in the early decades of this century, threatening, many people thought, the tranquility and stability of the Nation. See, e.g., [Lochner]. That formula [is] no less dangerous when used to enforce this Court's views about personal rights than those about economic rights. I had thought that we had laid that formula, as a means for striking down state legislation, to rest. [Apparently] my Brethren have less quarrel with state economic regulations than former Justices of their persuasion had. But any limitation upon their using the natural law due process philosophy to strike

---

2. See Hand, The Bill of Rights (1958) 70: "[J]udges are seldom content merely to annul the particular solution before them; they do not, indeed they may not, say that taking all things into consideration, the legislators' solution is too strong for the judicial stomach. On the contrary they wrap up their veto in a protective veil of adjectives such as 'arbitrary,' 'artificial,' 'normal,' 'reasonable,' 'inherent,' 'fundamental,' or 'essential,' whose office usually, though quite innocently, is to disguise what they are doing and impute to it a derivation far more impressive than their personal preferences, which are all that in fact lie behind the [decision]." [Footnote by Justice Black.]

down any state law, dealing with any activity whatever, will obviously be only self-imposed. [The] late Judge Learned Hand, after emphasizing his view that judges should not use the due process formula suggested in the concurring opinions today or any other formula like it to invalidate legislation offensive to their "personal preferences," made the statement, with which I fully agree, that: "For myself it would be most irksome to be ruled by a bevy of Platonic Guardians, even if I knew how to choose them, which I assuredly do not." [3] So far as I am concerned, Connecticut's law as applied here is not forbidden by any provision of the Federal Constitution as that Constitution was [written].

Mr. Justice STEWART, whom Mr. Justice BLACK joins, dissenting.

[I] think this is an uncommonly silly law. [But] we are not asked in this case to say whether we think this law is unwise, or even asinine. We are asked to hold that it violates [the] Constitution. And that I cannot do. In the course of its opinion the Court refers to no less than six Amendments to the Constitution [but] does not say which of these Amendments, if any, it thinks is infringed by this Connecticut law. We *are* told that the Due Process Clause of the 14th Amendment is not, as such, the "guide" in this case. With that much I agree. [As] to the First, Third, Fourth, and Fifth Amendments, I can find nothing in any of them to invalidate this Connecticut [law]. [To] say that the Ninth Amendment has anything to do with this case is to turn somersaults with history. The Ninth Amendment, like its companion the Tenth, [was] simply to make clear that the adoption of the Bill of Rights did not alter the plan that the *Federal* Government was to be a government of express and limited powers. [What] provision of the Constitution, then, does make this state law invalid? The Court says it is the right of privacy "created by several fundamental constitutional guarantees." With all deference, I can find no such general right of privacy in the Bill of Rights, in any other part of the Constitution, or in any case ever before decided by this Court.[1] At the oral argument [we] were told that the Connecticut law does not "conform to current community standards." But it is not the function of this Court to decide cases on the basis of community standards. [If], as I should surely hope, the law before us does not reflect the standards of the people of Connecticut, [they] can freely exercise their true Ninth and Tenth Amendment rights to persuade their elected representatives to repeal it. That is the constitutional way to take this law off the books.

GRISWOLD, PENUMBRAS, AND DOUBLE STANDARDS

1. *The constitutional basis of Griswold.* Consider the range of modes of constitutional adjudication disclosed by the opinions in Griswold. Is Justice Black right in charging that Griswold is of a piece with the free-wheeling, subjective variety of substantive due process adjudication long discredited in the economic regulation area? Or is Griswold distinguishable? How? Justice Douglas disavows Lochner as a guide. He relies instead on the "penumbras" and "emanations" of several specific guarantees in the Bill of Rights. Is the "right of privacy" he finds a legitimate derivation from the constitutional text?

3. [Hand, The Bill of Rights (1958)], at 73. While Judge Hand condemned as unjustified the invalidation of state laws under the natural law due process formula, he also expressed the view that this Court in a number of cases had gone too far in holding legislation to be in violation of specific guarantees of the Bill of Rights. Although I agree with his criticism of use of the due process formula, I do not agree with all the views he expressed about construing the specific guarantees of the Bill of Rights. [Footnote by Justice Black. See the comments on Justice Black's reliance on Judge Hand in the notes following this case.]

1. [The] Court does not say how far the new constitutional right of privacy announced today extends. I suppose, however, that even after today a State can constitutionally still punish at least some offenses which are not committed in public. [Footnote by Justice Stewart.]

Does that depend on what the content of that "right of privacy" is? (See note 2 below.) Does Justice Douglas' "penumbras-emanations" approach avoid subjective, idiosyncratic, extraconstitutional, "natural law" adjudication more effectively than the Lochner approach or the other opinions on the majority side in Griswold? Does Justice Douglas' approach channel judicial power more rigorously than the analyses of the other opinions? Than Justice Harlan's "basic values 'implicit in the concept of ordered liberty'" approach?[1] Than Justice Goldberg's Ninth Amendment-"fundamental rights" approach?[2] Does Justice Douglas' approach help distinguish "economic" and "personal" rights and justify the double standard? Are liberty of contract and the right to use property, the favored rights of the Lochner era, distinguishable because they are not specifically mentioned in the Constitution? But arguably liberty of contract could be seen as an emanation, or within the penumbra, of the contracts clause. And a general protection of property could be seen as within the penumbra of the specific mention of "property" in the condemnation clause of the Fifth Amendment—not to speak of the historical importance of property rights and the "specific" reference to property in the 14th Amendment itself.[3]

2. *The scope of "privacy" in Griswold.* What *is* the scope of the "right of privacy" recognized in Griswold? Is it the interest in preventing intrusions into the home? The interest in avoiding disclosure of personal information? The interest in the protection of the "intimacies of the marriage relationship"? A broader interest in personal autonomy—in freedom from governmental regulation of some range of personal activities that do not harm others? Consider the emphases of the various opinions in Griswold, and their implications for laws other than that banning the use of contraceptives in Griswold. And consider the distinction suggested in Note, "Roe and Paris:[4] Does Privacy Have a Principle?" 26 Stan.L.Rev. 1161 (1974)—a distinction between two meanings of privacy: (1) a "right of selective disclosure," or interest in control of information; and (2) a private "autonomy" of choice about performing acts or undergoing experiences.[5]

Between Griswold and Roe, the Court decided one other case involving the control of contraceptives: EISENSTADT v. BAIRD, 405 U.S. 438 (1972). One important passage in Eisenstadt clarified (more accurately, expanded) the nature of the right of privacy. In fact, the superficially quite modest sounding Eisenstadt opinion is widely seen in retrospect as a critical stepping point from the arguably narrow ruling in Griswold to the unmistakably broad one in Roe. Griswold involved the *use* of contraceptives by *married* persons; there, Justice Douglas had distinguished the regulation of the "manufacture or sale" of contraceptives from prohibitions of "use." But Eisenstadt overturned a conviction under a law banning the *distribution* of contraceptives; and, most significantly, marriage proved not to be a critical factor after all. Baird had distributed contraceptive foam, and the recipient was described by the state court as an *unmarried* person. The Court managed to avoid explicit decision of the

1. Compare Justice Stewart's comment on Griswold, eight years after his dissent in that case, when he concurred in Roe v. Wade, the abortion decision which follows: "Griswold stands as one in a long line of pre-Skrupa [Ferguson v. Skrupa, p. 468 above] cases decided under the doctrine of substantive due process, and I now accept it as such."

2. See Note, "The Uncertain Renaissance of the Ninth Amendment," 33 U.Chi.L.Rev. 814 (1966), and Beaney, "[The] Expanding Right to Privacy," 1966 Wis.L.Rev. 979.

3. See Kauper, "Penumbras, Peripheries, Emanations, Things Fundamental and Things

Forgotten: The Griswold Case," 64 Mich.L.Rev. 235 (1965).

4. The reference is to Paris Adult Theater I v. Slaton (1973; p. 1079 below), one of the Burger Court's major opinions on the problem of obscenity control.

5. Note the adoption of a similar distinction in Whalen v. Roe (1977; p. 564 below).

Consider what added light on the scope of constitutionally protected "privacy" and "autonomy" is shed by Roe v. Wade, which follows; and note the further examination of these concepts in the materials following that case.

questions whether the fundamental right recognized in Griswold extended beyond use to distribution and beyond married couples to unmarried persons. Instead, it purported to decide the case on a minimum rationality-equal protection ground.[6] Yet, despite Justice BRENNAN's asserted care to avoid writing a "fundamental rights" opinion, he made some significant comments on Griswold in his Eisenstadt opinion: "It is true that in Griswold the right of privacy in question inhered in the marital relationship. Yet the marital couple is not an independent entity with a mind and heart of its own, but an association of two individuals each with a separate intellectual and emotional make-up. If the right of privacy means anything, it is the right of the *individual,* married or single, to be free from unwarranted governmental intrusion into matters so fundamentally affecting a person as the decision whether to bear or beget a child. See Stanley v. Georgia [1969; banning prosecution for possessing obscene materials in the home; p. 1073 below]. See also [Skinner]."[7] And Justice WHITE's concurrence in Eisenstadt (joined by Justice Blackmun) commented: "Just as in Griswold, where the right of married persons to use contraceptives was 'diluted or adversely affected' by permitting a conviction for giving advice as to its exercise, [so] here to sanction a medical restriction upon distribution of a contraceptive not proved hazardous to health would impair the exercise of the constitutional right."

Justice Brennan's passing remarks in Eisenstadt proved important indeed. Not only were they relied on in Roe v. Wade, but, little more than a decade after Griswold, Justice Brennan was able to restate the holding of Griswold (in light of Eisenstadt and Roe) as follows: "Griswold may no longer be read as holding only that a State may not prohibit a married couple's use of contraceptives. Read in light of its progeny, the teaching of Griswold is that the Constitution protects individual decisions in matters of childbearing from unjustified intrusion by the State." After noting that "intrusion into 'the sacred precincts of marital bedrooms' made [the law in Griswold] particularly 'repulsive,' " he added that "subsequent decisions have made clear that the constitu-

---

6. In fact, however, the degree of equal protection rationality scrutiny exercised seemed a good deal stricter than the extremely deferential one of the post-Lochner era. See Gunther, "Foreword: [A] Model for a Newer Equal Protection," 86 Harv.L.Rev. 1 (1972).

7. Eisenstadt v. Baird involved a law making it a felony to distribute materials for prevention of conception, except by registered physicians or pharmacists to married persons. Purporting to apply a "lenient" equal protection standard, Justice Brennan's opinion held it unconstitutional, finding no "ground of difference that rationally explains the different treatment accorded married and unmarried persons." Among the flaws he found in a rather strained opinion (see the criticisms in the Gunther article cited above) were: (1) The law did not regulate the distribution of contraceptives when they were to be used for prevention of disease, and did make contraceptives available to married persons without regard to their intended use; thus, even assuming that "the fear of pregnancy operates as a deterrent to fornication, the [law] is so riddled with exceptions that deterrence of premarital sex cannot reasonably be regarded as its aim." (2) The purported health objective could not "reasonably be regarded" as the law's real purpose. If health were the rationale, it would "invidiously discriminate against the unmarried" and would be

"overbroad with respect to the married." Moreover, the law was not necessary as a health measure because of the many laws already regulating the distribution of harmful drugs. (3) The law could not be upheld "simply as a prohibition on contraception"—although "we [do] not" decide whether such a ban "conflicts with fundamental human rights," "whatever the rights of the individual to access to contraceptives, the rights must be the same for the unmarried and the married alike." In the discussion of this point, he included the passage quoted in text. (Only Chief Justice Burger dissented.) For a comment that Eisenstadt decided ("by assertion, without a pretext of reasoning") an issue left open by Griswold, the constitutionality of banning distribution of contraceptives to unmarried persons, see Wellington, "Common Law Rules and Constitutional Double Standards," 83 Yale L.J. 221 (1973). See also Posner, "The Uncertain Protection of Privacy by the Supreme Court," 1979 Sup.Ct.Rev. 173, arguing that Eisenstadt, unlike the arguably narrow Griswold ruling, was "a pure essay in substantive due process" and that Eisenstadt "unmasks Griswold as based on the idea of sexual liberty rather than privacy." (On whether the modern cases truly protect anything as broad as "sexual liberty," see the materials following Roe v. Wade, below.)

tional protection of individual autonomy in matters of childbearing is not dependent on that element." [8]

3. *Griswold and the double standard.* There is a common theme in all of the opinions supporting the majority result in Griswold, whatever the differences in the modes of constitutional interpretation and whatever the differences in the scope of the perceived fundamental rights: all agree that Griswold involves interests sufficiently special, sufficiently cherished, to warrant review at something beyond the deferential, minimum rationality stance of judicial scrutiny. And once a stricter degree of scrutiny is justified and applied, invalidation of the law becomes much more probable. That common theme provokes once again the recurrent question: What justifies that "double standard"—of strict scrutiny in some situations, hands off in others? The frequently invoked justification suggested by Justice Stone's footnote in Carolene Products (p. 473 above) is least helpful in a situation like Griswold. Stone suggested that greater scrutiny was justified when legislation conflicts with values expressed in the "specific" prohibitions of the Constitution or when it "restricts" the "political processes." That justification has created some difficulty even where First Amendment freedoms are involved. But the value protected in the Griswold decision does not fit those descriptions: even the Justices to whom the core of the penumbra is most visible would not call privacy a "specific" guarantee, or one central to the "political processes." Justice Stone also suggested special judicial solicitude for some "discrete and insular minorities." Is there anything in the Griswold context that satisfies that criterion? Is it arguable, for example, that Griswold is best seen as a women's rights case? (See the comments after the abortion cases, p. 530 below, and the sex discrimination materials, p. 642 below.) Or is there nothing more to be said for Griswold than could have been said for any of the Court's invalidations in the Lochner era? [9]

What is clear in Griswold is that all of the Justices in the majority found some ordering of constitutional values justified: *some* "fundamental values" *do* deserve special protection. That consensus poses a question common to all of the modern substantive due process cases: How does the Court determine the proper place of a particular right on the hierarchy of values? How does Justice White, for example, defend placing the right invoked in Griswold at a different place in the hierarchy from "mere" economic rights? Further consideration of this problem is postponed until after Roe v. Wade and the materials following it. Roe raises even more acutely the twin pervasive issues: What justifies a double standard in degrees of scrutiny? What *are* the proper sources of "fundamental values"?

---

8. That passage is from Carey (1977; p. 547 below). The Carey case involved state restrictions on the distribution and advertising of contraceptives. (The case is considered below because it reveals the impact of not only the earlier contraception decisions but also the later abortion decisions.)

9. Justice Black in his dissent obviously thought there was not. But ironically, he repeatedly quotes Judge Learned Hand. As Justice Black's footnote 3 hints, Judge Hand repudiated any double standard and was profoundly skeptical of the judicial enforceability of the due process clause in any context, whether of civil liberties or of economic regulation: he disapproved of Justice Black's variety of "absolute" enforcement of free speech (see chap. 11 below) as he did of the Lochner case. As he said of the shift in the Court after the 1937 Court crisis: "It began to seem as though, when 'personal rights' were in issue, something strangely akin to the discredited attitude toward the Bill of Rights of the old apostles of the institution of property was regaining recognition." Judge Hand thought that this was "an opportunistic reversion." To him, the principle of nonintervention via the due process clause of the 14th Amendment could not mean "that, when concerned with interests other than property, the Court should have a wider latitude for enforcing their own predilections." Do Griswold (and the later substantive due process cases, below) illustrate the validity of Hand's critique?

ROE v. WADE

410 U.S. 113, 93 S.Ct. 705, 35 L.Ed.2d 147 (1973).

[This was an attack on the Texas abortion laws—typical of those adopted by most states—making it a crime to "procure an abortion" except "by medical advice for the purpose of saving the life of the mother." [1] The challengers here were a pregnant single woman (Jane Roe), a childless couple, with the wife not pregnant (John and Mary Doe), and a licensed physician (Dr. Hallford). The suits by Roe and the Does were class actions. The three-judge District Court ruled the Does' complaint nonjusticiable, but granted declaratory relief to Roe and Dr. Hallford, holding the law unconstitutional under the Ninth Amendment.[2]]

Mr. Justice BLACKMUN delivered the opinion of the Court.

[We] forthwith acknowledge our awareness of the sensitive and emotional nature of the abortion controversy, of the vigorous opposing views, [and] of the deep and seemingly absolute convictions that the subject inspires. One's philosophy, one's experiences, one's exposure to the raw edges of human existence, one's religious training, one's attitudes toward life and family and their values, and the moral standards one establishes and seeks to observe, are all likely to [influence] one's thinking [about] abortion. In addition, population growth, pollution, poverty, and racial overtones tend to complicate and not to simplify the problem. Our task, of course, is to resolve the issue by constitutional measurement, free of emotion and of predilection. We seek earnestly to do this, and, because we do, we have inquired into, and in this opinion place some emphasis upon, medical and medical-legal history and what that history reveals about man's attitudes toward the abortion procedure over the centuries. We bear in mind, too, Mr. Justice Holmes' admonition in his now-vindicated dissent in [Lochner. The quotation from that dissent is omitted.] [The] principal thrust of appellant's attack on the Texas statutes is that they improperly invade a right, said to be possessed by the pregnant woman, to choose to terminate her pregnancy. [Before] addressing this claim, we feel it desirable briefly to survey, in several aspects, the history of abortion, for such insight as that history may afford us. [Justice Blackmun's review of that history is omitted. His survey began with "ancient attitudes"—starting with "Persian Empire abortifacients"—and continued through "the Hippocratic Oath," "the common law," "English statutory law," and "American law," to the positions of the American Medical, Public Health and Bar Associations. After stating the possible state interests in restricting abortions (summarized below), he continued:]

The Constitution does not explicitly mention any right of privacy. [However], the Court has recognized that a right of personal privacy, or a guarantee of certain areas or zones of privacy, does exist under the Constitution. In varying contexts, the Court or individual Justices have, indeed, found at least the roots of that right in the First Amendment [Stanley v. Georgia (obscenity; p. 1073 below)]; in the Fourth and Fifth Amendments; in the penumbras of the Bill of Rights [Griswold]; in the Ninth Amendment [id.]; or in the concept of liberty guaranteed [by] the 14th Amendment, see [Meyer]. These decisions make it clear that only personal rights that can be deemed "fundamental" or "implicit in the concept of ordered liberty" [Palko] are included in this guarantee of personal privacy. They also make it clear that the right has some extension to

---

1. In a companion case, Doe v. Bolton, 410 U.S. 179 (1973), which follows, the Court examined the constitutionality of the Georgia abortion laws, statutes with "a modern cast," reflecting "the influences of recent attitudinal change, of advancing medical knowledge and techniques and of new thinking about an old issue."

2. On the Court's handling of the justiciability problems, see p. 1589 below.

activities relating to marriage [Loving v. Virginia], procreation [Skinner], contraception [Eisenstadt v. Baird], family relationships [Prince v. Massachusetts], and child rearing and education [Pierce; Meyer].

This right of privacy, whether it be founded in the 14th Amendment's concept of personal liberty and restrictions upon state action, as we feel it is, or, as the District Court determined, in the [Ninth Amendment], is broad enough to encompass a woman's decision whether or not to terminate her pregnancy. The detriment that the State would impose upon the pregnant woman by denying this choice altogether is apparent. Specific and direct harm medically diagnosable even in early pregnancy may be involved. Maternity, or additional offspring, may force upon the woman a distressful life and future. Psychological harm may be imminent. Mental and physical health may be taxed by child care. There is also the distress, for all concerned, associated with the unwanted child, and there is the problem of bringing a child into a family already unable, psychologically and otherwise, to care for it. In other cases, as in this one, the additional difficulties and continuing stigma of unwed motherhood may be involved. All these are factors the woman and her responsible physician necessarily will consider in consultation.

On the basis of elements such as these, appellants and some amici argue that the woman's right is absolute and that she is entitled to terminate her pregnancy at whatever time, in whatever way, and for whatever reason she alone chooses. With this we do not agree. [The] Court's decisions recognizing a right of privacy also acknowledge that some state regulation in areas protected by that right is appropriate. [A] state may properly assert important interests in safeguarding health, in maintaining medical standards, and in protecting potential life.[3] At some point in pregnancy, these respective interests become sufficiently compelling to sustain regulation of the factors that govern the abortion decision. The privacy right involved, therefore, cannot be said to be absolute. In fact, it is not clear to us that the claim asserted by some amici that one has an unlimited right to do with one's body as one pleases bears a close relationship to the right of privacy previously articulated in the Court's decisions. The Court has refused to recognize an unlimited right of this kind in the past. [Jacobson v. Massachusetts (1905)] (vaccination); [Buck v. Bell (1927)] (sterilization). We, therefore, conclude that the right of personal privacy includes the abortion decision, but that this right is not unqualified and must be considered against important state interests in regulation. [Where] certain "fundamental rights" are involved, the Court has held that regulation limiting these rights may be justified only by a "compelling state interest" [and] that legislative enactments must be narrowly drawn to express only the legitimate state interests at stake. [Appellant claims] an absolute right that bars any state imposition of criminal penalties in the area. Appellee argues that the State's determination to recognize and protect prenatal life from and after conception constitutes a compelling state interest. [We] do not agree fully with either formulation.

---

3. In discussing these interests earlier in his opinion, Justice Blackmun had stated: "[The] State has a legitimate interest in seeing to it that abortion, like any other medical procedure, is performed under circumstances that ensure maximum safety for the patient. [The] State retains a definite interest in protecting the woman's own health and safety when an abortion is proposed at a late stage of pregnancy. [There is also] the State's interest [in] protecting prenatal life. Some of the argument for this justification rests on the theory that a new human life is present from the moment of conception. [Logically], of course, a legitimate state interest in this area need not stand or fall on acceptance of the belief that life begins at conception or at some other point prior to live birth. In assessing the State's interest, recognition may be given to the less rigid claim that as long as at least *potential* life is involved, the State may assert interests beyond the protection of the pregnant woman alone. [It] is with these interests, and the weight to be attached to them, that this case is concerned."

A. The appellee and certain amici argue that the fetus is a "person" within the language and meaning of the 14th Amendment. [If] this suggestion of personhood is established, the appellant's case, of course, collapses, for the fetus' right to life is then guaranteed specifically by the Amendment. [But] the appellee conceded [that] no case could be cited that holds that a fetus is a person within the meaning of the 14th Amendment. The Constitution does not define "person" in so many words. Section 1 of the 14th Amendment contains three references to "person." ["Person"] is used in other places in the Constitution.[4] [But] in nearly all these instances, the use of the word is such that it has application only postnatally. None indicates, with any assurance, that it has any possible prenatal application.[5] All this, together with our observation [that] throughout the major portion of the 19th century prevailing legal abortion practices were far freer than they are today, persuades us that the word "person," as used in the 14th Amendment, does not include the unborn. [We] pass on to other considerations.

B. The pregnant woman cannot be isolated in her privacy. She carries an embryo and, later, a [fetus]. The situation therefore is inherently different from marital intimacy, or bedroom possession of obscene material, or marriage, or procreation, or education, with which Eisenstadt, Griswold, Stanley, Loving, Skinner, Pierce, and Meyer [were] concerned. [I]t is reasonable and appropriate for a State to decide that at some point in time another interest, that of health of the mother or that of potential human life, becomes significantly involved. The woman's privacy is no longer sole and any right of privacy she possesses must be measured accordingly.

Texas urges that, apart from the 14th Amendment, life begins at conception and is present throughout pregnancy, and that, therefore, the State has a compelling interest in protecting that life from and after conception. We need not resolve the difficult question of when life begins. When those trained [in] medicine, philosophy, and theology are unable to arrive at any consensus, the judiciary, at this point in the development of man's knowledge, is not in a position to speculate as to the answer. It should be sufficient to note [the] wide divergence of thinking on this most sensitive and difficult question. [After reviewing a range of philosophical and religious beliefs, Justice Blackmun noted:] Physicians [have] tended to focus either upon conception, upon live birth, or upon the interim point at which the fetus becomes "viable," that is, potentially able to live outside the mother's womb, albeit with artificial aid. Viability is usually placed at about seven months (28 weeks) but may occur earlier, even at 24 weeks. [The modern official belief of the Catholic Church, recognizing the existence of life from the moment of conception,] is a view strongly held by many non-Catholics as well, and by many physicians. Substan-

---

4. At this point, Justice Blackmun recited all the other constitutional references to "person": "in the listing of qualifications for Representatives and Senators, Art. I, § 2, cl. 2, and § 3, cl. 3; in the Apportionment Clause, Art. I, § 2, cl. 3; in the Migration and Importation provision, Art. I, § 9, cl. 1; in the Emolument Clause, Art. I, § 9, cl. 8; in the Electors provisions, Art. II, § 1, cl. 2, and the superseded cl. 3; in the provision outlining qualifications for the office of President, Art. II, § 1, cl. 5; in the Extradition provisions, Art. IV, § 2, cl. 2, and the superseded Fugitive Slave Clause 3; and in the Fifth, Twelfth and Twenty-second Amendments, as well as in §§ 2 and 3 of the 14th Amendment." (After the second item listed in Justice Blackmun's catalogue, the Apportionment Clause, he added the following footnote: "We are not aware that in the taking of any census under this clause, a fetus has ever been counted.")

5. When Texas urges that a fetus is entitled to 14th Amendment protection as a person, it faces a dilemma. Neither in Texas nor in any other State are all abortions prohibited. Despite broad proscription, an exception always exists. The exception [in the Texas law], for an abortion procured or attempted by medical advice for the purpose of saving the life of the mother, is typical. But if the fetus is a person who is not to be deprived of life without due process of law, and if the mother's condition is the sole determinant, does not the Texas exception appear to be out of line with the Amendment's [command]?? [Footnote by Justice Blackmun.]

tial problems for precise definition of this view are posed, however, by new embryological data that purport to indicate that conception is a "process" over time, rather than an event, and by new medical techniques such as menstrual extraction, the "morning-after" pill, implantation of embryos, artificial insemination, and even artificial wombs. In areas other than criminal abortion, the law has been reluctant to endorse any theory that life, as we recognize it, begins before live birth or to accord legal rights to the unborn except in narrowly defined situations and except when the rights are contingent upon live birth. [Justice Blackmun noted illustrations in the law of torts and of inheritance.] In short, the unborn have never been recognized in the law as persons in the whole sense.

In view of all this, we do not agree that, by adopting one theory of life, Texas may override the rights of the pregnant woman that are at stake. We repeat, however, that the State does have an important and legitimate interest in preserving and protecting the health of the pregnant woman [and] that it has still another important and legitimate interest in protecting the potentiality of human life. These interests are separate and distinct. Each grows in substantiality as the woman approaches term and, at a point during pregnancy, each becomes "compelling."

With respect to the State's important and legitimate interest in the health of the mother, the "compelling" point, in the light of present medical knowledge, is at approximately the end of the first trimester. This is so because of the now established medical fact [that] until the end of the first trimester mortality in abortion is less than mortality in normal childbirth. It follows that, from and after this point, a State may regulate the abortion procedure to the extent that the regulation reasonably relates to the preservation and protection of maternal health. Examples of permissible state regulation in this area are requirements as to the qualifications of the person who is to perform the abortion; [as] to the facility in which the procedure is to be performed; and the like. This means, on the other hand, that, for the period of pregnancy prior to this "compelling" point, the attending physician, in consultation with his patient, is free to determine, without regulation by the State, that, in his medical judgment, the patient's pregnancy should be terminated. If that decision is reached, the judgment may be effectuated by an abortion free of interference by the State.

With respect to the State's important and legitimate interest in potential life, the "compelling" point is at viability. This is so because the fetus then presumably has the capability of meaningful life outside the mother's womb. State regulation protective of fetal life after viability thus has both logical and biological justifications. If the State is interested in protecting fetal life after viability, it may go so far as to proscribe abortion during that period, except when it is necessary to preserve the life or health of the mother.

Measured against these standards, [the Texas law] sweeps too broadly. The statute makes no distinction between abortions performed early in pregnancy and those performed later, and it limits to a single reason, "saving" the mother's life, the legal justification for the procedure. The statute, therefore, cannot survive the constitutional attack made upon it here. To summarize and repeat: A state criminal abortion statute of the current Texas type, that excepts from criminality only a *life saving* procedure on behalf of the mother, without regard to pregnancy stage and without recognition of the other interests involved, is violative of the [Due Process Clause]. (a) For the stage prior to approximately the end of the first trimester, the abortion decision and its effectuation must be left to the medical judgment of the pregnant woman's attending physician. (b) For the stage subsequent to approximately the end of the first trimester, the State, in promoting its interest in the health of the mother, may, if it chooses, regulate the abortion procedure in ways that are reasonably related to maternal health. (c) For the stage subsequent to viability, the State in promoting its interest in the potentiality of human life may, if it chooses, regulate, and even proscribe, abortion except where it is necessary, in appropriate medical judgment, for the preservation of the life or health of the mother. The State may define the term "physician" [to] mean only a physician currently licensed by the State, and may proscribe any abortion by a person who is not a physician as so defined. In Doe v. Bolton, post, procedural requirements contained in one of the modern abortion statutes are considered. That opinion and this one, of course, are to be read together.

This holding, we feel, is consistent with the relative weights of the respective interests involved, with the lessons and examples of medical and legal history, with the lenity of the common law, and with the demands of the profound problems of the present day. The decision leaves the State free to place increasing restrictions on abortion as the period of pregnancy lengthens, so long as those restrictions are tailored to the recognized state interests. The decision vindicates the right of the physician to administer medical treatment according to his professional judgment up to the points where important state interests provide compelling justifications for intervention. Up to those points, the abortion decision in all its aspects is inherently, and primarily, a medical decision, and basic responsibility for it must rest with the physician. If an individual practitioner abuses the privilege of exercising proper medical judgment, the usual remedies, judicial and intraprofessional, are [available].

It is so ordered.

Mr. Justice STEWART, concurring.

In 1963, this Court, in [Ferguson v. Skrupa, p. 468 above], purported to sound the death knell for the doctrine of substantive due process. Barely two years later, in [Griswold], the Court held a Connecticut birth control law unconstitutional. In view of what had been so recently said in Skrupa, the Court's opinion in Griswold understandably did its best to avoid reliance on the Due Process Clause. [Yet], the Connecticut law did not violate [any] specific provision of the Constitution. So it was clear to me then, and it is equally clear to me now, that the Griswold decision can be rationally understood only as a holding that the Connecticut statute substantively invaded "liberty". As so understood Griswold stands as one in a long line of pre-Skrupa cases decided under the doctrine of substantive due process, and I now accept it as such. [T]he "liberty" protected by the Due Process Clause of the 14th Amendment covers more than those freedoms explicitly named in the Bill of Rights. [Several] decisions of this Court make clear that freedom of personal choice in matters of marriage and family life is one of the liberties protected by the [Due Process Clause]. As recently as last Term, in [Eisenstadt], we recognized "the right of the individual, married or single, to be free from unwarranted governmental intrusion into matters so fundamentally affecting a person as the decision whether to bear or beget a child." That right necessarily includes the right of a woman to decide whether or not to terminate her [pregnancy]. It is evident that the Texas abortion statute infringes that right directly. [The] question then becomes whether the state interests advanced to justify this abridgment can survive the "particularly careful scrutiny" that the 14th Amendment here requires. The asserted state interests [are] legitimate objectives, amply sufficient to permit a State to regulate abortions as it does other surgical procedures, and perhaps sufficient to permit a State to regulate abortions more stringently or even to prohibit them in the late stages of pregnancy. But such legislation is not before us, and I think the Court today [has] demonstrated that these state interests cannot constitutionally support the broad abridgment of personal liberty worked by [the] Texas law. Accordingly, I join the Court's opinion holding that that law is invalid under the [Due Process Clause].

Mr. Justice DOUGLAS [joining the opinions in Doe v. Bolton, the Georgia case below, as well as in Roe v. Wade].[1]

[These cases] involve the right of privacy. [The] Ninth Amendment obviously does not create federally enforceable rights [but] a catalogue of [the rights acknowledged by the Ninth Amendment] includes customary, traditional and time-honored rights, amenities, privileges, and immunities that come within the sweep of "the Blessings of Liberty" mentioned in the preamble to the Constitution. Many of them in my view come within the meaning of the term "liberty" as used in the 14th Amendment.

First is the autonomous control over the development and expression of one's intellect, interests, tastes, and personality. These are rights protected by the First Amendment and in my view they are absolute, permitting of no [exceptions]. *Second is freedom of choice in the basic decisions of one's life respecting marriage, divorce, procreation, contraception, and the education and upbringing of children.* These ["fundamental"] rights, unlike those protected by the First Amendment, are subject to some control by the [police power].[2] *Third is the freedom to care for one's health and person, freedom from bodily restraint or compulsion, freedom to walk, stroll, or loaf.* These rights, though fundamental, are likewise subject to regulation on a showing of ["compelling state interest"]. [A] woman is free to make the basic decision whether to bear an unwanted child. [Childbirth] may deprive a woman of her preferred life style and force upon her a radically different and undesired future. [Such] reasoning is, however, only the beginning of the problem. The State has interests to protect. [While] childbirth endangers the lives of some women, voluntary abortion at any time and place regardless of medical standards would impinge on a rightful concern of society. The woman's health is part of that concern; as is the life of the fetus after quickening. These concerns justify the State in treating the procedure as [a medical one].[3]

Mr. Justice WHITE, with whom Mr. Justice REHNQUIST joins, dissenting [in Doe v. Bolton as well as in Roe v. Wade].

At the heart of the controversy in these cases are those recurring pregnancies that pose no danger whatsoever to the life or health of the mother but are nevertheless unwanted for any one or more of a variety of reasons—convenience, family planning, economics, dislike of children, the embarrassment of illegitimacy, etc. The common claim before us is that for any one of such reasons, or for no reason at all, and without asserting or claiming any threat to life or health, any woman is entitled to an abortion at her request if she is able to find a medical advisor willing to undertake the procedure. The Court for the most part sustains this position: During the period prior to the time the fetus becomes viable, the Constitution of the United States values the convenience, whim or caprice of the putative mother more than the life or potential life of the fetus; the Constitution, therefore, guarantees the right to an abortion as against any state law or policy seeking to protect the fetus from an abortion not prompted by more compelling reasons of the mother. [I] dissent. I find nothing in the language or history of the Constitution to support the Court's

---

1. Another concurring opinion applicable to both cases, by Chief Justice BURGER, is omitted.

2. My Brother Stewart [says] that our decision in Griswold reintroduced substantive due process that had been rejected in Ferguson v. Skrupa. [Decisions such as Griswold, Pierce and Meyer], with all respect, have nothing to do with substantive due process. One may think they are not peripheral rights to other rights that are expressed in the Bill of Rights. But that is not

enough to bring into play the protection of [substantive due process]. [Footnote by Justice Douglas.]

3. Later in his opinion, in commenting on the Georgia statute, Justice Douglas stated that a legislature may not equate "all phases of maturation preceding birth." One of the reasons for the law's overbreadth was accordingly that "it equates the value of embryonic life immediately after conception with the worth of life immediately before birth."

judgment. The Court simply fashions and announces a new constitutional right for pregnant mothers and, with scarcely any reason or authority for its action, invests that right with sufficient substance to override most existing state abortion statutes. The upshot is that the people and the legislatures of the 50 States are constitutionally disentitled to weigh the relative importance of the continued existence and development of the fetus on the one hand against a spectrum of possible impacts on the mother on the other hand. As an exercise of raw judicial power, the Court perhaps has authority to do what it does today; but in my view its judgment is an improvident and extravagant exercise of the power of [judicial review]. [In] a sensitive area such as this, involving as it does issues over which reasonable men may easily and heatedly differ, I cannot accept the Court's exercise of its clear power of choice by interposing a constitutional barrier to state efforts to protect human life and by investing mothers and doctors with the constitutionally protected right to exterminate it. This issue, for the most part, should be left with the people and to the political processes the people have devised to govern their [affairs].

Mr. Justice REHNQUIST, dissenting.[1]

[I] have difficulty in concluding [that] the right of "privacy" is involved in this case. [Texas] bars the performance of a medical abortion by a licensed physician on a plaintiff such as Roe. A transaction resulting in an operation such as this is not "private" in the ordinary usage of that word. Nor is the "privacy" which the Court finds here even a distant relative of the [Fourth Amendment freedom from searches and seizures]. If the Court means by the term "privacy" no more than that the claim of a person to be free from unwanted state regulation of consensual transactions may be a form of "liberty" protected by the 14th Amendment, there is no doubt that similar claims have been upheld in our earlier decisions on the basis of that liberty. I agree [that "liberty"] embraces more than the rights found in the Bill of Rights. But that liberty is not guaranteed absolutely against deprivation, but only against deprivation without due process of law. The test traditionally applied in the area of social and economic legislation is whether or not a law such as that challenged has a rational relation to a valid state objective. [Lee Optical.] [If] the Texas statute were to prohibit an abortion even where the mother's life is in jeopardy, I have little doubt that such a statute would lack a rational relation to a valid state objective under the test stated in [Lee Optical]. But the Court's sweeping invalidation of any restrictions on abortion during the first trimester is impossible to justify under that [standard].

The Court eschews the history of the 14th Amendment in its reliance on the "compelling state interest" test. But the Court adds a new wrinkle to this test by transporting it from the legal considerations associated with the [Equal Protection Clause] to this case arising under the [Due Process Clause]. While the Court's opinion quotes from the dissent of Mr. Justice Holmes in [Lochner], the result it reaches is more closely attuned to the majority opinion of Mr. Justice Peckham in that case. As in Lochner and similar cases applying substantive due process standards to economic and social welfare legislation, the adoption of the compelling state interest standard will inevitably require this Court to examine the legislative policies and pass on the wisdom of these policies in the very process of deciding whether a particular state interest put forward may or may not be "compelling." The decision here to break the term of pregnancy into three distinct terms and to outline the permissible restrictions the State may impose in each one, for example, partakes more of judicial legislation than it does of a determination of the intent of the drafters of the

---

1. Justice Rehnquist also submitted a separate, brief dissent in Doe v. Bolton, the Georgia case below.

14th Amendment. The fact that a majority of the [States] have had restrictions on abortions for at least a century is a strong indication, it seems to me, that the asserted right to an abortion is not "so rooted in the traditions and conscience of our people as to be ranked as fundamental" [Snyder v. Massachusetts, 291 U.S. 97 (1934)]. Even today, when society's views on abortion are changing, the very existence of the debate is evidence that the "right" to an abortion is not so universally accepted as the appellants would have us believe. To reach its result the Court necessarily has had to find within the scope of the 14th Amendment a right that was apparently completely unknown to the drafters of the Amendment. By the time of the adoption of the 14th Amendment in 1868, there were at least 36 laws enacted by state or territorial legislatures limiting abortion. [The] only conclusion possible from this history is that the drafters did not intend to have the 14th Amendment withdraw from the States the power to legislate with respect to this [matter].

DOE v. BOLTON, 410 U.S. 179 (1973), was the companion case to Roe v. Wade. The Georgia abortion law attacked in Doe—unlike the traditional ones invalidated in Roe—was a statute with "a modern cast," enacted in 1968, patterned after the American Law Institute's Model Penal Code, and similar to laws enacted by about one-fourth of the states. Nevertheless, the Court invalidated substantial portions of the Georgia statute. Georgia law made noncriminal an abortion performed by a licensed physician when, "based upon his best clinical judgment," an abortion was necessary because continued pregnancy would endanger the life or seriously injure the health of a pregnant woman; or the fetus would likely be born with serious defects; or if the pregnancy had resulted from rape. In addition to a requirement that the patient must be a Georgia resident, the scheme imposed procedural conditions regarding hospital accreditation and medical judgments beyond that of the performing physician. The three-judge District Court invalidated the statutory reference to the three situations in which the attending physician might undertake an abortion (leaving only the bare reference to "his best clinical judgment"), but sustained the procedural requirements regarding "manner of performance" of an abortion, relying partly on the state interest in the protection of a *potential of independent human existence.*" Justice BLACKMUN's majority opinion upheld the "best clinical judgment" provision but struck down the procedural conditions as well as the residence requirement. The Court rejected the argument that the lower court's interpretation of the provisions governing the physician's judgment had rendered the statute unconstitutionally vague. As the Court read the remaining reference to "best clinical judgment," it required the exercise of professional judgment "in the light of *all* the attendant circumstances. He is not now restricted to the three situations originally specified": judgment "may be exercised in light of all factors—physical, emotional, psychological, familial, and the woman's age—relevant to the well-being of the patient."

The three challenged procedural requirements ran into a variety of constitutional obstacles. (1) In striking down the requirement that abortion be performed in a hospital accredited by JCAH (Joint Commission on Accreditation of Hospitals), the Court invoked the 1957 equal protection ruling in Morey v. Doud (p. 607 below).[1] It insisted that "the State must show more than it has in order to prove that only the full resources of a licensed hospital, rather than those of some other appropriately licensed institution, satisfy [the] health interests." (2) The second requirement, requiring prior approval for an abortion by the hospital staff abortion committee, was also struck down. The

---

1. Morey v. Doud was overruled in 1976, in New Orleans v. Dukes (p. 607 below).

Court could find "no constitutionally justifiable pertinence" for that requirement. Committee review after the physician's approval would be review "once removed from diagnosis" and "basically redundant." No other surgical procedure required a similar review. Accordingly, the requirement was "unduly restrictive of the patient's rights and needs." (3) The final invalid procedural condition required "confirmation [of the abortion judgment] by two Georgia-licensed physicians in addition to the recommendation of the pregnant woman's own consultant (making under the statute, a total of six physicians involved, including the three on the hospital's abortion committee)." The Court concluded that the attending physician's "best clinical judgment" "should be sufficient." Though the reasons for the confirmation step were "perhaps apparent," "they are insufficient to withstand constitutional challenge." No other surgical procedure required similar confirmation. "Required acquiescence by co-practitioners has no rational connection with a patient's needs and unduly infringes on the physician's right to practice." [2]

ROE v. WADE AND THE LEGITIMATE SOURCES OF CONSTITUTIONAL VALUES

1. *The protected personal interest: "Privacy," "autonomy," and Roe.* What *is* the "privacy" right recognized in Roe? [1] Justice Blackmun finds the right of privacy "broad enough to encompass a woman's decision whether or not to terminate her pregnancy." It is not an "absolute" right, but neither is it one that can be overridden simply by merely "rational" state legislation. Rather, it is a prima facie, specially protected, qualified right to have an abortion that is subject to regulation only on the showing of a "compelling" state interest. What aspect of "privacy" explains this powerful interest? The interests in protecting the home against intrusions or in the marital relationship or in avoiding disclosures of information seem inapplicable here: as the Court recognizes, the situation here "is inherently different from marital intimacy, or bedroom possession of obscene material, or marriage, or procreation, or education" with which cases from Meyer to Eisenstadt were concerned. Is the relevant interest then that in personal "autonomy" of choice about performing acts or undergoing experiences? Yet Justice Blackmun expressed doubt that the claim "that one has an unlimited right to do with one's body as one pleases bears a close relationship to the right of privacy previously articulated in the Court's decisions." But surely the autonomy aspects of privacy have additional force after Roe. Roe involves not only the interest of the woman but some concern for the fetus—what the Court calls the state's "important and legitimate interest in protecting the potentiality of human life." That suggests that an autonomy claim should be even stronger when no other competing personal

---

2. Doe v. Bolton also struck down the requirement that the patient must be a Georgia resident. Justice Blackmun relied on the Privileges and Immunities Clause of Art. IV, § 2 (recall p. 307 above).

The post-Roe and Doe abortion decisions are noted below, beginning at p. 536.

1. Recall the questions about "privacy" in Griswold, at p. 514 above.

There has been extensive commentary on Roe and on the broader problems of constitutional interpretation it raises. For a particularly powerful criticism of the case, more elaborate than those in the dissenting opinions in Roe, see Ely,

"The Wages of Crying Wolf: A Comment on Roe v. Wade," 82 Yale L.J. 920 (1973). For a defense of the decision, see Heymann & Barzelay, "The Forest and the Trees: Roe v. Wade and Its Critics," 53 B.U.L.Rev. 765 (1973). See also Perry, "Abortion, the Public Morals, and the Police Power: The Ethical Function of Substantive Due Process," 23 U.C.L.A. L.Rev. 689 (1976), and Epstein, "Substantive Due Process by Any Other Name: The Abortion Cases," 1973 Sup.Ct.Rev. 159. (See also the sampling of the literature on the problems of interpretive methodology raised by Roe and its progeny, in note 5 below.)

interest, actual or potential, is involved—when only the claimant's body or life style, or only private consensual behavior is involved. But see note 6 below.

2. *"Balancing" the competing interests.* The Court finds that the woman's prima facie right to abort her pregnancy can be defeated only by "compelling" state interests. Justice Blackmun notes two relevant state interests: protecting the woman's health; and "protecting the potentiality of human life" of the fetus. At differing points in the trimester scheme, those interests become sufficiently "compelling" to justify state restraints. Consider how the Court determine when these interests become "compelling." Is it helpful to discuss whether the fetus is a "person" within the 14th Amendment—or within any other provision of the Constitution? Is it accurate to say: "We need not resolve the difficult question of when life begins"? Must not the Court at least determine when "the potentiality of human life" represents a sufficiently strong moral claim to justify curtailment of the woman's interest in autonomy? Justice Blackmun states that Texas may not, "by adopting one theory of life," "override the rights of the pregnant woman that are at stake." Yet Justice Blackmun also notes that there is wide disagreement, in medicine and philosophy and law, about when life begins. Why should not that lack of consensus lead the Court to defer to, rather than invalidate, the state's judgment?[2] Can the Court's judgment be supported by anything other than a judicial authority to infuse a particular set of moral values into the Constitution? Is it possible to articulate a more confining, disciplined approach to substantive due process? (Note the suggestions for emphasizing "traditional values" as a core ingredient, explored in the context of the family relations cases at p. 550 below.)

3. *Is Roe distinguishable from Lochner?* Is Roe v. Wade more justifiable than the value-laden interventions of the Lochner era? Are the judicially articulated values of Roe more defensible? Can it be argued that Roe—rather than being more defensible than Lochner, or at least as defensible—is even *less* defensible? John Hart Ely makes such an argument in "The Wages of Crying Wolf: A Comment on Roe v. Wade," 82 Yale L.J. 920 (1973). He insists that the "general philosophy of constitutional adjudication" is the same in Roe as in Lochner. To argue that noneconomic rights such as the right to abort a pregnancy accord more closely with "this generation's idealization of America"[3] does not help to distinguish Lochner: it was "precisely" the point of the Lochner philosophy, Ely argues, to "grant unusual protection to those 'rights' that somehow *seem* most pressing, regardless of whether the Constitution suggests any special solicitude for them." Ely goes on to argue, moreover, that Roe may be a "more dangerous precedent" than Lochner. At least the cases of

2. Compare Laurence Tribe's suggestion that the result of Roe v. Wade may be supportable on other grounds. In "Foreword: Toward a Model of Roles in the Due Process of Life and Law," 87 Harv.L.Rev. 1 (1973), he argued that "some types of choices ought to be remanded, on principle, to private decision-makers unchecked by substantive governmental control." As he viewed Roe in his 1973 article, the Court was not choosing simply between abortion and continued pregnancy, but "instead *choosing among alternative allocations of decisionmaking authority.*" And he suggested that the religion clauses of the First Amendment bar legislators from making judgments about potential life because, given the nature of the problem, "views of organized religious groups have come to play a pervasive role" in legislative considerations of that issue. Does Tribe's general "role allocation" approach help justify substantive due process adjudication?

Subsequently, Tribe said that he was not satisfied with that explanation of Roe. He suggested another one: the right of the judiciary to intervene when moral consensus is in flux, to permit a new moral consensus to evolve. (See, e.g., "Structural Due Process," 10 Harv.Civ.Rts.-Civ. Lib.L.Rev. 269 (1975), "Childhood, Suspect Classifications, and Conclusive Presumptions," 39 Law & Contemp.Prob. 8 (1975). Cf. Tribe, American Constitutional Law (1978).) Is principled justification for such judicial intervention possible? Can the existence of instability in society's consensus argue *for* rather than *against* judicial intervention? Recall the Holmesian arguments for withdrawal from the interventionism of the Lochner era.

3. That phrase is from Karst & Horowitz, "Reitman v. Mulkey: A Teleophase of Substantive Equal Protection," 1967 Sup.Ct.Rev. 39.

the Lochner era "did us the favor of sowing the seeds of their destruction." Lochner era invalidations rested either on the illegitimacy of the legislative goal or the lack of a "plausible argument" that legislative means furthered the permissible end. By contrast, Roe's rejection of the legislative judgment "takes neither of these forms." The state interest in protecting potential life is not denied, and the efficacy of the means is not questioned. Instead, Roe simply announces that the "goal is not important enough to sustain the restriction." Unlike the Lochner era cases, "Roe's 'refutation' of the legislative judgment [is] *not* obviously wrong, for the substitution of one nonrational judgment for another [can] be labeled neither wrong nor right. The problem with Roe is not so much that it bungles the question it sets itself, but rather that it sets itself a question the Constitution has not made the Court's business." [4] Is Ely's criticism persuasive?

4.   *The difference between Roe and Griswold (and other Warren Court decisions).* Ely also argues that Roe is even less defensible than Griswold. Does that depend upon how Griswold is read? Ely reads it as being a case "about likely invasions of the privacy of the bedroom," not one "directly enshrining a right to contraception." He finds "a general right of privacy" a legitimate constitutional inference, *"so long as some care is taken in defining the sort of right the inference will support."* In Griswold, the contraceptives use law was invalid because its enforcement ordinarily required "prying into the privacy of the home." According to Ely, in short, a general right of privacy regarding "governmental snooping" is justifiable; a general right of autonomy—"the freedom to live one's life without governmental interference"—is not, and was not asserted in Griswold. Does that reading of Griswold adequately take account of what Ely concedes to be "vague and openended" passages in Griswold?[5]

Can Roe v. Wade be criticized without calling into question many of the interventionist decisions of the Warren Court? (See especially the "new equal protection" decisions in the next chapter.) Ely insists that, despite the problems of some Warren Court opinions, their results can all be justified more persuasively than Roe: "What is frightening about Roe is that this super-protected right is not inferable from the language of the Constitution, the framers' thinking respecting the specific problem in issue, any general value derivable from the provisions they included, or the nation's governmental structure. Nor is it explainable in terms of the unusual political impotence of the group judicially protected vis-à-vis the interest that legislatively prevailed over it.[6]

---

4. See also Ely, "Foreword: On Discovering Fundamental Values," 92 Harv.L.Rev. 5 (1978), and Ely, Democracy and Distrust, chap. 3 (1980).

5. Compare the broader reading of Griswold in Eisenstadt and later cases, as noted at p. 514 above.

6. The reference here is to the rationale of Stone's Carolene Products footnote, p. 473 above, justifying special protection for "discrete and insular minorities" that do not receive adequate consideration in the political process. Ely argues that, "even assuming that that approach can be given principled content," it is only applicable to "those interests which, *as compared with the interest to which they have been subordinated,* constitute minorities unusually incapable of protecting themselves." He adds: "Compared with men, women may constitute such a 'minority'; compared with the unborn, they do not. I'm not sure I'd know a discrete and insular minority if I saw one, but confronted with a multiple choice question requiring me to designate (a) women or

(b) fetuses as one, I'd expect no credit for the former answer."

But see Karst, "Book Review," 89 Harv.L. Rev. 1028 (1976) (in the course of commenting on this section in a previous edition of this casebook): "[The] implicit message [is] that the issue of process and technique are *the* issues worth considering. [But what] is happening in these cases is a constitutional revolution comparable in scope and social importance to the Supreme Court's 1937 abdication from supervising economic regulation, and its intervention [to] secure the recognition of black Americans as fully participating members of the national community. Not merely the sex discrimination cases, but the cases on conception, abortion, and illegitimacy [p. 678] as well, present various faces of a single issue: the roles women are to play in our society. This is a *constitutional* issue, perhaps the most important of the 1970's. [It] is simply inconceivable that the majority Justices in Roe were indifferent to the question of 'woman's role.'" See also Karst, "Foreword: Equal Citi-

And that, I believe, [is] a charge that can responsibly be leveled at no other decision of the past twenty years. At times the inferences the Court has drawn from the values the Constitution marks for special protection have been controversial, even shaky, but never before has its sense of an obligation to draw one been so obviously lacking." [7]

5. *Roe and "noninterpretive" modes of adjudication.* Ely's criteria in criticizing Roe and distinguishing it from interventionist Warren era decisions once again suggest a pervasive problem of judicial review—a problem most acutely raised by the substantive due process cases in this chapter. Are those criteria the right ones? Must constitutional decisionmaking be "interpretive" rather than "noninterpretive"? [8] Must the Court limit itself to the sources of values Ely lists: is the Court's authority limited to values derived from text, history, structure, and perhaps, Stone's political process rationale? [9] Or does that unduly confine the Court?

For an argument that "noninterpretive" modes of adjudication *are* legitimate, see Grey, "Do We Have an Unwritten Constitution?" 27 Stan.L.Rev. 703 (1975). My colleague Thomas Grey disagrees with my colleague John Ely's type of criticism of Roe and with the Marbury v. Madison-Justice Black heritage of the "pure interpretive model" on which it rests. [10] Grey suggests

zenship Under the Fourteenth Amendment," 91 Harv.L.Rev. 1 (1977) (noting that abortion is "also a feminist issue, an issue going to women's position in society"), and Law, "Rethinking Sex and the Constitution," 132 U.Pa.L.Rev. 955 (1984) (emphasizing that "laws governing reproduction implicate equality concerns" and noting that "restrictions on access to abortion plainly oppress women"). These articles, like Karst's 1977 comment, are part of the growing body of literature tying the substantive due process issues raised in cases such as Roe to the sex discrimination ones considered in the next, equal protection chapter. See the additional materials at p. 642 below.

7. See also Ely's comment that Roe is "a very bad decision. Not because it will perceptively weaken the Court—it won't; and not because it conflicts with either my idea of progress or what the evidence suggests is society's—it doesn't. It is bad because it is bad constitutional law, or rather because it is *not* constitutional law and gives almost no sense of an obligation to try to be."

8. Recall the introductory comments on the "interpretive-noninterpretive" debate (and the difficulties of those labels as bases for categorization) in chap. 1, at p. 20 above.

9. Since his 1973 criticism of Roe, Ely has developed an elaborate approach that would allow considerable judicial intervention. Though he continues to reject "fundamental values" interpretation, he argues that unenumerated constitutional rights *were* contemplated (as shown, e.g., by the Ninth Amendment). But he insists that unspecified rights should *not* be open-ended ones; instead, they should be limited by an analysis akin to the framework of the Carolene Products footnote. He advocates a "representation-reinforcing" approach that would emphasize the maintaining of open political processes and the remedying of "malfunctions" that deny effective participation to minorities. See Ely, "Toward a

Representation-Reinforcing Mode of Judicial Review," 37 Md.L.Rev. 451 (1978), and, especially, Ely, Democracy and Distrust (1980).

10. For example, in his 1975 essay Grey took issue with Ely's statement: "A neutral and durable principle may be a thing of beauty and a joy forever. But if it lacks connection with any value the Constitution marks as special, it is not a constitutional principle and the Court has no business imposing it." Grey cited as other examples of "interpretive" criticism Bork, "Neutral Principles and Some First Amendment Problems," 47 Ind.L.J. 1 (1971) ("[T]he choice of 'fundamental values' by the Court cannot be justified. The judge must stick close to the text and the history, and their implications, and not construct new rights"), and Linde, "Judges, Critics, and the Realist Tradition," 82 Yale L.J. 227 (1972) ("The judicial responsibility begins and ends with determining the present scope and meaning of a decision that the nation, at an earlier time, articulated and enacted into constitutional text"). Grey did, however, distinguish the "interpretive" model from "literalism." For example, he includes inferences from structures and relationships within the "interpretive model." But the common denominator of all "unduly narrow," "purely interpretive" models, he finds, is the insistence "that the only norms used in constitutional adjudication must be those inferable from the text"; the interpretive model does not authorize courts "to articulate and apply contemporary norms not demonstrably expressed or implied by the Framers."

More recently, Grey has repented his origination of the "interpretive-noninterpretive" distinction, in "The Constitution as Scripture," 37 Stan. L.Rev. —— (1985). He now believes that that distinction "distorts the debate": "If the current interest in interpretive theory, or hermeneutics, does nothing else, at least it makes evident that the concept of interpretation is broad enough to encompass any plausible mode of constitutional

that the Court is not limited to enforcing "norms derived from the written Constitution": it may "also enforce principles of liberty and justice when the normative content of those principles is not to be found within the four corners of our founding document." He argues that "there was an original understanding, both implicit and textually expressed [in the Ninth Amendment], that unwritten higher law principles had constitutional status," and he claims that the courts have "enforced unwritten constitutional principles" from the beginning. He adds that an "extraordinarily radical purge of established constitutional doctrine would be required if we candidly and consistently applied the pure interpretive model." He recognizes a number of difficulties with the open avowal of the "noninterpretive" approach, especially: "Conceding the natural-rights origins of our Constitution, does not the erosion and abandonment of the 18th century ethics and epistemology on which the natural rights theory was founded require the abandonment of the mode of judicial review flowing from that theory? Is a 'fundamental law' judicially enforced in a climate of historical and cultural relativism the legitimate offspring of a fundamental law which its exponents felt expressed rationally demonstrable, universal and immutable human rights?"

Is it possible to develop a "legitimate pedigree of noninterpretive judicial review"? Can the Court's judicial review authority be defended on grounds other than the interpretive approach of Marbury v. Madison? Would a modern "natural rights" authority for the Court be within its institutional competence? Can a "higher law-natural rights" approach be reconciled with democratic theory? Is there a sufficient basis for finding a natural rights approach incorporated in the Constitution as a whole, or in the Ninth Amendment, or in the 14th Amendment? What guidance for judicial judgment can be articulated if a natural rights approach is openly adopted? As the post-Roe cases which follow indicate, the modern Court is clearly committed to substantive due process, "fundamental values" adjudication—at least in selected areas. That development in turn has been a major spur in producing the enormous flow of modern literature on the "interpretivist-noninterpretivist" dispute and on the proper sources for "noninterpretive" decisionmaking. These questions, then, are of pressing contemporary relevance.[11]

---

adjudication." (See Brest, "The Misconceived Quest for the Original Understanding," 60 B.U.L.Rev. 204 (1980).) Grey adds: "We are all interpretivists; and the real arguments are not over whether judges should stick to interpreting, but over what they should interpret and what interpretive attitudes they should adopt. Repenting past errors, I will therefore use the less misleading labels 'textualists' and 'supplementers' for, respectively, those who consider the text the sole legitimate source of operative norms in constitutional adjudication, and those who accept supplementary sources of constitutional law." Is that revision in terminology truly helpful? Pure "textualists," as commonly understood, is in any event a very underpopulated subgroup these days. (See also the next footnote.) Grey also identifies a recent development of a "third and fastgrowing group of constitutional theorists"— the "rejectionists," who argue that neither approach is satisfactory, since "the text if read with an appropriately generous notion of context provides as lively a constitution as the most activist judge might need." The rejectionist position, according to Grey, "summons sophisticated notions of the nature of interpretation in its support, and gains further appeal from the ennui

that the standard debate has come to induce in all but its most obsessive practitioners." Grey himself argues that, "for reasons that are largely political, we should reject rejectionism." Grey lists, among the "rejectionists," Wellington, "History and Morals in Constitutional Adjudication," 97 Harv.L.Rev. 326 (1983), as well as Perry's revised position, noted in the next footnote.

11. For a useful summary of the modern range of noninterpretivist arguments, see Wiseman, "The New Supreme Court Commentators: The Principled, the Political and the Philosophical," 10 Hastings Const.L.Q. 315 (1983). For critiques of noninterpretivism, see, e.g., Van Alstyne, "Interpreting *This* Constitution: The Unhelpful Contributions of Special Theories of Judicial Review," 35 U.Fla.L.Rev. 209 (1983), and Monaghan, "Our Perfect Constitution," 56 N.Y. U.L.Rev. 353 (1981). See also, generally, Tushnet, "Following the Rules Laid Down: A Critique of Interpretivism and Neutral Principles," 96 Harv.L.Rev. 781 (1983), Bennett, "Objectivity in Constitutional Law," 132 U.Pa.L. Rev. 445 (1984), Posner, "The Meaning of Judicial Self-Restraint," 59 Ind.L.J. 1 (1983), Sedler,

The implications of Roe and Griswold: Private autonomy and public morality.

The individual interest in autonomy. Has a basis for a fundamental general interest in personal autonomy now been established? Griswold arguably involved less than that (especially if it had been limited to the intrusion-into-the-home rationale); but Roe involves more than that—not only the pregnant woman's interest, but also that of the potential life of the fetus. But do the Griswold and Roe opinions and their general statements suggest the basis for a constitutionally recognized right of private autonomy—of private choice in performing acts or undergoing experiences—so long as there is no demonstrable harm to others? What varieties of laws would be threatened by recognition of such a right? Claims to autonomy have been advanced not only in Roe but in a wide range of other contexts. For example, should such a right apply to regulations of consensual sexual behavior? Note the Court's rejection of such a claim in Doe v. Commonwealth's Attorney (1976; p. 559 below). Regulations of dress and hair style? Note the Court's rejection of such a claim in Kelley v. Johnson (1976; p. 561 below). Requirements that motorcyclists wear helmets, see Note, "Motorcycle Helmets and the Constitutionality of Self-Protective Legislation," 30 Ohio St.L.J. 355 (1969)? Prohibitions of the possession or use of marijuana, see Comment, "The California Marijuana Possession [Statute]," 19 Hast.L.J. 758 (1968)? Access to nontoxic but unproven drugs such as Laetrile by cancer patients? [12] See generally Henkin, "Privacy and Autonomy," 74 Colum.L.Rev. 1410 (1974).

As the post-Roe decisions below indicate, the Court's considerable interventionism since Roe has fallen far short of any general recognition of a "fundamental value" in individual autonomy. Instead, the Court has used the Roe methodology to protect a selected number of "fundamental values." It is often unclear what animates the Court's selection of some, and rejection of other, values as "fundamental." A process rationale does not explain the post-Roe developments: as Ely has said, "No Carolene Products Court this." And as he has also commented, the Burger Court's "value-imposition methodology" has been manifested "principally though not exclusively in the 'area' (at least the Court sees it as an area) of sex-marriage-childbearing-childrearing—complete with all the apparent inconsistency [to] which such a 'we'll protect it because it seems important' approach is unusually susceptible." [13] True, some areas have

---

"The Legitimacy Debate in Constitutional Adjudication: An Assessment and a Different Perspective," 44 Ohio St.L.J. 93 (1983), Brest, "The Fundamental Rights [Controversy]," 90 Yale L.J. 1063 (1981), and Bobbitt, Constitutional Fate: Theory of the Constitution (1982).

A controversial argument for noninterpretive review appears in Perry, The Constitution, the Courts, and Human Rights (1982). Among the large amount of commentary generated by Perry's approach, see especially Symposium, "Judicial Review and the Constitution—The Text and Beyond," 8 U.Dayton L.Rev. 443 (1983). More recently, however, Perry has apparently moved from noninterpretivism to the third, "rejectionist" camp described in Grey's 1985 article noted in the preceding footnote. See Perry, "A Theory of Constitutional Interpretation," S.Cal.L.Rev. ___ (1985). Note also the recent interest in literary theory as a guide to problems of interpretation in constitutional law, reflected in some of the articles cited above. By contrast to that approach, there have been a growing number of arguments that, as Grey puts it, "scripture is more likely than literature to be an illuminating analog to law." In addition to Perry's 1985

article, he points to Levinson, " 'The Constitution' in American Civil Religion," 1979 Sup.Ct. Review 123. See also, on the analogy to theology, Cover, "Foreword: Nomos and Narrative," 97 Harv.L.Rev. 4 (1983), and Burt, "Constitutional Law and the Teaching of the Parables," 93 Yale L.J. 455 (1984). (The bibliography in this footnote is by no means exhaustive.)

12. Cf. United States v. Rutherford, 442 U.S. 544 (1979).

13. Ely, "Foreword: On Discovering Fundamental Values," 92 Harv.L.Rev. 5 (1978). Ely adds: "The Court has offered little assistance to one's understanding of what it is that makes all this a unit. Instead, it has generally contented itself with lengthy and undifferentiated string [cites]. There's no trick to finding some connections among these subjects. [You] can say a bunch of words, but a constitutional connection [should] require something more than this."

For a stimulating response to Ely's question about what "makes all this a unit," see Karst, "The Freedom of Intimate Association," 89 Yale L.J. 624 (1980). Karst urges the Court to acknowledge a "presumptive freedom of intimate

become quite regular occasions for heightened scrutiny. For example, extraordinary protection of individual rights in family contexts has become commonplace, as developed at p. 550 below. But if "sex" has become a part of the protected "area," it has certainly not encompassed all consensual sexual behavior, as the homosexuality decisions at p. 559 below, illustrate.[14]

    b. *The state interest in morality.* What legitimate countervailing governmental interests justify laws such as those noted at the beginning of this note? Are they constitutionally legitimate state interests? Is there a legitimate interest in preventing an individual from doing harm to himself or herself, or in regulating private consensual conduct deemed to be "immoral"? What, if anything, justifies the regulation of "morality"? Recall Justice Harlan's discussion (at p. 508 above) of Connecticut's claim that use of contraceptives could be banned "to protect the moral welfare of its citizenry": though Justice Harlan found the means impermissible, he suggested that the "morality" end was legitimate. He noted that the police power traditionally included the "morality objective":

association," a freedom he sees as lying behind many of the "recent decisions in the areas of marriage, procreation, and parent-child relationships." He defines "intimate association" as a "close and familiar personal relationship with another that is in the same significant way comparable to a marriage or family relationship." (Note the Court's recognition of a "freedom of intimate association" protected by due process in Roberts v. United States Jaycees (1984; p. 565 below).)

    14. Consider the suggestion in Grey, "Eros, Civilization and the Burger Court," 43 Law & Contemp.Prob. 83 (1980). Grey does not see the Court's decisions regarding sex as endorsing any "Millian" (see footnote 15) individual autonomy interest in sexual behavior. He states: "I believe that the contraception and abortion cases, and Stanley (the obscenity possession case, p. 1073 below) are, like the general run of the Court's decisions in this area, dedicated to the cause of social stability through the reinforcement of traditional institutions, and have nothing to do with the sexual liberation of the individual. The contraception and abortion cases [represent] two standard conservative views: that social stability is threatened by excessive population growth; and that family stability is threatened by unwanted pregnancies, with their accompanying fragile marriages, single-parent families, irresponsible youthful parents, and abandoned or neglected children. The conventions of constitutional adjudication of course demand that the decisions be justified, not on the basis of social stability, but in the language of individual rights. And so they were." True, Roe and Eisenstadt stressed the importance of the choice to the individual; but [the] choice was not sexual but procreational. [The] Court has consistently protected traditional familial institutions, bonds, and authority against the centrifugal forces of an anomic modern society. Where less traditional values have been directly protected [e.g., as to contraception and abortion], the decisions reflect not any Millian glorification of diverse individuality, but the stability-centered concerns of moderate conservative family and population policy."

    Grey adds: "I expect that within a few years fornication and sodomy laws will be found un-

constitutional, on something like the very dogma of the rights of consenting adults to control their own sex lives that the Court has until now so rigorously avoided. But the real reasons for the decisions will have little to do with any notion in the Justices' minds that sexual freedom is essential to the pursuit of happiness. Rather the decisions will respond to the same demands of order and social stability that have produced the contraception and abortion decisions. Thousands of couples are living together today outside of marriage. The fornication laws [stand] in the way of providing a stabilizing legal framework for these unions. [Therefore] those laws will be struck down. [Similarly], the homosexual community is becoming an increasingly public sector of our society. For that community to be governed effectively, it must be recognized as legitimate. [If legislatures do not change their laws, the Court will] step in and play its traditional role as enlightened conservator of the social interest in ordered stability, and will strike down those laws, in the glorious name of the individual."

    Consider an alternative explanation for the Court's decisions in the "sex" area, an alternative considered but rejected by Grey: "The alternative is to see the Court as engaged in the covert promotion of Mill's principle. The failure to carry the principle through, then, must represent a prudential guess that to place the protection of the Constitution behind what most people still reject as unnatural sexual practices would too much strain the Court's limited stock of public good will. Such a theory might indeed explain Doe v. Commonwealth's Attorney [p. 559 below]. Perhaps the Court [was] not ready to risk a foray into the explosive issue of gay rights. But if Mill's principle is in the wings, why have no hints of it appeared in opinions? [I believe] the Supreme Court's attitude toward sexual freedom is quite different from that of the liberal academic supporters of modern Millianism." (Grey's survey of over 40 pieces of law review commentary on Griswold and its progeny between 1965 and 1979 concludes that "almost all found support in the privacy cases for the libertarian position on sexual morals legislation.")

"Indeed to attempt a line between public behavior and that which is purely consensual or solitary would be to withdraw from community concern a range of subjects with which every society in civilized times has found it necessary to deal. Connecticut's judgment is no more demonstrably correct or incorrect than are the varieties of judgment, expressed in law, on marriage and divorce, on adult consensual homosexuality, abortion, and sterilization, or euthanasia and suicide." Can the traditional state interest in private morality nevertheless be found noncompelling under the modes of adjudication reflected in Griswold and Roe? Note the question in Brest, Processes of Constitutional Decisionmaking (1975), chap. 7: "If the Constitution does not enact Herbert Spencer's Social Statics, does it enact John Stuart Mill's On Liberty (1859)?" [15] (Compare the 1973 obscenity cases, p. 1076 below.)

7. *The political reaction to Roe: Proposed constitutional amendments; legislative efforts.* In the wake of Roe, well-publicized efforts to amend the Constitution were launched and several proposals were introduced in Congress. For one echoing Justice Rehnquist's position in his dissent, see the amendment introduced in the House in 1973, providing that nothing in the Constitution shall bar any State "from allowing, regulating, or prohibiting the practice of abortion." (H.J.Res. 427.) Contrast with this "neutral" provision two 1973 proposals in the Senate that are clearly anti-abortion in tendency. S.J.Res. 130, introduced by Senator Helms, sought to protect life "from the moment of conception." And S.J.Res. 119, introduced by Senator Buckley, protects unborn children "at every stage of their biological development," but is inapplicable "in an emergency when a reasonable medical certainty exists that continuation of the pregnancy will cause the death of the mother." [16]

Subsequently, the focus of some of the political responses to Roe shifted from constitutional amendments to legislative action. One type of response was to bar the use of public funds for many types of abortions. In decisions in 1977 and 1980 (p. 543 below), the Court held that such state and federal efforts were constitutional. A second legislative response was unveiled in 1981, when some members of Congress proposed a Human Life Statute, relying on power under § 5 of the 14th Amendment. (See the discussion of this proposal at p. 963 below.) But some "right to life" proponents doubted the constitutionality of such an approach and continued to attack Roe via the constitutional amendment route. The modern amendment proposals have fallen into two categories: first, those embodying a "States Rights" approach; second, those creating a new constitutional right to personhood in the unborn. The proposed amendments embodying a "States Rights" approach generally provide that no right to an abortion is secured by the Constitution; the states are thus left free to adopt restrictions on abortions as they see fit. Those amendments embodying the second approach expand the constitutional definition of "person." The right to personhood is declared variously to attach "from the moment of fertilization" or "conception" or "at any stage of biological development." Some of these proposed "right to life" amendments would permit abortions to prevent the death of the mother; others would not. And some of them would extend the

---

15. Mill's well-known argument elaborated "one very simple principle": "That the sole end to which mankind are warranted, individually or collectively, in interfering with the liberty of action of any of their number is self-protection"; that government may control the individual only "to prevent harm to others"; "His own good, either physical or moral, is not a sufficient warrant. [Over] himself, over his own body and mind, the individual is sovereign." [See also the

bearing of Mill's On Liberty on First Amendment theory, noted at p. 977 below.]

16. Abortion laws have produced controversial decisions around the world in recent years. Note, e.g., a decision by West Germany's Federal Constitutional Court in 1975 reaching a result quite contrary to Roe v. Wade: the German Court, relying on the protection of "life" in the German constitution, struck down a law making abortions more readily available.

right beyond the coverage of the Fifth and 14th Amendments to provide against the deprivation of life by "any person." [17]

8. *The 1980s challenge to (and reaffirmation of) Roe v. Wade on the Court.* A decade after Roe v. Wade (after years of cases carefully scrutinizing and often invalidating restrictions on access to abortions, as reviewed in the next group of notes), the majority had occasion to issue a firm reaffirmation of Roe, in the face of a new and major challenge to that ruling and its trimester framework—a challenge aired in a dissent written by Justice O'Connor, the newest appointee. AKRON v. AKRON CENTER FOR REPRODUCTIVE HEALTH, 462 U.S. 416 (1983). The majority, applying the strict scrutiny announced in Roe, struck down a range of municipal abortion regulations enacted by Akron; the dissenters, applying a more deferential standard, argued that all of the challenged regulations should stand. (The detailed nature and fate of the challenged Akron regulations are considered in the next group of notes.)

Justice POWELL's majority opinion noted that "arguments continue to be made [that] we erred in interpreting the Constitution" in Roe. He responded: "Nonetheless, the doctrine of stare decisis, while perhaps never entirely persuasive on a constitutional question, is a doctrine that demands respect in a society governed by the rule of law. We respect it today, and reaffirm Roe v. Wade." [18] Reviewing Roe, Justice Powell stated that an individual's "freedom of personal choice in matters of marriage and family life" was "central" among the liberties protected by due process and that "Roe was based firmly on this long-recognized and essential element of personal liberty." He also reiterated the basic trimester division set forth in Roe, including the insistence that the state's interest in safeguarding the health of women does not become compelling until "approximately the end of the first trimester" of pregnancy. Although he acknowledged that recent developments have altered some of the underlying premises for that scheme, he thought it unwise to make changes in the constitutional yardsticks. (Contrast the far more central role given to recent medical developments in Justice O'Connor's dissent.)

Justice O'CONNOR's dissent, joined by Justices White and Rehnquist, stopped short of urging an overruling of Roe,[19] but advocated a substantial change in the Court's approach to abortion cases. She claimed that it was apparent from the majority opinion that "neither sound constitutional theory

17. Although the Senate Judiciary Committee took favorable action on a proposed amendment of the "States Rights" variety during the 97th Congress, the proposal was withdrawn by its sponsor (Senator Hatch) before it could be voted on in the late summer of 1982. As modified and approved by a subcommittee in the 98th Congress, the proposal simply read: "A right to abortion is not secured by the Constitution." The full Senate Judiciary Committee deadlocked 9 to 9 on the amendment in April 1983 and sent it to the floor without a recommendation. In June 1983, the Senate rejected it on a 50 to 49 vote, with abortion foes falling 18 votes short of the two-thirds needed for proposing constitutional amendments.

18. He added in a footnote: "There are especially compelling reasons for adhering to stare decisis in applying the principles of Roe v. Wade. That case was considered with special [care]. Since Roe, [the] Court repeatedly and consistently has accepted and applied the basic principle that a woman has a fundamental right to make the highly personal choice whether or not to terminate her pregnancy." In this footnote, Jus-

tice Powell also responded to Justice O'Connor's dissent (which he described as rejecting "the basic premise of Roe and its progeny," although stopping short "of arguing flatly that Roe should be overruled"). Justice Powell's response to Justice O'Connor is noted in footnote 22 to her dissent, below.

19. Justice O'Connor did however air some doubts about the majority's emphasis on precedent: "Although respect for stare decisis cannot be challenged, 'this Court's considered practice [is] not to apply stare decisis as rigidly in constitutional as in nonconstitutional cases.' 'In constitutional questions, when correction depends on amendment and not upon legislative action, this Court throughout its history has freely exercised its power to reexamine the bases of its constitutional decisions.'" That attitude toward precedent helped provide the basis for her position that, even "assuming that there is a fundamental right to terminate a pregnancy in some situations, there is no justification in law or logic for the trimester framework adopted in Roe and employed by the Court today on the basis of stare decisis."

nor our need to decide cases based on the application of neutral principles can accommodate an analytical framework that varies according to the 'stages' of pregnancy, where those stages, and their concomitant standards of review, differ according to the level of medical technology available when a particular challenge to state regulation occurs." She argued that the majority's analysis was "inconsistent both with the [methods] employed in previous cases dealing with abortion, and with the Court's approach to fundamental rights in other areas." She advocated, as a substitute for the strict scrutiny-trimester approach of Roe, that an abortion regulation "is not unconstitutional unless it unduly burdens the right to seek an abortion." [20] She sketched her preferred approach as follows: "In my view, this 'unduly burdensome' standard should be applied to the challenged regulations throughout the entire pregnancy without reference to the particular 'stage' of pregnancy involved. If the particular regulation does not 'unduly burden' the fundamental right, then our evaluation of that regulation is limited to our determination that the regulation rationally relates to a legitimate state purpose. Irrespective of what we may believe is wise or prudent policy in this difficult area, 'the Constitution does not constitute us as 'Platonic Guardians'' nor does it vest in this Court the authority to strike down laws because they do not meet our standards of desirable social policy, "wisdom," or "common sense." ' " [21]

In justifying her opposition to continued reliance on the trimester approach, Justice O'Connor stated: "The Roe framework [is] clearly on a collision course with itself. As the medical risks of various abortion procedures decrease, the point at which the State may regulate for reasons of maternal health is moved further forward to actual childbirth. As medical science becomes better able to provide for the separate existence of the fetus, the point of viability is moved further back toward conception. Moreover, it is clear that the trimester approach violates the fundamental aspiration of judicial decisionmaking through the application of neutral principles. [The] Roe framework is inherently tied to the state of medical technology that exists whenever particular litigation ensues. Although legislatures are better suited to make the necessary factual judgments in this area, the Court's framework forces legislatures, as a matter of constitutional law, to speculate about what constitutes 'accepted medical practice' at any given time. Without the necessary expertise or ability, courts must then pretend to act as science review boards and examine those legislative judgments." [22]

20. As the source of the "unduly burdensome" standard, she cited Bellotti v. Baird (Bellotti I) (1977; note 1 in the next group of notes), as reiterated in Maher v. Roe (1977; an abortion funding case considered in note 3 of the next group of notes).

21. Justice O'Connor was quoting from the dissent of Chief Justice Burger in Plyler v. Doe (1982; in the equal protection chapter below, at p. 799). (Chief Justice Burger was with the majority in the Akron case. The "Platonic Guardians" reference came from Judge Learned Hand and had also been quoted in Justice Black's dissent in Griswold v. Connecticut, above.)

22. In illustrating the bases for her judgment that "technological improvements will move *backward* the point of viability at which the State may proscribe abortions except when necessary to preserve the life and health of the mother," Justice O'Connor noted that, in 1973, at the time of Roe, "viability before 28 weeks was considered unusual." Recent studies, however, "demonstrated increasingly earlier fetal viability. It is

certainly reasonable to believe that fetal viability in the first trimester of pregnancy may be possible in the not too distant future."

Justice Powell countered: "Roe identified the end of the first trimester as the compelling point because until that time—according to the medical literature available in 1973—'mortality in abortion may be less than mortality in normal childbirth.' There is substantial evidence that developments in the past decade, particularly the development of a much safer method for performing second-trimester abortions, have extended the period in which abortions are safer than childbirth. [He cited a medical journal article indicating that abortion may be safer than childbirth up to a gestational age of 16 weeks.] We think it prudent, however, to retain Roe's identification of the beginning of the second trimester as the approximate time at which the State's interest in maternal health becomes sufficiently compelling to justify significant regulation of abortion. We note that the medical evidence suggests that until approximately the end of the

Continuing her attack on the Roe framework, Justice O'Conr and accepting the legitimate state interests acknowledged by Roe, stated that, in her view, "the point at which these in compelling does not depend on the trimester of pregnancy. interests are present *throughout* pregnancy." She added: "The in the Roe framework is apparent: just because the State ha interest in ensuring maternal safety once an abortion may be n than childbirth, it simply does not follow that the State has *no* that point that justifies state regulation to ensure that first-trimester abortions are performed as safely as possible. The state interest in potential human life is likewise extant throughout pregnancy. [Under Roe, that interest does not become compelling until the point of viability.] The difficulty with this analysis is clear: *potential* life is no less potential in the first weeks of pregnancy than it is at viability or afterward. At any stage in pregnancy, there is the *potential* for human life. Although the Court refused [in Roe] to 'resolve the difficult question of when life begins,' the Court chose the point of viability—when the fetus is *capable* of life independent of its mother—to permit the complete proscription of abortion. The choice of viability as a point at which the state interest in *potential* life becomes compelling is no less arbitrary than choosing any point before viability or any point afterward. Accordingly, I believe that the State's interest in protecting potential human life exists throughout the pregnancy." That did not mean that every state regulation must be measured against a state's compelling interests and examined with strict scrutiny. In advocating, as the first step in the proper scrutiny, a determination of whether the State regulation was an "unduly burdensome" interference with the pregnant woman's choice, she insisted that such an initial finding "before heightened scrutiny is applied is not novel in our fundamental-rights jurisprudence, or restricted to the abortion context." [23] Only if the "undue burden" threshold were surmounted should a state be required to justify its regulations under the exacting "compelling state interest" standard. Moreover, even in that first step of the inquiry (regarding "undue burden"), respect for the judgment of the legislature was appropriate. And if no "undue burden" was found, a quite deferential rationale was appropriate. It was that regard for the competence of legislatures that produced her conclusion that all of the challenged Akron regulations should survive judicial scrutiny. [24]

---

first trimester, the State's interest in maternal health would not be served by regulations that restrict the manner in which abortions are performed by a licensed physician. [The] Roe trimester standard [continues] to provide a reasonable legal framework for limiting a State's authority to regulate abortions. Where the State adopts a health regulation governing the performance of abortions during the second trimester, the determinative question should be whether there is a reasonable medical basis for the regulation. The comparison between abortion and childbirth mortality rates may be relevant only where the State employs a health rationale as a justification for a complete prohibition on abortions in certain circumstances."

23. Justice O'Connor gave as illustrations of that standard Rodriguez (1973; equal protection; p. 789 below) and Gibson (1963; First Amendment; p. 1412 below).

24. Justice O'Connor noted in a footnote that the U.S. Solicitor General had argued in the Akron case that the Court should adopt the "unduly burdensome" standard and that, "in doing so, we should 'accord heavy deference to the legislative judgment' in determining what constitutes an 'undue burden.'" She commented: "The 'unduly burdensome' standard is appropriate *not* because it incorporates deference to legislative judgment at the threshold stage of analysis, but rather because of the limited *nature* of the fundamental right that has been recognized in the abortion cases. Although our cases do require that we 'pay careful attention' to the legislative judgment before we invoke strict scrutiny, it is not appropriate to *weigh* the state interests at the threshold stage."

STATE REGULATION OF ABORTIONS AND
CONTRACEPTIVES SINCE ROE v. WADE

Introduction. This group of notes focuses on the Court's handling of a range of state laws (primarily in the abortion area) enacted in response to the Roe ruling and allegedly designed to implement the compelling state interests recognized in Roe. So far, the Court's confrontations with efforts to limit access to abortion and contraceptives have usually produced defeats for the state laws. Typically, the Court has scrutinized the regulations very intensively. In the abortion area the Court has reiterated (and arguably expanded) the central role of the pregnant woman and her doctor in making the abortion decision. The Court's careful scrutiny of state laws is illustrated by its delineation in Akron, above, of the appropriate judicial stance on state and local laws allegedly furthering the interest in protecting the pregnant woman's health. Even though, under Roe, that interest does not become "compelling" until the second trimester, the majority noted in Akron that some regulations, those justified "by important state health objectives," are permissible even in the first trimester; but "even these minor regulations [may] not interfere with physician-patient consultation or with the woman's choice between abortion and childbirth." And with respect to second trimester regulations, when the state's interest in health regulation does become "compelling," the Court insists on strong demonstrations of justification: "The existence of a compelling state interest in health [is] only the beginning of the inquiry. The State's regulation may be upheld only if it is reasonably designed to further that state interest." As the notes below illustrate, a number of regulations have fallen for failure to survive the second step in that inquiry. However, the long series of cases striking down specific regulations of abortion have evoked increasingly strong dissents, culminating in the broad attack on the underpinnings of Roe in the Akron dissent, above.[1] (The most important area in which state power has been sustained rather than struck down is governmental refusals to fund certain abortions, note 3 below.)

1. *Consent requirements.* a. *Spousal consent.* In a number of cases the Court has considered state efforts to require the consent of relatives before a pregnant woman may obtain an abortion. Most cases involved *parental* consent requirements. But in the first major post-Roe abortion decision, the Court examined a requirement of *spousal* consent. Planned Parenthood of Missouri v. Danforth, 428 U.S. 52 (1976).[2] The Missouri provision barred a married woman from obtaining an abortion in most circumstances during the first 12 weeks of pregnancy without her husband's written consent. The 6 to 3 decision invalidated that requirement. Justice Blackmun's majority opinion insisted that "the State cannot delegate authority to any particular person, even the spouse, to prevent abortion" during the first trimester. That view, he acknowledged, made the woman's unilateral choice decisive, despite the husband's "deep and proper concern and interest [in] his wife's pregnancy." But since the woman "is the more directly and immediately affected by the pregnancy, as between the two, the balance weighs in her favor." [3]

---

1. The Court's elaborations of the implications of Roe have had an important general impact on the expansion of modern substantive due process. For example, in the course of passing on requirements that husbands or parents must consent to abortion decisions, the Court has made significant contributions to the expanding constitutionalization of family law—a subject more fully explored below at p. 550.

2. Danforth considered several varieties of regulation raising questions "secondary to those"

in Roe—questions described by the Court as "logical and anticipated corollar[ies]" of Roe. (Other issues raised in Danforth are summarized in the notes that follow.)

3. The dissent was by Justice White, joined by Chief Justice Burger and Justice Rehnquist. He attacked the majority's "delegation of State authority" approach, insisting that there had been no delegation of any power to vindicate the State's interest. Rather, Missouri had simply recognized "that the husband has an interest of

b. *Parental consent.* The role of parents regarding a child's abortion decision has come to the Court in a series of cases. The Court has refused to grant the parents anything resembling a veto power over the child's decision although it has sustained a provision merely requiring notice to the parents before an abortion is performed. The sequence began with the 1976 ruling in Danforth, above. There, the majority struck down a provision requiring an unmarried woman under 18 to obtain the consent of a parent (or a person in loco parentis) as a prerequisite to obtaining an abortion in most circumstances. As with the spousal consent provision, Justice Blackmun's majority opinion insisted that a state could not "give a third party an absolute, and possibly arbitrary, veto over the decision of the physician and his patient to terminate the patient's pregnancy." That did not mean that "every minor, regardless of age or maturity, may give effective consent for termination of her pregnancy." Rather, as he elaborated in a companion case to Danforth,[4] a blanket "parental veto" is "fundamentally different" from one permitting "a mature minor [to] obtain, without undue burden, an order permitting the abortion without parental consultation." In short, the parental consent requirement was unconstitutional only if "it unduly burdens the right to seek an abortion."[5]

Three years later, the Court undertook a fuller examination of state barriers to minors' access to abortions, in BELLOTTI v. BAIRD (BELLOTTI II), 443 U.S. 622 (1979). Once again, the Court struck down the law, with an 8 to 1 division; but the majority split 4 to 4 about the appropriate reasoning. Bellotti involved a Massachusetts effort to reconcile the rights of pregnant women "with the special interest of the State in encouraging an unmarried pregnant minor to seek the advice of her parents" in deciding about an abortion. The law required an unmarried minor to obtain the consent of both parents before she could have an abortion; and, if parental consent was refused, a state judge could authorize the abortion "for good cause shown."[6]

Justice POWELL's "guidelines" opinion announced that a state could involve the parents in a minor's abortion decision only if it also provided an "alternative procedure" (apparently not necessarily a judicial one, although that would presumably be the norm), in order that the parental involvement would not in fact amount to an "absolute, and possibly arbitrary, veto" impermissible under Danforth. He stated that a valid scheme must assure that "every minor [has] the opportunity—if she so desires—to go directly to a court without first consulting or notifying her parents. If she satisfies the court that she is mature and well-informed enough to make intelligently the abortion decision on her own, the court must authorize her to act without parental consultation or consent. If she fails to satisfy the court that she is competent to make this decision independently, she must be permitted to show that an abortion nevertheless would be in her best interest. If the court is persuaded that it is,

---

his own in the life of the fetus which should not be extinguished by the unilateral decision of the wife."

4. The companion case was Bellotti v. Baird (Bellotti I), 428 U.S. 132 (1976).

5. In this aspect of Danforth, Justice Stevens joined the three Justices who had dissented on the spousal consent provision. He argued that this provision was justified by "the State's interest in the welfare of its young citizens." Justice White's dissent, joined by Chief Justice Burger and Justice Rehnquist, emphasized that the provision served the parents', not only the State's, interest and also vindicated the woman's right to decide "whether *or not* to terminate her pregnancy."

6. The majority result was supported by two opinions, each representing the views of four of the Justices. Justice Powell, joined by Chief Justice Burger and Justices Stewart and Rehnquist, wrote very broadly in an attempt to provide "some guidance as to how a State constitutionally may provide for adult involvement—either by parents or a state official such as a judge—in the abortion decisions of minors." (Justice Rehnquist stated that he joined only until "this Court is willing to reconsider" Danforth.) Justice Stevens, joined by Justices Brennan, Marshall and Blackmun, branded that "guidelines" opinion as an "advisory" one addressed to "hypothetical" questions and argued for a narrower disposition, as noted below.

the court must authorize the abortion. If, however, the court is not persuaded by the minor that she is mature or that the abortion would be in her best interest, it may decline to sanction the operation." Moreover, in recognition of the "important state interest in encouraging a family rather than a judicial resolution of a minor's abortion decision," the court could deny the abortion request of an immature minor who had not consulted her parents "if [the court] concludes that her best interests would be served thereby." Alternatively, the court could "defer decision until there is parental consultation in which the court may participate." "But," Justice Powell insisted, "this is the full extent to which parental involvement may be required": "the constitutional right to seek an abortion may not be unduly burdened by state-imposed conditions upon initial access to court." Under these guidelines the Massachusetts law proved defective in two respects: "First, it permits judicial authorization for an abortion to be withheld from a minor who is found by the [court] to be mature and fully competent to make this decision independently. Second, it requires parental consultation or notification in every instance, without affording the pregnant minor an opportunity to receive an independent judicial determination that she is mature enough to consent or that an abortion would be in her best interests." [7]

In arguing for a narrower disposition, Justice STEVENS, joined by Justices Brennan, Marshall and Blackmun, argued that the case was governed by Danforth and added: "[To] the extent this statute differs from that in Danforth, it is potentially even more restrictive of the constitutional right to decide whether or not to terminate a pregnancy." Unlike the law in Danforth, for example, the law here potentially involved the consent of *both* parents. Moreover, authorizing state judges to be alternative sources of consent simply added another risk of "absolute veto over the minors' decisions." He found the judicial involvement "particularly troubling" because it threatened both aspects of privacy recognized in such cases as Whalen v. Roe (1977; p. 564 below)— the interest "in avoiding disclosure of personal matters" and that "in independence in making certain kinds of important decisions." He added: "It is inherent in the right to make the abortion decision that the right may be exercised without public scrutiny in defiance of the contrary opinion of the sovereign or other third parties." Yet the Massachusetts judicial procedure not only involved public scrutiny but also, given the vague "best interest of the minor" standard, risked a decision reflecting "personal and societal values and mores whose enforcement upon the minor [is] fundamentally at odds with privacy interests." [8]

7. In reaching these conclusions, Justice Powell provided an example of the modern Court's exploration of the constitutional status of children, parents, and the family. He commented that, though children have constitutional rights, "the status of minors under the law is unique in many respects. [The] unique role in our society of the family [requires] that constitutional principles be applied with sensitivity and flexibility to the special needs of parents and children. We have recognized three reasons justifying the conclusion that the constitutional rights of children cannot be equated with those of adults: the peculiar vulnerability of children; their inability to make critical decisions in an informed, mature manner; and the importance of the parental role in child-rearing." Commenting on the "tradition of parental authority," he insisted that it was "one of the basic presuppositions" of individual liberty. He noted, however, that the abortion context justified significant cur-

tailment of the traditional parental authority: "The need to preserve the constitutional right and the unique nature of the abortion decision, especially when made by a minor, require a State to act with particular sensitivity when it legislates to foster parental involvement in this matter." Accordingly, though "deference to parents may be permissible with respect to other choices facing a minor, the unique nature and consequences of the abortion decision make it inappropriate to give a third party an absolute and possibly arbitrary, veto over the decision of the physician and his patient to terminate the patient's pregnancy.'" (Note the fuller discussion of family relations at p. 550 below.)

8. Justice White, the sole dissenter, adhered to his Danforth position and argued further that the Massachusetts law was less objectionable than that in Danforth.

UPHELD

One kind of parental involvement that has been sustained by the Court was a parental *notice* requirement. H.L. v. Matheson, 450 U.S. 398 (1981), involved a Utah law requiring physicians to "[n]otify, if possible," the parents or guardian of any minor upon whom an abortion was to be performed. In a narrow ruling, the Court upheld the law as applied to a minor living with and dependent upon her parents (a minor not emancipated by marriage or otherwise), and where there was no showing as to her maturity or her relations with her parents.[9] Chief Justice Burger's majority opinion (in what the dissent described as a "cursory" examination of the merits) found that "the statute plainly serves important state interests, is narrowly drawn to protect only those interests, and does not violate any guarantees of the Constitution." He noted that the law did not involve a veto power over the minor's decision. As applied to immature and dependent minors, the law served "the important considerations of family integrity and protecting adolescents" as well as the "significant" state interest in providing "an opportunity for parents to supply essential medical and other information to a physician." He added that the possibility that the notice requirement might "inhibit some minors from seeking abortions" was no reason to strike it down: "The Constitution does not compel a state to fine-tune its statutes so as to encourage or facilitate abortions."[10] Justice Marshall's dissent, joined by Justices Brennan and Blackmun, insisted that the parental notice requirement "burdens the minor's privacy right" and argued that none of the proffered state justifications warranted "this intrusion, for the statute is not tailored to serve them." He noted, for example, that, rather than "respecting the private realm of family life, the statute invokes the criminal justice machinery of the State in an attempt to influence the interactions within the family."[11]

The Court also considered parental consent requirements in two 1983 decisions. In Akron, above, the majority struck down a requirement that an abortion could be performed on a woman under the age of 15 only if there was written consent of her parents or an order of the court. The Court, relying on Danforth and Bellotti II, emphasized that there was no procedure for an individualized determination of whether a minor was sufficiently mature to make the decision for herself. But in Planned Parenthood Ass'n of Kansas City v. Ashcroft, 462 U.S. 476 (1983), a majority *upheld* a requirement of parental consent or a judicial alternative, because there the judicial procedure comported with the requirement that "the State must provide an alternative procedure whereby a pregnant minor may demonstrate that she is sufficiently mature to make the abortion decision herself or that, despite her immaturity, an abortion would be in her best interests."

9. The lawsuit was initially an on-the-face attack on the law in a class action claiming to represent *all* unmarried minor women, including mature and emancipated ones. But the Court insisted that appellant lacked standing to bring such an overbreadth challenge and she had not shown that she was "mature or emancipated." Chief Justice Burger wrote for the majority. Justice Marshall's dissent, joined by Justices Brennan and Blackmun, argued that appellant did have standing to raise the broad challenge (by analogy to the generous standing rules in First Amendment overbreadth cases, see p. 1148 below).

10. Justice Powell, joined by Justice Stewart, supported the Chief Justice's opinion, but emphasized that it left open the question of the constitutionality of a parental notice requirement as applied to mature minors. In view of the numerous variables affecting minors' abortion decisions, "absolute rules—requiring parental notice in all cases or in none—would create an [undesirable] inflexibility." Justice Stevens, who concurred only in the judgment, thought the law constitutional on its face as applied to *all* minors, even mature ones.

11. Justice Marshall's comments on the asserted state interest in "protecting parental authority and family integrity" are of special interest because of the growing constitutionalization of family law, considered further at p. 550 below. He noted that the thrust of most earlier decisions had been "to protect the privacy of individual families from unwarranted state intrusion. Ironically, [Utah] invoke[s] these decisions in seeking to justify state interference in the normal functioning of the family. [Whatever] its motive, state intervention is hardly likely to resurrect parental authority that the parents themselves are unable to preserve." He was equally unimpressed by the related claim that the laws safeguarded the parents' "reserved right [to] know of the important activities of their children." He argued that, "when the threat to parental authority originates not from the State but from the minor child, invocation of 'reserved' rights of parents cannot sustain blanket state intrusion into family life [such as here]. Such a result [conflicts] with the limits traditionally placed on

2. *Regulations of medical practices.* In Roe v. Wade, the Court recognized compelling state interests, at varying points in a pregnancy, in the health of the mother and in the life of the viable fetus. In response, some state and local governments adopted regulations prescribing medical practices in abortion cases—regulations repeatedly challenged in the Court as unduly burdening the pregnant woman's access to abortions. As early as Doe v. Bolton, the companion case to Roe, the Court struck down several regulations largely relating to hospital care. Since then, the Court has continued to scrutinize regulations of medical practice carefully. In Danforth in 1976, above, the majority invalidated a provision prohibiting abortions by the method known as saline amniocentesis. Although that was the preferred method for abortions after the first trimester at the time the law was passed, the State considered the little used prostaglandin method the safer one. The majority concluded that, in view of the relative unavailability of the State's chosen technique, the requirement was not "a reasonable regulation for the protection of maternal health" but rather an "arbitrary regulation [inhibiting the] vast majority of abortions after the first 12 weeks." The Court also struck down a provision prescribing the physician's duty of care in abortions because, as read by the Court, the provision "impermissibly require[d] the physician to preserve the life and health of the fetus, whatever the stage of pregnancy." [12]

In 1979, in Colautti v. Franklin, 439 U.S. 379 (1979), the majority struck down, on vagueness grounds, a post-Roe law assertedly designed to further the state interest in protecting fetuses potentially able to survive. The state law subjected physicians performing abortions to criminal liability if they failed to follow a statutorily prescribed standard of care when the fetus was "viable" or when there was "sufficient reason to believe that the fetus may be viable." The majority found both the viability determination and the standard of care provision unconstitutionally vague. Emphasizing "the central role of the physician," Justice Blackmun insisted that the challenged scheme "created too many uncertainties about the exercise of medical judgment." He argued that the uncertainty created by the "ambiguous" viability provision was "aggravated by the absence of a scienter requirement with respect to the finding of viability." He also found "impermissibly vague" a standard of care provision requiring the physician to employ the abortion technique offering the greatest possibility of fetal survival, provided that some other technique would not be necessary in order to preserve the life or health of the mother. [13]

The Court's most significant modern encounter with the problem of permissible medical regulations came in 1983, in AKRON v. AKRON CENTER FOR REPRODUCTIVE HEALTH, 462 U.S. 416. In addition to the reaffirmation of (and challenge to) Roe v. Wade occasioned by the Akron litigation (noted at p. 533 above), the case also led the Court to confront a number of specific

parental authority." He added that "parental authority deserves de minimis legal reinforcement where the minor's exercise of a fundamental right is burdened."

12. However, the Court did sustain several other provisions of the law challenged in Danforth: certain record-keeping requirements imposed on physicians and hospitals as well as a definition of "viability." Moreover, the Court upheld the requirement for written, informed consent to an abortion by the pregnant woman during the first 12 weeks of pregnancy, even though no similar consent was required for other surgical procedures. (Compare Akron, below.)

13. A sharp dissent by Justice White, joined by Chief Justice Burger and Justice Rehnquist, charged that the ruling effectively withdrew from

the states "a substantial measure of the power to protect fetal life that was reserved to them in [Roe] and reaffirmed in [Danforth]." As he read the ruling, it constituted "a warning to the States, in the name of vagueness, that they should not attempt to forbid or regulate abortions when there is a chance for the survival of the fetus, but it is not sufficiently large that the abortionist considers the fetus to be viable. This edict has no constitutional warrant." He emphasized that "being *able*" to survive outside the womb and being "*potentially* able" to do so were not the same thing and that, under Roe, viability did not require a showing of the *actual* ability but merely of the *potential* ability of the fetus to survive.

restrictions on the abortion process.   Perhaps the most important was the City's requirement that any abortion performed after the first trimester had to be performed in a hospital, with the effect of preventing "the performance of abortions in outpatient facilities that are not part of an acute-care, full-service hospital."   That second trimester hospitalization requirement was invalidated because it placed "a significant obstacle in the path of women seeking an abortion," a burden not justifiable as a reasonable health regulation.   True, hospitalization for second-trimester abortions was recommended at the time of Roe, but the safety of such abortions had "increased dramatically" since then because the D&E (dilation-and-evacuation) procedure was now "widely and successfully used for second-trimester abortions."   Moreover, experience indicated that "D&E may be performed safely on an outpatient basis in appropriate nonhospital facilities."   Justice POWELL's opinion found data such as these "impressive evidence that—at least during the early weeks of the second trimester—D&E abortions may be performed as safely in an outpatient clinic as in a full-service hospital.   We conclude, therefore, that 'present medical knowledge' [Roe] convincingly undercuts Akron's justification for requiring that *all* second-trimester abortions be performed in a hospital." [14]   He also rejected Akron's argument that the entire regulation should not be struck down just because some mid-trimester abortions could be done in clinics.   Justice Powell responded: "It is true that a state abortion regulation is not unconstitutional simply because it does not correspond perfectly in all cases to the asserted state interest.   But the lines drawn in a state regulation must be reasonable, and this cannot be said of [this one].   [Akron] has imposed a heavy, and unnecessary, burden on women's access to a relatively inexpensive, otherwise accessible, and safe abortion procedure." [15]

14. Relying on Akron, Justice Powell's majority opinion in Planned Parenthood Ass'n of Kansas City v. Ashcroft, 462 U.S. 476 (1983), struck down a Missouri requirement that abortions after 12 weeks of pregnancy be performed in a hospital.   But Justice Powell was joined by Chief Justice Burger and Justices O'Connor, White, and Rehnquist in upholding a requirement that a second physician be present for abortions performed after viability: "Preserving the life of a viable fetus that is aborted may not often be possible, but the State legitimately may choose to provide safeguards for the comparatively few instances of live birth that occur.   We believe that the second-physician requirement reasonably furthers the State's compelling interest in protecting the lives of viable fetuses."   The same majority also upheld a requirement that any tissue removed be examined by a pathologist, and that the pathologist's report be filed with the state.   Justice Blackmun, joined by Justices Brennan, Marshall and Stevens, dissented with respect to the second-physician and pathology report holdings, arguing that in neither case had the state met its burden of showing that the requirements were "tailored to protect the State's legitimate interests."

Contrast Akron and Ashcroft with Simopoulos v. Virginia, 462 U.S. 506 (1983), sustaining a different hospitalization requirement.   There, Virginia's hospitalization requirement for second trimester abortions included a definition of "hospital" that included outpatient hospitals and clinics.   Justice Powell's majority opinion accordingly upheld the requirement.   "Unlike the provisions at issue in [Akron and Ashcroft], Virginia does not require that the patient be hospitalized as an inpatient or that the abortion be performed in a full-service, acute-care hospital.   Rather, the State's requirement that second-trimester abortions be performed in licensed clinics appears to comport with accepted medical practice, and leaves the method and timing of the abortion precisely where they belong—with the physician and the patient."

15. More generally, Justice Powell stated: "We reaffirm [that] a State's interest in health regulation becomes compelling at approximately the end of the first trimester.   The existence of a compelling state interest in health, however, is only the beginning of the inquiry.   The State's regulation may be upheld only if it is reasonably designed to further that state interest.   [Roe] did not hold that it always is reasonable for a State to adopt an abortion regulation that applies to the entire second trimester.   [If] it appears that during a substantial portion of the second trimester the State's regulation 'depart[s] from accepted medical practice,' the regulation may not be upheld simply because it may be reasonable for the remaining portion of the trimester.   Rather, the State is obligated to make a reasonable effort to limit the effect of its regulations to the period in the trimester during which its health interest will be furthered."

Justice O'CONNOR, joined by Justices White and Rehnquist, dissented from all of the majority's invalidations of Akron's regulations, applying the analytical framework she developed in the general portions of her dissent (p. 533 above).   Thus, with respect to the hospitalization require-

The Akron majority also struck down a requirement which, in order to ensure that the "informed written consent of the pregnant woman" to an abortion would be "truly informed," mandated a set of detailed guidelines regarding the information the attending physician had to convey to the woman. In 1976, in Danforth, the Court had sustained a general informed consent provision. But the range and nature of detail in the Akron ordinance prompted a different result. For example, Akron required that the woman must be informed of the status of the pregnancy, the development of the fetus, the date of possible viability, the physical and emotional complications that may result from an abortion, and the availability of agencies to provide her with assistance and information with respect to birth control, adoption, and childbirth.[16] Justice Powell's majority opinion found the mandated catalogue of information constitutionally defective. He acknowledged that, in the interest of protecting the health of the pregnant woman, a state could impose a general consent requirement, but insisted that this did not "justify abortion regulations designed to influence the woman's informed choice between abortion or childbirth."[17] He elaborated: "First, it is fair to say that much of the information required is designed not to inform the woman's consent but rather to persuade her to withhold it altogether. [An] additional, and equally decisive, objection [is the] intrusion upon the discretion of the pregnant woman's physician. This provision specifies a litany of information that the physician must recite to each woman regardless of whether in his judgment the information is relevant to her personal decision. [By] insisting upon recitation of a lengthy and inflexible list of information, Akron unreasonably has placed 'obstacles in the path of the doctor upon whom [the woman is] entitled to rely for advice in connection with her decision.'"

The majority also found other aspects of the consent scheme invalid. It struck down the requirement that only the woman's physician could provide the information, stating that the "critical factor" in implementing a state's interest in assuring a woman's informed consent was "whether she obtains the necessary information [from] a qualified person, not the identity of the person from whom she obtains it. [We] cannot say that the woman's consent to the abortion will not be informed if a physician delegates the counseling task to another qualified individual." Similarly, the majority rejected a provision barring a doctor from performing an abortion until 24 hours after the pregnant woman signed a consent form. Justice Powell concluded that Akron had "failed to demonstrate that any legitimate state interest is furthered by an arbitrary and inflexible waiting period. [If] a woman, after appropriate counseling, is prepared to give

ment, she concluded: "I find no justification for the trimester approach used by the Court to analyze this restriction. I would apply the 'unduly burdensome' test and find that the hospitalization requirement does not impose an undue burden on that decision." In her view, an "exacting standard of review" was not appropriate and the "rational relation" test of Lee Optical (sec. 1 above) was readily satisfied here.

16. Among the information the ordinance required to be conveyed was, for example, that "the unborn child is a human life from the moment of conception" as well as a detailed description of the "anatomical and physiological characteristics of the particular unborn child at the gestational point of development at which time the abortion is to be performed, including, but not limited to, appearance, mobility, tactile sensitivity, including pain, perception or re-

sponse, brain and heart function, the presence of internal organs and the presence of external members." Moreover, the attending physician had to inform the woman that "abortion is a major surgical procedure, which can result in serious [specified] complications," and that "abortion may leave essentially unaffected or may worsen any existing psychological problems she may have, and can result in severe emotional disturbances."

17. Maher v. Roe (1977; note 3 below) *did* recognize that such a state preference could be voiced in choosing whether to fund certain abortions. But Justice Powell reminded that legislation reflecting a preference of childbirth over abortion was permissible in the funding context only "because it did not add any 'restriction on access to abortion that was not already there.'"

her written informed consent and proceed with the abortion, a State may not demand that she delay the effectuation of that decision."[18]

3.   *Governmental refusals to fund abortions.*   As the preceding notes indicate, the Court has struck down most post-Roe efforts to restrict access to abortions. The most important exception to that generalization stems from decisions in 1977 and 1980 holding that, in structuring welfare programs, government may constitutionally choose not to fund abortions for financially needy pregnant women (even where it does pay for childbirth). In reaching that result, the Court relied on both due process and equal protection analyses. The issue presented a clash between two themes of the modern Court: the broad protection of the woman's right to choose whether or not to have an abortion, recognized in the Roe line of due process cases; and the reluctance to impose affirmative financial obligations on government, developed in equal protection cases (chap. 9 below).[19]   Arguably, the funding rulings suggest that the latter, equal protection theme carries greater weight with the Court than the former, substantive due process one.   In the 1980 case, the Court summarized the principle at the heart of Roe v. Wade (and explained the result regarding funding) as follows: "[Although] government may not place obstacles in the path of a woman's exercise of a freedom of choice, it need not remove those not of its own creation."   The 1977 cases sustained state refusals to fund nontherapeutic abortions; the 1980 decision extended that ruling to embrace medically necessary abortions as well, by upholding the congressional Hyde Amendment that had drastically limited federal spending for abortions.[20]

a.   The first major abortion funding case was MAHER v. ROE, 432 U.S. 464 (1977).   That 6 to 3 decision sustained a Connecticut law that did not include nontherapeutic, medically unnecessary abortions within a Medicaid-funded program.   According to Justice POWELL's majority opinion, the challengers claimed that Connecticut "must accord equal treatment to both abortion and childbirth, and may not evidence a policy preference by funding only the medical expenses incident to childbirth."   In rejecting the attack on that distinction, Justice Powell used an equal protection mode of analysis.   But determining whether strict scrutiny was warranted required in part a decision as to whether the scheme interfered with the fundamental right recognized in Roe. According to the majority, it did not; a more deferential "rationality" standard of review was therefore appropriate; and the law readily passed muster under that standard.

In rejecting the argument that the Connecticut law interfered with a fundamental right, Justice Powell explained: "[The] right [in Roe and its progeny] protects the woman from unduly burdensome interference with her freedom to decide whether to terminate her pregnancy.[21]   It implies no limitation on the authority of a State to make a value judgment favoring childbirth over abortion, and to implement that judgment by the allocation of public funds."   He insisted that the law attacked here was "different in kind

---

18. The Court also invalidated a provision requiring doctors performing abortions to ensure that "the remains of the unborn child are disposed of in a humane and sanitary manner." Justice Powell agreed with the lower court that the word "humane" was "impermissibly vague as a definition of conduct subject to criminal prosecution."

19. Because of the relevance that modern equal protection doctrine (regarding government's obligation to spend) has to the resolution of the abortion funding problem, consideration of these cases may at least in part be postponed to the next chapter, particularly sec. 4 at p. 787

below. But at least some attention is warranted at this point because of the light the funding cases shed on the scope of the right established in Roe v. Wade.

20. See the earlier comment on congressional consideration of abortion funding cut-offs in the wake of Roe, at p. 532 above. See also footnote 24 below.

21. Recall the reliance on this "unduly burdensome" language by Justice O'Connor in her dissent in Akron, arguing for less intrusive scrutiny in all abortion cases, as noted at p. 533 above.

from the laws invalidated in our previous abortion decisions": "The Connecticut regulation places no obstacles—absolute or otherwise—in the pregnant woman's path to an abortion. An indigent woman who desires an abortion suffers no disadvantage as a consequence of Connecticut's decision to fund childbirth; she continues as before to be dependent on private sources for the service she desires. The State may have made childbirth a more attractive alternative, thereby influencing the woman's decision, but it has imposed no restriction on access to abortions that was not already there. The indigency that may make it difficult—and in some cases, perhaps, impossible—for some women to have abortions is neither created nor in any way affected by the Connecticut regulation." Concluding that the state law did not "impinge upon the fundamental right recognized in Roe," he insisted that this signaled "no retreat from Roe or the cases applying it. There is a basic difference between direct state interference with a protected activity and state encouragement of an alternative activity consonant with legislative policy. Constitutional concerns are greatest when the State attempts to impose its will by force of law; the State's power to encourage actions deemed to be in the public interest is necessarily far broader." [22]

Justice BRENNAN's dissent, joined by Justices Marshall and Blackmun, accused the majority of "a distressing insensitivity to the plight of impoverished pregnant women." Moreover, the distinction in state funding coerced "indigent pregnant women to bear children they would not otherwise choose to have." He insisted that the ruling "seriously erodes the principles that Roe and Doe announced to guide the determination of what constitutes an unconstitutional infringement of the fundamental right of pregnant women to be free to decide whether to have an abortion." Financial pressure on indigent women to bear children, in his view, "unconstitutionally impinges upon [the] claim of privacy derived from the Due Process Clause." Justice Brennan was not persuaded by Justice Powell's efforts to distinguish the earlier abortion cases. Some of the post-Roe decisions, Justice Brennan noted, involved requirements which operated as less than "an absolute bar to elective abortions," yet the Court had struck them down. And in a wide range of situations outside the privacy area, the Court had found that "infringements of fundamental rights are not limited to outright denials of those rights." What was critical in those cases was that state law had "inhibited [the woman's] fundamental right to make [the] choice free from state interference." Nor did the funding context serve to distinguish this case: withholding financial benefits had been held to constitute invalid burdens on fundamental rights in other contexts. Justice MARSHALL's dissent argued that the regulations were "in reality intended to impose a moral viewpoint that no State may constitutionally enforce." He viewed the funding scheme as an attempt to circumvent Roe and its progeny, and he added: "I am appalled at the ethical bankruptcy of those who preach a 'right to life' that means [a] bare existence in utter misery for so many poor women and their children." He, too, was unpersuaded by the majority's efforts to avoid "any

---

22. Similarly, he found no strict scrutiny warranted on the ground that the law involved a "suspect class," recalling that the Court had never held that "financial need alone identifies a suspect class for purposes of equal protection analysis." (See the equal protection materials in the next chapter.) And the deferential scrutiny, "rationality" requirement was readily met here: "The subsidizing of costs incident to childbirth is a rational means of encouraging childbirth. [Our] cases uniformly have accorded the States a wider latitude in choosing among competing demands for limited public funds. [Dandridge v. Williams (1970; p. 850 below).]"

The majority also rejected attacks on similar funding schemes in two companion cases. Beal v. Doe, 432 U.S. 438 (1977), held that the federal laws establishing the Medicaid program did not require state funding of nontherapeutic first trimester abortions as a condition of participation in the federal-state program. And Poelker v. Doe, 432 U.S. 519 (1977), held, in reliance on Maher, that St. Louis could constitutionally choose to provide publicly financed hospital services for childbirth without providing corresponding services for nontherapeutic abortions.

meaningful scrutiny'': ''[The] Court pulls from thin air a distinction between laws that absolutely prevent exercise of the fundamental right to abortion and those that 'merely' make its exercise difficult for some people.'' He argued for application of his ''sliding scale'' equal protection approach (see p. 590 below) and found the asserted state interest plainly inadequate in light of ''the brutal effect'' of the challenged law.[23]

b.   Three years later, HARRIS v. McRAE, 448 U.S. 297 (1980), rejected constitutional challenges to public funding limitations that barred payments for most medically necessary abortions, and thus went well beyond the medically ''unnecessary,'' nontherapeutic ones involved in Maher. Nevertheless, relying heavily on Maher, the Court's 5 to 4 decision sustained the federal Hyde Amendment.[24]   In rejecting the substantive due process attack,[25] Justice STEW-ART's majority opinion concluded that ''it simply does not follow [from Roe] that a woman's freedom of choice carries with it a constitutional entitlement to the financial resources to avail herself of the full range of protected choices. The reason why was explained in Maher: although government may not place obstacles in the path of a woman's exercise of her freedom of choice, it need not remove those not of its own creation. Indigency falls in the latter category. The financial constraints that restrict an indigent woman's ability to enjoy the full range of constitutionally protected freedom of choice are the product not of governmental restrictions on access to abortions, but rather of her indigency. Although Congress has opted to subsidize medically necessary services generally [under Medicaid], but not certain medically necessary abortions, the fact remains that the Hyde Amendment leaves an indigent woman with at least the same range of choice in deciding whether to obtain a medically necessary abortion as she would have had if Congress had chosen to subsidize no health care costs at all.'' [26]

Justice Stewart added: ''Although the liberty protected by the Due Process Clause affords protection against unwarranted governmental interference with freedom of choice in the context of certain personal decisions, it does not confer an entitlement to such funds as may be necessary to realize all the advantages of that freedom. To hold otherwise would mark a drastic change in our understanding of the Constitution. It cannot be that because government may not prohibit the use of contraceptives [Griswold] or prevent parents from sending their child to a private school [Pierce], government, therefore, has an affirmative constitutional obligation to ensure that all persons have the financial resources to obtain contraceptives or send their children to private schools. To translate the limitation on governmental power implicit in the Due Process Clause into an affirmative funding obligation would require Congress to subsi-

---

23. A separate dissent by Justice BLACK-MUN, joined by Justices Brennan and Marshall, claimed that the majority's approach to the problems of indigent women was ''disingenuous and alarming, almost reminiscent of '[l]et them eat cake.' ''

24. The Hyde Amendment refers to a series of funding restrictions adopted by Congress between 1976 and 1980 to bar, except under specified circumstances, the use of federal funds for the reimbursement of abortion costs under the Medicaid program. (Starting in 1976, Congress was engaged in almost annual, bitter battles over the scope of cutoff provisions such as the Hyde Amendment. Recall p. 532 above.) The provision applicable for fiscal year 1980 permitted public payment only ''where the life of the mother would be endangered'' and for ''victims of rape or incest when such rape or incest has been

reported promptly.'' There had been an even more restrictive version for fiscal year 1977, which did not include the ''rape or incest'' exception. A more lenient version, applicable in 1978–79, had an additional exception for situations ''where severe and long-lasting physical health damage to the mother would result.''

25. The attack also relied on equal protection and on the religion clauses of the First Amendment, as noted in footnote 27 below.

26. Justice Stewart found the claim that the Hyde Amendment ''penalizes'' the woman's choice of an abortion worthy of no more than a footnote. He concluded: ''A refusal to fund protected activity, without more, cannot be equated with the imposition of a 'penalty' on that activity.''

dize the medically necessary abortion of an indigent woman even if Congress
had not enacted a Medicaid program to subsidize other medically necessary
services. Nothing in the Due Process Clause supports such an extraordinary
result. Whether freedom of choice that is constitutionally protected warrants
federal subsidization is a question for Congress to answer, not a matter of
constitutional entitlement." [27]

The dissenters were those who had been in dissent in Maher as well as
Justice Stevens, who had been with the majority in Maher. Each of the
dissenters submitted separate statements. Justice STEVENS insisted that this
case was "fundamentally different" from Maher because medically necessary
abortions were involved: "This case involve[s] a special exclusion of women
who, by definition, are confronted with a choice between two serious harms:
serious health damage to themselves on the one hand and abortion on the other.
The competing interests are the interest in maternal health and the interest in
protecting potential human life. It is now part of our law that the pregnant
woman's decision as to which of these conflicting interests shall prevail is
entitled to constitutional protection. [Government may not] exclude a woman
from medical benefits to which she would otherwise be entitled solely to further
an interest in potential life when a physician [certifies] that an abortion is
necessary 'for the preservation of the life or health of the mother.' Roe v.
Wade. The Court totally fails to explain why this reasoning is not dispositive
here." He added that Roe "squarely held that State interference is unreasonable if it attaches a greater importance to the interest in potential life than to the
interest in protecting the mother's health." He concluded: "Having decided to
alleviate some of the hardships of poverty by providing necessary medical care,
the Government must use neutral criteria in distributing benefits. It may not
deny benefits to a financially and medically needy person simply because he is a
Republican, a Catholic, or an Oriental—or because he has spoken against a
program the Government has a legitimate interest in furthering. In sum, it may
not create exceptions for the sole purpose of furthering a governmental interest
that is constitutionally subordinate to the individual interest that the entire
program was designed to protect. [The Hyde Amendment constitutes] an
unjustifiable, and indeed blatant, violation of the sovereign's duty to govern
impartially."

Justice BRENNAN, joined by Justices Marshall and Blackmun, criticized
"the Court's mischaracterization of the nature of the fundamental right recognized in [Roe], and its misconception of the manner in which that right is
infringed [by] withdrawing all funding for medically necessary abortions." He
commented: "The proposition for which [Roe and its progeny stand] is not that
the State is under an affirmative obligation to ensure access to abortions for all
who may desire them; it is that the State must refrain from wielding its
enormous power and influence in a manner that might burden the pregnant
woman's freedom to choose whether to have an abortion. [The Hyde Amend-

---

27. With respect to equal protection, Justice
Stewart followed the traditional "two-tier" approach discussed in the next chapter. Here, only
the deferential, "rationality" requirement applied,
and that standard was readily satisfied in this
case: "[The] Hyde Amendment, by encouraging
childbirth except in the most urgent circumstances, is rationally related to the legitimate
governmental objective of protecting potential
life. [Nor] is it irrational that Congress has
authorized federal reimbursement for medically
necessary services generally, but not for certain
medically necessary abortions. Abortion is inherently different from other medical procedures,
because no other procedure involves the pur-

poseful termination of a potential life. [We]
cannot [overturn] duly enacted statutes simply
'because they may be unwise, improvident, or out
of harmony with a particular school of thought.'
[Lee Optical.]" In rejecting an added claim
based on the religion clauses, Justice Stewart
reached only the Establishment Clause claim and
concluded that "the fact that the funding restrictions [may] coincide with the religious tenets of
the Roman Catholic Church does not, without
more, contravene the Establishment Clause."
(See chap. 14 below.) (Justice WHITE, who
agreed with Justice Stewart's "straightforward
analysis," also submitted a separate opinion.)

ment] intrudes upon this constitutionally protected decision, for both by design and in effect it serves to coerce indigent pregnant women to bear children that they would otherwise elect not to have." Stressing the "coercive financial incentives favoring childbirth," he accused the majority of failing to appreciate that "it is not simply the woman's indigency that interferes with her freedom of choice, but the combination of her own poverty and the government's unequal subsidization of abortion and childbirth." He insisted that the Court had "never hesitated to invalidate any scheme of granting or withholding financial benefits that incidentally or intentionally burdens one manner of exercising a constitutionally protected choice," pointing especially to Sherbert v. Verner (1963; p. 1514 below). He added: "The fundamental flaw in the Court's due process analysis [is] its failure to acknowledge that the discriminatory distribution of the benefits of governmental largesse can discourage the exercise of fundamental liberties just as effectively as can an outright denial of those rights through criminal and regulatory sanctions." [28]

4. *Restrictions on distribution of contraceptives after the Griswold and Roe line of cases.* In CAREY v. POPULATION SERVICES INTERNATIONAL, 431 U.S. 678 (1977), a divided Court invalidated a number of New York restrictions on the distribution and advertising of nonprescription contraceptives. The case provided opportunities both to clarify implications of the earlier cases and to elaborate the growing body of constitutionalized family law (see the next group of notes). The challenged prohibitions included (1) the distribution of contraceptives to persons over 16 by anyone other than a licensed pharmacist; and (2) the sale or distribution of contraceptives to minors under 16. [29] Justice BRENNAN announced early in his opinion that "strict scrutiny" was appropriate here: "The decision whether or not to beget or bear a child is at the very heart of [the] cluster of constitutionally protected choices"; "where a decision as fundamental as that whether to bear or beget a child is involved, regulations imposing a burden on it may be justified only by compelling state interests, and must be narrowly drawn to express only those interests." [30]

---

28. Justice MARSHALL's dissent reiterated his Maher approach and added: "If abortion is medically necessary and a funded abortion is unavailable, [the affected women] must resort to back-alley butchers, attempt to induce an abortion themselves by crude and dangerous methods, or suffer the serious medical consequences of attempting to carry the fetus to term. [The] denial of Medicaid benefits [solely] because the treatment that is medically necessary involves the exercise of the fundamental right to choose abortion [is] a form of discrimination repugnant to [equal protection]. The [decision] marks a retreat from [Roe] and represents a cruel blow to the most powerless members of our society." He concluded that the decision could ultimately be traced to "the Court's unwillingness to apply the constraints of the Constitution to decisions involving the expenditure of governmental funds." (Justice BLACKMUN also submitted a brief dissent, agreeing "wholeheartedly" with Justices Brennan and Stevens.)

29. A third provision, banning the advertising or display of contraceptives, was struck down on the basis of First Amendment "commercial speech" principles. See generally chap. 11, sec. 2, below.

Justice Brennan managed to gain majority support for all of his opinion except that part dis-

cussing the minors' ban. On that issue, his views were joined only by Justices Stewart, Marshall and Blackmun. Chief Justice Burger and Justice Rehnquist dissented from the entire decision; Justices White, Powell and Stevens submitted separate opinions concurring in the judgment while disagreeing with some of Justice Brennan's reasoning.

30. It was this case that provided Justice Brennan with the occasion to make explicit the broadening of Griswold that had taken place in Eisenstadt and later cases. (Recall p. 514 above.) After noting that Griswold had spoken of intrusion into "marital bedrooms," he stated that subsequent decisions had made clear that "the constitutional protection of individual autonomy in matters of childbearing is not dependent on that element. [Eisenstadt; Roe.] These decisions put Griswold in proper perspective. Griswold may no longer be read as holding only that a State may not prohibit a married couple's use of contraceptives. Read in light of its progeny, the teaching of Griswold is that the Constitution protects individual decisions in matters of childbearing from unjustified intrusion by the State."

expanded Griswold

a. *Channeling distribution to adults through pharmacists.* In invalidating provision (1), Justice Brennan wrote for a majority.[31] Though he conceded that no "independent fundamental 'right of access to contraceptives' " had been established, he insisted that strict scrutiny was nevertheless required for the access restriction, "because such access is essential to exercise of the constitutionally protected right of decision in matters of childbearing that is the underlying foundation of the holdings in Griswold, Eisenstadt, and Roe." He pointed to the post-Roe decisions to show "that the same test must be applied to state regulations that burden the individual's right to decide to prevent conception or terminate pregnancy by substantially limiting access to the means effectuating that decision as is applied to state statutes that prohibit the decision entirely." And he had no doubt that "[l]imiting the distribution of nonprescription contraceptives to licensed pharmacists clearly imposes a significant burden on the right of the individuals to use contraceptives if they choose to do so." Restricting distribution to a small number of retail outlets "renders contraceptive devices considerably less accessible to the public, reduces the opportunity for privacy of selection and purchase, and lessens the possibility of price competition." And there was no "compelling state interest" to justify that burden.

b. *Prohibiting distribution to minors.* On provision (2), which raised the most difficult issue in the case, Justice Brennan spoke only for a plurality. His opinion rejected the argument that the ban on distribution to persons under 16 could be justified "as a regulation of the morality of minors." He noted that the "question of the extent of state power to regulate conduct of minors not constitutionally regulable when committed by adults is a vexing one, perhaps not susceptible to precise answer." He recalled that minors have some constitutional rights, but that state power over children is greater than over adults.[32] Against that background, he was unpersuaded by the allegedly "significant" state interest in promoting its policy of discouraging sexual activity among the young. He was reluctant to attribute to the State a value scheme which would impose the burdens of pregnancy as "punishment for fornication" and he found "substantial reason for doubt [that] limiting access to contraceptives will in fact substantially discourage early sexual behavior." Nor was the law saved by the fact that another law permitted physicians to provide contraceptives to minors. As with the restrictions on distribution to adults, "less than total restrictions on access to contraceptives that significantly burden the right to decide whether to bear children must also pass constitutional scrutiny." And here, the only justification for the restriction was "to emphasize to young people the seriousness with which the State views the decision to engage in sexual intercourse at an early age." That was an unacceptable justification, weakened further by the fact that the State had delegated its authority "to disapprove of minors' sexual behavior to physicians, who may exercise it arbitrarily."

Justice WHITE's separate opinion concurred solely in the judgment with respect to distribution to minors, "primarily because the State has not demon-

---

31. That portion of his opinion was joined by Justices Stewart, White, Marshall, Blackmun and Stevens.

32. Justice Brennan found special guidance in Danforth, note 1 above. He noted that the Danforth standard was that "[s]tate restriction[s] inhibiting privacy rights of minors are valid only if they serve 'any significant state interest [that] is not present in the case of an adult.' " He commented that this test was "apparently less rigorous than the 'compelling state interest' test applied to restrictions on the privacy rights of adults." He added: "Such lesser scrutiny is appropriate both because of the States' greater latitude to regulate the conduct of children and because the right of privacy implicated here is the 'interest in independence in making certain kinds of decisions,' and the law has generally regarded minors as having a lesser capability for making important decisions." But since Danforth had barred blanket prohibitions and a blanket consent requirement regarding minors' abortions, "the constitutionality of a blanket prohibition of the distribution of contraceptives to minors is a fortiori foreclosed."

strated that the prohibition against distribution of contraceptives to minors measurably contributes to the deterrent purposes which the State advances as justification for the restriction." He emphasized that "the legality of state laws forbidding premarital intercourse is not at issue here." Justice STEVENS, in another separate opinion, thought the analogy to Danforth inappropriate because he "could not agree that the Constitution provides the same measure of protection to the minor's right to use contraceptives as to the pregnant female's right to abort." Moreover, he disapproved of leaving open the question "whether there is a significant state interest in discouraging sexual activity" among unmarried minors.[33] He added: "Indeed, I would describe as 'frivolous' appellee's argument that a minor has the constitutional right to put contraceptives to their intended use, notwithstanding the combined objection of both parents and the State." But he concurred in the invalidation of "the distribution to minors" provision because of the irrationality of the means employed: "Although the State may properly perform a teaching function [by communicating disapproval of sexual activity by minors, an] attempt to persuade by inflicting harm on the listener is an unacceptable means of conveying a message that is otherwise legitimate. The propaganda technique used in this case significantly increases the risk of unwanted pregnancy and venereal disease."

Justice POWELL concurred in the judgment in the longest of the separate opinions. He was "not persuaded that the Constitution requires the severe constraints [placed] upon legislative efforts to regulate the distribution of contraceptives, particularly to the young." With respect to distribution to adults, he thought application of the "strictest standard of judicial review" inappropriate. To him, the Court's "extraordinary protection" of what he described as "all personal decisions in matters of sex" was neither constitutionally required nor supported by the precedents. Cases like Griswold and Roe involved "direct and substantial interference with constitutionally protected rights"; this decision was an unnecessary extension of the reach of those cases, since strict scrutiny was not required where a regulation merely "implicates sexual freedom." Moreover, he found no justification for "heightened judicial review" of restrictions on "the sexual activity of the young." He read Justice Brennan's standard as "for all practical purposes approaching the 'compelling state interest' standard." In Justice Powell's view, it was enough to ask whether the restriction on the "action of young people in sexual matters" "rationally serves valid state interests." Examining the restrictions on the basis of those criteria, he found the restriction on the distribution to minors invalid on narrow grounds, although "properly framed legislation [would] meet constitutional standards." [34]

---

33. Note also the comments on state authority to prohibit minors' consensual sexual behavior in Michael M. v. Superior Court (1981; p. 652 below). Justice Rehnquist's plurality opinion rejected an equal protection attack on California's statutory rape law, a law that makes men alone criminally liable. He noted: "We do not understand petitioner to question a State's authority to make sexual intercourse among teenagers a criminal act, at least on a gender-neutral basis." Justice Brennan's dissent countered that "our cases would not foreclose [a] privacy challenge" to the state's power to criminalize consensual sexual activity. After quoting from Eisenstadt, he added: "Minors, too, enjoy a right of privacy in connection with decisions affecting procreation. Thus, despite the suggestion of the plurali-

ty to the contrary, it is not settled that a State may rely on a pregnancy-prevention justification to make consensual sexual intercourse among minors a criminal act." (On the fate of claims that adults have a fundamental right to engage in consensual sexual activity, see the note at p. 559 below. That note also summarizes the conflicting dicta in the opinions in Carey regarding the constitutional status of adult consensual sexual activity.)

34. Chief Justice BURGER dissented without opinion. Justice REHNQUIST submitted a brief, heated dissent invoking the memory of the patriots of Bunker Hill, Shiloh, Gettysburg and Cold Harbor: "If those responsible for [the Bill of Rights and the post-Civil War Amendments]

SUBSTANTIVE DUE PROCESS AND FAMILY RELATIONS

Introduction. A notable aspect of the Court's work since the late 1970s is the striking extent to which family relations have become a significant part of constitutional law. The Court has recognized a wide range of individual rights in the family context; and some of these rights persist even though they are not exercised in a traditional family unit. Repeatedly, the Court has been confronted with conflicts among the three potential centers of authority in the family context: the parents; the child; and the state. The problems that have surfaced have covered a wide range of functional problems and constitutional sources. Functionally, litigation has involved such problems as parent-child relationships, rights involved in divorce and child custody cases, procreative rights, and regulations of the marriage relationship. Legally, the process of constitutionalizing family law has drawn on such diverse sources as the First Amendment's speech [1] and religion [2] clauses and equal protection scrutiny of discriminations on the basis of sex [3] and illegitimacy. [4] But the central phenomenon since the

could have lived to know that their efforts had enshrined in the Constitution the right of commercial vendors of contraceptives to peddle them to unmarried minors, [it] is not difficult to imagine their reaction. I do not believe that the [prior cases] require any such result, but to debate the Court's treatment [on] a case-by-case basis would concede more validity to the [majority's result] than I am willing to do. There comes a point when endless and ill-considered extension of principles originally formulated in quite different cases produces such an indefensible result that no logic chopping can possibly make the fallacy of the result more obvious."

1. E.g., the Tinker case (1969; p. 1176 below) (children wearing Vietnam protest armbands in schools).

2. E.g., Wisconsin v. Yoder (1972; p. 1521 below) (application of compulsory school attendance law to Amish parents and children).

3. E.g., Caban v. Mohammed (1979; p. 666 below) (right of father to bar adoption of illegitimate children).

4. E.g., Lalli v. Lalli (1978; p. 681 below) (rights of illegitimate children to intestate inheritance). Note also a number of family law cases decided under procedural due process [e.g., Goss v. Lopez (1975; p. 583 below) (suspension of high school students)] and irrebuttable presumption analyses [e.g., Stanley v. Illinois (1972; p. 853 below) (claim of unwed father to custody of child)]. This introductory note by no means lists all of the modern family relations cases. The text notes that follow focus on the pervasive substantive due process emphasis that recurs in the modern cases.

Note that this group of notes also includes a few cases decided under doctrinal rubrics such as equal protection. These cases are noted here because they contribute importantly to the development of substantive due process law and can best be understood as in fact substantive due process cases decided under the guise of equal protection. Thus, Zablocki v. Redhail (1978; note 3 in this group of notes), the most important case on the "fundamental right to marry," was in form a strict scrutiny-"new equal protection"

case. See, generally, my colleague William Cohen's paper, "Is Equal Protection Like Oakland? Equality as a Surrogate for Other Rights," (forthcoming, in the Tulane Law Review). His examples of the use of equal protection analysis as a surrogate for substantive due process results include such cases as Skinner and Eisenstadt, already noted earlier in this section. He also lists Zablocki, below, as a use of "equal protection theory to resolve a constitutional problem that was, at bottom, one of substantive due process."

Cohen generally approves of such uses of equal protection as a way of avoiding direct confirmations with substantive due process problems, even though he recognizes that the equal protection analysis often makes sense only "if the Court has implicitly decided the avoided issues. The decision is narrower, however, precisely because the decision is only implicit, or summary and conclusory." (As Cohen recognizes, the author of this book is a good deal more troubled by the use of such avoidance—or obscuring—techniques.) Cohen does concede that using equal protection as an alternative theory in cases really involving substantive due process issues is not always satisfactory, since an "alternative equal protection theory may be as broad as, or even broader than, the theory for which it is a stand-in." (He gives Zablocki as an example, describing it as a case that "put a thin veneer of equality rhetoric over its construction of a due process right.") Moreover, he concedes that, if the Court "hides other substantive constitutional rights by using narrow equal protection decisions at the outset," problems may arise. For example, "[c]ontinued elaboration of a supposed equal protection theme will only complicate and obscure the decision process in hard cases." He gives as an example of a decisional area often handled at least in part in equal protection terms but ripe for "new explanations" the rights of fathers of children born outside of marriage. See, e.g., footnote 3, above. (Problems such as these—and especially the question of the substantive content, if any, of equal protection doctrine—are pursued in the next chapter.)

late 1970s, and the concern of these notes, is the increasingly commonplace reliance on substantive due process as the source of groundrules for constitutionalized family law, as the materials below illustrate.[5] These developments are controversial not only to those concerned with the appropriate policy ingredients in the realms of family and juvenile law. They also refocus attention on the pervasive problems of substantive due process methodology and "fundamental values" adjudication. The modern family law cases have produced sharp divisions on the Court and, to most observers, as yet no satisfactory and consistent resolutions of disputes among parents, children, and the state. But these cases provide important added evidence of the modern Court's commitment to substantive due process. Moreover, they cast added light on the recurrent problems regarding the appropriate sources for judicial identification of "fundamental values."[6]

    1. *Protected family relationships: Zoning restrictions and the "extended family."* MOORE v. EAST CLEVELAND, 431 U.S. 494 (1977), elicited an unusually explicit confrontation with the substantive due process underpinnings (and the appropriate "fundamental values" ingredients) of modern family law cases. Moore invalidated a zoning ordinance limiting occupancy of a dwelling to members of a single "family," narrowly defined as including only "a few categories of related individuals." Mrs. Moore was convicted because she shared her home with her two grandsons, who were first cousins. That relationship was not sufficiently close to constitute a "family" under the ordinance.[7] According to the City's position, "any constitutional right to live together as a family extends only to the nuclear family—essentially a couple and their dependent children." Justice Powell's plurality opinion invalidated the application of the ordinance to Mrs. Moore on substantive due process grounds. Two of the dissenters, Justices Stewart and White, took sharp issue with his substantive due process methodology.[8]

    Justice POWELL insisted that a scrutiny stricter than deferential review was appropriate "[w]hen a city undertakes such intrusive regulation of the family": "[W]hen the government intrudes on choices concerning family living arrangements, this Court must examine carefully the importance of the governmental interests advanced and the extent to which they are served by the challenged regulation." The ordinance could not survive that scrutiny: though such articulated city interests as "preventing overcrowding" and "minimizing traffic

---

    5. That substantive due process can contain ingredients for the resolution of family law problems is of course not a discovery of the modern Court. Recall the Meyer and Pierce cases of the Lochner era, p. 502 above, where Justice McReynolds' description of the protected "liberty" included not only liberty of contract but such family law-related freedoms as the right to "establish a home and bring up children" (Meyer; 1923) and "the liberty of parents and guardians to direct the upbringing and education of children under their control" (Pierce; 1925). Moreover, modern substantive due process-family law analyses have already surfaced in the preceding group of notes. Recall especially the discussion of state and parental control over minors' access to abortions and contraceptives, notes 1 and 4 above.

    6. For a useful review, largely approving of the Court's actions, see Developments, "The Constitution and the Family," 93 Harv.L.Rev. 1156 (1980) (hereinafter cited as "Developments"). For a more critical commentary on the Court's efforts, see Burt, "The Constitution of

the Family," 1979 Sup.Ct.Rev. 329. The "Developments" comment identifies the most frequently asserted state interest in the substantive due process-regulation of family life cases as follows: "the state's interest in strengthening the family as a valuable social institution, its police power interest in regulating the public morals, and its responsibility as parens patriae to intervene to promote the best interests of the child."

    7. Under the "unusual and complicated definitional section," the ordinance would have permitted the living arrangement if the grandsons had been brothers.

    8. Justice STEVENS, whose vote was necessary for the result in the 5 to 4 decision, applied the "limited standard of review" generally applicable in zoning cases (recall sec. 2A above) and found an unjustifiable restriction on Mrs. Moore's "right to use her own property as she sees fit." Chief Justice BURGER dissented because Mrs. Moore had failed to exhaust her state administrative remedies by not seeking a zoning variance.

and parking congestion" were "legitimate," the ordinance "serves them marginally, at best," and "has but a tenuous relation to them." The most difficult aspect of the case was presented by the city's argument that any "right to live together as a family" was limited to the situation of "the nuclear family—essentially a couple and its dependent children." Justice Powell held that the principles of the cases beginning with Meyer and Pierce covered "extended family" relationships such as Mrs. Moore's as well.

In articulating his substantive due process methodology, Justice Powell stated: "To be sure, [the Meyer-Pierce line of cases] did not expressly consider the family relationship presented here. They were immediately concerned with freedom of choice with respect to childbearing, e.g., [Roe; Griswold], or with the rights of parents to the custody and companionship of their own children [Stanley v. Illinois], or with traditional parental authority in matters of child rearing and education. [E.g., Yoder, Pierce, Meyer.] But unless we close our eyes to the basic reasons why certain rights associated with the family have been accorded shelter under the 14th Amendment's Due Process Clause, we cannot avoid applying the force and rationale of these precedents to the family choice involved in this case. Understanding those reasons requires careful attention to this Court's function under the Due Process Clause. Mr. Justice Harlan described it eloquently. [He quoted at length from Justice Harlan's opinion in Poe v. Ullman, printed at p. 508 above, and continued:]

"Substantive due process has at times been a treacherous field for this Court. There *are* risks when the judicial branch gives enhanced protection to certain substantive liberties without the guidance of the more specific provisions of the Bill of Rights. As the history of the Lochner era demonstrates, there is reason for concern lest the only limits to such judicial intervention become the predilections of those who happen at the time to be Members of this Court. That history counsels caution and restraint. But it does not counsel abandonment, nor does it require what the city urges here: cutting off any protection of family rights at the first convenient, if arbitrary boundary—the boundary of the nuclear family." In suggesting appropriate limits to guard against judicial excesses in exercising substantive due process review, he took a position challenged by the dissents. He stated: "Appropriate limits on substantive due process come not from drawing arbitrary lines but rather from 'careful respect for the teachings of history [and] solid recognition of the basic values that underlie our society.' [Griswold; Harlan, J., concurring.] Our decisions establish that the Constitution protects the sanctity of the family precisely because the institution of the family is deeply rooted in this Nation's history and tradition. It is through the family that we inculcate and pass down many of our most cherished values, moral and cultural."

"Ours is by no means a tradition limited to respect for the bonds uniting the members of the nuclear family. The tradition of uncles, aunts, cousins, and especially grandparents sharing a household along with parents and children has roots equally venerable and equally deserving of constitutional recognition. Over the years millions of our citizens have grown up in just such an environment. [Even] if conditions of modern society have brought about a decline in extended family households, they have not erased the accumulated wisdom of civilization [that] supports a larger conception of the family. Out of choice, necessity, or a sense of family responsibility, it has been common for close relatives to draw together and participate in the duties and satisfactions of a common home. [Especially] in times of adversity, such as the death of a spouse or economic need, the broader family has tended to come together for mutual sustenance and to maintain or rebuild a secure home life. This is apparently what happened here. Whether or not such a household is established because of personal tragedy, the choice of relatives in this degree of kinship to live together may not lightly be denied by the State. [See Pierce.] [The] Constitution prevents East Cleveland from standardizing its children—and its adults—by forcing all to live in certain narrowly defined family patterns."[9]

Justice WHITE's dissent argued that Justice Powell's emphasis on history and tradition would "broaden enormously the horizons" of substantive due process. He commented: "That the Court has ample precedent for the creation of new constitutional rights should not lead it to repeat the process at will. The judiciary [is] the most vulnerable and comes nearest to illegitimacy when it deals with judge-made constitutional law having little or no cognizable roots in the language or even the design of the Constitution." In his view, "the interest in residing with more than one set of grandchildren is [not] one that calls for any kind of heightened protection." He insisted that, under Palko, that interest was not a right "implicit in ordered liberty" or "one of which it could be said that 'neither liberty nor justice would exist if [it] were sacrificed.'" He added: "Mr. Justice Powell would apparently construe the Due Process Clause to protect from all but quite important state regulatory interests any right or privilege that in his estimate is deeply rooted in the country's traditions. For me, this suggests a far too expansive charter for this Court. [What] the deeply rooted traditions of the country are is arguable; which of them deserves the protection of the Due Process Clause is even more debatable. [If] the interest involved here is any measure of what the States would be forbidden to regulate, the courts would be substantively weighing and very likely invalidating a wide range of measures that Congress and state legislatures think appropriate to respond to a changing economic and social order." He recalled Justice Black's dissent in Griswold and urged the Court to be "extremely reluctant to breathe still further substantive content" into due process.[10]

---

9. In a separate opinion supporting Justice Powell's approach, Justice BRENNAN, joined by Justice Marshall, added that the ordinance reflected "cultural myopia" and displayed "a distressing insensitivity toward the economic and emotional needs of a very large part of our society." He noted that the "extended family" "remains not merely still a pervasive living pattern, but under the goad of brutal economic necessity, a prominent pattern—virtually a means of survival—for large numbers of the poor and deprived minorities of our society." He noted, too, that the "extended" form was "especially familiar among black families." (Justice Brennan added, however, that he was not implying that the ordinance was "motivated by a racially discriminatory purpose.") He concluded that the Constitution cannot "tolerate the imposition by government upon the rest of us of white suburbia's preference in patterns of family living."

[Compare a comment in Justice Stewart's dissent: "In point of fact, East Cleveland is a predominantly Negro community, with a Negro City Manager and City Commission." And note, Burt, "The Constitution of the Family," 1979 Sup.Ct.Rev. 329: "The plurality did not consider that the purpose of the ordinance was quite straightforward: to exclude from a middle-class, predominantly black [and nuclear family] community, that saw itself as socially and economically upwardly mobile, other black [extended] families most characteristic of lower-class ghetto life."]

10. Justice Powell responded by noting that "an approach grounded in history imposes limits on the judiciary that are more meaningful than any based on the abstract formula taken from [Palko]." (Justice STEWART, joined by Justice Rehnquist, argued, like Justice White, that Mrs. Moore's interest could not be considered "implicit in the concept of ordered liberty." He added: "To equate this interest with the fundamental decisions to marry and to bear and raise children is to extend the limited substantive contours of the Due Process Clause beyond recognition.")

Compare Belle Terre v. Boraas, 416 U.S. 1 (1974), where Justice Douglas' majority opinion, over Justice Marshall's dissent, found no privacy rights involved in a family-oriented zoning restriction excluding most *unrelated* groups from a village. Justice Douglas insisted the ordinance represented "economic and social legislation" and invoked the deferential judicial stance characteristic of zoning cases (see sec. 2A above). Justice Marshall argued that strict scrutiny was appropriate: "The choice of household companions—of whether a person's 'intellectual and emotional' needs are best met by living with family, friends, professional associates or others—involves deeply personal considerations as to the kind and quality of intimate relationships within the home. That decision surely falls within the ambit of the right to privacy protected by the Constitution. See [Roe; Eisenstadt; Griswold]." (Note the later decision in Roberts v. United States Jaycees (1984; p. 565 below), with dicta suggesting broad associational rights

  2. *The "fundamental right to marry": "Critical examination" of "significant" interferences with the right.* ZABLOCKI v. REDHAIL, 434 U.S. 374 (1978), invalidated a Wisconsin law which provided that any resident "having minor issue not in his custody and which he is under an obligation to support by any court order" could not marry without obtaining court approval. Under the statute, court permission required proof that the applicant's support obligation had been met and that children covered by the support order "are not then and are not likely thereafter to become public charges." Redhail's application for a marriage license was denied because he had not obtained court permission. He had not petitioned for permission because he could not satisfy the two requirements: he had not been paying court-ordered support for an illegitimate daughter, and the child had been receiving benefits under the AFDC program since her birth. The woman whom Redhail wished to marry was pregnant; they wanted to legalize their relationship before the birth of the child. He brought a class action challenging the law under the equal protection and due process clauses. Though the majority ultimately analyzed the case in terms of the "fundamental rights" strand of the "new equal protection," it was strongly influenced by substantive due process precedents which had asserted that the "right to marry" was "fundamental." In short, determining what qualifies as a "fundamental right" for purposes of triggering strict equal protection scrutiny turned, as it does quite frequently (though often more obscurely), on whether substantive due process precedents support such a "fundamental right." [11]

  In articulating the majority's standard of review, Justice MARSHALL's opinion stated that, since "the right to marry is of fundamental importance, and since the classification at issue here significantly interferes with the exercise of that right, we believe that 'critical examination' of the state interests advanced [is] required." In explaining why "the right to marry is of fundamental importance for all individuals"—the premise that triggered strict scrutiny—Justice Marshall pointed to Loving v. Virginia, the 1967 miscegenation decision (p. 626 below). He noted that Griswold and other recent decisions had "established that the right to marry is part of the fundamental 'right of privacy' implicit in [the] Due Process Clause." He elaborated: "It is not surprising that the decision to marry has been placed on the same level of importance as decisions relating to procreation, childbirth, child-rearing, and family relationships. As the facts of this case illustrate, it would make little sense to recognize a right of privacy with respect to other matters of family life and not with respect to the decision to enter the relationship that is the foundation of the family in our society. The woman whom appellee desired to marry had a

as an aspect of "liberty.") Justice Powell distinguished Belle Terre in Moore because it had affected "only unrelated individuals." Justice Stewart's dissent, by contrast, argued that the contentions in Moore were in large part answered by Belle Terre.

11. Although the judgment striking down the law was based on an 8 to 1 vote, the Justices differed widely as to the proper standard of scrutiny. Justice Marshall articulated a type of strict scrutiny, but his majority opinion was supported by only four of his colleagues—Chief Justice Burger and Justices Brennan, White and Blackmun. In separate concurring opinions, Justices Powell and Stevens rested on variations of an "intermediate" level of review. In another concurrence, Justice Stewart voted to invalidate the law on the basis of substantive due process rather than equal protection. Justice Rehnquist, the sole dissenter, advocated a deferential standard of review.

  That division illustrates a number of recurrent themes. First, though most of the Justices spoke in equal protection modes, the differences in intensity of review were clearly based on differences in evaluating the "fundamentalness" of the underlying due process "liberty" that warranted the heightened scrutiny. The case thus ultimately rests on a substantive due process analysis despite its equal protection form. (Recall footnote 4 at p. 550 above.) Second, the arguments about "strict" and "intermediate" standards of review foreshadow recurrent, divisive themes in modern equal protection law, examined in the next chapter. Third, the Court is more likely to resort openly to flexible, ad hoc, balancing varieties of heightened scrutiny in the substantive due process realm than in the equal protection area (where, as the next chapter shows, fairly rigid, two- or three-tier modes of review still prevail, at least in form).

fundamental right to seek an abortion of their expected child, see [Roe], or to bring the child into life to suffer the myriad social, if not economic, disabilities that the status of illegitimacy brings. Surely, a decision to marry and raise the child in a traditional family setting must receive equivalent protection. And, if appellee's right to procreate means anything at all, it must imply some right to enter the only relationship in which [the State] allows sexual relations legally to take place." But, after "reaffirming the fundamental character of the right to marry," Justice Marshall made clear that not "every state regulation which relates in any way to the incidents of or prerequisites for marriage must be subjected to rigorous scrutiny. [Reasonable] regulations that do not significantly interfere with decisions to enter into the marital relationship may legitimately be imposed. See Califano v. Jobst." [12] Here, however, the law "interfere[d] directly and substantially with the right to marry."

In engaging in his "critical examination" of the law, Justice Marshall stated that the classification in the law "cannot be upheld unless it is supported by sufficiently important state interests and is closely tailored to effectuate only those interests." He accepted, "for present purposes," that the asserted state interests were "legitimate and substantial," but found that "the means selected [for] achieving these interests unnecessarily impinge on the right to marry." The first asserted interest was the legislature's alleged intent to provide counseling before a person "entered into [a] new marital relationship [and] incurred further support obligations." Justice Marshall noted that the statute did not provide for counseling and that, even if counseling took place, the state interest could not "support the withholding of court permission to marry once counseling is completed." Another asserted state interest was "safeguarding the welfare of out-of-custody children," by providing an incentive to make support payments. Justice Marshall concluded that this "collection device" rationale could not justify the law's broad "infringement on the right to marry": he stated that the State had other, less intrusive means "for exacting compliance with support obligations," such as direct enforcement "via wage assignments, civil contempt proceedings, and criminal penalties." [13] He noted, finally, that "the net result of preventing the marriage is simply more illegitimate children."

Justice POWELL's concurrence insisted that the majority's rationale swept "too broadly in an area which traditionally has been subject to pervasive state regulation." He noted that the majority would subject a regulation to strict scrutiny if it "directly and substantially" interfered with the decision to marry; but if it did not "significantly interfere," the majority would consider it valid if "reasonable." He could see no "principled means for distinguishing between the two types of regulation." He commented: "Since state regulation in this area typically takes the form of a prerequisite or barrier to marriage or divorce, the degree of 'direct' interference with the decision to marry or to divorce is unlikely to provide either guidance for state legislatures or a basis for judicial oversight." Rejecting strict scrutiny, he argued that, "[a]lthough the cases cited [by the majority] indicate that there is a sphere of privacy or autonomy surrounding an existing marital relationship into which the State may not lightly intrude, they do not necessarily suggest that the same barrier of justification

12. Califano v. Jobst, 434 U.S. 47 (1977), sustained a Social Security Act provision which cuts off disabled children's benefits upon marriage to nonbeneficiaries but not upon marriage to beneficiaries, even if the nonbeneficiary is disabled. In Zablocki, Justice Marshall claimed that the "directness and substantiality of the interference with the freedom to marry" distinguished this case from Jobst.

13. Another asserted objective of the law was to prevent applicants from incurring new support obligations. In that respect, Justice Marshall found the law "grossly underinclusive," because it did not bar new financial commitments other than those arising out of the contemplated marriage, as well as "substantially overinclusive," because it prevented affected individuals "from improving their ability to satisfy their prior support obligations" through a new marriage.

blocks regulation of the conditions of entry into or the dissolution of the marital bond." He noted that "[a] 'compelling state purpose' inquiry would cast doubt on the network of restrictions that the States have fashioned to govern marriage and divorce," such as "bans on incest, bigamy, and homosexuality, as well as various preconditions to marriage, such as blood tests." [14]

Justice STEVENS stated that the Constitution permits "direct and substantial" restraints on the right to marry, such as prohibitions on marriage to a child or close relative. But in this case, there was "deliberate discrimination against the poor." Under the Wisconsin law, "a person's economic status may determine his eligibility to enter into a lawful marriage. A noncustodial parent whose children are 'public charges' may not marry even if he has met his court-ordered obligations. Thus, within the class of parents who have fulfilled their court-ordered obligations, the rich may marry and the poor may not. This type of statutory discrimination is, I believe, totally unprecedented, as well as inconsistent with our tradition of administering justice equally to the rich and to the poor." [15] Justice STEWART's concurring opinion was the only one which found substantive due process the sole appropriate basis for decision. He repudiated both strict and intermediate levels of equal protection scrutiny, insisting that to rely on equal protection in a case such as this was "no more than substantive due process by another name." [16] Instead, he found the law invalid "because it exceeds the bounds of permissible state regulation of marriage, and invades the sphere of liberty protected by the Due Process Clause." He relied especially on cases such as Boddie v. Connecticut (1971; p. 830 below),[17] which held that "a person's inability to pay money demanded by the State does not justify the total deprivation of a constitutionally protected liberty." He insisted that the law was an "irrational means" of effectuating the State's "legitimate interest in collecting delinquent support payments and reducing its welfare load" because it made "no allowance for the truly indigent." Although he conceded that the law was "substantially more rational" if viewed as a "means of assuring the financial viability of future marriages," he asserted that the State "must stop short of telling people they may not marry because they are too poor or because they might persist in their financial irresponsibility. The invasion of constitutionally protected liberty and the chance of erroneous prediction are simply too great. A legislative judgment so alien to our traditions and so offensive to our shared notions of fairness offends [due process]." [18]

14. Nevertheless, Justice Powell concluded that the law could not pass muster under either the due process or the equal protection standards he deemed appropriate, emphasizing especially the "intermediate level of scrutiny" he had articulated in Craig v. Boren, a 1976 sex discrimination-equal protection case (p. 647 below). The Craig formulation Justice Powell applied here requires that the classification "bear a fair and substantial relation to the object of the legislation."

15. Justice Stevens argued that "the public-charge provision is either futile or perverse insofar as it applies to childless couples, couples who will have illegitimate children if they are forbidden to marry, couples whose economic status will be improved by marriage, and couples who are so poor that the marriage will have no impact on the welfare status of their children in any event." (He did not try to articulate the appropriate standard of scrutiny except in a comment arguing that neither very strict nor very deferential review was appropriate.)

16. Justice Stewart added: "The Court is understandably reluctant to rely on substantive due process. But to embrace the essence of that doctrine under the guise of equal protection serves no purpose but obfuscation [and] invites mechanical or thoughtless application of misfocused doctrine. To bring it into the open forces a healthy and responsible recognition of the nature and purpose of the extreme power we wield."

17. Boddie found that indigents could not be compelled to pay filing fees in order to institute divorce actions in state courts. The case relied entirely on due process, but equal protection has played a major role (at least formally) in most other modern filing fee cases. Boddie is considered at p. 830 below, in order to examine it together with other filing fee decisions.

18. Justice REHNQUIST, the sole dissenter, found no basis for applying any "heightened standard of review," insisting on "the traditional presumption of validity" as expressed in such cases as Lee Optical. He concluded: "The stat-

3. *Commitment of children to mental hospitals.* In PARHAM v. J.R., 442 U.S. 584 (1979), the Court balanced "individual, family and social interests" in concluding that formal adversary hearings are not required when parents seek to commit their children to state mental institutions.[19] Challengers to Georgia's procedures for "voluntary" civil commitment of children by their parents had argued that "the constitutional rights of the child are of such magnitude and the likelihood of parental abuse is so great" that only a formal hearing prior to commitment would protect a child's rights adequately. Rejecting that claim, Chief Justice BURGER's majority opinion stressed that children's rights were circumscribed by the rights and duties of their parents. On balance, he gave greater weight to "the parents' traditional interests in and responsibility for the upbringing of their child." The Chief Justice emphasized the traditional concept of "the family as a unit with broad parental authority over minor children" and argued: "That some parents 'may at times be acting against the interests of their child' [creates] a basis for caution, but is hardly a reason to discard wholesale those pages of human experience that teach that parents generally do act in the child's best interests. The statist notion that governmental power should supersede parental authority in *all* cases because *some* parents abuse and neglect children is repugnant to American tradition." Although some decisions (e.g., Danforth, p. 536 above) had limited the traditional rights of parents, those cases did not justify a general mandate of formal hearings to curb parental discretion. Here, the informal preadmission procedures in the challenged Georgia scheme provided adequate safeguards: "In defining the respective rights and prerogatives of the child and parent in the voluntary commitment setting, we conclude that our precedents permit the parents to retain a substantial, if not the dominant, role in the decision, absent a finding of neglect or abuse, and that the traditional presumption that the parents act in the best interests of their child should apply. We also conclude, however, that the child's rights and the nature of the commitment decision are such that parents cannot always have absolute and unreviewable discretion to decide whether to have a child institutionalized."[20]

Justice BRENNAN's opinion, joined by Justices Marshall and Stevens, disagreed only partially about the result, but his underlying premises were sharply opposed to the majority's. He agreed that due process did not mandate *pre*-admission hearings, but objected to the majority's failure to require "at least one post-admission hearing." He especially objected to the argument that denial of hearings to juveniles could be justified "on the theory that parents act in their children's best interests and therefore may waive their children's due process rights," stating: "Notions of parental authority and family autonomy cannot stand as absolute and invariable barriers to the assertion of constitutional rights by children. [Danforth.]" He added: "The presumption that parents

---

ute [is] a permissible exercise of the State's power to regulate family life and to assure the support of minor children, despite its possible imprecision in the extreme cases envisioned in the concurring opinions."

19. Additional right to hearing cases are printed in sec. 4 below. The Parham case is noted here because of its unusually explicit consideration of the occasionally conflicting interests of parents and children. All of the cases in this group of notes involve interests of parents, children, and the state. In Moore and Zablocki, above, the conflict was essentially between the state and the family unit. Parham, by contrast, is one of the growing number of cases where there is potential or actual intrafamily conflict. (Danforth and Bellotti II, in the preceding group

of notes, provide the most relevant background to the situation in Parham. In those cases, the parent-child conflict was confronted in the context of laws requiring parental consent to minors' abortions.)

20. The Chief Justice emphasized that an informal "medical decisionmaking process" satisfied constitutional standards and that a formal hearing was not required: "[T]here is no reason to require a judicial-type hearing in all circumstances. As the scope of governmental action expands into new areas creating new controversies for judicial review, it is incumbent on courts to design procedures that protect the rights of the individual without unduly burdening the legitimate efforts of the states to deal with difficult social problems."

act in their children's best interests, while applicable to most child-rearing decisions, is not applicable in the commitment context. Numerous studies reveal that parental decisions to institutionalize their children often are the results of dislocation in the family unrelated to the children's mental condition." However, he conceded the inapplicability to children of the general rule requiring hearings preceding involuntary commitments of adults. He conclud-ed: "Children incarcerated in public mental institutions [are] entitled to some champion who can speak on their behalf and who stands ready to oppose a wrongful commitment. Georgia should not be permitted to deny that opportu-nity and that champion simply because the children's parents or guardians wish them to be confined without a hearing. The risk of erroneous commitment is simply too great unless there is some form of adversarial review." [21]

4. *Substantive due process methodology in light of the family relations cases: The role of tradition.* Recurrently, this section has raised the question whether the "fundamental values" search of modern substantive due process can be chan-neled in a manner that keeps it from becoming a wholly open-ended route for infusing subjective judicial values into the Constitution. Do the family law cases offer greater hope in that regard than Griswold, Roe, and their immediate progeny? Note especially the heavy reliance in Moore, above, on Justice Harlan's tradition-oriented approach. And consider the approving comments on such an approach in "Developments," 93 Harv.L.Rev. 1156 (1980): "In the family cases, the Court has consistently turned to tradition as a source of previously unrecognized aspects of [liberty]. Recognition of a traditional value as fundamental, however, does not mean that individual cases can be decided solely by reference to historical notions about the right. [Once] a traditional value has been accepted, [the] Court must give that value a consistent and principled interpretation. [While] tradition offers guidance, [due process] is not merely a mandate for the perpetuation of tradition with all its fortuitous historical attributes. Once it has been found that a particular right is an element of [liberty], the Court no longer looks exclusively to tradition to ascertain its contours. Instead, [the Court may adopt] a functional approach to the right, letting its rationale dictate its scope. [Because] a functional approach extends the scope of a traditional right beyond its historical contours, it may be criticized as manipulation of the level of generality of the relevant tradition so that rights not historically regarded as important liberties are brought within the scope of protection. This criticism misses the point. A court which extends the right of

---

21. In his critical analysis of a number of modern decisions on constitutionalized family law, Burt, in "The Constitution of the Family," 1979 Sup.Ct.Rev. 329, was especially caustic about both the majority and the minority posi-tions in the Parham case. He accused the major-ity of generally endorsing authority to suppress conflict, and the minority of somewhat naively appealing to the impact of reasoned justifications for calming discord. He viewed the majority as purporting to uphold "parental prerogatives against governmental intrusions," a formulation that obscured the real issue at stake: "Parents there were not seeking to resist governmental power over their children; they were invoking that power by attempting to confine their chil-dren in state psychiatric institutions." For the "liberal" dissenters in Parham, by contrast, "the familial guise of authority over children was not significant in principle. Authority required judicialized process to assure its [legitimacy], whether that authority was exercised by [parents or psychiatrists]." He adds: "[What] leads Mr.

Justice Brennan to believe that a child who protests his parents' decision to hospitalize and who resists the psychiatrists' custody will regard as 'fair' and 'legitimate' a proceeding that ends with a judge's ratification of the other adults' disposition?" He suggested that ultimately both sides are too preoccupied with striving for judi-cial, final solutions to complex problems, and suggests that the law would better protect the child's interests "if the dispute between him and the adult were prolonged in an orderly manner, rather than given the appearance of an abrupt conclusion." He accused both sides of having a "distaste for conflict," so that both suffer from "the concomitant failure to see its prolongation as a proper judicial technique." He suggested as the ultimate appropriate Court role in Parham and other family law cases that of provoking dispute not for its own sake but "to lead the contending parties to ward mutual accommoda-tion, toward abandoning the diametrically incon-sistent goals that lead each party to seek the others' total defeat."

procreative autonomy from a marital to a nonmarital context is not contending that the procreative rights of the unmarried are traditional. It is merely claiming that, given a longstanding cultural consensus that procreative activities comprise an area of human endeavor that should be regarded as within the realm of liberty, there must be some principled basis for treating the unmarried and married differently."

Does that approach adequately confine substantive due process adjudication? The "Developments" comment finds the "tradition-based approach" very appealing: "Recourse to traditional values enables the Court to afford protection to rights Americans traditionally have assumed to be part of our nation's scheme of liberty. [Not] all these rights would be preserved by exclusive resort to other theories, for example, one recognizing only rights essential to all possible systems of ordered liberty, or one concentrating on defects in the democratic process. Tradition ensures proper protection for important liberties that an abstract formula might overlook. The use of tradition [has] also appealed to the Court's need for a sense of impartiality. [Reference] to tradition does not involve the Court in the ambitious task of developing its own unified theory of political liberty; rather, the initial appeal is to a relatively objective history. While tradition is not always easy to ascertain, it is easier to tell that a value is deeply rooted in American tradition than to determine that it is a valid proposition of moral philosophy, or that it is supported by a convergence of contemporary views amounting to consensus." Does this position—essentially, an endorsement and elaboration of the Harlan-Powell methodology—adequately answer the charge of "Lochnerizing"?

EFFORTS TO ASSERT PRIVACY AND AUTONOMY INTERESTS IN ADDITIONAL CONTEXTS

1. *Unconventional sexual lifestyles.* a. *Homosexuality.* In 1976, without hearing argument or giving reasons for its decision, the Court summarily affirmed a three-judge federal court's dismissal of a challenge by male homosexuals to Virginia's sodomy law, in DOE v. COMMONWEALTH'S ATTORNEY, 425 U.S. 901.[1] In view of such cases as Roe, Griswold, Stanley v. Georgia and Eisenstadt, can it be said that the challengers' claim was so insubstantial as to warrant a summary disposition? Was the manner of disposition of the case (before the Court on appeal rather than certiorari) properly criticizable as "irresponsible" and "lawless"?[2] Consider the disposition not only against the background of the Court's privacy and autonomy rulings, but also in light of the lower court's decision on the issue:

The three-judge District Court divided 2 to 1 in rejecting the challenge. 403 F.Supp. 1199 (E.D.Va.1975). The plaintiffs sought a declaratory judgment that the sodomy law could not constitutionally be applied to a male homosexual's "active and regular homosexual relations with another adult male, consensually and in private." The majority distinguished the Court decisions relied on by the challengers as resting exclusively on interferences with "the privacy of the incidents of marriage," "the sanctity of the home," or "the nurture of family life." Homosexuality, by contrast, "is obviously no portion of marriage, home or family life," and may be prohibited, "even when committed in the home," when "appropriate in the promotion of morality and decency"; and the law had "a rational basis of State interests demonstrably legitimate and mirrored in the

---

1. Justices Brennan, Marshall and Stevens dissented from the summary disposition and urged that the case be set for oral argument.

2. See the comment by Gunther in The New York Times, April 3, 1976. Compare Grey's

analysis of the "sexual freedom" cases, at p. 531 above.

[Court's rulings]." The dissenting judge read the precedents as making it clear "that fundamental rights of such an intimate facet of an individual's life as sex, absent circumstances warranting intrusion by the state, are to be respected." He insisted that the majority had read the prior cases too narrowly: Eisenstadt showed that "the legal viability of a marital-nonmarital distinction in private sexual acts, if not eliminated, was at the very least seriously impaired." And under cases such as Roe, private "consensual sex acts between adults are matters, absent evidence that they are harmful, in which the state has no legitimate interest." In short, Roe and Eisenstadt demonstrated that "intimate personal decisions or private matters of substantial importance to the well-being of the individuals involved are protected by the Due Process Clause. The right to select consenting adult sexual partners must be considered within this category. The exercise of that right, whether heterosexual or homosexual, should not be proscribed by state regulation absent compelling justification." Here, the state had shown neither "a rational basis [nor] a compelling state interest" to justify the law.[3]

3. The significance of the summary affirmance in the homosexuality case elicited several comments in the course of the opinions in Carey (1977; p. 547 above; distribution of contraceptives). Justice Brennan's opinion insisted that "the Court has not definitively answered the difficult question whether and to what extent the Constitution prohibits state statutes regulating [private consensual sexual] behavior among adults." Justice Rehnquist's dissent challenged that remark, citing Doe v. Commonwealth's Attorney and stating: "While we have not ruled on every conceivable regulation affecting such conduct, the facial constitutional validity of criminal statutes prohibiting certain consensual acts has been 'definitively' established." Note also Justice Powell's concurrence, which criticized requiring strict scrutiny of a state regulation "whenever it implicates sexual freedom" or "affect[s] adult sexual relations." Justice Brennan claimed in response that his opinion did not go that far.

For a later examination (and rejection) of a homosexual's claim by a Court of Appeals, see Dronenburg v. Zech, 741 F.2d 1388 (D.C.Cir. 1984). That case was an unsuccessful attack on the Navy's policy of mandatory discharge for homosexual conduct. The challenge relied primarily on the line of cases beginning with Griswold and Roe. In rejecting the claim that "private consensual homosexual activity [falls] within the zone of constitutionally protected privacy," Judge Bork (a possible future Reagan nominee to the Court) noted Doe v. Commonwealth's Attorney, described it as a summary disposition on the merits "binding on lower federal courts," refused to distinguish it as possibly resting on plaintiffs' lack of standing, and insisted that even if it were a "somewhat ambiguous precedent," a lower court should not "extend the right of privacy" as claimed here. Examining the nature of the Court privacy decisions at length, he found in them "little guidance for lower courts." For example, Roe, while containing an illustrative list of privacy rights, "provided no explanatory principle that informs a lower court how to reason about what is and what is not encompassed by the right of privacy." To Judge Bork, the Court rulings posed a "peculiar jurisprudential problem": "When the [Court] decides cases under a specific provision [it] explicates the meaning and suggests the contours of a value already stated in the document or implied by the Constitution's structure and history," and that provides guidance for lower courts. "But when the Court creates new rights, [lower] courts have none of these materials available and can look only to what the [Court] has stated to be the principle involved." Yet the privacy rulings contained no "principle articulated even approaching in breadth" that claimed here. "The Court has listed as illustrative of the right of privacy such matters as activities relating to marriage, procreation, contraception, family relationships, and child rearing and education. It need hardly be said that none of these covers a right to homosexual conduct."

Judge Bork added: "We would find it impossible to conclude that a right to homosexual conduct is 'fundamental' or 'implicit in the concept of ordered liberty' unless any and all private sexual behavior falls within those categories, a conclusion we are unwilling to draw." He recognized that the Court's modern privacy cases had created new rights, but thought it certain that lower courts should not do so, if it was "in any degree doubtful that the [Court itself] should freely create new constitutional rights." (He added in a footnote: "It may be only candid to say at this point that the author of this opinion, when in academic life, expressed the view that no court should create new constitutional rights; that is, rights must be fairly derived by standard modes of legal interpretation from the text, structure, and history of the Constitution. [These] views are, however, completely irrelevant to the function of a circuit judge." The lower courts were indeed bound by the Court's assertion that it may create new rights; hence, the only question here was whether the Court's holdings or analyses, "honestly applied," reached the claim here.) He stated, too: "If the revolution in sexual mores that appellant proclaims is in fact ever to arrive, we think it must arrive through the moral choices of the people and their elected representatives, not through the ukase of this court." After finding that the precedents did not

b. *Adultery.* In HOLLENBAUGH v. CARNEGIE FREE LIBRARY, 439 U.S. 1052 (1978), the Court refused to review a decision sustaining the discharge of two public library employees for "living together in a state of 'open adultery.' " A male library custodian had left his wife and moved in with a female librarian after she became pregnant with his child. The library board fired the petitioners, claiming that it did not want to appear to condone the extramarital affair and the child's birth out of wedlock. Justice MARSHALL's dissent from the denial of certiorari stated that the lower federal court had sustained, "after the most minimal scrutiny, an unwarranted governmental intrusion into the privacy of public employees." He commented: "Petitioners' rights to pursue an open rather than a clandestine personal relationship and to rear their child together in this environment closely resemble the other aspects of personal privacy to which we have extended constitutional protection. That [their] arrangement was unconventional or socially disapproved does not negate the resemblance, particularly in the absence of a judgment that the arrangement so offends social norms as to evoke criminal sanctions." (The State had repealed its laws prohibiting adultery and fornication several years earlier.) He argued that the State "should at least be required to show that petitioners' discharge serves a substantial state interest"; and here, there had been no "meaningful showing that these private choices have any relation to job performance." He concluded: "I believe that individuals' choices concerning their private lives deserve more than token protection from this Court, regardless of whether we approve of those choices." [4]

2. *Personal appearance and hair style.* An effort to rely on privacy and autonomy concerns to invalidate a local regulation of the length and style of policemen's hair failed in KELLEY v. JOHNSON, 425 U.S. 238 (1976). The attack had succeeded in the lower federal courts after they had imposed the burden on the police department to establish "a genuine public need" for the regulation. Justice REHNQUIST's majority opinion disagreed with that approach and insisted that a much more deferential standard of review, of the Lee Optical variety, applied. And in his view, the hair grooming regulation easily met that "mere rationality standard." He argued that the "liberty" interest claimed here was "distinguishable" from the interests involved in cases from Meyer through Roe: "[W]hether the citizenry at large has some sort of 'liberty' interest [in] matters of personal appearance is a question on which this Court's cases offer little, if any, guidance. We can, nevertheless, assume an affirmative answer for purposes of deciding this case, because we find that assumption insufficient to carry the day" here. He emphasized that the claimant was a policeman, not "a member of the citizenry at large," and insisted that, even if citizens generally could demand strong justification for regulations of personal appearance, the state bore no such burden in the case of the police officers. It was the challenger who had to show that there was no "rational connection" between the regulation and "the promotion of safety." That burden could not be met here. Justice Rehnquist noted that most police forces were uniformed, and that similarity in appearance "may be based on a desire to make police officers readily recognizable to the members of the public, or a desire for the esprit de corps which such similarity is felt to inculcate within the police force itself." Justice MARSHALL's dissent, joined by Justice Brennan, found that the regulation could not pass scrutiny even under a "rational basis" standard, and went on to argue at

provide "even an ambiguous warrant" for the right claimed, he briefly rejected a broader theory as well: that "morality" was not a justifiable basis for legislation or at least naval regulations. Judge Bork replied: "This theory that majority morality and majority choice is always made presumptively invalid by the Constitution attacks

the very predicate of democratic government," although "this deference to democratic choice does not apply where the Constitution removes the choice from majorities."

4. Justice Brennan dissented from the denial of certiorari without writing an opinion.

length that personal appearance *is* an aspect of constitutionally protected liberty: "An individual's personal appearance may reflect, sustain, and nourish his personality and may well be used as a means of expressing his attitude and lifestyle.

In taking control over a citizen's personal appearance, the Government forces him to sacrifice substantial elements of his integrity and identity as well. To say that the liberty guarantee of the 14th Amendment does not encompass matters of personal appearance would be fundamentally inconsistent with the values of privacy, self-identity, autonomy, and personal integrity that I have always assumed the Constitution was designed to protect." [5]

3. *Substantive due process, the mentally retarded, and the mentally ill.* In YOUNGBERG v. ROMEO, 457 U.S. 307 (1982), the Court considered "for the first time the substantive [due process] rights of involuntarily-committed mentally retarded persons." Romeo, a "profoundly retarded" man with the mental capacity of an 18-month old child, had been committed to a state institution at the behest of his mother. After his commitment, his mother became concerned about injuries he had suffered in the institution. She filed a § 1983 action as his "best friend" claiming that officials of the institution had violated his constitutional rights by failing to take appropriate measures to protect him against injuries. That suit presented the Court with the question whether Romeo had "substantive rights under the Due Process Clause [to] (i) safe conditions of confinement; (ii) freedom from bodily restraints; and (iii) training or 'habilitation.' " [6]

Justice POWELL, in his opinion for the Court, had no difficulty finding constitutional support for the first two substantive rights claimed by Romeo: he found constitutionally protected liberty interests in "safety" and in "freedom of movement." But he found Romeo's third claim, to a "constitutional right to minimally adequate habilitation," more troubling. But that claim, too, was supportable to a limited extent. He explained: "In addressing the asserted right to training, we start from established principles. As a general matter, a State is under no constitutional duty to provide substantive services for those within its border. See [e.g., Harris v. McRae (publicly funded abortions)]. The record reveals that [Romeo's] primary needs are bodily safety and a minimum of physical restraint, and [Romeo] claims training related to these needs. As we have recognized that there is a constitutionally protected liberty interest in safety and freedom from restraint, training may be necessary to avoid unconstitutional infringement of those rights. [If], as seems the case, [Romeo] seeks only training related to safety and freedom from restraints, this case does not present the difficult question whether a mentally retarded person, involuntarily committed to a state institution, has some general constitutional right to training per se, even when no type or amount of training would lead to freedom. Here, we only conclude that [Romeo's] liberty interests require the State to provide minimally adequate or reasonable training to ensure safety and freedom from undue restraint." But the fact that a liberty interest was implicated, Justice Powell noted, did not necessarily demonstrate a due process violation. "[Whether Romeo's] constitutional rights have been violated must be determined by balancing his liberty interests against the relevant state interests. If there is to be any uniformity in protecting these interests, this balancing cannot be left to the unguided discretion of a judge or jury. We therefore turn to consider the proper standard for determining whether a State adequately has protected the rights of the involuntarily-committed mentally retarded."

5. Justice POWELL, who concurred in the majority opinion, stated that he, unlike the dissenters, found "no negative implication in the opinion with respect to a liberty interest [as] to matters of personal appearance."

6. "Habilitation," a term of art in programs for the mentally retarded, focuses upon "training and development of needed skills."

In articulating this standard, Justice Powell placed special emphasis on the need to defer to professional judgments. He relied heavily on an opinion in the Court of Appeals stating that the Constitution "only requires that the courts make certain that professional judgment in fact was exercised. It is not appropriate for the courts to specify which of several professionally acceptable choices should have been made." Although the involuntarily committed were entitled to "more considerate treatment" than criminals, the State did not have to meet a "compelling" or "substantial" necessity test. "In determining what is 'reasonable'—in this and in any case presenting a claim for training by a state— we emphasize that courts must show deference to the judgment exercised by a qualified professional. By so limiting judicial review, [interference] by the federal judiciary with the internal operations of [state] institutions should be minimized. Moreover, there certainly is no reason to think that judges or juries are better qualified than appropriate professionals in making such decisions. For these reasons, the decision, if made by a professional, is presumptively valid; liability may be imposed only when the decision by the professional is such a substantial departure from accepted professional judgment, practice or standards as to demonstrate that the person responsible actually did not base the decision on such a judgment. In an action for damages against a professional in his individual capacity, however, the professional will not be liable if he was unable to satisfy his normal professional standards because of budgetary constraints; in such a situation, good-faith immunity would bar liability."

A concurrence by Justice BLACKMUN, joined by Justices Brennan and O'Connor, noted "two difficult and important issues" which he thought properly left unresolved by the Court's opinion. The first was whether the State could accept Romeo for "care and treatment" and then "constitutionally refuse to provide him any 'treatment,' as that term is defined by state law."[7] The "second difficult question left open," Justice Blackmun noted, "is whether [Romeo] has an independent constitutional claim, grounded in the Due Process Clause, [to] that 'habilitation' or training necessary to *preserve* those basic self-care skills he possessed when he first entered [the state institution]—for example, the ability to dress himself and care for his personal hygiene. In my view, it would be consistent with the Court's reasoning today to include within the 'minimally adequate training required by the Constitution' such training as is reasonably necessary to prevent a person's pre-existing self-care skills from *deteriorating* because of his commitment." Chief Justice BURGER, concurring only in the judgment, emphasized that he "would hold flatly that respondent has no constitutional right to training, or 'habilitation,' per se." He agreed with Justice Powell "that some amount of self-care instruction may be necessary to avoid unreasonable infringement of a mentally-retarded person's interest in safety and freedom from restraint." But he added that "it seems clear to me that the Constitution does not otherwise place an affirmative duty on the State to provide any particular kind of training or habilitation—even such as might be encompassed under the essentially standardless rubric 'minimally adequate training' to which the Court refers."[8]

---

7. Chief Justice BURGER's opinion concurring only in the judgment thought it "frivolous" for Romeo to contend "that, because state law purportedly creates a right to 'care and treatment,' he has a *federal substantive* right under the Due Process Clause to enforcement of this state right": "[W]ere every substantive right created by state law enforceable under the Due Process Clause, the distinction between state and federal law would quickly be obliterated." Justice Blackmun insisted that the claim was not frivolous and argued: "If a state court orders a mentally retarded person committed for 'care *and* treatment,' [I] believe that due process might well bind the State to ensure that the conditions of his commitment bear some reasonable relation to each of these goals. In such a case, commitment without any 'treatment' whatsoever would not bear a reasonable relation to the purposes of the person's confinement."

8. In another case decided on the same day as Youngberg v. Romeo, the Court had granted review "to determine whether involuntarily com-

4. *Computerized data banks and "privacy."* WHALEN v. ROE, 429 U.S. 589 (1977), was the Court's first major encounter with the constitutional risks generated by governmental storage of personal data in computers. Patients and physicians made an on-the-face attack on a New York law under which the State recorded in a centralized computer file the names and addresses of all patients obtaining prescriptions for certain dangerous but legitimate drugs—drugs such as opium derivatives and amphetamines. The State acquired the information by requiring reports from doctors. A lower federal court held the patient identification provisions of the law unconstitutional on the ground that they invaded constitutionally protected "zones of privacy" with "a needlessly broad sweep." The Court unanimously reversed.

Justice STEVENS' prevailing opinion commented that prior "privacy" cases had "in fact involved at least two different kinds of interests. One is the individual interest in avoiding disclosure of personal matters [e.g., Griswold], and another is the interest in independence in making certain kinds of important decisions [e.g., Roe]." [9] He concluded, however, "that the New York program does not, on its face, pose a sufficiently grievous threat to either interest to establish a constitutional violation." With respect to disclosure of personal matters, he emphasized the careful security provisions in the law (which barred the disclosure of the identity of patients) and insisted that there was no justification for assuming that those provisions would be administered improperly. And the limited disclosure of the information to state health officials was not "meaningfully distinguishable from the host of other unpleasant invasions of privacy that are associated with many facets of health care." He was no more impressed with the claim of impingement on the "interest in making important decisions independently." The patients had argued that, even without unwarranted disclosures, "the knowledge that the information is readily available in a computerized file creates a genuine concern that causes some persons to decline needed medication." Justice Stevens responded that, despite the statute, about 100,000 prescriptions for the covered drugs were being filled each month and insisted that the law did not significantly inhibit the patient-physician decision regarding needed medication. [10]

4. *A general right of intimate association as an aspect of liberty?* Although most Court recognitions of fundamental privacy interests have occurred in marriage and family contexts, as the preceding materials illustrate, statements in a 1984

mitted mental patients have a constitutional right to refuse treatment with antipsychotic drugs." Mills v. Rogers, 457 U.S. 291 (1982). But the Court did not reach the merits of that issue. Instead, it remanded the case to the Court of Appeals to determine whether an intervening state court decision affected the proper disposition of the case. Justice Powell commented: "The parties agree that the Constitution recognizes a liberty interest in avoiding the unwanted administration of antipsychotic drugs. Assuming that they are correct in this respect, the substantive issue involves a definition of that protected constitutional interest, as well as identification of the conditions under which competing state interests might outweigh it. See [e.g., Youngberg v. Romeo]."

9. Note the similar distinction suggested in note 2 after Griswold, at p. 514 above.

10. Justice Stevens added: "We are not unaware of the threat to privacy implicit in the accumulation of vast amounts of personal information in computerized data banks." He noted, however, that New York's procedures showed a "proper concern" with protection of privacy: "We therefore need not, and do not, decide any question which might be presented by the unwarranted disclosure of accumulated private data [or] by a system that did not contain comparable security provisions." In a concurring opinion, Justice BRENNAN, while noting that limited medical reporting requirements were generally acceptable, added: "Broad dissemination [of] such information [would] clearly implicate constitutionally protected privacy rights, and would presumably be justified only by compelling state interests. [Roe.]" Finding the easy accessibility of computerized data here particularly "troubling," he commented: "I am not prepared to say that future developments will not demonstrate the necessity of some curb on such technology." Justice STEWART took a narrower view of the potential risks and constitutional challenges regarding such data banks and, criticizing Justice Brennan, insisted: "Whatever the ratio decidendi of Griswold, it does not recognize a general interest in freedom from disclosure of private information."

opinion suggest that the "freedom of association" protected by the due process clause may also extend to other relationships—relationships characterized by "relative smallness, a high degree of selectivity in decisions to begin and maintain the affiliation, and seclusion from others in critical aspects of the relationship." Those criteria were suggested by Justice BRENNAN writing for the Court in ROBERTS v. UNITED STATES JAYCEES, 468 U.S. ___ (1984) (more fully described below, at p. 1360).[11] Freedom of association keyed to the exercise of First Amendment rights has long been recognized by the Court, as later materials illustrate. But the Jaycees opinion also commented at some length on a broader associational right: it distinguished between the Jaycees members' "freedom of intimate association" and their "freedom of expressive association"; and the former was derived from the general concept of liberty rather than First Amendment needs. Noting that prior cases had referred to "freedom of association" in "two distinct senses," Justice Brennan spoke not only of First Amendment adjuncts but also of the safeguarding of "choices to enter into and maintain certain intimate human relationships." On the latter, he stated:

"The Court has long recognized that, because the Bill of Rights is designed to secure individual liberty, it must afford the formation and preservation of certain kinds of highly personal relationships a substantial measure of sanctuary from unjustified interference by the State. E.g., [Pierce; Meyer]. Without precisely identifying every consideration that may underlie this type of constitutional protection, we have noted that certain kinds of personal bonds have played a critical role in the culture and traditions of the Nation by cultivating and transmitting shared ideals and beliefs; they thereby foster diversity and act as critical buffers between the individual and the [State]. Moreover, the constitutional shelter afforded such relationships reflects the realization that individuals draw much of their emotional enrichment from close ties with others. Protecting these relationships from unwarranted state interference therefore safeguards the ability independently to define one's identity that is central to any concept of liberty. The personal affiliations that exemplify these considerations, and that therefore suggest some relevant limitations on the relationships that might be entitled to this sort of constitutional protection, are those that attend the creation and sustenance of a family—marriage; childbirth; the raising and education of children; and cohabitation with one's relatives. [Among] other things, [family relationships] are distinguished by such attributes as relative smallness, a high degree of selectivity in decisions to begin and maintain the affiliation, and seclusion from others in critical aspects of the relationship. As a general matter, only relationships with these sorts of qualities are likely to reflect the considerations that have led to an understanding of freedom of association as an intrinsic element of personal liberty. Conversely, an association lacking these qualities—such as a large business enterprise—seems remote from the concerns giving rise to this constitutional protection. [Between] these poles, of course, lies a broad range of human relationships that may make greater or lesser claims to constitutional protection from particular incursions by the State. Determining the limits of state authority over an individual's freedom to enter into a particular association therefore unavoidably entails a careful assessment of where that relationship's objective characteristics locate it on a spectrum from the most intimate to the most attenuated of personal attachments. We need not mark the potentially significant points on

---

11. The Jaycees case rejected a freedom of association challenge by the U.S. Jaycees, a formerly male-only organization, to the applicability of a Minnesota civil rights law banning sex discrimination in "public accommodations." There was no dissent from the holding. Justice Brennan wrote for the majority; Justice O'CONNOR concurred in only part of his opinion but joined the judgment; Justice REHNQUIST noted his concurrence in the judgment; Chief Justice BURGER and Justice BLACKMUN did not participate.

this terrain with any precision. We note only that factors that may be relevant include size, purpose, policies, selectivity, congeniality, and other characteristics that in a particular case may be pertinent." [12]

SECTION 4. THE SCOPE OF "LIBERTY" AND "PROPERTY": THE RIGHT TO HEARING CASES

Introduction. Since the beginning of the 1970s, the Court has decided a large number of cases involving claims that due process requires some form of adjudicatory hearing. In the typical situation, the claimant asserts a relationship or status vis-à-vis government—e.g., as employee or licensee or welfare recipient—and insists that it may not be terminated without a hearing. In deciding these cases, the Court has repeatedly confronted one of the central themes in the preceding sections: What constitutes constitutionally protected "liberty" and "property" under the due process clauses of the Fifth and 14th Amendments? True, the right to hearing cases deal with procedural due process, not substantive due process. But these procedural cases, like the substantive ones, ultimately involve resolution of the troublesome problem of identifying the appropriate sources for giving content to the meaning of "liberty" and "property." [1] This sampling of modern right to hearing cases offers an opportunity for further exploration of basic problems that surfaced repeatedly in the preceding materials. What light do these cases throw on the proper ingredients of the meaning of "liberty" and "property"? To what extent do their sources lie in federal constitutional law? To what extent are they determined instead by statutes (state as well as federal), or by common law?

Consider, for example, the question of "liberty." In the substantive due process cases, the Court adopted a very embracive view of the individual interests encompassed by the term "liberty." From Allgeyer and Lochner to Meyer and Pierce, the old Court extended "liberty" far beyond the freedom from physical restraint. And that legacy has been embraced by the modern Court: Griswold, Roe and their progeny have explicitly built upon the Lochner era's broad view of liberty. True, Justices have differed about what aspects of liberty are sufficiently "fundamental" to warrant special scrutiny by the Court. But those differences, examined above, have been accompanied by a widespread consensus that "liberty" includes just about every interest of significance to an individual—or, more accurately, that the phrase "life, liberty or property" in the due process clauses is "a unitary concept embracing all interests valued by sensible men." [2] In the substantive due process area, in short, the typical Court

---

12. The Court found that "several features of the Jaycees clearly place the organization outside of the category of relationships worthy of this kind of constitutional protection." For example, the local chapters of the Jaycees were "large and basically unselective groups"; they were "neither small nor selective." (For the Court's discussion of the Jaycees' claim of "freedom of expressive association," a freedom related to First Amendment rights, see the additional discussion of the case at p. 1360 below.)

1. Many of the procedural due process-right to hearing cases deal at length with the *kind* of hearing required when a hearing right is triggered because of an impingement upon liberty or property. The type of hearing required depends

on a number of variables pertaining to the context of the problem. Exploration of the details regarding the kind of hearing constitutionally mandated is beyond the scope of this book. The general considerations deemed important by the Court are articulated in Mathews v. Eldridge (1976; p. 584 below), but the detailed groundrules for hearings required in a range of administrative and civil contexts are left to other courses, especially those in administrative law. (On the procedural due process requirements to assure fair hearings in the *criminal* context, recall chap. 7 above.)

2. Monaghan, "Of 'Liberty' and 'Property'," 62 Cornell L.Rev. 405 (1977). This article, an unusually penetrating one amidst the flow of

focus has not been on whether a constitutionally protected interest has been impinged upon, but rather on what amount of justification the state must put forth to defend that impingement successfully.

Starting in the early 1970s, the procedural due process-right to hearing cases diverged from that pattern. In a growing number of cases (beginning with Roth, p. 569 below), the Court has found the claimed interest, albeit significant to the individual, not included within the constitutional notion of "liberty." Instead of readily assuming that a constitutionally protected interest is involved and dwelling primarily on the question of the appropriate contours of procedural due process in that context, the Court has increasingly paused at the outset to ask whether a constitutionally protected interest *is* presented. Moreover, in delineating "liberty" (and, even more often, "property") in the procedural due process context, the Court has repeatedly relied on state law or federal legislation—sources of guidance rarely drawn on in the substantive due process materials. The Court's course has been an uncertain, wavering one; but a sampling of the developments is warranted not only to inquire whether the modern Court's methodology in the right to hearing sphere justifiably departs from that familiar from the substantive due process area, but also to ask what impact the modern procedural due process analyses may have on future elaborations of substantive due process.

THE BACKGROUND OF THE MODERN DEVELOPMENTS: THE PROCEDURAL DUE PROCESS REVOLUTION OF THE EARLY 1970s

The major case launching the modern procedural due process revolution, a revolution that guaranteed hearing rights to those engaged in a variety of relations with government, was GOLDBERG v. KELLY, 397 U.S. 254 (1970). Justice BRENNAN's majority opinion held that due process required that a welfare recipient be afforded "an evidentiary hearing *before* the termination of benefits." He noted that the appellant, the Social Services Commissioner, had not claimed that "procedural due process is not applicable to the termination of welfare benefits" and added: "Such benefits are a matter of statutory entitlement for persons qualified to receive them." He commented, moreover, that welfare assistance is "not a mere charity, but a means to 'promote the general Welfare, and secure the Blessings of Liberty to ourselves and our Posterity,'" and added "that termination of aid pending resolution of the controversy over eligibility may deprive an *eligible* recipient of the very means by which to live while he waits."[1] A series of post-Goldberg cases in the early 1970s extended

modern commentary on the right to hearing cases, is cited hereinafter as Monaghan, "Of 'Liberty' and 'Property.'" See also, generally, Rabin, "Job Security and Due Process: Monitoring Administrative Discretion Through a Reasons Requirement," 44 U.Chi.L.Rev. 60 (1976), and the Van Alstyne and Tushnet articles cited in the next footnote.

1. In finding that a claim to welfare benefits could trigger procedural due process protection (even though there was no constitutional right to such benefits and the claim to them arose initially from a legislative decision), Justice Brennan quoted Charles Reich, the author of "The New Property," 73 Yale L.J. 733 (1964), and of "Individual Rights and Social Welfare: The Emerging Legal Issues," 74 Yale L.J. 1245 (1965) (as well as the widely sold 1970 book, The Greening of

America). Reich's "The New Property" traced the emergence of government as a major source of wealth, noting that it was pouring forth "money, benefits, services, contracts, franchises and licenses [on] a vast, imperial scale." He argued that, in view of the broad functions of the modern state, "it must be recognized that we are becoming a society based upon relationship and status—status deriving primarily from source of livelihood. Status is so closely linked to personality that destruction of one may well destroy the other. Status must therefore be surrounded with the kind of safeguards once reserved for personality." His claim that deprivations of governmental largess warranted protection similar to that given traditional property rights formed an important part of the background for the procedural due process revolution that began with Gold-

procedural due process guarantees to a wide range of other claimants: employees, students, prisoners, parolees, debtors, automobile drivers, and so forth.[2] The automobile driver case, BELL v. BURSON, 402 U.S. 535 (1971), was a particularly graphic illustration of the Court's initial eagerness to recognize a wide range of individual interests as triggering procedural due process protection. With Justice BRENNAN again writing for the Court, Bell held that a driver involved in an auto accident had an entitlement under state law to his driver's license; that entitlement triggered due process guarantees and required the state to hold a hearing to determine fault in the accident before the license could be suspended. He commented: "Once licenses are issued, [their] continued possession may become essential in the pursuit of livelihood. Suspension of issued licenses thus involves state action that adjudicates important interests of licensees. In such cases the licenses are not to be taken away without that procedural due process required by the 14th Amendment."

That recognition of a wide range of individual interests in the early 1970s soon triggered a partial reaction on the Court. Some of the Justices were evidently concerned that the requirement of adjudicatory hearings in a large number of settings would excessively constitutionalize government's relations with licensees, employees and persons of similar status. There may have been fear as well that imposing hearing requirements in an ever wider range of settings would ultimately prove so inconvenient and expensive that it might inhibit the state from granting benefits it concededly was not obliged to provide. It is the methodology of that partial counterrevolution that has caused special doctrinal patterns regarding the meaning of "liberty" and "property." Instead of finding that in some settings procedural due process requirements could be satisfied with very informal or truncated hearings, or none at all, the main focus of the majority's limiting efforts shifted to asking initially whether there was any "liberty" or "property" involved that warranted a triggering of procedural due process concerns. That has become the first step in the inquiry; the question of what process is due (see p. 584 below) is typically reached only if the first step produces an affirmative answer. The most significant case delineating the new position was Roth, which follows.[3]

---

berg v. Kelly. See Van Alstyne, "Cracks in 'The New Property': Adjudicative Due Process in the Administrative State," 62 Cornell L.Rev. 445 (1977); cf. Tushnet, "The Newer Property: Suggestion for the Revival of Substantive Due Process," 1975 Sup.Ct.Rev. 261.

Another important ingredient for the background of the early 1970s hearing cases was the effective abandonment, especially during the 1960s, of the traditional "right-privilege" distinction. The famous early expression of that distinction came from Justice Holmes while he was still a state judge, in McAuliffe v. Mayor of New Bedford (1892; p. 1361 below), rejecting any constitutional attack on the discharge of a public employee for political activities: "The petitioner may have the constitutional right to talk politics, but he has no constitutional right to be a policeman." The late 20th century cases make it clear that, even though an individual does not have a right to a public job or license or contract, he is protected by substantive constitutional guarantees when government seeks to terminate the relationship. For a tracing of that development in the First Amendment area, see p. 1361 below. See generally Van Alstyne, "The Demise of the Right-Privilege Distinction in Constitutional Law," 81 Harv.L.Rev. 1439 (1968).

2. See the review of the developments in Rendleman, "The New Due Process: Rights and Remedies," 63 Ky.L.J. 531 (1975). Some of the major cases are noted further below.

3. Roth and most major cases that follow involve public employees. Public employee cases are emphasized in this section because they produced most of the doctrinal innovations in the definition of "liberty" and "property" and because they illustrate the modern Court's methodology in a single functional context.

BOARD OF REGENTS v. ROTH

408 U.S. 564, 92 S.Ct. 2701, 33 L.Ed.2d 548 (1972).

Mr. Justice STEWART delivered the opinion of the Court.

[Roth, hired to teach for a one-year term at Wisconsin State University-Oshkosh, was informed without explanation that he would not be rehired for the following year. He had no tenure rights; under state law, "the decision whether to rehire a nontenured teacher [was left] to the unfettered discretion of university officials." Under the university rules "no reason for nonretention need be given." Roth brought a federal action claiming that the decision not to rehire him violated his First Amendment rights, alleging that "the true reason for the decision was to punish him for certain statements critical of the University administration" and asserting as well that the failure to give him "any reason for nonretention and an opportunity for a hearing" violated his procedural due process rights. The District Court granted summary judgment for Roth on the procedural due process claim, and the Court of Appeals affirmed.] The only question presented to us [is] whether [Roth] had a constitutional right to a statement of reasons and a hearing. [We] hold that he did not.

I. The requirements of procedural due process apply only to the deprivation of interests encompassed by the 14th Amendment's protection of liberty and property. When protected interests are implicated, the right to some kind of prior hearing is paramount. But the range of interests protected by procedural due process is not infinite. [Undeniably], the respondent's re-employment prospects were of major concern to him—[a] concern that we surely cannot say was insignificant. And a weighing process has long been a part of any determination of the *form* of hearing required in particular situations by procedural due process.[1] But, to determine whether due process requirements apply in the first place, we must look not to the "weight" but to the *nature* of the interest at stake. We must look to see if the interest is within the 14th Amendment's protection of liberty and property.

"Liberty" and "property" are broad and majestic terms. [For] that reason, the Court has fully and finally rejected the wooden distinction between "rights" and "privileges" that once seemed to govern the applicability of procedural due process rights. The Court has also made clear that the property interests protected by procedural due process extend well beyond actual ownership of real estate, chattels, or money. By the same token, the Court has required due process protection for deprivations of liberty beyond the sort of formal constraints imposed by the criminal process. Yet, while the Court has eschewed rigid or formalistic limitations on the protection of procedural due process, it has at the same time observed certain boundaries. For the words "liberty" and "property" in the Due Process Clause of the 14th Amendment must be given some meaning.

II. [After quoting Justice McReynolds' broad definition of "liberty" in Meyer v. Nebraska, the Court continued:] In a Constitution for a free people, there can be no doubt that the meaning of "liberty" must be broad indeed. There might be cases in which a State refused to re-employ a person under such circumstances that interests in liberty would be implicated. But this is not such a case. The State, in declining to rehire the respondent, did not make any charge against him that might seriously damage his standing and associations in his community, [for] example, that he had been guilty of dishonesty, or immorality. Had it done so, this would be a different case. For "[w]here a

---

1. "The formality and procedural requisites for the hearing can vary, depending upon the importance of the interests involved and the nature of the subsequent proceedings." Boddie v. Connecticut [1971; p. 830 below]. [Footnote by Justice Stewart.]

person's good name, reputation, honor, or integrity is at stake because of what the government is doing to him, notice and an opportunity to be heard are essential." Wisconsin v. Constantineau, 400 U.S. 433 [1971].[2] In such a case, due process would accord an opportunity to refute the charge before University officials. In the present case, however, there is no suggestion whatever that the respondent's "good name, reputation, honor, or integrity" is at stake. Similarly, there is no suggestion that the [State] imposed on him a stigma or other disability that foreclosed his freedom to take advantage of other employment [opportunities]. To be sure, the respondent has alleged that the non-renewal of his contract was based on his exercise of his right to freedom of speech. But this allegation is not now before us. [R]espondent has yet to prove that the decision not to rehire him was, in fact, based on his free speech activities. [Hence] all that clearly appears [here] is that the respondent was not rehired for one year at one university. It stretches the concept too far to suggest that a person is deprived of "liberty" when he simply is not rehired in one job but remains as free as before to seek another.

III. The 14th Amendment's procedural protection of property is a safeguard of the security of interests that a person has already acquired in specific benefits. These interests—property interests—may take many forms. Thus, the Court has held that a person receiving welfare benefits under statutory and administrative standards defining eligibility for them has an interest in continued receipt of those benefits that is safeguarded by procedural due process. Goldberg v. Kelly. Similarly, in the area of public employment, the Court has held that a public college professor dismissed from an office held under tenure provisions, Slochower [p. 1365 below], and college professors and staff members dismissed during the terms of their contracts, Wieman [p. 1364 below], have interests in continued employment that are safeguarded by [due process]. Certain attributes of "property" interests protected by procedural due process emerge from these decisions. To have a property interest in a benefit, a person clearly must have more than an abstract need or desire for it. He must have more than a unilateral expectation of it. He must, instead, have a legitimate claim of entitlement to it. [Property interests], of course, are not created by the Constitution. Rather, they are created and their dimensions are defined by existing rules or understandings that stem from an independent source such as state law—rules or understandings that secure certain benefits and that support claims of entitlement to those benefits. Thus, the welfare recipients in Goldberg v. Kelly had a claim of entitlement to welfare payments that was grounded in the statute defining eligibility for them. [Similarly], respondent's "property" interest in employment at [the University] was created and defined by the terms of his appointment [which] specifically provided that the respondent's employment was to terminate on June 30. They did not provide for contract renewal absent "sufficient cause." Indeed, they made no provision for renewal whatsoever. Thus, the terms of the respondent's appointment secured absolutely no interest in re-employment for the next year. They supported absolutely no possible claim of entitlement to re-employment. Nor, significantly, was there any state statute or University rule or policy that secured his interest in re-employment or that created any legitimate claim to it.[3] In these circumstances,

2. Wisconsin v. Constantineau invalidated a state law permitting a sheriff to label publicly a person as an alcoholic, by posting his name in a public place, without giving him prior notice and a hearing. But see the 1976 decision in Paul v. Davis (p. 578 below), straining to distinguish Constantineau and holding that "mere" injury to reputation did not fall within constitutionally protected "liberty." The narrow reading of "liberty" in Paul v. Davis was one symptom of the partial counterrevolution directed against the expansion of hearing rights after Goldberg v. Kelly.

3. To be sure, the respondent does suggest that most teachers hired on a year-to-year basis by [the University] are, in fact, rehired. But the District Court has not found that there is anything approaching a "common law" of re-employment, see Perry v. Sindermann [which follows], so strong as to require University officials to give the respondent a statement of reasons and

the respondent surely had an abstract concern in being rehired, but he did not have a *property* interest sufficient to require the University authorities to give him a hearing when they declined to renew his [contract].

Reversed and remanded.

Mr. Justice MARSHALL, dissenting.

[I] would go further than the Court does in defining the terms "liberty" and "property." [Prior decisions] establish [that] federal and state governments [are] restrained by the Constitution from acting arbitrarily with respect to employment opportunities that they either offer or control. [In] my view, every citizen who applies for a government job is entitled to it unless the government can establish some reason for denying the employment. This is the "property" right that I believe is protected by the 14th Amendment and that cannot be denied "without due process of law." And it is also liberty—liberty to work—which is the "very essence of the personal freedom and opportunity" secured by the 14th Amendment. [When] an application for public employment is denied or the contract of a government employee is not renewed, the government must say why, for it is only when the reasons underlying government action are known that citizens feel secure and protected against arbitrary government action. [I would] hold that respondent was denied due process when his contract was not renewed and he was not informed of the reasons and given an opportunity to respond.

It may be argued that to provide procedural due process to all public employees or prospective employees would [produce] an intolerable [burden]. The short answer [is] that it is not burdensome to give reasons when reasons exist. [Where] there are numerous applicants for jobs, it is likely that few will choose to demand reasons for not being hired. But, if the demand for reasons is exceptionally great, summary procedures can be devised that would provide fair and adequate [information]. It is only where the government acts improp-

---

a hearing on their decision not to rehire him. [Footnote by Justice Stewart.]

[PERRY v. SINDERMANN, 408 U.S. 593 (1972), was a companion case to Roth. Like Roth, Sindermann involved a claim of a nontenured college teacher who asserted a procedural due process right to a hearing where he might be informed of the grounds for his nonretention and challenge their sufficiency. But Sindermann, unlike Roth, won his case. Justice STEWART's majority opinion held that Sindermann's lack of a "tenure right to re-employment, taken alone, [did not defeat] his claim that the non-renewal of his contract violated due process." Clearly, his lack of tenure rights did not bar his speech claim, similar to the one made by Roth: "For at least a quarter-century, this Court has made clear that even though a person has no 'right' to a valuable governmental benefit and even though the government may deny him the benefit for any number of reasons, there are some reasons upon which the government may not rely," including reasons violating the First Amendment. Accordingly, Sindermann was entitled to the full trial court hearing on the alleged infringement of his First Amendment rights. [See also Mt. Healthy City Board of Education v. Doyle, 429 U.S. 274 (1977).] But on the issue closest to that discussed at length in Roth (the procedural due process claim), the question of Sindermann's job entitlement was of course central. The Court distinguished Roth. Although Sindermann could not claim (any more than Roth) that mere failure to rehire deprived him of liberty or property, Sindermann had alleged that his interest in continued employment, "though not secured by a formal contractual or tenure provision, was secured by a no less binding understanding fostered by the college administration": he claimed that "the college had a de facto tenure program, and that he had tenure under that program." Sindermann offered to prove that he, with several years of service at his college, had "no less a 'property' interest in continued employment than a formally tenured teacher" at colleges with a tenure system.

Justice Stewart agreed that Sindermann was entitled to a hearing on that de facto tenure claim. He recalled that in Roth the Court had said that "'property' denotes a broad range of interests that is secured by 'existing rules or understandings'" and added: "A person's interest in a benefit is a 'property' interest for due process purposes if there are such rules or mutually explicit understandings that support his claim of entitlement to the benefit and that he may invoke at a hearing." Reemphasizing that protected "property" interests were governed by state law, Justice Stewart concluded that Sindermann was entitled to an opportunity to prove "the existence of rules and understandings [that] may justify his legitimate claim of entitlement to continued employment absent 'sufficient cause.'"]

erly that procedural due process is truly burdensome. And that is precisely when it is most necessary. [It] might also be argued that to require a hearing and a statement of reasons is to require a useless act, because a government bent on denying employment to one or more persons will do so regardless of the procedural hurdles that are placed in its path. Perhaps this is so, but a requirement of procedural regularity at least renders arbitrary action more difficult. Moreover, proper procedures will surely eliminate some of the arbitrariness that results, not from malice, but from innocent error. [When] the government knows it may have to justify its decisions with sound reasons, its conduct is likely to be more cautious, careful, and [correct].[4]

"PROPERTY," "LIBERTY," AND HEARING RIGHTS OF PUBLIC EMPLOYEES IN LIGHT OF ROTH

1. *The Roth approach: Property and state law.* Monaghan, "Of 'Liberty' and 'Property,'" viewed Roth as working a "significant" analytical shift: the unitary, generous view of "life, liberty and property," encompassing "all interests valued by sensible men," was abandoned in the procedural due process area in favor of an approach examining each word of the phrase separately and reading "liberty" and "property" in a manner that did not include "the full range of state conduct having serious impact upon individual interests." Monaghan commented that "Roth's emphasis on the need for careful analysis of the *'nature* of the interest at stake' [has] not proved to be an isolated event," and the cases that follow illustrate the accuracy of that observation. What is objectionable about emphasizing the *"nature* of the interest" rather than the severity and importance of the challenged deprivation to the individual?

Consider especially the Court's emphasis on state law in determining the content of "property" in Roth. Is the central determinant the complainant's legitimate expectation or reliance? Or is the central question the less subjective one of identifying a reasonable interpretation of the state legislature's intentions with regard to creating entitlements? (Note the light thrown on these questions by Arnett and Bishop, which follow.) Monaghan notes that the role of state law in giving content to constitutionally protected "property" had been recognized before Roth, with the Court occasionally asking whether there was a "fair and substantial" basis in state law for the recognition of certain interests. But Monaghan adds an important comment: "The 'fair and substantial basis' rule [is] entirely consistent with the principle that there is a federal *content* to the word 'property.' To be sure, the *interests* must be initially created by state law," and state law ordinarily determinative on that question. "But the state court's *characterization* of those 'interests' is another matter altogether. The difference between the existence of an interest—a matter of state law—and its significance—a matter of federal law—is firmly established in other areas of law." To what extent does Roth adhere to that distinction? Do Arnett and Bishop, the post-Roth cases, erode it?

2. *The Arnett case: The "bitter with the sweet."* To what extent should the underlying statutory or common law from which the term "property" derives at least part of its content govern the question of whether a claimant is entitled to a hearing? May state law or federal legislation, in the process of delineating the existence of the property interest, include binding provisions barring hearings? An affirmative answer to that question was indicated by Justice REHNQUIST's

---

4. Chief Justice BURGER submitted a concurring statement. Justice DOUGLAS submitted a dissent. In another dissent, Justice BRENNAN, joined by Justice Douglas, stated that he agreed with Justice Marshall's conclusion that Roth was entitled to be "informed of the reasons and given an opportunity to respond." Justice POWELL did not participate in the case. (See generally the Rabin article cited at the beginning of this section.)

opinion in ARNETT v. KENNEDY, 416 U.S. 134 (1974), a decision rejecting a nonprobationary federal civil service employee's claim to a full hearing prior to dismissal. The governing federal law prescribed not only the grounds for removal but also set forth removal procedures. (The employee could be removed only for "cause"; but the procedures did not provide for an adversary hearing.) To Justice Rehnquist, those provisions were dispositive of the procedural due process claim. Although the law created a constitutionally protected property interest (an expectation of continued employment), "where the grant of a substantive right is inextricably intertwined with the limitations on the procedures which are to be employed in determining that right, a litigant [must] take the bitter with the sweet. [Here] the property interest which appellee had in his employment was itself conditioned by procedural limitations which had accompanied the grant of that interest."

But Justice Rehnquist's approach was not shared by the majority: he spoke only for three Justices, with Chief Justice Burger and Justice Stewart joining his opinion. Although a majority rejected the procedural due process claim, the remaining Justices, in several opinions, dissociated themselves from Justice Rehnquist's approach. Justice POWELL's concurrence, for example, found it incompatible with Roth and Sindermann and stated: "While the legislature may elect not to confer a property interest in federal employment, it may not constitutionally authorize the deprivation of such an interest, once conferred, without appropriate procedural safeguards." Has Justice Rehnquist's position become that of the majority *since* Arnett? That was the contention of the dissenters in the 5 to 4 decision in Bishop v. Wood (which follows), a case involving state rather than federal employment. The majority in Bishop denied that it was following the Rehnquist-Arnett approach. In examining Bishop, then, consider whether it makes state law determinative not only with respect to the initial creation of property interests but also with regard to the existence of hearing rights. Does Bishop obliterate the distinction suggested by Monaghan: Does it abandon any significant independent federal judicial role with regard to the "characterization" of state-created property interests? [1]

BISHOP v. WOOD

426 U.S. 341, 96 S.Ct. 2074, 48 L.Ed.2d 684 (1976).

Mr. Justice STEVENS delivered the opinion of the Court.

Acting on the recommendation of the Chief of Police, the City Manager of Marion, N.C., terminated petitioner's employment as a policeman without affording him a hearing to determine the sufficiency of the cause for his discharge. Petitioner brought suit contending that since a city ordinance

---

1. Compare the somewhat unusual situation in Logan v. Zimmerman Brush Co. (1982) (more fully considered, for its equal protection implications, at p. 619 below), where a unanimous Court found that the challenger had been deprived of a state-created property right without procedural due process, even though the state-created right had been surrounded with a range of procedural provisions. The Court held that when a state creates a remedy for an individual charging discrimination on the basis of physical handicap, it creates a property interest which cannot be eliminated without fair procedures. The Court stated that its position followed "logically from [its] more recent cases analyzing the nature of a property interest. The hallmark of property [is]

an individual entitlement grounded in state law, which cannot be removed except 'for cause.' Once that characteristic is found, the types of interests protected as 'property' are varied and, as often as not, intangible." In Logan, the deprivation resulted from a state agency's failure to take action within a defined length of time. The fact that the state law creating the right to bring a proceeding also provided a procedural framework did not eliminate the constitutional issue because minimal procedural requirements were a matter of federal rather than state law. Accordingly, the claimant's right to use the state statute's adjudicatory procedures was a constitutionally protected state-created property interest.

classified him as a "permanent employee," he had a constitutional right to a pretermination hearing. During pretrial discovery, [he] was advised that his dismissal was based on a failure to follow certain orders, poor attendance at police training classes, causing low morale, and conduct unsuited to an officer. Petitioner filed affidavits [denying the] charges. The District Court granted defendants' motion for summary judgment. [The] questions [are] (1) whether petitioner's employment status was a property interest protected by the Due Process Clause, [and] (2) assuming that the explanation for his discharge was false, whether that false explanation deprived him of an interest in liberty.

A city ordinance provides that a permanent employee may be discharged if he fails to perform work up to the standard of his classification, or if he is negligent, inefficient, or unfit to perform his duties.[1] Petitioner first contends that even though the ordinance does not expressly so provide, it should be read to prohibit discharge for any other reason, and therefore to confer tenure on all permanent employees. In addition, he contends that his period of service, together with his "permanent" classification, gave him a sufficient expectancy of continued employment to constitute a protected property interest.

A property interest in employment can, of course, be created by ordinance, or by an implied contract. In either case, however, the sufficiency of the claim of entitlement must be decided by reference to state law. [See Roth; Sindermann.] The North Carolina Supreme Court has held that an enforceable expectation of continued public employment in that State can exist only if the employer, by statute or contract, has actually granted some form of guarantee. [Still v. Lance.] Whether such a guarantee has been given can be determined only by an examination of the particular statute or ordinance in question. On its face the ordinance on which petitioner relies may fairly be read as conferring such a guarantee. However, such a reading is not the only possible interpretation; the ordinance may also be construed as granting no right to continued employment but merely conditioning an employee's removal on compliance with certain specified procedures.[2] We do not have any authoritative interpretation of this ordinance by [a] state court. We do, however, have the opinion of the [local] U.S. District Judge. Based on his understanding of state law, he concluded that petitioner "held his position at the will and pleasure of the city." [As] the District Court construed the ordinance, the City Manager's determination of the adequacy of the grounds for discharge is not subject to judicial review; the employee is merely given certain procedural rights which the District Court found not to have been violated in this case. The District Court's reading of the ordinance is tenable; it derives some support [from] Still v. Lance; and it was accepted by the Court of Appeals. [These] reasons are sufficient to foreclose our independent examination of the state-law issue. Under that view of the law, petitioner's discharge did not deprive him of a property interest protected by the 14th Amendment.

---

1. Article II, § 6, of the Personnel Ordinance of the city of Marion, reads as follows: "*Dismissal.* A permanent employee whose work is not satisfactory over a period of time shall be notified in what way his work is deficient and what he must do if his work is to be satisfactory. If a permanent employee fails to perform work up to the standard of the classification held, or continues to be negligent, inefficient, or unfit to perform his duties, he may be dismissed by the City Manager. Any discharged employee shall be given written notice of his discharge setting forth the effective date and reasons for his discharge if he shall request such a notice." [Footnote by Justice Stevens.]

2. This is not the construction which six Members of this Court placed on the federal regulations involved in Arnett v. Kennedy. In that case the Court concluded that because the employee could only be discharged for cause, he had a property interest which was entitled to constitutional protection. In this case, a holding that as a matter of state law the employee "held his position at the will and pleasure of the city" necessarily establishes that he had *no* property interest. The Court's evaluation of the federal regulations involved in Arnett sheds no light on the problem presented by this case. [Footnote by Justice Stevens.]

Petitioner's claim that he has been deprived of liberty has two components. He contends that the reasons given for his discharge are so serious as to constitute a stigma that may severely damage his reputation in the community; in addition, he claims that those reasons were false. In our appraisal of petitioner's claim we must accept his version of the facts since the District Court granted summary judgment against him. His evidence established that he was a competent police officer; that he was respected by his peers; that he made more arrests than any other officer on the force; that although he had been criticized for engaging in high-speed pursuits, he had promptly heeded such criticism; and that he had a reasonable explanation for his imperfect attendance at police training sessions. We must therefore assume that his discharge was a mistake and based on incorrect information.

In [Roth], we recognized that the nonretention of an untenured college teacher might make him somewhat less attractive to other employers, but nevertheless concluded that it would stretch the concept too far "to suggest that a person is deprived of 'liberty' when he simply is not rehired in one job but remains as free as before to seek another." This same conclusion applies to the discharge of a public employee whose position is terminable at the will of the employer when there is no public disclosure of the reasons for the discharge. In this case the asserted reasons for the City Manager's decision were communicated orally to the petitioner in private and also were stated in writing in answer to interrogatories after this litigation commenced. Since the former communication was not made public, it cannot properly form the basis for a claim that petitioner's interest in his "good name, reputation, honor, or integrity" [3] was thereby impaired. And since the latter communication was made in the course of a judicial proceeding which did not commence until after petitioner had suffered the injury for which he seeks redress, it surely cannot provide retroactive support for his claim. A contrary evaluation of either explanation would penalize forthright and truthful communication between employer and employee in the former instance, and between litigants in the latter.

Petitioner argues, however, that the reasons given for his discharge were false. Even so, the reasons stated to him in private had no different impact on his reputation than if they had been true. And the answers to his interrogatories, whether true or false, did not cause the discharge. The truth or falsity of the City Manager's statement determines whether or not his decision to discharge the petitioner was correct or prudent, but neither enhances nor diminishes petitioner's claim that his constitutionally protected interest in liberty has been impaired. A contrary evaluation of his contention would enable every discharged employee to assert a constitutional claim merely by alleging that his former supervisor made a mistake. The federal court is not the appropriate forum in which to review the multitude of personnel decisions that are made daily by public agencies.[4] We must accept the harsh fact that numerous individual mistakes are inevitable in the day-to-day administration of our affairs. [The] Constitution cannot feasibly be construed to require federal judicial review for every such error. In the absence of any claim that the public employer was motivated by a desire to curtail or to penalize the exercise of an employee's constitutionally protected rights, we must presume that official

3. [See] the discussion of the interest in reputation allied to employment in Paul v. Davis [p. 578 below]. [Footnote by Justice Stevens.]

4. [Unless] we were to adopt Mr. Justice Brennan's remarkably innovative suggestion that we develop a federal common law of property rights, or his equally far-reaching view that almost every discharge implicates a constitutionally protected liberty interest, the ultimate control of state personnel relationships is, and will remain, with the States; they may grant or withhold tenure at their unfettered discretion. In this case, whether we accept or reject the construction of the ordinance adopted by the two lower courts, the power to change or clarify that ordinance will remain in the hands of the City Council of the city of Marion. [Footnote by Justice Stevens.]

action was regular and, if erroneous, can best be corrected in other ways. The Due Process Clause [is] not a guarantee against incorrect or ill-advised personnel decisions.

Affirmed.

Mr. Justice BRENNAN, with whom Mr. Justice MARSHALL concurs, dissenting.

Petitioner was discharged as a policeman on the grounds of insubordination, "causing low morale," and "conduct unsuited to an officer." It is difficult to imagine a greater "badge of infamy" that could be imposed on one following petitioner's calling; in a profession in which prospective employees are invariably investigated, petitioner's job prospects will be severely constricted by the governmental action in this case. Although our case law would appear to require that petitioner thus be accorded an opportunity "to clear his name" of this calumny, see, e.g., [Roth], the Court [holds] that petitioner was deprived of no liberty interest. [The erroneous decision in Paul v. Davis (p. 578 below) confined] "liberty" to situations in which the State inflicts damage to a government employee's "good name, reputation, honor, or integrity" in the process of terminating his employment. Today the Court effectively destroys even that last vestige of protection for "liberty" by holding that a State may tell an employee that he is being fired for some nonderogatory reason, and then turn around and inform prospective employers that the employee was in fact discharged for a stigmatizing reason that will effectively preclude future employment. The Court purports to limit its holding to situations in which there is "no public disclosure of the reasons for the discharge," but in this case the stigmatizing reasons have been disclosed, and there is no reason to believe that respondents will not convey these actual reasons to petitioner's prospective employers. The Court responds by asserting that since the stigma was imposed "after petitioner had suffered the injury for which he seeks redress, it surely cannot provide retroactive support for his claim." But the "claim" does not arise until the State has officially branded petitioner in some way, and the purpose of the due process hearing is to accord him an opportunity to clear his [name]. This further expansion of those personal interests that the Court simply writes out of the "life, liberty, or property" Clauses of the Fifth and 14th Amendments is simply another curtailment of precious constitutional safeguards that marks too many recent decisions of the Court. [I] would only add that the strained reading of the local ordinance, which the Court deems to be "tenable," cannot be dispositive of the existence vel non of petitioner's "property" interest. There is certainly a federal dimension to the definition of "property" in the Federal Constitution. [At] least before a state law is definitively construed as not securing a "property" interest, the relevant inquiry is whether it was objectively reasonable for the employee to believe he could rely on continued employment. Cf. [Roth].[1] [At] a minimum, this would require in this case an analysis of the common practices utilized and the expectations generated by respondents, and the manner in which the local ordinance would reasonably be read by respondents' [employees].[2]

1. By holding that States have "unfettered discretion" in defining "property" for purposes of the Due Process Clause, [the] Court is, as my Brother White argues, effectively adopting the analysis rejected by a majority of the Court in [Arnett]. More basically, the Court's approach is a resurrection of the discredited rights/privileges distinction, for a State may now avoid all due process safeguards attendant upon the loss of even the necessities of life, cf. Goldberg v. Kelly, merely by labeling them as not constituting "property." [Footnote by Justice Brennan.]

2. For example, petitioner was hired for a "probationary" period of six months, after which he became a "permanent" employee. No reason appears on the record for this distinction, other than the logical assumption, confirmed by a reasonable reading of the local ordinance, that after completion of the former period, an employee may only be discharged [for "cause"]. [Footnote by Justice Brennan.]

Mr. Justice WHITE, with whom Mr. Justice BRENNAN, Mr. Justice MARSHALL, and Mr. Justice BLACKMUN join, dissenting.

[The] second sentence of [the] ordinance plainly conditions petitioner's dismissal on cause—i.e., failure to perform up to standard, negligence, inefficiency, or unfitness to perform the job. The District Court [did] not otherwise construe this portion of the ordinance. [In] concluding that petitioner had no "property interest" in his job entitling him to a hearing on discharge and that he held his position "at the will and pleasure of the city," the District Court relied on the fact that the ordinance described its own *procedures* for determining cause, which procedures did not include a hearing. The majority purports to read the District Court's opinion as construing the ordinance *not* to condition dismissal on cause, and, if this is what the majority means, its reading of the District Court's opinion is clearly erroneous for the reasons just stated. However, later in its opinion the majority [implicitly] concedes that the ordinance supplies the "grounds" for discharge and that the City Manager must determine them to be "adequate" before he may fire an employee. The majority's holding that petitioner had no property interest in his job in spite of the unequivocal language in the city ordinance that he may be dismissed only for certain kinds of cause rests, then, on the fact that state law provides no *procedures* for assuring that the City Manager dismiss him only for cause. The right to his job apparently given by the first two sentences of the ordinance is thus redefined, according to the majority, by the procedures provided for in the third sentence and as redefined is infringed only if the procedures are not followed. This is precisely the reasoning which was embraced by only three and expressly rejected by six Members of this Court in [Arnett]. [The] ordinance plainly grants petitioner a right to his job unless there is cause to fire him. Having granted him such a right it is the Federal Constitution,[1] not state law, which determines the process to be applied in connection with any state decision to deprive him of it.[2]

---

1. The majority intimates, [in its footnote 2] that the views of the three plurality Justices in Arnett were rejected because the other six Justices disagreed on the question of how the federal *statute* involved in that case should be construed. This is incorrect. All Justices agreed on the meaning of the statute. [It] was the constitutional significance of the statute on which the six disagreed with the plurality. Similarly, here, I do not disagree with the majority or the courts below on the meaning of the state law. [The] state law says that petitioner may be dismissed by the City Manager only for certain kinds of cause and then provides that he will receive notice and an explanation, but no hearing and no review. I agree that as a matter of state law petitioner has no remedy no matter how arbitrarily or erroneously the City Manager has acted. This is what the lower courts say the statute means. I differ with those courts and the majority only with respect to the constitutional significance of an unambiguous state law. A majority of the Justices in Arnett stood on the proposition that the Constitution requires procedures *not* required by state law when the state conditions dismissal on "cause." [Footnote by Justice White.]

2. Justice BLACKMUN, joined by Justice Brennan, also submitted a separate dissent, arguing that Still v. Lance was "by no means the authoritative holding on state law that the Court [thinks] it is."

Does Bishop v. Wood encourage a legislature to surround grants of benefits with explicit provision of minimal procedures? Is such a legislative power to control the scope of procedural guarantees a repudiation of the generous view (in Goldberg v. Kelly) of procedural due process rights attaching when government seeks to withdraw a benefit or status it has conferred? See Van Alstyne, "Cracks in ['The New Property']," 62 Cornell L.Rev. 445 (1977). Is this trend tantamount to a resurrection of the supposedly discredited "right-privilege" distinction?

Compare Codd v. Velger, 429 U.S. 624 (1977), where the majority's per curiam opinion held that an allegedly stigmatized former probationary police officer was not entitled to a hearing, because he had failed to allege that the purportedly harmful information was false. Justice Stevens, the author of the majority opinion in Bishop v. Wood, dissented in Codd.

THE SHRINKING SCOPE OF "LIBERTY" IN THE PROCEDURAL DUE PROCESS CASES

The preceding right to hearing cases make clear that the Court has increasingly deferred to legislative judgments in delineating constitutionally protected property rights. To what extent has there been a parallel development regarding hearing rights triggered by alleged infringements of liberty? Does and should state law play the central role with regard to liberty, as it has increasingly done with respect to property? Can the Court narrow the reading of liberty in the procedural due process context without casting doubt on its very broad interpretations of liberty in the substantive due process cases from Meyer to Roe and beyond?

1. *Paul v. Davis and its problems.* The problem of narrowing readings of "liberty" is foreshadowed in the preceding cases, which often involved liberty as well as property claims. But the most widely debated (and widely criticized) decision was PAUL v. DAVIS, 424 U.S. 693 (1976), where a sharply divided Court held, in a majority opinion by Justice REHNQUIST, that the plaintiff, whom the local police had named as an "active shoplifter" in flyers distributed to local merchants, had suffered no deprivation of liberty resulting from injury to his reputation. The plaintiff sued the local police under a federal civil rights law (42 U.S.C. § 1983; see p. 859 below) after the shoplifting charges were dismissed. Earlier cases had indicated that the personal interest in reputation is included within the constitutional protection of "liberty." (Note, e.g., Wisconsin v. Constantineau, 400 U.S. 433 (1971).) Justice Rehnquist found such cases distinguishable. He found that reputation alone was not a constitutionally protected interest and sought to distinguish all earlier cases speaking of "stigma" and damage to reputation as involving situations where some "more tangible interests such as employment were also present." [1]

Justice Rehnquist's explanation included the following passages: "The words 'liberty' and 'property' as used in the 14th Amendment do not in terms single out reputation as a candidate for special protection over and above other interests that may be protected by state law. While we have in a number of our prior cases pointed out the frequently drastic effect of the 'stigma' which may result from defamation by the government in a variety of contexts, this line of cases does not establish the proposition that reputation alone, apart from some more tangible interests such as employment, is either 'liberty' or 'property' by itself sufficient to invoke the procedural protection of the Due Process Clause. [There] exists a variety of interests which are difficult of definition but are nevertheless comprehended within the meaning of either 'liberty' or 'property' as meant in the Due Process Clause. These interests attain this constitutional status by virtue of the fact that they have been initially recognized and protected by state law,[2] and we have repeatedly ruled that the procedural guarantees of

---

1. With respect to Constantineau, for example, Justice Rehnquist claimed that the determinative fact was not the injury to reputation alone, but the consequence of the law in denying the alleged alcoholic the opportunity to purchase alcoholic beverages within city limits. (Recall also the reliance on Constantineau's discussion of reputation in Roth, where the reputation interest arose in the context of employment.)

Note the comment in Monaghan, "Of 'Liberty' and 'Property,' " on this aspect of Paul v. Davis: "The Court cavalierly distinguished Constantineau by noting that the state defamation there involved—posting by the sheriff—had the legal effect of cutting off the plaintiff's prior state-

created right to buy liquor, a factor which, the Court failed to add, played an obviously trivial role in the decision of that case. The Court's re-rationalization of the earlier cases is wholly startling to anyone familiar with those precedents. In many ways I find this Paul's most disturbing aspect. Fair treatment by the Court of its own precedents is an indispensable condition of judicial legitimacy."

2. "There are other interests, of course, protected not by virtue of their recognition by the law of a particular State but because they are guaranteed in one of the provisions of the Bill of Rights which has been 'incorporated' into the 14th Amendment. Section 1983 makes a depri-

the 14th Amendment apply whenever the State seeks to remove or significantly alter that protected status.[3] [In] each of these cases, as a result of the state action complained of, a right or status previously recognized by state law was distinctly altered or extinguished. It was this alteration, officially removing the interest from the recognition and protection previously afforded by the State, which we found sufficient to invoke the procedural guarantees contained in the [Due Process Clause]. But the interest in reputation alone which respondent seeks to vindicate in this action in federal court is quite different from the 'liberty' or 'property' recognized in those decisions. Kentucky law does not extend to respondent any legal guarantee of present enjoyment of reputation which has been altered as a result of petitioners' actions. Rather his interest in reputation is simply one of a number which the State may protect against injury by virtue of its tort law, providing a forum for vindication of those interests by means of damages actions.[4] And any harm or injury to that interest, even where as here inflicted by an officer of the State, does not result in a deprivation of any 'liberty' or 'property' recognized by state or federal law, nor has it worked any change of respondent's status as theretofore recognized under the State's laws. For these reasons we hold that the interest in reputation asserted in this case is neither 'liberty' nor 'property' guaranteed against state deprivation without due process of law."

Justice BRENNAN's dissent, joined by Justices Marshall and White, attacked the majority's alleged distortion of precedent, expressed the hope that the ruling would be but "a short-lived aberration," and stated: "The Court today holds that police officials [may] on their own initiative and without trial constitutionally condemn innocent individuals as criminals and thereby brand them with one of the most stigmatizing and debilitating labels in our society. If there are no constitutional restraints on such oppressive behavior, the safeguards constitutionally accorded an accused in a criminal trial are rendered a sham, and no individual can feel secure that he will not be arbitrarily singled out for similar ex parte punishment by those primarily charged with fair enforcement of the law. The Court accomplishes this result by excluding a person's interest in his good name and reputation from all constitutional protection, regardless of the character of or necessity for the government's actions. The result [is] demonstrably inconsistent with our prior case law and unduly restrictive in its construction of our precious Bill of Rights. [The] Court by mere fiat and with no analysis wholly excludes personal interest in reputation from the ambit of 'life, liberty, or property' under the Fifth and 14th Amendments, thus rendering due process concerns *never* applicable to the official stigmatization, however arbitrary, of an individual. The logical and disturbing corollary of this holding is that no due process infirmities would inhere in a statute constituting a commission to conduct ex parte trials of individuals, so long as the only official judgment

---

vation of such rights actionable independently of state law.

"[This part of our discussion] is limited to consideration of the procedural guarantees of the Due Process Clause and is not intended to describe those substantive limitations upon state action which may be encompassed within the concept of 'liberty' expressed in the 14th Amendment." [Footnote by Justice Rehnquist.]

3. See Bell v. Burson, 402 U.S. 535 (1971) (revoking driver's license); Morrissey v. Brewer, 408 U.S. 471 (1972) (altering status of parolee).

4. For an echo of the theme in this sentence, see Justice Rehnquist's majority opinion in Parratt v. Taylor, 451 U.S. 527 (1981), rejecting a prison inmate's claim against prison officials for

losing some hobby materials ordered by mail. Justice Rehnquist found that "the tort remedies which the [State] provides as a means of redress for property deprivations satisfy the requirements of procedural due process." And in Hudson v. Palmer, 468 U.S. ___ (1984), involving an alleged intentional rather than negligent destruction of a prisoner's property, the Court relied on Parratt and extended it to conclude that "intentional deprivations do not violate [due process] provided [that] adequate state postdeprivation remedies are available. [For] intentional, as for negligent deprivations of property by state employees, the State's action is not complete until and unless it provides or refuses to provide a suitable postdeprivation remedy."

pronounced was limited to the public condemnation and branding of a person as a Communist, a traitor, an 'active murderer,' a homosexual, or any other mark that 'merely' carries social opprobrium. The potential of today's decision is [frightening]." [5]

2. *The impact of the Paul v. Davis approach.* Paul v. Davis is by no means the only modern case that has been criticized as adopting an unduly narrow reading of "liberty" in the procedural due process context. Similar criticisms have been directed at the Roth and Bishop cases, above, for example. Moreover, soon after Paul, the Court decided Meachum v. Fano, 427 U.S. 215 (1976), rejecting a challenge to the procedures afforded when a state prisoner was transferred to a more restrictive prison. The Court emphasized that traditional, broad "liberty" was not implicated, because the original decision to imprison was clearly valid, and that state law created no independent liberty interest. See also the dissent by Justice Marshall, joined by Justices Brennan and Stevens, in Greenholtz v. Nebraska Penal Inmates, 442 U.S. 1 (1979), protesting the majority's "unduly narrow view of the liberty protected by the 14th Amendment." (Greenholtz involved parole release proceedings.) [6]

5. Consider Monaghan's criticisms of the Paul ruling in "Of 'Liberty' and 'Property,' ": "Taken at face value, Paul would radically reorient thinking about the nature of the 'liberty' protected by the due process clause. The case's rationale would confine the *federal content* of 'liberty' to specific constitutional guarantees and the Roe right of privacy, and perhaps, to the Framers' understanding of liberty as freedom from personal restraint. [The opinion] suggests that [only] state conduct imposing a new legal disability on any prior freedom would implicate 'liberty' in a constitutional sense. [E.g., heretofore, freedom of contract] had been viewed as part of the 'liberty' independently created by the due process clause. Under Paul, however, a state action interfering with that liberty could be challenged only if a new state-imposed disability 'officially remov[ed]' the interest from the recognition and protection previously afforded' it by state law.

"[Paul's] difficulties are deep ones. Even if the Court was free to view the question before it as an open one, it was surely not compelled to reject freedom from defamation as a protected interest. [The] opinion does more than repudiate the long-standing tradition of an expansive reading of the word 'liberty' as a matter of federal law. [It] seems to have proceeded from the premise that if the challenged conduct would constitute a common-law tort by a private person, it cannot constitute an interference with the 'liberty' protected by the 14th Amendment. Thus, the more reprehensible and subject to legal redress the conduct, the freer the state is to engage in it—at least until that conduct bumps up against some specific constitutional guarantee or the hodge-podge right of privacy.

"[Recent cases such as Paul] have narrowed the content of 'liberty.' [The] pressure to keep these cases out of the federal courts was great, and so a compromise was struck. Rather than facing the balancing question at the merits stage,

the Court struck a compromise at the definitional stage. But it has struck this balance on the uncritical assumption that every federal interference with state government undermines the values embodied by federalism. This is hardly self-evident."

6. Note the reliance on the cases in this paragraph in the 7 to 2 decision in Connecticut Board of Pardons v. Dumschat, 452 U.S. 458 (1981), holding that the Board's practice of granting about 75% of the applications for commutation of life sentences did *not* create a constitutionally protected "liberty interest" or "entitlement." Thus, the Board was not required to give reasons for denying an application. Following the post-Paul v. Davis approach of reading "liberty" narrowly, Chief Justice Burger stated: "The ground for a constitutional claim, if any, must be found in statutes or other rules defining the obligations of the authority charged with exercising clemency." Justice Stevens' dissent, joined by Justice Marshall, retorted that constitutionally protected liberty "is not merely 'a statutory creation of the State.' [Liberty] has far deeper roots."

Compare, however, Justice Stevens' comment welcoming the majority's generous reading of "liberty" in the course of his dissent in Bell v. Wolfish, 441 U.S. 520 (1979). There, the majority recognized a "liberty" interest of pretrial detainees in the conditions of their confinements (though rejecting the claims on the merits). Justice Stevens' dissent, joined by Justice Brennan, noted: "In recent years, the Court has mistakenly implied that the concept of liberty encompasses only those rights that are either created by statute or regulation or are protected by an express provision of the Bill of Rights. [E.g., Paul v. Davis.] Today, without the help of any statute, regulation, or express provision of the Constitution, the Court has derived the innocent person's right not to be punished from the Due Process Clause itself. It has accordingly aban-

The restrictive reading of "liberty" in Paul v. Davis and its progeny evidently stemmed from a range of institutional concerns, including the fear of excessive Court interference in the administration of state programs and Justice Rehnquist's related fear about reading the 14th Amendment as "a font of tort law to be superimposed upon whatever systems may already be administered by the States." But, assuming the substantiality of these concerns, were there no alternative routes to the result other than reading "liberty" more narrowly than its traditional broad reach? One possibility would have been to read 42 U.S.C. § 1983 (p. 859 below), the civil rights law relied on in Paul v. Davis, more narrowly than the reach of the due process clause: although § 1983 uses broad language (referring to rights "secured by the Constitution"), a limiting statutory interpretation would have made the Court's extensive discussion of constitutionally protected liberty unnecessary. Another source of the Court's concern was no doubt the burdens of administrative hearings that would flow from applications of Goldberg v. Kelly to a wide range of governmental activities. But it would have been possible to retain a more generous view of liberty and property and focus on the question of what procedural due process requires— and find that its requirements could be satisfied with informal hearings or no pretermination hearings at all in many circumstances.[7] See Friendly, " 'Some Kind of Hearing,' " 123 U.Pa.L.Rev. 1267 (1975), suggesting that the prior hearing theme in the area of mass administrative justice should be reconsidered.[8]

3. *State law as a source of "liberty" interests in the modern cases.* In thinking about the line of cases beginning with Paul v. Davis, consider not only the extent to which it has become established law that there is no "federal" interest in reputational injury but also the assertions that state law is an important source in delineating constitutionally protected liberty. The 1980 decision in VITEK v. JONES, 445 U.S. 480, suggested that the Court was somewhat ambivalent about these problems. Justice WHITE's majority opinion, in finding a protected liberty interest, spoke not only of a state-created right, but also of the Court's independent recognition of the "stigma" ingredient of liberty. Vitek held that "the involuntary transfer of a Nebraska state prisoner to a mental hospital implicates a liberty interest that is protected by the Due Process Clause." Here, there was an " 'objective expectation, firmly fixed in state law and official complex practice,' that a prisoner would not be transferred unless he suffered from a mental disease or defect that could not be adequately treated in the prison"; that "objective expectation" gave the prisoner "a liberty interest that entitled him to the benefits of appropriate procedures in connection with determining the conditions that warranted his transfer to a mental hospital." Justice White went on to comment: "We have recognized that for the ordinary citizen, commitment to a mental hospital produces 'a massive curtailment of

doned the parsimonious definition of the 'liberty' protected by the majestic words of the Clause. I concur in that abandonment." (See also the later cases, in note 3 below.)

7. Cf. Mathews v. Eldridge (1976, p. 584 below).

8. See Monaghan, above. Consider also Van Alstyne's suggestion, in "Cracks in ['The New Property']," 62 Cornell L.Rev. 445, urging a shift away from the "new property" approach that underlay Goldberg v. Kelly and advocating recognition of a *"freedom from arbitrary adjudicative procedures* as a substantive element of one's liberty." He argues that "the ideas of liberty and of substantive due process may easily accommodate a view that government may not adjudicate the claims of individuals by unreliable means" and that the "idea of freedom from adjudicative procedural arbitrariness as an element of personal liberty does not lack text, logic, flexibility, or precedent." Is there basis in the cases and in principle for avoiding the elaborate (if at times shaky) superstructure the Court has developed in the procedural due process cases and bluntly recognizing such an across-the-board "freedom from arbitrary adjudicative procedures"?

liberty' and in consequence 'requires due process protection.' The loss of liberty produced by an involuntary commitment is more than a loss of freedom from confinement. It is indisputable that commitment to a mental hospital 'can engender adverse social consequences to the individual' and that '[w]hether we label this phenomena "stigma" or choose to call it something else [we] recognize that it can occur and that it can have a very significant impact on the individual.' Also, '[a]mong the historic liberties' protected by the Due Process Clause is the 'right to be free from, and to obtain judicial relief for, unjustified intrusions on personal security.' Compelled treatment in the form of mandatory behavior modification programs, to which [the prisoner] was exposed in this case, was a proper factor to be weighed [here]. The District Court [was] sensitive to these concerns. [The lower court had mentioned, "for example" that a transfer to the mental hospital had "some stigmatizing consequences."] Were an ordinary citizen to be subjected involuntarily to these consequences, it is undeniable that protected liberty interests would be unconstitutionally infringed absent compliance with the procedures required by the Due Process Clause. We conclude that a convicted felon also is entitled to the benefit of procedures appropriate in the circumstances before he [is] transferred to a mental hospital." [9]

The Court's modern tendency to narrow the range of liberty interests independently recognized by the Constitution and to look to state law as determinative in many cases has not meant rejection of all claims of liberty triggering procedural due process questions. Rather, some of the modern cases have found that state-created rights and expectations created procedurally safeguarded liberty interests. Consider, for example, two 1983 decisions, Hewitt v. Helms, 459 U.S. 460 (1983), and Olim v. Wakinekona, 461 U.S. 238 (1983). In both cases, the Court found no liberty interest independently based on the Constitution, yet proceeded to examine quite carefully the possibility that state law had created interests in liberty triggering procedural protection.

In Hewitt, the issue arose in the context of a transfer of a prisoner from the general prison population to administrative segregation, a more restrictive environment. Justice Rehnquist's majority opinion (over the vigorous dissent of Justice Stevens, joined by Justices Marshall and Brennan) refused to find any deprivation of a liberty interest "independently protected by the Due Process Clause," noting that the transfer of an inmate to more restrictive quarters for nonpunitive reasons was "well within the terms of confinement ordinarily contemplated by a prison sentence." Similarly in Olim, involving transfer of a prisoner to an out-of-state prison, Justice Blackmun's majority opinion found no liberty independently recognized by the Constitution: "Just as an inmate has no justifiable expectation that he will be incarcerated in any particular prison within a State, he has no justifiable expectation that he will be incarcerated in any particular State. [And] interstate prison transfer, including one from Hawaii to

---

9. Note Justice Marshall's comment on Vitek v. Jones in the course of his concurring opinion in PruneYard Shopping Center v. Robins (1980; further noted below, esp. at p. 1294). In arguing that constitutional interests protected by due process do not turn wholly on underlying state law, he stated: "I do not understand the Court to suggest that rights of property are to be defined solely by state law. [The] constitutional terms 'life, liberty, and property' do not derive their meaning solely from the provisions of positive law. They have a normative dimension as well, establishing a sphere of private autonomy which government is bound to respect." He added in a footnote: "This understanding is embodied in cases in the procedural due process area holding that at least some 'grievous losses' amount to 'liberty' or 'property' within the meaning of the Due Process Clause, even if those losses are not protected by statutory or common law. See Vitek v. Jones."

California, does not deprive an inmate of any liberty interest protected by the Due Process Clause in and of itself."

Yet in both cases, the Court proceeded to an examination of state law to determine whether it had created a liberty interest. In Olim, the Court defined the focus of that inquiry as follows: "[A] State creates a protected liberty interest by placing substantive limitations on official discretion. An inmate must show 'that particularized standards or criteria guide the State's decisionmakers.' If the decisionmaker [instead] 'can deny the requested relief for any constitutionally permissible reason or for no reason at all,' the State has not created a constitutionally protected liberty interest." Application of this standard caused the Court to find no deprivation of any liberty in the Olim case, because "the prison Administrator's discretion to transfer an inmate is completely unfettered." But in Hewitt, the Court did find a state-created liberty interest, relying largely on the fact that the relevant Pennsylvania law had not only mandated such procedures prior to administrative segregation, but had also established "specific substantive predicates" before administrative segregation could be imposed. (However, despite the finding of a procedurally protected liberty in Hewitt, the Court found that the actual procedure afforded was constitutionally sufficient.) In its Hewitt discussion, the majority reaffirmed that "liberty interests protected by the 14th Amendment may arise from two sources—the Due Process Clause itself and the laws of the States." Although Hewitt and Olim both confirm the trend regarding the narrowing of "liberty" interests drawn from the former source, Hewitt also suggests that the latter source has potential for expanding.

PROCEDURAL DUE PROCESS IN OTHER CONTEXTS

Most of the cases in this section have focused on hearing rights in the employment context. But, as the immediately preceding materials indicate, the Court has confronted the definition of "liberty" and "property" in a range of other contexts as well. The public employment cases were examined in detail because they contain some of the most important modern doctrinal developments, and because they illustrate the modern Court's wavering methodology. Other areas that have prompted prolific litigation are the hearing rights of prisoners and others subject to the criminal justice system (e.g., Vitek v. Jones), and the procedural due process guarantees available in the school environment. A controversial example of the latter is Goss v. Lopez, 419 U.S. 565 (1975), where the divided Court afforded a right to an informal hearing to high school students threatened with brief disciplinary suspensions. Having created the public school system, the state had created an entitlement that it could not remove without due process.[1] See also Ingraham v. Wright, 430 U.S. 651 (1977), holding that corporal punishment in public schools "implicates a constitutionally protected liberty interest," but that procedural due process does not require a hearing before beatings can be inflicted, since the traditional

---

1. A strong dissent by Justice Powell in Goss, joined by Chief Justice Burger and Justices Blackmun and Rehnquist, charged the majority with excessive judicial interference in operating educational systems and insisted that state law had been inadequately heeded in defining the "entitlement" here: "The Ohio statute that creates the right to a 'free' education also explicitly authorizes a principal to suspend a student for as much as 10 days. Thus the very legislation which 'defines' the 'dimension' of the student's entitlement, while providing a right to education generally, does not establish this right free of discipline imposed in accord with Ohio law. Rather, the right is encompassed in the entire package of statutory provisions governing education in Ohio—of which the power to suspend is one."

common law after-the-fact remedies satisfied due process.[2] Moreover, as noted earlier, there has been extensive litigation regarding procedural guarantees when First Amendment interests are affected. See, e.g., the examination of limits on state authority to discharge employees in the First Amendment materials below.[3]

WHAT PROCESS IS DUE?

The focus of this section has been on the question of defining constitutionally protected "liberty" and "property" for procedural due process purposes. But another controversial question arises whenever the case involves an interest that is found protected by the due process clause and accordingly triggers the right to some sort of hearing. Exploring the details of the Court's methodology in delineating the nature of the hearing required in varied contexts is beyond the scope of this book.[1] It is worth noting, however, that the modern Court has reached agreement on a general balancing formula, albeit not a wholly informative one—a formula governing the identification of the procedural guarantees appropriate to a particular context. The source of the widely invoked modern balancing approach is Justice POWELL's majority opinion in MATHEWS v. ELDRIDGE, 424 U.S. 319 (1976). There, the Court held that pretermination evidentiary hearings were not required in the context of disability benefits (in contrast to the pretermination hearing required for welfare benefits by Goldberg v. Kelly, p. 567 above). In articulating the approach that has become the dominant one for determining what process is due, Justice Powell stated:

"In recent years this Court increasingly has had occasion to consider the extent to which due process requires an evidentiary hearing prior to the deprivation of some type of property interest even if such a hearing is provided thereafter. In only one case, Goldberg v. Kelly, has the Court held that a hearing closely approximating a judicial trial is necessary. In other cases requiring some type of pretermination hearing as a matter of constitutional right, the Court has spoken sparingly about the requisite procedures. [Our] decisions underscore the truism that ' "[d]ue process," unlike some legal rules, is not a technical conception with a fixed content unrelated to time, place and circumstances.' '[Due process] is flexible and calls for such procedural protections as the particular situation demands.' Accordingly, resolution of the issue whether the administrative procedures provided here are constitutionally sufficient requires analysis of the governmental and private interests that are affected. More precisely, our prior decisions indicate that identification of the specific dictates of due process generally requires consideration of three distinct

---

2. On the procedural safeguards necessary in the context of "academic" rather than "disciplinary" actions in the school context, see Board of Curators, Univ. of Mo. v. Horowitz, 435 U.S. 78 (1978), involving a student's dismissal from medical school because of her performance in the clinical program.

3. See, e.g., Branti v. Finkel (1980; p. 1393 below). See also the extensive and wavering line of cases challenging summary prejudgment remedies in civil litigation. The most important cases on hearing rights in the context of state-created creditors' remedies are reviewed in Flagg Bros., Inc. v. Brooks, (1978; p. 899 below). See especially Sniadach v. Family Finance Corp., 395 U.S. 337 (1969), Fuentes v. Shevin, 407 U.S. 67

(1972), and North Georgia Finishing, Inc. v. Di-Chem, 419 U.S. 601 (1975).

Note Ely's bemused comment on the right to hearing cases: "It turns out, you see, that whether [the asserted interest is] a property interest is a function of whether you are entitled to it, which means the Court has to decide whether you are entitled to it before it can decide whether you get a hearing on the question whether you are entitled to it." Ely, Democracy and Distrust (1980). Is this justifiable criticism? Can speculation about the merits be avoided so long as the Court follows the "nature-of-the-interest" test of Roth?

1. As noted earlier, that subject is typically explored in administrative law courses.

factors: First, the private interest that will be affected by the official action; second, the risk of an erroneous deprivation of such interest through the procedures used, and the probable value, if any, of additional or substitute procedural safeguards; and finally, the Government's interest, including the function involved and the fiscal and administrative burdens that the additional or substitute procedural requirement would entail." [2]

2. Do Justice Powell's three factors provide adequate guidance? Moreover, is it proper for judges to second-guess the legislature in weighing factors that presumably went into the formulation of the benefits scheme in the first place? For a criticism of the Mathews balancing test, see Mashaw, "The Supreme Court's Due Process Calculus for Administrative Adjudication in Mathews v. Eldridge: Three Factors in Search of a Theory of Value," 44 U.Chi.L.Rev. 28 (1976).

For examples of modern reliances on the Mathews v. Eldridge balancing analysis, see Dixon v. Love, 431 U.S. 105 (1977) (upholding the revocation of a driver's license without a prior hearing); Smith v. Organization of Foster Families, 431 U.S. 816 (1977) (informal procedures before a foster child may be removed from a foster home satisfied procedural due process guarantees, even assuming a constitutionally protected "liberty" was involved); and Memphis Light, Gas & Water Division v. Craft, 436 U.S. 1 (1978) (before municipal utility may cut off services to a customer, it must afford an opportunity to meet with an employee who has authority to settle billing disputes). See also Barry v. Barchi, 443 U.S. 55 (1979) (suspensions of horse trainer licenses), Mackey v. Montrym, 443 U.S. 1 (1979) (drivers' license), and Landon v. Plasencia, 459 U.S. 21 (1982) (deportation proceedings).

The modern constitutionalization of family law (reviewed in sec. 3 above) has also provided frequent occasions for applying the Mathews v. Eldridge balancing analysis. See, e.g., Little v. Streater, 452 U.S. 1 (1981) (state must pay for blood grouping tests in a state-involved paternity action against an indigent defendant); Lassiter v. Dept. of Social Services, 452 U.S. 18 (1981) (appointment of counsel not required for indigent parents in every proceeding to terminate parental status); and Santosky v. Kramer, 455 U.S. 745 (1982) (in proceedings to terminate parental rights over their natural children because of "permanent neglect," a "fair preponderance of the evidence" standard is inadequate and a state must instead support its allegations by "at least clear and convincing evidence").

Chapter 9

EQUAL PROTECTION

SECTION 1. AN OVERVIEW

Introduction. We now turn to the range of complex problems raised by the simple-sounding command of the 14th Amendment that no state shall "deny to any person within its jurisdiction the equal protection of the laws." Presumably, that command cannot mean that laws must deal in the same way with everyone. Almost all laws classify, by imposing special burdens or granting special benefits to some groups or individuals and not to others. But if legislation almost in its nature classifies, what content can be given to the equal protection guarantee? In its efforts to divine meanings, the Court has constructed a morass of doctrines, tried to identify types of situations warranting different degrees of judicial scrutiny (from the most deferential to the strictest), and purported to find in equal protection a range of specially protected fundamental values. The purpose of this introductory overview is to provide a rough road map through the maze. It surveys the historical changes in the significance of the equal protection clause; it outlines the most commonly invoked doctrinal tools, particularly the Court's efforts to delineate the occasions for particular intensities of judicial scrutiny of governmental actions; and it calls preliminary attention to some recurrent problems regarding the central content of constitutionally protected equality.

It may be surprising that, more than a century after the adoption of the 14th Amendment, the question of the inherent content of equal protection continues to be a subject of intense debate. In fact, the issue is very much in controversy. The strongest consensus about the meaning of equal protection is drawn from its historical origins: at the very least it was directed at racial discrimination against blacks. What, if anything, beyond that concern can equal protection be fairly read to include? In the earliest interpretation of the 14th Amendment, in the Slaughter-House Cases (1873; p. 410 above), the Court suggested that the racial concern exhausted the meaning of the clause: "We doubt very much whether any action of a State not directed by way of discrimination against the negroes as a class, or on account of their race, will ever be held to come within the purview of this provision." (Even in the area of race discrimination, controversies about the meaning and scope of the clause abound, as sec. 3 demonstrates.) Beyond the widely agreed-upon core, the widest agreement concerns the notion that equal protection imposes a variation of the "rationality" requirement already encountered in the examination of due process in the previous chapter. A classification, the argument goes, must be reasonably related to the purpose of the legislation. But even that widely supported minimum is not universally accepted; and those who support the existence of the rationality requirement disagree sharply about what it should mean in terms of judicial scrutiny of legislative action.

Beyond these points of quite wide consensus, equal protection is an embattled terrain. Particularly controversial are the modern Court's efforts to find some fundamental values inherent in equal protection. Can equal protection be viewed as an independent source of fundamental rights, or must all fundamental

586

rights be traceable to some other constitutional source, such as the First Amendment or substantive due process? One contemporary scholar has stirred a wide debate with his assertion that equality is an "empty idea." [1] Another has asked whether equal protection is really like Oakland (borrowing Gertrude Stein's quip that the trouble with Oakland is that "there is no there there").[2] These opening notes are designed to introduce the pervasive questions, from those dealing with doctrinal tools such as the appropriate levels of scrutiny to the more basic ones of what, if any, content there is to the constitutional command of equality. The complexity of the questions raised can best be appreciated in the context of the fuller exploration that follows, and a return to these introductory materials may be worthwhile after that exploration is concluded.[3]

　　1. *Modest origins: The "old equal protection" in the pre-Warren Court years.* Traditionally, equal protection supported only minimal judicial intervention in most contexts. Ordinarily, the command of equal protection was only that government must not impose differences in treatment "except upon some reasonable differentiation fairly related to the object of regulation," as Justice Jackson put it in the Railway Express case, p. 597 below. That "old" variety of equal protection scrutiny focused solely on the *means* used by the legislature: it insisted merely that the classification in the statute reasonably relate to the legislative purpose. Unlike substantive due process, equal protection scrutiny was not typically concerned with identifying "fundamental values" and restraining legislative ends. And usually that rational classification requirement was readily satisfied: the courts did not demand a tight fit between classification and purpose; perfect congruence between means and ends was not required; judges allowed legislators flexibility to act on the basis of broadly accurate generalizations and tolerated considerable overinclusiveness and underinclusiveness in classification schemes. Only in special, limited contexts was equal protection found to have a deeper bite during most of its history—most notably in racial discrimination cases, in view of the historical background of the 14th Amendment.

　　During the early 20th century era of extensive Court interference with state economic legislation under the 14th Amendment, it was usually due process, not equal protection, that provided the cutting edge. Thus, at the height of the Lochner era, Justice Holmes referred to equal protection as "the usual last resort of constitutional arguments." [4] Another comment, by Justice Jackson in the Railway Express case, also reflects the relatively narrow intrusion into the legislative domain traditionally associated with equal protection: "Invalidation of a statute or an ordinance on due process grounds leaves ungoverned and

1. Westen, "The Empty Idea of Equality," 95 Harv.L.Rev. 537 (1982).

2. Cohen, "Is Equal Protection Like Oakland? Equality as a Surrogate for Other Rights" (forthcoming, —— Tul.L.Rev. —— (1985)).

3. Although the equal protection requirement of the 14th Amendment literally applies only to state action, judicial interpretation has made it applicable to the federal government as well, as an aspect of Fifth Amendment due process. The most notable case announcing that de facto process of reverse incorporation is Bolling v. Sharpe, the District of Columbia school desegregation case (1954; p. 638 below). As a general (albeit not universal) rule, the Court's "approach to Fifth Amendment equal protection claims [has] been precisely the same as to equal protection claims under the 14th Amendment." Weinberger v. Wiesenfeld (1975; p. 735 below).

4. Buck v. Bell, 274 U.S. 200 (1927). The fact that due process was the favorite interventionist tool of the Lochner years does not mean, however, that equal protection invalidations were wholly unknown. As early as Gulf, C. & S. F. Ry. v. Ellis, 165 U.S. 150 (1897), for example, the Court relied on equal protection to strike down an economic regulation requiring railroads (but not other defendants) to pay attorneys' fees to successful plaintiffs in certain cases. Although the Court conceded the general legislative "power of classification," it insisted that the classification "must always rest upon some difference which bears a reasonable and just relation to the act in respect to which the classification is proposed." The "reasonable relation" requirement is examined in sec. 2, below.

ungovernable conduct which many people find objectionable. Invocation of the equal protection clause, on the other hand, does not disable any governmental body from dealing with the subject at hand. It merely means that the prohibition or regulation must have a broader impact." What Justice Jackson there emphasized is that the "old" equal protection ordinarily focused solely on legislative means, on the rationality of classifications, not on legislative objectives. Although due process also has a "rational means" ingredient, it is more commonly associated with restraints on legislative ends, in the era of Roe as well as of Lochner.

2. *From marginal intervention to major cutting edge: The Warren Court's "new equal protection" and the two-tier approach.* From its traditional modest role, equal protection burgeoned into a major interventionist tool during the Warren era, especially in the 1960s. The Warren Court did not abandon the deferential ingredients of the old equal protection: in most areas of economic and social legislation, the demands imposed by equal protection remained as minimal as ever. Indeed, the Warren Court's hands-off stance was even more lenient than that of its predecessors. But the Court launched an equal protection revolution by finding large new areas for strict rather than deferential scrutiny. A sharply differentiated two-tier approach evolved by the late 1960s: in addition to the deferential "old" equal protection, a "new" equal protection, connoting strict scrutiny, arose: "The Warren Court embraced a rigid two-tier attitude. Some situations evoked the aggressive 'new' equal protection, with scrutiny that was 'strict' in theory and fatal in fact; in other contexts, the deferential 'old' equal protection reigned, with minimal scrutiny in theory and virtually none in fact." [5] The intensive review associated with the new equal protection imposed two demands—a demand not only as to means but also one as to ends. Legislation qualifying for strict scrutiny required a far closer fit between classification and statutory purpose than the rough and ready flexibility traditionally tolerated by the old equal protection: means had to be shown "necessary" to achieve statutory ends, not merely "reasonably related" ones. Moreover, equal protection became a source of ends scrutiny as well: legislation in the areas of the new equal protection had to be justified by "compelling" state interests, not merely the wide spectrum of "legitimate" state ends.

The Warren Court identified the areas appropriate for strict scrutiny by searching for two characteristics: the presence of a "suspect" classification; or an impact on "fundamental" rights or interests. [6] In the category of "suspect classifications," the Warren Court's major contribution was to intensify the strict scrutiny in the traditionally interventionist area of racial classifications. But tantalizing statements also suggested that there might be other suspect categories as well: illegitimacy and wealth, for example. But it was the "fundamental interests" ingredient of the new equal protection that proved particularly dynamic, open-ended, and amorphous: "It was the element that bore the closest resemblance to freewheeling substantive due process, for it circumscribed legislative choices in the name of newly articulated values that lacked clear support in constitutional text and history. The list of interests identified as fundamental by the Warren Court was in fact quite modest: voting, criminal

5. Gunther, "Foreword: In Search of Evolving Doctrine on a Changing Court: A Model for a Newer Equal Protection," 86 Harv.L.Rev. 1 (1972) (hereinafter cited as Gunther, "Newer Equal Protection"). (All quotations in this overview, unless otherwise attributed, are from that article.) For a survey of the state of equal protection doctrine near the end of the Warren years, distinguishing the "restrained review" and "active review" spheres, see "Developments in the Law—Equal Protection," 82 Harv.L.Rev.

1065 (1969) (hereinafter cited as "Developments").

6. Whether suspect classifications and fundamental interests were separate or interrelated categories was often unclear. Note the commentaries cited in Gunther, "Newer Equal Protection," at 9, footnote 36, speculating that the two categories might be related gradients or intersecting variables or intertwined helices.

appeals, and the right of interstate travel were the prime examples. But in the extraordinary amount of commentary that followed, analysts searching for justifications for those enshrinements were understandably tempted to ponder analogous spheres that might similarly qualify. Welfare benefits, exclusionary zoning, municipal services and school financing came to be the most inviting frontiers."[7]

3. *The Burger Court and equal protection.* What has been the Burger Court's response to the legacy of the Warren era? There has been neither undiminished carrying forward nor wholesale turning back of the Warren Court approach. The response has been more complex than that. In form, the two-tier distinction between new, strict scrutiny and old, deferential review equal protection persists. In fact, the modern exercises of review in equal protection cases do not conform to that simple, bifurcated pattern. A summary of the early years of the Burger era stated, in terms that continue largely valid: "(1) The Burger Court is reluctant to expand the scope of the new equal protection, although its best established ingredients retain vitality. (2) There is mounting discontent with the rigid two-tier formulations of the Warren Court's equal protection doctrine. (3) The Court is prepared to use the clause as an interventionist tool without resorting to the strict scrutiny language of the new equal protection."[8]

a. *Blocking the expansion of the "new" equal protection.* The Burger Court's "thus far and no further" approach to the "new" equal protection has been especially notable with respect to the most amorphous aspect of Warren Court doctrine: the use of strict scrutiny where "fundamental interests" were affected. Those inclined to read Warren Court decisions most broadly had perceived in equal protection a potential tool on a wide front: there were suggestions that all legislation impinging on "necessities" (welfare, housing, education, etc.) might be subjected to strict scrutiny. Those hopes (or fears) did not materialize, perhaps in part because the Warren Court's doctrinal legacy was least well-fixed in those areas.[9] But refusal to expand has not meant that the Burger Court has scuttled the new equal protection. Its best established strands survive, as in the area of the fundamental interests in voting and access to the ballot. With respect to classifications, indeed, the Burger Court has not only maintained strict scrutiny of racial criteria but has added to the list of classifications triggering at least some heightened scrutiny those based on sex, alienage and illegitimacy.

b. *The unsettled state of modern equal protection doctrine: The discontent with two-tier formulations and the groping for new standards.* Even while the two-tier scheme

---

7. For a critical evaluation of new equal protection developments at the end of the Warren era, see Justice Harlan's dissent in Shapiro v. Thompson (1969; p. 832 below). For a more sympathetic view, see Karst & Horowitz, "Reitman v. Mulkey: A Telophase of Substantive Equal Protection," 1967 Sup.Ct.Rev. 39, noting that "some classifications although far from irrational [are] nonetheless unconstitutional because they produce inequities that are unacceptable in this generation's idealization of America" and praising the "egalitarian revolution" launched by the Warren Court. Note the comment by one of the authors of that article, in Karst, "Invidious Discrimination: Justice Douglas and the Return to the 'Natural-Law-Due-Process Formula,'" 16 U.C.L.A.L.Rev. 716 (1969), acknowledging: "The doctrine of invidious discrimination [as used in the new equal protection cases] does not permit an escape from the problems associated with substantive due process."

8. Gunther, "Newer Equal Protection," at 12.

9. Thus, Dandridge v. Williams, p. 850 below, made clear early in Chief Justice Burger's tenure that heightened scrutiny would not be employed with respect to welfare legislation generally and that equal protection would not be read as imposing substantial new affirmative obligations on government and as assuring equality of results. The cases rejecting efforts to invoke equal protection as an affirmative, broad-gauged weapon on behalf of the poor are symbolized by Rodriguez, the school financing case in 1973, where the majority rejected a claim that education was a "fundamental interest" and refused to find wealth a "suspect" classification (p. 789 below). But see Plyler v. Doe (1982; p. 799 below), holding that "undocumented" children (children of illegal aliens) could not be excluded from free public education.

has often been adhered to in form, there has also been an increasingly noticeable resistance to the sharp difference between deferential "old" and interventionist "new" equal protection. A number of Justices, from all segments of the Court, have sought formulations that would blur the sharp distinctions of the two-tiered approach or that would narrow the gap between strict scrutiny and deferential review. That mounting discontent with the two-tier scheme has sometimes been manifested in claims that a single standard applies to all equal protection cases.[10] But the most elaborate attacks on the two-tier notion have come from Justice Marshall. His frequently stated position was developed most elaborately in his dissent in the Rodriguez case (1973; p. 789 below): "The Court apparently seeks to establish [that] equal protection cases fall into one of two neat categories which dictate the appropriate standard of review—strict scrutiny or mere rationality. But this Court's [decisions] defy such easy categorization. A principled reading of what this Court has done reveals that it has applied a spectrum of standards in reviewing discrimination allegedly violative of the Equal Protection Clause. This spectrum clearly comprehends variations in the degree of care with which the Court will scrutinize particular classifications, depending, I believe, on the constitutional and societal importance of the interest adversely affected and the recognized invidiousness of the basis upon which the particular classification is drawn." [11]

Justice Marshall's "sliding scale" approach may describe many of the modern decisions, but it is a formulation that the majority has refused to embrace. But the Burger Court's results indicate at least two significant changes in equal protection law. *First,* invocation of the "old" equal protection formula no longer signals, as it did with the Warren Court, an extreme deference to legislative classifications and a virtually automatic validation of challenged statutes. Instead, several cases, even while voicing the minimal "rationality," "hands-off" standards of the old equal protection, proceed to find the statute unconstitutional: for the first time in years, old equal protection standards occasionally mean something other than perfunctory opinions sustaining the law under attack. Occasionally, moreover, reformulations of "mere rationality" standards hint at increased bite to the scrutiny.[12]

Second, in some areas the modern Court has put forth standards for equal protection review that, while clearly more intensive than the deference of the "old" equal protection, are less demanding than the strictness of the "new"

---

10. Justice Stevens has been the most frequent advocate of that position. See, e.g., his concurring opinion in Craig v. Boren (1976; p. 647 below), beginning: "There is only one Equal Protection Clause."

11. Justice White has occasionally endorsed much of Justice Marshall's analysis. See, e.g., his concurring opinion in Vlandis v. Kline, 412 U.S. 441 (1973) commenting that "it is clear that we employ not just one, or two, but, as my Brother Marshall has so ably demonstrated, a 'spectrum of standards.' "

12. Contrast the extremely deferential statements from the Warren Court with the occasionally more demanding versions of more recent years. Thus, Chief Justice Warren conveyed the deferential mood applied to the old equal protection category during the 1960s when he said that the equal protection clause was violated "only if the classification rests on grounds wholly irrelevant to the achievement of the State's objective," that a "statutory discrimination will not be set aside if any state of facts reasonably may be conceived to justify it." (McGowan [1961; p.

601 below].) By contrast, Burger Court Justices have sporadically articulated somewhat more demanding criteria, in two respects: first, they have suggested that the means, the classification, must *substantially* further the statutory objective; second, there has been the suggestion that the Court will no longer regularly hypothesize *conceivable* state purposes against which to test the rationality of the means—the hypothesizing familiar not only in the economic due process area but also in the Warren Court's "old" equal protection approach. Instead, there have been statements such as Justice Powell's opinion for the Court in McGinnis v. Royster, 410 U.S. 263 (1973), asking "whether the challenged distinction rationally furthers some legitimate, *articulated* state purpose"; insisting that the state objective be "nonillusory"; and claiming that the Court supplied "no imaginary basis or purpose" in sustaining the statutory scheme. For further discussion of the occasional surfacing of "new bite" for the "old" equal protection—the "newer equal protection" mode—see p. 604 below.

equal protection. Sex discrimination is the best established example of an "intermediate" level of review. In Craig v. Boren (1976; p. 647 below), the majority was able to agree that "classifications by gender must serve *important* governmental objectives and must be *substantially related* to achievement of those objectives." [13] That standard is "intermediate" with respect to both ends and means: where ends must be "compelling" to survive strict scrutiny and merely "legitimate" under the "old" mode, "important" objectives are required here; and where means must be "necessary" under the "new" equal protection, and merely "rationally related" under the "old" equal protection, they must be "substantially related" to survive the "intermediate" level of review. (There have been similar but far more erratic efforts to prescribe something in between the old and the new equal protection with respect to classifications based on illegitimacy and alienage.) [14]

4. *Modern equal protection: Summary and challenge.* Equal protection is in flux. Clearly, it has come a long way from being the "last resort of constitutional arguments"; instead, it is a prolific source of modern constitutional litigation. The Warren Court created a relatively clear, if not always well explained and justified, two-tiered approach. The gropings for new formulations by all wings of the Burger Court make for less clear doctrine: two-tiered analysis has not been formally abandoned, but the intensity of review under the lower tier has occasionally been sharpened, and varieties of intermediate levels of scrutiny have surfaced. At the end of the 1970s, the Court seemed to be retreating toward great deference for most varieties of economic and social legislation (e.g., Vance v. Bradley [1979; p. 609 below]), yet by the 1980s there remained ample basis for the widespread and justified charge that the modern Court's exercise of equal protection review has been erratic. Is the Burger Court's variety of equal protection simply an accumulation of ad hoc interventions? Is it most intelligible via Justice Marshall's sliding scale analysis? Does it offer promise for evolution toward a different variety of two-tier analysis, retaining the well established ingredients of the new equal protection and its strict scrutiny, but raising the level of scrutiny appropriate in the "old" equal protection sphere?

The search for coherence in the volatile, sometimes chaotic field of equal protection law, then, is the challenge—not only for the Court, but also in the examination of the materials that follow. Those materials reveal a doctrinal landscape strewn with not always reconcilable fragments. The doctrinal strands touched on in this introduction are examined at greater length in a variety of settings below. The recurrent questions are: Do the individual strands make sense? Do they provide ingredients for a coherent whole? Or is equal protection doctrine simply the modern Justices' garb for judicially selected value infusions, for Lochnerizing without wearing the occasionally discredited mantle of substantive due process? [15]

13. For a later reiteration of an intermediate scrutiny standard, after several intervening cases had cast doubt on the survival of the Craig v. Boren approach, see Mississippi University for Women v. Hogan (1982; p. 660 below).

14. Note the comment in Justice Marshall's dissent in Harris v. McRae, the 1980 abortion funding case (p. 543 above), stating that "the Court has adopted an 'intermediate' level of scrutiny for a variety of classifications." He cited Trimble v. Gordon (1977; illegitimacy; p. 680 below), Craig v. Boren (1976; sex discrimination; p. 647 below), and Foley v. Connelie (1979; alienage; p. 672 below). In examining the modern alienage and illegitimacy cases, consider whether Justice Marshall's "intermediate" label

for them, as for the sex discrimination cases, is accurate. (In his 1980 dissent in McRae, Justice Marshall, in addition to reiterating his earlier criticisms of two-tier analysis, called the two-tier approach "obsolete," noted that a number of Justices had "expressed discomfort" with it, and stated that he was "pleased to observe that its hold on the law may be waning.")

15. Modern equal protection developments have spurred an extraordinary flood of commentary. In addition to the materials cited in the preceding footnotes, see, e.g., Ely, Democracy and Distrust (1980); Wilkinson, "The Supreme Court, the Equal Protection Clause, and the Three Faces of Constitutional Equality," 61 Va. L.Rev. 945 (1975); Barrett, "Judicial Supervision

5. *Does equal protection protect core values of its own?* Once one gets beyond the hostility to racial discrimination that can be drawn from the historical origins of equal protection, is it possible to identify a value or a set of values that the constitutional equality principle is designed to implement? This question is a pervasive one in the materials that follow. The terms of the clause extend beyond the race background, and its applications similarly have gone well beyond. Value judgments underlie many of the decisions below, and not only those in the materials (starting with sec. 4) dealing with the "fundamental rights" implementation of the "new" equal protection. Yet the legitimacy of fundamental values adjudication under the guise of equal protection is not at all clear. To say that persons who are alike must be treated alike does not tell us how to determine whether persons are alike or not for the purposes of the classifications inherent in virtually all legislation.

Thus, in a series of articles in the early 1980s, Professor Westen has asserted that equality is in fact an "empty idea." As a matter of formal logic, he insists, a statement such as "people who are alike should be treated alike" is "entirely 'circular.'"[16] Westen suggests that the emphasis on "equality" distorts the analysis of underlying substantive rights and that, because "equality" is an "empty [and confusing] vessel with no substantive moral content of its own," it "should be banished from moral and legal discourse as an explanatory norm." In response, a number of scholars have sprung to the defense of the utility of the equality concept.[17] The typical responses are two-fold. First, it is argued that the equality notion at least creates a strong legal-moral presumption in favor of equal treatment of all persons, departures from which must be justified.[18] Moreover, there is a mounting argument that the inherent principle of equal protection is one that mandates equality of respect for individuals.[19] The extent to which equal protection permits value-free, process-oriented adjudication and the extent to which it inevitably involves governing assumptions about underlying (albeit often unarticulated) value choices, in short, is a problem to be borne in mind in examining the materials that follow.

6. *A note on organization.* The aim of this chapter is to look at the roots, contents, and implications of equal protection to see where we are, how we got here, and where we may be going. A body of law this volatile and diffuse is

of Legislative Classifications—A More Modest Role for Equal Protection?" 1976 B.Y.U.L.Rev. 89; Perry, "Modern Equal Protection: A Conceptualization and Appraisal," 79 Colum.L.Rev. 1023 (1979); O'Fallon, "Adjudication and Contested Concepts: The Case of Equal Protection," 54 N.Y.U.L.Rev. 19 (1979); and Bice, "Standards of Judicial Review under the Equal Protection and Due Process Clauses," 50 S.Cal.L.Rev. 689 (1977). Some of these, as well as additional writings, will be referred to at appropriate places below.

16. The major Westen article is "The Empty Idea of Equality," 95 Harv.L.Rev. 537 (1982). See also his elaborations in 91 Yale L.J. 1153 (1982), 81 Mich.L.Rev. 604 (1983), and 83 Colum.L.Rev. 1186 (1983).

17. See, e.g., Greenawalt, "How Empty is the Idea of Equality?" 83 Colum.L.Rev. 1167 (1983); Karst, "Why Equality Matters," 17 Ga.L.Rev. 245 (1983); Chemerinsky, "In Defense of [Equality]," 81 Mich.L.Rev. 575 (1983); and D'Amato, "Is Equality a Totally Empty Idea?" 81 Mich.L.Rev. 600 (1983).

18. See, e.g., Greenawalt and Chemerinsky, in the previous footnote.

19. See, e.g., Karst (cited in footnote 17) ("The Equal Citizenship principle [is] the presumptive right 'to be treated by the organized society as a respected, responsible, and participating member.' "); Baker, "Neutrality, Process, and Rationality: Flawed Interpretations of Equal Protection," 58 Tex.L.Rev. 1029 (1980) ("Society ought to respect the equality of worth of all its members and ought not to condone the subordination of any people."); and O'Fallon, "Adjudication and Contested Concepts: The Case of Equal Protection," 54 N.Y.U.L.Rev. 19 (1979) ("The guarantee of equal protection of the law is best understood in terms of a legal right to equal concern and respect from the legislature."). See also, generally, Lupu, "Untangling the Strands of the Fourteenth Amendment," 77 Mich.L.Rev. 981 (1979), and Cohen, "Is Equal Protection Like Oakland? Equality as a Surrogate for Other Rights" (forthcoming, —— Tul.L.Rev. —— (1985)). (The Cohen article is more fully noted at p. 550 above, in connection with the Zablocki case in chap. 8.)

difficult to organize: one cannot simultaneously bring to bear all of the relevant perspectives—chronological, functional, variations in modes of review, subgroups of substantive doctrine. In pursuing the multiple strands of equal protection, this chapter will proceed as follows: Sec. 2 examines the means-oriented focus of traditional equal protection: it pursues the ingredients of the requisite congruence or fit between classification and purpose in the context of modern economic and social legislation. Sec. 3 turns to the "suspect classifications" branch of heightened scrutiny. It begins with the historically most justified area of strict scrutiny, racial classifications, and then turns to a number of other classifying criteria that have at times triggered (or arguably should trigger) heightened scrutiny—especially the criteria of gender, alienage, and illegitimacy. Sec. 4 moves from the "suspect classifications" strand of heightened scrutiny to that turning on the presence of "fundamental interests" which are sought to be derived from the equal protection clause itself. That section includes both the developments in the relatively well established areas of equal protection—"fundamental rights" law regarding voting, the criminal process, and interstate migration—as well as those spheres where modern efforts to expand the range of fundamental values derivable from equal protection have proven unsuccessful—efforts primarily pertaining to problems of the poor.

SECTION 2. SCRUTINY OF MEANS IN ECONOMIC REGULATIONS: THE RATIONALITY REQUIREMENT

THE RATIONALITY REQUIREMENT: WHEN ARE CLASSIFICATIONS EXCESSIVELY "UNDER-INCLUSIVE" OR "OVERINCLUSIVE"?

Introduction. How does one determine whether a classification is "reasonably related" to the purposes of the legislation? In a sense, this ingredient of the equal protection command is an aspect of the broader constitutional requirement that there must be a "rational" connection between legislative means and ends—a requirement already foreshadowed as an element of due process, in chap. 8, sec. 1.[1] The added thrust provided by equal protection for that general

---

1. Recall also the very similar requirement (first elaborated in McCulloch, p. 72 above) that, under the necessary and proper clause, congressional means must have a rational connection to legislative ends. The Court's oftstated assertion that there *is* a rationality requirement has not gone unchallenged. For the most articulate modern attack on *any* "rationality" review, see Linde, "Due Process of Lawmaking," 55 Neb.L. Rev. 197 (1976). Linde argues that "the dogma that [the Constitution] requires every law to be a rational means to a legislative end [is] not a rational premise for judicial review [and is] even less plausible as a constitutional command to lawmakers." Others, without mounting so elaborate a challenge to the theory of rationality review, assert that the rationality requirement is "largely inconsequential" as a practical matter. See Perry, "Modern Equal Protection," 79 Colum.L.Rev. 1023 (1979). But Linde concedes that his approach "is likely to remain a heresy"; and Perry concedes that "the rationality require-

ment is not wholly unimportant." See also Michelman, "Politics and Values, or What's Really Wrong with Rationality Review," 13 Creighton L.Rev. 487 (1979); Posner, Economic Analysis of Law (2d ed. 1977); Bennett, " 'Mere' Rationality in [Constitutional Law]," 67 Calif.L. Rev. 1049 (1979); Bice, "Rationality Analysis in Constitutional Law," 65 Minn.L.Rev. 1 (1980); Baker, "Neutrality, Process, and Rationality: Flawed Interpretations of Equal Protection," 58 Tex.L.Rev. 1029 (1980); and Leedes, "The Rationality Requirement of the Equal Protection Clause," 42 Ohio St.L.J. 639 (1981).

The premise of this section is that the rationality requirement is worth exploring at least because the vast majority of Justices have persisted in articulating it for generations. (For an argument that it is a justifiable as well as an actual requirement, see, in addition to the cases and commentaries noted below, Gunther, "Newer Equal Protection.")

requirement of "rational" means focuses on legislative *classifications:* statutes are not all-embracive; legislatures characteristically classify; equal protection demands that there be some "rational" connection between classifications and objectives. A minimal "fit" or "congruence" must exist between the classifying means and the legislative ends. But the traditional, "old" equal protection standard does not demand anything approaching a perfect fit: legislatures must often act on the basis of generalizations; perfect congruence would often make legislative action impossible and would demand individualized hearings in every case. The deferential old equal protection, then, leaves considerable flexibility to the legislature.

The materials in this section involve economic and social legislation that does not evoke the heightened scrutiny associated with "suspect" or near-"suspect" classifications and "fundamental interests." What restraints on classifications-ends relationships should the Court impose in this area? A frequently quoted formulation of the basic standard came in a 1920 decision: "[T]he classification must be reasonable, not arbitrary, and must rest upon some ground of difference having a fair and substantial relation to the object of the legislation, so that all persons similarly circumstanced shall be treated alike." [2] That somewhat demanding standard coexisted, however, with a more deferential-sounding one, one also frequently cited. [3] In many later cases, from the 1940s through the 1960s, the Court veered quite consistently toward the more deferential direction and demanded far less than the "fair and substantial relation" formulation seemed to require—although even during that very deferential era, the Court never wholly abandoned articulating a rationality requirement. [4] During the Warren years, there was only one invalidation on the basis of traditional equal protection rationality criteria [Morey v. Doud (1957)], and Morey has been explicitly overruled [New Orleans v. Dukes (1976); see p. 607 below.]. Yet the Royster formulation, demanding a "fair and substantial relation" between classification and legislative objective, has once again become a recurrent citation by the Burger Court. [5] And, at least sporadically, the Burger Court has in fact been somewhat less deferential toward state economic legislation than the Warren Court: several Burger Court decisions have invalidated state laws even while reciting the traditional equal protection criteria. Thus, what emerges is that the modern Court has not formally abandoned the traditional equal protection requirement that legislative means must rationally further legislative ends. Accordingly, some examination of the rationality criteria and their meaning in theory and practice is justified by more than historical reasons. What, then, is signified by the old equal protection's demand for some but not perfect congruence between classifications and objectives?

1. *Classifications and adequate congruence: The Tussman-tenBroek analysis.* The classic discussion of the requisite relationship between classifications and legisla-

---

2. (Emphasis added.) F.S. Royster Guano Co. v. Virginia, 253 U.S. 412 (1920). (Note the similarity of the Royster Guano standard to that asserted for the rationality requirement in economic due process cases in Nebbia v. New York; 1934; p. 462 above.)

3. The more deferential formulation of equal protection rationality came in Lindsley v. Natural Carbonic Gas Co., 220 U.S. 61 (1911): "1. The equal protection clause of the 14th Amendment does not take from the State the power to classify in the adoption of police laws, but admits of the exercise of a wide scope of discretion in that regard, and avoids what is done only when it is without any reasonable basis and therefore is purely arbitrary. 2. A classification having some reasonable basis does not offend against that

clause merely because it is not made with mathematical nicety or because in practice it results in some inequality. 3. When the classification in such a law is called in question, if any state of facts reasonably can be conceived that would sustain it, the existence of that state of facts at the time the law was enacted must be assumed. 4. One who assails the classification in such a law must carry the burden of showing that it does not rest upon any reasonable basis, but is essentially arbitrary."

4. See, e.g., Williamson v. Lee Optical Co. (1955; p. 600 below).

5. See, e.g., Reed v. Reed (1971; p. 645 below).

tive objectives is in Tussman & tenBroek, "The Equal Protection of the Laws," 37 Calif.L.Rev. 341 (1949). Systematic analyses such as this are rare in the literature, and the article is especially useful in delineating the meaning of the "overinclusive-underinclusive" terminology that recurs frequently in the equal protection materials in this chapter. The following excerpts from the article accordingly provide useful background.[6]

"The measure of the reasonableness of a classification is the degree of its success in treating similarly those similarly situated. [W]here are we to look for the test of similarity of situation which determines the reasonableness of a classification? The inescapable answer is that we must look beyond the classification to the purpose of the law. A reasonable classification is one which includes all persons who are similarly situated with respect to the purpose of the [law]. The purpose of a law may be either the elimination of a public 'mischief' or the achievement of some positive public good. To simplify the discussion we shall refer to the purpose of a law in terms of the elimination of mischief, since the same argument holds in either case. We shall speak of the defining character or characteristics of the legislative classification as the trait. We can thus speak of the relation of the classification to the purpose of the law as the relation of the Trait to the Mischief. A problem arises at all because the classification in a law usually does not have as its defining Trait the possession of or involvement with the Mischief at which the law aims. [In the usual problem], we are really dealing with the relation of two classes to each other. The first class consists of all individuals possessing the defining Trait; the second class consists of all individuals possessing, or rather, tainted by, the Mischief at which the law aims. The former is the legislative classification; the latter is the class of those similarly situated with respect to the purpose of the law. We shall refer to these two classes as T and M respectively. Now, since the reasonableness of any class T depends entirely upon its relation to a class M, it is obvious that it is impossible to pass judgment on the reasonableness of a classification without taking into consideration, or identifying, the purpose of the [law].

"There are five possible relationships between the class defined by the Trait and the class defined by the Mischief. These relationships can be indicated by the following diagrams:

(1)	(MT)	: All T's are M's and all M's are T's
(2)	(T)(M)	: No T's are M's
(3)	(M over T)	: All T's are M's but some M's are not T's
(4)	(T over M)	: All M's are T's but some T's are not M's
(5)	(T ( ) M)	: Some T's are M's; some T's are not M's; and some M's are not T's

One of these five relationships holds in fact in any case of legislative classification, and we will consider each from the point of view of its 'reasonableness.'

"The first two situations represent respectively the ideal limits of reasonableness and unreasonableness. In the first case, the classification in the law coincides completely with the class of those similarly situated with respect to the purpose of the law. It is perfectly reasonable. In the second case, no member of the class defined in the law is tainted with the mischief at which the law aims. The classification is, therefore, perfectly unreasonable. These two situations need not detain us.

6. Reprinted with the permission of the publisher, © 1949, California Law Review, Inc.

"Classification of the third type may be called 'under-inclusive.' All who are included in the class are tainted with the mischief, but there are others also tainted whom the classification does not include. Since the classification does not include all who are similarly situated with respect to the purpose of the law, there is a prima facie violation of the equal protection requirement of reasonable classification. But the Court has recognized the very real difficulties under which legislatures operate—difficulties arising out of both the nature of the legislative process and of the society which legislation attempts perennially to reshape—and it has refused to strike down indiscriminately all legislation embodying the classificatory inequality here under consideration. In justifying this refusal, the Court has defended under-inclusive classifications on such grounds as: the legislature may attack a general problem in a piecemeal fashion; 'some play must be allowed for the joints of the machine'; '[the] law does all that is needed when it does all that it [can].'

"The fourth type of classification imposes a burden upon a wider range of individuals than are included in the class of those tainted with the mischief at which the law aims. It can thus be called 'over-inclusive.' [It] is exemplified by the quarantine and the dragnet. The wartime treatment of American citizens of Japanese ancestry [p. 642 below] is a striking recent instance of the imposition of burdens upon a large class of individuals because some of them were believed to be [disloyal].

"The final situation to be considered is one in which the previously discussed factors of under-inclusiveness and over-inclusiveness are both present. While it may seem paradoxical to assert that a classification can be at once over-inclusive and under-inclusive, many classifications do, in fact fall into this category, that is, they can be challenged separately on both grounds. For example, in [Hirabayashi v. United States, 320 U.S. 81 (1943)], the classification of 'American citizens of Japanese ancestry' for the purpose of meeting the dangers of sabotage can be challenged both on the grounds that it is under-inclusive, since others— American citizens of German or Italian ancestry—are equally under the strain of divided loyalties, and that it is over-inclusive, since it is not supposed that all American citizens of Japanese ancestry are disloyal. The sustaining of this classification, therefore, requires both the finding of sufficient emergency to justify the imposition of a burden upon a larger class than is believed tainted with the Mischief and the establishment of 'fair reasons' for failure to extend the operation of the law to a wider class of potential saboteurs."

    2. *Some preliminary observations on the requirements of congruence.* Consider the congruence demands of the traditional standard as applied in the modern economic and social regulation cases that follow. To what extent were the classifications involved in the cases "overinclusive" or "underinclusive"? Should they have survived scrutiny under the traditional criteria? Most in fact did survive. Which variety of imperfect classifications, overinclusive ones or those that are underinclusive, most warrant more careful scrutiny? Tussman and tenBroek claim there is a stronger prima facie case against overinclusive ones: in an underinclusive classification, they point out, "all who are included in the class are at least tainted by the mischiefs at which the law aims"; but overinclusive ones "reach out to the innocent bystander, the hapless victim of circumstance or association." Others (including Justice Jackson in the case below) argue instead that underinclusive classifications present the greater danger of arbitrary government. (As Justice Jackson said: "[Nothing] opens the door to arbitrary action so effectively as to allow [officials] to pick and choose only a few to whom they will apply legislation and thus to escape the political retribution that might be visited upon them if larger numbers were

affected.") [7] As Tussman and tenBroek recognized, the Court does not demand perfect congruence; the critical issue in the cases, then, is the degree to which a legislature shall be permitted to generalize or to deal with portions of a problem at a time, and thus to fall short of perfect congruence. What were the reasons offered by the Court for the failures to invalidate the noncongruent situations in the cases which follow? Are they persuasive reasons? Do those reasons, does that degree of deference to legislative discretion, ultimately remove all bite from the traditional equal protection standard? Could the Court have demanded more? Could it have done so by limiting itself simply to the question of legislative "means," without getting into the more difficult sphere of curtailing legislative discretion as to ends? Or must value judgments inevitably play a role when courts, in determining whether the rationality standard is met, make judgments about what "similarly situated" means and what the "purpose" of the law is?

RAILWAY EXPRESS AGENCY v. NEW YORK

336 U.S. 106, 69 S.Ct. 463, 93 L.Ed. 533 (1949).

Mr. Justice DOUGLAS delivered the opinion of the Court.

Section 124 of the [New York City Traffic Regulations] provides: "No person shall operate, or cause to be operated, in or upon any street an advertising vehicle; provided that nothing herein contained shall prevent the putting of business notices upon business delivery vehicles, so long as such vehicles are engaged in the usual business or regular work of the owner and not used merely or mainly for advertising." Appellant is engaged in a nationwide express business. It operates about 1,900 trucks in New York City and sells the space on the exterior sides of these trucks for advertising. That advertising is for the most part unconnected with its own business. It was convicted [and] fined. [The state court] concluded that advertising on [vehicles] constitutes a distraction to vehicle drivers and to pedestrians alike and therefore affects the safety of the public in the use of the streets. We do not sit to weigh evidence on the due process issue in order to determine whether the regulation is sound or appropriate; nor is it our function to pass judgment on its [wisdom].

The question of equal protection of the laws is pressed more strenuously on us. It is pointed out that the regulation draws the line between advertisements of products sold by the owner of the truck and general advertisements. It is argued that unequal treatment on the basis of such a distinction is not justified by the aim and purpose of the regulation. It is said, for example, that one of appellant's trucks carrying the advertisement of a commercial house would not cause any greater distraction of pedestrians and vehicle drivers than if the commercial house carried the same advertisement on its own truck. Yet the regulation allows the latter to do what the former is forbidden from doing. It is therefore contended that the classification which the regulation makes has no relation to the traffic problem since a violation turns not on what kind of advertisements are carried on trucks but on whose trucks they are carried. That, however, is a superficial way of analyzing the problem. [The] local authorities may well have concluded that those who advertise their own wares on their trucks do not present the same traffic problem in view of the nature or extent of the advertising which they use. It would take a degree of omniscience which we lack to say that such is not the case. If that judgment is correct, the

---

7. See also Tribe, American Constitutional Law (1978), 999, suggesting that underinclusiveness is especially dangerous from "the viewpoint of political accountability," because it may "exempt potentially powerful opponents from a law's reach." Contrast "Developments," 82 Harv.L. Rev. 1065 (1969).

advertising displays that are exempt have less incidence on traffic than those of appellants. We cannot say that that judgment is not an allowable one. Yet if it is, the classification has relation to the purpose for which it is made and does not contain the kind of discrimination against which [equal protection] affords protection. It is by such practical considerations based on experience rather than by theoretical inconsistencies that the question of equal protection is to be answered. And the fact that New York City sees fit to eliminate from traffic this kind of distraction but does not touch what may be even greater ones in a different category, such as the vivid displays on Times Square, is immaterial. It is no requirement of equal protection that all evils of the same genus be eradicated or none at [all].

Affirmed.[1]

Mr. Justice JACKSON, concurring.

[My] philosophy as to the relative readiness with which we should resort to [the due process and equal protection] clauses is almost diametrically opposed to the philosophy which prevails on this Court. While claims of denial of equal protection are frequently asserted, they are rarely sustained. But the Court frequently uses the due process clause to strike down measures taken by municipalities to deal with activities in their streets and public places which the local authorities consider as creating hazards, annoyances or discomforts to their inhabitants. [The] burden should rest heavily upon one who would persuade us to use the due process clause to strike down a substantive law or ordinance. Even its provident use against municipal regulations frequently disables all government—state, municipal and federal—from dealing with the conduct in question because the requirement of due process is also applicable to State and Federal Governments. Invalidation of a statute or an ordinance on due process grounds leaves ungoverned and ungovernable conduct which many people find objectionable.

Invocation of the equal protection clause, on the other hand, does not disable any governmental body from dealing with the subject at hand. It merely means that the prohibition or regulation must have a broader impact. I regard it as a salutary doctrine that [governments] must exercise their powers so as not to discriminate between their inhabitants except upon some reasonable differentiation fairly related to the object of regulation. This equality is not merely abstract justice. [T]here is no more effective practical guaranty against arbitrary and unreasonable government than to require that the principles of law which officials would impose upon a minority must be imposed generally. Conversely, nothing opens the door to arbitrary action so effectively as to allow those officials to pick and choose only a few to whom they will apply legislation and thus to escape the political retribution that might be visited upon them if larger numbers were affected. Courts can take no better measure to assure that laws will be just than to require that laws be equal in operation.

This case affords an illustration. Even casual observations from the sidewalks of New York will show that an ordinance which would forbid all advertising on vehicles would run into conflict with many interests, including some, if not all, of the great metropolitan newspapers, which use that advertising extensively. Their blandishment of the latest sensations is not less a cause of diverted attention and traffic hazard than the commonplace cigarette advertisement which this truckowner is forbidden to display. But any regulation applicable to all such advertising would require much clearer justification in local conditions to enable its enactment than does some regulation applicable to a few. I do not mention this to criticize the motives of those who enacted this

---

1. Justice RUTLEDGE "acquiesced" in the Court's opinion, stating that he was "dubitante on the question of [equal protection]."

ordinance, but it dramatizes the point that we are much more likely to find arbitrariness in the regulation of the few than of the [many].

In this case, if [New York] should assume that display of any advertising on vehicles tends and intends to distract the attention of persons using the highways and to increase the dangers of its traffic, I should think it fully within its constitutional powers to forbid it all. [Instead] of such general regulation of advertising, however, the City seeks to reduce the hazard only by saying that while some may, others may not exhibit such appeals. The same display, for example, advertising cigarettes, which this appellant is forbidden to carry on its trucks, may be carried on the trucks of a cigarette dealer. [The] City urges that this applies equally to all persons of a permissible classification, because, [while it] does not eliminate vehicular advertising, it does eliminate such advertising for hire and to this extent cuts down the hazard sought to be controlled. That the difference between carrying on any business for hire and engaging in the same activity on one's own is a sufficient one to sustain some types of regulations of the one that is not applied to the other, is almost elementary. But it is usual to find such regulations applied to the very incidents wherein the two classes present different problems, such as in charges, liability and quality of service. The difference, however, is invoked here to sustain a discrimination in a problem in which the two classes present identical dangers. The courts of New York have declared that the sole nature and purpose of the regulation before us is to reduce traffic hazards. There is not even a pretense here that the traffic hazard created by the advertising which is forbidden is in any manner or degree more hazardous than that which is [permitted].

I do not think differences of treatment under law should be approved on classification because of differences unrelated to the legislative purpose. The equal protection clause ceases to assure either equality or protection if it is avoided by any conceivable difference that can be pointed out between those bound and those left free. This Court has often announced the principle that the differentiation must have an appropriate relation to the object of the legislation or ordinance. [The] question in my mind comes to this. Where individuals contribute to an evil or danger in the same way and to the same degree, may those who do so for hire be prohibited, while those who do so for their own commercial ends but not for hire be allowed to continue? I think the answer has to be that the hireling may be put in a class by himself and may be dealt with differently than those who act on their own. But this is not merely because such a discrimination will enable the lawmaker to diminish the evil. That might be done by many classifications, which I should think wholly unsustainable. It is rather because there is a real difference between doing in self-interest and doing for hire, so that it is one thing to tolerate action from those who act on their own and it is another thing to permit the same action to be promoted for a price. [Of course], this appellant did not hold itself out to carry or display everybody's advertising, and its rental of space on the sides of its trucks was only incidental to the main business which brought its trucks into the streets. But it is not difficult to see that, in a day of extravagant advertising more or less subsidized by tax deduction, the rental of truck space could become an obnoxious enterprise. While I do not think highly of this type of regulation, that is not my business, and in view of the control I would concede to cities to protect citizens in quiet and orderly use for their proper purposes of the highways and public places, I think the judgment below must be affirmed.

THE WARREN COURT'S APPROACH IN OPERATION: RESTRICTIONS ON BUSINESS ENTRY

Some introductory questions. In the cases that follow, the Court rejected equal protection challenges to statutes charged with being "underinclusive" protections of a favored group. Were these situations in which Justice Jackson's Railway Express concern should have been heeded: Should the Court have insisted that the regulations "must have a broader impact," to safeguard against arbitrariness? Should the Court have used less imaginativeness to think of conceivable rationales that *might* have influenced a hypothetical legislature? Should it have used less imaginativeness in suggesting how the classifications *might* have furthered the legislative purposes? Should it have used less imaginativeness in determining what the legislative purpose *might* have been? Should it have tested the fit between means and ends on the basis of actual rather than conceivable purposes, and on the basis of demonstrated rather than imagined contributions of classifications to purposes? Could greater scrutiny of rationality of means or actuality of purposes have been undertaken without resuming the discredited substantive due process practice of unduly curtailing legislative ends in the economic regulation area? [1]

1. *Lee Optical and opticians.* In WILLIAMSON v. LEE OPTICAL CO., 348 U.S. 483 (1955) (noted earlier at p. 470 above), the challenge to Oklahoma's scheme for the regulation of opticians rested not only on due process but also on equal protection. But the Court, at the height of the deferential stance toward business regulation, rejected the equal protection claim even more summarily than the due process one. Justice DOUGLAS stated for a unanimous Court: "[T]he District Court held that it violated the Equal Protection Clause [to] subject opticians to this regulatory system and to exempt [all] sellers of ready-to-wear glasses. The problem of legislative classification is a perennial one, admitting of no doctrinaire definition. Evils in the same field may be of different dimensions and proportions, requiring different remedies. Or so the legislature may think. Or the reform may take one step at a time, addressing itself to the phase of the problem which seems most acute to the legislative mind. The legislature may select one phase of one field and apply a remedy there, neglecting the others. The prohibition of [equal protection] goes no further than the invidious discrimination. We cannot say that that point has been reached here. For all this record shows, the ready-to-wear branch of this business may not loom large in Oklahoma or may present problems of regulation distinct from the other branch." [2]

2. *McGowan and McDonald: The Warren Court's deferential approach at its extreme.* Judicial unwillingness to put any teeth into old equal protection

---

1. In one sense, the cases in this section are atypical: the Court *did* write an opinion in each of them. In most cases involving economic regulation during the Warren era, by contrast, the challenges were rejected summarily. (The cases in which the Court undertook plenary review were usually ones in which a lower court had invalidated a law.)

The Vinson Court of the late 1940s had been as deferential as the Warren Court of the 1950s and 1960s. See, in addition to Railway Express, Daniel v. Family Security Life Insurance Co., 336 U.S. 220 (1949), barring life insurance agencies from operating undertaking businesses and undertakers from serving as life insurance agents, and Kotch v. Board of River Pilot Commissioners, 330 U.S. 552 (1947), attacking the administration of Louisiana's pilotage laws on the

ground that only relatives and friends of incumbents were granted state certificates. Justice Black's majority opinion in the 5 to 4 decision in Kotch relied on the "entirely unique" nature of pilotage "in the light of its history in Louisiana." Justice Rutledge's dissent argued that "[blood was] the crux of selection" and that a standard of "race or consanguinity" was impermissible. See also Goesaert v. Cleary (1948; p. 644 below), a divided Court's rejection of a sex discrimination challenge to a bartender licensing scheme.

2. Was Justice Douglas' stance even more deferential than the "fair and substantial relation" criterion or the other rationality standards purportedly governing "old equal protection" scrutiny? Would adherence to his approach assure validation of virtually all departures from congruence in the business regulation area?

standards in the scrutiny of business regulations may have reached its most extreme form in two opinions written by Chief Justice Warren in the 1960s. Do these cases—even more than Lee Optical—reduce scrutiny under the old equal protection to "minimal scrutiny in theory and virtually none in fact"?[3]

a. *McGowan.* In a group of cases in 1961, state Sunday closing laws were sustained against challenges based not only on the religion clauses of the First Amendment but also on equal protection. The Court rejected the latter attack by applying traditional, permissive standards. In McGOWAN v. MARYLAND, 366 U.S. 420 (1961), Chief Justice WARREN spoke for a unanimous Court in rejecting the claim that the exemptions of certain businesses from the Maryland Sunday closing law violated equal protection. One of the provisions, for example, banned the Sunday "sale of all merchandise except the retail sale of tobacco products, confectioneries, milk, bread, fruits, gasoline, greases, drugs and medicines, and newspapers and periodicals." The Chief Justice stated: "[The] Court has held that the 14th Amendment permits the States a wide scope of discretion in enacting laws which affect some groups of citizens differently than others. The constitutional safeguard is offended only if the classification rests on grounds wholly irrelevant to the achievement of the State's objective. State legislatures are presumed to have acted within their constitutional power despite the fact that, in practice, their laws result in some inequality. A statutory discrimination will not be set aside if any state of facts reasonably may be conceived to justify it. It would seem that a legislature could reasonably find that the Sunday sale of the exempted commodities was necessary either for the health of the populace or for the enhancement of the recreational atmosphere of the day. [The] record is barren of any indication that this apparently reasonable basis does not exist, that the statutory distinctions are invidious, that local tradition and custom might not rationally call for this legislative treatment."

b. *McDonald.* Perhaps the most extremely deferential version of traditional equal protection criteria on the Warren Court—and one of the most graphic statements of the sharp difference between the strict scrutiny of the new equal protection and the leniency of the old—came in McDONALD v. BOARD OF ELECTION, 394 U.S. 802 (1969). That was a claim by qualified Cook County, Illinois, voters imprisoned in a County jail while awaiting trial that the state could not deny them absentee ballots when they were provided to other classes of persons.[4] Chief Justice WARREN's opinion for a unanimous Court first disposed of the claim that this was a case for the Warren Court's new equal protection criteria because the "fundamental interest" in voting was involved. Here, the Chief Justice replied, only a right to an absentee ballot, not an impact on "the fundamental right to vote," was in issue; conceivably, there were other opportunities for the challengers to vote. Accordingly, the lower level of the two-tier approach was invoked. The Chief Justice stated the "basic guidelines" governing the "more traditional standards for evaluating" equal protection claims as follows: "The distinctions drawn by a challenged statute must bear some rational relationship to a legitimate state end and will be set aside as violative of the Equal Protection Clause only if based on reasons totally unrelated to the pursuit of that goal. Legislatures are presumed to have acted constitutionally even if source materials normally resorted to for ascertaining their grounds for action are otherwise silent, and their statutory classifications will be set aside only if no grounds can be conceived to justify them. With this much discretion, a legislature traditionally has been allowed to take reform 'one

---

3. The quoted phrase is from Gunther, "Newer Equal Protection."

4. The four classes who were entitled to absentee ballots were: persons absent from their county of residency for any reason whatever; the "physically incapacitated"; those kept from the polls because of observance of a religious holiday; and those serving as poll watchers in precincts other than their own.

step at a time' [Lee Optical]; and a legislature need not run the risk of losing an entire remedial scheme simply because it failed, through inadvertence or otherwise, to cover every evil that might conceivably have been attacked." [5]

5. *The "one step at a time" justification.* Does even a commitment to a deferential stance justify leaning over backwards to quite the degree manifested by Chief Justice Warren's McDonald approach? (a) Is there significance to the Chief Justice's phrasing of the requisite means-ends nexus not in terms of "fair and substantial" relation but as "some rational relationship," with a reference to "reasons totally unrelated to the pursuit of [the] goal"? (b) Need judicial hypothesizing about the requisite relationship go so far as to say that invalidation will result "only if no grounds can be conceived to justify" classifications? (c) Is the "one step at a time" rationale ultimately subversive of *any* real judicial scrutiny under "old" equal protection standards? Some deference to legislative realities may be appropriate: legislators may want to experiment, or to respond to immediate needs or political pressures. But judicial blessing of every effort at piecemeal legislation would block all challenges based on underinclusiveness. What limits can and should the Court impose on justifying laws on the "one step at a time" ground? [6]

POSSIBILITIES OF GREATER SCRUTINY WITHIN THE RATIONALITY FRAMEWORK?

Introduction. As the preceding cases illustrate, at the end of the 1960s, the avowed deference of the "old" equal protection was greater than ever—even while the strict scrutiny of the "new" equal protection flourished in selected areas. Before turning to the Burger Court's execution of rationality review, two theories that offer potential bases for somewhat greater scrutiny within the framework of rationality standards warrant attention. The first draws on structural considerations pertaining to the Constitution and to representative government: it suggests heightened judicial concern for minorities with an inadequate say in the governmental process—including, arguably, minorities not entitled to invoke strict scrutiny under the suspect classifications branch of the "new" equal protection. The second position argues that, wherever the rationality standards of the "old" equal protection are appropriate, the Court can and should engage in more serious, less deferential review in order to assure that the legislative means *genuinely* promote *articulated* governmental purposes.

1. *"Selective intervention" on behalf of minorities (including economic minorities?): The relevance of the Carolene Products footnote.* Justice Douglas, the author of the

---

5. In searching for conceivable rationales to explain the "different treatment accorded unsentenced inmates incarcerated within and those incarcerated without their resident counties," the Chief Justice suggested that the difference "may reflect a legislative determination that without the protection of the voting booth, local officials might be too tempted to try to influence the local voter in-county inmates." But his justification for the law placed special reliance on the fact that this was "remedial legislation," the result of "a consistent and laudable state policy of adding, over a 50-year period, groups to the absentee coverage as their existence comes to the attention of the legislature." That "Illinois has not gone still further, as perhaps it might," was justified by the "one step at a time" rationale. Some classes of voters were entitled to absentee ballots,

to be sure; but the challengers' class was not the only one excluded. (He noted that among the other excluded were "mothers with children who cannot afford a babysitter" and "persons attending ill relations within their own county.")

Can the "remedial" purpose of legislation justify deferential scrutiny even in the context of suspect classifications and fundamental interests? For a similar reliance on the "remedial legislation" rationale to justify minimal scrutiny, see the last part of Justice Brennan's opinion in Katzenbach v. Morgan (1966; p. 946 below).

6. For a valiant modern effort to articulate curbs on the "one step at a time" justification, see Note, "Reforming the One Step at a Time Justification in Equal Protection Cases," 90 Yale L.J. 1777 (1981).

very deferential opinion in Lee Optical, voted to invalidate several regulatory laws during the three decades beginning with the 1940s.[1] Consider the explanation of Justice Douglas' move "from abdication to selective intervention" offered in Karst, "Invidious Discrimination: Justice Douglas and the Return of the 'Natural-Law-Due-Process Formula,'" 16 U.C.L.A.L.Rev. 716 (1969). Kenneth Karst noted that in each case the state was perpetuating "economic advantages for a favored group, at the expense of those who claimed to be relatively disadvantaged. The appeal of such an argument to a Justice with strong egalitarian views is great, great enough in these cases to overcome the inclination to keep the judiciary aloof from decisions about economic regulation." But what about Justice Douglas' opinion in Lee Optical? That, Karst suggests, is distinguishable because there "the losers in the legislature were not permanently disadvantaged minorities. The opticians might well have anticipated new legislative alliances" [though, he concedes in a footnote, "the opticians are still looking for such an alliance"]. In short, "consciously or not," the Douglas record accorded with "a principle of activism in the cause of economic opportunity"—a principle which is "the equal protection analogue of the double standard of judicial review under the due process clauses, enunciated in Justice Stone's footnote 4 [in the Carolene Products case], which made the legitimacy of judicial protection of the losers in the legislative process turn on the losers' long-term chances of becoming winners."

The Carolene Products footnote referred to by Karst (printed at p. 473 above) forms the starting point for most modern structural arguments urging special judicial solicitude for minorities. The third paragraph of that footnote, the "protecting losing minorities" aspect, is of special relevance to equal protection analysis. Recall that Justice Stone suggested a greater basis for judicial scrutiny where there might be "prejudice against discrete and insular minorities"—prejudice which "tends seriously to curtail the operation of those political processes ordinarily to be relied upon to protect minorities." That consideration clearly underlies some of the expansions of strict scrutiny for suspect classifications, considered in sec. 3 below. But can that rationale be applied as well to losing minorities that are not identified by "suspect" criteria— including losing *economic* minorities? Can economic minorities be protected without a return to the interventionism of the Lochner era?[2]

---

1. E.g., Kotch, the river pilots case, and Goesaert, the women bartenders case, p. 644 below, and Morey v. Doud (p. 607 below).

2. Note Karst's comment: "[Perhaps] activism offers no particular risk to a judiciary's independence unless it is directed at the wrong substantive ends."

Is the "minorities" rationale in any event as persuasive as the other portions of Justice Stone's footnote? Can it be an adequately limited rationale, since a majoritarian political process is *generally* an unreliable protector of minorities? Restrictions of the political process through curtailment of political debate or voting—Justice Stone's second category in his footnote—is a clear and readily persuasive concept. Can the same be said of restrictions on the "process" that are manifested solely by *results* that bear harshly on losing groups—even though all may speak and vote?

Compare the critical comments by Justice Rehnquist on the "minorities" aspect of the Carolene Products footnote, in objecting to the elevation of alienage into the category of "suspect classifications" triggering strict scrutiny. In his dissent in In re Griffiths (1973; p. 671 below), he stated: "The mere recitation of the words 'insular and discrete minority' is hardly a *constitutional* reason for prohibiting state legislative classifications such as are involved here, and is not necessarily consistent with the theory propounded in that footnote. The approach taken in [these cases] appears to be that whenever the Court feels that a societal group is 'discrete and insular,' it has the constitutional mandate to prohibit legislation that somehow treats the group differently from some other group. Our society, consisting of over 200 million individuals of multitudinous origins, customs, tongues, beliefs, and cultures, is, to say the least, diverse. It would hardly take extraordinary ingenuity for a lawyer to find 'insular and discrete' minorities at every turn in the road. Yet, unless the Court can precisely define and constitutionally justify both the terms and analysis it uses, these decisions today stand for the proposition that the Court can choose a 'minority' it 'feels' deserves 'solicitude' and thereafter prohibit the States from classifying that 'minority' differently from the 'majority.' I cannot find [any] constitutional

The major modern effort to articulate a theory of judicial review deriving protection of minorities from a "process" rationale akin to the Carolene Products footnote is John Hart Ely's. Ely's effort to give "principled content" to that suggestion culminated in his 1980 book, Democracy and Distrust.[3] Ely argued, inter alia, for heightened scrutiny in the interest of protecting minorities unable to participate fully in the political process. His "representation-reinforcing," minority-protecting theory emphasizes that "constitutional law appropriately exists for those situations where representative government cannot be trusted." Although Ely does not emphasize economic minorities as beneficiaries of his theory, can it be argued that, by analogy to his approach, the perennially losing opticians in Oklahoma should have received more careful Court scrutiny of their complaint than Lee Optical afforded? Rather than attempting to justify sporadic, "selective intervention" on behalf of some (perhaps even economic) minorities, would a more fruitful approach be to apply rationality criteria more seriously across the board? Consider the suggestions that follow.

2. *Rationality review "with bite": The "newer equal protection" argument.* A quite different approach, tied more directly to the traditional articulations of rationality review, is the argument for somewhat intensified scrutiny of means in economic and social regulations, set forth in Gunther, "Newer Equal Protection," 86 Harv.L.Rev. 1 (1972). That argument for a "new bite for the old equal protection" suggests that a less perfunctory scrutiny under the "mere rationality" standard could be achieved by viewing equal protection "as a means-focused, relatively narrow, preferred ground of decision in a broad range of cases." It would have the Court "less willing to supply justifying rationales by exercising its imagination. It would have the Court assess the means in terms of legislative purposes that have substantial basis in actuality, not merely in conjecture. Moreover, it would have the Justices gauge the reasonableness of questionable means on the basis of materials that are offered to the Court, rather than resorting to rationalizations created by perfunctory judicial hypothesizing."[4] The "newer equal protection" was not offered to replace strict

authority for such a 'ward of the Court' approach to equal protection."

3. Ely, "The Wages of Crying [Wolf]," 82 Yale L.J. 920 (1973), and Ely, "Toward a Representation-Reinforcing Mode of Judicial Review," 37 Md.L.Rev. 451 (1978).

4. The "newer equal protection" model was prompted by an unusual phenomenon that first emerged during the 1971 Term: in seven cases during that Term, the Burger Court, in sharp contrast to the Warren Court's pattern, found substantial bases for constitutional challenges even though the traditional equal protection criteria were recited. The "Newer Equal Protection" article did not claim that the Burger Court decisions in fact conformed to the model, but argued that the model offered justifiable bases for more genuine, across-the-board rationality review in a wide range of cases.

For a review of some efforts by lower courts to apply the "newer equal protection" model, see, e.g., Comment, " 'Newer' Equal Protection: The Impact of the Means-Focused Model," 23 Buffalo L.Rev. 665 (1974). For a skeptical view of the possibilities of means-oriented rationality review, see, e.g., Note, "Legislative Purpose, Rationality, and Equal Protection," 82 Yale L.J. 123 (1972); Linde, "Due Process of Lawmaking," 55 Neb.L. Rev. 197 (1976); and Justice Rehnquist's dissent

in Trimble v. Gordon, 430 U.S. 762 (1977). The Trimble dissent is probably Justice Rehnquist's fullest statement of his equal protection approach. The majority had applied heightened scrutiny to an illegitimacy classification, insisting that scrutiny in this area should be more than "toothless." That prompted Justice Rehnquist to launch an extensive attack on the Court's modern equal protection jurisprudence. He argued that, except where "classifications based on race or on national origin, the first cousin of race," were involved, heightened review was improper. He called the Court's "means" scrutiny a "self-imposed" task "stemming not from the Equal Protection Clause but from the Court's insistence on reading so much into it." The basic "purpose" of all legislation was simply "to make the language [in the enacted provision] a part of the law." The Court's approach "expands the normal reading of the word ['purpose'] into something more like motive." In determining how much "imperfection between means and ends is permissible," the Court deemed itself required to "throw into the judicial hopper the whole range of factors which were first thrown into the legislative hopper." That approach rested on a "fundamental flaw": "there is absolutely nothing to be inferred from the fact that we hold judicial commissions that would enable

scrutiny; rather, that means-focused model would impose some constraints on legislative action falling within the old equal protection and treated with extreme deference by the Warren Court.[5] It was defended not only on the ground that it would take seriously the rationality standard the Court has traditionally stated, but also because it could "improve the quality of the political process—without second-guessing the substantive validity of its results—by encouraging a fuller airing in the political arena of the grounds for legislative action." It argued, for example, that the Court could demand more of the state than it required in the Lee Optical case.[6] The model is clearly not problem-free. E.g., can it be applied without unduly scrutinizing legislative motivations and the actualities of legislative processes? Would it truly be beneficial to the legislative process? Would it truly encourage "a fuller airing in the political arena of the grounds for legislative action," or would it simply shift the burden of hypothesizing legislative rationales from the Court to counsel defending the challenged legislation? And, although the model purports to be concerned solely with means rather than ends, can it avoid undue intrusion into legislative value choices?[7]

Consider, in examining the materials that follow, the extent to which the Burger Court's equal protection decisions in the economic regulation area move in the direction of either the Ely "representation-reinforcing" or the Gunther "newer equal protection" model. With respect to "newer equal protection," a large number of Justices on the Burger Court have indeed spoken of testing legislation by articulated rather than hypothesized purposes, and have scrutinized the empiric underpinnings of the means-ends relationships more closely than the Warren Court had.[8] But resort to techniques akin to ingredients of the

us to answer [better] than the legislators." And he commented: "Without any antecedent constitutional mandate, we have created on the premises of the Equal Protection Clause a school for legislators, whereby opinions of this Court are written to instruct them in a better understanding of how to accomplish their ordinary legislative tasks."

5. The point of this sentence bears underlining, for it is occasionally misunderstood by judges and commentators (as well as students). The "newer equal protection" is *not* the same as the "intermediate" scrutiny developed in the modern cases for some quasi-suspect classifications such as gender. The "newer equal protection" theory does not take issue with the heightened scrutiny tiers of "strict" and "intermediate" review. Instead, it is solely addressed to the appropriate intensity of review to be exercised when the lowest tier, that of rationality review, is deemed appropriate. It is in the "mere rationality" cases that the Warren Court virtually abandoned effective scrutiny of any sort. What the "newer equal protection model" asks is that some teeth be put into that lowest level of scrutiny, that it be applied "with bite," focusing on means without second-guessing legislative ends. (Evaluating the importance of the ends is characteristic of all higher levels of scrutiny.) In short, "newer equal protection" seeks to raise slightly the lowest tier of review under the two- or three-tier models; but it does *not* seek to raise the "mere rationality" level appropriate for run-of-the-mill economic regulation cases all the way up to the level of "intermediate" or of "strict" scrutiny.

6. The model demanded that a demonstrable, "affirmative relation between means and ends" must be shown, and that the Court should assess the relationship "largely in terms of information presented by the defenders of the law rather than hypothesizing data of its own." Moreover, it urged the Court to "assess the rationality of the means in terms of the *state's* purposes, rather than hypothesizing conceivable justifications on its own initiative."

7. For discussions of additional problems with the model, see the "Newer Equal Protection" article and the Ninth Edition of this book, pp. 682–90.

8. For a review of some examples of the Burger Court's increasing—albeit sporadic—emphasis on articulated rather than hypothesized purposes, see Justice Brennan's comment in dissenting in Schlesinger v. Ballard, 419 U.S. 498 (1975): "While we have in the past exercised our imaginations to conceive of possible rational justifications for statutory classifications, see [McGowan], we have recently declined to manufacture justifications in order to save an apparently invalid statutory classification. Cf. James v. Strange, 407 U.S. 128 (1972); Weber (1972; p. 679 below). Moreover, we have analyzed asserted governmental interests to determine whether they were in fact the legislative purpose of a statutory classification, Eisenstadt v. Baird (1972; p. 514 above) [see also Weinberger v. Wiesenfeld, (1975; p. 739 below)]; and we have limited our inquiry to the legislature's stated purposes when these purposes are clearly set out in the statute or its legislative history. Johnson v. Robison, 415 U.S. 361 (1974). Never, to my knowledge, have

"newer equal protection" has been sporadic rather than consistent; and references to articulated purposes and actual contribution of means to ends are in many cases explainable by the fact that the issues arose in situations exerting special pressures toward some heightened scrutiny (e.g., sex discrimination), instead of the "run of the mill" context of economic regulations. Some of the Burger Court decisions that follow involve exercises of heightened scrutiny despite avowals of deferential, rationality standards. Other Burger Court cases, by contrast, involve review of economic regulations about as deferential as was common in the Warren era. Although, beginning in the mid-1970s, the Burger Court tended to swerve toward a deferential direction, there are enough 1980s opinions taking judicial scrutiny more seriously than that to suggest that the actual content of "rationality" equal protection review continues in flux.

RATIONALITY REVIEW ON THE BURGER COURT

1. *The early 1970s.* In its early years, the Burger Court repeatedly invalidated laws on equal protection grounds without asserting grounds for heightened scrutiny.[1] Thus, the 7 to 2 decision in U.S. Dept. of Agriculture v. Moreno, 413 U.S. 528 (1973), purporting to apply a rationality standard, struck down a provision of the federal food stamp program for assistance to "households"—households limited to groups of *related* persons. The exclusion of "unrelated persons" was found to be "irrational": it was not only "imprecise"; it was also "wholly without any rational basis." And in Jimenez v. Weinberger, 417 U.S. 628 (1974) another federal welfare program was struck down in an 8 to 1 ruling which scrutinized the law a good deal more carefully than the deferential stance dictated by Dandridge v. Williams (p. 852 below) for welfare programs.[2] (Note that in both cases grounds for heightened scrutiny arguably lurked in the background. On Moreno, compare Moore v. East Cleveland (1977; p. 551 above); on Jimenez, note the heightened scrutiny applied to

we endeavored to sustain a statute upon a supposition about the legislature's purpose in enacting it when the asserted justification can be shown conclusively *not* to have underlain the classification in any way." [Justice Brennan added in a footnote: "Indeed, to do so is to undermine the very premises of deference to legislative determination. If a legislature, considering the competing factors, determines that it is wise policy to treat two groups of people differently in pursuit of a certain goal, courts often defer to that legislative determination. But when a legislature has decided *not* to pursue a certain goal, upholding a statute on the basis of that goal is not properly deference to a legislative decision at all; it is deference to a decision which the legislature could have made but did not. See Gunther, 'Newer Equal Protection.'"]

See also the formulation in Justice Powell's opinion for the Court in McGinnis v. Royster, 410 U.S. 263 (1973), asking whether the challenged distinction furthered "some legitimate, *articulated* state purpose." Note, too, the examples of less deferential rationality review in some of the Burger Court decisions that follow, and the extensive debates about the relevance of the legislature's "actual purpose" in a number of cases in the 1980–81 term: the Fritz case (1980; p. 616 below), Schweiker v. Wilson, 450 U.S. 221

(1981; p. 619 below), and, in a non-equal protection, state regulation of commerce case, Kassel (1981; p. 255 above). Typically, Justice Brennan has contended that actual legislative purpose, not counsel's arguments or judicial hypothesizing, should be determinative, while Justice Rehnquist has continued to insist on a much more deferential stance, akin to that of Chief Justice Warren in the McDonald case above. [Compare Justice Brennan's majority opinion in Minnesota v. Clover Leaf Creamery Co. (1981; noted at p. 285 above on the commerce clause challenge), finding that the state court's review of the equal protection challenge had been unduly intrusive.]

1. In addition to the illustrative cases in the text, note the 1971–72 cases considered in Gunther, "Newer Equal Protection." See also Cohen, "Is Equal Protection Like Oakland? Equality as a Surrogate for Other Rights" (forthcoming, — Tul.L.Rev. — (1985)), and the indications of a move toward heightened scrutiny in the rationality cases in footnote 8 above.

2. Chief Justice Burger's majority opinion struck down a provision of the Social Security Act denying disability benefits to some but not all illegitimate children born after the onset of their wageearner parent's disability.

some illegitimacy classifications, see sec. 3 below—a basis for heightened scrutiny eschewed by the Court here.)

2. *The late 1970s.* In the late 1970s, the Burger Court seemed, most of the time, to retreat to a deferential variety of rationality review akin to that of the Warren era. NEW ORLEANS v. DUKES, 427 U.S. 297 (1976), was a harbinger of that trend. That per curiam opinion overruled Morey v. Doud, 354 U.S. 457 (1957), the only decision between the late 1930s and the 1970s in which the Court had struck down an economic regulation on equal protection grounds.[3] The Court stated that Morey had "so far depart[ed] from proper equal protection analysis in cases of exclusively economic regulation that it should be, and it is, overruled."[4] The Court sustained a 1972 New Orleans provision which exempted pushcart food vendors who had "continually operated the same business for eight years prior to January 1, 1972" from a prohibition against such vendors in the French Quarter (Vieux Carré). The ordinance was challenged by a pushcart vendor barred from continuing his business because he had been in business in the French Quarter for only two years at the time the provision was adopted. The Court emphasized that the grandfather clause was "solely an economic regulation aimed at enhancing the vital role of the French Quarter's tourist-oriented charm in the economy of New Orleans." The Court noted that economic regulations are subject to a deferential standard of review; that "the classification challenged [must be] rationally related to a legitimate state interest"; and that "rational distinctions may be made with substantially less than mathematical exactitude." The Court added that "the judiciary may not sit as a superlegislature to judge the wisdom or desirability of legislative policy determinations made in areas that neither affect fundamental rights nor proceed along suspect lines." Pointing to the "analogous situation" in Ferguson v. Skrupa [1963; economic due process; p. 468 above], the Court rejected the lower court's holding that the grandfather provision "failed even the rationality test," and found instead that "the city's classification rationally furthers the purpose which [the] city had identified as its objective in enacting the provisions, that is, '[preserving] the appearance and custom valued by the Quarter's residents and attractive to tourists.' "[5] The lower court had relied on Morey v. Doud in finding that "the hypothesis that a present eight-year veteran of the pushcart hot dog market in the Vieux Carre will continue to operate in a manner more consistent with the traditions of the Quarter than would any other operator is without foundation." But the Court found Morey no longer persuasive: it represented "a needlessly intrusive judicial infringement on the State's legislative powers": "Morey is the only case in the last half century to invalidate a wholly economic regulation solely on

---

3. In Morey, the Court invalidated an exemption by name of a company from a general regulatory scheme. The Illinois Community Currency Exchanges Act had imposed financial responsibility requirements on businesses issuing money orders but had explicitly exempted the American Express Company and several others. The American Express exemption was challenged by a local partnership which sought to sell money orders partially through drug and grocery stores. The 6 to 3 decision held the exemption unconstitutional. Justice Burton's majority opinion emphasized that the exemption created "a closed class," and that this grant of an economic advantage to a named company bore "no reasonable relation" to the purposes of the law. Justice Frankfurter, joined by Justices Harlan and Black, dissented.

4. Justice Marshall joined the judgment but not the per curiam opinion in this case. Justice Stevens did not participate.

5. Note that the Court sustained the law by reference to "the purpose which [the] city had identified as its purpose." Does that suggest that despite the deference to purely economic regulations on the Burger Court in the late 1970s, there was some tendency to test legislation in terms of the purpose articulated by the defenders of the law, rather than by reference to a hypothesized purpose, as was commonplace on the Warren Court? Note also the similar formulation in another equal protection deferential review case decided on the same day, Murgia, which follows.

equal protection grounds, and we are now satisfied that the decision was erroneous."

On the same day as Dukes, the Court, in another per curiam opinion, once again applied a very deferential stance in rejecting an equal protection challenge in MASSACHUSETTS BD. OF RETIREMENT v. MURGIA, 427 U.S. 307 (1976). That case sustained a Massachusetts law providing that a uniformed State police officer "shall be retired [upon] his attaining age fifty." After rejecting an argument that age should be viewed as a suspect classification triggering heightened scrutiny (as noted at p. 684 below), the majority applied the "relatively relaxed" rational basis standard: "Perfection in making the necessary classifications is neither possible nor necessary. Such action by a legislature is presumed to be valid. In this case, the [law] clearly meets the requirements of [equal protection], for the State's classification rationally furthers the purpose identified by the State: Through mandatory retirement at age 50, the legislature seeks to protect the public by assuring physical preparedness of its uniformed police. Since physical ability generally declines with age, mandatory retirement at 50 serves to remove from police service those whose fitness for uniformed work presumptively has diminished with age. This clearly is rationally related to the State's objective. There is no indication that [the law] has the effect of excluding from service so few officers who are in fact unqualified as to render age 50 a criterion wholly unrelated to the objective of the statute. That the State chooses not to determine fitness more precisely through individualized testing after age 50 is not to say that the objective of assuring physical fitness is not rationally furthered by a maximum age limitation. It is only to say that with regard to the interest of all concerned, the State perhaps has not chosen the best means to accomplish this purpose. But where rationality is the test, a State 'does not violate [equal protection] merely because the classifications made by its laws are imperfect.' Dandridge v. Williams."

Justice MARSHALL, the sole dissenter, used the case to launch one of his recurrent attacks on the "rigid two-tier model" of equal protection scrutiny. Although he thought that the "grasp on the law" of two-tier analysis was "weakening," he once again objected "to its perpetuation." He argued that the strict scrutiny and mere rationality tiers "simply do not describe the inquiry the Court has undertaken—or should undertake—in equal protection cases. Rather, the inquiry has been much more sophisticated and the Court should admit as much. It has focused upon the character of the classification in question, the relative importance to individuals in the class discriminated against of the governmental benefits that they do not receive, and the state interests asserted in support of the classification." He added: "[However] understandable the Court's hesitancy to invoke strict scrutiny, all remaining legislation should not drop into the bottom tier, and be measured by the mere rationality test." [6]

6. Justice Marshall noted that, while the traditional articulation of the rational basis test (as in McGowan, above) suggested a de facto abdication of judicial scrutiny, "happily the Court's deeds have not matched its words. Time and again, met with cases touching upon the prized rights and burdened classes of our society, the Court has acted only after a reasonably probing look at the legislative goals and means, and at the significance of the personal rights and interests invaded." (At this point, Justice Marshall cited a number of cases all noted elsewhere in this chapter, including Moreno, Reed, and Wiesenfeld, as well as Gunther, "Newer Equal Protection.") He added: "These cases make clear that the Court has rejected, albeit sub silentio, its most deferential statements of the rationality standard in assessing the validity under the Equal Protection Clause of much noneconomic legislation." But he objected to adherence to a standard not consistently followed in practice as "rudderless" and "unpredictable." Reiterating his own "flexible," sliding scale, multi-variable equal protection approach (for a full statement of his position, see his Rodriguez dissent, p. 689 below), he argued that applying his three critical factors ("the importance of the governmental benefits denied, the character of the class, and the asserted state interests") showed that the mandatory retirement law could not stand: "The elderly are undoubtedly discriminated against, and when legislation denies them an important benefit—employment—I conclude that to sustain the legislation [the state] must

Three years later, Vance v. Bradley, 440 U.S. 93 (1979), seemed to indicate that the Court had firmly embraced very deferential review. The case rejected an equal protection attack on a federal law requiring Foreign Service personnel to retire at age 60. Although Murgia had foreshadowed the decision, Justice White's majority opinion was noteworthy for illustrating how very little factual data the government needed to provide in order to defend a legislative classification under the rationality standard. He conceded that the classification was "to some extent both under- and over-inclusive," but held that "perfection is by no means required. [In] an equal protection case of this type, [those] challenging the legislative judgment must convince the court that the legislative facts on which the classification is apparently based could not reasonably be conceived to be true by the governmental decisionmaker." Yet only a few weeks after Vance, in New York City Transit Auth. v. Beazer, 440 U.S. 568 (1979), statements by several of the Justices indicated that the members of the Burger Court were not so clearly committed after all to as very deferential stance as Justice White's majority opinion in Vance had suggested. Indeed, Justice White himself, the author of the very deferential opinion in Vance, dissented in Beazer.[7]

3. *The 1980s.* The widespread anticipation that the Burger Court of the 1980s would return to exercising lowest tier rationality review in the very deferential manner of the Warren era has not been fulfilled. Instead, "old" equal protection review continues in flux, with frequent exercises at the very lenient level but with insistence from a substantial number of Justices in several cases that more serious scrutiny is warranted even in the area of economic and social legislation. The three cases that follow illustrate the modern pattern: some reiterations of deferential standards, accompanied by recurrent arguments for more serious review. Consider whether these cases suggest a continued potential for putting greater "bite" into rationality review—or whether they simply indicate instead that the Court is comfortable with using traditional equal protection standards as an occasional, ad hoc interventionist tool. Fritz, the first of the cases, seemed, to many, to announce a commitment to return to Warren Court deference:[8] it involved very lenient scrutiny; and it was a 7 to 2 decision

show a reasonably substantial interest and a scheme reasonably closely tailored to achieving that interest." Here, he found, the means chosen were so overinclusive that the law must fall: "I see no reason at all for automatically terminating those officers who have reached the age of 50; indeed, that action seems the height of irrationality," especially since the state was already individually testing its police officers for physical fitness.

7. Justice Stevens' majority opinion in Beazer upheld the exclusion of all methadone users from Transit Authority employment, rejecting the lower court's conclusion that, because about 75% of patients who have been on methadone treatment for at least a year were free of illicit drug use and because the exclusion applied to non-safety sensitive jobs, the exclusion had "no rational relation to the demands of the job to be performed." He viewed the exclusionary policy as "supported by the legitimate inference that as long as a treatment program (or other drug use) continues, a degree of uncertainty persists." The arguments that the exclusion rule was "broader than necessary" and arguably unwise involved "matters of personnel policy that do not implicate the principle safeguarded by the Equal Protection Clause." Since the rule did not "create or reflect any

special likelihood of bias on the part of the ruling majority," it was "of no constitutional significance that the degree of rationality is not as great with respect to certain ill-defined subparts of the classification as it is with respect to the classification as a whole." Justice White's dissent insisted that, given the facts in the record, the Court's result could be reached "only if [equal protection] imposes no real constraint at all in this situation. [The] rule's classification of successfully maintained persons as dispositively different from the general population is left without any justification and, with its irrationality and invidiousness thus uncovered, must fall before the Equal Protection Clause." (Justice Marshall joined Justice White's dissent. And in a separate opinion, Justice Powell submitted a partial dissent, also on rationality grounds. Justice Brennan's dissent did not reach the constitutional issue.)

8. For example, the annual Harvard Law Review study of the Court contained an extensive discussion of Fritz and proclaimed that it seemed "specifically designed to reject [the] notion of the 'newer equal protection'" and to reaffirm "the [Court's] pre-1970's posture of extreme deference," replacing the 1970s stance of giving "the historically toothless standard of minimum re-

written by Justice Rehnquist, the Court's most consistent advocate of deferential equal protection review. Yet, only a few months after Fritz, Schweiker v. Wilson demonstrated that Fritz had *not* marked the end of intense division on the Court about putting more "bite" into equal protection. Although the equal protection challenge was rejected in Schweiker, the Court was divided 5 to 4 instead of 7 to 2, and the dissent, in a tenor akin to that of rationality review "with bite," was written by Justice Powell, who had silently joined Justice Rehnquist's deferential opinion in Fritz. And in 1982, in Logan, a majority of Justices actually agreed that the challenged law violated equal protection. Logan was an unusual case, both on its facts and in its holding of invalidity under rationality standards, but it did once again demonstrate that rationality review retains potential for "bite" despite Fritz's deferential tone.[9] Thus, conflict persists on the Court about a number of recurring issues in rationality review. For example, to what extent should a challenged law be tested by the legislature's actual or articulated purposes rather than by purposes suggested by counsel, or by conceivable purposes hypothesized by the courts? Should rationality review have *any* "bite"?[10]

U.S. RAILROAD RETIREMENT BD. v. FRITZ

449 U.S. 166, 101 S.Ct. 453, 66 L.Ed.2d 368 (1980).

Justice REHNQUIST delivered the opinion of the Court.

[The District Court held unconstitutional a section of the Railroad Retirement Act of 1974.] The Act fundamentally restructured the railroad retirement system. The Act's predecessor statute, adopted in 1937, provided a system of retirement and disability benefits for persons who pursued careers in the railroad industry. Under that statute, a person who worked for both railroad and nonrailroad employers and who qualified for railroad retirement benefits and social security benefits received retirement benefits under both systems and an accompanying "windfall" benefit. [The] payment of windfall benefits threatened the railroad retirement system with [bankruptcy]. Congress therefore determined to place the system on a "sound financial basis" by eliminating future accruals of those benefits. Congress also enacted various transitional provisions, including a grandfather provision, § 231b(h), which expressly preserved windfall benefits for some classes of employees.

In restructuring the [Act], Congress divided employees into various groups. *First,* those employees who lacked the requisite 10 years of railroad employment

---

view [some] bite." Yet the Note failed to mention Schweiker, later in the same Term, with its far stronger signals of "bite." See Note, "The Supreme Court, 1980 Term," 95 Harv.L.Rev. 91, 152–61 (1981).

9. The 1980s have, as usual, also produced a number of cases rejecting equal protection rationality challenges. See, e.g., G.D. Searle & Co. v. Cohn, 455 U.S. 404 (1982); Schweiker v. Hogan, 457 U.S. 569 (1982); and Exxon Corp. v. Eagerton, 462 U.S. 176 (1983). Even these cases occasionally produced dissents arguing that the challenged classification was irrational, as in Justice Stevens' dissent in the Searle case. Compare Plyler v. Doe (1982; p. 799 below), and Zobel v. Williams (1982; p. 814 below).

10. Note the reflection of the continuing uncertainties in Justice Powell's dissent from the 5 to 4 ruling in Schweiker v. Wilson (1981; p. 616 below): "The Court has employed numerous formulations for the 'rational basis' test. Members of the Court continue to hold divergent views on the clarity with which a legislative purpose must appear [Fritz], and about the degree of deference afforded the legislature in suiting means to ends, compare [Lindsley] with [Royster Guano]." On the continued vitality of the Royster Guano standard (p. 594 above), whose "fair and substantial relation" test suggests greater rationality scrutiny than the more deferential Lindsley one, see also Mesquite v. Aladdin's Castle, Inc., 455 U.S. 283 (1982). (In Mesquite, Justice Stevens' majority opinion suggested that "it is unclear whether this Court would apply the Royster Guano standard," while Justice Powell's dissent argued that "[t]his Court has never rejected [Royster Guano].")

to qualify for railroad retirement benefits as of January 1, 1975, the changeover date, would have their retirement benefits computed under the new system and would not receive any windfall benefit. *Second,* those individuals already retired and already receiving dual benefits as of the changeover date would [continue] to receive a windfall benefit. *Third,* those employees who had qualified for both railroad and social security benefits as of the changeover date, but who had not yet retired as of that date (and thus were not yet receiving dual benefits), were entitled to windfall benefits if they had (1) performed some railroad service in 1974, or (2) had a "current connection" with the railroad industry as of December 31, 1974, or (3) completed 25 years of railroad service as of December 31, 1974.[1] [Thus], an individual who, as of the changeover date, was unretired and had 11 years of railroad employment and sufficient nonrailroad employment to qualify for social security benefits is eligible for the full windfall amount if he worked for the railroad in 1974 or had a current connection with the railroad as of December 31, 1974, or his later retirement date. But an unretired individual with 24 years of railroad service and sufficient nonrailroad service to qualify for social security benefits is not eligible for a full windfall amount unless he worked for the railroad in 1974, or had a current connection with the railroad as of December 31, 1974, or his later retirement date. [The] District Court agreed with appellees that a differentiation based solely on whether an employee was "active" in a railroad business as of 1974 was not "rationally related" to the congressional purposes of insuring the solvency of the railroad retirement system and protecting vested benefits. We disagree and reverse.

The initial issue [is] the appropriate standard of judicial review to be applied when social and economic legislation enacted by Congress is challenged as being violative of the ["equal protection component"] of the Fifth Amendment. [Because] the distinctions drawn in § 231b(h) do not burden fundamental constitutional rights or create "suspect" classifications, [we] may put cases involving judicial review of such claims to one side. [Despite] the narrowness of the issue, this Court in earlier cases has not been altogether consistent in its pronouncements in this area. In Lindsley [1911], the Court said that "when the classification in such a law is called in question, if any state of facts reasonably can be conceived that would sustain it, the existence of that state of facts at the time that the law was enacted must be assumed." On the other hand, only nine years later in [Royster Guano, 1920], the Court said that for a classification to be valid under the Equal Protection Clause it "must rest upon some ground of difference having a fair and substantial relation to the object of the legislation." In more recent years, however, the Court in cases involving social and economic benefits has consistently refused to invalidate on equal protection grounds legislation which it simply deemed unwise or unartfully drawn. [The Court noted, e.g., Dandridge v. Williams, Vance v. Bradley, Dukes, Flemming v. Nestor (p. 215 above), and Jefferson v. Hackney.][2]

Applying those principles to this case, the plain language of § 231b(h) marks the beginning and end of our inquiry.[3] There Congress determined that

---

1. A fourth category was comprised of those employees who had qualified for railroad benefits as of the changeover date, but lacked a current connection with the industry in 1974 and lacked 25 years of railroad employment. They could obtain a lesser amount of windfall benefits if they had qualified for Social Security benefits as of the year (prior to 1975) they had left railroad employment.

2. All of the cases cited in this opinion appear elsewhere in the casebook—mainly in this chapter.

3. This opinion and Justice Brennan's dissent cite a number of equal protection [cases]. The most arrogant legal scholar would not claim that all of these cases applied a uniform or consistent test under the Equal Protection Clause. And realistically speaking, we can be no more certain that this opinion will remain undisturbed than were those who joined the opinion in Lindsley, Royster Guano, or any of the other cases referred to in this opinion and in the dissenting opinion. But like our predecessors and our successors, we are obliged to apply the equal protection compo-

some of those who in the past received full windfall benefits would not continue to do so. Because Congress could have eliminated windfall benefits for all classes of employees, it is not constitutionally impermissible for Congress to have drawn lines between groups of employees for the purpose of phasing out those benefits. [Dukes.] The only remaining question is whether Congress achieved its purpose in a patently arbitrary or irrational way. [The] only eligible former railroad employees denied full windfall benefits are those, like appellees, who had no statutory entitlement to dual benefits at the time they left the railroad industry, but thereafter became eligible for dual benefits when they subsequently qualified for social security benefits. Congress could properly conclude that persons who had actually acquired statutory entitlement to windfall benefits while still employed in the railroad industry had a greater equitable claim to those benefits than the members of appellees' class who were no longer in railroad employment when they became eligible for dual benefits. Furthermore, the "current connection" test is not a patently arbitrary means for determining which employees are ["career railroaders"]. Congress could assume that those who had a current connection with the railroad industry when the Act was passed in 1974, or who returned to the industry before their retirement, were more likely than those who had left the industry prior to 1974 and who never returned, to be among the class of persons who pursue careers in the railroad industry, the class for whom the [Act] was designed.

Where, as here, there are plausible reasons for Congress' action, our inquiry is at an end. It is, of course, "constitutionally irrelevant whether this reasoning in fact underlay the legislative decision," Flemming v. Nestor, because this Court has never insisted that a legislative body articulate its reasons for enacting a statute. This is particularly true where the legislature must necessarily engage in a process of line drawing. The "task of classifying persons for [benefits] inevitably requires that some persons who have an almost equally strong claim to favorite treatment be placed on different sides of the line," and the fact that the line might have been drawn differently at some points is a matter for legislative, rather than judicial, consideration. Finally, we disagree with the District Court's conclusion that Congress was unaware of what it accomplished or that it was misled by the groups that appeared before it. If this test were applied literally to every member of any legislature that ever voted on a law, there would be very few laws which would survive it. The language of the statute is clear, and we have historically assumed that Congress intended what it enacted. To be sure, appellees lost a political battle in which they had a strong interest, but this is neither the first nor the last time that such a result will occur in the [legislative forum].

Reversed.

Justice STEVENS, concurring in the judgment.

In my opinion, Justice Brennan's criticism of the Court's approach to this case merits a more thoughtful response than that contained in footnote [3]. Justice Brennan correctly points out that if the analysis of legislative purpose requires only a reading of the statutory language in a disputed provision, and if any "conceivable basis" for a discriminatory classification will repel a constitutional attack on the statute, judicial review will constitute a mere tautological recognition of the fact that Congress did what it intended to do. Justice Brennan is also correct in reminding us that even though the statute is an

---

nent of the Fifth Amendment as we believe the Constitution requires and in so doing we have no hesitation in asserting, contrary to the dissent, that where social or economic regulations are involved, Dandridge v. Williams and Jefferson v. Hackney, together with this case, state the proper application of the test. The comments in the dissenting opinion about the proper cases for which to look for the correct statement of the equal protection rational basis standard, and about which cases limit earlier cases, are just that: comments in a dissenting opinion. [Footnote by Justice Rehnquist.]

concerned w/ "inconceivable" standard of review

example of "social and economic legislation," the challenge here is mounted by individuals whose legitimate expectations of receiving a fixed retirement income are being frustrated by, in effect, a breach of a solemn commitment by their government. When Congress deprives a small class of persons of vested rights that are protected [for] others who are in a similar though not identical position, I believe the Constitution requires something more than merely a "conceivable" or a "plausible" explanation for the unequal treatment.

But

I do not, however, share Justice Brennan's conclusion that every statutory classification must further an objective that can be confidently identified as the "actual purpose" of the legislature. Actual purpose is sometimes unknown. Moreover, undue emphasis on actual motivation may result in identically worded statutes being held valid in one State and invalid in a neighboring State. I therefore believe that we must discover a correlation between the classification and either the actual purpose of the statute or a legitimate purpose that we may reasonably presume to have motivated an impartial legislature. If the adverse impact on the disfavored class is an apparent aim of the legislature, its impartiality would be suspect. If, however, the adverse impact may reasonably be viewed as an acceptable cost of achieving a larger goal, an impartial lawmaker could rationally decide that that cost should be incurred. In this case, however, we need not look beyond the actual purpose of the legislature. As is often true, this legislation is the product of multiple and somewhat inconsistent purposes that led to certain compromises. One purpose was to eliminate in the future the benefit that is described by the Court as a "windfall benefit" and by Justice Brennan as an "earned dual benefit." That aim was incident to the broader objective of protecting the solvency of the entire railroad retirement program. Two purposes that conflicted somewhat with this broad objective were the purposes of preserving those benefits that had already vested and of increasing the level of payments to beneficiaries whose rights were not otherwise to be changed. As Justice Brennan emphasizes, Congress originally intended to protect *all* vested benefits, but it ultimately sacrificed some benefits in the interest of achieving other objectives. Given these conflicting purposes, I believe the decisive questions are (1) whether Congress can rationally reduce the vested benefits of some employees to improve the solvency of the entire program while simultaneously increasing the benefits of others; and (2) whether, in deciding which vested benefits to reduce, Congress may favor annuitants whose railroad service was more recent than that of disfavored annuitants who had an equal or greater quantum of employment.

dif from Br.

My answer to both questions is in the affirmative. The congressional purpose to eliminate dual benefits is unquestionably legitimate; that legitimacy is not undermined by the adjustment in the level of remaining benefits in response to inflation in the economy. As for the second question, some hardship—in the form of frustrated long-term expectations—must inevitably result from any reduction in vested benefits. Arguably, therefore, Congress had a duty—and surely it had the right to decide—to eliminate no more vested benefits than necessary to achieve its fiscal purpose. Having made that decision, any distinction it chose within the class of vested beneficiaries would involve a difference of degree rather than a difference in entitlement. I am satisfied that a distinction based upon currency of railroad employment represents an impartial method of identifying that sort of difference. Because retirement plans frequently provide greater benefits for recent retirees than for those who retired years ago—and thus give a greater reward for recent service than for past service of equal duration—the basis for the statutory discrimination is supported by relevant precedent. It follows, in my judgment, that the timing of the employees' railroad service is a "reasonable basis" for the classification as that term is used in Lindsley and Dandridge, as well as a "ground of difference having a fair and substantial relation to the object of the legislation" as those words are used in [Royster Guano].

Justice BRENNAN, with whom Justice MARSHALL joins, dissenting.

[The] legal standard applicable to this case is the "rational basis" test. [The] Court today purports to apply this standard, but in actuality fails to scrutinize the challenged classification in the manner established by [our] precedents. [The] mode of analysis employed by the Court [virtually] immunizes social and economic legislative classifications from judicial review.

[I.] Perhaps the clearest statement of this Court's present approach to "rational basis" scrutiny may be found in Johnson v. Robison, 415 U.S. 361 (1974). In considering the constitutionality of limitations on the availability of educational benefits under the Veterans' Readjustment Benefits Act of 1966, eight Members of this Court agreed [on the Royster Guano standard]. The enactments of Congress are entitled to a presumption of constitutionality, and the burden rests on those challenging a legislative classification to demonstrate that it does not bear the "fair and substantial relation to the object of the legislation" [Royster Guano] required under the Constitution. Nonetheless, the rational basis standard "is not a toothless one" [Mathews v. Lucas, p. 679 below] and will not be satisfied by flimsy or implausible justifications for the legislative classification, proffered after the fact by Government attorneys. See, e.g., [Jimenez; Moreno]. When faced with a challenge to a legislative classification under the rational basis test, the court should ask, first, what the purposes of the statute are, and second, whether the classification is rationally related to achievement of those purposes.

II. The purposes of the [Act] are clear, because Congress has commendably stated them in the House and Senate reports accompanying the Act. A section of the reports is entitled "Principal Purpose of the Bill." It notes generally that "[t]he bill [will] place [the Act] on a sound financial basis," and then states: "Persons who already have vested rights under both the Railroad Retirement and the Social Security systems will in the future be permitted to receive benefits computed under both systems just as is true under existing law." Moreover, Congress explained that this purpose was based on considerations of fairness and the legitimate expectations of the retirees. [Thus], a "principal purpose" of the [Act], as explicitly stated by Congress, was to preserve the vested earned benefits of retirees who had already qualified for them. The classification [here], which deprives some retirees of vested dual benefits that they had earned prior to 1974, directly conflicts with Congress' stated purpose. As such, the classification is not only rationally unrelated to the congressional purpose; it is inimical to it.

III. The [Court] avoids the conclusion that § 231b(h) must be invalidated by deviating in three ways from traditional rational basis analysis. First, the Court adopts a tautological approach to statutory [purpose]. Second, it disregards the actual stated purpose of Congress in favor of a justification which was never suggested by any [legislator], and which in fact conflicts with the stated congressional purpose. Third, it upholds the classification without any analysis of its rational relationship to the identified purpose.

A. The Court states that "the plain language of § 231b(h) marks the beginning and end of our inquiry." This statement is strange indeed, for the "plain language" of the statute can tell us only what the classification is; it can tell us nothing about the purpose of the classification let alone the relationship between the classification and that purpose. Since [§ 231b(h)] deprives appellees of their vested earned dual benefits, the Court apparently assumes that Congress must have intended that result. But by presuming purpose from result, the Court reduces analysis to tautology. It may always be said that Congress intended to do what it in fact did. If that were the extent of our analysis, we would find every statute, no matter how arbitrary or irrational, perfectly tailored to achieve its purpose. But equal protection scrutiny under the rational basis test requires the courts first to deduce the independent objectives of the statute, usually from statements of purpose and other evidence in the statute and legislative history, and second to analyze whether the challenged classification rationally furthers achievement of those objectives. The Court's tautological approach will not suffice.

B. The Court analyzes the rationality of § 231b(h) in terms of a justification suggested by Government attorneys, but never adopted by Congress. The Court states that it is "constitutionally irrelevant whether this reasoning in fact underlay the legislative decision" [quoting Flemming v. Nestor (1960)]. In fact, however, equal protection analysis has evolved substantially on this question since Flemming was decided. Over the past 10 years, this Court has frequently recognized that the actual purposes of Congress, rather than the post hoc justifications offered by Government attorneys, must be the primary basis for analysis under the rational basis test. E.g., [Wiesenfeld; Rodriguez; Murgia; Johnson v. Robison; Califano v. Goldfarb]. From these cases and others it is clear that this Court will no longer sustain a challenged classification under the rational basis test merely because Government attorneys can suggest a "conceivable basis" upon which it might be thought rational. The standard we have applied is properly deferential to the Legislative Branch: where Congress has articulated a legitimate governmental objective, and the challenged classification rationally furthers that objective, we must sustain the provision. In other cases, however, the courts must probe more deeply. Where Congress has expressly stated the purpose of a piece of legislation, but where the challenged classification is either irrelevant to or counter to that purpose, we must view any post hoc justifications proffered by Government attorneys with skepticism. A challenged classification may be sustained only if it is rationally related to achievement of an *actual* legitimate governmental purpose.

The Court argues that Congress chose to discriminate against appellees for reasons of equity, [but, as] I have shown, Congress expressed the view that it would be inequitable to deprive any retirees of any portion of the benefits they had been promised and that they had earned under prior law. The Court is unable to cite even one statement in the legislative history by a Representative or Senator that makes the equitable judgment it imputes to Congress. In the entire legislative history, [the] only persons to state that the equities justified eliminating appellees' earned dual benefits were representatives of railroad management and labor, whose self-serving interest in bringing about this result destroys any basis for attaching weight to their statements.

The factual findings of the District Court concerning the development of § 231b(h), amply supported by the legislative history, are revealing on this point. [Congress] asked railroad management and labor representatives to negotiate and submit a bill to restructure the Railroad Retirement [system]. The members of this Joint Labor-Management Negotiating Committee were not appointed by public officials, nor did they represent the interests of the appellee class, who were no longer active railroaders or union members. In an initial proposed restructuring of the system, the Joint Committee devised a means whereby the system's deficit could be completely eliminated without depriving retirees of vested earned benefits. However, labor representatives demanded that benefits be increased for their current members, the cost to be offset by divesting the appellee class of a portion of the benefits they had earned under prior law. [The] Joint Committee negotiators and Railroad Retirement Board members who testified at congressional hearings perpetuated the inaccurate impression that all retirees with earned vested dual benefits under prior law would retain their benefits unchanged. [Of course], a misstatement or several misstatements by witnesses before Congress would not ordinarily lead us to conclude that Congress misapprehended what it was doing. In this instance, however, where complex legislation was drafted by outside parties and Congress relied on them to explain it, where the misstatements are frequent and unrebutted, and where no Member of Congress can be found to have stated the effect of the classification correctly, we are entitled to suspect that Congress may have been misled. As the District Court found: "At no time during the hearings did Congress even give a hint that it understood that the bill by its language eliminated an earned benefit of plaintiff's class." Therefore, I do not think that this classification was rationally related to an *actual* governmental purpose.

C. The third way in which the Court has deviated from the principles of rational basis scrutiny is its failure to analyze whether the challenged classification is genuinely related to the purpose identified by the Court. Having suggested that "equitable considerations" underlay the challenged classification—in direct contradiction to Congress' evaluation of those considerations, and in the face of evidence that the classification was the product of private negotiation by interested parties, inadequately examined and understood by Congress—the Court proceeds to accept that suggestion without further analysis. An unadorned claim of "equitable" considerations is, of course, difficult to assess. It seems to me that before a court may accept a litigant's assertion of "equity," it must inquire what principles of equity or fairness might genuinely support such a judgment. But apparently the Court does not demand such inquiry, for it has failed to address any equitable considerations that might be relevant to the challenged classification. In my view, the following considerations are of greatest relevance to the equities of this case: (1) contribution to the system; (2) reasonable expectation and reliance; (3) need; and (4) character of service to the railroad industry. With respect to each of these considerations, I would conclude that appellees have as great an equitable claim to their earned dual benefits as do their more favored coworkers, who remain entitled to their earned dual benefits under [§ 231b(h)].[1] [I] therefore conclude that the Government's proffered justification of "equitable considerations," accepted without question by the Court, cannot be defended. [Rather], equity and fairness demand that appellees, like their coworkers, retain the vested dual benefits they earned prior to 1974. A conscientious application of rational basis scrutiny demands, therefore, that § 231b(h) be invalidated.

IV. Equal protection rationality analysis does not empower the courts to second-guess the wisdom of legislative classifications. On this we are [agreed]. On the other hand, we are not powerless to probe beneath claims by Government attorneys concerning the means and ends of Congress. Otherwise, we would defer not to the considered judgment of Congress, but to the arguments of litigators. The instant case serves as an example of the unfortunate consequence of such misplaced deference. Because the Court is willing to accept a tautological analysis of congressional purpose, an assertion of "equitable" considerations contrary to the expressed judgment of Congress, and a classification patently unrelated to achievement of the identified purpose, it succeeds in effectuating neither equity nor [congressional intent].

SCHWEIKER v. WILSON, 450 U.S. 221 (1981): As noted earlier, Schweiker, only a few months after Fritz, produced a much narrower, 5 to 4 decision and suggested that the alleged landmark case of Fritz had not, after all, settled the intense debate on the Court about the importance of actual legislative

---

1. Contrary to the Court's suggestion, this is not a "line-drawing" case, where the Congress must make a division at some point along an admittedly rationally conceived continuum. Here, Congress has isolated a particular class of retirees on the basis of a distinction that is utterly irrelevant to any actual or legitimate governmental purpose. [Footnote by Justice Brennan.]

purpose in rationality review. Justice Powell, who had subscribed to the deferential majority opinion in Fritz, now submitted a forceful dissent. He criticized the very deferential rationality cases (e.g., Flemming v. Nestor and McGowan v. Maryland): "[They] do not describe the importance of actual legislative purpose in our analysis." He argued, moreover, that "post hoc hypotheses about legislative purpose, unsupported by the legislative history," should be received skeptically. His scrutiny accordingly paid considerable attention to "discernable" or "identifiable" legislative purposes.

Schweiker upheld Congress' denial of federal "comfort allowances" to needy aged, blind, and disabled persons confined in public institutions unless the institutions receive federal Medicaid funds.[1] The challengers argued that the scheme bore "no rational relationship to any legitimate objective of the SSI program." Justice BLACKMUN's majority opinion rejected this challenge.[2] He explained: "[T]he pertinent inquiry is whether the [classification] advances legitimate legislative goals in a rational fashion. [Although] this rational basis standard is 'not a toothless one,' Mathews v. Lucas, it does not allow us to substitute our personal notions of good policy for those of Congress. [As] long as the classificatory scheme chosen by Congress rationally advances a reasonable and identifiable governmental objective, we must disregard the existence of other methods of allocation that we, as individuals, perhaps would have preferred." He found sufficient indication in the "sparse" legislative record that "the decision to incorporate the Medicaid eligibility standards into the SSI scheme must be considered Congress' deliberate, considered choice.' He proceeded: "Having found the adoption of the Medicaid standards intentional, we deem it logical to infer from Congress' deliberate action an intent to further the same subsidiary purpose [in framing the SSI exclusion] that lies behind the Medicaid exclusion, which [was] adopted because Congress believed the States to have a 'traditional' responsibility to care for those institutionalized in public mental institutions. [We] cannot say that the belief that the States should continue to have the primary responsibility for making this small 'comfort money' allowance available to those residing in state-run institutions is an irrational basis for withholding from them federal general welfare funds." He added: "This Court has granted a 'strong presumption of constitutionality' to legislation conferring monetary benefits, because it believes that Congress should have discretion in deciding how to expend necessarily limited resources. Awarding this type of benefit inevitably involves the kind of line-drawing that will leave some comparably needy person outside the favored circle. We cannot say that it was irrational of Congress, in view of budgetary constraints, to

---

1. The case arose in the following statutory context: The federal Supplemental Security Income program (SSI) provides subsistence payments for needy persons who are aged, blind, or disabled. Patients in public mental institutions are generally excluded from eligibility for full SSI payments. However, most patients in public institutions are eligible for smaller SSI payments—"comfort allowances" of $25.00 per month, to enable the institutionalized needy "to purchase small comfort items not supplied by the institution." But these "comfort payments" are offered only if a patient resides in a public institution that receives Medicaid funds on his or her behalf. This scheme was challenged in a class action representing all residents of public mental institutions between the ages of 21 and 65. This group is ineligible for Medicaid support; accordingly, under the SSI system, it is not entitled to the monthly comfort payments available to inmates of other medical institutions, including mental patients in public medical hospitals and private institutions.

2. The challengers also claimed that the classification warranted scrutiny at a level *higher* than that appropriate under rationality review, insisting that "because the statute classifies on the basis of mental illness, a factor that greatly resembles other characteristics that this Court has found inherently 'suspect,' [special] justification should be required for the congressional decision" to exclude most of the mentally ill. Justice Blackmun found it unnecessary to reach this issue, because he concluded "that this statute does not classify directly on the basis of mental health." This aspect of the case is further discussed below in sec. 3C3, at p. 684.

decide that it is the Medicaid recipients in public institutions that are the most needy and the most deserving of the small monthly supplement."

Justice POWELL's strong dissent, joined by Justices Brennan, Marshall and Stevens, countered: "Congress thoughtlessly has applied a statutory classification developed to further legitimate goals of one welfare program [Medicaid] to another welfare program [SSI] serving entirely different needs. The result is an exclusion of wholly dependent people from minimal benefits, serving no government interest. This irrational classification violates [equal protection]." He articulated his approach to rationality review as follows: "[The rationality] test holds two firmly established principles in tension. The Court must not substitute its view of wise or fair legislative policy for that of the duly elected representatives of the people, but the equal protection requirement does place a substantive limit on legislative power. At a minimum, the legislature cannot arbitrarily discriminate among citizens. Enforcing this prohibition while avoiding unwarranted incursions on the legislative power presents a difficult task. No bright line divides the merely foolish from the arbitrary law. Given this difficulty, legislation properly enjoys a presumption of rationality, which is particularly strong for welfare legislation where the apportionment of scarce benefits in accordance with complex criteria requires painful, but unavoidable, line drawing.

"The deference to which legislative accommodation of conflicting interests is entitled rests in part upon the principle that the political process of our majoritarian democracy responds to the wishes of the people. Accordingly, an important touchstone for equal protection review of statutes is how readily a policy can be discerned which the legislature intended to serve. See, e.g., [Moreno; McGinnis v. Royster]. When a legitimate purpose for a statute appears in the legislative history or is implicit in the statutory scheme itself, a court has some assurance that the legislature has made a conscious policy choice. [Yet], the question of whether a statutory classification discriminates arbitrarily cannot be divorced from whether it was enacted to serve an identifiable purpose. When a legislative purpose can be suggested only by the ingenuity of a government lawyer litigating the constitutionality of a statute, a reviewing court may be presented not so much with a legislative policy choice as its absence. In my view, the Court should receive with some skepticism post hoc hypotheses about legislative purpose, unsupported by the legislative history.[1] When no indication of legislative purpose appears other than the current position of the Secretary, the Court should require that the classification bear a 'fair and substantial relation' to the asserted purpose. See [Royster Guano]. This marginally more demanding scrutiny indirectly would test the plausibility of the tendered purpose, and preserve equal protection review as something more than 'a mere tautological recognition of the fact that Congress did what it intended to do.' Fritz (Stevens, J., concurring)."

Applying this approach to the challenged provision, Justice Powell commented: "Neither the structure of [the provision] nor its legislative history identifies or even suggests any policy plausibly intended to be served by denying appellees the small SSI allowance. [By] mechanically applying the criteria

---

1. "Some of our cases suggest that the actual purpose of a statute is irrelevant, Flemming v. Nestor, and that the statute must be upheld 'if any state of facts reasonably may be conceived to justify' its discrimination. McGowan v. Maryland. Although these cases preserve an important caution, they do not describe the importance of actual legislative purpose in our analysis. We recognize that a legislative body rarely acts with a single mind and that compromises blur pur-

pose. Therefore, it is appropriate to accord some deference to the executive's view of legislative intent, as similarly we accord deference to the consistent construction of a statute by the administrative agency charged with its enforcement. *Ascertainment of actual purpose to the extent feasible, however, remains an essential step in equal protection.*" [Footnote by Justice Powell. Emphasis added.]

developed for Medicaid, Congress appears to have avoided considering what criteria would be appropriate for deciding in which public institutions a person can reside and still be eligible for some SSI payment." The Government had argued: "Congress rationally could make the judgment that the States should bear the responsibility for any comfort allowance, because they already have the responsibility for providing treatment and minimal care." Justice Powell rejected this claim, stating: "There is no logical link [between] these two responsibilities." He elaborated: "[R]esidence in a *public mental* institution, as opposed to residence in a state *medical* hospital or a *private* mental hospital, bears no relation to any policy of the SSI program. [If] SSI pays a cash benefit relating to personal needs other than maintenance and medical care, it is irrelevant whether the State or the Federal Government is paying for the maintenance and medical care; the patients' need remains the same, the likelihood that the policies of SSI will be fulfilled remains the same." He accordingly concluded "that Congress had no rational reason for refusing to pay a comfort allowance to [the challengers], while paying it to numerous otherwise identically situated disabled indigents. This unexplained difference in treatment must have been a legislative oversight."

LOGAN v. ZIMMERMAN BRUSH CO., 455 U.S. 422 (1982): Logan, an unusual case both on its facts and in its manner of disposition, indicates that equal protection rationality review retains bite despite the deferential tone of the Fritz and Schweiker majority opinions. Justice Blackmun's "opinion of the Court" was devoted entirely to sustaining the challenger's procedural due process attack on a state statutory scheme; that opinion did not mention equal protection. But, in an unusual move, Justice Blackmun also submitted a separate opinion. That second opinion, joined by Justices Brennan, Marshall and O'Connor, stated: "Although the Court [in the opinion written by Justice Blackmun himself] considered that it was unnecessary to discuss and dispose of the equal protection claim when the due process issue was being decided in Logan's favor, I regard the equal protection issue as sufficiently important to require comment on my part, particularly inasmuch as a majority of the Members of the Court are favorably inclined toward the claim." Justice Blackmun's separate opinion then explained why the challenged provision did not satisfy the minimum rationality standards of equal protection. (Recall that he had written the deferential majority opinion in Schweiker less than a year earlier.) And, in another separate opinion, Justice Powell, joined by Justice Rehnquist (who is typically the strongest advocate of extremely deferential rationality review) stated that, even though he could not join Justice Blackmun's concurring opinion, he, too, agreed that the challenged law could not survive even the "minimal standard" of equal protection review. In short, six Justices voted to invalidate the law on "minimum rationality" equal protection grounds. Logan thus is a rare modern example of a case in which a majority agreed that a state law violated equal protection rationality standards.[1]

1. My colleague William Cohen—in his earlier cited article, "Is Equal Protection Like Oakland? Equality as a Surrogate for Other Rights," (forthcoming, —Tul.L.Rev. —— (1985))—argues that "it is hard to see how the [law] was 'unfair and irrational' unless one concluded that it did deny procedural due process." Cohen's position would endorse a Court's reliance solely on equal protection in a case such as Logan, since that "would provide a narrower precedent largely because it would obscure the reasons for [the] conclusion." He adds: "It is true that the equal protection analysis only makes sense in [such cases] if the Court has implicitly decided the avoided issues. The decision is narrower, however, precisely because the decision is only implicit, or summary and conclusory." Cohen largely approves of such uses of equal protection to avoid explicit confrontation with broader and more difficult constitutional problems. Gunther disagrees (even at the risk of being dubbed one of "the vestal virgins of the law schools," see Cohen's footnote 96). See Gunther, "The Subtle Vices of the 'Passive Virtues'—A Comment on Principle and Expediency in Judicial Review," 64 Colum.L.Rev. 1 (1964).

Logan had filed an employment discrimination complaint before an Illinois agency which inadvertently scheduled the hearing at a date after the statutory time period expired. The state court held that this deprived the agency of jurisdiction and dismissed Logan's claim.[2] Justice Blackmun's "opinion for the Court" held that this bar to considering the merits of Logan's claim was a violation of procedural due process (see p. 573 above). But, as noted, he then submitted a separate opinion as well, finding a violation of equal protection. Justice BLACKMUN, joined by Justices Brennan, Marshall and O'Connor, explained his equal protection analysis as follows: "On its face, Logan's equal protection claim is an unconventional one. The [Act] establishes no explicit classifications and does not expressly distinguish between claimants, and the company therefore argues that Logan has no more been deprived of equal protection than anyone would be who is injured by a random act of governmental misconduct. As the [state court] interpreted the statute, however, [it] unambiguously divides claims—and thus, necessarily, claimants—into two discrete groups that are accorded radically disparate treatment. Claims processed within 120 days are given full consideration on the merits. [In] contrast, otherwise identical claims that do not receive a hearing within the statutory period are unceremoniously, and finally, terminated. Because the Illinois court recognized, in so many words, that the [Act] establishes two categories of claims, one may proceed to determine whether the classification drawn by the statute is consistent with the [14th Amendment]. For over a century, the Court has engaged in a continuing and occasionally almost metaphysical effort to identify the precise nature of [equal protection] guarantees. [Here, Justice Blackmun cited the dissent in Schweiker.] At the minimum level, however, the Court 'consistently has required that legislation classify the persons it affects in a manner rationally related to legitimate governmental objectives.' Schweiker. This is not a difficult standard for a State to meet, when it is attempting to act sensibly and in good faith. But the 'rational-basis standard is "not a toothless one,"' id., quoting Mathews v. Lucas; the classificatory scheme must 'rationally advanc[e] a reasonable and identifiable governmental objective.' Schweiker. I see no need to explore the outer bounds of this test, for I find that the Illinois statute runs afoul of the lowest level of permissible equal protection scrutiny.'

Justice Blackmun proceeded to scrutinize the relationship between the statutory scheme and the State's purposes. He noted that the Act had "two express purposes: eliminating employment discrimination, and protecting [potential defendants] 'from unfounded charges of discrimination.'" He thought it "evident" that neither of these objectives was advanced by the Act's deadline provision. "Terminating potentially meritorious claims in a random manner obviously cannot serve to redress instances of discrimination. And it cannot protect employers from unfounded charges, for the frivolousness of a claim is entirely unrelated to the length of time the Commission takes to process that claim. [While] it may well be true that '[n]o bright line divides the merely foolish from the arbitrary law,' I have no doubt that [the Act] is patently irrational in the light of its stated purposes." He then turned to a "third rationale" recognized by Illinois' highest court: that the provision was "designed to further the 'just and expeditious resolutio[n]' of employment disputes." Justice Blackmun responded: "I cannot agree that terminating a claim that the State itself has misscheduled is a rational way of expediting the

2. Logan's claim was that his employer had discriminated against him on the basis of his physical handicap. Under the Illinois Fair Employment Practices Act, the State Commission was supposed to convene a "factfinding conference" within 120 days of the filing of the complaint. "Apparently through inadvertence, the [Commission] scheduled the conference for a date five days *after* the expiration of the statutory period." The state court found that the 120-day period was mandatory and that the Commission had therefore lost jurisdiction to consider Logan's complaint.

resolution of disputes." [3] He continued; "Most important, the procedure at issue does not serve generally to hasten the processing or ultimate termination of employment controversies. [It] is not enough, under [equal protection], to say that the legislature sought to terminate certain claims and succeeded in doing so, for that is 'a mere tautological recognition of the fact that [the legislature] did what it intended to do.' [Fritz (Stevens, J., concurring in the judgment).] This Court still has an obligation to view the classificatory *system*, in an effort to determine whether the disparate treatment accorded the affected classes is arbitrary. Here, that inquiry yields an affirmative result. So far as the State's purpose is concerned, every [claimant's] charge, when filed with the Commission, stands on the same footing. Yet certain randomly selected claims, because processed too slowly by the State are irrevocably terminated without review. In other words, the State converts similarly situated claims into dissimilarly situated ones, and then uses this distinction as the basis for its classification. This, I believe, is the very essence of arbitrary state action. [See Reed v. Reed.]" He added: "The State's rationale must be something more than the exercise of a strained imagination; while the connection between means and ends need not be precise, it, at the least, must have some objective basis. That is not so here."

Justice POWELL's concurrence in the judgment, joined by Justice Rehnquist, saw the case as "an isolated example of bureaucratic oversight," "of little importance except to the litigants." To him, the issues presented were "too simple and straightforward to justify broad pronouncements on the law of procedural due process or of equal protection." He stated that he was "particularly concerned by the potential implications of the Court's expansive due process analysis." He accordingly urged that the case "should be decided narrowly on its unusual facts." But he nevertheless spent three paragraphs placing himself on record as finding the challenged law a violation of equal protection. He thought "this unusual classification" was not "rationally related to a state interest that would justify it." He concluded: "This Court has held repeatedly that state created classifications must bear a rational relationship to legitimate governmental objectives. See, e.g., [Schweiker]. Although I do not join Justice Blackmun's separate opinion, I agree that the challenged statute, as construed and applied in this case, failed to comport with this minimal standard. I am concerned by the broad sweep of the Court's opinion, but I do join its judgment."

SECTION 3. SUSPECT CLASSIFICATIONS AND THE PROBLEMS OF FORBIDDEN DISCRIMINATION

Introduction. We now move from the realm of rationality review to those aspects of equal protection law that call for heightened scrutiny. This section focuses on the problems of "suspect" and "quasi-suspect" classifications as well as a range of related problems pertaining to the identification and remedying of forbidden discrimination. Racial discrimination was the major target of the 14th Amendment and thus racial classifications are ordinarily "suspect": this theme is among the few continuously voiced ones in equal protection doctrine.

---

3. In a footnote at this point, Justice Blackmun expressed some doubt that the state court had really defended the deadline provision on this ground. He added: "In light of my conclusions about the rationality of such a justification, however, it is irrelevant whether the [state court] intended to state that this was the actual or articulated rationale for ¶ 858(b)'s deadline proviso. I note that the rationales discussed in the text have not been expressed by the State's representatives; the Illinois Human Rights Commission, [the successor to the earlier Commission], by the State's Attorney General, has filed a brief in this Court supporting Logan."

But even racial discrimination, historically the clearest and most continuous target of equal protection, continues to give rise to differences on a host of questions. This section begins, in sec. 3A, with an examination of classifications disadvantaging racial (and ethnic) minorities (sec. 3A1) and of justifications for invalidating segregation in public facilities, despite the formal equivalence suggested by the "separate but equal" doctrine (sec. 3A2).[1] The occasions for strict scrutiny of disadvantaging racial classifications, and the meaning of "strict scrutiny," lie at the heart of sec. 3A. Secs. 3B and 3C turn to the question of whether there are other classifications, beyond race, that also trigger heightened scrutiny. Sec. 3B deals with sex discrimination. Gender is considered a "quasi-suspect" classification triggering an "intermediate" level of review. Sec. 3C turns to other classifications (alienage and illegitimacy) which also occasionally elicit heightened scrutiny and to additional criteria (e.g., mental illness) for which claims of more intensive scrutiny have been advanced. This subsection raises a recurrent question pertaining to the legitimacy of extrapolating from the characteristics that have elicited strict scrutiny: Is it permissible to reason by analogy from the well-established category of disadvantaging racial classifications to other classifications which share some, but not all, the characteristics of race?

The problems raised by the preceding subsections are complex enough. But the final two enter even more difficult and controversial domains. Sec. 3D deals with the frequently stated requirement that discrimination must be "purposeful" to be actionable under equal protection. If a showing of "purposeful," "intentional" discrimination is indeed necessary, how is it proven? And what is the relevance of discriminatory effects and disadvantaging impacts? The Court often states that impact data are at least usable to prove unconstitutional purpose or motive. Can equal protection also reach situations where governmental action, though not flowing from racial hostility, has the *effect* of producing a disproportionately harmful impact on a minority?[2] The last section, Sec. 3E, deals with the problems of "benign" discrimination and affirmative action. What standard of scrutiny should apply to the use of ordinarily suspect criteria invoked for the asserted purpose of helping rather than harming disadvantaged groups? What justifications and findings warrant governmental use of affirmative action programs? Sec. 3E accordingly examines the problems of ordinarily "suspect" or "quasi-suspect" classifications (gender as well as race) allegedly used for "benign" purposes.

A. RACE

---

1. THE INTENSIVE SCRUTINY OF DISADVANTAGING RACIAL AND ETHNIC CLASSIFICATIONS

---

1. *The Strauder case.* Seven years after the Slaughter-House Cases (p. 410 above) had emphasized the central anti-racial discrimination concern of the 14th Amendment, the Court recalled and applied that background in STRAUDER v.

---

1. As noted in sec. 1 above, efforts to expand the category of "suspect" or "quasi-suspect" classifications beyond race constitute one of the strands of the "new" equal protection.

Examination of racial classifications in this opening section is limited to situations where minorities are *disadvantaged.* Examination of the even more controversial constitutional debate about the use of racial factors for "benign" pur-

poses—the problems of "reverse discrimination" and affirmative action—are postponed to sec. 3E, in part to permit the consideration of "benign" racial classifications together with the problems of "benign" sex classifications.

2. Sec. 3D also deals with the problems of remedying unconstitutional segregation, because the "purpose"-"effect" distinction often arises in that context.

WEST VIRGINIA, 100 U.S. 303 (1880). Strauder, a black defendant, was convicted of murder by a jury from which blacks had been excluded because of the explicit command of a state law.[1] Strauder unsuccessfully sought to remove his case to a federal court. The Court held that removal should have been granted. Justice STRONG's majority opinion emphasized that the "common purpose" of the post-Civil War Amendments was the "securing to a race recently emancipated [all] the civil rights the superior race enjoy." He added: "[What is equal protection] but declaring [that] all persons, whether colored or white, shall stand equal before the laws of the States, and, in regard to the colored race, for whose protection the amendment was primarily designed, that no discrimination shall be made against them by law because of their color? The words of the amendment [contain] a necessary implication of a positive immunity, or right, most valuable to the colored race,—the right to exemption from unfriendly legislation against them distinctively as colored,—exemption from legal discriminations, implying inferiority in civil society, lessening the security of their enjoyment of the rights which others enjoy, and discriminations which are steps towards reducing them to the condition of a subject race.

"That the West Virginia statute respecting juries [is] such a discrimination ought not to be doubted. Nor would it be if the persons excluded by it were white men. If in those States where the colored people constitute a majority of the entire population a law should be enacted excluding all white men from jury service, [we] apprehend no one would be heard to claim that it would not be a denial to white men of the equal protection of the laws. Nor if a law should be passed excluding all naturalized Celtic Irishmen, would there be any doubt of its inconsistency with the spirit of the amendment. The very fact that colored people are singled out and expressly denied by a statute all right to participate in the administration of the law, as jurors, because of their color, [is] practically a brand upon them, affixed by the law, an assertion of their inferiority, and a stimulant to that race prejudice which is an impediment to securing to individuals of the race that equal justice which the law aims to secure to all others. [We] do not say that within the limits from which it is not excluded by the amendment a State may not prescribe the qualifications of its jurors, and in so doing make discriminations. It may confine the selection to males, to freeholders, to citizens, to persons within certain ages, or to persons having educational qualifications. We do not believe the 14th Amendment was ever intended to prohibit this. Looking at its history, it is clear it had no such purpose. Its aim was against discrimination because of race or color. [We] are not now called upon to affirm or deny that it had other purposes."[2]

Although Strauder involved discrimination against blacks (who were the historical focus of the 14th Amendment), the Court has readily found that *all* disadvantaging classifications resting on race and ethnicity are suspect. Indeed, even in Strauder, the first racial discrimination invalidation under the 14th Amendment, the Court mentioned laws directed at "all naturalized Celtic Irishmen" as falling within "the spirit of the amendment." Without much discussion, later Courts have treated discrimination based on national origin

---

1. The state law provided: "All white male persons who are twenty-one years of age and who are citizens of this State shall be liable to serve as [jurors]."

2. Note that in Strauder, the claim of racial discrimination was raised by a member of the excluded class. The law as to challenging discrimination in jury selection has changed since Strauder. For example, in Peters v. Kiff, 407 U.S. 493 (1972), a white defendant successfully challenged a conviction on the ground that blacks had been systematically excluded from jury service. And in Taylor v. Louisiana, 419 U.S. 422 (1975), a male defendant was permitted to raise the exclusion of women. That change in the jury selection context stems from the change in emphasis regarding the relevant "right" involved: the focus has shifted from equal protection to an aspect of the jury trial guarantee. In the Taylor case, the Court stated "that the selection of a petit jury from a representative cross section of the community is an essential component of the Sixth Amendment right to a jury trial."

(e.g., against Mexican-Americans) or on race generally (e.g., against Orientals) the same as discrimination against the black minority.[3]

     2. *Race as a "suspect" classification triggering "the most rigid scrutiny": The Korematsu case.* Although, as Strauder illustrates, the Court has long perceived special bite in equal protection when it is used as a weapon against racial discrimination, explicit reference to race as a "suspect" criterion did not come until well into the 20th century, in KOREMATSU v. UNITED STATES, 323 U.S. 214 (1944). Ironically, Korematsu was one of the very rare cases in which a classification based on racial ancestry survived scrutiny. The majority sustained a conviction for violating a military order during World War II excluding all persons of Japanese ancestry from designated West Coast areas.[4] Early in his majority opinion, Justice BLACK stated the governing standard: "[A]ll legal restrictions which curtail the civil rights of a single racial group are immediately suspect. That is not to say that all such restrictions are unconstitutional. It is to say that courts must subject them to the most rigid scrutiny. Pressing public necessity may sometimes justify the existence of such restrictions; racial antagonism never can." But here, the requisite "pressing public necessity" was found. He explained: "Like curfew, exclusion of those of Japanese origin was deemed necessary [by the military authorities] because of the presence of an unascertained number of disloyal members of the group, most of whom we have no doubt were loyal to this country." The military authorities had found "that it was impossible to bring about an immediate segregation of the disloyal from the loyal." The judgment that "exclusion of the whole group [was] a military imperative answers the contention that the exclusion was in the nature of group punishment based on antagonism to those of Japanese origin."[5] In a closing

---

3. E.g., Yick Wo v. Hopkins (1886; p. 688 below); Hernandez v. Texas, 347 U.S. 475 (1954). Hernandez struck down discrimination against Mexican-Americans in jury selection. Chief Justice Warren stated that "community prejudices are not static, and from time to time other differences [other than "differences in race and color"] from the community norm may define other groups which need the same protection. [The 14th Amendment] is not directed solely against discrimination due to a 'two-class theory'—that is, based upon differences between 'white' and Negro."

     Even Justice Rehnquist, the modern Justice who takes the least interventionist view of equal protection and who is the strongest opponent of the expansion of "suspect classifications" jurisprudence, acknowledged in Trimble v. Gordon (1977; p. 680 below) that classifications based on "national origin, the first cousin of race" (*not* only racial ones) were areas where "the Framers obviously meant [equal protection] to apply."

     4. Soon after the outbreak of war with Japan, President Roosevelt issued an Executive Order designed to protect "against espionage and against sabotage" and providing that certain military commanders might designate "military areas" in the United States "from which any or all persons may be excluded, and with respect to which the right of any person to enter, remain in, or leave shall be subject to whatever restrictions" the "Military Commander may impose in his discretion." The West Coast program established for persons of Japanese ancestry included curfews, detention in relocation centers, and exclusion from the West Coast area. After unani-

mously upholding the curfew orders in 1943 (Hirabayashi v. United States, 320 U.S. 81) the Court in the following year, in Korematsu, sustained the exclusion aspect of the program.

     5. Justice Black added: "That there were members of the group who retained loyalties to Japan has been confirmed by investigations made subsequent to the exclusion. Approximately 5000 American citizens of Japanese ancestry refused to swear unqualified allegiance to the United States and to renounce allegiance to the Japanese Emperor, and several thousand evacuees requested repatriation to Japan." (Compare Justice Murphy's dissent, especially in footnote 7 below.)

     The Court did not in this case—or any other— pass on the constitutionality of the detention and confinement programs. But see Ex parte Endo, 323 U.S. 283 (1944), decided on the same day as Korematsu, holding continued detention under the relocation program invalid for lack of statutory authority, without reaching the constitutional issues.

     Korematsu (and the evacuation program generally) have elicited extensive criticism. For reasonably contemporaneous comments, see, e.g., Rostow, "The Japanese American Cases—A Disaster," 54 Yale L.J. 489 (1945), and Grodzins, Americans Betrayed: Politics and the Japanese Evacuation (1949). For a thorough modern study, see Irons, Justice at War (1983). (Peter Irons' research for his book—and his participation as co-counsel—led to a 1984 District Court judgment vacating Korematsu's conviction. See Korematsu v. United States, 584 F.Supp. 1406 (N.D.Cal.1984).) Another of Korematsu's co-

passage, Justice Black reiterated that the Court had not endorsed racial discrimination: "Our task would be simple, our duty clear, were this a case involving the imprisonment of a loyal citizen in a concentration camp because of racial prejudice." Only the exclusion order was involved here, and to "cast this case into outlines of racial prejudice, without reference to the real military dangers which were presented, merely confuses the issue." Korematsu was excluded, he insisted, "because we are at war with the Japanese Empire, because the properly constituted military authorities feared an invasion of our West Coast and felt constrained to take proper security measures, because they decided that the military urgency of the situation demanded that all citizens of Japanese ancestry be segregated from the West Coast temporarily and finally, because Congress, reposing its confidence in this time of war in our military leaders—as inevitably it must—determined that they should have the power to do just this. There was evidence of disloyalty on the part of some, the military authorities considered that the need for action was great, and time was short. We cannot—by availing ourselves of the calm perspective of hindsight—now say that at that time these actions were unjustified." [6]

Justice MURPHY wrote the strongest dissent—even though he did not invoke the "suspect classification"-"strict scrutiny" test and purported to apply simply standards of "reasonableness." He acknowledged that "great respect" for military judgment in wartime was "appropriate." But "the military claim must subject itself to the judicial process of having its reasonableness determined." He was not persuaded that the deprivation of individual rights here was "reasonably related to a public danger that is so 'immediate, imminent, and impending' as not to admit of delay and not to permit the intervention of ordinary constitutional processes to alleviate the danger." The exclusion order applicable to "all persons of Japanese ancestry" seemed to him "an obvious racial discrimination" and hence a denial of equal protection. He conceded that there was "a very real fear of invasion," and fear of sabotage and espionage, on the West Coast in 1942. But he insisted that "the exclusion, either temporarily or permanently, of all persons with Japanese blood in their veins has [no] reasonable relation" to the "removal of the dangers." He explained: "[T]hat relation is lacking because the exclusion order necessarily must rely for its reasonableness upon the assumption that *all* persons of Japanese ancestry may have a dangerous tendency to commit sabotage and espionage." He found it "difficult to believe that reason, logic or experience could be marshalled in support of such an assumption." He argued that the "forced exclusion was the result in good measure of [an] erroneous assumption of racial guilt rather than bona fide military necessity." The justification for exclusion rested "mainly upon questionable racial and sociological grounds" not charged or proved—"an accumulation of much of the misinformation, half-truths and insinuations that for years have been directed against Japanese Americans by people with racial and economic prejudices—the same people who have been among the foremost advocates of the evacuation. A military judgment based upon such racial and sociological considerations is not entitled to the great weight ordinarily given

counsel stated that the 1984 ruling "sucked away the factual underpinnings" of the Court decision. But the Court ruling stays on the books, to be cited either for the "most rigid scrutiny" to which disadvantaging racial classifications ought to be subjected—or for the deference to the military in wartime that actually may, as in Korematsu, satisfy that scrutiny. [See also Personal Justice Denied (1982), the final Report of the Commission on Wartime Relocation and Internment of Civilians, a commission established by Congress in 1980.]

6. Note a comment on Korematsu 30 years later, by Justice Douglas, a member of the Korematsu majority. He stated in DeFunis v. Odegaard, (1974; p. 744 below): "It is, however, easy in retrospect to denounce what was done, as there actually was no attempted Japanese invasion of our country. [But] those making plans for defense of the Nation had no such knowledge and were planning for the worst."

the judgments based upon strictly military considerations." He accordingly dissented from "this legalization of racism." [7]

In a separate dissent, Justice JACKSON stated that the military orders may or may not have been "expedient military precautions"; but they should not be enforced by civil courts committed to the Constitution. He elaborated: "[A] judicial construction of the due process clause that will sustain this order is a far more subtle blow to liberty than the promulgation of the order itself. A military order, however unconstitutional, is not apt to last longer than the military emergency. [But] once a judicial opinion rationalizes such an order to show that it conforms to the Constitution, or rather rationalizes the Constitution to show that the Constitution sanctions such an order, the Court for all time has validated the principle of racial discrimination in criminal procedure and of transplanting American citizens. The principle then lies about like a loaded weapon ready for the hand of any authority that can bring forward a plausible claim of an urgent need. [A] military commander may overstep the bounds of constitutionality, and it is an incident. But if we review and approve, that passing incident becomes a doctrine of the Constitution." Earlier he had noted: "[I]f we cannot confine military expedients by the Constitution, neither would I distort the Constitution to approve all that the military may deem expedient." [8]

LOVING v. VIRGINIA

388 U.S. 1, 87 S.Ct. 1817, 18 L.Ed.2d 1010 (1967).

Mr. Chief Justice WARREN delivered the opinion of the Court.

This case presents a constitutional question never addressed by this Court: whether a statutory scheme adopted by [Virginia] to prevent marriages between persons solely on the basis of racial classifications violates [the] 14th Amendment. For reasons which seem to us to reflect the central meaning of those constitutional commands, we conclude that these statutes cannot stand. [The Virginia appellants, a black woman and a white man, were married in the District of Columbia, returned to Virginia, and were convicted of violating Virginia's ban on interracial marriages. The trial judge suspended their one year jail sentences for 25 years on the condition that they leave the state and not return to Virginia together for 25 years.]

Virginia is now one of 16 States which prohibit and punish marriages on the basis of racial classifications. Penalties for miscegenation arose as an incident to slavery and have been common in Virginia since the colonial period. [In] upholding the constitutionality of these provisions, [the highest state court] referred to its 1955 decision in Naim v. Naim [1] as stating the reasons supporting the validity of these laws. In Naim, the state court concluded that the State's legitimate purposes were "to preserve the racial integrity of its citizens" and to prevent "the corruption of blood," "a mongrel breed of citizens," and "the

---

7. Justice Murphy noted, too, that "not one person of Japanese ancestry was accused or convicted of espionage or sabotage after Pearl Harbor while they were still free, a fact which is some evidence of the loyalty of the vast majority of these individuals and of the effectiveness of the established methods of combating these evils." He added: "It seems incredible that under these circumstances it would have been impossible to hold loyalty hearings for the mere 112,000 persons involved—or at least for the 70,000 American citizens." He pointed out that the British government had been able to determine through individualized hearings whether 74,000 German

and Austrian aliens were genuine risks or only "friendly enemies." The British had accomplished that task in a six month period after the outbreak of war, and only 2,000 were ultimately interned.

8. Justice ROBERTS also submitted a dissent; Justice FRANKFURTER delivered a concurring opinion.

1. For criticism of the Court's refusal to confront the miscegenation issue in the mid-1950s (by dismissing the Naim appeal), see chap. 15, at p. 1595 below.

obliteration of racial pride," obviously an endorsement of the doctrine of White Supremacy. [T]he State does not contend [that] its powers to regulate marriage are unlimited notwithstanding the commands of the 14th Amendment [but] argues that the meaning of the Equal Protection Clause, as illuminated by the statements of the Framers, is only that state penal laws containing an interracial element as part of the definition of the offense must apply equally to whites and Negroes in the sense that members of each race are punished to the same degree. Thus, the State contends that, because its miscegenation statutes punish equally both the white and the Negro participants in an interracial marriage, these statutes, despite their reliance on racial classifications, do not constitute an invidious discrimination based upon [race]. Because we reject the notion that the mere "equal application" of a statute containing racial classifications is enough to remove the classifications from the 14th Amendment's proscription of all invidious racial discriminations,[2] we do not accept the State's contention that these statutes should be upheld if there is any possible basis for concluding that they serve a rational purpose. [W]e deal with statutes containing racial classifications, and the fact of equal application does not immunize the statute from the very heavy burden of justification which the 14th Amendment has traditionally required of state statutes drawn according to race.

The State argues that statements [in] Congress about the time of the passage of the 14th Amendment indicate that the Framers did not intend the Amendment to make unconstitutional state miscegenation laws. [W]e have said in connection with a related problem that although these historical sources "cast some light" they are not sufficient to resolve the problem; "[a]t best, they are inconclusive." Brown v. Board of Education [1954; p. 635 below]. We have rejected the proposition that the debates in the Thirty-ninth Congress or in the State legislatures which ratified the 14th Amendment supported the theory [that] the requirement of equal protection of the laws is satisfied by penal laws defining offenses based on racial classifications so long as white and Negro participants in the offense were similarly published. McLaughlin v. Florida.[3]

2. Note that in the preceding cases, the racial classification explicitly disadvantaged the minority. The "equal application" issue raised in this case is more fully pursued in the context of the segregation cases that follow in sec. 3A2: Is race-conscious action that purports to treat the races evenhandedly subject to strict scrutiny and to condemnation as invidious, unconstitutional discrimination? Why?

3. McLaughlin v. Florida, 379 U.S. 184 (1964), invalidated a criminal statute prohibiting cohabitation by interracial married couples. Justice White's majority opinion emphasized: "[We] deal here with a classification based upon the race of the participants, which must be viewed in light of the historical fact that the central purpose of the 14th Amendment was to eliminate racial discrimination emanating from official sources in the States. This strong policy renders racial classifications 'constitutionally suspect' and subject to the 'most rigid scrutiny' [Korematsu], and 'in most circumstances irrelevant' to any constitutionally acceptable legislative purpose [Hirabayashi]. Thus it is that racial classifications have been held invalid in a variety of contexts. We deal here with a racial classification embodied in a criminal statute. [Our] inquiry, therefore, is whether there clearly appears in the relevant materials some overriding statutory purpose requiring the proscription of the spec-

ified conduct when engaged in by a white person and a Negro, but not otherwise. Without such justification the racial classification [here] is reduced to an invidious discrimination forbidden by the Equal Protection Clause."

Compare a statement later in Justice White's opinion: "[A law] which trenches upon the constitutionally protected freedom from invidious official discrimination based on race [bears] a heavy burden of justification [and] will be upheld only if it is necessary, and not merely rationally related, to the accomplishment of a permissible state policy." Is there a significant shift in emphasis in that second passage? Most of the strict scrutiny formulations speak of legislative ends and require that there be compelling, overriding justification. But the second passage emphasizes means—"necessary" rather than merely rational means—to the accomplishment of a "permissible" state end. The exercises of strict scrutiny in the cases in the rest of this chapter typically insist upon both a "compelling" end and carefully tailored, "necessary means." [Compare a characteristic later statement, in In re Griffiths (1973; p. 671 below): "The Court has consistently emphasized that a State which adopts a suspect classification 'bears a heavy burden of justification' [McLaughlin], a burden which, variously formulated, requires the State to meet certain standards of proof. In order to

The State finds support for its "equal application" theory in the decision of the Court in Pace v. Alabama, 106 U.S. 583 (1883). In that case, the Court upheld a conviction under an Alabama statute forbidding adultery or fornication between a white person and a Negro which imposed a greater penalty than that of a statute proscribing similar conduct by members of the same race. The Court reasoned that the statute could not be said to discriminate against Negroes because the punishment for each participant in the offense was the same. However, as recently as the 1964 Term, in rejecting the reasoning of that case, we stated: "Pace represents a limited view of the Equal Protection Clause which has not withstood analysis in the subsequent decisions of this Court." McLaughlin. [The] clear and central purpose of the 14th Amendment was to eliminate all official state sources of invidious racial discrimination in the States. [E.g., Slaughter-House Cases; Strauder.] There can be no question but that Virginia's miscegenation statutes rest solely upon distinctions drawn according to race. The statutes proscribe generally accepted conduct if engaged in by members of different races. At the very least, the Equal Protection Clause demands that racial classifications, especially suspect in criminal statutes, be subjected to the "most rigid scrutiny" [Korematsu], and, if they are ever to be upheld, they must be shown to be necessary to the accomplishment of some permissible state objective, independent of the racial discrimination which it was the object of the 14th Amendment to eliminate. [There] is patently no legitimate overriding purpose independent of invidious racial discrimination which justifies this classification. The fact that Virginia prohibits only interracial marriages involving white persons demonstrates that the racial classifications must stand on their own justification, as measures designed to maintain White Supremacy.[4] We have consistently denied the constitutionality of measures which restrict the rights of citizens on account of race. There can be no doubt that restricting the freedom to marry solely because of racial classifications violates the central meaning of the [Equal Protection Clause].[5]

Reversed.

justify the use of a suspect classification, a State must show that its purpose or interest is both constitutionally permissible and substantial, and that its use of the classification is 'necessary [to] the accomplishment' of its purpose or the safeguarding of its interest." After the word "substantial" in that passage, the Court added as a footnote: "The state interest required has been characterized as 'overriding' [McLaughlin; Loving]; 'compelling' [Graham v. Richardson 1971; p. 670 below]; 'important' [Dunn v. Blumstein, 1972; p. 814 below], or 'substantial' [ibid.]. We attribute no particular significance to these variations in diction." Cf. also the standard articulated in Palmore v. Sidoti, which follows.]

Justice Stewart's concurrence in McLaughlin, joined by Justice Douglas, stated: "[T]he Court implies that a criminal law of the kind here involved might be constitutionally valid if a State could show 'some overriding statutory purpose.' This is an implication in which I cannot [join]. [I] think it is simply not possible for a state law to be valid under our Constitution which makes the criminality of an act depend upon the race of the actor. Discrimination of that kind is invidious per se."

4. Appellants point out that the State's concern in these statutes, as expressed in the words of the 1924 Act's title, "An Act to Preserve Racial Integrity," extends only to the integrity of the white race. While Virginia prohibits whites from marrying any nonwhite (subject to the exception for the descendants of Pocahontas), Negroes, Orientals, and any other racial class may intermarry without statutory interference. Appellants contend that this distinction renders Virginia's miscegenation statutes arbitrary and unreasonable even assuming the constitutional validity of an official purpose to preserve "racial integrity." We need not reach this contention because we find the racial classifications in these statutes repugnant to the 14th Amendment, even assuming an even-handed state purpose to protect the "integrity" of all races. [Footnote by Chief Justice Warren.]

5. In a brief concluding passage, Chief Justice Warren also found that the law had deprived the Lovings of liberty without due process: "Marriage is one of the 'basic civil rights of man,' fundamental to our very existence and survival. [Skinner v. Oklahoma (p. 503 above).] To deny this fundamental freedom on so unsupportable a basis as the racial classifications [employed here] is surely to deprive all the State's citizens of liberty without due process of law." [On the Court's elaborations of the "fundamental right to marry" in the course of the development of modern substantive due process doctrine, see chap. 8, at p. 554 above.]

Mr. Justice STEWART, concurring.

I have previously expressed [in McLaughlin] the belief that "it is simply not possible for a state law to be valid under our Constitution which makes the criminality of an act depend upon the race of the actor." Because I adhere to that belief, I concur in the [judgment].

PALMORE v. SIDOTI

466 U.S. ___, 104 S.Ct. 1879, 80 L.Ed.2d 421 (1984).

Chief Justice BURGER delivered the opinion of the Court.

We granted certiorari to review a judgment of a state court divesting a natural mother of the custody of her infant child because of her remarriage to a person of a different race.

I. When petitioner Linda Sidoti Palmore and respondent Anthony J. Sidoti, both Caucasians, were divorced in May 1980 in Florida, the mother was awarded custody of their three-year-old daughter. In September 1981 the father sought custody of the child by filing a petition to modify the prior judgment because of changed conditions. The change was that the child's mother was then cohabiting with a Negro, Clarence Palmore, Jr., whom she married two months later. Additionally, the father made several allegations of instances in which the mother had not properly cared for the child. After hearing testimony from both parties and considering a court counselor's investigative report, the court noted that the father had made allegations about the child's care, but the court made no findings with respect to these allegations. On the contrary, the court made a finding that "there is no issue as to either party's devotion to the child, adequacy of housing facilities, or respect[a]bility of the new spouse of either parent." The court then addressed the recommendations of the court counselor [and] noted the counselor's recommendation for a change in custody because "[t]he wife [petitioner] has chosen for herself and for her child, a life-style unacceptable to her father *and to society.* [The] child [is], or at school age will be, subject to environmental pressures not of choice." The court then concluded that the best interests of the child would be served by awarding custody to the father. The court's rationale is contained in the following: "The father's evident resentment of the mother's choice of a black partner is not sufficient to wrest custody from the mother. It is of some significance, however, that the mother did see fit to bring a man into her home and carry on a sexual relationship with him without being married to him. Such action tended to place gratification of her own desires ahead of her concern for the child's future welfare. *This Court feels that despite the strides that have been made in bettering relations between the races in this country, it is inevitable that Melanie will, if allowed to remain in her present situation and attains school age and thus more vulnerable to peer pressures, suffer from the social stigmatization that is sure to [come].*"

II. The judgment of a state court determining or reviewing a child custody decision is not ordinarily a likely candidate for review by this Court. However, the court's opinion [raises] important federal concerns arising from the Constitution's commitment to eradicating discrimination based on race. [The] court found that "there is no issue as to either party's devotion to the child, adequacy of housing facilities, or respect[a]bility of the new spouse of either parent." This, taken with the absence of any negative finding as to the quality of the care provided by the mother, constitutes a rejection of any claim of petitioner's unfitness to continue the custody of her child. The court correctly stated that the child's welfare was the controlling factor. But that court was entirely candid and made no effort to place its holding on any ground other than race. Taking the court's findings and rationale at face value, it is clear that the outcome would have been different had petitioner married a Caucasian male of similar respectability.

A core purpose of the [14th Amendment] was to do away with all governmentally-imposed discrimination based on race. Classifying persons according to their race is more likely to reflect racial prejudice than legitimate public concerns; the race, not the person, dictates the category. Such classifications are subject to the most exacting scrutiny; to pass constitutional muster, they must be justified by a compelling governmental interest and must be "necessary [to] the accomplishment" of its legitimate purpose [McLaughlin; see Loving]. The State, of course, has a duty of the highest order to protect the interests of minor children, particularly those of tender years. In common with most states, Florida law mandates that custody determinations be made in the best interests of the children involved. The goal of granting custody based on the best interests of the child is indisputably a substantial governmental interest for purposes of [equal protection].

It would ignore reality to suggest that racial and ethnic prejudices do not exist or that all manifestations of those prejudices have been eliminated. There is a risk that a child living with a step-parent of a different race may be subject to a variety of pressures and stresses not present if the child were living with parents of the same racial or ethnic origin. The question, however, is whether the reality of private biases and the possible injury they might inflict are permissible considerations for removal of an infant child from the custody of its natural mother. We have little difficulty concluding that they are not. The Constitution cannot control such prejudices but neither can it tolerate them. Private biases may be outside the reach of the law, but the law cannot, directly or indirectly, give them effect.

[This] is by no means the first time that acknowledged racial prejudice has been invoked to justify racial classifications. In Buchanan v. Warley, 245 U.S. 60 (1917), for example, this Court invalidated a Kentucky law forbidding Negroes from buying homes in white neighborhoods. "It is urged that this proposed segregation will promote the public peace by preventing race conflicts. Desirable as this is, and important as is the preservation of the public peace, this aim cannot be accomplished by laws or ordinances which deny [constitutional rights]." Whatever problems racially-mixed households may pose for children in 1984 can no more support a denial of constitutional rights than could the stresses that residential integration was thought to entail in 1917. The effects of racial prejudice, however real, cannot justify a racial classification removing an infant child from the custody of its natural mother found to be an appropriate person to have such custody.

[Reversed.]

SCRUTINIZING RACIAL CLASSIFICATIONS: SOME EXAMPLES AND QUESTIONS

Introduction. "Our Constitution is color-blind," insisted the first Justice Harlan's dissent in Plessy v. Ferguson (p. 633 below). Over the years, some Justices have suggested a per se rule invalidating all governmental distinctions among individuals because of race. And some commentators have argued that such a total ban on racial classifications is the most persuasive justification for a number of Court decisions—e.g., the invalidation of racial segregation in public facilities generally after the 1954 decision in Brown (p. 635 below). But, as the preceding cases illustrate, the Court has not stated so comprehensive a prohibition; rather, disadvantaging racial classifications are ordinarily "suspect," must be subjected to "the most rigid scrutiny," and bear a "very heavy burden of justification." When—if ever—are or should racial criteria be constitutionally permissible? What justification is strong enough to survive the strict scrutiny avowed by the Court in these cases?[1] Were the following cases proper exercises of strict scrutiny?

1. *Racial identification of political candidates.* ANDERSON v. MARTIN, 375 U.S. 399 (1964), invalidated a state law requiring that every candidate's race appear on the ballot. The Court rejected the defense that the requirement was nondiscriminatory because it applied to candidates of all races. Justice Clark's opinion for a unanimous Court stated that "by directing the citizen's attention to the single consideration of race or color, the State indicated that a candidate's race or color is an important—perhaps paramount—consideration in the citizen's choice, which may decisively influence the citizen to cast his ballot along racial lines. [The] vice lies [in] the placing of the power of the State behind a racial classification that induces racial prejudice at the polls." What if it were argued that racial designations helped elect more minority candidates—that, while making most voters more race conscious and inducing majority race voters to reject minority candidates, it induced minority voters to vote for more candidates of their own race? Should that argument satisfy the "very heavy burden of justification"?[2]

2. *Racial identification in official records.* In per curiam orders in Tancil v. Woolls and Virginia Board of Elections v. Hamm, 379 U.S. 19 (1964), the Court summarily affirmed decisions (a) invalidating laws requiring separate lists of whites and blacks in voting, tax and property records, but (b) sustaining a law requiring that every divorce decree indicate the race of the husband and wife. The District Judge stated that "the designation of race [may] in certain records serve a useful purpose"—for example, "for identification or statistical use." He found no such purpose in the separate records law: it served "no other purpose than to classify and distinguish official records on the basis of race." The divorce law requirement, on the other hand, aided "vital statistics."

3. *Public security as justification.* To what extent may arguments emphasizing national emergencies or local order justify racial classifications? Recall Korematsu, p. 624 above, and note LEE v. WASHINGTON, 390 U.S. 333 (1968), a per curiam approval of a federal court order holding unconstitutional Alabama statutes requiring racial segregation in prisons. The one paragraph affirmance noted Alabama's argument that the lower court order made "no allowance for the necessities of prison security and discipline" and commented that "we do not so read" the order, "which when read as a whole we find unexceptionable." A separate concurring paragraph, by Justices Black, Harlan, and Stewart, elaborated: "[W]e wish to make explicit [that] prison authorities have the right, acting in good faith and in particularized circumstances, to take into account racial tensions in maintaining security, discipline, and good order in prisons and jails. We are unwilling to assume that state or local prison authorities might mistakenly regard such an explicit pronouncement as evincing any dilution of this Court's firm commitment to the 14th Amendment's prohibition of racial discrimination."

4. *Racially specific traits.* Consider the comment by Justice Douglas in his book, We the Judges (1956): "Experience shows that liquor has a devastating effect on the North American Indian and Eskimo. It is, therefore, commonly provided [that] no liquor should be sold to those races. Other regulations based on race may likewise be justified by reason of the special traits of those races, such, for example, as their susceptibility to particular diseases. [W]hat at first blush may seem to be an invidious discrimination may on analysis be found

---

1. The relevance of strict scrutiny appropriate when racial criteria are used for "benign" purposes is considered in sec. 3E below.

2. See, e.g., Wright v. Rockefeller [1964; p. 691 below].

to have plausible grounds justifying it." Is a "plausible" justification sufficient? If the traits are not possessed by every member of the race, can such regulations be challenged for overinclusiveness under the strict scrutiny appropriate to racial classifications? [3]

5. *Racial classifications and lawmaking processes.* Under the Akron City Charter, most City Council measures became effective after a short time, subject to repeal by referendum initiated by 10 percent of the voters. After the City Council had adopted a fair housing ordinance, the City Charter was amended by popular vote to provide for an automatic referendum procedure in certain cases: the amendment, § 137, provided that any ordinance regulating real estate transactions "on the basis of race, color, religion, national origin or ancestry must first be approved by a majority of the electors voting on the question at a regular or general election before said ordinance shall be effective." That charter amendment was held unconstitutional in HUNTER v. ERICKSON, 393 U.S. 385 (1969). Justice WHITE's majority opinion stated that § 137 "makes an explicitly racial classification" which "obviously made it substantially more difficult to secure enactment of ordinances subject to § 137." Was there truly a "suspect" classification properly triggering strict scrutiny? Consider Justice White's explanation:

"It is true that the section draws no distinctions among racial and religious groups. [Nevertheless, the amendment] disadvantages those who would benefit from laws barring racial, religious, or ancestral discriminations as against those who would bar other discriminations or who would otherwise regulate the real estate market in their favor. The automatic referendum system does not reach housing discrimination on sexual or political grounds, or against those with children or dogs, nor does it affect tenants seeking more heat or better maintenance from landlords, nor those seeking rent control, urban renewal, public housing, or new building codes. Moreover, although the law on its face treats Negro and white, Jew and gentile in an identical manner, the reality is that the law's impact falls on the minority. The majority needs no protection against discrimination and, if it did, a referendum might be bothersome but no more than that. Like the law requiring specification of candidates' race on the ballot [(note 1 above), the amendment] places special burdens on racial minorities within the governmental process." [4]

---

3. See generally Dabbs, "Constitutional and Practical Considerations in Mandatory Sickle Cell Anemia Testing," 7 U.C.D.L.Rev. 509 (1974). Are racial generalizations ever permissible when a minority race is disadvantaged? Or does the "suspectness" of race compel government to act only on an individualized basis and avoid all disadvantaging generalizations? Note the similar problems with respect to gender-based generalizations, below; see especially the Manhart case (1978; p. 669 below).

4. In a concurring opinion, Justice HARLAN, joined by Justice Stewart, agreed that § 137 was "discriminatory on its face" and could not meet the heavy burden of justification. He emphasized that the charter amendment did not attempt to allocate governmental power on the basis of any general, neutral principle. But he pointed out that the 10 percent referendum provision, by contrast, was valid, even though it "might occasionally operate to disadvantage Negro political interests." That was a "neutral"

provision, and the mere fact that a minority group might lose an important political battle did not constitute a denial of equal protection. (Justice BLACK dissented.)

Suppose § 137 had included a number of other "delicate areas" in which the city had decided "to move slowly." Would such a broadened provision be invalid under the Hunter reasoning? Compare the Court's disposition of a "neutral" state constitutional amendment in effect barring fair housing laws, in Reitman v. Mulkey (1967; p. 890 below). Note also the reexamination of Hunter in the 1982 cases consideration of state efforts to curb school busing, p. 720 below. (For discussion of the validity under equal protection of facially neutral laws that have a discriminatory impact, see sec. 3D below. For additional consideration of why racial classifications are ordinarily "suspect," and whether they should always be subject to strict scrutiny, see the consideration of "benign" classifications in sec. 3E below.)

2. THE UNCONSTITUTIONALITY OF RACIAL SEGREGATION [1]

THE "SEPARATE BUT EQUAL" ERA

1. *Plessy v. Ferguson.* In PLESSY v. FERGUSON, 163 U.S. 537 (1896), the Court sustained a Louisiana law of 1890 that required "equal but separate accommodations" for "white" and "colored" railroad passengers.[2] Justice BROWN's majority opinion, after finding the 13th Amendment inapplicable, stated: "The object of the [14th] Amendment was undoubtedly to enforce the absolute equality of the two races before the law, but in the nature of things it could not have been intended to abolish distinctions based upon color, or to enforce social, as distinguished from political equality, or a commingling of the two races upon terms unsatisfactory to either. Laws [requiring] their separation in places where they are liable to be brought into contact do not necessarily imply the inferiority of either race to the other, and have been generally, if not universally, recognized as within the competency of the state legislatures in the exercise of their police power. The most common instance of this is connected with the establishment of separate schools for white and colored children, which have been [upheld] even by courts of States where the political rights of the colored race have been longest and most earnestly enforced.[3] [Laws] forbidding the intermarriage of the two races may be said in a technical sense to interfere with the freedom of contract, and yet have been universally recognized as within the police power of the state. [The] distinction between laws interfering with the political equality of the negro and those requiring the separation of the two races in schools, theaters, and railway carriages has been frequently drawn by this Court. [E.g., Strauder.]

"[It is suggested] that the same argument that will justify the state legislature in requiring railways to provide separate accommodations for the two races will also authorize them to require separate cars to be provided for people whose hair is of a certain color, or who are aliens, or who belong to certain nationalities, or to enact laws requiring colored people to walk upon one side of the street, and white people upon the other, or requiring white men's houses to be painted white, and colored men's black, or their vehicles or business signs to be of different colors, upon the theory that one side of the street is as good as the other, or that a house or vehicle of one color is as good as one of another color. The reply to all this is that every exercise of the police power must be reasonable, and extend only to such laws as are enacted in good faith for the promotion of the public good, and not for the annoyance or oppression of a particular class. [E.g., Yick Wo, p. 688 below.] [In] determining the question of reasonableness, [the legislature] is at liberty to act with reference to the established usages, customs, and traditions of the people, and with a view to the

1. The typical case in the preceding subsection (sec. 3A1) involved classifications *disadvantaging* racial or ethnic minorities. The problem of segregation in public facilities is treated separately in this subsection because segregation laws, at least in form, treated all races identically, and accordingly raised the question whether such "separate but equal" treatment could be considered disadvantaging discrimination. The problem was also raised by the miscegenation case, Loving, above. (The modern Court's holding that racial segregation is indeed unconstitutional has given rise to complex implementation problems. Most of those problems are postponed to sec. 3D below, for consideration in connection with other issues pertaining to the "purpose"-"impact" distinction in equal protection law.)

2. Plessy, the challenger, alleged that he was "seven-eighths Caucasian and one-eighth African blood; that the mixture of colored blood was not discernible in him; and that he was entitled to every right [of] the white race." He was arrested for refusing to leave a seat in a coach for whites.

3. See, e.g., Roberts v. Boston, 5 Cush. 198 (Mass. 1850).

promotion of their comfort, and the preservation of the public peace and good order. Gauged by this standard, we cannot say that [this law] is unreasonable, or more obnoxious to the [14th Amendment] than the [laws] requiring separate schools for colored children, [the] constitutionality of which does not seem to have been questioned.

"[We] consider the underlying fallacy of the plaintiff's argument to consist in the assumption that the enforced separation of the two races stamps the colored race with a badge of inferiority. If this be so, it is not by reason of anything found in the act, but solely because the colored race chooses to put that construction upon it. [The] argument also assumes that social prejudices may be overcome by legislation, and that equal rights cannot be secured to the negro except by an enforced commingling of the two races. We cannot accept this proposition. If the two races are to meet upon terms of social equality, it must be the result of natural affinities, a mutual appreciation of each other's merits, and a voluntary consent of individuals. [Legislation] is powerless to eradicate racial instincts or to abolish distinctions based upon physical differences, and the attempt to do so can only result in accentuating the difficulties of the present situation. If the civil and political rights of both races be equal one cannot be inferior to the other civilly or politically. If one race be inferior to the other socially, the [Constitution] cannot put them upon the same plane."

The first Justice HARLAN dissented: "[I] deny that any legislative body or judicial tribunal may have regard to the race of citizens when the civil rights of those citizens are involved. [It] was said in argument that the [law] does not discriminate against either race, but prescribes a rule applicable alike to white and colored citizens. But [every one] knows that [the law] had its origin in the purpose, not so much to exclude white persons from railroad cars occupied by blacks, as to exclude colored people from coaches [assigned] to white persons. [The] fundamental objection, therefore, to the statute is that it interferes with the personal freedom of citizens.

"The white race deems itself to be the dominant race in this country. And so it is, in prestige, in achievements, in education, in wealth and in power. So, I doubt not, it will continue to be for all time, if it remains true to its great heritage and holds fast to the principles of constitutional liberty. But in view of the Constitution, in the eye of the law, there is in this country no superior, dominant, ruling class of citizens. There is no caste there. Our Constitution is color-blind, and neither knows nor tolerates classes among citizens. [It] is, therefore, to be regretted that this high tribunal [has] reached the conclusion that it is competent for a State to regulate the enjoyment by citizens of their civil rights solely upon the basis of race. In my opinion, the judgment this day rendered will, in time, prove to be quite as pernicious as the decision made [in] the Dred Scott case. The present decision [will] encourage the belief that it is possible, by means of state enactments, to defeat the beneficent purposes which the [people] had in view when they adopted the recent amendments of the [Constitution]. Sixty millions of whites are in no danger from the presence here of eight millions of blacks. The destinies of the two races [are] indissolubly linked together, and the interests of both require that the common government of all shall not permit the seeds of race hate to be planted under the sanction of law. What can more certainly arouse race hate, what more certainly create and perpetuate a feeling of distrust between these races, than state enactments, which, in fact, proceed on the ground that colored citizens are so inferior and degraded that they cannot be allowed to sit in public coaches occupied by white citizens? [We] boast of the freedom enjoyed by our people above all other peoples. But it is difficult to reconcile that boast with a state of the law which, practically, puts the brand of servitude and degradation upon a large class of our fellow citizens,—our equals before the law. The thin disguise of 'equal' accommodations [will] not mislead any one, nor atone for the wrong this day done."

    2. *The 20th century attack on de jure segregation.* The modern legal attack on officially mandated segregation, led by the NAACP, began with efforts to show that the "separate but equal" doctrine of Plessy was vulnerable in the education provided for black students seeking graduate and professional school education. The first in the sequence of modern school segregation cases that culminated in Brown was Missouri ex rel. Gaines v. Canada, 305 U.S. 337 (1938). Gaines, a black applicant, had been refused admission to the University of Missouri Law School because of his race. Missouri's defense to his suit for admission was that, pending the establishment of a black law school in the state, it would pay Gaines' tuition in an out-of-state school. Chief Justice Hughes' majority opinion concluded that the State was obligated to furnish Gaines "within its borders facilities for legal education substantially equal to those which the State there offered for persons of the white race, whether or not other negroes sought the same opportunity." In the absence of such facilities, Gaines was entitled to be admitted to the existing state law school. Subsequent decisions dealing with segregated facilities in graduate and professional education are described in Brown, below.[4]

BROWN v. BOARD OF EDUCATION
[BROWN I—THE CONSTITUTIONAL RULING]

347 U.S. 483, 74 S.Ct. 686, 98 L.Ed. 873 (1954).

Mr. Chief Justice WARREN delivered the opinion of the Court.

    These cases come to us from the States of Kansas, South Carolina, Virginia, and Delaware.[1] [In] each of the cases, minors of the Negro race [seek] the aid of the courts in obtaining admission to the public schools of their community on a nonsegregated basis. In each instance, they had been denied admission to schools attended by white children under laws requiring or permitting segregation according to race. [In most of the cases, the courts below denied relief, relying on] the so-called "separate but equal" doctrine announced by this Court in Plessy.[2] [The] plaintiffs contend that segregated public schools are not "equal" and cannot be made "equal," and that hence they are deprived of the equal protection of the laws. [Argument] was heard in the 1952 Term, and reargument was heard this Term on certain questions propounded by the Court.[3]

---

4. For a detailed account of the background and Court consideration of Brown, see Kluger, Simple Justice: The History of Brown v. Board of Education and Black America's Struggle for Equality (1976).

1. The cases decided together with Brown v. Board of Education of Topeka were Briggs v. Elliott (South Carolina); Davis v. County School Board of Prince Edward County, Virginia; and Gebhart v. Belton (Delaware). See also Bolling v. Sharpe, the companion case from the District of Columbia, which follows.

2. The exception was the Delaware case, where the highest state court, while adhering to Plessy, ordered that plaintiffs be admitted to the white schools because of their superiority to the black schools.

3. The first three questions propounded by the Court follow:

"1. What evidence is there that the Congress which submitted and the State legislatures and conventions which ratified the 14th Amendment contemplated or did not contemplate, understood or did not understand, that it would abolish segregation in public schools?

"2. If neither the Congress in submitting nor the States in ratifying the 14th Amendment understood that compliance with it would require the immediate abolition of segregation in public schools, was it nevertheless the understanding of the framers of the Amendment *(a)* that future Congresses might, in the exercise of their power under section 5 of the Amendment, abolish such segregation, or *(b)* that it would be within the judicial power, in light of future conditions, to construe the Amendment as abolishing such segregation of its own force?

Reargument was largely devoted to the circumstances surrounding the adoption of the 14th Amendment in 1868. It covered exhaustively consideration of the Amendment in Congress, ratification by the states, then existing practices in racial segregation, and the views of proponents and opponents of the Amendment. This discussion and our own investigation convince us that, although these sources cast some light, it is not enough to resolve the problem with which we are faced. At best, they are inconclusive. The most avid proponents of the post-War Amendments undoubtedly intended them to remove all legal distinctions among "all persons born or naturalized in the United States." Their opponents, just as certainly, were antagonistic to both the letter and the spirit of the Amendments and wished them to have the most limited effect. What others in Congress and the state legislatures had in mind cannot be determined with any degree of certainty.

An additional reason for the inconclusive nature of the Amendment's history, with respect to segregated schools, is the status of public education at that time. In the South, the movement toward free common schools, supported by general taxation, had not yet taken hold. Education of white children was largely in the hands of private groups. Education of Negroes was almost nonexistent, and practically all of the race were illiterate. In fact, any education of Negroes was forbidden by law in some states. Today, in contrast, many Negroes have achieved outstanding success in the arts and sciences as well as in the business and professional world. It is true that public school education [had] advanced further in the North, but the effect of the Amendment on Northern States was generally ignored in the congressional debates. Even in the North, the conditions of public education did not approximate those existing today. The curriculum was usually rudimentary; ungraded schools were common in rural areas; [and] compulsory school attendance was virtually unknown. As a consequence, it is not surprising that there should be so little in the history of the 14th Amendment relating to its intended effect on public education.

In the first cases in this Court construing the 14th Amendment, decided shortly after its adoption, the Court interpreted it as proscribing all state-imposed discriminations against the Negro race.[4] The doctrine of "separate but equal" did not make its appearance in this Court until 1896 in [Plessy], involving not education but transportation. [In] this Court, there have been six cases involving the "separate but equal" doctrine in the field of public education. In Cumming v. County Board of Education, 175 U.S. 528, and Gong Lum v. Rice, 275 U.S. 78, the validity of the doctrine itself was not challenged.[5] In more recent cases, all on the graduate school level, inequality was found in that specific benefits enjoyed by white students were denied to Negro students of the same educational qualifications. Missouri ex rel. Gaines v. Canada; Sipuel v. Oklahoma, 332 U.S. 631; Sweatt v. Painter, 339 U.S. 629; McLaurin v. Oklahoma State Regents, 339 U.S. 637.[6] In none of these cases was it

"3. On the assumption that the answers to questions 2*(a)* and *(b)* do not dispose of the issue, is it within the judicial power, in construing the Amendment, to abolish segregation in public schools?" [Questions 4 and 5 were set for further argument in the Court's disposition of this case. Those questions appear in the footnote to the second Brown case, below.]

4. Slaughter-House Cases; [Strauder]. [Footnote by Chief Justice Warren.]

5. In the Cumming case, Negro taxpayers sought an injunction requiring the defendant school board to discontinue the operation of a high school for white children until the board resumed operation of a high school for Negro

children. Similarly, in the Gong Lum case, the plaintiff, a child of Chinese descent, contended only that state authorities had misapplied the doctrine by classifying him with Negro children and requiring him to attend a Negro school. [Footnote by Chief Justice Warren.]

6. The Sipuel case in 1948 reaffirmed the principles of Gaines, p. 635 above. The Sweatt case in 1950 required the admission of blacks to the University of Texas Law School even though the state had recently established a law school for blacks. Chief Justice Vinson's opinion for the Court found no "substantial equality in the educational opportunities offered white and Negro law students by the State. In terms of number of

necessary to reexamine the doctrine to grant relief to the Negro plaintiff. And in [Sweatt], the Court expressly reserved decision on the question whether [Plessy] should be held inapplicable to public education. In the instant cases, that question is directly presented. Here, unlike [Sweatt], there are findings below that the Negro and white schools involved have been equalized or are being equalized, with respect to buildings, curricula, qualifications and salaries of teachers, and other "tangible" factors. Our decision, therefore, cannot turn on merely a comparison of these tangible factors in the Negro and white schools involved in each of the cases. We must look instead to the effect of segregation itself on public education.

In approaching this problem, we cannot turn the clock back to 1868 when the Amendment was adopted, or even to 1896 when Plessy was written. We must consider public education in the light of its full development and its present place in American life throughout the Nation. Only in this way can it be determined if segregation in public schools deprives these plaintiffs of the equal protection of the laws. Today, education is perhaps the most important function of state and local governments. Compulsory school attendance laws and the great expenditures for education both demonstrate our recognition of the importance of education to our democratic society. It is required in the performance of our most basic public responsibilities, even service in the armed forces. It is the very foundation of good citizenship. Today it is a principal instrument in awakening the child to cultural values, in preparing him for later professional training, and in helping him to adjust normally to his environment. In these days, it is doubtful that any child may reasonably be expected to succeed in life if he is denied the opportunity of an education. Such an opportunity, where the state has undertaken to provide it, is a right which must be made available to all on equal terms.

We come then to the question presented: Does segregation of children in public schools solely on the basis of race, even though the physical facilities and other "tangible" factors may be equal, deprive the children of the minority group of equal educational opportunities? We believe that it does. In [Sweatt], this Court relied in large part on "those qualities which are incapable of objective measurement but which make for greatness in a law school." In McLaurin, the Court [again] resorted to intangible considerations: "[the] ability to study, to engage in discussions and exchange views with other students, and, in general, to learn [the] profession." Such considerations apply with added force to children in grade and high schools. To separate them from others of similar age and qualifications solely because of their race generates a feeling of

the faculty, variety of courses and opportunity for specialization, size of the student body, scope of the library, availability of law review and similar activities, the University of Texas Law School is superior. What is more important, the University of Texas Law School possesses to a far greater degree those qualities which are incapable of objective measurement but which make for greatness in a law school. Such qualities, to name but a few, include reputation of the faculty, experience of the administration, position and influence of the alumni, standing in the community, traditions and prestige." He added that a law school "cannot be effective in isolation from the individuals and institutions with which the law interacts," and he noted that the newly established black law school "excludes from its student body members of the racial groups which number 85% of the population of the state and include most of the lawyers, witnesses, jurors, judges and other officials with whom petitioner would inevitably be dealing when he becomes a member of the Texas Bar."

The McLaurin case in 1950, finally, involved a black student who had been admitted to a state university's graduate program not offered at the state's black school, but had been required to sit in separate sections in or adjoining the classrooms, library and cafeteria facilities. Chief Justice Vinson's opinion found that the restrictions impaired the "ability to study, to engage in discussions and exchange views with other students and, in general, to learn his profession." In rejecting the argument that petitioner might in any event be ostracized by his fellow students, the Chief Justice stated that "there is a vast difference—a Constitutional difference—between restrictions imposed by the state [and] the refusal of individuals to commingle."

inferiority as to their status in the community that may affect their hearts and minds in a way unlikely ever to be undone. The effect of this separation on their educational opportunities was well stated by a finding in the Kansas case by a court which nevertheless felt compelled to rule against the Negro plaintiffs: "Segregation of white and colored children in public schools has a detrimental effect upon the colored children. The impact is greater when it has the sanction of the law; for the policy of separating the races is usually interpreted as denoting the inferiority of the negro group. A sense of inferiority affects the motivation of a child to learn. Segregation with the sanction of law, therefore, has a tendency to [retard] the educational and mental development of negro children and to deprive them of some of the benefits they would receive in a [racially] integrated school system." [7] Whatever may have been the extent of psychological knowledge at the time of [Plessy], this finding is amply supported by modern authority.[8] Any language in [Plessy] contrary to this finding is rejected.

We conclude that in the field of public education the doctrine of "separate but equal" has no place. Separate educational facilities are inherently unequal. Therefore, we hold that the plaintiffs and others similarly situated for whom the actions have been brought are, by reason of the segregation complained of, deprived of [equal protection]. This disposition makes unnecessary any discussion whether such segregation also violates [due process]. Because these are class actions, because of the wide applicability of this decision, and because of the great variety of local conditions, the formulation of decrees in these cases presents problems of considerable complexity. On reargument, the consideration of appropriate relief was necessarily subordinated to the primary question—the constitutionality of segregation in public education. We have now announced that such segregation is a denial of the equal protection of the laws. In order that we may have the full assistance of the parties in formulating decrees, the cases will be restored to the docket, and the parties are requested to present further argument on Questions 4 and 5 [9] previously propounded by the Court for [reargument].

It is so ordered.

———

BOLLING v. SHARPE, 347 U.S. 497 (1954): In this case, decided on the same day as Brown, the Court held that racial segregation in the District of Columbia public schools violated the due process clause of the Fifth Amendment. Chief Justice Warren's opinion stated: "The Fifth Amendment [does] not contain an equal protection clause. [But] the concepts of equal protection and due process, both stemming from our American ideal of fairness, are not mutually exclusive. The 'equal protection of the laws' is a more explicit safeguard of prohibited unfairness than 'due process of law,' and, therefore, we do not imply that the two are always interchangeable phrases. But, as this

7. A similar finding was made in the Delaware case: "I conclude from the testimony that in our Delaware society, State-imposed segregation in education itself results in the Negro children, as a class, receiving educational opportunities which are substantially inferior to those available to white children otherwise similarly situated." [Footnote by Chief Justice Warren.]

8. K.B. Clark, Effect of Prejudice and Discrimination on Personality Development (Midcentury White House Conference on Children and Youth, 1950); Witmer and Kotinsky, Personality in the Making (1952), c. VI; Deutscher and Chein, The Psychological Effects of Enforced Segregation: A Survey of Social Science Opinion, 26 J. Psychol. 259 (1948); Chein, What are the Psychological Effects of Segregation Under Conditions of Equal Facilities?, 3 Int. J.Opinion and Attitude Res. 229 (1949); Brameld, Educational Costs, in Discrimination and National Welfare (McIver, ed., 1949), 44–48; Frazier, The Negro in the United States (1949), 674–681. And see generally Myrdal, An American Dilemma (1944). [Footnote by Chief Justice Warren.]

9. These questions appear in footnote 1 to Brown II, p. 641 below.

Court has recognized, discrimination may be so unjustifiable as to be violative of due process. Classifications based solely upon race must be scrutinized with particular care, since they are contrary to our traditions and hence constitutionally suspect. [E.g., Korematsu.] Although the Court has not assumed to define 'liberty' with any great precision, that term is not confined to mere freedom from bodily restraint. Liberty under law extends to the full range of conduct which the individual is free to pursue, and it cannot be restricted except for a proper governmental objective. Segregation in public education is not reasonably related to any proper governmental objective, and thus it imposes on Negro children of the District of Columbia a burden that constitutes an arbitrary deprivation of their liberty in violation of the Due Process Clause. In view of our decision that the Constitution prohibits the states from maintaining racially segregated public schools, it would be unthinkable that the same Constitution would impose a lesser duty on the Federal Government." [10]

SEGREGATION AND THE BROWN PRINCIPLE

1. *Legally mandated segregation in other public facilities.* After the 1954 decision in Brown, the Court found segregation unconstitutional in other public facilities as well. Despite the emphasis on the school context in Brown, the results in the later cases were reached in curt per curiam orders, most simply citing Brown.[1] It was not until 1963 that the Court was ready to articulate the import of these per curiam rulings. Johnson v. Virginia, 373 U.S. 61, reversed a contempt conviction for refusal to comply with a state judge's order to move to a section of a courtroom reserved for blacks. Now, the Court was willing to state: "Such a conviction cannot stand, for it is no longer open to question that a State may not constitutionally require segregation of public facilities."

2. *The Brown rationale.* In light of the school segregation opinion, and the public facilities cases in note 1, what are the bases and justifications for Brown? What is its scope?[2]

a. *History.* Do the history and "central purpose" of the 14th Amendment justify the decision? Was the Court's treatment of the historical understanding adequate? Consider Bickel's observation that the ban on segregation might well have been an improper implication if the 14th Amendment were a statute, but that "we are dealing with a constitutional amendment, not a statute."[3] He noted that the history of the 14th Amendment "rather clearly" demonstrates "that it was not expected in 1866 to apply to segregation." But his historical survey found "an awareness on the part of [the Framers of the 14th Amendment] that it was *a constitution* they were writing, which led to a choice of

10. Is it truly "unthinkable" that the Fifth Amendment imposed a "lesser duty" on the Federal government than the 14th did on the states?

1. See, e.g., Mayor of Baltimore v. Dawson, 350 U.S. 877 (1955) (beaches); Gayle v. Browder, 352 U.S. 903 (1956) (buses); Holmes v. Atlanta, 350 U.S. 879 (1955) (golf courses); New Orleans City Park Improvement Association v. Detiege, 358 U.S. 54 (1958) (parks). Cf. Turner v. Memphis, 369 U.S. 350 (1962) (municipal airport restaurant).

2. For a sampling of the extensive commentary generated by Brown, see Wechsler, "Toward Neutral Principles of Constitutional Law," 73 Harv.L.Rev. 1 (1959); Pollak, "Racial Discrimination and Judicial Integrity: A Reply to Professor Wechsler," 108 U.Pa.L.Rev. 1 (1959); C.L. Black, Jr., "The Lawfulness of the Segregation

Decisions," 69 Yale L.J. 421 (1960). See also Bickel, "The Original Understanding and the Segregation Decision," 69 Harv.L.Rev. 1 (1955).

For comments on the social science evidence in Brown, see Cahn, "Jurisprudence," 30 N.Y.U.L. Rev. 150 (1955); K.B. Clark, "The Desegregation Cases," 5 Vill.L.Rev. 224 (1959); and K.B. Clark, "The Social Scientists, the Brown Decision, and Contemporary Confusion," in Argument (Friedman ed. 1969). See also Stell v. Chatham Bd. of Ed., 220 F.Supp. 667 (S.D.Ga. 1963), rev'd, 333 F.2d 55 (5th Cir.1964), where the District Judge, after an extensive hearing to survey the social science data nearly a decade after Brown, unsuccessfully tried in effect to "reverse" Brown.

3. The sources of all of the comments referred to in this note are cited in footnote 2.

language capable of growth," and he concluded that "the record of history, properly understood, left the way open to, in fact invited, a decision based on the moral and material state of the nation in 1954, not 1866."

b. *Impact on educational and psychological development.* Was the critical element in Brown the Court's endorsement of the finding that state-imposed segregation "has a tendency to retard the educational and mental development of Negro children"? Were empirical data central to the Court's holding? The reliance on social science evidence—and the quality of those data, then and now [4]—have been criticized. See, e.g., Cahn's comment that "I would not have the constitutional rights of Negroes—or of other Americans—rest on any such flimsy foundation as some of the scientific demonstrations in these records. [Behavioral science findings] have an uncertain expectancy of life." Was the central element in the Court's decision the statement that segregation "generates a feeling of inferiority"? What are the critical elements in establishing such a conclusion? Social science data? Judicial notice? History? The intent of the legislators enacting segregation laws? The stereotypical assumption of black inferiority—the assumption which supposedly provided the underpinnings for the general system of segregation? The black community's perception of the stigma imposed by segregation? Note Cahn's emphasis on "the most familiar and universally accepted standards of right and wrong" as demonstrating that "racial segregation under government auspices inevitably inflicts humiliation" and that "official humiliation of innocent, law-abiding citizens is psychologically injurious and morally evil." Can the Court properly rest a decision on "universal" moral standards without added support in empirical data or history?

Compare Professor Black's defense of the "lawfulness" of Brown, emphasizing that the Southern cultural tradition during the period of enforced segregation makes it clear that "segregation is a massive intentional disadvantaging of the Negro race, as such, by state law." He commented: "[I]f a whole race of people finds itself confined within a system which is set up and continued for the very purpose of keeping it in an inferior station, and if the question is then solemnly propounded whether such a race is being treated 'equally,' I think we ought to exercise one of the sovereign prerogatives of philosophers—that of laughter." And the segregation system, he insisted, clearly met that description. He noted: "Segregation is historically and contemporaneously associated in a functioning complex with practices which are indisputably and grossly discriminatory." [5] Are positions such as Cahn's or Black's an adequate answer to Wechsler's argument: "For me, assuming equal facilities, the question posed by state-enforced segregation is not one of discrimination at all. Its human and its constitutional dimensions lie entirely elsewhere, in the denial by the state of freedom to associate, a denial that impinges in the same way on any groups or races that may be involved." He asked: "Given a situation where the state must practically choose between denying the association to those individuals who wish it or imposing it on those who would avoid it, is there a basis in

---

4. For a modern review of the available (and controversial) data, see Goodman, "De Facto School Segregation: A Constitutional and Empirical Analysis," 70 Calif.L.Rev. 275 (1972).

5. Black, who grew up in Texas, added that the "purpose and impact of segregation in the southern regional culture" were "matters of common notoriety, matters not so much for judicial notice as for the background knowledge of educated men who live in the world." Southern segregation at the time of Brown, he emphasized, was not "mutual separation of whites and Negroes," but rather "one in-group enjoying full

normal communal life and one out-group that is barred from this life and forced into an inferior life of its own." He concluded that the "regional culture" was properly determinative: the question was not whether segregation is inevitably discriminatory, but whether "discrimination inheres in that segregation which is imposed by law in the twentieth century in certain specific states in the American Union. And that question has meaning and can find an answer only on the ground of history and of common knowledge about the facts of life."

neutral principles for holding that the Constitution demands that the claims for association should prevail?"

c. *The scope of the holding.* In view of the emphasis on the impact of segregation on *educational* opportunity in Brown, should the Court have explained more fully the basis for its ultimate general principle "that a State may not constitutionally require segregation of public facilities," rather than resting that development largely on the per curiam orders in note 1, above? Do the considerations articulated in Brown, or other justifications for its result, support a claim that de facto as well as de jure segregation in public schools is unconstitutional? Is the major emphasis in Brown on the existence of *purposeful*, de jure discrimination, or does Brown focus on the *impact* of segregated schools (whether the segregation was "purposeful" or not) in limiting educational opportunity and in generating a sense of inferiority? (The question of the validity of de facto segregation is postponed to sec. 3D below, for consideration with other aspects of the "purpose"-"impact" distinction.)

BROWN v. BOARD OF EDUCATION
[BROWN II—THE IMPLEMENTATION DECISION]

349 U.S. 294, 75 S.Ct. 753, 99 L.Ed. 1083 (1955).

Mr. Chief Justice WARREN delivered the opinion of the Court.

These cases were decided on May 17, 1954. The opinions of that date, declaring the fundamental principle that racial discrimination in public education is unconstitutional, are incorporated herein by reference. All provisions of federal, state, or local law requiring or permitting such discrimination must yield to this principle. There remains for consideration the manner in which relief is to be accorded. Because these cases arose under different local conditions and their disposition will involve a variety of local problems, we requested further argument on the question of relief.[1] In view of the nation-wide importance of the decision, we invited the Attorney General of the United States and the Attorneys General of all states requiring or permitting racial discrimination in public education to present their views on that question. The parties, the United States, and [six states] participated [in the argument].

Full implementation of these constitutional principles may require solution of varied local school problems. School authorities have the primary responsibility for elucidating, assessing, and solving these problems; courts will have to consider whether the action of school authorities constitutes good faith implementation of the governing constitutional principles. Because of their proximity to local conditions and the possible need for further hearings, the courts

---

1. Further argument was requested on the following [questions], previously propounded by the Court:

"4. Assuming it is decided that segregation in public schools violates the 14th Amendment (*a*) would a decree necessarily follow providing that, within the limits set by normal geographic school districting, Negro children should forthwith be admitted to schools of their choice, or (*b*) may this Court, in the exercise of its equity powers, permit an effective gradual adjustment to be brought about from existing segregated systems to a system not based on color distinctions?

"5. On the assumption on which questions 4(*a*) and (*b*) are based, and assuming further

that this Court will exercise its equity powers to the end described in question 4(*b*), (*a*) should this Court formulate detailed decrees in these cases; (*b*) if so, what specific issues should the decrees reach; (*c*) should this Court appoint a special master to hear evidence with a view to recommending specific terms for such decrees; (*d*) should this Court remand to the courts of first instance with directions to frame decrees in these cases, and if so what general directions should the decrees of this Court include and what procedures should the courts of first instance follow in arriving at the specific terms of more detailed decrees?" [Footnote by Chief Justice Warren.]

which originally heard these cases can best perform this judicial appraisal. Accordingly, we believe it appropriate to remand the cases to those courts.

In fashioning and effectuating the decrees, the courts will be guided by equitable principles. Traditionally, equity has been characterized by a practical flexibility in shaping its remedies and by a facility for adjusting and reconciling public and private needs. These cases call for the exercise of these traditional attributes of equity power. At stake is the personal interest of the plaintiffs in admission to public schools as soon as practicable on a nondiscriminatory basis. To effectuate this interest may call for elimination of a variety of obstacles in making the transition to school systems operated in accordance with the constitutional principles set forth in [Brown I]. Courts of equity may properly take into account the public interest in the elimination of such obstacles in a systematic and effective manner. But it should go without saying that the vitality of these constitutional principles cannot be allowed to yield simply because of disagreement with them.

While giving weight to these public and private considerations, the courts will require that the defendants make a prompt and reasonable start toward full compliance with [Brown I]. Once such a start has been made, the courts may find that additional time is necessary to carry out the ruling in an effective manner. The burden rests upon the defendants to establish that such time is necessary in the public interest and is consistent with good faith compliance at the earliest practicable date. To that end, the courts may consider problems related to administration, arising from the physical condition of the school plant, the school transportation system, personnel, revision of school districts and attendance areas into compact units to achieve a system of determining admission to the public schools on a nonracial basis, and revision of local laws and regulations which may be necessary in solving the foregoing problems. They will also consider the adequacy of any plans the defendants may propose to meet these problems and to effectuate a transition to a racially nondiscriminatory school system. During this period of transition, the courts will retain jurisdiction of these cases. The [cases are accordingly remanded to the lower courts] to take such proceedings and enter such orders and decrees consistent with this opinion as are necessary and proper to admit to public schools on a racially nondiscriminatory basis with all deliberate speed the parties to these [cases].[2]

B. GENDER

---

1. *Introduction: Bases for expanding the categories of "suspect" classifications.* This section and the next turn to modern efforts to establish new categories of "suspect" or "quasi-suspect" classifications warranting heightened scrutiny. Three classifications have evoked varying, and often unstable, degrees of heightened scrutiny: gender; alienage; and illegitimacy. (These developments have been largely products of the Burger rather than the Warren era.) Still other classifications have been candidates for elevation to more intensive review. In examining the materials that follow, consider especially the extent to which the reasons which justify strict scrutiny of disadvantaging racial classifications are properly applicable to governmental action based on other criteria.

If the history and immediate purpose of the 14th Amendment were all that counted, only racial classifications directed against blacks would be suspect. But, as already noted, the Court has, without much discussion, treated ethnicity

---

2. As already noted, the problems of implementing desegregation since 1955 are considered in sec. 3D below.

like race. Is it possible to generalize more broadly? To what extent can one justify identification of additional classifications warranting heightened scrutiny by extrapolating from the characteristics that have elicited strict scrutiny of racial criteria? Is the critical element the possession of an unalterable trait? A trait distinguishing the possessor from the majority? A trait relied on by the classifier for the purpose—or the effect—of stigmatizing those possessing it? A trait frequently relied upon by the majority to signify its superiority vis-à-vis those possessing the trait? A trait rarely relevant to legitimate governmental objectives yet traditionally used to disadvantage those who possess it? A trait traditionally used and readily usable for "we-they" generalizations as opposed to "they-they" generalizations? [1]

What if the classifier relies on a trait which has some but not all of the characteristics that have made race traditionally suspect? Does a partial, incomplete resemblance to racial discrimination justify at least heightened, greater-than-minimal scrutiny? Are varying degrees of scrutiny warranted, depending upon the degree of "suspectness" of the classifying criterion? Is the Court implicitly applying such a sliding scale in some of the cases that follow? Is such a sliding scale approach justifiable? Or does it create an excessive risk of ad hoc, unprincipled judicial intervention?

2. *The changing attitude toward gender classifications.* While the battle for the ratification of the Equal Rights Amendment was under way in the early 1970s, the Court considered a growing number of cases challenging sex classifications under equal protection. A large number of these challenges succeeded, even though the Court at the outset purported to apply the rationality standard and even though the majority refused to assimilate gender criteria to the fully "suspect" status of racial ones. In the mid-1970s, in Craig v. Boren (1976; p.

---

1. See Ely, "The Wages of Crying Wolf: A Comment on Roe v. Wade," 82 Yale L.J. 920 (1973), suggesting special suspicion for classifications in which the decisionmakers (the "we"s) are particularly apt to resort to stereotypes resting on superiority-inferiority judgments when the "we"s resort to classifications disadvantaging the "they"s: "A decision to distinguish blacks from whites (or women from men) will therefore have its roots in a comparison between a 'we' stereotype and a 'they' stereotype, viz. They [blacks or women] are generally inferior to or not so well qualified as *we* [whites or men] are in the following respect(s), which we find sufficient to justify the [classification]." Ely adds: "The danger is therefore greater in we-they situations that we will overestimate the validity of the proposed stereotypical classification by seizing upon the positive myths about our own class and the negative myths about theirs—or indeed the realities respecting some or most members of the two classes—and too readily assuming that virtually the entire membership of the two classes fit the stereotypes and therefore that not many of 'them' will be unfairly deprived, nor many of 'us' unfairly benefitted, by the proposed classification. In short, I trust your generalizations about the differences between my gang and Wilfred's more than I do your generalizations about the differences between my gang and yours"—i.e., "there is less justification for special scrutiny of 'they-they' generalizations than for 'we-they' generalizations."

Recall the material at p. 604 above, on Ely's elaboration of this approach in his later writings, especially Democracy and Distrust (1980), urging a "representation-reinforcing," minority-protecting exercise of judicial review. Recall also the "discrete and insular," perennially "losing" minority ingredient in equal protection analysis, stemming from Justice Stone's Carolene Products footnote, as noted at p. 473 above.

Consider the passage in Justice Powell's majority opinion in Rodriguez (1973; p. 789 below) characterizing "the traditional indicia of suspectness" as follows: "[The] class [is] saddled with such disabilities, or subjected to such a history of purposeful unequal treatment, or relegated to such a position of political powerlessness as to command extraordinary protection from the majoritarian political process." Note the reference to "political powerlessness": it derives from the last paragraph of Justice Stone's Carolene Products footnote. Recall the earlier questions about the justifications for that aspect of the footnote, at p. 473 above. Should "political powerlessness" alone justify a conclusion of "suspectness"? (Note also the explicit reliance on Stone's footnote in the Court's occasional treatment of alienage as a suspect classification. See Graham v. Richardson (1971; p. 670 below)—and a criticism of that approach in Justice Rehnquist's dissent in In re Griffiths (1973; p. 671 below).) Note also Justice Brennan's 1982 effort to restate the rationale for "suspect classifications" analyses, in footnote 2 of his opinion in Plyler v. Doe (sec. 4A, p. 799, below).

647 below), a consensus was attained at last: the majority applied a heightened, intermediate level of scrutiny, a level reaffirmed in a restated manner in Hogan (1982; p. 660 below). Before turning to those modern cases, consider the following samples of sex classifications before the late 1970s. Consider especially the similarities and differences between race and sex discrimination.[2] Are the situations analogous in terms of a typical classifier's intent? Do sex classifications typically imply a sense of superiority by the classifier?[3] Consider, too, whether governmental reliance on deprecating stereotypes has become the central focus in the modern cases.

    3. *The deferential old equal protection in action.* For the Court's characteristic stance toward sex discrimination claims in an earlier era (not so long ago), see GOESAERT v. CLEARY, 335 U.S. 464 (1948), rejecting an attack on a Michigan law which provided that no woman could obtain a bartender's license unless she was "the wife or daughter of the male owner" of a licensed liquor establishment.[4] Justice FRANKFURTER stated: "Michigan could, beyond question, forbid all women from working behind a bar. This is so despite the vast changes in the social and legal position of women. The fact that women may now have achieved the virtues that men have long claimed as their prerogatives and now indulge in vices that men have long practiced, does not preclude the States from drawing a sharp line between the sexes, certainly in such matters as the regulation of the liquor traffic. [The] Constitution does not require legislatures to reflect sociological insight, or shifting social standards, any more than it requires them to keep abreast of the latest scientific standards. [While] Michigan may deny to all women opportunities for bartending, Michigan cannot play favorites among women without rhyme or reason. [Since] bartending by women may, in the allowable legislative judgment, give rise to moral and social problems against which it may devise preventive measures, the legislature need not go to the full length of the prohibition if it believes that as to a defined group of females other factors are operating which either eliminate or reduce the moral and social problems otherwise calling for prohibition. Michigan evidently believes that the oversight assured through ownership of a bar by a barmaid's husband or father minimizes hazards that may confront a barmaid without such protecting oversight. This Court is certainly not in a position to gainsay such belief by the Michigan legislature. [Since the line drawn] is not without a basis in reason, we cannot give ear to the suggestion that the real impulse behind this legislation was an unchivalrous desire of male bartenders to try to monopolize the calling."[5]

    2. Note the comment by Professor (now Judge) Ruth Bader Ginsburg (who had prime responsibility for appellant's brief in Reed v. Reed, below, and in many other sex discrimination cases of the 1970s) urging "recognition that generators of race and sex discrimination are often *different.*" She stated: "Neither ghettoized minorities nor women are well served by lumping their problems together for *all* purposes, by pretending that all are oppressed in the same way and for the same reasons. Prime among the differences: women are found in every economic class and in every neighborhood; they generally live and work in close physical contact with the men who, under traditional arrangements, held a control rein over them." Ginsburg, "Realizing the Equality Principle" (Keynote Address, 6th National Conference on Women and the Law, 1975). See also Ginsburg, "Gender and the Constitution," 44 U.Cinn.L.Rev. 1 (1975). Note also the comparisons between race and sex discrimination in Bakke, p. 745 below.

    3. See Ely, "The Wages of Crying Wolf: A Comment on Roe v. Wade," 82 Yale L.J. 920 (1973): "[L]egislators traditionally have not only not been black (or female); they have been white (and male). A decision to distinguish blacks from whites (or women from men) will therefore have its roots in a comparison between a 'we' stereotype and a 'they' stereotype." See also Ely, Democracy and Distrust (1980).

    4. For an even earlier example of the traditional attitude, see Bradwell v. State (1873), noted in Frontiero, p. 645 below. That case upheld a law denying women the right to practice law.

    5. Justice RUTLEDGE, joined by Justices Douglas and Murphy, dissented without challenging the majority's assumptions; instead, he focused on the inadequate fit between means and ends. The dissenters, like the majority, assumed that "benign," "protective" legislation regarding women was clearly constitutional. Recall that, during the Lochner era, one of the few types of laws regulating working conditions readily sus-

4. *Heightened scrutiny under a deferential, old equal protection guise.* In REED v. REED, 404 U.S. 71 (1971), the appellant's elaborate brief strenuously urged the Court to find sex a suspect classification. The Court declined. Yet, in an opinion discussed in Frontiero, below, the unanimous Court sustained the discrimination claim, while purporting to apply a traditional "rationality" standard of review. Chief Justice BURGER stated the question as "whether a difference in the sex of competing applicants for letters of administration bears a rational relationship to a state objective that is sought to be advanced by the operation of [the Idaho law]." [6] In Reed, the state courts had sustained the preference for men over women in the appointment of administrators of estates as a rational method "to resolve an issue that would otherwise require a hearing as to the relative merits" of the petitioning relatives. The Court stated: "Clearly the objective of reducing the work load on probate courts by eliminating one class of contests is not without some legitimacy." Nevertheless, there was a denial of equal protection: giving "a mandatory preference to members of either sex over members of the other, merely to accomplish the elimination of hearings on the merits, is to make the very kind of arbitrary legislative choice forbidden by [equal protection]; and whatever may be said as to the positive values of avoiding intrafamily controversy, the choice in this contest may not lawfully be mandated solely on the basis of sex." [7]

FRONTIERO v. RICHARDSON, 411 U.S. 677 (1973): Frontiero sustained an equal protection challenge to a federal law permitting male members of the armed forces an automatic dependency allowance for their wives but requiring servicewomen to prove that their husbands were dependent. Justice BRENNAN's opinion put forth the most elaborate judicial argument on the books for treating gender as a suspect classification, but he did not get majority support for his analysis. Joined by Justices Douglas, White and Marshall, Justice Brennan concluded that "classifications based upon sex, like [those] upon race, alienage, and national origin, are inherently suspect and must therefore be subjected to close judicial scrutiny." He found implicit support for that position in Reed's "departure from 'traditional' rational-basis analysis." He elaborated:

"[Our] Nation has had a long and unfortunate history of sex discrimination. Traditionally, such discrimination was rationalized by an attitude of 'romantic paternalism' which, in practical effect, put women, not on a pedestal, but in a cage.[1] As a result of notions such as these, our statute books gradually became laden with gross, stereotyped distinctions between the sexes and, indeed,

tained by the Court was the setting of maximum working hours for women. Muller v. Oregon (1908; p. 458 above) relied on women's alleged dependence and physical weakness to justify such legislation. (For an explicit modern disapproval of Goesaert, see footnote 4 in Craig v. Boren (1976; p. 647 below).)

6. He quoted as the applicable standard a statement in Royster Guano (1920; p. 596 above): a classification "must be reasonable, not arbitrary, and must rest upon some ground of difference having a fair and substantial relation to the object of the legislation."

7. Reed continued to be invoked to invalidate sex classifications in a number of cases after Frontiero, which follows, and before Craig v. Boren (p. 647 below). In each case, it seemed clear that a challenged statute *would* have survived scrutiny if a truly deferential, old equal protection approach had been applied and that the reference to Reed in fact signified an unar-

ticulated, heightened (but less than strict) scrutiny.

For an early interpretation of Reed, see Gunther, "Newer Equal Protection": "It is difficult to understand [the result in Reed] without an assumption that some special sensitivity to sex as a classifying factor entered into the analysis. [Only] by importing some special suspicion of sex-related means from the new equal protection area can the result be made entirely persuasive. Yet application of new equal protection criteria is precisely what Reed v. Reed purported to avoid." See also Justice Marshall's dissent in Rodriguez, p. 789 below: "[Reed] can only be understood as [an instance] in which the particularly invidious character of the classification caused the Court to pause and scrutinize with more than traditional care the rationality of state discrimination."

1. To illustrate the traditional "paternalistic attitude," Justice Brennan quoted from Justice Bradley's concurring opinion in Bradwell v.

throughout much of the 19th century the position of women in our society was, in many respects, comparable to that of blacks under the pre-Civil War slave codes. Neither slaves nor women could hold office, serve on juries, or bring suit in their own names, and married women traditionally were denied the legal capacity to hold or convey property or to serve as legal guardians of their own children. And although blacks were guaranteed the right to vote in 1870, women were denied even that right [until] adoption of the 19th Amendment half a century later.

It is true, of course, that the position of women in America has improved markedly in recent decades. Nevertheless, it can hardly be doubted that, in part because of the high visibility of the sex characteristic, women still face pervasive, although at times more subtle, discrimination in our educational institutions, in the job market and, perhaps most conspicuously, in the political arena.² Moreover, since sex, like race and national origin, is an immutable characteristic, the imposition of special disabilities upon the members of a particular sex because of their sex would seem to violate 'the basic concept of our system that legal burdens should bear some relationship to individual responsibility.' [Weber, an illegitimacy case, p. 679 below.] And what differentiates sex from such nonsuspect statuses as intelligence or physical disability, and aligns it with the recognized suspect criteria, is that the sex characteristic frequently bears no relation to ability to perform or contribute to society. As a result, statutory distinctions between the sexes often have the effect of invidiously relegating the entire class of females to inferior legal status without regard to the actual capabilities of its individual members."

Applying the "strict judicial scrutiny" he found appropriate, Justice Brennan found it "clear" that the law was unconstitutional. The Government had relied on promoting "administrative convenience": "[It] maintains that, as an empiri- cal matter, wives [frequently] are dependent upon their husbands, while hus- bands rarely are dependent upon their wives. Thus, the Government argues that [Congress] might reasonably have concluded that it would be both cheaper and easier simply conclusively to presume that wives of male members are financially dependent upon their husbands, while burdening female members with the task of establishing dependency in fact. The Government offers no

State, 16 Wall. 130 (1873), where the Court sustained a law denying to women the right to practice law: "Man is, or should be, woman's protector and defender. The natural and proper timidity and delicacy which belongs to the female sex evidently unfits it for many of the occupa- tions of civil life. The constitution of the family organization, which is founded in the divine ordi- nance, as well as in the nature of things, indicates the domestic sphere as that which properly be- longs to the domain and functions of woman- hood. The harmony, not to say identity, of interests and views which belong, or should be- long, to the family institution is repugnant to the idea of a woman adopting a distinct and indepen- dent career from that of her husband. [The] paramount destiny and mission of woman are to fulfil the noble and benign offices of wife and mother. This is the law of the Creator."

2. It is true, of course, that when viewed in the abstract, women do not constitute a small and powerless minority. Nevertheless, in part because of past discrimination, women are vastly underrepresented in this Nation's decisionmaking councils. [This] underrepresentation is present throughout all levels of our State and Federal Government. [Footnote by Justice Brennan.]

Compare Ely, Democracy and Distrust (1980), commenting on the relevance of "political powerlessness" to the scrutiny of gender classifi- cations. He suggests that the Court should strike down sex classifications only if they were enacted while women's access to the political process was blocked. But a legislature should then be free to reenact the law: "[In] the event— unlikely, precisely because access is no longer blocked—that the legislature after such a declara- tion of unconstitutionality" repassed the same law, it should be sustained: the "fact that due process of lawmaking was denied in 1908 [need not] imply that it was in 1982 as well." He adds: "To put on the group affected the burden of using its recently unblocked access to get the offending laws repealed would be to place in their path an additional hurdle that the rest of us do not have to contend with in order to protect ourselves. [But] if women don't protect them- selves from sex discrimination in the future, it [will be] because for one reason or another— substantive disagreement or more likely the as- signment of a low priority to the issue—they don't choose to." But see Note, "Sex Discrimi- nation and [Equal Protection]," 84 Harv.L.Rev. 1499 (1971).

concrete evidence, however, tending to support its view that such differential treatment in fact saves the Government any money. [Moreover], any statutory scheme which draws a sharp line between the sexes, *solely* for the purpose of achieving administrative convenience, [violates equal protection]. [Reed.]"

Justice POWELL, joined by Chief Justice Burger and Justice Blackmun, concurred only in the judgment, arguing that it was unnecessary "in this case to characterize sex as a suspect classification" because the case could and should be decided "on the authority of Reed" and "any expansion of its rationale" should be reserved for the future. Moreover, any general categorization of sex classifications as suspect should be postponed because of the pending Equal Rights Amendment ("which if adopted will resolve the substance of this precise question"): "[This] reaching out to pre-empt by judicial action a major political decision which is currently in process of resolution does not reflect appropriate respect for duly prescribed legislative processes." [3]

CRAIG v. BOREN

429 U.S. 190, 97 S.Ct. 451, 50 L.Ed.2d 397 (1976).

Mr. Justice BRENNAN delivered the opinion of the Court.[1]

The interaction of two sections of an Oklahoma statute prohibits the sale of "non-intoxicating" 3.2% beer to males under the age of 21 and to females under the age of 18. The question [is] whether such a gender-based differential constitutes a denial to males 18–20 years of age of [equal protection].

[To] withstand constitutional challenge, previous cases establish that classifications by gender must serve important governmental objectives and must be substantially related to achievement of those objectives. [Reed and subsequent decisions (e.g., Frontiero)] have rejected administrative ease and convenience as sufficiently important objectives to justify gender-based classifications. Reed has also provided the underpinning for decisions that have invalidated statutes employing gender as an inaccurate proxy for other, more germane bases of classification. Hence, "archaic and overbroad" generalizations, Schlesinger v. Ballard [1975], concerning the financial position of servicewomen, Frontiero, and working women, Weinberger v. Wiesenfeld [1975; p. 739 below], could not justify use of a gender line in determining eligibility for certain governmental entitlements. Similarly, increasingly outdated misconceptions concerning the

---

3. Justice STEWART, who also concurred solely in the judgment, stated merely that the law worked "an invidious discrimination in violation of the Constitution. [Reed.]" Justice REHNQUIST dissented "for the reasons stated by Judge Rives for the District Court." (Judge Rives, after doubting that the law classified on the basis of sex, insisted that it was valid even if it did so, since sex was not "suspect" and the classification satisfied the rationality standard of Reed by promoting administrative convenience.)

In the period between Frontiero and Craig v. Boren, which follows, the Court struck down several other sex classifications by invoking Reed. See, e.g., Stanton v. Stanton, 421 U.S. 7 (1975), involving a law that required child support for males to age 21 but for females only to age 18: "To distinguish between [male and female] on educational grounds is to be self-serving: if the female is not to be supported so long as the male, she hardly can be expected to attend school as long as he does, and bringing her

education to an end earlier coincides with the role-typing society has long imposed." (See also the additional sex discrimination cases in the period betwen 1971 and 1976 in the "benign" sex discrimination materials, sec. 3E1, p. 737 below.)

1. This case marks the emergence on the Court of a consensus about sex discrimination. Justice Brennan's majority opinion stated the new, "intermediate" scrutiny appropriate for gender classifications in the first sentence of the second paragraph of his opinion. Although some of the subsequent cases (e.g., Rostker v. Goldberg, p. 655 below) seemed to cast doubt upon it, the 1982 decision in Hogan (p. 660 below) made clear that intermediate scrutiny, slightly reformulated, retains majority support. (This case also was the first occasion to strike down discrimination that was clearly directed against males rather than females. The majority has continued to apply intermediate scrutiny whether the challenger is male or female.)

role of females in the home rather than in the "marketplace and world of ideas" were rejected as loose-fitting characterizations incapable of supporting state statutory schemes that were premised upon their accuracy. [E.g., Stanton.] In light of the weak congruence between gender and the characteristic or trait that gender purported to represent, it was necessary that the legislatures choose either to realign their substantive laws in a gender-neutral fashion, or to adopt procedures for identifying those instances where the sex-centered generalization actually comported to fact. In this case, too, "Reed, we feel, is controlling." [Stanton.] We turn then to the question whether, under Reed, the difference between males and females with respect to the purchase of 3.2% beer warrants the differential in age drawn by the Oklahoma statute. We conclude that it does not].

We accept for purposes of discussion the District Court's identification of the objective underlying [the law] as the enhancement of traffic safety. Clearly, the protection of public health and safety represents an important function of state and local governments. However, appellees' statistics in our view cannot support the conclusion that the gender-based distinction closely serves to achieve that objective and therefore the distinction cannot under Reed withstand equal protection challenge.

The appellees introduced a variety of statistical surveys. First, an analysis of arrest statistics for 1973 demonstrated that 18–20-year-old male arrests for "driving under the influence" and "drunkenness" substantially exceeded female arrests for that same age period. Similarly, youths aged 17–21 were found to be overrepresented among those killed or injured in traffic accidents, with males again numerically exceeding females in this regard. Third, a random roadside survey in Oklahoma City revealed that young males were more inclined to drive and drink beer than were their female counterparts. Fourth, [FBI] nationwide statistics exhibited a notable increase in arrests for "driving under the influence." Finally, statistical evidence gathered in other jurisdictions [was] offered to corroborate Oklahoma's experience by indicating the pervasiveness of youthful participation in motor vehicle accidents following the imbibing of [alcohol]. Even were this statistical evidence accepted as accurate, it nevertheless offers only a weak answer to the equal protection question presented here. The most focused and relevant of the statistical surveys, arrests of 18–20-year-olds for alcohol-related driving offenses, exemplifies the ultimate unpersuasiveness of this evidentiary record. Viewed in terms of the correlation between sex and the actual activity that Oklahoma seeks to regulate—driving while under the influence of alcohol—the statistics broadly establish that .18% of females and 2% of males in that age group were arrested for that offense. While such a disparity is not trivial in a statistical sense, it hardly can form the basis for employment of a gender line as a classifying device. Certainly if maleness is to serve as a proxy for drinking and driving, a correlation of 2% must be considered an unduly tenuous "fit." Indeed, prior cases have consistently rejected the use of sex as a decisionmaking factor even though the statutes in question certainly rested on far more predictive empirical relationships than this.

Moreover, the statistics exhibit a variety of other shortcomings that seriously impugn their value to equal protection analysis. Setting aside the obvious methodological problems,[2] the surveys do not adequately justify the salient features of Oklahoma's gender-based traffic-safety law. None purports to measure the use and dangerousness of 3.2% beer as opposed to alcohol [generally]. Moreover, many of the studies, while graphically documenting the

---

2. The very social stereotypes that find reflection in age differential laws are likely substantially to distort the accuracy of these comparative statistics. Hence "reckless" young men who drink and drive are transformed into arrest statistics, whereas their female counterparts are chivalrously escorted [home]. [Footnote by Justice Brennan.]

unfortunate increase in driving while under the influence of alcohol, make no effort to relate their findings to age-sex differentials as involved here. [There] is no reason to belabor this line of analysis. It is unrealistic to expect either members of the judiciary or state officials to be well versed in the rigors of experimental or statistical technique. But this merely illustrates that proving broad sociological propositions by statistics is a dubious business, and one that inevitably is in tension with the normative philosophy that underlies the Equal Protection Clause. Suffice to say that the showing offered by the appellees does not satisfy us that sex represents a legitimate, accurate proxy for the regulation of drinking and driving. In fact, when it is further recognized that Oklahoma's statute prohibits only the selling of 3.2% beer to young males and not their drinking the beverage once acquired (even after purchase by their 18–20-year-old female companions), the relationship between gender and traffic safety becomes far too tenuous to satisfy Reed's requirement that the gender-based difference be substantially related to achievement of the [statutory objective].

[Social science] studies that have uncovered quantifiable differences in drinking tendencies dividing along both racial and ethnic lines strongly suggest the need for application of the Equal Protection Clause in preventing discriminatory treatment that almost certainly would be perceived as invidious.[3] In sum, the principles embodied in the Equal Protection Clause are not to be rendered inapplicable by statistically measured but loose-fitting generalities concerning the drinking tendencies of aggregate groups. We conclude that [this] gender-based differential [is] a denial of the Equal Protection of the Laws [to males aged 18–20].[4]

Reversed.[5]

Mr. Justice POWELL, concurring.

I join the opinion of the Court [but] I do have reservations as to some of the discussion concerning the appropriate standard for equal protection analysis and the relevance of the statistical evidence. [I] agree that Reed is the most relevant precedent. But I find it unnecessary, in deciding this case, to read that decision as broadly as some of the Court's language may imply. Reed and subsequent cases involving gender-based classifications make clear that the Court subjects such classifications to a more critical examination than is normally applied when "fundamental" constitutional rights and "suspect classes" are not present.[1] I view this as a relatively easy case. [The] decision [turns] on whether the [state] has adopted a means that bears a "fair and substantial

---

3. Thus, if statistics were to govern the permissibility of state alcohol regulation without regard to the Equal Protection Clause as a limiting principle, it might follow that States could freely favor Jews and Italian Catholics at the expense of all other Americans, since available studies regularly demonstrate that the former two groups exhibit the lowest rates of problem drinking. Similarly, if a State were allowed simply to depend upon demographic characteristics of adolescents in identifying problem drinkers, statistics might support the conclusion that only black teenagers should be permitted to drink, followed by Asian- and [Spanish-Americans]. [Footnote by Justice Brennan.]

4. Insofar as Goesaert v. Cleary may be inconsistent, that decision is [disapproved]. [Footnote by Justice Brennan.]

5. Are gender-based generalizations permissible under the Constitution so long as they are valid rather than stereotypical ones? Note the important discussion of that issue, in Manhart (1978; p. 669 below), a case arising under Title VII of the 1964 Civil Rights Act.

1. As is evident from our opinions, the Court has had difficulty in agreeing upon a standard of equal protection analysis that can be applied consistently to the wide variety of legislative classifications. There are valid reasons for dissatisfaction with the "two-tier" approach that has been prominent in the Court's decisions in the past decade. Although viewed by many as a result-oriented substitute for more critical analysis, that approach—with its narrowly limited "upper-tier"—now has substantial precedential support. As has been true of Reed and its progeny, our decision today will be viewed by some as a "middle-tier" approach. While I would not endorse that characterization and would not welcome a further subdividing of equal protection analysis, candor compels the recognition that the relatively deferential "rational basis" standard of review normally applied takes on a sharper focus when we address a

relation" to this objective. Reed. It seems to me that the statistics offered by the [state] do tend generally to support the [classification]. Even so, I am not persuaded that these facts and the inferences fairly drawn from them justify this classification based on a three-year age differential between the sexes, and especially one that is so easily circumvented as to be virtually meaningless. Putting it differently, this gender-based classification does not bear a fair and substantial relation to the object of the legislation.

Mr. Justice STEVENS, concurring.

There is only one Equal Protection Clause. It requires every State to govern impartially. It does not direct the courts to apply one standard of review in some cases and a different standard in other cases. Whatever criticism may be levelled at a judicial opinion implying that there are at least three such standards applies with the same force to a double standard. I am inclined to believe that what has become known as the two-tiered analysis of equal protection claims does not describe a completely logical method of deciding cases, but rather is a method the Court has employed to explain decisions that actually apply a single standard in a reasonably consistent fashion. I also suspect that a careful explanation of the reasons motivating particular decisions may contribute more to an identification of that standard than an attempt to articulate it in all-encompassing terms. It may therefore be appropriate for me to state the principal reasons which persuaded me to join the Court's opinion.

In this case, the classification is not as obnoxious as some the Court has condemned,[1] nor as inoffensive as some the Court has accepted. It is objectionable because it is based on an accident at birth, because it is a mere remnant of the now almost universally rejected tradition of discriminating against males in this age bracket, and because, to the extent it reflects any physical difference between males and females, it is actually perverse.[2] The question then is whether the traffic safety justification put forward by the State is sufficient to make an otherwise offensive classification acceptable. The classification is not totally irrational. For the evidence does indicate that there are more males than females in this age bracket who drive and also more who drink. Nevertheless, there are several reasons why I regard the justification as unacceptable. It is difficult to believe that the statute was actually intended to cope with the problem of traffic safety,[3] since it has only a minimal effect on access to a not-very-intoxicating beverage and does not prohibit its consumption. Moreover, [the] legislation imposes a restraint on [100%] of the males in the class allegedly because about 2% of them have probably violated one or more laws relating to the consumption of alcoholic beverages. It is unlikely that this law will have a significant deterrent effect either on that 2% or on the law-abiding 98%. But even assuming some such slight benefit, it does not seem to me that an insult to all of the young men of the State can be justified by visiting the sins of the 2% on the 98%.[4]

gender-based [classification]. [Footnote by Justice Powell.]

1. Men as a general class have not been the victims of the kind of historic, pervasive discrimination that has disadvantaged other groups. [Footnote by Justice Stevens.]

2. Because males are generally heavier than females, they have a greater capacity to consume alcohol without impairing their driving ability than do females. [Footnote by Justice Stevens.]

3. [There is] no way of knowing what actually motivated this discrimination, but I would not

be surprised if it represented nothing more than the perpetuation of a stereotyped attitude about the relative maturity of the members of the two sexes in this age [bracket]. [Footnote by Justice Stevens.]

4. Justice Stewart, concurring in the judgment, stated that the law "amounts to total irrationality" and to "invidious discrimination. See [Reed]."

Mr. Justice REHNQUIST, *dissenting.*

The Court's disposition of this case is objectionable on two grounds. First is its conclusion that *men* challenging a gender-based statute which treats them less favorably than women may invoke a more stringent standard of judicial review than pertains to most other types of classifications. Second is the Court's enunciation of this standard, without citation to any source, as being that "classifications by gender must serve *important* governmental objectives and must be *substantially* related to achievement of those objectives." The only redeeming feature of the Court's opinion, to my mind, is that it apparently signals a retreat by those who joined the plurality opinion in Frontiero from their view that sex is a "suspect" classification. I think the [law] challenged here need pass only the "rational basis" equal protection analysis expounded in cases such as [McGowan] and [Lee Optical], and I believe that it is constitutional under that analysis.

I. [There] is no suggestion in the Court's opinion that males in this age group are in any way peculiarly disadvantaged, subject to systematic discriminatory treatment, or otherwise in need of special solicitude from the courts. It is true that a number of our opinions contain broadly phrased dicta implying that the same test should be applied to all classifications based on sex, whether affecting females or males. [E.g., Frontiero; Reed.] However, before today, no decision of this Court has applied an elevated level of scrutiny to invalidate a statutory discrimination harmful to males, except where the statute impaired an important personal interest protected by the Constitution. There being no such interest here, and there being no plausible argument that this is a discrimination against females,[1] the Court's reliance on our previous sex-discrimination cases is ill-founded.

[The] Court's conclusion that a law which treats males less favorably than females "must serve important governmental objectives and must be substantially related to achievement of those objectives" apparently comes out of thin air. [None] of our previous cases adopts that standard. I would think we have had enough difficulty with the two standards of [review]—the norm of "rational basis," and the "compelling state interest" required where a "suspect classification" is involved—so as to counsel weightily against the insertion of still another "standard" between those two. How is this Court to define what objectives are important? How is it to determine whether a particular law is "substantially" related to the achievement of such objective, rather than related in some other way to its achievement? Both of the phrases used are so diaphanous and elastic as to invite subjective judicial preferences or prejudices relating to particular types of legislation, masquerading as judgments whether such legislation is directed at "important" objectives or whether the relationship to those objectives is "substantial" enough. [E.g.], the introduction of the adverb "substantially" requires courts to make subjective judgments as to operational effects, for which neither their expertise nor their access to data fits [them].

II. The applicable rational basis test is [that described in the passage in McGowan (p. 601 above)]. I believe that [this] more traditional type of scrutiny is appropriate in this case, and I think that the Court would have done well here to heed its own warning that "[i]t is unrealistic to expect [the] judiciary [to] be well versed in the rigors of experimental or statistical technique." One need not immerse oneself in the fine-points of statistical analysis,

---

1. I am not unaware of the argument from time to time advanced, that all discriminations between the sexes ultimately redound to the detriment of females, because they tend to reinforce "old notions" restricting the roles and opportunities of women. As a general proposition applying equally to all sex categorizations, I believe that this argument was implicitly found to carry little weight in our decisions upholding gender-based differences. [See sec. 3E1 below.] Seeing no assertion that it has special applicability to the situation at hand, I believe it can be dismissed as an insubstantial consideration. [Footnote by Justice Rehnquist.]

however, in order to see the weakness in the Court's attempted denigration of the evidence at hand. [The] Court's criticism of the statistics [conveys] the impression that a legislature in enacting a new law is to be subjected to the judicial equivalent of a doctoral examination in statistics. Legislatures [are] entitled to draw factual conclusions on the basis of the determination of probable cause which an arrest by a police officer normally represents. In this situation, they could reasonably infer that the incidence of drunk driving is a good deal higher than the incidence of arrest. And while [such] statistics may be distorted as a result of stereotyping, the legislature is not required to prove before a court that its statistics are perfect. In any event, if stereotypes are as pervasive as the Court suggests, they may in turn influence the conduct of the men and women in question, and cause the young men to conform to the wild and reckless image which is their stereotype. [Our] only appropriate course is to defer to the reasonable inference supporting the statute—that taken in sufficient quantity this beer has the same effect as any alcoholic beverage. [The] rationality of a statutory classification for equal protection purposes does not depend upon the statistical "fit" between the class and the trait sought to be singled out. It turns on whether there may be a sufficiently higher incidence of the trait within the included class than in the excluded class to justify different treatment. [The statistical] evidence suggests clear differences between the drinking and driving habits of young men and women. Those differences are grounds enough for the State reasonably to conclude that young males pose by far the greater drunk driving hazard, both in terms of sheer numbers and in terms of hazard on a per-driver basis. The gender-based difference in treatment in this case is therefore not [irrational].[2]

MAJOR MODERN SEX DISCRIMINATION RULINGS

1. MICHAEL M. v. SUPERIOR COURT, 450 U.S. 464 (1981): This case rejected an attack on California's "statutory rape" law which punished the male, but not the female, participant in intercourse when the female was under 18 and not the male's wife.[1] Justice REHNQUIST's plurality opinion, joined by Chief Justice Burger and Justices Stewart and Powell, stated (five years after Craig v. Boren) that "the Court has had some difficulty in agreeing upon the proper approach and analysis in cases involving challenges to gender-based classifications. [We have held] that the traditional minimum rationality test takes on a somewhat 'sharper focus' when gender-based classifications are challenged. See [Craig; see also Reed]. [Underlying] these decisions is the principle that a legislature may not 'make overbroad generalizations based on sex which are entirely unrelated to any differences between men and women or which demean the ability or social status of the affected class.' But because [equal protection] does not [require] 'things which are different in fact [to] be treated in law as though they were the same,' this Court has consistently upheld statutes where the gender classification is not invidious, but rather realistically reflects the fact that the sexes are not similarly situated in certain circumstances. Parham v. Hughes; Califano v. Webster; Schlesinger v. Ballard; Kahn v. Shevin. As the

2. A dissenting notation by Chief Justice BURGER stated that he was "in general agreement with" Justice Rehnquist's dissent.

Note that Justice Rehnquist, the sole dissenter in Craig, wrote the prevailing opinions rejecting sex discrimination claims in the two 1981 cases that follow. Some read this to mean that the Court was retreating from intermediate scrutiny

for gender classifications. But in 1982, in Hogan (p. 660 below), the majority restated and reiterated the Craig approach, with Justice Rehnquist once more in dissent.

1. The challenger, at the time of the alleged statutory rape, was a 17½ year old male who had engaged in intercourse with a female under the age of 18.

Court has stated, a legislature may 'provide for the special problems of women.' Weinberger v. Wiesenfeld." [2]

Applying those principles, Justice Rehnquist sustained the law. He stated: "The justification for the statute offered by the State [is] that the legislature sought to prevent illegitimate teenage pregnancies. [We] are satisfied not only that the prevention of illegitimate pregnancy is at least one of the 'purposes' of the statute, but also that the State has a strong interest in preventing such pregnancy." [3] He continued: "[Young] men and young women are not similarly situated with respect to the problems and the risks of sexual intercourse. Only women may become pregnant, and they suffer disproportionately the profound physical, emotional, and psychological consequences of sexual activity. The [law here] protects women from sexual intercourse at an age when those consequences are particularly severe. [4] The question thus boils down to whether a State may attack the problem of sexual intercourse and teenage pregnancy directly by prohibiting a male from having sexual intercourse with a minor female. We hold that such a statute is sufficiently related to the State's objectives to pass constitutional muster.

"Because virtually all of the significant harmful and inescapably identifiable consequences of teenage pregnancy fall on the young female, a legislature acts well within its authority when it elects to punish only the participant who, by nature, suffers few of the consequences of his conduct. It is hardly unreasonable for a legislature acting to protect minor females to exclude them from punishment. Moreover, the risk of pregnancy itself constitutes a substantial deterrence to young females. No similar natural sanctions deter males. A criminal sanction imposed solely on males thus serves to roughly 'equalize' the deterrents on the sexes.

"We are unable to accept the contention that the statute is impermissibly underinclusive and must [be] *broadened* so as to hold the female as criminally liable as the male. It is argued that this statute is not *necessary* to deter teenage pregnancy because a gender-neutral statute [would] serve that goal equally well. The relevant inquiry, however, is not whether the statute is drawn as precisely as it might have been, but whether the line chosen by the [State] is within constitutional limitations. In any event, we cannot say that a gender-neutral statute would be as effective as the statute California has chosen to enact. The State persuasively contends that a gender-neutral statute would frustrate its interest in effective enforcement. Its view is that a female is surely less likely to report violations of the statute if she herself would be subject to criminal

2. All of the cases cited in these last two sentences appear either in this section or elsewhere in this chapter. Most appear in sec. 3E1 (on "benign" gender classifications), p. 737 below.

3. Justice Rehnquist commented in a footnote: "Although petitioner concedes that the State has a 'compelling' interest in preventing teenage pregnancy, he contends that the 'true' purpose of [the law] is to protect the virtue and chastity of young women. As such, the statute is unjustifiable because it rests on archaic stereotypes. [But the only] question for us [is] whether the legislation violates [equal protection], not whether its supporters may have endorsed it for reasons no longer generally accepted. Even if the preservation of female chastity were one of the motives of the statute, and even if that motive be impermissible, petitioner's argument must fail because '[i]t is a familiar practice of constitutional law that this Court will not strike down an

otherwise constitutional statute on the basis of an allegedly illicit legislative motive.' United States v. O'Brien [1968; see p. 1170 below and especially the passage quoted after Flemming v. Nestor, p. 215 above]." (Earlier in his opinion, Justice Rehnquist had stated that the Court had long recognized that "inquiries into congressional motives or purposes are a hazardous matter" and that the search for "actual" or "primary" purpose of a statute is likely to be "elusive" since, e.g., "the individual legislators may have voted for the statute for a variety of reasons." Moreover, the actual prohibition in the law was "a sure indication of its intent or purpose to discourage [the forbidden] conduct." See sec. 3D below, on "discriminatory purpose" inquiries.)

4. Earlier, Justice Rehnquist had noted that "approximately half of all teenage pregnancies end in abortion" and that, "of those children who are born, their illegitimacy makes them likely candidates to become wards of the State."

prosecution. In an area already fraught with prosecutorial difficulties, we decline to hold that [equal protection] requires a legislature to enact a statute so broad that it may well be incapable of enforcement.[5]

"In upholding the [law] we also recognize that this is not a case where a statute is being challenged on the grounds that it 'invidiously discriminates' against females. To the contrary, the statute places a burden on males which is not shared by females. But we find nothing to suggest that men, because of past discrimination or peculiar disadvantages, are in need of the special solicitude of the courts. Nor is this a case where the gender classification is made 'solely [for] administrative convenience,' as in [Frontiero], or rests on 'the baggage of sexual stereotypes,' as in Orr v. Orr [p. 738 below]. As we have held, the statute instead reasonably reflects the fact that the consequences of sexual intercourse and pregnancy fall more heavily on the female than on the male."[6]

Justice BRENNAN's dissent, joined by Justices White and Marshall, objected that none of the three opinions comprising the majority "fairly applies the equal protection analysis this Court has so carefully developed since [Craig]." He added that it was "perhaps because the gender classification in California's statutory rape law was initially designed to [further] outmoded sexual stereotypes [regarding the special need to protect young women's chastity], rather than to reduce the incidence of teenage pregnancies, that the State has been unable to demonstrate a substantial relationship between the classification and its newly asserted goal." In arguing that that relationship had not been shown, he rejected, for example, the State's assertion that law enforcement problems created by a gender-neutral statutory rape law would make such a law less effective than a gender-based statute in deterring sexual activity: "Even if fewer persons were prosecuted under the gender-neutral law, as the State suggests, it would still be true that twice as many persons would be *subject* to arrest."

A separate dissent by Justice STEVENS stated that laws prohibiting all teenagers from engaging in sexual intercourse would be permissible, but that a prohibition such as this, "applicable to only half of the joint participants in the risk-creating conduct," was impermissible sex discrimination—even though he agreed with the plurality's assumption "that the joint act that this law seeks to prohibit creates a greater risk of harm for the female than for the male." He stated: "The argument that a special need for protection provides a rational explanation for an exemption is one I simply do not comprehend."[1] The fact that a female confronted a greater risk of harm than a male was "a reason for applying the prohibition to her," not for exempting her. "Surely, if we examine the problem from the point of view of society's interest in preventing the risk-creating conduct from occurring at all, it is irrational to exempt 50% of the potential violators." Nor could this sex discrimination be adequately justified by a desire to encourage females to inform against their male partners: "Even if the concept of a wholesale informant's exemption were an acceptable enforcement device, what is the justification for defining the exempt class

---

5. "The question whether a statute is *substantially* related to its asserted goals is at best an opaque [one]." [Footnote by Justice Rehnquist.]

6. Justice STEWART, who joined Justice Rehnquist's opinion, also submitted a separate opinion. Justice BLACKMUN concurred in the judgment, stating that he voted to uphold the gender-based classification on the basis of the Reed and Craig tests "as exemplified by those two cases and by Schlesinger v. Ballard, Weinberger v. Wiesenfeld, and Kahn v. Shevin."

1. "A hypothetical racial classification will illustrate my point. Assume that skin pigmenta-

tion provides some measure of protection against cancer caused by exposure to certain chemicals in the atmosphere and, therefore, that white employees confront a greater risk than black employees in certain industrial settings. Would it be rational to require black employees to wear protective clothing but to exempt whites from that requirement? It seems to me that the greater risk of harm to white workers would be a reason for including them in the requirement—not for granting them an exemption." [Footnote by Justice Stevens.]

entirely by reference to sex rather than by reference to a more neutral criterion such as relative innocence?" He concluded: "Finally, even if my logic is faulty and there actually is some speculative basis for treating equally guilty males and females differently, I still believe that any such speculative justification would be outweighed by the paramount interest in even-handed enforcement of the law. A rule that authorizes punishment of only one of two equally guilty wrongdoers violates the essence of the constitutional requirement that the sovereign must govern impartially."

2. ROSTKER v. GOLDBERG, 453 U.S. 57 (1981): This 6 to 3 decision rejected a claim, under the equal protection aspect of Fifth Amendment due process, that the Military Selective Service Act was unconstitutional in "authorizing the President to require the registration of males and not females." Emphasizing that the purpose of draft registration was "to facilitate any eventual conscription," Justice REHNQUIST's majority opinion noted: "The case arises in the context of Congress' authority over national defense and military affairs, and perhaps in no other area has the Court accorded Congress greater deference. [Not] only is the scope of Congress' constitutional power in this area broad, but the lack of competence on the part of the courts is marked." He conceded that this did not mean that Congress was "free to disregard the Constitution when it acts in the area of military affairs," but insisted that "the tests and limitations to be applied may differ because of the military context. We of course do not abdicate our ultimate responsibility to decide the constitutional question, but simply recognize that the Constitution itself requires such deference to congressional choice. In deciding the question before us we must be particularly careful not to substitute our judgment of what is desirable for that of Congress, or our own evaluation of evidence for a reasonable evaluation by the Legislative Branch."

Against that background, Justice Rehnquist proceeded to apply "the heightened scrutiny with which we have approached gender-based discrimination, see [Michael M.; Craig; Reed]."[1] He stated: "No one could deny that under the test of [Craig], the Government's interest in raising and supporting armies is an 'important governmental interest.' Congress and its Committees carefully considered and debated two alternative means of furthering that interest: the first was to register only males for potential conscription, and the other was to register both sexes. Congress chose the former alternative. [In] light of the floor debate and the Report of the Senate Armed Services Committee, [it] is apparent that Congress was fully aware not merely of the many facts and figures presented to it by witnesses who testified, [but] of the current thinking as to the place of women in the Armed Services. In such a case, we cannot ignore Congress' broad authority [to] raise and support armies."

Turning to the sex discrimination claim, Justice Rehnquist noted that this case was "quite different" from several earlier ones because "Congress did not act 'unthinkingly' or 'reflexively and not for any considered reason.' The question of registering women for the draft not only received considerable national attention [but] also was extensively considered by Congress in hearings, floor debate, and in committee. [This] clearly establishes that the decision to exempt women from registration was not the 'accidental by-product of a traditional way of thinking about females.'" He continued: "[Any] assessment

---

1. Justice Rehnquist added: "We do not think that the substantive guarantee of due process or certainty in the law will be advanced by any further 'refinement' in the applicable tests as suggested by the Government. [The Government had argued that a mere rationality test should apply, given the military affairs context.] Announced degrees of 'deference' to legislative judgments, just as levels of 'scrutiny' which this Court announces that it applies to particular classifications made by a legislative body, may all too readily become facile abstractions used to justify a result. [Simply] labeling the legislative decision 'military' on the one hand or 'gender-based' on the other does not automatically guide a court to the correct constitutional result."

of the congressional purpose and its chosen means [must] consider the registration schemes as a prelude to a draft in a time of national emergency. [Congress] determined that any future draft, which would be facilitated by the registration scheme, would be characterized by a need for combat troops. [The] purpose of registration, therefore, was to prepare for a draft *of combat troops.* Women as a group, however, unlike men as a group, are not eligible for combat. [Since] women are excluded from combat, Congress concluded that they would not be needed in the event of a draft, and therefore decided [not to register them].[2] [This] is not a case of Congress arbitrarily choosing to burden one of two similarly situated groups, such as would be the case with an all-black or all-white, or an all-Catholic or all-Lutheran, or an all-Republican or all-Democratic registration. Men and women, because of the combat restrictions on women, are simply not similarly situated for purposes of a draft or registration for a draft. Congress' decision to authorize the registration of only men, therefore, does not violate the Due Process Clause. The exemption of women from registration is not only sufficiently but closely related to Congress' purpose in authorizing registration. See [Michael M. (plurality); Craig; Reed]. The fact that Congress and the Executive have decided that women should not serve in combat fully justifies Congress in not authorizing their registration, since the purpose of registration is to develop a pool of potential combat troops. As was the case in Schlesinger v. Ballard, 'the gender classification is not invidious, but rather realistically reflects the fact that the sexes are not similarly situated' in this case. The Constitution requires that Congress treat similarly situated persons similarly, not that it engage in gestures of superficial equality.

"In holding the MSSA constitutionally invalid the District Court relied heavily on the President's decision to seek authority to register women and the testimony of members of the Executive Branch and the military in support of that decision. [However], the President's 'decision to ask for authority to register women is based on equity.' This was also the basis for the testimony by military officials. The Senate Report, evaluating the testimony before the Committee, recognized that 'the argument for registration and induction of women [is] not based on military necessity, but on considerations of equity.' Congress was certainly entitled, in the exercise of its constitutional powers to raise and regulate armies and navies, to focus on the question of military need rather than ['equity']. Although the military experts who testified in favor of registering women uniformly opposed the actual drafting of women, there was testimony that in the event of a draft of 650,000 the military could absorb some 80,000 female inductees. The 80,000 would be used to fill noncombat positions, freeing men to go to the front. In relying on this testimony in striking down the MSSA, the District Court palpably exceeded its authority when it ignored Congress' considered response to this line of reasoning. In the first place, assuming that a small number of women could be drafted for noncombat roles, Congress simply did not consider it worth the added burdens of including women in draft and registration plans. [Congress] also concluded that whatever the need for women for noncombat roles during mobilization, whether 80,000 or less, it could be met by volunteers. Most significantly, Congress determined that staffing non-combat positions with women during a mobilization would be positively detrimental to the important goal of military flexibility. [In sum], Congress carefully evaluated the testimony that 80,000 women conscripts could be usefully employed in the event of a draft and rejected it in the permissible exercise of its constitutional responsibility. The

---

2. "Justice Marshall's suggestion that since Congress focused on the need for combat troops in authorizing male-only registration, the Court could "be forced to declare the male-only registration program unconstitutional" in the event of a peacetime draft misreads our opinion. The perceived need for combat or combat-eligible troops in the event of a draft was not limited to a wartime [draft]." [Footnote by Justice Rehnquist.]

District Court was quite wrong in undertaking an independent evaluation of this evidence, rather than adopting an appropriately deferential examination of *Congress'* evaluation of that evidence."

There were two dissenting opinions. Justice WHITE, joined by Justice Brennan, stated: "I assume what has not been challenged in this case—that excluding women from combat positions does not offend the Constitution. Granting that, it is self-evident that if during mobilization for war, all noncombat military positions must be filled by combat-qualified personnel available to be moved into combat positions, there would be no occasion whatsoever to have any women in the Army, whether as volunteers or inductees. The Court appears to say that Congress concluded as much and that we should accept that judgment even though the serious view of the Executive Branch, including the responsible military services, is to the contrary. The Court's position in this regard is most unpersuasive. I perceive little, if any, indication that Congress itself concluded that every position in the military, no matter how far removed from combat, must be filled with combat-ready men. Common sense and experience in recent wars, where women volunteers were employed in substantial numbers, belie this view of reality. It should not be ascribed to Congress, particularly in the face of the testimony of military authorities [that] there would be a substantial number of positions in the services that could be filled by women both in peacetime and during mobilization, even though they are ineligible for combat.

"I would also have little difficulty agreeing to a reversal if all the women who could serve in wartime without adversely affecting combat readiness could predictably be obtained through volunteers. In that event, [equal protection] would not require the United States to go through, and a large segment of the population to be burdened with, the expensive and essentially useless procedure of registering women. But [the] record as I understand it supports the District Court's finding that the services would have to conscript at least 80,000 persons to fill positions for which combat-ready men would not be required. [The] Court also submits that because the primary purpose of registration and conscription is to supply combat troops and because the great majority of noncombat positions must be filled by combat-trained men ready to be rotated into combat, the absolute number of positions for which women would be eligible is so small as to be de minimis and of no moment for equal protection purposes, especially in light of the administrative burdens involved in registering all women of suitable age. There is some sense to this; but at least on the record before us, the number of women who could be used in the military without sacrificing combat-readiness is not at all small or insubstantial, and administrative convenience has not been sufficient justification for the kind of outright gender-based discrimination involved in registering and conscripting men but no women at all. [I] discern no adequate justification for this kind of [discrimination]."

In another dissent, Justice MARSHALL, joined by Justice Brennan, stated: "The Court today places its imprimatur on one of the most potent remaining public expressions of 'ancient canards about the proper role of women.' [Although] the purpose of registration is to assist preparations for drafting civilians into the military, *we are not asked to rule on the constitutionality of a statute governing conscription.* [Consequently], we are not called upon to decide whether either men or women can be drafted at all, whether they must be drafted in equal numbers, in what order they should be drafted, or once inducted, how they are to be trained for their respective functions. In addition, this case does not involve a challenge to the statutes or policies that prohibit female members of the Armed Forces from serving in combat. It is with this understanding that I turn to the task at hand.

"[I] agree with the majority that 'none could deny that [the] Government's interest in raising and supporting armies is an important governmental interest.' Consequently, the first part of the [Craig] test is satisfied. But the question remains whether the discriminatory means employed itself substantially serves the statutory end. [Even] in the area of military affairs, deference to congressional judgments cannot be allowed to shade into an abdication of this Court's ultimate responsibility to decide constitutional questions. [In] my judgment, there simply is no basis for concluding in this case that excluding women from registration is substantially related to the achievement of a concededly important governmental interest in maintaining an effective defense. The Court reaches a contrary conclusion only by using an '[a]nnounced degre[e] of "deference" to legislative judgmen[t]' as a 'facile abstractio[n] [to] justify a particular result.' [Quoting majority opinion.]

"The Government does not defend the exclusion of women from registration on the ground that preventing women from serving in the military is substantially related to the effectiveness of the Armed Forces. Indeed, the successful experience of women serving in all branches of the Armed Services would belie any such claim. [The] justification for the MSSA's gender-based discrimination must therefore be found in considerations that are peculiar to the objectives of registration. The most authoritative discussion of Congress' reasons for declining to require registration of women is contained in the Report prepared by the Senate Armed Services Committee on the Fiscal Year 1981 Defense Authorization Bill.

"[The Court reasons] that since women are not eligible for assignment to combat, Congress' decision to exclude them from registration is not unconstitutional [discrimination]. There is a certain logic to this reasoning, but the Court's approach is fundamentally flawed. In the first place, although the Court purports to apply the [Craig] test, the 'similarly situated' analysis the Court employs is in fact significantly different from the [Craig] approach. Compare Kirchberg v. Feenstra (employing Craig v. Boren test) with id. (Stewart, J., concurring) (employing 'similarly situated' analysis).[1] The Court essentially reasons that the gender classification employed by the MSSA is constitutionally permissible because nondiscrimination is not necessary to achieve the purpose of registration to prepare for a draft of combat troops. In other words, the majority concludes that women may be excluded from registration because they will not be needed in the event of a draft.

"This analysis, however, focuses on the wrong question. The relevant inquiry under [Craig] is not whether a *gender-neutral* classification would substantially advance important governmental interests. Rather, the question is whether the gender-based classification is itself substantially related to the achievement of the asserted governmental interest. Thus, the Government's task in this case is to demonstrate that excluding women from registration substantially furthers the goal of preparing for a draft of combat troops. Or, to put it another way, the Government must show that registering women would substantially impede its efforts to prepare for such a draft. Under our precedents, the Government cannot meet this burden without showing that a gender-neutral statute would be a less effective means of attaining this end. [In] this case, the Government makes no claim that preparing for a draft of combat troops cannot be accomplished just as effectively by *registering* both men and women but *drafting* only

---

1. Kirchberg v. Feenstra, 450 U.S. 455 (1981) (decided on the same day as Michael M., above), struck down a now superseded provision of Louisiana's community property law that gave a husband the unilateral right to dispose of jointly owned community property without his spouse's consent. Justice Marshall's majority opinion applied the Craig intermediate scrutiny standard. Justice Stewart, joined by Justice Rehnquist, concurred only in the result, finding an equal protection violation because "men and women were similarly situated for all relevant purposes with respect to the management and disposition of community property."

men if only men turn out to be needed.[2] Nor can the Government argue that this alternative entails the additional cost and administrative inconvenience of registering women. This Court has repeatedly stated that the administrative convenience of employing a gender classification is not an adequate constitutional justification under the [Craig] test.

"The fact that registering women in no way obstructs the governmental interest in preparing for a draft of combat troops points up a second flaw in the Court's analysis. The Court essentially reduces the question of the constitutionality of male-only *registration* to the validity of a hypothetical program for *conscripting* only men. The Court posits a draft in which *all* conscripts are either assigned to those specific combat posts presently closed to women or must be available for rotation into such positions. By so doing, the Court is able to conclude that registering women would be no more than a 'gestur[e] of superficial equality,' since women are necessarily ineligible for every position to be filled in its hypothetical draft. If it could indeed be guaranteed in advance that conscription would be reimposed by Congress only in circumstances where, and in a form under which, all conscripts would have to be trained for and assigned to combat or combat rotation positions from which women are categorically excluded, then it could be argued that registration of women would be pointless. But of course, no such guarantee is possible. Certainly, nothing about the MSSA limits Congress to reinstituting the draft only in such circumstances. For example, Congress may decide that the All-Volunteer Armed Forces are inadequate to meet the Nation's defense needs even in times of peace and reinstitute peacetime conscription. In that event, the hypothetical draft the Court relied on to sustain the MSSA's gender-based classification would presumably be of little [relevance]. This difficulty comes about because both Congress and the Court have lost sight of the important distinction between *registration* and *conscription*. [The] fact that registration is a first step in the conscription process does not mean that a registration law expressly discriminating between men and women may be justified by a valid conscription program which would, in retrospect, make the current discrimination appear functionally related to the program that emerged.

"But even addressing the Court's reasoning on its own terms, its analysis is flawed because the entire argument rests on a premise that is demonstrably false. As noted, the majority simply assumes that registration prepares for a draft in which *every* draftee must be available for assignment to combat. But the majority's draft scenario finds no support in [the legislative record]. [For] my part, rather than join the Court in imagining hypothetical drafts, I prefer to examine the findings in the Senate Report and the testimony presented to Congress. [Testimony] about personnel requirements in the event of a draft established that women could fill at least 80,000 of the 650,000 positions for which conscripts would be inducted. Thus, with respect to these 80,000 or more positions, the statutes and policies barring women from combat do not provide a reason for distinguishing between male and female potential conscripts; the two groups are, in the majority's parlance, 'similarly situated.' As such, the combat restrictions cannot by themselves supply the constitutionally required justification for the MSSA's gender-based classification. Since the classification precludes women from being drafted to fill positions for which they would be qualified and useful, the Government must demonstrate that excluding women from those positions is substantially related to the achievement of an important governmental objective.

2. "Alternatively, the Government could employ a classification that is related to the statutory objective but is not based on gender, for example, combat eligibility. Under the current scheme, large subgroups of the male population who are ineligible for combat because of physical handicaps or conscientious objector status are nonetheless required to register." [Footnote by Justice Marshall.]

"[The] Court asserts that the President's decision to seek authority to register women was based on 'equity,' and concludes that 'Congress was certainly entitled [to] focus on the question of military need rather than "equity." ' In my view, a more careful examination of the concepts of 'equity' and 'military need' is required. [W]hat the majority so blithely dismisses as 'equity' is nothing less than the [guarantee of equal protection]. Moreover, whether Congress could subsume this constitutional requirement to 'military need' in part depends on precisely what the Senate Report meant by 'military need.' [However] the 'military need' statement in the Senate Report is understood, it does not provide the constitutionally required justification for the total exclusion of women from registration and draft plans. Recognizing the need to go beyond the 'military need' argument, the Court asserts that 'Congress determined that staffing noncombat positions with women during a mobilization would be positively detrimental to the important goal of military flexibility.' None would deny that preserving 'military flexibility' is an important governmental interest. But to justify the exclusion of women from registration and the draft on this ground, there must be a further showing that staffing even a limited number of noncombat positions with women would impede military flexibility. I find nothing in the Senate Report to provide any basis for the Court's representation that Congress believed this to be the case.

"[The] Senate Report concluded [that] drafting '*very large numbers* of women' would hinder military flexibility. The discussion does not, however, address the different question whether drafting only a *limited* number of women would similarly impede military flexibility. The testimony on this issue at congressional hearings was that drafting a limited number of women is quite compatible with [military flexibility]. In concluding that the Armed Services could usefully employ at least 80,000 women conscripts out of a total of 650,000 draftees that would be needed in the event of a major European war, the Defense Department took into account both the need for rotation of combat personnel and the possibility that some support personnel might have to be sent into combat. [There] is no reason why induction of a limited number of female draftees should any more divide the military into 'permanent combat' and 'permanent support' groups than is presently the case with the All-Volunteer Armed Forces.[3] After reviewing the discussion and findings contained in the Senate Report, the most I am able to say of the Report is that it [establishes] that induction of a large number of men but only a limited number of women [would be] substantially related to important governmental interests. But the discussion and findings in the Senate Report do not enable the Government to carry its burden of demonstrating that *completely* excluding women from the draft by excluding them from registration substantially furthers important governmental objectives."

3. MISSISSIPPI UNIVERSITY FOR WOMEN v. HOGAN, 458 U.S. 718 (1982): This 5 to 4 decision indicates that, despite the alleged weakening in Michael M. and Rostker, a majority of the Court continues to adhere to the intermediate level of scrutiny for sex classifications first established in Craig. The ruling sustained a male's equal protection challenge to the State's policy of excluding men from the Mississippi University for Women (MUW) School of Nursing. MUW, founded in 1884 (to provide for the "Education of White Girls"), is the oldest state-supported all-female university in the nation. Its

---

3. Moreover, Justice Marshall found no support in the legislative history for the majority's assertion that even "assuming that a small number of women could be drafted for noncombat roles, Congress simply did not consider it worth the added burdens of including women in draft and registration plans." All that the Senate Report had found, he insisted, was that there would be such burdens if "the law required women to be drafted *in equal numbers.*" The Senate Report had "simply failed to consider the possibility that a limited number of women could be drafted."

School of Nursing was established in 1971. Hogan, a registered nurse in Columbus, Miss., where MUW is located, was denied admission to the School's baccalaureate program. He was told he could only audit courses and would have to go to one of the State's coeducational nursing schools elsewhere in Mississippi to obtain credits toward a degree.

In sustaining Hogan's attack on the School of Nursing's single-sex admissions policy,[1] Justice O'CONNOR's majority opinion applied and restated the heightened level of scrutiny articulated in Craig and rejected the State's effort to justify its system as "benign" and "compensatory."[2] She sketched the framework for her analysis by stating "several firmly-established principles": "That this statute discriminates against males rather than against females does not exempt it from scrutiny or reduce the standard of review.[3] [Moreover], the party seeking to uphold a statute that classifies individuals on the basis of their gender must carry the burden of showing an 'exceedingly persuasive justification' for the classification. [Kirchberg v. Feenstra; Feeney (1979; p. 700 below).] The burden is met only by showing that the classification serves 'important governmental objectives and that the discriminatory means employed' are 'substantially related to the achievement of those objectives.' [Although] the test for determining the validity of a gender-based classification is straightforward, it must be applied free of fixed notions concerning the roles and abilities of males and females. Care must be taken in ascertaining whether the statutory objective itself reflects archaic and stereotypic notions. Thus, if the statutory objective is to exclude or 'protect' members of one gender because they are presumed to suffer from an inherent handicap or to be innately inferior, the objective itself is illegitimate. See [Frontiero (plurality opinion)]. If the State's objective is legitimate and important, we must next determine whether the requisite direct, substantial relationship between objective and means is present. The purpose of requiring that close relationship is to assure that the validity of a classification is determined through reasoned analysis rather than through the mechanical application of traditional, often inaccurate, assumptions about the proper roles of men and women. The need for the requirement is amply revealed by reference to the broad range of statutes already invalidated

1. Justice O'Connor repeatedly stated the ruling as a "narrow" one limited to MUW's professional nursing school: "[W]e decline to address the question of whether MUW's admissions policy, as applied to males seeking admission to schools other than the School of Nursing, violates the [14th Amendment]." But Justice Powell's dissent (noted more fully below) expressed doubt that the majority's analysis could be so limited. He thought the majority's limit on the scope of its ruling would be "welcome" if it left "MUW free to remain an all-women's university in each of its other schools and departments—which include four schools and more than a dozen departments." But in his view, the "logic of the Court's entire opinion [appears] to apply sweepingly to the entire university." As he saw it, "the issue properly before us is the single-sex policy of the University. [I] see no principled way—in light of the Court's rationale—to reach a different result with respect to other MUW schools and departments." But he added that, "given the Court's insistence that its decision applies only to the School of Nursing, it is my view that the Board and officials of MUW may continue to operate the remainder of the University on a single-sex basis without fear of personal liability."

2. Even though the Court focused on the "benign" justification, the case is noted here rather than in sec. 3E1 (with other "benign" sex discrimination cases) because of its importance in reiterating and restating the Craig standard for scrutiny of gender classifications. Most of the cases cited by the Court are printed either in this section or in sec. 3E1. This case can profitably be reexamined in considering the materials in sec. 3E1.

3. "Without question, MUW's admissions policy worked to Hogan's disadvantage. Although Hogan could have attended classes and received credit in one of Mississippi's state-supported coeducational nursing programs, none of which was located in Columbus, he could attend only by driving a considerable distance from his home. A similarly situated female would not have been required to choose between foregoing credit and bearing that inconvenience. [The] policy of denying males the right to obtain credit toward a baccalaureate degree [imposed] upon Hogan 'a burden he would not bear were he female.'" [Footnote by Justice O'Connor.]

by this Court, statutes that relied upon the simplistic, outdated assumption that gender could be used as a 'proxy for other, more germane bases of classification' [Craig] to establish a link between objective and classification." [4]

Justice O'Connor found that the MUW scheme could not survive scrutiny under this analysis. She rejected the State's primary justification, that the single-sex admissions policy "compensates for discrimination against women and, therefore, constitutes educational affirmative action." [5] She acknowledged that, in "limited circumstances, a gender-based classification favoring one sex can be justified if it intentionally and directly assists members of the sex that is disproportionately burdened." But such a "benign" justification requires "searching analysis." [E.g., Weinberger v. Wiesenfeld.] A state can establish a "compensatory purpose" justification "only if members of the gender benefited by the classification actually suffer a disadvantage related to the classification. [E.g., Califano v. Webster; Schlesinger v. Ballard.]" Here, however, the State had made "no showing that women lacked opportunities to obtain training in the field of nursing or to attain positions of leadership in that field when the MUW School of Nursing opened its doors or that women currently are deprived of such opportunities." She noted, for example, that, in 1970, "women earned 94 percent of the nursing baccalaureate degrees conferred in Mississippi and 98.6 percent of the degrees earned nationwide. [And] the labor force reflects the same predominance of women in nursing. [Accordingly], [r]ather than compensate for discriminatory barriers faced by women, MUW's policy of excluding males [tends] to perpetuate the stereotyped view of nursing as an exclusively woman's job. [MUW's] admissions policy lends credibility to the old view that women, not men, should become nurses, and makes the assumption that nursing is a field for women a self-fulfilling prophecy. Thus, we conclude that, although the State recited a 'benign, compensatory purpose,' it failed to establish that the alleged objective is the actual purpose underlying the discriminatory classification." [6]

Moreover, MUW's policy failed "the second part of the equal protection test, for the State has made no showing that the gender-based classification is substantially and directly related to its proposed compensatory objective. To the contrary, MUW's policy of permitting men to attend classes as auditors

---

4. There is some indication that the formulation in Hogan rather than Craig has become the Court's preferred phrasing of the "firmly-established principles" for evaluating gender-based classifications. In Heckler v. Mathews, 465 U.S. ___ (1984), Justice Brennan's opinion for a unanimous Court recited the above-quoted passage from Hogan, did not mention Craig, and stated that the Government had the burden of "(A) showing a legitimate and 'exceedingly persuasive justification' for the gender-based classification [and] (B) demonstrating 'the requisite direct, substantial relationship' between the classification and the important governmental objectives it purports to serve." In Heckler, the Court readily found that burden met. It sustained a provision pertaining to Social Security spousal benefits. The law had been passed in response to Califano v. Goldfarb (1977; p. 739 below), and it temporarily revived the gender classification found invalid in Goldfarb in order to protect the reasonable expectations of those who had planned retirement on the basis of the scheme invalidated in the earlier case. Here, the classification was adopted not to stereotype, but to protect reasonable expectations, and it was limited to a five-year period.

5. "In its Reply Brief, the State understandably retreated from its contention that MUW was founded to provide opportunities for women which were not available to men. Apparently, the impetus for founding MUW came not from a desire to provide women with advantages superior to those offered men, but rather [from] a desire to provide white women in Mississippi access to state-supported higher learning. [In] Mississippi, as elsewhere in the country, women's colleges were founded to provide some form of higher education for the academically disenfranchised." [Footnote by Justice O'Connor.]

6. "Even were we to assume that discrimination against women affects their opportunity to obtain an education or to obtain leadership roles in nursing, the challenged policy nonetheless would be invalid, for the State has failed to establish that the legislature intended the single-sex policy to compensate for any perceived discrimination. Cf. Califano v. Webster. The State has provided no evidence whatever that the Mississippi legislature has ever attempted to justify its differing treatment of men and women seeking nurses' [training]." [Footnote by Justice O'Connor.]

fatally undermines its claim that women, at least those in the School of Nursing, are adversely affected by the presence of men. [The] record in this case is flatly inconsistent with the claim that excluding men from the School of Nursing is necessary to reach any of MUW's educational goals. Thus, considering both the asserted interest and the relationship between the interest and the methods used by the State, we conclude that the State has fallen far short of establishing the 'exceedingly persuasive justification' needed to sustain the gender-based classification." [7]

Finally, Justice O'Connor rejected the argument that Congress had specifically authorized single-sex schools. Title IX of the Education Amendments Act of 1972, prohibiting gender discrimination in education programs that receive federal financial assistance, exempted undergraduate institutions if they "traditionally and continually from [their] establishment [have] had a policy of admitting only students of one sex." The State argued that this was a valid limit on the Equal Protection Clause enacted under the congressional power granted by § 5 of the 14th Amendment. Justice O'Connor expressed doubt that Congress had intended to exempt colleges "from any constitutional obligation"; she thought that the provision "at most" exempted colleges from the requirements of Title IX. But even if Congress "envisioned a constitutional exemption, the State's argument would fail." Congress' power under § 5, though "broad," was "limited to adopting measures to enforce the guarantees of the Amendment; § 5 grants Congress no power to restrict, abrogate, or dilute these guarantees" [quoting Justice Brennan's footnote [1] in Katzenbach v. Morgan (1966; p. 946 below)]. Justice O'Connor added: "The fact that the language of [the exemption] applies to MUW provides the State no solace: '[A] statute apparently governing a dispute cannot be applied by judges consistently with their obligations, when such an application of the statute would conflict with the Constitution. Marbury v. Madison.' Younger v. Harris (1971; p. 1602 below)." [8]

Justice POWELL, joined by Justice Rehnquist, submitted the most extensive dissent. He argued that the majority had unduly curtailed valuable diversity in higher education, that the heightened standard of review was inappropriate here, and that "[t]his simply is not a sex discrimination case. The Equal Protection Clause was never intended to be applied to this kind of case." In elaborating those conclusions, he objected to the Court's condemnation of the State's effort "to provide women with a traditionally popular and respected choice of educational environment. It does so in a case instituted by one man, who represents no class, and whose primary concern is personal convenience." The Court's emphasis on "sexual stereotyp[ing]," he insisted, had "no application whatever to [Hogan] or to the 'wrong' of which he complains. At best this is anomalous. And ultimately the anomaly reveals legal error—that of applying a heightened equal protection standard, developed in cases of genuine sexual stereotyping, to a narrowly utilized state classification that provides an *additional*

---

7. "Justice Powell's dissent suggests that a second objective is served by the gender-based classification in that Mississippi has elected to provide women a choice of educational environments. Since any gender-based classification provides one class a benefit or choice not available to the other class, however, that argument begs the question. The issue is not whether the benefited class profits from the classification, but whether the State's decision to confer a benefit only upon one class by means of a discriminatory classification is substantially related to achieving a legitimate and substantial goal." [Footnote by Justice O'Connor.]

Justice Powell responded to this comment as follows: "This is *not* the issue in this case. Hogan is not complaining about any benefit conferred upon women. Nor is he claiming discrimination because Mississippi offers no all-male college. As his brief states: 'Joe Hogan does not ask to attend an all-male college which offers a Bachelor of Science in nursing; he asks only to attend MUW' and he asks this only for his personal convenience."

8. See also the additional note on the important "Morgan power" aspect of this case at p. 971 below.

choice for women." Moreover, the Mississippi system should survive review even if a heightened standard of scrutiny were applied.

Reviewing the history of single-sex education, Justice Powell insisted that the "sexual segregation of students has been a reflection of, rather than an imposition upon, the preference of those subject to the policy." He noted that "generations of Americans, including scholars, have thought—wholly without regard to any discriminatory animus—that there were distinct advantages in this type of higher education." He conceded that coeducational institutions are now far more numerous, but argued that "their numerical predominance does not establish—in any sense properly cognizable by a court—that individual preferences for single-sex education are misguided or illegitimate, or that a State may not provide its citizens with a choice." He argued that the heightened standard of review generally applicable to sex discrimination was inappropriate here: "In no previous case have we applied it to invalidate state efforts to expand women's choices. Nor are there prior sex discrimination decisions by this Court in which a male plaintiff [had] the choice of an equal benefit." He insisted: "By applying heightened equal protection analysis to this case,[1] the Court frustrates the liberating spirit of the Equal Protection Clause. It forbids the States from providing women with an opportunity to choose the type of university they prefer."

Since Justice Powell did not view the case as "presenting a serious equal protection claim," he thought a "rational basis" analysis appropriate. But even if heightened scrutiny were applied, the record demonstrated that the gender-based distinction served "an important governmental objective by means that are substantially related to its achievement." He found the State's purpose of affording a choice "legitimate and substantial." And he rejected the majority's argument that MUW perpetuated stereotypes about nursing as a woman's job, noting that the School of Nursing was founded 90 years after the single-sex campus itself: "This hardly supports a link between nursing as a woman's profession and MUW's single-sex admission policy." He concluded: "[Mississippi's] accommodation [of] student choices is legitimate because it is completely consensual and is important because it permits students to decide for themselves the type of college education they think will benefit them most. Finally, Mississippi's policy is substantially related to its long-respected objective." The Court's decision ran counter to the traditional American "respect for diversity." All that was involved here was one man's claim to "a right to attend the college in his home community."[2]

---

1. "Even the Court does not argue that the appropriate standard here is 'strict scrutiny'—a standard that none of our 'sex discrimination' cases ever has adopted. Sexual segregation in education differs from the tradition typified by [Plessy v. Ferguson], of 'separate but equal' racial segregation. It was characteristic of racial segregation that segregated facilities were offered, not as alternatives to increase the choices available to blacks, but as the sole alternative. MUW stands in sharp contrast. Of Mississippi's eight public universities and 16 public junior colleges, only MUW considers sex as a criterion for admission. Women consequently are free to select a coeducational education environment for themselves if they so desire; their attendance at MUW is not a matter of coercion." [Footnote by Justice Powell.]

2. In a separate dissenting notation, Chief Justice BURGER, while agreeing generally with Justice Powell's dissent, emphasized that the holding was "limited to the context of a professional nursing school." He, unlike Justice Powell, read the majority opinion to suggest that "a State might well be justified in maintaining, for example, the option of an all-women's business school or liberal arts program." In another dissent, Justice BLACKMUN noted that the State had not "closed the doors of its educational system to males like Hogan" and added: "I have come to suspect that it is easy to go too far with rigid rules in this area of claimed sex discrimination, and to lose—indeed destroy—values that mean much to some people by forbidding the State from offering them a choice while not depriving others of an alternate choice. Justice Powell [advances] this theme well." Like Justice Powell, he was skeptical about the asserted narrowness of the majority opinion: "[T]here is inevitable spillover from the Court's ruling today.

ADDITIONAL PROBLEMS OF SEX DISCRIMINATION [1]

1. *What constitutes sex discrimination? The problem of sex-specific traits.* In GEDULDIG v. AIELLO, 417 U.S. 484 (1974), the majority held that exclusion of "disability that accompanies normal pregnancy and childbirth" from California's disability insurance system did not constitute "invidious discrimination." Stating that the challenged classification was not "based upon gender as such" (see footnote 2), Justice STEWART's majority opinion applied a very deferential standard of review: "California does not discriminate with respect [to] persons or groups. [The challenge is] to the asserted under-inclusiveness of the set of risks that the State has selected to insure. Although California has created a program to insure most risks of employment disability, it has not chosen to insure all such risks, and this decision is reflected in the level of annual contribution exacted from participating employees. [Under equal protection], a State 'may take one step at a time.' [Lee Optical.] Particularly with respect to social welfare programs, [the legislation need only be] rationally supportable.

"It is evident that a totally comprehensive program would be substantially more costly than the present program. [There] is nothing in the Constitution [that] requires the State to subordinate or compromise its legitimate interests solely to create a more comprehensive social security program than it already has. The State has a legitimate interest in maintaining the self-supporting nature of its insurance program [and] in distributing the available resources in such a way so as to keep benefit payments at an adequate level for disabilities that are covered rather than to cover all disabilities inadequately. [And it] has a legitimate concern in maintaining the contribution rate at a level that will not unduly burden participating employees. [These] policies provide an objective and wholly non-invidious basis for the State's decision not to create a more comprehensive insurance program than it has. There is no evidence in the record [that the selection of the risks] worked to discriminate against any definable group or class in terms of the aggregate risk protection derived by that group or class from the program.[2] There is no risk from which men are protected and women are not. Likewise, there is no risk from which women are protected and men are not."[3]

That ruling, it seems to me, places in constitutional jeopardy any state-supported educational institution that confines its student body in any area to members of one sex, even though the State elsewhere provides an equivalent program to the complaining applicant. [I] hope that we do not lose all values that some think are worthwhile (and are not based on differences of race or religion) and relegate ourselves to needless conformity."

1. In addition to the problems raised in this group of notes, note also the "benign" sex discrimination materials in sec. 3E1 below.

2. "The dissenting opinion to the contrary, this case is thus a far cry from cases like [Reed] and [Frontiero], involving discrimination based upon gender as such. The California insurance program does not exclude anyone from benefit eligibility because of gender but merely removes one physical condition—pregnancy—from the list of compensable disabilities. While it is true that only women can become pregnant, it does not follow that every legislative classification concerning pregnancy is a sex-based classification like those considered in Reed and Frontiero. Normal pregnancy is an objectively identifiable physical condition with unique characteristics. Absent a showing that distinctions involving pregnancy are mere pretexts designed to effect an invidious discrimination against the members of one sex or the other, lawmakers are constitutionally free to include or exclude pregnancy from the coverage of legislation such as this on any reasonable basis, just as with respect to any other physical condition. The lack of identity between the excluded disability and gender as such under this insurance program becomes clear upon the most cursory analysis. The program divides potential recipients into two groups—pregnant women and nonpregnant persons. While the first group is exclusively female, the second includes members of both sexes. The fiscal and actuarial benefits of the program thus accrue to members of both sexes." [Footnote by Justice Stewart.]

3. After the constitutional holding in Geduldig, the lower federal courts continued to hold in *statutory* claims based on Title VII of the 1964 Civil Rights Act that exclusions of pregnancies from private disability plans were illegal. But the Court put a stop to that trend in General Electric Co. v. Gilbert, 429 U.S. 125

Justice BRENNAN's dissent in Geduldig, joined by Justices Douglas and Marshall, concluded: "[B]y singling out for less favorable treatment a gender-linked disability peculiar to women, the State has created a double standard for disability compensation. [Such] dissimilar treatment of men and women, on the basis of physical characteristics inextricably limited to one sex, inevitably constitutes sex discrimination." Applying the strict scrutiny standard of his Frontiero opinion, he concluded that "the State's interest in preserving the fiscal integrity of [its] program simply cannot render the State's use of a suspect classification constitutional." [4]

2. *Discrimination against fathers of illegitimate children.* a. *Consent to adoptions.* The modern Court has repeatedly scrutinized, under the "intermediate" sex discrimination standard, discrimination against fathers of children born outside of marriage.[5] The 5 to 4 decision in CABAN v. MOHAMMED, 441 U.S. 380 (1979), invalidated a New York law granting the mother but not the father of an illegitimate child the right to block the child's adoption by withholding consent.[6] The provision was challenged by a father who had lived with his children and their mother as a natural family for several years. Justice POWELL's majority opinion concluded that the law was "another example of 'overbroad generalizations' in gender-based classifications" and that "no showing has been made that the [differentiation bears] a substantial relationship to the proclaimed interest of the State in promoting the adoption of illegitimate children." He dismissed the argument that the distinction could be justified by a fundamental difference between maternal and paternal relations—that 'a natural mother, absent special circumstances, bears a closer relationship with her child [than] a father does.'" He insisted that there was no "universal difference [at] every phase of a child's development," "even if unwed mothers as a class were closer than unwed fathers to their newborn infants." Although he conceded the importance of the State's interest in encouraging adoption, here the statutory scheme bore no "substantial relation" to that interest. While the "special difficulties attendant upon locating and identifying unwed fathers at

(1976). Although the Court recognized that the statutory ban on sex discrimination has a broader reach than the constitutional one, it closely tracked the Geduldig analysis in rejecting a claim that a private employer's plan violated the statute. But Gilbert was not read to bar all challenges to pregnancy-related schemes under Title VII. The Gilbert decision was distinguished in Nashville Gas Co. v. Satty, 434 U.S. 136 (1977), where pregnant employees were required not only to take pregnancy leaves and denied sick pay while on leave, but also lost all accumulated job seniority when they returned to work. That denial of accumulated seniority, according to Justice Rehnquist (who had written for the Court in Gilbert), violated the statute. He emphasized that here, unlike Gilbert, the employer had "not merely refused to extend to women a benefit that men cannot and do not receive, but has imposed on women a substantial burden that men do not suffer." (The Gilbert ruling was overturned by Congress when it amended Title VII in 1978. See 92 Stat. 2076.)

4. On what constitutes purposeful sex discrimination, note also the rejection of an equal protection attack on a state law granting an absolute preference to veterans for civil service positions, in Feeney (1979; p. 700 below).

5. Sex discrimination law has not been the only influence in these cases. To some extent,

the occasionally heightened scrutiny of illegitimacy classification (see sec. 3C1 below) has also played a role. Moreover, these cases are a part of the modern Court's tendency to find constitutional limits on family relations law, most often expressed in substantive due process developments, as noted in chap. 8, at p. 550 above. Could the cases in this note be analyzed more usefully as illegitimacy rather than sex discrimination cases? Or are they not truly equality cases at all, but rather substantive due process cases regarding the rights of parents? Note my colleague William Cohen's suggestion: "I conclude that defining the minimum rights of fathers of children born out of wedlock is a false equality problem, because the Due Process Clause would not permit achieving equality by denying rights to other parents. The issue thus is not one of discrimination. But, if that is so, are the cases dealing with the rights of non-marital children [sec. 3C2 below] also false equal protection cases? There may be no viable anti-discrimination principle that can be divorced from an inquiry into minimal natural rights." Cohen, "Is Equal Protection Like Oakland? Equality As a Surrogate for Other Rights," (forthcoming, —— Tul.L.Rev. —— 1985).)

6. The father could block adoption only by showing that the best interests of the child would not be served.

birth [might] justify a legislative distinction between mothers and fathers of newborns," "these difficulties need not persist past infancy. The State's interest in proceeding with adoption [of older children] can be protected by means that do not draw such an inflexible gender-based distinction as that made [here]." [7]

b. *Barring actions by the natural father for the wrongful death of an illegitimate child.* In a companion case to Caban, the Court rejected a sex discrimination attack on a Georgia law denying the father (but not the mother) the right to sue for his illegitimate child's wrongful death unless he had legitimated the child. PARHAM v. HUGHES, 441 U.S. 347 (1979). Once again, the Court divided 5 to 4; but here Justice Powell joined the Caban dissenters to reject the equal protection claim. Justice STEWART's plurality opinion, joined by Chief Justice Burger and Justices Rehnquist and Stevens, insisted that the law did not "invidiously discriminate against the [natural father] simply because he was of the male sex. The fact is that mothers and fathers of illegitimate children are not similarly situated. Under Georgia law, only a father can by voluntary unilateral action make an illegitimate child legitimate. Unlike the mother of an illegitimate child, [the] identity of the father will frequently be unknown. [Thus, the law] does not reflect any overbroad generalizations about men as a class, but rather the reality that in Georgia only a father can by unilateral action legitimate an illegitimate child. [The] statutory classification does not discriminate against fathers as a class but instead distinguishes between fathers who have legitimated their children and those who have not.[8] Such a classification is quite unlike those condemned in the Reed, Frontiero, and Stanton cases which were premised upon overbroad generalizations and excluded all members of one sex even though they were similarly situated with members of the other sex." Since the law did not "invidiously discriminate," only a more deferential review standard was appropriate, and that standard was readily met here.[9]

Justice WHITE's dissent, joined by Justices Brennan, Marshall and Blackmun, attacked the "startling circularity" in the plurality's argument: "The issue before the Court is whether Georgia may require unmarried fathers, but not unmarried mothers, to have pursued the statutory legitimization procedure in order to bring suit for the wrongful death of their children. Seemingly, it is

---

7. Justice STEWART's dissent emphasized that "gender-based classifications are not invariably invalid": "When men and women are not in fact similarly situated in the area covered by the legislation in question, the Equal Protection Clause is not violated. In my view, the gender-based distinction drawn by New York falls in [this] category. With respect to a large group of adoptions—those of newborn children and infants—unwed mothers and unwed fathers are simply not similarly situated." Here, to be sure, the father had established a paternal relationship with his children and was therefore "similarly situated to the mother." Though the sex discrimination challenge could therefore not be "lightly dismissed," he asserted that there was no invidious discrimination.

In another dissent, Justice STEVENS, joined by Chief Justice Burger and Justice Rehnquist, criticized the majority for imposing on the State "the burden not only of showing that the rule is generally justified [as he thought it clearly was] but also that the justification holds equally true for *all* persons disadvantaged by the rule." Since the law was justified in its most frequent applications (the adoption of very young children), the "mere fact that an otherwise valid general classification appears arbitrary in an isolated case is

not a sufficient reason for invalidating the entire rule." The Court's contrary approach, he charged, "can only be attributed to its own 'stereotyped reaction' to what is unquestionably, but in this case justifiably, a gender-based distinction." (Compare Lehr v. Robertson, 463 U.S. 248 (1983), where, with Justice Stevens writing for the majority, Caban was distinguished. The Court held that a father who had never had any significant relationship with his illegitimate child could be denied notice and hearing before the child's adoption.)

8. "The ability of a father to make his child legitimate under Georgia law distinguishes this case from Caban, [where] the father could neither change his children's status nor his own for purposes of the New York adoption statute." [Footnote by Justice Stewart.]

9. Justice POWELL's opinion concurring in the result purported to exercise the intermediate level of scrutiny of Craig, but found that standard met here. He concluded that "the gender-based distinction [is] substantially related to achievement of the important state objective of avoiding difficult problems in proving paternity after the death of an illegitimate child."

irrelevant that as a matter of state law mothers may not legitimate their children, for they are not required to do so in order to maintain a wrongful death action. That only fathers *may* resort to the legitimization process cannot dissolve the sex discrimination in *requiring* them to.[10] Under the plurality's bootstrap rationale, a State could require that women, but not men, pass a course in order to receive a taxi license, simply by limiting admission to the course to women."[11] Applying the Craig standard, he concluded that none of the moral and familial interests urged by the State warranted the sex discrimination in this case.[12]

3. *The proposed Equal Rights Amendment.* The proposed Equal Rights Amendment would provide that "[e]quality of rights under the law shall not be denied or abridged by the United States or by any State on account of sex" and would authorize Congress to enact implementing legislation. Although Congress submitted the Amendment to the states early in 1972 and about half the necessary number of states ratified it within a few months, the ratification effort ran into substantial obstacles thereafter. In 1978, Congress extended the period for ratification until 1982. On June 30, 1982, that extension period expired and the proposed amendment accordingly failed of ratification. Thirty-five states had ratified it, but the additional three required states could not be mustered. An identical amendment was introduced in Congress in 1983 and approved by the House Judiciary Committee in November 1983, after the Committee had rejected provisions that sought to narrow the scope of the ERA proposal by barring its applicability to such issues as abortion, military combat duty and the draft, and private or parochial education. The proposal was brought to the floor under suspension of the rules, a procedure designed to sharply curtail debate and bar changes. On November 15, 1983, the ERA proposal fell several votes short of the necessary two-thirds majority.

What would be the impact of the proposed Amendment?[13] Presumably, it would make sex a suspect classification. To what extent would that change the

10. "The plurality not only fails to examine whether required resort by fathers to the legitimization procedure bears more than a rational relationship to any state interest, but also fails even to address the constitutionality of the sex discrimination in allowing fathers but not mothers to legitimate their children. It is anomalous, at least, to assert that sex discrimination in one statute is constitutionally invisible because it is tied to sex discrimination in another statute, without subjecting *either* of these classifications on the basis of sex to an appropriate level of scrutiny." [Footnote by Justice White.]

11. "Men and women would therefore not be 'similarly situated.' Yet requiring a course for women but not for men is quite obviously a classification on the basis of sex." [Footnote by Justice White.]

12. For earlier decisions on the rights of fathers of illegitimate children, see Stanley v. Illinois, 405 U.S. 645 (1972), and Quilloin v. Walcott, 434 U.S. 246 (1978).

13. On the impact and desirability of the Amendment, see generally Brown, Emerson, Falk and Freedman, "The Equal Rights Amendment: A Constitutional Basis for Equal Rights for Women," 80 Yale L.J. 871 (1971), and "Equal Rights for Women: A Symposium on the Proposed Constitutional Amendment," 6 Harv. Civ.Rts.-Civ.Libs.L.Rev. 125 (1971).

On the Amendment and on the problems of sex discrimination generally, see Davidson, Gins-

burg and Kay, Cases and Materials on Sex-Based Discrimination (1974), and Babcock, Freedman, Norton and Ross, Sex Discrimination and the Law—Causes and Remedies (1975). These volumes also explore the details of statutory bans on sex discrimination—prohibitions which, like the details of statutes directed against racial discrimination, are beyond the scope of this book.

For modern and thoughtful efforts to reanalyze the problems of women and of sex discrimination, see, e.g., Freedman, "Sex Equality, Sex Differences, and the Supreme Court," 92 Yale L.J. 913 (1983); Williams, "The Equality Crisis: Some Reflections on Culture, Courts, and Feminism," 7 Women's Rts.L.Rep. 175 (1982); Karst, "Foreword: Equal Citizenship Under the Fourteenth Amendment," 91 Harv.L.Rev. 1 (1977); Karst, "Woman's Constitution," 1984 Duke L.J. 447; and Law, "Rethinking Sex and the Constitution," 132 U.Pa.L.Rev. 955 (1984). Note, e.g., Freedman's criticism of the dissenters in the Michael M. and Rostker cases for focusing on a means-ends analysis and on "irrationality" rather than on the moral and actual harms of sex discrimination. She argues that the Court should pursue an "explicitly normative theory of sex equality that identifies with some particularity the dynamics and harmful consequences of sexism." Law argues that sex equality doctrine must confront squarely the reality of categorical biological differences between men and women. She suggests: "To reconcile the ideal of human

results in the cases considered above? Would it bar all generalizations based on sex—even empirically valid ones? [14] Would it permit laws limited to physical sex differences? Classifications in the interests of privacy? [15]

---

equality with the reality of biological difference we must (1) begin to distinguish clearly between laws that classify on the basis of sex and laws that govern reproduction; (2) recognize that laws governing reproduction implicate equality concerns; and (3) establish a test that can determine when laws governing reproduction violate constitutional equality norms." (Recall the suggestion in chap. 8, sec. 3, above, that substantive due process-abortion issues should be viewed more clearly as sex equality concerns.)

Karst's 1984 article, above, is an especially creative and stimulating essay. In analyzing the present state of sex discrimination law (and its limitations), he notes that the "male conception of society underlies the very constitutional doctrine that women seek to use in effecting a reconstructed order of male-female relations." He explores the implication of an alternative constitutional approach, resting on the premise that women as a group "do tend to have a different perception of social relations and a different approach to moral issues." In that exploration, he stresses viewing the individual "as part of a network of relationships" that finds "security in connection" rather than separation and the competitive pursuit of individual power. One doctrinal consequence of such a view would have courts contribute to "the process of cooperative settlement" by "abandoning the requirement of a showing of discriminatory purpose, in favor of a principle recognizing a law's discriminatory impact as a constitutional harm requiring justification by the state." He also urges that constitutional law "should more overtly embrace the morality of care and responsibility," with consequences in a number of doctrinal areas (e.g., "renunciation of the 'state action' limitation in cases of discrimination"—see chap. 10, sec. 2— and recognizing broad affirmative state obligations to aid the poor, to fulfill state responsibility to alleviate "dehumanizing" harms).

14. In assessing claims of sex discrimination under the Constitution, the Court has frequently inveighed against differential treatment based on stereotypical, inaccurate generalizations. But what about *valid* generalizations? In Los Angeles Dept. of Water & Power v. Manhart, 435 U.S. 702 (1978), which arose in a statutory rather than a constitutional context, the Court gave its first careful consideration to differential treatment based on an *accurate* generalization—and found that the truth of the generalization did *not* justify different treatment of individuals on the basis of sex. Should the Manhart approach to Title VII govern in constitutional cases as well? Would it if the ERA were ratified?

The generalization in Manhart was that, "[a]s a class, women live longer than men." For that reason, a city pension plan required female employees to make larger contributions than male

workers; as a result, female employees received less take-home pay. Justice Stevens' majority opinion rejected the argument that the differential was defensible because the value of the pension benefits provided to males and females differed. He noted that the generalization here was "unquestionably true" but added: "It is equally true [that] all individuals in the respective classes do not share the characteristic which differentiates the average class representatives." Emphasizing that Title VII barred discrimination against "any *individual*," he concluded that the law barred "treatment of individuals as simply components of a racial, religious, sexual, or national class. [Even] a true generalization about the class is an insufficient reason for disqualifying an individual to whom the generalization does not apply." He added: "Even if the statutory language were less clear, the basic policy of the statute requires that we focus on fairness to individuals rather than fairness to classes. Practices which classify employees in terms of religion, race, or sex tend to preserve traditional assumptions about groups rather than thoughtful scrutiny of individuals." (Cf. Justice Stevens' opinion in Bakke, p. 745 below.)

Note also Arizona Governing Committee v. Norris, 463 U.S. 1073 (1983), applying the principles of Manhart to strike down Arizona's pension system for state employees that called for equal contributions by males and females. Employees were given the option of receiving benefits from one of several companies selected by the State. All of the companies paid lower pensions to females, using gender-based mortality tables. That violated Title VII, because "the classification of employees on the basis of sex is no more permissible at the pay-out stage of a retirement plan than at the pay-in stage [as in Manhart]." Although Manhart had recognized that equal employer contributions to all employees were permissible, with each retiree allowed to purchase pension plans on the open market, here the employer had selected the companies participating in the plan and thus was "legally responsible for the discriminatory terms" offered by the participating companies.

15. Note the responses to the "parade of horribles" raised against the Amendment, in Ginsburg, "The Fear of the Equal Rights Amendment" (The Washington Post, April 7, 1975). One of the allegedly baseless "horribles" Ginsburg mentioned was: "ERA will require unisex restrooms in public places." Her answer: "[N]ot so. Separate places to disrobe, sleep, perform personal bodily functions are permitted, in some situations required, by regard for individual privacy. Individual privacy, a right of constitutional dimension, is appropriately harmonized with the equality principle."

C. OTHER CLASSIFICATIONS ARGUABLY WARRANTING HEIGHTENED SCRUTINY

1. ALIENAGE

Introduction. In the early 1970s, the Burger Court elevated alienage classifications to the level of "suspect" ones warranting "strict scrutiny." In several cases, it invalidated state restrictions on aliens. By the late 1970s, however, the premises for considering alienage as a suspect classification came under increasing questioning, off and on the Court. A number of decisions sustained alienage classifications, state as well as federal ones. The modern Court's developing framework for scrutinizing alienage classifications represented a novel departure in equal protection doctrine: some alienage classifications continued to be subjected to strict scrutiny; but others, pertaining to "governmental functions" (or "political functions") were reviewed far more deferentially. That bifurcated scheme raises even more pressingly the recurrent questions about the Court's treatment of alienage: Is alienage justifiably a "suspect" classification under the various equal protection rationales for exercising special scrutiny regarding some classifying criteria? Would the Court have been wiser to deal with alienage issues in a different mode—e.g., by treating state alienage classifications not as "suspect" but as warranting special scrutiny because of the predominant federal interest in immigration and because of preemption principles? In examining these materials, consider especially whether the reasons justifying heightened scrutiny for race and sex classifications appropriately apply to alienage. Note that alienage is not an "unalterable" trait. Aliens are legitimately excluded from voting, as the Court has continued to recognize. Does the equal protection justification for careful scrutiny of alienage classifications rest solely, then, on the "political powerlessness" rationale and on the history of discrimination against some groups of aliens? And if heightened scrutiny for alienage classifications *is* justified, can the "political function" exception be defended—and how broadly can that exception be read without undermining the general suspectness of alienage classifications?

THE RISE OF STRICT SCRUTINY OF ALIENAGE CLASSIFICATIONS

1. *Graham v. Richardson and welfare benefits.* The Burger Court launched strict scrutiny in the alienage area in GRAHAM v. RICHARDSON, 403 U.S. 365 (1971), holding that states could not deny welfare benefits to aliens. Justice BLACKMUN's opinion announced: "[The] Court's decisions have established that classifications based on alienage, like those based on nationality or race, are inherently suspect and subject to close judicial scrutiny. Aliens as a class are a prime example of a 'discrete and insular' minority (see [the Carolene Products footnote]) for whom such heightened judicial solicitude is appropriate. Accordingly, it was said in [Takahashi v. Fish & Game Comm'n, 334 U.S. 410 (1948),[1] that] 'the power of a state to apply its laws exclusively to its alien inhabitants as a class is confined within narrow limits.'" Justice Blackmun was also unpersuaded by the effort to justify the restriction "on the basis of a State's 'special public interest' in favoring its own citizens over aliens in the distribution

---

1. Takahashi held that California's purported ownership of fish in its off-shore waters did not justify denying commercial fishing licenses to aliens. (Takahashi rested largely on preemption, federal supremacy grounds.)

of limited resources such as welfare benefits." He also offered a significant "additional" reason for the invalidation of the restriction: the "area of federal-state relations." Quoting from Takahashi, he stated: "The National Government has 'broad constitutional powers in determining what aliens shall be admitted to the United States, the period they may remain, [and the] regulation of their conduct before naturalization.'" Reviewing congressional control of immigration, he noted that "Congress has not seen fit to impose any burden or restriction on aliens who become indigent after their entry into the United States. [State] laws that restrict the eligibility of aliens for welfare benefits merely because of their alienage conflict with these overriding national policies in an area constitutionally entrusted to the Federal Government." [2]

2. *Bar admission and public employment.* Three years after Graham, a divided Court applied strict scrutiny to invalidate Connecticut's exclusion of resident aliens from law practice [IN RE GRIFFITHS, 413 U.S. 717 (1973)] and New York's law providing that only American citizens may hold permanent positions in the competitive classified civil service [SUGARMAN v. DOUGALL, 413 U.S. 634 (1973)]. Justice POWELL's majority opinion in Griffiths stated the appropriate scrutiny as follows: "In order to justify the use of a suspect classification, a State must show that its purpose or interest is both constitutionally permissible and substantial, and that its use of the classification is 'necessary [to] the accomplishment' of its purpose or the safeguarding of its interest." None of the asserted state interests was sufficiently substantial: neither the "undoubted interest in high professional standards" nor the role of lawyers in protecting clients' interests and serving as "officers of the Court" established that the State "must exclude all aliens from the practice of law." In Dougall, Justice BLACKMUN's majority opinion emphasized that the state barrier did not cover all high policymaking positions yet covered a number of menial ones. Accordingly, the restriction had "little, if any, relationship" to the State's "substantial" interest "in having an employee of undivided loyalty."

Justice Blackmun added a significant final section to his opinion in Dougall— a section that was to produce major inroads into the constitutional protection of aliens in the late 1970s. He stated that the Court had not held "that a State may not, in an appropriately defined class of positions, require citizenship as a qualification for office. [Such] power inheres in the State by virtue of its obligation [to] 'preserve the basic conception of a political community.' And this power and responsibility of the State applies, not only to the qualifications of voters, but also to persons holding state elective or important non-elective executive, legislative and judicial positions, for officers who participate directly in the formulation, execution, or review of broad public policy perform functions that go to the heart of representative government. [Such] state action [is] not wholly immune from scrutiny under [equal protection]. But our scrutiny will not be so demanding where we deal with matters resting firmly within a State's constitutional prerogatives. This is no more than a recognition of a State's historical power to exclude aliens from participation in its democratic political institutions." [3]

----

2. Justice HARLAN joined only the federal supremacy portion (not the equal protection part) of Justice Blackmun's opinion. [Despite the joint emphasis on equal protection and federalism principles in Graham, the major impact of the ruling in the immediately ensuing years was to encourage strict scrutiny under an equal protection rationale. That led to the invalidation of several state restrictions on aliens in such areas as employment and welfare, as the next text note illustrates.]

3. The "governmental function" or "political function" exception stated in Justice Blackmun's concluding passage was seen in the ensuing decade as increasingly undermining the general rule of strict scrutiny for alienage restrictions. See, e.g., Foley and Ambach, below; but see the 1984 ruling in Bernal v. Fainter at p. 673 below.

Justice REHNQUIST's dissent, applicable to both Griffiths and Dougall, questioned any extension of suspect classification analysis beyond the race area. He also objected to the reliance in

THE IMPAIRMENT OF STRICT SCRUTINY: DEFERENTIAL REVIEW UNDER THE "POLITICAL FUNCTION" EXCEPTION

1. In the late 1970s, the Court—drawing on the Dougall exception and typically reading it broadly—began to sustain a number of exclusions of aliens from public employment by exercising deferential review rather than strict scrutiny. The modern trend began with FOLEY v. CONNELIE, 435 U.S. 291 (1978), where Chief Justice BURGER's majority opinion held that New York could bar employment of aliens as state troopers. He conceded that the cases since Graham had struck down barriers to aliens on a strict scrutiny basis, but proceeded to state: "These exclusions struck at the noncitizen's ability to exist in the community, a position seemingly inconsistent with the congressional determination to admit the alien to permanent residence. It would be inappropriate, however, to require every statutory exclusion of aliens to clear the high hurdle of 'strict scrutiny' because to do so would 'obliterate all the distinctions between citizens and aliens, and thus depreciate the historic values of citizenship.' [The] practical consequence [is] that 'our scrutiny will not be so demanding where we deal with matters firmly within a State's constitutional prerogatives.' Dougall. The State need only justify its classification by a showing of some rational relationship between the interests sought to be protected and the limiting qualification." Recalling the Dougall exception regarding "important nonelective executive, legislative and judicial positions" held by "officers who participate directly in the formulation, execution, or review of broad public policy," he insisted that "we [must] examine each position in question to determine whether it involves discretionary decisionmaking, or execution of policy, which substantially affects members of the political community." Applying that approach, he found that the state police force fell within the Dougall exception: "Police officers in the ranks do not formulate policy, per se, but they are clothed with authority to exercise an almost infinite variety of discretionary powers. [Clearly] the exercise of police authority calls for a very high degree of judgment and discretion, the abuse or misuse of which can have serious impact on individuals. [It] would be as anomalous to conclude that citizens may be subjected to the broad discretionary powers of noncitizen police officers as it would be to say that judicial officers and jurors with power to judge citizens can be aliens. Police officers [are] engaged in the 'execution [of] broad public policy.'" He concluded: "In the enforcement and execution of the laws the police function is one where citizenship bears a rational relationship to the special demands of the particular position. A State may, therefore, [confine] the performance of this important public responsibility to citizens."[1]

Graham on the Carolene Products footnote rationale in order to include alienage within the suspect classifications category, as noted earlier. Moreover, he disagreed with the Court's suggestion that it was inappropriate to classify on the basis of alienage because it is a "status": "[There] is a marked difference between a status or condition such as illegitimacy, national origin, or race, which cannot be altered by an individual, and the 'status' of the [challengers here]." Insisting that the mere rationality test was applicable, he found it readily satisfied.

For examples of other decisions in which the application of equal protection strict scrutiny produced invalidation of restrictions on aliens, see Nyquist v. Mauclet, 432 U.S. 1 (1977) (state scholarships), and Examining Board v. Flores de Otero, 426 U.S. 572 (1976) (permission to practice civil engineering).

1. Justice STEWART's concurrence conceded that the judgment was "difficult if not impossible to reconcile" with "the full sweep of the reasoning and authority of some of our past decisions." Nevertheless, he joined the Chief Justice's opinion "because I have become increasingly doubtful about the validity of those decisions (in at least some of which I concurred)." A separate opinion by Justice BLACKMUN, concurring only in the result, stated that the decision was justified by the Dougall exception.

Justice MARSHALL's dissent, joined by Justices Brennan and Stevens, argued that state troopers did not perform functions placing them within the "narrow" Dougall exception, an ex-

2. AMBACH v. NORWICK, 441 U.S. 68 (1979), applied the Dougall exception and Foley to hold that a state may refuse to employ as elementary and secondary school teachers aliens who are eligible for citizenship but who refuse to seek naturalization. Justice POWELL, writing for the majority in the 5 to 4 decision, emphasized that, under the recent cases, a less demanding scrutiny was required when aliens were excluded from "state functions" that were "bound up with the operation of the State as a governmental entity." He noted: "The rule for governmental functions, which is an exception to the general standard applicable to classifications based on alienage, rests on important principles inherent in the Constitution": "[The] assumption of [citizenship status] denotes an association with a polity which, in a democratic republic, exercises the powers of governance. [It] is because of this special significance of citizenship that governmental entities [have] wider latitude in limiting the participation of noncitizens." Looking to the role of public education and "the degree of responsibility and discretion teachers possess in fulfilling that role," he found that "teaching in public schools constitutes a governmental function" for purposes of equal protection analysis. He stressed the importance of public schools in preparing individuals for participation as citizens and in "the preservation of the values on which our society rests," and he noted a teacher's "opportunity to influence the attitudes of students toward government, the political process, and a citizen's social responsibilities." Accordingly, it was "clear that public school teachers come well within the 'governmental function' principle recognized in [Dougall] and Foley." And the exclusion of aliens here was rationally related to the State's legitimate interest in furthering its educational goals.[2]

3. BERNAL v. FAINTER, 467 U.S. ___ (1984), identified a limit to the Dougall exception at last: The Court's 8 to 1 decision found that the exception could not justify the Texas barrier to aliens becoming notaries public.[3] Justice MARSHALL (who had dissented from all applications of the Dougall exception

ception he insisted "must be interpreted to include responsibility for actually setting government policy pursuant to a delegation of substantial authority from the legislature. [There] is a vast difference between the formulation and execution of broad public policy and the application of that policy to specific factual settings." And police officers' tasks fell in the latter category. Justice STEVENS, joined by Justice Brennan, also submitted a dissent.

2. Justice BLACKMUN's dissent, joined by Justices Brennan, Marshall and Stevens, stated: "There is [a] line [between] those employments that a State [may] restrict [to] citizens [and] those employments [that] the State may not deny to resident aliens. For me, the present case falls on the Dougall-Griffiths [side] of that line, rather than on the narrowly isolated Foley side." Moreover, he differed sharply with the majority's claim that the exclusion here could survive even rationality scrutiny. For example, New York was unconcerned with citizenship qualifications for teachers in private schools and permitted aliens to sit on certain local school boards. He also claimed the law swept indiscriminately and thought this ruling involving teachers was inconsistent with Griffiths, concerning attorneys. (Justice Powell answered these charges by noting, for example, that the exclusion of aliens from access to the bar implicated the right "to pursue a chosen occupation, not access to public employment," and that school board members

"teach no classes" and are typically unknown to the students.)

3. In the period between Ambach and Bernal, the Court had decided one other case involving the Dougall exception and found it applicable. In CABELL v. CHAVEZ-SALIDO, 454 U.S. 432 (1982) (further considered in Bernal v. Fainter), the majority sustained a California requirement that all "peace officers" be citizens as applied to resident aliens who sought to become "Deputy Probation Officer[s], Spanish-speaking." Reexamining the prior cases, Justice WHITE found the governing distinction to be that, "although citizenship is not a relevant ground for the distribution of economic benefits, it is a relevant ground for determining membership in the political community. [We] have concluded that strict scrutiny is out of place when the restriction primarily serves a political function. [The] exclusion of aliens from basic governmental processes is not a deficiency in the democratic system but a necessary consequence of the community's process of political self-definition." He emphasized the centrality of the "distinction between the economic and political functions of government," a distinction that he conceded "may be difficult to apply in particular cases." He outlined a two-step process to determine application of the political-economic distinction: "First, the specificity of the classification will be examined: a classification that is substantially overinclusive or underinclusive

to strict scrutiny) wrote for the majority and applied strict scrutiny. Justice Marshall's restatement of a law pertaining to exclusions of aliens included the following passages:

"As a general matter, a State law that discriminates on the basis of alienage can be sustained only if it can withstand strict judicial scrutiny. In order to withstand strict scrutiny, the law must advance a compelling State interest by the least restrictive means available. Applying this principle, we have invalidated an array of State statutes that denied aliens the right to pursue various occupations. [We] have, however, developed a narrow exception to the [rule]. This exception has been labelled the 'political function' exception and applies to laws that exclude aliens from positions intimately related to the process of democratic self-government. The contours of the 'political function' exception are outlined by our prior decisions. [Foley; Ambach; Cabell.] [We have] lowered our standard of review when evaluating the validity of exclusions that entrust only to citizens important elective and nonelective positions whose operations 'go to the heart of representative government.' [Dougall.] [We] have concluded that strict scrutiny is out of place when the restriction primarily serves a political function [rather than primarily affecting 'economic interests']. [Cabell.] To determine whether a restriction based on alienage fits within the narrow political function exception, we devised in Cabell a two-part test. 'First, the specificity of the classification will be examined: a classification that is substantially overinclusive or underinclusive tends to undercut the governmental claim that the classification serves legitimate political ends. [Second], even if the classification is sufficiently tailored, it may be applied in the particular case only to "persons holding state elective or important nonelective executive, legislative, and judicial positions," those officers who "participate directly in the formulation, execution, or review of broad public policy" and hence "perform functions that go right to the heart of representative government." ' " [4]

On the first part of that test, Justice Marshall found the law clearly not overinclusive, but thought the underinclusiveness issue less clear. For example, Texas law did not have a citizenship requirement for court reporters or its Secretary of State. But he found it unnecessary to decide this issue, because notaries public were not within the "political function" exception under the second part of the test. Even though they were designated as public officers by the state constitution, the Court had "never deemed the *source* of a position" dispositive; rather, "this Court has always looked to the actual *function* of the position as the dispositive factor. The focus of our inquiry has been whether a position was such that the officeholder would necessarily exercise broad discretionary power over the formulation or execution of public policies importantly affecting the citizen population—power of the sort that a self-governing community could properly entrust only to full-fledged members of that community."

tends to undercut the governmental claim that the classification serves legitimate political ends. [Second], even if the classification is sufficiently tailored, it may be applied in the particular case only to [those who] 'perform functions that go to the heart of representative government.' " He concluded that the restriction challenged here "passes both of [the] tests." He emphasized that all the categories of peace officers covered involved "law enforcement" functions. Moreover, deputy probation officers could be barred under that rationale. Justice White noted that "Foley and Ambach did not describe the outer limits of permissible citizenship requirements." Justice BLACKMUN, joined by Justices Brennan, Marshall and Stevens, dissented, arguing that the decision "rewrites the Court's precedents, ignores

history, defies common sense, and reinstates the deadening mantle of state parochialism in public employment. [I] find it ironic that the Court invokes the principle of democratic self-government to exclude from the law enforcement process individuals who have not only resided here lawfully, but who now desire merely to help the State enforce its laws."

4. "We emphasize, as we have in the past, that the political-function exception must be narrowly construed; otherwise the exception will swallow the rule and depreciate the significance that should attach to the designation of a group as a 'discrete and insular' minority for whom heightened judicial solicitude is appropriate." [Footnote by Justice Marshall.]

In applying this standard, Justice Marshall relied on the fact that the duties of notaries public, although important, were "essentially clerical and ministerial." In the absence of either policymaking responsibilities or broad discretion of the type exercised by teachers and other public employees, the duties would not be deemed to be within the Dougall exception.[5] Accordingly, strict scrutiny was required, and Justice Marshall readily found that the provision could not survive that scrutiny, finding that none of the asserted state interests was weighty enough to be considered "compelling."[6]

4. *Alienage restrictions and federal preemption: A more appropriate analysis?* Does the Court's course in alienage cases suggest that its equal protection emphasis is unwise? Note that in some of the cases, principles of federalism and preemption surfaced as alternate grounds of decision. At the end of the 1970s, commentators increasingly suggested that federalism concerns, not equal protection doctrine, provided the more satisfying explanation of the Court's rulings and the most persuasive basis for future development. Consider especially Note, "The Equal Treatment of Aliens: Preemption or Equal Protection?" 31 Stan.L.Rev. 1069 (1979), arguing that "suspect classifications" analyses "have not provided the Court with an intelligible basis for a review of restrictions based on alienage. Rather, the Court's opinions in this area seem to be following an unarticulated theory of preemption. Ironically, the Court had explicitly constructed much of this framework before its decision in Graham. Fundamental to this theory is the Court's belief that as the federal government, through the immigration scheme, 'invites' resident aliens to enter the country as permanent residents free of restriction—'on an equality of legal privileges with all citizens' [Takahashi]—it is not for the states to alter the terms of immigration with new burdens. Yet the Court appears to reason that since the federal government does not admit resident aliens to the *political* community—admission does not confer citizenship—the states may exclude resident aliens from state political offices and functions without offending federal power. [The] Court should recognize that its creation of a suspect classification of alienage has not been a successful experiment and should return to its pre-Graham theory of preemption for the equal treatment of aliens."[7]

For a rare modern Court decision striking down an alienage restriction on preemption rather than equal protection principles, see Toll v. Moreno, 458 U.S. 1 (1982). Although the District Court had relied on equal protection, Justice Brennan's majority opinion rested solely on the supremacy clause and therefore found it unnecessary to reach the equal protection issue. In the course of his opinion, he stated: "Commentators have noted [that] many of the

5. Recalling Griffiths, Justice Marshall commented: "If it is improper to apply the political function exception to a citizenship requirement governing eligibility for membership in a State bar, it would be anomalous to apply the exception to the citizenship requirement that governs eligibility to become a Texas notary."

6. In an earlier footnote, Justice Marshall had commented: "Only rarely are statutes sustained in the face of strict scrutiny. As one commentator observed, strict scrutiny review is 'strict' in theory but usually 'fatal' in fact. Gunther, 'Newer Equal Protection.' " (Justice REHNQUIST was the sole dissenter in Bernal, simply relying on his dissent in Dougall.)

All of the cases reviewed in the text involved legally resident aliens. One other case, involving illegal aliens, should be noted here, although it is printed later in this chapter. It is Plyler v. Doe, 457 U.S. 202 (1982), holding that Texas could

not deny free public education to "undocumented" alien children. It appears in sec. 4 below, at p. 787.

7. For an elaboration (and a pursuit of the implications) of the preemption model of the Stanford Note, see a later student Note, "State Burdens on Resident Aliens: A New Preemption Analysis," 89 Yale L.J. 940 (1980). The Yale Note proposes a standard "under which state laws that disproportionately burden aliens are preempted by the predominant federal interest in alienage, unless the state regulation is expressly authorized by Congress, or alternatively, can be analogized to a federal regulation from which an implicit authorization by Congress can be inferred." It concludes that "a preemption model better orders alienage jurisprudence than does equal protection analysis." [On preemption generally, see chap. 5, at p. 317 above.]

Court's decisions concerning alienage classifications, such as Takahashi, are better explained in preemption than equal protection terms." And he commented: "Takahashi and Graham stand for the broad principle that 'state regulation not congressionally sanctioned that discriminates against aliens lawfully admitted to the country is impermissible if it imposes additional burdens not contemplated by Congress.' " [8] The case struck down the University of Maryland's policy of granting preferential tuition and fees treatment to students with "in-state" status. "Nonimmigrant aliens" were not eligible for such status even if domiciled in Maryland. In reaching that result, Justice Brennan relied entirely on federal legislation: "In light of Congress' explicit decision not to bar [such] aliens from acquiring domicile, the State's decision to deny 'in-state' status to [such] aliens, *solely* on account of [the] alien's federal immigration status, surely amounts to an ancillary 'burden not contemplated by Congress' in admitting these aliens to the United States. [The] University's policy violates the Supremacy Clause." [9]

FEDERAL RESTRICTIONS ON ALIENS

1. *Public employment.* In HAMPTON v. MOW SUN WONG, 426 U.S. 88 (1976), the Court invalidated a Civil Service Commission (CSC) regulation barring resident aliens from employment in the federal competitive civil service—even while recognizing that "overriding national interests may provide a justification for a citizenship requirement in the federal service [though] an identical requirement may not be enforced by a State." Justice STEVENS' opinion found that the national interests offered in defense of the ban either (a) were not properly the concern of the CSC and had not explicitly emanated from Congress or the President, or (b) to the extent that they were within CSC competence, had not been evaluated fully by the CSC.

Though Justice Stevens recognized that "the paramount federal power over immigration and naturalization forecloses a simple extension" of Dougall to federal restrictions on aliens, he rejected the Government's "extreme position" that "federal power over aliens is so plenary that any agent of the National Government may arbitrarily subject all resident aliens to different substantive rules than those applied to citizens." He noted that the federal ban burdened a class "already subject to disadvantages not shared by the remainder of the community" and deprived "a discrete class of persons of an interest in liberty on a wholesale basis." Those considerations triggered constitutional concerns, and "some judicial scrutiny of the deprivation" accordingly was required. But he found it unnecessary to determine the substantive validity of the alien ban under the equal protection component of Fifth Amendment due process.[1] Instead, he

---

8. Justice Brennan added in a footnote: "Our cases do recognize, however, that a State, in the course of defining its political community, may, in appropriate circumstances, limit the participation of noncitizens in the State's political and governmental functions. See, e.g., [Cabell; Dougall]."

9. A lengthy dissent by Justice Rehnquist, joined by Chief Justice Burger, not only took exception to the majority's preemption approach but also challenged the equal protection argument relied on by the lower court. He argued that, in view of the Foley line of cases, there was "reason to doubt whether political powerlessness is any longer a legitimate reason for treating aliens as a 'suspect class.' " He argued that rationality review, easily met, was appropriate

here. Justice Rehnquist's comments on equal protection drew a strong response in a concurrence by Justice Blackmun, who noted that, "despite the vehemence with which his opinion is written, Justice Rehnquist has persuaded only one Justice to [join] his position. [I] cannot leave unchallenged his suggestion that the Court's decisions holding resident aliens to be a 'suspect class' no longer are good law."

1. Justice Stevens commented: "The concept of equal justice under law is served by the Fifth Amendment's guarantee of due process as well as by the Equal Protection Clause of the 14th Amendment. Although both Amendments require the same type of analysis, [the] two protections are not always coextensive. Not only does the language of the two Amendments differ, but

rested on the "narrower" ground that "essential procedures" had not been followed—"procedures" involving the source and the deliberativeness of the regulation. As he put it in his conclusion: "Since these residents were admitted as a result of decisions made by the Congress and the President, [due process] requires that the decision to impose [the] deprivation of an important liberty be made either at a comparable level of government or, if it is to be permitted to be made by the [CSC], that it be justified by reasons which are properly the concern of that agency." And those "structural due process" requirements had not been satisfied here.

Justice Stevens explained that when "an overriding national interest" is asserted as justification for a discriminatory rule which would be barred by equal protection if adopted by a state, "due process requires that there be a legitimate basis for presuming that the [federal] rule was actually intended to serve that interest." Here, there was no basis for such a presumption. He was willing to assume "that if the Congress or the President had expressly imposed the citizenship requirement, it would be justified by the national interest in providing an incentive for aliens to become naturalized, or possibly even as providing the President with an expendable token for treaty negotiating purposes." But those were not interests "which can reasonably be assumed to have influenced the CSC"; "we are not willing to presume that the [agency] was deliberately fostering an interest so far removed from [its] normal responsibilities." There was a third possible national interest, however, that *was* within the Commission's competence: "The administrative desirability of having one simple rule excluding all noncitizens when it is manifest that citizenship is an appropriate and legitimate requirement for some important and sensitive positions." That justification might make "administrative convenience" a "rational basis for the general rule," but it could not be given weight here, since there was nothing to indicate "that the Commission actually made any considered evaluation of the relative desirability of a simple exclusionary rule on the one hand, or the value to the service of enlarging the pool of eligible employees on the other." [2]

Justice REHNQUIST's dissent, joined by Chief Justice Burger and Justices White and Blackmun, charged the majority with enunciating "a novel conception" of procedural due process and evolving from it "a doctrine of delegation of legislative authority which [seems] quite contrary" to the precedents. Though the Court's "innovations" had some appeal in this case, he thought such appeal "outweighed by the potential mischief which the doctrine bids fair to make in other areas of the law." In his view, the majority "inexplicably melds together the concepts of equal protection, procedural and substantive due process." He argued that the majority had implicitly found "faulty" delegation of power to the CSC. That elaboration of delegation notions was not only unjustified by the due process precedents, but also "[flew] in the face of those cases which hold that the manner in which policies concerning aliens are made within the political branches of the government is not subject to judicial scrutiny." The "overriding national interest" involved here, he insisted, was not any "specific interest in excluding these particular aliens from the civil service, but a general interest in formulating policies toward aliens." He concluded: "Congress [could] have excluded aliens from the Civil Service.

more importantly, there may be overriding national interests which justify selective federal legislation that would be unacceptable for an individual State. On the other hand, when a federal rule is applicable to only a limited territory, such as the District of Columbia, and when there is no special national interest involved, the Due Process Clause has been construed as having the same significance as the Equal Protection Clause. [Bolling v. Sharpe.] [Here], we deal with a federal rule having nationwide impact [and involving a] paramount federal power."

2. Justices BRENNAN and MARSHALL joined the majority opinion "with the understanding that there are reserved the equal protection questions that would be raised by congressional or Presidential enactment of a bar on employment of aliens by the Federal Government."

The fact that it chose, in a separate political decision, to allow the [CSC] to make this determination does not render the governmental policy any less 'political' and, consequently, does not render it any more subject to judicial scrutiny."

2. *Medical benefits.* In MATHEWS v. DIAZ, 426 U.S. 67 (1976), the Court held that Congress may condition an alien's eligibility for participation in a federal Medicare program on (a) admission for permanent residence and (b) continuous residence in the United States for five years. Justice STEVENS once again wrote the prevailing opinion, but this time for a unanimous Court, emphasizing deferential standards of review. He reasoned that Congress, under its "broad power over naturalization and immigration," regularly makes rules that would be unacceptable if applied to citizens; disparate treatment of aliens and citizens does not demonstrate invidiousness. Turning to the welfare area, he insisted that congressional provision of some benefits to citizens "does not require it to provide like benefits for *all aliens.*" The "real question" was "not whether discrimination between citizens and aliens is permissible" but "whether the statutory discrimination *within* the class of aliens—allowing benefits to some aliens but not to others—" was valid. Justice Stevens' scrutiny was extremely deferential: "The reasons that preclude judicial review of political questions also dictate a narrow standard of review of decisions made by the Congress or the President in the area of immigration and naturalization." [This] case essentially involves nothing more than a claim that it would have been more reasonable for Congress to select somewhat different requirements of the same kind." [3]

2. ILLEGITIMACY

Introduction. The Court's course in reviewing state classifications based on illegitimacy has been (to put it mildly) a wavering one. In no area of classifications triggering occasional heightened scrutiny have the Court's actions been more unpredictable—and more inarticulate in explaining what degree of heightened scrutiny is warranted, and why. Does illegitimacy bear sufficient resemblance to race and sex to warrant the heightened scrutiny those classifications have elicited? This section surveys the Court's zigzag course and illustrates the uncertainties in this line of cases. What *is* clear is that, although the Court has never labelled illegitimacy a "suspect" classification, it has in fact exercised a degree of heightened scrutiny in most of the cases and has struck down illegitimacy classifications with some frequency. In examining these materials, consider whether a coherent approach can be drawn from the erratic pattern of uncertain reasoning and unpredictable results.

1. *The origin.* The modern Court's frequent encounters with illegitimacy classifications began in the late Warren years, in LEVY v. LOUISIANA, 391 U.S. 68 (1968), where the Court found a violation of equal protection in a law denying unacknowledged illegitimate children the right to recover for the wrongful death of their mother. The uncertain rationale of the cases is illustrated by this first one in the series: Justice DOUGLAS' majority opinion simultaneously hinted at rationality review and at heightened scrutiny. He stated: "[The] test [is] whether the line drawn is a rational one, [but] we have been extremely sensitive when it comes to basic civil rights and have not hesitated to strike down an invidious classification even though it had history

---

3. Note also the analogous deference to *illegitimacy* classifications in the immigration context, in Fiallo v. Bell (1977; p. 681 below).

and tradition on its side. The rights asserted here involve the intimate, familial relationship between a child and his own mother.[1] [Why], in terms of 'equal protection,' should the tortfeasors go free merely because the child is illegitimate? [Illegitimacy] has no relation to the nature of the wrong inflicted on the mother. [It] is invidious to discriminate against [the illegitimate children] when no action, conduct, or demeanor of theirs [2] is possibly relevant to the harm that was done the mother."

Justice HARLAN's dissent, joined by Justices Black and Stewart, called the decision a "constitutional curiosit[y]." Noting that "the interest one person has in the life of another is inherently intractable," he insisted that states could properly define eligible plaintiffs in wrongful death laws in terms of "their legal rather than their biological relation to the deceased." Emphasizing the biological rather than the legal relationship did not make a law "even marginally more 'rational,' [for] neither a biological relationship nor legal acknowledgement is indicative of the level of economic dependence that may exist between two persons." Moreover, the law had "obvious justification": to enforce requirements regarding acknowledgement of illegitimate children and to simplify proceedings "by reliance on formal papers."

2. *The wavering aftermath in the early 1970s.* Three years after Levy, Labine v. Vincent, 401 U.S. 532 (1971), indicated to many observers a substantial Court withdrawal from the heightened scrutiny suggested by Levy for state impositions of disadvantages on illegitimate children. In Labine, the dissenters in Levy joined with Chief Justice Burger and Justice Blackmun in distinguishing Levy and upholding an intestate succession provision which subordinated the rights of *acknowledged* illegitimate children to those of other relatives of the parent. Justice Black's brief majority opinion found remarkably little federal constitutional basis for review. One passage, indeed, suggested that there might not even be minimum rationality review, for he emphasized that, absent "a specific constitutional guarantee, it is for [the] legislature, not [this] Court, to select from among possible laws." But the post-Labine assertions of the demise of Levy proved exaggerated: one year later, in Weber v. Aetna Cas. & Sur. Co., 406 U.S. 164 (1972), Justice Powell's majority opinion followed Levy and distinguished Labine in holding that the claims of dependent unacknowledged illegitimate children to death benefits under a workmen's compensation law could not be subordinated to the claims of legitimate children. Justice Rehnquist was the sole dissenter.[3]

The wavering course continued in the mid-1970s. Mathews v. Lucas, 427 U.S. 495 (1976), sustained a Social Security Act provision disadvantaging many illegitimate children, explicitly rejected a plea to apply "strict scrutiny," and distinguished all prior rulings invalidating illegitimacy classifications. Justice Blackmun's majority opinion upheld a provision providing benefits for surviving dependent children. For many classes of children—all legitimate ones and some illegitimate ones—dependence was statutorily presumed; but other illegitimate children were subjected to an individualized burden of proving dependency. Although Justice Blackmun rejected the "suspect" label, he conceded that the

1. Recall the modern Court's increasing involvement with problems of family relations, under the aegis of substantive due process (chap. 8, at p. 550). Is it arguable that these illegitimacy cases fit better with a "fundamental rights" analysis, and that making such an approach explicit would provide greater coherence than the equal protection one that has typically been followed?

2. "We can say with Shakespeare: 'Why bastard, wherefore base? When my dimensions are as well compact, My mind as generous, and my shape as true, As honest madam's issue? Why brand they us With base? with baseness? bastardy? base, base?' King Lear, Act I, Scene 2." [Footnote by Justice Douglas.] [Compare the response in Justice Harlan's dissent: "Supposing that the Bard had any views on the law of legitimacy, they might more easily be discerned from Edmund's character than from the words he utters in defense of the only thing he cares for, himself."]

3. The Levy-Weber approach was solidified and applied in a series of subsequent cases. See, e.g., Gomez v. Perez, 409 U.S. 535 (1973).

"legal status of illegitimacy [is], like race or national origin, a characteristic determined by causes not within the control of the illegitimate individual, and it bears no relation to the individual's ability to participate in and to contribute to society. [Visiting] condemnation upon the child in order to express society's disapproval of the parents' liaisons 'is illogical and unjust.'" Laws based on such premises would be struck down as irrational; but "other, possibly rational, distinctions made in part on the basis of legitimacy [are not] inherently untenable." Moreover, "discrimination against illegitimates has never approached the severity or pervasiveness of the historic legal and political discrimination against women and Negroes," and distinctions based on illegitimacy do not "'command extraordinary protection from the majoritarian political process'" so as to require "exacting scrutiny." The Court's "possibly rational," less than "most exacting scrutiny," criterion was readily satisfied here. Though the Court insisted that its level of scrutiny was "not a toothless one," the challengers were required "to demonstrate the insubstantiality" of the means-ends relationship; and here, the statutory scheme reflected "reasonable empirical judgments." Unlike cases such as Weber and Levy, legitimacy here "was simply taken as an indication of dependency," a valid statutory criterion.[4]

3. *The late 1970s.* a. In TRIMBLE v. GORDON, 430 U.S. 762 (1977), the Court continued its uneasy search for an articulable (and consistently applied) standard of review of illegitimacy classifications. Trimble made clear that the Court's promise (in Mathews v. Lucas) that scrutiny of illegitimacy classifications would not be "toothless" was not an empty one. The 5 to 4 decision struck down a provision in the Illinois law governing intestate succession that barred inheritance by illegitimate children from their fathers.[5] Justice POWELL's majority opinion noted that the State had relied in part on its interest in "the promotion of [legitimate] family relationships," but stated that, in a case like this, equal protection "requires more than the mere incantation of a proper state purpose. [Since Labine], we have expressly [rejected] the argument that a State may attempt to influence the actions of men and women by imposing sanctions on the children born of their illegitimate relationships." The State had also relied on Labine "for another and more substantial justification": the "difficulty of proving paternity and the related danger of spurious claims." But Justice Powell insisted that, as in Lucas, a law relating to illegitimacy must be "carefully tuned to alternative considerations"; "[d]ifficulties of proving paternity in some situations do not justify the total statutory disinheritance of illegitimate children whose fathers die intestate." Here, the deceased had been found to be the father in a paternity action, and denying inheritance in such a context "graphically illustrate[d] the constitutional defect."[6]

4. Justice Stevens, joined by Justices Brennan and Marshall, dissented.

5. Justice Powell's opinion repeatedly deprecated the continuing vitality of Labine (the second case in the illegitimacy sequence, in 1971, above). At one point, he stated that Labine "is difficult to place in the pattern of this Court's equal protection decisions, and subsequent cases have limited its force as a precedent."

6. Justice Powell also rejected a State argument that its law mirrored the "presumed intention" of its citizens regarding the disposition of their property at death. He stated: "[We] do not think [the law] was enacted for this purpose [and] we will not hypothesize an additional state purpose" ignored by the highest state court. [Recall the "newer equal protection" theory, p.

691 above. Other facets of Trimble are considered in Lalli, which follows.]

A short dissenting statement by Chief Justice Burger and Justices Stewart, Blackmun and Rehnquist simply agreed with the highest court that the case was "constitutionally indistinguishable from Labine." Justice REHNQUIST submitted a long, separate dissent, a dissent that constitutes the most extensive attack by a Justice on the Court's modern equal protection jurisprudence. That dissent has been noted earlier, at p. 604 above. It argued that, beyond the area of clearly "suspect" classifications, very deferential rationality review (akin to Chief Justice Warren's in McGowan and McDonald (p. 601 above)) was all that was appropriate. Moreover, he articulated a particularly forceful challenge to the theory

b. The heightened scrutiny of Trimble did not produce stability in this area. Indeed, LALLI v. LALLI, 439 U.S. 259 (1978), cast doubt on the continuing vitality of Trimble and illustrates the divisions and uncertainties that illegitimacy classifications have generated on the modern Court. The decision upheld a New York law forbidding illegitimate children to inherit from their fathers by intestate succession (even though there was "convincing proof of paternity") unless there was a judicial finding of paternity during the father's lifetime. The Court was sharply divided. Justice Powell's plurality opinion was joined only by Chief Justice Burger and Justice Stewart; it found Trimble distinguishable. Justice Stewart, in a separate notation, stated that he agreed with Justice Powell. But Justice Rehnquist, who concurred solely in the judgment, rested on his *dissent* in Trimble. Justice Blackmun, in another concurrence in the judgment, was unconvinced by the effort to distinguish Trimble, urged that it be overruled, and stated that the Court "gratifyingly reverts to the principles set forth in Labine." Justice Brennan, joined by Justices White, Marshall and Stevens, insisted that Trimble warranted invalidating the law.

Justice POWELL found that the law was "substantially related" to the important state interests of providing for "the just and orderly disposition of property at death," in light of "the peculiar problems of proof [implicated] in paternal inheritance by illegitimate children." He added: "We do not question that there will be some illegitimate children who would be able to establish their relationship to their deceased fathers without serious disruption of the administration of estates and that, as applied to [them, the law] appears to operate unfairly. But few statutory classifications are entirely free from the criticism that they sometimes produce inequitable results. Our inquiry under [equal protection] does not focus on the abstract 'fairness' of a state law, but on whether the statute's relation to the state interests it is intended to promote is so tenuous that it lacks the rationality contemplated by the 14th Amendment. The Illinois statute in Trimble was constitutionally unacceptable because it effected a total statutory disinheritance of children born out of wedlock who were not legitimated by the subsequent marriage of their parents. [That law] was far in excess of its justifiable purposes. [The law here] does not share this defect. Inheritance is barred only where there has been a failure to secure evidence of paternity during the father's lifetime in the manner prescribed by the State. This is not a requirement that inevitably disqualifies an unnecessarily large number of children born out of wedlock." Justice BRENNAN's dissent argued that New York has available less drastic means of screening out fraudulent claims of paternity. In addition to requiring formal acknowledgments of paternity, New York might require illegitimates to prove paternity by an elevated standard of proof. "[In] any event, the fear that unknown illegitimates might assert belated claims hardly justifies cutting off the rights of known illegitimates such as [the claimant here]. The state interest in the speedy and efficient determination of paternity 'is completely served by public acknowledgment of parentage and simply [does not] apply to the case of acknowledged illegitimate children.' I see no reason to retreat from [Trimble]. The law discriminates against illegitimates through means not substantially related to the legitimate interests that the statute purports to promote."

and practice of means-oriented scrutiny such as that proposed by the "newer equal protection," as discussed in sec. 2 above.

In a case decided on the same day as Trimble, the Court made clear that deferential rather than heightened scrutiny was appropriate when the illegitimacy classification occurs in the federal immigration context. Fiallo v. Bell, 430 U.S. 787 (1977). (Recall the similarly deferential scrutiny for federal alienage classifications in Mathews v. Diaz (1976; p. 678 above).) Fiallo sustained the narrow definition of the "parent-child" relationship in federal immigration law, which excludes the relationship between an illegitimate child and the natural father from preferred immigration status, even though the relationship between an illegitimate child and the natural mother is included.

4. *The 1980s.* a. Despite the meandering course of decisions in the 1970s, the Court has continued to accord illegitimacy classifications more than deferential scrutiny. In MILLS v. HABLUETZEL, 456 U.S. 91 (1982), the Court struck down a Texas law requiring that a paternity suit to identify the natural father of an illegitimate child for the purpose of obtaining child support must be brought before the child is one year old. (Texas imposes no time limit on the right of a *legitimate* child to sue for support.) The one-year limit at issue in Mills was Texas' "less than generous" response to Gomez v. Perez, 409 U.S. 535 (1973), which had invalidated a Texas rule denying *any* support rights to illegitimate children. In Mills, the Justices once again found Texas' scheme unsatisfactory: the Court held that the special burden imposed on illegitimate children by the one-year limit was "not justified by the State's interest in avoiding the prosecution of stale or fraudulent claims."

Justice REHNQUIST (who had vehemently opposed any special scrutiny of illegitimacy classifications as recently as Trimble) wrote for the Court in Mills. He stated: "If Gomez and the equal protection principles which underlie it are to have any meaning, it is clear that the support opportunity provided by the State to illegitimate children must be more than illusory. The period for asserting the right to support must be sufficiently long to permit those who normally have an interest in such children to bring an action on their behalf despite the difficult personal, family, and financial circumstances that often surround the birth of a child outside of wedlock." He added, however, that the State was not required to "adopt procedures for illegitimate children that are coterminous with those accorded legitimate children. Paternal support suits on behalf of illegitimate children contain an element that such suits for legitimate children do not contain: proof of paternity. [Therefore], in support suits by illegitimate children more than in support suits by legitimate children, the State has an interest in preventing the prosecution of stale or fraudulent claims, and may impose greater restrictions on the former than it imposes on the latter. Such restrictions will survive equal protection scrutiny to the extent they are substantially related to a legitimate state interest. See [Lalli; Trimble; Lucas]. The State's interest in avoiding the litigation of stale or fraudulent claims will justify those periods of limitation that are sufficiently long to present a real threat of loss or diminution of evidence, or an increased vulnerability to fraudulent claims."

Applying these principles, Justice Rehnquist drew "two related requirements" from the Equal Protection Clause: "First, the period for obtaining support granted by Texas to illegitimate children must be sufficiently long in duration to present a reasonable opportunity for those with an interest in such children to assert claims on their behalf. Second, any time limitation placed on that opportunity must be substantially related to the State's interest in avoiding the litigation of stale or fraudulent claims." Under these criteria, the Texas one-year period was too short, in violation of equal protection. The time limit did not provide illegitimate children "with an adequate opportunity to obtain support," in light of the obvious "obstacles to such suits that confront unwed mothers during the child's first year." Moreover, "this unrealistically short time limitation is not substantially related to the State's interest in avoiding the prosecution of stale or fraudulent claims. [We] can conceive of no evidence essential to paternity suits that invariably will be lost in only one year, nor is it evident that the passage of twelve months will appreciably increase the likelihood of fraudulent claims."

Five of the Justices expressed concern that Justice Rehnquist might in the future be unduly deferential to longer time limits. Their concern was aroused by a concluding footnote to the Court's opinion in which Justice Rehnquist noted that, after the commencement of the Mills litigation, Texas had amended its time limit provision "to increase to four years the period for asserting paternity claims" on behalf of illegitimate children. Justice Rehnquist commented: "The restrictions imposed by States to control problems of proof [often] take the form of statutes of limitation. [Because] such statutes 'are by definition arbitrary,' they are best left to legislative determination and control. Normally, therefore, States are free to set periods of limitation without fear of violating some provision of the Constitution." In response, Justice O'CONNOR, joined by Chief Justice Burger and Justices Brennan, Blackmun, and (in a separate opinion) Powell, submitted a concurring opinion: "Although I agree with the Court's analysis and result, I write separately because I fear that the opinion may be misinterpreted as approving the four-year statute of limitation now used in Texas." She elaborated: "[I]t is not only birth-related circumstances that compel the conclusion that the statutory distinction in this case [is] unconstitutional. [E.g.], the strength of the asserted state interest is undercut by the countervailing state interest in ensuring that genuine claims for child support are satisfied. [It] is also significant to the result today that a paternity suit is one of the few Texas causes of action not tolled during the minority of the plaintiff. Of all the difficult proof problems that may arise in civil actions generally, paternity, an issue unique to illegitimate children, is singled out for special treatment." She thought there was reason "to question whether the burden placed on illegitimates is designed to advance permissible state interests." Moreover, "the practical obstacles to filing suit within one year of birth could as easily exist several years after the birth of the illegitimate child." She accordingly concluded: "A review of the factors used in deciding that the one-year statute of limitation cannot withstand an equal protection challenge indicates that longer periods of limitation for paternity suits also may be unconstitutional. [Because] I do not read the Court's decision as prejudging the constitutionality of longer periods of limitation, I join it."

b. The Court consolidated its Mills approach a year later, in PICKETT v. BROWN, 462 U.S. 1 (1983). It invalidated a Tennessee law that was, for all practical purposes, identical to the Texas one struck down in Mills, except that Tennessee set a two-year rather than a one-year limitation period. Writing for a now unanimous Court, Justice BRENNAN concluded that "the principles discussed in Mills require us to invalidate this limitations period on equal protection grounds." Relying heavily on Justice O'Connor's concurring opinion in Mills, Justice Brennan found that the two-year limitation was still insufficient to provide illegitimate children with "an adequate opportunity to gain support," and in addition also failed to meet the second, "substantial relationship" part of the Mills test. He held that the two-year period was not "substantially related to the State's interest in avoiding the litigation of stale or fraudulent claims" because it was too small a difference from a one-year period, because in some instances the same reasoning would apply to claims brought on behalf of legitimate children (who were nevertheless not restricted by the two-year period), and because "the State's interest in preventing the litigation of stale or fraudulent paternity claims has become more attenuated as scientific advances in blood testing have alleviated the problems of proof surrounding paternity actions."

---

3. ADDITIONAL "SUSPECT" OR "QUASI–SUSPECT" CLASSIFICATIONS?

1. *Age.* Recall the criteria suggested by the earlier materials in this sec. 3 for according heightened scrutiny to certain classifications.[1] An attempt to establish heightened scrutiny for age classifications failed in MASSACHUSETTS BD. OF RETIREMENT v. MURGIA, 427 U.S. 307 (1976). As noted at p. 608 above, the majority's per curiam opinion applied rationality standards in sustaining a mandatory retirement law for uniformed State Police Officers. Before applying its deferential criteria, the majority rejected a suspect classification contention: "[The] class of uniformed State Police Officers over 50 [does not] constitute a suspect class for purposes of equal protection analysis. [While] the treatment of the aged in this Nation has not been wholly free of discrimination, such persons, unlike, say, those who have been discriminated against on the basis of race or national origin, have not experienced a 'history of purposeful unequal treatment' or been subjected to unique disabilities on the basis of stereotyped characteristics not truly indicative of their abilities. The class subject to the compulsory retirement feature of the Massachusetts statute consists of uniformed state police officers over the age of 50. It cannot be said to discriminate only against the elderly. Rather, it draws the line at a certain age in middle life. But even old age does not define a 'discrete and insular' group [Carolene Products, fn. 4] in need of 'extraordinary protection from the majoritarian political process.' Instead, it marks a stage that each of us will reach if we live out our normal span."[2]

Justice MARSHALL, the sole dissenter, argued once again against the "rigid two-tier model" of equal protection review and urged adoption of his "flexible," "sliding scale" standard. As noted earlier, he would focus "upon the character of the classification in question, the relative importance to individuals in the class discriminated against of the governmental benefits that they do not receive, and the state interests asserted in the support of the classification." With respect to the age classification, he commented: "[The] Court is quite right in suggesting that distinctions exist between the elderly and traditional suspect classes such as Negroes, and between the elderly and 'quasi-suspect' classes such as women or illegitimates. The elderly are protected not only by certain anti-discrimination legislation, but by legislation that provides them with positive benefits not enjoyed by the public at large. Moreover, the elderly are not isolated in society, and discrimination against them is not pervasive but is centered primarily in employment. The advantage of a flexible equal protection standard, however, is that it can readily accommodate such variables. The elderly are undoubtedly discriminated against, and when legislation denies them an important benefit—employment—I conclude that to sustain the legislation [Massachusetts] must show a reasonably substantial interest and a scheme reasonably closely tailored to achieving that interest."

2. *Mental illness and mental retardation.* Recall, that in SCHWEIKER v. WILSON, 450 U.S. 221 (1981; p. 616 above), a divided Court sustained a provision of a federal welfare program excluding, among others, certain inmates of public mental institutions from "comfort payments." The District Court had struck down the provision after accepting the challengers' claim that the

---

1. Note also the suggestion in Ely, Democracy and Distrust (1980), that "the doctrine of suspect classifications is a roundabout way of uncovering official attempts to inflict inequality for its own sake—to treat a group worse not in the service of some overriding social goal but largely for the sake of simply disadvantaging its members." Do any of these reasons justify add-ing to the category of established "suspect" and "quasi-suspect" classifications?

2. Recall also Vance v. Bradley (1979; p. 609 above), applying rationality standards to uphold mandatory retirement at age 60 for federal Foreign Service personnel.

statutory scheme should be "subjected to a heightened standard of review" because the mentally ill "historically have been subjected to purposeful unequal treatment; they have been relegated to a position of political powerlessness; and prejudice against them curtails their participation in the pluralist political system and strips them of political protection against discriminatory legislation." The Court did not reach that issue. Justice BLACKMUN's majority opinion stated that "we [intimate] no view as to what standard of review applies to legislation expressly classifying the mentally ill as a discrete group" because "this statute does not classify directly on the basis of mental health." Justice POWELL's dissent in the 5 to 4 decision found the exclusion invalid under the rationality test but added that the majority "too quickly dispatches the argument that [the law] classifies on the basis of mental illness. While it is true that not all mentally ill people are denied the benefit, and that some people denied the benefit are not mentally ill, it is inescapable that appellees are denied the benefit because they are patients in mental institutions." [3]

3. *Poverty and wealth classifications.* Dicta by the Warren Court had suggested that de jure wealth classifications should trigger strict scrutiny and that even de facto wealth classifications—governmental action that has a differential impact dependent upon economic condition—should have that consequence (even though commentators were skeptical that the Court was in fact prepared to apply such an approach across the board). Burger Court developments have made clear that the mere presence of wealth classifications or the mere existence of a disadvantageous impact on the poor does not suffice to evoke heightened review. The Burger Court's attitude is best reflected in Rodriguez (1973; the first principal case in sec. 4 below, at p. 789). The most generous Warren Court dicta came in two cases. In Harper v. Virginia Bd. of Elections (1966; p. 808 below), Justice Douglas' majority opinion striking down Virginia's $1.50 poll tax as a precondition for voting had stated: "Lines drawn on the basis of wealth or property, like those of race, are traditionally disfavored." Three years later in McDonald (1969; p. 601 above), Chief Justice Warren stated that "a careful examination on our part is especially warranted where lines are drawn on the basis of wealth or race, two factors which independently render a classification highly suspect and thereby demand a more exacting judicial scrutiny." Yet Harper was a case which also involved the fundamental interest

3. The Court may soon decide the related issue whether classifications based on mental retardation (rather than mental illness) warrant heightened scrutiny. On November 13, 1984, the Court granted certiorari in Cleburne v. Cleburne Living Center, 726 F.2d 191 (5th Cir. 1984). The Fifth Circuit had struck down a Texas city's zoning ordinance excluding group homes for the mentally retarded from an "apartment house district." Judge Goldberg, for a unanimous panel, concluded that a "combination [of] factors—historical prejudice, political powerlessness, and immutability—calls for heightened scrutiny of classifications discriminating against the mentally retarded. We are not prepared to say that they are a full-fledged suspect class, however. Strict scrutiny has been reserved for classifications [that] 'tend to be irrelevant to any proper legislative goal.' Plyler v. Doe. Though mental retardation is irrelevant to many policies, it *is* a relevant distinction in some cases [e.g., school programs and employment]. [Therefore], we hold that mentally retarded persons are only a 'quasi-suspect' class and that laws discriminating against the mentally retarded should be given intermediate scrutiny." He added: "In deciding that classifications against the mentally retarded deserve heightened scrutiny, we express no view about classifications involving the mentally ill. Some courts and commentators have suggested that mentally ill persons are a suspect or quasi-suspect class. See, e.g., [Note], 'Mental Illness: A Suspect Classification,' 83 Yale L.J. 1237 (1974). [In] any event, mental retardation is functionally different from mental illness; and the differences cut in favor of heightened scrutiny for the retarded. Mental retardation is not an emotional disorder but a learning problem; it arguably invokes fewer safety concerns than does mental [illness]. More important, mental retardation, unlike many mental illnesses, is an immutable disorder. [Finally], mental illness covers a broader spectrum of disorders and is more difficult to define than mental retardation." [Many of the modern lower federal court decisions applying intermediate scrutiny to classifications based on mental retardation and mental illness have relied on Plyler v. Doe (1982; p. 799 below).]

in the franchise. And McDonald in fact applied deferential review.[4] The suspectness of wealth classifications, then, was not clearly established by the Warren Court, though there were many who hoped or feared that it was.[5]

That wealth classifications alone (even arguably de jure ones) would not trigger strict scrutiny by the Burger Court first became clear in JAMES v. VALTIERRA, 402 U.S. 137 (1971). There, Justice BLACK's majority opinion rejected an equal protection challenge to a California constitutional requirement that "[n]o low rent housing project shall hereafter be developed [by] any state public body" without prior approval in a local referendum. The provision defined "low rent housing project" as any development "for persons of low income"—"persons or families who lack the amount of income which is necessary [to] enable them, without financial assistance, to live in decent, safe and sanitary dwellings, without overcrowding." He emphasized that the provision did not involve "distinctions based on race," and noted: "Provisions for referendums demonstrate devotion to democracy, not to bias, discrimination, or prejudice." He also rejected the contention that the provision "singled out" advocates of low-income housing by mandating a referendum while many other referenda only take place upon citizen initiative. He replied that "a law making procedure that 'disadvantages' a particular group does not always deny equal protection." The Court should not undertake analysis of a variety of governmental structures to determine which "is likely to 'disadvantage' any of the diverse and shifting groups that make up the American people." Moreover, low-income housing advocates were not in fact singled out: mandatory referenda were required in a variety of areas—e.g., the issuance of long-term local

4. See also the Griffin and Douglas cases (in the portion of sec. 4 below dealing with access to courts as a "fundamental interest"). The Court's special concern with economic status in those cases came in that judicial access context.

For a rare pre-Warren Court statement akin to the Warren Court dicta, see Justice Jackson's concurrence in Edwards v. California (1941; p. 315 above), invalidating the California anti-Okie law barring the bringing of nonresident indigents into the state. He remarked that "mere property status, without more," cannot be used to limit the rights of citizens, adding: " 'Indigence' in itself [is] a neutral fact—constitutionally an irrelevance, like race, creed, or color."

5. For an examination of the difficulties in considering de facto wealth classifications as suspect, see the comment at the end of the Warren era by Michelman, "Foreword: On Protecting the Poor Through the Fourteenth Amendment," 83 Harv.L.Rev. 7 (1969). He stated that considering wealth a suspect classification is "endemically troublesome as a matter of principle" and added: "The trouble is that, unlike a de facto racial classification which usually must seek its justifications in purposes completely distinct from its race-related impacts, a de facto pecuniary classification typically carries a highly persuasive justification inseparable from the very effect which excites antipathy—i.e., the hard choices it forces upon the financially straitened. For the typical form assumed by such a classification is simply the charging of a price, reasonably approximating cost, for some good or service which the complaining person may freely choose to purchase or not to purchase. A de facto pecuniary classification, that is, is usually nothing more

or less than the making of a market (e.g., in trial transcripts) or the failure to relieve someone of the vicissitudes of market pricing (e.g., for appellate legal services). But the risk of exposure to markets and their 'decisions' is not normally deemed objectionable, to say the least, in our society. Not only do we not inveigh generally against unequal distribution of income or full-cost pricing for most goods. We usually regard it as both the fairest and most efficient arrangement to require each consumer to pay the full market price of what he consumes. [Exceptions], of course, exist. The point is precisely that such 'commodities' as a vote, an effective defense to criminal prosecution, perhaps education, conceivably some others, are exceptional, and that the exceptions depend on the special qualities of the excepted commodities. It is uninformative at best, and very likely misleading as well, to defend such exceptional holdings through formulas of disparagement [—invidious or suspect classification; lines [drawn] on the basis of wealth; discrimination against the indigent—] which apply nonselectively to the pricing practice and refer not at all to any exceptional attributes in the excepted commodities." (For elaboration of Michelman's "minimum protection" approach, see the additional note on his analysis at p. 850 below, in that part of sec. 4 dealing with the Court's refusal to find a strict scrutiny-triggering interest in "necessities." See also Winter, "Poverty, Economic Equality, and the Equal Protection Clause," 1972 Sup.Ct.Rev. 41; cf. Clune, "The Supreme Court's Treatment of Wealth Discriminations Under the Fourteenth Amendment," 1975 Sup.Ct.Rev. 289.)

bonds. Justice MARSHALL's dissent, joined by Justices Brennan and Blackmun, insisted that the provision "on its face constitutes invidious discrimination": it was "an explicit classification on the basis of poverty—a suspect classification which demands exacting judicial scrutiny." He argued that the provision "explicitly" burdened low-income persons: "Publicly assisted housing developments designed to accommodate the aged, veterans, state employees, persons of moderate income, or any class of citizens other than the poor, need not be approved by prior referenda." The majority, he objected, had treated the provision "as if it contained a totally benign, technical economic classification." He insisted that "singling out the poor to bear a burden not placed on any other class of citizens tramples the values the 14th Amendment was designed to protect." [6]

D. THE "PURPOSEFUL DISCRIMINATION" REQUIREMENT AND THE "PURPOSE"– "IMPACT" DISTINCTION

1. TYPES OF DISCRIMINATION

Introduction. We now turn to the meaning of a principle repeatedly stated by the modern Court: "the invidious quality of a law claimed to be racially discriminatory must ultimately be traced to a racially discriminatory purpose"; governmental action is not unconstitutional "*solely* because it has a racially disproportionate impact." [1] The materials in sec. 3D typically involve the racial discrimination context, but the principle has prompted controversy in other areas as well, as in cases claiming sex discrimination. [2] Sec. 3D1 surveys some of the types of unconstitutional purpose. For example, discriminatory purpose may be shown by data regarding the administration of a law, not merely by a disadvantaging racial classification on the face of the law. Moreover, a law neutral in language and application may have been enacted with a purpose or motive to discriminate. All these instances can be viewed as "de jure" discrimination. Sec. 3D1 also begins the exploration of the constitutional validity of so-called "de facto" discrimination—governmental action that is racially neutral in its language, administration and purpose but which has a disadvantaging impact or effect. That exploration provides background for an increasingly central issue in modern discrimination cases, pursued in sec. 3D2: What are the relevant data, and what are the burdens of proof for the challenger and the government, in cases in which nonobvious purposeful discrimination is sought to be demonstrated. The "purpose"-"impact" distinction is the pervasive theme of sec. 3D2. Sec. 3D3, finally, deals with a specific area which sheds

---

6. Note that in Rodriguez (1973; p. 789 below), Justice Powell's majority opinion and Justice Marshall's dissent agreed that wealth was not as suspect a classification as race, and that in Harris v. McRae, one of the abortion funding cases (1980; p. 543 above), the majority stated that "this Court has held repeatedly that poverty, standing alone, is not a suspect classification." See also Jefferson v. Hackney (1972; p. 692 below).

Are there additional classifying criteria that bear sufficient resemblance to, e.g., race and sex to warrant heightened scrutiny? With respect to the handicapped, see Burgdorf & Burgdorf,

"[The] Qualifications of Handicapped Persons as a ['Suspect Class']," 15 Santa Clara Law. 855 (1975). Note that congressional legislation bars discrimination against an "otherwise qualified handicapped individual" in federally funded programs "solely by reason of his handicap." For a Court consideration of that statutory ban, see Southeastern Community College v. Davis, 442 U.S. 397 (1979). On homosexuality, see the materials in chap. 8, sec. 3, at p. 559 above.

1. See Washington v. Davis (1976; p. 693 below).

2. E.g., Feeney (1979; p. 700 below).

important light on the "purpose"-"impact" distinction—the problems encountered in the implementation of Brown v. Board of Education, the school desegregation decision (p. 635 above).

1. *Discrimination in the administration of law.* a. *Yick Wo.* Cases such as Strauder v. West Virginia in sec. 3A involved explicit, disadvantaging racial classifications on the face of the law. Yick Wo is the leading early case illustrating that a facially neutral law can be purposeful discrimination because of the manner of its administration. A San Francisco ordinance prohibited operating a laundry without the consent of the Board of Supervisors except in a brick or stone building. The Board granted permits to operate laundries in wooden buildings to all but one of the non-Chinese applicants, but to none of about 200 Chinese applicants.[3] A Chinese alien who had operated a laundry for many years was refused a permit. In YICK WO v. HOPKINS, 118 U.S. 356 (1886), the Court, in a habeas corpus proceeding, held the challenger's imprisonment unjustified. Justice MATTHEWS' opinion found discrimination in the *administration* of the law: "[T]he cases present the ordinances in actual operation, and the facts shown establish an administration directed so exclusively against a particular class of persons as to warrant and require the conclusion, that, whatever may have been the intent of the ordinances as adopted, they are applied by the public authorities charged with their administration [with] a mind so unequal and oppressive as to amount to a practical denial by the State of [equal protection]. Though the law itself be fair on its face and impartial in appearance, yet, if it is applied and administered by public authority with an evil eye and an unequal hand, so as practically to make unjust and illegal discriminations between persons in similar circumstances, material to their rights, the denial of equal justice is still within the prohibition of the Constitution. The present cases [are] within this class. It appears that [petitioners] have complied with every requisite, deemed by the law or by the public officers charged with its administration, necessary for the protection of neighboring property from fire, or as a precaution against injury to the public health. No reason whatever, except the will of the supervisors, is assigned why they should not be permitted to [carry on] their harmless and useful occupation, on which they depend for a livelihood. And while this consent of the supervisors is withheld from them and from two hundred others who have also petitioned, all of whom happen to be Chinese subjects, eighty others, not Chinese subjects, are permitted to carry on the same business under similar conditions. The fact of this discrimination is admitted. No reason for it is shown, and the conclusion cannot be resisted, that no reason for it exists except hostility to the race and nationality to which the petitioners belong, and which in the eye of the law is not justified."

b. *Proof of purposeful discrimination.* Yick Wo illustrates a frequent phenomenon: purposeful, hostile discrimination is inferred from data regarding administration of a facially neutral law. Reliance on statistical data showing a discriminatory pattern of administration has become commonplace in modern cases. Discrimination in jury selection was the earliest area;[4] the practices

---

3. There were about 320 laundries in the city (about 310 of them constructed of wood); 240 had Chinese owners. The challenger and more than 150 other Chinese had been arrested for violating the ordinance; the 80 or so non-Chinese operating laundries under similar conditions had been left alone by the law enforcement authorities.

4. See, e.g., Castaneda v. Partida, 430 U.S. 482 (1977), Carter v. Jury Comm'n, 396 U.S. 320 (1970), Hernandez v. Texas, 347 U.S. 475 (1954), and Avery v. Georgia, 345 U.S. 559 (1953).

In Castaneda, the respondent challenged the grand jury that indicted him in 1972. He showed that, although nearly 80% of the county's population had Spanish surnames, the average percentage of Spanish-surnamed grand jurors in the preceding decade was only 39%. (In 1972, 52.5% of persons on the grand jury list had such surnames.) Justice Blackmun's majority opinion in the 5 to 4 decision held that respondent had established a prima facie case of discrimination against Mexican-Americans, stating that "substantial underrepresentation of the

spread to other fields as well, such as discrimination in voting and employment.[5] The use of statistical and other empirical data allegedly showing purposeful discrimination has become not only an increasingly frequent practice but also an ever more controversial one. The Court's position on what data are relevant (and how much must be shown to prove purposeful discrimination) has become a critical issue in equal protection litigation, particularly in view of the modern Court's insistence that mere discriminatory effect does not suffice to show the constitutional violation, but that impact may provide probative data regarding the requisite discriminatory purpose. The cases after this group of introductory notes focus on that controversial issue of proof of purposeful discrimination.

2. *Discriminatory motivation.* In a number of modern cases, the Court has spoken at length about the relevance of proof of improper "motive" rather than "purpose." Often, the terms are used interchangeably. Does a focus on "motive" differ from the more common emphasis on discriminatory "purpose"? Typical "purpose" inquiries focus on "objective" empirical data about the administration of law. "Motive" inquiries, at first glance, seem to focus on the

group constitutes a constitutional violation, [if] it results from purposeful discrimination. [The] degree of underrepresentation must be proved by comparing the proportion of the group in the total population to the proportion called to serve as grand jurors, over a significant period of time. (He added in a footnote: "[If] a disparity is sufficiently large, then it is unlikely that it is due solely to chance or accident, and, in the absence of evidence to the contrary, one must conclude that racial or other class-related factors entered into the selection process.") [Once] the defendant has shown substantial underrepresentation of his group, he has made out a prima facie case of discriminatory purpose, and the burden then shifts to the State to rebut that case." He went on to hold that the State had not dispelled the presumption of purposeful discrimination by showing that "a governing majority of elected officials" in the county was Mexican-American. Similarly, he did not find dispositive the fact that three of the five jury commissioners in respondent's case were Mexican-American: he refused to assume that "human beings would not discriminate against their own kind" and insisted that the prima facie case of discriminatory purpose "can be rebutted only with evidence in the record about the way in which the commissioners operated and their reasons for doing so. It was the State's burden to supply such evidence, once respondent established his prima facie case. The State's failure in this regard leaves unchallenged respondent's proof of purposeful discrimination."

The major dissent was by Justice Powell, who argued that here, "where Mexican-Americans control both the selection of jurors and the political process, rational inferences from the most basic facts in a democratic society render improbable respondent's claim of an intent to discriminate against him and other Mexican-Americans. [I] am compelled to say that the Court today *has* 'lightly' concluded that the grand jury commissioners of this county have disregarded not only their sworn duty but also their likely inclination to assure fairness to Mexican-Americans." [Note, however, the divided Court's holding in Swain v. Alabama, 380 U.S. 202 (1965), that, without violating equal protection, a prosecutor

may use peremptory challenges to strike all blacks from the jury in a particular case. The majority emphasized that the peremptory challenge was, in the words of Blackstone, "'an arbitrary and capricious right; and it must be exercised with full freedom, or it fails of its full purpose.' [To] subject the prosecutor's challenge in any particular case to the demands [of equal protection] would entail a radical change in [its] nature and [operation]. [But] when the prosecutor, [in] case after case, whatever the circumstances, whatever the crime and whoever the defendant or the victim may be, is responsible for the removal of Negroes [with] the result that no Negroes ever serve on petit juries, [the] purposes of the peremptory challenge are being perverted." But the latter showing had not been made here. See Comment, "[A] Constitutional Blueprint for the Perpetuation of the All-White Jury," 52 Va. L.Rev. 1157 (1966).]

5. May the government, in cases claiming violations of equal protection, assert that individual variations in administration of law were not deliberate discriminations? See Snowden v. Hughes, 321 U.S. 1 (1944), stating that "unequal application" of statutes fair on their face is not a violation of equal protection "unless there is shown an element of intentional or purposeful discrimination." See also Oyler v. Boles, 368 U.S. 448 (1962), where the Court rejected a challenge to sentencing under a habitual criminal statute. The challenger claimed that there had been failure to prosecute other habitual offenders. Justice Clark noted that the allegations did not state whether the failure to prosecute was due to a deliberate policy or to lack of knowledge. If there was lack of knowledge, there would clearly be no equal protection violation, he insisted. He added: "Moreover, the conscious exercise of some selectivity in enforcement is not in itself a federal constitutional violation. Even though the statistics in this case might imply a policy of selective enforcement, it was not stated that the selection was deliberately based upon an unjustifiable standard such as race, religion, or other arbitrary classification. Therefore grounds supporting a finding of denial of equal protection were not alleged."

subjective state of mind of the defendant. May courts strike down otherwise valid official action because it was adopted for motives of racial hostility? Suppose there is proof of bad motive that contributed to the challenged action, but there is also a showing that the action would have been justifiable on grounds that are not constitutionally improper: should courts invalidate in that situation? This problem is explored further in some of the modern cases below.[6] Note as a preliminary matter, however, that pleas for judicial scrutiny in this area encounter the Court's institutional inhibitions regarding inquiries into improper motives.[7]

As background for consideration of that problem, consider the 5 to 4 decision in PALMER v. THOMPSON, 403 U.S. 217 (1971), holding that the city of Jackson, Mississippi, had *not* acted unconstitutionally in closing its public swimming pools after they had been ordered desegregated. Justice BLACK's majority opinion, after noting that there was no "affirmative duty" to operate swimming pools, rejected the argument that the closing was unconstitutional because it "was motivated by a desire to avoid integration." He asserted that "no case in this Court had held that a legislative act may violate equal protection solely because of the motivations of the men who voted for it." Ascertaining motivation was "extremely difficult." Though there was some evidence that the city had acted in part because of "ideological opposition to racial integration," there was also substantial evidence that the city had thought that the pools "could not be operated safely and economically on an integrated basis." He added that it was "difficult or impossible for any court to determine the 'sole' or 'dominant' motivation behind the choices of a group of legislators. Furthermore, there is an element of futility in a judicial attempt to invalidate a law because of the bad motives of its supporters. If the law is struck down for this reason, rather than because of its facial content or effect, it would presumably be valid as soon as the legislature or relevant governing body repassed it for different reasons." He conceded that there was "language in some of our cases" suggesting "that the motive or purpose behind a law is relevant to its constitutionality." "But," he added, "the focus in those cases was on the actual effect of the enactments, not upon the motivation which led the States to behave as they did." The record here showed "no state action affecting blacks differently from whites." Justice WHITE's dissent insisted that whites and blacks were not being treated alike when both were denied use of public services: "The fact is that closing the pools is an expression of official policy that Negroes are unfit to associate with whites." He asserted that forbidden "racial motive or animus" was a common focus of judicial inquiry—in the context of federal civil rights legislation, for example. He found that here "desegregation, and desegregation alone," was the cause of the closing. (Can Palmer be squared with the later cases, below, emphasizing the centrality of "discriminatory purpose"? See, e.g., the comments on Palmer in Washington v. Davis, the next principal case.[8])

6. See especially the first footnote in the Arlington Heights case (1977; p. 698 below).

7. Recall the earlier consideration of these inhibitions in chap. 4, sec. 2, above. See generally Brest, "Palmer v. Thompson: An Approach to the Problem of Unconstitutional Legislative Motive," 1971 Sup.Ct.Rev. 95; Ely, "Legislative and Administrative Motivation in Constitutional Law," 79 Yale L.J. 1205 (1970); and Symposium, "Legislative Motivation," 15 San Diego L.Rev. 925 (1978).

8. Compare Griffin v. County School Board of Prince Edward County, 377 U.S. 218 (1964), where the Court found the closing of public schools unconstitutional in one of the counties involved in the first group of school desegregation cases decided together with Brown v. Board of Education. The public school closing scheme included grants of public funds to white children to attend private schools. Justice Black emphasized that "public schools were closed and private schools operated in their place with state and county assistance, for one reason, and one reason only: to ensure [that] white and colored children in Prince Edward County would not, under any circumstances, go to the same school. Whatever nonracial grounds might support a State's allowing a county to abandon public schools, the object must be a constitutional one,

3. *De facto discrimination: Should differential effect be sufficient?* Suppose that no purposeful discrimination appears on the face of a statute or can be inferred from the manner in which it is administered, and that there is no evidence of racially hostile motivation by the lawmakers or administrators. Suppose, moreover, that the challenged action, taken for reasons independent of racial considerations, has a differential impact and disadvantaging effect on racial minorities. Is such action unconstitutional? Should such de facto, adventitious "discrimination" be treated like de jure, purposeful discrimination? By 1980, the answer was clear: the Court insists on proof of purposeful discrimination to establish a constitutional violation. And that had been clear at least since 1976, when Washington v. Davis, below, was decided. But in the early 1970s, a considerable number of lower courts had assumed that "de facto" discrimination was a constitutional violation. To some extent, that assumption was spurred by the Court's handling of discrimination claims resting on congressional statutes rather than the Constitution.

In a number of cases, the Court held that Congress had validly decided that discriminatory effect is adequate to establish a prima facie statutory claim. Note, e.g., GRIGGS v. DUKE POWER CO., 401 U.S. 424 (1971), a case arising under Title VII, the employment discrimination provision of the Civil Rights Act of 1964. Chief Justice BURGER's opinion for a unanimous Court read the Act as prohibiting an employer from subjecting job applicants to a general intelligence test and from requiring high school diplomas, where the effect was to disadvantage black applicants and where the criteria had not been shown by the employer to predict job performance. He stated that the Act required "the removal of artificial, arbitrary, and unnecessary barriers to employment where the barriers operate invidiously to discriminate on the basis of racial or other impermissible classification. [The Act] proscribes not only overt discrimination but also practices that are fair in form, but discriminatory in operation. [Good] intent or absence of discriminatory intent does not redeem employment procedures or testing mechanisms that operate as 'built-in headwinds' for minority groups and are unrelated to measuring job capability. Congress directed the thrust of the Act to the *consequences* of employment practices, not simply their motivation. More than that, Congress has placed on the employer the burden of showing that any given requirement must have a manifest relationship to the employment in question."[9] (In Griggs, the em-

---

and grounds of race and opposition to desegregation do not qualify as constitutional." (In Palmer, Justice Black distinguished Griffin because, "unlike the 'private schools,' in [there] there is nothing here to show the city is directly or indirectly involved in the funding or operation" of the swimming pools.)

See also Gomillion v. Lightfoot, 364 U.S. 339 (1960), finding that an Alabama law redefining the city boundaries of Tuskegee was a device to disenfranchise blacks in violation of the 15th Amendment. The statute, which altered "the shape of Tuskegee from a square to an uncouth twenty-eight-sided figure," was alleged to result in removing from the city "all save only four or five of its 400 Negro voters while not removing a single white voter or resident." Justice Frankfurter's opinion found that the allegations, if proved, would "abundantly establish" that the law "was not an ordinary geographic redistricting measure even within familiar abuses of gerrymandering." If the claims were proved, "the conclusion would be irresistible, tantamount for all practical purposes to a mathematical demon-

stration, that the legislation is solely concerned with segregating white and colored voters by fencing Negro citizens out of town so as to deprive them of their preexisting municipal vote."

Compare Wright v. Rockefeller, 376 U.S. 52 (1964), rejecting a claim that congressional districts in Manhattan were racially gerrymandered: appellants failed to prove that the legislature "was either motivated by racial considerations or in fact drew the districts on racial lines." For later Court considerations of claims that redistricting schemes—especially multimember districting—discriminated unfairly against racial minorities, compare Whitcomb v. Chavis (1971; p. 1632 below) with White v. Regester (1973; p. 1630 below). The latter case for the first time sustained a claim that a multimember district unconstitutionally tended "to cancel out or minimize the voting strength of racial groups."

9. Note also the congressional effect to impose an "effect" rather than a "purpose" requirement in the Voting Rights Act of 1965 and its

ployer had discriminated openly and purposefully prior to the adoption of the
1960 Act, but that background apparently was not central to the decision.
Accordingly, many lower courts read the Act as requiring simply an "effect"
showing for a prima facie case, and some applied a similar standard to
constitutional claims.)

But, as Washington v. Davis, below, made clear, while Congress may go a
long way toward substituting "effect" for "purpose," a showing of a violation of
the Constitution still requires proof that the discrimination was purposeful.
That holding was partly foreshadowed by a decision a year after Griggs,
JEFFERSON v. HACKNEY, 406 U.S. 535 (1972) (further noted at p. 852
below), rejecting a de facto discrimination claim in the welfare benefits context.
The case was an attack on a Texas scheme for computing AFDC benefits in
allocating the state's fixed amount of welfare money. A lower percentage of
"need" was granted to AFDC recipients than to beneficiaries of other categorical assistance programs. One of the grounds for attacking that scheme was that
"there is a larger percentage of Negroes and Mexican-Americans in AFDC than
in other programs." Justice REHNQUIST's majority opinion was not moved
by that "naked statistical argument." He noted that "the number of minority
members in all categories is substantial" and added that, "given the heterogeneity of the Nation's population, it would be only an infrequent coincidence that
the racial composition of each grant class was identical to that of the others."
And he went on to state a broader ground: "The acceptance of appellants'
constitutional theory would render suspect each difference in treatment among
the grant classes, however lacking in racial motivation and however otherwise
rational the treatment might be. Few legislative efforts to deal with the difficult
problems posed by current welfare programs could survive such scrutiny, and
we do not find it required by the 14th Amendment." [10]

PROVING PURPOSEFUL DISCRIMINATION:
THE MODERN COURT'S POSITION

Introduction. The following cases, from Washington v. Davis in 1976 to
Rogers v. Lodge in 1982, illustrate the modern Court's struggles with the
purposeful discrimination requirement. That purposeful discrimination is a
necessary basis to demonstrate a constitutional violation was settled fairly readily
in Washington v. Davis; but that ruling simply shifted the focus to another

successors, considered in chap. 10, sec. 4, below,
especially in Rome v. United States (1980; p. 937
below). Those materials also explore the *power*
of Congress to impose an "effect" criterion where
the constitutional prohibition is limited to "purposeful" discrimination.

The details of federal antidiscrimination laws
are beyond the scope of this book. On post-
Griggs interpretations of Title VII, see Lerner,
"Employment Discrimination: Adverse Impact,
Validity, and Equality," 1979 Sup.Ct.Rev. 17,
and, generally, Abernathy, Civil Rights—Cases
and Materials (1980).

10. The "purpose-effect" tension permeates
this and the following group of cases. Not only
the "purpose-effect" dichotomy, but also the
"process-result," "individual-group," and, of
course, "de jure-de facto" themes, reflect variants
of that tension. A recurrent underlying question
is whether the major focus of equal protection
should be on purifying the *processes* of decisionmaking from improper considerations (such as

racial hostility) or whether it should strive to
assure greater equality in *result* and condition.
Compare, e.g., Brest, "Foreword: In Defense of
the Antidiscrimination Principle," 90 Harv.L.
Rev. 1 (1976), with Fiss, "The Fate of an Idea
Whose Time Has [Come]," 41 U.Chi.L.Rev. 742
(1974), and Fiss, "Groups and the Equal Protection Clause," 5 Phil. & Pub. Affairs 107 (1976).
See also Perry, "The Disproportionate Impact
Theory of Racial Discrimination," 125 U.Pa.L.
Rev. 540 (1977). Perry notes: "[Laws] employing a racial criterion are usually difficult if not
impossible to justify on legitimate grounds. By
contrast, laws having a disproportionate racial
impact are quite easy to explain on legitimate
grounds because such laws serve a legitimate
function in addition to the function of racial
selection. Accordingly the standard of review
[for "disproportionate impact" cases should be]
more rigorous than that required by the rational
relationship test but less rigorous than that required by the strict scrutiny test."

battleground. How difficult is the plaintiff's burden of proving purposeful discrimination, and what data are relevant in meeting that burden? And what is the defendant's burden of justification after the plaintiff has established a prima facie case of discrimination? That the Court is indeed divided about these questions is demonstrated by the 1980s decisions, below.[1] Washington v. Davis reaffirmed that discrimination could be inferred from effects and contextual data, but its guidelines, and those in Arlington Heights a year later, could not wholly clarify the issue for the entire range of circumstances and for all types of constitutional claims. For example, those cases left room for dispute about the reach of the purposeful discrimination requirement. Do the "purpose" criteria apply only where the underlying claim is an individual one to be free from racial discrimination in such areas as employment and housing? Is it arguable that in other areas (such as jury discrimination or school desegregation or minority representation in the governmental structure), the underlying claim should be seen as one of group representation, with the consequence that a less burdensome "purpose" showing or even a mere "effect" showing might suffice?[2]

WASHINGTON v. DAVIS

426 U.S. 229, 96 S.Ct. 2040, 48 L.Ed.2d 597 (1976).

Mr. Justice WHITE delivered the opinion of the Court.

This case involves the validity of a qualifying test administered to applicants for positions as police officers in the District of Columbia Metropolitan Police Department. The test was sustained by the District Court but invalidated by the Court of Appeals. We are in agreement with the District Court and hence reverse the judgment of the Court of Appeals. [To] be accepted by the Department and to enter an intensive 17-week training program, the police recruit was required to satisfy certain physical and character standards, to be a high school graduate or its equivalent, and to receive a grade of at least 40 out of 80 on "Test 21," which is "an examination that is used generally throughout the federal service," which "was developed by the Civil Service Commission, not the Police Department," and which was "designed to test verbal ability, vocabulary, reading and comprehension." [Respondents'] evidence, the District Court said, warranted three conclusions: "(a) The number of black police officers, while substantial, is not proportionate to the population mix of the city. (b) A higher percentage of blacks fail the Test than whites. (c) The Test has not been validated to establish its reliability for measuring subsequent job performance." This showing was deemed sufficient to shift the burden of proof to the defendants in the action, petitioners here; but the court nevertheless

---

1. See especially Rogers v. Lodge (1982; p. 703 below) and Mobile v. Bolden (1980; discussed in Rogers v. Lodge).

These cases repeatedly raise questions similar to those noted in the text. Consider also whether the burden of showing purposeful discrimination does and should vary with the type of right asserted. For example, should a purposeful discrimination requirement apply as rigidly when the plaintiff asserts "group rights" (such as representational rights in the governmental structure—e.g., Rogers v. Lodge and Mobile v. Bolden, below) as it does in the context of "individual" rights (such as those against racial or sexual discrimination in employment, e.g., Washington v. Davis and Feeney, below)? Or should the plaintiff carry a lesser burden than purposefulness in "group rights" cases? The cases

printed in this section 3D2 are not the only ones to raise such issues. Note especially the quite lenient application of the purposeful discrimination requirement in the context of school desegregation, especially in the 1979 decisions in the Dayton and Columbus cases, in sec. 3D3 below, at p. 726. (For additional materials on the representational rights issue, see also the UJO case (p. 752 below) and the statutory cases under the Voting Rights Act in chap. 10, below (especially the 1980 decision in Rome v. United States, at p. 937).)

2. Recall the questions raised in the preceding footnote and see, e.g., Justice Stevens' concurrence in Washington v. Davis, which follows: "[The] burden of proving a prima facie case may well involve differing evidentiary considerations [in] different contexts."

concluded that on the undisputed facts respondents were not entitled to relief. The District Court relied on several factors. Since August 1969, 44% of new police force recruits had been black; that figure also represented the proportion of blacks on the total force and was roughly equivalent to 20- to 29-year-old blacks in the 50-mile radius in which the recruiting efforts of the Police Department had been concentrated. It was undisputed that the Department had systematically and affirmatively sought to enroll black officers many of whom passed the test but failed to report for duty. The District Court rejected the assertion that Test 21 was culturally slanted to favor whites and was "satisfied that the undisputable facts prove the test to be reasonably and directly related to the requirements of the police recruit training program and that it is neither so designed nor operates [sic] to discriminate against otherwise qualified blacks." It was thus not necessary to show that Test 21 was not only a useful indicator of training school performance but had also been validated in terms of job performance. [The Court of Appeals] announced that it would be guided by Griggs [the Title VII case at p. 691 above] [and] held that the statutory standards elucidated in that case were to govern the [constitutional] question tendered in this one. The court went on to declare that lack of discriminatory intent in designing and administering Test 21 was irrelevant; the critical fact was rather that a far greater proportion of blacks—four times as many—failed the test than did whites. This disproportionate impact, standing alone and without regard to whether it indicated a discriminatory purpose, was held sufficient to establish a constitutional violation, absent proof by petitioners that the test was an adequate measure of job performance in addition to being an indicator of probable success in the training program, a burden which the court ruled petitioners had failed to discharge.

[We] have never held that the constitutional standard for adjudicating claims of invidious racial discrimination is identical to the standards applicable under Title VII, and we decline to do so today. The central purpose of the Equal Protection Clause [is] the prevention of official conduct discriminating on the basis of race. [But] our cases have not embraced the proposition that a law or other official act, without regard to whether it reflects a racially discriminatory purpose, is unconstitutional *solely* because it has a racially disproportionate impact.

Almost 100 years ago, [Strauder] established that the exclusion of Negroes from grand and petit juries in criminal proceedings violated [equal protection], but the fact that a particular jury or a series of juries does not statistically reflect the racial composition of the community does not in itself make out an invidious discrimination forbidden by the Clause. "A purpose to discriminate must be present which may be proven by systematic exclusion of eligible jurymen of the proscribed race or by unequal application of the law to such an extent as to show intentional discrimination." Akins v. Texas, 325 U.S. 398 (1945). [See also, as to racial gerrymandering, Wright v. Rockefeller (1964; p. 691 above).] The school desegregation cases have also adhered to the basic equal protection principle that the invidious quality of a law claimed to be racially discriminatory must ultimately be traced to a racially discriminatory purpose. That there are both predominantly black and predominantly white schools in a community is not alone violative of [equal protection]. The essential element of de jure segregation is "a current condition of segregation resulting from intentional state action. [The] differentiating factor between de jure segregation and so-called de facto segregation [is] *purpose* or *intent* to segregate." [Keyes (p. 725 below).] [See also, in the welfare benefits context, Jefferson v. Hackney (1972; p. 692 above).]

This is not to say that the necessary discriminatory racial purpose must be express or appear on the face of the statute, or that a law's disproportionate impact is irrelevant in cases involving Constitution-based claims of racial discrimination. A statute, otherwise neutral on its face, must not be applied so as invidiously to discriminate on the basis of race. Yick Wo. It is also clear from the cases dealing with racial discrimination in the selection of juries that the systematic exclusion of Negroes is itself such an "unequal application of the law [as] to show intentional discrimination." A prima facie case of discriminatory purpose may be proved as well by the absence of Negroes on a particular jury combined with the failure of the jury commissioners to be informed of eligible Negro jurors in a community or with racially nonneutral selection procedures. With a prima facie case made out, "the burden of proof shifts to the State to rebut the presumption of unconstitutional action by showing that permissible racially neutral selection criteria and procedures have produced the monochromatic result."

Necessarily, an invidious discriminatory purpose may often be inferred from the totality of the relevant facts, including the fact, if it is true, that the law bears more heavily on one race than another. It is also not infrequently true that the discriminatory impact—in the jury cases for example, the total or seriously disproportionate exclusion of Negroes from jury venires—may for all practical purposes demonstrate unconstitutionality because in various circumstances the discrimination is very difficult to explain on nonracial grounds. Nevertheless, we have not held that a law, neutral on its face and serving ends otherwise within the power of government to pursue, is invalid under [equal protection] simply because it may affect a greater proportion of one race than of another. Disproportionate impact is not irrelevant, but it is not the sole touchstone of an invidious racial discrimination forbidden by the Constitution. Standing alone, it does not trigger the rule that racial classifications are to be subjected to the strictest scrutiny and are justifiable only by the weightiest of considerations.

There are some indications to the contrary in our cases. [See Palmer v. Thompson (1971; the swimming pool closing case at p. 690 above).] [Palmer] warned against grounding decision on legislative purpose or motivation, thereby lending support for the proposition that the operative effect of the law rather than its purpose is the paramount factor. But the holding of the case was that the legitimate purposes of the ordinance—to preserve peace and avoid deficits—were not open to impeachment by evidence that the councilmen were actually motivated by racial considerations. Whatever dicta the opinion may contain, the decision did not involve, much less invalidate, a statute or ordinance having neutral purposes but disproportionate racial consequences. That [Palmer] was not understood to have changed the prevailing rule is apparent from [Keyes]. [See also Jefferson v. Hackney.][1]

Both before and after [Palmer], however, various Courts of Appeals have held in several contexts, including public employment, that the substantially disproportionate racial impact of a statute or official practice standing alone and without regard to discriminatory purpose, suffices to prove racial discrimination violating [equal protection] absent some justification going substantially beyond what would be necessary to validate most other legislative classifications.[2] The cases impressively demonstrate that there is another side to the issue; but, with

1. To the extent that Palmer suggests a generally applicable proposition that legislative purpose is irrelevant in constitutional adjudication, our prior cases—as indicated in the text—are to the [contrary]. [Footnote by Justice White.]

2. At this point, a footnote by Justice White listed—and seemingly repudiated—16 such cases, mainly from the public employment area, but also from such contexts as urban renewal, zoning, public housing, and municipal services.

Among the cases he listed with apparent disapproval was the Arlington Heights case, a zoning case in which the Court had granted certiorari just a few months earlier. The inclusion of that case prompted Justice Brennan in dissent to question the "propriety" of Justice White's footnote and its "laundry list of lower court decisions." [The Court's 1977 decision in Arlington Heights is noted at p. 698 below.]

all due respect, to the extent that those cases rested on or expressed the view that proof of discriminatory racial purpose is unnecessary in making out an equal protection violation, we are in disagreement. [Test 21] seeks to ascertain whether those who take it have acquired a particular level of verbal skill; and it is untenable that the Constitution prevents the Government from seeking modestly to upgrade the communicative abilities of its employees rather than to be satisfied with some lower level of competence, particularly where the job requires special ability to communicate orally and in writing. Respondents, as Negroes, could no more successfully claim that the test denied them equal protection than could white applicants who also failed. The conclusion would not be different in the face of proof that more Negroes than whites had been disqualified by Test 21. That other Negroes also failed to score well would, alone, not demonstrate that respondents individually were being denied [equal protection] by the application of an otherwise valid qualifying test being administered to prospective police recruits.

Nor on the facts of the case before us would the disproportionate impact of Test 21 warrant the conclusion that it is a purposeful device to discriminate against Negroes. [The] test is neutral on its face and rationally may be said to serve a purpose the Government is constitutionally empowered to pursue. Even agreeing with the District Court that the differential racial effect of Test 21 called for further inquiry, we think the District Court correctly held that the affirmative efforts of the Metropolitan Police Department to recruit black officers, the changing racial composition of the recruit classes and of the force in general, and the relationship of the test to the training program negated any inference that the Department discriminated on the basis of [race].

Under [Title VII of the Civil Rights Act of 1964], Congress provided that when hiring and promotion practices disqualifying substantially disproportionate numbers of blacks are challenged, discriminatory purpose need not be proved, and that it is an insufficient response to demonstrate some rational basis for the challenged practices. It is necessary, in addition, that they be "validated" in terms of job performance in any one of several ways, perhaps by ascertaining the minimum skill, ability, or potential necessary for the position at issue and determining whether the qualifying tests are appropriate for the selection of qualified applicants for the job in question. However this process proceeds, it involves a more probing judicial review of, and less deference to, the seemingly reasonable acts of administrators and executives than is appropriate under the Constitution where special racial impact, without discriminatory purpose, is claimed. We are not disposed to adopt this more rigorous standard for the purposes of applying the Fifth and the 14th Amendments in cases such as this. A rule that a statute designed to serve neutral ends is nevertheless invalid, absent compelling justification, if in practice it benefits or burdens one race more than another would be far reaching and would raise serious questions about, and perhaps invalidate, a whole range of tax, welfare, public service, regulatory, and licensing statutes that may be more burdensome to the poor and to the average black than to the more affluent white.[3] Given that rule, such consequences would perhaps be likely to follow. However, in our view, extension of the rule beyond those areas where it is already applicable by reason

3. Goodman, De Facto School Segregation: A Constitutional and Empirical Analysis, 60 Calif.L.Rev. 275, 300 (1972) suggests that disproportionate-impact analysis might invalidate "tests and qualifications for voting, draft deferment, public employment, jury service, and other government-conferred benefits and [opportunities]; [s]ales taxes, bail schedules, utility rates, bridge tolls, license fees, and other state-imposed charges." It has also been argued that minimum wage and usury laws as well as professional licensing requirements would require major modifications in light of the unequal-impact rule. Silverman, Equal Protection, Economic Legislation, and Racial Discrimination, 25 Vand.L.Rev. 1183 (1972). [Footnote by Justice White.]

of statute, such as in the field of public employment, should await legislative prescription.[4]

Mr. Justice STEVENS, concurring [and joining the Court's opinion].

[The] requirement of purposeful discrimination is a common thread running through the cases summarized [by the Court]. Although it may be proper to use the same language to describe the constitutional claim in each of these contexts, the burden of proving a prima facie case may well involve differing evidentiary considerations. The extent of deference that one pays to the trial court's determination of the factual issue, and indeed, the extent to which one characterizes the intent issue as a question of fact or a question of law, will vary in different contexts. Frequently the most probative evidence of intent will be objective evidence of what actually happened rather than evidence describing the subjective state of mind of the actor. For normally the actor is presumed to have intended the natural consequences of his deeds. This is particularly true in the case of governmental action which is frequently the product of compromise, of collective decisionmaking, and of mixed motivation. It is unrealistic, on the one hand, to require the victim of alleged discrimination to uncover the actual subjective intent of the decisionmaker or, conversely, to invalidate otherwise legitimate action simply because an improper motive affected the deliberation of a participant in the decisional process. A law conscripting clerics should not be invalidated because an atheist voted for it. My point in making this observation is to suggest that the line between discriminatory purpose and discriminatory impact is not nearly as bright, and perhaps not quite as critical, as the reader of the Court's opinion might assume. I agree, of course, that a constitutional issue does not arise every time some disproportionate impact is shown. On the other hand, when the disproportion is as dramatic as in Gomillion or Yick Wo, it really does not matter whether the standard is phrased in terms of purpose or effect. Therefore, although I accept the statement of the general rule in the Court's opinion, I am not yet prepared to indicate how that standard should be applied in the many cases which have formulated the governing standard in different language.[1]

My agreement with the [Court's conclusion] rests on a ground narrower than the Court describes. I do not rely at all on the evidence of good-faith efforts to recruit black police officers. In my judgment, neither those efforts nor the subjective good faith of the District administration, would save Test 21 if it were otherwise invalid. There are two reasons why I am convinced that the challenge to Test 21 is insufficient. First, the test serves the neutral and legitimate purpose of requiring all applicants to meet a uniform minimum standard of literacy. Reading ability is manifestly relevant to the police function, there is no evidence that the required passing grade was set at an arbitrarily high level, and there is sufficient disparity among high schools and high school graduates to justify the use of a separate uniform test. Second, the same test is used throughout the federal service. The applicants for employment in the [D.C.] Police Department represent such a small fraction of the total number of persons who have taken the test that their experience is of minimal probative value in assessing the neutrality of the test itself. That evidence, without more, is not sufficient to overcome the presumption that a test which is this widely used by the Federal Government is in fact neutral in its

---

4. Justice White also rejected the statutory claim. Justice Stewart joined the constitutional part of Justice White's opinion. Justice Brennan, joined by Justice Marshall, dissented on the statutory issue and did not reach the constitutional claim. [The detailed interpretations of Title VII and similar statutes are beyond the scope of this book; they are noted only when they bear closely on an ongoing constitutional debate, as in Griggs, above.]

1. Specifically, I express no opinion on the merits of the cases listed [in footnote [2] to] the Court's opinion. [Footnote by Justice Stevens.]

effect as well as its "purpose" as that term is used in constitutional [adjudication].[2]

ARLINGTON HEIGHTS v. METROPOLITAN HOUSING CORP., 429 U.S. 252 (1977), reaffirmed the Washington v. Davis principle that "official action will not be held unconstitutional solely because it results in a racially disproportionate impact" and elaborated on the "subjects of proper inquiry" in determining whether an unconstitutional discriminatory purpose exists. The case involved a challenge to a Chicago suburb's refusal to grant a request to rezone certain property from a single-family to a multiple-family classification. A nonprofit developer planned to build federally subsidized townhouse units in the largely white suburb, so that low and moderate income tenants, including members of racial minorities, might live there. Though the lower federal courts found that the suburb's officials were motivated by a concern for the integrity of the zoning plan rather than by racial hostility, the Court of Appeals held the denial of the rezoning request unconstitutional because its "ultimate effect" was racially discriminatory. In reversing that decision, Justice POWELL's majority opinion repudiated the Court of Appeals' emphasis on effect rather than purpose, discussed some of the evidentiary data generally relevant to a search for the kind of "discriminatory purpose" required under Washington v. Davis, and found no showing of unconstitutional behavior in the record here. In his discussion of the Davis requirement of "[p]roof of racially discriminatory intent or purpose," he elaborated the ingredients of such an "intent or purpose":

"Davis does not require a plaintiff to prove that the challenged action rested solely on racially discriminatory purposes. Rarely can it be said that a legislature or administrative body operating under a broad mandate made a decision motivated solely by a single concern, or even that a particular purpose was the 'dominant' or 'primary' one." It was enough to show "that a discriminatory purpose has been a motivating factor in the decision."[1] But he made clear that proving such a motivating factor would not be easy: "Determining whether invidious discriminatory purpose was a motivating factor demands a sensitive

---

2. See also Justice Stevens' separate opinion in Rogers v. Lodge (1982; p. 703 below).

1. Note a significant footnote added by Justice Powell later in his opinion. He stated: "Proof that the decision by the Village was motivated in part by a racially discriminatory purpose would not necessarily have required invalidation of the challenged decision. Such proof would, however, have shifted to the Village the burden of establishing that the same decision would have resulted even had the impermissible purpose not been considered. If this were established, the complaining party in a case of this kind no longer fairly could attribute the injury complained of to improper consideration of a discriminatory purpose. In such circumstances, there would be no justification for judicial interference with the challenged decision. But in this case respondents failed to make the required threshold showing." [Justice Powell cited the articulation of a similar theme in a First Amendment context in Mt. Healthy City Bd. of Educ. v. Doyle, 429 U.S. 274 (1977).

Why should proof of discriminatory purpose not produce an immediate invalidation of the law, instead of merely shifting the burden of justification to the government, as Justice Powell states? If the "discriminatory purpose" inquiry is largely designed to cleanse or purify the decisionmaking process, what justifies validating a governmental decision that has been found to have been discriminatorily motivated? Arguably, the reason is similar to that often given to avoid *any* motivation inquiries—the futility of invalidating a law when the lawmakers could enact the very same law if their motives were pure. But would not true adherence to the process-cleansing rationale—the rationale that in part underlies the modern Court's emphasis on "purpose" rather than "effect"—warrant in effect a remand of the issue to the lawmakers for reconsideration on the basis of purely legitimate factors? Some legislators, "after being informed that they initially acted unconstitutionally, may refuse to vote for reenactment. [And] if a statute is invalidated on judicial review, the legislature often will decline or fail to consider a new law. In many situations, therefore, judicial action on the basis of motive results in an effective, not a futile, invalidation." Eisenberg, "Disproportionate Impact and Illicit Motive: Theories of Constitutional Adjudication," 52 N.Y.U. L.Rev. 36 (1977).

inquiry into such circumstantial and direct evidence of intent as may be available. The impact of the official action [may] provide an important starting point. Sometimes a clear pattern, unexplainable on grounds other than race, emerges from the effect of the state action even when the governing legislation appears neutral on its face. [E.g., Yick Wo; Gomillion.] The evidentiary inquiry is then relatively easy.[2] But such cases are rare. Absent a pattern as stark as that in Gomillion or Yick Wo, impact alone is not determinative,[3] and the Court must look to other evidence.[4]

"The historical background of the decision is one evidentiary source, particularly if it reveals a series of official actions taken for invidious purposes. The specific sequence of events leading up to the challenged decision also may shed some light on the decisionmaker's purposes. [E.g., Reitman v. Mulkey (1967; p. 890 below).] For example, if the property involved here always had been zoned [for multiple-family housing] but suddenly was changed to [a single-family classification] when the town learned of [the developer's] plans to erect integrated housing, we would have a far different case. Departures from the normal procedural sequence also might afford evidence that improper purposes are playing a role. Substantive departures too may be relevant, particularly if the factors usually considered important by the decisionmaker strongly favor a decision contrary to the one reached. The legislative or administrative history may be highly relevant, especially where there are contemporary statements by members of the decisionmaking body, minutes of its meetings, or reports. In some extraordinary instances the members might be called to the stand at trial to testify concerning the purpose of the [official action]."[5]

After summarizing those "subjects of proper inquiry," "without purporting to be exhaustive," Justice Powell turned to the record in this case and found (as had the lower courts) no demonstration of a "racially discriminatory intent." Though the refusal to rezone "arguably" bore more heavily on racial minorities, there was "little about the sequence of events leading up to the decision that would spark suspicion." The area in which the tract lay had long been zoned for single family use, and the rezoning request was handled according to the usual procedures. He concluded that the challengers had "simply failed to carry their burden of proving that discriminatory purpose was a motivating factor in the Village's decision. This conclusion ends the constitutional inquiry. The Court of Appeals' further finding that the Village's decision carried a discriminatory 'ultimate effect' is without independent constitutional significance."[6]

---

2. "Several of our jury selection cases fall into this category. Because of the nature of the jury selection task, however, we have permitted a finding of constitutional violation even when the statistical pattern does not approach the extremes of Yick Wo or Gomillion." [Footnote by Justice Powell.]

3. "This is not to say that a consistent pattern of official racial discrimination is a necessary predicate to a violation of [equal protection]. A single invidiously discriminatory governmental act [would] not necessarily be immunized by the absence of such discrimination in the making of other comparable decisions." [Footnote by Justice Powell.]

4. "In many instances, to recognize the limited probative value of disproportionate impact is merely to acknowledge the 'heterogeneity' of the nation's population. [Jefferson v. Hackney]" [Footnote by Justice Powell.]

5. "This Court has recognized [that] judicial inquiries into legislative or executive motivation represent a substantial intrusion into the workings of other branches of government. Placing a decisionmaker on the stand is therefore 'usually to be [avoided].'" [Footnote by Justice Powell.]

6. The challengers had also claimed violation of the Fair Housing Act; but since the Court of Appeals had not reached that issue, the Court remanded the case for consideration of the statutory claim.

Three of the Justices disagreed with the majority's handling of the case (Justice Stevens did not participate.) In a partial dissent, Justice MARSHALL, joined by Justice Brennan, thought that the entire case should have been remanded for further proceedings in light of the intervening decision in Davis. And in a separate dissent, Justice WHITE similarly objected to the majority's "failure to follow our usual practice in this

PERSONNEL ADMINISTRATOR OF MASS. v. FEENEY, 442 U.S. 256 (1979): This decision relied on Davis and Arlington Heights to reject a sex discrimination attack on Massachusetts' law granting "absolute lifetime" preference to veterans for state civil service positions, even though "the preference operates overwhelmingly to the advantage of males." Under the State's Veterans Preference Statute, "all veterans who qualify for state civil service positions must be considered for appointment ahead of any qualifying nonveterans." (Over 98% of the veterans in Massachusetts were male; only 1.8% were female.) Challenger Helen B. Feeney, who was not a veteran, claimed that the law denied equal protection to women. In rejecting her challenge, Justice STEWART's majority opinion noted that the statute "defined the term 'veterans' in gender-neutral language," but that the law had a "severe" impact on the public employment opportunities of women: "This is attributable in some measure to the variety of federal [policies] that have restricted the number of women who could enlist in the [Armed Forces], and largely to the simple fact that women have never been subjected to a military draft." Turning to the governing standards, Justice Stewart stated that Washington v. Davis and Arlington Heights "signalled no departure from the settled rule that the 14th Amendment guarantees equal laws, not equal results. [Those principles] apply with equal force to a case involving alleged gender discrimination. When a statute gender-neutral on its face is challenged on the ground that its effects upon women are disproportionately adverse, a two-fold inquiry is thus appropriate. The first question is whether the statutory classification is indeed neutral in the sense that it is not gender-based. If the classification itself, covert or overt, is not based upon gender, the second question is whether the adverse effect reflects invidious gender-based discrimination. In this second inquiry, impact provides an 'important starting point' [Arlington Heights], but purposeful discrimination is 'the condition that offends the Constitution.'"

Engaging in the first step of that inquiry—whether the law "establishes a classification that is overtly or covertly based upon gender"—Justice Stewart noted that appellee had "acknowledged that state hiring preferences for veterans are not per se invalid, for she has limited her challenge to the absolute lifetime preference." He continued: "The District Court made two central findings that are relevant here: first, that [the law] serves legitimate and worthy purposes; second, that the absolute preference was not established for the purpose of discriminating against women. [Thus], the distinction between veterans and nonveterans [here] is not a pretext for gender discrimination. [If] the impact of this statute could not be plausibly explained on a neutral ground, impact itself would signal that the real classification made by the law was in fact not neutral. But there can be but one answer to the question whether this veteran preference excludes significant numbers of women from preferred state jobs because they are women or because they are nonveterans. [T]his is not a law that can plausibly be explained only as a gender-based classification. Indeed, it is not a law that can rationally be explained on that ground. Veteran status is not uniquely male. Although few women benefit from the preference, the nonveteran class is not substantially all-female. To the contrary, significant numbers of nonveterans are men, and all nonveterans—male as well as female—are placed at a disadvantage. Too many men are affected by [the law] to permit the inference that the statute is but a pretext for preferring men over women."

situation" by remanding for reconsideration in light of Davis. He thought that course especially appropriate because a remand was necessary in any event on the statutory issue. Justice White, the author of Davis, added that he thought it "wholly unnecessary for the Court to embark on a lengthy discussion of the standards for proving

the racially discriminatory purpose required by Davis": in light of the lower courts' findings that the suburb's decision rested on legitimate grounds, there was no need "for this Court to list various 'evidentiary sources' or 'subjects of proper inquiry' in determining whether a racially discriminatory purpose existed."

Moreover, [the] purposes of the statute provide the surest explanation for its impact. Just as there are cases in which impact alone can unmask an invidious classification, cf. [Yick Wo], there are others, in which—notwithstanding impact—the legitimate noninvidious purposes of a law cannot be missed. This is one. The distinction made by [the law] is, as it seems to be, quite simply between veterans and nonveterans, not between men and women."

On the second part of the inquiry, Justice Stewart stated: "The dispositive question [is] whether the appellee has shown that a gender-based discriminatory purpose has, at least in some measure, shaped the Massachusetts veterans' preference legislation. [She] points to two basic factors which in her view distinguish [the law] from the neutral rules at issue in [Washington v. Davis and Arlington Heights]. The first is the nature of the preference, which is said to be demonstrably gender-biased in the sense that it favors a status reserved under federal military policy primarily to men. The second concerns the impact of the absolute lifetime preference upon the employment opportunities of women, an impact claimed to be too inevitable to have been unintended. The appellee contends that these factors, coupled with the fact that the preference itself has little if any relevance to actual job performance, more than suffice [to prove discriminatory intent].

"The contention that [the law] is 'inherently non-neutral' or 'gender-biased' presumes that the State, by favoring veterans, intentionally incorporated into its public employment policies the panoply of sex-based and assertedly discriminatory federal laws that have prevented all but a handful of women from becoming veterans. There are two serious difficulties with this argument. First, it is wholly at odds with the District Court's central finding that Massachusetts has not [acted] for the purpose of discriminating against women. Second, it cannot be reconciled with the assumption made by both the appellee and the District Court that a more limited hiring preference for veterans could be sustained. Taken together, these difficulties are fatal. To the extent that the status of veteran is one that few women have been enabled to achieve, every hiring preference for veterans, however modest or extreme, is inherently gender-biased. If Massachusetts by offering such a preference can be said intentionally to have incorporated into its state employment policies the historical gender-based federal military personnel practices, the degree of the preference would or should make no constitutional difference. Invidious discrimination does not become less so because the discrimination accomplished is of a lesser magnitude.[1] Discriminatory intent is simply not amenable to calibration. It either is a factor that has influenced the legislative choice or it is not. The District Court's conclusion that the [law] was not originally enacted or subsequently reaffirmed for the purpose of giving an advantage to males as such necessarily compels the conclusion that the State intended nothing more than to prefer 'veterans.' Given this finding, simple logic suggests that an intent to exclude women from significant public jobs was not at work in this law. To reason that it was, by describing the preference as 'inherently non-neutral' or 'gender-biased,' is merely to restate the fact of impact, not to answer the question of intent.

"To be sure, this case is unusual in that it involves a law that by design is not neutral. The law overtly prefers veterans as such. As opposed to the written test at issue in Davis, it does not purport to define a job related characteristic. To the contrary, it confers upon a specifically described group—perceived to be particularly deserving—a competitive head start. But the District Court found,

---

1. "This is not to say that the degree of impact is irrelevant to the question of intent. But it is to say that a more modest preference, while it might well lessen impact and, as the State argues, might lessen the effectiveness of the statute in helping veterans, would not be any more or less 'neutral' in the constitutional sense." [Footnote by Justice Stewart.]

appellee has not disputed, that this legislative choice was legitimate. ...sic distinction between veterans and nonveterans, having been found not ...r-based, and the goals of the preference having been found worthy, [the ... must be analyzed as is any other neutral law that casts a greater burden ...n women as a group than upon men as a group. The enlistment policies of the armed services may well have discriminated on the basis of sex. But the history of discrimination against women in the military is not on trial in this case.

"The appellee's ultimate argument rests upon the presumption, common to the criminal and civil law, that a person intends the natural and foreseeable consequences of his voluntary actions. [It] would [be] disingenuous to say that the adverse consequences of this legislation for women were unintended, in the sense that they were not volitional or in the sense that they were not foreseeable. 'Discriminatory purpose,' however, implies more than intent as volition or intent as awareness of consequences. See [UJO, p. 752 below] (concurring opinion). It implies that the decisionmaker, in this case a state legislature, selected or reaffirmed a particular course of action at least in part 'because of,' not merely 'in spite of,' its adverse effects upon an identifiable group.[2] Yet nothing in the record demonstrates that this preference for veterans was originally devised or subsequently re-enacted because it would accomplish the collateral goal of keeping women in a stereotypic and predefined place in the Massachusetts Civil Service. [When] the totality of legislative actions establishing and extending the Massachusetts veterans' preference are considered, the law remains what it purports to be: a preference for veterans of either sex over nonveterans of either sex, not for men over women. [The] substantial edge granted to veterans by [the law] may reflect unwise policy. The appellee, however, has simply failed to demonstrate that the law in any way reflects [purposeful sex discrimination]."

Justice STEVENS, joined by Justice White, concurred in the opinion and added: "I confess that I am not at all sure that there is any difference between the two questions [posed]. If a classification is not overtly based on gender, I am inclined to believe the question whether it is covertly gender-based is the same as the question whether its adverse effects reflect invidious gender-based discrimination. However the question is phrased, for me the answer is largely provided by the fact that the number of males disadvantaged by Massachusetts' Veterans Preference (1,867,000) is sufficiently large—and sufficiently close to the number of disadvantaged females (2,954,000)—to refute the claim that the rule was intended to benefit males as a class over females as a class."

Justice MARSHALL, joined by Justice Brennan, dissented: "In my judgment, [the law] evinces purposeful gender-based discrimination [and is unconstitutional]." He elaborated: "I find the Court's logic neither simple nor compelling. That a legislature seeks to advantage one group does not, as a matter of logic or of common sense, exclude the possibility that it also intends to disadvantage another. Individuals in general and lawmakers in particular frequently act for a variety of reasons. [Since] reliable evidence of subjective intentions is seldom obtainable, resort to inference based on objective factors is generally unavoidable. To discern the purposes underlying facially neutral

---

2. This is not to say that the inevitability or foreseeability of consequences of a neutral rule has no bearing upon the existence of discriminatory intent. Certainly, when the adverse consequences of a law upon an identifiable group are as inevitable as the gender-based consequences of [this law], a strong inference that the adverse effects were desired can reasonably be drawn. But in this inquiry—made as it is under the Constitution—an inference is a working tool, not a synonym for proof. When as here, the impact is essentially an unavoidable consequence of a legislative policy that has in itself always been deemed to be legitimate, and when, as here, the statutory history and all of the available evidence affirmatively demonstrate the opposite, the inference simply fails to ripen into proof. [Footnote by Justice Stewart.]

policies, this Court has therefore considered the degree, inevitability, and foreseeability of any disproportionate impact as well as the alternatives reasonably available. See, [e.g., Gomillion]. In the instant case, the impact of the [law] on women is undisputed. [The] absolute preference formula has rendered desirable state civil service employment an almost exclusively male prerogative. [T]his consequence followed foreseeably, indeed inexorably, from the long history of policies severely limiting women's participation in the military.[1] Although neutral in form, the statute is anything but neutral in application. [Where] the foreseeable impact of a facially neutral policy is so disproportionate, the burden should rest on the State to establish that sex-based considerations played no part in the choice of the particular legislative scheme.

"Clearly, that burden was not sustained here. The legislative history of the statute reflects the Commonwealth's patent appreciation of the impact the preference system would have on women, and an equally evident desire to mitigate that impact only with respect to certain traditionally female occupations. Until 1971, the statute and implementing civil service regulations exempted from operation of the preference any job requisitions 'especially calling for women.' In practice, this exemption, coupled with the absolute preference for veterans, has created a gender-based civil service hierarchy, with women occupying low grade clerical and secretarial jobs and men holding more responsible and remunerative positions. Thus, for over 70 years, the Commonwealth has maintained, as an integral part of its veterans' preference system, an exemption relegating female civil service applicants to occupations traditionally filled by women. Such a statutory scheme both reflects and perpetuates precisely the kind of archaic assumptions about women's roles which we have previously held invalid. Particularly when viewed against the range of less discriminatory alternatives available to assist veterans, Massachusetts' choice of a formula that so severely restricts public employment opportunities for women cannot reasonably be thought gender-neutral.[2] The Court's conclusion to the contrary—that 'nothing in the record' evinces a 'collateral goal of keeping women in a stereotypic and predefined place in the Massachusetts Civil Service'—displays a singularly myopic view of the facts established below." [3]

ROGERS v. LODGE

458 U.S. 613, 102 S.Ct. 3272, 73 L.Ed.2d 1012 (1982).

Justice WHITE delivered the opinion of the Court.

The issue in this case is whether the at-large system of elections in Burke County, Ga., violates the 14th Amendment rights of Burke County's black citizens.

I. Burke County is a large, predominantly rural county located in eastern Georgia. [According] to the 1980 census, Burke County had a total population

1. "[Unlike] the employment examination in Washington v. Davis, which the Court found to be demonstrably job-related, the Massachusetts preference statute incorporates the results of sex-based military policies irrelevant to women's current fitness for civilian public employment." [Footnote by Justice Marshall.]

2. "Only four States afford a preference comparable in scope to that of Massachusetts. Other States and the Federal Government grant point or tie-breaking preferences that do not foreclose opportunities for women." [Footnote by Justice Marshall.]

3. "Although it is relevant that the preference statute also disadvantages a substantial group of men, it is equally pertinent that 47% of Massachusetts men over 18 are veterans, as compared to 0.8% of Massachusetts women. Given this disparity, and the indicia of intent noted above, the absolute number of men denied preference cannot be dispositive, especially since they have not faced the barriers to achieving veteran status confronted by women." [Footnote by Justice Marshall.]

of 19,349, of whom 10,385, or 53.6%, were black. The average age of blacks living there is lower than the average age of whites and therefore whites constitute a slight majority of the voting age population. As of 1978, 6,373 persons were registered to vote in Burke County, of whom 38% were black. The Burke County Board of Commissioners governs the county. It was created in 1911 [under state law] and consists of five members elected at large to concurrent 4-year terms by all qualified voters in the county. The county has never been divided into [districts]. In order to be nominated or elected, a candidate must receive a majority of the votes cast in the primary or general election, and a runoff must be held if no candidate receives a majority in the first primary or general election. [There is no residency requirement for candidates.] Each candidate must run for a specific seat on the Board, and a voter may vote only once for any candidate. No Negro has ever been elected to the [Board].

Appellees, eight black citizens, filed this suit in 1976 in [the District Court] on behalf of all black citizens in Burke County. The complaint alleged that the county's system of at-large elections violates appellees' [constitutional] rights [by] diluting the voting power of black citizens. [The] court issued an order [stating] that appellees were entitled to prevail and ordering that Burke County be divided into five districts for purposes of electing County Commissioners. The court later issued detailed findings of fact and conclusions of law in which it stated that while the present method of electing County Commissioners was "racially neutral when adopted, [it] is being *maintained* for invidious purposes" in violation of appellees' 14th and 15th Amendment rights. The Court of Appeals affirmed. It stated that while the proceedings in the District Court took place prior to the decision in Mobile v. Bolden, 446 U.S. 55 (1980), the District court correctly anticipated Mobile and required appellees to prove that the at-large voting system was maintained for a discriminatory purpose, [and] that the District Court's findings were not clearly erroneous, and that its conclusion that the at-large system was maintained for invidious purposes was "virtually mandated by the overwhelming proof." [We] affirm.

II. At-large voting schemes and multimember districts tend to minimize the voting strength of minority groups by permitting the political majority to elect *all* representatives of the district. A distinct minority, whether it be a racial, ethnic, economic, or political group, may be unable to elect any representatives in an at-large election, yet may be able to elect several representatives if the political unit is divided into single-member districts. The minority's voting power in a multimember district is particularly diluted when bloc voting occurs and ballots are cast along strict majority-minority lines. While multimember districts have been challenged for "their winner-take-all aspects, their tendency to submerge minorities and to overrepresent the winning party," Whitcomb v. Chavis [1971; p. 1632 below], this Court has repeatedly held that they are not unconstitutional per se. The Court has recognized, however, that multimember districts violate the 14th Amendment if "conceived or operated as purposeful devices to further racial discrimination" by minimizing, cancelling out or diluting the voting strength of racial elements in the voting population. Cases charging that multimember districts unconstitutionally dilute the voting strength of racial minorities are thus subject to the standard of proof generally applicable to [equal protection] cases. Washington v. Davis and [Arlington Heights] made it clear that in order for the Equal Protection Clause to be violated, "the invidious quality of a law claimed to be racially discriminatory must ultimately be traced to a racially discriminatory purpose." Neither case involved voting dilution, but in both cases the Court observed that the requirement that racially discriminatory purpose or intent be proved applies to voting cases by relying upon, among others, Wright v. Rockefeller [1964; p. 691 above], a districting case, to illustrate that a showing of discriminatory intent has long been required in all types of equal protection cases charging racial discrimination.[1] Arlington Heights and [Davis] both rejected the notion that a law is invalid under [equal protection] simply because it may affect a greater proportion of one race than another. However, both cases recognized that discriminatory intent need not be proved by direct evidence. [Thus] determining the existence of a discriminatory purpose "demands a sensitive inquiry into such circumstantial and direct evidence of intent as may be available."

In Mobile v. Bolden, the Court was called upon to apply these principles to the at-large election system in Mobile, Ala. Mobile is governed by three commissioners who exercise all legislative, executive, and administrative power in the municipality. Each candidate for the City Commission runs for one of three numbered posts in an at-large election and can only be elected by a majority vote. Plaintiffs brought a class action on behalf of all Negro citizens of Mobile alleging that the at-large scheme diluted their voting [strength]. The District Court [ordered] that the commission form of government be replaced by a mayor and a nine-member City Council elected from single-member districts. The Court of Appeals affirmed. This Court reversed. Justice Stewart, writing for himself and three other Justices, noted that to prevail in their contention that the at-large voting system violates [equal protection], plaintiffs had to prove the system was " 'conceived or operated as [a] purposeful devic[e] to further [racial] discrimination.' "[2] [Another] Justice agreed with the standard of proof recognized by the plurality. (White, J., dissenting).[3]

The plurality went on to conclude that the District Court had failed to comply with this standard. The District Court had analyzed plaintiffs' claims in light of the standard which had been set forth in Zimmer v. McKeithen, 485 F.2d 1297 (CA5 1973), aff'd on other grounds, 424 U.S. 636 (1975). Zimmer set out a list of factors[4] gleaned from Whitcomb v. Chavis and White v. Regester [1973; p. 1630 below], that a court should consider in assessing the constitutionality of at-large and multimember district voting schemes. Under

1. Purposeful racial discrimination invokes the strictest scrutiny of adverse differential treatment. Absent such purpose, differential impact is subject only to the test of rationality. [Davis]. [Footnote by Justice White.]

2. With respect to the 15th Amendment, the plurality held that the Amendment prohibits only direct, purposefully discriminatory interference with the freedom of Negroes to vote. [Three] Justices disagreed with the plurality's basis for putting aside the 15th Amendment. (Stevens, White and Marshall, JJ.) [We] express no view on the application of the 15th Amendment to this case.

The plurality noted that plaintiffs' claim under § 2 of the Voting Rights Act [added] nothing to their 15th Amendment claim because the "legislative history of § 2 makes clear that it was intended to have an effect no different from that of the 15th Amendment itself." [Footnote by Justice White. See footnote 7 below.]

3. In Mobile v. Bolden, Justice Stewart's plurality opinion had been joined by Chief Justice Burger and Justices Powell and Rehnquist. Justice White's dissent endorsed the "purposeful discrimination" standard, but insisted (as he did in Rogers v. Lodge) that "the findings of the District Court amply support an inference of purposeful discrimination." The critical votes to make up a majority for Justice Stewart's result in Mobile had come from Justices Blackmun and

Stevens. Justice Blackmun stated: "Assuming that proof of intent is a prerequisite, [I] am inclined to agree with [Justice White that the District Court findings support an inference of purposeful discrimination]." He concurred in the judgment "because I believe that the relief afforded appellees by the District Court was not commensurate with the sound exercise of judicial discretion. [I] do not believe that, in order to remedy the unconstitutional vote dilution, [it] was necessary to convert Mobile's city government to a mayor-council system." Justice Stevens' concurrence in the judgment rested on an opinion similar to that of his dissent, below, in Rogers. (See also Justice Powell's summary, below, of Justice Stevens' position.) The dissenters in Mobile, in addition to Justice White, were Justices Marshall and Brennan.

4. The primary factors listed in Zimmer include a lack of minority access to the candidate selection process, unresponsiveness of elected officials to minority interests, a tenuous state policy underlying the preference for multimember or at-large districting, and the existence of past discrimination which precludes effective participation in the electoral process. Factors which enhance the proof of voting dilution are the existence of large districts, anti-single-shot voting provisions, and the absence of any provision for at-large candidates to run from geographic subdistricts. [Footnote by Justice White.]

Zimmer, voting dilution is established "upon proof of the existence of an aggregate of these factors." The plurality in Mobile was of the view that Zimmer was "decided upon the misunderstanding that it is not necessary to show a discriminatory purpose in order to prove a violation of the Equal Protection Clause—that proof of a discriminatory effect is sufficient." The plurality observed that while "the presence of the indicia relied on in Zimmer may afford some evidence of a discriminatory purpose," the mere existence of those criteria is not a substitute for a finding of discriminatory purpose. The District Court's standard in Mobile was likewise flawed. Finally, the plurality concluded that the evidence upon which the lower courts had relied was "insufficient to prove an unconstitutionally discriminatory purpose in the present case."

[Because] the District Court in the present case employed the evidentiary factors outlined in Zimmer, it is urged that its judgment is infirm for the same reasons that led to the reversal in Mobile. We do not agree. First, and fundamentally, we are unconvinced that the District Court in this case applied the wrong legal standard. Not only was the District Court's decision rendered a considerable time after [Davis] and Arlington Heights, but the trial judge also had the benefit of Nevett v. Sides, 571 F.2d 209 (1978), where the Court of Appeals for the Fifth Circuit assessed the impact of [Davis] and Arlington Heights and held that "a showing of racially motivated discrimination is a necessary element in an equal protection voting dilution claim." The court stated that "[t]he ultimate issue in a case alleging unconstitutional dilution of the votes of a racial group is whether the districting plan under attack exists because it was intended to diminish or dilute the political efficacy of that group." The Court of Appeals also explained that although the evidentiary factors outlined in Zimmer were important considerations in arriving at the ultimate conclusion of discriminatory intent, the plaintiff is not limited to those factors. "The task before the fact finder is to determine, under all the relevant facts, in whose favor the 'aggregate' of the evidence preponderates. This determination is peculiarly dependent upon the facts of each case."

The District Court referred to Nevett v. Sides and demonstrated its understanding of the controlling standard by observing that a determination of discriminatory intent is "a requisite to a finding of unconstitutional vote dilution" under the 14th and 15th Amendments. Furthermore, while recognizing that the evidentiary factors identified in Zimmer were to be considered, the District Court was aware that it was "not limited in its determination only to the Zimmer factors" but could consider other relevant factors as well. [It] then proceeded to deal with what it considered to be the relevant proof and concluded that the at-large scheme of electing commissioners, "although racially neutral when adopted, is being *maintained* for invidious purposes." That system, "while neutral in origin, [has] been subverted to invidious purposes." For the most part, the District Court dealt with the evidence in terms of the factors set out in Zimmer and its progeny, but as the Court of Appeals stated: "Judge Alaimo employed the constitutionally required standard [and] did not treat the Zimmer criteria as absolute, but rather considered them only to the extent they were relevant to the question of discriminatory intent." Although a tenable argument can be made to the contrary, we are not inclined to disagree with the Court of Appeals' conclusion that the District Court applied the proper legal standard.

III. A. We are also unconvinced that we should disturb the District Court's finding that the at-large system in Burke County was being maintained for the invidious purpose of diluting the voting strength of the black population. In White v. Regester, we stated that we were not inclined to overturn the District Court's factual findings, "representing as they do a blend of history and an intensely local appraisal of the design and impact of the Bexar County multimember district in the light of past and present reality, political and otherwise." See also Columbus Board of Education v. Penick [(1979; p. 726 below) (Burger, C.J., concurring in judgment)].[5] Our recent decision in Pullman-Standard v. Swint, 456 U.S. 273 (1982), emphasizes the deference [FRCP] 52 requires reviewing courts to give a trial court's findings of fact. "Rule 52(a) broadly requires that findings of fact not be set aside unless clearly [erroneous]." The Court held that the issue of whether the differential impact of a seniority system resulted from an intent to discriminate on racial grounds "is a pure question of fact, subject to Rule 52(a)'s clearly erroneous standard." The Swint Court also noted that issues of intent are commonly treated as factual matters. We are of the view that the same clearly-erroneous standard applies to the trial court's finding in this case that the at-large system in Burke County is being maintained for discriminatory purposes, as well as to the court's subsidiary findings of fact. The Court of Appeals did not hold any of the District Court's findings of fact to be clearly erroneous, and this Court has frequently noted its reluctance to disturb findings of fact concurred in by two lower courts. We agree with the Court of Appeals that on the record before us, none of the factual findings [is] clearly erroneous.

B. The District Court found that blacks have always made up a substantial majority of the population in Burke County, but that they are a distinct minority of the registered voters. There was also overwhelming evidence of bloc voting along racial lines. Hence, although there had been black candidates, no black had ever been elected to the Burke County Commission. These facts bear heavily on the issue of purposeful discrimination. Voting along racial lines allows those elected to ignore black interests without fear of political consequences, and without bloc voting the minority candidates would not lose elections solely because of their race. Because it is sensible to expect that at least some blacks would have been elected in Burke County, the fact that none [has] ever been elected is important evidence of purposeful exclusion. Under our cases, however, such facts are insufficient in themselves to prove purposeful discrimination absent other evidence such as proof that blacks have less opportunity to participate in the political processes and to elect candidates of their choice. Both the District Court and the Court of Appeals thought the supporting proof in this case was sufficient to support an inference of intentional discrimination. The supporting evidence was organized primarily around the factors which Nevett v. Sides had deemed relevant to the issue of intentional discrimination. These factors were primarily those suggested in [Zimmer].

The District Court began by determining the impact of past discrimination on the ability of blacks to participate effectively in the political process. Past discrimination was found to contribute to low black voter registration because prior to the Voting Rights Act of 1965, blacks had been denied access to the political process by means such as literacy tests, poll taxes, and white primaries. The result was that "Black suffrage in Burke County was virtually non-existent." Black voter registration in Burke County has increased following the [Act] to the point that some 38% of blacks eligible to vote are registered to do so. On that basis the District Court inferred that "past discrimination has had an adverse effect on black voter registration which lingers to this date." Past discrimination against blacks in education also had the same effect. Not only did Burke County schools discriminate against blacks as recently as 1969, but also some schools still remain essentially segregated and blacks as a group have

---

5. The Columbus case, noted at p. 726 below, endorsed a systemwide school desegregation remedy. As in this case, the majority opinion in Columbus was written by Justice White. Note the similarity of his technique in Columbus and in this case (deference to lower court fact findings so long as he was generally satisfied that the lower court understood the proper legal standard).

completed less formal education than whites. The District Court found further evidence of exclusion from the political process. Past discrimination had prevented blacks from effectively participating in Democratic Party affairs and in primary elections. Until this lawsuit was filed, there had never been a black member of the County Executive Committee of the Democratic Party. There were also property ownership requirements that made it difficult for blacks to serve as chief registrar in the county. There had been discrimination in the selection of grand jurors, the hiring of county employees, and in the appointments to boards and committees which oversee the county government. The District Court thus concluded that historical discrimination had restricted the present opportunity of blacks effectively to participate in the political process. Evidence of historical discrimination is relevant to drawing an inference of purposeful discrimination, particularly in cases such as this one where the evidence shows that discriminatory practices were commonly utilized, that they were abandoned when enjoined by courts or made illegal by civil rights legislation, and that they were replaced by laws and practices which, though neutral on their face, serve to maintain the status quo.

Extensive evidence was cited by the District Court to support its finding that elected officials of Burke County have been unresponsive and insensitive to the needs of the black community,[6] which increases the likelihood that the political process was not equally open to blacks. This evidence ranged from the effects of past discrimination which still haunt the county courthouse to the infrequent appointment of blacks to county boards and committees; the overtly discriminatory pattern of paving county roads; the reluctance of the county to remedy black complaints, which forced blacks to take legal action to obtain school and grand jury desegregation; and the role played by the County Commissioners in the incorporation of an all-white private school to which they donated public funds for the purchase of band uniforms. The District Court also considered the depressed socioeconomic status of Burke County blacks. It found that proportionately more blacks than whites have incomes below the poverty level. [Not] only have blacks completed less formal education than whites, but also the education they have received "was qualitatively inferior to a marked degree." Blacks tend to receive less pay than whites, even for similar work, and they tend to be employed in menial jobs more often than whites. Seventy-three per cent of houses occupied by blacks lacked all or some plumbing facilities; only 16% of white-occupied houses suffered the same deficiency. The District Court concluded that the depressed socioeconomic status of blacks results in part from "the lingering effects of past discrimination."

Although finding that the state policy behind the at-large electoral system in Burke County was "neutral in origin," the District Court concluded that the policy "has been subverted to invidious purposes." As a practical matter, maintenance of the state statute providing for at-large elections in Burke County is determined by Burke County's state representatives, for the legislature defers to their wishes on matters of purely local application. The court found that Burke County's state representatives "have retained a system which has minimized the ability of Burke County Blacks to participate in the political system."

The trial court considered, in addition, several factors which this Court has indicated enhance the tendency of multimember districts to minimize the voting

---

6. The Court of Appeals held that "proof of unresponsiveness by the public body in question to the group claiming injury" is an *essential* element of a claim of voting dilution under the 14th Amendment. Under our cases, however, unresponsiveness is an important element but only one of a number of circumstances a court should consider in determining whether discriminatory purpose may be inferred. [Footnote by Justice White.]

strength of racial minorities. See Whitcomb v. Chavis. It found that th
geographic size of the county, which is nearly two-thirds the size of
Island, "has made it more difficult for Blacks to get to polling places or
campaign for office." The court concluded, as a matter of law, that the size of
the county tends to impair the access of blacks to the political process. The
majority vote requirement was found "to submerge the will of the minority"
and thus "deny the minority's access to the system." The court also found the
requirement that candidates run for specific seats enhances appellees' lack of
access because it prevents a cohesive political group from concentrating on a
single candidate. Because Burke County has no residency requirement, "[a]ll
candidates could reside in Waynesboro, or in 'lilly-white' neighborhoods. To
that extent, the denial of access becomes enhanced." None of the District
Court's findings underlying its ultimate finding of intentional discrimination
appears to us to be clearly erroneous; and as we have said, we decline to
overturn the essential finding of the District Court, agreed to by the Court of
Appeals, that the at-large system in Burke County has been maintained for the
purpose of denying blacks equal access to the political processes in the [county].

IV.   We also find no reason to overturn the relief ordered by the District
Court. Neither the District Court nor the Court of Appeals discerned any
special circumstances that would militate against utilizing single-member districts. Where "a constitutional violation has been found, the remedy does not
'exceed' the violation if the remedy is tailored to cure the 'condition that
offends the Constitution.' "

[Affirmed.] [7]

Justice POWELL, with whom Justice REHNQUIST joins, dissenting.

I.   Mobile v. Bolden establishes that an at-large voting system must be
upheld against constitutional attack unless maintained for a discriminatory
purpose. In Mobile we reversed a finding of unconstitutional vote dilution
because the lower courts had relied on factors insufficient as a matter of law to
establish discriminatory intent. See (plurality opinion of Stewart, J.). The
District Court and Court of Appeals in this case based their findings of
unconstitutional discrimination on the same factors held insufficient in Mobile.
Yet the Court now finds their conclusion unexceptionable. The Mobile plurality also affirmed that the concept of "intent" was no mere fiction, and held that
the District Court had erred in "its failure to identify the state officials whose
intent it considered relevant." Although the courts below did not answer that
question in this case, the Court today affirms their decision. Whatever the
wisdom of Mobile, the Court's opinion cannot be reconciled persuasively with
that case. There are some variances in the largely sociological evidence
presented in the two cases. But Mobile held that this *kind* of evidence was not
enough. Such evidence, we found in Mobile, did not merely fall short, but
"fell *far* short of showing that [an at-large electoral scheme was] 'conceived or

---

7. The Mobile v. Bolden decision led to important legislative consequences. As Justice
White noted in Rogers (see fn. 2 above), the
Mobile plurality had stated that the claim under
§ 2 of the Voting Rights Act "added nothing to
[the] 15th Amendment claim" because § 2 was
"intended to have an effect no different from that
of the 15th Amendment itself." Efforts to
change the § 2 standard to one of "effect" rather
than "purpose" followed soon after the decision
in Mobile. The House voted to substitute a

"results" test, but the Senate balked. Ultimately,
in extending the Voting Rights Act, Congress
approved a compromise provision. President
Reagan signed the extension on June 29, 1982—
two days before Rogers v. Lodge was handed
down. (No § 2 claim was involved in Rogers.)
For the terms of the compromise provision
(clearly intended to change the interpretation of
§ 2 in Mobile) see the note in the next chapter,
at p. 936 below.

operated [as a] purposeful devic[e] to further [racial] discrimination.' " Because I believe that Mobile controls this case, I dissent.

II.   The Court's decision today relies heavily on the capacity of the federal district courts—essentially free from any standards propounded by this Court—to determine whether at-large voting systems are "being maintained for the invidious purpose of diluting the voting strength of the black population." Federal courts thus are invited to engage in deeply subjective inquiries into the motivations of local officials in structuring local governments. Inquiries of this kind not only can be "unseemly," see Karst, The Costs of Motive-Centered Inquiry, 15 San Diego L.Rev. 1163, 1164 (1978); they intrude the federal courts—with only the vaguest constitutional direction—into an area of intensely local and political concern. Emphasizing these considerations, Justice Stevens argues forcefully that the Court's focus of inquiry is seriously mistaken. I agree with much of what he says. As I do not share his views entirely, however, I write separately.

A.   As I understand it, Justice Stevens' critique of the Court's approach rests on three principles with which I am in fundamental agreement. First, it is appropriate to distinguish between "state action that inhibits an individual's right to vote and state action that affects the political strength of various groups." Mobile v. Bolden (Stevens, J., concurring in judgment); see [his dissent in this case]. Under this distinction, this case is fundamentally different from cases involving direct barriers to voting. There is no claim here that blacks may not register freely and vote for whom they choose. This case also differs from one-man, one-vote cases [p. 1621 below], in which districting practices make a person's vote less weighty in some districts than in others. Second, I agree with Justice Stevens that vote dilution cases of this kind are difficult if not impossible to distinguish—especially in their remedial aspect—from other actions to redress gerrymanders. Finally, Justice Stevens clearly is correct in arguing that the standard used to identify unlawful racial discrimination in this area should be defined in terms that are judicially manageable and reviewable. In the absence of compelling reasons of both law and fact, the federal judiciary is unwarranted in undertaking to restructure state political systems. This is inherently a political area, where the identification of a seeming violation does not necessarily suggest an enforceable judicial remedy—or at least none short of a system of quotas or group representation. Any such system, of course, would be antithetical to the principles of our democracy.

B.   Justice Stevens would accommodate these principles by holding that subjective intent is irrelevant to the establishment of a case of racial vote dilution under the 14th Amendment. Despite sharing the concerns from which his position is developed, I would not accept this view. "The central purpose of the Equal Protection Clause [is] the prevention of official conduct discriminating on the basis of race." [Davis]. Because I am unwilling to abandon this central principle in cases of this kind, I cannot join Justice Stevens' opinion. Nonetheless, I do agree with him that what he calls "objective" factors should be the focus of inquiry in vote-dilution cases. Unlike the considerations on which the lower courts relied in this case and in Mobile, the factors identified by Justice STEVENS as "objective" in fact are direct, reliable, and unambiguous indices of discriminatory *intent*. If we held, as I think we should, that the district courts must place primary reliance on these factors to establish discriminatory intent, we would prevent federal-court inquiries into the *subjective* thought processes of local officials—at least until enough objective evidence had been presented to warrant discovery into subjective motivations in this complex, politically charged area. By prescribing such a rule we would hold federal courts to a standard that was judicially manageable. And we would remain faithful to the central protective purpose of the Equal Protection Clause. In the absence of proof of discrimination by reliance on the kind of objective factors identified by Justice Stevens, I would hold that the factors cited by the Court of Appeals are too attenuated as a matter of law to support an inference of discriminatory intent. I would reverse its judgment on that basis.[1]

Discriminatory purpose and the 13th Amendment. The question of whether the 13th Amendment, like the 14th, includes a purposeful discrimination requirement was raised in MEMPHIS v. GREENE, 451 U.S. 100 (1981), but the majority did not reach that issue. In Greene, black residents sued Memphis because it had closed a street at the border between a white and a black

---

1. Justice STEVENS' lengthy dissent, akin to the opinion he had submitted in Mobile v. Bolden, stated—in addition to the highlights summarized by Justice Powell—that "I do not believe that the subjective intent of the persons who adopted the system in 1911, or the intent of those who have since declined to change it, can determine its constitutionality. Even if the intent of the political majority were the controlling constitutional consideration, I could not agree that the only political groups that are entitled to protection under the Court's rule are those defined by racial characteristics." He stated, too: "Ever since I joined the Court, I have been concerned about the Court's emphasis on subjective intent as a criterion for constitutional adjudication"—both because of "the quantum of power it confers upon the judiciary" and especially, because of "the quality of that power": "[Constitutional] adjudication that is premised on a case-by-case appraisal of the subjective intent of local decisionmakers cannot possibly satisfy the requirement of impartial administration of the law that is embodied in [equal protection]." He concluded: "My conviction that all minority groups are equally entitled to constitutional protection against the misuse of the majority's political power does not mean that I would abandon judicial review of such action. [E.g., the gerrymander in Gomillion.] But if the standard the Court applies today extends to all types of minority groups, it is either so broad that virtually every political device is vulnerable or it is so undefined that federal judges can pick and choose almost at will among those that will be upheld and those that will be condemned. There are valid reasons for concluding that certain minority groups—such as the black voters [here]—should be given special protection from political oppression by the dominant majority. But those are reasons that justify the application of a legislative policy choice rather than a constitutional principle that cannot be confined to special circumstances or to a temporary period in our history. Any suggestion that political groups in which black leadership predominates are in need of a permanent constitutional shield against the tactics of their political opponents underestimates the resourcefulness, the wisdom, and the demonstrated capacity of such leaders. I cannot accept the Court's constitutional holding."

Earlier, Justice Stevens had noted: "It is incongruous that subjective intent is identified as the constitutional standard and yet the persons who allegedly harbored an improper intent are never identified or mentioned." He stated, moreover: "A rule that would invalidate all governmental action motivated by racial, ethnic, or political considerations is too broad. Moreover, in my opinion the Court is incorrect in assuming that the intent of elected officials is invidious when they are motivated by a desire to retain control of the local political machinery. For such an intent is surely characteristic of politicians throughout the country."

With respect to the objective criteria that he would rely on, Justice Stevens had drawn, in his dissent in Mobile v. Bolden, on the characteristics that invalidated the gerrymander in Gomillion (p. 691 above). He explained: "These characteristics suggest that a proper test should focus on the objective effects of the political decision rather than the subjective motivation of the decisionmaker. In this case, if the commission form of government in Mobile were extraordinary, or if it were nothing more than a vestige of history, with no greater justification than the grotesque figure in Gomillion, it would surely violate the Constitution. That conclusion would follow simply from its adverse impact on black voters plus the absence of any legitimate justification for the system, without reference to the subjective intent of the political body that has refused to alter it. Conversely, I am also persuaded that a political decision that affects group voting rights may be valid even if it can be proved that irrational or invidious factors have played some part in its enactment or retention. [A] political decision that is supported by valid and articulable justifications cannot be invalid simply because some participants in the decisionmaking process were motivated by a purpose to disadvantage a minority group."

neighborhood.[1] Justice STEVENS' opinion for the Court found that the street closing had only caused "slight inconvenience" to black motorists and was motivated simply by an interest in protecting the tranquility of a residential neighborhood. The City had "merely required black residents to use one public street rather than another." The "inconvenience" imposed by the City, he concluded, was not "in any sense comparable to the odious practice the 13th Amendment was designed to eradicate" and could not be considered as imposing a stigma amounting to a "badge of slavery."

Justice WHITE, who concurred in the judgment, was the only member of the Court to reach the discriminatory purpose question and insisted that "purposeful racial discrimination" was essential to showing a violation of § 1982, the 13th Amendment-implementing law. (Justice MARSHALL's dissent, while purporting not to reach that issue, nevertheless noted that he disagreed with Justice White's position.) The issue left open by most of the Justices in Greene was settled by the Court two years later, in General Building Contractors Ass'n, Inc. v. Pa., 458 U.S. 375 (1982), where the majority (over the dissent of Justices Marshall and Brennan) held that, in an action under § 1981 (another post-Civil War 13th Amendment-implementing law), "proof of discriminatory intent" *is* required; the law does not reach "practices that merely result in a disproportionate impact on a particular class."

---

3. THE DE JURE–DE FACTO DISTINCTION IN THE SCHOOL DESEGREGATION CONTEXT

THE IMPLEMENTATION OF BROWN: FROM DESEGREGATION TO INTEGRATION

Introduction. We now return to the problem of school desegregation (pursued through Brown II, the 1955 implementation decision, in sec. 3A1, p. 641, above). The notes that follow consider the aftermath of Brown II. These problems are considered here because they repeatedly raise, in a particular context, the distinction between purposeful discrimination and disadvantaging distinctions in impact or effect. Most relevantly, they raise a question similar to that raised by Rogers v. Lodge, above: even though the Court continues to insist, at least in form, that purposeful, de jure discrimination is essential to establishing an equal protection claim, do its actual practices (e.g., deferring to lower court findings of purposeful discrimination so long as there is some indication that those courts were aware of the purposefulness requirement, as in Rogers v. Lodge above and in the Columbus and Dayton cases below, p. 726) suggest that the Court has in fact gone very far toward substituting an impact, de facto principle in some contexts?

After its promulgation of general guidelines in Brown II, with its insistence on "a prompt and reasonable start" and the demand for full transition to nondiscriminatory school admissions "with all deliberate speed," the Court remained silent about implementation for several years. Enforcement of the desegregation requirement was left largely to lower court litigation—and to the political arena. During the early post-Brown years of "massive resistance" in the South, the Court broke its silence only rarely, though firmly: in Cooper v. Aaron (1958; p. 26 above), all of the Justices signed an opinion reaffirming the

---

1. The case involved both a 13th Amendment claim and a claim under 42 U.S.C. § 1982, one of the post-Civil War laws designed to implement the Amendment. The coverage of the Amend- ment and the implementing legislation is more fully considered in the next chapter at p. 924 below.

Brown principle in the face of the official resistance in Little Rock, Arkansas. And in Griffin (1964; p. 690 above), the Court held unconstitutional an effort to avoid desegregation "by a combination of closed public schools and county grants to white children" to attend private schools. During the 1960s (after the doctrine of Brown had been adopted by the other branches of the national government, beginning with the Civil Rights Act of 1964), Court rulings on implementation came with greater frequency, specificity, and urgency. Court actions during the early sixties were limited to invalidations of impermissible student transfer plans and expressions of mounting impatience with the pace of desegregation.[1] But that pace remained slow during most of the sixties: widely used and officially approved "freedom of choice" plans had relatively little impact on the racial composition of schools. The first major reentry by the Court into implementation problems came in 1968, in the Green case (note 1 below), which rejected freedom of choice plans where they failed to produce a "unitary, nonracial system of public education." And beginning with the Swann case in 1971 (p. 715), the Court has repeatedly spoken in detail about remedial requirements.

In all of these cases—even the 1970s ones involving northern communities— the Court has purported to speak solely about remedies for prior purposeful discrimination: dismantling the dual school systems established by statewide de jure segregation in the South; undoing the effects of hostile racial action by local officials in the North. But the Court has been willing to pursue the consequences of past de jure discrimination very far, in time and in impact. And the Court has put an increasing emphasis on *results* in measuring success of efforts to eliminate past discrimination. In examining those developments, consider whether the purportedly "remedial" decisions in fact rest on changing perceptions of substantive rights. Do the far-reaching demands for eliminating past discrimination make the distinction between de jure and de facto segregation increasingly unjustifiable, as Justice Powell suggested in his dissent in Keyes, p. 725 below? Or is the continued insistence on finding some formal evidence of past de jure discrimination an indication that condemnation of purposeful discrimination exhausts the command of the 14th Amendment in the school segregation area as in most others?[2]

In the 1950s, a lower court, echoing the dominant theme at the time of Brown, stated that the Constitution "does not require integration. It merely forbids [segregation]." Is that still true, in view of the emphasis in Green, below, on producing a "unitary" system? In view of the handling of the purposeful discrimination requirement in the Columbus and Dayton cases, p.

---

1. E.g., in 1963, the Court unanimously struck down minority-to-majority transfer plans in Goss v. Board of Education, 373 U.S. 683 (1963), holding unconstitutional "transfer plans [based] solely on racial factors which, under their terms, inevitably lead toward segregation of the students by race." The Court stated that it was now eight years after Brown II and that "the context in which we must interpret and apply [its] language [has] been significantly altered." For a contemporaneous expression of Court impatience with the pace of desegregation, see Watson v. Memphis, 373 U.S. 526 (1963).

2. For a useful general survey of the post-Brown developments, see Wilkinson, From Brown to Bakke—The Supreme Court and School Integration: 1954–1978 (1979). For critical evaluations of the post-Brown developments, see Graglia, Disaster by Decree—The Supreme Court Decisions on Race and the Schools (1976),

and Kurland, " 'Brown v. Board of Education Was the Beginning': The School Desegregation Cases in the United States Supreme Court, 1954–1979," 1979 Wash.U.L.Q. 309. Compare Gunther, "Of Rights and Remedies, Legitimacy and Competence," 1979 Wash.U.L.Q. 815.

For a survey of the experience in the lower courts in the years immediately after Brown, see McKay, "With All Deliberate Speed," 31 N.Y. U.L.Rev. 991 (1956) and 43 Va.L.Rev. 1205 (1957). For a review of the problems in the years before the Court reentered the picture, see Bickel, "A Decade of School Desegregation," 64 Colum.L.Rev. 193 (1964). For a subsequent evaluation by that observer, see The Supreme Court and the Idea of Progress (1970). See generally Read, "Judicial Evolution of the Law of School Integration Since [Brown]," 39 Law & Contemp.Probs. 7 (1975).

726 below? Note the distinction between "process-oriented" and "result-oriented" antidiscrimination remedies by Owen Fiss: [3] the process orientation "emphasizes the purification of the decisional process," banning decisions based on racial criteria; the result-oriented approach "emphasizes the achievement of certain results"—for example, achieving racial integration rather than merely refraining from racially-based pupil assignments. Do the implementation decisions which follow indicate a shift from process orientation to result orientation? Does the Constitution justify an exclusive emphasis on result, whether or not there was past impurity in the process—the impurity of purposeful discrimination?

2. *"Freedom of choice."* The decision in GREEN v. COUNTY SCHOOL BOARD, 391 U.S. 430 (1968), marked a major turning point in the Court's role in—and requirements for—desegregation. For the first time since Brown II, the Court issued a detailed opinion on the question of remedies. And that opinion, in focusing on the *effects* rather than the purpose and good faith of desegregation efforts, raised important new questions about underlying substantive doctrine as well as the remedies. At the time of Green, freedom of choice plans had become commonplace in the South. School districts argued that good faith plans of that variety, employing no improper pressures on students and parents, adequately complied with the Brown mandate. Opponents of the plans emphasized that desegregation under "freedom of choice" had not significantly changed the racial composition of schools and insisted that the constitutional mandate was not merely the elimination of formal racial barriers but the abolition of racially identifiable schools. Thus, the freedom of choice issue in the context of formerly de jure segregated schools sharply presented the question of whether the 14th Amendment merely required desegregation (the elimination of formal racial barriers) or compelled integration (the creation of racially mixed schools). The Court's answer was clear: its emphasis shifted from "purification of the decisional process" to "achievement of a certain result," [4] albeit on the theory that achieving results was the only acceptable evidence that the process had been purified.

The Green case involved a small school district with two schools, in a county where about half the population was black and where there was no significant residential segregation. The district had adopted a freedom of choice plan in 1965 to remain eligible for federal financial aid. After three years of operation, no white child had chosen to attend the former black school and about 85% of the black children remained in the all-black school. Under these circumstances, the unanimous Court found the plan to be an inadequate compliance with desegregation requirements. Justice BRENNAN's opinion emphasized that "[r]acial identification of the system's schools" remained "complete" and that "the transition to a unitary, nonracial system of public education was and is the ultimate end to be brought about." He stated: "It is against this background [that] we must measure the effectiveness of respondent School Board's 'freedom-of-choice' plan to achieve that end. The School Board contends that it has fully discharged its obligation by adopting a plan by which every student, regardless of race, may 'freely' choose the school he will attend. The Board

3. Fiss, "The Fate of an Idea Whose Time Has Come: Antidiscrimination Law in the Second Decade After Brown v. Board of Education," 41 U.Chi.L.Rev. 742 (1974). See also Fiss, "School Desegregation: The Uncertain Path of the Law," 4 Phil. & Pub.Affairs 3 (1974). Compare, Brest, "Foreword: In Defense of the Antidiscrimination Principle," 90 Harv.L.Rev. 1 (1976).

4. See Fiss, 41 U.Chi.L.Rev. 742 (1974) (footnote 3 above). [The growing emphasis on

affirmative obligations to overcome past de jure segregation, on results rather than process, had come somewhat earlier in lower courts and in HEW guidelines issued under the 1964 Civil Rights Act. See, e.g., the extensive discussion of the "duty to desegregate-duty to integrate" distinction in United States v. Jefferson County Board of Education, 372 F.2d 836 (5th Cir.1966). See Note, "The Courts, HEW, and Southern School Desegregation," 77 Yale L.J. 321 (1967).]

attempts to cast the issue in its broadest form by arguing that its 'freedom-of-choice' plan may be faulted only by reading the 14th Amendment as universally requiring 'compulsory integration,' a reading it insists the wording of the Amendment will not support. But [what] is involved here is the question whether the Board has achieved the 'racially nondiscriminatory school system' Brown II held must be effectuated. [School] boards such as the respondent then operating state-compelled dual systems [were] clearly charged with the affirmative duty to take whatever steps might be necessary to convert to a unitary system in which racial discrimination would be eliminated root and branch. [It] is relevant that [the Board's] first step did not come [until] 10 years after Brown II directed the making of a 'prompt and reasonable start.' [Such] delays are no longer tolerable. [The] burden on a school board today is to come forward with a plan that promises realistically to work, and promises realistically to work *now*. [There] may well be instances in which [freedom of choice] can serve as an effective device. [But] if there are reasonably available other ways, such for illustration as zoning, promising speedier and more effective conversion to a unitary, nonracial school system, 'freedom of choice' must be held unacceptable." Given the experience here, with "a dual system" still in existence and the availability of other courses "such as zoning," the school officials were required to "fashion steps which promise realistically to convert promptly to a system without a 'white' school and a 'Negro' school, but just schools."[5]

In rural and small town areas with no significant residential segregation, the elimination of "freedom of choice" plans and their variants and the adoption of geographic zoning largely eliminated racially identifiable schools. But in large Southern cities with substantial residential segregation—as in the North—geographic zoning alone could not substantially alter the racial composition of schools. In 1971, the Court turned to the problem of metropolitan areas in the South, in Swann, which follows. Swann addressed such problems as the permissibility of seeking racial balance and of ordering widespread busing, and at last provided a detailed guidelines opinion.

SWANN v. CHARLOTTE–MECKLENBURG BOARD OF EDUCATION

402 U.S. 1, 91 S.Ct. 1267, 28 L.Ed.2d 554 (1971).

Mr. Chief Justice BURGER delivered the opinion of the [Court].

[This case involved desegregation in the school district covering the Charlotte, North Carolina, metropolitan area. Nearly 30% of the students were black. By 1969, after several years of operation under a court-approved desegregation plan, about half of the black students were in formerly white schools; the others remained in virtually all-black schools. After Green, the District Court ordered that the school authorities prepare a more effective plan. After rejecting several of the proposals, that court appointed its own expert and accepted his plan, which involved some grouping of outlying white schools with

---

5. In several other decisions from 1968 to 1970, the Court reemphasized the implications of Green and its "at once" requirement. See, e.g., Alexander v. Holmes County Bd. of Educ., 396 U.S. 19 (1969). Note also Monroe v. Board of Commissions, 391 U.S. 450 (1968), a companion case to Green, invalidating a "free transfer" plan in a geographically zoned system. Though the plan was not limited to minority-to-majority transfers, it permitted students to return, "at the implicit invitation of the Board," to "the comfortable security of the old, established discriminatory pattern." The Court was unpersuaded by the school officials' argument that without the "free transfer" choice, "white students will flee the school system altogether." (On the problem of "white flight" and resegregation, note, e.g., Bickel, The Supreme Court and the Idea of Progress (1970), and Graglia, Disaster by [Decree] (1976).)

inner city black schools, and some busing of elementary school students in both directions. The Court of Appeals set aside that provision on the ground that "pairing and grouping of elementary schools would place an unreasonable burden on the board and the system's pupils."]

The problems encountered by the [lower courts] make plain that we should now try to amplify guidelines, however incomplete and imperfect, for the assistance of school authorities and courts. [Elimination of dual school systems] has been rendered more difficult by changes since 1954 in the structure and patterns of communities, the growth of student population, movement of families, and other changes, some of which had marked impact on school planning, sometimes neutralizing or negating remedial action before it was fully implemented. Rural areas accustomed for half a century to the consolidated school systems implemented by bus transportation could make adjustments more readily than metropolitan areas. [The] objective today remains to eliminate from the public schools all vestiges of state-imposed segregation. [If] school authorities fail in their affirmative obligations under [Brown and later] holdings, judicial authority may be invoked. Once a right and a violation have been shown, the scope of a district court's equitable powers to remedy past wrongs is broad. [The] task is to correct, by a balancing of the individual and collective interests, the condition that offends the Constitution. [But] it is important to remember that judicial powers may be exercised only on the basis of a constitutional violation. [School authorities] are traditionally charged with broad power to formulate and implement educational policy and might well conclude, for example, that in order to prepare students to live in a pluralistic society each school should have a prescribed ratio of Negro to white students reflecting the proportion for the district as a whole. To do this as an educational policy is within the broad discretionary powers of school authorities; absent a finding of a constitutional violation, however, that would not be within the authority of a federal court. [In] default by the school authorities of their obligation to proffer acceptable remedies, a district court has broad power to fashion a remedy that will assure a unitary school system. [The] central issue in this case is that of student assignment, and there are essentially four problem [areas].[1]

(1) *Racial Balances or Racial Quotas.* [We] do not reach in this case the question whether a showing that school segregation is a consequence of other types of state action, without any discriminatory action by the school authorities, is a constitutional violation requiring remedial action by a school desegregation decree. [Our aim in] these cases is to see that school authorities exclude no people of a racial minority from any school, directly or indirectly, on account of race; it does not and cannot embrace all the problems of racial prejudice, even when those problems contribute to disproportionate racial concentrations in some schools. In this case it is urged that the District Court has imposed a racial balance requirement of 71%–29% on individual schools. [The District Court opinion] contains intimations that the "norm" is a fixed mathematical

---

1. The Court rejected the argument that federal judicial authority had been limited by Title IV of the Civil Rights Act of 1964. For example, that Title had defined "desegregation" as "the assignment of students to public schools and within such schools without regard to their race, color, religion, or national origin, but 'desegregation' shall not mean the assignment of students to public schools in order to overcome racial imbalance." The Court read that provision as simply intended "to foreclose any interpretation of the Act as expanding the *existing* powers of federal courts to enforce the Equal Protection Clause.

There is no suggestion of an intention to restrict those powers." Chief Justice Burger found in the legislative history a concern that the Act "might be read as creating a right of action under the 14th Amendment in the situation of so-called 'de facto segregation,' where racial imbalance exists in the schools but with no showing that this was brought about by discriminatory action of state authorities." In that view, the Act provided no "material assistance in answering the question of remedy for state-imposed segregation in violation of Brown I."

racial balance reflecting the pupil constituency of the system. If we were to read the holding of the District Court to require, as a matter of substantive constitutional right, any particular degree of racial balance or mixing, that approach would be [disapproved]. The constitutional command to desegregate schools does not mean that every school in every community must always reflect the racial composition of the school system as a whole. [But] the use made of mathematical ratios was no more than a starting point in the process of shaping a remedy, rather than an inflexible requirement. [As] we said in Green, a school authority's remedial plan or a district court's remedial decree is to be judged by its effectiveness. Awareness of the racial composition of the whole school system is likely to be a useful starting point in shaping a remedy to correct past constitutional violations. In sum, the very limited use made of mathematical ratios was within the equitable remedial discretion of the District Court.

(2) *One-Race Schools.* The record in this case reveals the familiar phenomenon that in metropolitan areas minority groups are often found concentrated in one part of the city. In some circumstances certain schools may remain all or largely of one race until new schools can be provided or neighborhood patterns change. Schools all or predominantly of one race in a district of mixed population will require close scrutiny to determine that school assignments are not part of state-enforced segregation. [It] should be clear that the existence of some small number of one-race, or virtually one-race, schools within a district is not in and of itself the mark of a system which still practices segregation by law. [But the] court should scrutinize such schools, and the burden upon the school authorities will be to satisfy the court that their racial composition is not the result of present or past discriminatory action on their part. An optional majority-to-minority transfer provision [is] an indispensable remedy for those students willing to transfer to other schools in order to lessen the impact on them of the state-imposed stigma of segregation. In order to be effective, such a transfer arrangement must grant the transferring student free transportation and space must be made available in the school to which he desires to [move].

(3) *Remedial Altering of Attendance Zones.* The maps submitted in these cases graphically demonstrate that one of the principal tools employed by school planners and by courts to break up the dual school system has been a frank—and sometimes drastic—gerrymandering of school districts and attendance zones. An additional step was pairing, "clustering," or "grouping" of schools with attendance assignments made deliberately to accomplish the transfer of Negro students out of formerly segregated Negro schools and transfer of white students to formerly all-Negro schools. More often than not, these zones are neither compact [2] nor contiguous; indeed they may be on opposite ends of the city. As an interim corrective measure, this cannot be said to be beyond the broad remedial powers of a court. Absent a constitutional violation there would be no basis for judicially ordering assignment of students on a racial basis. All things being equal, with no history of discrimination, it might well be desirable to assign pupils to schools nearest their homes. But all things are not equal in a system that has been deliberately constructed and maintained to enforce racial segregation. The remedy for such segregation may be administratively awkward, inconvenient, and even bizarre in some situations and may impose burdens on some; but all awkwardness and inconvenience cannot be avoided in the interim period when remedial adjustments are being made to

---

2. The reliance of school authorities on the reference to the "revision [of] attendance areas into *compact* units," Brown II, is misplaced. The enumeration in that opinion of considerations to be taken into account by district courts was patently intended to be suggestive rather than exhaustive. The decision in Brown II to remand the cases decided in Brown I to local courts for the framing of specific decrees was premised on a recognition that this Court could not at that time foresee the particular means which would be required to implement the constitutional principles [announced]. [Footnote by Chief Justice Burger.]

eliminate the dual school systems. No fixed or even substantially fixed guidelines can be established as to how far a court can go, but it must be recognized that there are limits. The objective is to dismantle the dual school system. "Racially neutral" assignment plans [may] fail to counteract the continuing effects of past school segregation resulting from discriminatory location of school sites or distortion of school size in order to achieve or maintain an artificial racial separation. When school authorities present a district court with a "loaded game board," affirmative action in the form of remedial altering of attendance zones is proper to achieve truly nondiscriminatory assignments. [We] hold that the pairing and grouping of non-contiguous school zones is a permissible tool and such action is to be considered in light of the objectives [sought].

(4) *Transportation of Students.* [No rigid guidelines are possible about the scope] of permissible transportation of students as an implement of a remedial decree. [Bus] transportation has been an integral part of the public education system for [years]. Eighteen million of the Nation's public school children, approximately 39%, were transported to their schools by bus in 1969–1970 in all parts of the country. The importance of bus transportation as a normal and accepted tool of educational policy is readily discernible in this and the companion case. [The] decree provided that [the] trips for elementary school pupils average about seven miles and the District Court found that they would take "not over 35 minutes at the most." This system compares favorably with the transportation plan previously operated in Charlotte under which each day 23,600 students on all grade levels were transported an average of 15 miles one way for an average trip requiring over an hour. In these circumstances, we find no basis for holding that the local school authorities may not be required to employ bus transportation as one tool of school desegregation. Desegregation plans cannot be limited to the walk-in school. An objection to transportation of students may have validity when the time or distance of travel is so great as to risk either the health of the children or significantly impinge on the educational process. District courts must weigh the soundness of any transportation plan in light of what is said in subdivisions (1), (2), and (3) above. [The] reconciliation of competing values in a desegregation case is, of course, a difficult task with many sensitive facets but fundamentally no more so than remedial measures courts of equity have traditionally [employed].

At some point, these school authorities and others like them should have achieved full compliance with this Court's decision in Brown I. The systems will then be "unitary" in the sense required by our decisions in Green and Alexander. It does not follow that the communities served by such systems will remain demographically stable, for in a growing, mobile society, few will do so. Neither school authorities nor district courts are constitutionally required to make year-by-year adjustments of the racial composition of student bodies once the affirmative duty to desegregate has been accomplished and racial discrimination through official action is eliminated from the system.[3] This does not mean

---

3. For an application of the guidelines in this passage to the problem of resegregation (because of population movements) of a previously judicially desegregated school system, see Pasadena City Bd. of Educ. v. Spangler, 427 U.S. 424 (1976), a rare example of a Court holding in the 1970s that a District Judge had imposed excessively harsh intradistrict desegregation remedies. In 1970, the lower court had found de jure segregation in Pasadena schools and had imposed a system-wide desegregation plan, which included a provision requiring reassignment of students in such a way that there would be no school with "a majority of any minority students." After the first year, population movements undermined that racial mix in some schools. In 1974, school officials sought a modification of the requirement. The District Judge refused, stating that the 1970 order meant "that at least during my lifetime there would be no majority of any minority in any school in Pasadena." Justice Rehnquist's majority opinion found this to be an abuse of discretion and insisted that the annual reassignment requirement was inconsistent with Swann. He noted that there had been no showing that the post-1971 changes in the racial mix

that federal courts are without power to deal with future problems; but in the absence of a showing that either the school authorities or some other agency of the State has deliberately attempted to fix or alter demographic patterns to affect the racial composition of the schools, further intervention by a district court should not be necessary.

[So ordered.] [4]

ANTI–BUSING MEASURES

1. *Congressional efforts.* In the wake of Swann, proposals for congressional curbs on busing proliferated. The first major enactment came in 1974, in response to messages from President Nixon.[1] The Education Amendments of 1974, 88 Stat. 484, established "a priority of remedies" to be used by federal courts and agencies in implementing desegregation, endorsed neighborhood schools, and barred any order "that would require the transportation of any student to a school other than the school closest or next closest to his place of residence." The congressional findings repeatedly condemned "excessive transportation of students" and stated a purpose of providing "appropriate remedies for the elimination of the vestiges of dual school systems." The 1974 Act contained an important proviso, however: it stated that the provisions were "not intended to modify or diminish the authority of the courts of the United States to enforce fully the fifth and fourteenth amendments." Would the 1974 Act have been within congressional power without that proviso?[2] Annual congressional efforts to impose further limitations on desegregation remedies, especially busing, continued throughout the late 1970s. The most important enactments were a series of riders to appropriation laws. See, e.g., the rider in 1976 (90 Stat. 1434) barring the use of federal funds to "force" any "desegregated" school district "to take any action to force the busing of students."

In the early 1980s, supporters of efforts to curb busing were encouraged by the more conservative composition of Congress and by the Reagan Administration's anti-busing position. The most widely discussed proposals followed the pattern of the 1970s: the addition of anti-busing riders to funding bills. Such a rider came close to enactment in 1981, but ultimately failed. In the course of Senate debate on the 1981 rider, Senator Johnston of Louisiana proposed an anti-busing amendment that rested on a different, broader approach. Instead of simply curbing executive action to achieve busing via riders to funding bills, he

---

"were in any manner caused by segregative actions" by the school officials; instead, they had "apparently resulted from people randomly moving into, out of, and around" the school district. He concluded that the trial court had fully performed its function of remedying de jure segregation once it had implemented a racially neutral attendance pattern in 1970. Justice Marshall, joined by Justice Brennan, dissented.

4. In a companion case noted below (p. 743), the Court held unconstitutional North Carolina's Anti-Busing Law prohibiting school assignments on the basis of race: that purportedly "color blind" directive was found to be an impermissible restraint on the implementation of Brown. North Carolina State Board of Education v. Swann, 402 U.S. 43 (1971).

1. An earlier, 1972 provision had been criticized by the President as unduly mild. The Higher Education Act of 1972 included a moratorium on court orders adopted "for the purpose of achieving a balance among students with re-

spect to race, sex, religion, or socioeconomic status." In Drummond v. Acree, 409 U.S. 1228 (1972), Justice Powell as Circuit Justice refused to stay a desegregation decree "entered [in] accordance with the mandate of Swann and not for the purpose of achieving a racial balance." He viewed the statutory provision as inapplicable: if Congress had decided to stay all busing orders, "it could have used clear and explicit language appropriate to that result."

2. What constitutional bases could Congress draw on? Article III? Sec. 5 of the 14th Amendment (see sec. 4 of the next chapter)? In advocating the antecedent of the 1974 law, President Nixon had stated (in 1972): "The Constitution in the 14th Amendment explicitly grants power to the Congress to set up the remedies to accomplish the right of equal protection of the law." He emphasized the "fundamental difference" between "a remedy" and "a right." See also Bork, Constitutionality of the President's Busing Proposals (1972).

relied on congressional power under § 5 of the 14th Amendment as interpreted in Katzenbach v. Morgan (p. 946 below). The Johnston Amendment, known as the Neighborhood School Act, would have barred the courts from ordering busing in school cases except in narrowly defined circumstances. In most cases, the amendment would have prevented any federal court from ordering a student to be assigned or bused to a public school other than the one closest to the student's home.[3] The Johnston Amendment was adopted by the Senate in a 57–37 vote in March, 1982, but the House failed to act on it before the 97th Congress adjourned. Was it justifiable under the Morgan power?[4]

Additional anti-busing proposals to restrict federal court power to order busing were before Congress in 1984. These proposals relied both on congressional power under Art. III and under § 5 of the 14th Amendment. Although a Senate subcommittee approved one of these proposals in March 1984, none was enacted by the 98th Congress. Starting in the late 1970s, and contemporaneous with legislative efforts, constitutional amendments to curb busing were proposed in Congress. The first to reach the floor of the House, in July 1979, was an amendment to bar busing and assure neighborhood schools. However, the amendment fell far short of the necessary support in the House. Similar amendment proposals were introduced in the early 1980s, but none made it out of committee.

2. *State efforts to curb busing remedies for de facto segregation.* In two 1982 cases, the Court considered state measures adopted to curb mandatory busing programs through which states had sought to eliminate racial imbalance in schools and to end de facto school segregation. The 5 to 4 decision in

3. During the early 1980s, congressional committees also had under consideration bills to curb federal court jurisdiction in a number of controversial areas, including busing. None of these jurisdiction-curbing proposals was enacted into law. See chap. 1, at p. 48, above.

4. The Johnston proposal rested not only on § 5 of the 14th Amendment, but also on congressional power, under Art. III, § 1, pertaining to the jurisdiction of the lower federal courts. That aspect of the bill is noted above, in chap. 1, at p. 48.

Just before adopting the Johnston Amendment in 1982, the Senate turned down an alternative bill sponsored by Senator Gorton, Republican of Washington. Senator Gorton's proposal, unlike Johnston's, rested exclusively on the remedial power of Congress under § 5 of the 14th Amendment. Moreover, the Gorton proposal specifically recognized the right, acknowledged by the Court ever since Brown, to be free from de jure segregated schools. Senator Gorton's approach was to deal more directly with the problem of providing remedies for that constitutionally recognized right, in the exercise of congressional remedial power, and to avoid tampering with lower federal court jurisdiction. Was the Gorton approach on more solid constitutional footing than Johnston's invocation of the power over jurisdiction? Can the Court decisions regarding busing be viewed as delineations of "remedies" rather than creation of "rights"?

Consider Attorney General Smith's letter of May 6, 1982, to Congressman Rodino, endorsing the constitutionality of Johnston's S. 951, both on grounds of Art. III, § 1, as noted above (in chap. 1) and (somewhat ambivalently and ambiguous-

ly) under § 5 of the 14th Amendment. With respect to the latter, the Attorney General stated: "The limitation on busing remedies contained in the Neighborhood School Act would be authorized under § 5 to the extent that it does not prevent the inferior federal courts from adequately vindicating constitutional rights." He argued that under the Morgan case, the courts "would probably pay considerable deference to the congressional factfinding upon which the bill is ultimately based," although he conceded that there apparently was "no particularized research [presented] to the Senate which might have supported or undermined the specific limitations on federal court decrees." In his view, the Act would not be "interpreted to 'dilute' 14th Amendment rights merely because it denies a certain form of relief in the inferior federal courts." He added, however, that, "although Congress can express its view through factfinding [that] busing is an ineffective remedial tool and that extensive busing is not necessary to remedy a constitutional violation, it is ultimately the responsibility of the courts to determine, after giving due consideration to the congressional findings, [whether] in a given case an effective remedy requires the use of mandatory busing in excess of the limitations set forth in [the bill]." [The Attorney General conceded that Congress could not, under § 5 of the 14th Amendment, bar inferior federal courts from ordering mandatory busing when, in the judgment of the courts, "such busing is necessary to remedy a constitutional violation." That concession apparently led him to rely with greater confidence on Art. III, § 1, as the ultimate constitutional support for the Johnston Amendment.]

WASHINGTON v. SEATTLE SCHOOL DIST. NO. 1, 458 U.S. 457, held such a state effort unconstitutional, despite Justice Powell's vehement opinion for the dissenters. But in CRAWFORD v. LOS ANGELES BOARD OF EDUCATION, 458 U.S. 527, it was Justice Powell who wrote for the majority. The 8 to 1 decision in Crawford sustained California's prohibition of court-ordered busing to alleviate de facto segregation. Was the Washington ruling justifiable? If so, was the California case distinguishable?

    a.   *Washington v. Seattle School Dist. No. 1.*   The Washington case invalidated a state initiative law (Initiative 350) adopted in response to the Seattle School District's integration plan. The Seattle Plan had been designed to eliminate "racial imbalance" in the District's schools, in part through mandatory busing.[5] Justice BLACKMUN, in his opinion for the majority, relied heavily on Hunter v. Erickson (1969, p. 632 above), the case that involved obstacles to adopting fair housing legislation in Akron, Ohio. The central principle of Hunter, in Justice Blackmun's view, was that, although "the political majority may generally restructure the political process to place obstacles in the path of everyone seeking to secure the benefits of governmental action, [a] different analysis is required when the State allocates governmental power non-neutrally, by explicitly using the *racial* nature of a decision to determine the decisionmaking process. State action of this [kind] 'places *special* burdens on racial minorities within the governmental process,' thereby 'making it *more* difficult for certain racial and religious minorities [than for other members of the community] to achieve legislation that is in their interest.'" He concluded: "Initiative 350 must fall because it does 'not attemp[t] to allocate governmental power on the basis of any general principle.' [Hunter (Harlan, J., concurring).] Instead, it uses the racial nature of an issue to define the governmental decisionmaking structure, and thus imposes substantial and unique burdens on racial minorities."[6] Justice Blackmun rejected the argument that the initiative had no racial overtones: "[It] is beyond reasonable dispute [that] the initiative was enacted ' "because of," not merely "in spite of," its adverse effects upon' busing for integration. [Feeney.]" Nor did he accept the view that "busing for integration, unlike the fair housing ordinance involved in Hunter, is not a peculiarly 'racial' issue at all." He conceded that "proponents of mandatory integration cannot be classified by race," but insisted that "desegregation of the public schools [at] bottom inures primarily to the benefit of the minority, and is designed for that purpose. [For] present purposes, it is enough that minorities may consider busing for integration to be 'legislation that is in their interest.' Given the racial focus of Initiative 350, this suffices to trigger application of the Hunter doctrine."

    Justice Blackmun emphasized that the practical effect of Initiative 350 was to work a reallocation of power similar to the kind condemned in Hunter. He explained: "Those favoring the elimination of de facto school segregation now must seek relief from the state legislature or from the statewide electorate. Yet authority over all other student assignment decisions, as well as over most other areas of educational policy, remains vested in the local school board. [As] in

---

    5. Initiative 350 stated that "no school board [shall] directly or indirectly require any student to attend a school other than the school which is geographically nearest or next nearest the student's place of residence [and] which offers the course of study pursued by such student." (The initiative also enumerated several exceptions to this prohibition.) However, the initiative did not "prevent any court of competent jurisdiction from adjudicating constitutional issues relating to the public schools" and thus did *not* bar judicial orders requiring mandatory busing in order to eliminate constitutionally prohibited de jure segregation.

    6. Justice Blackmun rejected the dissent's charge that, under the majority's view, "the State's attempt to repeal a desegregation program creates a racial classification, while 'identical action' by the Seattle School Board does not": "It is the State's race-conscious restructuring of its decisionmaking process that is impermissible, not the simple repeal of the Seattle Plan."

Hunter, then, the community's political mechanisms are modified to place effective decisionmaking authority over a racial issue at a different level of government." He rejected the arguments that the initiative had "not worked *any* reallocation of power," that it amounted "to nothing more than an unexceptional example of a State's intervention in its own school system," and that, "if the State is the body that usually makes decisions in this area, Initiative 350 worked a simple change in policy rather than a forbidden reallocation of power. Cf. [Crawford]." Justice Blackmun conceded that this seemed, "at first glance," a "potent argument." But he insisted that the issue here was "not whether Washington has the authority to intervene in the affairs of local school boards; it is, rather, whether the state has exercised that authority in a manner consistent with [equal protection]." In this case, Washington, by analogy to Hunter, had "chosen to make use of a more complex governmental structure, and a close examination both of the Washington statutes and of the Court's decisions in related areas convinces us that Hunter is fully applicable here." He noted, for example, that Washington had, until the passage of the initiative, in fact "established the local school board, rather than the State, as the entity charged with making decisions of the type at issue here." Justice Blackmun conceded, quoting from Crawford, that "the simple repeal or modification of desegregation or anti-discrimination laws, without more, never has been viewed as embodying a presumptively invalid racial classification." But Initiative 350, he insisted, "works something more than the 'mere repeal' of a desegregation law by the political entity that created it. It burdens all future attempts to integrate Washington schools in districts throughout the State, by lodging decisionmaking authority over the question at a new and remote level of government. [One] group cannot be subjected to a debilitating and often insurmountable disadvantage." [7]

Justice POWELL's dissent, joined by Chief Justice Burger and Justices Rehnquist and O'Connor, objected to "the Court's unprecedented intrusion into the structure of a state government." He emphasized that there was no federal constitutional duty "to adopt mandatory busing [in] the absence of [de jure segregation]." Thus, "a neighborhood school policy and a decision *not* to assign students on the basis of their race does not offend the 14th Amendment." [8] He noted that the school district itself constitutionally could have canceled its integration program at any time, "yet this Court holds that neither the legislature nor the people of [Washington] could alter what the District had

---

7. Justice Blackmun also rejected the argument that Hunter had in effect been overruled by more recent decisions. The defenders of the initiative argued that "Hunter applied a simple 'disparate impact' analysis" and had therefore been swept away by the purposeful discrimination approach of Washington v. Davis and Arlington Heights. But this, Justice Blackmun insisted, "misapprehends the basis of the Hunter doctrine": "There is one immediate and crucial difference between Hunter and the [purposeful discrimination cases]": Cases such as Arlington Heights involved facially neutral classifications: the Hunter provision "dealt in explicitly racial terms. [When] the political process or the decisionmaking mechanism used to *address* racially conscious legislation [is] singled out for peculiar and disadvantageous treatment, the governmental action plainly 'rests on "distinctions based on race." ' And when the State's allocation of power places unusual burdens on the ability of racial groups to enact legislation specifically designed to overcome the 'special condition' of prejudice,

the governmental action seriously 'curtail[s] the operation of those political processes ordinarily to be relied upon to protect minorities.' [Carolene Products footnote.]" Hunter accordingly rested on a central principle of the 14th Amendment—"the prevention of meaningful and unjustified official distinctions based on race"— and that principle had been violated here.

8. "[Indeed], in the absence of a finding of segregation by the School District, mandatory busing on the basis of race raises constitutional difficulties of its own. Extensive pupil transportation may threaten liberty or privacy interests. See [Bakke (Powell opinion); Keyes (Powell opinion)]. Moreover, when a State or school board assigns students on the basis of their race, it acts on the basis of a racial classification, and we have consistently held that '[a] racial classification, regardless of purported motivation, is presumptively invalid and can be upheld only upon an extraordinary justification.' [Feeney.]" [Footnote by Justice Powell.]

decided. [The Constitution] does not require such a bizarre result." [9] He insisted that Hunter was "simply irrelevant" : The Washington initiative "simply does not place unique political obstacles in the way of racial minorities. In this case, unlike in Hunter, the political system has *not* been redrawn or altered. The authority of the State over the public school system [is] plenary. Thus, the State's political system is not altered when it adopts for the first time a policy, concededly within the area of its authority, for the regulation of local school districts. [Under the Court's] unprecedented theory of a vested constitutional right to local decisionmaking, the State apparently is now forever barred from addressing the perplexing problems of how best to educate fairly *all* children in a multiracial society where, as in this case, the local school board has acted first."

     b. *Crawford v. Los Angeles Board of Education.* In Crawford, the majority rejected an attack on a California constitutional amendment (Proposition I) designed to conform the state courts' power to order busing to that exercised by the federal courts under the 14th Amendment.[10] The amendment to the California Constitution provided that state courts could not order mandatory pupil assignment or transportation unless a federal court would do so to remedy a violation of the federal Equal Protection Clause. In writing the majority opinion which rejected the 14th Amendment attack on the state constitutional amendment, Justice POWELL disagreed with the challengers' contention (as stated by Justice Powell) that "once a State chooses to do 'more' than the 14th Amendment requires, it may never recede. We reject an interpretation of the 14th Amendment so destructive of a state's democratic processes and of its ability to experiment. This interpretation has no support in the decisions of this Court." He thought it would be "paradoxical" to conclude that California, by adopting federal equal protection standards that provided for mandatory busing, had thereby violated the 14th Amendment.[11]

     Justice Powell rejected the challengers' claim that Proposition I employed an "explicit racial classification" and imposed a "race-specific" burden on minorities seeking to vindicate state-created rights. The claim was that, by limiting the power of state courts to enforce the state-created right to desegregated schools in de facto segregation situations, Proposition I created a "dual court system" which discriminated on the basis of race. The challengers emphasized that "other state created rights may be vindicated by the state courts without limitation on remedies." But Justice Powell insisted that Proposition I did not

9. In a footnote, Justice Powell stated: "The policies in support of neighborhood schooling are various but all of them are racially neutral. The people of the State legitimately could decide that unlimited mandatory busing places too great a burden on the liberty and privacy interests of families and students of all races. It might decide that the reassignment of students to distant schools, on the basis of race, was too great a departure from the ideal of racial neutrality in State action. And, in light of the experience with mandatory busing in other cities, the State might conclude that such a program ultimately would lead to greater racial imbalance in the schools."

10. Proposition I was ratified by the California voters in 1979. Prior to the adoption of the constitutional amendment, the California courts (relying on their interpretation of the state constitution's equal protection provision) had ordered busing in cases of de facto, not only de jure, segregation. (The amendment was adopted in the midst of controversy over court-ordered

mandatory busing in Los Angeles. The state trial court's busing order had been affirmed by the state Supreme Court on the basis of an interpretation of the state constitution's equal protection provision, an interpretation which barred de facto, not merely de jure, school segregation.)

11. Justice Powell noted that, "even after Proposition I, the California Constitution still imposes a greater duty of desegregation than does the Federal Constitution. The state courts [continue] to have an obligation under state law to order segregated school districts to use voluntary desegregation techniques, whether or not there has been a finding of intentional segregation. The school districts themselves retain a state law obligation to take reasonably feasible steps to desegregate, and they remain free to adopt reassignment and busing plans to effectuate desegregation." He added: "In this respect this case differs from the situation presented in [Washington]."

"embody a racial classification"[12]: "It neither says nor implies that persons are to be treated differently on account of their race. [The] benefit it seeks to confer—neighborhood schooling—is made available regardless of race in the discretion of school boards. Indeed, even if Proposition I had a racially discriminatory effect, in view of the demographic mix of the [Los Angeles] District it is not clear which race or races would be affected the most or in what way." (White students are in a minority in the Los Angeles school district.) Moreover, "discriminatory purpose" was necessary to show a 14th Amendment violation. He added that "the simple repeal or modification of desegregation or anti-discrimination laws, without more, never has been viewed as embodying a presumptively valid racial classification."[13]

The challengers' central argument, however, was that Proposition I was not a "mere repeal" but rather was invalid under Hunter. Justice Powell replied: "We do not view Hunter as controlling here, nor are we persuaded by [the] characterization of Proposition I as something more than a mere repeal." Proposition I was less than a "repeal" of the California equal protection provision, since the California Constitution still placed upon school boards "a greater duty to desegregate than does the 14th Amendment." Nor did Proposition I "distort[t] the political process for racial reasons" or "allocat[e] governmental or judicial power on the basis of a discriminatory principle. [Remedies] appropriate in one area of legislation may not be desirable in another. [A] 'dual court system'—one for the racial majority and one for the racial minority—is not established simply because civil rights remedies are different from those available in other areas. [In short], having gone beyond the requirements of the Federal Constitution, the State was free to return in part to the standard prevailing generally throughout the United States." Finally, Justice Powell, like the California appellate court, rejected the challengers' claim that "Proposition I, if facially valid, was nonetheless unconstitutional because enacted with a discriminatory purpose." The state court had found that the voters might have been motivated by the amendment's stated purposes, "chief among them the educational benefits of neighborhood schooling," and that they might also have considered "that the extent of mandatory busing, authorized by state law, actually was aggravating rather than ameliorating the desegregation problem." The state court characterized the challengers' "claim of discriminatory intent on the part of millions of voters as but 'pure speculation.'" Justice Powell saw "no reason to differ with the conclusions of the state appellate court," pointing by analogy to the Court's deference to a state court's identification of discriminatory purpose in Reitman v. Mulkey. "Even if we could assume that Proposition I had a disproportionate, adverse affect on racial minorities, we see no reason to challenge the [state appellate court's] conclusion that the voters of the State were not motivated by a discriminatory purpose."[14]

---

12. Justice Powell noted that, in Hunter, the Court had found that, although the law was neutral on its face, "the reality [was] that the law's impact [fell] on the minority." Justice Powell added: "In light of this reality and the distortion of the political process worked by the charter amendment [in Hunter], the Court considered that the amendment employed a racial classification despite its facial neutrality."

13. "Of course, if the purpose of repealing legislation is to disadvantage a racial minority, the repeal is unconstitutional for this reason. See Reitman v. Mulkey [1967; p. 890 below]." [Footnote by Justice Powell.]

14. A concurring opinion by Justice BLACKMUN, joined by Justice Brennan, supported Justice Powell's opinion and emphasized

the "critical distinctions" between this case and Washington. In Crawford, by contrast to Washington, there had been no restructuring of the state's decisionmaking process: "State courts do not create the rights they enforce; those rights originate elsewhere—in the state legislature, in the State's political subdivisions, or in the state constitution itself. When one of those rights is repealed, and therefore is rendered unenforceable in the courts, that action hardly can be said to restructure the State's decisionmaking mechanism. While the California electorate may have made it more difficult to achieve desegregation when it enacted Proposition I, to my mind it did so not by working a structural change in the political *process* so much as by simply repealing the right to invoke a judicial busing remedy.

Justice MARSHALL, the sole dissenter, insisted at length that this case was indistinguishable from the Washington one: "[Because] I fail to see how a fundamental redefinition of the governmental decisionmaking structure with respect to the same racial issue can be unconstitutional when the state seeks to remove the authority from local school boards, yet constitutional when the state attempts to achieve the same result by limiting the power of its courts, I must dissent." He thought Proposition I was sufficiently "racial" to invoke the Hunter doctrine because "minorities may consider busing for integration to be 'legislation that is in their interest'" [quoting the Washington opinion]. Indeed, he insisted that California's provision was even more vulnerable than the Hunter scheme: "Proposition I, by denying full access to the only branch of government [the judiciary] that has been willing to address this issue meaningfully, is far worse for those seeking to vindicate the plainly unpopular cause of racial integration in the public schools than a simple reallocation of an often unavailable and unresponsive legislative process." [15]

DESEGREGATION IN THE NORTH

1. *Broad intradistrict remedies for de jure segregation.* The Denver school case, KEYES v. SCHOOL DISTRICT, 413 U.S. 189 (1973), was the Court's first decision on school desegregation in the North. Justice BRENNAN's majority opinion purported to adhere to the de jure-de facto distinction. (He stated: "We emphasize that the differentiating factor between de jure and so-called de facto segregation [is] *purpose* or *intent* to segregate.") But he set forth criteria that would facilitate a finding of purposeful discrimination in Northern districts without a background of state-mandated segregation; and he announced standards that would permit court orders for districtwide remedies to rest on findings of intentional discrimination in only *part* of the district. The immediate charges of purposeful discrimination were limited to one portion of the citywide Denver school district. The lower court found that the school board (by such techniques as manipulation of attendance zones, and schoolsite selection) had "engaged over almost a decade after 1960 in an unconstitutional policy of deliberate racial segregation" with respect to schools in the Park Hill area, and ordered their desegregation. There was also a heavy concentration of black students in the core city area, but the lower court found that the school board had no deliberate segregative policy as to that area and refused to order desegregation there.

Justice Brennan's opinion provided guidelines that would permit *districtwide* desegregation on the basis of the finding regarding the Park Hill area. He sketched two routes to such a result. First, "where plaintiffs prove that the school authorities have carried out a systematic program of segregation affecting a substantial proportion of the students, schools, teachers and facilities," a finding that the entire district is a dual, segregated one is authorized, absent a

Indeed, ruling for the [challengers] on a Hunter theory seemingly would mean that statutory affirmative action or antidiscrimination programs never could be repealed." Justice Blackmun also noted that the "political mechanisms that create and repeal the rights ultimately enforced by the courts were left entirely unaffected by Proposition I."

15. Justice Marshall insisted, moreover, that Proposition I was not a "mere repeal" within the meaning of any other prior decisions. He claimed that the only time that the Court had held that a "mere repeal" was not unconstitu-

tional was in the Dayton school case (p. 726 below), "a situation where a governmental entity rescinded *its own* prior statement of policy without affecting any existing educational policy." By contrast, in the three cases in which the Court had rejected "mere repeal" defenses—the Washington, Reitman v. Mulkey, and Hunter decisions—"the alleged rescission was accomplished by a governmental entity other than the entity that had taken the initial action, and resulted in a drastic alteration of the substantive effect of existing policy. This case falls squarely within this latter category."

showing that the district is divided into clearly unrelated units. And once such a districtwide finding is made, the usual remedies evolved in the southern context, from Brown II to Swann, are applicable. He explained that "common sense dictates the conclusion that racially inspired school board actions have an impact beyond the particular schools that are the subjects of those actions." Second, even if the areas within a district are treated separately, a showing of intentional segregation in one area may be probative as to intentional segregation in other areas. Accordingly, the finding as to Park Hill was usable in the efforts to prove segregative intent in the core city area. He added: "We have no occasion to consider [here] whether a 'neighborhood school policy' of itself will justify racial or ethnic concentrations in the absence of a finding that school authorities have committed acts constituting de jure segregation." [1]

Justice REHNQUIST was the only member of the Court in total disagreement with the majority. He concluded: "The Court has taken a long leap [in] equating the district-wide consequences of gerrymandering individual attendance zones in a district where separation of the races was never required by law with statutes or ordinances in other jurisdictions which did so require. It then adds to this potpourri a confusing enunciation of evidentiary rules in order to make it more likely that the trial court will on remand reach the result which the Court apparently wants it to reach." He also criticized the "drastic extension" of Brown in Green—an extension which "was barely, if at all, explicated in the latter opinion." He elaborated: "To require that a genuinely 'dual' system be disestablished, in the sense of the assignment of a child to a particular school is not made to depend on his race, is one thing. To require that school boards affirmatively undertake to achieve racial mixing in schools where such mixing is not achieved in sufficient degree by neutrally drawn boundary lines is quite obviously something else." [2]

2. *Demonstrating "discriminatory purpose" and imposing intradistrict systemwide remedies in 1979: Reaffirmation of Keyes, or drastic expansion?* Despite considerable speculation that the Court would take the occasion to cut back on Keyes, the majority affirmed Court of Appeals decisions mandating broad desegregation remedies in COLUMBUS BOARD OF EDUCATION v. PENICK, 443 U.S. 449 (1979), and DAYTON BOARD OF EDUCATION v. BRINKMAN (Dayton II), 443 U.S. 526 (1979). Justice White's majority opinion showed great deference to the Court of Appeals and rejected the argument that the lower court had misused Keyes. To some of the dissenters, by contrast, the majority's "Delphic" pronouncements marked "a radical new approach to desegregation cases in systems without a history of statutorily mandated separation of the races." As Justice Rehnquist's dissent in Columbus claimed: "Keyes [is] not overruled, yet [its "essential message" is] ignored." His dissent in Dayton added that the "Court's cascade of presumptions in this case sweeps away the distinction between de facto and de jure segregation." Objecting to the Court's "cavalier treatment of causality," he claimed that the majority's approach "reliev[ed] school desegregation plaintiffs from any showing of a causal nexus between intentional segregative actions and the conditions they seek to remedy." (Justice White denied that charge, pointing out that the lower courts had found "that the [Columbus] Board's purposefully discriminato-

---

1. An elaborate separate opinion by Justice POWELL went considerably further on the issue of rights as well as on remedies. As to the former, he advocated abandonment of the de jure-de facto distinction and urged recognition of a uniform, nationwide right to have local school boards operate "integrated school systems." (See note 3 below.) On the question of remedies, Justice Powell urged greatly reduced use of massive busing as a desegregation tool. (In a sepa-

rate opinion, Justice DOUGLAS agreed with Justice Powell on the issue of rights: he, too, advocated scrapping the de jure-de facto distinction. Chief Justice BURGER concurred only in the majority's result. (Justice REHNQUIST dissented, as noted below. Justice White did not participate.)

2. See also his dissents in the Dayton and Columbus cases, which follow.

ry conduct and policies had current, systemwide impact—an essential predicate, as both courts recognized, for a systemwide remedy.")

Justice WHITE's majority opinion in Columbus endorsed the conclusion of the lower federal courts that the school authorities' conduct "not only was animated by an unconstitutional, segregative purpose, but also had current, segregative impact that was sufficiently systemwide to warrant the [systemwide] remedy." Though there had been no statutorily mandated segregation in the 20th century, the trial court found that in 1954, when Brown I was decided, "the Columbus Board was not operating a racially neutral, unitary school system, but was conducting 'an enclave of separate, black schools on the near east side of Columbus' and that '[t]he then-existing racial separation was the direct result of cognitive acts or omissions of those school board members and administrators who had originally intentionally caused and later perpetuated the racial isolation.'" Emphasizing and supporting that finding, Justice White stated: "Proof of purposeful and effective maintenance of a body of separate black schools in a substantial part of the system itself is prima facie proof of a dual school system and supports a finding to this effect absent sufficient contrary proof by the Board, which was not forthcoming in this case. Keyes."

With that finding of de jure segregation in 1954 as the underpinning, Justice White agreed with the lower courts' statement that the Board had, since Brown II (1955), "been under a continuous constitutional obligation to disestablish its dual school system." He emphasized: "The Board's continuing 'affirmative duty to disestablish the dual school system' [is] beyond question, and it has pointed to nothing in the record persuading us that at the time of trial the dual school system and its effects had been disestablished." He also approved the District Court's finding that, in the years since 1954, "there had been a series of Board actions and practices[3] that could not 'reasonably be explained without reference to racial concerns' and that 'intentionally aggravated, rather than alleviated,' racial separation in the schools." In short, "'[s]ince the 1954 Brown decision, the Columbus defendants or their predecessors were adequately put on notice of the fact that action was required to correct and to prevent the increase in' segregation, yet failed to heed their duty to alleviate racial separation in the schools." Against that background, he concluded that "we cannot fault the conclusion of the [lower courts] that at the time of trial there was systemwide segregation in the Columbus schools that was the result of recent and remote intentionally segregative actions of the Columbus Board."

Justice White rejected the claim that the desegregation decree rested on misapprehension of the controlling law. It was argued, for example, that the courts below had ignored Washington v. Davis and Arlington Heights by considering the "purposeful discrimination" requirement satisfied "if it were shown that disparate impact would be the natural and foreseeable consequence of the practices and policies of the Board, which, it is said, is nothing more than equating impact with intent, contrary to the controlling precedent." In Justice White's view, however, the trial court had recognized that disparate impact and foreseeable consequence did not alone establish a constitutional violation; it had simply "correctly noted that actions having foreseeable and anticipated disparate impact are relevant evidence to prove the ultimate fact, forbidden purpose." That approach "stayed well within the requirements of [Davis] and Arlington Heights." Moreover, there had been no "misuse of Keyes": "There was no undue reliance here on the inferences permitted by Keyes, or upon those recognized by Swann. Furthermore, the Board was given ample opportunity to

---

3. The improper "actions and practices" since 1954 included "the intentionally segregative use of optional attendance zones, discontinuance of attendance areas, and boundary changes; and the selection of sites for new school construction that had the foreseeable and anticipated effect of maintaining the racial separation of the schools."

counter the evidence of segregative purpose and current, systemwide impact, and the findings of the courts below were against it in both respects."

In the Dayton case, unlike Columbus, the District Court had decided *against* the plaintiffs, finding that they "had failed to prove that acts of intentional segregation over 20 years old had any current incremental segregative effects." The Court of Appeals, emphasizing the existence of a dual school system at the time of Brown I, reversed and ordered a systemwide remedy. Justice White's opinion stated: "Given intentionally segregated schools in 1954, [the] Court of Appeals was quite right in holding that the Board was thereafter under a continuing duty to eradicate the effects of that system [Columbus] and that the systemwide nature of the violation furnished prima facie proof that current segregation in the Dayton schools was caused at least in part by prior intentionally segregative official acts. Thus, judgment for the plaintiffs was authorized and required absent sufficient countervailing evidence by the defendant school officials. [Keyes; Swann.]" He noted, moreover, that the Dayton Board "had engaged in many post-Brown actions that had the effect of increasing or perpetuating segregation." He added: "The District Court [ignored] this compounding of the original constitutional breach on the ground that there was no direct evidence of continued discriminatory purpose. But the measure of a post-Brown conduct of a school board under an unsatisfied duty to liquidate a dual system is the effectiveness, not the purpose, of the actions in decreasing or increasing the segregation caused by the dual system. As was clearly established in Keyes and Swann, the Board had to do more than abandon its prior discriminatory purpose. The Board has had an affirmative responsibility to see that pupil assignment policies and school construction and abandonment practices 'are not used and do not serve to perpetuate or re-establish the dual school system' [Columbus], and the Board has a 'heavy burden' of showing that actions that increased or continued the effects of the dual system serve important and legitimate ends." He added: "The Court of Appeals was also quite justified in utilizing the Board's total failure to fulfill its affirmative duty—and indeed its conduct resulting in increased segregation—to trace the current, systemwide segregation back to the purposefully dual system of the 1950's and to the subsequent acts of intentional discrimination."

Justice STEWART, joined by Chief Justice Burger, concurred in the result in the Columbus case (where the District Court had found for the plaintiffs) but dissented in Dayton. To him, the critical difference was that the Court of Appeals had "ignored the crucial role of the federal district courts in school desegregation litigation": in desegregation cases, "appellate courts should accept even more readily than in most cases the factual findings of the courts of first instance." Justice Stewart also disagreed with important elements of the majority's approach. He argued that "the Court has attached far too much importance in each case to the question whether there existed a 'dual school system' in 1954." The Board's duty to desegregate in 1954, he claimed, "does not justify a complete shift of the normal burden of proof" in a 1970s case. In his view, current racial separation in the schools could not be presumed to have been caused by unconstitutional acts committed as long ago as 1954. He commented: "Much has changed in 25 years. [The] prejudices of the school boards of 1954 (and earlier) cannot realistically be assumed to haunt the school boards of today. [It] is unrealistic to assume that the hand of 1954 plays any major part in shaping the current school systems in either [Dayton or Columbus]. [I] simply cannot accept [this] shift in the litigative burden of proof." Turning to the question of the basis for systemwide remedies in post-1954 developments, he concluded that "[t]he plaintiffs in the Columbus case, unlike those in the Dayton case, proved what the Court in Keyes defined as a prima facie case" which the Board had not rebutted.

Justice REHNQUIST, joined by Justice Powell, submitted the longest dissent in the Columbus case, and reiterated his views in a brief dissenting statement (again joined by Justice Powell) in Dayton. In Columbus, he claimed that the lower courts had "emasculate[d] the key determinants set down in Keyes": "The lower courts' methodology would all but eliminate the distinction between de facto and de jure segregation and render all school systems captives of a remote and ambiguous past." In exploring the implications of the majority opinions, he offered two suggestions for fathoming them. First, "the Court, possibly chastened by the complexity and emotion that accompanies school desegregation cases, wishes to relegate the determination of a [constitutional violation] in any plan of pupil assignment, and the formulation of a remedy for its violation, to a judgment of a single District Judge," with both "discriminatory purpose" and "systemwide violation" to be treated "as talismanic phrases which, once invoked, warrant only the most superficial scrutiny by appellate courts." But such an approach, he argued, would disparage "both this Court's oft-expressed concern for the important role of local autonomy in educational matters and the significance of the constitutional rights involved." The second and only other possible interpretation of the opinions, he insisted, was a "literal reading," and that he found "even more disquieting": "Such a reading would require embracing a novel analytical approach to school segregation in systems without a history of statutorily mandated separation of the races—an approach that would have dramatic consequences for urban school systems in this country." In his view, there were "glaring deficiencies both in the Court's new framework and in its decision to subject [school systems to a] sweeping racial balance remedy."

Justice Rehnquist attacked the majority's emphasis on 1954 violations to justify current systemwide remedies, insisting that "[a]s a matter of history, case law, or logic, there is nothing to support the novel proposition that the primary inquiry in school desegregation cases involving systems without a history of statutorily mandated racial assignment is what happened in those systems before 1954. As a matter of history, 1954 makes no more sense as a benchmark—indeed it makes *less* sense—than 1968, 1971 or 1973. Perhaps the latter year has the most to commend it, [because] in Keyes this Court first confronted the problem of school segregation in the context of systems without a history of statutorily mandated separation of the races." In Keyes, causality was central: the School Board's past acts were relevant only if "segregation resulting from those actions continues to exist." Justice Rehnquist added: "That inquiry is not central under the approach approved by the Court today. Henceforth, the question is apparently whether pre-1954 acts contributed in some unspecified manner to segregated conditions that existed in 1954. If the answer is yes, then the only question is whether the school board has exploited all integrative opportunities that presented themselves in the subsequent 25 years. If not, a systemwide remedy is in order despite the plaintiff's failure to demonstrate a link between those past acts and current racial imbalance." He argued, moreover, that the Keyes "presumption" had been misused: it had not only been applied to a situation "remote in time" but also invoked in a manner which "essentially makes the Keyes presumption irrebuttable." To him, the majority's analysis of the alleged post-1954 violations underlined its "departure from established doctrines of causation and discriminatory purpose." He commented: "[O]bjective evidence must be carefully analyzed, for it may otherwise reduce the 'discriminatory purpose' requirement to a 'discriminatory impact' test by another name." Claiming that "foreseeability was not one kind of evidence, but the whole ball game" in the District Court's examination of post-1954 actions in the Columbus case, he thought it "somewhat misleading for the Court to refer to these actions as in some sense independent of the constitutional duty it suggests that the Columbus Board assumed in 1954." [4]

In another dissent, Justice POWELL, joined by Justice Rehnquist, found the majority opinions "profoundly disturbing": they seemed "remarkably insensitive to the now widely accepted view that a quarter of a century after [Brown I], the federal judiciary should be limiting rather than expanding the extent to which courts are operating the public school systems of our country." He argued that experience in many cities demonstrated that it was "an illusion" to expect school boards to be "capable of bringing about and maintaining the desired racial balance." He insisted, moreover, that judicial mandates would probably generate "responses that will defeat the integrative purpose of the courts' order": "Parents, unlike school officials, are not bound by these decrees and may frustrate them through the simple expedient of withdrawing their children from a public school system in which they have lost confidence. [W]here inner city populations comprise a large proportion of racial minorities and surrounding suburbs remain white, [the] demonstrated effect of compulsory integration is a substantial exodus of whites from the system." This cast "serious doubt upon the efficacy of far-reaching judicial remedies directed not against specific constitutional violations, but rather imposed on an entire school system on the fictional assumption that the existence of identifiable black or white schools is caused entirely by intentional segregative conduct, and is evidence of systemwide discrimination." He accordingly urged: "The time has come for a thoughtful re-examination of the proper limits of the role of courts in confronting the intractable problems of public education in our complex society. [Courts] are the branch least competent to provide long-range solutions acceptable to the public. [It] is now reasonably clear that the goal of diversity that we call integration, if it is to be lasting and conducive to quality education, must have the support of parents who so frequently have the option to choose where their children will attend school. Courts, of course, should confront discrimination wherever it is found to exist. But they should recognize limitations on judicial action inherent in our system and also the limits of effective judicial power." [5]

3. *How much vitality does the de jure-de facto distinction retain in school desegregation cases?* In the Northern intradistrict desegregation cases in the preceding notes, the Court has, at least in form, adhered to the "purposeful discrimination" requirement considered in sec. 3D2 above. Yet in these school cases— Keyes, Columbus, and Dayton—the Court has also been quite lenient in allowing inferences of purposeful discrimination, in much the same way (and by use of very much the same technique of deferring to the "fact findings" of lower federal courts) as it had been in Rogers v. Lodge, the multimember district minority representation case at p. 703 above. In examining these Northern school cases, consider whether the Court's guidelines regarding burdens of proof, presumptions, and deference to lower federal courts are

4. In a concluding passage, Justice Rehnquist stated: "The Court does not intimate that it has fathomed the full implications of the analysis it has sanctioned—an approach that would certainly make school desegregation litigation a 'loaded game board,' Swann, [and] one at which a school board could never win. A school system's only hope of avoiding a judicial receivership would be voluntary dismantling of its neighborhood school program. If that is the Court's intent today, it has indeed accepted the role of Judge Learned Hand's feared 'Platonic Guardians' and intellectual integrity—if not the Constitution or the interests of our beleaguered urban school systems and their students of all races—would be better

served by discarding the pretextual distinction between de facto and de jure segregation."

5. For a critical comment on the Dayton and Columbus cases [as well as on Weber, p. 785 below], see Kitch, "The Return of Color-Consciousness to the Constitution: Weber, Dayton, and Columbus," 1979 Sup.Ct.Rev. 1. Kitch argued that the remedies imposed by these cases "focus not on racial discrimination but on redressing racial [imbalance]. They acknowledge that separate but unequal treatment under law is warranted by our history, because they deal with classes of persons and not with individuals." (See also the materials in sec. 3E below.)

consistent with the "purposefulness" criteria articulated in such cases as Davis, Arlington Heights, and Feeney, sec. 3D2 above. Is there merit to Justice Rehnquist's dissenting claim in the 1979 cases that the "lower court's methodology [approved by the Court] would all but eliminate the distinction between de facto and de jure segregation"? Is there justification for applying more lenient standards regarding proof of purposeful discrimination in the school desegregation (and representational) context than in such earlier contexts as employment and zoning (Davis and Arlington Heights)? (Recall the comments at p. 693 above.)

a. Consider also the partial anticipation (and elaboration) of Justice Rehnquist's 1979 dissents in Justice POWELL's arguments in his separate opinion in the Denver school case, KEYES v. SCHOOL DISTRICT, 413 U.S. 189 (1973). In Keyes, Justice Powell claimed that the modern desegregation cases since Green in 1968 had undercut the justifications for maintaining a constitutional distinction between de jure and de facto school desegregation. Has the Court's treatment of burdens of proof regarding discriminatory purpose (and of desegregation remedies) substantially undercut the practical significance of that distinction? Justice Powell stated in Keyes: "The focus of the school desegregation problem has now shifted from the South to the country as a whole. Unwilling and footdragging as the process was in most places, substantial progress toward achieving integration has been made in Southern States. No comparable progress has been made in many nonsouthern cities, [primarily] because of the de facto/de jure distinction nurtured by the courts and accepted complacently by many of the same voices which denounced the evils of segregated schools in the South. But if our national concern is for those who attend such schools, rather than for perpetuating a legalism rooted in history rather than present reality, we must recognize that the evil of operating separate schools is no less in Denver than in Atlanta.

"In my view we should abandon a distinction which long since has outlived its time, and formulate constitutional principles of national rather than merely regional application. [The] doctrine of Brown [did] not retain its original meaning. In a series of decisions extending from 1954 to 1971 the concept of state neutrality was transformed into the present constitutional doctrine requiring affirmative state action to desegregate school systems. The keystone case was Green. [The] language in Green imposing an affirmative duty to convert to a unitary system was appropriate [in the rural setting of that case]. There was, however, reason to question to what extent this duty would apply in the vastly different factual setting of a large city with extensive areas of residential [segregation]. [The] doubt as to whether the affirmative-duty concept would flower into a new constitutional principle of general application was laid to rest by Swann. [Swann] refrained from even considering whether the evolution of constitutional doctrine from Brown I to Green/Swann undercut whatever logic once supported the de facto/de jure distinction. In imposing on metropolitan southern school districts an affirmative duty, entailing large-scale transportation of pupils, to eliminate segregation in the schools, the Court required these districts to alleviate conditions which in large part did *not* result from historic, state-imposed de jure segregation. Rather, the familiar root cause of segregated schools in *all* the biracial metropolitan areas of our country is essentially the same: one of segregated residential and migratory patterns the impact of which on the racial composition of the schools was often perpetuated and rarely ameliorated by action of public school authorities. This is a national, not a southern, phenomenon. And it is largely unrelated to whether a particular State had or did not have segregative school laws. Whereas Brown I rightly decreed the elimination of state-imposed segregation in that particular section of the country where it did exist, Swann imposed obligations on southern school districts to eliminate conditions which are not regionally unique but are similar both in origin and effect to conditions in the rest of the [country].

"The Court's decision today, while adhering to the de jure/de facto distinction, will require the application of the Green/Swann doctrine of "affirmative duty" to the Denver School Board despite the absence of any history of state-mandated school segregation. [I] concur in the Court's position that [if] the affirmative-duty doctrine is sound constitutional law for Charlotte, it is equally so for Denver. I would not, however, perpetuate the de jure/de facto distinction nor would I leave to petitioners the initial tortuous effort of identifying 'segregative acts' and deducing 'segregative intent.' I would hold, quite simply, that where segregated public schools exist within a school district to a substantial degree, there is a prima facie case that the duly constituted public authorities, [usually, the school board,] are sufficiently responsible [6] to warrant imposing upon them a nationally applicable burden to demonstrate they nevertheless are operating a genuinely integrated school system.

"The principal reason for abandonment of the de jure/de facto distinction is that, in view of the evolution of the holding in Brown I into the affirmative-duty doctrine, the distinction no longer can be justified on a principled basis. [And], as the Court's opinion today abundantly demonstrates, the facts deemed necessary to establish de jure discrimination present problems of subjective intent which the courts cannot fairly resolve. [In] the evolutionary process since 1954, decisions of this Court have added a significant gloss to [the] original right [in Brown]. Although nowhere expressly articulated in these terms, I would now define it as the right, derived from [equal protection], to expect that once the State has assumed responsibility for education, local school boards will operate *integrated school systems* within their respective districts. This means that school authorities [must] make and implement their customary decisions with a view toward enhancing integrated school opportunities. [A] system would be integrated in accord with constitutional standards if the responsible authorities had taken appropriate steps to (i) integrate faculties and administration; (ii) scrupulously assure equality of facilities, instruction, and curriculum opportunities throughout the district; (iii) utilize their authority to draw attendance zones to promote integration; and (iv) locate new schools, close old ones, and determine the size and grade categories with this same objective in mind. Where school authorities decide to undertake the transportation of students, this also must be with integrative opportunities in mind. [Courts] judging past school board actions with a view to their *general integrative effect* will be best able to assure an absence of [racial] discrimination while avoiding the murky, subjective judgments inherent in the Court's search for 'segregative intent.' [School board] decisions obviously are not the sole cause of segregated school conditions. But if, after such detailed and complete public supervision, substantial school segregation still persists, the presumption is strong that the school board, by its acts or omissions, is in some part responsible [and] this Court is justified in finding a prima facie case of a constitutional violation. The burden then must fall on the school board to demonstrate it is operating an 'integrated school system.' [The] history of state-imposed segregation is more widespread in our country than the de jure/de facto distinction has traditionally cared to [recognize].[7] [In] addition, there are reasons of policy and prudent judicial

6. "A prima facie case of constitutional violation exists when segregation is found to a substantial degree in the schools of a particular district. It is recognized, of course, that this term is relative and provides no precise standards. But circumstances, demographic and otherwise, vary from district to district and hard-and-fast rules should not be formulated. The existence of a substantial percentage of schools populated by students from one race only or predominantly so populated, should trigger the inquiry." [Footnote by Justice Powell.]

7. "Indeed, if one goes back far enough, it is probable that all racial segregation, wherever occurring and whether or not confined to the

administration which point strongly toward the adoption of a uniform national rule. [Today's decision], emphasizing [the] elusive element of segregative intent, will invite numerous desegregation suits in which there can be little hope of uniformity of result. [We] should acknowledge that whenever public school segregation exists to a substantial degree there is prima facie evidence of a constitutional violation by the responsible school board."

b. Justice Powell's argument in Keyes rested largely on the Court's increasing emphasis, since Green, on *results* in cases from southern communities in which formal de jure school segregation once existed—and on the increasingly tenuous search for evidence of deliberate discrimination in the North. (Despite Justice Powell's argument against the de jure-de facto distinction in Keyes, he has been at the forefront in insisting on the "purposeful discrimination" requirement outside the school segregation field. For example, he wrote the majority opinion in Arlington Heights, the zoning case.) Despite Justice Powell's conclusions from the ever lighter "purpose" burden in the school desegregation cases, the course of decisions from Green to Columbus and Dayton may simply show, as Justice Rehnquist argues, that the Court has gone too far in imposing affirmative obligations on school authorities.

Can it be argued that, for reasons other than Justice Powell's, de facto segregation should be considered a constitutional wrong? To what extent do the factors relied on in Brown I (to demonstrate the harm inherent in school segregation) apply to the de facto situation? Can it be argued that Brown rested at least as much on the *impact* of segregated schools in diminishing educational opportunities and in fostering feelings of inferiority as on the purpose behind the dual school system? Is the stigma stemming from de facto segregated schools as great as that from de jure segregated schools? Is there similar impairment of educational opportunity? Is condemnation of de facto segregation justified by the purposes of the 14th Amendment? Can de facto school desegregation be considered unconstitutional without undercutting the "purposeful discrimination" requirement reiterated in most of the materials in sec. 3D2? Can de facto school segregation be considered unconstitutional without bringing all de facto "discriminations," all differential impacts of governmental action, within the constitutional ban? Can the 14th Amendment be read as safeguarding not only the purity of the process—the elimination of racial hostility from decisionmaking—but also the quality of results, the assurance of equality of condition?[8] Has school segregation law moved steadily, and justifiably, from concern with elimination of racial factors in student assignments to achievement of racial integration as the constitutionally mandated result?

4. *Limits on remedies for de jure segregation: Interdistrict remedies.* In 1974, a sharply divided Court addressed the question of the permissible extent of multidistrict remedies for situations in which de jure segregation had been found to exist in only one of the districts. MILLIKEN v. BRADLEY, 418 U.S. 717 (1974). Milliken reversed lower court orders that had directed interdistrict remedies in the Detroit metropolitan area after a finding of de jure segregation in the city of Detroit: the majority concluded "that absent an interdistrict violation there is no basis for an inter-district remedy."[9]

schools, has at some time been supported or maintained by government [action]." [Footnote by Justice Powell.]

in Nationwide Application," 1972 Wash.U.L.Q. 383.

8. For an extensive examination of developments and problems, see Goodman, "De Facto School Segregation: A Constitutional and Empirical Analysis," 60 Calif.L.Rev. 275 (1972). See also Karst, "Not One Law at Rome and Another at Athens: The Fourteenth Amendment

9. Chief Justice Burger wrote for the majority in the 5 to 4 decision. Justice Stewart submitted a concurring opinion. The dissenters were Justices Douglas, Brennan, White and Marshall. (There were lengthy dissents by Justices White and Marshall; each of those opinions was joined

In the Detroit area, the city constituted one school district and there were separate districts for the suburban areas. Blacks were concentrated in the city. The trial court found that there was de jure segregation in the Detroit school system because of acts of state and city officials, and the Court saw no reason to disturb that finding in view of the 1973 standards of Keyes. But the trial court, in fashioning remedies, concluded that desegregation could not be effective if it were limited to the city boundaries and accordingly issued an order including 53 surrounding school districts. In justifying its multidistrict remedy, the lower court pointed not only to the practical obstacles to a narrower order, but also to other considerations: the Detroit district was an agent of the state; the state had power to prevent segregation there—by changing district boundaries, for example. Moreover, the state had contributed to segregation in the city—e.g., by prohibiting the use of state funds for busing in the city. Concluding that "district lines are simply matters of political convenience and may not be used to deny constitutional rights," the trial judge designated 53 of the 85 suburban school districts and Detroit as the "desegregation area" and, without any finding that there had been de jure segregation in any of the suburban districts, directed the preparation of "an effective desegregation plan" for the entire area. The Court reversed, insisting that the remedy exceeded the scope of the constitutional wrong.

Chief Justice BURGER's majority opinion concluded: "Boundary lines may be bridged where there has been a constitutional violation calling for interdistrict relief, but, the notion that school district lines may be casually ignored or treated as a mere administrative convenience is contrary to the history of public education in our country." In delineating the limited circumstances in which inter-district remedies were permissible, he stated: "The controlling principle [is] that the scope of the remedy is determined by the nature and extent of the constitutional violation. Swann. Before the boundaries of separate and autonomous school districts may be set aside by consolidating the separate units for remedial purposes or by imposing a cross-district remedy, it must first be shown that there has been a constitutional violation within one district that produces a significant segregative effect in another district. Specifically it must be shown that racially discriminatory acts of the state or local school districts, or of a single school district, have been a substantial cause of inter-district segregation.[10] Thus an inter-district remedy might be in order where the racially discriminatory acts of one or more school districts caused racial segregation in an adjacent district, or where district lines have been deliberately drawn on the basis of race. [Conversely], without an inter-district violation and inter-district effect, there is no constitutional wrong calling for an inter-district remedy."

The Chief Justice emphasized that the interdistrict remedy "could disrupt and alter the structure of public education in Michigan. [Apart] from the logistical and other serious problems attending large-scale transportation of students, the consolidation would give rise to an array of other problems in financing and operating this new school system." He added: "With no showing of significant violation by the 53 outlying school districts and no evidence of any inter-district violation or effect, the [lower court] mandated a metropolitan area remedy. To approve the remedy ordered by the court would impose on the outlying districts, not shown to have committed any constitutional violation, a wholly impermissible remedy based on a standard not hinted at [in] any holding of this Court." He was not persuaded by the dissenters' argument that the participation of state officials in maintaining de jure segregation in

by all of the other dissenters. There was also a brief separate dissent by Justice Douglas.)

10. Is this burden of proof allocation consistent with Keyes? Are there good reasons for different presumptions of segregative effects in

intradistrict rather than an interdistrict situation? See generally Sedler, "Metropolitan Desegregation in the Wake of [Milliken]," 1975 Wash.U.L. Q. 535, and Strickman, "School Desegregation at the Crossroads," 70 Nw.U.L.Rev. 725 (1975).

Detroit justified interdistrict relief. Even assuming that there was significant state participation, "established doctrine" required focusing on particular districts. He continued: "The constitutional right of the Negro respondents residing in Detroit is to attend a unitary school system in that district. [The] view of the dissenters, that the existence of a dual system *in Detroit* can be made the basis for a decree requiring cross-district transportation of pupils cannot be supported on the grounds that it represents merely the devising of a suitably flexible remedy for the violation of rights already established by our prior decisions. It can be supported only by drastic expansion of the constitutional right itself, an expansion without any support in [either] principle or precedent." [11]

The most extensive dissent came from Justice MARSHALL. He stated: "Today's holding, I fear, is more a reflection of a perceived public mood that we have gone far enough in enforcing the Constitution's guarantee of equal justice than it is the product of neutral principles of law. In the short run, it may seem to be the easier course to allow our great metropolitan areas to be divided up each into two cities—one white, the other black—but it is a course, I predict, our people will ultimately regret." He thought the decision "a giant step backwards" and an "emasculation" of equal protection. He insisted that "where, as here, state-imposed segregation has been demonstrated, it becomes the duty of the State to eliminate root and branch all vestiges of racial discrimination and to achieve the greatest possible degree of actual desegregation." The lower courts had been right in finding that "this duty cannot be fulfilled unless [Michigan] involves outlying metropolitan area school districts in its desegregation remedy." He added that he saw "no basis either in law or in the practicalities of the situation justifying the State's interposition of school district boundaries as absolute barriers to the implementation of an effective desegregation remedy."

Justice WHITE stated in dissent: "The core of my disagreement is that deliberate acts of segregation and their consequences will go unremedied, not because a remedy will be infeasible or unreasonable in terms of the usual criteria governing school desegregation cases, but because an effective remedy would cause what the Court considers to be undue administrative inconvenience to the State. The result is that [Michigan], the entity at which the 14th Amendment is directed, has successfully insulated itself from its duty to provide effective desegregation remedies by vesting sufficient power over its public schools in its local school districts." He insisted that the Court had fashioned "out of whole cloth an arbitrary rule that remedies for constitutional violations occurring in a single Michigan school district must stop at the school district line. Apparently, no matter how much less burdensome or more effective [in] many respects, such as transportation, the metropolitan plan might be, the school district line may not be crossed." He concluded that the majority had compelled "an intracity desegregation plan more expensive to the district, more burdensome for many of Detroit's Negro students and surely more conducive to

---

11. The majority in Milliken emphasized that the remedy must be tailored to the wrong in the sense that "absent an inter-district violation there is no basis for an inter-district remedy." Consider another aspect of tailoring the remedy to the wrong that is raised by the desegregation cases. Note that the requirement of showing purposeful discrimination focuses primarily on the defendant. In the school desegregation context, the effect of a finding of de jure segregation may therefore be the granting of a remedy to a plaintiff pupil who was *not* a direct, immediate victim of the original unconstitutional action. Should

such a principle apply *outside* of the context of public schools? Does the law normally grant remedies to parties that have not been injured? But is it arguable that the narrow view of injury is inappropriate in the racial segregation context? (Note that in the context of a statutory rather than a constitutional claim, the modern Court has suggested that only those employees who have themselves been the victims of illegal discrimination are entitled to remedial hiring and seniority awards. See Firefighters v. Stotts (1984; p. 786 below).)

white flight than a metropolitan plan would be—all of this merely to avoid what the [lower courts] considered to be the very manageable and quite surmountable difficulties that would be involved in extending the desegregation remedy to the suburban school districts." [12]

E. THE BENIGN USE OF QUASI–SUSPECT AND SUSPECT CRITERIA: GENDER; RACE

Introduction. To what extent may racial classifications be used for "benign" purposes? The problem of "benign" or "reverse" discrimination, of affirmative action and preferential programs, is difficult and controversial. The pervasive problems are: Should the strict scrutiny of racial classifications be relaxed when they are employed for the asserted purpose of aiding a minority? What justifications will suffice to permit the benign use of racial criteria? The earlier materials in this section frequently stated that racial classifications are "suspect" and are permissible only for "compelling" justifications. Is benignness of purpose a compelling justification? Or is a lower level of scrutiny appropriate when the objective is benign? When *may* government be color conscious rather than color blind? When *must* it be color conscious? Can courts adequately distinguish between truly benign purposes and hostile ones masquerading behind a "benign" facade? May benign classifications be used to remedy only the effects of past purposeful discrimination? Or may they also be used to compensate for past societal injustices? Questions such as these have produced the greatest controversy and difficulty in the context of benign *racial* classifications. But before turning to that context, it is instructive to begin with a look at the Court's treatment of related problems that have surfaced in the setting of

---

12. Contrast, with the disapproval of an interdistrict school desegregation remedy in Milliken, the Court's unanimous holding in Hills v. Gautreaux, 425 U.S. 284 (1976), authorizing consideration of a metropolitan area remedy in a housing discrimination case. Justice Stewart's opinion stated: "Nothing in the Milliken decision suggests a per se rule that federal courts lack authority to order parties found to have violated the Constitution to undertake remedial efforts beyond the municipal boundaries of the city where the violation occurred."

In Hills, the U.S. Department of Housing and Urban Development (HUD) had violated constitutional and statutory prohibitions of racial discrimination in connection with the selection of sites for public housing in Chicago. [HUD was found to have assisted the Chicago Housing Authority (CHA) in carrying out a racially discriminatory housing program.] The Court found that, in those circumstances, a federal court's remedial order against HUD could properly extend to activities beyond Chicago's city boundaries. The Court rejected both of HUD's major arguments: first, that a metropolitan area order "would constitute the grant of relief incommensurate with the constitutional violation to be repaired"; second, "that a decree regulating HUD's conduct beyond Chicago's boundaries" would unduly in-

terfere with local autonomy, because it would "inevitably have the effect of 'consolidat[ing] for remedial purposes' governmental units not implicated in HUD's and CHA's violations." In rejecting HUD's second contention, the Court concluded that "there is no basis for the [claim] that court-ordered metropolitan relief in this case would be impermissible as a matter of law under the Milliken decision. [Here], by contrast, the metropolitan relief order would not consolidate or in any way restructure local units.

[Note also an aftermath of the Milliken decision, known as Milliken II: Milliken v. Bradley, 433 U.S. 267 (1977). There, the Court held for the first time that "federal courts can order remedial education programs as part of a school desegregation decree." Rejecting the State's argument that the lower court order exceeded the scope of constitutional violations, Chief Justice Burger emphasized that "the remedy does not 'exceed' the violation if the remedy is tailored to cure the '*condition* that offends the Constitution.' Milliken I." Here, the "condition" requiring the remedial education program was a consequence of the constitutional violation, unlawful segregation of students; the lower court was not limited to directing its remedies solely to unlawful pupil assignments.]

gender-based classifications that are sought to be justified as benign efforts to make up for past injustices to women.

---

1. THE BENIGN USE OF SEX CLASSIFICATIONS

Background and overview. As the materials in sec. 3B show, the majority of the Court has not treated gender as a "suspect" classification triggering "strict" scrutiny. However, sex classifications clearly disadvantaging women do evoke a heightened, intermediate level of scrutiny. With respect to *benign* sex classifications, the Court, after some initial stumbling, achieved a consensus that is clearer than the doctrine regarding benign racial classifications. When sex classifications are defended as benign aids to women, the Court applies exactly the *same* level of scrutiny as it does to disadvantaging classifications: the Craig and Hogan levels of intermediate scrutiny govern, as Wengler (1980; p. 740 below) and other cases below demonstrate.[1] What, if any, lessons for the treatment of benign racial classifications can be drawn from these developments in the sex classification area? To the extent that the pattern of the benign sex discrimination cases is an appropriate framework for the scrutiny of benign racial classifications, what *is* that pattern? Is it the use of the *same* level of scrutiny for benign as for disadvantaging classifications? That pattern would encourage the use of strict scrutiny for benign racial classifications as well as for hostile ones. (See Justice Powell's opinion in Bakke, p. 745 below.) Or is it the use of an intermediate, rather than strict, level of scrutiny for benign classifications, in race cases as in gender ones? (See Justice Brennan's opinion in Bakke.)

1. *The early approach.* In the modern Court's first encounter with benign sex classifications, the majority applied an extremely deferential standard of review. In KAHN v. SHEVIN, 416 U.S. 351 (1974)—decided two years before Craig mandated intermediate scrutiny for sex classifications—Justice DOUGLAS' majority opinion held that a state property tax exemption for widows (but not for widowers) was easily sustainable, because it rested " 'upon some ground of difference having a fair and substantial relation to the subject of the legislation.' Reed." He noted that "gender has never been rejected as an impermissible classification in all instances" and stated that the state tax law was "reasonably designed to further the state policy of cushioning the financial impact of spousal loss upon the sex for which that loss imposes a disproportionately heavy burden." He emphasized the Court's traditional leeway to state tax classifications challenged under the equal protection clause. Under that approach, laws "designed to rectify the effects of past discrimination against women" readily passed muster.[2] Justice BRENNAN's dissent, joined by Justice

---

1. Moreover, the Court insists on considerable proof that the "benign" justification is genuinely rooted in the *actual* legislative purpose. See, e.g., Justice Brennan's frequently reiterated statement in Weinberger v. Wiesenfeld (1975; p. 739 below): "[T]he mere recitation of a benign, compensatory purpose is not an automatic shield which protects against any inquiry into the actual purposes underlying a statutory scheme." Justice Brennan's analysis of a Social Security Act survivors' benefits provision in Wiesenfeld emphasized "actual" and "articulated" legislative purposes and carefully scrutinized "the statutory scheme itself" and "the legislative history."

2. Note that, not long before Kahn, Justice Douglas had joined Justice Brennan's opinion in

Frontiero (p. 645 above) urging strict scrutiny for sex classifications. His very deferential approach in Kahn suggests that he perceived a sharp difference in the levels of scrutiny for disadvantaging and benign sex classifications. His stance in Kahn is all the more striking because, just one day earlier, he had applied strict scrutiny to a "benign" racially preferential law school admissions program in DeFunis (1974; p. 744 below). Were Justice Douglas' positions in DeFunis, Frontiero and Kahn reconcilable? Was his emphasis on the fact that Kahn was a tax case an adequate explanation?

Marshall, urged "close judicial scrutiny" of gender-based classifications, even benign ones. He thought the law served a "compelling governmental interest," but thought the statute invalid because it had not resorted to the most narrowly available means. Although "this country's history of pervasive sex discrimination against women" justified "remedial measures to correct the resulting economic imbalances," "less drastic means" were available to achieve that objective, since the property tax exemption was granted to all widows, whatever their financial status: "[The] State could readily narrow the class of beneficiaries to those widows for whom the effects of past economic discrimination against women have been a practical reality." [3]

2. *Benignness in alimony laws.* In ORR v. ORR, 440 U.S. 268 (1979), the Court struck down laws which authorized the Alabama courts to impose alimony obligations on husbands but not on wives. Justice BRENNAN's opinion, applying the intermediate scrutiny standard of Craig, found that Alabama's scheme did not meet the requirement that gender-based classifications "must serve important governmental objectives and must be substantially related to achievement of those objectives." In examining the "benign" justification, he conceded that helping needy spouses and "compensating women for past discrimination during marriage" were "legitimate and important" objectives. But the "means" aspect of that test had not been satisfied: "even if sex were a reliable proxy for need, and even if the institution of marriage did discriminate against women, these factors still would not 'adequately justify the salient features of' Alabama's statutory scheme. [Craig.] Under the statute, individualized hearings at which the parties' relative financial circumstances are considered *already* occur. [Since these] hearings can determine which women were in fact discriminated against vis-à-vis their husbands, as well as which family units defied the stereotype and left the husband dependent on the wife, Alabama's alleged compensatory purpose may be effectuated without placing burdens solely on husbands. Progress toward fulfilling such a purpose would not be hampered, and it would cost the State nothing more, if it were to treat men and women equally by making alimony burdens independent of sex. 'Thus, the gender-based distinction is gratuitous.' " Here, moreover, Alabama's "use of a gender classification actually produces perverse results," by giving "an advantage only to the financially secure wife whose husband is in need." Such a scheme was clearly irrational since nondependent wives are "precisely those who are not 'needy spouses' and who are 'least likely to have been victims [of] discrimination' by the institution of marriage." Finally, Justice Brennan commented generally on the dangers latent in "benign" gender classifications: "[Even] statutes purportedly designed to compensate for and ameliorate the effects of past discrimination must be carefully tailored," since they "carry the inherent risk of reinforcing stereotypes about the 'proper place' of women and their need for special protection." Since here "the State's compensatory and ameliorative purposes are as well served by a gender-neutral classification as one that gender-classifies and therefore carries with it the baggage of sexual stereotypes, the State cannot be permitted to classify on the basis of sex." [4]

3. *Benefits programs.* CALIFANO v. WEBSTER, 430 U.S. 313 (1977), a per curiam decision, sustained as a valid benign classification, the Social

3. Another dissent, by Justice WHITE, focused primarily on the fact that the tax exemption was available "to all widows but not to widowers": "[The State] has not adequately explained why women should be treated differently from men."

The more recent cases that follow illustrate that the Court's approach to benign sex discrimination has changed significantly since Kahn.

4. Justices Blackmun and Stevens submitted separate, brief concurrences. Lengthier dissents, by Justices Powell and Rehnquist (joined by Chief Justice Burger), insisted that the majority had treated Art. III jurisdictional barriers "too casually" and accordingly objected to the Court reaching the merits.

Security Act's formula for computing old age benefits. Under the challenged statutory formula, a female wage earner could exclude from the computation of her "average monthly wage" three more lower earning years than a similarly situated male wage earner could exclude. This resulted in a slightly higher "average monthly wage" and a correspondingly higher level of monthly old-age benefits for the retired female wage earner. (In this case, for example, the male challenger was awarded a monthly benefit of $185.70, but a similarly situated female wage earner would have been awarded $240 per month.) In sustaining that scheme, the Court stated:

"To withstand scrutiny under [equal protection] 'classifications by gender must serve important governmental objectives and must be substantially related to achievement of those objectives.' [Craig.] Reduction of the disparity in economic condition between men and women caused by the long history of discrimination against women has been recognized as such an important governmental objective. Schlesinger v. Ballard; [Kahn]. But 'the mere recitation of a benign, compensatory purpose is not an automatic shield that protects against any inquiry into the actual purposes underlying a legislative scheme.' [Wiesenfeld.] Accordingly, we have rejected attempts to justify gender classifications as compensation for past discrimination against women when the classifications in fact penalized women wage earners, Califano v. Goldfarb; [Wiesenfeld], or when its legislative history revealed that the classification was not enacted as compensation for past discrimination. [Goldfarb; Wiesenfeld.] The statutory scheme involved here is more analogous to those upheld in Kahn and Ballard than to those struck down in Wiesenfeld and Goldfarb.[1] The more favorable

---

1. Kahn is described in note 1 above. Schlesinger v. Ballard, 419 U.S. 498 (1975), rejected a male officer's attack on sex distinctions in the Navy's promotion system. The system accorded to women officers a 13-year tenure before mandatory discharge for want of promotion; males, by contrast, had to be discharged if they had been twice passed over for promotion, even though they might have had less than 13 years of commissioned service. Justice Stewart's majority opinion purported to apply deferential rationality standards. Justice Brennan's dissent, joined by Justices Douglas and Marshall, insisted that strict scrutiny was applicable, but argued further that the scheme should not even survive rationality review. Justice Stewart insisted that the different treatment of men and women officers reflected "not archaic and overbroad generalizations, but, instead, the demonstrable fact that male and female line officers in the Navy are *not* similarly situated with respect to opportunities for professional service." Justice Brennan's dissent insisted that the majority had conjured up a legislative purpose: "I find nothing in the statutory scheme or the legislative history to support the supposition that Congress intended [to] compensate women for other forms of disadvantage visited upon them by the Navy."

Weinberger v. Wiesenfeld, 420 U.S. 636 (1975), invalidated a Social Security provision applicable when a covered wage earner dies. In the case of a deceased husband and father, benefits were payable both to the widow and to the couple's minor children in her care. But in the case of a deceased wife and mother, benefits were payable only to the minor children and not to the widower. The Court sustained the widower's challenge, finding an unjustifiable discrimination

against covered women wage earners by affording them less protection for their survivors than that provided for survivors of men wage earners. The Court rejected the effort to defend the classification as a benign one because that had not been the actual purpose of Congress.

Califano v. Goldfarb, 430 U.S. 199 (1977), was a companion case to Califano v. Webster. It set aside a gender-based distinction in a federal benefits program under which survivors' benefits based on the earnings of a deceased husband covered by the Act were payable to his widow, but benefits on the basis of the earnings of a deceased wife were payable to a widower only if he "was receiving at least one-half of his support" from his deceased wife. Justice Brennan's plurality opinion found the scheme, "burdening a widower but not a widow with the task of proving dependency upon the deceased spouse," indistinguishable from that struck down in Wiesenfeld. He found the discrimination to be directed against female workers, whose social security taxes produced less protection for their spouses than was produced by the efforts of men. He also considered the argument that the discrimination should be viewed as being directed not against the covered wage earning female, but as against the surviving widower, and that, so viewed, it could be justified as benign. But an "inquiry into the actual purposes" of the distinction showed that Congress had not been so motivated: there was no "deliberate congressional intention to remedy the arguably greater needs of [widows] but [simply] an intention to aid the dependent spouses of deceased wage earners, coupled with a presumption that wives are usually dependent." Justice Stevens concurred in the judgment on a very different ground: he insisted

treatment of the female wage earner enacted here was not a result of 'archaic and overbroad generalizations' about women or of 'the role-typing society has long imposed' upon women, such as casual assumptions that women are 'the weaker sex' or are more likely to be child-rearers or dependents. Rather, 'the only discernible purpose of [the law's more favorable treatment is] the permissible one of redressing our society's longstanding disparate treatment of women.' The challenged statute operated directly to compensate women for past economic discrimination. Retirement benefits under the Act are based on past earnings. But as we have recognized, '[w]hether from overt discrimination or from the socialization process of a male-dominated culture, the job market is inhospitable to the woman seeking any but the lowest paid jobs.' [Kahn.] Thus, allowing women, who as such have been unfairly hindered from earning as much as men, to eliminate additional low-earning years from the calculation of their retirement benefits works directly to remedy some part of the effect of past discrimination. The legislative history [also] reveals that Congress directly addressed the justification for differing treatment of men and women in the former version of that section and purposely enacted the more favorable treatment for female wage earners to compensate for past employment discrimination against women. [T]he legislative history is clear that the differing treatment of men and women [was] not 'the accidental byproduct of a traditional way of thinking about females,' but rather was deliberately enacted to compensate for particular economic disabilities suffered by women.''

WENGLER v. DRUGGISTS MUTUAL INS. CO.

446 U.S. 142, 100 S.Ct. 1540, 64 L.Ed.2d 107 (1980).

Mr. Justice WHITE delivered the opinion of the [Court].

I. [In 1977], Ruth Wengler, wife of appellant Paul J. Wengler, died in a work-related accident in the parking lot of her employer. [Appellant] filed a claim for death benefits under Missouri's workers' compensation law, under which a widower is not entitled to death benefits unless he either is mentally or physically incapacitated from wage earning or proves actual dependence on his wife's earnings. In contrast, a widow qualifies for death benefits without having to prove actual dependence on her husband's earnings. Appellant stipulated that he was neither incapacitated nor dependent on his wife's earnings, but argued that, owing to its disparate treatment of similarly situated widows and widowers, [the law] violated [equal protection]. [The state rejected the challenge] because "the substantive difference in the economic standing of

---

that "the relevant discrimination [is] against surviving male spouses, rather than against deceased female wage earners." But he found the discrimination against males an impermissible "accidental byproduct of a traditional way of thinking about females." He insisted that Wiesenfeld was inconsistent with Kahn and thought the later, Wiesenfeld analysis should govern.

Justice Rehnquist's dissent, joined by Chief Justice Burger and Justices Stewart and Blackmun, argued, inter alia, that the deferential approach of Kahn should be followed with respect to benign sex classifications, that discrimination against men should not be treated as an "invidious discrimination," and that heightened scrutiny of sex distinctions should apply only when they disadvantage women, because it was women who had "in the past been the victims of unfair treatment."

Note that Justice Brennan, in the racially preferential medical school admissions case, Bakke (p. 745 below), specifically relies on Goldfarb and Webster as providing the appropriate standard of scrutiny for benign race classifications. Recall the questions at p. 737 above: What *is* the lesson of modern benign sex discrimination cases for the benign race discrimination area? That the intermediate standard of cases such as Goldfarb and Webster (and Wengler, which follows) should govern in the race area, or that the same level of scrutiny that has applied to disadvantaging classifications should be applied to benign ones (which, in the race context, would mean strict scrutiny, as Justice Powell's opinion in Bakke argued)?

working men and women justifies the advantage that [the law] gives to a widow." [We] reverse.

II. The Missouri law indisputably mandates gender-based discrimination. Although the [state court] was of the view that the law favored, rather than disfavored, women, it is apparent that the statute discriminates against both men and women. The provision discriminates against a woman [because the benefits] that the working woman can expect to be paid to her spouse in the case of her work-related death are less than those payable to the spouse of the deceased male wage earner. It is this kind of discrimination against working women that our cases have identified and in the circumstances found unjustified. [Wiesenfeld; Goldfarb.] The Missouri law [also] discriminates against men who survive their employed wives dying in work-related accidents. To receive benefits, the surviving male spouse must prove his incapacity or dependency. The widow of a deceased wage earner, in contrast, is presumed dependent and is guaranteed a weekly benefit for life or until remarriage. It was this discrimination against the male survivor as compared with a similarly situated female that Mr. Justice Stevens identified in [Goldfarb] as resulting in a denial of equal protection.

III. However the discrimination is described in this case, our precedents require that gender-based discriminations must serve important governmental objectives and that the discriminatory means employed must be substantially related to the achievement of those objectives. [E.g., Orr; Webster; Craig.] Providing for needy spouses is surely an important governmental objective, and the [law] effects that goal by paying benefits to all surviving female spouses and to all surviving male spouses who prove their dependency. But the question remains whether the discriminatory means employed—discrimination against women wage earners and surviving male spouses—itself substantially serves the statutory end. Surely the needs of surviving widows and widowers would be completely served either by paying benefits to all members of both classes or by paying benefits only to those members of either class who can demonstrate their need. Why, then, employ the discriminatory means of paying all surviving widows without requiring proof of dependency, but paying only those widowers who make the required demonstration? The only justification offered [for] not treating males and females alike, whether viewed as wage earners or survivors of wage earners, is the assertion that most women are dependent on male wage earners and that it is more efficient to presume dependency in the case of women than to engage in case-to-case determination, whereas individualized inquiries in the postulated few cases in which men might be dependent are not prohibitively costly. The burden, however, is on those defending the discrimination to make out the claimed justification, and this burden is not carried simply by noting that in 1925 the state legislature thought widows to be more in need of prompt help than men or that today "the substantive difference in the economic standing of working men and women justifies the advantage given to widows." It may be that there is empirical support for the proposition that men are more likely to be the principal supporters of their spouses and families, Wiesenfeld, but the bare assertion of this argument falls far short of justifying gender-based discrimination on the grounds of administrative convenience. Yet neither the court below nor appellees in this Court essay any persuasive demonstration as to what the economic consequences to the State or to the beneficiaries might be if, in one way or another, men and women, whether as wage earners or survivors, were treated equally under the workers' compensation law, thus eliminating the double-edged discrimination described [above]. We think, then, that the claimed justification of administrative convenience fails, just as it has in our prior cases. It may be that there are levels of administrative convenience that will justify discriminations that are subject to heightened scrutiny under the Equal Protection Clause, but the requisite showing has not been made here by the mere claim that it would be inconvenient to individualize determinations about widows as well as [widowers].

[Reversed and remanded.] [1]

Mr. Justice STEVENS, concurring.

Nothing has happened since the decision in [Goldfarb] to persuade me that this kind of gender-based classification can simultaneously disfavor the male class and the female class. To illustrate my difficulty with the analysis in Part II of the Court's opinion, it should be noted that there are three relevant kinds of marriages: (1) those in which the husband is dependent on the wife; (2) those in which the wife is dependent on the husband; and (3) those in which neither spouse is dependent on the other. Under the Missouri statute, in either of the first two situations, if the dependent spouse survives, a death benefit will be paid regardless of whether the survivor is male or female; conversely, if the working spouse survives, no death benefit will be paid. The only difference in the two situations is that the surviving male, unlike the surviving female, must undergo the inconvenience of proving dependency. That surely is not a discrimination against females. In the third situation, if one spouse dies, benefits are payable to a surviving female but not to a surviving male. In my view, that is a rather blatant discrimination against males. While both spouses remain alive, the prospect of receiving a potential death benefit upon the husband's demise reduces the wife's need for insurance on his life, whereas the prospect of *not* receiving a death benefit upon the wife's demise increases the husband's need for insurance on her life. That difference again places the husband at a disadvantage. No matter how the statute is viewed, the class against which it discriminates is the male class. I therefore cannot join Part II of the Court's opinion. I do, however, agree that Missouri has failed to justify the disparate treatment of persons who have as strong a claim to equal treatment as do similarly situated surviving spouses, see [Goldfarb] (Stevens, J., concurring), and that its statute violates [equal protection].[2]

---

1. The remand was the result of the Court's brief consideration, in a closing passage, of the question "whether the defect [in the Missouri law] should be cured by extending the presumption of dependence to widowers or by eliminating it for widows." This is a frequent problem flowing from the invalidation of a provision under equal protection: Should the entire statute be struck, or should its coverage be extended to cover the unconstitutionally excluded category? Justice White's response in Wengler was as follows: "Because state legislation is at issue, and because a remedial outcome consonant with the state legislature's overall purpose is preferable, we believe that state judges are better positioned to choose an appropriate method of remedying the constitutional violation." Accordingly, the case was remanded.

By contrast, in federal legislation, where the Court *does* have the statutory interpretation power, the Court has most often extended the coverage of the benefits program after finding a particular limitation of benefits unconstitutional under equal protection. For a division on the Court on the remedial issue in a federal case, see Califano v. Westcott, 443 U.S. 76 (1979). On the merits, the Court was unanimous in finding sex discrimination in a provision of the Aid to Families with Dependent Children program that provided benefits only to families where children were dependent because of the father's (not the mother's) unemployment. But on the remedy, the Court divided 5 to 4. Justice Blackmun, for the majority, adhered to the Court's approach in earlier "equal protection challenges to underinclusive federal benefits statutes, [that] extension, rather than nullification, is the proper course." Justice Powell, joined by Chief Justice Burger and Justices Stewart and Rehnquist, thought that, in light of the congressional desire to reduce expenditures under the program, nullification was appropriate here: "Rather than frustrate the clear intent of Congress, the [District Court] simply should have enjoined any further payment of benefits under the provision found to be unconstitutional."

2. The only dissenter was Justice REHNQUIST, who stated that he continued to believe that Goldfarb "was wrongly decided, and that constitutional issues should be more readily reexamined under the doctrine of stare decisis than other issues."

For additional discussions of "benign" justifications for gender classifications, recall Michael M. (1981; p. 652 above) and Hogan (1982; p. 660 above). See generally Kanowitz, " 'Benign' Sex Discrimination: Its Troubles and Their Cure," 31 Hast.L.J. 1379 (1980).

2. RACIAL CRITERIA AND BENIGN PURPOSES

Introduction. In light of the preceding materials on the Court's quite clear standards in reviewing benign sex classifications, consider the materials that follow on the Court's more uncertain response to the reliance on racial criteria to aid minorities. Recall the introductory questions at p. 736 above: Should the standard of review of benign racial classifications be the same as that applied to disadvantaging ones? Or is a more lenient standard warranted? Should the standard be the intermediate level of scrutiny applied by the Court in such sex discrimination cases as Wengler? Should the standard be even more lenient than that: should it be as deferential as the "mere rationality" standard applied to economic regulations under the old equal protection? Can "rationality" review be defended on the ground that the 14th Amendment's original purpose was directed at hostile legislation imposing a stigma on the disadvantaged minority? Or does the evolution of equal protection criteria since the 19th century warrant a broader suspicion of *all* racial classifications, benign as well as hostile, so that heightened scrutiny is warranted even in the benign context? These problems generated an enormous flood of commentary even before the first major Court consideration in Bakke in 1978 (p. 745 below). The large amount of commentary has continued since, while the Court continues to struggle with the problems. Bakke and later cases air the contending positions at length. These introductory materials are limited to some of the relevant background materials available to the Court when it confronted the Bakke problem. (Additional background materials are aired in the opinions in Bakke.)

1. *Color consciousness to remedy purposeful discrimination: The school desegregation context.* As the materials in sec. 3D3 demonstrated, there is at least one area where government need not be color blind and indeed must be color conscious. The Court's requirements for eliminating the effects of de jure segregation have emphasized the *results* of desegregation efforts—results measured by the racial identification of schools, as the cases since Green and Swann illustrate. Moreover, in a companion case to Swann (p. 715 above), the Court unanimously struck down a state law mandating color blindness as an undue interference with desegregation requirements. In NORTH CAROLINA STATE BOARD OF EDUCATION v. SWANN, 402 U.S. 43 (1971), the Court held unconstitutional North Carolina's Anti-Busing Law [1] prohibiting student assignments on the basis of race. Chief Justice BURGER stated that "if a state-imposed limitation on a school authority's discretion operates to inhibit or obstruct the operation of a unitary school system, [it] must fall; state policy must give way when it operates to hinder vindication of federal constitutional guarantees." He commented that "the statute exploits an apparently neutral form to control school assignment plans by directing that they be 'color blind'; that requirement, against the background of segregation, would render illusory the promise" of Brown I. He elaborated: "Just as the race of students must be considered in determining whether a constitutional violation has occurred, so also must race be considered in formulating a remedy. To forbid, at this stage, all assignments made on the basis of race would deprive school authorities of the one tool absolutely essential to fulfillment of their [constitutional obligation]."

Is that endorsement of color consciousness limited to the remedying of de jure segregation? Or may school authorities also consider racial factors in

---

1. The Law provided: "No student shall be assigned or compelled to attend any school on account of race, creed, color or national origin, or for the purpose of creating a balance or ratio of race, religion or national origins. Involuntary bussing of students in contravention of this article is prohibited, and public funds shall not be used for any such bussing."

efforts to eliminate de facto segregation—efforts not mandated by the Constitution? In dicta in the Swann cases, Chief Justice Burger suggested that such voluntary use of racial criteria in the discretion of school officials was permissible. Recall that in the major Swann case, p. 715 above, the Chief Justice stated: "School authorities are traditionally charged with broad power to formulate and implement educational policy and might well conclude, for example, that in order to prepare students to live in a pluralistic society each school should have a prescribed ratio of Negro to white students reflecting the proportion for the district as a whole. To do this as an educational policy is within the broad discretionary powers of school authorities." (Cf. Bakke, p. 745 below.) What justifies such dicta? Is administrative use of race in the elimination of de facto segregation "suspect," with the "educational policy" providing the "compelling" justification? Or is the use of race in that context not subject to strict scrutiny and sustainable upon more lenient, perhaps even "mere rationality," scrutiny?[2] Do the arguments for color consciousness in public school desegregation efforts apply to other "benign" classifications as well? Do they justify preferential admissions programs in law schools, for example? Preferential, "affirmative action" employment programs?[3]

2. *Preferential admissions programs.* Preferential admissions programs in higher education, adopted without specific findings of past purposeful discrimination, began to be challenged in the courts in the early 1970s. The Court avoided decision on a challenge to a law school preferential admissions program in DeFunis v. Odegaard, 416 U.S. 312 (1974): in a 5 to 4 decision, the Court held the case moot on the ground that DeFunis, who had attended the law school while the case was in the courts, was about to graduate. Only Justice Douglas reached the merits. His opinion contained strong passages condemning racial factors in admissions programs but also suggested possible cultural bias in the ordinary admissions criteria and urged that the case be remanded. On the broad constitutional issue, he opposed reliance on racial criteria even for benign purposes and insisted that the 14th Amendment required "the consideration of each application *in a racially neutral way.*" Several years passed before the Court was compelled to reach the merits—and in Bakke, which follows, it divided sharply. In the period between DeFunis and Bakke, the solutions proposed in academic commentary ranged over the entire spectrum. For example, Ely suggested: "When the group that controls the decision making process classifies so as to advantage a minority and disadvantage itself, the reasons for being unusually suspicious, and, consequently, employing a stringent brand of review are lacking."[4] Kaplan argued that "any legal classification by race weakens the government as an educative force."[5] Others offered a range of intermediate positions between those two polar ones.[6] What justifications

2. For earlier decisions rejecting attacks on "color conscious" voluntary school integration programs, see, e.g., Balaban v. Rubin, 14 N.Y.2d 193, cert. denied, 379 U.S. 881 (1964), and School Comm. v. Board of Educ., 352 Mass. 693 (1967), appeal dismissed, 389 U.S. 572 (1968). Some of these cases explicitly applied a deferential, "mere rationality" standard of scrutiny. What justification was there for abandoning the strict scrutiny of "suspect" classifications? Because race *is* "relevant" here? Because the aim is to "help"? Should "relevance" and "helpfulness" go to the issue of whether justification is "compelling" rather than lowering the strict scrutiny justification requirement to a merely "reasonable" one?

3. See generally Kaplan, "Equal Justice in an Unequal World: Equality for the Negro—The Problem of Special Treatment," 61 Nw.U.L.Rev. 363 (1966); "Developments," 82 Harv.L.Rev. 1065 (1969); Ely, "The Constitutionality of Reverse Racial Discrimination," 41 U.Chi.L.Rev. 723 (1974).

4. See the Ely article cited in fn. 3.

5. Note Kaplan's comment in the article cited in fn. 3. He stated: "Preference for Negroes can [be] expected to be a major factor in preventing the education [toward color blindness] we are trying to bring about through a host of other laws."

6. For a sampling of the extensive pre-Bakke commentary on the constitutionality of color conscious admissions programs, see O'Neil, "Preferential Admissions: Equalizing the Access of Minority Groups to Higher Education," 80

should suffice when a preferential program is subjected to a heightened level of scrutiny, whether of the strict or intermediate variety? That question is pursued at length in Bakke.

3. *Benign programs and objecting members of minority groups.* What if doubts about the benignness of a program arise because of alleged harm to individual members of the supposedly aided minority? One aspect of that problem has been discussed in connection with quota and "tipping point" programs designed to promote integrated housing. E.g., may racial exclusion of a black person from a housing project be justified on the ground that the exclusion is pursuant to a quota designed to provide integrated housing for blacks generally?[7] Even if the benign purpose of a program is adequately demonstrated, must it be measured against the costs of the stigma that may be asserted by some members of the benefited group? More generally, may courts view programs that are clearly pro-integration in purpose and effect as "benign" when some segments of the "benefited" minority assert that separation is desirable in the long run or at least temporarily, to develop the group's cohesiveness and pride?[8]

REGENTS OF UNIV. OF CALIFORNIA v. BAKKE

438 U.S. 265, 98 S.Ct. 2733, 57 L.Ed.2d 750 (1978).

Mr. Justice POWELL announced the judgment of the Court.

This case presents a challenge to the special admissions program of the petitioner, the Medical School of the University of California at Davis, which is designed to assure the admission of a specified number of students from certain minority groups. [The] Supreme Court of California [held] the special admissions program unlawful, [enjoined] petitioner from considering the race of any

Yale L.J. 699 (1971); Graglia, "Special Admission of the 'Culturally Deprived' to Law School," 119 U.Pa.L.Rev. 351 (1970); Bell, "In Defense of Minority [Admissions Programs]," 119 U.Pa. L.Rev. 364 (1970); Sandalow, "Racial Preferences in Higher [Education]," 42 U.Chi.L.Rev. 653 (1975); Posner, "The DeFunis [Case]," 1974 Sup.Ct.Rev. 1; and Greenawalt, "Judicial Scrutiny of 'Benign' Racial Classifications in Law School Admissions," 75 Colum.L.Rev. 559 (1975). See also the symposia on DeFunis in 60 U.Va.L.Rev. 917 (1974) and in 75 Colum.L.Rev. 483 (1975).

7. See Bittker, The Case of the Checker-Board [Ordinance]," 71 Yale L.J. 1387 (1962); Navasky, "The Benevolent Housing Quota," 6 Howard L.J. 30 (1960); Ackerman, "Integration for Subsidized Housing and the Question of Racial Occupancy Controls," 26 Stan.L.Rev. 245 (1975); and Note, "Benign Steering and Benign [Quotas]," 93 Harv.L.Rev. 938 (1980). See also Otero v. N.Y.C. Hous. Auth., 484 F.2d 1122 (2d Cir.1973).

In 1980 the Court granted review in a case raising a related issue, but managed to dispose of it without reaching the merits. The case was Johnson v. Chicago Bd. of Ed., 604 F.2d 504 (7th Cir.1979), sustaining a maximum quota on minorities in certain high schools as part of a plan to prevent de facto segregation resulting from "white flight." The school board's "Student Racial Stabilization Quota Plan" was a response to the fact that white enrollment in two

neighborhood high schools had dropped by 10% in three years. The plan was designed to assure that minority enrollment in the schools would not go beyond about 60%. The lower court concluded that the racial quotas were "a necessary means of arresting de facto segregation in the public schools." The Court handed down two rulings in the case, but without reaching the merits. In 1981 (449 U.S. 915), the Court remanded the case "for further consideration in light of the subsequent development described in the suggestion of mootness filed by respondents." (The parties had tentatively agreed on a revised plan in a related case after the Court had granted review.) A year later [457 U.S. 52 (1982)], the case was once again in the Court, and the Court once again failed to reach the merits. In a 5 to 3 per curiam ruling, the majority, while agreeing with the lower court that the controversy was not moot, once again remanded so that Johnson could be consolidated with the related case, in order to develop a "complete factual record."

8. See "Developments," 82 Harv.L.Rev. 1065 (1969): "A state program permitting or encouraging racial separatism could also be used to create a system of segregation." That comment notes the occasional "division of opinion within the Black community itself" on the desirability of integration. Do the school desegregation cases in sec. 3D3 commit the Court to adhering to integration as the only legitimate goal, and to opposing separateness as an ideal, whether it is called "separatism" or "segregation"?

applicant,[1] [and ordered Bakke's] admission. For the reasons stated in the following opinion, I believe that so much of the judgment of the California court as holds petitioner's special admissions program unlawful and directs that respondent be admitted to the Medical School must be affirmed. For the reasons expressed in a separate opinion, my Brothers The Chief Justice [Burger], Mr. Justice Stewart, Mr. Justice Rehnquist, and Mr. Justice Stevens concur in this judgment. I also conclude for the reasons stated in the following opinion that the portion of the court's judgment enjoining petitioner from according any consideration to race in its admissions process must be reversed. For reasons expressed in separate opinions, my Brothers Mr. Justice Brennan, Mr. Justice White, Mr. Justice Marshall, and Mr. Justice Blackmun concur in this judgment.

Affirmed in part and reversed in part.

I.[2] [In Part I of his opinion, Justice Powell summarized the facts and the proceedings below. The admissions procedure challenged by Allan Bakke, an unsuccessful white applicant to the U.C. Davis Medical School in 1973 and 1974, was designed to admit 16 minority students into each entering class of 100. There were about 3,000 applicants in all. Davis operated two admissions programs in selecting its entering classes—a regular admissions program and a special admissions program. Under the regular admissions procedure, candidates with undergraduate grade point averages below 2.5 were summarily rejected. Applicants invited for a personal interview were rated by the regular admissions committee to achieve a "benchmark" score. The special admissions program operated with a separate committee; members of minority groups constituted a majority of that committee. The 2.5 grade point average cut-off did not apply to special admissions applicants. Bakke's applications in 1973 and 1974 were rejected even though "[i]n both years, applicants were admitted under the special program with grade point averages, MCAT scores, and benchmark scores significantly lower than Bakke's."[3] After his second rejection, Bakke filed suit in the state courts, relying on a state constitutional provision, Title VI of the 1964 Civil Rights Act, and the Equal Protection Clause. The trial court, relying on all three grounds, held that the University could not take race into account in making admission decisions. However, it refused to order Bakke's admission because he had failed to carry his burden of proving that he would have been admitted but for the existence of the special program. Both sides appealed to the California Supreme Court. The decision there was described by Justice Powell as follows:]

1. Mr. Justice Stevens views the judgment of the California court as limited to prohibiting the consideration of race only in passing upon Bakke's application. [But the highest state court's opinion] left no doubt that the reason for its holding was petitioner's use of race in consideration of *any candidate's* application. [This] makes it unreasonable to assume that the reach of the California court's judgment can be limited in the manner suggested by Mr. Justice Stevens. [Footnote by Justice Powell.]

2. Mr. Justice Brennan, Mr. Justice White, Mr. Justice Marshall, and Mr. Justice Blackmun join Parts I and V–C of this opinion. Mr. Justice White also joins Part III–A of this opinion. [Footnote by Justice Powell.]

3. According to the 1973 application forms, the special program was open to those "economically and/or educationally disadvantaged"; on the 1974 forms, the special program was available to applicants who were members of a "minority group"—a designation which Davis applied to "Blacks," "Chicanos," "Asians," and "American Indians." Justice Powell noted: "Although disadvantaged whites applied to the special program in large numbers, none received an offer of admission through that process. Indeed, in 1974, at least, the special committee explicitly considered only 'disadvantaged' special applicants who were members of one of the designated minority groups."

In describing eligibility for the special admissions program, Justice Powell noted: "No formal definition of 'disadvantaged' was ever produced, but the chairman of the special committee screened each application to see whether it reflected economic or educational deprivation. The chairman normally checked to see if, among other things, the applicant had been granted a waiver of the school's application fee, which required a means test; whether the applicant had worked during college or interrupted his education in order to support himself or his family; and whether the applicant was a member of a minority group."

Because the special admissions program involved a racial classification, the supreme court held itself bound to apply strict scrutiny. It then turned to the goals the University presented as justifying the special program. Although the court agreed that the goals of integrating the medical profession and increasing the number of physicians willing to serve members of minority groups were compelling state interests, it concluded that the special admissions program was not the least intrusive means of achieving those goals.[4] Without passing on the state constitutional or the federal statutory grounds cited in the trial court's judgment, the California court held that the Equal Protection Clause [required] that "no applicant may be rejected because of his race, in favor of another who is less qualified, as measured by standards applied without regard to race." [5]

II. [Justice Powell began with a consideration of Title VI of the Civil Rights Act of 1964.] At the outset we face the question whether a right of action for private parties exists under Title VI. We find it unnecessary to resolve this question in the instant case. [We] assume only for the purposes of this case that respondent has a right of action under Title VI.[6] [The] legislative history of Title VI reveals a congressional intent to halt federal funding of entities that violate a prohibition of racial discrimination similar to that of the Constitution. Although isolated statements of various legislators, taken out of context, can be marshalled in support of the proposition that § 601 enacted a purely colorblind scheme, without regard to the reach of the Equal Protection Clause, these comments must be read against the background of both the problem that Congress was addressing and the broader view of the statute that emerges from a full examination of the legislative debates. In view of the clear legislative intent, Title VI must be held to proscribe only those racial classifications that would violate [equal protection].

III. A. [The parties] disagree as to the level of judicial scrutiny to be applied to the special admissions program. [En route] to this crucial battle over the scope of judicial review, the parties fight a sharp preliminary action over the proper characterization of the special admissions program. Petitioner prefers to view it as establishing a "goal" of minority representation in the medical school. Respondent, echoing the courts below, labels it a racial quota.[7] This semantic

---

4. In delineating a range of "less detrimental" means, the majority of the California Supreme Court suggested that the University could place less emphasis on quantitative measures of test scores and grade point averages for all applicants, increase the size of its medical schools, resort to "aggressive programs" to recruit applicants and "provide remedial schooling for disadvantaged students of all races," or design special admissions programs for "disadvantaged applicants of all races." Justice Mosk added: "So far as the record discloses, the University has not considered the adoption of these or other nonracial alternatives to the special admissions program."

5. Justice Powell summarized the subsequent proceedings in California as follows: "[The court also] ruled that since Bakke had established that the University had discriminated against him on the basis of his race, the burden of proof shifted to the University to demonstrate that he would not have been admitted even in the absence of the special admissions program. [T]he court initially ordered a remand for the purpose of determining whether, under the newly allocated burden of proof, Bakke would have been admitted to either the 1973 or the 1974 entering class in the absence of the special admissions program.

In its petition for rehearing below, however, the University conceded its inability to carry that burden. The California court thereupon amended its opinion to direct that the trial court enter judgment ordering Bakke's admission to the medical school. That order was stayed pending review in this Court."

6. Title VI provides: "No person in the United States shall, on the ground of race, color, or national origin, be excluded from participation in, be denied the benefits of, or be subjected to discrimination under any program or activity receiving Federal financial assistance."

Compare the decision a year later in Cannon v. University of Chicago, 441 U.S. 677 (1979), a sex discrimination case finding an implied right of action under Title IX of the Education Amendments of 1972. (Title IX was patterned after Title VI of the 1964 Act.) Justice Stevens' majority opinion in Cannon placed great emphasis on the large number of lower court opinions that had long read Title VI as creating a private right of action.

7. Petitioner defines "quota" as a requirement which must be met but can never be exceeded, regardless of the quality of the minority applicants. Petitioner declares that there is no

distinction is beside the point: the special admissions program is undeniably a classification based on race and ethnic background. To the extent that there existed a pool of at least minimally qualified minority applicants to fill the 16 special admissions seats, white applicants could compete only for 84 seats in the entering class, rather than the 100 open to minority applicants. Whether this limitation is described as a quota or a goal, it is a line drawn on the basis of race and ethnic status.

The guarantees of the 14th Amendment extend to persons. Its language is explicit. [Shelley v. Kraemer (1948; p. 877 below).] [The] guarantee of equal protection cannot mean one thing when applied to one individual and something else when applied to a person of another color. [Nevertheless], petitioner argues that the court below erred in applying strict scrutiny [because white males] are not a "discrete and insular minority" requiring extraordinary protection from the majoritarian political process. [Carolene Products, n. 4.] This rationale, however, has never been invoked in our decisions as a prerequisite to subjecting racial or ethnic distinctions to strict scrutiny. Nor has this Court held that discreteness and insularity constitute necessary preconditions to a holding that a particular classification is invidious. These characteristics may be relevant in deciding whether or not to add new types of classifications to the list of "suspect" categories or whether a particular classification survives close examination. See, e.g., [Murgia (age); Graham (aliens)]. Racial and ethnic classifications, however, are subject to stringent examination without regard to these additional characteristics. We declared as much in the first cases explicitly to recognize racial distinctions as suspect [Hirabayashi; Korematsu]. Racial and ethnic distinctions of any sort are inherently suspect and thus call for the most exacting judicial examination.

B. This perception of racial and ethnic distinctions is rooted in our Nation's constitutional and demographic history. The Court's initial view of the 14th Amendment was that its "one pervading purpose" was "the freedom of the slave race." [Slaughter-House Cases.] [Equal protection], however, was "[v]irtually strangled in its infancy by post-civil-war judicial reactionism." It was relegated to decades of relative desuetude while [due process flourished] as a cornerstone in the Court's defense of property and liberty of contract. In that cause, the 14th Amendment's "one pervading purpose" was displaced. It was only as the era of substantive due process came to a close that [equal protection] began to attain a genuine measure of vitality. By that time it was no longer possible to peg the guarantees of the 14th Amendment to the struggle for equality of one racial minority. During the dormancy of [equal protection], the United States had become a nation of minorities. Each had to struggle—and to some extent struggles still [8]—to overcome the prejudices not of a monolithic majority, but of a "majority" composed of various minority groups of whom it was said—perhaps unfairly in many cases—that a shared characteristic was a willingness to disadvantage other groups. As the Nation filled with the stock of many lands, the reach of the Clause was gradually extended to all ethnic groups seeking protection from official discrimination. See [Strauder (Celtic Irishmen); Yick Wo (Chinese); Truax v. Raich (Austrian resident aliens); Korematsu

"floor" under the total number of minority students admitted; completely unqualified students will not be admitted simply to meet a "quota." Neither is there a "ceiling," since an unlimited number could be admitted through the general admissions process. On this basis the special admissions program does not meet petitioner's definition of a quota. The court below found [that] white applicants could not compete for the 16 places reserved solely for the special admissions program. Both courts below characterized this as a "quota" system. [Footnote by Justice Powell.]

8. "Members of various religious and ethnic groups, primarily but not exclusively of eastern, and middle and southern European ancestry, such as Jews, Catholics, Italians, Greeks and Slavic groups [continue] to be excluded from executive, middle-management and other job levels because of discrimination based upon their religion and/or national origin." 41 CFR § 60–50.1(b) (1977). [Footnote by Justice Powell.]

(Japanese); Hernandez v. Texas (Mexican-Americans)]. [Although] many of the Framers of the 14th Amendment conceived of its primary function as bridging the vast distance between members of the Negro race and the white "majority," the Amendment itself was framed in universal terms, without reference to color, ethnic origin, or condition of prior servitude. [I]t is not unlikely that among the Framers were many who would have applauded a reading of [equal protection] which states a principle of universal application and is responsive to the racial, ethnic and cultural diversity of the Nation.

Over the past 30 years, this Court has embarked upon the crucial mission of interpreting the Equal Protection Clause with the view of assuring to all persons "the protection of equal laws," in a Nation confronting a legacy of slavery and racial discrimination. See, e.g., [Brown]. Because the landmark decisions in this area arose in response to the continued exclusion of Negroes from the mainstream of American society, they could be characterized as involving discrimination by the "majority" white race against the Negro minority. But they need not be read as depending upon that characterization for their results. It suffices to say that "[o]ver the years, this Court consistently repudiated '[d]istinctions between citizens solely because of their ancestry' as being 'odious to a free people whose institutions are founded upon the doctrine of equality.' " [Loving v. Virginia, quoting Hirabayashi.] Petitioner urges us to adopt for the first time a more restrictive view of [equal protection] and hold that discrimination against members of the white "majority" cannot be suspect if its purpose can be characterized as "benign." [9] The clock of our liberties, however, cannot be turned back to 1868. Brown. It is far too late to argue that the guarantee of equal protection to all persons permits the recognition of special wards entitled to a degree of protection greater than that accorded others.[10]

Once the artificial line of a "two-class theory" of the 14th Amendment is put aside, the difficulties entailed in varying the level of judicial review according to a perceived "preferred" status of a particular racial or ethnic minority are intractable. The concepts of "majority" and "minority" necessarily reflect temporary arrangements and political judgments. As observed above, the white "majority" itself is composed of various minority groups, most of which can lay claim to a history of prior discrimination at the hands of the state and private individuals. Not all of these groups can receive preferential treatment and

9. In the view of Mr. Justice Brennan [et al.] the pliable notion of "stigma" is the crucial element in analyzing racial classifications. The Equal Protection Clause is not framed in terms of "stigma." Certainly the word has no clearly defined constitutional meaning. It reflects a subjective judgment that is standardless. *All* state-imposed classifications that rearrange burdens and benefits on the basis of race are likely to be viewed with deep resentment by the individuals burdened. The denial to innocent persons of equal rights and opportunities may outrage those so deprived and therefore may be perceived as invidious. These individuals are likely to find little comfort in the notion that the deprivation they are asked to endure is merely the price of membership in the dominant majority and that its imposition is inspired by the supposedly benign purpose of aiding others. One should not lightly dismiss the inherent unfairness of, and the perception of mistreatment that accompanies, a system of allocating benefits and privileges on the basis of skin color and ethnic origin. Moreover, Mr. Justice Brennan [et al.] offer no principle for deciding whether preferential classifications reflect a benign remedial purpose or a malevolent stigmatic classification, since they are willing in this case to accept mere post hoc declarations by an isolated state entity—a medical school faculty—unadorned by particularized findings of past discrimination, to establish such a remedial purpose. [Footnote by Justice Powell.]

10. Professor Bickel noted the self-contradiction of that view: "The lesson of the great decisions of the Supreme Court and the lesson of contemporary history have been the same for at least a generation: discrimination on the basis of race is illegal, immoral, unconstitutional, inherently wrong, and destructive of democratic society. Now this is to be unlearned and we are told that this is not a matter of fundamental principle but only a matter of whose ox is gored. Those for whom racial equality was demanded are to be more equal than others. Having found support in the Constitution for equality, they now claim support for inequality under the same Constitution." A. Bickel, The Morality of Consent 133 (1975). [Footnote by Justice Powell.]

corresponding judicial tolerance of distinctions drawn in terms of race and nationality, for then the only "majority" left would be a new minority of White Anglo-Saxon Protestants. There is no principled basis for deciding which groups would merit "heightened judicial solicitude" and which would not.[11] Courts would be asked to evaluate the extent of the prejudice and consequent harm suffered by various minority groups. Those whose societal injury is thought to exceed some arbitrary level of tolerability then would be entitled to preferential classifications at the expense of individuals belonging to other groups. Those classifications would be free from exacting judicial scrutiny. As these preferences began to have their desired effect, and the consequences of past discrimination were undone, new judicial rankings would be necessary. The kind of variable sociological and political analysis necessary to produce such rankings simply does not lie within the judicial [competence].

Moreover, there are serious problems of justice connected with the idea of preference itself. First, it may not always be clear that a so-called preference is in fact benign. Courts may be asked to validate burdens imposed upon individual members of particular groups in order to advance the group's general interest. See United Jewish Organizations v. Carey [hereinafter UJO (1977; see fn. 17 below)] [Brennan, J.]. Nothing in the Constitution supports the notion that individuals may be asked to suffer otherwise impermissible burdens in order to enhance the societal standing of their ethnic groups. Second, preferential programs may only reinforce common stereotypes holding that certain groups are unable to achieve success without special protection based on a factor having no relationship to individual worth. Third, there is a measure of inequity in forcing innocent persons in respondent's position to bear the burdens of redressing grievances not of their making. By hitching the meaning of [equal protection] to these transitory considerations, we would be holding, as a constitutional principle, that judicial scrutiny of classifications touching on racial and ethnic background may vary with the ebb and flow of political forces. Disparate constitutional tolerance of such classifications well may serve to exacerbate racial and ethnic antagonisms rather than alleviate them. UJO [Brennan, J.]. Also, the mutability of a constitutional principle, based upon shifting political and social judgments, undermines the chances for consistent application of the Constitution from one generation to the next, a critical feature of its coherent [interpretation].

If it is the individual who is entitled to judicial protection against classifications based upon his racial or ethnic background because such distinctions impinge upon personal rights, rather than the individual only because of his

---

11. As I am in agreement with the view that race may be taken into account as a factor in an admissions program, I agree with my Brothers Brennan [et al.] that the portion of the judgment that would proscribe all consideration of race must be reversed. See Part V, infra. But I disagree with much that is said in their opinion.

They would require as a justification for a program such as petitioner's only two findings: (i) that there has been some form of discrimination against the preferred minority groups "by society at large" (it being conceded that petitioner had no history of discrimination), and (ii) that "there is reason to believe" that the disparate impact sought to be rectified by the program is the "product" of such discrimination. The breadth of this hypothesis is unprecedented in our constitutional system. The first step is easily taken. No one denies the regrettable fact that there has been societal discrimination in this

country against various racial and ethnic groups. The second step, however, involves a speculative leap; but for this discrimination by society at large, Bakke "would have failed to qualify for admission" because Negro applicants—nothing is said about Asians—would have made better scores. Not one word in the record supports this conclusion, and the plurality offers no standard for courts to use in applying such a presumption of causation to other racial or ethnic classifications. This failure is a grave one, since if it may be concluded *on this record* that each of the minority groups preferred by the petitioner's special program is entitled to the benefit of the presumption, it would seem difficult to determine that any of the dozens of minority groups that have suffered "societal discrimination" cannot also claim it, in any area of social intercourse. See Part IV–B, infra. [Footnote by Justice Powell.]

membership in a particular group, then constitutional standards may be applied consistently. Political judgments regarding the necessity for the particular classification may be weighed in the constitutional balance [Korematsu], but the standard of justification will remain constant. This is as it should be, since those political judgments are the product of rough compromise struck by contending groups within the democratic process. When they touch upon an individual's race or ethnic background, he is entitled to a judicial determination that the burden he is asked to bear on that basis is precisely tailored to serve a compelling governmental [interest].

C. Petitioner contends that on several occasions this Court has approved preferential classifications without applying the most exacting scrutiny. Most of the cases upon which petitioner relies are drawn from three areas: school desegregation, employment discrimination, and sex discrimination. Each of the cases cited presented a situation materially different from the facts of this case. The school desegregation cases are inapposite. Each involved remedies for clearly determined constitutional violations.[12] [E.g., Swann.] Racial classifications thus were designed as remedies for the vindication of constitutional entitlement. Moreover, the scope of the remedies was not permitted to exceed the extent of the violations. Here, there was no judicial determination of constitutional violation as a predicate for the formulation of a remedial classification.

The employment discrimination cases also do not advance petitioner's cause. For example, in Franks v. Bowman Transportation Co., 424 U.S. 747 (1976), we approved a retroactive award of seniority to a class of Negro truck drivers who had been the victims of discrimination—not just by society at large, but by the respondent in that case. While this relief imposed some burdens on other employees, it was held necessary " 'to make [the victims] whole for injuries suffered on account of unlawful employment discrimination.' " The courts of appeals have fashioned various types of racial preferences as remedies for constitutional or statutory violations resulting in identified, race-based injuries to individuals held entitled to the preference.[13] Such preferences also have been upheld where a legislative or administrative body charged with the responsibility made determinations of past discrimination by the industries affected, and fashioned remedies deemed appropriate to rectify the discrimination. E.g., [Contractors Ass'n v. Secretary of Labor, 442 F.2d 159 (3rd Cir.), cert. denied, 404 U.S. 854 (1971).][14] But we have never approved preferential classifications in the absence of proven constitutional or statutory violations.[15]

12. [Respondent's] position is wholly dissimilar to that of a pupil bused from his neighborhood school to a comparable school in another neighborhood in compliance with a desegregation decree. Petitioner did not arrange for respondent to attend a different medical school in order to desegregate Davis Medical School; instead, it denied him admission and may have deprived him altogether of a medical education. [Footnote by Justice Powell.]

13. E.g., Bridgeport Guardians, Inc. v. Civil Service Commission, 482 F.2d 1333 (2d Cir. 1973); Carter v. Gallagher, 452 F.2d 315, 327 (8th Cir.1972).

14. Every decision upholding the requirement of preferential hiring under the authority of Exec. Order No. 11246 has emphasized the existence of previous discrimination as a predicate for the imposition of a preferential remedy. [Footnote by Justice Powell.]

15. This case does not call into question congressionally authorized administrative actions, such as consent decrees under Title VII or approval of reapportionment plans under § 5 of the Voting Rights Act of 1965. In such cases, there has been detailed legislative consideration of the various indicia of previous constitutional or statutory violations, e.g., South Carolina v. Katzenbach [p. 933 below], and particular administrative bodies have been charged with monitoring various activities in order to detect such violations and formulate appropriate remedies.

Furthermore, we are not here presented with an occasion to review legislation by Congress pursuant to its powers under § 2 of the 13th Amendment and § 5 of the 14th Amendment to remedy the effects of prior discrimination. Katzenbach v. Morgan; Jones v. Alfred H. Mayer Co. [chap. 10 below]. We have previously recognized the special competence of Congress to make findings with respect to the effects of iden-

Nor is petitioner's view as to the applicable standard supported by the fact that gender-based classifications are not subjected to this level of scrutiny. E.g., Califano v. Webster. Gender-based distinctions are less likely to create the analytical and practical problems present in preferential programs premised on racial or ethnic criteria. With respect to gender there are only two possible classifications. The incidence of the burdens imposed by preferential classifications is clear. There are no rival groups who can claim that they, too, are entitled to preferential treatment. Classwide questions as to the group suffering previous injury and groups which fairly can be burdened are relatively manageable for reviewing courts. See, e.g., [Goldfarb; Wiesenfeld]. The resolution of these same questions in the context of racial and ethnic preferences presents far more complex and intractable problems than gender-based classifications. More importantly, the perception of racial classifications as inherently odious stems from a lengthy and tragic history that gender-based classifications do not share. In sum, the Court has never viewed such classification as inherently suspect or as comparable to racial or ethnic classifications for the purpose of equal-protection analysis.

[In] a similar vein,[16] petitioner contends that [UJO] indicates a willingness to approve racial classifications designed to benefit certain minorities, without denominating the classifications as "suspect." [New York] had redrawn its reapportionment plan to meet objections of the Department of Justice under § 5 of the Voting Rights Act of 1965. Specifically, voting districts were redrawn to enhance the electoral power of certain "nonwhite" voters found to have been the victims of unlawful "dilution" under the original reapportionment plan. [UJO] properly is viewed as a case in which the remedy for an administrative finding of discrimination encompassed measures to improve the previously disadvantaged group's ability to participate, without excluding individuals belonging to any other group from enjoyment of the relevant opportunity—meaningful participation in the electoral process.[17] In this case, unlike

tified past discrimination and its discretionary authority to take appropriate remedial measures. [Footnote by Justice Powell.]

16. Petitioner also cites our decision in Morton v. Mancari, 417 U.S. 535 (1974), for the proposition that the State may prefer members of traditionally disadvantaged groups. In Mancari, we approved a hiring preference for qualified Indians in the Bureau of Indian [Affairs] (BIA). We observed in that case, however, that the legal status of BIA is sui generis. Indeed, we found that the preference was not racial at all, but "an employment criterion reasonably designed to further the cause of Indian self-government and to make the BIA more responsive to [groups] whose lives are governed by the BIA in a unique fashion." [Footnote by Justice Powell.]

17. As this passage in the text indicates, United Jewish Organizations v. Carey, 430 U.S. 144 (1977), gave rise to some speculation that the Court was willing to apply deferential review to benign racial classifications. UJO, as Justice Powell notes, was a redistricting case under the Voting Rights Act. [For further discussion of UJO, see the materials in chap. 10, sec. 4, below.] In UJO, New York had redrawn districts in Brooklyn in order to maintain black representation in the state legislature, in an attempt to comply with the Voting Rights Act. The redistricting affected an area where about 30,000

Hasidic Jews lived. In order to create substantial nonwhite majorities in a few districts, New York's revision split the Hasidic community into several districts. The Hasidic Jews attacked the redistricting as unconstitutional racial reapportionment under the 14th and 15th Amendments. In rejecting that challenge, Justice White's opinion (entirely joined by Justice Stevens and partly joined by Justices Brennan, Blackmun and Rehnquist) emphasized two reasons. First, New York had done no more than the Attorney General was authorized to require under the Voting Rights Act. His second, "independent" ground went further: in a portion of the opinion supported only by Justices Stevens and Rehnquist, Justice White gave rise to the speculation about the permissibility of benign racial criteria by stating: "[W]hether or not the plan was authorized [by] the Voting Rights Act, New York was entitled to consider racial factors in redistricting under the Constitution." He noted that New York's plan "represented no racial slur or stigma with respect to whites or any other race." Although, in the redrawn districts, black representatives were more likely to be elected, "as long as whites in [Brooklyn], as a group, were provided with fair representation, we cannot conclude that there was a cognizable discrimination against whites." He concluded that a state may, quite apart from the Voting Rights Act, constitutionally "attempt to prevent racial minorities from

[UJO], there has been no determination by the legislature or a responsible administrative agency that the University engaged in a discriminatory practice requiring remedial efforts. Moreover, the operation of petitioner's special admissions program is quite different from the remedial measures approved [there]. It prefers the designated minority groups at the expense of other individuals who are totally foreclosed from competition for the 16 special admissions seats in every medical school class. Because of that foreclosure, some individuals are excluded from enjoyment of a state-provided benefit—admission to the medical school—they otherwise would receive. When a classification denies an individual opportunities or benefits enjoyed by others solely because of his race or ethnic background, it must be regarded as suspect.

IV. We have held that in "order to justify the use of a suspect classification, a State must show that its purpose or interest is both constitutionally permissible and substantial, and that its use of the classification is 'necessary [to] the accomplishment' of its purpose or the safeguarding of its interest." [E.g., Loving.] The special admissions program purports to serve the purposes of: (i) "reducing the historic deficit of traditionally disfavored minorities in medical schools and the medical profession"; (ii) countering the effects of societal discrimination; [18] (iii) increasing the number of physicians who will practice in

being repeatedly outvoted by creating districts that would afford fair representation to the members of those racial groups who are sufficiently numerous and whose residential patterns afford the opportunity of creating districts in which they will be in the majority." (Justice White paid relatively little attention to the claim that the Hasidic Jews were themselves a "discrete and insular" minority who were being discriminated against by the reapportionment. He noted that the Hasidic Jews had not challenged the lower court's holding that they "had no constitutional right to separate community recognition in reapportionment.")

Justice Brennan's concurrence rested solely on the Voting Rights Act but spoke at length about the potential abuses of "benign" racial factors in state action, in a fashion similar to his discussion in his Bakke opinion, below. He concluded: "However the Court ultimately decides the constitutional legitimacy of 'reverse discrimination' pure and simple, I am convinced that the application of the Voting Rights Act substantially minimizes the objections to preferential treatment, and legitimates the use of even overt, numerical racial devices in electoral redistricting." A separate opinion by Justice Stewart, joined by Justice Powell, concurred in the judgment, finding no "purposeful discrimination" under the 14th Amendment standard of Washington v. Davis: "The clear purpose with which the New York Legislature acted—in response to the position of the [U.S.] Department of Justice under the Voting Rights Act—forecloses any finding that it acted with the invidious purpose of discriminating against white voters." Chief Justice Burger's dissent concluded: "While petitioners may have no constitutional right to remain unified within a single political district, they do have [the] constitutional right not to be carved up so as to create a voting bloc composed of some other ethnic or racial group through the kind of racial gerrymandering the Court condemned in Gomillion v. Lightfoot (p. 691 above).

[I] cannot square the mechanical racial gerrymandering in this case with the mandate of the Constitution."

18. A number of distinct subgoals have been advanced as falling under the rubric of "compensation for past discrimination." For example, it is said that preferences for Negro applicants may compensate for harm done them personally, or serve to place them at economic levels they might have attained but for discrimination against their forebears. Another view of the "compensation" goal is that it serves as a form of reparation by the "majority" to a victimized group as a whole. B. Bittker, The Case for Black Reparations (1973). [Finally], it has been argued that ethnic preferences 'compensate' the group by providing examples of success whom other members of the group will emulate, thereby advancing the group's interest and society's interest in encouraging new generations to overcome the barriers and frustrations of the past. For purposes of analysis these subgoals need not be considered separately.

Racial classifications in admissions conceivably could serve a fifth purpose, one which petitioner does not articulate: fair appraisal of each individual's academic promise in the light of some cultural bias in grading or testing procedures. To the extent that race and ethnic background were considered only to the extent of curing established inaccuracies in predicting academic performance, it might be argued that there is no "preference" at all. Nothing in this record, however, suggests either that any of the quantitative factors considered by the Medical School were culturally biased or that petitioner's special admissions program was formulated to correct for any such biases. Furthermore, if race or ethnic background were used solely to arrive at an unbiased prediction of academic success, the reservation of fixed numbers of seats would be inexplicable. [Footnote by Justice Powell.]

communities currently underserved; and (iv) obtaining the educational benefits that flow from an ethnically diverse student body. It is necessary to decide which, if any, of these purposes is substantial enough to support the use of a suspect classification.

A.   If petitioner's purpose is to assure within its student body some specified percentage of a particular group merely because of its race or ethnic origin, such a preferential purpose must be rejected not as insubstantial but as facially invalid. Preferring members of any one group for no reason other than race or ethnic origin is discrimination for its own sake. This the Constitution forbids. E.g., Loving; Brown.

B.   The State certainly has a legitimate and substantial interest in ameliorating, or eliminating where feasible, the disabling effects of identified discrimination. [The] school desegregation cases [attest] to the importance of this state goal, [which is] far more focused than the remedying of the effects of "societal discrimination," an amorphous concept of injury that may be ageless in its reach into the past. We have never approved a classification that aids persons perceived as members of relatively victimized groups at the expense of other innocent individuals in the absence of judicial, legislative, or administrative findings of constitutional or statutory violations. After such findings have been made, the governmental interest in preferring members of the injured groups at the expense of others is substantial, since the legal rights of the victims must be vindicated. In such a case, the extent of the injury and the consequent remedy will have been judicially, legislatively, or administratively defined. Also, the remedial action usually remains subject to continuing oversight to assure that it will work the least harm possible to other innocent persons competing for the benefit. Without such findings of constitutional or statutory violations,[19] it cannot be said that the government has any greater interest in helping one individual than in refraining from harming another. Thus, the government has no compelling justification for inflicting such harm.

Petitioner does not purport to have made, and is in no position to make, such findings. Its broad mission is education, not the formulation of any legislative policy or the adjudication of particular claims of illegality. For reasons similar to those stated in Part III of this opinion, isolated segments of our vast governmental structures are not competent to make those decisions, at least in the absence of legislative mandates and legislatively determined criteria.[20] Cf. Hampton v. Mow Sun Wong [p. 676 above]. Compare n. [15], supra. Before relying upon these sorts of findings in establishing a racial classification, a governmental body must have the authority and capability to

---

19. Mr. Justice Brennan [et al.] misconceive the scope of this Court's holdings under Title VII when they suggest that "disparate impact" alone is sufficient to establish a violation of that statute, and, by analogy, other civil rights measures. That this was not the meaning of Title VII was made quite clear in the seminal decision in this area, [Griggs]. [D]isparate impact is a basis for relief under Title VII only if the practise in question is not founded on "business necessity," or lacks "a manifest relationship to the employment in question." Nothing *in this record*—as opposed to some of the general literature cited by Mr. Justice Brennan [et al.]—even remotely suggests that the disparate impact of the general admissions program at Davis Medical School, resulting primarily [from] disparate test scores and grades, [is] without educational justification.

Moreover, the presumption in Griggs—that disparate impact without any showing of business justification established the existence of discrimination in violation of the statute—was based on legislative determinations, wholly absent here, that past discrimination had handicapped various minority groups to such an extent that disparate impact could be traced to identifiable instances of past discrimination. [Thus], Title VII principles support the proposition that findings of identified discrimination must precede the fashioning of remedial measures embodying racial classifications. [Footnote by Justice Powell.]

20. For example, the University is unable to explain its selection of only the three favored groups—Negroes, Mexican-Americans, and Asians—for preferential treatment. The inclusion of the last group is especially curious in light of the substantial numbers of Asians admitted through the regular admissions process. [Footnote by Justice Powell.]

establish, in the record, that the classification is responsive to identified discrimination. See, e.g., [Webster; Goldfarb]. Lacking this capability, petitioner has not carried its burden of justification on this issue. Hence, the purpose of helping certain groups whom the faculty of the Davis Medical School perceived as victims of "societal discrimination" does not justify a classification that imposes disadvantages upon persons like respondent, who bear no responsibility for whatever harm the beneficiaries of the special admissions program are thought to have suffered. To hold otherwise would be to convert a remedy heretofore reserved for violations of legal rights into a privilege that all institutions throughout the Nation could grant at their pleasure to whatever groups are perceived as victims of societal discrimination. That is a step we have never approved.

C. Petitioner identifies, as another purpose of its program, improving the delivery of health care services to communities currently underserved. It may be assumed that in some situations a State's interest in facilitating the health care of its citizens is sufficiently compelling to support the use of a suspect classification. But there is virtually no evidence in the record indicating that petitioner's special admissions program is either needed or geared to promote that goal. [Petitioner] simply has not carried its burden of demonstrating that it must prefer members of particular ethnic groups over all other individuals in order to promote better health care delivery to deprived citizens. Indeed, petitioner has not shown that its preferential classification is likely to have any significant effect on the problem.

D. The fourth goal asserted by petitioner is the attainment of a diverse student body. This clearly is a constitutionally permissible goal for an institution of higher education. Academic freedom, though not a specifically enumerated constitutional right, long has been viewed as a special concern of the First Amendment. The freedom of a university to make its own judgments as to education includes the selection of its student body. [E.g., Sweezy (1957; p. 1406 below), Frankfurter, J., concurring.] [Thus], in arguing that its universities must be accorded the right to select those students who will contribute the most to the "robust exchange of ideas," petitioner invokes a countervailing constitutional interest, that of the First Amendment. In this light, petitioner must be viewed as seeking to achieve a goal that is of paramount importance in the fulfillment of its mission. It may be argued that there is greater force to these views at the undergraduate level than in a medical school where the training is centered primarily on professional competency. But even at the graduate level, our tradition and experience lend support to the view that the contribution of diversity is substantial. [Physicians] serve a heterogeneous population. An otherwise qualified medical student with a particular background—whether it be ethnic, geographic, culturally advantaged or disadvantaged—may bring to a professional school of medicine experiences, outlooks and ideas that enrich the training of its student body and better equip its graduates to render with understanding their vital service to humanity. Ethnic diversity, however, is only one element in a range of factors a university properly may consider in attaining the goal of a heterogeneous student body. Although a university must have wide discretion in making the sensitive judgments as to who should be admitted, constitutional limitations protecting individual rights may not be disregarded. Respondent urges—and the courts below have held—that petitioner's dual admissions program is a racial classification that impermissibly infringes his rights under the 14th Amendment. As the interest of diversity is compelling in the context of a university's admissions program, the question remains whether the program's racial classification is necessary to promote this interest.

V. A. It may be assumed that the reservation of a specified number of seats in each class for individuals from the preferred ethnic groups would contribute to the attainment of considerable ethnic diversity in the student body. But petitioner's argument that this is the only effective means of serving the interest of diversity is seriously flawed. In a most fundamental sense the argument misconceives the nature of the state interest that would justify consideration of race or ethnic background. It is not an interest in simple ethnic diversity, in which a specified percentage of the student body is in effect guaranteed to be members of selected ethnic groups, with the remaining percentage an undifferentiated aggregation of students. The diversity that furthers a compelling state interest encompasses a far broader array of qualifications and characteristics of which racial or ethnic origin is but a single though important element. Petitioner's special admissions program, focused *solely* on ethnic diversity, would hinder rather than further attainment of genuine diversity. Nor would the state interest in genuine diversity be served by expanding petitioner's two-track system into a multitrack program with a prescribed number of seats set aside for each identifiable category of applicants. Indeed, it is inconceivable that a university would thus pursue the logic of petitioner's two-track program to the illogical end of insulating each category of applicants with certain desired qualifications from competition with all other applicants.

The experience of other university admissions programs, which take race into account in achieving the educational diversity valued by the First Amendment, demonstrates that the assignment of a fixed number of places to a minority group is not a necessary means toward that end. An illuminating example is found in the Harvard College program: "In recent years Harvard College has expanded the concept of diversity to include students from disadvantaged economic, racial and ethnic groups. Harvard College now recruits not only Californians or Louisianans but also blacks and Chicanos and other minority students. [In] practice, this new definition of diversity has meant that race has been a factor in some admission decisions. When the Committee on Admissions reviews the large middle group of applicants who are 'admissible' and deemed capable of doing good work in their courses, the race of an applicant may tip the balance in his favor just as geographic origin or a life spent on a farm may tip the balance in other candidates' cases. A farm boy from Idaho can bring something to Harvard College that a Bostonian cannot offer. Similarly, a black student can usually bring something that a white person cannot offer. In Harvard college admissions the Committee has not set target-quotas for the number of blacks, or of musicians, football players, physicists or Californians to be admitted in a given year.[21] [But in] choosing among thousands of applicants who are not only 'admissible' academically but have other strong qualities, the Committee, with a number of criteria in mind, pays some attention to distribution among many types and categories of students."[22]

In such an admissions program, race or ethnic background may be deemed a "plus" in a particular applicant's file, yet it does not insulate the individual from

---

21. A fuller statement of the Harvard program appeared as an Appendix to Justice Powell's opinion. In a passage omitted by Justice Powell at this point in the text of his opinion, the description stated: "At the same time the Committee is aware that if Harvard College is to provide a truly heterogeneous environment that reflects the rich diversity of the United States, it cannot be provided without some attention to numbers. It would not make sense, for example, to have 10 or 20 students out of 1,100 whose homes are west of the Mississippi. Comparably, 10 or 20 black students could not begin to bring to their classmates and to each other the variety of points of view, backgrounds and experiences of blacks in the United States. Their small num-

bers might also create a sense of isolation among the black students themselves and thus make it more difficult for them to develop and achieve their potential. Consequently, when making its decisions, the Committee on Admissions is aware that there is some relationship between numbers and achieving the benefits to be derived from a diverse student body, and between numbers and providing a reasonable environment for those students admitted."

22. Brief for Columbia University, Harvard University, Stanford University, and the University of Pennsylvania, as Amici Curiae, App. 2, 3. [Citation by Justice Powell.]

comparison with all other candidates for the available seats. The file of a particular black applicant may be examined for his potential contribution to diversity without the factor of race being decisive when compared, for example, with that of an applicant identified as an Italian-American if the latter is thought to exhibit qualities more likely to promote beneficial educational pluralism. Such qualities could include exceptional personal talents, unique work or service experience, leadership potential, maturity, demonstrated compassion, a history of overcoming disadvantage, ability to communicate with the poor, or other qualifications deemed important. In short, an admissions program operated in this way is flexible enough to consider all pertinent elements of diversity in light of the particular qualifications of each applicant, and to place them on the same footing for consideration, although not necessarily according them the same weight. Indeed, the weight attributed to a particular quality may vary from year to year depending upon the "mix" both of the student body and the applicants for the incoming class. This kind of program treats each applicant as an individual in the admissions process. The applicant who loses out on the last available seat to another candidate receiving a "plus" on the basis of ethnic background will not have been foreclosed from all consideration for that seat simply because he was not the right color or had the wrong surname. It would mean only that his combined qualifications, which may have included similar nonobjective factors, did not outweigh those of the other applicant. His qualifications would have been weighed fairly and competitively, and he would have no basis to complain of unequal treatment under the 14th Amendment.[23]

It has been suggested that an admissions program which considers race only as one factor is simply a subtle and more sophisticated—but no less effective—means of according racial preference than the Davis program. A facial intent to discriminate, however, is evident in petitioner's preference program and not denied in this case. No such facial infirmity exists in an admissions program where race or ethnic background is simply one element—to be weighed fairly against other elements—in the selection process. "A boundary line," as Mr. Justice Frankfurter remarked in another connection, "is none the worse for being narrow." And a Court would not assume that a university, professing to employ a facially nondiscriminatory admissions policy, would operate it as a cover for the functional equivalent of a quota system. In short, good faith would be presumed in the absence of a showing to the contrary in the manner permitted by our cases. See, e.g., [Arlington Heights; Washington v. Davis].[24]

B. In summary, it is evident that the Davis special admissions program involves the use of an explicit racial classification never before countenanced by this Court. It tells applicants who are not Negro, Asian, or "Chicano" that they

23. The denial to respondent of this right to individualized consideration without regard to his race is the principal evil of petitioner's special admissions program. Nowhere in the opinion of Mr. Justice Brennan [et al.] is this denial even addressed. [Footnote by Justice Powell.]

24. Universities [may] make individualized decisions, in which ethnic background plays a part, under a presumption of legality and legitimate educational purpose. So long as the university proceeds on an individualized, case-by-case basis, there is no warrant for judicial interference in the academic process. If an applicant can establish that the institution does not adhere to a policy of individual comparisons, or can show that a systematic exclusion of certain groups results, the presumption of legality might be overcome, creating the necessity of proving legitimate educational purpose.

There also are strong policy reasons that correspond to the constitutional distinction between petitioner's preference program and one that assures a measure of competition among all applicants. Petitioner's program will be viewed as inherently unfair by the public generally as well as by applicants for admission to state universities. Fairness in individual competition for opportunities, especially those provided by the State, is a widely cherished American ethic. Indeed, in a broader sense, an underlying assumption of the rule of law is the worthiness of a system of justice based on fairness to the individual. As Mr. Justice Frankfurter declared in another connection, "[j]ustice must satisfy the appearance of justice." [Footnote by Justice Powell.]

are totally excluded from a specific percentage of the seats in an entering class. No matter how strong their qualifications, quantitative and extracurricular, including their own potential for contribution to educational diversity, they are never afforded the chance to compete with applicants from the preferred groups for the special admission seats. At the same time, the preferred applicants have the opportunity to compete for every seat in the class. The fatal flaw in petitioner's preferential program is its disregard of individual rights as guaranteed by the 14th Amendment. Such rights are not absolute. But when a State's distribution of benefits or imposition of burdens hinges on the color of a person's skin or ancestry, that individual is entitled to a demonstration that the challenged classification is necessary to promote a substantial state interest. Petitioner has failed to carry this burden. For this reason, that portion of the California court's judgment holding petitioner's special admissions program invalid under the 14th Amendment must be affirmed.

C. In enjoining petitioner from ever considering the race of any applicant, however, the courts below failed to recognize that the State has a substantial interest that legitimately may be served by a properly devised admissions program involving the competitive consideration of race and ethnic origin. For this reason, so much of the judgment as enjoins petitioner from any consideration of the race of any applicant must be reversed.

VI. With respect to respondent's entitlement to an injunction directing his admission to the Medical School, petitioner has conceded that it could not carry its burden of proving that, but for the existence of its unlawful special admissions program, respondent still would not have been admitted. Hence, respondent is entitled to the injunction, and that portion of the judgment must be affirmed.

Opinion of Mr. Justice BRENNAN, Mr. Justice WHITE, Mr. Justice MARSHALL, and Mr. Justice BLACKMUN, concurring in the judgment in part and dissenting.

The Court [today] affirms the constitutional power of [government] to act affirmatively to achieve equal opportunity for all. The difficulty of the issue presented [has] resulted in many opinions, no single one speaking for the Court. But this should not and must not mask the central meaning of today's opinions: Government may take race into account when it acts not to demean or insult any racial group, but to remedy disadvantages cast on minorities by past racial prejudice, at least when appropriate findings have been made by judicial, legislative, or administrative bodies with competence to act in this area. [We] agree with Mr. Justice Powell that, as applied to the case before us, Title VI goes no further in prohibiting the use of race than [equal protection] itself. We also agree that the effect of the [decision below] would be to prohibit the University from establishing in the future affirmative action programs that take race into account. Since we conclude that the affirmative admissions program [is] constitutional, we would reverse the judgment below in all respects. Mr. Justice Powell agrees that some uses of race in university admissions are permissible and, therefore, he joins with us to make five votes to reverse the judgment below insofar as it prohibits the University from establishing race-conscious programs in the future.[1]

I. [Even] today officially sanctioned discrimination is not a thing of the past. Against this background, claims that law must be "colorblind" or that the datum of race is no longer relevant to public policy must be seen as aspiration rather than as description of reality. This is not to denigrate aspiration; for

---

1. We also agree with Mr. Justice Powell that a plan like the "Harvard" plan is constitutional under our approach, at least so long as the use of race to achieve an integrated student body is necessitated by the lingering effects of past discrimination. [Footnote by Justice Brennan et al.]

reality rebukes us that race has too often been used by those who would stigmatize and oppress minorities. Yet we [cannot] let color blindness become myopia which masks the reality that many "created equal" have been treated within our lifetimes as inferior both by the law and by their fellow citizens.

II. [On Title VI, we] join Parts I and V–C of our Brother Powell's opinion and three of us agree with his conclusion in Part II that this case does not require us to resolve the question whether there is a private right of action under Title VI.[2] [Title VI] prohibits only those uses of racial criteria that would violate the 14th Amendment if employed by a State or its agencies; it does not bar the preferential treatment of racial minorities as a means of remedying past societal discrimination to the extent that such action is consistent with the 14th Amendment. [The] legislative history shows that Congress specifically eschewed any static definition of discrimination in favor of broad language that could be shaped by experience, administrative necessity, and evolving judicial doctrine. [Cf. Weber, p. 785 below.] [A]ny claim that the use of racial criteria is barred by the plain language of the statute must fail in light of the remedial purpose of Title VI and its legislative [history].

III. A. [Our] cases have always implied that an "overriding statutory purpose" could be found that would justify racial classifications. See, e.g., [Loving; Korematsu]. We conclude, therefore, that racial classifications are not per se invalid under the 14th Amendment. Accordingly, we turn to the problem of articulating what our role should be in reviewing state action that expressly classifies by race.

B. Respondent argues that racial classifications are always suspect. [Petitioner] states that our proper role is simply to accept [its] determination that the racial classifications used by its program are reasonably related to what it tells us are its benign purposes. We reject petitioner's view, but, because our prior cases are in many respects inapposite to that before us now, we find it necessary to define with precision the meaning of that inexact term, "strict scrutiny." Unquestionably we have held that a government practice or statute which restricts "fundamental rights" or which contains "suspect classifications" is to be subjected to "strict scrutiny." [But] no fundamental right is involved here. Nor do whites as a class have any of the "traditional indicia of suspectness: the class is not saddled with such disabilities, or subjected to such a history of purposeful unequal treatment, or relegated to such a position of political powerlessness as to command extraordinary protection from the majoritarian political process." Rodriguez [p. 789 below]; see Carolene Products, n. 4.[3] Moreover, if the University's representations are credited, this is not a case where racial classifications are "irrelevant and therefore prohibited." Hirabayashi. Nor has anyone suggested that the University's purposes contravene the cardinal principle that racial classifications that stigmatize—because they are drawn on the presumption that one race is inferior to another or because they put the weight of government behind racial hatred and separatism—are invalid without more. On the other hand, the fact that this case does not fit neatly into our prior analytic framework for race cases does not mean that it should be analyzed by applying the very loose rational-basis [standard]. " '[T]he mere recitation of a benign, compensatory purpose is not an automatic shield which protects against any inquiry into the actual purposes underlying a statutory scheme.' " [Webster, quoting Wiesenfeld.] Instead, a number of considerations—developed in gender discrimination cases but which carry even more

2. Mr. Justice White believes we should address the private right of action issue. Accordingly, he has filed a separate opinion stating his view that there is no private right of action under Title VI. [Footnote by Justice Brennan et al.] [Justice White's concurrence is omitted.]

3. Of course, the fact that whites constitute a political majority in our Nation does not necessarily mean that active judicial scrutiny of racial classifications that disadvantage whites is inappropriate. [Footnote by Justice Brennan et al.]

force when applied to racial classifications—lead us to conclude that racial classifications designed to further remedial purposes "must serve important governmental objectives and must be substantially related to achievement of those objectives." [Craig.] [4]

First, race, like "gender-based classifications, too often [has] been inexcusably utilized to stereotype and stigmatize politically powerless segments of society." [Kahn] (dissenting opinion). While a carefully tailored statute designed to remedy past discrimination could avoid these vices, see, [e.g., Webster; Ballard], we nonetheless have recognized that the line between honest and thoughtful appraisal of the effects of past discrimination and paternalistic stereotyping is not so clear and that a statute based on the latter is patently capable of stigmatizing all women with a badge of inferiority. State programs designed ostensibly to ameliorate the effects of past racial discrimination obviously create the same hazard of stigma, since they may promote racial separatism and reinforce the views of those who believe that members of racial minorities are inherently incapable of succeeding on their own.

Second, race, like gender and illegitimacy, is an immutable characteristic which its possessors are powerless to escape or set aside. While a classification is not per se invalid because it divides classes on the basis of an immutable characteristic, it is nevertheless true that such divisions are contrary to our deep belief that "legal burdens should bear some relationship to individual responsibility or wrongdoing" and that advancement sanctioned, sponsored, or approved by the State should ideally be based on individual merit or achievement, or at the least on factors within the control of an individual. [5] Because this principle is so deeply rooted it might be supposed that it would be considered in the legislative process and weighed against the benefits of programs preferring individuals because of their race. But this is not necessarily so: The "natural consequence of our governing processes [may well be] that the most 'discrete and insular' of whites [will] be called upon to bear the immediate, direct costs of benign discrimination." UJO (concurring opinion). Moreover, it is clear from our cases that there are limits beyond which majorities may not go when they classify on the basis of immutable characteristics. Thus, even if the concern for individualism is weighed by the political process, that weighing cannot waive the personal rights of individuals under the 14th Amendment.

4. We disagree with our Brother Powell's suggestion that the presence of "rival groups who can claim that they, too, are entitled to preferential treatment" distinguishes the gender cases or is relevant to the question of scope of judicial review of race classifications. We are not asked to determine whether groups other than those favored by the Davis program should similarly be favored. All we are asked to do is to pronounce the constitutionality of what Davis has done.

But, were we asked to decide whether any given rival group—German-Americans for example—must constitutionally be accorded preferential treatment, we do have a "principled basis" for deciding this question, one that is well-established in our cases: The Davis program expressly sets out four classes which receive preferred status. The program clearly distinguishes whites, but one cannot reason from this to a conclusion that German-Americans, as a national group, are singled out for invidious treatment. And even if the Davis program had a differential impact on German-Americans, they would have no constitutional claim unless they could prove that Davis intended invidiously to discriminate against German-Americans. [See Arlington Heights; Washington v. Davis.] If this could not be shown, then "the principle that calls for the closest scrutiny of distinctions in laws denying fundamental rights [is] inapplicable," Katzenbach v. Morgan, and the only question is whether it was rational for Davis to conclude that the groups it preferred had a greater claim to compensation than the groups it excluded. See ibid.; Rodriguez (applying Katzenbach test to state action intended to remove discrimination in educational opportunity). Thus, claims of rival groups, although they may create thorny political problems, create relatively simple problems for the courts. [Footnote by Justice Brennan et al.]

5. But note Karst & Horowitz, "Affirmative Action and Equal Protection," 60 Va.L.Rev. 955 (1974): "['Merit'] includes a large and hard-to-isolate ingredient of native talents. These talents resemble race in that they are beyond the control of the [individual]. If racial classifications are 'suspect' partly for this reason, then it may be appropriate to insist that public rewards for native talents be justified by a showing of compelling necessity."

In sum, because of the significant risk that racial classifications established for ostensibly benign purposes can be misused, causing effects not unlike those created by invidious classifications, it is inappropriate to inquire only whether there is any conceivable basis that might sustain such a classification. Instead, to justify such a classification an important and articulated purpose for its use must be shown. In addition, any statute must be stricken that stigmatizes any group or that singles out those least well represented in the political process to bear the brunt of a benign program. Thus our review under the 14th Amendment should be strict—not " 'strict' in theory and fatal in fact," [6] because it is stigma that causes fatality—but strict and searching nonetheless.

IV. Davis' articulated purpose of remedying the effects of past societal discrimination [is] sufficiently important to justify the use of race-conscious admissions programs where there is a sound basis for concluding that minority underrepresentation is substantial and chronic, and that the handicap of past discrimination is impeding access of minorities to the medical school.

A. At least since [Green], it has been clear that a public body which has itself been adjudged to have engaged in racial discrimination cannot bring itself into compliance with the Equal Protection Clause simply by ending its unlawful acts and adopting a neutral stance. Three years later, Swann [held] both that courts could enter desegregation orders which assigned students and faculty by reference to race, and that local school boards could *voluntarily* adopt desegregation plans which made express reference to race if this was necessary to remedy the effects of past discrimination. Moreover, we stated that school boards, even in the absence of a judicial finding of past discrimination, could voluntarily adopt plans which assigned students with the end of creating racial pluralism by establishing fixed ratios of black and white students in each [school].

Finally, the conclusion that state educational institutions may constitutionally adopt admissions programs designed to avoid exclusion of historically disadvantaged minorities, even when such programs explicitly take race into account, finds direct support in our cases construing congressional legislation designed to overcome the present effects of past discrimination. Congress can and has outlawed actions which have a disproportionately adverse and unjustified impact upon members of racial minorities and has required or authorized race-conscious action to put individuals disadvantaged by such impact in the position they otherwise might have enjoyed. See [e.g., Franks v. Bowman]. Such relief does not require as a predicate proof that recipients of preferential advancement have been individually discriminated against; it is enough that each recipient is within a general class of persons likely to have been the victims of discrimination. [Cases such as these] cannot be distinguished simply by the presence of judicial findings of discrimination, for race-conscious remedies have been approved where such findings have not been made. [E.g., UJO; Webster; Ballard.] Indeed, the requirement of a judicial determination of a constitutional or statutory violation as a predicate for race-conscious remedial actions would be self-defeating. Such a requirement would severely undermine efforts to achieve voluntary compliance with the requirements of law. And, our society and jurisprudence have always stressed the value of voluntary efforts to further the objectives of the law. Judicial intervention is a last resort to achieve cessation of illegal conduct or the remedying of its effects rather than a prerequisite to action.[7]

Nor can our cases be distinguished on the ground that the entity using explicit racial classifications had itself violated § 1 of the 14th Amendment or

---

6. Gunther, ["Newer Equal Protection"]. [Footnote by Justice Brennan et al.]

7. Indeed, Titles VI and VII of the Civil Rights Act of 1964 put great emphasis on volun-

tarism in remedial [action]. [Footnote by Justice Brennan et al.] [See Weber, below.]

an antidiscrimination regulation, for again race-conscious remedies have been approved where this is not the case. See UJO (opinion of White [et al.]); cf. [Webster; Kahn]. Moreover, the presence or absence of past discrimination by universities or employers is largely irrelevant to resolving respondent's constitutional claims. The claims of those burdened by the race-conscious actions of a university or employer who has never been adjudged in violation of an antidiscrimination law are not any more or less entitled to deference than the claims of the burdened nonminority workers in Franks v. Bowman, in which the employer had violated Title VII, for in each case the employees are innocent of past discrimination. And, although it might be argued that, where an employer has violated an antidiscrimination law, the expectations of nonminority workers are themselves products of discrimination and hence "tainted" and therefore more easily upset, the same argument can be made with respect to respondent. If it was reasonable to conclude—as we hold that it was—that the failure of minorities to qualify for admission at Davis under regular procedures was due principally to the effects of past discrimination, then there is a reasonable likelihood that, but for pervasive racial discrimination, respondent would have failed to qualify for admission even in the absence of Davis' special admissions program.[8] Thus, our cases under [Title VII] have held that, in order to achieve minority participation in previously segregated areas of public life, Congress may require or authorize preferential treatment for those likely disadvantaged by societal racial discrimination. Such legislation has been sustained even without a requirement of findings of intentional racial discrimination by those required or authorized to accord preferential treatment, or a case-by-case determination that those to be benefited suffered from racial discrimination. These decisions compel the conclusion that States also may adopt race-conscious programs designed to overcome substantial, chronic minority underrepresentation where there is reason to believe that the evil addressed is a product of past racial discrimination.[9]

Title VII was enacted pursuant to Congress' power under the Commerce Clause and § 5 of the 14th Amendment. To the extent that Congress acted under the Commerce Clause power, it was restricted in the use of race in

---

8. Our cases cannot be distinguished by suggesting, as our Brother Powell does, that in none of them was anyone deprived of "the relevant benefit." Our school cases have deprived whites of the neighborhood school of their choice; our Title VII cases have deprived nondiscriminating employees of their settled seniority expectations; and UJO deprived the Hasidim of bloc voting strength. Each of these injuries was constitutionally cognizable as is respondent's here. [Footnote by Justice Brennan et al.]

9. We do not understand Mr. Justice Powell to disagree that providing a remedy for past racial prejudice can constitute a compelling purpose sufficient to meet strict scrutiny. Yet, because petitioner is a university, he would not allow it to exercise such power in the absence of "judicial, legislative, or administrative findings of constitutional or statutory violations." While we agree that reversal in this case would follow a fortiori had Davis been guilty of invidious racial discrimination or if a federal statute mandated that universities refrain from applying any admissions policy that had a disparate and unjustified racial impact, we do not think it of constitutional significance that Davis has not been so adjudged.

Generally, the manner in which a State chooses to delegate governmental functions is for it to decide. California, by constitutional provision, has chosen to place authority over the operation of the [University] in the Board of Regents [who] have been vested with full legislative (including policymaking), administrative, and adjudicative powers by the citizens of California. This is certainly a permissible choice and we, unlike our Brother Powell, find nothing in [equal protection] that requires us to depart from established principle by limiting the scope of power the Regents may exercise more narrowly than the powers that may constitutionally be wielded by the Assembly.

Because the Regents can exercise plenary legislative and administrative power, it elevates form over substance to insist that Davis could not use race-conscious remedial programs until it had been adjudged in violation of the Constitution or an antidiscrimination statute. For, if [equal protection] required such a violation as a predicate, the Regents could simply have promulgated a regulation prohibiting disparate treatment not justified by the need to admit only qualified students, and could have declared Davis to have been in violation of such a regulation on the basis of the exclusionary effect of the admissions policy applied during the first two years of its operation. [Footnote by Justice Brennan et al.]

governmental decisionmaking by the equal protection component of the Due Process Clause of the Fifth Amendment precisely to the same extent as are the States by § 1 of the 14th Amendment. Therefore, to the extent that Title VII rests on the Commerce Clause power, our decisions such as [Franks] implicitly recognize that the affirmative use of race is consistent with the equal protection component of the Fifth Amendment and therefore of the 14th Amendment. To the extent that Congress acted pursuant to § 5 of the 14th Amendment, those cases impliedly recognized that Congress was empowered under that provision to accord preferential treatment to victims of past discrimination in order to overcome the effects of segregation, and we see no reason to conclude that the States cannot voluntarily accomplish under § 1 of the 14th Amendment what Congress under § 5 of the 14th Amendment validly may authorize or compel either the States or private persons to do. A contrary position would conflict with the traditional understanding recognizing the competence of the States to initiate measures consistent with federal policy in the absence of congressional pre-emption of the subject matter. Nothing whatever in the legislative history of either the 14th Amendment or the Civil Rights Act even remotely suggests that the States are foreclosed from furthering the fundamental purpose of [equal opportunity]. Indeed, voluntary initiatives by the States to achieve the national goal of equal opportunity have been recognized to be essential to its attainment. [We] therefore conclude that Davis' goal of admitting minority students disadvantaged by the effects of past discrimination is sufficiently important to justify use of race-conscious admissions criteria.

B.　Properly construed, therefore, our prior cases unequivocally show that a state government may adopt race-conscious programs if the purpose of such programs is to remove the disparate racial impact its actions might otherwise have and if there is reason to believe that the disparate impact is itself the product of past discrimination, whether its own or that of society at large. There is no question that Davis' program is valid under this test. [Certainly], Davis had a sound basis for believing that the problem of underrepresentation of minorities was substantial and chronic and that the problem was attributable to handicaps imposed on minority applicants by past and present racial discrimination. Until at least 1973, the practice of medicine in this country was, in fact, if not in law, largely the prerogative of whites. In 1950, for example, while Negroes comprised 10% of the total population, Negro physicians constituted only 2.2% of the total number of physicians. [By] 1970, the gap between the proportion of Negroes in medicine and their proportion in the population had widened: The number of Negroes employed in medicine remained frozen at 2.2% while the Negro population had increased to 11.1%. The number of Negro admittees to predominantly white medical schools, moreover, had declined in absolute numbers during the years 1955 to 1964. Moreover, Davis had very good reason to believe that the national pattern of underrepresentation of minorities in medicine would be perpetuated if it retained a single admissions standard. For example, the entering classes in 1968 and 1969, the years in which such a standard was used, included only one Chicano and two Negroes out of 100 admittees. Nor is there any relief from this pattern of underrepresentation in the statistics for the regular admissions program in later years.

Davis clearly could conclude that the serious and persistent underrepresentation of minorities in medicine depicted by these statistics is the result of handicaps under which minority applicants labor as a consequence of a background of deliberate, purposeful discrimination against minorities in education and in society generally, as well as in the medical profession. From the inception of our national life, Negroes have been subjected to unique legal disabilities impairing access to equal educational opportunity. Under slavery, penal sanctions were imposed upon anyone attempting to educate Negroes. After enactment of the 14th Amendment the States continued to deny Negroes equal educational opportunity, enforcing a strict policy of segregation that itself stamped Negroes as [inferior]. [Green] gave explicit recognition to the fact that the habit of discrimination and the cultural tradition of race prejudice cultivated by centuries of legal slavery and segregation were not immediately dissipated [by] Brown I. Rather, massive official and private resistance prevented, and to a lesser extent still prevents, attainment of equal opportunity in education at all levels and in the professions. The generation of minority students applying to Davis Medical School since it opened in 1968—most of whom were born before or about the time Brown I was decided—clearly have been victims of this discrimination. Judicial decrees recognizing discrimination in public education in California testify to the fact of widespread discrimination suffered by California-born minority applicants; many minority group members living in California, moreover, were born and reared in school districts in southern States segregated by law. [The] conclusion is inescapable that applicants to medical school must be few indeed who endured the effects of de jure segregation, the resistance to Brown I, or the equally debilitating pervasive private discrimination fostered by our long history of official discrimination, and yet come to the starting line with an education equal to whites.

Moreover, [HEW has] also reached the conclusion that race may be taken into account in situations where a failure to do so would limit participation by minorities in federally funded programs, and regulations promulgated by the Department expressly contemplate that appropriate race-conscious programs may be adopted by universities to remedy unequal access to university programs caused by their own or by past societal discrimination. It cannot be questioned that, in the absence of the special admissions program, access of minority students to the Medical School would be severely limited and, accordingly, race-conscious admissions would be deemed an appropriate response under these federal regulations. Moreover, the Department's regulatory policy is not one that has gone unnoticed by Congress. Indeed, although an amendment to an appropriations bill was introduced just last year that would have prevented [HEW] from mandating race-conscious programs in university admissions, proponents of this measure, significantly, did not question the validity of voluntary implementation of race-conscious admissions criteria. In these circumstances, the conclusion implicit in the regulations—that the lingering effects of past discrimination continue to make race-conscious remedial programs appropriate means for ensuring equal educational opportunity in universities—deserves considerable judicial deference.

C. The second prong of our test—whether the Davis program stigmatizes any discrete group or individual and whether race is reasonably used in light of the program's objectives—is clearly satisfied by the Davis program. It is not even claimed that Davis' program in any way operates to stigmatize or single out any discrete and insular, or even any identifiable, nonminority group. Nor will harm comparable to that imposed upon racial minorities by exclusion or separation on grounds of race be the likely result of the program. It does not, for example, establish an exclusive preserve for minority students apart from and exclusive of whites. Rather, its purpose is to overcome the effects of segregation by bringing the races together. True, whites are excluded from participation in the special admissions program, but this fact only operates to reduce the number of whites to be admitted in the regular admissions program in order to permit admission of a reasonable percentage—less than their proportion of the California population [10]—of otherwise underrepresented qualified minority applicants.[11]

---

10. Negroes and Chicanos alone comprise approximately 22% of California's population. [Footnote by Justice Brennan et al.]

11. The constitutionality of the special admissions program is buttressed by its restriction to only 16% of the positions in the Medical School,

Nor was Bakke in any sense stamped as inferior by the Medical School's [rejection]. Indeed, it is conceded [that] he satisfied those criteria regarded by the School as generally relevant to academic performance better than most of the minority members who were admitted. Moreover, there is absolutely no basis for concluding that Bakke's rejection [will] affect him throughout his life in the same way as the segregation of the Negro school children in Brown I would have affected them. Unlike discrimination against racial minorities, the use of racial preferences for remedial purposes does not inflict a pervasive injury upon individual whites in the sense that wherever they go or whatever they do there is a significant likelihood that they will be treated as second-class citizens because of their color. This distinction does not mean that the exclusion of a white resulting from the preferential use of race is not sufficiently serious to require justification; but it does mean that the injury inflicted by such a policy is not distinguishable from disadvantages caused by a wide range of government actions, none of which has ever been thought impermissible for that reason alone.

In addition, there is simply no evidence that the Davis program discriminates intentionally or unintentionally against any minority group which it purports to benefit. The program does not establish a quota in the invidious sense of a ceiling on the number of minority applicants to be admitted. Nor can the program reasonably be regarded as stigmatizing the program's beneficiaries or their race as inferior. The Davis program does not simply advance less qualified applicants; rather it compensates applicants, whom it is uncontested are fully qualified to study medicine, for educational disadvantage which it was reasonable to conclude was a product of state-fostered discrimination. Once admitted, these students must satisfy the same degree requirements as regularly admitted students; and their performance is evaluated by the same standards by which regularly admitted students are judged. Under these circumstances, their performance and degrees must be regarded equally with the regularly admitted [students]. Since minority graduates cannot justifiably be regarded as less well qualified than nonminority graduates by virtue of the special admissions program, there is no reasonable basis to conclude that minority graduates at schools using such programs would be stigmatized as inferior by the existence of such programs.

D. We disagree with the lower courts' conclusion that the Davis program's use of race was unreasonable in light of its objectives. First, [there] are no practical means by which it could achieve it ends in the foreseeable future without the use of race-conscious measures. With respect to any factor (such as poverty or family educational background) that may be used as a substitute for race as an indicator of past discrimination, whites greatly outnumber racial minorities simply because whites make up a far larger percentage of the total population and therefore far outnumber minorities in absolute terms at every socio-economic level. For example, of a class of recent medical school applicants from families with less than $10,000 income, at least 71% were white. Of all 1970 families headed by a person *not* a high school graduate which

a percentage less than that of the minority population in California, and to those minority applicants deemed qualified for admission and deemed likely to contribute to the medical school and the medical profession. This is consistent with the goal of putting minority applicants in the position they would have been in if not for the evil of racial discrimination. Accordingly, this case does not raise the question whether even a remedial use of race would be unconstitutional if it admitted unqualified minority applicants in preference to qualified applicants or admitted, as a result of preferential consideration, racial minorities in numbers significantly in excess of their proportional representation in the relevant population. Such programs might well be inadequately justified by the legitimate remedial objectives. Our allusion to the proportional percentage of minorities in the population of the State administering the program is not intended to establish either that figure or that population universe as a constitutional [benchmark]. [Footnote by Justice Brennan et al.]

included related children under 18, 80% were white and 20% were racial minorities. Moreover, while race is positively correlated with differences in GPA and MCAT scores, economic disadvantage is not. Thus, it appears that economically disadvantaged whites do not score less well than economically advantaged whites, while economically advantaged blacks score less well than do disadvantaged whites. These statistics graphically illustrate that the University's purpose [could] not be achieved by a general preference for the economically disadvantaged or the children of parents of limited education unless such groups were to make up the entire class.

Second, the Davis admissions program does not simply equate minority status with disadvantage. Rather, Davis considers on an individual basis each applicant's personal history to determine whether he or she has likely been disadvantaged by racial discrimination. The record makes clear that only minority applicants likely to have been isolated from the mainstream of American life are considered in the special program; other minority applicants are eligible only through the regular admissions program. True, the procedure by which disadvantage is detected is informal, but we have never insisted that educators conduct their affairs through adjudicatory [proceedings]. A case-by-case inquiry into the extent to which each individual applicant has been affected, either directly or indirectly, by racial discrimination, would seem to be, as a practical matter, virtually impossible, despite the fact that there are excellent reasons for concluding that such effects generally exist. When individual measurement is impossible or extremely impractical, there is nothing to prevent a State from using categorical means to achieve its ends, at least where the category is closely related to the goal. Cf. [e.g.] Katzenbach v. Morgan. And it is clear from our cases that specific proof that a person has been victimized by discrimination is not a necessary predicate to offering him relief where the probability of victimization is great.

E.   Finally, Davis' special admissions program cannot be said to violate the Constitution simply because it has set aside a predetermined number of places for qualified minority applicants rather than using minority status as a positive factor to be considered in evaluating the applications of disadvantaged minority applicants. For purposes of constitutional adjudication, there is no difference between the two approaches. In any admissions program which accords special consideration to disadvantaged racial minorities, a determination of the degree of preference to be given is unavoidable, and any given preference that results in the exclusion of a white candidate is no more or less constitutionally acceptable than a program such as that at Davis. Furthermore, the extent of the preference inevitably depends on how many minority applicants the particular school is seeking to admit in any particular year so long as the number of qualified minority applicants exceeds that number. There is no sensible, and certainly no constitutional, distinction between, for example, adding a set number of points to the admissions rating of disadvantaged minority applicants as an expression of the preference with the expectation that this will result in the admission of an approximately determined number of qualified minority applicants and setting a fixed number of places for such applicants as was done here.[12] The "Harvard" program openly and successfully employs a racial [criterion]. That the Harvard approach does not also make public the extent of the preference and the precise workings of the system while the Davis program employs a specific, openly stated number, does not condemn the latter plan for purposes of 14th Amendment adjudication. It may be that the Harvard plan is more acceptable to the public than is the Davis "quota." If it is, any State [is]

12.   The excluded white applicant, despite Mr. Justice Powell's contention to the contrary, receives no more or less "individualized consider- ation" under our approach than under his. [Footnote by Justice Brennan et al.]

free to adopt it in preference to a less acceptable alternative, just as it is generally free [to] abjure granting any racial preferences in its admissions program. But there is no basis for preferring a particular preference program simply because in achieving the same goals that [Davis] is pursuing, it proceeds in a manner that is not immediately apparent to the [public].

Mr. Justice MARSHALL.

[It] must be remembered that, during most of the past 200 years, the Constitution as interpreted by this Court did not prohibit the most ingenious and pervasive forms of discrimination against the Negro. Now, when a State acts to remedy the effects of that legacy of discrimination, I cannot believe that this same Constitution stands as a barrier. [The] position of the Negro today in America is the tragic but inevitable consequence of centuries of unequal treatment. Measured by any benchmark of comfort or achievement, meaningful equality remains a distant dream for the Negro. [Justice Marshall listed statistics on health, employment, and income.] The relationship between those figures and the history of unequal treatment afforded to the Negro cannot be denied. At every point from birth to death the impact of the past is reflected in the still disfavored position of the Negro. In light of the sorry history of discrimination and its devastating impact on the lives of Negroes, bringing the Negro into the mainstream of American life should be a state interest of the highest order. To fail to do so is to ensure that America will forever remain a divided society. [I] do not believe that the 14th Amendment requires us to accept that fate. Neither its history nor our past cases lend any support to the conclusion that a University may not remedy the cumulative effects of society's discrimination by giving consideration to race in an effort to increase the number and percentage of Negro doctors. [Since] the Congress that considered and rejected the objections to the 1866 Freedmen's Bureau Act concerning special relief to Negroes also proposed the 14th Amendment, it is inconceivable that the 14th Amendment was intended to prohibit all race-conscious relief measures. [T]o hold that it barred state action to remedy the effects [of] discrimination [would] pervert the intent of the framers by substituting abstract equality for the genuine equality the amendment was intended to achieve.

[While] I applaud the judgment of the Court that a university may consider race in its admissions process, it is more than a little ironic that, after several hundred years of class-based discrimination against Negroes, the Court is unwilling to hold that a class-based remedy for that discrimination is permissible. In declining to so hold, today's judgment ignores the fact that for several hundred years Negroes have been discriminated against, not as individuals, but rather solely because of the color of their skins. It is unnecessary in 20th century America to have individual Negroes demonstrate that they have been victims of racial discrimination; the racism of our society has been so pervasive that none, regardless of wealth or position, has managed to escape its impact. The experience of Negroes in America has been different in kind, not just in degree, from that of other ethnic groups. It is not merely the history of slavery alone but also that a whole people were marked as inferior by the law. And that mark has endured. The dream of America as the great melting pot has not been realized for the Negro; because of his skin color he never even made it into the pot. [Had] the Court been willing in 1896, in [Plessy], to hold that [equal protection] forbids differences in treatment based on race, we would not be faced with this dilemma in 1978. We must remember, however, that the principle that the "Constitution is color-blind" appeared only in the opinion of the lone dissenter. [For] the next 60 years, from Plessy to Brown, ours was a Nation where, *by law,* an individual could be given "special" treatment based on the color of his skin. It is because of a legacy of unequal treatment that we now must permit the institutions of this society to give consideration to race in making decisions about who will hold the positions of influence, affluence and prestige in [America].

I fear that we have come full circle. After the Civil War our government started several "affirmative action" programs. This Court in the Civil Rights Cases and [Plessy] destroyed the movement toward complete equality. For almost a century no action was taken, and this nonaction was with the tacit approval of the courts. Then we had Brown and the Civil Rights Acts of Congress, followed by numerous affirmative action programs. *Now,* we have this Court again stepping in, this time to stop affirmative action programs of the type used by the University of California.

Mr. Justice BLACKMUN.

[I] yield to no one in my earnest hope that the time will come when an "affirmative action" program is unnecessary and is, in truth, only a relic of the past. I would hope that we could reach this stage within a decade at the most. But the story of Brown [suggests] that that hope is a slim one. At some time, however, beyond any period of what some would claim is only transitional inequality, the United States must and will reach a stage of maturity where action along this line is no longer necessary. Then persons will be regarded as persons, and discrimination of the type we address today will be an ugly feature of history that is instructive but that is behind [us].

It is somewhat ironic to have us so deeply disturbed over a program where race is an element of consciousness, and yet to be aware of the fact, as we are, that institutions of higher learning, albeit more on the undergraduate than the graduate level, have given conceded preferences up to a point to those possessed of athletic skills, to the children of alumni, to the affluent who may bestow their largess on the institutions, and to those having connections with celebrities, the famous, and the [powerful]. I, of course, accept the propositions that (a) 14th Amendment rights are personal; (b) racial and ethnic distinctions where they are stereotypes are inherently suspect and call for exacting judicial scrutiny; (c) academic freedom is a special concern of the First Amendment; and (d) the 14th Amendment has expanded beyond its original 1868 [conception]. This enlargement does not mean for me, however, that the 14th Amendment has broken away from its moorings and its original intended purposes. Those original aims persist. And that, in a distinct sense, is what "affirmative action," in the face of proper facts, is all about. If this conflicts with idealistic equality, that tension is original 14th Amendment tension, [and] it is part of the Amendment's very nature until complete equality is achieved in the area. In this sense, constitutional equal protection is a shield.

I am not convinced [that] the difference between [the Davis and Harvard programs] is very profound or constitutionally significant. [The] cynical [may] say that under a program such as Harvard's one may accomplish covertly what Davis concedes it does openly. I need not go that far, for despite its two-track aspect, the Davis program, for me, is within constitutional bounds, though perhaps barely so. [I] suspect that it would be impossible to arrange an affirmative action program in a racially neutral way and have it successful. To ask that this be so is to demand the impossible. In order to get beyond racism, we must first take account of race. There is no other way. And in order to treat some persons equally, we must treat them differently. We cannot—we dare not—let the Equal Protection Clause perpetuate [racial supremacy].

Mr. Justice STEVENS, with whom The Chief Justice [BURGER], Mr. Justice STEWART, and Mr. Justice REHNQUIST join, concurring in the judgment in part and dissenting in part.

[This] is not a class action. [Bakke] challenged petitioner's special admissions program [and the] California Supreme Court upheld his challenge and ordered him admitted. If the state court was correct in its view that the

University's special program was illegal, and that Bakke was therefore unlawfully excluded from the medical school because of his race, we should affirm its judgment, regardless of our views about the legality of admissions programs that are not now before the Court. [After construing the state court ruling as containing "no outstanding injunction forbidding any consideration of racial criteria in processing applications," he stated:] "It is therefore perfectly clear that the question whether race can ever be used as a factor in an admissions decision is not an issue in this case, and that discussion of that issue is inappropriate. [He proceeded to interpret Title VI (see footnote 6 to Justice Powell's opinion) as containing a "crystal clear" meaning:[1] "Race cannot be the basis of excluding anyone from participation in a federally funded program."][2]

FULLILOVE v. KLUTZNICK

448 U.S. 448, 100 S.Ct. 2758, 65 L.Ed.2d 902 (1980).

Mr. Chief Justice BURGER announced the judgment of the Court and delivered an opinion in which Mr. Justice WHITE and Mr. Justice POWELL joined.

[This case involves] a facial constitutional challenge to a requirement in a congressional spending program that, absent an administrative waiver, 10% of the federal funds granted for local public works projects must be used by the state or local grantee to procure services or supplies from businesses owned and controlled by members of statutorily identified minority [groups].[1] [Parts I and II of the opinion are summarized in footnote 1.]

---

1. Justice Stevens commented: "Both Title VI and Title VII express Congress' belief that, in the long struggle to eliminate social prejudice and the effects of prejudice, the principle of *individual* equality, without regard to race or religion, was one on which there could be a 'meeting of the minds' among all races and a common national purpose. See [Manhart, p. 669 above] ('the basic policy of the statute [Title VII] requires that we focus on fairness to individuals rather than fairness to classes'). This same principle of *individual* fairness is embodied in Title VI." (Compare Weber, p. 785 below.)

2. The Bakke decision has spawned a new round of academic commentary on the constitutional aspects of preferential admissions and affirmative action programs. For a representative sampling, see Symposium, 67 Calif.L.Rev. 1 (1979). See also Karst & Horowitz, "The Bakke Opinions and Equal Protection Doctrine," 14 Harv.C.R.–C.L.L.Rev. 7 (1979).

1. The challenge was to the "minority business enterprise" (MBE) provision, § 103(f)(2) of the Public Works Employment Act of 1977. The general purpose of the Act was to alleviate national unemployment and to stimulate the economy by distributing $4 billion dollars to state and local governments for public works projects. The "minority set-aside" provision stated: "Except to the extent that the Secretary [of Commerce] determines otherwise, no grant shall be made under this Act for any local public works project unless the applicant gives satisfactory assurance to the Secretary that at least 10 per centum of the amount of each grant shall be expended for minority business enterprises. For purposes of this paragraph, the term 'minority business enterprise' means a business at least 50 per centum of which is owned by minority group members. [For] the purposes of the preceding sentence, minority group members are citizens of the United States who are Negroes, Spanish-speaking, Orientals, Indians, Eskimos and Aleuts." The provision originated in an amendment offered on the floor of the House by Rep. Mitchell of Maryland. The sparse 1977 debates on the provision contained no explicit reference to past discrimination in the construction industry. The lower courts upheld the provision. (The case was brought by a firm engaged in heating and air conditioning work and by several associations of construction contractors and subcontractors. The major defendant was the Secretary of Commerce.)

In reviewing the legislative history, the Chief Justice noted that the provision was not "a new concept, but rather one building upon prior administrative practice." He noted, moreover, that Sen. Brooke of Massachusetts, who had introduced a similar amendment in the Senate, "summarized the various expressions on the House side that the amendment was necessary to ensure that minority businesses were not deprived of access to the government contracting opportunities generated by the public works program."

In examining the 1977 amendment, the Chief Justice commented that the purposes of the MBE provision "must be considered against the back-

III. [A] program that employs racial or ethnic criteria, even in a remedial context, calls for close examination; yet we are bound to approach our task with appropriate deference to the Congress. [Here], we pass, not on a choice made by a single judge or a school board, but on a considered decision of the Congress and the President. However, in no sense does that render it immune from judicial scrutiny, [nor would we] hesitate to invoke the Constitution should we determine that Congress has overstepped the bounds of its constitutional power. [The] clear objective of the MBE provision is disclosed by [our] extended review of its legislative and administrative background. The program was designed to ensure that, to the extent federal funds were granted under the [Act], grantees who elect to participate would not employ procurement practices that Congress had decided might result in perpetuation of the effects of prior discrimination which had impaired or foreclosed access by minority businesses to public contracting opportunities. The MBE program does not mandate the allocation of federal funds according to inflexible percentages solely based on race or ethnicity. Our analysis proceeds in two steps. At the outset, we must inquire whether the *objectives* of this legislation are within the power of Congress. If so, we must go on to decide whether the limited use of racial and ethnic criteria, in the context presented, is a constitutionally permissible *means* for achieving the congressional objectives and does not violate [equal protection].

A. [In] enacting the MBE provision, it is clear that Congress employed an amalgam of its specifically delegated powers. The [Act], by its very nature, is primarily an exercise of the Spending Power. [The] reach of the Spending Power [is] at least as broad as the regulatory powers of Congress. If, pursuant to its regulatory powers, Congress could have achieved the objectives of the MBE program, then it may do so under the Spending Power. And we have no difficulty perceiving a basis for accomplishing the objectives of the MBE program through the Commerce Power insofar as the program objectives pertain to the action of private contracting parties, and through the power to enforce the equal protection guarantees of the 14th Amendment insofar as the program objectives pertain to the action of state and local grantees.

[On the commerce power, the] legislative history [shows] that there was a rational basis for Congress to conclude that the subcontracting practices of prime contractors could perpetuate the prevailing impaired access by minority businesses to public contracting opportunities, and that this inequity has an effect on interstate commerce. [In] certain contexts, there are limitations on the reach of the Commerce Power to regulate the actions of state and local governments.

ground of ongoing efforts directed toward deliverance of the century-old promise of equality of economic opportunity." He referred especially to a program—in operation since 1968 and administered by the Small Business Administration (SBA)—designed to assist small business concerns owned and controlled by "socially or economically disadvantaged" persons to achieve a competitive position in the economy. (The SBA regulations stated that the relevant "disadvantage may arise from cultural, social, chronic economic circumstances or background, or other similar cause. Such persons include, but are not limited to, black Americans, American Indians, Spanish-Americans, oriental Americans, Eskimos, and Aleuts." Note the similarities and differences between this provision and the 1977 MBE amendment. See footnote 2 to Justice Stevens' dissent, below.) The Chief Justice emphasized a 1977 House Committee evaluation of the SBA program. That evaluation included a reference to a 1975 assessment of the SBA program by a House Subcommittee. The 1975 report contained a rare reference to past discrimination in the construction industry, including the statement: "The effects of past inequities stemming from racial prejudice have not remained in the past. The Congress has recognized the reality that past discriminatory practices have, to some degree, adversely affected our present economic system." The Chief Justice concluded: "Against this backdrop of legislative and administrative programs, it is inconceivable that Members of both Houses were not fully aware of the objectives of the MBE provision and of the reasons prompting its enactment." (The Chief Justice also noted that the MBE program included a provision "for an administrative waiver where application of the program is not feasible." For other references to arguably relevant portions of the legislative history, see the several opinions in this case.)

[National League of Cities (1976; p. 170 above).] To avoid such complications, we look to § 5 of the 14th Amendment for the power to regulate the procurement practices of state and local grantees of federal funds. Fitzpatrick v. Bitzer [1976; p. 173 above]. A review of our cases persuades us that the objectives of the MBE program are within the power of Congress under § 5 "to enforce by appropriate legislation" the equal protection guarantees of the 14th Amendment. See Katzenbach v. Morgan [1966; p. 946 below]; Oregon v. Mitchell [1970; p. 953 below]. Our cases reviewing the parallel power of Congress to enforce the provisions of the 15th Amendment confirm that congressional authority extends beyond the prohibition of purposeful discrimination to encompass state action that has discriminatory impact perpetuating the effects of past discrimination. South Carolina v. Katzenbach [1966; p. 953 below]; cf. Rome v. United States [1980; p. 937 below].

With respect to the MBE provision, Congress had abundant evidence from which it could conclude that minority businesses have been denied effective participation in public contracting opportunities by procurement practices that perpetuated the effects of prior discrimination. Congress, of course, may legislate without compiling the kind of "record" appropriate with respect to judicial or administrative proceedings. Congress had before it, among other data, evidence of a long history of marked disparity in the percentage of public contracts awarded to minority business enterprises. This disparity was considered to result not from any lack of capable and qualified minority businesses, but from the existence and maintenance of barriers to competitive access which had their roots in racial and ethnic discrimination, and which continue today, even absent any intentional discrimination or other unlawful conduct. Although much of this history related to the experience of minority businesses in the area of federal procurement, there was direct evidence before the Congress that this pattern of disadvantage and discrimination existed with respect to state and local construction contracting as well. In relation to the MBE provision, Congress acted within its competence to determine that the problem was national in scope. Although the Act recites no preambulary "findings" on the subject, we are satisfied that Congress had abundant historical basis from which it could conclude that traditional procurement practices, when applied to minority businesses, could perpetuate the effects of prior discrimination. Accordingly, Congress reasonably determined that the prospective elimination of these barriers to minority firm access to public contracting opportunities generated by the 1977 Act was appropriate to ensure that those businesses were not denied equal opportunity to participate in federal grants to state and local governments, which is one aspect of the equal protection of the laws. Insofar as the MBE program pertains to the actions of state and local grantees, Congress could have achieved its objectives by use of its power under § 5 of the 14th Amendment. We conclude that in this respect the objectives of the MBE provision are within the scope of the [Spending Power].

B. We now turn to the question whether, as a *means* to accomplish these plainly constitutional objectives, Congress may use racial and ethnic criteria, in this limited way, as a condition attached to a federal grant. [Congress] may employ racial or ethnic classifications in exercising its Spending or other legislative Powers only if those classifications do not violate [equal protection]. We recognize the need for careful judicial evaluation to assure that any congressional program that employs racial or ethnic criteria to accomplish the objective of remedying the present effects of past discrimination is narrowly tailored to the achievement of that goal. Again, we stress the limited scope of our inquiry. Here we are not dealing with a remedial decree of a court but with the legislative authority of Congress. Furthermore, petitioners have challenged the constitutionality of the MBE provision on its face; they have not sought damages or other specific relief for injury allegedly flowing from specific applications of the program; nor have they attempted to show that as applied in identified situations the MBE provision violated the constitutional or statutory rights of any party to this case.

[Our] review of the [administrative] regulations [reveals] that Congress enacted the program as a strictly remedial [measure]. As a threshold matter, we reject the contention that in the remedial context the Congress must act in a wholly "color-blind" fashion. [E.g., Swann.] In another setting, we have held that a state may employ racial criteria that are reasonably necessary to assure compliance with federal voting rights legislation, even though the state action does not entail the remedy of a constitutional violation. [UJO (1977; p. 752 above).] [Here] we deal [not] with the limited remedial powers of a federal court [but] with the broad remedial powers of Congress. It is fundamental that in no organ of government [does] there repose a more comprehensive remedial power than in the Congress, expressly charged by the Constitution with competence and authority to enforce equal protection guarantees. Congress not only may induce voluntary action to assure compliance with existing federal statutory or constitutional antidiscrimination provisions, but also, where Congress has authority to declare certain conduct unlawful, it may, as here, authorize and induce state action to avoid such [conduct].

A more specific challenge to the MBE program is the charge that it impermissibly deprives nonminority businesses of access to at least some portion of the government contracting opportunities generated by the Act. [It] is not a constitutional defect in this program that it may disappoint the expectations of nonminority firms. When effectuating a limited and properly tailored remedy to cure the effects of prior discrimination, such "a sharing of the burden" by innocent parties is not impermissible. The actual "burden" shouldered by nonminority firms is relatively light in this connection when we consider the scope of this public works program as compared with overall construction contracting opportunities.[2] Moreover, although we may assume that the complaining parties are innocent of any discriminatory conduct, it was within congressional power to act on the assumption that in the past some nonminority businesses may have reaped competitive benefit over the years from the virtual exclusion of minority firms from these contracting opportunities. [Another] challenge to the validity of the MBE program is the assertion that it is underinclusive—that it limits its benefit to specified minority groups rather than extending its remedial objectives to all businesses whose access to government contracting is impaired by the effects of disadvantage or discrimination. [The] well-established concept that a legislature may take one step at a time to remedy only part of a broader problem is not without relevance. See [e.g., Lee Optical]. [Congress] has not sought to give select minority groups a preferred standing in the construction industry, but has embarked on a remedial [program]. There has been no showing in this case that Congress has inadvertently effected an invidious discrimination by excluding from coverage an identifiable minority group that has been the victim of a degree of disadvantage and discrimination equal to or greater than that suffered by the groups encompassed by the MBE program. It is not inconceivable that on very special facts a case might be made to challenge the congressional decision to limit MBE eligibility to the particular minority groups identified in the Act. But on this record we find no basis to hold that Congress is without authority to undertake the kind of limited remedial [effort].

---

2. The Court of Appeals relied upon Department of Commerce statistics to calculate that the $4.2 billion in federal grants conditioned upon compliance with the MBE provision amounted to about 2.5% of the total of nearly $170 billion spent on construction in the United States during 1977. Thus, the 10% minimum minority business participation contemplated by this program would account for only 0.25% of the annual expenditure for construction work in the United States. [Footnote by the Chief Justice.]

It is also contended that the MBE program is overinclusive—that it bestows a benefit on businesses identified by racial or ethnic criteria which cannot be justified on the basis of competitive criteria or as a remedy for the present effects of identified prior discrimination. It is conceivable that a particular application of the program may have this effect; however, the peculiarities of specific applications are not before us in this case. [This] does not mean that the claim of overinclusiveness is entitled to no consideration in the present case. The history of governmental tolerance of practices using racial or ethnic criteria for the purpose or with the effect of imposing an invidious discrimination must alert us to the deleterious effects of even benign racial or ethnic classifications when they stray from narrow remedial justifications. [T]he MBE provision cannot pass muster unless, with due account for its administrative program, it provides a reasonable assurance that application of racial or ethnic criteria will be limited to accomplishing the remedial objectives of Congress and that misapplications of the program will be promptly and adequately remedied administratively.

It is significant that the administrative scheme provides for waiver and exemption. [The] fundamental congressional assumptions [that] underlie the MBE program [may] be rebutted in the administrative process. [There] is administrative scrutiny to identify and eliminate from participation in the program MBE's who are not "bona-fide" within the regulations and guidelines; for example, spurious minority-front entities can be exposed.[3] [Grantees] are given the opportunity to demonstrate that their best efforts [cannot achieve] the statutory 10% target for minority firm participation. [In] these circumstances a waiver or partial waiver is available once compliance has been demonstrated. That the use of racial and ethnic criteria is premised on assumptions rebuttable in the administrative process gives reasonable assurance that application of the MBE program will be limited to accomplishing the remedial objectives contemplated by Congress and that misapplications of the racial and ethnic criteria can be remedied. In dealing with this facial challenge to the statute, doubts must be resolved in support of the congressional judgment that this limited program is a necessary step to effectuate the constitutional mandate for equality of economic opportunity. The MBE provision may be viewed as a pilot project, appropriately limited in extent and duration, and subject to reassessment and reevaluation by the Congress prior to any extension or re-enactment. Miscarriages of administration could have only a transitory economic impact on businesses not encompassed by the program, and would not be irremediable.

IV. Congress, after due consideration, perceived a pressing need to move forward with new approaches in the continuing effort to achieve the goal of equality of economic opportunity. In this effort, Congress has necessary latitude to try new techniques such as the limited use of racial and ethnic criteria to accomplish remedial objectives; this is especially so in programs where voluntary cooperation with remedial measures is induced by placing conditions on federal expenditures. That the program may press the outer limits of congressional authority affords no basis for striking it down. Petitioners have mounted a facial challenge to a program developed by the politically responsive branches of Government. For its part, the Congress must proceed only with programs narrowly tailored to achieve its objectives, subject to continuing evaluation and reassessment; administration of the programs must be vigilant and flexible; and, when such a program comes under judicial review, courts must be satisfied that the legislative objectives and projected administration give

---

3. [The] specific inclusion of [the named minority] groups in the MBE provision demonstrates that Congress concluded they were victims of discrimination. Petitioners did not press any challenge to Congress' classification catego-ries in the Court of Appeals; there is no reason for this Court to pass upon the issue at this time. [Footnote by the Chief Justice, earlier in his opinion.]

reasonable assurance that the program will function within constitutional [limitations].

Any preference based on racial or ethnic criteria must necessarily receive a most searching examination to make sure that it does not conflict with constitutional guarantees. This case is one which [has received] that kind of examination. This opinion does not adopt, either expressly or implicitly, the formulas of analysis articulated in such cases as Bakke. However, our analysis demonstrates that the MBE provision would survive judicial review under either "test" articulated in the several Bakke [opinions].[4]

Affirmed.

Mr. Justice POWELL, concurring.

Although I would place greater emphasis than The Chief Justice on the need to articulate judicial standards of review in conventional terms, I view his opinion [as] substantially in accord with my own views. Accordingly, I join that opinion and write separately to apply the analysis set forth by my opinion in Bakke. [The MBE law] employs a racial classification that is constitutionally prohibited unless it is a necessary means of advancing a compelling governmental interest. [I] believe that § 103(f)(2) is justified as a remedy that serves the compelling governmental interest in eradicating the continuing effects of past discrimination identified by Congress.

I. [Because] the distinction between permissible remedial action and impermissible racial preference rests on the existence of a constitutional or statutory violation, the legitimate interest in creating a race-conscious remedy is not compelling unless an appropriate governmental authority has found [such] a violation. [In] other words, two requirements must be met. First, the governmental body that attempts to impose a race-conscious remedy must have the authority to act in response to identified discrimination. Second, the governmental body must make findings that demonstrate the existence of illegal discrimination. In Bakke, the Regents failed both requirements. [Our] past cases also establish that even if the government proffers a compelling interest to support reliance upon a suspect classification, the means selected must be narrowly drawn to fulfill the governmental purpose. [In] reviewing the constitutionality of § 103(f)(2), we must decide: (i) whether Congress is competent to make findings of unlawful discrimination; (ii) if so, whether sufficient findings have been made to establish that unlawful discrimination has affected adversely minority business enterprises; and (iii) whether the 10% set-aside is a permissible means for redressing identifiable past [discrimination].

II. The history of this Court's review of congressional action demonstrates beyond question that [Congress] is competent to find constitutional and statutory violations. Unlike the Regents [in Bakke], Congress properly may—and indeed must—address directly the problems of discrimination in our society. [Congress] has been given the unique constitutional power of legislating to enforce the provisions of the 13th, 14th, and 15th Amendments. [Implicit in the holding in Katzenbach v. Morgan] was the Court's belief that Congress had the authority to find, and had found, that members of [the Puerto Rican] minority group had suffered governmental discrimination. Congress' authority to find and provide for the redress of constitutional violations also has been confirmed in cases construing the enforcement clause of the 15th Amendment. [South Carolina v. Katzenbach.] [It] is beyond question, therefore, that Congress has the authority to identify unlawful discriminatory practices, to

---

4. [We] perceive no inconsistency between the requirements of Title VI and those of the MBE provision. To the extent any statutory inconsistencies might be asserted, the MBE provision—the later, more specific enactment—must be deemed to control. [Footnote by the Chief Justice.]

prohibit those practices, and to prescribe remedies to eradicate their continuing [effects].

III. A. The petitioners contend that the legislative history [reflects] no congressional finding of statutory or constitutional violations. Crucial to that contention is the assertion that a reviewing court may not look beyond the legislative history of the [Act] itself for evidence that Congress believed it was combatting invidious discrimination. But petitioners' theory would erect an artificial barrier to full understanding of the legislative process. Congress is not an adjudicatory body called upon to resolve specific disputes between competing adversaries. [Petitioners'] contention that this Court should treat the debates on § 103(f)(2) as the complete "record" of congressional decisionmaking underlying that statute is essentially a plea that we treat Congress as if it were a lower federal court. [But the] creation of national rules for the governance of our society simply does not entail the same concept of recordmaking that is appropriate to a judicial or administrative proceeding. Congress has no responsibility to confine its vision to the facts and evidence adduced by particular parties. Instead, its special attribute as a legislative body lies in its broader mission to investigate and consider all facts and opinions that may be relevant to the resolution of an issue. One appropriate source is the information and expertise that Congress acquires in the consideration and enactment of earlier legislation. [Acceptance] of petitioners' argument would force Congress to make specific factual findings with respect to each legislative action. [Neither] the Constitution nor our democratic tradition warrants such a constraint on the legislative process. I therefore conclude that [we] properly may examine the total contemporary record of congressional action dealing with the problems of racial discrimination against minority business enterprises.

B. In my view, the legislative history of § 103(f)(2) demonstrates that Congress reasonably concluded that private and governmental discrimination had contributed to the negligible percentage of public contracts awarded minority contractors.[1] In light of [the] legislative materials,[2] [I] believe that a court must accept as established the conclusion that purposeful discrimination contributed significantly to the small percentage of federal contracting funds that minority business enterprises have received. [Although] the discriminatory activities were not identified with the exactitude expected in judicial or administrative adjudication, it must be remembered that "Congress may paint with a much broader brush than may this Court."[3]

IV. [The] conclusion that Congress found a compelling governmental interest in redressing identified discrimination against minority contractors

---

1. I cannot accept the suggestion of the Court of Appeals [quoting Katzenbach v. Morgan] that § 103(f)(2) must be viewed as serving a compelling state interest if the reviewing court can "perceive a basis" for legislative action. The "perceive a basis" standard refers to congressional authority to act, not to the distinct question whether that action violates [the] Fifth Amendment. In my view, a court should uphold a reasonable congressional finding of discrimination. A more stringent standard of review would impinge upon Congress' ability to address problems of discrimination; a standard requiring a court to "perceive a basis" is essentially meaningless in this context. Such a test might allow a court to justify legislative action even in the absence of affirmative evidence of congressional findings. [Footnote by Justice Powell.]

2. Justice Powell's comments on the legislative history placed special emphasis on the refer-

ence to past discrimination in a House Committee report on the Small Business Administration program. See footnote 1 to the Chief Justice's opinion, above.

3. Although this record suffices to support the congressional judgment that minority contractors suffered identifiable discrimination, Congress need not be content with findings that merely meet constitutional standards. Race-conscious remedies, popularly referred to as affirmative action programs, almost invariably affect some innocent persons. Respect and support for the law, especially in an area as sensitive as this, depend in large measure upon the public's perception of fairness. It therefore is important that the legislative record supporting race-conscious remedies contain evidence that satisfies fair minded people that the congressional action is just. [Footnote by Justice Powell.]

[leads] to the inquiry whether use of a 10% set-aside is a constitutionally appropriate means of serving that interest. In the past, this "means" test has been virtually impossible to satisfy. Only two of this Court's modern cases have held the use of racial classifications to be constitutional. [Korematsu; Hirabayashi.] Indeed, the failure of legislative action to survive strict scrutiny has led some to wonder whether our review of racial classifications has been strict in theory, but fatal in fact. See Gunther, ["Newer Equal Protection"].

A. Application of the "means" test necessarily demands an understanding of the type of congressional action at issue. This is not a case in which Congress has employed a racial classification solely as a means to confer a racial preference. Such a purpose plainly would be unconstitutional. Nor has Congress sought to employ a racially conscious means to further a nonracial goal. In such instances, a nonracial means should be available to further the legitimate governmental purpose. See Bakke. Enactment of the set-aside is designed to serve the compelling governmental interest in redressing racial discrimination. [The] implementation of any affirmative remedy for redress of racial discrimination is likely to affect persons differently depending upon their race. Although federal courts may not order or approve remedies that exceed the scope of a constitutional violation, this Court has not required remedial plans to be limited to the least restrictive means of implementation. We have recognized that the choice of remedies to redress racial discrimination is "a balancing process left, within appropriate constitutional or statutory limits, to the sound discretion of the trial court."

I believe that the enforcement clauses of the 13th and 14th Amendments give Congress a similar measure of discretion to choose a suitable remedy for the redress of racial discrimination. [I] conclude [that these clauses] confer upon Congress the authority to select reasonable remedies to advance the compelling state interest in repairing the effects of discrimination. But that authority must be exercised in a manner that does not erode the guarantees of these Amendments. The Judicial Branch has the special responsibility to make a searching inquiry into the justification for employing a race-conscious remedy. Courts must be sensitive to the possibility that less intrusive means might serve the compelling state interest equally as well. I believe that Congress' choice of a remedy should be upheld, however, if the means selected are equitable and reasonably necessary to the redress of identified discrimination. Such a test allows the Congress to [exercise] discretion but preserves [the] safeguard of judicial review of racial classifications.

B. When reviewing the selection by Congress of a race-conscious remedy, it is instructive to note the factors upon which the Courts of Appeals have relied in a closely analogous area. Courts reviewing the proper scope of race-conscious hiring remedies have considered (i) the efficacy of alternative remedies, (ii) the planned duration of the remedy, (iii) the relationship between the percentage of minority workers to be employed and the percentage of minority group members in the relevant population or work force, and (iv) the availability of waiver provisions if the hiring plan could not be met. By the time Congress enacted § 103(f)(2) in 1977, it knew that other remedies had failed to ameliorate the effects of racial discrimination in the construction industry. [Moreover, the] temporary nature of this remedy ensures that a race-conscious program will not last longer than the discriminatory effects it is designed to eliminate. [The] percentage chosen for the set-aside is within the scope of congressional discretion. [The] choice of a 10% set-aside [falls] roughly halfway between the present percentage of minority contractors and the percentage of minority group members in the Nation. Although the set-aside is pegged at a reasonable figure, its effect might be unfair if it were applied rigidly in areas of the country where minority group members constitute a small percentage of the population. To meet this concern, Congress enacted a waiver [provision].

C. A race-conscious remedy should not be approved without consideration of an additional crucial factor—the effect of the set-aside upon innocent third parties. [The] petitioners contend with some force that they have been asked to bear the burden of the set-aside even though they are innocent of wrongdoing. I do not believe, however, that their burden is so great that the set-aside must be disapproved. [The] effect of the set-aside is limited and so widely dispersed that its use is consistent with fundamental fairness.[4] Consideration of these factors persuades me that the set-aside is a reasonably necessary means of furthering the compelling governmental interest in redressing the discrimination that affects minority contractors. Any marginal unfairness to innocent nonminority contractors is not sufficiently significant—or sufficiently identifiable—to outweigh the governmental interest [served].[5]

V. [In] our quest to achieve a society free from racial classification, we cannot ignore the claims of those who still suffer from the effects of identifiable discrimination. Distinguishing the rights of all citizens to be free from racial classifications from the rights of some citizens to be made whole is a perplexing, but necessary, judicial task. [As I made clear in Bakke], I believe that the use of racial classifications [cannot] be imposed simply to serve transient social or political goals, however worthy they may be. But the issue here turns on the scope of congressional power, and Congress has been given a unique constitutional role in the enforcement of the post-Civil War Amendments. In this case, where Congress determined that minority contractors were victims of purposeful discrimination and where Congress chose a reasonably necessary means to effectuate its purpose, I find no constitutional reason to invalidate § 103(f)(2).

Mr. Justice MARSHALL, with whom Mr. Justice BRENNAN and Mr. Justice BLACKMUN join, concurring in the judgment.

[It] is clear to me that the racial classifications employed in the set-aside provision are substantially related to the achievement of the important and congressionally articulated goal of remedying the present effects of past racial discrimination. The provision, therefore, passes muster under the equal protection standard I adopted in Bakke. [Doors that have been shut to Negroes] cannot be fully opened without the acceptance of race-conscious remedies. [I] applaud this [result].

Mr. Justice STEWART, with whom Mr. Justice REHNQUIST joins, dissenting.

[I] think today's decision is wrong for the same reason that [Plessy] was wrong. [Equal protection] has one clear and central meaning—it absolutely prohibits invidious discrimination by government. [Any] official action that treats a person differently on account of his race or ethnic origin is inherently suspect and presumptively invalid. [Our] cases have made clear that the Constitution is wholly neutral in forbidding such racial discrimination, whatever

---

4. Although I believe that the burden placed upon nonminority contractors is not unconstitutional, I reject the suggestion that it is legally irrelevant. Apparently on the theory that Congress could have enacted no set-aside and provided $400 million less in funding, the Secretary of Commerce argues that "[n]onminorities have lost no right or legitimate expectation by the addition of Section 103(f)(2) to the 1976 Act." But the United States may not employ unconstitutional classifications, or base a decision upon unconstitutional considerations, when it provides a bene-fit to which a recipient is not legally entitled. [Footnote by Justice Powell.]

5. [I do not conclude] that use of a set-aside always will be an appropriate remedy or that the selection of a set-aside by any other governmental body would be constitutional. See Bakke. The degree of specificity required in the findings of discrimination and the breadth of discretion in the choice of remedies may vary with the nature and authority of a governmental body. [Footnote by Justice Powell.]

the race may be of those who are its victims.[1] [Under] our Constitution, the government may never act to the detriment of a person solely because of that person's race. The color of a person's skin and the country of his origin are immutable facts that bear no relation to ability, disadvantage, moral culpability, or any other characteristics of constitutionally permissible interest to government. [In] short, racial discrimination is by definition invidious discrimination. The rule cannot be any different when the persons injured by a racially biased law are not members of a racial minority. [From] the perspective of a person detrimentally affected by a racially discriminatory law, the arbitrariness and unfairness is entirely the same, whatever his skin color and whatever the law's purpose, be it purportedly "for the promotion of the public good" or otherwise.

No one disputes the self-evident proposition that Congress has broad discretion under its Spending Power to disburse the revenues of the United States as it deems [best]. No one disputes that Congress has the authority under the Commerce Clause to regulate contracting practices on federally funded public works projects, or that it enjoys broad powers under § 5 of the 14th Amendment "to enforce by appropriate legislation" the provisions of that Amendment. But these self-evident truisms do not begin to answer the question before us in this case. For in the exercise of its powers, Congress must obey the Constitution just as the legislatures of all the States must obey the Constitution in the exercise of their powers. If a law is unconstitutional, it is no less unconstitutional just because it is a product of [Congress].

On its face, [the MBE provision] denies [equal protection]. [It] bars a class to which the petitioners belong from having the opportunity to receive a government benefit, and bars the members of that class solely on the basis of their race or ethnic background. This is precisely the kind of law [that] equal protection forbids. The Court's attempt to characterize the law as a proper remedial measure to counteract the effects of past or present racial discrimination is remarkably unconvincing. The Legislative Branch of government is not a court of equity. It has neither the dispassionate objectivity nor the flexibility that are needed to mold a race-conscious remedy around the single objective of eliminating the effects of past or present discrimination. But even assuming that Congress has the power [to] remedy previous illegal racial discrimination, there is no evidence that Congress has in the past engaged in racial discrimination in its disbursement of federal contracting funds. The MBE provision thus pushes the limits of any such justification far beyond the equal protection [standard]. Certainly, nothing in the Constitution gives Congress any greater authority to impose detriments on the basis of race than is afforded the Judicial Branch.[2] And a judicial decree that imposes burdens on the basis of race can be upheld only where its sole purpose is to eradicate the actual effects of illegal race discrimination.

The provision at issue here does not satisfy this condition. Its legislative history suggests that it had at least two other objectives in addition to that of counteracting the effects of past or present racial discrimination in the public

---

1. [UJO (p. 752 above) does] not suggest a different rule. [There], a state legislature had apportioned certain voting districts with an awareness of their racial composition. Since the plaintiffs there had "failed to show that the legislative reapportionment plan had either the purpose or the effect of discriminating against them on the basis of their race," no constitutional violation had occurred. No person in that case was deprived of his electoral franchise.

More than 35 years ago, during the Second World War, this Court did find constitutional a governmental program imposing injury on the basis of race. See Korematsu; Hirabayashi. Significantly, those cases were decided not only in time of war, but in an era before the Court had held that the Due Process Clause of the Fifth Amendment imposes the same equal protection standard upon the Federal Government that the 14th Amendment imposes upon the States. [Footnote by Justice Stewart.]

2. [The enforcement clauses of the 13th and 14th Amendments do not grant] to Congress the [power] to enact legislation that itself violates the equal protection component of the Fifth Amendment. [Footnote by Justice Stewart.]

works construction industry.[3] One such purpose appears to have been to assure to minority contractors a certain percentage of federally funded public works contracts. But, since the guarantee of equal protection immunizes from capricious governmental treatment "persons"—not "races"—it can never countenance laws that seek racial balance as a goal in and of itself. [Second], there are indications that the MBE provision may have been enacted to compensate for the effects of social, educational, and economic "disadvantage." No race, however, has a monopoly on social, educational, or economic disadvantage, and any law that indulges in such a presumption clearly violates [equal protection]. Since the MBE provision was in whole or in part designed to effectuate objectives other than the elimination of the effects of racial discrimination, it cannot stand as a remedy that comports with the strictures of equal protection, even if it otherwise [could].[4]

[Today], the Court [places] its imprimatur on the creation once again by government of privileges based on birth. The Court, moreover, takes this drastic step [without] seriously considering the ramifications of its decision. [Our] statute books will once again have to contain laws that reflect the odious practice of delineating the qualities that make one person a Negro and make another white. Moreover, racial discrimination, even "good faith" racial discrimination, is inevitably a two-edged sword. [By] making race a relevant criterion once again in its own affairs, the Government implicitly teaches the public that the apportionment of rewards and penalties can legitimately be made according to race—rather than according to merit or ability—and that people can, and perhaps should, view themselves and others in terms of their racial characteristics. Notions of "racial entitlement" will be fostered, and private discrimination will necessarily be encouraged. See [e.g.] Van Alstyne, Rites of Passage: Race, the Supreme Court, and the Constitution, 46 U.Chi.L.Rev. 775 (1979). There are those who think that we need a new Constitution, and their views may someday prevail. But under the Constitution we have, one practice in which government may never engage is the practice of racism—not even "temporarily" and not even as an "experiment."

Mr. Justice STEVENS, dissenting.

3. The legislative history of the MBE provision itself contains not one mention of racial discrimination or the need to provide a mechanism to correct the effects of such discrimination. From the context of the Act, however, it is reasonable to infer that the program was enacted, at least in part, to remedy perceived past and present racial discrimination. In 1977, Congress knew that many minority business enterprises had historically suffered racial discrimination in the economy as a whole and in the construction industry in [particular]. [Footnote by Justice Stewart.]

4. Moreover, even a properly based judicial decree will be struck down if the scope of the remedy it provides is not carefully tailored to fit the nature and extent of the violation. Here, assuming that the MBE provision was intended solely as a remedy for past and present racial discrimination, it sweeps far too broadly. It directs every state and local government covered by the program to set aside 10% of its grant for minority business enterprises. Waivers from that requirement are permitted, but only where insufficient numbers of minority businesses capable of doing the work at nonexorbitant prices are located in the relevant contracting area. No waiver is provided for any governmental entity that can prove a history free of racial discrimination. Nor is any exemption permitted for nonminority contractors that are able to demonstrate that they have not engaged in racially discriminatory behavior. Finally, the statute makes no attempt to direct the aid it provides solely toward those minority contracting firms that arguably still suffer from the effects of past or present discrimination. These are not the characteristics of a racially conscious remedial decree that is closely tailored to the evil to be corrected. In today's society, it constitutes far too gross an oversimplification to assume that every single Negro, Spanish-speaking citizen, Oriental, Indian, Eskimo, and Aleut potentially interested in construction contracting currently suffers from the effects of past or present racial discrimination. Since the MBE set-aside must be viewed as resting upon such an assumption, it necessarily paints with too broad a brush. Except to make whole the identified victims of racial discrimination, the guarantee of equal protection prohibits the government from taking detrimental action against innocent people on the basis of the sins of others of their own race. [Footnote by Justice Stewart.]

The 10% set-aside [creates] monopoly privileges in a $400,000,000 market for a class of investors defined solely by racial characteristics. The direct beneficiaries of these monopoly privileges are the relatively small number of persons within the racial classification who represent the entrepreneurial sub-class—those who have, or can borrow, working capital. [When] government accords different treatment to different persons, there must be a reason for the difference. Because racial characteristics so seldom provide a relevant basis for disparate treatment, and because classifications based on race are potentially so harmful to the entire body politic,[1] it is especially important that the reasons for any such classification be clearly identified and unquestionably legitimate. The statutory definition of the preferred class includes "citizens of the United States who are Negroes, Spanish-speaking, Orientals, Indians, Eskimos, and Aleuts." [There] is not one word [that] explains why any Congressman or Senator favored this particular definition over any other or that identifies the common characteristics that every member of the preferred class was believed to share.[2] Nor does the Act or its history explain why 10% of the total appropriation was the proper amount to set aside for investors in each of the six racial subclasses. Four different, though somewhat interrelated, justifications for the racial classification in this Act have been advanced: first, that the 10% set aside is a form of reparation for past injuries to the entire membership of the class; second, that it is an appropriate remedy for past discrimination against minority business enterprises that have been denied access to public contracts; third, that the members of the favored class have a special entitlement to "a piece of the action" when government is distributing benefits; and, fourth, that the program is an appropriate method of fostering greater minority participation in a competitive economy. Each of these asserted justifications merits separate scrutiny.

I. Racial characteristics may serve to define a group of persons who have suffered a special wrong and who, therefore, are entitled to special reparations. [E.g., laws regarding "Indian tribes."] In his eloquent separate opinion in Bakke, Mr. Justice Marshall recounted the tragic class-based discrimination against Negroes that is an indelible part of America's history. I assume that the wrong committed against the Negro class is both so serious and so pervasive that it would constitutionally justify an appropriate classwide recovery measured by a sum certain for every member of the injured class. [But] that serious classwide wrong cannot in itself justify the particular classification Congress has made in this Act. Racial classifications are simply too pernicious to permit any but the most exact connection between justification and classification. Quite obviously, the history of discrimination against black citizens in America cannot

---

1. Indeed, the very attempt to define with precision a beneficiary's qualifying racial characteristics is repugnant to our constitutional ideals. The so-called guidelines [administratively developed here] are so general as to be fairly innocuous; as a consequence they are too vague to be useful. [If] the National Government is to make a serious effort to define racial classes by criteria that can be administered objectively, it must study precedents such as the First Regulation to the Reich Citizenship Law of November 14, 1935 [defining "a Jew" in great detail]. [Footnote by Justice Stevens.]

2. In 1968, almost 10 years before the Act was passed, the Small Business Administration had developed a program to assist small business concerns owned or controlled by "socially or economically disadvantaged persons." The Agency's description of persons eligible for such assistance stated that such "persons include, but are not limited to, black Americans, American Indians, Spanish-Americans, oriental Americans, Eskimos and Aleuts." This may be the source of the definition of the class at issue in this case. But the SBA's class of socially or economically disadvantaged persons neither included all persons in the racial class nor excluded all nonmembers of the racial class. Race was used as no more than a factor in identifying the class of the disadvantaged. The difference between the statutory quota involved in this case and the SBA's 1968 description of those whose businesses were to be assisted under [the] Small Business Act is thus at least as great as the difference between the University of California's racial quota and the Harvard admissions system that Mr. Justice Powell regarded as critical in Bakke. [Footnote by Justice Stevens.]

justify a grant of privileges to Eskimos or Indians. Even if we assume that each of the six racial subclasses has suffered its own special injury at some time in our history, surely it does not necessarily follow that each of those subclasses suffered harm of identical magnitude. Although "the Negro was dragged to this country in chains to be sold in slavery," the "Spanish-speaking" subclass came voluntarily, frequently without invitation, and the Indians, the Eskimos and the Aleuts had an opportunity to exploit America's resources before most American citizens arrived. There is no reason to assume, and nothing in the legislative history suggests, much less demonstrates, that each of these subclasses is equally entitled to reparations from the United States Government. At best, the statutory preference is a somewhat perverse form of reparation for the members of the injured classes. For those who are the most disadvantaged within each class are the least likely to receive any benefit from the special privilege even though they are the persons most likely still to be suffering the consequences of the past wrong. A random distribution to a favored few is a poor form of compensation for an injury shared by many.

My principal objection to the reparation justification for this legislation, however, cuts more deeply than my concern about its inequitable character. We can never either erase or ignore the history that Mr. Justice Marshall has recounted. But if that history can justify such a random distribution of benefits on racial lines as that embodied in this statutory scheme, it will serve not merely as a basis for remedial legislation, but rather as a permanent source of justification for grants of special privileges. For if there is no duty to attempt either to measure the recovery by the wrong or to distribute that recovery within the injured class in an evenhanded way, our history will adequately support a legislative preference for almost any ethnic, religious, or racial group with the political strength to negotiate "a piece of the action" for its members. Although I do not dispute the validity of the assumption that each of the subclasses identified in the Act has suffered a severe wrong at some time in the past, I cannot accept this slapdash statute as a legitimate method of providing class-wide relief.

II.　The Act may also be viewed [as] designed to grant relief to the specific minority business enterprises that have been denied access to public contracts by discriminatory practices. But the statute grants the special preference to a class that includes (1) those minority owned firms that have successfully obtained business in the past on a free competitive basis and undoubtedly are capable of doing so in the future as well; (2) firms that have never attempted to obtain any public business in the past; (3) firms that were initially formed after the Act was passed, including those that may have been organized simply to take advantage of its provisions; (4) firms that have tried to obtain public business but were unsuccessful for reasons that are unrelated to the racial characteristics of their stockholders; and (5) those firms that have been victimized by racial discrimination. Since there is no reason to believe that any of the firms in the first four categories had been wrongfully excluded from the market for public contracts, the statutory preference for those firms cannot be justified as a remedial measure. And since a [statutory] remedy was already available for the firms in the fifth category, it seems inappropriate to regard the preference as a remedy designed to redress any specific wrongs.[3] In any event, since it is highly

---

3. I recognize that the [administrator] has issued a technical bulletin, relied on heavily by The Chief Justice, which distinguishes between higher bids quoted by minority subcontractors which are attributable to the effects of disadvantage or discrimination and those which are not. That is, according to the bulletin, if it is determined that a subcontractor's uncompetitive high price is not attributable to the effects of discrimination, a contractor may be entitled to relief from the 10% set-aside requirement. But even assuming that the technical bulletin accurately reflects Congress' intent in enacting the set-aside, it is not easy to envision how one could realistically demonstrate with any degree of precision, if at all, the extent to which a bid has been inflated

unlikely that the composition of the fifth category is at all representative of the entire class of firms to which the statute grants a valuable preference, it is ill-fitting to characterize this as a "narrowly tailored" remedial measure.

III.   The legislative history of the Act discloses that there is a group of legislators in Congress identified as the "Black Caucus" and that members of that group argued that if the Federal Government was going to provide $4,000,000,000 of new public contract business, their constituents were entitled to "a piece of the action." [In] the short run our political processes might benefit from legislation that enhanced the ability of representatives of minority groups to disseminate patronage to their political backers. But in the long run any rule that authorized the award of public business on a racial basis would be just as objectionable as one that awarded such business on a purely partisan basis. [See Elrod v. Burns (1976; p. 1393 below).] The legislators' interest in providing their constituents with favored access to benefits distributed by the Federal Government is, in my opinion, a plainly impermissible justification for this racial classification.

IV.   The interest in facilitating and encouraging the participation by minority business enterprises in the economy is unquestionably legitimate. Any barrier to such entry and growth [should] be vigorously and thoroughly removed. [This] statute, however, is not designed to remove any barriers to entry. Nor does its sparse legislative history detail any insuperable or even significant obstacles to entry into the competitive market.

[The] question whether the history of past discrimination has created barriers that can only be overcome by an unusual measure of this kind is [the most] difficult to evaluate. In analyzing this question, I think it is essential to draw a distinction between obstacles placed in the path of minority business enterprises by others and characteristics of those firms that may impair their ability to compete. It is [true] that irrational racial prejudice persists today and continues to obstruct minority participation in a variety of economic pursuits, presumably including the construction industry. But there are two reasons why this legislation will not eliminate, or even tend to eliminate, such prejudice. First, prejudice is less likely to be a significant factor in the public sector of the economy than in the private sector because both federal and state laws have prohibited discrimination in the award of public contracts for many years. Second, and of greater importance, an absolute preference that is unrelated to a minority firm's ability to perform a contract inevitably will engender resentment on the part of competitors excluded from the market for a purely racial reason and skepticism on the part of customers and suppliers aware of the statutory classification. It thus seems clear to me that this Act cannot be defended as an appropriate method of reducing racial prejudice.

The argument that our history of discrimination has left the entire membership of each of the six racial classes identified in the Act less able to compete in a free market than others is more easily stated than proved. The reduction in prejudice that has occurred during the last generation has accomplished much less than was anticipated; it nevertheless remains true that increased opportunities have produced an ever increasing number of demonstrations that members of disadvantaged races are entirely capable not merely of competing on an equal basis, but also of excelling in the most demanding professions. But, even though it is not the actual predicate for this legislation, a statute of this kind inevitably is perceived by many as resting on an assumption that those who are granted this special preference are less qualified in some respect that is identified purely by their race. Because that perception—especially when

by the effects of disadvantage or past discrimination. Consequently, while The Chief Justice describes the set-aside as a remedial measure, it plainly operates as a flat quota. [Footnote by Justice Stevens.]

fostered by [Congress]—can only exacerbate rather than reduce racial prejudice, it will delay the time when race will become a truly irrelevant, or at least insignificant, factor. Unless Congress clearly articulates the need and basis for a racial classification, and also tailors the classification to its justification, the Court should not uphold this kind of statute.[4] [The] ultimate goal must be to eliminate entirely from governmental decisionmaking such irrelevant factors as a human being's race. The removal of barriers to access to political and economic processes serves that goal. But the creation of new barriers can only frustrate true progress. For [such] protective barriers reinforce habitual ways of thinking in terms of classes instead of individuals. Preferences based on characteristics acquired at birth foster intolerance and antagonism against the entire member- ship of the favored classes. For this reason, I am firmly convinced that this "temporary measure" will disserve the goal of equal opportunity.

V. [Unlike Justices Stewart and Rehnquist], I am not convinced that the Clause contains an absolute prohibition against any statutory classification based on race. I am nonetheless persuaded that it does impose a special obligation to scrutinize any governmental decisionmaking process that draws nationwide distinctions between citizens on the basis of their race and incidentally also discriminates against noncitizens in the preferred racial classes.[5] For just as procedural safeguards are necessary to guarantee impartial decisionmaking in the judicial process, so can they play a vital part in preserving the impartial character of the legislative process. In both its substantive and procedural aspects this Act is markedly different from the normal product of the legislative decisionmaking process. The very fact that Congress for the first time in the Nation's history has created a broad legislative classification for entitlement to benefits based solely on racial characteristics identifies a dramatic difference between this Act and the thousands of statutes that preceded it. This dramatic point of departure is not even mentioned in the statement of purpose of the Act or in the reports of either the House or the Senate Committee that processed the legislation,[6] and was not the subject of any testimony or inquiry in any

---

4. Justice Stevens added: "This Act has a character that is fundamentally different from a carefully drafted remedial measure like the Vot- ing Rights Act of 1965. [See chap. 10, sec. 4, below.] A consideration of some of the dramatic differences between these two legislative re- sponses to racial injustice reveals not merely a difference in legislative craftsmanship but a dif- ference of constitutional significance. Whereas the enactment of the Voting Rights Act was preceded by exhaustive hearings and debates con- cerning discriminatory denial of access to the electoral process, and became effective in specific States only after specific findings were made, this statute authorizes an automatic nationwide pref- erence for all members of a diverse racial class regardless of their possible interest in the particu- lar geographic areas where the public contracts are to be performed. [The] Voting Rights Act addressed the problem of denial of access to the electoral process, [removed] old barriers to equal access [and] precluded the erection of new barri- ers. The Act before us today does not outlaw any existing barriers to access to the economic market and does nothing to prevent the erection of new barriers. On the contrary, it adopts the fundamentally different approach of creating a new set of barriers of its own.

"A comparable approach in the electoral con- text would support a rule requiring that at least

10% of the candidates elected to the legislature be members of specified racial minorities. Surely that would be an effective way of ensuring black citizens the representation that has long been their due. Quite obviously, however, such a measure would merely create the kind of inequal- ity that an impartial sovereign cannot tolerate. Yet that is precisely the kind of 'remedy' that this Act authorizes. In both political and eco- nomic contexts, we have a legitimate interest in seeing that those who were disadvantaged in the past may succeed in the future. But neither an election nor a market can be equally accessible to all if race provides a basis for placing a special value on votes or dollars."

5. See Hampton v. Mow Sun Wong [1976; p. 676 above]. [Footnote by Justice Stevens.]

6. [The] Court quotes three paragraphs from a lengthy report issued by the House Committee on small business in 1977, implying that the contents of that report were considered by Con- gress when it enacted the 10% minority set aside. But that report was not mentioned by anyone during the very brief discussion of the set-aside amendment. When one considers the vast quan- tity of written material turned out by the dozens of congressional committees and subcommittees these days, it is unrealistic to assume that a significant number of legislators read, or even

legislative hearing on the bill that was enacted. [The floor debate was] a perfunctory consideration of an unprecedented policy decision of profound constitutional importance to the Nation. [Although] it is traditional for judges to accord the same presumption of regularity to the legislative process no matter how obvious it may be that a busy Congress has acted precipitately, I see no reason why the character of their procedures may not be considered relevant to the decision whether the legislative product has caused a deprivation of liberty or property without due process of law.[7] Whenever Congress creates a classification that would be subject to strict scrutiny under [equal protection] if it had been fashioned by a state legislature, it seems to me that judicial review should include a consideration of the procedural character of the decisionmaking process. A holding that the classification was not adequately preceded by a consideration of less drastic alternatives or adequately explained by a statement of legislative purpose would be far less intrusive than a final determination that the substance of the decision is not "narrowly tailored to the achievement of that [goal]."

[I] would hold this statute unconstitutional on a narrower ground [than Justice Stewart's dissent]. It cannot fairly be characterized as a "narrowly tailored" racial classification because it simply raises too many serious questions that Congress failed to answer or even to address in a responsible way.[8] The risk that habitual attitudes toward classes of persons, rather than analysis of the relevant characteristics of the class, will serve as a basis for a legislative classification is present when benefits are distributed as well as when burdens are imposed. In the past, traditional attitudes too often provided the only explanation for discrimination against women, aliens, illegitimates, and black citizens. Today there is a danger that awareness of past injustice will lead to automatic acceptance of new classifications that are not in fact justified by attributes characteristic of the class as a whole. When Congress creates a special preference, or a special disability, for a class of persons, it should identify the characteristic that justifies the special treatment. When the classification is defined in racial terms, I believe that such particular identification is imperative. In this case, only two conceivable bases for differentiating the preferred classes from society as a whole have occurred to me: (1) that they were the victims of unfair treatment in the past and (2) that they are less able to compete in the future. Although the first of these factors would justify an appropriate remedy for past wrongs, for reasons that I have already stated, this statute is not such a remedial measure. The second factor is simply not true. Nothing in the record of this case, the legislative history of the Act, or experience that we may notice judicially provides any support for such a proposition. It is up to Congress to

---

were aware of that report. Even if they did, the report does not contain an explanation of this 10% set-aside for six racial subclasses. Indeed, the broad racial classification in this Act is totally unexplained. Although the legislative history [explains] why Negro citizens are included within the preferred class, there is absolutely no discussion of why Spanish-speaking, Orientals, Indians, Eskimos, and Aleuts were also included. [Footnote by Justice Stevens.]

7. [See] Linde, Due Process of Lawmaking, 55 Neb.L.Rev. 197 (1976). [Footnote by Justice Stevens.]

8. For example, why were these six racial classifications, and no others, included in the preferred class? Why are aliens excluded from the preference although they are not otherwise ineligible for public contracts? What percentage of Oriental blood or what degree of Spanish-

speaking skill is required for membership in the preferred class? How does the legacy of slavery and the history of discrimination against the descendants of its victims support a preference for Spanish-speaking citizens who may be directly competing with black citizens in some overpopulated communities? Why is a preference given only to owners of business enterprises and why is that preference unaccompanied by any requirement concerning the employment of disadvantaged persons? Is the preference limited to a subclass of persons who can prove that they are subject to a special disability caused by past discrimination, as the Court's opinion indicates? Or is every member of the racial class entitled to a preference as the statutory language seems plainly to indicate? Are businesses formed just to take advantage of the preference eligible? [Footnote by Justice Stevens.]

demonstrate that its unique statutory preference is justified by a relevant characteristic that is shared by the members of the preferred class. In my opinion, because it has failed to make that demonstration, it has also failed to discharge its duty to govern impartially embodied in the [Fifth Amendment].[9]

STATUTORY INTERPRETATIONS BEARING ON THE BENIGN CLASSIFICATIONS PROBLEM

1.   UNITED STEELWORKERS v. WEBER, 443 U.S. 193 (1979): The 5 to 2 decision in Weber held that "voluntary" affirmative action programs did not violate Title VII of the 1964 Civil Rights Act. In this case, "an affirmative action plan—collectively bargained by an employer and a union—that reserves for black employees 50% of the openings in an in-plant craft-training program until the percentage of black craftworkers in the plant is commensurate with the percentage of blacks in the local labor force" was not vulnerable under Title VII.[1] Justice BRENNAN's majority opinion held that the Act "left employers and unions in the private sector free to take such race-conscious steps to

9. That the Court did not think that Fullilove had disposed of all constitutional questions about the permissibility of race-conscious remedies (including, e.g., the status of affirmative action programs emanating from a source other than Congress) was indicated by its grant of review, on the very day it decided Fullilove, in two additional "benign" classification cases. But in both cases, the Court managed to avoid decision on the merits. The first, Johnson v. Chicago Board of Education, has already been noted, at p. 745 above. The second was Minnick v. Department of Corrections, 452 U.S. 105 (1981), where the state court had upheld a California Corrections Department affirmative action program that had as its "over-all" objective a workforce of 38% women and 36% minorities. (The percentages were based on prison inmate population rather than the relevant labor market.) The challengers claimed that the state agency had adopted the program solely on the basis of its "conclusory allegations" that its past employment practices had a discriminatory impact on minorities and women. The Court dismissed the writ of certiorari on the ground that the state court decision was not "final" in the sense of the jurisdictional statute. This conclusion was heavily influenced by "significant ambiguities" in the record and by "significant developments" in the law since the trial (which had taken place before Bakke).

Justice Stewart was the only one to reach the merits. He dissented, claiming the program unconstitutionally considered "a person's race in making promotion decisions." Relying on his Fullilove dissent, he added that, while "a private person may engage in any racial discrimination he wants" [see Weber, which follows], a state may not do so. He added: "It is self-evident folly to suppose that a person's race may constitutionally be taken into account, but that it must not be controlling." And he thought it "wholly irrelevant whether the State gives a 'plus' or 'minus' value to a person's race." (In a separate notation, Justice Rehnquist agreed with the dismissal but added that if he, too, had viewed the

judgment as "final," he would have joined Justice Stewart's dissent.

1. Sec. 703(a) of Title VII provides: "It shall be an unlawful employment practice for an employer—

"(1) to fail or refuse to hire or to discharge any individual, or otherwise to discriminate against any individual with respect to his compensation, terms, conditions, or privileges of employment, because of such individual's race, color, religion, sex, or national origin; or

"(2) to limit or classify his employees or applicants for employment in any way which would deprive or tend to deprive any individual of employment opportunities or otherwise adversely affect his status as an employee, because of such individual's race, color, religion, sex, or national origin."

Sec. 703(d) provides: "It shall be an unlawful employment practice for any employer, labor organization, or joint labor-management committee controlling apprenticeship or other training or retraining, including on-the-job training programs, to discriminate against any individual because of his race, color, religion, sex, or national origin in admission to, or employment in, any program established to provide apprenticeship or other training."

Justice Brennan noted that, since the plan did not involve state action, the case did not present an alleged violation of equal protection. He noted, too, that Title VII could not be "read in pari materia" with Title VI (considered in Bakke), because of their different aims. Title VI was concerned with discrimination in federal spending programs; Title VII, by contrast, was enacted pursuant to the commerce power "to regulate purely private decisionmaking and was not intended to incorporate and particularize the commands of the Fifth and 14th Amendments." Moreover, he was not persuaded by the argument that assurance of color-blindness was a dominant theme in the enactment of the 1964 Act.

eliminate manifest racial imbalances in traditionally segregated job categories." He rejected the argument that the law should be read literally "to prohibit all race-conscious affirmative action plans." Although he conceded that the argument was "not without force," he concluded that the law must be "read against the background of the legislative history [and] the historical context. [It] would be ironic indeed if a law triggered by a Nation's concern over centuries of racial injustice [constituted] the first legislative prohibition of all voluntary, private, race-conscious efforts to abolish traditional patterns of racial segregation and hierarchy." He added: "We need not today define in detail the line of demarcation between permissible and impermissible affirmative action plans. It suffices to hold that the challenged [plan] falls on the permissible side of the line. [It] does not unnecessarily trammel the interests of the white employees. [It] does not require the discharge of white workers and their replacement with new black hires. Nor does [it] create an absolute bar to the advancement of white employees; half of those trained [will] be white. Moreover, [it] is a temporary measure [not] to maintain racial balance, but simply to eliminate a manifest racial imbalance. Preferential selection of craft trainees at [the] plant will end as soon as the percentage of black skilled craft workers [approximates] the percentage of blacks in the local labor force." Accordingly, the plan fell "within the area of discretion left by Title VII to the private sector voluntarily to adopt affirmative action plans."

An extensive and vehement dissent by Justice REHNQUIST, joined by Chief Justice Burger, reviewed the legislative history in detail and concluded that that history was "as clear as the language of §§ 703(a) and (d), and it irrefutably demonstrates that Congress meant precisely what it [said]—that *no* racial discrimination in employment is permissible under Title VII, not even preferential treatment of minorities to correct racial imbalance. [By] a tour de force reminiscent not of jurists such as Hale, Holmes, and Hughes, but of escape artists such as Houdini, the Court eludes clear statutory language, 'uncontradicted' legislative history, and uniform precedent in concluding that employers are, after all, permitted to consider race in making employment decisions." [2]

2. FIREFIGHTERS v. STOTTS, 467 U.S. —— (1984): Like Weber, Stotts involved Title VII; unlike Weber, it was a rare case in which the proponents of affirmative action remedies did not prevail. It arose in the following context: In the early 1970s, Memphis adopted a seniority system for all city employees. Subsequently, as a result of a suit by black employees charging discrimination, the city entered into a consent decree to increase black employment. (The city did not admit past purposeful discrimination.) In 1981, a budget shortfall required reduction of city personnel. The layoff plan was based on the "last hired, first fired" rule for seniority. Although the plan was not adopted with the intent to discriminate, it had an adverse proportionate impact on blacks.

---

2. Chief Justice BURGER also submitted a separate dissent. Justice BLACKMUN, who joined the majority opinion, also submitted a separate concurrence. (Justices Powell and Stevens did not participate.)

Consider the critical comment, addressed not only to Weber but also to the 1979 Dayton and Columbus school desegregation decisions (p. 726 above), in Kitch, "The Return of Color-Consciousness to the Constitution: Weber, Dayton and Columbus," 1979 Sup.Ct.Rev. 1: "Twenty-five years after [Brown], the [Court] has assured us that the answer to the 'American dilemma' will not come through the first Mr. Justice Harlan's 'color blindness' but rather by acknowl-

edging differences between blacks and whites as the basis for 'affirmative action.' That is the cumulative message of Weber, Columbus, and Dayton. [Their] remedies focus not on racial discrimination but on redressing racial imbalance in the work force and the school population. They acknowledge that separate but unequal treatment under law is warranted by our history, because they deal with classes of persons and not with individuals." (See also Fullilove, above. Compare Mishkin, "The Uses of Ambivalence: Reflections on the Supreme Court and the Constitutionality of Affirmative Action," 131 U.Pa. L.Rev. 907 (1983).)

The lower court issued an injunction forbidding the use of the layoff plan because it would have a racially discriminatory effect. The Court, in an opinion by Justice WHITE, held that Title VII precluded the lower federal court from modifying the consent decree so as to displace "a non-minority employee with seniority under the contractually established seniority system absent either a finding that the seniority system was adopted with discriminatory intent or a determination that such a remedy was necessary to make whole a proven victim of discrimination." He stated: "Title VII protects bona fide seniority systems, and it is inappropriate to deny an innocent employee the benefits of his seniority in order to provide a remedy in [a] suit such as this." Relying on Teamsters v. United States, 431 U.S. 324 (1977), he held that § 703(h) "permits the routine application of a seniority system absent proof of an intention to discriminate." [1] And he stressed that a finding of intent to discriminate must be made with reference to the individuals seeking the remedy: "If individual members of a plaintiff class demonstrate that they have been actual victims of the discriminatory practice, they may be awarded competitive seniority. [But] mere membership in the disadvantaged class is insufficient to warrant a seniority award; each individual must prove that the discriminatory practice had an impact on him." He also relied on the general policies behind § 706(g), which deals with remedies generally in Title VII cases. He described the policy of Title VII as being "to provide make-whole relief only to those who have been actual victims of illegal discrimination." [2]

SECTION 4. THE "FUNDAMENTAL RIGHTS AND INTERESTS" STRAND OF STRICT SCRUTINY

Introduction. As noted at the beginning of this chapter, the Warren Court's "new" equal protection-strict scrutiny framework contained two major elements: not only the "suspect classifications" theme traced in sec. 3, but also the position that intensive review is justified whenever governmental action seriously burdens "fundamental rights or interests." This section focuses on that latter strand. The novel aspect of the fundamental interests theme lay in the Warren Court's suggestions that specially protected constitutional rights could be derived directly from the equal protection clause itself.[1] That characteristic should be distinguished from the traditional notion that an equal protection mode of analysis may be applied when governmental action discriminatorily burdens a right clearly embodied elsewhere in the Constitution—e.g., the First Amendment.[2] The distinctive feature in most of the fundamental interests-"new"

---

1. Sec. 703(h) provides that "it shall not be an unlawful employment practice to apply different standards of compensation, or different terms [of] employment pursuant to a bona fide seniority system, [provided] that such differences are not the result of an intention to discriminate because of race."

2. Justice BLACKMUN, joined by Justices Brennan and Marshall, dissented, arguing that the case was moot, that the nature of the case made it impossible for the named plaintiffs to prove their individual claims of injury, and that, on the merits, the legislative history demonstrated that Congress had not intended to prohibit all race-conscious remedies, but only those that were "broader than necessary." (He interpreted the majority opinion as relying only on this narrower proposition.) Justice O'CONNOR filed a separate opinion in concurring with the majority. Justice STEVENS joined only in the judgment.

1. Recall the controversy generated by Westen's thesis that equality is an "empty idea," as noted in sec. 1 above. See also Cohen, "Is Equal Protection Like Oakland? Equality as a Surrogate for Other Rights" (forthcoming, — Tul.L. Rev. — (1985).)

2. Thus, the view that the First Amendment protects against discriminatory regulations based on the content of expression is a well established one, as later chapters repeatedly illustrate. See, e.g., Police Dept. v. Mosley (1972; p. 1164 below), and Karst, "Equality as a Central Principle in the First Amendment," 43 U.Chi.L.Rev. 20 (1975). Moreover, when a "fundamental" constitutional right is identified via substantive due

equal protection cases in *this* section is that the justification for heightened scrutiny purports to stem *entirely* from equal protection itself, *not* from any independent source elsewhere in the Constitution.

The Warren Court's derivation of fundamental interests directly from the equal protection clause was a novel and wide-ranging departure. Potentially, it promised to raise many of the institutional and interpretive difficulties that have marked the history of substantive due process; indeed, the search for "fundamental values" that inhered in this strand of equal protection analysis led some to refer to it as "substantive equal protection." [3] Others commented that the fundamental interests strand of the "new" equal protection was especially attractive to the Warren Court because some Justices were reluctant to cloak their desire to identify new fundamental values in the then-discredited cloak of substantive due process; equal protection, far less identified with much-criticized "Lochnerizing," seemed a tempting alternative route. [4]

In fact, the implementation of fundamental interests-"new" equal protection analysis by the Warren Court was limited to a very few areas. The Burger Court has generally adhered to these well-established strands of the Warren Court's fundamental interests-"new" equal protection. But the Burger Court has refused to expand that analysis into new spheres: "thus far and no further" has been its response to the Warren Court's fundamental interests legacy under the equal protection clause. [5]

This section begins, in sec. 4A, with the 1973 decision in Rodriguez, the decision which most fully and clearly reveals the characteristic Burger Court reluctance to expand fundamental interests-"new" equal protection analysis. [6] Rodriguez is followed by, and should be contrasted with, a later Burger Court decision, Plyler v. Doe, which, despite the Rodriguez holding that education is not a "fundamental interest," manages to exercise heightened scrutiny in striking down the Texas exclusion of illegal "undocumented" alien children from free public education. (Are Rodriguez and Plyler reconcilable?) The focus then shifts to the three strands of fundamental interests-"new" equal protection analysis that became solidly established on the Warren Court and that have been adhered to by the Burger Court: the fundamental interest in equal access to voting, which has produced the striking down of a wide range of barriers to the voting booth and the ballot (sec. 4B); access to the judicial process (sec. 4C); and the right of interstate migration, most often impeded by

process analysis, impingements on that right are often subjected to an equal protection mode of review. Recall, e.g., Zablocki v. Redhail (1978; p. 554 above), where most of the Justices scrutinized a restriction on the "fundamental" right to marry in an equal protection mode.

3. The phrase is from Karst & Horowitz, "Reitman v. Mulkey: A Teleophase of Substantive Equal Protection," 1967 Sup.Ct.Rev. 39.

4. Moreover, the language of equality lends itself more readily to the achievement of the aims of those advocates and judges who sought to find constitutional mandates for affirmative governmental obligations to equalize economic conditions. The legacy of substantive due process was far more associated with an Adam Smith-John Stuart Mill notion of negative restraints on government—a hands-off philosophy rather than one imposing affirmative, egalitarian obligations.

5. See Gunther, "Newer Equal Protection."

6. Rodriguez did not mean Burger Court abandonment of the expansion of "fundamental values" modes of adjudication outside the equal

protection sphere. Ironically, in the very year that Rodriguez called a halt to further fundamental value searches under the aegis of equal protection, the Court announced its willingness to engage in fundamental value searches under the formerly discredited mode of substantive due process. Recall Roe v. Wade and its progeny, in chap. 8, sec. 3.

Rodriguez reflects both the Burger Court's unwillingness to find new fundamental interests in the equal protection clause and its readiness to accept the well-established ingredients of fundamental interests-equal protection analysis as developed by the Warren Court. Examining Rodriguez at the outset of this section not only provides a useful overview of the modern Court's reluctance to expand, but also focuses special attention on the Court's (occasionally strained) efforts to justify and distinguish the "well-established" fundamental interests in such areas as voting rights—areas more fully pursued in the later subsections.

durational residence requirements (sec. 4D). The final group of materials, sec. 4E, returns to one of the themes of Rodriguez by focusing on the most amorphous and controversial aspect of fundamental interests analysis, the unsuccessful effort to derive from equal protection fundamental interests in such "necessities" as welfare benefits and housing.

A. THE BURGER COURT'S GENERAL STANCE: RODRIGUEZ AND PLYLER

SAN ANTONIO IND. SCHOOL DIST. v. RODRIGUEZ
411 U.S. 1, 93 S.Ct. 1278, 36 L.Ed.2d 16 (1973).

[This was an attack on the Texas system of financing public education, which relied heavily on local property taxes. The targets of the attack were the substantial interdistrict disparities in per-pupil expenditures resulting primarily from differences in taxable property values among the districts. The appellees who brought the class action were Mexican-American parents of children attending schools in the Edgewood Independent School District in San Antonio, suing on behalf of children of poor families residing in districts having a low property tax base. Texas public schools, like those in most states, are largely financed through a combination of state and local funds. A statewide Minimum Foundation School Program serves to reduce disparities among district tax bases, but district spending varies considerably on the basis of local property wealth.[1] The District Court, exercising strict scrutiny, invalidated the Texas financing system.]

Mr. Justice POWELL delivered the opinion of the [Court].

[I.] We must decide, first whether the Texas system of financing public education operates to the disadvantage of some suspect class or impinges upon a fundamental right explicitly or implicitly protected by the Constitution, thereby requiring strict judicial scrutiny. If so, the judgment of the District Court [which had found wealth a "suspect" classification and education a "fundamental interest"] should be affirmed. If not, the Texas scheme must still be examined to determine whether it rationally furthers some legitimate, articulated state purpose and therefore does not constitute an invidious discrimination in violation of [equal protection].

II. [We] find neither the suspect-classification nor the fundamental-interest analysis persuasive. A. The wealth discrimination discovered by the District Court, [and] by several other courts that have recently struck down school financing laws in other States,[2] is quite unlike any of the forms of wealth discrimination heretofore reviewed by this Court. [The] individuals or groups

---

1. For example, as the Court's opinion pointed out, a spending comparison between appellees' Edgewood district and the Alamo Heights district—the "most affluent district in the San Antonio area"—indicated "the extent to which substantial disparities exist despite the State's impressive progress in recent years." During the 1967–68 school year, Edgewood had an average assessed property value per pupil of $5960. By taxing itself at about 1%—the highest rate in the metropolitan area—the district raised $26 for the education of each child, after paying its share to the statewide Foundation Program. State and federal support brought Edgewood per pupil ex-

penditures to $356. By contrast, the Alamo Heights district had a property tax base of more than $49,000 per pupil. By taxing itself at only .85%, it raised $333 per pupil over and above its contribution to the Foundation Program. State and federal support brought Alamo Heights spending to $594 per pupil.

2. Serrano v. Priest, 487 P.2d 1241, 5 Cal.3d 584 (1971); Van Dusartz v. Hatfield, 334 F.Supp. 870 (Minn.1971); Robinson v. Cahill, 118 N.J.Super. 223, 287 A.2d 187 (1972); Milliken v. Green, [Mich.S.Ct.1973]. [Footnote by Justice Powell.]

of individuals who constituted the class discriminated against in our prior cases shared two distinguishing characteristics: because of their impecunity they were completely unable to pay for some desired benefit, and as a consequence, they sustained an absolute deprivation of a meaningful opportunity to enjoy that benefit.[3] [Even] a cursory examination, however, demonstrates that neither of the two distinguishing characteristics of wealth classifications can be found here. First, [there] is reason to believe that the poorest families are not necessarily clustered in the poorest property districts. [A recent] Connecticut study found, not surprisingly, that the poor were clustered around commercial and industrial areas—those same areas that provide the most attractive sources of property tax income for school districts. [T]here is no basis on the record [for] assuming that the poorest people [are] concentrated in the poorest districts [in Texas]. [Second], lack of personal resources has not occasioned an absolute deprivation of the desired benefit. The argument here is not that the children [are] receiving no public education; rather, it is that they are receiving a poorer quality education [than] children in districts having more assessable wealth. Apart from the unsettled and disputed question whether the quality of education may be determined by the amount of money expended for it, a sufficient answer to appellees' argument is that, at least where wealth is involved, [equal protection] does not require absolute equality or precisely equal advantages. Nor, indeed, in view of the infinite variables affecting the educational process, can any system assure equal quality of education except in the most relative sense. [For] these two reasons—the absence of any evidence that the financing system discriminates against any definable category of "poor" people or that it results in the absolute deprivation of education—the disadvantaged class is not susceptible of identification in traditional terms.[4]

[This] brings us [to] the third way in which the classification scheme might be defined—*district* wealth discrimination. Since the only correlation indicated by the evidence is between district property wealth and expenditures, it may be argued that discrimination might be found without regard to the individual income characteristics of district residents. [However] described, it is clear that appellees' suit asks this Court to extend its most exacting scrutiny to review a system that allegedly discriminates against a large, diverse, and amorphous class, unified only by the common factor of residence in districts that happen to have less taxable wealth than other districts. The system of alleged discrimination and the class it defines have none of the traditional indicia of suspectness: the class is not saddled with such disabilities, or subjected to such a history of purposeful unequal treatment, or relegated to such a position of political powerlessness as to command extraordinary protection from the majoritarian political process. We thus conclude that the Texas system does not operate to the peculiar disadvantage of any suspect class. [Recognizing] that this Court has never heretofore held that wealth discrimination alone provides an adequate basis for invoking strict scrutiny, appellees [also] assert that the State's system impermissibly interferes with the exercise of a "fundamental" right [requiring] the strict standard of judicial [review].

B. In [Brown v. Board of Education], a unanimous Court recognized that "education is perhaps the most important function of state and local govern-

---

3. At this point, Justice Powell discussed Griffin v. Illinois, Douglas v. California, Williams v. Illinois, Tate v. Short and Bullock v. Carter, all noted below (mainly in sec. 4C).

4. [If] elementary and secondary education were made available by the State only to those able to pay a [tuition], there would be a clearly defined class of "poor" people—definable in terms of their inability to pay the prescribed sum—who would be absolutely precluded from receiving an education. That case would present a far more compelling set of circumstances for judicial assistance than the case before us today. [But] Texas [has] provided what it considers to be an adequate base education for all children [and no proof was offered at trial persuasively discrediting the State's assertion]. [Footnote by Justice Powell.]

ments." Nothing this Court holds today in any way detracts from our historic dedication to public education. [But] the importance of a service performed by the State does not determine whether it must be regarded as fundamental for purposes of examination under the Equal Protection Clause. [After discussing Shapiro v. Thompson, Lindsey v. Normet, and Dandridge v. Williams (and noting Jefferson v. Hackney and Richardson v. Belcher),[5] Justice Powell continued:] The lesson of these cases [is that it] is not the province of this Court to create substantive constitutional rights in the name of guaranteeing [equal protection]. Thus the key to discovering whether education is "fundamental" is not to be found in comparisons of the relative societal significance of education as opposed to subsistence or housing. Nor is it to be found by weighing whether education is as important as the right to travel. Rather, the answer lies in assessing whether there is a right to education explicitly or implicitly guaranteed by the Constitution. [Eisenstadt v. Baird; Dunn v. Blumstein;[6] Police Dept. of Chicago v. Mosley;[7] Skinner v. Oklahoma.[8]]

Education, of course, is not among the rights afforded explicit protection under our Federal Constitution. Nor do we find any basis for saying it is implicitly so protected. As we have said, the undisputed importance of education will not alone cause this Court to depart from the usual standard for reviewing a State's social and economic legislation. It is appellees' contention, however, that education is distinguishable from other services and benefits provided by the State because it bears a peculiarly close relationship to other rights and liberties accorded protection under the Constitution. Specifically, they insist that education is itself a fundamental personal right because it is essential to the effective exercise of First Amendment freedoms and to intelligent utilization of the right to vote. In asserting a nexus between speech and education, appellees urge that the right to speak is meaningless unless the speaker is capable of articulating his thoughts intelligently and persuasively. The "marketplace of ideas" is an empty forum for those lacking basic communicative tools. [A] similar line of reasoning is pursued with respect to the right to

5. All of these decisions are noted below, especially in sec. 4E, on modern welfare and other "necessities" cases. In the course of his review of the cases, Justice Powell recalled Justice Harlan's dissent in Shapiro v. Thompson, p. 832 below: "[I]f the degree of judicial scrutiny of state legislation fluctuated depending on a majority's view of the importance of the interest affected, we would have gone 'far toward making this Court a "superlegislature." ' " Justice Powell added: "We would, indeed, then be assuming a legislative role and one for which the Court lacks both authority and competence."

In discussing Shapiro, Justice Powell also commented that the "right to interstate travel had long been recognized as a right of constitutional significance, and the Court's decision, therefore, did not require an ad hoc determination as to the social or economic importance of that right." [Consider this explanation in examining the right to travel-migration cases in Sec. 4D.]

6. Dunn [p. 814 below] fully canvasses this Court's voting rights cases and explains that "this Court has made clear that a citizen has a *constitutionally protected right* to participate in elections on an equal basis with other citizens in the jurisdiction." [Emphasis supplied.] The constitutional underpinnings of the right to equal

treatment in the voting process can no longer be doubted even though, as the Court noted in [Harper], "the right to vote in state elections is nowhere expressly mentioned." [Footnote by Justice Powell.] [Consider this explanation in exploring the voting cases in sec. 4B below. Compare footnote 1 to Justice Stewart's concurrence, below; footnote 2 to Justice Marshall's dissent, below; and footnote 3 in Justice Brennan's opinion in Plyler v. Doe (p. 799 below).]

7. In Mosley [p. 1164 below], the Court struck down a Chicago antipicketing ordinance that exempted labor picketing from its prohibitions. The ordinance was held invalid under [equal protection] after subjecting it to careful scrutiny and finding that the ordinance was not narrowly drawn. The stricter standard of review was appropriately applied since the ordinance was one "affecting First Amendment interests." [Footnote by Justice Powell.]

8. Skinner [p. 503 above] applied the standard of close scrutiny to a state law permitting forced sterilization of "habitual criminals." Implicit in the Court's opinion is the recognition that the right of procreation is among the rights of personal privacy protected under the Constitution. See [Roe v. Wade]. [Footnote by Justice Powell.]

vote.[9] Exercise of the franchise, it is contended, cannot be divorced from the educational foundation of the voter. [We] need not dispute any of these propositions. [Yet] we have never presumed to possess either the ability or the authority to guarantee to the citizenry the most *effective* speech or the most *informed* electoral choice. That these may be desirable goals [is] not to be doubted. [But] they are not values to be implemented by judicial intrusion into otherwise legitimate state activities.

Even if it were conceded that some identifiable quantum of education is a constitutionally protected prerequisite to the meaningful exercise of either right, we have no indication that the [Texas] system fails to provide each child with an opportunity to acquire the basic minimal skills necessary. [Furthermore], the logical limitations on appellees' nexus theory are difficult to perceive. How, for instance, is education to be distinguished from the significant personal interests in the basics of decent food and shelter? Empirical examination might well buttress an assumption that the ill-fed, ill-clothed, and ill-housed are among the most ineffective participants in the political process and that they derive the least enjoyment from the benefits of the First Amendment. If so appellees' thesis would cast serious doubt on the authority of Dandrige v. Williams and Lindsey v. Normet [sec. 4E].

[The] present case, in another basic sense, is significantly different from any of the cases in which [we have] applied strict scrutiny [to] legislation touching upon constitutionally protected rights. Each of our prior cases involved legislation which "deprived," "infringed," or "interfered" with the free exercise of some such fundamental personal right or liberty. [See Skinner; Shapiro; Dunn.] A critical distinction between those cases and the one now before us lies in what Texas is endeavoring to do with respect to education. [Every] step leading to the establishment of the system Texas utilizes today [was] implemented in an effort to *extend* [public education]. Of course, every reform that benefits some more than others may be criticized for what it fails to accomplish. But we think it plain that [the] thrust of the Texas system is affirmative and reformatory and, therefore, should be scrutinized under judicial principles sensitive to the nature of the State's efforts and to the rights reserved to the States under the Constitution.

C. [We] need not rest our decision, however, solely on the inappropriateness of the strict scrutiny test. A century of Supreme Court adjudication under the Equal Protection Clause affirmatively supports the application of the traditional standard of review, which requires only that the State's system be shown to bear some rational relationship to legitimate state purposes. [We] have here nothing less than a direct attack on the way in which Texas has chosen to raise and disburse state and local tax revenues. [A]ppellees would have the Court intrude in an area in which it has traditionally deferred to state legislatures. This Court has often admonished against such interferences with the State's fiscal policies under [equal protection]. [Thus] we stand on familiar ground when we continue to acknowledge that the Justices of this Court lack both the expertise and the familiarity with local problems so necessary to the making of wise decisions with respect to the raising and disposition of public revenues. Yet we are urged to direct the States either to alter drastically the present system or to throw out the property tax altogether in favor of some other form of taxation. No scheme of taxation [has] yet been devised which is free of all discriminatory impact. In such a complex arena in which no perfect alternatives

9. Since the right to vote, per se, is not a constitutionally protected right, we assume that appellees' references to that right are simply shorthand references to the protected right, implicit in our constitutional system, to participate in state elections on an equal basis with other qualified voters whenever the State has adopted an elective process for determining who will represent any segment of the State's population. See n. [6] supra [and sec. 4B below]. [Footnote by Justice Powell.]

exist, the Court does well not to impose too rigorous a standard of scrutiny lest all local fiscal schemes become subjects of criticism under [equal protection]. In addition to matters of fiscal policy, this case also involves the most persistent and difficult questions of educational policy, another area in which this Court's lack of specialized knowledge and experience counsels against premature interference with the informed judgments made at the state and local levels. [Educational] experts are divided. Indeed, one of the hottest sources of controversy concerns the extent to which there is a demonstrable correlation between educational expenditures and the quality of education—an assumed correlation underlying virtually every legal conclusion drawn by the [District Court]. [The] foregoing considerations buttress our conclusion that Texas' system of public school finance is an inappropriate candidate for strict judicial scrutiny. These same considerations are relevant to the determination whether that system, with its conceded imperfections, nevertheless bears some rational relationships to a legitimate state [purpose].

III. [The] Texas system of school finance, [w]hile assuring a basic education for every child in the State, [encourages] a large measure of participation in and control of each district's schools at the local level. [Appellees] suggest that local control could be preserved and promoted under other financing systems that resulted in more equality in educational expenditures. While it is no doubt true that reliance on local property taxation for school revenues provides less freedom of choice with respect to expenditures for some districts than for others,[10] the existence of "some inequality" in the manner in which the State's rationale is achieved is not alone a sufficient basis for striking down the entire system. [Nor] must the financing system fail because, as appellees suggest, other methods of satisfying the State's interest, which occasion "less drastic" disparities in expenditures, might be conceived. Only where state action impinges on the exercise of fundamental constitutional rights or liberties must it be found to have chosen the least restrictive alternative. It is also well to remember that even those districts that have reduced ability to make free decisions with respect to how much they spend on education still retain under the present system a large measure of authority as to how available funds will be allocated. They further enjoy the power to make numerous other decisions with respect to the operation of the schools.[11] The people of Texas may be justified in believing [that] along with increased control of the purse strings at the State level will go increased control over local policies.

Appellees further urge that the Texas system is unconstitutionally arbitrary because it allows the availability of local taxable resources to turn on "happenstance." [But] any scheme of local taxation—indeed the very existence of identifiable local governmental units—requires the establishment of jurisdictional boundaries that are inevitably arbitrary. It is equally inevitable that some localities are going to be blessed with more taxable assets than others. Nor is local wealth a static quantity. [Moreover], if local taxation for local expenditure

---

10. [Justice White's dissent] suggests [that] the Texas system violates [equal protection] because the means it has selected to effectuate its interest in local autonomy fail to guarantee complete freedom of choice to every district. He places special emphasis on the statutory provision that establishes a maximum rate of $1.50 per $100 valuation at which a local school district may tax for school maintenance. The maintenance rate in Edgewood when this case was litigated in the District Court was $.55 per $100, barely one-third of the allowable rate. [Appellees] do not claim that the ceiling presently bars desired tax increases in Edgewood or in any other Texas district. Therefore, the constitutionality of that statutory provision is not [before us]. [Footnote by Justice Powell.]

11. [Justice Marshall's] assertion, that genuine local control does not exist in Texas, simply cannot be supported. [Although] policy decision-making and supervision in certain areas are reserved to the State, the day-to-day authority over the "management and control" of all public elementary and secondary schools is squarely placed on the local [school boards]. [Footnote by Justice Powell.]

is an unconstitutional method of providing for education, then it may be an equally impermissible means of providing other necessary services customarily financed largely from local property taxes, including local police and fire protection, public health and hospitals, and public utility facilities of various kinds. We perceive no justification for such a severe denigration of local property taxation and control as would follow from appellees' contentions. [In] sum, [we] cannot say that [the Texas interdistrict] disparities are the product of a system that is so irrational as to be invidiously discriminatory. [The equal protection standard] is whether the challenged state action rationally furthers a legitimate state purpose or interest. [We] hold that the Texas plan abundantly satisfies this standard.

IV. [A] cautionary postscript seems appropriate. [Affirmance here] would occasion in Texas and elsewhere an unprecedented upheaval in public education. [The] complexity of [the] problems is demonstrated by the lack of consensus with respect to whether it may be said with any assurance that the poor, the racial minorities, or the children in overburdened core-city school districts would be benefitted by abrogation of traditional modes of financing education. These practical considerations [serve] to highlight the wisdom of the traditional limitations on this Court's function. [We] hardly need add that this Court's action today is not to be viewed as placing its judicial imprimatur on the status quo. The need is apparent for reform in tax systems which may well have relied too long and too heavily on the local property tax. And certainly innovative new thinking as to public education, its methods and its funding, is necessary to assure both a higher level of quality and greater uniformity of opportunity. [But] the ultimate solutions must come from the lawmakers and from the democratic pressures of those who elect them.

Reversed.

Mr. Justice STEWART, concurring.

[I] join the opinion [because] I am convinced that any other course would mark an extraordinary departure from principled adjudication under [equal protection]. The uncharted directions of such a departure are suggested, I think, by [Justice Marshall's] imaginative [dissent]. Unlike other provisions of the Constitution, the Equal Protection Clause confers no substantive rights and creates no substantive liberties.[1] The function of [equal protection], rather, is simply to measure the validity of *classifications* created by state laws. [Quite] apart from [equal protection], a state law that impinges upon a substantive right or liberty created or conferred by the Constitution is, of course, presumptively invalid, whether or not the law's purpose or effect is to create any classifications. [Numerous] cases in this Court illustrate this principle.[2] In refusing to invalidate the Texas system of financing its public schools, the Court today applies with thoughtfulness and understanding the basic principles [of equal protection].

Mr. Justice WHITE, with whom Mr. Justice DOUGLAS and Mr. Justice BRENNAN join, [dissenting].

[T]his case would be quite different if it were true that the Texas system, while insuring minimum educational expenditures in every district through state funding, extended a meaningful option to all local districts to increase their per-pupil [expenditures]. But for districts with a low per-pupil real estate tax base,

1. There is one notable exception to the above statement: It has been established in recent years that [equal protection] confers the substantive right to participate on an equal basis with other qualified voters whenever the State has adopted an electoral process for determining who will represent any segment of the State's population. [But] there is no constitutional right to vote, as [such]. [Footnote by Justice Stewart.] [See sec. 4B below.]

2. See, [e.g.], Mosley v. Police Dept. of City of Chicago, 408 U.S. 92 (free speech); Shapiro v. Thompson, 394 U.S. 618 (freedom of interstate travel); Skinner v. Oklahoma, 316 U.S. 535 ("liberty" conditionally protected by [due process]). [Footnote by Justice Stewart.]

[the] Texas system utterly fails to extend a realistic choice to parents because the property tax, which is the only revenue-raising mechanism extended to school districts, is practically and legally unavailable. [Requiring] the State to establish only that unequal treatment is in furtherance of a permissible goal, without also requiring the State to show that the means chosen to effectuate that goal are rationally related to its achievement, makes equal protection analysis no more than an empty [gesture].[1]

Mr. Justice MARSHALL, with whom Mr. Justice DOUGLAS concurs, [dissenting].

[I] must once more voice my disagreement with the Court's rigidified approach to equal protection analysis. [The] Court apparently seeks to establish today that equal protection cases fall into one of two neat categories which dictate the appropriate standard of review—strict scrutiny or mere rationality. But this Court's [decisions] defy such easy categorization. A principled reading of what this Court has done reveals that it has applied a spectrum of standards in reviewing discrimination allegedly violative of [equal protection]. This spectrum clearly comprehends variations in the degree of care with which the Court will scrutinize particular classifications, depending, I believe, on the constitutional and societal importance of the interest adversely affected and the recognized invidiousness of the basis upon which the particular classification is drawn. [In fact], many of the Court's recent decisions embody the very sort of reasoned approach to [equal protection] for which I previously argued.[1] [I] therefore cannot accept the majority's labored efforts to demonstrate that fundamental interests, which call for [strict scrutiny], encompass only established rights which we are somehow bound to recognize from the text of the Constitution itself. To be sure, some interests which the Court has deemed to be fundamental for purposes of [equal protection] are themselves constitutionally protected rights. [E.g., Shapiro v. Thompson.] But it will not do to suggest that the "answer" to whether an interest is fundamental for purposes of equal protection analysis is *always* determined by whether that interest "is a [right] explicitly or implicitly guaranteed by the Constitution." I would like to know where the Constitution guarantees the right to procreate [Skinner v. Oklahoma], or the right to vote in state elections [e.g., Reynolds v. Sims (p. 1621 below)],[2] or the right to an appeal from a criminal conviction [e.g., Griffin v. Illinois].[3] These are instances in which, due to the importance of the interests at stake, the Court has displayed

1. [The State] insists that districts have a choice. [Like] the majority, however, the State fails to explain why [equal protection] is not violated [where] the system makes it much more difficult for some than for others to provide additional educational funds and where as a practical and legal matter it is impossible for some districts to provide the educational budgets that other districts can make available from real property tax revenues. [Footnote by Justice White. Earlier, Justice White had pointed out that, in order to equal the highest yield in any other school district, "Alamo Heights would be required to tax at the rate of 68¢ per $100 of assessed valuation. Edgewood would be required to tax at the prohibitive rate of $5.76 per $100. But state law places a $1.50 per $100 ceiling on the maintenance tax rate."]

1. Justice Marshall referred to his "sliding scale" dissent in Dandridge v. Williams (1970; sec. 4E, at p. 850 below).

2. It is interesting that in its effort to reconcile the state voting rights cases with its theory of fundamentality the majority can muster nothing

more than the contention that "[t]he constitutional underpinnings of the right to equal treatment in the voting *process* can no longer be doubted" (emphasis added). If, by this, the Court intends to recognize a substantive constitutional "right to equal treatment in the voting process" independent of the Equal Protection Clause, the source of such a right is certainly a mystery to me. [Footnote by Justice Marshall—later in the opinion.]

3. It is true that Griffin [also] involved discrimination against indigents, that is, wealth discrimination. But, as the majority points out, [the] Court has never deemed wealth discrimination alone to be sufficient to require strict judicial scrutiny; rather, such review of wealth classifications has been applied only where the discrimination affects an important individual interest, see, e.g., [Harper]. Thus, I believe Griffin [can] only be understood as premised on a recognition of the fundamental importance of the criminal appellate process. [Footnote by Justice Marshall—later in the opinion.]

a strong concern with the existence of discriminatory state treatment. But the Court has never said or indicated that these are interests which independently enjoy full-blown constitutional [protection].

The majority is, of course, correct when it suggests that the process of determining which interests are fundamental is a difficult one. But I do not think the problem is insurmountable. And I certainly do not accept the view that the process need necessarily degenerate into an unprincipled, subjective "picking-and-choosing" between various interests or that it must involve this Court in creating "substantive constitutional rights in the name of guaranteeing equal protection of the laws." Although not all fundamental interests are constitutionally guaranteed, the determination of which interests are fundamental should be firmly rooted in the text of the Constitution. The task in every case should be to determine the extent to which constitutionally guaranteed rights are dependent on interests not mentioned in the Constitution. As the nexus between the specific constitutional guarantee and the nonconstitutional interest draws closer, the nonconstitutional interest becomes more fundamental and the degree of judicial scrutiny applied when the interest is infringed on a discriminatory basis must be adjusted accordingly. Thus, it cannot be denied that interests such as procreation, the exercise of the state franchise, and access to criminal appellate processes are not fully guaranteed to the citizen by our Constitution. But these interests have nonetheless been afforded special judicial consideration in the face of discrimination because they are, to some extent, interrelated with constitutional guarantees. Procreation is now understood to be important because of its interaction with the established constitutional right of privacy. The exercise of the state franchise is closely tied to basic civil and political rights inherent in the First Amendment. And access to criminal appellate processes enhances the integrity of the range of rights implicit in the 14th Amendment guarantee of due process of law. Only if we closely protect the related interests from state discrimination do we ultimately ensure the integrity of the constitutional guarantee itself. This is the real lesson that must be taken from our previous decisions involving interests deemed to be fundamental.

The effect of the interaction of individual interests with established constitutional guarantees upon the degree of care exercised by this Court in reviewing state discrimination affecting such interests is amply illustrated [by Eisenstadt v. Baird (1972; p. 514 above)]. [Justice Marshall also discussed James v. Strange, 407 U.S. 128 (1972) (on state recoupment statutes; Justice Marshall stated that, though the Court purported to apply the traditional "some rationality" requirement, it scrutinized the law "with less than the traditional deference and restraint") and Reed v. Reed (p. 645 above) (Justice Marshall commented that the Court, despite its statement of the rationality standard, was "unwilling to consider a theoretical and unsubstantiated basis for distinction—however reasonable it might appear—sufficient to sustain a statute discriminating on the basis of sex").] James and Reed can only be understood as instances in which the particularly invidious character of the classification caused the Court to pause and scrutinize with more than traditional care the rationality of state discrimination. Discrimination on the basis of past criminality and on the basis of sex posed for the Court the spectre of forms of discrimination which it implicitly recognized to have deep social and legal roots without necessarily having any basis in actual differences. Still, the Court's sensitivity to the invidiousness of the basis for discrimination is perhaps most apparent in its decisions protecting the interests of [illegitimate children]. See [Levy and Weber, p. 679 above].

In summary, it seems to me inescapably clear that this Court has consistently adjusted the care with which it will review state discrimination in light of the constitutional significance of the interests affected and the invidiousness of the particular classification. [The] majority suggests, however, that a variable standard of review would give this Court the appearance of a "super-legislature." I cannot agree. Such an approach seems to me a part of the guarantees of our Constitution and of the historic experiences with oppression of and discrimination against discrete, powerless minorities which underlie that document. In truth, the Court itself will be open to the criticism raised by the majority so long as it continues on its present course of effectively selecting in private which cases will be afforded special consideration without acknowledging the true basis of its action.[4] Opinions such as those in Reed and James seem drawn more as efforts to shield rather than to reveal the true basis of the Court's decisions. Such obfuscated action may be appropriate to a political body such as a legislature, but it is not appropriate to this Court. [It] is true that this Court has never deemed the provision of free public education to be required by the Constitution. Nevertheless, the fundamental importance of education is amply indicated by the prior decisions of this Court, by the unique status accorded public education by our society, and by the close relationship between education and some of our most basic constitutional values. [Education] directly affects the ability of a child to exercise his First Amendment [interests]. [Of] particular importance is the relationship between education and the political process and the demonstrated effect of education on the exercise of the franchise by the electorate. [It] is this very sort of intimate relationship between a particular personal interest and specific constitutional guarantees that has heretofore caused the Court to attach special significance, for purposes of equal protection analysis, to individual interests such as procreation and the exercise of the state franchise.[5] [These factors] compel us to recognize the fundamentality of education and to scrutinize with appropriate care the bases for state discrimination affecting equality of educational opportunity in Texas school districts—a conclusion which is only strengthened when we consider the character of the classification in this [case].

[We] are told that in every prior case involving a wealth classification, the members of the disadvantaged class have "shared two distinguishing characteristics: because of their impecunity they were completely unable to pay for some desired benefit, and as a consequence, they sustained an absolute deprivation of a meaningful opportunity to enjoy that benefit." I cannot agree. [Harper, Griffin and Douglas] refute the majority's contention that we have in the past required an absolute deprivation before subjecting wealth classifications to strict scrutiny. [This] is not to say that the form of wealth classification in this case does not differ significantly from those recognized [in previous decisions]. Here, the children [are] being discriminated against not necessarily because of their personal wealth or the wealth of their families, but because of the taxable property wealth of the residents of the district in which they happen to live. The appropriate question, then, is whether the same degree of judicial [scrutiny]

---

4. See generally Gunther, ["Newer Equal Protection"]. [Footnote by Justice Marshall. See also his footnote [6] below.]

5. I believe that the close nexus between education and our established constitutional values with respect to freedom of speech and participation in the political process makes this a different case than our prior decisions concerning discrimination affecting public welfare, see, e.g., [Dandridge v. Williams], or housing, see, e.g., [Lindsey v. Normet]. [See sec. 4E below.] There can be no question that, as the majority suggests, constitutional rights may be less meaningful for someone without enough to eat or without decent housing. But the crucial difference lies in the closeness of the relationship.

Whatever the severity of the impact of insufficient food or inadequate housing on a person's life, they have never been considered to bear the same direct and immediate relationship to constitutional concerns for free speech and for our political processes as education has long been recognized to bear. Perhaps the best evidence of this fact is the unique status which has been accorded public education as the single public service nearly unanimously guaranteed in the constitutions of our States. Education, in terms of constitutional values, is much more analogous, in my judgment, to the right to vote in state elections than to public welfare or [public housing]. [Footnote by Justice Marshall.]

that has previously been afforded wealth classifications is warranted here. [That] wealth classifications alone have not necessarily been considered to bear the same high degree of suspectness as have classifications based on, for instance, race or alienage may be explainable on a number of grounds. The "poor" may not be seen as politically powerless as certain discrete and insular minority groups. Personal poverty may entail much the same social stigma as historically attached to certain racial or ethnic groups [but it] is not a permanent disability; its shackles may be escaped. Perhaps, most importantly, though, personal wealth may not necessarily share the general irrelevance as a basis for legislative action that race or nationality is recognized to have. While the "poor" have frequently been a legally disadvantaged group, it cannot be ignored that social legislation must frequently take cognizance of the economic status of our citizens. Thus, we have generally gauged the invidiousness of wealth classifications with an awareness of the importance of the interests being affected and the relevance of personal wealth to those interests. [See Harper, p. 808 below.]

When evaluated with these considerations in mind, it seems to me that discrimination on the basis of group wealth in this case likewise calls for careful judicial scrutiny. First, [local district wealth] bears no relationship whatsoever to the interest of Texas school children in the educational opportunity afforded them [by] Texas. Given the importance of that interest, we must be particularly sensitive to the invidious characteristics of any form of discrimination that is not clearly intended to serve it, as opposed to some other distinct state interest. Discrimination on the basis of group wealth may not, to be sure, reflect the social stigma frequently attached to personal poverty. Nevertheless, insofar as group wealth discrimination involves wealth over which the disadvantaged individual has no significant control, it represents in fact a more serious basis of discrimination than does personal wealth. For such discrimination is no reflection of the individual's characteristics or his abilities. And thus—particularly in the context of a disadvantaged class composed of children—we have previously treated discrimination on a basis which the individual cannot control as constitutionally disfavored. Cf. [Weber; Levy, sec. 3C2 above]. The disability of the disadvantaged class in this case extends as well into the political processes upon which we ordinarily rely as adequate for the protection and promotion of all interests. [Moreover, prior] cases have dealt with discrimination on the basis of indigency which was attributable to the operation of the private sector. But we have no such simple de facto wealth discrimination here. The means for financing public education in Texas are [specified] by the State. [At] the same time, governmentally imposed land use controls have undoubtedly encouraged and rigidified natural trends in the allocation of particular areas for residential or commercial use, and thus determined each district's amount of taxable property wealth. In short, this case, in contrast to the Court's previous wealth discrimination decisions, can only be seen as "unusual in the extent to which governmental action *is* the cause of the wealth classifications."

[Here], both the nature of the interest and the classification dictate close judicial scrutiny of the purposes which Texas seeks to serve with its present educational financing scheme and of the means it has selected to serve that purpose. [I] need not now decide how I might ultimately strike the balance were we confronted with a situation where the State's sincere concern for local control inevitably produced educational inequality. For on this record, it is apparent that the State's purported concern with local control is offered primarily as an excuse rather than as a justification for interdistrict inequality. [School districts] cannot choose to have the best education in the State by imposing the highest tax rate. Instead, the quality of the educational opportunity offered by any particular district is largely determined by the amount of taxable property located in the district—a factor over which local voters can exercise no [control]. In my judgment, any substantial degree of scrutiny [reveals] that the State has selected means wholly inappropriate to secure its purported interest in assuring its school districts local fiscal control.[6] At the same time, appellees have pointed out a variety of alternative financing schemes which may serve the State's purported interest in local control as well as, if not better than, the present scheme without the current impairment of the educational opportunity of vast numbers of Texas school children.[7] I see no need, however, to explore the practical or constitutional merits of those suggested alternatives at this time for, whatever their positive or negative features, experience with the present financing scheme impugns any suggestion that it constitutes a serious effort to provide local fiscal [control].[8]

PLYLER v. DOE

457 U.S. 202, 102 S.Ct. 2382, 72 L.Ed.2d 786 (1982).[1]

Justice BRENNAN delivered the opinion of the Court.

The question presented by these cases is whether, consistent with [equal protection], Texas may deny to undocumented school-age children the free public education that it provides to children who are citizens of the United States or legally admitted aliens.

6. [Although] my Brother White purports to reach this result by application of that lenient standard of mere rationality traditionally applied in the context of commercial interests, it seems to me that the care with which he scrutinizes the practical effectiveness of the present local property tax as a device for affording local fiscal control reflects the application of a more stringent standard of review, a standard which at the least is influenced by the constitutional significance of the process of public education. [Footnote by Justice Marshall.]

7. Centralized educational financing [is] one alternative. [A] second possibility is the much discussed theory of district power equalization put forth by Professors Coons, Clune, and Sugarman in their seminal work, Private Wealth and Public Education 201–242 (1970). [Under] their system, each school district would receive a fixed amount of revenue per pupil for any particular level of tax effort regardless of the level of local property tax [base]. District wealth reapportionment is yet another alternative which would accomplish directly essentially what district power equalization would seek to do [artificially]. A fourth possibility would be to remove commercial, industrial, and mineral property from local tax rolls, to tax this property on a state-wide basis, and to return the resulting revenues to the local districts in a fashion that would compensate for remaining variations in the local tax bases. None of these particular alternatives [is] necessarily constitutionally compelled; rather, they indicate the breadth of choice which remains to the State if the present interdistrict disparities were eliminated. [Footnote by Justice Marshall—elsewhere in the opinion.]

8. In a brief dissent, Justice BRENNAN agreed with Justice White's view that the Texas scheme "is devoid of any rational basis" and stated his disagreement with "the Court's rather distressing assertion that a right may be deemed 'fundamental' for the purposes of equal protection analysis only if it is 'explicitly or implicitly guaranteed by the Constitution.' As my Brother Marshall convincingly demonstrates, our prior cases stand for the proposition that 'fundamentality' is, in large measure, a function of the right's importance in terms of the effectuation of those rights which are in fact constitutionally guaranteed."

Contrast Justice White's approach in this case with his occasional later statements that Justice Marshall's "sliding scale" analysis accurately reflected the Court's decisionmaking in the equal protection area. See, e.g., his concurrence in Vlandis v. Kline, 412 U.S. 441 (1973), commenting that "it is clear that we employ not just one, or two, but, as my Brother Marshall has so ably demonstrated, a 'spectrum of standards.'"

1. Plyler v. Doe was a class action on behalf of certain school-age children of Mexican origin residing in Smith County, Texas, who could not establish that they had been legally admitted into the United States. The suit attacked the exclusion of the children from the public schools of the Tyler Independent School District. Since 1977, the District had required "undocumented" children to pay a "full tuition fee" in order to enroll. The lower federal courts held that the exclusion of the children from free public education violated equal protection.

A companion case, Texas v. Certain [Undocumented] Alien Children, was a consolidated action against state and local officials. There, too, the District Court and the Court of Appeals found an equal protection violation. The Court of Appeals rejected claims that Texas law was preempted by federal law and policy. The Supreme Court did not reach the preemption argument.

I. Since the late nineteenth century, the United States has restricted immigration into this country. Unsanctioned entry into the United States is a crime, and those who have entered unlawfully are subject to deportation. But despite the existence of these legal restrictions, a substantial number of persons have succeeded in unlawfully entering the United States, and now live within various States, including [Texas]. In May 1975, the Texas legislature revised its education laws to withhold from local school districts any state funds for the education of children who were not "legally admitted" into the United States. The 1975 revision also authorized local school districts to deny enrollment in their public schools to children not "legally admitted" to the [country].

II. The 14th Amendment provides that "No State [shall] deprive any person of life, liberty, or property, without due process of law; nor deny to *any person within its jurisdiction* the equal protection of the laws." Appellants argue at the outset that undocumented aliens, because of their immigration status, are not "persons within the jurisdiction" of [Texas], and that they therefore have no right to the equal protection of Texas law. We reject this argument. [Justice Brennan's reasons for rejecting this argument are omitted.] Our conclusion that the illegal aliens who are plaintiffs in these cases may claim the benefit of the 14th Amendment's guarantee of equal protection only begins the inquiry. The more difficult question is whether [equal protection] has been violated [here].

III. [In] applying [equal protection] to most forms of state action, [we] seek only the assurance that the classification at issue bears some fair relationship to a legitimate public purpose. But we would not be faithful to our obligations [if] we applied so deferential a standard to every classification. [Equal protection] was intended as a restriction on state legislative action inconsistent with elemental constitutional premises. Thus we have treated as presumptively invidious those classifications that disadvantage a "suspect class," [2] or that impinge upon the exercise of a "fundamental right." [3] With respect to such classifications, it is appropriate to enforce the mandate of equal protection by requiring the State to demonstrate that its classification has been precisely tailored to serve a compelling governmental interest. In addition, we have recognized that certain forms of legislative classification, while not facially invidious, nonetheless give rise to recurring constitutional difficulties; in these limited circumstances we have sought the assurance that the classification reflects a reasoned judgment consistent with the ideal of equal protection by inquiring whether it may fairly be viewed as furthering a substantial interest of the State. [4]

2. Several formulations might explain our treatment of certain classifications as "suspect." Some classifications are more likely than others to reflect deep-seated prejudice rather than legislative rationality in pursuit of some legitimate objective. Legislation predicated on such prejudice is easily recognized as incompatible with the constitutional understanding that each person is to be judged individually and is entitled to equal justice under the law. Classifications treated as suspect tend to be irrelevant to any proper legislative goal. Finally, certain groups, indeed largely the same groups, have historically been "relegated to such a position of political powerlessness as to command extraordinary protection from the majoritarian political process." [Carolene Products.] [Legislation] imposing special disabilities upon groups disfavored by virtue of circumstances beyond their control suggests the kind of "class or caste" treatment that the 14th Amendment was designed to abolish. [Footnote by Justice Brennan.]

3. In determining whether a class-based denial of a particular right is deserving of strict scrutiny under [equal protection], we look to the Constitution to see if the right infringed has its source, explicitly or implicitly, therein. But we have also recognized the fundamentality of participation in state "elections on an equal basis with other citizens in the jurisdiction" even though "the right to vote, per se, is not a constitutionally protected right." With respect to suffrage, we have explained the need for strict scrutiny as arising from the significance of the franchise as the guardian of all other rights. [Footnote by Justice Brennan.]

4. See Craig v. Boren; Lalli v. Lalli. This technique of "intermediate" scrutiny permits us to evaluate the rationality of the legislative judgment with reference to well-settled constitutional principles. [Only] when concerns sufficiently absolute and enduring can be clearly ascertained from the Constitution and our cases do we employ this standard to aid us in determining the

We turn to a consideration of the standard appropriate for the evaluation of [the Texas law].

A. Sheer incapability or lax enforcement of the laws barring entry into this country, coupled with the failure to establish an effective bar to the employment of undocumented aliens, has resulted in the creation of a substantial "shadow population" of illegal migrants—numbering in the millions—within our borders. This situation raises the specter of a permanent caste of undocumented resident aliens, encouraged by some to remain here as a source of cheap labor, but nevertheless denied the benefits that our society makes available to citizens and lawful residents. The existence of such an underclass presents most difficult problems for a Nation that prides itself in adherence to principles of equality under law.[5] The children who are plaintiffs in these cases are special members of this underclass. Persuasive arguments support the view that a State may withhold its beneficence from those whose very presence within the United States is the product of their own unlawful conduct. These arguments do not apply with the same force to classifications imposing disabilities on the minor *children* of such illegal entrants. [Their] "parents have the ability to conform their conduct to societal norms," and presumably the ability to remove themselves from the State's jurisdiction; but the children who are plaintiffs in these cases "can affect neither their parents' conduct nor their own status." Trimble v. Gordon. Even if the State found it expedient to control the conduct of adults by acting against their children, legislation directing the onus of a parent's misconduct against his children does not comport with fundamental conceptions of justice. [Weber.][6] Of course, undocumented status is not irrelevant to any proper legislative goal. Nor is undocumented status an absolutely immutable characteristic since it is the product of conscious, indeed unlawful, action. But [the Texas law] is directed against children, and imposes its discriminatory burden on the basis of a legal characteristic over which children can have little control. It is thus difficult to conceive of a rational justification for penalizing these children for their presence within the United States. Yet that appears to be precisely the effect of [the law].

Public education is not a "right" granted to individuals by the Constitution. [Rodriguez.] But neither is it merely some governmental "benefit" indistinguishable from other forms of social welfare legislation. Both the importance of education in maintaining our basic institutions, and the lasting impact of its deprivation on the life of the child, mark the distinction. [In] addition, education provides the basic tools by which individuals might lead economically productive lives to the benefit of us all. In sum, education has a fundamental role in maintaining the fabric of our society. We cannot ignore the significant social costs borne by our Nation when select groups are denied the means to absorb the values and skills upon which our social order rests. In addition to the pivotal role of education in sustaining our political and cultural heritage, denial of education to some isolated group of children poses an affront to one of the goals of [equal protection]: the abolition of governmental barriers presenting unreasonable obstacles to advancement on the basis of individual merit. Paradoxically, by depriving the children of any disfavored group of an education, we foreclose the means by which that group might raise the level of esteem in which it is held by the majority. But more directly, "education prepares

rationality of the legislative choice. [Footnote by Justice Brennan.]

5. We reject the claim that "illegal aliens" are a "suspect class." No case in which we have attempted to define a suspect class has addressed the status of persons unlawfully in our country. Unlike most of the classifications that we have recognized as suspect, entry into this class, by virtue of entry into this country, is the product of voluntary action. Indeed, entry into the class is itself a crime. In addition, it could hardly be suggested that undocumented status is a ["constitutional irrelevancy"]. [Footnote by Justice Brennan.]

6. Trimble and Weber are illegitimacy cases, in sec. 3C2 above.

individuals to be self-reliant and self-sufficient participants in society." [Yoder, p. 1521 below.] Illiteracy is an enduring disability. The inability to read and write will handicap the individual deprived of a basic education each and every day of his life. The inestimable toll of that deprivation on the social, economic, intellectual and psychological well-being of the individual, and the obstacle it poses to individual achievement, makes it most difficult to reconcile the cost or the principle of a status-based denial of basic education with the framework of equality embodied in [equal protection].[7] What we said 28 years ago in [Brown] still holds true: "Today, education is perhaps the most important function of state and local [governments]."

B. These well-settled principles allow us to determine the proper level of deference to be afforded [here]. Undocumented aliens cannot be treated as a suspect class because their presence in this country in violation of federal law is not a "constitutional irrelevancy." Nor is education a fundamental [right]. But more is involved in this case than the abstract question whether [this law] discriminates against a suspect class, or whether education is a fundamental right. [This law] imposes a lifetime hardship on a discrete class of children not accountable for their disabling status. The stigma of illiteracy will mark them for the rest of their lives. By denying these children a basic education, we deny them the ability to live within the structure of our civic institutions, and foreclose any realistic possibility that they will contribute in even the smallest way to the progress of our Nation. In determining the rationality of [this law], we may appropriately take into account its costs to the Nation and to the innocent children who are its victims. In light of these countervailing costs, the discrimination contained in [this law] can hardly be considered rational unless it furthers some substantial goal of the State.

IV. It is the State's principal argument, and apparently the view of the dissenting Justices, that the undocumented status of these children *vel non* establishes a sufficient rational basis for denying them benefits that a State might choose to afford other residents. The State notes that while other aliens are admitted "on an equality of legal privileges with all citizens under non-discriminatory laws" [Takahashi], the asserted right of these children to an education can claim no implicit congressional imprimatur.[8] Indeed, on the State's view, Congress' apparent disapproval of the presence of these children [provides] authority for its decision to impose upon them special disabilities. Faced with an equal protection challenge respecting the treatment of aliens, we agree that the courts must be attentive to congressional [policy]. But we are unable to find in the congressional immigration scheme any statement of policy that might weigh significantly in arriving at an equal protection balance concern-

---

7. Because the State does not afford noncitizens the right to vote, and may bar noncitizens from participating in activities at the heart of its political community, appellants argue that denial of a basic education to these children is of less significance than the denial to some other group. Whatever the current status of these children, the courts below concluded that many will remain here permanently and that some indeterminate number will eventually become citizens. The fact that many will not is not decisive, even with respect to the importance of education to participation in core political institutions. [In] addition, although a noncitizen "may be barred from full involvement in the political arena, he may play a role—perhaps even a leadership role—in other areas of import to the community." Moreover, the significance of education to our society is not limited to its political and cultural fruits.

The public schools are an important socializing institution, imparting those shared values through which social order and stability are maintained. [Footnote by Justice Brennan.]

8. If the constitutional guarantee of equal protection was available only to those upon whom Congress affirmatively granted its benefit, the State's argument would be virtually unanswerable. But [equal protection] operates of its own force to protect anyone [from] the State's arbitrary action. The question we examine in text is whether the federal *disapproval* of the presence of these children assists the State in overcoming the presumption that denial of education to innocent children is not a rational response to legitimate state concerns. [Footnote by Justice Brennan.]

ing the State's authority to deprive these children of an education. [Congress] has developed a complex scheme governing admission to and status within our borders. The obvious need for delicate policy judgments has counselled the Judicial Branch to avoid intrusion into this field. But this traditional caution does not persuade us that unusual deference must be shown the classification embodied [in the Texas law]. The States enjoy no power with respect to the classification of aliens. [Unlike] De Canas v. Bica, [there] is no indication that the disability imposed by [Texas] corresponds to any identifiable congressional policy. [To] be sure, [these] children are subject to deportation. But there is no assurance that a child subject to deportation will ever be deported. [We] are reluctant to impute to Congress the intention to withhold from these children, for so long as they are present in this country through no fault of their own, access to a basic education. In other contexts, undocumented status, coupled with some articulable federal policy, might enhance State authority with respect to the treatment of undocumented aliens. But in the area of special constitutional sensitivity presented by this case, and in the absence of any contrary indication fairly discernible in the present legislative record, we perceive no national policy that supports the State in denying these children an elementary education. The State may borrow the federal classification. But to justify its use as a criterion for its own discriminatory policy, the State must demonstrate that the classification is reasonably adapted to *"the purposes for which the state desires to use it."* Oyama v. California, 332 U.S. 633, 664 (1948) (emphasis added). We therefore turn to the state objectives that are said to support [the Texas law].

　　　V. Appellants argue that the classification at issue furthers an interest in the "preservation of the state's limited resources for the education of its lawful residents." [Apart] from the asserted state prerogative to act against undocumented children solely on the basis of their undocumented status—an asserted prerogative that carries only minimal force in the circumstances of this case—we discern three colorable state interests that might support [this law]. First, appellants appear to suggest that the State may seek to protect [itself] from an influx of illegal immigrants. While a State might have an interest in mitigating the potentially harsh economic effects of sudden shifts in population,[9] [this law] hardly offers an effective method of dealing with an urgent demographic or economic problem. There is no evidence in the record suggesting that illegal entrants impose any significant burden on the State's economy. To the contrary, the available evidence suggests that illegal aliens underutilize public services, while contributing their labor to the local economy and tax money to the State fisc. The dominant incentive for illegal entry into [Texas] is the availability of employment; few if any illegal immigrants come [in] order to avail themselves of a free education. [Thus], we think it clear that "[c]harging tuition to undocumented children constitutes a ludicrously ineffectual attempt to stem the tide of illegal immigration," at least when compared with the alternative of prohibiting the employment of illegal aliens.

　　　Second, [appellants] suggest that undocumented children are appropriately singled out for exclusion because of the special burdens they impose on the State's ability to provide high quality public education. But the record in no way supports the claim that exclusion of undocumented children is likely to improve the overall quality of education in the State. [Of course], even if improvement in the quality of education were a likely result of barring some *number* of children from the schools of the State, the State must support its selection of *this* group as the appropriate target for exclusion. In terms of

---

9. [Despite] the exclusive federal control of this Nation's borders, we cannot conclude that the States are without any power to deter the influx of persons entering the United States against Federal law, and whose numbers might have a discernible impact on traditional state concerns. [Footnote by Justice Brennan.]

educational cost and need, however, undocumented children are "basically indistinguishable" from legally resident alien children. Finally, appellants suggest that undocumented children are appropriately singled out because their unlawful presence within the United States renders them less likely than other children to remain within the boundaries of the State, and to put their education to productive social or political use within the State. Even assuming that such an interest is legitimate, it is an interest that is most difficult to quantify. The State has no assurance that any child, citizen or not, will employ the education provided by the State within the confines of the State's borders. In any event, the record is clear that many of the undocumented children disabled by this classification will remain in this country indefinitely, and that some will become lawful residents or citizens of the United States. It is difficult to understand precisely what the State hopes to achieve by promoting the creation and perpetuation of a subclass of illiterates within our boundaries, surely adding to the problems and costs of unemployment, welfare, and crime. It is thus clear that whatever savings might be achieved by denying these children an education, they are wholly insubstantial in light of the costs involved to these children, the State, and the Nation.

VI. If the State is to deny a discrete group of innocent children the free public education that it offers to other children residing within its borders, that denial must be justified by a showing that it furthers some substantial state interest. No such showing was made here.

[Affirmed.] [10]

Justice BLACKMUN, concurring.

I join the opinion and judgment of the Court. Like Justice Powell, I believe that the children involved in this litigation "should not be left on the streets uneducated." I write separately, however, because in my view the nature of the interest at stake is crucial to the proper resolution of this case. [I] joined Justice Powell's opinion [in] Rodriguez, and I continue to believe that it provides the appropriate model for resolving most equal protection disputes. Classifications infringing substantive constitutional rights necessarily will be invalid, if not by force of [equal protection], then through operation of other provisions of the Constitution. Conversely, classifications bearing on nonconstitutional interests—even those involving "the most basic economic needs of impoverished human beings," Dandridge v. Williams—generally are not subject to special treatment under [equal protection], because they are not distinguishable in any relevant way from other regulations in "the area of economics and social welfare."

With all this said, however, I believe the Court's experience has demonstrated that the Rodriguez formulation does not settle every issue of "fundamental rights" arising under the Equal Protection Clause. Only a pedant would insist that there are no meaningful distinctions among the multitude of social and political interests regulated by the States, and Rodriguez does not stand for quite so absolute a proposition. To the contrary, Rodriguez implicitly acknowledged that certain interests, though not constitutionally guaranteed, must be accorded a special place in equal protection analysis. Thus, the Court's decisions long have accorded strict scrutiny to classifications bearing on the right to

---

10. In a separate notation, Justice MARSHALL stated that he joined the Court's opinion "without in any way retreating from my opinion in [Rodriguez]." He reiterated his belief stated there that the interest in education is "fundamental." He added that the facts here once again demonstrated "the wisdom of rejecting a rigidified approach to equal protection analysis." As in Rodriguez, he advocated "varying levels of scrutiny" on the basis of a sliding scale, multifactor analysis.

Does the Plyler result represent the strongest vindication yet of Justice Marshall's long-maintained position? (Recall that a number of lower courts, in finding mental illness and mental retardation suspect classifications, relied heavily on Plyler. See p. 685 above.)

vote in state elections. [The] right to vote is accorded extraordinary treatment because it is, in equal protection terms, an extraordinary right: a citizen cannot hope to achieve any meaningful degree of individual political equality if granted an inferior right of participation in the political process. Those denied the vote are relegated, by state fiat, in a most basic way to second-class status. It is arguable, of course, that the Court never should have applied fundamental rights doctrine in the fashion outlined above. [But] it is too late to debate that point, and I believe that accepting the principle of the voting cases—the idea that state classifications bearing on certain interests pose the risk of allocating rights in a fashion inherently contrary to any notion of "equality"—dictates the outcome [here].

In my view, when the State provides an education to some and denies it to others, it immediately and inevitably creates class distinctions of a type fundamentally inconsistent with [equal protection]. Children denied an education are placed at a permanent and insurmountable competitive disadvantage, for an uneducated child is denied even the opportunity to achieve. And when those children are members of an identifiable group, that group—through the State's action—will have been converted into a discrete underclass. Other benefits provided by the State, such as housing and public assistance, are of course [important]. But classifications involving the complete denial of education are in a sense unique, for they strike at the heart of equal protection values by involving the State in the creation of permanent class distinctions. Cf. Rodriguez (Marshall, J., dissenting). In a sense, then, denial of an education is the analogue of denial of the right to vote: the former relegates the individual to second-class social status; the latter places him at a permanent political disadvantage. This conclusion is fully consistent with Rodriguez. The Court there reserved judgment on the constitutionality of a state system that "occasioned an absolute denial of educational opportunities to any of its children." [It] is undeniable that education is not a "fundamental right" in the sense that it is constitutionally guaranteed. Here, however, the State has undertaken to provide an education to most of the children residing within its borders. And, in contrast to the situation in Rodriguez, it does not take an advanced degree to predict the effects of a complete denial of education upon those children targeted by the State's classification. In such circumstances, the voting decisions suggest that the State must offer something more than a rational basis for its classification.[1] [The] statute at issue here sweeps within it a substantial number of children who will in fact, and who may well be entitled to, remain in the United States. Given the extraordinary nature of the interest involved, this makes the classification here fatally imprecise. And, as the Court demonstrates, the Texas legislation is not otherwise supported by any substantial [interests].

Justice POWELL, concurring.

I join the opinion of the Court, and write separately to emphasize the unique character of the case before us. The classification in question severely disadvantages children who are the victims of a combination of circumstances. [Illegal] aliens are attracted by our employment opportunities, and perhaps by other benefits as well. [Congress] has not provided effective leadership in dealing with this problem. It therefore is certain that illegal aliens will continue to enter the United States [and] an unknown percentage of them will remain here. I agree with the Court that their children should not be left on the streets uneducated. Although the analogy is not perfect, our holding today does find support in decisions of this Court with respect to the status of illegitimates.

1. The Court concludes that [the law] must be invalidated "unless it furthers some substantial goal of the State." Since the statute fails to survive this level of scrutiny, as the Court demonstrates, there is no need to determine whether a more probing level of review would be appropriate. [Footnote by Justice Blackmun.]

[See Weber.] [In] this case, [Texas] effectively denies to the school age children of illegal aliens the opportunity to attend the free public schools that the State makes available to all residents. They are excluded only because of a status resulting from the violation by parents or guardians of our immigration laws and the fact that they remain in our country unlawfully. The respondent children are innocent in this respect. They can "affect neither their parents' conduct nor their own status." Trimble v. Gordon.

Our review in a case such as this is properly heightened. Cf. Craig v. Boren. [These] children [have] been singled out for a lifelong penalty and stigma. A legislative classification that threatens the creation of an underclass of future citizens and residents cannot be reconciled with one of the fundamental purposes of the 14th Amendment. In these unique circumstances, the Court properly may require that the State's interests be substantial and that the means bear a "fair and substantial relation" to these interests.[1] [The] State's denial of education to these children bears no substantial relation to any substantial state interest. [The] exclusion of [these] children from state-provided education is a type of punitive discrimination based on status that is impermissible under [equal protection]. I am not unmindful of what must be the exasperation of responsible citizens and government authorities in Texas and other states similarly situated. [But] it hardly can be argued rationally that anyone benefits from the creation within our borders of a subclass of illiterate persons many of whom will remain in the State, adding to the problems and costs of both State and National Governments attendant upon unemployment, welfare and crime.

Chief Justice BURGER, with whom Justice WHITE, Justice REHNQUIST, and Justice O'CONNOR join, dissenting.

Were it our business to set the Nation's social policy, I would agree without hesitation that it is senseless for an enlightened society to deprive any children— including illegal aliens—of an elementary education. I fully agree that it would be folly—and wrong—to tolerate creation of a segment of society made up of illiterate persons, many having a limited or no command of our language. However, [we] trespass on the assigned function of the political branches [when] we assume a policymaking role as the Court does today. [The] holding today manifests the justly criticized judicial tendency to attempt speedy and wholesale formulation of "remedies" for the failures—or simply the laggard pace—of the political [processes]. The Court [abuses] the 14th Amendment in an effort to become an omnipotent and omniscient [problem solver].

[The] dispositive issue [is] whether, for purposes of allocating its finite resources, a State has a legitimate reason to differentiate between persons who are lawfully within the State and those who are unlawfully there. The distinction [Texas] has drawn—based not only upon its own legitimate interests but on classifications established by the federal [government]—is not unconstitutional. [The] Court [correctly] rejects any suggestion that illegal aliens are a suspect class or that education is a fundamental right. Yet by patching together bits and pieces of what might be termed quasi-suspect-class and quasi-fundamental-rights analysis, the Court spins out a theory custom-tailored to the facts of these cases. In the end, we are told little more than that the level of scrutiny employed to strike down the Texas law applies only when illegal alien children are deprived

---

1. The Chief Justice argues in his dissenting opinion that this heightened standard of review is inconsistent with the Court's decision in [Rodriguez]. But in Rodriguez no group of children was singled out by the State and then penalized because of their parent's status. Rather, funding for education varied across the State because of the tradition of local control. Nor, in that case, was any group of children totally deprived of all education as in this case. If the resident children of illegal aliens were denied welfare assistance, made available by government to all other children who qualify, this also—in my opinion— would be an impermissible penalizing of children because of their parents' status. [Footnote by Justice Powell.]

of a public education. If ever a court was guilty of an unabashedly result-oriented approach, this case is a prime example.

[Equal protection is] not an all-encompassing "equalizer" designed to eradicate every distinction for which persons are not "responsible." The Court does not [suggest] that appellees' purported lack of culpability for their illegal status prevents them from being deported or otherwise "penalized" under federal law. Yet would deportation be any less a "penalty" than denial of privileges provided to legal residents? The Court's analogy to cases involving discrimination against illegitimate children [is] grossly misleading. The State has not thrust any disabilities upon appellees due to their "status of birth." Rather, appellees' status is predicated upon the circumstances of their concededly illegal presence in this country, and is a direct result of Congress' obviously valid exercise of its "broad constitutional powers" in the field of [immigration].

The second strand of the Court's analysis rests on the premise that, although public education is not a constitutionally-guaranteed right, "neither is it merely some governmental 'benefit' indistinguishable from other forms of social welfare legislation." Whatever meaning or relevance this opaque observation might have in some other context, it simply has no bearing on the issues at hand. Indeed, it is never made clear what the Court's opinion means on this score. [We] have held repeatedly that the importance of a governmental service does not elevate it to the status of a "fundamental right" for purposes of equal protection analysis. [Rodriguez.] Moreover, the Court points to no meaningful way to distinguish between education and other governmental benefits in this context. Is the Court suggesting that education is more "fundamental" than food, shelter, or medical care? [Equal protection] does not mandate a constitutional hierarchy of governmental services. [The] central question [is] whether there is some legitimate basis for a legislative distinction between different classes of persons. The fact that the distinction is drawn in legislation affecting access to public education—as opposed to legislation allocating other important governmental benefits, such as public assistance, health care, or housing—cannot make a difference in the level of scrutiny applied.

Once it is conceded—as the Court does—that illegal aliens are not a suspect class, and that education is not a fundamental right, our inquiry should focus on and be limited to whether the legislative classification at issue bears a rational relationship to a legitimate state purpose. [E.g., Vance v. Bradley; Dandridge v. Williams.] [It] simply is not "irrational" for a State to conclude that it does not have the same responsibility to provide benefits for persons whose very presence in the State and this country is illegal as it does to provide for persons lawfully present. By definition, illegal aliens have no right whatever to be here, and the State may reasonably, and constitutionally, elect not to provide them with governmental services at the expense of those who are lawfully in the State. [The] Court has failed to offer even a plausible explanation why illegality of residence in this country is not a factor that may legitimately bear upon the bona fides of state residence and entitlement to the benefits of lawful residence. It is significant that the federal government has seen fit to exclude illegal aliens from numerous social welfare [programs]. Although these exclusions do not conclusively demonstrate the constitutionality of the State's use of the same classification for comparable purposes, at the very least they tend to support the rationality of excluding illegal alien residents of a State from such programs so as to preserve the State's finite revenues for the benefit of lawful residents. [The] State need not show, as the Court implies, that the incremental cost of educating illegal aliens will send it into bankruptcy, or have a "grave impact on the quality of education"; that is not dispositive under a "rational basis" scrutiny. In the absence of a constitutional imperative to provide for the education of illegal aliens, the State may "rationally" choose to take advantage of whatever savings will accrue from limiting access to the tuition-free public schools to its own lawful [residents]. Denying a free education to illegal alien children is not a choice I would make were I a legislator. Apart from compassionate considerations, the long-range costs of excluding any children from the public schools may well outweigh the costs of educating them. But that is not the issue; the fact that there are sound *policy* arguments against the Texas legislature's choice does not render that choice an unconstitutional one.

Congress [bears] primary responsibility for addressing the problems occasioned by the millions of illegal aliens flooding across our southern border. [While] the "specter of a permanent caste" of illegal Mexican residents of the United States is indeed a disturbing one, it is but one segment of a larger problem, which is for the political branches to solve. I find it difficult to believe that Congress would long tolerate such a self-destructive result—that it would fail to deport these illegal alien families or to provide for the education of their children. Yet instead of allowing the political processes to run their course—albeit with some delay—the Court seeks to do Congress' job for it, compensating for congressional inaction. It is not unreasonable to think that this encourages the political branches to pass their problems to the judiciary. The solution to this seemingly intractable problem is to defer to the political processes, unpalatable as that may be to some.[1]

B.　VOTING AND ACCESS TO THE BALLOT

HARPER v. VIRGINIA BOARD OF ELECTIONS

383 U.S. 663, 86 S.Ct. 1079, 16 L.Ed.2d 169 (1966).

[Virginia imposed an annual $1.50 poll tax on all residents over 21. The state made payment of the poll taxes a precondition for voting. The tax proceeds supported local governmental activities, including schools. Appellants' suit to have the poll tax declared unconstitutional was dismissed by a

---

1.　Contrast with Plyler v. Doe the decision a year later in Martinez v. Bynum, 461 U.S. 321 (1983). Justice Powell's majority opinion rejected a facial challenge to a Texas residency requirement regarding minors who wished to attend free public schools while living apart from their parents or guardians. (The case was brought on behalf of a minor American citizen whose Mexican parents were nonresident aliens, but the Court considered only the facial challenge.) Justice Powell emphasized that the sole Texas exclusion was for minors living apart from their parents or guardians if the minors' presence in the school district was "for the primary purpose of attending the public free schools." He construed that as being a bona fide residence provision which required both physical presence and an intention to remain. He noted that, although the Court had repeatedly invalidated minimum residence requirements as conditions for receipt of state benefits (see sec. 4D below), "it always has been careful to distinguish such durational residence requirements from bona fide residence requirements." He found such a bona fide residence requirement justified under equal protection because it was rationally related to "the substantial state interest in assuring that

services provided for its residents are enjoyed only by residents" and by the interest in "proper planning and operation of the schools": "The State [has] a substantial interest in imposing bona fide residence requirements to maintain the quality of local public schools." (He made clear that he was applying a deferential rationality requirement: "A bona fide residence requirement implicates no 'suspect' classification" and "public education is not a 'right' granted [by] the Constitution. [Plyler.]" Justice Brennan, who joined the majority opinion, stressed that the majority was not considering the validity of the requirement as it applied "to children in a range of specific factual contexts": "If this question were before the Court, I believe that a different set of considerations would be implicated which might affect significantly an analysis of [constitutionality]." Justice Marshall was the sole dissenter. He reiterated the sliding scale approach of his Rodriguez dissent, accordingly insisted on "careful scrutiny," stated that the interest in education was "fundamental" (and noted that Plyler was "the most recent decision [to] recognize the special importance of education"), and found that the law was "not narrowly tailored to achieve a substantial state interest."

three-judge district court on the authority of Breedlove v. Suttles, 302 U.S. 277 (1937), where the Court had unanimously rejected an equal protection attack on the Georgia poll tax.]

Mr. Justice DOUGLAS delivered the opinion of the [Court].

[The] right to vote in state elections is nowhere expressly mentioned [in the Constitution]. It is argued that the right to vote in state elections is implicit, particularly by reason of the First Amendment. [We] do not stop to canvass the relation between voting and political expression. For it is enough to say that once the franchise is granted to the electorate, lines may not be drawn which are inconsistent with [equal protection].[1] [We] conclude that a State violates [equal protection] whenever it makes the affluence of the voter or payment of any fee an electoral standard. Voter qualifications have no relation to wealth nor to paying or not paying this or any other tax. Our cases demonstrate that [equal protection] restrains the States from fixing voter qualifications which invidiously discriminate. Thus, [we] held in Carrington v. Rash, 380 U.S. 89 [1965], that a State may not deny the opportunity to vote to a bona fide resident merely because he is a member of the armed services. [We] think that requirements of wealth or affluence or payment of a fee [are not permissible voting qualifications].

Long ago in [Yick Wo] the Court referred to "the political franchise of voting" as a "fundamental political right, because preservative of all rights." [It] is argued that a State may exact fees from citizens for many different kinds of licenses; that if it can demand from all an equal fee for a driver's license, it can demand from all an equal poll tax for voting. But we must remember that the interest of the State, when it comes to voting, is limited to the power to fix qualifications. Wealth, like race, creed, or color, is not germane to one's ability to participate intelligently in the electoral process. Lines drawn on the basis of wealth or property, like those of race, are traditionally disfavored. See [e.g., Griffin; Douglas (sec. 4C below)]. To introduce wealth or payment of a fee as a measure of a voter's qualifications is to introduce a capricious or irrelevant factor. [In] this context—that is, as a condition of obtaining a ballot—the requirement of fee paying causes an "invidious" discrimination [that] runs afoul of [equal protection]. [Breedlove sanctioned the use of a poll tax] as "a prerequisite of voting." To that extent [it] is overruled.

We agree, of course, with Mr. Justice Holmes that the Due Process Clause of the 14th Amendment "does not enact Mr. Herbert Spencer's Social Statics" [Lochner]. Likewise, the Equal Protection Clause is not shackled to the political theory of a particular era. In determining what lines are unconstitutionally discriminatory, we have never been confined to historic notions of equality, any more than we have restricted due process to a fixed catalogue of what was at a given time deemed to be the limits of fundamental rights. Notions of what constitutes equal treatment for purposes of the Equal Protection Clause *do* change. [See Brown.] In a recent searching re-examination of [equal protection], we [held] that "the opportunity for equal participation by all voters in the election of state legislators" is required. [Reynolds v. Sims.] We decline to qualify that principle by sustaining this poll tax. Our conclusion [is] founded not on what we think governmental policy should be, but on what [equal protection] requires. We have long been mindful that where fundamental rights and liberties are asserted under [equal protection], classifications which might invade or restrain them must be closely scrutinized and carefully confined. See [e.g., Skinner]. Those principles apply here. For to repeat, wealth or fee

---

1. [While] the "Virginia poll tax was born of a desire to disenfranchise the Negro" (Harman v. Forssenius, 380 U.S. 528), we do not stop to determine whether on this record the Virginia tax in its modern setting serves the same end. [Footnote by Justice Douglas.]

paying [has] no relation to voting qualifications; the right to vote is too precious, too fundamental to be so burdened or conditioned.

Reversed.

Mr. Justice BLACK [dissenting].

[It] would be difficult to say that the poll tax requirement is "irrational" or "arbitrary" or works "invidious discriminations." State poll tax legislation can "reasonably," "rationally" and without an "invidious" or evil purpose to injure anyone be found to rest on a number of state policies including (1) the State's desire to collect its revenue, and (2) its belief that voters who pay a poll tax will be interested in furthering the State's welfare when they vote. [And] history is on the side of "rationality" of the State's poll tax policy. [Another] reason for my dissent [is] that it seems to be using the old "natural-law-due-process formula" to justify striking down state laws as violations of [equal protection]. There is no more constitutional support for this Court to use [equal protection than to use due process] to write into the Constitution its notions of what it thinks is good governmental [policy].

Mr. Justice HARLAN, whom Mr. Justice STEWART joins, dissenting.

[The Court uses] captivating phrases, but they are wholly inadequate to satisfy the standard governing adjudication of the equal protection issue: Is there a rational basis for Virginia's poll tax as a voting qualification? I think the answer to that question is undoubtedly "yes." Property qualifications and poll taxes have been a traditional part of our political structure. [It] is certainly a rational argument that payment of some minimal poll tax promotes civic responsibility, weeding out those who do not care enough about public affairs to pay $1.50 or thereabouts a year for the exercise of the franchise. It is also arguable, indeed it was probably accepted as sound political theory by a large percentage of Americans through most of our history, that people with some property have a deeper stake in community affairs, and are consequently more responsible, more educated, more knowledgeable, more worthy of confidence, than those without means, and that the community and Nation would be better managed if the franchise were restricted to such citizens. Property and poll-tax qualifications [are] not in accord with current egalitarian notions of how a modern democracy should be organized. [But] it is all wrong [for] the Court to adopt the political doctrines popularly accepted at a particular moment of our history and to declare all others to be irrational and [invidious]. It was not too long ago that Mr. Justice Holmes felt impelled to remind the Court that the Due Process Clause of the 14th Amendment does not enact the laissez-faire theory of society [Lochner]. The times have changed, and perhaps it is appropriate to observe that neither does [equal protection] of that Amendment rigidly impose upon America an idelogy of unrestrained [egalitarianism].

THE BASES AND IMPACT OF HARPER

The Harper decision rested on dual grounds: "fundamental interests" and "suspect classifications" analyses evidently *both* played a role. The former theme has proved the sturdier one, and the focus of this subsection is on the elaboration of strict scrutiny of laws burdening participation in the electoral process.[1] The "fundamental interest" in voting and the electoral process suggested (somewhat obscurely) by Harper has flourished vigorously since that decision, as the following materials illustrate. (The strict scrutiny of limits on the franchise has not been confined to financial barriers, as the next case, from

----

1. Harper also contained the first of the War- ren Court dicta suggesting that classifications based on wealth, like those based on race, were suspect. The limited impact of that aspect of Harper has already been considered, in sec. 3C3 above.

the close of the Warren era, demonstrates.) In examining the materials that follow, consider: What *is* the fundamental interest established by these cases? What is the source of the right? (Recall the discussion of the right in the opinions in Rodriguez.) Harper acknowledges that the Constitution does not guarantee a right to vote in state elections; instead, the 1787 Constitution left it to the states to determine who should have the right to vote in national as well as state elections. Is the fundamental right in these cases derived solely (and legitimately) from equal protection? Are there other possible sources in the Constitution? [2]

KRAMER v. UNION FREE SCHOOL DISTRICT NO. 15

395 U.S. 621, 89 S.Ct. 1886, 23 L.Ed.2d 583 (1969).

Mr. Chief Justice WARREN delivered the opinion of the Court.

[Sec. 2012 of the New York Education Law] provides that in certain New York school districts residents [may] vote in the school district election only if they (1) own (or lease) taxable real property within the district, or (2) are parents (or have custody of) children enrolled in the local public schools.[1] [We] must give the statute a close and exacting examination. [See Reynolds v. Sims.] This is necessary because statutes distributing the franchise constitute the foundation of our representative society. Any unjustified discrimination in determining who may participate in political affairs or in the selection of public officials undermines the legitimacy of representative government. [Rigid] examination is applicable to statutes *denying* the franchise to citizens who are otherwise qualified by residence and age. Statutes granting the franchise to residents on a selective basis always pose the danger of denying some citizens any effective voice in the governmental affairs which substantially affect their lives. [Such laws] must be carefully scrutinized by the Court to determine whether each resident citizen has, as far as is possible, an equal voice in the selections. [The] presumption of constitutionality and the approval given "rational" classifications in other types of enactments are based on an assumption that the institutions of state government are structured so as to represent fairly all the people. However, when the challenge to the statute is in effect a challenge of this basic assumption, the assumption can no longer serve as the basis for presuming constitutionality. [The] need for exacting judicial scrutiny of statutes distributing the franchise is undiminished simply because, under a different statutory scheme, the offices subject to election might have been filled

---

2. The "Republican Form of Government" guarantee, Art. IV, § 4, has been held to be nonjusticiable. Would that provision be a more plausible source of the right developed in these cases? Does the right ultimately rest in general structural considerations drawn from the Constitution? Note Ely's comment (in Democracy and Distrust (1980), 117) that "unblocking stoppages in the democratic process is what judicial review ought preeminently to be about, and denial of the vote seems the quintessential stoppage." Recall also the Carolene Products footnote. (Note also the references to the First Amendment in some of the cases in this section.)

The recognition of the fundamental interests in voting actually predates Harper. Harper itself cites Reynolds v. Sims, the basic legislative districting case establishing the "one person-one vote" rule (chap. 15, p. 1621 below). Reynolds

was decided in a strict scrutiny-equal protection mode.

In addition to the voting rights materials in this section and Reynolds v. Sims and its progeny in the final chapter, note also the attacks on literacy tests considered in sec. 4 of the next chapter (p. 931 below)—attacks that were largely unsuccessful when based on equal protection, but that proved sweepingly effective after Congress entered the field with the Voting Rights Act of 1965.

1. The law was unsuccessfully challenged in the lower court by "a bachelor who neither owns nor leases taxable real property": appellant was "a thirty-one-year-old college-educated stockbroker who lives in his parents' home" in the district.

through appointment.[2] "[O]nce the franchise is granted to the electorate, lines may not be drawn which are inconsistent with [equal protection]." [Harper.]

We turn therefore to question whether the exclusion is necessary to promote a compelling state interest. First, appellees argue that the State has a legitimate interest in limiting the franchise in school district elections [to] those "primarily interested in such elections." Second, appellees urge that the State may reasonably and permissibly conclude that "property taxpayers" [and] parents of the children enrolled in the district's schools are those "primarily interested" in school affairs.[3] [We] need express no opinion as to whether the State in some circumstances might limit the exercise of the franchise to those "primarily interested" or "primarily affected." [For], assuming, arguendo, that New York legitimately might limit the franchise in these school district elections to those "primarily interested in school affairs," close scrutiny of the § 2012 classifications demonstrates that they do not accomplish this purpose with sufficient precision to justify denying appellant the franchise. Whether classifications allegedly limiting the franchise to those resident citizens "primarily interested" deny those excluded [equal protection] depends, inter alia, on whether all those excluded are in fact substantially less interested or affected than those the statute includes. In other words, the classifications must be tailored so that the exclusion of appellant and members of his class is necessary to achieve the articulated state goal.[4] Section 2012 does not meet the exacting standard of precision we require of statutes which selectively distribute the franchise. [Its] classifications [permit] inclusion of many persons who have, at best, a remote and indirect interest in school affairs and, on the other hand, exclude others who have a distinct and direct interest in the school meeting [decisions].[5]

Reversed.

Mr. Justice STEWART, with whom Mr. Justice BLACK and Mr. Justice HARLAN join, [dissenting].

[Clearly] a State may reasonably assume that its residents have a greater stake in the outcome of elections held within its boundaries than do other persons [and] that residents, being generally better informed regarding state affairs than are nonresidents, will be more likely [to] vote responsibly. And the same may be said of legislative assumptions regarding the electoral competence of adults and literate persons on the one hand, and of minors and illiterates on the other. It is clear, of course, that lines thus drawn cannot infallibly perform their intended legislative function. Just as "[i]lliterate people may be intelligent voters," nonresidents or minors might also in some instances be interested, informed, and intelligent participants in the electoral process. Persons who commute across a state line to work may well have a great stake in the affairs of the State in which they are employed; some college students under 21 may be both better informed and more passionately interested in political affairs than many adults. But such discrepancies are the inevitable concomitant of the line

2. Similarly, no less a showing of a compelling justification for disenfranchising residents is required merely because the questions scheduled for the election need not have been submitted to the voters. [Footnote by Chief Justice Warren.]

3. Appellees argued that it was necessary to limit the franchise to those "primarily interested" in school affairs because "the ever increasing complexity of the many interacting phases of the school system and structure make it extremely difficult for the electorate fully to understand the whys and wherefores of the detailed operations of the school system."

4. Of course, if the exclusions are necessary to promote the articulated state interest, we must then determine whether the interest promoted by limiting the franchise constitutes a compelling state interest. We do not reach that issue in this case. [Footnote by Chief Justice Warren.]

5. For example, appellant resides with his parents in the school district, pays state and federal taxes and is interested in and affected by school board decisions; however, he has no vote. On the other hand, an uninterested unemployed young man who pays no state or federal taxes, but who rents an apartment in the district, can participate in the election. [Footnote by Chief Justice Warren.]

drawing that is essential to law making. So long as the classification is rationally related to a permissible legislative end, [there] is no denial of equal protection. Thus judged, the statutory classification involved here seems to me clearly to be valid [and the] Court does not really argue the contrary. Instead, it [asserts] that the traditional equal protection standard is inapt in this case. [But] the asserted justification for applying [its stricter] standard cannot withstand analysis. [The] voting qualifications at issue have been promulgated, not by [the school district], but by the New York State Legislature, and the appellant is of course fully able to participate in the election of representatives in that body. [And the law] does not involve racial classifications [nor impinge] upon a constitutionally protected right and that consequently can be justified only by a "compelling" state interest. [For] "the Constitution of the United States does not confer the right of suffrage upon any one." Minor v. Happersett, 21 Wall. 162 [1874]. In any event, it seems to me that under *any* equal protection standard, short of a doctrinaire insistence that universal suffrage is somehow mandated by the Constitution, the appellant's claim must be [rejected].

ADDITIONAL RESTRICTIONS ON THE FRANCHISE

Introduction. Kramer sought to explain more adequately than Harper why "equal" participation in the electoral process is a "fundamental interest" triggering equal protection strict scrutiny, even though there is no constitutional "right" to vote. Recall that both Justices Powell and Stewart in Rodriguez, despite their opposition to further expansion of the fundamental interests strand of equal protection, accepted the electoral process cases—and tried valiantly to state the newly found right in terms consistent with their equal protection theory. In examining the post-Kramer cases that follow, consider especially what state interests are sufficiently "compelling" to survive strict scrutiny in this area, and what means are sufficiently narrowly tailored. Note that in this area, unlike most other spheres of strict scrutiny, some laws *do* survive judicial review. Does that indicate that a "sliding scale" or "balancing" approach has made significant inroads in the voting rights area?

1. *Efforts to limit the franchise in the contexts of limited purpose elections and special purpose governmental units.* In CIPRIANO v. HOUMA, 395 U.S. 701 (1969), decided on the same day as Kramer, the unanimous Court invalidated provisions of a Louisiana law granting only property taxpayers the right to vote in elections called to approve the issuance of revenue bonds by a municipal utility. The per curiam opinion noted that the revenue bonds were to be financed from the operations of the utilities, not from property taxes, and concluded: "The challenged statute contains a classification which excludes otherwise qualified voters who are as substantially affected and directly interested in the matter voted upon as are those who are permitted to vote."[1] A year later, in PHOENIX v. KOLODZIEJSKI, 399 U.S. 204 (1970), the majority extended Cipriano, holding that the restriction of the franchise to real property taxpayers was no more valid in elections on general obligation bonds (which looked only to property tax revenues for servicing) than in elections to approve the issuance of revenue bonds. Justice WHITE's majority opinion concluded that the differences between the interests of property owners and of nonproperty owners were not "sufficiently substantial to justify excluding the latter from the franchise."[2]

---

1. In a concurring notation, Justices BLACK and Stewart stated that this case, unlike Kramer, "involves a voting classification 'wholly irrelevant to achievement' of the State's objective."

2. Justice STEWART, joined by Chief Justice Burger and Justice Harlan, dissented.

Three years later, the majority found the Kramer-Cipriano-Kolodziejski line of cases inapplicable and sustained an election scheme for a water storage district under which only landowners were permitted to vote and in which votes were proportioned according to the assessed valuation of the land. SALYER LAND CO. v. TULARE LAKE BASIN WATER STORAGE DISTRICT, 410 U.S. 719 (1973). Justice REHNQUIST's majority opinion noted that the district's main purpose was to assure water for farming, and that project costs were assessed against the land in proportion to benefits received. He found the demanding requirements of such cases as Kramer and Reynolds v. Sims inapplicable to the district "by reason of its special limited purpose and of the disproportionate effect of its activities on landowners as a group." Accordingly, the details of the election scheme were subjected only to the minimal scrutiny of the old equal protection, and those details—the exclusion of mere residents and lessees, and weighting the votes according to the value of the land—easily survived that scrutiny. There was a vigorous dissent by Justice DOUGLAS, joined by Justices Brennan and Marshall. He especially objected to voting by the large land-owning corporations which farmed 85% of the land in the district: "The result is a corporation political kingdom undreamed of by those who wrote our Constitution." Compare BALL v. JAMES, 451 U.S. 355 (1981), where a sharply divided Court applied the Salyer exception to the "one person-one vote" rule and sustained the constitutionality of a "one acre-one vote" scheme for electing the directors of a large water reclamation district in Arizona. The dissenters in the 5 to 4 decision insisted that the majority had unjustifiably departed from the Kramer-Cipriano-Kolodziejski line of cases. The majority applied the deferential rationality review of Salyer rather than the strict scrutiny of Kramer.[3]

   2. *Durational residence requirements.* The 6 to 1 decision in DUNN v. BLUMSTEIN, 405 U.S. 330 (1972), invalidated Tennessee's durational residence requirements for voters. (Tennessee required one year residence in the state and three months in the county as a condition of voting.) Justice MARSHALL's majority opinion—while recognizing the state's strong interest in limiting voting to residents—held that durational residence requirements were subject to strict scrutiny both because they curtailed the fundamental interest in voting and because they burdened the right to travel.[4] His discussion of the appropriate standard of review afforded him his first opportunity to articulate his multi-variable, "sliding scale" approach which he has reiterated and elaborated frequently. (See, e.g., his Rodriguez dissent.) He stated: "[W]hether we

3. The Salt River District (involved in Ball v. James) finances most of its water operations by sending electricity to several hundred thousand Arizona residents, including those inhabiting a large part of metropolitan Phoenix. (The district in Salyer, by contrast, covered a sparsely populated agricultural area.) Justice STEWART's majority opinion nevertheless concluded that the Salyer restriction of voting to landowners was also valid in the Salt River District. He conceded that the services provided by the Arizona District in this case were "more diverse and affect far more people" than those in Salyer, but insisted that the Arizona District "simply does not exercise the sort of governmental powers that invoke" the one person-one vote principle. And he rejected the argument that "the sheer size of the power operations and the great number of people they affect serve to transform the District into an entity of general governmental power." Accordingly, the voting scheme was valid because "it bears a reasonable relationship to its statutory objectives." (In a separate notation agreeing with the majority, Justice POWELL insisted that Kramer survived Salyer and Ball, but that "it must be evident that some of the reasoning in [Kramer] has been questioned.") Justice WHITE's dissent, joined by Justices Brennan, Marshall and Blackmun, insisted that the majority had misapplied the Salyer exception: "An analysis of the two relevant factors required by Salyer [limited purpose and insubstantial effect on nonvoters] demonstrates that the [District here] possesses significant governmental authority and has a sufficiently wide effect on nonvoters to require application of the strict scrutiny mandated by Kramer. [To analogize the District here] to that in Salyer ignores reality."

4. For additional consideration of the right to travel or migrate from state to state (and the invalidation of other durational residence requirements), see sec. 4D, p. 832 below.

look to the benefit withheld by the classification (the opportunity to vote) or the basis for the classification (recent interstate travel), we conclude that the state must show a substantial and compelling reason for imposing durational residence requirements." Such requirements could not stand "unless the State can demonstrate that such laws are '*necessary* to promote a *compelling* government interest.'" That equal protection approach, Justice Marshall explained, was not mathematically precise, but rather one "of degree."

The "least restrictive means" ingredient of strict scrutiny proved fatal to the Tennessee laws. Tennessee asserted two basic justifications: insuring "purity of the ballot box" and furthering the goal of having "knowledgeable voters." Neither proved sufficient. With respect to preventing fraud, "30 days appears to be an ample period of [time]—and a year, or three months, too much." (The State closed its registration books 30 days before election.) And with regard to knowledgeability, "the conclusive presumptions of durational residence requirements are much too crude." He added: "By requiring classifications to be tailored to their purpose, we do not secretly require the impossible." Here, the relationship between method and purpose was "simply too attenuated." [5]

3. *Disenfranchisement of felons.* California, like many of the states, disenfranchises convicted felons who have served their sentences and completed their parole. In RICHARDSON v. RAMIREZ, 418 U.S. 24 (1974), the highest state court had struck down that barrier under the assumed compulsion of the higher decree of scrutiny demanded by modern voting cases. But the Court reversed: it found an exception to the equal protection standards usual in the voting area in the recognition of ex-felons' disenfranchisement in the rarely invoked § 2 of the 14th Amendment. The reduced representation sanction of § 2 is specifically inapplicable to denials of the vote "for participation in rebellion, or other crime." Justice REHNQUIST's majority opinion drew on the language and history of that provision to conclude that "the exclusion of felons from the vote has an affirmative sanction in § 2 of the 14th Amendment." He found textually and historically "persuasive" the argument "that those who framed and adopted the 14th Amendment could not have intended to prohibit outright in § 1 of that Amendment that which was expressly exempted from the lesser sanction of reduced representation imposed by § 2 of the Amendment." He accordingly concluded that "the exclusion of felons from the vote has an affirmative sanction [which] was not present in the case of the other restrictions on the franchise" invalidated in the Harper-Kramer line of cases. [6]

---

5. Chief Justice BURGER was the only dissenter: "Some lines must be drawn. To challenge such lines by the 'compelling state interest' standard is to condemn them all. So far as I am aware, no state law has ever satisfied this seemingly insurmountable standard, and I doubt one ever will."

But some laws challenged in subsequent cases did survive such scrutiny. See, e.g., two decisions in which the Court found 50-day residency requirements constitutional. Marston v. Lewis, 410 U.S. 679 (1973); Burns v. Fortson, 410 U.S. 686 (1973). The per curiam decisions accepted the states' judgments that the 50-day period was "necessary" to serve the states' "important interest in accurate voter lists." Justice Marshall's dissents, joined by Justices Douglas and Brennan, insisted that 30 days gave the states ample time to achieve their objectives.

6. Justice MARSHALL, joined by Justice Brennan, dissented on the merits. (Justice Douglas dissented on jurisdictional grounds.) Justice Marshall viewed § 2 of the 14th Amendment as a provision of limited purpose which should not be viewed as "the exclusive remedy for all forms of electoral discrimination" and should not be invoked to avoid the strict scrutiny compelled by § 1. Applying the standards he had articulated in Dunn v. Blumstein, he readily concluded that the burden of showing that the restriction was "*necessary* to promote a *compelling* state interest" had not been met.

Note also the Court's repeated encounters with claims to absentee ballots by persons in jail. Recall that in McDonald (1969; p. 601 above), Chief Justice Warren applied deferential equal protection standards to a "remedial law" which failed to provide absentee ballots to jail inmates

4. *Anti-"raiding" cutoff requirements for party enrollment: The appropriate level of scrutiny.* a. The 5 to 4 decision in ROSARIO v. ROCKEFELLER, 410 U.S. 752 (1973), sustained New York's unusually lengthy enrollment time prerequisite for voting in party primaries. The provisions required a voter to register affiliation 30 days before a general election in order to be eligible to vote in the following year's party primary. That scheme in effect prevented a change in party affiliation for up to eleven months to retain eligibility to vote in primaries. In rejecting the constitutional attack, Justice STEWART's majority opinion insisted that the challengers' reliance on cases such as Dunn v. Blumstein was not "apposite," since the New York scheme "did not absolutely disenfranchise the class to which the petitioners belong." Rather, it "merely imposed a time deadline." The requirement was not "unreasonably long" and did not unduly burden the exercise of rights of voting and free association. Though the period was "lengthy," it was "not an arbitrary time limit unconnected to any important state goal." The justifiable purpose of the system was "to inhibit party 'raiding' whereby voters in sympathy with one party designate themselves as voters of another party so as to influence or determine the results of the other party's primary." Justice POWELL's dissent, joined by Justices Douglas, Brennan and Marshall, objected especially to the majority's lack of clarity about applicable standards and insisted that the strict scrutiny of Blumstein was appropriate here. He concluded that the law imposed "substantial and unnecessary restrictions" on voting and associational rights. More than a mere "time deadline" was involved: "Deferment of a right [can] be tantamount to its denial." He added: "The Court's formulation [resembles the] 'rational basis' test." That was an inappropriate standard under Blumstein; the requirements of "strict judicial scrutiny" were not met here. It was not enough that the lower court had found the state interest in deterring "raiding" a "compelling" one: the "least restrictive alternatives" inquiry was not satisfied because the majority had failed "to address the critical question of whether [the state] interest may be protected adequately by lesser measures."

b. Justice Powell's advocacy of a clear-cut strict scrutiny approach soon bore fruit. In KUSPER v. PONTIKES, 414 U.S. 51 (1973), Justice STEWART's majority opinion distinguished Rosario and invalidated an Illinois scheme prohibiting a person from voting in the primary election of a political party if he had voted in the primary of any other party within the preceding 23 months. The Court emphasized that the provision "substantially restricts an Illinois voter's freedom to change his political party affiliation" and thus significantly encroached upon First Amendment associational freedoms. The Illinois system was found to differ from the New York delayed-enrollment law sustained in Rosario in a number of respects. In New York, disenfranchisement was caused by the voters' own failure to take timely measures to enroll; the Illinois law, by contrast, " 'locks' voters into a preexisting party affiliation from one primary to the next, and the only way to break the 'lock' is to forego voting in *any* primary for a period of almost two years." The Court concluded that "the legitimate interest of Illinois in preventing 'raiding' cannot justify the device it has chosen to effect its goal."

---

awaiting trial in their county of residence. But later lower court efforts to rely on McDonald in considering absentee ballot claims were unsuccessful. For example, O'Brien v. Skinner, 414 U.S. 524 (1974), held unconstitutional a New York system which failed to provide absentee registration or voting for pre-trial detainees and convicted misdemeanants confined in the county of their residence. Chief Justice Burger's majority opinion found the scheme "wholly arbitrary."

ACCESS TO THE BALLOT: RESTRICTIONS ON CANDIDATES AND PARTIES

Introduction. At least partially as an outgrowth of the cases noted above, the Court has, for nearly 20 years, examined a series of state restrictions on candidates and parties seeking access to the ballot. The cases that follow are of special interest for two reasons. First, they illustrate that, on issues of this sort, the First Amendment, not only equal protection, may be relevant.[1] Second, these cases—although in their equal protection aspects a consequence of the earlier voting rights-strict scrutiny cases—show an especially pervasive degree of uncertainty and instability as to the appropriate level of scrutiny. Although, throughout the 1970s, the Court continued to apply strict scrutiny at least in form, a number of restrictions were sustained. And in one of the cases of the 1980s, Clements v. Fashing (note 6 below), the plurality opinion announced that "[n]ot all ballot access restrictions require 'heightened' equal protection scrutiny." Would it be more appropriate to analyze these cases consistently in First Amendment rather than equal protection terms?[2]

1. *The Williams case.* Beginning with WILLIAMS v. RHODES, 393 U.S. 23 (1968), the Court has had repeated occasion to delineate the states' authority to curtail access to ballots by independent candidates and third parties. In Williams, the Court held that Ohio's election laws created unduly burdensome obstacles to third party candidates seeking a place on presidential ballots. The challenge came from a new party, the American Independent Party supporting George Wallace, as well as from an established minor party. Under the Ohio system, major parties retained their positions on the ballot simply by obtaining 10% of the votes in the last gubernatorial election. Parties newly seeking access to the presidential election ballot, by contrast, faced greater obstacles: early in the presidential election year, they were required to file petitions signed by 15% of the number of ballots cast in the last gubernatorial election; they had to erect an elaborate party structure; and they had to conduct primaries. Justice BLACK's majority opinion stated that these requirements "made it virtually impossible for a new political party, even though it has hundreds of thousands of members, or an old party, which has a very small number of members," to gain a place on the ballot. As a result, the two established major parties had "a decided advantage over any new parties struggling for existence." He found strict scrutiny appropriate. Here the state scheme placed "unequal burdens" on "two different, although overlapping, kinds of rights—the right of individuals to associate for the advancement of political beliefs, and the right of qualified voters [to] cast their votes effectively." He found that the state had "failed to show any 'compelling interest' which justifie[d] imposing such heavy burdens" on such "precious freedoms." Encouraging a two party system to promote compromise and political stability could not support giving the two major parties a permanent monopoly. And the interest in avoiding run-off elections and preventing voter confusion could not support the crippling restrictions here: those dangers were too remote; and the experience of other states showed that "no more than a handful of parties attempts to qualify for ballot positions even where a very low number of signatures, such as 1% of the electorate, is required."[3]

1. Indeed, in the most recent case, the 1983 decision in Anderson v. Celebrezze (below), the majority relied primarily on the First Amendment, although it continued to consider relevant earlier decisions analyzed in an equal protection mode.

2. See also the discussion of election regulations in the First Amendment materials below.

See, e.g., the Court's discussion of the ballot access cases in its examination of the Federal Election Campaign Act in Buckley v. Valeo (1976; p. 1301 below).

3. There were dissents by Justices STEWART and WHITE and by Chief Justice WARREN. A concurrence by Justice HARLAN stated that he would rest "entirely" on First

2. *Jenness v. Fortson.* Three years after Williams, a unanimous Court found that decision distinguishable in rejecting challenges to Georgia's nominating procedures in JENNESS v. FORTSON, 403 U.S. 431 (1971). Unlike Ohio, Georgia permits write-in votes and allows independent candidates to appear on the ballots without third party endorsement if they have filed nominating petitions signed by at least 5% of those eligible to vote in the last election for the office. Petitions can be filed as late as June of the election year, and there are no requirements for establishing an elaborate primary election machinery. Justice STEWART found that scheme "vastly different" from that in Williams. The Georgia system did not unduly "freeze the political status quo." And the different treatment of established large parties and new small parties was justifiable: "There is surely an important state interest in requiring some preliminary showing of a significant modicum of support before printing the name of a political organization and its candidates on the ballot—the interest, if no other, in avoiding confusion, deception, and even frustration of the democratic process at the general election."

3. *The 1974 decisions.* In STORER v. BROWN, 415 U.S. 724 (1974), and AMERICAN PARTY OF TEXAS v. WHITE, 415 U.S. 767 (1974), the Court reexamined ballot access barriers to independent candidates and small political parties, found them of a magnitude somewhere between Williams v. Rhodes and Jenness v. Fortson, and rejected most of the challenges. The majority acknowledged, however, that a strict scrutiny standard was applicable: as the Court put it in the Texas case, "whether the qualifications for ballot positions are viewed as substantial burdens on the right to associate or as discriminations against [small parties], their validity depends upon whether they are necessary to further compelling state interests." In Storer, the Court sustained a California provision denying a ballot position to an independent candidate if he had registered with a political party within a year prior to the immediately preceding primary election or if he had voted in that election. That barrier was not found discriminatory against independents. The one-year disaffiliation provision furthered the state's "compelling" interest in the "stability of its political system." In the Texas case, the Court sustained most of that state's provisions regarding independents and minor parties, but invalidated a provision under which only names of major parties were included on absentee ballots. Justice WHITE's majority opinion noted that the Texas scheme "affords minority political parties a real and substantially equal opportunity for ballot qualification" and found most of the regulations were "valid measures, reasonably taken in pursuit of vital state objectives that cannot be served equally well in significantly less burdensome ways." [4]

4. *The Socialist Workers case.* The Court reiterated its commitment to strict scrutiny in ballot access cases in ILLINOIS ELECTIONS BD. v. SOCIALIST WORKERS PARTY, 440 U.S. 173 (1979). Justice MARSHALL's opinion for the Court struck down the Illinois system requiring new political parties and independent candidates to gather more voter signatures in order to appear on the ballot in Chicago elections than in statewide ones. After examining this "incongruous result," Justice Marshall found that the "discrepancy" could not

---

Amendment associational rights and insisted that reliance on equal protection was "unnecessary."

How far-reaching is the Williams principle? What was the "voting" interest protected? The right to "vote effectively"—i.e., for a particular candidate—rather than simply access to the ballot or equality of votes? Does that suggest a constitutional "right to write-in space," see Note, 83 Harv.L.Rev. 96 (1969)? Is the basic concern in Williams with *groups* rather than with *individuals*? Should the elaborations of the new princi-

ples move in the direction of encouraging third parties, or in the direction of encouraging the major parties to represent divergent viewpoints more effectively? See generally Barton, "The General-Election Ballot: More Nominees or More Representative Nominees?" 22 Stan.L. Rev. 165 (1970).

4. Justices DOUGLAS, BRENNAN and MARSHALL dissented in the California case; Justice DOUGLAS was the sole dissenter in the Texas case.

survive strict scrutiny. He emphasized the "least drastic means" aspect of strict scrutiny, commenting that it was "particularly important where restrictions on access to the ballot are involved": "The States' interest in screening out frivolous candidates must be considered in light of the significant role that third parties have played in the political development of the Nation. [As the records of past third parties demonstrate], an election campaign is a means of disseminating ideas as well as attaining political office. [Overbroad] restrictions on ballot access jeopardize this form of political expression." Here, in view of the less burdensome prerequisite for statewide elections, the Chicago requirements were "plainly not the least restrictive means of protecting" the State's interest in avoiding overloaded ballots; and the State had "advanced no reason, much less a compelling one," why "a more stringent requirement" was needed for Chicago.

5. *Financial barriers to ballot access.* In BULLOCK v. CARTER, 405 U.S. 134 (1972), and LUBIN v. PANISH, 415 U.S. 709 (1974), the unanimous Court invalidated a filing fee requirement for candidates. Chief Justice BURGER wrote the prevailing opinion in each case. Each opinion was marked by some obscurity about the appropriate standard of review: though there were several references to strict scrutiny, there were also invocations of traditional rationality standards. The results, in any event, are clear: the Court is reluctant to sustain financial barriers burdensome not only to voters (as in Harper) but also to candidates. The Texas scheme invalidated in Bullock required candidates for local office to pay fees as high as $8900 to get on the primary ballot. The Chief Justice emphasized that "the very size of the fees" indicated a "patently exclusionary system" with an obviously immediate impact on voters. He concluded that the state had not established the "requisite justification" either in its concern about regulating the size of the ballot or in its interest in financing the election. Lubin v. Panish invalidated a California requirement of a fee fixed at a percentage of the salary for the office sought. Petitioner, an indigent, was unable to get on the primary ballot for County Supervisor because he could not pay a filing fee of about $700. The Chief Justice identified the critical problem as the accommodation of "the desire for increased ballot access with the imperative of protecting the integrity of the electoral system from the recognized dangers of ballots listing so many candidates as to undermine the process of giving expression to the will of the majority." He concluded that California had "chosen to achieve the important and legitimate interest of maintaining the integrity of elections by means which can operate to exclude some potentially serious candidates from the ballot without providing them with any alternative means of coming before the voters." He accordingly held "that in the absence of reasonable alternative means of valid access, a State may not, consistently with constitutional standards, require from an indigent candidate filing fees he cannot pay." [5]

6. *More deferential scrutiny in ballot access cases: Public officials' candidacies.* In CLEMENTS v. FASHING, 457 U.S. 957 (1982), Justice REHNQUIST's plurality opinion announced that "[n]ot all ballot access restrictions require

---

5. The Bullock and Lubin cases are of special interest for their wavering course in attempting to articulate the appropriate standard of review. Do they represent "strict scrutiny"? Traditional scrutiny? Minimum scrutiny "with bite"? A "sliding scale" approach? Chief Justice Burger employed varying formulations. He began his Bullock opinion by stating: "[We] must determine whether the strict standard of review of the Harper case should be applied." And at the end of that discussion, he stated that "we conclude, as in Harper, that the laws must be 'closely

scrutinized.'" Compare his description of Bullock v. Carter two years later, in a footnote to his opinion in Lubin v. Panish: "Bullock, of course, does not completely resolve the present attack [because] it involved filing fees that were so patently exclusionary as to violate traditional equal protection concepts." Compare Justice Douglas' concurrence in Lubin, which advocated strict scrutiny and relied in part on Harper—a decision that the Chief Justice had invoked in Bullock but did not mention in Lubin.

'heightened' equal protection scrutiny" and sustained two Texas constitutional provisions limiting a public official's ability to become a candidate for another public office. One provision (§ 19) required certain officeholders to complete their current terms of office before they could be eligible to serve in the state legislature. Another, "automatic resignation" provision (§ 65) mandated that, if holders of certain state and county offices whose unexpired term exceeded one year became candidates for any other state or federal office, "such announcement or such candidacy [would] constitute an automatic resignation of the office then held." The "automatic resignation" provision was challenged by four officials whose candidacies for higher judicial office were allegedly inhibited by the state barrier. One of the challengers (a Justice of the Peace) also attacked the state restriction on candidacies for the legislature.

In rejecting the equal protection attack, Justice REHNQUIST's plurality opinion (joined by Chief Justice Burger and Justices Powell and O'Connor) began by explaining why the challenged provisions did not "deserve 'scrutiny' more vigorous than that which the traditional [equal protection rationality principles of McDonald and McGowan] would require." He insisted that, in recent years, the Court had departed from "traditional equal protection analysis" only in "two essentially separate, although similar, lines of ballot access cases. One line [involves] classifications based on wealth. [Clearly], the challenged provisions in the instant case involve neither filing fees nor restrictions that invidiously burden those of lower economic status. [Bullock; Lubin.] The second line [involves] classification schemes that impose burdens on new or small political parties or independent candidates. See, e.g., [Socialist Workers Party; Storer; American Party of Texas; Jenness; Williams v. Rhodes]." He added: "The provisions [challenged here] do not contain any classification that imposes special burdens on minority political parties or independent candidates. The burdens placed on [these] candidates [in] no way depend upon political affiliation or political viewpoint." In determining whether heightened scrutiny should nevertheless apply here, he examined "the nature of the interests that are affected and the extent of the burden these provisions place on candidacy." He limited his examination of § 19, the barrier to candidacies for the legislature, solely to the situation of the challenger who was a Justice of the Peace. The Justice of the Peace served for a four-year term. To Justice Rehnquist, the length of the term in effect established "a maximum 'waiting period' of two years for candidacy by a Justice of the Peace for the Legislature" and therefore placed only "a de minimis burden on the political aspirations of a *current* officeholder." He insisted: "A 'waiting period' is hardly a significant barrier to candidacy. [This] sort of insignificant interference with access to the ballot need only rest on a rational predicate in order to survive a challenge under [equal protection]." And the rationality requirement was readily met here: "[The] provision furthers Texas' interests in maintaining the integrity of the State's Justices of the Peace.[6] By prohibiting candidacy for the Legislature until completion of one's term of office, § 19 seeks to ensure that a Justice of the Peace will neither abuse his position nor neglect his duties because of his aspirations for higher office." Nor did he find any flaw in the provision "because it burdens only those officeholders who desire to run for the Legislature." Here, he relied on the "one step at a time" philosophy of Lee Optical. Justice Rehnquist disposed of the equal protection challenge to the "automatic resignation" provision even more summarily: "The burdens that § 65 imposes on candidacy are even less substantial than those imposed by § 19. The two provisions [serve] essentially the same state interests." He was not impressed by the District Court's view that the classification was unconstitutional "because

---

6. "The State's particular interest in maintaining the integrity of the judicial system could support § 19 even if such a restriction could not survive constitutional scrutiny with regard to any other officeholder." [Footnote by Justice Rehnquist.]

Texas has failed to explain sufficiently why some elected public officials are subject to [the barrier] and why others are not." The challengers had failed to show "that there is no rational predicate to the classification scheme." Again, he invoked the "one step at a time" rationale: the barrier had been enacted in connection with the extension of certain terms of office from two to four years; "that the State did not go further in applying the automatic resignation provision to those officeholders whose terms were not extended, [absent] an invidious purpose, is not the sort of malfunctioning of the State's lawmaking process forbidden by [equal protection]. A regulation is not devoid of a rational predicate simply because it happens to be incomplete. See [Lee Optical]."[7]

In a separate opinion, Justice STEVENS agreed with the rejection of the equal protection claim but gave different reasons for doing so. He objected to the general discussion of the "level of scrutiny" problem: "Unfortunately that analysis may do more to obfuscate than to clarify the inquiry. This case suggests that a better starting point may be a careful identification of the character of the federal interest in equality that is implicated by the State's discriminatory classification. In my opinion, the disparate treatment in this case is not inconsistent with any federal interest that is protected by [equal protection]." Here, "the disparate treatment of different officeholders [was] entirely a function of the different offices that they occupy"; there was "no suggestion that the attributes of the offices have been defined to conceal an intent to discriminate on the basis of personal characteristics." The central question, then, was "whether there is any federal interest in requiring a State to define the benefits and burdens of different elective state offices in any particular manner. In my opinion there is not. [There] may be no explanation for these classifications that a federal judge would find to be 'rational.' But they do not violate [equal protection] because there is no federal requirement that a State fit the emoluments or the burdens of different elective state offices into any particular pattern. The reason, then, that appellees may be treated differently from other officeholders is that they occupy different offices." He added: "As in so many areas of the law, it is important to consider each case individually. In the situation presented, however, I believe that there is no federal interest in equality that requires the [State] to treat the different classes as if they were the same. This reasoning brings me to the same conclusion that Justice Rehnquist has reached. It avoids, however, the danger of confusing two quite different questions.[8] Justice Rehnquist has demonstrated that there is a 'rational basis' for imposing the burdens at issue [here]. He has not, however, adequately explained the reasons, if any, for imposing those burdens on some offices but not others. With respect to the latter inquiry, the plurality is satisfied to note that the State may approach its goals 'one step at a time.' In my judgment, this response is simply another way of stating that there need be no justification at all

---

7. In the only portion of Justice Rehnquist's discussion of the merits that gained majority rather than plurality support (because Justice Stevens joined that part of the opinion), Justice Rehnquist also rejected a First Amendment challenge. Relying on his discussion of the equal protection arguments, he stated: "The State's interests in this regard are sufficient to warrant the de minimis interference with appellees' interests in candidacy." He cited "another reason" for rejecting the First Amendment challenge: "Appellees are *elected* state officeholders who contest restrictions on partisan political activity. [The barriers here] represent a far more limited restriction on political activity than this Court has upheld with regard to *civil servants.* See

CSC v. Letter Carriers; Broadrick v. Oklahoma; United Public Workers v. Mitchell [all considered in the First Amendment chapters below]."

8. "See Westen, The Empty Idea of Equality, 95 Harv.L.Rev. 537 (1982). Professor Westen's article is valuable because it illustrates the distinction between concern with the substantive import of a state restriction and concern with any disparate impact that it may produce. In recognizing that distinction, however, it is important not to lose sight of the fact that the Equal Protection Clause has independent significance in protecting the federal interest in requiring States to govern impartially." [Footnote by Justice Stevens.]

for treating two classes differently during the interval between the first step and the second step—an interval that, of course, may well last forever. Although such an approach is unobjectionable in a case involving the differences between different public offices, I surely could not subscribe to Justice Rehnquist's formulation of the standard to be used in evaluating state legislation that treats different classes of persons differently." [9]

Justice BRENNAN, joined by Justices Marshall, Blackmun and White, strongly disagreed with Justice Rehnquist's rejection of the equal protection claim. He concluded that the challenged provisions could not "survive even minimal equal protection scrutiny." [10] Even applying rationality review, he could find "no genuine justification" for "*differential* treatment of various classes of officeholders, and the search for such justification makes clear that the classifications embodied in these provisions lack any meaningful relationship to the State's asserted or supposed interests." He also objected at length to Justice Rehnquist's use of the "one step at a time" approach: "the plurality today gives new meaning to the term 'legal fiction.' " The "one step at a time" justification was available only "where the record demonstrates that such 'one step at a time' regulation is in fact being undertaken. I cannot subscribe [to] the plurality's wholly fictional one-step-at-a-time justification. [The] haphazard reach and isolated existence [of this barrier] strikes me as the very sort of 'arbitrary scheme or plan' that we distinguished from an as-yet-uncompleted design in [McDonald]. Similarly, the "automatic resignation" provision could not "in any realistic sense be upheld as one step in an evolving scheme." [11]

7. *Hints of a new approach: Emphasizing the First Amendment rather than equal protection in ballot access cases.* Justice STEVENS' majority opinion in ANDERSON v. CELEBREZZE, 460 U.S. 780 (1983), suggests a rather different methodology for ballot access cases. At issue was an Ohio statute that required independent candidates to file their petitions and related materials by March 20 if they wished a place on the November ballot. John Anderson, independent candidate for President in 1980, challenged the statute on two grounds. First, he claimed that the early filing deadline was so early that it represented an excess restriction on access to the ballot, one that was not justified by any legitimate state interest. Second, by imposing a filing deadline for independ-

---

9. Justice Brennan's dissent took issue with a portion of this passage in Justice Stevens' opinion: "I agree [that] the State may define *many* of the 'benefits and burdens of different elective state offices' in a dissimilar manner without [persuading a federal judge that it is acting rationally], so long as such classifications do not mask any racial or otherwise impermissible discrimination. But where the differential treatment concerns a restriction on the right to seek public office—a right protected by the First Amendment—that Amendment supplies the federal interest in equality that may be lacking where the State is simply determining salary, hours, or working conditions of its own employees."

10. Justice Brennan addressed the "level of scrutiny" problem in ballot access cases generally only in a footnote: "It is worth noting [that] the plurality's analysis of the level of scrutiny to be applied to these restrictions gives too little consideration to the impact of our prior cases. Although we have never defined candidacy as a fundamental right, we have clearly recognized that restrictions on candidacy impinge on First Amendment rights of candidates and voters. See, e.g., [Socialist Workers Party; Lubin; Bullock; Williams v. Rhodes]. With this considera-

tion in mind, we have applied strict scrutiny in reviewing most restrictions on ballot access. [The] plurality dismisses our prior cases as dealing with only two kinds of ballot access [restrictions]. But strict scrutiny was required in those cases because of their impact on the First Amendment *rights* of candidates and voters, not because the *class* of candidates or voters that was burdened was somehow suspect. The plurality offers no explanation as to why the restrictions at issue here, which completely bar some candidates from running and require other candidates to give up their present employment, are less 'substantial' in their impact on candidates and supporters than, for example, the $700 filing fee at issue in Lubin. In my view, some greater deference may be due the State because these restrictions affect only public employees, but this does not suggest that, in subjecting these classifications to equal protection scrutiny, we should completely disregard the vital interests of the candidates and the citizens whom they represent in a political campaign."

11. Justice Brennan also sustained the separate First Amendment challenge to § 19, but Justice White did not join that part of his opinion.

ents without requiring comparable action for the nominee of a political party, the statute impermissibly discriminated against independent candidates. The Court upheld Anderson's claim, finding that Ohio's asserted interests in voter education, equal treatment for partisan and independent candidates, and political stability were either illegitimate or too remotely related to the early filing deadline to justify such a substantial barrier to independent candidates. More important than the particular result, however, were two significant departures in approach from previous ballot access cases.

Most noteworthy, especially in light of the skepticism evidenced in Rodriguez with respect to fundamental rights analysis in the equal protection area, was the Court's specific decision to rely on First Amendment and not equal protection grounds. "[We] base our conclusions directly on the First and 14th Amendments and do not engage in a separate [equal protection] analysis. We rely, however, on the analysis in a number of our prior election cases resting on [equal protection]. [These] cases, applying the 'fundamental rights' strand of equal protection analysis, have identified the [First Amendment] rights implicated by restrictions on the eligibility of voters and candidates, and have considered the degree to which the State's restrictions further legitimate state interests. [Williams; Bullock; Lubin; Socialist Workers Party.]" The Court also made clear that ballot access cases would be decided by an individualized weighing of the various interests involved: "Constitutional challenges to specific provisions of a State's election laws [cannot] be resolved by any 'litmus-paper test' that will separate valid from invalid restrictions. Storer. Instead, a court [must] first consider the character and magnitude of the asserted injury to the [First Amendment rights] that the plaintiff seeks to vindicate. It then must identify and evaluate the precise interests put forward by the State as justifications for the burden imposed. [The] Court must not only determine the legitimacy and strength of each of those interests; it also must consider the extent to which those interests make it necessary to burden the plaintiff's rights. Only after weighing all these factors is the reviewing court in a position to decide whether the challenged provision is unconstitutional." [12]

C. ACCESS TO COURTS

Introduction. In the cases that follow, the Court carefully scrutinizes and frequently invalidates economic barriers impeding access to the criminal and civil processes. What is the proper constitutional basis for this line of cases? The Court has repeatedly divided on the issue of whether procedural due process or equal protection provides the appropriate framework for analysis. Justice Harlan was the leading advocate of the due process approach. The majority has most commonly emphasized the relevance of equal protection; and that strand of the new equal protection has retained considerable vitality on the Burger Court, at least in the criminal area.

Which provision *does* provide the most appropriate basis for these developments? Does either due process or equal protection provide an adequate basis? The core of procedural due process notions is adequate notice and opportunity

---

12. Justice REHNQUIST's dissenting opinion, joined by Justices White, Powell, and O'Connor, focused primarily on the similarities between this case and Storer. The dissenters were unpersuaded by the Court's attempts to distinguish Storer, and were also unconvinced that this restriction in fact impeded the efforts of Anderson or other independent candidates. Interestingly, however, the dissent expressed no disagreement with the Court's characterization of the case as a First Amendment case rather than an equal protection case, and did not take issue with the generalized balancing approach set forth by Justice Stevens.

to be heard. (Recall chap. 7, p. 420.) Do the results in the cases below flow plausibly from those core concepts? In several of the cases, the Court holds that a state may not impose fee requirements and must provide counsel when defendants seek to appeal criminal convictions. Yet the Court continues to maintain that there is no constitutional *right* to appeal a conviction: no such right has been found "fundamental" in the evolution of criminal procedure guarantees. Does a due process right to access and participation nevertheless arise once the state chooses to establish an appellate structure? Do access and participation rights then flow from the "opportunity to be heard" ingredient of due process? Even though, on appeal and unlike at trial, the initiative to invoke the judicial process comes from the defendant rather than the state? Or does equal protection provide a more plausible rationale? Do such economic barriers as fee requirements in filing appeals contravene traditional equal protection standards? Justice Black said in Griffin, which follows, that there is "no rational relationship" between "the ability to pay costs" and "a defendant's guilt or innocence." But are there not other legitimate state objectives to which fee requirements do bear a rational relationship? Since wealth has not been accepted as a suspect classification, something more than the mere existence of economic barriers must be involved to explain the Court interventions. What is that "something more"? Is the stricter scrutiny triggered by the existence of a "fundamental interest" in these cases? Is there a "fundamental interest," for example, in effective participation in the criminal appellate process—even though there is no constitutional "right" to a criminal appeal?[1] What are the plausible limits on the principles implicit in these cases?

The Griffin case. The evolution of this strand of the new equal protection had its origin in GRIFFIN v. ILLINOIS, 351 U.S. 12 (1956). Griffin held that a state must provide a trial transcript or its equivalent to an indigent criminal defendant appealing a conviction on nonfederal grounds, even though the state ordinarily required that, in order to obtain review, appellants must furnish transcripts to the appellate court. The challengers in Griffin attacked the failure to provide them the free transcripts and claimed that the resulting "refusal to afford appellate reviews solely because of poverty" was unconstitutional.[2] Justice BLACK's opinion, joined by Chief Justice Warren and Justices Douglas and Clark, stated: "Providing equal justice for poor and rich, weak and powerful alike is an age-old problem. [D]ue process and equal protection both call for procedures in criminal trials which allow no invidious discriminations. [Both] equal protection and due process emphasize the central aim of our entire judicial system—all people charged with crime [must] 'stand on an equality before the bar of justice in every American court.' [In] criminal trials a State can no more discriminate on account of poverty than on account of religion, race, or color. Plainly the ability to pay costs in advance bears no rational relationship to a defendant's guilt or innocence and could not be used as an excuse to deprive a defendant of a fair trial. [There] is no meaningful distinction between a rule which would deny the poor the right to defend themselves in a trial court and one which effectively denies the poor an adequate appellate review accorded to all who have money enough to pay the costs in advance. It is true that a State is not required by the Federal Constitution to provide appellate courts or a right to

---

1. Recall the effort to explain Griffin, Douglas, and their progeny in the several opinions in the Rodriguez case.

See generally Goodpaster, "The Integration of Equal Protection, Due Process Standards, and the Indigent's Right of Free Access to the Courts," 56 Iowa L.Rev. 223 (1970), and Michelman, "The Supreme Court and Litigation Access [Fees]," 1973 Duke L.J. 1153 and 1974 Duke L.J. 527.

2. In denying their request for a free transcript, Illinois stated that it provided free transcripts only to indigent defendants sentenced to death. The petitioners in Griffin had been sentenced to prison for armed robbery. Originally, their discrimination claim focused primarily on the distinction between capital and noncapital cases; but the Court's approach rested on broader grounds.

appellate review at all. See, e.g., McKane v. Durston, 153 U.S. 684 [1894]. But that is not to say that a State that does grant appellate review can do so in a way that discriminates against some convicted defendants on account of their poverty. [All] States now provide some method of appeal from criminal convictions. [To] deny adequate review to the poor means that many of them may lose their life, liberty or property because of unjust convictions which appellate courts would set aside. [There] can be no equal justice where the kind of trial a man gets depends on the amount of money he has. Destitute defendants must be afforded as adequate appellate review as defendants who have money enough to buy transcripts."[3]

Justice HARLAN's dissent sketched an approach he was to reiterate and elaborate in a number of later cases. (See, e.g., Douglas, which follows.) He thought the equal protection emphasis misplaced and found no violation of due process. On equal protection, he noted: "All that Illinois has done is to fail to alleviate the consequences of differences in economic circumstances that exist wholly apart from any state action. The Court thus holds that, at least in this area of criminal appeals, [equal protection] imposes on the States an affirmative duty to lift the handicaps flowing from differences in economic circumstances. That holding produces the anomalous result that a constitutional admonition to the States to treat all persons equally means in this instance that Illinois must give to some what it requires others to pay for. [T]he real issue in this case is not whether Illinois *has* discriminated but whether it has a duty *to* discriminate. [T]he issue here is not the typical equal protection question of the reasonableness of a 'classification' on the basis of which the State has imposed legal disabilities, but rather the reasonableness of the State's failure to remove natural disabilities. [I] submit that the basis for that holding is simply an unarticulated conclusion that it violates 'fundamental fairness' for a State which provides for appellate review [not] to see to it that such appeals are in fact available to those it would imprison for serious crimes. That of course is the traditional language of due process." Turning to the due process issue, he asked: "Can it be that, while it was not unconstitutional for Illinois to afford no appeals, its steady progress in increasing the safeguards against erroneous convictions has resulted in a constitutional decline?" He noted that "there is no 'right' to an appeal in the same sense that there is a right to a trial." The only due process guarantee was "simply the right not to be denied an appeal for arbitrary or capricious reasons," and "[n]othing of that kind" appeared here.[4]

---

3. Justice Black added, however, that the transcript might not be necessary in every case: the state courts "may find other means of affording adequate and effective appellate review to indigent defendants. For example, it may be that bystanders' bills of exceptions or other methods of reporting trial proceedings could be used in some cases." Justice FRANKFURTER concurred in the result: "[N]either the fact that a State may deny the right of appeal altogether nor the right of a State to make an appropriate classification, based on differences in crimes and their punishment, nor the right of a State to lay down conditions it deems appropriate for criminal appeals, sanctions differentiations by a State that have no relation to a rational policy of criminal appeal or authorize the imposition of conditions that offend the deepest presupposi-

tions of our society." A dissent by Justices BURTON and MINTON, joined by Justices Reed and Harlan, commented: "We think the distinction [between] capital cases and noncapital cases is a reasonable and valid one. [Illinois] is not bound to make the defendants economically equal before its bar of justice."

4. The view that equal protection imposes on government "an affirmative duty to lift the handicaps flowing from differences in economic circumstances" (as Justice Harlan charged the majority with doing here) became a central premise of those advocating the expansion of fundamental interests-"new" equal protection analysis into such areas as "necessities" in the late 1960s and early 1970s. (See especially sec. 4E below.)

DOUGLAS v. CALIFORNIA

372 U.S. 353, 83 S.Ct. 814, 9 L.Ed.2d 811 (1963).

[Petitioners, indigent criminal defendants, unsuccessfully sought appointed counsel to represent them in their direct appeal as of right to an intermediate appellate court in California. In denying their requests, the appellate court relied on the state procedure under which it made "an independent investigation of the record" to "determine whether it would be of advantage to the defendant or helpful to the appellate court to have counsel appointed." The appellate court stated that it had "gone through" the record and had come to the conclusion that "no good whatever would be served by appointment of counsel." The Court reversed.]

Mr. Justice DOUGLAS delivered the opinion of the [Court].

We agree [with] Justice Traynor of the California Supreme Court, who said that the "[d]enial of counsel on appeal [to an indigent] would seem to be a discrimination at least as invidious as that condemned in Griffin." [The] evil is the same: discrimination against the indigent. For there can be no equal justice where the kind of an appeal a man enjoys "depends on the amount of money he has." [Griffin.] [We] are not here concerned with problems that might arise from the denial of counsel for the preparation of a petition for discretionary or mandatory review beyond the stage in the appellate process at which the claims have once been presented by a lawyer and passed upon by an appellate court. We are dealing only with the *first appeal,* granted [by state law] as a matter of right to rich and poor alike.[1] [Absolute] equality is not required; lines can be and are drawn and we often sustain them. But where the merits of *the one and only appeal* an indigent has as of right are decided without benefit of counsel, we think an unconstitutional line has been drawn between rich and poor. When an indigent is forced to run this gauntlet of a preliminary showing of merit, the right to appeal does not comport with fair procedure. [This case] shows that the discrimination is not between "possibly good and obviously bad cases," but between cases where the rich man can require the court to listen to argument of counsel before deciding on the merits, but a poor man cannot. There is lacking that equality demanded by the 14th Amendment where the rich man, who appeals as of right, enjoys the benefit of counsel's examination into the record, research of the law, and marshalling of arguments on his behalf, while the indigent, already burdened by a preliminary determination that his case is without merit, is forced to shift for himself. The indigent, where the record is unclear or the errors are hidden, has only the right to a meaningless ritual, while the rich man has a meaningful appeal.

Reversed and remanded.

Mr. Justice HARLAN, whom Mr. Justice STEWART joins, dissenting.

[Equal protection] is not apposite, and its application to cases like the present one can lead only to mischievous results. This case should be judged solely under the Due Process Clause, and I do not believe that the California procedure violates that provision. [As to equal protection, the] States, of course, are prohibited [from] discriminating between "rich" and "poor" *as such* in the formulation and application of their laws. But it is a far different thing to suggest that [this] prevents the State from adopting a law of general applicability that may affect the poor more harshly than it does the rich, or, on the other hand, from making some effort to redress economic imbalances while not eliminating them entirely. Every financial exaction which the State imposes on a uniform basis is more easily satisfied by the well-to-do than by the indigent.

---

1. Eleven years later, a divided Court held that the considerations underlying Douglas did not require appointment of counsel in discretionary appeals. Ross v. Moffit (below).

Yet I take it that no one would dispute the constitutional power of the State to levy a uniform sales tax, to charge tuition at a state university, to fix rates for the purchase of water from a municipal corporation, to impose a standard fine for criminal violations, or to establish minimum bail for various categories of offenses. Nor could it be contended that the State may not classify as crimes acts which the poor are more likely to commit then are the rich. And surely, there would be no basis for attacking a state law which provided benefits for the needy simply because those benefits fell short of the goods or services that others could purchase for themselves. Laws such as these do not deny equal protection to the less fortunate for one essential reason: [equal protection] does not impose on the States "an affirmative duty to lift the handicaps flowing from differences in economic circumstances." To so construe it would be to read into the Constitution a philosophy of leveling that would be foreign to many of our basic concepts of the proper relations between government and society. The State may have a moral obligation to eliminate the evils of poverty, but it is not required by [equal protection] to give to some whatever others can afford. [No] matter how far the state rule might go in providing counsel for indigents, it could never be expected to satisfy an affirmative duty—if one existed—to place the poor on the same level as those who can afford the best legal talent [available].

[As to due process], appellate review is in itself not required by the 14th Amendment [and] thus the question presented is the narrow one whether the State's rules with respect to the appointment of counsel are so arbitrary or unreasonable, *in the context of the particular appellate procedure that it has established,* as to require their invalidation. [What] the Court finds constitutionally offensive here bears a striking resemblance to the rules of this Court and many state courts of last resort on petitions for certiorari or for leave to appeal filed by indigent defendants pro se. [This Court] has never deemed itself constitutionally required to appoint counsel to assist in the preparation of each [pro se certiorari petition]. The Court distinguishes our review from the present case on the grounds that the California rule relates to "the *first appeal,* granted as a matter of right." But I fail to see the significance of this difference. Surely, it cannot be contended that the requirements of fair procedure are exhausted once an indigent has been given one appellate review. Nor can it well be suggested that having appointed counsel is more necessary to the fair administration of justice in an initial appeal taken as a matter of right, which the reviewing court on the full record has already determined to be frivolous, than in a petition asking a higher appellate court to exercise its discretion to consider what may be a substantial constitutional claim. [I] cannot agree that the Constitution prohibits a State, in seeking to redress economic imbalances at its bar of justice and to provide indigents with full review, from taking reasonable steps to guard against needless expense. This is all that California has [done].[2]

---

2. Justice CLARK also submitted a dissenting opinion in Douglas.

In a large number of later decisions, the Court has extended the principles of Griffin and Douglas to transcript claims in a range of settings and to the invalidation of filing fee requirements. In Roberts v. LaVallee, 389 U.S. 40 (1967), the Court stated the constitutional requirement in very broad terms: "Our decisions for more than a decade now have made clear that differences in access to the instruments needed to vindicate legal rights, when based upon the financial situation of the defendant, are repugnant to the Constitution." Should there be any limits on the "instruments" to which the indigent defendant is entitled?

ECONOMIC DIFFERENTIATIONS AND THE CRIMINAL PROCESS: THE REACH OF THE GRIFFIN–DOUGLAS PRINCIPLES

1. *Counsel.* ROSS v. MOFFITT, 417 U.S. 600 (1974), refused to extend *Douglas* to discretionary appeals. Justice REHNQUIST's majority opinion emphasized that *Douglas* was limited to the "appointment of counsel for indigent state defendants on their first appeal as of right" and found no constitutional mandate "to require counsel for discretionary state appeals and for applications for review in this Court." He reviewed the Griffin-Douglas line of cases and noted that their "precise rationale" had "never been explicitly stated, some support being derived from [equal protection], and some from [due process]." He added: "Neither clause by itself provides an entirely satisfactory basis for the result reached." Turning to the clauses separately, he disposed of the due process contention in a brief passage. He emphasized the "significant differences between the trial and appellate stages," noting that "it is ordinarily the defendant, rather than the State, who initiates the appellate process. [The] defendant needs an attorney on appeal not as a shield, [but] rather as a sword to upset the prior determination of guilt." This was a "significant" difference. Defendants were entitled to a trial, but there was no right to an appeal: "The fact that an appeal *has* been provided does not automatically mean that a State then acts unfairly by refusing to provide counsel to indigent defendants at every stage of the way. Unfairness results only if indigents are singled out by the State and denied meaningful access to the appellate system because of their poverty. That question is more profitably considered under an equal protection analysis."

Turning to equal protection, he emphasized that the guarantee "does not require absolute equality" but merely appellate systems "free of unreasoned distinctions" and assurance that "indigents have an adequate opportunity to present their claims fairly within the adversarial system." States could not deprive indigents of a "meaningful appeal," but that question was "one of degree." And here, where there had been one appeal as of right, not providing counsel to assist in seeking discretionary review did not deny indigents "meaningful access" to the highest state court. He conceded that a skilled lawyer would "prove helpful to any litigant able to employ him." But this was only a "relative handicap," one "far less than the handicap borne by the indigent defendant denied counsel on his initial appeal as of right in *Douglas*. And the fact that a particular service might be of benefit to an indigent defendant does not mean that the service is constitutionally required. The duty of the State under our cases is not to duplicate the legal arsenal that may be privately retained by a criminal defendant, [but] only to assure the indigent defendant an adequate opportunity to present his claims fairly in the context of the State's appellate process." [1]

2. *State recoupment of funds expended for indigents.* When a state expends funds to assist indigents in the criminal process—e.g., as a result of the constitutional mandate of the Griffin-Douglas line of cases—may it claim

---

1. Justice DOUGLAS' dissent, joined by Justices Brennan and Marshall, drew on due process as well as equal protection, stated that "*Douglas* was grounded on concepts of fairness and equality," and insisted that the "same concepts of fairness and equality, [which] require counsel in a first appeal of right, require counsel in other and subsequent discretionary appeals."

Douglas has not been extended to require provision of counsel to state prisoners in applying for collateral post-conviction relief. But in Bounds v. Smith, 430 U.S. 817 (1977), the majority held that "the fundamental constitutional right of access to the courts requires prison authorities to assist inmates in the preparation and filing of meaningful legal papers by providing prisoners with adequate law libraries or adequate assistance from persons trained in the law."

reimbursement of those expenditures? An equal protection challenge to a recoupment law failed in FULLER v. OREGON, 417 U.S. 40 (1974). The Court sustained a scheme under which the state sought recoupment of legal expenses to the extent a convicted defendant became able to repay, and conditioned a solvent defendant's probation on his reimbursement of the county's legal and investigatory expenses incurred because of his indigency. The Court rejected the claim that that obligation to repay might impel the defendant "to decline the services of an appointed attorney and thus 'chill' his constitutional right to counsel." Justice Stewart responded: "We live in a society where the distribution of legal assistance, like the distribution of all goods and services, is generally regulated by the dynamics of private enterprise. A defendant in a criminal case who is just above the line separating the indigent from the nonindigent must borrow money, sell off his meager assets, or call upon his family or friends in order to hire a lawyer. We cannot say that the Constitution requires that those only slightly poorer must remain forever immune from any obligation to shoulder the expenses of their legal defense, even when they are able to pay without hardship." [2]

3. *Jail sentences to "work off" fines.* Several Burger Court decisions have relied in part on the Griffin-Douglas principles to bar imprisonment for inability to pay fines. For example, in Williams v. Illinois, 399 U.S. 235 (1970), the criminal judgment provided that if the defendant was in default of payments at the expiration of his sentence, he would remain in jail to "work off" his obligations at the rate of $5 per day. That judgment exposed the indigent appellant to confinement for 101 days beyond the statutory maximum sentence for the crime. Chief Justice Burger's majority opinion concluded, on the basis of the Griffin equal protection emphasis, "that an indigent criminal defendant may not be imprisoned in default of payment of a fine beyond the maximum authorized by the statute regulating the substantive offense." To imprison beyond the maximum statutory term solely because of "involuntary nonpayment of a fine or court cost" constituted "an impermissible discrimination that rests on ability to pay." Justice Harlan concurred in the result, but wrote separately in order "to dissociate myself from the 'equal protection' rationale" and once again to urge a due process analysis.[3]

---

2. Though a direct challenge to recoupment provisions does not lie under the Griffin-Douglas principles, traditional equal protection principles—especially the application of minimum scrutiny "with bite"—make the classifications in some recoupment statutes vulnerable. Though such an attack failed in Fuller, it succeeded with respect to another recoupment law in James v. Strange, 407 U.S. 128 (1972). (The case is discussed in Gunther, "Newer Equal Protection.") See also Rinaldi v. Yeager, 384 U.S. 305 (1966).

3. See also Tate v. Short, 401 U.S. 395 (1971), where Williams was extended to cover the case of an indigent who was unable to pay fines of $425 for traffic offenses and was ordered to a prison farm for a period to "work off" the fines at $5 a day. Justice Brennan's opinion stated: "[This] imprisonment for nonpayment constitutes precisely the same unconstitutional discrimination [as in Williams, since] petitioner was subjected to imprisonment solely because of his indigency." The Court noted, however, that Williams might not bar imprisonment "as an enforcement method when alternative means are unsuccessful despite the defendant's reasonable efforts to satisfy the fines by those means." And Williams left open the question whether impris-

onment for nonpayment of fines is permissible when the total jail sentence is no greater than the statutory maximum.

In Bearden v. Georgia, 461 U.S. 660 (1983), the Court relied on Williams and Tate to hold that probation may be revoked for nonpayment of a fine only if it is determined that there had been no bona fide efforts to pay, "or that adequate alternative forms of punishment did not exist." Of particular interest in Justice O'Connor's majority opinion is the discussion of the relationship between due process and equal protection principles: "There is no doubt that the State has treated the petitioner differently from a person who did not fail to pay the imposed fine and therefore did not violate probation. To determine whether this differential treatment violates the Equal Protection Clause, one must determine whether, and under what circumstances, a defendant's indigent status may be considered in the decision whether to revoke probation. This is substantially similar to asking directly the due process question of whether and when it is fundamentally unfair or arbitrary for the State to revoke probation when an indigent is unable to pay the fine." At this point Justice O'Connor added a footnote that articulated a

4. *Noneconomic distinctions and the criminal process.* Does the unusual degree of scrutiny manifested in Griffin, Douglas and their progeny stem from the impact of the challenged state practices on a "fundamental interest"? Is there a "fundamental interest" here analogous to the interest in participation in the electoral process? In the cases in sec. 4B, the presence of the fundamental interest triggered strict scrutiny whether or not economic distinctions were present. The thrust of the Griffin-Douglas principles, by contrast, usually has been more limited. Intense scrutiny has been exercised only where the interest in access to the criminal process was combined with differential economic impacts. Yet the modern Court has not always treated noneconomic classifications in the criminal area with the extreme deference of the old equal protection. Rather, it has steered a somewhat uncertain course, occasionally invalidating classifications by announcing traditional equal protection standards but applying them "with bite." More commonly, the Court has sustained challenged classifications, yet with occasional restatements of "old" equal protection criteria in the direction of the "newer" equal protection. As suggested earlier, it may be the hovering background presence of a quasi-fundamental interest that has induced the Court to voice somewhat more intrusive review criteria in these cases. For an example of an invalidation pursuant to traditional criteria applied "with bite," see Jackson v. Indiana, 406 U.S. 715 (1972), invalidating provisions for the pretrial commitment of incompetent criminal defendants.[4] Since 1972, equal protection challenges have proved less successful, even though standards somewhat more interventionist than those of the old equal protection have sometimes been voiced.[5]

ECONOMIC BARRIERS AND CIVIL LITIGATION: THE BASES (AND LIMITS) OF BODDIE

1. *Boddie.* The appellants in BODDIE v. CONNECTICUT, 401 U.S. 371 (1971), were indigent welfare recipients who sought to file divorce actions in the state courts but were unable to pay the required court fees and costs for services of process. (The amount involved was $60.) They claimed that this financial barrier unconstitutionally restricted their access to the courts. Justice HARLAN's majority opinion sustained that claim, relying entirely on due process rather than equal protection. He concluded "that, given the basic position of the marriage relationship in this society's hierarchy of values[1] and the concomitant state monopolization of the means for legally dissolving this relationship, due process [prohibits] a State from denying, solely because of inability to pay, access to its courts to individuals who seek judicial dissolution of their marriages." He noted that "this Court has seldom been asked to view

preference for a due process inquiry: "A due process approach has the advantage in this context of directly confronting the intertwined question of the role that a defendant's financial background can play in determining an appropriate sentence. When the court is initially considering what sentence to impose, a defendant's level of financial resources is a point on a spectrum rather than a classification. Since indigency in this context is a relative term rather than a classification, [the] more appropriate question is whether consideration of a defendant's financial background in setting or resetting a sentence is so arbitrary or unfair as to be a denial of due process."

4. Decisions such as Jackson are discussed in Gunther, "Newer Equal Protection."

5. See, e.g., McGinnis v. Royster, 410 U.S. 263 (1973). There, even though the challenged statutory scheme was upheld, Justice Powell's majority opinion used language (quoted at p. 606 above) which tested the law by its actual, articulated purposes rather than by hypothesized ones frequently invoked in the deferential review of the old equal protection. But see Marshall v. United States, 414 U.S. 417 (1974), where the standards, as articulated and applied, seemed to retreat to the deferential review of the "old" equal protection.

1. On the substantive due process development of the "fundamental" right to marry, see chap. 8, sec. 3, p. 554 above.

access to the courts as an element of due process"; but that was because "resort to the courts is not usually the only available, legitimate means of resolving private disputes." Here, however, the claims asserted by would-be plaintiffs were "akin to that of defendants faced with exclusion from the only forum effectively empowered to settle their disputes." Accordingly, the applicable principles were those stated "in our due process decisions that delimit rights of defendants compelled to litigate their differences in the judicial forum." He emphasized one of these "settled principles": "due process requires, at a minimum, that absent a countervailing state interest of overriding significance, persons forced to settle their claims of right and duty through the judicial process must be given a meaningful opportunity to be heard." He concluded with an attempt to limit the scope of the decision: "We do not decide that access for all individuals to the courts is a right that is, in all circumstances, guaranteed [by due process, for] in the case before us this right is the exclusive precondition to the adjustment of the fundamental human relationship. The requirement that these appellants resort to the judicial process is entirely a state-created matter." [2]

2. *Kras and Ortwein.* Two months after Boddie, Justice Black, who had dissented there, found broad implications in it. In disagreeing with the Court's disposition of eight other cases "in which indigents were denied access to civil courts because of their poverty," he argued that if Boddie were to continue to be the law, it should be "expanded to all civil cases." Relying on equal protection, he insisted: "Persons seeking a divorce are no different from other members of society who must resort to the judicial process for resolution of their disputes." Meltzer v. LeCraw, 402 U.S. 954 (1971). Lower courts, too, read Boddie broadly. But when the issue of the applicability of Boddie in other civil contexts finally reached the Court, the majority called a halt to that trend. Are the distinctions between Boddie and the later cases justifiable?

In the first post-Boddie ruling, the Court refused to extend "the principle of Boddie to the no-asset bankruptcy proceeding." UNITED STATES v. KRAS, 409 U.S. 434 (1973). An indigent had challenged the $50 filing fee requirement in voluntary bankruptcy proceedings. Justice BLACKMUN's majority opinion emphasized that Boddie "obviously stopped short of an unlimited rule that an indigent at all times and in all cases has the right to relief without the payment of fees." And the bankruptcy situation was sufficiently distinguishable from divorce: Boddie involved the "fundamental" marital relationship; the interest in discharge in bankruptcy did "not rise to the same constitutional level." Moreover, Boddie had emphasized the "utter exclusiveness" of a court remedy; governmental control over debts is not "nearly so exclusive." [3] In ORTWEIN v. SCHWAB, 410 U.S. 656 (1973), the same 5 to 4 majority found Kras rather than Boddie applicable in rejecting an attack by indigents on Oregon's $25 filing fee prerequisite to judicial review of administrative denials

---

2. Justice DOUGLAS' concurring opinion insisted that the equal protection principle of the Griffin line of cases, not due process, was the appropriate ground of decision. He opposed the revival of the elastic, uncertain notions of substantive due process. In another concurring opinion, Justice BRENNAN joined the Court's opinion to the extent that it rested on "procedural due process" grounds. Justice BLACK was the only dissenter, emphasizing that his opinion in Griffin did not suggest that its requirements for criminal defendants were applicable to "the quite different field of civil cases."

3. Justice STEWART's dissent, joined by Justices Douglas, Brennan, and Marshall,

thought the Boddie due process rationale "equally" applicable here. In a separate dissent, Justice MARSHALL went further: "I view the case as involving the right of access to the courts, the opportunity to be heard when one claims a legal right, and not just the right to a discharge in bankruptcy. When a person raises a claim of right or entitlement under the laws, the only forum in our legal system empowered to determine that claim is a court." In another dissent, Justice DOUGLAS, joined by Justice Brennan, emphasized that "discrimination based on wealth" is "particularly 'invidious.'"

of welfare benefits. The Court noted, per curiam, that the interest in welfare payments, like that in a bankruptcy discharge, "has far less constitutional significance than the interest of the Boddie appellants." Moreover, the claim of discrimination against the poor must fail because welfare payments are "in the area of economics and social welfare" and no suspect classification was involved.[4]

3. *Little.* In the 1980s, however, Boddie was followed and Kras and Ortwein distinguished in the unanimous decision in LITTLE v. STREATER, 452 U.S. 1 (1981), holding that due process entitled an indigent defendant in a paternity action to state-subsidized blood grouping tests. Chief Justice BURGER emphasized the unique quality of blood grouping tests as a "source of exculpatory evidence" and "the State's prominent role in litigation." He insisted that "the State's involvement [was] considerable and manifest, giving rise to a constitutional duty." Moreover, paternity proceedings in Connecticut, where this case arose, in fact had "quasi-criminal" overtones, even though they were characterized as "civil" by the State. Accordingly, "an indigent defendant, who faces the State as an adversary [and] who must overcome the evidentiary burden Connecticut imposes, lacks 'a meaningful opportunity to be heard' [Boddie]." Thus, the "fundamental fairness" requirement of due process had not been satisfied. According to the Chief Justice, because defendant had "no choice of an alternative forum and his interests, as well as those of the child, are constitutionally significant [because the creation of a parent-child relationship was at stake], this case is comparable to Boddie rather than to Kras and Ortwein."[5]

D. DURATIONAL RESIDENCE REQUIREMENTS "PENALIZING" THE RIGHT OF INTERSTATE MIGRATION

SHAPIRO v. THOMPSON

394 U.S. 618, 89 S.Ct. 1322, 22 L.Ed.2d 600 (1969).

Mr. Justice BRENNAN delivered the opinion of the Court.

[Each of these three appeals is from a federal court decision] holding unconstitutional [Pa., Conn., and D.C. provisions denying] welfare assistance to residents [who] have not resided within their jurisdictions for at least one year immediately preceding their applications for such assistance. We affirm. [There] is no dispute that the effect of the waiting-period requirement [is] to create two classes of needy resident families indistinguishable from each other except that one is composed of residents who have resided a year or more, and the second of residents who have resided less than a year, in the jurisdiction. [The] first class is granted and the second class is denied welfare aid upon which may depend the ability of the families to obtain the very means to subsist—food, shelter, and other necessities of life. We agree [that the laws violate equal protection]. The interests which appellants assert are promoted by the classification either may not constitutionally be promoted by government or are not compelling governmental interests.

---

4. There were separate dissents by Justices DOUGLAS, BRENNAN, MARSHALL and STEWART. Most of the dissenters insisted that the case was closer to Boddie than to Kras.

5. Compare with Little the divided Court's decision on the same day, in Lassiter v. Department of Social Services, 452 U.S. 18 (1981), rejecting the claim of an indigent mother involved in a state court parental status determination proceeding that she was entitled to counsel. [Little and Lassiter are also noted in the previous chapter, at p. 585 above.]

Primarily, appellants justify the waiting-period requirement as a protective device to preserve the fiscal integrity of state public assistance programs. It is asserted that people who require welfare assistance during their first year of residence in a State are likely to become continuing burdens on state welfare programs. Therefore, the argument runs, if such people can be deterred from entering the jurisdiction by denying them welfare benefits during the first year, state programs to assist long-time residents will not be impaired by a substantial influx of indigent [newcomers].

[The] purpose of inhibiting migration by needy persons into the State is constitutionally impermissible. This Court long ago recognized that the nature of our Federal Union and our constitutional concepts of personal liberty unite to require that all citizens be free to travel throughout the length and breadth of our land uninhibited by statutes, rules, or regulations which unreasonably burden or restrict this movement. [We] have no occasion to ascribe the source of this right to travel interstate to a particular constitutional provision.[1] [See Guest (chap. 10, p. 905 below).] [Thus], the purpose of deterring the in-migration of indigents cannot serve as justification for the classification created by the one-year waiting period, since that purpose is constitutionally [impermissible]. Alternatively, appellants argue that even if it is impermissible for a State to attempt to deter the entry of all indigents, the challenged classification may be justified as a permissible state attempt to discourage those indigents who would enter the State solely to obtain larger benefits. We observe first that none of the statutes before us is tailored to serve that objective. More fundamentally, a State may no more try to fence out those indigents who seek higher welfare benefits than it may try to fence out indigents generally. [We] do not perceive why a mother who is seeking to make a new life for herself and her children should be regarded as less deserving because she considers, among other factors, the level of a State's public assistance. [Appellants] argue further that the challenged classification may be sustained as an attempt to distinguish between new and old residents on the basis of the contribution they have made to the community through the payment of taxes. [This] reasoning would logically permit the State to bar new residents from schools, parks, and libraries or deprive them of police and fire protection. Indeed it would permit the State to apportion all benefits and services according to the past tax contributions of its citizens. [Equal protection] prohibits such an apportionment of state services.[2] We recognize that a State has a valid interest in preserving the fiscal integrity of its programs. It may legitimately attempt to limit its expenditures, whether for public assistance, public education, or any other program. But a State may not accomplish such a purpose by invidious distinctions between

---

1. Recall the discussion of the "right to travel interstate"—and the reasons why it can usually be better understood as a right to migrate from state to state—in chap. 5 above, at p. 315. At this point in his Shapiro opinion, Justice Brennan cited a variety of sources for the "right to travel interstate"—the Privileges and Immunities Clause of Art. IV, § 2 (e.g., Corfield v. Coryell), the commerce clause (e.g., Edwards v. California), and the Privileges and Immunities Clause of the 14th Amendment (e.g., Edwards v. California).

Given the uncertain underpinnings of the right of interstate travel, would it be preferable to rest decisions such as those in this section on the Art. IV, § 2, provision? See the discussion of that provision in chap. 5, at p. 307 above, and in Justice O'Connor's concurrence in Zobel v. Williams, p. 842 below. Note also Doe v. Bolton

(1973; p. 524 above), the companion case to Roe v. Wade. One of the provisions of the Georgia law struck down in Doe was that a patient must be a Georgia resident. The provision was attacked as violative of the right to travel discussed in Shapiro, but the Court relied instead on Art. IV, § 2. Justice Blackmun stated that, just as the Clause "protects persons who enter other States to ply their trade, [so] must it protect persons who enter Georgia seeking the medical services that are available there. [A] contrary holding would mean that a State could limit to its own residents the general medical care available within its borders. This we could not approve."

2. We are not dealing here with state insurance programs which may legitimately tie the amount of benefits to the individual's contributions. [Footnote by Justice Brennan.]

classes of its citizens. It could not, for example, reduce expenditures for education by barring indigent children from its schools. Similarly, [appellants] must do more than show that denying welfare benefits to new residents saves money. The saving of welfare costs cannot justify an otherwise invidious [classification].

Appellants next advance as justification certain administrative and related governmental objectives allegedly served by the waiting-period requirement. [At] the outset, we reject [the] argument that a mere showing of a rational relationship between the waiting period and [the] four admittedly permissible state objectives will suffice, [for] in moving from State to State or to the District of Columbia appellees were exercising a constitutional right, and any classification which serves to penalize the exercise of that right, unless shown to be necessary to promote a *compelling* governmental interest, is unconstitutional. [Cf., e.g., Skinner; Korematsu.] The argument that the waiting-period requirement facilitates budget predictability is wholly unfounded. The records [are] utterly devoid of evidence [of the use of] the one-year requirement as a means to predict the number of people who will require assistance in the budget year. [The] argument that the waiting period serves as an administratively efficient rule of thumb for determining residency similarly will not withstand scrutiny. [Before] granting an application, the welfare authorities investigate the applicant [and] in the course of the inquiry necessarily learn the facts upon which to determine whether the applicant is a resident. [Similarly], there is no need for a State to use the one-year waiting period as a safeguard against fraudulent receipt of benefits; for less drastic means are available, and are employed, to minimize that hazard. [And a] state purpose to encourage employment provides no rational basis for imposing a one-year waiting-period restriction on new residents only [because "this logic would also require a similar waiting period for long-term residents of the State"]. We conclude therefore that appellants [do] not use and have no need to use the one-year requirement for the governmental purposes suggested. Thus, even under traditional equal protection tests a classification of welfare applicants according to whether they have lived in the State for one year would seem irrational and unconstitutional. But, [since] the classification here touches on the fundamental right of interstate movement, its constitutionality must be judged by the stricter standard of whether it promotes a *compelling* state interest. Under this standard, the waiting period requirement clearly violates [equal protection].[3]

Affirmed.[4]

---

3. We imply no view of the validity of waiting-period or residence requirements determining eligibility to vote, eligibility for tuition-free education, to obtain a license to practice a profession, to hunt or fish, and so forth. Such requirements may promote compelling state interests on the one hand, or, on the other, may not be penalties upon the exercise of the constitutional right of interstate travel. [Footnote by Justice Brennan. See the cases that follow.]

The Court also rejected the argument that the constitutional challenge "must fail because Congress expressly approved the imposition" of such a requirement as part of the federal-state funded benefit programs. The Court found no such approval and added that, "even if we were to assume, arguendo," that Congress had approved a one-year waiting period, such an approval "would be unconstitutional. Congress may not authorize the States to violate [equal protection]." In reaching this conclusion, Justice Brennan cited Katzenbach v. Morgan (1966; p.

946 below) and his controversial footnote in that case. (The problem of the power of Congress to determine the substantive content of equal protection is considered in sec. 4 of the next chapter.)

4. Does Shapiro v. Thompson really belong with this fundamental interest-"new" equal protection group of cases? Does it rest on a right derived solely from equal protection? Does it rest on suspect classification analysis? Or does it simply involve an undue burden on a right protected by parts of the Constitution other than equal protection? Recall that Justice Powell, in Rodriguez (p. 789 above), distinguished Shapiro from voting rights and equal protection cases. He stated the basis of Shapiro as follows: "The right to interstate travel had long been recognized as a right of constitutional significance, and the Court's decision, therefore, did not require an ad hoc determination as to the social or economic importance of that right." Compare Justice

Mr. Chief Justice WARREN, with whom Mr. Justice BLACK joins, [dissenting].

[Congress] has imposed a residence requirement in the District of Columbia and authorized the States to impose similar requirements. [I] am convinced that the extent of the burden on interstate travel when compared with the justification for its imposition requires the Court to uphold this exertion of federal power. Congress, pursuant to its commerce power, has enacted a variety of restrictions upon interstate travel. [Recall chap. 3.] [Their] constitutionality appears well settled. [The] Court's right-to-travel cases lend little support to the view that congressional action is invalid merely because it burdens the right to travel. [Here], travel itself is not prohibited. Any burden inheres solely in the fact that a potential welfare recipient might take into consideration the loss of welfare benefits for a limited period of time if he changes his residence. Not only is this burden of uncertain degree, but appellees themselves assert there is evidence that few welfare recipients have in fact been deterred by residence requirements. [The] insubstantiality of the restriction imposed by residence requirements must then be evaluated in light of the possible congressional reasons for such requirements. Our cases require only that Congress have a rational basis for finding that a chosen regulatory scheme is necessary to the furtherance of interstate commerce. Certainly, a congressional finding that residence requirements allowed each State to concentrate its resources upon new and increased programs of rehabilitation ultimately resulting in an enhanced flow of commerce as the economic condition of welfare recipients progressively improved is rational and would justify imposition of residence requirements under the Commerce Clause. [Although] the Court dismisses [the federal permission] with the remark that Congress cannot authorize the States to violate equal protection, I believe that the dispositive issue is whether under its commerce power Congress can impose [residence requirements].

Mr. Justice HARLAN, [dissenting].

In upholding the equal protection argument, the Court has applied an equal protection doctrine of relatively recent vintage: the rule that statutory classifications which either are based upon certain "suspect" criteria or affect "fundamental rights" will be held to deny equal protection unless justified by a "compelling" governmental interest. The "compelling interest" doctrine, which today is articulated more explicitly than ever before, constitutes an increasingly significant exception to the long-established rule that a statute does not deny equal protection if it is rationally related to a legitimate governmental objective. The "compelling interest" doctrine has two branches. The branch which requires that classifications based upon "suspect" criteria be supported by a compelling interest apparently had its genesis in cases involving racial classifications. Today the list [of "suspect" criteria] apparently has been further enlarged to include classifications based upon recent interstate movement, and perhaps those based upon the exercise of *any* constitutional right. [I] think that

Harlan's dissent, below, on which Justice Powell's opinion in Rodriguez relied heavily.

Even though Shapiro can be read as resting ultimately on the right of interstate migration, it did encourage assertions of an equal protection right to "necessities of life." That encouragement came in part from Justice Brennan's passing reference, in the first paragraph of the opinion above, to "the very means to subsist—food, shelter, and other necessities of life." It also came in part from the special attention to that passage in Justice Harlan's dissent (which follows), in the course of his general criticism of

most of the "new" equal protection methodology. But the Warren Court never specifically held that there was a fundamental equal protection interest in "necessities," any more than it clearly held that wealth was a suspect classification. The failure to develop those Warren Court dicta is traced in sec. 4E below. (Even though Shapiro failed to spur an expansion of welfare and "necessities" rights, it has retained some vitality with respect to its actual holding, regarding the impact of durational residence requirements on the right to travel. See the notes at p. 838 below.)

this branch of the "compelling interest" doctrine is sound when applied to racial classifications [because of the historical purpose of equal protection]. However, I believe that the more recent extensions have been unwise. [I] do not consider wealth a "suspect" statutory criterion. And [when] a classification is based upon the exercise of rights guaranteed against state infringement by [the] Constitution, then there is no need for any resort to [equal protection]; in such instances, this Court may properly and straightforwardly invalidate any undue burden upon those rights under the 14th Amendment's Due Process Clause.

The second branch of the "compelling interest" principle is even more troublesome. For it has been held that a statutory classification is subject to the "compelling interest" test if the result of the classification may be to affect a "fundamental right," regardless of the basis of the classification. This rule was foreshadowed in [Skinner] and reemerged in Reynolds v. Sims. [See also e.g., Harper; Williams v. Rhodes.][1] It has reappeared today in the Court's cryptic suggestion that the "compelling interest" test is applicable merely because the result of the classification may be to deny the appellees "food, shelter, and other necessities of life," as well as in the Court's statement that "[s]ince the classification here touches on the fundamental right of interstate movement, its constitutionality must be judged by the stricter standard of whether it promotes a *compelling* state interest." I think this branch of the "compelling interest" doctrine particularly unfortunate and unnecessary. It is unfortunate because it creates an exception which threatens to swallow the standard equal protection rule. Virtually every state statute affects important rights. This Court has repeatedly held, for example, that the traditional equal protection standard is applicable to statutory classifications affecting such fundamental matters as the right to pursue a particular occupation, the right to receive greater or smaller wages or to work more or less hours, and the right to inherit property. Rights such as these are in principle indistinguishable from those involved here, and to extend the "compelling interest" rule to all cases in which such rights are affected would go far toward making this Court a "super-legislature." This branch of the doctrine is also unnecessary. When the right affected is one assured by the federal Constitution, any infringement can be dealt with under [due process]. But when a statute affects only matters not mentioned in the Federal Constitution and is not arbitrary or irrational, I must reiterate that I know of nothing which entitles this Court to pick out particular human activities, characterize them as "fundamental," and give them added protection under an unusually stringent equal protection test.[2]

[If] the issue is regarded purely as one of equal protection, then, [this] nonracial classification should be judged by ordinary equal protection standards. [For] reasons hereafter set forth, a legislature might rationally find that the imposition of a welfare residence requirement would aid in the accomplishment

---

1. Analysis is complicated when the statutory classification is grounded upon the exercise of a "fundamental" right. For then the statute may come within the first branch of the "compelling interest" doctrine because exercise of the right is deemed a "suspect" criterion and also within the second because the statute is considered to affect the right by deterring its exercise. Williams v. Rhodes [p. 817 above] is such a case insofar as the statutes involved both inhibited exercise of the right of political association and drew distinctions based upon the way the right was exercised. The present case is another instance, insofar as welfare residence statutes both deter interstate movement and distinguish among welfare applicants on the basis of such movement. Consequently, I have not attempted to specify the branch of the doctrine upon which these decisions rest. [Footnote by Justice Harlan.]

2. Justice STEWART, who joined the majority opinion, criticized this passage in a separate concurring notation. He claimed that Justice Harlan had "quite misapprehended" the majority opinion: "The Court today does *not* 'pick out particular human activities, characterize them as fundamental,' and give them added protection. To the contrary, the Court simply recognizes [an] established constitutional right [the right to travel]. [The] Court today, therefore, is not 'contriving new constitutional principles.' It is deciding these cases under the aegis of established constitutional law."

of at least four valid governmental objectives. It might also find that residence requirements have advantages not shared by other methods of achieving the same goals. [Thus], it cannot be said that the requirements are "arbitrary" or "lacking in rational justification." Hence, I can find no objection to these residence requirements under [equal protection]. The next issue, which I think requires fuller analysis than that deemed necessary by the Court under its equal protection rationale, is whether a one-year welfare residence requirement amounts to an undue burden upon the right of interstate travel. Four considerations are relevant: *First,* what is the constitutional source and nature of the right to travel which is relied upon? *Second,* what is the extent of the interference with that right? *Third,* what governmental interests are served by welfare residence requirements? *Fourth,* how should the balance of the competing considerations be struck? [I conclude] that the right to travel interstate is a "fundamental" right which, for present purposes, should be regarded as having its source in [due process]. [On "the extent of the interference" with that right, Justice Harlan noted: "The number or proportion of persons who are actually deterred from changing residence by the existence of these provisions is unknown."]

[Turning to the "governmental interests" served by the requirements, Justice Harlan stated:] There appear to be four such interests. First, it is evident that a primary concern [of the legislatures] was to deny welfare benefits to persons who moved into the jurisdiction primarily in order to collect those benefits. This seems to me an entirely legitimate objective. [A] second possible purpose of residence requirements is the prevention of fraud. A residence requirement provides an objective and workable means of determining that an applicant intends to remain indefinitely within the jurisdiction. [Third], the requirement of a fixed period of residence may help in predicting the budgetary amount which will be needed for public assistance in the future. [Fourth], the residence requirements conceivably may have been predicated upon a legislative desire to restrict welfare payments financed in part by state tax funds to persons who have recently made some contribution to the State's economy. [This] too would appear to be a legitimate purpose.

The next question is the decisive one: whether the governmental interests served by residence requirements outweigh the burden imposed upon the right to travel. In my view, a number of considerations militate in favor of constitutionality. [He noted the "legitimate governmental interests" listed above; the "indirect" and "insubstantial" impact on travel; the state-federal cooperation; and the "mature deliberation" on the competing arguments by the legislatures. He added:] Fifth, and of longer-range importance, the field of welfare assistance is one in which there is a widely recognized need for fresh solutions and consequently for experimentation. Invalidation of welfare residence requirements might have the unfortunate consequence of discouraging the Federal and State Governments from establishing unusually generous welfare programs in particular areas on an experimental basis, because of fears that the program would cause an influx of persons seeking higher welfare payments. Sixth and finally, a strong presumption of constitutionality attaches to statutes of the types now before us. [A]lthough the appellees assert that the same objectives could have been achieved by less restrictive means, this is an area in which the judiciary should be especially slow to fetter the judgment of Congress and of some 46 state legislatures in the choice of [methods]. Today's decision reflects to an unusual degree the current notion that this Court possesses a peculiar wisdom all its own whose capacity to lead this Nation out of its present troubles is contained only by the limits of judicial ingenuity in contriving new constitutional principles to meet each problem as it arises. For anyone who, like myself, believes that it is an essential function of this Court to maintain the constitutional divisions between state and federal authority and among the three branches of the Federal Government, today's decision is a step in the wrong direction. This resurgence of the expansive view of "equal protection" carries the seeds of more judicial interference with the state and federal legislative process, much more indeed than does the judicial application of "due process" according to traditional concepts, about which some members of this Court have expressed fears as to its potentialities for setting us up as judges ["at large"].

DURATIONAL RESIDENCE REQUIREMENTS

Introduction. Shapiro v. Thompson was an important step in the Warren Court's development of the "fundamental rights and interests" strand of the "new" equal protection in two respects. First, it launched strict scrutiny of durational residence requirements "penalizing" the "right" of interstate mobility. That strand proved a quite sturdy one, and its evolution is traced in this group of notes. Second, Shapiro hinted at an amorphous, new fundamental interest with potentially far-reaching implications in imposing affirmative governmental obligations to redress economic inequalities—the hint Justice Harlan's dissent referred to as the "cryptic suggestion that the 'compelling interest' test is applicable merely because the result of the classification may be to deny appellees food, shelter, and other necessities of life." That strand proved far less sturdy: as Rodriguez confirmed, the Burger Court refused to extend the strict scrutiny of the new equal protection to a broad range of "necessities." [1]

Consider, then, the impact of Shapiro on durational residence requirements. Shapiro applies the strict scrutiny variety of equal protection to "penalties" on the right of interstate travel. (The right of interstate mobility or interstate migration might be more descriptive terms.) When are restraints on interstate mobility permissible? And what are the criteria for determining when a state restriction "penalizes" the constitutional right? For determining whether an asserted state justification is adequately "compelling"? One case considered earlier throws light on the implications of Shapiro. In Dunn v. Blumstein (1972; p. 814 above), the strict scrutiny invalidation of a state one-year residence requirement for voting rested not only on the interference with the "fundamental interest" in participation in the electoral process, but also on the "right" to travel. In Blumstein, Justice Marshall noted that the state sought to avoid "the clear command of Shapiro" by claiming "that durational residence requirements for voting neither seek to nor actually do deter such travel." He insisted that that argument reflected "a fundamental misunderstanding": "Shapiro did not rest upon a finding that denial of welfare actually deterred travel." Rather, Shapiro found strict scrutiny triggered by "any classification which serves to *penalize* the exercise" of the right to travel. Justice Marshall emphasized that the Shapiro majority had "found no need to dispute the 'evidence that few welfare recipients have in fact been deterred [from moving] by residence requirements.'" He added: "Only last Term, it was specifically noted that because a durational residence requirement for voting 'operates to *penalize* those persons, and only those persons, who have exercised their constitutional right of interstate migration, [it] may withstand constitutional scrutiny only upon a clear showing that the burden imposed is necessary to protect a compelling and substantial governmental interest.' " [2]

If the suspiciously viewed residence requirements are those that "serve to *penalize*," and if the notion of "penalty" does not necessarily rest on legislative purpose or effect, how are the occasions for strict scrutiny to be identified?

---

1. The refusal to establish fundamental equal protection rights regarding "necessities" is traced in sec. 4E below.

2. That quotation was from the separate opinion of Justices Brennan, White and Marshall in Oregon v. Mitchell (1970; p. 953 below).

Justice Marshall elaborated on that theme in Maricopa, which follows. Ironically, in the context of distinguishing permissible from impermissible residence requirements as to eligibility for state benefits, the "necessities of life" concept of Shapiro continues to play a role. As Rodriguez and sec. 4E show, "necessities of life" did not become a full-blown new "fundamental interest," as Justice Harlan in Shapiro had feared, and as others had hoped. Shapiro's major impact has been confined to the context of residence requirements; but in the evolution of that impact, requirements barring eligibility for "necessities" have proved to be particularly vulnerable.

1. *Medical care for indigents.* Justice MARSHALL's majority opinion in MEMORIAL HOSPITAL v. MARICOPA COUNTY, 415 U.S. 250 (1974), reexamined and relied on Shapiro in invalidating an Arizona requirement of a year's residence in a county as a condition to an indigent's receiving free nonemergency hospitalization or medical care. In that reexamination, it emerged that not all residence requirements were impermissible: Shapiro had cautioned that some "waiting periods [may] not be penalties"; in other cases, the Court had sustained durational residence requirements as a condition to lower tuition at state universities.[3] The critical ingredient for triggering strict scrutiny and probable invalidation proved to be the existence of a "penalty"; and whether there was a "penalty" apparently turned largely on whether there was an effect on a "necessity of life."

Justice Marshall noted that the constitutional right of interstate travel "was involved in only a limited sense in Shapiro." Both Shapiro and Blumstein had endorsed "bona fide residence requirements"; yet even those requirements "would burden the right to travel, if travel meant merely movement." Not mere travel but the right to "migrate with intent to settle and abide" had been central in Shapiro. And though any durational residence requirement "impinges to some extent" on that right, Shapiro had not condemned all such requirements. Instead, Shapiro mandated intensive review only when the requirements were "penalties." And whether a durational residence requirement was a "penalty" depended on the impact of the requirement. He acknowledged that the "amount of impact required to give rise to the compelling-state-interest test was not made clear" in Shapiro. Shapiro had suggested two criteria: first, "whether the waiting period would deter migration"; second, "the extent to which the residency requirement served to *penalize* the exercise of the right to travel." In Justice Marshall's view, the second, not the first, criterion was critical. And whether a residence requirement was a "penalty" depended on the nature of the benefits affected: in Shapiro "the Court found denial of the basic 'necessities of life' to be a penalty"; on the other hand, state college tuition differentials between residents and nonresidents had not been invalidated. Accordingly, "[w]hatever the ultimate parameters of the Shapiro penalty analysis, it is at least clear that medical care is as much 'a basic necessity of life' to an indigent as welfare assistance. And, governmental [benefits] necessary to basic sustenance have often been viewed as being of greater constitutional significance than less essential forms of governmental entitlements." That analysis led to the ultimate conclusion about the appropriate standard of scrutiny: "[The] right of interstate travel must be seen as insuring new residents the same right to vital government benefits and privileges in the States to which they migrate as are enjoyed by other residents. [Arizona's] durational residency requirement for free medical care penalizes indigents for exercising their right to migrate to and settle in that State. Accordingly, the classification created by the residence requirement, 'unless shown to be necessary to promote a *compelling* [state] interest, is unconstitutional.' Shapiro." Justice Marshall had little difficulty in concluding that the

---

3. See footnote 5 below.

Arizona scheme could not survive the strict scrutiny demanded by that standard: the defenders of the durational residence requirement had not "met their heavy burden of justification, or demonstrated that the State, in pursuing legitimate objectives, has chosen means which do not unnecessarily impinge on constitutionally protected interests." [4]

2. *Divorce laws.* A year later, in rejecting another attack on a residence requirement, Justice Rehnquist wrote for the majority and Justice Marshall was in dissent. In SOSNA v. IOWA, 419 U.S. 393 (1975), the Court upheld a requirement that a party reside in the state for one year before bringing a divorce action against a nonresident. In rejecting the challenge based on the line of cases from Shapiro to Maricopa, Justice REHNQUIST noted that most states had "durational residency requirements for divorce" and that the area of domestic relations "has long been regarded as a virtually exclusive province of the States." He found ample justification for the requirement here: "What [the earlier] cases had in common was that the durational residency requirements they struck down were justified on the basis of budgetary or record-keeping considerations which were held insufficient to outweigh the constitutional claims of the individuals. But Iowa's divorce residency requirement is of a different stripe. Appellant was not irretrievably foreclosed from obtaining some part of what she sought, as was the case with the welfare recipients in Shapiro, the voters in Blumstein, or the indigent patient in Maricopa County. She would eventually qualify for the same sort of adjudication which she demanded virtually upon her arrival in the State. Iowa's requirement delayed her access to the courts, but, by fulfilling it, a plaintiff could ultimately obtain the same opportunity for adjudication which she asserts ought to be hers at an earlier point in time. Iowa's residency requirement may reasonably be justified on grounds other than purely budgetary considerations or administrative convenience. A decree of divorce is not a matter in which the only interested parties are the State [and] a plaintiff. [Both] spouses are obviously interested [and] a decree of divorce [often includes] provisions [for] custody and support. With consequences of such moment riding on a divorce decree, [Iowa] may insist that one seeking to initiate such a proceeding have the modicum of attachment to the State required here. Such a requirement additionally furthers the State's parallel interests in both avoiding officious intermeddling in matters in which another State has a paramount interest, and in minimizing the susceptibility of its own divorce decrees to collateral attack. A State such as Iowa may quite reasonably decide that it does not wish to become a divorce mill."

Justice MARSHALL, joined by Justice Brennan, dissented, insisting that the decision "departs sharply from the course we have followed in analyzing durational residency requirements since Shapiro." He thought the majority's approach suggested "a new distaste for the mode of analysis we have applied to this corner of equal protection law." The majority had substituted "an ad hoc

---

4. Justice REHNQUIST was the sole dissenter. However, several other Justices also withheld full support from Justice Marshall's rationale. Chief Justice BURGER and Justice BLACKMUN simply noted their concurrence in the result. And Justice DOUGLAS' concurrence stated that he shared Justice Rehnquist's doubts about "interstate travel per se." He concluded: "The political processes rather than equal protection litigation are the ultimate solution of the present problem. But in the setting of this case the invidious discrimination against the poor [Harper], not the right to travel interstate, is in my view the critical issue." (Justice Rehnquist criticized the majority's inadequate exploration of a travel rationale and offered his own

alternative: "It seems to me that the line to be derived from our prior cases is that some financial impositions on interstate travelers [e.g., toll charges on interstate bridges] have such indirect inconsequential impact on travel that they simply do not constitute the type of direct purposeful barrier struck down in [e.g., Shapiro]. Where the impact is that remote, a State can reasonably require that the citizen bear some proportion of the State's cost in its facilities. I would think that this standard is not only supported by this Court's decisions, but would be eminently sensible and workable. But the Court not only rejects this approach, but leaves it entirely without guidance as to the proper standard to be applied.")

balancing test." He was especially critical of the majority's failure to make what "should be the first inquiry: whether the right to obtain a divorce is of sufficient importance that its denial to recent immigrants constitutes a penalty on interstate travel." He added: "In my view, it clearly meets that standard." Accordingly, [I] would scrutinize Iowa's durational residency requirement to determine whether it constitutes a reasonable means of furthering important interests asserted by the State." The majority, by contrast, had not only declined to apply the "compelling interest" test, but had also "conjured up possible justifications for the State's restriction in a manner much more akin to the lenient standard we have in the past applied in analyzing equal protection challenges to business regulations." [5]

---

5. Justice Marshall found only one justification for the law of "any real force": the claim that "the State has interests both in protecting itself from use as a 'divorce mill' and in protecting its judgments from possible collateral attack in other States." But he found that these interests would "adequately be protected by a simple requirement of domicile—physical presence plus intent to remain—which would remove the rigid one-year barrier while permitting the State to restrict the availability of its divorce process to citizens who are genuinely its own."

What is the constitutional status of other state durational residence requirements in light of Shapiro, Maricopa, and Sosna? All Justices agree that some residence requirements are valid; yet the cases also indicate that others may be vulnerable to constitutional challenge—if they affect "important interests," under Justice Marshall's approach, or if they lack adequate justification, under Justice Rehnquist's analysis. One of the barriers to nonresidents frequently mentioned as permissible is a state tuition preference for local students at state universities. In 1971, a summary affirmance suggested the futility of a Shapiro-based attack on such a preference scheme: the Court sustained Minnesota's one-year durational residence requirement for receipt of in-state tuition benefits. Starns v. Malkerson, 326 F.Supp. 234, aff'd, 401 U.S. 985 (1971). Yet implementation of such a scheme proved vulnerable via another route, in Vlandis v. Kline, 412 U.S. 441 (1973). There, the Court found the Connecticut scheme for implementing in-state students' tuition preferences invalid by purporting to resort to procedural due process principles, finding in the scheme a reliance on forbidden "irrebuttable presumptions" (see p. 853 below). Recall also the sustaining of a bona fide residence requirement (as applied to bar free public education for children who were American citizens but whose parents were non-resident aliens and who had come to the State "for the primary purpose of attending the public free schools"), in Martinez v. Bynum (1983; noted in sec. 4A above, at p. 808).

For rare modern cases examining right to travel claims in contexts other than durational residence requirements, see not only the principal case that follows, but also Jones v. Helms, 452 U.S. 412 (1981). That decision unanimously upheld a Georgia law making a parent's willful abandonment of a dependent child a crime. Such behavior is a misdemeanor if all the events take place intrastate, but becomes a felony if the parent leaves the State after abandoning the child in Georgia. The lower court upheld the challenge, applying strict scrutiny in the belief that the law constituted an infringement of the "fundamental right to travel." But Justice Stevens' opinion reversing that judgment emphasized that the defendant's criminal behavior "necessarily qualified his right" to travel interstate. Unlike the earlier cases, moreover, this did not involve disparate treatment of residents and nonresidents or old and new residents. The question was simply a narrower one of whether a state could enhance criminal punishment if the offender left after committing the crime: "[Although] a simple penalty for leaving a State is plainly impermissible, if departure aggravates the consequences of conduct [otherwise] punishable, the State may treat the entire sequence of events [as] more serious than its separate components." Since there was no impermissible infringement of the right to travel, rationality review applied, and that was easily satisfied. (In a separate statement, Justice White contended that the Court had vindicated his position at the time of Shapiro: that such cases could be decided directly on right to travel grounds "without implicating [equal protection] at all." He claimed that the Court had in essence followed such an approach here. Justice Blackmun concurred only in the judgment.) Note also the next principal case, another unusual right to travel context: there, eligibility for state benefits was not conditioned on minimal residence, but rather was allocated on the basis of length of residence.

ZOBEL v. WILLIAMS

457 U.S. 55, 102 S.Ct. 2309, 72 L.Ed.2d 672 (1982).

Chief Justice BURGER delivered the opinion of the Court.

The question presented [is] whether a statutory scheme by which a State distributes income derived from its natural resources to the adult citizens of the State in varying amounts, based on the length of each citizen's residence, violates the equal protection rights of newer state citizens. The 1967 discovery of large oil reserves on state-owned land in the Prudhoe Bay Area of Alaska resulted in a windfall to the State. The State, which had a total budget of $124 million in 1969, before the oil revenues began to flow into the state coffers, received $3.7 billion in petroleum revenues during the 1981 fiscal year.[1] This income will continue, and most likely grow for some years in the future. Recognizing that its mineral reserves, although large, are finite and that the resulting income will not continue in perpetuity, the State took steps to assure that its current good fortune will bring long range benefits. To accomplish this Alaska in 1976 adopted a constitutional amendment establishing the Permanent Fund into which the State must deposit at least 25% of its mineral income each year. The amendment prohibits the legislature from appropriating any of the principal of the Fund but permits use of the Fund's earnings for general governmental purposes.

In 1980, the legislature enacted a dividend program to distribute annually a portion of the Fund's earnings directly to the State's adult residents. Under the plan, each citizen 18 years of age or older receives one dividend unit for each year of residency subsequent to 1959, the first year of statehood. The statute fixed the value of each dividend unit at $50 for the 1979 fiscal year; a one-year resident thus would receive one unit, or $50, while a resident of Alaska since it became a State in 1959 would receive 21 units, or $1,050. The value of a dividend unit will vary each year depending on the income of the Permanent Fund and the amount of that income the State allocates for other purposes. The State now estimates that the 1985 fiscal year dividend will be nearly four times as large as that for 1979. Appellants, residents of Alaska since 1978, brought this suit in 1980 challenging the dividend distribution plan as violative of their right to [equal protection] and their constitutional right to migrate to Alaska, to establish residency there and thereafter to enjoy the full rights of Alaska citizenship on the same terms as all other citizens of the [State].

[The] Alaska dividend distribution law is quite unlike the durational residency requirements we examined in [Sosna; Maricopa; Blumstein; Shapiro]. Those cases involved laws which required new residents to reside in the State a fixed minimum period to be eligible for certain benefits available on an equal basis to all other residents. [The] Alaska statute does not impose any threshold waiting period on those seeking dividend [benefits]. Nor does the statute purport to establish a test of the bona fides of state residence. Instead, the dividend statute creates fixed, permanent distinctions between an ever increasing number of perpetual classes of concededly bona fide residents, based on how long they have been in the State. The distinctions appellants attack include the preference given to persons who were residents when Alaska became a State in 1959 over all those who have arrived since then, as well as the distinctions made between all bona fide residents who settled in Alaska at different times during the 1959 to 1980 period.[2] When a State distributes benefits unequally,

---

1. [The] 1980 census reports that Alaska's adult population is 270,265; per capita 1981 oil revenues amount to $13,632 for each adult resident. Petroleum revenues now amount to 89% of the State's total government revenue. [Footnote by Chief Justice Burger.]

2. The Alaska statute does not simply make distinctions between native born Alaskans and

the distinctions it makes are subject to scrutiny under [equal protection].[3] Generally, a law will survive that scrutiny if the distinction it makes rationally furthers a legitimate state purpose. Some particularly invidious distinctions are subject to more rigorous scrutiny. Appellants claim that the distinctions made by the Alaska law should be subjected to the higher level of scrutiny applied to the durational residency requirements in [Shapiro and Maricopa]. The State, on other hand, asserts that the law need only meet the minimum rationality test. In any event, if the statutory scheme cannot pass even the minimal test proposed by the State, we need not decide whether any enhanced scrutiny is called for.

[The] State advanced [three] purposes justifying the distinctions made by the dividend program: (a) creation of a financial incentive for individuals to establish and maintain residence in Alaska; (b) encouragement of prudent management of the Permanent Fund; and (c) apportionment of benefits in recognition of undefined "contributions of various kinds, both tangible and intangible, which residents have made during their years of residency." [The] first two state objectives [are] not rationally related to the distinctions Alaska seeks to make between newer residents and those who have been in the State since 1959. Assuming arguendo that granting increased dividend benefits for each year of continued Alaska residence might give some residents an incentive to stay in the state in order to reap increased dividend benefits in the future, the State's interest is not in any way served by granting greater dividends to persons for their residency during the 21 years prior to the enactment. Nor does the State's purpose of furthering the prudent management of the Permanent Fund and the state's resources support retrospective application of its plan to the date of statehood. [Even] if we assume that the state interest is served by increasing the dividend for each year of residency beginning with the date of enactment, is it rationally served by granting greater dividends in varying amounts to those who resided in Alaska during the 21 years prior to enactment? We think not.

The last of the State's objectives—to reward citizens for past contributions—alone was relied upon by the Alaska Supreme Court to support the retrospective application of the law to 1959. However, that objective is not a legitimate state purpose. A similar "past contributions" argument was made and rejected in [Shapiro]: "[This] reasoning would permit the State to apportion all benefits and services according to the past tax [or intangible] contributions of its citizens. *The Equal Protection Clause prohibits such an apportionment of state services.*" (Em-

those who migrate to Alaska from other states; it does not discriminate only against those who have recently exercised the right to travel, as did the statute involved in [Shapiro]. The Alaska statute also discriminates among long-time residents and even native born residents. For example, a person born in Alaska in 1962 would have received $100 less than someone who was born in the State in 1960. Of course the native Alaskan born in 1962 would also receive $100 less than the person who moved to the State in 1960.

The statute does not involve the kind of discrimination which the Privileges and Immunities Clause of Art. IV was designed to prevent. That Clause "was designed to insure to a citizen of State A who ventures into State B the same privileges which the citizens of State B enjoy." Toomer v. Witsell. The Clause is thus not applicable to this case. [Footnote by Chief Justice Burger. Compare Justice O'Connor's concurrence, below, and the Camden case in chap. 5, at p. 308.]

3. The Alaska courts considered whether the dividend distribution law violated appellants'

constitutional right to travel. The right to travel and to move from one state to another has long been accepted, yet both the nature and the source of that right has remained obscure. In addition to protecting persons against the erection of actual barriers to interstate movement, the right to travel, when applied to residency requirements, protects new residents of a state from being disadvantaged because of their recent migration or from otherwise being treated differently from longer-term residents. In reality, right to travel analysis refers to little more than a particular application of equal protection analysis. Right to travel cases have examined, in equal protection terms, state distinctions between newcomers and longer-term residents. See [Maricopa; Blumstein; Shapiro]. This case also involves distinctions between residents based on when they arrived in the State and is therefore also subject to equal protection analysis. [Footnote by Chief Justice Burger.]

phasis added.) [If] the States can make the amount of a cash dividend depend on length of residence, what would preclude varying university tuition on a sliding scale based on years of residence—or even limiting access to finite public facilities, eligibility for student loans, for civil service jobs, or for government contracts by length of domicile? Could States impose different taxes based on length of residence? Alaska's reasoning could open the door to state apportionment of other rights, benefits and services according to length of residency.[4] It would permit the states to divide citizens into expanding numbers of permanent classes. Such a result would be clearly [impermissible].[5]

The only apparent justification for the retrospective aspect of the program, "favoring established residents over new residents," is constitutionally unacceptable. In our view Alaska has shown no valid state interests which are rationally served by the distinction it makes between citizens who established residence before 1959 and those who have become residents since then. We hold that the Alaska dividend distribution plan violates the guarantees of [equal protection].

[Reversed.]

Justice BRENNAN, with whom Justice MARSHALL, Justice BLACKMUN, and Justice POWELL join, concurring.

I join the opinion of the [Court]. I write separately only to emphasize that the pervasive discrimination embodied in the Alaska distribution scheme gives rise to constitutional concerns of somewhat larger proportions than may be evident on a cursory reading of the Court's opinion. In my view, these concerns might well preclude even the prospective operation of Alaska's scheme.[1] [I] agree with Justice O'Connor that these more fundamental defects in the Alaska dividend-distribution law are, in part, reflected in what has come to be called the "right to travel." [2] That right—or, more precisely, the federal interest in free interstate migration—is clearly, though indirectly, affected by the Alaska dividend-distribution law, and this threat to free interstate migration provides an independent rationale for holding that law unconstitutional. At the outset, however, I note that the frequent attempts to assign the right to travel some textual source in the Constitution seem to me to have proven both inconclusive and unnecessary. [As] is clear from our cases, the right to travel achieves its most forceful expression in the context of equal protection analysis. But if, finding no citable passage in the Constitution to assign as its source, some might be led to question the independent vitality of the principle of free interstate migration, I find its unmistakable essence in that document that transformed a loose confederation of States into one Nation. A scheme of the sort adopted by Alaska is inconsistent with the Federal structure even in its prospective operation.

The Court today reaffirms the important principle that, at least with respect to a durational-residency discrimination, a State's desire "to reward citizens for

---

4. Apportionment would thus be prohibited only when it involves "fundamental rights" and services deemed to involve "basic necessities of life." See [Maricopa]. [Footnote by Chief Justice Burger.]

5. Starns v. Malkerson [p. 841 above] cannot be read as a contrary decision of this Court. First, summary affirmance by this Court is not to be read as an adoption of the reasoning supporting the judgment under review. Moreover, [we] considered the Minnesota one-year residency requirement [for in-state tuition benefits] examined in Starns a test of bona fide residence, not a return on prior contributions to the commonwealth. [Footnote by Chief Justice Burger.]

1. Chief Justice Burger found it unnecessary to consider whether the dividend program could operate prospectively.

2. What is notably at stake in this case, and what clearly must be taken into account in determining the constitutionality of this legislative scheme, is the *national* interest in a fluid system of interstate movement. It may be that national interests are not always easily translated into individual rights, but where the "right to travel" is involved, our cases leave no doubt that it will trigger intensified equal protection [scrutiny]. [Footnote by Justice Brennan.]

past contributions" is "clearly not a legitimate state purpose." I do not think it "odd" [see Justice O'Connor's concurrence] that the Court disclaims reliance on the "right to travel" as the source of this limitation on state power. In my view, the acknowledged illegitimacy of that state purpose has a different heritage—it reflects not the structure of the Federal Union but the idea of constitutionally protected equality. See [e.g., Shapiro]. [T]he Alaska plan discriminates against the recently naturalized citizen, in favor of the Alaska citizen of longer duration; it discriminates against the eighteen year old native resident, in favor of all residents of longer duration. If the Alaska plan were limited to discriminations such as these, and did not purport to apply to migrants from sister States, interstate travel would not be noticeably burdened—yet those discriminations would surely be constitutionally suspect. [The 14th] Amendment does not suggest by its terms that equal treatment might be denied a person depending upon how long that person *has been* within the jurisdiction of the State. [It] does, however, expressly recognize one elementary basis for distinguishing between persons who may be within a State's jurisdiction at any particular time—by setting forth the requirements for state citizenship. But it is significant that the Citizenship Clause of the 14th Amendment expressly equates citizenship only with simple residence. That Clause does not provide for, and does not allow for, degrees of citizenship based on length of residence. And the Equal Protection Clause would not tolerate such distinctions. In short, as much as the right to travel, equality of citizenship is of the essence in our republic.

[It] is, of course, elementary that the Constitution does not bar the States from making reasoned distinctions between citizens. Insofar as those distinctions are rationally related to the legitimate ends of the State they present no constitutional difficulty, as our equal protection jurisprudence attests. But we have never suggested that duration of residence *vel non* provides a valid justification for discrimination. To the contrary, discrimination on the basis of residence must be supported by a valid state interest independent of the discrimination itself. To be sure, allegiance and attachment may be rationally measured by length of residence—length of residence may, for example, be used to test the bona fides of citizenship—and allegiance and attachment may bear some rational relationship to a very limited number of legitimate state purposes. [E.g., the seven year citizenship requirement to run for governor in New Hampshire.] But those instances in which length of residence could provide a legitimate basis for distinguishing one citizen from another are rare. Permissible discriminations between persons must bear a rational relationship to their *relevant* characteristics. [The] ideal of equal protection requires attention to individual merit, to individual need. In almost all instances, the business of the State is not with the past, but with the [present]. The past actions of individuals may be relevant in assessing their present needs; past actions may also be relevant in predicting current ability and future performance. In addition, to a limited extent, recognition and reward of past public service has independent utility for the State, for such recognition may encourage other people to engage in comparably meritorious service. But even the idea of rewarding past public service offers scarce support for the "past contribution" justification for durational residence classifications since length of residence has only the most tenuous relation to the *actual* service of individuals to the State.

Thus, the past contribution rationale proves much too little to provide a rational predicate for discrimination on the basis of length of residence. But it also proves far too much, for "it would permit the State to apportion all benefits and services according to the [past] contributions of its citizens." [Shapiro.] In effect, then, the past-contribution rationale is so far-reaching in its potential application, and the relationship between residence and contribution to the State so vague and insupportable, that it amounts to little more than a restatement of the criterion for discrimination that it purports to justify. But while duration of residence has minimal utility as a measure of things that are, in fact, constitutionally relevant, resort to duration of residence as the basis for a distribution of state largesse does closely track the constitutionally untenable position that the longer one's residence, the worthier one is of the State's favor. In my view, it is difficult to escape from the recognition that underlying any scheme of classification on the basis of duration of residence, we shall almost invariably find the unstated premise that "some citizens are more equal than others." We rejected that premise and, I believe, implicitly rejected most forms of discrimination based upon length of residence, when we adopted the Equal Protection Clause.

Justice O'CONNOR, concurring in the judgment.

The Court strikes Alaska's distribution scheme, purporting to rely solely upon [equal protection]. The phrase "right to travel" appears only fleetingly in the Court's analysis. [The] Court's reluctance to rely explicitly on a right to travel is odd, because its holding depends on the assumption that Alaska's desire "to reward citizens for past contributions [is] not a legitimate state purpose." Nothing in the Equal Protection Clause itself, however, declares this objective illegitimate. Instead, as a full reading of [Shapiro] and Vlandis v. Kline reveals, the Court has rejected this objective only when its implementation would abridge an interest in interstate travel or migration.

I respectfully suggest, therefore, that the Court misdirects its criticism when it labels Alaska's objective illegitimate. A desire to compensate citizens for their prior contributions is neither inherently invidious nor irrational. Under some circumstances, the objective may be wholly reasonable.[1] Even a generalized desire to reward citizens for past endurance, particularly in a State where years of hardship only recently have produced prosperity, is not innately improper. The difficulty is that plans enacted to further this objective necessarily treat new residents of a State less favorably than the longer-term residents who have past contributions to "reward." This inequality [conflicts] with the constitutional purpose of maintaining a Union rather than a mere "league of States." The Court's task, therefore, should be (1) to articulate this constitutional principle, explaining its textual sources, and (2) to test the strength of Alaska's objective against the constitutional imperative. By choosing instead to declare Alaska's purpose wholly illegitimate, the Court establishes an uncertain jurisprudence. What makes Alaska's purpose illegitimate? Is the purpose illegitimate under all circumstances? What other state interests are wholly illegitimate? Will an "illegitimate" purpose survive review if it becomes "important" or "compelling"?[2] These ambiguities in the Court's analysis prompt me to develop my own approach to Alaska's scheme.

---

1. A State, for example, might choose to divide its largesse among all persons who previously have contributed their time to volunteer community organizations. [Alternatively], a State might enact a tax credit for citizens who contribute to the State's ecology by building alternative fuel sources or establishing recycling plants. If the State made this credit retroactive, to benefit those citizens who launched these improvements before they became fashionable, the State once again would be rewarding past contributions. The Court's opinion would dismiss these objectives as wholly illegitimate. I would recognize them as valid goals and inquire only whether their implementation infringed any constitutionally protected interest. [Footnote by Justice O'Connor.]

2. The Court's conclusion that Alaska's scheme lacks a rational basis masks a puzzling aspect of its analysis. By refusing to extend any legitimacy to Alaska's objective, the Court implies that a program designed to reward prior contributions will never survive equal protection scrutiny. For example, the programs described in n. 1, supra, could not survive the Court's analysis even if the State demonstrated a compelling interest in rewarding volunteer activity or promoting conservation measures. The Court's opinion, although purporting to apply a deferential standard of review, actually insures that any governmental program depending upon a "past contributions" rationale will violate [equal protection]. [Footnote by Justice O'Connor.]

Alaska's distribution plan distinguishes between long-term residents and recent arrivals. Stripped to its essentials, the plan denies non-Alaskans settling in the State the same privileges afforded longer-term residents. The Privileges and Immunities Clause of Article IV [addresses] just this type of discrimination. [See chap. 5, p. 307 above.] Accordingly, I would measure Alaska's scheme against the principles implementing that Clause. In addition to resolving the particular problems raised by Alaska's scheme, this analysis supplies a needed foundation for many of the "right to travel" claims discussed in the Court's prior opinions.

I. Our opinions teach that Article IV's Privileges and Immunities Clause "was designed to insure to a citizen of State A who ventures into State B the same privileges which the citizens of State B enjoy." Toomer v. Witsell. [In] this case, Alaska forces nonresidents settling in the State to accept a status inferior to that of old-timers. In effect, [the] State told its citizens: "Your status depends upon the date on which you established residence here. Those of you who migrated to the State cannot share its bounty on the same basis as those who were here before you." Surely this scheme imposes one of the "disabilities of alienage" prohibited by [the] Clause. It could be argued that Alaska's scheme does not trigger the [Clause] because it discriminates among classes of residents, rather than between residents and nonresidents. This argument, however, misinterprets the force of Alaska's distribution system. Alaska's scheme classifies citizens on the basis of their former residential status, imposing a relative burden on those who migrated to the State after 1959. [The] fact that this discrimination unfolds after the nonresident establishes residency does not insulate Alaska's scheme from scrutiny under [the] Clause. Each group of citizens who migrated to Alaska in the past, or chooses to move there in the future, lives in the State on less favorable terms than those who arrived earlier. The circumstance that some of the disfavored citizens already live in Alaska does not negate the fact that "the citizen of State A who ventures into [Alaska]" to establish a home labors under a continuous disability.

If the [Clause] applies to Alaska's distribution system, then our prior opinions describe the proper standard of review. [See Baldwin (p. 310 above).] [Once] the Court ascertains that discrimination burdens an "essential activity," it will test the constitutionality of the discrimination under a two-part test. [See Hicklin, (p. 311 above).] First, there must be "something to indicate that non-citizens constitute a peculiar source of the evil at which the statute is aimed." Second, the Court must find a "substantial relationship" between the evil and the discrimination practiced against the noncitizens. Certainly the right infringed in this case is "fundamental." [Alaska's] encumbrance on the right of nonresidents to settle in that State, therefore, must satisfy the dual standard identified [above]. Alaska has not shown that its new residents are the "peculiar source" of any evil addressed by its disbursement scheme. [Even] if new residents were the peculiar source of these evils, Alaska has not chosen a cure that bears a "substantial relationship" to the malady. [Alaska's] scheme gives the largest dividends to residents who have lived longest in the State. The dividends awarded to new residents may be too small to encourage them to stay in Alaska. The size of these dividends appears to give new residents only a weak interest in prudent management of the State's resources. As a reward for prior contributions, finally, Alaska's scheme is quite ill-suited. While the phrase "substantial relationship" does not require mathematical precision, it demands at least some recognition of the fact that persons who have migrated to Alaska may have contributed significantly more to the State, both before and after their arrival, than have some natives. For these reasons, I conclude that Alaska's disbursement scheme violates [the] Clause. I thus reach the same destination as the Court, but along a course that more precisely identifies the evils of the challenged statute.

II.   The analysis outlined above might apply to many cases in which a litigant asserts a right to travel or migrate interstate.[3]   To historians, this would come as no surprise.   The Clause has enjoyed a long association with the rights to travel and migrate interstate.   [History], therefore, supports assessment of Alaska's scheme, as well as other infringements of the right to travel, under [the] Clause.   This Clause may not address every conceivable type of discrimination that the Court previously has denominated a burden on interstate travel. I believe, however, that application of [the Clause] to controversies involving the "right to travel" would at least begin the task of reuniting this elusive right with the constitutional principles it embodies.   Because I believe that Alaska's distribution scheme violates [the Clause], I concur in the [judgment].

Justice REHNQUIST, dissenting.

Alaska's dividend distribution scheme represents one State's effort to apportion unique economic benefits among its citizens.   [The] distribution scheme being in the nature of economic regulation, I am at a loss to see the rationality behind the Court's invalidation of it as a denial of equal protection.   [Despite] the highly deferential approach which we invariably have taken toward state economic regulations, the Court today finds the retroactive aspect of the Alaska distribution scheme violative of the [14th] Amendment.   [But] the illegitimacy of a State's recognizing the past contributions of its citizens has been established by the Court only in certain cases considering an infringement of the right to travel, and the majority itself rightly declines to apply the strict scrutiny analysis of those right-to-travel cases.   The distribution scheme at issue in this case impedes no person's right to travel to and settle in Alaska; if anything, the prospect of receiving annual cash dividends would encourage immigration to Alaska.   The State's [reward-for-past-contributions] justification cannot, therefore, be dismissed simply by quoting language [from] right-to-travel cases which have no relevance to the question before us.   So understood, this case clearly passes equal protection muster.   There can be no doubt that the state legislature acted rationally when it concluded that dividends retroactive to the year of statehood would "recognize the 'contributions of various kinds, both tangible and intangible,' which residents have made during their years of state residency."   Nor can there be any doubt that Alaska, perhaps more than any other State in the Union, has good reason for recognizing such contributions.   Because the distribution scheme is thus rationally based, I dissent from its invalidation under the guise of equal protection [analysis].[1]

---

3.   Any durational residency requirement, for example, treats nonresidents who have exercised their right to settle in a State differently from longer-term residents.   This is not to say, however, that all such requirements would fail scrutiny under the Privileges and Immunities Clause. The durational residency requirement upheld in [Sosna], for example, would have survived under the analysis outlined above.   [I] am confident that the analysis developed [above and in Hicklin v. Orbeck (p. 311)] will adequately identify other legitimate durational residency requirements. [Footnote by Justice O'Connor.]

Would Justice O'Connor's analysis apply to a state's preference for employing its own resi-

dents?   See Camden (1984; p. 308 above) and White (1983; p. 305 above).   See generally Simson, "Discrimination Against Nonresidents and the Privileges and Immunities Clause of Article IV," 128 U.Pa.L.Rev. 379 (1979).

1.   I also disagree with the suggestion of Justice O'Connor that the Alaska distribution scheme contravenes the Privileges and Immunities [Clause].   That Clause assures that *nonresidents* of a State shall enjoy the same privileges and immunities as residents enjoy.   We long ago held that the Clause has no application to a citizen of the State whose laws are complained of.   [Slaughter-House Cases.]   [Footnote by Justice Rehnquist.]

E. REFUSALS TO EXPAND FUNDAMENTAL INTERESTS ANALYSIS TO REDRESS ECONOMIC INEQUALITIES

Introduction. This group of materials traces the Burger Court developments regarding welfare legislation and "necessities" that anteceded and culminated in Rodriguez: the Court's refusal to fashion equal protection into a broad-ranging tool to redress economic inequalities and impose affirmative obligations on government. As Rodriguez symbolizes, the modern Court has been reluctant to elaborate either strand of the "new" equal protection toward those ends: it has refused to consider wealth or economic status a suspect classification;[1] and it has refused to elevate welfare benefits or other "necessities of life" into the realm of fundamental interests. The latter phenomenon is the subject of this subsection. By adopting that stance, the Burger Court has disappointed those who perceived in Warren Court dicta the potential for vast expansion of the new equal protection; but it is not at all clear that the Warren Court itself would have been able to resolve the problems of institutional competence and doctrinal justification such an expansion would entail.[2]

1. *The potentials and problems at the end of the Warren era.* More than any other case, the dicta in Shapiro v. Thompson prompted wide-ranging speculation and advocacy regarding the potential fundamental interest in "necessities" such as welfare aid and housing. What interests might be found to be "fundamental"? What were the limits, in principle and in institutional capabilities, to such an extension of the new equal protection? Much of the commentary supported further expansion.[3] But doubts and reservations were also voiced.[4]

---

1. The Court's refusal to consider wealth as a suspect classification is examined in sec. 3C3, at p. 685, above.

2. Note the assessment in Gunther, "Newer Equal Protection" (1972): "The Warren Court left a legacy of anticipations as well as accomplishments. Its new equal protection was a dynamic concept, and the radiations encouraged hopes of further steps toward egalitarianism. 'Once loosed, the idea of Equality is not easily cabined,' Archibald Cox noted in the mid-sixties. The commentators' speculations, even more than the Court's results, confirmed the validity of that observation. The fundamental interests ingredient of the new equal protection was particularly open-ended. It was the element which bore the closest resemblance to freewheeling substantive due process, for it circumscribed legislative choices in the name of newly articulated values that lacked clear support in constitutional text and history. The list of interests identified as fundamental by the Warren Court was in fact quite modest: voting, criminal appeals and the right of interstate travel were the prime examples. But in the extraordinary amount of commentary that followed, analysts searching for justifications for those enshrinements were understandably tempted to ponder analogous spheres that might similarly qualify. Welfare benefits, exclusionary zoning, municipal services and school financing came to be the most inviting frontiers." See also, e.g., Krislov, "The OEO Lawyers Fail to Constitutionalize a Right to [Welfare]," 58 Minn.L.Rev. 211 (1973), Michelman, "Welfare Rights in a Constitutional

Democracy," 1979 Wash.U.L.Q. 659 (compare Bork's comment, id., at 695), and other articles noted below.

3. See, e.g., Karst, "Invidious Discrimination: Justice Douglas and the Return of the 'Natural-Law-Due-Process Formula,'" 16 U.C.L.A.L. Rev. 716 (1969), suggesting a three-part formulation for identifying whether a classification is an unconstitutional "invidious discrimination": (1) does it "discriminate" against a "disadvantaged group"; (2) does that discrimination relate to an interest that is "basic" or "fundamental" or "critical"; if so, (3) is the state's justification "'compelling' enough to overcome the presumptive invalidity implied in a phrase like 'strict scrutiny.'" (Compare Justice Marshall's "sliding scale" approach, most fully developed in his dissent in Rodriguez, p. 789.) [See also the introductory overview in sec. 1 and the commentaries cited in Gunther, "Newer Equal Protection."]

4. Note, e.g., the comment in "Developments," 82 Harv.L.Rev. 1065 (1969): "[The] suggestion that government has an affirmative duty to raise everyone to a minimum acceptable standard of living has not yet assumed the dignity of a constitutional proposition. Three major reasons for this lack of development may be suggested. The first is the conceptual difficulty of finding support for the proposition in the Constitution. [T]he guarantee of a minimum standard of living appears to be on a completely different level from the guarantee of effectively equal access to the criminal process, to the politi-

Perhaps the most imaginative analysis of "new" equal protection frontiers at the end of the Warren era came in Michelman, "Foreword: On Protecting the Poor Through the [14th Amendment]," 83 Harv.L.Rev. 7 (1969). As noted at p. 686, he criticized language suggesting that wealth was a suspect classification on the ground that that was an unacceptable principle in a society generally committed to a market pricing system. But he drew from the fundamental interests analysis a somewhat different approach, arguing that even in a market economy persons were entitled to "minimum protection" against economic deprivations in certain areas. He suggested as an appropriate doctrinal tool to bar certain payment requirements: "It is no justification for deprivation of a fundamental right (i.e., involuntary nonfulfillment of a just want) that the deprivation results from a general practice of requiring persons to pay for what they get." His "minimum protection" approach would emphasize "severe deprivations" rather than "inequalities." It would identify "instances in which persons have important needs or interests which they are prevented from satisfying because of traits or predicaments not adopted by free and proximate choice"; it would then seek to determine which of these instances are intolerable ones by asking which risks of deprivation would be consensually deemed unacceptable in a "just society." [5] Michelman recognized that the notion of "minimum protection is more readily assimilated to the due process than to the equal protection clause." Nevertheless, courts might decide to invoke "the verbiage of inequality and discrimination" in developing a "minimum protection" analysis, because, for example, "detecting a failure to provide the required minimum may nonetheless depend in part upon the detection of inequalities; and elimination or reduction of inequality may be entailed in rectifying such a failure, insofar as the just minimum is understood to be a function (in part) of the existing maximum. [W]idening inequalities become increasingly suggestive of failure to furnish the just minimum." [6]

1. *Welfare benefits.* The first indication that the Burger Court would not build on the Shapiro v. Thompson dicta regarding special scrutiny of classifications affecting "necessities" came in DANDRIDGE v. WILLIAMS, 397 U.S. 471 (1970), a decision relied on three years later in Rodriguez. The Court rejected a challenge to Maryland's implementation of the Aid to Families with Dependent Children (AFDC) program, jointly financed by the state and federal governments. Maryland granted most eligible families their "standard of need," but imposed a "maximum grant" limit of $250 per month per family, regardless of the family size or computed standard of need. In rejecting the equal protection attack on that limitation, Justice STEWART's majority opinion stated: "[Here] we deal with state regulation in the social and economic field,

cal process, to education, or even to other state activities. The latter find their sources primarily, if not exclusively, in the state. One seeking income, housing, or a job, on the other hand, is remitted primarily to the private sector for satisfaction of his needs. Second, the practical problems in reallocating resources according to an infinite variety of needs, and in establishing acceptable minimum norms, would be far greater than those which have already attended judicial efforts to impose precise standards of equality on the states. Finally, [legislatures] themselves have taken significant, if as yet small, strides through social security and other welfare measures to provide minimum standards for selected groups of people." (See also Cox, "Foreword: Constitutional Adjudication and the Promotion of Human Rights," 80 Harv.L.Rev. 91 (1966), and Sager, "Tight Little Islands: Exclusionary Zon-

ing, Equal Protection, and the Indigent," 21 Stan.L.Rev. 767 (1969); cf. Winter, "Poverty, Economic Equality, and the Equal Protection Clause," 1972 Sup.Ct.Rev. 51.)

5. Cf. Rawls, A Theory of Justice (1971). Professor Rawls' earlier writings heavily influenced Michelman's "just wants" analysis. [But see Nozick, Anarchy, State, and Utopia (1975).]

6. Do the Burger Court developments leave any room for adoption of Michelman's "minimum protection against economic hazards" approach? Note especially the reference in Justice Powell's opinion in Rodriguez (p. 789) to the possibility that "some identifiable quantum of education is a constitutionally protected prerequisite to the meaningful exercise" of other rights. See also Plyler v. Doe (p. 799 above).

not affecting freedoms guaranteed by the Bill of Rights, and claimed to violate the 14th Amendment only because the regulation results in some disparity in grants of welfare payments to the largest AFDC families.[7]　For this Court to approve the invalidation of state economic or social regulation [here] would be far too reminiscent of an era when the Court thought the 14th Amendment gave it power to strike down state laws 'because they may be unwise, improvident, or out of harmony with a particular school of thought.' [Lee Optical.].　That era long ago passed into history.　In the area of economics and social welfare, a State does not violate [equal protection] merely because the classifications made by its laws are imperfect.　If the classification has some 'reasonable basis,' it does not offend the Constitution.　[E.g., McGowan.]　To be sure, [the cases] enunciating this fundamental standard under [equal protection] have in the main involved state regulation of business or industry.　The administration of public welfare assistance, by contrast, involves the most basic economic needs of impoverished human beings.　We recognize the dramatically real factual difference between the cited cases and this one, but we can find no basis for applying a different constitutional standard.　It is a standard that has consistently been applied to state legislation restricting the availability of employment opportunities.　[E.g., Kotch.]　And it is a standard that is true to the principle that the 14th Amendment gives the federal courts no power to impose upon the States their views of what constitutes wise economic or social policy.　[The] intractable economic, social, and even philosophical problems presented by public welfare assistance programs are not the business of this Court.　The Constitution may impose certain procedural safeguards upon systems of welfare administration. [See chap. 8, sec. 4.]　But the Constitution does not empower this Court to second-guess state officials charged with the difficult responsibility of allocating limited public welfare funds among the myriad of potential recipients."[8]

Justice MARSHALL's dissent, joined by Justice Brennan, insisted that the Maryland regulation could not be sustained even under the majority's "reasonableness" test.　But he devoted most of his opinion to advocating a stricter standard of review, even while finding the Warren Court's rigid two-tier analysis inappropriate here.　(His dissent marked an important step in the evolution of his "sliding scale" approach, more fully elaborated in his Rodriguez dissent.)　He criticized the majority for "focusing upon the abstract dichotomy between two different approaches to equal protection problems that have been utilized by this Court": "This case simply defies easy characterization in terms of one or the other of these 'tests.'　The cases relied on by the Court, in which a 'mere rationality' [rather than 'compelling interest'] test was actually used, are most accurately described as involving the application of equal protection reasoning to the regulation of [business interests].　This case, involving the literally vital interests of a powerless minority—poor families without breadwinners—is far removed from the area of business regulation, as the Court concedes.　Why then is the standard used in those cases imposed

7.　"Cf. Shapiro v. Thompson, where, by contrast, the Court found state interference with the constitutionally protected freedom of interstate travel." [Footnote by Justice Stewart.]

8.　Justice Stewart readily found a "reasonable basis" for the challenged regulation "in the State's legitimate interest in encouraging employment and in avoiding discrimination between welfare families and the families of the working poor."　He added: "It is true that in some AFDC families there may be no person who is employable.　It is also true that with respect to AFDC families whose determined standard of need is below the regulatory maximum, [the] employment incentive is absent.　But [equal pro-

tection] does not require that a State must choose between attacking every aspect of a problem or not attacking the problem at all.　It is enough that the State's action be rationally based and free from invidious discrimination.　The regulation before us meets that test."

Justices HARLAN and BLACK (joined by Chief Justice Burger) joined the Court's opinion with separate notations.　Justice DOUGLAS dissented solely on the basis of "the inconsistency of the Maryland maximum grant regulation with the Social Security Act." (Justice Marshall's opinion endorsed that statutory argument before moving on to the constitutional discussion noted in the text.)

here? In my view, equal protection analysis of this case is not appreciably advanced by the a priori definition of a 'right,' fundamental or otherwise.[9] Rather, concentration must be placed upon the character of the classification in question, the relative importance to individuals in the class discriminated against of the governmental benefits that they do not receive, and the asserted state interests in support of the classification. [It] is the individual interests here at stake that [most] clearly distinguish this case from the 'business regulation' equal protection cases. AFDC support to needy dependent children provides the stuff that sustains those children's lives: food, clothing, shelter. And this Court has already recognized several times that when a benefit, even a 'gratuitous' benefit, is necessary to sustain life, stricter constitutional standards, both procedural and substantive, are applied to the deprivation of that benefit." [10]

2. *Housing.* An effort to establish a "fundamental interest" in "decent shelter" and "possession of one's home" failed in LINDSEY v. NORMET, 405 U.S. 56 (1972). That 5 to 2 decision sustained provisions of Oregon's Forcible Entry and Wrongful Detainer statute prescribing judicial procedures for eviction of tenants after alleged nonpayment of rent. Justice WHITE's majority opinion rejected the argument "that a more stringent standard than mere rationality should be applied both to the challenged classification and its stated purpose." One of the rejected contentions was that "the 'need for decent shelter' and the 'right to retain peaceful possession of one's home' are fundamental interests which are particularly important to the poor and which may be trenched upon only after the State demonstrates some superior interest." He replied: "We do not denigrate the importance of decent, safe and sanitary housing. But the Constitution does not provide judicial remedies for every social and economic ill. We are unable to perceive in that document any constitutional guarantee of access to dwellings of a particular quality or any recognition of the right of a tenant to occupy the real property of his landlord beyond the term of his lease, without the payment of [rent]. Absent constitutional mandate, the assurance of adequate housing and the definition of landlord-tenant relationships is a legislative not a judicial function." Exercising deferential review, he found no constitutional flaw in the fact that eviction actions "differ substantially from other litigation, where the time between complaint and trial is substantially longer, and where a broader range of issues may be considered." Here, there were "unique factual and legal characteristics of the landlord-tenant relationship that justify special statutory treatment." Accordingly, such features as limiting the issue at trial to that of the tenant's default and barring such defenses as the landlord's failure to maintain the premises were found rational.[11]

---

9. "[The] Court's insistence that equal protection analysis turns on the basis of a closed category of 'fundamental rights' involves a curious value judgment. It is certainly difficult to believe that a person whose very survival is at stake would be comforted by the knowledge that his 'fundamental' rights are preserved [intact]." [Footnote by Justice Marshall.]

10. Justice Marshall found none of the asserted rationales for the State's scheme persuasive.

The Dandridge approach to claims that "necessities" are a fundamental interest (and its deferential stance) also surfaced in several other cases between Dandridge and the Rodriguez decision. See, e.g., Richardson v. Belcher, 404 U.S. 78 (1971) (disability benefits), and Jefferson v.

Hackney, 406 U.S. 535 (1972) (grant of lower percentage of "need" to AFDC recipients than to beneficiaries of other categorical assistance programs). (In the latter case, Justice Rehnquist's majority opinion also rejected a de facto race discrimination argument, as noted at p. 692 above.)

11. One feature of the Oregon system was invalidated, however: a requirement that the tenant desiring to appeal a decision post a bond of twice the rent that would accrue pending decision, with the bond to be forfeited if the tenant lost the appeal. Relying on the Griffin v. Illinois strand of equal protection doctrine, Justice White found that special burden on appeals unjustified by any desire to eliminate frivolous claims.

DO ANY BASES REMAIN FOR HEIGHTENED SCRUTINY OF WELFARE LAWS?

1. *A review.* The developments traced in this final section apparently dashed any possibility that the Burger Court would apply the strict scrutiny of the new equal protection to laws bearing on welfare benefits and other "necessities." Are challenges to such laws accordingly doomed to the very deferential review of the old equal protection? A few bases for more intensive review may remain. First, as Justice Stewart noted in Dandridge, procedural, right-to-hearing claims may succeed in the welfare context as in other areas. (See chap. 8, sec. 4.) Second, the Burger Court occasionally, albeit quite sporadically, has applied rationality review with unusual bite, using analyses akin to the "newer equal protection." (See sec. 2.) And that tendency has sometimes surfaced in the welfare area.[1] Most often, however, the Court has manifested a quite deferential stance.

2. *The brief and troubled life of "irrebuttable presumptions" analysis.* For a brief period in the mid-1970s, the Court opened a route toward heightened scrutiny of legislative classifications via an approach avoiding the language of equal protection. The Court ventured into "irrebuttable presumptions" analysis, purportedly an aspect of procedural due process but in substance similar to very intensive scrutiny of legislative generalizations. In practice, application of the irrebuttable presumptions analysis meant invalidation of the generalization and produced a requirement for individualized hearings. The 1970s manifestation of the irrebuttable presumptions approach was launched by Justice Stewart's majority opinion in Vlandis v. Kline, 412 U.S. 441 (1973), involving tuition preferences for in-state students at a state university. The majority stated: "[S]ince Connecticut purports to be concerned with residency in allocating the rates for tuition, [it] is forbidden by the Due Process Clause to deny an individual the resident rates on the basis of a permanent and irrebuttable presumption of non-residence, when the presumption is not *necessarily or universally true in fact.* [Due process requires] that the State allow such an individual to present evidence showing that he is a bona fide resident entitled to the in-state rates." [Emphasis added.] The italicized passage was the most extreme statement of the irrebuttable presumptions doctrine, and it was invoked in several cases to strike down legislative generalizations because they were not "universally true in fact."[2] From the outset, most commentators thought the irrebuttable presumptions doctrine puzzling and unjustifiable. The critics argued that the finding of an unconstitutional irrebuttable presumption was essentially the same as holding a classification overbroad under the equal protection clause. The irrebuttable presumptions analysis imposed extraordinarily strict safeguards against "overinclusive" classifications. Under equal protection standards—even under most varieties of strict scrutiny—an absolutely perfect fit between classification and purpose is not demanded. But just that seemed to be required by the Vlandis complaint that the "presumption" there was "not necessarily or universally true in fact." In short, irrebuttable presumption analysis seemed to many to be the equivalent of an extremely strict variety of "means" scrutiny.[3]

1. See, e.g., Jimenez v. Weinberger (1974; p. 606 above), and U.S. Dept. of Agriculture v. Moreno (1973; p. 606 above).

2. See, e.g., Cleveland Bd. of Educ. v. La-Fleur, 414 U.S. 632 (1974) (mandatory pregnancy leaves for school teachers); Department of Agriculture v. Murry, 413 U.S. 508 (1973) (a provision in the federal Food Stamp Act); cf. Stanley v. Illinois, 405 U.S. 645 (1972) (right of father to custody of his illegitimate children);

but see Mourning v. Family Publications Serv., Inc., 411 U.S. 356 (1973).

3. See, e.g., Note, "The Irrebuttable Presumption Doctrine in the Supreme Court," 87 Harv.L.Rev. 1534 (1974): "The Court's analysis manifests a misunderstanding of the nature of such presumptions. It has treated them as evidentiary rules involved in the process of factfinding, failing to recognize that irrebuttable presumptions are nothing more than statutory classi-

The irrebuttable presumptions doctrine, never consistently applied during its brief life, was soon killed by the Court as a generally acceptable approach.[4] The death blow came in WEINBERGER v. SALFI, 422 U.S. 749 (1975), setting aside a lower court decision that had invalidated on irrebuttable presumptions grounds a duration-of-relationship Social Security eligibility requirement for surviving wives and stepchildren of deceased wageearners. Justice REHNQUIST's majority opinion insisted that the deferential standard of Dandridge was applicable to such claims and distinguished most of the earlier cases on the ground that they involved interests with "constitutionally protected status." To extend the irrebuttable presumptions line of cases to the eligibility requirement here "would turn the doctrine of those cases into a virtual engine of destruction for countless legislative judgments which have heretofore been thought wholly consistent with [the Constitution]." That would "represent a degree of judicial involvement in the legislative function which we have eschewed except in the most unusual circumstances." He elaborated: "[If] the Fifth and 14th Amendments permit [the Lee Optical variety of broad] latitude to legislative decisions regulating the private sector of the economy, they surely allow no less latitude in prescribing the conditions upon which funds shall be dispensed from the public treasury. [Under] those standards, the question raised is not whether a statutory provision precisely filters out those, and only those, who are in the factual position which generated the congressional concern reflected in the statute. Such a rule would ban all prophylactic provisions. [Nor] is the question whether the provision filters out a substantial part of the class which caused congressional concern, or whether it filters out more members of the class than non-members. The question is whether Congress [could] rationally have concluded both that a particular limitation [would] protect against [the occurrence of the feared abuse], and that the expense and other difficulties of individual determinations justify the inherent imprecision of a prophylactic rule. We conclude that the duration-of-relationship test meets this constitutional standard. [There is] no basis for our requiring individualized determinations when Congress can rationally conclude not only that generalized rules are appropriate to its purposes and concerns, but also that the difficulties of individual determinations outweigh the marginal increments in the precise effectuation of congressional concern which they might be expected to produce."[5]

---

fications." The "exacting standard of precision" imposed by this approach "reflects a fundamental confusion between legislative prescription and adjudicatory application of statutory classifications." The Note called the irrebuttable presumptions analysis a "strange hybrid," "if not simply a confusion," of equal protection and procedural due process scrutiny. See also Note, "Irrebuttable Presumptions: An Illusory Analysis," 27 Stan.L.Rev. 449 (1975), viewing the doctrine as "fundamentally misconceived," seeing it as "logically equivalent to an equal protection argument," and finding it a "standardless, illusory" approach.

4. The approach may survive for use where there are independent reasons for heightened scrutiny, as when "fundamental interests" are affected. See the discussion in Justice Brennan's majority opinion in Elkins v. Moreno, 435 U.S. 647 (1978), where the Court managed to avoid deciding whether Vlandis should be overruled. But there is no longer basis for claiming that heightened scrutiny across the board can be trig-

gered simply by asserting an irrebuttable presumptions claim. (See also Usery v. Turner Elkhorn Mining Co., 428 U.S. 1 (1976); cf. Toll v. Moreno, 441 U.S. 458 (1979), a per curiam ruling "supplement[ing]" Elkins v. Moreno, above.)

5. Justice STEWART, the chief architect of the irrebuttable presumptions doctrine, joined the Salfi majority without comment. Justice Brennan's dissent, joined by Justice Marshall, viewed the decisions as "flatly contrary" to several earlier cases. He conceded, however, that the Court had never held "that all statutory provisions based on assumptions about underlying facts were per se unconstitutional unless individual hearings are provided. But in this case, as in others in which we have stricken down conclusive presumptions, it *is* possible to specify those factors which, if proved in a hearing, would disprove a rebuttable presumption." Accordingly, individualized hearings were required. Justice DOUGLAS also dissented.

Chapter 10

THE POST–CIVIL WAR AMENDMENTS AND CIVIL RIGHTS LEGISLATION: CONSTITUTIONAL RESTRAINTS ON PRIVATE CONDUCT; CONGRESSIONAL POWER TO IMPLEMENT THE AMENDMENTS

AN INTRODUCTORY OVERVIEW

In the preceding chapters on due process and equal protection, the actions challenged on constitutional grounds have clearly been actions by an arm of *state government;* and the virtually exclusive focus has been on the role of the *Court* in elaborating constitutional guarantees. This chapter broadens the focus, adding two significant dimensions. First, the concern here extends beyond limits on official *state* action to restraints against seemingly *private* conduct. Second, concern here extends beyond the Court's role to that of *Congress* in enforcing and elaborating the provisions of the post-Civil War Amendments.

1. *"State action" limits and private actors.* The first new theme—the applicability of constitutional guarantees to seemingly private conduct—reflects the fact that the 14th and 15th Amendments, like most limits in the Constitution, are addressed to government, not to private behavior. For example, the prohibitions of § 1 of the 14th Amendment begin with "No State shall." From the beginning, the Court's interpretations of that Amendment have emphasized "the essential dichotomy set forth in that Amendment between deprivation by the State, subject to scrutiny under its provisions, and private conduct, 'however discriminatory and wrongful,' against which the 14th Amendment offers no shield." But the state-private distinction is deceptively simple. As governmental involvement in the private sector has become more pervasive, traditional notions as to what activity constitutes "state action" have become blurred. Under what circumstances is arguably private behavior subject to such restraints as those in the 14th Amendment? When may a challenger relying on the 14th Amendment insist that the Court impose constitutional restraints on a seemingly "private" actor—or at least require that government withdraw from involvement with "private" actors' conduct? The materials in sec. 2 below pursue such questions.[1]

2. *Congress and the Amendments.* The second theme—the role of Congress—reflects the fact that each of the three post-Civil War amendments grants Congress authority to protect civil rights: the final sections of the 13th, 14th, and 15th Amendments give "power to enforce" each amendment "by appropriate legislation." These are of course not the only sources of congressional power to enact civil rights laws: e.g. the commerce power has been invoked on behalf of civil rights. (Recall chap. 3, at p. 157 above.) But the post-Civil War additions, unlike the original grants, were born of a special concern with racial

---

1. Note that the 13th Amendment, banning slavery and involuntary servitude, does *not* contain a state action limitation. The absence of that limit has especially important implications for the scope of congressional power to prohibit private racial discrimination, as explored in sec. 3C below.

discrimination; and the civil rights powers they confer are potentially the most far-reaching. The reach of these powers is pursued in secs. 3 and 4 below.

3. *Court-Congress interactions.* The two themes, of Court elaboration and congressional power, are combined in this chapter because the evolution of the post-Civil War Amendments has evoked a pattern of institutional interactions unlike most under the Art. I powers. Early congressional action under the post-Civil War Amendments stimulated Court responses that helped inhibit further legislative enforcement; subsequent Court elaborations in turn influenced the modern pattern of more vigorous congressional action. Congress has resorted to these Amendments during only two periods of our history: there was a spurt of activity soon after the adoption of the Amendments, and then again in recent years. For the near-century intervening, the Amendments were effectively in the Court's sole keeping. And the most recent spurt of legislative activity in turn provoked new, broader Court statements of the scope of congressional powers. This historical sequence of Court-Congress interactions yielded the institutional collaborations and tensions pursued in this chapter.

4. *A note on organization.* To explore these interrelated themes, this chapter is organized to focus on two specific, climactic problems. The first deals with the reach of the Amendments and the state action-private action dichotomy: Does Congress have power to expand the *reach* of the Amendments and to reach private rather than governmental invasions of individual rights? That inquiry culminates in the materials in sec. 3 below. The second is the problem of the congressional power to modify the *substantive content* of the Amendments: Is congressional enforcement power limited to providing remedies for substantive rights perceived by the Court, or may it "reinterpret" constitutional rights? That inquiry is pursued in sec. 4 below.

As background, sec. 1 sketches the statutory framework of the post-Civil War laws and their modern counterparts. And as further background—and because of its independent significance as a problem of continuing vitality—sec. 2 examines the Court's evolution of the "state action" concept. Sec. 3 examines the modern efforts to apply the remnants of the post-Civil War laws to private action. That section concludes with the late 1960s varieties of congressional action based on the 14th Amendment, as well as with the rediscovery, in the Jones case, of the 13th Amendment (which is not saddled with a state action limitation) as a far-reaching source of congressional power over private racial discrimination. Sec. 4, finally, focuses on the question of congressional power to provide remedies for, and perhaps to modify, the substantive rights unearthed by the Court in its interpretations. The major context for that examination is voting rights legislation—legislation beginning in 1965 that went beyond prior, Court-imposed restrictions on voting discrimination in several respects. Are the modern laws "remedial" (providing legislative remedies for judicially identified rights) or "substantive" (resting on a nearly autonomous congressional authority to delineate and reinterpret rights, not merely provide remedies)? In 1966, Katzenbach v. Morgan (p. 946) suggested a broad legislative power to reinterpret the substantive contours of constitutional rights. Other cases—e.g., Rome v. United States in 1980 (p. 937)—indicate that even if congressional power is viewed as merely "remedial" rather than "substantive," its reach can be great indeed. These materials, then, are not only an essential supplement to an understanding of due process and equal protection guarantees, but also a provocative manifestation of Court-Congress interactions raising questions reaching back all the way to those considered in connection with Marbury v. Madison—questions about institutional autonomy and ultimate authority in the interpretation of constitutional rights.

SECTION 1. THE STATUTORY FRAMEWORK

THE LAWS OF THE RECONSTRUCTION ERA

Introduction: The historical background and the Slaughter-House Cases. There was an intimate interrelationship among the emancipation of slaves during the Civil War, the adoption of the 13th, 14th, and 15th Amendments, and the enactment of the Civil Rights Acts of 1866, 1870, 1871, and 1875. The central purpose of the Amendments was articulated in the Court's first encounter with them, in 1873. Recall Justice Miller's majority opinion in the Slaughter-House Cases (1873; p. 410 above), stating the "one pervading purpose" underlying all of the Amendments: "[W]e mean the freedom of the slave race, the security and firm establishment of that freedom, and the protection of the newly-made freeman and citizen from the oppressions of those who had formerly exercised unlimited dominion over him."

1. *The 1866 Act.* The 13th Amendment, in 1865, gave constitutional support to the wartime Emancipation Proclamation. Congress considered additional protection of the newly freed black necessary, however—partly because of the "black codes" enacted in several states, which imposed severe legal restrictions just short of formal slavery. The Civil Rights Act of 1866 sought to end these restrictions. Section 1 stated that all persons born in the United States were "citizens of the United States" and proceeded to list certain rights of "such citizens, of every race and color, without regard to any previous condition of slavery." [See the modern counterparts, 42 U.S.C. §§ 1981, 1982.][1] That listing of rights was followed by a criminal enforcement provision, § 2. [Its modern counterpart is 18 U.S.C. § 242.] During the debates on the 1866 Act, constitutional doubts were raised about the adequacy of the 13th Amendment to support the constitutionality of the law. These doubts were reflected in President Johnson's veto: "[W]here can we find a Federal prohibition against the power of any State to discriminate[?]" Congress overrode the veto, but the amendment machinery was immediately put in motion. The 14th Amendment—designed in part to validate the 1866 Act—was ratified in 1868.

2. *The 1870 Act.* In 1870, the 15th Amendment was ratified. It prohibits denial of the franchise "on account of race, color, or previous condition of servitude"; unlike § 1 of the 14th Amendment, it explicitly mentions the race-slavery problem that provoked all of the post-Civil War Amendments. Congress promptly passed enforcement legislation. The 1870 Enforcement Act dealt primarily with denials of voting rights. [The development of voting rights laws is traced in sec. 4 below.] Section 6, however, contained broader terms: it provided criminal sanctions for private conspiracies to violate federal rights. [The current version of this criminal provision is 18 U.S.C. § 241.]

3. *The 1871 and 1875 Acts.* In 1871, Congress not only amended the 1870 Act, but also enacted a new law, the Civil Rights Act of 1871. The 1871 Act "to enforce [the] 14th Amendment," known as the Ku Klux Klan Act, was "among the last of the reconstruction legislation to be based on the 'conquered province' theory which prevailed in Congress for a period following the Civil War. This statute [established] civil liabilities, together with parallel criminal liabilities." Collins v. Hardyman (1951; p. 918 below). The substance of these civil provisions has been preserved [2]—and has given rise to important cases. For example, 42 U.S.C. § 1983 creates a cause of action for depriva-

---

1. The texts of the modern statutory counterparts noted in this survey, together with indications of their post-Civil War antecedents, follow.

2. Another provision of the 1871 Act, subsequently repealed, dealt with private criminal con-

spiracies. This provision was found to exceed the "state action" limit of the 14th Amendment in United States v. Harris (1882; p. 865 below).

tions, under color of state law, of rights secured by the Constitution and federal laws. And 42 U.S.C. § 1985(3) provides for civil actions for certain private anti-civil rights conspiracies. Finally, the Civil Rights Act of 1875, which contained, inter alia, "public accommodations" provisions, is discussed in the 1883 Civil Rights Cases (p. 860 below), holding the provisions unconstitutional.[3]

THE SURVIVING REMNANTS OF THE POST–CIVIL WAR LAWS: THE MODERN COUNTERPARTS

1. Criminal provisions:

18 U.S.C. § 241.[1] *"Conspiracy against rights of citizens.* If two or more persons conspire to injure, oppress, threaten, or intimidate any citizen in the free exercise or enjoyment of any right or privilege secured to him by the Constitution or laws of the United States, or because of his having so exercised the same; or

"If two or more persons go in disguise on the highway, or on the premises of another, with intent to prevent or hinder his free exercise or enjoyment of any right or privilege so secured—

"They shall be fined not more than $10,000 or imprisoned not more than ten years, or both; and if death results, they shall be subject to imprisonment for any term of years or for life."

18 U.S.C. § 242.[2] *"Deprivation of rights under color of law.* Whoever, under color of any law, statute, ordinance, regulation, or custom, willfully subjects any inhabitant of any State, Territory, or District to the deprivation of any rights, privileges, or immunities secured or protected by the [Constitution or laws], or to different punishments, pains, or penalties, on account of such inhabitant being an alien, or by reason of his color, or race, than are prescribed for the punishment of citizens, shall be fined not more than $1,000 or imprisoned not more than one year, or both; and if death results shall be subject to imprisonment for any term of years or for life."

2. Civil provisions:

42 U.S.C. § 1981.[3] *"Equal rights under the law.* All persons within the jurisdiction of the United States shall have the same right in every State and Territory to make and enforce contracts, to sue, be parties, give evidence, and to the full and equal benefit of all laws and proceedings for the security of persons and property as is enjoyed by white citizens, and shall be subject to like punishment, pains, penalties, taxes, licenses, and exactions of every kind, and to no other."

3. For a review of the post-Civil War laws, and their fate in later decades, see Gressman, "The Unhappy History of Civil Rights Legislation," 50 Mich.L.Rev. 1323 (1952). See also Carr, Federal Protection of Civil Rights (1947), and U.S. Civil Rights Comm'n, Enforcement (1965). For a useful compilation, see Federal Civil Rights Laws: A Sourcebook (1984), published by a Subcommittee of the Senate Judiciary Committee (S.Prt. 98–245, 98th Cong., 2d Sess.).

1. Derived from § 6 of the 1870 Act, via § 5508 of Rev.Stats., 1874–78, § 19 of the Criminal Code of 1909, and § 51 of the 1946 edition of 18 U.S.C. It is referred to by its earlier designations in some of the cases below. [The concluding portions of the penalty provisions in §§ 241 and 242 were added by the 1968 Civil Rights Act.] For modern applications of § 241, see the Guest and Price cases, at pp. 905, 911 below.

2. Derived from § 2 of the 1866 Act, as amended by § 17 of the 1870 Act. The section was § 5510 of Rev.Stats., 1874–78; § 20 of the 1909 Criminal Code; and § 52 of the 1946 edition of 18 U.S.C. The section is discussed and applied in the Price case, at p. 911 below.

3. Derived from the 1866 and 1870 Acts. It was § 1977 of Rev.Stats., 1874–78.

42 U.S.C. § 1982.[4] *"Property rights of citizens.* All citizens of the United States shall have the same right, in every State and Territory, as is enjoyed by white citizens thereof to inherit, purchase, lease, sell, hold, and convey real and personal property."

42 U.S.C. § 1983.[5] *"Civil action for deprivation of rights.* Every person who, under color of any statute, ordinance, regulation, custom, or usage, of any State or Territory, subjects, or causes to be subjected, any citizen of the United States or other persons within the jurisdiction thereof to the deprivation of any rights, privileges or immunities secured by the Constitution and laws, shall be liable to the person injured in an action of law, suit in equity, or other proper proceedings for redress."

42 U.S.C. § 1985(c).[6] *"Conspiracy to interfere with civil rights.* [If] two or more persons in any State or Territory conspire or go in disguise on the highway or on the premises of another, for the purpose of depriving, either directly or indirectly, any person or class of persons of the equal protection of the laws, or of equal privileges and immunities under the laws; [the] party so injured or deprived may have an action for the recovery of damages, occasioned by such injury or deprivation, against any one or more of the conspirators." [7]

MODERN CIVIL RIGHTS LEGISLATION

The modern revival of congressional civil rights activity began with the Civil Rights Act of 1957; that law, like the Civil Rights Act of 1960, was primarily designed to expand remedies against racial discrimination in voting.[1] The Civil Rights Act of 1964—the first comprehensive modern civil rights law—moved substantially beyond the area of voting rights. The 1964 provisions based primarily on Art. I powers of Congress have already been considered. (Recall, e.g., the Public Accommodations Title, chap. 3, at p. 158 above.) In addition, the 1964 Act included several provisions primarily rooted in the post-Civil War Amendments: e.g., Titles I and VIII contained new voting rights provisions, and Titles III and IV dealt with desegregation of schools and other public facilities. After the 1965 Voting Rights Act was adopted,[2] Johnson Administration proposals for additional omnibus civil rights laws were repeatedly blocked in the Senate. In 1968, however—after the assassination of Dr. Martin Luther King that April—new legislation was enacted.[3]

---

4. Derived from the 1866 Act. It was § 1978 of Rev.Stats., 1874–78. This section was found to have a broad sweep and a solid constitutional base (in the 13th Amendment) in Jones v. Alfred H. Mayer Co. (1968; p. 924 below).

5. Derived from § 1 of the Civil Rights Act of 1871, Rev.Stats. § 1979 (1875). See, e.g., the Monroe and Adickes cases, p. 923 below.

6. Derived from Civil Rights Act of 1871, Rev.Stats. § 1980. For interpretations, see Collins (1951; p. 918 below), Griffin (1971; p. 918 below), and the Carpenters case (1983; p. 920 below).

7. See also the following, less frequently litigated, provisions of 42 U.S.C.: § 1986 (derived from the 1871 Act) (neglecting to prevent acts wrongful under § 1985); § 1994 (the anti-peonage law of 1867). The provisions specifically dealing with voting are considered in sec. 4, p. 929 below. (See also 28 U.S.C. § 1443, autho-

rizing defendants to remove certain civil rights cases from state to federal courts.)

1. The voting aspects of the 1957 and 1960 Acts are considered in sec. 4, at p. 929, below, together with the broader provisions of the Voting Rights Acts of 1965, 1970 and 1975.

2. The modern Voting Rights Acts are more fully examined in sec. 4 below. See especially the decisions in South Carolina v. Katzenbach, Katzenbach v. Morgan, Oregon v. Mitchell, and Rome v. United States.

3. The provisions of the 1968 Act of special concern in this chapter are the elaborate additions to federal criminal laws dealing with civil rights violence in the new 18 U.S.C. § 245 (p. 916 below). Among the important civil rights laws adopted since 1968 are the Education Amendments of 1972 (Title IX) directed at sex discrimination in federally funded educational

SECTION 2.   THE PROBLEM OF STATE ACTION

A.   STATE ACTION IN THE 19TH CENTURY:
THE COLLAPSE OF EARLY CONGRESSIONAL EFFORTS
TO REACH PRIVATE CONDUCT

*finds § 1 unconst.
by 14th (& 15th)*

CIVIL RIGHTS CASES

109 U.S. 3, 3 S.Ct. 18, 27 L.Ed. 835 (1883).

[Sec. 1 of the Civil Rights Act of 1875 provided: "[A]ll persons within the jurisdiction of the United States shall be entitled to the full and equal enjoyment of the accommodations, advantages, facilities, and privileges of inns, public conveyances on land or water, theatres, and other places of public amusement; subject only to the conditions and limitations established by law, and applicable alike to citizens of every race and color, regardless of any previous condition of servitude."   Sec. 2 made violation a misdemeanor and also authorized aggrieved persons to recover $500 "for every such offense."   This decision involved five cases, from Kansas, California, Missouri, New York and Tennessee.   Four of the cases were criminal indictments; the fifth, an action for the civil penalty.   The cases grew out of exclusions of blacks from hotels, theaters and railroads.]

Mr. Justice BRADLEY delivered the opinion of the [Court].

Has Congress constitutional power to make such a law?   The power is sought, first, in the 14th Amendment.   [It] is State action of a particular character that is prohibited [by the first section of the 14th Amendment]. Individual invasion of individual rights is not the subject-matter of the amendment.   [It] nullifies and makes void all State legislation, and State action of every kind, which impairs the privileges and immunities of citizens of the United States, or which injures them in life, liberty or property without due process of law, or which denies to any of them the equal protection of the laws. [The] last section of the amendment invests Congress with power to enforce it by appropriate legislation.   To enforce what?   To enforce the prohibition.   To adopt appropriate legislation for correcting the effects of such prohibited State laws and State acts, and thus to render them effectually null, void, and innocuous.   This is the legislative power conferred upon Congress, and this is the whole of it.   It does not invest Congress with power to legislate upon subjects which are within the domain of State legislation; but to provide modes of relief against State legislation, or State action, of the kind referred to.   It does not authorize Congress to create a code of municipal law for the regulation of private rights; but to provide modes of redress against the operation of State laws, and the action of State officers executive or judicial, when these are subversive of the fundamental rights specified in the amendment.   [Until] some State law has been passed, or some State action through its officers or agents has been taken, adverse to the rights of citizens sought to be protected by the 14th Amendment, no legislation [under] said amendment, nor any proceeding under such legislation, can be called into activity: for the prohibitions of the amendment are against State laws and acts done under State [authority].

An inspection of the law shows that [it] proceeds ex directo to declare that certain acts committed by individuals shall be deemed offences, and shall be prosecuted and punished by proceedings in the [federal courts].   It does not

absence of State denying private parties from disc. can't invoke 14

programs (86 Stat. 373), and the Age Discrimination Act of 1975 (Title III) (89 Stat. 728).

must be a conflict of State laws — the CRA by CRA invoked?

profess to be corrective of any constitutional wrong committed by the States; [it] applies equally to cases arising in States which have the justest laws respecting the personal rights of citizens, and whose authorities are ever ready to enforce such laws, as to those which arise in States that may have violated the prohibition of the amendment. In other words, it steps into the domain of local jurisprudence, and lays down rules for the conduct of individuals in society towards each [other], without referring in any manner to any supposed action of the State or its authorities.

[C]ivil rights, such as are guaranteed by the Constitution against State aggression, cannot be impaired by the wrongful acts of individuals, unsupported by State authority in the shape of laws, customs, or judicial or executive proceedings. The wrongful act of an individual, unsupported by any such authority, is simply a private wrong, or a crime of that individual. [I]f not sanctioned in some way by the State, or not done under State authority, [the injured party's] rights remain in full force, and may presumably be vindicated by resort to the laws of the State for redress. An individual cannot deprive a man of his right to vote, to hold property, to buy and sell, to sue in the courts, or to be a witness or a juror; he may, by force or fraud, interfere with the enjoyment of the right in a particular case; he may commit an assault against the person, or commit murder, or use ruffian violence at the polls, or slander the good name of a fellow citizen; but, unless protected in these wrongful acts by some shield of State law or State authority, he cannot destroy or injure the right; he will only render himself amenable to satisfaction or punishment; and amenable therefor to the laws of the State where the wrongful acts are committed. [The] abrogation and denial of rights, for which the States alone were or could be responsible, was the great seminal and fundamental wrong which was intended to be remedied. And the remedy to be provided must necessarily be predicated upon that wrong. [Of course], these remarks do not apply to those cases in which Congress is clothed with direct and plenary powers of legislation over the whole subject [as] in the regulation of commerce. [I]t is clear that the law in question cannot be sustained by any grant of legislative power made to Congress by the 14th Amendment. [This] is not corrective legislation; it is primary and direct. [Whether] Congress, in the exercise of its power to regulate commerce amongst the several States, might or might not pass a law regulating rights in public conveyances passing from one State to another, [is] a question which is not now before us, as the sections in question are not conceived in any such view.

But the power of Congress to adopt direct and primary, as distinguished from corrective legislation on the subject in hand, is sought, in the second place, from the 13th Amendment. [Such] legislation may be primary and direct in its character; for the amendment is not a mere prohibition of State laws establishing or upholding slavery, but an absolute declaration that slavery or involuntary servitude shall not exist in any part of the United States. [I]t is assumed, that the power vested in Congress to enforce the article by appropriate legislation, clothes Congress with power to pass all laws necessary and proper for abolishing all badges and incidents of slavery in the United States: and upon this assumption it is claimed, that this is sufficient authority for [enacting this law]; the argument being, that the denial of such equal accommodations and privileges is, in itself, a subjection to a species of servitude within the meaning of the amendment. [Can] the act of a mere individual, the owner of the inn, the public conveyance or place of amusement, refusing the accommodation, be justly regarded as imposing any badge of slavery or servitude upon the applicant, or only as inflicting an ordinary civil injury, properly cognizable by the laws of the State, and presumably subject to redress by those laws until the contrary appears? [W]e are forced to the conclusion that such an act of refusal has nothing to do with slavery or involuntary servitude, and that if it is violative of any right of the party, his redress is to be sought under the laws of the State; or if those laws are adverse to his rights and do not protect him, his remedy will be found in the corrective legislation which Congress has adopted, or may adopt, for counteracting the effect of State laws, or State action, prohibited by the 14th Amendment.   It would be running the slavery argument into the ground to make it apply to every act of discrimination which a person may see fit to make as to the guests he will entertain, or as to the people he will take into his coach or cab or car, or admit to his concert or theatre, or deal with in other matters of intercourse or business.   Innkeepers and public carriers, by the laws of all the States, so far as we are aware, are bound, to the extent of their facilities, to furnish proper accommodation to all unobjectionable persons who in good faith apply for them.   If the laws themselves make any unjust discrimination, amenable to the prohibitions of the 14th Amendment, Congress has full power to afford a remedy under that amendment and in accordance with it.[1] When a man has emerged from slavery, and by the aid of beneficent legislation has shaken off the inseparable concomitants of that state, there must be some stage in the progress of his elevation when he takes the rank of a mere citizen, and ceases to be the special favorite of the laws.   [There] were thousands of free colored people in this country before the abolition of slavery.   [Mere] discriminations on account of race or color were not regarded as badges of slavery.   If, since that time, the enjoyment of equal rights in all these respects has become established by constitutional enactment, it is not by force of the 13th Amendment (which merely abolishes slavery), but by force of the [14th] and 15th Amendments.   [The challenged law is unconstitutional.]

So ordered.

Mr. Justice HARLAN dissenting.

The opinion in these cases proceeds, it seems to me, upon grounds entirely too narrow and artificial.   I cannot resist the conclusion that the substance and spirit of the recent amendments of the Constitution have been sacrificed by a subtle and ingenious verbal criticism.   [Was] it the purpose of the [13th Amendment] simply to destroy the institution [of slavery], and then remit the race, theretofore held in bondage, to the several States for such protection, in their civil rights, [as] those States, in their discretion, might choose to provide? [That] there are burdens and disabilities which constitute badges of slavery and servitude, and that the power to enforce by appropriate legislation the 13th Amendment may be exerted by legislation of a direct and primary character, for the eradication, not simply of the institution, but of its badges and incidents, are propositions which ought to be deemed indisputable.   [I] do not contend that the 13th Amendment invests Congress with authority, by legislation, to define and regulate the entire body of the civil rights which citizens enjoy, or may enjoy, in the several States.   But I hold that since slavery [was] the moving or principal cause of the adoption of that amendment, and since that institution rested wholly upon the inferiority, as a race, of those held in bondage, their freedom necessarily involved immunity from, and protection against, all discrimination against them, because of their race, in respect of such civil rights as belong to freemen of other races.   Congress, therefore, under its express power to enforce that amendment, [may] enact laws to protect that people against the deprivation, *because of their race,* of any civil rights granted to other freemen in the same State; and such legislation may be of a direct and primary character

---

1.   Can it be argued that Justice Bradley assumed that state laws would bar racial discrimination in public accommodations?   If so, would a state's failure to safeguard against such discrimination constitute "state action" and justify federal corrective remedial legislation?   See, e.g., Peters, "Civil Rights and State Non-Action," 34 Notre Dame Law. 303 (1959), and Frank & Munro, "The Original Understanding of 'Equal Protection of the Laws,'" 1972 Wash.U.L.Q. 421.   [Justice Bradley's narrow view of 13th Amendment power was in effect overturned by Jones (1968, p. 924 below).]

operating upon States, their officers and agents, and, also, upon, at least, such individuals and corporations as exercise public functions and wield power and authority under the [State].

It remains now to inquire what are the legal rights of colored persons in respect of the accommodations, privileges and facilities of public conveyances, inns and places of public amusement? *First,* as to public conveyances on land and water. [In] Olcott v. Supervisors, 16 Wall. 678, it was ruled that railroads [are] none the less public highways, because controlled and owned by private corporations; that it is a part of the function of government to make and maintain highways for the convenience of the public; that no matter who is the agent, or what is the agency, the function performed is *that of the State.* [The] sum of the adjudged cases is that a railroad corporation is a governmental agency, created primarily for public purposes, and subject to be controlled for the public benefit. [Such] being the relations these corporations hold to the public, it would seem that the right of a colored person to use an improved public highway, upon the terms accorded to freemen of other races, is as fundamental [as] are any of the rights which my brethren concede to be so far fundamental as to be deemed the essence of civil [freedom]. *Second,* as to inns. [A] keeper of an inn is in the exercise of a quasi-public employment. The law gives him special privileges and he is charged with certain duties and responsibilities to the public. The public nature of his employment forbids him from discriminating against any person asking admission as a guest on account of the race or color of that person. *Third.* As to places of public amusement. [Within] the meaning of the act of 1875, [they] are such as are established and maintained under direct license of the law. [The] local government granting the license represents [the colored race] as well as all other races within its jurisdiction. A license from the public to establish a place of public amusement, imports, in law, equality of right, at such places, among all the members of that public. [I] am of the opinion that [racial] discrimination practised by corporations and individuals in the exercise of their public or quasi-public functions is a badge of servitude the imposition of which Congress may prevent under its power, by appropriate legislation, to enforce the [13th Amendment].

[Much] that has been said as to the power of Congress under the 13th Amendment is applicable [to the 14th]. [The] assumption that this amendment consists wholly of prohibitions upon State laws and State proceedings in hostility to its provisions, is unauthorized by its language. The first clause of the first section [is] of a distinctly affirmative character. [It granted to blacks state as well as national citizenship, and brought them within the protection of the privileges and immunities clause of Art. IV, § 2.] The citizenship thus acquired, by [the colored] race [may] be protected, not alone by the [judiciary], but by congressional legislation of a primary, direct character; this, because the power of Congress is not restricted to the enforcement of prohibitions upon State laws or State action. It is, in terms distinct and positive, to enforce "the *provisions of this article*" of [amendment]—all of the provisions—affirmative and prohibitive. But what was secured to colored citizens of the United States—as between them and their respective States—by the national grant to them of State citizenship? With what rights, privileges, or immunities did this grant invest them? There is one, if there be no other—exemption from race discrimination in respect of any civil right belonging to citizens of the white race in the same State. It is fundamental in American citizenship that, in respect of such rights, there shall be no discrimination by the State, or its officers, or by individuals or corporations exercising public functions or authority.

[But] if it were conceded that the power of Congress could not be brought into activity until the rights specified in the act of 1875 had been abridged or denied by some State law or State action, I maintain that the decision of the court is erroneous. [In] every material sense applicable to the practical enforcement of the 14th Amendment, railroad corporations, keepers of inns, and managers of places of public amusement are agents or instrumentalities of the State, because they are charged with duties to the public, and are amenable, in respect of their duties and functions, to governmental regulation. [I] agree that if one citizen chooses not to hold social intercourse with another, he is not and cannot be made amenable to the [law]; for no legal right of a citizen is violated by the refusal of others to maintain merely social relations with [him]. [But the] rights which Congress [endeavored] to secure and protect [here] are legal, not social rights. The right, for instance, of a colored citizen to use the accommodations of a public highway, upon the same terms as are permitted to white citizens, is no more a social right than his right, under the law, to use the public streets of a city or a town, or a turnpike road, or a public market, or a post office, or his right to sit in a public building with others, of whatever race, for the purpose of hearing the political questions of the day discussed.

THE AFTERMATH OF THE CIVIL RIGHTS CASES

1. *Cruikshank, the 14th Amendment limitation to state action—and the recognition of rights outside the 14th Amendment against private action.* UNITED STATES v. CRUIKSHANK, 92 U.S. 542 (1875), involved an indictment under § 6 of the 1870 Act, the predecessor of 18 U.S.C. § 241. Three persons were convicted of participating in a lynching of two blacks. One of the charges was interference with the "right and privilege peaceably to assemble together." The Court held the application of the law unconstitutional. Chief Justice WAITE stated that the indictment would have been adequate if it had charged interference with the right to assemble "for the purpose of petitioning Congress for a redress of grievances," an "attribute of national citizenship"; but the charge was merely a conspiracy "to prevent a meeting for any lawful purpose whatever." Another charge (depriving citizens of "lives and liberty of person without due process of law") was found "even more objectionable": "It is no more the duty or within the power of the United States to punish for a conspiracy to falsely imprison or murder within a State, than it would be to punish for false imprisonment or murder itself. The 14th amendment [adds] nothing to the rights of one citizen as against another." A final charge ("injur[ing]" for having voted at an election) was also insufficient: the election might have been a state election, and there was no claim of a conspiracy based on race; the charge, then, "is really of nothing more than a conspiracy to commit a breach of the peace within a State. Certainly it will not be claimed that the United States have the power or are required to do mere police duty in the States."

Note that even under Cruikshank private misconduct was not wholly outside congressional reach: the opinion also recognized that there might be constitutional rights derived from sources not subject to the state action limitation, and that those might accordingly be protected against private as well as state interferences. That distinction—between constitutional rights against the state and constitutional rights not limited by the state action concept—remains an important one in the search for bases of congressional action against private misconduct. As the materials in sec. 3 will show, congressional power to reach private conduct under the 14th Amendment still presents substantial difficulties, though the power is not so tightly confined today as it was in the 19th century. That continuing state action difficulty makes the Court's efforts to articulate constitutional rights not based on the 14th and 15th Amendments (and hence

not subject to the state action limitation) of special importance. That proble[
pursued more fully in sec. 3.[1]

2. *The legacy of the Civil Rights Cases: A transitional note.* Most of
remaining materials in this chapter will discuss the contemporary vitality of the
Civil Rights Cases. Bear in mind the varied ingredients of the majority's
position. *First,* it insisted that the 14th Amendment's self-executing impact did
not reach beyond state action to private discrimination. The Court continues to
reiterate that position—and continues to cite the Civil Rights Cases for it. Yet
notions of what discrimination may fairly be attributed to the state have
expanded considerably in recent decades. The ingredients of modern state
action concepts—the extent to which the Amendment by its own force *may*
reach arguably private action—is the theme of sec. 2B. *Second,* the Civil Rights
Cases insisted that congressional enforcement powers under § 5 of the 14th
Amendment could not reach beyond the state action limits of § 1 of the
Amendment: Congress did not have power to forbid private discrimination.
Modern cases, considered in secs. 3 and 4 below, have taken a more expansive
view of congressional powers under § 5 of the 14th Amendment. *Third,* the
majority in the Civil Rights Cases recognized that the 13th Amendment is not
limited to state action and extends to private actors as well. But that majority
sharply limited congressional enforcement power; it refused to find in § 2 of
the 13th Amendment a general congressional power to deal with private racial
discrimination as "badges of servitude." That view has in effect been overruled
by the 1968 decision in Jones, p. 924 below.

B. COURT ELABORATIONS OF THE STATE ACTION CONCEPT IN THE 20TH CENTURY

Introduction. Beginning in the 1940s, while congressional power under the
14th Amendment lay dormant (because of political reasons as well as constitutional obstacles), the Court began to expand the boundaries of the state action
concept. The results were often clearer than the contents and limits of the
principles. In many cases, arguably private conduct was treated as state action;
the result was either that the private actor was subjected to constitutional
prohibitions or that the state was required to disengage itself from the private
activity. What was often obscure was the extent to which additional seemingly
private activities could be reached on the basis of those holdings. Yet it seemed
all along that the Court's principles were not intended to be limitless. And the
Burger Court's decisions have made it increasingly clear that a state action limit
persists and that not every effort to impose constitutional restraints on arguably
private actors will receive judicial support.[1]

1. Another early decision, United States v.
Harris, 106 U.S. 629 (1882), held unconstitutional a criminal provision of the 1875 Act prohibiting private conspiracies to deprive any person of
"the equal protection of the laws or of equal
privileges and immunities under the law." (That
criminal provision was repealed in 1909. Compare the civil counterpart, derived from the 1871
Act and still on the books, 42 U.S.C. § 1985(c),
considered in sec. 3B below.) The Court stated
in Harris: "When the State has been guilty of no
violation [of the provisions of the 14th Amend-
ment]; [when], on the contrary, the laws of the
State, as [enacted, construed, and administered],
recognize and protect the rights of all persons,
the amendment [confers] no power upon Congress."

See also, on 14th Amendment power, e.g.,
Virginia v. Rives, 100 U.S. 313 (1879), and Baldwin v. Franks, 120 U.S. 678 (1887). There were
parallel obstacles to reaching private action under the 15th Amendment. See, e.g., James v.
Bowman, 190 U.S. 127 (1903).

1. Most of the cases from the 1940s to the
1960s involved claims of racial discrimination
(and most found the 14th Amendment applicable). Since the rediscovery of the 13th Amendment (which does not have a state action limit) in
the late 1960s (and the enactment of modern
legislation based on congressional spending and
commerce powers), Congress has been able to
reach discrimination in the private sector without
relying on the 14th Amendment. But, as the
1970s cases, below, illustrate, that development

What must be shown to subject seemingly private actors to the constitutional guarantees ordinarily applicable only to government? The cases of the last four decades present recurrent themes. Note especially the relative emphases on two distinguishable lines of inquiry: first, whether the private actor is sufficiently entangled with or sufficiently like the state to consider the private conduct "state action"; second, whether applicability of constitutional guarantees to the private actor unduly impinges on the private interest in being free to behave in ways constitutionally barred to the state.

The second inquiry rests on the assumption that there is a sphere of private behavior in which individuals are free to discriminate.[2] That there are such areas, and that some legitimate freedom in the private sector acts as a limit to expansions of the applicability of 14th Amendment guarantees, is recognized even by those Justices who have advocated the broadest extensions of the state action concept.[3] Freedoms of association, rights of privacy, perhaps interests in personal property, all have some claim to recognition. But what is the relevance of those competing individual interests to the delineation of the boundaries of the state action concept? Is the individual freedom of association or of privacy the central ingredient in determining what behavior is not state action for 14th Amendment purposes? Or does the emphasis on individual interests suggest that the support of the "state"—at least in maintaining a legal order—is to be found throughout the entire private sector; that the search for indicia of "state action" is therefore irrelevant; and that the underlying question about the reach of constitutional guarantees is really one of balancing the impact on the aggrieved against the proper area of unrestrained choice and privacy of the discriminator?

Though many of the results in the cases can be explained on such "balancing" grounds, and though explicit consideration of the privacy interests of the discriminator occasionally surfaces in the opinions, most of the cases are preoccupied with the search for adequate elements of the "state." That search for indicia of state action follows two distinguishable routes. One may be called

has by no means made state action problems of historical interest only. As the two preceding chapters show, the Court's interpretations of the due process and equal protection clauses have brought a wide range of rights that are not race-related within the 14th Amendment, with resulting efforts to apply those constitutional guarantees to private actors. See, e.g., Jackson (1974; p. 895 below.) Since the 1970s, the Court has been far more reluctant to find state action. Consider whether the Court would have been wise and justified to have varied the requirements for finding state action with the type of constitutional claim involved—e.g., by being more willing to find it in racial discrimination cases than in others. (See Justice Marshall's dissent in Jackson, below.)

The literature on the state action problem is extensive. See generally Lewis, "The Meaning of State Action," 60 Colum.L.Rev. 1083 (1960); Wechsler, "Toward Neutral Principles of Constitutional Law," 73 Harv.L.Rev. 1 (1959); and Pollak, "Racial Discrimination and Judicial [Integrity]," 108 U.Pa.L.Rev. 1 (1959). See also, e.g., Williams, "The Twilight of State Action," 41 Texas L.Rev. 347 (1963); Van Alstyne & Karst, "State Action," 14 Stan.L.Rev. 3 (1961); Horowitz, "The Misleading Search for ['State Action']," 30 So.Cal.L.Rev. 208 (1957); Henkin, "Shelley v. Kraemer: Notes for a Revised Opin-

ion," 110 U.Pa.L.Rev. 473 (1962); Note, "State [Action]," 74 Colum.L.Rev. 656 (1974); Glennon & Nowak, "A Functional Analysis of [the] 'State Action' Requirement," 1976 Sup.Ct.Rev. 221; and Choper, "Thoughts on State [Action]," 1979 Wash.U.L.Q. 757. For a critical review of the literature as well as of the entire state action concept (urging that it go into "honored retirement as an innocuous truism"), see C.L. Black, Jr., "Foreword: "'State [Action']," 81 Harv.L. Rev. 69 (1967). (Despite that plea for "retirement," the state action concept remains in active service, as the 1970s cases below illustrate with special force).

2. The terms "discriminate" and "discriminator" are used here as shorthand for the private actor engaging in allegedly unconstitutional behavior. Bear in mind, however, that racial discrimination is not the only focus of the 14th Amendment.

3. See, e.g., Justice Douglas' dissent, joined by Justice Marshall, in the Moose Lodge case in 1972 (p. 888 below): "The associational rights which our system honors permit all white, all black, all brown, and all yellow clubs to be formed. [Government] may not tell a man or woman who his or her associates must be. The individual can be as selective as he desires."

the "nexus" approach: it seeks to identify sufficient points of contact between the private actor and the state to justify imposing constitutional restraints on the private actor or commanding state disentanglement. That approach is exemplified by Burton (1961; p. 884 below), which states "that private conduct abridging individual rights does no violence to [equal protection] unless to some significant extent the State in any of its manifestations has been found to have become involved in it." That search for "significant" state involvements permeates most of the cases—and raises numerous problems. The Burton approach assumes that a genuinely neutral state tolerance of private discrimination is permissible. But how much active, affirmative engagement by the state is necessary under that approach? Is it enough that the state "authorize" the private discrimination? Can authorization be distinguished from mere tolerance, where the state has power to forbid private discrimination and does not exercise that power? What varieties of more active state involvement satisfy the state action requirement? Must the state be shown to approve discrimination? To encourage discrimination? Is it enough that the state confers some benefits on the private discriminator? Must there be special benefits, such as a grant of a monopoly? Is state regulation of the discriminator enough? State licensing? State leasing or sale of property? Is it enough that the state judicial system enforces the private discriminator's wishes, as part of a general system of property and contract law? Questions such as these are characteristic of the "significant state involvements" approach.

The alternative to that "nexus" analysis is the "public function" approach. Instead of searching for formal contacts between the state and the private discriminator, it focuses on the nature of the activity the private discriminator engages in. Marsh v. Alabama, the company town case which follows, illustrates that approach. Basically, the "public function" analysis treats private enterprises whose "operation is essentially a public function" as sufficiently state-like to be treated as a state for purposes of applying constitutional guarantees. This was one of the earliest, most amorphous, and potentially most far-reaching themes in the expansion of the state action concept, but the cases since the early 1970s have curtailed it sharply. An examination of the "public function" cases follows, as the first group of the materials exploring the varying strands of state action analysis.

THE "PUBLIC FUNCTION" STRAND OF STATE ACTION ANALYSIS

1. *Marsh v. Alabama and modern "public function" analysis.* a. *The decision.* A major source of the view that the private performance of "public functions" can make 14th Amendment guarantees applicable was MARSH v. ALABAMA, 326 U.S. 501 (1946).[1] Marsh arose in the context of First Amendment rights and held that a state cannot "impose criminal punishment on a person who undertakes to distribute religious literature on the premises of a company-owned town contrary to the wishes of the town's management." Chickasaw, Alabama, was owned by the Gulf Shipbuilding Corporation. Except for that private ownership, it had "all the characteristics of any other American town." Marsh, a Jehovah's Witness, was convicted under the state criminal trespass law because she distributed religious literature without permission. Justice BLACK's majority opinion noted that an ordinary town could not have prohibited her activities, in view of cases such as Lovell v. Griffin (p. 1201 below). That a corporation owned title to the town could not justify impairing the public's interest "in the

---

1. Recall also the "public function" discussion in Justice Harlan's dissent in the Civil Rights Cases, p. 860 above, and compare the evolution of "public function" analysis in the White Primary Cases, p. 875 below.

functioning of the community in such a manner that the channels of communication remain free." Accordingly, he rejected the argument that "the corporation's right to control the inhabitants of Chickasaw is coextensive with the right of a homeowner to regulate the conduct of his guests." He stated: "Ownership does not always mean absolute dominion. The more an owner, for his advantage, opens up his property for use by the public in general, the more do his rights become circumscribed by the statutory and constitutional rights of those who use it. Thus, the owners of privately held bridges, ferries, turnpikes and railroads may not operate them as freely as a farmer does his farm. Since these facilities are built and operated primarily to benefit the public and *since their operation is essentially a public function,* it is subject to state regulation." (Emphasis added.) Justice Black also noted that many Americans "live in company-owned towns," and that to act "as good citizens, they must be informed." He added: "When we balance the Constitutional rights of owners of property against those of the people to enjoy freedom of press and religion, as we must here, we remain mindful of the fact that the latter occupy a preferred position." He noted, moreover, that "the town and its shopping district are accessible to and freely used by the public in general and there is nothing to distinguish them from any other town and shopping center except the fact that the title to the property belongs to a private corporation." And that property interest could not justify infringement of First Amendment rights: "The 'business block' serves as the community shopping center and is freely accessible and open to the people in the area and those passing through. The managers appointed by the corporation cannot curtail the liberty of press and religion of these people consistently with the purposes of the Constitutional guarantees, and a state statute [which] enforces such action by criminally punishing those who attempt to distribute religious literature clearly violates the [Constitution]." [2]

b. *Some questions.* What satisfied the state action requirement in Marsh? Apparently, the invocation of a state trespass law was not important to the finding of state action.[3] Rather, Marsh rested largely on the nature of the private activity—the fact that Chickasaw was "a town" which in "its community aspects [did] not differ from other towns" and which therefore exercised a "public function." Is the aim of the "public function" discussion to demonstrate an adequate relationship with the state—i.e., does it rest on an implicit view that the state had "delegated" a nondelegable function to the private entity? Or is the "public function" discussion really a substitute for (rather than part of the search for) formal state involvement? In the latter view, "public function" analysis focuses on a balancing of competing interests—those of the First Amendment claimant and those of the private property owner. Consider the relative emphases on nexus and balancing approaches in the evolution of the public function approach, below.

2. Justice FRANKFURTER's concurrence stated that, in view of First Amendment rights in ordinary municipalities, "I am unable to find legal significance in the fact that a town in which the Constitutional freedoms of religion and speech are invoked happens to be company-owned." He added: "Title to property as defined by State law controls property relations; it cannot control issues of civil liberties which arise precisely because a company town is a town as well as a congeries of property relations."

Justice REED's dissent, joined by Chief Justice Stone and Justice Burton, noted that this was "the first case to extend by law the privilege of religious exercises beyond public places or to

private places without the assent of the owner" and disagreed with this "novel Constitutional doctrine." He added: "The [constitutionally protected] rights of the owner [are] not outweighed by the interests of the trespasser, even though he trespasses in behalf of religion or free speech."

3. Should that state "nexus" have played a more prominent role? Compare Shelley v. Kraemer (p. 877 below) where, two years later, the Court placed great emphasis on state judicial enforcement of a private restrictive covenant. Shelley, viewed as a far-reaching and novel approach to state action, barely mentioned Marsh.

2. *The refusal to extend Marsh: The modern shopping center cases.* More than 20 years later, the Court returned to the Marsh problem to consider claims that shopping centers, which were replacing downtown business areas throughout the country, should be subjected to First Amendment constitutional restraints, just as the company town had been in Marsh. In the first of the series of cases, Amalgamated Food Employees Union v. Logan Valley Plaza, Inc., 391 U.S. 308 (1968), that effort succeeded. Justice Marshall's opinion concluded that the shopping center involved in that case was "clearly the functional equivalent to the business district of Chickasaw involved in Marsh." But in 1976, in Hudgens v. NLRB (below), the Court made clear that Logan Valley was no longer the law and that shopping center owners were not engaged in "state action." Between Logan Valley and Hudgens, the 1972 decision in Lloyd Corp. v. Tanner had sought to distinguish Logan Valley; but Hudgens announced that Lloyd had in effect overruled the Logan Valley case. Marsh, it had become clear, would be limited to its immediate context, the company town situation.[4]

In Logan Valley, the majority noted the "large-scale movement of this country's population from the cities to the suburbs [that had been] accompanied by the advent of the suburban shopping center," insisted that "the State may not delegate the power, through the use of its trespass laws, wholly to exclude those members of the public wishing to exercise their First Amendment rights," and argued that the shopping center was "unlike a situation involving a person's home," because the shopping center owner could advance "no meaningful claim to protection of a right of privacy." That case involved labor union picketing. Justice Black, the author of Marsh, dissented in Logan Valley, insisting that, under Marsh, private property could be treated as though it were public only "when that property has taken on *all* the attributes of a town." Four years later, in Lloyd Corp. v. Tanner, 407 U.S. 551 (1972), the majority tried to distinguish Logan Valley and permitted a shopping center to exclude anti-war leafleters. Justice Powell's majority opinion stressed that, unlike the Logan Valley picketing, the handbilling "had no relation to any purpose for which the center was [used]."

HUDGENS v. NLRB, 424 U.S. 507 (1976), brought the short-lived era of treating shopping centers like company towns to an end: Justice STEWART, who had dissented in Lloyd, now announced that Lloyd had in effect overruled Logan Valley. Like Logan Valley, Hudgens arose in the labor picketing context. Justice POWELL, who had written Lloyd, agreed with Justice Stewart, stating that, "upon more mature thought," he had concluded that it would have been "wiser" in Lloyd not to have drawn "distinctions based upon rather attenuated factual differences." Justice MARSHALL, the author of Logan Valley, tried unsuccessfully to preserve Logan Valley by distinguishing Lloyd. His dissent insisted that the majority had taken an "overly formalistic view of the relationship [between] private ownership of property" and the First Amendment. He commented: "Not only employees with a labor dispute, but also consumers with complaints against business establishments, may look to the location of a retail store as the only reasonable avenue for effective communication with the public. As far as these groups are concerned, the shopping center owner has assumed the traditional role of the state in its control of historical First Amendment forums." But the late Justice Black's narrow view of Marsh, as expressed in his Logan Valley dissent, in effect carried the day.[5]

4. This series of company town and shopping center cases is more fully discussed, together with other First Amendment problems, at p. 1291 below.

5. To what extent does the position that prevailed in Lloyd and Hudgens rest on constitu-

tionally protected property rights that are protected not only against Court expansions of state action and free speech principles but also against restrictions by other organs of government, be they Congress, state legislatures, or state courts? That question was considered in PruneYard

3. *The reach of the "public function" rationale: The parks context.* Efforts to rely on the "public function" analysis in areas beyond company towns (and, briefly, shopping centers) have encountered considerable difficulties. But the public function theme was relied on as an alternative ground in Justice DOUG-LAS' majority opinion in EVANS v. NEWTON, 382 U.S. 296 (1966). That case involved a park created in Macon, Ga., pursuant to a trust established in the 1911 will of Senator Bacon. The trust provided that the park, Baconsfield, be used by whites only. The city originally acted as trustee and enforced the racial exclusion, but decided after the racial segregation decisions beginning with Brown that it could no longer participate in discrimination. In the Newton litigation, the state court accepted the city's resignation as trustee and appointed private trustees instead. The Court held that Baconsfield nevertheless could not be operated on a racially restrictive basis. In explaining why the 14th Amendment prohibition continued to apply to the park despite the substitution of private trustees, Justice DOUGLAS relied in part on the ground that, so far as the record showed, "there has been no change in municipal maintenance and concern over this facility." But he suggested a "public function" ground as additional support: "This conclusion is buttressed by the nature of the service rendered the community by a park. The service rendered even by a private park of this character is municipal in nature. It is open to every white person, there being no selective element other than race. Golf clubs, social centers, luncheon clubs, schools such as Tuskegee was at least in origin, and other like organizations in the private sector are often racially oriented. A park, on the other hand, is more like a fire department or police department that traditionally serves the community. Mass recreation through the use of parks is plainly in the public domain; and state courts that aid private parties to perform that public function on a segregated basis implicate the State in conduct proscribed by the 14th Amendment. Like the streets of the company town in [Marsh] [and] the elective process of Terry [p. 876 below], the predominant character and purpose of this park are municipal." [6]

4. *Public function and private power.* Does the intermittent reliance on the public function analysis rest ultimately on the notion that 14th Amendment restraints become applicable whenever private action has substantial impact on important interests of individuals? How does that "private government"

Shopping Center v. Robins (1980; more fully considered below, at p. 1294). The state court had interpreted the California Constitution as guaranteeing access to a privately owned shopping center for persons seeking signatures for a petition to the White House. The state court emphasized a dictum in Hudgens acknowledging that "statutory or common law in some situations may extend protection or provide redress against a private corporation or person who seeks to abridge the free expression of others." The Court affirmed the Robins decision but Justice Powell's concurring opinion, below, indicated that there might be constitutional defenses—First Amendment ones as well as ones based on property rights—if a state granted broad access rights to private property in other contexts.

6. The expansive potential of Justice Douglas' public function rationale evoked special criticism in Justice Harlan's dissent, joined by Justice Stewart: "Its failing as a principle of decision [can] be shown by comparing [the] 'public function' of privately established schools with that of privately owned parks. [Despite the majority's disavowal, I] find it difficult [to] avoid the con-

clusion that this decision, [at] least in logic, jeopardizes the existence of denominationally restricted schools while making of every college entrance rejection letter a potential 14th Amendment question. [While] this process of analogy might be spun out to reach privately owned orphanages, libraries, garbage collection companies, detective agencies, and a host of other functions commonly regarded as nongovernmental though paralleling fields of governmental activity, the example of schools is, I think, sufficient to indicate the pervasive potentialities of this 'public function' [theory]. [It entails] a catch-phrase approach as vague and amorphous as it is far-reaching." (Note the narrow reading of Evans v. Newton—and the implicit rejection of Justice Douglas' public function argument—in Justice Rehnquist's opinion for the Court in Flagg Bros. in 1978, at p. 899 below.)

After the reversal in Evans v. Newton, the state courts held that the trust had failed because the Senator's intention had become impossible to fulfill; the property accordingly reverted to his heirs. A divided Court affirmed that decision. Evans v. Abney (1970; p. 880 below).

emphasis satisfy the "state action" requirement? Does it rest simply on a balancing of competing interests, with the power and impact of the challenged enterprise playing a large role? Or is the requisite formal state involvement provided by the probability that the "private government" is chartered by the state? (Compare the licensing and regulation cases below.) Is an adequate involvement with the state shown simply by the state's tolerance of the challenged practice? If mere state failure to prohibit suffices, is the approach inconsistent with any genuine effort to preserve a "state action"-"private action" distinction? Would expansion of a "public function" or "private government" approach unduly constitutionalize all operations of "private" groups found subject to the 14th Amendment? [7]

5. *The Burger Court's curtailment of public function analysis: The limitation to powers "exclusively reserved to the State."* Two decisions of the 1970s make it especially clear that the modern Court does not look with favor upon efforts to expand the "public function" analysis launched by Marsh. a. JACKSON v. METROPOLITAN EDISON CO., 419 U.S. 345 (1974) (noted more fully at p. 895 below), was a federal suit against a privately owned utility licensed and regulated by a state public utilities commission. Petitioner sought relief against the company's termination of her electric service for nonpayment. She claimed that the company was bound by the 14th Amendment and that her procedural due process rights had been denied by the failure to give adequate notice and a hearing. Among the various state action theories she relied on was one urging that "state action is present because respondent provides an essential public service required to be supplied on a reasonably continuous basis by [state law] and hence performs a 'public function.'" Justice REHNQUIST's majority opinion rejected this as well as all other state action claims. As to public function, he stated: "We have, of course, found state action present in the exercise by a private entity of powers traditionally *exclusively reserved to the State.* [Emphasis added. He cited Marsh and the White Primary Cases, p. 875 below.] If we were dealing with the exercise by [the company] of some power delegated to it by the State which is traditionally associated with sovereignty, such as eminent domain, our case would be quite a different one. [Perhaps] in recognition of the fact that the supplying of utility service is not traditionally the exclusive prerogative of the State, petitioner invites the expansion of a doctrine of this limited line of cases into a broad principle that all businesses 'affected with a public interest' are state actors in all their actions. We decline the invitation for reasons stated long ago in Nebbia [p. 462 above], in the course of rejecting a substantive due process attack on state legislation: 'It is clear that there is no closed class or category of businesses affected with a public interest. [The] phrase "affected with a public interest" can, in the nature of things, mean

---

7. See Wellington, "The Constitution, the Labor Union, and 'Governmental Action,'" 70 Yale L.J. 345 (1961). On the obligation of unions designated as exclusive bargaining representatives under federal labor legislation to avoid racial discrimination, see, e.g., Steele v. Louisville & Nashville Railroad Co., 323 U.S. 192 (1944). In Steele, the Court stated: "We think that the Railway Labor Act imposes upon the statutory representative of a craft at least as exacting a duty to protect equally the interests of the members of the craft as the Constitution imposes upon a legislature to give equal protection."

Consider the assertion of an "emerging principle" in Berle, "Constitutional Limitations on Corporate Activity—Protection of Personal Rights from Invasion through Economic Power," 100 U.Pa.L.Rev. 933 (1952). Berle suggested

that "principle" to be that a corporation may be "as subject to constitutional limitations as is the state itself." He notes two prerequisites: the "undeniable fact" of the state's action in chartering the corporation, and "the existence of sufficient economic power [to] invade the constitutional rights of the individual to a material degree." Berle offered as one of the justifications the fact that the state relies upon "the corporate system to carry out functions for which in modern life by community demand the government is held ultimately responsible." See also Robert L. Hale's anticipation of many of the post-World War II theories on this issue in "Force and the State: A Comparison of 'Political' and 'Economic' Compulsion," 35 Colum.L.Rev. 149 (1935). To what extent is Berle's "emerging principle" supported by the cases since his 1952 article?

no more than that an industry, for adequate reason, is subject to control for the public good.' Doctors, optometrists, lawyers, Metropolitan [the utility here], and Nebbia's upstate New York grocery selling a quart of milk are all in regulated businesses, providing arguably essential goods and services, 'affected with a public interest.' We do not believe that such a status converts their every action, absent more, into that of the State." [8]

Justice MARSHALL's dissent argued that the presence of "a service uniquely public in nature" had been important in past state action cases. The fact that the utility "supplies an essential public service that is in many communities supplied by the government weighs more heavily for me than for the majority." He elaborated: "The Court concedes that state action might be present if the activity in question were 'traditionally associated with sovereignty,' but it then undercuts that point by suggesting that a particular service is not a public function if the State in question has not required that it be governmentally operated. This reads the 'public function' argument too narrowly. The whole point of the 'public function' cases is to look behind the State's decision to provide public services through private parties. See [Evans v. Newton; Terry; Marsh]. In my view, utility service is traditionally identified with the State through universal public regulation or ownership to a degree sufficient to render it a 'public function.' [I agree] that it requires more than a finding that a particular business is 'affected with the public interest' before constitutional burdens can be imposed on that business. But when the activity in question is of such public importance that the State invariably either provides the service itself or permits private companies to act as state surrogates in providing it, much more is involved than just a matter of public interest. In those cases, the State has determined that if private companies wish to enter the field, they will have to surrender many of the prerogatives normally associated with private enterprise and behave in many ways like a governmental body. And when the State's regulatory scheme has gone that far, it seems entirely consistent to impose on the public utility the constitutional burdens normally reserved for the State." [9]

    b. Justice REHNQUIST reemphasized the "carefully confined bounds" of the public function doctrine on the modern Court in FLAGG BROS., INC. v. BROOKS, 436 U.S. 149 (1978), holding that a warehouseman's proposed sale of goods entrusted to him for storage to satisfy a warehouseman's lien under the Uniform Commercial Code did not constitute state action.[10] The plaintiffs'

---

8. Justice Rehnquist added that the argument had been "impliedly rejected by this Court on a number of occasions." He cited the Civil Rights Cases and the disavowal of intrusion into parochial schools, despite the "public interest" nature of schools, in a dictum in Evans v. Newton.

Compare Justice Rehnquist's dissent in Central Hudson Gas v. Public Service Comm'n (1980; p. 1139 below), arguing that, "for purposes of First Amendment analysis, a utility is far closer to a state-controlled enterprise than is an ordinary corporation."

9. In another dissent, Justice DOUGLAS commented more briefly on the majority's rejection of the public function argument: "I agree that doctors, lawyers, and grocers are not transformed into state actors simply because they provide arguably essential goods and services and are regulated by the State. In the present case, however, respondent is not just one person among many; it is the only public utility furnishing electric power to the town."

10. The claim was that warehousemen's sales' pursuant to the UCC were subject to the procedural due process guarantees of the 14th Amendment. The plaintiffs argued that the UCC procedures would be constitutionally inadequate if the sales were conducted by state officials and that a warehouseman utilizing the UCC was engaged in state action. In a series of earlier cases, the Court *had* held constitutional guarantees regarding minimal hearings applicable to a range of summary creditors' remedies. See, e.g., the Sniadach (garnishment), Fuentes (repossession), and North Georgia Finishing (garnishment) cases, all noted in chap. 8, at p. 584 above, and all distinguished by Justice Rehnquist in this case. But note a 1982 creditors' summary remedies case, Lugar (p. 901 below), where the majority distinguished Flagg Bros. (and Justice Rehnquist was among the dissenters).

main claim was that the State had delegated to the warehouseman "a power 'traditionally exclusively reserved to the State.' Jackson. They argued that the resolution of private disputes is a traditional function of civil government." Justice Rehnquist replied that the plaintiffs had "read too much into the language of our previous cases": "While many functions have been traditionally performed by governments, very few have been 'exclusively reserved to the State.'" Reviewing the White Primary Cases (which follow) and Marsh, he elaborated:

"These two branches of the public function doctrine have in common the feature of exclusivity.[11] Although the elections held by the Democratic Party and its affiliates were the only meaningful elections in Texas [in Smith v. Allwright and Terry, below] and the streets owned by the Gulf Shipbuilding Corporation were the only streets in Chickasaw [in Marsh], the proposed sale by Flagg Brothers [is] not the only means of resolving this purely private dispute. [Brooks] has never alleged that state law barred her from seeking a waiver of Flagg Brothers' right to sell her goods at the time she authorized their storage. Presumably, respondent Jones, who alleges that she never authorized the storage of her goods, could have sought to replevy her goods at any time under state law. The challenged statute itself provides a damage remedy against the warehouseman for violations of its provisions. This system of rights and remedies, recognizing the traditional place of private arrangements in ordering relationships in the commercial world, can hardly be said to have delegated to Flagg Brothers an exclusive prerogative of the sovereign.[12] [Creditors] and debtors have had available to them historically a far wider number of choices than has one who would be an elected public official, or a member of Jehovah's Witnesses who wished to distribute literature in Chickasaw, Ala., at the time Marsh was decided. Our analysis requires no parsing of the difference between various commercial liens and other remedies to support the conclusion that this entire field of activity is outside the scope of Terry and Marsh. This is true whether these commercial rights and remedies are created by statute or decisional law. To rely upon the historical antecedents of a particular practice would result in the constitutional condemnation in one State of a remedy found perfectly permissible in another. Thus, even if we were inclined to extend the sovereign function doctrine outside of its present carefully confined bounds, the field of private commercial transactions would be a particularly inappropriate area into which to expand it. We conclude that our sovereign function cases do not support a finding of state action here. [W]e would be remiss if we did not note that there are a number of state and municipal functions not covered by our election cases nor governed by the reasoning of Marsh which have been administered with a greater degree of exclusivity by States and municipalities than has the function of so-called 'dispute resolution.' Among these are such functions as education, fire and police protection, and tax collection. We express no view as to the extent, if any, to which a city or State might be free to delegate to private parties the performance of such functions and thereby avoid

---

11. "Respondents also contend that Evans v. Newton [p. 870 above] establishes that the operation of a park for recreational purposes is an exclusively public function. We doubt that Newton intended to establish any such broad doctrine in the teeth of the experience of several American entrepreneurs who amassed great fortunes by operating parks for recreational purposes. We think Newton rests on a finding of ordinary state action under extraordinary circumstances. The Court's opinion emphasizes that the record showed [that the] transfer of title to private trustees [had not] eliminated the actual involvement of the city in the daily maintenance and care of the park." [Footnote by Justice Rehnquist. Cf. footnote 16 below.]

12. "[It] would intolerably broaden, beyond the scope of any of our previous cases, the notion of state action under the 14th Amendment to hold that the mere existence of a body of property law in a State, whether decisional or statutory, itself amounted to 'state action' even though no state officials or state process were ever involved in enforcing that body of [law]." [Footnote by Justice Rehnquist.]

the strictures of the 14th Amendment. The mere recitation of these possible permutations and combinations of factual situations suffices to caution us that their resolution should abide the necessity of deciding them." [13]

Justice STEVENS' dissent, joined by Justices White and Marshall, responded to the majority's public function analysis as follows: "[The State] has authorized the warehouseman to perform what is clearly a state function. The test of what is a state function for purposes of [due process] has been variously phrased. Most frequently the issue is presented in terms of whether the State has delegated a function traditionally and historically associated with sovereignty. See, e.g., Jackson; Newton. [Petitioners argue] that the nonconsensual transfer of property rights is not a traditional function of the sovereign. The overwhelming historical evidence is to the contrary, however,[14] and the Court wisely does not adopt this position. Instead, the Court reasons that state action cannot be found because the State has not delegated to the warehouseman an *exclusive* sovereign function.[15] This distinction, however, is not consistent with our prior decisions on state action;[16] is not even adhered to by the Court in this case;[17] and, most importantly, is inconsistent with the line of cases beginning with Sniadach. Since Sniadach this Court has scrutinized various state statutes regulating the debtor-creditor relationship for compliance with [due process]. In each of these cases a finding of state action was a prerequisite to the Court's decision. The Court today seeks to explain these findings on the ground that in each case there was some element of 'overt official involvement.' Given the facts of those cases, this explanation is baffling. In North Georgia Finishing, for instance, the official involvement of the State of Georgia consisted of a court clerk who issued a writ of garnishment based solely on the affidavit of the creditor. The clerk's actions were purely ministerial, and until today, this Court had never held that purely ministerial acts of 'minor governmental functionaries' were sufficient to establish state action. The suggestion that this was the basis for due process review in [North Georgia Finishing etc.] marks a major and, in

---

13. The Court also rejected the claim that the warehouseman's proposed sale constituted state action "because the State has authorized and encouraged it in enacting [the UCC]." The discussion of that claim is noted further below, at p. 899.

14. "The New York State courts have recognized that the execution of a lien is a traditional function of the State. See also Blackstone, Commentaries, which notes that the right of self-help at common law was severely limited. [Some] reference to history and well-settled practice is necessary to determine whether a particular action is a 'traditional state function.' See [Jackson]." [Footnote by Justice Stevens.]

15. "As I understand the Court's notion of 'exclusivity,' the sovereign function here is not exclusive because there may be other state remedies, under different statutes or common-law theories, available to respondents. Even if I were to accept the notion that sovereign functions must be 'exclusive,' the Court's description of exclusivity is incomprehensible. The question is whether a particular action is a uniquely sovereign function, not whether state law forecloses any possibility of recovering for damages for such activity. For instance, it is clear that the maintenance of a police force is a unique sovereign function, and the delegation of police power to a private party will entail state action. Under the Court's analysis, however, there would be no state action if the

State provided a remedy, such as an action for wrongful imprisonment, for the individual injured by the 'private' policeman. This analysis is not based on 'exclusivity,' but on some vague, and highly inappropriate, notion that respondents should not complain about this state statute if the state offers them a glimmer of hope of redeeming their possessions, or at least the value of the goods, through some other state action. Of course, the availability of other state remedies may be relevant in determining whether the statute provides sufficient procedural protections under [due process], but it is not relevant to the state action issue." [Footnote by Justice Stevens.]

16. "The Court, for instance, attempts to distinguish Evans v. Newton. Newton concededly involved a function which is not exclusively sovereign—the operation of a park—but the Court claims that Newton actually rested on a determination that the City was still involved in the 'daily maintenance and care of the park.' This [is a] stark attempt to rewrite the rationale of the Newton [opinion]." [Footnote by Justice Stevens.]

17. "As the Court is forced to recognize, its notion of exclusivity simply cannot be squared with the wide range of functions that are typically considered sovereign functions, such as 'education, fire and police protection, and tax collection.'" [Footnote by Justice Stevens.]

my judgment, unwise expansion of the state action doctrine. The number of private actions in which a governmental functionary plays some ministerial role is legion; to base due process review on the fortuity of such governmental intervention would demean the majestic purposes of [due process]. Instead, cases such as North Georgia Finishing must be viewed as reflecting this Court's recognition of the significance of the State's role in defining *and controlling* the debtor-creditor relationship. [The] very defect that made the [laws in North Georgia Finishing etc.] unconstitutional—lack of state control—is, under today's decision, the factor that precludes constitutional review of the state statute. [Due process] cannot command such incongruous results. If it is unconstitutional for a State to allow a private party to exercise a traditional state power because the state supervision of that power is purely mechanical, the State surely cannot immunize its actions from constitutional *scrutiny* by removing even the mechanical supervision. [Whether] termed 'traditional,' 'exclusive,' or 'significant,' the state power to order binding, nonconsensual resolution of a conflict between debtor and creditor is exactly the sort of power with which [due process] is concerned. And the State's delegation of that power to a private party is, accordingly, subject to due process scrutiny." [18]

THE WHITE PRIMARY CASES

The White Primary Cases were decisions culminating in the 1950s holding that Democratic Party groups in southern one-party states could not exclude blacks from pre-general election candidate selection processes, despite repeated efforts to eliminate all formal indicia of state involvement in the primary schemes. Although the cases are frequently referred to in discussions of the public function approach, they may represent a distinctive, separable line of development. Arguably, they are explainable on the basis of their special context of voting and elections. Moreover, they may be supportable on the basis of the 15th Amendment and its specific reference to racial discrimination in voting rather than on the 14th Amendment. Moreover, the tradition of state regulation of primaries may help explain the White Primary Cases.

The sequence of cases began with Nixon v. Herndon, 273 U.S. 536 (1927), where the exclusion of blacks from Democratic primaries was expressed on the face of a state law. That was held to be state racial discrimination in violation of the 14th Amendment. Texas responded by granting the power to prescribe membership qualifications to party executive committees. A resultant racial exclusion was again found unconstitutional under the 14th Amendment, in Nixon v. Condon, 286 U.S. 73 (1932), on the ground that the law had made the committee an agent of the state. This time, Texas enacted no new law. Instead, a third round of racial exclusions stemmed from action of the state party convention. That exclusion survived constitutional attack in Grovey v. Townsend, 295 U.S. 45 (1935): the convention was found to be an organ of a voluntary, private group, not of the state; the state was no longer unconstitutionally involved. But Grovey v. Townsend was overruled nine years later, in SMITH v. ALLWRIGHT, 321 U.S. 649 (1944). Where the Nixon cases had relied on the 14th Amendment, Smith found that the white primary established by the state convention violated the 15th Amendment. The Smith Court pointed to an intervening decision, United States v. Classic, 313 U.S. 299 (1941), which held that Art. I, § 4, authorized congressional control of

---

18. Justice MARSHALL, one of those joining Justice Stevens' dissent, also submitted a separate dissenting opinion. He accused the majority of once again demonstrating "an attitude of callous indifference to the realities of life for the poor," and he objected to the Court's "cavalier treatment of the place of historical factors" in identifying functions "traditionally reserved to the State." (Justice Brennan did not participate in the case.)

primaries "where the primary is by law made part of the election machinery." Classic was relevant in Smith, according to Justice REED's majority opinion, "not because exclusion of Negroes from primaries is any more or less state action by reason of the unitary character of the electoral process but because the recognition of the place of the primary in the electoral scheme makes clear that state delegation to a party of the power to fix the qualifications of primary elections is delegation of a state function that may make the party's action the action of the State. [O]ur ruling in Classic as to the unitary character of the electoral process calls for a re-examination as to whether or not the exclusion of Negroes from a Texas party primary was state action." The Court examined the Texas laws and concluded: "We think that this statutory system for the selection of party nominees for inclusion on the general election ballot makes the party which is required to follow these legislative directions an agency of the State in so far as it determines the participants in a primary election." [1]

The issue came to the Supreme Court in its most extreme "private" form in TERRY v. ADAMS, 345 U.S. 461 (1953). Terry involved racial exclusion in the "pre-primary" elections of the Jaybird Democratic Association, a "voluntary club" of white Democrats. Candidates who won the Jaybird elections typically ran unopposed in the Democratic primaries. The trial court found a "complete absence" of state involvement in the Jaybirds' operations. The Court nevertheless found the 15th Amendment violated by the exclusion of black voters from the pre-primary. There was no opinion on which a majority could agree, but only one Justice dissented from the result. Justice BLACK, joined by Justices Douglas and Burton, found that "the combined Jaybird-Democratic-general election machinery" was unconstitutional. Though the Amendment "excludes social or business clubs," it "includes any election in which public officials are elected. Any election machinery with the 'purpose or effect' of denying "Negroes on account of their race an effective voice in governmental affairs" was barred: "For a State to permit such a duplication of its election processes" as the Jaybird pre-primary was unconstitutional. In a separate opinion, Justice FRANKFURTER stated that the "vital requirement is State responsibility—that somewhere, somehow, to some extent, there be an infusion by conduct by officials [into] any scheme" denying the franchise because of race. Nevertheless, he found a constitutional violation here: he thought that county election officials were in effect "participants in the scheme." They had participated by voting in the primary, and that indicated that they "condone[d]" the effectiveness of the exclusionary pre-primary; the "action and abdication" of state officials had in effect permitted a procedure "which predetermines the legally devised primary." Justice CLARK, joined by Chief Justice Vinson and Justices Reed and Jackson, concurred on the ground that the Jaybirds operated "as an auxiliary of the local Party" and were therefore subject to the principles of Smith v. Allwright. He emphasized the Jaybirds' "decisive power" in the county's electoral process and concluded that "when a state structures its electoral apparatus in a form which devolves upon a political organization the uncontested choice of public officials, that organization itself, in whatever disguise, takes on those attributes of government which draw the Constitution's safeguards into play." [2]

---

1. After Smith v. Allwright, several efforts to preserve "private" white primaries by abandoning much of the state statutory framework of the primary election process were thwarted in the lower courts. Note especially the language in Rice v. Ellmore, 165 F.2d 387 (4th Cir.1947), cert. denied 333 U.S. 875 (1948), where South Carolina had repealed all primary laws. The Court of Appeals concluded: "Having undertaken to perform an important function relating to the exercise of sovereignty by the people, [a political party] may not violate the fundamental principles laid down by the Constitution for its exercise."

2. Justice MINTON was the sole dissenter: he thought that the Jaybirds' activities, like those

STATE ACTION THROUGH STATE "INVOLVEMENT": THE "NEXUS" STRAND OF STATE ACTION ANALYSIS

SHELLEY v. KRAEMER

334 U.S. 1, 68 S.Ct. 836, 92 L.Ed. 1161 (1948).

[These cases (from Missouri and Michigan) were successful challenges to judicial enforcement of the once widely used practice of restrictive covenants—agreements among property owners to exclude persons of designated races.[1] In the Missouri case, for example, a 1911 agreement signed by 30 out of 39 property owners in the area restricted occupancy for 50 years to persons of "the Caucasian race" and excluded "people of the Negro or Mongolian race." The petitioners in these cases were blacks who had purchased houses from white owners despite the racially restrictive covenants. Respondents, owners of other properties subject to the terms of the covenants, sued to enjoin black purchasers from taking possession of the property and to divest them of title. The state courts granted the relief.]

Mr. Chief Justice VINSON delivered the opinion of the [Court].

Whether the equal protection clause [inhibits] judicial enforcement by state courts of restrictive covenants based on race or color is a question which this Court has not heretofore been called upon to consider. [It] cannot be doubted that among the civil rights intended to be protected from discriminatory state action by the 14th Amendment are the rights to acquire, enjoy, own and dispose of property. Equality in the enjoyment of property rights was regarded by the framers of that Amendment as an essential precondition to the realization of other basic civil rights and liberties which the Amendment was intended to guarantee. Thus, [the present 42 U.S.C. § 1982[2]], derived from § 1 of the Civil Rights Act of 1866 which was enacted by Congress while the 14th Amendment was also under consideration, provides: "All citizens of the United States shall have the same right, in every State and Territory, as is enjoyed by white citizens thereof to inherit, purchase, lease, sell, hold, and convey real and personal property." This Court has given specific recognition to the same principle. Buchanan v. Warley, 245 U.S. 60 (1917).[3] It is likewise clear that restrictions on the right of occupancy of the sort sought to be created by the private agreements in these cases could not be squared with the requirements of the 14th Amendment if imposed by state statute or local ordinance. [But] the present cases [do] not involve action by state legislatures or city councils. Here the particular patterns of discrimination and the areas in which the restrictions are to operate, are determined, in the first instance, by the terms of agreements among private individuals. Participation of the State consists in the enforcement of the restrictions so defined. The crucial issue [is] whether this distinction removes these cases from [the 14th Amendment].

Since [the Civil Rights Cases, the principle has become firmly [established] that the action inhibited by the first section of the 14th Amendment is only such action as may fairly be said to be that of the States. That Amendment erects no

of other pressure groups, were protected private "attempts to influence or obtain state action."

1. For a history of the litigation strategy in the battle against restrictive covenants, see Vose, Caucasians Only: The Supreme Court, the NAACP, and the Restrictive Covenant Cases (1959).

2. On the modern interpretation (and reinvigoration) of § 1982, see Jones (1968; p. 924 below).

3. Buchanan v. Warley held unconstitutional a city ordinance making it unlawful for any "colored person" to move in and occupy a house on a block where the majority of residents were whites.

shield against merely private conduct, however discriminatory or wrongful. We conclude, therefore, that the restrictive agreements standing alone cannot be regarded as violative of any rights guaranteed to petitioners by the 14th Amendment. So long as the purposes of those agreements are effectuated by voluntary adherence to their terms, it would appear clear that there has been no action by the State and the provisions of the Amendment have not been violated. But here there was more. These are cases in which the purposes of the agreements were secured only by judicial enforcement by state courts of the restrictive terms of the agreements. The respondents urge that judicial enforcement of private agreements does not amount to state action; or, in any event, the participation of the State is so attenuated in character as not to amount to state action within the meaning of the 14th Amendment. Finally, it is suggested, even if the States in these cases may be deemed to have acted in the constitutional sense, their action did not deprive petitioners of rights guaranteed by the 14th [Amendment].

That the action of state courts and judicial officers in their official capacities is to be regarded as action of the State within the meaning of the 14th Amendment, is a proposition which has long been established by decisions of this Court. [E.g., in] Bridges v. California [1941; p. 1338 below], enforcement of the state's common-law rule relating to contempts by publication was held to be state action inconsistent with the prohibitions of the 14th Amendment. [We] have no doubt that there has been state action in these cases in the full and complete sense of the phrase. The undisputed facts disclose that petitioners were willing purchasers of properties upon which they desired to establish homes. The owners of the properties were willing sellers; and contracts of sale were accordingly consummated. It is clear that but for the active intervention of the state courts, supported by the full panoply of state power, petitioners would have been free to occupy the properties in question without restraint. These are not cases, as has been suggested, in which the States have merely abstained from action, leaving private individuals free to impose such discriminations as they see fit. Rather, these are cases in which the States have made available to such individuals the full coercive power of government to deny to petitioners, on the grounds of race or color, the enjoyment of property rights in premises which petitioners are willing and financially able to acquire and which the grantors are willing to sell. The difference between judicial enforcement and non-enforcement of the restrictive covenants is the difference to petitioners between being denied rights of property available to other members of the community and being accorded full enjoyment of those rights on an equal footing.

The enforcement of the restrictive agreements by the state courts in these cases was directed pursuant to the common-law policy of the States as formulated by those courts in earlier decisions. [The] judicial action in each case bears the clear and unmistakable imprimatur of the State. We have noted that previous decisions of this Court have established the proposition that judicial action is not immunized from the operation of the 14th Amendment simply because it is taken pursuant to the state's common-law policy. Nor is the Amendment ineffective simply because the particular pattern of discrimination, which the State has enforced, was defined initially by the terms of a private agreement. State action, as that phrase is understood for the purposes of the 14th Amendment, refers to exertions of state power in all forms. And when the effect of that action is to deny rights subject to the protection of the 14th Amendment, it is the obligation of this Court to enforce the constitutional commands. We hold that in granting judicial enforcement of the restrictive agreements in these cases, the States have denied petitioners the equal protection of the laws and that, therefore, the action of the state courts cannot stand. We have noted that freedom from discrimination by the States in the enjoyment of property rights was among the basic objectives sought to be effectuated by the framers of the 14th Amendment. That such discrimination has occurred in these cases is [clear].

Respondents urge, however, that since the state courts stand ready to enforce restrictive covenants excluding white [persons], enforcement of covenants excluding colored persons may not be deemed a denial of equal protection of the laws to the colored persons who are thereby affected. This contention does not bear scrutiny. The parties have directed our attention to no case in which a court, state or federal, has been called upon to enforce a covenant excluding members of the white majority from ownership or occupancy of real property on grounds of race or color. But there are more fundamental considerations. The rights created by the first section of the 14th Amendment are, by its terms, guaranteed to the individual. The rights established are personal rights. It is, therefore, no answer to these petitioners to say that the courts may also be induced to deny white persons rights of ownership and occupancy on grounds of race or color. Equal protection of the laws is not achieved through indiscriminate imposition of [inequalities].

Reversed.[4]

SHELLEY v. KRAEMER: THE APPLICATIONS AND THE SEARCH FOR LIMITS

Introduction. If Shelley were read at its broadest, a simple citation of the case would have disposed of most subsequent state action cases. Some seemingly "neutral" state nexus with a private actor can almost always be found: at least by way of the usual state law backdrop for exercises of private choices; usually via more concrete state involvement than that. Given the entanglement of private choices with law, a broad application of Shelley might in effect have left no private choices immune from constitutional restraints. But, as the cases that follow illustrate, the Court has rejected so expansive a reading and has taken seriously the Shelley assurance that, despite some of its analysis, a state-private distinction was to be retained. The efforts to find principled limits on the broadest implications of Shelley have produced extensive commentary on and off the Court.

In considering Shelley in light of the subsequent cases, bear in mind some pervasive questions: Is the Shelley opinion's emphasis on the role of the state persuasive? Is "neutral" judicial enforcement a more significant benefit to the private actor than "neutral" provision of police and fire services? Is it as significant a benefit as a grant of governmental funds or monopoly status (considered below)? Denial of "neutral" judicial enforcement may spur the private actor to resort to self-help. Suppose there is violent resistance to that self-help: may the private property owner call on the police for help? Would that in turn provide the requisite state involvement? Does the Shelley approach give adequate weight to competing interests in privacy, association and property?[1] Over the years, a number of narrower readings of Shelley have been

---

4. Justices Reed, Jackson, and Rutledge did not participate in the case.

In a companion case to Shelley, Hurd v. Hodge, 334 U.S. 24 (1948), the Court held that courts in the District of Columbia could not enforce restrictive covenants even though the 14th Amendment is not applicable to the federal government. Chief Justice Vinson stated that such action would deny "rights [protected] by the Civil Rights Act"; moreover, it would be contrary to the public policy of the United States

to allow a federal court to enforce an agreement constitutionally unenforceable in state courts. (Cf. Bolling v. Sharpe, the companion case to Brown v. Board of Education, p. 638 above.)

1. See Henkin, "Shelley v. Kraemer: Notes for a Revised Opinion," 110 U.Pa.L.Rev. 473 (1962): "If the competing claims of liberty and the possibility that they may sometimes prevail are recognized, [Shelley] must be given [a] limited reading." Henkin argues that "there are circumstances where the discriminator can in-

advanced. It has been argued, for example, that Shelley is limited to situations where the state intervention has the effect of blocking a transaction between willing seller and buyer. It has also been urged that Shelley can be explained on the basis of 42 U.S.C. § 1982, cited by the Court. (Cf. Jones, p. 924 below.) Can Shelley also be explained via a "public function" rationale, on the ground that restrictive covenants covering a large area are equivalent to impermissible racial zoning laws? [2] Some applications of Shelley, and some efforts to limit it, follow.

1. *Restrictive covenants and damage actions.* Chief Justice Vinson, who wrote Shelley, dissented five years later when the Court applied it to block enforcement of a restrictive covenant via a damage suit against a co-covenantor. BARROWS v. JACKSON, 346 U.S. 249 (1953). The Court noted that permitting damage judgments would induce prospective sellers either to refuse to sell to non-Caucasians or to "require non-Caucasians to pay a higher price to meet the damages which the seller may incur." The Court "will not permit or require" the state "to coerce respondent to respond in damages for failure to observe a restrictive covenant that this Court would deny [the state] the right to enforce in equity." [3]

2. *Reverter provisions in deeds.* The Court's 5 to 2 decision in EVANS v. ABNEY, 396 U.S. 435 (1970), demonstrated that Shelley had not barred all state involvement in enforcing private restrictions on property. Senator Bacon's will had conveyed property in trust to Macon, Ga., for use as a park "for white people only." After Evans v. Newton (1966; p. 870 above) had held that the park could not be operated on a racially discriminatory basis, the state court ruled that "Senator Bacon's intention to provide a park for whites only had become impossible to fulfill and that accordingly the trust had failed and the parkland and other trust property had reverted by operation of Georgia law to the heirs of the Senator." The Court, in a majority opinion by Justice BLACK, held that this ruling did not constitute state discrimination under the 14th Amendment. The state court concluded that "Senator Bacon would have rather had the whole trust fail than have Baconsfield integrated" and rejected arguments that it should save the trust by applying the cy pres doctrine to alter the will by striking the racial restriction. Justice Black found that terminating the trust and enforcing the reverter violated no federal rights: "[A]ny harshness that may have resulted from the State court's decision can be attributed solely to its intention to effectuate as nearly as possible the explicit terms of Senator Bacon's will." He insisted that the situation presented in this case was "easily distinguishable from [Shelley], where we held unconstitutional state judicial action which had affirmatively enforced a private scheme of discrimination

voke a protected liberty which is not constitutionally inferior to the claim of equal protection. There, the Constitution requires or permits the state to favor the right to discriminate over the victim's claim to equal protection; the state, then, is not in violation of the 14th amendment when it legislates or affords a remedy in support of the discrimination." He suggests as those "special cases" where the discriminator should prevail "those few where the state supports that basic liberty, privacy, autonomy, which outweighs even the equal protection of the laws." Are the only competing interests which limit the application of the Shelley principle those that are themselves of constitutional dimensions? In other words, is the Shelley principle applicable, and must state action be found, in every situation in which state or federal legislatures have the *power* to outlaw racial discrimination without impinging on constitutional guarantees? Or is Shelley's reach narrower than that?

2. Note Justice Douglas' concurring opinion in Reitman (1967; p. 890 below): "Leaving the zoning function to groups [e.g., real estate brokers] which practice discrimination and are [state-licensed] constitutes state action in the narrowest sense in which Shelley can be construed."

3. Do Shelley and Barrows bar recognition of a restrictive covenant as a defense in actions for damages for breach of contract? See Rice v. Sioux City Memorial Park Cemetery, 245 Iowa 147, 60 N.W.2d 110 (1953), affirmed by an equally divided Court, 348 U.S. 880 (1954), vacated and cert. dismissed as improvidently granted 349 U.S. 70 (1955). Cf. Black v. Cutter Laboratories, 351 U.S. 292 (1956).

against Negroes. Here the effect of the Georgia decision eliminated all discrimination against Negroes in the park by eliminating the park itself, and the termination of the park was a loss shared equally by the white and Negro citizens of Macon."[4]

Only Justice BRENNAN's dissent[5] mentioned Shelley: "[Shelley] stands at least for the proposition that where parties of different races are willing to deal with one another a state court cannot keep them from doing so by enforcing a privately authored racial restriction." But he placed greater emphasis on other, related, arguments: "The exculpation of the State and city from responsibility for the closing of the park is simply indefensible on this record. This discriminatory closing is permeated with state action: at the time Senator Bacon wrote his will Georgia statutes expressly authorized and supported the precise kind of discrimination provided for by him; in accepting title to the park, public officials of [Macon] entered into an arrangement vesting in private persons the power to enforce a reversion if the city should ever incur a constitutional obligation to desegregate the park; it is a *public* park that is being closed for a discriminatory reason after having been operated for nearly half a century as a segregated *public* facility. [T]here is state action whenever a State enters into an arrangement which creates a private right to compel or enforce the reversion of a public facility. Whether the right is a possibility of reverter, a right of entry, an executory interest, or a contractual right, it can be created only with the consent of a public body or official."

   3. *Other testamentary provisions: The Girard College litigation.* Evans v. Abney dampened the speculation over the preceding two decades about the impact of Shelley on the enforcement of restrictive provisions in wills. For example, there had been doubt about whether a court could enforce a restrictive testamentary provision by cutting off a beneficiary when he or she married someone of another religion or race.[6] Abney may cast doubt on the ultimate outcome of the lengthy Girard College litigation. In PENNSYLVANIA v. BOARD OF TRUSTS, 353 U.S. 230 (1957), petitioners were denied admission to the school on the basis of race, pursuant to Stephen Girard's will, probated in 1831, setting up a trust for a school for "poor white male orphans." The will named the City of Philadelphia as trustee; subsequently, a "Board of Directors of City Trusts," composed of city officials and persons named by local courts, was established to administer the trust and the college. The state court refused to order admission. The Supreme Court reversed per curiam: "The Board which operates Girard College is an agency of the State. [Therefore], even though the Board was acting as trustee, its refusal to admit [petitioners] was discrimination by the State." After that ruling, the state courts substituted private trustees to carry out Girard's will. The Court denied certiorari in 1958. Ten years later, however, the Court of Appeals held that this substitution was unconstitutional state action.[7]

   4. *Trespass actions and the sit-in cases.* Does Shelley bar the enforcement of state trespass laws against persons excluded from private property on racial

   4. The challengers also argued that the state court had done more than merely giving effect to a clear-cut private intent, because they had exercised choice in interpreting that intent as requiring a reverter. But Justice Black rejected "the idea that the Georgia courts had a constitutional obligation in this case to resolve any doubt about the testator's intent in favor of preserving the trust. [The] Constitution imposes no requirement upon the Georgia courts to approach Bacon's will any differently than they would approach any will creating a charitable trust of any kind."

   5. Justice DOUGLAS also dissented. (Justice Marshall did not participate.)

   6. See Gordon v. Gordon, 332 Mass. 197, 124 N.E.2d 228, cert. denied 349 U.S. 947 (1955), where the state court enforced such a will and summarily distinguished Shelley and similar cases as involving "quite different considerations from the right to dispose of property by will."

   7. Pennsylvania v. Brown, 392 F.2d 120 (3d Cir.1968), cert. denied 391 U.S. 921. See generally Clark, "Charitable Trusts, the 14th Amendment and the Will of Stephen Girard," 66 Yale L.J. 979 (1957).

grounds? Is the state's enforcement of the property owner's restrictions sufficient state action to make the 14th Amendment applicable? That was the broadest issue inherent in a number of sit-in convictions of demonstrators who had protested discrimination by restaurants and other businesses prior to the enactment of the public accommodations provisions of the 1964 Civil Rights Act. The broadest reading of Shelley would have covered these cases with ease. Yet, in a series of decisions in the early 1960s, the Court set aside all of the convictions without relying on Shelley. The failure to rely on Shelley suggested that more state involvement than even-handed enforcement of private biases was necessary to find unconstitutional state action. For example, in Peterson v. Greenville, 373 U.S. 244 (1963)—one of five sit-in cases reversed at that time—the Court found official segregation policies in the background of the private action and refused to inquire whether the restaurant manager would have excluded the demonstrators had the state been wholly silent: the unconstitutional ingredients "cannot be saved by attempting to separate the mental urges of the discriminators." Justice Harlan's separate opinion asserted that the "ultimate substantive question" was whether "the character of the State's involvement in an arbitrary discrimination is such that it should be held *responsible* for the discrimination." In another sit-in case resting on narrow grounds, Lombard v. Louisiana, 373 U.S. 267 (1963), Justice Douglas argued that state courts cannot "put criminal sanctions behind racial discrimination in public places." He distinguished the restaurant situation from "an intrusion of a man's home or yard or farm or garden," where "the property owner could seek and obtain the aid of the State against the intruder." But the restaurant had "no aura of constitutionally protected privacy about it." (Compare Justice Harlan's opinion in Peterson, insisting that the sit-in problem involved "a clash of competing constitutional claims of a high order: liberty and equality." He emphasized the restaurant proprietor's freedom to "use and dispose of his property as he sees fit.")

Another group of five sit-in cases reached the Court in 1964. The trespass convictions were once again reversed on narrow grounds; but this time six of the Justices reached the broader issues at last—and divided 3 to 3. BELL v. MARYLAND, 378 U.S. 226 (1964). None of the opinions took a "simple" view of Shelley. For example, Justice DOUGLAS, joined by Justice Goldberg, reiterated his approach in Lombard and emphasized that restaurant discrimination "did not reflect 'personal' prejudices but business reasons." This was not property associated with privacy interests, but "property that is serving the public." And he argued that Shelley should govern here: "The preferences involved in [Shelley] were far more personal than the motivations of the corporate managers in the present case."[8] Justice BLACK's dissent in Bell, joined by Justices Harlan and White, viewed Shelley and the reach of § 1 of the 14th Amendment more narrowly.[9] Justice Black insisted that § 1 "does not of

8. Justice GOLDBERG, joined by Chief Justice Warren and Justice Douglas, also submitted a separate opinion. He concluded that "the Constitution guarantees to all Americans the right to be treated as equal members of the community with respect to public accommodations. [The post-Civil War Amendments] do not permit Negroes to be considered as second-class citizens in any aspect of our public life. [We] make no racial distinctions between citizens in exacting from them the discharge of public [responsibilities]. [Our] fundamental law which insures such an equality of public burdens, in my view, similarly insures an equality of public benefits." In a lengthy historical discussion supporting that conclusion, he noted, e.g., that the first

sentence of the 14th Amendment was designed "to ensure that the constitutional concept of citizenship with all attendant rights and privileges would henceforth embrace Negroes. It follows that Negroes as citizens necessarily became entitled to share the right, customarily possessed by other citizens, of access to public accommodations. [Under] the Constitution no American can, or should, be denied rights fundamental to freedom and citizenship." Cf. Karst, "Foreword: Equal Citizenship under the 14th Amendment," 91 Harv.L.Rev. 1 (1977).

9. Justice Black's opinion also included an important suggestion of a congressional power to reach further into the private sphere under § 5 of

itself, standing alone, in the absence of some cooperative state action or compulsion, forbid property holders, including restaurant owners, to ban people from entering or remaining upon their premises, even if the owners act out of racial prejudice." He elaborated: "The Amendment does not forbid a State to prosecute for crimes committed against a person or his property, however prejudiced or narrow the victim's views may be. Nor can whatever prejudice and bigotry the victim of a crime may have be automatically attributed to the State that prosecutes. Such a doctrine would not only be based on a fiction; it would also severely handicap a State's efforts to maintain a peaceful and orderly society. [It] would betray our whole plan for a tranquil and orderly society to say that a citizen, because of his personal prejudices, habits, attitudes, or beliefs, is cast outside the law's protection. [R]eliance [on Shelley] is misplaced. [The] reason judicial enforcement of the restrictive covenants in Shelley was deemed state action was not merely the fact that a state court had acted, but rather that state enforcement of the covenants had the effect of denying to the parties their federally guaranteed right to own, occupy, enjoy, and use their property without regard to race or color. Thus, the line of cases from [Buchanan v. Warley, the racial zoning ordinance case,] through Shelley establishes these propositions: (1) When an owner of property is willing to sell and a would-be purchaser is willing to buy, then the Civil Rights Act of 1866, which gives all persons the same right to 'inherit, lease, sell, hold and convey' property, prohibits a State [from] preventing the sale on the grounds of the race or color of one of the [parties]. (2) Once a person has become a property owner, then he acquires all the rights that go with ownership. [When] *both* parties are willing parties, then the principles stated in Buchanan and Shelley protect this right. But equally, when one party is unwilling, as when the property owner chooses *not* to sell to a particular person or *not* to admit that person, then [he] is entitled to rely on the guarantee of due process of law [to] protect his free use and enjoyment of property." [10]

5. *Transitional note.* Recall the questions raised at the beginning of this group of notes about the possible explanations for, and limits upon, the Shelley principle. What are the limits suggested by the materials in these notes? Do the cases below indicate additional limits on broad readings of Shelley and suggest different directions for delineating the scope of the state action concept? The Burton case, which follows, requires state involvement "to some significant extent" to convert private action into unconstitutional discrimination. What constitutes the requisite state involvement? What is the relevance of the use of state property? Of state regulation? Of licensing? Of conferral of other state benefits? Does Reitman, p. 890 below, indicate that state "encouragement" is enough? When does the state "encourage" private discrimination? Is state authorization enough? Can state "authorization" be distinguished from mere failure to prohibit private discrimination when the state has the power to do so?

---

the 14th Amendment than the Court itself could properly go in its interpretations of § 1. He stated that § 1, "unlike [the congressional enforcement power under § 5], is a prohibition against certain conduct only when done by a State." See sec. 3 below.

10. Soon after this decision, the Court held in Hamm v. Rock Hill, 379 U.S. 306 (1964), that the enactment of the 1964 Civil Rights Act abated prosecutions against persons who (if the Act had been in force at the time of the sit-in) would have been entitled to service.

BURTON v. WILMINGTON PARKING AUTHORITY

365 U.S. 715, 81 S.Ct. 856, 6 L.Ed.2d 45 (1961).

Mr. Justice CLARK delivered the opinion of the Court.

In this action for declaratory and injunctive relief it is admitted that the Eagle Coffee Shoppe, Inc., a restaurant located within an off-street automobile parking building in Wilmington, Delaware, has refused to serve appellant food or drink solely because he is a Negro. The parking building is owned and operated by the Wilmington Parking Authority, an agency of the State of Delaware, and the restaurant is the Authority's lessee. [The Supreme Court of Delaware] held that Eagle was acting in "a purely private capacity" under its lease; that its action was not that of the Authority and was not, therefore, state action. [It] also held that under 24 Del.Code § 1501 [1] Eagle was a restaurant, not an inn, and that as such it "is not required [under Delaware law] to serve any and all persons entering its place of business." [We conclude] that the exclusion of appellant [was] discriminatory state action.

The Authority was created [to] provide adequate parking facilities for the convenience of the public. [Its] first project [was] the erection of a parking facility. [T]he Authority was advised by its retained experts that the anticipated revenue from the parking of cars and proceeds from sale of its bonds would not be sufficient to finance the construction costs of the facility. [To] secure additional capital [the] Authority decided it was necessary to enter long-term leases with responsible tenants for commercial use of some of the space available in the projected "garage building." [In] April 1957 such a private lease, for 20 years, [was] made with [Eagle] for use as a "restaurant." [The lease] contains no requirement that [the] restaurant services be made available to the general public on a nondiscriminatory basis, in spite of the fact that the Authority has power to adopt rules and regulations respecting the use of its facilities. [Other] portions of the structure were leased to other tenants, including a bookstore, a retail jeweler, and a food store. Upon completion of the building, the Authority located at appropriate places thereon official signs indicating the public character of the building, and flew from mastheads on the roof both the state and national flags.

[It has always been clear] since the Civil Rights Cases [that] private conduct abridging individual rights does no violence to [equal protection] unless to some significant extent the State in any of its manifestations has been found to have become involved in it. Because the virtue of the right to [equal protection] could only lie in the breadth of its application, its constitutional assurance was reserved in terms whose imprecision was necessary if the right were to be enjoyed in the variety of individual-state relationships which the Amendment was designed to embrace. For the same reason, to fashion and apply a precise formula for recognition of state responsibility under [equal protection] is "an impossible task" which "this Court has never attempted." Only by sifting facts and weighing circumstances can the nonobvious involvement of the State in private conduct be attributed its true significance.

[T]he Delaware Supreme Court seems to have placed controlling emphasis on its conclusion that only some 15% of the total cost of the facility was "advanced" from public funds; that the cost of the entire facility was allocated three-fifths to the space for commercial leasing and two-fifths to parking space; that anticipated revenue from parking was only some 30.5% of the total

---

1. The statute provided that: "No keeper of an inn, tavern, hotel, or restaurant, or other place of public entertainment or refreshment of travelers, guests, or customers shall be obliged by law, to furnish entertainment or refreshment to persons whose reception or entertainment by him would be offensive to the major part of his customers, and would injure his [business]." [Footnote by Justice Clark. Cf. the separate opinions, below.]

income, the balance of which was expected to be earned by the leasing; [that] the restaurant's main and marked public entrance is on Ninth Street without any public entrance direct from the parking area; and that "the only connection Eagle has with the public facility [is] the furnishing [of] rent which is used by the Authority to defray a portion of the operating expense of an otherwise unprofitable enterprise." While these factual considerations are indeed validly accountable aspects of the [enterprise], we cannot say that they lead inescapably to the conclusion that state action is not present. Their persuasiveness is diminished when evaluated in the context of other factors which must be acknowledged.

The land and building were publicly owned. As an entity, the building was dedicated to "public uses" in performance of the Authority's "essential governmental functions." The costs of land acquisition, construction, and maintenance are defrayed entirely from donations by the City of Wilmington, from loans and revenue bonds and from the proceeds of rentals and parking services out of which the loans and bonds were payable. Assuming that the distinction would be significant, cf. Derrington v. Plummer [note 1 below], the commercially leased areas were not surplus state property, but constituted a physically and financially integral and, indeed, indispensable part of the State's plan to operate its project as a self-sustaining unit. [It] cannot be doubted that the peculiar relationship of the restaurant to the parking facility in which it is located confers on each an incidental variety of mutual benefits. [Neither] can it be ignored, especially in view of Eagle's affirmative allegation that for it to serve Negroes would injure its business, that profits earned by discrimination not only contribute to, but are indispensable elements in, the financial success of a governmental agency.

Addition of all these activities, obligations and responsibilities of the Authority, the benefits mutually conferred, together with the obvious fact that the restaurant is operated as an integral part of a public building devoted to a public parking service, indicates that degree of state participation and involvement in discriminatory action which it was the design of the 14th Amendment to condemn. It is irony amounting to grave injustice that in one part of a single building, erected and maintained with public funds by an agency of the State to serve a public purpose, all persons have equal rights, while in another portion, also serving the public, a Negro is a second-class citizen. [In] its lease with Eagle the Authority could have affirmatively required Eagle to discharge the responsibilities under the 14th Amendment imposed upon the private enterprise as a consequence of state participation. But no State may effectively abdicate its responsibilities by either ignoring them or by merely failing to discharge them whatever the motive may be. It is of no consolation to an individual denied [equal protection] that it was done in good faith. [By] its inaction, the Authority, and through it the State, has not only made itself a party to the refusal of service, but has elected to place its power, property and prestige behind the admitted discrimination. The State has so far insinuated itself into a position of interdependence with Eagle that it must be recognized as a joint participant in the challenged activity, which, on that account, cannot be considered to have been so "purely private" as to fall without the scope of the 14th Amendment.

Because readily applicable formulae may not be fashioned, the conclusions drawn [from] this record are by no means declared as universal truths on the basis of which every state leasing agreement is to be tested. Owing to the very "largeness" of government, a multitude of relationships might appear to some to fall within the Amendment's embrace, but that, it must be remembered, can be determined only in the framework of the peculiar facts or circumstances present. Therefore respondents' prophecy of nigh universal application of a constitutional precept so peculiarly dependent for its invocation upon appropriate facts fails to take into account "Differences in circumstances [which] beget appropriate differences in law." [Specifically] defining the limits of our inquiry, what we hold today is that when a State leases public property in the manner and for the purpose shown to have been the case here, the proscriptions of the 14th Amendment must be complied with by the lessee as certainly as though they were binding covenants written into the agreement [itself].

Reversed and remanded.

Mr. Justice STEWART, concurring.

I agree that the judgment must be reversed, but I reach that conclusion by a route much more direct than the one traveled by the Court. In upholding Eagle's right to deny service to the appellant solely because of his race, the [state court] relied upon a [state law] which permits the proprietor of a restaurant to refuse to serve "persons whose reception or entertainment by him would be offensive to the major part of his customers." There is no suggestion in the record that the appellant as an individual was such a person. The [Delaware court] has thus construed this legislative enactment as authorizing discriminatory classification based exclusively on color. Such a law seems to me clearly violative of the 14th [Amendment].

Mr. Justice HARLAN, whom Mr. Justice WHITTAKER joins, dissenting.

The Court's opinion, by a process of first undiscriminatingly throwing together various factual bits and pieces and then undermining the resulting structure by an equally vague disclaimer, seems to me to leave completely at sea just what it is in this record that satisfies the requirement of "state action." I find it unnecessary, however, to inquire into the matter at this stage, for it seems to me apparent [that] the case should first be sent back to the state court for clarification as to the precise basis of its decision. [If Justice Stewart is correct], I would certainly agree [with his conclusion]. [If], on the other hand, the state court meant no more than that under the statute, as at common law, Eagle was free to serve only those whom it pleased, then, and only then, would the question of "state action" be presented in full-blown [form].[2]

STATE INVOLVEMENT IN PRIVATE ACTION—"TO SOME SIGNIFICANT EXTENT"

Does the Burton majority retreat from the broadest implications of Shelley, by insisting that the state must be involved "to some significant extent" to bring private conduct under the 14th Amendment? Under Burton, it is not enough to find merely *some* nexus between the state and the private discriminator. Does Burton provide adequate guidance for evaluating the "significance" of state involvement?[1] In pursuing the search for indicia of "significant" state involvement, consider the factors appraised in the cases in the following notes.

1. *Leases and sales of public property.* Was the critical factor in Burton the lease of public property? The Burton majority cited Derrington v. Plummer, 240 F.2d 922 (5th Cir.1956), cert. denied, 353 U.S. 924 (1957), where a county had equipped a courthouse basement as a cafeteria and leased it to a private party who refused to serve blacks. The lease required that the cafeteria be open during courthouse hours and that the operator give a discount to county employees. The court held that an injunction against renewal of the lease should be granted: although "a county may in good faith [lawfully] dispose of its surplus property," the property here was not surplus and the

---

2. Justice FRANKFURTER's dissent also urged that the case should be sent back to the state court.

1. See Lewis, "Burton v. Wilmington Parking Authority—A Case Without Precedent," 61 Colum.L.Rev. 1458 (1961).

purpose of the lease was to furnish service to courthouse users. The court concluded that the county was providing services "through the instrumentality" of the lease and that the lessee accordingly "stands in the place of the County."[2]

2. *Use of public property by private groups.* The question in GILMORE v. MONTGOMERY, 417 U.S. 556 (1974), was the propriety of a federal court injunction barring a city from permitting private segregated school groups and racially discriminatory non-school groups to use its recreational facilities. The Court had little difficulty in sustaining that portion of the injunction that barred *exclusive* temporary use of public recreational facilities by segregated private schools; that clearly interfered with an outstanding federal court school desegregation order.[3] But the Court had greater difficulty with *nonexclusive* use of recreational facilities by private schools and other segregated groups. Justice BLACKMUN's prevailing opinion remanded that problem for further consideration: "Upon this record, we are unable to draw a conclusion as to whether the use of zoos, museums, parks, and other recreational facilities by private school groups in common with others, and by private nonschool organizations, involves government so directly in the actions of those users as to warrant court intervention on constitutional grounds." The Court emphasized the need for a particularized examination of the circumstances in accordance with the approach of Burton. If the uses could be identified as undermining outstanding desegregation orders for public schools and parks, the case would be relatively easy. But the "problem of private group use is much more complex" if the decision had to turn solely on state action principles. He elaborated: "[The] portion of the District Court's order prohibiting the mere use of such facilities by *any* segregated 'private group, club or organization' is invalid because it was not predicated upon a proper finding of state action. [If], however, the city or other governmental entity rations otherwise freely accessible recreational facilities, the case for state action will naturally be stronger than if the facilities are simply available to all comers without condition or reservation. Here, for example, petitioners allege that the city engages in scheduling softball games for an all-white church league and provides balls, equipment, fields and lighting. The city's role in that situation would be dangerously close to what was found to exist in Burton."[4]

2. Compare Tonkins v. Greensboro, 276 F.2d 890 (4th Cir.1960), holding that a bona fide sale of a public swimming pool to private parties was not unconstitutional state involvement in discrimination by the private owners. But Hampton v. Jacksonville, 304 F.2d 320 (5th Cir.1962), barred the exclusion of blacks from a golf course sold by a city to a private owner, where the sale included a provision that the property would revert to the city if it was not used as a golf course. The court found the case closer to Derrington than to Tonkins.

3. Does that suggest that a governmental body under a duty to undo the effects of past de jure segregation is less free to make public property available to private discriminatory groups than bodies which have not practiced de jure segregation? See generally chap. 9 above; and note Norwood v. Harrison, 413 U.S. 455 (1973), holding that Mississippi could not lend textbooks to students in private segregated schools under a long-established program for providing books to all public and private school students.

Compare McGlotten v. Connally, 338 F.Supp. 448 (D.D.C.1972), holding that the Government could neither grant tax exemptions nor allow charitable deductions for gifts to discriminating fraternal orders. Though every tax deduction confers benefits, that is not enough to impose constitutional restraints on the beneficiary; here, however, the Government was "sufficiently entwined with private parties" to make the Constitution applicable, in part because of the extensive control by the government over the purposes of exempt organizations and "the aura of government approval inherent in an exempt ruling." See also Green v. Connally, 330 F.Supp. 1150 (D.D.C.), affirmed, 404 U.S. 997 (1971); Bittker & Kaufman, "Taxes and Civil Rights: 'Constitutionalizing' the Internal Revenue Code," 82 Yale L.J. 51 (1972). Note also the ruling, in partial reliance on Green, sustaining the IRS's denial of tax exemptions to racially discriminatory private schools, in Bob Jones University v. United States, 461 U.S. 574 (1983).

4. There were several concurring opinions. Note especially the comments on the Burton problem in Justice WHITE's concurrence, joined by Justice Douglas: "[There] is very plainly state action of some sort involved in the leasing, rental or extending the use of scarce city-owned recreation facilities to [private groups]. The question [is] whether the conceded state action [is] such that the State must be deemed to have denied

3. *Governmental involvement through licensing.* Does governmental licensing of a private actor constitute sufficient governmental involvement to warrant the application of constitutional restraints? Does the nature of the licensing scheme make a difference? For example, are licenses that certify qualifications distinguishable from licenses that grant special rights to use scarce resources? In Garner v. Louisiana, 368 U.S. 157 (1961), one of the sit-in cases, Justice Douglas' separate opinion suggested that licensing and regulation of a restaurant made it a "public facility" and constituted adequate state action. (The majority disposed of the case on narrower grounds.)

a. *Liquor licenses.* The full Court confronted the relevance of licensing a decade later, in MOOSE LODGE NO. 107 v. IRVIS, 407 U.S. 163 (1972). That 6 to 3 decision rejected a claim that a private club's racial discrimination was unconstitutional because the club held a state liquor license. In Moose Lodge, the club had refused service in its dining room and bar to a Lodge member's black guest. The lower federal court sustained Irvis' state action claim and declared the Lodge's liquor license invalid. But the Court found that, with one exception, the operation of the state liquor regulation scheme did "not sufficiently implicate the State in the discriminatory guest policies of Moose Lodge so as to make the latter 'State action.'" Justice REHNQUIST, citing Shelley, conceded that "the impetus for the forbidden discrimination need not originate with the State if it is state action that enforces privately originated discrimination." But that did not mean "that discrimination by an otherwise private entity would be violative of [equal protection] if the private entity receives any sort of benefit or service at all from the state, or if it is subject to state regulation in any degree whatever. Since state-furnished services include such necessities of life as electricity, water, and police and fire protection, such a holding would utterly emasculate the distinction between private as distinguished from State conduct." To find unconstitutional state action in situations "where the impetus for the discrimination is private, the State must have 'significantly involved itself with invidious discriminations.'" And he found no such involvement here. He emphasized the distinctions between the Lodge situation and Burton. Here, for example, there was "nothing approaching the symbiotic relationship between lessor and lessee" in Burton. That was "a public restaurant in a public building"; this was "a private social club in a private building." The lower court had emphasized that the liquor regulations were "pervasive." Justice Rehnquist responded: "However detailed this type of regulation may be in some particulars, it cannot be said to in any way foster or encourage racial discrimination." And that conclusion was not undercut by the fact that Pennsylvania limited the number of liquor licenses in each city, since that fell "far short of conferring upon club licensees a monopoly in the dispensing of liquor."[5]

[equal protection]. [Under Burton], it is perfectly clear that to violate [equal protection] the State itself need not make, advise or authorize the private decision to discriminate that involves the State in the practice of segregation or would appear to do so in the minds of ordinary citizens."

5. The Court did find one constitutional defect: An administrative regulation required that "every club licensee shall adhere to all the provisions of its constitution and by-laws." That regulation was defended as a means to prevent the subterfuge of a place of public accommodation masquerading as a private club. But the Court found the regulation unconstitutional,

though "neutral in its terms," because "the result of its application" in a case such as this "would be to invoke the sanctions of the State to enforce a concededly discriminatory private rule," and that was barred by Shelley. The Court accordingly directed an injunction against the enforcement of that regulation; but Irvis "was entitled to no more."

When do freedom of association barriers bar imposition of 14th Amendment commands on private clubs? Cf. Roberts v. United States Jaycees (1984; p. 565 above), sustaining the application of a state ban on sex discrimination to a formerly all-male national civic organization.

Justice DOUGLAS' dissent explained that he would *not* apply constitutional restrictions to private clubs simply because they had a state license of some kind. He noted that First Amendment and related guarantees create "a zone of privacy"; accordingly, the fact that the Lodge had a racially restrictive policy was "constitutionally irrelevant." Moreover, earlier cases in which he had emphasized a state nexus because of licensing (see Garner, above) were inapposite, because a private club "is not in the public domain," and its getting "some kind of permit from the [state] does not make it ipso facto a public [enterprise], any more than the grant to a householder of a permit to operate an incinerator puts the householder in the public domain." But here, there were "special circumstances" distinguishable from the ordinary licensing situation. Here, the State was "putting the weight of its liquor license, concededly a valued and important adjunct to a private club, behind racial discrimination." Had the specific regulation invalidated by the majority been the only problem, he might have agreed with the Court's narrow injunction. But "another flaw in the scheme not so easily cured" was that "state-enforced scarcity of licenses restricts the ability of blacks to obtain liquor." A group desiring to form a nondiscriminatory club would have to "purchase a license held by an existing club, which can exact a monopoly price for the transfer." And "without a liquor license a fraternal organization would be hard-pressed to survive."[6]

b. *Broadcasting licenses.* In CBS, INC. v. DEMOCRATIC NAT. COMM., 412 U.S. 94 (1973), the majority sustained the FCC's refusal to compel broadcasters to accept editorial advertisements. (The Court's analysis of the First Amendment issues is considered at p. 1296 below.) In the course of the disposition, several of the Justices also considered the "novel question" whether "the action of a broadcast licensee such as that challenged here is 'governmental action' for purposes of the First Amendment." Chief Justice BURGER concluded "that the policies complained of do not constitute governmental action violative of the First Amendment"; but the Chief Justice was joined only by Justices Stewart and Rehnquist in that conclusion.[7] The Chief Justice noted that the FCC had not "fostered the licensee policy challenged here; it [had] simply declined to command particular action because it fell within the area of journalistic discretion." He concluded: "Thus, it cannot be said that the government is a 'partner' to the action of the broadcast licensee complained of here, nor is it engaged in a 'symbiotic relationship' with the licensee, profiting from the invidious discrimination of its proxy. Compare [Moose Lodge] with [Burton]. The First Amendment does not reach acts of private parties in every instance where the Congress or the Commission has merely permitted or failed to prohibit such acts." In supporting that position in his concurrence, Justice STEWART explained his reasons for rejecting the suggested analogies to such cases as Logan Valley, Marsh and Public Utilities Commission v. Pollak, 343 U.S. 451 (1952), "where a policy of a privately owned but publicly regulated

---

6. Justice Marshall joined Justice Douglas' dissent, as well as one by Justice Brennan. Justice BRENNAN stressed the "pervasive regulatory schemes under which the State dictates and continually supervises virtually every detail of the operation of a licensee's business." He thought this state involvement sufficient to fall within the principle banning all state efforts "to authorize, encourage, or otherwise support racial discrimination in a particular facet of life."

Soon after the Irvis decision, Mr. Irvis won his battle on the basis of state law. The Pennsylvania Supreme Court sustained an administrative ruling under the state public accommodations law ordering the Harrisburg Moose Lodge to end its ban on black guests.

7. The other Justices who supported the Chief Justice in his discussion of the statutory and First Amendment issues withheld approval of the "governmental action" part of his opinion. Justice BRENNAN's dissent, joined by Justice Marshall, found ample "governmental involvement" to justify application of the First Amendment. He recited the "myriad indicia" of governmental involvement, "including the public nature of the airwaves, the governmentally preferred status of broadcasters, the extensive Government regulation of broadcast programming, and the specific governmental approval of the challenged policy."

bus company that had been approved by the regulatory commission was held to activate First Amendment review." [8]

   c. Transitional Note: The relevance of governmental licensing, regulation, and benefits. Reexamine, in the light of these cases, what the relevance of governmental licensing and regulation should be in determining whether constitutional guarantees are applicable to private actors. Should licensing be sufficient only when special benefits, such as monopolies, are conferred? Should regulation or grants of benefits be adequate only when the regulation or benefits are immediately relevant to the particular challenged practices of the private actor? [9] The Court reexamined these problems in 1974, in Jackson, p. 895 below. Consideration of that case is postponed until after Reitman, which follows. Reitman considered the problem of state "encouragement" of private discrimination, and raised again an issue first suggested by the separate opinions in Burton: the extent to which state failure to prohibit private discrimination constitutes "authorization."

REITMAN v. MULKEY

387 U.S. 369, 87 S.Ct. 1627, 18 L.Ed.2d 830 (1967).

Mr. Justice WHITE delivered the opinion of the Court.

   The question here is whether Art. I, § 26 of the California Constitution [violates the 14th Amendment]. Section 26, [an] initiated measure submitted to the people as Proposition 14 in a statewide ballot in 1964, provides in part as follows: "Neither the State nor any subdivision or agency thereof shall deny, limit or abridge, directly or indirectly, the right of any person, who is willing or desires to sell, lease or rent any part or all of his real property, to decline to sell, lease or rent such property to such person or persons as he, in his absolute discretion, chooses." The real property covered by § 26 is limited to residential property and contains an exception for state-owned real estate. [Respondents] sued under [state laws prohibiting racial and certain other discrimination "in all business establishments"], alleging that petitioners had refused to rent them an apartment solely on account of their race. Petitioners moved for summary judgment on the ground that [the state laws] had been rendered null and void by the adoption of Proposition 14 after the filing of the complaint. The trial court granted the motion [but] the California Supreme Court [held] that Art. I, § 26, was invalid as denying [equal protection]. We affirm [that judgment, which] quite properly undertook to examine the constitutionality of § 26 in terms of its "immediate objective," its "ultimate effect," and its "historical context and the conditions existing prior to its enactment." Judgments such as these we have frequently undertaken ourselves. But here the California Supreme Court has addressed itself to these matters and we should give careful consideration to its views because they concern the purpose, scope, and operative effect of a provision of the California Constitution.

---

   8. In Pollak, the Court held that a private bus company did not violate the First Amendment by subjecting its captive audiences to radio broadcasts. See p. 1211 below. However, the Court apparently did find the company subject to constitutional limits. But it did not simply rely on the company's operating a public utility or enjoying a substantial monopoly of transit in the District of Columbia. Rather, it emphasized the regulatory supervision by the Public Utilities Commission and particularly "the fact that that agency, pursuant to protests against the radio program, ordered an investigation of it, and after formal public hearings, ordered its investigation dismissed on the ground that the public safety, comfort, and convenience were not impaired thereby." (See the further consideration of Pollak in Jackson (1974, p. 895 below).)

   9. See Powe v. Miles, 407 F.2d 73 (2d Cir. 1968): "[The] state must be involved not simply with some activity of the institution [but] with the activity that caused the injury."

First, the court considered whether § 26 was concerned at all with private discriminations in residential housing. This involved a review of past efforts by the California Legislature to regulate such discriminations. The Unruh Act, on which respondents based their cases, was passed in 1959. [I]n 1963 came the Rumford Fair Housing Act, [prohibiting] racial discriminations in the sale or rental of any private dwelling containing more than four units. [It] was against this background that Proposition 14 was enacted. Its immediate design and intent, the California court said, was "to overturn state laws that bore on the right of private sellers and lessors to discriminate," the Unruh and Rumford Acts, and "to forestall future state action that might circumscribe this right." Second, the court conceded that the State was permitted a neutral position with respect to private racial discriminations and that the State was not bound by the Federal Constitution to forbid them. But [the] court deemed it necessary to determine whether Proposition 14 invalidly involved the State in racial discriminations in the housing market. Its conclusion was that it did. To reach this result, the state court examined certain prior decisions in this Court in which discriminatory state action was identified. Based on these cases, it concluded that a prohibited state involvement could be found "even where the State can be charged only with encouraging," rather than commanding discrimination. Also of particular interest to the court was Mr. Justice Stewart's concurrence in [Burton], where it was said that the Delaware courts had construed an existing Delaware statute as "authorizing" racial discrimination in restaurants and that the statute was therefore invalid. To the California court "the instant case presents an undeniably analogous situation" wherein the State had taken affirmative action designed to make private discriminations legally possible. Section 26 was said to have changed the situation from one in which discriminatory practices were restricted "to one where it is encouraged, within the meaning of the cited decisions"; § 26 was legislative action "which authorized private discrimination" and made the State "at least a partner in the instant act of discrimination." The court could "conceive of no other purpose for an application of § 26 aside from authorizing the perpetration of a purported private discrimination."

[There] is no sound reason for rejecting this judgment. Petitioners contend that the California court has misconstrued the 14th Amendment since the repeal of any statute prohibiting racial discrimination, which is constitutionally permissible, may be said to "authorize" and "encourage" discrimination because it makes legally permissible that which was formerly proscribed. But [the California court] did not read either our cases or the 14th Amendment as establishing an automatic constitutional barrier to the repeal of an existing law prohibiting racial discriminations in housing; nor did the court rule that a State may never put in statutory form an existing policy of neutrality with respect to private discriminations. [It] dealt with § 26 as though it expressly authorized and constitutionalized the private right to discriminate. [And] the court assessed the ultimate impact of § 26 in the California environment and concluded that the section would encourage and significantly involve the State in private racial discrimination contrary to the 14th Amendment. The California court could very reasonably conclude that § 26 would and did have wider impact than a mere repeal of existing [laws]. Private discriminations in housing were now not only free from Rumford and Unruh but they also enjoyed a far different status than was true before the passage of those statutes. The right to discriminate [was] now embodied in the State's basic charter, immune from legislative, executive, or judicial regulation at any level of the state government. Those practicing racial discriminations need no longer rely solely on their personal choice. They could now invoke express constitutional authority, free from censure or interference of any kind from official [sources].

This Court has never attempted the "impossible task" of formulating an infallible test for determining whether the State "in any of its manifestations" has become significantly involved in private discriminations. [Burton.] Here the California court, armed as it was with the knowledge of the facts and circumstances concerning the passage and potential impact of § 26, and familiar with the milieu in which that provision would operate, has determined that the provision would involve the State in private racial discriminations to an unconstitutional degree. We accept this holding of the California court. The assessment of § 26 by the California court is similar to what this Court has done in appraising state statutes or other official actions in other contexts. [None of our prior cases] squarely controls [this case]. But they [do] exemplify the necessity for a court to assess the potential impact of official action in determining whether the State has significantly involved itself with invidious discriminations. Here we are dealing with a provision which does not just repeal an existing law forbidding private racial discriminations. Section 26 was intended to authorize, and does authorize, racial discrimination in the housing market. The right to discriminate is now one of the basic policies of the State. The California Supreme Court believes that the section will significantly encourage and involve the State in private discriminations. We have been presented with no persuasive considerations indicating that this judgment should be overturned.

Affirmed.[1]

Mr. Justice HARLAN, whom Mr. Justice BLACK, Mr. Justice CLARK, and Mr. Justice STEWART join, [dissenting].

[California] has decided to remain "neutral." [All] that has happened is that California has effected a pro tanto repeal of its prior statutes forbidding private discrimination. This runs no more afoul of the 14th Amendment than would have California's failure to pass any such antidiscrimination statutes in the first instance. The fact that such repeal was also accompanied by a constitutional prohibition against future enactment of such laws [cannot] affect [the] validity of what California has [done].

The Court attempts to fit § 26 within the coverage of [equal protection] by characterizing it as in effect an affirmative call to residents of California to discriminate. The main difficulty with this viewpoint is that it depends upon a characterization of § 26 that cannot fairly be made. The provision is neutral on its face, and it is only by in effect asserting that this requirement of passive official neutrality is camouflage that the Court is able to reach its conclusion. In depicting the provision as tantamount to active state encouragement of discrimination, the Court essentially relies on the fact that the California Supreme Court so concluded. [I] agree of course, that *findings of fact* by a state court should be given great weight, but this familiar proposition hardly aids the Court's holding [here]. There were no disputed issues of fact at all. [There] was no finding, for example, that the defendants' actions were anything but the product of their own private choice. [There] were no findings as to the general effect of § 26.

---

1. Justice DOUGLAS joined the Court's opinion but added a comment "to indicate the dimensions of our problem." He considered the actions of brokers in the real estate market as akin to zoning and invoked the analogy of the public function cases. Since real estate brokers were state-regulated and state-licensed, their business "must be dedicated, like the telephone companies and the carriers and the hotels and motels," to nondiscriminatory service.

Recall and compare Hunter v. Erickson (1969; p. 632 above), invalidating an Akron charter amendment requiring that any local ordinance banning racial discrimination in housing must be submitted to a referendum of the voters. The City sought to distinguish Reitman, but Justice White did not pursue that argument in Hunter: elaboration of Reitman was unnecessary because in Hunter, unlike Reitman, "there was an explicitly racial classification treating racial housing matters differently from other racial and housing matters." Recall also the further discussion of Hunter in the 1982 Seattle and Los Angeles cases considering state measures designed to curb mandatory busing which had been designed to eliminate de facto school segregation (p. 720 above).

The Court declares that the California court "held the purpose and intent of § 26 was to authorize private racial discriminations," [but] there is no supporting fact in the record for this characterization. Moreover, the grounds which prompt legislators or state voters to repeal a law do not determine its constitutional validity. [The] only "factual" matter relied on by the [state court] was the context in which Proposition 14 was adopted, namely, that several strong antidiscrimination acts had been passed by the legislature, and opposed by many of those who successfully led the movement for adoption of Proposition 14 by popular referendum. These circumstances, and these alone, the California court held, made § 26 unlawful under this Court's cases interpreting [equal protection]. This, of course, is nothing but a legal conclusion as to federal constitutional law. [Accepting] all the suppositions under which the state court acted, I cannot see that its conclusion is entitled to any special weight in the discharge of our own responsibilities. [It] seems to me manifest that the state court decision rested entirely on what that court conceived to be the compulsion of the 14th Amendment, not on any factfinding by the state courts.

[The] core of the Court's opinion is that § 26 is offensive to the 14th Amendment because it effectively *encourages* private discrimination. By focusing on "encouragement" the Court, I fear, is forging a slippery and unfortunate criterion by which to measure the constitutionality of a statute simply permissive in purpose and effect, and inoffensive on its face. It is true that standards in this area have not been definitely formulated, and that acts of discrimination have been included within the compass of [equal protection] not merely when they were compelled by a state statute or other governmental pressures, but also when they were said to be "induced" or "authorized" by the State. Most of these cases, however, can be approached in terms of the impact and extent of affirmative state governmental activities, e.g., the action of a sheriff [Lombard v. Louisiana]; the official supervision over a park [Evans v. Newton]; a joint venture with a lessee in a municipally owned building [Burton]. In situations such as these the focus has been on positive state cooperation or partnership in affirmatively promoted activities, an involvement that could have been avoided. Here, in contrast, we have only the straightforward adoption of a neutral provision restoring to the sphere of free choice, left untouched by the 14th Amendment, private behavior within a limited area of the racial problem. The denial of equal protection emerges only from the conclusion reached by the Court that the implementation of a new policy of governmental neutrality [has] the effect of lending encouragement to those who wish to discriminate. In the context of the actual facts of the case, this conclusion appears to me to state only a truism: people who want to discriminate but were previously forbidden to do so by state law are now left free because the State has chosen to have no law on the subject at all. Obviously whenever there is a change in the law it will have resulted from the concerted activity of those who desire the change, and its enactment will allow those supporting the legislation to pursue their private goals.

A moment of thought will reveal the far-reaching possibilities of the Court's new doctrine, which I am sure the Court does not intend. Every act of private discrimination is either forbidden by state law or permitted by it. There can be little doubt that such permissiveness—whether by express constitutional or statutory provision, or implicit in the common law—to some extent "encourages" those who wish to discriminate to do so. Under this theory "state action" in the form of laws that do nothing more than passively permit private discrimination could be said to tinge *all* private discrimination with the taint of unconstitutional state encouragement. [I] believe the state action required to bring the 14th Amendment into operation must be affirmative and purposeful, actively fostering discrimination. [I] think that this decision is not only constitutionally unsound, but in its practical potentialities short-sighted. Opponents of state antidiscrimination statutes are now in a position to argue that such legislation should be defeated because, if enacted, it may be unrepealable. More fundamentally, the doctrine underlying this decision may hamper, if not preclude, attempts to deal with the delicate and troublesome problems of race relations through the [legislative process].

STATE ACTION THROUGH STATE "ENCOURAGEMENT" AND "AUTHORIZATION"

1. *State "encouragement."* What is the reach of the "encouragement" theme of Reitman? Can a state provision that keeps hands off private discrimination, or "authorizes"—by failing to forbid—private discrimination, be deemed an "encouragement"? Was § 26 truly distinguishable from a mere repeal of an anti-discrimination law? Was there a significant difference here because California did not merely repeal anti-discrimination laws but incorporated that repeal in a constitutional provision? Was the flaw the effect of § 26 in disadvantaging racial minorities, and the lack of the heavy justification required to support such an impact? (Recall the equal protection "purpose" and "effect" principles in the racial discrimination area in chap. 9.) Or does Reitman ultimately rest on the notion that a state may not "authorize" racial discrimination? (See below.)

2. *"Authorization" of racial discrimination.* Recall the separate opinions in Burton, indicating that a finding of a state "authorization" of private discrimination would be a "more direct," "easy road to decision." Was that truly an easier route? Justice Stewart in Burton was willing to find "authorization." And Justice Harlan in Burton suggested that a finding of "authorization," if the state statute could be construed that way, would indeed be a narrower ground. Yet both Justices dissented in Reitman. What kind of "authorization" did they have in mind in Burton? Is "authorization" really any different from failure to prohibit where the state has power to prohibit? Is the "authorization" rationale tantamount to imposing an affirmative duty on the state to prevent private discrimination? Is such "authorization" of unrestrained private choices, by constitutional provision, statute, or common law, "significant involvement" by the state?

3. *Transitional Note.* Despite the far-reaching statements about "authorization" and "encouragement" in the cases of the 1960s, the modern Court has refused to apply those concepts broadly. For example, the enforcement of the reverter in the Baconsfield park case, Evans v. Abney, above, could have been considered "authorization" in the sense of some of the earlier cases. And Justice Brennan's dissent in that 1970 case recited "significant" state involvements that were arguably as substantial as those in Burton and Reitman. After Reitman and before Abney, some commentators, noting that no modern Court decision had rejected a discrimination claim because of the state action barrier, suggested that the concept was moribund.[1] But Abney made it clear that the state action barrier was very much alive. And the more recent Burger Court decisions, beginning with the Moose Lodge case in 1974 and continuing with the later rulings, below, make it even clearer that the state action barrier remains and, indeed, has gained new strength.

Reexamine the various, often inchoate, strands that contributed to the expansion of the state action principle through the 1960s in light of the 1974 decision in Jackson, which follows. Note that the rejections of the state action claims in Jackson (and in Flagg Bros., in 1978) occurred in the context of

----

1. See e.g., C.L. Black, Jr., "Foreword: 'State Action,' Equal Protection and California's Proposition 14," 81 Harv.L.Rev. 69 (1967).

procedural due process assertions, not racial discrimination claims. Should state action criteria be interpreted differently depending on the claims involved? For example, would the public utility in Jackson be subjected to constitutional restraints if it cut off services on racially discriminatory bases? (Note Justice Marshall's dissent in Jackson.) As noted earlier, the Court's unwillingness to intrude further into the private sphere under § 1 of the 14th Amendment may well be related to the increasing scope and exercise of congressional power to reach private activities under § 5 of that Amendment. The modern Court's curtailment of state action coverage may also be related to the newly recognized, very broad congressional power to deal with private racial discrimination under § 2 of the 13th Amendment.[2]

JACKSON v. METROPOLITAN EDISON CO.

419 U.S. 345, 95 S.Ct. 449, 42 L.Ed.2d 477 (1974).

[Petitioner Catherine Jackson brought a federal civil rights action under 42 U.S.C. § 1983 against respondent Metropolitan Edison Co., a private company holding a certificate of public convenience from the Pennsylvania Public Utilities Commission (PUC) empowering it to deliver electricity to a specific service area. She sought damages and injunctive relief against the Company for terminating her electric service for alleged nonpayment, claiming that she had not been afforded notice, hearing, and an opportunity to pay any amounts found due. She claimed that under state law she was entitled to reasonably continuous electrical service and that the Company's termination was state action depriving her of property without procedural due process. The lower federal courts dismissed her complaint.]

Mr. Justice REHNQUIST delivered the opinion of the [Court].

While the principle that private action is immune from the restrictions of the 14th Amendment is well established and easily stated, the question whether particular conduct is "private," on the one hand, or "state action," on the other, frequently admits of no easy answer. Here the action complained of was taken by a utility company which is privately owned, [but] which in many particulars of its business is subject to extensive state regulation. The mere fact that a business is subject to state regulation does not by itself convert its action into that of the State for purposes of the 14th Amendment. [Moose Lodge.] Nor does the fact that the regulation is extensive and detailed, as in the case of most public utilities, do so. [PUC v. Pollak.] It may well be that acts of a heavily regulated utility with at least something of a governmentally protected monopoly will more readily be found to be "state" acts than will the acts of an entity lacking these characteristics. But the inquiry must be whether there is a sufficiently close nexus between the State and the challenged action of the regulated entity so that the action of the latter may be fairly treated as that of the State itself. The true nature of the State's involvement may not be immediately obvious, and detailed inquiry may be required in order to determine whether the test is met. [Burton.]

Petitioner advances a series of contentions which, in her view, lead to the conclusion that this case should fall on the Burton side of the line drawn in the Civil Rights Cases, rather than on the Moose Lodge side of that line. We find none of them persuasive. Petitioner first argues that "state action" is present

---

2. The scope of congressional enforcement power to move beyond where the Court has gone under the post-Civil War Amendments is the focus of the remaining sections of this chapter. See, e.g., Jones v. Alfred H. Mayer Co. (1968; p. 924 below), analyzed by the lower courts on the basis of 14th Amendment state action analysis but decided by the Court under the 13th Amendment-based 42 U.S.C. § 1982.

because of the monopoly status allegedly conferred upon [Metropolitan]. As a factual matter, it may well be doubted that the State ever granted or guaranteed Metropolitan a monopoly.[1] But assuming that it had, this fact is not determinative in considering whether Metropolitan's termination of service to petitioner was "state action." In Pollak, where the Court dealt with the activities of the District of Columbia Transit Company, a congressionally established monopoly, we expressly disclaimed reliance on the monopoly status of the transit authority. Similarly, although certain monopoly aspects were presented in [Moose Lodge], we found that the lodge's action was not subject to the provisions of the 14th Amendment. In each of those cases, there was insufficient relationship between the challenged actions of the entities involved and their monopoly status. There is no indication of any greater connection here. Petitioner next urges that state action is present because respondent provides an essential public service [and] hence performs a "public function." [The Court rejected that argument.[2]]

We also reject the notion that Metropolitan's termination is state action because the State "has specifically authorized and approved" the termination practice. In the instant case, Metropolitan filed with the [PUC] a general tariff—a provision of which states Metropolitan's right to terminate service for nonpayment. This provision has appeared in Metropolitan's previously filed tariffs for many years and has never been the subject of a hearing or other scrutiny by the [PUC].[3] Although the Commission did hold hearings on portions of Metropolitan's general tariff relating to a general rate increase, it never even considered the reinsertion of this provision in the newly filed general tariff. The case most heavily relied on by petitioner is [Pollak]. There the Court dealt with the contention that Capital Transit's installation of a piped music system on its buses violated the First Amendment rights of the bus riders. [T]he nature of the state involvement there was quite different than it is here. The [D.C. PUC], on its own motion, commenced an investigation of the effects of the piped music, and after a full hearing concluded not only that Capital Transit's practices were "not inconsistent with public convenience, comfort, and safety," but that the practice "in fact through the creation of better will among passengers, [tends] to improve the conditions under which the public rides." Here, on the other hand, there was no such imprimatur placed on the practice of Metropolitan about which petitioner complains. The nature of governmental regulation of private utilities is such that a utility may frequently be required by the state regulatory scheme to obtain approval for practices a business regulated in less detail would be free to institute without any approval from a regulatory body. Approval by a state utility commission of such a request from a regulated utility, where the Commission has not put its own weight on the side of the proposed practice by ordering it, does not transmute a practice initiated by the utility and approved by the Commission into "state action." At most, the Commission's failure to overturn this practice amounted to no more than a determination that a Pennsylvania utility was authorized to employ such a practice if it so desired. Respondent's exercise of the choice allowed by state law, where the initiative comes from it and not from the State, does not make its action in doing so "state action" for purposes of the 14th Amendment.

We also find absent in the instant case the symbiotic relationship presented in [Burton.] There [the Court] cautioned [that] differences in circumstances

---

1. [Such] public utility companies are natural monopolies created by the economic forces of high threshold capital requirements and virtually unlimited economy of scale. Regulation was superimposed on such natural monopolies as a substitute for competition and not to eliminate [it]. [Footnote by Justice Rehnquist.]

2. The portion of the opinion rejecting the "public function" argument is printed above, at p. 871.

3. Petitioner [concedes] that Metropolitan had this right, before the advent of regulation, at common law. [Footnote by Justice Rehnquist.]

beget differences in law, limiting the actual holding to lessees of public property. Metropolitan is a privately owned corporation, and it does not lease its facilities from [Pennsylvania]. It [is] subject to a form of extensive regulation by the State in a way that most other business enterprises are not. But this was likewise true of [the] club in [Moose Lodge], where we said: "However detailed this type of regulation may be in some particulars, it cannot be said to in any way foster or encourage racial discrimination. Nor can it be said to make the state in any realistic sense a partner or even a joint venturer in the club's enterprise." All of petitioner's arguments taken together show no more than that Metropolitan was a heavily regulated private utility, enjoying at least a partial monopoly in the providing of electrical service within its territory, and that it elected to terminate service to petitioner in a manner which the [PUC] found permissible under state law. Under our decision this is not sufficient to connect the [State] with respondent's action so as to make the latter's conduct attributable to the State for purposes of the 14th [Amendment].

Affirmed.[4]

Mr. Justice MARSHALL, [dissenting].

I. Our state action cases have repeatedly relied on several factors clearly presented by this case: a state-sanctioned monopoly; an extensive pattern of cooperation between the "private" entity and the state; and a service uniquely public in nature. Today the Court takes a major step in repudiating this line of authority and adopts a stance that is bound to lead to mischief when applied to problems beyond the narrow sphere of due process objections to utility terminations.

A. When the State confers a monopoly on a group or organization, this Court has held that the organization assumes many of the obligations of the State. [The] majority distinguishes [prior] cases with a cryptic assertion that public utility companies are "natural monopolies." The theory behind the distinction appears to be that since the State's purpose in regulating a natural monopoly is not to aid the company but to prevent its charging monopoly prices, the State's involvement is somehow less significant for state action purposes. I cannot agree that so much should turn on so narrow a distinction. [The] difficulty inherent [in] economic analysis counsels against excusing natural monopolies from the reach of state action principles. To invite inquiry into whether a particular state-sanctioned monopoly might have survived without the State's express approval grounds the analysis in hopeless speculation. Worse, this approach ignores important implications of the State's policy of utilizing private monopolies to provide electric service. Encompassed within this policy is the State's determination not to permit governmental competition with the selected private company, but to cooperate with and regulate the company in a multitude of ways to ensure that the company's service will be the functional equivalent of service provided by the State.

B. The pattern of cooperation between Metropolitan Edison and the State has led to significant state involvement in virtually every phase of the company's business. [I] disagree with the majority's position on three separate grounds.

4. A dissent by Justice DOUGLAS argued, inter alia, that Metropolitan's actions were "sufficiently intertwined with those of the State [to] warrant a holding [of] 'state action.'" He insisted that, under Burton, it was "not enough to examine seriatim each of the factors [and] to dismiss each individually as being insufficient to support a finding of state action. It is the aggregate that is controlling." Here, by contrast, the Court's underlying analysis was "fundamentally sequential rather than cumulative" and therefore constituted "a significant departure" from previous cases. (A dissent by Justice BRENNAN, finding that on the facts of this case "no controversy existed between petitioner and respondent," is omitted. Justice Marshall thought those factual complexities were such that certiorari should have been dismissed as improvidently granted. But, since the majority had reached the state action issue, he submitted a dissent on that problem, which follows.)

First, the suggestion that the State would have to "put its own weight on the side of the proposed practice by ordering it" seems to me to mark a sharp departure from our previous state action cases. From the Civil Rights Cases to Moose Lodge, we have consistently indicated that state authorization and approval of "private" conduct would support a finding of state action.[1] Second, I question the wisdom of giving such short shrift to the extensive interaction between the company and the State, and focusing solely on the extent of state support for the particular activity under challenge. In cases where the State's only significant involvement is through financial support or limited regulation of the private entity, it may be well to inquire whether the State's involvement suggests state approval of the objectionable conduct. See [e.g.] Powe v. Miles, 407 F.2d 73, 81 (C.A.2 1968) [university context]. But where the State has so thoroughly insinuated itself into the operations of the enterprise, it should not be fatal if the State has not affirmatively sanctioned the particular practice in question. Finally, it seems to me in any event that the State *has* given its approval to Metropolitan Edison's termination procedures. [That the termination provision] was not seriously questioned before approval does not mean that it was not approved. It suggests, instead, that the commission was satisfied to permit the company to proceed in the termination area as it had done in the past. [Apparently], authorization and approval would require the kind of hearing that was held in [Pollak]. I am afraid that the majority has in effect restricted Pollak to its facts if it has not discarded it altogether.[2]

II. The majority's conclusion that there is no state action in this case is likely guided in part by its reluctance to impose on a utility company burdens that might ultimately hurt consumers more than they would help them. Elaborate hearings prior to termination might be quite expensive, and for a responsible company there might be relatively few cases in which such hearings would do any good. The solution to this problem, however, is to require only abbreviated pretermination procedures for all utility companies, not to free the "private" companies to behave however they see [fit].

III. What is perhaps most troubling about the Court's opinion is that it would appear to apply to a broad range of claimed constitutional violations by the company. The Court has not adopted the notion [that] different standards should apply to state action analysis when different constitutional claims are presented. Thus, the majority's analysis would seemingly apply as well to a company that refused to extend service to Negroes, welfare recipients, or any other group that the company preferred, for its own reasons, not to serve. I cannot believe that this Court would hold that the State's involvement with the utility company was not sufficient to impose upon the company an obligation to meet the constitutional mandate of nondiscrimination. Yet nothing in the analysis of the majority opinion suggests [otherwise].

---

1. In the Civil Rights Cases, the Court suggested that state action might be found if the conduct in question were "sanctioned in some way by the State." Later cases made it clear that the State's sanction did not need to be in the form of an affirmative command. In Burton, the Court noted that by its inaction, the State had "elected to place its power, property, and prestige behind the admitted discrimination," although the State did not actually order the discrimination. See id. (Stewart, J., concurring). And in [Reitman], the Court based its "state action" ruling on the fact that the California constitutional provision "was intended to authorize, and does authorize, racial discrimination in the housing market." Even in Moose Lodge the Court suggested that if the State's regulation had in any way fostered or encouraged racial discrimination, a state action finding might have been justified. Certainly this is a less rigid standard than the Court's requirement in this case that the public utility commission be shown to have ordered the challenged conduct, not merely to have approved it. [Footnote by Justice Marshall.]

2. Part IC of Justice Marshall's dissent, applying the "public function" analysis, is printed at p. 872 above.

FLAGG BROS., INC. v. BROOKS, 436 U.S. 149 (1978): As noted at p. 872 above, this decision reaffirmed the Burger Court majority's determination to view the state action concept narrowly. It held that a warehouseman's sale of bailed goods to satisfy a warehouseman's lien under the UCC was not state action. Most of the opinion, as noted earlier, rejected the "public function" argument. But the Court also rejected the claim that the warehouseman's proposed sale was "properly attributable to the State because the State has authorized and encouraged it in enacting [the UCC]." Justice REHNQUIST's majority opinion responded: "Our cases state 'that a State is responsible for [the] act of a private party when the State, by its law, has compelled the act.' This Court, however, has never held that a State's mere acquiescence in a private action converts that action into that of the State. The Court rejected a similar argument in [Jackson]. The clearest demonstration of this distinction appears in [Moose Lodge]. These cases clearly rejected the notion that our prior cases permitted the imposition of 14th Amendment restraints on private action by the simple device of characterizing the State's inaction as 'authorization' or 'encouragement.' It is quite immaterial that the State has embodied its decision not to act in statutory form. If New York had no commercial statutes at all, its courts would still be faced with the decision whether to prohibit or permit the sort of sale threatened here the first time an aggrieved bailor came before them for relief. A judicial decision to deny relief would be no less an 'authorization' or 'encouragement' of that sale than the legislature's decision embodied in this statute. [If] the mere denial of judicial relief is considered sufficient encouragement to make the State responsible for those private acts, all private deprivations of property would be converted into public acts whenever the State, for whatever reason, denies relief sought by the putative property owner. Not only is this notion completely contrary to [the] 'essential dichotomy' between public and private acts, but it has been previously rejected by this Court. [Abney.] [New York] is in no way responsible for [the warehouseman's] decision, a decision which the state in [the UCC] permits but does not compel, to threaten to sell these respondents' belongings. Here, [New York] has not compelled the sale of a bailor's goods, but has merely announced the circumstances under which its courts will not interfere with the private sale. Indeed, the crux of the respondent's complaint is not that the State *has* acted, but that it has *refused* to act. This statutory refusal to act is no different in principle from the ordinary statute of limitations whereby the State declines to provide a remedy for private deprivations of property after the passage of a given period of time."

Justice STEVENS' dissent, joined by Justices White and Marshall, criticized this "permission"-"compulsion" distinction as follows: "Under this approach a State could enact laws authorizing private citizens to use self-help in countless situations without any possibility of federal challenge. A state statute could authorize the warehouseman to retain all proceeds of the lien sale, even if they far exceeded the amount of the alleged debt; it could authorize finance companies to enter private homes to repossess merchandise; or indeed, it could authorize 'any person with sufficient physical power' to acquire and sell the property of his weaker neighbor. An attempt to challenge the validity of any such outrageous statute would be defeated by the reasoning the Court uses today: The Court's rationale would characterize action pursuant to such a statute as purely private action, which the State permits but does not compel. [As] these examples suggest, the [distinction] between 'permission' and 'compulsion' [cannot be the determinative factor] in state-action analysis. There is no great chasm between 'permission' and 'compulsion' requiring particular state action to fall within one or the other definitional camp. [New York], by enacting [the UCC provision], has acted in the most effective and unambiguous way a State can act. This section specifically authorizes petitioner to sell respondents' possessions; it details the procedures that petitioner must follow; and it grants petitioner the power to convey good title to goods that are now owned by respondents to a third party. While Members of this Court have suggested that statutory authorization alone may be sufficient to establish a state action, it is not necessary to rely on those suggestions in this case because New York has authorized the warehouseman to perform what is clearly a state function." [1]

STATE ACTION DOCTRINE IN THE 1980s

In three 1982 cases, the Court returned to the complexities of state action doctrine. In two of the cases, Blum and Rendell-Baker, the majority followed in the footsteps of the Burger Court's earlier efforts to circumscribe the scope of the state action concept. Thus, Justice Rehnquist, the author of the major narrowing opinions of the prior decade, Jackson and Flagg Bros., was in the majority, and Justice Marshall dissented. But the third 1982 case, Lugar, produced a strikingly different alignment: Justices Brennan and Marshall were in the majority; Justice Rehnquist was among the dissenters.[1] In examining these cases, consider whether the reformulations in Blum and Rendell-Baker clarify the reach of the modern state action doctrine; and whether Lugar is inconsistent with the usual Burger Court approach.

1. *Blum.* In BLUM v. YARETSKY, 457 U.S. 991 (1982), the Court held that certain privately owned nursing homes receiving reimbursements from the state for caring for Medicaid patients were not state actors for purposes of the 14th Amendment claim raised here. A class of Medicaid patients had sued the nursing homes claiming their procedural due process rights had been violated when they were transferred (by decisions of the physicians and administrators in the nursing homes) from "skilled nursing facilities" to less expensive "health related facilities." The transfer decisions resulted in lower Medicaid benefits for the patients. In rejecting the claim that the transfer decision triggered the 14th Amendment's procedural due process requirements, Justice REHNQUIST's majority opinion rejected the argument that the State "affirmatively commands" the transfer: he was "not satisfied that the State is responsible for those decisions." Rather, the decisions ultimately turned "on medical judgments made by private parties according to professional standards that are not established by the State." The plaintiffs had sued state officials responsible for administering the Medicaid program in the State, but Justice Rehnquist emphasized that the plaintiffs were not challenging particular state regulations but rather private decisions. The mere fact of extensive state regulation of the nursing homes did not invoke 14th Amendment guarantees. Citing Jackson, he stated that "constitutional standards are invoked only when it can be said that the State is *responsible* for the specific conduct of which the plaintiff complains"; here, by contrast, "the complaining party seeks to hold the State liable for the actions of private parties." He added that a state "normally can be held responsible for a private decision only when it has exercised a coercive power or has provided such significant encouragement, either overt or covert, that the choice must in law be deemed to be that of the State. Mere approval of or acquiescence in the initiatives of a private party is not sufficient to justify holding the State responsible [under the] 14th Amendment." Nor was the Burton standard satisfied here simply because the State subsidized the operating

---

1. Justice Stevens' "state function" argument is printed at p. 874 above.

1. Justice POWELL's dissent in Lugar accused the majority of undermining "fundamental distinctions between the common-sense categories of state and private conduct." (As an added illustration of the unusual voting pattern in Lugar, note that Justice White, who had dissented in Flagg Bros., wrote for the majority. He had concurred in the judgments in the other two 1982 cases.)

and capital costs of the facilities, licensed them, and paid the medical expenses of more than 90% of the patients: "[Privately] owned enterprises providing services that the State would not necessarily provide, even though they are extensively regulated, do not fall within the ambit of Burton." He also rejected the plaintiffs' "public function" argument.[2]

2. *Rendell-Baker.* In RENDELL–BAKER v. KOHN, 457 U.S. 830 (1982), the majority, closely tracking Justice Rehnquist's approach in Blum, held that "a private school, whose income is derived primarily from public sources and which is regulated by public authorities," could not be considered as engaging in state action when it discharged certain employees. The employees had brought a federal civil rights action under § 1983 claiming that school officials, in firing them from the staff of a small private school for "maladjusted" students, had violated their constitutional rights to free speech and procedural due process. After examining all of the alleged indicia of state action, Chief Justice BURGER's majority opinion concluded that the school's action did not fall within the 14th Amendment. He noted that, even though public funds accounted for almost all of the school's operating budget, it was "not fundamentally different from many private corporations whose business depends primarily on contracts [with] the government. Acts of such private contractors do not become acts of the government by reason of their significant or even total engagement in performing public contracts."[3]

3. *Lugar.* In LUGAR v. EDMONDSON OIL CO., 457 U.S. 922, the third of the 1982 state action trilogy, the majority found the state action requirement satisfied. Lugar was the latest of a long series of cases (from Sniadach in 1969 through Flagg Bros. in 1978) considering procedural due process rights in creditors' summary remedies proceedings. The authors of the majority opinions in Blum and Rendell-Baker were among the dissenters in Lugar. In Lugar, a creditor, pursuant to a state law, had attached the debtor's property in an ex parte proceeding, alleging that the debtor might dispose of the property to defeat creditors. The attachment writ was issued by a state clerk, and the writ was executed by the Sheriff. In a later hearing, a state judge dismissed the attachment. The debtor brought suit against the creditor under § 1983 (p. 859 above), which authorizes damage actions for deprivation of constitutional rights "under color of any statute [of] any State." Justice

---

2. Justice WHITE concurred in the judgment on the basis of the analysis he developed most fully in Lugar, note 3 below. He argued that "respondents must show that the transfer [is] made on the basis of some rule of decision for which the State is responsible." Justice BRENNAN, joined by Justice Marshall, submitted a lengthy dissent, insisting that the majority had departed from Burton, had ignored "the nature of the regulatory framework," and had accordingly failed to perceive "the decisive involvement of the State in the private conduct challenged [here]." He insisted that the "imprint of state power on the private party's actions" was "even more significant" here than in Lugar. He concluded: "[With] respect to the level-of-care determination, the State does everything but pay the nursing home operator a fixed salary" and was "clearly responsible for the specific conduct" complained of here.

3. As in Blum, Justice WHITE concurred only in the judgment, emphasizing "the absence of any allegation that the employment decision was itself based upon some rule of conduct or policy put forth by the State." Justice MAR-

SHALL's dissent, joined by Justice Brennan, insisted that the State had "delegated to the [school] its statutory duty to educate children with special needs. The school receives almost all of its funds from the State, and is heavily regulated. This nexus between the school and the State is so substantial that the school's action must be considered state action." He relied especially on the "symbiotic relationship" approach of Burton: "it is difficult to imagine a closer relationship between a government and a private enterprise." He also noted that the school was "performing a vital public function." He concluded: "[The] decision in this case marks a return to empty formalism in state action doctrine. Because I believe that the state action requirement must be given a more sensitive and flexible interpretation, [I] dissent." (He objected to the Chief Justice's analogy between the school and other contractors: although other contractors "may be dependent on government funds, they are not so closely supervised by the government. And unlike most private contractors, the school is performing a statutory duty of the State.")

WHITE's majority opinion began by holding that if the creditor's conduct was "state action" it also satisfied the "under color of state law" requirement of § 1983. On the state action issue, he stated:

"[The] first question is whether the claimed deprivation has resulted from the exercise of a right or privilege having its source in state authority. The second question is whether, under the facts of this case, [the creditors], who are private parties, may be appropriately characterized as 'state actors.'" On the first question, Justice White focused on the debtor's claim that the state statute was "procedurally defective under the 14th Amendment." [4] That claim satisfied Justice White's first requirement: "[The] procedural scheme created by the statute obviously is the product of state action [and] properly may be addressed in a § 1983 action, if the second element of the state-action requirement is met as well." And that second requirement was also met: "[We] have consistently held that a private party's joint participation with state officials in the seizure of disputed property is sufficient to characterize that party as a 'state actor' for purposes of the 14th Amendment. [The lower court] erred in holding that in this context 'joint participation' required something more than invoking the aid of state officials to take advantage of state-created attachment procedures. That holding is contrary to the conclusions we have reached as to the applicability of due process standards to such procedures. Whatever may be true in other contexts, this is sufficient when the State has created a system whereby state officials will attach property on the ex parte application of one party to a private dispute." [5]

Chief Justice BURGER's dissent insisted that the creditor "did no more than invoke a presumptively valid state prejudgment attachment procedure available to all. Relying on a dubious 'but for' analysis, the Court erroneously concludes that the subsequent procedural steps taken by the State in attaching a putative debtor's property in some way transforms [the creditor's] acts into actions of the State. This case is no different from the situation in which a private party commences a lawsuit and secures injunctive relief which, even if temporary, may cause significant injury to the defendant. Invoking a judicial process, of course, implicates the State and its officers but does not transform essentially private conduct into actions of the State." In a longer dissent, Justice POWELL, joined by Justices Rehnquist and O'Connor, stated: "[This] decision is as unprecedented as it is unjust." He insisted that "our cases do not establish that a private party's mere invocation of state legal procedures constitutes 'joint participation' or 'conspiracy' with state officials satisfying the § 1983 requirement of action under color of law. [Instead], recent decisions make clear that independent,

4. The debtor's complaint was construed as alleging a due process violation both from a misuse of the attachment procedure and from the statutory procedure itself. Justice White concluded that the debtor "did present a valid cause of action under § 1983 insofar as he challenged the constitutionality of the [statute]; he did not insofar as he alleged only misuse or abuse of the statute."

5. "Contrary to the suggestion of the dissent, we do not hold today that 'a private party's mere invocation of state legal procedures constitutes "joint participation" or "conspiracy" with state officials satisfying the § 1983 requirement of action under color of law.' The holding today, as the above analysis makes clear, is limited to the particular context of prejudgment attachment." [Footnote by Justice White.]

In finding Flagg Bros. distinguishable, the majority relied in part on the fact that the creditor's

remedy involved in Flagg Bros. (a warehouseman's sale pursuant to a statutory warehouseman's lien) could be exercised without the intervention of a state official, but simply pursuant to state procedures. Here, by contrast, the issuance and execution of the writ of attachment pursuant to the creditor's suit was undertaken by state officials. Distinguishing the Flagg Bros. case further, Justice White stated that there the state was undoubtedly "responsible for the statute. The response of the Court [in Flagg Bros.], however, focused not on the terms of the statute but on the character of the defendant to the § 1983 suit: Action by a private party pursuant to this statute, without something more, was not sufficient to justify a characterization of that party as a 'state actor.'"

private decisions made in the context of litigation cannot be said to occur under color of law." [6]

SECTION 3.   CONGRESSIONAL POWER TO REACH PRIVATE INTERFERENCES WITH CONSTITUTIONAL RIGHTS: MODERN SCOPE AND PROBLEMS

THE INGREDIENTS OF THE PROBLEM: AN INTRODUCTORY SKETCH

To what extent may Congress provide criminal and civil sanctions against private interferences with constitutional rights? The question is complex; the answer, unclear. The question is pursued here by focusing on the background and implications of United States v. Guest (1966; p. 905). Careful examination of these materials suggests answers to some problems and highlights the substantial additional ones as yet unresolved. Before doing so, it may be useful to sketch the recurrent clusters of problems presented by cases of this nature, to aid in disentangling the constitutional and statutory issues. At the outset, it should be noted that the central questions are the constitutional and statutory reaches of the modern counterparts of the post-Civil War civil rights laws (printed at p. 858 above). Recall that those modern counterparts contain both criminal and civil provisions and that they fall into two groups: one reaches only action "under color" of law; the other reaches private conspiracies, without any state nexus requirement on the face of the statutes. Thus, on the criminal side, 18 U.S.C. § 242 covers action "under color" of law, while § 241 is directed at private conspiracies. There is a similar distinction in the major civil provisions: 42 U.S.C. § 1983 is the state action-related statute; § 1985(c) is the civil conspiracy provision. What persons are covered by these provisions? What rights are protected by them? What is the statutory and constitutional reach of the laws? A number of variables require attention in exploring these issues. These introductory notes focus on an intertwined trilogy of concerns: the sources of constitutional rights; vagueness; and statutory construction. This overview of that trilogy is designed to aid understanding of the opinions below. But bear in mind that the trilogy is offered as background and that the primary emphasis here is on the question foreshadowed by the preceding section: the power of Congress to safeguard 14th Amendment rights against interferences by seemingly private actors, either by relying on the Court's interpretations of the state action concept or, more controversially, by invoking a claimed congressional power under § 5 of the 14th Amendment to reach private actors the Court would not reach on its own.

1. *The sources of constitutional rights.* The most important recurrent theme in analyzing the scope of congressional power to reach private interferences with constitutional rights is the problem of identifying the sources of the covered rights. Note especially three types of rights, with quite different implications regarding their potential reach to private behavior.

a. *14th and 15th Amendment rights against the "state."* First, there are the rights presenting problems introduced in sec. 2: due process and equal protection rights under the 14th, as well as 15th Amendments rights—rights in terms applicable only to *state* interferences. Under the Court's interpretations of the

---

6. "The Court avers that its holding 'is limited to the particular context of prejudgment attachment.' However welcome, this limitation lacks a principled basis. It is unclear why a private party engages in state action when filing papers seeking an attachment of property, but not when seeking other relief (e.g., injunction), or when summoning police to investigate a suspected crime." [Footnote by Justice Powell.]

state action concept, some seemingly private behavior is reachable under the 14th and 15th Amendments. But may Congress go beyond the Court's view of "state action" and reach additional private actors? For example, can the private conspiracies provisions, §§ 241 and 1985(c), be applied to private actors who interfere with 14th Amendment rights? That problem is discussed, but not resolved, in Guest, p. 905 below.[1]

   b. *13th Amendment rights.* The other post-Civil War Amendment, the 13th, is not limited to state action; it applies to private interferences generally. And under the Jones case, p. 924 below, Congress, may, under § 2 of that Amendment, deal broadly with private acts of racial discrimination. The 13th Amendment, then, provides an independent constitutional basis for congressional sanctions against private interferences with rights (see, e.g., Griffin, p. 918 below). But its scope is limited by its racial discrimination emphasis; it probably does not help with non-racial interferences with rights.

   c. *Rights stemming from sources other than the post-Civil War Amendments.* Third, the Court has recognized a number of constitutional rights, based on sources other than the post-Civil War Amendments, that are not subject to the state action limitation. Those rights provide additional sources of congressional power to reach private conduct. As the cases below illustrate, the rights involved are largely rights derived from structures and relationships found implicit in the Constitution (recall McCulloch v. Maryland). Note, for example, the reliance on the right to travel in Guest, p. 905.[2]

   2. *Specificity and vagueness.* Provisions such as 18 U.S.C. § 242 speak in very general terms: they contain broad references to "rights, privileges, or immunities" under the "Constitution or laws." Even assuming congressional power to reach private interferences with constitutional rights, are those statuto-

1. For the special status of rights under the privileges and immunities provision of the 14th Amendment, see footnote 2 below.

2. Justice Harlan—a Justice often skeptical of broad interpretations—recognized the existence of some constitutional rights of that variety applicable to private action in his separate opinion in Guest. After expressing his doubt that the Constitution was generally intended to create "rights of private individuals as against other private individuals," he conceded: "It is true that there is a very narrow range of rights against individuals which have been read into the Constitution. In Ex parte Yarbrough, 110 U.S. 651 [1884], the Court held that implicit in the Constitution is the right of citizens to be free of private interference in federal elections. United States v. Classic, 313 U.S. 299 [1941], extended this coverage to primaries. Logan v. United States, 144 U.S. 263 [1892], applied the predecessor of § 241 to a conspiracy to injure someone in the custody of a United States marshal. [The] Court in In re Quarles, 158 U.S. 532 [1895], extending Logan, declared that there was a right of federal citizenship to inform federal officials of violations of federal law. See also United States v. Cruikshank, 92 U.S. 542 [1875; p. 864 above], which announced in dicta a federal right to assemble to petition the Congress for a redress of grievances."

In effect, the state action limitation does not apply to the currently recognized privileges of national citizenship under the 14th Amendment, even though in terms these, too, appear to be subject to the state action limits. The development of that strange situation traces back to the narrow reading of the 14th Amendment in the Slaughter-House Cases (1873; p. 810 above). Recall the catalogue of national citizenship privileges in Twining (1908; p. 418 above), similar to the privileges acknowledged by Justice Harlan in Guest. In the Slaughter-House Cases, the majority defined the privileges of national citizenship as those "which owe their existence to the Federal government, its National character, its Constitution, or its laws." Under that view, those privileges were not created by the 14th Amendment but really antedated it and have their roots in structural implications of the Constitution. Therefore, the privileges are protected against *all* interferences, private as well as state. [Presumably, if some of the modern suggestions for a broader reading of the largely forgotten privileges and immunities clause of the 14th Amendment *were* adopted by the Court (and privileges other than those derived from structural considerations were recognized), the state action limitation *would* apply.]

These materials emphasize federal *constitutional* rights. But note that the rights-protecting statutes considered in this section typically speak not only of rights under the Constitution but also of rights under the "laws of the United States." To the extent that Congress acts under powers applicable to private individuals—e.g., the commerce and spending powers—Congress may protect the statutory rights it has created against private interferences. Recall, e.g., the public accommodations provisions of the 1964 Civil Rights Act (p. 158) and note 18 U.S.C. § 245, p. 916 below.

ry references sufficiently specific to give adequate notice to those subjected to them? To the extent that such phrases appear in criminal provisions, do they risk invalidation for vagueness? That concern may inhibit the Court in searching out new varieties of rights to read into those broadly phrased remnants of the post-Civil War laws. Screws (p. 913) illustrates the Court's difficulties in finding adequate specificity in such broad formulations.[3]

3. *Statutory interpretation.* Another pervasive theme in these materials—a theme related to those noted in the preceding paragraphs—is that of statutory construction. In construing the general civil rights statutes, what varieties of constitutional rights can be read into such phrases as "rights, privileges, or immunities secured or protected by the Constitution"? Thus, when Congress purports to reach private actors in a statute originally enacted soon after adoption of the 14th Amendment, should the Court read a state action limitation into the statute? Or should the statute be read broadly, in accordance with its apparent terms—thereby including in it constitutional rights *not* subject to the state action limitation (as well as state action-limited 14th Amendment rights made applicable to private interferences only because of an arguable congressional power to reach beyond Court-announced state action limits)?[4]

A. PRIVATE INTERFERENCES WITH FEDERAL RIGHTS: CRIMINAL SANCTIONS

UNITED STATES v. GUEST

383 U.S. 745, 86 S.Ct. 1170, 16 L.Ed.2d 239 (1966).

Mr. Justice STEWART delivered the opinion of the Court.

The six defendants [were indicted] for criminal conspiracy in violation of 18 U.S.C. § 241. [The] indictment alleged a single conspiracy by the defendants to deprive Negro citizens of the free exercise and enjoyment of several specified rights secured by the Constitution and laws of the United States.[1] The defendants [successfully] moved to dismiss the indictment on the ground that it did not charge an offense under the laws of the United States. [We] reverse. [W]e deal here with issues of statutory construction, not with issues of constitutional [power].

II. The second numbered paragraph of the indictment alleged that the defendants conspired to injure, oppress, threaten, and intimidate Negro citizens of the United States in the free exercise and enjoyment of: "The right to the

---

3. A suggestion in Justice Brennan's opinion in Guest, urging greater specificity in congressional formulations, in turn helped produce the new 1968 civil rights provisions, 18 U.S.C. § 245, p. 916 below. That more specific enumeration of protected rights—rights Congress *explicitly* sought to protect against private interferences—raises anew the problem of congressional powers, and invites reference back to the distinctions among the constitutional sources of rights summarized here.

4. In the cases of the early 1950s—e.g., the Williams cases on the criminal side and Collins v. Hardyman on the civil side—there was strong support on the Court for narrow readings of the statutes to avoid constitutional doubts. More recent cases, by contrast—e.g., Griffin and Price—take a broader view of the meaning of the statutes, in part because of diminished constitutional doubts. These cases are noted below.

1. The indictment was in five numbered paragraphs. The critical three paragraphs (paragraphs 2, 3 and 4) are quoted in Justice Stewart's opinion. Justice Stewart noted that, beyond the indictment, the "only additional indication in the record concerning the factual details of the conduct with which the defendants were charged is the statement of the District Court that: 'it is common knowledge that two of the [defendants] have already been prosecuted in [a Georgia court] for the murder of Lemuel A. Penn and by a jury found not guilty.'" (The killing of Lemuel Penn in 1964 was one of the widely publicized incidents of civil rights violence in the South in the 1960s.)

equal utilization, without discrimination upon the basis of race, of public facilities in the vicinity of Athens, Georgia, owned, operated or managed by or on behalf of the State of Georgia or any subdivision thereof." Correctly characterizing this paragraph as embracing rights protected by the Equal Protection Clause, [the] District Court held as a matter of statutory construction that § 241 does not encompass any 14th Amendment rights. [This] was in error, as our opinion in United States v. Price [p. 911 below], decided today, makes abundantly [clear]. Moreover, inclusion of 14th Amendment rights within the compass of § 241 does not render the statute unconstitutionally vague. Since the gravamen of the offense is conspiracy, the requirement that the offender must act with a specific intent to interfere with the federal rights in question is satisfied. [Screws; Williams (dissenting opinion) (p. 913 below)]. And the rights under the Equal Protection Clause described by this paragraph of the indictment have been so firmly and precisely established by a consistent line of decisions in this Court, that the lack of specification of these rights in the language of § 241 itself can raise no serious constitutional question on the ground of vagueness or indefiniteness.

Unlike the indictment in Price, however, the indictment in the present case names no person alleged to have acted in any way under the color of state law. The argument is therefore made that, since there exist no [equal protection] rights against wholly private action, the judgment [on] this branch of the case must be affirmed. On its face, the argument is unexceptionable. [Equal protection] speaks to the State or to those acting under the color of its authority. In this connection, we emphasize that § 241 by its clear language incorporates no more than the Equal Protection Clause itself; the statute does not purport to give substantive, as opposed to remedial, implementation to any rights secured by that Clause. Since we therefore deal here only with the bare terms of the [Clause] itself, nothing said in this opinion goes to the question of what kinds of other and broader legislation Congress might constitutionally enact under § 5 of the 14th Amendment to implement that [Clause].

[It] is a commonplace that rights under the Equal Protection Clause itself arise only where there has been involvement of the State or of one acting under the color of its authority. [This] is not to say, however, that the involvement of the State need be either exclusive or direct. In a variety of situations the Court has found state action of a nature sufficient to create rights under the [Clause] even though the participation of the State was peripheral, or its action was only one of several co-operative forces leading to the constitutional violation. This case, however, requires no determination of the threshold level that state action must attain in order to create rights under the [Clause]. This is so because [the] indictment in fact contains an express allegation of state involvement sufficient at least to require the denial of a motion to dismiss. One of the means of accomplishing the object of the conspiracy, according to the indictment, was "By causing the arrest of Negroes by means of false reports that such Negroes had committed criminal acts." [T]he extent of official involvement [alleged here] is not clear. [T]he allegation is broad enough to cover a charge of active connivance by agents of the State in the making of the "false reports," or other conduct amounting to official discrimination clearly sufficient to constitute denial of rights protected by [equal protection]. Although it is possible that [the] proof if the case goes to trial would disclose no co-operative action of that kind by officials of the State, the allegation is enough to prevent dismissal of this branch of the indictment.

III. The fourth numbered paragraph of the indictment alleged that the defendants conspired to injure, oppress, threaten, and intimidate Negro citizens of the United States in the free exercise and enjoyment of: "The right to travel freely to and from [Georgia] and to use highway facilities and other instrumentalities of interstate commerce within [Georgia]."[2] The District Court was in error in dismissing the indictment as to this paragraph. The constitutional right to travel from one State to another, and necessarily to use the highways and other instrumentalities of interstate commerce in doing so, occupies a position fundamental to the concept of our Federal Union. It is a right that has been firmly established and repeatedly recognized.[3] [Although] there have been recurring differences in emphasis within the Court as to the source of the constitutional right of interstate travel, there is no need here to canvass those differences further. All have agreed that the right exists. Its explicit recognition as one of the federal rights protected by what is now 18 U.S.C. § 241 goes back at least as far as 1904. United States v. Moore, 129 F. 630, 633. We reaffirm it now.[4] This does not mean, of course, that every criminal conspiracy affecting an individual's right of free interstate passage is within the sanction of § 241. A specific intent to interfere with the federal right must be proved, and at a trial the defendants are entitled to a jury instruction phrased in those terms. [Screws.] Thus, for example, a conspiracy to rob an interstate traveler would not, of itself, violate § 241. But if the predominant purpose of the conspiracy is to impede or prevent the exercise of the right of interstate travel, or to oppress a person because of his exercise of that right, then, whether or not motivated by racial discrimination, the conspiracy becomes a proper object of the federal law under which the indictment in this case was [brought].

Reversed and remanded.

Mr. Justice CLARK, with whom Mr. Justice BLACK and Mr. Justice FORTAS join, concurring.

I join the opinion of the Court in this case, but believe it worthwhile to comment on its Part II. [The] Court's interpretation of the indictment clearly avoids the question whether Congress, by appropriate legislation, has the power to punish private conspiracies that interfere with 14th Amendment [rights]. My Brother Brennan, however, [suggests] that the Court indicates sub silentio that Congress does not have the power to outlaw such conspiracies. Although the Court specifically rejects any such connotation, it is, I believe, both appropriate and necessary under the circumstances here to say that there now can be no doubt that the specific language of § 5 empowers the Congress to enact laws punishing all conspiracies—with or without state action—that interfere with 14th Amendment rights.

Mr. Justice HARLAN, concurring in part and dissenting in part.

I join [Part II][1] of the Court's opinion, but I cannot subscribe to Part III in its full sweep. To the extent that it is there held that § 241 reaches conspiracies, embracing only the action of private persons, [to] interfere with the right

---

2. The third numbered paragraph alleged that the defendants conspired to injure, oppress, threaten, and intimidate Negro citizens of the United States in the free exercise and enjoyment of: "The right to the full and equal use on the same terms as white citizens of the public streets and highways in the vicinity of Athens, Georgia." Insofar as the third paragraph refers to the use of local public facilities, it is covered by the discussion of the second numbered paragraph of the indictment in Part II of this opinion. Insofar as the third paragraph refers to the use of streets or highways in interstate commerce, it is covered by the present discussion of the fourth numbered paragraph of the indictment. [Footnote by Justice Stewart.]

3. Recall also the discussion of the right to move from state to state in chap. 9, at p. 832 above.

4. As emphasized in Mr. Justice Harlan's separate opinion, § 241 protects only against interference with rights secured by other federal laws or by the Constitution itself. The right to interstate travel is a right that the Constitution itself guarantees. Although [the cases recognizing that right] in fact involved governmental interference with the right of free interstate travel, their reasoning fully supports the conclusion that the constitutional right of interstate travel is a right secured against interference from any source whatever, whether governmental or private. In this connection, it is important to reiterate that the right to travel freely from State to State finds constitutional protection that is quite independent of the 14th Amendment. [Footnote by Justice Stewart.]

1. The action of three of the Justices who join the Court's opinion in nonetheless cursorily

of citizens freely to engage in interstate travel, I am constrained to dissent. On the other hand, I agree that § 241 does embrace state interference with such interstate travel, and I therefore consider that this aspect of the indictment is sustainable on the reasoning of Part II of the Court's opinion.

This right to travel must be found in the Constitution itself. This is so because [no] "right to travel" can be found in § 241 or in any other law of the United States. [While] past cases do indeed establish that there is a constitutional "right to travel" between States free from unreasonable *governmental* interference, today's decision is the first to hold that such movement is also protected against *private* interference, and, depending on the constitutional source of the right, I think it either unwise or impermissible so to read the [Constitution]. As a general proposition it seems to me very dubious that the Constitution was intended to create certain rights of private individuals as against other private individuals. [It] is true that there is a very narrow range of rights against individuals which have been read into the Constitution. [See the passage from this opinion quoted at p. 904 above.] [These cases] are narrow, and are essentially concerned with the vindication of important relationships with the Federal Government—voting in federal elections, involvement in federal law enforcement, communicating with the Federal Government. The present case stands on a considerably different footing. It is arguable that the same considerations which led the Court on numerous occasions to find a right of free movement against oppressive state action now justify a similar result with respect to private impediments. [I] do not think [this argument] is particularly persuasive. There is a difference in power between States and private groups so great that analogies between the two tend to be misleading. If the State obstructs free intercourse of goods, people, or ideas, the bonds of the union are threatened; if a private group effectively stops such communication, there is at most a temporary breakdown of law and order, to be remedied by the exercise of state authority or by appropriate federal legislation. [I] do not gainsay that the immunities and commerce provisions of the Constitution leave the way open for the finding of this "private" constitutional right, since they do not speak solely in terms of governmental action. Nevertheless, I think it wrong to sustain a criminal indictment on such an uncertain ground. To do so subjects § 241 to serious challenge on the score of vagueness and serves in effect to place this Court in the position of making criminal law under the name of constitutional [interpretation].

Mr. Justice BRENNAN, with whom The Chief Justice [WARREN] and Mr. Justice DOUGLAS join, concurring in part and dissenting in part.

[I] reach the same result as the Court on that branch of the indictment discussed in Part III of its opinion but for other reasons. See footnote [1] infra. And I agree with so much of Part II as construes § 241 to encompass conspiracies to injure, oppress, threaten or intimidate citizens in the free exercise or enjoyment of 14th Amendment rights and holds that, as so construed, § 241 is not void for indefiniteness. I do not agree, however, with the remainder of Part II which holds, as I read the opinion, that a conspiracy to interfere with the exercise of the right to equal utilization of state facilities is not, within the meaning of § 241, a conspiracy to interfere with the exercise of a "right [secured] by the Constitution" unless discriminatory conduct by state officers is involved in the alleged conspiracy.

I. [I believe that] a conspiracy to interfere with the right to equal utilization of state facilities [is] a conspiracy [within] the meaning of § 241—without regard to whether state officers participated in the alleged conspiracy. I believe that § 241 reaches such a private conspiracy, not because the 14th Amendment

---

pronouncing themselves on the far-reaching constitutional questions deliberately not reached in   Part II seems to me, to say the very least, extraordinary. [Footnote by Justice Harlan.]

of its own force prohibits such a conspiracy, but because § 241, as an exercise of congressional power under § 5 of that Amendment, prohibits *all* conspiracies to interfere with the exercise of a "right [secured] by the Constitution" and because the right to equal utilization of state facilities is a "right [secured] by the Constitution" within the meaning of that phrase as used in § 241.[1] My difference with the Court stems from its construction of the term "secured" as used in § 241. The Court tacitly construes the term "secured" so as to restrict the coverage of § 241 to those rights that are "fully protected" by the Constitution or another federal law. Unless private interferences with the exercise of the right in question are prohibited by the Constitution itself or another federal law, the right cannot, in the Court's view, be deemed ["secured"] so as to make § 241 applicable to a private conspiracy to interfere with the exercise of that right. The Court then premises that neither the 14th Amendment nor any other federal law prohibits private interferences with the exercise of the right to equal utilization of state facilities.

In my view, however, a right can be deemed "secured [by] the Constitution or laws of the United States," within the meaning of § 241, even though only governmental interferences with the exercise of the right are prohibited by the Constitution itself (or another federal law). The term "secured" means "created by, arising under or dependent upon," rather than "fully protected." A right is "secured [by] the Constitution" within the meaning of § 241 if it emanates from the Constitution, if it finds its source in the Constitution. Section 241 must thus be viewed, in this context, as an exercise of congressional power to amplify prohibitions of the Constitution addressed, as is invariably the case, to government officers; contrary to the view of the Court, I think we are dealing here with a statute that seeks to implement the Constitution, not with the "bare terms" of the Constitution. Section 241 is not confined to protecting rights against private conspiracies that the Constitution or another federal law also protects against private interferences. Many of the rights that have been held to be encompassed within § 241 are not additionally the subject of protection of specific federal legislation or of any provision of the Constitution addressed to private individuals.[2] [The] full import of our decision in [Price] regarding § 241 is to treat the rights purportedly arising from the 14th Amendment in parity with those rights just enumerated, arising from other constitutional provisions. The reach of § 241 should not vary with the particular constitutional provision that is the source of the [right].

For me, the right to use state facilities without discrimination on the basis of race is, within the meaning of § 241, a right created by, arising under and dependent upon the 14th Amendment and hence is a right "secured" by that Amendment. It finds its source in that Amendment. [The] 14th Amendment commands the State to provide the members of all races with equal access to the public facilities it owns or manages, and the right of a citizen to use those facilities without discrimination on the basis of race is a basic corollary of this command. Cf. Brewer v. Hoxie School District No. 46, 238 F.2d 91 (C.A.8th Cir.1956) [p. 915 below]. Whatever may be the status of the right to equal

1. Similarly, I believe that § 241 reaches a private conspiracy to interfere with the right to travel from State to State. I therefore need not reach the question whether the Constitution of its own force prohibits private interferences with that right; for I construe § 241 to prohibit such interferences, and as so construed I am of the opinion that § 241 is a valid exercise of congressional power. [Footnote by Justice Brennan.]

2. Justice Brennan gave the following examples: "[The] remedies of § 241 have been declared to apply, without regard to whether the alleged violator was a government officer, to interferences with the right to vote in a federal election, Ex parte Yarbrough, or primary, United States v. Classic; the right to discuss public affairs or petition for redress of grievances [United States v. Cruikshank; cf. Collins v. Hardyman (dissenting opinion)]; the right to be protected against violence while in the lawful custody of a federal officer, Logan v. United States; and the right to inform of violations of federal law [In re Quarles]."

utilization of *privately owned facilities,* it must be emphasized that we are here concerned with the right to equal utilization of *public facilities owned or operated by or on behalf of the State.* To deny the existence of this right or its constitutional stature is to deny the history of the last decade, or to ignore the role of federal power, predicated on the 14th Amendment, in obtaining nondiscriminatory access to such facilities. [I] would therefore hold that proof [of] the conspiracy charged to the defendants in [the second] paragraph will establish a violation of § 241 without regard to whether there is also proof that state law enforcement officers actively connived in causing the arrests of Negroes by means of false reports.

II. My view as to the scope of § 241 requires that I reach the question of constitutional power—whether § 241 or legislation indubitably designed to punish entirely private conspiracies to interfere with the exercise of 14th Amendment rights constitutes a permissible exercise of the power granted to Congress by § 5 of the 14th Amendment. [A] majority of the members of the Court [3] expresses the view today that § 5 empowers Congress to enact laws punishing *all* conspiracies to interfere with the exercise of 14th Amendment rights, whether or not state officers or others acting under the color of state law are implicated in the conspiracy. Although the 14th Amendment [itself], "speaks to the State or to those acting under the color of its authority," legislation protecting rights created by that Amendment, such as the right to equal utilization of state facilities, need not be confined to punishing conspiracies in which state officers participate. Rather, § 5 authorizes Congress to make laws that it concludes are reasonably necessary to protect a right created by and arising under that Amendment; and Congress is thus fully empowered to determine that punishment of private conspiracies interfering with the exercise of such a right is necessary to its full protection. It made that determination in enacting § 241, [and] therefore § 241 is constitutional legislation as applied [here].

I acknowledge that some of the decisions of this Court, most notably an aspect of the Civil Rights Cases, have declared that Congress' power under § 5 is confined to the adoption of "appropriate legislation for correcting the effects [of] prohibited State laws and State [acts]." I do not accept—and a majority of the Court today rejects—this interpretation of § 5. It reduces the legislative power to enforce the provisions of the Amendment to that of the judiciary; and it attributes a far too limited objective to the Amendment's sponsors. Moreover, the language of § 5 of the 14th Amendment and § 2 of the Fifteenth Amendment are virtually the same, and we recently held in South Carolina v. Katzenbach [p. 933 below] that "[t]he basic test to be applied in a case involving § 2 of the Fifteenth Amendment is the same as in all cases concerning the express powers of Congress with relation to the reserved powers of the States." The classic formulation of that test by Chief Justice Marshall in [McCulloch] was there adopted. [It] seems to me that this is also the standard that defines the scope of congressional authority under [§ 5]. Viewed in its proper perspective, [§ 5] appears as a positive grant of legislative power, authorizing Congress to exercise its discretion in fashioning remedies to achieve civil and political equality for all citizens. No one would deny that Congress could enact legislation directing state officials to provide Negroes with equal access to state schools, parks and other [state] facilities. [Nor] could it be denied that Congress has the power to punish state officers who [conspire] to threaten, harass and murder Negroes for attempting to use these facilities. And I can find no principle of federalism nor word of the Constitution that denies Congress power to determine that in order adequately to protect the right to

---

3. The majority consists of the Justices join-ing my Brother Clark's opinion and the Justices joining this [opinion]. [Footnote by Justice Brennan.]

equal utilization of state facilities, it is also appropriate to punish other individuals—not state officers themselves and not acting in concert with state officers—who engage in the same brutal conduct for the same misguided purpose.

III.   Section 241 is certainly not model legislation for punishing private conspiracies to interfere with the exercise of the right of equal utilization of state facilities.   It deals in only general language [which] plainly brings § 241 close to the danger line of being void for vagueness.   But, as the Court holds, a stringent scienter requirement saves § 241 from condemnation as a criminal statute failing to provide adequate notice of the proscribed conduct.   [We] have construed § 241 to require proof that the persons charged conspired to act in defiance, or in reckless disregard, of an announced rule making the federal right specific and definite.   [See Screws.]   Since this case reaches us on the pleadings, there is no occasion to decide now whether the Government will be able on trial to sustain the burden of proving the requisite specific [intent].   In any event, we may well agree that the necessity to discharge that burden can imperil the effectiveness of § 241 where, as is often the case, the pertinent constitutional right must be implied from a grant of congressional power or a prohibition upon the exercise of governmental power.   But since the limitation on the statute's effectiveness derives from Congress' failure to define—with any measure of specificity—the rights encompassed, the remedy is for Congress to write a law without this [defect].[4]

SOME PROBLEMS OF APPLYING CRIMINAL SANCTIONS TO STATE-INVOLVED DEFENDANTS INTERFERING WITH 14TH AMENDMENT RIGHTS

Introduction.   This group of notes focuses on one cluster of problems raised by the Guest case.   Note Part II of Justice Stewart's opinion in Guest: that part sustains a portion of the indictment (covering interference with 14th Amendment rights) without reaching the question whether § 5 of the 14th Amendment may reach purely private actors; it does so by finding the allegation "broad enough to cover a charge of active connivance by agents of the State" or "other conduct amounting to official discrimination."   Under that theory, "private" defendants may be reached if they are sufficiently involved with state officials.   That approach thus relies on the Court's interpretations of § 1 of the 14th Amendment considered above (e.g., Burton), without asserting any independent congressional power to expand the reach of the 14th Amendment.   But even this rationale of reaching private actors because of state "involvement" is not without difficulty, as this group of notes illustrates.   There is, first, the problem of *how much* state involvement with the private actors needs to be shown—a problem akin to those considered in sec. 2B.   There is, moreover, the question of construing §§ 241 and 242 as reaching 14th Amendment rights and state-involved private actors.   There is, finally, the concern (voiced in Guest) about vagueness problems raised by broad constructions of these general statutes.[1]

1.   *The Price case.*   UNITED STATES v. PRICE, 383 U.S. 787 (1966), arose out of a widely publicized murder of three civil rights workers near Philadelphia, Mississippi, in 1964.   The defendants were three local law enforcement officials (Deputy Sheriff Price of Neshoba County, the Sheriff, and a

---

4.   See 18 U.S.C. § 245, p. 916 below, enacted two years after the decision in this case.

1.   Guest of course raises additional, more far-reaching problems as well: e.g., congressional authority to reach purely private actors under § 5 of the 14th Amendment, and congressional authority to reach private actors by drawing upon federal rights derived from sources outside the 14th and 15th Amendments and thus not limited by the state action concept.   Those problems are postponed until the next group of notes.

policeman) and fifteen private individuals, all allegedly involved in the killing of civil rights workers Schwerner, Chaney and Goodman. There were two indictments against the 18 defendants: one based on 18 U.S.C. § 242; the other on § 241. The alleged conspiracy involved releasing the victims from jail at night, intercepting and killing them, and disposing of their bodies—all with the purpose to "punish" the victims summarily and thus to deprive them of their 14th Amendment right "not to be summarily punished without due process of law by persons acting under color of the laws of the State of Mississippi." The District Court dismissed most of the charges. The Court reversed all of the dismissals. Justice FORTAS wrote for the Court, stating (like Justice Stewart in Guest) that the case involved only issues "of construction, not of constitutional power."

a. The first indictment charged substantive violations of 18 U.S.C. § 242 (the "under color" of law provision) as well as a conspiracy to violate that Section. The District Court sustained the conspiracy count against all of the defendants. As to the private defendants, the lower court found it "immaterial" that they were "not acting under color of law" because the charge was "that they were conspiring with persons who were so acting." But the trial court sustained the substantive counts only against the three official defendants; it dismissed those against the private defendants since they were not "officers in fact." The Court reversed the dismissal of the substantive charges against the private defendants. Sec. 242 concededly required that the "person indicted has acted 'under color' of law," and "under color" of law should be treated, as it had been under its civil counterpart (see sec. 3B below), "as the same thing as the 'state action' required under the 14th Amendment." But that did not bar reaching private individuals, in view of the Court's interpretations of the state action coverage of the 14th Amendment: "Private persons, jointly engaged with state officials in the prohibited action, are acting 'under color' of law for purposes of the statute. To act 'under color' of law does not require that the accused be an officer of the State. It is enough that he is a willful participant in joint activity with the State or its agents." Justice Fortas particularly emphasized the relevance of the Burton "involvement" analysis. Here, he noted, "state officers participated in every phase of the alleged [joint adventure]: the release from jail, the interception, assault and murder. [Those] who took advantage of participation by state officers in accomplishment of the foul purpose alleged must suffer the consequences of that participation. In effect, if the allegations are true, they were participants in official lawlessness, acting in willful concert with state officers and hence under color of law."

b. The second indictment charged all 18 defendants with a conspiracy under 18 U.S.C. § 241, the "private conspiracy" section. Fifteen years earlier, the Court, in one of the Williams cases (note 2 below) had left in doubt whether that provision applied to interferences with 14th Amendment rights. But in Price, the Court had no difficulty in holding that § 241 did apply, and that its reach in this context presented no constitutional difficulty because of the presence of state action. The District Court, relying on Justice Frankfurter's opinion in Williams, had dismissed the indictment against all the defendants, holding that the section did not apply to rights under the 14th Amendment. But in Price, the Court, noting that the 4 to 4 division in 1951 had left the construction of § 241 "an open question," adopted Justice Douglas' position in that case: "[Section 241] includes rights or privileges protected by the 14th Amendment; [and] it extends to conspiracies otherwise within the scope of the section, participated in by officials alone or in collaboration with private persons." [2]

2. Cf. the more expansive modern interpretation of § 1985(c) in Griffin (1971; p. 918 below).

2. *The Williams cases.* The 1951 Williams cases, referred to in Price, throw light on two problems: first, they provide another example of using Court-developed state action analyses of § 1 of the 14th Amendment to reach private individuals; second, they raise the problem of statutory construction resolved in Price. One of the cases, WILLIAMS v. UNITED STATES, 341 U.S. 97 (1951), was a prosecution under the predecessor of § 242, the "under color" of law provision. Williams, a private detective who had been issued a special police officer's badge, was employed by a lumber company to investigate thefts of its property. Flashing his badge and accompanied by a regular police officer, he beat four suspects until they confessed to the thefts. He was convicted of depriving his victims of the right to be tried by due process of law. The Court affirmed. Justice DOUGLAS' majority opinion concluded that the jury could find that the defendant was "no mere interloper but had a semblance of policeman's power," and that "the manner of his conduct of the interrogations [made] clear that he was asserting the authority granted him and not acting in the role of a private person." [3] In a companion case, UNITED STATES v. WILLIAMS, 341 U.S. 70 (1951), the same defendant, two of his employees who participated in the beatings, and the police officer detailed to assist him, were convicted of conspiracy under the predecessor of § 241, the private conspiracy provision. The Court reversed the convictions; but only eight of the Justices reached the critical issue of statutory construction, and they divided 4 to 4, leaving the uncertainty that was clarified by the Price case.[4] Justice FRANK-FURTER's opinion, joined by Chief Justice Vinson and Justices Jackson and Minton, argued that § 241 should *not* be read as covering 14th Amendment rights: § 242 was intended to deal fully with conspiracies under color of state law to deprive persons of 14th Amendment rights; § 241 covered conspiracies by private persons; accordingly, § 241 should be construed as protecting only those rights "which Congress can beyond doubt constitutionally secure against interference by private individuals." The other four Justices—Justice DOUG-LAS, joined by Justices Reed, Burton and Clark—took a broader view of § 242, and their view was adopted by the Court in Price. They insisted that § 241, like § 242, was applicable to 14th Amendment rights as well as others. They thought it "strange to hear" that, though § 242 "extends to rights guaranteed against state action by the 14th Amendment, [§ 241] is limited to rights which the Federal Government can secure against invasion by private persons."

3. *The Screws case: Vagueness and civil rights laws.* The broad references in 18 U.S.C. §§ 241 and 242 to rights "secured" by the Constitution have stimulated recurrent challenges that the statutes do not give adequate notice of what is prohibited and are therefore void for vagueness. The Court has repeatedly rejected those challenges by reading what Justice Brennan in Guest called "a strict scienter requirement" into the criminal provisions. That reading stems from one of the earliest of the modern cases under the civil rights laws, SCREWS v. UNITED STATES, 321 U.S. 91 (1945). That case involved a "shocking and revolting episode in law enforcement." The defendants were police officers (Screws was sheriff of Baker County, Ga.) who arrested the black victim for theft and beat him "with their fists and with a solid-bar blackjack" after he allegedly reached for a gun and used insulting language. The victim was knocked on the ground and beaten until he was unconscious. He died soon after. "There was evidence that Screws held a grudge against [the victim] and had threatened to 'get' him."

The defendants were convicted under 18 U.S.C. § 242 for "willfully" and "under color of law" depriving the victim of his 14th Amendment rights,

---

3. Justices Frankfurter, Jackson and Minton dissented for the reasons set forth in the dissent in Screws, note 3 below. Justice Black also dissented.

4. Justice Black cast the decisive vote for the result, relying on res judicata grounds.

including "the right not to be deprived of life without due process of law." Justice DOUGLAS' opinion, joined by Chief Justice Stone and Justices Black and Reed, conceded that there would be a serious vagueness problem if "the customary standard of guilt for statutory crimes" were adopted: "If a man intentionally adopts certain conduct in certain circumstances known to him, and that conduct is forbidden by the law under those circumstances, he intentionally breaks the law." Under such a test, "a local law enforcement officer violates [§ 242] if he does an act which some court later holds deprives a person of due process of law. And he is a criminal though his motive was pure and though his purpose was unrelated to the disregard of any constitutional guarantee." Under such a view, state officials would indeed walk on "treacherous ground," given the "character and closeness of decisions of this Court interpreting the due process clause." But he found it possible to read § 242 "more narrowly" to avoid the vagueness difficulty: "[I]f we construe 'willfully' in [§ 242] as connoting a purpose to deprive a person of a specific constitutional right, we would introduce no innovation. [W]here the punishment imposed is only for an act knowingly done with the purpose of doing that which the statute prohibits, the accused cannot be said to suffer from lack of warning or knowledge that the act which he does is a violation of law. [T]he presence of a bad purpose or evil intent alone may not be sufficient. [But] a requirement of a specific intent to deprive a person of a federal right made definite by decision or other rule of law saves the Act from any charge of unconstitutionality on the grounds of [vagueness].[5]

"It is said, however, that this construction of the Act will not save it from the infirmity of vagueness since neither a law enforcement official nor a trial judge can know with sufficient definiteness the range of rights that are constitutional. But that criticism is wide of the mark. For the specific intent required by the Act is an intent to deprive a person of a right which has been made specific either by the express terms of the Constitution or laws of the United States or by decisions interpreting them. [He] who defies a decision interpreting the Constitution knows precisely what he is doing. If sane, he hardly may be heard to say that he knew not what he did. [Acting "willfully" in the sense in which we use the word means acting] in open defiance or in reckless disregard of a constitutional requirement which has been made specific and definite. [The] fact that the defendants may not have been thinking in constitutional terms is not material where their aim was not to enforce local law but to deprive a citizen of a right and that right was protected by the Constitution. When they so act they at least act in reckless disregard of constitutional prohibitions or guarantees. [Those] who decide to take the law into their own hands and act as prosecutor, jury, judge, and executioner plainly act to deprive a prisoner of the trial which [due process] guarantees him. And such a purpose need not be expressed; it may at times be reasonably inferred from all the circumstances attendant on the act." But in this case, the trial judge had not instructed the jury properly on the question of intent, and the conviction was accordingly reversed.[6]

---

5. On the vagueness defense to criminal prosecutions, see also p. 1156 below.

6. Justice RUTLEDGE cast the decisive vote to make that disposition possible: though he (like Justice Murphy) considered the trial judge's instructions adequate and thought that the conviction should be affirmed, he noted that the case "cannot have disposition" if each Justice adhered to his belief; he accordingly voted to remand for disposition in accordance with Justice Douglas' views. Justices ROBERTS, FRANKFURTER, and JACKSON dissented, insisting that the "intrinsic vagueness" of the statute "surely cannot be removed by making the statute applicable only where the defendant has the 'requisite bad purpose.' Does that not amount to saying that the black heart of the defendant enables him to know what are the constitutional rights deprivation of which the statute forbids, although we as judges are not able to define their classes or their limits, or, at least, are not prepared to state what they are unless it be to say that [§ 242] protects

THE REACH OF CONGRESSIONAL POWER, THE GUEST CASE, AND THE 1968 LAW

1. *Congressional power to reach private actors under § 5 of the 14th Amendment.* Price, Williams and Screws all involved applications of the criminal sanctions of the civil rights laws to actors reachable under the Court's own interpretations of the state action concept. But Justice Brennan's opinion in Guest (and presumably Justice Clark's comment) suggest that Congress under § 5 of the 14th Amendment may go further in reaching private behavior than the Court would under § 1. How far-reaching is that congressional power? Justice Clark's opinion stated that "the specific language of § 5 empowers the Congress to enact laws punishing all conspiracies—with or without state action—that interfere with 14th Amendment rights." And Justice Brennan insisted that "legislation protecting rights created by [the 14th] Amendment, such as the right to equal utilization of state facilities, need not be confined to punishing conspiracies in which state officers participate"; Congress is "fully empowered to determine that punishment of private conspiracies interfering with the exercise of such a right is necessary to its full protection." Note that the Brennan and Clark opinions in Guest continue to assume that 14th Amendment rights are rights against the state. Thus, Justice Brennan notes that the 14th Amendment "commands the State to provide the members of all races with equal access" to public facilities. He draws from this obligation a "basic corollary": "the right of a citizen to use those facilities without discrimination on the basis of race." What kinds of private interferences with the relationship between the state and the individual *are* reachable under the broad view of § 5? Are the private interferences limited to those directly aimed at state officials, in order to hamper them from carrying out their 14th Amendment obligations? Or may Congress also reach private interferences directed against the private citizen who has a "corollary" right against the state? May Congress go even further than that?

The Brennan theory in Guest is most readily applicable where the private interference is directed against the state officials themselves. That was the situation in a case cited by Justice Brennan in Guest, Brewer v. Hoxie School District No. 46, 238 F.2d 91 (8th Cir.1956). Brewer sustained federal power to reach private actors who intimidate state officials in the performance of their 14th Amendment obligations. It upheld an injunction restraining private persons from intimidating school officials who were trying to carry out a plan to desegregate schools. The court noted that the school officials were trying to apply the Constitution as interpreted in Brown and that it followed "as a necessary corollary that they have a federal right to be free from direct and deliberate interference with the performance of the constitutionally imposed duty. The right arises by necessary implication from the imposition of the duty." But Justice Brennan was clearly willing to give that theory a broader reach in Guest: he was prepared to sustain the application of § 241 to a private interference with the private citizen who had a right of access to public facilities. In short, he found power to reach the private actor interfering with the state-victim relationship by intimidations directed not against the state official but against the victim. Under that theory, is it essential that the defendant intends to interfere with the victim's access to state facilities? Or is it enough that murder of the victim has the *effect* of interfering with the victim's use of state facilities?

Is the theory even more far-reaching than that? *Is* a special relationship between the victim and the state an essential ingredient for invoking § 5? Or may Congress act directly under § 5 to prevent private interferences with access

whatever rights the Constitution protects?" (At the second trial, Screws was acquitted.)

Gunther Const.Law 11th Ed. UCB—22

to *private* facilities as well? E.g., may Congress move directly to reach private interferences with access to private housing, on the ground that that is appropriate legislation to protect access to public housing? The Guest rationale presumably does not go that far. But may justification for such a law be found in either the "remedial" or "substantive" rationales under § 5, considered in sec. 4 below? E.g., is such a power supported by the approach of Katzenbach v. Morgan, p. 946 below—an approach that seems to give Congress some power to "reinterpret" the content of 14th Amendment guarantees, and perhaps, analogously, some power to redraw the lines between state action and private action under the 14th Amendment?[1]

2. *Criminal sanctions against private conduct: Sources outside the 14th Amendment.* The Guest case and related materials point to sources of congressional authority beyond 14th Amendment rights. A number of constitutional provisions run against private behavior as well as state conduct. (Recall the listing of such rights at pp. 864 and 904 above.) Moreover, private interferences may be reached when Congress establishes new statutory rights under powers that clearly reach private behavior—e.g., the commerce power, used as a basis for the public accommodations provisions of the Civil Rights Act of 1964. Against that background, consider the 1968 provisions affording criminal sanctions against private actors, 18 U.S.C. § 245 which follows. These modern provisions can be viewed as a response to Justice Brennan's suggestion in Guest of more specific legislation. Do the specifications in § 245 cure the vagueness concerns aroused by §§ 241 and 242? What explains the differences in intent requirements for (b)(1) violations and (b)(2) acts? What explains the grouping of § 245(b) into two subsections? What are the sources of the various rights specified? Which are 14th Amendment rights? Which stem from other sources? Does § 245 raise any constitutional questions?[2]

THE 1968 CRIMINAL PROVISIONS: § 245

§ 245. Federally protected activities. . . .

(b) Whoever, whether or not acting under color of law, by force or threat of force willfully injures, intimidates or interferes with, or attempts to injure, intimidate or interfere with—

(1) any person because he is or has been, or in order to intimidate such person or any other person or any class of persons from—

   (A) voting or qualifying to vote, qualifying or campaigning as a candidate for elective office, or qualifying or acting as a poll watcher, or any legally authorized election official, in any primary, special, or general election;

---

1. Recall also the justifications for regulations of intrastate commerce in the interest of protecting interstate commerce, under the Necessary and Proper Clause, in chap. 3.

See generally Cox, "Foreword: Constitutional Adjudication and the Promotion of Human Rights," 80 Harv.L.Rev. 91 (1966); Feuerstein, "Civil Rights [Crimes]," 19 Vand.L.Rev. 641 (1966); Brest, "The Federal Government's Power to Protect Negroes and Civil Rights Workers Against Privately Inflicted Harm," 1 Harv.C.R.-C.L.L.Rev. 1 (1966); and Note, "Federal Power to Regulate Private [Discrimination]," 74 Colum. L.Rev. 451 (1974). See also the development of these theories in the notes in sec. 4 below.

2. The background of § 245 vividly reveals interactions between the Court and the other branches. Thus, President Johnson in January 1966 asked for new laws "to try those who murder, attack, or intimidate either civil rights workers or others exercising federal rights." But implementation of that Administration proposal was delayed, in part to await the Court's decisions in Guest and Price. These cases came down on March 28, 1966. Exactly a month later, the President submitted a special Civil Rights Message to Congress, accompanied by detailed proposals to prescribe "penalties for certain acts of violence or intimidation." The 1966 legislative efforts ended in a Senate filibuster. A slightly revised version of the 1966 proposal was included in the Johnson Administration's 1967 civil rights bill. That bill, as substantially amended, became the Civil Rights Act of 1968, which included § 245.

(B) participating in or enjoying any benefit, service, privilege, program, facility or activity provided or administered by the United States;

(C) applying for or enjoying employment, or any perquisite thereof, by any agency of the United States;

(D) serving, or attending upon any court of any State in connection with service, as a grand or petit juror in any court of the United States;

(E) participating in or enjoying the benefits of any program or activity receiving Federal financial assistance; or

(2) any person because of his race, color, religion or national origin and because he is or has been—

(A) enrolling in or attending any public school or public college;

(B) participating in or enjoying any benefit, service, privilege, program, facility or activity provided or administered by any State or subdivision thereof;

(C) applying for or enjoying employment, or any perquisite thereof, by any private employer or any agency of any State or subdivision thereof, or joining or using the services or advantages of any labor organization, hiring hall, or employment agency;

(D) serving, or attending upon any court of any State in connection with possible service, as a grand or petit juror;

(E) traveling in or using any facility of interstate commerce, or using any vehicle, terminal, or facility of any common carrier by motor, rail, water, or air;

(F) enjoying the goods, services, facilities, privileges, advantages, or accommodations of any inn, hotel, motel, or other establishment which provides lodging to transient guests, or of any restaurant, cafeteria, lunchroom, lunch counter, soda fountain, or other facility which serves the public and which is principally engaged in selling food or beverages for consumption on the premises, or of any gasoline station, or of any motion picture house, theater, concert hall, sports arena, stadium, or any other place of exhibition or entertainment which serves the public, or of any other establishment which serves the public and (i) which is located within the premises of any of the aforesaid establishments or within the premises of which is physically located any of the aforesaid establishments, and (ii) which holds itself out as serving patrons of such establishments; or

(3) during or incident to a riot or civil disorder, any person engaged in a business in commerce or affecting commerce, including, but not limited to, any person engaged in a business which sells or offers for sale to interstate travelers a substantial portion of the articles, commodities, or services which it sells or where a substantial portion of the articles or commodities which it sells or offers for sale have moved in commerce; or

(4) any person because he is or has been, or in order to intimidate such person or any other person or any class of persons from—

(A) participating, without discrimination on account of race, color, religion or national origin, in any of the benefits or activities described in subparagraphs (1)(A) through (1)(E) or subparagraphs (2)(A) through (2)(F); or

(B) affording another person or class of persons opportunity or protection to so participate; or

(5) any citizen because he is or has been, or in order to intimidate such citizen or any other citizen from lawfully aiding or encouraging other persons to participate, without discrimination on account of race, color, religion or national origin, in any of the benefits or activities described in subparagraphs (1)(A) through (1)(E) or subparagraphs (2)(A) through (2)(F), or participating lawfully in speech or peaceful assembly opposing any denial of the opportunity to so participate—

shall be fined not more than $1,000, or imprisoned not more than one year, or both; and if bodily injury results shall be fined not more than $10,000, or imprisoned not more than ten years, or both; and if death results shall be subject to imprisonment for any term of years or for life. As used in this section, the term "participating lawfully in speech or peaceful assembly" shall not mean the aiding, abetting, or inciting of other persons to [riot].

B. PRIVATE INTERFERENCES WITH FEDERAL RIGHTS: CIVIL SANCTIONS

Introduction. As the statutory survey in sec. 1 indicated, several of the laws of the Civil War era afforded civil rather than criminal sanctions; and their modern remnants give rise to problems of statutory scope and constitutional authority analogous to those considered in sec. 3A in connection with the criminal provisions. Thus, 42 U.S.C. § 1983, the civil counterpart of 18 U.S.C. § 242, provides civil remedies for deprivations of rights "under color" of law. And 42 U.S.C. § 1985(c) grants civil remedies for certain private conspiracies, as 18 U.S.C. § 241 does in the criminal sphere. The notes that follow first consider the more difficult statutory and constitutional problems raised by that civil private conspiracy provision (problems analogous to those raised by Guest) before examining some issues raised by the "under color" of law provision.

PRIVATE CONSPIRACIES AND GRIFFIN v. BRECKENRIDGE

1. *The Griffin interpretation of § 1985(c).* In Collins v. Hardyman, 341 U.S. 651 (1951),[1] the Court, beset by constitutional doubts, gave a narrow interpretation to the conspiracy provision in § 1985(c)—the provision granting a civil remedy for conspiracies to deny "the equal protection of the laws, or of equal privileges and immunities under the laws." Collins in effect construed § 1985(c) as reaching only conspiracies under color of state law. Twenty years later, however, in GRIFFIN v. BRECKENRIDGE, 403 U.S. 88 (1971), a unanimous Court discarded that interpretation and found that "many of the constitutional problems" perceived in Collins "simply do not exist," and held § 1985(c) applicable to certain private conspiracies. On the congressional power issue, the Court found it unnecessary to reach the 14th Amendment question. Instead, Justice Stewart relied on the power to reach private conduct under the 13th Amendment and in protection of the right of interstate travel.[2]

---

1. In Collins, plaintiffs, members of a political club, stated that defendants broke up their meeting (held to adopt a resolution opposing the Marshall Plan) and thus interfered with their rights to petition the national government for redress of grievances and to equal privileges under the laws. There was no allegation that defendants acted under color of law. Justice Jackson's majority opinion concluded that no cause of action under § 1985(c) had been stated. He stated: "The only inequality suggested is that the defendants broke up plaintiffs' meetings and did not break up meetings of others with whose sentiments they agreed. [Such] private discrimination is not inequality before the law unless there is some manipulation of the law or its agencies to give sanction or sanctuary for doing so." He added: "We do not say that no conspiracy by private individuals could be of such magnitude and effect as to work a deprivation of [equal protection]. Indeed, the post-Civil War Ku Klux Klan [may have] done so. [It] may well be that a conspiracy, so far-flung and embracing such numbers, [was] able effectively to deprive Negroes of their equal rights and to close all avenues [of] redress or vindication. [H]ere

nothing of that sort appears. We have a case of a lawless political brawl, precipitated by a handful of white citizens against other white citizens. California courts are open to plaintiffs." Justice Burton, joined by Justices Black and Douglas, dissented. The right to petition the federal government for a redress of grievances, he noted, was a constitutional right, under United States v. Cruikshank (p. 864 above), and it was not a right limited to state interferences. He added that cases holding that the 14th Amendment was directed only at state action "are not authority for the contention that Congress may not pass laws supporting rights which exist apart from [the 14th Amendment]."

2. Justice Harlan's concurrence dissociated himself from the reliance on the right to travel rationale.

Note the parallels in the evolution of the civil and criminal conspiracy provisions: Collins was decided in the same year as the Williams cases, p. 913 above. In Williams, Justice Frankfurter's opinion had read § 241 narrowly; that statutory interpretation was repudiated in the Price case in 1966. Similarly, Justice Jackson's narrow read-

The petitioners in Griffin were Mississippi blacks who were passengers in an automobile operated by a Tennesseean in Mississippi, near the Mississippi-Alabama border. They charged that respondents, white Mississippians, had conspired to detain, assault and beat them for the purpose of preventing them and other blacks "from seeking the equal protection of the laws and from enjoying the equal rights, privileges and immunities of citizens," including their rights to free speech, movement, association, assembly, and "their rights not to be enslaved nor deprived of life and liberty other than by due process of law." They claimed that the respondents, mistakenly believing the driver to be a civil rights worker, blocked the car, forced the inhabitants to get out of it, and threatened and clubbed them. The lower federal courts dismissed the complaint on the authority of Collins. Justice STEWART's opinion concluded, without deciding whether Collins was decided correctly "on its own facts," that, "in the light of the evolution of decisional law," the statute should now be given its "apparent meaning." Not only the text but "companion provisions, and legislative history" pointed "unwaveringly to [§ 1985(c)'s] coverage of private conspiracies." Reading the law to cover private action did not, however, mean that it would apply "to all tortious, conspiratorial interferences with the rights of others." He explained: "The constitutional shoals that would lie in the path of interpreting § 1985(c) as a general federal tort law can be avoided by giving full effect to the congressional purpose—by requiring, as an element of the cause of action," an "invidiously discriminatory motivation." He added: "The language requiring intent to deprive of *equal* protection, or *equal* privileges and immunities, means that there must be some racial, or perhaps otherwise class-based, invidiously discriminatory animus behind the conspirators' action." [3]

After finding that petitioners' complaint easily fell within that new construction of § 1985(c)—"[i]ndeed, the conduct here alleged lies so close to the core of the coverage intended by Congress that it is hard to conceive of wholly private conduct that would come within the statute if this does not"—Justice Stewart turned to the question of congressional power to reach this private conspiracy. He noted: "That § 1985(c) reaches private conspiracies to deprive others of legal rights can, of itself, cause no doubts of its constitutionality. It has long been settled that 18 U.S.C. § 241 [reaches] wholly private conspiracies and is constitutional. Our inquiry, therefore, need go only to identifying a source of congressional power to reach the private conspiracy alleged by the complaint in this case." He found one adequate constitutional basis in the 13th Amendment, concluding "that Congress was wholly within its powers under § 2 of [that] Amendment in creating a statutory cause of action for Negro citizens who have been the victims of conspiratorial, racially discriminatory private action aimed at depriving them of the basic rights that the law secures to all free men." (See Jones, p. 924 below.) He also found an independent basis in "the right of interstate travel," relying, inter alia, on his opinion in Guest. He added: "In identifying these two constitutional sources of congressional power, we do not imply the absence of any other. More specifically, the allegations of the complaint in this case have not required consideration of the scope of the power of Congress under § 5 of the 14th Amendment. By the same token, since the allegations of the complaint bring this cause of action so close to the

ing of § 1985(c) was overturned in Griffin in 1971.

3. Justice Stewart added in a footnote: "We need not decide, given the facts of this case, whether a conspiracy motivated by invidiously discriminatory intent other than racial bias would be actionable under the portion of § 1985(c) before us." He noted, too, that the motivation requirement stemming from the reference to "equal" in the statute "must not be confused with" the scienter test of Screws. "Willfulness" was not an element of § 1985(c), unlike § 242. Justice Stewart added: "The motivation aspect of § 1985(c) focuses not on scienter in relation to deprivation of rights but on invidiously discriminatory animus."

constitutionally authorized core of the statute, there has been no occasion here to trace out its constitutionally permissible periphery."

2. *The potential reach of § 1985(c) and the Carpenters case.* What *is* the "constitutionally permissible periphery" of 42 U.S.C. § 1985(c)? To what extent *may* Congress reach "invidiously discriminatory intent other than racial bias"? To what extent may Congress reach private interferences with 14th Amendment rights—an issue not reached in Griffin? For more than a decade after Griffin, the Court had no occasion to engage in a full scale reexamination of § 1985(c).[4] In the meanwhile, lower federal courts divided about its scope.[5] But in the 1980s, the Court went a long way towards clarifying the reach of § 1985(c).

CARPENTERS v. SCOTT, 463 U.S. 825 (1983), arose out of a labor dispute that involved a claim that a union had violently interfered with non-union workers. This, it was alleged, constituted a conspiracy to interfere with the non-union workers' First Amendment rights not to associate with a union. Justice WHITE's majority opinion in the 5 to 4 ruling found that the claim did not state a cause of action under § 1985(c). He concluded that an alleged conspiracy to infringe First Amendment rights is not a violation of § 1985(c) unless it is proved that "the state is involved in the conspiracy or that the aim of the conspiracy is to influence the activity of the state." Moreover, "the kind of animus that § 1985(c) requires" was not present here. The Court of Appeals, relying on its reading of the implications of Griffin, had concluded that it was not necessary to show "some state involvement" to demonstrate an infringement of First Amendment rights. Justice White disagreed, relying on the emphasis on the state action requirement in Justice Stewart's opinion in Guest as well as in Price. Moreover, Griffin was "not to the contrary." There was no state action requirement on the face of the statute, because the statute was not limited to 14th Amendment rights; and the conspiracy alleged in Griffin was actionable because it involved the right to travel as well as 13th Amendment rights. But "Griffin did not hold that even when the alleged conspiracy is aimed at a right that is by definition a right only against state interference the plaintiff in a § 1985(c) suit nevertheless need not prove that the conspiracy contemplated state involvement of some sort." He added: "Neither is respondents' position

---

4. In Great American Federal Savings & Loan Association v. Novotny, 442 U.S. 366 (1979), some Justices touched upon the un-resolved issues tangentially. Novotny dealt mainly with the question of the applicability of § 1985(c) to statutory rather than constitutional rights. Justice Stewart found that rights created by the employment discrimination provision of the 1964 Civil Rights Act (Title VII) could not be the basis for a suit under § 1985(c). Two Justices who joined Justice Stewart's majority opinion (Justices Powell and Stevens) were willing to go further, arguing that the section should not cover *any* statutory rights and should be "limited to conspiracies to violate those fundamental rights derived from the Constitution." Justice Stevens' separate opinion was the only one to consider the constitutionally permissible scope of the section. He noted that the "rights secured by the 14th Amendment are rights to protection against unequal or unfair treatment by the State, not by private parties." Thus, there could be no claim for relief "based on a violation of the 14th Amendment if there has been no involvement by the State. The requirement of state action, in this context, is no more than a requirement that there be a constitutional viola-

tion"—a necessary ingredient of a § 1985(c) cause of action, in his view.

5. A number of Courts of Appeals considered the constitutional boundaries of § 1985(c) more directly. Thus, in Action v. Gannon, 450 F.2d 1227 (8th Cir.1971), the Eighth Circuit affirmed an injunction enjoining civil rights groups from disrupting services at a Roman Catholic cathedral. Reading Griffin and Guest very broadly, the court insisted that plaintiffs' rights to "the freedom of assembly and worship" were covered by the law and that "Congress was given the power in § 5 [to] enforce the rights guaranteed by the [14th Amendment] against private conspiracies." See also Westberry v. Gilman Paper Co., 507 F.2d 206 (5th Cir.1975). Contrast the Fourth Circuit's decision in Bellamy v. Mason's Stores, Inc., 508 F.2d 504 (4th Cir.1974), insisting (in a case where an employee sued his employer because he had been discharged for membership in the KKK) that the law could not be applied to "persons who conspire without involvement of government to deny another person the right of free association," because First Amendment rights limit only the government.

helped by the assertion that even if the 14th Amendment does not provide authority to proscribe exclusively private conspiracies, precisely the same conduct could be proscribed by the Commerce Clause. That is no doubt the case; but § 1985(c) is not such a provision, since it 'provides no substantial rights itself' to the class conspired against. The rights, privileges, and immunities that § 1985(c) vindicates must be found elsewhere, and here the right claimed to have been infringed has its source in the First Amendment. Because that Amendment restrains only official conduct, to make out [their] case, it was necessary for respondents to prove that the state was somehow involved in or affected by the conspiracy."

Justice White next turned to the lower courts' claim that § 1985(c) "not only reaches conspiracies other than those motivated by racial bias but also forbids conspiracies against workers who refuse to join a union." He stated: "We disagree with the latter conclusion and do not affirm the former." On the first of these issues, the Court of Appeals had reasoned that, "because [Radical] Republicans [of the Reconstruction era] were among the objects of the Klan's conspiratorial activities, Republicans in particular and political groups in general were to be protected by § 1985(c)," the anti-KKK law. The lower court had concluded that "animus against non-union employees [here] was sufficiently similar to the animus against a political party to satisfy the requirements of § 1985(c)." Justice White replied: "We are unpersuaded. In the first place, it is a close question whether § 1985(c) was intended to reach any class-based animus other than animus against Negroes and those who championed their cause, most notably Republicans. [Although] we have examined with some care the legislative history, [we] find difficult the question whether § 1985(c) provided a remedy for every concerted effort by one political group to nullify the influence of or do other injury to a competing group by use of otherwise unlawful means. To accede to that view would go far toward making the federal courts, by virtue of § 1985(c), the monitors of campaign tactics in both state and federal elections, a role that the courts should not be quick to assume." He noted that in Griffin, the Court had "withheld judgment on the question whether [§ 1985(c)] went any farther than its central concern—combatting the violent and other efforts of the Klan and its allies to resist and frustrate the intended effects of the [post-Civil War Amendments]. Lacking other evidence of congressional intention, we follow the same course here."

Justice White was more decisive on the issue of the provision's applicability to conspiracies against nonunion workers: "Even if the section must be construed to reach conspiracies aimed at any class or organization on account of its political views, [we] find no convincing support in the legislative history for the proposition that the provision was intended to reach conspiracies motivated by bias towards others on account of their *economic* views, status or activities. Such a construction would extend § 1985(c) into the economic life of the country in a way that we doubt that the 1871 Congress would have intended." Accordingly, he refused to construe the section to "reach conspiracies motivated by economic or commercial animus," explaining: "Were it otherwise, for example, § 1985(c) could be brought to bear on any act of violence resulting from union efforts to organize an employer or from the employer's efforts to resist it," so long as unionization-related animus was shown. "[It] would be an unsettling event to rule that strike and picket-line violence must now be considered in the light of the strictures of § 1985(c)," particularly in view of the detailed regulation of union activities in the NLRA. "[We] think that such a construction of the statute, which is at best only arguable and surely not compelled by either its language or legislative history, should be [eschewed]. Economic and commercial conflicts, we think, are best dealt with by statutes, federal or state, specifically addressed to such problems, as well as by the general law proscribing injuries to persons and property."

Justice BLACKMUN's dissent, joined by Justices Brennan, Marshall and O'Connor, read the legislative history quite differently and found "no basis for the Court's crabbed and uninformed reading of the words of § 1985(c)." He claimed that the legislators who adopted the provision in 1871 believed that Congress did have "authority to reach private conduct by virtue of [congressional] power to protect the rights of national citizenship" guaranteed "directly to the people" and existing "independently of any state action," and that "Congress did not intend any requirement of state involvement in either a civil or criminal action." [6] He accordingly concluded that, properly interpreted, the section "prohibits private conspiracies designed to interfere with persons' equal enjoyment and exercise of their civil rights even if those conspiracies have no state involvement of any kind." [At this point, he appended a brief footnote with his only reference to the source of congressional power for so broad a reading: "The Constitution poses no obstacle to this exercise of congressional power. The Court correctly recognizes that Congress has the power under the Commerce Clause to ban such conspiracies." (Recall the very brief reference to the commerce power in the majority opinion.)] He conceded that, under Griffin, the statute was limited to private conspiracies "involving class-based animus," and that "the types of classes covered by the statute are far from clear." Griffin had "reserved the question whether nonracial classes are covered." His own reading was that "Congress intended to provide a federal remedy for all *classes* that seek to exercise their legal rights in unprotected circumstances similar to those of the victims of Klan violence." Moreover, one of the groups subject to Klan violence had been "economic migrants." In short, Congress in 1871 was responding generally to "the problem of Klan violence—a problem with political, racial, and economic overtones. [Congress] intended to provide a remedy to any class of persons, whose beliefs or associations placed them in danger of not receiving equal protection of the laws from local authorities. While certain class traits, such as race, religion, sex, and national origin, per se meet this requirement, other traits also may implicate the functional concerns in particular situations." That approach justified application of the statute here. The victims had been attacked "because of their preexisting nonunion association." And this conspiracy was "similar to the Klan conspiracies Congress desired to [punish]. In this union town, the effectiveness of local law enforcement protection for nonunion workers was open to question." In short, the defendants in this § 1985(c) action "intended to hinder a particular group in the exercise of their legal rights because of their membership in a specific class."

CIVIL REMEDIES AGAINST ACTIONS "UNDER COLOR" OF LAW

a.   42 U.S.C. § 1983—like its criminal counterpart, 18 U.S.C. § 242—provides remedies against actions "under color" of law. It has given rise to

---

6. Justice Blackmun claimed that the Court had misinterpreted the statutory scope of the provision by its "subtle confusion of statutory construction with constitutional interpretation": "Determining the scope of § 1985(c) is a matter of statutory construction and has nothing to do with current interpretations of the First or 14th Amendments. [Congress'] view of its constitutional authority in 1871 to reach private conduct under the 14th Amendment is relevant in interpreting the reach of § 1985(c)." He conceded that the Court in Novotny (footnote 5 above) had viewed the provision as "a remedial statute" not providing "substantive rights." But he explained that the 1871 Congress "also believed it was providing a remedy—a remedy for violations of the right to equal protection which it believed was guaranteed against both state and private action. To the extent that the language of [the statute] incorporated that interpretation of the scope of the right, it is not strictly remedial from the current perspective on constitutional law. [See] Note, Private Conspiracies to Violate Civil [Rights], 61 B.U.L.Rev. 1007 (1981)."

problems similar to those presented by § 242, considered in sec. 3A. A major decision accounting for the widespread modern invocation of § 1983 was Monroe v. Pape, 365 U.S. 167 (1960), permitting a damage action against police officers for unlawful invasion of petitioners' home and for illegal search, seizure and detention. Justice Douglas' majority opinion emphasized that the "specific intent" requirement of Screws for criminal cases was not applicable here: "[§ 1983] should be read against the background of tort liability that makes a man responsible for the natural consequences of his actions." [1] Under Monroe, however, local governments were immune from § 1983 actions. That immunity has substantially evaporated in light of more recent decisions, Monell v. Department of Social Services, 436 U.S. 658 (1978), and Owen v. Independence, 445 U.S. 622 (1980).[2] The Court has repeatedly been confronted with problems of defenses (such as "good faith") and implied official immunities (e.g., for judges and legislators) under § 1983. In reading a variety of absolute and qualified defenses into § 1983, the Court has typically relied on "common-law tradition" and "public policy reasons." Moreover, the readings of § 1983 have been repeatedly influenced by the Court's concern that the provision might turn into a general federal action for all torts committed by state and local officials. See, e.g., the fears expressed in the prevailing opinion in Paul v. Davis (1976; p. 578 above). (The details of the statutory issues under § 1983 are beyond the scope of this book.)

b. One additional problem under § 1983 warrants mention here—a problem arising from the fact that its language covers not only action "under color" of law, but refers also to "custom, or usage, of any State." In the Court's first extensive consideration of that phrase, in Adickes v. S.H. Kress & Co., 398 U.S. 144 (1970), Justice Harlan's majority opinion concluded that it "requires state involvement and is not simply a practice that reflects longstanding social habit." "Custom," he insisted, "must have the force of law by virtue of the persistent practices of state officials." Justice Brennan's dissent argued that "custom" means "custom of the people of a State, not custom of state officials"—"a widespread and longstanding practice," not necessarily "backed by the force of the State." [3]

---

1. See generally Klitgaard, "The Civil Rights Acts and Mr. Monroe," 49 Calif.L.Rev. 144 (1961), and Note, "The Proper Scope of the Civil Rights Acts," 66 Harv.L.Rev. 1285 (1953). (The Court reexamined Monroe in Parratt v. Taylor, 451 U.S. 527 (1981), and concluded that, in some circumstances, negligent (not merely intentional) deprivations of rights may be actionable under § 1983.)

Note also the *judicially created* civil damages remedy for constitutional violations by *federal* law enforcement officials (who are not covered by § 1983), in the line of cases beginning with Bivens v. Six Unknown Named Agents, 403 U.S. 388 (1971).

2. Newport v. Fact Concerts, Inc., 453 U.S. 247 (1981), ruled that a municipality may *not* be held liable for punitive damages under § 1983. However, apart from this municipal immunity, punitive damages are generally available in § 1983 actions. See Smith v. Wade, 461 U.S. 30 (1983).

3. Justice Brennan did not reach the question whether the "custom" he described would itself constitute state action under the 14th Amendment. Justice Douglas, whose dissent supported a similar view of the law, relied on the 13th Amendment for constitutional authority.

Congress can deal w/ private
racial discrim
as "badges" of servitude "border"
★
(overrules Civil Rights Cases)
13th

C. CONGRESSIONAL POWER TO REACH PRIVATE CONDUCT UNDER THE 13TH AMENDMENT

JONES v. ALFRED H. MAYER CO.

392 U.S. 409, 88 S.Ct. 2186, 20 L.Ed.2d 1189 (1968).

Mr. Justice STEWART delivered the opinion of the Court.

In this case we are called upon to determine the scope and the constitutionality [of] 42 U.S.C. § 1982.* [P]etitioners filed a complaint [that] respondents had refused to sell them a home [for] the sole reason that petitioner [is] a Negro. Relying in part upon § 1982, the petitioners sought injunctive and other relief. [The lower federal courts dismissed the complaint], concluding that § 1982 applies only to state action and does not reach private refusals to sell. [We] reverse. [We] hold that § 1982 bars *all* racial discrimination, private as well as public, in the sale or rental of property, and that the statute, thus construed, is a valid exercise of the power of Congress to enforce the 13th Amendment.[1]

At the outset, it is important to make clear precisely what this case does *not* involve. Whatever else it may be, 42 U.S.C. § 1982 is not a comprehensive open housing law, [unlike] the Fair Housing Title (Title VIII) of the Civil Rights Act of 1968.[2] [Thus], although § 1982 contains none of the exemptions that Congress included in the Civil Rights Act of 1968,[3] it would be a serious mistake to suppose that § 1982 in any way diminishes the significance of the law recently enacted by [Congress]. On its face, [§ 1982] appears to prohibit *all* discrimination against Negroes in the sale or rental of property—discrimination by private owners as well as discrimination by public [authorities].[4] Stressing what they consider to be the revolutionary implications of so literal a reading of § 1982, respondents argue that Congress cannot possibly have intended any such result. Our examination of the relevant history, however, persuades us that Congress meant exactly what it said. In its original form, § 1982 was part [of] the Civil Rights Act of 1866. [The Court examined the legislative history at length.] Nor was the scope of the 1866 Act altered when it was re-enacted in 1870, some two years after the ratification of the 14th

---

* As noted at p. 859 above, § 1982 states: "All citizens of the United States shall have the same right, in every State and Territory, as is enjoyed by white citizens thereof to inherit, purchase, lease, sell, hold, and convey real and personal property."

1. Because we have concluded that the discrimination alleged in the petitioners' complaint violated a federal statute that Congress had the power to enact under the 13th Amendment, we find it unnecessary to decide whether that discrimination also violated [equal protection]. [Footnote by Justice Stewart. The 14th Amendment state action issue had been the major focus in the lower courts.]

2. Justice Stewart elaborated: "In sharp contrast to Title VIII, [§ 1982] deals only with racial discrimination and does not address itself to discrimination on grounds of religion or national origin. It does not deal specifically with discrimination in the provision of services or facilities in connection with the sale or rental of a dwelling. It does not prohibit advertising or other representations that indicate discriminatory

preferences. It does not refer explicitly to discrimination in financing arrangements or in the provision of brokerage services. It does not empower a federal administrative agency to assist aggrieved parties. It makes no provision for intervention by the Attorney General. And, although it can be enforced by injunction, it contains no provision expressly authorizing a federal court to order the payment of damages."

3. As an illustration of the exemptions under the Fair Housing Title of the 1968 Act, see § 803(b)(2), making the law inapplicable to "rooms or units in dwellings containing living quarters occupied or intended to be occupied by no more than four families living independently of each other, if the owner actually maintains and occupies one of such living quarters as his residence."

4. Justice Stewart acknowledged that earlier dicta—e.g., Hurd v. Hodge (1948; p. 879 above)—had stated that § 1982 was limited to state action, but emphasized that none of the earlier cases had "presented [the] precise issue for adjudication."

Amendment. It is quite true that some members of Congress supported the 14th Amendment "in order to eliminate doubt as to the constitutional validity of the Civil Rights Act as applied to the States." But it certainly does not follow that the adoption of the 14th Amendment or the subsequent readoption of the Civil Rights Act were meant somehow to *limit* its application to state action. The legislative history furnishes not the slightest factual basis for any such speculation, and the conditions prevailing in 1870 make it highly [implausible].

The remaining question is whether Congress has power under the Constitution to do what § 1982 purports to do: to prohibit all racial discrimination, private and public, in the sale and rental of property. Our starting point is the 13th Amendment, for it was pursuant to that constitutional provision that Congress originally enacted what is now § 1982. It has never been doubted "[that] the power vested in Congress to enforce the article by appropriate legislation" includes the power to enact laws "direct and primary, operating upon the acts of individuals, whether sanctioned by State legislation or not." [Civil Rights Cases.] Thus, the fact that § 1982 operates upon the unofficial acts of private individuals, whether or not sanctioned by state law, presents no constitutional problem. [The] constitutional question in this case, therefore, comes to this: Does the authority of Congress to enforce the 13th Amendment "by appropriate legislation" include the power to eliminate all racial barriers to the acquisition of real and personal property? We think the answer to that question is plainly yes.

"By its own unaided force and effect," the 13th Amendment "abolished slavery, and established universal freedom." [Civil Rights Cases.] Whether or not the Amendment *itself* did any more than that—a question not involved in this case—it is at least clear that the Enabling Clause of that Amendment empowered Congress to do much more. For that clause clothed "Congress with power to pass *all laws necessary and proper for abolishing all badges and incidents of slavery in the United States.*" Ibid. (Emphasis added.) [Surely] Congress has the power under the 13th Amendment rationally to determine what are the badges and the incidents of slavery, and the authority to translate that determination into effective legislation. Nor can we say that the determination Congress has made is an irrational one. For this Court recognized long ago that, whatever else they may have encompassed, the badges and incidents of slavery—its "burdens and disabilities"—included restraints upon "those fundamental rights which are the essence of civil freedom, namely, the same right [to] inherit, purchase, lease, sell and convey property, as is enjoyed by white citizens." [Civil Rights Cases.] Just as the Black Codes, enacted after the Civil War to restrict the free exercise of those rights, were substitutes for the slave system, so the exclusion of Negroes from white communities became a substitute for the Black Codes. And when racial discrimination herds men into ghettos and makes their ability to buy property turn on the color of their skin, then it too is a relic of slavery. [At] the very least, the freedom that Congress is empowered to secure under the 13th Amendment includes the freedom to buy whatever a white man can buy, the right to live wherever a white man can live. If Congress cannot say that being a free man means at least this much, then the 13th Amendment made a promise the Nation cannot [keep].

Reversed.[5]

Mr. Justice HARLAN, whom Mr. Justice WHITE joins, dissenting.

[This decision] appears to me to be most ill-considered and ill-advised. [I] believe that the Court's construction of § 1982 as applying to purely private action is almost surely wrong, and at the least is open to serious doubt. The

---

5. A concurring opinion by Justice DOUG-LAS is omitted.

issue of the constitutionality of § 1982, as construed by the Court, and of liability under the 14th Amendment alone,[1] also present formidable difficulties. Moreover, the political processes of our own era have, since the date of oral argument in this case, given birth to a civil rights statute embodying "fair housing" provisions which would at the end of this year make available to others, though apparently not to the petitioners themselves, the type of relief which the petitioners now seek.[2] It seems to me that this latter factor so diminishes the public importance of this case that by far the wisest course would be [to] dismiss the writ as improvidently granted.

[The Court] finds it "plain and unambiguous" [that the language of § 1982] forbids purely private as well as state-authorized discrimination. [I] do not find it so. For me, there is an inherent ambiguity in the term "right," as used in § 1982. The "right" referred to may either be a right to equal status under the law, in which case the statute operates only against state-sanctioned discrimination, or it may be an "absolute" right enforceable against private individuals. To me, the words of the statute, taken alone, suggest the former interpretation, not the latter. [The] Court rests its opinion chiefly upon the legislative history of the Civil Rights Act of 1866. I shall endeavor to show that those debates do [not] overwhelmingly support the result reached by the Court, and in fact that a contrary conclusion may equally well be drawn. [A discussion of the legislative history is omitted.] [In] holding that the 13th Amendment is sufficient constitutional authority for § 1982 as interpreted, the Court also decides a question of great importance. Even contemporary supporters of the aims of the 1866 Civil Rights Act doubted that those goals could constitutionally be achieved under the 13th Amendment, and this Court has twice expressed similar [doubts].

13TH AMENDMENT POWERS AND THE 1866 ACT

1. *The scope of congressional power after the Jones case.* a. How far-reaching is the 13th Amendment power recognized in Jones? Is it an adequate constitutional basis for all conceivable civil rights legislation directed at private conduct? Did it in effect make the public accommodations and employment discrimination provisions of the 1964 Civil Rights Act superfluous? Did it do so especially in view of § 1981, another legacy of the Civil Rights Act of 1866?[1] See Runyon v. McCrary (1976; note 2b below).

b. Is there any action against racial discrimination that Congress may not consider a remedy for the "badges of servitude"? May Congress deal with discrimination against groups other than blacks? See Note, 69 Colum.L.Rev. 1019 (1969), suggesting that the Jones reading indicates that "slavery" now includes "the second class citizenship imposed on members of disparate minority groups. [A] victim's people need not have been enslaved in order to invoke its protection. He need only be suffering today under conditions that could reasonably be called symptoms of a slave society."[2]

1. Justice Harlan noted, in a footnote at another point, that the 14th Amendment "state action" argument—not reached by the majority in Jones—had emphasized "the respondents' role as a housing developer who exercised continuing authority over a suburban housing complex with about 1,000 inhabitants."

2. Elsewhere in his opinion, Justice Harlan commented: "In effect, this Court, by its construction of § 1982, has extended the coverage of federal 'fair housing' laws far beyond that which Congress in its wisdom chose to provide in the Civil Rights Act of 1968."

1. As noted at p. 858 above, § 1981 guarantees all persons "the same right [to] make and enforce contracts, to sue, be parties, give evidence, and to the full and equal benefits of all laws and proceedings for the security of persons and property as is enjoyed by white citizens."

2. Cf. Note, "The 'New' 13th [Amendment]," 82 Harv.L.Rev. 1294 (1969), and Calhoun, "The 13th and 14th Amendments: Consti-

c. For an extensive criticism of the Jones majority's reading of history, see Fairman, Reconstruction and Reunion: 1864–1888, Part One (6 History of the Supreme Court of the United States) (1971).[3] Compare Levinson, Book Review, 26 Stan.L.Rev. 461 (1974), concluding that Fairman clearly demonstrates the "slipshod" nature of the majority's historical analysis but adding that its conclusion may nevertheless be warranted, "for the Civil Rights Act of 1866 *did* manifest, however imperfectly and ambivalently, a vision of a new order of freedom for the black man." The real issue, Levinson argues, is not whether the text of the law "dictated" the decision, but "whether the decision was *permitted*." On that issue, the historical background "need not be conclusive regarding its present application."[4]

2. *Modern interpretations of the 1866 Act.* a. The Court applied the newly discovered 1866 Act—and expanded its broad interpretation—in SULLIVAN v. LITTLE HUNTING PARK, INC., 396 U.S. 229 (1969). There, a "nonstock corporation" operated a community park and playground facilities for the benefit of residents in an area of Virginia. Subject to the board's approval, a member who rented his house could assign his share to his tenant. Sullivan leased his house to Freeman and assigned his membership share to him. The board "refused to approve the assignment, because Freeman was a Negro." Sullivan was expelled for protesting that decision. The Court found that Sullivan and Freeman could sue under § 1982 for damages and injunctive relief. Justice DOUGLAS' majority opinion, reversing a state court's dismissal of their action, found the corporation's refusal an interference with the right to "lease" within the terms of the 1866 Act. He rejected the state court's finding that the case involved a private social club: "There was no plan or purpose of exclusiveness. It is open to every white person within the geographic area, there being no selective element other than race."[5]

Justice HARLAN's dissent, joined by Chief Justice Burger and Justice White, urged that certiorari be dismissed as improvidently granted because of the "complexities" under the 1866 Act and the existence of the 1968 fair housing law. He noted that the Court had gone beyond the Jones case, above, "(1) by implying a private right to damages for violations of § 1982; (2) by interpreting § 1982 to prohibit a community recreation association from withholding, on the basis of race, approval of an assignment of a membership that was transferred incident to a lease of real property; and (3) by deciding that a white person who is expelled from a recreation association 'for the advocacy of [a

tutional Authority for Federal Legislation Against Private Sex Discrimination," 61 Minn.L. Rev. 313 (1977).

In McDonald v. Sante Fe Trail Transportation Co., 427 U.S. 273 (1976), the Court implicitly suggested that congressional power under the 13th Amendment can be invoked to curb discrimination against whites. In his majority opinion, Justice Marshall found that § 1981 (as well as the 1964 Civil Rights Act) "affords protection from racial discrimination in private employment to white persons as well as nonwhites." The Court's discussion was limited to statutory issues; the implicit constitutional premise—that the antislavery Amendment could benefit races who had never been enslaved—was not discussed by the Justices. (The Court merely noted that it "has previously ratified the view that Congress is authorized under the [13th] Amendment to legislate in regard to 'every race and individual.'" The Court emphasized, moreover, that it was not

considering the constitutionality of affirmative action programs.)

3. See also Casper, "Jones v. Mayer: Clio, Bemused and Confused Muse," 1968 Sup.Ct.Rev. 89; compare Kohl, "The Civil Rights Act of 1866, Its Hour Come Round at Last," 55 Va.L. Rev. 272 (1969).

4. Similar arguments have been made to justify modern interpretations of equal protection. See Bickel, "The Original Understanding and the Segregation Decision," 69 Harv.L.Rev. 1 (1955). Assuming such open-ended readings are appropriate for constitutional provisions, are they also appropriate for legislative enactments? Compare Weber (1979; p. 785 above).

5. Recall also the reliance on congressional power under the 13th Amendment in justifying the application of § 1985(c) in Griffin v. Breckenridge (1971; p. 918 above).

Negro's] cause' has 'standing' to maintain an action for relief under § 1982." He commented, moreover: "[Lurking] in the background are grave constitutional issues should § 1982 be extended too far into some types of private discrimination." He cited the Civil Rights Cases. What are those "grave constitutional issues"? Which concerns of the Civil Rights Cases are relevant to 13th Amendment legislation? There is no state action limitation under the 13th Amendment. Is there nevertheless a limitation stemming from the privacy and associational interests of the discriminator? Recall the comments at p. 866 above, on balancing the competing interests of the discriminator and the victim. Is that variety of balancing relevant to 13th Amendment interpretation? Was there such balancing in Runyon, which follows?

b. In RUNYON v. McCRARY, 427 U.S. 160 (1976), the Court held that § 1981 (derived from the 1866 Act; see footnote 1) "prohibits private, commercially operated, nonsectarian schools from denying admission to prospective students because they are Negroes" and that § 1981 was constitutional as so applied. Justice STEWART's majority opinion relied on his approach in Jones for the statutory interpretation, and he found no violation of "constitutionally protected rights of free association and privacy, or a parent's right to direct the education of his children." With respect to freedom of association, he noted that "it may be assumed that parents have a First Amendment right to send their children to educational institutions that promote the belief that racial segregation is desirable, and that the children have an equal right to attend such institutions." But "it does not follow that the *practice* of excluding racial minorities from such institutions is also protected by the same principle." With respect to privacy, he stated that "it does not follow that because government is [largely] precluded from regulating the child-bearing decision, it is similarly restricted [from] regulating the implementation of parental decisions concerning a child's education." Nor could he find any infringement of any "parental right" as recognized in such cases as Meyer (1923; p. 502 above) and Yoder (1972; p. 1521 below).[6]

Justice WHITE's dissent, joined by Justice Rehnquist, argued that, despite the broad reading of § 1982 in Jones, § 1981 ought not to be given the majority's construction. He argued that the legislative history of § 1981 "confirms that the statute means what it says and no more, i.e., that it outlaws any legal rule disabling any person from making or enforcing a contract, but does not prohibit private racially motivated refusals to contract." The holding, he added, "threatens to embark the judiciary on a treacherous course. [W]hites and blacks will undoubtedly choose to form a variety of associational relationships pursuant to [racially exclusionary contracts]. Social clubs, black and white, and associations designed to further the interests of blacks or whites are but two examples. [As] the associational or contractual relationships become more private, the pressures to hold § 1981 inapplicable to them will increase. Imaginative judicial construction of the word 'contract' is foreseeable; [13th Amendment] limitations on Congress' power to ban 'badges and incidents of slavery' may be discovered; the doctrine of the right to association may be bent to cover a given situation. [Courts] will be called upon to balance sensitive policy considerations against each other, [all] under the guise of 'construing' a statute. This is a task appropriate for the legislature, not for the judiciary." (He added that he did not "question at this point" the congressional power to

6. In light of the broad readings of §§ 1981 and 1982 by the modern Court, consider the extent to which the revived 1866 laws in effect make unnecessary not only the modern laws against racial discrimination but also the struggles regarding state action theories in the cases in sec. 2 above. See Henkin, "On Drawing Lines," 82 Harv.L.Rev. 63 (1968). Bear in mind, however, that state action analysis remained significant outside the race discrimination area, as noted earlier.

ban racial discrimination in private school admission decisions; but "as I see it, Congress has not yet chosen to exercise that power.")[7]

c. Do §§ 1981 and 1982 require a finding of purposeful discrimination to justify recovery? Although that was the question on which certiorari had been granted in Memphis v. Greene (1981; noted in chap. 9, at p. 711), the majority did not reach the issue. However, Justice White's separate opinion argued that "[p]urposeful racial discrimination" was required under § 1982. (Justice Marshall disagreed.) The issue was in effect settled by the full Court a year later, in General Building Contractors Ass'n v. Pennsylvania, 458 U.S. 375 (1982), where Justice Rehnquist's majority opinion held that a suit under § 1981 requires "proof of discriminatory intent" and does not reach "practices that merely result in a disproportionate impact on a particular class."[8] Justice Marshall's dissent, joined by Justice Brennan, insisted that there was nothing in the statutory language implying that "a right denied because of sheer insensitivity, or a pattern of conduct that disproportionately burdens the protected class of persons, is entitled to any less protection than one denied because of racial animus." Moreover, he argued that the majority had "virtually ignore[d] Congress' broad remedial purposes." He claimed, finally, that the majority had "[shut] its eyes to reality, ignoring the manner in which racial discrimination most often infects our society. Today, although flagrant examples of intentional discrimination still exist, discrimination more often occurs 'on a more sophisticated and subtle level,' the effects of which are often as cruel and 'devastating as the most crude form of discrimination.'"

SECTION 4. CONGRESSIONAL POWER TO CHANGE THE CONTENT OF CONSTITUTIONAL RIGHTS?—"REMEDIAL" AND "SUBSTANTIVE" POWER UNDER § 5 OF THE 14TH AMENDMENT

Introduction. Historically, most of the laws enacted by Congress under its powers to "enforce" the 14th and 15th Amendments were clearly "remedial":

7. In separate concurrences, Justices STEVENS and POWELL indicated that, if the question were a new one, they would agree with Justice White's statutory construction. But they thought the broad Jones view of § 1982 was indistinguishable, and that Jones should not be overruled at this late date. That, Justice Stevens stated, "would be a significant step backwards" and would be "contrary to my understanding of the mores of today." Justice Powell, moreover, warned about an excessively broad construction of the holding: he insisted that it did not imply "the intrusive investigation into the motives of every refusal to contract by a private citizen that is suggested by the dissent." Some contracts are so personal "as to have a discernible rule of exclusivity which is inoffensive to § 1981." He added that in certain personal contractual relationships, such as those "where the offeror selects those with whom he desires to bargain on an individualized basis, or where the contract is the foundation of a close association (such as, for example, that between an employer and a private tutor, babysitter, or housekeeper), there is reason to assume that, although the choice by the offeror is selective, it reflects 'a purpose of exclusiveness' other than the desire to bar members of the Negro race. Such a purpose, certainly in most cases, would invoke associational rights long respected." This case, however, involved strictly commercial schools. "A small kindergarten or music class, operated on the basis of personal invitations extended to a limited number of pre-identified students, for example, would present a far different case." There was no "bright line" to identify contracts within § 1981, but this case "is clearly on one side of the line [and] the kindergarten and music school examples are clearly on the other side. [The] open offer to the public generally involved [in this case] is simply not a 'private' contract" in the sense of § 1981."

On the limits associational rights may place on governmental power to ban discriminations by private entities, recall also the discussion in chap. 8 of Roberts v. United States Jaycees (1984; p. 565), permitting application of a state ban on sex discrimination to a formerly all-male national civic organization.

8. There were also separate opinions by Justice Stevens and by Justice O'Connor, joined by Justice Blackmun.

Congress simply provided enforcement mechanisms to implement judicially declared rights. For example, the post-Civil War "under color of law" criminal and civil provisions, now § 242 and § 1983, afforded remedies for the deprivation of rights as secured by the Constitution and interpreted by the Court. The Guest case suggested a potentially broader congressional authority: the authority to extend the reach of the 14th Amendment to cover private behavior not within the state action concept delineated by the Court. But even there, Congress did not purport to modify the *content* of the rights it protected. This section examines congressional authority to go beyond that: not merely to provide sanctions against practices independently held unconstitutional under Court-announced doctrine, but also to determine on its own that certain practices are unlawful even though no court has found them unconstitutional.

This novel variety of congressional action has arisen largely in the voting rights context.[1] Most of the cases below involve the Voting Rights Act, first adopted in 1965 and extended (and expanded) since. Thus, in South Carolina v. Katzenbach (1966; p. 933 below), the Court sustained a provision, applicable largely to the South, suspending literacy tests—even though the Lassiter case (1959; p. 933 below) had unanimously rejected an on-the-face equal protection attack on literacy tests. Oregon v. Mitchell (1970; p. 953 below) unanimously sustained the nationwide suspension of literacy tests accomplished by the 1970 Act: that was not seen as a significant extension of the South Carolina case. Those laws were sustained on the view that Congress had enacted valid "remedial" legislation—albeit "remedial" actions more far-reaching than the traditional ones. Katzenbach v. Morgan (1966; p. 946 below) upheld another provision of the 1965 Act, barring literacy tests for Puerto Ricans educated in Spanish-language schools—even though, in a companion case, Cardona v. Power (1966; p. 950 below), the Court avoided deciding whether the application of New York's English literacy requirement to those literate in Spanish was unconstitutional under the equal protection clause. The Morgan case was more difficult to explain on a "remedial" rationale; and Justice Brennan's majority opinion indeed contained controversial language indicating that Congress had some power to determine on its own the substantive content of constitutional rights. Morgan—in passages suggesting that congressional power could be "substantive," not merely "remedial"—suggested great judicial deference not only to congressional creation of remedies but also to congressional refashioning of rights.

The controversial "substantive" theory suggested by Morgan has produced extensive commentary on and off the Court. Justice Brennan's Morgan opinion sought to limit it to "expansions" of constitutional rights: he insisted in a footnote that Congress could only expand, not "dilute," rights. But others have argued that his bases for recognizing a congressional "substantive" power can cut both ways; and that, if Congress can in fact dilute Court-delineated rights, Morgan's new congressional authority runs counter to the views of judicial autonomy in Marbury v. Madison and Cooper v. Aaron. In Oregon v. Mitchell (1970; p. 953 below), the Morgan rationale did not prove adequate to sustain a congressional effort to lower the minimum voting age in state elections to 18: there was no majority for the broadest possible reading of Morgan. But a decade after that apparent confinement of Morgan, the Court sustained a farreaching aspect of the Voting Rights Act in Rome v. United States (1980; p. 937 below). The Rome case held that Congress, acting under its 15th Amendment enforcement power, could constitutionally bar a city from making any governmental changes that were found to be racially discriminatory in

---

1. Because of that voting rights context, these cases frequently involve the 15th as well as the 14th Amendment.

effect, even though the city had not engaged in any purposeful discrimination for nearly two decades. But the Court did *not* rely on the novel "substantive" power of Morgan. Instead, the Rome decision rested on a broad reading of the expanded "remedial" power recognized in the South Carolina case.[2]

This section focuses on that series of cases and their implications. How farreaching is congressional power under the enforcement clauses of the 14th and 15th Amendments? To what extent does it go beyond the providing of sanctions for violations of judicially-declared rights? Can the provisions sustained in the Voting Rights Act cases beginning with South Carolina v. Katzenbach be justified as merely "remedial," as earlier enactments undoubtedly were? Are the suggestions in the Morgan case truly distinguishable as recognizing a "substantive" rather than "remedial" power of Congress? If the "remedial" power is read as broadly as in the Rome case, does it make resort to the apparently more controversial "substantive" rationale of Morgan unnecessary? Can Congress, in short, play a powerful role in determining the effective content of constitutional rights by asserting the power to act "remedially," without needing to resort to a "substantive" rationale? In what contexts outside the voting rights area may Congress invoke the broad powers recognized in the Rome and Morgan cases? In pursuing those questions, this section begins with the background of judicial and congressional action in the voting rights field culminating in the statutory provisions sustained on "remedial" grounds in the cases from South Carolina to Rome.

PROTECTION OF VOTING RIGHTS: THE BACKGROUND AND THE SOUTH CAROLINA CASE

1. *Chief Justice Warren's summary of the background.* [Prior to the Voting Rights Act of 1965, congressional legislation directed against racial discrimination in voting was quite clearly remedial. Congress merely provided enforcement mechanisms; the rights guaranteed were stated in the very general terms of the Constitution.[1] Delineation of the content of the rights was left to the courts; and implementation was left to litigation. Frustration with that case-by-case approach led to the enactment of the 1965 Act. Chief Justice Warren's opinion in South Carolina v. Katzenbach, 383 U.S. 301 (1966; further considered below), contained a summary of the "historical experience" that led Congress to two basic conclusions: "First: Congress felt itself confronted by an insidious and pervasive evil which had been perpetuated in certain parts of our country through unremitting and ingenious defiance of the Constitution. Second: Congress concluded that the unsuccessful remedies which it had prescribed in the past would have to be replaced by sterner and more elaborate measures in order to satisfy the clear commands of the 15th Amendment." Excerpts from the Chief Justice's account of the historical background follow:]

The 15th Amendment [was] ratified in 1870. Promptly thereafter Congress passed the Enforcement Act of 1870, which made it a crime for public officers and private persons to obstruct exercise of the right to vote. [E]nforcement of

---

2. Recall also the reliance on Morgan and Oregon in the 1980 decision in Fullilove v. Klutznick (chap. 9, p. 769 above). More recently, however, a majority endorsed Justice Brennan's anti-dilution footnote in Morgan and insisted that neither Congress nor a state can validate a law that denies the rights guaranteed by the 14th Amendment. See Justice O'Connor's majority opinion in Mississippi University for Women v. Hogan (1982; p. 660 above and p. 971 below).

1. See, e.g., the echoing of the terms of the 15th Amendment in the only remnant of the post-Civil War voting laws that remained on the books as of 1957, 42 U.S.C. § 1971(a): "All citizens of the United States who are otherwise qualified to vote at any election by the people in any State [shall] be entitled [to] vote at all such elections, without distinction of race, color, or previous condition of servitude; any constitution, law, custom, usage, or regulation of any State [to] the contrary notwithstanding."

the laws became spotty and ineffective, and most of their provisions were repealed in 1894. [Meanwhile], beginning in 1890, the States of Alabama, Georgia, Louisiana, Mississippi, North Carolina, South Carolina, and Virginia enacted tests still in use which were specifically designed to prevent Negroes from voting. Typically, they made the ability to read and write a registration qualification and also required completion of a registration form. These laws were based on the fact that as of 1890 in each of the named States, more than two-thirds of the adult Negroes were illiterate while less than one-quarter of the adult whites were unable to read or write. At the same time, alternate tests were prescribed in all of the named States to assure that white illiterates would not be deprived of the franchise. These included grandfather clauses, property qualifications, "good character" tests, and the requirement that registrants "understand" or "interpret" certain matter. The course of subsequent 15th Amendment litigation [2] [demonstrates] the variety and persistence of these and similar institutions designed to deprive Negroes of the right to vote. [According-ing to] the evidence in recent Justice Department voting suits, [discriminatory enforcement of voting qualifications] is now the principal method used to bar Negroes from the polls. [White] applicants for registration have often been excused altogether from the literacy and understanding tests or have been given easy versions, have received extensive help from voting officials, and have been registered despite serious errors in their answers. Negroes, on the other hand, have typically been required to pass difficult versions of all the tests, without any outside assistance and without the slightest error. The good-morals require-ment is so vague and subjective that it has constituted an open invitation to abuse at the hands of voting officials. [In recent years], Congress has repeated-ly tried to cope with the problem by facilitating case-by-case litigation against voting discrimination. The Civil Rights Act of 1957 authorized the Attorney General to seek injunctions against public and private interference with the right to vote on racial grounds. Perfecting amendments in the Civil Rights Act of 1960 permitted the joinder of States as parties defendant, gave the Attorney General access to local voting records, and authorized courts to register voters in areas of systematic discrimination. Title I of the Civil Rights Act of 1964 expedited the hearing of voting cases before three-judge courts and outlawed some of the tactics used to disqualify Negroes from voting in federal elections. [The] previous legislation has proved ineffective for a number of reasons. Voting suits are unusually onerous to prepare. [Litigation] has been exceeding-ly slow. [Even when] favorable decisions have finally been obtained, some of the States affected have merely switched to discriminatory devices not covered by the federal decrees or have enacted difficult new tests. [Alternatively], certain local officials have defied and evaded court orders or have simply closed their registration offices to freeze the voting rolls.

2. *The constitutional status of literacy tests before the 1965 Act.* It was against that background that Congress enacted the Voting Rights Act of 1965 "to rid the country of racial discrimination in voting." One controversial provision of that "complex scheme of stringent remedies aimed at areas where voting discrimination has been most flagrant" suspended literacy tests in covered localities—including many localities where there had been no judicial finding of discriminatory practices. In that sense, Congress moved beyond where the

---

2. The Chief Justice summarized the Court decisions as follows: "Grandfather clauses were invalidated in Guinn v. United States, 238 U.S. 347, and Myers v. Anderson, 238 U.S. 368. Procedural hurdles were struck down in Lane v. Wilson, 307 U.S. 268. The white primary was outlawed in Smith v. Allwright, 321 U.S. 649, and Terry v. Adams, 345 U.S. 461. Improper challenges were nullified in United States v. Thomas, 362 U.S. 58. Racial gerrymandering was forbidden by Gomillion v. Lightfoot, 364 U.S. 339. Finally, discriminatory application of voting tests was condemned in Schnell v. Davis, 336 U.S. 933; Alabama v. United States, 371 U.S. 37; and Louisiana v. United States, 380 U.S. 145."

courts had gone. A few years earlier, the Court had refused to strike down literacy tests on their face. In LASSITER v. NORTHAMPTON ELECTION BD., 360 U.S. 45 (1959), Justice DOUGLAS, for a unanimous Court, rejected a black citizen's attack on the North Carolina literacy test. The operative part of the state provision stated: "Every person presenting himself for registration shall be able to read and write any section of the [North Carolina] Constitution in the English language." Justice Douglas stated: "The States have long been held to have broad powers to determine the conditions under which the right of suffrage may be exercised, absent of course the discrimination which the Constitution condemns. [We] do not suggest that any standards which a State desires to adopt may be required of voters. But there is wide scope for exercise of its jurisdiction. Residence requirements, age, previous criminal record are obvious examples indicating factors which a State may take into consideration in determining the qualifications of voters. The ability to read and write likewise has some relation to standards designed to promote intelligent use of the ballot. Literacy and illiteracy are neutral on race, creed, color, and sex, as reports around the world show. Literacy and intelligence are obviously not synonymous. Illiterate people may be intelligent voters. Yet in our society where newspapers, periodicals, books, and other printed matter canvass and debate campaign issues, a State might conclude that only those who are literate should exercise the franchise. It was said last century in Massachusetts that a literacy test was designed to insure an 'independent and intelligent' exercise of the right of suffrage. North Carolina agrees. We do not sit in judgment on the wisdom of that policy. We cannot say, however, that it is not an allowable one measured by constitutional standards. Of course a literacy test, fair on its face, may be employed to perpetuate that discrimination which the 15th Amendment was designed to uproot. No such influence is charged here." [3] But Lassiter proved no obstacle to Congress' broad-gauged moves against literacy tests that began 1965.

     3. *The South Carolina case.* SOUTH CAROLINA v. KATZENBACH, 383 U.S. 301 (1966), sustained several controversial provisions of the Voting Rights Act of 1965, largely directed at racial discrimination in the South, as a proper exercise of congressional power under § 2 of the 15th Amendment.[4] In his general passages, Chief Justice WARREN stated: "Congress may use any rational means to effectuate the constitutional prohibition of racial discrimination in voting. The basic test to be applied [under § 2] is the same as in all cases concerning the express powers of Congress with relation to the reserved powers of the States. [McCulloch.]" That led him to conclude: "[We] reject South Carolina's argument that Congress may appropriately do no more than to forbid violations of the 15th Amendment in general terms—that the task of fashioning specific remedies or of applying them to particular localities must necessarily be left entirely to the courts. Congress is not circumscribed by any such artificial rules under § 2 of the 15th Amendment. [Cf. Gibbons v.

---

3. Justice Douglas added: "On the other hand, a literacy test may be unconstitutional on its face," and the Court had so ruled. He referred to Davis v. Schnell, 81 F.Supp. 872 (D.Ala.1949), affirmed, 336 U.S. 933 (1949). There, the test was the citizen's ability to "understand and explain" an Article of the U.S. Constitution. That was struck down on its face because the "legislative setting [and] the great discretion it vested in the registrar made it clear that [the] literacy requirement was merely a device to make racial discrimination easy." Justice Douglas added that no such discriminatory inference could be made about the North Carolina test challenged in Lassiter: that seemed to be

"one fair way of determining whether a person is literate, not a calculated scheme to lay springes for the citizen. Certainly we cannot condemn it on its face as a device unrelated to the desire of North Carolina to raise the standards for people of all races who cast the ballot." (In Lassiter, the Court evidently applied a rationality standard. On the Court's later "strict scrutiny" of state restrictions on voting, recall chap. 9, p. 808 above.)

4. Only a brief summary of the South Carolina case appears here; additional aspects are discussed in the Rome case (1980; p. 937 below).

Ogden.]" That broad discretion validated the "inventive" use of congressional powers here. Prescribing remedies for voting discrimination "which go into effect without any need for prior adjudication" was "clearly a legitimate response to the problem, for which there is ample precedent under other constitutional provisions. [See McClung; Darby (commerce power cases in chap. 3 above).]" Congress "had found that case-by-case litigation was inadequate to combat widespread and persistent discrimination in voting"; accordingly, it "might well decide to shift the advantage of time and inertia from the perpetrators of the evil to its victims." And the "specific remedies" in the Act were "appropriate means of combating the evil."

Turning to those specific remedies, the Court focused on the coverage formula for determining the localities in which literacy tests and similar voting qualifications were to be suspended for a period of five years.[5] The Court found that the areas covered by the Act "were an appropriate target for the new remedies." He noted that the law "intentionally confines these remedies to a small number of States and political subdivisions which in most instances were familiar to Congress by name." Congress had properly chosen "to limit its attention to the geographic areas where immediate action seemed necessary." The Court was not persuaded by the argument "that the coverage formula is awkwardly designed in a number of respects and that it disregards various local conditions which have nothing to do with racial discrimination." The Chief Justice replied: "Congress began work with reliable evidence [in judicial proceedings and in findings by the Justice Department and the Civil Rights Commission] of actual voting discrimination in a great majority of the [areas] affected by the new remedies of the Act. The formula eventually evolved to describe these areas was relevant to the problem of voting discrimination, and Congress was therefore entitled to infer a significant danger of the evil in the few remaining States and political subdivisions covered." All of the areas for which there was evidence of actual voting discrimination shared the "two characteristics incorporated by Congress into the coverage formula." The Chief Justice elaborated: "Tests and devices are relevant to voting discrimination because of their long history as a tool for perpetrating the evil; a low voting rate is pertinent for the obvious reason that widespread disenfranchisement must inevitably affect the number of actual voters. Accordingly, the coverage formula is rational in both practice and theory. It was therefore permissible to impose the new remedies on the few remaining States and political subdivisions covered by the formula, at least in the absence of proof that they have been free of substantial voting discrimination in recent years." And it was "irrelevant that the coverage formula excludes certain localities which do not employ voting tests and devices but for which there is evidence of voting discrimination by other means": "Legislation need not deal with all phases of a problem in the same way, so long as the distinctions drawn have some basis in practical experience." Moreover, the existence of the termination procedure was an adequate safeguard against overbreadth of the Act. And South Carolina's

5. Under that formula, the Act was applicable to any state or political subdivision "for which two findings have been made: (1) the Attorney General has determined that on November 1, 1964, it maintained a 'test or device,' and (2) the Director of the Census has determined that less than 50 percent of its voting-age residents were registered on November 1, 1964, or voted in the presidential election of November, 1964." These findings were not reviewable. Statutory coverage could be terminated if the covered area obtained a declaratory judgment from the District Court of the District of Colum-

bia, "determining that tests and devices have not been used during the preceding five years to abridge the franchise on racial grounds." (See the Rome case, p. 937 below.) Pursuant to administrative determinations, a number of areas were promptly brought under the coverage of the Act. (The areas that had been brought under the Act by the time this case reached the Court were South Carolina, Alabama, Alaska, Georgia, Louisiana, Mississippi, Virginia, 26 counties in North Carolina, and three counties in Arizona, one county in Hawaii, and one county in Idaho.)

argument "that these termination procedures are a nullity because they impose an impossible burden of proof" were not persuasive. The rejection of the constitutional attack on literacy tests in Lassiter did not bar these congressional remedies: Lassiter itself had recognized that literacy tests could be used as discriminatory devices. The record here showed "that in most of the States [covered], various tests and devices have been instituted with the purpose of disenfranchising Negroes, have been framed in such a way as to facilitate this aim, and have been administered in a discriminatory fashion for many years. Under these circumstances, the 15th Amendment has clearly been violated."

In the covered areas, the Act suspended literacy tests for five years from the last occurrence of substantial voting discrimination. Moreover, § 5 barred any new "standard, practice, or procedure with respect to voting" pending scrutiny by federal authorities to determine whether their use would violate the 15th Amendment.[6] These were found to be "legitimate" remedies, since continuance of the tests "would freeze the effect of past discrimination in favor of unqualified white registrants" and since Congress knew that some of the covered states "had resorted to the extraordinary strategem of contriving new rules of various kinds for the sole purpose of perpetuating voting discrimination in the face of adverse federal court decrees."[7]

4. *The nationwide suspension of literacy tests in the 1970 Act and later extensions of the Voting Rights Act.* The Voting Rights Act Amendments of 1970 not only extended the 1965 Act for five years but added a number of new provisions. In one of the 1970 provisions, Congress suspended the use of literacy tests on a nationwide basis, not just in the areas subject to the coverage formula of the 1965 Act. The 1970 Act produced another major Court decision on congressional powers. In Oregon v. Mitchell (1970; p. 953 below), although the Court divided on all other provisions of the 1970 Act (and held the 18 year-old-vote provision for state elections unconstitutional), it was unanimous in one respect: every Justice found the nationwide literacy test suspension constitutional. (The various justifications offered by the Justices are considered in Rome, p. 937 below.) Even Justice Harlan, the member of the Warren Court who took the most restrictive view of congressional powers under the post-Civil War Amendments, agreed that the expanded reach of the literacy test provision fell within the "remedial" powers of Congress.[8] Other Justices found additional

6. The impact of § 5 is examined at length in the Rome case (1980; p. 937 below). [Other provisions of the Act included authorization for the appointment of federal examiners to list qualified applicants as "eligible voters." That, like all other remedies considered by the Court, was found to be a "valid means for carrying out the commands of the 15th Amendment."]

In a series of subsequent cases, the majority gave a broad reading to the types of changes subject to the prior approval requirement of § 5. See, e.g., Allen v. State Board of Elections, 393 U.S. 544 (1969), and Beer v. United States, 425 U.S. 130 (1976). See also the UJO case (chap. 9, p. 752 above). These broad readings of § 5 are further discussed in Rome, p. 937 below.

In the South Carolina case, a partial dissent by Justice BLACK objected to § 5, the prior approval requirement. That remedy, he insisted, utilized means "that conflict with the most basic principles of the Constitution": requiring states "to beg federal authorities to approve their policies [distorts] our constitutional structure." Moreover, the federal approval requirement conflicted with the "Republican Form of Govern-

ment" guarantee, Art. VI, § 4, since it created the impression that states were "little more than conquered provinces." (For an elaboration of views similar to some of Justice Black's, see the dissents in Rome, below.)

7. For an attempt by a county to reinstate a literacy test suspended pursuant to the Act, see Gaston County v. United States, 395 U.S. 285 (1969). Though the Court did not question the county's claim that it had administered its tests in a fair and impartial manner, it rejected the county's reinstatement effort in view of past unequal educational opportunities. (See the discussion in the Rome case, p. 937 below.)

8. Justice Harlan stated: "Despite the lack of evidence of specific instances of discriminatory application or effect, Congress could have determined that racial prejudice is prevalent throughout the Nation, and that literacy tests unduly lend themselves to discriminatory application, either conscious or unconscious. The danger of violation of § 1 of the [15th Amendment] was sufficient to authorize the exercise of congressional power under § 2. [While] a less sweeping approach in this delicate area might well have

justifications for the 1970 extension in the congressional interest in nationwide uniformity and in "this country's history of discriminatory educational opportunities in both the North and the South." [9]

been appropriate, the choice which Congress made was within the range of the reasonable." [Note also Justice Harlan's dissent in Morgan (1966; p. 946 below), where he distinguished South Carolina as involving merely "remedial" provisions. He claimed that the South Carolina decision involved "appropriate remedial legislation to cure an established violation of a constitutional command." The "substantive" rather than "remedial" power—reflected in his view in the majority opinion in Morgan—by contrast sought to determine "whether there has in fact been an infringement" of equal protection. That attempted distinction raises again the questions, considered in note 5 and pursued below, about the distinction between Congressional "remedial" and "substantive" powers.]

9. In 1975, the Voting Rights Act was once again amended, and extended for 7 years, until 1982. One of its provisions was to make permanent the nationwide ban on literacy tests.

The 1982 extension of the Voting Rights Act. With § 5 of the Voting Rights Act of 1965 scheduled to expire in August 1982, efforts began in Congress early in 1981 to extend it once again, this time for ten years. The debate began with consideration of § 5, the "preclearance" provision. But the focus of controversy soon shifted to § 2 and the issue of the appropriate standard of proof for identifying laws that "deny or abridge" the right to vote. The Court's ruling in 1980, in Mobile v. Bolden [discussed in Rogers v. Lodge (1981; p. 703 above)] had determined that § 2 was coextensive with equal protection standards and therefore required proof of discriminatory purpose, not merely discriminatory result. Civil rights groups, arguing for a "results" standard, maintained that the Court's purposefulness test imposed an unduly burdensome litigation obstacle. Supporters of the Court's decision countered that discrimination, by its very nature, must be intentional and that the "results" standard would eventually lead to the establishment of racial quotas and proportional representation in elections.

In November 1981, the House, siding with civil rights advocates, adopted the results standard for § 2 and indefinitely extended § 5's "preclearance" requirement. In the Senate, conservative lawmakers mounted strong opposition to the House's "results" language until Kansas Republican Robert Dole proposed a compromise. The Dole Compromise in effect endorsed judicial attention to "results" as one factor in the consideration of the "totality of circumstances" relevant to a § 2 discrimination claim. However, the Compromise qualified the results standard in order to mollify concerns about racial quotas and proportional representation. The amended version of § 2 resulting from that compromise provides, in § 2(a), that "[n]o voting qualification or prerequisite to voting or standard, practice, or procedure shall be imposed or applied [in] a manner which results in a denial or abridgement of the right [to] vote on account of race or color, or in contravention of the guarantees [provided in subsection (b)]." Sec. 2(b) stated that a violation of § 2(a) is established "if, based on the totality of circumstances, it is shown that the political processes leading to nomination or election [are] not equally open to participation by members of a [protected] class of citizens [in] that its members have less opportunity than other members of the electorate to participate in the political process and to elect representatives of their choice. The extent to which members of a protected class have been elected to office [is] one circumstance which may be considered: *Provided,* That nothing in this section establishes a right to have members of a protected class elected in numbers equal to their proportion in the population." [On the preclearance issue, the indefinite extension of § 5 by the House was reduced to 25 years. After 1984, moreover, a jurisdiction now subject to § 5 may "bail out" (under § 4) upon demonstrating a history of affirmative voting rights policies.] After nearly unanimous approval in both houses, the compromise extension of the Voting Rights Act was signed into law by President Reagan on June 29, 1982. See 96 Stat. 131. (Recall the discussion in the previous chapter about the "purpose"-"effect" distinction and on the 1982 extension of the Act, at p. 709 above.)

For a useful discussion of the underlying principles in conflict during the debate over the modification of § 2, and about the probable consequences of the extension, see Blumstein, "Defining and Proving Race Discrimination: Perspectives on the Purpose vs. Results Approach from the Voting Rights Act," 69 Va.L.Rev. 633 (1983). (Blumstein concludes that the amended § 2 "gives minorities an affirmative entitlement to ballot access but that Congress did not intend the revised [§ 2] to give minorities an affirmative entitlement to proportional representation." He states that Congress, in 1982, "found a race-based entitlement approach 'repugnant to our democratic principles.' [The] proposed principle of 'fair and effective political participation' should govern the Court's interpretation of section 2. [That principle rejects] race-based entitlements to actual governmental representation, but acknowledges a substantial public interest in enriching the political process by expanding the electorate.") Cf. Howard & Howard, "The Dilemma of the Voting Rights Act—Recognizing the Emerging Political Equality Norm," 83 Colum.L.Rev. 1615 (1983).

Is there any doubt about the constitutionality of the amended § 2 under the majority rationale in the Rome case, which follows? Under the analysis of Justice Rehnquist's dissent? Can the § 2 amendment be justified simply under the "remedial" rationale? Or must a justification

5. *Some questions about "remedial" legislation and the "remedial"-"substantive" distinction.* Was the "remedial" power of Congress asserted in the South Carolina case significantly different from that sustained in the earlier, more traditional civil rights laws? Can the exercise of congressional power sustained in South Carolina and Oregon be justified as "remedial"; or were those assertions of power practically indistinguishable from the more controversial "substantive" power suggested in Morgan, below? At the heart of the "remedial" case for the treatment of the literacy provisions in the 1965 and 1970 Acts is the premise that Congress acted on the basis of Court-endorsed rules that discriminatory "tests and devices" *are* unconstitutional. True, Lassiter refused to find literacy tests unconstitutional per se. But Chief Justice Warren did say in the South Carolina case, after examining the evidence before Congress: "Under these circumstances, the Fifteenth Amendment has clearly been violated." Can the South Carolina decision, then, be viewed as an implicit overruling of Lassiter, in view of the new information before Congress? Can a similar rationale support the Oregon expansion of the literacy test ban? The Rome case, which follows, takes an even broader view of "remedial" powers of Congress than South Carolina and Oregon had. Does Rome make it even more difficult to maintain a practical distinction between the reach of the "remedial" and "substantive" rationales? These questions should be borne in mind when examining Rome; and they will warrant renewed attention after examining the Morgan-related problems printed after Rome.

ROME v. UNITED STATES

446 U.S. 156, 100 S.Ct. 1548, 64 L.Ed.2d 119 (1980).

Mr. Justice MARSHALL delivered the opinion of the [Court].

At issue in this case is the constitutionality of the Voting Rights Act of 1965 [as amended] and its applicability to electoral changes and annexations made by the city of Rome, Ga. [In 1966, Rome's electoral system changed in several ways, as a result of a state law: e.g., each of the nine members of its city commission would be elected by majority rather than plurality vote, the number of wards would be reduced from nine to three, and each commissioner would henceforth be elected at-large to one of three posts established in each ward. Moreover, the city made a number of annexations to its territory between 1964 and 1975. Because Georgia had been designated a covered jurisdiction under the 1965 Act, the State and its municipalities were required to comply with the preclearance, prior approval provisions of § 5 of the Act. The Attorney General refused to approve the electoral changes, concluding that in a city such as Rome, with a predominantly white population and a norm of racial bloc voting, the changes would deprive black voters of the opportunity to elect a candidate of their choice.[1] The Attorney General also refused to preclear 13 of the annexations for purposes of city commission elections, finding that Rome had not carried its burden of proving that these annexations would not dilute the black vote. The city then sought declaratory relief in a three-judge District Court. That court rejected all of the city's challenges, finding that the disapproved changes and annexations, while not made for any discriminatory pur-

---

also draw on the "substantive" rationale of the Morgan case, below?

1. Under § 5, the Attorney General may clear a change in voting practice only if it "does not have the purpose *and* will not have the effect of denying or abridging the right to vote on account of race or color." (Emphasis added.) In the Rome case, the Attorney General found no forbidden "purpose" but relied on the "effect" provision.

pose, did have a discriminatory effect. The Supreme Court affirmed in a 6 to 3 decision.][2]

II. [The city contends that it] may exempt itself from the coverage of the Act. [The city] comes within the preclearance requirement of [§ 4(a)] because it is a political unit in a covered jurisdiction, the State of Georgia. [But § 4(a) also provides] a procedure for exemption from the Act. This so-called "bail out" provision allows a covered jurisdiction to escape the preclearance requirement of § 5 by bringing a declaratory judgment action before [a three-judge court] and proving that no "test or device" has been used in the jurisdiction "during the seventeen years preceding the filing of the action for the purpose or with the effect of denying or abridging the right to vote on account of race or color." The District Court refused to allow the city to "bail out" of the Act's coverage, holding that the political units of a covered jurisdiction cannot independently bring a § 4(a) bailout action. We agree [because of the] unambiguous congressional intent.

III. The appellants raise [several] issues of law in support of their contention that the Act may not properly be applied to the electoral changes and annexations disapproved by the Attorney General. [A. The city argues] that [§ 5] may not be read as prohibiting voting practices that have only a discriminatory effect. By describing the elements of discriminatory purpose and effect in the conjunctive, Congress plainly intended that a voting practice not be precleared unless *both* discriminatory purpose and effect are absent. Our decisions have consistently interpreted § 5 in this fashion. [The city urges] that we abandon this settled interpretation because in their view § 5, to the extent that it prohibits voting changes that have only a discriminatory effect, is unconstitutional. Because the statutory meaning and congressional intent are plain, [we] reject [the] suggestion that we engage in a saving construction and avoid the constitutional issues they raise. Instead, [we turn to the] constitutional contentions.

B. Congress passed the Act under [the 15th Amendment]. [The city claims] that § 1 of the Amendment prohibits only purposeful racial discrimination in voting, and that in enforcing that provision pursuant to § 2, Congress may not prohibit voting practices lacking discriminatory intent even if they are discriminatory in effect. We hold that, even if § 1 of the Amendment prohibits only purposeful discrimination, the prior decisions of this Court foreclose any argument that Congress may not, pursuant to § 2, outlaw voting practices that are discriminatory in effect.

The [city is] asking us to do nothing less than overrule our decision in [South Carolina, where] we upheld the constitutionality of the Act. [We there] examined the interplay between the judicial remedy created by § 1 of the Amendment and the legislative authority conferred by § 2. [Congress'] authority under § 2, [we] held, was no less broad than its authority under the Necessary and Proper Clause, see [McCulloch]. This authority, as applied by longstanding precedent to congressional enforcement of the Civil War Amendments, is defined in these terms: "'Whatever legislation is appropriate, that is, adapted to carry out the objects the [Civil War] amendments have in view, [if] not prohibited, is brought within the domain of congressional power.' Ex parte Virginia [100 U.S. 339 (1880)]." Applying this standard, the Court held that [the challenged provisions, including] the requirement that new voting rules

---

2. On the same day, the Court rejected a *constitutional* attack on the electoral system of Mobile, Ala., in Mobile v. Bolden, considered in Rogers v. Lodge (1982; p. 703 above). Since the Mobile case did not involve a change of a prior electoral system, it was not subject to § 5 of the Voting Rights Act; the attack rested mainly on the equal protection clause of the 14th Amendment. Four of the Justices in the Mobile majority found that the "purposeful discrimination" standard under the Constitution had not been met; § 5 of the Act, by contrast, is satisfied by a showing of either "effect" *or* "purpose."

must be precleared and must lack both discriminatory purpose and effect, [were] all appropriate methods for Congress to use to enforce the 15th Amendment.

The Court's treatment in [South Carolina] of the Act's ban on literacy tests demonstrates that, under the 15th Amendment, Congress may prohibit voting practices that have only a discriminatory effect. [In] upholding the Act's per se ban on [nondiscriminatory literacy tests] in South Carolina, the Court found no reason to overrule Lassiter. Instead, the Court recognized that the prohibition was an appropriate method of enforcing the 15th Amendment because for many years most of the covered jurisdictions had imposed such tests to effect voting discrimination and the continued use of even nondiscriminatory, fairly administered literacy tests would "freeze the effect" of past discrimination by allowing white illiterates to remain on the voting rolls while excluding illiterate Negroes. This holding makes clear that Congress may, under the authority of § 2 of the 15th Amendment, prohibit state action that, though in itself not violative of § 1, perpetuates the effects of past discrimination. Other decisions of this Court also recognize Congress' broad power to enforce the Civil War Amendments. [See Katzenbach v. Morgan and Oregon v. Mitchell. These cases follow, below.]

It is clear, then, that under § 2 of the 15th Amendment Congress may prohibit practices that in and of themselves do not violate § 1 of the Amendment, so long as the prohibitions attacking racial discrimination in voting are "appropriate," as that term is defined in [McCulloch] and Ex parte Virginia. In the present case, we hold that the Act's ban on electoral changes that are discriminatory in effect is an appropriate method of promoting the purposes of the 15th Amendment, even if it is assumed that § 1 of the Amendment prohibits only intentional discrimination in voting. Congress could rationally have concluded that, because electoral changes by jurisdictions with a demonstrable history of intentional racial discrimination in voting create the risk of purposeful discrimination,[3] it was proper to prohibit changes that have a discriminatory impact. We find no reason, then, to disturb Congress' considered judgment that banning electoral changes that have a discriminatory impact is an effective method of preventing States from " 'undo[ing] or defeat[ing] the rights recently won' by Negroes."

C. [The city next asserts] that, even if the 15th Amendment authorized Congress to enact the Voting Rights Act, that legislation violates principles of federalism articulated in National League of Cities v. Usery [1976; p. 170 above]. This contention necessarily supposes that [Usery] signifies a retreat from our decision in South Carolina. [The] decision in [Usery] was based solely on an assessment of congressional power under the Commerce Clause, and we explicitly reserved the question "whether different results might obtain if Congress seeks to affect integral operations of State governments by exercising authority granted it under other sections of the Constitution such [as] § 5 of the 14th Amendment." The answer to this question came four days later in Fitzpatrick v. Bitzer [1976; p. 173 above]. [Fitzpatrick] stands for the proposition that principles of federalism that might otherwise be an obstacle to congressional authority are necessarily overridden by the power to enforce the Civil War Amendments "by appropriate legislation." Those Amendments were specifically designed as an expansion of federal power and an intrusion on state sovereignty. Applying this principle, we hold that Congress had the authority to regulate state and local voting through the provisions of the Voting Rights Act.

[D.] The city contends in the alternative that, even if the Act and its preclearance requirement were appropriate means of enforcing the 15th Amendment in 1965, they had outlived their usefulness by 1975, when

---

3. See [South Carolina]. [Footnote by Justice Marshall.]

Congress extended the Act for another seven years. We decline this invitation to overrule Congress' judgment that the 1975 extension was warranted. In considering the 1975 extension, Congress acknowledged that, largely as a result of the Act, Negro voter registration had improved dramatically since 1965. Congress determined, however, [that significant] disparity persisted between the percentages of whites and Negroes registered in at least several of the covered jurisdictions. In addition, though the number of Negro elected officials had increased since 1965, most held only relatively minor positions [and] their number in the state legislatures fell far short of being representative of the number of Negroes residing in the covered jurisdictions. Congress concluded [that] extension of the Act was warranted. Congress [not] only determined that § 5 should be extended for another seven years, [but] gave that provision [a] ringing endorsement. [Congress'] considered determination that at least another seven years of statutory remedies were necessary to counter the perpetuation of 95 years of pervasive voting discrimination is both unsurprising and unassailable. The extension of the Act, then, was plainly a constitutional method of enforcing the 15th Amendment.

IV. Now that we have reaffirmed our holdings in [South Carolina], we must address [the] contentions that the 1966 electoral changes and the annexations disapproved by the Attorney General do not, in fact, have a discriminatory effect. [We] conclude that the District Court did not clearly err in finding that the city had failed to prove that the 1966 electoral changes would not dilute the effectiveness of the Negro vote in Rome.[4] [The lower court's holding is] consistent with our statement in Beer v. United States [425 U.S. 130 (1976)] that "the purpose of § 5 has always been to insure that no voting procedure changes would be made that would lead to retrogression in the position of racial minorities with respect to their effective exercise of the electoral process." [The] District Court also found that the city had failed to meet its burden of proving that the thirteen disapproved annexations did not dilute the Negro vote in Rome. [Particularly] in light of the inadequate evidence introduced by the city, this determination cannot be considered to be clearly erroneous.

[Affirmed.][5]

Mr. Justice POWELL, [dissenting].

The Court [holds] that no subdivision may bail out so long as its State remains subject to preclearance. [There is] more involved here than incorrect construction of the statute. The Court's interpretation of § 4(a) renders the Voting Rights Act unconstitutional as applied to the city of Rome. The preclearance requirement both intrudes on the prerogatives of state and local governments and abridges the voting rights of all citizens in States covered under the Act. Under § 2 of the 15th Amendment Congress may impose such constitutional deprivations only if it is acting to remedy violations of voting rights. See [South Carolina; Morgan (Harlan dissent).] In view of the District Court finding that Rome has not denied [the] voting rights of blacks, the 15th

---

4. Under § 5, the city bears the burden of proving lack of discriminatory purpose and effect. [Footnote by the Court.]

5. Justice BLACKMUN, who joined the Court's opinion, submitted a separate statement about the affirmance of the lower court's holding regarding the 13 disputed annexations. Justice Stevens, who also joined the Court's opinion, submitted a separate statement defending (in response to the dissents, below) the statutory and constitutional bases for the Act's "statewide rem-edy that denies local political units within a covered State the right to 'bail out' separately." With respect to the constitutional issue, he stated: "Congress has the constitutional power to regulate voting practices in Rome, so long as it has the power to regulate such practices in the entire State of Georgia. Since there is no claim that the entire State is entitled to relief from the federal restrictions, Rome's separate claim must fail."

Amendment provides no authority for continuing those deprivations until the entire State of Georgia satisfies the bailout standards of § 4(a).[1]

When this Court first sustained the [1965 Act], it recognized that preclearance under the Act implicates serious federalism concerns. [South Carolina] upheld the imposition of preclearance as a prophylactic measure based on the remedial power of Congress to enforce the 15th Amendment. But the Court emphasized that preclearance, like any remedial device, can be imposed only in response to some harm. When Congress approved the Act, the Court observed, there was "reliable evidence of actual voting discrimination in a great majority of the States and political subdivisions affected by the new remedies of the Act." Since the coverage formula in § 4(b) purported to identify accurately those jurisdictions that had engaged in voting discrimination, the imposition of preclearance was held to be justified "at least in the absence of proof that [the state or local government has] been free of substantial voting discrimination in recent years."[2] [South Carolina] emphasized, however, that a government subjected to preclearance could be relieved of federal oversight if voting discrimination in fact did not continue or materialize during the prescribed period. [As] long as the bailout option is available, there is less cause for concern that the [Act] may overreach congressional powers by imposing preclearance on a nondiscriminating government. Without bailout, the problem of constitutional authority for preclearance becomes acute.

The Court today decrees that the citizens of Rome will not have direct control over their city's voting practices until the entire State of Georgia can free itself from the Act's restrictions. Under the current interpretation of the word "State" in § 4(a), Georgia will have to establish not only that it has satisfied the standards in § 4(a), but also that each and every one of its political subdivisions meets those criteria. This outcome makes every city and county in Georgia a hostage to the errors, or even the deliberate intransigence, of a single subdivision.[3] Since the statute was enacted, only one State has succeeded in bailing out—Alaska in 1966, and again in 1971. That precedent holds out little or no hope for more populous States such as Georgia. [Today's] ruling therefore will seal off the constitutionally necessary safety valve in the [Act]. The preclearance requirement enforces a presumption against voting changes by certain state and local governments. If that presumption is restricted to those governments meeting § 4(b)'s coverage criteria, and if the presumption can be rebutted by a proper showing in a bailout suit, the Act may be seen, as the [South Carolina] Court saw it, as action by Congress at the limit of its authority under the 15th Amendment. But if governments like the city of Rome may not

---

1. In view of the narrower focus of my approach to the statutory and constitutional issues raised in this case, I do not reach the broad analysis offered by Mr. Justice Rehnquist's dissent. [Footnote by Justice Powell.]

2. [The] Court took a similar approach when it affirmed the temporary suspension of all literacy tests by Congress in 1970. Oregon v. Mitchell. The entire Court agreed with Mr. Justice Black's view that the congressional action was justified by the "long history of the discriminatory use of literacy tests to disenfranchise voters on account of their race." That history supported temporary suspension of those few literacy tests still in use, without providing any bailout-like option. In contrast, preclearance involves a broad restraint on all state and local voting practices, regardless of whether they have been, or even could be, used to discriminate. [Footnote by Justice Powell.]

3. The Court's position dictates this eccentric result by insisting that subdivisions in covered States can be relieved of preclearance only when their State bails out. In my view this also would cast serious doubt on the Act's constitutionality as applied to any State which could not bail out due to the failings of a single subdivision. A rational approach would treat the states and local governments independently for purposes of bailout. If subdivisions in Georgia were free to seek bailout on their own, then a bailout action by the State could properly focus on the State's voting policies. Then, if Georgia were entitled to bail out, preclearance would continue to apply to subdivisions that by their own noncompliance met the coverage criteria of § 4(b). Of course, the situation would be different if the State had contributed, overtly or covertly, to the subdivision's failure to comply. [Footnote by Justice Powell.]

bail out, the statute oversteps those limits. [If] there were reason to believe that today's decision would protect the voting rights of minorities in any way, perhaps this case could be viewed as one where the Court's ends justify dubious analytical means. But the District Court found, and no one denies, that for at least 17 years there has been no voting discrimination by [Rome]. Despite this record, the Court today continues federal rule over the most local decisions made by this small city in Georgia. Such an outcome must vitiate the incentive for any local government in a State covered by the Act to meet diligently the Act's requirements. Neither the Framers of the 15th Amendment nor the Congress that enacted the [Act] could have intended that result.

Mr. Justice REHNQUIST, with whom Mr. Justice STEWART joins, [dissenting].

[Rome] is prevented from instituting precisely the type of structural changes which the Court says Mobile may maintain consistently with the Civil War Amendments,[1] [because] Congress has prohibited these changes under the Voting Rights Act as an exercise of its "enforcement" power conferred by those Amendments. It is not necessary to hold that Congress is limited to merely providing a forum in which aggrieved plaintiffs may assert rights under the Civil War Amendments in order to disagree with the Court's decision permitting Congress to strait-jacket the city of Rome in this manner. [Congress] is granted only the power to "enforce" by "appropriate" legislation the limitations on state action embodied in those Amendments. While the presumption of constitutionality is due to any act of a coordinate branch of the Federal Government or of one of the States, it is this Court which is ultimately responsible for deciding challenges to the exercise of power by those entities. [Marbury; Nixon.] Today's decision is nothing less than a total abdication of that authority, rather than an exercise of the deference due to a coordinate branch of the [government].[2]

While I agree with Mr. Justice Powell's conclusion that requiring localities to *submit* to preclearance is a significant intrusion on local autonomy, it is an even greater intrusion on that autonomy to *deny* preclearance sought. The facts of this case signal the necessity for this Court to carefully scrutinize the alleged source of congressional power to intrude so deeply in the governmental structure of [cities]. There are three theories of congressional enforcement power relevant to this case. First, it is clear that if the proposed changes would violate the Constitution, Congress could certainly prohibit their implementation. It has never been seriously maintained, however, that Congress can do no more than the judiciary to enforce the Amendments' commands. Thus, if the electoral changes in issue do not violate the Constitution, as judicially interpreted, it must be determined whether Congress could nevertheless appropriately prohibit these changes under the other two theories of congressional power. Under the second theory, Congress can act remedially to enforce the judicially established substantive prohibitions of the Amendments. If not properly remedial, the exercise of this power could be sustained only if this Court accepts the premise of the third theory that Congress has the authority under its enforcement powers to determine, without more, that electoral changes with a disparate impact on race violate the Constitution, in which case Congress by a legislative Act could effectively amend the Constitution. I think it is apparent that neither of the first two theories for sustaining the exercise of congressional power support this application of the Voting Rights Act. After our decision in

---

1. Mobile v. Bolden, decided on the same day as Rome, is considered in Rogers v. Lodge (1982; p. 703 above).

2. [The] nature of the enforcement powers conferred by the 14th and 15th Amendments has always been treated as coextensive. For this reason, it is not necessary to differentiate between the 14th and 15th Amendment powers for the purposes of this opinion. [Footnote by Justice Rehnquist.]

[Mobile] there is little doubt that Rome has not engaged in *constitutionally* prohibited conduct. I also do not believe that prohibition of these changes can genuinely be characterized as a remedial exercise of congressional enforcement powers. Thus, the result of the Court's holding is that Congress effectively has the power to determine for itself that this conduct violates the Constitution. This result violates previously well-established distinctions between the Judicial Branch and the Legislative or Executive Branches of the Federal Government.

A. If the enforcement power is construed as a "remedial" grant of authority, it is this Court's duty to ensure that a challenged congressional act does no more than "enforce" the limitations on state power established in the 14th and 15th Amendments. The Court has not resolved the question of whether it is an appropriate exercise of remedial power for Congress to prohibit local governments from instituting structural changes in their government, which, although not racially motivated, will have the effect of decreasing the ability of a black voting bloc to elect a black candidate. This Court has found, as a matter of statutory interpretation, that Congress intended to prohibit governmental changes on the basis of no more than disparate impact under the [Act]. These cases, however, have never directly presented the constitutional questions implicated by the lower court finding in this case that the city has engaged in no purposeful discrimination in enacting these changes, or otherwise, for almost two decades. In none of these cases was the Court squarely presented with a constitutional challenge to congressional power to prohibit state electoral practices after the locality has *disproved* the existence of any purposeful discrimination. The cases in which this Court has actually examined the constitutional questions relating to congressional exercise of its powers [also] did not purport to resolve this issue.[3] But the principles which can be distilled from those precedents require the conclusion that the limitations on state power at issue cannot be sustained as a remedial exercise of power. While [the] Amendments prohibit only purposeful discrimination, the decisions of this Court have recognized that in some circumstances, congressional prohibition of state or local action which is not purposefully discriminatory may nevertheless be appropriate remedial legislation under the [Amendments]. See [e.g., Oregon]. Those circumstances, however, are not without judicial limits. These decisions indicate that congressional prohibition of some conduct which may not itself violate the Constitution is "appropriate" legislation "to enforce" [the] Amendments if that prohibition is necessary to remedy prior constitutional violations by the governmental unit, or if necessary to effectively prevent purposeful discrimination by a governmental unit. In both circumstances, Congress would still be legislating in response to the incidence of state action violative of [the] Amendments. These precedents are carefully formulated around a historic tenet of the law that in order to invoke a remedy, there must be a wrong—and under a remedial construction of congressional power to enforce [the] Amendments, that wrong must amount to a constitutional violation. Only when the wrong is identified can the appropriateness of the remedy be measured.

The Court today identifies the constitutional wrong which was the object of this congressional exercise of power as purposeful discrimination by local

---

3. This issue was also not squarely presented or resolved in [UJO (1977; p. 752 above)]. In UJO, the issue was whether the State could constitutionally take racial criteria into account in drawing its district lines where such redistricting was not strictly necessary to eliminate the effects of past discriminatory districting or apportionment. The Court found that use of this criterion was proper, for differing reasons. [The] only question, however, was the constitutionality of state use of racial criteria, vis-à-vis other citizens, and not the constitutionality of congressional acts which required state governments to use racial criteria against their will. [While] States may be empowered to voluntarily use racial criteria in order to minimize the effects of racial bloc voting, that conclusion does not determine the constitutional authority of Congress to require States to use racial criteria in structuring their governments. [Footnote by Justice Rehnquist.]

governments in structuring their political processes in an effort to reduce black voting strength. The Court goes on to hold that the prohibitions imposed in this case represent an "appropriate" means of preventing such constitutional violations. The Court does not rest this conclusion on any finding that this prohibition is necessary to remedy any prior discrimination by the locality. Rather, the Court reasons that prohibition of changes discriminatory in effect prevent the incidence of changes which are discriminatory in purpose: "Congress could rationally have concluded that, because electoral changes by jurisdictions with a demonstrable history of intentional racial discrimination in voting create the risk of purposeful discrimination, it was proper to prohibit changes that have a discriminatory impact." What the Court explicitly ignores is that in this case the city has proven that these changes are not discriminatory in purpose. Neither reason nor precedent support the conclusion that here it is "appropriate" for Congress to attempt to prevent purposeful discrimination by prohibiting conduct which a locality proves is *not* purposeful discrimination. Congress had before it evidence that various governments were enacting [electoral changes] to prevent the participation of blacks in local government by measures other than outright denial of the franchise. Congress could of course remedy and prevent such purposeful discrimination on the part of local governments. And given the difficulties of proving that an [electoral change] has been undertaken for the purpose of discriminating against blacks, Congress could properly conclude that as a remedial matter it was necessary to place the burden of proving lack of discriminatory purpose on the localities. See [South Carolina]. But all of this does not support the conclusion that Congress is acting remedially when it continues the presumption of purposeful discrimination even after the locality has disproved that presumption. Absent other circumstances, it would be a topsy-turvy judicial system which held that electoral changes which have been affirmatively proven to be permissible under the Constitution nonetheless violate the Constitution.

The precedent on which the Court relies simply does not support its remedial characterization. Neither [Oregon] nor [South Carolina] legitimize the use of an irrebuttable presumption that "vote diluting" changes are motivated by a discriminatory animus. The principal electoral practice in issue in those cases was the use of literacy tests. Yet, the Court simply fails to make any inquiry as to whether the particular electoral practices in issue here are encompassed by the "preventive" remedial rationale invoked in South Carolina and Oregon. The rationale does support congressional prohibition of some electoral practices, but simply has no logical application to the "vote-dilution" devices in issue. [In sustaining the nationwide ban of literacy tests in Oregon], the Court established that under some circumstances, a congressional remedy may be constitutionally overinclusive by prohibiting some state action which might not be purposefully discriminatory. That possibility does not justify the overinclusiveness countenanced by the Court in this case, however. Oregon by no means held that Congress could simply use discriminatory effect as a proxy for discriminatory purpose, as the Court seems to imply. Instead, the Court opinions identified the factors which rendered this prohibition properly remedial. The Court found the nationwide ban to be an appropriate means of effectively preventing purposeful discrimination in the application of the literacy tests as well as an appropriate means of remedying prior constitutional violations by state and local governments in the administration of education to minorities. The presumption that the literacy tests were either being used to purposefully discriminate, or that the disparate effects of those tests were attributable to discrimination in state-administered education, was not very wide of the mark. [Even] if not adopted with a discriminatory purpose, the tests could readily be applied in a discriminatory fashion. Thus a demonstration by the State that it sought to reinstate the tests for legitimate purposes did not eliminate the substantial risk of discrimination in application. Only a ban could effectively prevent the occurrence of purposeful discrimination. The [ban] was also found necessary [to] remedy past constitutional violations [in education]. Finally, [Justice Stewart in Oregon] found that a uniform prohibition had definite advantages for enforcement and [federal relations].[4]

Presumptive prohibition of vote diluting procedures is not similarly an "appropriate" means of exacting state compliance with the Civil War Amendments. First, these prohibitions are quite unlike the literacy ban, where the disparate effects were traceable to the discrimination of governmental bodies in education even if their present desire to use the tests was legitimate. Any disparate impact associated with the nondiscriminatory electoral changes in issue here results from bloc voting—private rather than governmental discrimination. It is clear therefore that these prohibitions do not implicate congressional power to devise an effective remedy for prior constitutional violations by local governments. Nor does the Court invoke this aspect of congressional remedial powers. It is also clear that while most States still utilizing literacy tests may have been doing so to discriminate, a similar generalization could not be made about all government structures which have some disparate impact on black voting strength. At the time Congress passed the Act, one study demonstrated that 60% of all cities nationwide had at-large elections for city officials, for example. This form of government was adopted by many cities throughout this century as a reform measure designed to overcome wide-scale corruption in the ward system of government. [Nor] does the prohibition of all practices with a disparate impact enhance congressional prevention of purposeful discrimination. The changes in issue are not, like literacy tests, though fair on their face, subject to discriminatory application by local authorities. They are either discriminatory from the outset or not. Finally, the advantages supporting the imposition of a nationwide ban are simply not implicated in this case. No added administrative burdens are in issue since Congress has provided the mechanism for preclearance suits in any event, and the burden of proof for this issue is on the locality. And it is certain that the only constitutional wrong implicated— purposeful dilution—can be effectively remedied by prohibiting it where it occurs. For all these reasons, I do not think that the present case is controlled by the result in Oregon. By prohibiting all electoral changes with a disparate impact, Congress has attempted to prevent disparate impacts—not purposeful discrimination.

[Unless congressional enforcement] powers are to be wholly uncanalized, it cannot be appropriate remedial legislation [to] prohibit Rome from structuring its government in the manner as its population sees fit absent a finding or unrebutted presumption that Rome has, or is, intentionally discriminating against its black citizens. Rome has simply committed no constitutional violations, as this Court has defined them. More is at stake than sophistry at its worst in the Court's conclusion that requiring the local government to structure its political system in a manner that most effectively enhances black political strength serves to remedy or prevent constitutional wrongs on the part of the local government. The need to prevent this disparate impact is premised on the assumption that white candidates will not represent black interests, and that States should devise a system encouraging blacks to vote in a bloc for black candidates. The findings in this case alone demonstrate the tenuous nature of these assumptions. The court below expressly found that white officials have ably represented the interests of the black community. Even blacks who testified admitted no dissatisfaction, but expressed only a preference to be represented by officials of their own race. The enforcement provisions of the

---

4. Reconsider this explanation when examining Oregon v. Mitchell, p. 953 below.

Civil War Amendments were not premised on the notion that Congress could empower a later generation of blacks to "get even" for wrongs inflicted on their forebears. What is now at stake in the city of Rome is the preference of the black community to be represented by a black. This Court has never elevated such a notion, by no means confined to blacks, to the status of a constitutional right.[5] The Constitution imposes no obligation on local governments to erect institutional safeguards to ensure the election of a black candidate. Nor do I believe that Congress can do so, absent a finding that this obligation would be necessary to remedy constitutional violations on the part of the local government. It is appropriate to add that even if this Court could find a remedial relationship between the prohibition of all state action with a disparate impact on black voting strength and the incidence of purposeful discrimination, this Court should exercise caution in approving the remedy in issue here absent purposeful dilution. Political theorists can readily differ on the advantages inherent in different governmental structures. As Justice Harlan noted in his dissent in Farley v. Patterson, 393 U.S. 544 (1969): "It is not clear to me how a court would go about deciding whether an at-large system is to be preferred over a district system. Under one system, Negroes have some influence in the election of all officers; under the other, minority groups have more influence in the selection of fewer officers."

B. The result reached by the Court today can be sustained only upon the theory that Congress was empowered to determine that structural changes with a disparate impact on a minority group's ability to elect a candidate of their race violates the 14th or 15th Amendments. [Justice Rehnquist's argument that a majority of the Court has never endorsed a "substantive" (rather than "remedial") theory of congressional enforcement powers is printed at p. 968 below, after the Morgan and Oregon cases.]

KATZENBACH v. MORGAN

384 U.S. 641, 86 S.Ct. 1717, 16 L.Ed.2d 828 (1966).

Mr. Justice BRENNAN delivered the opinion of the Court.

Section 4(e) of the Voting Rights Act of 1965 [provides] that no person who has successfully completed the sixth primary grade in [an accredited school in] Puerto Rico in which the language of instruction was other than English shall be denied the right to vote in any election because of his inability to read or write English. Appellees, registered voters in New York City, brought this suit to challenge the constitutionality of § 4(e) insofar as it pro tanto prohibits the enforcement of the election laws of New York requiring an ability to read and write English. [We hold that] § 4(e) is a proper exercise of the powers granted to Congress by § 5 of the 14th Amendment.

[Under the Constitution], the qualifications established by the States for voting for members of the most numerous branch of the state legislature also determine who may vote for [U.S.] Representatives and Senators [Art. I, § 2; 17th Amendment]. But, of course, the States have no power to grant or withhold the franchise on conditions that are forbidden by the 14th Amendment. [New York] argues that an exercise of congressional power under § 5 of the 14th Amendment that prohibits the enforcement of a state law can only be sustained if the judicial branch determines that the state law is prohibited by the provisions of the Amendment that Congress sought to enforce. More specifically, [it] urges that § 4(e) cannot be sustained as appropriate legislation

5. Justice Rehnquist here cited Whitcomb v. Chavis (1971; p. 1632 below; also considered in Rogers v. Lodge, p. 703 above).

to enforce [equal protection] unless the judiciary decides—even with the guidance of a congressional judgment—that the application of the English literacy requirement prohibited by § 4(e) is forbidden by [equal protection] itself. We disagree. Neither the language nor history of § 5 supports such a construction. [A] construction [that] would require a judicial determination that the enforcement of the state law precluded by Congress violated the Amendment, as a condition of sustaining the congressional enactment, [would] confine the legislative power in this context to the insignificant role of abrogating only those state laws that the judicial branch was prepared to adjudge unconstitutional, or of merely informing the judgment of the judiciary by particularizing the "majestic generalities" of § 1 of the Amendment. Thus our task in this case is not to determine whether the New York English literacy requirement as applied [violates equal protection]. Accordingly, our decision in [Lassiter] is inapposite. Lassiter did not present the question before us here: Without regard to whether the judiciary would find that [equal protection] itself nullifies New York's English literacy requirement [as] applied, could Congress prohibit the enforcement of the state law by legislating under § 5 of the 14th Amendment? In answering this question, our task is limited to determining whether such legislation is, as required by § 5, appropriate legislation to enforce [equal protection].

By including § 5 the draftsmen sought to grant to Congress, by a specific provision applicable to the 14th Amendment, the same broad powers expressed in the Necessary and Proper Clause. The classic formulation of the reach of those powers was established [in McCulloch]. [Ex parte Virginia], decided 12 years after the adoption of the 14th Amendment, held that congressional power under § 5 had this same broad scope. Section 2 of the 15th Amendment grants Congress a similar [power]. Correctly viewed, § 5 is a positive grant of legislative power authorizing Congress to exercise its discretion in determining whether and what legislation is needed to secure the guarantees of the 14th Amendment. We therefore proceed to the consideration whether § 4(e) is "appropriate legislation" to enforce the Equal Protection Clause, that is, under the [McCulloch] standard, whether § 4(e) may be regarded as an enactment to enforce [equal protection], whether it is "plainly adapted to that end" and whether it is not prohibited by but is consistent with "the letter and spirit of the Constitution." [1]

There can be no doubt that § 4(e) may be regarded as an enactment to enforce [equal protection]. [Specifically], § 4(e) may be viewed as a measure to secure for the Puerto Rican community residing in New York nondiscriminatory treatment by government—both in the imposition of voting qualifications and the provision or administration of governmental services, such as public schools, public housing and law enforcement. Section 4(e) may be readily seen as "plainly adapted" to furthering these aims of [equal protection]. The practical effect of § 4(e) is to prohibit New York from denying the right to vote to large segments of its Puerto Rican community. [This] enhanced political power will be helpful in gaining nondiscriminatory treatment in public services for the entire Puerto Rican community.[2] Section 4(e) thereby enables

---

1. Contrary to the suggestion of the dissent, § 5 does not grant Congress power to exercise discretion in the other direction and to enact "statutes so as in effect to dilute equal protection and due process decisions of this Court." We emphasize that Congress' power under § 5 is limited to adopting measures to enforce the guarantees of the Amendment; § 5 grants Congress no power to restrict, abrogate, or dilute these guarantees. Thus, for example, an enactment authorizing the States to establish racially segre-

gated systems of education would not be—as required by § 5—a measure "to enforce" the Equal Protection Clause since that clause of its own force prohibits such state laws. [Footnote by Justice Brennan. Compare Justice Brennan's footnote [1] in Oregon, which follows, and note the comments on these footnotes in the materials following Oregon.]

2. [Cf.] the settled principle applied in the Shreveport Rate Case [p. 109] and expressed in

the Puerto Rican minority better to obtain "perfect equality of civil rights and equal protection of the laws." It was well within congressional authority to say that this need of the Puerto Rican minority for the vote warranted federal intrusion upon any state interests served by the English literacy requirement. It was for Congress, as the branch that made this judgment, to assess and weigh the various conflicting considerations—the risk or pervasiveness of the discrimination in governmental services, the effectiveness of eliminating the state restriction on the right to vote as a means of dealing with the evil, the adequacy or availability of alternative remedies, and the nature and significance of the state interest that would be affected by the nullification of the English literacy requirement as applied to residents who have successfully completed the sixth grade in a Puerto Rican school. It is not for us to review the congressional resolution of these factors. It is enough that we be able to perceive a basis upon which the Congress might resolve the conflict as it did. There plainly was such a basis [here]. Any contrary conclusion would require us to be blind to the realities familiar to the legislators.

The result is no different if we confine our inquiry to the question whether § 4(e) was merely legislation aimed at the elimination of an invidious discrimination in establishing voter qualifications. We are told that New York's English literacy requirement originated in the desire to provide an incentive for non-English speaking immigrants to learn the English language and in order to assure the intelligent exercise of the franchise. Yet Congress might well have questioned, in light of the many exemptions provided,[3] and some evidence suggesting that prejudice played a prominent role in the enactment of the requirement [4] whether these were actually the interests being served. Congress might have also questioned whether denial of a right deemed so precious and fundamental in our society was a necessary or appropriate means of encouraging persons to learn English, or of furthering the goal of an intelligent exercise of the franchise.[5] Finally, Congress might well have concluded that as a means of furthering the intelligent exercise of the franchise, an ability to read or understand Spanish is as effective as ability to read English for those to whom Spanish-language newspapers and Spanish-language radio and television programs are available to inform them of election issues and governmental affairs. Since Congress undertook to legislate so as to preclude the enforcement of the state law, and did so in the context of a general appraisal of literacy requirements for voting, see [South Carolina], to which it brought a specially informed legislative competence, it was Congress' prerogative to weigh these competing

[Darby] [p. 138] that the power of Congress to regulate interstate commerce "extends to those activities intrastate which so affect interstate commerce or the exercise of the power of Congress over it as to make regulation of them appropriate means to the attainment of a legitimate end." Accord, Heart of Atlanta Motel [p. 164]. [Footnote by Justice Brennan.]

3. The principal exemption complained of is that for persons who had been eligible to vote before January 1, 1922. [Footnote by Justice Brennan.]

4. This evidence consists in part of statements made in the Constitutional Convention first considering the English literacy requirement [during World War I]. [Congress] was aware of this [evidence]. [Footnote by Justice Brennan.]

5. Other States have found ways of assuring an intelligent exercise of the franchise short of total disenfranchisement of persons not literate in English. For example, in Hawaii, where literacy in either English or Hawaiian suffices, candidates' names may be printed in both languages; New York itself already provides assistance for those exempt from the literacy requirement and are literate in no language; and, of course, the problem of assuring the intelligent exercise of the franchise has been met by those States, more than 30 in number, that have no literacy requirement at all. Section 4(e) does not preclude resort to these alternative methods of assuring the intelligent exercise of the franchise. True, the statute precludes, for a certain class, disenfranchisement and thus limits the States' choice of means of satisfying a purported state interest. But our cases have held that the States can be required to tailor carefully the means of satisfying a legitimate state interest when fundamental liberties and rights are threatened [see chaps. 8 and 9, above], and Congress is free to apply the same principle in the exercise of its powers. [Footnote by Justice Brennan.]

considerations. Here again, it is enough that we perceive a basis upon which Congress might predicate a judgment that the application of New York's [requirement] constituted an invidious discrimination in violation of [equal protection].

There remains the question whether the congressional remedies adopted in § 4(e) constitute means which are not prohibited by, but are consistent "with the letter and spirit of the constitution." [Appellees claim that § 4(e)] works an invidious discrimination in violation of the Fifth Amendment by prohibiting the enforcement of the English literacy requirement only for those educated in American-flag schools [in] which the language of instruction was other than English, and not for those educated in schools beyond the territorial limits of the United States in which the language of instruction was also other than English. This is not a complaint that Congress [has] unconstitutionally denied or diluted anyone's right to vote but rather that Congress violated the Constitution by not extending the relief effected in § 4(e) to those educated in non-American-flag schools. We need not pause to determine whether appellees have a sufficient personal interest to have § 4(e) invalidated on this ground, [since the argument] falls on the merits. Section 4(e) does not restrict or deny the franchise but in effect extends the franchise to persons who otherwise would be denied it by state law. Thus we need not decide whether a state literacy law conditioning the right to vote on achieving a certain level of education in an American-flag school (regardless of the language of instruction) discriminates invidiously against those educated in non-American-flag schools. We need only decide whether the challenged limitation on the relief effected in § 4(e) was permissible. In deciding that question, the principle that calls for the closest scrutiny of distinctions in laws *denying* fundamental rights [is] inapplicable; for the distinction challenged [here] is presented only as a limitation on a reform measure aimed at eliminating an existing barrier to the exercise of the franchise. Rather, in deciding the constitutional propriety of the limitations in such a reform measure we are guided by the familiar principles [that] "reform may take one step at a time" [Lee Optical]. Guided by these principles, we are satisfied that [the] challenge to this limitation in § 4(e) is without merit. [The] congressional choice to limit the relief effected in § 4(e) may, for example, reflect Congress' greater familiarity with the quality of instruction in American-flag schools, a recognition of the unique historic relationship between the Congress and the Commonwealth of Puerto Rico, an awareness of the Federal Government's acceptance of the desirability of the use of Spanish as the language of instruction in Commonwealth schools, and the fact that Congress has fostered policies encouraging migration from the Commonwealth to the States. We have no occasion to determine in this case whether such factors would justify a similar distinction embodied in a voting-qualification law that denied the franchise to persons educated in non-American-flag schools. We hold only that the limitation on relief effected in § 4(e) does not constitute a forbidden discrimination since these factors might well have been the basis for the decision of Congress to go "no farther than it [did]."

Reversed.[6]

Mr. Justice HARLAN, whom Mr. Justice STEWART joins, dissenting.

Worthy as its purposes may be thought by many, I do not see how § 4(e) can be sustained except at the sacrifice of fundamentals in the American constitutional system—the separation between the legislative and judicial function and the boundaries between federal and state political authority. By the same token I think that the validity of New York's literacy test, a question

---

6. Justice Douglas joined Justice Brennan's opinion except for its last paragraph, reserving judgment on that issue "until such time as it is presented by a member of the class against which that particular discrimination is directed."

which the Court considers *only* in the context of the federal statute, must be upheld. It will conduce to analytical clarity if I discuss the second issue first.

I. [Applying] the basic equal protection standard, the issue in [CARDONA v. POWER][1] is whether New York has shown that its English-language literacy test is reasonably designed to serve a legitimate state interest. I think that it has. [The] same interests recounted in [Lassiter] indubitably point toward upholding the rationality of the New York voting test. [The] range of material available to a resident of New York literate only in Spanish is much more limited than what is available to an English-speaking resident [and] the business [of] government is conducted in English. [The] ballot [is] likewise in English. It is also true that most candidates [make] their speeches in English. New York may justifiably want its voters to be able to understand candidates directly, rather than through possibly imprecise translations or summaries reported in a limited number of Spanish news media. [Given] the State's legitimate concern with promoting and safeguarding the intelligent use of the ballot, and given also New York's long experience with the process of integrating non-English-speaking residents into the mainstream of American life, I do not see how it can be said that this [requirement] is unconstitutional. I would uphold the validity of the [law], unless the federal statute prevents that result, the question to which I now turn.

II. [The] pivotal question in [Morgan] is what effect the added factor of a congressional enactment has on the straight equal protection [argument]. The Court declares that [under § 5] the test for judicial review [is] simply one of rationality; that is, in effect, was Congress acting rationally in declaring that the New York statute is irrational? [The] Court has confused the issue of how much enforcement power Congress possesses under § 5 with the distinct issue of what questions are appropriate for congressional determination and what questions are essentially judicial in nature.

When recognized state violations of federal constitutional standards have occurred, Congress is of course empowered by § 5 to take appropriate remedial measures to redress and prevent the wrongs. But it is a judicial question whether the condition with which Congress has thus sought to deal is in truth an infringement of the Constitution, something that is the necessary prerequisite to bringing the § 5 power into play at all. [Thus, in South Carolina, we] reviewed first the "voluminous legislative history" as well as judicial precedents supporting the basic congressional finding that the clear commands of the 15th Amendment had been infringed by various state subterfuges. Given the existence of the evil, we held the remedial steps taken by the legislature under [the 15th] Amendment to be a justifiable exercise of congressional initiative. Section 4(e), however, presents a significantly different type of congressional enactment. The question here is not whether the statute is appropriate remedial legislation to cure an established violation of a constitutional command, but whether there has in fact been an infringement of that constitutional command,

---

1. CARDONA v. POWER, 384 U.S. 672 (1966), a companion case to Morgan, was an appeal from an unsuccessful state court equal protection challenge to the New York literacy requirement. The plaintiff was a New York resident educated in Puerto Rico who did not allege that she had completed sixth grade education—the minimum under § 4(e). The state courts, prior to the enactment of § 4(e), rejected her equal protection attack. Justice BRENNAN's majority opinion vacated that judgment and remanded the case: appellant might be covered by § 4(e) and her case "might therefore be moot"; even if she were not so covered, the state court should determine whether "in light of this federal enactment, those applications of the New York English literacy requirement not in terms prohibited by § 4(e) have continuing validity." Justice DOUGLAS, joined by Justice Fortas, reached the merits of the equal protection claim and dissented, arguing that the requirement could not survive the strict scrutiny mandated in voting cases by Harper (chap. 9, p. 808). Justice HARLAN's dissent, joined by Justice Stewart, rejected the constitutional attack in Cardona before turning to the problems of Morgan, as noted in text.

that is, whether a particular state practice or, as here, a statute is so arbitrary or irrational as to offend [equal protection]. That question is one for the judicial branch ultimately to determine. Were the rule otherwise, Congress would be able to qualify this Court's constitutional decisions under the 14th and 15th Amendments, let alone those under other provisions of the Constitution, by resorting to congressional power under the Necessary and Proper Clause. In view of [Lassiter], I do not think it is open to Congress to limit the effect of that decision as it has undertaken to do by § 4(e). In effect the Court reads § 5 of the 14th Amendment as giving Congress the power to define the *substantive* scope of the Amendment. If that indeed be the true reach of § 5, then I do not see why Congress should not be able as well to exercise its § 5 "discretion" by enacting statutes so as in effect to dilute equal protection and due process decisions of this Court. In all such cases there is room for reasonable men to differ as to whether or not a denial of equal protection or due process has occurred, and the final decision is one of judgment. Until today this judgment has always been one for the judiciary to resolve.

I do not mean to suggest [that] a legislative judgment of the type incorporated in § 4(e) is without any force whatsoever. Decisions on questions of equal protection and due process are based not on abstract logic, but on empirical foundations. To the extent "legislative facts" are relevant to a judicial determination, Congress is well equipped to investigate them, and such determinations are of course entitled to due respect. In [South Carolina], such legislative findings were made to show that racial discrimination in voting was actually occurring. Similarly, in [Heart of Atlanta Motel and McClung (pp. 164, 165 above)], the congressional determination that racial discrimination in a clearly defined group of public accommodations did effectively impede interstate commerce was based on "voluminous testimony," which had been put before the Congress and in the context of which it passed remedial legislation. But no such factual data provide a legislative record supporting § 4(e)[2] by way of showing that Spanish-speaking citizens are fully as capable of making informed decisions in a New York election as are English-speaking citizens. Nor was there any showing whatever to support the Court's alternative argument that § 4(e) should be viewed as but a remedial measure designed to cure or assure against unconstitutional discrimination of other varieties, e.g., in "public schools, public housing and law enforcement." [There] is simply no legislative record supporting such hypothesized discrimination of the sort we have hitherto insisted upon when congressional power is brought to bear on constitutionally reserved state concerns. [Thus], we have here not a matter of giving deference to a congressional estimate, based on its determination of legislative facts, bearing upon the validity *vel non* of a statute, but rather what can at most be called a legislative announcement that Congress believes a state law to entail an unconstitutional deprivation of equal protection. Although this kind of declaration is of course entitled to the most respectful consideration, I do not believe it lessens our responsibility to decide the fundamental issue of whether in fact the state enactment violates federal constitutional rights.

In assessing the deference we should give to this kind of congressional expression of policy, it is relevant that the judiciary has always given to congressional enactments a presumption of validity. However, it is also a canon of judicial review that state statutes are given a similar presumption. Whichever way this case is decided, one statute will be rendered inoperative in whole or in part, and although it has been suggested that this Court should give somewhat

2. There were no committee hearings or reports referring to this section, which was introduced from the floor during debate on the full Voting Rights Act. [Footnote by Justice Harlan.]

more deference to Congress than to a state legislature,[3] such a simple weighing of presumptions is hardly a satisfying way of resolving a matter that touches the distribution of state and federal power in an area so sensitive as that of the regulation of the franchise. Rather it should be recognized that while the 14th Amendment is a "brooding omnipresence" over all state legislation, the substantive matters which it touches are all within the primary legislative competence of the States. Federal authority, legislative no less than judicial, does not intrude unless there has been a denial by state action of 14th Amendment limitations. [At least] in the area of primary state concern a state statute that passes constitutional muster under the judicial standard of rationality should not be permitted to be set at naught by a mere contrary congressional pronouncement unsupported by a legislative record justifying that conclusion. [To] hold on this record that § 4(e) overrides the New York literacy requirement seems to me tantamount to allowing the 14th Amendment to swallow the State's constitutionally ordained primary authority in this field. For if Congress by what, as here, amounts to mere ipse dixit can set that otherwise permissible requirement partially at naught I see no reason why it could not also substitute its judgment for that of the States in other fields of their exclusive primary competence [as well].

CONGRESSIONAL POWER AND THE MORGAN CASE

a. How far-reaching is the § 5 power recognized in Morgan? Though full discussion of the scope of the Morgan rationale is best postponed until after Oregon v. Mitchell, which follows, some preliminary questions are in order here. Is there merit in the following assessment of Morgan in Burt, "Miranda and Title II: A Morganatic Marriage," 1969 Sup.Ct.Rev. 81?: "In effect, the Court is saying that—at least in some circumstances—where Congress and the Court disagree about the meaning of the 14th Amendment, the Court will defer to Congress' version. The Court is suggesting that, to some extent at least, § 5 exempts the 14th Amendment from the principle of Court-Congress relationships expressed by Marbury v. Madison, that the judiciary is the final arbiter of the meaning of the Constitution." If so, to what "extent" and under what "circumstances"?

b. In exploring that question, note that Morgan rests on alternative rationales: First, § 4(e) is a measure to secure for Puerto Ricans in New York nondiscriminatory treatment in the "provision or administration of governmental services." Second, § 4(e) eliminates "an invidious discrimination in establishing voter qualifications." (Under the second theory, the Court permits Congress to find—because the Court perceives "a basis" for the "finding"—that application of New York's English literacy requirement to covered Puerto Ricans itself constitutes "an invidious discrimination in violation of [equal protection].")

The second theory seems the more far-reaching. Discrimination against Puerto Ricans in providing public services is clearly unconstitutional under Court-developed interpretations of equal protection; under the first theory, then, Congress can be viewed as implementing judicially-determined constitutional rights. (Even under that theory, Congress is making the factual determination that New York is discriminating in public services, and that Puerto Rican voting is an appropriate remedy for such discrimination.) Under the second theory, Congress does more than that. The Court has not held that requiring English literacy tests of Puerto Ricans literate in Spanish is itself unconstitutional

---

3. See Thayer, The Origin and Scope of the American Doctrine of Constitutional Law, 7   Harv.L.Rev. 129, 154–155 (1893). [Footnote by Justice Harlan.]

discrimination in voting. Under that theory, then, Congress is making the initial determination that an English literacy test in these circumstances is unconstitutional; and the Court readily defers to that determination. Arguably, then, Congress (not the Court) makes a determination about the substantive content of rights under § 1 of the 14th Amendment. Does Morgan, then, recognize a "substantive" power of Congress under § 5 of the 14th Amendment? Is that power distinctively different (and broader than) the expanding "remedial" power considered in the Rome case, above? Can the congressional determination endorsed in Morgan be justified as resting simply on legislative findings of fact? Or does it involve a resolution of competing values and a delineation of substantive constitutional rights by Congress rather than by the Court? Justice Brennan stated that it "was for Congress" to "assess and weigh the various conflicting considerations," including such considerations as the "significance of the state interest." Did he mean to authorize Congress to make the value choices typically involved in judicial, "strict scrutiny" interpretations of equal protection? Does his rationale (that it is "not for us to review the congressional resolution of these factors," so long as the Justices can "perceive a basis upon which the Congress might resolve the conflict as it did") give Congress a general power to resolve the value conflicts in constitutional interpretation with a result different from that the Court might reach—or has reached? May Congress use that rationale to dilute as well as expand constitutional rights? These questions are pursued further after [Oregon], below.*

OREGON v. MITCHELL

400 U.S. 112, 91 S.Ct. 260, 27 L.Ed.2d 272 (1970).

[These cases—in the Court's original jurisdiction—involved constitutional challenges by several states to three provisions of the Voting Rights Act Amendments of 1970. (1) Sec. 302 prohibited denying to any citizen the right to vote in any election "on account of age if such citizen is eighteen years of age or older." [1] By a 5 to 4 vote, that provision was upheld for federal elections; but another 5 to 4 division held the 18-year-old vote provision unconstitutional as applied to state elections. [2] (2) Section 201 expanded the ban on literacy tests

---

* The major constitutional controversy in Oregon stemmed from the 1970 Act provision lowering the voting age to 18 in state elections. Enactment came after an extensive constitutional debate in Congress. In Congress, the proponents of the 18-year-old vote provision relied heavily on a statement by Archibald Cox resting on Morgan for the proposition that "Congress has constitutional power to determine what [equal protection] requires," though cautioning that "some constitutional scholars would not share my view. [Possibly], my reasoning runs the logic of [Morgan] into the ground." Opponents of the lowering of the voting age by statute rather than by constitutional amendment introduced a statement by Louis H. Pollak noting that Morgan "provides the basis for a modestly plausible, but not for an ultimately persuasive, case for the constitutionality of the statute."

1. The congressional findings accompanying § 302 stated that a requirement that a voter be 21 years old "(1) denies and abridges the inherent constitutional rights of citizens eighteen years of age but not yet twenty-one years of age to vote—a particularly unfair treatment of such citi-

zens in view of the national defence responsibilities imposed upon such citizens; (2) has the effect of denying to citizens eighteen years of age [the] due process and equal protection of the laws; [and] (3) does not bear a reasonable relationship to any compelling State interest." 42 U.S.C. § 1973bb.

2. Justices Douglas, Brennan, White and Marshall thought the provision valid as applied to all elections, state as well as federal; Chief Justice Burger and Justices Harlan, Stewart and Blackmun thought the provision exceeded congressional power as applied to any election, federal or state; Justice Black cast the deciding vote—he thought it constitutional as applied to federal elections but not to state elections.

The decision was handed down on Dec. 21, 1970. Three months later, on March 23, 1971, Congress submitted the 26th Amendment to the states for ratification. Three months after that, on June 30, 1971, the ratification process was completed. The 26th Amendment provides that the federal and state governments may not deny

in the 1965 Act by making the suspension applicable nationwide. That provision was upheld unanimously as discussed at p. 935 above. (3) Section 202 prohibited the application of state durational residency requirements in presidential elections and established uniform standards for registration and absentee balloting. It included a provision that voters could register within 30 days of a presidential election. Those provisions were sustained by an 8 to 1 vote, with Justice Harlan the only dissenter.[3]]

Mr. Justice BLACK announcing the judgments of the Court in an opinion expressing his own view of the [cases].

[T]he responsibility of the States for setting the qualifications of voters in congressional elections [Art. I, § 2] was made subject to the power of Congress to make or alter such regulations if it deemed it advisable to do so [Art. I, § 4]. Moreover, the power of Congress to make election regulations in national elections is augmented by the Necessary and Proper Clause. [In short], the Constitution allotted to the States the power to make laws regarding national elections, but provided that if Congress became dissatisfied with the state laws, Congress could alter them. I would hold [that] Congress has ultimate supervisory power over congressional elections. Similarly, it is the prerogative of Congress to oversee the conduct of presidential and vice-presidential elections and to set the qualifications for voters for [them]. It cannot be seriously contended that Congress has less power over the conduct of presidential elections than it has over congressional elections.[1] On the other hand, [no] function is more essential to the separate and independent existence of the States [than] the power to determine within the limits of the Constitution the qualifications of their own voters for state, county, and municipal [offices. See Art. I, § 2.] My Brother Brennan's opinion, if carried to its logical conclusion, would, under the guise of insuring equal protection, blot out all state [power]. [Of course, where] Congress attempts to remedy racial discrimination under its enforcement powers, its authority is enhanced by the avowed intention of the Framers of the 13th, 14th, and 15th Amendments. In enacting the 18-year-old vote provisions [here], Congress made no legislative findings that the 21-year-old vote requirement was used by the States to disenfranchise voters on account of race. I seriously doubt that such a finding, if made, could be supported by substantial evidence. Since Congress has attempted to invade an area preserved to the States by the Constitution without a foundation for enforcing the Civil War Amendments' ban on racial discrimination, I would hold that Congress has exceeded its powers in attempting to lower the voting age in state and local elections. On the other hand, where Congress legislates in a domain not exclusively reserved [to] the States, its enforcement power need not be tied so closely to the goal of eliminating discrimination on account of [race].

Mr. Justice BRENNAN, Mr. Justice WHITE, and Mr. Justice MARSHALL dissent from the judgments insofar as they declare § 302 unconstitutional as applied to state and local elections.

the vote "on account of age" to citizens "eighteen years of age or older."

3. The portions of the Oregon opinions printed here focus on the discussion of the 18-year-old vote provision, because that provision provided the major test of the scope of the Morgan power. (Recall the earlier discussion, at p. 935, of the literacy test ban, as well as the discussion of the Oregon disposition in the Rome case (1980, p. 937 above).)

1. [This] Court in Burroughs v. United States, 290 U.S. 534 (1934), [rejected] a construc-

tion of Art. II, § 1, that would have curtailed the power of Congress to regulate [presidential] elections. [Most] important, inherent in the very concept of a supreme national government with national officers is a residual power in Congress to insure that those officers represent their national constituency as responsively as possible. This power arises from the nature of our constitutional system of government and from the Necessary and Proper Clause. [Footnote by Justice Black.]

[We] easily perceive a rational basis for the congressional judgments. [We] believe there is serious question whether a statute [denying the franchise to citizens] between the ages of 18 and 21 [could] withstand present scrutiny under [equal protection]. Regardless of the answer to this question, however, it is clear to us that proper regard for the special function of Congress in making determinations of legislative fact compels this Court to respect those determinations unless they are contradicted by evidence far stronger than anything that has been adduced in these [cases].

A. [W]hen exclusions from the franchise are challenged as violating [equal protection], "the Court must determine whether the exclusions are necessary to promote a compelling state interest." [See chap. 9.] In the present cases, the States justify exclusion of 18- to 21-year-olds from the voting rolls solely on the basis of the States' interests in promoting intelligent and responsible exercise of the franchise. [We must] examine with particular care the asserted connection between age limitations and the admittedly laudable state purpose to further intelligent and responsible voting. [Every State] has concluded [that] citizens 21 years of age and over are capable of responsible and intelligent voting. Accepting this judgment, there remains the question whether citizens 18 to 21 years of age may fairly be said to be less able. State practice itself in other areas casts doubt upon any such proposition. Each of the 50 States has provided special mechanisms for dealing with persons who are deemed insufficiently mature and intelligent to understand, and to conform their behavior to, the criminal laws of the State. Forty-nine of the States have concluded that, in this regard, 18-year-olds are invariably to be dealt with according to precisely the same standards prescribed for their elders. This at the very least is evidence of a nearly unanimous legislative judgment on the part of the States themselves that differences in maturity and intelligence between 18-year-olds and persons over the age of 21 are too trivial to warrant specialized treatment for *any* of the former class in the critically important matter of criminal responsibility. Similarly, every State permits 18-year-olds to marry. [No State] requires attendance at school beyond the age of 18. [T]hat 18-year-olds as a class may be less educated than some of their elders cannot justify restriction of the franchise, for the States themselves have determined that this incremental education is irrelevant to voting qualifications. And finally, we have been cited to no material whatsoever that would support the proposition that intelligence, as opposed to educational attainment, increases between the ages of 18 and 21. [No] State seeking to uphold its denial of the franchise to 18-year-olds has adduced anything beyond the mere difference in age. [As noted], the relevance of this difference is contradicted by nearly uniform state practice in other areas. But perhaps more important is the uniform experience of those States—Georgia since 1943, and Kentucky since 1955—that have permitted 18-year-olds to vote. [E]very person who spoke to the issue in [Congress] was agreed that 18-year-olds in both States were at least as interested, able, and responsible in voting as were their elders. In short, we are faced with [a] restriction upon the franchise supported only by bare assertions and long practice, in the face of strong indications that the States themselves do not credit the factual propositions upon which the restriction is asserted to rest. But there is no reason for us to decide whether, in a proper case, we would be compelled to hold this restriction a violation of [equal protection]. [For] the question we face today [is] the scope of congressional power under [§ 5].

B. As we have often indicated, questions of constitutional power frequently turn in the last analysis on questions of fact. This is particularly the case when an assertion of state power is challenged under [equal protection]. When a state legislative classification is subjected to judicial challenge as violating [equal protection], it comes before the courts cloaked by the presumption that the legislature has, as it should, acted within constitutional limitations. Accordingly, "[a] statutory discrimination will not be set aside as the denial of equal protection of the laws if any state of facts reasonably may be conceived to justify it." [But] this limitation on judicial review of state legislative classifications is a limitation stemming, not from the 14th Amendment itself, but from the nature of judicial review. The nature of the judicial process makes it an inappropriate forum for the determination of complex factual questions of the kind so often involved in constitutional adjudication. Courts, therefore, will overturn a legislative determination of a factual question only if the legislature's finding is so clearly wrong that it may be characterized as "arbitrary," "irrational," or "unreasonable." Limitations stemming from the nature of the judicial process, however, have no application to [Congress]. Should Congress, pursuant to [§ 5], undertake an investigation in order to determine whether the factual basis necessary to support a state legislative discrimination actually exists, it need not stop once it determines that some reasonable men could believe the factual basis exists. Section 5 empowers Congress to make its own determination on the matter. [Morgan.] It should hardly be necessary to add that if the asserted factual basis necessary to support a given state discrimination does not exist, [§ 5] vests Congress with power to remove the discrimination by appropriate means. The scope of our review in such matters has been established by a long line of consistent decisions. "[W]here we find that the legislators, in light of the facts and testimony before them, have a rational basis for finding a chosen regulatory scheme necessary [our] investigation is at an end." [E.g., McClung; Morgan.][1]

This scheme is consistent with our prior decisions in related areas. The core of dispute [here] is a conflict between state and federal legislative determinations of the factual issues upon which depends decision of a federal constitutional question—the legitimacy, under [equal protection], of state discrimination against persons between the ages of 18 and 21. Our cases have repeatedly emphasized that, when state and federal claims come into conflict, the primacy of federal power requires that the federal finding of fact control. The Supremacy Clause requires an identical result when the conflict is one of legislative, not judicial, findings. Finally, it is no answer to say that [the law] intrudes upon a domain reserved to the States—the power to set qualifications for voting. It is no longer open to question that the 14th Amendment applies to this, as to any other, exercise of [state power].

C. [A lengthy discussion rejected Justice Harlan's historical argument that the 14th Amendment "was never intended to restrict the authority of the States to allocate their political power as they see fit." It concluded:] We could not accept [Justice Harlan's] thesis even if it were supported by historical evidence far stronger than anything adduced today. But in our view, [his] historical analysis is flawed by his ascription of 20th-century meanings to the words of 19th-century legislators. In consequence, his analysis imposes an artificial simplicity upon a complex era, and presents, as universal, beliefs that were held by merely one of several groups competing for political power. [The] historical record left by the framers of the 14th Amendment, because it is a product of differing and conflicting political pressures and conceptions of federalism, is thus too vague and imprecise to provide us with sure guidance in deciding the pending cases. We must therefore conclude that its framers understood their Amendment to be a broadly worded injunction capable of being interpreted by

---

1. As we emphasized in [Morgan], "§ 5 does not grant Congress power [to] enact 'statutes so as in effect to dilute equal protection and due process decisions of this Court.'" As indicated above, a decision of this Court striking down a state statute expresses, among other things, our conclusion that the legislative findings upon which the statute is based are so far wrong as to be unreasonable. Unless Congress were to unearth new evidence in its investigation, its identical findings on the identical issue would be no more reasonable than those of the state legislature. [Footnote by Justice Brennan et al.]

future generations in accordance with the vision and needs of those generations. We would be remiss in our duty if, in an attempt to find certainty amidst uncertainty, we were to misread the historical record and cease to interpret the Amendment as this Court has always interpreted it.

D.   There remains only the question whether Congress could rationally have concluded that denial of the franchise to citizens between the ages of 18 and 21 was unnecessary to promote any legitimate interests of the States in assuring intelligent and responsible [voting]. Congress was aware, of course, of the facts and state practices already discussed. [E.g., it] was aware that 18-year-olds today make up a not insubstantial proportion of the adult work force. [As] Congress recognized, its judgment that 18-year-olds are capable of voting is consistent with its practice of entrusting them with the heavy responsibilities of military service. Finally, Congress was presented with evidence that the age of social and biological maturity in modern society has been consistently decreasing. [Perhaps] more important, Congress had before it information on the experience of two States, Georgia and Kentucky, which have allowed 18-year-olds to vote. [In sum], Congress had ample evidence upon which it could have based the conclusion that exclusion of citizens 18 to 21 years of age from the franchise is wholly unnecessary to promote any legitimate interest the States may have in assuring intelligent and responsible voting. [Morgan.] If discrimination is unnecessary to promote any legitimate state interest, it is plainly unconstitutional under [equal protection], and Congress has ample power to forbid it under [§ 5].[2]

Mr. Justice STEWART, with whom The Chief Justice [BURGER] and Mr. Justice BLACKMUN join, concurring in part and dissenting in part.

[Congress] was wholly without constitutional power to alter—for the purpose of *any* elections—the voting age qualifications now determined by the several States. In my view, neither the Morgan case, nor any other case, [establishes] such congressional power, even assuming that all those cases were rightly decided. Mr. Justice Black is surely correct when he writes, "[The] whole Constitution reserves to the States the power to set voter qualifications in state and local elections, except to the limited extent that the people through constitutional amendments have specifically narrowed the powers of the States." [It] is equally plain to me that the Constitution just as completely withholds from Congress the power to alter by legislation qualifications for voters in federal elections, in view of the explicit provisions of [Art. I, § 2, Art. II, and the 17th Amendment]. To be sure, recent decisions have established that state action regulating suffrage is not immune from the impact of [equal protection]. But we have been careful in those decisions to note the undoubted power of a State to establish a qualification for voting based on age. Indeed, none of the opinions filed today suggests that the States have anything but a constitutionally unimpeachable interest in establishing some age qualification as such. Yet to test the power to establish an age qualification by the "compelling interest" standard is really to deny a State any choice at all, because no State could demonstrate a "compelling interest" in drawing the line with respect to age at one point rather than another. Obviously, the power to establish an age qualification must carry with it the power to choose 21 as a reasonable voting age, as the vast majority of the States have done.[1]

---

2. Justice DOUGLAS' separate statement insisted that the grant of the franchise to 18-year-olds was valid across the board: "Congress might well conclude that a reduction in the voting age from 21 to 18 was needed in the interest of equal protection. [There] is not a word of limitation in § 5 which would restrict its applicability to matters of race alone."

1. If the Government is correct in its submission that a particular age requirement must meet the "compelling interest" standard, then, of course, a substantial question would exist whether a 21-year-old voter qualification is constitutional even in the absence of congressional action, as my Brothers point out. Yet it is inconceivable to me that this Court would ever

[Morgan] does not hold that Congress has the power to determine what are and what are not "compelling state interests" for equal protection purposes. [Morgan upheld] the statute on two grounds: that Congress could conclude that enhancing the political power of the Puerto Rican community by conferring the right to vote was an appropriate means of remedying discriminatory treatment in public services; and that Congress could conclude that the New York statute was tainted by the impermissible purpose of denying the right to vote to Puerto Ricans, an undoubted invidious discrimination under [equal protection]. Both of these decisional grounds were farreaching. The Court's opinion made clear that Congress could impose on the States a remedy for the denial of equal protection that elaborated upon the direct command of the Constitution, and that it could override state laws on the ground that they were in fact used as instruments of invidious discrimination even though a court in an individual lawsuit might not have reached that factual conclusion. But it is necessary to go much further to sustain § 302. The state laws that it invalidates do not invidiously discriminate against any discrete and insular minority. Unlike the statute considered in Morgan, § 302 is valid only if Congress has the power not only to provide the means of eradicating situations that amount to a violation of [equal protection], but also to determine as a matter of substantive constitutional law what situations fall within the ambit of the clause, and what state interests are "compelling." I concurred in Mr. Justice Harlan's dissent in Morgan. That case, as I now read it, gave congressional power under § 5 the furthest possible legitimate reach. Yet to sustain the constitutionality of § 302 would require an enormous extension of that decision's [rationale].

Mr. Justice HARLAN, concurring in part and dissenting in [part].

I think that the history of the 14th Amendment makes it clear beyond any reasonable doubt that no part of the legislation now under review can be upheld as a legitimate exercise of congressional power under that Amendment. [Justice Harlan's extensive examination of the historical data is omitted.*] [I] must confess to complete astonishment at the position of some of my Brethren that the history of [the] Amendment has become irrelevant. [T]he very fact that constitutional amendments were deemed necessary to bring about federal abolition of state restrictions on voting by reason of race, sex, and [the] failure to pay state poll taxes, is itself forceful evidence of the common understanding in 1869, 1919, and 1962, respectively, that the 14th Amendment did not empower Congress to legislate in these respects. It must be recognized, of course, that [the] judiciary has long been entrusted with the task of applying the Constitution in changing circumstances, and as conditions change the Constitution in a sense changes as well. But when the Court disregards the express intent and understanding of the Framers, it has invaded the realm of the political process to which the amending power was committed, and it has violated the constitutional structure which it is its highest duty to protect.

---

hold that the denial of the vote to those between the ages of 18 and 21 constitutes such an invidious discrimination as to be a denial of [equal protection]. The establishment of an age qualification is not state action aimed at any discrete and insular minority. Cf. [Carolene Products, fn. 4]. Moreover, so long as a State does not set the voting age higher than 21, the reasonableness of its choice is confirmed by the very 14th Amendment upon which the Government relies. Section 2 of that Amendment provides for sanctions when the right to vote "is denied to any of the male inhabitants of such State, *being twenty-one years of age,* and citizens of the United States." [Footnote by Justice Stewart.]

* Justice Harlan argued that history made it clear that § 1 of the 14th Amendment was not intended to "reach discriminatory voting qualifications." He emphasized § 2 of the 14th Amendment—see the footnote to Justice Stewart's opinion, above. He concluded: "The only sensible explanation of § 2 [is] that the racial voter qualifications it was designed to penalize were understood to be permitted by § 1 of the 14th Amendment." [See also Justice Harlan's dissents in the voting cases in chap. 9, and in Reynolds v. Sims (1964; p. 1621 below).]

As the Court is not justified in substituting its own views of wise policy for the commands of the Constitution, still less is it justified in allowing Congress to disregard those commands as the Court understands them. Although Congress' expression of the view that it does have power to alter state suffrage qualifications is entitled to the most respectful consideration by the judiciary, [this] cannot displace the duty of this Court to make an independent determination whether Congress has exceeded its powers. The reason for this goes beyond Marshall's assertion that: "It is emphatically the province and duty of the judicial department to say what the law is." [Marbury.][1] It inheres in the structure of the constitutional system itself. Congress is subject to none of the institutional restraints imposed on judicial decision-making; it is controlled only by the political process. In Article V, the Framers expressed the view that the political restraints on Congress alone were an insufficient control over the process of constitution making. [To] allow a simple majority of Congress to have final say on matters of constitutional interpretation is therefore fundamentally out of keeping with the constitutional structure. Nor is that structure adequately protected by a requirement that the judiciary be able to perceive a basis for the congressional interpretation, the only restriction laid down in [Morgan].

It is suggested that the proper basis for the doctrine enunciated in Morgan lies in the relative factfinding competence of Court, Congress, and state legislatures. [In] the first place, this argument has little or no force as applied to the issue whether the 14th Amendment covers voter qualifications. Indeed, I do not understand the adherents of Morgan to maintain the contrary. But even on the assumption that the 14th Amendment does place a limit on the sorts of voter qualifications which a State may adopt, I still do not see any real force in the reasoning. When my Brothers refer to "complex factual questions," they call to mind disputes about primary, objective facts dealing with such issues as the number of persons between the ages of 18 and 21, the extent of their education, and so forth. [But the] disagreement in these cases revolves around the evaluation [of] largely uncontested factual material. On the assumption that maturity and experience are relevant to intelligent and responsible exercise of the elective franchise, are the immaturity and inexperience of the average 18-, 19-, or 20-year-old sufficiently serious to justify denying such a person a direct voice in decisions affecting his or her life? Whether or not this judgment is characterized as "factual," it calls for striking a balance between incommensurate interests. Where the balance is to be struck depends ultimately on the values and the perspective of the decisionmaker. It is a matter as to which men of good will can and do reasonably differ. I fully agree that judgments of the sort involved here are beyond the institutional competence and constitutional authority of the judiciary. They are pre-eminently matters for legislative [discretion]. But the same reasons which in my view would require the judiciary to sustain a reasonable state resolution of the issue also require Congress to abstain from entering the picture. Judicial deference is based, not on relative factfinding competence, but on due regard for the decision of the body constitutionally appointed to decide. Establishment of voting qualifications is a matter for state legislatures. Assuming any authority at all, only when the Court can say with some confidence that the legislature has demonstrably erred in adjusting the competing interests is it justified in striking down the legislative judgment.

[The] same considerations apply [to] Congress' displacement of state decisions with its own ideas of wise policy. The sole distinction between Congress

---

1. In fact, however, I do not understand how the doctrine of deference to rational constitutional interpretation by Congress espoused by the majority in [Morgan] is consistent with this state- ment of Chief Justice Marshall or with our reaffirmation of it in Cooper v. Aaron, [chap. 1, p. 26]. [Footnote by Justice Harlan.]

and the Court in this regard is that Congress presumptively has popular authority for the value judgment it makes.   But since the state legislature has a like authority, this distinction between Congress and the judiciary falls short of justifying a congressional veto on the state judgment.   The perspectives and values of national legislators on the issue of voting qualifications are likely to differ from those of state legislators, but I see no reason a priori to prefer those of the national figures, whose collective decision, applying nationwide, is necessarily less able to take account of peculiar local conditions.   Whether one agrees with this judgment or not, it is the one expressed by the Framers in leaving voter qualifications to the States.   The Supremacy Clause does [not] represent a judgment that federal decisions are superior to those of the States whenever the two may differ.

To be sure, my colleagues do not expressly say that Congress or this Court is empowered by the Constitution to substitute its own judgment for those of the States.   However, before sustaining a state judgment they require a "clear showing that the burden imposed is necessary to protect a compelling and substantial governmental interest." [2]   I should think that if [a state voter qualification met that test], no reasonable person would think the qualification undesirable.   Equivalently, if my colleagues or a majority of Congress deem a given voting qualification undesirable as a matter of policy, they must consider that the state interests involved are not "compelling" or "substantial" or that they can be adequately protected in other ways.   It follows that my colleagues must be prepared to hold invalid as a matter of federal constitutional law all state voting qualifications which they deem unwise, as well as all such qualifications which Congress reasonably deems unwise.   For this reason, I find their argument subject to the same objection as if it explicitly acknowledged such a conclusion.   It seems to me that the notion of deference to congressional interpretation of the Constitution, which the Court promulgated in Morgan, is directly related to this higher standard of constitutionality which the Court [brought] to fruition in Kramer [chap. 9, p. 811].   When the scope of federal review of state determinations became so broad as to be judicially unmanageable, it was natural for the Court to seek assistance from the national legislature.   [In] this area, to rely on Congress would make that body a judge in its own cause.   The role of final arbiter belongs to this [Court].

CONGRESSIONAL POWER AND CONSTITUTIONAL RIGHTS AFTER MORGAN, OREGON, AND ROME

Introduction.   The main purpose of this group of notes is to explore the reach of the congressional "substantive" or "interpretive" (as distinguished from "remedial") power under the 14th and 15th Amendments—the power suggested by Justice Brennan's opinion for the Court in Morgan and by the opinion signed by Justices Brennan, White and Marshall in Oregon.   The central problems are: How broad is that power?   Does it risk a congressional undercutting of the Court's traditional role in delineating the content of constitutional rights?   Can it be invoked to dilute as well as expand constitutional rights?   Is it a justifiable power?   Has the Morgan power been curtailed by the developments of the 1980s?   Is the Morgan power truly broader than the "remedial" power as construed in Rome?

In exploring the ramifications of this controversial "substantive" enforcement power, it is well to bear in mind two additional considerations.   First, how

---

2. It might well be asked why this standard is not equally applicable to the congressional expansion of the franchise before us. Lowering of voter qualifications dilutes the voting power of those who could meet the higher [standard]. [Footnote by Justice Harlan.]

well established is the Morgan power that Justice Brennan has had so large a hand in formulating?   Note 5 below contains the concluding passages from Justice Rehnquist's dissent in the 1980 decision in Rome.   Consider his argument there that a "substantive" enforcement power has *not* been embraced by a majority of the Court.   Second, is the "substantive" power truly broader than the traditionally less controversial "remedial" power exemplified by the South Carolina case in 1965 and applied very broadly by the majority in Rome in 1980?   Arguably, if the "remedial" power is as broad as Rome suggests, Congress, in many circumstances, may be able to play a very significant role in giving effective meaning to constitutional rights without any need to resort to the "substantive" power that is the subject of this set of notes.

1.   *Some pervasive problems.*   What, then, *is* the scope of congressional power to modify the content of constitutional rights?   Recall the comments (at p. 952) about the two alternative theories in Morgan.   Do both of those theories retain vitality after Oregon?   To what extent does the congressional action considered in Oregon rest on Justice Brennan's first theory in Morgan—congressional judgments about remedies that might be appropriate to implement judicially-declared rights?   To what extent did the 18-year-old vote provision need the support of his second theory—congressional determination of the substantive content of constitutional rights?   In Morgan, Justice Brennan was ready to validate a congressional determination that the English literacy requirement as applied to Puerto Ricans was itself unconstitutional under equal protection standards governing voting.   In Oregon, does Justice Brennan support a congressional determination that denial of the vote to 18-year-olds itself violates equal protection?   Only if such a determination rested on such legislative factfinding?   Even if it rested on resolution of conflicting "values"?   Are equal protection determinations ever wholly "factual," or do they always involve value choices?

If Congress is permitted to make determinations that state practices are "unconstitutional," should the Court accord them the deference associated with McCulloch or the even greater deference suggested by the "perceive a basis" test of Morgan?   Can such deference be squared with Marbury and Cooper v. Aaron?   What principled limits on congressional authority (and judicial deference) are possible?   Is congressional modification of constitutional rights permissible only in special circumstances—circumstances taking proper account of congressional competence and judicial authority?[1]   [Consider the limits on the congressional "substantive" power suggested by Justice Brennan (in note 2) and by several commentators (note 4).]

2.   *Limiting congressional power to "dilute" constitutional rights: Justice Brennan's footnotes.*   a.   Can the Court recognize a congressional power in effect to reinterpret constitutional provisions and yet avoid deference to congressional judgments diluting or contracting (rather than expanding) rights?   Justice Brennan's footnote [1] in Morgan tried to safeguard against the risk of dilution: Justice Brennan insisted that § 5 "grants Congress no power to restrict, abrogate, or dilute these guarantees."   Thus, if Congress were to try to authorize the states to establish racial segregation in schools, justification could not be found in § 5 in the power "to enforce" equal protection "since that clause of its own force prohibits such state laws."   Can that footnote be squared with Justice Brennan's rationale in the Morgan text, deferring to congressional resolution of "the various conflicting considerations" if the Court can "perceive a basis upon which the Congress might resolve the conflict as it did"?   What does equal protection prohibit "by its own force"?   What does that phrase

1.   Consider the limits on the congressional "substantive" power suggested by Justice Brennan (in note 2 below), as well as the somewhat different ones advanced by several commentators (see note 4 below).

mean: that the Court has ruled, *and* that no different evaluation of competing considerations is possible? Is that true of the typical due process and equal protection interpretations? In Oregon, the opinion joined by Justice Brennan also contained a footnote that tried to safeguard against uses of the § 5 power to dilute constitutional rights. This footnote purported to reiterate the Morgan footnote's limit on congressional power; but it carried a somewhat different emphasis: it focused on deference to congressional fact-finding capacity as the critical element in § 5 power. Was that a retreat from Morgan's deference to congressional resolution of value conflicts? [2]

Are fact-findings actually critical in typical equal protection controversies? Note the criticism of Justice Brennan's "modified ratchet theory" in Cohen, "Congressional Power to Interpret Due Process and Equal Protection," 27 Stan. L.Rev. 603 (1975): "This new [Oregon footnote] rationale for the ratchet theory is as unpersuasive as the first [in the Morgan footnote]. If Congress is a more appropriate forum than the courts for determining issues of legislative fact, it is hard to understand why a congressional determination that there exists a sufficient 'factual' basis to [justify] discrimination by the state should, in the absence of new evidence, be entitled to no weight at all." Moreover, Cohen notes that the new footnote in fact recognizes "that the ratchet may be released—that in some cases Congress can turn back the clock on equal protection and due process on the basis of new evidence."

b. Even if Justice Brennan's distinction between "dilution" and "expansion" in the Morgan footnote is persuasive, how is it to be applied? Recall the Court's disposition (in the last part of Morgan) of the claim that § 4(e) of the 1965 Act unfairly discriminated against those literate in foreign languages who were not covered by § 4(e). Justice Brennan's scrutiny of that claim was very deferential, supposedly because § 4(e) was "a reform measure" rather than a restriction on existing rights. Is that "reform" rationale, permitting a legislature to "take one step at a time," persuasive as applied in Morgan? [3]

3. *Potential applications of the Morgan rationale.* a. Would the Morgan rationale justify the anti-busing legislative proposals that followed in the wake of the 1971 Swann decision (chap. 9, at p. 715)? President Nixon based his 1972 proposals to limit busing in the desegregation of schools on the ground that the proposed legislation "deals with a remedy and not a right." Is the "remedial" theory of the South Carolina and Rome cases adequate to support anti-busing laws? [4] If busing is not viewed as a mere remedy, is congressional action nevertheless supportable on the basis of the "substantive" rationale of Morgan? [5] Suppose Congress were to enact legislation accepting the principle of

2. The Oregon footnote stated that "a decision of this Court striking down a state statute expresses, among other things, our conclusion that the legislative findings upon which the statute is based are so wrong as to be unreasonable. Unless Congress were to unearth new evidence in its investigation, its identical findings on the identical issue would be no more reasonable than those of the state legislature." (In the text, however, Justices Brennan et al. emphasized Congress' superior capacity to "determine whether the factual basis necessary to support a state legislative discrimination actually exists.")

3. Note the criticism of the Morgan "ratchet theory" in the Cohen article cited above. He finds two problems: "it does not satisfactorily explain why Congress may move the due process and equal protection handle in only one direction"; and there is "difficulty in determining the direction in which the handle is turning."

4. See Bork, Constitutionality of the President's Busing Proposals (1972).

5. Consider, e.g., the 1974 proposals in Congress to prohibit any court to require "the transportation of any student to a school other than the school closest or next closest to his place of residence which provides an appropriate grade level and type of education for such student." Yet the Court in the Swann case (1971; p. 715 above), suggested that busing at a greater distance is justifiable as a remedy for de jure segregation. And in a companion case, North Carolina Board of Education v. Swann (p. 743 above), the Court struck down a state law prohibiting assignment of students by race: the state prohibition impeded "the operation of a unified school system" and hindered "vindication of federal constitutional guarantees." Would a congressionally established barrier to dismantling de jure segregated school systems be entitled to greater

Brown but determining, after extensive hearings, that busing is an ineffective remedy and that alternative remedies are available and should be used? [6]

What other congressional legislation might find support in Morgan? Applying to private conduct all restrictions governing "state action" under § 1 of the 14th Amendment? (Recall sec. 3 above, and note Leedes, "State Action Limitations on Courts and Congressional Power," 60 N.C.L.Rev. 747 (1982).) The civil rights violence provisions of the 1968 Act (p. 916 above)? Prohibitions of de facto segregation in public education? Modifications of the Court's criminal procedure due process decisions (chap. 7 above)? Altering the "one person-one vote" theme of the Court's reapportionment decisions (p. 1621 below)? (See also the additional examples noted below.)

b.　Can Congress use the Morgan rationale to readjust the balance when constitutional values compete? Are such "balancing" readjustments "expansions" or "dilutions" of constitutional guarantees? For example, may Congress redefine the boundaries between the rights of the free press and the accused? Consider the reliance on the Morgan rationale in an opinion in Welsh v. United States (1970; at p. 1529 below). In the Welsh case, Justice White, joined by Chief Justice Burger and Justice Stewart, thought the "religious training and belief" limitation on the conscientious objector exemption in the draft law constitutional on the ground that the Court, by analogy to Morgan, "should respect congressional judgment accommodating the Free Exercise Clause and the power to raise armies." [7]

c.　More than a decade after Morgan, the scope of the legislative power suggested by that ruling attracted an unprecedented degree of interest in Congress. Opponents of various decisions turned to the Morgan rationale in framing legislative responses to the Court rulings. The most controversial proposal was the proposed "Human Life Statute," introduced by Senator Helms and Congressman Hyde. [8] The Helms-Hyde bill was designed to authorize broader state control of abortions or, at least, to express congressional displeasure with the Roe v. Wade decision and to prompt the Court to reconsider it. [9] Sec. 1 of the bill provides: "The Congress finds that present-day scientific evidence indicates a significant likelihood that actual human life exists from conception. [10] The Congress further finds that the fourteenth amendment [was] intended to protect all human beings. Upon the basis of these findings, and in the exercise of the powers of the Congress, including its power under [§ 5], the Congress hereby declares that for the purpose of enforcing the obligation of the States under the fourteenth amendment not to deprive persons of life without due process of law, human life shall be deemed to exist from conception,

---

deference than the North Carolina law, either as an exercise of congressional authority to readjust "*remedies*" for the violation of constitutional rights or as an exercise of congressional authority to "weigh competing considerations" in determining the *content* of constitutional *rights*?

6.　Recall Senator Gorton's alternative to Senator Johnston's anti-busing bill, submitted in the Senate in 1982, as noted in chap. 9, at p. 719 above.

7.　Note also another reliance on the Morgan rationale by Justice White, in Trafficante (1972; p. 1573 below). In a concurring opinion joined by Justices Blackmun and Powell, he cited Morgan as well as Oregon in explaining his agreement with the Court's "generous construction" of the standing provisions regarding housing discrimination complaints under the Civil Rights Act of 1968. Absent the statute, he explained, he would have had serious constitutional doubts

based on the Art. III case or controversy requirement. But he concluded—invoking the Morgan analogy—that the statute was adequate to overcome those doubts. [Note that Justice Rehnquist's survey of the Justices' views on the Morgan "substantive" rationale (in the Rome excerpt in note 5a below) does not mention these opinions by Justice White.]

8.　S. 158, H.R. 900, 97th Cong., 1st Sess.

9.　Court-ordered busing in school desegregation cases was a second major area for congressional invocation of the Morgan rationale. (Recall chap. 9, at p. 719, above.)

10.　Before S. 158 was approved by a Senate Subcommittee in July 1981, the first paragraph of § 1 was revised to read: "The Congress finds that the life of each human being begins at conception."

without regard to race, sex, age, health, defect, or condition of dependency; and for this purpose 'person' shall include all human life as defined herein." [11]

Senator East's Subcommittee on the Separation of Powers of the Senate Judiciary Committee approved the bill by a 3 to 2 vote on July 9, 1981. However, full Senate consideration was postponed because of the position of Senator Hatch, one of the Senators in the majority. He stated that he had "serious constitutional reservations" about the bill and that he preferred the constitutional amendment route. Although the 97th Congress took no final action on the proposal, the proposal was reintroduced in substantially the same form in the 98th Congress. However, no further action has been taken.

Is the proposed "Human Life Statute" constitutional? Before approving the proposal, Senator East's Subcommittee held extensive hearings on that question. Among the proponents was Stephen H. Galebach, a young Washington lawyer who had advocated such legislation in an article. [12] Galebach argued that § 1 of the proposal is constitutional despite Roe v. Wade. He claimed that the Court's refusal in Roe to treat the fetus as a person was merely a decision resting on the incapacity of the judiciary to decide the question of when human life begins, and that, under § 5, Congress was the appropriate body to resolve that question. He explored at length the line of cases beginning with Morgan. He stated, for example: "A [congressional] determination that unborn children are human life [fully] justifies the correlative determination that they are persons. The latter determination, however, collides with the [Court's] holding in [Roe] that the unborn are not persons. But that holding makes sense only in light of the Court's inability to decide whether the unborn are human life. Informed by a congressional determination that life begins at conception, the Court might well reach a different conclusion. Still, the potential conflict raises serious constitutional questions. Does the [Roe] holding as to 'person' deprive Congress of power to pass contrary legislation? If Congress does pass legislation declaring unborn children to be human life and persons, should the Court defer to Congress' determination?" Galebach answered these questions by defending congressional power: under the Morgan line of cases, he insisted, Congress is the "co-enforcer of the 14th Amendment." He claimed that *both* rationales in Morgan permit Congress to include unborn children within the protections of the 14th Amendment without regard to whether the judiciary would find them to be persons. And he viewed such legislation as consistent with the Morgan dissent as well: "[W]hether the Court follows the standard of the Morgan majority, or the stricter review standard of the minority, the result in this case is the same: the [Court's] interpretation of 'person' in [Roe] does not bar Congress from taking a different view based on its determination that human life begins or is likely to begin at conception." Finally, in discussing the impact of the proposal, he commented that "the suggested statute would create a situation in which states have a compelling state interest in the protection of unborn life sufficient to justify anti-abortion statutes should states choose to enact them." [13]

---

11. Sec. 2 of the bill, which would eliminate lower federal court jurisdiction in abortion cases, is noted in chap. 1, at p. 52, above.

12. Galebach, "A Human Life Statute," The Human Life Review 5 (1981) [reprinted in 127 Cong.Rec. S 288 (daily ed. Jan. 19, 1981)].

13. Galebach elaborated: "The task of adjusting the meaning of 'life' and 'person' to accord with changing evidence and views of life is properly a task for Congress. Not only is the line between life and non-life a difficult one, more appropriately drawn by the legislature than by the courts; it is a line that [Roe] itself explicitly declared the courts unable to draw. If Congress draws the line at conception, the courts have no independent basis on which to draw a line different from that drawn by Congress. Under the approach of [Morgan], the Court's prior definition of 'person in [Roe] poses no greater barrier to congressional enforcement action than the Lassiter holding posed to Congress' nationwide prohibition of literacy tests."

Is Galebach's reasoning persuasive? Sharp criticisms of his proposed invocation of the Morgan power were voiced by pro-choice groups and by some legal scholars. Laurence H. Tribe, for example, stated that if the proposal were read as overruling Roe, it would be clearly unconstitutional.[14] Is such a position defensible without repudiating some of the statements in Morgan? Other scholars, such as former Solicitor General (now Judge) Robert H. Bork, rested their assertions that the proposal was unconstitutional on their conclusion that some of the broad statements regarding congressional power in Morgan are themselves wrong.[15]

4. *Limits on (and justifications for) congressional power to "interpret" constitutional rights: Some alternative views.* Most commentators on Morgan and Oregon have found Justice Brennan's footnotes unpersuasive efforts to articulate limits on a "substantive" congressional power under § 5 of the 14th Amendment. In addition to Cohen's comments noted earlier, see, e.g., Cox, "Foreword: Constitutional Adjudication and the Promotion of Human Rights," 80 Harv.L.Rev. 91 (1966): "It is hard to see how the Court can persistently give weight to the congressional judgment in expanding the definition of equal protection in the area of human rights and refuse to give it weight in narrowing the definition where the definition depends upon appraisal of facts. The footnote, therefore, may not be the end of the argument." See also Burt, "Miranda and Title II: A Morganatic Marriage," 1969 Sup.Ct.Rev. 81, suggesting that "the Court was wrong to erect its apparently rigid footnote [1] limitation on § 5 legislation." But those commentators have also tried their hands at justifying a limited congressional authority to determine the content of constitutional rights, and at suggesting safeguards other than those in Justice Brennan's footnotes. Consider the alternative justifications and limits they suggest. Are they adequate and persuasive?

a. *"Line-drawing" capacities and congressional power "around the edges" of Court doctrine—consistent with judicial "value preferences."* Burt, after recognizing that the Morgan rationale "to some extent" exempts the 14th Amendment from "the principle of Court-Congress relationships expressed by Marbury," endorses *some* congressional autonomy, in situations where principled lines to accommodate competing interests are difficult to draw. He notes that "Congress is less burdened by the principled constraints under which courts labor," and suggests that Congress may impose restrictions on states "where the Court does not feel able to do so itself" because of line-drawing difficulties—so long as Congress follows the Court's value preferences rather than imposing its own on the states. Thus, he supports a congressional "revisory authority" that "would be 'around the edges' of the Court's proclaimed doctrine"—i.e., a congressional power to redefine doctrine, but not too much: "As in Morgan, the Court would independently characterize the measure as a 'reform' that it approved or a 'restriction' that it did not." Burt suggests as an example of potential congres-

---

14. See also Ely & Tribe, "Let There Be Life," The New York Times (March 17, 1981): "Senator Jesse A. Helms wasn't conceived yesterday, and his constitutional advisers undoubtedly have explained to him why an attempt to overrule Roe v. Wade by statute must fail."

15. For a careful review of the arguments for and against the proposal, see Lewis & Rosenberg, "Legal Analysis of Congress' Authority to Enact a Human Life Statute" (Congressional Research Service, The Library of Congress, Feb. 20, 1981).

See also Gordon, "The Nature and Uses of Congressional Power under Section Five of the 14th Amendment to Overcome Decisions of the Supreme Court," 72 Nw.U.L.Rev. 656 (1977).

Professor Gordon states: "Congress has power to overturn the empirical findings of the Court; but it can do so only as long as it does not infringe on the normative component of the judicial decision. Were Congress to make an empirical 'finding' that an abortion procedure that was difficult or relatively unavailable was safer, thereby banning the generally available one, its legislation could not stand. In that case its empirical finding would undermine the normative principle of the woman's autonomy over her body." Compare Note, "Congressional Power to Enforce Due Process Rights," 80 Colum.L.Rev. 1265 (1980).

sional authority the difficulties of delineating the reach of the 14th Amendment to private discrimination: the Court "could not independently proscribe some private discrimination without its proclaimed principle extending to proscribe all discrimination," and that would unduly sacrifice competing values such as privacy. Congress, by contrast, could "arbitrarily" exempt some private choice, as it did in the Fair Housing Act of 1968. Thus, he endorses a congressional role where "the legislative mechanism is greatly superior to the Court's." (Cf. Jones, p. 924 above.) [16]

Would Burt's approach significantly limit congressional opportunities to resolve conflicts among competing interests in constitutional interpretation? How would the Court determine whether the congressional resolution was in accord with its "value preferences"? E.g., would that approach authorize Congress to "reinterpret" due process by curtailing the situation in which abortions are permissible after Roe v. Wade? Would it permit Congress to "interpret" due process to ban all state legislation regulating consensual sexual conduct? Would it authorize federal legislation to define the scope of a journalist's privilege in state courts, despite the Court's rejection of such a privilege under the First Amendment in Branzburg v. Hayes (1972; p. 1431 below).[17]

b. *Fact-finding capacities and the Morgan power.* Rather than endorsing a congressional power to resolve contests among competing interests, so long as they are in accord with the Court's "value preferences," would it be preferable to insist that any congressional power must be justified by its superior fact-finding capacity? The latter emphasis is increasingly prominent in Archibald Cox's comments on the § 5 power. In 1966, he drew from the second part of the Morgan rationale "the generalization that Congress, in the field of state activities except as confined by the Bill of Rights, has the power to enact any law which may be viewed as a measure for correction of any condition which Congress might believe involves a denial of equality or other 14th Amendment rights." Cox, "Foreword: Constitutional Adjudication and the Promotion of Human Rights," 80 Harv.L.Rev. 91 (1966). In 1971, in "The Role of Congress in Constitutional Determinations," 40 U.Cinn.L.Rev. 199, he argued that "the Morgan decision follows logically from the basic principles determining the respective functions of the legislative and judicial branches outside the field of preferred constitutional rights. Whether a state law denies equal protection depends to a large extent upon the finding and appraisal of the practical importance of relevant facts." He emphasized the "presumption that facts exist which sustain federal legislation" and the "principle of deference to congressional judgment upon questions of proportion and degree, as illustrated by the Due Process and Commerce Clause cases."

Are the actual and potential uses of the Morgan rationale in fact limited to determinations resting on factual grounds? Or may they involve congressional value choices as well? Even if they rest solely on factual bases, why should there be greater deference to congressional rather than to state legislative

---

16. Note, however, that Burt recognizes the "substantial risk for the Court" in such a view of Morgan: though the Court "retains ample doctrinal handles to disapprove congressional action, nonetheless its presentational rhetoric—that Congress has, to whatever degree, an 'independent' role in interpreting the Constitution—is likely to remove an important restraint on Congress which has, in the past, counseled great wariness in trespassing on the Court's prerogatives."

Given that risk, is the "presentational rhetoric" of South Carolina and Rome preferable to that of Morgan? Does the "remedial" (rather than "substantive") rationale of South Carolina and Rome give the Court a better "doctrinal handle" to disapprove congressional actions that a majority of the Justices find unacceptable?

17. In Branzburg, Justice White's majority opinion commented that Congress had freedom at the federal level "to determine whether a statutory newsman's privilege is necessary and desirable and to fashion standards and rules as narrow or broad as deemed necessary [and] to refashion those rules as experience from time to time may dictate."

judgments? (Recall Justice Harlan's dissent in Oregon.) And if there should be greater deference to congressional assessments, should the Court hypothesize facts that might justify congressional resolutions, or should it insist on a factual record in Congress? Was there such a factual record for § 4(e) in the Morgan case? Was there for the provisions involved in Oregon? Arguably, judicial deference should turn on the degree to which the congressional findings truly involve issues of fact, and on the degree to which those factual issues are spelled out in the legislative record.[18] What § 5 legislation would be permissible if Congress' special competence in fact determinations is emphasized? Would it justify "a comprehensive code of criminal procedure applicable to prosecutions in state courts," as Cox suggested in 80 Harv.L.Rev. 91: "Congress would seem to have the power, under the second branch of the Morgan decision, not only to enforce the specifics but also to make its own findings of fact and evaluation of the competing considerations in determining what constitutes due process and what measures are necessary to secure it in practice."[19]

c. *A distinction between "federalism" and "liberty" issues?* William Cohen's search for limits on congressional power under § 5 of the 14th Amendment looks in a different direction. In 27 Stan.L.Rev. 603 (1975) (noted above), he found Justice Brennan's efforts to articulate limits in Morgan and Oregon unsatisfactory because they gave Congress "an ill-defined power to dilute judicially declared protections of section 1 of the 14th Amendment." Cohen claims that a "viable theory concerning the limits of Congress' enforcement power under [§ 5]—one that realistically assesses the different strengths of Congress and the courts—can be formulated. [The] theory turns partly on considerations of federalism, distinguishing the relative capacity of Congress to draw the lines between national and state power from the courts' sensitivity to the rights of racial, religious, and political minorities." In short, he "distinguishes between congressional competence to make 'liberty' and 'federalism' judgments." Drawing on Wechsler's emphasis on the "political safeguards of federalism" (p. 95 above), he argues that "a congressional judgment resolving at the national level an issue that could—without constitutional objection—be decided in the same way at the state level, ought normally to be binding on the courts, since Congress presumably reflects a balance between both national and state interests and hence is better able to adjust such conflicts." But a "congressional judgment rejecting a judicial interpretation of the due process or equal protection clauses—an interpretation that had given the individual procedural or substantive protection from state and federal government alike—is entitled to no more deference than the identical decision of the state legislature." Is that approach persuasive? Does it actually differ from Justice Brennan's "ratchet" theory?[20] Is the "political safeguards" factor the only one

---

18. But see the majority's position on the need for congressional articulation of the power it relies on, in EEOC v. Wyoming (1983; p. 970 below).

19. See Title II of the Omnibus Crime Control Act of 1968, which included a partial overturning of the Court's required safeguards in the questioning of suspects, established in Miranda v. Arizona, 384 U.S. 436 (1966). The Burt article noted above sees the statute supportable under Morgan because the differences between Miranda and Title II "are limited in scope, and do not entrench upon the basic purposes which the Court was pursuing." Is such legislation nevertheless barred by the anti-"dilution" footnote [1] in Morgan?

Could modifications of the Miranda requirements be justified more readily under the "reme-

dial" rationale? Recall that even the dissenters in Morgan—and the unanimous Court in Oregon, with respect to the nationwide suspension of literacy tests—endorsed congressional remedial measures, and that the majority gave the "remedial" power a very broad reading in Rome.

20. Cohen recognizes that the two theories will typically produce the same results: congressional "extensions" of due process and equal protection would usually involve "federalism" decisions; congressional "dilutions" will ordinarily raise "liberty" decisions. But he insists that the outcomes under the two approaches would not always be the same.

For a restatement (and slight modification) of Cohen's position, see his later article, "Congressional Power to Validate Unconstitutional State Laws: A Forgotten Solution to an Old Enigma,"

that explains judicial deference to congressional judgments when the exercise of Art. I powers allegedly impinges on federalism concerns? Or is there a special breadth to those powers—a breadth not necessarily applicable to congressional "interpretations" of 14th Amendment rights? And even under Art. I powers, does Congress clearly have the power to determine what is interstate commerce, rather than merely deciding what is appropriate to regulate that commerce?

5. *The state of the Morgan "substantive" rationale in the 1980s.* a. [After all these speculations about congressional "substantive" enforcement power suggested by Morgan, it is useful to scrutinize the actual support for such a power on the modern Court. Justice REHNQUIST addressed that question in the closing passages of his dissent (joined by Justice Stewart) in ROME v. UNITED STATES (1980; p. 937 above). Most of his dissent, printed earlier, argued that the "remedial" power of the South Carolina case could not justify the application of the Voting Rights Act's preclearance provisions to Rome. He then turned to the "substantive" theory (which the majority had not thought it necessary to rely on) and argued that it was an untenable theory not supported by a majority of the Justices. Do you agree with Justice Rehnquist's reading of the prior cases? (Note especially his view of Morgan in his footnote [1].) He stated:]

The result reached by the Court today can be sustained only upon the theory that Congress was empowered to determine that structural changes with a disparate impact on a minority group's ability to elect a candidate of their race violate the 14th or 15th Amendments. This construction of the 14th Amendment was rejected in the Civil Rights Cases. The Court emphasized that the power conferred was "remedial" only. [This] interpretation is consonant with the legislative history surrounding the enactment of the Amendment. This construction has never been refuted by a majority of the Members of this Court. Support for this construction in current years has emerged in South Carolina and Oregon.[21] See also opinion of Powell, J., [in Rome]. In South Carolina, the Court observed that Congress could not attack evils not comprehended by the 15th Amendment. In Oregon, five Members of the Court were unwilling to conclude that Congress had the power to determine that establishing the age limitation for voting at 21 denied equal protection to those between the ages of 18 and 20. The opinion of Mr. Justice Stewart in that case [reaffirmed] that Congress only has the power under the 14th Amendment to "provide the means of eradicating situations that amount to a violation of [equal protection]" but not to "determine as a matter of substantive constitutional law that situations fall within the ambit of the clause." Mr. Justice Harlan, in a separate opinion,

---

35 Stan.L.Rev. 387 (1983). In this later article, Cohen states that "Congress should be able to remove constitutional limits on state power if those limits stem solely from divisions of power within the federal system. [It] should be able to approve unconstitutional policy choices in state laws when [it] is not constitutionally prohibited from directly adopting the same policy itself. In appropriate circumstances, Congress should be able to authorize the states to enact legislation that, in the absence of congressional consent, would run afoul of the due process or equal protection clauses" as well as the privileges and immunities clause of Art. IV and the contracts clause. "[But] my thesis would *not* permit Congress to ignore constitutional limits on its own power. [Ordinary] federal legislation cannot eliminate constitutional guarantees of individual liberty that are applicable to the states and Congress alike."

21. Explicit support can also be derived from Mr. Justice Harlan's dissenting opinion in [Morgan]. Mr. Justice Harlan clarified the need for the remedial construction of congressional powers. It is also unnecessary, however, to read the majority opinion as establishing the Court's rejection of the remedial construction of the Civil Rights Cases. While Mr. Justice Brennan's majority opinion did contain language suggesting a rejection of the "remedial" construction of the enforcement powers, the opinion also advanced a remedial rationale which supports the determination reached by the Court. It would be particularly inappropriate to construe [Morgan] as a rejection of the remedial interpretation of congressional powers in view of this Court's subsequent decision in [Oregon]. [Footnote by Justice Rehnquist. Compare with Justice Rehnquist's view the discussion of the Morgan power in Fullilove (1980; chap. 9, p. 769 above).]

reiterated his belief that it is the duty of the Court, and not the Congress, to determine when States have exceeded constitutional limitations imposed upon their powers. [Cf.] Cooper v. Aaron. Mr. Justice Black also was unwilling to accept the broad construction of enforcement powers formulated in the opinion of Mr. Justice Brennan, joined by Justices White and Marshall.[22]

The Court today fails to heed this prior precedent. To permit congressional power to prohibit the conduct challenged in this case requires state and local governments to cede far more of their powers to the Federal Government than the Civil War Amendments ever envisioned; and it requires the judiciary to cede far more of its power to interpret and enforce the Constitution than ever envisioned. The intrusion is all the more offensive to our constitutional system when it is recognized that the only values fostered are debatable assumptions about political theory which should properly be left to the local democratic process.

b. A year after his dissent in Rome, Justice Rehnquist found another context in which to suggest a narrow view of the Morgan power. This time, however, he spoke for a majority. The case, PENNHURST STATE SCHOOL v. HALDERMAN, 451 U.S. 1 (1981), involved the interpretation of the Developmentally Disabled Assistance and Bill of Rights Act of 1975. The Act established a federal-state grant program providing financial assistance to programs for the care and treatment of the mentally retarded. The Act's "bill of rights" provision states that mentally retarded persons "have a right to appropriate treatment, services, and habilitation" in "the setting that is least restrictive [of] personal liberty." The Court of Appeals found that Congress had enacted the law "pursuant to both § 5 of the 14th Amendment and the Spending Power," and that the "bill of rights" provision created substantive rights judicially enforceable by private litigants.

Justice REHNQUIST's majority opinion reversed, holding that the "bill of rights" provision "simply does not create substantive rights." He accordingly found it unnecessary to address the constitutional issue of whether Congress had the power to impose such affirmative obligations on states. But in the course of "discerning congressional intent," Justice Rehnquist discussed "the appropriate test for determining when Congress intends to enforce [14th Amendment] guarantees." He stated: "Because [enforcing] legislation imposes congressional policy on a State involuntarily, and because it often intrudes on traditional state authority, we should not quickly attribute to Congress an unstated intent to act under its authority to enforce the Fourteenth Amendment. Our previous cases are wholly consistent with that view, since Congress in those cases expressly articulated its intent to legislate pursuant to § 5. [See, e.g., Morgan.] Those cases, moreover, involved statutes which simply prohibited certain kinds of state conduct. The case for inferring intent is at its weakest where, as here, the rights asserted impose *affirmative* obligations on the States to fund certain services, since we may assume that Congress will not implicitly attempt to impose massive financial obligations on the States."[23]

---

22. Since Mr. Justice Black found that congressional powers were more circumscribed when not acting to counter racial discrimination under the 14th Amendment, he did not have to determine the precise nature of congressional powers when they were exercised in the field of racial relations. His analysis of the nationwide ban on literacy tests, also presented in [Oregon], however, is consistent with a remedial interpretation of those powers. [Footnote by Justice Rehnquist.]

23. In a footnote to this passage, Justice Rehnquist added: "There is of course a question whether Congress would have the power to create the rights and obligations found by the court below. Although the court below held that '[the provision] does not go beyond what has been judicially declared to be the limits of the 14th Amendment,' this Court has never found that the involuntarily committed have a constitutional 'right to treatment,' much less the voluntarily committed. Thus, [several parties] argue that legislation which purports to create against the States not only a right to treatment, but one in the least restrictive setting, is not 'appropriate' legislation within the meaning of § 5. Because we conclude that [the provision] creates no rights

c. In EEOC v. WYOMING, 460 U.S. 226 (1983), the Court clarified its position regarding the evidence necessary to show congressional reliance on § 5. (The case involved the application of the federal Age Discrimination in Employment Act to state governments.) Although the Court's disposition of the commerce clause and Tenth Amendment issues (p. 187 above) made it possible to avoid the § 5 issue, Justice BRENNAN's majority opinion nevertheless sought to correct a significant misconception. The lower court had taken Pennhurst to require of Congress an explicit reliance on § 5 in plain § 5 language. In response, Justice Brennan described Pennhurst as containing no such requirement: "It is in the nature of our review of congressional legislation defended on the basis of Congress's powers under § 5 of the 14th Amendment that we be able to discern some legislative purpose or factual predicate that supports the exercise of that power. That does not mean, however, that Congress need anywhere recite the words 'section 5' or '14th Amendment' or 'equal protection.' [The] rule of statutory construction invoked in Pennhurst was, like all rules of statutory construction, a tool with which to divine the meaning of otherwise ambiguous statutory intent."

The majority did not deal further with the § 5 question, but Chief Justice BURGER's dissent, joined by Justices Powell, Rehnquist, and O'Connor, contended that imposing restrictions on the mandatory retirement laws of the states was beyond Congress' § 5 power: "Since it was ratified after the Tenth Amendment, the 14th Amendment is not subject to the constraints [of National League of Cities.] [But] this does not mean that Congress has been given a 'blank check' to intrude into details of states' governments at will. [Congress] may act [under § 5] only where a violation lurks. The flaw in the [EEOC's] analysis is that in this instance, no one—not the Court, not the Congress—has determined that mandatory retirement plans violate any rights protected by [the post-Civil War] amendments." The Chief Justice then outlined the Court's deferential rationality approach to age discrimination claims, as embodied in Murgia (p. 608 above). Concluding that the Act accordingly could not be viewed as enforcing the Court's definition of equal protection, the Chief Justice also rejected the argument that this case came within the scope of Morgan: "Nor can appellant claim that Congress has used the powers we recognized in [Rome; Oregon; Jones; South Carolina; Morgan] to enact legislation that prohibits conduct not in itself unconstitutional because it considered the prohibition necessary to guard against encroachment of guaranteed rights or to rectify past discrimination. There has been no finding [that] the abrogated state law infringed on rights identified by this Court. Nor did Congress use, as it did in [Morgan], its 'specially informed legislative competence' to decide that the state law it invalidated was too intrusive on federal rights to be an appropriate means to achieve the ends sought by the state. [Allowing] Congress to protect constitutional rights statutorily that it has independently defined fundamentally alters our scheme of government." The Chief Justice went on to refer to the Court's refusal in Oregon to allow congressional control over state elections. This provided ample precedent to refuse to allow the § 5 power to be used to encroach on areas traditionally left to the states: "[This] same reasoning leads inevitably to the conclusion that Congress lacked power to apply the Age Act to the states. There is no hint in the body of the Constitution ratified in 1789 or in the relevant amendments that every classification based on age is outlawed. Yet there is much in the Constitution and the relevant amendments to indicate that states retain sovereign powers not expressly surrendered, and these surely

whatsoever, we find it unnecessary to consider that question." (Justice White's partial dissent, joined by Justices Brennan and Marshall, agreed that the provision was not enacted pursuant to congressional power under the 14th Amendment, but rather under the Spending Power. For the Court's comments on the Spending Power aspects of the case, see p. 213 above.)

include the power to choose the employees they feel are best able to serve and protect their citizens."

d. Note, finally, the potentially important, narrow view of the Morgan power (with heavy reliance on footnote [1] of Justice Brennan's opinion in Morgan) in Justice O'CONNOR's majority opinion in MISSISSIPPI UNIVER-SITY FOR WOMEN v. HOGAN (1982; p. 660 above). Justice O'Connor found that a state university had unconstitutionally excluded a male applicant from its women-only School of Nursing. The State offered as an added justification the argument that Congress, in Title IX of the Education Amendments of 1972, had authorized the university's discrimination by exempting undergraduate institutions that traditionally have used single-sex admissions policies from the gender discrimination prohibition of Title IX. The exemption provision in Title IX, the State argued, was "a congressional limitation upon the broad prohibitions of [equal protection]." Justice O'Connor rejected that claim summarily: Even if the statute were read as attempting to provide a "constitutional exemption, the State's argument would fail." Sec. 5 gave Congress broad power, to be sure; but Congress' power " 'is limited to adopting measures to enforce the guarantees of the Amendment; § 5 grants Congress no power to restrict, abrogate, or dilute these guarantees' [Morgan, quoting Justice Brennan's footnote]. Although we give deference to congressional decisions and classifications, neither Congress nor a State can validate a law that denies the rights guaranteed by the 14th Amendment. The fact that the language of [the exemption provision] applies to the [University] provides the State no solace: '[A] statute apparently governing a dispute cannot be applied by judges, consistently with their obligations, when such an application of the statute would conflict with the Constitution. [Marbury].' "

Chapter 11

FREEDOM OF EXPRESSION: SOME BASIC THEMES—REGULATION OF SPEECH BECAUSE OF ITS CONTENT

Introduction. The history of Supreme Court litigation regarding First Amendment freedoms is brief in years but enormous in volume. The Court's first major encounters with free speech claims did not come until after World War I; yet, in the less than 70 years since, claimed infringements of First Amendment rights have become a staple of Court business—and a source of frequent controversy. What are the ingredients and the dimensions of the concerns protected by the First Amendment? What analyses and techniques are helpful? An often bewildering array of slogans and standards abounds in the cases. What, for example, is the meaning and scope of the "clear and present danger" test? What are the alternative judicial approaches? Is it helpful to talk about "preferred positions" of certain freedoms, or about presumptions of unconstitutionality? How significant is the clash between judicial positions of "balancing" and of "absolute" guarantees? Is it useful to distinguish between regulations of "speech" and of "conduct"? Between "direct" and "indirect" restraints on free expression?

The problems of freedom of expression are too varied to lend themselves to solution by any single, simple, all-embracing formula. The cases typically involve more than one value of constitutional dimension, and the resolution of value clashes cannot be a mechanical process. But, after nearly seven decades of First Amendment litigation, there is special need to examine the diffuse and complex materials in an orderly manner. The purpose of the next three chapters is to facilitate that examination.

Chap. 11 explores some important recurrent themes in First Amendment analyses and is designed to provide building blocks for thinking about First Amendment issues. It deals with the relevance of the *content* of expression to the coverage of the First Amendment. As written, the First Amendment is simple and unqualified. But there has been a broad consensus that not all expression or communication is included within "the freedom of speech." Thus, bribery, perjury, and counseling to murder are widely considered unprotected by the First Amendment. This chapter considers the extent to which the content of speech should be a central consideration in determining the scope of the First Amendment. Are some types of speech clearly *within* its coverage, while others are entitled to less protection, or excluded altogether? After an introductory survey of the values allegedly underlying the First Amendment, sec. 1 turns to a variety of speech that is, by wide agreement, most clearly within the First Amendment—"political" speech, or speech critical of governmental policies and officials. This initial encounter with political speech issues emphasizes the problem of subversive advocacy and focuses on congressional efforts to deal with speech allegedly creating serious risks to national security and survival. Sec. 2 shifts attention from the most clearly protected variety of speech to those types of expression that have been the most frequently mentioned candidates for *lesser* protection under the First Amendment, or for total exclusion from it: "fighting words," defamation, obscenity and other offensive expressions, and commercial speech.

Chapter 12 turns to another group of basic, "building block" problems in First Amendment analysis. It begins, in the opening sections, with an introductory look at several additional techniques frequently utilized by the Court. Sec. 1A examines the meanings of the overbreadth, less restrictive means, and vagueness concepts. Sec. 1B considers the Court's special hostility to prior restraints. Sec. 2 introduces judicial concern, of growing importance on the Burger Court, with discrimination in the regulation of expression. A pervasive question is whether content-based distinctions should be subjected to stricter scrutiny than content-neutral ones. Sec. 3 examines the problems of symbolic expression. Sec. 4, the final section, addresses the permissibility of regulation of expression in public places such as streets and parks, and in some privately owned places (e.g., shopping centers) as well. To what extent are regulations of the "time, place, and manner" of speech more tolerable than those openly directed at the content of speech? This section deals mainly with the problems of the so-called "public forum."[1]

Chap. 13, the last of the free expression chapters, applies some of the analyses developed in the preceding building block segments and introduces several additional clusters of First Amendment problems as well. It considers "incidental" restraints on speech and association. The restraints here, like several in the earlier chapters, are sought to be justified by governmental interests that allegedly stem from concerns not with speech as such but with non-speech interests in, e.g., governmental efficiency. That section includes a variety of restraints on government employees—both efforts to elicit information about their associations and attempts to restrain their political activities. It also deals with such controversial areas as the regulation of the financing of political campaigns. The chapter concludes with an examination of the constitutional status of the media. It focuses on problems such as whether the media may be restrained from publishing materials in their hands and whether the First Amendment includes a media right of access to some kinds of governmental information. One reason for treating the problems of the media separately is the fact that the First Amendment protects not only "the freedom of speech" but also "the freedom of the press." What is the significance of that special mention of the media? Does it entitle the press to preferential rights under the First Amendment?[2]

THE FIRST AMENDMENT AND THE JUDICIAL ROLE— AN INTRODUCTION TO SOME RECURRENT THEMES

The problems of what constitutes "the freedom of speech" and what amounts to an "abridging" of that freedom are best examined in the particular-

---

1. Sec. 4 illustrates a recurrent principle in the organization of these materials. The materials seek to be both descriptive and critical: they seek to portray the judicial techniques most typically resorted to by the Court, and also to offer criticisms and alternative analyses when the Court's approaches seem unsatisfactory.

2. The literature on the First Amendment is voluminous. Some useful articles in the periodicals will be referred to in the materials below, at appropriate places. This footnote is limited to some useful books on the subject, as well as one article.

The article is Van Alstyne, "A Graphic Review of the Free Speech Clause," 70 Calif.L.Rev. 107 (1982) (reprinted as revised in chap. 1 of Van

Alstyne's book, Interpretations of the First Amendment (1984)). Van Alstyne's graphic overview may be useful to students as a survey of some commonly voiced alternatives in interpreting the First Amendment.

The most recent of the books devoted to the First Amendment are Nimmer, Nimmer on Freedom of Speech: A Treatise on the Theory of the First Amendment (1984), and Redish, Freedom of Expression: A Critical Analysis (1984). Additional especially useful works are Schauer, Free Speech: A Philosophical Enquiry (1982); Emerson, The System of Freedom of Expression (1970); Shapiro, Freedom of Speech: The Supreme Court and Judicial Review (1966); and Chafee, Free Speech in the United States (1941).

ized context of the materials that follow.   But a cluster of pervasive, related problems warrant introductory attention here.   What rationales justify the protection of freedom of expression?   What justifies special solicitude for free speech values?   And what judicial techniques serve best to manifest that solicitude? [1]   These questions address both the underlying policies that are claimed to animate the First Amendment and the judicial responsibility for articulating and protecting speech values.   In the materials below, there are frequent controversies over "double standards," the alleged preferred position of the First Amendment, its claimed "absoluteness," and the legitimacy of "balancing" First Amendment interests against competing societal concerns. More obscured in the cases but equally important are the searches for the roots of the values reflected in the First Amendment.   To what extent do historical and philosophical judgments, and those drawing on contemporary moral and social values, provide appropriate guidelines for judicial implementation of the First Amendment?   These introductory materials sketch some of the themes to be borne in mind in examining the particularized contexts that follow.

1.   *Justifying the special protection of speech: The Carolene Products footnote.*   One of the most influential statements of the modern Court's double standard—of its justifications for intervening in some areas (e.g., freedom of expression) while keeping hands off others (e.g., economic rights)—came in footnote 4 in Justice Stone's opinion in United States v. Carolene Products Co. (1938;   printed at p. 473 above).   Although, as noted earlier, Stone's argument extends beyond the First Amendment area, two of its three paragraphs suggest justifications for special scrutiny of restraints on freedom of expression.   In his first paragraph, Stone spoke of a "narrower scope for operation of the presumption of constitutionality when legislation appears on its face to be within a specific prohibition of the Constitution, such as those of the first ten amendments, which are deemed equally specific when held to be embraced within the 14th."   And in his second paragraph, he suggested, more tentatively, a "more exacting judicial scrutiny" of legislation restricting the "political processes";   and he listed "restraints upon the dissemination of information" among his examples under that head.   How persuasive are those "specific right" and "political process" rationales?   And what are their implications?   Are First Amendment rights truly more "specific" than constitutional guarantees that do not elicit special judicial solicitude from the modern Court—e.g., the contracts clause and protections of "property"?   Are they still "specific" when they are "incorporated" into the "liberty" of the 14th Amendment?   Is the scope of First Amendment rights unduly narrowed when primary reliance is placed on the "political process" rationale: does that argument suggest a greater protection for "political" than for "nonpolitical" speech (e.g., obscenity or "commercial speech" or "private" defamations)?   Is it helpful in analyses of First Amendment problems to think of a core area of "political" speech with less protection for nonpolitical expressions at the penumbras?   Note Alexander Meiklejohn's argument suggesting that "public" speech—speech on public issues, speech affecting "self-government"— must be wholly immune from regulation, while "private" speech is entitled to less complete protection.   See Meiklejohn, Free Speech and Its Relation to Self-Government (1948).   Compare the majority's statement in New York Times Co. v. Sullivan (1964; p. 1052 below), discussing the "central meaning of the

---

1.   A special judicial solicitude for free speech means at least that governmental action directed at expression or communication must satisfy a greater burden of justification than governmental action directed at most other forms of behavior. Whether that greater burden should involve across-the-board unitary, "strict scrutiny" (demanding a showing of "compelling" ends and "necessary" means) whenever First Amendment interests are affected, or whether the burden of justification should sometimes involve a somewhat lower level of scrutiny (e.g., for "indirect" restraints, or for restraints based on nonspeech rather than speech concerns) is a pervasive issue in the materials that follow.

First Amendment" and emphasizing the "broad consensus" that the Sedition Act of 1798 was unconstitutional "because of the restraint it imposed upon criticism of government and public officials."

2. *Justifying special protection for speech: The uses of history.*   In Palko v. Connecticut (p. 423 above), Justice Cardozo characterized protection of speech as a "fundamental" liberty in part because "our history, political and legal," recognized "freedom of thought and speech" as "the indispensable condition of nearly every other form of freedom."   Does history in fact support special protection of First Amendment rights?   And what is the scope of "the freedom of speech" enshrined by the Framers of the Bill of Rights?   When the Court has invoked history to justify special protection for criticism of government, the Justices have typically turned *not* to the thinking of the time the First Amendment was ratified in 1791, but rather to an episode a decade later—the Jeffersonian response to the Sedition Act of 1798.   See, e.g., the New York Times case, note 1 above, and Justice Holmes' dissent in Abrams, p. 991 below. But what of the intent of the Framers?

The Framers' intent.   a.   *Prior restraints.*   The scope of "the freedom of speech" the adopters of the First Amendment intended to protect is uncertain. What evils of pre-Constitution history was the Amendment designed to avert? The most prominent technique of restraint in English law had been the licensing of printers and the prosecutions for seditious libel.   But prior restraint through licensing was abandoned in England a century before the adoption of the American Bill of Rights.   Nevertheless, a barrier to licensing was at one time viewed as the major thrust of the First Amendment.   See, e.g., Justice Holmes' opinion in Patterson v. Colorado, 205 U.S. 454 (1907), embracing the Blackstonian view that freedom of expression was protected solely against prior restraints.   Compare his grudging recognition 12 years later, in Schenck, p. 986 below, that "[i]t well may be that the prohibition of laws abridging the freedom of speech is not confined to previous restraints, although to prevent them may have been the main purpose." [2]

b.   *Seditious libel.*   Zechariah Chafee, Jr.'s influential work on free speech [see Free Speech in the United States (1941), a revision of Freedom of Speech (1920)] argued that the Framers of the First Amendment had more in mind than the banning of the long-gone censorship through licensing: he insisted that they "intended to wipe out the common law of sedition and make further prosecutions for criticism of the government, without any incitement to lawbreaking, forever impossible."   There had been frequent prosecutions in pre-Revolutionary England for seditious libel—"the intentional publication, without lawful excuse or justification, of written blame of any public man, or of the law, or of any institution established by law."   Compare, however, Leonard Levy's careful historical study—Legacy of Suppression: Freedom of Speech and Press in Early American History (1960)—denying that the First Amendment was "intended to wipe out the common law of sedition."   His "revisionist interpretation" claims that 18th century Americans "did not believe in a broad scope for freedom of expression, particularly in the realm of politics." [3]   He concludes that "libertarian theory from the time of Milton to the ratification of the First Amendment substantially accepted the right of the state to suppress seditious libel," claims that the First Amendment framers' main concern was with states' rights and the fear of national power rather than with individual liberty, and argues that a "broad libertarian theory of freedom of speech and press did not

2.   On the Court's continued concern about the special dangers of prior restraints, see sec. 2 of chap. 12 and the final section of chap. 13 below.

3.   Note also that obscenity and blasphemy laws and civil actions for defamation were in existence during that period.

emerge in the United States" until the Jeffersonian battle against the Sedition Act of 1798.[4]

3. *The rationales for special protection of free speech: Values from philosophy.* The sources of the values that may guide interpretations of the First Amendment (and justify the primacy of free speech) typically extend well beyond the uncertain light cast by history. What *are* the values and functions of free speech? Assumptions about answers to this question typically underlie the resolution of the concrete problems raised by the materials that follow—even though most of the opinions fail to articulate those assumptions. Two themes are prominent in the judicial and philosophical justifications: one emphasizes the value of free speech in promoting individual self-expression and self-realization; the other stresses the value of freedom of expression for a system of representative democracy and self-government. Another frequent argument for speech, partly related to these themes, is the utility of free expression in promoting the search for knowledge and "truth" in the "marketplace of ideas."[5] What is the consequence of one emphasis or another for the implementation of First Amendment values in the materials that follow? Consider, e.g., the implications of the varying emphases for a position that would extend greater protection to political than to nonpolitical speech.[6]

a. *Articulating the values and functions of speech: Some judicial efforts.* Although efforts to state the special values and functions of speech are relatively rare in the Court's opinions, Justice Stone's Carolene Products footnote is by no means the only one. Some rationales have already surfaced in earlier materials. Recall, for example, Justice Cardozo on "freedom of thought and speech" in Palko (1937; p. 423 above): "Of that freedom one may say that it is the matrix, the indispensable condition, of nearly every other form of freedom."

4. Levy adds that the Jeffersonians in power "were not much more tolerant of their political critics than the Federalists had been." (For an effective elaboration of that thesis, see his Jefferson and Civil Liberties: The Darker Side (1963).)

See also the revised and enlarged edition of Levy's 1960 book, Emergence of a Free Press (1985), where Levy concludes that "the American experience with a free press was as broad as the theoretical inheritance was narrow." Note also Levy, "The Legacy Reexamined: A Response to Critics," 37 Stan.L.Rev. —— (1985); Hamburger, "The Origin and Development of the Law of Seditious Libel," 37 Stan.L.Rev. —— (1985); cf. Mayton, "Seditious Libel and the Lost Guarantee of a Freedom of Expression," 84 Colum.L.Rev. 91 (1984).

5. Note also the summary of these and related rationales for the protection of speech in text note 4 below.

6. For a modern effort to summarize the values and functions of freedom of expression, see Emerson, The System of Freedom of Expression (1970), 6: "First, freedom of expression is essential as a means of assuring individual self-fulfillment. [Second, it] is an essential process for advancing knowledge and discovering truth. [Third, it] is essential to provide for participation in decision making by all members of society. This is particularly significant for political decisions." Compare the varying emphases on these several strands in the selections below from judges' and philosophers' efforts to articulate the values of speech.

Emerson draws from his articulation a "fundamental distinction between belief, opinion, and communication of ideas on the one hand, and different forms of conduct on the other"—a distinction between specially protected "expression" and regulatable "action." For comments (and criticisms) of such "speech"-"conduct" or "expression"-"action" distinctions, see the materials that follow. Note also Ely, Democracy and Distrust (1980), suggesting that "absolutists" such as Justices Black and Douglas would nevertheless justify restraint of a speaker urging on a lynch mob by resorting to distinctions similar to the "speech"-"conduct" one: "To judge from performances elsewhere, Justice Douglas would say that that was 'speech brigaded with action' and therefore not protected, while Justice Black would call it 'speech plus' or perhaps 'not speech' and similarly deny it protection. The justices do themselves no credit here, for 'answers' like this are simply not responsible. They refuse to display whatever reasoning in fact underlies the denial of protection, and by their transparent lack of principle substantially attenuate whatever hortatory value there was in the pronouncement that speech is always protected." On Douglas, see, e.g., his concurrence in Brandenburg v. Ohio (1969; p. 1037 below); on Black, see, e.g., his dissent in Street v. New York (1969; p. 1178 below). Note also the comments on Justice Goldberg's opinion in Cox v. Louisiana I (1965), at p. 1230 below.

Probably the most eloquent judicial defense of free speech is that by Justice Brandeis in his concurrence in Whitney v. California (1927; p. 1007 below). His defense reflects most of the rationales—from the functioning of democratic government to individual self-expression—that have been advanced over the years. Note especially his passage explaining "why a State is, ordinarily, denied the power to prohibit dissemination of social, economic and political doctrine which a vast majority of its citizens believes to be false and fraught with evil consequence":

"Those who won our independence believed that the final end of the State was to make men free to develop their faculties; and that in its government the deliberative forces should prevail over the arbitrary. They valued liberty both as an end and as a means. They believed liberty to be the secret of happiness and courage to be the secret of liberty. They believed that freedom to think as you will and to speak as you think are means indispensable to the discovery and spread of political truth; that without free speech and assembly discussion would be futile; that with them, discussion affords ordinarily adequate protection against the dissemination of noxious doctrine; that the greatest menace to freedom is an inert people; that public discussion is a political duty; and that this should be a fundamental principle of the American government. They recognized the risks to which all human institutions are subject. But they knew that order cannot be secured merely through fear of punishment for its infraction; that it is hazardous to discourage thought, hope and imagination; that fear breeds repression; that repression breeds hate; that hate menaces stable government; that the path of safety lies in the opportunity to discuss freely supposed grievances and proposed remedies; and that the fitting remedy for evil counsels is good ones. Believing in the power of reason as applied through public discussion, they eschewed silence coerced by law—the argument of force in its worst form. Recognizing the occasional tyrannies of governing majorities, they amended the Constitution so that free speech and assembly should be guaranteed."

Ranking with Justice Brandeis' among the best known articulations of the values of speech is Justice Holmes' dissent in Abrams (1919; p. 991 below): "[W]hen men have realized that time has upset many fighting faiths, they may come to believe even more than they believe the very foundations of their own conduct that the ultimate good desired is better reached by free trade in ideas— that the best test of truth is the power of the thought to get itself accepted in the competition of the market and that truth is the only ground upon which their wishes safely can be carried out. That at any rate is the theory of our constitution." [7] See also Judge Learned Hand in the Masses case (1917; p. 997 below), insisting that the "right to criticize either by temperate reasoning, or by immoderate and indecent invective, [is] normally the privilege of the individual in countries dependent upon the free expression of opinion as the ultimate source of authority." [8]

---

7. See also Holmes' dissent in Gitlow v. New York (1925; p. 1002 below), and his dissent in United States v. Schwimmer, 279 U.S. 644 (1929), defending the right of a pacifist to become a naturalized citizen: "[I]f there is any principle of the Constitution that more imperatively calls for attachment than any other it is the principle of free thought—not free thought for those who agree with us but freedom for the thought that we hate."

8. For later statements, see, e.g., Justice Jackson's opinion in the second Flag Salute Case, Barnette (1943; p. 1510 below): "If there is any fixed star in our constitutional constellation, it is that no official, high or petty, can prescribe what shall be orthodox in politics, nationalism, religion, or other matters of opinion or force citizens to confess by word or act their faith therein." See also Justice Brennan's reference, in New York Times Co. v. Sullivan (1964; p. 1052 below), to "a profound national commitment to the principle that debate on public issues should be uninhibited, robust, and wide-open, and that it may well include vehement, caustic, and sometimes unpleasantly sharp attacks on government and public officials."

b. *Articulating the values and functions of speech: Some philosophers' comments.*
Though the Court opinions rarely refer to nonjudicial writings explicitly, some
of the Justices' articulations echo the themes of philosophers and political
theorists. The classic speech-protective statements are those of John Milton and
John Stuart Mill. John Milton wrote in 1644, protesting a licensing scheme for
books: "And though all the winds of doctrine were let loose to play upon the
earth, so Truth be in the field, we do injuriously, by licensing and prohibiting,
to misdoubt her strength. Let her and Falsehood grapple; who ever knew
Truth put to the worst, in a free and open encounter?" [9] John Stuart Mill's
classic libertarian argument came two centuries after Milton's, in On Liberty
(1859). Mill's central argument was that the suppression of opinion is wrong,
whether or not the opinion is true: if it is true, society is denied the truth; if it
is false, society is denied the fuller understanding of truth which comes from its
conflict with error; and when the received opinion is part truth and part error,
society can know the whole truth only by allowing the airing of competing
views.[10] What are the implications of Mill's classic defense of freedom of
opinion? Does it bar all restraints on speech? Even incitement to violation of
law—the problem pursued in sec. 1 below? Note Mill's own elaboration in On
Liberty: "No one pretends that actions should be as free as opinions. On the
contrary, even opinions lose immunity, when the circumstances in which they
are expressed are such as to constitute their expression a positive instigation to
some mischievous act. An opinion that corn-dealers are starvers of the poor, or
that private property is robbery, ought to be unmolested when simply circulated
through the press, but may justly incur punishment when delivered orally to an
excited mob assembled before the house of a corn-dealer, or when handed
about among the same mob in the form of a placard. Acts of whatever kind,
which, without justifiable cause, do harm to others, may be, and in the more
important cases absolutely require to be, controlled by the unfavorable sentiments, and, when needful, by the active interference of mankind. The liberty
of the individual must be thus far limited; he must not make himself a nuisance
to other people." [11]

4. *The major rationales for protecting speech, and some variations: An overview.*
The preceding excerpts illustrate the major rationales for protecting free speech.
(Most of them are reflected in the excerpt from Justice Brandeis' opinion in
Whitney.) As the materials below illustrate, emphasis on one rationale rather
than another may have important consequences for the scope of First Amendment protection. Thus, an emphasis on speech as an essential of representative
government tends to reserve the highest protection for political speech and
raises questions about the appropriateness of protecting such arguably "nonpolitical" areas as literary and artistic expression and commercial speech.[12] A second

---

9. Milton, Areopagitica—A Speech for the
Liberty of Unlicensed Printing (1644). (Compare Milton's battle metaphor with Holmes' reference to "the competition of the market," in the
Abrams passage quoted above.)

10. As Mill summarized his argument in
chapter II of On Liberty: "First, if any opinion
is compelled to silence, that opinion may, for
aught we can certainly know, be true. To deny
this is to assume our own infallibility. Secondly,
though the silenced opinion be in error, it may,
and very commonly does, contain a portion of
the truth; and since the general or prevailing
opinion on any subject is rarely or never the
whole truth, it is only by the collision of adverse
opinions that the remainder of the truth has any
chance of being supplied. Thirdly, even if the
received opinion be not only true, but the whole

truth; unless it is suffered to be, and actually is,
vigorously and earnestly contested, it will, by
most of those who receive it, be held in the
manner of a prejudice, with little comprehension
or feeling of its rational grounds. And not only
this, but, fourthly, the meaning of the doctrine
itself will be in danger of being lost, or en-
feebled."

11. Compare Hand's "incitement" standard
in Masses with Holmes' "clear and present danger" test in Schenck, pp. 997 and 986 below.

12. The political speech concern is associated
with Meiklejohn's position. Note also Justice
Brennan's emphasis on "debate on public issues"
and criticism of public officials in the New York
Times case, footnote 8 above, as well as Justice
Black's opinion in Mills v. Alabama, 384 U.S.

recurrent theme was echoed in the Brandeis statement in Whitney that "freedom to think as you will and to speak as you think are means indispensable to the discovery and spread of political truth." This theme is also illustrated by Justice Holmes' "marketplace of ideas" metaphor in his Abrams dissent, and it reflects arguments made in the Milton and Mill statements noted above.[13] The third widely voiced, and often more farreaching, rationale for protecting speech is the emphasis on the values of individual liberty, autonomy, and self-development. That theme, too, is reflected in the Brandeis passage from Whitney, with its explication of the value of liberty "as an end." The individual self-realization emphasis facilitates extension of First Amendment protection to speech that is artistic or literary rather than purely political, but it has been criticized as being too broad: arguably, it becomes indistinguishable from the autonomy aspects of substantive due process and covers a range of behavior far broader than speech.[14]

5. *The appropriate judicial stance.* Assuming that freedom of expression warrants protection because of its values to society and the individual, what *is* the appropriate judicial responsibility in protecting it? Is it useful to speak in

214 (1966), stating that "there is practically universal agreement that a major purpose of [the First Amendment] was to protect the free discussion of governmental affairs." For an endorsement of the political speech emphasis that finds broad implications in that rationale, see BeVier, "The First Amendment and Political Speech: An Inquiry Into the Substance and Limits of Principle," 30 Stan.L.Rev. 299 (1978). For a narrower view of the implications of an emphasis on political speech, see Bork, "Neutral Principles and Some First Amendment Problems," 47 Ind.L.J. 1 (1971). (Many scholars who reject the notion that sustaining the process of representative, democratic self-government is the *sole* purpose of the First Amendment nevertheless recognize the importance of that function.)

For a variant on or supplement to the First Amendment values drawn from the theory of representative government, see Blasi's thoughtful monograph, "The Checking Value in First Amendment Theory," 1977 A.B. Found. Research J. 521. Blasi offers as an additional basic value warranting a central place in First Amendment theory "the value that free speech, a free press, and free assembly can serve in checking the abuse of power by public officials." He argues that "the role of the ordinary citizen is not so much to contribute on a continuing basis to the formation of public policy as to retain a veto power to be employed when the decisions of officials pass certain bounds." Note also Schauer's defense of free speech on the basis of an "argument from governmental incompetence"— an emphasis on "a distrust of the ability of government to make the necessary distinctions, a distrust of governmental determinations of truth and falsity." Schauer, Free Speech: A Philosophical Enquiry (1982).

13. A number of commentators have criticized the "marketplace" rationale on the ground that its assumptions do not fit the realities of contemporary society. See e.g., Barron, "Access to the Press—A New First Amendment Right," 80 Harv.L.Rev. 1641 (1967), arguing (in the course of developing a claim of right of access to

the media) that the notion of a "self-operating marketplace of ideas [has] long ceased to exist" and insisting that a "realistic view of the first amendment requires recognition that a right of expression is somewhat thin if it can be exercised only at the sufferance of the managers of mass communications." Note also Herbert Marcuse's more extreme assertion that, "[u]nder the rule of monopolistic media—themselves the mere instruments of economic and political power—a mentality is created for which right and wrong, true and false are predefined wherever they affect the vital interests of the society." Marcuse's solution is to argue for "liberating tolerance"— "intolerance against movements from the Right and toleration of movements from the Left." See Marcuse, "Repressive Tolerance," in Robert Wolff et al., A Critique of Pure Tolerance 95 (1965). Cf. Powe, "Mass Speech and the Newer First Amendment," 1982 Sup.Ct.Rev. 243.

14. For modern elaborations of the self-development, autonomy, libertarian emphases, see e.g., Richards, "Free Speech and Obscenity Law: Toward a Moral Theory of the First Amendment," 123 U.Pa.L.Rev. 45 (1974) (cf. Richards, "Unnatural Acts and the Constitutional Right to Privacy: A Moral Theory," 45 Fordham L.Rev. 1281 (1977)); Baker, "Scope of the First Amendment Freedom of Speech," 25 U.C.L.A. L.Rev. 964 (1978). See also Redish, "The Value of Free Speech," 130 U.Pa.L.Rev. 591 (1982), and Scanlon, "A Theory of Freedom of Expression," 1 Phil. & Pub.Aff. 204 (1972) (but see Scanlon, "Freedom of Expression and Categories of Expression," 40 U.Pitt.L.Rev. 519 (1979)).

Among the general reviews of the competing rationales for protecting speech, see Schauer, Free Speech: A Philosophical Enquiry (1982) (Part I—surveying, e.g., the arguments from "truth," "democracy," and "individuality"); see also Nimmer, Nimmer on Freedom of Speech (1984) (esp. chap. 1, emphasizing as central the "enlightenment function"—the "search for all forms of 'truth,' which is to say the search for all aspects of knowledge and the formulation of enlightened opinion on all subjects").

general terms of an appropriate judicial approach—e.g., of speech as a "preferred" freedom? Is it useful to speak generally about whether the First Amendment guarantee is "absolute," or one that requires "balancing" of competing interests? This note illustrates the recurrent disputes these problems have produced, and introduces some widely used judicial techniques for evaluating First Amendment claims.

a. *The "preferred position" talk and Justice Frankfurter's critique.* In the excerpts from a 1949 opinion that follow, Justice Frankfurter reviewed (and attacked) statements in Court opinions asserting that the First Amendment is entitled to a "preferred position." He was especially critical of such statements because they suggested a presumption of unconstitutionality for impingement on speech rights. Note that Justice Frankfurter's attack falls short of Judge Hand's total repudiation, in some extrajudicial statements, of any double standard regarding judicial scrutiny of "personal rights" and "property" claims.[15] Note that Justice Frankfurter does not go quite so far as to suggest that judicial review should be as deferential in the free speech area as in that of economic regulation.[16] Thus, Frankfurter, too, recognized a hierarchy of values, with freedom of speech high on the list. In short, he, too, found that First Amendment rights were specially protected ones. Justice FRANKFURTER said, in a concurring opinion in KOVACS v. COOPER, 336 U.S. 77 (1949) (p. 1208 below):

"My brother Reed speaks of 'the preferred position of freedom of speech.' [This] is a phrase that has uncritically crept into some recent opinions of this Court. I deem it a mischievous phrase, if it carries the thought [that] any law touching communication is infected with presumptive invalidity. [I] say the phrase is mischievous because it radiates a constitutional doctrine without avowing it. Clarity and candor in these matters [make] it appropriate to trace the history of the phrase 'preferred position.' The following is a chronological account of the evolution of talk about ['preferred position']. [Frankfurter's review of the cases included the following comment on the Carolene Products footnote: "A footnote hardly seems to be an appropriate way of announcing a new constitutional doctrine, and the Carolene footnote did not purport to announce any new doctrine; incidentally, it did not have the concurrence of a majority of the Court." After reviewing the cases, Frankfurter added:]

"In short, the claim that any legislation is presumptively unconstitutional which touches the field of the First Amendment [has] never commended itself to a majority of this Court. Behind the notion sought to be expressed by the formula as to 'the preferred position of freedom of speech' lies a relevant consideration in determining whether an enactment relating to [free speech is unconstitutional]. In law also, doctrine is illuminated by history. The ideas now governing the constitutional protection of freedom of speech derive essentially from the opinions of Mr. Justice Holmes, [who] seldom felt justified in opposing his own opinion to economic views which the legislature embodied in law. But since he also realized that the progress of civilization is to a considerable extent the displacement of error which once held sway as official truth by beliefs which in turn have yielded to other beliefs, for him the right to search for truth was of a different order than some transient economic dogma.

---

15. See, e.g., Judge Hand's essay, "Chief Justice Stone's Concept of the Judicial Function," in The Spirit of Liberty (3d ed. Dilliard 1960). In his last years, Hand went further: he viewed the Bill of Rights primarily as merely "admonitory or hortatory, not definite enough to be guides on concrete occasions." See Hand, The Bill of Rights (1958). But see his opinion in the Masses case, p. 997 below.

16. It is true, however, that Justice Frankfurter rarely found laws invalid on First Amendment grounds. See, e.g., his dissent in Barnette (1943; p. 1510 below) and his opinion in Dennis (1951; p. 1017 below). But see his concurrence in the Sweezy case (1957; p. 1406 below).

And without freedom of expression, thought becomes checked and atrophied. Therefore, in considering what interests are so fundamental as to be enshrined in the Due Process Clause, those liberties of the individual which history has attested as the indispensable conditions of an open as against a closed society come to this Court with a momentum for respect lacking when appeal is made to liberties which derive merely from shifting economic arrangements. Accordingly, [he] was far more ready to find legislative invasion where free inquiry was involved than in the debatable area of economics. The objection to summarizing this line of thought by the phrase 'the preferred position of freedom of speech' is that it expresses a complicated process of constitutional adjudication by a deceptive formula. [Such] a formula makes for mechanical jurisprudence."

b. *"Absolutes" or "balancing"?* A recurrent theme in modern First Amendment adjudication has been the debate as to whether First Amendment rights are "absolute," or whether First Amendment interpretation requires the "balancing" of competing interests. Justice Black was the most eloquent advocate of the former position;[17] Justices Frankfurter, Harlan and Powell have been especially identified with the latter. One of the classic confrontations between Justices Black and Harlan came in KONIGSBERG v. STATE BAR OF CALIFORNIA, 366 U.S. 36 (1961) (p. 1367 below). Justice Harlan's majority opinion sustained the State's denial of bar admission to an applicant who had refused to answer questions about Communist Party membership. Justice Black dissented from that 5 to 4 decision. Justice HARLAN'S opinion included the following passage: "[W]e reject the view that freedom of speech and association [are] 'absolutes,' not only in the undoubted sense that where the constitutional protection exists it must prevail, but also in the sense that the scope of that protection must be gathered solely from a literal reading of the First Amendment.[18] Throughout its history this Court has consistently recognized at least two ways in which constitutionally protected freedom of speech is narrower than an unlimited license to talk. On the one hand, certain forms of speech, or speech in certain contexts, has been considered outside the scope of constitutional protection.[19] See, e.g., [Schenck; Chaplinsky; Dennis; Beauharnais; Yates; Roth]. On the other hand, general regulatory statutes, not intended to control the content of speech but incidentally limiting its unfettered exercise, have not been regarded as the type of law the First or 14th Amendment forbade Congress or the States to pass, when they have been found justified by subordinating valid governmental interests, a prerequisite to constitutionality which has necessarily involved a weighing of the governmental interest involved. See, e.g., [Schneider; Cox v. New Hampshire]. It is in the latter class of cases that this Court has always placed rules compelling disclosure of prior association as an incident of the informed exercise of a valid governmental function. Bates v. Little Rock. Whenever, in such a context, these constitu-

---

17. For elaboration of Justice Black's view of "absolutes" and "balancing"—in addition to his opinions—see his lectures, "The Bill of Rights," 35 N.Y.U.L.Rev. 865 (1960), and A' Constitutional Faith (1968). See also Cahn, "Justice Black and First Amendment 'Absolutes': A Public Interview," 37 N.Y.U.L.Rev. 549 (1962).

18. "That view [cannot] be reconciled with the law relating to libel, slander, misrepresentation, obscenity, perjury, false advertising, solicitation of crime, complicity by encouragement, conspiracy, and the [like]." [Footnote by Justice Harlan.]

19. "That the First Amendment immunity for speech, press and assembly has to be reconciled with valid but conflicting governmental interests was clear to Holmes, J. ('I do not doubt

for a moment that by the same reasoning that would justify punishing persuasion to murder, the United States constitutionally may punish speech that produces or is intended to produce a clear and imminent danger that it will bring about forthwith certain substantive evils that the United States constitutionally may seek to prevent.' [Abrams v. United States]; to Brandeis, J. ('But, although the rights of free speech and assembly are fundamental, they are not in their nature absolute.' [Whitney v. California]; and to Hughes, C.J. ('[T]he protection [of free speech] even as to previous restraint is not absolutely unlimited.' [Near v. Minnesota]." [Footnote by Justice Harlan. All of the cases cited in the text and footnotes are considered below.]

tional protections are asserted against the exercise of valid governmental powers a reconciliation must be effected, and that perforce requires an appropriate weighing of the respective interests involved."

Justice BLACK'S dissent countered: "I do not subscribe to ['the doctrine that permits constitutionally protected rights to be "balanced" away when a majority of the Court thinks that a State might have interest sufficient to justify abridgment of those freedoms'] for I believe that the First Amendment's unequivocal command that there shall be no abridgment of the rights of free speech and assembly shows that the men who drafted our Bill of Rights did all the 'balancing' that was to be [done]. [I] fear that the creation of 'tests' by which speech is left unprotected under certain circumstances is a standing invitation to abridge [it]. The Court suggests that a 'literal reading of the First Amendment' would be totally unreasonable because it would invalidate many widely accepted laws. I do not know to what extent this is true. I do not believe, for example, that it would invalidate laws resting upon the premise that where speech is an integral part of unlawful conduct that is going on at the time, the speech can be used to illustrate, emphasize and establish the unlawful conduct.[20] On the other hand, it certainly would invalidate all laws that abridge the right of the people to discuss matters of religious or public interest, in the broadest meaning of those terms, for it is clear that a desire to protect this right was the primary purpose of the First Amendment. Some people have argued with much force, that the freedoms guaranteed by the First Amendment are limited to somewhat broad areas like those.[21] But I believe this Nation's security and tranquility can best be served by giving the First Amendment the same broad construction that all Bill of Rights guarantees [deserve].

"Whatever may be the wisdom [of] an approach that would reject exceptions to the plain language of the First Amendment based upon such things as 'libel,' 'obscenity' or 'fighting words,' such is not the issue in this case. [T]he only issue presently before us is whether speech that must be well within the protection of the Amendment should be given complete protection or whether it is entitled only to such protection as is consistent in the minds of a majority of this Court with whatever interest the Government may be asserting to justify its abridgment. The Court, by stating unequivocally that there are no 'absolutes' under the First Amendment necessarily takes the position that even speech that is admittedly protected by the First Amendment is subject to the 'balancing test' and that therefore no kind of speech is to be protected if the Government can assert an interest of sufficient weight to induce this Court to uphold its abridgment. [Such] a sweeping denial of the existence of any inalienable right to speak undermines the very foundation upon which the First Amendment, the Bill of Rights, and, indeed, our entire structure of government rest. [I] cannot believe that this Court would adhere to the 'balancing test' to the limit of its logic. [Strict] adherence to it would necessarily mean that there would be only a conditional right, not a complete right, for any American to express his views to his neighbors—or for his neighbors to hear those views. [It] seems to me that the Court's 'absolute' statement that there are no 'absolutes' under the First Amendment must be an exaggeration of its own views.

"[There is a difference] between the sort of 'balancing' that the majority has been doing and the sort of 'balancing' that was intended when that concept was first accepted as a method for insuring the complete protection of First Amendment freedoms even against purely incidental or inadvertent consequences. The term came into use chiefly as a result of cases in which the power of municipalities to keep their streets open for normal traffic was attacked by

20. "Roth v. United States (dissenting opinion). See also [e.g.] Giboney v. Empire Storage Co." [Footnote by Justice Black.]

21. "See, e.g., Meiklejohn, What Does the First Amendment Mean? 20 U.Chi.L.Rev. 461, 464." [Footnote by Justice Black.]

groups wishing to use those streets for religious or political purposes.[22] When those cases came before this Court, we did not treat the issue posed by them as one primarily involving First Amendment rights. Recognizing instead that public streets are avenues of travel which must be kept open for that purpose, we upheld various city ordinances designed to prevent unnecessary noises and congestions that disrupt the normal and necessary flow of traffic. In doing so, however, we recognized that the enforcement of even these ordinances, which attempted no regulation at all of the content of speech and which were neither openly nor surreptitiously aimed at speech, could bring about an 'incidental' abridgment of speech. So we went on to point out that even ordinances directed at and regulating only conduct might be invalidated if, after 'weighing' the reasons for regulating the particular conduct, we found them insufficient to justify diminishing 'the exercise of rights so vital to the maintenance of democratic institutions' as those of the First Amendment. But those cases never intimated that we would uphold as constitutional an ordinance which purported to rest upon the power of a city to regulate traffic but which was aimed at speech or attempted to regulate the content of speech. None of them held, nor could they constitutionally have held, that a person rightfully walking or riding along the streets and talking in a normal way could have his views controlled, licensed or penalized in any way by the city—for that would be a direct abridgment of speech itself. Those cases have only begun to take on that meaning by being relied upon, [as] they are here, to justify the application of the 'balancing test' to governmental action that is aimed at speech and depends for its application upon the content of speech."

There may be somewhat less to the "absolutes"-"balancing" debate than meets the eye. See, e.g., Kalven, "Upon Rereading Mr. Justice Black on the First Amendment," 14 U.C.L.A.L.Rev. 428 (1967): The "absolutes"-"balancing" controversy "seems to me on the whole to have been an unfortunate, misleading, and unnecessary one." Justice Black, for example, did not support every freedom of expression claim, as the passage from Konigsberg and some of his opinions below illustrate; he only urged protection from "direct" infringements of those aspects of expression he considered to be within "the freedom of speech." Justice Harlan's "balancing," on the other hand, was not necessarily deferential. In one of the flag burning cases, Street v. New York, p. 1178 below, for example, he wrote the majority opinion sustaining the First Amendment challenge while Justice Black dissented on the ground that the prosecution was not for "spoken words," but for speech "used as an integral part of conduct" in burning the flag in public. Similarly, in Cohen v. California (1971; p. 1101 below), the "Fuck the Draft" case, Justice Harlan's statement for the majority was one of the most speech-protective (albeit largely "balancing" in approach) on the books, while Justice Black was once again in dissent.

The "absolutes"-"balancing" debate is best pursued and evaluated in the context of the materials below. But some preliminary remarks are appropriate here in the interest of clarification. The "absolute" position associated with Justices Black and Douglas has been criticized for not protecting all speech in practice and as resting instead on covert balancing judgments to justify the "absolute" results.[23] "Balancing," on the other hand, has been criticized for

---

22. "Typical of such cases [are, e.g., Schneider; Cox v. New Hampshire; Kovacs v. Cooper]." [Footnote by Justice Black.]

23. See, e.g., Mendelson, "The First Amendment and the Judicial Process: A Reply to Mr. Frantz," 17 Vand.L.Rev. 479 (1964): "Balancing seems to me the essence of the judicial process— the nexus between abstract law and concrete [life]. Surely the choice is simply this: shall the balancing be done 'intuitively' or rationally; covertly or out in the open?" [That comment is part of an extended debate between Mendelson and Frantz on the "absolutes"-"balancing" controversy. See also Frantz, 71 Yale L.J. 1424 (1962), Mendelson, 50 Calif.L.Rev. 821 (1962), and Frantz, 51 Calif.L.Rev. 729 (1963).] See also Ely's criticism of the "absolutist" approach, in footnote 6 above, and note Henkin, "Infallibil-

being too deferential to governmental judgments and as providing inadequate guidance to decisionmakers. The latter attack is reflected in the (usually pejorative) label "ad hoc balancing" and the suggestion that all balancing simply focuses on the particular facts of a particular case. But even balancing opinions, in addition to being arguably more candid in disclosing competing considerations, can provide guidance.[24]

Another frequently advocated approach which recurs below is that of "categorization," an approach that strives for "bright line" rules that distinguish what is within the First Amendment from that which is outside "the freedom of speech"—e.g., "political" speech is "in," "fighting words" or "obscenity" are "out." "Categorization" may be more acceptable if it rests on an adequate explanation of why certain varieties of expression are "in" or "out"—i.e., when it rests on a type of "balancing," exploring the free speech values and the competing interests regarding a variety of speech before determining whether it is included within or excluded from First Amendment coverage. But when categorization consists largely of conclusory statements, it is subject to some of the criticisms of the "absolutist" approach (including not disclosing the covert balancing on which it rests); and it may also suffer from the flaws of overgeneralization, with resultant demands that the Court retreat from overly broad exclusionary categories.[25]

A final judgment about the merits of the "preferred position," "absolutes"-"balancing," and "categorizing" debates is best reserved until an exploration of the arguments in the particularized contexts below. The same may be said about the appropriate levels of scrutiny in First Amendment cases (e.g., should strict scrutiny follow *whenever* government impinges on an expression interest, or should there be lower levels of scrutiny when restraints on speech are "indirect" rather than "direct," or when the variety of speech is not the "political" speech that most would put at the core of the First Amendment?)[26] May the debate at

---

ity under Law: Constitutional Balancing," 78 Colum.L.Rev. 1022 (1978).

24. See e.g., the discussion of "First Amendment balancing in the Harlan manner" in Gunther, "In Search of Judicial Quality on a Changing Court: The Case of Justice Powell," 24 Stan. L.Rev. 1001 (1972), concluding: "In the finest manifestations of Justice Harlan's approach to first amendment problems, [he] viewed balancing not as an escape from judicial responsibility, but as a mandate to perceive every free speech interest in a situation and to scrutinize every justification for a restriction of individual liberty. Moreover, after the closest possible analysis had isolated the crucial conflicts of values, [he] strove for unifying principles that might guide future decisions."

For an example of an "ad hoc" balancing statement note the "reformulation" of the clear and present danger test by Judge Hand, embraced by Chief Justice Vinson's plurality opinion in Dennis v. United States (1951; p. 1017 below): "In each case [courts] must ask whether the gravity of the 'evil,' discounted by its improbability, justifies such invasion of free speech as is necessary to avoid the danger." That does indeed suggest a case-by-case analysis; yet a modern commentator has noted "the compelling capacity of the Hand formulation to answer an immense number of first amendment disputes": "It is [a] very powerful formula for resolving 'the freedom' of speech, and is used more frequently

than is generally acknowledged because its approach figures in time, place, and manner cases and in indirect effects cases as well." Van Alstyne, "A Graphic Review of the Free Speech Clause," 70 Calif.L.Rev. 107, 128 (1982). See also the similarity to the Hand formulation in Van Alstyne's more embracive one, id. at footnote 57: "The question in each case is whether the circumstances were sufficiently compelling to justify the degree of infringement resulting from the law, given the relationship of the speech abridged to the presuppositions of the first amendment." (The last part of that formulation, Van Alstyne explains, "takes into account an implied, first amendment rank-ordering of speech, ranging from the most protected 'political' to the less protected 'aesthetic' and 'commercial' to the least protected 'obscene' and 'criminal' [e.g., perjury and solicitation to commit a crime].")

25. See sec. 2 below.

26. See, e.g., the widely used two-track model of justification advanced in the draft card burning case, O'Brien (1968; p. 1170 below). Contrast with the two-track models of justifications approach of O'Brien the two-tier models for evaluating the First Amendment side of the balance (valuing some types of speech less highly than other varieties) advocated by Justice Stevens in such cases as American Mini Theatres (1976; p. 1110 below) and Pacifica (1978; p. 1114 below).

these general levels nevertheless be important for what they say about judicial "attitudes"? That has been repeatedly suggested. Robert McKay, for example, argues that the notion of a "preferred position" for speech is a useful concept because it suggests an attitude, "a whole manner of approaching" free speech.[27] Similarly as to "absolutes": for example, Charles L. Black, Jr., while conceding that Justice Black's "absolutes" position cannot be taken literally, has suggested: "Attitude is what is at stake between Mr. Justice Black and his adversaries." [28] Is it fruitful to engage in extended discussions of general "attitudes"? These broad controversies surface repeatedly in the following materials; and evaluation of the competing positions requires examination of concrete conflicts and disparate judicial techniques. For example, if (as McKay suggests) "preferred position" consists of "a variety of devices" to protect speech—including "the clear and present danger test" and "prohibitions against prior restraint and subsequent punishment"—it may be more important to examine those varied "devices" in detail, in the context of recurrent problems, than to debate moods and attitudes at length.

SECTION 1. REGULATION OF POLITICAL SPEECH BECAUSE OF ITS CONTENT: THE PROBLEM OF SUBVERSIVE ADVOCACY

A. THE WORLD WAR I CASES: "CLEAR AND PRESENT DANGER"—ORIGINS, WEAKNESSES, ALTERNATIVES

Introduction. The Court's first significant encounter with the problem of articulating the scope of constitutionally protected expression came in a series of cases involving agitation against the war and the draft during World War I. The issues presented by these cases are a useful beginning for exploring the problem of the meaning of "the freedom of speech." Typically, the speaker presents claims at the core of First Amendment concerns: expression critical of government policies. The government asserts especially strong interests for restraining speech: protecting governmental operations, even assuring the survival of government. In the materials in this sec. 1, the Court has developed quite speech-protective doctrines. The materials in this section contrast sharply with those in sec. 2, where the Court has frequently endorsed claims that a particular variety of expression should be excluded from First Amendment protection altogether, or warrant at most a sharply curtailed degree of protection.

Sec. 1A introduces the "clear and present danger" test, a standard that has been a prominent and controversial ingredient of First Amendment law. The language stems from the first of these cases, Justice Holmes' opinion in Schenck. When is restriction on speech permissible? "Clear and present danger" has been hailed as an answer that avoids extremes. At one extreme, it can be argued that restriction on speech, at least political speech, is *never* legitimate— that punishment must be limited to illegal action, even if the speech directly "incites" that action. Holmes rejected that "perfect immunity" for speech. But, as one of the strongest defenders of "clear and present danger" emphasized, Holmes also rejected a far more restrictive, far more widely supported

---

27. McKay, "The Preference for Freedom," 34 N.Y.U.L.Rev. 1182 (1959).

28. See C.L. Black, Jr., "Mr. Justice Black, the Supreme Court, and the Bill of Rights," in The Occasions of Justice (1963).

alternative: that "any tendency in speech to produce bad acts, no matter how remote, would suffice to validate a repressive statute." [1] "Clear and present danger" purports to draw the line somewhere in between, but with a strong leaning toward protection of speech. But what is the meaning of "clear and present danger"? What are its uses, what its weaknesses? The test has been criticized as too simplistic. It has been charged with being insensitive to legitimate state interests for curtailing speech. It has been criticized from another direction as too flexible, as permitting too much incursion on speech, as a shield too likely to collapse under stress. It has been employed far outside its original context. It has had periods of disfavor as well as of popularity with Justices and commentators. [2] It is less widely invoked today than it once was. Yet it remains an important strain at the core of Court efforts to protect expression; and later doctrinal variations have grown from it.

Attention to the origins and meaning of clear and present danger is one of the justifications for beginning this chapter with an examination of the post-World War I cases. The Schenck case gave birth to the language; but Schenck was followed within a week by two other Holmes decisions, Frohwerk and Debs, which purported to follow Schenck, and those opinions are important to an understanding of the original Schenck criterion. Later in the same year came Holmes' dissent in Abrams. Did the Abrams dissent simply apply the Schenck standard, or did it give a new meaning to clear and present danger? District Judge Learned Hand's opinion in Masses is printed to promote critical examination of the Schenck-Abrams criterion. Does Hand's analysis, dealing with the same World War I statute about two years before Schenck, suggest a useful alternative to that of Holmes? And doctrinal significance is not the only justification for beginning with these cases: their factual context—agitation against war and the draft—is a recurrent one in our history. [3]

SCHENCK v. UNITED STATES

249 U.S. 47, 39 S.Ct. 247, 63 L.Ed. 470 (1919).

Mr. Justice HOLMES delivered the opinion of the court.

This is an indictment in three counts. The first charges a conspiracy to violate the Espionage Act of June 15, 1917, by causing and attempting to cause insubordination, &c., in the military and naval forces of the United States, and to obstruct the recruiting and enlistment service of the United States, when the United States was at war with the German Empire, to-wit, that the defendants wilfully conspired to have printed and circulated to men who had been called and accepted for military service [a document] alleged to be calculated to cause such insubordination and obstruction. [The] second count alleges a conspiracy

---

1. See Chafee, Book Review, 62 Harv.L.Rev. 891 (1949).

2. See, e.g., Strong, "Fifty Years of 'Clear and Present Danger': From Schenck to Brandenburg—and Beyond," 1969 Sup.Ct.Rev. 41, and Linde, " 'Clear and Present Danger' Reexamined," 22 Stan.L.Rev. 1163 (1970).

For a useful review of the state of free speech law in the years immediately *before* the issue reached the Court, see Rabban, "The First Amendment in Its Forgotten Years," 90 Yale L.J. 514 (1981).

3. Most of the cases below arose under section 3 of Title I of the 1917 Espionage Act. (The Abrams case involved 1918 amendments to the law.) The 1917 Act created three new of-

fenses: "[1] Whoever, when the United States is at war, shall willfully make or convey false reports or false statements with intent to interfere with the operation or success of the military or naval forces of the United States or to promote the success of its enemies, and [2] whoever, when the United States is at war, shall willfully cause or attempt to cause insubordination, disloyalty, mutiny, or refusal of duty, in the military or naval forces of the United States, or [3] shall willfully obstruct the recruiting or enlistment service of the United States, to the injury of the service or of the United States, shall be punished by a fine of not more than $10,000 or imprisonment for not more than twenty years, or both."

to commit an offence against the United States, to-wit, to use the mails for the transmission of matter declared to be non-mailable by [the 1917 Espionage Act], to-wit, the above mentioned document. [The] third count charges an unlawful use of the mails for the transmission of the same matter. [The] defendants were found guilty on all the counts. They set up the First Amendment to the Constitution, [and] bringing the case here on that ground have argued some other points [also].

The document in question upon its first printed side recited the first section of the 13th Amendment, said that the idea embodied in it was violated by the Conscription Act and that a conscript is little better than a convict. In impassioned language it intimated that conscription was despotism in its worst form and a monstrous wrong against humanity in the interest of Wall Street's chosen few. It said "Do not submit to intimidation," but in form at least confined itself to peaceful measures such as a petition for the repeal of the act. The other and later printed side of the sheet was headed "Assert Your Rights." It stated reasons for alleging that any one violated the Constitution when he refused to recognize "your right to assert your opposition to the draft," and went on "If you do not assert and support your rights, you are helping to deny or disparage rights which it is the solemn duty of all citizens and residents of the United States to retain." It described the arguments on the other side as coming from cunning politicians and a mercenary capitalist press, and even silent consent to the conscription law as helping to support an infamous conspiracy. It denied the power to send our citizens away to foreign shores to shoot up the people of other lands, and added that words could not express the condemnation such cold-blooded ruthlessness deserves, &c., &c., winding up "You must do your share to maintain, support and uphold the rights of the people of this country." Of course the document would not have been sent unless it had been intended to have some effect, and we do not see what effect it could be expected to have upon persons subject to the draft except to influence them to obstruct the carrying of it out. The defendants do not deny that the jury might find against them on [this].

But it is said, suppose that that was the tendency of this circular, it is protected by the [First Amendment]. Two of the strongest expressions are said to be quoted respectively from well-known public men. It well may be that the prohibition of laws abridging the freedom of speech is not confined to previous restraints, although to prevent them may have been the main purpose, as intimated in Patterson v. Colorado, 205 U.S. 454 [1907]. We admit that in many places and in ordinary times the defendants in saying all that was said in the circular would have been within their constitutional rights. But the character of every act depends upon the circumstances in which it is done. The most stringent protection of free speech would not protect a man in falsely shouting fire in a theatre and causing a panic. [The] question in every case is whether the words used are used in such circumstances and are of such a nature as to create a clear and present danger that they will bring about the substantive evils that Congress has a right to prevent. It is a question of proximity and degree. When a nation is at war many things that might be said in time of peace are such a hindrance to its effort that their utterance will not be endured so long as men fight, and that no Court could regard them as protected by any constitutional right. It seems to be admitted that if an actual obstruction of the recruiting service were proved, liability for words that produced that effect might be enforced. [The 1917 law] punishes conspiracies to obstruct as well as actual obstruction. If the act (speaking, or circulating a paper), its tendency and the intent with which it is done are the same, we perceive no ground for saying that success alone warrants making the act a [crime].

Judgments affirmed.

————

FROHWERK v. UNITED STATES, 249 U.S. 204 (1919): In this case and in Debs, which follows (both decided a week after Schenck), Justice Holmes once again spoke for the Court in affirming convictions under the 1917 Act. Consider what light these cases throw on the meaning of the clear and present danger standard he had stated in Schenck. In Frohwerk, Justice Holmes stated: "This is an indictment in thirteen counts. The first alleges a conspiracy between [Frohwerk] and one Carl Gleeser, they then being engaged in the preparation and publication of a newspaper, the Missouri Staats Zeitung, to violate the [1917 Act]. It alleges as overt acts the preparation and circulation of twelve articles, &c. in the said newspaper at different dates from July 6, 1917, to December 7 of the same year. The other counts allege attempts to cause disloyalty, mutiny and refusal of duty in the military and naval forces of the United States, by the same publications, each count being confined to the publication of a single date. [A motion to dismiss based on the First Amendment was overruled.] Frohwerk was found [guilty].

"[With regard to the constitutional argument] we think it necessary to add to what has been said in [Schenck] only that the First Amendment while prohibiting legislation against free speech as such cannot have been, and obviously was not, intended to give immunity for every possible use of language. [We] venture to believe that neither Hamilton nor Madison, nor any other competent person then or later, ever supposed that to make criminal the counselling of a murder within the jurisdiction of Congress would be an unconstitutional interference with free speech. [We] have decided in [Schenck] that a person may be convicted of a conspiracy to obstruct recruiting by words of persuasion. [S]o far as the language of the articles goes there is not much to choose between expressions to be found in them and those before us in [Schenck]. The first begins by declaring it a monumental and inexcusable mistake to send our soldiers to France, says that it comes no doubt from the great trusts, and later that it appears to be outright murder without serving anything practical; speaks of the unconquerable spirit and undiminished strength of the German nation, and characterizes its own discourse as words of warning to the American people. [A]fter deploring 'the draft riots in Oklahoma and elsewhere' in language that might be taken to convey an innuendo of a different sort, it is said that the previous talk about legal remedies is all very well for those who are past the draft age and have no boys to be [drafted]. Who then, it is asked, will pronounce a verdict of guilty upon him if he stops reasoning and follows the first impulse of nature: self-preservation; and further, whether, while technically he is wrong in his resistance, he is not more sinned against than sinning; and yet again whether the guilt of those who voted the unnatural sacrifice is not greater than the wrong of those who now seek to escape by ill-advised resistance. [There] is much more to the general effect that we are in the wrong and are giving false and hypocritical reasons for our course, but the foregoing is enough to indicate the kind of matter with which we have to deal.

"It may be that all this might be said or written even in time of war in circumstances that would not make it a crime. We do not lose our right to condemn either measures or men because the Country is at war. It does not appear that there was any special effort to reach men who were subject to the draft, and if the evidence should show that the defendant was a poor man, turning out copy for Gleeser, his employer, at less than a day laborer's pay, for Gleeser to use or reject as he saw fit, in a newspaper of small circulation, there would be a natural inclination to test every question of law to be found in the record very thoroughly before upholding the very severe penalty imposed.[1]

1. Frohwerk was sentenced to a fine and to ten years imprisonment on each count with the imprisonment on the substantive counts to run concurrently with that on the conspiracy charge.

But [on this] record it is impossible to say that it might not have been found that the circulation of the paper was in quarters where a little breath would be enough to kindle a flame and that the fact was known and relied upon by those who sent the paper out. Small compensation would not exonerate the defendant if it were found that he expected the result, even if pay were his chief desire. When we consider that we do not know how strong the Government's evidence may have been we find ourselves unable to say that the articles could not furnish a basis for a conviction upon the first count at least. We pass therefore to the other points that are raised. [The Court rejected all other arguments, including:] It is argued that there is no sufficient allegation of intent, but intent to accomplish an object cannot be alleged more clearly than by stating that parties conspired to accomplish [it]."

DEBS v. UNITED STATES, 249 U.S. 211 (1919): In this companion case to Frohwerk, the defendant was Eugene V. Debs, the long-time leader and frequent presidential candidate of the Socialist party.[1] The Court considered two counts of the indictment under which Debs had been convicted. The first alleged that, in June 1918, Debs had "caused and incited and attempted to cause and incite insubordination, disloyalty, mutiny and refusal of duty in the [armed] forces" and "with intent so to do delivered, to an assembly of people, a public speech." The second alleged that he "obstructed and attempted to obstruct the recruiting and enlistment service" of the U.S. and "to that end and with that intent delivered the same speech." In affirming that conviction, Justice HOLMES wrote:

"The main theme of the speech was socialism, its growth, and a prophecy of its ultimate success. With that we have nothing to do, but if a part or the manifest intent of the more general utterances was to encourage those present to obstruct the recruiting service and if in passages such encouragement was directly given, the immunity of the general theme may not be enough to protect the speech. The speaker began by saying that he had just returned from a visit to the workhouse in the neighborhood where three of their most loyal comrades were paying the penalty for their devotion to the working class—[persons] who had been convicted of aiding and abetting another in failing to register for the draft. He said that he had to be prudent and might not be able to say all that he thought, thus intimating to his hearers that they might infer that he meant more, but he did say that those persons were paying the penalty for standing erect and for seeking to pave the way to better conditions for all mankind. Later he added further eulogies and said that he was proud of them. [There] followed personal experiences and illustrations of the growth of socialism, a glorification of minorities, and a prophecy of the success of the international socialist crusade, with the interjection that 'you need to know that you are fit for something better than slavery and cannon fodder.' The rest of the discourse had only the indirect though not necessarily ineffective bearing on the offences alleged that is to be found in the usual contrasts between capitalists and laboring men, sneers at the advice to cultivate war gardens, attribution to plutocrats of the high price of coal, &c. [The] defendant addressed the jury himself, and while contending that his speech did not warrant the charges said 'I have been accused of obstructing the war. I admit it. Gentlemen, I abhor war. I would oppose the war if I stood alone.' The statement was not necessary to warrant the jury in finding that one purpose of the speech, whether incidental or not does not matter, was to oppose not only war in general but this war, and that

1. In 1912, Debs had gotten over 900,000 votes, nearly 6% of the total. In 1920 (while Debs was in jail because of the conviction affirmed in this case) he again received over 900,000 votes, 3.4% of the total vote. Debs did not serve the full ten-year term to which he was sentenced: in 1921, he was released, on order of President Harding. (Note Kalven, "Professor Ernst Freund and [Debs]," 40 U.Chi.L.Rev. 235 (1973): "To put the case in modern context, it is somewhat as though George McGovern had been sent to prison for his criticism of the war.")

the opposition was so expressed that its natural and intended effect would be to obstruct recruiting. If that was intended and if, in all the circumstances, that would be its probable effect it would not be protected by reason of its being part of a general program and expressions of a general and conscientious belief.

"[The chief defense is] that based upon the First Amendment, [disposed of in Schenck]. There was introduced [in evidence] an 'Anti-war Proclamation and Program' adopted at St. Louis in April, 1917, coupled with testimony that about an hour before his speech the defendant had stated that he approved of that platform in spirit and in substance. [Counsel] argued against its admissibility, at some length. This document contained the usual suggestion that capitalism was the cause of the war and that our entrance into it 'was instigated by the predatory capitalists in the United States.' [Its] first recommendation was, 'continuous, active, and public opposition to the war, through demonstrations, mass petitions, and all other means within our power.' Evidence that the defendant accepted this view and this declaration of his duties at the time that he made his speech is evidence that if in that speech he used words tending to obstruct the recruiting service he meant that they should have that effect. [We] should add that the jury were most carefully instructed that they could not find the defendant guilty for advocacy of any of his opinions unless the words used had as their natural tendency and reasonably probable effect to obstruct the recruiting service, &c., and unless the defendant had the specific intent to do so in his mind. Without going into further particulars we are of opinion that the verdict on the fourth count, for obstructing and attempting to obstruct the recruiting service of the United States, must be sustained. Therefore it is less important to consider whether that upon the third count, for causing and attempting to cause insubordination, &c., in the military and naval forces, is equally impregnable. The jury were instructed that for the purposes of the statute the persons designated by the Act of May 18, 1917, registered and enrolled under it, and thus subject to be called into the active service, were a part of the military forces of the United States. The Government presents a strong argument from the history of the statutes that the instruction was correct and in accordance with established legislative usage. We see no sufficient reason for differing from the [conclusion]."

SOME QUESTIONS ABOUT THE SCHENCK–FROHWERK–DEBS APPROACH

Clear and present danger supposedly assures special attention to the time dimension: speech may not be curtailed until there is an immediate risk of an evil; speech with a remote tendency to cause danger cannot be curtailed. Is that sense conveyed by the language of these early 1919 cases? By the facts and results?

1. *Schenck.* What showing was there that the substantive evil had come about, or that the words would "bring about" the evils? Does Schenck clearly reject a "bad tendency" criterion and replace it with one of "clear and present" immediacy? Note the reference to "the act, [its] tendency and the intent" at the end of the opinion. What is the relevance of "intent" to immediate risk of harm? "Tendency"? Is the "shouting fire" analogy apt? To political speech? Are truth and falsity relevant? What if the speaker thought there was a fire?

2. *Frohwerk.* Was the Frohwerk "counselling of a murder" reference helpful in delineating the requisite "proximity and degree"? Was the language used by Frohwerk indistinguishable from that in Schenck? The Frohwerk opinion refers to "language that might be taken to convey an innuendo of a different sort." Is talk of risks of "innuendos" consistent with a sensitive regard

for speech? Is talk of the possibility of evidence about "a little breath" that might "kindle a flame"? Does that suggest insistence on showing a high probability of harm? Is that talk more protective of speech than the "bad tendency" test?

3. *Debs.* Did Holmes demonstrate the "clear and present danger" of Debs' speeches? Did he deprecate the "general theme" unduly? Did he unduly emphasize what "his hearers [might] infer"? Does the talk of "natural tendency and reasonably probable effect" sound like an immediacy-emphasizing alternative to a "bad tendency" approach?

THE ABRAMS CASE—EVOLUTION OR REBIRTH OF THE CLEAR AND PRESENT DANGER TEST?

1. *The facts of the Abrams case.* In 1918, the Espionage Act was amended to add to the provisions relied on in the Schenck group of cases a new series of offenses, including urging any curtailment of production of materials necessary to the prosecution of the war against Germany with intent to hinder its prosecution. The convictions of the defendants in ABRAMS v. UNITED STATES, 250 U.S. 616 (1919), rested in part on that amendment: they were found guilty of unlawfully writing and publishing language "intended to incite, provoke and encourage resistance to the United States" during World War I, and of conspiring "to urge, incite and advocate curtailment of production [of] ordnance and ammunition, necessary [to] the prosecution of the war." The Court sustained the convictions, rejecting the constitutional attack summarily on the basis of Schenck and finding the proof sufficient to sustain the charges. Justice CLARKE's majority opinion noted that it was part of the charge "that the defendants would attempt to accomplish their unlawful purpose by printing, writing and distributing in the City of New York many copies of a leaflet or circular, printed in the English language, and of another printed in the Yiddish language." He added: "All of the five defendants were born in Russia. They were intelligent, had considerable schooling, and at the time they were arrested they had lived in the United States terms varying from five to ten years, but none of them had applied for naturalization. Four of them testified as witnesses in their own behalf and of these, three frankly avowed that they were 'rebels,' 'revolutionists,' 'anarchists.' [It] was admitted on the trial that the defendants had united to print and distribute the described circulars and that five thousand of them had been printed and distributed [in] August, 1918. [The] circulars were distributed some by throwing them from a window of a building where one of the defendants was employed and others secretly, in New York City."[1]

2. *The Holmes dissent in Abrams.* [The Abrams affirmance provoked one of the most famous Holmes dissents, joined by Brandeis. Justice HOLMES stated:] This indictment is founded wholly upon the publication of two leaflets which I shall describe in a moment. [There were four counts; the majority found sufficient evidence to justify conviction under the third and fourth.] The third count alleges a conspiracy to encourage resistance to the United States in the [war with Germany] and to attempt to effectuate the purpose by publishing the [two] leaflets. The fourth count lays a conspiracy to incite curtailment of production of things necessary to the prosecution of the war and to attempt to accomplish it by publishing the second [leaflet]. The first of these leaflets says that the President's cowardly silence about the intervention in Russia reveals the hypocrisy of the plutocratic gang in Washington. It intimates that "German militarism combined with allied capitalism to crush the Russian revolution"—

---

1. The contents of the circulars are summarized in Justice Holmes' dissent, note 2 below.

See also the additional excerpts from the majority opinion, in note 3 below.

goes on that the tyrants of the world fight each other until they see a common enemy—working class enlightenment, when they combine to crush it; and that now militarism and capitalism combined, though not openly, to crush the Russian revolution. It says that there is only one enemy of the workers of the world and that is capitalism; that it is a crime for workers of America, &c., to fight the workers' republic of Russia, and ends "Awake! Awake, you Workers of the World! Revolutionists." A note adds "It is absurd to call us pro-German. We hate and despise German militarism more than do you hypocritical tyrants. We have more reasons for denouncing German militarism than has the coward of the White House."

The other leaflet, headed "Workers—Wake Up," with abusive language says that America together with the Allies will march for Russia to help the Czecko-Slovaks in their struggle against the Bolsheviki, and that this time the hypocrites shall not fool the Russian emigrants and friends of Russia in America. It tells the Russian emigrants that they now must spit in the face of the false military propaganda by which their sympathy and help to the prosecution of the war have been called forth and says that with the money they have lent or are going to lend "they will make bullets not only for the Germans but also for the Workers Soviets of Russia," and further, "Workers in the ammunition factories, you are producing bullets, bayonets, cannon, to murder not only the Germans, but also your dearest, best, who are in Russia and are fighting for freedom." It then appeals to the same Russian emigrants at some length not to consent to the "inquisitionary expedition to Russia," and says that the destruction of the Russian revolution is "the politics of the march to Russia." The leaflet winds up by saying "Workers, our reply to this barbaric intervention has to be a general strike!," and after a few words on the spirit of revolution, exhortations not to be afraid, and some usual tall talk ends "Woe unto those who will be in the way of progress. Let solidarity live! The Rebels."

[With regard to the fourth count] it seems too plain to be denied that the suggestion to workers in the ammunition factories that they are producing bullets to murder their dearest, and the further advocacy of a general strike, both in the second leaflet, do urge curtailment of production of things necessary to the prosecution of the war within the meaning of the Act of May 16, 1918, amending § 3 of the earlier Act of 1917. But to make the conduct criminal that statute requires that it should be "with intent by such curtailment to cripple or hinder the United States in the prosecution of the war [with Germany]." It seems to me that no such intent is proved. I am aware of course that the word intent as vaguely used in ordinary legal discussion means no more than knowledge at the time of the act that the consequences said to be intended will ensue. Even less than that will satisfy the general principle of civil and criminal liability. A man may have to pay damages, may be sent to prison, at common law might be hanged, if at the time of his act he knew facts from which common experience showed that the consequences would follow, whether he individually could foresee them or not. But, when words are used exactly, a deed is not done with intent to produce a consequence unless that consequence is the aim of the deed. It may be obvious, and obvious to the actor, that the consequence will follow, and he may be liable for it even if he regrets it, but he does not do the act with intent to produce it unless the aim to produce it is the proximate motive of the specific act, although there may be some deeper motive behind. It seems to me that this statute must be taken to use its words in a strict and accurate sense. They would be absurd in any other. A patriot might think that we were wasting money on aeroplanes, or making more cannon of a certain kind than we needed, and might advocate curtailment with success, yet even if it turned out that the curtailment hindered and was thought by other minds to have been obviously likely to hinder the United States in the prosecution of the war, no one would hold such conduct a crime. I admit that my illustration does not answer all that might be said but it is enough to show what I think and to let me pass to a more important aspect of the case. I refer to the [First Amendment].

I never have seen any reason to doubt that the questions of law that alone were before this Court in the cases of [Schenck, Frohwerk, and Debs] were rightly decided. I do not doubt for a moment that by the same reasoning that would justify punishing persuasion to murder, the United States constitutionally may punish speech that produces or is intended to produce a clear and imminent danger that it will bring about forthwith certain substantive evils that the United States constitutionally may seek to prevent. The power undoubtedly is greater in time of war than in time of peace because war opens dangers that do not exist at other times. But as against dangers peculiar to war, as against others, the principle of the right to free speech is always the same. It is only the present danger of immediate evil or an intent to bring it about that warrants Congress in setting a limit to the expression of opinion where private rights are not concerned. Congress certainly cannot forbid all effort to change the mind of the country. Now nobody can suppose that the surreptitious publishing of a silly leaflet by an unknown man, without more, would present any immediate danger that its opinions would hinder the success of the government arms or have any appreciable tendency to do so. Publishing those opinions for the very purpose of obstructing, however, might indicate a greater danger and at any rate would have the quality of an attempt. So I assume that the second leaflet if published for the purposes alleged in the fourth count might be punishable. But it seems pretty clear to me that nothing less than that would bring these papers within the scope of this law. An actual intent in the sense that I have explained is necessary to constitute an attempt, where a further act of the same individual is required to complete the substantive crime. [It] is necessary where the success of the attempt depends upon others because if that intent is not present the actor's aim may be accomplished without bringing about the evils sought to be checked. An intent to prevent interference with the revolution in Russia might have been satisfied without any hindrance to carrying on the war in which we were engaged.

I do not see how anyone can find the intent required by the statute in any of the defendants' words. The second leaflet is the only one that affords even a foundation for the charge, and there, without invoking the hatred of German militarism expressed in the former one, it is evident from the beginning to the end that the only object of the paper is to help Russia and stop American intervention there against the popular government—not to impede the United States in the war that it was carrying on. To say that two phrases taken literally might import a suggestion of conduct that would have interference with the war as an indirect and probably undesired effect seems to me by no means enough to show an attempt to produce that effect. I [turn] for a moment to the third count. That charges an intent to provoke resistance to the United States in its war with Germany. Taking the clause in the statute that deals with that in connection with the [other] provisions of the act, I think that resistance to the United States means some forcible act of opposition to some proceeding of the United States in pursuance of the war. I think the intent must be the specific intent that I have described [and] I think that no such intent was proved or existed in fact. I also think that there is no hint at resistance to the United States as I construe the phrase.

In this case sentences of twenty years imprisonment have been imposed for the publishing of two leaflets that I believe the defendants had as much right to publish as the Government has to publish the Constitution of the United States now vainly invoked by them. Even if I am technically wrong and enough can be squeezed from these poor and puny anonymities to turn the color of legal litmus paper; I will add, even if what I think the necessary intent were shown; the most nominal punishment seems to me all that possibly could be inflicted, unless the defendants are to be made to suffer not for what the indictment alleges but for the creed that they avow—a creed that I believe to be the creed of ignorance and immaturity when honestly held, as I see no reason to doubt that it was held here, but which, although made the subject of examination at the trial, no one has a right even to consider in dealing with the charges before the Court.

Persecution for the expression of opinions seems to me perfectly logical. If you have no doubt of your premises or your power and want a certain result with all your heart you naturally express your wishes in law and sweep away all opposition. To allow opposition by speech seems to indicate that you think the speech impotent, as when a man says that he has squared the circle, or that you do not care whole-heartedly for the result, or that you doubt either your power or your premises. But when men have realized that time has upset many fighting faiths, they may come to believe even more than they believe the very foundations of their own conduct that the ultimate good desired is better reached by free trade in ideas—that the best test of truth is the power of the thought to get itself accepted in the competition of the market, and that truth is the only ground upon which their wishes safely can be carried out. That at any rate is the theory of our Constitution. It is an experiment, as all life is an experiment. Every year if not every day we have to wager our salvation upon some prophecy based upon imperfect knowledge. While that experiment is part of our system I think that we should be eternally vigilant against attempts to check the expression of opinions that we loathe and believe to be fraught with death, unless they so imminently threaten immediate interference with the lawful and pressing purposes of the law that an immediate check is required to save the country. I wholly disagree with the argument of the Government that the First Amendment left the common law as to seditious libel in force. History seems to me against the notion. I had conceived that the United States through many years had shown its repentance for the Sedition Act of 1798, by repaying fines that it imposed. Only the emergency that makes it immediately dangerous to leave the correction of evil counsels to time warrants making any exception to the sweeping command, "Congress shall make no [law] abridging the freedom of speech." Of course I am speaking only of expressions of opinion and exhortations, which were all that were uttered here, but I regret that I cannot put into more impressive words my belief that in their conviction upon this indictment the defendants were deprived of their rights under the [Constitution].

3. *The majority's evaluation of the evidence in Abrams.* Compare with Justice Holmes' evaluation of the circulars the following comments in the majority opinion's review of the evidence. Which evaluation seems closer to the approach of Schenck-Frohwerk-Debs: the majority's or the dissent's? Justice CLARKE's majority opinion stated: "It will not do to say [that] the only intent of these defendants was to prevent injury to the Russian cause. Men must be held to have intended, and to be accountable for, the effects which their acts were likely to produce. Even if their primary purpose and intent was to aid the cause of the Russian Revolution, the plan of action which they adopted necessarily involved, before it could be realized, defeat of the war program of the United States, for the obvious effect of this appeal, if it should become effective, as they hoped it might, would be to persuade persons of character such as those whom they regarded themselves as addressing not to aid government loans and not to work in ammunition factories where their work would produce 'bullets, bayonets, cannon' and other munitions of war, the use of which would cause the 'murder' of Germans and [Russians]. That the interpretation we have put upon these articles circulated in the greatest port of our land,

from which great numbers of soldiers were at the time taking ship daily, and in which great quantities of war supplies of every kind were at the time being manufactured for transportation overseas, is not only the fair interpretation of them, but that it is the meaning which their authors consciously intended should be conveyed by them to others is further shown by the additional writings found in the meeting place of the defendant group and on the person of one of them. One of these circulars is headed: 'Revolutionists! Unite for Action!' [These excerpts sufficiently show, that while the immediate occasion for this particular outbreak of lawlessness, on the part of the defendant alien anarchists, may have been resentment caused by our Government sending troops into Russia as a strategic operation against the Germans on the eastern battle front, yet the plain purpose of their propaganda was to excite, at the supreme crisis of the war, disaffection, sedition, riots, and, as they hoped, revolution, in this country for the purpose of embarrassing and if possible defeating the military plans of the Government in Europe." [2]

4. *The impact of Abrams.* Does Abrams give new content to "clear and present danger"? Can it be said that the Schenck phrase was not turned into an effective safeguard of speech until the Abrams dissent? A great admirer of Holmes has suggested about the Schenck-Abrams sequence that the Justice "was biding his time until the Court should have before it a conviction so clearly wrong as to let him speak out his deepest thoughts about the First Amendment." [3] *Were* the Abrams convictions more "clearly wrong" than those in the Schenck group of cases?

How useful is the approach of the Abrams dissent? It emphasizes immediacy more than the predecessors. Does it concentrate adequately on immediate proximity of speech to danger? Note the comment about a "silly leaflet" that would not present "any immediate danger" or "have any appreciable tendency to do so." Is "tendency" enough? Note also the reference to "the present danger of immediate evil" or "an intent to bring it about." Should "intent" be enough? Are "tendency" and "intent" reliable indicia of immediacy of danger?

Is Holmes' approach applicable only in contexts (as with the 1917 Act) [4] where the law is mainly directed at an evil other than speech (e.g., obstruction of military recruiting), and where speech is evidence of the risk of that evil? Or is it also useful when the legislature proscribes speech directly, as in Gitlow and Whitney, below? Does Holmes accept the legislative statement of the evil? Must speech create immediate risk of causing the legislatively determined evil— e.g., interference with recruiting? Or does the Court define the evil? Note the

2. Soon after Abrams, Justice Holmes also joined in dissents from other decisions affirming convictions under the 1917 Act. See Pierce v. United States, 252 U.S. 239 (1920), and Schaefer v. United States, 251 U.S. 466 (1920). In his Schaefer dissent, Justice Brandeis said of the Schenck standard: "This is a rule of reason. Correctly applied, it will preserve the right of free speech both from suppression by tyrannous, well-meaning majorities and from abuse by irresponsible, fanatical minorities. Like many other rules for human conduct, it can be applied correctly only by the exercise of good judgment; and to the exercise of good judgment, calmness is, in times of deep feeling and on subjects which excite passion, as essential as fearlessness and honesty. The question whether in a particular instance the words spoken or written fall within the permissible curtailment of free speech is, under the rule enunciated by this court, one of degree. And because it is a question of degree

the field in which the jury may exercise its judgment is, necessarily, a wide one. But its field is not unlimited. [In] my opinion, no jury acting in calmness could reasonably say that any of the publications set forth in the indictment was of such a character or was made under such circumstances as to create a clear and present danger either that they would obstruct recruiting or that they would promote the success of the enemies of the United States."

Although relatively few cases under the 1917 and 1918 laws reached the Supreme Court, there were over two thousand convictions in the lower federal courts.

3. Chafee, Free Speech in the United States (1941), 86.

4. Note, however, that the 1918 Act, unlike the 1917 one, included "urging" the curtailment of war production within its prohibitions.

reference to "an immediate [check] required to save the country," in Holmes' last paragraph. Is Holmes concerned with the gravity of the evil? Do immediacy requirements vary with gravity? What light is cast on these questions by the elaborations of clear and present danger in Gitlow and Whitney? Before turning to those cases, consider the historical data on the Schenck-Abrams evolution in note 5 below and the alternative analysis suggested by Hand's Masses opinion, which follows that note.

5. *The evolution of Holmes' approach from Schenck to Abrams: Some data from history.* That Justice Holmes' thinking did undergo considerable change in the period between the Schenck trilogy of cases in the spring of 1919 and the Abrams dissent in the fall of that year is suggested by some of Justice Holmes' correspondence. Note Gunther's conclusion "that Holmes was [at the time of Schenck] quite insensitive to any claim for special judicial protection of free speech; that the Schenck standard was not truly speech-protective; and that it was not until the fall of 1919, with his famous dissent in [Abrams], that Holmes put some teeth into the clear and present danger formula, at least partly as a result of probing criticism by acquaintances such as Learned Hand."[5] In the summer of 1918, for example, Holmes, in a letter to Hand espoused the "natural right" to silence "the other fellow when he disagrees": free speech, he insisted, "stands no differently than freedom from vaccination"—a freedom that the state could legitimately curtail, as demonstrated in Jacobson v. Massachusetts, 197 U.S. 11 (1905), a decision consistent with Justice Holmes' generally deferential due process philosophy. (Recall chap. 8 above.) In 1918, Holmes seemed impervious to Hand's arguments that the "natural right" to silence dissenters must be curbed by the law in the interests of democratic presuppositions and the search for truth. In the spring of 1919, after Debs, Hand insisted to Holmes that liability for speech should not rest on guesses about the future impact of the words: "in nature the causal sequence is perfect, but responsibility does not go pari passu"; the legal responsibility of the speaker should not turn "upon reasonable forecast." Instead, Hand argued, the punishability of speech should begin only "when the words [are] directly an incitement." But, once again, Holmes was impervious to the criticism. As Hand wrote to another critic of the Debs decision, "I have so far been unable to make [Holmes] see that he and we have any real differences." Holmes' insensitivity to free speech values and his lack of concern for tailoring doctrine to implement those values as of the spring of 1919 is supported by Holmes' own letters: as Holmes began his letter in response to Hand's critique of the Debs approach, "I don't quite get your point." But by the fall of 1919, with the Abrams dissent and its infusion of a genuine immediacy element, the clear and present danger test became a more speech-protective doctrine. Was it an adequate doctrine in that refurbished form? Compare Hand's continued criticism, in the notes following Masses, below.

---

5. See Gunther, "Learned Hand and the Origins of Modern First Amendment Doctrine: Some Fragments of History," 27 Stan.L.Rev. 719 (1975) [hereinafter cited as "Hand and the First Amendment"]. See also Kalven, "Professor Ernst Freund and Debs v. United States," 40 U.Chi.L.Rev. 235 (1973); Ginsburg, "Afterword to Ernst Freund and the First Amendment Tradition," 40 U.Chi.L.Rev. 243 (1973); Ragan, "Justice Oliver Wendell Holmes, Jr., Zechariah Chafee, Jr., and the Clear and Present Danger Test for Free Speech: The First Year, 1919," 58 J.Am.Hist. 24 (1971); Rabban, "The Emergence of Modern First Amendment Doctrine," 50 U.Chi.L.Rev. 1205 (1983); and O'Fallon & Rogat, "Mr. Justice Holmes: A Dissenting Opinion," 36 Stan.L.Rev. —— (1984). See also Cover, "The Left, the Right and the First Amendment: 1918–1928," 40 Md.L.Rev. 349 (1981). Cf. Kairys, "Freedom of Speech," in The Politics of Law: A Progressive Critique (Kairys ed., 1982).

LEARNED HAND AND THE MASSES CASE: DIFFERENT FROM, AND PREFERABLE TO, CLEAR AND PRESENT DANGER?

Introduction. Two years before the issue reached the Court in Schenck, the problem of interpreting the Espionage Act of 1917 arose in a case before Learned Hand, then a District Judge. The Hand opinion plainly reveals considerable solicitude for speech, but it does so without mentioning clear and present danger. Consider the advantages and disadvantages of Hand's approach in the World War I context. How would Schenck, Debs, or Abrams have gone under that standard? Would Hand's approach have avoided some of the difficulties of the clear and present danger test?

MASSES PUBLISHING CO. v. PATTEN

244 Fed. 535 (S.D.N.Y.1917).

LEARNED HAND, District Judge. The plaintiff applies for a preliminary injunction against the postmaster of New York to forbid his refusal to accept its magazine in the mails under the following circumstances: The plaintiff is a publishing company in the city of New York engaged in the production of a monthly revolutionary journal called "The Masses," containing both text and cartoons.[1] [In] July, 1917, the postmaster of New York, acting upon the direction of the Postmaster General, advised the plaintiff that the August [issue] to which he had had access would be denied the mails under the Espionage Act of June 15, 1917. [T]he defendant, while objecting generally that the whole purport of the [issue] was in violation of the law, since it tended to produce a violation of the law, to encourage the enemies of the United States, and to hamper the government in the conduct of the war, specified four cartoons and four pieces of text as especially falling within [the 1917 Act].[2] [In] this case there is no dispute of fact which the plaintiff can successfully challenge except the meaning of the words and pictures in the magazine. As to these the query must be: What is the extreme latitude of the interpretation which must be placed upon them, and whether that extremity certainly falls outside any of the provisions of the [1917 Act]. Unless this be true, the decision of the postmaster must stand. It will be necessary, first, to interpret the law, and, next, the words and pictures. [N]o question arises touching the war powers of Congress. [Here] is presented solely the question of how far Congress after much discussion has up to the present time seen fit to exercise a power which may extend to measures not yet even considered, but necessary to the existence of the state as [such].

Coming to the act itself, [I] turn directly to section 3 of title 1, which the plaintiff is said to violate. That section contains three provisions. The first is, in substance, that no one shall make any false statements with intent to interfere with the operation or success of the military or naval forces of the United States or to promote the success of its enemies. The defendant says that the cartoons and text of the magazine, constituting, as they certainly do, a virulent attack upon the war, [may] interfere with the success of the military forces of the

---

1. On the background of the magazine, see Fishbein, Rebels in Bohemia: The Radicals of The Masses, 1911–1917 (1982), and Zurier, Art for The Masses (1911–1917): A Radical Magazine and its Graphics (1985).

2. Sec. 3 of Title I of the Act—the same provision that was involved in the Schenck line of cases—is noted above, in the footnote at p. 986. (It is also summarized in Judge Hand's opinion.) Title XII of the Act declared to be "nonmailable" every "writing," "newspaper," or "any other publication" violating any other provision of the Act.

United States. That such utterances may have the effect so ascribed to them is unhappily true. [Dissension] within a country is a high source of comfort and assistance to its [enemies]. All this, however, is beside the question whether such an attack is a willfully false statement. That phrase properly includes only a statement of fact which the utterer knows to be false, and it cannot be maintained that any of these statements are of fact, or that the plaintiff believes them to be false. They are all within the range of opinion and of criticism; they are all certainly believed to be true by the utterer. As such they fall within the scope of that right to criticise either by temperate reasoning, or by immoderate and indecent invective, which is normally the privilege of the individual in countries dependent upon the free expression of opinion as the ultimate source of authority. The argument may be trivial in substance, and violent and perverse in manner, but so long as it is confined to abuse of existing policies or laws, it is impossible to class it as a false statement of facts of the kind here in question. To modify this provision, so clearly intended to prevent the spreading of false rumors which may embarrass the military, into the prohibition of any kind of propaganda, honest or vicious, is to disregard the meaning of the language, established by legal construction and common use, and to raise it into a means of suppressing intemperate and inflammatory public discussion, which was surely not its purpose.

The next phrase relied upon is that which forbids any one from willfully causing insubordination, disloyalty, mutiny, or refusal of duty in the military or naval forces of the United States. The defendant's position is that to arouse discontent and disaffection among the people with the prosecution of the war and with the draft tends to promote a mutinous and insubordinate temper among the troops. This, too, is true; men who become satisfied that they are engaged in an enterprise dictated by the unconscionable selfishness of the rich, and effectuated by a tyrannous disregard for the will of those who must suffer and die, will be more prone to insubordination than those who have faith in the cause and acquiesce in the means. Yet to interpret the word "cause" so broadly would, as before, involve necessarily as a consequence the suppression of all hostile criticism, and of all opinion except what encouraged and supported the existing policies, or which fell within the range of temperate argument. It would contradict the normal assumption of democratic government that the suppression of hostile criticism does not turn upon the justice of its substance or the decency and propriety of its temper. Assuming that the power to repress such opinion may rest in Congress in the throes of a struggle for the very existence of the state, its exercise is so contrary to the use and wont of our people that only the clearest expression of such a power justifies the conclusion that it was intended.

The defendant's position, therefore, in so far as it involves the suppression of the free utterance of abuse and criticism of the existing law, or of the policies of the war, is not, in my judgment, supported by the language of the statute. Yet there has always been a recognized limit to such expressions, incident indeed to the existence of any compulsive power of the state itself. One may not counsel or advise others to violate the law as it stands. Words are not only the keys of persuasion, but the triggers of action, and those which have no purport but to counsel the violation of law cannot by any latitude of interpretation be a part of that public opinion which is the final source of government in a democratic state. The defendant asserts not only that the magazine indirectly through its propaganda leads to a disintegration of loyalty and a disobedience of law, but that in addition it counsels and advises resistance to existing law, especially to the draft. The consideration of this aspect of the case more properly arises under the third phrase of section 3, which forbids any willful obstruction of the recruiting or enlistment service of the United States, but, as the defendant urges that the magazine falls within each phrase, it is as well to take it up now. To counsel or advise a man to an act is to urge upon him either that it is his intere. or his duty, to do it. While, of course, this may be accomplished as well by indirection as expressly, since words carry the meaning that they impart, the definition is exhaustive, I think, and I shall use it. Political agitation, by the passions it arouses or the convictions it engenders, may in fact stimulate men to the violation of law. Detestation of existing policies is easily transformed into forcible resistance of the authority which puts them in execution, and it would be folly to disregard the causal relation between the two. Yet to assimilate agitation, legitimate as such, with direct incitement to violent resistance, is to disregard the tolerance of all methods of political agitation which in normal times is a safeguard of free government. The distinction is not a scholastic subterfuge, but a hard-bought acquisition in the fight for freedom, and the purpose to disregard it must be evident when the power exists. If one stops short of urging upon others that it is their duty or their interest to resist the law, it seems to me one should not be held to have attempted to cause its violation. If that be not the test, I can see no escape from the conclusion that under this section every political agitation which can be shown to be apt to create a seditious temper is illegal. I am confident that by such language Congress had no such revolutionary purpose in view.

It seems to me, however, quite plain that none of the language and none of the cartoons in this paper can be thought directly to counsel or advise insubordination or mutiny, without a violation of their meaning quite beyond any tolerable understanding. I come, therefore, to the third phrase of the section, which forbids any one from willfully obstructing the recruiting or enlistment service of the United States. [Here] again, [since] the question is of the expression of opinion, I construe the sentence, so far as it restrains public utterance, as I have construed the other two, and as therefore limited to the direct advocacy of resistance to the recruiting and enlistment service. If so, the inquiry is narrowed to the question whether any of the challenged matter may be said to advocate resistance to the draft, taking the meaning of the words with the utmost latitude which they can bear. As to the cartoons it seems to me quite clear that they do not fall within such a test. Certainly the nearest is that entitled "Conscription," and the most that can be said of that is that it may breed such animosity to the draft as will promote resistance and strengthen the determination of those disposed to be recalcitrant. There is no intimation that, however hateful the draft may be, one is in duty bound to resist it, certainly none that such resistance is to one's [interest].

The text offers more embarrassment. The poem to Emma Goldman and Alexander Berkman, at most, goes no further than to say that they are martyrs in the cause of love among nations. Such a sentiment holds them up to admiration, and hence their conduct to possible emulation. [The] paragraphs upon conscientious objectors are of the same kind. [It] is plain enough that the paper has the fullest sympathy for these people, that it admires their courage, and that it presumptively approves their conduct. [Moreover], these passages [occur] in a magazine which attacks with the utmost violence the draft and the war. That such comments have a tendency to arouse emulation in others is clear enough but that they counsel others to follow these examples is not so plain. Literally at least they do not, and while, as I have said, the words are to be taken, not literally, but according to their full import, the literal meaning is the starting point for interpretation. One may admire and approve the course of a hero without feeling any duty to follow him. There is not the least implied intimation in these words that others are under a duty to follow. The most that can be said is that, if others do follow, they will get the same admiration and the same approval. Now, there is surely an appreciable distance between esteem and emulation; and unless there is here some advocacy of such emulation, I cannot see how the passages can be said to fall within [the law]. The question

666

quite the same as what would arise upon a motion to dismiss an ~~in~~ the close of the proof: Could any reasonable man say, not that the ~~result~~ of the language might be to arouse a seditious disposition, for that ~~would be~~ enough, but that the language directly advocated resistance to the ~~draft? Can~~not think that upon such language any verdict would [stand].[3]

COMPARING THE HOLMES AND HAND APPROACHES

1. *The differences between Hand and Holmes: The strengths and weaknesses of Hand's "incitement" approach.* Is the Masses "incitement" standard distinctively different from "clear and present danger"? How would Eugene Debs have fared under the Masses approach? Arguably, Hand was more sensitive than Holmes to the risk of sustaining convictions based on the "natural tendency" and "probable effect" of words. Arguably, Hand was more sensitive because he focused less on forecasts about the likelihood that the speech would produce danger (e.g., draft obstruction) and focused more on the speaker's words and the value of free speech (and on the protection that must be afforded to speech if widespread critical debate of governmental policy is to be maintained).

Does the shift in focus from proximity of danger to content of speech promote greater protection of speech? Arguably, courts are more competent to scrutinize words for evidence of incitement than to hazard guesses about the possible future impact of words in complex contexts. Arguably, the incitement inquiry requires less judicial inquiry into "circumstances" and variable degrees of danger. Moreover, the incitement approach may draw on more traditional, more manageable judicial tools: courts may be better at concentrating on what the defendant said than on how near (and how serious) the danger is. Similarly, they may be more competent to identify "counseling" than to assess risks. Can it also be argued that Masses articulates speech values more effectively than Schenck and even Abrams? But Hand's Masses approach may have had weaknesses as well as strengths. One arguable weakness was that "it could not easily deal with the indirect but purposeful incitement of Marc Anthony's oration over the body of Caesar." There was the possible additional weakness that Hand did not "fully deal with the problem of the harmless inciter, the speaker explicitly urging law violation but with little realistic hope of success." [1]

2. *The differences between Hand and Holmes: Some historical data.* Learned Hand's correspondence reveals that he perceived a considerable difference between his Masses approach and Holmes' clear and present danger test, even as refined in the Abrams dissent.[2] (Although Hand welcomed Holmes' greater sensitivity to free speech values in the Abrams dissent, he questioned Holmes' doctrinal implementation.) In a series of letters from 1919 to 1921 to Professor Zechariah Chafee, Jr.,[3] Hand elaborated the differences between the Masses

---

3. District Judge Hand's decision was reversed on appeal. Masses Publishing Co. v. Patten, 246 Fed. 24 (2d Cir.1917). The Circuit Court not only emphasized the broad administrative discretion of the Postmaster General, but also disagreed with Hand's incitement test: "This court does not agree that such is the law. If the natural and reasonable effect of what is said is to encourage resistance to a law, and the words are used in an endeavor to persuade to resistance, it is immaterial that the duty to resist is not mentioned, or the interest of the persons addressed in resistance is not suggested." As Hand wrote in one of his letters, his opinion "seemed to meet with practically no professional approval whatever." (All otherwise unattributed

quotations in this and the following notes are from Gunther, "Hand and the First Amendment.")

1. Compare the cure suggested for these weaknesses by the standards of the Brandenburg case, p. 1037 below.

2. See the documents and commentary in Gunther, "Hand and the First Amendment."

3. Professor Chafee, for more than three decades after Schenck and Abrams, was the most prominent commentator on First Amendment problems. See especially his Freedom of Speech (1920) and the revisions of that volume in Free Speech in the United States (1941). Though the 1920 volume was dedicated to Judge Hand, Chaf-

analysis and the alternatives. As Hand wrote to Chafee, soon after Abrams: "I do not altogether like the way Justice Holmes put the limitation. I myself think it is a little more manageable and quite adequate a distinction to say that there is an absolute and objective test to language. [I] still prefer that which I attempted to state in my first 'Masses' opinion, rather than to say that the connection between the words used and the evil aimed at should be 'immediate and direct.' " And as he elaborated later, "I prefer a test based upon the nature of the utterance itself. If, taken in its setting, the effect upon the hearers is only to counsel them to violate the law, it is unconditionally illegal. [As] to other utterances, it appears to me that regardless of their tendency they should be permitted." Hand's major objection to formulations such as "clear and present danger" or "natural and reasonable tendency" was that they were too slippery in "practical administration": "I think it is precisely at those times when alone the freedom of speech becomes important as an institution, that the protection of a jury on such an issue is illusory." And, as he said in still another letter, "I am not wholly in love with Holmesy's test and the reason is this. Once you admit that the matter is one of degree, while you may put it where it genuinely belongs, [you] so obviously make it a matter of administration. [I] should prefer a qualitative formula, hard, conventional, difficult to evade." His incitement test was intended to be such a formula.[4]

After 1921, Hand gave up on his advocacy of the Masses approach: he no longer had any real hope that that standard "would ever be recognized as law." Compare that prophecy with the evolution of doctrine in the 1950s and 1960s cases, especially Yates, Scales, and Brandenburg, below. Note the evaluation by Gunther that that course of decisions represents "a belated adoption by the Supreme Court of aspects of the Masses approach—long after Hand himself had lost confidence in it, after the rise and decline of Schenck's clear and present danger standard, after Hand had contributed to Schenck's disintegration [in his Court of Appeals opinion in Dennis, see p. 1016 below]."[5] That comment also suggests that the 1969 decision in Brandenburg v. Ohio "combines the most protective ingredients of the Masses incitement emphasis with the most useful elements of the clear and present danger heritage."[6]

---

ee's writings tended to minimize the differences between Hand and Holmes and were the single most important academic source for the widely held view that clear and present danger was the best possible speech-protective doctrine.

4. See also the evaluation of the Hand letters to Chafee in Gunther, "Hand and the First Amendment"; "These letters make clear what has long been doubted or ignored: that the Masses approach was indeed a distinctive, carefully considered alternative to the prevalent analyses of free speech issues. According to the usual arguments, the punishability of speech turned on an evaluation of its likelihood to cause forbidden consequences. [All of the prevalent approaches] shared the common characteristic of requiring factfinders—typically, juries—to assess circumstances and to guess about the risks created by the challenged speech. Learned Hand thought this [characteristic] too slippery, too dangerous to free expression, too much at the mercy of factfinders reflecting majoritarian sentiments—hostile to dissent. Instead, he urged, in Masses and for several years thereafter, the adoption of a strict, 'hard,' 'objective' test focusing on the speaker's words: if the language used was solely that of direct incitement to illegal action,

speech could be proscribed; otherwise, it was protected."

5. Privately, however, Hand expressed adherance to his Masses approach as late as 1951, when the Dennis case came before the Court—and when the Court's plurality opinion sustained the conviction of Communist Party leaders on the basis of Hand's diluted restatement of the clear and present danger test.

6. Would the models regarding inchoate crimes be adequate to accommodate the competing speech and governmental interests as well as the Holmes or Hand approaches? See generally Greenawalt, "Speech and Crime," 1980 A.B. Found.Research J. 645. Compare with Hand's formulation the definition of criminal solicitation in the ALI Model Penal Code, § 5.02(1): "A person is guilty of solicitation to commit a crime if with the purpose of promoting or facilitating its commission he commands, encourages, or requests another person to engage in specific conduct which would constitute such crime or an attempt to commit such crime or which would establish his complicity in its commission or attempted commission." (See also the definitions

B. LEGISLATION AGAINST FORBIDDEN ADVOCACY IN THE TWENTIES AND THIRTIES

GITLOW, WHITNEY, AND THE INCREASING PROTECTION OF SPEECH

GITLOW v. NEW YORK

268 U.S. 652, 45 S.Ct. 625, 69 L.Ed. 1138 (1925).

Mr. Justice SANFORD delivered the opinion of the Court.

 Benjamin Gitlow was indicted [and convicted] for the statutory crime of criminal anarchy. New York Penal Law, §§ 160, 161.[1] [The] contention here is that the statute, by its terms and as applied in this case, is repugnant to the due process clause of the [14th Amendment]. The indictment was in two counts. The first charged that the defendant had advocated, advised and taught the duty, necessity and propriety of overthrowing and overturning organized government by force, violence and unlawful means, by certain writings therein set forth entitled "The Left Wing Manifesto"; the second that he had printed, published and knowingly circulated and distributed a certain paper called "The Revolutionary Age," containing the writings set forth in the [first count]. The following facts were established on the trial by undisputed evidence and admissions: The defendant is a member of the Left Wing Section of the Socialist Party, a dissenting branch or faction of that party formed [in 1919] in opposition to its dominant policy of "moderate Socialism." The conference elected a National Council, of which the defendant was a member, and left to it the adoption of a "Manifesto." This was published in The Revolutionary Age, the official organ of the Left Wing. The defendant was on the board of managers of the paper and was its business manager. He arranged for the printing of the paper and took to the printer the manuscript of the first issue which contained the Left Wing Manifesto. [16,000 copies were printed.] It was admitted that the defendant signed a card subscribing to the Manifesto and Program of the Left Wing; [that] he went to different parts of the State to speak to branches of the Socialist Party about the principles of the Left Wing and advocated their adoption; and that he was responsible for the Manifesto as it appeared that "he knew of the publication, in a general way and he knew of its publications afterwards, and is responsible for its circulation." There was no evidence of any effect resulting from the publication and circulation of the Manifesto. [The Manifesto] condemned the dominant "moderate Socialism" for its recognition of the necessity of the democratic parliamentary state [and]

of attempt and conspiracy in Model Penal Code §§ 5.01(1)(c) and 5.03(1).)

1. The New York statute—enacted in 1902, after the assassination of President McKinley—provided:

"§ 160. *Criminal anarchy defined.* Criminal anarchy is the doctrine that organized government should be overthrown by force or violence, or by assassination of the executive head or of any of the executive officials of government, or by any unlawful means. The advocacy of such doctrine either by word of mouth or writing is a felony.

"§ 161. *Advocacy of criminal anarchy.* Any person who:

"1. By word of mouth or writing advocates, advises or teaches the duty, necessity or propriety of overthrowing or overturning organized government by force or violence, or by assassination of the executive head or of any of the executive officials of government, or by any unlawful means; or,

"2. Prints, publishes, edits, issues or knowingly circulates, sells, distributes or publicly displays any book, paper, document, or written or printed matter in any form, containing or advocating, advising or teaching the doctrine that organized government should be overthrown by force, violence or any unlawful [means],

"Is guilty of a [felony]."

advocated [the] necessity of accomplishing the "Communist Revolution" by a militant and "revolutionary Socialism," based on "the class struggle" and mobilizing the "power of the proletariat in action," through mass industrial revolts developing into mass political strikes and "revolutionary mass action," for the purpose of conquering and destroying the parliamentary state and establishing in its place, through a "revolutionary dictatorship of the proletariat," the system of [Communist Socialism].

The court [charged] the jury, in substance, that they must determine what was the intent, purpose and fair meaning of the Manifesto; [that] a mere statement or analysis of social and economic facts and historical incidents, in the nature of an essay, accompanied by prophecy as to the future course of events, but with no teaching, advice or advocacy of action, would not constitute the advocacy, advice or teaching of a doctrine for the overthrow of government within the meaning of the statute; that a mere statement that unlawful acts might accomplish such a purpose would be insufficient, unless there was a teaching, advising and advocacy of employing such unlawful acts for the purpose of overthrowing [government]. The defendant's counsel submitted two requests to charge which embodied in substance the statement that to constitute criminal anarchy within the meaning of the statute it was necessary that the language used or published should advocate, teach or advise the duty, necessity or propriety of doing "some definite or immediate act or acts" of force, violence or unlawfulness directed toward the overthrowing of organized government. These were denied further than had been charged. [The] sole contention here [is] that as there was no evidence of any concrete result flowing from the publication of the Manifesto or of circumstances showing the likelihood of such result, the statute as construed and [applied] penalizes the mere utterance, as such, of "doctrine" having no quality of incitement, without regard either to the circumstances of its utterance or to the likelihood of unlawful [consequences].

The statute does not penalize the utterance or publication of abstract "doctrine" or academic discussion having no quality of incitement to any concrete action. It is not aimed against mere historical or philosophical essays. It does not restrain the advocacy of changes in the form of government by constitutional and lawful means. What it prohibits is language advocating, advising or teaching the overthrow of organized government by unlawful means. These words imply urging to [action]. The Manifesto, plainly, is neither the statement of abstract doctrine [nor] mere prediction that industrial disturbances and revolutionary mass strikes will result spontaneously in an inevitable process of evolution in the economic system. It advocates and urges in fervent language mass action which shall progressively foment industrial disturbances and through political mass strikes and revolutionary mass action overthrow and destroy organized parliamentary government. It concludes with a call to action in these words: "The proletarian revolution and the Communist reconstruction of society—*the struggle for these*—is now indispensable. [The] Communist International calls the proletariat of the world to the final struggle!" This is not the expression of philosophical abstraction, the mere prediction of future events; it is the language of direct incitement. The means advocated for bringing about the destruction of organized parliamentary government, namely, mass industrial revolts usurping the functions of municipal government, political mass strikes directed against the parliamentary state, and revolutionary mass action for its final destruction, necessarily imply the use of force and violence, and in their essential nature are inherently unlawful in a constitutional government of law and order. That the jury were warranted in finding that the Manifesto advocated not merely the abstract doctrine of overthrowing organized government by force, violence and unlawful means, but action to that end, is clear.

For present purposes we may and do assume that freedom of speech and of the press—which are protected by the First Amendment from abridgment by Congress—are among the fundamental personal rights and "liberties" protected by the due process clause of the 14th Amendment from impairment by the States.[2] [It] is a fundamental principle, long established, that the freedom of speech and of the press which is secured by the Constitution, does not confer an absolute right to speak or publish, without responsibility, whatever one may choose. [A] State may punish utterances endangering the foundations of organized government and threatening its overthrow by unlawful means. [In] short this freedom does not deprive a State of the primary and essential right of [self preservation]. By enacting the present statute the State has determined, through its legislative body, that utterances advocating the overthrow of organized government by force, violence and unlawful means, are so inimical to the general welfare and involve such danger of substantive evil that they may be penalized in the exercise of its police power. That determination must be given great weight. Every presumption is to be indulged in favor of the validity of the statute. Mugler v. Kansas [p. 447 above]. That utterances inciting to the overthrow of organized government by unlawful means, present a sufficient danger of substantive evil to bring their punishment within the range of legislative discretion, is clear. Such utterances, by their very nature, involve danger to the public peace and to the security of the State. They threaten breaches of the peace and ultimate revolution. And the immediate danger is none the less real and substantial, because the effect of a given utterance cannot be accurately foreseen. The State cannot reasonably be required to measure the danger from every such utterance in the nice balance of a jeweler's scale. A single revolutionary spark may kindle a fire that, smouldering for a time, may burst into a sweeping and destructive conflagration. It cannot be said that the State is acting arbitrarily or unreasonably when in the exercise of its judgment as to the measures necessary to protect the public peace and safety, it seeks to extinguish the spark without waiting until it has enkindled the flame or blazed into the conflagration. It cannot reasonably be required to defer the adoption of measures for its own peace and safety until the revolutionary utterances lead to actual disturbances of the public peace or imminent and immediate danger of its own destruction; but it may, in the exercise of its judgment, suppress the threatened danger in its incipiency. [We] cannot hold that the present statute is an arbitrary or unreasonable exercise of the police power of the State unwarrantably infringing the freedom of speech or press; and we must and do sustain its constitutionality.

This being so it may be applied to every utterance—not too trivial to be beneath the notice of the law—which is of such a character and used with such intent and purpose as to bring it within the prohibition of the statute. [In] other words, when the legislative body has determined generally, in the constitutional exercise of its discretion, that utterances of a certain kind involve such danger of substantive evil that they may be punished, the question whether any specific utterance coming within the prohibited class is likely, in and of itself, to bring about the substantive evil, is not open to consideration. It is sufficient that the statute itself be constitutional and that the use of the language comes within its prohibition. It is clear that the question in such cases is entirely different from that involved in those cases where the statute merely prohibits certain acts involving the danger of substantive evil, without any reference to language itself, and it is sought to apply its provisions to language used by the defendant for the purpose of bringing about the prohibited results. There, if it be contended that the statute cannot be applied to the language used

---

2. This passage was the Court's first indication that First Amendment guarantees are "incorporated" in the 14th Amendment.

by the defendant because of its protection by the freedom of speech or press, it must necessarily be found, as an original question, without any previous determination by the legislative body whether the specific language used involved such likelihood of bringing about the substantive evil as to deprive it of the constitutional protection. In such cases it has been held that the general provisions of the statute may be constitutionally applied to the specific utterance of the defendant if its natural tendency and probable effect was to bring about the substantive evil which the legislative body might prevent. [Schenck; Debs.] And the ["clear and present danger" passage in Schenck]—upon which great reliance is placed in the defendant's argument—was manifestly intended, as shown by the context, to apply only in cases of this class, and has no application to those like the present, where the legislative body itself has previously determined the danger of substantive evil arising from utterances of a specified character. [It] was not necessary, within the meaning of the statute, that the defendant should have advocated "some definite or immediate act or acts" of force, violence or unlawfulness. It was sufficient if such acts were advocated in general terms; and it was not essential that their immediate execution should have been advocated. Nor was it necessary that the language should have been "reasonably and ordinarily calculated to incite certain persons" to acts of force, violence or unlawfulness. The advocacy need not be addressed to specific persons. Thus, the publication and circulation of a newspaper article may be an encouragement or endeavor to persuade to murder, although not addressed to any person in [particular].

Affirmed.

Mr. Justice HOLMES (dissenting). Mr. Justice Brandeis and I are of opinion that this judgment should be reversed. The general principle of free speech, it seems to me, must be taken to be included in the 14th Amendment, in view of the scope that has been given to the word "liberty" as there used, although perhaps it may be accepted with a somewhat larger latitude of interpretation than is allowed to Congress by the sweeping language that governs or ought to govern the laws of the United States. If I am right, then I think that the criterion sanctioned by the full Court in [Schenck] applies. [It] is true that in my opinion this criterion was departed from in [Abrams], but the convictions that I expressed in that case are too deep for it to be possible for me as yet to believe that it [has] settled the law. If what I think the correct test is applied, it is manifest that there was no present danger of an attempt to overthrow the government by force on the part of the admittedly small minority who shared the defendant's views. It is said that this manifesto was more than a theory, that it was an incitement. Every idea is an incitement. It offers itself for belief and if believed it is acted on unless some other belief outweighs it or some failure of energy stifles the movement at its birth. The only difference between the expression of an opinion and an incitement in the narrower sense is the speaker's enthusiasm for the result. Eloquence may set fire to reason. But whatever may be thought of the redundant discourse before us it had no chance of starting a present conflagration. If in the long run the beliefs expressed in proletarian dictatorship are destined to be accepted by the dominant forces of the community, the only meaning of free speech is that they should be given their chance and have their way. If the publication of this document had been laid as an attempt to induce an uprising against government at once and not at some indefinite time in the future it would have presented a different question.[1]

1. For Holmes' views on criminal attempts while a Massachusetts judge, see generally Rogat's articles (cited earlier and below) and note Holmes' comments on the law of attempts in Commonwealth v. Peaslee, 59 N.E. 55 (Mass. 1901): "The question on the evidence [is] whether the defendant's acts come near enough to the accomplishment of the substantive offense to be punishable. [It] is a question of degree. [The] degree of proximity held sufficient may vary with [circumstances]."

The object would have been one with which the law might deal, subject to the doubt whether there was any danger that the publication could produce any result, or in other words, whether it was not futile and too remote from possible consequences. But the indictment alleges the publication and nothing more.

THE GITLOW PROBLEM AND THE HOLMES DISSENT

Was the majority right in claiming that the question in a case such as Gitlow "is entirely different from that involved in those cases where the statute merely prohibits certain acts involving the danger of substantive evil, without any reference to language itself, and it is sought to apply its provisions to language used by the defendant for the purpose of bringing about the prohibited results"? Was the majority correct in saying that the Schenck standard only applied to those cases, "and has no application to those like the present, where the legislative body itself has previously determined the danger of substantive evil arising from utterances of a specified character"? Or *did* the clear and present danger test of Schenck apply to the Gitlow (and Whitney, below) problem? Recall that, in his dissents from Court invalidations of state economic regulations on substantive due process grounds, Holmes repeatedly urged deference to legislative judgments, in cases beginning with Lochner. In his Gitlow dissent, Holmes began by stating that free speech is a legitimate ingredient of the "liberty" protected by the 14th Amendment. Would it accordingly not have been appropriate for Holmes to say something about the weight to be given legislative judgments in situations such as Gitlow? [1]

Consider Rogat's comment: "In Gitlow, Holmes was confronted by, and evaded, the difficulty of applying his Schenck remark without modification to this different kind of problem." [2] Rogat argued that when the legislature prohibits advocacy of a specific doctrine, the question is no longer "proximity" to a specified act: "Here a court may have to establish [the] importance (or the legitimacy) of forbidding the completed act." The important question, he argues, may well not be "proximity," but "which 'evils' a legislature may prohibit." Does the Brandeis opinion in Whitney, which follows, adequately confront the issue Holmes "evaded"?

Arguably, the clear and present danger test made it inherently difficult for judges to confront and set aside a legislative judgment that a particular variety of speech is dangerous. The clear and present danger test puts great emphasis on context and guesses about future harm; to the extent that this involves an empirical judgment, judges may feel particularly incompetent and inhibited in second-guessing legislative judgments. Would adoption of the Masses approach have alleviated those judicial difficulties? By emphasizing what speech is protected (and the speaker's words rather than guesses about future harms), are courts in a better position to protect speech without direct confrontations with legislative judgments that particular types of speech present a "clear and present danger" of an especially grave evil? The problem of judicial confrontations

1. Is it arguable that the case for judicial deference to the legislative judgment in Gitlow was weak because the law was enacted in 1902, long before the evolution of the post-World War I radicalism that gave rise to the Gitlow prosecution? Compare Whitney, which follows, involving prosecution for 1919 behavior under a 1919 law. Consider especially how the Brandeis concurrence sidesteps the risk of direct confrontation with the legislative assertion that particular expressive behavior is dangerous. Note that Brandeis does not challenge the California law in Whitney on its face; instead, he insists that the defendant is entitled to raise an "as applied" challenge under the free speech guarantee. Compare the judicial techniques in response to legislative prohibitions of speech in the post-World War II cases below.

2. Rogat, "The Judge as Spectator," 31 U.Chi.L.Rev. 213 (1964).

with prior legislative judgments regarding harmful speech is pursued further in connection with later materials.

WHITNEY v. CALIFORNIA

274 U.S. 357, 47 S.Ct. 641, 71 L.Ed. 1095 (1927).

Mr. Justice SANFORD delivered the opinion of the [Court].

[Miss Whitney was convicted under the Criminal Syndicalism Act of California, enacted in 1919.[1] The charge was that she "did [organize] and assist in organizing, and was, is, and knowingly became a member of an organization [organized] to advocate, teach, aid and abet criminal syndicalism." In its summary of the facts, the Court stated that she had attended the 1919 national convention of the Socialist Party as a delegate from the Oakland branch. The convention split, and the "radicals"—including Miss Whitney—went to another hall and formed the Communist Labor Party [CLP]. Later in 1919, she was a branch delegate to a convention called to organize a California unit of the CLP. As a member of that convention's resolutions committee, she supported a resolution endorsing "the value of political action" and urging workers "to cast their votes for the party which represents their immediate and final interest—the [CLP]—at all elections." The proposed resolution was defeated on the floor and a more extreme program was adopted. Miss Whitney remained a member of the Party and testified at the trial "that it was not her intention that the [CLP] of California should be an instrument of terrorism or violence."]

1. While it is not denied that the evidence warranted the jury in finding that the defendant became a member of and assisted in organizing the [CLP] of California, and that this was organized to advocate, teach, aid or abet criminal syndicalism as defined by the Act, it is urged that the Act, as here construed and applied, deprived the defendant of her liberty without due process of law. [The] argument is, in effect, that the character of the state organization could not be forecast when she attended the convention; that she had no purpose of helping to create an instrument of terrorism and violence; that she "took part in formulating and presenting to the convention a resolution which, if adopted, would have committed the new organization to a legitimate policy of political reform by the use of the ballot"; that it was not until after the majority of the convention turned out to be "contrary-minded, and other less temperate policies prevailed" that the convention could have taken on the character of criminal syndicalism; and that as this was done over her protest, her mere presence in the convention, however violent the opinions expressed therein, could not thereby become a crime. This contention, while advanced in the form of a constitutional objection to the Act, is in effect nothing more than an effort to review the weight of the evidence for the purpose of showing that the defendant did not join and assist in organizing the [CLP] with a knowledge of its unlawful character and purpose. This question, which is foreclosed by the verdict of the jury, [is] one of fact merely which is not open to review in this Court, involving as it does no constitutional question [whatever].

1. The pertinent provisions of the Act stated:

"Section 1. The term 'criminal syndicalism' as used in this act is hereby defined as any doctrine or precept advocating, teaching or aiding and abetting the commission of crime, sabotage, [or] unlawful acts of force and violence or unlawful methods of terrorism as a means of accomplishing a change in industrial ownership or control, or effecting any political change.

"Sec. 2. Any person who: . . . . [4.] Organizes or assists in organizing, or is or knowingly becomes a member of, any organization, society, group or assemblage of persons organized or assembled to advocate, teach or aid and abet criminal syndicalism];

"Is guilty of a [felony]."

2. It is clear that the Syndicalism Act is not repugnant to the due process clause by reason of vagueness and uncertainty of [definition].

[4.] Nor is the [Act] as applied in this case repugnant to the due process clause as a restraint of the rights of free speech, assembly, and association. That [a state] may punish those who abuse [freedom of speech] by utterances inimical to the public welfare, tending to incite to crime, disturb the public peace, or endanger the foundations of organized government and threaten its overthrow by unlawful means, is not open to question. [Gitlow.] [The legislative] determination must be given great weight. [The] essence of the offense [is] the combining with others in an association for the accomplishment of the desired ends through the advocacy and use of criminal and unlawful methods. It partakes of the nature of a criminal conspiracy. [That] such [united] action involves even greater danger to the public peace and security than the isolated utterances and acts of individuals, is clear. We cannot hold that, as here applied, the Act is an unreasonable or arbitrary exercise of the police power of the State, unwarrantably infringing any right of free speech, assembly or association, or that those persons are protected from punishment by [due process] who abuse such rights by joining and furthering an organization thus menacing the peace and welfare of the [State].

Affirmed.

Mr. Justice BRANDEIS, [joined by Justice HOLMES, concurring].

The felony which the statute created is a crime very unlike the old felony of conspiracy or the old misdemeanor of unlawful assembly. The mere act of assisting in forming a society for teaching syndicalism, of becoming a member of it, or of assembling with others for that purpose is given the dynamic quality of crime. There is guilt although the society may not contemplate immediate promulgation of the doctrine. Thus the accused is to be punished, not for attempt, incitement or conspiracy, but for a step in preparation, which, if it threatens the public order at all, does so only remotely. The novelty in the prohibition introduced is that the statute aims, not at the practice of criminal syndicalism, nor even directly at the preaching of it, but at association with those who propose to preach it.

Despite arguments to the contrary which had seemed to me persuasive, it is settled that the due process clause of the 14th Amendment applies to matters of substantive law as well as to matters of procedure. Thus all fundamental rights comprised within the term liberty are protected by the [Constitution] from invasion by the States. The right of free speech, the right to teach and the right of assembly are, of course, fundamental rights. These may not be denied or abridged. But, although the rights of free speech and assembly are fundamental, they are not in their nature absolute. Their exercise is subject to restriction, if the particular restriction proposed is required in order to protect the State from destruction or from serious injury, political, economic or moral. That the necessity which is essential to a valid restriction does not exist unless speech would produce, or is intended to produce, a clear and imminent danger of some substantive evil which the State constitutionally may seek to prevent has been settled. See [Schenck].

It is said to be the function of the legislature to determine whether at a particular time and under the particular circumstances the formation of, or assembly with, a society organized to advocate criminal syndicalism constitutes a clear and present danger of substantive evil; and that by enacting the law here in question the legislature of California determined that question in the affirmative. Compare [Gitlow]. The legislature must obviously decide, in the first instance, whether a danger exists which calls for a particular protective measure. But where a statute is valid only in case certain conditions exist, the enactment of the statute cannot alone establish the facts which are essential to its validity.

Prohibitory legislation has repeatedly been held invalid because unnecessary, where the denial of liberty involved was that of engaging in a particular business. The power of the courts to strike down an offending law is no less when the interests involved are not property rights, but the fundamental personal rights of free speech and assembly.

This Court has not yet fixed the standard by which to determine when a danger shall be deemed clear; how remote the danger may be and yet be deemed present; and what degree of evil shall be deemed sufficiently substantial to justify resort to abridgment of free speech and assembly as the means of protection. To reach sound conclusions on these matters, we must bear in mind why a State is, ordinarily, denied the power to prohibit dissemination of social, economic and political doctrine which a vast majority of its citizens believes to be false and fraught with evil consequence.

Those who won our independence believed that the final end of the State was to make men free to develop their faculties; and that in its government the deliberative forces should prevail over the arbitrary. They valued liberty both as an end and as a means. They believed liberty to be the secret of happiness and courage to be the secret of liberty. They believed that freedom to think as you will and to speak as you think are means indispensable to the discovery and spread of political truth; that without free speech and assembly discussion would be futile; that with them, discussion affords ordinarily adequate protection against the dissemination of noxious doctrine; that the greatest menace to freedom is an inert people; that public discussion is a political duty; and that this should be a fundamental principle of the American government. They recognized the risks to which all human institutions are subject. But they knew that order cannot be secured merely through fear of punishment for its infraction; that it is hazardous to discourage thought, hope and imagination; that fear breeds repression; that repression breeds hate; that hate menaces stable government; that the path of safety lies in the opportunity to discuss freely supposed grievances and proposed remedies; and that the fitting remedy for evil counsels is good ones. Believing in the power of reason as applied through public discussion, they eschewed silence coerced by law—the argument of force in its worst form. Recognizing the occasional tyrannies of governing majorities, they amended the Constitution so that free speech and assembly should be guaranteed.

Fear of serious injury cannot alone justify suppression of free speech and assembly. Men feared witches and burned women. It is the function of speech to free men from the bondage of irrational fears. To justify suppression of free speech there must be reasonable ground to fear that serious evil will result if free speech is practiced. There must be reasonable ground to believe that the danger apprehended is imminent. There must be reasonable ground to believe that the evil to be prevented is a serious one. Every denunciation of existing law tends in some measure to increase the probability that there will be violation of it. Condonation of a breach enhances the probability. Expressions of approval add to the probability. Propagation of the criminal state of mind by teaching syndicalism increases it. Advocacy of law-breaking heightens it still further. But even advocacy of violation, however reprehensible morally, is not a justification for denying free speech where the advocacy falls short of incitement and there is nothing to indicate that the advocacy would be immediately acted on. The wide difference between advocacy and incitement, between preparation and attempt, between assembling and conspiracy, must be borne in mind. In order to support a finding of clear and present danger it must be shown either that immediate serious violence was to be expected or was advocated, or that the past conduct furnished reason to believe that such advocacy was then contemplated.

Those who won our independence by revolution were not cowards. They did not fear political change. They did not exalt order at the cost of liberty. To courageous, self-reliant men, with confidence in the power of free and fearless reasoning applied through the processes of popular government, no danger flowing from speech can be deemed clear and present, unless the incidence of the evil apprehended is so imminent that it may befall before there is opportunity for full discussion. If there be time to expose through discussion the falsehood and fallacies, to avert the evil by the processes of education, the remedy to be applied is more speech, not enforced silence. Only an emergency can justify repression. Such must be the rule if authority is to be reconciled with freedom. Such, in my opinion, is the command of the Constitution. It is therefore always open to Americans to challenge a law abridging free speech and assembly by showing that there was no emergency justifying it. Moreover, even imminent danger cannot justify resort to prohibition of these functions essential to effective democracy, unless the evil apprehended is relatively serious. Prohibition of free speech and assembly is a measure so stringent that it would be inappropriate as the means for averting a relatively trivial harm to society. A police measure may be unconstitutional merely because the remedy, although effective as a means of protection, is unduly harsh or oppressive. Thus, a State might, in the exercise of its police power, make any trespass upon the land of another a crime, regardless of the results or of the intent or purpose of the trespasser. It might, also, punish an attempt, a conspiracy, or an incitement to commit the trespass. But it is hardly conceivable that this Court would hold constitutional a statute which punished as a felony the mere voluntary assembly with a society formed to teach that pedestrians had the moral right to cross unenclosed, unposted, waste lands and to advocate their doing so, even if there was imminent danger that advocacy would lead to a trespass. The fact that speech is likely to result in some violence or in destruction of property is not enough to justify its suppression. There must be the probability of serious injury to the State. Among free men, the deterrents ordinarily to be applied to prevent crime are education and punishment for violations of the law, not abridgment of the rights of free speech and assembly.

[The California] legislative declaration satisfies the requirement of the constitution of the State concerning emergency legislation. [But] it does not preclude enquiry into the question whether, at the time and under the circumstances, the conditions existed which are essential to validity under the Federal Constitution. As a statute, even if not void on its face, may be challenged because invalid as applied, the result of such an inquiry may depend upon the specific facts of the particular case. Whenever the fundamental rights of free speech and assembly are alleged to have been invaded, it must remain open to a defendant to present the issue whether there actually did exist at the time a clear danger; whether the danger, if any, was imminent; and whether the evil apprehended was one so substantial as to justify the stringent restriction interposed by the legislature. The legislative declaration, like the fact that the statute was passed and was sustained by the highest court of the State, creates merely a rebuttable presumption that these conditions have been satisfied.

Whether in 1919, when Miss Whitney did the things complained of, there was in California such clear and present danger of serious evil, might have been made the important issue in the case. She might have required that the issue be determined either by the court or the jury. She claimed below that the statute as applied to her violated the [Constitution]; but she did not claim that it was void because there was no clear and present danger of serious evil, nor did she request that the existence of these conditions of a valid measure thus restricting the rights of free speech and assembly be passed upon by the court or a jury. On the other hand, there was evidence on which the court or jury might have found that such danger existed. I am unable to assent to the suggestion in the opinion of the Court that assembling with a political party, formed to advocate the desirability of a proletarian revolution by mass action at some date necessarily far in the future, is not a right within the protection of the 14th Amendment. In the present case, however, there was other testimony which tended to establish the existence of a conspiracy, on the part of members of the International Workers of the World, to commit present serious crimes; and likewise to show that such a conspiracy would be furthered by the activity of the society of which Miss Whitney was a member. Under these circumstances the judgment of the state court cannot be disturbed. Our power of review in this case [from a state court] is limited not only to the question whether a right guaranteed by the Federal Constitution was denied, but to the particular claims duly made below, and denied. [We] lack here the power occasionally exercised on review of judgments of lower federal courts to correct in criminal cases vital errors, although the objection was not taken in the trial court. Because we may not enquire into the errors now alleged, I concur in affirming the judgment of the state court.

OTHER CASES OF THE TWENTIES AND THIRTIES

Introduction. Most states enacted anti-sedition laws in the immediate post-World War I years—some patterned on the New York and California ones in Gitlow and Whitney, some going off in different and often more extreme directions. In the cases in the 1920s and 1930s that follow, the Court set aside convictions under such laws.[1] Although in these cases First Amendment claimants prevailed in the Court at last, the holdings most arguably rested on constitutional bases other than the First Amendment. Moreover, these cases did not contribute greatly to providing answers to the problems raised by the Schenck and Gitlow lines of decision.

1. FISKE v. KANSAS, 274 U.S. 380 (1927): This case, decided on the same day as Whitney, held unconstitutional an application of the Kansas version of criminal syndicalism legislation. Fiske was convicted for soliciting new members for a branch of the IWW (Industrial Workers of the World). The only trial evidence of IWW doctrine was the preamble to its constitution, containing such statements as: "Between [the working and employing] classes a struggle must go on until the workers of the World organize as a class, take possession of the earth, and the machinery of production and abolish the wage system." Fiske insisted that the preamble taught "peaceful," not "criminal or unlawful," action, and that he had not advocated criminal syndicalism or sabotage. In affirming the conviction, the highest state court said: "The language quoted from the I.W.W. preamble need not—in order to sustain the judgment—be held, necessarily and as a matter of law, to advocate, teach or even affirmatively suggest physical violence as a means of accomplishing industrial or political ends. It is open to that interpretation and is capable of use to convey that meaning." The Court unanimously reversed, in an opinion by Justice SANFORD:

"[T]his Court will review the finding of facts by a State court where a Federal right has been denied as the result of a finding shown by the record to be without evidence to support it; or where a conclusion of law as to a Federal right and a finding of fact are so intermingled as to make it necessary, in order

---

1. In addition to the decisions considered here, note also Stromberg v. California, 283 U.S. 359 (1931) (holding unconstitutional a version of a widely adopted red flag law), and two cases not directly involving "Red Scare," antisubversion concerns: Near v. Minnesota (1931; invalidating injunctive remedies against "malicious, scandalous and defamatory" periodicals, p. 1157 below); and Hague v. CIO, 307 U.S. 496 (1939; invalidating a licensing requirement for meetings on public property, p. 1197 below).

to pass upon the Federal question, to analyze the facts. [No] substantial inference can, in our judgment, be drawn from the language of this preamble, that the organization taught, advocated or suggested the duty, necessity, propriety, or expediency of crime, criminal syndicalism, sabotage, or other unlawful acts or methods. [S]tanding alone, [there] was nothing which warranted the court or jury in ascribing to this language, either as an inference of law or fact, 'the sinister meaning attributed to it by the state.' In this respect the language of the preamble is essentially different from that of the manifesto involved in [Gitlow]. The result is that the Syndicalism Act has been applied in this case to sustain the conviction of the defendant, without any charge or evidence that the organization in which he secured members advocated any crime, violence or other unlawful acts or methods as a means of effecting industrial or political changes or revolution. Thus applied the Act is an arbitrary and unreasonable exercise of the police power of the State, unwarrantably infringing the liberty of the defendant in violation of the due process clause of the 14th Amendment."

Arguably, Fiske was not truly a First Amendment decision and did not rest on the constitutionally protected nature of the defendant's conduct. Rather, it may be explainable simply as an example of the Lochner-substantive due process approach. Alternatively, it may have rested on procedural due process grounds: the impermissibility of drawing conclusory inferences from inadequate factual bases. Cf. the Thompson v. Louisville principle.[2]

2. DE JONGE v. OREGON, 299 U.S. 353 (1937): This was the first of these cases to rest squarely on substantive First Amendment grounds. It set aside a conviction under Oregon's criminal syndicalism law.[3] Appellant was charged with assisting in the conduct of a meeting "which was called under the auspices of the Communist Party, an organization advocating criminal syndicalism." He argued that "the meeting was public and orderly and was held for a lawful purpose; that while it was held under the auspices of the Communist Party, neither criminal syndicalism nor any unlawful conduct was taught or advocated at the [meeting]." The highest state court rejected that defense, noting that there was no charge that criminal syndicalism was advocated at the meeting; rather, the charge had simply been that DeJonge had conducted a meeting called by the Party, and that the Party advocated criminal syndicalism. Accordingly, lack of proof of illegal advocacy at the meeting itself was immaterial. The Court unanimously reversed the conviction. Chief Justice HUGHES stated:

"[De Jonge] was not indicted for participating in its organization, or for joining it, or for soliciting members or for distributing its literature. He was not charged with teaching or advocating criminal syndicalism or sabotage or any unlawful acts, either at the meeting or elsewhere. [His] sole offense [was] that he had assisted in the conduct of a public meeting, albeit otherwise lawful,

2. In Thompson v. Louisville, 362 U.S. 199 (1960), Justice Black's opinion for the Court reversed a conviction for loitering and disorderly conduct on the ground that the charges "were so totally devoid of evidentiary support as to render [petitioner's] conviction unconstitutional under [due process]." He insisted that the decision turned "not on the sufficiency of the evidence, but on whether this conviction rests upon any evidence at all." Note that Thompson purports to be a procedural due process decision. It does not say that petitioner's conduct was constitutionally protected or could not be made a crime. Instead, it claims that the state could not infer from the evidence shown that he had committed the crime charged.

The Thompson v. Louisville principle was applied by the Warren Court in a variety of contexts, especially as a procedural technique for the indirect protection of substantive rights. In a number of instances, it was relied on to reverse convictions without the necessity of reaching underlying First Amendment issues. See, e.g., Gregory v. Chicago (1969; p. 1222 below) and Shuttlesworth v. Birmingham (1965; p. 1236 below). Cf. Jackson v. Virginia, 443 U.S. 307 (1979).

3. The law defined criminal syndicalism as "the doctrine which advocates crime, physical violence, sabotage, or any unlawful acts or methods as a means of accomplishing or effecting industrial or political change or revolution."

which was held under the auspices of the Communist Party. The broad reach of the statute as thus applied is plain. While defendant was a member of the Communist Party, that membership was not necessary to conviction on such a charge. A like fate might have attended any speaker, although not a member, who 'assisted in the conduct' of the meeting. However innocuous the object of the meeting, however lawful the subjects and tenor of the addresses, however reasonable and timely the discussion, all those assisting in the conduct of the meeting would be subject to imprisonment as felons if the meeting were held by the [Party].

"The right of peaceable assembly is a right cognate to those of free speech and free press and is equally fundamental. [These] rights may be abused by using speech or press or assembly in order to incite to violence and crime. [But] the legislative intervention can find constitutional justification only by dealing with the abuse. [It] follows [that] peaceable assembly for lawful discussion cannot be made a crime. The holding of meetings for peaceable political action cannot be proscribed. Those who assist in the conduct of such meetings cannot be branded as criminals on that score. The question, if the rights of free speech and peaceable assembly are to be preserved, is not as to the auspices under which the meeting is held but as to its purpose; not as to the relations of the speakers, but whether their utterances transcend the bounds of the freedom of speech which the Constitution [protects]. We are not called upon to review the findings of the state court as to the objectives of the Communist Party. Notwithstanding those objectives, the defendant still enjoyed his personal right of free speech and to take part in a peaceable assembly having a lawful purpose, although called by that Party. [We] hold that the [state law] as applied to the particular charge as defined by the state court is repugnant to the due process clause of the 14th Amendment."

3.   HERNDON v. LOWRY, 301 U.S. 242 (1937): Herndon, a black organizer for the Communist party in the South, was convicted of an "attempt to incite insurrection" under a Georgia law.[4] In overturning that conviction, the Court rested in part on substantive First Amendment grounds and in part on grounds of vagueness.[5] The conviction was based largely on documents found in Herndon's possession. One document listed the aims for which members of the Communist Party were to vote. The Court found none of these aims was criminal on its face, but Georgia argued that one of them—"equal rights for the Negroes and self-determination of the Black Belt"—showed criminality "because of extrinsic facts." The major item of "extrinsic facts" was a booklet elaborating the Party's position on "self-determination" for blacks in the South—a booklet that had on its cover a map of the United States "having a dark belt across certain Southern states." The Court's 5 to 4 decision overturned the conviction because (1) the construction and application of the law deprived Herndon of his constitutional rights of free speech and assembly, and (2) the law as construed and applied did not furnish "a reasonably definite and ascertainable standard of guilt."

Justice ROBERTS' majority opinion emphasized that there was no evidence that Herndon had ever advocated "forcible subversion." Turning to the construction of the law, he noted that the highest state court had stated: "Force must have been contemplated, [but] the statute does not include either its occurrence or its imminence as an ingredient of the particular offense charged." Herndon's challenge rested on the clear and present danger test of Schenck; Georgia's argument stressed Gitlow. But the Court found Gitlow inapplicable:

---

4. The Georgia law defined "insurrection" as "any combined resistance to the lawful authority of the State, with intent to the denial thereof, when the same is manifested or intended to be manifested by acts of violence."

5. Vagueness objections in First Amendment cases are considered further in sec. 1 of chap. 12, especially at p. 1156.

according to Justice Roberts, the law in Gitlow, unlike the one here, "denounced as criminal certain acts carefully and adequately described." Gitlow, he insisted, "furnishes no warrant for [Georgia's] contention that under a law general in its description of the mischief to be remedied and equally general in respect of the intent of the actor, the standard of guilt may be made the 'dangerous tendency' of his words."

In explaining the first basis of the Court's reversal of the conviction—the violation of Herndon's First Amendment rights—Justice Roberts emphasized the application of the law: "In its application the offense made criminal is that of soliciting members for a political party and conducting meetings of a local unit of that party when one of the doctrines of the party, established by reference to a document not shown to have been exhibited to anyone by the accused, may be said to be ultimate resort to violence at some indefinite future time against organized government. It is to be borne in mind that the law has not made membership in the Communist Party unlawful by reason of its supposed dangerous tendency even in the remote future. The question is not whether Georgia might, in analogy to what other states have done, so declare. [See the Gitlow and Whitney statutes.] The appellant induced others to become members of the Communist Party. Did he thus incite to insurrection by reason of the fact that they agreed to abide by the tenets of the party, some of them lawful, others, as may be assumed, unlawful, in the absence of proof that he brought the unlawful aims to their notice, that he approved them, or that the fantastic program they envisaged was conceived of by anyone as more than an ultimate ideal? Doubtless circumstantial evidence might affect the answer to the question if appellant had been shown to have said that the Black Belt should be organized at once as a separate state and that that objective was one of his principal aims. But here circumstantial evidence is all to the opposite effect. [His] membership in the Communist Party and his solicitation of a few members wholly fail to establish an attempt to incite others to insurrection. [In] these circumstances, to make membership in the party and solicitation of members for that party a criminal offense, punishable by death, in the discretion of a jury, is an unwarranted invasion of the right of freedom of speech."

Turning to the second ground for the reversal—that the law as construed and applied did not furnish "a sufficiently ascertainable standard of guilt"—Justice Roberts stated: "The Act does not prohibit incitement to violent interference with any given activity or operation of the state. By force of it, as construed, the judge and jury trying an alleged offender cannot appraise the circumstances and character of the defendant's utterances or activities as begetting a clear and present danger of forcible obstruction of a particular state function. Nor is any specified conduct or utterance of the accused made an offense. [If] the jury conclude that the defendant should have contemplated that any act or utterance of his in opposition to the established order or advocating a change in that order, might, in the distant future, eventuate in a combination to offer forcible resistance to the State, or as the State says, if the jury believe he should have known that his words would have 'a dangerous tendency' then he may be convicted. To be guilty under the law, as construed, a defendant need not advocate resort to force. He need not teach any particular doctrine. [If], by the exercise of prophesy, he can forecast that, as a result of a chain of causation, following his proposed action a group may arise at some future date which will resort to force, he is bound to make the prophesy and abstain, under pain of punishment, possibly of execution. Every person who attacks existing conditions, who agitates for a change in the form of government, must take the risk that if a jury should be of opinion he ought to have foreseen that his utterances might contribute in any measure to some future forcible resistance to the existing government he may be convicted of [the] offense. [It] would be sufficient if the jury thought he reasonably might foretell that those he persuaded to join the party might, at some time in the indefinite future, resort to forcible resistance of government. The question thus proposed to a jury involves pure speculation as to future trends of thought and action. Within what time might one reasonably expect that an attempted organization of the Communist Party in the United States would result in violent action by that party? If a jury returned a special verdict saying twenty years or even fifty years the verdict could not be shown to be wrong. The law, as thus construed, licenses the jury to create its own standard in each case. [The law], as construed and applied, amounts merely to a dragnet which may enmesh anyone who agitates for a change of government if a jury can be persuaded that he ought to have foreseen his words would have some effect in the future conduct of others. So vague and indeterminate are the boundaries thus set to the freedom of speech and assembly that the law necessarily violates the guaranties of liberty embodied in the 14th Amendment." [6]

C. THE SMITH ACT PROSECUTIONS

CLEAR AND PRESENT DANGER IN THE FORTIES: WIDENING USE; RISING DISSATISFACTION

Introduction. The post-World War II prosecutions of Communist Party leaders were brought under the Smith Act of 1940, a law quite similar to the New York statute sustained in Gitlow. When the first group of defendants brought their appeals to the Court, in the 1951 Dennis case below, they relied extensively on clear and present danger; and the opinions in Dennis reexamine that standard at length. The defendants' reliance on the test was understandable: the Court had spoken of it with increasing frequency during the 1940s. The test had most commonly surfaced in contexts far removed from subversive advocacy. For example, an early use in a majority opinion was Schneider v. State (1939; p. 1206 below), involving an ordinance against littering streets. And the most consistent use of the test had been to strike down contempt of court penalties imposed for newspaper comments allegedly interfering with the administration of justice. See, e.g., Craig v. Harney (1947; p. 1338 below). Moreover, there had been increasing criticism of the standard itself. Some critics, then and later, thought clear and present danger afforded either too

---

6. Justice VAN DEVANTER, joined by Justices McReynolds, Sutherland and Butler, dissented. The dissent stated that the "purpose and probable effect" of the literature carried by Herndon should be determined "with appropriate regard to the capacity and circumstances of those who are sought to be influenced." He added: "In this instance the literature is largely directed to a people whose past and present circumstances would lead them to give unusual credence to its inflaming and inciting features."

These three cases did set aside convictions by First Amendment claimants, but they left unsettled many questions regarding the punishability of subversive advocacy. Accordingly, there was no clear guidance when the Court confronted the issue once more in the post-World War II cases, below. De Jonge was the only decision based solely on substantive First Amendment grounds. However, one of the grounds in Herndon did stress the temporal "immediacy" ingredient of clear and present danger—an ingredient not emphasized in Gitlow and Whitney. Arguably, some of these cases, more than the majority rulings in the earlier ones, began to articulate the contours of political agitation protected by the First Amendment. Thus, the centrality of the First Amendment protection in De Jonge may suggest that judicial efforts to define the protected area of debate at the core of the First Amendment are more productive than the proximity-of-danger preoccupations of clear and present danger. So viewed, De Jonge seems closer to Hand's focus in Masses than to Holmes' analyses. In examining the later cases, below, consider which approach predominates. Consider, too, whether the preceding group of cases speaks more directly to the Gitlow-Whitney problem (the problem of the weight to be given to prior *legislative* judgments regarding the danger of specified speech) than the Gitlow dissent had. Did they provide adequate guidance when the Smith Act prosecutions, below, came before the Court after World War II?

much or too little protection to free speech: the Vinson plurality opinion in Dennis, for example, finds the immediacy emphasis too restrictive on government; the Douglas opinion in Brandenburg (1969; p. 1037 below), illustrates the dissatisfaction with the use of the standard to "balance away" liberties. But much of the criticism dealt less with the scope of protection afforded by the Schenck phrase than with its suitability: it was argued that the standard was used in inappropriate contexts, that it was too simplistic, that in any event it did not deal adequately with the type of problem presented by Gitlow and Dennis.

1. *Clear and present danger and legislative balancing.* As early as 1941—a few months after the Smith Act was enacted, eight years before the Dennis trial— Herbert Wechsler suggested not only that the Smith Act variety of statute had "little positive merit" as a legislative formula but also that the clear and present danger judicial formula urged as a protection of speech had "little positive content" and "prescribes no rigid limitation on legislative action."[1] As a legislative approach, the Smith Act, an "advocacy of violent overthrow" statute, was unresponsive to current dangers: it was "an uncritical acceptance of a formula devised during the days when the Communist manifesto represented the technique of revolution; when revolutionaries operated by declaring rather than disguising their principles." And as a judicial technique, clear and present danger was of limited utility: what it "can do, and all that it can do, is to require an extended judicial review in the fullest legislative sense of the competing values which the particular situation presents"; but that review "may be limited" by a "deference to legislative judgment, at least where the legislation condemns specific doctrine."

2. *Clear and present danger as oversimplification.* Compare an evaluation of clear and present danger near the end of the 1940s, just before Dennis (an evaluation quoted by Justice Frankfurter in Dennis): "The truth is that the clear-and-present-danger test is an oversimplified judgment unless it takes account also of a number of other factors: the relative seriousness of the danger in comparison with the value of the occasion for speech or political activity; the availability of more moderate controls than those which the state has imposed; and perhaps the specific intent with which the speech or activity is launched. No matter how rapidly we utter the phrase 'clear and present danger,' or how closely we hyphenate the words, they are not a substitute for the weighing of values. They tend to convey a delusion of certitude when what is most certain is the complexity of the strands in the web of freedoms which the judge must disentangle."[2]

3. *Clear and present danger and Learned Hand.* Among the critics of clear and present danger was Judge Learned Hand. His "Bill of Rights" lectures in 1958 included a skeptical aside on Holmes' Schenck formulation: "Homer nodded." More generally, these lectures revealed deep skepticism that substantive constitutional guarantees were judicially enforceable at all. Yet as District Judge in Masses, Hand had tried to articulate judicial criteria of his own. And it fell to him on the Court of Appeals to pass on the Dennis defendants' clear and present danger defense—and reformulate it in words adopted by the plurality opinion in the Supreme Court.[3]

Note Judge Hand's puzzled comment on the variety of clear and present danger invocations, in the course of his effort to restate the test in the Dennis case, 183 F.2d 201 (2d Cir.1950): "[Cases such as Gitlow] concerned the validity of statutes which had made it unlawful to stir up opposition to [government] in the discharge of some vital function. There followed several

1. Wechsler, in "Symposium on Civil Liberties," 9 Am.L.Sch.Rev. 881 (1941).

2. Freund, On Understanding the Supreme Court (1949), 27.

3. Even at the time of the Court's decision in Dennis in 1951, Judge Hand, privately, continued to prefer his 1917 Masses "incitement" standard.

which held that an ordinance or statute might not trench upon freedom of speech in order to promote minor public convenience: e.g., preventing the streets from being littered by broadsides, Schneider v. State (1939; p. 1206 below); requiring a license to solicit contributions for societies, Cantwell v. Connecticut (1940; p. 1204 below); requiring a union leader to register his name and union affiliation with the Secretary of State, Thomas v. Collins, 323 U.S. 516 (1945). The opinions in all these cases did however repeat the rubric of [Schenck], though none of them attempted to define how grave, or how imminent the danger must be, or whether the two factors are mutually interdependent. Moreover, the situation in all was wholly different from that in the preceding decisions. It is one thing to say that the public interest in keeping streets clean, or in keeping a register of union leaders, or in requiring solicitors to take out licenses, will not justify interference with freedom of utterance; [but] it is quite another matter to say that an organized effort to inculcate the duty of revolution may not be repressed. It does not seem to us therefore that these decisions help towards a solution here."

4. *Clear and present danger and Dennis.* Consider the use of clear and present danger in Dennis, below, against the background of these criticisms. Does Dennis give inadequate protection to speech? If so, is that because it failed to apply clear and present danger? Or because of problems inherent in clear and present danger? Was a greater emphasis on immediacy in Dennis compelled by the earlier cases? What different approach to speech would have been preferable in Dennis?

5. *Clear and present danger as inadequate protection of Meiklejohn's "public" speech.* While the clarity and suitability of clear and present danger were being questioned during the forties, another—and increasingly influential—challenge attacked it for protecting speech insufficiently. In 1948, philosopher Alexander Meiklejohn took direct issue with Schenck because its standard authorized some suppression of speech that should be wholly immune. The First Amendment, he insisted, "means that certain substantive evils which, in principle, Congress has a right to prevent, must be endured if the only way of avoiding them is by the abridging of that freedom of speech upon which the entire structure of our free institutions rests." Meiklejohn distinguished among varieties of speech: only "public" speech—speech on public issues, speech connected with "self-government"—should be immune from regulation; "private" speech was entitled to less complete protection.[4] Would the Meiklejohn approach have been preferable in Dennis? Has it had greater acceptance in the cases since Dennis? [5]

DENNIS v. UNITED STATES

341 U.S. 494, 71 S.Ct. 857, 95 L.Ed. 1137 (1951).

Mr. Chief Justice VINSON announced the judgment of the Court and an opinion in which Mr. Justice REED, Mr. Justice BURTON and Mr. Justice MINTON join.

Petitioners were indicted in July, 1948, for violation of the conspiracy provisions of the Smith Act during the period of April, 1945, to July, 1948. [The Second Circuit affirmed petitioners' conviction.] We granted certiorari, limited to the following two questions: (1) Whether either § 2 or § 3 of the

---

4. Meiklejohn, Free Speech and Its Relation to Self-Government (1948), 48, reprinted in Meiklejohn, Political Freedom (1960).

5. Consider this question especially in connection with New York Times v. Sullivan (1964;

p. 1052 below) and Brandenburg v. Ohio (1969; p. 1037 below). See generally Brennan, "The Supreme Court and the Meiklejohn Interpretation of the First Amendment," 79 Harv.L.Rev. 1 (1965).

Smith Act,[1] inherently or as construed and applied in the instant case, violates the First Amendment and other provisions of the Bill of Rights; (2) whether either § 2 or § 3 of the Act inherently or as construed and applied in the instant case, violates the First and Fifth Amendments because of indefiniteness. [The] indictment charged the petitioners with wilfully and knowingly conspiring (1) to organize as the Communist Party of the United States of America a society, group and assembly of persons who teach and advocate the overthrow and destruction of the Government of the United States by force and violence, and (2) knowingly and wilfully to advocate and teach the duty and necessity of overthrowing and destroying the Government of the United States by force and [violence]. The trial of the case extended over nine months, [resulting] in a record of 16,000 pages. Our limited grant of the writ of certiorari has removed from our consideration any question as to the sufficiency of the [evidence]. [T]he Court of Appeals held that the record supports the following broad conclusion: [that] the Communist Party is a highly disciplined organization, adept at infiltration into stragetic positions, use of aliases, and double-meaning language; that the Party is rigidly controlled; that Communists, unlike other political parties, tolerate no dissension from the policy laid down by the guiding forces; [that] the literature of the Party and the statements and activities of its leaders, petitioners here, advocate, and the general goal of the Party was, during the period in question, to achieve a successful overthrow of the existing order by force and [violence].

A "right" to rebellion against dictatorial governments is without force where the existing structure of the government provides for peaceful and orderly change. We reject any principle of governmental helplessness in the face of preparation for revolution. [No] one could conceive that it is not within the power of Congress to prohibit acts intended to overthrow the Government by force and violence. The question with which we are concerned here is not whether Congress has such *power,* but whether the *means* which it has employed conflict with [the] Constitution. One of the bases for the contention that the means which Congress has employed are invalid takes the form of an attack on the face of the statute on the grounds that by its terms it prohibits academic discussion of the merits of Marxism-Leninism, that it stifles ideas and is contrary to all concepts of a free speech and a free press. [The] very language of the Smith Act negates the interpretation which petitioners would have us impose on that Act. It is directed at advocacy, not discussion. Thus, the trial judge properly charged the jury that they could not convict if they found that petitioners did "no more than pursue peaceful studies and discussions or teaching and advocacy in the realm of ideas." [But the application of the Act] in this case has resulted in convictions for the teaching and advocacy of the overthrow of the Government by force and violence, which, even though coupled with the intent to accomplish that overthrow, contains an element of speech. For this reason, we must pay special heed to the demands of the First Amendment marking out the boundaries of speech.

---

1. Sections 2 and 3 of the Smith Act provide as follows:

"Sec. 2. (a) It shall be unlawful for any person—

"(1) to knowingly or willfully advocate, abet, advise, or teach the duty, necessity, desirability, or propriety of overthrowing or destroying any government in the United States by force or violence, or by the assassination of any officer of any such [government];

"(3) to organize or help to organize any society, group, or assembly of persons who teach, advocate, or encourage the overthrow or destruction of any government in the United States by force or violence; or to be or become a member of, or affiliate with, any such society, group, or assembly of persons, knowing the purposes [thereof].

"Sec. 3. It shall be unlawful for any person to attempt to commit, or to conspire to commit, any of the acts prohibited [by] this title."

[T]he basis of the First Amendment is the hypothesis that speech can rebut speech, propaganda will answer propaganda, free debate of ideas will result in the wisest governmental policies. [An] analysis of the leading cases in this Court which have involved direct limitations on speech, however, will demonstrate that both the majority of the Court and the dissenters in particular cases have recognized that this is not an unlimited, unqualified right, but that the societal value of speech must, on occasion, be subordinated to other values and considerations. [Although] no case subsequent to Whitney and Gitlow has expressly overruled the majority opinions in those cases, there is little doubt that subsequent opinions have inclined toward the Holmes-Brandeis rationale. [But] neither Justice Holmes nor Justice Brandeis ever envisioned that a shorthand phrase should be crystallized into a rigid rule to be applied inflexibly without regard to the circumstances of each case. Speech is not an absolute, above and beyond control by the legislature when its judgment, subject to review here, is that certain kinds of speech are so undesirable as to warrant [criminal sanction].

In this case we are squarely presented with the application of the "clear and present danger" test, and must decide what that phrase imports. We first note that many of the cases in which this Court has reversed convictions by use of this or similar tests have been based on the fact that the interest which the State was attempting to protect was itself too insubstantial to warrant restriction of [speech]. Overthrow of the Government by force and violence is certainly a substantial enough interest for the Government to limit speech. [If], then, this interest may be protected, the literal problem which is presented is what has been meant by the use of the phrase "clear and present danger" of the utterances bringing about the evil within the power of Congress to punish. Obviously, the words cannot mean that before the Government may act, it must wait until the putsch is about to be executed, the plans have been laid and the signal is awaited. If Government is aware that a group aiming at its overthrow is attempting to indoctrinate its members and to commit them to a course whereby they will strike when the leaders feel the circumstances permit, action by the Government is required. The argument that there is no need for Government to concern itself, for Government is strong, it possesses ample powers to put down a rebellion, it may defeat the revolution with ease needs no answer. For that is not the question. Certainly an attempt to overthrow the Government by force, even though doomed from the outset because of inadequate numbers or power of the revolutionists, is a sufficient evil for Congress to prevent. The damage which such attempts create both physically and politically to a nation makes it impossible to measure the validity in terms of the probability of success, or the immediacy of a successful attempt. In the instant case the trial judge charged the jury that they could not convict unless they found that petitioners intended to overthrow the Government "as speedily as circumstances would permit." This does not mean, and could not properly mean, that they would not strike until there was certainty of success. What was meant was that the revolutionists would strike when they thought the time was ripe. We must therefore reject the contention that success or probability of success is the criterion.

The situation with which Justices Holmes and Brandeis were concerned in Gitlow was a comparatively isolated event, bearing little relation in their minds to any substantial threat to the safety of the community. [They] were not confronted with any situation comparable to the instant one—the development of an apparatus designed and dedicated to the overthrow of the Government, in the context of world crisis after crisis. Chief Judge Learned Hand, writing for the majority below, interpreted the phrase as follows: "In each case [courts] must ask whether the gravity of the 'evil,' discounted by its improbability, justifies such invasion of free speech as is necessary to avoid the danger." We adopt this statement of the rule. As articulated by Chief Judge Hand, it is as succinct and inclusive as any other we might devise at this [time]. Likewise, we are in accord with the court below, which affirmed the trial court's finding that the requisite danger existed. The mere fact that from the period 1945 to 1948 petitioners' activities did not result in an attempt to overthrow the Government by force and violence is of course no answer to the fact that there was a group that was ready to make the attempt. The formation by petitioners of such a highly organized conspiracy, with rigidly disciplined members subject to call when the leaders, these petitioners, felt that the time had come for action, coupled with the inflammable nature of world conditions, similar uprisings in other countries, and the touch-and-go nature of our relations with countries with whom petitioners were in the very least ideologically attuned, convince us that their convictions were justified on this score. And this analysis disposes of the contention that a conspiracy to advocate, as distinguished from the advocacy itself, cannot be constitutionally restrained, because it comprises only the preparation. It is the existence of the conspiracy which creates the danger. [If] the ingredients of the reaction are present, we cannot bind the Government to wait until the catalyst is added.

Although we have concluded that the finding that there was a sufficient danger to warrant the application of the statute was justified on the merits, there remains the problem of whether the trial judge's treatment of the issue was correct. [The trial judge (Medina)] reserved the question of the existence of the danger for his own determination, and the question becomes whether the issue is of such a nature that it should have been submitted to a jury. [Petitioners' claim] rests on the theory that a jury must decide a question of the application of the First Amendment. We do not agree. When facts are found that establish the violation of a statute, the protection against conviction afforded by the First Amendment is a matter of law. The doctrine that there must be a clear and present danger of a substantive evil that Congress has a right to prevent is a judicial rule to be applied as a matter of law by the courts. The guilt is established by proof of facts. Whether the First Amendment protects the activity which constitutes the violation of the statute must depend upon a judicial determination of the scope of the First Amendment applied to the circumstances of the [case].[2]

[Petitioners] intended to overthrow the Government of the United States as speedily as the circumstances would permit. Their conspiracy to organize the Communist Party and to teach and advocate the overthrow of the [Government] by force and violence created a "clear and present danger" of an attempt to overthrow the Government by force and [violence].

Affirmed.[3]

Mr. Justice FRANKFURTER, concurring in affirmance of the judgment.

[The] historic antecedents of the First Amendment preclude the notion that its purpose was to give unqualified immunity to every expression that touched on matters within the range of political interest. [Absolute] rules would inevitably lead to absolute exceptions, and such exceptions would eventually corrode the rules. The demands of free speech in a democratic society as well as the interest in national security are better served by candid and informed weighing of the competing interests, within the confines of the judicial process, than by announcing dogmas too inflexible for the non-Euclidian problems to be solved. But how are competing interests to be assessed? Since they are not subject to quantitative ascertainment, the issue necessarily resolves itself into

2. Chief Justice Vinson also rejected the claim that the Act as interpreted was "too vague, not sufficiently advising those who would speak of the limitations upon their activity."

3. Justice Clark did not participate in the decision.

asking, who is to make the adjustments?　—who is to balance[?]　Full responsibility for the choice cannot be given to the courts.　Courts are not representative bodies.　[Their] judgment is best informed, and therefore most dependable, within narrow limits.　Their essential quality is detachment, founded on independence.　History teaches that the independence of the judiciary is jeopardized when courts become embroiled in the passions of the day and assume primary responsibility in choosing between competing political, economic and social pressures.　Primary responsibility for adjusting the interests which compete in the situation before us of necessity belongs to the Congress.　[We] are to set aside the judgment [of legislators] only if there is no reasonable basis for [it].

In all fairness, [defendants' clear and present danger] argument cannot be met by reinterpreting the Court's frequent use of "clear" and "present" to mean an entertainable "probability."　In giving this meaning to the phrase "clear and present danger," the Court of Appeals was fastidiously confining the rhetoric of opinions to the exact scope of what was decided by them.　We have greater responsibility for having given constitutional support, over repeated protests, to uncritical libertarian generalities.　[If past] decisions are to be used as a guide and not as an argument, it is important to view them as a whole and to distrust the easy generalizations to which some of them lend themselves.　[Viewed as a whole, these] decisions express an attitude toward the judicial function and a standard of values which for me are decisive of the case before us.

A survey of the relevant decisions indicates that the results which we have reached are on the whole those that would ensue from careful weighing of conflicting interests.　The complex issues presented by regulation of speech in public places, by picketing, and by legislation prohibiting advocacy of crime have been resolved by scrutiny of many factors besides the imminence and gravity of the evil threatened.[1]　It is a familiar experience in the law that new situations do not fit neatly into legal conceptions that arose under different circumstances to satisfy different needs.　[So] it is with the attempt to use the direction of thought lying behind the criterion of "clear and present danger" wholly out of the context in which it originated, and to make of it an absolute dogma and definitive measuring rod for the power of Congress to deal with assaults against security through devices other than overt physical attempts.　[It] would be a distortion, indeed a mockery, of [Holmes'] reasoning to compare the "puny anonymities" [to] which he was addressing himself in [Abrams] or the publication that was "futile and too remote from possible consequences" [in Gitlow] with the setting of events [in this case].　Not every type of speech occupies the same position on the scale of values.　[On] any scale of values which we have hitherto recognized, [the defendants' sort of speech] ranks low.

These general considerations underlie decision of the case before us.　On the one hand is the interest in security.　The Communist Party was not designed by these defendants as an ordinary political party.　For the circumstances of its organization, its aims and methods, and the relation of the defendants to its organization and aims we are concluded by the jury's verdict.　[The] jury found that the Party advocates the theory that there is a duty and necessity to overthrow the Government by force and violence.　It found that the Party entertains and promotes this view, not as a prophetic insight, [but] as a program for winning adherents and as a policy to be translated into action.　In finding that the defendants violated the statute, we may not treat as established fact that the Communist Party in this country is of significant size, well-organized, well-disciplined, conditioned to embark on unlawful activity when given the com-

---

1. At this point, Justice Frankfurter quoted the Freund comment on clear and present danger, printed at p. 1016 above.

mand. But in determining whether application of the statute to the defendants is within the constitutional powers of Congress, we are not limited to the facts found by the jury. We must view such a question in the light of whatever is relevant to a legislative judgment. We may take judicial notice that the Communist doctrines which these defendants have conspired to advocate are in the ascendency in powerful nations who cannot be acquitted of unfriendliness to the institutions of this country. We may take account of evidence brought forward at this trial and elsewhere, much of which has long been common knowledge. In sum, it would amply justify a legislature in concluding that recruitment of additional members for the Party would create a substantial danger to national security.

In 1947, it has been reliably reported, at least 60,000 members were enrolled in the Party. Evidence was introduced in this case that the membership was organized in small units [protected] by elaborate precautions designed to prevent disclosure of individual identity. There are no reliable data tracing acts of sabotage or espionage directly to these defendants. But a Canadian Royal Commission [in 1946 reported] that "the Communist movement was the principal base in which the espionage network was recruited." The most notorious spy within recent history [Klaus Fuchs] was led into the service of the Soviet Union through Communist indoctrination. Evidence supports the conclusion that members of the Party seek and occupy positions of importance in political and labor organizations. Congress was not barred by the Constitution from believing that indifference to such experience would be an exercise not of freedom but of irresponsibility.

On the other hand is the interest in free speech. The right to exert all governmental powers in aid of maintaining our institutions and resisting their physical overthrow does not include intolerance of opinions and speech that cannot do harm although opposed and perhaps alien to dominant, traditional opinion. [It] is better for those who have almost unlimited power of government in their hands to err on the side of freedom. [No] matter how clear we may be that the defendants now before us are preparing to overthrow our Government at the propitious moment, it is self-delusion to think that we can punish them for their advocacy without adding to the risks run by loyal citizens who honestly believe in some of the reforms these defendants advance. It is a sobering fact that in sustaining the convictions before us we can hardly escape restriction on the interchange of [ideas].

[But it] is not for us to decide how we would adjust the clash of interests which this case presents were the primary responsibility for reconciling it ours. Congress has determined that the danger created by advocacy of overthrow justifies the ensuing restriction on freedom of speech. The determination was made after due deliberation, and the seriousness of the congressional purpose is attested by the volume of legislation passed to effectuate the same ends. [Can] we hold that the First Amendment deprives Congress of what it deemed necessary for the Government's protection? To make validity of legislation depend on judicial reading of events still in the womb of time—a forecast, that is, of the outcome of forces at best appreciated only with knowledge of the topmost secrets of nations—is to charge the judiciary with duties beyond its [equipment]. [It] is relevant to remind that in sustaining the power of Congress in a case like this nothing irrevocable is done. The democratic process at all events is not impaired or restricted. Power and responsibility remain with the people and immediately with their representatives. All the Court says is that Congress was not forbidden by the Constitution to pass this enactment and that a prosecution under it may be brought against a conspiracy such as the one before [us].

Mr. Justice JACKSON, concurring.

[E]ither by accident or design, the Communist strategem outwits the anti-anarchist pattern of statutes aimed against "overthrow by force and violence" if qualified by the doctrine that only "clear and present danger" of accomplishing that result will sustain the prosecution. The "clear and present danger" test was an innovation by Mr. Justice Holmes in [Schenck, refined] in later cases, all arising before the era of World War II revealed the subtlety and efficacy of modernized revolutionary techniques used by totalitarian parties. [I] would save it, unmodified, for application as a "rule of reason" in the kind of case for which it was devised. When the issue is criminality of a hotheaded speech on a street corner, or circulation of a few incendiary pamphlets, or parading by some zealots behind a red flag, or refusal of a handful of school children to salute our flag, it is not beyond the capacity of the judicial process to gather, comprehend, and weigh the necessary materials for decision whether it is a clear and present danger of substantive evil or a harmless letting off of steam. It is not a prophecy, for the danger in such cases has matured by the time of trial or it was never present. The test applies and has meaning where a conviction is sought to be based on a speech or writing which does not directly or explicitly advocate a crime but to which such tendency is sought to be attributed by construction or by implication from external circumstances. The formula in such cases favors freedoms that are vital to our society, and, even if sometimes applied too generously, the consequences cannot be grave. But its recent expansion has extended, in particular to Communists, unprecedented immunities. Unless we are to hold our Government captive in a judge-made verbal trap, we must approach the problem of a well-organized, nation-wide conspiracy, such as I have described, as realistically as our predecessors faced the trivialities that were being prosecuted until they were checked with a rule of reason.

I think reason is lacking for applying that test to this case. If we must decide that this Act and its application are constitutional only if we are convinced that petitioner's conduct creates a "clear and present danger" of violent overthrow, we must appraise imponderables, including international and national phenomena which baffle the best informed foreign offices and our most experienced politicians. [No] doctrine can be sound whose application requires us to make a prophecy of that sort in the guise of a legal decision. The judicial process simply is not adequate to a trial of such far-flung issues. The answers given would reflect our own political predilections and nothing more. The authors of the clear and present danger test never applied it to a case like this, nor would I. If applied as it is proposed here, it means that the Communist plotting is protected during its period of incubation; its preliminary stages of organization and preparation are immune from the law; the Government can move only after imminent action is manifest, when it would, of course, be too [late].

The highest degree of constitutional protection is due to the individual acting without conspiracy. But even an individual cannot claim that the Constitution protects him in advocating or teaching overthrow of government by force or violence. I should suppose no one would doubt that Congress has power to make such attempted overthrow a crime. But the contention is that one has the constitutional right to work up a public desire and will to do what it is a crime to attempt. I think direct incitement by speech or writing can be made a crime, and I think there can be a conviction without also proving that the odds favored its success by 99 to 1, or some other extremely high [ratio]. What really is under review here is a conviction of conspiracy, after a trial for conspiracy, on an indictment charging conspiracy, brought under a statute outlawing conspiracy. With due respect to my colleagues, they seem to me to discuss anything under the sun except the law of conspiracy. [The] Constitution does not make conspiracy a civil right. [Although] I consider criminal conspiracy a dragnet device capable of perversion into an instrument of injustice in the hands of a partisan or complacent judiciary, it has an established place in our system of law, and no reason appears for applying it only to concerted action claimed to disturb interstate commerce and withholding it from those claimed to undermine our whole [Government]. I do not suggest that Congress could punish conspiracy to advocate something, the doing of which it may not punish. Advocacy or exposition of the doctrine of communal property ownership, or any political philosophy unassociated with advocacy of its imposition by force or seizure of government by unlawful means could not be reached through conspiracy prosecution. But it is not forbidden to put down force or violence, it is not forbidden to punish its teaching or advocacy, and the end being punishable, there is no doubt of the power to punish conspiracy for the [purpose].

Mr. Justice BLACK [dissenting].

[I] cannot agree that the First Amendment permits us to sustain laws suppressing freedom of speech and press on the basis of Congress' or our own notions of mere "reasonableness." Such a doctrine waters down the First Amendment so that it amounts to little more than an admonition to Congress. The Amendment as so construed is not likely to protect any but those "safe" or orthodox views which rarely need its protection. I must also express my objection to the holding [because] it sanctions the determination of a crucial issue of fact by the judge rather than by the [jury]. Public opinion being what it now is, few will protest the conviction of these Communist petitioners. There is hope, however, that in calmer times, when present pressures, passions and fears subside, this or some later Court will restore the First Amendment liberties to the high preferred place where they belong in a free society.

Mr. Justice DOUGLAS, dissenting.

[I]f this were a case where those who claimed protection under the First Amendment were teaching the techniques of sabotage, the assassination of the President, the filching of documents from public files, the planting of bombs, the art of street warfare, and the like, I would have no doubts. The freedom to speak is not absolute; the teaching of methods of terror and other seditious conduct should be beyond the pale along with obscenity and immorality. This case was argued as if those were the facts. The argument imported much seditious conduct into the record. That is easy and it has popular appeal, for the activities of Communists in plotting and scheming against the free world are common knowledge. But the fact is that no such evidence was introduced at the trial. There is a statute which makes a seditious conspiracy unlawful. Petitioners, however, were not charged with a "conspiracy to overthrow" the Government. They were charged with a conspiracy to form a party and groups and assemblies of people who teach and advocate the overthrow of our Government by force or violence and with a conspiracy to advocate and teach its overthrow by force and violence. It may well be that indoctrination in the techniques of terror to destroy the Government would be indictable under either statute. But the teaching which is condemned here is of a different character.

So far as the present record is concerned, what petitioners did was to organize people to teach and themselves teach the Marxist-Leninist doctrine contained chiefly in four books: Foundations of Leninism by Stalin (1924), The Communist Manifesto by Marx and Engels (1848), State and Revolution by Lenin (1917), History of the Communist Party of the Soviet Union (B) (1939). Those books are to Soviet Communism what Mein Kampf was to Nazism. If they are understood, the ugliness of Communism is revealed, its deceit and cunning are exposed, the nature of its activities becomes apparent, and the chances of its success less likely. That is not, of course, the reason why petitioners chose these books for their classrooms. They are fervent Communists to whom these volumes are gospel. They preached the creed with the hope that some day it would be acted upon. The opinion of the Court does not outlaw these texts nor condemn them to the fire, as the Communists do literature offensive to their creed. But if the books themselves are not outlawed, if they can lawfully remain on library shelves, by what reasoning does their use in a classroom become a crime? [The] Act, as construed, requires the element of intent—that those who teach the creed believe in it. The crime then depends not on what is taught but on who the teacher is. That is to make freedom of speech turn not on *what is said,* but on the *intent* with which it is said. Once we start down that road we enter territory dangerous to the liberties of every [citizen].

There comes a time when even speech loses its constitutional immunity. Speech innocuous one year may at another time fan such destructive flames that it must be halted in the interests of the safety of the Republic. That is the meaning of the clear and present danger test. When conditions are so critical that there will be no time to avoid the evil that the speech threatens, it is time to call a halt. Otherwise, free speech which is the strength of the Nation will be the cause of its destruction. Yet free speech is the rule, not the exception. The restraint to be constitutional must be based on more than fear, on more than passionate opposition against the speech, on more than a revolted dislike for its contents. There must be some immediate injury to society that is likely if speech is [allowed].

I had assumed that the question of the clear and present danger, being so critical an issue in the case, would be a matter for submission to the jury. [The] Court, I think, errs when it treats the question as one of law. Yet, whether the question is one for the Court or the jury, there should be evidence of record on the issue. This record, however, contains no evidence whatsoever showing that the acts charged, viz., the teaching of the Soviet theory of revolution with the hope that it will be realized, have created any clear and present danger to the Nation. The Court, however, rules to the contrary. That ruling is [not] responsive to the issue in the case. We might as well say that the speech of petitioners is outlawed because Soviet Russia and her Red Army are a threat to world peace.

The nature of Communism as a force on the world scene would, of course, be relevant to the issue of clear and present danger of petitioners' advocacy within the United States. But the primary consideration is the strength and tactical position of petitioners and their converts in this country. On that there is no evidence in the record. If we are to take judicial notice of the threat of Communists within the nation, it should not be difficult to conclude that *as a political party* they are of little consequence. [Communism] in the world scene is no bogeyman; but Communism as a political faction or party in this country plainly is. Communism has been so thoroughly exposed in this country that it has been crippled as a political force. Free speech has destroyed it as an effective political party. [In] days of trouble and confusion, when bread lines were long, when the unemployed walked the streets, when people were starving, the advocates of a short-cut to revolution might have a chance to gain adherents. But today there are no such conditions. [How] it can be said that there is a clear and present danger that this advocacy will succeed is, therefore, a mystery. [I]n America [Communists] are miserable merchants of unwanted ideas; their wares remain unsold. [If] we are to proceed on the basis of judicial notice, it is impossible for me to say that the Communists in this country are so potent or so strategically deployed that they must be suppressed for their speech. [This] is my view if we are to act on the basis of judicial notice. But the mere statement of the opposing views indicates how important it is that we know the facts before we act. Neither prejudice nor hate nor senseless fear should be the basis of this solemn act. Free speech [should] not be sacrificed on anything less than plain and objective proof of danger that the evil advocated is [imminent].[1]

SMITH ACT CASES AFTER DENNIS: DELINEATING PROTECTED SPEECH RATHER THAN GUESSING ABOUT DANGERS?

1. *The problems of Dennis.* Recall the questions immediately preceding Dennis. Did Dennis ignore clear and present danger? Distort clear and present danger? Or fall prey to the inherent weaknesses of clear and present danger? What did the Holmes standard say about the Dennis problem? What "substantive evil" was relevant? Actual overthrow? Risk of overthrow? Conspiracy to overthrow? Conspiracy to advocate overthrow? What weight did the legislative judgment deserve? Should it have been weighed in terms of the 1940 circumstances, when the Smith Act became law? 1948? Should the Court have insisted on greater record evidence of the 1948 situation? Should it have ignored the world situation? Did the Court unduly deemphasize the temporal dimension—i.e., the *immediacy* of the risk? Did it consider risks more remote than the Abrams dissent would permit? Than the Whitney concurrence? [1]

What alternative approaches would have been preferable in Dennis? Consider the subsequent Smith Act cases "clarifying" Dennis—and, in the view of many, assuring greater protection of speech (notes 4 and 5 below). Does the emphasis in Yates, Scales, and Noto, below, on the distinction between advocacy of abstract doctrine and advocacy of action, and on the need for scrutiny of the evidence, repudiate Dennis? Do these cases return to an earlier clear and present danger approach? Or do they move toward the Masses approach—of defining the contours of protected speech and of using traditional judicial techniques of construing statutes and scrutinizing evidence? Arguably, these post-Dennis cases suggest that courts are more competent and effective in defining protected speech than in second-guessing legislatures about the risks of dangerous consequences.

2. *Free speech theory and the advocacy of overthrow and of totalitarian government.* Dennis, even more sharply than the earlier subversive speech cases, raises questions as to why the First Amendment should protect those who, were they

---

1. Justice Douglas reiterated his attack on the Dennis decision in many later cases. See especially the evolution of his views reflected in his concurrence in Brandenburg v. Ohio (1969, p. 1037 below): "Though I doubt if the 'clear and present danger' test is congenial to the First Amendment in time of a declared war, I am certain it is not reconcilable with the First Amendment in days of peace. [I] see no place in the regime of the First Amendment for any 'clear and present danger' test, whether strict and tight as some would make it, or free-wheeling as the Court in Dennis rephrased it. When one reads the opinions closely and sees when and how the 'clear and present danger' test has been applied, great misgivings are aroused. First, the threats were often loud but always puny and made serious only by judges so wedded to the status quo that critical analysis made them nervous. Second, the test was so twisted and perverted in Dennis as to make the trial of those teachers of Marxism an all-out political trial which was part and parcel of the cold war that has eroded substantial parts of the First Amendment. [The] line between what is permissible and not subject to control and what may be made impermissible and subject to regulation is the line between ideas and overt acts. The example usually given by those who would punish speech is the case of one who falsely shouts fire in a crowded theatre. This is, however, a classic case where speech is brigaded with action."

1. For a sampling of the extensive commentary on Dennis, see Richardson, "Freedom of Expression and the Function of Courts," 65 Harv.L. Rev. 1 (1951), Mendelson, "Clear and Present Danger—From Schenck to Dennis," 52 Colum. L.Rev. 313 (1952), Gorfinkel & Mack, "Dennis v. United States and the Clear and Present Danger Rule," 39 Calif.L.Rev. 475 (1951), and Konefsky, The Legacy of Holmes and Brandeis (1956). See generally "Developments in the Law: The National Security Interest and Civil Liberties," 85 Harv.L.Rev. 1130 (1972).

in power, would deny free speech rights to others. That problem has engendered considerable debate among the commentators. Thus, Bork argues that "advocacy of law violation does not qualify as political speech. [Advocacy] of law violation is a call to set aside the results that political speech has produced." More specifically, he insists that speech advocating "forcible overthrow of the government" is not entitled to protection: "Speech advocating violent overthrow [is] not 'political speech' as that term must be defined by a Madisonian system of government [because] it violates constitutional truths about processes and because it is not aimed at a new definition of political truth by a legislative majority." Violent overthrow of government breaks the premises of our system concerning the ways in which truth is defined, and yet those premises are the only reasons for protecting political speech." [2] And Auerbach states that, "in suppressing totalitarian movements a democratic society is not acting to protect the status quo, but the very same interests which freedom of speech itself seeks to secure—the possibility of peaceful progress under freedom. [One] type of constitutional change in the constitutional system is excluded—'a change which would endanger its democratic character.' This [is] the basic postulate which should control [the] interpretation of the [First Amendment]." [3] Nevertheless, the Court's interpretations of the First Amendment protect advocacy of overthrow to a considerable extent, as the cases that follow reveal especially well. And most commentators support that position. For example, Emerson argues that "democratic society should tolerate opinion which attacks the fundamental institutions of democracy for much the same reasons that it tolerates other opinion." He notes: "Suppression of any group in a society destroys the atmosphere of freedom essential to the life and progress of a healthy community. [It] is not possible for a society to practice both freedom of expression and suppression of expression at the same time." [4]

3. *Judicial confrontations with legislative determinations of danger: A modern view of the Whitney problem.* Compare the Dennis disposition of the recurrent, Gitlow-Whitney problem (of judicial responsibility in the face of legislative judgments regarding the dangerousness of speech) with Chief Justice Burger's majority opinion in LANDMARK COMMUNICATIONS, INC. v. VIRGINIA, 435 U.S. 829 (1978). In Landmark, the Court held that a criminal statute barring accurate disclosure of information about confidential proceedings before a Judicial Inquiry Commission could not constitutionally be applied to "third persons who are strangers to the inquiry, including news media." As noted below (p. 1341), the Chief Justice concluded that the state interests were not sufficient to justify the restraints on First Amendment expression. But in the last part of his opinion, he turned to the "clear and present danger" standard relied on by the highest state court. That court had relied on the legislature's explicit finding "that a clear and present danger to the orderly administration of justice would be created by divulgence of the confidential proceedings of the Commission." The Chief Justice was not impressed by the argument for special deference to the legislature. He replied: "Deference to a legislative finding cannot limit judicial inquiry when First Amendment rights are at stake." He quoted the passage from Justice Brandeis' concurrence in Whitney beginning: "[A legislative declaration] does not preclude enquiry into the question whether, at the time and under the circumstances, the conditions existed which are essential to validity under the [Constitution]" and added: "A legislature appropriately inquires into and may declare the reasons impelling legislative

2. Bork, "Neutral Principles and Some First Amendment Problems," 47 Ind.L.J. 1 (1971).

3. Auerbach, "The Communist Control Act of 1954: A Proposed Legal-Political Theory of Free Speech," 23 U.Chi.L.Rev. 173 (1956). See also Chase, "The Libertarian Case for Making it

a Crime to be a Communist," 29 Temp.L.Q. 121 (1956).

4. Emerson, The System of Freedom of Expression (1970). Cf. Scanlon, "A Theory of Freedom of Expression," 1 Phil. & Pub.Aff. 204 (1971).

action but the judicial function commands analysis of whether the specific conduct charged falls within the reach of the statute and if so whether the legislation is consonant with the Constitution. Were it otherwise, the scope of freedom of speech and of the press would be subject to legislative definition and the function of the First Amendment as a check on legislative power would be nullified. It was thus incumbent upon the [state court] to go behind the legislative determination and examine for itself 'the particular utterance here in question and the circumstances of [its] publication to determine to what extent the substantive evil of unfair administration of justice was a likely consequence, and whether the degree of likelihood was sufficient to justify [subsequent] punishment.' Bridges v. California. Our precedents leave little doubt as to the proper outcome of such an inquiry." [5]

4. *The Yates case.* After Dennis, the Government brought Smith Act cases against a number of Communists who were "lower echelon" rather than "first string" leaders. In YATES v. UNITED STATES, 354 U.S. 298 (1957), the Court set aside the convictions of 14 defendants. In "explaining" the requirements of Dennis, the Court made it clear that Smith Act convictions would not be easy to sustain. On an examination of the record, Justice HARLAN's majority opinion concluded that the lower courts had given too broad a meaning to the term "organize" in the Smith Act; that the trial court's instructions to the jury gave inadequate guidance on the distinction between advocacy of abstract doctrine and advocacy of action; and that the evidence was insufficient to support the convictions. [6] Some excerpts from this important opinion follow:

"Petitioners contend that the instructions to the jury were fatally defective in that the trial court refused to charge that, in order to convict, the jury must find that the advocacy which the defendants conspired to promote was of a kind calculated to 'incite' persons to action for the forcible overthrow of the Government. [The Government argues] that the true constitutional dividing line is not between inciting and abstract advocacy of forcible overthrow, but rather between advocacy as such, irrespective of its inciting qualities, and the mere discussion or exposition of violent overthrow as an abstract theory. [The trial court charged:] 'Any advocacy or teaching which does not include the urging of force and violence as the means of overthrowing and destroying the [Government] is not within the issue of the indictment here and can constitute no basis for any finding against the defendants. The kind of advocacy and teaching which is charged and upon which your verdict must be reached is not merely a desirability but a necessity that the [Government] be overthrown and destroyed by force and violence and not merely a propriety but a duty to overthrow and destroy the [Government] by force and violence.' There can be no doubt from the record that in so instructing the jury the court regarded as immaterial, and intended to withdraw from the jury's consideration, any issue as to the character of the advocacy in terms of its capacity to stir listeners to forcible action. [We] are thus faced with the question whether the Smith Act prohibits advocacy and teaching of forcible overthrow as an abstract principle, divorced from any effort to instigate action to that end, so long as such advocacy or teaching is engaged in with evil intent. We hold that it does not.

"The distinction between advocacy of abstract doctrine and advocacy directed at promoting unlawful action is one that has been consistently recognized in

5. Note that the standard of the Bridges case invoked by the Chief Justice was articulated in a contempt of court context and, unlike Landmark, did *not* involve a prior legislative finding that a clear and present danger existed. Bridges and other contempt of court cases, involving punishments based on inherent judicial power rather than on legislative proscriptions, are discussed in Wood v. Georgia, p. 1337 below.

6. Justices BURTON and BLACK, joined by Justice Douglas, submitted separate opinions. Justice CLARK dissented.

the opinions of this Court. [We] need not, however, decide the issue before us in terms of constitutional compulsion, for our first duty is to construe this statute.[7] In doing so we should not assume that Congress chose to disregard a constitutional danger zone so clearly marked, or that it used the words 'advocate' and 'teach' in their ordinary dictionary meanings when they had already been construed as terms of art carrying a special and limited [connotation].

"In failing to distinguish between advocacy of forcible overthrow as an abstract doctrine and advocacy of action to that end, the District Court appears to have been led astray by the holding in Dennis that advocacy of violent action to be taken at some future time was enough. It seems to have considered that, since 'inciting' speech is usually thought of as something calculated to induce immediate action, and since Dennis held advocacy of action for future overthrow sufficient, this meant that advocacy, irrespective of its tendency to generate action, is punishable, provided only that it is uttered with a specific intent to accomplish overthrow. In other words, the District Court apparently thought that Dennis obliterated the traditional dividing line between advocacy of abstract doctrine and advocacy of action. This misconceives the situation confronting the Court in Dennis and what was held there. Although the jury's verdict, interpreted in light of the trial court's instructions, did not justify the conclusion that the defendants' advocacy was directed at, or created any danger of, immediate overthrow, it did establish that the advocacy was aimed at building up a seditious group and maintaining it in readiness for action at a propitious time. In such circumstances, said Chief Justice Vinson, the Government need not hold its hand 'until the putsch is about to be executed, the plans have been laid and the signal is awaited.' [The] essence of the Dennis holding was that indoctrination of a group in preparation for future violent action, as well as exhortation to immediate action, by advocacy found to be directed to 'action for the accomplishment' of forcible overthrow, to violence as 'a rule or principle of action,' and employing 'language of incitement,' [is] not constitutionally protected when the group is of sufficient size and cohesiveness, is sufficiently oriented towards action, and other circumstances are such as reasonably to justify apprehension that action will occur. This is quite a different thing from the view of the District Court here that mere doctrinal justification of forcible overthrow, if engaged in with the intent to accomplish overthrow, is punishable per se under the Smith Act. That sort of advocacy, even though uttered with the hope that it may ultimately lead to violent revolution, is too remote from concrete action to be regarded as the kind of indoctrination preparatory to action which was condemned in Dennis. [Dennis was] not concerned with a conspiracy to engage at some future time in seditious advocacy, but rather with a conspiracy to advocate presently the taking of forcible action in the future. It was action, not advocacy, that was to be postponed until 'circumstances' would 'permit.'

"[In] light of the foregoing we are unable to regard the District Court's charge upon this aspect of the case as adequate. The jury was never told that the Smith Act does not denounce advocacy in the sense of preaching abstractly the forcible overthrow of the Government. We think that the trial court's statement that the proscribed advocacy must include the 'urging,' 'necessity,' and 'duty' of forcible overthrow, and not merely its 'desirability' and 'propriety,' may not be regarded as a sufficient substitute for charging that the Smith Act reaches only advocacy of action for the overthrow of government by force and violence. The essential distinction is that those to whom the advocacy is addressed must be urged to *do* something, now or in the future, rather than

---

7. Note the similarity to Learned Hand's approach in Masses; and compare the "restatement" of Yates in Brandenburg, p. 1037 below.

merely to *believe* in [something]. We recognize that distinctions between advocacy or teaching of abstract doctrines, with evil intent, and that which is directed to stirring people to action, are often subtle and difficult to grasp, for in a broad sense, as Mr. Justice Holmes said in his dissenting opinion in [Gitlow]: 'Every idea is an incitement.' But the very subtlety of these distinctions required the most clear and explicit instructions with reference to them, for they concerned an issue which went to the very heart of the charges against these petitioners. The need for precise and understandable instructions on this issue is further emphasized by the equivocal character of the evidence in this [record]. Instances of speech that could be considered to amount to 'advocacy of action' are so few and far between as to be almost completely overshadowed by the hundreds of instances in the record in which overthrow, if mentioned at all, occurs in the course of doctrinal disputation so remote from action as to be almost wholly lacking in probative value. Vague references to 'revolutionary' or 'militant' action of an unspecified character, which are found in the evidence, might in addition be given too great weight by the jury in the absence of more precise instructions. Particularly in light of this record, we must regard the trial court's charge in this respect as furnishing wholly inadequate guidance to the jury on this central point in the case."[8]

5. *The Scales and Noto cases.* a. In SCALES v. UNITED STATES, 367 U.S. 203 (1961), the Court sustained the membership clause of the Smith Act and clarified the evidentiary requirements of Yates. The challenged clause, as described in Justice HARLAN's majority opinion, "makes a felony the acquisition or holding of knowing membership in any organization which advocates the overthrow of the Government of the United States by force or violence." Petitioner was charged with having been a member of the Communist Party "with knowledge of the Party's illegal purpose and a specific intent to accomplish overthrow 'as speedily as circumstances would permit.'" The Court found that the trial judge had properly construed the statute to require "specific intent" and "active" rather than merely "nominal" membership. As so construed, the Court rejected the claim that the statute violated the Fifth Amendment "in that it impermissibly imputes guilt to an individual merely on the basis of his associations and sympathies, rather than because of some concrete personal involvement in criminal conduct." Moreover, the majority refused to find a First Amendment violation:

"It was settled in Dennis that the advocacy with which we are here concerned is not constitutionally protected speech, and it was further established that a combination to promote such advocacy, albeit under the aegis of what purports to be a political party, is not such association as is protected by the First Amendment. We can discern no reason why membership, when it constitutes a purposeful form of complicity in a group engaging in this same forbidden advocacy, should receive any greater degree of protection from the guarantees of that Amendment. If it is said that the mere existence of such an enactment tends to inhibit the exercise of constitutionally protected rights, in that it engenders an unhealthy fear that one may find himself unwittingly embroiled in criminal liability, the answer surely is that the statute provides that a defendant must be proven to have knowledge of the proscribed advocacy before he may be convicted. [The] clause does not make criminal all association with an organization which has been shown to engage in illegal advocacy. There must be clear proof that a defendant 'specifically intend[s] to accomplish [the aims of the organization] by resort to violence.' [Noto, below.] Thus the member for

---

8. The Yates Court ordered acquittals of five of the defendants and remanded the indictments of the remaining nine for new trials. On remand, those indictments were dismissed at the Government's request, because of expected inability to meet the Yates evidentiary requirements. (Note the clarifying comments in Scales, which follows, on the evaluation of the evidence in Yates.)

whom the organization is a vehicle for the advancement of legitimate aims and policies does not fall within the ban of the statute: he lacks the requisite specific intent 'to bring about the overthrow of the government as speedily as circumstances would permit.' Such a person may be foolish, deluded, or perhaps merely optimistic, but he is not by this statute made a criminal." [9]

The Court, in an especially important part of its opinion, then proceeded to examine the sufficiency of the evidence in considerable detail, "to make sure that substantive constitutional standards have not been thwarted." Justice Harlan stated that the evidentiary question was "controlled in large part by Yates" and explained at some length the Yates criteria for the evaluation of evidence. He noted: "The decision in Yates rested on the view (not articulated in the opinion, though perhaps it should have been) that the Smith Act offenses, involving as they do subtler elements than are present in most other crimes, call for strict standards in assessing the adequacy of the proof needed to make out a case of illegal advocacy." He continued: "The impact of Yates with respect to this petitioner's evidentiary challenge is not limited, however, to that decision's requirement of strict standards of proof. Yates also articulates general criteria for the evaluation of evidence in determining whether this requirement is met. The Yates opinion [indicates] what type of evidence is needed to permit a jury to find that (a) there was 'advocacy of action' and (b) the Party was responsible for such advocacy.

"First, Yates makes clear what type of evidence is not *in itself* sufficient to show illegal advocacy. This category includes evidence of the following: the teaching of Marxism-Leninism and the connected use of Marxist 'classics' as textbooks; the official general resolutions and pronouncements of the Party at past conventions; dissemination of the Party's general literature, including the standard outlines on Marxism; the Party's history and organizational structure; the secrecy of meetings and the clandestine nature of the Party generally; statements by officials evidencing sympathy for and alliance with the U.S.S.R. It was the predominance of evidence of this type which led the Court to order the acquittal of several Yates defendants. [However], this kind of evidence, while insufficient in itself to sustain a conviction, is not irrelevant. Such evidence, in the context of other evidence, may be of value in showing illegal advocacy.

"Second, the Yates opinion also indicates what kind of evidence is sufficient. There the Court pointed to two series of events which justified the denial of directed acquittals as to nine of the Yates defendants. The Court noted that with respect to seven of the defendants, meetings in San Francisco might be considered to be 'the systematic teaching and advocacy of illegal action which is condemned by the statute.' In those meetings, a small group of members were not only taught that violent revolution was inevitable, but they were also taught techniques for achieving that end. For example, the Yates record reveals that members were directed to be prepared to convert a general strike into a revolution and deal with Negroes so as to prepare them specifically for revolution. [Yates also] referred to certain activities in the Los Angeles area 'which might be considered to amount to "advocacy of action"' and with which two Yates defendants were linked. Here again, the participants did not stop with teaching of the inevitability of eventual revolution, but went on to explain techniques, both legal and illegal, to be employed in preparation for or in connection with the revolution. [Viewed together], these events described in Yates indicate at least two patterns of evidence sufficient to show illegal advocacy: (a) the teaching of forceful overthrow, accompanied by directions as to the type of illegal action which must be taken when the time for the

9. For additional consideration of the problem of forbidden membership and associations, in the context of regulations of government employees and licensees, see chap. 13, p. 1363 below.

revolution is reached; and (b) the teaching of forceful overthrow, accompanied by a contemporary, though legal, course of conduct clearly undertaken for the specific purpose of rendering effective the later illegal activity which is advocated." Justice Harlan found these evidentiary criteria satisfied in the Scales record: "[T]his evidence sufficed to make a case for the jury on the issue of illegal Party advocacy. Dennis and Yates have definitely laid at rest any doubt that present advocacy of *future* action for violent overthrow satisfies statutory and constitutional requirements equally with advocacy of *immediate* action to that end. Hence this record cannot be considered deficient because it contains no evidence of advocacy for immediate overthrow." [10]

b. Though the Court found the evidentiary criteria of Yates satisfied in the conviction of Scales, it reversed a conviction under the membership clause in a companion case because "the evidence of illegal Party advocacy was insufficient." NOTO v. UNITED STATES, 367 U.S. 290 (1961). With Justice HARLAN once again writing for the Court, the opinion noted that the evidence of "advocacy of action" was "sparse indeed," was not "broadly based" geographically, and "lacked the compelling quality which in Scales was supplied by the petitioner's own utterances and systematic course of conduct as a high Party official." He added: "It need hardly be said that it is upon the particular evidence in a particular record that a particular defendant must be judged, and not upon the evidence in some other record or upon what may be supposed to be the tenets of the [Party]." Here, the record "bears much of the infirmity that we found in the Yates record."

6. *The impact of Yates and Scales.* Were the Yates and Scales decisions truly restatements of Dennis, or did they mark a significant shift in emphasis? Can Justice Harlan's opinions be viewed as the beginning of a "long-delayed vindication of Masses"? Consider Gunther's comment: "[Harlan] reinvigorated free speech protection in the post-Dennis years by exhibiting the best qualities of judicial craftsmanship so long associated with Learned Hand. Harlan found a way to curtail prosecutions under the Smith Act even though the constitutionality of the Act had been sustained in Dennis. He did it by invoking techniques very similar to those applied by Hand in Masses to the World War I Espionage Act he read the statute in terms of constitutional presuppositions; and he strove to find standards 'manageable' by judges and capable of curbing jury discretion. He insisted on strict statutory standards of proof emphasizing the actual speech of the defendants—a variation on the 'hard,' 'objective,' words-oriented focus of Masses. Harlan claimed to be interpreting Dennis. In fact, Yates and Scales represented doctrinal evolution in a new direction, a direction in the Masses tradition." [11]

---

10. The Scales decision elicited dissenting opinions from Justices Black, Douglas and Brennan (joined by Chief Justice Warren and Justice Douglas). Justice BLACK once again objected to the "balancing test." Justice DOUGLAS emphasized that the "membership" clause of the Smith Act did not require a finding of conspiracy and added: "The case is not saved by showing that petitioner was an active member. None of the activity constitutes a crime. [Not] one single illegal act is charged to petitioner. That is why the essence of the crime covered by the indictment is merely belief—belief in the proletarian revolution, belief in Communist creed." Justice BRENNAN's dissent insisted that Congress had legislated immunity from prosecution under the membership clause of the Smith Act by enacting

the Internal Security Act of 1950. See sec. 1D below.

11. Gunther, "Hand and the First Amendment." (On the evolution of the Yates and Scales criteria from statutory to constitutional standards, see Brandenburg, p. 1037 below.)

To what extent does Yates return to Hand's incitement test? Note Harlan's comment: "We recognize that distinctions between advocacy or teaching of abstract doctrines, with evil intent, and that which is directed to stirring people to action, are often subtle and difficult to grasp. [But] the very subtlety of these distinctions requires the most clear and explicit instructions with reference to them." Contrast Holmes' comment in Gitlow: "Every idea is an incitement."

D. THE COURT AND ANTI–COMMUNIST LAWS
OF THE FIFTIES

Introduction. Before turning (in sec. 1E below) to the modern Court's variations on the contending techniques traced above, these materials briefly consider the Court's responses to the largely ineffectual congressional laws of the fifties. These laws complete the survey of major legislation against Communists. Unlike the Smith Act, the laws of the fifties did not follow the traditional pattern of the Gitlow-Whitney sedition-syndicalism statutes. For example, the 1950 Act looked mainly to registration and disclosure rather than direct "prohibition of speech because of its content."[1] The Subversive Activities Control Act of 1950, the major federal anti-Communist law of the fifties, was an intricate scheme for registration and disclosure to be administered by the Subversive Activities Control Board (SACB). After the Board's registration orders to "Communist-action" organizations became final, a variety of sanctions were to be imposed on the organizations and their members, including passport denials and prohibitions of employment in defense facilities. In its first encounter with the statute, a divided Court sustained the basic legislative scheme (note 1 below). However, the registration provisions were never successfully implemented (and were ultimately repealed), the Court found most of the sanctions unconstitutional, and, after extensive litigation, the SACB was disbanded. Another law of the fifties, the Communist Control Act of 1954, proved even more ineffectual. (Note 4 below.)[2]

1. *The validity of the registration requirement of the 1950 Act.* In COMMUNIST PARTY v. SACB, 367 U.S. 1 (1961), the majority sustained an SACB order requiring the Communist Party to register with the Attorney General as a "Communist-action organization" under the 1950 Act.[3] Justice FRANKFURTER insisted that freedom of speech and of association did not prevent Congress "from requiring the registration and filing of information, including membership lists, by organizations substantially dominated or controlled by the foreign powers controlling the world Communist movement." Though requirements of registration "as a condition upon the exercise of speech may in some circumstances" violate the First Amendment,[4] the majority noted that here the requirement did not attach "to the incident of speech, but to the incidents of foreign domination and of operation to advance the objectives of the world Communist movement—operation which, the Board has found here, includes

Compare Brandeis' greater sensitivity to the potential utility of the incitement concept in his concurrence in Whitney: "The wide difference between advocacy and incitement [must] be borne in mind." Is the incitement ingredient in Brandenburg, p. 1037 below, more speech-protective than Harlan's emphasis in Yates? More so than Hand's in Masses?

1. For further examination of disclosure requirements, see chap. 13 below.

2. The 1950s laws were more important for their doctrinal than their practical consequences. For example, challenges to some of the sanctions in the 1950 Act provided the Warren Court with the opportunity to elaborate the relatively new judicial technique of "overbreadth." See note 3 below. (A fuller analysis of the "overbreadth" technique is postponed to sec. 1 of the next chapter, for consideration together with other techniques such as "vagueness" that gained spe-

cial popularity during the last decade of the Warren Court.)

3. The statute contained extensive legislative findings, concluding: "The Communist movement in the United States is an organization numbering thousands of adherents, rigidly and ruthlessly disciplined. [The] Communist organization in the United States, pursuing its stated objectives, the recent successes of Communist methods in other countries, and the nature and control of the world Communist movement itself, present a clear and present danger to the security of the United States and to the existence of free American institutions, and make it necessary that Congress [enact] appropriate legislation recognizing the existence of such world-wide conspiracy and designed to prevent it from accomplishing its purpose in the United States."

4. See chap. 13 below.

extensive, long-continuing organizational, as well as 'speech,' activity." Justice Frankfurter emphasized the detailed legislative findings: they reflected a permissible "appraisal by Congress of the threat which Communist organizations pose." Though "[i]ndividual liberties fundamental to American institutions are not to be destroyed under pretext of preserving those institutions, even from the gravest external dangers," "where the problems of accommodating the exigencies of self-preservation and the values of liberty are as complex and intricate [as here], the legislative judgment as to how that threat may best be met consistently with the safeguarding of personal freedom is not to be set aside merely because the judgment of judges would, in the first instance, have chosen other methods." He also insisted that the decision did not imply that "Congress may impose similar requirements upon any group which pursues unpopular political objectives": the Act applied "only to *foreign-dominated* organizations which work primarily to advance the objectives of a world movement controlled by the government of a *foreign* country." [5]

2. *Subsequent efforts to implement registration requirements of the 1950 Act.* As a result of the 1961 decision above, the SACB order finding the Party to be a "Communist-action organization" became final. Under the Act, the Party was accordingly under duty to register. But, as a result of several subsequent decisions, this and other registration orders were never implemented. (However, a final order to register, even without actual registration, triggered additional sanctions under the Act, see note 3 below.) The Party's refusal to register on self-incrimination grounds was sustained: the Court of Appeals set aside the conviction of the Party for failure to register.[6] After the Party's successful resistance to registration, a lower court sustained a Board order directing two members of the Party to register. That decision was unanimously reversed by the Court.[7] Justice Brennan's opinion found that the Board orders violated the privilege against self-incrimination, and that the challenge was no longer one that could be rejected as "premature." The Court noted that an admission of Party membership "may be used to prosecute the registrant under the membership clause of the Smith Act" as well as other provisions.

3. *The invalidation of other sanctions under the 1950 Act on overbreadth grounds.*
a. *Aptheker.* One of the sanctions triggered by the existence of a final registration order was § 6 of the 1950 Act, prohibiting any "member" of a "Communist organization" from using a passport with "knowledge or notice" that a registration order had become final. The State Department tried to revoke the passports of two Party leaders. In APTHEKER v. SECRETARY

---

5. The majority also held that the Act was not a bill of attainder. It found most other constitutional challenges premature—including a claim that compelling Party officials to file registration statements would violate the privilege against self-incrimination. There were dissenting opinions by Chief Justice WARREN and Justices BLACK, DOUGLAS and BRENNAN. They all found merit in the self-incrimination claim. Moreover, Justice Black insisted that the Act was a bill of attainder by inflicting "pains, penalties and punishments in a number of ways without a judicial trial."

A passage on the First Amendment issue in Justice Douglas' dissent is of special interest: although he was persuaded by the Fifth Amendment challenge, he conceded that "the bare requirement that the Communist Party register and disclose the names of its officers and directors is in line with the most exacting adjudications touching First Amendment activities." He ex-

plained: "When an organization is used by a foreign power to make advances here, questions of security are raised beyond the ken of disputation and debate between the people resident here. Espionage, business activities, formation of cells for subversion, as well as the exercise of First Amendment rights, are then used to pry open our society and make intrusions of a foreign power easy. These machinations of a foreign power add additional elements to free speech just as marching up and down adds something to picketing that goes beyond free speech." (Justice Black was the only dissenter who found the First Amendment challenge persuasive.)

6. Communist Party v. United States, 331 F.2d 807 (D.C.Cir.1963), cert. denied, 377 U.S. 968 (1964).

7. Albertson v. SACB, 332 F.2d 317 (D.C. Cir.1964), reversed, 382 U.S. 70 (1965).

OF STATE, 378 U.S. 500 (1964), the Court held § 6 "unconstitutional on its face" because it "too broadly and indiscriminately restricts the right to travel and thereby abridges the liberty guaranteed by the Fifth Amendment." [8] Justice GOLDBERG's majority opinion rejected the Government's argument that "surely § 6 was reasonable as applied to the top-ranking Party leaders involved here." He insisted that, because of its sweeping impact on protected activity, the Section had to be invalidated, without regard to whether the particular challengers were protected by the Constitution.[9] He added: "The clarity and preciseness of the provision in question make it impossible to narrow its indiscriminately cast and overly broad scope without substantial rewriting." Justice Goldberg emphasized that § 6 "sweeps within its prohibition both knowing and unknowing members" and "renders irrelevant the member's degree of activity in the organization and his commitment to its purpose." [10] He insisted that § 6 could not be saved by an interpretation analogous to the reading of the membership clause of the Smith Act in Scales—the reading limiting the Smith Act's prohibition to "active" members having a "guilty knowledge and intent." He stated: "With regard to the [1950 Act], 'neither the words nor history of [§] 6 suggests limiting its application to active members.' " [11]

b. *Robel.* Another consequence of a final registration order under the 1950 Act was that specified in § 5(a)(1)(D): it made it a crime for any member of a Communist-action organization "to engage in any employment in any defense facility," with knowledge or notice that there was in effect a final order requiring the organization to register. In UNITED STATES v. ROBEL, 389 U.S. 258 (1967), as in Aptheker, the majority invalidated that sanction on "overbreadth" grounds; but unlike Aptheker, Robel emphasized the infringement of the First Amendment right of association rather than the impairment of the Fifth Amendment "liberty" to travel. Chief Justice WARREN noted that it was irrelevant under the Act "that an individual may be a passive or inactive member of a designated organization, that he may be unaware of the organization's unlawful aims, or that he may disagree with those unlawful aims." Moreover, the statute made it irrelevant that an individual subject to it "may occupy a nonsensitive position in a defense facility." He concluded that the provision "contains the fatal defect of overbreadth because it seeks to bar employment both for association which may be proscribed and for association which may not be proscribed consistently with First Amendment rights." [12]

8. In relying on the "right to travel abroad" aspect of "liberty," rather than on free speech, Justice Goldberg's majority opinion cited Kent v. Dulles, 357 U.S. 116 (1958).

9. A dissent by Justice CLARK, joined by Justices Harlan and White, would have accepted the argument that the statute was valid as applied to the top-ranking Party members involved here. (Justices Clark and Harlan would also have sustained the statute on its face, as a restriction reasonably related to national security.)

10. Note also the Aptheker opinion's argument that "Congress has within its power 'less drastic' means of achieving the congressional objective of safeguarding our national security." Justice Goldberg added that the "broad and enveloping prohibition" applying to all members "indiscriminately excludes plainly relevant considerations such as the individual's knowledge, activity, commitment, and purposes in and places for travel." (The "less drastic means" analysis in First Amendment cases is more fully consid-

ered—together with "overbreadth" analysis—in sec. 1 of the next chapter.)

Does the Aptheker approach suggest that the statutory interpretation views regarding membership in Scales had become constitutional requirements by the time of Aptheker? (Note also the evolution of Scales and Yates statutory requirements into constitutional limits in government employees' noncriminal security cases such as Keyishian (1967; p. 1377 below).)

11. The emphasis on "overly broad" means in Aptheker—and in Robel, which follows—was important in the development of the "overbreadth" technique. The overbreadth approach is more fully discussed in sec. 1 of the next chapter. (For later decisions on passport regulations, see Haig v. Agee (1981) and Regan v. Wald (1984; p. 1040 below).

12. In resorting to the overbreadth and less restrictive alternatives technique in Robel, Chief Justice Warren explicitly disavowed that he was engaging in any kind of "balancing." For ex-

(Justices WHITE and HARLAN dissented, emphasizing the "public interest in national security.")

4. *The Communist Control Act of 1954.* Federal legislation directed at the Communist Party culminated in the 1954 Communist Control Act, a law with more sweeping provisions but fewer practical and legal consequences than the 1950 Act. The congressional "findings" included a statement that the Communist Party, "although purportedly a political party, is in fact an instrumentality of a conspiracy to overthrow the Government of the United States," and concluded: "Therefore, the Communist Party should be outlawed." One section of the law stated that the Party was "not entitled to any of the rights, privileges, and immunities attendant upon legal bodies created under [the] laws of the United States or [any] subdivision thereof." In the only case involving the 1954 Act to reach the Court, the Justices avoided decision on any constitutional challenges. In Communist Party v. Catherwood, 367 U.S. 389 (1961), New York courts had relied on the "rights, privileges, and immunities" provision in upholding the termination of the Party's registration and its liability to state taxation as an employer under the State Unemployment Insurance Law. Justice Harlan's opinion held that the constitutional challenges did not have to be reached because the state courts' interpretation, "raising as it does novel constitutional questions, the answers to which are not necessarily controlled by decisions of this Court in connection with other legislation dealing with the [Party], must [be] rejected." [13]

E. SUBVERSIVE ADVOCACY AND THE COURT AFTER NEARLY SEVEN DECADES: OLD PRECEDENTS AND NEW APPROACHES

Introduction. This section returns to the statutory and factual contexts of the Schenck-Gitlow-Whitney era. Do the modern Court's free speech doctrines deal satisfactorily with those problems? Brandenburg, which follows, is the Warren Court's response to a Whitney-type criminal syndicalism statute. And the anti-Vietnam war protests considered in the materials after Brandenburg involve modern variations on the setting of the World War I Espionage Act prosecutions. What are the roles of clear and present danger and the Masses approach in the modern handling of these questions?

---

cerpts from Chief Justice Warren's disavowal— and for a criticism of his assertions—see p. 1150 below, in the discussion of the overbreadth technique.

13. The 1954 Act stemmed from a Democratic proposal that membership in the Party be made a crime—a proposal introduced by Senator Humphrey with the statement: "I am tired of reading headlines about being 'soft' toward communism." President Eisenhower opposed the proposal because it might obstruct enforcement of the Smith Act and the 1950 law. The final version of the 1954 Act was a compromise substituted by Republicans.

Note also the Court's invalidation of a 1962 law under which the Post Office screened foreign unsealed mail, detained "communist political propaganda," and notified the addressee that the mail would be destroyed unless the addressee requested delivery by returning a reply card. The Court, in Lamont v. Postmaster General, 381 U.S. 301 (1965), relied on a First Amendment right to "receive information and ideas" (a right explored further in later sections). Justice Douglas' majority opinion thought the reply card requirement was "almost certain to have a deterrent effect" and imposed an impermissible affirmative obligation on the addressee. But the right to "receive information and ideas" was not sufficient to curtail the government's broad power over the exclusion of aliens in Kleindienst v. Mandel, 408 U.S. 753 (1972), sustaining a provision of the 1950 Act making foreign Communists "ineligible" to receive visas.

[handwritten margin note: Ohio Stat. overturned b/c mere advocacy of unlawful action NOT enough; need intent to imminent lawlessness]

BRANDENBURG v. OHIO

395 U.S. 444, 89 S.Ct. 1827, 23 L.Ed.2d 430 (1969).

PER CURIAM.

The appellant, a leader of a Ku Klux Klan group, was convicted under the Ohio Criminal Syndicalism statute for "advocat[ing] the duty, necessity, or propriety of crime, sabotage, violence, or unlawful methods of terrorism as a means of accomplishing industrial or political reform" and for "voluntarily assembl[ing] with any society, group, or assemblage of persons formed to teach or advocate the doctrines of criminal syndicalism." He was fined $1,000 and sentenced to one to 10 years' imprisonment. The Supreme Court of Ohio dismissed his appeal [because] "no substantial constitutional question exists herein." [We] reverse.

The record shows that a man, identified at trial as the appellant, telephoned an announcer-reporter on the staff of a Cincinnati television station and invited him to come to a Ku Klux Klan "rally" to be held at a [farm]. With the cooperation of the organizers, the reporter and a cameraman attended the meeting and filmed the events. Portions of the films were later broadcast on the local station and on a national network. The prosecution's case rested on the films and on testimony identifying the appellant as the person who communicated with the reporter and who spoke at the [rally]. One film showed 12 hooded figures, some of whom carried firearms. They were gathered around a large wooden cross, which they burned. No one was present other than the participants and the newsmen who made the film. Most of the words uttered during the scene were incomprehensible when the film was projected, but scattered phrases could be understood that were derogatory of Negroes and, in one instance, of Jews.[1] Another scene on the same film showed the appellant, in Klan regalia, making a speech. The speech, in full, was as follows: "This is an organizers' meeting. We have had quite a few members here today which are—we have hundreds, hundreds of members throughout [Ohio]. I can quote from a newspaper clipping from the Columbus, Ohio Dispatch, five weeks ago Sunday morning. The Klan has more members in [Ohio] than does any other organization. We're not a revengent organization, but if our President, our Congress, our Supreme Court, continues to suppress the white, Caucasian race, it's possible that there might have to be some revengeance taken. We are marching on Congress July the Fourth, four hundred thousand strong. From there we are dividing into two groups, one group to march on St. Augustine, Florida, the other group to march into Mississippi. Thank you." The second film showed six hooded figures one of whom, later identified as the appellant, repeated a speech very similar to that recorded on the first film. The reference to the possibility of "revengeance" was omitted, and one sentence was added: "Personally, I believe the nigger should be returned to Africa, the Jew returned to Israel." Though some of the figures in the films carried weapons, the speaker did not.

---

1. The significant portions that could be understood were:

"How far is the nigger going to—yeah."

"This is what we are going to do to the niggers."

"A dirty nigger."

"Send the Jews back to Israel."

"Let's give them back to the dark garden."

"Save America."

"Let's go back to constitutional betterment."

"Bury the niggers."

"We intend to do our part."

"Give us our state rights."

"Freedom for the whites."

"Nigger will have to fight for every inch he gets from now on." [Footnotes 1 through 4 are by the Court.]

The Ohio [law] was enacted in 1919. From 1917 to 1920, identical or quite similar laws were adopted by 20 States and two territories. [In 1927], this Court sustained the constitutionality of California's Criminal Syndicalism Act, the text of which is quite similar to that of the laws of Ohio [Whitney]. The Court upheld the statute on the ground that, without more, "advocating" violent means to effect political and economic change involves such danger to the security of the State that the State may outlaw it. Cf. [Fiske v. Kansas]. But Whitney has been thoroughly discredited by later decisions. See [Dennis]. These later decisions have fashioned the principle that the constitutional guarantees of free speech and free press do not permit a State to forbid or proscribe advocacy of the use of force or of law violation except where such advocacy is directed to inciting or producing imminent lawless action and is likely to incite or produce such action.[2] As we said in [Noto], "the mere abstract teaching [of] the moral propriety or even moral necessity for a resort to force and violence, is not the same as preparing a group for violent action and steeling it to such action." See also [Herndon v. Lowry; Bond v. Floyd (which follows)]. A statute which fails to draw this distinction impermissibly intrudes upon the freedoms guaranteed by the First and 14th Amendments. It sweeps within its condemnation speech which our Constitution has immunized from governmental control. Cf. [Yates; De Jonge].

Measured by this test, Ohio's [Act] cannot be sustained. The Act punishes persons who "advocate or teach the duty, necessity, or propriety" of violence "as a means of accomplishing industrial or political reform"; or who publish or circulate or display any book or paper containing such advocacy; or who "justify" the commission of violent acts "with intent to exemplify, spread or advocate the propriety of the doctrines of criminal syndicalism"; or who "voluntarily assemble" with a group formed "to teach or advocate the doctrines of criminal syndicalism." Neither the indictment nor the trial judge's instructions to the jury in any way refined the statute's bald definition of the crime in terms of mere advocacy not distinguished from incitement to imminent lawless action.[3] Accordingly, we are here confronted with a statute which, by its own words and as applied, purports to punish mere advocacy and to forbid, on pain of criminal punishment, assembly with others merely to advocate the described type of action.[4] Such a statute falls within the condemnation of the First and 14th Amendments. The contrary teaching of [Whitney] cannot be supported, and that decision is therefore overruled.

Reversed.[5]

---

2. It was on the theory that the Smith Act embodied such a principle and that it had been applied only in conformity with it that this Court sustained the Act's constitutionality. [Dennis.] That this was the basis for Dennis was emphasized in [Yates], in which the Court overturned convictions for advocacy of the forcible overthrow of the Government under the Smith Act, because the trial judge's instructions had allowed conviction for mere advocacy, unrelated to its tendency to produce forcible action.

3. The first count of the indictment charged that appellant "did unlawfully by word of mouth advocate the necessity, or propriety of crime, violence, or unlawful methods of terrorism as a means of accomplishing political [reform]." The second count charged that appellant "did unlawfully voluntarily assemble with a group or assemblage of persons formed to advocate the doctrines of [criminal syndicalism]." The trial judge's

charge merely followed the language of the indictment. No construction of the statute by the Ohio courts has brought it within constitutionally permissible [limits].

4. Statutes affecting the right of assembly, like those touching on freedom of speech, must observe the established distinctions between mere advocacy and incitement to imminent lawless action, for as Chief Justice Hughes wrote in [De Jonge]: "The right of peaceable assembly is a right cognate to those of free speech and free press and is equally fundamental."

5. Justices Black and Douglas submitted concurring opinions. Justice DOUGLAS' opinion, quoted in part above (at p. 1026, with Dennis), objected to "any 'clear and present danger' test, whether strict and tight as some would make it, or free-wheeling as the Court in Dennis rephrased it." He stated, moreover, that "there is

THE IMPACT OF BRANDENBURG

1. *The implications of Brandenburg: The best of Hand and Holmes?* To what extent does the Brandenburg standard change rather than restate First Amendment doctrine? Are the Brandenburg Court's descriptions of the prior cases accurate? See, e.g., the reference in footnote 4 to "the established distinctions between mere advocacy and incitement to imminent lawless action." Where were these distinctions "established"?[1] Recall the question raised earlier: Can Brandenburg be viewed as combining "the most protective ingredients of the Masses incitement emphasis with the most useful elements of the clear and present danger heritage"? Can Brandenburg be viewed as building on Yates and Scales "to produce [the Warren Court's] clearest and most protective standard under the first amendment"? Can Brandenburg be viewed as resting "ultimately on the insight Learned Hand urged without success at the end of World War I"?[2]

2. *The vitality of Brandenburg: The Hess case.* a. The Brandenburg decision came during the last Term of Chief Justice Warren's tenure (and shortly after Justice Fortas' resignation), but the case has several times been cited with approval in the Burger era. For a modern reliance on the Brandenburg incitement standard, note its invocation as the primary ground for reversal of a disorderly conduct conviction in HESS v. INDIANA, 414 U.S. 105 (1973). After a campus anti-war demonstration during which there had been arrests, over 100 demonstrators blocked the street until they were moved to the curb by the police. Appellant, standing off the street, said: "We'll take the fucking street later (or again)." The state court relied primarily on a finding that this statement was "intended to incite further lawless action on the part of the crowd in the vicinity of appellant and was likely to produce such action." The Court summarily reversed on "as applied" grounds, in a per curiam opinion. The majority disagreed with the state court's evaluation of appellant's speech: "At best, [the] statement could be taken as counsel for present moderation; at worst, it amounted to nothing more than advocacy of illegal action at some indefinite future time." The Court added that "since there was no evidence, or rational inference from the import of the language, that his words were intended to produce, and likely to produce, *imminent* disorder, those words could not be punished by the State on the ground that they had 'a tendency to lead to violence.'"[3]

no constitutional line between advocacy of abstract ideas as in Yates and advocacy of political action as in Scales." Finally, he objected to the Court's decision in O'Brien, the 1968 draft card burning case, p. 1170 below. Justice BLACK's concurrence agreed with Justice Douglas' condemnation of "clear and present danger" and stated that, in his understanding, the Brandenburg citation of Dennis did not "indicate any agreement [with] the 'clear and present danger' doctrine on which Dennis purported to rely."

1. Consider the comment in Gunther, "Hand and the First Amendment": "An incitement-nonincitement distinction had only fragmentary and ambiguous antecedents in the pre-Brandenburg era; it was Brandenburg that really 'established' it; and, it was essentially an establishment of the legacy of Learned Hand."

2. Consider Gunther, above: "The incitement emphasis is Hand's; the reference to 'imminent' reflects a limited influence of Holmes, combined with later experience; and 'the likely to incite or produce such action' addition in the

Brandenburg standard is the only reference to the need to guess about future consequences of speech, so central to the Schenck approach. Under Brandenburg, probability of harm is no longer the central criterion for speech limitations. The inciting language of the speaker—the Hand focus on 'objective' words—is the major consideration. And punishment of the harmless inciter is prevented by the Schenck-derived requirement of a likelihood of dangerous consequences."

3. Justice REHNQUIST's dissent in Hess, joined by Chief Justice Burger and Justice Blackmun, thought the majority had improperly substituted "a different complex of factual inferences for the inferences reached by the courts below" and had accordingly "exceeded the proper scope of our review." He thought appellant's words were "susceptible of characterization as an exhortation, particularly when uttered in a loud voice while facing a crowd." Perhaps, he added, Hess had simply expressed his views "to the world at large, but that is surely not the only rational explanation."

3. *The reach of Brandenburg.* a. *The 1980s passport cases.* Should the Court have considered Brandenburg relevant in modern cases sustaining restrictions on travel? (Recall the 1964 passport case, Aptheker, sec. 1D, p. 1034 above.) HAIG v. AGEE, 453 U.S. 280 (1981), sustained the application of a State Department regulation permitting the Secretary of State to revoke a passport if he determines that the national's activities "abroad are causing or are likely to cause serious damage to the national security or the foreign policy of the United States." Relying on this, the Secretary revoked the passport of Philip Agee, a former CIA agent who was engaged in a campaign "to expose CIA officers and agents." The majority rejected Agee's challenge to the revocation on both statutory and constitutional grounds. Chief Justice BURGER gave only brief consideration to the constitutional challenges, which included, inter alia, First Amendment and freedom to travel claims.[4] On the travel issue, the Chief Justice emphasized that "the *freedom* to travel outside the United States must be distinguished from the *right* to travel within the United States." Citing Aptheker, he remarked: "It is 'obvious and unarguable' that no governmental interest is more compelling than the security of the Nation. [Measures] to protect the secrecy of our Government's foreign intelligence operations plainly serve these interests."

Turning to the free speech claim, the Chief Justice stated: "Assuming arguendo that First Amendment protections reach beyond our national bounda-

The contrast between the majority and the dissent in Hess presents a recurrent and important issue in First Amendment law. It is now well entrenched in First Amendment theory that an appellate court can conduct an independent review of the factual findings below in order to assure that protected material is not penalized. That review power extends not only to the incitement cases, but also, e.g., to appellate review of lower court findings of obscenity and defamation. For a recent general discussion of the issue in the defamation context, see Bose Corp. v. Consumers Union, 466 U.S. ___ (1984). Recall the antecedents to this appellate review authority, in, e.g., Fiske v. Kansas (1927; p. 1011 above).

For a subsequent discussion of the Brandenburg incitement standard, see NAACP v. Claiborne Hardware Co. (1982; more fully discussed at p. 1345 below). There, the Court set aside, on First Amendment grounds, a large damage award against alleged participants in an economic boycott by black citizens of white merchants in a Mississippi county. The boycott sought to secure compliance with a list of demands for racial justice. One of the defendants was Charles Evers, the Field Secretary of the NAACP, who took a leading role in the boycott. One of the arguments advanced to defend the imposition of liability on Evers was that "a finding that his public speeches were likely to incite lawless action could justify holding him liable for unlawful conduct that in fact followed within a reasonable period." In one speech, Evers had stated that boycott violators would be "disciplined" by their own people. The portion of Justice Stevens' opinion rejecting the incitement rationale for imposing liability on Evers follows. Is that passage a persuasive application of Brandenburg and the concept of incitement, or does it significantly modify the Brandenburg incitement standard? Justice Stevens stated:

"While many of the comments in Evers' speeches might have contemplated 'discipline' in the permissible form of social ostracism, it cannot be denied that references [e.g.] to the possibility that necks would be [broken] implicitly conveyed a sterner message. In the passionate atmosphere in which the speeches were delivered, they might have been understood as inviting an unlawful form of discipline or, at least, as intending to create a fear of violence whether or not improper discipline was specifically intended. [This] Court has made clear, however, that *mere advocacy* of the use of force or violence does not remove speech from the protection of the First Amendment. [The] emotionally charged rhetoric of Charles Evers' speeches did not transcend the bounds of protected speech set forth in Brandenburg. The lengthy addresses generally contained an impassioned plea for black citizens to unify, to support and respect each other, and to realize the political and economic power available to them. In the course of those pleas, strong language was used. *If that language had been followed by acts of violence, a substantial question would be presented whether Evers could be held liable for the consequences of that unlawful conduct.* In this case, however, [almost all] acts of violence identified in 1966 occurred weeks or months after the April 1, 1966 speech; the chancellor made no finding of any violence after the challenged 1969 speech. Strong and effective extemporaneous rhetoric cannot be nicely channeled in purely dulcet phrases. An advocate must be free to stimulate his audience with spontaneous and emotional appeals for unity and action in a common cause. When such appeals do not incite lawless action, they must be regarded as protected speech." [Emphasis added.]

4. Justice Brennan's dissent criticized the Chief Justice's "whirlwind treatment of Agee's constitutional claims."

ries, Agee's First Amendment claim has no foundation." He conceded that the revocation of Agee's passport rested in part on the content of his speech— "specifically, his repeated disclosures of intelligence operations and names of intelligence personnel." He added, citing Near v. Minnesota (p. 1157 below), that "Agee's disclosures, among other things, have the declared purpose of obstructing intelligence operations and the recruiting of intelligence personnel. They are clearly not protected by the Constitution. The mere fact that Agee is also engaged in criticism of the Government does not render his conduct beyond the reach of the law. To the extent the revocation of his passport operates to inhibit Agee, it is an inhibition of *action,*' rather than of speech." [5] Moreover, the Chief Justice stated (relying once again on Aptheker): "The protection accorded beliefs standing alone is very different from the protection accorded conduct. [E.g., Aptheker.]" He elaborated: "Beliefs and speech are only part of Agee's 'campaign to fight the United States CIA.' In that sense, this case contrasts markedly with the facts in [Aptheker]."

Justice BRENNAN's dissent, joined by Justice Marshall, rested largely on disagreement with the majority's statutory interpretation approach and addressed the Court's treatment of the constitutional issues only in a footnote. He asserted that the Court's handling of Agee's constitutional claims was unwarranted, "either because [the majority's statements] are extreme oversimplifications of constitutional doctrine or mistaken views of the law and facts of this case." One of his complaints was that "the Court seems to misunderstand the prior precedents of this Court, for Agee's speech is undoubtedly protected by the Constitution. However, it may be that [his] First Amendment right to speak is outweighed by the Government's interest in national security. The point [Agee] makes, and one that is worthy of plenary consideration, is that revocation of his passport obviously does implicate First Amendment rights by chilling his right to speak, and therefore the Court's responsibility must be to balance that infringement against the asserted governmental interests to determine whether the revocation contravenes the First Amendment." [6]

5. In support of the last sentence, Chief Justice Burger cited (and quoted from) Chief Justice Warren's opinion in an earlier passport case, Zemel v. Rusk, 381 U.S. 1 (1965). For an additional comment on the use of the "speech"-"conduct" distinction in the Agee case, see p. 1232 below.

In Regan v. Wald, 468 U.S. ___ (1984), the Court relied on both Haig and Zemel in upholding travel restrictions to Cuba. After determining that the restrictions on travel to Cuba imposed by the President had indeed been authorized by Congress, Justice Rehnquist's majority opinion rejected claims based both on the First Amendment and on the right to travel: "The Secretary of State in Zemel, as here, made no effort selectively to deny passports on the basis of political belief or affiliation, but simply imposed a general ban on travel to Cuba following the break in diplomatic and consular relations with that country in 1961." He concluded that no constitutional rights were violated by the similar "across-the-board" travel restrictions here: "Both have the practical effect of preventing travel to Cuba by most American citizens, and both are justified by weighty concerns of foreign policy." Nor did Justice Rehnquist find the current absence of an emergency equivalent to the Cuban missile crisis relevant: "Our holding in Zemel was merely an example of [the]

classical deference to the political branches in matters of foreign policy." (Justices Blackmun, Brennan, Marshall, and Powell dissented, relying solely on what they took to be a lack of legislative authorization for the President's action.)

6. In June 1982, as a response to the problem of "naming names" reflected in the Agee case, Congress enacted the Intelligence Identities Protection Act, 50 U.S.C. § 421. The Act imposes fines and jail terms for divulging information that is sufficient to identify intelligence operatives. Its most controversial provision extends the sanctions beyond former government employees such as Agee to anyone who, "with reason to believe that such activities would impair or impede the foreign intelligence activities of the United States, discloses any information that identifies an individual as a covert agent," provided that the disclosure is part of a "pattern of activities intended to identify or expose covert action." [Some supporters of the law admitted that their major target was publications such as the "Covert Action Information Bulletin," whose revelations of agents' names had allegedly resulted in several injuries and at least one death.]

The congressional consideration of the Act spurred an extensive First Amendment debate. Opponents argued that, in any appropriate First Amendment balancing, only an *intent* to endan-

b. *Is Brandenburg applicable to the disclosure of factual information allegedly harming the national security?* The "incitement" and "advocacy" language of Brandenburg describes speech that in some way *urges* people to action. Does Brandenburg apply as well to the communication of *information* that may lead to criminal acts, such as instructions for manufacturing illegal drugs, plans for the security system at Fort Knox, or information allegedly endangering national security because it relates to the construction of illegal (in private hands) bombs or weapons? Do the dangers involved in the dissemination of this type of information fit into the Brandenburg model? Does the relevance of Brandenburg turn at least on the presence of some "political" component in the information? Consider the problems raised by the Intelligence Identities Protection Act of 1982, in the preceding footnote. Note also the problems raised by the attempts to stop the media from disseminating information in their possession allegedly endangering national security. That problem is explored further in chap. 13, in New York Times Co. v. United States (the Pentagon Papers case; 1971; p. 1420 below), and United States v. The Progressive, Inc. (hydrogen bomb design; 1979; p. 1426 below). See also Snepp v. United States (1980; p. 1394 below) (remedies against former employees who publish secret information).[7]

Apart from the distinction between statements of political opinion and statements of fact, can it be argued that some dangers, some evils against which government may act, are so great as to outweigh even the strongest First Amendment values, and cannot be analyzed in Brandenburg terms? Note that this problem is related to those pursued in sec. 2, where arguments are made that some varieties of expression are entitled to little or no protection under the First Amendment. See, e.g., the Ferber case (1982; p. 1090 below), where the Court speaks of the "compelling" interest in protecting children and concludes that child pornography is *not* "freedom of speech." As the later materials illustrate, the range of compelling interest may be broader than those involved in the incitement to riot situation considered in Brandenburg and those in subversive speech cases prior to Brandenburg.

OPPOSITION TO VIETNAM POLICY AND TO THE DRAFT: SOME CASES OF THE BRANDENBURG ERA

Consider the scope given to freedom of expression (and the criteria applied) in the following modern draft and war protest cases decided, like Brandenburg, in the late 1960s. All involve modern counterparts of the milieu of the World War I Espionage Act cases.

1. *Criticism of governmental policy and state legislators' oaths.* In BOND v. FLOYD, 385 U.S. 116 (1966), the Court held that a Georgia House of Representatives resolution excluding Julian Bond from membership violated the First Amendment. The State's justification was that Bond could not conscientiously take the required oath to "support the Constitution of this State and of

---

ger the national security should outbalance the protections of the First Amendment. They also objected to what they feared was a precedent for criminalizing the publication of nonclassified information. Proponents of the law insisted that simple negligence—"reason to know" of the risk created—was sufficient to tip the constitutional scales in favor of the validity of the law. Congress adopted the negligence standard; but the Conference Committee Report made special efforts to interpret the statutory language as exempting routine news reporting.

7. For an argument that Snepp, together with Haig v. Agee and the Progressive case, is part of a recent return to "our nation's dark tradition of repression" (including the post-World War I and II campaigns against dissidents) and that they illustrate the "new seditious libel" that restrains speech critical of "the secrecy state," see Koffler & Gershman, "The New Seditious Libel," 69 Cornell L.Rev. 816 (1984).

the United States." The House relied on Bond's endorsement of a SNCC statement and his supplementary remarks critical of the draft and of Vietnam policy. Chief Justice WARREN's opinion for a unanimous Court is of special interest for the problems considered in this section because of its discussion of the question whether Bond's statements would have been protected by the First Amendment if they had been made by a private citizen. In explaining that Bond's statements *were* protected criticisms, the Chief Justice stated:

"Bond could not have been constitutionally convicted under 50 U.S.C. § 462(a), which punishes any person who 'counsels, aids, or abets another to refuse or evade registration.' Bond's statements were at worst unclear on the question of the means to be adopted to avoid the draft. While the SNCC statements said 'We are in sympathy with, and support, the men in this country who are unwilling to respond to a military draft,' this statement alone cannot be interpreted as a call to unlawful refusal to be drafted. Moreover, Bond's supplementary statements tend to resolve the opaqueness in favor of legal alternatives to the draft, and there is no evidence to the contrary. On the day the statement was issued, Bond explained that he endorsed it 'because I like to think of myself as a pacifist and one who opposes that war and any other war and eager and anxious to encourage people not to participate in it for any reason that they choose.' [He] further stated 'I oppose the Viet Cong fighting in Viet Nam as much as I oppose the United States fighting in Viet Nam.' At the hearing before [a committee] of the Georgia House, when asked his position on persons who burned their draft cards, Bond replied that he admired [their] courage. [When pressed, he] stated: 'I have never suggested or counseled or advocated that any one other person burn their draft card. In fact, I have mine in my pocket and will produce it if you wish. I do not advocate that people should break laws. What I simply [tried] to say was that I admired the courage of someone who could act on his convictions knowing that he faces pretty stiff consequences.' Certainly this clarification does not demonstrate any incitement to violation of law. No useful purpose would be served by discussing the many decisions of this Court which establish that Bond could not have been convicted for these statements consistently with the First Amendment." [1]

2. *Counselling draft evasion and the Bond case.* Consider the First Amendment comments in Bond in light of the Spock-Coffin prosecution, see United States v. Spock, 416 F.2d 165 (1st Cir. 1969); [2] and compare United States v. O'Brien, the 1968 draft-card burning case, p. 1170 below. Compare the Bond opinion with the "counselling" and "admiration" approaches in Hand's Masses opinion and Holmes' Debs opinion, respectively.[3]

1. According to the Chief Justice, Bond's position as an elected legislator did not change the situation: "[W]hile the State has an interest in requiring its legislators to swear to a belief in constitutional processes of government, surely the oath gives it no interest in limiting its legislators' capacity to discuss their views of local or national policy."

2. That decision reversed Dr. Spock's conviction for conspiring to counsel registrants to violate the draft law. He signed a document entitled "A Call to Resist Illegitimate Authority," which included a public call to resist draft law duties. Later, he attended a demonstration where, after a large number of draft cards had been collected, there was an unsuccessful attempt to present these cards to the Attorney General. In ordering Spock's acquittal, the Court of Appeals majority stated that his words were "limit-

ed to condemnation of the war and the draft, and lacked any words or content of counselling. The jury could not find proscribed advocacy from the mere fact [that] he hoped the frequent stating of his views might give young men 'courage to take active steps in draft resistance.' This is a natural consequence of vigorous speech." The majority added: "The [dissent] forgets the teaching of Bond v. Floyd that expressing one's views in broad areas is not foreclosed by knowledge of the consequences."

3. Also compare Bond's statements with the statements found punishable in the Schenck-Frohwerk-Debs triology. Note one commentator's reaction: "[T]he distance traversed in First Amendment interpretation is quite apparent." Emerson, "Freedom of Expression in Wartime," 116 U.Pa.L.Rev. 975 (1968).

3. *Threats against the President and the Watts case.* For a per curiam decision considering anti-draft comments in an unusual context, note the Court's reversal without argument in WATTS v. UNITED STATES, 394 U.S. 705 (1969). Petitioner had been convicted under a 1917 law making it a felony "knowingly and willfully" to make "any threat to take the life" of the President. Petitioner had said at a public rally (after it had been urged that young people get more education before speaking): "They always holler at us to get an education. And now I have already received my draft classification as 1–A and I have got to report for my physical this Monday coming. I am not going. If they ever make me carry a rifle, the first man I want to get in my sights is L.B.J. They are not going to make me kill my black brothers." The opinion (joined by four Justices) stated: "Certainly the statute [is] constitutional on its face. The Nation undoubtedly has a valid, even an overwhelming, interest in protecting the safety of its Chief Executive and in allowing him to perform his duties without interference from threats of physical violence. Nevertheless, a statute such as this one, which makes criminal a form of pure speech, must be interpreted with the commands of the First Amendment clearly in mind. What is a threat must be distinguished from what is constitutionally protected speech.

"[W]hatever the 'willfulness' requirement implies, the statute initially requires the Government to prove a true 'threat.' We do not believe that the kind of political hyperbole indulged in by petitioner fits within that statutory term. For we must interpret the language Congress chose 'against the background of a profound national commitment to the principle that debate on public issues should be uninhibited, robust, and wide-open, and that it may well include vehement, caustic, and sometimes unpleasantly sharp attacks on government and public officials.' New York Times Co. v. Sullivan [p. 1052 below]. The language of the political arena, like the language used in labor disputes, [is] often vituperative, abusive, and inexact. We agree with petitioner that his only offense [was] 'a kind of very crude offensive method of stating a political opposition to the President.' Taken in context, and regarding the expressly conditional nature of the statement and the reaction of the listeners [laughter], we do not see how it could be interpreted otherwise." [4]

SECTION 2. CONTENT REGULATIONS ASSERTEDLY WARRANTING REDUCED OR NO FIRST AMENDMENT PROTECTION: CATEGORIZATION OR BALANCING?

Introduction. The content regulations considered in sec. 1 were carefully scrutinized by the Court and a wide range of expression was protected. This section presents a largely contrasting set of problems. In the materials that follow, the recurrent claim by the defenders of the regulations is that the

4. Does the Watts case comply with the incitement or clear and present danger standards? Or does it authorize greater restrictions on speech than those standards would permit? Is there an "overwhelming" national interest in protecting the President from threats as well as from actual harm? Does the Court view threats against the President as something other than "speech"? Is that justifiable when the threats are uttered in the context of political criticism of the President? Does Watts suggest that the standards of Brandenburg and its predecessors are representative rather than exclusive? Compare the cases in sec. 2 below, repeatedly advocating a categorizing approach to First Amendment adjudication.

Consider also whether the applicable judicial criteria should change when anti-war protest is expressed symbolically, through behavior rather than words. Is the First Amendment inapplicable there because "conduct" rather than "speech" is involved? Such "symbolic speech" issues have repeatedly come before the modern Court and are examined in the materials below. See generally sec. 3 of Chap. 12, including O'Brien, the draft card burning case, at p. 1170, and the cases involving mutilation of the American flag, at p. 1183 below.

asserted First Amendment interest warrants either no constitutional protection at all, or a reduced degree of protection. Repeatedly, the Court insists that some varieties of expression are wholly outside "the freedom of speech" safeguarded by the First Amendment. A recurrent question is whether the diminished or non-existent protection of certain varieties of expression is justified.

In the cases that follow, the asserted state interests differ from those in sec. 1. The interests include, e.g., avoiding outbreaks of local violence and disorder, protecting children or the sensibilities of audiences, and safeguarding individual concerns with reputation and privacy. On the question of judicial methodology, the pervasive problem is whether the reduced protection should be analyzed in terms of "categorization" or of "balancing." Categorization would, on a wholesale basis, find certain varieties of speech unprotected because the claim simply does not belong in the First Amendment ballpark—either because, as it is often put (as in Chaplinsky, which follows), because some "utterances are no essential part of any exposition of ideas, and are of such slight social value as a step to truth," or because, as is often suggested more implicitly, there are such powerful state interests justifying restrictions that the type of expression can be wholly excluded from "the freedom of speech." The balancing approach, by contrast, asserts (in its speech-protective form) that a very broad range of expression is presumptively within the First Amendment and can be found unprotected only after the restrictions are subjected to strict judicial scrutiny—a scrutiny which requires both a showing of "compelling" state ends (or a showing of grave evil stemming from the speech) and a demonstration that the means are carefully tailored to achieve those ends. A balancing approach, in short, permits judicial evaluations only on the state interest side of the balance, and would not shortcut the balancing process by encouraging judicial evaluations on the First Amendment side, excluding certain varieties of speech from protection at the threshold, on a wholesale basis. The types of expression considered in this section are "fighting words," defamation, obscenity and other varieties of offensive speech, and commercial speech.

A. "FIGHTING WORDS" AND THE CHAPLINSKY CATEGORIZATION APPROACH

---

1. *The Chaplinsky decision.* The brief opinion in CHAPLINSKY v. NEW HAMPSHIRE, 315 U.S. 568 (1942), unanimously upheld a conviction under a state law stating that no person "shall address any offensive, derisive or annoying word to any other person who is lawfully in any street or other public place, nor call him by any offensive or derisive name." The state court interpreted the law to ban words that "men of common intelligence would understand would be words likely to cause an average addressee to fight"— "face-to-face words plainly likely to cause a breach of the peace by the addressee, words whose speaking constitute a breach of the peace by the speaker." Chaplinsky, a Jehovah's Witness engaged in distributing literature on the streets of Rochester, New Hampshire, had allegedly attracted a "restless" crowd by denouncing all religion as a "racket." When a disturbance broke out, a police officer escorted Chaplinsky away. The police officer and Chaplinsky encountered the City Marshal. Chaplinsky claimed that he asked the Marshal to arrest the ones responsible for the disturbance. The Marshal insisted that he merely told Chaplinsky that the crowd had gotten restless. In the ensuing argument between Chaplinsky and the City Marshal, Chaplinsky called the Marshal a "God damned racketeer" and "a damned Fascist" (and added that

the whole government of Rochester are fascists or agents of Fascists"). The conviction was based on using these words to the Marshal.

Justice MURPHY's opinion found it obvious that "the appellations 'damned racketeer' and 'damned Fascist' are epithets likely to provoke the average person to retaliation, and thereby cause a breach of the peace." In his most important passage, Justice Murphy stated more generally: "There are certain well-defined and narrowly limited classes of speech, the prevention and punishment of which have never been thought to raise any Constitutional problem. These include the lewd and obscene, the profane, the libelous, and the insulting or 'fighting' words—those which by their very utterance inflict injury or tend to incite an immediate breach of the peace. It has been well observed that such utterances are no essential part of any exposition of ideas, and are of such slight social value as a step to truth that any benefit that may be derived from them is clearly outweighed by the social interest in order and morality. 'Resort to epithets or personal abuse is not in any proper sense communication of information or opinion safeguarded by the [Constitution].' Cantwell v. Connecticut, 310 U.S. 296 [1940]." [1]

2. *The Court's methodology in excluding "fighting words" from First Amendment protection.* In speaking about certain "classes of speech, the prevention and punishment of which have never been thought to raise any Constitutional problem" (and in identifying fighting words as such a class), the Chaplinsky court took an extreme categorization approach: it indicated that some varieties of speech are wholly outside of First Amendment coverage. Such an approach has the attraction of clarity and of providing guidance to judges and other government officials. But it also risks substantial dangers to First Amendment values and adequate First Amendment analysis. It may cast entire classes of speech outside the First Amendment on a wholesale basis and without adequate examination of the bases for the categorization conclusion; and it may, in its striving for general and bright-line rules, unduly slight the distinctions among types of speech within the category and the differences in contexts (and competing state interests) that particular examples of excluded speech may in fact present.

Some types of communication are indeed widely viewed as unprotected by the First Amendment via such a route, on the ground that they are quite unrelated to the purposes of the First Amendment. For example, crimes such as perjury, bribery or solicitation (at least of nonpolitical criminal behavior) are viewed as legitimately punishable because they do not raise the concerns of the First Amendment.[2] But beyond readily explainable categories such as those, a threshold exclusionary categorization analysis is a risky one. The risk of peremptory, ill-considered, overly broad exclusions from First Amendment protection is reflected in the Chaplinsky dicta. To Justice Murphy, not only "fighting words," but also "the lewd and obscene," the "profane," and the "libelous" raised no constitutional problem. That categorical list has not fared well over the years. The "fighting words" category survives to a limited extent. The others—"the lewd and obscene, the profane, the libelous"—have been afforded at least some degree of First Amendment protection, as the materials that follow illustrate.

Categorization is sometimes defended as a welcome recognition of the diversity of the types of speech. It is also defended as a welcome alternative to the undue flexibility of balancing: by avoiding the assessment of every allegedly

---

1. The Cantwell case, reversing the breach of the peace conviction of another proselytizing Jehovah's Witness, but not involving "[r]esort to epithets or personal abuse," is considered more fully in the next chapter, together with other "public forum" cases, at p. 1204.

2. See generally Van Alstyne, "A Graphic Review of the Free Speech Clause," 70 Calif.L. Rev. 107 (1982); Schauer, "Codifying the First Amendment: New York v. Ferber," 1982 Sup. Ct.Rev. 285.

protected speech manifestation against all relevant state interests, the argument goes, manipulation of balancing standards by those who apply the law is sharply curtailed. But, as Chaplinsky illustrates, the line between categorization and balancing is not so clear-cut. The extreme categorization approach discussed in the preceding paragraph is reflected only in the opening of Justice Murphy's passage in Chaplinsky. The rest of that paragraph has avowed balancing ingredients. It openly attaches a low value to the speech claiming protection ("no essential part of any exposition of ideas"; "slight social value as a step to truth"), and it proceeds to measure that weak variety of "speech" against the competing state interests ("any benefit that may be derived [is] clearly outweighed by the social interest in order and morality"). That indeed reflects balancing considerations—balancing at a very general, wholesale level, producing a total exclusion of a class of speech from First Amendment coverage and avoiding any more particularized inquiry.[3]

The risk of wholesale balancing (akin to "definitional balancing") is illustrated not only by the subsequent fate of the non-"fighting words" categories mentioned in Chaplinsky but also by the Chaplinsky facts themselves. Chaplinsky's own words came in the context of criticizing the City Marshal for the allegedly inadequate police protection he had received. Can it really be said that "fighting words" such as Chaplinsky's are not useful to the "exposition of ideas" and have only very slight social value? Was not Chaplinsky's speech a variety of political criticism of public officials? Note, too, that the addressee in Chaplinsky was a law enforcement officer. Should that affect the permissibility of "fighting words"?[4] Moreover, for lack of a more particularized identifica-

3. Additional examples of this variety of extreme categorizing, excluding certain varieties of speech from First Amendment coverage at the threshold because of their alleged lack of relationship to the purposes of the First Amendment, are Roth (1957; p. 1068 below; obscenity), and Beauharnais (1952; p. 1050 below; libel). Note also another category not mentioned in Chaplinsky, but peremptorily cast outside First Amendment coverage a month later, in the unanimous Court's even briefer opinion in Valentine v. Chrestensen (1942; p. 1128 below; commercial advertising)—another categorical exclusion from which the Court has since beaten a substantial retreat, as sec. 2D illustrates.

Contrast a different variety of threshold classification, increasingly resorted to in modern cases and discussed below. This variety does not result in total exclusion from First Amendment coverage, but rather merely uses initial classifications of some types of speech as less valuable than "core" value speech as a basis for imposing a lesser burden on government to justify restrictions on "lower value" speech. Thus, Justice Stevens has suggested that offensive speech is less important than strongly protected varieties such as political speech. See Pacifica (1978; p. 1114 below). A similar mode of analysis has been adopted by the Court for commercial speech, see Central Hudson (1980; p. 1139 below), and arguably for defamation as well (see, e.g., Gertz, 1974; p. 1060 below).

One of the questions raised by this development is whether it represents an unfortunate dilution of First Amendment protections (by establishing a hierarchy of types of speech and justifying lesser protection for some marginal varieties) or whether it ultimately assures better

protection of "core" speech by realistically recognizing that judges *will* react differently to these more marginal areas and that the strict scrutiny protection of core speech will be diluted if it is not modified in order to distinguish the core from the more penumbral varieties of speech. See, e.g., Schauer, footnote 2 above: "Categorization, in the sense of treating different forms of speech differently, [is] not necessarily speech restrictive. It is inconceivable that we will ignore such well-established governmental concerns as safety, reputation, protection against fraud, and protection of children. [Certain] state interests are inevitably going to be recognized, and the alternatives then are diluting those tests that are valuable precisely because of their strength, or formulating new tests and categories that leave existing standards strong within their narrower range. [A] narrow but strong First Amendment, with its strong principle universally available for all speech covered by the First Amendment, has much to be said for it. First Amendment protection can be like an oil spill, thinning out as it broadens. But excess precautions against this danger might lead to a First Amendment that is so narrow as to thwart its major purposes." Schauer endorses "the Court's continuing recognition of the diversity of speech and the diversity of state interests. It is unrealistic to expect that one test, one category, or one analytical approach can reflect this diversity." But he concedes that it "possible to go too far. Because no two speech acts or governmental concerns are identical, categorization is in one way artificial," and "excess categorization can reduce flexibility."

4. Note Justice Powell's concurrence in Lewis v. New Orleans (1972; p. 1105 below), where the petitioner had addressed a police of-

*higher threshold for dealing with insult & less protected counter my intuition — I don't want all to see officers [*suggests police officer should have] humiliated officer*

tion of the social interests involved, Chaplinsky leaves on the books very broad endorsements not only of a social interest in "order" but also a much more diffuse interest in "morality," an interest that has recurrently produced difficult Court reexaminations, as materials below illustrate. In examining the Court's additional efforts at exclusionary categorization in the materials that follow, it is useful to bear in mind Justice Brennan's skeptical admonition, two decades after Chaplinsky, in a case that, contrary to the Chaplinsky dicta, found some instances of libel within the First Amendment. He stated in New York Times Co. v. Sullivan (1964; p. 1052 below): "Like 'insurrection,' contempt, advocacy of unlawful acts, breach of the peace, obscenity, solicitation of legal business, and the various other formulae for the repression of expression that have been challenged in this Court, libel can claim no talismanic immunity from constitutional limitations. It must be measured by standards that satisfy the First Amendment." (Note that applying First Amendment standards rather than excluding the class of speech entirely from its protection wholesale is *not* synonymous with ultimate protection under the First Amendment. All it does do is to seek more particularized attention to the First Amendment ingredients of the speech, and the state interests asserted as justifications for restraints.) [5]

3. *The contemporary vitality of the "fighting words" exception.* Although the Court has repudiated the notion of broad exceptions from First Amendment concerns for most of the types of speech listed by Justice Murphy in Chaplinsky, the specific holding of Chaplinsky with regard to the non-protected nature of "fighting words" continues to be cited by the modern Court, albeit in diluted form. The major modern case is GOODING v. WILSON, 405 U.S. 518 (1972). That 4 to 3 ruling reversed a conviction under a Georgia statute providing that any person "who shall, without provocation, use to or of [another], opprobrious words or abusive language, tending to cause a breach of the peace," was guilty of a misdemeanor. Appellee and others, anti-war picketers at an Army building, refused a police request to stop blocking access to inductees. In the ensuing scuffle, appellee said to a police officer, "White son of a bitch, I'll kill you," "You son of a bitch, I'll choke you to death," and "You son of a bitch, if you ever put your hands on me again, I'll cut you all to pieces." Justice BRENNAN's majority opinion found that statute void on its face, primarily on overbreadth grounds. He rejected the State's argument that the state courts had construed the statute so as to cover only the "fighting words" punishable under Chaplinsky. Justice Brennan replied: "We have [made] our own examination of the Georgia cases [and conclude that] Georgia appellate decisions have not construed [the statute] to be limited in application, as in Chaplinsky, to words that 'have a direct tendency to cause acts of violence by the person to whom, individually, the remark is addressed.'" Accordingly, the statute was overbroad: it was "susceptible of application to protected expression." [6] In reaching that conclusion, Justice Brennan noted that the

ficer who was arresting her son with the words, as the Court put them, "g _ _ d _ _ _ m _ _ _ _ _ f _ _ _ _ _." She was convicted under a breach of the peace law making it unlawful "for any person wantonly to curse, or revile or to use obscene or inappropriate language toward a police officer on duty." In an opinion concurring in the majority's summary remand of the conviction, Justice Powell stated that he would have no doubt that the words would have been "fighting words" if they "had been addressed by one citizen to another, face to face and in a hostile manner." But he added that "the situation may be different where such words are addressed to a police officer trained to exercise a higher degree of restraint than the average citizen."

5. For additional comments on categorization, see e.g., Schauer, "Categories and the First Amendment: A Play in Three Acts," 34 Vand.L. Rev. 265 (1981); Schauer, "Speech and 'Speech'—Obscenity and 'Obscenity': An Exercise in the Interpretation of Constitutional Language," 67 Geo.L.J. 899 (1979); Scanlon, "Freedom of Expression and Categories of Expression," 40 U.Pitt.L.Rev. 519 (1979); and Ely "Flag Desecration: A Case Study in the Roles of Categorization and Balancing in First Amendment Analysis," 88 Harv.L.Rev. 1482 (1975).

6. For discussion of the overbreadth technique used in Gooding, see chap. 12, sec. 1, below.

dictionary definitions of "opprobrious" and "abusive" were broader than "fighting words" and that the state courts (largely in pre-Chaplinsky cases) had applied the law to utterances that were not " 'fighting' words as Chaplinsky defines them"—words " 'which by their very utterance [tended] to incite an immediate breach of the peace.' [Chaplinsky.]."

Note that the "fighting words" term as used by Justice Murphy in Chaplinsky included not only those that "tend to incite an immediate breach of the peace" but also "those which by their very utterance inflict injury." In short, Justice Murphy's version was not limited to avoidance of disorder and violence but included as well offensive speech sought to be restrained in order to protect the sensibilities of the audience from shock. Chaplinsky has not been relied upon in the Court's subsequent examinations of "offensive speech" problems, problems considered further in sec. 2C2 below. Moreover, subsequent cases may have partially undermined Chaplinsky in other respects. Note especially Terminiello v. Chicago (1949; p. 1218 below), reversing the breach of the peace conviction of an abrasive speaker who had condemned an angry crowd outside the auditorium as "snakes," "slimy snakes," "slimy scum," etc. The reversal rested on an improper charge to the jury and did not reach the fighting words issue directly; but Justice Douglas' opinion stated that free speech may "best serve its high purpose when it induces a condition of unrest, creates dissatisfaction with conditions as they are, or even stirs people to anger." Note also Justice Harlan's majority opinion in Cohen v. California (1969; p. 1101 below), including its emphasis on the emotive power of words. Finally, the state interest typically relied on to justify the exclusion of fighting words—the interest in avoiding disorder and violence—has recurrently come before the Court in subsequent cases, especially those involving the "hostile audience" problem. These cases are considered in chap. 12, sec. 4D, below, at p. 1217. The "hostile audience" cases do not involve face-to-face epithets to a particular addressee, but rather the hostile, violence-threatening reactions of the general audience to an abrasive speaker; and the Court typically addresses those problems through balancing rather than categorization analyses.[7]

B. PROTECTION OF REPUTATION AND PRIVACY

Introduction. In 1942, the Court in Chaplinsky readily categorized libel with other types of speech properly cast outside the First Amendment. Ten years later, in Beauharnais, which follows, the Court followed that lead in the group libel context. But in the 1960s, beginning with New York Times v. Sullivan, the Court turned its back on the peremptory categorical exclusion of libel and, ever since, has exercised more careful First Amendment scrutiny. This subsection examines some of the highlights of this development. It does not cover suits for injuries to reputation (and to privacy) in detail; that is left to courses in torts and media law. The focus here is on the Court's methodology in bringing these areas into the First Amendment ballpark, and on the bearing of the Court's analyses on other First Amendment problems.

---

7. Note, however, the reliance on the Chaplinsky categorization approach in New York v. Ferber (1982; p. 1090 below), viewing "child pornography as a category of material outside the protection of the First Amendment."

1. BEAUHARNAIS AND GROUP LIBEL

1. *The Beauharnais case.* The 5 to 4 decision in BEAUHARNAIS v. ILLINOIS, 343 U.S. 250 (1952), sustained an Illinois criminal group libel law prohibiting the publishing, selling, or exhibiting in any public place of any publication which "portrays depravity, criminality, unchastity, or lack of virtue of a class of citizens, of any race, color, creed or religion, [or which] exposes the citizens of any race, color, creed or religion to contempt, derision, or obloquy, or which is productive of breach of the peace or riots." Beauharnais, president of the White Circle League, had organized the circulation of a leaflet calling on Chicago officials "to halt the further encroachment, harassment and invasion of white people, their property, neighborhoods and persons, by the Negro." The leaflet called on Chicago's white people to unite and warned that if "persuasion and the need to prevent the white race from becoming mongrelized by the negro will not unite us, then the [aggressions], rapes, robberies, knives, guns and marijuana of the negro surely will." The trial court refused to give a "clear and present danger" charge requested by petitioner. Moreover, it refused offered evidence on the issue of truth, in accordance with its position that the statute was "a form of criminal libel law." Justice FRANKFURTER's majority opinion, after quoting Justice Murphy's Chaplinsky passage about nonprotected classes of speech, stated:

"No one will gainsay that it is libelous falsely to charge another with being a rapist, robber, carrier of knives and guns, and user of marijuana. The precise question before us, then, is whether [the 14th Amendment] prevents a State from punishing such libels—as criminal libel has been defined, limited and constitutionally recognized time out of mind—directed at designated collectivities and flagrantly disseminated. [We] cannot say [that] the question is concluded by history and practice. But if an utterance directed at an individual may be the object of criminal sanctions, we cannot deny to a State power to punish the same utterance directed at a defined group, unless we can say that this is a wilful and purposeless restriction unrelated to the peace and well-being of the State. Illinois [could] conclude that wilful purveyors of falsehood concerning racial and religious groups promote strife and tend powerfully to obstruct the manifold adjustments required for free, ordered life in a metropolitan, polyglot community. From the murder of the abolitionist Lovejoy in 1837 to the Cicero riots of 1951, Illinois has been the scene of exacerbated tension between races, often flaring into violence and destruction. In many of these outbreaks, utterances of the character here in question, so the Illinois legislature could conclude, played a significant part. [In] the face of this history and its frequent obligato of extreme racial and religious propaganda, we would deny experience to say that the Illinois legislature was without reason in seeking ways to curb false or malicious defamation of racial and religious groups, made in public places and by means calculated to have a powerful emotional impact on those to whom it was presented. [It] may be argued, and weightily, that this legislation will not help matters. [But it] is not within our competence to confirm or deny claims of social scientists as to the dependence of the individual on the position of his racial or religious group in the community. [W]e are precluded from saying that speech concededly punishable when immediately directed at individuals cannot be outlawed if directed at groups with whose position and esteem in society the affiliated individual may be inextricably involved. [Libelous] utterances not being within the area of constitutionally protected speech, it is unnecessary, either for us or for the State courts, to consider the issues behind the phrase 'clear and present danger.' Certainly no one would contend that obscene speech, for example, may be punished only upon a showing of such circumstances.   Libel, as we have seen, is in the same class." [1]

There were four dissenting opinions.   Justice BLACK, joined by Justice Douglas, stated: "[Reliance upon the 'group libel law'] label may make the Court's holding more palatable for those who sustain it, but the sugar-coating does not make the censorship less deadly.   However tagged, the Illinois law is not that criminal libel which has been 'defined, limited and constitutionally recognized time out of mind.'   For as 'constitutionally recognized' that crime has provided for punishment of false, malicious, scurrilous charges against individuals, not against huge groups.   This limited scope of the law of criminal libel [has] confined state punishment of speech and expression to the narrowest of areas involving nothing more than purely private feuds.   Every expansion of the law of criminal libel so as to punish discussion of matters of public concern means a corresponding invasion of the area dedicated to free expression by the First Amendment."   Justice DOUGLAS' dissent insisted: "My view is that if in any case other public interests are to override the plain command of the First Amendment, the peril of speech must be clear and present, leaving no room for argument, raising no doubts as to the necessity of curbing speech in order to prevent disaster." [2]   In still another dissent, Justice JACKSON argued at length that the 14th Amendment's restraints on the states were less confining than the First Amendment's limits on Congress.   He argued that "because Congress probably could not enact this law it does not follow that the States may not." [3]   He noted the "tolerance of state libel laws by the very authors and partisans" of the 14th Amendment and insisted that the Palko analysis (p. 423 above) provided the appropriate standard.   But he nevertheless found the Illinois law unconstitutional: "If one can claim to announce the judgment of legal history on any subject, it is that criminal libel laws are consistent with the concept of ordered liberty only when applied with safeguards evolved to prevent their invasion of freedom of expression."   Under the challenged law, he emphasized, there was no requirement "to find any injury to any person, or group, or to the public peace, nor to find any probability, let alone any clear and present danger, of injury to any of these.   [The] leaflet was simply held punishable as criminal libel per se irrespective of its actual or probable consequences."

2.   *The vitality of Beauharnais.*   Have the First Amendment developments of recent decades drained Beauharnais of all vitality?   Some of the measures adopted by Skokie, Illinois, in the late 1970s to block planned demonstrations by American Nazis relied on the approach sustained in Beauharnais.   As noted in the fuller treatment of the Skokie controversy at p. 1237 below, state and lower federal courts struck down all of the ordinances designed to block the Nazi marchers, including one that prohibited the "dissemination of any materials within [Skokie] which [intentionally] promotes and incites hatred against persons by reasons of their race, national origin, or religion."   Most of the judges found Beauharnais no longer controlling.   The Seventh Circuit, for example, stated: "It may be questioned, after cases such as Cohen v. California, Gooding v. Wilson, and Brandenburg v. Ohio, whether the *tendency to induce violence* approach sanctioned implicitly in Beauharnais would pass constitutional

1. See generally Riesman, "Democracy and Defamation: Control of Group Libel," 42 Colum.L.Rev. 727 (1942), cited by both majority and minority.   See also Tanenhaus, "Group Libel," 35 Cornell L.Q. 261 (1950); Beth, "Group Libel and Free Speech," 39 Minn.L.Rev. 167 (1955).   Note also Kalven's comment that the level of scrutiny applied by Beauharnais was even "less exacting than would be applied to purely economic regulations."   Kalven, The Negro and the First Amendment (1965), 37.

2. Justice REED's dissent, joined by Justice Douglas, emphasized the vagueness of the statutory words "virtue," "derision," and "obloquy."

3. Note the similar argument in Justice Harlan's separate opinion in the first major obscenity case, Roth (1957; p. 1068 below).   During the 1970s, Justice Rehnquist expressed a similar position.

muster today." Collin v. Smith, 578 F.2d 1197 (7th Cir.1978). But note Justice Blackmun's dissent, joined by Justice Rehnquist, from a denial of a stay of the Court of Appeals order: "Beauharnais has never been overruled or formally limited in any way." Smith v. Collin, 436 U.S. 953 (1978).

Despite its apparent undercutting by later developments, arguments resting on Beauharnais continue to be voiced. A controversial recent example is the advocacy of ordinances to curb sexually explicit but not necessarily obscene materials by asserting that pornography contributes to the subordination of women. These anti-pornography efforts invoked an equality, civil rights model to justify curbs on speech: the argument is in part that Beauharnais demonstrates that the promotion of equality is a compelling state objective justifying restrictions on expression. This anti-pornography effort is more fully considered in sec. 1C below, at p. 1097.

---

2. INJURY TO INDIVIDUAL REPUTATION AND PRIVACY

NEW YORK TIMES CO. v. SULLIVAN

376 U.S. 254, 84 S.Ct. 710, 11 L.Ed.2d 686 (1964).

Mr. Justice BRENNAN delivered the opinion of the Court.

We are required in this case to determine for the first time the extent to which the constitutional protections for speech and press limit a State's power to award damages in a libel action brought by a public official against critics of his official conduct. [This libel action stemmed from a paid, full-page, fund-raising advertisement in The New York Times in March 1960 by the Committee to Defend Martin Luther King and the Struggle for Freedom in the South. The ad, headed "Heed Their Rising Voices," charged the existence of "an unprecedented wave of terror" against blacks engaged in nonviolent demonstrations in the South. Sullivan, the Montgomery, Ala., police commissioner, sued the Times and several black clergymen who had signed the ad. Sullivan objected especially to the claim that "truckloads of police armed with shotguns and teargas ringed the Alabama State College Campus" in Montgomery and that Dr. King had been assaulted and arrested seven times. Sullivan's witnesses testified that they took the charges to implicate Sullivan, and that he did not participate in the events regarding Dr. King. Sullivan offered no proof that he had suffered actual pecuniary loss. He recovered a judgment for $500,000 under Alabama libel law. The judgment was based on several inaccurate statements in the ad—e.g., the statement that Dr. King had been arrested seven times: in fact he had been arrested four times. The Court rejected the argument that First Amendment guarantees were inapplicable because the statements were published as part of a "paid 'commercial'" ad and concluded: "We hold that the rule of law applied by the Alabama courts is constitutionally deficient for failure to provide the safeguards for freedom of speech and of the press that are required by the [First Amendment] in a libel action brought by a public official against critics of his official conduct. We further hold that under the proper safeguards the evidence presented in this case is constitutionally insufficient to support the judgment." In explaining that conclusion, Justice Brennan stated:]

Under Alabama law, [a] publication is "libelous per se" if the words "tend to injure a person [in] his reputation" or to "bring [him] into public contempt." [Once] "libel per se" has been established, the defendant has no defense as to stated facts unless he can persuade the jury that they were true in all their particulars. [Unless] he can discharge the burden of proving truth, general damages are presumed, and may be awarded without proof of pecuniary injury.

The question before us is whether this rule of liability, as applied to an action brought by a public official against critics of his official conduct, abridges the freedom of speech and of the [press].

Respondent [and] the Alabama courts [rely heavily] on statements of this Court to the effect that the Constitution does not protect libelous publications. Those statements do not foreclose our inquiry here.   None of the cases sustained the use of libel laws to impose sanctions upon expression critical of the official conduct of public officials.   [Like] insurrection, contempt, advocacy of unlawful acts, breach of the peace, obscenity, solicitation of legal business, and the various other formulae for the repression of expression that have been challenged in this Court, libel can claim no talismanic immunity from constitutional limitations.   It must be measured by standards that satisfy the [First Amendment].

[W]e consider this case against the background of a profound national commitment to the principle that debate on public issues should be uninhibited, robust, and wide-open, and that it may well include vehement, caustic, and sometimes unpleasantly sharp attacks on government and public officials.   The present advertisement, as an expression of grievance and protest on one of the major public issues of our time, would seem clearly to qualify for the constitutional protection.   The question is whether it forfeits that protection by the falsity of some of its factual statements and by its alleged defamation of respondent.   Authoritative interpretations of the First Amendment guarantees have consistently refused to recognize an exception for any test of truth—whether administered by judges, juries, or administrative officials—and especially not one that puts the burden of proving truth on the speaker.   "The constitutional protection does not turn upon the truth, popularity, or social utility of the ideas and beliefs which are offered."   [E]rroneous statement is inevitable in free debate and [must] be protected if the freedoms of expression are to have the "breathing space" that they "need [to] survive" [NAACP v. Button, p. 1353 below].   [Injury] to official reputation affords no more warrant for repressing speech that would otherwise be free than does factual error.   [If] judges are to be treated as "men of fortitude, able to thrive in a hardy climate" [Craig v. Harney, p. 1338 below], surely the same must be true of other government officials, such as elected city commissioners.   Criticism of their official conduct does not lose its constitutional protection merely because it is effective criticism and hence diminishes their official reputations.

If neither factual error nor defamatory content suffices to remove the constitutional shield from criticism of official conduct, the combination of the two elements is no less inadequate.   This is the lesson to be drawn from the great controversy over the Sedition Act of 1798, which first crystallized a national awareness of the central meaning of the First Amendment.   [Although] the Sedition Act was never tested in this Court, the attack upon its validity has carried the day in the court of history.   Fines levied in its prosecution were repaid by Act of Congress on the ground that it was unconstitutional.   [President Jefferson] pardoned those who had been convicted and sentenced under the Act and remitted their fines.   [Its] invalidity [has] also been assumed by Justices of this Court.   [These] views reflect a broad consensus that the Act, because of the restraint it imposed upon criticism of government and public officials, was inconsistent with the [First Amendment].

What a State may not constitutionally bring about by means of a criminal statute is likewise beyond the reach of its civil law of libel.   The fear of damage awards under a rule such as that invoked by the Alabama courts here may be markedly more inhibiting than the fear of prosecution under a criminal statute. [The] judgment awarded in this case—without the need for any proof of actual pecuniary loss—was [100] times greater than that provided by the Sedition Act.

And since there is no double jeopardy limitation applicable to civil lawsuits, this is not the only judgment that may be awarded against petitioners for the same publication. Whether or not a newspaper can survive a succession of such judgments, the pall of fear and timidity imposed upon those who would give voice to public criticism is an atmosphere in which the First Amendment freedoms cannot [survive].

The state rule of law is not saved by its allowance of the defense of truth. A defense for erroneous statements honestly made is no less essential here than was the requirement of proof of guilty knowledge which, in [Smith v. California, p. 1161 below], we held indispensable to a valid conviction of a bookseller for possessing obscene writings for sale. [A] rule compelling the critic of official conduct to guarantee the truth of all his factual assertions—and to do so on pain of libel judgments virtually unlimited in amount—leads to a comparable "self-censorship." Allowance of the defense of truth, with the burden of proving it on the defendant, does not mean that only false speech will be deterred.[1] [Under] such a rule, would-be critics of official conduct may be deterred from voicing their criticism, even though it is believed to be true and even though it is in fact true, because of doubt whether it can be proved in court or fear of the expense of having to do so. They tend to make only statements which "steer far wider of the unlawful zone." The rule thus dampens the vigor and limits the variety of public debate. It is inconsistent with the [First Amendment].

The constitutional guarantees require, we think, a federal rule that prohibits a public official from recovering damages for a defamatory falsehood relating to his official conduct unless he proves that the statement was made with "actual malice"—that is, with knowledge that it was false or with reckless disregard of whether it was false or not.[2] [We] consider that the proof presented to show actual malice lacks the convincing clarity which the constitutional standard demands, and hence that it would not constitutionally sustain the judgment for respondent under the proper rule of law. [E.g., we] think the evidence against the Times supports at most a finding of negligence in failing to discover the misstatements, and is constitutionally insufficient to show the recklessness that is required for a finding of actual malice. We also think the evidence was constitutionally defective in another respect: it was incapable of supporting the jury's finding that the allegedly libelous statements were made "of and concerning" respondent. [There] was no reference to respondent in the advertisement, either by name or official position. [As the Supreme Court of Alabama made clear, reliance was placed solely] on the bare fact of respondent's official position. [This] has disquieting implications for criticism of governmental conduct. [It raises] the possibility that a good-faith critic of government will be penalized for his criticism [and] strikes at the very center of the constitutionally protected area of free expression. We hold that such a proposition may not constitutionally be utilized to establish that an otherwise impersonal attack on governmental operations was a libel of an official responsible for those operations. Since it was relied on exclusively, [the] evidence was constitutionally insufficient to support a finding that the statements referred to [respondent].

Reversed and remanded.[3]

---

1. Even a false statement may be deemed to make a valuable contribution to public debate, since it brings about "the clearer perception and livelier impression of truth, produced by its collision with error." Mill, On Liberty; see also Milton, Areopagitica. [Footnote by Justice Brennan.]

2. We have no occasion here to determine how far down into the lower ranks of govern-

ment employees the "public official" designation would extend for purposes of this rule, or otherwise to specify categories of persons who would or would not be included. [Nor] need we here determine the boundaries of the "official conduct" [concept]. [Footnote by Justice Brennan, elsewhere in the opinion.]

3. Two years after New York Times, the Court had little difficulty in extending its princi-

Mr. Justice BLACK, with whom Mr. Justice DOUGLAS joins (concurring).
[I] base my vote to reverse on the belief that the First and 14th Amendments not merely "delimit" a State's power to award damages to "public officials against critics of their official conduct" but completely prohibit a State from exercising such a [power]. "Malice," even as defined by the Court, is an elusive, abstract concept, hard to prove and hard to disprove. The requirement that malice be proved provides at best an evanescent protection for the right critically to discuss public affairs. [Therefore], I vote to reverse exclusively on the ground that the [defendants] had an absolute, unconditional constitutional right to publish in the Times advertisement their criticisms of the Montgomery agencies and [officials]. [4]

FIRST AMENDMENT ANALYSIS AND DEFAMATION CASES

1. *The Court's methodology: Was New York Times a breakthrough?* As noted earlier, the emphasis of this section is on the Court's mode of analysis rather than the details of defamation law. Consider Harry Kalven's comment, soon after the New York Times decision, that it "may prove to be the best and most important opinion [the Court] has ever produced in the realm of freedom of speech." [1] Justice Brennan's emphasis on "the principle that debate on public issues should be uninhibited, robust, and wide-open" has indeed surfaced in later cases. But can greater novelty than that be claimed for the case? Kalven's perception of "exciting possibilities" in the opinion stemmed especially from "its emphasis on seditious libel and the Sedition Act of 1798 as the key to the meaning of the First Amendment." Kalven argued that "the importance of the free-speech provision of the Constitution rests on the rejection of seditious libel as an offense," and that that key theme had been ignored in traditional analyses before New York Times. Accordingly, he found the "special virtue of the Times opinion" in "its restoration of seditious libel to its essential role, thus suddenly and dramatically changing the idiom of free-speech analysis." And he added, even more broadly, "that the effect of the Times opinion is necessarily to discard or diminish in importance the clear-and-present danger test, the balancing formula, the two-level speech theory of Beauharnais and Roth [obscenity; p. 1068 below], and the two-tier theory of different effects of the First Amendment on federal and state action." [2] Have those tests and formulas and theories been "discarded," have they truly "diminished in importance," since New York Times? [3] Would free speech analysis be in better shape today if they had?

ples to state criminal libel cases. Garrison v. Louisiana, 379 U.S. 64 (1964).

4. In another concurrence, Justice GOLDBERG, joined by Justice Douglas, stated that the Constitution afforded "an absolute, unconditional privilege to criticize official conduct" of public officials, but did not protect "defamatory statements directed against the private conduct of a public official or private citizen." He insisted: "Purely private defamation has little to do with the political ends of a self-governing society." Although he recognized that there would be difficulties in applying "a public-private standard," he insisted that those difficulties were "certainly of a different genre from those attending the differentiation between a malicious and nonmalicious state of mind." He, too, objected to "the elusive concept of malice."

1. Kalven, "The New York Times Case: A Note on 'The Central Meaning of the First Amendment,'" 1964 Sup.Ct.Rev. 191.

2. Kalven urged, moreover, that "analysis of free-speech issues should hereafter begin with the significant issue of seditious libel and defamation of government by its critics rather than with the sterile example of a man falsely yelling fire in a crowded theater." Kalven added that the hostility to seditious libel did not "represent the whole meaning of the Amendment. There are other freedoms protected by it. But at the center there is no doubt what speech is being protected and no doubt why it is being protected. The theory of the freedom of speech clause was put right side up for the first time."

3. Compare Schauer's comment, in the course of discussing New York v. Ferber, the 1982 child pornography case at p. 1090 below: Schauer sees in the exclusion of child pornography from First Amendment protection "a growing consensus within the Court on a doctrinal proposition of great importance in First Amendment theory—that the diversity of communica-

2. *New York Times, the varieties of "balancing," and the First Amendment interest in false statements of fact.* Kalven noted that "the idiom of balancing was eschewed in the Times case." True, there was no "ad hoc balancing": no resort to the view "that the court, in each case, balance the individual and social interest in freedom of expression against the social interest sought by the regulation." [4] But was New York Times truly *not* a balancing case? As Kalven himself recognized, there was, "of course, a sense in which the Court did indulge in balancing. It did not go the whole way and give an absolute privilege to the 'citizen-critic' "; it did balance "two obvious conflicting interests." Despite the avoidance of "the idiom of balancing" in the Times case, the Court in Times and its progeny has balanced the interest in protecting personal reputation against the First Amendment values implicated by the law of libel.

But what *are* the First Amendment values in the false statements of fact inherent in defamatory statements? In addition to the New York Times opinion, note Justice Powell's statement in Gertz (p. 1060 below): "Under the First Amendment there is no such thing as a false idea. [But] there is no constitutional value in false statements of fact." (Justice Powell acknowledged, however, that "some falsehood" needs to be protected "in order to protect speech that matters.") Compare Justice Brennan's reliance on John Stuart Mill in footnote 1 of his opinion in New York Times: "Even a false statement may be deemed to make a valuable contribution to public [debate]." [5]

The New York Times line of cases, then, reflects balancing, albeit not ad hoc balancing. Thus, Nimmer, the formost advocate of "definitional balancing," uses the New York Times case as his prime example.[6] The decisions reflect a search for standards or rules to balance the competing interests.[7] What have been the important variables in that search?

tive activity and governmental concerns is so wide as to make it implausible to apply the same tests or analytical tools to the entire range of First Amendment problems. [Ferber], in carving out yet another distinct category of material unprotected by the First Amendment, [is] a significant milestone on the road toward elaborate codification of the First Amendment. At the same time it may warn us of the dangers of going much farther." Schauer, "Codifying the First Amendment: New York v. Ferber," 1982 Sup. Ct.Rev. 285.

4. That description is from a critic of balancing, Emerson, "Toward a General Theory of the First Amendment," 72 Yale L.J. 877, 912 (1963). (Recall the comments on the varieties of balancing in the introductory materials to this chapter.)

5. Compare, however, Justice Brennan's statement two years after New York Times, in Garrison v. Louisiana, 379 U.S. 64 (1964): "Although honest utterance, even if inaccurate, may further the fruitful exercise of the right of free speech, it does not follow that the lie, knowingly and deliberately published about a public official, should enjoy a like immunity. [That] speech is used as a tool for political ends does not automatically bring it under the protective mantle of the Constitution. For the use of the known lie as a tool is at once at odds with the premises of democratic government and with the orderly manner in which economic, social, or political change is to be effected. Calculated falsehood falls into that class of utterances [which are excluded under Chaplinsky]. Hence the knowingly false statement and the false statement

made with reckless disregard of the truth do not enjoy constitutional protection."

6. Note also Nimmer's comments on "definitional balancing," in his article, "The Right to Speak from Times to [Time]," 56 Calif.L.Rev. 935 (1968), Nimmer suggested that New York Times represented "a third approach which avoids the all or nothing implications of absolutism versus ad hoc balancing. Times points the way to the employment of the balancing process on the definitional rather than the litigation or ad hoc level." He adds that, by "in effect holding that knowingly and recklessly false speech was not 'speech' within the meaning of the First Amendment, the Court must have implicitly (since no explicit explanation was offered) referred to certain competing policy considerations." He argues that defitional balancing, unlike ad hoc balancing, produces "a rule [that] can be employed in future cases." Is that a characteristic limited to "definitional" balancing? Is that not a distinctive feature of all balancing when it goes beyond ad hoc balancing? Compare the next footnote.

7. Note the comment by Justice Powell in a later libel case, Gertz, p. 1060 below: "Theoretically, of course, the balance between [the First Amendment] and the individual's claim to compensation [might] be struck on a case-by-case basis. [But] this approach would lead to unpredictable results and uncertain expectations, and it could render our duty to supervise the lower courts unmanageable. Because an ad hoc resolution of the competing interests [in] each particu-

3. *The ingredients of balancing in the defamation cases: The significant variables in the resulting standards.*   In examining the progeny of New York Times that follow, note especially the types of rules and standards that emerge as a result of the Court's efforts to accommodate the competing interests through a balancing technique.   The Court's efforts to delineate constitutional limits in the defamation area have focused on two recurrent and sometimes interrelated questions: (1) When does the First Amendment impose limits on liability?   (2) What remedies—especially with respect to damages—are constitutionally permissible for the defamation plaintiff?   Which emphasis—substantive limits on liability or limits on remedies—is likely to be more productive in accommodating the competing interests?

With respect to substantive limits on liability, the Court has most often emphasized the status of the plaintiff: for example, the New York Times case limit on liability, which originated in a case involving a public official, has been extended to "public figures" (in Butts and Walker, p. 1058 below).[8]   For a brief period, the Court's emphasis shifted to the nature of the issue discussed in the allegedly libelous communication: Rosenbloom (p. 1059 below) extended the New York Times "malice" test to libel actions by private individuals where the alleged defamation involved a matter of public or general interest.   But the majority rejected that position a few years later, in Gertz (p. 1060 below). Most recently, the Court has added the extent of the relief granted—the permissible bases of damages—as an important variable in the rules applicable to the libel area, as Gertz again illustrates.   Do the rules that have evolved strike a proper balance between First Amendment values and the interest in protecting individual reputations?   There have been recurrent attacks on New York Times on the ground that it gives inadequate protection to defamation plaintiffs. More recently, there have been mounting complaints from the other side: that the principles of accommodation give inadequate protection to defamation defendants.   These critics have complained of the ease with which defamation cases under the New York Times standard can get to a jury (and the reluctance of courts to direct summary judgments for defendants), the increasingly large verdicts against defendants, and the "chilling effects" caused by the litigation burdens and legal fees even in cases where defendants ultimately prevail on appeal.   Some of these issues are considered further below, at p. 1062.

Consider the light thrown by the post-New York Times cases, below, on the importance and utility of balancing.   Does the attempt to evolve standards through multiple variables, from standards of liability to scope of relief, risk developing into such fine-tuned balancing that the resulting rules become ultimately unmanageable by judges and juries?   See, e.g., the intellectually sophisticated but, arguably, practically unadministrable approach of Justice Harlan—a Justice often admired for his balancing prowess—in the Butts and Walker cases that follow.

---

lar case is not feasible, we must lay down broad rules of general application."

8. To what extent should the nature of the *defendant* rather than the plaintiff be significant in the application of New York Times and its progeny?   Typically, defendants in the Court's cases have been media defendants; at this writing, the Court has not yet decided whether private defendants can assert variants of the New York Times privilege.   In New York Times itself, however, private defendants were joined with the New York Times.   And in Hutchinson

v. Proxmire (1979; p. 1061 below), the defendant was a Senator.   In a footnote in that case, the Court stated that the Court had never decided whether the New York Times defense could be raised by an individual rather than a media defendant and added that "our conclusion that Hutchinson is not a public figures makes it unnecessary to do so in this case."   See Shiffrin, "Defamatory Non-Media Speech and First Amendment Methodology," 25 U.C.L.A.L.Rev. 915 (1978).   That issue may be decided by the Court in the 1984–85 Term.

EXPLORING THE IMPLICATIONS OF NEW YORK TIMES FOR OTHER DEFAMATION ACTIONS

1. *Extending New York Times to "public figures."* After New York Times, the Court was confronted with recurrent pleas to extend its constitutional immunities to other areas of defamation law. Although a divided Court took some steps to extend the applicability of the New York Times rule, it has repeatedly rejected additional expansions. The developments began with CUR-TIS PUBLISHING CO. v. BUTTS and ASSOCIATED PRESS v. WALKER, decided together at 388 U.S. 130 (1967). Those cases applied the New York Times rule to libel actions "instituted by persons who are not public officials, but who are 'public figures' and involved in issues in which the public has a justified and important interest." [1]

Butts grew out of a Saturday Evening Post article which claimed that the University of Georgia athletic director (and former football coach) had fixed a football game. In Walker, a retired general challenged an AP report that he had led a violent crowd in opposition to the enforcement of a desegregation decree at the University of Mississippi. The Court was sharply divided in its reasoning,[2] but the result was that the New York Times rule was extended to "public figures" cases. In announcing the view that became the Court position, Chief Justice WARREN stated that "differentiation between 'public figures' and 'public officials' and adoption of separate standards of proof for each have no basis in law, logic, or First Amendment policy. Increasingly in this country, the distinctions between governmental and private sectors are blurred. [It] is plain that although they are not subject to the restraints of the political process, 'public figures,' like 'public officials,' often play an influential role in ordering society. And surely as a class these 'public figures' have as ready access as 'public officials' to mass media, [both] to influence policy and to counter criticism of their views and activities. Our citizenry has a legitimate and substantial interest in the conduct of such persons, and freedom of the press to engage in uninhibited debate about their involvement in public issues and events is as crucial as it is in the case of 'public officials.'"

In announcing the position of the four Justices who opposed extension of the New York Times rule, Justice HARLAN examined the similarities and differences between "public officials" and other "public figures"; agreed that "public figures" actions "cannot be left entirely to state libel laws"; but insisted that "the rigorous federal requirements of New York Times are not the only appropriate accommodation of the conflicting interests at stake." He concluded: "We [would] hold that a 'public figure' who is not a public official may also recover damages for a defamatory falsehood whose substance makes substantial danger to reputation apparent, on a showing of highly unreasonable conduct constituting an extreme departure from the standards of investigation and reporting ordinarily adhered to by responsible publishers." [3] Was Justice Harlan's effort to evolve three different standards of liability—for "public

---

1. As the Court put it in Gertz, p. 1060 below, the result of Curtis and Butts is that the New York Times rule applies to those "who, by reason of the notoriety of their achievements or the vigor and success with which they seek the public's attention, are properly classified as public figures."

2. Four of the Justices (Harlan, Clark, Stewart and Fortas) opposed extending the New York Times rule; three (Chief Justice Warren, and Justices Brennan and White) urged application of New York Times to public figures; the remaining two (Black and Douglas) urged a broader

press immunity, as they did ever since New York Times.

3. Although the New York Times standard gives considerable protection to the media when they utter defamatory statements about public officials or public figures, it leaves them open to wide-ranging inquiries on the issue of whether they were guilty of knowing or reckless falsity. In Herbert v. Lando, 441 U.S. 153 (1979), the Court rejected a television producer's claim to a broad First Amendment-based privilege that would preclude questions in pretrial discovery proceedings pertaining to his liability under the

officials" (the New York Times "malice" rule), for "public figures" (the "highly unreasonable conduct" variant on gross negligence), and for private plaintiffs—an example of highly sophisticated balancing that would have produced unadministrable rules? [4]

2. *Defamation actions by private plaintiffs: The Rosenbloom experiment and the Gertz resolution.* After extending the New York Times standard to "public figures," the divided Court's balancing approach encountered new challenges when publishers claimed First Amendment defenses to defamation suits by *private* individuals. At first, in the 1971 decision in Rosenbloom, the Court extended the New York Times rule to that situation; but it made that extension by shifting the focus of its balancing from the status of the plaintiff to the "general interest" content of the publication. But in Gertz, three years later, that experiment was abandoned and a rule permitting recovery more easily than under the New York Times standard was adopted for "private" plaintiffs. In Rosenbloom, Justice Brennan's plurality opinion extended the New York Times privilege to a "private" plaintiff's action claiming defamation in a report "about the individual's involvement in an event of public or general interest." But in Gertz, Justice Powell spoke for a majority holding that state libel law could impose liability in suits by private individuals "on a less demanding showing" than that required by New York Times "so long as [states] do not impose liability without fault." The Gertz decision, in addition to authorizing standards of liability such as negligence, also imposed restrictions on damages. In lessening the constitutional restraints on standards of liability and in focusing on damages as an important new variable in its balancing, the new majority generally followed the approach advocated by the dissents of Justices Marshall and Harlan in Rosenbloom.

a. In ROSENBLOOM v. METROMEDIA, INC., 403 U.S. 29 (1971), Justice BRENNAN's plurality opinion, joined by Chief Justice Burger and Justice Blackmun, argued that the critical criterion should be the subject matter of the allegedly defamatory report rather than the status of the plaintiff.[5] He insisted that experience since New York Times had "disclosed the artificiality, in terms of the public's interest, of a simple distinction between 'public' and 'private' individuals" and concluded: "If a matter is a subject of public or general interest, it cannot suddenly become less so merely because a private individual is involved, or because in some sense the individual did not 'voluntarily' choose to become involved. The public's primary interest is in the event; the public focus is on the conduct of the participant and the content, effect, and significance of the conduct, not the participant's prior anonymity or notoriety. [We] honor the commitment to robust debate on public issues [by] extending constitutional protection to all discussion and communication involving matters of public or general concern without regard to whether the persons involved are famous or anonymous." [6]

Times "malice" standard. Although the press vehemently criticized that ruling, none of the Justices was prepared to uphold all of the broad media claims. Even Justices Marshall and Brennan were only willing to grant a limited privilege. In rejecting all First Amendment claims, Justice White's majority opinion noted that "according an absolute privilege to the editorial process of a media defendant in a libel case is not required, authorized or presaged by our prior cases, and would substantially enhance the burden of proving actual malice, contrary to the expectations of New York Times, Butts, and similar cases." (For additional discussion of media claims in the Court, see the material on the press in chap. 13, at p. 1416 below.)

4. See generally Kalven, "The Reasonable Man and the First Amendment: Hill, Butts, and Walker," 1967 Sup.Ct.Rev. 267. (In a number of cases since Butts and Walker, the Court has construed the "public figure" category quite narrowly. See footnote 8 below.)

5. Rosenbloom was a libel action by a distributor of nudist magazines, based on radio reports about police action against his allegedly obscene books, about his lawsuit, and about police interference with his business. Some of the news reports referred to "girlie book peddlers" and the "smut literature racket."

6. Justice BLACK's brief concurrence in the judgment reiterated his support of an unqualified

b. In GERTZ v. ROBERT WELCH, INC., 418 U.S. 323 (1974), the Court abandoned the Rosenbloom course and held that a private person should be able to recover without meeting the New York Times standard.[7] Justice POWELL's majority opinion stated the new standard of liability for private libel actions as follows: "We hold that, so long as they do not impose liability without fault, the States may define for themselves the appropriate standard of liability for a publisher or broadcaster of defamatory falsehoods injurious to a private individual. This approach provides a more equitable boundary between the competing concerns involved here. It recognizes the strength of the legitimate state interest in compensating private individuals for wrongful injury to reputation, yet shields the press and broadcast media from the rigors of strict liability for defamation. At least this conclusion obtains where, as here, the substance of the defamatory statement 'makes substantial danger to reputation apparent.' Our inquiry would involve [different] considerations [if] a State purported to condition civil liability on a factual misstatement whose content did not warn a reasonably prudent editor or broadcaster of its defamatory potential." Regarding the new constitutional restraints on damage awards, Justice Powell announced that states may ordinarily go no further "than compensation for actual injury": "[W]e hold that the States may not permit recovery of presumed or punitive damages, at least when liability is not based on a showing of knowledge of falsity or reckless disregard for the truth."

Justice Powell explained that the state interest in compensating injuries to private individuals was stronger than in the case of "public figures," and that distinction made a less demanding standard of liability appropriate here. Public figures could use the remedy of "self-help" more effectively because of their "significantly greater access" to the media. Private persons, by contrast, were "more vulnerable to injury." Moreover, there was "a compelling normative consideration" for a stronger defamation remedy by private persons: unlike public figures, they had not "voluntarily exposed themselves to increased risk of injury from defamatory falsehoods concerning them." In short, "private individuals are not only more vulnerable to injury than public officials and public figures; they are also more deserving of recovery." The Rosenbloom plurality rule had abridged the legitimate state concern with private plaintiffs' injuries "to a degree that we find unacceptable." Moreover, Rosenbloom had unwisely imposed the task on judges of deciding "on an ad hoc basis which publications address issues of 'general or public interest' and which do not." Accordingly, the new Gertz rule, leaving states free to impose any standard of liability short of "liability without fault" in private person cases, seemed preferable.[8]

First Amendment privilege. Justice WHITE's concurrence in the judgment thought the other opinions in Rosenbloom displaced "more state libel law than is necessary for the decision." He urged applying the New York Times rule to "discussion of the official actions of public servants such as the police."

Justice MARSHALL's dissent, joined by Justice Stewart, took a different tack—one that closely resembled the majority position that emerged in Gertz, below. He urged a focus on damages rather than on liability because "the size of the potential judgment that may be rendered against the press must be the most significant factor in producing self censorship." Justice HARLAN's dissent agreed with most of Justice Marshall's approach; but, unlike Justice Marshall, he thought that punitive as well as actual damages were permissible in some cases.

7. This was a libel action by Elmer Gertz, a Chicago lawyer, against the publisher of "American Opinion," an "outlet for the views of the John Birch Society." Gertz had been retained by a victim's family in a civil suit against a Chicago policeman who had been convicted of murder. The magazine charged Gertz with being an architect of the "frame-up" of the policeman in the murder trial and called Gertz, inter alia, a "Communist-fronter." The Court found that Gertz was not a "public figure." (See the further discussion in the next footnote.)

8. In finding that Gertz was not "a public figure," the Court began a trend which intensified in later years—a trend to read the "public figure" category narrowly. Gertz, for example, had "long been active in community and professional affairs" and was "well-known in some circles." But the Court emphasized that "he had

In explaining the conclusion that "the private defamation plaintiff who establishes liability under a less demanding standard than that stated by New York Times may recover only such damages as are sufficient to compensate him for actual injury," Justice Powell stated: "Like the doctrine of presumed damages, jury discretion to award punitive damages unnecessarily exacerbates the danger of media self-censorship." He noted, however, that "actual injury" is "not limited to out-of-pocket loss": "Indeed, the more customary types of actual harm inflicted by defamatory falsehood included impairment of reputation and standing in the community, personal humiliation, and mental anguish and suffering." [9]

Justice BRENNAN's dissent was the only opinion in Gertz to adhere fully to the Rosenbloom plurality approach. He insisted that the claim that public figures had greater access to the media to clear their names was unrealistic: "In the vast majority of libels involving public officials or public figures, the ability to respond through the media will depend on the same complex factor on which the ability of a private individual depends: the unpredictable event of the media's continuing interest in the story." Moreover, "the idea that certain 'public' figures have voluntarily exposed their entire lives to public inspection, while private individuals have kept theirs carefully shrouded from public view is, at best, a legal fiction." The new rule, he argued, denied "free expression its needed 'breathing space.'" Widespread adoption of a reasonable care standard in private defamations—"the probable result of today's decision"—will "lead to self-censorship."

Justice WHITE's lengthy dissent argued that even the Gertz protection of the media went too far: "I fail to see how the quality or quantity of public debate will be promoted by further emasculation of state libel laws [protecting non-public persons] for the benefit of the news media." He argued that traditional libel laws should be permitted to stand, particularly in view of "the increasingly prominent role [and power of the] mass media." He conceded

achieved no general fame or notoriety in the community." Justice Powell added: "We would not lightly assume that a citizen's participation in community and professional affairs rendered him a public figure for all purposes. Absent clear evidence of general fame or notoriety in the community, and pervasive involvement in the affairs of society, an individual should not be deemed a public personality for all aspects of his life. It is preferable to reduce the public figure question to a more meaningful context by looking to the nature and extent of an individual's participation in the particular controversy giving rise to the defamation." And in the course of the policeman's murder trial, Gertz had played only "a minimal role."

The Court elaborated Gertz's narrow view of the "public figure" category in Time, Inc. v. Firestone, 424 U.S. 448 (1976). There, Time had erroneously reported that Ms. Firestone's divorce had been granted on grounds of adultery as well as extreme cruelty. The Court found that Firestone was not a "public figure" because she had not assumed "any role of especial prominence in the affairs of society, other than perhaps Palm Beach society," and because she had not "thrust herself to the forefront of any particular public controversy." Accordingly, she was not a person who had "voluntarily exposed [herself] to increased risk of injury from defamatory falsehoods. [Gertz.]"

Two 1979 decisions evidenced the Court's continuing determination to view the "public figure" category narrowly. Hutchinson v. Proxmire, 443 U.S. 111 (1979), was a defamation suit by a scientist whose federally funded research on monkey behavior had been characterized by the defendant Senator as an egregious example of wasteful government spending. As in Firestone, the majority opinion emphasized that the plaintiff had not "thrust himself or his views into public controversy to influence others." And in Wolston v. Reader's Digest Ass'n, Inc., 443 U.S. 157 (1979), Wolston sued for libel because a 1974 book had listed him as a "Soviet agent." Wolston had been in the public eye briefly in 1958, after a criminal contempt conviction for failure to appear before a grand jury investigating Soviet espionage. The majority emphasized that Wolston had not "voluntarily thrust" or "injected" himself into the controversy: "We decline to hold that his mere citation for contempt rendered him a public figure for purposes of comment on the investigation of Soviet espionage."

9. Justice BLACKMUN, a member of the Rosenbloom plurality, explained in a brief notation that he thought the Rosenbloom rule more logical than the new approach, but had decided to vote with Justice Powell "to create a majority": "A definitive ruling [is] paramount."

that the New York Times rule itself was justifiable because "seditious libel—criticism of government and public officials—falls beyond the police power of the State." But traditional standards of liability and the authorization of punitive as well as general damages should be permitted to stand when private citizens were defamed. He argued that experience showed "that some publications are so inherently capable of injury, and actual injury so difficult to prove, that the risk of falsehood should be borne by the publisher, not the victim."[10]

3. INVASIONS OF PRIVACY AND THE NEW YORK TIMES RULE

1. *The Time, Inc. v. Hill decision.* The New York Times rule was developed as a limited barrier to defamation actions, designed to vindicate the plaintiff's interest in reputation. Should it also shield against liability when the plaintiff seeks to vindicate an interest in privacy rather than reputation? "True" privacy actions, though widely discussed, are relatively rare: in those actions, the plaintiff does not claim falsity, but rather that *true* disclosures about the plaintiff's personal life are embarrassing invasions of privacy, not newsworthy, and subject to liability.[1] More common are "false light" privacy cases, where the claim is

---

10. Justice DOUGLAS' dissent came from the opposite direction: he continued to insist that the First Amendment barred all libel suits "for public discussion of public issues." Chief Justice BURGER also submitted a dissent.

Contrast with Justice White's position (that New York Times and its progeny had curtailed defamation actions unduly "for the benefit of the news media") the mounting criticism from the other side of the spectrum. The latter criticism maintains that, given the ease with which even actions subject to the New York Times standard can get to the jury and the time and cost of litigation, the standard is unduly burdensome to the media. Moreover, this criticism asserts that defamation actions, especially by major public figures, unduly move the forum of public debate from the political marketplace to the courtroom and permit the use of libel actions claiming enormous damages to "chill" criticism by the media. The lengthy trial of General Westmoreland's claim against CBS (and General Sharon's suit against Time) have been special spurs to this variety of criticism in 1985.

On the Court's reluctance to impose barriers to jury consideration of libel cases, note Hutchinson v. Proxmire (1979; footnote 8 above). There, the trial court had stated that in determining whether a plaintiff had made an adequate showing of "actual malice," summary judgment might well be the rule rather than the exception. But a comment in Chief Justice Burger's majority opinion rejected that suggestion: "[We] are constrained to express some doubt about the so-called 'rule.' The proof of 'actual malice' calls a defendant's state of mind into question, and does not readily lend itself to summary disposition." (Note, however, Bose Corp. v. Consumers Union, 466 U.S. — (1984), emphasizing that findings that statements were made with "malice" must be independently reexamined on appeal to determine whether the evidence established "malice" with convincing clarity.)

The Chief Justice's response in Proxmire is typical of the Court's general unwillingness to modify procedural rules in the interest of the First Amendment in the New York Times line of cases. Herbert v. Lando (1979; footnote 3 above) similarly suggests that New York Times and its progeny themselves provide, in their substantive rules, the appropriate degree of accommodation of First Amendment interests, making unnecessary any First Amendment modifications of procedural rules. See also Calder v. Jones, 465 U.S. — (1984), a unanimous ruling that due process principles regulating the exercise of personal jurisdiction will not be modified in actions for defamation against media defendants: "[The] potential chill on protected First Amendment activity stemming from libel and defamation actions is already taken into account in the constitutional limitations on the substantive law governing such suits. To reintroduce those concerns at the jurisdictional stage would be a form of double counting."

In light of the recent claimed abuses of defamation actions against the media, is adequate regard for First Amendment interests truly assured by the Court's primary concern with substantive rules of liability—and by its willingness, in this as in other areas, to engage in an independent review of the factual findings below in order to assure that protective material is not penalized (see Bose Corp. v. Consumers Union, above)? Or should the Court be more ready to modify procedural rules to protect defamation defendants, and to review damages for possible excessiveness?

1. See the much-discussed article by Warren and Brandeis, "The Right to Privacy," 4 Harv.L. Rev. 193 (1890). Compare Prosser, "Privacy," 48 Calif.L.Rev. 383 (1960). (For situations where the media are sued for reporting true matters, but on grounds other than invasion of privacy, see the Zacchini and Cox Broadcasting cases, below.)

that the disclosure not only invaded privacy but was also false—though not necessarily injurious to reputation, the gist of defamation actions. The decision in TIME, INC. v. HILL, 385 U.S. 374 (1967), focused primarily on "false light" privacy actions, and the result from a divided Court was that the New York Times standard should be applicable to such actions. (Does Hill survive Gertz? See the additional comments below.)

The Hill suit against Time, Inc., was based on a New York "right of privacy" statute generally prohibiting anyone from using "for advertising purposes, or for the purposes of trade, the name, portrait or picture of any living person without having first obtained the written consent of such person." Under the statute, truth was a defense in actions "based upon newsworthy people or events," but a "newsworthy person" could recover when he or she was the subject of a "fictitious" report—a report involving "material and substantial falsification." Justice BRENNAN's "opinion of the Court" concluded that "the constitutional protections for speech and press preclude the application of the New York statute to redress false reports of matters of public interest in the absence of proof that the defendant published the report with knowledge of its falsity or in reckless disregard of the truth." [2] Moreover, Justice Brennan went on to indicate in a much-debated dictum that "newsworthiness" would offer similar protection even in a "true" privacy action. [3]

2. *Some comments.* Does the Hill principle (announced in 1967) survive the Court's retreat in Gertz (the 1974 decision above) from Justice Brennan's position that the New York Times principle applies to all "newsworthy" matters? Is the extension of New York Times to the Hill situation persuasive? Does Hill move well beyond the seditious libel-political speech emphasis that was seen as the "central meaning" of the First Amendment in the New York Times case? Nimmer criticized the Court for failing to "pierce the superficial similarity between false light invasion of privacy and defamation" and urged that disclosure of nondefamatory matters interfering with privacy not be afforded First Amendment protection. He noted, for example, that, unlike

2. The Hill suit arose from the following circumstances: In 1952, the Hill family had been held hostage by three escaped convicts for 19 hours but was released unharmed. Three years later, a play portrayed the incident as involving considerable violence, though in fact there had been none. Life magazine's story on the play posed the actors in the original Hill home and indicated that the play accurately portrayed the actual incident. The original incident had been widely reported, but the Hills had tried to stay out of the public eye thereafter. Though the Life magazine report that was the subject of the action did not substantially damage the Hills' reputation—they were portrayed as courageous —, they ultimately recovered a $30,000 judgment under the New York privacy law.

3. For still another interest put forth as justifying imposition of liability on the media, see Zacchini v. Scripps-Howard Broadcasting Co., 433 U.S. 562 (1977). That suit was based on the plaintiff's "right of publicity" rather than any interest in privacy or in reputation. The Court distinguished Time and held that the First Amendment does not "immunize the media [from liability for damages] when they broadcast a performer's entire act without his consent." Zacchini performed a "human cannonball" act in which he was shot from a cannon into a net some 200 feet away. The defendant filmed Zacchini's

performance at a county fair and showed the entire 15-second act on a television news program. In allowing recovery, Justice White emphasized that the Court in Hill "was aware that it was adjudicating a 'false light' privacy case, [not] a case involving 'intrusion'" or "private details" about a nonnewsworthy person. And neither did Hill involve a claim of a "right of publicity" as here; this kind of claim was a "discrete kind of 'appropriation.'" Unlike "false light" cases designed to protect the interest in reputation, suits such as this one rested on the state interest "in protecting the proprietary interest of the individual in his act in part to encourage such entertainment," an interest "closely analogous to those of patent and copyright law." Moreover, a "right of publicity" case did not significantly intrude on dissemination of information to the public: "the only question is who gets to do the publishing." Accordingly, Justice White found the performer's claim a strong one, and the media arguments weak. By contrast, Justice Powell's dissent, joined by Justices Brennan and Marshall, concluded that "the First Amendment protects the station from a 'right of publicity' or 'appropriation' suit, absent a strong showing by the plaintiff that the news broadcast was a subterfuge or a cover for private or commercial exploitation."

"injury arising from defamation, 'more speech' is irrelevant in mitigating the injury due to an invasion of privacy." [4] Does the Hill approach afford too much immunity to the press, without adequate regard to competing interests? The Court has not yet confronted a "true" privacy case involving materials not a matter of public record. Cf. Cox Broadcasting, which follows.

3. *Cox Broadcasting.* A "true" privacy case did reach the Court in COX BROADCASTING CORP. v. COHN, 420 U.S. 469 (1975), but the decision did not reach the question of whether Hill and its dictum had survived Gertz. The Court merely held that civil liability in a "true" privacy action could not be imposed upon a broadcaster for truthfully publishing information released to the public in official court records.[5] However, the Court recognized that a plaintiff's interest in a "true" privacy case was an especially strong one. Moreover, the opinions revealed disagreement on the Court about the implications of Gertz in the defamation context. Justice WHITE's opinion for the Court commented: "In this sphere of collision between claims of privacy and those of the free press, the interests on both sides are plainly rooted in the traditions and significant concerns of our society." But he found it unnecessary to decide "the broader question whether truthful publication may ever be subjected to civil or criminal liability," or "whether the State may ever define and protect an area of privacy free from unwanted publicity in the press." Moreover, he recognized the "impressive credentials for a right of privacy." In addition, he claimed that earlier cases had "carefully left open the question" whether the Constitution requires "that truth be recognized as a defense in a defamation action brought by a private person," as well as "the question whether truthful publication of very private matters unrelated to public affairs could be constitutionally proscribed." [6]

C. OBSCENITY AND OTHER VARIETIES OF OFFENSIVE OR INDECENT COMMUNICATION

Introduction. This subsection pursues two additional themes raised by Justice Murphy's 1942 statement in Chaplinsky (sec. 2A above). First, recall that the Court there categorized obscenity, like libel and "fighting words," as expressions outside of First Amendment protection. Second, Justice Murphy's definition of "fighting words" covered not only words that "tend to incite an immediate breach of the peace" but also words "which by their very utterance inflict injury." The justification for restraint in the latter category does not rest primarily on an interest in averting violence and disorder. Rather, the apparent interest justifying restraint is that in protecting the sensibilities of the audience from shock (or, more broadly, protecting the moral standards of the communi-

---

4. See Nimmer, "The Right to Speak From Times to Time: First Amendment Theory Applied to Libel and Misapplied to Privacy," 56 Calif.L.Rev. 935 (1968). See also Kalven, "The Reasonable Man and the First Amendment: Hill, Butts, and Walker," 1967 Sup.Ct.Rev. 267, suggesting that "the logic of New York Times and Hill taken together grants the press some measure of constitutional protection for anything the press thinks is a matter of public interest."

5. In Cox, a father had sued because of the broadcasting of the fact that his daughter had been a rape victim. Barring liability, the Court relied especially on "the public interest in a vigorous press."

6. A concurring opinion by Justice POWELL disagreed with that reading of prior decisions. He insisted that "the constitutional necessity of recognizing a defense of truth" in defamation actions by private plaintiffs was "implicit" in Gertz and other cases. He noted, however, that "causes of action grounded in a State's desire to protect privacy generally implicate interests that are distinct from those protected by defamation actions." He commented, moreover, that Gertz "calls into question the conceptual basis of Time, Inc. v. Hill."

ty). The concern with shock to the audience raises a general problem of permissible restraints on offensive or indecent speech. Sec. 2C1 focuses on the problem of restraining obscenity or pornography. Sec. 2C2 deals with the Court's encounters with questions of offensiveness and indecency. As before, a major concern here is the Court's methodology. With respect to obscenity, sec. 2C1 reveals that the categorization approach of Chaplinsky still carries considerable weight, although in the modern cases, unlike the earlier ones, the Court has articulated the state interests justifying restraint. In its treatment of offensiveness and indecency, by contrast, the Court's analysis does not adhere to the conclusory, broad categorization approach of Chaplinsky. Instead, as the materials in sec. 2C2 illustrate, an approach much more resembling explicit balancing (with a far greater protection of speech) has predominated. What explains the different analyses, and the differing protections of speech? Note that the Court has protected speech concerning sex—speech offending cultural sensibilities— less than speech used in situations where what might otherwise be sexually offensive words or images are used in a clearly political context. These materials, then, provide another opportunity to compare the relative merits of categorization and balancing.

---

1. OBSCENITY AND PORNOGRAPHY: WHAT JUSTIFIES RESTRAINTS?

Introduction. The Court's first direct encounter with the constitutionality of obscenity control did not come until 15 years after Chaplinsky, in Roth, which follows. Roth, even while reasserting that obscenity is not "speech" and thereby theoretically casting it outside the First Amendment ballpark, made clear that the regulation of obscenity *can* raise First Amendment issues. But it set about doing so by focusing on the proper constitutional definition of obscenity—the proper delineation of the area excluded from constitutional protection, the proper determination of boundaries—so that constitutionally protected speech would not be infringed. The flood of divided rulings and groping opinions in the wake of Roth made obscenity control one of the most troublesome areas of First Amendment litigation.[1]

For nearly two decades after Roth, the obscenity opinions—plausibly, in light of Roth's categorization approach—dealt mainly with the definition of obscenity and rarely hinted at the reasons justifying its prohibition. Typically, the Court did not address the question central in other areas of First Amendment law: "What state interests justify restraint?" Does that course of decision suggest that the categorization approach too readily obscures the typical First Amendment analysis that involves identification of speech ingredients and articulation of state interests? After a tortuous course of decisions in the post-Roth years, a new definition of obscenity was agreed upon at last in 1973, in Miller and Paris, p. 1076 below. In one sense, these Burger Court decisions are in the tradition of Roth, though they modified the ingredients of obscenity. But the majority opinions in the 1973 cases at last confronted the question of what state interests justify the control of obscenity—and answered the question in a way that may cast shadows over other First Amendment areas. In those 1973 cases, moreover, Justice Brennan, the author of the Roth opinion and the

---

1. As Justice Harlan commented a little more than a decade after Roth: "The subject of obscenity has produced a variety of views among the members of the Court unmatched in any other course of constitutional adjudication. [In] the 13 obscenity cases [since Roth] in which signed opinions were written [as of 1968], [there] has been a total of 55 separate opinions among the Justices." Ginsberg v. New York, 390 U.S. 629 (1968).

Court's leading voice on obscenity in ensuing years, turned his back on the Roth approach.[2] This group of materials does not trace all of the Court's difficult and divided struggles with the obscenity problem in the years between Roth and the Burger Court's 1973 rulings. The focus here is on the search for the interests allegedly justifying obscenity control, on the appropriate weight of those interests, on the First Amendment values that may justify at least some protection of obscenity, as well as on the definition of obscenity. Obscenity may well be a relatively "foolish and trivial problem"[3] in the universe of free speech concerns; yet the Court's struggles with it have been so continuous and extensive that they warrant attention, particularly for the light they throw—or shadows they cast—on the development of a coherent body of First Amendment analysis.

In examining the materials that follow, then, consider especially (a) what objectives may justify obscenity regulation, and (b) which, if any, First Amendment values may justify some protection for obscenity. As to relevant state interests: Which objectives are identified by the Court? What additional ones may be implicit in the various opinions? To protect society's moral standards against erosion?[4] To preserve or improve "the quality of life" and "a decent community environment"?[5] To promote equality values barring sex discrimination, by curbing materials that contribute to the subordination of women (by analogy to the group libel theme in Beauharnais) and by banning stimuli that may encourage sexual harassment?[6] To avoid the "corrupting" of individual morals and character by the "sin of obscenity"[7]—whether or not improper behavior results? To safeguard against the stimulation of (incitement of? creating a clear and present danger of?) illegal or improper behavior? To protect the sensibilities of the audience by safeguarding against the risk of shock from offensive obscene materials?[8] To protect children against exposure to obscene materials, because of the alleged greater susceptibility of the immature to the harmful effects of obscenity?[9]

Questions such as these assume that obscenity may belong in the First Amendment ballpark, thus triggering a requirement of some justification. But

2. As Justice Brennan stated in his Paris dissent (p. 1079 below): "I am convinced that [the Roth approach] cannot bring stability to this area of the law without jeopardizing fundamental First Amendment values, and I have concluded that the time has come to make a significant departure from that approach." Justices Stewart and Marshall joined that dissent. (After Justice Stevens joined the Court in 1975, he, too, voiced disagreement with the 1973 majority's approach. See p. 1087 below.)

3. The phrase is the late Harry Kalven's, in a comment regretting the 1973 decisions as indicating that the problem "will be with us for some time to come." Kalven, "A Step Backward," Chicago Tribune, Aug. 31, 1973. See also his earlier piece, Kalven, "The Metaphysics of the Law of Obscenity," 1960 Sup.Ct.Rev. 1, one of the best of the many commentaries on the Roth era obscenity decisions. That article contains a thoughtful criticism of the "two-level speech theory" which Kalven saw reflected in Beauharnais as well as Roth. He viewed that approach as "a strained effort to trap a problem." As he described the approach, it first required determination of whether the communication belonged in "a category that has any social utility." If it did not, "it may be banned." "If it does, there is a further question of measuring the clarity and

proximity and gravity of any danger from it." (Is a concern with the second question really clear on the face of Beauharnais or Roth?)

4. As several of the questions in this paragraph suggest, the problems about potentially relevant state interests regarding obscenity echo themes raised elsewhere in these materials. Recall, e.g., chap. 8, on society's interest in maintaining standards of morality (in the context of claims to personal autonomy as in the abortion cases); and recall especially Justice Harlan's dissent in Poe v. Ullman, printed with the contraception decision, Griswold v. Connecticut (p. 503 above).

5. See e.g., Bickel's comment, quoted in the majority opinion in Paris, p. 1079 below.

6. See the modern advocacy of ordinances defended on those grounds—especially the consideration of the Indianapolis ordinance at p. 1097 below.

7. See Henkin, "Morals and the Constitution: The Sin of Obscenity," 63 Colum.L.Rev. 391 (1963).

8. Regarding the appropriate degree of concern with the sensibilities of the audience, see the "offensiveness" cases in sec. 2C2 below.

9. See, e.g., the Pacifica case, p. 1114 below.

is obscenity properly considered a variety of "speech"? Or does its restriction warrant only very deferential scrutiny, or none at all? (Recall Beauharnais.) Which if any of the values underlying First Amendment protection, surveyed in the introduction to this chapter, justify the imposition of any scrutiny at all? The arguments from self-government and democracy seem largely directed at political speech. The arguments from the marketplace of ideas and the search for truth are broader and seem to include scientific debate as well. But do they also extend to artistic and literary communication? Note that the Court's definitions of obscenity in the cases that follow exclude materials of certain "literary, artistic, political, or scientific value" and that the obscenity category typically focuses on hard-core pornography. Can such materials nevertheless claim First Amendment protection? Most of the arguments of that variety stem from the autonomy, self-realization rationale for protecting speech.[10] Contrast Schauer's argument (more fully considered at p. 1089 below, after the 1963 cases) that inclusion of obscenity within "speech" is not justified by any other rationale underlying the First Amendment, and emphasizing that hardcore pornography is "designed to produce a purely physical effect" rather than an appeal to the intellectual process, thus resembling more "the characteristics of sexual activity than of the communicative process."[11]

---

10. See especially the writings of David Richards—e.g., "Free Speech and Obscenity Law: Toward a Moral Theory of the First Amendment," 123 U.Pa.L.Rev. 45 (1974)—emphasizing that the First Amendment rests on "the moral liberties of expression, conscience and thought," "liberties [that] are fundamental conditions of the integrity and competence of a person in mastering his life and expressing this mastery to others." Richards adds: "There is no reason whatsoever to believe that the freedom to determine the sexual contents of one's communications or to be an audience to such communications is not as fundamental to this self mastery as the freedom to decide upon any other communicative contents." Cf. Stanley v. Georgia (1969; p. 1073 below), affording constitutional protection to the *private possession* of pornography.

11. This subsection is limited to the substantive concerns regarding obscenity control. The concern with obscenity has also been a prolific source of litigation about the *methods* of regulation, particularly in the context of licensing and censorship of motion pictures. Consideration of procedural issues pertaining to obscenity control is postponed to later chapters. See, e.g., the discussion of prior restraints at p. 1157 below.

Recall Schauer's emphasis, in his Free Speech: A Philosophical Enquiry (1982), on skepticism about governmental ability to distinguish between permissible and impermissible speech as an independent, "negative justification" for the protection of speech (see p. 979 above). Schauer states: "Even if there is nothing especially good about speech compared to other conduct, the state may have less ability to regulate speech than it has to regulate other forms of conduct, or the attempt to regulate speech may entail special harms or special dangers not present in regulation of other conduct. [Throughout] history the process of regulating speech has been marked with what we now see to be fairly plain errors"—including "the banning of numerous admittedly great works of art because someone thought them obscene." He adds that "acts of suppression that have been proved erroneous seem to represent a disproportionate percentage of the governmental mistakes of the past. [Experience] arguably shows that governments are particularly bad at censorship." He concludes there, as noted earlier: "Freedom of speech is based in large part on a distrust of the ability of government to make the necessary distinctions, a distrust of governmental determinations of truth and falsity, an appreciation the fallibility of political leaders, and of somewhat deeper distrust of governmental power in a more general sense. [Accordingly], the power of government to regulate speech should, for a number of reasons, be more limited than are its powers in other areas of governance." He adds that "the most persuasive argument for a Free Speech Principle is what may be characterized as the argument from governmental incompetence." Does that "argument from governmental incompetence" provide an added, independent reason not to exclude obscenity from the First Amendment ballpark?

THE WARREN COURT AND OBSCENITY

ROTH v. UNITED STATES
ALBERTS v. CALIFORNIA

354 U.S. 476, 77 S.Ct. 1304, 1 L.Ed.2d 1498 (1957).

[In these cases, the Court sustained the validity of federal and state obscenity laws without reaching the question of whether any particular materials were obscene. Roth, a New York publisher and seller, was convicted of mailing obscene advertising and an obscene book in violation of the federal obscenity statute. Alberts, engaged in the mail order business, was convicted under a California law for "lewdly keeping for sale obscene and indecent books" and "publishing an obscene advertisement of them."]

Mr. Justice BRENNAN delivered the opinion of the [Court].

The dispositive question is whether obscenity is utterance within the area of protected speech and press.[1] Although this is the first time the question has been squarely presented [here], expressions found in numerous opinions indicate that this Court has always assumed that obscenity is not protected by the freedoms of speech and press. In light [of] history, it is apparent that the unconditional phrasing of the First Amendment was not intended to protect every utterance. [T]here is sufficiently contemporaneous evidence to show that obscenity [like libel, see Beauharnais] was outside the protection intended for speech and [press]. All ideas having even the slightest redeeming social importance—unorthodox ideas, controversial ideas, even ideas hateful to the prevailing climate of opinion—have the full protection of the guaranties, unless excludable because they encroach upon the limited area of more important interests. But implicit in the history of the First Amendment is the rejection of obscenity as utterly without redeeming social importance. This rejection for that reason is mirrored in the universal judgment that obscenity should be restrained, reflected in the international agreement of over 50 nations, in the obscenity laws of all of the 48 States, and in the 20 obscenity laws enacted by the Congress from 1842 to 1956. [We] hold that obscenity is not within the area of constitutionally protected speech or press.

It is strenuously urged that these obscenity statutes offend the constitutional guaranties because they punish incitation to impure sexual *thoughts,* not shown to be related to any overt antisocial conduct which is or may be incited in the persons stimulated to such *thoughts.* It is insisted that the constitutional guaranties are violated because convictions may be had without proof either that obscene material will perceptibly create a clear and present danger of antisocial conduct, or will probably induce its recipients to such conduct. But, in light of our holding that obscenity is not protected speech, the complete answer to this argument is in the holding [in Beauharnais].

However, sex and obscenity are not synonymous. Obscene material is material which deals with sex in a manner appealing to prurient interest.[2] The

1. No issue is presented in either case concerning the obscenity of the material involved. [Footnote by the Court.]

2. I.e., material having a tendency to excite lustful thoughts. Webster's New International Dictionary (Unabridged, 2d ed., 1949) defines *prurient,* in pertinent part, as follows: "Itching; longing; uneasy with desire or longing; of persons, having itching, morbid, or lascivious longings; of desire, curiosity or propensity, lewd."

[We] perceive no significant difference between the meaning of obscenity developed in the case law and the definition of the A.L.I., Model Penal Code (Tent.Draft No. 6, 1957): "[A] thing is obscene if, considered as a whole, its predominant appeal is to prurient interest, i.e., a shameful or morbid interest in nudity, sex, or excretion, and if it goes substantially beyond customary limits of candor in description or representation

portrayal of sex, e.g., in art, literature and scientific works, is not itself sufficient reason to deny material the constitutional protection of freedom of speech and press. [It] is therefore vital that the standards for judging obscenity safeguard the protection of freedom of speech and press for material which does not treat sex in a manner appealing to prurient interest.

The early leading standard of obscenity allowed material to be judged merely by the effect of an isolated excerpt upon particularly susceptible persons. Regina v. Hicklin, [1868] L.R. 3 Q.B. 360. Some American courts adopted this standard but later decisions have rejected it and substituted this test: whether to the average person, applying contemporary community standards, the dominant theme of the material taken as a whole appeals to prurient interest. The Hicklin test, judging obscenity by the effect of isolated passages upon the most susceptible persons, might well encompass material legitimately treating with sex, and so it must be rejected as unconstitutionally restrictive of the freedoms of speech and press. On the other hand, the substituted standard provides safeguards adequate to withstand the charge of constitutional infirmity. Both trial courts below sufficiently followed the proper [standard]. [W]e hold that these statutes, applied according to the proper standard for judging obscenity, do not offend constitutional safeguards against convictions based upon protected material, or fail to give men in acting adequate notice of what is [prohibited].

Affirmed.[3]

Mr. Justice HARLAN, concurring in the result in [Alberts] and dissenting in [Roth].

[My] basic difficulties with the Court's opinion are three-fold. First, the opinion paints with such a broad brush that I fear it may result in a loosening of the tight reins which state and federal courts should hold upon the enforcement of obscenity statutes. Second, the Court fails to discriminate between the different factors which, in my opinion, are involved in the constitutional adjudication of state and federal obscenity cases. Third, relevant distinctions between the two obscenity statutes here involved, and the Court's own definition of "obscenity," are ignored. [The] Court seems to assume that "obscenity" is a peculiar *genus* of "speech and press," which is as distinct, recognizable, and classifiable as poison ivy is among other plants. On this basis the *constitutional* question before us simply [becomes] whether "obscenity," as an abstraction, is protected by the [First Amendment], and the question whether a *particular* book may be suppressed becomes a mere matter of classification, of "fact," to be entrusted to a fact-finder and insulated from independent constitutional judgment. But surely the problem cannot be solved in such a generalized fashion. Every communication has an individuality and "value" of its own. The suppression of a particular writing or other tangible form of expression is, therefore, an *individual* matter, and in the nature of things every such suppression raises an individual constitutional problem, in which a reviewing court must determine for *itself* whether the attacked expression is suppressable within constitutional standards. [I] do not understand how the Court can resolve the constitutional problems now before it without making its own independent judgment upon the character of the material upon which these convictions were [based].

[T]he Court has not been bothered by the fact that the two cases involved different statutes. [The] two statutes do not seem to me to present the same

of such matters." [Footnote by Justice Brennan.]

3. Chief Justice WARREN concurred in the result, stating that the defendants were "engaged in the commercial exploitation of the morbid and shameful craving for materials with prurient effect. I believe that [government] can constitutionally punish such conduct. That is all [we] need to decide."

problems. Yet the Court compounds confusion when it superimposes on these two statutory definitions a third, drawn from the [ALI's] Model Penal Code. [The] bland assurance that this definition is the same as the ones with which we deal flies in the face of the authors' express rejection of the "depraved and corrupt" and "sexual thoughts" tests. [The Court] merely assimilates the various tests into one indiscriminate [potpourri].

I concur in [Alberts]. We can inquire only whether the state action so subverts the fundamental liberties implicit in the Due Process Clause that it cannot be sustained as a rational exercise of power. [T]he state legislature has made the judgment that printed words *can* "deprave or corrupt" the reader— that words can incite to antisocial or immoral action. [The] validity of this assumption is a matter of dispute among critics, sociologists, psychiatrists, and penologists. [I]t is not our function to decide this question. [It] seems to me clear that it is not irrational, in our present state of knowledge, to consider that pornography can induce a type of sexual conduct which a State may deem obnoxious to the moral fabric of society. [E]ven assuming that pornography cannot be deemed ever to cause, in an immediate sense, criminal sexual conduct, other interests within the proper cognizance of the States may be protected by the prohibition placed on such materials. The State can reasonably draw the inference that over a long period of time the indiscriminate dissemination of materials, the essential character of which is to degrade sex, will have an eroding effect on moral standards. And the State has a legitimate interest in protecting the privacy of the home against invasion of unsolicited obscenity. Above all stands the realization that we deal here with an area where knowledge is small, data are insufficient, and experts are divided. Since the domain of sexual morality is pre-eminently a matter of state concern, this Court should be slow to interfere with state legislation calculated to protect that morality. [That], however, does not dispose of the case. It still remains for us to decide whether the state court's determination that this material should be suppressed is consistent with the 14th Amendment; and that, of course, presents a federal question as to which we, and not the state court, have the ultimate responsibility. And so, in the final analysis, I concur in the judgment because, upon an independent perusal of the material involved, and in light of the considerations discussed above, I cannot say that its suppression would so interfere with the communication of "ideas" in any proper sense of that term that it would offend [due process].

I dissent in [Roth]. [The Roth question] is of quite a different order than one where we are dealing with state legislation under the 14th Amendment. [I]n every case where we are called upon to balance the interest in free expression against other interests, it seems to me important that we should keep in the forefront the question of whether those other interests are state or federal. [W]hether a particular limitation on speech or press is to be upheld because it subserves a paramount governmental interest must, to a large extent, I think, depend on whether that government has, under the Constitution, a direct substantive interest, that is, the power to act, in the particular area involved. [T]he interests which obscenity statutes purportedly protect are primarily entrusted to the care, not of the Federal Government, but of the States. Congress has no substantive power over sexual morality. Such powers as the Federal Government has in this field are but incidental to its other powers, here the [postal power].

I judge this case, then, in view of what I think is the attenuated federal interest in this field, in view of the very real danger of a deadening uniformity which can result from nation-wide federal censorship, and in view of the fact that the constitutionality of this conviction must be weighed against the First and not the 14th Amendment. So viewed, I do not think that this conviction can be upheld. [I] cannot agree that any book which tends to stir sexual impulses and lead to sexually impure thoughts necessarily is "utterly without redeeming social importance." [M]uch of the great literature of the world could lead to conviction under such a view of the statute. Moreover, in no event do I think that the limited federal interest in this area can extend to mere "thoughts." The Federal Government has no business, whether under the postal or commerce power, to bar the sale of books because they might lead to any kind of "thoughts." It is no answer to say, as the Court does, that obscenity is not protected speech. The point is that this statute, as here construed, defines obscenity so widely that it encompasses matters which might very well be protected speech. I do not think that the federal statute can be constitutionally construed to reach other than what the Government has termed as "hard-core" [pornography].

Mr. Justice DOUGLAS, with whom Mr. Justice BLACK concurs, dissenting.

When we sustain these convictions, we make the legality of a publication turn on the purity of thought which a book or tract instills in the mind of the reader. I do not think we can approve that standard and be faithful to the command of the First Amendment. [I] do not think that the problem can be resolved by the Court's statement that "obscenity is not expression protected by the First Amendment." With the exception of [Beauharnais], none of our cases has resolved problems of free speech and free press by placing any form of expression beyond the pale of the absolute prohibition of the First Amendment. [I] reject too the implication that problems of freedom of speech and of the press are to be resolved by weighing against the values of free expression, the judgment of the Court that a particular form of that expression has "no redeeming social importance." The First Amendment, its prohibition in terms absolute, was designed to preclude courts as well as legislatures from weighing the values of speech against [silence].

THE STRUGGLE TO DEFINE OBSCENITY IN THE YEARS AFTER ROTH

[The Court's tortured efforts to define prohibitable obscenity in the years after Roth were summarized in a dissenting opinion by Justice Brennan in one of the 1973 cases, Paris Adult Theatre I v. Slaton, 413 U.S. 49, 73. Justice Brennan's summary portrays the highlights—and reflects the Justices' sense of futility and malaise. Ironically, Justice Brennan was the Court's leading spokesman in the efforts at definition of obscenity, but was moved to conclude at last, in 1973, that the task was a hopeless one, as the additional excerpts from his dissent (p. 1082 below) elaborate. Justice Brennan's summary of the definitional search follows:]

[Our] efforts to implement [the Roth] approach demonstrate that agreement on the existence of something called "obscenity" is still a long and painful step from agreement on a workable definition of the term. [W]e have demanded that "sensitive tools" be used to carry out the "separation of legitimate from illegitimate speech." The essence of our problem in the obscenity area is that we have been unable to provide "sensitive tools" to separate obscenity from other sexually oriented but constitutionally protected speech, so that efforts to suppress the former do not spill over into the suppression of the [latter].

To be sure, five members of the Court did agree in Roth that obscenity could be determined by asking "whether to the average person, applying contemporary community standards, the dominant theme of the material taken as a whole appeals to prurient interest." But agreement on that test—achieved in the abstract and without reference to the particular material before the

Court—was, to say the least, short lived. By 1967 the following views had emerged: Mr. Justice Black and Mr. Justice Douglas consistently maintained that government is wholly powerless to regulate any sexually oriented matter on the ground of its obscenity. Mr. Justice Harlan, on the other hand, believed that the Federal Government in the exercise of its enumerated powers could control the distribution of "hard core" pornography, while the States were afforded more latitude to "[ban] any material which, taken as a whole, has been reasonably found in state judicial proceedings to treat with sex in a fundamentally offensive manner, under rationally established criteria for judging such material." Jacobellis v. Ohio, [378 U.S. 184 (1964)]. Mr. Justice Stewart regarded "hard core" pornography as the limit of both federal and state power. See, e.g., Ginzburg v. United States, 383 U.S. 463 (1966) (dissenting opinion); [Jacobellis] (concurring opinion.)[1]

The view that, until today, enjoyed the most, but not majority, support was an interpretation of Roth adopted by Mr. Chief Justice Warren, Mr. Justice Fortas, and the author of this opinion in Memoirs v. Massachusetts, 383 U.S. 413 (1966). We expressed the view that Federal or State Governments could control the distribution of material where "three [elements] coalesce: it must be established that (a) the dominant theme of the material taken as a whole appeals to a prurient interest in sex; (b) the material is patently offensive because it affronts contemporary community standards relating to the description or representation of sexual matters; and (c) the material is utterly without redeeming social value." Even this formulation, however, concealed differences of opinion.[2] Moreover, it did not provide a definition covering all situations.[3] Nor, finally, did it ever command a majority of the [Court].

In the face of this divergence of opinion the Court began the practice in Redrup v. New York, 386 U.S. 767 (1967), of per curiam reversals of convictions for the dissemination of materials that at least five members of the Court, applying their separate tests, deemed not to be obscene.[4] [Today, in Paris], a majority of the Court offers a slightly altered formulation of the basic Roth test, while leaving entirely unchanged the underlying approach. [W]e have failed to formulate a standard that sharply distinguishes protected from unprotected speech, and out of necessity, we have resorted to the Redrup approach, which resolves cases as between the parties, but offers only the most obscure guidance to legislation, adjudication by other courts, and primary conduct. By disposing of cases through summary reversal or denial of certiorari

---

1. Justice Stewart's concurrence in Jacobellis said of "hard-core pornography": "I shall not today attempt further to define the kinds of material I understand to be embraced within that shorthand description; and perhaps I could never succeed in intelligibly doing so. But I know it when I see it, and the motion picture involved in this case is not that." (Jacobellis involved a French film, "The Lovers.") Justice Stewart tried to elaborate that "definition" in his dissent in Ginzburg two years later, using a description in the Solicitor General's brief to explain "the kind of thing to which I have reference": "Such materials include photographs, both still and motion picture, with no pretense of artistic value, graphically depicting acts of sexual intercourse, including various acts of sodomy and sadism, and sometimes involving several participants in scenes of orgy-like character. They also include strips of drawings in comic-book format grossly depicting similar activities in an exaggerated fashion. There are, in addition, pamphlets and booklets, sometimes with photographic illustrations, ver-

bally describing such activities in a bizarre manner with no attempt whatsoever to afford portrayals of character or situation and with no pretense to literary value."

2. In supporting this statement, Justice Brennan noted: "Compare Jacobellis v. Ohio, supra, at 192–195 (Brennan, J., joined by Goldberg, J.) (community standards national), with id., at 200–201 (Warren, C.J., joined by Clark, J., dissenting) (community standards local)."

3. In supporting this comment, Justice Brennan stated: "See Mishkin v. New York, 383 U.S. 502 (1966) (prurient appeal defined in terms of a deviant sexual group); Ginzburg v. United States, supra ('pandering' probative evidence of obscenity in close cases). See also Ginsberg v. New York, 390 U.S. 629 (1968) (obscenity for juveniles)."

4. No fewer than 31 cases have been disposed of in this fashion. [Footnote by Justice Brennan.]

we have deliberately and effectively obscured the rationale underlying the decisions. It comes as no surprise that judicial attempts to follow our lead conscientiously have often ended in hopeless [confusion].

THE EFFORTS TO ARTICULATE THE JUSTIFICATIONS FOR OBSCENITY CONTROL IN THE YEARS AFTER ROTH

Most of the cases after Roth were conspicuously silent about the interests thought to justify control of obscenity: the preoccupation was almost entirely with definition. But some articulations of justifications did occasionally surface. An early and rare example was Kingsley Pictures, note 1 below: it did not deal directly with an obscenity law; but its examination of "immorality" concerns bore at least a tangential relation to the obscenity area. Finally, in 1969, in Stanley v. Georgia (protecting the possession of obscenity, note 2 below), state justifications were explicitly discussed. But the expectations of some that Stanley would be the precursor of a new approach to the distribution of obscene materials were cut short by Reidel two years later (note 3 below). Justifications for obscenity control were considered at length in the Report of the Commission on Obscenity and Pornography (1970) (note 4 below). Its conclusions were similar to those reached by some of the dissenters in 1973: it urged that obscenity restraints be limited to displays offensive to unwilling adults and to the protection of children.

1. *Kingsley Pictures and sexual immorality.* One case in the post-Roth years—though not dealing directly with "obscenity" (and perhaps *because* it was not an "obscenity" case)—spoke more explicitly than most about the justifications for state regulations of expression pertaining to sex. KINGSLEY INT'L PICTURES CORP. v. REGENTS, 360 U.S. 684 (1959), invalidated a New York motion picture licensing law. The law banned any "immoral" film, defined as a film that "portrays acts of sexual immorality [or] which expressly or impliedly presents such acts as desirable, acceptable, or proper patterns of behavior." The state denied a license to the film "Lady Chatterley's Lover" under this law because "its subject matter is adultery presented as being right and desirable for certain people under certain circumstances." The Court reversed. Justice STEWART's opinion emphasized that "sexual immorality" under the New York scheme was "entirely different from" concepts like "obscenity" or "pornography," and that New York had not claimed that "the film would itself operate as an incitement to illegal action." He concluded that the state had prevented the exhibition of the film "because that picture advocates an idea—that adultery under certain circumstances may be proper behavior. Yet the First Amendment's basic guarantee is of freedom to advocate ideas. The State, quite simply, has thus struck at the very heart of constitutionally protected liberty. [The constitutional] guarantee is not confined to the expression of ideas that are conventional or shared by a majority. It protects advocacy of the opinion that adultery may sometimes be proper, no less than advocacy of socialism or the single tax."

2. *Stanley and possession of obscene materials.* In STANLEY v. GEORGIA, 394 U.S. 557 (1969), the Court reversed a conviction for knowing "possession of obscene matter," holding that the First Amendment prohibits "making the private possession of obscene material a crime." Justice MARSHALL's opinion, in striking contrast to the approach of the earlier obscenity cases, systematically canvassed the asserted state justifications. Some read Stanley as presaging a new era of greater restraints on laws governing the distribution of obscenity. But in Reidel, which follows, the Court made clear that Stanley would not be read as

undercutting the reign of Roth.[1] In Stanley, a search of a home for bookmaking evidence had uncovered obscene films. Georgia defended its law on the basis of Roth and with the argument: "If the State can protect the body of the citizen, may it [not] protect his mind?" Justice Marshall replied: "[The constitutional] right to receive information and ideas, regardless of their social worth, [is] fundamental to our free society. Moreover, in the context of this case—a prosecution for mere possession [in] the privacy of a person's own home—that right takes on an added dimension. For also fundamental is the right to be free, except in very limited circumstances, from unwanted governmental intrusions into one's privacy. [W]e think that mere categorization of these films as 'obscene' is insufficient justification for such a drastic invasion of personal liberties guaranteed by the [First Amendment]. Whatever may be the justifications for other statutes regulating obscenity, we do not think they reach into the privacy of one's own home. If the First Amendment means anything, it means that a State has no business telling a man, sitting alone in his own house, what books he may read or what films he may watch.

"[Y]et in the face of these traditional notions of individual liberty, Georgia asserts the right to protect the individual's mind from the effects of obscenity. We are not certain that this argument amounts to anything more than the assertion that the State has the right to control the moral content of a person's thoughts.[2] To some, this may be a noble purpose, but it is wholly inconsistent with the philosophy of the First Amendment. [Kingsley Pictures.] Whatever the power of the state to control public dissemination of ideas inimical to the public morality, it cannot constitutionally premise legislation on the desirability of controlling a person's private thoughts. Perhaps recognizing this, Georgia asserts that exposure to obscenity may lead to deviant sexual behavior or crimes of sexual violence. [Given] the present state of knowledge, the State may no more prohibit mere possession of [obscenity] on the ground that it may lead to antisocial conduct than it may prohibit possession of chemistry books on the ground that they may lead to the manufacture of homemade spirits. It is true that in Roth this Court rejected the necessity of proving that exposure to obscene material would create a clear and present danger of antisocial conduct or would probably induce its recipients to such conduct. But that case dealt with public distribution of obscene materials and such distribution is subject to different objections. For example, there is always the danger that obscene material might fall into the hands of children or that it might intrude upon the sensibilities or privacy of the general public. No such dangers are present in this case. Finally, we are faced with the argument that prohibition of possession of [obscenity] is a necessary incident to statutory schemes prohibiting distribution. That argument is based on alleged difficulties of proving an intent to distribute or in producing evidence of actual distribution. We are not convinced that such difficulties exist, but even if they did we do not think that they would justify infringement of the individual's right to read or observe what he pleases. Because that right is so fundamental to our scheme of individual liberty, its restriction may not be justified by the need to ease the administration of otherwise valid criminal laws."[3]

1. Stanley had noted privacy as well as First Amendment interests; in Reidel, the privacy interests were emphasized as the dominant if not exclusive ones explaining the result in Stanley.

2. " 'Communities believe, and act on the belief, that obscenity is immoral, is wrong for the individual, and has no place in a decent society. They believe, too, that adults as well as children are corruptible in morals and character, and that obscenity is a source of corruption that should be eliminated. Obscenity is not suppressed primari-

ly for the protection of others. Much of it is suppressed for the purity of the community and for the salvation and welfare of the "consumer." Obscenity, at bottom, is not crime. Obscenity is sin.' Henkin, Morals and the Constitution: The Sin of Obscenity, 63 Colum.L.Rev. 391, 395 (1963)." [Footnote by Justice Marshall.]

3. Despite his concern with the evaluation of asserted state interests, Justice Marshall concluded his opinion by stating that the Roth line of cases was "not impaired" by Stanley. Justice

3. *Reidel: Roth survives Stanley.* Two years after Stanley, the Court made clear (over the objections of the author of Stanley) that lower courts had been wrong in finding reasons in Stanley to question the validity of obscenity *distribution* laws. In UNITED STATES v. REIDEL, 402 U.S. 351 (1971), a District Court had relied on Stanley to dismiss an indictment under the federal law prohibiting the mailing of obscene materials—the law involved in Roth. The lower court had reasoned that "if a person has the right to receive and possess this material, then someone must have the right to deliver it to him," and had concluded that the federal prohibition could not be applied "where obscene material is not directed at children, or it is not directed at an unwilling public, where the material such as this case is solicited by adults." Justice WHITE's majority opinion gave short shrift to that argument: "To extrapolate from Stanley's right to have and peruse obscene material in the privacy of his own home a First Amendment right in Reidel to sell it to him would effectively scuttle Roth, the precise result that the Stanley opinion abjured." As the Reidel Court read Stanley, its "focus" was "on freedom of mind and thought and on the privacy of one's home." Reidel could not claim infringement of those rights. "Roth has squarely placed obscenity and its distribution outside the reach of the First Amendment and they remain there today. Stanley did not overrule [Roth]."

Justice MARSHALL's separate opinion in Reidel disagreed strongly with Justice White's narrow reading of Stanley. He insisted that "Stanley turned on an assessment of which state interests may legitimately underpin governmental action." Stanley merely approved "regulatory action taken to protect children and unwilling adults from exposure to materials deemed to be obscene." But Stanley, he maintained, made an "assessment of state interests" approach appropriate for distribution cases as well. Applying that approach, Justice Marshall concurred in Reidel. Mail distribution "poses the danger that obscenity will be sent to children"; though Reidel himself planned to sell only to adults who requested his materials, "the sole safeguard designed to prevent the receipt of his merchandise by minors was his requirement that buyers declare their age." He accordingly concluded "that distributors of purportedly obscene merchandise may be required to take more stringent steps to guard against possible receipt by minors."

4. *The Obscenity Commission's Report, 1970.* One other major consideration of the interests justifying obscenity control should be noted before turning to the Court's major reexamination of the obscenity problem in 1973. The U.S. Commission on Obscenity and Pornography was established by Congress in 1967. Its Report, submitted in 1970, rested in part on empirical studies of the impact of sexual literature. It concluded, for example, that patterns of sexual behavior were "not altered substantially by exposure to erotica"; that the available data did not demonstrate that "erotic material is a significant cause of sex crime"; and that exposure to erotica has "little or no effect" on attitudes regarding sexuality or sexual morality.[4] The Commission majority's legislative

STEWART, joined by Justices Brennan and White, concurred only in the result, on the ground that the films were seized in violation of the Fourth Amendment; they accordingly did not reach the issue of the validity of the obscenity possession law.

Four years later, in his dissent in Paris (p. 1082 below), Justice Brennan announced his delayed adherence to the Stanley approach, although he ultimately rested his dissent on somewhat different grounds. He commented: "[I]f a person has the right to receive information without regard to its social worth, [then] it would

seem to follow that a State could not constitutionally punish one who undertakes to provide this information to a *willing, adult recipient.*"

4. The scope and quality of the Commission's empirical studies have been criticized. Did the empirical studies ask the right questions? Are all of the interests allegedly justifying obscenity control susceptible to empirical studies? See generally Sunderland, Obscenity—The Court, the Congress and the President's Commission (Amer. Enterprise Inst., 1975), summarizing some of the criticisms. Note, e.g., his comment: "The complexities and subtleties of human sexuality within

recommendations included one urging that laws "prohibiting the sale, exhibition, or distribution of sexual materials to consenting adults should be repealed." The Commission also recommended the adoption of state laws "prohibiting the commercial distribution or display for sale of certain sexual materials to young persons," as well as laws "prohibiting public displays of sexually explicit pictorial materials." [5]

THE BURGER COURT AND OBSCENITY

MILLER v. CALIFORNIA

413 U.S. 15, 93 S.Ct. 2607, 37 L.Ed.2d 419 (1973).

Mr. Chief Justice BURGER delivered the opinion of the Court.

This is one of a group of "obscenity-pornography" cases being reviewed [in] a re-examination of standards enunciated in earlier cases involving what Mr. Justice Harlan called "the intractable obscenity problem." [1] [This] case involves the application of a State's criminal obscenity statute to a situation in which sexually explicit materials have been thrust by aggressive sales action upon unwilling recipients who had in no way indicated any desire to receive such materials. This Court has recognized that the States have a legitimate interest in prohibiting dissemination or exhibition of obscene material when the mode of dissemination carries with it a significant danger of offending the sensibilities of unwilling recipients or of exposure to juveniles. [Stanley.] It is in this context that we are called on to define the standards which must be used to identify obscene material that a State may regulate.

[Justice Brennan's dissent] reviews the background of the obscenity problem, but since the Court now undertakes to formulate standards more concrete than those in the past, it is useful for us to focus on two of the landmark cases in the somewhat tortured history of the Court's obscenity decisions. [While] Roth presumed "obscenity" to be "utterly without redeeming social value," [Memoirs v. Massachusetts, 383 U.S. 413 (1966)] required that to prove obscenity it must be affirmatively established that the material is *utterly* without redeeming social value." Thus, even as they repeated the words of Roth, the Memoirs plurality produced a drastically altered test that called on the prosecution to prove a negative, i.e., that the material was *utterly* without redeeming social value"—a burden virtually impossible to discharge. [Apart] from the initial formulation in [Roth], no majority of the Court has at any given time been able to agree on a standard to determine what constitutes obscene, pornographic material subject to regulation under the States' police power.

society are extremely difficult to duplicate in the laboratory." Note also his discussion of "indirect effects neglected by the Commission"—including "the influence exerted on attitudes by public law, qua law," and "the long-term effects of pornography."

5. Note the similarity between the Commission's recommendations and Justice Brennan's conclusions in his dissent in the 1973 cases, which follow. Might the course of obscenity law have been different if Justice Brennan had reached those conclusions a few years earlier, during the Warren era?

1. As the Chief Justice described the facts, appellant "conducted a mass mailing campaign to advertise the sale of illustrated books, euphemistically called 'adult' material. [H]e was convicted of violating California Penal Code § 311.2(a), a misdemeanor, by knowingly distributing obscene matter. [Appellant had caused] five unsolicited advertising brochures to be sent through the mail. [While] the brochures contain some descriptive printed material, primarily they consist of pictures and drawings very explicitly depicting men and women in groups of two or more engaging in a variety of sexual activities with genitals often prominently displayed."

[The variety of views] is not remarkable, for in the area of freedom of speech and press the courts must always remain sensitive to any infringement on genuinely serious literary, artistic, political, or scientific expression. This is an area in which there are few eternal verities. The case we now review was tried on the theory that the [California law] approximately incorporates the three-stage Memoirs test. But now the Memoirs test has been abandoned as unworkable by its author [see Justice Brennan's Paris dissent, below] and no member of the Court today supports the Memoirs formulation.

This much has been categorically settled by the Court, that obscene material is unprotected by the First Amendment. [We] acknowledge, however, the inherent dangers of undertaking to regulate any form of expression. State statutes designed to regulate obscene materials must be carefully limited. As a result, we now confine the permissible scope of such regulation to works which depict or describe sexual conduct. That conduct must be specifically defined by the applicable state law, as written or authoritatively construed.[2] A state offense must also be limited to works which, taken as a whole, appeal to the prurient interest in sex, which portray sexual conduct in a patently offensive way, and which, taken as a whole, do not have serious literary, artistic, political, or scientific value.

The basic guidelines for the trier of fact must be: (a) whether "the average person, applying contemporary community standards" would find that the work, taken as a whole, appeals to the prurient interest [Roth], (b) whether the work depicts or describes, in a patently offensive way, sexual conduct specifically defined by the applicable state law, and (c) whether the work, taken as a whole, lacks serious literary, artistic, political, or scientific value. We do not adopt as a constitutional standard the "*utterly* without redeeming social value" test of [Memoirs]. If a state law that regulates obscene material is thus limited, as written or construed, [First Amendment values] are adequately protected by the ultimate power of appellate courts to conduct an independent review of constitutional claims when necessary.

We emphasize that it is not our function to propose regulatory schemes for the States. [It] is possible, however, to give a few plain examples of what a state statute could define for regulation under the second part (b) of the standard announced in this opinion: (a) Patently offensive representations or descriptions of ultimate sexual acts, normal or perverted, actual or simulated. (b) Patently offensive representations or descriptions of masturbation, excretory functions, and lewd exhibition of the genitals.

Sex and nudity may not be exploited without limit by films or pictures exhibited or sold in places of public accommodation any more than live sex and nudity can be exhibited or sold without limit in such public places.[3] At a minimum, prurient, patently offensive depiction or description of sexual conduct must have serious literary, artistic, political, or scientific value to merit First Amendment protection. For example, medical books for the education of physicians and related personnel necessarily use graphic illustrations and descriptions of human anatomy. In resolving the inevitably sensitive questions of fact and law, we must continue to rely on the jury system, accompanied by the safeguards that judges, rules of evidence, presumption of innocence and other

2. See, e.g., [Oregon Laws] and [Hawaii Penal Code] as examples of state laws directed at depiction of defined physical conduct, as opposed to [expression]. We do not hold, as Mr. Justice Brennan intimates, that all States other than Oregon must now enact new obscenity statutes. Other existing state statutes, as construed heretofore or hereafter, may well be [adequate]. [Footnote by Chief Justice Burger.]

3. Although we are not presented here with the problem of regulating lewd public conduct itself, the States have greater power to regulate nonverbal, physical conduct than to suppress depictions or descriptions of the same behavior. [United States v. O'Brien (1968; p. 1170 below).] [Footnote by Chief Justice Burger.]

protective features provide, as we do with rape, murder and a host of other offenses against society and its individual members.

Mr. Justice Brennan, author of the opinions of the Court, or the plurality opinions, in [Roth, Jacobellis, Ginzburg, Mishkin, and Memoirs], has abandoned his former position and now maintains that no formulation of this Court, the Congress, or the States can adequately distinguish obscene material unprotected by the First Amendment from protected expression. Paradoxically, [he] indicates that suppression of unprotected obscene material is permissible to avoid exposure to unconsenting adults, as in this case, and to juveniles, although he gives no indication of how the division between protected and nonprotected materials may be drawn with greater precision for these purposes than for regulation of commercial exposure to consenting adults only. Nor does he indicate where in the Constitution he finds the authority to distinguish between a willing "adult" one month past the state law age of majority and a willing "juvenile" one month younger.

Under the holdings announced today, no one will be subject to prosecution for the sale or exposure of obscene materials unless these materials depict or describe patently offensive "hard core" sexual conduct specifically defined by the regulating state law, as written or construed. We are satisfied that these specific prerequisites will provide fair notice to a dealer in such materials that his public and commercial activities may bring prosecution. If the inability to define regulated materials with ultimate, god-like precision altogether removes the power of the States or the Congress to regulate, then "hard core" pornography may be exposed without limit to the juvenile, the passerby, and the consenting adult alike, as, indeed, Mr. Justice Douglas contends. [In] this belief, however, [he] now stands alone. [Today], for the first time since [Roth], a majority of this Court has agreed on concrete guidelines to isolate "hard core" pornography from expression protected by the First Amendment. Now we may abandon the casual practice of [Redrup] and attempt to provide positive guidance to the federal and state courts [alike].

Under a national Constitution, fundamental First Amendment limitations on the powers of the States do not vary from community to community, but this does not mean that there are, or should or can be, fixed, uniform national standards of precisely what appeals to the "prurient interest" or is "patently offensive." These are essentially questions of fact, and our nation is simply too big and too diverse for this Court to reasonably expect that such standards could be articulated for all 50 States in a single formulation, even assuming the prerequisite consensus exists. [To] require a State to structure obscenity proceedings around evidence of a *national* "community standard" would be an exercise in futility. [N]either the State's alleged failure to offer evidence of "national standards," nor the trial court's charge that the jury consider state community standards, were constitutional errors [in this case]. It is neither realistic nor constitutionally sound to read the First Amendment as requiring that the people of Maine or Mississippi accept public depiction of conduct found tolerable in Las Vegas, or New York City. [People] in different States vary in their tastes and attitudes, and this diversity is not to be strangled by the absolutism of imposed [uniformity].

The dissenting Justices sound the alarm of repression. But, in our view, to equate the free and robust exchange of ideas and political debate with commercial exploitation of obscene material demeans the grand conception of the First Amendment and its high purposes in the historic struggle for freedom. [The] First Amendment protects work which, taken as a whole, have serious literary, artistic, political, or scientific value, regardless of whether the government or a majority of the people approve of the ideas these works represent. [But] the public portrayal of hard core sexual conduct for its own sake, and for the ensuing commercial gain, is a different matter.

There is no evidence, empirical or historical, that the stern 19th century American censorship of public distribution and display of material relating to sex in any way limited or affected expression of serious literary, artistic, political, or scientific ideas. [We] do not see the harsh hand of censorship of ideas—good or bad, sound or unsound—and "repression" of political liberty lurking in every state regulation of commercial exploitation of human interest in sex. [Justice Brennan's Paris dissent, below,] finds "it is hard to see how state-ordered regimentation of our minds can ever be forestalled." These doleful anticipations assume that courts cannot distinguish commerce in ideas, protected by the First Amendment, from commercial exploitation of obscene material. [One] can concede that the "sexual revolution" of recent years may have had useful byproducts in striking layers of prudery from a subject long irrationally kept from needed ventilation. But it does not follow that no regulation of patently offensive "hard core" materials is needed or permissible; civilized people do not allow unregulated access to heroin because it is a derivative of medicinal morphine. In sum we (a) reaffirm the Roth holding that obscene material is not protected by the First Amendment; (b) hold that such material can be regulated by the States, subject to the specific safeguards enunciated above, without a showing that the material is *"utterly* without redeeming social value"; and (c) hold that obscenity is to be determined by applying "contemporary community standards," [not "national standards"].

Vacated and remanded.

Mr. Justice DOUGLAS, [dissenting].

[To] send men to jail for violating standards they cannot understand, construe, and apply is a monstrous thing to do in a Nation dedicated to fair trials and due process. [We] deal with highly emotional, not rational, questions. To many the Song of Solomon is obscene. I do not think we, the judges, were ever given the constitutional power to make definitions of obscenity. If it is to be defined, let the people [decide] by a constitutional amendment what they want to ban as obscene and what standards they want the legislatures and the courts to apply. [Whatever] the choice, the courts will have some guidelines. Now we have none except our own predilections.

Mr. Justice BRENNAN, with whom Mr. Justice STEWART and Mr. Justice MARSHALL join, dissenting.

In my dissent in [Paris, below], I noted that I had no occasion to consider the extent of state power to regulate the distribution of sexually oriented material to juveniles or the offensive exposure of such material to unconsenting adults. [I] need not now decide whether a statute might be drawn to impose, within the requirements of the First Amendment, criminal penalties for the precise conduct at issue here [—mailing unsolicited brochures]. For it is clear that under my dissent in [Paris], the statute [here] is unconstitutionally overbroad, and therefore invalid on its [face].

PARIS ADULT THEATRE I v. SLATON

413 U.S. 49, 93 S.Ct. 2628, 37 L.Ed.2d 446 (1973).

Mr. Chief Justice BURGER delivered the opinion of the [Court].[1]

1. This was a Georgia civil proceeding to enjoin the showing of two allegedly obscene films at two "adult" theaters. At a trial before a judge, the evidence consisted primarily of the films and of photographs of the entrance to the theaters. As described by the Chief Justice, these photographs "show a conventional, inoffensive theatre entrance, without any pictures, but

We categorically disapprove the theory, apparently adopted by the trial judge, that obscene, pornographic films acquire constitutional immunity from state regulation simply because they are exhibited for consenting adults only. [The] States have a long-recognized legitimate interest in regulating the use of obscene material in local commerce and in all places of public accommodation. [In] particular, we hold that there are legitimate state interests at stake in stemming the tide of commercialized obscenity, even assuming it is feasible to enforce effective safeguards against exposure to juveniles and to passersby.[2] [These] include the interest of the public in the quality of life and the total community environment, the tone of commerce in the great city centers, and, possibly, the public safety itself. The Hill-Link Minority Report of the Commission on Obscenity and Pornography indicates that there is at least an arguable correlation between obscene material and crime. Quite apart from sex crimes, however, there remains one problem of large proportions aptly described by Professor Bickel: "It concerns the tone of the society, the mode, or to use terms that have perhaps greater currency, the style and quality of life, now and in the future. A man may be entitled to read an obscene book in his room, or expose himself indecently there. [We] should protect his privacy. But if he demands a right to obtain the books and pictures he wants in the market, and to foregather in public places—discreet, if you will, but accessible to all—with others who share his tastes, *then to grant him his right is to affect the world about the rest of us, and to impinge on other privacies.* Even supposing that each of us can, if he wishes, effectively avert the eye and stop the ear (which, in truth, we cannot), what is commonly read and seen and heard and done intrudes upon us all, want it or not." 22 The Public Interest 25–26 (Winter, 1971). (Emphasis added.) As Mr. Chief Justice Warren stated, there is a "right of the Nation and of the States to maintain a decent society" [Jacobellis dissent].

But, it is argued, there is no scientific data which conclusively demonstrate that exposure to obscene materials adversely affects men and women or their society. It is [urged] that, absent such a demonstration, any kind of state regulation is "impermissible." We reject this argument. It is not for us to resolve empirical uncertainties underlying state legislation, save in the exceptional case where that legislation plainly impinges upon rights protected by the Constitution itself. [Although] there is no conclusive proof of a connection between antisocial behavior and obscene material, the legislature of Georgia could quite reasonably determine that such a connection does or might exist. In deciding Roth, this Court implicitly accepted that a legislature could legitimately act on such a conclusion to protect *"the social interest in order and morality."*

From the beginning of civilized societies, legislators and judges have acted on various unprovable assumptions. Such assumptions underlie much lawful

---

with signs indicating that the theatres exhibit 'Atlanta's Finest Mature Feature Films.' On the door itself is a sign saying: 'Adult Theatre—You must be 21 and able to prove it. If viewing the nude body offends you, Please Do Not Enter.'" (Two state investigators who saw the films testified that the signs did not indicate "the full nature of what was shown. In particular, nothing indicated that the films depicted—as they did—scenes of simulated fellatio, cunnilingus, and group sex intercourse.") The trial judge dismissed the complaint. He held the showing of obscene films permissible where there was "requisite notice to the public" and "reasonable protection against the exposure of these films to minors." The Georgia Supreme Court reversed.

Before turning to the issues discussed in the text, the Chief Justice found that it was not error

"to fail to require 'expert' affirmative evidence that the materials were obscene when the materials themselves were placed in evidence." Moreover, he praised the civil injunction procedure because it provides an exhibitor "the best possible notice, prior to any criminal indictments," as to whether the materials are obscene.

2. It is conceivable that an "adult" theatre can—if it really insists—prevent the exposure of its obscene wares to juveniles. An "adult" bookstore, dealing in obscene books, magazines, and pictures, cannot realistically make this claim. [The] legitimate interest in preventing exposure of juveniles to obscene materials cannot be fully served by simply barring juveniles from the immediate physical premises of "adult" bookstores, when there is a flourishing "outside business" in these materials. [Footnote by the Court.]

state regulation of commercial and business affairs. See [e.g., Ferguson v. Skrupa; Lincoln Federal Labor Union (economic due process cases in chap. 8, above)]. The same is true of the federal securities and antitrust laws and a host of federal regulations. [Understandably] those who entertain an absolutist view of the First Amendment find it uncomfortable to explain why rights of association, speech, and press should be severely restrained in the marketplace of goods and money, but not in the marketplace of pornography. Likewise, when legislatures and administrators act to protect the physical environment from pollution and to preserve our resources of forests, streams and parks, they must act on such imponderables as the impact of a new highway near or through an existing park or wilderness area. [The] fact that a congressional directive reflects unprovable assumptions about what is good for the people, including imponderable aesthetic assumptions, is not a sufficient reason to find that statute unconstitutional.

If we accept the unprovable assumption that a complete education requires certain books and the well nigh universal belief that good books, plays, and art lift the spirit, improve the mind, enrich the human personality and develop character, can we then say that a state legislature may not act on the corollary assumption that commerce in obscene books, or public exhibitions focused on obscene conduct, have a tendency to exert a corrupting and debasing impact leading to antisocial behavior? [The sum of experience] affords an ample basis for legislatures to conclude that a sensitive, key relationship of human existence, central to family life, community welfare, and the development of human personality, can be debased and distorted by crass commercial exploitation of sex. Nothing in the Constitution prohibits a State from reaching such a conclusion and acting on it legislatively simply because there is no conclusive evidence or empirical [data].

It is asserted, however, that standards for evaluating state commercial regulations are inapposite in the present context, as state regulation of access by consenting adults to obscene material violates the constitutionally protected right to privacy enjoyed by petitioners' customers. [I]t is unavailing to compare a theater open to the public for a fee, with the private home of [Stanley] and the marital bedroom of [Griswold]. This Court, has, on numerous occasions, refused to hold that commercial ventures such as a motion-picture house are "private" for the purpose [of] civil rights statutes. Our prior decisions recognizing a right to privacy [protect] the personal intimacies of the home, the family, marriage, motherhood, procreation, and child rearing. Nothing, however, in this Court's decisions intimates that there is any "fundamental" privacy right "implicit in the concept of ordered liberty" to watch obscene movies in places of public accommodation. [The] idea of a "privacy" right and a place of public accommodation are, in this context, mutually exclusive. Conduct or depictions of conduct that the state police power can prohibit on a public street do not become automatically protected by the Constitution merely because the conduct is moved to a bar or a "live" theatre stage, any more than a "live" performance of a man and woman locked in a sexual embrace at high noon in Times Square is protected by the Constitution because they simultaneously engage in a valid political dialogue. [We also] reject the claim that [Georgia] is here attempting to control the minds or thoughts of those who patronize theaters. [Where] communication of ideas, protected by the First Amendment, is not involved, or the particular privacy of the home protected by Stanley, or any of the other "areas or zones" of constitutionally protected privacy, the mere fact that, as a consequence, some human "utterances" or "thoughts" may be incidentally affected does not bar the State from acting to protect legitimate state interests. Cf. [Roth; Beauharnais]. [Finally, for] us to say that our Constitution incorporates the proposition that conduct involving consenting adults only is always beyond state regulation, is a step we are unable to take. [W]e hold that the States have a legitimate interest in regulating commerce in obscene material and in regulating exhibition of obscene material in places of public accommodation, including so-called "adult" theaters from which minors are [excluded].

Vacated and remanded.[3]

Mr. Justice BRENNAN, with whom Mr. Justice STEWART and Mr. Justice MARSHALL join, dissenting.

[I] am convinced that the approach initiated 16 years ago in [Roth], and culminating in the Court's decision today, cannot bring stability to this area of the law without jeopardizing fundamental First Amendment values, and I have concluded that the time has come to make a significant departure from that approach. [The] essence of our problem in the obscenity area is that we have been unable to provide "sensitive tools" to separate obscenity from other sexually oriented but constitutionally protected speech, so that efforts to suppress the former do not spill over into the suppression of the latter.[1] [I] am reluctantly forced to the conclusion that none of the available formulas, including the one announced today, can reduce the vagueness [of our obscenity standards] to a tolerable level. [Any] effort to draw a constitutionally acceptable boundary on state power must resort to such indefinite concepts as "prurient interest," "patent offensiveness," "serious literary value," and the like. The meaning of these concepts necessarily varies with the experience, outlook, and even idiosyncracies of the person defining them. [Added] to the "perhaps inherent residual vagueness" of each of the current multitude of standards is the further complication that the obscenity of any particular item may depend upon nuances of presentation and the context of its [dissemination].[2]

The vagueness of the standards in the obscenity area produces a number of separate problems, and any improvement must rest on an understanding that the problems are to some extent distinct. First, a vague statute fails to provide adequate notice to persons who are engaged in the type of conduct that the statute could be thought to proscribe. [In addition], a vague statute in the areas of speech and press creates a second level of difficulty [—that of "chilling protected speech"]. [Moreover], a vague statute in this area creates a third, although admittedly more subtle, set of problems. These problems concern the institutional stress that inevitably results where the line separating protected from unprotected speech is excessively vague. [T]he uncertainty of the standards creates a continuing source of tension between state and federal courts, since the need for an independent determination by this Court seems to render superfluous even the most conscientious analysis by state tribunals. And our inability to justify our decisions with a persuasive rationale—or indeed, any rationale at all—necessarily creates the impression that we are merely second-guessing state court judges. The severe problems arising from the lack of fair notice, from the chill on protected expression, and from the stress imposed on the state and federal judicial machinery persuade me that a significant change in direction is urgently required.[3] I turn, therefore, to the alternatives that are now open.

3. A dissent by Justice DOUGLAS is omitted.

1. At this point, Justice Brennan reviewed the cases that sought to define obscenity during the 1957–73 period. Excerpts from his summary are printed above, at p. 1071.

2. In a footnote at this point, Justice Brennan explained why he was "now inclined to agree" with much of Stanley v. Georgia, even though he had not joined that opinion. (See p. 1073 above.)

3. For further discussion of the vagueness problem in First Amendment cases, see the next chapter, at p. 1156 below.

1.   The approach requiring the smallest deviation from our present course would be to draw a new line between protected and unprotected speech, still permitting the States to suppress all material on the unprotected side of the line. In my view, clarity cannot be obtained pursuant to this approach except by drawing a line that resolves all doubt in favor of state power and against the guarantees of the [First Amendment].

2.   The alternative adopted by the Court today recognizes that a prohibition against any depiction or description of human sexual organs could not be reconciled with the guarantees of the First Amendment.   But the Court does retain the view that certain sexually oriented material can be considered obscene and therefore [unprotected].   To describe that unprotected class of expression, the Court adopts a restatement of the Roth-Memoirs definition of obscenity. [In] my view, the restatement leaves unresolved the very difficulties that compel our rejection of the underlying Roth approach, while at the same time contributing substantial difficulties of its own.   [T]he Court today permits suppression if the government can prove that the materials lack *"serious* literary, artistic, political or scientific value."   But [Roth] held that certain expression is obscene, and thus outside the protection of the First Amendment, precisely *because* it lacks even the slightest redeeming social value.   The Court's approach necessarily assumes that some works will be deemed obscene—even though they clearly have *some* social value—because the State was able to prove that the value, measured by some unspecified standard, was not sufficiently "serious" to warrant constitutional protection.   That result [is] nothing less than a rejection of the fundamental First Amendment premises and rationale of the Roth opinion and an invitation to widespread suppression of sexually oriented speech.   Before today, the protections of the First Amendment have never been thought limited to expressions of *serious* literary or political value.   [E]ven if the Court's approach left undamaged the conceptual framework of Roth, and even if it clearly barred the suppression of works with at least some social value, I would nevertheless be compelled to reject it.   For it is beyond dispute that the approach can have no ameliorative impact on the cluster of problems that grow out of the vagueness of our current [standards].

Of course, the Court's restated Roth test does limit the definition of obscenity to depictions of physical conduct and explicit sexual acts.   And that limitation may seem, at first glance, a welcome and clarifying addition to the Roth-Memoirs formula.   [But] the mere formulation of a "physical conduct" test is no assurance that it can be applied with any greater facility.   [T]he valiant attempt of one lower federal court to draw the constitutional line at depictions of explicit sexual conduct seems to belie any suggestion that this approach marks the road to clarity.[4]   The Court surely demonstrates little sensitivity to our own institutional problems, much less the other vagueness-related difficulties, in establishing a system that requires us to consider whether a description of human genitals is sufficiently "lewd" to deprive it of constitutional protection; whether a sexual act is "ultimate"; whether the conduct depicted in materials before us fits within one of the categories of conduct whose depiction the state or federal governments have attempted to suppress; and a host of equally pointless inquiries.   [Ultimately], the reformulation must fail because it still leaves to this Court the responsibility of determining in each case whether the materials are protected by the First Amendment.   [In addition], I am convinced that a definition of obscenity in terms of physical conduct cannot provide sufficient clarity to afford fair notice, to avoid a chill on protected expression, and to minimize the institutional stress, so long as that definition is used to

---

4.   Huffman v. United States, 470 F.2d 386 (D.C.Cir.1971).   The test apparently requires an effort to distinguish between "singles" and "duals," between "erect penises" and "semi-erect penises," and between "ongoing sexual activity" and "imminent sexual activity."   [Footnote by Justice Brennan.]

justify the outright suppression of any material that is asserted to fall within its terms.

3. I have also considered the possibility of reducing our own role, and the role of appellate courts generally, in determining whether particular matter is obscene. Thus, [we] might adopt the position that where a lower federal or state court has conscientiously applied the constitutional standard, its finding of obscenity will be no more vulnerable to reversal by this Court than any finding of fact. [But] it is implicit in [Redrup] that the First Amendment requires an independent review by appellate courts of the constitutional fact of obscenity. [In any event, while this approach would mitigate institutional stress,] it would neither offer nor produce any cure for the other vices of vagueness. [Plainly], the institutional gain would be more than offset by the unprecedented infringement of First Amendment rights.

4. Finally, I have considered the view, urged so forcefully since 1957 by our Brothers Black and Douglas, that the First Amendment bars the suppression of any sexually oriented expression. [But that would strip] the States of power to an extent that cannot be justified by the commands of the Constitution, at least so long as there is available an alternative approach that strikes a better balance between the guarantee of free expression and the States' legitimate interests.

Our experience since Roth requires us not only to abandon the effort to pick out obscene materials on a case-by-case basis, but also to reconsider a fundamental postulate of Roth: that there exists a definable class of sexually oriented expression that may be totally suppressed by [government]. Assuming that such a class of expression does in fact exist, I am forced to conclude that the concept of "obscenity" cannot be defined with sufficient specificity and clarity to provide fair notice to persons who create and distribute sexually oriented materials, to prevent substantial erosion of protected speech as a byproduct of the attempt to suppress unprotected speech, and to avoid very costly institutional harms. Given these inevitable side-effects of state efforts to suppress what is assumed to be *unprotected* speech, we must scrutinize with care the state interest that is asserted to justify the suppression. For in the absence of some very substantial interest in suppressing such speech, we can hardly condone the ill-effects that seem to flow inevitably from the [effort].

Because we assumed—incorrectly, as experience has proven—that obscenity could be separated from other sexually oriented expression without significant costs, [we] had no occasion in Roth to prove the asserted state interest in curtailing unprotected, sexually oriented speech. Yet, as we have increasingly come to appreciate the vagueness of the concept of obscenity, we have begun to recognize and articulate the state interests at stake. [The] opinions in Redrup and [Stanley] reflected our emerging view that the state interests in protecting children and in protecting unconsenting adults may stand on a different footing from the other asserted state interests. It may well be, as one commentator has argued, that "exposure to [erotic material] is for some persons an intense emotional experience. A communication of this nature, imposed upon a person contrary to his wishes, has all the characteristics of a physical assault. [It] constitutes an invasion of his privacy." [5] But cf. [Cohen v. California (sec. 2C2 below)]. Similarly, if children are "not possessed of that full capacity for individual choice which is the presupposition of First Amendment guarantees," [the] State may have a substantial interest in precluding the flow of obscene materials even to consenting juveniles. [But whatever the strength of those interests, they] cannot be asserted in defense of the holding of the Georgia

5. T. Emerson, The System of Freedom of Expression 496 (1970). [Footnote by Justice Brennan.]

Supreme Court. [The justification here] must be found [in] some independent interest in regulating the reading and viewing habits of consenting adults.

At the outset it should be noted that virtually all of [those interests] were also posited in [Stanley]. That decision presages the conclusions I reach here today. [Of course, a State need not] remain utterly indifferent to—and take no action bearing on—the morality of the community. The traditional description of state police power does embrace the regulation of morals as well as health, safety, and general welfare of the citizenry. And much legislation—compulsory public education laws, civil rights laws, even the abolition of capital punishment—is grounded, at least in part, on a concern with the morality of the community. But the State's interest in regulating morality by suppressing obscenity, while often asserted, remains essentially unfocused and ill-defined. And, since the attempt to curtail unprotected speech necessarily spills over into the area of protected speech, the effort to serve this speculative interest through the suppression of obscene material must tread heavily on rights protected by the First Amendment. [Like] the proscription of abortions, the effort to suppress obscenity is predicated on unprovable, although strongly held, assumptions about human behavior, morality, sex, and religion. The existence of these assumptions cannot validate a statute that substantially undermines the guarantees of the First Amendment, any more than the existence of similar assumptions on the issue of abortion can validate a statute that infringes the constitutionally-protected privacy interests of a pregnant woman.

If, as the Court today assumes, "a state legislature may [act on the assumption that obscenity has] a tendency to exert a corrupting and debasing impact leading to antisocial behavior," then it is hard to see how state-ordered regimentation of our minds can ever be forestalled. [W]e have held that so-called thematic obscenity—obscenity which might persuade the viewer or the reader to engage in "obscene" conduct—is not outside the protection of the First Amendment. [Kingsley Pictures.] Even a legitimate, sharply focused state concern for the morality of the community cannot, in other words, justify an assault on the protections of the First Amendment. Where the state interest in regulation of morality is vague and ill-defined, interference with the guarantees of the First Amendment is even more difficult to justify.

In short, while I cannot say that the interest of the State—apart from the question of juveniles and unconsenting adults—are trivial or nonexistent, I am compelled to conclude that these interests cannot justify the substantial damage to constitutional rights and to [the] judicial machinery that inevitably results from state efforts to bar the distribution even of unprotected material to consenting adults. I would hold, therefore, that at least in the absence of distribution to juveniles or obtrusive exposure to unconsenting adults, the [First Amendment prohibits governments] from attempting wholly to suppress sexually oriented materials on the basis of their allegedly "obscene" contents. Nothing in this approach precludes [governments] from taking action to serve what may be strong and legitimate interests through regulation of the manner of distribution of sexually oriented material. [I] do not pretend to have found a complete and infallible [answer]. Difficult questions must still be faced, notably in the areas of distribution to juveniles and offensive exposure to unconsenting adults. Whatever the extent of state power to regulate in those areas,[6] it should be clear that the view I espouse today would introduce a large measure of clarity to this troubled area, would reduce the institutional pressure on this Court and the rest of the State and Federal Judiciary, and would guarantee fuller freedom

6. The Court erroneously states [in Miller] that the author of this opinion "indicates that suppression of unprotected obscene material is permissible to avoid exposure to unconsenting adults [and] to juveniles." [I] defer expression of my views as to the scope of state power in these areas until cases squarely presenting these questions are before the Court. [Footnote by Justice Brennan.]

of expression while leaving room for the protection of legitimate governmental [interests].[7]

THE BURGER COURT AND OBSCENITY SINCE MILLER AND PARIS

1. *Continued Court review.* Although the number of obscenity cases decided by the Court has diminished since the 1973 rulings, the Miller-Paris standards have not wholly extricated the Court from the unwelcome task of case-by-case review in obscenity cases.[1] JENKINS v. GEORGIA, 418 U.S. 153 (1974), illustrates the Court's continued involvement. That ruling reversed a state conviction for showing the film "Carnal Knowledge." The state court had mistakenly thought that, under the new standards, a jury verdict virtually precluded further review regarding most elements of obscenity. Justice REHN-QUIST countered: "Even though questions of appeal to the 'prurient interest' or of patent offensiveness are 'essentially questions of fact,' it would be a serious misreading of Miller to conclude that juries have unbridled discretion in determining what is 'patently offensive.' [While the Miller illustrations] did not purport to be an exhaustive catalog of what juries might find patently offensive, [they were] certainly intended to fix substantive constitutional limitations [on] the type of material subject to such a determination."[2] He concluded that, under Miller, "Carnal Knowledge" "could not be found to depict sexual conduct in a patently offensive way. [While] the subject matter of the picture is, in a broader sense, sex, and there are scenes in which sexual conduct including 'ultimate sexual acts' is to be understood to be taking place, the camera does not focus on the bodies of the actors at such time. There is no exhibition whatever of the actors' genitals, lewd or otherwise, during these scenes. There are occasional scenes of nudity, but nudity alone is not enough to make material legally obscene under the Miller standards."[3]

---

7. In three additional decisions handed down together with Miller and Paris, the Court, with the same 5 to 4 division, sustained obscenity controls in other contexts. In United States v. Twelve 200-Foot Reels, 413 U.S. 123 (1973), the majority held that federal laws could be applied to prevent the importation of obscene material for private use. In United States v. Orito, 413 U.S. 139 (1973), the Court sustained the federal ban on interstate transportation of obscene materials as applied to transport for private use. And in Kaplan v. California, 413 U.S. 115 (1973), the majority upheld the application of a state obscenity law to a book without pictorial contents.

1. As noted earlier, the First Amendment obligation of an appellate court to conduct an independent review of the factual findings below in order to assure that protected material is not penalized is a pervasive and widely accepted theme in First Amendment litigation. Recall the comments in connection with Hess v. Indiana at p. 1039 above.

2. That the Miller examples are not "an exhaustive catalog" of "patently offensive" materials is illustrated by two later decisions finding that bases for liability acknowledged prior to Miller continue to be applicable, even though not mentioned in Miller itself. Ward v. Illinois, 431 U.S. 767 (1977), sustained a state conviction for selling "sado-masochistic" materials of the kind proscribed in the 1966 decision in Mishkin v. New York. Splawn v. California, 431 U.S. 595 (1977), sustained a conviction resting on the "pandering" concept of the 1966 decision in Ginzburg v. United States and reiterated that "evidence of pandering to prurient interests [is] relevant in determining whether the material is obscene."

3. In Jenkins, there were separate opinions concurring in the result by Justice BRENNAN, joined by Justices Stewart and Marshall, and by Justice DOUGLAS.

A companion case to Jenkins, Hamling v. United States, 418 U.S. 87 (1974), illustrates the modern Court's recurrent struggles with the problem of the proper scope of the "community" whose standards govern in obscenity cases. In Hamling, the Court opted for local rather than statewide or national standards in federal obscenity prosecutions and rejected the argument that application of local standards would unduly inhibit producers of materials for a national market. The Hamling ruling was again by a 5 to 4 vote. (In Jenkins, the Court had similarly refused to require that statewide standards be applied in state prosecutions, even though a statewide standard had been used in Miller.)

But the determination of the composition of the appropriate "community" is not left wholly to lower courts. Pinkus v. United States, 436

2. *Justice Stevens' dissenting position.* Soon after he succeeded Justice Douglas in 1975, Justice Stevens began to develop a position that has led him to join those opposing criminal prosecutions for obscenity. However, his position is a distinctive one, differing both from the approach of Justice Douglas and that of Justice Brennan. Indeed, he has led the way in justifying *civil* sanctions restraining not only obscene but also nonobscene offensive or indecent displays, and in arguing for a lower First Amendment status of indecent speech than of political speech.[4] It is only with respect to *criminal* prosecutions for obscenity that he has voiced strong objections. He set forth his position most fully in his dissent in SMITH v. UNITED STATES, 431 U.S. 291 (1977).[5]

Justice STEVENS' separate dissent in Smith questioned at length "the suitability of criminal prosecution as the mechanism for regulating the distribution of erotic material." He commented: "The question of offensiveness to community standards, whether national or local, is not one that the average juror can be expected to answer with evenhanded consistency. The average juror may well have one reaction to sexually oriented materials in a completely private setting and an entirely different reaction in a social context. Studies have shown that an opinion held by a large majority of a group concerning a neutral and objective subject has a significant impact in distorting the perceptions of group members who would normally take a different position. Since obscenity is by no means a neutral subject, and since the ascertainment of the community standard is such a subjective task, the expression of individual jurors' sentiments will inevitably influence the perceptions of other jurors, particularly those who would normally be in the minority. Moreover, because the record never discloses the obscenity standards which the jurors actually apply, their decisions in these cases are effectively unreviewable by an appellate court. In the final analysis, the guilt or innocence of a criminal defendant in an obscenity trial is determined primarily by individual jurors' subjective reactions to the materials in question rather than by the predictable application of rules of law. This conclusion is especially troubling because the same image—whether created by words, sounds, or pictures—may produce such a wide variety of reactions. As Mr. Justice Harlan noted: '[It is] often true that one man's vulgarity is another's lyric. Indeed, we think it is largely because government officials [or jurors] cannot make principled distinctions in this area that the Constitution leaves matters of taste and style so largely to the individual.' Cohen v. California. In my judgment, the line between communications which 'offend'

U.S. 293 (1978), held that children cannot be considered part of the relevant community when there was no distribution to children. The Court found error in an instruction to the jury that, in determining community standards, "you are to consider the community as a whole, [men], women and *children.*" Chief Justice Burger's opinion for a unanimous Court found that reference to "children" impermissible. He noted that the "average person" by whose standard obscenity is to be judged (see Smith, which follows) "would reach a much lower 'average' when children are part of the equation than it would if [consideration is restricted] to the effect of allegedly obscene materials on adults." He relied in part on Butler v. Michigan, 352 U.S. 380 (1957), decided shortly before Roth, which struck down a conviction under a state law banning the dissemination of books "found to have a potentially deleterious influence on youth" on the ground that the impact was "to reduce the adult population [to] reading only what is fit for children."

(Pinkus noted however that nothing prevented a court "from giving an instruction on prurient appeal to deviant sexual groups as part of an instruction pertaining to appeal to the average person when the evidence, as here, would support such a charge.")

4. See Justice Stevens' opinions in the American Mini Theatres and Pacifica cases, pp. 1114 and 1110 below.

5. In Smith, the majority held that determination of local "community standards" in federal obscenity prosecutions was for the jury, even where the defendant had mailed the allegedly obscene materials solely intrastate, in a state which had no law prohibiting sales to adults. Justice Blackmun's majority opinion concluded that state law, although relevant, "is not conclusive as to the issue of contemporary community standards for appeal to the prurient interest and patent offensiveness."

and those which do not is too blurred to identify criminal conduct. It is also too blurred to delimit the protections of the First Amendment."

While condemning criminal sanctions, Justice Stevens strongly endorsed the civil route: "Although the variable nature of a standard dependent on local community attitudes is critically defective when used to define a federal crime, that very flexibility is a desirable feature of a civil rule designed to protect the individual's right to select the kind of environment in which he wants to live." Criticizing the Roth categorization approach, he argued that it rested in part "on the assumed premise that all communications within the protected area are equally immune from governmental restraint, whereas those outside that area are utterly without social value and, hence, deserving of no protection. Last Term the Court expressly rejected that premise.[6] The fact that speech is protected by the First Amendment does not mean that it is wholly immune from state regulation. Although offensive or misleading statements in a political oration cannot be censored, offensive language in a courtroom or misleading representations in a securities prospectus may surely be regulated. Nuisances such as sound trucks and erotic displays in a residential area may be abated under appropriately flexible civil standards even though the First Amendment provides a shield against criminal prosecution.

"As long as the government does not totally suppress protected speech and is faithful to its paramount obligation of complete neutrality with respect to the point of view expressed in a protected communication, I see no reason why regulation of certain types of communication may not take into account obvious differences in subject matter.[7] It seems to me ridiculous to assume that no regulation of the display of sexually oriented material is permissible unless the same regulation could be applied to political comment. On the other hand, I am not prepared to rely on either the average citizen's understanding of an amorphous community standard or on my fellow judges' appraisal of what has serious artistic merit as a basis for deciding what one citizen may communicate to another by appropriate means. I do not know whether the ugly [8] pictures in this record have any beneficial value. The fact that there is a large demand for comparable materials indicates that they do provide amusement or information, or at least satisfy the curiosity of interested persons. Moreover, there are serious well-intentioned people who are persuaded that they serve a worthwhile purpose. Others believe they arouse passions that lead to the commission of crimes; if that be true, surely there is a mountain of material just within the protected zone that is equally capable of motivating comparable conduct. Moreover, the dire predictions about the baneful effects of these materials are disturbingly reminiscent of arguments formerly made about the availability of what are now valued as works of art. In the end, I believe we must rely on the capacity of the free marketplace of ideas to distinguish that which is useful or beautiful from that which is ugly or worthless."[9]

---

6. Justice Stevens referred not only to American Mini Theatres, p. 1110 below, but also to a commercial speech case, Virginia Pharmacy, in sec. 2D, at p. 1130 below.

7. For further development of this position, see Justice Stevens' subsequent opinion in Pacifica, p. 1114 below.

8. "If First Amendment protection is properly denied to materials that are 'patently offensive' to the average citizen, I question whether the element of erotic appeal is of critical importance. For the average person may find some portrayals of violence, of disease, or of intimate bodily functions (such as the birth of a child) equally offensive—at least when they are viewed for the

first time. It is noteworthy that one of the examples of an unprotected representation identified by the Court [in Miller] surely would have no erotic appeal to the average person." [Footnote by Justice Stevens. Recall that Miller's examples had included "patently offensive representations" of "excretory functions."]

9. Are Justice Stevens' reasons for opposing obscenity prosecutions more persuasive than those of Justice Brennan or of Justice Douglas? Is his distinction between civil "environmental" regulation and criminal prosecution persuasive? Note the materials on procedural problems in obscenity control in chap. 12; and see especially the Kingsley Books case, p. 1162 below. Is

3. *Some comments and questions.*   a.   Consider the Court's handling of obscenity problems since Roth in light of the well-established justifications for protecting and restraining speech. The obscenity issue raises special difficulties pertaining to the proper scope of the First Amendment coverage and the legitimate dimensions of state interests. Do any of the rationales for protecting speech justify the exclusion of obscene materials from the First Amendment? Do the rationales drawn from notions of representative government (recall Meiklejohn's position) and from the free marketplace of ideas metaphor (recall Justice Holmes' Abrams dissent) justify the protection of art and literature generally and of obscenity in particular? [10] As noted earlier, it may be necessary to resort to the individual self-expression, autonomy rationale to bring literature and the arts within the First Amendment.[11] But is the autonomy rationale a proper First Amendment ingredient? And does the autonomy rationale prove too much? [12]

b.   Consider the argument by Frederick Schauer, one of the most prolific modern commentators on obscenity problems, that proper First Amendment theory *can* justify denial of constitutional protection to pornography.[13] Schauer takes issue with the widespread academic criticism of the exclusion of obscenity from First Amendment protection. He argues that individual self-expression has not been recognized as a fundamental purpose of the First Amendment and that freedom of speech is not "merely an individual subset of a broader notion of individual liberty." Limiting himself to Holmes' marketplace of ideas and to Meiklejohn's representative theory rationales, Schauer suggests that pornography "has no value in the context of the justifications underlying the first amendment." "Speech," he claims, should be limited to "communication of a mental stimulus," to "communication designed to appeal to the intellectual process." Hard-core pornography, by contrast, is "designed to produce a purely physical effect." Accordingly, "the realization that the primary purpose of pornography is to produce sexual excitement" is essential to an understanding of the Court's treatment of pornography as non-speech.[14] He concludes that the Court's exclusion of pornography from constitutional protection "is consistent

---

Justice Stevens' endorsement of civil sanctions, and his downgrading of the First Amendment value of "indecent" speech in American Mini Theatres and Pacifica (pp. 1110 and 1114 below), significantly less harmful to First Amendment analysis than the Miller-Paris endorsement of criminal prosecution that he so vehemently opposes in his Smith dissent?

10. See Kalven, "The Metaphysics of the Law of Obscenity," 1960 Sup.Ct.Rev. 1: "The classic defense of John Stuart Mill and the modern defense of Alexander Meiklejohn do not help much when the question is why the novel, the poem, the painting, the drama, or the piece of sculpture falls within the protection of the First Amendment." Compare Meiklejohn's later extension of his "public," political speech emphasis to encompass not only speech pertaining to the political process but also literature and art, as aspects of speech within the public domain. See Meiklejohn, "The First Amendment Is an Absolute," 1961 Sup.Ct.Rev. 245.

11. Recall David Richards' reliance on that rationale, as noted at p. 1067 above.

12. Recall that in the modern substantive due process cases since Roe v. Wade (in chap. 8 above), the Court has been unwilling to adopt the position that "liberty" is broad enough to protect all individual behavior that does not harm others.

Is there a stronger argument for protecting all such behavior under the First Amendment?

13. See especially "Speech and 'Speech'—Obscenity and 'Obscenity': An Exercise in the Interpretation of Constitutional Language," 67 Geo.L.J. 899 (1979). See also Schauer's "Response: Pornography and the First Amendment," 40 U.Pitt.L.Rev. 605 (1979), and his The Law of Obscenity (1976).

14. Schauer elaborates: "Thus the refusal to treat pornography as speech is grounded in the assumption that the prototypical pornographic item on closer analysis shares more of the characteristics of sexual activity than of the communicative process. The pornographic item is in a real sense a sexual surrogate." Schauer argues that his emphasis on communication designed to appeal to the intellectual process would not exclude "emotive" communication from First Amendment coverage. (See Cohen v. California, p. 1101 below.) "[T]he emotive, as well as the propositional or cognitive, is implicitly encompassed by the intellectual or communicative interpretation of the first amendment. [The] emotive is essentially an intellectual or mental process. Thus the emotive and the cognitive are distinguishable from the physical." He adds: "Cohen, in telling us what obscenity is *not*, explains legal obscenity better than any of the cases

with a vision [of the First Amendment] that emphasizes intellectual (and perhaps public) communication and not self-expression." Does Schauer's "non-speech" argument regarding obscenity adequately safeguard against the risk that it may encourage the Court to exclude whole categories of speech from First Amendment protection? In his argument at least preferable to the argument that some "indecent" displays, even though within the First Amendment, are entitled to less constitutional protection than other types of speech? [15]

c. Consider, finally, the impact of the Court's analysis of obscenity on the evaluation of state interests that may justify restrictions of speech in other areas. What are the interests underlying the Court's endorsement of a legitimate state concern with maintaining a "decent society"? Recall the questions at p. 1066 above, and note especially Chief Justice Burger's discussion in the 1973 cases. Can "offensiveness" notions (a part of the Court's definition of obscenity) and "nuisance" rationales (see American Mini Theatres, p. 1110 below) be recognized in the sphere of sexual materials without threatening the protection of controversial speech in other areas? Can the interest in public morality be accepted as a justification to bar obscenity without undercutting Justice Harlan's speech-protective approach in Cohen v. California, p. 1101 below? Should the narrow range of interests suggested in Justice Brennan's dissents in the 1973 cases be the only ones tolerable in the obscenity sphere?

CHILD PORNOGRAPHY

1. *The Ferber decision.* In NEW YORK v. FERBER, 458 U.S. 747 (1982), the Court unanimously rejected a First Amendment attack on a New York law designed to deal with the problem of child pornography. The law prohibits the distribution of material depicting children engaged in sexual conduct; it does not require that the material be legally obscene. In reaching that result, Justice WHITE, who wrote the majority opinion, echoed the Chaplinsky approach by "classifying child pornography as a category of material outside the protection of the First Amendment." [1] Ferber, the owner of a bookstore specializing in sexually oriented products, was convicted under § 263.15 of the New York Penal Law for selling two films devoted almost exclusively to depicting young boys masturbating. The provision states: "A person is guilty of promoting a sexual performance by a child when, knowing the character and content thereof, he produces, directs or promotes any performance which includes sexual

---

that purport to tell us what obscenity *is.*" Note also Schauer's comment on the "prurient interest" test: "The concept fundamental to the Miller test is that material appealing to the prurient interest *is* sex, and not merely describing or advocating sex. Material that appeals to the prurient interest is material that turns you on. Period." Schauer does not, however, endorse all of the Court's analysis of obscenity, and is especially critical of the emphasis on "offensiveness" in the Roth and Miller tests: "If the prurient interest test isolates material that has physical as opposed to mental effect, and if the 'value' test restricts regulation to material that is *solely* physical in nature, what is left is not speech in the constitutional sense, regardless of whether anyone is offended, and regardless of whether any community's standards are affronted." (Contrast, once again, Schauer's 1982 argument, in Free Speech: A Philosophical Enquiry, resting his Free Speech Principle heavily on "the argument from governmental incompetence," govern-

ment's inability to "make the necessary distinctions," as noted at p. 1067 above.)

15. See the American Mini Theatres and Pacifica cases, pp. 1110 and 1114 below. (As noted earlier, the special "procedural" problems raised by regulatory methods used in the control of obscenity are postponed for consideration in the next chapter, at p. 1160.)

1. Although the Court reached a unanimous judgment, only four other Justices (Chief Justice Burger and Justices Powell, Rehnquist and O'Connor) fully supported Justice White's opinion. (Justice O'Connor also submitted a separate concurrence.) Justice Blackmun simply noted his concurrence in the result. Justice Brennan, joined by Justice Marshall, filed an opinion concurring in the judgment. Justice Stevens also submitted a separate opinion concurring in the judgment. (The separate opinions are noted further below.)

conduct by a child less than sixteen years of age." [2] The Court found Ferber's conviction constitutional.

Justice White noted that this case was the Court's "first examination of a statute directed at and limited to depictions of sexual activity involving children. [3] We believe our inquiry should begin with the question of whether a State has somewhat more freedom in proscribing works which portray sexual acts or lewd exhibitions of genitalia by children [than in regulating obscenity]." In developing his affirmative answer to that question, Justice White began by noting that Chaplinsky had "excis[ed]" obscenity "from the realm of constitutionally protected expression." But in his view the 1973 Miller obscenity standard did not delineate the extent of state power over child pornography. The portions of his opinion explaining why states have "greater leeway" over child pornography warrant extensive quotation:

"*First.* It is evident [that] a state's interest in 'safeguarding the physical and psychological well being of a minor' is 'compelling.' [Globe Newspapers (1982; p. 1449 below).] Accordingly, we have sustained legislation aimed at protecting the physical and emotional well-being of youth even when the laws have operated in the sensitive area of constitutionally protected rights. [E.g. Ginsberg v. New York; see also Pacifica.] The prevention of sexual exploitation and abuse of children constitutes a government objective of surpassing importance. The legislative findings accompanying passage of the New York laws reflect this concern: '[The] public policy of the state demands the protection of children from exploitation through sexual performances.' We shall not second-guess this legislative judgment. [The] legislative judgment [is] that the use of children as subjects of pornographic materials is harmful to the physiological, emotional, and mental health of the child. That judgment, we think, easily passes muster under the First Amendment.

"*Second.* The distribution of photographs and films depicting sexual activity by juveniles is intrinsically related to the sexual abuse of children in at least two ways. First, the materials produced are a permanent record of the children's participation and the harm to the child is exacerbated by their circulation. Second, the distribution network for child pornography must be closed if the production of material which requires the sexual exploitation of children is to be effectively controlled. [While] the production of pornographic materials is a low-profile, clandestine industry, the need to market the resulting products requires a visible apparatus of distribution. The most expeditious if not the only practical method of law enforcement may be to dry up the market for this

---

2. Another section of the law defines "sexual conduct" as "actual or simulated sexual intercourse, deviate sexual intercourse, sexual bestiality, masturbation, sadomasochistic abuse, or lewd exhibition of the genitals." The law defines the term "promote" as "to procure, manufacture, issue, sell, give, provide, lend, mail, deliver, transfer, transmute, publish, distribute, circulate, disseminate, present, exhibit or advertise, or to offer or agree to do the same."

Ferber was also indicted under a companion provision, which was solely directed at obscenity. He was acquitted of the charge of promoting an obscene sexual performance, but found guilty of violating § 263.15, the child pornography provision, which did not require proof that the films were obscene. (Justice Stevens' concurring opinion noted that Ferber's counsel "conceded at oral argument that a finding that the films are obscene would have been consistent with the Miller definition.")

3. Justice White had noted earlier that, "[i]n recent years, the exploitive use of children in the production of pornography has become a serious national problem." The federal government and 47 states had enacted statutes "specifically directed at the production of child pornography." At least half of these did not require "that the materials produced be legally obscene." Moreover, 35 states and Congress had passed legislation prohibiting the distribution of such materials. Twenty of these states prohibited the distribution of material depicting children engaged in sexual conduct without requiring that the material be legally obscene. New York was one of these 20 states. (The laws in the other 15 states, as well as the federal law, prohibited dissemination of such material only if it was obscene.)

material by imposing severe criminal penalties on persons selling, advertising, or otherwise promoting the product.

"Respondent [argues] that it is enough for the State to prohibit the distribution of materials that are legally obscene under the Miller test. While some States may find that this approach properly accommodates [their interests], it does not follow that the First Amendment prohibits a State from going further. The Miller [standard] does not reflect the State's particular and more compelling interest in prosecuting those who promote the sexual exploitation of children. Thus, the question under the Miller test of whether a work, taken as a whole, appeals to the prurient interest of the average person bears no connection to the issue of whether a child has been physically or psychologically harmed in the production of the work. Similarly, a sexually explicit depiction need not be 'patently offensive' in order to have required the sexual exploitation of a child for its production. In addition, a work which, taken on the whole, contains serious literary, artistic, political, or scientific value may nevertheless embody the hardest core of child pornography. 'It is irrelevant to the child [who has been abused] whether or not the material [has] a literary, artistic, political, or [social value].'

"*Third.* The advertising and selling of child pornography provides an economic motive for and is thus an integral part of the production of such materials, an activity illegal throughout the nation. 'It rarely has been suggested that the constitutional freedom for speech and press extends its immunity to speech or writing used as an integral part of conduct in violation of a valid criminal statute.' Giboney v. Empire Storage & Ice Co. [1948; p. 1343 below]. We note that were the statutes outlawing the employment of children in these films and photographs fully effective, and the constitutionality of these laws have not been questioned, the First Amendment implications would be no greater than that presented by laws against distribution: enforceable production laws would leave no child pornography to be marketed.

"*Fourth.* The value of permitting live performances and photographic reproductions of children engaged in lewd sexual conduct is exceedingly modest, if not de minimis. We consider it unlikely that visual depictions of children performing sexual acts or lewdly exhibiting their genitals would often constitute an important and necessary part of a literary performance or scientific or educational work. [If] it were necessary for literary or artistic value, a person over the statutory age who perhaps looked younger could be utilized. Simulation outside of the prohibition of the statute could provide another alternative. Nor is there any question here of censoring a particular literary theme or portrayal of sexual activity. The First Amendment interest is limited to that of rendering the portrayal somewhat more 'realistic' by utilizing or photographing children.

"*Fifth.* Recognizing and classifying child pornography as a category of material outside the protection of the First Amendment is not incompatible with our earlier decisions. 'The question whether speech is, or is not protected by the First Amendment often depends on the content of the speech.' 'It is the content of an utterance that determines whether it is a protected epithet or an unprotected "fighting comment."' [American Mini Theatres.] See [e.g., Chaplinsky; Beauharnais]. [Thus], it is not rare that a content-based classification of speech has been accepted because it may be appropriately generalized that within the confines of the given classification, the evil to be restricted so overwhelmingly outweighs the expressive interests, if any, at stake, that no process of case-by-case adjudication is required. When a definable class of material, such as that covered by § 263.15, bears so heavily and pervasively on the welfare of children engaged in its production, we think the balance of competing interests is clearly struck and that it is permissible to consider these materials as without the protection of the First Amendment.

"C. There are, of course, limits on the category of child pornography which, like obscenity, is unprotected by the First Amendment. As with all legislation in this sensitive area, the conduct to be prohibited must be adequately defined by the applicable state law, as written or authoritatively construed. Here the nature of the harm to be combatted requires that the state offense be limited to works that *visually* depict sexual conduct by children below a specified age. The category of 'sexual conduct' proscribed must also be suitably limited and described. The test for child pornography is separate from the obscenity standard enunciated in Miller, but may be compared to it for purpose of clarity. The Miller formulation is adjusted in the following respects: A trier of fact need not find that the material appeals to the prurient interest of the average person; it is not required that sexual conduct portrayed be done so in a patently offensive manner; and the material at issue need not be considered as a whole. We note that the distribution of descriptions or other depictions of sexual conduct, not otherwise obscene, which do not involve live performance or photographic or other visual reproduction of live performances, retains First Amendment protection. As with obscenity laws, criminal responsibility may not be imposed without some element of scienter on the part of the defendant. [Smith v. California, 361 U.S. 147 (1959).]

"D. [The law's] prohibition incorporates a definition of sexual conduct that comports with the above-stated principles. [We] hold that § 263.15 sufficiently describes a category of material the production and distribution of which is not entitled to First Amendment protection. It is therefore clear that there is nothing unconstitutionally 'underinclusive' about a statute that singles out this category of material for proscription.[4] It also follows that the State is not barred by the First Amendment from prohibiting the distribution of unprotected materials produced outside the State."

After elaborating these central premises, Justice White turned to the claim that the New York law was "unconstitutionally overbroad because it would forbid the distribution of material with serious literary, scientific or educational value or material which does not threaten the harms sought to be combatted by the State." In rejecting that attack, Justice White relied heavily upon—and elaborated—the "substantial overbreadth" approach of Broadrick v. Oklahoma (a 1973 decision written by Justice White and discussed at length at p. 1151 below). In finding the law "not substantially overbroad," Justice White stated: "We consider this the paradigmatic case of a state statute whose legitimate reach dwarfs its arguably impermissible applications. New York, as we have held, may constitutionally prohibit dissemination of material specified in [the law]. While the reach of the statute is directed at the hard core of child pornography, the [highest New York court] was understandably concerned that some protected expression, ranging from medical textbooks to pictorials in National Geographic, would fall prey to the statute. How often, if ever, it may be necessary to employ children to engage in conduct clearly within the reach of the [law] in order to produce educational, medical or artistic works cannot be known with certainty. Yet we seriously doubt [that] these arguably impermissible applications of the statute amount to more than a tiny fraction of the materials within

---

4. "[Erznoznik (1975; p. 1107 below), relied upon by the highest New York court,] struck down a law against drive-in theaters showing nude scenes if movies could be seen from a public place. Since nudity, without more, is protected expression we proceeded to consider the underinclusiveness of the ordinance. The Jacksonville ordinance impermissibly singled out movies with nudity for special treatment while failing to regulate other protected speech which created the same alleged risk to traffic. Today, we hold that child pornography as defined in § 263.15 is unprotected speech subject to content-based regulation. Hence, it cannot be underinclusive or unconstitutional for a State to do precisely that." [Footnote by Justice White.]

the statute's reach. [Under] these circumstances, § 263.15 is 'not substantially overbroad and whatever overbreadth exists should be cured through case-by-case analysis of the fact situations to which its sanctions, assertedly, may not be applied.' [Broadrick.] He accordingly concluded: "Because § 263.15 is not substantially overbroad, it is unnecessary to consider its application to material that does not depict sexual conduct of a type that New York may restrict consistent with the First Amendment. As applied to Paul Ferber and to others who distribute similar material, the statute does not violate the First Amendment." [5]

Justice BRENNAN, joined by Justice Marshall, submitted an opinion concurring in the judgment. He stated that he agreed "with much of what is said in the Court's opinion" and that he had long held the view that "the State has a special interest in protecting the well-being of its youth." That "special and compelling interest, and the particular vulnerability of children," afforded the State leeway to regulate pornographic material harmful to children "even though the State does not have such leeway when it seeks only to protect consenting adults from exposure to such material." He also agreed with the rejection of the overbreadth attack because the "tiny fraction" of arguably protected serious material that could conceivably fall within the statute was insufficient to strike the law on overbreadth grounds even under his dissenting view in Broadrick. But he proceeded to add an important qualification. He insisted that application of a law such as New York's to "depictions of children that in themselves do have serious literary, artistic, scientific or medical value, would violate the First Amendment." He explained that "the limited classes of speech, the suppression of which does not raise serious First Amendment concerns, have two attributes": they are "of exceedingly 'slight social value,'" and the state has a compelling interest in their regulation. See [Chaplinsky]." He elaborated: "The First Amendment value of depictions of children that are in themselves serious contributions to art, literature or science, is, by definition, simply not 'de minimis.' At the same time, the State's interest in suppression of such materials is likely to be far less compelling. For the Court's assumption of harm to the child [lacks] much of its force where the depiction is a serious contribution to art or science. [In] short, it is inconceivable how a depiction of a child that is itself a serious contribution to the world of art or literature or

---

5. Justice O'CONNOR, while joining Justice White's opinion, also submitted a separate concurrence. She emphasized that the Court had not held that "New York must except 'material with serious literary, scientific or educational value' from its statute. The Court merely holds that, even if the First Amendment shelters such material, New York's current statute is not sufficiently overbroad to support [Ferber's] facial attack." She went on to suggest that the compelling state interests involved here "might in fact permit New York to ban knowing distribution of works depicting minors engaged in explicit sexual conduct, regardless of the social value of the depictions. For example, a 12-year-old child photographed while masturbating surely suffers the same psychological harm whether the community labels the photograph 'edifying' or 'tasteless.' The audience's appreciation of the depiction is simply irrelevant to New York's asserted interest in protecting children from psychological, emotional, and mental harm." She noted that an "exception for depictions of serious social value [would] actually increase opportunities for the content-based censorship disfavored by the

First Amendment." The New York law sought "to protect minors from abuse without attempting to restrict the expression of ideas by those who might use children as live models."

She added: "On the other hand, it is quite possible that New York's statute is overbroad because it bans depictions that do not actually threaten the harms identified by the Court. For example, clinical pictures of adolescent sexuality, such as those that might appear in medical textbooks, might not involve the type of sexual exploitation and abuse targeted by New York's statute. Nor might such depictions feed the poisonous 'kiddie porn' market that New York and other States have attempted to regulate. Similarly, pictures of children engaged in rites widely approved by their cultures, such as those that might appear in issues of National Geographic, might not trigger the compelling interests identified by the Court. It is not necessary to address these possibilities further today, however, because this potential overbreadth is not sufficiently substantial to warrant facial invalidation of [the law]."

science can be deemed 'material outside the protection of the First Amendment.' "

The longest and most distinctive of the separate opinions came from Justice STEVENS, who concurred only in the judgment. That opinion warrants noting at some length: "Two propositions seem perfectly clear to me. First, the specific conduct that gave rise to this criminal prosecution is not protected by the Federal Constitution; second, the state statute that respondent violated prohibits some conduct that is protected by the First Amendment. The critical question, then, is whether this respondent, to whom the statute may be applied without violating the Constitution, may challenge the statute on the ground that it conceivably may be applied unconstitutionally to others in situations not before the Court. I agree with the Court's answer to this question but not with its method of analyzing the issue.

"[A holding] that respondent may be punished for selling these two films does not require us to conclude that other users of these very films, or that other motion pictures containing similar scenes, are beyond the pale of constitutional protection. Thus, the exhibition of these films before a legislative committee studying a proposed amendment to a state law, or before a group of research scientists studying human behavior, could not, in my opinion, be made a crime. Moreover, it is at least conceivable that a serious work of art, a documentary on behavioral problems, or a medical or psychiatric teaching device, might include a scene from one of these films and, when viewed as a whole in a proper setting, be entitled to constitutional protection. The question whether a specific act of communication is protected by the First Amendment always requires some consideration of both its content and its context. The Court's holding that this respondent may not challenge New York's statute as overbroad follows its discussion of the contours of the category of nonobscene child pornography that New York may legitimately prohibit. Having defined that category in an abstract setting, the Court makes the empirical judgment that the arguably impermissible application of the New York statute amounts to only a 'tiny fraction of the materials within the statute's reach.' Even assuming that the Court's empirical analysis is sound,[6] I believe a more conservative approach to the issue would adequately vindicate the State's interest in protecting its children and cause less harm to the federal interest in free expression.

"A hypothetical example will illustrate my concern. Assume that the operator of a New York motion picture theater specializing in the exhibition of foreign feature films is offered a full-length movie containing one scene that is plainly lewd if viewed in isolation but that nevertheless is part of a serious work of art. If the child actor resided abroad, New York's interest in protecting its young from sexual exploitation would be far less compelling than in the case before us. The federal interest in free expression would, however, be just as strong as if an adult actor had been used. There are at least three different ways to deal with the statute's potential application to that sort of case.

"First, at one extreme and as the Court appears to hold, the First Amendment inquiry might be limited to determining whether the offensive scene, viewed in isolation, is lewd. When the constitutional protection is narrowed in this drastic fashion, the Court is probably safe in concluding that only a tiny

---

6. "The Court's analysis is directed entirely at the permissibility of the statute's coverage of nonobscene material. Its empirical evidence, however, is drawn substantially from congressional committee reports that ultimately reached the conclusion that a prohibition against *obscene* child pornography—coupled with sufficiently stiff sanctions—is an adequate response to this social problem. The Senate Committee on the Judiciary concluded that 'virtually all of the materials that are normally considered child pornography are obscene under the current standards,' and that '[i]n comparison with this blatant pornography, non-obscene materials that depict children are very few and very inconsequential.' The coverage of the federal statute is limited to obscene material." [Footnote by Justice Stevens.]

fraction of the materials covered by the New York statute is protected. And with respect to my hypothetical exhibitor of foreign films, he need have no uncertainty about the permissible application of the statute; for the one lewd scene would deprive the entire film of any constitutional protection. Second, at the other extreme, [the] application of this Court's cases requiring that an obscenity determination be based on the artistic value of a production taken as a whole would afford the exhibitor constitutional protection and result in a holding that the statute is invalid because of its overbreadth. Under that approach, the rationale for invalidating the entire statute is premised on the concern that the exhibitor's understanding about its potential reach could cause him to engage in self censorship. This Court's approach today substitutes broad, unambiguous state-imposed censorship for the self censorship that an overbroad statute might produce. Third, as an intermediate position, I would refuse to apply overbreadth analysis for reasons unrelated to any prediction concerning the relative number of protected communications that the statute may prohibit. Specifically, I would postpone decision of my hypothetical case until it actually arises. Advocates of a liberal use of overbreadth analysis could object to such postponement on the ground that it creates the risk that the exhibitor's uncertainty may produce self censorship. But that risk obviously interferes less with the interest in free expression than does an abstract, advance ruling that the film is simply unprotected whenever it contains a lewd scene, no matter how brief.

"My reasons for avoiding overbreadth analysis in this case are more qualitative than quantitative. When we follow our traditional practice of adjudicating difficult and novel constitutional questions only in concrete factual situations, the adjudications tend to be crafted with greater wisdom. Hypothetical rulings are inherently treacherous and prone to lead us into unforeseen errors; they are qualitatively less reliable than the products of case-by-case adjudication. Moreover, it is probably safe to assume that the category of speech that is covered by the New York statute generally is of a lower quality than most other types of communication. On a number of occasions, I have expressed the view that the First Amendment affords some forms of speech more protection from governmental regulation than other forms of speech.[7] Today the Court accepts this view, putting the category of speech described in the New York statute in its rightful place near the bottom of this hierarchy. Although I disagree with the Court's position that such speech is totally without First Amendment protection, I agree that generally marginal speech does not warrant the extraordinary protection afforded by the overbreadth doctrine. Because I have no difficulty with the statute's application in this case, I concur in the Court's judgment."[8]

    2. *Some comments on the Court's methodology.* Although the Justices were unanimous in supporting the Ferber result, there were significant differences in the roads they took to that end. Of special interest is the majority's analysis. On its face, this is a rare modern case in the tradition of the Chaplinsky exclusionary categorization approach: the majority simply casts outside the First

    7. "E.g., [Schad; Consolidated Edison; Pacifica; American Mini Theatres—all noted below]. "[Footnote by Justice Stevens.]

    8. In response to Ferber, Congress and a number of states have enacted or proposed legislation that would conform to the Court's opinion. In May 1984 Congress passed the Child Protection Act of 1984, which would eliminate the requirement currently found in federal law (18 U.S.C. § 2252) that sexually explicit materials be obscene in order to be subject to the strictures against child pornography. President Reagan signed the bill into law in May, 1984 (P.L. 98–

292). An earlier version of the bill had provided that in any prosecution for child pornography, "it shall be an affirmative defense that the medium, when taken as a whole, possesses serious literary, artistic, scientific, social, or educational values." At the insistence of the Senate, this provision was deleted. Assuming that a defendant is shown to have distributed material depicting sexual activity by a child, is this affirmative defense required by Ferber? If at least this much is required by Ferber, is an affirmative defense sufficient?

Amendment the entire class of child pornography, even though the class concededly includes materials not "obscene." But that technique produces vastly more discussion in this case than it had in Chaplinsky, and the Court also draws on a variety of other First Amendment techniques. In contrast to the Chaplinsky approach, the majority speaks at length not only about the limited social value of the communication involved but also, and most notably, about the state interests justifying restraint. So seen, Ferber contains earmarks of the "definitional balancing" technique involved in New York Times v. Sullivan (p. 1052 above), in the sense that that case held "malicious" defamation of public officials unprotected.[9] The codification emphasis of Ferber is also diluted by the reference to the rationale of the Giboney case for restricting speech—that it is "an integral part of [illegal] conduct." (See Justice White's paragraph beginning with "Third." The Giboney rationale is a much criticized notion in First Amendment law, as later materials will illustrate.) Note too that in his paragraph "Fourth," Justice White, in examining the First Amendment side of the balance, finds the value of child pornography "exceedingly modest, if not de minimis" by stating that child pornography does not constitute "an important and necessary part of a literary performance or scientific or educational work." Does that mark a departure from prior analyses? Does communication have to be "necessary" to literary or similar expression to qualify for First Amendment coverage?

PORNOGRAPHY AS SUBORDINATION OF WOMEN

In recent years, opponents of sexually explicit materials have advocated a novel theory for restrictive legislation. The theory seeks to invoke the civil rights, equality-seeking model by arguing that pornography promotes sex discrimination and subordination of women. The argument is reflected in an ordinance drafted in 1983 by two feminist theorists for the Minneapolis City Council and enacted, in revised form, by Indianapolis in 1984.[1] The basic constitutional premise of the ordinance is that promoting civil rights and equality, itself a constitutional value under the 14th Amendment, provides a "compelling" interest outweighing any First Amendment interest in the communication. The early arguments for the law rested heavily on cases such as Beauharnais. More recently, the primary reliance has been on Ferber above, as well as on American Mini Theatres and Pacifica, the two cases that follow. The Indianapolis ordinance was struck down in November 1984 by U.S. District

---

9. See generally Schauer, "Codifying the First Amendment: New York v. Ferber," 1982 Sup.Ct.Rev. 285. Schauer further argues that "Ferber can be viewed as partially relying on [a] 'covered but outweighed' path to nonprotection" and adds that defamation cases provide one of the closest parallels to the Ferber methodology. (Schauer adds: "The product of this process was the creation of yet another comparatively distinct area of First Amendment doctrine. [The] First Amendment is becoming increasingly intricate, which has prompted one scholar to observe pejoratively that First Amendment doctrine is beginning to resemble the Internal Revenue Code. The metaphor rings true, and maybe we are moving toward codification of the First Amendment." Schauer does not think that direction necessarily a bad one.)

1. The drafters of the Minneapolis ordinance were Catherine A. MacKinnon, University of Minnesota law professor, and Andrea Dworkin,

feminist author (including the book Pornography: Men Possessing Women (1981)). The Minneapolis ordinance was adopted by the Minneapolis City Council at the end of 1983, but vetoed by Mayor Fraser on the ground that the "remedy sought [is] neither appropriate nor enforceable within our cherished tradition and constitutionally protected right of free speech." See generally the symposium, "The Proposed Minneapolis Pornography Ordinance: Pornography Regulation Versus Civil Rights or Pornography Regulation as Civil Rights?," 11 Wm. Mitchell L.Rev. 39 (1985). In addition to printing the text of the ordinance, the symposium contains an article defending its constitutionality—Gershel, "Evaluating a Proposed Civil Rights Approach to Pornography: Legal Analysis As If Women Mattered"—and an argument challenging its constitutionality—Tigue, "Civil Rights and Censorship—Incompatible Bedfellows."

Judge Sarah Evans Barker in AMERICAN BOOKSELLERS ASSOCIATION v. HUDNUT, 598 F.Supp. 1316 (S.D.Ind.1984).[2] In examining the Indianapolis ordinance and the District Court ruling on it, consider especially whether the civil rights model adequately avoids the First Amendment concerns raised by the ordinance.

A major focus of the ordinance is "the impact of pornography on women's status and treatment."[3] As adopted in Indianapolis, the target of the ordinance goes beyond sexually explicit materials considered obscene under the Miller standards. "Pornography" is defined by the ordinance as "the graphic sexually explicit subordination of women, whether in pictures or in words," that also satisfies "one or more" stated criteria. These criteria include not only, e.g., the presentation of women "as sexual objects who experience sexual pleasure in being raped" but also the presentation of women "as sexual objects for domination, conquest, violation, exploitation, possession, or use, or through postures or positions of servility or submission or display." The ordinance rested on findings stating: "Pornography is a discriminatory practice based on sex which denies women equal opportunities in society. Pornography is central in creating and maintaining sex as a basis for discrimination. Pornography is a systematic practice of exploitation and subordination based on sex which differentially harms women." The purpose of the ordinance is to "prevent and prohibit all discriminatory practices of sexual subordination or inequality through pornography." Under the ordinance, the behavior made actionable includes "trafficking in pornography" and the "forcing of pornography on any woman, man, child, or transsexual in any place of employment, in education, in a home, or in any public place."[4]

In invalidating the ordinance, Judge Barker concluded that the proscriptions of the ordinance "are not limited to categories of speech, such as obscenity or child pornography, which have been excepted from First Amendment protections. [The ordinance seeks] to regulate expression, that is, to suppress speech, [and] although the State has a recognized interest in prohibiting sex discrimination, that interest does not outweigh the constitutionally protected interest of free speech."[5] In her lengthy opinion, Judge Barker found it "difficult to quarrel either with the Council's underlying concern [with pornography and sex discrimination] or with its premise that some legislative controls are in order," but she found the measure unacceptable under the First Amendment. She rejected the defenders' alleged argument that the ordinance "regulates conduct, not speech."[6] She also rejected the claim that the ordinance could be justified by the obscenity cases, stating that "defendants concede that the 'pornography'

---

2. Mayor Hudnut of Indianapolis announced soon after the decision that the ruling would be appealed. Ordinances based on the MacKinnon-Dworkin model are under consideration by other communities, from New York to California. See New York Times, Nov. 21, 1984.

3. Memorandum by MacKinnon & Dworkin to Minneapolis City Council, December 26, 1983.

4. Under the Indianapolis ordinance, enforcement is largely through complaints to and action by a city-county agency, which may award injunctive relief and damages. The Minneapolis ordinance had also provided for private lawsuits against the prohibited behavior.

5. Judge Barker added: "Assuming arguendo that the state's interest in prohibiting sex discrimination does outweigh the First Amendment interest of free speech, the Ordinance is nonetheless unconstitutional" because "it is unconstitutionally vague" and, as applied to some of the pro-

scribed activity, "it constitutes an unconstitutional prior restraint on speech."

6. Judge Barker stated: "[The defenders] contend (one senses with a certain sleight of hand) that the production, dissemination, and use of sexually explicit words and pictures is the actual subordination of women and not an expression of ideas deserving of First Amendment protection. [They] claim support for their theory by analogy, arguing that it is an [established] legal distinction that has allowed other courts to find that advocacy of a racially 'separate but equal' doctrine [is] protected speech [though] 'segregation' is not constitutionally [protected]. Accordingly, [they] characterize their Ordinance here as a civil rights measure, through which they seek to prevent the distribution [etc.] of 'pornography' [in] order to regulate and control the underlying unacceptable conduct. The content-versus-conduct approach espoused [is] not

they seek to control goes beyond obscenity, as defined by the [Court] and excepted from First Amendment protections." She was also unpersuaded by the claim that Ferber lent support to the ordinance because the "interests" of protecting women from sex-based discrimination are "analogous to and every bit as compelling and fundamental as those which the [Court] upheld in Ferber for the benefit of children." She thought Ferber "clearly distinguishable from the instant case on both the facts and law."

Judge Barker conceded that the state has "a well-recognized interest in preventing sex discrimination," but she did not think that that interest was "so compelling as to be fundamental" and therefore outweighing the free speech interest.[7] In broadly rejecting the claim that the state interest here was so compelling to justify "an exception to free speech," she noted that the ordinance was directed at "sociological harm, i.e., the discrimination, which results from 'pornography' to degrade women as a class. The Ordinance does not presume or require specifically defined, identifiable victims for most of its proscriptions. The Ordinance seeks to protect adult women [from] the diminution of their legal and sociological status as women, that is, from the discriminatory stigma which befalls women as women as a result of 'pornography.'" In reply, Judge Barker stated:

"This is a novel theory, [an] issue of first impression in the courts. If this Court were to accept defendants' argument—that the State's interest in protecting women from the humiliation and degradation which comes from being depicted in a sexually subordinate context is so compelling as to warrant the regulation of otherwise free speech to accomplish that end—one wonders what would prevent the [Council] (or any other legislative body) from enacting protections for other equally compelling claims against exploitation and discrimination as are presented here. Legislative bodies, finding support here, could also enact legislation prohibiting other unfair expression—the publication and distribution of racist material, for instance, on the grounds that it causes racial discrimination,[8] [or] legislation prohibiting ethnic or religious slurs on the grounds that they cause discrimination against particular ethnic or religious groups, or legislation barring literary depictions which are uncomplimentary or oppressive to handicapped persons on the grounds that they cause discrimination against that group of people, and so on. If this Court were to extend to this case the rationale in Ferber, [it] would signal so great a potential encroachment upon First Amendment freedoms that the precious liberties reposed within those guarantees would not survive. The compelling state interest [asserted here], though important and valid as that interest may be in other contexts, is not so fundamental an interest as to warrant a broad intrusion into otherwise free expression." Later, she added: "This Court cannot legitimately embark on

persuasive [and] is contrary to accepted First Amendment principles. Accepting as true the [Council's] finding that pornography conditions society to subordinate women, the means by which the Ordinance attempts to combat this sex discrimination is nonetheless through the regulation of speech. [Though] the purpose of the Ordinance is cast in civil rights terminology, [it] is clearly aimed at controlling the content of the speech and ideas which the [Council] has found harmful and offensive. [Despite the defenders'] attempt to redefine offensive speech as harmful action, the clear wording of the Ordinance discloses that they seek to control speech, and those restrictions must be analyzed in light of applicable constitutional requirements and standards."

7. Distinguishing the interest of children in Ferber from that asserted here, she noted:

"Adult women generally have the capacity to protect themselves from participating in and being personally victimized by [pornography]." She also found the Pacifica and American Mini Theatres cases, which follow, distinguishable— the former because the Indianapolis ordinance involved an effort to ban, not merely to channel, sexually explicit materials, and the latter because this case lacked the features of Pacifica with respect to protecting children and the intrusion of broadcasting into the privacy of the home.

8. In a footnote, she cited Beauharnais and noted that its "underlying reasoning" had been "questioned in many recent cases." She cited the Court of Appeals decision in Collin v. Smith in 1978, one of the cases arising from Skokie's effort to ban Nazi demonstrations (see p. 1237 below).

judicial policy-making, carving out a new exception to the First Amendment simply to uphold the Ordinance, even when there may be many good reasons to support legislative action. To permit every interest group, especially those who claim to be victimized by unfair expression, their own legislative exceptions to the First Amendment so long as they succeed in obtaining a majority of legislative votes in their favor demonstrates the potentially predatory nature of what defendants seek. [It] ought to be remembered by defendants and all others who would support such a legislative initiative that, in terms of altering sociological patterns, much as alteration may be necessary and desirable, free speech, rather than being the enemy, is a long-tested and worthy ally. To deny free speech in order to engineer social change in the name of accomplishing a greater good for one sector of our society erodes the freedoms of all and, as such, threatens tyranny and injustice for those subjected to the rule of such laws. The First Amendment protections presuppose the evil of such tyranny and prevent a finding by this Court upholding the Ordinance."

---

2. OFFENSIVENESS AND INDECENCY

Introduction. This subsection focuses on a problem first raised by one of the definitions of "fighting words" Justice Murphy stated in Chaplinsky (p. 1045 above). He spoke of words "which by their very utterance inflict injury" (not only the face-to-face insults which "tend to incite an immediate breach of the peace"), and he asserted that suppression was justified not only by the "social interest" in "order" but also by that in "morality." This group of materials concentrates on words and displays—typically with sexual connotations—that offend. The primary state interest usually asserted in curbing offensiveness and indecency is not the fear of immediate disorder.[1] Rather, it is the concern with the psychological or emotional injury inflicted on the audience (and sometimes a broader, vaguer concern with the minimum level of "morality" in public discourse). In a series of modern cases, the Court has confronted efforts to curtail offensiveness. Consider the adequacy of the Court's responses in terms of a persuasive First Amendment theory. Does recognition of a strong interest in protecting the sensitivity of the audience risk curtailment of the First Amendment interest in protecting even abrasive speech?

In the cases that follow, the Justices typically do not resort to the categorization approach pervasive in the preceding subsection on obscenity and pornography. More commonly they have engaged in inquiries akin to balancing, seeking to identify the First Amendment values inherent in the communication and to articulate and evaluate the state interests allegedly justifying restraint. Should the categorization approach have been followed more widely in the cases that follow? Or does the avoidance of that methodology here cast added doubt on the ready resort to exclusionary classifications in the preceding materials? Cohen, the next case, was the Court's first major encounter with the offensive language problem. Consider whether the Harlan opinion in Cohen deserves some of the praise it has received: some commentators view it as a model speech-protective balancing opinion;[2] others see it in part as a speech-protective

---

1. The line between "offensive words" and "fighting words" (in the narrower sense) is not clear-cut: a sensitive audience shocked by the speaker's words may be so outraged as to resort to vigilante tactics.

Note that a speaker may also be "offensive" because the *message* (rather than its form) may provoke audience hostility. Such situations are considered in the material on the "hostile audience" problem in the next chapter, at p. 1217.

2. E.g., Gunther, "[The] Case of Justice Powell," 24 Stan.L.Rev. 1001 (1972). See also Farber, "Civilizing Public Discourse: [The] Enduring Significance of Cohen v. California," 1980 Duke L.J. 283. For criticisms of Cohen, see Bickel, The Morality of Consent (1975), and Cox, The Role of the Supreme Court in American Government (1976).

use of the categorization approach.[3] To what extent has the Cohen approach survived the later decisions? Erznoznik, p. 1107 below, reflects the Cohen analysis at least in part. But in American Mini Theatres and Pacifica, pp. 1110 and 1114 below, some Justices in the majority endorsed an approach extending to some varieties of speech (the offensive and the indecent) less First Amendment protection than to other kinds of speech (e.g., political). Does such a "less valuable speech" approach, imposing a lesser burden of justification for restraints with respect to the less protected variety of speech, assure adequate safeguards for free expression?[4] Or should all expression within the First Amendment receive equally strong judicial protection?[5]

COHEN v. CALIFORNIA

403 U.S. 15, 91 S.Ct. 1780, 29 L.Ed.2d 284 (1971).

Mr. Justice HARLAN delivered the opinion of the Court.

This case may seem at first blush too inconsequential to find its way into our books, but the issue it presents is of no small constitutional significance.

[Cohen] was convicted [of violating a California law] which prohibits "maliciously and willfully disturb[ing] the peace or quiet of any neighborhood or person [by] offensive conduct." He was given 30 days' imprisonment. The facts upon which his conviction rests are detailed in the opinion of the [state court]: "On April 26, 1968, the defendant was observed in the Los Angeles County Courthouse in the corridor outside of Division 20 of the Municipal Court wearing a jacket bearing the words 'Fuck the Draft' which were plainly visible. There were women and children present in the corridor. The defendant was arrested. The defendant testified that he wore the jacket as a means of informing the public of the depth of his feelings against the Vietnam War and the draft. The defendant did not engage in, nor threaten to engage in, nor did anyone as the result of his conduct in fact commit or threaten to commit any act of violence." In affirming the conviction the [state court] held that "offensive conduct" means "behavior which has a tendency to provoke *others* to acts of violence or to in turn disturb the peace," and that the State had proved this element because, on the facts of this case, "[i]t was certainly reasonably foreseeable that such conduct might cause others to rise up to commit a violent

---

3. Ely, "Flag Desecration: A Case Study in the Roles of Categorization and Balancing in First Amendment Analysis," 88 Harv.L.Rev. 1482 (1975). See also Ely, Democracy and Distrust (1980), 114.

4. Note the distinctions between this lower level of "less valuable speech" approach and the Chaplinsky variety of categorization. Under Chaplinsky, some types of communication are wholly excluded from First Amendment coverage. Under the "lower value" speech approach, the type of communication involved is also the first subject of inquiry, but not for the purpose of determining whether it is wholly "out" of the First Amendment, but only to determine whether it is sufficiently far removed from the core values of the First Amendment (e.g., political speech) so that it should receive a lower level (albeit some) constitutional protection.

5. As noted earlier, the central argument against a unitary theory of the First Amendment (which would extend similar, strong protection to all varieties of communication) is that it would ultimately dilute First Amendment protections, because some types of speech (e.g., advertising, see sec. 2D below, or indecency) will inevitably receive less protection, with the result that even the protection of core, political speech will suffer. A central counterargument is that any variation in the levels of protection by assigning hierarchies of values on the First Amendment side of the balance for speech concededly within the First Amendment ballpark results ultimately in a myriad, increasingly ad hoc range of First Amendment rules and an excessive codification harmful to long range protection of First Amendment values. Those who make the latter claim argue that any adjustments in the actual protection of communication should take place by careful evaluation of the state interests asserted on the justification side of the balance, rather than by assigning variable weights not only to that side of the scale but also to the First Amendment side.

act against the person of the defendant or attempt to forceably remove his jacket." [We reverse.]

I. In order to lay hands on the precise issue which this case involves, it is useful first to canvass various matters which this record does *not* present.

The conviction quite clearly rests upon the asserted offensiveness of the *words* Cohen used to convey his message to the public. The only "conduct" which the State sought to punish is the fact of communication. Thus, we deal here with a conviction resting solely upon "speech," not upon any separately identifiable conduct which allegedly was intended by Cohen to be perceived by others as expressive of particular views but which, on its face, does not necessarily convey any message and hence arguably could be regulated without effectively repressing Cohen's ability to express himself. Cf. [United States v. O'Brien, p. 1170 below]. Further, the State certainly lacks power to punish Cohen for the underlying content of the message the inscription conveyed. At least so long as there is no showing of an intent to incite disobedience to or disruption of the draft, Cohen [could not] be punished for asserting the evident position on the inutility or immorality of the draft his jacket reflected. [Yates.]

[Cohen's] conviction, then, rests squarely upon his exercise of the "freedom of speech" [and] can be justified, if at all, only as a valid regulation of the manner in which he exercised that freedom, not as a permissible prohibition on the substantive message it conveys. This does not end the inquiry, of course, for the [First Amendment has] never been thought to give absolute protection to every individual to speak whenever or wherever he pleases, or to use any form of address in any circumstances that he chooses. In this vein, too, however, we think it important to note that several issues typically associated with such problems are not presented here.

In the first place, Cohen was tried under a statute applicable throughout the entire State. Any attempt to support this conviction on the ground that the statute seeks to preserve an appropriately decorous atmosphere in the court-house where Cohen was arrested must fail in the absence of any language in the statute that would have put appellant on notice that certain kinds of otherwise permissible speech or conduct would nevertheless [not] be tolerated in certain places. See [Edwards, p. 1221 below; cf. Adderley, p. 1243 below.] No fair reading of the phrase "offensive conduct" can be said sufficiently to inform the ordinary person that distinctions between certain locations are thereby created.

In the second place, as it comes to us, this case cannot be said to fall within those relatively few categories of instances where prior decisions have established the power of government to deal more comprehensively with certain forms of individual expression simply upon a showing that such a form was employed. This is not, for example, an obscenity case. Whatever else may be necessary to give rise to the States' broader power to prohibit obscene expression, such expression must be, in some significant way, erotic. [Roth; p. 1068 below.] It cannot plausibly be maintained that this vulgar allusion to the [draft] would conjure up such psychic stimulation in anyone likely to be confronted with Cohen's crudely defaced jacket.

This Court has also held that the States are free to ban the simple use, without a demonstration of additional justifying circumstances, of so-called "fighting words," those personally abusive epithets which, when addressed to the ordinary citizen, are, as a matter of common knowledge, inherently likely to provoke violent reaction. [Chaplinsky.] While the four-letter word displayed by Cohen in relation to the draft is not uncommonly employed in a personally provocative fashion, in this instance it was clearly not "directed to the person of the hearer." No individual actually or likely to be present could reasonably have regarded the words on appellant's jacket as a direct personal insult. Nor do we have here an instance of the exercise of the State's police power to prevent a speaker from intentionally provoking a given group to hostile reaction. Cf. [e.g., Feiner; p. 1219 below]. There is, as noted above, no showing that anyone who saw Cohen was in fact violently aroused or that [Cohen] intended such a result.

Finally, [much] has been made of the claim that Cohen's distasteful mode of expression was thrust upon unwilling or unsuspecting viewers, and that the State might therefore legitimately act as it did in order to protect the sensitive from otherwise unavoidable exposure to appellant's crude form of protest. Of course, the mere presumed presence of unwilling listeners or viewers does not serve automatically to justify curtailing all speech capable of giving offense. See, e.g., [Keefe; p. 1212 below]. While this Court has recognized that government may properly act in many situations to prohibit intrusion into the privacy of the home of unwelcome views and ideas which cannot be totally banned from the public dialogue, e.g., [Rowan; p. 1211 below], we have at the same time consistently stressed that "we are often 'captives' outside the sanctuary of the home and subject to objectionable speech." Id. The ability of government, consonant with the Constitution, to shut off discourse solely to protect others from hearing it is, in other words, dependent upon a showing that substantial privacy interests are being invaded in an essentially intolerable manner. Any broader view of this authority would effectively empower a majority to silence dissidents simply as a matter of personal predilections.

In this regard, persons confronted with Cohen's jacket were in a quite different posture than, say, those subjected to the raucous emissions of sound trucks blaring outside their residences. [See, e.g., Saia; p. 1208 below.] Those in the Los Angeles courthouse could effectively avoid further bombardment of their sensibilities simply by averting their eyes. And, while it may be that one has a more substantial claim to a recognizable privacy interest when walking through a courthouse corridor than, for example, strolling through Central Park, surely it is nothing like the interest in being free from unwanted expression in the confines of one's own home. Given the subtlety and complexity of the factors involved, if Cohen's "speech" was otherwise entitled to constitutional protection, we do not think the fact that some unwilling "listeners" in a public building may have been briefly exposed to it can serve to justify this breach of the peace conviction where, as here, there was no evidence that persons powerless to avoid appellant's conduct did in fact object to it, and where [the statute] evinces no concern [with] the special plight of the captive auditor, but, instead, indiscriminately sweeps within its prohibitions all "offensive conduct" that disturbs "any neighborhood or person."

II. Against this background, the issue flushed by this case stands out in bold relief. It is whether California can excise, as "offensive conduct," one particular scurrilous epithet from the public discourse, either upon the theory of the court below that its use is inherently likely to cause violent reaction or upon a more general assertion that the States, acting as guardians of public morality, may properly remove this offensive word from the public vocabulary. The rationale of the California court is plainly untenable. At most it reflects an "undifferentiated fear or apprehension of disturbance [which] is not enough to overcome the right to freedom of expression." [Tinker; p. 1176 below.] We have been shown no evidence that substantial numbers of citizens are standing ready to strike out physically at whoever may assault their sensibilities with execrations like that uttered by Cohen. There may be some persons about with such lawless and violent proclivities, but that is an insufficient base upon which to erect, consistently with constitutional values, a governmental power to force persons who wish to ventilate their dissident views into avoiding particular forms of expression. The argument amounts to little more than the self-defeating proposition that to avoid physical censorship of one who has not sought to provoke such a response by a hypothetical coterie of the violent and lawless, the States may more appropriately effectuate that censorship themselves.

Admittedly, it is not so obvious that the [First Amendment] must be taken to disable the States from punishing public utterance of this unseemly expletive in order to maintain what they regard as a suitable level of discourse within the body politic. We think, however, that examination and reflection will reveal the shortcomings of a contrary viewpoint. At the outset, we cannot overemphasize that, in our judgment, most situations where the State has a justifiable interest in regulating speech will fall within one or more of the various established exceptions, discussed above but not applicable here, to the usual rule that governmental bodies may not prescribe the form or content of individual expression. Equally important to our conclusion is the constitutional backdrop against which our decision must be made. The constitutional right of free expression is powerful medicine in a society as diverse and populous as ours. It is designed and intended to remove governmental restraints from the arena of public discussion, putting the decision as to what views shall be voiced largely into the hands of each of us, in the hope that use of such freedom will ultimately produce a more capable citizenry and more perfect polity and in the belief that no other approach would comport with the premise of individual dignity and choice upon which our political system rests. See [Whitney concurrence].

To many, the immediate consequence of this freedom may often appear to be only verbal tumult, discord, and even offensive utterance. These are, however, within established limits, in truth necessary side effects of the broader enduring values which the process of open debate permits us to achieve. That the air may at times seem filled with verbal cacophony is, in this sense, not a sign of weakness but of strength. We cannot lose sight of the fact that, in what otherwise might seem a trifling and annoying instance of individual distasteful abuse of a privilege, these fundamental societal values are truly [implicated].

Against this perception of the constitutional policies involved, we discern certain more particularized considerations that peculiarly call for reversal of this conviction. First, the principle contended for by the State seems inherently boundless. How is one to distinguish this from any other offensive word? Surely the State has no right to cleanse public debate to the point where it is grammatically palatable to the most squeamish among us. Yet no readily ascertainable general principle exists for stopping short of that result were we to affirm the judgment below. For, while the particular four-letter word being litigated here is perhaps more distasteful than most others of its genre, it is nevertheless often true that one man's vulgarity is another's lyric. Indeed, we think it is largely because governmental officials cannot make principled distinctions in this area that the Constitution leaves matters of taste and style so largely to the individual.

Additionally, we cannot overlook the fact, because it is well illustrated by the episode involved here, that much linguistic expression serves a dual communicative function: it conveys not only ideas capable of relatively precise, detached explication, but otherwise inexpressible emotions as well. In fact, words are often chosen as much for their emotive as their cognitive force. We cannot sanction the view that the Constitution, while solicitous of the cognitive content of individual speech, has little or no regard for that emotive function which, practically speaking, may often be the more important element of the overall message sought to be [communicated]. Finally, and in the same vein, we cannot indulge the facile assumption that one can forbid particular words without also running a substantial risk of suppressing ideas in the process. Indeed, governments might soon seize upon the censorship of particular words as a convenient guise for banning the expression of unpopular views. [It] is, in sum, our judgment that, absent a more particularized and compelling reason for its actions, the State may not, consistently with the [First Amendment], make the simple public display here involved of this single four-letter expletive a [criminal offense].

Reversed.

Mr. Justice BLACKMUN, with whom The Chief Justice [BURGER] and Mr. Justice BLACK join.

I dissent, and I do so for two reasons: 1. Cohen's absurd and immature antic, in my view, was mainly conduct and little speech. See [Street v. New York (p. 1178 below); Cox I (p. 1225 below); Giboney (p. 1343 below)]. Further, the case appears to me to be well within the sphere of [Chaplinsky], where Mr. Justice Murphy, a known champion of First Amendment freedoms, wrote for a unanimous bench. As a consequence, this Court's agonizing over First Amendment values seems misplaced and unnecessary.

2. I am not at all certain that the California Court of Appeal's construction of [the law] is now the authoritative California construction. [A month after the ruling below], the State Supreme Court in another case construed § 415, evidently for the first time. In re Bushman. [The Bushman decision stated:] "[The law] makes punishable only wilful and malicious conduct that is violent and endangers public safety and order or that creates a clear and present danger that others will engage in violence of that nature. [It] does not make criminal any nonviolent act unless the act incites or threatens to incite others to violence." Cohen was cited in Bushman, but I am not convinced that its description there and Cohen itself are completely consistent with the "clear and present danger" standard enunciated in Bushman. [This case] ought to be remanded in the light of [Bushman].[1]

THE BURGER COURT AND OFFENSIVE LANGUAGE

1. *The 1972 trilogy.* In three 1972 decisions, ROSENFELD v. NEW JERSEY, LEWIS v. NEW ORLEANS, and BROWN v. OKLAHOMA, reported at 408 U.S. 901, 913, and 914, the majority summarily vacated and remanded three convictions for use of offensive language.[1] These orders provided several Justices with the opportunity to voice their concerns about the majority's unduly narrow view of governmental power to restrain offensive words. Rosenfeld had addressed a school board meeting attended by about 150 people, including women and children, and had "used the adjective 'm_ _ _ _ _ f_ _ _ _ _' [sic] on four occasions, to describe the teachers, the school board, the town and his own country." He was convicted under a "disorderly person" statute prohibiting "indecent" and "offensive" language in public places and interpreted to cover words "of such a nature as to be likely to incite the hearer to an immediate breach of the peace or to be likely, in the light of the gender and age of the listener and the setting of the utterance, to affect the sensibilities of a hearer." Lewis had addressed police officers who were arresting her son as "g_ _ d_ _ _ m_ _ _ _ _ f_ _ _ _ _ _." She was convicted under a breach of the peace statute prohibiting anyone from wantonly cursing, reviling, or using

---

1. Justice WHITE concurred only in the second paragraph of Justice Blackmun's dissent. Justice Harlan's majority opinion commented on that paragraph as follows: "We perceive no difference of substance between the Bushman construction and that of the [court below in Cohen], particularly in light of the Bushman court's approving citation of Cohen."

1. Rosenfeld and Brown were remanded in light of Cohen v. California as well as Gooding v.

Wilson, a "fighting words" overbreadth case noted in sec. 2A, at p. 1048 above. Lewis was remanded for reconsideration only in light of Gooding, the overbreadth case. Chief Justice Burger and Justices Blackmun and Rehnquist dissented in all three cases. Justice Powell concurred in the results in Lewis and Brown and dissented in Rosenfeld.

"obscene or opprobrious language" toward a police officer on duty. Brown, in a meeting at a university chapel, had referred to some policemen as "m_ _ _ _ _ f_ _ _ _ _ _ fascist pig cops" and to a particular policeman as that "black m_ _ _ _ _ f_ _ _ _ _ _ pig." He was convicted under a statute barring "any obscene or lascivious language or word in any public place, or in the presence of females."

Justice POWELL's separate opinions explained his differing votes in the three situations. In Rosenfeld, he thought Cohen distinguishable and described the words as a "gross abuse of the respected privilege in this country of allowing every citizen to speak his mind." He conceded that the language "perhaps" did not constitute "fighting words" in the Chaplinsky sense. Physical retaliation against the speaker was unlikely. Nor were the words directed at a specific individual. But the Chaplinsky principle was not so limited, he insisted: "It also extends to the willful use of scurrilous language calculated to offend the sensibilities of an unwilling audience." He stated that "a verbal assault on an unwilling audience may be so grossly offensive and emotionally disturbing as to be the proper subject of criminal proscription, whether under a statute denominating it [to be] disorderly conduct, or, more accurately, a public nuisance." In the other two cases, Justice Powell concurred with the majority. In Lewis, he urged remand solely in light of Chaplinsky, not Gooding.[2] And in Brown, he emphasized that the language had been used in the course of "a political meeting to which appellant had been invited to present the Black Panther viewpoint. In these circumstances language of the character charged might well have been anticipated by the audience."[3]

The other dissenters took broader positions. Chief Justice BURGER's opinion stated: "When we undermine the general belief that the law will give protection against fighting words and profane and abusive language such as the utterances involved in these cases, we take steps to return to the law of the jungle." In a case like Rosenfeld, there might not be instantaneous retaliation, but it was imaginable that "some justifiably outraged parent whose family were exposed to the foul mouthings of the speaker would 'meet him outside' [and] resort to the 19th Century's vigorous modes of dealing with such people." Justice REHNQUIST insisted that Lewis' words were "fighting words," and that the words in the other two cases were "lewd and obscene" and "profane" in the Chaplinsky sense.[4]

---

2. Justice Powell's central ground—that "the situation may be different where [what otherwise might be fighting words] are addressed to a police officer trained to exercise a higher degree of restraint than the average citizen"—has been noted earlier, in sec. 2A at p. 1047 above. Two years later, when the Lewis case returned to the Court, Justice Powell changed his position. Lewis v. New Orleans, 415 U.S. 130 (Lewis II) (1974), produced an outright reversal on overbreadth grounds, with Justice Powell now joining the support of that technique in this context. Justice Powell emphasized that the law "confers on police a virtually unrestrained power."

3. Contrast with Justice Powell's emphasis on the factual setting in Brown and Lewis, his silence about the context in Rosenfeld (involving a white school teacher supporting black claims at a school board meeting). At his trial, Rosenfeld had testified (echoing Harlan's emphasis in Cohen on the "emotive force" of certain language) that he had used his offensive words to show his sympathy with the black position and to express his deep concern about racial problems. See

Gunther, "[The] Case of Justice Powell," 24 Stan.L.Rev. 1001 (1972). Note Justice Powell's suggestion in these cases that the legitimacy of restraints on offensive language should turn on the context of the particular audience. Is Justice Powell's effort to pull together the three notions of "nuisance, audience expectations, and policeman's higher degree of restraint" a useful approach to the offensive language problem? See Gunther, above.

4. Note also the decision in Papish v. Board of Curators of Univ. of Missouri, 410 U.S. 667 (1973), where the majority summarily set aside the expulsion of a graduate student for distributing on campus a publication which, inter alia, used the "M_ _ _ _ _ f_ _ _ _ _" language. Justice Rehnquist's dissent, joined by Chief Justice Burger and Justice Blackmun, insisted that even if Rosenfeld were correct, this case, not involving criminal sanctions, was distinguishable. And a separate dissent by the Chief Justice thought the extension of the Cohen-Rosenfeld precedents to the campus situation was "curious—even bizarre."

2. *Some questions.* Reconsider, in light of these offensive language cases of the early 1970s, whether anything other than words risking violent retaliation from a particular individual justify restraint on offensive language. Do these cases still endorse restrictions on words that, as Chaplinsky put it, "by their very utterance inflict injury"? Or was that prong of Chaplinsky overturned by the cases of the Cohen era? Has it been revived to some extent by the late 1970s decisions that follow? Note that none of the cases in this section involves expression falling within the "obscenity" rubric; all of these cases involve "offensive" or "indecent" expression falling short of obscenity. To what extent do any of the Justices in the preceding cases recognize not only a sensitive audience, risk-of-violence interest but also a general legitimate state interest in "morality"—or, as Justice Harlan put it in Cohen, an interest in maintaining a "suitable level of discourse within the body politic"? Recall also the open acknowledgement of an interest in a moral, decent environment in the obscenity context. Is recognition of an audience sensitivity concern as a restraint on offensive language more justifiable than a general interest in morality?

ERZNOZNIK AND OFFENSIVE DISPLAYS: DEVELOPING THE COHEN APPROACH

In ERZNOZNIK v. JACKSONVILLE, 422 U.S. 205 (1975), the Court sustained a challenge to the facial validity of an ordinance prohibiting drive-in movie theaters with screens visible from public streets from showing films containing nudity. The ordinance prohibited exhibitions of "the human male or female bare buttocks, human female bare breasts, or human bare pubic areas." Concededly, the ban applied to nonobscene films. The city's major defense was that "it may protect its citizens against unwilling exposure to materials that may be offensive." In rejecting that claim, Justice POWELL's majority opinion developed and applied the approach articulated by Justice Harlan in Cohen. He stated:

"This Court has considered analogous issues—pitting the First Amendment rights of speakers against the privacy rights of those who may be unwilling viewers or auditors—in a variety of contexts. See, e.g., [Kovacs v. Cooper; Cohen]. Such cases demand delicate balancing. [Although] each case ultimately must depend on its own specific facts, some general principles have emerged. A State or municipality may protect individual privacy by enacting reasonable time, place, and manner regulations applicable to all speech irrespective of content. But when the government, acting as censor, undertakes selectively to shield the public from some kinds of speech on the ground that they are more offensive than others, the First Amendment strictly limits its power. See, e.g., [Mosley].[1] Such selective restrictions have been upheld only when the speaker intrudes on the privacy of the home or the degree of captivity makes it impractical for the unwilling viewer or auditor to avoid exposure. See [Lehman (p. 1247 below); Cohen]. The plain, if at times disquieting, truth is that in our pluralistic society, [with] constantly proliferating new and ingenious forms of expression, 'we are inescapably captive audiences for many purposes.' [Rowan.] Much that we encounter offends our esthetic, if not our political and moral, sensibilities. Nevertheless, the Constitution does not permit government

---

1. Police Dept. v. Mosley (1972; p. 1164 below) is a major case in the development of judicial hostility to content discrimination as a central concern in free speech cases. Mosley emphasized the relationship between the First Amendment and equal protection in the analysis of discriminatory regulations of speech. Mosley and other cases dealing with varieties of discrimination in the speech area are considered more fully below, in chap. 12, sec. 2, at p. 1164. See generally Karst, "Equality as a Central Principle in the First Amendment," 43 U.Chi.L.Rev. 20 (1975), and other materials noted in chap. 12.

to decide which types of otherwise protected speech are sufficiently offensive to require protection for the unwilling listener or viewer. Rather, absent the narrow circumstances described above,[2] the burden normally falls upon the viewer to 'avoid further bombardment of [his] sensibilities simply by averting [his] eyes.' [Cohen; see also Spence v. Washington (p. 1183 below).]

"The Jacksonville ordinance discriminates among movies solely on the basis of content.[3] Its effect is to deter drive-in theaters from showing movies containing any nudity, however innocent or even educational. This discrimination cannot be justified as a means of preventing significant intrusions on privacy. The ordinance seeks only to keep these films from being seen from public streets and places where the offended viewer readily can avert his eyes. In short, the screen of a drive-in theater is not 'so obtrusive as to make it impossible for an unwilling individual to avoid exposure to it.' [Redrup.] Thus, we conclude that the limited privacy interest of persons on the public streets cannot justify this censorship of otherwise protected speech on the basis of its content."

Justice Powell also rejected two other proffered justifications. With respect to the claim that the ordinance was intended to regulate expression accessible to minors, he found the law "overbroad in its proscription." He noted that it was not limited to sexually explicit nudity and applied to all films "containing *any* uncovered buttocks or breasts, irrespective of context or pervasiveness." That would bar films "containing a picture of a baby's buttocks, the nude body of a war victim, or scenes from a culture in which nudity is indigenous." Justice Powell commented: "Clearly all nudity cannot be deemed obscene even as to minors. [Speech] that is neither obscene as to youths nor subject to some other legitimate proscription cannot be suppressed solely to protect the young from ideas or images that a legislative body thinks unsuitable for them." The city also defended the ordinance as a traffic regulation, claiming that "nudity on a drive-in movie screen distracts passing motorists, thus slowing the flow of traffic and increasing the likelihood of accidents." Noting that nothing in the record indicated that the law was in fact aimed at traffic regulation, Justice Powell commented: "[E]ven if this were the purpose of the ordinance, it nonetheless would be invalid. By singling out movies containing even the most fleeting and innocent glimpses of nudity the legislative classification is strikingly underinclusive. There is no reason to think that a wide variety of other scenes in the customary screen diet [would] be any less distracting to the passing motorist.

2. "It has also been suggested that government may proscribe, by a properly framed law, 'the willful use of scurrilous language calculated to offend the sensibilities of an unwilling audience.' [Rosenfeld (Powell, J., dissenting).] In such cases the speaker may seek to 'force public confrontation with the potentially offensive aspects of the work.' It may not be the content of the speech, as much as the deliberate 'verbal [or visual] assault,' Rosenfeld, that justifies proscription. In the present case, however, appellant is not trying to reach, much less shock, unwilling viewers. Appellant manages a commercial enterprise which depends for its success on *paying* customers, not on freeloading passersby. Presumably, where economically feasible, the screen of a drive-in theater will be shielded from those who do not pay." [Footnote by Justice Powell.]

3. "Scenes of nudity in a movie, like pictures of nude persons in a book, must be considered as a part of the whole work. In this respect such nudity is distinguishable from the kind of public nudity traditionally subject to indecent exposure laws.

"The Chief Justice's dissent, in response to this point, states that '[u]nlike persons reading books, passersby cannot consider fragments of drive-in movies as a part of the "whole work" for the simple reason that they *see* but do not *hear* the [performance].' At issue here, however, is not the viewing rights of unwilling viewers but rather the rights of those who operate drive-in theaters and the public that attends these establishments. The effect of the Jacksonville ordinance is to increase the cost of showing films containing nudity. In certain circumstances theaters will avoid showing these movies rather than incur the additional costs. As a result persons who want to see such films at drive-ins will be unable to do so. It is in this regard that a motion picture must be considered as a whole, and not as isolated fragments or scenes of nudity." [Footnote by Justice Powell.]

[Even] a traffic regulation cannot discriminate on the basis of content unless there are clear reasons for the distinctions."

Chief Justice BURGER's dissent, joined by Justice Rehnquist, accused the majority of taking a "rigidly simplistic approach" and concluded that the ordinance was "narrowly drawn to regulate only certain unique public exhibitions of nudity; it would be absurd to suggest that it operates to suppress expression of *ideas*." He elaborated: "The conclusion that only a limited interest of persons on the public streets is at stake here can be supported only if one completely ignores the unique visual medium to which the Jacksonville ordinance is directed. Whatever validity the notion that passersby may protect their sensibilities by averting their eyes may have when applied to words printed on an individual's jacket, see [Cohen], or a flag hung from a second-floor apartment window, see [Spence], it distorts reality to apply that notion to the outsize screen of a drive-in movie theater. Such screens are invariably huge. [Moreover], when films are projected on such screens the combination of color and animation against a necessarily dark background is designed to, and results in, attracting and holding the attention of all observers. No more defensible is the Court's conclusion that Jacksonville's ordinance is defective because it regulates only nudity. The significance of this fact is explained only in [footnote 3]. Both the analogy and the distinction are flawed. Unlike persons reading books, passersby cannot consider fragments of drive-in movies as a part of the 'whole work' for the simple reason that they *see* but do not *hear* the [performance]. The communicative value of such fleeting exposure falls somewhere in the range of slight to nonexistent. Moreover, those persons who legitimately desire to consider the 'work as a whole' are not foreclosed from doing so. [The] First Amendment interests involved in this case are trivial at best. On the other hand, assuming arguendo that there could be a play performed in a theater by nude actors involving genuine communication of ideas, the same conduct in a public park or street could be prosecuted under an ordinance prohibiting indecent exposure. [Whether] such regulation is justified as necessary to protect public mores or simply to insure the undistracted enjoyment of open areas by the greatest number of people—or for traffic safety—its rationale applies a fortiori to giant displays which through technology are capable of revealing and emphasizing the most intimate details of human anatomy." [4]

TOWARD A THEORY OF "LOWER VALUE" SPEECH?

Introduction. In the two cases that follow, Justice Stevens' plurality opinions support a kind of content regulation of offensive displays and speech that falls short of outright exclusion of that type of communication from the First Amendment, but that insists that such expression is less valuable than core, political speech and accordingly more readily restrainable. The cases involve (1) a zoning regulation regarding the sale or display of sexually explicit (but not necessarily obscene) materials, and (2) a broadcasting prohibition of offensive words in a comedian's monologue. In the later cases that conclude this subsection, Justice Stevens articulates limits on the restrictions permissible under his approach, but he adheres to the general notion that some varieties of speech are entitled to less protection than others. (A similar position has been adopted by the entire Court with regard to commercial speech, considered in sec. 2D below.) In examining these materials, consider whether this less valuable, lower level of speech methodology is a justifiable, realistic approach (a viewing

---

    4. Justice WHITE submitted a separate dissent. There was also a concurring opinion by Justice DOUGLAS.

of the First Amendment as covering widely differing varieties of speech, varieties that must be aligned in a hierarchy, with resultant differing degrees of protection) or whether this departure from a unitary approach to First Amendment problems (protecting all varieties of speech via a single, heavy burden of justification) unduly fragmentizes First Amendment analysis.

YOUNG v. AMERICAN MINI THEATRES, 427 U.S. 50 (1976): This decision upheld portions of a Detroit "Anti-Skid Row Ordinance" that differentiates between motion picture theaters which exhibit sexually explicit "adult movies" and those which do not. The Court rejected the claim that the statutory classification was unconstitutional because it was based on the content of communication protected by the First Amendment. The impact of the classification was to channel the display of the sexually explicit (but not necessarily obscene) materials into limited portions of the city, not to ban the display from the city entirely. In his plurality opinion, Justice STEVENS launched his theory that differing levels of speech warrant different degrees of First Amendment protection. He identified the communication here as being of lower value than core, political speech. (He developed that theory further in another prevailing but less than majority opinion in Pacifica, the next principal case.)[1]

The Detroit ordinance required dispersal of "adult" theaters and bookstores—e.g., it stated that an "adult" theater may not be located within 1,000 feet of any two other "regulated uses" or within 500 feet of a residential area.[2] Theaters are classified as "adult" on the basis of the character of the motion pictures they exhibit. If a theater presents "material distinguished or characterized by emphasis on matters depicting, describing or relating to 'specified sexual activities' or 'specified anatomical areas,'"[3] it is an "adult" establishment. The ordinance was challenged by the operators of two adult motion picture theaters located within 1,000 feet of two other "regulated uses." The city argued that the ordinance was a zoning law needed because the location of several "regulated uses" in the same neighborhood tended to attract undesirable transients, adversely affected property values, and caused an increase in crime.

At the outset of his opinion, Justice Stevens rejected the arguments that the ordinance was unconstitutionally vague and constituted a prior restraint. He then turned to the central issue in the case, the validity of the classifications in the ordinance, and stated: "A remark attributed to Voltaire characterizes our zealous adherence to the principle that the Government may not tell the citizen what he may or may not say. Referring to a suggestion that the violent

---

1. Justice Stevens spoke only for a plurality of the Court in the central part of his opinion. Justice Powell, whose vote was necessary for the 5 to 4 result, wrote separately to voice his doubts about Justice Stevens' approach, as noted below. For additional development of the differences between Justices Powell and Stevens, see Pacifica, the next case.

2. In addition to adult motion picture theaters and "mini" theaters, which contain less than 50 seats, the regulated uses include adult bookstores; cabarets; establishments for the sale of beer or intoxicating liquor for consumption on the premises; hotels or motels; pawnshops; pool or billiard halls; public lodging houses; second-hand stores; shoeshine parlors; and taxi dance halls.

3. The ordinance defined these terms as follows: "For the purpose of this Section, 'Specified Sexual Activities' is defined as:

"1. Human Genitals in a state of sexual stimulation or arousal;

"2. Acts of human masturbation, sexual intercourse or sodomy;

"3. Fondling or other erotic touching of human genitals, pubic region, buttock or female breast.

"And 'Specified Anatomical Areas' is defined as:

"1. Less than completely and opaquely covered: (a) human genitals, pubic region, (b) buttock, and (c) female breast below a point immediately above the top of the areola; and

"2. Human male genitals in a discernibly turgid state, even if completely and opaquely covered."

overthrow of tyranny might be legitimate, he said: 'I disapprove of what you say, but I will defend to the death your right to say it.' The essence of that comment has been repeated time after time in our decisions invalidating attempts [to] impose selective controls upon the dissemination of ideas. [Some of our statements], read literally and without regard for the facts of the case in which [they were] made, would absolutely preclude any regulation of expressive activity predicated in whole or in part on the content of the communication. [But the] question whether speech is, or is not, protected by the First Amendment often depends on the content of the speech. Thus, the line between permissible advocacy and impermissible incitation to crime or violence depends, not merely on the setting in which the speech occurs, but also on exactly what the speaker had to say. Similarly, it is the content of the utterance that determines whether it is a protected epithet or an unprotected ['fighting comment']. Even within the area of protected speech, a difference in content may require a different governmental response. [After reviewing libel and commercial speech cases, he continued:] More directly in point are opinions dealing with the question whether the First Amendment prohibits government from wholly suppressing sexually oriented materials on the basis of their "obscene character." [Indeed], the Members of the Court who would accord the greatest protection to such materials have repeatedly indicated that the State could prohibit the distribution or exhibition of such materials to juveniles and unconsenting adults. [Such] a line may be drawn on the basis of content without violating the Government's paramount obligation of neutrality in its regulation of protected communication. For the regulation of the places where sexually explicit films may be exhibited is unaffected by whatever social, political, or philosophical message the film may be intended to communicate; whether the motion picture ridicules or characterizes one point of view or another, the effect of the ordinances is exactly the same.

"Moreover, even though we recognize that the First Amendment will not tolerate the total suppression of erotic materials that have some arguably artistic value, it is manifest that society's interest in protecting this type of expression is of a wholly different, and lesser, magnitude than the interest in untrammeled political debate that inspired Voltaire's immortal comment. Whether political oratory or philosophical discussion moves us to applaud or to despise what is said, every schoolchild can understand why our duty to defend the right to speak remains the same. But few of us would march our sons and daughters off to war to preserve the citizen's right to see 'Specified Sexual Activities' exhibited in the theaters of our choice. Even though the First Amendment protects communication in this area from total suppression, we hold that the State may legitimately use the content of these materials as the basis for placing them in a different classification from other motion pictures.

"The remaining question is whether the line drawn by these ordinances is justified by the city's interest in preserving the character of its neighborhoods. [The] record discloses a factual basis for the [Council's] conclusion that this kind of restriction will have the desired effect.[4] It is not our function to appraise the wisdom of its decision to require adult theaters to be separated rather than concentrated in the same areas. In either event, the city's interest in attempting to preserve the quality of urban life is one that must be accorded high respect.

---

4. "The City Council's determination was that a concentration of 'adult' movie theaters causes the area to deteriorate and become a focus of crime, effects which are not attributable to theaters showing other types of films. It is this secondary effect which this zoning ordinance attempts to avoid, not the dissemination of 'offensive' speech. In contrast, in Erznoznik, the justi-fications offered by the city rested primarily on the city's interest in protecting its citizens from exposure to unwanted, 'offensive' speech. The only secondary effect relied on to support that ordinance was the impact on traffic—an effect which might be caused by a distracting open-air movie even if it did not exhibit nudity." [Foot-note by Justice Stevens.]

Moreover, the city must be allowed a reasonable opportunity to experiment with solutions to admittedly serious problems. Since what is ultimately at stake is nothing more than a limitation on the place where adult films may be exhibited,[5] even though the determination of whether a particular film fits that characterization turns on the nature of its content, we conclude that the city's interest in the present and future character of its neighborhoods adequately supports its classification of [motion pictures]."

Justice POWELL, whose vote was necessary to support the majority judgment, stated in a separate opinion: "[My] approach to the resolution of this case is sufficiently different to prompt me to write separately.[1] I view the case as presenting an example of innovative land-use regulation, implicating First Amendment concerns only incidentally and to a limited [extent]. [This zoning] situation is not analogous [to] any other prior case. The unique situation presented by this ordinance calls [for] a careful inquiry into the competing concerns of the State and the interests protected by the guaranty of free expression. Because a substantial burden rests upon the State when it would limit in any way First Amendment rights, it is necessary to identify with specificity the nature of the infringement in each [case].

"The inquiry for First Amendment purposes [looks] only to the effect of this ordinance upon freedom of expression. This prompts essentially two inquiries: (i) does the ordinance impose any content limitation on the creators of adult movies or their ability to make them available to whom they desire, and (ii) does it restrict in any significant way the viewing of these movies by those who desire to see them? On the record in this case, these inquiries must be answered in the negative. At most the impact of the ordinance on these interests is incidental and minimal.[2] [The] ordinance is addressed only to the places at which this type of expression may be presented, a restriction that does not interfere with content. Nor is there any significant overall curtailment of adult movie presentations, or the opportunity for a message to reach an audience. [In] these circumstances, it is appropriate to analyze the permissibility of Detroit's action under the four-part test of United States v. O'Brien [p. 1170 below]. There [is] no question that the Ordinance was within the power of the Detroit Common Council to enact. Nor is there doubt that the interests furthered by this Ordinance are both important and substantial. The third and fourth tests of O'Brien also are met on this record. It is clear both from the chronology and from the facts that Detroit has not embarked on an effort to suppress free expression. The Ordinance was already in existence, and its purposes clearly set out, for a full decade before adult establishments were brought under it. When this occurred, it is clear [that] the governmental interest prompting the inclusion in the ordinance of adult establishments was wholly unrelated to any suppression of free expression. Nor is there reason to question that the degree of incidental encroachment upon such expression was the minimum necessary to further the purpose of the [ordinance].[3]

---

5. "The situation would be quite different if the ordinance had the effect of suppressing, or greatly restricting access to, lawful speech. Here, however, the District Court [found]: 'There are myriad locations in the City of Detroit which must be over 1,000 feet from existing regulated establishments. This burden on First Amendment rights is [slight].'" [Footnote by Justice Stevens.]

1. "I do not think we need reach, nor am I inclined to agree with, the [holding] that nonobscene, erotic materials may be treated differently under First Amendment principles from other forms of protected [expression]." [Footnote by

Justice Powell. See also Justice Powell's separate opinion in Pacifica, which follows, where he criticized Justice Stevens' lesser value speech approach at greater length.]

2. "The communication involved here is not a kind in which the content or effectiveness of the message depends in some measure upon where or how it is conveyed. Cf. [Cox I; Brown v. Louisiana; Mosley—all in the next chapter]." [Footnote by Justice Powell.]

3. "In my view the dissent misconceives the issue in this case by insisting that it involves an impermissible time, place and manner restriction

"The dissent perceives support for its position in [Erznoznik]. I believe this perception is a clouded one. [T]he ordinance in Erznoznik was a misconceived attempt directly to regulate content of expression. The Detroit zoning ordinance, in contrast, affects expression only incidentally and in furtherance of governmental interests wholly unrelated to the regulation of expression. [Although] courts must be alert to the possibility of direct rather than incidental effects of zoning on expression, and especially to the possibility of pretextual use of the power to zone as a means of suppressing expression, it is clear that this is not such a case."

Justice STEWART, joined by Justices Brennan, Marshall and Blackmun, dissented: "[This] case does not involve a simple zoning ordinance, or a content-neutral time, place, and manner restriction, or a regulation of obscene expression or other speech that is entitled to less than the full protection of the First Amendment. The kind of expression at issue here is no doubt objectionable to some, but that fact does not diminish its protected [status]. What this case does involve is the constitutional permissibility of selective interference with protected speech whose content is thought to produce distasteful effects. It is elementary that a prime function of the First Amendment is to guard against just such interference. By refusing to invalidate Detroit's ordinance the Court rides roughshod over cardinal principles of First Amendment law, which require that time, place and manner regulations that affect protected expression be content-neutral except in the limited context of a captive or juvenile audience. In place of these principles the Court invokes a concept wholly alien to the First Amendment. [The Court] stands 'Voltaire's immortal comment' on its head. For if the guarantees of the First Amendment were reserved for expression that more than a 'few of us' would take up arms to defend, then the right of free expression would be defined and circumscribed by current popular [opinion].[1]

"The fact that the 'offensive' speech here may not address 'important' topics—'ideas of social and political significance,' in the Court's terminology—does not mean that it is less worthy of constitutional protection [e.g., Cohen]. Moreover, in the absence of a judicial determination of obscenity, it is by no means clear that the speech is not 'important' even on the Court's terms. I can only interpret today's decision as an aberration. The Court is undoubtedly sympathetic, as am I, to the well-intentioned efforts of Detroit to 'clean up' its streets and prevent the proliferation of 'skid rows.' But it is in those instances where protected speech grates most unpleasantly against the sensibilities that judicial vigilance must be at its height. [The] factual parallels between [Erznoznik] and this [case] are [striking]."[2]

would have met Stevens' high standard anyway

---

based on the content of expression. It involves nothing of the kind. We have here merely a decision by the city to treat certain movie theaters differently because they have markedly different effects upon their surroundings. Moreover, even if this were a case involving a special governmental response to the content of one type of movie, it is possible that the result would be supported by a line of cases recognizing that the government can tailor its reaction to different types of speech according to the degree to which its special and overriding interests are implicated. See, e.g., Tinker; Procunier v. Martinez; Greer v. Spock (Powell, J., concurring) [all below]. It is not analogous to [Mosley], in which no governmental interest justified a distinction between the types of messages permitted in the public forum there involved." [Footnote by Justice Powell.]

1. "The Court stresses that Detroit's content-based regulatory system does not preclude altogether the display of sexually oriented films. But as the Court noted in a similar context in Southeastern Promotions, Ltd. v. Conrad [p. 1251 below], this is constitutionally irrelevant for 'one is not to have the exercise of his liberty of expression in appropriate places abridged on the plea that it may be exercised in some other place.' Id., quoting Schneider v. State." [Footnote by Justice Stewart.]

2. Justice BLACKMUN, in addition to joining Justice Stewart's dissent, submitted a separate dissent (joined by Justices Brennan, Stewart and Marshall) objecting to the ordinance on vagueness grounds.

FCC v. PACIFICA FOUNDATION

438 U.S. 726, 98 S.Ct. 3026, 57 L.Ed.2d 1073 (1978).

[This decision held that the Federal Communications Commission has power to regulate radio broadcasts that are indecent but not obscene. It arose from the following circumstances: In a mid-afternoon weekday broadcast, respondent's New York radio station aired a 12-minute monologue called "Filthy Words" by George Carlin, a satiric humorist. The monologue, recorded before a live audience that frequently interrupted with laughter, began by referring to Carlin's thoughts about "the words you couldn't say on the public, ah, airwaves, um, the ones you definitely wouldn't say, ever." Carlin listed those words and repeated them in a variety of colloquialisms.[1] The monologue was aired as part of a program on contemporary attitudes toward the use of language. Immediately before the broadcast, the station had advised listeners that it would include "sensitive language which might be regarded as offensive to some."

[The FCC received a complaint from a man who stated that he had heard the broadcast while driving with his young son. In response, the FCC issued a Declaratory Order granting the complaint and holding that Pacifica "could have been the subject of administrative sanctions." However, the FCC did not impose formal sanctions; instead, it stated that the Order would be "associated with the station's license file, and in the event that subsequent complaints are received, the [FCC] will then decide whether it should utilize any of the available sanctions it has been granted by Congress." The FCC explained that Carlin's "patently offensive," though *not* obscene, language should be regulated by principles analogous to those found in the law of nuisance where the "law generally speaks to *channeling* -behavior more than actually prohibiting it." Later, the FCC explained that its regulation of certain words depicting sexual and excretory activity was designed to channel them "to times of day when children most likely would not be exposed." The Court of Appeals overturned the FCC Order.

[In sustaining the FCC's action, Justice STEVENS, in Part I of his opinion, found the administrative action an adjudication rather than rulemaking and stated that "the focus of our review must be on the Commission's determination that the Carlin monologue was indecent as broadcast." In Part II, he concluded that the statutory prohibition of "censorship" by the FCC did not limit the Commission's authority to impose sanctions "on licensees who engage in obscene, indecent, or profane broadcasting." In Part III, he found Carlin's monologue "indecent" within the meaning of the governing statute and rejected Pacifica's argument that "indecent" broadcasts should be limited to those with prurient appeal and, accordingly, "obscene." In Part IV(A), he found an overbreadth analysis inappropriate and concluded that review should be on an "as applied" basis: "whether the Commission has the authority to proscribe this particular broadcast." With that background, Justice Stevens turned to the central First Amendment issues:][2]

---

1. The transcript of Carlin's "Filthy Words" monologue in the five-page Appendix to Justice Stevens' opinion includes the following passage:

"I was thinking about the curse words and the swear words, the cuss words and the words that you can't say, that you're not supposed to say all the time. [I] was thinking one night about the words you couldn't say on the public, ah, airwaves, um, the ones you definitely wouldn't say, ever. [B]astard you can say, and hell and damn so I have to figure out which ones you couldn't and ever and it came down to seven but the list is open to amendment, and in fact, has been changed, uh, by now. [The] original seven words were shit, piss, fuck, cunt, cocksucker, motherfucker, and tits. Those are the ones that will curve your spine, grow hair on your hands and (laughter) maybe, even bring us, God help us, peace without honor (laughter) um, and a bourbon."

2. Justice Stevens' opinion on the central constitutional issues (in Part IV of his opinion) was (as in the preceding case, American Mini Theatres) only a plurality opinion: only Chief

IV(B). When the issue is narrowed to the facts of this case, the question is whether the First Amendment denies government any power to restrict the public broadcast of indecent language in any circumstances. For if the government has any such power, this was an appropriate occasion for its exercise. The words of the Carlin monologue are unquestionably "speech" within the meaning of the First Amendment. It is equally clear that the [FCC's] objections to the broadcast were based in part on its content. The order must therefore fall if, as Pacifica argues, the First Amendment prohibits all governmental regulation that depends on the content of speech. Our past cases demonstrate, however, that no such absolute rule is mandated by the Constitution. [See, e.g., the cases on "fighting words," obscenity, libel, and commercial speech, as well as Mini Theatres.]

The question in this case is whether a broadcast of patently offensive words dealing with sex and excretion may be regulated because of its content. [T]he fact that society may find speech offensive is not a sufficient reason for suppressing it. Indeed, if it is the speaker's opinion that gives offense, that consequence is a reason for according it constitutional protection. [If] there were any reason to believe that the Commission's characterization of the Carlin monologue as offensive could be traced to its political content—or even to the fact that it satirized contemporary attitudes about four letter words[3]—First Amendment protection might be required. But that is simply not this case. These words offend for the same reasons that obscenity offends.[4] Their place in the hierarchy of First Amendment values was aptly sketched by Mr. Justice Murphy [in Chaplinsky].

Although these words ordinarily lack literary, political, or scientific value, they are not entirely outside the protection of the First Amendment. Some uses of even the most offensive words are unquestionably protected. [E.g., Hess v. Indiana.] Indeed, we may assume, arguendo, that this monologue would be protected in other contexts. Nonetheless, the constitutional protection accorded to a communication containing such patently offensive sexual and excretory language need not be the same in every context. It is a characteristic of speech such as this that both its capacity to offend and its "social value" [Chaplinsky] [vary] with the circumstances. Words that are commonplace in one setting are shocking in another. To paraphrase Mr. Justice Harlan, one occasion's lyric is another's vulgarity. Cf. [Cohen].[5] In this case it is undisputed that the content of Pacifica's broadcast was "vulgar," "offensive," and "shocking." Because content of that character is not entitled to absolute constitutional protection under all circumstances, we must consider its context in order to determine whether the Commission's action was constitutionally permissible.

Justice Burger and Justice Rehnquist joined Parts IV(A) and IV(B) of his opinion. Justice Powell, joined by Justice Blackmun, wrote separately, and their votes were necessary for the majority result on the central constitutional issues. Justice Powell stated more elaborately than in American Mini Theatres his disagreement with Justice Stevens' "less valuable speech" approach.

3. The monologue does present a point of view; it attempts to show that the words it uses are "harmless" and that our attitudes toward them are "essentially silly." The Commission objects, not to this point of view, but to the way in which it is expressed. The belief that these words are harmless does not necessarily confer a First Amendment privilege to use them while proselytizing, just as the conviction that obscenity is harmless does not license one to communicate that conviction by the indiscriminate distribution of an obscene leaflet. [Footnote by Justice Stevens.]

4. The Commission stated: "Obnoxious, gutter language describing these matters has the effect of debasing and brutalizing human beings by reducing them to their mere bodily functions." Our society has a tradition of performing certain bodily functions in private, and of severely limiting the public exposure or discussion of such matters. Verbal or physical acts exposing those intimacies are offensive irrespective of any message that may accompany the exposure. [Footnote by Justice Stevens.]

5. The importance of context is illustrated by the Cohen case. [So] far as the evidence showed, no one in the courthouse was offended by his jacket. [In] contrast, in this case the Commission was responding to a listener's strenuous [complaint]. [Footnote by Justice Stevens.]

IV(C). We have long recognized that each medium of expression presents special First Amendment problems. And of all forms of communication, it is broadcasting that has received the most limited First Amendment protection. [The] reasons for these distinctions are complex, but two have relevance to the present case. First, the broadcast media have established a uniquely pervasive presence in the lives of all Americans. Patently offensive, indecent material presented over the airwaves confronts the citizen, not only in public, but also in the privacy of the home, where the individual's right to be let alone plainly outweighs the First Amendment rights of an intruder. [Rowan, p. 1211 below.] Because the broadcast audience is constantly tuning in and out, prior warnings cannot completely protect the listener or viewer from unexpected program content. To say that one may avoid further offense by turning off the radio when he hears indecent language is like saying that the remedy for an assault is to run away after the first blow. One may hang up on an indecent phone call, but that option does not give the caller a constitutional immunity or avoid a harm that has already taken place.[6]

Second, broadcasting is uniquely accessible to children, even those too young to read. Although Cohen's written message might have been incomprehensible to a first grader, Pacifica's broadcast could have enlarged a child's vocabulary in an instant. Other forms of offensive expression may be withheld from the young without restricting the expression at its source. Bookstores and motion picture theaters, for example, may be prohibited from making indecent material available to children. [Ginsberg v. New York].[7] The ease with which children may obtain access to broadcast material, coupled with the concerns recognized in Ginsberg, amply justify special treatment of indecent broadcasting.

It is appropriate [to] emphasize the narrowness of our holding. This case does not involve a two-way radio conversation between a cab driver and a dispatcher, or a telecast of an Elizabethan comedy. We have not decided that an occasional expletive in either setting would justify any sanction or, indeed, that this broadcast would justify a criminal prosecution. The [FCC's] decision rested entirely on a nuisance rationale under which context is all-important. The concept requires consideration of a host of variables. The time of day was emphasized by the [FCC]. The content of the program in which the language is used will also affect the composition of the audience, and differences between radio, television, and perhaps closed-circuit transmissions, may also be relevant. As Mr. Justice Sutherland wrote, a "nuisance may be merely a right thing in the wrong place—like a pig in the parlor instead of the barnyard." Euclid v. Ambler Realty Co. We simply hold that when the Commission finds that a pig has entered the parlor, the exercise of its regulatory power does not depend on proof that the pig is obscene.

Reversed.

Mr. Justice POWELL, with whom Mr. Justice BLACKMUN joins, concurring.[1]

---

6. Outside the home, the balance between the offensive speaker and the unwilling audience may sometimes tip in favor of the speaker, requiring the offended listener to turn away. See [Erznoznik and Cohen]. [Footnote by Justice Stevens.]

7. The Commission's action does not by any means reduce adults to hearing only what is fit for children. Cf. Butler v. Michigan, 352 U.S. 380 (1957). Adults who feel the need may purchase tapes and records or go to theaters and nightclubs to hear these words. In fact, the Commission has not unequivocally closed even broadcasting to speech of this sort; whether broadcast audiences in the late evening contain so few children that playing this monologue would be permissible is an issue neither the Commission nor this Court has decided. [Footnote by Justice Stevens.]

1. Justice Powell stated that he wrote separately because "I do not subscribe to all that is said in [Parts IV(A) and (B)]" of Justice Stevens' opinion.

I.   [T]he Commission sought to "channel" the monologue to hours when the fewest unsupervised children would be exposed to it. In my view, this consideration provides strong support for the Commission's holding. [In] most instances, the dissemination of this kind of speech to children may be limited without also limiting willing adults' access to it. [The] difficulty is that such a physical separation of the audience cannot be accomplished in the broadcast media. During most of the broadcast hours [the] broadcaster cannot reach willing adults without also reaching children. This [is] one of the distinctions between the broadcast and other media. [The] Commission was entitled to give substantial weight to this [difference].

A second difference [is] that broadcasting—unlike most other forms of communication—comes directly into the home, the one place where people ordinarily have the right not to be assaulted by uninvited and offensive sights and sounds. Although the First Amendment may require unwilling adults to absorb the first blow of offensive but protected speech when they are in public before they turn away, a different order of values obtains in the home. [The] Commission also was entitled to give this factor appropriate weight in the circumstances of the instant case. This is not to say, however, that the Commission has an unrestricted license to decide what speech, protected in other media, may be banned from the airwaves in order to protect unwilling adults from momentary exposure to it in their homes. Making the sensitive judgments required in these cases is not easy. But this responsibility has been reposed initially in the Commission, and its judgment is entitled to respect. [It] is said that this ruling will have the effect of "reduc[ing] the adult population [to hearing] only what is fit for children." This argument is not without force. The Commission certainly should consider it as it develops standards in this area. But it is not sufficiently strong to leave the Commission powerless to act in circumstances such as those in this case. The Commission's holding does not prevent willing adults from purchasing Carlin's record, from attending his performances, or indeed, from reading the transcript reprinted as an appendix to the Court's opinion. On its face, it does not prevent respondent from broadcasting the monologue during late evening hours. [The decision] does not speak to cases involving the isolated use of a potentially offensive word in the course of a radio broadcast, as distinguished from the verbal shock treatment administered by respondent [here].

II.   [I] do not join Part IV(B), however, because I do not subscribe to the theory that the Justices of this Court are free generally to decide on the basis of its content which speech protected by the First Amendment is most "valuable" and hence deserving of the most protection, and which is less "valuable" and hence deserving of less protection.[2] In my view, the result in this case does not turn on whether Carlin's monologue, viewed as a whole, or the words that comprise it, have more or less "value" than a candidate's campaign speech. This is a judgment for each person to make, not one for the judges to impose upon him.[3] The result turns instead on the unique characteristics of the broadcast media, combined with society's right to protect its children from speech generally agreed to be inappropriate for their years, and with the interest of unwilling adults in not being assaulted by such offensive speech in their homes. Moreover, I doubt whether today's decision will prevent any adult who wishes to receive Carlin's message in Carlin's own words from doing so, and

2. The Court has, however, created a limited exception to this rule in order to bring commercial speech within the protection of the First Amendment. [Footnote by Justice Powell. See, Sec. 2D below.]

3. For much the same reason, I also do not join Part IV(A). I had not thought that the application *vel non* of overbreadth analysis should depend on the Court's judgment as to the value of the protected speech that might be deterred. Except in the context of commercial speech, it has not in the past. [However], I agree [that] respondent's overbreadth challenge is meritless. [Footnote by Justice Powell.]

from making for himself a value judgment as to the merit of the message and words. These are the grounds upon which I join the judgment [as] to Part IV.

Mr. Justice BRENNAN, with whom Mr. Justice MARSHALL joins, dissenting.

I agree with Mr. Justice Stewart that [the statutory term "indecent"] must be construed to prohibit only obscene speech. I would, therefore, normally refrain from expressing my views on any constitutional issues implicated in this case. However, I find the Court's misapplication of fundamental First Amendment principles so patent, and its attempt to impose *its* notions of propriety on the whole of the American people so misguided, that I am unable to remain silent.

I. For the second time in two years, see [American Mini Theatres], the Court refuses to embrace the notion, completely antithetical to basic First Amendment values, that the degree of protection the First Amendment affords protected speech varies with the social value ascribed to that speech by five Members of this Court. See opinion of Mr. Justice Powell. [Yet despite] our unanimous agreement that the Carlin monologue is protected speech, a majority of the Court nevertheless finds that, on the facts of this case, the FCC is not constitutionally barred from imposing sanctions on Pacifica for its airing of the Carlin monologue. This majority apparently believes that the FCC's disapproval of Pacifica's afternoon broadcast of Carlin's "Dirty Words" recording is a permissible time, place, and manner regulation. Both the opinion of my Brother Stevens and the opinion of my Brother Powell rely principally on two factors in reaching this conclusion: (1) the capacity of a radio broadcast to intrude into the unwilling listener's home, and (2) the presence of children in the listening audience. Dispassionate analysis, removed from individual notions as to what is proper and what is not, starkly reveals that these justifications [simply] do not support even the professedly moderate degree of governmental homogenization of radio communications [that] the Court today permits.

A. [In finding] the privacy interests of an individual in his home [sufficient] to justify the content regulation of protected speech, [the] Court commits two errors. First, it misconceives the nature of the privacy interests involved where an individual voluntarily chooses to admit radio communications into his home. Second, it ignores the constitutionally protected interests of both those who wish to transmit and those who desire to receive broadcasts that many [might] find offensive.

[An] individual's actions in switching on and listening to communications transmitted over the public airways and directed to the public at large do not implicate fundamental privacy interests, even when engaged in within the home. Instead, because the radio is undeniably a public medium, these actions are more properly viewed as a decision to take part, if only as a listener, in an ongoing public discourse. Although an individual's decision to allow public radio communications into his home undoubtedly does not abrogate all of his privacy interests, the residual privacy interest he retains vis-à-vis the communication he voluntarily admits into his home are surely no greater than those of the people present in the corridor of the Los Angeles courthouse in Cohen who bore witness to the words "Fuck the Draft" emblazoned across Cohen's [jacket]. Even if an individual who voluntarily opens his home to radio communications retains privacy interests of sufficient moment to justify a ban on protected speech if those interests are "invaded in an essentially intolerable manner," Cohen, the very fact that those interests are threatened only by a radio broadcast precludes any intolerable invasion of privacy; for unlike other intrusive modes of communication, such as sound trucks, "[t]he radio can be turned off"—and with a minimum of effort. As Judge Bazelon aptly observed below, "having elected to receive public air waves, the scanner who stumbles onto an offensive program is in the same position as the unsuspecting passers-by in Cohen and

Erznoznik; he can avert his attention by changing channels or turning off the set." Whatever the minimal discomfort suffered by a listener who inadvertently tunes into a program he finds offensive during the brief interval before he can simply extend his arm and switch stations or flick the "off" button, it is surely worth the candle to preserve the broadcaster's right to send, and the right of those interested to receive, a message entitled to full First Amendment protection. To reach a contrary balance, as does the Court, is clearly, to follow Mr. Justice Stevens' reliance on animal metaphors, "to burn the house to roast the pig."

The Court's balance, of necessity, fails to accord proper weight to the interests of listeners who wish to hear broadcasts the FCC deems offensive. It permits majoritarian tastes completely to preclude a protected message from entering the homes of a receptive, unoffended minority. No decision of this Court supports such a result. Where the individuals comprising the offended majority may freely choose to reject the material being offered, we have never found their privacy interests of such moment to warrant the suppression of speech on privacy grounds. [Rowan] confirms rather than belies this conclusion. [The] determination of offensiveness *vel non* under the statute involved in Rowan was completely within the hands of the individual householder; no governmental evaluation of the worth of the mail's content stood between the mailer and the householder. In contrast, the visage of the censor is all too discernible here.

B. [The] government unquestionably has a special interest in the well-being of children. [But here] the Court, for the first time, allows the government to prevent minors from gaining access to materials that are not obscene, and are therefore protected, as to them. It thus ignores our recent admonition that "[s]peech that is neither obscene as to youths nor subject to some other legitimate proscription cannot be suppressed solely to protect the young from ideas or images that a legislative body thinks unsuitable for them." [Erznoznik.] The Court's refusal to follow its own pronouncements is especially lamentable since it has the anomalous subsidiary effect, at least in the radio context at issue here, of making completely unavailable to adults material which may not constitutionally be kept even from children. This result violates in spades the principle of Butler v. Michigan. [I] am far less certain than my Brother Powell [that] faith in the Commission is warranted; and even if I shared it, I could not so easily shirk the responsibility assumed by each Member of this Court jealously to guard against encroachments on First Amendment freedoms.

[T]he opinions of my Brother Powell and my Brother Stevens both stress the time-honored right of a parent to raise his child as he sees fit—a right this Court has consistently been vigilant to protect. [E.g., Wisconsin v. Yoder, p. 1521 below.] Yet this principle supports a result directly contrary to that reached by the Court. Yoder [holds] that parents, *not* the government, have the right to make certain decisions regarding the upbringing of their children. As surprising as it may be to individual Members of this Court, some parents may actually find Mr. Carlin's unabashed attitudes towards the seven "dirty words" healthy, and deem it desirable to expose their children to the manner in which Mr. Carlin defuses the taboo surrounding the words. Such parents may constitute a minority of the American public, but the absence of great numbers willing to exercise the right to raise their children in this fashion does not alter the right's nature or its existence. Only the Court's regrettable decision does that.[1]

---

1. The opinions of my Brothers Powell and Stevens rightly refrain from relying on the notion of "spectrum scarcity" to support their result. As Chief Judge Bazelon noted below, "although scarcity has justified *increasing* the diversity of speakers and speech, it has never been held to justify censorship." [Footnote by Justice Brennan.]

C. As demonstrated above, [the] intrusive nature of radio and the presence of children in the listening audience [cannot] support the FCC's disapproval of the Carlin monologue. These two asserted justifications are further plagued by a common failing: the lack of principled limits on their use as a basis for FCC censorship. [Taken] to their logical extreme, these rationales would support the cleansing of public radio of any "four-letter words" whatsoever, regardless of their context. The rationales could justify the banning from radio of a myriad of literary works, novels, poems, and plays by the likes of Shakespeare, Joyce, Hemingway, Ben Jonson, Henry Fielding, Robert Burns, and Chaucer; they could support the suppression of a good deal of political speech, such as the Nixon tapes; and they could even provide the basis for imposing sanctions for the broadcast of certain portions of the Bible. In order to dispel the spectre of the possibility of so unpalatable a degree of censorship, and to defuse Pacifica's overbreadth challenge, the FCC insists that it desires only the authority to reprimand a broadcaster on facts analogous to those present in this case. [To] insure that the FCC's regulation of protected speech does not exceed [limited] bounds, my Brother Powell is content to rely upon the judgment of the Commission while my Brother Stevens deems it prudent to rely on this Court's ability accurately to assess the worth of various kinds of speech.[2] For my own part, even accepting that this case is limited to its facts,[3] I would place the responsibility and the right to weed worthless and offensive communications from the public airways where it belongs and where, until today, it resided: in a public free to choose those communications worthy of its attention from a marketplace unsullied by the censor's hand.

II. [I] find the reasoning by which my Brethren conclude that the FCC censorship they approve will not significantly infringe on First Amendment values both disingenuous as to reality and wrong as a matter of law. My Brother Stevens, in reaching a result apologetically described as narrow, takes comfort in his observation that "[a] requirement that indecent language be avoided will have its primary effect on the form, rather than the content, of serious communication" and finds solace in his conviction that "[t]here are few, if any, thoughts that cannot be expressed by the use of less offensive language." The idea that the contents of a message and its potential impact on any who might receive it can be divorced from the words that are the vehicle for its expression is transparently fallacious. A given word may have a unique capacity to capsule an idea, evoke an emotion, or conjure up an image. Indeed, for those of us who place an appropriately high value on our cherished First Amendment rights, the word "censor" is such a word. Mr. Justice Harlan, speaking for the Court, recognized the truism that a speaker's choice of words cannot surgically be separated from the ideas he desires to express when he warned that "we cannot indulge the facile assumption that one can forbid particular words without also running a substantial risk of suppressing ideas in

2. Although ultimately dependent upon the outcome of review in this Court, the approach taken by my Brother Stevens would not appear to tolerate the FCC's suppression of any speech, such as political speech, falling within the core area of First Amendment concern. The same, however, cannot be said of the approach taken by my Brother Powell, which, on its face, permits the Commission to censor even political speech if it is sufficiently offensive to community standards. A result more contrary to rudimentary First Amendment principles is difficult to imagine. [Footnote by Justice Brennan.]

3. Having insisted that it seeks to impose sanctions on radio communications only in the limited circumstances present here, I believe that the FCC is estopped from using either this decision or its own orders in this case as a basis for imposing sanctions on any public radio broadcast other than one aired during the daytime or early evening and containing the relentless repetition, for longer than a brief interval, of "language that describes, in terms patently offensive as measured by contemporary community standards for the broadcast medium, sexual or excretory activities and organs." For surely broadcasters are not now on notice that the Commission desires to regulate any offensive broadcast other than the type of "verbal shock treatment" condemned here, or even this "shock treatment" type of offensive broadcast during the late evening. [Footnote by Justice Brennan.]

the process." Cohen. Moreover, even if an alternative phrasing may communicate a speaker's abstract ideas as effectively as those words he is forbidden to use, it is doubtful that the sterilized message will convey the emotion that is an essential part of so many communications. This too, was apparent to Mr. Justice Harlan and the Court in Cohen. [The] opinions of my Brethren [suggesting alternatives to hearing the broadcast, such as buying Carlin's record,] display both a sad insensitivity to the fact that [the] alternatives involve the expenditure of money, time, and effort that many of those wishing to hear Mr. Carlin's message may not be able to afford, and a naive innocence of the reality that in many cases, the medium may well be the message. The Court apparently believes that the FCC's actions here can be analogized to the zoning ordinances upheld in American Mini Theatres. For two reasons, it is wrong. First, the zoning ordinances found to pass constitutional muster [there] had valid goals other than the channeling of protected speech. [Second], the ordinances did not restrict the access of distributors or exhibitors to the market or impair the viewing public's access to the regulated [material].

   III. [There] runs throughout the opinions of my Brothers Powell and Stevens another vein I find equally disturbing: a depressing inability to appreciate that in our land of cultural pluralism, there are many who think, act, and talk differently from the Members of this Court, and who do not share their fragile sensibilities. It is only an acute ethnocentric myopia that enables the Court to approve the censorship of communications solely because of the words they contain. [The] words [found] so unpalatable may be the stuff of everyday conversations in some, if not many, of the innumerable subcultures that comprise this Nation. [As] one researcher concluded, "[w]ords generally considered obscene like 'bullshit' and 'fuck' are considered neither obscene nor derogatory in the [black] vernacular except in particular contextual situations and when used with certain intonations." Cf. Keefe v. Geanakos, 418 F.2d 359, 361 (CA1 1969) (finding the use of the word "motherfucker" commonplace among young radicals and protestors). Today's decision will thus have its greatest impact on broadcasters desiring to reach, and listening audiences comprised of, persons who do not share the Court's view as to which words or expressions are acceptable and who, for a variety of reasons, including a conscious desire to flout majoritarian conventions, express themselves using words that may be regarded as offensive by those from different socio-economic backgrounds.[4] In this context, the Court's decision may be seen for what, in the broader perspective, it really is: another of the dominant culture's inevitable efforts to force those groups who do not share its mores to conform to its way of thinking, acting, and speaking. Pacifica [explained to the FCC] that "Carlin is not mouthing obscenities, he is merely using words to satirize as harmless and essentially silly our attitudes towards those words." In confirming Carlin's prescience as a social commentator by the result it reaches today, the Court evinces an attitude towards the "seven dirty words" that many others besides Mr. Carlin and Pacifica might describe as "silly." Whether today's decision will similarly prove "harmless" remains to be seen. One can only hope that it will.[5]

---

4. Under the approach taken by my Brother Powell, the availability of broadcasts *about* groups whose members comprise such audiences might also be affected. Both news broadcasts about activities involving these groups and public affairs broadcasts about their concerns are apt to contain interviews, statements, or remarks by group leaders and members which may contain offensive language to an extent my Brother Powell finds unacceptable. [Footnote by Justice Brennan.]

5. In a separate dissent, Justice STEWART, joined by Justices Brennan, White and Marshall, argued that the constitutional questions in the case could be avoided by holding that Congress intended, by using the word "indecent," "to prohibit nothing more than obscene speech." Since Carlin's monologue was concededly not obscene, the FCC action could not stand.

   In reviewing the offensiveness and indecency cases from Cohen through Pacifica, consider whether the Cohen legacy has been substantially

THE LIMITS OF THE PRIVACY INVASION RATIONALE OF PACIFICA: THE CONSOLIDATED EDISON CASE

The Court reexamined the permissibility of content controls and of restrictions on speech intruding into the privacy of the home in CONSOLIDATED EDISON v. PUBLIC SERV. COMM'N [PSC], 447 U.S. 530 (1980), holding that the First Amendment barred an order of the New York PSC prohibiting the inclusion in monthly electric bills of inserts that discussed controversial issues of public policy. A state attempt to rely on an "invasion of privacy rationale" proved unavailing; and, in a separate opinion, Justice Stevens, the author of Pacifica, rejected any reliance on the Pacifica rationale here. The PSC order had barred "utilities from using bill inserts to discuss political matters, including the desirability of future development of nuclear power,"[1] and the highest state court had sustained the order as a valid time, place, and manner regulation designed to protect the privacy of the utility's customers. In reversing, Justice POWELL's majority opinion concluded that the ban could not be sustained as "(i) a reasonable time, place, or manner restriction, (ii) a permissible subject-matter regulation, or (iii) a narrowly tailored means of serving a compelling state interest." With respect to (i), he stated that "a constitutionally permissible time, place, or manner restriction may not be based upon either the content or subject matter of speech." Nor was the ban permissible because it was "related to subject matter rather than to the views of a particular speaker." He stated: "The First Amendment's hostility to content-based regulation extends not only to restrictions on particular viewpoints, but also to prohibition of public discussion of an entire topic. [To] allow a

eroded by the later cases noted above. Compare the cases that follow. Do they adequately curb the risks to the First Amendment created by cases such as Pacifica? Note also the comment by Gunther in an interview ("The Highest Court, the Toughest Issues," Stanford Magazine, Fall-Winter 1978, 34), a comment finding Pacifica a "most troublesome" decision: "The significant thing about the case [is] precisely the fact that the Court did not and could not put it under the obscenity exception to First Amendment protection. Nor did it resort to the usual arguments given for broadcast regulations, that there is a scarce spectrum of broadcast frequencies. Instead, the case was handled as a general First Amendment one, and that makes it more threatening to the entire free speech area. What the case comes down to ultimately is a majority support of a prohibition of speech because it is offensive to the audience. [And] that is startingly bad news. [True,] the Court said that it [might] rule differently in the case of a political speaker. [But] I am most worried by the legitimation of the offensiveness rationale. It is no wonder that Julian Bond is outraged about the FCC's doing nothing to stop an announcer on a radio station in the South who frequently uses the word 'nigger.' Bond argued that if the FCC can stop people who use four-letter words that are offensive, they surely ought to stop someone who uses a word that is offensive to half the audience in the South. It is not that I think that Julian Bond ought to have prevailed in his complaint. What Bond's complaint illustrates to me is that once you open the door to punishing a station broadcasting George Carlin's 'filthy

words,' the next step may be that you will permit Skokie to ban the swastika (see p. 1237 below) and will support Bond's claim to ban derogatory racial expletives."

Consider whether there are genuine spill-over risks in the Pacifica decision for the entire First Amendment area. Recall the partial reliance on Pacifica in the Ferber case, above. Do the post-Pacifica cases that follow satisfactorily safeguard against the spill-over risks?

For a later, unsuccessful effort to rely on Pacifica, see Bolger v. Youngs Drug Products Corp., 463 U.S. 60 (1983), invalidating a federal law barring the mailing of unsolicited advertisements for contraceptives (further discussed with the commercial speech materials in sec. 2D, at p. 1145 below). One of the proffered justifications was to protect recipients from offense. The Court rejected that argument: "[We] have never held that [government] can shut off the flow of mailings to protect those recipients who might potentially be offended." Pacifica was distinguished on the ground that the receipt of mail is "far less intrusive and uncontrollable" than are radio and television broadcasts.

1. The order stemmed from the following background: After the utility had included pro-nuclear power inserts in its bills, the Natural Resources Defense Council asked the Commission to order the utility to include contrasting views on controversial issues with its bills. Instead of granting that "fairness" access request, see Red Lion (p. 1295 below), the Commission issued the challenged blanket ban.

government the choice of permissible subjects for public debate would be to [allow] government control over the search for political truth." In the most significant part of his opinion, Justice Powell rejected the claim that the prohibition should survive strict First Amendment scrutiny because it was "a precisely drawn means of serving a compelling state interest." The court below had rested largely on the state interest in protecting individual privacy, asserting that the customers "have no choice whether to receive the insert and the views expressed in the insert may inflame their sensibilities." Justice Powell replied that the state court had "erred in its assessment of the seriousness of the intrusion." He explained:

"Even if a short exposure to Consolidated Edison's views may offend the sensibilities of some consumers, the ability of government 'to shut off discourse solely to protect others from hearing it [is] dependent upon a showing that substantial privacy interests are being invaded in an essentially intolerable manner.' Cohen. [Where] a single speaker communicates to many listeners, the First Amendment does not permit the government to prohibit speech as intrusive unless the 'captive' audience cannot avoid objectionable speech. Passengers on public transportation or residents of a neighborhood disturbed by the raucous broadcasts from a passing soundtruck may well be unable to escape an unwanted message. But customers who encounter an objectionable billing insert may 'effectively avoid further bombardment of their sensibilities simply by averting their eyes.' Cohen. The customer of Consolidated Edison may escape exposure to objectionable material simply by transferring the bill insert from envelope to wastebasket." [2]

In an important opinion concurring only in the judgment, Justice STEVENS reiterated his "lesser value speech" theory of American Mini Theatres and Pacifica (insisting that content control *was* widely permissible) but also forcefully rejected the notion that the offensiveness rationale of the earlier cases could be invoked as justification here. He stated: "Instead of trying to justify our conclusion by reasoning from honeycombed premises [e.g., that all content-based restrictions are impermissible], I prefer to identify the basis of decision in more simple terms. See American Mini Theatres. A regulation of speech that is motivated by nothing more than a desire to curtail expression of a particular point of view on controversial issues of general interest is the purest example of a 'law abridging the freedom of speech, or of the press.' A regulation that denies one group of persons the right to address a selected audience on 'controversial issues of public policy' is plainly such a regulation.

"The only justification relied on by [the state court] is that the utilities' bill inserts may be 'offensive' to some of their customers. But a communication may be offensive in two different ways. Independently of the message the speaker intends to convey, the form of his communication may be offensive— perhaps because it is too loud [Kovacs (p. 1208 below)] or too ugly in a particular setting. [Pacifica.] Other speeches, even though elegantly phrased in dulcet tones, are offensive simply because the listener disagrees with the speaker's message. The fact that the offensive form of some communication may subject it to appropriate regulation surely does not support the conclusion that the offensive character of an idea can justify an attempt to censor its expression. Since the [PSC] has candidly put forward this impermissible

2. "Although this Court has recognized the special privacy interests that attach to persons who seek seclusion within their own homes, see Rowan, the arrival of a billing envelope is hardly as intrusive as the visit of a door-to-door solici- tor. Yet the Court has rejected the contention that a municipality may ban door-to-door solici- tors because they may invade the privacy of households. Martin v. Struthers [p. 1213 be- low]." [Footnote by Justice Powell.]

justification for its censorial regulation, it plainly violates the First Amendment." [3]

LIMITS OF THE LESS VALUABLE SPEECH RATIONALE OF AMERICAN MINI THEATRES

SCHAD v. MT. EPHRAIM, 452 U.S. 61 (1981): Like American Mini Theatres, this case involved the use of a zoning ordinance to curb displays, including sexually oriented ones. The state court sustained the restraint on the basis of Mini Theatres, viewing that case as a broad endorsement of the zoning power in this area. But the Court reversed. Emphasizing that this case presented a total ban rather than a mere channeling of displays in a community, the Court—not only in the majority opinion by Justice White but also in a concurring one by Justice Stevens, the author of the controversial opinion in Mini Theatres—found Mini Theatres distinguishable. The challenge was brought by the operators of a store selling "adult" materials who, in 1976, had added a coin-operated mechanism permitting customers to watch a live, nude dancer performing behind a glass panel. The ordinance of the Borough of Mt. Ephraim, N.J., described the "permitted uses" in the small community's commercial zone and barred all other uses. As construed by the state courts, the ban covered all "live entertainment." Justice WHITE's majority opinion stated:

"By excluding live entertainment throughout [the] Borough, [the ordinance] prohibits a wide range of expression that has long been held to be within the protections of the [First Amendment]. Entertainment, as well as political and ideological speech, is protected; motion pictures, programs broadcast by radio and television and live entertainment, such as musical and dramatic works, fall within the First Amendment guarantee. Nor may an entertainment program be prohibited solely because it displays the nude human figure. 'Nudity alone' does not place otherwise protected material outside the mantle of the First Amendment. [E.g.], Jenkins v. Georgia; Erznoznik. [Furthermore], nude dancing is not without its First Amendment protections from official regulation. Whatever First Amendment protection should be extended to nude dancing, live or on film, however, [the] ordinance prohibits all live [entertainment]. Because appellants' claims are rooted in the First Amendment, they are entitled to rely on the impact of the ordinance on the expressive activities of others as well as their own [and accordingly may make an overbreadth challenge].

"The power of local governments to zone and control land use is undoubtedly broad and its proper exercise is an essential aspect of achieving a satisfactory quality of life in both urban and rural communities. But the zoning [power] 'must be exercised within constitutional limits.' [When] a zoning law infringes upon a protected liberty, it must be narrowly drawn and must further a

---

3. A dissent by Justice BLACKMUN argued that, because of the utility's monopoly status and its rate structure, "the use of the insert amounts to an exaction from the utility's customers by way of forced aid for the utility's speech. [And an] allocation of the insert's cost between the utility's shareholders and the ratepayers would not eliminate this coerced subsidy." In the concluding passages of his opinion (the only portion of his dissent not joined by Justice Rehnquist), he added that he hoped that the decision "ha[d] not completely tied a State's hands in preventing this type of abuse of monopoly power." He suggested, as alternatives open to the states, that they "might use their power to define property rights

so that the billing envelope is the property of the ratepayers and not of the utility's shareholders, cf. PruneYard [p. 1294 below]," and that, through cost allocation, they could charge the shareholders for all of the mailing costs, to eliminate "the most offensive aspects of the forced subsidization of the utility's speech."

Justice MARSHALL's comment joining the Court's opinion emphasized that the decision "in no way addresse[d] the question whether the Commission may exclude the costs of bill inserts from the rate base, nor does it intimate any view on the appropriateness of any allocation of such costs the Commission might choose to make."

sufficiently substantial government interest. Because the ordinance challenged in this case significantly limits communicative activity within the Borough, we must scrutinize both the interests advanced by the Borough to justify this limitation on protected expression and the means chosen to further those interests.

"As an initial matter, this case is not controlled by American Mini Theatres. Although the Court there stated that a zoning ordinance is not invalid merely because it regulates activity protected under the First Amendment, it emphasized that the challenged restriction on the location of adult movie theaters imposed a minimal burden on protected speech. The restriction did not affect the number of adult movie theaters that could operate in the city; it merely dispersed them. The Court did not imply that a municipality could ban all adult theaters—much less all live entertainment or all nude dancing—from its commercial districts citywide. Moreover, it was emphasized in that case that the evidence [indicated] that the concentration of adult movie theaters in limited areas led to deterioration of surrounding neighborhoods, and it was concluded that the city had justified the incidental burden on First Amendment interests resulting from merely dispersing, but not excluding, adult theaters.

"In this case, however, Mount Ephraim has not adequately justified its substantial restriction of protected activity.[1] None of the justifications [withstands] scrutiny. First, the Borough contends that permitting live entertainment would conflict with its plan to create a commercial area that caters only to the 'immediate needs' of its residents and that would enable them to purchase at local stores the few items they occasionally forgot to buy outside the Borough. No evidence was introduced below to support this assertion, and it is difficult to reconcile this characterization of the Borough's commercial zones with the provisions of the ordinance, [which] expressly states that the purpose of creating commercial zones was to provide areas for 'local and *regional* commercial operations.' The range of permitted uses goes far beyond providing for the 'immediate needs' of the residents. [Virtually] the only item or service that may not be sold in a commercial zone is entertainment, or at least live entertainment.[2] The Borough's first justification is patently insufficient.

"Second, Mount Ephraim contends that it may selectively exclude commercial live entertainment from the broad range of commercial uses permitted in the Borough for reasons normally associated with zoning in commercial districts, that is, to avoid the problems that may be associated with live entertainment, such as parking, trash, police protection, and medical facilities. The Borough has presented no evidence, and it is not immediately apparent as a matter of experience, that live entertainment poses problems of this nature more significant than those associated with various permitted uses; nor does it appear that the Borough's zoning authority has arrived at a defensible conclusion that unusual problems are presented by live entertainment. Cf. [American Mini Theatres].[3] [The] Borough also suggests that [the ordinance] is a reasonable

---

1. "If the New Jersey courts had expressly interpreted this ordinance as banning all entertainment, we would reach the same result." [Footnote by Justice White.]

2. "At present, this effect is somewhat lessened by the presence of at least three establishments that are permitted to offer live entertainment as a nonconforming use. These uses apparently may continue indefinitely, since the Mount Ephraim Code does not require nonconforming uses to be terminated within a specified period of time. The Borough's decision to permit live entertainment as a nonconforming use only undermines the Borough's contention that

live entertainment poses inherent problems that justify its exclusion." [Footnote by Justice White.]

3. "Mount Ephraim also speculates that the Borough may have concluded that live nude dancing is undesirable. [This] speculation lends no support to the challenged ordinance. [The ordinance] excludes all live entertainment, not just live nude dancing. Even if Mount Ephraim might validly place restrictions on certain forms of live nude dancing under a narrowly drawn ordinance, this would not justify the exclusion of all live entertainment or, insofar as this record

'time, place and manner' restriction; yet it does not identify the municipal interests making it reasonable to exclude all commercial live entertainment but to allow a variety of other commercial uses in the Borough. [The] initial question in determining the validity of the exclusion as a time, place and manner restriction is whether live entertainment is 'basically incompatible with the normal activity [in the commercial zones].' [No] evidence has been presented to establish that live entertainment is incompatible with the uses presently permitted by the Borough. Mount Ephraim asserts that it could have chosen to eliminate all commercial uses within its boundaries. Yet we must assess the exclusion of live entertainment in light of the commercial uses Mount Ephraim allows, not in light of what the Borough might have done.[4] To be reasonable, time, place and manner restrictions not only must serve significant state interests but also must leave open adequate alternative channels of communication. Here, the Borough totally excludes all live entertainment, including nonobscene nude dancing that is otherwise protected by the First Amendment. [American Mini Theatres] did not purport to approve the total exclusion from the city of theaters showing adult, but not obscene, materials. It was carefully noted in that case that the number of regulated establishments was not limited and that '[t]he situation would be quite different if the ordinance had the effect of suppressing, or greatly restricting access to, lawful speech.'

"The Borough nevertheless contends that live entertainment in general and nude dancing in particular are amply available in close-by areas outside the limits of the Borough. Its position suggests the argument that if there were countywide zoning, it would be quite legal to allow live entertainment in only selected areas of the county and to exclude it from primarily residential communities, such as the [Borough]. This may very well be true, but the Borough cannot avail itself of that argument in this case. There is no countywide zoning in Camden County, and Mount Ephraim is free under state law to impose its own zoning restrictions, within constitutional limits. Furthermore, there is no evidence in this record to support the proposition that the kind of entertainment appellants wish to provide is available in reasonably nearby [areas]. '[O]ne is not to have the exercise of his liberty of expression in appropriate places abridged on the plea that it may be exercised in some other place.' [Schneider v. State, p. 1206 below.]." [5]

Justice STEVENS concurred only in the judgment. He stated: "The record in this case leaves so many relevant questions unanswered that the outcome, in my judgment, depends on the allocation of the burden of persuasion. If the case is viewed as a simple attempt by a small residential community to exclude the commercial exploitation of nude dancing from a 'setting of tranquility' (Burger, C.J., dissenting), it would seem reasonable to require appellants to overcome the usual presumption that a municipality's zoning enactments are constitutionally valid. [On] the other hand, if one starts, as the Court does, from the premise that 'appellants' claims are rooted in the First Amendment,' it

reveals, even the nude dancing involved in this [case]." [Footnote by Justice White.]

4. "Thus, our decision today does not establish that every unit of local government entrusted with zoning responsibilities must provide a commercial zone in which live entertainment is permitted." [Footnote by Justice White.]

5. Justice BLACKMUN, who joined the Court's opinion, wrote separately to emphasize two points. First, the usual deference to zoning laws when only economic rights are affected does not apply in the First Amendment area: "[Where] protected First Amendment interests are at stake, zoning regulations have no ['talis-

manic] immunity from constitutional challenge.'" Second, he rejected any notion that a community could "eliminate a particular form of expression so long as that form is available in areas reasonably nearby." Such a view would be "a substantial step beyond Mini Theatres." Justice POWELL, joined by Justice Stewart, also joined the Court's opinion but wrote separately to emphasize that a community could, in a carefully drawn ordinance, ban all commercial entertainment. But the ordinance here was not carefully drawn, so that "any argument about the need to maintain the residential nature of this community fails as a justification."

would seem reasonable to require the Borough to overcome a presumption of invalidity. [Neither] of these characterizations provides me with a satisfactory approach to this case. For appellants' business is located in a commercial zone, and the character of that zone is not unequivocally identified either by the text of the Borough's zoning ordinance or by the evidence in the record. And even though the foliage of the First Amendment may cast protective shadows over some forms of nude dancing, its roots were germinated by more serious concerns that are not necessarily implicated by a content-neutral zoning ordinance banning commercial exploitation of live entertainment. Cf. [American Mini Theatres].

"One of the puzzling features of this case is that the character of the prohibition the Borough seeks to enforce is so hard to ascertain.[1] Without more information about this commercial [enclave], one cannot know whether the change in appellants' business in 1976 introduced cacophony into a tranquil setting or merely a new refrain in a local replica of Place Pigalle. If I were convinced that the former is the correct appraisal of this commercial zone, I would have no hesitation in agreeing with The Chief Justice that even if the live nude dancing is a form of expressive activity protected by the First Amendment, the Borough may prohibit it. But when the record is opaque, as this record is, I believe the Borough must shoulder the burden of demonstrating that appellants' introduction of live entertainment had an identifiable adverse impact on the neighborhood or on the Borough as a whole. It might be appropriate to presume that such an adverse impact would occur if the zoning plan itself were narrowly drawn to create categories of commercial uses that unambiguously differentiated this entertainment from permitted uses. However, this open-ended ordinance affords no basis for any such presumption.

"The difficulty in this case is that we are left to speculate as to the Borough's reasons for proceeding against appellants' business, and as to the justification for the distinction the Borough has drawn between live and other forms of entertainment. While a municipality need not persuade a federal court that its zoning decisions are correct as a matter of policy, when First Amendment interests are implicated, it must at least be able to demonstrate that a uniform policy in fact exists and is applied in a content-neutral fashion. Presumably, municipalities may regulate expressive activity—even protected activity—pursuant to narrowly-drawn content-neutral standards; however, they may not regulate protected activity when the only standard provided is the unbridled discretion of a municipal official. Compare Saia v. New York with Kovacs v. Cooper [loudspeaker regulations; p. 1208 below]. Because neither the text of the zoning ordinance, nor the evidence in the record, indicates that Mount Ephraim applied narrowly-drawn content-neutral standards to the appellants' business, for me this case involves a criminal prosecution of appellants simply because one of their employees has engaged in expressive activity that has been assumed arguendo to be protected by the First Amendment. Accordingly, and without endorsing the overbreadth analysis employed by the Court, I concur in its judgment."

The dissent by Chief Justice BURGER, joined by Justice Rehnquist, stated: "At issue here is the right of a small community to ban an activity incompatible with a quiet, residential atmosphere. [Mount Ephraim] did nothing more than employ traditional police power to provide a setting of tranquility. [T]he issue *in the case that we have before us* is not whether Mount Ephraim may ban traditional live entertainment, but whether it may ban nude dancing, which is used as the 'bait' to induce customers into the appellants' book store. When,

---

1. Justice Stevens noted, for example, that the small commercial zone in which the bookstore was located included three establishments which offered live entertainment (permitted as prior non-conforming uses) as well as an inn, one or more restaurants, and a movie theater.

and if, this ordinance is used to prevent a high school performance of 'The Sound of Music,' for example, the Court can deal with that problem. An overconcern about draftsmanship and overbreadth should not be allowed to obscure the central question before us. It is clear that, in passing the statute challenged here, the citizens [of] Mount Ephraim meant only to preserve the basic character of their community. It is just as clear that, by thrusting its live nude dancing shows on this community, the appellant alters and damages that community over its objections. As applied in this case, therefore, the statute speaks directly and unequivocally. It may be that, as applied in some other case, this statute would violate the First Amendment, but, since such a case is not before us, we should not decide it. Even assuming that the 'expression' manifested in the nude dancing that is involved here is somehow protected speech under the First Amendment, [Mount Ephraim] is entitled to regulate it. Here, as in American Mini Theatres, the zoning ordinance imposes a minimal intrusion on genuine rights of expression; only by contortions of logic can it be made [otherwise]. [That] a community is willing to tolerate such a commercial use as a convenience store, a gas station, a pharmacy, or a delicatessen does not compel it also to tolerate every other 'commercial use,' including pornography peddlers and live nude shows. [To] invoke the First Amendment to protect the activity involved in this case trivializes and demeans that great Amendment."

D. COMMERCIAL SPEECH

Introduction. We now turn, as the final group of materials in this section, to one more category of speech which, because of its content, has been treated at various times as either wholly outside the First Amendment or as being a variety of "less valuable" speech not entitled to the high degree of protection afforded to "core" speech. Before the mid-1970s, the Court assumed that most types of commercial speech—commercial advertising, or speech that merely proposes a commercial transaction—fell wholly outside the First Amendment. The doctrine had its origin in a case decided soon after the classic exclusionary categorization case, Chaplinsky. Valentine v. Chrestensen, 316 U.S. 52 (1942)—a ruling Justice Douglas was later to call "casual, almost offhand"— stated that the First Amendment imposed no "restraint on government as respects purely commercial advertising" similar to that governing restrictions on protected speech.[1]

The Valentine approach did not mean that First Amendment protection was barred simply because the speaker had a commercial motive. Recall, e.g., New York Times v. Sullivan (sec. 2B), rejecting the argument that the First Amendment did not apply to a "paid 'commercial' advertisement": "That the Times was paid for publishing the advertisement is as immaterial [here] as is the fact that newspapers and books are sold. Any other conclusion would discourage newspapers from carrying 'editorial advertisements' of this type." Moreover, as sec. 2C illustrates, movies and books have long enjoyed First Amendment protections even though they are produced and distributed for profit. Nevertheless, the commercial-noncommercial distinction played a significant role in

---

   1. Valentine sustained a ban on distribution of a handbill advertisement soliciting customers to pay admission to tour a privately owned submarine. The entrepreneur in Valentine printed his advertising message on one side of the circular; on the other side, he published a protest against the city's denial of permission to use a municipal pier for his exhibit. The Court viewed the ban as a regulation of business activity rather than protected speech, and considered the political protest as merely an attempt to evade the city regulation forbidding distribution of advertisements in the streets.

the cases after Valentine.[2] In the early 1970s, moreover, the Court gave more weight to Valentine's commercial speech doctrine than it had in years. For example, the 5 to 4 decision in Pittsburgh Press Co. v. Human Relations Comm'n, 413 U.S. 376 (1973), sustained a local order prohibiting a newspaper from listing advertisements for jobs covered by a sex discrimination ordinance in sex-designated help-wanted columns. Justice Powell's majority opinion found that the advertisements resembled the "Chrestensen rather than the [New York Times] advertisement. None expresses a position on whether, as a matter of social policy, certain positions ought to be filled by members of one or the other sex, nor does any of them criticize [the sex discrimination ordinance]. Each is no more than a proposal of possible employment. The advertisements are thus classic examples of commercial speech [not protected by the First Amendment]."[3] But shortly after that indication of vigor in the commercial speech doctrine, the Court changed course.

The new trend began with Bigelow v. Virginia, 421 U.S. 809 (1975),[4] and flourished a year later in Virginia Pharmacy, which follows. According to the Court in Virginia Pharmacy, "the notion of unprotected 'commercial speech' all but passed from the scene" in Bigelow. That was an overstatement of the impression at the time Bigelow was decided: Bigelow had arisen in the special setting of newspaper ads about the availability of out-of-state abortions, a subject involving constitutionally protected activities. But Virginia Pharmacy spoke far more broadly and made it clear that the commercial speech exception had indeed shrunk drastically. Virginia Pharmacy in turn spawned a series of cases, below, in which the Court has struggled to delineate the contours of permissible restrictions on commercial advertising.

From the beginning of the Court's modern ventures into this area, it has been clear that commercial advertising does not enjoy as much constitutional protection as most types of speech, although it is no longer wholly excluded from First Amendment coverage. With respect to commercial speech (as with the indecent words and displays that are considered "less valuable speech" under Justice Stevens' position in some of the preceding cases), the Court has found the First Amendment interests weaker and the case for state restraints stronger than in other areas of speech. Was inclusion of commercial advertising within the First Amendment a mistake? Should it be excluded from the First Amendment in light of the underlying purposes of the constitutional concern with "speech"? Would total exclusion of commercial speech encourage a Court return to wholesale exclusionary categorization in the Chaplinsky manner? Does treatment of commercial advertising as a less valuable variety of speech produce even greater risks to the First Amendment than total exclusion would, by increasing the legitimacy of a methodology allocating differing and often lower weights to particular types of speech on the First Amendment balancing scale? Issues such as these are more fully pursued in the comments below, esp. at p. 1137.

---

2. E.g., contrast Martin v. Struthers (1943; p. 1213 below), barring the application of a city ordinance prohibiting uninvited door-to-door solicitors for Jehovah's Witnesses, with Breard v. Alexandria (1951; p. 1213 below), sustaining a conviction of magazine subscription solicitors (and emphasizing the householders' interests in privacy and repose).

3. See also the nearly contemporaneous, unusual invocation of the commercial speech exception in Southeastern Promotions, Ltd. v. Conrad (1975; p. 1251 below).

4. Bigelow is summarized in Virginia Pharmacy, which follows.

VIRGINIA PHARMACY BOARD v. VIRGINIA CONSUMER COUNCIL

425 U.S. 748, 96 S.Ct. 1817, 48 L.Ed.2d 346 (1976).

Mr. Justice BLACKMUN delivered the opinion of the [Court].

[A Virginia law provided that pharmacists were guilty of "unprofessional conduct" if they advertised the prices of prescription drugs. Since only pharmacists were authorized to dispense such drugs, the law effectively prevented the dissemination of prescription drug price information in the State. About 95% of all prescription drugs were prepared by pharmaceutical manufacturers rather than by the pharmacists themselves. The Court affirmed a lower court's invalidation of the law on First Amendment grounds. Justice Blackmun began by noting that the challenge to the law came not from a pharmacist but from prescription drug consumers who claimed that the First Amendment entitled them to drug price information. He commented: "Certainly that information may be of value. Drug prices [in the state] strikingly vary from outlet to outlet even within the same locality." He found that the audience for drug price information could assert a First Amendment interest: "[W]here a speaker exists [as here], the protection afforded [by the First Amendment] is to the communication, to its source and to its recipients both. [If] there is a right to advertise, there is a reciprocal right to receive the advertising, and it may be asserted by [the consumers here]." He continued:]

IV. The appellants contend that the advertisement of prescription drug prices is outside the protection of the First Amendment because it is "commercial speech." There can be no question that in past decisions the Court has given some indication that commercial speech is unprotected. [E.g., Valentine; Breard.] [Last] Term, in [Bigelow], the notion of unprotected "commercial speech" all but passed from the scene. We reversed a conviction for violation of a Virginia statute that made the circulation of any publication to encourage or promote the processing of an abortion in Virginia a misdemeanor. The defendant had published in his newspaper the availability of abortions in New York. The advertisement in question, in addition to announcing that abortions were legal in New York, offered the services of a referral agency in that State. We rejected the contention that the publication was unprotected because it was commercial. [Some] fragment of hope for the continuing validity of a "commercial speech" exception arguably might have persisted because of the subject matter of the advertisement in Bigelow. We noted that in announcing the availability of legal abortions in New York, the advertisement "did more than simply propose a commercial transaction. It contained factual material of clear 'public interest.'" And, of course, the advertisement related to activity with which, at least in some respects, the State could not interfere. See [e.g., Roe v. Wade]. [We] concluded that "the Virginia courts erred in their assumptions that advertising, as such, was entitled to no First Amendment protection," and we observed that the "relationship of speech to the marketplace of products or of services does not make it valueless in the marketplace of ideas."

Here, in contrast, the question whether there is a First Amendment exception for "commercial speech" is squarely before us. Our pharmacist does not wish to editorialize on any subject, cultural, philosophical, or political. He does not wish to report any particularly newsworthy fact, or to make generalized observations even about commercial matters. The "idea" he wishes to communicate is simply this: "I will sell you the X prescription drug at the Y price." Our question, then, is whether this communication is wholly outside the protection of the First Amendment.

V. [It] is clear [that] speech does not lose its First Amendment protection because money is spent to project it, as in a paid [advertisement]. [E.g., New York Times v. Sullivan.] [Our] question is whether speech which does "no more than propose a commercial transaction" [Pittsburgh Press] is so removed from any "exposition of ideas" [Chaplinsky] and from "truth, science, morality, and arts in general, in its diffusion of liberal sentiments on the administration of Government" [Roth], that it lacks all protection. Our answer is that it is not. Focusing first on the individual parties to the transaction that is proposed in the commercial advertisement, we may assume that the advertiser's interest is a purely economic one. That hardly disqualifies him for protection under the First Amendment. The interests of the contestants in a labor dispute are primarily economic, but it has long been settled that both the employee and the employer are protected by the First Amendment where they express themselves on the merits of the dispute in order to influence its outcome. [As] to the particular consumer's interest in the free flow of commercial information, that interest may be as keen, if not keener by far, than his interest in the day's most urgent political debate. [Those] whom the suppression of prescription drug price information hits the hardest are the poor, the sick, and particularly the aged. [When] drug prices vary as strikingly as they do, information as to who is charging what becomes more than a convenience. It could mean the alleviation of physical pain or the enjoyment of basic necessities.

Generalizing, society also may have a strong interest in the free flow of commercial information. Even an individual advertisement, though entirely "commercial," may be of general public interest. The facts of decided cases furnish illustrations: [e.g.,] advertisements stating that referral services for legal abortions are available [and] that a manufacturer of artificial furs promotes his product as an alternative to the extinction by his competitors of fur-bearing mammals. [Obviously], not all commercial messages contain the same or even a very great public interest element. There are few to which such an element, however, could not be added. Our pharmacist, for example, could cast himself as a commentator on store-to-store disparities in drug prices, giving his own and those of a competitor as proof. We see little point in requiring him to do so, and little difference if he does not.

Moreover, there is another consideration that suggests that no line between publicly "interesting" or "important" commercial advertising and the opposite kind could ever be drawn. Advertising, however tasteless and excessive it sometimes may seem, is nonetheless dissemination of information as to who is producing and selling what product, for what reason, and at what price. So long as we preserve a predominantly free enterprise economy, the allocation of our resources in large measure will be made through numerous private economic decisions. It is a matter of public interest that those decisions, in the aggregate, be intelligent and well informed. To this end, the free flow of commercial information is indispensable. And if it is indispensable to the proper allocation of resources in a free enterprise system, it is also indispensable to the formation of intelligent opinions as to how that system ought to be regulated or altered. Therefore, even if the First Amendment were thought to be primarily an instrument to enlighten public decisionmaking in a democracy, we could not say that the free flow of information does not serve that goal.

Arrayed against these substantial individual and societal interests are a number of justifications for the advertising ban. These have to do principally with maintaining a high degree of professionalism on the part of licensed pharmacists. [Price] advertising, it is argued, will place in jeopardy the pharmacist's expertise and, with it, the customer's health. It is claimed that the aggressive price competition that will result from unlimited advertising will make it impossible for the pharmacist to supply professional services in the compounding, handling, and dispensing of prescription drugs. [The] strength of these proffered justifications is greatly undermined by the fact that high professional standards, to a substantial extent, are guaranteed by the close regulation to which pharmacists in Virginia are subject. [At] the same time, we cannot discount the Board's justifications entirely. The Court regarded justifications of this type sufficient to sustain the advertising bans challenged on due process and equal protection grounds in [several cases].[1]

The challenge now made, however, is based on the First Amendment. This casts the Board's justifications in a different light, for on close inspection it is seen that the State's protectiveness of its citizens rests in large measure on the advantages of their being kept in ignorance. [It] appears to be feared that if the pharmacist who wishes to provide low cost, and assertedly low quality, services is permitted to advertise, he will be taken up on his offer by too many unwitting customers. [There] is, of course, an alternative to this highly paternalistic approach. That alternative is to assume that this information is not in itself harmful, that people will perceive their own best interests if only they are well enough informed, and that the best means to that end is to open the channels of communication rather than to close them. If they are truly open, nothing prevents the "professional" pharmacist from marketing his own assertedly superior product, and contrasting it with that of the low-cost, high-volume prescription drug retailer. But the choice among these alternative approaches is not ours to make or the Virginia General Assembly's. It is precisely this kind of choice, between the dangers of suppressing information, and the dangers of its misuse if it is freely available, that the First Amendment makes for us. Virginia is free to require whatever professional standards it wishes of its pharmacists; it may subsidize them or protect them from competition in other ways. But it may not do so by keeping the public in ignorance of the entirely lawful terms that competing pharmacists are offering. In this sense, the justifications Virginia has offered for suppressing the flow of prescription drug price information, far from persuading us that the flow is not protected by the First Amendment, have reinforced our view that it is. We so hold.

VI.   In concluding that commercial speech, like other varieties, is protected, we of course do not hold that it can never be regulated in any way. Some forms of commercial speech regulation are surely permissible. We mention a few. [There] is no claim, for example, that the prohibition on prescription drug price advertising is a mere time, place, and manner restriction. We have often approved restrictions of that kind provided that they are justified without reference to the content of the regulated speech, that they serve a significant governmental interest, and that in so doing they leave open ample alternative channels for communication of the information. [But this law] singles out speech of a particular content and seeks to prevent its dissemination completely. Nor is there any claim that prescription drug price advertisements are forbidden because they are false or misleading in any way. Untruthful speech, commercial or otherwise, has never been protected for its own sake. [E.g., Gertz.] Obviously, much commercial speech is not provably false, or even wholly false, but only deceptive or misleading. We foresee no obstacle to a State's dealing effectively with this problem.[2]   The First Amendment, as we construe it today,

1.   Justice Blackmun cited several modern economic regulation, deferential review cases (see chap. 8 above): Head v. New Mexico Board, 374 U.S. 424 (1963) (optometrists' services); Williamson v. Lee Optical Co., 348 U.S. 483 (1955) (eyeglass frames); and Semler v. Dental Examiners, 294 U.S. 608 (1935) (dentists' services).

2.   In concluding that commercial speech enjoys First Amendment protection, we have not held that it is wholly undifferentiable from other forms. There are commonsense differences between speech that does "no more than propose a commercial transaction" and other varieties. Even if the differences do not justify the conclusion that commercial speech is valueless, and thus subject to complete suppression by the State, they nonetheless suggest that a different degree of protection is necessary to insure that the flow of

does not prohibit the State from insuring that the stream of commercial information flows cleanly as well as freely. Also, there is no claim that the transactions proposed in the forbidden advertisements are themselves illegal in any way. [Cf., e.g., Pittsburgh Press.] Finally, the special problems of the electronic broadcast media are likewise not in this case. What is at issue is whether a State may completely suppress the dissemination of concededly truthful information about entirely lawful activity, fearful of that information's effect upon its disseminators and its recipients. Reserving other questions [3] we conclude that the answer to this one is in the negative.

Affirmed.[4]

Mr. Justice REHNQUIST, dissenting.

The logical consequences of the Court's decision in this case, a decision which elevates commercial intercourse between a seller hawking his wares and a buyer seeking to strike a bargain to the same plane as has been previously reserved for the free marketplace of ideas, are far reaching indeed. Under the Court's opinion the way will be open not only for dissemination of price information but for active promotion of prescription drugs, liquor, cigarettes and other products the use of which it has previously been thought desirable to discourage. Now, however, such promotion is protected by the First Amendment so long as it is not misleading or does not promote an illegal product or [enterprise].

The Court speaks of the consumer's interest in the free flow of commercial [information]. It goes on to observe that "society also may have a strong interest in the free flow of commercial information." [But these interests] should presumptively be the concern of the [Virginia Legislature]. The Court speaks of the importance in a "predominantly free enterprise economy" of intelligent and well-informed decisions as to allocation of resources. While there is again much to be said for [this] as a matter of desirable public policy, there is certainly nothing in the [Constitution] which requires [Virginia] to hew to the teachings of Adam Smith in its legislative decisions regulating the pharmacy profession. E.g., [Nebbia, chap. 8 above]. [I]f the sole limitation on permissible state proscription of advertising is that it may not be false or misleading, surely the difference between pharmacists' advertising and lawyers' and doctors' advertising can be only one of degree and not of [kind].

truthful and legitimate commercial information is unimpaired. The truth of commercial speech, for example, may be more easily verifiable by its disseminator than, let us say, news reporting or political commentary, in that ordinarily the advertiser seeks to disseminate information about a specific product or service that he himself provides and presumably knows more about than anyone else. Also, commercial speech may be more durable than other kinds. Since advertising is the sine qua non of commercial profits, there is little likelihood of its being chilled by proper regulation and foregone entirely.

Attributes such as these, the greater objectivity and hardiness of commercial speech, may make it less necessary to tolerate inaccurate statements for fear of silencing the speaker. They may also make it appropriate to require that a commercial message appear in such a form, or include such additional information, warnings and disclaimers as are necessary to prevent its being deceptive. They also make inapplicable the prohibition against [prior restraints]. [Footnote by Justice Blackmun.]

3. We stress that we have considered in this case the regulation of commercial advertising by pharmacists. Although we express no opinion as to other professions, the distinctions, historical and functional, between professions, may require consideration of quite different factors. Physicians and lawyers, for example, do not dispense standardized products; they render professional *services* of almost infinite variety and nature, with the consequent enhanced possibility for confusion and deception if they were to undertake certain kinds of advertising. [Footnote by Justice Blackmun. (Note the cases which follow, involving regulations of other professions, including lawyers.)]

4. Chief Justice Burger's concurrence emphasized the reservation in footnote [3] of the opinion regarding advertising by physicians and lawyers. Justice Stewart, concurring, wrote separately to explain "why I think today's decision does not preclude [regulation of false or deceptive advertising]." Justice Stevens did not participate.

The Court insists that the rule it lays down is consistent even with the view that the First Amendment is "primarily an instrument to enlighten public decisionmaking in a democracy." I had understood this view to relate to public decisionmaking as to political, social, and other public issues, rather than the decision of a particular individual as to whether to purchase one or another kind of shampoo. It is undoubtedly arguable that many people in the country regard the choice of shampoo as just as important as who may be elected to local, state, or national political office, but that does not automatically bring information about competing shampoos within the protection of the First Amendment. It is one thing to say that the line between strictly ideological and political commentaries and other kinds of commentary is difficult to draw, and that the mere fact that the former may have in it an element of commercialism does not strip it of First Amendment protection. See New York Times v. Sullivan. But it is another thing to say that because that line is difficult to draw, we will stand at the other end of the [spectrum].

In the case of "our" hypothetical pharmacist, he may now presumably advertise not only the prices of prescription drugs, but may attempt to energetically promote their sale so long as he does so truthfully. Quite consistently with Virginia law requiring prescription drugs to be available only through a physician, "our" pharmacist might run any of the following representative advertisements in a local newspaper: "Pain getting you down? Insist that your physician prescribe Demerol. You pay a little more than for aspirin, but you get a lot more relief." "Can't shake the flu? Get a prescription for tetracycline from your doctor today." "Don't spend another sleepless night. Ask your doctor to prescribe Seconal without delay." Unless the State can show that these advertisements are either actually untruthful or misleading, it presumably is not free to restrict in any way commercial efforts on the part of those who profit from the sale of prescription drugs to put them in the widest possible circulation. But such a line simply makes no allowance whatever for what appears to have been a considered legislative judgment in most States that while prescription drugs are a necessary and vital part of medical care and treatment, there are sufficient dangers attending their widespread use that they simply may not be promoted in the same manner as hair creams, deodorants, and toothpaste. The very real dangers that general advertising for such drugs might create in terms of encouraging, even though not sanctioning, illicit use of them by individuals for whom they have not been prescribed, or by generating patient pressure upon physicians to prescribe them, are simply not dealt with in the Court's [opinion].

This case presents a fairly typical First Amendment problem—that of balancing interests in individual free speech against public welfare determinations embodied in a legislative enactment. [Here] the rights of the appellees seem to me to be marginal at best. There is no ideological content to the information which they seek and it is freely available to them—they may even publish it if they so desire. [On] the other hand, the societal interest against the promotion of drug use for every ill, real or imaginery, seems to me extremely strong. I do not believe that the First Amendment mandates the Court's "open door policy" toward such commercial advertising.*

---

* Note the majority's heavy reliance on Virginia Pharmacy a year later, in Carey v. Population Services Int'l (1977; chap. 8; p. 547 above), invalidating a New York ban on the advertising or display of nonprescription contraceptives. Justice Brennan noted that here, as in Virginia Pharmacy, there were "substantial individual and societal interests in the free flow of commercial information," and, as in Bigelow, the information suppressed "related to activity with which, at least in some respects, the State could not interfere."

Justice Brennan's opinion in Carey also summarily rejected other state defenses: that advertisements of contraceptives "would be offensive

SOME COMMERCIAL SPEECH RULINGS SINCE
VIRGINIA PHARMACY

1. *Regulating the legal profession.* Virginia Pharmacy had left some doubt about whether it would apply to commercial communications by lawyers. But the Court soon made it clear that the Virginia Pharmacy principles would apply to lawyers' advertising as well. The course of decisions began with the 5 to 4 ruling in Bates v. State Bar of Arizona, 433 U.S. 350 (1977), holding that states could not prohibit lawyers from price advertising of "routine legal services." [1] Justice Blackmun's majority opinion noted that the case did not involve advertising relating to the *"quality* of legal services" or to "in-person solicitation of clients." He rejected a variety of justifications for the restraint, including "adverse effect on professionalism" and the claim that attorney advertising was "inherently misleading." [2] The major dissent was by Justice Powell, joined by Justice Stewart, who claimed that the decision would "effect profound changes in the practice of law" and who argued that the majority had given inadequate weight to "the two fundamental ways in which the advertising of professional services [differs] from that of tangible products: the vastly increased potential for deception and the enhanced difficulty of effective regulation in the public interest." [3]

A year later, two cases involving lawyers' solicitation of clients came to the Court. In these cases, the distinction between commercial and non-commercial speech proved critical. In Ohralik v. Ohio State Bar Association, 436 U.S. 447 (1978), involving "classic examples of 'ambulance chasing,' " the Court sustained a suspension from law practice for violating anti-solicitation rules. The case involved an attorney soliciting contingent fee employment from accident victims. Justice Powell's majority opinion stated that "the State may proscribe in-person solicitation for pecuniary gain under circumstances likely to result in adverse consequences" without a showing of actual harm and with some leeway for prophylactic rules. But in In re Primus, 436 U.S. 412 (1978), the Court set aside disciplinary action in a case involving an attorney who did volunteer work for the ACLU. She had been reprimanded for writing a letter asking a woman who had been sterilized whether she wanted to become a plaintiff in a lawsuit against a doctor who had allegedly participated in a program of sterilizing pregnant mothers as a condition of continued receipt of Medicaid benefits. Justice Powell's majority opinion there emphasized that the attorney's letter fell within "the generous zone of First Amendment protection reserved for associational freedoms" [see NAACP v. Button (p. 1353 below)] and concluded that a state may not punish a lawyer "who, seeking to further political and ideological goals through associational activity, including litigation, advises a lay person of her legal rights and discloses in a subsequent letter that free legal assistance is available from a nonprofit organization." Accordingly, more "exacting" scruti-

---

and embarassing to those exposed to them, and that permitting them would legitimize sexual activity of young people." With respect to offensiveness, he cited Cohen v. California, p. 1101 above. And with respect to legitimizing sexual activity, he noted that the advertisements were not incitements in the sense of Brandenburg p. 1037 above. [See also Bolger (1983, p. 1145 below).]

1. The case involved a state disciplinary rule against lawyers' advertising as applied to ads for a "legal clinic" providing services at low fees by accepting only routine cases.

2. Justice Blackmun's opinion in Bates added an important new difference between the protec-

tion of commercial and non-commercial speech. (Recall footnote [2] to his Virginia Pharmacy opinion.) In Bates, he stated that the challengers could not make an overbreadth attack, explaining that "the justification for the application of overbreadth analysis applies weakly, if at all, in the ordinary commercial context. [Since] advertising is linked to commercial well-being, it seems unlikely that such speech is particularly susceptible to being crushed by overbroad regulation."

3. Chief Justice Burger and Justice Rehnquist also dissented in part.

ny was justified in Primus than in Ohralik; and in the "political expression or association" context of Primus—unlike the commercial speech one of Ohralik—the First Amendment required a showing that the attorney's solicitation had "in fact" produced harm, a showing not made here. Justice Rehnquist's dissent insisted that there was "no principled distinction" between the cases and suggested that the majority had developed "a jurisprudence of epithets and slogans [in] which 'ambulance chasers' suffer one fate and 'civil liberties lawyers' another." [4]

Bates and its progeny were explored and applied in In re R.M.J., 455 U.S. 191 (1982), where the Court unanimously held unconstitutional a range of Missouri restrictions on lawyer advertising. The restrictions limited such advertising to certain categories of information and, in some instances, to certain specified language. Justice Powell's opinion sustained all of the First Amendment challenges. Among the regulations struck down were those barring lawyers from deviating from a prescribed list of 23 specific terms describing areas of practice. Justice Powell emphasized that the challenger's differently worded listing had not been shown to be "misleading." Another invalid regulation was the ban on mailing cards announcing the opening of a law office to a larger audience than the permitted one: "lawyers, clients, former clients, personal friends and relatives." Once again, Justice Powell emphasized that there was no finding that the speech was actually or inherently "misleading." [5]

2. *The risk of misleading advertising: The use of trade names by optometrists.* The 7 to 2 decision in Friedman v. Rogers, 440 U.S. 1 (1979), rejected a First Amendment attack on a Texas law prohibiting the practice of optometry under a trade name. Justice Powell's majority opinion concluded: "It is clear that the State's interest in protecting the public from the deceptive and misleading use of optometrical trade names is substantial and well-demonstrated. We are convinced that [the law] is a constitutionally permissible state regulation in furtherance of this interest." He distinguished the statements protected in Virginia Pharmacy and Bates on the ground that they were "self-contained and self-explanatory." Here, by contrast, "we are concerned with a form of commercial speech that has no intrinsic meaning. A trade name conveys no information about the price and nature of the services offered by an optometrist until it acquires meaning over a period of time by associations formed in the minds of the public between the name and some standard of price or quality. Because these ill-defined associations of trade names with price and quality information can be manipulated by the users of trade names, there is a significant possibility

4. A separate opinion by Justice Marshall suggested that he would find First Amendment protection for most solicitations short of the Ohralik extreme.

5. In an earlier passage, Justice Powell summarized the current state of commercial speech doctrine as follows: "Commercial speech doctrine, in the context of advertising for professional services, may be summarized generally as follows: Truthful advertising related to lawful activities is entitled to the protections of the First Amendment. But when the particular content or method of the advertising suggests that it is inherently misleading or when experience has proven that in fact such advertising is subject to abuse, the states may impose appropriate restrictions. Misleading advertising may be prohibited entirely. But the states may not place an absolute prohibition on certain types of potentially misleading information, e.g., a listing of areas of practice, if the information also may be presented in a way that is not deceptive. [Although] the

potential for deception and confusion is particularly strong in the context of advertising professional services, restrictions upon such advertising may be no broader than reasonably necessary to prevent the deception. Even when a communication is not misleading, the state retains some authority to regulate. But the state must assert a substantial interest and the interference with speech must be in proportion to the interest served. [Central Hudson, below.] Restrictions must be narrowly drawn, and the state lawfully may regulate only to the extent regulation furthers the state's substantial interest." He added in a footnote: "We recognize, of course, that the generalizations summarized above do not afford precise guidance to the Bar and the courts. They do represent the general principles that may be distilled from our decisions in this developing area of the law. As they are applied on a case by case basis [as in this opinion], more specific guidance will be available."

that trade names will be used to mislead the public."[6] He pointed out that, even though trade names were barred, "factual information associated with trade names may be communicated freely and explicitly to the public" by the kind of advertising protected under Virginia Pharmacy and Bates.[7]

3. *Real estate "For Sale" signs as protected speech.* In Linmark Associates, Inc. v. Willingboro, 431 U.S. 85 (1977), the unanimous Court relied in part on Virginia Pharmacy to strike down an ordinance prohibiting the posting of real estate "For Sale" and "Sold" signs.[8] Justice Marshall's opinion agreed that the town's objectives—to promote a stable, racially integrated community and to stem the flight of white homeowners—were important ones, but insisted that the law could not survive the "means" prong of judicial scrutiny: the town had failed to demonstrate that the ordinance was "necessary" to achieve its objectives. He continued: "The constitutional defect in this ordinance, however, is far more basic. The [town here, like the State in Virginia Pharmacy,] acted to prevent its residents from obtaining certain information. That information [is] of vital interest to Willingboro residents, since it may bear on one of the most important decisions they have a right to make: where to live and raise their families. The [town] has sought to restrict the free flow of this data because it fears that otherwise, homeowners will make decisions inimical to what the [town] views as the homeowners' self-interest and the corporate interest of the township: they will choose to leave town. The [town's] concern, then, was not with any commercial aspect of 'For Sale' signs—with offerors communicating offers to offerees—but with the substance of the information communicated to Willingboro citizens. If dissemination of this information can be restricted, then every locality in the country can suppress any facts that reflect poorly on the locality, so long as a plausible claim can be made that disclosure would cause the recipients of the information to act 'irrationally.' Virginia Pharmacy denies government such sweeping powers [to deny its citizens] information that is neither false nor misleading."

IS CONSTITUTIONAL PROTECTION OF COMMERCIAL ADVERTISING JUSTIFIED? TO WHAT EXTENT IS IT PROTECTED?

1. *Commercial advertising as "speech."* Recall the varying rationales for protecting expression under the First Amendment.[1] Does speech that does "no more than propose a commercial transaction" warrant protection under any of these rationales? Does commercial advertising contribute to better decision-making in a representative form of government (recall the Meiklejohn rationale)? Is it a part of the free marketplace of ideas (recall the Holmes rationale)? Is protection of advertising justifiable only under the quite open-ended autonomy, individual self-realization rationale? If the primary purpose of commercial advertising is to contribute to a more efficient operation of the free *economic* market, is that a quality relevant to First Amendment theory? Can

6. In listing some of the "numerous" "possibilities for deception," Justice Powell noted that a trade name can remain unchanged despite changes in the staff of optometrists in the business. Moreover, by using different trade names at shops under its common ownership, "an optometrist can give the public a false impression of competition." He added: "The use of a trade name also facilitates the advertising essential to large-scale commercial practices with numerous branch offices, conduct the State rationally may wish to discourage while not prohibiting com-

mercial optometrical practice altogether." He emphasized, moreover, that the State's concerns about the misleading uses of trade names "were not speculative or hypothetical, but were based on experience in Texas with which the legislature was familiar."

7. Justice Blackmun wrote the dissent.

8. Justice Rehnquist did not participate.

1. See especially the introductory materials to this chapter.

protection of the economic market under the First Amendment be reconciled with the modern Court's "hands-off" attitude in economic regulation cases (see esp. chap. 8 above)? Recall that Justice Blackmun in Virginia Pharmacy cited a number of cases of the post-Lochner era that had deferentially sustained economic regulations of the profession. Does adherence to Virginia Pharmacy warrant reexamination of those economic regulation cases?

Consider the critical comments on the developments beginning with Virginia Pharmacy in Jackson & Jeffries, "Commercial Speech: Economic Due Process and the First Amendment," 65 Va.L.Rev. 1 (1979). The authors accept both the representative government and the individual self-fulfillment rationales for protecting free speech but insist that neither justifies protection of commercial speech. To them, Virginia Pharmacy "is inexplicable under traditional First Amendment principles. Ordinary business advertising does not advance the goal of individual self-fulfillment through free expression, nor does it contribute to political decisionmaking in a representative democracy. Commercial advertising simply is not relevant to either of these commonly accepted bases for construing the First Amendment. Moreover, there is no evidence of a strategic necessity to protect constitutionally irrelevant speech 'in order to protect speech that matters.' [Recall Gertz, p. 1060 above.] Both reason and experience suggest that the distinction between commercial speech and protected speech is relatively easy to maintain." To Jackson and Jeffries, Virginia Pharmacy rests not on traditional First Amendment rationales but on "two basic values of economic liberty": "the opportunity of the individual producer or consumer to maximize his own economic utility"; and "the aggregate economic efficiency of a free market economy." They agree with the Court's economic analysis but add: "It is surprising to discover [that] these economic considerations add up to a *constitutional* impediment to legislative control of the marketplace" under the First Amendment. To them, the essence of the Virginia Pharmacy line of cases is that "the [Court] has reconstituted the values of [Lochner] as components of freedom of speech." [2]

2. *The extent of protection of commercial speech.* In the years since Virginia Pharmacy, the Court has sometimes expressed doubt about its inclusion of commercial speech within the First Amendment; but it has not reverted to its earlier total exclusion of advertising from constitutional protection. Thus, in Friedman, above, Justice Blackmun, the author of Virginia Pharmacy, dissented and charged the majority with retreating from the spirit of Virginia Pharmacy. And Justice Powell, the author of many of the modern commercial speech cases, has repeatedly emphasized the especially limited protection of commercial speech under the First Amendment. Moreover, Justice Powell suggested in Ohralik, above, that the challenger's speech was entitled to less protection than the legal clinic advertising in Bates, above. Does this multi-level view of First Amendment values—not only ranking commercial speech as lower than non-commercial speech, but also ranking some varieties of commercial speech as lower than others—itself invite a dilution of the normal force of the First Amendment guarantee? [3] Justice Powell once again wrote for the Court in

2. The authors add: "Exactly the same values that are impaired by Virginia's ban against drug price advertising are also invaded by [most] other instances of governmental regulation of the economy." They conclude that Virginia Pharmacy was "decided wrongly" and urge that "the line of development begun by [it] should be cut short." Would acceptance of their position strengthen or weaken First Amendment doctrine?

3. A year after Ohralik, Justice Powell expressed even stronger reservations about First Amendment protection of commercial speech. In a footnote in Friedman, above, he commented that the extension of the First Amendment to commercial speech "has been recognized generally as a substantial extension of traditional free-speech doctrine which poses special problems not presented by other forms of protected speech. [Our] decisions dealing with more traditional First Amendment problems do not extend automatically to this as yet uncharted area." In that footnote, Justice Powell cited the Jackson & Jeffries article, see text note 1 above.)

1980, in the Central Hudson case which follows. There, he promulgated a new four-step analysis for commercial speech cases—an analysis that Justice Blackmun's concurrence described as providing "intermediate scrutiny" (and that he criticized as diluting the protection promised by Virginia Pharmacy and its progeny). In examining Central Hudson, consider especially in what respects, if any, its four-step analysis dilutes normal First Amendment protections.

CENTRAL HUDSON GAS v. PUBLIC SERVICE COMM'N
447 U.S. 557, 100 S.Ct. 2343, 65 L.Ed.2d 341 (1980).

Mr. Justice POWELL delivered the opinion of the Court.

This case presents the question whether a regulation of the [N.Y. Public Service Commission (PSC)] violates the [First Amendment] because it completely bans promotional advertising by an electrical utility. [The PSC's 1977 Policy Statement declared all promotional advertising contrary to the national policy of conserving energy.[1]]

[II.]. The Commission's order restricts only commercial speech, that is, expression related solely to the economic interests of the speaker and its audience. The First Amendment [protects] commercial speech from unwarranted governmental regulation. Virginia Pharmacy. Commercial expression not only serves the economic interest of the speaker, but also assists consumers and furthers the societal interest in the fullest possible dissemination of information. [Even] when advertising communicates only an incomplete version of the relevant facts, the First Amendment presumes that some accurate information is better than no information at all. Bates. Nevertheless, our decisions have recognized "the 'commonsense' distinction between speech proposing a commercial transaction [and] other varieties of speech." Ohralik. The Constitution therefore accords a lesser protection to commercial speech than to other constitutionally guaranteed expression. The protection available for particular commercial expression turns on the nature both of the expression and of the governmental interests served by its regulation.

The First Amendment's concern for commercial speech is based on the informational function of advertising. Consequently, there can be no constitutional objection to the suppression of commercial messages that do not accurately inform the public about lawful activity. The government may ban forms of communication more likely to deceive the public than to inform it, Friedman; Ohralik, or commercial speech related to illegal activity, Pittsburgh Press. If the communication is neither misleading nor related to unlawful activity, the government's power is more circumscribed. The State must assert a substantial interest to be achieved by restrictions on commercial speech. Moreover, the regulatory technique must be in proportion to that interest. The limitation on expression must be designed carefully to achieve the State's goal. Compliance with this requirement may be measured by two criteria. First, the restriction must directly advance the state interest involved; the regulation may not be sustained if it provides only ineffective or remote support for the government's purpose. Second, if the governmental interest could be served as well by a more limited restriction on commercial speech, the excessive restrictions cannot survive. Under the first criterion, the Court has declined to uphold regulations

---

1. The Statement divided advertising expenses "into two broad categories: promotional—advertising intended to stimulate the purchase of utility services—and institutional and informational, a broad category inclusive of all advertising not clearly intended to promote sales." Only "promotional" advertising was prohibited.

The 1977 ban was a continuation of one initiated in 1973, at the time of a severe fuel shortage. The PSC continued the ban in 1977 even though the fuel shortage had eased.

that only indirectly advance the state interest involved. Bates; Virginia Pharmacy. [The] second criterion recognizes that the First Amendment mandates that speech restrictions be "narrowly drawn." Primus. The regulatory technique may extend only as far as the interest it serves. The State cannot regulate speech that poses no danger to the asserted state interest, nor can it completely suppress information when narrower restrictions on expression would serve its interest [as well].

In commercial speech cases, then, a four-part analysis has developed. At the outset, we must determine whether the expression is protected by the First Amendment. For commercial speech to come within that provision, it at least must concern lawful activity and not be misleading. Next, we ask whether the asserted governmental interest is substantial. If both inquiries yield positive answers, we must determine whether the regulation directly advances the governmental interest asserted, and whether it is not more extensive than is necessary to serve that interest.

III. We now apply this four-step analysis for commercial speech to the [PSC's] arguments in support of its ban on promotional advertising. A. [Because] appellant holds a monopoly over the sale of electricity in its service area, the state court suggested that the [PSC's] order restricts no commercial speech of any worth. [This] reasoning falls short of establishing that appellant's advertising is not commercial speech protected by the First Amendment. Monopoly over the supply of a product provides no protection from competition with substitutes for that product. Electric utilities compete with suppliers of fuel oil and natural gas in several markets, such as those for home heating and industrial power. [For] consumers in those competitive markets, advertising by utilities is just as valuable as advertising by unregulated [firms]. B. The [PSC argues] that the State's interest in conserving energy is sufficient to support suppression of advertising designed to increase consumption of electricity. [Plainly], the state interest asserted is substantial. The [PSC] also argues that promotional advertising will aggravate inequities caused by the failure to base the utility's rates on marginal cost. [The] choice among rate structures involves difficult and important questions of economic supply and distributional fairness. The State's concern that rates be fair and efficient represents a clear and substantial governmental interest.

C. Next, we focus on the relationship between the State's interests and the advertising ban. [The] Commission's laudable concern over the equity and efficiency of appellant's rates does not provide a constitutionally adequate reason for restricting protected speech. The link between the advertising prohibition and appellant's rate structure is, at most, tenuous. The impact of promotional advertising on the equity of appellant's rates is highly speculative. [In] contrast, the State's interest in energy conservation is directly advanced by the Commission order at issue here. There is an immediate connection between advertising and demand for electricity. [Thus], we find a direct link between the state interest in conservation and the [PSC's] order.

D. We come finally to the critical inquiry in this case: whether the Commission's complete suppression of speech ordinarily protected by the First Amendment is no more extensive than necessary to further the State's interest in energy conservation. The Commission's order reaches all promotional advertising, regardless of the impact of the touted service on overall energy use. But the energy conservation rationale, as important as it is, cannot justify suppressing information about electric devices or services that would cause no net increase in total energy use. In addition, no showing has been made that a more limited restriction on the content of promotional advertising would not serve adequately the State's interests. Appellant insists that but for the ban, it would advertise products and services that use energy efficiently. These include the "heat pump," which both parties acknowledge to be a major improvement in electric heating, and the use of electric heat as a "backup" to solar and other heat sources. [In] the absence of authoritative findings to the contrary, we must credit as within the realm of possibility the claim that electric heat can be an efficient alternative in some circumstances.

The Commission's order prevents appellant from promoting electric services that would reduce energy use by diverting demand from less efficient sources, or that would consume roughly the same amount of energy as do alternative sources. In neither situation would the utility's advertising endanger conservation or mislead the public. To the extent that the Commission's order suppresses speech that in no way impairs the State's interest in energy conservation, the Commission's order violates the [First Amendment]. The Commission also has not demonstrated that its interest in conservation cannot be protected adequately by more limited regulation of appellant's commercial expression. To further its policy of conservation, the Commission could attempt to restrict the format and content of Central Hudson's advertising. It might, for example, require that the advertisements include information about the relative efficiency and expense of the offered service.[2] In the absence of a showing that more limited speech regulation would be ineffective, we cannot approve the complete suppression of Central Hudson's [advertising].[3]

Reversed.

Mr. Justice BLACKMUN, with whom Mr. Justice BRENNAN joins, concurring [in the judgment].

[I] concur only in the Court's judgment, [because] I believe the test now evolved and applied by the Court is not consistent with our prior cases and does not provide adequate protection for truthful, nonmisleading, noncoercive commercial speech. I agree with the Court that [its] level of intermediate scrutiny is appropriate for a restraint on commercial speech designed to protect consumers from misleading or coercive speech, or a regulation related to the time, place, or manner of commercial speech. I do not agree, however, that the Court's four-part test is the proper one to be applied when a State seeks to suppress information about a product in order to manipulate a private economic decision that the State cannot or has not regulated or outlawed directly. [I] disagree with the Court [when] it says that suppression of speech may be a permissible means to achieve [energy conservation]. [I] seriously doubt whether suppression of information concerning the availability and price of a legally offered product is ever a permissible way for the State to "dampen" demand for or use of the product. Even though "commercial" speech is involved, such a regulatory measure strikes at the heart of the First Amendment. This is because it is a covert attempt by the State to manipulate the choices of its citizens, not by persuasion or direct regulation, but by depriving the public of the information needed to make a free choice.

If the First Amendment guarantee means anything, it means that, absent clear and present danger, government has no power to restrict expression because of the effect its message is likely to have on the public. [Virginia Pharmacy] held that the State "may *not* [pursue its goals] by keeping the public in ignorance." Until today, this principle has governed.[1] [We] have not

---

2. The Commission also might consider a system of previewing advertising campaigns to insure that they will not defeat conservation policy. [We] have observed that commercial speech is such a sturdy brand of expression that traditional prior restraint doctrine may not apply to [it]. [Footnote by Justice Powell.]

3. [The] Commission makes no claim that an emergency now exists. We do not consider the

powers that the State might have over utility advertising in emergency circumstances. [Footnote by Justice Powell.]

1. In my view, the Court today misconstrues the holdings of both Virginia Pharmacy and Linmark by implying that those decisions were based on the fact that the restraints were not closely enough related to the governmental interests asserted. [The] holding of each clearly

suggested that the "commonsense differences" between commercial speech and other speech justify relaxed scrutiny of restraints that suppress truthful, nondeceptive, noncoercive commercial speech. [No] differences between commercial speech and other protected speech justify suppression of commercial speech in order to influence public conduct through manipulation of the availability of [information].

Mr. Justice STEVENS, with whom Mr. Justice BRENNAN joins, concurring [in the judgment].

Because "commercial speech" is afforded less constitutional protection than other forms of speech, it is important that the commercial speech concept not be defined too broadly lest speech deserving of greater constitutional protection be inadvertently suppressed. The issue in this case is whether New York's prohibition on the promotion of the use of electricity through advertising is a ban on nothing but commercial speech. In my judgment one of the two definitions the Court uses in addressing that issue is too broad and the other may be somewhat too narrow. The Court first describes commercial speech as "expression related solely to the economic interests of the speaker and its audience." [It] seems clear to me that [this] encompasses speech that is entitled to the maximum protection afforded by the First Amendment. Neither a labor leader's exhortation to strike, nor an economist's dissertation on the money supply, should receive any lesser protection because the subject matter concerns only the economic interests of the audience. Nor should the economic motivation of a speaker qualify his constitutional protection; even Shakespeare may have been motivated by the prospect of pecuniary reward. Thus, the Court's first definition of commercial speech is unquestionably too broad. The Court's second definition refers to "speech proposing a commercial transaction." [Whatever] the precise contours of the concept, [I] am persuaded that it should not include the entire range of communication that is embraced within the term "promotional advertising."

This case involves a governmental regulation that completely bans promotional advertising by an electric utility. This ban encompasses a great deal more than mere proposals to engage in certain kinds of commercial transactions. It prohibits all advocacy of the immediate or future use of electricity. It curtails expression by an informed and interested group of persons of their point of view on questions relating to the production and consumption of electrical energy—questions frequently discussed and debated by our political leaders. For example, an electric company's advocacy of the use of electric heat for environmental reasons, as opposed to wood-burning stoves, would seem to fall squarely within New York's promotional advertising ban and also within the bounds of maximum First Amendment protection. The breadth of the ban thus exceeds the boundaries of the commercial speech concept, however that concept may be defined. The justification for the regulation is nothing more than the expressed fear that the audience may find the utility's message persuasive. Without the aid of any coercion, deception, or misinformation, truthful communication may persuade some citizens to consume more electricity than they otherwise would. I assume that such a consequence would be undesirable and that government may therefore prohibit and punish the unnecessary or excessive use of electricity. But if the perceived harm associated with greater electrical usage is not sufficiently serious to justify direct regulation, surely it does not constitute the kind of clear and present danger that can justify the suppression of speech. [I] concur in the result because I do not consider this to be a "commercial speech" case. Accordingly, I see no need to decide whether the

rested on a much broader principle. [Footnote by Justice Blackmun.]

Court's four-part analysis adequately protects commercial speech—as properly defined—in the face of a blanket ban of the sort involved in this case.[1]

Mr. Justice REHNQUIST, [dissenting].

The Court's analysis [is] wrong in several respects. Initially, I disagree with the Court's conclusion that the speech of a state-created monopoly, which is the subject of a comprehensive regulatory scheme, is entitled to protection under the First Amendment. I also think that the Court errs here in failing to recognize that the state law is most accurately viewed as an economic regulation and that the speech involved (if it falls within the scope of the First Amendment at all) occupies a significantly more subordinate position in the hierarchy of First Amendment values than the Court gives it today. Finally, the Court in reaching its decision improperly substitutes its own judgment for that of the State in deciding how a proper ban on promotional advertising should be drafted. With regard to this latter point, the Court adopts as its final part of a four-part test a "no more extensive than necessary" analysis that will unduly impair a state legislature's ability to adopt legislation reasonably designed to promote interests that have always been rightly thought to be of great importance to the State.

I. [When] the source of the speech is a state-created monopoly such as this, traditional First Amendment concerns, if they come into play at all, certainly do not justify the broad interventionist role adopted by the Court today. [The] consequences of this natural monopoly [justify] much more wide-ranging supervision and control of a utility under the First Amendment than this Court held in Bellotti [p. 1316 below] to be permissible with regard to ordinary corporations. [The] extensive regulations governing decisionmaking by public utilities suggest that for purposes of First Amendment analysis, a utility is far closer to a state-controlled enterprise than is an ordinary corporation.[1] Accordingly, I think a State has broad discretion in determining the statements that a utility may make in that such statements emanate from the entity created by the State to provide important and unique public services. [I] also think New York's ban on such advertising falls within the scope of permissible state regulation of an economic activity by an entity that could not exist in corporate form, say nothing of enjoy monopoly status, were it not for the laws of New York.

II. [The] Court's decision today fails to give due deference to [the] subordinate position of commercial speech. The Court in so doing returns to the bygone era of [Lochner]. [The] test adopted by the [Court] elevates the protection accorded commercial speech that falls within the scope of the First Amendment to a level that is virtually indistinguishable from that of noncommercial speech. I think [that] by labeling economic regulation of business conduct as a restraint on "free speech" [the Court has] gone far to resurrect the discredited doctrine of cases such as [Lochner]. New York's order here is in my view more akin to an economic regulation to which virtually complete deference should be accorded by this Court. I doubt there would be any question as to the constitutionality of New York's conservation effort if the [PSC] had chosen to raise the price of electricity, to condition its sale on specified terms, or to restrict its production. In terms of constitutional values, I think that such controls are virtually indistinguishable from the State's ban on promotional advertising.

While [an] important objective of the First Amendment is to foster the free flow of information, identification of speech that falls within its protection is not aided by the metaphorical reference to a "marketplace of ideas." There is no

---

1. Justice BRENNAN also submitted a separate statement explaining his agreement with the opinions of Justices Blackmun and Stevens.

1. Compare Justice Rehnquist's majority opinion in Jackson v. Metropolitan Edison Co. (1974; chap. 10, p. 895 above), holding that a public utility's termination of service is not "state action" and is therefore not subject to 14th Amendment restrictions.

reason for believing that the marketplace of ideas is free from market imperfections any more than there is to believe that the invisible hand will always lead to optimum economic decisions in the commercial market. [Even] if I were to agree that commercial speech is entitled to some First Amendment protection, I would hold here that the State's decision to ban promotional advertising, in light of the substantial state interest at stake, is a constitutionally permissible exercise of its power to adopt regulations designed to promote the interests of its citizens.

The plethora of opinions filed in this case highlights the doctrinal difficulties that emerge from this Court's decisions granting First Amendment protection to commercial speech. [The Court's] reasons for invalidating New York's ban on promotional advertising make it quite difficult for a legislature to draft a statute regulating promotional advertising that will satisfy the First Amendment requirements established by the Court in this context. [I] remain of the view that the Court unleashed a Pandora's box when it "elevated" commercial speech to the level of traditional political speech by according it First Amendment protection. The line between "commercial speech," and the kind of speech that those who drafted the First Amendment had in mind, may not be a technically or intellectually easy one to draw, but it surely produced far fewer problems than has the development of judicial doctrine in this area since Virginia Pharmacy. For in the world of political advocacy and *its* marketplace of ideas, there is no such thing as a "fraudulent" idea. [The] free flow of information is important in this context not because it will lead to the discovery of any objective "truth," but because it is essential to our system of self-government. The notion that more speech is the remedy to expose falsehood and fallacies is wholly out of place in the commercial bazaar, where if applied logically the remedy of one who was defrauded would be merely a statement, available upon request, reciting the Latin maxim "caveat emptor." But since "fraudulent speech" in this area is to be remediable under Virginia Pharmacy, the remedy of one defrauded is a lawsuit or an agency proceeding based on common law notions of fraud that are separated by a world of difference from the realm of politics and government. What time, legal decisions, and common sense have so widely severed, I declined to join in Virginia Pharmacy, and regret now to see the Court reaping the seeds that it there sowed. For in a democracy, the economic is subordinate to the [political].

III. [The] final part of the Court's [test] leaves room for so many hypothetical "better" ways that any ingenious lawyer will surely seize on one of them to secure the invalidation of what the state agency actually did. [It] is in my view inappropriate for the Court to invalidate the State's ban on commercial advertising here based on its speculation that in some cases the advertising may result in a net savings in electrical energy use, and in the cases in which it is clear a net energy savings would result from utility advertising the [PSC] would apply its ban so as to proscribe such advertising. Even assuming that the Court's speculation is correct, I do not think it follows that facial invalidation of the ban is the appropriate [course].

COMMERCIAL SPEECH SINCE CENTRAL HUDSON

1. *Commercial advertising on billboards.* In METROMEDIA, INC. v. SAN DIEGO, 453 U.S. 490 (1981) (more fully discussed below, at p. 1287), Justice WHITE's plurality opinion dealt extensively with the permissibility of restricting billboards containing commercial advertisements. Although the Court struck down the ordinance at issue for excessively restricting *non*-commercial speech, the plurality made it clear that restricting commercial billboards would be permissible. Applying the Central Hudson test, Justice White found little

problem with the ban on commercial billboards as satisfying its first, second, and fourth criteria, but found more problematic the question of whether such a ban "directly advanced" the acknowledged governmental interests "in traffic safety and the appearance of the city." Finding no ulterior motives, the plurality proceeded to apply a deferential attitude to the determinations made by San Diego, especially that relating to traffic safety. And although there was an indication that aesthetic justifications might be scrutinized slightly more closely, the plurality had little doubt that the ban on commercial billboards satisfied all aspects of the Central Hudson test. Because the dissenting opinions of Chief Justice BURGER and Justices REHNQUIST and STEVENS would have upheld the restriction in its entirety, it is clear that a majority of the Court agrees that restriction of *commercial* billboards for both aesthetic and traffic safety reasons satisfies the Central Hudson standard.[1]

2. *Defining commercial speech.* In BOLGER v. YOUNGS DRUG PRODUCTS CORP., 463 U.S. 60 (1983), the Court had the opportunity not only to apply the Central Hudson analysis, but also to provide some important clarification on the threshold issue of what does and does not count as "commercial speech." At issue in Bolger was a First Amendment challenge to a federal statute, 39 U.S.C. § 3001(e)(2), prohibiting the mailing of unsolicited advertisements for contraceptives. Because the degree of First Amendment protection afforded the mailings depended on whether they were characterized as commercial or non-commercial speech, classification of the materials was the Court's first task. Justice MARSHALL's opinion for the Court dealt with the classification of the materials in the context of a "drug store flyer" as well as two informational pamphlets, "Condoms and Human Sexuality" and "Plain Talk about Venereal Disease." One of the informational pamphlets repeatedly referred to Youngs' products by name, and the other emphasized generic descriptions of condoms, a product in which Youngs has a leading market position. Justice Marshall's analysis of whether these materials constituted commercial speech warrants full quotation:

"Most of appellee's mailings fall within the core notion of commercial speech—'speech which does "no more than propose a commercial transaction."' Youngs' informational pamphlets, however, cannot be characterized merely as proposals to engage in commercial transactions. Their proper classification as commercial or non-commercial speech thus presents a closer question. The mere fact that these pamphlets are conceded to be advertisements clearly does not compel the conclusion that they are commercial speech. Similarly, the reference to a specific product does not by itself render the pamphlets commercial speech. Finally, the fact that Youngs has an economic motivation for mailing the pamphlets would clearly be insufficient by itself to turn the materials into commercial speech. The combination of *all* these characteristics, however, provides strong support for the District Court's conclusion that the informational pamphlets are properly characterized as commercial speech. The mailings constitute commercial speech notwithstanding the fact that they contain discussions of important public issues such as venereal disease and family planning. [Central Hudson.] A company has the full panoply of protections available

---

1. Note the deferential scrutiny employed by the plurality in applying the Central Hudson standard in Metromedia. Arguably, the stringency of a standard of review is a function of the factors that must be examined, the strength of the state justifications required by the verbal formulation of the standard, and the rigor with which an appellate court will examine legislative or lower court determinations with respect to those justifications. If in fact an appellate court (such as the Court in Metromedia) is extremely deferential in exercising its scrutiny, does the detailed formulation of the test really matter? Is the Metromedia plurality's evident deference regarding the commercial speech aspects of the case a further indication of the significance of the differences in treatment between "core" First Amendment speech and "lower value" speech such as commercial speech? In view of the plurality position in Metromedia, can it be said that the impact of Virginia Pharmacy has been as much as was originally imagined—or feared?

[for] its direct comments on public issues, so there is no reason for providing similar constitutional protection when such statements are made in the context of commercial transactions. [We] conclude [that] all of the mailings in this case are entitled to the qualified but nonetheless substantial protection accorded to commercial speech."[2]

Having found the materials to be commercial speech, the Court applied the Central Hudson analysis. Because the speech was neither misleading nor concerned with unlawful activity, and in fact dealt with "substantial individual and societal interests," it was covered by the First Amendment. The Court then had to evaluate the substantiality of the government's interest. While agreeing that aiding parents' efforts to discuss birth control with their children constituted a substantial interest, Justice Marshall found that the statute provided "only the most limited incremental support for the interest asserted. We can reasonably assume that parents already exercise substantial control over the disposition of mail once it enters their mailbox. [And parents] must already cope with a multitude of external stimuli that color their children's perception of sensitive subjects."[3] The Court also found the reach of the statute far more extensive than necessary. The advertisements were "entirely suitable for adults. [The] level of discourse reaching a mailbox cannot be limited to that which would be suitable for a sandbox."[4]

Justice REHNQUIST, joined by Justice O'Connor, concurred in the judgment. He noted the substantial governmental interest in preventing intrusion into the home, but argued that the statute here imposed an unduly large restriction in view of the extent of the intrusion. Justice STEVENS, also concurring in the judgment, took issue with the majority's "virtually complete rejection of offensiveness as a possibly legitimate justification for the suppression of speech." He also was less certain that this material was properly classified as commercial speech. But to him the important question was "whether a law regulates communications for their ideas or for their style. [Regulations] of form and context may strike a constitutionally appropriate balance between the advocate's right to convey a message and the recipient's interest in the quality of his environment. [But the] statute at issue [censors] ideas, not style." To Justice Stevens, a crucial distinction was that this statute dealt only with contraception and not with conception, thus excluding "one advocate from a forum to which adversaries have unlimited access."

---

2. "[Of course], a different conclusion may be appropriate in a case where the pamphlet advertises an activity itself protected by the First Amendment." [Footnote by Justice Marshall.]

3. "For example, many magazines contain advertisements for contraceptives. § 3001(e)(2) itself permits the mailing of publications containing contraceptive advertisements to subscribers. Similarly, drug stores commonly display contraceptives. And minors taking a course in sex education will undoubtedly be exposed to the subject of contraception." [Footnote by Justice Marshall.]

4. As noted above, the Court distinguished Pacifica on the ground that the receipt of mail is "far less intrusive and uncontrollable" than are radio and television broadcasts.

Chapter 12

FREEDOM OF EXPRESSION: ADDITIONAL PERVASIVE THEMES; THE PUBLIC FORUM PROBLEM

Introduction. As previewed in the introductory pages to chap. 11, this chapter continues the pursuit of basic, "building block" problems in First Amendment analysis. It turns from the problems of coverage or noncoverage under the First Amendment because of the content of speech to a range of techniques and issues that are also pervasive in the modern cases. Sec. 1A provides an introduction to a range of judicial techniques already tangentially encountered in some of the preceding materials and even more prominent in the cases that follow. It focuses on the relevance of "overbreadth" in First Amendment challenges to regulations, and it introduces as well some related but at times distinctive themes—the demand that government regulate speech by utilizing "less restrictive means" and the concept of "vagueness." Sec. 1B provides an overview of the Court's often announced special hostility to "prior restraints." Sec. 2 turns to another theme that frequently surfaces in the materials below, especially Burger Court decisions: the concern with actual or potential discrimination in the regulation of expression. "Discrimination" in the First Amendment area has chameleonic tendencies, as it did in earlier chapters concerned with inequality (e.g., chaps. 5 and 9). This section tries to examine, in a preliminary way, the varying colorations which the term manifests, with particular emphasis on the increasingly invoked distinction between content-neutral and content-based regulations. Sec. 3 turns to the problem of "symbolic speech" and the influential two-track standard of O'Brien, the 1968 draft card burning case. "Symbolic speech" refers to expression communicated not primarily through words but rather through behavior, be it burning of draft cards or mutilating the flag or wearing arm bands or camping near the White House to dramatize the treatment of the homeless. The two-track approach of O'Brien—relating to different levels of justification dependent on whether the regulation stems from a concern with the communicative impact of the regulation or with the nonspeech elements of the expression—is emphasized because, as the later materials illustrate, that approach is widely invoked in areas well beyond that of "symbolic speech."

Sec. 4 turns to a set of functional problems in which many of these techniques, from overbreadth to discrimination and two-track justification theories, have played a prominent role. The underlying issue here is that of First Amendment access to public property such as streets and parks, and to some privately owned places (e.g., shopping centers) as well. These problems are often viewed as those of the "public forum"; the recurrent issue is the extent of governmental power to regulate access to the public forum. When speakers wish to express themselves in public places and when government asserts a regulatory interest generally related to the maintenance of peace and order, the clashes often produce controversy and litigation. To what extent may government prevail when it purports to regulate the "time, place and manner" rather than the content of speech in the "public forum"? All of the judicial techniques surveyed in this and the preceding chapter play a role in the resolution of these conflicts.

SECTION 1. ADDITIONAL PERVASIVE THEMES

A. OVERBREADTH, VAGUENESS, LESS RESTRICTIVE MEANS

THE FIRST AMENDMENT OVERBREADTH DOCTRINE AND RELATED TECHNIQUES

Introduction. We begin this examination of additional judicial techniques for protecting speech with an introduction to the use of overbreadth analysis in the First Amendment area. That approach has already surfaced briefly above, as in the Aptheker and Robel cases at p. 1034; it is more fully developed in later materials. This introduction delineates the contours of the technique, and suggests some of its strengths and weaknesses. The overbreadth technique has been praised as a particularly effective one for the protection of freedom of expression. It is a technique that proved especially popular with the Warren Court. It has encountered mounting criticism and some curtailment on the Burger Court; but it continues to be quite widely invoked. The examination of its central features here invites comparison with the quite different, content-oriented approaches explored in the preceding chapter.

1. *The distinctive features of overbreadth.* The modern Court has repeatedly invoked the principle that "a governmental purpose to control or prevent activities constitutionally subject [to] regulation may not be achieved by *means which sweep unnecessarily broadly and thereby invade the area of protected freedoms."* (Emphasis added.)[1] The most distinctive feature of the overbreadth technique is that it marks an exception to some of the usual rules of constitutional litigation. Ordinarily, a particular litigant claims that a statute is unconstitutional as applied to him or her; if the litigant prevails, the courts carve away the unconstitutional aspects of the law by invalidating its improper applications on a case-by-case basis. Ordinarily, moreover, challengers to a law are not permitted to raise the rights of third parties and can only assert their own interests.[2] In overbreadth analysis, those rules give way: challengers *are* permitted to raise the rights of third parties; and the court invalidates the entire statute "on its face" or "as construed," not merely "as applied," so that the overbroad law becomes unenforceable until a properly authorized court construes it more narrowly.[3] The factor that motivates courts to depart from the normal adjudicatory rules is the concern with the "chilling," deterrent effect of the overbroad statute on third parties not courageous enough to bring suit. The Court assumes that an overbroad law's "very existence may cause others not before the court to refrain from constitutionally protected speech or expression." An overbreadth ruling is designed to remove that deterrent effect on the speech of those third parties.[4]

1. The quotation is from Justice Harlan's opinion for the Court in NAACP v. Alabama (1964; p. 1350 below).

2. See generally Note, "Standing to Assert Constitutional Jus Tertii," 88 Harv.L.Rev. 423 (1974), and the materials on "standing to sue" in chap. 15, at p. 1574 below.

3. As the Court summarized the "overbreadth" approach in Schaumburg v. Citizens for a Better Environment (1980; p. 1215 below): "Given a case or controversy, a litigant whose own activities are unprotected may nevertheless challenge a statute by showing that it substantial-

ly abridges the First Amendment rights of other parties not before the court. In these First Amendment contexts, the courts are inclined to disregard the normal rule against permitting one whose conduct may validly be prohibited to challenge the proscription as it applies to others because of the possibility that protected speech or associative activities may be inhibited by the overly broad reach of the statute."

4. See generally Note, "The First Amendment Overbreadth Doctrine," 83 Harv.L.Rev. 844 (1970); cf. Note, "The Chilling Effect in

To restate the distinctive procedural aspects of the overbreadth approach somewhat more fully: in the usual "as applied" situation, the Court asks simply whether the challenger's activities are protected by the First Amendment. In that typical "as applied" case, the holding is that the challenger's speech *is* protected. As a result, the challenged statute is constitutionally inapplicable to the challenger; in effect, the challenged law is pro tanto trimmed down. The overbreadth technique, by contrast, does not reach the question whether the *challenger's* speech is constitutionally protected; instead it strikes down the statute entirely, because it *might* be applied to others not before the Court whose activities *are* constitutionally protected. Typically, the Court assumes that the challenger's behavior is *not* protected by the First Amendment and *is* reachable by the state under a more "narrowly drawn" law. The challenged statute is struck down because the challenger is permitted to argue that *other* conceivable statutory applications *might* constitutionally burden protected activity. One of the pervasive problems in the application of the doctrine is how far the Court should seek out *possible* unconstitutional applications of the law as a basis for reversing a conviction of someone whose behavior could presumably be punished by a more narrowly drawn law.[5]

2. *The attractiveness of the overbreadth technique.* Overbreadth analysis has been especially attractive to some Justices because it gives the appearance of leaving alternatives open to the legislature. By holding out the prospect that narrower means may be available to achieve legislative objectives, it conveys the appearance of intervening in legislative choices more marginally than outright "balancing" would. What else may account for the popularity of the overbreadth technique, especially in the late Warren years? Its attractiveness may be attributable in part to its relatively technical, tentative appearance. It strikes down the law at the behest of challenger A without saying much about the First Amendment dimensions of A's behavior; it strikes down the law because of a possible application to third party B not before the Court, an application that is

Constitutional Law," 69 Colum.L.Rev. 808 (1969).

For careful modern efforts to reexamine the contours and distinctiveness of overbreadth, see Monaghan, "Overbreadth," 1981 Sup.Ct.Rev. 1, and Monaghan, "Third Party Standing," 84 Colum.L.Rev. 277 (1984). Monaghan argues that, correctly understood, "overbreadth challenges involve first, not third, party standing." He states that "overbreadth challenges are best understood as invoking the conventional principle that a litigant's conduct may be regulated only in accordance with a valid rule. Where the substantive constitutional standard is more stringent than the rational basis test, this demand translates into a requirement of significant congruence between the boundaries of the rule and constitutionally acceptable governmental ends. [In] sum, overbreadth decisions are simply determinations *on the merits* of the litigant's substantive constitutional claim. [He adds in a footnote: "In other words, the litigant's assertion always takes the following form: 'I am being subjected to an invalid rule.' "] What differentiates a first amendment case from other cases is not a special standing principle but the substantive content of the applicable constitutional law." He adds, however: "To be sure, overbreadth methodology, even as properly understood, requires consideration of the impact of a rule on third parties. In assessing the constitutional validity of the opera-

tive rule, the court's attention is drawn away from the litigant's conduct to the rule's reasonably foreseeable applications to persons not before the court. In that sense we have third party standing. But, rhetoric aside, the 'rights' of third persons are not implicated." Note also Redish, "The Warren Court, the Burger Court, and the First Amendment Overbreadth Doctrine," 78 Nw.L.Rev. 1031 (1983).

5. It is that problem which has contributed to the Burger Court's "substantial overbreadth" limitation on the technique. See notes 4 and 5 below.

When the Court finds that the particular challenger's behavior may constitutionally be curtailed, yet the means chosen by the legislature are "too broad" because of the potential application of the statute to protected conduct, should the Justices be under an obligation to explain what narrower means are available to achieve the state's objective? In a considerable number of overbreadth decisions, the Court has been largely silent about such alternatives; and that silence—while it may account for the popularity of the overbreadth technique with some Justices—has been criticized. See, e.g., Gunther, "Reflections on [Robel]," 20 Stan.L.Rev. 1140 (1968); compare Tribe, American Constitutional Law (1978), 723. (See also text note 6, below.)

often only briefly discussed rather than fully explored. Unlike most of the techniques considered earlier, overbreadth opinions frequently do not deal explicitly and elaborately with the substantive dimensions of protected speech; they purport to be concerned with *means* to legitimate ends, not ultimate quasi-legislative choices; they often do not pursue the reasons for the constitutionality of government regulation of A's behavior or for the unconstitutionality of regulating B's conduct; and they typically avoid explicit "balancing." [6]

Yet an overbreadth opinion necessarily involves *some* delineation of protected expression under the First Amendment, albeit more obliquely and less explicitly than do some other techniques. To strike down an excessively broad "means" because it impinges on an "area of protected freedom" presupposes, after all, at least an implicit judgment about what the contours of that "area" are. To strike down a law at A's behest because of its potential invalid application to B involves at least implicit assumptions about *why* B is protected by the First Amendment. Some of the popularity of the overbreadth technique on the Court may stem, then, from its usefulness in deciding speech problems somewhat more indirectly, often more sketchily, than the more open confrontations of ultimate speech issues noted earlier—even though the Court's overbreadth opinions often emphasize that it is not denying legislative power to reach challenger A's behavior through more "narrowly drawn" legislation. (The popularity of the technique for the challenger is evident: when successfully invoked, it produces not a limited holding that the law is invalid "as applied" to the particular challenger, but rather that it is void "on its face" or "as construed" and hence unenforceable against *anyone,* until an authorized court narrows it.)[7]

3. *The mounting criticisms of the overbreadth technique.* The overbreadth technique for finding statutes invalid on their face was resorted to with considerable frequency during the final years of the Warren era. In addition to its use in the Aptheker and Robel cases, p. 1034 above, other prominent examples include Keyishian (1967; government employees' security program; p. 1377 below), and Gooding v. Wilson (1972; law prohibiting "opprobrious words or abusive language"; p. 1048 above). But in more recent years, there

---

6. Chief Justice Warren's opinion in United States v. Robel (1967; p. 1035 above) illustrates the problematical type of overbreadth opinion discussed in the text: it discusses only sketchily the constitutional dimensions of A's and B's conduct; and it explicitly disavows that it is engaging in "balancing." Chief Justice Warren stated: "It has been suggested that this case should be decided by 'balancing' the governmental interests [against] the First Amendment rights asserted. [This] we decline to do. We recognize that both interests are substantial, but we deem it inappropriate for this Court to label one as being more important or more substantial than the other. Our inquiry is more circumscribed. [We] have confined our analysis to whether Congress has adopted a constitutional means in achieving its concededly legitimate [goal]. In making this determination we have found it necessary to measure the validity of the means [against] both the goal [and] the First Amendment. But we have in no way 'balanced' those respective interests. We have ruled only that the Constitution requires that the conflict between congressional power and individual rights be accommodated by legislation drawn more narrowly to avoid the conflict. There is, of course, nothing novel in that analysis. [McCulloch v. Maryland.]"

Note the comment in Gunther, "Reflections on [Robel]," 20 Stan.L.Rev. 1140 (1968): "The Court's disavowals are, of course, not persuasive. [Perhaps] someday the Court will be able to assess alternatives, as it does here at least implicitly, without the compulsion to deny that it is doing so; perhaps some day it will be able to confront competing ultimate values, as it does here, without denying that it is doing so—whether the process is called 'balancing' or has another label to which the majority is less allergic." Note also Ely's comment on Chief Justice Warren's statement in Robel, in Democracy and Distrust (1980), 106: "That may be good propaganda, but it does not accurately reflect what was going on in Robel and similar cases." (For an example of an overbreadth opinion that *does* explore the reasons why B's behavior cannot be regulated, see Schaumburg (1980; p. 1215 below).)

7. See Dombrowski v. Pfister (1965; p. 1602 below).

Recall that the Court has explicitly refused to apply the overbreadth technique in some areas of First Amendment litigation. See Bates v. State Bar of Arizona (1977; p. 1135 above; commercial speech).

has been increasing criticism of invocations of overbreadth. See, e.g., Justice Black's opinion in Younger v. Harris (1971; p. 1602 below), including the comment that "the existence of a 'chilling effect' even in the area of First Amendment rights has never been considered a sufficient basis, in and of itself, for prohibiting state action." In curtailing federal injunctive relief against a law claimed to be "on its face" vague or overly broad, Justice Black also emphasized a "more basic consideration": "the function of the federal courts in our constitutional plan." The federal judicial power to resolve "concrete disputes," he noted, "does not amount to an unlimited power to survey the statute books and pass judgment on laws before the courts are called upon to enforce them." Implicitly attacking a characteristic of overbreadth review—the consideration of *potential* applications of a statute, to parties not before the Court—he commented: "The combination of the relative remoteness of the controversy, the impact on the legislative process of the relief sought, and above all the speculative and amorphous nature of the required line-by-line analysis of detailed statutes ordinarily results in a kind of case that is wholly unsatisfactory for deciding constitutional questions." [8]

4. *The curtailment of overbreadth attacks: Broadrick and "substantial overbreadth."* Criticisms such as those bore fruit by 1973, when a new majority apparently endorsed a curtailment of the overbreadth technique, though not its elimination. In BROADRICK v. OKLAHOMA, 413 U.S. 601 (1973), Justice White—who dissented from some earlier overbreadth invalidations—wrote for the majority, and Justice Brennan—who had written some of the major overbreadth opinions of the Warren era—wrote for most of the dissenters. Justice White emphasized a "substantial overbreadth" theme, and he suggested that overbreadth invalidations were generally inappropriate when the allegedly impermissible applications of the challenged statute affected "conduct" rather than "speech." [9] Though Broadrick arose in the context of government employees' conduct (see chap. 13, p. 1392 below), a look at the overbreadth discussion in the Broadrick opinions is appropriate here to round out this preliminary survey of the nature, attractions, problems and status of the overbreadth technique.

The Broadrick case was a challenge to § 818 of Oklahoma's Merit System Act restricting political activities by classified civil servants. Among the challenged provisions was one prohibiting employees from "tak[ing] part in the management or affairs of any political party or in any political campaign, except to exercise his right as a citizen privately to express his opinion and to cast his vote." Other provisions more specifically prohibited soliciting for campaign contributions. Appellants, who had campaigned for a superior, challenged § 818 on vagueness and overbreadth grounds. The Court's 5 to 4 decision rejected those challenges. Justice WHITE's majority opinion devoted most attention to the overbreadth issue:

"Appellants assert that § 818 has been construed as applying to such allegedly protected political expression as the wearing of political buttons or the displaying of bumper stickers. But appellants did not engage in any such activity. They are charged with actively engaging in partisan political activi-

---

8. Note also Justice White's dissent from an invalidation for vagueness and overbreadth in Coates v. Cincinnati (1971; p. 1234 below), and Chief Justice Burger's dissent from the overbreadth invalidation in Gooding v. Wilson (1972; p. 1048 above). Building on Justice Black's comments in Younger v. Harris, Chief Justice Burger in Gooding argued that the more proper, narrower approach would be to invalidate only for "*substantial*" overbreadth." He urged that courts not invalidate for overbreadth "because of some insubstantial or imagined potential for occasional and isolated applications that go beyond constitutional bounds." ("Substantial overbreadth" gained majority support in Broadrick in 1973, which follows.)

9. The "speech"-"conduct" distinction is repeatedly criticized in these materials. See, e.g., the comments on the Cox v. Louisiana cases (1965; p. 1225 below).

ties—including the solicitation of money—among their co-workers for the benefit of their superior. Appellants concede [that] § 818 would be constitutional as applied to this type of conduct. They nevertheless maintain that the statute is overbroad and purports to reach protected, as well as unprotected conduct, and must therefore be struck down on its face and held to be incapable of any constitutional application. We do not believe that the overbreadth doctrine may appropriately be invoked in this manner here."

Justice White then proceeded to justify and delineate a "substantial overbreadth" approach at some length: "Embedded in the traditional rules governing constitutional adjudication is the principle that a person to whom a statute may constitutionally be applied will not be heard to challenge that statute on the ground that it may conceivably be applied unconstitutionally to others, in other situations not before the Court. [This principle reflects] the conviction [that] our constitutional courts are not roving commissions assigned to pass judgment on the validity of the Nation's laws. [In] the past, the Court has recognized some limited exceptions to these principles, but only because of the most 'weighty countervailing policies.' [One such exception] has been carved out in the area of the First Amendment. It has long been recognized that the First Amendment needs breathing space and that statutes attempting to restrict or burden the exercise of First Amendment rights must be narrowly drawn and represent a considered legislative judgment that a particular mode of expression has to give way to other compelling needs of society. [E.g., Shelton v. Tucker (1960; p. 1371 below).] As a corollary, the Court has altered its traditional rules of standing to permit—in the First Amendment area—'attacks on overly broad statutes with no requirement that the person making the attack demonstrate that his own conduct could not be regulated by a statute drawn with the requisite narrow specificity.' [Dombrowski v. Pfister (1965; p. 1602 below).] Litigants, therefore, are permitted to challenge a statute not because their own rights of free expression are violated, but because of a judicial prediction or assumption that the statute's very existence may cause others not before the court to refrain from constitutionally protected speech or expression.

"Such claims of facial overbreadth have been entertained in cases involving statutes which, by their terms, seek to regulate 'only spoken words.' [Gooding v. Wilson (p. 1048 above).] In such cases, it has been the judgment of this Court that the possible harm to society in permitting some unprotected speech to go unpunished is outweighed by the possibility that protected speech of others may be muted and perceived grievances left to fester because of the possible inhibitory effects of overly broad statutes. Overbreadth attacks have also been allowed where the Court thought rights of association were ensnared in statutes which, by their broad sweep, might result in burdening innocent associations. [See, e.g., Keyishian; Robel; Aptheker.] Facial overbreadth claims have also been entertained where statutes, by their terms, purport to regulate the time, place, and manner of expressive or communicative conduct, see [e.g., Grayned v. Rockford],[10] and where such conduct has required official approval under laws that delegated standardless discretionary power to local functionaries, resulting in virtually unreviewable prior restraints on First Amendment rights. See [e.g., Shuttlesworth; Cox I; Kunz; Lovell v. Griffin].

"The consequence of our departure from traditional rules of standing in the First Amendment area is that any enforcement of a statute thus placed at issue is totally forbidden until and unless a limiting construction or partial invalidation so narrows it as to remove the seeming threat or deterrence to constitutionally protected expression. Application of the overbreadth doctrine in this manner is, manifestly, strong medicine. It has been employed by the Court sparingly

---

10. Most of the cases cited by Justice White in this and the following passages—cases regulat- ing "time, place and manner" of expression—are considered in sec. 4 below.

and only as a last resort. Facial overbreadth has not been invoked when a limiting construction has been or could be placed on the challenged statute. See [e.g., Cox v. New Hampshire].[11] Equally important, overbreadth claims, if entertained at all, have been curtailed when invoked against ordinary criminal laws that are sought to be applied to protected conduct. In Cantwell v. Connecticut, [we] did not hold that the offense 'known as breach-of-the-peace' must fall in toto because it was capable of some unconstitutional application. In [Edwards v. South Carolina] and [Cox v. Louisiana I, we] concluded that the conduct at issue could not itself be punished under a breach of the peace statute. On that basis, the convictions were reversed.[12] [O]verbreadth scrutiny has [also] generally been somewhat less rigid in the context of statutes regulating conduct in the shadow of the First Amendment, but doing so in a neutral, noncensorial manner.

"It remains a 'matter of no little difficulty' to determine when a law may properly be held void on its face and when 'such summary action' is inappropriate. [But] the plain import of our cases is, at the very least, that facial overbreadth adjudication is an exception to our traditional rules of practice and that its function, a limited one at the outset, attenuates as the otherwise unprotected behavior that it forbids the State to sanction moves from 'pure speech' towards conduct and that conduct—even if expressive—falls within the scope of otherwise valid criminal laws that reflect legitimate state interests in maintaining comprehensive controls over harmful, constitutionally unprotected conduct. Although such laws, if too broadly worded, may deter protected speech to some unknown extent, there comes a point where that effect—at best a prediction—cannot, with confidence, justify invalidating a statute on its face and so prohibiting a State from enforcing the statute against conduct that is admittedly within its power to proscribe. [To] put the matter another way, particularly where conduct and not merely speech is involved, we believe that the overbreadth of a statute must not only be real, but substantial as well, judged in relation to the statute's plainly legitimate sweep. It is our view that § 818 is not substantially overbroad and that whatever overbreadth may exist should be cured through case-by-case analysis of the fact situations to which its sanctions, assertedly, may not be applied.[13]

"Unlike ordinary breach-of-the-peace statutes or other broad regulatory acts, § 818 is directed, by its terms, at political expression which if engaged in by private persons would plainly be protected by the [First Amendment]. But at the same time, § 818 is not a censorial statute, directed at particular groups or viewpoints. The statute, rather, seeks to regulate political activity in an even-handed and neutral manner. As indicated, such statutes have in the past been subject to a less exacting overbreadth scrutiny. Moreover, the fact remains that § 818 regulates a substantial spectrum of conduct that is as manifestly subject to

11. Note that, in review of decisions involving state statutes, the Court lacks authority to construe the statute narrowly to avoid overbroad applications. Instead, it must take the state statute as construed by the state courts.

12. "In both Edwards and Cox I, at the very end of the discussions, the Court also noted that the statutes would be facially unconstitutional for overbreadth. In Cox I, the Court termed this discussion an 'additional reason' for its reversal. These 'additional' holdings were unnecessary to the dispositions of the cases, so much so that only one Member of this Court relied on Cox's 'additional' holding in [Brown v. Louisiana], which involved convictions under the very same breach-of-the-peace statute." [Footnote by Justice White.]

13. "My Brother Brennan asserts that in some sense a requirement of substantial overbreadth is already implicit in the doctrine. This is a welcome observation. It perhaps reduces our differences to our differing views of whether the Oklahoma statute is substantially overbroad. The dissent also insists that [Coates v. Cincinnati] must be taken as overruled. But we are unpersuaded that Coates stands as a barrier to a rule that would invalidate statutes for overbreadth only when the flaw is a substantial concern in the context of the statute as a whole. Our judgment is that the Oklahoma statute, when authoritative administrative constructions are accepted, is not invalid under such a rule." [Footnote by Justice White.]

state regulation as the public peace or criminal trespass. Without question, the conduct appellants have been charged with falls squarely within those proscriptions. Appellants assert that § 818 goes much farther. [They point to] interpretive rules purporting to restrict such allegedly protected activities as the wearing of political buttons or the use of bumper stickers. It may be that such restrictions are impermissible and that § 818 may be susceptible of some other improper applications. But, as presently construed, we do not believe that § 818 must be discarded in toto because some persons' arguably protected conduct may or may not be caught or chilled by the statute. Section 818 is not substantially overbroad and is not, therefore, unconstitutional on its face."

The major dissent was by Justice BRENNAN, joined by Justices Stewart and Marshall. (Justice Douglas dissented separately.) Justice Brennan thought the decision a "wholly unjustified retreat from fundamental and previously well-established" principles. The "substantial overbreadth" approach, he insisted, was unsupported by prior decisions and "effectively overrules" the 1971 decision in Coates (p. 1234 below). The majority had conceded the possibility of some "improper applications." "[T]hat assumption requires a finding that the statute is unconstitutional on its face."

Justice Brennan summarized the majority's curtailment of overbreadth challenges as follows: "Where conduct is involved, a statute's overbreadth must henceforth be 'substantial' before the statute can properly be found invalid on its face." He objected to that approach in the following passage: "I cannot accept the validity of [the majority's] analysis. In the first place, the Court makes no effort to define what it means by 'substantial overbreadth.' We have never held that a statute should be held invalid on its face merely because it is possible to conceive of a single impermissible application, and in that sense a requirement of substantial overbreadth is already implicit in the doctrine. [Whether] the Court means to require some different or greater showing of substantiality is left obscure by today's opinion, in large part because the Court makes no effort to explain why the overbreadth of the Oklahoma Act, while real, is somehow not quite substantial. [More] fundamentally, the Court offers no rationale to explain its conclusion that, for purposes of overbreadth analysis, deterrence of conduct should be viewed differently from deterrence of speech, even where both are equally protected by the [First Amendment].[14] At this stage, it is obviously difficult to estimate the probable impact of today's decision. If the requirement of 'substantial' overbreadth is construed to mean only that facial review is inappropriate where the likelihood of an impermissible application of the statute is too small to generate a 'chilling effect' on protected speech or conduct, then the impact is likely to be small. On the other hand, if today's decision necessitates the drawing of artificial distinctions between protected speech and protected conduct, and if the 'chill' on protected conduct is rarely, if ever, found sufficient to require the facial invalidation of an overbroad statute, then the effect could be very grave indeed."

5. *The impact of the modern skepticism about overbreadth.* To what extent does the skepticism about overbreadth manifested in Broadrick curtail the availability of that technique? Since Broadrick, the Court has indicated that overbreadth remains available in certain circumstances, especially in challenging some regulations of "speech" rather than "conduct."[15] But in other contexts, a divided

---

14. "The Court has applied overbreadth review to many other statutes that assertedly had a 'chilling effect' on protected conduct, rather than on 'pure speech.' See, e.g., [Robel; Aptheker]." [Footnote by Justice Brennan.]

15. For post-Broadrick indications that overbreadth challenges continue to be available in proper circumstances, see, e.g., Erznoznik (1975;

ban on showing nude films in drive-ins; p. 1107 above); Schaumburg (1980; ban on solicitation of contributions by charitable organizations that do not use at least 75% of their receipts for "charitable purposes"; majority opinion by Justice White, the author of Broadrick; p. 1215 below); Schad (1981; another majority opinion by Justice White; ban on live entertainment; p.

Court has rejected several overbreadth attacks since Broadrick.[16]   And in a number of modern cases, the Court has reiterated Broadrick and attempted to restate it.   Thus, in New York v. Ferber (1982; child pornography; p. 1090 above), Justice White's majority opinion rejected an overbreadth attack, reiterated that "the rationale of Broadrick is sound," insisted that "a law should not be invalidated for overbreadth unless it reaches a substantial number of impermissible applications," and noted that the arguably impermissible applications of the law challenged there amounted to only a "tiny fraction of the materials within the statute's reach." [17]   Note also City Council v. Taxpayers for Vincent (1984; p. 1277 below; ban on posting of signs on public property), where Justice Stevens' majority opinion stated: "The concept of 'substantial overbreadth' is not readily reduced to an exact definition.   It is clear, however, that the mere fact that one can conceive of some impermissible applications of a statute is not sufficient to render it susceptible to an overbreadth challenge.   On the contrary, the requirement of substantial overbreadth stems from the underlying justification for the overbreadth exception itself—the interest in preventing an invalid statute from inhibiting the speech of third parties who are not before the Court." [18]

1124 below).   Moreover, Gooding v. Wilson (1972; p. 1048 above) retains vitality, at least in its "fighting words" context.   See Lewis (1974; p. 1105 above).

16.   See, e.g., Arnett v. Kennedy, 416 U.S. 134 (1974), and Parker v. Levy, 417 U.S. 733 (1974).   Justice Rehnquist wrote for the majority in both cases.   In Arnett, he rejected an overbreadth challenge to a law providing for the discharge of federal civil service employees for "such cause as will promote the efficiency of the service."   The employee had been removed for making allegedly false and defamatory statements about fellow employees.   Although Justice Rehnquist's opinion conceded that the law undoubtedly "intended to authorize dismissal for speech as well as other conduct," he construed the federal law as not authorizing "discharge [for] speech which is constitutionally protected."   Accordingly, it was not overbroad.   Justice Marshall's dissent, joined by Justices Douglas and Brennan, thought that this approach would "functionally [eliminate] overbreadth from the First Amendment lexicon.   No statute can [punish] constitutionally protected speech.   The majority has not given the statute a limiting construction but merely repeated the obvious."   He insisted that the majority had misunderstood the overbreadth principle by overlooking the "potential deterrent effect on constitutionally protected speech of a statute that is overbroad.   [For] every employee who risks his job by testing the limits of the statute, many more will choose the cautious path and not speak at all."

17.   In an opinion concurring in the judgment, Justice Stevens objected to the majority's quantitative approach.   He stated: "My reasons for avoiding overbreadth analysis in this case are more qualitative than quantitative.   When we follow our traditional practice of adjudicating difficult and novel constitutional questions only in concrete factual situations, the adjudications tend to be crafted with greater wisdom.   Hypothetical rulings are inherently treacherous and prone to lead us into unforeseen errors; they are

qualitatively less reliable than the products of case-by-case adjudication.   Moreover, it is probably safe to assume that the category of speech that is covered by the New York statute generally is of a lower quality than most other types of communication," and "generally marginal speech does not warrant the extraordinary protection afforded by the overbreadth doctrine."

18.   In the Court's view, the lower court in this case had relied on overbreadth, but Justice Stevens found that this was not "an appropriate case" to entertain such a challenge, because "we have found nothing in the record to indicate that the ordinance will have any different impact on any third parties' interests in free speech than it has on [the challengers here]."

Note also the extensive discussion of overbreadth in Secretary of State v. J.H. Munson Co., 468 U.S. ___ (1984), striking down a restriction on charitable solicitations in reliance on Schaumburg (1980; p. 1217 below).   There, Justice Blackmun's majority opinion suggested a distinction between two types of overbreadth claims.   In one (primarily discussed in the text above), the challenger's own conduct is unprotected, but the challenge is permitted in order to protect the First Amendment rights of third parties not before the Court (even though " 'as applied' to [the challenger] the statute would be constitutional").   He added: " 'Overbreadth' has also been used to describe a challenge to a statute that in all its applications directly restricts protected First Amendment activity and does not employ means narrowly tailored to serve a compelling governmental interest." [E.g., Schaumburg; cf. City Council v. Taxpayers for Vincent (1984; p. 1277 below), Central Hudson (1980; p. 1139 above).]   Recall Monaghan's analysis of overbreadth claims, footnote 4, p. 1149 above.   Is the latter type of case, stressing "narrowly tailored" or least restrictive means, truly an "overbreadth" case?   See the next note in the text.

In the Munson case, Justice Rehnquist's dissent, joined by Chief Justice Burger and Justices

6. *"Less restrictive means" analysis and its relation to overbreadth.* Overbreadth cases typically emphasize the availability of more carefully tailored, narrower means to achieve legislative ends. This emphasis is an aspect of "less restrictive means" analysis which is commonplace in the substantive law governing scrutiny of means in the First Amendment area. The strict scrutiny often associated with First Amendment analysis asks not only about the "compelling" nature of the ends but also inserts upon carefully tailored means. "Less restrictive means" analysis is not limited to the overbreadth context; it also surfaces in First Amendment cases using other techniques. For an early example of such analysis, see Shelton v. Tucker (1960; p. 1371 below), invalidating a law compelling a teacher to list every organization with which the teacher had been affiliated over a five-year period. The Court explained: "[E]ven though the governmental purpose be legitimate and substantial, that purpose cannot be pursued by means that broadly stifle fundamental personal liberties when the end can be more narrowly achieved. The breadth of legislative abridgment must be viewed in the light of *less drastic means* for achieving the same basic purpose." (Emphasis added.)[19]

A footnote in Shelton suggested an analogy to the less-drastic-alternatives rationale of Dean Milk Co. v. Madison, the 1951 state regulation of commerce case in chap. 5 above. Recall Monaghan's argument that much if not all of overbreadth doctrine is in fact simply a reflection of substantive rules where the judicial stance towards means is stricter than deferential, and that it does not involve special standing rules at all. See footnote 4 above. Note also that, even though the Court insists that overbreadth analysis is inappropriate for commercial speech cases (see p. 1132 above), a commercial speech case such as Central Hudson (1980; p. 1139 above) finds the State's means "more extensive than necessary to further the State's interest." Indeed, under the four-part analysis for the commercial speech area propounded by Central Hudson—in an area where overbreadth is allegedly unavailable—one of the steps in the analysis asks whether the regulation "is not more extensive than is necessary to serve [the State] interest."

7. *Vagueness.* An "overbreadth" challenge should not be confused with one based on "vagueness," though a challenger will often assert both grounds of invalidity. An unconstitutionally vague statute, like an overbroad one, creates risks of "chilling effect" to protected speech and produces rulings of facial invalidity. But a statute can be quite specific—i.e., *not* "vague"—and yet be overbroad. The vagueness challenge rests ultimately on the procedural due process requirement of adequate notice, though it is a challenge with special bite in the First Amendment area.[20] Note the emphasis on the distinction between

Powell and O'Connor, once again objected to excessive receptiveness to overbreadth challenges and emphasized the "obvious" advantages of case-by-case adjudication. He noted that, in the case of a successful overbreadth challenge, enforcement of the law is suspended, and the "interests underlying the law, however substantial, are simply negated until the statute is either rewritten by the legislature or 'reinterpreted' by an authorized court to serve those interests more narrowly. [This is more] intrusive on the legislative prerogative and [more] disruptive of state policy." Note that his position, like many criticisms of excessive uses of overbreadth, parallels judicial reluctance to give advisory opinions (see chap. 15, sec. 1, below). Can it be argued in response that an excessive reliance on case-by-case, "as applied" adjudication will provide insufficient guidance for lower courts and government

officials who look to Court opinions in planning their conduct—especially in view of the small number of cases the Court actually decides each Term?

19. Shelton was characteristically silent on explaining what narrower means might be available. Bickel, in The Least Dangerous Branch (1962), argued that a decision such as Shelton, in failing to spell out possible alternative means, "lacks intellectual coherence." Note the similar criticism directed at modern overbreadth cases in the First Amendment area in Gunther, "Reflections on [Robel]," 20 Stan.L.Rev. 1140 (1968).

20. The due process requirement of a minimum degree of definiteness in the statutory prescription of standards demands language which conveys "sufficiently definite warning as to the proscribed conduct when measured by common

"overbreadth" and "vagueness" in Zwickler v. Koota, 389 U.S. 241 (1967), a challenge to a ban on the distribution of anonymous handbills. Justice Brennan noted that the attack was not based on grounds of vagueness, "that is, that it is a statute 'which either forbids or requires the doing of an act in terms so vague that men of common intelligence must necessarily guess at its meaning and differ as to its application' "; instead, the attack was based on the ground "that the statute, although lacking neither clarity nor precision, is void for 'overbreadth,' that is, that it offends the constitutional principle that 'a governmental purpose to control or prevent activities constitutionally subject to state regulation may not be achieved by means which sweep unnecessarily broadly and thereby invade the area of protected freedoms.' " [21]

B. PRIOR RESTRAINTS

Introduction. This subsection turns to a theme frequently voiced by the Court: that prior restraints are especially disfavored under the First Amendment.[1] That theme has strong historical roots. As noted early in the previous chapter, the licensing system for English presses against which Milton protested played a central role in the development of free speech theories. Blackstone, indeed, argued that prior restraint was the *only* evil to be guarded against, and that subsequent punishment was permissible; and Holmes initially embraced that idea and abandoned it only grudgingly in Schenck. But the question whether there is contemporary justification for greater suspicion of prior restraints than of subsequent punishment is far more controversial. In examining these introductory materials, consider especially whether the special hostility to prior restraints is justified, as a theoretical or practical matter.[2]

NEAR v. MINNESOTA

283 U.S. 697, 51 S.Ct. 625, 75 L.Ed. 1357 (1931).

Mr. Chief Justice HUGHES delivered the opinion of the [Court].

understanding and practices." Jordan v. De-George, 341 U.S. 223 (1951). But, as an astute commentator on "vagueness" has remarked, the doctrine is "most frequently employed as an implement for curbing legislative invasion of constitutional rights *other* than that of fair notice," though there is "an actual vagueness component in the vagueness decisions." Amsterdam, "The Void-for-Vagueness Doctrine in the Supreme Court," 109 U.Pa.L.Rev. 67 (1960). Vagueness challenges in the First Amendment area surface frequently in the cases below. See, e.g., Coates v. Cincinnati (1971; p. 1234 below; ordinance unconstitutionally vague as well as overbroad).

21. Note also Justice Powell's articulation of one special purpose of the vagueness doctrine in the First Amendment context, in Smith v. Goguen (1974; p. 1185 below; mistreatment of the flag): "[It] requires legislatures to set reasonably clear guidelines for law enforcement officials and triers of fact in order to prevent 'arbitrary and discriminatory enforcement.' Where a statute's literal scope, unaided by a narrowing state court interpretation, is capable of reaching expression sheltered by the First Amendment, the

[vagueness] doctrine demands a greater degree of specificity than in other contexts."

1. See, e.g., Bantam Books, Inc. v. Sullivan, 372 U.S. 58 (1963): "Any system of prior restraints of expression comes to this Court bearing a heavy presumption against its constitutional validity."

2. This introductory survey is limited to some high points: Near v. Minnesota, which is the most frequently cited case symbolizing the special suspicion of prior restraints; Freedman v. Maryland, involving censorship of movies for obscenity—an area where prior restraint has been of special functional significance; and the Kingsley Books case, also involving obscenity controls but of particular interest here because it raises the question of the justifiability of the prior restraint-subsequent punishment dichotomy. (Problems of prior restraint recur in the later materials. Note, especially, problems of injunctions to ban publication by the media, considered in detail in the materials dealing with freedom of the press in chap. 13, at p. 1419 below.)

[A Minnesota law authorized abatement, as a public nuisance, of a "malicious, scandalous and defamatory newspaper, or other periodical." Pursuant to that law, a local prosecutor sought to abate publication of "The Saturday Press." The "Press" had published articles charging in substance "that a Jewish gangster was in control of gambling, bootlegging and racketeering in Minneapolis, and that law enforcing officers and agencies were not energetically performing their duties." A state court order "abated" the "Press" and perpetually enjoined the defendants from publishing or circulating "any publication whatsoever which is a malicious, scandalous or defamatory newspaper." In setting aside the state injunction, the Court noted that the law was "unusual if not unique," reminded that "the liberty of the press, and of speech," was protected by the 14th Amendment, and stated:]

If we cut through mere details of procedure, the operation and effect of the statute in substance is that public authorities may bring the owner or publisher of a newspaper or periodical before a judge upon a charge of conducting a business of publishing scandalous and defamatory matter—in particular that the matter consists of charges against public officers of official dereliction—and unless the owner or publisher is able and disposed to bring competent evidence to satisfy the judge that the charges are true and are published with good motives and for justifiable ends, his newspaper or periodical is suppressed and further publication is made punishable as a contempt. This is of the essence of censorship.

The question is whether a statute authorizing such proceedings in restraint of publication is consistent with the conception of the liberty of the press as historically conceived and guaranteed. In determining the extent of the constitutional protection, it has been generally, if not universally, considered that it is the chief purpose of the guaranty to prevent previous restraints upon publication. The struggle in England, directed against the legislative power of the licenser, resulted in renunciation of the censorship of the press. The liberty deemed to be established was thus described by Blackstone: "The liberty of the press is indeed essential to the nature of a free state; but this consists in laying no *previous* restraints upon publications, and not in freedom from censure for criminal matter when published. Every freeman has an undoubted right to lay what sentiments he pleases before the public; to forbid this, is to destroy the freedom of the press; but if he publishes what is improper, mischievous or illegal, he must take the consequence of his own temerity." [The] criticism upon Blackstone's statement has not been because immunity from previous restraint upon publication has not been regarded as deserving of special emphasis, but chiefly because that immunity cannot be deemed to exhaust the conception of the liberty guaranteed by state and federal [constitutions].

The objection has also been made that the principle as to immunity from previous restraint is stated too broadly, if every such restraint is deemed to be prohibited. That is undoubtedly true; the protection even as to previous restraint is not absolutely unlimited. But the limitation has been recognized only in exceptional cases. [No] one would question but that a government might prevent actual obstruction to its recruiting service or the publication of the sailing dates of transports or the number and location of troops.[1] On similar grounds, the primary requirements of decency may be enforced against obscene publications. The security of the community life may be protected against incitements to acts of violence and the overthrow by force of orderly government. [See Schenck.] These limitations are not applicable [here].

---

1. This passage has been widely discussed in cases seeking to enjoin the press from publishing information allegedly endangering the national security. See, e.g., New York Times Co. v. United States, the Pentagon Papers Case (1971; chap. 13, at p. 1420 below).

The exceptional nature of its limitations places in a strong light the general conception that liberty of the press [has] meant, principally although not exclusively, immunity from previous restraints, or censorship. [The] fact that for approximately [150] years there has been almost an entire absence of attempts to impose previous restraints upon publications relating to the malfeasance of public officers is significant of the deep-seated conviction that such restraints would violate constitutional right. Public officers, whose character and conduct remain open to debate and free discussion in the press, find their remedies for false accusations in actions under libel laws providing for redress and punishment, and not in proceedings to restrain the publication of newspapers and periodicals. [The] fact that the liberty of the press may be abused by miscreant purveyors of scandal does not make any the less necessary the immunity of the press from previous restraint in dealing with official misconduct. Subsequent punishment for such abuses as may exist is the appropriate remedy, consistent with constitutional privilege.

The statute in question cannot be justified by reason of the fact that the publisher is permitted to show, before injunction issues, that the matter published is true and is published with good motives and for justifiable ends. If such a statute [is] valid, it would be equally permissible for the legislature to provide that at any time the publisher of any newspaper could be brought before a court, or even an administrative officer, and required to produce proof of the truth of his publication, or of what he intended to publish and of his motives, or stand enjoined. If this can be done, the legislature may provide the machinery for determining in the complete exercise of its discretion what are justifiable ends and restrain publication accordingly. And it would be but a step to a complete system of censorship. [We] hold the statute, so far as it authorized the proceedings in this action, [to] be an infringement of the liberty of the press guaranteed by the [14th Amendment].

Judgment reversed.

Mr. Justice BUTLER [dissenting].[1]

[T]he *previous restraint* referred to by [Blackstone] subjected the press to the arbitrary will of an administrative officer. [The] Minnesota statute does not operate as a *previous* restraint on publication within the proper meaning of that phrase. It does not authorize administrative control in advance such as was formerly exercised by the licensers and censors but prescribes a remedy to be enforced by a suit in equity. In this case there was previous publication made in the course of the business of regularly producing malicious, scandalous and defamatory periodicals. The business and publications unquestionably constitute an abuse of the right of free press. The statute denounces the things done as a nuisance on the ground, as stated by the state supreme court, that they threaten morals, peace and good order. There is no question of the power of the State to denounce such transgressions. The restraint authorized is only in respect of continuing to do what has been duly adjudged to constitute a nuisance. [It] is fanciful to suggest similarity between the granting or enforcement of the decree authorized by this statute to prevent *further* publication of malicious, scandalous and defamatory articles and the *previous restraint* upon the press by licensers as referred to by Blackstone and described in the history of the times to which he [alludes].[2]

---

1. Justices Van Devanter, McReynolds and Sutherland joined Justice Butler's dissent.

2. On the background of Near v. Minnesota, see Friendly, Minnesota Rag: The Dramatic Sto-

ry of the Landmark Supreme Court Case That Gave New Meaning to Freedom of the Press (1981).

1. *Motion picture censorship and the Freedman case.* The Court's hostility to prior restraints, and its special suspicion of use of the discretion by administrators authorized to exercise censorship authority, has had especially frequent airings in the context of licensing of motion pictures, under censorship schemes that were widely in use in earlier decades. Beginning with Joseph Burstyn, Inc. v. Wilson, 343 U.S. 495 (1952), the Court scrutinized the statutory standards in film licensing schemes with special care, to avoid abuse of discretion by the administrator. The Burstyn case set the pattern: the Court had no difficulty finding that movies were protected by the First Amendment, even though they were designed for entertainment and distributed for profit; but the Court refused to impose a ban on all prior restraints of films. Instead, the Court repeatedly invalidated particular laws because they lacked adequate specificity.[1] In Times Film Corp. v. Chicago, 365 U.S. 43 (1961), an on-the-face attack on a prior submissions scheme for movies failed: the Court refused to hold "that the public exhibition of motion pictures must be allowed under any circumstances." But in the Freedman case in 1965, the Court announced "procedural safeguards designed to obviate the dangers of a censorship system"—safeguards which have proven important in the protection of First Amendment interests in contexts far beyond the obscenity area.[2]

FREEDMAN v. MARYLAND, 380 U.S. 51 (1965), was a successful constitutional attack on the procedural aspects of a Maryland motion picture censorship law. The challenger exhibited a movie without first submitting the picture to the state censorship board. He was convicted for failure to submit the film for licensing (even though the State conceded that the movie would have been licensed if it had been properly submitted). He argued that the censorship scheme was an invalid prior restraint. He focused particularly on the procedure for an initial decision by the censorship board which, without any judicial participation, effectively barred exhibition of any disapproved film unless and until the exhibitor undertook a time-consuming appeal to the state courts in order to get the censorship agency's decision reversed. The statute did not impose a time limit for completion of judicial review. The Court, in an opinion by Justice BRENNAN, found the statutory procedure, especially its long time delays for the review process, unconstitutional. Noting that "[risk] of delay is built into the Maryland procedure," Justice Brennan stressed the "heavy presumption" against the validity of prior restraints, noted that a state "is not free to adopt whatever procedures it pleases for dealing with obscenity [without] regard to the possible consequences for constitutionally protected speech," and added: "The administration of a censorship system for motion pictures presents peculiar dangers to constitutionally protected speech. Unlike a prosecution for obscenity, a censorship proceeding puts the initial burden on the exhibitor or distributor. Because the censor's business is to censor, there inheres the danger that he may well be less responsive than a court [to] the constitutionally protected interests in free expression. And if it is made unduly

---

1. In Burstyn, for example, New York had banned the movie "The Miracle" as "sacrilegious"—i.e., treating religion "with contempt, mockery, scorn and ridicule." The Court condemned that "broad and all-inclusive definition" because it set the censor adrift "upon a boundless sea amid a myriad of conflicting currents of religious views." Burstyn was followed by a series of similar per curiam decisions concerning other vague standards. E.g., Commercial Pictures Corp. v. Regents, 346 U.S. 587 (1954) ("immoral" and "tend to corrupt morals").

2. See, e.g., the reliance on the Freedman criteria in Carroll v. President & Comm'rs of Princess Anne (1968; p. 1236 below), referring to the "careful procedural provisions" of Freedman in delineating the limits on ex parte restraining orders against demonstrations. See also Southeastern Promotions, Ltd. v. Conrad (1975; p. 1251 below).

The stricter requirements of Freedman (and the invalidation of a number of vague censorship standards) have helped to diminish sharply the practical importance of governmental licensing of movies. But Freedman, as noted, remains important because of its impact outside the movie censorship area, and because of its illustration of a manifestation of the special concern with prior restraints.

onerous, by reason of delay or otherwise, to seek judicial review, the censor's determination may in practice be final.

"Applying the settled rule of our cases, we hold that a noncriminal process which requires the prior submission of a film to a censor avoids constitutional infirmity only if it takes place under procedural safeguards designed to obviate the dangers of a censorship system. First, the burden of proving that the film is unprotected expression must rest on the censor. As we said in Speiser v. Randall, 357 U.S. 513 [1958], 'Where the transcendent value of speech is involved, due process certainly requires [that] the State bear the burden of persuasion to show that the appellants engaged in criminal speech.' Second, while the State may require advance submission of all films, in order to proceed effectively to bar all showings of unprotected films, the requirement cannot be administered in a manner which would lend an effect of finality to the censor's determination whether a film constitutes protected expression. The teaching of our cases is that, because only a judicial determination in an adversary proceeding ensures the necessary sensitivity to freedom of expression, only a procedure requiring a judicial determination suffices to impose a valid final restraint. To this end, the exhibitor must be assured [that] the censor will, within a specified brief period, either issue a license or go to court to restrain showing the film. Any restraint imposed in advance of a final judicial determination on the merits must similarly be limited to preservation of the status quo for the shortest fixed period compatible with sound judicial resolution. Moreover, we are well aware that, even after expiration of a temporary restraint, an administrative refusal to license [may] have a discouraging effect on the exhibitor. Therefore, the procedure must also assure a prompt final judicial decision, to minimize the deterrent effect of an interim and possibly erroneous denial of a license.

"It is readily apparent that the Maryland procedural scheme does not satisfy these criteria. First, once the censor disapproves the film, the exhibitor must assume the burden of instituting judicial proceedings and of persuading the courts that the film is protected expression. Second, once the Board has acted against a film, exhibition is prohibited pending judicial review, however protracted. Under the statute, appellant could have been convicted if he had shown the film after unsuccessfully seeking a license, even though no court had ever ruled on the obscenity of the film. Third, it is abundantly clear that the Maryland statute provides no assurance of prompt judicial determination. We hold, therefore, that [the] scheme fails to provide adequate safeguards against undue inhibition of protected expression, and this renders the § 2 requirement of prior submission of films to the Board an invalid previous restraint." [3]

3. Justice Brennan commented in the course of his opinion: "How or whether Maryland is to incorporate the required procedural safeguards in the statutory scheme is, of course, for the State to decide. But a model is not lacking: In [Kingsley Books], we upheld a New York injunctive procedure designed to prevent the sale of obscene books." The procedure sustained in Kingsley Books against the prior restraint challenge is considered in the next note. (In Freedman, a concurring statement by Justice DOUGLAS, joined by Justice Black, stated: "I do not believe any form of censorship—no matter how speedy or prolonged it may be—is permissible.")

The procedural safeguards established by Freedman illustrate a wider phenomenon: procedural safeguards often have a special bite in the First Amendment context; the concern with substantive free speech values frequently evokes an auxiliary judicial scrutiny of procedures. See generally Monaghan, "First Amendment 'Due Process,' " 83 Harv.L.Rev. 518 (1970). Regulatory methods in the obscenity context have been an especially prolific source of such special procedural First Amendment safeguards. As the Court put it in another obscenity case, Smith v. California, 361 U.S. 147 (1959): "Our decisions furnish examples of legal devices and doctrines, in most applications consistent with the Constitution, which cannot be applied in settings where they have the collateral effect of inhibiting the freedom of expression." (In Smith, the Court held that states could not impose "strict or absolute criminal responsibility" for obscenity law violations. The decision overturned the conviction of a bookseller for having an obscene book in his shop under a statute which "included no element of scienter—knowledge by appellant of the contents of the book." Justice Brennan commented that the "bookseller's self-censorship,

2. *Does the prior restraint-subsequent punishment distinction make sense?—The Kingsley Books case.* The preceding materials introduced the Court's special hostility to prior restraints. But a special, rigid hostility to prior restraints—as distinguished from subsequent punishment—is questionable, even though it is frequently reiterated by the Court. For example, may not some "prior" speedy mechanisms be ultimately more protective of free speech interests than subsequent criminal sanctions? Consider the Court's approval of a limited injunctive remedy in the face of a "prior restraint" attack in KINGSLEY BOOKS, INC. v. BROWN, 354 U.S. 436 (1957). That 5 to 4 decision sustained a New York procedure which authorized an injunction to prevent the sale and distribution of obscene printed matter and an order for its seizure and destruction upon entry of final judgment. Under the statute, § 22–a, an ex parte injunction could be obtained before trial, but the person sought to be enjoined was entitled to trial within one day after joinder of issue, and to a decision within two days of the end of the trial. Kingsley, the publisher of booklets entitled "Nights of Horror," consented to an injunction pendente lite. After trial, the booklets were found obscene, their further distribution was enjoined, and they were ordered destroyed. Kingsley did not challenge the finding of obscenity, but objected to the injunction as a prior restraint. In sustaining the procedure, Justice FRANKFURTER's opinion stated:

"The phrase 'prior restraint' is not a self-wielding sword. Nor can it serve as a talismanic test. The duty of closer analysis and critical judgment in applying the thought behind the phrase has thus been authoritatively put by one who brings weighty learning to his support of constitutionally protected liberties: 'What is needed,' writes Professor Paul A. Freund, 'is a pragmatic assessment of its operation in the particular circumstances. The generalization that prior restraint is particularly obnoxious in civil liberties cases must yield to more particularistic analysis.' The Supreme Court and Civil Liberties, 4 Vand. L.Rev. 533, 539. Wherein does § 22–a differ in its effective operation from the type of statute upheld in Alberts [the state companion obscenity case to Roth, p. 1068 above]? One would be bold to assert that the in terrorem effect of [criminal sanctions] less restrains booksellers in the period before the law strikes than does § 22–a. Instead of requiring the bookseller to dread that the offer for sale of a book may, without prior warning, subject him to a criminal prosecution, [the] civil procedure assures him that such consequences cannot follow unless he ignores a court order specifically directed to him for a prompt and carefully circumscribed determination of the issue of obscenity. Until then, he may keep the book for sale and sell it on his own judgment rather than steer 'nervously among the treacherous shoals.'

"[Criminal] enforcement and the proceeding under § 22–a interfere with a book's solicitation of the public precisely at the same stage. In each situation the law moves after publication; the book need not in either case have yet passed into the hands of the public. [In] each case the bookseller is put on notice by the complaint that sale of the publication charged with obscenity in the period before trial may subject him to penal consequences. In the one case he may suffer fine and imprisonment for violation of the criminal statute, in the other, for disobedience of the temporary injunction. The bookseller may of course stand his ground and confidently believe that in any judicial proceeding

compelled by the State, would be a censorship affecting the whole public, hardly less virulent for being privately administered.") See also Marcus v. Search Warrants, 367 U.S. 717 (1961) (search and seizure); cf. Bantam Books, Inc. v. Sullivan, 372 U.S. 58 (1963) (informal censorship through blacklists). (For a modern partial reliance on Freedman in the context of restraints on obscene movies, see the majority's per curiam ruling in Vance v. Universal Amusement Co., 445 U.S. 308 (1980), invalidating a Texas procedure authorizing injunctions against unnamed "obscene" motion pictures as public nuisances and rejecting the argument that the restraint was "no more serious than that imposed [by] criminal statutes.")

the book could not be condemned as obscene, but both modes of procedure provide an effective deterrent against distribution prior to adjudication of the book's content—the threat of subsequent penalization. [In] each case a judge is the conventional trier of fact; in each, a jury may as a matter of discretion be summoned." Justice Frankfurter argued, moreover, that the impact of the New York scheme was in fact *less* harsh than the California criminal provision sustained in Alberts: "Not only was [Alberts] completely separated from society for two months but he was also seriously restrained from trafficking in all obscene publications for a considerable time. [The Kingsley appellants], on the other hand, were enjoined from displaying for sale or distributing only the particular booklets theretofore published and adjudged to be obscene. Thus, the restraint upon appellants as merchants in obscenity was narrower than that imposed on Alberts." He noted, too, that § 22–a "studiously withholds restraint upon matters not already published and not yet found to be offensive."

The disposition in Kingsley Books highlights a recurrent question: Is the Court's special suspicion of prior restraints justified? Kingsley Books argues that prior restraints—in a scheme with clear standards and speedy judicial hearings—are not inevitably more harmful to speech than subsequent punishments, and indeed that a scheme of the Kingsley Books variety may be preferable to some subsequent punishment laws. Yet, as the materials below repeatedly illustrate, the Court's special hostility to prior restraints persists.[1] A growing amount of modern commentary is critical of the Court's broad-gauged special presumption against prior restraints, both for the oversimplification of the statement and the inconsistency in its applications. See, e.g., Schauer's argument that the distinction "appears on closer analysis to be without justification." He concludes: "The doctrine of prior restraint focuses on the largely irrelevant *timing* of the restraint, to the detriment of attention to those flaws that are the actual source of the objection. It is the identity and discretion of the restrainers and not the timing of the restraint that is important. Unfortunately, this factor remains obscured by continuing obeisance to the doctrine of prior restraint."[2] Note also Redish's analysis of the doctrine that, while opposed to the Court's "traditional reflexive rhetoric against prior restraints," tries to restate it in terms of its ultimate substantive evils. To Redish, the only legitimate basis for hostility to interim prior restraints is that "they authorize abridgment of expression prior to a full and fair determination of the constitutionally protected nature of the expression by an independent judicial forum." He accordingly urges that the validity of a prior restraint "be measured by comparison to the ultimate ideal of no abridgment prior to a full and fair judicial hearing." Under that analysis, nonjudicial administrative licensing schemes would be most disfavored, "while the least problematic would be permanent judicial injunctions issued after trial. Somewhere in between are judicially issued preliminary injunctions and temporary restraining orders."[3]

---

1. The most common forms of prior restraints are schemes requiring a speaker to obtain prior permission from a licensing official and court injunctions restricting future expression. In licensing cases, the judicial suspicion of prior restraints is typically joined with concern over the particular abuse of discretion by a government official. See generally Emerson, "The Doctrine of Prior Restraint," 20 Law & Contemp. Probs. 648 (1955); Blasi, "Prior Restraints on Demonstrations," 68 Mich.L.Rev. 1481 (1970); Blasi, "Toward a Theory of Prior Restraint: The Central Linkage," 66 Minn.L.Rev. 11 (1981); Jeffries, "Rethinking Prior Restraint," 92 Yale L.J. 409 (1983); and Redish "The Proper Role of the Prior Restraint Doctrine in First Amendment Theory" 70 Va.L.Rev. 53 (1984). See also Mayton, "Toward a Theory of First Amendment Process: Injunctions of Speech, Subsequent Punishment, and the Costs of the Prior Restraint Doctrine," 67 Cornell L.Rev. 245 (1982).

2. Schauer, Free Speech: A Philosophical Enquiry (1982), 150, 152.

3. Redish, footnote 1 above. Redish condemns many of the past invocations of prior restraint analysis as "oversimplified formulas" used "to avoid the hard questions." He argues: "The prior restraint doctrine as it presently stands crudely sweeps within its reach all forms

SECTION 2. DISCRIMINATORY RESTRAINTS ON EXPRESSION: THE DISTINCTION BETWEEN CONTENT–BASED AND CONTENT–NEUTRAL REGULATIONS

An increasingly common theme in modern First Amendment analysis is the widely invoked distinction between content-based and content-neutral restrictions on expression. Increasingly, the modern Court has scrutinized content-based distinctions more carefully than those it considers content-neutral. This section calls attention to this pervasive theme. The materials here are not designed to be exhaustive; fuller exploration is best pursued in some of the materials that follow.[1] The limited purpose of these introductory materials is to note the existence of this theme, and to raise some questions about its meaning and its justifiability. The section begins with two widely cited modern cases that state the theme explicitly. These are followed by some comments and questions designed to raise some recurrent questions about the distinction.[2]

SOME LEADING CASES

1. POLICE DEPT. v. MOSLEY, 408 U.S. 92 (1972): Mosley is probably the most widely cited case in modern decisions focusing on discriminatory

of direct governmental restraint of expression—those issued administratively and judicially, those issued prior to an adversarial hearing, as well as those issued following such a hearing. Ironically, such an unbending, sweeping approach has led the Court both to condemn restraints when they perhaps should not have been condemned and to allow restraints, particularly in the areas of obscenity regulation and demonstrations, when they were actually harmful and could not be justified by truly compelling interests."

1. See especially the preoccupation with the discrimination issue in the public forum cases, sec. 4 of this chapter. The preoccupation with the content-based/content-neutral distinction has been called "the Burger Court's foremost contribution to first amendment analysis" (as well as "the most pervasively employed doctrine in the jurisprudence of free expression"). Stone, "Content Regulation and the First Amendment," 25 Wm. & Mary L.Rev. 189 (1983). In fact, the distinction gained considerable popularity in the latter years of the Warren Court as well. See, e.g., Cox v. Louisiana I (1965; p. 1225 below), and contrast the readiness of the Court in earlier years to apply strict scrutiny even in situations where no obvious content discrimination was involved, as in Schneider v. State (1939; p. 1206 below).

Although the theme is most fully developed in the materials that follow, it has already surfaced in earlier materials. Recall, e.g., the reliance on it in Erznoznik (1975; p. 1107 above) and in Central Hudson (1980; p. 1139 above). Moreover, the variety of content-based justifications for extending lesser protection to some varieties of "less valuable" speech (in sec. 2 of chap. 11) can be viewed as exceptions to the hostility toward content-based distinctions, even though there the Court did not typically resort to that technique in form. Recall, e.g., the limited pro-

tection of commercial speech as in Central Hudson, p. 1139 above, and Justice Stevens' unwillingness to grant full First Amendment protection to offensive speech, as in Pacifica, p. 1114 above.

2. The theme raised in this section has been the subject of an increasing amount of academic commentary. For a defense of the content-based/content-neutral distinction (a defense which candidly recognizes the many sub-questions and ambiguities that lurk in the simple statement of the distinction), see Stone, "Content Regulation and the First Amendment," 25 Wm. & Mary L.Rev. 189 (1983). For an especially effective criticism of the distinction, see Redish, "The Content Distinction in First Amendment Analysis," 34 Stan.L.Rev. 113 (1981) (reprinted, like other First Amendment articles by Redish, in his 1984 book, Freedom of Expression—A Critical Analysis). (Note also the articulation of similar criticisms in Justice Marshall's dissent in Clark v. Community for Creative Non-Violence (1984; sec. 3, p. 1188 below).) Other useful articles are Stephan, "The First Amendment and Content Discrimination," 68 Va.L.Rev. 203 (1982); Farber, "Content Regulation and the First Amendment: A Revisionist View," 68 Geo. L.J. 727 (1980); and Stone, "Restrictions of Speech Because of Its Content: The Peculiar Case of Subject-Matter Restrictions," 46 U.Chi. L.Rev. 81 (1978). See also Ely, "Flag Desecration: A Case Study in the Roles of Categorization and Balancing in First Amendment Analysis," 88 Harv.L.Rev. 1482 (1975); Emerson, "First Amendment Doctrine and the Burger Court," 68 Calif.L.Rev. 422 (1980); and Tribe, American Constitutional Law (1978). For a useful student comment criticizing the distinction, see Note, "A Unitary Approach to Claims of First Amendment Access to Publicly Owned Property," 35 Stan.L.Rev. 121 (1982).

regulations of speech—especially for its passage stating that "[Above] all else, the First Amendment means that government has no power to restrict expression because of its message, its ideas, its subject matter, or its content." Mosley invalidated a Chicago disorderly conduct ordinance which barred picketing within 150 feet of a school, but exempted "peaceful picketing of any school involved in a labor dispute." Justice MARSHALL's opinion found this "selective exclusion from a public place" unconstitutional. He stated: "Because Chicago treats some picketing differently from others, we analyze this ordinance in terms of the Equal Protection Clause of the 14th Amendment. Of course, the equal protection claim in this case is closely intertwined with First Amendment interests: the Chicago ordinance affects picketing, which is expressive conduct; moreover, it does so by classifications formulated in terms of the subject of the picketing." He proceeded:

"The central problem with Chicago's ordinance is that it describes the permissible picketing in terms of its subject matter. [The] operative distinction is the message on a picket sign. [After making the "above all" statement quoted above, he continued:] To permit the continued building of our politics and culture, and to assure self-fulfillment for each individual, our people are guaranteed the right to express any thought, free from government censorship. The essence of this forbidden censorship is content control. [Necessarily], then, under [equal protection], not to mention the First Amendment itself, government may not grant the use of a forum to people whose views it finds acceptable, but deny use to those wishing to express less favored or more controversial views. And it may not select which issues are worth discussing or debating in public facilities. There is an 'equality of status in the field of ideas' [Meiklejohn, Political Freedom (1948)], and government must afford all points of view an equal opportunity to be heard. Once a forum is opened up to assembly or speaking by some groups, government may not prohibit others from assembling or speaking on the basis of what they intend to say. Selective exclusions from a public forum may not be based on content alone, and may not be justified by reference to content alone. [See, e.g., Cox v. Louisiana I (1965) (Black, J., concurring) (p. 1225 below).]"

Justice Marshall noted that "reasonable 'time, place and manner' regulations of picketing may be necessary to further significant governmental interests." But this was not a time, place, and manner regulation, but rather one "in terms of subject matter," and this was "never permitted." He rejected the argument that preventing school disruption justified the ordinance: "If peaceful labor picketing is permitted, there is no justification for prohibiting all nonlabor picketing, both peaceful and nonpeaceful. 'Peaceful' nonlabor picketing [is] obviously no more disruptive than 'peaceful' labor picketing. But Chicago's ordinance permits the latter and prohibits the former." Moreover, he rejected the argument that a city could prohibit all nonlabor picketing "because, as a class, nonlabor picketing is more prone to produce violence than labor picketing": "Predictions about imminent disruption from picketing involve judgments appropriately made on an individualized basis, not by means of broad classifications, especially those based on subject matter. Freedom of expression, and its intersection with the guarantee of equal protection, would rest on a soft foundation indeed if government could distinguish among picketers on such a wholesale and categorical basis." Here, instead of "being tailored to a substantial governmental interest, the discrimination among pickets is based on the content of their expression."[1]

1. In a concurring notation, Chief Justice BURGER joined Justice Marshall's opinion but with a "reservation" about the potentially misleading nature of the statement that we "are guaranteed the right to express any thought, free from government censorship." He stated: "This statement is subject to some qualifications, as for example those of [Roth and Chaplinsky]. See also [New York Times v. Sullivan]." Justices

2. CAREY v. BROWN, 447 U.S. 455 (1980): The majority in this 6 to 3 decision found another picketing restriction unconstitutional and thought the case basically indistinguishable from Mosley; but the dissenters claimed that the majority had mischaracterized the law. According to Justice BRENNAN's majority view, the case involved a state law "that generally bars picketing of residences or dwellings, but exempts from its prohibition 'the peaceful picketing of a place of employment involved in a labor dispute.'" He insisted that the law "discriminates between lawful and unlawful conduct based upon the content of the demonstrator's communication. [The] permissibility of residential picketing under the [law is based] solely on the nature of the message being conveyed." Accordingly, the law suffered "from the same constitutional infirmities" as that in Mosley.[2] He rejected the argument that the state interests here were "especially compelling"—the interests in protecting residential privacy and providing special protection for labor protests.[3]

In a lengthy dissent, Justice REHNQUIST, joined by Chief Justice Burger and Justice Blackmun, argued that the majority had misstated the scope of the law. He noted that there were four exemptions rather than only one from the general ban on residential picketing. He pointed out that the law's exemptions applied "when the residence has been used as a place of business, a place for public meetings, or a place of employment, or is occupied by the picket himself"—all situations in which the state has "determined that the resident has waived some measure of privacy through voluntary use of his home for these purposes." In short, "the principal determinant of a person's right to picket a residence [is] not content, [but] rather the character of the residence sought to be picketed. Content is relevant only in one of the categories established by the legislature." Accordingly, the Mosley prohibition of regulation on the basis of *"content alone"* was inapplicable here; the appropriate governing precedents should be those "involving state impositions of time, place, and manner restrictions on speech activities," not content discrimination cases. Here, the State had avoided "an outright ban on all residential picketing" and any "reliance on any vague or discretionary standards," and had permitted picketing at residences where "the resident's own actions have substantially reduced his interest in privacy"; and yet the Court had struck down the effort: "Under the Court's approach today, the State would fare better by adopting *more* restrictive means"—i.e., a flat ban. "This can only mean that the hymns of praise in prior opinions celebrating carefully drawn statutes are no more than sympathetic clucking, and in fact the State is damned if it does and damned if it doesn't."[4]

SOME COMMENTS ON THE SCOPE AND PROBLEMS OF THE CONTENT–NEUTRAL/CONTENT–BASED DISTINCTION

On its face, the principle announced in Mosley and reiterated in Carey seems simple: content-based restrictions are very strictly scrutinized; content-neutral

BLACKMUN and REHNQUIST concurred only in the result.

2. In a footnote, Justice Brennan pointed out that "Mosley was neither the Court's first nor its last pronouncement that the [14th Amendment forbids] discrimination in the regulation of expression on the basis of the content of that expression. See [Cox v. Louisiana I (1965; p. 1225 below; Black, J., concurring)]. See also [e.g., Erznoznik (1975; p. 1107 above); Consolidated Edison (1980; p. 1122 above)]."

3. Justice STEWART's concurrence objected to the reliance on equal protection rather than the First Amendment. He argued that "what was actually at stake in Mosley, and is at stake here, is the basic meaning of the constitutional protection of free speech."

4. Applying the analysis he considered appropriate, Justice Rehnquist concluded, inter alia, that it was "quite clear that the statute does not prohibit the appellees [from] engaging in conduct which must be protected under the First Amendment, the state interests would not be satisfied by a statute employing less restrictive means, [and] the statute is not facially overbroad."

distinctions survive judicial scrutiny more readily. In fact, the justifications for, meaning of, and applications of the distinction raise a host of problems. Some of the problems are previewed here; other variants will emerge in later materials.

1. *Justifications.* a. *Equal protection or First Amendment?* Note first that in Mosley and Carey, the Court draws on equal protection as well as the First Amendment. What, if anything, does the equal protection clause add? Recall the discussion of the fundamental-interests strict-scrutiny strand of the "new" equal protection in chap. 9 above. Often, Court condemnations of content discriminations rely solely on the First Amendment without mentioning equal protection.[1] Karst argues that the concept of equality lies at the heart of the First Amendment's protections against government regulation of the content of speech.[2] But does reliance on the equality principle truly further exploration of the contours of the content-based/content-neutral distinction?[3]

b. *First Amendment justifications.* What First Amendment considerations warrant imposing particularly high standards of justification for content-based regulations, and less intensive scrutiny of content-neutral ones? Stone, one of the leading theoretical defenders of the distinction, finds little difficulty with obvious discriminations against a particular *viewpoint:* "Any law that substantially prevents the communication of a particular idea, viewpoint, or item of information violates the first amendment except, perhaps, in the most extraordinary of circumstances. This is so, not because such a law restricts 'a lot' of speech, but because by effectively excising a specific message from public debate, it mutilates 'the thinking process of the community' and is thus incompatible with the central precepts of the first amendment."[4] Yet the intensive scrutiny of content-based distinctions is applied even though only some, not all, expressions of a viewpoint are limited. In justifying that pattern, Stone relies not only on the "distortion" rationale, but also on a judicial concern with ferreting out improper motivations (in the sense that content-based restrictions are more likely to reflect governmental disapproval of the ideas expressed) and on a "communicative impact" rationale. The latter rationale draws on the principle that "government ordinarily may not restrict speech because of its *communicative impact* —that is, because of 'a fear of how people will react to what the speaker is saying' [quoting Ely, Democracy and Distrust (1980)]." Stone identifies the underlying concern of such arguments as the hostility to "paternalistic" measures by government: ordinarily government "may not restrict the expression of particular ideas, viewpoints, or items of information because it does not trust its citizens to make wise or desirable decisions if they are exposed to such expression."[5] And content-based distinctions, Stone argues, are likely to reflect such an improper "paternalistic" concern.

But one may concede the legitimacy of all such First Amendment concerns and still question the justifiability of *special* scrutiny of content-based restrictions. As will more fully appear in the materials below, so-called "content-neutral"

1. See, e.g., Consolidated Edison (1980; p. 1122 above), and Widmar v. Vincent (1981; p. 1265 below).

2. See Karst, "Equality as a Central Principle in the First Amendment," 43 U.Chi.L.Rev. 20 (1975).

3. See the comment in Stone, "Content Regulation and the First Amendment," 25 Wm. & Mary L.Rev. 189 (1983), that, "although the concern with equality may support the content-based/content-neutral distinction, it does not in itself have much explanatory power. To determine why some inequalities are more bothersome than others, we must look elsewhere." Stone

also comments that the invocation of equal protection "adds nothing constructive to the analysis. It may, however, by appearing to 'simplify' matters, deflect attention from the central constitutional issue"; and that central issue is "fundamentally a first amendment issue."

4. Stone, "Content Regulation and the First Amendment," 25 Wm. & Mary L.Rev. 189 (1983). [For a clear example of a viewpoint discrimination, recall Kingsley Pictures (1959; p. 1073 above).]

5. Recall, e.g., Virginia Pharmacy (1976; p. 1130 above).

restrictions may in their impact also reflect paternalism or improper motivations. Moreover, they may in fact do more substantial damage to the permissible quantity, and effective exercise, of speech than content-based ones. Additionally, a primary judicial preoccupation with content-based restrictions may imply that governmental flat bans may fare better than partial prohibitions, despite their greater impact on the total quantity and diversity of speech.[6] Redish, a major critic of the distinction, finds the content-based/content-neutral dichotomy permeated by "conceptual and practical awkwardness": "While governmental attempts to regulate the content of expression undoubtedly deserve strict judicial review, it does not logically follow that equally serious threats to first amendment freedoms cannot derive from restrictions imposed to regulate expression in a manner unrelated to content."[7] Redish urges a unitary approach: "[That] all governmental regulations of expression be subjected to a unified 'compelling interest' analysis. To be sure, various types of expression often give rise to harmful consequences, and any judicial attempt to reconcile these competing interests will face a myriad of obstacles. In certain instances, the courts will mold the elements of the 'compelling interest' analysis into categorical rules that may be applied with relative ease. In other cases the courts will be forced to apply the analysis in an ad hoc fashion. [But] this distinction need not and should not turn on whether the regulation of expression is content-based or content-neutral." He insists: "Whatever rationale one adopts for the constitutional protection of speech, the goals behind that rationale are undermined by *any* limitation on expression, content-based or not."

2. *The meaning and applications of the distinction: The problem of subject-matter distinctions.* Even when the content-based/content-neutral distinction is accepted, its precise scope and its appropriate applications have given rise to great difficulties. For example, the advocates of the distinction agree that the highest scrutiny is warranted for clear discriminations based on viewpoint. Yet seminal cases such as Mosley and Carey, in which this strict scrutiny was applied, seem more obviously subject-matter distinctions than viewpoint distinctions.[8] The Court's course on subject-matter distinctions has been, to put it mildly, wavering. Thus, Mosley is an example of a case where a subject-matter restriction—the distinction between labor picketing and other picketing—is treated as viewpoint-based.[9] Yet, other subject-matter restrictions have been treated as essentially content-neutral and scrutinized under a less stringent standard.[10]

3. *The problem of format discrimination.* An especially troublesome aspect of the content-based/content-neutral distinction is raised when government bans resort to a particular format of expression. [Consider, for example, a total ban on billboards on private property, a question left open by Metromedia (1981; p. 1144 above and p. 1287 below), or a ban on posting signs on public property—a ban sustained in City Council v. Taxpayers for Vincent (1984; p. 1277 below).[11]

---

6. Recall Justice Rehnquist's dissent in Carey, above, and note the further pursuit of this theme in the public forum access cases in sec. 4 below.

7. Redish, "The Content Distinction in First Amendment Analysis," 34 Stan.L.Rev. 113 (1981). See also Note, "A Unitary Approach to Claims of First Amendment Access to Publicly Owned Property," 35 Stan.L.Rev. 121 (1982). Note the echoing of Redish's criticism in Justice Marshall's dissent in Clark v. Community for Creative Non-Violence (1984; sec. 3, p. 1188 below).

8. Thus, Stone agrees that "subject matter distinctions" are an example of "ambiguous restrictions"—restrictions that are neither clearly "content-neutral" nor clearly "viewpoint-based."

He suggests that such subject-matter restrictions "fall between viewpoint-based and content-neutral restrictions, sharing some of the characteristics of each."

9. See also, e.g., Carey; Erznoznik (1975; p. 1107 above); Consolidated Edison (1980; p. 1122 above); and Widmar v. Vincent (1981; p. 1265 below).

10. See, e.g., Lehman v. Shaker Heights (1974; p. 1247 below) and Greer v. Spock (1976; p. 1252 below). See also Broadrick (1973; p. 1151 above); Mini Theatres (1976; p. 1110 above).

11. Justice Stevens wrote the majority opinion in the 1984 case, sustaining the ban in part because of the absence of any discrimination on

Contrast the Court's treatment of a total ban on handbills in Schneider v. State (1939; p. 1206 below), and its scrutiny of restrictions on loudspeakers (p. 1208 below).] A total ban on a particular format may in fact have a major effect on the quantity of communication. Moreover, it may in fact discriminate against particular groups in the society who are financially unable to resort to the more conventional (and more expensive) means of communication, such as newspapers and the broadcasting media. Note also the Court's consideration of a ban on sleeping in a public park to attempt to dramatize the plight of the homeless, in Clark v. Community for Creative Non-Violence (1984; p. 1188 below). (See especially footnote 14 to Justice Marshall's dissent in that case, dealing in effect with the inequalities that may result from format discriminations.) Most of the modern prohibitions on particular formats have been sustained by the Court and have *not* been treated as content-based discriminations—and accordingly have been subjected to less intense scrutiny than content-based distinctions. Does that pattern make sense in terms of First Amendment values? [12]

SECTION 3. SYMBOLIC EXPRESSION AND THE O'BRIEN TWO-TRACK ANALYSIS

Introduction and background. In the materials that follow, critics of public policies sought to express their views in part through symbolic *behavior* rather than words: by burning draft cards; by wearing a black armband in a classroom; by mutilating the flag; by sleeping in a park. In each case, the critic claimed immunity from governmental restraint on the ground that the expression, albeit partly nonverbal, was constitutionally protected "speech." Can the critic claim First Amendment protection? Can the critic claim as much protection as would be afforded if the criticism had been expressed through the more traditional modes—through the spoken or printed word?

The problems of symbolic expression are the focus of this final section of introductory, building block materials. These materials are presented here for two major reasons. The first theme involves the existence and extent of First Amendment protection. The Justices initially encountered these problems in

the basis of viewpoint. As already noted, Justice Stevens takes a particularly narrow view of the content-based discrimination ban, applying it by and large only to situations where there is a clear discrimination against a particular viewpoint. In addition to Vincent, see his separate opinions in Metromedia, Consolidated Edison, and Bolger v. Youngs Drug Products (most noted earlier). Justice Stevens not only sees discrimination on the basis of viewpoint as a central concern of the First Amendment, but may view that kind of discrimination as the First Amendment's *only* concern. Is that position tenable?

12. The point flagged preliminarily here (and to be examined further below) is that format discriminations involve neither discrimination on the basis of viewpoint nor discrimination on the basis of subject matter, yet *do* involve singling out for special treatment activities of First Amendment concern. (Even if explicit discriminations against formats important to First Amendment expression were scrutinized more carefully, additional difficulties would arise if government were to raise the level of generality of the restrictions. Consider the following pairs of regulations: A prohibition on all bookstores in a certain area; and a prohibition on all commercial establishments in a certain area, implicitly including bookstores. A prohibition on parades, designed to prevent obstruction of traffic; and a prohibition on obstructing traffic, which is applied evenhandedly to trucks that take excessively long to make a delivery, to people who park illegally in intersections, and to organizers of parades. A prohibition on soundtrucks, designed to prevent excess noise; and a prohibition on making excess noise, applied to motorcycles, jackhammers, and soundtrucks. A prohibition on billboards; and a prohibition on all structures higher than a certain height and thus implicitly prohibiting billboards along with other structures. Is the first example in each of these pairs more troublesome than the second? Why? Does it have something to do with testing the legitimacy and sincerity of the motives of the regulators? Questions such as these should be considered further in the materials below, in connection with the additional examples of the currently popular discrimination emphasis in the Court's First Amendment analyses.)

large numbers as a result of the anti-war protests of the 1960s, and they had unusual difficulty finding the critics' behavior entitled to at least some First Amendment protection. The proper standard of judicial scrutiny for restraints on symbolic expression is the most pervasive theme in this group of materials. The second reason for considering these materials here stems from the Court's analysis in the principal case that follows, O'Brien, the draft card burning case. The Court there laid the basis for a two-track theory regarding the strength of justifications necessary to validate governmental restraints—a theory which has proven important in areas well beyond that of symbolic expression, as the later materials repeatedly illustrate. The applicability and the merits of this two-track justification analysis constitute the second major problem introduced by this section.

The perception that "speech" may be nonverbal antedates the modern cases. Earlier decisions had given First Amendment protection to some varieties of symbolic expression. For example, as early as 1931, in Stromberg v. California, 283 U.S. 359, the Court held unconstitutional a state prohibition on displaying a red flag "as a sign, symbol or emblem of opposition to organized government." The Court stated that the law curtailed "the opportunity for free political discussion." In the following decade, moreover, Barnette (1943; p. 1510 below) held that public school children could not be compelled to salute the flag in violation of their religious scruples. And the prevailing opinion in Brown v. Louisiana (1966; public library sit-in; p. 1241 below), emphasized that First Amendment rights "are not confined to verbal expression" and "embrace appropriate types of action." The constitutional claims in the symbolic expression cases that follow sought to build on those premises.

UNITED STATES v. O'BRIEN

391 U.S. 367, 88 S.Ct. 1673, 20 L.Ed.2d 672 (1968).

Mr. Chief Justice WARREN delivered the opinion of the Court.

On the morning of March 31, 1966, David Paul O'Brien and three companions burned their Selective Service registration certificates on the steps of the South Boston Courthouse. A sizable crowd, including several [FBI agents], witnessed the event. [O'Brien] stated to FBI agents that he had burned his registration certificate because of his beliefs, knowing that he was violating federal law. [For this act, O'Brien was convicted. He stated] to the jury that he burned the certificate publicly to influence others to adopt his antiwar beliefs, as he put it, "so that other people would reevaluate their positions with Selective Service, with the armed forces, and reevaluate their place in the culture of today, to hopefully consider my position."

The indictment upon which he was tried charged that he "willfully and knowingly did mutilate, destroy, and change by burning [his] Registration Certificate" in violation of [§ 462(b)(3) of the Universal Military Training and Service Act of 1948], amended by Congress in 1965 (adding the words italicized below), so that at the time O'Brien burned his certificate an offense was committed by any person "who forges, alters, *knowingly destroys, knowingly mutilates,* or in any manner changes any such certificate." (Italics supplied.) [The Court of Appeals] held the 1965 Amendment unconstitutional as a law abridging freedom of speech. At the time the Amendment was enacted, a regulation of the Selective Service System required registrants to keep their registration certificates in their "personal possession at all times." Wilful violations of regulations promulgated pursuant to the Universal Military Training and Service Act were made criminal by statute. The Court of Appeals, therefore, was of the opinion that conduct punishable under the 1965 Amendment was already punishable under the nonpossession regulation, and consequently that the Amendment served no valid purpose; further, that in light of the prior regulation, the Amendment must have been "directed at public as distinguished from private destruction." On this basis, the court concluded that the 1965 Amendment ran afoul of the First Amendment by singling out persons engaged in protests for special treatment. [We] hold that the 1965 Amendment is constitutional both as enacted and [as applied].

When a male reaches the age of 18, he is required by the [Act] to register with a local draft board. He is assigned a Selective Service number, and within five days he is issued a registration certificate. Subsequently, and based on a questionnaire completed by the registrant, he is assigned a classification denoting his eligibility for induction, and "[a]s soon as practicable" thereafter he is issued a Notice of Classification. [Both] the registration and classification certificates bear notices that the registrant must notify his local board [of] every change in address, physical condition, [etc.].

We note at the outset that the 1965 Amendment plainly does not abridge free speech on its face. [On its face, it] deals with conduct having no connection with speech. [It] does not distinguish between public and private destruction, and it does not punish only destruction engaged in for the purpose of expressing views. [Cf. Stromberg.] [1] A law prohibiting destruction of Selective Service certificates no more abridges free speech on its face than a motor vehicle law prohibiting the destruction of drivers' licenses, or a tax law prohibiting the destruction of books and records.

[O'Brien nonetheless] first argues that the 1965 Amendment is unconstitutional as applied to him because his act of burning his registration certificate was protected "symbolic speech" within the First Amendment. His argument is that the freedom of expression which the First Amendment guarantees includes all modes of "communication of ideas by conduct," and that his conduct is within this definition because he did it in "demonstration against the war and against the draft." We cannot accept the view that an apparently limitless variety of conduct can be labeled "speech" whenever the person engaging in the conduct intends thereby to express an idea. However, even on the assumption that the alleged communicative element in O'Brien's conduct is sufficient to bring into play the First Amendment, it does not necessarily follow that the destruction of a registration certificate is constitutionally protected activity. This Court has held that when "speech" and "non-speech" elements are combined in the same course of conduct, a sufficiently important governmental interest in regulating the nonspeech element can justify incidental limitations on First Amendment freedoms. To characterize the quality of the governmental interest which must appear, the Court has employed a variety of descriptive terms: compelling; substantial; subordinating; paramount; cogent; strong. *[We] think it clear that a government regulation is sufficiently justified if it is within the constitutional power of the Government; if it furthers an important or substantial governmental interest; if the governmental interest is unrelated to the suppression of free expression; and if the incidental restriction on alleged First Amendment freedoms is no greater than is essential to the furtherance of that interest.* [2] We find that the 1965 Amendment [meets] all of these requirements, and consequently that O'Brien can be constitutionally convicted for violating it. [Pursuant to its power] to classify and conscript manpower for military service, [Congress] may establish a system of registration

---

1. Compare the comment in the opinion of the Court of Appeals for the First Circuit, 376 F.2d at 541: "We would be closing our eyes [if] we did not see on the face of the amendment that it was precisely directed at public as distinguished from private destruction. [In] singling out persons engaging in protest for special treat-

ment the amendment strikes at the very core of what the First Amendment protects."

2. (Emphasis supplied.) This passage is the foundation of the widely discussed two-track justification analysis associated with O'Brien (further discussed below).

[and] may require such individuals within reason to cooperate in the registration system. The issuance of certificates indicating the registration and eligibility classification of individuals is a legitimate and substantial administrative aid in the functioning of this system. And legislation to insure the continuing availability of issued certificates serves a legitimate and substantial purpose in the system's administration.

O'Brien's argument to the contrary is necessarily premised upon his unrealistic characterization of Selective Service certificates. He essentially adopts the position that such certificates are so many pieces of paper designed to notify registrants of their registration or classification, to be retained or tossed in the wastebasket according to the convenience or taste of the registrant. [However, the registration and classification certificates serve] purposes in addition to initial notification. Many of these purposes would be defeated by the certificates' destruction or mutilation. Among these are [verifying the registration and classification of suspected delinquents, facilitating communication between registrants and local boards, demonstrating availability for induction in times of national crisis, and reminding registrants to notify local boards of changes in status]. The many functions performed by Selective Service certificates establish beyond doubt that Congress has a legitimate and substantial interest in preventing their wanton and unrestrained destruction and assuring their continuing availability by punishing people who knowingly and wilfully destroy or mutilate them. And we are unpersuaded that the pre-existence of the nonpossession regulations in any way negates this interest. In the absence of a question as to multiple punishment, it has never been suggested that there is anything improper in Congress' providing alternative statutory avenues of prosecution to assure the effective protection of one and the same [interest].

Equally important, a comparison of the regulations with the 1965 Amendment indicates that they protect overlapping but not identical governmental interests, and that they reach somewhat different classes of wrongdoers. The gravamen of the offense defined by the statute is the deliberate rendering of certificates unavailable for the various purposes which they may serve. Whether registrants keep their certificates in their personal possession at all times, as required by the regulations, is of no particular concern under the 1965 Amendment, as long as they do not mutilate or destroy the certificates so as to render them unavailable. [And] the 1965 Amendment [is] concerned with abuses involving *any* issued Selective Service certificates, not only with the registrant's own certificates. The knowing destruction or mutilation of someone else's certificates would therefore violate the statute but not the nonpossession regulations. We think it apparent that the continuing availability to each registrant of his Selective Service certificates substantially furthers the smooth and proper functioning of the system that Congress has established to raise [armies].

It is equally clear that the 1965 Amendment specifically protects this substantial governmental interest. We perceive no alternative means that would more precisely and narrowly assure the continuing availability of issued Selective Service certificates than a law which prohibits their wilful mutilation or destruction. The 1965 Amendment prohibits such conduct and does nothing more. In other words, both the governmental interest and the operation of the 1965 Amendment are limited to the noncommunicative aspect of O'Brien's conduct. The governmental interest and the scope of the 1965 Amendment are limited to preventing harm to the smooth and efficient functioning of the Selective Service System. When O'Brien deliberately rendered unavailable his registration certificate, he wilfully frustrated this governmental interest. For this noncommunicative impact of his conduct, and for nothing else, he was convicted. The case [is] therefore unlike one where the alleged governmental interest in regulating conduct arises in some measure because the communication allegedly integral to the conduct is itself thought to be harmful. In Stromberg [the 1931 "red flag" case], for example, the statute was aimed at suppressing communication [and therefore] could not be sustained as a regulation of noncommunicative conduct. [We] find that because of the Government's substantial interest in assuring the continuing availability of issued Selective Service certificates, because amended § 462(b) is an appropriately narrow means of protecting this interest and condemns only the independent noncommunicative impact of conduct within its reach, and because the noncommunicative impact of O'Brien's act of burning his registration certificate frustrated the Government's interest, a sufficient governmental interest has been shown to justify O'Brien's conviction.

O'Brien finally argues that the 1965 Amendment is unconstitutional as enacted because what he calls the "purpose" of Congress was "to suppress freedom of speech." We reject this argument because under settled principles the purpose of Congress, as O'Brien uses that term, is not a basis for declaring this legislation [unconstitutional].[3]

Reversed.[4]

THE SIGNIFICANCE OF O'BRIEN

1. *O'Brien and symbolic expression.* Is Chief Justice Warren's treatment of O'Brien's symbolic speech claim adequate? Note that he does little more than reject "the view that an apparently limitless variety of conduct can be labeled 'speech' whenever the person engaging in the conduct intends thereby to express an idea" and then finds the conviction justifiable "even on the assumption that the alleged communicative element in O'Brien's conduct is sufficient to bring into play the First Amendment." Most commentators have echoed the criticism that the Court's disposition of O'Brien's "by no means frivolous" claim is "astonishingly cavalier."[1] (That critical review asserts that the Court "chose not to deal with the complexities" of the problem, "made no attempt to discuss, let alone to answer, the difficult and disturbing constitutional questions presented," and instead "trivialized the issues and handed down an opinion that has all the deceptive simplicity and superficial force that can usually be achieved by

3. See the additional passages from this opinion, on the asserted impropriety of judicial invalidation because of "an alleged illicit legislative motive," printed in chap. 4, at p. 217 above.

4. A concurring notation by Justice HARLAN stated: "I wish to make explicit my understanding that [the Court's criteria do] not foreclose consideration of First Amendment claims in those rare instances when an 'incidental' restriction upon expression, imposed by a regulation which furthers an 'important or substantial' governmental interest and satisfies the Court's other criteria, in practice has the effect of entirely preventing a 'speaker' from reaching a significant audience with whom he could not otherwise lawfully communicate. This is not such a case, since O'Brien manifestly could have conveyed his message in many ways other than by burning his draft card."

A dissent by Justice DOUGLAS thought that the "underlying and basic problem" was "whether conscription is permissible in the absence of a declaration of war." He urged reargument on "the question of the constitutionality of a peace-

time draft." [Recall chap. 6, at p. 372 above.] (Justice Douglas did not reach the First Amendment issues in O'Brien until his concurring opinion a year later, in Brandenburg v. Ohio, p. 1037 above. In Brandenburg, he insisted that O'Brien's conviction was inconsistent with the First Amendment. He stated more generally that action "is often a method of expression and within the protection of the First Amendment." But he added: "Picketing [is] 'free speech plus.' [Therefore], it can be regulated when it comes to the 'plus' or 'action' side of the protest. It can be regulated as to the number of pickets and the place and hours, because traffic and other community problems would otherwise suffer. But none of these considerations are implicated in the symbolic protest of the Vietnam war in the burning of a draft card.")

1. That critical comment appears in Alfange, "Free Speech and Symbolic Conduct: The Draft-Card Burning Case," 1968 Sup.Ct.Rev. 1 (which concludes, however, that "the result in O'Brien is defensible despite the deficiencies of manifest oversimplification in the Court's opinion").

begging the question." [2]) Note that O'Brien, like Tinker and Street (which follow), came near the close of the Warren era. The Warren Court had upheld a large number of First Amendment claims; and it had been almost as prolific in its doctrinal innovations as in its speech-protective results. Yet the Warren Court's symbolic speech decisions suggest not only uncertainty of results but also instability of doctrinal foundations.[3]

2. *The O'Brien multi-step analysis and the implicit two-track justification approach.* a. In the passage italicized in the O'Brien opinion, the Court suggested what Ely has described as essentially a three-step process: a governmental regulation is justified "[1] if it furthers an important or substantial governmental interest; [2] if the governmental interest is unrelated to the suppression of free expression; and [3] if the incidental restriction on alleged First Amendment freedoms is no greater than is essential to the furtherance of that interest."[4] As applied in O'Brien, that three-step approach did not prove very speech-protective. For example, the "substantial" governmental interests identified by the Court were in fact, as Ely notes, only "plausible but little more." And criterion [3] was very weakly applied: although its formulation suggests the quite careful scrutiny of the "less restrictive means" analysis, see p. 1156 above, in fact the Court applied a quite deferential scrutiny. As Ely notes, a weak version of the "less restrictive alternative" approach would "require only that there be no less restrictive alternative capable of serving the state's interest *as efficiently as it is served by the regulation under attack.* But [in] virtually every case involving real legislation, a more perfect fit involves some added cost. In effect, therefore, this weak formulation would reach only laws that engage in the gratuitous inhibition of expression, requiring only that a prohibition not outrun the interest it is designed to serve."[5] In O'Brien, in contrast to other less restrictive alternative cases, the mere absence of "gratuitous inhibition" satisfied the Court that criterion [3] was met. However, with respect to steps [1] and [3] of the O'Brien formulation, the approach does have speech-protective potential, *if* the

2. See also, e.g., Velvel, "Freedom of Speech and the Draft Card Burning Cases," 16 U.Kan.L. Rev. 149 (1968); Nimmer, "The Meaning of Symbolic Speech Under the First Amendment," 21 UCLA L.Rev. 29 (1973) and Note, "First Amendment Protection of Ambiguous Conduct," 84 Colum.L.Rev. 467 (1984).

3. The First Amendment claim did prevail in two of the three cases in the O'Brien-Tinker-Street sequence, to be sure. But in one of them—Street—a tortured reading of the legal posture of the case was necessary to assure reversal of the conviction. And, more important, the opinions by several members of the usual Warren Court majority indicated that—despite a half century of talk about "absolute" rights, "preferred" positions, and "immediate" risks—a comprehensive, coherent framework for First Amendment protection had not yet emerged. Contrast Spence (1974; p. 1183 below), a decision of the post-Warren era that is widely viewed as setting forth a far more speech-protective and intellectually satisfying treatment of symbolic expression claims. The O'Brien opinion's evident reluctance to acknowledge that symbolic expression is entitled to First Amendment protection no doubt reflects in part a fear that, as Chief Justice Warren put it, an "apparently limitless variety of conduct" might be labeled "speech" if the claim of symbolic speech to First Amendment protection were acknowledged. But does

that fear of a "slippery slope" warrant exclusion of symbolic expression from the First Amendment, rather than a consideration of competing (and no doubt at times "compelling") state interests under the usual First Amendment scrutiny? Cf. Clark v. Community for Creative Non-Violence (1984; p. 1188 below).

4. See Ely, "Flag Desecration: A Case Study in the Roles of Categorization and Balancing in First Amendment Analysis," 88 Harv.L.Rev. 1482 (1975). In Ely's view, the O'Brien Court assigned a "trivial functional significance [to] criterion [1]'s critical word 'substantial.' "

5. Ely contrasts, as an example of a "less restrictive alternative test" with a "significantly stronger meaning" than the "weak" version applied in O'Brien, a case such as Schneider v. State (1939; p. 1206 below), holding that an anti-handbill distribution law cannot be justified by the concededly legitimate state interest in preventing litter, because of the damage done to First Amendment values by a total prohibition of handbills. The more common use of the "less restrictive alternative" test is one that engages in "serious balancing of interests: the question is whether the marginally greater effectiveness of an anti-handbill ordinance relative to alternative means of litter control justifies the greater burden on communication."

"substantial" interest requirement of [1] is taken more seriously and *if* the "less restrictive alternatives" approach of [3] is applied in its strong rather than its weak form.

But it is step [2]—whether the "governmental interest is unrelated to the suppression of free expression"—that has had the most imaginative elaborations and that is the central basis of the two-track justification theory.[6] Where criterion [2] *is* satisfied—where the "governmental interest *is* unrelated to" the suppression of free expression—the regulation is subject only to a fairly serious balancing scrutiny (more serious than in fact took place in O'Brien). As Ely puts it, where "the evil the state is seeking to avert is one that is independent of the message being regulated, where it arises from something other than a fear of how people will react to what the speaker is saying," a balancing approach (demanding a "specific threat" to the asserted state interest) is appropriate. But Ely finds implicit in O'Brien a second track as well: in situations where the governmental interest is *not* "unrelated to the suppression of free expression"— where "the evil the state is seeking to avert is one that *is* thought to arise from the particular dangers of the message being conveyed"—the restriction is unconstitutional *unless* it falls within a specifically and narrowly defined category of *unprotected* speech.[7]

Thus, to Ely, step [2] of O'Brien is centrally important and performs a critical switching function: in situations where the state interest is "related to free expression," the First Amendment assures protection *unless* the speech is in an excluded category; but where the state interest is *unrelated* to the suppression of free expression, a mere balancing review (albeit reasonably strong balancing) is the appropriate response. The Court, in cases since O'Brien, has relied on such a distinction in a number of different contexts—often, by scrutinizing restrictions unrelated to the suppression of expression a good deal less seriously than state restrictions resting on an interest in the communicative impact of the speaker's statement. One manifestation of this two-tier level of scrutiny—most protective of restraints resting on state interests related to the "suppression of free expression"—is the content-based/content-neutral distinction considered in sec. 2 above.[8] In examining the materials that follow, consider especially

6. See especially Ely's "Flag Desecration" article noted above, and the summary of his position in Ely, Democracy and Distrust (1980), 110–116. See also Tribe, American Constitutional Law (1978).

7. As Ely explains, "restrictions on free expression are seldom defended on the ground that the state simply didn't like what the defendant was saying: reference will generally be made to some danger beyond the message, such as the danger of riot, unlawful action, or violent overthrow of the government. The constitutional reference [in determining whether the second track, of restrictions based on a governmental interest that *is* related to the suppression of free expression, comes into play] must therefore be not to the ultimate interest to which the state points, for that will always be unrelated to expression, but rather to the causal connection the state asserts. If, for example, the state asserts an interest in discouraging riots, the Court should ask why that interest is implicated in the case at bar. If the answer is, as in such cases it will likely have to be, that the danger of riot was created by what the defendant was saying, the state's interest is not unrelated to the suppression of free expression, and the inhibition should be upheld only in the event the expression falls

within one of the few unprotected categories." (Ely strongly denies that his distinction is the "functional equivalent" of "the shopworn distinction between 'regulation of content' and 'regulation of time, place, and manner' [see sec. 4 below]. That would be a mistaken equation, however, one with serious costs for free expression. For the state obviously can move, and often does, 'simply' to control the time, place, or manner of communication out of a concern for the likely effect of the message on its audience. Thus in Tinker [which follows] the state regulated only the place and manner of expression—no armbands in school—but it did so [because] it feared the way the other students would react to the message those armbands conveyed.")

8. Note, e.g., the extensive discussion of the two-track model of justification in the two commentaries on the content-based/content-neutral distinction discussed at greatest length in sec. 2 above—those by Stone and Redish.

Ely finds in this two-track approach a useful, speech-protective combination of categorization and balancing approaches. Critical to that speech-protective quality is Ely's narrow and specific categorization approach, limiting the occasions for unprotected categories of speech, and

whether the two-track approach is preferable to a unitary approach in First Amendment analysis.[9]

TINKER v. DES MOINES SCHOOL DISTRICT, 393 U.S. 503 (1969): In Tinker, the Warren Court had another opportunity to confront the question of First Amendment protection for symbolic expression. This time, unlike O'Brien, the First Amendment claimant prevailed. But the ruling did relatively little to further the development of symbolic speech analysis: the majority found the restriction unconstitutional because the claimant's behavior "was closely akin to 'pure speech.'" The case arose out of the following circumstances: In December 1965, two high school students and one junior high school student wore black armbands to school to publicize their objections to the Vietnam war. They were asked to remove their armbands and refused. In accordance with a school policy adopted two days earlier in anticipation of such a protest, the students were suspended until they were ready to return without the armbands. The lower federal courts refused to enjoin the disciplinary action. They declined to follow another Circuit's holding that the wearing of symbols such as armbands cannot be prohibited unless it "materially and substantially interfere[s] with the requirements of appropriate discipline in the operation of the school."[1]

In reversing, Justice FORTAS' majority opinion stated that "[t]he wearing of armbands in the circumstances of this case was entirely divorced from actually or potentially disruptive conduct. [It] was closely akin to 'pure speech.'" He added: "First Amendment rights, applied in light of the special characteristics of the school environment, are available to teachers and students." He elaborated: "The problem [here] does not relate to regulation of the length of skirts or the type of clothing, to hair style, or deportment. It does not concern aggressive, disruptive action or even group demonstrations. Our problem involves direct, primary First Amendment rights akin to 'pure speech.' The school officials [banned] petitioners for a silent, passive expression of opinion, unaccompanied by any disorder or disturbance on the part of petitioners. There is here no evidence whatever of petitioners' interference, actual or nascent, with the schools' work or of collision with the rights of other students to be secure and to be let alone. Accordingly, this case does not concern speech or action that intrudes upon the work of the school or the rights of other students. [In] our system, undifferentiated fear or apprehension of disturbance is not enough to overcome the right to freedom of expression. [Any] word spoken [in school] that deviates from the views of another person may start an argument or cause a disturbance. But our Constitution says we must take this risk [Terminiello]; and our history says that it is this sort of hazardous freedom—this kind of openness—that is the basis of our national strength and of

---

his reasonably rigorous approach to balancing on the other track (where balancing is appropriate). As the comments in the preceding section indicate, and as the later materials will illustrate, the Court has not always been as speech-protective in its application of the lower level of justification— the level called for by the "interest [unrelated] to the suppression of free expression" track. As noted earlier, Cohen v. California (1971; p. 1101 above) is to Ely a model example of speech-protective categorization illustrating his two-track approach. (He also invokes Brandenburg v. Ohio (1969; p. 1037 above) as an admirable categorization case. Do you agree?)

9. Recall, e.g., Redish's preference for a unitary approach to the content-based/content-neu-

tral distinction in First Amendment analysis, 34 Stan.L.Rev. 113 (1981), quoted in sec. 2. Note, moreover, that the two-track approach raises a host of difficulties of its own in definition and application—particularly with respect to identifying whether the asserted interest is or is not "related to the suppression of free expression." Note Ely's admonition, footnote 7 above, against taking governmental assertions of interest "unrelated to suppression of free expression" at face value.

1. The language is from Burnside v. Byars, 363 F.2d 744 (1966), where the Fifth Circuit blocked high school authorities from enforcing a regulation forbidding students to wear "freedom buttons."

the independence and vigor of Americans who grow up and live in this relatively permissive, often disputatious, society.

"In order for the State in the person of school officials to justify prohibition of a particular expression of opinion, it must be able to show that its action was caused by something more than a mere desire to avoid the discomfort and unpleasantness that always accompany an unpopular viewpoint. Certainly where there is no finding and no showing that engaging in the forbidden conduct would 'materially and substantially interfere with the requirements of appropriate discipline in the operation of the school,' the prohibition cannot be sustained. [Burnside, above.]. [Here, there was no] evidence that the school authorities had reason to anticipate that the wearing of the armbands would substantially interfere with the work of the school or impinge upon the rights of other students. On the contrary, the action of the school authorities appears to have been based upon an urgent wish to avoid the controversy which might result from the expression, even by the silent symbol of armbands, of opposition to this Nation's part in the conflagration in Vietnam. It is also relevant that the school authorities did not purport to prohibit the wearing of all symbols of political or controversial significance. The record shows that students in some of the schools wore buttons relating to national political campaigns, and some even wore the Iron Cross, traditionally a symbol of Nazism. The order prohibiting the wearing of armbands did not extend to these. Instead, a particular symbol [was] singled out for prohibition.

"[In] the absence of a specific showing of constitutionally valid reasons to regulate their speech, students are entitled to freedom of expression of their views. [The] principle of [past] cases is not confined to the supervised and ordained discussion which takes place in the classroom. The principal use to which the schools are dedicated is to accommodate students during prescribed hours for the purpose of certain types of activities. Among those activities is personal intercommunication among the students.[2] [A] student's rights, therefore, do not embrace merely the classroom hours. When he is in the cafeteria, or on the playing field, or on the campus during the authorized hours, he may express his opinions, even on controversial subjects like the conflict in Vietnam, if he does so without 'materially and substantially interfer[ing] with the requirements of appropriate discipline in the operation of the school' and without colliding with the rights of others. Burnside."[3]

A caustic dissent by Justice BLACK charged the majority with taking over from school officials "the power to control pupils." He commented: "Assuming that the Court is correct in holding that the conduct of wearing armbands for the purpose of conveying political ideas is protected by the First Amendment, compare, e.g., [Giboney, p. 1343 below],[4] the crucial remaining ques-

2. "In Hammond v. South Carolina State College, 272 F.Supp. 947 (D.C.S.C.1967), District Judge Hemphill had before him a case involving a meeting on campus of 300 students to express their views on school practices. He pointed out that a school is not like a hospital or a jail enclosure. Cf. [Cox I; Adderley]. It is a public place, and its dedication to specific uses does not imply that the constitutional rights of persons entitled to be there are to be gauged as if the premises were purely private property. Cf. [Edwards; Brown v. Louisiana]." [Footnote by Justice Fortas.]

3. Concurring notations by Justices STEWART and WHITE are omitted. Compare, with Justice Fortas' analysis in Tinker, his approach in the dissent in Street, which follows. Can his positions be reconciled?

On the specific Tinker problem of students' free speech, compare Justice Fortas' notation—a few weeks after Tinker—concurring in the denial of certiorari in Barker v. Hardway, 394 U.S. 905 (1969): "The petitioners were suspended from college *not* for expressing their opinions on a matter of substance, but for violent and destructive interference with the rights of others. [They] engaged in an aggressive and violent demonstration, and not in peaceful, nondisruptive expression, such as was involved in [Tinker]."

4. In Giboney v. Empire Storage & Ice Co., 336 U.S. 490 (1949), a decision frequently cited in First Amendment cases by Justices Black and Douglas, Justice Black found labor picketing enjoinable on the ground that First Amendment freedoms typically do not extend "to speech or writing used as an integral part of conduct in

tions are whether students and teachers may use the schools at their whim as a platform for the exercise of free speech—'symbolic' or 'pure'—and whether the courts will allocate to themselves the function of deciding how the pupils' school day will be spent. [I] have never believed that any person has a right to give speeches or engage in demonstrations where he pleases and when he pleases." He argued, moreover, that "the record overwhelmingly shows that the armbands did exactly what [the school officials] foresaw it would, that is, took the students' minds off their classwork and diverted them to thoughts about the highly emotional subject of the Vietnam war. [One] does not need to be a prophet or the son of a prophet to know that after the Court's holding today some students [will] be ready, able, and willing to defy their teachers on practically all orders. This is the more unfortunate for the schools since groups of students all over the land are already running loose, conducting break-ins, sit-ins, lie-ins, and smash-ins." [5]

STREET v. NEW YORK

394 U.S. 576, 89 S.Ct. 1354, 22 L.Ed.2d 572 (1969).

Mr. Justice HARLAN delivered the opinion of the Court.

[Appellant Street was convicted of violating a New York provision] which makes it a misdemeanor "publicly [to] mutilate, deface, defile, or defy, trample upon, or cast contempt upon either by words or act [any flag of the United States]." [The] events which led to the conviction were these: [During] the afternoon of June 6, 1966, [appellant] was listening to the radio in his Brooklyn apartment. He heard a news report that civil rights leader James Meredith had been shot by a sniper in Mississippi. Saying to himself, "They didn't protect him," appellant, himself a Negro, took from his drawer a neatly folded, 48-star American flag which he formerly had displayed on national holidays. Appellant left his apartment and carried the still-folded flag to the nearby intersection of St. James Place and Lafayette Avenue. Appellant stood on the northeast corner of the intersection, lit the flag with a match, and dropped the flag on the pavement when it began to burn. Soon thereafter, a police officer halted his patrol car and found the burning flag. The officer testified that he then crossed to the northwest corner of the intersection, where he found appellant "talking out loud" to a small group of persons. The officer estimated that there were some 30 persons on the corner near the flag and five to 10 on the corner with appellant. The officer testified [that] he heard appellant say, "We don't need no damn flag," and that when he asked appellant whether he had burned the flag appellant replied: "Yes, that is my flag; I burned it. If they let that happen to Meredith we don't need an American flag."

[We] deem it unnecessary to consider [Street's overbreadth and vagueness] arguments, for we hold that [the provision] was unconstitutionally applied in [his] case because it permitted him to be punished merely for speaking defiant or contemptuous words about the American flag. In the face of an information explicitly setting forth appellant's words as an element of his alleged crime, and of appellant's subsequent conviction under a statute making it an offense to speak words of that sort, we find this record insufficient to eliminate the

violation of a valid criminal statute." (Note, e.g., the reliance on Giboney in his dissent in Street, which follows.) The Giboney case is discussed further in Teamsters Union v. Vogt, Inc. (1957; p. 1342 below).

5. In a separate dissent, Justice HARLAN recognized that the First Amendment applied in the school context but concluded: "I would, in cases like this, cast upon those complaining the burden of showing that a particular school measure was motivated by other than legitimate school concerns—for example, a desire to prohibit the expression of an unpopular point of view, while permitting expression of the dominant opinion."

possibility either that appellant's words were the sole basis of his conviction or that appellant was convicted for both his words and his deed.

We come finally to the question whether, in the circumstances of this case, New York may constitutionally inflict criminal punishment upon one who ventures "publicly [to] defy [or] cast contempt upon [any American flag] by words." [We] can think of four governmental interests which might conceivably have been furthered by punishing appellant for his words: (1) an interest in deterring appellant from vocally inciting others to commit unlawful acts; (2) an interest in preventing appellant from uttering words so inflammatory that they would provoke others to retaliate physically against him, thereby causing a breach of the peace; (3) an interest in protecting the sensibilities of passers-by who might be shocked by appellant's words about the American flag; and (4) an interest in assuring that appellant, regardless of the impact of his words upon others, showed proper respect for our national emblem.

In the circumstances of this case, we do not believe that any of these interests may constitutionally justify appellant's conviction [for] speaking as he did. We begin with the interest in preventing incitement. Appellant's words, taken alone, did not urge anyone to do anything unlawful. They amounted only to somewhat excited public advocacy of the idea that the United States should abandon, at least temporarily, one of its national symbols. It is clear that the 14th Amendment prohibits the States from imposing criminal punishment for public advocacy of peaceful change in our institutions. See, e.g., [Cox I, Edwards, Terminiello; cf. Yates]. Even assuming that appellant's words might be found incitive when considered together with his simultaneous burning of the flag, [the law] does not purport to punish only those defiant or contemptuous words which amount to incitement. [Hence], a conviction for words could not be upheld on this [basis].

Nor could such a conviction be justified on the second ground: [the] possible tendency of appellant's words to provoke violent retaliation. Though it is conceivable that some listeners might have been moved to retaliate upon hearing appellant's disrespectful words, we cannot say that appellant's remarks were so inherently inflammatory as to come within that small class of "fighting words" which are "likely to provoke the average person to retaliation, and thereby cause a breach of the peace." [Chaplinsky.] And even if [his] words might be found within that category, [the law] is not narrowly drawn to punish only words of that character, and there is no indication that it was so interpreted by the state courts. [Moreover, the conviction cannot] be sustained on the ground that appellant's words were likely to shock passers-by. Except perhaps for appellant's incidental use of the word "damn," upon which no emphasis was placed at trial, any shock effect of appellant's speech must be attributed to the content of the ideas expressed. It is firmly settled that under our Constitution the public expression of ideas may not be prohibited merely because the ideas are themselves offensive to some of their hearers. See, e.g., [Cox I, Edwards, Terminiello; cf. Cantwell].[1] And even if such a conviction might be upheld on the ground of "shock," there is again no indication that the state courts regarded the statute as limited to that purpose.

Finally, such a conviction could not be supported on the theory that by making [his] remarks about the flag appellant failed to show the respect for our national symbol which may properly be demanded of every citizen. In [Barnette (1943; p. 1510 below)], this Court held that to require unwilling schoolchildren to salute the flag would violate rights of free expression assured by the 14th Amendment. [There], Mr. Justice Jackson wrote words which are

---

1. Recall Justice Harlan's elaboration of this point in his opinion two years later in Cohen v. California, the "offensive language" case at p. 1101 above. Note the similarity between Harlan's approaches in Cohen and in this case.

especially apposite here.[2] [We] have no doubt that the constitutionally guaranteed "freedom to be intellectually [diverse] or even contrary," and the "right to differ as to things that touch the heart of the existing order," encompass the freedom to express publicly one's opinions about our flag, including those opinions which are defiant or contemptuous.

Since appellant could not constitutionally be punished under [the statute] for his speech, and since we have found that he may have been so punished, his conviction cannot be permitted to stand. In so holding, we reiterate that we have no occasion to pass upon the validity of this conviction insofar as it was sustained by the state courts on the basis that Street could be punished for his burning of the flag, even though the burning was an act of protest. [W]e add that disrespect for our flag is to be deplored no less in these vexed times than in calmer periods of our history. Cf. Halter v. Nebraska, 205 U.S. 34 (1907). Nevertheless, we are unable to sustain a conviction that may have rested on a form of expression, however distasteful, which the Constitution tolerates and [protects].

Reversed.

Mr. Chief Justice WARREN [dissenting].

[A]ppellant was convicted for his act not his words. [I] believe that the States and the Federal Government do have the power to protect the flag from acts of desecration and disgrace. But because the Court has not met the issue, it would serve no purpose to delineate my reasons for this view. However, it is difficult for me to imagine that, had the Court faced this issue, it would have concluded [otherwise].

Mr. Justice BLACK [dissenting].

[If] I could agree with the Court's interpretation of the record as to the possibility of the conviction's resting on these spoken words, I would firmly and automatically agree that the law is unconstitutional. I would not feel constrained, as the Court seems to be, to search my imagination to see if I could think of interests the State may have in suppressing this freedom of speech. I would not balance away the First Amendment mandate that speech not be abridged in any fashion whatsoever. But I accept the unanimous opinion of the New York Court of Appeals that the conviction does not and could not have rested merely on the spoken words but that it rested entirely on the fact that the defendant had publicly burned the American [flag]. It passes my belief that anything in the Federal Constitution bars a State from making the deliberate burning of the American flag an offense. It is immaterial to me that words are spoken in connection with the burning. It is the *burning* of the flag that the State has set its face against. "It rarely has been suggested that the constitutional freedom for speech and press extends its immunity to speech or writing used as an integral part of conduct in violation of a valid criminal statute." [Giboney (1949; p. 1343 below).] In my view this [quotation] precisely applies here. The talking that was done took place "as an integral part of conduct in violation of a valid criminal statute" against burning the American flag in [public].

Mr. Justice WHITE [dissenting].

2. Justice Harlan quoted the following language from the Jackson opinion in Barnette: "The case is made difficult not because the principles of its decision are obscure but because the flag involved is our own. Nevertheless, we apply the limitations of the Constitution with no fear that freedom to be intellectually and spiritually diverse or even contrary will disintegrate the social organization. [F]reedom to differ is not limited to things that do not matter much. [The] test of its substance is the right to differ as to things that touch the heart of the existing order.

"If there is any fixed star in our constitutional constellation, it is that no official, high or petty, can prescribe what shall be orthodox in politics, nationalism, religion, or other matters of opinion or force citizens to confess by word or act their faith therein. If there are any circumstances which permit an exception, they do not now occur to us."

[Before] Street's conviction can be either reversed or affirmed, the Court *must* reach and decide the validity of a conviction for flag burning. The Court is obviously wrong in reversing the judgment below because it believes that Street was unconstitutionally convicted for speaking. Reversal can follow only if the Court reaches the conviction for flag burning and finds that conviction, as well as the assumed conviction for speech, to be violative of the First Amendment.[1] For myself, without the benefit of the majority's thinking if it were to find flag burning protected by the First Amendment, I would sustain such a [conviction].

Mr. Justice FORTAS, dissenting.

I agree with the dissenting opinion filed by The Chief Justice, but I believe that it is necessary briefly to set forth the reasons why the States and the Federal Government have the power to protect the flag from acts of desecration committed in public. If the national flag were nothing more than a chattel, subject only to the rules governing the use of private personalty, its use would nevertheless be subject to certain types of state regulation. For example, regulations concerning the use of chattels which are reasonably designed to avoid danger to life or property, or impingement upon the rights of others to the quiet use of their property and of public facilities, would unquestionably be a valid exercise of police power. They would not necessarily be defeated by a claim that they conflicted with the rights of the owner of the regulated property.[1]

If a state statute provided that it is a misdemeanor to burn one's shirt or trousers or shoes on the public thoroughfare, it could hardly be asserted that the citizen's constitutional right is violated. If the arsonist asserted that he was burning his shirt or trousers or shoes as a protest against the Government's fiscal policies, for example, it is hardly possible that his claim to First Amendment shelter would prevail against the State's claim of a right to avert danger to the public and to avoid obstruction to traffic as a result of the fire. This is because action, even if clearly for serious protest purposes, is not entitled to the pervasive protection that is given to speech alone. See [Cantwell]. It may be subjected to reasonable regulation that appropriately takes into account the competing interests involved. The test that is applicable in every case where conduct is restricted or prohibited is whether the regulation or prohibition is reasonable, due account being taken of the paramountcy of First Amendment values. If, as I submit, it is permissible to prohibit the burning of personal property on the public sidewalk, there is no basis for applying a different rule to flag burning. And the fact that the law is violated for purposes of protest does not immunize the violator. [O'Brien; see Giboney.]

Beyond this, however, the flag is a special kind of personalty. Its use is traditionally and universally subject to special rules and regulation. As early as 1907, this Court affirmed the constitutionality of a state statute making it a crime to use a representation of the United States flag for purposes of advertising. Halter v. Nebraska. Statutes prescribe how the flag may be

---

1. Arguably, under today's decision any conviction for flag burning where the defendant's words are critical to proving intent or some other element of the crime would be invalid since the conviction would be based in part on speech. The Court disclaims this result, but without explaining why it would not reverse a conviction for burning where words spoken at the time are necessarily used to prove a case and yet reverse burning convictions on precisely the same evidence simply because on that evidence the defendant might also have been convicted for [speaking]. [Footnote by Justice White.]

Justice Harlan responded to this by stating that he perceived no basis for Justice White's "fears": "Assuming that such a conviction would otherwise pass constitutional muster, a matter about which we express no view, nothing in this opinion would render the conviction impermissible merely because an element of the crime was proved by the defendant's words rather than in some other way. See [O'Brien]."

1. At this point, Justice Fortas cited Euclid (1926; p. 480 above) and Berman v. Parker (1954; p. 485 above)—decisions sustaining zoning and eminent domain actions.

displayed; how it may lawfully be disposed of; when, how, and for what purposes it may and may not be used. A person may "own" a flag, but ownership is subject to special burdens and responsibilities. A flag may be property, in a sense; but it is property burdened with peculiar obligations and restrictions. Certainly, as [Halter] held, these special conditions are not per se arbitrary or beyond governmental power under our Constitution.

One may not justify burning a house, even if it is his own, on the ground, however sincere, that he does so as a protest. One may not justify breaking the windows of a government building on that basis. Protest does not exonerate lawlessness. And the prohibition against flag burning on the public thorough-fare being valid, the misdemeanor is not excused merely because it is an act of flamboyant protest.

SOME COMMENTS ON THE WARREN COURT'S HANDLING OF SYMBOLIC EXPRESSION

As noted earlier, the O'Brien opinion has been criticized as "question begging," especially in the application of its standards to the facts in that case. Is it arguable that O'Brien's weaknesses were a reflection of the doctrinal techniques in vogue rather than a mere aberration, or a response to the perceived pressures of de facto war? Note especially the reliance, in varying ways, on the "speech"-"conduct" distinction in all of the cases in the O'Brien-Tinker-Street sequence. Does that distinction tend to avoid subtle judgments and to evoke overstatements? Compare, for example, Justice Fortas majority opinion in Tinker with his dissent in Street. Does his Tinker opinion convey a sense of greater protection of student behavior than intended because the "akin to 'pure speech'" categorization generates speech-protective rhetoric—which requires later qualification regarding punishable "conduct"? Does the same oversimplified and obscuring "speech"-"conduct" premise in turn give rise to the equally extreme—albeit restrictive rather than libertarian—rhetoric in For-tas' Street dissent, which apparently finds a "mere rationality" requirement appropriate via the easy route of an "action"-"speech alone" distinction?[1] Does his Street dissent give the "due" recognition to the "paramountcy" of First Amendment values that he professes to be necessary? A protest purpose does not "immunize" against law violation, to be sure—but was that the issue? What should be the scope of "symbolic expression" entitled to First Amendment protection?[2]

The readiness of several Justices of the Warren era to invoke the simplistic "speech"-"conduct" distinction may be attributable to their aversion to "balancing." Yet do not these cases illustrate the need for discriminating, sensitive, articulate balancing for many speech problems? Justice Fortas and Chief Justice Warren were among those generally identified with the "liberal" wing during the closing years of the Warren Court; Justice Harlan, by contrast, was viewed as a "conservative" and was a chief target of those who, like Justice Black, saw in "balancing" a frittering away of First Amendment rights.[3] Is it not ironic, then, that Justice Harlan should write the majority opinion in Street—with Chief

---

1. For further criticisms of the "speech"-"conduct" distinction in First Amendment analysis, see the later materials, especially the comments on the Cox cases (1965; p. 1225 below).

2. Note Henkin, "Foreword: On Drawing Lines," 82 Harv.L.Rev. 63 (1968): "The meaningful constitutional distinction is not between speech and conduct, but between conduct that speaks, communicates, and other kinds of con-duct. If it is intended as expression, if in fact it communicates, especially if it becomes a common comprehensible form of expression, it is 'speech.'" [Note the reflection of that approach in Spence, the 1974 decision which follows.]

3. Recall the Harlan-Black "balancing"-"absolutes" clash in the Konigsberg excerpts, in the introductory materials to chap. 11, at p. 981 above.

Justice Warren as well as Justices Fortas and Black finding little difficulty in sustaining the conviction? Would Justice Harlan have applied his analysis if he had focused on the flag-burning, and not just the words, in Street—i.e., would he have sought to identify the governmental interests and to determine whether any were sufficiently furthered to justify the conviction? Would a conviction for the act of burning have been sustainable under that approach? Compare the Court's confrontations with symbolic expression problems (including flag mutilation ones) in the post-Warren era, in the materials that follow.

SPENCE v. WASHINGTON

418 U.S. 405, 94 S.Ct. 2727, 41 L.Ed.2d 842 (1974).

PER CURIAM. [Spence] displayed a United States flag, which he owned, out the window of his apartment. Affixed to both surfaces of the flag was a large peace symbol fashioned of removable tape. [He] was convicted under a Washington statute forbidding the exhibition of a United States flag to which is attached or superimposed figures, symbols, or other extraneous material. [W]e reverse on the ground that as applied to appellant's activity the [law] impermissibly infringed protected expression.

[Spence] was not charged under Washington's flag desecration statute.[1] Rather, the State relied on the so-called "improper use" statute.[2] [He] testified that he put a peace symbol on the flag and displayed it to public view as a protest to the invasion of Cambodia and the killings at Kent State University, events which occurred a few days prior to his arrest [in May, 1970]. He said that his purpose was to associate the American flag with peace instead of war and violence: "I felt there had been so much killing and that this was not what America stood for. I felt that the flag stood for America and I wanted people to know that I thought America stood for peace." [He] further testified that he chose to fashion the peace symbol from tape so that it could be removed without damaging the flag.

A number of factors are important in the instant case. First, this was a privately owned flag. In a technical property sense it was not the property of any government. [Second, Spence] displayed his flag on private property. He engaged in no trespass or disorderly conduct. Nor is this a case that might be analyzed in terms of reasonable time, place, or manner restraints on access to a public area. Third, the record is devoid of proof of any risk of breach of the peace. [Fourth], the State concedes [that Spence] engaged in a form of communication. [That] concession is inevitable on this record. [To] be sure, [Spence] did not choose to articulate his views through printed or spoken words. It is therefore necessary to determine whether his activity was sufficiently imbued with elements of communication to fall within the scope of the First [Amendment]. [The] nature of [Spence's] activity, combined with the factual context and environment in which it was undertaken, lead to the conclusion that he engaged in a form of protected expression.

---

1. This [flag desecration] statute provides in part:

"No person shall knowingly cast contempt upon any flag, standard, color, ensign or shield [by] publicly mutilating, defacing, defiling, burning, or trampling upon said flag, standard, color, ensign or shield." [Footnote by the Court.]

2. This statute provides: "No person shall, in any manner, for exhibition or display:

"(1) Place or cause to be placed any word, figure, mark, picture, design, drawing or advertisement of any nature upon any flag, standard, color, ensign or shield of the United States or of this state [or]

"(2) Expose to public view any such flag, standard, color, ensign or shield upon which shall have been printed, painted or otherwise produced, or to which shall have been attached, appended, affixed or annexed any such word, figure, mark, picture, design, drawing or [advertisement]."

Moreover, the context in which a symbol is used for purposes of expression is important, for the context may give meaning to the symbol. In this case, [Spence's] activity was roughly simultaneous with and concededly triggered by the Cambodian incursion and the Kent State tragedy, [issues] of great public moment. A flag bearing a peace symbol and displayed upside down by a student today might be interpreted as nothing more than bizarre behavior, but it would have been difficult for the great majority of citizens to miss the drift of [Spence's] point at the time that he made it. It may be noted, further, that this was not an act of mindless nihilism. Rather, it was a pointed expression of anguish [about] the then current domestic and foreign affairs of his government. An intent to convey a particularized message was present, and in the surrounding circumstances the likelihood was great that the message would be understood by those who viewed it.

We are confronted then with a case of prosecution for the expression of an idea through activity. Moreover, the activity occurred on private property. [Accordingly], we must examine with particular care [the] range of various state interests that might be thought to support the challenged conviction, drawing upon the arguments before us, the opinions below, and the Court's opinion in [Street].[3] The first interest at issue is prevention of breach of the peace. [It] is totally without support in the record.

We are also unable to affirm the judgment below on the ground that the State may have desired to protect the sensibilities of passersby. "It is firmly settled that under our Constitution the public expression of ideas may not be prohibited merely because the ideas are themselves offensive to some of their hearers." [Street.] Moreover, appellant did not impose his ideas upon a captive audience. Anyone who might have been offended could easily have avoided the display. See [Cohen]. Nor may appellant be punished for failing to show proper respect for our national emblem. [Street; Barnette.][4]

We are brought, then, to the state court's thesis that Washington has an interest in preserving the national flag as an unalloyed symbol of our country. The court did not define this interest; it simply asserted it. The dissenting opinion today adopts essentially the same approach. Presumably, this interest might be seen as an effort to prevent the appropriation of a revered national symbol by an individual, interest group, or enterprise where there was a risk that association of the symbol with a particular product or viewpoint might be taken erroneously as evidence of governmental endorsement.[5] Alternatively, it might be argued that the interest asserted by the state court is based on the uniquely universal character of the national flag as a symbol. For the great majority of us, the flag is a symbol of patriotism, of pride in the history of our country, and of the service, sacrifice, and valor of the millions of Americans who in peace and war have joined together to build and to defend a Nation in which self-government and personal liberty endure. It evidences both the unity and diversity which are America. For others the flag carries in varying degrees a

---

3. [A] subsidiary ground relied on by the Washington Supreme Court must be rejected summarily. It found the inhibition on appellant's freedom of expression "miniscule and trifling" because there are "thousands of other means available to [him] for the dissemination of his personal [views]."

As the Court noted in, e.g., [Schneider], "one is not to have the exercise of his liberty of expression in appropriate places abridged on the plea that it may be exercised in some other place." [Footnote by the Court to an earlier passage.]

4. Counsel for the State conceded that promoting respect for the flag is not a legitimate state interest. [Footnote by the Court.]

5. Undoubtedly such a concern underlies that portion of the improper-use statute forbidding the utilization of representations of the flag in a commercial context. [There] is no occasion in this case to address the application of the challenged statute to commercial behavior. Cf. [Halter]. The dissent places major reliance on Halter, despite the fact that Halter was decided nearly 20 years before the Court concluded that the First Amendment applies to the [states]. [Footnote by the Court.]

different message. "A person gets from a symbol the meaning he puts into it, and what is one man's comfort and inspiration is another's jest and scorn." [Barnette.] It might be said that we all draw something from our national symbol, for it is capable of conveying simultaneously a spectrum of meanings. If it may be destroyed or permanently disfigured, it could be argued that it will lose its capability of mirroring the sentiments of all who view it.

But we need not decide in this case whether the interest advanced by the court below is valid.[6] We assume, arguendo, that it is. The statute is nonetheless unconstitutional as applied to appellant's activity.[7] There was no risk that appellant's acts would mislead viewers into assuming that the Government endorsed his viewpoint. To the contrary, he was plainly and peacefully[8] protesting the fact that it did not. Appellant was not charged under the desecration statute, nor did he permanently disfigure the flag or destroy it. He displayed it as a flag of his country in a way closely analogous to the manner in which flags have always been used to convey ideas. Moreover, his message was

6. If this interest is valid, we note that it is directly related to expression in the context of activity like that undertaken by appellant. For that reason and because no other governmental interest unrelated to expression has been advanced or can be supported on this record, the four-step analysis of [O'Brien] is inapplicable. [Footnote by the Court.]

7. Because we agree with appellant's as-applied argument, we do not reach the more comprehensive overbreadth contention he also advances. But it is worth noting the nearly limitless sweep of the Washington improper-use flag statute. Read literally, it forbids a veteran's group from attaching, e.g., battalion commendations to a United States flag. It proscribes photographs of war heroes standing in front of the flag. It outlaws newspaper mastheads composed of the national flag with superimposed print. Other examples could easily be listed. Statutes of such sweep suggest problems of selective enforcement. We are, however, unable to agree with appellant's void-for-vagueness argument. The statute's application is quite mechanical, particularly when implemented with jury instructions like the ones given in this case. The law in Washington, simply put, is that *nothing* may be affixed to or superimposed on a United States flag or a representation thereof. Thus, if selective enforcement has occurred, it has been a result of prosecutorial discretion, not the language of the statute. Accordingly, this case is unlike Smith v. Goguen, 415 U.S. 566 (1974), where the words of the statute at issue ("publicly [treats] contemptuously") were themselves sufficiently indefinite to prompt subjective treatment by prosecutorial authorities. [Footnote by the Court.]

[SMITH v. GOGUEN, decided three months before Spence, was a 6 to 3 decision reversing a Massachusetts conviction for wearing a small United States flag sewn to the seat of appellee's trousers. Justice POWELL's majority opinion found it unnecessary to reach a variety of First Amendment claims and rested instead on "the due process doctrine of vagueness." Though appellee's behavior seemed to reflect "immaturity" and "silly conduct," Justice Powell observed

that "casual treatment of the flag in many contexts has become a widespread contemporary phenomenon." Here, the statutory language "fails to draw reasonably clear lines between the kinds of nonceremonial treatment (of the flag) that are criminal and those that are not." Fair notice standards were not met, given "today's tendencies to treat the flag unceremoniously." Justice Powell added: "Statutory language of such standardless sweep allows policemen, prosecutors, and juries to pursue their personal predilections."

[Justice WHITE disagreed with the majority's reasoning, though not its result. He defended the constitutionality of flag mutilation laws, but objected to the conviction for being contemptuous of the flag: "To convict on this basis is not to protect the physical integrity or to protect against acts interfering with the proper use of the flag, but to punish for communicating ideas about the flag unacceptable to the controlling majority." Justice REHNQUIST, joined by Chief Justice Burger, dissented at length, describing the flag as a "unique physical object" and emphasizing the strong state interest in protecting "the physical integrity of a unique national symbol." There was also a second, briefer dissenting opinion, by Justice BLACKMUN, joined by the Chief Justice.]

8. Appellant's activity occurred at a time of national turmoil over the introduction of United States forces into Cambodia and the deaths at Kent State University. It is difficult now, more than four years later, to recall vividly the depth of emotion that pervaded most colleges and universities at the time, and that was widely shared by young Americans everywhere. A spontaneous outpouring of feeling resulted in widespread action, not all of it rational when viewed in retrospect. This included the closing down of some schools, as well as other disruptions of many centers of education. It was against this highly inflamed background that appellant chose to express his own views in a manner that can fairly be described as gentle and restrained as compared to the actions undertaken by a number of his peers. [Footnote by the Court.]

direct, likely to be understood, and within the contours of the First Amendment. Given the protected character of his expression and in light of the fact that no interest the State may have in preserving the physical integrity of a privately-owned flag was significantly impaired on these facts, the conviction must be invalidated.

Reversed.[9]

Mr. Justice REHNQUIST, with whom The Chief Justice [BURGER] and Mr. Justice WHITE join, [dissenting].[1]

Since a State concededly may impose some limitations on speech directly, it would seem to follow a fortiori that a State may legislate to protect important state interests even though an incidental limitation on free speech results. Virtually any law enacted by a State, when viewed with sufficient ingenuity, could be thought to interfere with some citizen's preferred means of expression. But no one would argue, I presume, that a State could not prevent the painting of public buildings simply because a particular class of protesters believed their message would best be conveyed through that medium. [Yet] the Court today holds that [the State] cannot limit use of the American flag, at least insofar as its statute prevents appellant from using a privately owned flag to convey his personal message. [The Court] demonstrates a total misunderstanding of the State's interest in the integrity of the American flag, and [places itself] in the position either of ultimately favoring appellant's message because of its [non-commercial] subject matter [or], alternatively, of making the flag available for a limitless succession of political and commercial messages. I shall treat these issues in reverse order.

The statute under which appellant was convicted is no stranger to this Court, a virtually identical statute having been before the Court in [Halter, where] the Court held that Nebraska could enforce its statute to prevent use of a flag representation on beer bottles, [stating]: "Such use tends to degrade and cheapen the flag in the estimation of the people, as well as to defeat the object of maintaining it as an emblem of National power and National honor." The Court today finds Halter irrelevant. [Insofar] as Halter assesses the State's interest, of course, the Court's argument is simply beside the point. [Yet] if the Court is suggesting that Halter would now be decided differently, and that the State's interest in the flag falls before any speech which is "direct, likely to be understood, and within the contours of the First Amendment," that view would mean the flag could be auctioned as a background to anyone willing and able to buy or copy one. I find it hard to believe the Court intends to presage that result.

---

9. Justices BLACKMUN and DOUGLAS concurred in the result.

Does the opinion in Spence, in the post-Warren era, go further than any Warren Court opinion in delineating the contours of what is protected symbolic expression? Note the Court's emphasis on two factors: the speaker's intent; and the context indicating that the message would be understood by the audience. Is that a useful approach? Is it adequate? What about conduct more ambiguous than that in Spence? See Note, "First Amendment Protection of Ambiguous Conduct," 84 Colum.L.Rev. 467 (1984). Can the Court protect all such conduct without risking the slippery slope Chief Justice Warren feared in O'Brien? Compare the Clark case, which follows.

Note the extent to which the Spence opinion echoes Justice Harlan's approach in Street as well

as in Cohen. Does that variety of balancing lay bare the competing values, including the "speech" ingredients, more effectively than alternative techniques? (Ely, "[Flag Desecration]," 88 Harv.L.Rev. 1482 (1975), considers Spence another model combination of categorization and balancing.) Does Street cast further doubt on the "conduct"-"speech" distinction? Does Spence at least suggest that "absolutes," "balancing," and "speech"-"conduct" analyses and their offshoots are not wholly adequate to the task of supplying principled, intellectually respectable, and pragmatically effective tools for the implementation of First Amendment values?

1. Chief Justice BURGER also submitted a brief separate dissent.

Turning to the question of the State's interest in the flag, it seems to me that the Court's treatment lacks all substance. The suggestion that the State's interest somehow diminishes when the flag is decorated with *removable* tape trivializes something which is not trivial. The [State] is hardly seeking to protect the flag's resale value. [Unlike] flag-desecration statutes, the Washington statute challenged here seeks to prevent personal *use* of the flag, not simply particular forms of *abuse*. The [State] has chosen to set the flag apart for a special purpose, and has directed that it not be turned into a common background for an endless variety of superimposed messages. The physical condition of the flag itself is irrelevant to that purpose.

The true nature of the State's interest in this case is not only one of preserving "the physical integrity of the flag," but also one of preserving the flag as "an important symbol of nationhood and unity." [2] Although the Court treats this important interest with a studied inattention, it is hardly one of recent invention and has previously been accorded considerable respect by this Court. There was no question in Halter of physical impairment of a flag since no actual flag was even involved. And it certainly would have made no difference to the Court's discussion of the State's interest if the [challenger] in that case had chosen to advertise his product by decorating the flag with beer bottles fashioned from some removable substance. It is the character, not the cloth, of the flag which the State seeks to protect. The value of this interest has been emphasized in recent as well as distant times. [After noting Justice Fortas' dissent in Street, Justice Rehnquist quoted Justice White's statement in Smith v. Goguen that "the flag is a national property, and the Nation may regulate those who would make, imitate, sell, possess, or use it."] I agree. What appellant here seeks is simply license to use the flag however he pleases, so long as the activity can be tied to a concept of speech, regardless of any state interest in having the flag used only for more limited purposes. I find no reasoning in the Court's opinion which convinces me that the Constitution requires such license to be given.

The fact that the State has a valid interest in preserving the character of the flag does not mean, of course, that it can employ all conceivable means to enforce it. It certainly could not require all citizens to own the flag or compel citizens to salute one. [Barnette.] It presumably cannot punish criticism of the flag, or the principles for which it stands, any more than it could punish criticism of this country's policies or ideas. But the statute in this case demands no such allegiance. Its operation does not depend upon whether the flag is used for communicative or noncommunicative purposes; upon whether a particular message is deemed commercial or political; upon whether the use of the flag is respectful or contemptuous; or upon whether any particular segment of the State's citizenry might applaud or oppose the intended message. It simply withdraws a unique national symbol from the roster of materials that may be used as a background for communications. Since I do not believe the Constitution prohibits Washington from making that decision, I dissent. [3]

------

2. The quoted phrases are from the opinions of Justices Blackmun and White in Smith v. Goguen (footnote 7 above).

3. Compare with Spence the Burger Court's avoidance and apparent deprecation of a "symbolic speech" ground in Wooley v. Maynard, 430 U.S. 705 (1977) (p. 1511 below). Wooley sustained Jehovah's Witnesses' objections to displaying the New Hampshire motto, "Live Free or Die," on their automobile license plates. Chief Justice Burger found that requirement a coerced affirmation of belief, in violation of the principles of Barnette, the second Flag Salute Case (p. 1510 below). In the District Court, by contrast, the challengers had prevailed on symbolic speech grounds. But the Chief Justice found it "unnecessary" to pass on that issue. Yet he added in a footnote that the challengers' "claim of symbolic expression is substantially undermined by their prayer in the District Court for issuance of special license plates not bearing the state motto. This is hardly consistent with the stated intent to communicate affirmative opposition to the motto." Justice Brennan, who joined the majority

CLARK v. COMMUNITY FOR CREATIVE NON–VIOLENCE

468 U.S. —, 104 S.Ct. 3065, 82 L.Ed.2d 221 (1984).

Justice WHITE delivered the opinion of the Court.

The issue in this case is whether a National Park Service regulation prohibiting camping in certain parks violates the First Amendment when applied to prohibit demonstrators from sleeping in Lafayette Park and the Mall in connection with a demonstration intended to call attention to the plight of the homeless. We hold that it does [not].

I. The Interior Department, through the National Park Service, is charged with responsibility for the management and maintenance of the National Parks and is authorized to promulgate rules and regulations for the use of the parks in accordance with the purposes for which they were established. The network of National Parks includes the National Memorial-core parks [Lafayette Park and the Mall].[1] Under the regulations involved in this case, camping in National Parks is permitted only in campgrounds designated for that purpose. No such campgrounds have ever been designated in Lafayette Park or the Mall.[2] [Demonstrations] for the airing of views or grievances are permitted in the Memorial-core parks, but for the most part only by Park Service permits. Temporary structures may be erected for demonstration purposes but may not be used for camping.[3]

In 1982, the Park Service issued a renewable permit to respondent Community for Creative Non-Violence (CCNV) to conduct a wintertime demonstration in Lafayette Park and the Mall for the purpose of demonstrating the plight of the homeless. The permit authorized the erection of two symbolic tent cities:

opinion in other respects, stated explicitly that he did not join in that footnote. And Justice Rehnquist's dissent viewed that footnote as an "implicit recognition that there is no protected 'symbolic speech' in this case."

Does Justice Rehnquist's dissent in Spence adequately identify precisely what the special governmental interest in the flag is? Is it a legitimate and compelling one? Note Ely, "[Flag Desecration]," 88 Harv.L.Rev. 1482 (1975), suggesting that the interest promoted by a flag misuse law is not an interest "unrelated to the suppression of free expression" in the sense of O'Brien's two-track approach and that reliance on that interest is accordingly unconstitutional (because the varieties of speech it is likely to curtail do not fall within any narrow, clear category of unprotected speech). He concedes that improper flag use laws "do not single out certain messages for proscription," but insists that "they *do* single out one set of messages, namely the set of messages conveyed by the American flag, for protection." He argues that O'Brien's step [2] should not be limited to "situations where the harm the state seeks to avert is one that arises from the defendant's communication." That formulation (note the comments on his analysis after O'Brien, above) is "incomplete": that criterion should also "encompass the case in which the government singles out a specific message or set of messages." He notes: "Orthodoxy of thought can be fostered not simply by placing unusual restrictions on 'deviant' expression but also by granting unusual protection to expression that is officially acceptable." In effect, he argues

that special protection of the flag distorts "the free marketplace of ideas."

1. Lafayette Park is a seven-acre square located across Pennsylvania Avenue from the White House. The Mall is a stretch of land running westward from the Capitol to the Lincoln Memorial some two miles away. (It includes the Washington Monument as well as a series of pools, trees, lawns, and other greenery.) Both park areas are visited by "vast numbers of visitors."

2. The regulation defined "camping" as "the use of park land for living accommodation purposes such as sleeping activities, or making preparations to sleep (including the laying down of bedding for the purpose of sleeping), or storing personal belongings, or making any fire, or using any tents or [other] structure [for] sleeping or doing any digging or earth breaking or carrying on cooking activities." Under the regulations, these activities "constitute camping when it reasonably appears, in light of all the circumstances, that the participants, in conducting these activities, are in fact using the area as a living accommodation regardless of the intent of the participants or the nature of any other activities in which they may also be engaging."

3. The regulations state: "In connection with permitted demonstrations or special events, temporary structures may be erected for the purpose of symbolizing a message or meeting logistical needs such as [first aid facilities]. Temporary structures may not be used outside designated camping areas for [camping activities]."

20 tents in Lafayette Park that would accommodate 50 people and 40 tents in the Mall with a capacity of up to 100. The Park Service, however, relying on [the] regulations, specifically denied CCNV's request that demonstrators be permitted to sleep in the symbolic tents. CCNV and several individuals then filed an action to prevent the application of the anti-camping regulations to the proposed [demonstration].[4]

II. We need not differ with the view of the Court of Appeals that overnight sleeping in connection with the demonstration is expressive conduct protected to some extent by the First Amendment.[5] We assume for present purposes, but do not decide, that such is the case, cf. [O'Brien], but this assumption only begins the inquiry. Expression, whether oral or written or symbolized by conduct, is subject to reasonable time, place, and manner restrictions. We have often noted that restrictions of this kind are valid provided that they are justified without reference to the content of the regulated speech, that they are narrowly tailored to serve a significant governmental interest, and that they leave open ample alternative channels for communication of the information. [E.g., Taxpayers for Vincent; Grace; Perry; Heffron; Consolidated Edison.[6]] It is also true that a message may be delivered by conduct that is intended to be communicative and that, in context, would reasonably be understood by the viewer to be communicative. [Spence; Tinker.] Symbolic expression of this kind may be forbidden or regulated if the conduct itself may constitutionally be regulated, if the regulation is narrowly drawn to further a substantial governmental interest, and if the interest is unrelated to the suppression of free speech. [O'Brien.]

The United States submits [that] the regulation forbidding sleeping is defensible either as a time, place, or manner restriction or as a regulation of symbolic conduct. We [agree]. The permit that was issued authorized the demonstration but required compliance with [the regulation] which prohibits "camping" on park lands, that is, the use of park lands for living accommodations, such as sleeping, storing personal belongings, making fires, digging, or cooking. These provisions, including the ban on sleeping, are clearly limitations on the manner in which the demonstration could be carried out. That sleeping, like the symbolic tents themselves, may be expressive and part of the message delivered by the demonstration does not make the ban any less a limitation on the manner of demonstrating, for reasonable time, place, and manner regulations normally have the purpose and direct effect of limiting expression but are nevertheless valid. [Taxpayers for Vincent; Heffron; Kovacs v. Cooper (all noted below).] Neither does the fact that sleeping, arguendo, may be expressive conduct, rather than oral or written expression, render the sleeping prohibition any less a time, place, or manner regulation. To the contrary, the Park Service neither attempts to ban sleeping generally nor to ban it everywhere in the Parks. It has established areas for camping and forbids it elsewhere, including Lafayette Park and the Mall. Considered as

---

4. The District Court granted summary judgment for the Park Service. The Court of Appeals reversed in an en banc decision. Community for Creative Non-Violence v. Watt, 703 F.2d 586 (D.C.Cir.1983). By a 6 to 5 vote, the Court of Appeals found the regulations invalid as applied. (The eleven judges produced six opinions.) The Supreme Court reversed that ruling.

5. We reject the suggestion of the plurality below, however, that the burden on the demonstrators is limited to "the advancement of a plausible contention" that their conduct is expressive. Although it is common to place the burden upon the Government to justify impinge-

ments on First Amendment interests, it is the obligation of the person desiring to engage in assertedly expressive conduct to demonstrate that the First Amendment even applies. To hold otherwise would be to create a rule that all conduct is presumptively expressive. In the absence of a showing that such a rule is necessary to protect vital First Amendment interests, we decline to deviate from the general rule that one seeking relief bears the burden of demonstrating that he is entitled to it. [Footnote by Justice White.]

6. Consolidated Edison appears at p. 1122 above. All of the other cases are noted below.

such, we have very little trouble concluding that the Park Service may prohibit overnight sleeping in the parks involved here.

The requirement that the regulation be content neutral is clearly satisfied. [It] is not disputed here that the prohibition on camping, and on sleeping specifically, is content neutral and is not being applied because of disagreement with the message presented. Neither was the regulation faulted, nor could it be, on the ground that without overnight sleeping the plight of the homeless could not be communicated in other ways. The regulation otherwise left the demonstration intact, with its symbolic city, signs, and the presence of those who were willing to take their turns in a day-and-night vigil. Respondents do not suggest that there was, or is, any barrier to delivering to the media, or to the public by other means, the intended message concerning the plight of the homeless. It is also apparent to us that the regulation narrowly focuses on the Government's substantial interest in maintaining the parks in the heart of our capital in an attractive and intact condition, readily available to the millions of people who wish to [enjoy them]. To permit camping [would] be totally inimical to these purposes, as would be readily understood by those who have frequented the National Parks across the country and observed the unfortunate consequences of the activities of those who refuse to confine their camping to designated areas.

[The Court of Appeals held] that if the symbolic city of tents was to be permitted and if the demonstrators did not intend to cook, dig, or engage in aspects of camping other than sleeping, the incremental benefit to the parks could not justify the ban on sleeping, which was here an expressive activity said to enhance the message concerning the plight of the poor and homeless. We cannot agree. In the first place, we seriously doubt that the First Amendment requires the Park Service to permit a demonstration in Lafayette Park and the Mall involving a 24-hour vigil and the erection of tents to accommodate 150 people. Furthermore, although we have assumed for present purposes that the sleeping banned in this case would have an expressive element, it is evident that its major value to this demonstration would be facilitative. Without a permit to sleep, it would be difficult to get the poor and homeless to participate or to be present at all. This much is apparent from the permit application filed by respondents: "Without the incentive of sleeping space or a hot meal, the homeless would not come to the site." The sleeping ban, if enforced, would thus effectively limit the nature, extent, and duration of the demonstration and to that extent ease the pressure on the Parks.

Beyond this, however, it is evident from our cases that the validity of this regulation need not be judged solely by reference to the demonstration at hand. [Heffron.] Absent the prohibition on sleeping, there would be other groups who would demand permission to deliver an asserted message by camping in Lafayette Park. Some of them would surely have as credible a claim in this regard as does CCNV, and the denial of permits to still others would present difficult problems for the Park Service. With the prohibition, however, as is evident in the case before us, at least some around-the-clock demonstrations lasting for days on end will not materialize, others will be limited in size and duration, and the purposes of the regulation will thus be materially served. Perhaps these purposes would be more effectively and not so clumsily achieved by preventing tents and 24-hour vigils entirely in the core areas. But the Park Service's decision to permit non-sleeping demonstrations does not, in our view, impugn the camping prohibition as a valuable, but perhaps imperfect, protection to the parks. If the Government has a legitimate interest in ensuring that the National Parks are adequately protected, which we think it has, and if the parks would be more exposed to harm without the sleeping prohibition than with it, the ban is safe from invalidation under the First Amendment as a reasonable regulation on the manner in which a demonstration may be carried out. As in [Taxpayers for Vincent], the regulation "responds precisely to the substantive problems which legitimately concern the [Government]."

[We] have difficulty, therefore, in understanding why the prohibition against camping, with its ban on sleeping overnight, is not a reasonable time, place, and manner regulation that withstands constitutional scrutiny. Surely the regulation is not unconstitutional on its face. None of its provisions appears unrelated to the ends that it was designed to serve. Nor is it any less valid when applied to prevent camping in Memorial-core parks by those who wish to demonstrate and deliver a message to the public and the central government. Damage to the parks as well as their partial inaccessibility to other members of the public can as easily result from camping by demonstrators as by non-demonstrators. In neither case must the Government tolerate it. All those who would resort to the parks must abide by otherwise valid rules for their use, just as they must observe the traffic laws, sanitation regulations, and laws to preserve the public peace.[7] This is no more than a reaffirmation that reasonable time, place, and manner restrictions on expression are constitutionally acceptable.

Contrary to the conclusion of the Court of Appeals, the foregoing analysis demonstrates that the Park Service regulation is sustainable under the four-factor standard of [O'Brien] for validating a regulation of expressive conduct, which, in the last analysis is little, if any, different from the standard applied to time, place, and manner restrictions.[8] No one contends that aside from its impact on speech a rule against camping or overnight sleeping in public parks is beyond the constitutional power of the Government to enforce. And for the reasons we have discussed above, there is a substantial government interest in conserving park property, an interest that is plainly served by, and requires for its implementation, measures such as the proscription of sleeping that are designed to limit the wear and tear on park properties. That interest is unrelated to suppression of expression.

We are unmoved by the Court of Appeals' view that the challenged regulation is unnecessary, and hence invalid, because there are less speech-restrictive alternatives that could have satisfied the government interest in preserving park lands. There is no gainsaying that preventing overnight sleeping will avoid a measure of actual or threatened damage to Lafayette Park and the Mall. The Court of Appeals' suggestions that the Park Service minimize the possible injury by reducing the size, duration, or frequency of demonstrations would still curtail the total allowable expression in which demonstrators could engage, whether by sleeping or otherwise, and these suggestions represent no more than a disagreement with the Park Service over how much protection the core parks require or how an acceptable level of preservation is to be attained. We do not believe, however, that either

7. When the Government seeks to regulate conduct that is ordinarily non-expressive it may do so regardless of the situs of the application of the regulation. Thus, even against people who choose to violate Park Service regulations for expressive purposes, the Park Service may enforce regulations relating to grazing animals; flying model planes; gambling; hunting and fishing; setting off fireworks; and urination. [Footnote by Justice White.]

8. Reasonable time, place, and manner restrictions are valid even though they directly limit oral or written expression. It would be odd to insist on a higher standard for limitations aimed at regulable conduct and having only an incidental impact on speech. Thus, if the time, place, and manner restriction on expressive sleeping, if that is what is involved in this case, sufficiently and narrowly serves a substantial enough governmental interest to escape First Amendment condemnation, it is untenable to invalidate it under O'Brien on the ground that the governmental interest is insufficient to warrant the intrusion on First Amendment concerns or that there is an inadequate nexus between the regulation and the interest sought to be served. We note that only recently, in a case dealing with the regulation of signs, the Court framed the issue under O'Brien and then based a crucial part of its analysis on the time, place, and manner cases. [Taxpayers for Vincent; 1984; p. 1277 below.] [Footnote by Justice White.]

[O'Brien] or the time, place, and manner decisions assign to the judiciary the authority to replace the Park Service as the manager of the Nation's parks or endow the judiciary with the competence to judge how much protection of park lands is wise and how that level of conservation is to be attained.

[Reversed.] [9]

Justice MARSHALL, with whom Justice BRENNAN joins, dissenting.

The Court's disposition of this case is marked by two related failings. First, the majority is either unwilling or unable to take seriously the First Amendment claims advanced by respondents. [They] are citizens raising issues of profound public importance who have properly turned to the courts for the vindication of their constitutional rights. Second, the majority misapplies the test for ascertaining whether a restraint on speech qualifies as a reasonable time, place, and manner regulation. In determining what constitutes a sustainable regulation, the majority fails to subject the alleged interests of the Government to the degree of scrutiny required to ensure that expressive activity protected by the First Amendment remains free of unnecessary limitations.

I. The proper starting point for analysis [is] a recognition that the activity in which respondents seek to engage [is] symbolic speech protected by the First Amendment. The majority [so] assumes, without deciding. [The] problem with this assumption is that the Court thereby avoids examining closely the reality of [the] planned expression. The majority's approach denatures respondents' asserted right and thus makes all too easy identification of a government interest sufficient to warrant its abridgement. A realistic appraisal of the competing interests at stake in this case requires a closer look at the nature of the expressive conduct at issue and the context in which that conduct would be displayed. [E.g., missing] from the majority's description is any inkling that Lafayette Park and the Mall have served as the sites for some of the most rousing political demonstrations in the Nation's history. [The] primary [1] purpose for making *sleep* an integral part of the demonstration was "to re-enact the central reality of homelessness" and to impress upon public consciousness, in as dramatic a way as possible, that homelessness is a widespread problem, often ignored, that confronts its victims with life-threatening [deprivations].

In a long line of cases, this Court has afforded First Amendment protection to expressive conduct that qualifies as symbolic speech. [Tinker; Brown v. Louisiana (1966; p. 1241 below); Stromberg.] In light of the surrounding context, respondents' proposed activity meets the qualifications. The Court has previously acknowledged the importance of context in determining whether an act can properly be denominated as "speech" for First Amendment purposes and has provided guidance concerning the way in which courts should "read" a context in making this determination. The leading case is [Spence], where this

---

9. In a separate statement, Chief Justice BURGER concurred "fully in the Court's opinion" and added: "The actions here claimed as speech [simply] are not speech; rather, they constitute conduct." After quoting from Justice Black's concurrence with a similar emphasis in Cox v. Louisiana I (1965; p. 1225 below), the Chief Justice continued: "Respondents' attempt at camping [is] a form of 'picketing'; it is conduct, not speech. Moreover, it is conduct that interferes with the rights of others to use Lafayette Park for the purposes for which it was created. Lafayette Park and others like it are for all the people, and their rights are not to be trespassed even by those who have some 'statement' to make. [Of course], the Constitution guarantees that people may make their 'state-

ments,' but Washington has countless places for the kind of 'statement' these respondents sought to make. It trivializes the First Amendment to seek to use it as a shield in the manner asserted here. And it tells us something about why many people must wait for their 'day in court' when the time of the courts is preempted by frivolous proceedings that delay the causes of litigants who have legitimate, nonfrivolous claims."

1. Another purpose for making sleep part of the demonstration was to enable participants to weather the rigors of the round-the-clock vigil and to encourage other homeless persons to participate in the [demonstration]. [Footnote by Justice Marshall.]

Court [looked] first to the intent of the speaker and second to the perception of the audience. Here respondents clearly intended to protest the reality of homelessness by sleeping outdoors in the winter in the near vicinity of the [White House].

Nor can there be any doubt that in the surrounding circumstances the likelihood was great that the political significance of sleeping in the parks would be understood by those who viewed it. [This] likelihood stems from the remarkably apt fit between the activity in which respondents seek to engage and the social problems they seek to highlight.[2] [It] is true that we all go to sleep as part of our daily regimen and that, for the most part, sleep represents a physical necessity and not a vehicle for expression. But these characteristics need not prevent an activity that is normally devoid of expressive purpose from being used as a novel mode of communication. Sitting or standing in a library is a commonplace activity necessary to facilitate ends usually having nothing to do with making a statement. Moreover, sitting or standing is not conduct that an observer would normally construe as expressive conduct. However, for Negroes to stand or sit in a "whites only" library in Louisiana in 1965 was powerfully expressive; in that particular context, those acts became "monuments of protest" against segregation. [Brown.]

The Government contends that a forseeable difficulty of administration counsels against recognizing sleep as a mode of expression protected by the First Amendment. The predicament the Government envisions can be termed "the imposter problem": the problem of distinguishing bona fide protesters from imposters whose requests for permission to sleep in Lafayette Park or the Mall on First Amendment grounds would mask ulterior designs—the simple desire, for example, to avoid the expense of hotel lodgings. The Government maintains that such distinctions cannot be made without inquiring into the sincerity of demonstrators and that such an inquiry would itself pose dangers to First Amendment values because it would necessarily be content-sensitive. I find this argument unpersuasive. First, a variety of circumstances *already* require government agencies to engage in the delicate task of inquiring into the sincerity of claimants asserting First Amendment rights. [Justice Marshall referred to several cases involving religious claims—see chap. 14 below.] Second, the administrative difficulty the Government envisions is now nothing more than a vague apprehension. [The Government also] contends that the Spence approach is overinclusive because it accords First Amendment status to a wide variety of acts that, although expressive, are obviously subject to prohibition. As the Government notes, "[a]ctions such as assassination of political figures and the bombing of government buildings can fairly be characterized as intended to convey a message that is readily perceived by the public." The Government's argument would pose a difficult problem were the determination whether an act constitutes "speech" the end of First Amendment analysis. But such a determination is not the end. If an act is defined as speech, it must still be balanced against countervailing government interests. The balancing which the First Amendment requires would doom any argument seeking to protect anti-social acts such as assassination or destruction of government property from government interference because compelling interests would outweigh the expressive value of such conduct.

II. Although sleep in the context of this case is symbolic speech protected by the First Amendment, it is nonetheless subject to reasonable time, place, and manner restrictions. I agree with the standard enunciated by the majority [at

---

2. For a somewhat similar emphasis on this factor, see the comment on the decision in the Court of Appeals in Note, "First Amendment Protection of Ambiguous Conduct," 84 Colum.L. Rev. 467 (1984).

the beginning of Part II of Justice White's opinion].[3] I conclude, however, that the regulations at issue [here], as applied to respondents, fail to satisfy this standard. [The] issue posed by this case is not whether the Government is constitutionally compelled to permit the erection of tents and the staging of a continuous 24-hour vigil; rather, the issue is whether any substantial government interest is served by banning sleep that is part of a political demonstration.

What the Court may be suggesting is that if the tents and the 24-hour vigil are permitted, but not constitutionally required to be permitted, then respondents have no constitutional right to engage in expressive conduct that supplements these activities. Put in arithmetical terms, the Court appears to contend that if x is permitted by grace rather than by constitutional compulsion, x + 1 can be denied without regard to the requirements the Government must normally satisfy in order to restrain protected activity. This notion, however, represents a misguided conception of the First Amendment. The First Amendment requires the Government to justify *every* instance of abridgement. [The] stringency of that requirement is not diminished simply because the activity the Government seeks to restrain is supplemental to other activity that the Government may have permitted out of grace but was not constitutionally compelled to [allow]. [The majority also suggests] that, although sleeping contains an element of expression, "its major value to [the] demonstration would have been facilitative." While this observation does provide a hint of the weight the Court attaches to respondents' First Amendment claims,[4] it is utterly irrelevant to whether the Government's ban on sleeping advances a substantial government interest. [Moreover, the] majority fails to offer any evidence indicating that the absence of an absolute ban on sleeping would present administrative problems to the Park Service that are substantially more difficult than those it ordinarily confronts. A mere apprehension of difficulties should not be enough to overcome the right to free expression. [E.g., Tinker.]

The Court's erroneous application of the standard for ascertaining a reasonable time, place, and manner restriction is also revealed by the majority's conclusion that a substantial governmental interest is served by the sleeping ban because it will discourage "around-the-clock demonstrations for days" and thus further the regulation's purpose "to limit wear and tear on park properties." The majority cites no evidence indicating that sleeping engaged in as symbolic speech will cause *substantial* wear and tear on park property. Furthermore, the Government's application of the sleeping ban in the circumstances of this case is strikingly underinclusive. The majority acknowledges that a proper time, place, and manner restriction must be "narrowly tailored." Here, however, the tailoring requirement is virtually forsaken inasmuch as the Government offers no justification for applying its absolute ban on sleeping yet is willing to allow respondents to engage in activities—such as feigned sleeping—that is no less burdensome. In short, there are no substantial governmental interests advanced by the Government's regulations as applied to respondents. All that the Court's decision advances are the prerogatives of a bureaucracy that over the years has

---

3. I also agree with the majority that no substantial difference distinguishes the test applicable to time, place, and manner restrictions and the test articulated in United States v. O'Brien. [Footnote by Justice Marshall.]

4. The facilitative purpose of the sleep-in takes away nothing from its independent status as symbolic speech. Moreover, facilitative conduct that is closely related to expressive activity is itself protected by First Amendment considerations. I therefore find myself in agreement with Judge Ginsburg [of the D.C. Circuit] who noted that "the personal non-communicative aspect of

sleeping in symbolic tents at a demonstration site bears a close, functional relationship to an activity that is commonly comprehended as 'free speech.'" "[S]leeping in the tents rather than simply standing or sitting down in them allows the demonstrator to sustain his or her protest without stopping short of the officially-granted round-the-clock permission." For me, as for Judge Ginsburg, that linkage itself "suffices to require a genuine effort to balance the demonstrators' interests against other concerns for which the government bears responsibility." [Footnote by Justice Marshall.]

shown an implacable hostility towards citizens' exercise of First Amendment rights.

III.　　The disposition of this case impels me to make two additional observations.　First, in this case, as in some others involving time, place, and manner restrictions,[5] the Court has dramatically lowered its scrutiny of governmental regulations once it has determined that such regulations are content neutral. The result has been the creation of a two-tiered approach to First Amendment cases: while regulations that turn on the content of the expression are subjected to a strict form of judicial review,[6] regulations that are aimed at matters other than expression receive only a minimal level of scrutiny.　The minimal scrutiny prong of this two-tiered approach has led to an unfortunate diminution of First Amendment protection.　By narrowly limiting its concern to whether a given regulation creates a content-based distinction, the Court has seemingly overlooked the fact that content-neutral restrictions are also capable of unnecessarily restricting protected expressive activity.[7]　To be sure, the general prohibition against content-based regulations is an essential tool of First Amendment analysis.　[Mosley.]　The Court, however, has transformed the ban against content-distinctions from a floor that offers all persons at least equal liberty under the First Amendment into a ceiling that restricts persons to the protection of First Amendment equality—but nothing more.[8]　The consistent imposition of silence upon all may fulfill the dictates of an even-handed content-neutrality. But it offends our "profound national commitment to the principle that debate on public issues should be uninhibited, robust, and wide-open." [New York Times v. Sullivan.]

Second, the disposition of this case reveals a mistaken assumption regarding the motives and behavior of government officials who create and administer content-neutral regulations.　The Court's salutary skepticism of governmental decisionmaking in First Amendment matters suddenly dissipates once it determines that a restriction is not content-based.　The Court evidently assumes that the balance struck by officials is deserving of deference so long as it does not appear to be tainted by content discrimination.　What the Court fails to recognize is that public officials have strong incentives to overregulate even in the absence of an intent to censor particular views.　This incentive stems from

---

5.　See, e.g., [Taxpayers for Vincent; Heffron].　But see [United States v. Grace; Tinker; Brown v. Louisiana.]　[Footnote by Justice Marshall.　All of these cases—with the exception of Tinker, above—are considered below.]

6.　[It] should be noted, however, that there is a context in which regulations that are facially content-neutral are nonetheless subjected to strict scrutiny.　This situation arises when a regulation vests standardless discretion in officials empowered to dispense permits for the use of public forums.　[See, e.g., Lovell; Hague; Shuttlesworth—all in sec. 4 below.]　[Footnote by Justice Marshall.]

7.　See Redish, The Content Distinction in First Amendment Analysis, 34 Stan.L.Rev. 113 (1981).　[Footnote by Justice Marshall.]

8.　Furthermore, a content-neutral regulation does not necessarily fall with random or equal force upon different groups or different points of view.　A content-neutral regulation that restricts an inexpensive mode of communication will fall most heavily upon relatively poor speakers and the points of view that such speakers typically espouse.　See, e.g., [Taxpayers for Vincent]. This sort of latent inequality is very much in

evidence in this case for respondents lack the financial means necessary to buy access to more conventional modes of persuasion.

A disquieting feature about the disposition of this case is that it lends credence to the charge that judicial administration of the First Amendment, in conjunction with a social order marked by large disparities in wealth and other sources of power, tends systematically to discriminate against efforts by the relatively disadvantaged to convey their political ideas.　In the past, this Court has taken such considerations into account in adjudicating the First Amendment rights of those among us who are financially deprived. See, e.g., [Martin v. Struthers; Marsh v. Alabama].　Such solicitude is noticeably absent from the majority's opinion, continuing a trend that has not escaped the attention of commentators. See, e.g., Dorsen & Gora, Free Speech, Property, and the Burger Court: Old Values, New Balances, 1982 Sup.Ct.Rev. 195; Van Alstyne, The Recrudescence of Property Rights as the Foremost Principle of [Civil Liberties], 43 Law & Contemp.Prob. 66 [1980].　[Footnote by Justice Marshall.]

the fact that of the two groups whose interests officials must accommodate—on the one hand, the interests of the general public and on the other, the interests of those who seek to use a particular forum for First Amendment activity—the political power of the former is likely to be far greater than that of the latter. The political dynamics likely to lead officials to a disproportionate sensitivity to regulatory as opposed to First Amendment interests can be discerned in the background of this case. [It illustrates] concretely that government agencies by their very nature are driven to overregulate public forums to the detriment of First Amendment rights, that facial viewpoint-neutrality is no shield against unnecessary restrictions on unpopular ideas or modes of expression, and that in this case in particular there was evidence readily available that should have impelled the Court to subject the Government's restrictive policy to something more than minimal [scrutiny].[9]

SECTION 4. EXPRESSION IN PUBLIC PLACES AND THE MAINTENANCE OF LOCAL PEACE AND ORDER: NEUTRAL "TIME, PLACE, AND MANNER" REGULATIONS RATHER THAN CONTENT–BASED RESTRAINTS IN THE "PUBLIC FORUM"?

A. ASSURED MINIMUM ACCESS OR MERELY EQUAL ACCESS TO THE PUBLIC FORUM?—AN OVERVIEW

Introduction. To what extent may government regulate those who want to march in city streets or ring doorbells or speak in the parks to publicize their views? To what extent does concern with such values as order and quiet and traffic control and audience sensibilities justify curbs on expression? Restraints on speech in the interest of local tranquility did not reach the Court until the late 1930s. But since then, these problems have produced a constant flow of litigation as a variety of minorities, from Jehovah's Witnesses at the outset to anti-war and civil rights demonstrators in later years, sought to use streets, parks, and other public places to change views and induce action. What legal analyses

9. The principal case warrants especially careful examination, for it bears importantly not only on the introductory materials above, but also on the materials that follow in sec. 4. First, the case involves the symbolic expression problem, the immediate focus of this section, and raises the question whether the fairly generous attitude toward symbolic speech established since Spence has been eroded. Second, it addresses the content-based/content-neutral distinction considered (and criticized) in sec. 2 above and pursued more fully below. Note especially Justice Marshall's criticism that the Court's solicitude about content-based distinctions risks undue judicial deference to content-neutral ones. Third, it considers the problems of "time, place, and manner" restrictions and of access to the public forum that are the focus of sec. 4. Note that the majority and the dissent agree on the formulation of the appropriate standard for reviewing time, place, and manner restrictions—a standard that is not as strict as that applicable to restrictions directly aimed at the content of speech. Importantly, however, Justice Marshall insists that the exercise of that lower level scrutiny for time, place and manner restrictions by the majority is too casual and lenient. Fourth, the majority relies not only on the standard for time, place, and manner restrictions but also on the criteria set forth in the O'Brien multi-step analysis, considered earlier in this section. Note that the majority and the dissent agree that the lower level of scrutiny of the O'Brien analysis for regulations "unrelated to the suppression of free speech" is not substantially different from the lower level scrutiny prescribed for time, place, and manner regulations. Fifth, note that Justice Marshall (in his footnote 14), considers (as the majority does not) the substantial and unequal impact that even a content-neutral regulation may have on the opportunity of relatively poor speakers to utilize inexpensive modes of communication. Recall the comments on "format discrimination" at p. 1168, in sec. 2, above.

are appropriate in evaluating the claims of those who seek access to public places—who seek to use the "public forum"—to air their views?

1. *The First Amendment "right" to a public forum: A presumptive* right *of assured access to some public places, or mere opportunity for equal, non-discriminatory access?* In view of the range of variables presented by the materials in this section, it is useful to bear in mind a pervasive problem often obscured in the Court opinions. What *are* the plausible dimensions of a presumptive First Amendment claim to use streets, parks, and other public places?[1] A broad public forum position might argue, for example, that government *must* make some public places available for the expression of ideas. It would insist that access to places such as streets and parks is of special importance as the "poor man's printing press," for those who cannot afford to resort to other means of communication, who cannot effectively reach audiences through alternative, often costlier channels. A narrower public forum theory would limit government's obligation to that of providing *equal* access to public places: it would require only that government not use its power over public places to impose content-based restrictions and discriminate among competing views. The broad, "assured minimum access" issue arises, for example, when a city decides that *no one* can use streets or parks for meetings; the narrower, "equal access" view concentrates scrutiny on situations where a city allows some speakers but not others to use public property.

Those who urge the broader, guaranteed access view frequently quote a statement in Justice ROBERTS' opinion in HAGUE v. CIO, 307 U.S. 496 (1939): "Wherever the title of streets and parks may rest they have immemorially been held in trust for the use of the public and, time out of mind, have been used for purposes of assembly, communicating thoughts between citizens, and discussing public questions. Such use of the streets and public places has, from ancient times, been a part of the privileges, immunities, rights and liberties of citizens. The privilege [to] use the streets and parks for communication of views on national questions may be regulated in the interest of all; [but] it must not, in the guise of regulation, be abridged or denied."[2] Contrast a narrower view at the polar extreme from that of Justice Roberts—a view articulated by Justice Holmes while sitting on the highest Massachusetts court. HOLMES said in MASSACHUSETTS v. DAVIS (1895):[3] "For the legislature absolutely or conditionally to forbid public speaking in a highway or public park is no more an infringement of the rights of a member of the public than for the owner of a private house to forbid it in his house." No modern Justice views a city's control of its public property as broadly as Justice Holmes did. In the narrow, equal access public forum position, there is at least recognition that a city may not grant access on a discriminatory basis, may not use its control of public places to impose content-based restraints on speech. A recurrent question pursued in this section concerns the contours of that position, and whether a

---

1. A "presumptive First Amendment claim" as used here does not mean that all restrictions on access would be impermissible. It suggests only that, whenever a speaker seeks access to public places for First Amendment activities, government may not restrict that access without meeting a standard akin to strict scrutiny—a standard requiring "compelling" ends and carefully tailored means (e.g., a resort to "less restrictive alternatives").

2. The ultimate holding in Hague rested on narrower grounds. Justice Roberts (citing Lovell v. Griffin, the next principal case) found a Jersey City, N.J., ordinance "void upon its face" because access to streets and parks required a permit, and the standards of the ordinance governing issuance of the permit did not adequately curb the possible use of discretion. Thus, a permit could be refused on the "mere opinion [of the head of the police] that such refusal will prevent 'riots, disturbances or disorderly assemblage.' It can thus [be] made the instrument of arbitrary suppression of free expression of views on [national affairs]." That risked "uncontrolled official suppression."

3. 162 Mass. 510, 39 N.E. 113 (1895), affirmed 167 U.S. 43 (1897—before free speech was recognized as an aspect of liberty protected by the 14th Amendment).

First Amendment public forum claim should imply more than that. Put another way, this question is an aspect of the theme raised in sec. 2, above: Are First Amendment interests adequately protected if the primary or sole concern of the Court is with the elimination of content-based restrictions, or does the First Amendment also require serious scrutiny of the impact on free speech of content-neutral restraints?

Under the narrower, equal access view, flat bans on the use of at least some public places may be permissible. "Time, place, and manner" regulations would be sustained so long as they were framed and applied in a content-neutral manner—or at least would be subjected to a relatively low level of scrutiny. Judicial scrutiny of regulations would mainly seek to assure that they are not devices to exercise control over the content of speech. The broader, assured access view would worry not only about the neutrality of "time, place, and manner" regulations, but would also strike down evenhanded regulations when they unduly curtailed a "public forum" right of assured access—i.e., unduly impinged upon the opportunities of the speaker to express views and reach an audience. In examining the cases that follow, note when the Court is concerned merely with assuring the evenhandedness of access controls and when it recognizes that a broader claim—denominated here as an assured minimum access claim—is entitled to consideration.

The underlying tensions between the broad view of the public forum concept as one that supports an assured minimum access claim and the narrower view that would largely safeguard against only nonneutral, unequal restraints on access help to explain the emphases and conflicts in many of the cases below. Analysis of these cases in terms of those contending positions is complicated by the fact that the broad, guaranteed access argument is not advocated by any Justice as one applicable to all public property at all times. For example, some public places—the Senate gallery? courtrooms? libraries? jails?—may be so anomalous as places for speech as to justify total exclusion of "public forum" uses. And in other public places where the broad view would recognize some assured access, some "time, place, and manner" restraints may nevertheless be permissible: e.g., prohibitions of noisy parades in residential areas late at night or of mass gatherings on heavily travelled streets during the rush hour. In short, even the broad, assured access public forum position typically requires the balancing of competing interests. But the broad view would argue that such "time, place, and manner" restraints warrant more than deferential or intermediate scrutiny and must satisfy the strict scrutiny, as to both ends and means, that is appropriate in other First Amendment areas.[4]

4. For useful analyses of the competing views, see Note, "The Public Forum: Minimum Access, Equal Access, and the First Amendment," 28 Stan.L.Rev. 117 (1975), and Note, "A Unitary Approach to Claims of First Amendment Access to Publicly Owned Property," 35 Stan.L.Rev. 121 (1982).

The 1982 Note urges "a unitary approach that requires direct examination and evaluation of the competing [interests]." It argues that the Court "should uphold restrictions on expressions only when the restrictions are the least restrictive means of serving a compelling state interest." In examining the materials that follow, consider the differences between that approach and the analyses used by the modern Court; and consider as well whether the proposed "unitary approach" would be a more manageable as well as a more speech-protective one. (The Note states that the modern Court "has used a categorization approach" by classifying "some places as public forums and other places as nonforums. In places classified as public forums, the validity of restrictions on expression depends on how the Court further classifies the restrictions. A law that relates to the content of expression requires greater justification than a law that is content-neutral. A law that restricts expression in a nonforum requires still less justification." The Note suggests that the Court abolish not only "the distinction between public forums and nonforums," but also "the distinction between content-based and content-neutral restrictions. By incorrectly implying that content-neutral restrictions are inherently less serious matters than content-based restrictions, this system of categorization [tends] to trivialize serious restrictions on expression." For cases elaborating the public

Many of the opinions that follow (e.g., Justice Frankfurter's survey, note 2 below) speak of "the primary use of streets and parks" as a legitimate interest limiting expression in public places. Does this formulation suggest that use of streets and parks for speech is ordinarily a secondary use, to be subordinated whenever traffic or recreation are threatened? Does it imply that a state can completely bar the use of public places for expression, for the purpose of protecting the "primary" use? Is its concern solely with assuring that whatever access the city chooses to permit is delineated and applied evenhandedly? In short, the "primary use of streets and parks" emphasis may reflect the narrower, equal access position, rather than the broad, assured minimum access one. Are there nevertheless occasions when free speech values and public forum claims compel traffic and recreation to give way to speech? Cf. Schneider (1939, p. 1206 below). Do the Court's analyses adequately promote inquiry into the question of when free speech values should prevail? Does the Roberts statement in Hague v. CIO suggest that "discussing public questions," not simply traffic and recreation, deserves recognition as a "primary use" of streets and parks? In short, to what extent do the cases in this section adequately recognize the importance of a right of access to public forums? [5]

2. *Justice Frankfurter's survey of contexts and problems.* [For an overview of the range of problems presented by regulations of expression in public places, consider the following suggestions for classification and analysis. They are from a survey of the background written by Justice Frankfurter in 1951, after only a little more than a decade of Court experience with these questions. Justice Frankfurter undertook this review in a concurring opinion (in NIEMOTKO v. MARYLAND, 340 U.S. 268, 273) reexamining the problem of "how to reconcile the interest in allowing free expression of ideas in public places with the protection of the public peace and of the primary uses of streets and parks." [6] Justice FRANKFURTER stated in Niemotko:]

[Previous decisions primarily] concerned with restrictions upon expression in its divers forms in public places have answered problems varying greatly in content and difficulty. The easiest cases have been those in which the only interest opposing free communication was that of keeping the streets of the community clean. This could scarcely justify prohibiting the dissemination of information by handbills or censoring their contents. [In] a group of related cases, regulation of solicitation has been the issue. Here the opposing interest is more substantial—protection of the public from fraud and from criminals who use solicitation as a device to enter homes. [Control] of speeches made in streets and parks draws on still different considerations—protection of the public

forum-nonpublic forum distinction, see the decisions beginning with Greer v. Spock (1976; military bases; p. 1252 below).

5. For an especially thoughtful discussion of the public forum problem (and an endorsement of a broad, guaranteed access view), see Kalven, "The Concept of the Public Forum: Cox v. Louisiana," 1965 Sup.Ct.Rev. 1. Kalven suggested three interrelated themes for the examination of public forum problems: "First, that in an open democratic society the streets, the parks, and other public places are an important facility for public discussion and political process. They are in brief a public forum that the citizen can commandeer." (Kalven suggests later, however, that use of some public places for expression would be "anomalous": "Certainly it is easy to think of public places, swimming pools, for example, so clearly dedicated to recreational use

that talk of their use as a public forum would in general be totally unpersuasive.") "Second, that only confusion can result from distinguishing sharply between 'speech pure' and 'speech plus.' And, third, that what is required is in effect a set of Robert's Rules of Order for the new uses of the public forum, albeit the designing of such rules poses a problem of formidable practical difficulty." Is the "Robert's Rules" concept a "happy analogy" because, as Kalven suggested, "concern ought not to be with censorship, or with the content of what is said; what is needed is a phasing or timing of the activity, not a ban on it"?

6. Justice Frankfurter's opinion was one concurring in the result in three cases (all considered below, at pp. 1219 and 1224): Feiner v. New York, and Kunz v. New York, as well as Niemotko v. Maryland.

peace and of the primary uses of travel and recreation for which streets and parks exist. [An attempt to assert] the right of a city to exercise any power over its parks, however arbitrary or discriminatory, was rejected in [Hague v. CIO]. Cox v. New Hampshire made it clear that the [Constitution] does not deny localities the power to devise a licensing system if the exercise of discretion by the licensing officials is appropriately confined. Two cases have involved the additional considerations incident to the use of [sound trucks].

The results in these multifarious cases have been expressed in language looking in two directions. While the Court has emphasized the importance of "free speech," it has recognized that "free speech" is not in itself a touchstone. The Constitution is not unmindful of other important interests, such as public order, if interference with free expression of ideas is not found to be the overbalancing consideration. More important than the phrasing of the opinions are the questions on which the decisions appear to have turned.

(1) What is the interest deemed to require the regulation of speech? The State cannot of course forbid public proselyting or religious argument merely because public officials disapprove the speaker's views. It must act in patent good faith to maintain the public peace, to assure the availability of the streets for their primary purposes of passenger and vehicular traffic, or for equally indispensable ends of modern community life.

(2) What is the method used to achieve such ends as a consequence of which public speech is constrained or barred? A licensing standard which gives an official authority to censor the content of a speech differs *toto coelo* from one limited by its terms, or by nondiscriminatory practice, to considerations of public safety and the like. Again, a sanction applied after the event assures consideration of the particular circumstances of a situation. The net of control must not be cast too broadly.

(3) What mode of speech is regulated? A sound truck may be found to affect the public peace as normal speech does not. A man who is calling names or using the kind of language which would reasonably stir another to violence does not have the same claim to protection as one whose speech is an appeal to reason.

(4) Where does the speaking which is regulated take place? Not only the general classifications—streets, parks, private buildings—are relevant. The location and size of a park; its customary use for the recreational, esthetic and contemplative needs of a community; the facilities, other than a park or street corner, readily available in a community for airing views, are all pertinent [considerations].

Transitional note. As Justice Frankfurter's survey reminds, the themes suggested in note 1 are not the only ones that pervade the materials that follow. Additional variables abound. For example, what competing interests justify curtailment of the speaker: The interest in preventing outbreaks of violence? In protecting the sensibilities and repose of listeners, willing and unwilling? In safeguarding the "primary uses" of the public places? Even if a broad, assured access view is accepted, interference with other uses may become an especially important restraining factor when the focus of the cases shifts from traditional public forums such as streets and parks to more novel environments such as libraries, jails and transit facilities. Moreover, the appropriate standards may vary with the nature of the regulatory scheme: Is licensing properly more suspect than subsequent restraint? When may a speaker ignore an apparently invalid licensing scheme, and when must he or she show compliance with it as a precondition to a court challenge? The materials that follow are designed to aid pursuit of the basic themes raised in these introductory notes.[7]

B. DOCTRINAL FOUNDATIONS: THE LEGACY OF THE EARLY CASES

The cases in this subsection illustrate the Court's earliest encounters with the problem of regulating access to public places. The cases continue to be widely cited by the modern Court. What do they contribute in the search for answers to the questions posed above? Lovell and Cox are early guideposts regarding the impermissible and the permissible in permit schemes; Cantwell is an early example of the control of street use through a breach of the peace prosecution. Both techniques of control—prior licensing and subsequent punishment—recur in the later materials. What did these early cases contribute to analysis of the validity of the regulatory schemes invoked—and to the delineation of the scope of a justifiable First Amendment public forum access claim?[1]

LOVELL v. GRIFFIN, 303 U.S. 444 (1938): An ordinance of the city of Griffin, Georgia, prohibited the distribution of "circulars, handbooks, advertising, or literature of any kind" within the city "without first obtaining written permission from the City Manager." Alma Lovell, a Jehovah's Witness, distributed religious tracts without applying for a permit. She challenged her conviction on free press and free exercise of religion grounds. Chief Justice Hughes' opinion for a unanimous Court, in reversing her conviction, stated:

"The ordinance is not limited to 'literature' that is obscene or offensive to public morals or that advocates unlawful conduct. [It] embraces 'literature' in the widest sense. The ordinance is comprehensive with respect to the method of distribution. There is thus no restriction in its application with respect to time or place. It is not limited to ways which might be regarded as inconsistent with the maintenance of public order or as involving disorderly conduct, the molestation of the inhabitants, or the misuse or littering of the streets. The ordinance prohibits the distribution of literature of any kind at any time, at any place, and in any manner without a permit from the City Manager.

"We think that the ordinance is invalid on its face. Whatever the motive which induced its adoption, its character is such that it strikes at the very foundation of the freedom of the press by subjecting it to license and censorship. The struggle for the freedom of the press was primarily directed against the power of the licensor. It was against that power that John Milton directed

---

7. The organizational scheme is partly topical, partly chronological. Both emphases are needed for adequate exploration of the Court's responses to disparate public places problems. The materials below accordingly begin (sec. 4B) with a group of cases from the period in which the Court first encountered public forum issues— cases on which the modern Court places frequent reliance despite their occasionally ambiguous content. The materials then turn to a largely topical organization, considering a range of competing interests that have been asserted as justifications for curtailing the speaker—from protecting residents from noise and annoyance (sec. 4C) to avoiding violence because of hostile audience reactions (sec. 4D). Sec. 4E examines the

Court's response to the protest demonstrations of the 1960s in the traditional street setting; sec. 4F surveys access claims to nontraditional public forums—to public places other than parks and streets. (It concludes with two modern decisions set forth at length, in order to survey and contrast the range of techniques in vogue on the contemporary Court.) Sec. 4G focuses on the modern Court's responses to access claims in contexts other than public property, from the use of private shopping centers as a "forum" to problems of access to the privately owned media.

1. See the questions about these cases at p. 1205 below.

his [assault]. And the liberty of the press became initially a right to publish *'without* a license what formerly could be published only *with* one.' While this freedom from previous restraint upon publication cannot be regarded as exhausting the guaranty of liberty, the prevention of that restraint was a leading purpose in the adoption of the [constitutional provision]. [Near v. Minnesota.] As the ordinance is void on its face, it was not necessary for appellant to seek a permit under it. She was entitled to contest its validity in answer to the charge against [her]." *

COX v. NEW HAMPSHIRE, 312 U.S. 569 (1941): In this case, Chief Justice HUGHES, once again writing for a unanimous Court, affirmed a conviction of several Jehovah's Witnesses for violating a state law prohibiting a "parade or procession" upon a public street without a special license issued by local authorities.[1] Chief Justice Hughes stated the facts as follows: "The sixty-eight defendants and twenty other persons met at a hall in the City of Manchester on the evening of Saturday, July 8, 1939, 'for the purpose of engaging in an information march.' The company was divided into four or five groups, each with about fifteen to twenty persons. Each group then proceeded to a different part of the business district of the city and there 'would line up in single-file formation and then proceed to march along the sidewalk, "single-file," that is, following one another.' Each of the defendants carried a small staff with a sign reading 'Religion is a Snare and a Racket' and on the reverse 'Serve God and Christ the King.' Some of the marchers carried placards bearing the statement 'Fascism or Freedom. Hear Judge Rutherford and Face the Facts.' The marchers also handed out printed leaflets announcing a meeting to be held at a later time in the hall from which they had started, where a talk on government would be given to the public free of charge. Defendants did not apply for a permit and none was issued. [The] state court thus summarizes the effect of the march: 'Manchester had a population of over 75,000 in 1930, and there was testimony that on Saturday nights in an hour's time 26,000 persons passed one of the intersections where the defendants marched. The marchers interfered with the normal sidewalk travel, but no technical breach of the peace occurred.' "

In explaining the reasons for affirming the convictions, Chief Justice Hughes stated: "Civil liberties imply the existence of an organized society maintaining

---

* The issue noted in the last two sentences of Lovell is a recurrent and difficult one. May a person ignore an allegedly unconstitutional permit scheme and still challenge it in court (as a defense to a prosecution for speaking without a permit)? Must the speaker seek to comply with the permit requirement in order to challenge it? The problem is considered in light of later cases in the note on compliance with permit requirements, p. 1235 below. See also the next case, Cox v. New Hampshire, and compare Poulos v. New Hampshire, 345 U.S. 395 (1953), where a conviction for holding a meeting in a park without a required permit was sustained without considering the argument that the denial had been arbitrary, because the speakers had not gone to court to challenge the denial of the permission. In Poulos, unlike Lovell, the law requiring a permit was valid on its face; it was the administrative denial of the permit that was claimed to be unconstitutional.

Under cases like Lovell, then, speakers need not challenge the denial of permission in advance—or even to seek permission—where the claim is that the law is unconstitutional *on its*

face. But if the challenge is that a valid law is unconstitutionally *applied,* the challengers cannot go ahead and hold their meeting or parade if they want to preserve their constitutional defenses. See also the problem of compliance with court orders restraining parades or meetings, in Walker v. Birmingham, p. 1236 below.

1. The statute provided: "No theatrical or dramatic representation shall be performed or exhibited, and no parade or procession upon any public street or way, and no open-air public meeting upon any ground abutting thereon, shall be permitted, unless a special license therefor shall first be obtained from the selectmen of the town, or from a licensing committee for cities hereinafter provided for." New Hampshire law also provided for the creation of licensing boards by cities and included a licensing and fee section stating: "Every such special license shall be in writing, and shall specify the day and hour of the permit to perform or exhibit or of such parade, procession or open-air public meeting. Every licensee shall pay in advance for such license, for the use of the city or town, a sum not more than three hundred dollars for each [day]."

public order without which liberty itself would be lost in the excesses of unrestrained abuses. The authority of a municipality to impose regulations in order to assure the safety and convenience of the people in the use of public highways has never been regarded as inconsistent with civil liberties. [The] control of travel on the streets of cities is the most familiar illustration of this recognition of social need. Where a restriction of the use of highways in that relation is designed to promote the public convenience in the interest of all, it cannot be disregarded by the attempted exercise of some civil right which in other circumstances would be entitled to protection. One would not be justified in ignoring the familiar red traffic light because he thought it his religious duty to disobey the municipal command or sought by that means to direct public attention to an announcement of his opinions. As regulation of the use of the streets for parades and processions is a traditional exercise of control by local government, the question in a particular case is whether that control is exerted so as not to deny or unwarrantedly abridge the right of assembly and the opportunities for the communication of thought and the discussion of public questions immemorially associated with resort to public places.

"In the instant case, we are aided by the opinion of the Supreme Court of the State, [which] defined the limitations of the authority conferred for the granting of licenses. [T]he state court considered and defined the duty of the licensing authority and the rights of the appellants to a license for their parade, with regard only to considerations of time, place and manner so as to conserve the public convenience. The obvious advantage of requiring application for a permit was noted as giving the public authorities notice in advance so as to afford opportunity for proper policing. And the court further observed that, in fixing time and place, the license served 'to prevent confusion by overlapping parades or processions, to secure convenient use of the streets by other travelers, and to minimize the risk of disorder.' But the court held that the licensing board was not vested with arbitrary power or an unfettered discretion; that its discretion must be exercised with 'uniformity of method of treatment upon the facts of each application, free from improper or inappropriate consider-ations and from unfair discrimination'; that a 'systematic, consistent and just order of treatment, with reference to the convenience of public use of the highways, is the statutory mandate.' The defendants, said the court, 'had a right, under the Act, to a license to march when, where and as they did, if after a required investigation it was found that the convenience of the public in the use of the streets would not thereby be unduly disturbed, upon such conditions or changes in time, place and manner as would avoid disturbance.'

"If a municipality has authority to control the use of its public streets for parades or processions, as it undoubtedly has, it cannot be denied authority to give consideration, without unfair discrimination, to time, place and manner in relation to the other proper uses of the streets. We find it impossible to say that the limited authority conferred by the licensing provisions of the statute in question as thus construed by the state court contravened any constitutional right.[2] [There] is no evidence that the statute has been administered otherwise

---

2. The Court also sustained the license fee requirement, noting that it was "not a revenue tax, but one to meet the expense incident to the administration of the Act." It concluded: "There is nothing contrary to the Constitution in the charge of a fee limited to the purpose stated."

Should municipalities be permitted to impose fees—even very large fees—so long as they are designed to defray the cost of policing? Could such a scheme be attacked as imposing an undue

financial burden on the exercise of a constitution-al right? See generally Blasi, "Prior Restraints on Demonstrations," 68 Mich.L.Rev. 1481 (1970). Are advance payment conditions—e.g., insurance requirements—more clearly vulnerable to a First Amendment attack? See the litigation pertaining to the planned Nazi demonstrations in Skokie and Chicago in the late 1970s, p. 1237 below.

than in the fair and non-discriminatory manner which the state court has construed it to [require]."[3]

CANTWELL v. CONNECTICUT

310 U.S. 296, 60 S.Ct. 900, 84 L.Ed. 1213 (1940).

Mr. Justice ROBERTS delivered the opinion of the [Court].

[Jesse Cantwell, a Jehovah's Witness, was arrested in the course of his proselytizing activities on the streets of New Haven, Conn., and was convicted of the common law offense of inciting a breach of the peace.] We hold that, in the circumstances disclosed, the conviction [must] be set aside.[1] [We] must determine whether the alleged protection of the State's interest [in "peace and good order"] has been pressed, in this instance, to a point where it has come into fatal collision with the overriding interest [in the First Amendment] protected by the federal compact.

Conviction [was] not pursuant to a statute evincing a legislative judgment that street discussion of religious affairs, because of its tendency to provoke disorder, should be regulated, or a judgment that the playing of a phonograph on the streets should in the interest of comfort or privacy be limited or prevented. Violation of an Act exhibiting such a legislative judgment and narrowly drawn to prevent the supposed evil, would pose a question differing from what we must here answer. Such a declaration of the State's policy would weigh heavily in any challenge of the law as infringing constitutional limitations. Here, however, the judgment is based on a common law concept of the most general and undefined [nature]. The offense known as breach of the peace embraces a great variety of conduct [menacing] public order and tranquility. It includes not only violent acts but acts and words likely to produce violence in others. No one would have the hardihood to suggest that the principle of freedom of speech sanctions incitement to riot or that religious liberty connotes the privilege to exhort others to physical attack upon those belonging to another sect. When clear and present danger of riot, disorder, interference with traffic upon the public streets, or other immediate threat to public safety, peace, or order appears, the power of the State to prevent or punish is obvious. Equally obvious is it that a State may not unduly suppress free communication of views, religious or other, under the guise of conserving desirable conditions. Here we have a situation analogous to a conviction under a statute sweeping in a great

---

3. The Court also rejected the claim that the law violated appellants' freedom of worship under the religion clauses of the First Amendment.

Why could the appellants in Cox not claim (as Lovell had, successfully) that the statute was void on its face because of the vague standards at the time of their march, and that this vagueness could not be cured as to them by the state court's subsequent construction of the statute? Compare the Court's explanation and distinction of this aspect of Cox in Shuttlesworth v. Birmingham, (1969; p. 1236 below). Note the Court's frequent reliance on Cox in later cases with respect to the state's power to regulate "time, place or manner" through "properly drawn" licensing statutes. See, e.g., Cox v. Louisiana I (1965; p. 1225 below).

1. In another part of the opinion, the Court also set aside the conviction of Jesse Cantwell, his brother, and his father for violation of a statute banning solicitation without a permit. Justice Roberts concluded: "[T]o condition the solicitation of aid for the perpetuation of religious views or systems upon a license, the grant of which rests in the exercise of a determination by state authority as to what is a religious cause, is to lay a forbidden burden upon the exercise of liberty protected by the Constitution." The religious freedom aspect of that holding is noted below, chap. 14, p. 1510. The aspect of that ruling pertaining to regulation of solicitations is noted later in this chapter. See, e.g., Schaumburg (1980; p. 1215 below). (On the role of Cantwell in the development of the "fighting words" doctrine, recall sec. 2A of the previous chapter.)

variety of conduct under a general and indefinite characterization, and leaving to the executive and judicial branches too wide a discretion in its application.

Having these considerations in mind, we note that Jesse Cantwell, on April 26, 1938, was upon a public street, where he had a right to be, and where he had a right peacefully to impart his views to others. There is no showing that his deportment was noisy, truculent, overbearing or offensive. [It] is not claimed that he intended to insult or affront the hearers by playing the record. It is plain that he wished only to interest them in his propaganda. The sound of the phonograph is not shown to have disturbed residents of the street, to have drawn a crowd, or to have impeded traffic. Thus far he had invaded no right or interest of the public or of the men accosted.

The record played by Cantwell embodies a general attack on all organized religious systems as instruments of Satan and injurious to man; it then singles out the Roman Catholic Church for strictures couched in terms which naturally would offend not only persons of that persuasion, but all others who respect the honestly held religious faith of their fellows. The hearers were in fact highly offended. One of them said he felt like hitting Cantwell and the other that he was tempted to throw Cantwell off the street. The one who testified he felt like hitting Cantwell said, in answer to the question "Did you do anything else or have any other reaction?" "No, sir, because he said he would take the victrola and he went." The other witness testified that he told Cantwell he had better get off the street before something happened to him and that was the end of the matter as Cantwell picked up his books and walked up the street. Cantwell's conduct, in the view of the court below, considered apart from the effect of his communication upon his hearers, did not amount to a breach of the peace. One may, however, be guilty of the offense if he commit acts or make statements likely to provoke violence and disturbance of good order, even though no such eventuality be intended. [But in practically all such cases], the provocative language which was held to amount to a breach of the peace consisted of profane, indecent, or abusive remarks directed to the person of the hearer. Resort to epithets or personal abuse is not in any proper sense communication of information or opinion safeguarded by the [Constitution].

We find in the instant case no assault or threatening of bodily harm, no truculent bearing, no intentional discourtesy, no personal abuse. On the contrary, we find only an effort to persuade a willing listener to buy a book or to contribute money in the interest of what Cantwell, however misguided others may think him, conceived to be true religion. [Although] the contents of the record not unnaturally aroused animosity, we think that, in the absence of a statute narrowly drawn to define and punish specific conduct as constituting a clear and present danger to a substantial interest of the State, the petitioner's communication, considered in the light of the constitutional guarantees, raised no such clear and present menace to public peace and order as to render him liable to conviction of the common law offense [in question].

Reversed.

SOME QUESTIONS ON THE EARLY CASES

1. *Lovell, Cox, and Cantwell.* What was the central vice in the licensing scheme in Lovell? Prior restraint, the risk of abuse of discretion, censorship, content control? Or the ban on *all* distribution? Does Lovell reinforce the Hague v. CIO support for a claim of guaranteed access to a public forum (see also note 3 below)? Or is it primarily concerned with the risks to equal access under the licensing scheme? What is the emphasis of Cox? Does *it* reinforce the guaranteed access claim? Or is it primarily concerned with safeguarding

against inequality and censorship risks by assuring adequate standards in licensing? Does Cox suggest that judicial scrutiny will not extend much beyond assurance that the restraints are truly directed at "time, place and manner," and that they are neutrally framed and administered?[1]

What is the thrust of Cantwell? Does *it* guarantee access to streets? Or does it concern also center on restraints that risk content-oriented, unequal applications? What local interests would be sufficiently strong to justify punishment of speakers such as Cantwell under a narrowly drawn statute? Fear of violence? Actual violence? Sensibilities of the audience? What, in short, is the holding in Cantwell? That the First Amendment protected Cantwell's behavior and barred *any* state regulation? Or only that Cantwell's behavior could not be punished without more evidence of violence, or risk of violence, or injury to listeners' sensibilities? Or only that Cantwell's behavior could not be punished in the absence of a narrowly drawn statute?

2. *The Schneider case.* In addition to the three cases above, one other decision from the Court's early encounters with public places problems is frequently cited by the modern Court: SCHNEIDER v. STATE, 308 U.S. 147 (1939). The majority opinion by Justice ROBERTS, the author of Hague v. CIO, invalidated the ordinances of four different New Jersey communities forbidding distribution of leaflets. The cities' central defense was that flat bans were necessary to prevent littering of its streets. The Court replied: "[Although] the alleged offenders were not charged with themselves scattering paper in the streets, their convictions were sustained upon the theory that distribution by them encouraged or resulted in such littering. We are of opinion that the purpose to keep the streets clean [is] insufficient to justify an ordinance which prohibits a person rightfully on a public street from handing literature to one willing to receive it. Any burden imposed upon the city authorities in cleaning and caring for the streets as an indirect consequence of such distribution results from the constitutional protection of the freedom of speech and press. This constitutional protection does not deprive a city of all power to prevent street littering. There are obvious methods of preventing littering. Amongst these is the punishment of those who actually throw papers on the street." [2]

Note some important aspects of Schneider: No doubt a city's interest in preventing littering and keeping its streets clean is a legitimate local interest. Moreover, distributing leaflets undoubtedly creates a "clear and present danger" of littering. In addition, the flat ban on distribution of leaflets was plainly

1. Note Kalven's comment on the case, in "The Concept of the Public Forum," 1965 Sup. Ct.Rev. 1: "Of course, Cox v. New Hampshire did no more than to give a general standard for accommodation of the conflicting interests. It did not tell us whether certain congested areas or certain times of the day might not always be held unavailable for parading, nor whether the size of some crowds might always be too large. But it seems to me to symbolize the ideal of Robert's Rules of Order for use of the public forum of the streets."

2. Note also Justice Roberts' response in Schneider to the argument on behalf of some of the ordinances that they applied only to streets and left open other public places: "[T]he streets are natural and proper places for the dissemination of information and opinion; and one is not to have the exercise of his liberty of expression in appropriate places abridged on the plea that it may be exercised in some other place."

That passage from Schneider is often quoted in modern public forum cases. Is Justice Roberts' approach persuasive? Should this aspect of the Roberts approach be limited to traditional public places such as streets and parks? Consider whether, in evaluating access to nontraditional public places—e.g., public libraries, as in Brown v. Louisiana, p. 1241 below—adequate analysis of the access claim *requires* consideration of the availability of adequate alternative forums in which the speaker may reach the desired audience. Should the claimant to a nontraditional public forum be required to demonstrate a special interest in the particular location—i.e., that there *is* no adequate alternative channel to communicate the views the claimant seeks to express? Or does Justice Roberts' statement bar such an inquiry?

content-neutral on its face, not content-based. Yet the Court struck down the ban, by applying a variety of strict scrutiny balancing. Invalidating the ban might cast a burden on the city in cleaning streets; yet that was a cost that had to be borne as a consequence of the First Amendment. In examining the later cases that follow, consider whether subsequent Courts have forgotten some of the lessons of Schneider (and of Hague) in their preoccupation with the search for potential abuses of discretion, and for content-based regulations. Note Kalven, "The Concept of the Public Forum," 1965 Sup.Ct.Rev. 1, noting the "impressive bite" of Schneider: "Leaflet distribution in public places [is] a method of communication that carries as an inextricable and expected consequence substantial littering of the [streets]. It is also a method of communication of some annoyance to a majority of people so [addressed]. Yet the constitutional balance in Schneider was struck emphatically in favor of keeping the public forum open for this mode of communication. [The] operative theory of the Court, at least for the leaflet situation, is that, although it is a method of communication that interferes with the public use of the streets, the right to the streets as a public forum is such that leaflet distribution cannot be prohibited and can be regulated only for weighty reasons." (See also the comments in the next note.)[3]

3. *The significance of the leaflet cases for the development of a theory of presumptive minimum access to the public forum.* For an argument that Schneider strengthened the case for an assured minimum access right to the streets as a public forum, see Kalven's emphasis in 1965 Sup.Ct.Rev. 1. Kalven noted that Schneider did not involve simply "freedom from arbitrariness in the states' control of public places," but rather "reasonable regulation of the immemorial claim of the free man to use the streets as a forum. The regulation in order to be deemed reasonable, the Court was telling us, must recognize the special nature and value of that claim to be on the street." He suggested that the leafleting cases were "the relevant model for analysis of the complex speech issues involved" in the mass demonstration public forum cases, sec. 4E below, and commented: "Mr. Justice Roberts really had it all worked out in Schneider. Since all speech was 'speech plus,' it was subject to regulation of time, place, manner, and circumstance, but to be acceptable the regulation had to weigh heavily the fact that communication was involved."[4] Did Justice Roberts really have it "all worked out" in Schneider? Have later cases undone that work?

----

3. Note that Schneider mentioned that a city could achieve its "clean streets" objective by punishing "those who actually throw papers on the streets." Should Schneider accordingly be viewed as a "less drastic means" case? (Recall sec. 1 above.) Note Kalven's comment: "It is difficult to take seriously so impractical an alternative." Kalven saw the alternatives emphasis in Schneider as an additional flaw in the regulations, not the "decisive flaw."

4. Note also Kalven's comment on the problem of the possible "unwanted overtones for free-speech enthusiasts" in the Schneider rationale. He asked: "Does it not embrace two hobgoblins, a balancing test of First-Amendment interests, and a commitment to prior restraints by licensing?" Kalven answered that the balancing test *is* appropriate, especially "with the Schneider mandate that the thumb of the Court be on the speech side of the scales." He considered the controversy over balancing (p. 941 above) "fruitless" and he reminded "how awkward for many speech problems the clear-and-present-danger test has proved." Moreover, he noted that in public forum access cases, "Mr. Justice Black has always been willing to balance." See, e.g., Cox v. Louisiana I, p. 1225 below. And as to prior restraint, Kalven argued that "there is little, if anything, left today to the idea that prior licensing is bad per se, regardless of the criteria used. It now appears that the historical reaction was against general licensing with unlimited or unspecified grounds for exercise of discretion." He suggested that Cox v. New Hampshire "stands as a strong and healthy precedent for use of a prior restraint, at least in regulating the public forum." In examining the modern cases below, consider whether they support Kalven's observations.

C. THE INTRUSIVE SPEAKER AND THE UNWILLING LISTENER: THE AUDIENCE INTEREST IN BEING LEFT ALONE AS A JUSTIFICATION FOR RESTRAINING SPEECH

THE NOISY SPEAKER'S INTERFERENCE WITH AUDIENCE REPOSE: THE LOUDSPEAKER CASES

Introduction. The materials now turn from early doctrinal developments to a series of asserted *audience* interests that are frequently put forth as justifications for curtailing speech. They begin with the audience interest in its privacy and repose before moving to problems of hostile listeners.[1] Consider first two decisions of the late 1940s dealing with control of amplified sound. They bear not only on the specific loudspeaker question and the audience interest in being free from noise, but also suggest evolving approaches to more general problems: the audience response justifications that may support bans on some manifestation of speech; the significance of a city's methods of control as well as the speaker's method of communication; and the Justices' sensitivities toward claims that a particular forum is necessary to enable the speaker—especially the poor speaker unable to pay for access to the costlier media—to reach an audience.

1. *Saia.* In SAIA v. NEW YORK, 334 U.S. 558 (1948), the Court's 5 to 4 decision held invalid a Lockport, N.Y., ordinance prohibiting the use of amplification devices without the permission of the police chief. Relying on Lovell, Hague, and Cantwell, Justice DOUGLAS' majority opinion found the ordinance unconstitutional "on its face" for establishing a standardless "previous restraint" on free speech. He stated: "Loud-speakers are today indispensable instruments of effective public speech. The sound truck has become an accepted method of political campaigning. It is the way people are reached. Must a candidate for governor or the Congress depend on the whim or caprice of the Chief of Police in order to use his sound truck for campaigning? Must he prove to the satisfaction of that official that his noise will not be annoying to people? The present ordinance would be a dangerous weapon if it were allowed to get a hold on our public life. Noise can be regulated by regulating decibels. The hours and place of public discussion can be controlled. But to allow the police to bar the use of loud-speakers because their use can be abused is like barring radio receivers because they too make a noise. [Any] abuses which loud-speakers create can be controlled by narrowly drawn statutes. When a city allows an official to ban them in his uncontrolled discretion, it sanctions a device for suppression of free communication of ideas. In this case a permit is denied because some persons were said to have found the sound annoying. In the next one a permit may be denied because some people find the ideas annoying. Annoyance at ideas can be cloaked in annoyance at sound. The power of censorship inherent in this type of ordinance reveals its vice."[2]

2. *Kovacs.* In KOVACS v. COOPER, 336 U.S. 77 (1949), one year after Saia, the Court examined a subsequent punishment rather than prior restraint scheme and sustained application of a Trenton, N.J., ordinance designed to

---

1. Note also the asserted justifications for restraining speakers because of the interest of the *offended* (rather than the hostile or repose-seeking audience), considered in sec. 2C2 of the previous chapter, in cases such as Cohen v. California and Pacifica.

2. Justice FRANKFURTER's dissent, joined by Justices Reed and Burton, emphasized that

"no arbitrary action or discrimination" had been shown and stated: "[M]odern devices for amplifying the range and volume of the voice [afford] easy, too easy, opportunities for aural aggression. If uncontrolled, the result is intrusion into cherished privacy. [Surely] there is not a constitutional right to force unwilling people to listen." Justice JACKSON also dissented.

regulate loudspeakers. Kovacs was convicted of violating a ban on "any device known as a sound truck, loud speaker or sound amplifier [which] emits therefrom loud and raucous noises and is attached to and upon any vehicle operated or standing [upon] streets or public places."

Justice REED's opinion announcing the judgment of the Court was joined only by Chief Justice Vinson and Justice Burton. He indicated that absolute prohibition of loudspeakers would probably be unconstitutional but found that the ordinance was valid because, as construed by the state court, it applied only to loudspeakers emitting "loud and raucous" noises. He explained: "City streets are recognized as a normal place for the exchange of ideas by speech or paper. But this does not mean the freedom is beyond all control. We think it is a permissible exercise of legislative discretion to bar sound trucks with broadcasts of public interest, amplified to a loud and raucous volume, from the public ways of municipalities. On the business streets of cities like Trenton, with its more than 125,000 people, such distractions would be dangerous to traffic at all hours useful for the dissemination of information, and in the residential thoroughfares the quiet and tranquility so desirable for city dwellers would likewise be at the mercy of advocates of particular religious, social or political persuasions. We cannot believe that rights of free speech compel a municipality to allow such mechanical voice amplification on any of its streets. [The] preferred position of freedom of speech [does] not require legislators to be insensible to claims by citizens to comfort and convenience. [That] more people may be more easily and cheaply reached by sound trucks [is] not enough to call forth constitutional protection for what those charged with public welfare reasonably think is a nuisance when easy means of publicity are open. [We] think that the need for reasonable protection in the homes or business houses from the distracting noises of vehicles equipped with such sound amplifying devices justifies the ordinance."

Justice JACKSON concurred in the result even though, unlike Justice Reed, he viewed the ordinance as a flat ban on loudspeakers. He thought the prohibition was justified because loudspeakers conflict "with quiet enjoyment of home and park": loudspeaker regulations were permissible so long as they did not seek "to censor the contents." He agreed with the Kovacs dissenters' position that it was a repudiation of Saia. Saia, he noted, "struck down a more moderate exercise of the state's police power" than the one sustained here. He added: "I do not agree that, if we sustain regulations or prohibitions of sound trucks, they must therefore be valid if applied to other methods of 'communication of ideas.' The moving picture screen, the radio, the newspaper, the handbill, the sound truck and the street corner orator have differing natures, values, abuses and dangers. Each, in my view, is a law unto itself, and all we are dealing with now is the sound truck." [3]

Justice BLACK, joined by Justices Douglas and Rutledge, dissented: "The appellant was neither charged with nor convicted of operating a sound truck that emitted 'loud and raucous noises.' The charge [was] that he violated the city ordinance 'in that he [used] a device known as a sound truck.' The record reflects not even a shadow of evidence to prove that the noise was either 'loud or raucous,' unless these words of the ordinance refer to any noise coming from an amplifier, whatever its volume or tone. [This] ordinance wholly bars the use of all loud speakers mounted upon any vehicle in any of the city's public streets.

3. In another opinion concurring in the result, Justice FRANKFURTER also sustained the ordinance as a flat ban, in accordance with his Saia dissent. He emphasized that, so long as a city does not seek to censor or discriminate among ideas, "it is not for us to supervise the limits the legislature may impose in safeguarding the steadily narrowing opportunities for serenity and reflection." He devoted most of his opinion to "observations" on Justice Reed's reference to "the preferred position of freedom of speech." Some of his "observations" are printed above, at p. 980.

In my view this repudiation of [Saia] makes a dangerous and unjustifiable breach in the constitutional barriers designed to insure freedom of expression. Ideas and beliefs are today chiefly disseminated to the masses of people through the press, radio, moving pictures, and public address systems. To some extent at least there is competition of ideas between and within these groups. The basic premise of the First Amendment is that all present instruments of communication, as well as others that inventive genius may bring into being, shall be free from governmental censorship or prohibition. Laws which hamper the free use of some instruments of communication thereby favor competing channels. Thus, unless constitutionally prohibited, laws like [this] can give an overpowering influence to views of owners of legally favored instruments of communication. This favoritism, it seems to me, is the inevitable result of today's decision. For the result of today's [decision] would surely not be reached by this Court if such channels of communication as the press, radio, or moving pictures were similarly attacked.

"There are many people who have ideas that they wish to disseminate but who do not have enough money to own or control publishing plants, newspapers, radios, moving picture studios, or chains of show places. Yet everybody knows the vast reaches of these powerful channels of communication which from the very nature of our economic system must be under the control and guidance of comparatively few people. On the other hand, public speaking is done by many men of divergent minds with no centralized control over the ideas they entertain so as to limit the causes they espouse. It is no reflection on the value of preserving freedom for dissemination of the ideas of publishers of newspapers [etc.] to believe that transmission of ideas through public speaking is also essential. [Criticism] of governmental action [should] not be limited to criticisms by press, radio, and moving pictures. [For] the press, the radio, and the moving picture owners have their favorites. [And] it is an obvious fact that public speaking today without sound amplifiers is a wholly inadequate way to reach the people on a large scale. Consequently, to tip the scales against transmission of ideas through public speaking, as the Court does today, is to deprive the people of a large part of the basic advantages of the receipt of ideas that the First Amendment was designed to protect.

"There is no more reason that I can see for wholly prohibiting one useful instrument of communication than another. If Trenton can completely bar the streets to the advantageous use of loud speakers, all cities can do the same. In that event preference in the dissemination of ideas is given those who can obtain the support of newspapers [etc.] or those who have money enough to buy advertising from newspapers [etc.]. This Court should no more permit this invidious prohibition against the dissemination of ideas by speaking than it would permit a complete blackout of the press, the radio, or moving pictures. [A] city ordinance that reasonably restricts the volume of sound, or the hours during which an amplifier may be used, does not [infringe] free speech. [But this] ordinance does none of these things, but is instead an absolute prohibition of all uses of an amplifier on any of the streets of Trenton at any time." [4]

    3. *The noisy speaker's public forum in light of Saia and Kovacs.* Would a flat ban on all sound trucks be constitutional? Should it be? Given the disagreement on the Court about the scope of the ordinance in Kovacs, the impact of the case is unclear. What do Saia and Kovacs say about a guaranteed access public forum claim of a loudspeaker user? Are the access claims of loudspeaker users entitled to special weight because of the importance of sound trucks (like leaflets) as a form of "poor man's printing press"? If the Kovacs ordinance is read in accordance with the Jackson and Black views—that it authorized a flat ban—do the results in Saia and Kovacs make sense? Is the vice of the

---

4. Justice MURPHY also dissented.

administrative censorship risk in a vague licensing ordinance greater than the vice of total silencing of the medium of communication? Should a total ban on loudspeakers be invalidated because it constitutes impermissible "format discrimination" (see sec. 2 above)—because it bans resort to a medium of special importance to those who cannot afford to pay for access to more expensive ones? Is a ban on loudspeakers justifiable because of a legislative judgment that the particular method of communication is obnoxious? Would a specific ban on all speeches or marches in residential neighborhoods be similarly supportable on grounds of deference to legislative judgment? A ban on all street demonstrations? Would it depend on the available alternative communication channels? Was the Kovacs ban permissible only because the speaker had other adequate outlets? Or was it enough that a legislative body had deemed this method of communication too annoying?

4. *The captive audience interest as a basis for an affirmative constitutional claim: The Pollak case.* Can the unwilling listener make a First Amendment or privacy claim to protection from "aural aggression"? Can there be both a listener's right not to be disturbed and a speaker's right to reach an unwilling listener? In Saia, Justice Douglas endorsed the latter right; yet in dissenting in Pollak a few years later, he strongly endorsed the former. In PUBLIC UTILITIES COMM'N v. POLLAK, 343 U.S. 451 (1952), the PUC found that the use of radio receivers on city buses was "not inconsistent with public convenience, comfort and safety." That ruling came in response to complaints about a D.C. bus company's installation of radio receivers that broadcast programs of music, news and advertising in the buses. The Court found no First or Fifth Amendment (privacy) flaws, but Justice Douglas' dissent emphasized the right to be let alone: he insisted that subjecting the captive audience of bus passengers to radio programs violated their constitutional right of privacy.[5]

5. *Modern considerations of the right "to be let alone" as a restriction on the right to communicate.* a. *The Rowan case.* In ROWAN v. POST OFFICE DEPARTMENT, 397 U.S. 728 (1970), appellants, in the mail order business, unsuccessfully claimed that a federal law violated their right to communicate. The law provides that a person who has received in the mail "a pandering advertisement" which offers for sale "matter which the addressee in his sole discretion believes to be erotically arousing or sexually provocative" may request a post office order requiring the mailer to remove his name from his mailing list and stop all future mailings to the addressee. The law was enacted in response to concern "with use of mail facilities to distribute unsolicited advertisements that recipients found to be offensive because of their lewd and salacious character" and which "was found to be pressed upon minors as well as adults who did not seek and did not want it."

Chief Justice BURGER's opinion found the constitutional challenge unpersuasive: "[T]he right of every person 'to be let alone' must be placed in the scales with the right of others to communicate. In today's complex society we are inescapably captive audiences for many purposes, but a sufficient measure of individual autonomy must survive to permit every householder to exercise control over unwanted mail. [Weighing] the highly important right to communicate [against] the very basic right to be free from sights, sounds and tangible matter we do not want, it seems to us that a mailer's right to communicate must stop at the mailbox of an unreceptive addressee. [In] effect the power of a householder under the statute is unlimited; he may prohibit the mailing of a dry

5. For further consideration of efforts to reconcile public forum access claims with the captive audience's privacy interests, see Lehman v. Shaker Heights (1974; p. 1247 below), where Justice Douglas' Pollak-like concern for the audience proved the decisive vote in rejecting an access claim by a political candidate who wanted to advertise in a city bus. On the Pollak problem, see Black, "He Cannot Choose But Hear: The Plight of the Captive Auditor," 53 Colum.L. Rev. 960 (1953).

goods catalog because he objects to the contents—or indeed the text of the language touting the merchandise. Congress provided the sweeping power not only to protect privacy but to avoid possible constitutional questions that might arise from vesting the power to make any discretionary evaluation of the material in a governmental official." The Chief Justice added: "If this prohibition operates to impede the flow of even valid ideas, the answer is that no one has a right to press even 'good' ideas on an unwilling recipient. That we are often 'captives' outside the sanctuary of the home and subject to objectionable speech and other sound does not mean we must be captives everywhere. See [Pollak]." [6]

   b. *The Keefe case.* Chief Justice Burger had no difficulty distinguishing the Rowan case in ORGANIZATION FOR A BETTER AUSTIN v. KEEFE, 402 U.S. 415 (1971). A real estate broker had obtained from the Illinois courts an injunction enjoining a racially integrated Chicago community organization from distributing its literature criticizing his alleged "block-busting" and "panic peddling" activities. His business activities were in Chicago but he resided in a suburb, and the injunction prevented distribution of the literature in that suburb. The state courts viewed petitioners' activities "as coercive and intimidating, rather than informative," and relied on the state's policy favoring "protection of the privacy of home and family." Chief Justice BURGER found these arguments insufficient to justify the injunction. He emphasized that the "heavy burden of showing justification" for the imposition of a prior restraint had not been met here: "No prior decisions support the claim that the interest of an individual in being free from public criticism of his business practices in pamphlets or leaflets warrants use of the injunctive power of a court. Designating the conduct as an invasion of privacy [is] not sufficient to support an injunction against peaceful distribution of informational literature of the nature revealed by this record. [Rowan] is not in point; the right of privacy involved in that case is not shown here. Among other important distinctions, respondent is not attempting to stop the flow of information into his own household, but to the public." [7]

THE REGULATION OF SOLICITORS AND CANVASSERS: THE BACKGROUND AND THE MODERN APPROACH— FROM CONCERN ABOUT DISCRETION TO ASSURANCE OF ACCESS

   Introduction. For decades, the Court has had to deal with efforts by local governments to regulate the pursuit of financial contributions by door-to-door canvassers and street solicitors. The defenders of solicitation restrictions have invoked not only the interests in privacy and tranquility but also the governmental concerns with preventing fraud and crime. Over the years, the most common Court ground for invalidating such regulations has reflected the equal access rather than the guaranteed access approach: typically, the Court has

---

   6. Recall that Rowan (as well as Kovacs) were distinguished in Cohen v. California (1971; p. 1101 above).

   7. Recall that Carey v. Brown (1980; p. 1166 below) invalidated a law banning residential picketing, emphasizing the exclusion of labor picketing from the ban; but that the majority pointed out that it did not reach the question of the validity of a law "barring all residential picketing regardless of its subject matter." Justice Brennan's majority opinion stated: "We are not to be understood to imply [that] residential picketing is

beyond the reach of uniform and nondiscriminatory regulation. For the right to communicate is not limitless. [The] State's interest in protecting the well-being, tranquility, and privacy of the home is certainly of the highest order in a free and civilized society." [Compare the rejection of an intrusion-into-the-privacy-of-the-home justification in Consolidated Edison v. Public Serv. Comm'n (1980; p. 1122 below), invalidating a state order prohibiting the inclusion in monthly electric bills of inserts that discussed controversial issues of public policy.]

invalidated schemes for licensing solicitors by finding that the administrator had been given too much discretion because of inadequate standards—discretion that risked discriminatory enforcement.[1]　Only rarely, however, has the Court confronted the guaranteed access aspect of the problem: Are excessive restrictions on solicitation impermissible interferences with free speech even when the standards are clear and the risks of abuse of discretion are absent?　An early decision, Martin v. Struthers (note 1 below), suggested that flat governmental bans on door-to-door canvassers were impermissible, and implied that protection of individual interests in privacy and repose could be adequately achieved by authorizing the individual resident to bar those who would ring doorbells.[2]　But the message of Martin was clouded by two features: Martin involved religious rather than political canvassers; and it did not involve the collection of money, but only the distribution of handbills.　Court dicta over the years hinted that governmental bans on solicitors might be permissible to safeguard against fraud and crime.[3]　Accordingly, the constitutional status of broad prohibitions on solicitations remained unclear throughout the 1950s and 1960s; and it was still unclear as recently as 1976, as the Hynes case (note 2 below) shows.　But in 1980, the Schaumburg decision (note 3 below) drew on the Martin legacy and gave the solicitor unusually explicit substantive constitutional protection.　In Schaumburg, atypically, the guaranteed access rather than equal access theme emerged as the dominant one.

　　1.　*The legacy of Martin v. Struthers.*　The majority ruling in MARTIN v. STRUTHERS, 319 U.S. 141 (1943), invalidated an ordinance prohibiting the distribution of handbills to residences by ringing doorbells or otherwise summoning residents to the door.　The City of Struthers, an Ohio industrial community, argued that the law was necessary to protect residents from annoyance and crime; and it emphasized that many of the residents worked night shifts and slept days, making them especially vulnerable to "casual bell pushers" disrupting their sleep.　The ordinance was challenged by a Jehovah's Witness who had gone door-to-door to distribute leaflets advertising a religious meeting.　Justice BLACK's majority opinion noted that permission to engage in door-to-door canvassing had traditionally depended "upon the individual master of each household, and not upon the determination of the community," and indicated that that approach was mandated by the Constitution.　He stated: "The dangers of distribution [such as annoyance and crime] can so easily be controlled by traditional legal methods, leaving to each householder the full right to decide whether he will receive strangers as visitors, that stringent prohibition can serve no purpose but that forbidden by the Constitution, the

1.　Typical of such cases is Staub v. Baxley, 355 U.S. 313 (1958), striking down an ordinance prohibiting the solicitation of membership in dues-paying organizations without a permit from city officials. In finding the regulation "invalid on its face," the Court stated: "It is settled [that] an ordinance which, like this one, makes the peaceful enjoyment of [constitutional freedoms] contingent upon the uncontrolled will of an official [is] an unconstitutional censorship or prior restraint upon the enjoyment of those freedoms." See also Cantwell v. Connecticut, p. 1204 above, which invalidated a law requiring official approval for the solicitation of contributions to religious causes. Troubled by the requirement of an official determination of what was a "religious cause," the Court found the scheme an invalid prior restraint on the free exercise of religion. Although the Court rested on the free exercise clause, chap. 14 below, subsequent rulings have viewed Cantwell as implying that the soliciting of funds involved interests protected by the free speech guarantee as well. The Hynes case, note 2 in the text below, is a modern illustration of that equal access, feared-abuse-of-discretion theme.

2.　The same theme—reliance on individual residents' choice rather than on governmental bans—is reflected in the Rowan-Keefe sequence, in the preceding note.

3.　Added doubt was cast on Martin by the decision in Breard v. Alexandria, 341 U.S. 622 (1951), *sustaining* an ordinance barring door-to-door solicitation for magazine subscriptions without the prior consent of the homeowners. The majority emphasized the "householders' desire for privacy" in rejecting First Amendment as well as commerce clause challenges to the ordinance.

naked restriction of the dissemination of ideas." He thought it permissible to make it an offense "for any person to ring the bell of a householder who has appropriately indicated that he is unwilling to be disturbed": regulations of that sort "leave the decision as to whether distributors of literature may lawfully call at a home where it belongs—with the homeowner himself. A city can punish those who call at a home in defiance of the previously expressed will of the occupant and, in addition, can by identification devices control the abuse of the privilege by criminals posing as canvassers." [4]

2. *A modern emphasis on abuse of discretion in the regulation of canvassing: The Hynes case.* HYNES v. MAYOR OF ORADELL, 425 U.S. 610 (1976), invalidated an ordinance requiring advance notice to police in writing, "for identification only," by "any person desiring to canvass, solicit or call from house to house [for] a recognized charitable [or] political campaign or cause." The ordinance was challenged by political canvassers. Chief Justice BURGER's majority opinion struck it down solely on vagueness grounds, finding it defective in several respects: its coverage was unclear because, e.g., it failed to explain the precise meaning of "*recognized* charitable cause"; and it did not sufficiently specify what would be considered adequate "identification." The Chief Justice added: "To the extent that these ambiguities [give] police the *effective* power to grant or deny permission to canvass for political causes, the Ordinance suffers in its practical effect from the vice condemned in Lovell, Schneider, Cantwell, and Staub." [5] The Chief Justice's dicta in the case generated far more controversy than the holding. His general comments included the statement that past cases had "consistently recognized a municipality's power to protect its citizens from crime and undue annoyance by regulating soliciting and canvassing. A narrowly drawn ordinance, that does not vest in municipal officials the undefined power to determine what messages residents will hear, may serve these important interests without running afoul of the First Amendment." [6]

A separate opinion by Justice BRENNAN, joined by Justice Marshall, objected to the Chief Justice's suggestion that an equal access approach was adequate and that the guaranteed access interest was minimal. In Justice Brennan's view, the Chief Justice's discussion could be "read as suggesting that, vagueness defects aside, an ordinance of this kind would ordinarily withstand constitutional attack." Justice Brennan countered that such ordinances, even though "precisely drafted to avoid the pitfalls of vagueness, must present substantial First Amendment questions." He emphasized the special threat of canvassing regulations to political expression. Commenting that the work of volunteers was "the lifeblood of today's political campaigning," he found that identification requirements, "even in their least intrusive form, must discourage

---

4. The Martin case is often cited as an early example of "less drastic means" analysis. But note that it is doubtful that the individual resident's decision is as "effective" in safeguarding against annoyance, fraud and crime as a governmental ban on all canvassers. If that is so, the decision suggests a constitutionally mandated, substantive First Amendment preference for individual choice rather than governmental rule in safeguarding residents' privacy and tranquility. In Kovacs, p. 1208 above, Justice Reed distinguished the problem of loudspeakers from other intrusions into privacy. In sustaining a governmental ban on loudspeakers, he noted that Martin had rejected governmental controls and had found the individual resident's "no canvassing" sign adequate assurance of privacy protection. But the Kovacs situation was different: "In his

home or on the street he is practically helpless to escape this interference with his privacy by loud speakers except through the protection of the municipality."

5. Only Justice REHNQUIST dissented, insisting that the challengers lacked standing to raise vagueness claims and arguing that the language of the ordinance was in any event sufficiently clear.

6. The Chief Justice's discussion included a quotation from Zechariah Chafee's articulation of "the householder's right-to-be-let-alone": "Of all the methods of spreading unpopular ideas, [house-to-house canvassing] seems the least entitled to extensive protection. The possibilities of persuasion are slight compared with [the] certainties of annoyance."

that participation." He argued, too, that the restraints implicit in identification requirements "extend beyond restrictions on time and place—they chill discussion itself." [7] Four years after Hynes, the Schaumburg case, which follows, presumably allayed most of Justice Brennan's concerns by making clear that First Amendment problems about regulations of canvassing persist even when all risk of abuse of discretion is absent.

3. *Emphasizing First Amendment assured access rights in reviewing regulations of solicitation.* a. The 8 to 1 decision in SCHAUMBURG v. CITIZENS FOR BETTER ENVIRON., 444 U.S. 620 (1980), struck down an ordinance barring door-to-door and on-street solicitations of contributions by charitable organizations that did not use at least 75% of their receipts for "charitable purposes." "Charitable purposes" were defined to exclude solicitation expenses. Because of that 75% rule, Citizens for a Better Environment (CBE), an environmental protection group, was denied permission to solicit contributions in Schaumburg, a suburb of Chicago. In its federal court challenge to the ban, CBE raised no questions about vague standards or abuse of discretion. Instead, CBE argued that the ban interfered with substantive First Amendment access rights.

In sustaining the attack, Justice WHITE's majority opinion began by articulating the First Amendment interests at stake. He rejected the argument that the solicitation ban was permissible because it only dealt with the collection of money and did not restrict the expression of views. Reviewing prior cases from Cantwell to Hynes, Justice White concluded that they "clearly establish that charitable appeals for funds, on the street or door to door, involve a variety of speech interests—communication of information, the dissemination and propagation of views and ideas, and the advocacy of causes—that are within the protection of the First Amendment. Soliciting financial support is undoubtedly subject to reasonable regulation but the latter must be undertaken with due regard for the reality that solicitation is characteristically intertwined with informative and perhaps persuasive speech seeking support for particular causes or for particular views on economic, political or social issues, and for the reality that without solicitation the flow of such information and advocacy would likely cease. Canvassers in such contexts are necessarily more than solicitors for money." In short, "charitable solicitations in residential neighborhoods [are clearly] within the protections of the First Amendment." And the regulation here unduly intruded on free speech rights.

In exploring the constitutional flaws of the regulation, Justice White pursued an overbreadth analysis. He found that CBE was entitled to a "judgment of facial invalidity if the ordinance purported to prohibit canvassing by a substantial category of charities to which the 75-percent limitation could not be applied consistently with the [First Amendment], even if there was no demonstration that CBE itself was one of these organizations." The organizations to whom the 75% rule could not be applied were found to be those whose "primary purpose is not to provide money or services for the poor, the needy or other worthy objects of charity, but to gather and disseminate information about and advocate positions on matters of public concern." Typically, these organizations have

---

7. In arguing that identification requirements discouraged free speech, Justice Brennan relied on Talley v. California, 362 U.S. 60 (1960). Talley invalidated a Los Angeles ordinance that prohibited the distribution of any handbill in the city unless it had printed on it the name and address of the person who prepared, distributed, or sponsored it. Holding the ordinance "void on its face," the Court noted that the identification requirement would tend to restrict freedom of expression. The Court rejected the argument that the law was a justifiable "way to identify those responsible for fraud, false advertising and libel," stating that "the ordinance is in no manner so limited." Writing for the three dissenters, Justice Clark stated: "I stand second to none in supporting Talley's right of free speech—but not his freedom of anonymity." [See also the further discussions below of disclosure requirements challenged as inhibitions of speech, as in Buckley v. Valeo (1976; p. 1301 below), and with the materials on disclosure by public employees and licensees (p. 1387 below).]

paid employees not only to solicit funds but also to gather information and advocate positions. "Organizations of this kind, although they might pay only reasonable salaries, would necessarily spend more than 25% of their budgets on salaries and administrative expenses and would be completely barred from solicitation in [Schaumburg]." And as to such organizations, the ordinance constituted "a direct and substantial limitation of protected activity that cannot be sustained unless it serves a sufficiently strong, subordinating interest that the Village is entitled to protect." Here, Justice White concluded, "the Village's preferred justifications are inadequate and [the] ordinance cannot survive scrutiny under the First Amendment."

The Court found that the asserted interests "in protecting the public from fraud, crime and undue annoyance" were "indeed substantial," but were "only peripherally promoted by the 75-percent requirement and could be sufficiently served by measures less destructive of First Amendment interests." With respect to the prevention of fraud, the Court found the 75% rule not a justifiable device for distinguishing charitable from commercial enterprises: organizations primarily engaged in research, advocacy or publication that use their own paid staffs to carry out these functions could not be labeled as presumptively "fraudulent" or as using the "charitable" label as a cloak for profit making. Under the First Amendment, Schaumburg had to employ more precise measures to separate genuine charitable organizations from profitmaking ones: "The Village's legitimate interest in preventing fraud can be better served by measures less intrusive than a direct prohibition on solicitation"—e.g., by prohibiting fraudulent misrepresentations or by requiring disclosure of the finances of charitable organizations.

With respect to the interests in the protection of safety and of residential privacy, the Court was unable to "perceive any substantial relationship" between the 75% rule and the governmental ends. Organizations devoting more than 25% of their funds to administrative expenses were no more likely "to employ solicitors who would be a threat to public safety than are other charitable organizations." And "householders are equally disturbed by solicitation on behalf of organizations satisfying the 75-percent requirement as they are by solicitation on behalf of other organizations. The 75-percent requirement protects privacy only by reducing the total number of solicitors." Moreover, the ordinance was "not directed to the unique privacy interests of persons residing in their homes because it applies not only to door-to-door solicitation, but also to solicitation on 'public streets and public ways.' Other provisions of the ordinance, [such as those] permitting homeowners to bar solicitors from their property by posting signs, [suggest] the availability of less intrusive and more effective measures to protect privacy. See [Rowan; Martin]."

Justice REHNQUIST, the sole dissenter, argued that the decision unduly hampered local regulation of door-to-door activities. He denied that earlier decisions justified the ruling: most regulations invalidated in the past involved either denials of permits on the basis of inadequate criteria (e.g., Hynes) or distribution of information rather than requests for contributions (e.g., Martin). He insisted that the majority's position imposed an excessive practical burden by requiring local governments to search for criteria to identify constitutionally protected organizations.[8] And he concluded that "the Court overestimates the

---

8. Justice Rehnquist also criticized the majority for being inadequately sensitive to the abuse of discretion risk while pursuing its substantive First Amendment course. He noted that the majority had referred approvingly to a Fort Worth ordinance which, like Schaumburg's, authorized denial of charitable solicitation permits to organizations with excessive solicitation costs,

but which, unlike Schaumburg's, permitted organizations to obtain permits if they demonstrated the reasonableness of the excess costs. National Foundation v. Fort Worth, 415 F.2d 41 (5th Cir. 1969), cert. denied, 396 U.S. 1040 (1970). Justice Rehnquist commented: "Given the potential for abuse of this open-ended grant of discretion, I would think that Fort Worth's ordinance would

value, in a constitutional sense, of door-to-door solicitation for financial contributions and simultaneously underestimates the reasons why a village board might conclude that regulation of such activity was necessary. [A] simple request for money lies far from the core protections of the First Amendment. [Nothing in the Constitution] should prevent residents of a community from making the collective judgment that certain worthy charities may solicit door to door while at the same time insulating themselves against panhandlers, profiteers, and peddlers."

b. In SECRETARY OF STATE v. J.H. MUNSON CO., 468 U.S. ___ (1984), the Court followed Schaumburg in striking down a similar restriction on charitable solicitations. The law at issue in Munson differed from that in Schaumburg in two respects. First, it did not contain a permit requirement, but exercised control only through subsequent criminal penalties. Second, the 25% limitation on the amount of proceeds that could be used for other than charitable purposes was not absolutely rigid; it could be waived whenever that limitation "would effectively prevent the charitable organization from raising contributions." The law was challenged by a professional fundraiser who claimed primarily the First Amendment rights of his customers, who were not parties to the action.[9] But the Court, in an opinion by Justice BLACKMUN, found these factors insufficient to distinguish this case from Schaumburg, for the possibility of gaining an exemption was deemed to be inadequate to prevent the inhibition of activity itself protected by the First Amendment. "The flaw in the statute is not simply that it includes within its sweep some impermissible applications, but that in all its applications, it operates on a fundamentally mistaken premise that high solicitation costs are an accurate measure of fraud. That the statute in some of its applications actually prevents the misdirection of funds from the organization's charitable goal is little more than fortuitous. It is equally likely that the statute will restrict First Amendment activity that results in high costs but is itself a part of the charity's goal or that is simply attributable to the fact that the charity's cause proves to be unpopular."[10]

D. HOSTILE AUDIENCE REACTIONS AS JUSTIFICATIONS FOR CURTAILING SPEECH

PROVOCATIVE SPEECH AND THE "HECKLER'S VETO"

Introduction. In this group of cases, the state seeks to stop the speaker in order to promote the interest in assuring order and avoiding violence. The typical claim is that a speaker's provocative message so outrages the audience that some listeners are likely to resort to violence in response. Does the apprehension of hostile audience reaction justify restricting the speaker? Only if the speaker uses extremely provocative words? Even if the audience is very

---

be more, not less, suspect than Schaumburg's." [For a later Court consideration of a regulation of solicitors—in a state fair grounds context—see the Heffron case (1981; p. 1255 below).]

9. The majority permitted the fundraiser to make an on-the-face attack. This prompted a dissent by Justice Rehnquist, joined by Chief Justice Burger and Justices Powell and O'Connor. Justice Rehnquist insisted: "[Given] the extensive legitimate application of this statute, both to fundraising expenses not attributable to public education or advocacy and to the fees charged by professional fundraisers who, like

Munson, are not themselves engaged in advocating any causes, I see no basis for concluding that the Maryland statute is substantially overbroad." (Recall the majority's effort in this case to differentiate between two types of overbreadth, as noted in sec. 1 above, at p. 1155.)

10. Compare Heffron v. Int'l Soc. for Krishna Consc., 452 U.S. 640 (1981), sustaining a ban on, inter alia, solicitation of funds on state fairgrounds except in specified booths. Consideration of this case is postponed to sec. 4F at p. 1255, for consideration with other claims to access to non-traditional public forums.

easily provoked? Does the First Amendment impose an obligation on the government to protect the speaker from the angry crowd? Must government preserve order by restraining listeners rather than speakers? Or may government stop the speaker simply by showing that his words created an immediate danger of disorder? Would recognition of that justification legitimate a "heckler's veto"? Must some protection of the provocative speaker be assured lest the public forum be blocked by the "heckler's veto"? How effectively have the cases dealt with this Robert's Rules problem?[1]

1. *Terminiello and "provocative" speech which "invites dispute."* In TERMINIELLO v. CHICAGO, 337 U.S. 1 (1949), the Court reversed the breach of the peace conviction of an abrasive speaker, but on the basis of an improper charge to the jury and without directly reaching the "hostile words" issue. The speaker viciously denounced various political and racial groups; outside the auditorium, an angry crowd gathered; the speaker then condemned the crowd as "snakes," "slimy scum," etc. After the disturbance, he was convicted under a breach of the peace statute construed by the trial judge to include speech which "stirs the public to anger, invites dispute, brings about a condition of unrest, or creates a disturbance." Justice DOUGLAS' majority opinion found that standard unconstitutional: "[A] function of free speech under our system of government is to invite dispute. It may indeed best serve its high purpose when it induces a condition of unrest, creates dissatisfaction with conditions as they are, or even stirs people to anger. Speech is often provocative and challenging. It may strike at prejudices and preconceptions and have profound unsettling effects as it presses for acceptance of an idea. That is why freedom of speech, though not absolute [Chaplinsky], is nevertheless protected against censorship or punishment, unless shown likely to produce a clear and present danger of a serious substantive evil that rises far above public inconvenience, annoyance, or unrest." Do the "heckler's veto" cases that follow give adequate weight to the First Amendment interests of the abrasive speaker in the public forum, or do they give undue weight to audience reactions as justifications for curtailment of speech?[2] By what standards can the competing interests best be reconciled? By what mechanisms? Subsequent punishment? Permit systems? Protective custody but not punishment of the speaker in violent situations?

3. *The Feiner problem: Focus on protected words or on audience context?* The Feiner case, which follows, elicited extensive consideration of the hostile audience problem. In examining it, consider: To what extent should protection of speech turn on the response of the particular audience? To what extent should it turn on the words and content of the speech? Can the Court delineate the protected area by stating, e.g., that words short of "incitement" are

---

1. Recall Chaplinsky v. New Hampshire (1942; p. 1045 above) and its "fighting words" exception to First Amendment coverage. Although the fighting words exception rests in part on the interest in preventing disorder and violence, it has been construed narrowly to cover only face-to-face insults and epithets "which by their very utterance [tend] to incite an immediate breach of the peace." The materials in this section typically do not involve fighting words in that face-to-face sense, but rather the threat of reactions by an audience hostile to the speaker. Note, e.g., Terminiello, which follows, reversing the conviction of a provocative speaker without reaching the fighting words issue.

2. What about the First Amendment interests of the heckler? See In re Kay, 464 P.2d 142 (Cal.1970), setting aside a conviction for disturbing a lawful meeting. A small part of a large crowd at a Fourth of July celebration "engaged in rhythmical clapping and some shouting for about five or ten minutes. This demonstration did not affect the program"—the speaker finished his speech despite the protest. The California Supreme Court opinion commented: "Audience activities, such as heckling, interrupting, harsh questioning, and booing, even though they may be impolite and discourteous, can nonetheless advance the goals of the First Amendment." To construe the law within constitutional limits, the Court interpreted it to require "that the defendant substantially impaired the conduct of the meeting by intentionally committing acts in violation of implicit customs or usages or of explicit rules for governance of the meeting, of which he knew, or as a reasonable man should have known."

protected, no matter what their probable impact? Or must the boundaries of protection depend on the context and environment, including the actual response of the audience? Does the First Amendment impose responsibility on the state to restrain the hostile audience, or does the speaker bear the risk of having his provocative words stopped by the hecklers' response? Was Feiner's speech an "incitement" in the sense of Brandenburg, p. 1037 above, or were his words made punishable by reason of the audience reaction? Contrast the Court's response in Feiner with that in Edwards, p. 1221 below, a case growing out of a modern mass demonstration in a hostile environment.

FEINER v. NEW YORK

340 U.S. 315, 71 S.Ct. 303, 95 L.Ed. 295 (1951).

[Feiner's disorderly conduct conviction stemmed from the following circumstances: In March 1949, Feiner addressed a crowd of 75 to 80 persons, black and white, on a street corner in a predominantly black residential section of Syracuse, N.Y. Soon after he began, two policemen, summoned by a telephone complaint, arrived to investigate. They found the crowd filling the sidewalk and spreading into the street. In the course of Feiner's speech urging his listeners to attend a meeting of the Young Progressives of America at a hotel that evening, he protested the cancellation of a permit to hold the meeting in a public school and made derogatory remarks about President Truman and the Mayor of Syracuse (calling them both "bums") and about the American Legion ("a Nazi Gestapo"). He also said: "The Negroes don't have equal rights; they should rise up in arms and fight for them."

[Feiner's statements, delivered in a "loud, highpitched voice," "stirred up a little excitement," and there was "some pushing, shoving and milling around" in the crowd. After Feiner had been speaking about 20 minutes, one of the onlookers said to the arresting policeman: "If you don't get that son of a bitch off, I will go over and get him off there myself." The policeman finally "stepped in to prevent it resulting in a fight." After Feiner ignored two police requests to stop speaking, he was arrested. The specifications underlying the disorderly conduct charge included the following: "By ignoring and refusing to heed and obey reasonable police orders issued [to] regulate and control said crowd and to prevent a breach [of] the peace and to prevent injuries to pedestrians attempting to use said walk, [and] prevent injury to the public generally."]

Mr. Chief Justice VINSON delivered the opinion of the [Court].

We are not faced here with blind condonation by a state court of arbitrary police action. [The state courts] found that the officers in making the arrest were motivated solely by a proper concern for the preservation of order and protection of the general welfare, and that there was no evidence which could lend color to a claim that the acts of the police were a cover for suppression of petitioner's views and opinions. Petitioner was thus neither arrested nor convicted for the making or the content of his speech. Rather, it was the reaction which it actually engendered.

The language of [Cantwell] is appropriate here. "[Nobody would suggest that free speech] sanctions incitement to riot. [When] clear and present danger of riot, disorder, interference with traffic upon the public streets, or other immediate threat to public safety, peace, or order, appears, the power of the State to prevent or punish is obvious." [This] Court respects [the] interests of the community in maintaining peace and order on its streets. [We] cannot say that the preservation of that interest here encroaches on the constitutional rights of this petitioner.

We are well aware that the ordinary murmurings and objections of a hostile audience cannot be allowed to silence a speaker, and are also mindful of the possible danger of giving overzealous police officials complete discretion to break up otherwise lawful public meetings. [But] we are not faced here with such a situation. It is one thing to say that the police cannot be used as an instrument for the suppression of unpopular views, and another to say that, when as here the speaker passes the bounds of argument or persuasion and undertakes incitement to riot, they are powerless to prevent a breach of the peace. Nor in this case can we condemn the considered judgment of three New York courts approving the means which the police, faced with a crisis, used in the exercise of their power and duty to preserve peace and order. The findings of the state courts as to the existing situation and the imminence of greater disorder coupled with petitioner's deliberate defiance of the police officers convince us that we should not reverse this conviction in the name of free speech.

Affirmed.

Mr. Justice FRANKFURTER, concurring in the [result].[1]

[U]ncontrolled official suppression of the speaker 'cannot be made a substitute for the duty to maintain order.' [Hague.] Where conduct is within the allowable limits of free speech, the police are peace officers for the speaker as well as for his hearers. But the power effectively to preserve order cannot be displaced by giving a speaker complete immunity. Here, [the officers] interfered only when they apprehended imminence of violence. It is not a constitutional principle that, in acting to preserve order, the police must proceed against the crowd, whatever its size and temper, and not against the [speaker].

Mr. Justice BLACK, dissenting.

The record before us convinces me that petitioner, a young college student, has been sentenced to the penitentiary for the unpopular views he expressed on matters of public interest while lawfully making a street-corner speech. [It] seems far-fetched to suggest that the "facts" show any imminent threat of riot or uncontrollable disorder. It is neither unusual nor unexpected that some people at public street meetings mutter, mill about, push, shove, or disagree, even violently, with the speaker. [Nor] does one isolated threat to assault the speaker forebode disorder. [Moreover], assuming that the "facts" did indicate a critical situation, I reject the implication of the Court's opinion that the police had no obligation to protect petitioner's constitutional right to talk. The police of course have power to prevent breaches of the peace. But if, in the name of preserving order, they ever can interfere with a lawful public speaker, they first must make all reasonable efforts to protect him. Here the policemen did not even pretend to try to protect petitioner. According to the officers' testimony, the crowd was restless but there is no showing of any attempt to quiet it; pedestrians were forced to walk into the street, but there was no effort to clear a path on the sidewalk; one person threatened to assault petitioner but the officers did nothing to discourage this when even a word might have sufficed. Their duty was to protect petitioner's right to talk, even to the extent of arresting the man who threatened to interfere.[2] Instead, they shirked that duty and acted only to suppress the right to speak.

---

1. Justice Frankfurter's opinion was applicable not only to Feiner but also to two companion cases, Kunz (1951; p. 1224 below), and Niemotko v. Maryland, 340 U.S. 268 (1951). In Niemotko, a disorderly conduct conviction of Jehovah's Witnesses for holding a meeting in a park without a permit was reversed on the ground that the denial of the permit had rested not on fear of disorder but rather on official dislike of the appellants and their views. (Other portions of this Frankfurther opinion, surveying the public forum cases, are printed in the introductory materials to this section, at p. 980 above.)

2. [The] threat of one person to assault a speaker does not justify suppression of the speech. There are obvious available alternative methods of preserving public order. One of

Finally, I cannot agree with the Court's statement that petitioner's disregard of the policeman's unexplained request amounted to such "deliberate defiance" as would justify an arrest or conviction for disorderly conduct. On the contrary, I think that the policeman's action was a "deliberate defiance" of ordinary official duty as well as of the constitutional right of free speech. For at least where time allows, courtesy and explanation of commands are basic elements of good official conduct in a democratic society. [Today's] holding means that as a practical matter, minority speakers can be silenced in any city. [For] whatever is thought to be guaranteed in [Kunz, p. 1224 below] is taken away by what is done here. [While] previous restraints probably cannot be imposed on an unpopular speaker, the police have discretion to silence him as soon as the customary hostility to his views [develops].

Mr. Justice DOUGLAS, with whom Mr. Justice MINTON concurs, [dissenting].

A speaker may not, of course, incite a riot. [But] this record shows no such extremes. It shows an unsympathetic audience and the threat of one man to haul the speaker from the stage. It is against that kind of threat that speakers need police protection. If they do not receive it and instead the police throw their weight on the side of those who would break up the meetings, the police become the new censors of speech. Police censorship has all the vices of the censorship from city halls which we have repeatedly [struck down].

EDWARDS: A "FAR CRY" FROM FEINER?

1. *The decision.* In EDWARDS v. SOUTH CAROLINA, 372 U.S. 229 (1963), the Court reversed breach of peace convictions of 187 black student demonstrators. Petitioners had walked along the South Carolina State House grounds to protest against racial discrimination. After a large crowd of onlookers gathered, they were ordered to disperse within 15 minutes; when they did not do so, they were arrested. The Court, in an opinion by Justice STEWART, held that "South Carolina infringed the petitioners' constitutionally protected rights." He added: "The 14th Amendment does not permit a State to make criminal the peaceful expression of unpopular views. [Terminiello.]" He noted that there had been no violence by the demonstrators or the onlookers; that there was no evidence of "fighting words"; and that the circumstances were "a far cry from the situation" in Feiner. He noted, too, that the convictions did not arise "from the evenhanded application of a precise and narrowly drawn regulatory statute evincing a legislative judgment that certain specific conduct be limited or proscribed. If, for example, the petitioners had been convicted upon evidence that they had violated a law regulating traffic, or had disobeyed a law reasonably limiting the periods during which the State House grounds were open to the public, this would be a different case."

Justice CLARK's dissent viewed the record differently. To him, this "was by no means the passive demonstration which this Court relates. [The question is] whether a State is constitutionally prohibited from enforcing laws to prevent breach of the peace in a situation where city officials in good faith believe, and the record shows, that disorder and violence are imminent, merely because the activities constituting that breach contain claimed elements of constitutionally protected speech and assembly. To me the answer under our cases is clearly in the negative." The situation in Feiner was "no more dangerous than that found

---

these is to arrest the person who threatens an assault. Cf. Dean Milk Co. v. Madison [1951; p. 270 above], decided today, in which the Court invalidates a municipal health ordinance under the Commerce Clause because of a belief that the city could have accomplished its purposes by reasonably adequate alternatives. The Court certainly should not be less alert to protect freedom of speech than it is to protect freedom of trade. [Footnote by Justice Black.]

here. [It] is my belief that anyone conversant with the almost spontaneous combustion in some Southern communities in such a situation will agree that the City Manager's action may well have averted a major catastrophe."

2. *Some questions.* Why was the protest march in Edwards "a far cry" from Feiner? Because here there was "peaceful expression of unpopular views" (rather than "incitement to riot," as the Court had described Feiner's speech)? Was that a persuasive distinction? Have the bounds of protected provocative speech changed since Feiner? Note the references to Edwards in the cases that follow.

Does the difference lie in the fact that the onlookers in Edwards in fact remained peaceful and that ample police were at hand? What if there had been some disorder: Would the speech still have been protected because most onlookers in most cities would remain peaceful? Should the focus be on the reasonable audience's reaction, or on the actual audience's response? The demonstrators carried placards with such messages as "Down with segregation," and engaged in "chanting," "stamping feet," and "clapping hands"—conduct that, according to the dissent, created a "much greater danger of riot and disorder" than in Feiner, given the atmosphere in "some Southern communities." Would an outbreak of disorder in these circumstances simply show police failure to protect "peaceful" speech? Or would it suggest that the speakers had used "fighting words"? Did the Court clarify the modern Robert's Rules for the hostile audience problem in the later cases arising from modern street demonstrations (especially Cox I (1965; p. 1225 below))?

What kind of a "precise and narrowly drawn regulatory statute" would survive judicial scrutiny in light of Edwards? Could the state house grounds be declared off limits to demonstrations entirely, on a legislative finding that the risk of interference with legislative business was too great and that alternative places for demonstrations were available? Or does Edwards imply a guaranteed access to the state house grounds as a public forum at least during some hours? Could a statute such as that sustained with respect to court house picketing in Cox II (1965; p. 1228 below) constitutionally curtail state house demonstrations?

GREGORY: STREET DEMONSTRATIONS AND THE UNSOLVED PROBLEM OF THE HOSTILE AUDIENCE

Claims that speakers may be restrained because of the risk of violence in hostile audience responses have come to the Court recurrently. Feiner was the Vinson Court's reaction to the problem. Edwards was a Warren Court effort of the early sixties. The street demonstration cases of the mid-sixties, in sec. 4E below, reflect additional encounters with the problem. A brief look at a 1969 decision appears here to illustrate that the hostile audience problem had not been solved by the end of the Warren era. What problems remain for solution if an adequate set of Robert's Rules is to be achieved?

1. *The decision.* In GREGORY v. CHICAGO, 394 U.S. 111 (1969), petitioners had "marched in a peaceful and orderly procession from city hall to the mayor's residence to press their claims for desegregation of the public schools." When "the number of bystanders increased" and "the onlookers became unruly," Chicago police, "to prevent what they regarded as an impending civil disorder," demanded that the demonstrators disperse. When petitioners refused to do so, they were arrested for disorderly conduct. Chief Justice WARREN's very brief opinion justifying the Court's reversal of the convictions asserted that this was "a simple case": as in Edwards, petitioners' peaceful conduct was activity protected by the First Amendment; as in Thompson v. Louisville, p. 1012 above, the convictions were "totally devoid of evidentiary

support" to show that the conduct was disorderly; and the trial judge's charge permitted the jury to convict for acts clearly entitled to First Amendment protection. Nor could the conviction rest on refusal to follow the dispersal request: petitioners were convicted for the demonstration, "not for a refusal to obey a police officer."

2. *The concurrence.* Justice BLACK's concurrence, joined by Justice Douglas, found lurking complexities in the "simple case." He noted that "both police and demonstrators made their best efforts faithfully to discharge their responsibilities as officers and citizens, but they were nevertheless unable to restrain the hostile hecklers within decent and orderly bounds." More generally, he commented "that when groups with diametrically opposed, deep-seated views are permitted to air their emotional grievances, side by side, on city streets, tranquility and order cannot be maintained even by the joint efforts of the finest and best officers and of those who desire to be the most law-abiding protestors of their grievances." Here, he emphasized, the disorderly conduct convictions were especially vulnerable because the ordinance was not a narrowly drawn law, but rather "a meat-ax ordinance": the Court had repeatedly warned against the "use of sweeping, dragnet statutes that may, because of vagueness, jeopardize" First Amendment freedoms. But, he added, the Court had also been careful to assure that "the Constitution does not bar enactment of laws regulating conduct, even though connected with speech, press, assembly, and petition, if such laws specifically bar only the conduct deemed obnoxious and are carefully and narrowly aimed at that forbidden conduct. The dilemma revealed by this record is a crying example of a need for some such narrowly drawn law."

3. *Some questions.* Is Gregory—either in the Warren or the Black emphasis—a step forward toward evolution of Robert's Rules for the hostile audience problem? Is the Black reliance on the speech-conduct distinction helpful? What "specific ban on conduct" would do, in his view? Would a specific ban on marches in all residential areas be a constitutional "narrowly drawn" law? A ban on processions during certain hours? A specific ban on demonstrations near the mayor's residence? A limit on the number of participants? What "conduct," in short, may a "narrowly drawn" ordinance "deem obnoxious"? Anything, so long as it is "conduct," not pure speech, and so long as it is identified in a "narrowly drawn" statute? If so, what of streets as a public forum? When subsequent restraints on provocative speakers are invoked, should the permissible sanction be limited to protective custody rather than punishment? Despite the Court's special hostility to prior restraints, could a permit scheme be a more speech-protective mechanism to deal with the hostile audience problem?

PERMIT REQUIREMENTS AND THE KUNZ CASE

Introduction. The cases from Feiner to Gregory considered efforts to deal with the hostile audience problem through the device of subsequent restraints. But can even "narrowly drawn" laws adequately deal with the problem if those laws must be applied after the fact? Can subsequent punishment laws adequately restrain on-the-spot police discretion? Would it be preferable to use a permit scheme, with prior notice of planned uses of public places, with the aim of providing adequate police protection for the speaker, and with clear standards to govern the issuance of permits? Should it be permissible to deny a permit for a meeting or parade because of anticipated fears of violence and hostile audience reactions? [1]

The recurrent problem of prior restraints and permit requirements, raised as early as Lovell and Cox, above, reemerged in one of the cases decided together with Feiner. Note especially the Jackson dissent in the Kunz case which follows, and consider the parallel to the Saia-Kovacs contrast in the Loudspeaker Cases above: Does it make sense to be so suspicious of prior licensing schemes (Saia, Kunz) when the state may penalize the speech by other, after-the-fact punishment routes (Kovacs, Feiner)? The problems raised by Kunz and licensing schemes are reexamined in the modern street demonstration context in the notes in sec. 4E below. [2]

The Kunz case. KUNZ v. NEW YORK, 340 U.S. 290 (1951), reversed a conviction for violating a New York City ordinance which prohibited public worship meetings in the street "without first obtaining a permit" from the police commissioner. The ordinance also made it unlawful "to ridicule or denounce any form of religious belief" or to "expound atheism or agnosticism [in] any street." Kunz, a Baptist minister, was convicted for holding a meeting in 1948 without a permit. He had obtained a permit in 1946, but that was revoked in the same year after an administrative hearing: there had been complaints that Kunz had engaged in "scurrilous attacks on Catholics and Jews," and the revocation was based on "evidence that he had ridiculed and denounced other religious beliefs in his meetings." Kunz's application for permits in 1947 and 1948 were "disapproved," without stated reasons. Chief Justice VINSON's majority opinion included the following passage:

"Disapproval of the 1948 permit application by the police commissioner was justified by the New York courts on the ground that a permit had previously been revoked 'for good reasons.' It is noteworthy that there is no mention in the ordinance of reasons for which such a permit application can be refused. This interpretation allows the police commissioner, an administrative official, to exercise discretion in denying subsequent permit applications on the basis of his interpretation, at that time, of what is deemed to be conduct condemned by the ordinance. We have here, then, an ordinance which gives an administrative official discretionary power to control in advance the right of citizens to speak on religious matters on the streets of New York. As such, the ordinance is clearly invalid as a prior restraint on the exercise of First Amendment rights. [The] court below has mistakenly derived support for its conclusion from the evidence [that] appellant's religious meetings had, in the past, caused some disorder. There are appropriate public remedies to protect the peace and order of the community if appellant's speeches should result in disorder or violence." [3]

Justice JACKSON's lengthy dissent included the following passage: "[It] seems hypercritical to strike down local laws on their faces for want of standards when we have no standards. [I]f the Court conceives, as Feiner indicates, that upon uttering insulting, provocative or inciting words the policeman on the beat may stop the meeting, then its assurance of free speech in this decision is 'a promise to the ear to be broken to the hope,' if the patrolman on the beat happens to have prejudices of his own. [It] seems to me that this [permit] procedure better protects freedom of speech than to let everyone speak without leave, but subject to surveillance and to being ordered to stop in the discretion of the police."

---

1. See generally Blasi, "Prior Restraints on Demonstrations," 68 Mich.L.Rev. 1481 (1970).

2. See also the note on permit requirements in the modern street demonstration context, p. 1235 below, and especially the lower courts' ef-

forts to deal with the problems of threatened American Nazi demonstrations in Illinois in the late 1970s, p. 1237 below.

3. Justices BLACK and FRANKFURTER concurred in the result.

E. MASS DEMONSTRATIONS IN TRADITIONAL PUBLIC PLACES SUCH AS STREETS: THE MODERN CONTEXT OF THE PUBLIC FORUM

Introduction. How useful are the analyses developed in the public places cases of the thirties and forties for the solution of modern street demonstration problems? Most early cases were stimulated by the "robust evangelism" of the Jehovah's Witnesses. During the fifties, as Professor Kalven remarked, "the story of the streets became a bit quaint." But by the sixties, with the rise of the civil rights and anti-war movements, it became clear "that the story [was] not over."[1] The Jehovah's Witnesses' evangelism may have been "robust," but it was largely the proselytizing of the single evangelist, selling magazines, ringing doorbells, speaking at street corners. The "evangelism" that began in the sixties was one of numbers, of parades in streets and vigils in parks, of protest meetings in front of and inside public buildings. With a greater need than ever for Robert's Rules, how did the Court respond? The Edwards and Gregory cases, above, illustrate some Warren Court answers. Are the modern cases more adequate? Are old Rules clarified and adapted to new circumstances? Are the judicial techniques responsive and satisfactory? The doctrinal tools developed in the preceding pages intertwine in the cases that follow; new techniques emerge; but the problems of principle and practice raised earlier persist as challenges in the modern cases that follow.

COX v. LOUISIANA [COX I]

379 U.S. 536, 85 S.Ct. 453, 13 L.Ed.2d 471 (1965).

[This case arose from the following circumstances: In December, 1961, 23 students from a black college were arrested in Baton Rouge, La., for picketing stores that maintained segregated lunch counters. The students were placed in a jail on the third floor of a local courthouse. The next day, appellant, the Rev. Cox, a Field Secretary of CORE, led about 2,000 students in a peaceful march toward the courthouse in order to protest the jailing. As Cox, at the head of the group, approached the vicinity of the courthouse, he was met by the police chief, who, according to Cox, permitted the demonstration but insisted that it must be confined to the west side of the street, across from the courthouse. The students lined up on the sidewalk 101 feet from the courthouse steps. They were about five deep and spread almost the entire length of the block. About 100 to 300 whites gathered on the opposite sidewalk. About 75 policemen were stationed on the street between the two groups. Some demonstrators carried picket signs advocating boycotts of "unfair" stores and the group sang songs and hymns, including "We Shall Overcome." The jailed students, out of sight of the demonstrators, responded by singing, and this in turn was greeted by cheers from the demonstrators.

[Cox gave a speech protesting the "illegal arrest" of the jailed students and urged the demonstrators to sit at segregated lunch counters. This evoked some "muttering" and "grumbling" from the white onlookers across the street. The sheriff viewed Cox's appeal to sit in at lunch counters as "inflammatory" and ordered the demonstration "broken up immediately." When the demonstrators did not disperse, policemen exploded tear gas shells. The demonstrators ran away. The next day, Cox was arrested and charged with several offenses. In

---

1. Kalven, "The Concept of the Public Forum: Cox v. Louisiana," 1965 Sup.Ct.Rev. 1.

this case, the Court reviewed convictions for breach of the peace and for obstructing the sidewalk.][1]

Mr. Justice GOLDBERG delivered the opinion of the [Court].

[*The breach of the peace conviction.*][2] It is clear to us that on the facts of this case, which are strikingly similar to those present in [Edwards], Louisiana infringed appellant's rights of free speech and free assembly by convicting him under this statute. [We] hold that Louisiana may not constitutionally punish appellant under this statute for engaging in the type of conduct which this record reveals, and also that the statute as authoritatively interpreted by the Louisiana Supreme Court is unconstitutionally broad in scope.

[O]ur independent examination of the [record] shows no conduct which the State had a right to prohibit as a breach of the peace. [The State argues] that while the demonstrators started out to be orderly, the loud cheering and clapping by the students in response to the singing from the jail converted the peaceful assembly into a riotous one. The record, however, does not support this assertion. [Our] conclusion that the entire meeting from the beginning until its dispersal by tear gas was orderly and not riotous is confirmed by a film of the events. [The] State contends that the conviction should be sustained because of fear expressed [that] "violence was about to erupt" because of the demonstration. [But] the students themselves were not violent and threatened no violence. [There] is no indication [that] any member of the white group threatened violence. And [the] policemen [could] have handled the crowd. This situation, like that in Edwards, is "a far cry from the situation in [Feiner]." Nor is there any evidence here of ["fighting words"].

There is an additional reason why this conviction cannot be sustained. The statute at issue in this case, as authoritatively interpreted by the Louisiana Supreme Court, is unconstitutionally vague in its overly broad scope. The statutory crime consists of two elements: (1) congregating with others "with intent to provoke a breach of the peace, or under circumstances such that a breach of the peace may be occasioned," and (2) a refusal to move on after having been ordered to do so by a law enforcement officer. While the second part of this offense is narrow and specific, the first element is not. The Louisiana Supreme Court in this case defined ["breach of the peace"] as "to agitate, to arouse from a state of repose, to molest, to interrupt, to hinder, to disquiet." [That] would allow persons to be punished merely for peacefully expressing unpopular views. [Therefore], as in Terminiello and Edwards the conviction [must] be reversed as the statute is unconstitutional in that it sweeps within its broad scope activities that are constitutionally [protected].

[*The obstructing public passages conviction.*][3] From [our] decisions certain clear principles emerge. The rights of free speech and assembly, while fundamental in our democratic society, still do not mean that everyone with opinions or

---

1. In a companion case (Cox II, which follows), the Court reviewed a conviction under a law banning courthouse picketing. Although the courthouse context moves into the sphere of nontraditional public forums considered in sec. 4F below—forums other than the traditional streets and parks—, Cox II is printed here with Cox I because of the similarity in the analyses of the companion cases.

2. The conviction was under Louisiana's "disturbing the peace" statute, which provided: "Whoever with intent to provoke a breach of the peace, or under circumstances such that a breach of the peace may be occasioned thereby, [crowds or congregates with others upon] a public street or a public highway, or upon a public sidewalk,

or any other public place or building [and] who fails or refuses to disperse and move on, [when] ordered to do so by any law enforcement officer, [shall] be guilty of disturbing the peace."

3. Cox's conviction for leading the meeting on the sidewalk across the street from the courthouse was based on a Louisiana law prohibiting the obstruction of "the free, convenient and normal use of any public sidewalk, street, [or] other passageway [by] impeding, hindering, stifling, retarding or restraining traffic or passage thereon." The statute added: "Providing, however, nothing herein contained shall apply to a bona fide legitimate labor organization or to any of its legal activities such as picketing."

beliefs to express may address a group at any public place and at any time. The constitutional guarantee of liberty implies the existence of an organized society maintaining public order, without which liberty itself would be lost in the excesses of anarchy. The control of travel on the streets is a clear example of governmental responsibility to insure this necessary order. A restriction in that relation, designed to promote the public convenience in the interest of all, and not susceptible to abuses of discriminatory application, cannot be disregarded by the attempted exercise of some civil right which, in other circumstances, would be entitled to protection. One would not be justified in ignoring the familiar red light because this was thought to be a means of social protest. Nor could one, contrary to traffic regulations, insist upon a street meeting in the middle of Times Square at the rush hour as a form of freedom of speech or assembly. Governmental authorities have the duty and responsibility to keep their streets open and available for movement. A group of demonstrators could not insist upon the right to cordon off a street, or entrance to a public or private building, and allow no one to pass who did not agree to listen to their [exhortations]. We emphatically reject the notion urged by appellant that the [First Amendment affords] the same kind of freedom to those who would communicate ideas by conduct such as patrolling, marching, and picketing on streets and highways, as these amendments afford to those who communicate ideas by pure speech. [We] reaffirm the statement of the Court in Giboney v. Empire Storage & Ice Co. [p. 1343 below] that "it has never been deemed an abridgment of freedom of speech or press to make a course of conduct illegal merely because the conduct was in part initiated, evidenced, or carried out by means of language, either spoken, written, or printed."

We have no occasion in this case to consider the constitutionality of the uniform, consistent, and nondiscriminatory application of a statute forbidding all access to streets and other public facilities for parades and meetings. Although the statute here involved on its face precludes all street assemblies and parades, it has not been so applied and enforced by the Baton Rouge authorities. City officials [indicated] that certain meetings and parades are permitted in Baton Rouge, even though they have the effect of obstructing traffic, provided prior approval is obtained. [The] statute itself provides no standards for the determination of local officials as to which assemblies to permit or which to prohibit. [It] appears that the authorities in Baton Rouge permit or prohibit parades or street meetings in their completely uncontrolled discretion. The situation is thus the same as if the statute itself expressly provided that there could only be peaceful parades or demonstrations in the unbridled discretion of the local officials. The pervasive restraint on freedom of discussion by the practice of the authorities under the statute is not any less effective than a statute expressly permitting such selective [enforcement]. [Such] broad discretion in a public official [permits] the official to act as a censor. [Also] inherent in such a system [is] the obvious danger to the right of a person or group not to be denied equal protection of the laws. [It] is clearly unconstitutional to enable a public official to determine which expressions of view will be permitted and which will not or to engage in invidious discrimination among persons or groups either by use of a statute providing a system of broad discretionary licensing power or, as in this case, the equivalent of such a system by selective enforcement of an extremely broad prohibitory [statute].

Reversed.[4]

---

4. The separate opinions applicable to Cox I are printed with Cox II, which follows. (See also the comments and questions about the Cox cases, in the notes after Cox II.)

COX v. LOUISIANA [COX II]

379 U.S. 559, 85 S.Ct. 476, 13 L.Ed.2d 487 (1965).

[This conviction of Cox, under a courthouse picketing statute, arose from the same demonstration as that in Cox I. The Court reversed the conviction. Although it rejected Cox's First Amendment challenge, it found another ground to set aside his conviction.]

Mr. Justice GOLDBERG delivered the opinion of the [Court].

This statute [1] was passed by Louisiana in 1950 and was modeled after a [federal law of 1950] pertaining to the federal judiciary [—a law which] resulted from the picketing of federal courthouses by partisans of the defendants during trials involving leaders of the Communist Party. This statute, unlike the two [in Cox I], is a precise, narrowly drawn regulatory statute which proscribes certain specific behavior. [There] can be no question that a State has a legitimate interest in protecting its judicial system from the pressures which picketing near a courthouse might create. Since we are committed to a government of laws and not of men, it is of the utmost importance that the administration of justice be absolutely fair and orderly. This Court has recognized that the unhindered and untrammeled functioning of our courts is part of the very foundation of our constitutional democracy. See Wood v. Georgia [p. 1337 below]. [M]ob law is the very antithesis of due process. [A] State may adopt safeguards necessary and appropriate to assure that the administration of justice at all stages is free from outside control and influence. A narrowly drawn statute such as the one under review is obviously a safeguard both necessary and appropriate to vindicate the State's interest in assuring justice under law. Nor does such a statute infringe upon the constitutionally protected rights of free speech and free assembly. The conduct which is the subject of this statute—picketing and parading—is subject to regulation even though intertwined with expression and association. The examples are many of the application by this Court of the principle that certain forms of conduct mixed with speech may be regulated or [prohibited].

Bridges v. California and Pennekamp v. Florida [cases, like Wood above, applying the clear and present danger test in reversing contempt of court convictions, p. 1338 below] do not hold to the contrary. [Here] we deal not with the contempt power [but with] a statute narrowly drawn. We are not concerned here with such a pure form of expression as newspaper comment or a telegram by a citizen to a public official. We deal in this case not with free speech alone, but with expression mixed with particular conduct. [We] hold that this statute on its face is a valid law dealing with conduct subject to regulation so as to vindicate important interests of society and that the fact that free speech is intermingled with such conduct does not bring with it constitutional protection.

We now deal with the Louisiana statute as applied to the conduct in this case. The group of 2,000, led by appellant, paraded and demonstrated before the courthouse. Judges and court officers were in attendance to discharge their respective functions. It is undisputed that a major purpose of the demonstration was to protest what the demonstrators considered an "illegal" arrest of 23 students the previous day. [It] is, of course, true that most judges will be influenced only by what they see and hear in court. However, judges are human; and the legislature has the right to recognize the danger that some

---

1. The law provided: "Whoever, with the intent of interfering with, obstructing, or impeding the administration of justice, or with the intent of influencing any judge, juror, witness, or court officer, in the discharge of his duty, pickets or parades in or near a building housing a court of the State of Louisiana [shall] be fined not more than five thousand dollars or imprisoned not more than one year, or both."

judges, jurors, and other court officials, will be consciously or unconsciously influenced by demonstrations in or near their courtrooms both prior to and at the time of the trial. A State may also properly protect the judicial process from being misjudged in the minds of the public. Suppose demonstrators paraded and picketed for weeks with signs asking that indictments be dismissed, and that a judge completely uninfluenced by these demonstrations, dismissed the indictments. A State may protect against the possibility of a conclusion by the public under these circumstances that the judge's action was in part a product of intimidation and did not flow only from the fair and orderly working of the [judicial process].

Appellant invokes the clear and present danger doctrine in support of his argument that the statute cannot constitutionally be applied to the conduct involved here, [relying upon Pennekamp and Bridges]. He defines the standard to be applied [to] be whether the expression of opinion presents a clear and present danger to the administration of justice. We have already pointed out the important differences between the contempt cases and the present one. [Here] we deal not with the contempt power but with a narrowly drafted statute and not with speech in its pristine form but with conduct of a totally different character. Even assuming the applicability of a general clear and present danger test, it is one thing to conclude that the mere publication of a newspaper editorial or a telegram to a Secretary of Labor, however critical of a court, presents no clear and present danger to the administration of justice and quite another thing to conclude that crowds, such as this, demonstrating before a courthouse may not be prohibited by a legislative determination based on experience that such conduct inherently threatens the judicial process. We therefore reject the clear and present danger [argument].

[However, Justice Goldberg did find "substantial constitutional objections" to the conviction. Noting that the police officials had permitted the demonstration to take place across the street from the courthouse, he commented: "In effect, [Cox] was advised that a demonstration at the place it was held would not be one 'near' the courthouse within the terms of the statute." Under those circumstances, subsequent conviction constituted "an indefensible sort of entrapment" in violation of due process. Moreover, he found that the later dispersal order did not remove the protection accorded Cox by the original grant of permission.]

Nothing we have said here or in [Cox I] is to be interpreted as sanctioning riotous conduct in any form or demonstrations, however peaceful their conduct or commendable their motives, which conflict with properly drawn statutes and ordinances designed to promote law and order, protect the community against disorder, regulate traffic, safeguard legitimate interests in private and public property, or protect the administration of justice and other essential governmental functions. We reaffirm the repeated holdings of this Court that our constitutional command of free speech and assembly [encompasses] peaceful social protest. [We] also reaffirm [that] there is no place for violence in a democratic society dedicated to liberty under law, and that the right of peaceful protest does not mean that everyone with opinions or beliefs to express may do so at any time and at any place. There is a proper time and place for even the most peaceful protest and a plain duty and responsibility on the part of all citizens to obey all valid [laws].

Reversed.

Mr. Justice BLACK, concurring in [Cox I] and dissenting in [Cox II].

[The First Amendment takes] away from government [all] power to restrict freedom of speech, press, and assembly *where people have a right to be for such purposes.* This does not mean, however, that [it also grants] a constitutional right to engage in the conduct of picketing or patrolling, whether on publicly owned streets or on privately owned property. [Were] the law otherwise, people on the streets, in their homes and anywhere else could be compelled to listen against their will to speakers they did not want to hear. Picketing, though it may be utilized to communicate ideas, is not speech, and therefore is not of itself protected by the First Amendment. [However], because Louisiana's breach-of-peace statute is not narrowly drawn to assure nondiscriminatory application, I think it is constitutionally invalid under our holding in [Edwards]. [As to the obstructing-public-passages conviction], I believe that the [First Amendment requires] that if the streets of a town are open to some views, they must be open to all. [B]y specifically permitting picketing for the publication of labor union views, Louisiana is attempting to pick and choose among the views it is willing to have discussed on its [streets].

I would sustain the conviction [for picketing near a courthouse]. Certainly the most obvious reason for their protest at the courthouse was to influence the judge and other court officials. [The] Court attempts to support its holding by its inference that the Chief of Police gave his consent to picketing the courthouse. But quite apart from the fact that a police chief cannot authorize violations of his State's criminal laws, there was strong, emphatic testimony that if any consent was given it was limited to telling Cox and his group to come no closer to the courthouse than they had already come without the consent of any [official]. [I] fail to understand how the Court can justify the reversal of this conviction because of a permission which testimony in the record denies was given, which could not have been authoritatively given anyway, and which even if given was soon afterwards [revoked].

[Those] who encourage minority groups to believe that the [Constitution gives] them a right to patrol and picket in the streets whenever they choose, in order to advance what they think to be a just and noble end, do no service to those minority groups, their cause, or their country. I am confident from this record that this appellant violated the Louisiana statute because of a mistaken belief that he and his followers had a constitutional right to do so, because of what they believed were just grievances. But the history of the past 25 years if it shows nothing else shows that his group's constitutional and statutory rights have to be protected by the courts, which must be kept free from intimidation and coercive pressures of any [kind].[2]

DEMONSTRATIONS AND COX: ADEQUATE GUIDELINES FOR THE PUBLIC FORUM? ADEQUATE TECHNIQUES FOR DEVELOPING GUIDELINES?

1. *Cox and the public forum.* Do the Cox cases make significant progress in developing Robert's Rules? Adequate progress? Are the Rules suggested sound? How should the gaps be filled? Is Professor Kalven persuasive in perceiving "a certain scheme of legal results" from the opinions: (1) at one extreme, it is "clear" that "this kind of use" of public places cannot be summarily suppressed as a breach of the peace, though there is some risk of violence; (2) at the other extreme, all picketing of courthouses can be prohibited; (3) "in the middle" is the "obstructing" streets question—a question the Court "colored with dicta but studiously avoided deciding."[1] Is (1) "clear", in

---

2. Justice CLARK also concurred in Cox I and dissented in Cox II. In another separate opinion, Justice WHITE, joined by Justice Harlan, dissented in Cox II and concurred with the reversal of the breach of the peace conviction in Cox I, on the basis of Edwards. Moreover, he dissented with respect to the reversal of the conviction for obstruction of public passages in Cox I.

1. Kalven, "The Concept of a Public Forum: Cox v. Louisiana," 1965 Sup.Ct.Rev. 1.

view of the efforts to distinguish Feiner in Edwards and Cox I? Is (2) sound? How should (3) be decided?

What do the Cox cases contribute to the concept of a public forum? Recall the distinction between an "assured minimum access" right to some public places and a narrower "equal access" view. What is the Cox Court's emphasis? Is the preoccupation with overbreadth and abuses of discretion so great that it produces an overwhelming emphasis on the equal access view? Do Justice Goldberg's opinions adequately reflect the legacy of Hague v. CIO and other cases on assured access? Note Justice Goldberg's comment in Cox I: "We have no occasion in this case to consider the constitutionality of the uniform, consistent, and nondiscriminatory application of a statute forbidding all access to streets and other public facilities for parades and meetings." Is that a surprising statement in a 1965 decision by the Warren Court? Should this have been an open question, after Hague and its progeny? Does the emphasis on discriminatory application (as well as on the "speech"-"conduct" distinction) obscure the underlying assured access problem? [2] Does the hesitancy about a presumptive First Amendment interest in access to streets and parks contribute to the uncertainties of the Court when the issues move to more novel places for public meetings, such as courts in Cox II and libraries, jails and military bases in the cases in sec. 4F below? [3]

2. *Cox and the "speech"-"conduct" distinction.* The majority opinions in the Cox cases not only suggest a far greater concern with "equal access" rather than "assured minimum access" to public places (and with greater scrutiny of "content-based" rather than "content-neutral" distinctions). They also repeatedly stress the much greater permissibility of regulating "conduct" rather than "speech." The "speech"-"conduct" distinction has already surfaced: recall especially the symbolic expression cases in sec. 3 above, and the criticism of that distinction as used in O'Brien and the Street dissent. Moreover, the distinction has surfaced frequently in the public forum cases, as the later materials illustrate. Does the distinction tend to extend exaggerated protection to the (slim) "pure speech" category—and tend to give inadequate protection to communication

2. Recall the comments in sec. 2 of this chapter about the distinction between content-based and content-neutral distinctions. Note that some commentators (see, e.g., p. 1166 above) maintain that this distinction is a special contribution by the Burger Court. However, as the Cox rulings of the Warren Court illustrate with particular force, the distinction was popular even earlier. Recall the criticisms of the distinction noted earlier. One of these criticisms suggests that the distinction may channel most if not all judicial energies into the search for content-based distinctions and give very much lower scrutiny—or no scrutiny at all—to content-neutral restraints, despite the impact the latter restraints may have on speech interests. Again, the Cox cases may provide particularly graphic early illustrations of these risks.

3. Contrast with the Warren Court's hesitancy about recognizing an assured minimum access right to streets the Burger Court's recognition that flat bans on access to streets are *im*permissible. Note, e.g., Greer v. Spock (1976; p. 1252 below), where the majority, while denying access for speech activities to military bases, stated as "the long-established constitutional rule" that "there cannot be a blanket exclusion of First Amendment activity from a municipality's open streets, sidewalks, and parks for the reasons stated in the familiar words of Mr. Justice Roberts in Hague v. CIO." However, this belated recognition of the thrust of the Roberts dictum was accompanied by a less speech-protective aspect of the case. In decisions such as Greer v. Spock, as the later materials illustrate, the Court began an approach of categorizing public places into those which qualify as "public forums" and those which do not. In the relatively narrow (and largely closed) category of traditional public forums, the modern Court has been ready to strike down flat bans and has recognized an assured minimum access interest under the First Amendment. But most instances of public places that have come before the modern Court have involved places *not* traditionally used for expression, and the Court has tended to apply quite deferential review of restrictions in these contexts. In most modern cases, the nontraditional forums have been characterized as not being "public forums"; in these contexts, the Court has tended to avoid not only the lower level review typically afforded to content-neutral regulations of "time, place, and manner," but has suggested that an even lower, even more deferential standard (of "reasonableness") is the appropriate judicial stance. See, e.g., United States Postal Service v. Greenburgh Civic Ass'ns, (1981; p. 1259 below).

outside that category? Does the "conduct" label unduly minimize the expression elements (and exaggerate the permissibility of restrictions)? Does the "speech"-"conduct" distinction promote insensitivity to free expression ingredients in situations that in fact involve *some* First Amendment elements? In short, the all-or-nothing distinction between the "speech" and "conduct" categories may artificially compartmentalize what are in fact matters of degree—and thereby promote inadequate judicial scrutiny of the "conduct" category. (See also the next note.) [4]

3. *Cox and the threat to courts.* Was the rejection of clear and present danger in Cox II sound? Would the clear and present danger test have been relevant here? At least as useful as in the contempt by publication cases distinguished in Cox II? [5] Compare the comments on the contempt cases, p. 1340 below. What *does* justify the ban on courthouse picketing? Is the "speech"-"conduct" distinction helpful? Kalven comments: "[A]ll speech is necessarily 'speech plus.'" He also suggests that the "essential feature" of most civil rights demonstrations in public places is "appeal to public opinion." If that is so, can the Court respond to the communicative element by labeling it conduct? If there is justification for restricting these forms of communication, should it not be explicitly stated why this form of expression is controllable, rather than suggesting that something other than speech is involved? Was the Warren Court more sensitive in the Brown and Adderley cases, below?

4. *Protection of courts in the 1980s.* In UNITED STATES v. GRACE, 461 U.S. 171 (1983), the challengers attacked a provision of 40 U.S.C. § 13k which prohibits the "display [of] any flag, banner, or device designed or adapted to bring into public notice any party, organization, or movement" in the U.S.

---

4. The "speech"-"conduct" distinction was especially popular during the Warren era, as the Cox cases, O'Brien, and Justice Black's position (see the introduction to the preceding chapter) illustrate. On the Burger Court, it has been invoked less often, sometimes because of reliance on other, arguably equally criticizable distinctions, such as those between places that are "public forums" and those that are not (see the preceding footnote). But the Burger Court has not been wholly free of a readiness to rely on a "speech"-"conduct" distinction. See, e.g., Chief Justice Burger's majority opinion in Haig v. Agee (1981; considered at p. 1040 above).

That case involved the revocation of the passport of a former CIA agent whose activities abroad had resulted in exposure of alleged undercover CIA agents and intelligence sources in foreign countries. Chief Justice Burger devoted most of his opinion to demonstrating that the executive action had been authorized by Congress and gave only cursory attention to the constitutional challenges. One of these challenges rested on the First Amendment. The Chief Justice stated in part: "To the extent the revocation of [Agee's] passport operates to inhibit [him], 'it is an inhibition of *action,*' rather than of speech. Zemel v. Rusk, 381 U.S. 1 (1965). Agee is as free to criticize the United States Government as he was when he held the passport." [Ironically, Chief Justice Burger relied on the language of his predecessor, Chief Justice Warren, the author of Zemel. In Zemel, another passport case, Chief Justice Warren had stated: "There are few restrictions on action which could not be clothed by ingenious argument in the garb

of decreased data flow." Contrast Justice Powell's comment on this approach in Saxbe v. Washington Post Co. (1974; p. 1440 below): "[T]he dichotomy between speech and action, while often helpful to analysis, is too uncertain to serve as the dispositive factor in charting the outer boundaries of First Amendment concerns." Justice Brennan's dissent in Haig v. Agee objected to the majority's "whirlwind treatment of Agee's constitutional claims" and its "extreme oversimplifications of constitutional doctrine." With respect to the use of the "speech"-"action" distinction, Justice Brennan commented: "Under the Court's rationale, I would suppose that a 40-year prison sentence imposed upon a person who criticized the Government's food stamp policy would represent only an 'inhibition of action.' After all, the individual would remain free to criticize the United States Government, albeit from a jail cell."

5. The contempt by publication cases are considered in sec. 2 of chap. 13 below. Compare with Justice Goldberg's opinion in Cox II Chief Justice Burger's opinion in Landmark Communications, Inc. v. Virginia (1978; p. 1341 below). Landmark, unlike Cox II, *invalidated* a law based on a legislatively perceived threat to the fair administration of justice; and Landmark, unlike Cox II, found that the contempt of court cases such as Bridges v. California *were* relevant in the review of state legislation. In Landmark, the conviction was reversed in the face of a legislative finding "that a clear and present danger to the orderly administration of justice would be created by divulgence of the confidential proceedings of the [Judicial Inquiry] Commission."

Supreme Court building and on its grounds. However, the Court did not reach the problem of restricting expression in the interest of promoting the administration of justice. Instead, since the controversy "concerned [the challengers' right] to use the public sidewalks surrounding the Court building for the communicative activities they sought to carry out," the Court addressed "only whether the proscriptions [are] constitutional as applied to the public sidewalks." [6]

In holding § 13k unconstitutional as applied to the sidewalks adjacent to the Court, Justice WHITE stated: "The sidewalks comprising the outer boundaries of the Court grounds are indistinguishable from any other sidewalks in Washington, D.C., and we can discern no reason why they should be treated any differently. Sidewalks, of course, are among those areas of public property that traditionally have been held open to the public for expressive activities and are clearly within those areas of public property that may be considered, generally without further inquiry, to be public forum property. [This case is unlike Greer v. Spock, p. 1252 below, where] the streets and sidewalks [were] located within an enclosed military reservation. [Here, there is] no separation, no fence, and no indication whatever to persons stepping from the street to the curb and sidewalks that serve as the perimeter of the Court grounds that they have entered some special type of enclave. [Traditional] public forum property occupies a special position in terms of First Amendment protection and will not lose its historically recognized character for the reason that it abuts government property that has been dedicated to a use other than as a forum for public expression. Nor may the government transform the character of the property by the expedient of including it within the statutory definition of what might be considered a nonpublic forum parcel of property." Justice White rejected the Government's argument that the ban could be justified as "a reasonable time, place, and manner restriction" on public forum property. He found no sufficient connection with any of the asserted state interests to warrant the restriction. For example, he questioned whether the statutory ban substantially served the purpose of maintaining proper order and decorum within the Court grounds. The Government also relied (as Justice Goldberg had in Cox II) on the claim that the restraint should stand lest it "*appear* to the public that the Supreme Court is subject to outside influence or that picketing or marching, singly or in groups, is an acceptable or proper way of appealing to or influencing the Supreme Court." Justice White recognized "the importance of this proffered purpose," but was "unconvinced that the prohibitions [at] issue here sufficiently serve that purpose to sustain its validity insofar as the public sidewalks on the perimeter of the grounds are concerned." Here, he explained: "Those sidewalks are used by the public like other public sidewalks. [We] seriously doubt that the public would draw a different inference from a lone picketer carrying a sign on the sidewalks around the building than it would from a similar picket on the sidewalks across the street."

In a separate opinion, Justice MARSHALL argued that the ban should be found "unconstitutional on its face": "The statute in no way distinguishes the sidewalks from the rest of the premises, and excising the sidewalks from its purview does not bring it into conformity with the First Amendment. [Since] the continuing existence of the statute will inevitably have a chilling effect on freedom of expression, there is no virtue in deciding its constitutionality on a piecemeal basis. [Every] citizen lawfully present in a public place has a right to engage in peaceable and orderly expression that is not incompatible with the primary activity of the place in [question]. I see no reason why the premises of

---

6. Appellee Thaddeus Zywicki had distributed leaflets to passersby on the sidewalk. The leaflets were reprints of a letter to a newspaper from a Senator concerning the removal of unfit judges from the bench. Appellee Mary Grace displayed on the sidewalk a four foot by two-and-a-half foot sign on which was inscribed the verbatim text of the First Amendment.

this Court should be exempt from this basic principle." He added: "The statute is not a reasonable regulation of time, place, and manner, for it applies at all times, covers the entire premises, and, as interpreted by the Court, proscribes even the handing out of a leaflet and, presumably, the wearing of a campaign button as well. Nor does the statute merely forbid conduct that is incompatible with the primary activity being carried out in this Court. [Nor is it] limited to expressive activities that are intended to interfere with, obstruct, or impede the administration of justice." [7]

USES OF THE STREETS SINCE COX

This group of cases samples decisions since Cox involving restraints on street use. Consider the range of judicial techniques employed. To what extent does this mix of overbreadth, vagueness, and "as applied" adjudication significantly further the search for guidelines regarding access to traditional public forums? [1]

BACHELLAR v. MARYLAND, 397 U.S. 564 (1970): Petitioners were convicted under a law which prohibits "acting in a disorderly manner to the disturbance of the public peace, upon any public street." The state courts affirmed their convictions against a challenge that their conduct was constitutionally protected under the First Amendment. The Court unanimously reversed. The prosecutions arose out of an antiwar demonstration in front of an Army Recruiting Station. After participating in a march in front of the station, petitioners staged a brief sit-in inside the station, were removed, and ended up on the sidewalk in front of the station. The instructions to the jury offered alternative grounds for conviction under the statute: the jury might find petitioners had engaged in "the doing or saying or both of that which offends, disturbs, incites or tends to incite a number of people gathered in the same area"; or a guilty verdict under the disorderly conduct charge might be based on "refusal to obey a policeman's command to move on when not to do so may endanger the public peace." Justice BRENNAN's opinion concluded: "On this record, if the jury believed the State's evidence, petitioners' convictions could constitutionally have rested on a finding that they sat or lay across a public sidewalk with the intent of fully blocking passage along it, or that they refused to obey police commands to stop obstructing the sidewalk in this manner and move on. See, e.g., [Cox I]. It is impossible to say, however, that either of these grounds was the basis for the verdict. On the contrary, so far as we can tell, it is equally likely that the verdict resulted 'merely because [petitioners' views about the Vietnam war were] themselves offensive to some of their hearers.' Thus, since petitioners' convictions may have rested on an unconstitutional ground, they must be set aside."

COATES v. CINCINNATI, 402 U.S. 611 (1971): An ordinance made it illegal for "three or more persons to assemble [on] any of the sidewalks [and] there conduct themselves in a manner annoying to persons passing by." Justice STEWART's opinion found the ordinance "unconstitutionally vague because it subjects the exercise of the right of assembly to an unascertainable standard, and unconstitutionally broad because it authorizes the punishment of constitutionally protected conduct." On the vagueness point, he stated that the "annoying" criterion meant that "no standard of conduct is specified at all." With respect to overbreadth, he emphasized that the right of assembly could not be restricted

---

7. In another separate opinion, Justice STEVENS urged avoiding the constitutional question and deciding the case on statutory grounds: "I see no reason to stretch the language of the statute to encompass the activities of [the challengers here]."

1. These cases also help illustrate the overbreadth and vagueness techniques surveyed in sec. 1 of this chapter.

"simply because its exercise may be 'annoying' to some people." And such a prohibition "contains an obvious invitation to discriminatory enforcement against those whose association together is 'annoying' because their ideas, their lifestyle or their physical appearance is resented by the majority of their fellow citizens." [2]

COMPLIANCE WITH PERMIT REQUIREMENTS AND INJUNCTIONS IN THE MASS DEMONSTRATION CONTEXT

Introduction. A procedural theme of great practical importance has recurrently surfaced in the preceding materials: When may a speaker ignore the existence of a permit requirement, or the refusal of permission under such a scheme, and proceed to make a speech? May a speaker who has spoken or demonstrated without a permit raise constitutional challenges to the permit scheme or the permit denial in a prosecution for speaking without a permit? To what extent do the doctrines of the early licensing cases (e.g., Lovell, Cox v. New Hampshire and Kunz) govern the modern regulations of mass meetings and parades through permit requirements and other "prior restraints"?

The Warren Court considered these questions in the late sixties, in connection with two efforts to challenge a Birmingham parade permit ordinance. Both efforts involved the Good Friday civil rights protest march in Birmingham in 1963, led by several black ministers, including Martin Luther King, Jr. The ordinance was ultimately found to be unconstitutional, but the first effort to

---

2. The pure "on the face" rather than "as applied" analysis in Coates was emphasized by the majority's ability to state all of the facts known to the Court in a portion of a single sentence: the record "tells us no more than that [Coates] was a student involved in a demonstration and the other appellants were pickets involved in a labor dispute." To the four dissenters, that lack of record data was a major factor counseling against a ruling of unconstitutionality. Justice WHITE's dissent thought the law was not vague on its face and added: "Even accepting the overbreadth doctrine with respect to statutes clearly reaching speech, the Cincinnati ordinance does not purport to bar or regulate speech as such." (In Broadrick v. Oklahoma (1973; p. 1151 above), the "substantial overbreadth" case, the dissenters claimed that Broadrick had "effectively overrule[d]" Coates.)

Compare with Coates a decision a year later in Papachristou v. Jacksonville, 405 U.S. 156 (1972), where a unanimous Court held a local vagrancy ordinance unconstitutional on its face on vagueness grounds. The ordinance included among its definition of vagrants "rogues and vagabonds, or dissolute persons who go about begging," "common drunkards," "common night walkers," "habitual loafers," and "persons wandering or strolling around from place to place without any lawful purpose or object." Justice Douglas concluded that the law was vague both in the sense that it failed to give fair notice and because it encouraged "arbitrary and erratic arrests and convictions."

See also Kolender v. Lawson, 461 U.S. 352 (1983), striking down on vagueness grounds a California law "that requires persons who loiter or wander on the streets to provide a 'credible and reliable' identification and to account for their presence when requested by a peace officer." Justice O'Connor's majority opinion relied heavily on the special justifications for the vagueness doctrine articulated in Smith v. Goguen (1974; sec. 3 at p. 1185 above): "Although the [vagueness] doctrine focuses both on actual notice to citizens and arbitrary enforcement, we have recognized [that] the more important aspect of the vagueness doctrine 'is not actual notice, but the other principal element of the doctrine—the requirement that the legislature establish minimal guidelines to govern law enforcement.'" She noted: "Our concern here is based upon the 'potential for arbitrarily suppressing First Amendment [liberties],' Shuttlesworth v. Birmingham [1969; p. 1236 below]." Justice White, joined by Justice Rehnquist, dissented, insisting that in the absence of specific identification of the way in which a law might implicate the First Amendment, it should not be struck down on vagueness grounds "unless it is 'impermissibly vague in all of its applications.'"

The Coates vagueness ruling was distinguished in Grayned v. Rockford (1972; p. 1264 below), where Justice Marshall's opinion rejected a vagueness attack on an anti-noise ordinance applicable to places adjacent to school buildings. Confident that the state courts would interpret the law "to prohibit only actual or imminent interference with the 'peace or good order' of the school," Justice Marshall argued that it was distinguishable from general breach of the peace ordinances because it was "written specifically for the school context, where the prohibited disturbances are easily measured by their impact on the normal activities of the school."

challenge it failed. In WALKER v. BIRMINGHAM, 388 U.S. 307 (1967), the demonstrators had marched in the face of an ex parte injunction directing compliance with the ordinance. The Court held that the demonstrators (who had not challenged the injunction in court before marching) could not defend contempt charges by asserting the unconstitutionality of the ordinance or the injunction. But two years later, in SHUTTLESWORTH v. BIRMINGHAM, 394 U.S. 147 (1969), one of the demonstrators in the same march was successful in having his constitutional challenge to the ordinance heard and sustained: in Shuttlesworth, the charge was parading without a permit in violation of the ordinance, not disobeying an injunction; and in that context, the Court held the ordinance unconstitutional.

1. *Walker.* In Walker, the 5 to 4 decision sustained a state court's refusal to consider constitutional challenges to the injunction and to the ordinance at the contempt hearing: petitioners had openly flouted the injunction because they considered it "raw tyranny"; Alabama had justifiably relied on the general rule that court orders must be obeyed until "reversed for error by orderly review." Justice STEWART concluded: "This Court cannot hold that the petitioners were constitutionally free to ignore all the procedures of the law and carry their battle to the streets." Justice BRENNAN's dissent, joined by Chief Justice Warren and Justices Douglas and Fortas, insisted that the Court had elevated a "rule of judicial administration above the right of free expression." [1]

2. *Shuttlesworth.* In Shuttlesworth, however, one of the petitioners in Walker was permitted to challenge the parade ordinance in attacking his conviction for marching without a permit. The ordinance directed the city commission to issue a permit "unless in its judgment the public welfare, peace, safety, health, decency, good order, morals, or convenience require that it be refused." Justice STEWART's opinion for the Court had "no doubt" that, as written, the ordinance was unconstitutional because it conferred "virtually unbridled and absolute power." The state countered that the conviction should nevertheless stand because the highest state court here—following the pattern accepted by the Court in Cox v. New Hampshire, p. 1202 above—had given a narrow construction to the broadly written law in reviewing petitioner's case. The Court conceded that the Alabama judges' "remarkable job of plastic surgery upon the face of the ordinance" had transformed it into one "authorizing no more than the objective and even-handed regulation of traffic." But here, unlike Cox, the narrowing effort came too late. Here, it was difficult to anticipate the subsequent construction: it "would have taken extraordinary clairvoyance for anyone" in 1963 to perceive that the ordinance meant what the highest state court construed it to mean in 1967. Moreover, the city officials had indicated in 1963 that they thought "the ordinance meant exactly what it said" on its face: they had given petitioner to understand that "under no circumstances" would he be permitted to demonstrate in Birmingham. In Cox, unlike here, there had been no prior administrative practice different from the state court's subsequent narrowing construction.

3. *Carroll.* Contrast with the impact of the injunction in Walker the restrictions imposed on injunctions in a properly raised challenge, in CARROLL v. PRESIDENT & COMM'RS OF PRINCESS ANNE, 393 U.S. 175 (1968). There, the Court found unconstitutional the ex parte procedure followed in issuing a 10-day temporary restraining order against holding a public rally. Petitioners had held a meeting at which they made "aggressively and militantly racist" speeches to a crowd of both whites and blacks. They announced that they would resume the rally the following night. Before that time, local

---

1. Compare the First Amendment limits imposed on ex parte injunctions a year later in Carroll, note 3 below, where petitioners obeyed the injunction and then challenged it successfully in court.

officials obtained the order restraining petitioners and their "white supremacist" National States Rights Party from holding meetings "which will tend to disturb and endanger the citizens of the County." There was no notice to petitioners prior to the issuance of the order. The rally was cancelled and petitioners (rather than ignoring the injunction as in Walker) challenged the injunction in court. Justice FORTAS' opinion for the Court found no adequate justification for the ex parte nature of the proceedings. In the rare situations where prior restraints were permissible (see Freedman v. Maryland, p. 1160 above), "the Court has insisted upon careful procedural provisions." "There is a place in our jurisprudence for ex parte issuance, without notice, of temporary restraining orders of short duration; but there is no place within the area of basic freedoms guaranteed by the First Amendment for such orders where no showing is made that it is impossible to serve or to notify the opposing parties and to give them an opportunity to participate." Here, procedural care was even more important than in the obscenity context of Freedman: "The present case involves a rally and 'political' speech in which the element of timeliness may be important." Without an adversary hearing, there was "insufficient assurance of the balanced analysis and careful conclusions which are essential in the area of First Amendment adjudication."

4. *Some questions and comments.* Does the distinction between Walker and Shuttlesworth make sense? Does the distinction between Shuttlesworth and Cox v. New Hampshire make sense? What are the operative guidelines in light of the modern cases for demonstrators trying to evaluate the risks of marching without seeking a permit or after denial of a permit: When can they expect to be able to raise constitutional defenses to the permit scheme or permit denial in subsequent prosecutions?[2] Is it still true that, as in Lovell, a facially invalid law may be ignored by the speaker? Is it still true that, as in Cox v. New Hampshire, a speaker takes the risk that a facially questionable law may be construed narrowly and constitutionally by the state courts? Why did that state technique not succeed in Shuttlesworth? Is it still true that a speaker may not ignore a permit scheme where the constitutional objection goes not to the constitutionality of the law but rather to the arbitrariness of its administration? Recall Poulos v. New Hampshire (1953; p. 1202 above), where a speaker had been arbitrarily denied a permit under a valid law. The Court rejected the speaker's argument "that he may risk speaking without a license and defeat prosecution by showing the license was arbitrarily withheld." Justice Reed was unpersuaded by the defendant's objection that "his right to preach may be postponed until a case, possibly after years, reaches this Court for final adjudication of constitutional rights." He answered: "Delay is unfortunate, but the expense and annoyance of litigation is a price citizens must pay for life in an orderly society where the rights of the First Amendment have a real and abiding meaning." Is the delay permitted in the Poulos context sharply curtailed by the "careful procedural provisions"—including time requirements—required by Freedman v. Maryland (1965; p. 1160 above)?

THE SKOKIE CONTROVERSY:
FIRST AMENDMENT PROBLEMS IN EFFORTS
TO RESTRAIN NAZI DEMONSTRATIONS

Introduction. In the late 1970s, plans by American Nazis to hold marches and meetings in Illinois spurred a range of efforts by local governments to block the demonstrations and prompted the courts to reexamine the procedural and

---

2. See generally Blasi, "Prior Restraints on Demonstrations," 68 Mich.L.Rev. 1481 (1970), and Monaghan, "First Amendment 'Due Process,'" 83 Harv.L.Rev. 518 (1970).

substantive principles governing access to traditional public forums. Most of the litigation took place in the state and lower federal courts; the Court's encounters with the emotional controversy were tangential. Ultimately, all local efforts to stop the Nazis were struck down by the courts. But the tensions felt by the judges were reflected in a comment by Justice Blackmun in dissenting from the denial of certiorari in Smith v. Collin, 439 U.S. 916 (1978). Noting the "pervading sensitivity of the litigation," he commented: "On the one hand, we have precious First Amendment rights vigorously asserted and an obvious concern that, if those asserted rights are not recognized, the precedent of a 'hard' case might offer a justification for repression in the future. On the other hand, we are presented with evidence of a potentially explosive and dangerous situation, enflamed by unforgettable recollections of traumatic experiences in the second world conflict." Consider, in light of the preceding materials, the proper resolution of the constitutional disputes engendered by the Nazis' plans. Consider, too, in light of the failures of all the efforts to stop the Nazis' demonstrations, whether any other measures of control could have withstood First Amendment attacks.[1]

1. *Injunctions against demonstrations and the need for speedy judicial review.* Most of the Nazi plans focused on a proposed march in Skokie, Illinois, a community with a large Jewish population, including many survivors of Nazi persecutions. In the first round of the Skokie efforts to stop the demonstration, a state trial court issued an injunction prohibiting the National Socialist Party from engaging in a number of activities in the town—e.g., "parading in the uniform" of the Party; "displaying the swastika"; and "[d]istributing pamphlets [that] incite or promote hatred against persons of Jewish faith or ancestry or hatred against any person of any faith or ancestry, race or religion." The Illinois appellate courts refused to stay the injunction pending appeal, and the Illinois Supreme Court denied a petition for direct expedited appeal to that court. The Party then sought a stay in the U.S. Supreme Court. The Court treated the stay petition as a petition for certiorari, granted the writ, and summarily reversed the highest state court's denial of the stay. In its per curiam disposition in NATIONAL SOCIALIST PARTY v. SKOKIE, 432 U.S. 43 (1977), the Court emphasized the need for "strict procedural safeguards" in the First Amendment area.

The 5–4 decision found the state court action to be a reviewable "final judgment" under the jurisdictional statute, noting that it "finally determined the merits of appellants' claim that the outstanding injunction would deprive them of rights protected by the First Amendment during the period of appellate review which, in the normal course, may take a year or more to complete." And that probable delay, the majority concluded, was intolerable in the First Amendment area: "If a State seeks to impose a restraint of this kind, it must provide strict procedural safeguards, Freedman v. Maryland, including immediate appellate review. Absent such review, the State must instead allow a stay. The order of the Illinois Supreme Court constituted a denial of that right."[2] In response to that ruling, the Illinois courts ultimately set aside the preliminary

1. Recall the materials in sec. 2B of the preceding chapter, at p. 1097 above, on the modern efforts to curb pornography on the ground that it subordinates and degrades women. Consider what arguments raised in support of such ordinances are relevant to Skokie's efforts to curb Nazi demonstrations. Recall also the District Court opinion, noted above, striking down the Indianapolis pornography ordinance on First Amendment grounds.

2. Justice Rehnquist's dissent, joined by Chief Justice Burger and Justice Stewart, conceded that the injunction was "extremely broad." In light of prior First Amendment decisions, he added, the Illinois courts could be expected to "at least substantially modif[y]" it. But he disagreed with the majority's action because "I simply do not see how [the refusal of a stay below] can be described as a 'final judgment'" in the sense of the jurisdictional statute. He noted: "No Illinois appellate court has heard or decided the merits of applicants' federal claim." Justice White also dissented, without opinion.

injunction that had barred the Nazis' march. In the first instance, the interme-diate appellate court modified the injunction, leaving in effect only a provision enjoining the defendants from "displaying the swastika" during the march. (366 N.E.2d 347.) Thereafter, the Illinois Supreme Court held that the entire injunction, including the swastika provision, was unconstitutional. The majority concluded, "albeit reluctantly," that "the display of the swastika cannot be enjoined under the fighting-words exception to free speech, nor can anticipation of a hostile audience justify the prior restraint. Furthermore, Cohen and Erzonoznik direct the citizens of Skokie that it is their burden to avoid the offensive symbol if they can do so without unreasonable inconvenience." (373 N.E.2d 21.)

2. *Other devices to curb the Nazi demonstrations.* By the time the injunction dispute ended, a second round of efforts to block the Nazi demonstration had gotten under way. In May 1977, Skokie enacted three ordinances to prohibit demonstrations such as the one the Nazis contemplated. The first established a comprehensive permit system for parades and public assemblies, requiring permit applicants to obtain $300,000 in public liability insurance and $50,000 in property damage insurance. The second prohibited the "dissemination of any materials within [Skokie] which [intentionally] promotes and incites hatred against persons by reason of their race, national origin, or religion." (Compare the Illinois group libel law sustained by the Court in 1952, in Beauharnais v. Illinois, p. 1050 above.) The third ordinance prohibited public demonstrations by members of political parties while wearing "military-style" uniforms.

Represented by a Jewish ACLU attorney, the National Socialist Party of America and its leader at that time, Frank Collin, brought a federal court action to challenge the Skokie ordinances on First Amendment grounds. In Collin v. Smith [447 F.Supp. 676 (1978)], the District Court held the ordinances unconstitutional, commenting that "it is better to allow those who preach racial hate to expend their venom in rhetoric rather than to be panicked into embarking on the dangerous course of permitting the government to decide what its citizens may say and hear." The Court of Appeals affirmed that decision in almost all respects. In invalidating the ban on dissemination of materials promoting and inciting hatred, the majority found Beauharnais not binding. It commented: "It may be questioned, after cases such as Cohen v. California, Gooding v. Wilson, and Brandenburg v. Ohio, whether the *tendency to induce violence* approach sanctioned implicitly in Beauharnais would pass constitutional muster today." And it added that the Skokie ordinance could not be sustained on the basis of "blind obeisance to uncertain implications from an opinion issued years before the Supreme Court itself rewrote the rules." [3] [Collin v. Smith, 578 F.2d 1197 (7th Cir., 1978).] [4] With the Nazi demonstra-tion scheduled June 25, 1978, Skokie sought a Supreme Court stay of the Court of Appeals ruling, pending review. On June 12, 1978, however, the Supreme Court denied the stay. Justice Blackmun, joined by Justice Rehnquist, dissented from that order, stating that the Court of Appeals decision "is in some tension with this Court's decision, 25 years ago, in Beauharnais," and noting that

3. In ruling on the insurance requirement, the Court of Appeals majority found it unconsti-tutional as applied rather than embracing the trial judge's view that it was invalid on its face. The Court of Appeals commented that "we do not need to determine now that no insurance requirement could be imposed in any circum-stances, which would be a close question."

4. After the Court of Appeals decision in May, 1978, opponents of the march introduced two bills in the Illinois legislature designed to replace the invalidated Skokie ordinances. The bills were approved by the Illinois Senate but rejected by the House in mid-June 1978. One bill would have made it unlawful to engage in "criminal group defamation" by displaying in public any sign, slogan, or symbol defaming citi-zens of any race, creed, or color. The other bill would have banned demonstrations by groups that arouse "reasonable apprehensions" that they are organized for the purpose of using or display-ing physical force to promote their beliefs.

"Beauharnais has never been overruled or formally limited in any way." Smith v. Collin, 436 U.S. 953.

With all legal obstacles to the Skokie march removed by the Court's denial of the stay, Collin cancelled the planned demonstration three days before it was to take place. Relying on the rulings in the Skokie litigation, the Nazis had obtained a federal court order setting aside the Chicago Park District's $60,000 liability insurance requirement which had previously blocked Nazi demonstrations in city parks there. Collin explained that the aim of the Nazis' Skokie efforts had been "pure agitation to restore our right to free speech." He stated that "he had used the threat of the Skokie march to win the right to rally in [Chicago]." No serious violence occurred when about 25 Nazis held a rally in a Chicago park on July 9, 1978.

The final scene in the Skokie drama took place in October, 1978, when the Court refused to review the Seventh Circuit decision invalidating the Skokie ordinances. SMITH v. COLLIN, 439 U.S. 916. Justice BLACKMUN, joined by Justice White, dissented, urging that certiorari be granted "in order to resolve any possible conflict that may exist between the ruling of the Seventh Circuit here and Beauharnais." He added: "I also feel that the present case affords the Court an opportunity to consider whether, in the context of the facts that this record appears to present, there is no limit whatsoever to the exercise of free speech. There indeed may be no such limit, but when citizens assert, not casually but with deep conviction, that the proposed demonstration is scheduled at a place and in a manner that is taunting and overwhelmingly offensive to the citizens of that place, that assertion, uncomfortable though it may be for judges, deserves to be examined. It just might fall into the same category as one's 'right' to cry 'fire' in a crowded theater, for 'the character of every act depends upon the circumstances in which it is done.' Schenck."

F. ACCESS TO NONTRADITIONAL PUBLIC PLACES: SHOULD THE CONTOURS OF THE PUBLIC FORUM EXTEND BEYOND THE TRADITIONAL STREETS AND PARKS?

Introduction. In Hague v. CIO, Justice Roberts, in speaking of public places which have "immemorially" and "time out of mind" been used for "discussing public questions," mentioned only "streets and parks." And most of the preceding materials involved access to and regulation of streets and parks as a public forum. What of other public places? In Cox II, the Court rejected efforts to demonstrate near a courthouse. Was that because of the special protection of the judicial process? Or was that a signal that places that were not "immemorially" public forums could be kept free of meetings and demonstrations? In a series of modern cases, the Court has confronted claims of speakers seeking access to such nontraditional forums as libraries, jail environs, buses, and schools. Should an assured minimum access claim be recognized in these contexts as well? At least an equal access claim? The modern Court has increasingly limited its serious scrutiny of denials of both minimum access and equal access to public places it labels "public forums." With respect to "non-public forums," judicial review tends to be at a very deferential level—even more deferential than that afforded to content-neutral "time, place, and manner" restrictions. Is the Court's rigid "public forum"-"non-public forum" distinction persuasive? Or should the Court apply a unitary First Amendment approach to all access claims to public property?[1]　If the prevailing Court approach is to persist—an approach that considers the first and often decisive inquiry whether the public property to which access is sought is or is not a "public forum"—what should be the governing criteria in making that determination?　Solely tradition?　The compatibility of expressive activities with other ("primary"?) uses of the property?　The availability to the First Amendment claimant of alternative forums for expression?　The relationship between the subject matter of the protest and the nontraditional forum of protest?　Cf. Brown, which follows.

DEMONSTRATIONS IN LIBRARIES AND NEAR JAILS

BROWN v. LOUISIANA, 383 U.S. 131 (1966): The events giving rise to this case took place at a branch public library in Louisiana.　The branch did not serve blacks.　Five young blacks entered the reading room and one of them, Brown, asked branch assistant Reeves for a book.　Reeves told Brown that she did not have the book but would request it from the state library and would notify him upon receipt.　When Reeves asked the young black men to leave, they refused.　Instead, Brown, in protest against the library's discriminatory policy, sat down and the others stood near him.　There was no noise or boisterous talking.　After about 10 minutes, the sheriff arrived and asked the blacks to leave; when they did not, he arrested them.　Brown and his companions were convicted under Louisiana's breach of the peace statute.[1]

The Court's 5 to 4 decision reversed the convictions.　Justice FORTAS' plurality opinion, joined only by Chief Justice Warren and Justice Douglas, stated: "The issue, asserts the State, is simply that petitioners were using the library room 'as a place in which to loaf or make a nuisance of themselves.' The State argues that the 'test'—the permissible civil rights demonstration—was concluded when petitioners entered the library, asked for service and were served.　Having satisfied themselves, the argument runs, that they could get service, they should have departed.　Instead, they simply sat there, 'staring vacantly,' and this was 'enough to unnerve a woman in the situation Mrs. Reeves was in.'　This is a piquant version of the affair, but the matter is hardly to be decided on points.　It was not a game.　It could not be won so handily by the gesture of service to this particular request.　There is no dispute that the library system was segregated, and no possible doubt that these petitioners were there to protest this fact.　But even if we were to agree with the State's ingenuous characterization of the events, we would have to reverse.　There was no violation of the statute which petitioners are accused of breaching; no disorder, no intent to provoke a breach of the peace and no circumstances indicating that a breach might be occasioned by petitioners' actions.　The sole statutory provision invoked by the State contains not a word about occupying the reading room of a public library for more than 15 minutes.

"[But] there is another and sharper answer which is called for.　We are here dealing with an aspect of a basic constitutional right—the right under the First and Fourteenth Amendments guaranteeing freedom of speech and of assembly, and freedom to petition the Government for a redress of grievances.　[These]

---

1. Such an approach is advocated in Note, "A Unitary Approach to Claims of First Amendment Access to Publicly Owned Property," 35 Stan.L.Rev. 121 (1982).　The conclusions of that Note are summarized above, at p. 1198.　Cf. Justice Marshall's dissent in Clark v. Community for Creative Non-Violence (1984; sleeping in Washington parks; p. 1188 above).

1. This was the same breach of the peace statute involved in Cox I, p. 1225 above.　The Louisiana Supreme Court had affirmed the convictions in Brown before the decision in Cox I was announced.

rights are not confined to verbal expression. They embrace appropriate types of action which certainly include the right in a peaceable and orderly manner to protest by silent and reproachful presence, in a place where the protestant has every right to be, the unconstitutional segregation of public facilities. Accordingly, even if the accused action were within the scope of the [law], [we] would have to hold that the statute cannot constitutionally be applied to punish petitioners' actions in the circumstances of this case. See [Edwards]. The statute was deliberately and purposefully applied solely to terminate the reasonable, orderly, and limited exercise of the right to protest the unconstitutional segregation of a public facility. Interference with this right, so exercised, by state action is intolerable under our Constitution. [Fortunately], the circumstances here were such that no claim can be made that use of the library by others was disturbed by the demonstration. Perhaps the time and method were carefully chosen with this in mind. Were it otherwise, a factor not present in this case would have to be considered. Here, there was no disturbance of others, no disruption of library activities, and no violation of any library regulations." [2]

Justice BLACK's dissent, joined by Justices Clark, Harlan and Stewart, insisted that Cox I was irrelevant here: "The problems of state regulation of the streets on the one hand, and public buildings on the other, are quite obviously separate and distinct. Public buildings such as libraries, schoolhouses, fire departments, courthouses, and executive mansions are maintained to perform certain specific and vital functions. Order and tranquility of a sort entirely unknown to the public streets are essential to their normal operation. [I]t is incomprehensible to me that a State must measure disturbances in its libraries and on the streets with identical standards." He insisted that there was no racial discrimination in this case and that there was adequate evidence to support conviction under the statute: "A tiny parish branch library, staffed by two women, is not a department store [nor] a bus terminal [nor] a public thoroughfare as in Edwards and Cox." He continued: "Apparently unsatisfied with or unsure of the 'no evidence' ground for reversing the convictions, the prevailing opinion goes on to state that the statute was used unconstitutionally [here] because it was 'deliberately and purposefully applied solely to terminate the reasonable, orderly, and limited exercise of the right to protest the unconstitutional segregation of a public facility.' [This] statement is wholly unsupported by the record in this case. [Moreover, the conclusion] establishes a completely new constitutional doctrine. In this case this new constitutional principle means that even though these petitioners did not want to use the [library] for library purposes, they had a constitutional right nevertheless to stay there over the protest of the librarians who had lawful authority to keep the library orderly for the use of people who wanted to use [it]. But the principle espoused also has a far broader meaning. It means that the [Constitution] requires the [supervisors] of the public libraries in this country to stand helplessly by while protesting groups advocating one cause or another, stage 'sit-ins' or 'stand-ups' to dramatize their particular views on particular issues. And it should be remembered that if one group can take over libraries for one cause, other groups will assert the right to do so for causes which, while wholly legal, may not be so appealing to this Court. The States are thus paralyzed with reference to control of their libraries for library purposes, and I suppose that inevitably the next step will be to paralyze the schools. [The First Amendment] does not guarantee to any person the right to use someone else's property, even that owned by govern-

2. Justice BRENNAN concurred in the judgment solely on overbreadth grounds. Justice WHITE concurred in the result. He found that petitioners' actions did not "depart significantly from what normal library use would contem-

plate" and concluded: "On this record, it is difficult to avoid the conclusion that petitioners were asked to leave the library because they were Negroes. If they were, their convictions deny them [equal protection]."

ment and dedicated to other purposes, as a stage to express dissident ideas. The novel constitutional doctrine of the prevailing opinion nevertheless exalts the power of private nongovernmental groups to determine what use shall be made of governmental property over the power of the elected governmental officials." [3]

ADDERLEY v. FLORIDA

385 U.S. 39, 87 S.Ct. 242, 17 L.Ed.2d 149 (1966).

Mr. Justice BLACK delivered the opinion of the Court.

Petitioners [32 students at Florida A. & M. University in Tallahassee] were convicted [of] "trespass with a malicious and mischievous intent" upon the premises of the county jail contrary to [Florida law].[1] [They] had gone from the school to the jail about a mile away, along with many other students, to "demonstrate" at the jail their protests of arrests of other protesting students the day before, and perhaps to protest more generally against state and local policies and practices of racial segregation, including segregation of the jail. The county sheriff, legal custodian of the [jail], tried to persuade [them to leave]. When this did not work he notified them that they must leave, that if they did not leave he would arrest them for trespassing, and that if they resisted he would charge them with that as well. Some of the students left but others, including petitioners, [remained].

Petitioners [insist that these cases] are controlled [by Edwards and Cox I]. We cannot agree. [As to Edwards:] Traditionally, state capitol grounds are open to the public. Jails, built for security purposes, are not. [The Edwards demonstrators were charged with] breach of the peace. [That law was struck down as too] broad and all-embracing. [It] was on this same ground of vagueness that [the] Louisiana breach-of-the-peace law [in Cox I] was invalidated. [But the Florida trespass law here] cannot be challenged on this ground. It is aimed at conduct of one limited kind, that is, [trespassing] upon the property of another with a malicious and mischievous intent. There is no lack of notice in this law, nothing to entrap or fool the unwary. [Petitioners] here

---

3. In a closing passage, Justice Black added remarks akin to those of his dissent in Cox II, above. (See also his majority opinion in Adderley, which follows.) At the end of this Brown dissent, Justice Black stated: "I am deeply troubled with the fear that powerful private groups throughout the Nation will read the Court's action, as I do—that is, as granting them a license to invade the tranquility and beauty of our libraries whenever they have quarrel with some state policy which may or may not exist. It is an unhappy circumstance in my judgment that the group, which more than any other has needed a government of equal laws and equal justice, is now encouraged to believe that the best way for it to advance its cause, which is a worthy one, is by taking the law into its own hands from place to place and from time to time. Governments like ours were formed to substitute the rule of law for the rule of force. Illustrations may be given where crowds have gathered together peaceably by reason of extraordinarily good discipline reinforced by vigilant officers. 'Demonstrations' have taken place without any manifestations of force at the time. But I say once more that the crowd moved by noble ideals today can

become the mob ruled by hate and passion and greed and violence tomorrow."

Consider the comment in Kalven, "Upon Re-reading Mr. Justice Black on the First Amendment," 14 U.C.L.A.L.Rev. 428 (1967): "[I]t remains something of a puzzle how Justice Black, who has been so sympathetic to the 'poor man's printing press' and so tolerant of noise in Kovacs, the intrusion in [Martin v. Struthers], the anonymity in [Talley v. California], can be so impatient with this kind of communication. It is as though his strategy of protecting all speech just because it was something other than conduct traps him when he is confronted by conduct which is symbolic." (Recall also the symbolic speech cases in sec. 3 above—especially Justice Black's dissent in Street v. New York, the flag burning case.)

1. "Every trespass upon the property of another, committed with a malicious and mischievous intent, the punishment of which is not specially provided for, shall be punished by imprisonment not exceeding three months, or by fine not exceeding one hundred dollars." [Footnote by Justice Black.]

contend that "[their] convictions are based on a total lack of relevant evidence." If true, this would be a denial of due process, Thompson v. Louisville [p. 1012 above]. [P]etitioners' summary of facts [shows] an abundance of facts to support the jury's verdict of [guilty].[2]

[The only remaining question is whether the conviction violates petitioners' First Amendment rights.] We hold it does not. The sheriff, as jail custodian, had power [to] direct that this large crowd of people get off the grounds. There is not a shred of evidence in this record that this power was exercised [because] the sheriff objected to what was being sung or said by the demonstrators or because he disagreed with the objectives of their protest. The record reveals that he objected only to their presence on that part of the jail grounds reserved for jail uses. There is no evidence at all that on any other occasion had similarly large groups of the public been permitted to gather on this portion of the jail grounds for any purpose. Nothing in the [Constitution] prevents Florida from even-handed enforcement of its general trespass statute against those refusing to obey the sheriff's order to remove themselves from what amounted to the curtilage of the jailhouse. The State, no less than a private owner of property, has power to preserve the property under its control for the use to which it is lawfully dedicated. For this reason there is no merit to the petitioners' argument that they had a constitutional right to stay on the property, over the jail custodian's objections, because this "area chosen for the peaceful civil rights demonstration was not only 'reasonable' but also particularly appropriate." Such an argument has as its major unarticulated premise the assumption that people who want to propagandize protests or views have a constitutional right to do so whenever and however and wherever they please. That concept of constitutional law was vigorously and forthrightly rejected in two of the cases petitioners rely on, [Cox I and II]. We reject it again. The [Constitution] does not forbid a State to control the use of its own property for its own lawful nondiscriminatory purpose.

Affirmed.

Mr. Justice DOUGLAS, with whom The Chief Justice [WARREN], Mr. Justice BRENNAN, and Mr. Justice FORTAS concur, [dissenting].

[T]he Court errs in treating the case as if it were an ordinary trespass case or an ordinary picketing case. The jailhouse, like an executive mansion, a legislative chamber, a courthouse, or the statehouse itself [Edwards], is one of the seats of government, whether it be the Tower of London, the Bastille, or a

---

2. Justice Black stated the facts as follows: "In summary both [of the] statements show testimony ample to prove this: Disturbed and upset by the arrest of their schoolmates the day before, a large number of Florida A. & M. students assembled on the school grounds and decided to march down to the county jail. Some apparently wanted to be put in jail too, along with the students already there. A group of around 200 marched from the school and arrived at the jail singing and clapping. They went directly to the jail-door entrance where they were met by a deputy sheriff, evidently surprised by their arrival. He asked them to move back, claiming they were blocking the entrance to the jail and fearing that they might attempt to enter the jail. They moved back part of the way, where they stood or sat, singing, clapping and dancing, on the jail driveway and on an adjacent grassy area upon the jail premises. This particular jail entrance and driveway were not normally used by the public, but by the sheriff's department for transporting prisoners to and from the courts several

blocks away and by commercial concerns for servicing the jail. Even after their partial retreat, the demonstrators continued to block vehicular passage over this driveway up to the entrance of the jail. [The sheriff told two] of the leaders that they were trespassing upon jail property and that he would give them 10 minutes to leave or he would arrest them. Neither of the leaders did anything to disperse the crowd, and one of them told the sheriff that they wanted to get arrested. [After] about 10 minutes, the sheriff, in a voice loud enough to be heard by all, told the demonstrators that he was the legal custodian of the jail and its premises, that they were trespassing on county property in violation of the law, that they should all leave forthwith or he would arrest them, and that if they attempted to resist arrest, he would charge them with that as a separate offense. Some of the group then left. Others, including all petitioners, did not leave. Some of them sat down. In a few minutes, [the remaining 107 demonstrators were arrested]."

small county jail. And when it houses political prisoners or those whom many think are unjustly held, it is an obvious center for protest. The right to petition for the redress of grievances has an ancient history and is not limited to writing a letter or sending a telegram to a congressman; it is not confined to appearing before the local city council, or writing letters to the President or Governor or Mayor.[1] Conventional methods of petitioning may be, and often have been, shut off to large groups of our citizens. Legislators may turn deaf ears; formal complaints may be routed endlessly through a bureaucratic maze; courts may let the wheels of justice grind very slowly. Those who do not control television and radio, those who cannot afford to advertise in newspapers or circulate elaborate pamphlets may have only a more limited type of access to public officials. Their methods should not be condemned as tactics of obstruction and harassment as long as the assembly and petition are peaceable, as these were.

There is no question that petitioners had as their purpose a protest against the arrest of Florida A. & M. students for trying to integrate public theatres. [The] group was protesting the arrests, and state and local policies of segregation, including segregation of the jail. [The] group [sang] "freedom" songs. And history shows that a song can be a powerful tool of protest. [There] was no violence; no threat of violence; no attempted jail break; no storming of a prison; no plan or plot to do anything but protest. The evidence is uncontradicted that the petitioners' conduct did not upset the jailhouse routine. [There] was no shoving, no pushing, no disorder or threat of riot. It is said that some of the group blocked part of the driveway leading to the jail entrance. [If] there was congestion, the solution was a further request to move to lawns or parking areas, not complete ejection and arrest. [Finally], the fact that some of the protestants may have felt their cause so just that they were willing to be arrested for making their protest outside the jail seems wholly irrelevant. A petition is nonetheless a petition, though its futility may make martyrdom attractive.

We do violence to the First Amendment when we permit this "petition for redress of grievances" to be turned into a trespass action. It does not help to analogize this problem to the problem of picketing. Picketing is a form of protest usually directed against private interests. I do not see how rules governing picketing in general are relevant to this express constitutional right to assemble and to [petition]. In the first place the jailhouse grounds were not marked with "NO TRESPASSING!" signs, nor does respondent claim that the public was generally excluded from the grounds. Only the sheriff's fiat transformed lawful conduct into an unlawful trespass. To say that a private owner could have done the same if the rally had taken place on private property is to speak of a different case, as an assembly and a petition for redress of grievances run to government, not to private proprietors.

The Court forgets that prior to this day our decisions have drastically limited the application of state statutes inhibiting the right to go peacefully on public property to exercise First Amendment rights [quoting Hague v. CIO]. When we allow Florida to construe her "malicious trespass" statute to bar a person from going on property knowing it is not his own and to apply that prohibition to public property, we discard [Cox v. New Hampshire and Edwards]. Would the case be any different if, as is common, the demonstration took place outside a building which housed both the jail and the legislative body? I think not.

There may be some public places which are so clearly committed to other purposes that their use for the airing of grievances is anomalous. There may be some instances in which assemblies and [petitions] are not consistent with other necessary purposes of public property. A noisy meeting may be out of keeping

---

1. For a modern discussion of the right to petition, see Note "The Misapplication of the *Noerr-Pennington* Doctrine in Non-Antitrust Right to Petition Cases," 36 Stan.L.Rev. 1243 (1984).

with the serenity of the statehouse or the quiet of the courthouse. No one, for example, would suggest that the Senate gallery is the proper place for a vociferous protest rally. And in other cases it may be necessary to adjust the right to [petition] to the other interest inhering in the uses to which the public property is normally put. But this is quite different from saying that all public places are off limits to people with grievances. And it is farther yet from saying that the "custodian" of the public property in his discretion can decide when public places shall be used for the communication of ideas. [For] to place such discretion in any public official [is] to place those who assert their First Amendment rights at his mercy. [Such] power is out of step with all our decisions prior to today where we have insisted that before a First Amendment right may be curtailed under the guise of a criminal law, any evil that may be collateral to the exercise of the right, must be isolated and defined in a "narrowly drawn" statute [lest] the power to control excesses of conduct be used to suppress the constitutional right itself. [It] is said that the sheriff did not make the arrests because of the views which petitioners espoused. That excuse is usually given, as we know from the many cases involving arrests of minority groups for breaches of the peace, unlawful assemblies, and parading without a permit. [By] allowing these orderly and civilized protests against injustice to be suppressed, we only increase the forces of frustration which the conditions of second-class citizenship are generating amongst us.

THE WARREN COURT AND THE PUBLIC FORUM IN LIGHT OF BROWN AND ADDERLEY

a. The claimants in cases such as Cox II and Brown and Adderley sought access to public places beyond the traditional forums of streets and parks. Are these nontraditional public places anomalous areas for speech? And do the Court's responses adequately heed the assured access view of the public forum suggested by Hague v. CIO and other early cases? Do these Warren Court rulings on public forum claims in novel contexts retreat entirely to an equal access view of the public forum? Do they retreat even further than that?

b. What does Justice Black mean in Adderley when he says: "The State, no less than a private owner of property, has power to preserve the property under its control for the use to which it is lawfully dedicated." Is that a retreat all the way to Justice Holmes' analogy of the state and the private property owner in Davis v. Massachusetts, p. 1197 above? Does Justice Black at least recognize the equal access notion when he says at the end of the opinion: "[The] Constitution does not forbid a state to control the use of its own property for its own lawful nondiscriminatory purpose." Would Justice Black sustain a blanket prohibition of the use of streets and parks for meetings and parades? Or are his broad comments applicable only to such nontraditional forums as jailhouses?

c. Arguably, Justice Douglas' dissent in Adderley is the first opinion from the Warren Court adequately responsive to assured minimum access public forum claims. Is it surprising that an adequate opinion came so late in the Warren era? Was that delay an understandable consequence of the Warren Court's preoccupation with risks of discrimination in administration and with overbreadth and with the "speech"-"conduct" distinction?[1] Is the majority position in Adderley reconcilable with the statehouse case, Edwards? Does Adderley indicate that assured access claims are to be rejected whenever the claim goes beyond the traditional streets and parks? Or is there access to

---

1. For another articulate public forum opinion in the late years of the Warren Court, see Justice Marshall's opinion in the Logan Valley Plaza case (1968; p. 1291 below). See also Justice Marshall's opinion in Grayned (1972; p. 1264 below).

nontraditional forums so long as there is no showing of substantial disruption of or interference with the functioning of their primary uses? Is that the message of the Brown case?

d. To what extent is the "substantial disruption" criterion a major theme of the Burger Court decisions examining access claims to nontraditional public places, in the materials that follow? Can a claim to a nontraditional public forum be adequately analyzed without inquiries as to the availability of adequate alternative forums in which the speaker may reach the desired audience?[2] Should the public forum claimant be required to demonstrate his special interest in the particular location? Was there special justification for the protest near the jailhouse in Adderley, and in the library in Brown? (Compare the distinction attempted in the shopping center cases, Logan Valley and Lloyd, p. 1291 below.)

THE BURGER COURT AND ACCESS TO NONTRADITIONAL PUBLIC PLACES

ACCESS TO BUSES, THEATERS, AND MILITARY BASES *

LEHMAN v. SHAKER HEIGHTS

418 U.S. 298, 94 S.Ct. 2714, 41 L.Ed.2d 770 (1974).

[Petitioner Lehman was a candidate for election to the Ohio General Assembly in 1970. He attempted to buy car card space for campaign advertisements on the Shaker Heights city-owned buses. His ads were refused because of the city's rule against political advertising. Although the transit system accepted commercial ads, it had always barred *"any* political or public issue advertising" on the buses, pursuant to city council action. Lehman unsuccessfully sought relief in the state courts on the basis of the First Amendment and the equal protection clause.]

Mr. Justice BLACKMUN announced the judgment of the Court and an opinion, in which The Chief Justice [BURGER], Mr. Justice WHITE, and Mr. Justice REHNQUIST join.

[It] is urged that the car cards here constitute a public forum protected by the First Amendment, and that there is a guarantee of nondiscriminatory access to such publicly owned and controlled areas of communication "regardless of the primary purpose for which the area is dedicated." We disagree. [This situation is] different from the traditional settings where First Amendment values inalterably prevail. "[T]he truth is that open spaces and public places

---

2. Is an inquiry about the availability of adequate alternative forums barred by the Court's comment in Schneider v. State (1939; p. 1206 above) that "one is not to have the exercise of his liberty of expression in appropriate places abridged on the plea that it may be exercised in some other place"? Should that Schneider statement, made in the context of traditional public places, apply in situations where nontraditional public places are at issue? Note the repeated reliance on the Schneider statement in later opinions—e.g., Justice Brennan's dissent in Lehman, p. 1247 below, and the per curiam opinion in Spence, p. 1183 above.

* This first group of Burger Court cases deals with decisions of the early Burger era and reviews the gropings for standards in those years. See also Grayned v. Rockford (1972; p. 1264 below). The last of the cases in this group, Greer v. Spock, significantly foreshadows the approach that has prevailed during the most recent decade: the initial inquiry as to whether the property is a "public forum"; the unwillingness to extend that status to most nontraditional public forums; and the very deferential review the Burger Court exercises when it finds the "public forum" label inappropriate.

differ very much in their character, and before you could say whether a certain thing could be done in a certain place you would have to know the history of the particular place." Although American constitutional jurisprudence, in the light of the First Amendment, has been jealous to preserve access to public places for purposes of free speech, the nature of the forum and the conflicting interests involved have remained important in determining the degree of protection afforded by the Amendment to the speech in [question]. Here, we have no open spaces, no meeting hall, park, street corner, or other public thoroughfare. Instead, the city is engaged in commerce. [The] car card space, although incidental to the provision of public transportation, is a part of the commercial venture. In much the same way that a newspaper or periodical, or even a radio or television station, need not accept every proffer of advertising from the general public, a city transit system has discretion to develop and make reasonable choices concerning the type of advertising that may be displayed in its [vehicles].

Because state action exists, however, the policies and practices governing access to the transit system's advertising space must not be arbitrary, capricious, or invidious. Here, the city has decided that "[p]urveyors of goods and services saleable in commerce may purchase advertising space on an equal basis, whether they be house builders or butchers." This decision is little different from deciding to impose a 10-, 25-, or 35-cent fare, or from changing schedules or the location of bus stops. Revenue earned from long-term commercial advertising could be jeopardized by a requirement that short-term candidacy or issue-oriented advertisements be displayed on car cards. Users would be subjected to the blare of political propaganda. There could be lurking doubts about favoritism, and sticky administrative problems might arise in parceling out limited space to eager politicians. In these circumstances, the managerial decision to limit car card space to innocuous and less controversial commercial and service oriented advertising does not rise to the dignity of a First Amendment violation. Were we to hold to the contrary, display cases in public hospitals, libraries, office buildings, military compounds, and other public facilities immediately would become Hyde Parks open to every would-be pamphleteer and politician. This the Constitution does not require. No First Amendment forum is here to be found. The city consciously has limited access to its transit system advertising space in order to minimize chances of abuse, the appearance of favoritism, and the risk of imposing upon a captive audience. These are reasonable legislative objectives advanced by the city in a [proprietary capacity].

[Affirmed.]

Mr. Justice DOUGLAS, concurring in the [judgment].

My Brother Brennan would find that "[a] forum for communication was voluntarily established." If the streetcar or bus were a forum for communication akin to that of streets or public parks, considerable problems would be presented. But a streetcar or bus is plainly not a park or sidewalk or other meeting place for discussion, any more than is a highway. It is only a way to get to work or back home. The fact that it is owned and operated by the city does not without more make it a forum. Bus and streetcar placards are in the category of highway billboards, [a] form of communication [that] has been significantly curtailed by state regulation. [The] fact that land on which a billboard rests is municipal land does not curtail or enhance such regulatory schemes.

If a bus is a forum it is more akin to a newspaper than to a park. Yet if a bus is treated as a newspaper, then, as we hold this date [Tornillo, p. 1300 below], the owner cannot be forced to include in his offerings news or other items which outsiders may desire but which the owner abhors. [And] if we are to turn a bus or streetcar into either a newspaper or a park, we take great liberties with people who because of necessity become commuters and at the same time captive viewers or listeners. [The constitutional] right of the commuters to be free from forced intrusions on their privacy precludes the city from transforming its vehicles of public transportation into forums for the dissemination of ideas upon this captive audience. Buses are not recreational vehicles used for Sunday chautauquas as a public park might be used on holidays for such a purpose; they are a practical necessity for millions in our urban centers. I have already stated this view in my dissent in [PUC v. Pollak, p. 1211 above]: "[T]he man on the streetcar has no choice but to sit and listen, or perhaps to sit and to try *not* to listen." There is no difference when the message is visual, not auricular. In each the viewer or listener is captive. [I] do not view the content of the message as relevant either to petitioner's right to express it or to the commuters' right to be free from it. Commercial advertisements may be as offensive and intrusive to captive audiences as any political message. But the validity of the commercial advertising program is not before [us]. Since I do not believe that petitioner has any constitutional right to spread his message before this captive audience, I concur in the Court's judgment.

Mr. Justice BRENNAN, with whom Mr. Justice STEWART, Mr. Justice MARSHALL, and Mr. Justice POWELL join, [dissenting].

[The] city created a forum for the dissemination of information and expression of ideas when it accepted and displayed commercial and public service advertisements on its rapid transit vehicles. Having opened a forum for communication, the city is barred by the [First Amendment] from discriminating among forum users solely on the basis of message content. [The city] attempts to justify its ban [by] arguing that the interior advertising space of a transit car is an inappropriate forum for political expression and debate. To be sure, there are some public places which are so clearly committed to other purposes that their use as public forums for communication is anomalous. [See Adderley (Douglas, J., dissenting).] The determination of whether a particular type of public property or facility constitutes a "public forum" requires the Court to strike a balance between the competing interests of the government, on the one hand, and the speaker and his audience, on the other. Thus, the Court must assess the importance of the primary use to which the public property or facility is committed, and the extent to which that use will be disrupted if access for free expression is permitted. Applying these principles, the Court has long recognized the public's right of access to public streets and parks for expressive activity. [Hague v. CIO]. More recently, the Court has added state capitol grounds to the list of public forums compatible with free speech [Edwards], but denied similar status to the curtilage of a jailhouse [Adderley].[1] In the circumstances of this case, however, we need not decide whether public transit cars *must* be made available as forums for the exercise of First Amendment rights. By accepting commercial and public service advertising, the city effectively waived any argument that advertising in its transit cars is incompatible with the rapid transit system's primary function of providing transportation. A forum for communication was voluntarily established.

[The] plurality opinion, however, contends that as long as the city limits its advertising space to "innocuous and less controversial commercial and service oriented advertising," no First Amendment forum is created. I find no merit in that position. [While] it is possible that commercial advertising may be accorded *less* First Amendment protection than speech concerning political and

1. Contrast this passage with Justice Brennan's approach to the public forum problem in his dissent, two years later in Greer v. Spock, which follows. Consider whether the change in Justice Brennan's approach from Lehman to Spock contributes to greater protection of free speech.

social issues of public importance [see chap. 11, sec. 2D], it is "speech" nonetheless, often communicating information and ideas found by many persons to be controversial. [Once] such messages have been accepted and displayed, the existence of a forum for communication cannot be gainsaid. To hold otherwise, and thus sanction the city's preference for bland commercialism and noncontroversial public service messages over "uninhibited, robust, and wide-open" debate on public issues, would reverse the traditional priorities of the First Amendment. Once a public forum for communication has been established, both free speech and equal protection principles prohibit discrimination based *solely* upon subject matter or content. [That] the discrimination is among entire classes of ideas, rather than among points of view within a particular class, does not render it any less odious. Subject matter or content censorship in any form is [forbidden].[2]

The [city's] solicitous regard for "captive riders" [has] a hollow ring in the present case, where the city has voluntarily opened its rapid transit system as a forum for communication. [By] accepting commercial and public service advertisements, the city opened the door to "sometimes controversial or unsettling speech" and determined that such speech does not unduly interfere with the rapid transit system's primary purpose of transporting passengers. In the eyes of many passengers, certain commercial or public service messages are as profoundly disturbing as some political advertisements might be to other passengers. [Moreover], even if it were possible to draw a manageable line between controversial and noncontroversial messages, the city's practice of censorship for the benefit of "captive audiences" still would not be justified. [The] advertisements [are] not broadcast over loudspeakers in the transit cars. [Pollak.] Rather, all advertisements [are] in *written* form. Should passengers chance to glance at advertisements they find offensive, they can "effectively avoid further bombardment of their sensibilities simply by averting their eyes." [Cohen.] Surely that minor inconvenience is a small price to pay for the continued preservation of so precious a liberty as free speech.

The city's remaining justification [that acceptance of political ads would suggest political favoritism or city support of the candidate] is equally unpersuasive. [Such] ephemeral concerns do not provide the city with *carte blanche* authority to exclude an entire category of speech from a public forum. [Moreover,] neutral regulations, which do not distinguish among advertisements on the basis of subject matter, can be narrowly tailored to allay the city's fears. The impression of city endorsement can be dispelled by requiring disclaimers to appear prominently on the face of every advertisement. And [the] appearance of favoritism can be avoided by the even-handed regulation of time, place, and manner for all advertising, irrespective of [subject matter].

BUSES, THEATERS, AND PUBLIC FORUM THEORY

1. *Transportation facilities and the public forum.* Lehman presents primarily an issue of "equal access," not "guaranteed access." As Justice Brennan's dissent noted, it was unnecessary to decide here "whether public transit cars *must* be made available as forums." What if the transit system had excluded *all* advertising, commercial as well as noncommercial? By what criteria should a guaranteed access claim under such circumstances be decided? Is a city bus an "anomalous" place for messages?[1] Note that the government property involved here (bus advertising) and in the next note (municipal theater) is

2. The existence of other public forums for the dissemination of political messages is, of course, irrelevant. [Schneider v. State.] [Footnote by Justice Brennan.]

1. Compare Justice Blackmun's majority opinion a few months later, in the Southeastern Promotions case, note 2 below. And on the Lehman problem, see Note, "The Public Forum:

property designed for communicative purposes, in contrast to the primary *non*communicative purposes of the public property involved in such contexts as jails in the earlier cases. Should that make a difference in the analysis?

Would Justice Douglas' position in Lehman, building on his Pollak dissent (p. 1211 above), bar all advertising on buses, commercial as well as noncommercial? Can Justice Douglas' solicitude for the "captive audience" here be reconciled with his statements in Saia, the loudspeaker case, p. 1208 above? Can the majority's solicitude for the "captive audience"—in Justice Blackmun's opinion as well as in Justice Douglas'—be reconciled with the weight accorded to the interests of the audience in the offensive language cases (in sec. 2B of chap. 11)? In the hostile audience cases, p. 1213 above?

2. *Municipal theaters and the public forum.* Contrast Justice Blackmun's reluctance to recognize a public forum claim in Lehman with his majority opinion less than a year later in SOUTHEASTERN PROMOTIONS, LTD. v. CONRAD, 420 U.S. 546 (1975). There, the Court found that the challenger's First Amendment rights were violated when the municipal board managing city theaters in Chattanooga refused permission to present "the controversial rock musical 'Hair.'" The refusal was based on the ground that the production would not be "in the best interest of the community." Although the alleged obscenity of "Hair" had been the major issue in the lower courts, Justice Blackmun did not reach that question. Instead, he found that the refusal constituted a prior restraint imposed without affording the "rigorous procedural safeguards" required by Freedman v. Maryland, p. 1160 above.

In the course of reaching that conclusion, Justice Blackmun commented that the municipal theaters were "public forums designed for and dedicated to expressive activities." He added: "None of the circumstances qualifying as an established exception to the doctrine of prior restraint was present. Petitioner was not seeking to use a facility primarily serving a competing use. [E.g., Adderley; Brown.] Nor was rejection of the application based on any regulation of time, place, or manner related to the nature of the facility or applications from other users. [E.g., Cox v. New Hampshire.] No rights of individuals in surrounding areas were violated by noise or any other aspect of the production. [Kovacs v. Cooper.] There was no captive audience. See [Lehman; Pollak]. Whether the petitioner might have used some other, privately owned, theater in the city for the production is of no consequence. [Even] if a privately owned forum had been available, that fact alone would not justify an otherwise impermissible prior restraint. [Schneider.]"

Justice DOUGLAS' separate opinion thought the majority's procedural holding did not go far enough: he insisted that no prior screening process of any sort was permissible. And he added: "A municipal theater is no less a forum for the expression of ideas than is a public park, or a sidewalk." A dissent by Justice WHITE, joined by Chief Justice Burger, concluded that, whether or not "Hair" was obscene, the city "could constitutionally forbid exhibition of the musical for children" and could "reserve its auditorium for productions suitable for exhibition to all the citizens of the city, adults and children alike." Another dissent, by Justice REHNQUIST, argued that a public auditorium should not be equated with public streets and parks. He feared that the majority had given "no constitutionally permissible role in the way of selection to the municipal authorities" and asked: "May a municipal theater devote an entire season to Shakespeare, or is it required to book any potential producer on a first-come, first-served basis?" He concluded that a city policy not to show attractions "of the kind that would offend any substantial number of potential theater goers" was not "arbitrary or unreasonable." He concluded:

Minimum Access, Equal Access, and the First Amendment," 28 Stan.L.Rev. 119 (1975), and

Stone, "Fora Americana: Speech in Public Places," 1974 Sup.Ct.Rev. 233.

"A municipal theater may not be run by municipal authorities as if it were a private theater, free to judge on a content basis alone which plays it wished to have performed and which it did not. But, just as surely, that element of it which is 'theater' ought to be accorded some constitutional recognition along with that element of it which is 'municipal.' "

ACCESS TO MILITARY BASES

To what extent may a First Amendment claimant gain access to a military base that has been opened up to the general public for some purposes? The per curiam decision in Flower v. United States, 407 U.S. 197 (1972) held out some hope that military bases could be treated as nontraditional public forums. There, the 7 to 2 decision reversed a conviction for distributing peace leaflets on a street within the boundaries of an Army base in San Antonio: "Whatever power the authorities may have to restrict general access to a military facility, here the fort commander chose not to exclude the public from the street where petitioner was arrested." But when the Court confronted the issue more fully four years later, in GREER v. SPOCK, 424 U.S. 828 (1976), the majority interpreted Flower narrowly and in effect barred access to bases by political speakers. The decision is of general interest for a number of reasons. Note, first, the majority's rejection of the access claim: in focusing initially on the question of whether a military base is a "public forum," and in deciding that quite deferential scrutiny is justified for public places that are not designated as "public forums," the majority adopted an approach echoed in later Burger Court decisions involving nontraditional forums. Note, second, Justice Brennan's effort in dissent to articulate a new, more flexible, allegedly more speech-protective analysis of access claims. In examining Greer v. Spock, consider whether the majority's mode of rejecting the First Amendment claim is persuasive. Consider also whether Justice Brennan's analysis, though speech-protective as applied here, risks eroding past assurances of assured access to some public places. Or is Justice Brennan's approach in this case preferable to his analysis in Lehman, the preceding case?

Greer v. Spock upheld two regulations at Fort Dix, a large Army post in rural New Jersey. The regulations barred political activities on the base: the first prohibited, inter alia, speeches and demonstrations of a partisan political nature; the second, distribution of literature without prior approval of the base commander.[1] Justice STEWART's majority opinion emphasized that the business of a base such as Fort Dix was "to train soldiers, not to provide a public forum," and rejected any claim to a generalized constitutional right to "make political speeches or distribute leaflets" there. He observed that in Spock, unlike in Flower, the military authorities had never "abandoned any claim of special interest" in regulating political activities.[2] Noting "the special constitutional function of the military in our national life," he stated: "The notion that federal military reservations, like municipal streets and parks, have traditionally served as a place for free public assembly and communication of thoughts by private citizens [is] historically and constitutionally false."[3] After using these

1. The challengers included the candidates for national office of two minor parties in the 1972 campaign—the People's Party and the Socialist Workers' Party.

2. Distinguishing Flower, Justice Stewart noted that it had rested on the Court's understanding that the street there was "no different from all other public thoroughfares" in San Antonio and that the military had abandoned any right to exclude leafleteers. But, citing Ad-

derley, he insisted that Flower did not mean "that whenever members of the public are permitted freely to visit a place owned or operated by the Government, then that place becomes a 'public forum' for purposes of the First Amendment."

3. However, as noted earlier, Justice Stewart, in the course of rejecting the access claim to military bases, furnished in dictum a relatively

broad grounds to reject the "on the face" challenges, the majority turned down the "as applied" attacks with similar deference and brevity. With respect to the ban on speeches and demonstrations, Justice Stewart noted that the regulation had been applied evenhandedly rather than discriminatorily, in accordance with a policy of "keeping official military activities there wholly free of entanglement with partisan political campaigns of any kind"—a policy "wholly consistent with the American constitutional tradition of a politically neutral military establishment under civilian control." And with respect to the prior approval requirement for the distribution of literature, he noted that it did not authorize bans on "conventional political campaign literature," but only prohibitions of literature constituting "a clear danger to [military] loyalty, discipline, or morale." And since the challengers had not submitted any material for approval, they could not claim that that regulation had been arbitrarily applied.[4]

Justice POWELL's concurrence sought to sketch "the appropriate framework of analysis" more fully. He thought the central question was "whether the manner of expression is basically incompatible with the normal activity of a particular place at a particular time." But "it is not sufficient that the area in which the right of expression is sought to be exercised be dedicated to some purpose other than use as a 'public forum,' or even that the primary business to be carried on in the area may be disturbed by the unpopular viewpoint expressed. Our inquiry must be more carefully addressed to the intrusion on the specific activity involved and to the degree of infringement on the First Amendment rights of the private parties. Some basic incompatibility must be discerned between the communication and the primary activity of an area." Here, it was significant that access was sought to an "enclave of [the military] system that stands apart from and outside of many of the rules that govern ordinary civilian life in our country." In that context, "our inquiry is not limited to claims that the exercise of First Amendment rights is disruptive of base activity. We also must consider *functional and symbolic incompatibility* with the 'specialized society separate from civilian society' that has its home on the base." [Emphasis added.][5]

Using that analytical framework, Justice Powell found the ban on political meetings justified by "the legitimate interests of the public in maintaining the reality and appearance of the political neutrality of the Armed Services," interests which "outweigh [those] of political candidates and their servicemen audience in the availability of a military base for campaign activities." He noted that the candidates had "alternative means of communicating with those who live and work on the Fort." Turning to the requirement of prior approval to distribute literature, he found it justified, not by the public interest in military neutrality, but rather by "the unique need of the military to 'insist upon a respect for duty and a discipline without counterpart in civilian life.'"[6]

rare, unusually strong statement of an "assured access" right to *traditional* public places.

4. In later cases following Justice Stewart's "public forum"-"non-public forum" distinction, the scrutiny of access claims to "non-public forum" public property seems even more deferential than that exercised by Justice Stewart in Greer v. Spock. See, e.g., U.S. Postal Service v. Greenburgh Civic Assns. (1981; home letter boxes; p. 1259 below).

5. Justice Brennan's dissent, while praising Justice Powell for at least recognizing "the need for a careful inquiry," criticized his emphasis on "symbolic incompatibility." To Justice Brennan, that emphasis pointed to an admittedly valid interest in assuring the neutrality of the military.

But he thought Justice Powell's concurrence "so devoid of limiting principle as to contravene fundamentals of First Amendment jurisprudence. This Court many times has held protected by the First Amendment conduct which was 'symbolically incompatible' with the activity upon which it impacted. Indeed, the very symbolisms of many of our institutions have been the subject of criticisms held to be unassailably protected by the First Amendment."

6. In addition to Justice Brennan's dissent, which follows, there were also two brief additional opinions: a concurrence by Chief Justice BURGER and a separate dissent by Justice MARSHALL.

Justice BRENNAN's lengthy dissent, joined by Justice Marshall, focused on the "public forum" issue and developed it in an unusual way. He noted that the challengers had not made absolute claims, but rather had expressed their willingness to confine political rallies "to such times and places as might reasonably be designated" by the military officials, and had "sought only to distribute leaflets in unrestricted areas." Moreover, the challengers' claims had carefully distinguished "between a military base considered as a whole and those portions of a military base open to the public." He continued, in the most novel part of his dissent: "Not only do [the challengers] not go so far as to contend that open places constitute a 'public forum,' but also they need not go so far. [The] determination that a locale is a 'public forum' has never been erected as an absolute prerequisite to all forms of demonstrative First Amendment activity. [It] bears special note that the notion of 'public forum' has never been the touchstone of public expression, for a contrary approach blinds the Court to any possible accommodation of First Amendment values in this case. In [Brown v. Louisiana], for example, [there] was no finding by the Court that the library was a public forum. Similarly, in [Edwards], the Court never expressly determined that the state capitol grounds constituted a public forum. [Cf. his dissent in Lehman.] [Moreover], none of the opinions that have expressly characterized locales as public forums has really gone that far, for a careful reading of those opinions reveals that the characterizations were always qualified, indicating that not every conceivable form of public expression would be protected.

"Those cases permitting public expression without characterizing the locale involved as a public forum, together with those cases recognizing the existence of a public forum, albeit qualifiedly, evidence the desirability of a flexible approach to determining when public expression should be protected. Realizing that the permissibility of a certain form of public expression at a given locale may differ depending on whether it is asked if the locale is a public forum or if the form of expression is compatible with the activities occurring at the locale, it becomes apparent that there is need for a flexible approach. Otherwise, with the rigid characterization of a given locale as not a public forum, there is the danger that certain forms of public speech at the locale may be suppressed, even though they are basically compatible with the activities otherwise occurring at the locale." Applying his more flexible test, Justice Brennan concluded that the proposed leaflet distribution should be permitted "in those streets and lots unrestricted to civilian traffic," since those areas did not "differ in their nature and use from city streets and lots where open speech long has been protected." By contrast, the claimed "political rallies" did "present some difficulty," because of the "potential for disruption even in unrestricted areas." Even so, the proposed rally should have been permitted: "[That] a rally is disruptive of the usual activities in an unrestricted area is not to say that it is necessarily disruptive so as significantly to impair training or defense, thereby requiring its prohibition.[7] Additionally, this Court has recognized that some quite disruptive

---

7. Note also Justice Brennan's sharp attack on the majority's heavy reliance on the interest in assuring military neutrality. He insisted that "it borders on casuistry to contend that by even-handedly permitting public expression to occur in unrestricted portions of a military installation, the military will be viewed as sanctioning the causes there espoused." He added: "More fundamentally, however, the specter of partiality does not vanish with the severing of all partisan contact. It is naive to believe that any organization, including the military, is value neutral. More than this, where the interest and purpose of an organization are peculiarly affected by national affairs, it becomes highly susceptible to politicization. For this reason, it is precisely the nature of a military organization to tend toward that end. That tendency is only facilitated by action that serves to isolate the organization's members from the opportunity for exposure to the moderating influence of other ideas, particularly where, as with the military, the organization's activities pervade the lives of its members. For this reason, any unnecessary isolation only erodes neutrality and invites the danger that neutrality seeks to avoid."

forms of public expression are protected by the First Amendment. [E.g., Edwards.] In view of [the challengers'] willingness to submit to reasonable regulation as to time, place, and manner, it hardly may be argued that Fort Dix's purpose was threatened here." [8]

ACCESS TO NONTRADITIONAL FORUMS IN THE EARLY 1980s: FAIRGROUNDS AND HOME LETTER BOXES

Introduction. In the two major cases below, the claimants sought First Amendment access in the context of state fairgrounds and home letter boxes, respectively. The cases illustrate the development of public forum access theory by the early 1980s. In Heffron, the majority found that state fairgrounds constituted "a limited public forum" distinguishable from such traditional ones as streets. It applied the variety of intermediate scrutiny considered appropriate for content-neutral time, place, and manner regulations. In Greenburgh, the letter box case, by contrast, the majority found no public forum at all and applied an even more deferential level of review.

HEFFRON v. INT'L SOC. FOR KRISHNA CONSC. (ISKCON), 452 U.S. 640 (1981): This case upheld, as a permissible time, place, and manner regulation, a rule that distribution and sale of literature and solicitation of funds at the Minnesota State Fair could be conducted only from a duly licensed booth on the fairgrounds. The rule was challenged by ISKCON, a religious society espousing the views of the Krishna religion. The Court noted that the booth restriction was applicable to all non-profit, charitable, and commercial enterprises, and that booths were rented on a first-come, first-served basis in a nondiscriminatory fashion. Nevertheless, Krishna claimed that barring its members from walking about the grounds distributing and selling religious literature and soliciting funds violated its First Amendment rights. (The restriction did not prevent ISKCON representatives from walking about the fairgrounds and communicating their views in face-to-face discussions; it barred only the distribution and sale of literature and the solicitation of donations outside of booths.) Although the highest state court had sustained that claim, Justice WHITE's majority opinion found the restriction permissible. He explained: "[The] First Amendment does not guarantee the right to communicate one's views at all times and places or in any manner that may be desired. [E.g., Adderley; see Cox I.] [T]he activities of ISKCON, like those of others protected by the First Amendment, are subject to reasonable time, place, and manner restrictions. [Grayned; Adderley; Cox v. New Hampshire.] "We have often approved restrictions of that kind provided that they are justified without reference to the content of the regulated speech, that they serve a significant governmental interest, and that in doing so they leave open ample alternative channels for communication of the information." [Virginia Pharmacy (commercial speech).] Under that standard, the Rule was valid. Justice White noted:

8. The Court relied on Greer v. Spock in Brown v. Glines, 444 U.S. 348 (1980), rejecting a challenge to Air Force regulations requiring Air Force personnel to obtain approval from their commanders before circulating petitions on Air Force bases. Justice Powell wrote for the majority; Justices Stevens and Stewart, joined by Justice Brennan, submitted dissents on statutory grounds; Justice Brennan submitted an additional dissent based on the First Amendment [a dissent also applicable to a companion case, Sec- retary of Navy v. Huff, 444 U.S. 453 (1980)]; Justice Marshall did not participate. Justice Brennan's dissent, in addition to criticizing the majority's "unquestioning acceptance of the very flawed assumption that discipline and morale are enhanced by restricting peaceful communication," argued that Greer v. Spock was distinguishable. He noted, for example, that the regulations here applied to military personnel, not to civilians seeking access to military bases.

"A major criterion for a valid time, place, and manner restriction is that the restriction 'may not be based upon either the content or subject matter of the speech.' [The Rule here] qualifies in this respect, since [it] applies evenhandedly to all who wish to distribute and sell written materials or to solicit funds. Nor does Rule 6.05 suffer from the more covert forms of discrimination that may result when arbitrary discretion is vested in some governmental authority. The method of allocating space is a straightforward first-come, first-served system. [A] valid time, place, and manner regulation must also 'serve a significant governmental interest.' Here, the principal justification asserted by the State in support of Rule 6.05 is the need to maintain the orderly movement of the crowd given the large number of exhibitors and persons attending the Fair.[1] [Because] the Fair attracts large crowds—an average of 115,000 patrons on weekdays and 160,000 on Saturdays and Sundays—it is apparent that the State's interest in the orderly movement and control of such an assembly of persons is a substantial consideration.

"As a general matter, it is clear that a State's interest in protecting the 'safety and convenience' of persons using a public forum is a valid governmental objective. Furthermore, consideration of a forum's special attributes is relevant to the constitutionality of a regulation since the significance of the governmental interest must be assessed in light of the characteristic nature and function of the particular forum involved. See, e.g., [Grayned; Lehman]. This observation bears particular import in the present case since respondents make a number of analogies between the fairgrounds and city [streets]. [But] it is clear that there are significant differences between a street and the fairgrounds. [The] flow of the crowd and demands of safety are more pressing in the context of the Fair. As such, any comparisons to public streets are necessarily inexact.

"[In focusing solely on] whatever disorder would likely result from granting members of ISKCON an exemption, [and in striking down the restriction because such an exemption was not necessary to serve the State's interest, the highest state court] took too narrow a view of the State's [interest]. The justification for the Rule should not be measured by the disorder that would result from granting an exemption solely to ISKCON. [If Rule 6.05] is an invalid restriction on the activities of ISKCON, it is no more valid with respect to the other social, political, or charitable organizations that have rented booths at the Fair and confined their distribution, sale, and fund solicitation to those locations. [ISKCON] desires to proselytize at the fair because it believes it can successfully communicate and raise funds. [This] consequence would be multiplied many times over if [the Rule] could not be applied to confine such transactions by ISKCON and others to fixed locations. [Obviously, there would be a larger threat] to the State's interest in crowd control if all other religious, nonreligious, and noncommercial organizations could likewise move freely about the fairgrounds distributing and selling literature and soliciting funds at will.

"Given these considerations, we hold that the State's interest in confining distribution, selling, and fund solicitation activities to fixed locations is sufficient to satisfy the requirement that a place or manner restriction must serve a substantial state interest. By focusing on the incidental effect of providing an exemption from Rule 6.05 to ISKCON, the Minnesota Supreme Court did not

---

1. "Petitioners assert two other state interests in support of the Rule. First, petitioners claim that the Rule forwards the State's valid interest in protecting its citizens from fraudulent solicitations, deceptive or false speech, and undue annoyance. See [Schaumburg; Cantwell]. Petitioners also forward the State's interest in protecting the fairgoers from being harrassed or otherwise bothered, on the grounds that they are a captive audience. In light of our holding that the Rule is justified solely in terms of the State's interest in managing the flow of the crowd, we do not reach whether these other two purposes are constitutionally sufficient to support the imposition of the Rule." [Footnote by Justice White.]

take into [account] the fact that any such exemption cannot be meaningfully limited to ISKCON, and as applied to similarly situated groups would prevent the State from furthering its important concern with managing the flow of the crowd. In our view, the Society may apply its Rule and confine the type of transactions at issue to designated locations without violating the First Amendment. For similar reasons, we cannot agree with the [highest state court that the Rule] is an unnecessary regulation because the State could avoid the threat to its interest posed by ISKCON by less restrictive means, such as penalizing disorder or disruption, limiting the number of solicitors, or putting more narrowly drawn restrictions on the location and movement of ISKCON's representatives. As we have indicated, the inquiry must involve not only ISKCON, but also all other organizations that would be entitled to distribute, sell or solicit if the booth rule may not be enforced with respect to ISKCON. Looked at in this way, it is quite improbable that [alternative means] would deal adequately with the problems posed by the much larger number of distributors and solicitors that would be present on the fairgrounds if the judgment below were affirmed.

"For [the Rule] to be valid as a place and manner restriction, it must also be sufficiently clear that alternative forums for the expression of respondents' protected speech exist despite the effects of the Rule. [The Rule] is not vulnerable on this ground. [It] does not exclude ISKCON from the fairgrounds, nor does it deny that organization the right to conduct any desired activity at some point within the forum. Its members may mingle with the crowd and orally propagate their views. The organization may also arrange for a booth and distribute and sell literature and solicit funds from that location on the fairgrounds itself. The Minnesota State Fair is a limited public forum in that it exists to provide a means for a great number of exhibitors temporarily to present their products or views, be they commercial, religious, or political, to a large number of people in an efficient fashion. Considering the limited functions of the Fair and the [confined] area within which it operates, we are unwilling to say that [the Rule] does not provide ISKCON and other organizations with an adequate means to sell and solicit on the fairgrounds. The First Amendment protects the right of every citizen to 'reach the minds of willing listeners and to do so there must be opportunity to win their attention.' Kovacs v. Cooper. [The Rule] does not unnecessarily limit that right within the fairgrounds." [2]

Four Justices were in partial dissent. Justice BRENNAN, joined by Justices Marshall and Stevens, agreed with the result regarding the limitation of literature sales and funds solicitation to fixed booths, but dissented regarding the ban on *distribution* of literature outside of booths. He emphasized the State's "significant interest in protecting its fairgoers from fraudulent or deceptive solicitation practices" and found this interest "substantially furthered" by the booth requirement regarding sales and solicitations. But, "because I believe that the [booth rule] is an overly intrusive means of achieving the State's interest in crowd control, and because I cannot accept the validity of the State's

---

2. "Given this understanding of the nature of the Fair, we reject respondents' claim that Rule 6.05 effects a total ban on protected First Amendment activities in the open areas of the fairgrounds. In effect, respondents seek to separate, for constitutional purposes, the open areas of the fairgrounds from that part of the fairgrounds where the booths are located. For the reasons stated in text, we believe respondents' characterization of the Rule is plainly incorrect. The booths are not secreted away in some nonac-

cessible location, but are located within the area of the fairgrounds where visitors are expected, and indeed encouraged, to pass. Since respondents are permitted to solicit funds and distribute and sell literature from within the fairgrounds, albeit from a fixed location, it is inaccurate to say that Rule 6.05 constitutes a ban on such protected activity in the relevant public forum. Accordingly, the only question is the Rule's validity as a time, place, and manner restriction." [Footnote by Justice White.]

third asserted justification [harassment of a captive audience],[1] I dissent from the Court's approval of [the] restriction on the distribution of literature." He stated his general approach as follows:

"[Once] a governmental regulation is shown to impinge upon basic First Amendment rights, the burden falls on the government to show the validity of its asserted interest and the absence of less intrusive alternatives. See, e.g., [Schneider]. The challenged 'regulation must be narrowly tailored to further the State's legitimate interest.' [The Rule] does not meet this test. [Significantly], each and every fairgoer, whether political candidate, concerned citizen, or member of a religious group, is free to give speeches, engage in face-to-face advocacy, campaign, or proselytize. No restrictions are placed on any fairgoer's right to speak at any time, at any place, or to any person.[2] [Because of the Rule], however, as soon as a proselytizing member of ISKCON hands out a free copy of the Bhagavad-Gita to an interested listener, or a political candidate distributes his campaign brochure to a potential voter, he becomes subject to arrest and removal from the fairgrounds. This constitutes a significant restriction on First Amendment rights.

"In support of its crowd control justification, the State contends that if fairgoers are permitted to distribute literature, large crowds will gather, blocking traffic lanes and causing safety problems. [But] the State has failed to provide any support for these assertions. It has made no showing that relaxation of its booth rule would create additional disorder in a fair that is already characterized by the robust and unrestrained participation of hundreds of thousands of wandering fairgoers. If fairgoers can make speeches, engage in face-to-face proselytizing, and buttonhole prospective supporters, they can surely distribute literature to members of their audience without significantly adding to the State's asserted crowd control problem. The record is devoid of any evidence that the 125-acre fairgrounds could not accommodate peripatetic distributors of literature just as easily as it now accommodates peripatetic speechmakers and proselytizers.

"Relying on a general, speculative fear of disorder [see Tinker], the [State] has placed a significant restriction on respondents' ability to exercise core First Amendment rights. This restriction is not narrowly drawn to advance the State's interests, and for that reason is unconstitutional. [If] the State had a reasonable concern that distribution in certain parts of the fairgrounds—for example, entrances and exits—would cause disorder, it could have drafted its rule to prohibit distribution of literature at those points. If the State felt it necessary to limit the number of persons distributing an organization's literature, it could, within reason, have done that as well. It had no right, however, to ban all distribution of literature outside the booths."[3]

---

1. "Because fairgoers are fully capable of saying 'no' to persons seeking their attention and then walking away, they are not members of a captive audience. They have no general right to be free from being approached. See [Schaumburg; Martin v. Struthers]." [Footnote by Justice Brennan.]

2. "A state fair is truly a marketplace of ideas and a public forum for the communication of ideas and information. [Despite] the Court's suggestion to the contrary, a fair is surely a 'natural and proper place[ ] for the dissemination of information and opinion.' [Schneider.] In no way could I agree that respondents' desired 'manner of expression is basically incompatible with the normal activity' of the fair." [Footnote by Justice Brennan.]

3. In a separate opinion, Justice BLACKMUN agreed with Justice Brennan's result but for somewhat different reasons. He did not find that the interest in preventing fraud justified the restrictions on solicitations and sales. As to the fraud rationale, he relied on Schaumburg (p. 1215 above) and stated: "There is nothing in this record to suggest that it is more difficult to police fairgrounds for fraudulent solicitations than it is to police an entire community's streets." But, unlike Justice Brennan, he found that the crowd control and safety justification warranted the restriction on solicitations and sales: "I think that common-sense differences between literature distribution, on the one hand, and solicitation and sales, on the other, suggest that the latter activities present greater crowd control problems than the former."

U.S. POSTAL SERVICE v. GREENBURGH CIVIC ASSNS., 453 U.S. 114 (1981): This case rejected a First Amendment challenge to a federal law (18 U.S.C. § 1725) which prohibits the deposit of unstamped "mailable matter" in home letter boxes. It was challenged by a group of civic associations who asserted that the ban on their delivering messages to local residents by placing unstamped notices and pamphlets in the letter boxes of private homes unduly inhibited their communications with the residents. Justice REHNQUIST's majority opinion found the challenge without merit. Finding that a letter box "is not traditionally [a] 'public forum,' " he insisted that that made it unnecessary to apply the principles governing time, place, and manner restrictions on the use of public forums. Instead, it was enough to be satisfied, as the majority was, that this was a "reasonable," "content-neutral" regulation.

In rejecting the "public forum" claim, Justice Rehnquist noted that a "letterbox provided by a postal customer which meets the Postal Service's specifications [becomes] part of the [Service's] nationwide system for the receipt and delivery of mail." He continued: "What is at issue in this case is solely the constitutionality of [a law] which makes it unlawful for persons to use, without payment of a fee, a letter box which has been designated an 'authorized depository' of the mail by the Postal Service. [W]hen a letter box is so designated, it becomes an essential part of the Postal Service's nationwide system for the delivery and receipt of mail. In effect, the postal customer, although he pays for the physical components of the 'authorized depository,' agrees to abide by the Postal Service's regulations in exchange for the Postal Service agreeing to deliver and pick up his mail. Appellees' claim is undermined by the fact that a letter box, once designated an 'authorized depository,' does not at the same time undergo a transformation into a 'public forum' of some limited nature to which the First Amendment guarantees access to all comers. There is neither historical nor constitutional support for the characterization of a letter box as a public forum. [It] is difficult to accept appellees' assertion that because it may be somewhat more efficient to place their messages in letter boxes there is a First Amendment right to do so. The underlying rationale of appellees' argument would seem to foreclose Congress or the Postal Service from requiring in the future that all letter boxes contain locks with keys being available only to the homeowner and the mail carrier. [Letter boxes] which lock, however, have the same effect on civic associations who wish access to them as does the enforcement of § 1725. Such letter boxes also accomplish the same purpose—that is, they protect mail revenues while at the same time facilitating the secure and efficient delivery of the mails. We do not think the First Amendment prohibits Congress from choosing to accomplish these purposes through legislation as opposed to lock and key.

"Indeed, it is difficult to conceive of any reason why this Court should treat a letter box differently for First Amendment access purposes than it has in the past treated the military base in Greer v. Spock, the jail or prison in [e.g., Adderley], or the advertising space made available in city rapid transit cars in [Lehman]. In all these cases, this Court recognized that the First Amendment does not guarantee access to property simply because it is owned or controlled by the government. In Greer v. Spock, the Court cited approvingly from its earlier opinion in [Adderley], wherein it explained that 'The State, no less than a private owner of property, has power to preserve the property under its control for the use to which it is lawfully dedicated.'[1] This Court has not

---

1. Justice Brennan argues that a letter box is a public forum because: "[the] mere deposit of mailable matter without postage is not 'basically incompatible' with the 'normal activity' for which a letter box is used, i.e., deposit of maila-ble matter with proper postage or mail delivery by the postal service. On the contrary, the mails and the letter boxes are specifically used for the communication of information and ideas and thus surely constitute a public forum appropriate

hesitated in the past to hold invalid laws which it concluded granted too much discretion to public officials as to who might and who might not solicit individual homeowners, or which too broadly inhibited the access of persons to traditional First Amendment forums such as the public streets and parks. See, [e.g., Schaumburg; Lovell; Mosley]. But it is a giant leap from the traditional 'soap box' to the letter box designated as an authorized depository of the United States mails, and we do not believe the First Amendment requires us to make that leap.[2] "

After finding that a letter box was not a public forum, Justice Rehnquist found only a very limited scope of review appropriate: "It is thus unnecessary for us to examine § 1725 in the context of a 'time, place, and manner' restriction on the use of the traditional 'public forums' referred to above. This Court has long recognized the validity of reasonable time, place, and manner regulations on such a forum so long as the regulation is content neutral, serves a significant governmental interest, and leaves open adequate alternative channels for communication. But since a letter box is not traditionally such a 'public forum,' the elaborate analysis engaged in by the District Court was, we think, unnecessary.[3] To be sure, if a governmental regulation is based on the content

for the exercise of First Amendment rights subject to reasonable time, place, and manner restrictions such as those embodied in § 1725." Justice Brennan's analysis assumes that simply because an instrumentality "is used for the communication of ideas or information," it thereby becomes a public forum. Our cases provide no support for such a sweeping proposition. Certainly, a bulletin board in a cafeteria at Fort Dix is "specifically used for the communication of information and ideas," but such a bulletin board is no more a "public forum" than are the street corners and parking lots found not to be so at the same military base. Greer v. Spock. Likewise, the advertising space made available in public transportation in the City of Shaker Heights is "specifically used for the communication of information and ideas," but that fact alone was not sufficient to transform that space into a "public forum" for First Amendment purposes. [Lehman.]

[For] the reasons we have stated at length in our opinion, we think the appellees' First Amendment activities are wholly incompatible with the maintenance of a nationwide system for the safe and efficient delivery of mail. The history of the postal system and the role the letter box serves within that system supports this conclusion, and even Justice Brennan acknowledges that a "significant governmental interest" is advanced by the restriction imposed by § 1725. [Footnote by Justice Rehnquist.]

2. Justice Marshall in his dissent states that he disagrees "with the Court's assumption that if no public forum is involved, the only First Amendment challenges to be considered are whether the regulation is content-based [and] reasonable." The First Amendment prohibits Congress from "abridging freedom of speech, or of the press," and its ramifications are not confined to the "public forum" first noted in Hague v. CIO. What we hold is the principle reiterated by cases such as Adderley v. Florida and Greer v. Spock, that property owned or controlled by the government which is *not* a public forum may

be subject to a prohibition of speech, leafleting, picketing, or other forms of communication without running afoul of the First Amendment. Admittedly, the government must act reasonably in imposing such restrictions, and the prohibition must be content-neutral. But, for the reasons stated in our opinion, we think it cannot be questioned that § 1725 is both a reasonable and content-neutral [regulation]. [Footnote by Justice Rehnquist.]

3. In the District Court, the Government had offered three justifications: protecting mail revenues; facilitating the efficient and secure delivery of the mail; and promoting the privacy of mail patrons. In finding § 1725 unconstitutional as applied, the District Court rested on several related grounds: Since civic associations generally have limited financial resources and cannot afford to pay for postage, they would find it "financially burdensome" to use the mails. Moreover, given the "relatively slow pace of the mail," use of the mail would impede their "ability to communicate quickly with their constituents." Most important, the District Court found that "none of the alternative means of delivery suggested by the Postal Service were 'nearly as effective as placing civic association flyers in approved mail boxes; so that restriction on [their] delivery methods to such alternatives also constitutes a serious burden on [their] ability to communicate with their constituents.' "

The District Court reasoned that the alternative methods suggested by the Postal Service were inadequate because they can result in the civic notices either being lost or damaged as a result of wind, rain or snow. Weatherstripping on doors may prevent the flyers from being placed under the door. Use of plastic bags for protection of the civic notices is both time consuming and "relatively expensive for a small volunteer organization." Deposit of materials outside may cause litter problems as well as arouse resentment among residents because it informs burglars that no one is home. Alternative methods which depend on reaching the occu-

of the speech or the message, that action must be scrutinized more carefully to ensure that communication has not been prohibited 'merely because public officials disapprove the speakers' view.' [Consolidated Edison Co. v. PSC.] But in this case there simply is no question that § 1725 does not regulate speech on the basis of content. While the analytical line between a regulation of the 'time, place, and manner' in which First Amendment rights may be exercised in a traditional public forum, and the question of whether a particular piece of personal or real property owned or controlled by the government is in fact a 'public forum' may blur at the edges, we think the line is nonetheless a workable one. We likewise think that Congress may, in exercising its authority to develop and operate a national postal system, properly legislate with the generality of cases in mind, and should not be put to the test of defending in one township after another the constitutionality of a statute under the traditional 'time, place, and manner' analysis. This Court has previously acknowledged that the 'guarantees of the First Amendment' have never meant 'that people who want to propagandize their protests or views have a constitutional right to do so whenever and however they please.' Greer v. Spock, quoting [Adderley]. If Congress and the Postal Service are to operate as efficiently as possible a system for the delivery of mail, [they] must obviously adopt regulations of general character having uniform [applicability]. [While] Congress no more than a suburban township may not by its own ipse dixit destroy the 'public forum' status of streets and parks which have historically been public forums, we think that for the reasons stated a letter box may not properly be analogized to streets and parks. It is enough for our purposes that neither the enactment nor the enforcement of § 1725 was geared in any way to the content of the message sought to be placed in the letter box."

Justice BRENNAN, concurring in the judgment, insisted that a letter box is a public forum, but that the law was a reasonable time, place, and manner regulation. As to the latter, he noted that the restraint was "content-neutral" and that it advanced "a significant governmental interest—preventing loss of mail revenues." [1] Moreover, there were "ample alternative channels for communication"—e.g., placing circulars under doors or attaching them to doorknobs. Most of his opinion, however, was devoted to objecting to the majority's analysis: "The Court declines to analyze § 1725 as a time, place, and manner restriction. Instead, it concludes that a letterbox is not a public forum. [I] believe that [this] ignores the proper method of analysis in determining whether property owned or directly controlled by the Government is a public forum. Moreover, even if the Court were correct that a letter box is not a public forum, the First Amendment would still require the Court to determine whether the burden on appellees' exercise of their First Amendment rights is supportable as a reasonable time, place, and manner restriction." He elaborated:

"For public forum analysis, '[t]he crucial question is whether the manner of expression is basically incompatible with the normal activity of a particular place

---

pant personally are less effective because their success depends on the mere chance that the person called or visited will be home at any given time. The court also found that enforcement of § 1725 against civic associations "does not appear so necessary or contribute to enforcement of the anti-theft, anti-fraud, or Private Express statutes that this interest outweighs the [appellees'] substantial interest in expedient and economical communication with their constituents." The District Court accordingly concluded that "the cost to free expression of imposing this burden on [appellees] outweighed the showing made by the

Postal Service of its need to enforce the statute to promote effective delivery and protection of the mails."

1. Justice Brennan conceded that the District Court might well be right in saying that there would not be "a *substantial* loss of revenue" if the law were not enforced against the challengers, but added that "that conclusion overlooks the obvious cumulative effect that the District Court's ruling would have if applied across the country."

at a particular time.' [Grayned (p. 1264 below).] Our cases have recognized generally that public properties are appropriate fora for exercise of First Amendment rights. While First Amendment rights exercised on public property may be subject to reasonable time, place, and manner restrictions, that is very different from saying that government-controlled property, such as a letter box, does not constitute a public forum. Only where the exercise of First Amendment rights is incompatible with the normal activity occurring on public property have we held that the property is not a public forum. See [e.g., Greer v. Spock; Adderley]. [I] believe that the mere deposit of mailable matter without postage is not 'basically incompatible' with the 'normal activity' for which a letter box is [used]. On the contrary, the mails and the letter box are specifically used for the communication of information and ideas, and thus surely constitute a public forum appropriate for the exercise of First Amendment rights subject to reasonable time, place, and manner restrictions such as those embodied in § 1725 or in the requirement that postage be affixed to mailable matter to obtain access to the postal system. The history of the mails as a vital national medium of expression confirms this conclusion. [Moreover, the Court] relies on inapposite cases to reach its result. Greer v. Spock [and Adderley] rested on the inherent incompatibility between the rights sought to be exercised and the physical location in which the exercise was to occur. [Lehman] rested in large measure on the captive audience doctrine and in part on the transportation purpose of the city bus system. These cases, therefore, provide no support for the Court's conclusion that a letter box is not a public forum.

"Having determined that a letter box is not a public forum, the Court inexplicably terminates its analysis. Surely, however, the mere fact that property is not a public forum does not free government to impose unwarranted restrictions on First Amendment rights. [Even] where property does not constitute a public forum, government regulation that is content-neutral must still be reasonable as to time, place, and manner. The restriction in § 1725 could have such an effect on First Amendment rights—and does for Justice Marshall—that it should be struck down. The Court, therefore, cannot avoid analyzing § 1725 as a time, place, and manner restriction.[2]"

Justice MARSHALL's dissent insisted that, although the law sought to achieve the legitimate and important congressional objective of assuring the economic viability and efficiency of the postal service, it was "inconsistent with the underlying commitment to communication." He objected to the majority's result, its analysis, and its "premise" that "private persons lose their prerogatives over the letterboxes they own and supply for mail service." He elaborated: "First, I disagree with the Court's assumption that if no public forum is involved, the only First Amendment challenges to be considered are whether the regulation is content-based and reasonable. Even if the Postal Service were not a public forum, which [I] do not accept, the statute advanced in its aid is a law challenged as an abridgment of free expression. [The] question, then, is whether this statute burdens any First Amendment rights enjoyed by appellees.

2. "Even if the letter box were characterized as purely private property that is being regulated by the Government, rather than property which has become incorporated into the 'Postal Service's nationwide system for the receipt and delivery of mail,' § 1725 would still be subject to time, place, and manner analysis. See, e.g., Young v. American Mini Theatres." [Footnote by Justice Brennan.]

In another opinion concurring in the judgment, Justice WHITE insisted that "the validity of user fees does not necessarily depend on satisfying typical time, place or manner requirements. Equally bootless is the inquiry whether the postal system is a public forum. For all who pay the fee, it obviously is, and the only question is whether a user fee may be [charged]. [I] am quite sure that the fee is a valid charge."

If so, it must be determined whether this burden is justified by a significant governmental interest substantially advanced by the statute. See [e.g., Consolidated Edison Co. v. PSC; Grayned].

"[I] cannot agree with the Court's conclusion that we need not ask whether the ban against [placing] messages in letter boxes is a restriction on appellees' free expression rights. I see no ground to disturb [the] factual determinations of the trier of fact [the District Court]. And, given these facts, the Postal Service bears a heavy burden to show that its interests are legitimate and substantially served by the restriction of appellees' freedom of expression. Here, the District Court concluded that the Postal Service 'has not shown that failure to enforce the statute as to [appellees] would result in a substantial loss of revenue, or a significant reduction in the government's ability to protect the mails by investigating and prosecuting mail theft, mail fraud, or unauthorized private mail delivery service.' In light of this failure of proof, I cannot join the Court's conclusion that [the] Government may thus curtail appellees' ability to inform community residents about local civic matters. That decision, I fear, threatens a departure from this Court's belief that free expression [must] not yield unnecessarily before such governmental interests as economy or efficiency. Certainly, free expression should not have to yield here, where the intruding statute has seldom been enforced. [T]he statute's asserted purposes easily could be advanced by less intrusive alternatives, such as a nondiscriminatory permit requirement for depositing unstamped circulars in letter boxes.

"[Even] apart from the result in this case, I must differ with the Court's use of the public forum concept to avoid application of the First Amendment. Rather than a threshold barrier that must be surmounted before reaching the terrain of the First Amendment, the concept of a public forum has more properly been used to open varied governmental locations to equal public access for free expression, subject to the constraints on time, place or manner necessary to preserve the governmental function. [Given] its pervasive and traditional use as purveyor of written communication, the Postal Service [may] properly be viewed as a public forum. The Court relies on easily distinguishable cases in reaching the contrary conclusion. For the Postal Service's very purpose is to facilitate communication, which surely differentiates it from the military bases, jails, and mass transportation discussed in cases relied on by the Court. [The] inquiry in our public forum cases has instead asked whether 'the manner of expression is basically incompatible with the normal activity of a particular place at a particular time.' [Grayned.] Assuming for the moment that the letter boxes, as 'authorized depositories,' are under governmental control and thus part of the governmental enterprise, their purpose is hardly incompatible with appellees' use. For the letter boxes are intended to receive written communication directed to the residents and to protect such materials from the weather or the intruding eyes of would-be burglars.

"Reluctance to treat the letter boxes as public forums might stem not from the Postal Service's approval of their form but instead from the fact that their ownership and use remain in the hands of private individuals. Even that hesitation, I should think, would be misguided, for those owners necessarily retain the right to receive information as a counterpart of the right of speakers to speak. On that basis alone, I would doubt the validity of 18 U.S.C. § 1725, for it deprives residents of the information which civic groups or individuals may wish to deliver to these private receptacles. [And I] remain troubled by the Court's effort to transform the letter boxes entirely into components of the governmental enterprise despite their private ownership. [Instead] of starting with the scope of governmental control, I would adhere to our usual analysis which looks to whether the exercise of a First Amendment right is burdened by the challenged governmental action, and then upholds that action only where it is necessary to advance a substantial and legitimate governmental interest." [1]

ACCESS TO SCHOOLS AND SCHOOL ENVIRONS

Introduction. This subsection briefly samples some access claims that have arisen in the school context. The first case, of the early 1970s, is of special importance for its suggestion of the concept of "basic incompatibility" in delineating First Amendment access claims to public places. The second case, of the early 1980s, illustrates the modern Court's special, intense scrutiny of content-based restrictions.[1]

GRAYNED v. ROCKFORD, 408 U.S. 104 (1972): This decision sustained an ordinance barring a demonstration near a school. The Court affirmed a conviction under an "antinoise" ordinance stating that no person on grounds "adjacent to any [school] building" in which a class is in session "shall willfully make or assist in the making of any noise or diversion which disturbs or tends to disturb the peace or good order of such school session." As understood by the Court, the ordinance prohibited "only actual or imminent interference with the 'peace or good order' of the school." Appellant had participated in a mass demonstration promoting a Black cause in front of a high school. Justice MARSHALL's majority opinion, after rejecting a vagueness attack, turned to an overbreadth claim; and his discussion of the relevance of "incompatibility" in delineating public forum principles came in the course of that examination. He emphasized that it was "the nature of a place" which determines the reasonableness of "time, place and manner" restrictions: "The crucial question is whether the manner of expression is basically incompatible with the normal activity of a particular place at a particular time." And here, he found the restraint appropriate to the school environment. He elaborated: "Although a silent vigil may not unduly interfere with a public library [Brown], making a speech in the reading room almost certainly would. That same speech should be perfectly appropriate in a park. [Our] cases make clear that in assessing the reasonableness of a regulation, we must weigh heavily the fact that communication is involved [Schneider; Hague]; the regulation must be narrowly tailored to further the State's legitimate interest. Access to the 'streets, sidewalks, parks, and other similar public places [for] the purpose of exercising [First Amendment rights] cannot constitutionally be denied broadly.' [Logan Valley, p.

---

1. Justice STEVENS, in a separate dissent, agreed with Justice Marshall's result, but by a different reasoning. He stated that he could not "accept the proposition that these private receptacles are the functional equivalent of public fora." He viewed the letter boxes as private property, but insisted that the law "interferes with the owner's receipt of information that he may want to receive. [The law] deprives millions of homeowners of the legal right to make a simple decision affecting their ability to receive communications from others." He added: "The Government seeks to justify the prohibition on three grounds: avoiding the loss of federal revenues, preventing theft from the mails, and maintaining the efficiency of the Postal Service. In my judgment the first ground is frivolous and the other two, though valid, are insufficient to overcome the presumption that this impediment to communication is invalid."

1. This is not the only place in these free expression chapters in which school contexts are involved. For another "access to public places" claim in the school context, recall Police Dept. v. Mosley (1972), considered in sec. 2 of this chapter, at p. 1164 above. Mosley is a major case in the development of judicial hostility to content-based distinctions. It struck down a ban on picketing near school buildings during school hours because it discriminatorily exempted labor picketing. For additional school context cases, see, e.g., Tinker (1969; symbolic expression; wearing black armbands in school as an anti-war protest; p. 1176 above), and Perry Ed. Assn. v. Perry Local Educators' Assn. (1983; p. 1268 below) (access to public school system's internal communication system). See also the group of problems dealing with the First Amendment in the school context in the next chapter, especially Board of Education v. Pico (1982; p. 1323 below) (removal of books from school libraries).

1291 below.] In light of these general principles, we do not think that Rockford's ordinance is an unconstitutional regulation of activity around a school."

Turning to that school context, Justice Marshall stated: "Tinker (p. 1176 below) made clear that school property may not be declared off-limits for expressive activity by students. [Similarly] we think it clear that the public sidewalk adjacent to school grounds may not be declared off-limits for expressive activity by members of the public. But in each case, expressive activity may be prohibited if it 'materially disrupts classwork or involves substantial disorder or invasion of the rights of others.' [Tinker.] We would be ignoring reality if we did not recognize that the public schools [are] often the focus of significant grievances. Without interfering with normal school activities, daytime picketing and handbilling on public grounds near a school can effectively publicize those grievances. [Some] picketing to that end will be quiet and peaceful, and will in no way disturb the normal functioning of the school. [On] the other hand, schools could hardly tolerate boisterous demonstrators who drown out classroom conversation, make studying impossible, block entrances, or incite children to leave the schoolhouse. [This] ordinance goes no further than Tinker says a municipality may go to prevent interference with its schools. It is narrowly tailored to further Rockford's compelling interest in having an undisrupted school session conducive to the students' learning, and does not unnecessarily interfere with First Amendment rights." [2]

WIDMAR v. VINCENT, 454 U.S. 263 (1981): In this case, the Court exercised the strict scrutiny it typically applies to content-based exclusions from public places. It held that a state university that makes its facilities generally available for the activities of registered student groups may not constitutionally bar a group desiring to use the facilities for religious worship and discussion. The case arose when the University of Missouri at Kansas City, relying on its policy of prohibiting the use of its facilities "for purposes of religious worship or religious teaching," barred a student religious group from meeting anywhere on its grounds. The Court rejected the University's argument that its interest in promoting the separation of church and state was adequate to survive strict scrutiny. [3]

In explaining the application of free speech principles here, Justice POWELL's majority opinion stated: "Through its policy of accommodating their meetings, the University has created a forum generally open for use by student groups. Having done so, the University has assumed an obligation to justify its discriminations and exclusions under applicable constitutional norms. [4] The Constitution forbids a State to enforce certain exclusions from a forum generally

---

2. Note also a further comment by Justice Marshall: "We recognize that the ordinance prohibits some picketing which is neither violent nor physically obstructive. Noisy demonstrations that disrupt or are incompatible with normal school activities are obviously within the ordinance's reach. Such expressive conduct may be constitutionally protected at other places or other times [Edwards; Cox I], but next to a school, while classes are in session, it may be prohibited." Elsewhere, Justice Marshall stated that Cox II "indicated that, because of the special nature of the place, persons could be constitutionally prohibited from picketing 'in or near' a courthouse. [Similarly] Rockford's modest restriction [represents] a considered and specific legislative judgment that some kind of expressive activity should be restricted at a particular time and place, here in order to protect the schools.

Such a reasonable regulation is not inconsistent with the [First Amendment]."

3. The Court's discussion of separation of church and state principles is noted in chap. 14, below.

4. Justice Powell elaborated in a footnote: "This Court has recognized that the campus of a public university, at least for its students, possesses many of the characteristics of a public forum. See generally [Mosley]. At the same time, however, our cases have recognized that First Amendment rights must be analyzed 'in light of the special characteristics of the school environment.' [Tinker.] We continue to adhere to that view. A university differs in significant respects from public forums such as streets or parks or even municipal theaters. A university's mission is education, and decisions of this Court have

open to the public, even if it was not required to create the forum in the first place. The University's institutional mission, which it describes as providing a '*secular* education' to its students, does not exempt its actions from constitutional scrutiny. With respect to persons entitled to be there, our cases leave no doubt that the First Amendment rights of speech and association extend to the campuses of state universities. Here the [University] has discriminated against student groups and speakers based on their desire to use a generally open forum to engage in religious worship and discussion. These are forms of speech and association protected by the First Amendment. See, e.g., [Heffron; Saia]. In order to justify discriminatory exclusion from a public forum based on the religious content of a group's intended speech, the University must therefore satisfy the standard of review appropriate to content-based exclusions. It must show that its regulation is necessary to serve a compelling state interest and that it is narrowly drawn to achieve that end. See Carey v. Brown [1980, sec. 2, at p. 1166 above]."

After rejecting the University's separation of church and state defense (as discussed in chap. 14 below), Justice Powell concluded by returning to free speech principles. He emphasized: "Our holding in this case in no way undermines the capacity of the University to establish reasonable time, place, and manner regulations. [See, e.g., Grayned.] Nor do we question the right of the University to make academic judgments as to how best to allocate scarce resources or 'to determine for itself on academic grounds who may teach, what may be taught, how it shall be taught, and who may be admitted to study.' [Sweezy v. New Hampshire, chap. 13, p. 1406 below.] Finally, we affirm the continuing validity of cases that recognize a University's right to exclude even First Amendment activities that violate reasonable campus rules or substantially interfere with the opportunity of other students to obtain an education. The basis for our decision is narrow. Having created a forum generally open to student groups, the University seeks to enforce a content-based exclusion of religious speech. Its exclusionary policy violates the fundamental principle that a state regulation of speech should be content-neutral, and the University is unable to justify this violation under applicable constitutional standards."

In an opinion concurring only in the judgment, Justice STEVENS took issue with the majority's approach: "In my opinion, the use of the terms 'compelling state interest' and 'public forum' to analyze the question presented in this case may needlessly undermine the academic freedom of public universities."[5] He elaborated: "Today most major colleges and universities are operated by public authority. Nevertheless, their facilities are not open to the public in the same way that streets and parks are. University facilities—private or public—are maintained primarily for the benefit of the student body and the faculty. In performing their learning and teaching missions, the managers of the university routinely make countless decisions based on the content of communicative materials. They select books for inclusion in the library, they hire professors on the basis of their academic philosophies, they select courses for inclusion in the curriculum, and they reward scholars for what they have written. In addition, in encouraging students to participate in extracurricular activities, they necessarily make decisions concerning the content of these activities. Because every university's resources are limited, an educational institution must routinely make decisions concerning the use of the time and space that is available for

never denied its authority to impose reasonable regulations compatible with that mission upon the use of its campus and facilities. We have not held, for example, that a campus must make all of its facilities equally available to students and nonstudents alike, or that a university must grant free access to all of its grounds or buildings."

[Cf. Princeton University v. Schmid, 455 U.S. 100 (1982).]

5. Justice Powell responded to this concern by calling it "unjustified": "Our holding is limited to the context of a public forum created by the University itself."

extracurricular activities. In my judgment, it is both necessary and appropriate for those decisions to evaluate the content of a proposed student activity. I should think it obvious, for example, that if two groups of 25 students requested the use of a room at a particular time—one to view Mickey Mouse cartoons and the other to rehearse an amateur performance of Hamlet—the First Amendment would not require that the room be reserved for the group that submitted its application first. Nor do I see why a university should have to establish a 'compelling state interest' to defend its decision to permit one group to use the facility and not the other. In my opinion, a university should be allowed to decide for itself whether a program that illuminates the genius of Walt Disney should be given precedence over one that may duplicate material adequately covered in the classroom. Judgments of this kind should be made by academicians, not by federal judges, and their standards for decision should not be encumbered with ambiguous phrases like 'compelling state interest.'

"Thus, I do not subscribe to the view that a public university has no greater interest in the content of student activities than the police chief has in the content of a soap box oration on Capitol Hill. A university legitimately may regard some subjects as more relevant to its educational mission than others. But the university, like the police officer, may not allow its agreement or disagreement with the viewpoint of a particular speaker to determine whether access to a forum will be granted. If a state university is to deny recognition to a student organization—or is to give it a lesser right to use school facilities than other student groups—it must have a valid reason for doing so." Despite his different standard of review, Justice Stevens found the University decision unjustified. He explained: "[The] University could not allow a group of Republicans or Presbyterians to meet while denying Democrats or Mormons the same privilege. It seems apparent that the policy under attack would allow groups of young philosophers to meet to discuss their skepticism that a Supreme Being exists, or a group of political scientists to meet to debate the accuracy of the view that religion is the 'opium of the people.' If school facilities may be used to discuss anti-clerical doctrine, it seems to me that comparable use by a group desiring to express a belief in God must also be permitted. The fact that their expression of faith includes ceremonial conduct is not, in my opinion, a sufficient reason for suppressing their discussion entirely."

Justice WHITE, the sole dissenter, disagreed not only with the majority's Establishment Clause approach (as discussed in the additional note below) but also with its free speech analysis. He objected to the argument that, "because religious worship uses speech, it is protected by the Free Speech Clause of the First Amendment.[6] Not only is it protected, [the challengers] argue, but religious worship qua speech is not different from any other variety of protected speech as a matter of constitutional principle. I believe that this proposition is plainly wrong. Were it right, the Religion Clauses would be emptied of any independent meaning in circumstances in which religious practice took the form of speech. Although the majority describes this argument as 'novel,' I believe it to be clearly supported by our previous cases." He added: "There may be instances in which a state's attempt to disentangle itself from religious worship would intrude upon secular speech about religion. In such a case the state's action would be subject to challenge under the Free Speech [Clause]. This is not such a case. This case involves religious worship only; the fact that that worship is accomplished through speech does not add anything to [the challengers'] argument. That argument must rely upon the claim that the state's action

---

6. In a footnote at this point, Justice White commented that it was "surprising that the majority assumes this proposition to require no argument." The precedents did not support Justice Powell's reasoning, he insisted. For example, "Heffron and Saia involved the communication of religious views to a non-religious public audience. Talk about religion and about religious beliefs, however, is not the same as religious services of worship."

impermissibly interferes with the free exercise of respondents' religious practices. Although this is a close question, I conclude that it does not." In explaining that conclusion, Justice White insisted that in this instance the burden on free exercise was "minimal" and that therefore "the state need do no more than demonstrate that the regulation furthers some permissible state end. [I] believe the interest of the state is sufficiently strong to justify the imposition of the minimal burden on [the challengers'] ability freely to exercise their religious beliefs."[7]

ACCESS TO NONTRADITIONAL PUBLIC PLACES IN THE MID–1980s: A SURVEY OF THE MODERN COURT'S PREDOMINANT TECHNIQUES

Introduction. The two principal cases in this final subsection involving claims of access to public property illustrate the wide range of analyses available to the modern Court and invite not only review but also critical examination of the adequacy of the techniques currently in vogue. Perry, the first of the cases, presented a claim of equal access to an internal mail distribution system in public schools. It prompted Justice White, who wrote for the majority, to set forth an elaborate public forum analysis for the resolution of access claims. Taxpayers for Vincent, the second principal case, involved a ban on posting signs on public property. There, Justice Stevens deemphasized public forum analysis, concentrated on an application of the O'Brien multi-part standard, and stressed the absence of viewpoint discrimination. (The First Amendment claimants lost in both cases.) These cases, in addition to illustrating the approaches of (and divisions on) the contemporary Court, invite reexamination of most of the techniques considered earlier in this chapter.[1] In addition to the assured minimal access-equal access dichotomy that permeates this sec. 4, recall especially the examination of (and critical comments on) the content-based/content-neutral distinction in sec. 2 and the O'Brien two-track justification scheme in sec. 3 above.

PERRY ED. ASSN. v. PERRY LOCAL EDUCATORS' ASSN.

460 U.S. 37, 103 S.Ct. 948, 74 L.Ed.2d 794 (1983).

Justice WHITE delivered the opinion of the Court.

Perry Education Association is the duly elected exclusive bargaining representative for the teachers of the Metropolitan School District of Perry Township, Indiana. A collective bargaining agreement with the Board of Education provided that Perry Education Association [PEA], but no other union, would have access to the interschool mail system and teacher mailboxes in the Perry Township schools. The issue in this case is whether the denial of similar access to the Perry Local Educators' Association [PLEA], a rival teacher group, violates the [First Amendment].

7. Note also Justice White's comment in a footnote: "I know of no precedent holding that simply because a public forum is open to all kinds of speech—including speech about religion—it must be open to regular religious worship services as well. I doubt that the state need stand by and allow its public forum to become a church for any religious sect that chooses to stand on its right of access to that forum." [See also the additional materials on free speech in the school context in chap. 13, sec. 2, at p. 1323 below.]

1. Together with the survey of the modern analyses presented by the two principal cases which follow, it may be useful at this point to reexamine a third modern case examining contemporary analyses—Clark v. Community for Creative Non-Violence (1984; printed in sec. 3, at p. 1188 above).

I. The School District operates a public school system of thirteen separate schools. Each school building contains a set of mailboxes for the teachers. Interschool delivery by school employees permits messages to be delivered rapidly to teachers in the district. The primary function of this internal mail system is to transmit official messages among the teachers and between the teachers and the school administration. In addition, teachers use the system to send personal messages and individual school building principals have allowed delivery of messages from various private organizations. Prior to 1977, both PEA and PLEA represented teachers in the school district and apparently had equal access to the interschool mail system. In 1977, PLEA challenged PEA's status as de facto bargaining representative for the Perry Township teachers by filing an election petition with the Indiana Education Employment Relations Board (Board). PEA won the election and was certified as the exclusive representative, as provided by Indiana law.

The Board permits a school district to provide access to communication facilities to the union selected for the discharge of the exclusive representative duties of representing the bargaining unit and its individual members without having to provide equal access to rival unions. Following the election, PEA and the school district negotiated a labor contract in which the school board gave PEA "access to teachers' mailboxes in which to insert material" and the right to use the interschool mail delivery system to the extent that the school district incurred no extra expense by such use. The labor agreement [still in force] noted that these access rights were being accorded to PEA "acting as the representative of the teachers" and went on to stipulate that these access rights shall not be granted to any other ["school employee organization"]. [The] exclusive access policy applies only to use of the mailboxes and school mail system. PLEA is not prevented from using other school facilities to communicate with teachers. [E.g.,] PLEA may post notices on school bulletin boards; may hold meetings on school property after school hours; and may, with approval of the building principals, make announcements on the public address [system].[1]

[III.] The primary question presented is whether the First Amendment is violated when a union that has been elected by public school teachers as their exclusive bargaining representative is granted access to certain means of communication, while such access is denied to a rival union. There is no question that constitutional interests are implicated by denying PLEA use of the interschool mail system. [The] First Amendment's guarantee of free speech applies to teacher's mailboxes as surely as it does elsewhere within the school [Tinker] and on sidewalks outside [Mosley]. But this is not to say that the First Amendment requires equivalent access to all parts of a school building in which some form of communicative activity occurs. [Grayned.] The existence of a right of access to public property and the standard by which limitations upon such a right must be evaluated differ depending on the character of the property at issue.

A. In places which by long tradition or by government fiat have been devoted to assembly and debate, the rights of the state to limit expressive activity are sharply circumscribed. At one end of the spectrum are streets and parks which "have immemorially been held in trust for the use of the public, and, time out of mind, have been used for purposes of assembly, communicating thoughts between citizens, and discussing public questions." Hague v. CIO. In these quintessential public forums, the government may not prohibit all communicative activity. For the state to enforce a content-based exclusion it

---

1. This action was brought by PLEA against PEA and the School Board. PLEA claimed that PEA's preferential access to the internal mail system violates the First Amendment and equal protection. The District Court ruled for the defendants, but the Seventh Circuit reversed, finding the system invalid under both the First Amendment and equal protection.

must show that its regulation is necessary to serve a compelling state interest and that it is narrowly drawn to achieve that end. Carey v. Brown. The state may also enforce regulations of the time, place, and manner of expression which are content-neutral, are narrowly tailored to serve a significant government interest, and leave open ample alternative channels of communication. [E.g., Greenburgh; Consolidated Edison.]

A second category consists of public property which the state has opened for use by the public as a place for expressive activity. The Constitution forbids a state to enforce certain exclusions from a forum generally open to the public even if it was not required to create the forum in the first place. [E.g., Widmar; Southeastern Promotions.] [2] Although a state is not required to indefinitely retain the open character of the facility, as long as it does so it is bound by the same standards as apply in a traditional public forum. Reasonable time, place and manner regulations are permissible, and a content-based prohibition must be narrowly drawn to effectuate a compelling state interest.

Public property which is not by tradition or designation a forum for public communication is governed by different standards. We have recognized that the "First Amendment does not guarantee access to property simply because it is owned or controlled by the government." [Greenburgh.] In addition to time, place, and manner regulations, the state may reserve the forum for its intended purposes, communicative or otherwise, as long as the regulation on speech is reasonable and not an effort to suppress expression merely because public officials oppose the speaker's view. [Ibid.] As we have stated on several occasions, "the State, no less than a private owner of property, has power to preserve the property under its control for the use to which it is lawfully dedicated." [Id.; Greer; Adderley.]

The school mail facilities at issue here fall within this third category. [The] School District's interschool mail system is not a traditional public forum. [On] this point the parties agree. [The] internal mail system [is] not held open to the general public. It is instead PLEA's position that the school mail facilities have become a "limited public forum" from which it may not be excluded because of the periodic use of the system by private non-school connected groups, and PLEA's own unrestricted access to the system prior to PEA's certification as exclusive representative.

Neither of these arguments is persuasive. The use of the internal school mail by groups not affiliated with the schools is no doubt a relevant consideration. If by policy or by practice the Perry School District has opened its mail system for indiscriminate use by the general public, then PLEA could justifiably argue a public forum has been created. This, however, is not the case. [There] is no indication [that] the school mailboxes and interschool delivery system are open for use by the general public. Permission to use the system to communicate with teachers must be secured from the individual building principal. There is no [evidence that] this permission has been granted as a matter of course to all who seek to distribute material. We can only conclude that the schools do allow some outside organizations such as the YMCA, Cub Scouts, and other civic and church organizations to use the facilities. This type of selective access does not transform government property into a public forum. [Greer; Lehman.] Moreover, even if we assume that by granting access to [some groups], the school district has created a "limited" public forum, the constitutional right of access would in any event extend only to other entities of similar character. While the school mail facilities thus might be a forum

---

2. A public forum may be created for a limited purpose such as use by certain groups, e.g., Widmar v. Vincent (student groups), or for the discussion of certain subjects, e.g., Madison Joint School District v. Wisconsin Public Employment Relations Comm'n, 429 U.S. 167 (1976) (school board business). [Footnote by Justice White.]

generally open for use by the Girl Scouts, the local boys' club and other organizations that engage in activities of interest and educational relevance to students, they would not as a consequence be open to an organization such as PLEA, which is concerned with the terms and conditions of teacher employment.

PLEA also points to its ability to use the school mailboxes and delivery system on an equal footing with PEA prior to the collective bargaining agreement signed in 1978. Its argument appears to be that the access policy in effect at that time converted the school mail facilities into a limited public forum generally open for use by employee organizations, and that once this occurred, exclusions of employee organizations thereafter must be judged by the constitutional standard applicable to public forums. The fallacy in the argument is that it is not the forum, but PLEA itself, which has changed. Prior to 1977, there was no exclusive representative for the Perry school district teachers. PEA and PLEA each represented its own members. Therefore the school district's policy of allowing both organizations to use the school mail facilities simply reflected the fact that both unions represented the teachers and had legitimate reasons for use of the system. PLEA's previous access was consistent with the school district's preservation of the facilities for school-related business, and did not constitute creation of a public forum in any broader sense.

Because the school mail system is not a public forum, the School District had no "constitutional obligation per se to let any organization use the school mail boxes." In the Court of Appeals' view, however, the access policy adopted by the Perry schools favors a particular viewpoint, that of the PEA, on labor relations, and consequently must be strictly scrutinized regardless of whether a public forum is involved. There is, however, no indication that the school board intended to discourage one viewpoint and advance another. We believe it is more accurate to characterize the access policy as based on the *status* of the respective unions rather than their views. Implicit in the concept of the nonpublic forum is the right to make distinctions in access on the basis of subject matter and speaker identity. These distinctions may be impermissible in a public forum but are inherent and inescapable in the process of limiting a nonpublic forum to activities compatible with the intended purpose of the property. The touchstone for evaluating these distinctions is whether they are reasonable in light of the purpose which the forum at issue serves.[3]

---

3. [Justice Brennan insists] that the Perry access policy is a forbidden exercise of viewpoint discrimination. [We] disagree. [The] access policy applies not only to PLEA but to all unions other than the recognized bargaining representative, and there is no indication in the record that the policy was motivated by a desire to suppress the PLEA's views. Moreover, under Justice Brennan's analysis, if PLEA and PEA were given access to the mailboxes, it would be equally imperative that any other citizen's group or community organization with a message for school personnel—the chamber of commerce, right-to-work groups, or any other labor union—also be permitted access to the mail system. Justice Brennan's attempt to build a public forum with his own hands is untenable; it would invite schools to close their mail systems to all but school personnel. Although his viewpoint-discrimination thesis might indicate otherwise, Justice Brennan apparently would not forbid the school district from closing the mail system to all outsiders for the purpose of discussing labor matters while permitting such discussion by ad-

ministrators and teachers. We agree that the mail service could be restricted to those with teaching and operational responsibility in the schools. But, by the same token—and upon the same principle—the system was properly opened to PEA, when it, pursuant to law, was designated the collective bargaining agent for all teachers in the Perry schools. PEA thereby assumed an official position in the operational structure of the District's schools, and obtained a status that carried with it rights and obligations that no other labor organization could share. Excluding PLEA from the use of the mail service is therefore not viewpoint discrimination barred by the [First Amendment]. [Footnote by Justice White.]

[Note the recurrent modern emphasis on the presence or absence of viewpoint discrimination, not only in separate opinions by Justice Stevens (who, as noted earlier, has occasionally indicated that he considers this the *only* concern of the First Amendment) but also in opinions of the Court. In addition to the examples noted else-

B. The differential access provided PEA and PLEA is reasonable because it is wholly consistent with the district's legitimate interest in "preserv[ing] the property [for] the use to which it is lawfully dedicated." [Greenburgh.] Use of school mail facilities enables PEA to perform effectively its obligations as exclusive representative of *all* Perry Township teachers. Conversely, PLEA does not have any official responsibility in connection with the school district and need not be entitled to the same rights of access to school mailboxes. [Moreover], exclusion of the rival union may reasonably be considered a means of insuring labor-peace within the [schools].[4] The Court of Appeals accorded little or no weight to PEA's special responsibilities. In its view these responsibilities, while justifying PEA's access, did not justify denying equal access to PLEA. The Court of Appeals would have been correct if a public forum were involved here. But the internal mail system is not a public forum. As we have already stressed, when government property is not dedicated to open communication the government may—without further justification—restrict use to those who participate in the forum's official business.

Finally, the reasonableness of the limitations on PLEA's access to the school mail system is also supported by the substantial alternative channels that remain open for union-teacher communication to take place. These means range from bulletin boards to meeting facilities to the United States mail. During election periods, PLEA is assured of equal access to all modes of communication. There is no showing here that PLEA's ability to communicate with teachers is seriously impinged by the restricted access to the internal mail system. The variety and type of alternative modes of access present here compare favorably with those in other nonpublic forum cases where we have upheld restrictions on access. [E.g., Greer] (servicemen free to attend political rallies off base).

IV. The Court of Appeals also held that the differential access provided the rival unions constituted impermissible content discrimination in violation of [equal protection]. We have rejected this contention when cast as a First Amendment argument, and it fares no better in equal protection garb. As we have explained above, PLEA did not have a First Amendment or other right of access to the interschool mail system. The grant of such access to PEA, therefore, does not burden a fundamental right of the PLEA. Thus, the decision to grant such privileges to the PEA need not be tested by the strict scrutiny applied when government action impinges upon a fundamental right protected by the Constitution. See [Rodriguez]. The school district's policy need only rationally further a legitimate state purpose. That purpose is clearly found in the special responsibilities of an exclusive bargaining representative.

The Seventh Circuit and PLEA rely on [Mosley and Carey v. Brown]. In Mosley and Carey, we struck down prohibitions on peaceful picketing in a public forum. [In] both cases, we found the distinction between classes of speech violative of [equal protection]. The key to those decisions, however, was the presence of a public forum. In a public forum, by definition, all parties have a constitutional right of access and the state must demonstrate compelling reasons for restricting access to a single class of speakers, a single viewpoint, or a single subject. When speakers and subjects are similarly situated, the state may not pick and choose. Conversely on government property that has not been made a public forum, not all speech is equally situated, and the state may draw

where in this chapter, see, e.g., the rejection of a claim of unconstitutional viewpoint discrimination, in the context of the Internal Revenue Code, in Regan v. Taxation with Representation (1983; noted below, chap. 13, p. 1402).]

4. [This] factor was discounted by the Court of Appeals because there is no showing in the record of past disturbances stemming from

PLEA's past access to the internal mail system or evidence that future disturbance would be likely. We have not required that such proof be present to justify the denial of access to a nonpublic forum on grounds that the proposed use may disrupt the property's intended function. [Footnote by Justice White.]

distinctions which relate to the special purpose for which the property is used. As we have explained above, for a school mail facility, the difference in status between the exclusive bargaining representative and its rival is such a distinction. [The Seventh Circuit misapplied] our cases that have dealt with the rights of free expression on streets, parks, and other fora generally open for assembly and debate.

[Reversed.]

Justice BRENNAN, with whom Justice MARSHALL, Justice POWELL, and Justice STEVENS join, dissenting.

[Because] the exclusive access provision in the collective bargaining agreement amounts to viewpoint discrimination that infringes the respondents' First Amendment rights and fails to advance any substantial state interest, I dissent.

I. The Court properly acknowledges that teachers have protected First Amendment rights within the school context. [From] this point of departure the Court veers sharply off course. Based on a finding that the interschool mail system is not a "public forum," the Court states that the respondents have no right of access to the system, and that the school board is free "to make distinctions in access on the basis of subject matter and speaker identity," if the distinctions are "reasonable in light of the purpose which the forum at issue serves." According to the Court, the petitioner's status as the exclusive bargaining representative provides a reasonable basis for the exclusive access policy. The Court fundamentally misperceives the essence of the respondents' claims. [This] case does not involve an "absolute access" claim. It involves an "equal access" claim. As such it does not turn on whether the internal school mail system is a "public forum." In focusing on the public forum issue, the Court disregards the First Amendment's central proscription against censorship, in the form of viewpoint discrimination, in any forum, public or nonpublic.

A. The First Amendment's prohibition against government discrimination among viewpoints on particular issues falling within the realm of protected speech has been noted extensively in the opinions of this Court. [E.g., Tinker.] There is another line of cases, closely related to those implicating the prohibition against viewpoint discrimination, that have addressed the First Amendment principle of subject matter, or content, neutrality. Generally, the concept of content neutrality prohibits the government from choosing the subjects that are appropriate for public discussion. The content neutrality cases frequently refer to the prohibition against viewpoint discrimination and both concepts have their roots in the First Amendment's bar against censorship. But unlike the viewpoint discrimination concept, which is used to strike down government restrictions on speech by particular speakers, the content neutrality principle is invoked when the government has imposed restrictions on speech related to an entire subject area. The content neutrality principle can be seen as an outgrowth of the core First Amendment prohibition against viewpoint discrimination.[1]

We have invoked the prohibition against content discrimination to invalidate government restrictions on access to public forums. [E.g., Carey; Mosley.] We also have relied on this prohibition to strike down restrictions on access to a limited public forum. [Widmar.] Finally, we have applied the doctrine of content neutrality to government regulation of protected speech in cases in which no restriction of access to public property was involved. [E.g., Consolidated Edison; Erznoznik.] Admittedly, this Court has not always required content neutrality in restrictions on access to government property. We upheld content-based exclusions in [e.g., Lehman and Greer]. [These] involved an

---

1. Justice Brennan cited Stone, "Restrictions of Speech Because of its Content: The Peculiar Case of Subject-Matter Restrictions," 46 U.Chi. L.Rev. 81 (1978).

unusual forum, which was found to be nonpublic, and the speech was determined for a variety of reasons to be incompatible with the forum. These cases provide some support for the notion that the government is permitted to exclude certain subjects from discussion in nonpublic forums. They provide no support, however, for the notion that government, once it has opened up government property for discussion of specific subjects, may discriminate among viewpoints on those topics. Although [e.g., Greer and Lehman] permitted content-based restrictions, none of the cases involved viewpoint discrimination. All of the restrictions were viewpoint-neutral.

[Once] the government permits discussion of certain subject matter, it may not impose restrictions that discriminate among viewpoints on those subjects whether a nonpublic forum is involved or not. This prohibition is implicit in the Mosley line of cases, in [Tinker], and in those cases in which we have approved content-based restrictions on access to government property that is not a public forum. We have never held that government may allow discussion of a subject and then discriminate among viewpoints on that particular topic, even if the government for certain reasons may entirely exclude discussion of the subject from the forum. In this context, the greater power does not include the lesser because for First Amendment purposes exercise of the lesser power is more threatening to core values. Viewpoint discrimination is censorship in its purest form and government regulation that discriminates among viewpoints threatens the continued vitality of "free speech."

B.   Against this background, it is clear that the Court's approach to this case is flawed. By focusing on whether the interschool mail system is a public forum, the Court disregards the independent First Amendment protection afforded by the prohibition against viewpoint discrimination. This case does not involve a claim of an absolute right of access to the forum to discuss any subject whatever. If it did, public forum analysis might be relevant. This case involves a claim of equal access to discuss a subject that the board has approved for discussion in the forum. In essence, the respondents are not asserting a right of access at all; they are asserting a right to be free from discrimination. The critical inquiry, therefore, is whether the board's grant of exclusive access to the petitioner amounts to prohibited viewpoint discrimination.

II.   [The] Court responds to the allegation of viewpoint discrimination by suggesting that there is no indication that the board intended to discriminate and that the exclusive access policy is based on the parties' status rather than on their views. In this case, [the] intent to discriminate can be inferred from the effect of the policy, which is to deny an effective channel of communication to the respondents. In addition, the petitioner's status has nothing to do with whether viewpoint discrimination in fact has occurred. If anything, the petitioner's status is relevant to the question of whether the exclusive access policy can be justified, not to whether the board has discriminated among viewpoints.

Addressing the question of viewpoint discrimination directly, free of the Court's irrelevant public forum analysis, it is clear that the exclusive access policy discriminates on the basis of viewpoint. The Court of Appeals found that "the access policy [here], in form a speaker restriction, favors a particular viewpoint on [labor relations]; the teachers inevitably will receive from [the petitioner] self-laudatory descriptions of its activities on their behalf and will be denied the critical perspective offered by [the respondents]." [On] a practical level, the only reason for the petitioner to seek an exclusive access policy is to deny its rivals access to an effective channel of communication. No other group is explicitly denied access to the mail system. In fact, [many] other groups have been granted access to the system. Apparently, access is denied to the respondents because of the likelihood of their expressing points of view different from the petitioner's on a range of subjects. The very argument the petitioner advances in support of the policy, the need to preserve labor peace, also indicates that the access policy is not viewpoint-neutral. In short, the exclusive access policy discriminates against the respondents based on their viewpoint. The board has agreed to amplify the speech of the petitioner, while repressing the speech of the respondents based on the respondents' point of view. This sort of discrimination amounts to censorship and infringes the First Amendment rights of the respondents. [The] policy can survive only if the petitioner can justify it.

III.　A.　[The] petitioner attempts to justify the exclusive access provision based on its status as the exclusive bargaining representative for the teachers and on the state's interest in efficient communication between collective bargaining representatives and the members of the unit. The petitioner's status and the state's interest in efficient communication are important considerations. They are not sufficient, however, to sustain the exclusive access policy.

As the Court of Appeals pointed out, the exclusive access policy is both "overinclusive and underinclusive" as a means of serving the state's interest in the efficient discharge of the petitioner's legal duties to the teachers. The policy is overinclusive because it does not strictly limit the petitioner's use of the mail system to performance of its special legal duties and underinclusive because the board permits outside organizations with no special duties to the teachers, or to the students, to use the system. [Putting] aside the difficulties with the fit between this policy and the asserted interests, the Court of Appeals properly pointed out that the policy is invalid "because it furthers no discernible state interest." While the board may have a legitimate interest in granting the petitioner access to the system, it has no legitimate interest in making that access exclusive by denying access to the [respondents].[2]

B.　The petitioner also argues, and the Court agrees, that the exclusive access policy is justified by the state's interest in preserving labor peace. [Although] the state's interest in preserving labor peace in the schools in order to prevent disruption is unquestionably substantial, merely articulating the interest is not enough to sustain the exclusive access policy in this case. There must be some showing that the asserted interest is advanced by the policy. In the absence of such a showing, the exclusive access policy must [fall].

C.　Because the grant to the petitioner of exclusive access to the internal school mail system amounts to viewpoint discrimination that infringes the respondents' First Amendment rights and because the petitioner has failed to

---

2. A variant of the "special legal duties" justification for the exclusive access policy is the "official business" justification. [The] government has a legitimate interest in limiting access to a nonpublic forum to those involved in the "official business" of the agency. This interest may justify restrictions based on speaker identity, as for example, when a school board denies access to a classroom to persons other than teachers. Such a speaker identity restriction may have a viewpoint discriminatory effect, but it is justified by the government's interest in clear, definitive classroom instruction.

In this case, an "official business" argument is inadequate to justify the exclusive access policy. [The] exclusive access policy is both overinclusive and underinclusive with respect to an "official business" justification. First, [the] school board neither monitors nor endorses the petitioner's messages. In this light, it is difficult to consider the petitioner an agent of the board. Moreover, in light of the virtually unlimited scope of a union's collective bargaining duties, it expands the definition of "official business" beyond any clear meaning to suggest that the petitioner's messages are always related to the school system's "official business."

More importantly, however, the only board policy discernible from this record involves a denial of access to one group: the respondents. The board has made no explicit effort to restrict access to those involved in the "official business" of the schools. In fact, access has been granted to outside groups such as parochial schools, church groups, YMCAs, and Cub Scout units. [The] provision of access to these groups strongly suggests that the denial of access to the respondents was not based on any desire to limit access to the forum to those involved in the "official business" of the schools; instead, it suggests that it was based on hostility to the point of view likely to be expressed by the [respondents]. [Footnote by Justice Brennan.]

show that the policy furthers any substantial state interest, the policy must be invalidated as violative of the [First Amendment].[3]

A NOTE ON GOVERNMENT SPEECH AND THE FIRST AMENDMENT

Although the majority and the dissent in Perry differ as to the proper characterization of PEA's activities, both agree that granting preferential access to someone clearly performing "official business" would create no significant First Amendment problems.[1] Implicit is the view that government *as speaker* is not constrained by the First Amendment, nor need it provide access to the channels of communication employed by government. This view of the First Amendment as restricting the government only when it plays the role of regulator and not when it itself communicates is an accurate generalization of current law.[2] Several commentators, however, have maintained that the First Amendment ought to impose some limitations on government speech,[3] at least

---

3. Contrast with the access to public property issue in Perry the problem in MINNESOTA BD. FOR COMMUNITY COLLEGES v. KNIGHT, 465 U.S. 271 (1984). Knight raised the issue whether there can be a right of access to government itself—to government officials rather than government property. The case concerned the Minnesota Public Employment Labor Relations Act, which authorized public employee collective bargaining. The statute also "requires public employers to engage in official exchanges of views with their professional employees on policy questions relating to employment but outside the scope of mandatory bargaining." But if those employees "have selected an exclusive representative for mandatory bargaining, their employer may exchange views on nonmandatory subjects only with the exclusive representative." This last provision provided the focus for the constitutional challenge, for it had the effect of denying access to these "meet and confer" sessions to anyone except certain designated representatives. The challenge was brought by a number of community college faculty members who were *not* members of the faculty union and claimed that they therefore not only had no right to attend these meet and confer sessions, but also had no right to participate in the selection of faculty representatives to those sessions.

The challengers did not claim that the meet and confer sessions were a public forum; they relied largely on claims that principles of academic freedom (see below, chap. 13, sec. 4) derived from the First Amendment granted them rights of access and rights to participate in college governance that might not in general be available. Justice O'CONNOR's majority opinion rejected these claims, holding that nothing in the first amendment granted rights to a governmental audience, either for members of the public, public employees, or public college teachers: "Even assuming that speech rights guaranteed by the First Amendment take on a special meaning in an academic setting, they do not require government to allow teachers employed by it to participate in institutional policymaking. Faculty involvement in academic governance has much to recommend it as a matter of academic policy, but it finds no basis in the Constitution."

Justice MARSHALL concurred in the judgment, urging a more contextual inquiry that took greater account of the particular nature of an academic setting. But even taking the special nature of academic institutions and academic governance as relevant was insufficient for him to disagree with the majority's conclusion. Justice BRENNAN, dissenting, also focused closely on the particular setting. To him, "principles of academic freedom" required "the freedom of faculty members to express their views to the administration concerning matters of academic governance." But the most intriguing opinion was the dissent of Justice STEVENS, joined partially by Justice Brennan and partially by Justice Powell: "There can be no question but that the First Amendment secures the right of individuals to communicate with their government. And the First Amendment was intended to secure something more than an exercise in futility—it guarantees a *meaningful* opportunity to express one's views." But Justice Stevens did not in the final analysis rely on these and similar sweeping statements about a meaningful opportunity to be heard. Rather, he found the particular preference for the union in the meet and confer sessions an impermissible form of viewpoint discrimination, which to him went to the heart of the First Amendment: "Here, by giving the union exclusive rights with respect to the primary avenue for communication with college administration, the Minnesota statutory scheme plainly advances the union's viewpoint at the expense of all others."

1. See, e.g., the discussion of the "official business" argument in footnote 2 of Justice Brennan's Perry opinion.

2. See, e.g., Muir v. Alabama Education Television Comm'n, 688 F.2d 1033 (5th Cir.1982); P.A.M. News Corp. v. Butz, 514 F.2d 272 (D.C. Cir.1975).

3. See, e.g., Yudof, When Government Speaks: Politics, Law, and Government Expression in America (1983); Kamenshine, "The First

in those cases in which the nature or extent of governmental communication can be said to distort the political process or the marketplace of ideas.[4] But is the First Amendment truly relevant to government speech? Are any of the dangers that prompted the First Amendment present when government is speaking rather than restricting? Are certain types of government speech more dangerous than others? If so, can lines be drawn that would allow some government speech but not others? Is there room for a content-neutrality obligation, for example, when government subsidizes speech, as in campaign financing?[5] Additional problems pertaining to government speech and an arguable mandate of governmental neutrality surface in the later materials. See especially the several opinions in Board of Education v. Pico (removal of books from school libraries), noted in sec. 2 of the next chapter, at p. 1323.

CITY COUNCIL v. TAXPAYERS FOR VINCENT

466 U.S. ——, 104 S.Ct. 2118, 80 L.Ed.2d 772 (1984).

Justice STEVENS delivered the opinion of the Court.

Section 28.04 of the Los Angeles Municipal Code prohibits the posting of signs on public property. The question presented is whether that prohibition abridges appellees' freedom of speech within the meaning of the First Amendment.

In March 1979, Roland Vincent was a candidate for election to the Los Angeles City Council. A group of his supporters known as Taxpayers for Vincent ("Taxpayers") entered into a contract with a political sign service company known as Candidates Outdoor Graphics Service ("COGS") to fabricate and post signs with Vincent's name on them. COGS produced 15 × 44 inch cardboard signs and attached them to utility poles at various locations by draping them over cross-arms which support the poles and stapling the cardboard together at the bottom. The signs' message was: "Roland Vincent—City Council." Acting under the authority of § 28.04, [city employees] routinely removed all posters attached to utility poles and similar objects covered by the ordinance, including the COGS signs. The weekly sign removal report covering the period March 1—March 7, 1979, indicated that among the 1,207 signs removed from public property during that week, 48 were identified as "Roland Vincent" signs. Most of the other signs identified in that report were apparently commercial in character. [Taxpayers and COGS brought suit challenging the constitutionality of the ordinance. The District Court dismissed the action, but the Court of Appeals reversed.]

Amendment's Implied Political Establishment Clause," 67 Calif.L.Rev. 1104 (1979); Shiffrin, "Government Speech," 27 U.C.L.A.L.Rev. 565 (1980); Ziegler, "Government Speech and the Constitution: The Limits of Official Partisanship," 21 B.C.L.Rev. 578 (1980).

4. The examples most frequently cited relate to active governmental involvement in an issue then before the electorate. In Bonner-Lyons v. School Committee, 480 F.2d 442 (1st Cir.1973), school authorities were prohibited from using the internal distribution system of the Boston city schools to disseminate to parents notices advertising anti-busing rallies, unless the authorities granted an equal opportunity to pro-busing proponents. Is this outcome called into question by Perry?

5. See e.g., Buckley v. Valeo (1976; p. 1301 below), where the Court rejected an attack on public financing of presidential election campaigns. The Government rejected the argument that, by analogy to the separation of church and state and the governmental neutrality regarding religion mandated by the First Amendment (chap. 14 below), there is a similar obligation to be wholly neutral regarding political speech. The Court responded that the provision was "a congressional effort, not to abridge [speech], but rather to use public money to facilitate and enlarge public discussion and participation in the electoral process, goals vital to a self-governing people. Thus, [the provision] furthers, not abridges, pertinent First Amendment values."

In its appeal to this Court the City challenges the Court of Appeals' holding that § 28.04 is unconstitutional on its face. Taxpayers and COGS defend that holding and also contend that the ordinance is unconstitutional as applied to their [actions]. There are two quite different ways in which a statute or ordinance may be considered invalid "on its face"—either because it is unconstitutional in every conceivable application, or because it seeks to prohibit such a broad range of protected conduct that it is unconstitutionally "overbroad." We shall analyze the "facial" challenges to the ordinance, and then address its specific application to appellees.

I. The seminal cases in which the Court held state legislation unconstitutional "on its face" did not involve any departure from the general rule that a litigant only has standing to vindicate his own constitutional rights. In [Stromberg and Lovell], the statutes were unconstitutional as applied to the defendants' conduct, but they were also unconstitutional on their face because it was apparent that any attempt to enforce such legislation would create an unacceptable risk of the suppression of ideas. In cases of this character a holding of facial invalidity expresses the conclusion that the statute could never be applied in a valid manner. Such holdings invalidated entire statutes, but did not create any exception from the general rule that constitutional adjudication requires a review of the application of a statute to the conduct of the party before the Court.

Subsequently, however, the Court did recognize an exception to this general rule for laws that are written so broadly that they may inhibit the constitutionally protected speech of third parties. [The] Court has repeatedly held that such a statute may be challenged on its face even though a more narrowly drawn statute would be valid as applied to the party in the case before it. This exception from the general rule is predicated on "a judicial prediction or assumption that the statute's very existence may cause others not before the court to refrain from constitutionally protected speech or expression." [Broadrick; 1973; sec. 1 above.] In the development of the overbreadth doctrine the Court has been sensitive to the risk that the doctrine itself might sweep so broadly that the exception to ordinary standing requirements would swallow the general rule. In order to decide whether the overbreadth exception is applicable in a particular case, we have weighed the likelihood that the statute's very existence will inhibit free expression. The concept of "substantial overbreadth" [stated in Broadrick] is not readily reduced to an exact definition. It is clear, however, that the mere fact that one can conceive of some impermissible applications of a statute is not sufficient to render it susceptible to an overbreadth challenge. On the contrary, the requirement of substantial overbreadth stems from the underlying justification for the overbreadth exception itself—the interest in preventing an invalid statute from inhibiting the speech of third parties who are not before the Court.

[The] Court of Appeals concluded that the ordinance was vulnerable to an overbreadth challenge because it was an "overinclusive" response to traffic concerns and not the "least drastic means" of preventing interference with the normal use of public property. This conclusion rested on an evaluation of the assumed effect of the ordinance on third parties, rather than on any specific consideration of the impact of the ordinance on the parties before the Court. This is not, however, an appropriate case to entertain a facial challenge based on overbreadth. For we have found nothing in the record to indicate that the ordinance will have any different impact on any third parties' interests in free speech than it has on Taxpayers and COGS.

Taxpayers and COGS apparently would agree that the prohibition against posting signs on most of the publicly owned objects mentioned in the ordinance is perfectly reasonable. Thus, they do not dispute the City's power to proscribe the attachment of any handbill or sign to any sidewalk, cross-walk, curb, lamppost, hydrant, or lifesaving equipment. Their position with respect to utility poles is not entirely clear, but they do contend that it is unconstitutional to prohibit the attachment of their cardboard signs to the horizontal cross-arms supporting utility poles during a political campaign. They have, in short, failed to identify any significant difference between their claim that the ordinance is invalid on overbreadth grounds and their claim that it is unconstitutional when applied to their political signs. Specifically, Taxpayers and COGS have not attempted to demonstrate that the ordinance applies to any conduct more likely to be protected by the First Amendment than their own cross-arm signs. Indeed, the record suggests that many of the signs posted in violation of the ordinance are posted in such a way that they may create safety or traffic problems that COGS has tried to avoid. Accordingly, on this record it appears that if the ordinance may be validly applied to COGS, it can be validly applied to most if not all of the signs of parties not before the Court. Appellees have simply failed to demonstrate a realistic danger that the ordinance will significantly compromise recognized First Amendment protections of individuals not before the Court. It would therefore be inappropriate in this case to entertain an overbreadth challenge to the ordinance.

Taxpayers and COGS do argue generally that the City's interest in eliminating visual blight is not sufficiently weighty to justify an abridgment of speech. If that were the only interest the ordinance advanced, then this argument would be analogous to the facial challenges involved in cases like Stromberg and Lovell. But as previously observed, appellees acknowledge that the ordinance serves safety interests in many of its applications, and hence do not argue that the ordinance can never be validly applied. Instead, appellees argue that they have placed their signs in locations where only the esthetic interest is implicated. [Accordingly], appellees' attack [is] basically a challenge to the ordinance as applied to their activities. We therefore limit our analysis [to] the concrete case before [us].

II. The ordinance prohibits appellees from communicating with the public in a certain manner, and presumably diminishes the total quantity of their communication in the City. The application of the ordinance to appellees' expressive activities surely raises the question whether the ordinance abridges their ["freedom of speech"]. [But it] has been clear since this Court's earliest decisions concerning the freedom of speech that the state may sometimes curtail speech when necessary to advance a significant and legitimate state interest. [Schenck.]

As Stromberg and Lovell demonstrate, there are some purported interests— such as a desire to suppress support for a minority party or an unpopular cause, or to exclude the expression of certain points of view from the marketplace of ideas—that are so plainly illegitimate that they would immediately invalidate the rule. The general principle is that the First Amendment forbids the government from regulating speech in ways that favor some viewpoints or ideas at the expense of [others]. That general rule has no application to this case. For there is not even a hint of bias or censorship in the City's enactment or enforcement of this ordinance. There is no claim that the ordinance was designed to suppress certain ideas that the City finds distasteful or that it has been applied to appellees because of the views that they express. The text of the ordinance is neutral—indeed it is silent—concerning any speaker's point of view and [it] has been applied to appellees and others in an evenhanded manner.

In [O'Brien] the Court set forth the appropriate framework for reviewing a viewpoint neutral regulation of this kind: "[A] government regulation is sufficiently justified if it is within the constitutional power of the Government;

if it furthers an important or substantial governmental interest; if the governmental interest is unrelated to the suppression of free expression; and if the incidental restriction on alleged First Amendment freedoms is no greater than is essential to the furtherance of that interest." It is well settled that the state may legitimately exercise its police powers to advance esthetic values. [In] this case, Taxpayers and COGS do not dispute that it is within the constitutional power of the City to attempt to improve its appearance, or that this interest is basically unrelated to the suppression of ideas. Therefore the critical inquiries are whether that interest is sufficiently substantial to justify the effect of the ordinance on appellees' expression, and whether that effect is no greater than necessary to accomplish the City's purpose.

III. In Kovacs v. Cooper, the Court rejected the notion that a city is powerless to protect its citizens from unwanted exposure to certain methods of expression which may legitimately be deemed a public nuisance. [The] cases indicate that the municipalities have a weighty, essentially esthetic interest in proscribing intrusive and unpleasant formats for expression. Metromedia, Inc. v. San Diego dealt with San Diego's prohibition of certain forms of outdoor billboards.[1] There the Court considered the city's interest in avoiding visual clutter, and seven Justices explicitly concluded that this interest was sufficient to justify a prohibition of billboards. Justice White, writing for the plurality, expressly concluded that the city's esthetic interests were sufficiently substantial to provide an acceptable justification for a content neutral prohibition against the use of billboards; San Diego's interest in its appearance was undoubtedly a substantial governmental goal. We reaffirm the conclusion of the majority in Metromedia. The problem addressed by this ordinance—the visual assault on the citizens of Los Angeles presented by an accumulation of signs posted on public property—constitutes a significant substantive evil within the City's power to prohibit. [See also Mini Theatres.]

IV. We turn to the question whether the scope of the restriction on appellees' expressive activity is substantially broader than necessary to protect the City's interest in eliminating visual clutter. The incidental restriction on expression which results from the City's attempt to accomplish such a purpose is considered justified as a reasonable regulation of the time, place, or manner of expression if it is narrowly tailored to serve that interest. [By] banning these signs, the City did no more than eliminate the exact source of the evil it sought to remedy. It is true that the esthetic interest in preventing the kind of litter that may result from the distribution of leaflets on the public streets and sidewalks cannot support a prophylactic prohibition against the citizens' exercise of that method of expressing his views. In Schneider v. State [1939; p. 1206 above] the Court held that ordinances that absolutely prohibited handbilling on the streets were invalid. The Court explained that cities could adequately protect the esthetic interest in avoiding litter without abridging protected expression merely by penalizing those who actually litter. Taxpayers contend that their interest in supporting Vincent's political campaign, which affords them a constitutional right to distribute [leaflets] on the public streets of Los Angeles, provides equal support for their asserted right to post temporary signs on objects adjacent to the streets and sidewalks. They argue that the mere fact that their temporary signs "add somewhat" to the city's visual clutter is entitled to no more weight than the temporary unsightliness of discarded handbills and the additional street cleaning burden that were insufficient to justify the ordinances reviewed in Schneider.

---

1. The Metromedia case (1981) has been noted briefly earlier, in connection with its commercial speech aspects (chap. 11, sec. 2, p. 1144 above). It will be considered somewhat more fully in a note at the end of this case. It involved largely a ban on erecting billboards on private property, with certain exceptions. The Court divided sharply and produced several opinions; there was no majority opinion.

The rationale of Schneider is inapposite in the context of the instant case. There, individual citizens were actively exercising their right to communicate directly with potential recipients of their message. The conduct continued only while the speakers or distributors remained on the scene. In this case, appellees posted dozens of temporary signs throughout an area where they would remain unattended until removed. As the Court expressly noted in Schneider, the First Amendment does not "deprive a municipality of power to enact regulations against throwing literature broadcast in the [streets]." A distributor of leaflets has no right simply to scatter his pamphlets in the air—or to toss large quantities of paper from the window of a tall building or a low flying airplane. Characterizing such an activity as a separate means of communication does not diminish the state's power to condemn it as a public nuisance.

[With] respect to signs posted by appellees, [it] is the tangible medium of expressing the message that has the adverse impact on the appearance of the landscape. In Schneider, an anti-littering statute could have addressed the substantive evil without prohibiting expressive activity, whereas application of the prophylactic rule actually employed gratuitously infringed upon the right of an individual to communicate directly with a willing listener. Here, the substantive evil—visual blight—is not merely a possible by-product of the activity, but is created by the medium of expression itself. In contrast to Schneider, therefore, the application of [the] ordinance in this case responds precisely to the substantive problem which legitimately concerns the City. The ordinance curtails no more speech than is necessary to accomplish its purpose.

V. The Court of Appeals accepted the argument that a prohibition against the use of unattractive signs cannot be justified on esthetic grounds if it fails to apply to all equally unattractive signs wherever they might be located. A comparable argument was categorically rejected in Metromedia. In that case it was argued that the city could not simultaneously permit billboards to be used for on-site advertising and also justify the prohibition against offsite advertising on esthetic grounds, since both types of advertising were equally unattractive. The Court held, however, that the city could reasonably conclude that the esthetic interest was outweighed by the countervailing interest in one kind of advertising even though it was not outweighed by the other. So here, the validity of the esthetic interest in the elimination of signs on public property is not compromised by failing to extend the ban to private property. The private citizen's interest in controlling the use of his own property justifies the disparate treatment. Moreover, by not extending the ban to all locations, a significant opportunity to communicate by means of temporary signs is preserved, and private property owners' esthetic concerns will keep the posting of signs on their property within reasonable bounds. Even if some visual blight remains, a partial, content-neutral ban may nevertheless enhance the City's appearance. Furthermore, there is no finding that in any area where appellees seek to place signs, there are already so many signs posted on adjacent private property that the elimination of appellees' signs would have an inconsequential effect on [esthetic values].

VI. While the First Amendment does not guarantee the right to employ every conceivable method of communication at all times and in all places [Heffron], a restriction on expressive activity may be invalid if the remaining modes of communication are inadequate. [Grace; Heffron; Consolidated Edison; Linmark.] The Los Angeles ordinance does not affect any individual's freedom to exercise the right to speak and to distribute literature in the same place where the posting of signs on public property is prohibited. To the extent that the posting of signs on public property has advantages over these forms of expression, there is no reason to believe that these same advantages cannot be obtained through other means. To the contrary, the findings [indicate] that there are ample alternative modes of communication in Los Angeles. Notwithstanding appellees' general assertions [concerning] the utility of political posters, nothing in the findings indicates that the posting of political posters on public property is a uniquely valuable or important mode of communication, or that appellees' ability to communicate effectively is threatened by ever-increasing restrictions on expression.

VII. Appellees suggest that the public property covered by the ordinance is either itself a "public forum" for First Amendment purposes, or at least should be treated in the same respect as the "public forum" in which the property is located. "Traditional public forum property occupies a special position in terms of First Amendment protection" [Grace] and appellees maintain that their sign-posting activities are entitled to this protection. [Appellees'] reliance on the public forum doctrine is misplaced. They fail to demonstrate the existence of a traditional right of access respecting such items as utility poles for purposes of their communication comparable to that recognized for public streets and parks, and it is clear that "the First Amendment does not guarantee access to government property simply because it is owned or controlled by the government." [Greenburgh.] Rather, the "existence of a right of access to public property and the standard by which limitations upon such a right must be evaluated differ depending on the character of the property at issue." [Perry.]

Lampposts can of course be used as signposts, but the mere fact that government property can be used as a vehicle for communication does not mean that the Constitution requires such uses to be permitted. Cf. [Greenburgh].[2] Public property which is not by tradition or designation a forum for public communication may be reserved by the state "for its intended purposes, communicative or otherwise, as long as the regulation on speech is reasonable and not an effort to suppress expression merely because public officials oppose the speaker's view." [Perry.] Given our analysis of the legitimate interest served by the ordinance, its viewpoint neutrality, and the availability of alternative channels of communication, the ordinance is certainly constitutional as applied to appellees under this standard.[3]

VIII. Finally, Taxpayers and COGS argue that Los Angeles could have written an ordinance that would have had a less severe effect on expressive activity such as theirs, by permitting the posting of any kind of sign at any time on some types of public property, or by making a variety of other more specific exceptions to the ordinance: for signs carrying certain types of messages (such as political campaign signs), for signs posted during specific time periods (perhaps during political campaigns), for particular locations (perhaps for areas already cluttered by an excessive number of signs on adjacent private property), or for signs meeting design specifications (such as size or color). Plausible

---

2. Any tangible property owned by the government could be used to communicate—bumper stickers may be placed on official automobiles—and yet appellees could not seriously claim the right to attach "Taxpayer for Vincent" bumper stickers to City-owned automobiles. At some point, the government's relationship to things under its dominion and control is virtually identical to a private owner's property interest in the same kinds of things, and in such circumstances, the State, "no less than a private owner of property, has power to preserve the property under its control for the use to which it is lawfully dedicated." Adderley v. Florida. [Footnote by Justice Stevens.]

3. Just as it is not dispositive to label the posting of signs on public property as a discrete medium of expression, it is also of limited utility in the context of this case to focus on whether the tangible property itself should be deemed a public forum. Generally an analysis of whether property is a public forum provides a workable analytical tool. However, "the analytical line between a regulation of the 'time, place, and manner' in which First Amendment rights may be exercised in a traditional public forum, and the question of whether a particular piece of personal or real property owned or controlled by the government is in fact a 'public forum' may blur at the edges" [Greenburgh], and this is particularly true in cases falling between the paradigms of government property interests essentially mirroring analogous private interests and those clearly held in trust, either by tradition or recent convention, for the use of citizens at large. [Footnote by Justice Stevens.]

public policy arguments might well be made in support of any such exception, but it by no means follows that it is therefore constitutionally mandated, nor is it clear that some of the suggested exceptions would even be constitutionally permissible. For example, even though political speech is entitled to the fullest possible measure of constitutional protection, there are a host of other communications that command the same respect. An assertion that "Jesus Saves," that "Abortion is Murder," that every woman has the "Right to Choose," or that "Alcohol Kills," may have a claim to a constitutional exemption from the ordinance that is just as strong as "[Roland] Vincent—City Council." To create an exception for appellees' political speech and not these other types of speech might create a risk of engaging in constitutionally forbidden content discrimination. [Carey; Mosley.] Moreover, the volume of permissible postings under such a mandated exemption might so limit the ordinance's effect as to defeat its aim of combatting visual blight.

Any constitutionally mandated exception to the City's total prohibition against temporary signs on public property would necessarily rest on a judicial determination that the City's traffic control and safety interests had little or no applicability within the excepted category, and that the City's interests in esthetics are not sufficiently important to justify the prohibition in that category. But the findings of the District Court provide no basis for questioning the substantiality of the esthetic interest [or] for believing that a uniquely important form of communication has been abridged for the categories of expression engaged in by [the challengers]. Therefore, we accept the City's position that it may decide that the esthetic interest in avoiding "visual clutter" justifies a removal of signs creating or increasing that clutter. [As] is true of billboards [see Metromedia], the esthetic interests that are implicated by temporary signs are presumptively at work in all parts of the city, including those where appellees posted their signs, and there is no basis in the record in this case upon which to rebut that presumption. These interests are both psychological and economic. [We] hold that on this record these interests are sufficiently substantial to justify this content neutral, impartially administered prohibition against the posting of appellees' temporary signs on public property and that such an application of the ordinance does not create an unacceptable threat to the "profound national commitment to the principle that debate on public issues should be uninhibited, robust, and wide-open." New York Times v. Sullivan.

[Reversed.]

Justice BRENNAN, with whom Justice MARSHALL and Justice BLACKMUN join, dissenting.

The plurality opinion in [Metromedia] concluded that [San Diego] could, consistently with the First Amendment, restrict the commercial use of billboards in order to "preserve and improve the appearance of the City." Today, the Court sustains the constitutionality of Los Angeles' similarly motivated ban on the posting of political signs on public property. Because the Court's lenient approach towards the restriction of speech for reasons of aesthetics threatens seriously to undermine the protections of the First Amendment, I dissent. The Court finds that the City's "interest [in eliminating visual clutter] is sufficiently substantial to justify the restrictive effect of the ordinance on appellees' expression" and that the effect of the ordinance on speech is "no greater than necessary to accomplish the City's purpose." These are the right questions to consider when analyzing the constitutionality of the challenged ordinance, but the answers that the Court provides reflect a startling insensitivity to the principles embodied in the First Amendment. In my view, [Los Angeles] has not shown that its interest in eliminating "visual clutter" justifies its restriction of appellees' ability to communicate with the local electorate.

I. The Court recognizes that each medium for communicating ideas and information presents its own particular problems. Our analysis of the First Amendment concerns implicated by a given medium must therefore be sensitive to these particular problems and characteristics. The posting of signs is, of course, a time-honored means of communicating a broad range of ideas and information, particularly in our cities and towns. At the same time, the unfettered proliferation of signs on public fixtures may offend the public's legitimate desire to preserve an orderly and aesthetically pleasing urban environment. In deciding this First Amendment question, the critical importance of the posting of signs as a means of communication must not be overlooked. Use of this medium of communication is particularly valuable in part because it entails a relatively small expense in reaching a wide audience, allows flexibility in accommodating various formats, typographies, and graphics, and conveys its message in a manner that is easily read and understood by its reader or viewer. There may be alternative channels of communication, but the prevalence of a large number of signs in Los Angeles is a strong indication that, for many speakers, those alternatives are far less satisfactory.

Nevertheless, [the City] asserts that ample alternative avenues of communication are available. The City notes that, although the posting of signs on public property is prohibited, the posting of signs on private property and the distribution of handbills are not. But there is no showing that either of these alternatives would serve appellees' needs nearly as well as would the posting of signs on public property. First, there is no proof that a sufficient number of private parties would allow the posting of signs on their property. Indeed, common sense suggests the contrary at least in some instances. A speaker with a message that is generally unpopular or simply unpopular among property owners is hardly likely to get his message across if forced to rely on this medium. [Similarly], the adequacy of distributing handbills is dubious, despite certain advantages of handbills over signs. Particularly when the message to be carried is best expressed by a few words or a graphic image, a message on a sign will typically reach far more people than one on a handbill. The message on a posted sign remains to be seen by passersby as long as it is posted, while a handbill is typically read by a single reader and discarded. Thus, not only must handbills be printed in large quantity, but many hours must be spent distributing them. [Because] the City has completely banned the use of this particular medium of communication, and because, given the circumstances, there are no equivalent alternative media that provide an adequate substitute, the Court must examine with particular care the justifications that the City proffers for its ban.

II. [The] Court's first task is to determine whether the ordinance is aimed at suppressing the content of speech, and, if it is, whether a compelling state interest justifies the suppression. If the restriction is content-neutral, the court's task is to determine (1) whether the governmental objective advanced by the restriction is substantial, and (2) whether the restriction imposed on speech is no greater than is essential to further that objective. Unless both conditions are met the restriction must be invalidated.

My suggestion in Metromedia was that courts should exercise special care in addressing these questions when a purely aesthetic objective is asserted to justify a restriction of speech. Specifically, "before deferring to a city's judgment, a court must be convinced that the city is seriously and comprehensively addressing aesthetic concerns with respect to its environment." I adhere to that view. Its correctness—premised largely on my concern that aesthetic interests are easy for a city to assert and difficult for a court to evaluate—is, for me, reaffirmed by this case.

The fundamental problem in this kind of case is that a purely aesthetic state interest offered to justify a restriction on speech—that is, a governmental objective justified solely in terms like "proscribing intrusive and unpleasant formats for expression,"—creates difficulties for a reviewing court in fulfilling its obligation to ensure that government regulation does not trespass upon protections secured by the First Amendment. The source of those difficulties is the unavoidable subjectivity of aesthetic judgments—the fact that "beauty is in the eye of the beholder." As a consequence of this subjectivity, laws defended on aesthetic grounds raise problems for judicial review that are not presented by laws defended on more objective grounds—such as national security, public health, or public safety. In practice, therefore, the inherent subjectivity of aesthetic judgments makes it all too easy for the government to fashion its justification for a law in a manner that impairs the ability of a reviewing court meaningfully to make the required inquiries.

Initially, a reviewing court faces substantial difficulties determining whether the actual objective is related to the suppression of speech. The asserted interest in aesthetics may be only a facade for content-based suppression. [For example], in evaluating the ordinance before us in this case, the City might be pursuing either of two objectives, motivated by two very different judgments. One objective might be the elimination of "visual clutter," attributable in whole or in part to signs posted on public property. The aesthetic judgment underlying this objective would be that the clutter created by these signs offends the community's desire for an orderly, visually pleasing environment. A second objective might simply be the elimination of the messages typically carried by the signs. In that case, the aesthetic judgment would be that the signs' messages are themselves displeasing. The first objective is lawful, of course, but the second is not. Yet the City might easily mask the second objective by asserting the first and declaring that signs constitute visual clutter. In short, we must avoid unquestioned acceptance of the City's bare declaration of an aesthetic objective lest we fail in our duty to prevent unlawful trespasses upon First Amendment [protections].

Similarly, when a total ban is justified solely in terms of aesthetics, the means inquiry necessary to evaluate the constitutionality of the ban may be impeded by deliberate or unintended government manipulation. Governmental objectives that are purely aesthetic can usually be expressed in a virtually limitless variety of ways. Consequently, objectives can be tailored to fit whatever program the government devises to promote its general aesthetic interests. Once the government has identified a substantial aesthetic objective and has selected a preferred means of achieving its objective, it will be possible for the government to correct any mismatch between means and ends by redefining the ends to conform with the means. In this case, for example, any of several objectives might be the City's actual substantial goal in banning temporary signs: (1) the elimination of all signs throughout the City, (2) the elimination of all signs in certain parts of the City, or (3) a reduction of the density of signs. Although a total ban on the posting of signs on public property would be the least restrictive means of achieving only the first objective, it would be a very effective means of achieving the other two as well. It is quite possible, therefore, that the City might select such a ban as the means by which to further its general interest in solving its sign problem, without explicitly considering which of the three specific objectives is really substantial. Then, having selected the total ban as its preferred means, the City would be strongly inclined to characterize the first objective as the substantial one. This might be done purposefully in order to conform the ban to the least-restrictive-means requirement, or it might be done inadvertently as a natural concomitant of considering means and ends together. But regardless of why it is done, a reviewing court will be confronted with a statement of substantiality the subjectivity of which makes it impossible to question on its face.

This possibility of interdependence between means and ends in the development of policies to promote aesthetics poses a major obstacle to judicial review of the availability of alternative means that are less restrictive of speech. Indeed, when a court reviews a restriction of speech imposed in order to promote an aesthetic objective, there is a significant possibility that the court will be able to do little more than pay lip service to the First Amendment inquiry into the availability of less restrictive alternatives.

III. The fact that there are difficulties inherent in judicial review of aesthetics-based restrictions of speech does not imply that government may not engage in such activities. As I have said, improvement and preservation of the aesthetic environment are often legitimate and important governmental functions. But because the implementation of these functions creates special dangers to our First Amendment freedoms, there is a need for more stringent judicial scrutiny than the Court seems willing to exercise. In cases like this, where a total ban is imposed on a particularly valuable method of communication, a court should require the government to provide tangible proof of the legitimacy and substantiality of its aesthetic objective. Justifications for such restrictions articulated by the government should be critically examined to determine whether the government has committed itself to addressing the identified aesthetic problem.

In my view, such statements of aesthetic objectives should be accepted as substantial and unrelated to the suppression of speech only if the government demonstrates that it is pursuing an identified objective seriously and comprehensively and in ways that are unrelated to the restriction of speech. [Metromedia (Brennan, J., concurring in judgment).] Without such a demonstration, I would invalidate the restriction as violative of the First Amendment. By requiring this type of showing, courts can ensure that governmental regulation of the aesthetic environment remains within the constraints established by the First Amendment. First, we would have a reasonably reliable indication that it is not the content or communicative aspect of speech that the government finds unaesthetic. Second, when a restriction of speech is part of a comprehensive and seriously pursued program to promote an aesthetic objective, we have a more reliable indication of the government's own assessment of the substantiality of its objective. And finally, when an aesthetic objective is pursued on more than one front, we have a better basis upon which to ascertain its precise nature and thereby determine whether the means selected are the least restrictive ones for achieving the objective. This does not mean that a government must address all aesthetic problems at one time or that a government should hesitate to pursue aesthetic objectives. What it does mean, however, is that when such an objective is pursued, it may not be pursued solely at the expense of First Amendment freedoms, nor may it be pursued by arbitrarily discriminating against a form of speech that has the same aesthetic characteristics as other forms of speech that are also present in the community.

Accordingly, in order for Los Angeles to succeed in defending its total ban on the posting of signs, the City would have to demonstrate that it is pursuing its goal of eliminating visual clutter in a serious and comprehensive manner. Most importantly, the City would have to show that it is pursuing its goal through programs other than its ban on signs, that at least some of those programs address the visual clutter problem through means that do not entail the restriction of speech, and that the programs parallel the ban in their stringency, geographical scope, and aesthetic focus. In this case, however, there is no indication that the City has addressed its visual clutter problem in any way other than by prohibiting the posting of signs—throughout the City and without regard to the density of their presence. Therefore, I would hold that the prohibition violates appellees' First Amendment rights.

In light of the extreme stringency of Los Angeles' ban—barring all signs from being posted—and its wide geographical scope—covering the entire City— it might be difficult for Los Angeles to make the type of showing I have suggested. A more limited approach to the visual clutter problem, however, might well pass constitutional muster. I have no doubt that signs posted on public property in certain areas—including, perhaps, parts of Los Angeles— could contribute to the type of eyesore that a city would genuinely have a substantial interest in eliminating. These areas might include parts of the City that are particularly pristine, reserved for certain uses, designated to reflect certain themes, or so blighted that broad gauged renovation is necessary. Presumably, in these types of areas the City would also regulate the aesthetic environment in ways other than the banning of temporary signs. The City might zone such areas for a particular type of development or lack of development; it might actively create a particular type of environment; it might be especially vigilant in keeping the area clean; it might regulate the size and location of permanent signs; or it might reserve particular locations, such as kiosks, for the posting of temporary signs. Similarly, Los Angeles might be able to attack its visual clutter problem in more areas of the City by reducing the stringency of the ban, perhaps by regulating the density of temporary signs, and coupling that approach with additional measures designed to reduce other forms of visual clutter. There are a variety of ways that the aesthetic environment can be regulated, some restrictive of speech and others not, but it is only when aesthetic regulation is addressed in a comprehensive and focused manner that we can ensure that the goals pursued are substantial and that the manner in which they are pursued is no more restrictive of speech than is necessary. In the absence of such a showing in this case, I believe that Los Angeles' total ban sweeps so broadly and trenches so completely on appellees' use of an important medium of political expression that it must be struck down as violative of the [First Amendment].

VISUAL POLLUTION AND THE PROBLEM OF FORMAT DISCRIMINATION: REGULATION OF SIGNS AND BILLBOARDS

In Taxpayers for Vincent, above, the Justices referred repeatedly to the 1981 decision in METROMEDIA, INC. v. SAN DIEGO, 453 U.S. 490. Rather than dealing with the posting of signs on public property, Metromedia focused on the regulation of billboards placed on private property. At issue in Metromedia was a San Diego ordinance imposing substantial restrictions on outdoor advertising displays, largely in the interest of curtailing visual pollution. The Justices produced five major opinions; none spoke for the majority. Designed "to eliminate hazards to pedestrians and motorists brought about by distracting sign displays" and "to preserve and improve the appearance of the City," the ordinance prohibited all billboards, with certain exceptions. These exceptions were the centerpiece of the litigation. One exception was for on-site signs, those that advertised products or services rendered on the premises on which the sign was placed. (Among the other exceptions were those for government signs, temporary political campaign signs, for-sale and for-lease signs, and signs within shopping malls.)

The ordinance was challenged by Metromedia and other companies engaged in the ownership of billboards and the sale of advertising space on those billboards. Justice WHITE's plurality opinion, joined by Justices Stewart, Marshall and Powell, struck down the ordinance, finding the content regulation implicit in the exceptions to be a fatal constitutional infirmity. Justice White acknowledged that billboards "are a well-established medium of communication, used to convey a broad range of different kinds of messages." But he also recognized that unmodified First Amendment principles cannot easily be applied to such "unique forums of expression." Because billboards are "large, immobile, and permanent" structures, and because they are "designed to stand out and apart" from their surroundings, the "billboard creates a unique set of problems for land-use planning and development. [Billboards] combine communicative and noncommunicative aspects. As with other media, the government has legitimate interests in controlling the noncommunicative aspects of the medium, but [the First Amendment forecloses] a similar interest in controlling the communicative aspects. Because regulation of the noncommunicative aspects of a medium often impinges to some degree on the communicative aspects, it has been necessary for the courts to reconcile the government's regulatory interests with the individual's right to expression."

It was the regulatory impact on the communicative aspects that enabled Justice White to avoid having to decide whether a *total* prohibition of outdoor advertising would be permissible. He relied instead upon the content distinctions contained in the ordinance as the basis for finding the ordinance unconstitutional. He found the regulation of *commercial* billboards permissible because of the lesser protection provided to commercial speech.[1] Justice White reached the opposite result with respect to noncommercial billboards. Of particular importance in reaching this conclusion was the exception for on-site commercial billboards: "[O]ur recent commercial speech cases have consistently accorded noncommercial speech a greater degree of protection than commercial speech. San Diego effectively inverts this judgment, by affording a greater degree of protection to commercial than to noncommercial speech. There is a broad exception for on-site commercial advertisements, but there is no similar exception for noncommercial speech. [Insofar] as the city tolerates billboards at all, it cannot choose to limit their content to commercial messages; the city may not conclude that the communication of commercial information concerning goods and services connected with a particular site is of greater value than the communication of noncommercial messages." Moreover, some of the other exceptions, such as those for religious symbols, signs telling the time and temperature, and historical commemorative plaques, created a separate constitutional defect: "Although the city may distinguish between the relative value of different categories of commercial speech, the city does not have the same range of choice in the area of noncommercial speech to evaluate the strength of, or distinguish between, various communicative interests. [Mosley.] With respect to noncommercial speech, the city may not choose the appropriate subjects for public discourse. [Consolidated Edison.] Because some noncommercial messages may be conveyed on billboards throughout the commercial and industrial zones, San Diego must similarly allow billboards conveying other noncommercial messages throughout those zones."

Justice White relied on the exceptions in the ordinance not only to identify an impermissible content distinction, but also to cast doubt on the need or justifications for regulating billboards in this case: "[T]he exceptions to the general prohibition are of great significance in assessing the strength of the city's interest in prohibiting billboards." "Governmental interests are only revealed and given concrete force by the steps taken to meet those interests. If the city has concluded that its official interests are not as strong as private interests in commercial communications, may it nevertheless claim that those same official interests outweigh private interests in noncommercial communications? Our answer, which is consistent with our cases, is in the negative."

---

1. Recall the discussion of First Amendment protection of commercial speech in sec. 2D of the preceding chapter, and note especially the consid-   eration of the commercial speech aspects of Metromedia at p. 1144 above.

Justice BRENNAN, joined by Justice Blackmun, concurred in the judgment. He was troubled by the plurality's extensive reliance on the distinction between commercial and noncommercial speech, and he viewed the case as presenting squarely the problem of a total ban on billboards. He argued that "the *practical* effect of the San Diego ordinance is to eliminate the billboard as an effective medium of communication." That prompted him to adopt an analysis quite different from the plurality's: "Instead of relying on the exceptions to the ban to invalidate the ordinance, I would apply the tests [developed] to analyze content-neutral prohibitions of particular media of communication."[2] He relied especially on Schad (p. 1124 above), where, in striking down a total ban on live commercial entertainment, the Court had examined "the substantiality of the governmental interests asserted" and "whether those interests could be served by means that would be less intrusive on activity protected by the First Amendment."[3] Applying that analysis here, he stated that, "[in] the case of billboards, I would hold that a city may totally ban them if it can show that a sufficiently substantial governmental interest is directly furthered by the total ban, and that any more narrowly drawn restriction, i.e., anything less than a total ban, would promote less well the achievement of that goal."

Applying that standard, Justice Brennan found the ban unjustified. He was dissatisfied with the evidentiary support for the traffic safety claims, and he was especially skeptical of the asserted aesthetic interests: "Of course, it is not for a court to impose its own notion of beauty on San Diego. But before deferring to a city's judgment, a court must be convinced that the city is seriously and comprehensively addressing aesthetic concerns with respect to its environment." This, he noted, could be shown by an effort, not shown here, to address *other* "obvious contributors to an unattractive environment. In this sense the ordinance is underinclusive, [and] the commitment of the city to improving its physical environment is placed in doubt." (Compare his opinion in Taxpayers for Vincent, above.)

Chief Justice BURGER, Justice REHNQUIST, and Justice STEVENS each filed a separate dissent. The Chief Justice's angry opinion chided the plurality for undervaluing the importance of local control over local problems: "This is the long arm and voracious appetite of federal power—this time judicial power—with a vengeance, reaching and absorbing concepts [of] local authority." Because ample alternative channels of communications were available, he would not have the First Amendment interfere with San Diego's justifiable and reasonable effort to do something about "what it perceives—and what it has a right to perceive—as ugly and dangerous eyesores thrust upon its citizens." Justice Stevens' dissent disagreed that completely effective alternative channels of communication were available. But he did not see the diminution of communications opportunities as fatal. "The essential concern embodied in the First Amendment is that government not impose its viewpoint on the public or select the topics on which public debate is permissible." In short, as he has in a number of his First Amendment opinions, Justice Stevens claimed that the central focus should be on the existence of viewpoint discrimination.[4] Finding

2. "Different factors come into play when the challenged legislation is simply a time, place, or manner regulation rather than a total ban of a particular medium of expression." [Footnote by Justice Brennan.]

3. Justice Brennan stated that Schad "merely articulated an analysis applied in previous cases concerning total bans of media of expression. E.g., [Schneider; Martin v. Struthers]."

4. Recall the comments in sec. 2, at p. 1168 above, on viewpoint discrimination, and the sug-

gestion there that Justice Stevens may view viewpoint discrimination as the *only* concern of the First Amendment. Is that a justifiable approach? For other recent Stevens opinions with that emphasis, recall his opinion in Taxpayers for Vincent, above, and in Consolidated Edison (p. 1122 above). See also Minnesota Bd. for Community Colleges v. Knight (1984; p. 1276 above) and Bolger v. Youngs Drug Products Co. (1983; p. 1145 above).

no viewpoint discrimination here, Justice Stevens argued for a much less stringent standard of review, a standard readily satisfied by the San Diego ordinance.[5]

Given the division on the Court in Metromedia, the question of whether a total, content-neutral, prohibition of billboards is permissible was left unresolved. (Cf. Taxpayers for Vincent.) This raises once again the question of the permissibility of format discriminations. That question has been encountered repeatedly. As Justice Brennan's opinion in Metromedia notes, it arose in Schad, banning live commercial entertainment. He also points to such earlier cases as the ban on leaflets in Schneider. Note also the consideration of format discrimination in connection with the loudspeaker cases at p. 1208 above; and recall Justice Marshall's dissent in Clark v. Community for Creative Non-Violence (1984; p. 1188 above), the symbolic speech case involving sleeping in parks. By and large, the majority of the modern Court has been unconcerned with format discrimination, despite its growing emphasis on the search for content discriminations and its ambivalent treatment of subject matter discriminations.[6] (But see, on singling out the press, Minneapolis Star and Tribune (1983; p. 1453 below).) Recall the discussions of the variety of possible discriminatory regulations in sec. 2, at p. 1164 above. In light of the modern cases, is the Court's treatment of the range of discriminatory regulations satisfactory? Has it unduly forgotten the lessons of Schneider (p. 1206 above) and its unitary First Amendment balancing approach?[7]

---

5. Justice REHNQUIST's dissent, which agreed generally with the positions of Chief Justice Burger and Justice Stevens, noted that "it is a genuine misfortune to have the Court's treatment of the subject be a virtual Tower of Babel, from which no definitive principles can be clearly drawn."

6. For a relatively straightforward recent application of the Court's aversion to content regulation, see Regan v. Time, Inc., 468 U.S. ___ (1984). At issue were 18 U.S.C. §§ 474 and 504, which together prohibit the photographing of United States currency, but which provide an exception for "printing, publishing, or importation [of] illustrations of [any] obligation or other security of the United States for philatelic, numismatic, educational, historical or newsworthy purposes in articles, books, journals, newspapers, or albums." Because the statute was designed to prevent counterfeiting, the exception was limited to black-and-white reproductions less than three-fourths or more than one and one-half the size of the original; and the original negatives and plates had to be destroyed after the permitted use. The challenge to the statute occurred in the context of a Sports Illustrated cover that "carried a photographic color reproduction of $100 bills pouring into a basketball hoop."

In a complicated alignment of opinions, a majority of the Court agreed that the purpose requirement of the exception was an impermissible distinction on the basis of content: "A determination concerning the newsworthiness or educational value of a photograph cannot help but be based on the content of the photograph and the message it [delivers]. Regulations which permit the Government to discriminate on the basis of the content of the message cannot be tolerated under the First Amendment." (As to the pur-

pose requirement, only Justice Stevens believed that the First Amendment was not offended.) As to the balance of the statute, in particular the color and size restrictions, a different majority upheld the restrictions, finding them to be a content-neutral and reasonable time, place, and manner regulation that substantially served the Government's compelling interest in preventing counterfeiting. Justice White's plurality opinion on this issue noted: "It is enough that the color restriction substantially serves the Government's legitimate ends." "The less-restrictive-alternative analysis invoked by Time has never been a part of the inquiry into the validity of a time, place, and manner regulation." Justice Powell, joined by Justice Blackmun, dissented from upholding the color and size requirements because he found them not capable of severance from the purpose requirement. Justice Brennan, joined by Justice Marshall, also found the statute's provisions nonseverable, and in addition found the general statutory approach here excessively restrictive on publication. He would have struck down the entire statute and required Congress to draft a statute much more narrowly tailored to the goals of prohibiting counterfeiting.

7. Recall also the two-track approach of O'Brien (sec. 3, p. 1170 above), on the closely related problem of exercising varying levels of scrutiny depending on whether the governmental interest is speech-related (i.e., turning on the effect on recipients of a particular message or class of messages) or whether it is unrelated to free expression (i.e., is merely incidental to governmental interests unrelated to the speaker's message). Note that the O'Brien approach has surfaced widely outside the symbolic speech area, including in the analysis of problems dealing with access to the public forum, as the most recent

G.   FIRST AMENDMENT ACCESS RIGHTS TO PRIVATE PROPERTY?

Introduction. The preceding materials primarily considered claimed rights of equal and assured minimal access to *public* property. Do the principles of those cases aid in developing a claim of access by a speaker who wants to use *privately* owned property to air a message? Is there a "private forum" counterpart to the public forum developments? Do the private forum cases throw light on the appropriate ingredients of a public forum doctrine? In recent years, claims of access to private property have been voiced in a variety of contexts. Typically, these cases involve not only First Amendment principles, but also the delineation of the applicability of constitutional norms to the private sector and the possible constraints imposed by the constitutional safeguards of private property. Recall chap. 10 and its "state action" problem, p. 860 above. Ordinarily constitutional guarantees limit only government; in several of the private property cases below, accordingly, questions regarding not only the applicability of constitutional guarantees to the private sector but also the constitutional limits on interfering with private property are intertwined with the dimensions of First Amendment assurances of access.

That intertwining is especially reflected in the first group of cases, involving claimed rights of access to privately owned shopping centers as a forum for expression. The second group of cases presents claims of access to the heavily regulated broadcasting media: May government impose access requirements on the holders of broadcasting licenses? May First Amendment claimants assert rights against licensees to air messages? And the final case in this group asks whether government may enforce access rights against the privately owned, largely unregulated print media, in the interest of making newspapers the forums for the airing of a wider range of views. In each of these contexts, the access principles developed in the preceding materials are reexamined and, occasionally, clarified.

A RIGHT OF ACCESS TO PRIVATELY OWNED SHOPPING CENTERS?

1. *Logan Valley.* More than a generation ago, in Marsh v. Alabama, 326 U.S. 501 (1946) (p. 867 above), the Court initiated the "public function" state action theory by holding that Jehovah's Witnesses could claim a constitutional right of access to distribute religious literature in a company-owned town. In 1968, the 5 to 4 decision in AMALGAMATED FOOD EMPLOYEES v. LOGAN VALLEY PLAZA, 391 U.S. 308, relied in part on Marsh to hold that a state trespass law could not be applied to enjoin peaceful union picketing of a supermarket in a privately owned shopping center.[1] Justice MARSHALL's majority opinion found that the ban on picketing could not be justified on the ground that picketing constituted an unconsented invasion of private property rights: "The shopping center here is clearly the functional equivalent of the

cases above illustrate. Is it possible to follow the O'Brien approach without looking closely at governmental motives? If it is not, what remains of the Court's statement in O'Brien that it would *not* look at congressional purpose or motive?

The question of illicit governmental purposes is closely tied to the issue of content regulation. To ask which governmental purposes are illicit is essentially similar to as asking, e.g., to what extent subject matter discrimination is as much a First Amendment evil as discrimination on the

basis of viewpoint. Similarly, the concerns noted in the text about format discrimination can be asked in terms of whether discrimination on the basis of the format reflects an illicit governmental purpose.

1. This group of shopping center cases is considered at greater length in chap. 10, in connection with the "state action" problem. See p. 869 above. Other First Amendment aspects of labor union picketing are considered in chap. 13, at p. 1342 below.

business district of Chickasaw involved in Marsh. [We] see no reason why access to a business district in a company town for the purpose of exercising First Amendment rights should be constitutionally required, while access for the same purpose to property functioning as a business district should be limited simply because the property surrounding the 'business district' is not under the same ownership." [2]

Having established the applicability of constitutional restraints to the shopping center, Justice Marshall proceeded to examine the scope of First Amendment public forum principles in this context: "The essence of [such cases as Lovell, Hague, and Schneider] is that streets, sidewalks, parks, and other similar public places are so historically associated with the exercise of First Amendment rights that access to them for the purpose of exercising such rights cannot constitutionally be denied broadly and absolutely. The fact that [decisions such as Schneider] were concerned with handbilling rather than picketing is immaterial so far as the question is solely one of right of access for the purpose of expression of views." He distinguished decisions sustaining restrictions on access to public property—such as the jail in Adderley—by noting that, "where property is not ordinarily open to the public, this Court has held that access to it for the purpose of exercising First Amendment rights may be denied altogether. Even where municipal or state property is open to the public generally, the exercise of First Amendment rights may be regulated so as to prevent interference with the use to which the property is ordinarily put by the State. [And] the exercise of First Amendment rights may be regulated where such exercise will unduly interfere with the normal use of the public property by other members of the public with an equal right of access to it."

The detailed scope of permissible restrictions was not at issue here, however: "Because the Pennsylvania courts have held that 'picketing and trespassing' can be prohibited absolutely on respondents' premises, we have no occasion to consider the extent to which respondents are entitled to limit the location and manner of the picketing or the number of picketers within the mall in order to prevent interference with either access to the market building or vehicular use of the parcel pickup area and parking lot. [The] fact that the nonspeech aspects of petitioners' activity are also rendered less effective is not particularly compelling in light of the absence of any showing [that] the patrolling accompanying the picketing sought to be carried on was significantly interfering with the use to which the mall property was being put by both respondents and the general public. [T]he mere fact that speech is accompanied by conduct does not mean that the speech can be suppressed under the guise of prohibiting the conduct. Here it is perfectly clear that a prohibition against trespass on the mall operates to bar all speech within the shopping center to which respondents object. Yet this Court stated many years ago, '[O]ne is not to have the exercise of his liberty of expression in appropriate places abridged on the plea that it may be exercised in some other place.' [Schneider]." [3]

2. *Lloyd.* The Logan Valley decision was "distinguished" four years later, in the 5 to 4 decision in LLOYD CORP. v. TANNER, 407 U.S. 551 (1972)—

---

2. In this line of shopping center cases, all of the opinions supporting an access claim emphasized the functional importance of shopping centers in modern society. For example, Justice Marshall noted in Logan Valley: "It has been estimated that by the end of 1966 there were between 10,000 and 11,000 shopping centers in the United States and Canada, accounting for approximately 37% of the total retail sales in these two countries."

3. Justice BLACK's dissent included the comment: "[O]f course, picketing, that is patrol-

ling, is not free speech and not protected as such." Justice WHITE's dissent stated, in partial reliance on Adderley: "[S]ome public property is available for some uses and not for others; some public property is neither designed nor dedicated for use by pickets or for other communicative activities. [W]hether Logan Valley Plaza is public or private property, it is a place for shopping and not a place for picketing."

although, on second thought four years after, the majority concluded that Lloyd should be read as overruling Logan Valley. In Lloyd, the lower federal courts had relied on Marsh and Logan Valley in holding unconstitutional the application to anti-war leafleteers of a shopping center ban on the distribution of handbills. In a 5 to 4 decision, the Supreme Court reversed, finding the facts in its earlier cases "significantly different." Justice POWELL found reliance on the "functional equivalent of a public business district" language in Logan Valley unjustifiable. There, the First Amendment activity—union picketing of a store—"was related to the shopping center's operations" and the store was "in the center of a large private enclave with the consequence that no other reasonable opportunities" to convey the picketers' message existed. Here, by contrast, the handbilling "had no relation to any purpose for which the center was built and being used" and alternative means of communication were available. Patrons of the large shopping center had to cross public streets to get into the private areas: "Handbills may be distributed conveniently [from] these public sidewalks and streets." More generally, Justice Powell commented that the free speech guarantees are "limitations on *state* action, not on action by the owner of private property used nondiscriminatorily for private purposes only." And he emphasized that the protections of property in the due process clauses were "also relevant": "Although accommodations between [speech and property values] are sometimes necessary, and the courts properly have shown a special solicitude for the [First Amendment], this Court has never held that a trespasser or an uninvited guest may exercise general rights of free speech on property privately owned." ·

Justice MARSHALL's sharp dissent, joined by Justice Douglas, Brennan and Stewart, insisted that Logan Valley was not truly distinguishable, that the majority opinion was "an attack" on the rationale of Marsh as well as Logan Valley, and that "one may suspect from reading the [majority opinion] that it is Logan Valley itself that the Court finds bothersome." [See the excerpts in chap. 10 above.] Of special interest to the development of "assured minimal access" public forum principles is Justice Marshall's explanation in Lloyd of the "tremendous need" of the handbillers to have access to the private shopping center: "For many persons who do not have easy access to television, radio, the major newspapers, and the other forms of mass media, the only way they can express themselves to a broad range of citizens on issues of general public concern is to picket, or to handbill, or to utilize other free or relatively inexpensive means of communication. The only hope that these people have to be able to communicate effectively is to be permitted to speak in those areas in which most of their fellow citizens can be found. One such area is the business district of a city or town or its functional equivalent."

3. *Hudgens.* Even though Lloyd had purported to distinguish Logan Valley, HUDGENS v. NLRB, 424 U.S. 507 (1976), announced that Lloyd had in effect overruled Logan Valley. Hudgens involved labor picketing of a store in a private shopping center. The picketers were employees of a warehouse maintained by the store owner at a location outside of the shopping center. Justice Stewart's majority opinion concluded that "the constitutional guarantee of free expression has no part to play in a case such as this." He explained his refusal to apply First Amendment protections to private shopping centers as follows: "If a large self-contained shopping center *is* the functional equivalent of a municipality, as Logan Valley held, then the [First Amendment] would not permit control of speech within such a center to depend upon the speech's content. [It] conversely follows, therefore, that if the respondent in the Lloyd case did not have a First Amendment right to enter that shopping center to distribute handbills concerning Vietnam, then the respondents in the present case did not have a First Amendment right to enter this shopping center for the purpose of advertising their strike."

Justice MARSHALL's dissent, joined by Justice Brennan, claimed that the majority's invocation of cases banning municipal control of the content of speech was "simply inapposite." In his view, determining whether First Amendment guarantees are applicable when "the primary regulator is a private entity" rather than the government properly depended "on the subject of the speech the private entity seeks to regulate, because the degree to which the private entity monopolizes the effective channels of communication may depend upon what subject is involved." He added: "This limited reference to the subject matter of the speech poses none of the dangers of government suppression or censorship that lay at the heart" of the decisions barring governmental content control. He argued, moreover, that, in opening private property to use by the public, a shopping center owner "necessarily surrendered" a "degree of privacy." He concluded: "The interest of members of the public in communicating with one another on subjects relating to the businesses that occupy a modern shopping center is substantial. Not only employees with a labor dispute, but also consumers with complaints against business establishments, may look to the location of a retail store as the only reasonable avenue for effective communication with the public. As far as these groups are concerned, the shopping center owner has assumed the traditional role of the state in its control of historical First Amendment forums. Lloyd and Logan Valley recognized the vital role the First Amendment has to play in such cases, and I believe that this Court errs when it holds otherwise." [4]

4. *May states grant access to shopping centers without violating federal rights?—The PruneYard case.* In PRUNEYARD SHOPPING CENTER v. ROBINS, 447 U.S. 74 (1980), California's highest court had interpreted its *state* constitution to guarantee access to a privately owned shopping center, asserting that Lloyd's discussion of property rights did not bar a state from granting broader access under its own free speech guarantee than the Court had found in the First Amendment. PruneYard, in accordance with its nondiscriminatory policy of barring all expressive activity not directly related to its commercial purposes, had excluded several high school students who sought to solicit signatures for a petition protesting a UN resolution against "Zionism"; the highest state court, abandoning its earlier policy of following Lloyd and adopting an approach akin to Logan Valley, interpreted the state constitution as protecting the students' activities. Justice REHNQUIST's opinion for the Court concluded that "state constitutional provisions, which permit individuals to exercise free speech and petition rights on the property of a privately owned shopping center to which the public is invited, [do not] violate the shopping center owner's [federal] property rights [or] his free speech rights."

The shopping center, echoing the state court dissenters, argued that Lloyd rested on the federal "constitutional private property rights of the owner." Justice Rehnquist disagreed: "Our reasoning in Lloyd [does not] ex proprio vigore limit the authority of the State to exercise its police power or its sovereign right to adopt in its own Constitution individual liberties more expansive than those conferred by the Federal Constitution." Federal guarantees of property and speech rights of course limited that power; but those limitations had not been transgressed here. With respect to property rights, the Court found no violation of the federal guarantee against taking of property

---

4. In his effort to preserve the Logan Valley-Lloyd distinction, Justice Marshall stated: "Lloyd retained the availability of First Amendment protection when the picketing is related to the function of the shopping center, and when there is no other reasonable opportunity to convey the message to the intended audience. Preserving Logan Valley subject to Lloyd's two re-lated criteria guaranteed that the First Amendment would have application in those situations in which the shopping center owner had most clearly monopolized the forums essential for effective communication. This result, although not the optimal one in my view, is nonetheless defensible."

without just compensation. Although "one of the essential sticks in the bundle of property rights is the right to exclude others," here there was "nothing to suggest that preventing [the shopping center] from prohibiting [the students'] activity will unreasonably impair the value or use of [the] property as a shopping center. [The students] were orderly, and they limited their activity to the common area of the [large] shopping center. In these circumstances, the fact that they may have 'physically invaded' appellants' property cannot be viewed as determinative. [Appellants] have failed to demonstrate that the 'right to exclude others' is so essential to the use or economic value of their property that the state-authorized limitation of it amounted to a 'taking.' " Moreover, the state-granted access right did not violate the rationality requirement of Nebbia (p. 462 above): a state could reasonably conclude that access furthered its "asserted interest in promoting more expansive rights of free speech and petition than conferred by the Federal Constitution." (The Court also rejected the property owner's claim of a "First Amendment right not to be forced by the State to use his property as a forum for the speech of others.")

Although the Court was unanimous about the result, several Justices submitted separate opinions. Justice MARSHALL, who joined in the Court's opinion, reiterated his view that Logan Valley was correct and Lloyd wrong and "applaud[ed]" the California court's adoption of the Logan Valley approach, viewing it as "a part of a very healthy trend of affording state constitutional provisions a more expansive interpretation than this Court has given to the Federal Constitution." Justice POWELL's partial concurrence, joined by Justice White, supported the majority's discussion of property rights "on the understanding that [it] is limited to the type of shopping center involved in this case." He added: "Significantly different questions would be presented if a State authorized strangers to picket or leafleteer in privately owned, freestanding stores and commercial premises." He warned, moreover, that the decision did not apply to all "shopping centers": "Even large establishments may be able to show that the number or type of persons wishing to speak on their premises would create a substantial annoyance to customers that could be eliminated only by elaborate, expensive, and possibly unenforceable time, place, and manner restrictions." [5]

A RIGHT OF ACCESS TO THE BROADCASTING MEDIA?

1. *Government regulations to assure a right to reply on the broadcasting media: The Red Lion case.* May government safeguard individual reputations by requiring a broadcaster to afford reply time to the target of an attack? Does that requirement in turn violate the First Amendment rights of the broadcaster? When government has sought to vindicate the interest in private reputation by authorizing defamation actions, the Court has sharply curtailed suits against the press. (See chap. 11, p. 1052 above.) But when the FCC sought to provide rights of access for individuals attacked on the air and imposed requirements that radio and television stations give reply time, the Court sustained the regulations. RED LION BROADCASTING CO. v. FCC, 395 U.S. 367 (1969).

The FCC traditional "fairness doctrine" requires stations to present discussion of public issues, and to assure fair coverage for each side. Later FCC

---

5. Justice Powell devoted most of his concurrence to possible First Amendment defenses of shopping center owners. He insisted that the decision did not constitute "blanket approval for state efforts to transform privately owned commercial property into public forums."

In a separate opinion, Justice WHITE elaborated on his agreement with Justice Powell's position. In an additional, brief notation, Justice BLACKMUN noted his agreement with virtually all of the Court's opinion.

rulings elaborated the personal attack and political editorials aspects of the fairness doctrine by specifying the circumstances in which free reply time had to be made available by licensees. In sustaining those regulations in the Red Lion case, Justice WHITE's opinion for a unanimous Court supported a limited right of access to the broadcasting media. He found that access would "enhance rather than abridge the freedoms of speech and press." He emphasized the "scarcity of broadcast frequencies, the Government's role in allocating those frequencies, and the legitimate claims of those unable without governmental assistance to gain access to those frequencies for expression of their views." In response to the broadcasters' First Amendment claims, the Court stressed the speech interests of the public. The Court added: "[D]ifferences in the characteristics of news media justify differences in the First Amendment standards applied to them. Just as the Government may limit the use of sound amplifying equipment potentially so noisy that it drowns out civilized private speech, so may the Government limit the use of broadcast equipment. The right of free speech of a broadcaster, the user of a sound truck, or any other individual does not embrace a right to snuff out the free speech of others." It would be "a serious matter," to be sure, if the FCC requirements induced self-censorship by licensees and made their coverage of controversial public issues "ineffective." But that was only a speculative possibility.[1]

2. *A First Amendment right of access to the broadcasting media for editorial advertisements?* That the right of access to the broadcasting media is a very limited one was made clear three years after Red Lion, when the Court decided CBS, INC. v. DEMOCRATIC NAT. COMM., 412 U.S. 94 (1973). The CBS case involved a broadcasting context counterpart to the access claim presented in the city bus context in Lehman, p. 1247 above. The CBS case originated with complaints filed before the FCC in 1970 by the Democratic National Committee and an anti-war group challenging certain broadcasters' policies of refusing all editorial advertisements. The FCC sustained the broadcasters' position, but the Court of Appeals reversed, holding that "a flat ban on paid public issue announcements is in violation of the First Amendment, at least when other sorts of paid announcements are accepted." The divided Court's resolution of that controversy in 1973 produced a series of elaborate opinions. In resolving conflicting emanations from First Amendment values, the majority emphasized the broadcasters' right to control the content of their programs, while the dissenters gave greater weight to the public's right of access to the airwaves.[2]

Chief Justice BURGER's opinion rejected the argument that a broad right of access could be drawn from the Red Lion ruling. Instead, he emphasized the statutory indications "that Congress intended to permit private broadcasting to develop with the widest journalistic freedom consistent with its public obliga-

---

1. Despite the Court's endorsement of part of the "fairness doctrine" in Red Lion, the doctrine continues to receive wide criticism. Note, however, the continued reliance on Red Lion in FCC v. National Citizens Comm. for Broadcasting, 436 U.S. 775 (1978), upholding FCC regulations prospectively barring common ownership of broadcasting stations and daily newspapers located in the same community.

Note also the Court's continued reliance on Red Lion and the scarcity rationale in FCC v. League of Women Voters, 468 U.S. ___ (1984). That case suggested a lower standard of review for content regulations of broadcast media than would be permissible for other media. Nevertheless, in applying the less-than-strict scrutiny considered appropriate for the broadcasting media,

the Court found that the content regulation in this case could not survive judicial scrutiny. The case is more fully noted in chap. 13 below, at p. 1461. (Note, however, that the scarcity rationale was *not* invoked in justifying FCC restrictions on broadcasts of offensive speech in Pacifica, p. 1114 above.)

2. The majority's position on most issues was stated by Chief Justice Burger. Justice Brennan, joined by Justice Marshall, dissented. Justice Douglas submitted an extensive opinion concurring in the majority's result. Justice Stewart, who concurred with parts of the Chief Justice's opinion, also submitted an extensive concurrence. Moreover, there were brief partial concurring opinions by Justice White and by Justice Blackmun, joined by Justice Powell.

tions." [3]　He concluded: "To agree that debate on public issues should be 'robust, and wide-open' does not mean that we should exchange 'public trustee' broadcasting, with all its limitations, for a system of self-appointed editorial commentators."　The Chief Justice emphasized: "The Commission's responsibilities under a right-of-access system would tend to draw it into a continuing case-by-case determination of who should be heard and when."　Moreover, he noted "the reality that in a very real sense listeners and viewers constitute a 'captive audience.'"

Justice DOUGLAS' concurrence took a far firmer constitutional position on the side of the broadcasters: "My conclusion is that TV and radio stand in the same protected position under the First Amendment as do newspapers and magazines."　The Red Lion case, in which he had not participated, curtailed broadcasters' rights unduly, he insisted, since "the First Amendment puts beyond the reach of government federal regulation of news agencies save only business or financial practices which do not involve First Amendment rights." Justice BRENNAN's extensive dissent, joined by Justice Marshall, concluded, in "balancing" the competing interests, that the broadcasters' "absolute ban on editorial advertising" could "serve only to inhibit, rather than to further" robust public debate.　He insisted that the fairness doctrine was "insufficient" to provide that kind of debate.　He noted not only the interests of broadcasters and of the listening and viewing public, "but also the independent First Amendment interest of groups and individuals in effective self-expression." Drawing on access principles developed in the public forum context, he commented: "[F]reedom of speech does not exist in the abstract.　On the contrary, the right to speak can flourish only if it is allowed to operate in an effective forum—whether it be a public park, a schoolroom, a town meeting hall, a soapbox, or a radio and television frequency.　For in the absence of an effective means of communication, the right to speak would ring hollow indeed."　Accordingly, "in light of the current dominance of the electronic media as the most effective means of reaching the public, any policy that *absolutely* denies citizens access to the airwaves" was unjustifiable.

3.　*A statutory right of access to the broadcasting media for candidates seeking federal elective office.*　Sec. 312(a)(7) of the Communications Act of 1934, as added by the Federal Election Campaign Act of 1971, authorizes the FCC to revoke a broadcaster's license "for willful or repeated failure to allow reasonable access to or to permit purchase of reasonable amounts of time for the use of a broadcasting station by a legally qualified candidate for Federal elective office on behalf of his candidacy."　The 6 to 3 decision in CBS, INC. v. FCC, 453 U.S. 367 (1981), found that this provision created a major new right of access— a right that enlarged the political broadcasting responsibilities of licensees.　The Court also held that the FCC's interpretation and application of the provision did not violate broadcasters' First Amendment rights.　The controversy originated in October 1979, when the Carter-Mondale Presidential Committee asked each of the three major television networks to sell the Committee a half-hour of early December 1979 air time.　The Committee sought to broadcast a documentary on the record of the Carter Administration, to augment President Carter's planned announcement of his candidacy for re-election.　All three networks denied the request, relying on their across-the-board rules about

---

3.　Chief Justice Burger considered the First Amendment problems despite his earlier conclusion that the broadcasters' policy did not constitute "governmental action" for purposes of the First Amendment.　(That "state action" aspect of his opinion is more fully considered in chap. 10, sec. 2, above.)　In explaining his justifications for discussing the First Amendment issues—a discussion which the dissenters branded as dicta—the Chief Justice noted that the "public interest" standard of the Federal Communications Act "invites reference to First Amendment principles."

political broadcasts.[4] The Committee filed a complaint, and the FCC ruled that the networks' reasons were "deficient" under the FCC's interpretation of the statute. The FCC concluded that the networks had violated the law by failing to provide "reasonable access."

Chief Justice BURGER—who had emphasized "the widest journalistic freedom" for broadcasters when he argued in 1973 (in CBS v. Democratic National Committee, above) that Red Lion did *not* support a First Amendment right of access for editorial advertisements—wrote the majority opinion in the 1981 case. He agreed with the FCC's view that § 312(a)(7) created a major new access right, and he found that this broad reading of the statute did not interfere with the broadcasters' First Amendment rights. He acknowledged that, prior to the enactment of § 312(a)(7) in 1971, candidates' access rights were governed simply by the general "public interest" requirement of the Act. Under this standard, licensees, in order to assure license renewal, had to allocate some time to political issues; but an individual candidate could claim no personal right of access unless an opponent had used the station. But the 1971 provision changed all that, in the majority's view: "By its terms, [the provision] singles out legally qualified candidates for *federal* elective office and grants them a special right of access on an individual basis, violation of which carries the serious consequence of license revocation. The conclusion is inescapable that the statute did more than simply codify the pre-existing public interest standard. [The] legislative history supports the plain meaning of the statute that individual candidates for federal elective office have a right of reasonable access to the use of stations for paid political broadcasts on behalf of their candidacies, without reference to whether an opponent has secured time."

The FCC had developed an elaborate set of standards, "evolved principally on a case-by-case basis and [not] embodied in formalized rules," to implement § 312(a)(7). The Court found that implementation justified. The Chief Justice explained that, under these standards, "once a campaign has begun, [broadcasters] must give reasonable and good faith attention to access requests. [Such] requests must be considered on an individualized basis, and broadcasters are required to tailor their responses to accommodate, as much as reasonably possible, a candidate's stated purposes in seeking air time. [To] justify a negative response, broadcasters must cite a realistic danger of substantial program disruption—perhaps caused by insufficient notice to allow adjustments in the schedule—or of an excessive number of equal time requests [under § 315 of the Act]." Under the Chief Justice's view of the standards, "[i]f broadcasters take the appropriate factors into account and act reasonably and in good faith, their decisions will be entitled to deference even if the Commission's analysis would have differed in the first instance. But if broadcasters adopt 'across-the-board policies' and do not attempt to respond to the individualized situation of a particular candidate, the Commission is not compelled to sustain their denial of access." The FCC had relied on such standards when it ruled that CBS, NBC and ABC had illegally denied the Carter-Mondale Committee's requests.

The networks challenged certain aspects of the standards, but the Court was unsympathetic. Chief Justice Burger rejected the claim that the FCC, by requiring the broadcasters to respond to access requests on an individualized basis, had "attached inordinate significance to candidates' needs" and had unfairly belittled "broadcasters' concerns." Moreover, he upheld the FCC's authority to "independently determine whether a campaign has begun and the obligations imposed by § 312(a)(7) have attached." In sum, the Chief Justice concluded that the FCC had engaged in "a reasoned attempt to effectuate [the

---

4. ABC and NBC indicated that December 1979 was "too early in the political season." CBS contended that programming disruption   would result if it abandoned its policy of selling only 5-minute spots to candidates.

statutory] access requirement." In the majority's view, the Commission had not "abused its discretion" in finding that the networks had violated the statute. Nor had the FCC violated the broadcasters' First Amendment rights. Quoting from Red Lion, the Chief Justice stated: "There is nothing in the First Amendment which prevents the Government from requiring a licensee to share his frequency with others." He elaborated: "Although the broadcasting industry is entitled under the First Amendment to exercise 'the widest journalistic freedom consistent with its public [duties],' CBS, Inc. v. Democratic National Committee, the Court has made clear that: '*it is the right of the viewers and listeners, not the right of the broadcasters which is paramount.*' [The] First Amendment interests of candidates and voters, as well as broadcasters, are implicated by § 312(a)(7). [The provision] makes a significant contribution to freedom of expression by enhancing the ability of candidates to present, and the public to receive, information necessary for the effective operation of the democratic process." He added: "[The networks] are correct that the Court has never approved a *general* right of access to the media. See, e.g., [Tornillo; CBS, Inc. v. Democratic National Committee]. Nor do we do so today. Section 312(a) (7) creates a *limited* right to 'reasonable' access. [Further], § 312(a)(7) does not impair the discretion of broadcasters to present their views on any issue or to carry any particular type of programming." He concluded: "Section 312(a) (7) represents an effort by Congress to assure that an important resource—the airwaves—will be used in the public interest. We hold that the statutory right of access [properly] balances the First Amendment rights of federal candidates, the public, and broadcasters."

Justice WHITE's dissent, joined by Justices Rehnquist and Stevens, strongly disagreed with the Chief Justice's broad reading of the statute and with the Court's endorsement of the FCC's standards and their application. Justice White argued that the majority's approach "conceals the fundamental issue in this case, which is whether Congress intended not only to create a right of reasonable access but also to negate the long-standing statutory policy of deferring to editorial judgments that are not destructive of the goals of the Act. In this case, such a policy would require acceptance of network or station decisions on access as long as they are within the range of reasonableness, even if the Commission would have preferred different responses by the networks. It is demonstrable that Congress did not intend to set aside this traditional policy, and the Commission seriously misconstrued the statute when it assumed that it had been given authority to insist on its own views as to reasonable access even though this entailed rejection of media judgments representing different but nevertheless reasonable reactions to access requests. As this case demonstrates, the result is an administratively created right of access which, in light of the pre-existing statutory policies concerning access, is far broader than Congress could have intended to allow." Developing that position at length, Justice White claimed that it is "as clear as can be that the regulation of the broadcast media has been and is marked by a clearly defined 'legislative desire to preserve values of private journalism.' [CBS, Inc. v. Democratic National Committee.] The corollary legislative policy has been not to recognize [individual] rights of access to the broadcast media. These policies have been so clear and are so obviously grounded in constitutional considerations that, in the absence of unequivocal legislative intent to the contrary, it should not be assumed that § 312(a)(7) was designed to make the kind of substantial inroads in these basic considerations that the Commission has now mandated." [5]

---

5. Justice White's evaluation of the FCC's application of its standards differed sharply from that of the Chief Justice. The contrast was particularly well illustrated by Justice White's comment that "the Commission's assertions of deference to editorial judgment are palpably incredible." He charged: "While both the Court and the Commission describe [several] factors

MAY GOVERNMENT IMPOSE A RIGHT OF ACCESS TO NEWSPAPERS?—"RIGHT OF REPLY" LAWS

Direct judicial enforcement of any First Amendment right of access against private newspapers is presumably barred by the "state action" principle. But is a legislature's interest in protecting "right of access" First Amendment values sufficiently strong to impose upon newspapers an obligation to grant a "right of reply"? In 1974, a unanimous Court found any such interest easily overcome by the powerful protection newspapers enjoy because of the freedom of the press guaranteed by the First Amendment.[1] The decision in MIAMI HERALD PUB. CO. v. TORNILLO, 418 U.S. 241 (1974), held unconstitutional Florida's "right of reply" law and rejected efforts to justify it on the basis of a First Amendment right of access. The law granted political candidates a right to equal space to reply to criticism and attacks on their record by a newspaper. The state court had sustained the law because it furthered the "broad societal interest in the free flow of information." Chief Justice Burger's opinion concluded, however, that the law violated the First Amendment.

Chief Justice BURGER reviewed at some length the modern evolution of arguments for "an enforceable right of access to the press" and the concomitant claim "that Government has an obligation to ensure that a wide variety of views reach the public."[2] He noted that "access advocates" emphasize the concentration of power in the newspaper business and the shrinking number of newspapers; claim that the public has consequently lost its ability to contribute meaningfully to public debate; note the disappearance of real opportunity to form competing newspapers by dissidents; and accordingly urge "that the only effective way to insure fairness and accuracy" is "for government to take affirmative action." But the Chief Justice was not persuaded: "However much validity may be found in these arguments, at each point the implementation of a remedy such as an enforceable right of access necessarily calls for some mechanism, either governmental or consensual. If it is governmental coercion, this at once brings about a confrontation with the [First Amendment]. [A] responsible press is an undoubtedly desirable goal, but press responsibility is not mandated by the Constitution and like many other virtues it cannot be legislated." The fact that the newspaper was not being prevented from giving its own views did not help the defenders of the law: "The Florida statute exacts a penalty on the basis of the content of a newspaper. [G]overnment-enforced right of access inescapably 'dampens the vigor and limits the variety of public debate.'" And even if there were no such consequences to the law, it would nevertheless be invalid "because of its intrusion into the function of editors."[3]

considered relevant, [the] overarching focus is directed to the perceived needs of the individual candidate." He called this a "highly skewed approach" and charged the majority with abandoning "the traditionally recognized discretion of the broadcaster." He concluded that "[there] is no basis in the statute for this very broad unworkable scheme of access."

A brief separate dissent by Justice STEVENS (who also joined Justice White's opinion) argued that the FCC's approach here "creates an impermissible risk that the Commission's evaluation of a given refusal by a licensee will be biased—or will appear to be biased—by the character of the office held by the candidate making the request."

1. The scope of the free press guarantee of the First Amendment is considered at greater length in chap. 13, sec. 6, below.

2. The Chief Justice noted two law review articles on the position of "access advocates": Barron, "Access to the Press—A New First Amendment Right," 80 Harv.L.Rev. 1641 (1967), and Lange, "The Role of the Access Doctrine in the Regulation of the Mass Media," 52 N.Car.L.Rev. 1 (1973).

3. In a brief concurring notation, Justice BRENNAN, joined by Justice Rehnquist, noted that the Court "implies no view upon the constitutionality of 'retraction' statutes affording plaintiffs able to prove defamatory falsehoods a statutory action to require publication of a retraction." Justice WHITE also submitted a concurring opinion.

Chapter 13

FREEDOM OF EXPRESSION
IN SOME SPECIAL CONTEXTS

Scope Note. The preceding two chapters considered a range of pervasive, building block themes in First Amendment analysis. This final chapter on free expression presents an opportunity to apply the techniques considered earlier and to examine the relevance of additional variables as well. In many of the contexts that follow, government asserts interests allegedly justifying restraints on expression that go beyond those typically put forth in the earlier chapters. Moreover, in many of the materials below, the First Amendment claimant expresses views in modes that differ, arguably significantly, from those encountered above. Thus, sec. 1 deals with the efforts to regulate the use of money in political campaigns. The "speech" involved is manifested in funds directed to the support of candidates and causes; the typical regulatory interest asserted is that in assuring the integrity and openness of the electoral process. Sec. 2 examines First Amendment claims in a variety of other special environments: schools; the administration of justice; labor picketing; and economic boycotts. Sec. 3 considers the First Amendment right of association, a right allegedly impinged by regulations compelling disclosure of membership lists or restrictions on group activities. In sec. 4, the central problems turn on the special interest government may have in dealing with its own employees, either in compelling disclosure of political associations or in otherwise curtailing the First Amendment activities of the employees. Sec. 5 turns to a special context of governmental demands for information—demands through the legislative investigation process. Sec. 6, finally, surveys a series of problems involving the media. A pervasive question in that section is whether the media are entitled to special protection because, for example, "the press" is separately mentioned in the text of the First Amendment.

SECTION 1. MONEY IN THE POLITICAL CAMPAIGN PROCESS

BUCKLEY v. VALEO

424 U.S. 1, 96 S.Ct. 612, 46 L.Ed.2d 659 (1976).

PER CURIAM.[1]

These appeals present constitutional challenges to the key provisions of the Federal Election Campaign Act of 1971 [and] related provisions, [as] amended in 1974.[2] [The challenged laws] in broad terms [provide]: (a) individual

---

1. The Court of Appeals for the District of Columbia Circuit had sustained almost all provisions of the complex Act. Only Justices Brennan, Stewart, and Powell joined all portions of the per curiam opinion reversing the Court of Appeals judgment in part. There were separate opinions by Chief Justice Burger and Justices White, Marshall, Blackmun and Rehnquist, all joining the opinion in part and dissenting in part,

though in differing respects. Justice Stevens did not participate. Excerpts from the separate opinions are printed below.

2. The Court identified the challengers as follows: "Plaintiffs included a candidate for the Presidency of the United States [Eugene McCarthy], a United States Senator who is a candidate for reelection, a potential contributor, the Com-

political contributions are limited to $1,000 to any single candidate per election, with an overall annual limitation of $25,000 by any contributor; independent expenditures by individuals and groups "relative to a clearly identified candidate" are limited to $1,000 a year; campaign spending by candidates for various federal offices and spending for national conventions by political parties are subject to prescribed limits; (b) contributions and expenditures above certain threshold levels must be reported and publicly disclosed; (c) a system for public funding of Presidential campaign activities is established; [and] (d) a Federal Election Commission is established to administer and enforce the [Act].

[The majority summarized its conclusions as follows: "[W]e sustain the individual contribution limits, the disclosure and reporting provisions, and the public financing scheme. We conclude, however, that the limitations on campaign expenditures, on independent expenditures by individuals and groups, and on expenditures by a candidate from his personal funds are constitutionally infirm." Moreover, the composition of the Federal Election Commission was held unconstitutional. The excerpts that follow focus on the contribution and expenditure provisions. Other parts of the decision are noted elsewhere in this book.[3]

I.   *Contribution and Expenditure [Limitations].*

A.   *General Principles.* The Act's contribution and expenditure limitations operate in an area of the most fundamental First Amendment activities. Discussion of public issues and debate on the qualifications of candidates are integral to the operation of the system of government established by our Constitution. [In] upholding the constitutional validity of the Act's contribution and expenditure provisions on the ground that those provisions should be viewed as regulating conduct not speech, the Court of Appeals relied upon United States v. O'Brien. [We] cannot share the view that the present Act's contribution and expenditure limitations are comparable to the restrictions on conduct upheld in O'Brien. The expenditure of money simply cannot be equated with such conduct as destruction of a draft card. Some forms of communication made possible by the giving and spending of money involve speech alone, some involve conduct primarily, and some involve a combination of the two. Yet, this Court has never suggested that the dependence of a communication on the expenditure of money operates itself to introduce a nonspeech element or to reduce the exacting scrutiny required by the [First Amendment].

Even if the categorization of the expenditure of money as conduct were accepted, the limitations challenged here would not meet the O'Brien test because the governmental interests advanced in support of the Act involve "suppressing communication." The interests served by the Act include restricting the voices of people and interest groups who have money to spend and reducing the overall scope of federal election campaigns. Although the Act does not focus on the ideas expressed by persons or groups subjected to its regulations, it is aimed in part at equalizing the relative ability of all voters to affect electoral outcomes by placing a ceiling on expenditures for political expression by citizens and groups. Unlike [the situation in O'Brien], it is beyond dispute that the interest in regulating the alleged "conduct" of giving or spending money "arises in some measure because the communication allegedly integral to the conduct is itself thought to be harmful." Nor can the Act's

mittee for a Constitutional Presidency-McCarthy '76, the Conservative Party of the State of New York, the Mississippi Republican Party, the Libertarian Party, the New York Civil Liberties Union, Inc., the American Conservative Union, the Conservative Victory Fund, and Human Events, Inc." [Among the organizations filing

amici curiae briefs was the Socialist Labor Party.]

3. See especially the excerpts from the discussion of the disclosure provisions, at p. 1387 below. On the unconstitutionality of the composition of the Commission under the Appointments Clause, Art. II, § 2, cl. 2, see chap. 6, p. 378 above.

contribution and expenditure limitations be sustained [by] reference to the constitutional principles reflected in such decisions as Cox v. Louisiana II, Adderley v. Florida, and Kovacs v. Cooper. [The] critical difference between this case and those time, place and manner cases is that the present Act's contribution and expenditure limitations impose direct quantity restrictions on political communication and association by persons, groups, candidates and political parties in addition to any reasonable time, place, and manner regulations otherwise imposed.[4]

A restriction on the amount of money a person or group can spend on political communication during a campaign necessarily reduces the quantity of expression by restricting the number of issues discussed, the depth of their exploration, and the size of the audience reached.[5] This is because virtually every means of communicating ideas in today's mass society requires the expenditure of money. [The] expenditure limitations contained in the Act represent substantial rather than merely theoretical restraints on the quantity and diversity of political speech. [E.g., the] $1,000 ceiling on spending "relative to a clearly identified candidate" would appear to exclude all citizens and groups except candidates, political parties and the institutional press from any significant use of the most effective means of [communication].

By contrast with a limitation upon expenditures for political expression, a limitation upon the amount that any one person or group may contribute to a candidate or political committee entails only a marginal restriction upon the contributor's ability to engage in free communication. A contribution serves as a general expression of support for the candidate and his views, but does not communicate the underlying basis for the support. The quantity of communication by the contributor does not increase perceptibly with the size of his contribution, since the expression rests solely on the undifferentiated, symbolic act of contributing. At most, the size of the contribution provides a very rough index of the intensity of the contributor's support for the candidate. A limitation on the amount of money a person may give to a candidate or campaign organization thus involves little direct restraint on his political communication, for it permits the symbolic expression of support evidenced by a contribution but does not in any way infringe the contributor's freedom to discuss candidates and issues. While contributions may result in political expression if spent by a candidate or an association to present views to the voters, the transformation of contributions into political debate involves speech by someone other than the contributor.

Given the important role of contributions in financing political campaigns, contribution restrictions could have a severe impact on political dialogue if the limitations prevented candidates and political committees from amassing the resources necessary for effective advocacy. There is no indication, however, that the contribution limitations imposed by the Act would have any dramatic adverse effect on the funding of campaigns and political associations.[6] The

---

4. The nongovernmental appellees argue that just as the decibels emitted by a sound truck can be regulated consistent with the First Amendment, Kovacs, the Act may restrict the volume of dollars in political campaigns without impermissibly restricting freedom of speech. See Freund, Commentary, in A. Rosenthal, Federal Regulation of Campaign Finance: Some Constitutional Questions 72 (1971). This comparison underscores a fundamental misconception. The decibel restriction upheld in Kovacs limited the *manner* of operating a sound truck but not the *extent* of its proper use. By contrast, the Act's dollar ceilings restrict the extent of the reasonable use

of virtually every means of communicating information. [Footnote by the Court.]

5. Being free to engage in unlimited political expression subject to a ceiling on expenditures is like being free to drive an automobile as far and as often as one desires on a single tank of gasoline. [Footnote by the Court.]

6. Statistical findings agreed to by the parties reveal that approximately 5.1% of the $73,483,613 raised by the 1161 candidates for Congress in 1974 was obtained in amounts in excess of $1,000. In 1974, two major-party senatorial candidates, Ramsey Clark and Senator

overall effect of the Act's contribution ceilings is merely to require candidates and political committees to raise funds from a greater number of persons and to compel people who would otherwise contribute amounts greater than the statutory limits to expend such funds on direct political expression, rather than to reduce the total amount of money potentially available to promote political expression.

The Act's contribution and expenditure limitations also impinge on protected associational freedoms [see sec. 3 below]. Making a contribution, like joining a political party, serves to affiliate a person with a candidate. In addition, it enables likeminded persons to pool their resources in furtherance of common political goals. The Act's contribution ceilings thus limit one important means of associating with a candidate or committee, but leave the contributor free to become a member of any political association and to assist personally in the association's efforts on behalf of candidates. And the Act's contribution limitations permit associations and candidates to aggregate large sums of money to promote effective advocacy. By contrast, the Act's $1,000 limitation on independent expenditures "relative to a clearly identified candidate" precludes most associations from effectively amplifying the voice of their adherents. [In] sum, although the Act's contribution and expenditure limitations both implicate fundamental First Amendment interests, its expenditure ceilings impose significantly more severe restrictions on protected freedoms of political expression and association than do its limitations on financial contributions.

B. *Contribution Limitations.* 1. *The $1,000 Limitation on Contributions by Individuals and Groups to Candidates and Authorized Campaign Committees.* [T]he primary First Amendment problem raised by the Act's contribution limitations is their restriction of one aspect of the contributor's freedom of political association. [G]overnmental "action which may have the effect of curtailing the freedom to associate is subject to the closest scrutiny." NAACP v. Alabama [1958; p. 1350 below]. Yet, [e]ven a " 'significant interference' with protected rights of political association" may be sustained if the State demonstrates a sufficiently important interest and employs means closely drawn to avoid unnecessary abridgment of associational [freedoms].

It is unnecessary to look beyond the Act's primary purpose—to limit the actuality and appearance of corruption resulting from large individual financial contributions—in order to find a constitutionally sufficient justification for the $1,000 contribution limitation. [To] the extent that large contributions are given to secure political quid pro quos from current and potential officeholders, the integrity of our system of representative democracy is undermined. Although the scope of such pernicious practices can never be reliably ascertained, the deeply disturbing examples surfacing after the 1972 election demonstrate that the problem is not an illusory one. [Of] almost equal concern as the danger of actual quid pro quo arrangements is the impact of the appearance of corruption stemming from public awareness of the opportunities for abuse inherent in a regime of large individual financial contributions. [Appellants] contend that the contribution limitations must be invalidated because bribery laws and narrowly-drawn disclosure requirements constitute a less restrictive means of dealing with "proven and suspected quid pro quo arrangements." But laws making criminal the giving and taking of bribes deal with only the most blatant and specific attempts of those with money to influence governmental action. And [Congress] was surely entitled to conclude that disclosure was only a partial measure, and that contribution ceilings were a necessary legislative concomitant to deal with the reality or appearance of [corruption].

Charles Mathias, Jr., operated large-scale campaigns on contributions raised under a voluntarily imposed $100 contribution limitation. [Footnote by the Court.]

The Act's $1,000 contribution limitation focuses precisely on the problem of large campaign contributions—the narrow aspect of political association where the actuality and potential for corruption have been identified—while leaving persons free to engage in independent political expression, to associate actively through volunteering their services, and to assist to a limited but nonetheless substantial extent in supporting candidates and committees with financial resources. Significantly, the Act's contribution limitations in themselves do not undermine to any material degree the potential for robust and effective discussion of candidates and campaign issues by individual citizens, associations, the institutional press, candidates, and political parties. We find that, under the rigorous standard of review established by our prior decisions, the weighty interests served by restricting the size of financial contributions to political candidates are sufficient to justify the limited effect upon First Amendment freedoms caused by the $1,000 contribution ceiling.

Appellants' first overbreadth challenge to the contribution ceilings rests on the proposition that most large contributors do not seek improper influence over a candidate's position or an officeholder's action. Although the truth of that proposition may be assumed, it does not undercut the validity of the $1,000 contribution limitation. Not only is it difficult to isolate suspect contributions but, more importantly, Congress was justified in concluding that the interest in safeguarding against the appearance of impropriety requires that the opportunity for abuse inherent in the process of raising large monetary contributions be eliminated. A second, related overbreadth claim is that the $1,000 restriction is unrealistically low because much more than that amount would still not be enough to enable an unscrupulous contributor to exercise improper influence over a candidate or officeholder, especially in campaigns for statewide or national office. While the contribution limitation provisions might well have been structured to take account of the graduated expenditure limitations for House, Senate and Presidential campaigns, Congress' failure to engage in such fine tuning does not invalidate the [legislation].

Apart from these First Amendment concerns, appellants argue that the contribution limitations work such an invidious discrimination between incumbents and challengers that the statutory provisions must be declared unconstitutional on their face. There is [no] evidence to support the claim that the contribution limitations in themselves discriminate against major-party challengers to incumbents. The charge of discrimination against minor-party and independent candidates is more troubling, but the record provides no basis for concluding that the Act invidiously disadvantages such candidates. [T]he restriction would appear to benefit minor-party and independent candidates relative to their major-party opponents because major-party candidates receive far more money in large contributions. Although there is some force to appellants' response that minor-party candidates are primarily concerned with their ability to amass the resources necessary to reach the electorate rather than with their funding position relative to their major-party opponents, the record is virtually devoid of support for the claim that the $1,000 contribution limitation will have a serious effect on the initiation and scope of minor-party and independent [candidacies]. [The Court also rejected similar challenges to the $5000 limit on contributions by "political committees," the limits on volunteers' incidental expenses, and the $25,000 limit on total contributions by an individual during a calendar year.]

C. *Expenditure Limitations.* The Act's expenditure ceilings impose direct and substantial restraints on the quantity of political speech. [It] is clear that a primary effect of these expenditure limitations is to restrict the quantity of campaign speech by individuals, groups, and candidates. The restrictions, while neutral as to the ideas expressed, limit political expression "at the core of our electoral process and of First Amendment freedoms."

1. *The $1,000 limitation on expenditures "relative to a clearly identified candidate."* Section 608(e)(1) provides that "[n]o person may make any expenditure [relative] to a clearly identified candidate during a calendar year which, when added to all other expenditures made by such person during the year advocating the election or defeat of such candidate, exceeds $1,000." The plain effect of § 608(e)(1) is to prohibit all individuals, who are neither candidates nor owners of institutional press facilities, and all groups, except political parties and campaign organizations, from voicing their views "relative to a clearly identified candidate" through means that entail aggregate expenditures of more than $1,000 during a calendar year. The provision, for example, would make it a federal criminal offense for a person or association to place a single one-quarter page advertisement "relative to a clearly identified candidate" in a major metropolitan [newspaper].

[Unconstitutional vagueness] can be avoided only by reading § 608(e)(1) as limited to communications that include explicit words of advocacy of election or defeat of a candidate. [We] turn then to the basic First Amendment question— whether § 608(e)(1), even as thus narrowly and explicitly construed, impermissibly burdens the constitutional right of free expression. The Court of Appeals summarily held the provision constitutionally valid on the ground that "section 608(e) is a loophole-closing provision only" that is necessary to prevent circumvention of the contribution limitations. We cannot agree. [T]he constitutionality of § 608(e)(1) turns on whether the governmental interests advanced in its support satisfy the exacting scrutiny applicable to limitations on core First Amendment rights of political expression.

We find that the governmental interest in preventing corruption and the appearance of corruption is inadequate to justify § 608(e)(1)'s ceiling on independent expenditures. First, assuming arguendo that large independent expenditures pose the same dangers of actual or apparent quid pro quo arrangements as do large contributions, § 608(e)(1) does not provide an answer that sufficiently relates to the elimination of those dangers. Unlike the contribution limitations' total ban on the giving of large amounts of money to candidates, § 608(e)(1) prevents only some large expenditures. So long as persons and groups eschew expenditures that in express terms advocate the election or defeat of a clearly identified candidate, they are free to spend as much as they want to promote the candidate and his views. [It] would naively underestimate the ingenuity and resourcefulness of persons and groups desiring to buy influence to believe that they would have much difficulty devising expenditures that skirted the restriction on express advocacy of election or defeat but nevertheless benefited the candidate's campaign. [Second], the independent advocacy restricted by the provision does not presently appear to pose dangers of real or apparent corruption comparable to those identified with large campaign contributions. The parties defending § 608(e)(1) contend that it is necessary to prevent would-be contributors from avoiding the contribution limitations by the simple expedient of paying directly for media advertisements or for other portions of the candidate's campaign activities. [But] controlled or coordinated expenditures are treated as contributions rather than expenditures under the Act [and are restricted by the valid § 608(b)]. By contrast, § 608(e)(1) limits expenditures for express advocacy of candidates made totally independently of the candidate and his campaign. Unlike contributions, such independent expenditures may well provide little assistance to the candidate's campaign and indeed may prove counterproductive. The absence of prearrangement and coordination of an expenditure with the candidate or his agent not only undermines the value of the expenditure to the candidate, but also alleviates the danger that expenditures will be given as a quid pro quo for improper commitments from the candidate. Rather than preventing circumvention of the contribution limitations, § 608(e)(1) severely restricts all independent advocacy despite its substantially diminished potential for abuse. While the independent expenditure ceiling thus fails to serve any substantial governmental interest in stemming the reality or appearance of corruption in the electoral process, it heavily burdens core First Amendment expression. [Advocacy] of the election or defeat of candidates for federal office is no less entitled to protection under the First Amendment than the discussion of political policy generally or advocacy of the passage or defeat of legislation.

It is argued, however, that the ancillary governmental interest in equalizing the relative ability of individuals and groups to influence the outcome of elections serves to justify [this limitation]. But the concept that government may restrict the speech of some elements of our society in order to enhance the relative voice of others is wholly foreign to the First Amendment, which was designed "to secure 'the widest possible dissemination of information from diverse and antagonistic sources,'" and "'to assure unfettered interchange of ideas for the bringing about of political and social changes desired by the people.'" New York Times v. Sullivan. The First Amendment's protection against governmental abridgment of free expression cannot properly be made to depend on a person's financial ability to engage in public discussion.

The Court's decisions in Mills v. Alabama, 384 U.S. 214 (1966), and in Tornillo [1974; p. 1300 above)] held that legislative restrictions on advocacy of the election or defeat of political candidates are wholly at odds with the guarantees of the First Amendment. In Mills, the Court addressed the question whether "a State [can] make it a crime for the editor of a daily newspaper to write and publish an editorial *on election day* urging people to vote a certain way on issues submitted to them." We held that "no test of reasonableness could save [such] a state law from invalidation as a violation of the First Amendment." Yet the prohibition on election day editorials invalidated in Mills is clearly a lesser intrusion on constitutional freedom than a $1,000 limitation on the amount of money any person or association can spend *during an entire election year* in advocating the election or defeat of a candidate for public office. [The] legislative restraint [invalidated] in Tornillo [also] pales in comparison to the limitations imposed by § 608(e)(1). [We] conclude that § 608(e)(1)'s independent expenditure limitation is unconstitutional under the First Amendment.

2. *Limitation on expenditures by candidates from personal or family resources.* The Act also sets limits on expenditures by a candidate "from his personal funds, or the personal funds of his immediate family, in connection with his campaigns during any calendar year." § 608(a)(1). These ceilings vary from $50,000 for Presidential or Vice Presidential candidates to $35,000 for Senate candidates, and $25,000 for most candidates for the House of Representatives. [The] candidate, no less than any other person, has a First Amendment right to engage in the discussion of public issues and vigorously and tirelessly to advocate his own election and the election of other candidates. [The] ceiling on personal expenditures by a candidate in furtherance of his own candidacy thus clearly and directly interferes with constitutionally protected freedoms. The primary governmental interest served by the Act—the prevention of actual and apparent corruption of the political process—does not support the limitation on the candidate's expenditure of his own personal funds. [T]he use of personal funds reduces the candidate's dependence on outside contributions and thereby counteracts the coercive pressures and attendant risks of abuse to which the Act's contribution limitations are directed.

The ancillary interest in equalizing the relative financial resources of candidates competing for elective office, therefore, provides the sole relevant rationale for Section 608(a)'s expenditure ceiling. That interest is clearly not sufficient to justify the provision's infringement of fundamental First Amendment rights. First, the limitation may fail to promote financial equality among candidates. A candidate who spends less of his personal resources on his campaign may nonetheless outspend his rival as a result of more successful fundraising efforts. Indeed, a candidate's personal wealth may impede his efforts to persuade others that he needs their financial contributions or volunteer efforts to conduct an effective campaign. Second, and more fundamentally, the First Amendment simply cannot tolerate § 608(a)'s restriction upon the freedom of a candidate to speak without legislative limit on behalf of his own [candidacy].

3. *Limitations on campaign expenditures.* Section 608(c) of the Act places limitations on overall campaign expenditures by candidates seeking nomination for election and election to federal office. Presidential candidates may spend $10,000,000 in seeking nomination for office and an additional $20,000,000 in the general election campaign. [There are also ceilings for campaigns for the House and Senate.] [No] governmental interest that has been suggested is sufficient to justify [these restrictions] on the quantity of political expression. [The] campaign expenditure ceilings appear to be designed primarily to serve the governmental interests in reducing the allegedly skyrocketing costs of political campaigns. [T]he mere growth in the cost of federal election campaigns in and of itself provides no basis for governmental restrictions on the quantity of campaign spending and the resulting limitation on the scope of federal campaigns. The First Amendment denies government the power to determine that spending to promote one's political views is wasteful, excessive, or unwise. In the free society ordained by our Constitution it is not the government but the people—individually as citizens and candidates and collectively as associations and political committees—who must retain control over the quantity and range of debate on public issues in a political campaign.[7] [W]e hold that § 608(c) is constitutionally invalid.

In sum, the [contribution limits] are constitutionally valid. These limitations along with the disclosure provisions, constitute the Act's primary weapons against the reality or appearance of improper influence stemming from the dependence of candidates on large campaign contributions. The contribution ceilings thus serve the basic governmental interest in safeguarding the integrity of the electoral process without directly impinging upon the rights of individual citizens and candidates to engage in political debate and discussion. By

7. For the reasons discussed in Part III, Congress may engage in public financing of election campaigns and may condition acceptance of public funds on an agreement by the candidate to abide by specified expenditure limitations. Just as a candidate may voluntarily limit the size of the contributions he chooses to accept, he may decide to forego private fundraising and accept public funding. [Footnote by the Court.]

[In Part III, the Court sustained the provisions for public financing of Presidential election campaigns. It rejected the argument that the law was not spending for the "general welfare" under Art. I, § 8 (see chap. 4 above). Moreover, it rejected the claim that, by analogy to the religion clauses of the First Amendment (see the next chapter), public financing of election campaigns violated the First Amendment. The Court replied: "[T]he analogy is patently inapplicable to our issue here [because the law] furthers, not abridges, pertinent First Amendment values." Moreover, the Court rejected a series of equal

protection attacks on public financing. The Court found no unconstitutional discrimination against candidates of minor and new parties and noted that "public financing is generally less restrictive of access to the electoral process than the ballot-access regulations dealt with in prior cases." (Recall chap. 9, sec. 4, above.)

[Chief Justice Burger and Justice Rehnquist dissented from the upholding of the public financing provisions. The Chief Justice emphasized that the inappropriateness of federal subsidies to political campaigns was "as basic to our national tradition as the separation of church and state [or] the separation of civilian and military authority." Justice Rehnquist emphasized that the scheme invidiously discriminated against minor parties. He argued that Congress had "enshrined the Republican and Democratic parties in a permanently preferred position." (Recall the note on government speech in the preceding chapter, at p. 1276 above.)]

contrast, the First Amendment requires the invalidation of the Act's independent expenditure ceiling, its limitation on a candidate's expenditures from his own personal funds, and its ceilings on overall campaign expenditures. These provisions place substantial and direct restrictions on the ability of candidates, citizens, and associations to engage in protected political expression, restrictions that the First Amendment cannot [tolerate].

Affirmed in part and reversed in part.

Mr. Chief Justice BURGER, concurring in part and dissenting [in part].

Contribution and expenditure limits. I agree fully with that part of the Court's opinion that holds unconstitutional the limitations the Act puts on campaign expenditures. [Yet] when it approves similarly stringent limitations on contributions, the Court ignores the reasons it finds so persuasive in the context of expenditures. For me contributions and expenditures are two sides of the same First Amendment [coin]. The Court attempts to separate the two communicative aspects of political contributions—the "moral" support that the gift itself conveys, which the Court suggests is the same whether the gift is of $10 or $10,000, and the fact that money translates into communication. The Court dismisses the effect of the limitations on the second aspect of contributions. [On the premise] that contribution limitations restrict only the speech of "someone other than the contributor" [rests] the Court's justification for treating contributions differently from expenditures. The premise is demonstrably flawed; the contribution limitations will, in specific instances, limit exactly the same political activity that the expenditure ceilings limit, and at least one of the "expenditure" limitations the Court finds objectionable operates precisely like the "contribution" limitations.[1] The Court's attempt to distinguish the communication inherent in political *contributions* from the speech aspects of political *expenditures* simply will not wash. We do little but engage in word games unless we recognize that people—candidates and contributors—spend money on political activity because they wish to communicate ideas, and their constitutional interest in doing so is precisely the same whether they or someone else utter the words. The Court attempts to make the Act seem less restrictive by casting the problem as one that goes to freedom of association rather than freedom of speech. I have long thought freedom of association and freedom of expression were two peas from the same pod. [It] is not simply speculation to think that the limitations on contributions will foreclose some candidacies.[2] The limitations will also alter the nature of some electoral contests drastically.

At any rate, the contribution limits are a far more severe restriction on First Amendment activity than the sort of "chilling" legislation for which the Court has shown such extraordinary concern in the past. [After] a bow to the "weighty interests" Congress meant to serve, the Court then forsakes this analysis in one sentence: "Congress was surely entitled to conclude that disclosure was only a partial measure, and that contribution ceilings were a necessary legislative concomitant to deal with the reality or appearance of corruption." In striking down the limitations on campaign expenditures, the Court relies in part on its conclusion that other means—namely, disclosure and contribution ceilings—will adequately serve the statute's aim. It is not clear why the same analysis is not also appropriate in weighing the need for

---

1. The Court treats the Act's provisions limiting a candidate's spending from his personal resources as *expenditure* limits, as indeed the Act characterizes them, and holds them unconstitutional. As Mr. Justice Marshall points out, infra, by the Court's logic these provisions could as easily be treated as limits on *contributions,* since they limit what the candidate can give to his own campaign. [Footnote by Chief Justice Burger.]

2. Candidates who must raise large initial contributions in order to appeal for more funds to a broader audience will be handicapped. It is not enough to say that the contribution ceilings "merely require candidates [to] raise funds from a greater number of persons," where the limitations will effectively prevent candidates without substantial personal resources from doing just that. [Footnote by Chief Justice Burger.]

contribution ceilings in addition to disclosure requirements. Congress may well be entitled to conclude that disclosure was a "partial measure," but I had not thought until today that Congress could enact its conclusions in the First Amendment area into laws immune from the most searching review by this [Court].

Finally, it seems clear to me that in approving these limitations on contributions the Court must rest upon the proposition that "pooling" money is fundamentally different from other forms of associational or joint activity. I see only two possible ways in which money differs from volunteer work, endorsements, and the like. Money can be used to buy favors, because an unscrupulous politician can put it to personal use; second, giving money is a less visible form of associational activity. With respect to the first problem, the Act does not attempt to do any more than the bribery laws to combat this sort of corruption. In fact, the Act does not reach at all, and certainly the contribution limits do not reach, forms of "association" that can be fully as corrupt as a contribution intended as a quid pro quo—such as the eleventh hour endorsement by a former rival, obtained for the promise of a federal appointment. [As to the second problem, disclosure laws are the "wholly efficacious" answer.][3]

Mr. Justice WHITE, concurring in part and dissenting [in part].

I dissent [from] the Court's view that the expenditure limitations [violate] the First Amendment. Concededly, neither the limitations on contributions nor those on expenditures directly or indirectly purport to control the content of political speech by candidates or by their supporters or detractors. What the Act regulates is giving and spending money, acts that have First Amendment significance not because they are themselves communicative with respect to the qualifications of the candidate, but because money may be used to defray the expenses of speaking or otherwise communicating about the merits or demerits of federal candidates for election. The act of giving money to political candidates, however, may have illegal or other undesirable consequences: it may be used to secure the express or tacit understanding that the giver will enjoy political favor if the candidate is elected. Both Congress and this Court's cases have recognized this as a moral danger against which effective preventive and curative steps must be taken.

Since the contribution and expenditure limitations are neutral as to the content of speech and are not motivated by fear of the consequences of the political speech of particular candidates or of political speech in general, this case depends on whether the nonspeech interests of the Federal Government in regulating the use of money in political campaigns are sufficiently urgent to justify the incidental effects that the limitations visit upon the First Amendment interests of candidates and their supporters. Despite its seeming struggle with the standard by which to judge this case, this is essentially the question the Court asks and answers in the affirmative with respect to the limitations on contributions. [The] Court thus accepts the congressional judgment that the evils of unlimited contributions are sufficiently threatening to warrant restriction regardless of the impact of the limits on the contributor's opportunity for effective speech and in turn on the total volume of the candidate's political communications by reason of his inability to accept large sums from those willing to give.

The congressional judgment, which I would also accept, was that other steps must be taken to counter the corrosive effects of money in federal election campaigns. One of these steps is § 608(e) [the expenditure limits]. Congress

---

3. In a separate opinion, Justice BLACK-MUN also dissented from the majority's upholding of the contribution restrictions. He found no "principled constitutional distinction" between limits on contributions and limits on expenditures and concluded: "I therefore do not join Part I–B of the Court's opinion or those portions of Part I–A that are consistent with Part I–B."

was plainly of the view that these expenditures also have corruptive potential; but the Court strikes down the provision, strangely enough claiming more insight as to what may improperly influence candidates than is possessed by the majority of Congress that passed this Bill and the President who signed it. [It] would make little sense to me, and apparently made none to Congress, to limit the amounts an individual may give to a candidate or spend with his approval but fail to limit the amounts that could be spent on his behalf. Yet the Court permits the former while striking down the latter [limitation]. Let us suppose that each of two brothers spends one million dollars on TV spot announcements that he has individually prepared and in which he appears, urging the election of the same named candidate in identical words. One brother has sought and obtained the approval of the candidate; the other has not. The former may validly be prosecuted under § 608(e); under the Court's view, the latter may not, even though the candidate could scarcely help knowing about and appreciating the expensive favor. For constitutional purposes it is difficult to see the difference between the two situations. I would take the word of those who know—that limiting independent expenditures is essential to prevent transparent and widespread evasion of the contribution limits.

In sustaining the contribution limits, the Court recognizes the importance of avoiding public misapprehension about a candidate's reliance on large contributions. It ignores that consideration in invalidating § 608(e). In like fashion, it says that Congress was entitled to determine that the criminal provisions against bribery and corruption, together with the disclosure provisions, would not in themselves be adequate to combat the evil and that limits on contributions should be provided. Here, the Court rejects the identical kind of judgment made by Congress as to the need for and utility of expenditure limits. I would not do so.

The Court also rejects Congress' judgment manifested in § 608(c) that the federal interest in limiting total campaign expenditures by individual candidates justifies the incidental effect on their opportunity for effective political speech. I disagree both with the Court's assessment of the impact on speech and with its narrow view of the values the limitations will serve. [As] an initial matter, the argument that money is speech and that limiting the flow of money to the speaker violates the First Amendment proves entirely too much. Compulsory bargaining and the right to strike, both provided for or protected by federal law, inevitably have increased the labor costs of those who publish newspapers, which are in turn an important factor in the recent disappearance of many daily papers. [Justice White also referred to tax, antitrust, and price control legislation.] But it has not been suggested, nor could it be successfully, that these laws, and many others, are invalid because they siphon off or prevent the accumulation of large sums that would otherwise be available for communicative activities.

In any [event], money is not always equivalent to or used for speech, even in the context of political campaigns. There [are] many expensive campaign activities that are not themselves communicative or remotely related to speech. Furthermore, campaigns differ among themselves. Some seem to spend much less money than others and yet communicate as much or more than those supported by enormous bureaucracies with unlimited financing. The record before us no more supports the conclusion that the communicative efforts of congressional and Presidential candidates will be crippled by the expenditure limitations than it supports the contrary. The judgment of Congress was that reasonably effective campaigns could be conducted within the limits established by the Act and that the communicative efforts of these campaigns would not seriously suffer. In this posture of the case, there is no sound basis for invalidating the expenditure limitations, so long as the purposes they serve are legitimate and sufficiently substantial, which in my view they are.

In the first place, expenditure ceilings reinforce the contribution limits and help eradicate the hazard of corruption. [It] should be added that many successful candidates would also be saved from large, overhanging campaign debts which must be paid off with money raised while holding public office and at a time when they are already preparing or thinking about the next campaign. The danger to the public interest in such situations is self-evident. Besides backing up the contribution [limits], expenditure limits have their own potential for preventing the corruption of federal elections themselves. [The] corrupt use of money by candidates is as much to be feared as the corrosive influence of large contributions. [I] have little doubt in addition that limiting the total that can be spent will ease the candidate's understandable obsession with fundraising, and so free him and his staff to communicate in more places and ways unconnected with the fundraising function. [It] is also important to restore and maintain public confidence in federal elections. It is critical to obviate or dispel the impression that federal elections are purely and simply a function of money, that federal offices are bought and sold or that political races are reserved for those who have the facility—and the stomach—for doing whatever it takes to bring together those interests, groups, and individuals that can raise or contribute large fortunes in order to prevail at the polls. The ceiling on candidate expenditures represents the considered judgment of Congress that elections are to be decided among candidates none of whom has an overpowering advantage by reason of a huge campaign war chest. At least so long as the ceiling placed upon the candidates is not plainly too low, elections are not to turn on the difference in the amounts of money that candidates have to spend. This seems an acceptable purpose and the means chosen a common sense way to achieve [it].

I also disagree with the Court's judgment that § 608(a), which limits the amount of money that a candidate or his family may spend on his campaign, violates the Constitution. Although it is true that this provision does not promote any interest in preventing the corruption of candidates, the provision does, nevertheless, serve salutary purposes related to the integrity of federal campaigns. By limiting the importance of personal wealth, § 608(a) helps to assure that only individuals with a modicum of support from others will be viable candidates. This in turn would tend to discourage any notion that the outcome of elections is primarily a function of money. Similarly, § 608(a) tends to equalize access to the political arena, encouraging the less wealthy, unable to bankroll their own campaigns, to run for political office. As with the campaign expenditure limits, Congress was entitled to determine that personal wealth ought to play a less important role in political campaigns than it has in the past. Nothing in the First Amendment stands in the way of that [determination].[4]

---

4. In another separate opinion, Justice MARSHALL dissented from that part of the Court's opinion which prohibited limiting the amount a candidate may spend from his own funds. He emphasized the governmental interest "in promoting the reality and appearance of equal access to the political arena," insisting that even if the wealthy candidate's initial advantage can be overcome, "the perception that personal wealth wins elections may not only discourage potential candidates without significant personal wealth [but] also undermine public confidence in the integrity of the electoral process." (He noted: "In the Nation's seven largest States in 1970, 11 of the 15 major senatorial candidates were millionaires. The four who were not millionaires lost their bid for election.") He added that the concern about the appearance that only the wealthy can become candidates was heightened by the impact of the contribution limits sustained by the Court: "Large contributions are the less wealthy candidate's only hope of countering the wealthy candidate's immediate access to substantial sums of money. With that option removed, the less wealthy candidate is without the means to match the large initial expenditures of money of which

CALIFORNIA MEDICAL ASSN. v. FEC, 453 U.S. 182 (1981): Certain provisions of the Federal Election Campaign Act limit the amount an unincorporated association may contribute to a multicandidate political committee. In California Medical Association v. FEC, the Court rejected constitutional challenges to these provisions. The central target of the attack was 2 U.S.C. § 441a(a)(1)(C), which prohibits individuals and unincorporated associations from contributing more than $5,000 per calendar year to any multicandidate political committee.[1] This provision was challenged by the California Medical Association (CMA), a not-for-profit unincorporated association of approximately 25,000 California physicians. CMA had formed the California Medical Political Action Committee (CALPAC), a multicandidate political committee within the meaning of the Act. The Federal Election Commission claimed that CMA had violated the Act by making annual contributions to CALPAC in excess of $5,000. CMA's defense relied mainly on the First Amendment and the alleged implications of Buckley v. Valeo. The Court rejected the First Amendment claim, but could not muster a majority opinion to justify its judgment. Justice Marshall submitted a plurality opinion, joined by Justices Brennan, White and Stevens. Justice Blackmun's concurring opinion, resting on a different analysis, was necessary to achieve the majority result.[2]

In disposing of the First Amendment challenge, Justice MARSHALL stated: "Although the $5,000 annual limit [on] the amount that individuals and unincorporated associations may contribute to political committees is, strictly speaking, a contribution limitation [and although Buckley sustained several contribution limitations], appellants seek to bring their challenge [within] the reasoning of Buckley. First, they contend that § 441a(a)(1)(C) is akin to an unconstitutional expenditure limitation because it restricts the ability of CMA to engage in political speech through a political committee, CALPAC. Appellants further contend that even if the challenged provision is viewed as a contribution limitation, it is qualitatively different from the contribution restrictions we upheld in Buckley. Specifically, appellants assert that because the contributions here flow to a political committee, rather than to a candidate, the danger of actual or apparent corruption of the political process recognized by this Court in Buckley as a sufficient justification for contribution restrictions is not present in this case.

"While these contentions have some surface appeal, they are in the end unpersuasive. The type of expenditures that this Court in Buckley considered constitutionally protected were those made *independently* by a candidate, individ-

---

the wealthy candidate is capable. In short, the limitations on contributions put a premium on a candidate's personal wealth." Accordingly, the restriction on candidates' use of their own resources was not merely a device to reduce the natural advantages of the wealthy, but "a provision providing some symmetry to a regulatory scheme that otherwise enhances the natural advantage of the wealthy. Regardless of whether the goal of equalizing access would justify a legislative limit on personal candidate expenditures standing by itself, I think it clear that goal justifies [the limits here] when they are considered in conjunction with the remainder of the Act."

The Court's ruling in Buckley v. Valeo spurred extensive commentary. See, e.g., Polsby, "Buckley v. Valeo: The Special Nature of Political Speech," 1976 Sup.Ct.Rev. 1; Wright, "Politics and the Constitution: Is Money Speech?" 85 Yale L.J. 1001 (1976); and Clagett & Bolton, "Buckley v. Valeo: Its Aftermath and its [Pros-

pects]," 29 Vand.L.Rev. 1327 (1976). In examining the case, consider especially whether the Court applied a lower level of scrutiny to the contribution limitations than it did to the expenditure ones, and whether that difference is persuasively explained by the Court.

1. A related provision of the Act makes it unlawful for political committees to knowingly accept contributions exceeding this limit.

The Act defines a "multicandidate political committee" as a "political committee [which] has received contributions from more than 50 persons, and [has] made contributions to 5 or more candidates for Federal Office."

2. Justice STEWART's dissent, joined by Chief Justice Burger and Justices Powell and Rehnquist, argued that, under the complex judicial review provisions of the Act, the Court lacked authority to review, given the posture of the case. The dissenters accordingly did not reach the merits.

ual or group in order to engage directly in political speech. Nothing in § 441a(a)(1)(C) limits the amount CMA or any of its members may independently expend in order to advocate political views; rather, the statute restrains only the amount that CMA may contribute to CALPAC. Appellants nonetheless insist that CMA's contributions to CALPAC should receive the same constitutional protection as independent expenditures because, according to appellants, this is the manner in which CMA has chosen to engage in political speech.

"We would naturally be hesitant to conclude that CMA's determination to fund CALPAC rather than to engage directly in political advocacy is entirely unprotected by the First Amendment.[3] Nonetheless, the 'speech by proxy' that CMA seeks to achieve through its contributions to CALPAC is not the sort of political advocacy that this Court in Buckley found entitled to full First Amendment protection. CALPAC, as a multicandidate political committee, receives contributions from more than 50 persons during a calendar year. Thus, appellants' claim that CALPAC is merely the mouthpiece of CMA is untenable. CALPAC instead is a separate legal entity that receives funds from multiple sources and that engages in independent political advocacy. Of course, CMA would probably not contribute to CALPAC unless it agreed with the views espoused by CALPAC, but this sympathy of interests alone does not convert CALPAC's speech into that of CMA.

"Our decision in Buckley precludes any argument to the contrary. In that case, the limitations on the amount individuals could contribute to candidates and campaign organizations were challenged on the ground that they limited the ability of the contributor to express his political views, albeit through the speech of another. The Court, in dismissing the claim, noted: 'While contributions may result in political expression if spent by a candidate or an association to present views to the voters, the transformation of contributions into political debate *involves speech by someone other than the contributors.*' (Emphasis added). This analysis controls the instant case. If the First Amendment rights of a contributor are not infringed by limitations on the amount he may contribute to a campaign organization which advocates the views and candidacy of a particular candidate, the rights of a contributor are similarly not impaired by limits on the amount he may give to a multicandidate political committee, such as CALPAC, which advocates the views and candidacies of a number of candidates.[4]

"We also disagree with appellants' claim that the contribution restriction challenged here does not further the governmental interest in preventing the actual or apparent corruption of the political process. Congress enacted § 441a(a)(1)(C) in part to prevent circumvention of the very limitations on contributions that this Court upheld in Buckley. Under the Act, individuals and unincorporated associations such as CMA may not contribute more than $1,000 to any single candidate in any calendar year. Moreover, individuals may not make more than $25,000 in aggregate annual political contributions. If appellants' position—that Congress cannot prohibit individuals and unincorporated associations from making unlimited contributions to multicandidate political

---

3. "In Buckley, this Court concluded that the act of contribution involved some limited element of protected speech. [Under the Buckley analysis], CMA's contributions to CALPAC symbolize CMA's general approval of CALPAC's role in the political process. However, this attenuated form of speech does not resemble the direct political advocacy to which this Court in Buckley accorded substantial constitutional protection." [Footnote by Justice Marshall.]

4. "Amicus American Civil Liberties Union suggests that § 441a(a)(1)(C) would violate the First Amendment if construed to limit the amount individuals could jointly expend to express their political views. We need not consider this hypothetical application of the Act. The case before us involves the constitutionality of § 441a(a)(1)(C) as it applies to contributions to multicandidate political committees. [Contributions] to such committees [are] distinguishable from expenditures made jointly by groups of individuals in order to express common political views." [Footnote by Justice Marshall.]

committees—is accepted, then both these contribution limitations could be easily evaded. Since multicandidate political committees may contribute up to $5,000 per year to any candidate, an individual or association seeking to evade the $1,000 limit on contributions to candidates could do so by channelling funds through a multicandidate political committee. Similarly, individuals could evade the $25,000 limit on aggregate annual contributions to candidates if they were allowed to give unlimited sums to multicandidate political committees, since such committees are not limited in the aggregate amount they may contribute in any year. These concerns prompted Congress to enact § 441a(a) (1)(C), and it is clear that this provision is an appropriate means by which Congress could seek to protect the integrity of the contribution restrictions upheld by this Court in Buckley."

Justice BLACKMUN's separate opinion explained why he supported the plurality's result, but could not endorse its reasoning: "[Justice Marshall's approach] appears to rest on the premise that the First Amendment test to be applied to contribution limitations is different from the test applicable to expenditure limitations. I do not agree with that proposition. Although I dissented in part in [Buckley], I am willing to accept as binding the Court's judgment in that case that the contribution limitations challenged there were constitutional. But it does not follow that I must concur in the plurality conclusion today that political contributions are not entitled to full First Amendment protection. It is true that there is language in Buckley that might suggest that conclusion. [At] the same time, however, Buckley states that 'contribution and expenditure limitations both implicate fundamental First Amendment interests,' and that 'governmental "action which may have the effect of curtailing the freedom to associate is subject to the closest scrutiny,"' quoting NAACP v. Alabama. Thus, contribution limitations can be upheld only 'if the State demonstrates a sufficiently important interest and employs means closely drawn to avoid unnecessary abridgment of associational freedoms.' [Buckley.]

"Unlike the plurality, I would apply this 'rigorous standard of review' to the instant case, rather than relying on what I believe to be a mistaken view that contributions are 'not the sort of political advocacy [entitled] to full First Amendment protection.' Respondents claim that § 441a(a)(1)(C) is justified by the governmental interest in preventing apparent or actual political corruption. That this interest is important cannot be doubted. It is a closer question, however, whether the statute is narrowly drawn to advance that interest. Nonetheless, I conclude that contributions to multicandidate political committees may be limited to $5,000 per year as a means of preventing evasion of the limitations on contributions to a candidate or his authorized campaign committee upheld in Buckley. The statute challenged here is thus analogous to the $25,000 limitation on total contributions in a given year that Buckley held to be constitutional.

"I stress, however, that this analysis suggests that a different result would follow if § 441a(a)(1)(C) were applied to contributions to a political committee established for the purpose of making independent expenditures, rather than contributions to candidates. By definition, a multicandidate political committee like CALPAC makes contributions to five or more candidates for federal office. Multicandidate political committees are therefore essentially conduits for contributions to candidates, and as such they pose a perceived threat of actual or potential corruption. In contrast, contributions to a committee that makes only independent expenditures pose no such threat. The Court repeatedly has recognized that '[e]ffective advocacy of both public and private points of view, particularly controversial ones, is undeniably enhanced by group association.' NAACP v. Alabama. By pooling their resources, adherents of an association amplify their own voices. [I] believe that contributions to political committees can be limited only if those contributions implicate the governmental interest in preventing actual or potential corruption, and if the limitation is no broader than necessary to achieve that interest. Because this narrow test is satisfied here, I concur in the result reached [by Justice Marshall on the First Amendment issue]." [5]

CORPORATE SPENDING AND REFERENDA

The 5 to 4 decision in FIRST NATIONAL BANK OF BOSTON v. BELLOTTI, 435 U.S. 765 (1978), invalidated a Massachusetts criminal law prohibiting certain expenditures by banks and business corporations for the purpose of influencing the vote on referendum proposals. The law barred banks and business corporations from making expenditures to influence the outcome of referenda on any question "other than one materially affecting any of the property, business or assets of the corporation." The statute provided further that no referendum question "solely concerning" taxation of individuals "shall be deemed materially to affect the property, business or assets of the corporation." Accordingly, the challengers—banks and business corporations— were prevented from spending money on a proposed state constitutional amendment to authorize a graduated individual income tax. The Court found that the statute could not survive the strict scrutiny appropriate under the First Amendment because the law prohibited "protected speech in a manner unjustified by a compelling state interest." [1]

The highest state court had sustained the statute by viewing corporate free speech rights as narrower than those of individuals: corporations could assert

---

5. The majority also rejected an equal protection challenge. (On this issue, Justice Blackmun joined Justice Marshall's opinion.) This challenge arose because the Act imposes no limits on contributions by corporations or unions to their segregated political funds. The challengers claimed that such contributions are "directly analogous to an unincorporated association's contributions to a multicandidate political committee." Justice Marshall insisted, however, that the Act did not discriminate between contributions by unincorporated associations and contributions by corporations and unions: "Appellants' claim of unfair treatment ignores the plain fact that the statute as a whole imposes far *fewer* restrictions on individuals and unincorporated associations than it does on corporations and unions." In his view, the differing restrictions simply reflected the congressional judgment that entities with differing structures and purposes "may require different forms of regulation in order to protect the integrity of the electoral process."

Note also FEC v. National Right to Work Committee, 459 U.S. 197 (1982), where a unanimous Court upheld the solicitation limitations in § 441(b)(4)(C) of the Federal Election Campaign Act. That provision allows corporations to establish separate funds "to receive and make contributions on behalf of federal candidates," but limits solicitations for funds to stockholders and executive and administrative personnel of the corporation. For a corporation without capital stock, such as the National Right to Work Committee, solicitation is limited to "members." The Committee claimed that this included all those who had responded in some way to their previous solicitations, but the Court, in an opinion by Justice Rehnquist, held that such a construction would be inconsistent with both the language and the purpose of the provision, which was designed to allow corporations without stockholders to solicit on the same basis as those with stockholders. In holding that this construction of the Act raised no constitutional problems, the Court relied heavily on Buckley v. Valeo in deferring to the congressional judgment that the limitations on solicitation were necessary to prevent actual or apparent corruption by corporations and labor organizations. The Court relied as well on the California Medical Association case for the proposition that different structures or entities might require different forms of regulation.

Another First Amendment challenge to provisions of federal campaign regulations reached the Court in Common Cause v. Schmitt, 455 U.S. 129 (1982), but produced no opinions on the merits. Instead, an equally divided Court (with Justice O'Connor not participating) affirmed a lower court invalidation of § 9012(f) of the Presidential Election Campaign Fund Act which, inter alia, imposed spending limits on "unauthorized" political committees seeking to further the election of presidential candidates.

1. Although the problems of this case and aspects of Buckley v. Valeo overlap, the majority opinion in this case did not place heavy reliance on the Buckley ruling.

only "property" rather than "liberty" interests; corporate speech claims were merely "an incident" of the protection of corporate "property"; corporations were therefore entitled to free speech only "when a general political issue materially affects the corporation's business, property or assets." Since in that view the state restriction was coextensive with corporate First Amendment rights and did not impinge on protected speech interests, the state court exercised deferential review rather than strict scrutiny and readily sustained the law. Justice POWELL's majority opinion rejected the state court's premises and conclusions. To begin inquiry with the extent of corporate free speech rights, he insisted, was to pose "the wrong question": "The proper question [is] not whether corporations 'have' First Amendment rights and, if so, whether they are coextensive with those of natural persons. Instead, the question must be whether [the statute] abridges expression that the First Amendment was meant to protect. We hold that it does."

In explaining the view that substantial First Amendment interests triggering strict scrutiny were implicated, Justice Powell noted that the expression the challengers wanted to engage in—publicizing their views on a proposed constitutional amendment—lay "at the heart of the First Amendment's protection." He commented: "If the speakers here were not corporations, no one would suggest that the State could silence their proposed speech. It is the type of speech indispensable to decisionmaking in a democracy. [The] inherent worth of the speech in terms of its capacity for informing the public does not depend on the identity of its [source]." Against that background, the state court's "novel and restrictive gloss on the First Amendment"—protecting corporate speech "only when it pertains directly to the corporation's business interests"— was indefensible: the "corporate identity of the speaker" could not deprive speech "of what otherwise would be its clear entitlement to protection." The state court's insistence that a corporation's First Amendment rights "derive from its property rights under the 14th" was rejected as "an artificial mode of analysis, untenable under the decisions of this Court." Though most past decisions protecting corporate speech—especially decisions involving media corporations and commercial speech—were consistent with the novel "materially affecting" theory, "the effect on the business of the corporation was not the governing rationale in any of these decisions." The Constitution and the case law accordingly did not support "the proposition that speech that otherwise would be within the protection of the First Amendment loses that protection simply because its source is a corporation that cannot prove, to the satisfaction of a court, a material effect on its business or property." The law therefore amounted to "an impermissible legislative prohibition of speech": "In the realm of protected speech, the legislature is constitutionally disqualified from dictating the subjects about which persons may speak and the speakers who may address a public issue. [Mosley.] If a legislature may direct business corporations to 'stick to business,' it also may limit other corporations—religious, charitable, or civic—to their respective 'business' when addressing the public. Such power in government to channel the expression of views is unacceptable under the First Amendment. Especially where, as here, the legislature's suppression of speech suggests an attempt to give one side of a debatable public question an advantage in expressing its views to the people, the First Amendment is plainly offended."

Having articulated the case for First Amendment protection, Justice Powell turned to the State's claim that "its action [was] necessitated by governmental interests of the highest order" and found that the law could not survive the requisite "exacting scrutiny." After reciting the "compelling interests" and "closely drawn means" prongs of strict scrutiny, Justice Powell examined the two principal state justifications: (1) "the State's interest in sustaining the active role of the individual citizen in the electoral process and thereby preventing diminution of the citizen's confidence in government"; and (2) "the interest in protecting the rights of shareholders whose views differ from those expressed by management on behalf of the corporation." He concluded: "However weighty these interests may be in the context of partisan candidate elections,[2] they either are not implicated in this case or are not served at all, or in other than a random manner, by the prohibition."

With respect to the democratic process interests, Justice Powell concluded that "there had been no showing that the relative voice of corporations has been overwhelming or even significant in influencing referenda in Massachusetts, or that there has been any threat to the confidence of the citizenry in government." In short, that state interest had not been shown to be adequately "implicated in this case." Moreover, the risk of corruption recognized in cases involving candidate elections "simply is not present in a popular vote on a public issue." Although corporate advertising might influence the outcome, "the fact that advocacy may persuade the electorate is hardly a reason to suppress it." It was for the voters to evaluate the relative merits of conflicting arguments; the government "is forbidden to assume the task of ultimate judgment lest the people lose their ability to govern themselves"; the "State's paternalism evidenced by this statute" was inconsistent with the First Amendment's emphasis on the people's right to hear.

The asserted state interest in protecting shareholders also provided inadequate justification, on somewhat different grounds: the claim that the statute prevented "the use of corporate resources in furtherance of views with which some shareholders may disagree" was "belied" by the law's scope, which was found to be "both underinclusive and overinclusive." Underinclusiveness was shown, for example, by the fact that the law barred only corporate expenditures with respect to referenda and not with regard to "the passage or defeat of legislation," "even though corporations may engage in lobbying more often than they take positions on ballot questions submitted to the voters." Justice Powell commented: "The fact that a particular kind of ballot question has been singled out for special treatment undermines the likelihood of a genuine state interest in protecting shareholders. It suggests instead that the legislature may have been concerned with silencing corporations on a particular subject." And overinclusiveness was demonstrated by the fact that the statutory prohibition applied "even if [shareholders] unanimously authorized the contribution or expenditure." Justice Powell concluded: "Assuming, arguendo, the protection of shareholders is a 'compelling' interest under the circumstances of this case,

2. In a footnote, Justice Powell distinguished the problem of laws regulating corporate participation in partisan candidate elections. The overriding concern in those statutes, he noted, was "the problem of corruption of elected representatives through the creation of political debts." Here, there was no "comparable problem, and our consideration of a corporation's right to speak on issues of general public interest implies no comparable right in the quite different context of participation in a political campaign for election to public office. [The legislature] might well be able to demonstrate the existence of a danger of real or apparent corruption in independent expenditures by corporations to influence candidate elections. Cf. Buckley v. Valeo."

Is Justice Powell's distinction persuasive? Or do Bellotti and Buckley presage constitutional limits on the widely adopted laws limiting corporate spending in candidate elections? Justice White in dissent was not persuaded by the dis-

tinction: he suggested that the decision casts "considerable doubt upon the constitutionality of the legislation passed by some 31 States restricting corporate political activity, as well as upon the Federal Corrupt Practices Act." He noted that Buckley had already held that the interest in preventing corruption was insufficient to justify restrictions on *individual* expenditures and added: "If the corporate identity of the speaker makes no difference, all the Court has done is to reserve the formal interment of the Corrupt Practices Act and similar state statutes for another day. As I understand the view that has now become part of First Amendment jurisprudence, the use of corporate funds, even for causes irrelevant to the corporation's business, may be no more limited than that of individual funds. Hence, corporate contributions to and expenditures on behalf of political candidates may be no more limited than those of individuals."

we find 'no substantially relevant correlation between the governmental interest asserted and the State's effort' to prohibit appellants from speaking. Shelton v. Tucker (p. 1371 below)."[3]

In a lengthy dissent, Justice WHITE, joined by Justices Brennan and Marshall, insisted that the majority's "fundamental error" was "its failure to realize that the state regulatory interests [are] themselves derived from the First Amendment"—primarily, the value of promoting the free marketplace of ideas by preventing corporate domination. Although Justice White conceded that corporate communications were within the First Amendment, he insisted that "an examination of the First Amendment values corporate expression furthers and the threat to the functioning of a free society it is capable of posing reveals that it is not fungible with communications emanating from individuals and is subject to restrictions which individual expression is not." Corporate communications, he commented, do not further "what some have considered to be the principal function of the First Amendment, the use of communication as a means of self-expression, self-realization and self-fulfillment." True, the right to receive information and the protection of the interchange of ideas were also First Amendment values. But that recognition did not establish "that the right of the general public to receive communications financed by means of corporate expenditures is of the same dimensions as that to hear other forms of expression": "Ideas which are not a product of individual choice are entitled to less First Amendment protection." Moreover, "the restriction of corporate speech concerned with political matters impinges much less severely upon the availability of ideas to the general public than do restrictions upon individual speech."

Justice White argued further that the "governmental interest in regulating corporate political communications, especially those relating to electoral matters, [raises] considerations which differ significantly from those governing the regulation of individual speech. [T]he special status of corporations has placed them in a position to control vast amounts of economic power which may, if not regulated, dominate not only the economy but also the very heart of our democracy, the electoral process. Although [Buckley] provides support for the position that the desire to equalize the financial resources available to candidates does not justify the limitation upon the expression of support which a restriction upon individual contributions entails, the interest of [the states] which have restricted corporate political activity is quite different. It is not one of equalizing the resources of opposing candidates or opposing positions but rather of preventing institutions which have been permitted to amass wealth as a result of special advantages extended by the State for certain economic purposes from using that wealth to acquire an unfair advantage in the political process, especially where, as here, the issue involved has no material connection with the business of the corporation. The State need not permit its own creation to consume it. Massachusetts could permissibly conclude that not to impose limits upon political activities of corporations would have placed it in a position of departing from neutrality and indirectly assisting the propagation of corporate views because of the advantages its law gave to the corporate acquisition of funds to finance such activities. Such expenditures may be viewed as seriously threatening the role of the First Amendment as a guarantor of a free marketplace of ideas." Moreover, Justice White was impressed by an "additional overriding interest": "assuring that shareholders are not compelled to support and financially further beliefs with which they disagree where, as is the case here, the issue involved does not materially affect the business, property, or other affairs of the corporation." He was not persuaded by the majority's

---

3. Chief Justice BURGER joined the majority opinion but submitted a controversial concurring opinion on an issue "implicated only indirectly by this case"—"the meaning of the Press Clause, as a provision separate and apart from the Speech Clause" of the First Amendment. That concurring opinion is considered with other materials on the media in sec. 6 below, at p. 1417.

criticism of the State's choice of means to protect shareholders. He noted, too, that preventing corporate management from using corporate funds that would ultimately promote "the purely personal views of the management" was a policy not only consistent with the First Amendment "but one which protects the very freedoms that this Court has held to be guaranteed by the First Amendment." [4]

A separate dissent by Justice REHNQUIST concluded "that the 14th Amendment does not require a State to endow a business corporation with the power of political speech." He emphasized that corporations were created by the state and were limited to rights explicitly or implicitly guaranteed as part of the state-granted charter. He insisted that it could not be readily concluded that "the right of political expression is [necessary] to carry out the functions of a corporation organized for commercial purposes." He explained: "[I]t might be argued that liberties of political expression are not at all necessary to effectuate the purposes for which States permit commercial corporations to exist. [Indeed], the States might reasonably feel that the corporation would use its economic power to obtain further benefits beyond those already bestowed." And he emphasized: "I can see no basis for concluding that the liberty of a corporation to engage in political activity with regard to matters having no material effect on its business is necessarily incidental to the purposes for which the Commonwealth permitted these corporations to be organized or admitted within its boundaries." Accordingly, the Massachusetts law provided "at least as much protection as the 14th Amendment requires." [5]

THE SCRUTINY OF STATE REGULATIONS OF ELECTIONS IN THE 1980s

1. *Contributions regarding local ballot measures.* In CITIZENS AGAINST RENT CONTROL v. BERKELEY, 454 U.S. 290 (1981), the Court invalidated a Berkeley, Calif., ordinance imposing a $250 limit on personal contributions to committees formed to support or oppose ballot measures. A local association, formed to oppose a ballot initiative measure to establish rent control in the city, challenged that restriction. The highest state court, applying strict scrutiny and

---

4. Justice White pointed to cases prohibiting organizations to which individuals are compelled to belong as a condition of employment from using compulsory dues to support candidates, political parties, or other forms of political expression with which members disagree. See, e.g., the 1977 decision in Abood v. Detroit Board of Educ. (p. 1352 below). Justice Powell's majority opinion countered that cases such as Abood were "irrelevant to the question presented in this case. [The] critical distinction here is that no shareholder has been 'compelled' to contribute anything."

5. Justice Rehnquist once again noted that he views the First Amendment as having only a "limited application" to the states—a view, he acknowledged, "which I share with the two immediately preceding occupants of my seat on the Court [Justices Harlan and Jackson], but not with my present colleagues."

In a footnote to his opinion, Justice Rehnquist added some noteworthy comments about the actual purposes of the Massachusetts restriction. Although he had no difficulty finding "a rational basis" for the law, he disagreed with the "intimation" that the justification Justice White had articulated was "*in fact* the reason that the Mas-

sachusetts [legislature] enacted this legislation." Justice Rehnquist explained: "If inquiry into legislative motives were to determine the outcome of cases such as this, I think a very persuasive argument could be made that the [legislature], desiring to impose a personal income tax but more than once defeated in that desire by the combination of the Commonwealth's referendum provision and corporate expenditures in opposition to such a tax, simply decided to muzzle corporations on this sort of issue so that it would succeed in its desire. If one believes, as my Brother White apparently does, that a function of the First Amendment is to protect the interchange of ideas, he cannot readily subscribe to the idea that, if the desire to muzzle corporations played a part in the enactment of this legislation, the [legislature] was simply engaged in deciding *which* First Amendment values to promote." But, Justice Rehnquist added, that speculation about legislative motivation did not disturb his conclusion: in his view, the highest state court "was correct in concluding that, whatever may have been the motive of the [legislature], the law thus challenged did not violate [the] Constitution."

citing Buckley, upheld the contribution limit. It identified the requisite compelling governmental interest as that of assuring that special interest groups could not "corrupt" the initiative process and thereby cause voter apathy. Chief Justice BURGER's opinion for the Court found the limit on contributions unconstitutional: "The restraint imposed by the Berkeley Ordinance on rights of association and in turn on individual and collective rights of expression plainly contravenes both the right of association and the speech guarantees of the First Amendment." He stated that "regulation of First Amendment rights is always subject to exacting judicial review." Although Buckley had sustained limits on contributions in candidate elections (because of the "risk of corruption" rationale), the Chief Justice insisted that "Buckley does not support limitations on contributions to committees formed to favor or oppose *ballot measures.*" He pointed out, moreover, that Bellotti had relied on Buckley "to strike down state legislative limits on advocacy relating to ballot measures." He rejected the City's effort to distinguish those cases on the ground that the Berkeley limit was "necessary as a prophylactic measure to make known the identity of supporters and opponents of ballot measures." He found that interest "insubstantial" in this case because the disclosure provisions of the ordinance assured that the identities of contributors would be known. Moreover, there was no evidence in the record that the limit was necessary to preserve voters' confidence in the initiative process.[1]

The sole dissenter, Justice WHITE, reiterated his dissenting positions in Buckley and Bellotti. He insisted, moreover, that the Berkeley limit was "a less encompassing regulation of campaign activity" than those involved in the earlier cases and that the challenged ordinance was "tailored to the odd measurements of Buckley and Bellotti." For example, Berkeley had followed those decisions by regulating "contributions but not expenditures" and by limiting personal but not corporate spending. He commented: "It is for that very reason perhaps that the effectiveness of the ordinance in preserving the integrity of the referendum process is debatable. Even so, the result here illustrates that the Buckley framework is most problematical and strengthens my belief that there is a proper role for carefully drafted limitations on expenditures."[2]

---

1. Chief Justice Burger also found that the ordinance imposed "a significant restraint on the freedom of expression," not only on freedom of association. He noted that, under the ordinance, "an individual may make expenditures without limit [but] may not contribute beyond the $250 limit when joining with others to advocate common views. The contribution limit thus automatically affects expenditures, and limits on expenditures operate as a direct restraint on freedom of expression of a group or committee desiring to engage in political dialogue concerning a ballot measure. [Placing] limits on contributions which in turn limit expenditures plainly impairs freedom of expression."

In a concurring statement, Justice REHNQUIST, who had dissented in Bellotti, emphasized that Bellotti did not help the defenders of the Berkeley ordinance because it "was not aimed only at corporations." Justice MARSHALL, concurring only in the judgment, noted that the Court had failed "to indicate whether or not it attaches any constitutional significance to the fact that the Berkeley ordinance seeks to limit *contributions* as opposed to direct *expenditures,*" even though, beginning with Buckley, "this Court has *always* drawn a distinction between restrictions on contributions and direct

limitations on the amount an individual can expend for his own speech." He accordingly stated: "Because the Court's opinion is silent on the standard of review it is applying to this contributions limitation, I must assume that the Court is following our consistent position that this type of governmental action is subjected to less rigorous scrutiny than a direct restriction on expenditures." Justice Marshall joined the result only because the city had failed to disclose "sufficient evidence to justify the conclusion that large contributions to ballot measure committees undermined the 'confidence of the citizenry in government.'" Another separate opinion concurring in the judgment, by Justices BLACKMUN and O'CONNOR, insisted that "exacting scrutiny," a "rigorous standard of review," was appropriate here and concluded "that Berkeley has neither demonstrated a genuine threat to its important governmental interests nor employed means closely drawn to avoid unnecessary abridgment of protected activity."

2. Justice White devoted most of his dissent to arguing that, even under Buckley, "the Berkeley ordinance represents such a negligible intrusion on expression and association that the measure should be upheld." He elaborated: "When the infringement is as slight and ephemeral as it

2. *Candidates' promises in election campaigns.* In BROWN v. HARTLAGE, 456 U.S. 45 (1982), the Court once again examined the limited reach of the state interest in preventing corruption. A candidate for a county office had made a campaign statement that salaries were too high and that, if elected, he would serve at a salary below that "fixed by law" by lowering his salary. Shortly after making the statement, he learned that it arguably violated the Kentucky Corrupt Practices Act, which prohibited candidates from offering material benefits to voters in consideration for their votes. The candidate retracted the statement and was elected. Thereafter, a suit was brought to set aside his election because of his "illegal" promise. The state court granted the relief, finding that a candidate's promise to serve at a salary below that "fixed by law" was "an attempt to buy votes or to bribe the voters." In reversing that judgment, Justice BRENNAN's opinion found strict scrutiny appropriate. He noted three possible bases which might conceivably justify the law: "first, as a prohibition on buying votes; second, as facilitating the candidacy of persons lacking independent wealth; and third, as an application of the State's interests [with] respect to factual misstatements." He found none of these justifications adequate under the First Amendment.

Justice Brennan noted that "there is no *constitutional* basis upon which [a pledge to reduce one's salary] might be equated with a candidate's promise to pay voters for their support from his own pocketbook." He added that the candidate's promise could not be "considered as inviting the kind of corrupt arrangement the appearance of which a State may have a compelling interest in avoiding. See Buckley v. Valeo. [A] candidate's promise to confer some ultimate benefit on the voter, qua taxpayer, citizen, or member of the general public, does not lie beyond the pale of First Amendment protection." On the interest in facilitating candidacies by those lacking independent wealth he noted that, if the law "was designed to further this interest, it chooses a means unacceptable under the First Amendment. [The] State's fear that voters might make an ill-advised choice does not provide the State with a compelling justification for limiting speech." As to the interest regarding factual misstatements, finally, he conceded that it was "somewhat different from the state interest in protecting individuals from defamatory falsehoods," but insisted that "the principles underlying the First Amendment remain paramount." He concluded that nullifying the election victory was "inconsistent with the atmosphere of robust political debate protected by the First Amendment."[1]

3. *Ballot access and related issues.* Cases involving claims of ballot access and related electoral issues have traditionally been argued and decided under the "fundamental rights" strand of equal protection analysis, as noted in chap. 9, sec. 4. More recently, however, the Court has veered away from equal protection in favor of deciding ballot access cases directly on the basis of First Amendment rights to political choice and political association. See especially Anderson v. Celebrezze (1983; discussed in chap. 9, at p. 822 above).

---

is here, the requisite state interest to justify the regulation need not be so high." He pointed out that the historic purpose of the initiative in California was to prevent "the dominance of special interests" and added: "Perhaps [the City cannot] 'prove' that elections have been or can be unfairly won by special interest groups spending large sums of money, but there is a widespread conviction in legislative halls, as well as among citizens, that the danger is real. I regret that the Court continues to disregard that hazard."

1. Justice REHNQUIST's concurrence in the result stated that he could not join "the Court's analogy between [anti-corruption laws] and state defamation laws." Instead, he argued that Mills v. Alabama (1966; invalidating a law prohibiting press endorsements of candidates on election day; considered in Buckley) afforded "ample basis" for the result here. Chief Justice BURGER also noted his concurrence solely in the judgment.

SECTION 2. THE FIRST AMENDMENT IN SOME ADDITIONAL SPECIAL ENVIRONMENTS *

A. THE SCHOOL CONTEXT: REMOVAL OF BOOKS FROM SCHOOL LIBRARIES †

BOARD OF EDUCATION v. PICO

457 U.S. 853, 102 S.Ct. 2799, 73 L.Ed.2d 435 (1982).

Justice BRENNAN announced the judgment of the Court, and delivered an opinion in which Justice MARSHALL and Justice STEVENS joined, and in which Justice BLACKMUN joined except for Part II–A–(1).

The principal question presented is whether the First Amendment imposes limitations upon the exercise by a local school board of its discretion to remove library books from high school and junior high school libraries.

I. Petitioners are the Board of Education of the Island Trees Union Free School District No. 26 in New York, and [the members of the Board]. [The Board operates the District's schools, including a high school and a junior high school. Respondents are five high school students and one junior high school student.] In September 1975, [three Board members] attended a conference sponsored by Parents of New York United (PONYU), a politically conservative organization of parents concerned about education legislation. [At] the conference these [Board members] obtained lists of books described by [one member]

---

* The sampling of materials in this section does not exhaust the problems of First Amendment rights in special, restricted environments. For other illustrations, considered elsewhere in this book, note especially the special state interests asserted in the environments of military bases and prisons. On military bases, recall especially Greer v. Spock (1976; p. 1252 above). On prisons, see the cases involving press claims of access for the purpose of interviewing prisoners, in Pell v. Procunier and Saxbe v. Washington Post Co. (1974; p. 1440 below) and in Houchins v. KQED, Inc. (1978; p. 1441 below). On interferences with prisoners' mail, see Procunier v. Martinez, 416 U.S. 396 (1974), and Bell v. Wolfish, 441 U.S. 520 (1979). Note also the majority's very deferential attitude towards prison regulations designed to inhibit organizing efforts by a prisoners' union, in Jones v. North Carolina Prisoners' Labor Union, 433 U.S. 119 (1977).

† Board of Education v. Pico, the principal case here, is of special interest because of the unresolved questions it presents regarding the accommodation between the school's interest in communicating and inculcating community values and the First Amendment interests in avoiding censorship and in access to information. Pico is of course not the only case arising in the school context. For considerations of students' rights in the school environment, recall especially Tinker (1969; p. 1176 above), protecting the wearing of black armbands by students as a

symbolic protest, and Grayned v. Rockford (1972; p. 1264 above), discussing the permissible restraints on a student demonstration in front of a high school. Note also Healy v. James, 408 U.S. 169 (1972), striking down a state college's denial of official recognition to a local chapter of the SDS. See generally Wright, "The Constitution on the Campus," 22 Vand.L.Rev. 1027 (1969), and Gunther, "[The] Case of Justice Powell," 24 Stan.L.Rev. 1001 (1972). On procedural due process limitations imposed on disciplinary suspensions of students, see Goss v. Lopez, 419 U.S. 565 (1975); compare chap. 8, sec. 4, above.

In addition to those materials on students' rights, note the Court's occasional consideration of teachers' rights. On academic freedom and the First Amendment, see especially Sweezy v. New Hampshire (1957; p. 1406 below); cf. Justice Powell's opinion in the Bakke case, p. 745 above. On teachers' free speech rights, see the Pickering case, p. 1392 below, and generally Schauer, " 'Private' Speech and the 'Private' [Forum]," 1979 Sup.Ct.Rev. 217. See also Connick v. Myers (1983; p. 1395 below). On teachers' First Amendment and procedural rights in challenging dismissals from employment, see the Roth and Sindermann cases (1972; p. 569 above). Recall also the Perry case (1983; p. 1268 above), involving access to a school system's internal mail system, and Widmar v. Vincent (1981; p. 1265 above), on content controls regarding access to public university facilities.

as "objectionable" and by [another] as "improper fare for school students." [1] It was later determined that the High School library contained nine of the listed books, and that another listed book was in the Junior High School library.[2] In February 1976, [the] Board gave an "unofficial direction" that the listed books be removed from the library shelves and delivered to the Board's offices, so that Board members could read them. When this directive was carried out, it became publicized, and the Board issued a press release justifying its action. It characterized the removed books as "anti-American, anti-Christian, anti-Semitic, and just plain filthy," and concluded that "It is our duty, our moral obligation, to protect the children in our schools from this moral danger as surely as from physical and medical dangers." A short time later, the Board appointed a "Book Review Committee," consisting of [several parents and members of the school staff] to recommend [whether] the books should be retained. [The Committee recommended that some (but not all) of the listed books be retained.] The Board substantially rejected the Committee's report later that month, deciding that only one book [Slaughter House Five] should be returned to the High School library without restriction. [The] Board gave no reasons for rejecting the recommendations of the Committee that it had appointed. Respondents reacted to the Board's decision by bringing the present action under 42 U.S.C. § 1983. They alleged that petitioners had "ordered the removal of the books from school libraries and proscribed their use in the curriculum because particular passages in the books offended their social, political and moral tastes and not because the books, taken as a whole, were lacking in educational value." Respondents claimed that the Board's actions denied them their rights under the First Amendment.[3]

II. We emphasize at the outset the limited nature of the substantive question presented by the case before us. Our precedents have long recognized certain constitutional limits upon the power of the State to control even the curriculum and classroom. For example, Meyer v. Nebraska [1923; p. 502 above] struck down a state law that forbade the teaching of modern foreign languages in public and private schools, and Epperson v. Arkansas [1968; p. 1492 below] declared unconstitutional a state law that prohibited the teaching of the Darwinian theory of evolution in any state-supported school. But the current action does not require us to re-enter this difficult terrain, which Meyer and Epperson traversed without apparent misgiving. For as this case is presented to us, it does not involve textbooks, or indeed any books that Island Trees students would be required to read. Respondents do not seek in this Court to impose limitations upon their school board's discretion to prescribe the curricula of the Island Trees schools. On the contrary, the only books at issue in this case are *library* books, books that by their nature are optional rather than required reading. Our adjudication of the present case thus does not intrude into the classroom, or into the compulsory courses taught there. Furthermore, even as to library books, the action before us does not involve the *acquisition* of books.

---

1. The District Court noted, however, that petitioners "concede that the books are not obscene." [Footnote by Justice Brennan.]

2. The nine books in the High School library were: Slaughter House Five, by Kurt Vonnegut, Jr.; The Naked Ape, by Desmond Morris; Down These Mean Streets, by Piri Thomas; Best Short Stories of Negro Writers, edited by Langston Hughes; Go Ask Alice, of anonymous authorship; Laughing Boy, by Oliver LaFarge; Black Boy, by Richard Wright; A Hero Ain't Nothin' But A Sandwich, by Alice Childress; and Soul On Ice, by Eldridge Cleaver. The book in the Junior High School library was A Reader for Writers, edited by Jerome Archer. Still an-

other listed book, The Fixer, by Bernard Malamud, was found to be included in the curriculum of a twelfth grade literature course. [Footnote by Justice Brennan.]

3. The respondents asked for declaratory and injunctive relief ordering the Board to return the nine books to the school libraries. The District Court granted summary judgment for the Board. A three-judge panel of the Court of Appeals for the Second Circuit reversed and remanded for a trial on respondents' allegations. Each judge on the panel wrote a separate opinion. Judges Sifton and Newman were in the majority; Judge Mansfield dissented.

Respondents have not sought to compel their school board to add to the school library shelves any books that students desire to read. Rather, the only action challenged in this case is the *removal* from the school libraries of books originally placed there by the school authorities, or without objection from them.

The substantive question before us is still further constrained by the procedural posture of this case. [We can] grant petitioners' request for reinstatement of the summary judgment in their favor only if we determine that "there is no genuine issue as to any material fact," and that petitioners are "entitled to a judgment as a matter of law." Fed.Rule Civ.Proc. 56(c). In making our determination, any doubt as to the existence of a genuine issue of material fact must be resolved against petitioners as the moving party. [In] sum, the issue before us in this case is a narrow one, both substantively and procedurally. It may best be restated as two distinct questions. First, Does the First Amendment impose *any* limitations upon the discretion of petitioners to remove library books from the Island Trees [schools]? Second, If so, do the affidavits and other evidentiary materials before the District Court, construed most favorably to respondents, raise a genuine issue of fact whether petitioners might have exceeded those [limitations]?

A. (1) The Court has long recognized that local school boards have broad discretion in the management of school affairs. [E.g., Meyer; Pierce; Epperson; Tinker.] We have also acknowledged that public schools are vitally important [as] vehicles for "inculcating fundamental values necessary to the maintenance of a democratic political system." Ambach v. Norwick [1979; p. 673 above]. We are therefore in full agreement with petitioners that local school boards must be permitted "to establish and apply their curriculum in such a way as to transmit community values," and that "there is a legitimate and substantial community interest in promoting respect for authority and traditional values be they social, moral, or political." At the same time, however, we have necessarily recognized that the discretion of the States and local school boards in matters of education must be exercised in a manner that comports with the transcendent imperatives of the First Amendment. In West Virginia v. Barnette [1943; p. 1510 below], we held that under the First Amendment a student in a public school could not be compelled to salute the flag. [See also, e.g., Epperson; Tinker.] In sum, students do not "shed their rights to freedom of speech or expression at the schoolhouse gate" [Tinker] and therefore local school boards must discharge their "important, delicate, and highly discretionary functions" within the limits and constraints of the First Amendment.

The nature of students' First Amendment rights in the context of this case requires further examination. [Barnette] is instructive. There the Court held that students' liberty of conscience could not be infringed in the name of "national unity" or "patriotism." [See also Tinker.] Of course, courts should not "intervene in the resolution of conflicts which arise in the daily operations of school systems" unless "basic constitutional values" are "directly and sharply implicate[d]" in those conflicts. [Epperson.] But we think that the First Amendment rights of students may be directly and sharply implicated by the removal of books from the shelves of a school library. Our precedents have focused "not only on the role of the First Amendment in fostering individual self-expression but also on its role in affording the public access to discussion, debate, and the dissemination of information and ideas." [Bellotti.] And we have recognized that "the State may not, consistently with the spirit of the First Amendment, contract the spectrum of available knowledge." Griswold v. Connecticut. In keeping with this principle, we have held that in a variety of contexts "the Constitution protects the right to receive information and ideas." Stanley v. Georgia. This right is an inherent corollary of the rights of free speech and press that are explicitly guaranteed by the Constitution, in two senses. First, the right to receive ideas follows ineluctably from the *sender's* First Amendment right to send them. [More] importantly, the right to receive ideas is a necessary predicate to the *recipient's* meaningful exercise of his own rights of speech, press, and political freedom. [Students] too are beneficiaries of this principle. [In] sum, just as access to ideas makes it possible for citizens generally to exercise their rights of free speech and press in a meaningful manner, such access prepares students for active and effective participation in the pluralistic, often contentious society in which they will soon be adult members. Of course all First Amendment rights accorded to students must be construed "in light of the special characteristics of the school environment." [Tinker.] But the special characteristics of the school *library* make that environment especially appropriate for the recognition of the First Amendment rights of students.

A school library, no less than any other public library, is "a place dedicated to quiet, to knowledge, and to beauty." Brown v. Louisiana. [Keyishian; 1967; p. 1377 below] observed that "students must always remain free to inquire, to study and to evaluate, to gain new maturity and understanding." The school library is the principal locus of such freedom. [Petitioners] emphasize the inculcative function of secondary education, and argue that they must be allowed *unfettered* discretion to "transmit community values" through [the] schools. But that sweeping claim overlooks the unique role of the school library. It appears from the record that use of the Island Trees school libraries is completely voluntary on the part of students. Their selection of books from these libraries is entirely a matter of free choice; the libraries afford them an opportunity at self-education and individual enrichment that is wholly optional. Petitioners might well defend their claim of absolute discretion in matters of *curriculum* by reliance upon their duty to inculcate community values. But we think that petitioners' reliance upon that duty is misplaced where, as here, they attempt to extend their claim of absolute discretion beyond the compulsory environment of the classroom, into the school library and the regime of voluntary inquiry that there holds sway.

(2) In rejecting petitioners' claim of absolute discretion to remove books from their school libraries, we do not deny that local school boards have a substantial legitimate role to play in the determination of school library content. We thus must turn to the question of the extent to which the First Amendment places limitations upon the discretion of petitioners to remove books from their libraries. In this inquiry we enjoy the guidance of several precedents. [E.g., Barnette; Keyishian; Epperson.] With respect to the present case, the message of these precedents is clear. Petitioners rightly possess significant discretion to determine the content of their school libraries. But that discretion may not be exercised in a narrowly partisan or political manner. If a Democratic school board, motivated by party affiliation, ordered the removal of all books written by or in favor of Republicans, few would doubt that the order violated the constitutional rights of the students denied access to those books. The same conclusion would surely apply if an all-white school board, motivated by racial animus, decided to remove all books authored by blacks or advocating racial equality and integration. Our Constitution does not permit the official suppression of *ideas*. Thus whether petitioners' removal of books from their school libraries denied respondents their First Amendment rights depends upon the motivation behind petitioners' actions. If petitioners *intended* by their removal decision to deny respondents access to ideas with which petitioners disagreed, and if this intent was the decisive factor in petitioners' decision,[4] then petitioners

---

4. By "decisive factor" we mean a "substantial factor" in the absence of which the opposite decision would have been reached. See Mt. Healthy City Board of Ed. v. Doyle, 429 U.S. 274 (1977). [Footnote by Justice Brennan.]

have exercised their discretion in violation of the Constitution. To permit such intentions to control official actions would be to encourage the precise sort of officially prescribed orthodoxy unequivocally condemned in Barnette. On the other hand, respondents implicitly concede that an unconstitutional motivation would *not* be demonstrated if it were shown that petitioners had decided to remove the books at issue because those books were pervasively vulgar. And again, respondents concede that if it were demonstrated that the removal decision was based solely upon the "educational suitability" of the books in question, then their removal would be "perfectly permissible." In other words, in respondents' view such motivations, if decisive of petitioners' actions, would not carry the danger of an official suppression of ideas, and thus would not violate respondents' First Amendment rights.

As noted earlier, nothing in our decision today affects in any way the discretion of a local school board to choose books to *add* to the libraries of their schools. Because we are concerned in this case with the suppression of ideas, our holding today affects only the discretion to *remove* books. In brief, we hold that local school boards may not remove books from school library shelves simply because they dislike the ideas contained in those books and seek by their removal to "prescribe what shall be orthodox in politics, nationalism, religion, or other matters of opinion." [Barnette.] Such purposes stand inescapably condemned by our precedents.

B. We now turn to the remaining question presented by this case: Do the evidentiary materials that were before the District Court, when construed most favorably to respondents, raise a genuine issue of material fact whether petitioners exceeded constitutional limitations in exercising their discretion to remove the books from the school libraries? We conclude that the materials do raise such a question, which forecloses summary judgment in favor of petitioners. The evidence plainly does not foreclose the possibility that petitioners' decision to remove the books rested decisively upon disagreement with constitutionally protected ideas in those books, or upon a desire on petitioners' part to impose upon the students [a] political orthodoxy to which petitioners and their constituents adhered. Of course, some of the evidence before the District Court might lead a finder of fact to accept petitioners' claim that their removal decision was based upon constitutionally valid concerns. But that evidence at most creates a genuine issue of material fact on the critical question of the credibility of petitioners' justifications for their decision. On that issue, it simply cannot be said that there is no genuine issue as to any material fact.

[Affirmed.]

Justice BLACKMUN, concurring in part and concurring in the judgment.

While I agree with much in today's plurality opinion, and while I accept the standard laid down by the plurality to guide proceedings on remand, I write separately because I have a somewhat different perspective on the nature of the First Amendment right involved.

I. To my mind, this case presents a particularly complex problem because it involves two competing principles of constitutional stature. On the one hand, [it] seems entirely appropriate that the State use "public schools [to] inculcat[e] fundamental values necessary to the maintenance of a democratic political system." Ambach v. Norwick. On the other hand, as the plurality demonstrates, it is beyond dispute that schools and school boards must operate within the confines of the First Amendment. [The cases yield] a general principle: the State may not suppress exposure to ideas—for the sole *purpose* of suppressing exposure to those ideas—absent sufficiently compelling reasons. [This] principle necessarily applies in at least a limited way to public education. [In] my view, then, the principle involved here is both narrower and more basic than the "right to receive information" identified by the plurality. I do not suggest that the State has any affirmative obligation to provide students with information or ideas, something that may well be associated with a "right to receive." And I do not believe, as the plurality suggests, that the right at issue here is somehow associated with the peculiar nature of the school library; if schools may be used to inculcate ideas, surely libraries may play a role in that process.[1] Instead, I suggest that certain forms of state discrimination *between* ideas are improper. In particular, our precedents command the conclusion that the State may not act to deny access to an idea simply because state officials disapprove of that idea for partisan or political reasons.[2]

Certainly, the unique environment of the school places substantial limits on the extent to which official decisions may be restrained by First Amendment values. But that environment also makes it particularly important that *some* limits be imposed. The school is designed to, and inevitably will, inculcate ways of thought and outlooks; if educators intentionally may eliminate all diversity of thought, the school will "strangle the free mind at its source and teach youth to discount important principles of our government as mere platitudes." Barnette. As I see it, then, the question in this case is how to make the delicate accommodation between the limited constitutional restriction that I think is imposed by the First Amendment, and the necessarily broad state authority to regulate education. In starker terms, we must reconcile the schools' "inculcative" function with the First Amendment's bar on "prescriptions of orthodoxy."

II. In my view, we strike a proper balance here by holding that school officials may not remove books for the *purpose* of restricting access to the political ideas or social perspectives discussed in them, when that action is motivated simply by the officials' disapproval of the ideas involved. [The] school board must "be able to show that its action was caused by something more than a mere desire to avoid the discomfort and unpleasantness that always accompany an unpopular viewpoint" [Tinker] and that the board had something in mind in addition to the suppression of partisan or political views it did not share. As I view it, this is a narrow principle. School officials must be able to choose one book over another, without outside interference, when the first book is deemed more relevant to the curriculum, or better written, or when one of a host of other politically neutral reasons is present. [And] even absent space or financial limitations, First Amendment principles would allow a school board to refuse to make a book available to students because it contains offensive

1. As a practical matter, however, it is difficult to see the First Amendment right that I believe is at work here playing a role in a school's choice of curriculum. The school's finite resources—as well as the limited number of hours in the day—require that education officials make sensitive choices between subjects to be offered and competing areas of academic emphasis; subjects generally are excluded simply because school officials have chosen to devote their resources to one rather than to another subject. As is explained below, a choice of this nature does not run afoul of the First Amendment. In any event, the Court has recognized that students' First Amendment rights in most cases must give way if they interfere "with the schools' work or [with] the rights of other students to be secure and to be let alone" [Tinker] and such interference will rise to intolerable levels if public participation in the management of the curriculum becomes commonplace. In contrast, library books on a shelf intrude not at all on the daily operation of a school.

I also have some doubt that there is a theoretical distinction between removal of a book and failure to acquire a book. But as Judge Newman observed, there is a profound practical and evidentiary distinction between the two actions: "removal, more than failure to acquire, is likely to suggest that an impermissible political motivation may be present. There are many reasons why a book is not acquired, the most obvious being limited resources, but there are few legitimate reasons why a book, once acquired, should be removed from a library not filled to capacity." [Footnote by Justice Blackmun.]

2. In effect, my view presents the obverse of the plurality's analysis: while the plurality focuses on the failure to provide information, I find crucial the State's decision to single out an idea for disapproval and then deny access to it. [Footnote by Justice Blackmun.]

language, cf. [Pacifica], or because it is psychologically or intellectually inappropriate for the age group, or even, perhaps, because the ideas it advances are "manifestly inimical to the public welfare." [Pierce.] And, of course, school officials may choose one book over another because they believe that one subject is more important, or is more deserving of emphasis.

[I] do not share Justice Rehnquist's view that the notion of "suppression of ideas" is not a useful analytical concept. [And] I believe that tying the First Amendment right to the *purposeful* suppression of ideas makes the concept more manageable than Justice Rehnquist acknowledges. Most people would recognize that refusing to allow discussion of current events in Latin class is a policy designed to "inculcate" Latin, not to suppress ideas. Similarly, removing a learned treatise criticizing American foreign policy from an elementary school library because the students would not understand it is an action unrelated to the *purpose* of suppressing ideas. In my view, however, removing the same treatise because it is "anti-American" raises a far more difficult issue. It is not a sufficient answer to this problem that a State operates a school in its role as "educator," rather than its role as "sovereign" [see Justice Rehnquist's dissent], for the First Amendment has application to all the State's activities. While the State may act as "property owner" when it prevents certain types of expressive activity from taking place on public lands, for example, few would suggest that the State may base such restrictions on the content of the speaker's message, or may take its action for the purpose of suppressing access to the ideas involved. See [Mosley].

[Concededly], a tension exists between the properly inculcative purposes of public education and any limitation on the school board's absolute discretion to choose academic materials. But that tension demonstrates only that the problem here is a difficult one, not that the problem should be resolved by choosing one principle over another. [School] officials may seek to instill certain values "by persuasion and example" [Barnette] or by choice of emphasis. That sort of positive educational action, however, is the converse of an intentional attempt to shield students from certain ideas that officials find politically distasteful. [The] principle involved here may be difficult to apply in an individual case. But on a record as sparse as the one before us, the plurality can hardly be faulted for failing to explore every possible ramification of its decision. [Because] I believe that the plurality has derived a standard similar to the one compelled by my analysis, I join all but Part IIA(1) of the plurality opinion.

Justice WHITE, concurring in the judgment.

[The Court of Appeals concluded] that there was a material issue of fact that precluded summary judgment sought by petitioners. The unresolved factual issue [is] the reason or reasons underlying the school board's removal of the books. I am not inclined to disagree with the Court of Appeals on such a fact-bound issue and hence concur in the judgment of affirmance. Presumably this will result in a trial and the making of a full record and findings on the critical issues. The Court seems compelled to go further and issue a dissertation on the extent to which the First Amendment limits the discretion of the school board to remove books from the school library. I see no necessity for doing so at this [point].

Chief Justice BURGER, with whom Justice POWELL, Justice REHNQUIST, and Justice O'CONNOR join, dissenting.

[In] an attempt to deal with a problem in an area traditionally left to the states, a plurality of the Court, in a lavish expansion going beyond any prior holding under the First Amendment, expresses its view that a school board's decision concerning what books are to be in the school library is subject to federal court review. Were this to become the law, this Court would come perilously close to becoming a "super censor" of school board library decisions.

[If], as we have held, schools may legitimately be used as vehicles for "inculcating fundamental values necessary to the maintenance of a democratic political system," Ambach v. Norwick, school authorities must have broad discretion to fulfill that obligation. [How] are "fundamental values" to be inculcated except by having school boards make content-based decisions about the appropriateness of retaining materials in the school library and curriculum? In order to fulfill its function, an elected school board *must* express its views on the subjects which are taught to its students. In doing so those elected officials express the views of their community; they may err, of course, and the voters may remove them. It is a startling erosion of the very idea of democratic government to have this Court arrogate to itself the power the plurality asserts today.

[No] amount of "limiting" language could rein in the sweeping "right" the plurality would create. [Through] use of bits and pieces of prior opinions unrelated to the issue of this case, the plurality demeans our function of constitutional adjudication. Today the plurality suggests that the *Constitution* distinguishes between school libraries and school classrooms, between *removing* unwanted books and *acquiring* books. Even more extreme, the plurality concludes that the Constitution *requires* school boards to justify to its teenage pupils the decision to remove a particular book from a school library. I categorically reject this notion that the Constitution dictates that judges, rather than parents, teachers, and local school boards, must determine how the standards of morality and vulgarity are to be treated in the classroom.[1]

Justice POWELL, dissenting.

[It] is fair to say that no single agency of government at any level is closer to the people whom it serves than the typical school board. I therefore view today's decision with genuine dismay. Whatever the final outcome of this suit and suits like it, the resolution of educational policy decisions through litigation, and the exposure of school board members to liability for such decisions, can be expected to corrode the school board's authority and effectiveness. As is evident from the generality of the plurality's "standard" for judicial review, the decision as to the educational worth of a book is a highly subjective one. Judges rarely are as competent as school authorities to make this decision; nor are judges responsive to the parents and people of the school district. [The plurality's] new constitutional right ["to receive ideas"] is framed in terms that approach a meaningless generalization. [The] plurality does announce the following standard: A school board's "discretion may not be exercised in a narrowly partisan or political manner." But this is a standardless standard that affords no more than subjective guidance to school boards, their counsel, and to courts that now will be required to decide whether a particular decision was made in a "narrowly partisan or political manner." Even the "chancellor's foot" standard in ancient equity jurisdiction was never this [fuzzy].[1]

Justice REHNQUIST, with whom The Chief Justice [BURGER] and Justice POWELL, join, dissenting.

[The] District Court was correct in granting summary judgment. [I] agree fully with the views expressed by The Chief Justice, and concur in his opinion. I disagree with Justice Brennan's opinion because it is largely hypothetical in character, failing to take account of the facts as admitted by the parties pursuant to local rules of the District Court, and because it is analytically unsound and internally inconsistent.

---

1. Justice O'CONNOR, who joined the Chief Justice's dissent, stated in a separate notation: "I do not personally agree with the board's action with respect to some of the books in question here, but it is not the function of the courts to make the decisions that have been properly relegated to the elected members of school boards."

1. As an appendix to his opinion, Justice Powell reprinted a seven-page summary (compiled by Court of Appeals Judge Mansfield) of "excerpts from the books at issue in this case."

I. A. Justice Brennan's opinion deals far more sparsely with the procedural posture of this case than it does with the constitutional issues. [When] Justice Brennan finally does address the state of the record, he refers to snippets and excerpts of the relevant facts to explain why a grant of summary judgment was improper. But he totally ignores the effect of Rule 9(g) of the local rules of the District Court, under which the parties set forth their version of the disputed facts in this case. Since summary judgment was entered against respondents, they are entitled to have their version of the facts, as embodied in their Rule 9(g) statement, accepted for purposes of our review. Since the parties themselves are presumably the best judges of the extent of the factual dispute between them, however, respondents certainly are not entitled to any more favorable version of the facts than that contained in their own Rule 9(g) statement. Justice Brennan's combing through the record of affidavits, school bulletins, and the like for bits and snatches of dispute is therefore entirely beside the point at this stage of the case.

[Respondents agreed that petitioners] "have not precluded discussion about the themes of the books or the books themselves." Justice Brennan's concern with the "suppression of ideas" thus seems entirely unwarranted on this state of the record, and his creation of constitutional rules to cover such eventualities is entirely gratuitous. [The] nine books removed undoubtedly did contain "ideas," [but] it is apparent that eight of them contained demonstrable amounts of vulgarity and profanity, and the ninth contained nothing that could be considered partisan or political. [Petitioners] did not, for the reasons stated hereafter, run afoul of the [First Amendment] by removing these particular books from the library in the manner in which they did. I would save for another day—feeling quite confident that that day will not arrive—the extreme examples posed in Justice Brennan's opinion.

B. [Had] petitioners been the members of a town council, I suppose all would agree that, absent a good deal more than is present in this record, they could not have prohibited the sale of these books by private booksellers within the municipality. But we have also recognized that the government may act in other capacities than as sovereign, and when it does the First Amendment may speak with a different voice. [E.g., Pickering v. Board of Education (1968; government as employer; p. 1392 below); Adderley v. Florida (government as property owner).] [With] these differentiated roles of government in mind, it is helpful to assess the role of government as educator, as compared with the role of government as sovereign. When it acts as an educator, at least at the elementary and secondary school level, the government is engaged in inculcating social values and knowledge in relatively impressionable young people. Obviously there are innumerable decisions to be made as to what courses should be taught, what books should be purchased, or what teachers should be employed. In every one of these areas the members of a school board will act on the basis of their own personal or moral values, will attempt to mirror those of the community, or will abdicate the making of such decisions to so-called "experts." [In] the very course of administering the many-faceted operations of a school district, the mere decision to purchase some books will necessarily preclude the possibility of purchasing others. The decision to teach a particular subject may preclude the possibility of teaching another subject. A decision to replace a teacher because of ineffectiveness may by implication be seen as a disparagement of the subject matter taught. In each of these instances, however, the book or the exposure to the subject matter may be acquired elsewhere. The managers of the school district are not proscribing it as to the citizenry in general, but are simply determining that it will not be included in the curriculum or school library. In short, actions by the government as educator do not raise the same First Amendment concerns as actions by the government as sovereign.

II. [It] is the very existence of a right to receive information, in the junior high school and high school setting, which I find wholly unsupported by our past decisions and inconsistent with the necessarily selective process of elementary and secondary education.

A. The right described by Justice Brennan has never been recognized in the decisions of this Court and is not supported by their rationale. [O]ur past decisions in this area have concerned freedom of speech and expression, not the right of access to particular ideas. [Tinker; Barnette.] But these decisions scarcely control the case before us. [Despite] Justice Brennan's suggestion to the contrary, this Court has never held that the First Amendment grants junior high school and high school students a right of access to certain information in school. It is true that the Court has recognized a limited version of that right in other settings, and Justice Brennan quotes language from [several] such decisions [in order to] demonstrate the viability of the right-to-receive doctrine. But not one of these cases concerned or even purported to discuss elementary or secondary educational institutions.

Nor does the right-to-receive doctrine recognized in our past decisions apply to schools by analogy. Justice Brennan correctly characterizes the right of access to ideas as "an inherent corollary of the rights of free speech and press" which "follows ineluctably from the *sender*'s First Amendment right to send them." But he then fails to recognize the predicate right to speak from which the students' right to receive must follow. It would be ludicrous, of course, to contend that all authors have a constitutional right to have their books placed in [school] libraries. And yet without such a right our prior precedents would not recognize the reciprocal right to receive information. Justice Brennan disregards this inconsistency with our prior cases and fails to explain the constitutional or logical underpinnings of a right to hear ideas in a place where no speaker has the right to express them. [Moreover], the denial of access to ideas inhibits one's own acquisition of knowledge only when that denial is relatively complete. [Our] past decisions [are] unlike this case where the removed books are readily available to students and non-students alike at the corner bookstore or the public library.

B. There are even greater reasons for rejecting Justice Brennan's analysis, however. [Public schools] fulfill the vital role of "inculcating fundamental values necessary to the maintenance of a democratic political system." [Ambach v. Norwick.] The idea that such students have a right of access, *in the school,* to information other than that thought by their educators to be necessary is contrary to the very nature of an inculcative education. Education consists of the selective presentation and explanation of ideas. The effective acquisition of knowledge depends upon an orderly exposure to relevant information. Nowhere is this more true than in elementary and secondary schools, where, unlike the broad-ranging inquiry available to university students, the courses taught are those thought most relevant to the young students' individual development. Of necessity, elementary and secondary educators must separate the relevant from the irrelevant, the appropriate from the inappropriate. Determining what information *not* to present to the students is often as important as identifying relevant material. This winnowing process necessarily leaves much information to be discovered by students at another time or in another place, and is fundamentally inconsistent with any constitutionally required eclecticism in public education.

Justice Brennan rejects this idea, claiming that it "overlooks the unique role of the school library." But the unique role referred to appears to be one of Justice Brennan's own creation. [In his] paean of praise to [school] libraries as the "environment especially appropriate for the recognition of the First Amendment rights of students," [he] turns to language about *public* libraries from

Brown v. Louisiana and to language about universities and colleges from [Keyishian]. Not only is his authority thus transparently thin, but also, and more importantly, his reasoning misapprehends the function of libraries in our public school system. [E]lementary and secondary schools are inculcative in nature. The libraries of such schools serve as supplements to this inculcative role. Unlike university or public libraries, elementary and secondary school libraries are not designed for free-wheeling inquiry; they are tailored, as the public school curriculum is tailored, to the teaching of basic skills and ideas. Thus, Justice Brennan cannot rely upon the nature of school libraries to escape the fact that the First Amendment right to receive information simply has no application to the one public institution which, by its very nature, is a place for the selective conveyance of ideas. After all else is said, however, the most obvious reason that petitioners' removal of the books did not violate respondents' right to receive information is the ready availability of the books [elsewhere]. The government as educator does not seek to reach beyond the confines of the school. Indeed, following the removal from the school library of the books at issue in this case, the local public library put all nine books on display for public inspection. Their contents were fully accessible to any inquisitive student.

C. Justice Brennan's own discomfort with the idea that students have a right to receive information from their elementary or secondary schools is demonstrated by the artificial limitations which he places upon the right— limitations which are supported neither by logic nor authority and which are inconsistent with the right itself. The attempt to confine the right to the library is one such [limitation]. As a second limitation, Justice Brennan distinguishes the act of removing a previously acquired book from the act of refusing to acquire the book in the first place. [If] Justice Brennan truly has found a "right to receive ideas," however, this distinction between acquisition and removal makes little sense. The failure of a library to acquire a book denies access to its contents just as effectively as does the removal of the book from the library's shelf.

[The] justification for this limiting distinction is said [to be the] concern in this case with "the suppression of ideas." Whatever may be the analytical usefulness of this appealing sounding phrase, see subpart D, infra, the suppression of ideas surely is not the identical twin of the denial of access to information. Not every official act which denies access to an idea can be characterized as a suppression of the idea. Thus unless the "right to receive information" and the prohibition against "suppression of ideas" are each a kind of mother-hubbard catch phrase for whatever First Amendment doctrines one wishes to cover, they would not appear to be interchangeable. Justice Brennan's reliance on the "suppression of ideas" to justify his distinction between acquisition and removal of books has additional logical pitfalls. Presumably the distinction is based upon the greater visibility and the greater sense of conscious decision thought to be involved in the removal of a book, as opposed to that involved in the refusal to acquire a book. But if "suppression of ideas" is to be the talisman, one would think that a school board's public announcement of its refusal to acquire certain books would have every bit as much impact on public attention as would an equally publicized decision to remove the books. And yet only the latter action would violate the First Amendment under Justice Brennan's analysis.

The final limitation placed by Justice Brennan upon his newly discovered right is a motive requirement: the First Amendment is violated only "[i]f petitioners *intended* by their removal decision to deny respondents access to ideas with which petitioners disagreed." But bad motives and good motives alike deny access to the books removed. If [there truly is] a constitutional right to receive information, it is difficult to see why the reason for the denial makes any difference. Of course Justice Brennan's view is that intent matters because the First Amendment does not tolerate an officially prescribed orthodoxy. But this reasoning mixes First Amendment apples and oranges. The right to receive information differs from the right to be free from an officially prescribed orthodoxy. Not every educational denial of access to information casts a pall of orthodoxy over the classroom.

It is difficult to tell from Justice Brennan's opinion just what motives he would consider constitutionally impermissible. I had thought that the First Amendment proscribes content-based restrictions on the marketplace of ideas. Justice Brennan concludes, however, that a removal decision based solely upon the "educational suitability" of a book or upon its perceived vulgarity is " 'perfectly permissible.' " But such determinations are based as much on the content of the book as determinations that the book espouses pernicious political views. Moreover, Justice Brennan's motive test is difficult to square with his distinction between acquisition and removal. If a school board's removal of books might be motivated by a desire to promote favored political or religious views, there is no reason that its acquisition policy might not also be so motivated. And yet the "pall of orthodoxy" cast by a carefully executed book-acquisition program apparently would not violate the First Amendment under Justice Brennan's view.

D. Intertwined as a basis for Justice Brennan's opinion, along with the "right to receive information," is the statement that "our Constitution does not permit the official suppression of *ideas*." [My] difficulty is not with the admittedly appealing catchiness of the phrase, but with my doubt that it is really a useful analytical tool in solving difficult First Amendment problems. Since the phrase appears in the opinion "out of the blue," [it] would appear that the Court for years has managed to decide First Amendment cases without it. I would think that prior cases decided under established First Amendment doctrine afford adequate guides in this area without resorting to a phrase which seeks to express "a complicated process of constitutional adjudication by a deceptive formula." A school board which publicly adopts a policy forbidding the criticism of United States foreign policy by any student, any teacher, or any book on the library shelves is indulging in one kind of "suppression of ideas." A school board which adopts a policy that there shall be no discussion of current events in a class for high school sophomores devoted to second-year Latin "suppresses ideas" in quite a different context. A teacher who had a lesson plan consisting of 14 weeks of study of United States history from 1607 to the present time, but who because of a week's illness is forced to forego the most recent 20 years of American history, may "suppress ideas" in still another way. I think a far more satisfactory basis for addressing these kinds of questions is found in the Court's language in [Tinker]. [In] the case before us the petitioners may in one sense be said to have "suppressed" the "ideas" of vulgarity and profanity, but that is hardly an apt description of what was done. They ordered the removal of books containing vulgarity and profanity, but they did not attempt to preclude discussion about the themes of the books or the books themselves. Such a decision [is] sufficiently related to "educational suitability" to pass muster under the First Amendment.

E. The inconsistencies and illogic of the limitations placed by Justice Brennan upon his notion of the right to receive ideas in school are not here emphasized in order to suggest that they should be eliminated. They are emphasized because they illustrate that the right itself is misplaced in the elementary and secondary school setting. Likewise, the criticism of Justice Brennan's newly found prohibition against the "suppression of ideas" is by no means intended to suggest that the Constitution permits the suppression of ideas; it is rather to suggest that such a vague and imprecise phrase, while perhaps wholly consistent with the First Amendment, is simply too diaphanous to assist careful decision of cases such as these.

I think the Court will far better serve the cause of First Amendment jurisprudence by candidly recognizing that the role of government as sovereign is subject to more stringent limitations than is the role of government as employer, property owner, or educator. [With] respect to the education of children in elementary and secondary schools, the school board may properly determine in many cases that a particular book, a particular course, or even a particular area of knowledge is not educationally suitable for inclusion within the body of knowledge which the school seeks to impart. Without more, this is not a condemnation of the book or the course; it is only a determination akin to that referred to by the Court in [Euclid v. Ambler Realty Co.; 1926; chap. 8 above]: "A nuisance may be merely a right thing in the wrong place—like a pig in the parlor instead of the barnyard."

III. Accepting as true respondents' assertion that petitioners acted on the basis of their own "personal values, morals, and tastes," I find the actions taken in this case hard to distinguish from the myriad choices made by school boards in the routine supervision of elementary and secondary schools. [In] this case respondents' rights of free speech and expression were not infringed, and by respondents' own admission no ideas were "suppressed." I would leave to another day the harder cases.

———

WHAT SOLUTION TO THE UNRESOLVED PROBLEMS OF PICO?

The multiple opinions in Board of Education v. Pico raise but do not resolve the conflicts between the schools' inculcative function and the limiting First Amendment interests. There was no majority opinion; and the remand disposition was made possible by the concurring vote of Justice White, who expressed no view at all on the constitutional merits.[1] But the several opinions—especially those of Justices Brennan, Blackmun and Rehnquist—do reveal the clash of competing principles and the difficulties of formulating a resolution. What *should* be the proper resolution? To some extent, the case raises issues previewed in the note on government speech (p. 1276 above), and particularly the concern with excessive governmental communicative power, especially in the school setting. As noted earlier, one recurrent question is whether First Amendment protections are at all applicable to government speech.

The Pico division produced extensive commentary. For a particularly thoughtful discussion, critical of most of the opinions in Pico, see Note, "State Indoctrination and the Protection of Non-State Voices in the Schools: Justifying a Prohibition of School Library Censorship," 35 Stan.L.Rev. 497 (1983). The Note criticizes the "confusion and the appearance of arbitrariness" in most judicial confrontations of problems of library book removals and curriculum controls. The Note argues that "courts have recognized an undefined, potentially all-encompassing state indoctrinative interest and have balanced it against an undefined, potentially all-encompassing first amendment interest." The Note argues that "a more satisfying analysis would come from an understanding that both the scope of state indoctrinative interests and the scope of first amendment interests are aspects of the same social interest in approximating an ideal of communal self-government." With respect to Justice Brennan's analysis in Pico, the Note claims that "the opinion's confusion stems from its uncritical

---

1. Moreover, the remand produced no resolution: the case was abandoned after the remand; there was no further hearing on the merits. See New York Times, Aug. 13, 1982.

acceptance of the validity of the very broad interest in indoctrination and from its willingness to juxtapose that interest and a supposedly unrelated student first amendment right. That approach gave rise to a need for limiting in some way the areas where the state interest applied, but the shape of those limits could not be derived from the student right as it was stated in the opinion."

In its search for a more plausible basis for limiting state inculcative goals, the Note relies heavily on Meiklejohn's self-government rationale for freedom of expression. (Recall the introductory passages to chap. 11, above.) The central role of representative self-government assertedly can serve both to delineate the proper scope of state indoctrination and the proper First Amendment limits on that state role. The Note concludes that Meiklejohn's rationale would "support a government interest in inculcating values that would promote the community's continued capacity to govern itself through critical and independent intellectual inquiry, public debate, and participation in elections." But that rationale "would prohibit [a] government interest in inculcating values for the purpose of influencing the outcomes of future public debates." Thus, "the constitutional ideal of citizen self-government precludes recognizing a broad state indoctrinative interest in using education to instill in children whatever values might be chosen by the local community according to majoritarian preferences," but "does legitimize certain indoctrinative goals." The Note insists that the Meiklejohn rationale "clearly demonstrates the need for limits on the state." However the distinction the Note finds inherent in Meiklejohn—the distinction between legitimate and illegitimate indoctrination—may be a judicially unmanageable distinction. The Note views Justice Blackmun's concurrence as a plausible " 'second best' solution that indirectly and imperfectly serves many of the same concerns as the analyses derived from the self-government ideal," while still providing a judicially usable approach.[2] Is that a persuasive analysis? A judicially manageable one? An approach at least useful to conscientious school officials seeking constitutional guidance?

B. INTERFERENCE WITH THE ADMINISTRATION OF JUSTICE

WOOD v. GEORGIA

370 U.S. 375, 82 S.Ct. 1364, 8 L.Ed.2d 569 (1962).

Mr. Chief Justice WARREN delivered the opinion of the Court.

2. The Note finds Justice Blackmun's approach, although leading to much the same results as the plurality's, resting on a "less complex and more coherent" analysis. Moreover, Justice Blackmun's approach "offers guidance for other issues of free speech in the schools." Thus, Justice Blackmun viewed "the principle that the state may not seek to suppress ideas as theoretically applicable to *all* aspects of education, even if in some contexts practical constraints or problems of evidence might prevent the effective [judicial] enforcement of this principle." The Note stresses that Justice Blackmun's approach "allows a change in the focus of first amendment inquiry with regard to the schools." Justice Blackmun pushes towards "the proper concern: Does the state have compelling reasons for denying access to an idea? Unlike the plurality, Justice Blackmun does not put the question in terms of an ill-defined student 'right to receive information.' "

The Note insists that any First Amendment limits on the state should not rest on the individual student's right but on "the societal need to prohibit the government from pursuing ends destructive to our ideal of the self-governing sovereign citizenry." The Note concludes: "In essence, the premise of the school boards' defenders has been that the state's interest in conforming education to the majority's indoctrinative goals outweighs the minimal dignitary harm done to any individual. But under the self-government view of the first amendment, the legitimacy of that state interest is not unlimited and the purpose of applying the first amendment is, in fact, to define appropriate limits. Just as the self-government rationale justifies protecting the voices of parents, teachers, and students elsewhere in the educational system [as illustrated by cases from Barnette through Tinker], it justifies protecting books in the school library."

We granted certiorari to consider the scope of the constitutional protection to be enjoyed by persons when the publication of their thoughts and opinions is alleged to be in conflict with the fair administration of justice in state courts. The petitioner, an elected sheriff in Bibb County, Georgia, contends that the Georgia courts, in holding him in contempt of court for expressing his personal ideas on a matter that was presently before the grand jury for its consideration, have abridged his liberty of [free speech].

On June 6, 1960, a judge of the Bibb Superior Court [instructed a grand jury] to conduct an investigation into a political situation which had allegedly arisen in the county [—apparently] "an inane and inexplicable pattern of Negro bloc voting" [and] "rumors and accusations" [that] candidates for public office had paid large sums of money [to] obtain the Negro vote. [The] instructions were given in the midst of a local political campaign and the [judges], in order to publicize the investigation, requested reporters for all local news media to be present in the courtroom when the charge was delivered. The following day, [petitioner issued a news release] in which he criticized the judges' action and in which he urged the citizenry to take notice when their highest judicial officers threatened political intimidation and persecution of voters in the county under the guise of law enforcement.[1]

[A] month later, [petitioner] was cited [for] contempt based on the above statements. The citation charged that the language used by the petitioner was designed and calculated to be contemptuous of the court, to ridicule the investigation ordered by the charge, and "to hamper, hinder, interfere with and obstruct" the grand jury in its investigation. [An] amendment to the citation alleged that the statements "in and of [themselves] created [a] clear, present and imminent danger to the investigation being conducted [and] to the proper administration of justice in Bibb Superior Court." The next day the petitioner issued a further press release in which he repeated substantially the charges he had made in the release on June 7, and in which he asserted that his defense to the contempt citation would be that he had spoken the truth. The contempt citation was thereupon amended by including [a] count based on this latter statement. [No] witnesses were presented at the hearing [before the trial judge] and no evidence was introduced to show that the publications resulted in any actual interference or obstruction of the court or the work of the grand jury. The gravamen of [the] case against the petitioner was that the mere publishing

---

1. The news release stated:

"Whatever the Judges' intention, the action [ordering the grand jury] to investigate 'negro block voting' will be considered one of the most deplorable examples of race agitation to come out of Middle Georgia in recent years.

"At a time when all thinking people want to preserve the good will and cooperation between the races in Bibb County, this action appears either as a crude attempt at judicial intimidation of negro voters and leaders, or, at best, as agitation for a 'negro vote' issue in local politics.

"Negro people will find little difference in principle between attempted intimidation of their people by judicial summons and inquiry and attempted intimidation by physical demonstration such as used by the K.K.K. [It] is hoped that the present Grand Jury will not let its high office be a party to any political attempt to intimidate the negro people in this community.

"It seems incredible that all three of our Superior Court Judges, who themselves hold high political office, are so politically nieve [naive] as to actually believe that the negro voters in Bibb County sell their votes in any fashion, either to candidates for office or to some negro leaders.

"If anyone in the community [should] be free of racial prejudice, it should be our Judges. It is shocking to find a Judge charging a Grand Jury in the style and language of a race baiting candidate [for political office]. However politically popular the judges' action may be at this time, they are employing a practice far more dangerous to free elections than anything they want investigated.

"James I. Wood."

of the news release and defense statement constituted a contempt of court, and in and of itself was a clear and present danger to the administration of [justice].

We start with the premise that the right of courts to conduct their business in an untrammeled way lies at the foundation of our system of government and that courts necessarily must possess the means of punishing for contempt when conduct tends directly to prevent the discharge of their functions. While courts have continuously had the authority and power to maintain order in their courtrooms and to assure litigants a fair trial, the exercise of that bare contempt power is not what is questioned in this case. Here it is asserted that the exercise of the contempt power, to commit a person to jail for an utterance out of the presence of the court, has abridged the accused's liberty of free expression. In this situation the burden upon this Court is to define the limitations upon the contempt power according to the terms of the Federal Constitution.

In Bridges v. California, 314 U.S. 252 [1941], [we] held that out-of-court publications were to be governed by the clear and present danger standard, described as "a working principle that the substantive evil must be extremely serious and the degree of imminence extremely high before utterances can be punished." [2] Subsequently, in Pennekamp v. Florida, 328 U.S. 331 [1946], [the] Court reaffirmed its belief that the "essential right of the courts to be free of intimidation and coercion [is] consonant with a recognition that freedom of the press must be allowed in the broadest scope compatible with the supremacy of order." [3] The Court's last occasion to consider the application of the clear and present danger principle to a case of the type under review was in Craig v. Harney, 331 U.S. 367 [1947]. There the Court held that to warrant a sanction "[t]he fires which [the expression] kindles must constitute an imminent, not merely a likely, threat to the administration of justice. The danger must not be remote or even probable; it must immediately imperil." [4]

It is with these principles in mind that we consider the case before us. [Despite] its conclusion that the petitioner's conduct created [a clear and present danger to the fair administration of justice], the Court of Appeals did not cite or

2. Bridges reversed contempt convictions in two cases. In the first, a newspaper—while a decision was pending on the sentencing of union members for assault on nonunion workers—had attacked the convicted defendants and had stated that the trial judge would "make a serious mistake if he [granted] probation." In the second, union leader Harry Bridges—while a motion for a new trial in a labor dispute was pending—had caused the newspaper publication of his telegram to the Secretary of Labor threatening a strike if the "outrageous" court decision were enforced. The lower courts had rested their contempt findings on the "tendency" of the publications to interfere with the "orderly administration of justice." Justice Black's majority opinion in the 5 to 4 decision reversing these convictions concluded that punishment was permissible only where there was a clear and present danger that justice would be obstructed. Justice Frankfurter's dissent stated: "A trial is not 'a free trade in ideas,' nor is the best test of truth in a courtroom 'the power of the thought to get itself accepted in the competition of the market.'"

3. In the Pennekamp case, a newspaper involved in an anti-vice crusade published editorials and a cartoon implying that the judges were using legal technicalities to hinder the prosecution of several rape and gambling cases. The newspaper and its associate editor, Pennekamp,

were held in contempt and fined by a Florida court. As in Bridges, the Court applied the clear and present danger test and reversed.

4. Craig v. Harney reversed contempt convictions of a newspaper editor who, in an effort to influence an elected lay judge on a pending motion for a new trial in a private lawsuit, published inaccurate reports and unfair criticisms of the judge's action in directing a verdict for a landlord. Justice Douglas' majority opinion commented: "[T]he law of contempt is not made for the protection of judges who may be sensitive to the winds of public opinion. Judges are supposed to be men of fortitude, able to thrive in a hardy climate." One of the dissenters, Justice Jackson, retorted: "From our sheltered position, fortified by life tenure, [it] is easy to say that this local judge ought to have shown more fortitude in the face of criticism. [Of] course, the blasts of these little papers in this small community do not jolt us, but I am not so confident that we would be indifferent if a news monopoly in our entire jurisdiction should perpetrate this kind of an attack on us."

Note the efforts to distinguish Bridges, Pennekamp, and Craig in Justice Harlan's dissent, below. Compare the approach in Cox v. Louisiana [Cox II; 1965; p. 1228 above and note 2 below].

discuss the Bridges, Pennekamp or Harney cases, nor did it display an awareness of the standards enunciated in those cases to support a finding of clear and present danger. [The] court did not indicate in any manner *how* the publications interfered with the grand jury's investigation. [Thus] we have simply been told, as a matter of law without factual support, that if a State is unable to punish persons for expressing their views on matters of great public importance when those matters are being considered in an investigation by the grand jury, a clear and present danger to the administration of justice will be created. We find no such danger in the record before us. The type of "danger" evidenced by the record is precisely one of the types of activity envisioned by the [framers of the First Amendment]. Men are entitled to speak as they please on matters vital to them; errors in judgment or unsubstantiated opinions may be exposed, of course, but not through punishment for contempt for the expression. [In] the absence of some other showing of a substantive evil actually designed to impede the course of justice in justification of the exercise of the contempt power to silence the petitioner, his utterances are entitled to be protected.

[We find the state court's "clear and present danger" conclusion] unpersuasive. First, it is important to emphasize that this case does not represent a situation where an individual is on trial. [Moreover], we need not pause here to consider the variant factors that would be present in a case involving a petit jury. Neither Bridges, Pennekamp nor Harney involved a trial by jury. [The] grand jury here was conducting a general investigation into a matter touching each member of the community. [Particularly] in matters of local political corruption and investigations is it important that freedom of communication be kept open and that the real issues not become obscured to the grand jury. [The] necessity to society of an independent and informed grand jury becomes readily apparent in the context of the present case. For here a panel of judges, themselves elected officers and charged under state law with the responsibility of instructing a grand jury to investigate political corruption, have exercised the contempt power to hold in contempt another elected representative of the people for publishing views honestly held and contrary to those contained in the charge. And, an effort by the petitioner to prove the truth of his allegations was rejected, the court holding irrelevant the truth or falsity of the facts and opinions expressed in the publications. If the petitioner could be silenced in this manner, the problem to the people in [Georgia] and indeed in all the States becomes evident.

The administration of the law is not the problem of the judge or prosecuting attorney alone, but necessitates the active cooperation of an enlightened public. Nothing is to be gained by an attitude on the part of the citizenry of civic irresponsibility and apathy in voicing their sentiments on community problems. The petitioner's attack on the charge to the grand jury would have been likely to have an impeding influence on the outcome of the investigation only if the charge was so manifestly unjust that it could not stand inspection. In this sense discussion serves as a corrective force to political, economic and other influences which are inevitably present in matters of grave [importance]. Moreover, it is difficult to imagine how the voting problem may be alleviated by an abridgment of talk and comment regarding its solution. [When] the grand jury is performing its investigatory function into a general problem area, without specific regard to indicting a particular individual, society's interest is best served by a thorough and extensive investigation, and a greater degree of disinterestedness and impartiality is assured by allowing free expression of contrary opinion. [In] the absence of any showing of an actual interference with the undertakings of the grand jury, this record lacks persuasion in illustrating the serious degree of harm to the administration of law necessary to justify exercise of the [contempt power].

Reversed.[5]

Mr. Justice HARLAN, whom Mr. Justice CLARK joins, dissenting.

[Even] under the most expansive view of Bridges and its offshoots the contempt judgment against this sheriff should be upheld. [The] right of free speech [is] not absolute; when the right to speak conflicts with the right to an impartial judicial proceeding, an accommodation must be made to preserve the essence of both. [The Bridges clear and present danger test] is amply met here. Petitioner, a public official connected with the court, accused, from his office in the courthouse, the Superior Court judges of fomenting race hatred; of misusing the criminal law to persecute and to intimidate political and racial minorities; of political naiveté, racial prejudice, and hypocrisy. He compared the calling of the grand jury to the activities of the Ku Klux Klan. He made an undisguised effort to influence the outcome of the investigation by declaring that only the politically naive could believe Bibb County Negroes might be guilty of selling votes. It was stipulated that both of petitioner's formal statements were read by the grand jurors during the course of their investigation. The Court considers this evidence insufficient because there was no showing of "an actual interference with the undertakings of the jury." [Surely] the Court cannot mean that attempts to influence judicial proceedings are punishable only if they are successful. Speech creating sufficient danger of an evil which the State may prevent may certainly be punished regardless of whether that evil materializes. [Any] expression of opinion on the merits of a pending judicial proceeding is likely to have an impact on deliberations. In this instance that likelihood was increased by two factors which were not present in Bridges, Pennekamp, or Craig. [None] of those cases involved statements by officers of the court; and all concerned statements whose alleged interference was with the deliberations of a judge rather than a [jury].

Of equal if not greater importance is the fact that petitioner's statements were calculated to influence, not a judge chosen because of his independence, integrity, and courage and trained by experience and the discipline of law to deal only with evidence properly before him, but a grand jury of laymen chosen to serve for a limited term from the general population of Bibb County. It cannot be assumed with grand jurors, as it has been with judges [Craig v. Harney], that they are all "men of fortitude, able to thrive in a hardy climate." What may not seriously endanger the independent deliberations of a judge may well jeopardize those of a grand or petit jury. [Finally], petitioner's case is not saved by the fact that both he and the judges he attacked are elected officials, or by the fact that the statement concerned an issue of some political moment. There was ample opportunity to bring the judges' performance to the voters after the investigation was closed. "Political interest" cannot be used as an excuse for affecting the result of a [judicial inquiry].

CONTEMPT BY PUBLICATION, CLEAR AND PRESENT DANGER, AND THE PROBLEM OF IDENTIFYING AND EVALUATING THE "SUBSTANTIVE EVILS"

1. *Clear and present danger of what?* In no other area has the Court more consistently invoked clear and present danger language than in the Bridges-Pennekamp-Craig-Wood line of cases. Recall the questions raised about the test in chap. 11, sec. 1. How useful is emphasis on immediacy of harm in this area? To what extent is the problem that of identifying the "substantive evil," and of assessing its gravity? Is the "evil" that of *any* impact on judicial processes? Is it

---

5. Justices FRANKFURTER and WHITE did not participate in the case.

serious impact, distortion, interruption? Is it the *appearance* of impact? Which of these are grave enough to justify restricting speech?

2. *The contrast with Cox II.* Compare the contempt cases from Bridges to Wood with Cox v. Louisiana (Cox II, p. 1228 above), the 1965 decision upholding a ban on courthouse picketing. In Cox II, the Court distinguished these contempt cases: "We are not concerned here with such a pure form of expression as a newspaper comment. [We] deal in this case not with free speech alone but with expression mixed with particular conduct." Moreover, the Cox Court insisted that, "even assuming" clear and present danger was the applicable test, "mere publication" in these contempt cases was "quite another thing" from demonstrators barred "by a legislative determination based on experience that such conduct inherently threatens the judicial process." Recall, moreover, the Cox Court's statements about "evils" the legislature might legitimately consider: the danger that "some judges [will] be consciously or unconsciously influenced by demonstrations"; the risk of "the judicial process [being] misjudged in the minds of the public" even if the judge was "completely uninfluenced"—the danger, in other words, of "the possibility of a conclusion by the public [that] the judge's action was in part a product of intimidation." Were there such risks in the contempt cases? Were those dangers "clear and present" there? Was the Cox Court persuasive in distinguishing the contempt situations?

3. *The Landmark case.* Consider the extent to which the Burger Court repudiated the Cox II analysis and returned to the more speech-protective approach of the Bridges line of cases in LANDMARK COMMUNICATIONS, INC. v. VIRGINIA, 435 U.S. 829 (1978). Landmark, a newspaper publisher, had printed an accurate report of a pending inquiry by the Virginia Judicial Inquiry and Review Commission and had identified the state judge under investigation. A state law deemed information before the Commission confidential and made disclosure a crime. Chief Justice BURGER's opinion held that Landmark's conviction violated the First Amendment, concluding that the information lay near "the core of the First Amendment" and that the "interests advanced by the imposition of criminal sanctions [were] insufficient to justify the actual and potential encroachments on freedom of speech and of the press." Noting that the operation of judicial inquiry commissions, like the operation of the judicial system itself, was a matter of public interest, he insisted that the State's "legitimate" interests were not "sufficient to justify the subsequent punishment of speech at issue here." The asserted interests were promoting efficient Commission proceedings, protecting the reputation of Virginia's judges, and maintaining the institutional integrity of its courts. In the course of his discussion, the Chief Justice commented that "injury to official reputation is an insufficient reason 'for repressing speech that would otherwise be free.'" Recall that the Court had given considerable weight to just such an interest in protecting the reputation of the judiciary in Cox II; Cox II in turn had distinguished the Bridges line of contempt of court cases. In Landmark, however, the Court relied heavily on that line of cases, even though the state sanctions in Landmark rested on a legislative finding of clear and present danger rather than on the inherent contempt power of the courts.[1]

The Chief Justice based his conclusion primarily on strict scrutiny First Amendment balancing and questioned the relevance of the clear and present danger test that had been so predominant in the Bridges line of cases and in Virginia's law. But even if that test were relevant, he insisted, the state courts had applied it too mechanically here: "Properly applied, the test requires a

---

1. The Chief Justice's important response to the claim that the state legislature's finding of clear and present danger was entitled to special weight is quoted above, with the Gitlow-Whitney line of cases, at p. 1027.

court to make its own inquiry into the imminence and magnitude of the danger said to flow from a particular utterance and then to balance the character of the evil, as well as its likelihood, against the need for free and unfettered expression. The possibility that other methods will serve the State's interests should also be weighed." Moreover, he insisted that the state courts' efforts to distinguish the Bridges line of cases were "unpersuasive" and added: "The threat to the administration of justice posed by the speech and publications in Bridges, Pennekamp, Craig, and Wood was, if anything, more direct and substantial than the threat posed by Landmark's article." [2]

C. LABOR PICKETING

TEAMSTERS UNION v. VOGT, INC.

354 U.S. 284, 77 S.Ct. 1166, 1 L.Ed.2d 1347 (1957).

Mr. Justice FRANKFURTER delivered the opinion of the Court.

This is one more in the long series of cases in which this Court has been required to consider the limits [on] the power of a State to enjoin picketing. [Vogt] owns and operates a gravel pit in Oconomowoc, Wisconsin, where it employs 15 to 20 men. Petitioner unions sought unsuccessfully to induce some of respondent's employees to join the unions and commenced to picket the entrance to respondent's place of business with signs reading, "The men on this job are not 100% affiliated with the A.F.L." "In consequence," drivers of several trucking companies refused to deliver and haul goods to and from respondent's plant, causing substantial damage to respondent. Respondent thereupon sought [to enjoin] the picketing. [In affirming the trial court's injunction, the Wisconsin Supreme Court, drawing its own inferences from the undisputed facts, found that the picketing had been for the "unlawful purpose" of coercing the employer to induce its employees to join the union and was therefore an "unfair labor practice" under state law.]

[The Court's decisions on 14th Amendment limits on state uses of injunctions in labor controversies] disclose an evolving, not a static, course of decision. [In 1940], the Court made sweeping pronouncements about the right to picket in holding unconstitutional a statute that had been applied to ban all picketing [Thornhill v. Alabama, 310 U.S. 88 (1940)]. As the statute dealt at large with all picketing, so the Court broadly assimilated peaceful picketing in general to freedom of speech, and as such protected against abridgment by the 14th Amendment. These principles were applied by the Court in A.F. of L. v. Swing, 312 U.S. 321 [1941], to hold unconstitutional an injunction against peaceful picketing, based on a State's common-law policy against picketing when there was no immediate dispute between employer and employee. On the same day, however, the Court upheld a generalized injunction against picketing where there had been violence because "it could justifiably be concluded that the momentum of fear generated by past violence would survive even though future picketing might be wholly peaceful." Milk Wagon Drivers Union v. Meadowmoor Dairies, 312 U.S. 287 [1941]. Soon, however, the Court came to realize that the broad pronouncements, but not the specific holding, of Thornhill had to yield "to the impact of facts unforeseen," or at least not sufficiently appreciated. [Cases] reached the Court in which a State had

---

2. Justice STEWART's opinion concurring in the judgment relied on the special protection of the press rather than on free speech principles. See his views on the Press Clause of the First Amendment in sec. 6, at p. 1418 below. (Justices Brennan and Powell did not participate in the case.)

designed a remedy to meet a specific situation or to accomplish a particular social policy. These cases made manifest that picketing, even though "peaceful," involved more than just communication of ideas and could not be immune from all state regulation. "Picketing by an organized group is more than free speech, since it involves patrol of a particular locality and since the very presence of a picket line may induce action of one kind or another, quite irrespective of the nature of the ideas which are being disseminated." Bakery Drivers Local v. Wohl, 315 U.S. 769, 776 [1942] (concurring opinion). [The] strong reliance on the particular facts in [these cases] demonstrated a growing awareness that these cases involved not so much questions of free speech as review of the balance struck by a State between picketing that involved more than "publicity" and competing interests of [state policy].

The implied reassessments of the broad language of the Thornhill case were finally generalized in a series of cases sustaining injunctions against peaceful picketing, even when arising in the course of a labor controversy, when such picketing was counter to valid state policy in a domain open to state regulation. The decisive reconsideration came in Giboney v. Empire Storage & Ice Co., 336 U.S. 490 [1949]. A union, seeking to organize peddlers, picketed a wholesale dealer to induce it to refrain from selling to nonunion peddlers. The state courts, finding that such an agreement would constitute a conspiracy in restraint of trade in violation of the state antitrust laws, enjoined the picketing. This Court affirmed, [rejecting the argument that the injunction was] "an unconstitutional abridgment of free speech because the picketers were attempting peacefully to publicize truthful facts about a labor dispute. [Here], the sole immediate object of the [picketing and other activities] was to compel Empire to agree to stop selling ice to nonunion peddlers. [In] this situation, the injunction did no more than enjoin an offense against Missouri law, a felony." The Court therefore concluded that it was "clear that appellants were doing more than exercising a right of free speech or press. [Their "single and integrated course of conduct" violated a valid state antitrust law.] They were exercising their economic power together with that of their allies to compel Empire to abide by union rather than by state regulation of trade." [1]

The following Term, the Court decided a group of cases applying and elaborating on the theory of Giboney. [E.g.], Hughes v. Superior Court, 339 U.S. 460 [1950], held that the 14th Amendment did not bar use of the injunction to prohibit picketing of a place of business solely to secure compliance with a demand that its employees be hired in proportion to the racial origin of its customers. [This] series of cases, then, established a broad field in which a State, in enforcing some public policy, [could] constitutionally enjoin peaceful picketing aimed at preventing effectuation of that policy.

In the light of this background, the Maine Supreme Judicial Court in 1955 decided [Pappas v. Stacey]. [Three] union employees went on strike and picketed a restaurant peacefully "for the sole purpose of seeking to organize other employees of the Plaintiff, ultimately to have the Plaintiff enter into collective bargaining and negotiations with the Union." [A state law granted workers] full liberty of self-organization, free from restraint by employers or

---

1. The unanimous opinion in Giboney was written by Justice Black. In later cases, Justices Black and Douglas frequently cited Giboney to illustrate their views of regulations not barred by the First Amendment, in the context of their premise that "speech" is absolutely protected. Recall, e.g., Justice Black's quotation from Giboney in his dissent in Street v. New York, the flag burning case at p. 1178 above. The Giboney statement he quoted was: "It rarely has been suggested that the constitutional freedom for speech and press extends its immunity to speech or writing used as an integral part of conduct in violation of a valid criminal statute." Recall also Justice Douglas' concurrence in Brandenburg v. Ohio, p. 1037 above: "Picketing, as we have said on numerous occasions, is 'free speech plus.' That means it can be regulated when it comes to the 'plus' or 'action' side of the protest."

other persons. The Maine Supreme Judicial Court [noting "the pressure upon the employer to interfere with the free choice of the employees"] enjoined the picketing, and an appeal was taken to this Court. The whole series of cases discussed above allowing, as they did, wide discretion to a State in the formulation of domestic policy, and not involving a curtailment of free speech in its obvious and accepted scope, led this Court, without the need of further argument, to grant appellee's motion to dismiss the appeal in that it no longer presented a substantial federal question. [The] Stacey case is this [case].

Of course, the mere fact that there is "picketing" does not automatically justify its restraint without an investigation into its conduct and purposes. State courts, no more than state legislatures, can enact blanket prohibitions against picketing. [Thornhill; Swing.] The series of cases following Thornhill and Swing demonstrate that the policy of Wisconsin enforced by the prohibition of this picketing is a valid one. In this case, the circumstances [afforded] a rational basis for the inference [the Wisconsin Supreme Court] drew concerning the purpose of the [picketing].

Affirmed.[2]

Mr. Justice DOUGLAS, with whom The Chief Justice [WARREN] and Mr. Justice BLACK concur, dissenting.

The Court has now come full circle. In [Thornhill] we struck down a state ban on picketing on the ground that "the dissemination of information concerning the facts of a labor dispute must be regarded as within that area of free discussion that is guaranteed by the Constitution." Less than one year later, we held that the First Amendment protected organizational picketing on a factual record which cannot be distinguished from the one now before us. [Swing.] Of course, we have always recognized that picketing has aspects which make it more than speech. [That] difference underlies our decision in [Giboney]. There, picketing was an essential part of "a single and integrated course of conduct, which was in violation of Missouri's valid law" [and] "there was clear danger, imminent and immediate, that unless restrained, appellants would succeed in making [the state] policy a dead letter." [Speech] there was enjoined because it was an inseparable part of conduct which the State constitutionally could and did regulate. But where, as here, there is no rioting, no mass picketing, no violence, no disorder, no fisticuffs, no coercion—indeed nothing but speech—the principles announced in Thornhill and Swing should give the advocacy of one side of a dispute First Amendment protection.

The retreat began [when] four members of the Court announced that all picketing could be prohibited if a state court decided that that picketing violated the State's public policy. The retreat became a rout in [Plumbers Union v. Graham, 345 U.S. 192 (1953)]. It was only the "purpose" of the picketing which was relevant. The state court's characterization of the picketers' "purpose" had been made well-nigh conclusive. Considerations of the proximity of picketing to conduct which the State could control or prevent were abandoned and no longer was it necessary for the state court's decree to be narrowly drawn to proscribe a specific [evil]. Today, the Court signs the formal surrender. State courts and state legislatures cannot fashion blanket prohibitions on all picketing. But, for practical purposes, [they] are free to decide whether to permit or suppress any particular picket line for any reason other than a blanket policy against all picketing. I would adhere to the principle announced in Thornhill. I would adhere to the result reached in Swing. I would return to the test enunciated in Giboney—that this form of expression can be regulated or

---

2. Justice Whittaker did not participate in the case.

prohibited only to the extent that it forms an essential part of a course of conduct which the State can regulate or [prohibit].

LABOR PICKETING AND THE CONSTITUTION

The declining significance of the First Amendment in the labor picketing area, after the broad statements in Thornhill, is traced in Vogt. That decline was not only attributable to First Amendment interpretations permitting limits on picketing; also important was the congressional occupation of the field and the growing displacement of state control of picketing because of preemption principles. Nevertheless, the picketing cases remain an important source of First Amendment doctrine.[1] And the First Amendment continues to play some direct role in labor picketing as well. Recall the materials on union picketers' access rights to "private forums" such as shopping centers in the Logan Valley case, p. 1291 above.[2]

D. ECONOMIC BOYCOTTS FOR POLITICAL PURPOSES

NAACP v. CLAIBORNE HARDWARE CO., 458 U.S. 886 (1982): This case arose from a boycott of white merchants by black citizens in Claiborne County, Mississippi. The boycott, begun in 1966, sought to persuade white civic and business leaders to comply with a long list of black citizens' demands for equality and racial justice. The boycott was conducted by largely peaceful means, but it included some incidents of violence as well. In a civil action brought by some of the merchants to recover economic losses allegedly caused by the boycott, a state trial court imposed a judgment for more than $1,000,000 on a large group of defendants (including the NAACP). The Mississippi Supreme Court, although not accepting all of the lower court's reasons, upheld the judgment of liability and remanded for a recomputation of damages.[1]

1. See note 1 to Vogt above, on the frequent invocation of Giboney by those who, like Justices Black and Douglas, urged "absolute" protection of "speech" but found restraints on "speech plus" or "conduct" permissible.

2. For a modern example of a summary rejection of a First Amendment claim in a labor law context, see Longshoremen v. Allied International, Inc., 456 U.S. 212 (1982). The longshoremen's union, protesting the Russian invasion of Afghanistan, refused to unload cargoes shipped from the Soviet Union. The Court found the union's protest to be an illegal secondary boycott under the National Labor Relations Act. The unanimous Court rejected the claim that, because the union boycott "was not a labor dispute with a primary employer but a political dispute with a foreign nation," the Act should be found inapplicable. Justice Powell dispatched the argument that application of the law violated the First Amendment in one brief passage: "We have consistently rejected the claim that secondary picketing by labor unions in violation of [the Act] is a protected activity under the First Amendment. It would seem even clearer that conduct designed not to communicate but to coerce merits still less consideration under the First Amendment. The labor laws reflect a careful balancing of interests. There are many ways in which a union and its individual members may express

their opposition to Russian foreign policy without infringing upon the rights of others." Contrast the summary disposition of the First Amendment claim in the Longshoremen's case with the full examination (and sustaining) of the constitutional challenge in Claiborne, the following case, involving an economic boycott for political ends, but *not* in a labor relations context.

1. In somewhat fuller detail, the background of the case was as follows: The boycott by black citizens of Port Gibson, Miss., and other areas of Claiborne County began after white elected officials had turned down a long list of demands by black citizens. (The demands included desegregation of public facilities, hiring of black policemen, the end of verbal abuse by the police, and the hiring of more black employees by local stores.) In April 1966, at a local NAACP meeting, several hundred black people voted unanimously to boycott the area's white merchants.

The suit was brought in 1969 by 17 white merchants—many of them civic leaders. In 1973, a state equity court conducted a lengthy trial. Ultimately, the chancellor held the petitioners liable for all of the respondents' lost earnings during a seven-year period, from 1966 to the end of 1972. The chancellor found all but 18 of the original 148 defendants jointly and severally liable for the entire judgment of

Without dissent,[2] the U.S. Supreme Court reversed, holding "that the nonviolent elements of petitioners' activities are entitled to the protection of the First Amendment" and that, "[w]hile the State legitimately may impose damages for the consequences of violent conduct, it may not award compensation for the consequences of nonviolent, protected activity. Only those losses proximately caused by unlawful conduct may be recovered." The Court remanded the case for further proceedings in accordance with its guidelines.

Justice STEVENS, in his opinion for the Court, summarized his conclusions as follows: "Concerted action is a powerful weapon. History teaches that special dangers are associated with conspiratorial activity. And yet one of the foundations of our society is the right of individuals to combine with other persons in pursuit of a common goal by lawful means. At times the difference between lawful and unlawful collective action may be identified easily by reference to its purpose. In this case, however, petitioners' ultimate objectives were unquestionably legitimate. The charge of illegality—like the claim of constitutional protection—derives from the means employed by the participants to achieve those goals. The use of speeches, marches, and threats of social ostracism cannot provide the basis for a damage award. But violent conduct is beyond the pale of constitutional protection.

"The taint of violence colored the conduct of some of the petitioners. They, of course, may be held liable for the consequences of their violent deeds. The burden of demonstrating that it colored the entire collective effort, however, is not satisfied by evidence that violence occurred or even that violence contributed to the success of the boycott. A massive and prolonged effort to change the social, political, and economic structure of a local environment cannot be characterized as a violent conspiracy simply by reference to the ephemeral consequences of relatively few violent acts. Such a characterization must be supported by findings that adequately disclose the evidentiary basis for concluding that specific parties agreed to use unlawful means, that carefully identify the impact of such unlawful conduct, and that recognize the importance of avoiding the imposition of punishment for constitutionally protected activity. The burden of demonstrating that fear rather than protected conduct was the dominant force in the movement is heavy. A court must be wary of a claim that the true color of a forest is better revealed by reptiles hidden in the weeds than by the foliage of countless free-standing trees. The findings of [the trial court] are constitutionally insufficient to support the judgment that all petitioners are liable for all losses resulting from the boycott."

In supporting these conclusions, Justice Stevens began by explaining why "the nonviolent elements of petitioners' activities" were entitled to First

---

$1,250,699 plus interest and costs. The chancellor imposed liability on the basis of three separate conspiracy theories.

The Mississippi Supreme Court rejected two of these conspiracy theories, but upheld the imposition of liability on the basis of the chancellor's common law tort theory—the tort of malicious interference with the plaintiffs' businesses. The highest Mississippi court emphasized that there had been some violence and quoted the lower court finding that "the volition of many black persons was overcome out of sheer fear, and they were forced and compelled against their personal wills to withhold their trade and business intercourse from the complainants." On the basis of this finding, the State Supreme Court concluded that the entire boycott was unlawful: "If any of these factors—force, violence, or threats—is present, then the boycott is illegal regardless of

whether it is primary, secondary, economical, political, social or other." Summarily rejecting a First Amendment defense, the court stated: "The agreed use of illegal force, violence, and threats against the peace to achieve a goal makes the present state of facts a conspiracy. We know of no instance [wherein] it has been adjudicated that free speech guaranteed by the First Amendment includes in its protection the right to commit crime." (The Mississippi Supreme Court did find that liability had not been demonstrated in the case of 38 of the defendants and that there had been inadequate proof of some of the damages. It accordingly remanded for further proceedings on the damages issue.)

2. Justice Stevens' opinion of the Court had the support of seven Justices. Justice REHNQUIST concurred only in the result. Justice MARSHALL did not participate in the case.

Amendment protection. He noted that the boycott "took many forms" and that its "acknowledged purpose was to secure compliance by both civic and business leaders with a lengthy list of demands for equality and racial justice. The boycott was supported by speeches and nonviolent picketing. Participants repeatedly encouraged others to join in its cause." He found that each of these elements was "a form of speech or conduct that is ordinarily entitled to protection under the [First Amendment]. The right to associate does not lose all constitutional protection merely because some members of the group may have participated in conduct or advocated doctrine that itself is not protected. [De Jonge v. Oregon.]"

Justice Stevens conceded that the petitioners "did more than assemble peaceably and discuss among themselves their grievances against governmental and business policy." But he insisted that "[o]ther elements of the boycott [also] involved activities ordinarily safeguarded by the First Amendment. [E.g., Thornhill v. Alabama (peaceful picketing).]" Justice Stevens continued: "Speech itself was used to further the aims of the boycott. Nonparticipants repeatedly were urged to join the common cause, both through public address and through personal solicitation. These elements of the boycott involve speech in its most direct form. In addition, [petitioners] sought to persuade others to join the boycott through social pressure and the 'threat' of social ostracism. Speech does not lose its protected character, however, simply because it may embarrass others or coerce them into action. [In sum], the boycott clearly involved constitutionally protected activity. The established elements of speech, assembly, association and petition, 'though not identical, are inseparable.' Thomas v. Collins. Through exercise of these First Amendment rights, petitioners sought to bring about political, social, and economic change. Through speech, assembly, and petition—rather than through riot or revolution—petitioners sought to change a social order that had consistently treated them as second-class citizens."

True, the "presence of protected activity [did] not end the relevant constitutional inquiry": "Governmental regulation that has an incidental effect on First Amendment freedoms may be justified in certain narrowly defined instances. See United States v. O'Brien. A nonviolent and totally voluntary boycott may have a disruptive effect on local economic conditions. This Court has recognized the strong governmental interest in certain forms of economic regulation, even though such regulation may have an incidental effect on rights of speech and association. See [e.g., Giboney]. The right of business entities to 'associate' to suppress competition may be curtailed. Unfair trade practices may be restricted. Secondary boycotts and picketing by labor unions may be prohibited, as part of 'Congress' striking of the delicate balance between union freedom of expression and the ability of neutral employers, employees, and consumers to remain free from coerced participation in industrial strife.' See [the Longshoremen case; 1982; p. 1345 above]." But, Justice Stevens added, "[w]hile States have broad power to regulate economic activity, we do not find a comparable right to prohibit peaceful political activity such as that found in the boycott in this case. This Court has recognized that expression on public issues 'has always rested on the highest rung of the hierarchy of First Amendment values.' Carey v. Brown." [3]

Applying these principles, Justice Stevens suggested that the purpose of affecting governmental action was protected by the First Amendment even if there was also an anti-competitive effect: "[A] major purpose of the boycott in

---

3. "We need not decide in this case the extent to which a narrowly tailored statute designed to prohibit certain forms of anticompetitive conduct or certain types of secondary pressure may restrict protected First Amendment activity. No such statute is involved in this case. Nor are we presented with a boycott designed to secure aims that are themselves prohibited by a valid state law." [Footnote by Justice Stevens.]

this case was to influence governmental action. [The] petitioners certainly foresaw—and directly intended—that the merchants would sustain economic injury as a result of their campaign. [However], the purpose of petitioners' campaign was not to destroy legitimate competition. Petitioners sought to vindicate rights of equality and of freedom that lie at the heart of the 14th Amendment itself. The right of the State to regulate economic activity could not justify a complete prohibition against a nonviolent, politically-motivated boycott designed to force governmental and economic change and to effectuate rights guaranteed by the Constitution itself." [4]

Turning to the specific bases for the Mississippi Supreme Court's imposition of liability here, Justice Stevens conceded that the judgment did not rest "on a theory that state law prohibited a nonviolent, politically-motivated boycott." He added, however: "The fact that such activity is constitutionally protected [imposes] a special obligation on this Court to examine critically the basis on which liability was imposed. In particular, we consider here the effect of our holding that much of petitioners' conduct was constitutionally protected on the ability of the State to impose liability for elements of the boycott that were not so protected." Clearly, there were unprotected aspects of the boycott: "The First Amendment does not protect violence. [There] is no question that acts of violence occurred. No federal rule of law restricts a State from imposing tort liability for business losses that are caused by violence and by threats of violence. When such conduct occurs in the context of a constitutionally protected activity, however, 'precision of regulation' is demanded. NAACP v. Button.[5] Specifically, the presence of activity protected by the First Amendment imposes restraints on the grounds that may give rise to damage liability and on the persons who may be held accountable for those damages."

In articulating these "restraints," Justice Stevens emphasized: "Only those losses proximately caused by unlawful conduct may be recovered. The First Amendment similarly restricts the ability of the State to impose liability on an individual solely because of his association with another.[6] [See, e.g., Scales; Noto.] [The] principles announced in these cases are relevant to this case. Civil liability may not be imposed merely because an individual belonged to a group, some members of which committed acts of violence. For liability to be imposed by reason of association alone, it is necessary to establish that the group itself possessed unlawful goals and that the individual held a specific intent to further those illegal aims. 'In this sensitive field, the State may not employ "means that broadly stifle fundamental personal liberties when the end can be more narrowly achieved." Shelton v. Tucker.' Carroll v. Princess Anne."

Under these principles, the award of damages on the view that petitioners were liable for all damages "resulting from the boycott" could not be sustained. The state court's opinion itself demonstrated "that all business losses were not proximately caused by the violence and threats of violence. [To] the extent that the court's judgment rests on the ground that 'many' black citizens were 'intimidated' by 'threats' of 'social ostracism, vilification, and traduction,' it is flatly inconsistent with the First Amendment. The ambiguous findings of the

---

4. Justice Stevens also quoted with approval a comment by a U.S. Court of Appeals judge in a related proceeding: "[All] of the picketing, speeches, and other communication associated with the boycott were directed to the elimination of racial discrimination in the town. This differentiates this case from a boycott organized for economic ends, for speech to protest racial discrimination is essential political speech lying at the core of the First Amendment." (Compare the materials in the preceding subsection of this chapter.)

5. "Although this is a civil lawsuit between private parties, the application of state rules of law by the Mississippi state courts in a manner alleged to restrict First Amendment freedoms constitutes 'state action' under the 14th Amendment. New York Times v. Sullivan." [Footnote by Justice Stevens.]

6. On freedom of association, see sec. 3 of this chapter, which follows.

Mississippi Supreme Court are inadequate to assure the 'precision of regulation' demanded by that constitutional provision." Moreover, the record demonstrated that all of the merchants' losses were not proximately caused by violence or threats of violence: the record showed that many boycotters acted voluntarily. "It is indeed inconceivable that a boycott launched by the unanimous vote of several hundred persons succeeded solely through fear and intimidation." The state court had "completely failed to demonstrate that business losses suffered in 1972 [were] proximately caused by the isolated acts of violence found in 1966. It is impossible to conclude that state power has not been exerted to compensate respondents for the direct consequences of nonviolent, constitutionally protected activity." [7]

With respect to most of the petitioners, moreover, the record failed to show an adequate basis to sustain the judgments against them. For example, mere participation in the local meetings of the NAACP was "an insufficient predicate on which to impose liability." That would "not even constitute 'guilt by association,' since there is no evidence that the association possessed unlawful aims. Rather, liability could only be imposed on a 'guilt *for* association' theory. Neither is permissible under the First Amendment." Similarly, there was no basis for imposing liability on "store watchers"—boycott participants who stood outside of the stores and recorded the names of those not heeding the boycott. True, there was evidence that some "store watchers" engaged in violence or threats of violence. "Unquestionably, these individuals may be held responsible for the injuries that they caused; a judgment tailored to the consequences of their unlawful conduct may be sustained." [8]

SECTION 3. FREEDOM OF ASSOCIATION

Introduction. This section focuses on the concept of freedom of association, a concept which has surfaced occasionally in earlier cases and which is central in many of the cases in the next two sections. As early as De Jonge v. Oregon (1937; p. 1012 above), the Court relied on the First Amendment reference to "the right of the people peaceably to assemble" in invalidating a conviction. In NAACP v. Alabama, the 1958 decision which follows, the Court began to develop that right vigorously. In that case, Justice Harlan spoke of an independent constitutional "right of association" that included "privacy in group

---

7. Justice Stevens distinguished Milk Wagon Drivers Union v. Meadowmoor Dairies (1941; noted in Vogt, p. 1342 above), where the Court had held that the presence of violence justified an injunction against both violent and nonviolent activity. In that case, he noted, the violent conduct was "pervasive." Here, by contrast, the Mississippi Supreme Court had "relied on isolated acts of violence during a limited period to uphold respondents' recovery of *all* business losses sustained over a seven-year span. No losses are attributed to the voluntary participation of individuals determined to secure 'justice and equal opportunity.' The court's judgment 'screens reality' and cannot stand."

8. Justice Stevens also found no basis for sustaining the judgments against Charles Evers or, because of his activities, the national NAACP. Charles Evers, the Field Secretary of the NAACP, had helped organize the Claiborne County Branch of the NAACP, at whose meet-

ings the boycott was born. The State claimed, inter alia, that Evers' speeches constituted punishable "incitement." Justice Stevens found that Evers' statements were protected under the First Amendment. His explanation of that conclusion is printed above, with other materials on "incitement" in sec. 1 of chap. 11.

The alleged liability of the NAACP derived solely from the asserted liability of Evers. But that was not adequate: "To impose liability without a finding that the NAACP authorized—either actually or apparently—or ratified unlawful conduct would impermissibly burden the rights of political association that are protected by the First Amendment." Since the chancellor had made no finding that Charles Evers or any other NAACP member "had either actual or apparent authority to commit acts of violence or to threaten violent conduct," his findings were not "adequate" to support the judgment against the NAACP.

association." In that case, the right was protected in the context of state demands for information about a group's membership lists. In NAACP v. Button, below, the impairment of the right stemmed from restrictions on the activities of the group. Invocations of that right against similar state demands are involved in a number of the cases in the next two sections as well. In NAACP v. Alabama and NAACP v. Button, the exercise of the right involved political activities—"association for the advancement of beliefs and ideas." But is there an associational right that does not require an immediate nexus with First Amendment activities? Note the cases in the notes following Button. More recently, moreover, the Court has suggested (in Roberts, the final case in this introductory section) that an associational right may also be derived from the "liberty" protected by the due process clauses. (Recall also Griswold v. Connecticut and other modern substantive due process cases such as Moore v. East Cleveland, in sec. 3 of chap. 8 above.) [1]

NAACP v. ALABAMA

357 U.S. 449, 78 S.Ct. 1163, 2 L.Ed.2d 1488 (1958).

[In this case, the Court held unconstitutional Alabama's demand that the NAACP reveal the names and addresses of all of its Alabama members and agents. The State's demand was made in the course of an injunction action brought in 1956 to stop the NAACP from conducting activities in Alabama, on the ground that it had failed to comply with the requirement that foreign corporations qualify before "doing business" in the State. The NAACP, a New York membership corporation, operated in Alabama largely through local affiliates that were unincorporated associations. It considered itself exempt from the State's foreign corporation registration law. While the injunction action was pending, the State moved for the production of a large number of the NAACP's records. The NAACP "produced substantially all the data called for [except] its membership lists, as to which it contended that Alabama could not constitutionally compel disclosure." The trial court adjudged the NAACP in contempt and imposed a $100,000 fine.]

Mr. Justice HARLAN delivered the opinion of the [Court].*

Effective advocacy of both public and private points of view, particularly controversial ones, is undeniably enhanced by group association, as this Court has more than once recognized by remarking upon the close nexus between the freedoms of speech and assembly. [E.g., De Jonge.] It is beyond debate that freedom to engage in association for the advancement of beliefs and ideas is an inseparable aspect of the "liberty" assured by the Due Process Clause of the 14th Amendment, which embraces freedom of speech. Of course, it is immaterial whether the beliefs sought to be advanced by association pertain to political, economic, religious or cultural matters, and state action which may have the effect of curtailing the freedom to associate is subject to the closest scrutiny. The fact that Alabama [has] taken no direct action [to] restrict the right of petitioner's members to associate freely does not end inquiry into the effect of the production order. [I]n the domain of these indispensable liberties, whether of speech, press, or association, the decisions of this Court recognize that abridgment of such rights, even though unintended, may inevitably follow from varied forms of governmental [action]. It is hardly a novel perception that

---

1. See generally Nathanson, "The Right of Association," in Dorsen, ed., The Rights of Americans (1970).

* Before reaching the merits, the Court rejected several jurisdictional arguments, including the State's claim that the NAACP had no standing to assert the constitutional rights of its members. See chap. 15, p. 1575 below.

compelled disclosure of affiliation with groups engaged in advocacy may constitute [an effective] restraint on freedom of association. [The] Court has recognized the vital relationship between freedom to associate and privacy in one's associations. [Inviolability] of privacy in group association may in many circumstances be indispensable to preservation of freedom of association, particularly where a group espouses dissident [beliefs].

We think that the production order [must] be regarded as entailing the likelihood of a substantial restraint upon the exercise by petitioner's members of their right to freedom of association. Petitioner has made an uncontroverted showing that on past occasions revelation of the identity of its rank-and-file members has exposed these members to economic reprisal, loss of employment, threat of physical coercion, and other manifestations of public hostility. Under these circumstances, we think it apparent that compelled disclosure of petitioner's Alabama membership is likely to affect adversely the ability of petitioner and its members to pursue their collective effort to foster beliefs which they admittedly have the right to advocate, in that it may induce members to withdraw from the Association and dissuade others from joining it because of fear of exposure of their beliefs shown through their associations and of the consequences of this [exposure].

We turn to the [question] whether Alabama has demonstrated an interest in obtaining the disclosures it seeks from petitioner which is sufficient to justify the deterrent effect which we have concluded these disclosures may well have on the free exercise by petitioner's members of their constitutionally protected right of association. [Such a] "subordinating interest of the State must be compelling" Sweezy v. New Hampshire [1957; (concurring opinion by Justice Frankfurter); p. 1406 below].[1] It is important to bear in mind that petitioner asserts no right to absolute immunity from state investigation, and no right to disregard Alabama's laws. As shown by its substantial compliance with the production order, petitioner does not deny Alabama's right to obtain from it such information as the State desires concerning the purposes of the Association and its activities within the State. Petitioner has not objected to divulging the identity of its members who are employed by or hold official positions with it. It has urged the rights solely of its ordinary rank-and-file [members].

Whether there was "justification" in this instance turns solely on the substantiality of Alabama's interest in obtaining the membership lists. [The] exclusive purpose [claimed by the state] was to determine whether petitioner was conducting intrastate business in violation of the Alabama foreign corporation registration statute, and the membership lists were expected to help resolve this question. [W]e are unable to perceive that the disclosure of the names of petitioner's rank-and-file members has a substantial bearing on [the state interest]. [W]hatever interest the State may have in obtaining names of ordinary members has not been shown to be sufficient to overcome petitioner's constitutional objections to the production order.[2] [W]e conclude that Alabama has fallen short of showing a controlling justification for the deterrent effect on the

1. The "compelling interest" language used here by Justice Harlan—borrowed from an earlier concurring opinion by Justice Frankfurter—marks an important step in the formulation of the modern First Amendment strict scrutiny of alleged infringements of First Amendment interests. (The modern test requires "compelling" ends as well as "less restrictive" means.)

2. Justice Harlan distinguished Bryant v. Zimmerman, 278 U.S. 63 (1926), where the Court had upheld a New York law requiring disclosure of membership lists of any organization requiring an oath as a condition of membership. That law had been challenged by a member of the Ku Klux Klan. One of the distinctions noted by Justice Harlan was that Bryant had rested on "the peculiar character of the Klan's activities, involving acts of unlawful intimidation and violence." Moreover, the KKK, unlike the NAACP here, had refused to give the state "*any* information as to its local activities."

free enjoyment of the right to associate which disclosure of membership lists is likely to [have].

Reversed.[3]

THE RIGHT *NOT* TO ASSOCIATE

Soon after NAACP v. Alabama launched the modern elaboration of a First Amendment "right of association," claims were made that there was a similar right *not* to associate. Typically, the claims came from individuals who objected to compulsory contributions to organizations—e.g., employees subject to union shop agreements and lawyers attacking dues requirements under integrated bar systems. For more than a decade, the Court managed to avoid the central constitutional issues in cases raising such First Amendment claims.[1] Finally in ABOOD v. DETROIT BOARD OF EDUC., 431 U.S. 209 (1977), the Court confronted some of these constitutional claims in the context of public employees' unions.

Abood, unlike the earlier cases, involved employees in the public rather than private sector and an agency shop rather than a union shop agreement. Under an agreement adopted by a school board and a union pursuant to state law, every nonunion employee was required to pay to the union "a service fee equal in amount to union dues" as a condition of employment. That scheme was challenged by dissenting employees who objected to (1) fees for "collective bargaining in the public sector" and (2) "ideological union expenditures not directly related to collective bargaining." Justice STEWART's majority opinion, while recognizing a right to "refus[e] to associate," rejected the first challenge and sustained only the second objection. A separate opinion by Justice POWELL, joined by Chief Justice Burger and Justice Blackmun, as well as another separate opinion by Justice REHNQUIST, argued that the first challenge should also be sustained.

Justice Stewart relied in part on earlier cases that had sustained, largely on statutory grounds, compulsory dues in the private sector. He insisted that in the public sector, as in the private sector, the interests in the operation of a collective bargaining system, in assuring labor peace, and in avoiding the risk of "free riders" overcame the objectors' First Amendment interests "in not being compelled to contribute to the costs of exclusive union representation." Justice Powell's opinion countered that the earlier cases had not explored the constitutional issues and that the majority here had adopted an unnecessary, "sweeping limitation of First Amendment rights" by failing to apply "strict scrutiny." He concluded: "I would [require] the State to come forward and demonstrate, as to each union expenditure for which it would exact support from minority employees, that the compelled contribution is necessary to serve overriding governmental objectives."

---

3. NAACP v. Alabama was followed by a similar ruling in a similar context in Bates v. Little Rock, 361 U.S. 516 (1960). In Bates, the city demanded certain information from the NAACP, including a list of all persons contributing money, allegedly in aid of its effort to collect license taxes imposed on all businesses and professions. Bates, the custodian of the records of a local NAACP branch, was convicted for failing to turn over the information. Justice Stewart's opinion reversing the conviction noted that no plausible claim could be made that the NAACP was subject to the tax, found that disclosure "would work a significant interference with the freedom of association," and concluded that there was a "complete failure [to] demonstrate a controlling justification" for such interference. (For additional progeny of NAACP v. Alabama in the compelled disclosure context, see secs. 4 and 5 below. See, e.g.,—in addition to Button, the next principal case—the Gibson case, on legislative investigations, at p. 1412 below).

1. See Railway Employes' Dept. v. Hanson, 351 U.S. 225 (1956), International Ass'n of Machinists v. Street, 367 U.S. 740 (1961), Lathrop v. Donohue, 367 U.S. 820 (1961), and Brotherhood of Railway Clerks v. Allen, 373 U.S. 113 (1963).

In sustaining the second claim, Justice Stewart's majority opinion concluded that the First Amendment barred requiring dissidents to contribute to the support of an objectionable ideological cause. He accordingly remanded for development of remedies to prevent "compulsory subsidization of ideological activities by employees who object thereto without restricting the union's ability to require every employee to contribute to the cost of collective-bargaining activities." Justice Powell objected to that aspect of the majority's disposition as well: he opposed placing the burden on the dissenting employee. Instead, he insisted, "the State should bear the burden of proving that any union dues or fees that it requires of nonunion employees are needed to serve paramount governmental interests." He argued that a governmental collective bargaining agreement, "like any other enactment of state law, is fully subject to the constraints that the Constitution imposes on coercive governmental regulation." [2]

NAACP v. BUTTON

371 U.S. 415, 83 S.Ct. 328, 9 L.Ed.2d 405 (1963).

[This case held unconstitutional a Virginia prohibition of "the improper solicitation of any legal or professional business" as applied to NAACP litigation activities. Virginia had long regulated unethical and nonprofessional conduct by attorneys. Among the traditional regulations was a ban on the solicitation of legal business in the form of "running" or "capping." Before 1956, there was no attempt to apply those regulations to curb the NAACP's activities in sponsoring litigation directed at racial segregation. But in 1956, the laws were amended by adding a Chapter 33 to include, in the definition of "runner" or "capper," an agent for any organization which "employs, retains or compensates" any lawyer "in connection with any judicial proceeding in which it has no pecuniary right or liability." Virginia's highest court stated that the amendment's purpose "was to strengthen the existing statutes to further control the evils of solicitation of legal business." It held that the NAACP's Virginia

---

2. The separate opinions of Justices Powell and Rehnquist argued that compulsory contribution requirements were inconsistent with Elrod v. Burns, the 1976 decision at p. 1393 below invalidating aspects of political patronage systems, and with Buckley v. Valeo, the 1976 decision at p. 1301 above on contributions and expenditures in political campaigns. Justice Rehnquist, focusing on Elrod v. Burns, stated: "I am unable to see a constitutional distinction between a governmentally imposed requirement that a public employee be a Democrat or a Republican or else lose his job, and a similar requirement that a public employee contribute to the collective-bargaining expenses of a labor union." (Justice Stevens also submitted a separate opinion, on the question of remedies.)

For a recent examination of "the line between union expenditures that all employees must help defray and those that are not sufficiently related to collective bargaining to justify their being imposed on dissenters," see Justice White's majority opinion in Ellis v. Railway Clerks, 466 U.S. ___ (1984). Justice White announced that, when employees subject to the Railway Labor

Act object to the use of compelled dues or fees for union activities, "the test must be whether the challenged expenditures are necessarily or reasonably incurred for the purpose of performing the duties of an exclusive [bargaining] representative of the employees." Relying largely on statutory interpretation, Justice White found a lack of authority for compelled employee payments for certain union litigation and organization expenses. But as to union expenses for conventions, social activities and publications, he found neither statutory nor First Amendment barriers to compel payments by union members pursuant to a union shop agreement. Although acknowledging the First Amendment implications, he ultimately found "little additional infringement of First Amendment rights beyond that already accepted, and none that is not justified by the interests behind the union shop itself." He noted: "The First Amendment does limit the uses to which the union can put funds obtained from dissenting employees. See generally Abood. But by allowing the union shop at all, we have already countenanced a significant impingement on First Amendment rights."

activities violated Chapter 33 as well as Canons 35 and 47 of the ABA's Canons of Professional Ethics, which the court had adopted in 1938.[1]

[As described by the Court, the Virginia Conference of NAACP branches employed 15 lawyers; each lawyer "must agree to abide by the policies of the NAACP, which [limit] the kinds of litigation which the NAACP will assist." The Conference also used some non-staff lawyers in NAACP-assisted cases. In litigation involving public school segregation, cases were typically not initiated by aggrieved persons applying to the Conference for assistance. Instead, a local NAACP branch usually invited a member of the Conference legal staff to explain to a meeting of parents and children the legal steps necessary to achieve desegregation. The staff member would bring printed forms authorizing NAACP attorneys to represent the signers in desegregation suits. "In effect, then, the prospective litigant retains not so much a particular attorney as the 'firm' " of NAACP lawyers. The Conference paid for the costs of the litigation, but a litigant was free to withdraw from a suit at any time.]

Mr. Justice BRENNAN delivered the opinion of the Court.

[We] hold that the activities of the NAACP, its affiliates and legal staff shown on this record are modes of expression and association protected by the [First Amendment] which Virginia may not prohibit, under its power to regulate the legal profession, as improper solicitation of legal business. [We] meet at the outset the contention that "solicitation" is wholly outside the area of freedoms protected by the First Amendment. To this contention there are two answers. The first is that a State cannot foreclose the exercise of constitutional rights by mere labels. The second is that abstract discussion is not the only species of communication which the Constitution protects; the First Amendment also protects vigorous advocacy, certainly of lawful ends, against governmental intrusion. [In] the context of NAACP objectives, litigation is not a technique of resolving private differences; it is a means for achieving the lawful objectives of equality of treatment by all government, federal, state and local, for the members of the Negro community in this country. It is thus a form of political expression. Groups which find themselves unable to achieve their objectives through the ballot frequently turn to the courts. Just as it was true of the opponents of New Deal legislation during the 1930's, for example, no less is it true of the Negro minority today. And under the conditions of modern government, litigation may well be the sole practicable avenue open to a minority to petition for redress of grievances. We need not, in order to find constitutional protection [for the activity described], subsume such activity under a narrow, literal conception of freedom of speech, petition or assembly. For there is no longer any doubt that the [First Amendment protects] certain forms of orderly group activity. Thus we have affirmed the right "to engage in association for the advancement of beliefs and ideas." NAACP v. Alabama. We have deemed privileged, under certain circumstances, the efforts of a union official to organize workers. [The] NAACP is not a conventional political party, but the litigation it assists, while working to vindicate the legal rights of members of the American Negro community, at the same time and perhaps more importantly, makes possible the distinctive contribution of a minority

1. Canon 35 read in part as follows: "*Intermediaries.*—The professional services of a lawyer should not be controlled or exploited by any lay agency, personal or corporate, which intervene between client and lawyer. A lawyer's responsibilities and qualifications are individual. He should avoid all relations which direct the performance of his duties by or in the interest of such intermediary. A lawyer's relation to his client should be personal, and the responsibility should be directed to the client. Charitable societies rendering aid to the indigent are not deemed such intermediaries."

Canon 47 read as follows: "*Aiding the Unauthorized Practice of Law.*—No lawyer shall permit his professional services, or his name, to be used in aid of, or to make possible, the unauthorized practice of law by any lay agency, personal or corporate."

group to the ideas and beliefs of our society.   For such a group, association for litigation may be the most effective form of [political association].

[The Virginia decree proscribes] any arrangement by which prospective litigants are advised to seek the assistance of particular attorneys.   [We] cannot accept the reading suggested [that the state court] construed Chapter 33 as proscribing control only of the actual litigation by the NAACP after it is instituted.   [S]imple referral to or recommendation of a lawyer may be solicitation within the meaning of Chapter 33.   [We] conclude that under Chapter 33, as authoritatively construed, a person who advises another that his legal rights have been infringed and refers him to a particular attorney or group of attorneys (for example, to the Virginia Conference's legal staff) for assistance has committed a crime, as has the attorney who knowingly renders assistance under such circumstances.   There thus inheres in the statute the gravest danger of smothering all discussion looking to the eventual institution of litigation on behalf of the rights of members of an unpopular minority.   Lawyers on the legal staff or even mere NAACP members or sympathizers would understandably hesitate [to] do what the decree purports to allow, namely, acquaint "persons with what they believe to be their legal rights and [advise] them to assert their rights by commencing or further prosecuting a suit."   For if the lawyers, members or sympathizers also appeared in or had any connection with any litigation supported with NAACP funds contributed under the provision of the decree by which the NAACP is not prohibited "from contributing money to persons to assist them in commencing or further prosecuting such suits," they plainly would risk (if lawyers) disbarment proceedings and, lawyers and nonlawyers alike, criminal prosecution for the offense of "solicitation," to which the Virginia court gave so broad and uncertain a meaning.   It makes no difference whether such prosecutions or proceedings would actually be commenced.   It is enough that a vague and broad statute lends itself to selective enforcement against unpopular causes.   We cannot close our eyes to the fact that the militant Negro civil rights movement has engendered the intense resentment and opposition of the politically dominant white community of Virginia; litigation assisted by the NAACP has been bitterly fought.   In such circumstances a statute broadly curtailing group activity leading to litigation may easily become a weapon of oppression, however evenhanded its terms [appear].

[We reject the contention] that Virginia has a subordinating interest in the regulation of the legal profession [that] justifies limiting petitioner's First Amendment rights.   [We] have consistently held that only a compelling state interest in the regulation of a subject within [a state's power] can justify limiting First Amendment freedoms.[2]   [However] valid may be Virginia's interest in regulating the traditionally illegal practices of barratry, maintenance and champerty, that interest does not justify the prohibition of the NAACP activities disclosed by this record.   Malicious intent was of the essence of the common-law offenses of fomenting or stirring up litigation.   [T]he exercise [of] First Amendment rights to enforce constitutional rights through litigation [cannot] be deemed malicious.   [More modern regulations not involving malice] which reflect hostility to stirring up litigation have been aimed chiefly at those who urge recourse to the courts for private gain, serving no [public interest].

Objection to the intervention of a lay intermediary, who may control litigation or otherwise interfere with the rendering of legal services in a confidential relationship, also derives from the element of pecuniary gain.   Fearful of dangers thought to arise from that element, the courts of several States have sustained regulations aimed at these activities.   We intimate no view

---

2. This reference to the "compelling" state interest is often cited in modern cases to express one aspect of the strict scrutiny required of state regulations in the First Amendment area.   See also Justice Harlan's formulation a few years earlier in NAACP v. Alabama, as noted above.

one way or the other as to the merits of those decisions with respect to the particular arrangements against which they are directed. It is enough that the superficial resemblance in form between those arrangements and that at bar cannot obscure the vital fact that here the entire arrangement employs constitutionally privileged means of expression to secure constitutionally guaranteed civil rights. There has been no showing of a serious danger here of professionally reprehensible conflicts of interest which rules against solicitation frequently seek to prevent. This is so partly because no monetary stakes are involved, and so there is no danger that the attorney will desert or subvert the paramount interests of his client to enrich himself or an outside sponsor. And the aims and interests of NAACP have not been shown to conflict with those of its members and nonmember Negro litigants. [Resort] to the courts to seek vindication of constitutional rights is a different matter from the oppressive, malicious, or avaricious use of the legal process for purely [private gain].

We conclude that although the petitioner has amply shown that its activities fall within the First Amendment's protections, the State has failed to advance any substantial regulatory interest in the form of substantive evils flowing from petitioner's activities, which can justify the broad prohibitions which it has imposed. [Because] our disposition is rested on the First Amendment, [we] do not reach the considerations of race or racial discrimination which are the predicate of petitioner's challenge to the statute under [equal protection]. That the petitioner happens to be engaged in activities of expression and association on behalf of the rights of Negro children to equal opportunity is constitutionally irrelevant to the ground of our decision. The course of our decisions in the First Amendment area makes plain that its protections would apply as fully to those who would arouse our society against the objectives of the [petitioner].

Reversed.[3]

Mr. Justice HARLAN, whom Mr. Justice CLARK and Mr. Justice STEWART join, [dissenting].

[Justice Harlan's dissent agreed that freedom of expression includes not only the individual's right to speak but also "his right to advocate and his right to join with his fellows in an effort to make that advocacy effective." (See his opinion in NAACP v. Alabama, above.) Moreover, it includes "the right to join together for purposes of obtaining judicial redress." But, he added, "to declare that litigation is a form of conduct that may be associated with political expression does not resolve this case." He reminded that the Court had "repeatedly held that certain forms of speech are outside the scope of the protection of [the First Amendment] and that, in addition, 'general regulatory statutes, not intended to control the content of speech but incidentally limiting its unfettered exercise,' are permissible 'when they have been found justified by subordinating valid governmental interests.'" He suggested an analogy between this case and "the rights of workingmen in labor disputes." (See sec. 2C above.) He noted that "as we move away from speech alone and into the sphere of conduct—even conduct associated with speech or resulting from it—the area of legitimate governmental interest expands," citing, inter alia, the Giboney case. Here, he agreed, the NAACP members' rights "to associate, to discuss, and to advocate [must] remain free from frontal attack or suppression," absent "the gravest danger to the community." But he added that "litigation, whether or not associated with the attempt to vindicate constitutional rights, is

3. Justice DOUGLAS' concurrence joining the opinion of the Court argued that the Virginia law reflected "a legislative purpose to penalize the NAACP because it promotes desegregation of the races." A separate opinion by Justice WHITE stated that he would support "a narrowly drawn statute proscribing only the actual day-ly drawn statute proscribing only the actual day-to-day management and dictation of the tactics, strategy and conduct of litigation by a lay entity such as the NAACP." He joined only in the result here because it was not clear to him that the majority opinion "would not also strike down such a narrowly drawn statute."

conduct. It is speech *plus.* Although the State surely may not broadly prohibit individuals with a common interest from joining together to petition a court for redress of their grievances, it is equally certain that the State may impose reasonable regulations limiting the permissible form of litigation and the manner of legal representation within its borders." And the "regulation of conduct concerning litigation" challenged here, he concluded, "has a reasonable relation to the furtherance of a proper state interest, and [that] interest outweighs any foreseeable harm to the furtherance of protected freedoms." He explained:]

The interest which Virginia has here asserted is that of maintaining high professional standards among those who practice law within its borders. [The Court's efforts to distinguish this case from the traditional area of state control "are too facile."] [Although] these professional standards may have been born in a desire to curb malice and self-aggrandizement by those who would use clients and the courts for their own pecuniary ends, they have acquired a far broader significance during their long development. *First,* with regard to the claimed absence of the pecuniary element. [A] State's felt need for regulation of professional conduct may reasonably extend beyond mere "ambulance chasing." [Of] particular relevance here is a series of nationwide adjudications culminating in 1958 in In re Brotherhood of Railroad Trainmen, 13 Ill.2d 391, 150 N.E.2d 163. [The] practices of the Brotherhood, similar in so many respects to those engaged in by the petitioner here, have been condemned by every state court which has considered them.[1] Underlying this impressive array of relevant precedent is the widely shared conviction that avoidance of improper pecuniary gain is not the only relevant factor in determining standards of professional conduct. Running perhaps even deeper is the desire of the profession, of courts, and of legislatures to prevent any interference with the uniquely personal relationship between lawyer and client and to maintain untrammeled by outside influences the responsibility which the lawyer owes to the courts he serves. When an attorney is employed by an association or corporation to represent individual litigants, two problems arise, whether or not the association is organized for profit and no matter how unimpeachable its motives. The lawyer becomes subject to the control of a body that is not itself a litigant and that, unlike the lawyers it employs, is not subject to strict professional discipline as an officer of the court. In addition, the lawyer necessarily finds himself with a divided allegiance—to his employer and to his client—which may prevent full compliance with his basic professional obligations.

Second, it is claimed that the interests of petitioner and its members are sufficiently identical to eliminate any "serious danger" of "professionally reprehensible conflicts of interest." [The] NAACP may be no more than the sum of the efforts and views infused in it by its members; but the totality of the separate interests of the members and others whose causes the petitioner champions, even in the field of race relations, may far exceed in scope and variety that body's views of policy, as embodied in litigating strategy and tactics. Thus it may be in the interest of the Association in every case to make a frontal attack on segregation, to press for an immediate breaking down of racial barriers, and to sacrifice minor points that may win a given case for the major points that may win other cases too. But in a particular litigation, it is not impossible that after authorizing action in his behalf, a Negro parent, concerned that a continued frontal attack could result in schools closed for years, might prefer to wait with his fellows a longer time for good-faith efforts by the local school board than is permitted by the centrally determined policy of the NAACP. Or he might see a greater prospect of success through discussions

1. But see Brotherhood of Railroad Trainmen v. Virginia, 377 U.S. 1 (1964), in the notes that follow.

with local school authorities than through the litigation deemed necessary by the Association. The parent, of course, is free to withdraw his authorization, but is his lawyer, retained and paid by petitioner and subject to its directions on matters of policy, able to advise the parent with that undivided allegiance that is the hallmark of the attorney-client relation? I am afraid [not]. *Third,* it is said that the practices involved here must stand on a different footing because the litigation that petitioner supports concerns the vindication of constitutionally guaranteed rights. But surely state law is still the source of basic regulation of the legal profession, whether an attorney is pressing a federal or a state claim within its borders. [The] true question is whether the State has taken action which unreasonably obstructs the assertion of federal rights. Here, it cannot be said that the underlying state policy is inevitably inconsistent with [federal interests].

THE GROUNDS AND APPLICATIONS OF BUTTON: REGULATING THE FURNISHING OF LEGAL SERVICES

1. *The broad applications of Button.* a. A year after Button, the Court relied on it outside the area of litigation involving racial discrimination or other constitutional rights, to invalidate a Virginia injunction against a union's alleged solicitation and unauthorized practice of law. BROTHERHOOD OF RAILROAD TRAINMEN v. VIRGINIA, 377 U.S. 1 (1964). The Brotherhood advised its members to obtain legal advice before making settlements of their personal injury claims, and recommended particular attorneys; the result of its plan was "to channel legal employment to the particular lawyers approved by the Brotherhood." Justice BLACK's majority opinion concluded that First Amendment rights had been violated: "The State can no more keep these workers from using their cooperative plan to advise one another than it could use more direct means to bar them from resorting to the courts to vindicate their legal rights." As in the Button case, "the State again has failed to show any appreciable public interest in preventing the Brotherhood from carrying out its plan to recommend the lawyers it selects to represent injured workers. [The] Constitution protects the associational rights of the members of the union precisely as it does those of the NAACP."[1]

b. The Button and Trainmen cases in turn provided the basis for setting aside a state order against another variety of allegedly unauthorized practice of law by a union. UNITED MINE WORKERS v. ILLINOIS BAR ASS'N, 389 U.S. 217 (1967). The Union had employed a salaried attorney to assist its members with workmen's compensation claims. Justice BLACK's majority opinion concluded that the state ban "substantially impairs the associational rights of the Mine Workers and is not needed to protect the State's interest in high standards of legal ethics." Justice HARLAN dissented: "Although I agree with the balancing approach employed by the majority, I find the scales tipped differently."

c. The Court relied on the Button, Trainmen, and United Mine Workers cases in UNITED TRANSPORTATION UNION v. STATE BAR OF MICHIGAN, 401 U.S. 576 (1971), setting aside a broad state court injunction against

---

1. Justice CLARK's dissent, joined by Justice Harlan, claimed that the decision "overthrows state regulation of the legal profession and relegates the practice of law to the level of a commercial enterprise." He insisted that Button was distinguishable: "Personal injury litigation is not a form of political expression, but rather a procedure for the settlement of damage claims. [Here], the question involves solely the regulation of the profession, a power long recognized as belonging peculiarly to the State. [No] substantive evil would result from the activity permitted in Button. But here the past history of the union indicates the contrary. [Virginia] has sought only to halt the gross abuses of channeling and soliciting litigation which have been going on [for] 30 years."

a union's plan purportedly designed to protect union members from excessive fees by incompetent attorneys in FELA actions. In the concluding paragraph of his majority opinion, Justice BLACK emphasized the general principle upon which he relied—"the basic right to group legal action, a right first asserted in this Court by an association of Negroes seeking the protection of freedoms guaranteed by the Constitution." He added: "The common thread running through our decisions in NAACP v. Button, Trainmen, and United Mine Workers is that collective activity undertaken to obtain meaningful access to the courts is a fundamental right within the protection of the First Amendment. [That] right would be a hollow promise if courts could deny associations of workers or others the means of enabling their members to meet the costs of legal representation." [2]

d. Although Button describes litigation as often "the sole practicable avenue open to a minority to petition for a redress of grievances," the case and its successors rely strongly on group or associational activity. By contrast, a recent series of labor cases has recognized litigation as an aspect of the first amendment right to petition for redress of grievances [3] independent of concepts of freedom of association. Bill Johnson's Restaurants v. NLRB, 461 U.S. 731 (1983); Sure-Tan, Inc. v. NLRB, 468 U.S. —— (1984). Both cases recognize (although only the former finds applicable) that the first amendment limits the extent to which filing litigation can be considered an unfair labor practice in the context of a labor dispute.

2. *Regulating the legal profession: The Button line of associational rights cases and the impact of commercial speech decisions.* The Button line of cases rests explicitly on the First Amendment freedom of association. Were the associational rights concerns protected in the NAACP context of Button equally applicable in the union cases that followed? Would refusal to apply Button in the union cases have shown Button to be a non-neutral decision? (Recall the last paragraph of Button, reflecting the Court's concern about neutrality.) Would a distinction between "personal injury litigation" and "civil rights litigation" have been non-neutral? Should the Court have inquired further into (and explicitly relied upon) the State's motives in Button? May reluctance to identify improper motives in cases such as Button have led the Court to give inadequate weight in other cases to "purer" state concerns regarding professional ethics and conflicts of interest? [4]

More than a decade after Button, the Court began the development of modern First Amendment protections of commercial speech. (Recall chap. 11, sec. 2.) Beginning with the Bates case protecting lawyers' advertising (p. 1135 above), commercial speech principles have provided another route for imposing First Amendment limitations on state regulation of the legal profession. But the Button line of cases, resting on associational rights rather than commercial speech developments, retains vitality. Recall especially the contrast between the Ohralik and Primus rulings, p. 1135 above: in Ohralik, commercial speech notions did not bar regulation of in-person solicitation of clients; but in Primus, the companion case, the Court relied on the Button legacy to protect an ACLU lawyer against solicitation charges for seeking a client to bring a suit against alleged compulsory sterilization. Primus illustrates that the neutrality concern that has marked the Button line of cases persists: recall Justice Rehnquist's dissent in Primus charging the majority with developing "a jurisprudence of

---

2. Justices HARLAN, WHITE and BLACKMUN dissented in part.

3. See generally Note, "The Misapplication of the Noerr-Pennington Doctrine in Non-Antitrust Right to Petition Cases," 36 Stan.L.Rev. 1243 (1984).

4. See generally Kalven, The Negro and the First Amendment (1965); Symposium, "Group Legal Services in Perspective," 12 U.C.L.A.L. Rev. 279 (1965); and Birkby & Murphy, "Interest Group Conflict in the Judicial [Arena]," 42 Tex.L.Rev. 1018 (1964).

epithets and slogans" distinguishing between "ambulance-chasers" and "civil liberties lawyers."

IS THERE A GENERAL RIGHT TO FREEDOM OF ASSOCIATION?

Is there a general right to freedom of association, or is it only a right that is keyed to the exercise of First Amendment activities? This was the question before the Court in ROBERTS v. UNITED STATES JAYCEES, 468 U.S. —— (1984). At issue was a Minnesota statute prohibiting sex discrimination in a "place of public accommodation." The law had been applied to the Jaycees, a national civic organization which restricted full voting membership to men between the ages of 18 and 35. The Jaycees argued that this restriction on their membership policies interfered with their members' freedom of association.

In rejecting that claim, Justice BRENNAN's opinion for the Court distinguished two different varieties of freedom of association. Regarding the first variety (noted in the earlier discussion of this case, with the substantive due process materials in sec. 3 of chap. 8, at p. 565 above), the Court had protected some "choices to enter into and maintain certain intimate human relationships." In that respect, "freedom of association receives protection as a fundamental element of personal liberty." The relevant features in applying this right beyond existing cases, Justice Brennan stated, were the presence of "relative smallness, a high degree of selectivity in decisions to begin and maintain the affiliation, and seclusion from others." The Court found that right inapplicable here because the Jaycees were found to be "neither small nor selective," and because "much of the activity central to the formation and maintenance of the association involves the participation of strangers to that relationship."

Justice Brennan also identified a separate associational right: to engage in group activities themselves protected by the First Amendment. Because the Jaycees engaged in various civic, educational, and related activities, the Court found this latter associational right "plainly implicated in this case": "There can be no clearer example of an intrusion into the internal structure or affairs of an association than a regulation that forces the group to accept members it does not desire. Such a regulation may impair the ability of the original members to express only those views that brought them together. Freedom of association therefore plainly presupposes a freedom not to associate. Abood." But Justice Brennan did not find that right dispositive in this case: "The right to associate for expressive purposes is [not] absolute. Infringements on that right may be justified by regulations adopted to serve compelling state interests, unrelated to the suppression of ideas, that cannot be achieved through means significantly less restrictive of associational freedoms." Justice Brennan found that standard satisfied here. There was no indication of any distinctions drawn on the basis of the content of the expression involved; rather, this was merely a restriction incidental to Minnesota's "compelling interest in eradicating discrimination against its female citizens." Moreover, there was no indication that the law imposed "any serious burden on the male members' freedom of expressive association." In the absence of a showing far more substantial than that attempted here, "we decline to indulge in the sexual stereotyping that underlies appellee's contention that, by allowing women to vote, application of the Minnesota Act will change the content or impact of an organization's speech."[1]

---

1. Justice O'CONNOR's concurring opinion drew a distinction between rights of commercial association and rights of expressive association. As to the former, state regulation should be "readily permit[ted]," but there remained "the ideal of complete protection for purely expressive association." Because the Jaycees, in her view, were primarily commercial, she concurred in

SECTION 4. GOVERNMENTAL RESTRICTIONS ON ITS EMPLOYEES (AND ON OTHERS IN A SPECIAL RELATIONSHIP WITH GOVERNMENT)

Introduction. To what extent does the First Amendment limit governmental power to regulate the behavior of its employees or remove the "privileges" of those in a special relationship with the government (e.g., lawyers and contractors)? Does the government's status as employer or licensor or contractor or grantor of tax deductions add a significant variable to First Amendment analysis and justify regulations and disqualifications because of political beliefs, associations or conduct? Even if political activities cannot be made the basis for restricting employees or denying benefits, may government nevertheless inquire and compel disclosure about the individual's associations, on the ground that the answers are "relevant" to fitness for a government job or license or benefit? Pursuit of these questions is the aim of this section.

The questions would not have been viewed as substantial constitutional ones if Oliver Wendell Holmes' views as a state court judge had prevailed. In 1892, he said: "The petitioner may have a constitutional right to talk politics, but he has no constitutional right to be a policeman. There are few employments for hire in which the servant does not agree to suspend his constitutional right of free speech, as well of idleness, by the implied terms of his contract. The servant cannot complain, as he takes the employment on the terms which are offered him." [1] But the Holmes position has not prevailed: it has long been recognized that, even though there is no "right" to public employment or to a license, constitutional restrictions apply when government attempts to discharge employees, revoke licenses, or seek disclosure from those in a special relationship to it. [2] This section traces the changing contours of the constitutional restraints regarding demands for disclosure and grounds for disqualification.

Much of the law in this area was developed in the context of governmental concern with internal security and subversion. That concern is the focus of sec. 4A. The materials in sec. 4A form important background for the problem of government regulation in the modern context, outside the subversion area, pursued in sec. 4B. Loyalty-security programs and oath requirements were an especially prolific source of litigation during the 1950s and 1960s, and that litigation is the central concern of sec. 4A. The subversion context of many of those cases resembles that of the criminal laws against subversive advocacy considered in sec. 1 of chap. 11. Like cases of the Dennis-Scales variety, some of the materials that follow raise questions of what speech may be barred and what associations may be forbidden. But the sec. 4A materials differ in important respects. The criminal provisions considered earlier were immediately concerned with the content of speech. In the cases in sec. 4A, by contrast, the governmental concern often purports to be with issues such as fitness of

---

finding the associational challenge to be without merit. Justice REHNQUIST concurred only in the judgment. (Chief Justice Burger and Justice Blackmun did not participate in the case.) See generally Linder, "Freedom of Association after [Roberts]," 82 Mich.L.Rev. 1878 (1984). (Note also the cursory rejection of a law firm's freedom of association claim in a Title VII sex discrimination case, in Hishon v. King & Spalding, 467 U.S. — (1984).)

1. McAuliffe v. Mayor of New Bedford, 155 Mass. 216, 29 N.E. 517 (1892). (Compare Holmes' view as a state court judge in Davis v.

Massachusetts, p. 1197 above—a view that treated government's right to exclude speakers from public property as identical to the right of an owner to control private property, a view that would have seen no substantial constitutional issues in most of the "public forum" cases discussed in sec. 4 of the preceding chapter.)

2. See generally Van Alstyne, "The Demise of the Right-Privilege Distinction in Constitutional Law," 81 Harv.L.Rev. 1439 (1968), and "Developments—The National Security Interest and Civil Liberties," 85 Harv.L.Rev. 1130 (1972).

employees and integrity of lawyers and contractors, rather than immediately with the content of the speech and associations. Are state inquiries and disqualifications constitutionally more tolerable because their impact on First Amendment interests is "indirect" rather than "direct"? To what extent are questions about beliefs and associations relevant to legitimate governmental concerns regarding public employment? May an individual refuse to answer even a "relevant" question because the effect on First Amendment rights outweighs the government's need to know? Is the scope of inquiry identical to the scope of the permissible bases for disqualification—i.e., may a state ask a question only if an answer would justify dismissal of an employee, or is the state's right to know broader than the permissible bases for dismissal? May a state demand an answer on the ground that the information elicited would be a useful step in an inquiry as to fitness for a government job or benefit? In short, in examining the materials that follow, consider especially the extent to which the Court distinguishes between permissible areas of *inquiry* and permissible substantive grounds for *disqualification* of an individual from government employment or from a "privileged" status.[3] In exploring these questions and the materials that follow, sec. 4A1 concentrates on the Court responses during the 1950s, the first decade of frequent encounters for these problems; sec. 4A2 traces the sharply changing analyses of later years, particularly the 1960s and early 1970s.[4]

Sec. 4B turns to governmental restraints on its employees in the modern context. Since the early 1970s, the concern with subversion has subsided (although the subversion cases form important background for consideration of contemporary restrictions). Instead, the typical modern cases involve such issues as whether government may discharge an employee who, in the asserted exercise of freedom of expression, criticizes employer policies. The recurrent issue in cases raising that question is the extent to which a public employee has free speech rights *as an employee*.[5] This question should be distinguished from that concerning the extent to which an employee's free speech rights *as a citizen* may be restricted because of the demands of public employment, an issue that has been before the Court over the decades and that continues to arise.[6] Questions such as these are central to the contours of modern First Amendment problems regarding government employees, the central focus of sec. 4B.

---

3. See, e.g., the 1971 Bar Admission Cases, p. 1381 below.

4. The First Amendment is the dominant limitation in the cases in sec. 4A, but other guarantees also surface—especially the Fifth Amendment privilege against self-incrimination.

Although the concern with subversion provides the most common context in the materials in sec. 4A, the cases are not restricted to that context. For example, some of the most important developments in a more speech-protective direction stemmed from the context of demands for information about civil rights activities. Indeed, the relationship between inquiry cases involving alleged subversion on the one hand (the major theme of sec. 4A) and NAACP activities on the other (as already illustrated by NAACP v. Ala-

bama, p. 1350 above) suggests a series of provocative comparisons between the materials in this section and those in sec. 5, on legislative investigations. See, e.g., the Gibson case, p. 1412 below, involving a legislative committee's demand for information about NAACP membership in the course of an investigation into alleged Communist infiltration.

5. See especially the 1983 decision in Connick v. Myers, p. 1395 below.

6. See especially the Letter Carriers and Pickering cases, p. 1392 below. The modern Court has also faced the problem of whether patronage in public employment violates employee rights to political association. See especially the Elrod and Branti cases, p. 1393 below.

A. GOVERNMENT DEMANDS FOR INFORMATION AND AFFIRMATION: SCOPE OF INQUIRY AND GROUNDS FOR DISQUALIFICATION OF PUBLIC EMPLOYEES AND LICENSEES, ESPECIALLY IN THE SUBVERSION CONTEXT

1. THE BACKGROUND OF THE FIFTIES

THE GARNER AND WIEMAN CASES: RELEVANT INQUIRIES; SUSPECT METHODS

Introduction. Demands for information and assurances relating to subversion are relevant and legitimate so long as the methods of inquiry are clear and limited: that was the usual theme at the beginning of the modern Court's encounters with these problems. The Garner and Wieman cases illustrate that approach of the early 1950s.[1]

1. *Garner.* GARNER v. LOS ANGELES BOARD OF PUBLIC WORKS, 341 U.S. 716 (1951), involved a 1941 state legislative amendment of the Los Angeles City Charter which barred from public employment anyone who (1) within the past 5 years had "advised, advocated or taught," or thereafter should "advise, advocate or teach," the "overthrow by force or violence" of the state or national government; or (2) within the past 5 years had, or thereafter should, become a member of or affiliated with an organization engaging in such advocacy. A 1948 city ordinance implemented that legislation by requiring each employee to take an oath (covering the 5 years prior to 1948) regarding the forbidden activities, as well as to execute an affidavit disclosing whether or not he or she was or had ever been a Communist Party member and, if so, for what period.

The Court sustained both requirements of the ordinance. Justice CLARK's majority opinion found the affidavit inquiry relevant: a city may inquire of its employees "as to matters that may prove relevant to their fitness and suitability for the public service. Past conduct may well relate to present fitness; past loyalty may have a reasonable relationship to present and future trust." The Court noted, however, that it was not deciding whether the city could say that disclosure of Party membership by an employee "justifies his discharge"; the category of relevant questions was apparently broader than the category of grounds for disqualification from employment. The oath requirement was also found valid: it had no retroactive effect, given the 1941 and 1948 dates for state and local provisions; the 1948 oath obligation applied only to those engaging in the forbidden advocacy or association after the 1941 state law: "The provisions operating thus prospectively were a reasonable regulation to protect the municipal service by establishing an employment qualification of

---

1. Note that, by the time these government employee cases in the subversion area reached the Court, the Court had already decided that the public employment context justified some greater restraints on the speech and association of government workers than on the citizenry generally. See especially the sustaining of the Hatch Act, prohibiting federal employees from taking "any active part in political management or in political campaigns," in United Public Workers v. Mitchell (1947; p. 1391 below). The Hatch Act and similar state provisions were again sustained against First Amendment attacks in two 1973 decisions, despite the broadening First Amendment protections of the cases of the sixties, below. The two 1973 decisions were Civil Service Comm'n v. Letter Carriers and Broadrick v. Oklahoma, noted at p. 1151 above and p. 1392 below. Compare the modern patronage decisions, p. 1392 below.

loyalty." Finally, the oath was found sufficiently narrow by being read as limited to *knowing* membership: "We have no reason to suppose that the oath [will be] construed [to apply to members of organizations who were] innocent of its purpose."

2. *Wieman.* In WIEMAN v. UPDEGRAFF, 344 U.S. 183 (1952), by contrast, a unanimous Court struck down an Oklahoma loyalty oath requiring employees to state that they were not "affiliated directly or indirectly," and for the previous 5 years had "not been a member of," any organization "which has been officially determined by the United States Attorney General or other authorized public agency of the United States to be a communist front or subversive organization." Justice CLARK again wrote the opinion. He noted that the state had construed the oath so that here, unlike Garner, "knowledge is not a factor" and continued: "We are thus brought to the question touched on in Garner, Adler[2] and Gerende:[3] whether [due process] permits a state, in attempting to bar disloyal individuals from its employ, to exclude persons solely on the basis of organizational membership, regardless of their knowledge concerning the organizations to which they had belonged. For, under the statute before us, the fact of membership alone disqualifies. But membership may be innocent. [E.g.], a state servant may have joined a proscribed organization unaware of its activities and purposes. [There] can be no dispute about the consequences visited upon a person excluded from public employment on disloyalty grounds. In the view of the community, the stain is a deep one; indeed, it has become a badge of infamy. [Yet] under the Oklahoma Act, [it] matters not whether association existed innocently or knowingly. To thus inhibit individual freedom of movement is to stifle the flow of democratic expression and controversy at one of its chief sources. We hold that the distinction observed between the case at bar and Garner, Adler and Gerende is decisive. Indiscriminate classification of innocent with knowing activity must fall as an assertion of arbitrary power. The oath offends due process."[4]

THE CONSEQUENCE OF SILENCE IN THE FACE OF RELEVANT INQUIRIES: DISMISSALS FROM EMPLOYMENT AND DENIALS OF BAR ADMISSION FOR FAILURE TO DISCLOSE

Introduction. Court consideration of constitutional claims by state employees and licensees who had refused to answer questions relating to subversion continued in a series of cases in the late 1950s. The Court most often rejected the claims. Typically, the state insisted that the dismissal or license refusal was

---

2. Adler v. Board of Education, 342 U.S. 485 (1952), sustained the New York Feinberg law directed at subversive teachers and stated that teachers could be barred for "knowing membership" in the Communist Party. Adler is discussed in—and largely overruled by—Keyishian v. Board of Regents, (1967; p. 1377 below).

3. Gerende v. Board of Supervisors, 341 U.S. 56 (1951), was a per curiam decision sustaining the Maryland Ober Law requirement that any candidate for public office file an affidavit that he was not a "subversive person." In sustaining it, the Court expressed its understanding that the candidate "need only make oath that he is not a person who is engaged 'in one way or another in the attempt to overthrow the government *by force or violence,*' and that he is not knowingly a member of an organization engaged in such an

attempt." Compare the frequent invalidation of loyalty oath requirements, especially on vagueness grounds, in the cases of the 1960s, p. 1373 below.

4. In a separate concurring opinion in Wieman, Justice FRANKFURTER, joined by Justice Douglas, may have been the first to use the "chilling effects" metaphor that played such a prominent role in First Amendment analysis, and especially in the overbreadth technique, in later decades. He said: "Such unwarranted inhibition upon the free spirit of teachers affects not only those who, like the appellants, are immediately before the Court. It has an unmistakable tendency to chill that free play of the spirit which all teachers ought especially to cultivate and practice; it makes for caution and timidity in their associations by potential teachers."

based on the failure to answer questions "relevant" to a legitimate state interest (in the sense of cases such as Garner, above): the usual claim was that the government's action was a permissible response to the individual's lack of candor vis-à-vis relevant inquiries. The individual, by contrast, characteristically insisted that the real basis for the state's action was hostility to dissident political views and suspicious inferences about the claimant's beliefs. The divisions on the Court were often differences about assessments of the record: there was agreement in principle that penalties for political beliefs would violate First Amendment rights and that inferences of guilt from invocations of the self-incrimination privilege would violate the Fifth; the immediately troublesome issues were problems such as the scope of permissible Court inquiry into "real" state motives and purposes, and the deference appropriate for state judgments in this area. There were other underlying difficulties, to be sure: the contours of relevance, both for inquiries and for grounds of disqualification; the probable cause a state should show to justify questions in a sensitive area; the nature of beliefs and associations that would permit a state to bar employment or deny licenses. But questions of that variety were more obscured in the decisions of the 1950s than in the First Amendment cases of later decades. The materials that follow illustrate the mood of the Court in the 1950s in the subversion context: Slochower and Lerner involved claims of discharged state employees who had invoked the Fifth Amendment in federal inquiries (note 1);[1] Schware and Konigsberg involved applicants for bar admission who had relied on the First Amendment in refusing to answer questions (note 2).

1. *Discharging employees who refused to answer inquiries for "lack of candor":* *Justice Harlan in Slochower and Lerner.* a. SLOCHOWER v. BOARD OF HIGHER EDUC., 350 U.S. 551 (1956), held unconstitutional § 903 of the New York City Charter which provided that whenever an employee of the City invoked the self-incrimination privilege in refusing to answer a question relating to his official conduct, "his term or tenure of office or employment shall terminate." Pursuant to that provision, Slochower, a tenured city college faculty member, was summarily discharged for relying on the Fifth Amendment in refusing to testify about his associations in 1940–41 at a 1952 hearing of the congressional committee investigating subversion in education. The 5 to 4 decision held that the summary dismissal violated due process. As Justice CLARK read the record, application of § 903 "falls squarely within the prohibition of [Wieman, above]." He explained: "In practical effect the questions asked are taken as confessed and made the basis of the discharge. No consideration is given to such factors as the subject matter of the questions, remoteness of the period to which they are directed, or justification for exercise of the privilege." In his view, § 903 had converted the privilege "into a conclusive presumption of guilt."

Justice HARLAN's dissent sketched an approach that became the dominant one in a series of later cases (including Lerner, which follows). His basic argument was that a state's legitimate scope of inquiry was broader than the scope of grounds for disqualification—and that refusal to answer a legitimate question was itself a justifiable ground for discharge, whatever the grounds for refusal. He implied that a state might not be able to fire an employee who acknowledged allegedly subversive associations in years long past; but that did not bar a state from asking questions about such associations if they were relevant to an inquiry into present associations that *were* grounds for disqualification. He noted that the Court had already held that a state could bar a teacher for "knowing membership" in the Communist Party (in the Adler decision, the

---

1. At the time these cases were decided, the Fifth Amendment was not yet applicable to the states. For the impact on state employees' rights of the early 1960s rulings making the federal self-incrimination privilege available in state proceedings, see the materials at p. 1369 below.

1952 ruling noted above). Accordingly, an inquiry as to past membership in the Party was proper because it was "relevant" to that basis for discharge, though mere membership as such would not be a constitutionally adequate ground for disqualification from public employment: "A requirement that public school teachers shall furnish information as to their past or present membership in the Communist Party is a relevant step in the implementation of [a state policy of discharging for "knowing membership"], and a teacher may be discharged for refusing to comply with that requirement. [Garner.]" [2]

b. Two years after Slochower, Justice Harlan wrote the majority opinion when the Court, in a 5 to 4 decision, sustained a discharge of a subway conductor who had refused to answer on self-incrimination grounds questions put by local inquirers about present subversive associations. LERNER v. CASEY, 357 U.S. 468 (1958). Lerner was dismissed on the stated ground that "reasonable grounds exist for belief that because of his doubtful trust and reliability" he was a "security risk" under state law. As Justice HARLAN's majority opinion read the record, Lerner "had been discharged neither because of any inference of Communist Party membership which was drawn from the exercise of the Fifth Amendment privilege, nor because of the assertion of that constitutional protection, but rather because of the doubt created as to his 'reliability' by his refusal to answer a relevant question put by his employer, a doubt which the court held justifiable quite independently of appellant's reasons for his silence. In effect, administrative action was interpreted to rest solely on the refusal to respond. It was this lack of candor which provided the evidence of appellant's doubtful trust and reliability which under the New York statutory scheme constituted him a security risk." He added: "We think it scarcely debatable that had there been no claim of Fifth Amendment privilege, New York would have been constitutionally entitled to conclude from appellant's refusal to answer what must be conceded to have been a question relevant to the purposes of the statute and his employment, cf. [Garner], that he was of doubtful trust and reliability." Lerner's reliance on the Fifth Amendment did not change that outcome: "The federal privilege against self-incrimination was not available to appellant through the 14th Amendment in this state investigation."

Justice DOUGLAS' dissent, joined by Justice Black, concluded: "[W]e have here only a bare refusal to testify; and the Court holds that sufficient to show these employees are unfit to hold their public posts. That makes qualification for public office turn solely on a matter of belief—a notion very much at war with the Bill of Rights." Earlier, he noted: "I would allow no inference of wrongdoing to flow from the invocation of any constitutional right. If it be said that we deal not with guilt or innocence but with frankness, the answer is the same. There are areas where government may not probe. [G]overnment has no business penalizing a citizen merely for his beliefs or associations." Justice BRENNAN's dissent argued that the state's true motivation in firing Lerner was its unfounded conclusion that he was disloyal.[3]

2. Justice REED, joined by Justices Burton and Minton, dissented on similar grounds. Compare Nelson v. County of Los Angeles, 362 U.S. 1 (1960), where Justice Clark, the author of Slochower, distinguished that ruling in sustaining the dismissal of an employee for "insubordination" because he had refused to answer questions about present Communist membership. Noting that the employee had been discharged for "failure [to] answer" rather than "the invocation of any constitutional privilege"—even though Nelson had relied on the First and Fifth Amendments—Justice Clark found Lerner (which fol-

lows) controlling. The dissenters insisted that Slochower controlled. Was Justice Clark's distinction persuasive?

3. Chief Justice WARREN also dissented. Note also the decision, by an identical division, in a companion case, Beilan v. Board of Public Educ., 357 U.S. 399 (1958), involving a school teacher dismissed for "incompetency" after refusing to answer school officials' questions. On the pervasiveness of loyalty-security programs during this period, see generally Brown, Loyalty and

2. *The early bar admission cases: Schware and Konigsberg.* In its first encounter with bar admission cases in the subversion context, in 1957, the Court set aside state refusals to admit applicants to the bar by finding that the states' alleged inferences regarding moral character were irrational on the basis of the records adduced and accordingly violated due process. SCHWARE v. BOARD OF BAR EXAMINERS, 353 U.S. 232 (1957); KONIGSBERG v. STATE BAR, 353 U.S. 252 (1957). But when the second of those cases, Konigsberg, returned to the Court four years later, in KONIGSBERG v. STATE BAR OF CALIFORNIA, 366 U.S. 36 (1961), the Court affirmed the denial of admission with an analysis similar to that developed by Justice Harlan in the state employee cases in the preceding note.

a. In Schware, the New Mexico Board had refused to let the applicant take the bar examination because, "taking into consideration [his] use of aliases, [his] former connection with subversive organizations, and his record of arrests, he has failed to satisfy the board as to the requisite moral character for admission to the bar." The grounds of that decision rested on events prior to 1940; at a state hearing, Schware had offered evidence of his excellent moral character since then. Justice BLACK noted for the Court that "a person cannot be prevented from practicing except for valid reasons." And here the reasons were insufficient: in light of Schware's strong showing of good moral character in recent years, the State's evidence could not be said "to raise substantial doubts about his present good moral character." Justice FRANKFURTER, joined by Justices Clark and Harlan, concurred, concluding that the state court's holding "that a Communist affiliation for six to seven years up to 1940 [in] and of itself made the petitioner 'a person of questionable character' is so dogmatic an inference as to be wholly unwarranted."

b. The approach of Schware led to a similar result in the companion case, Konigsberg I. Were those grounds appropriate in Konigsberg I? Konigsberg was denied admission to the California bar because he "failed to demonstrate that he was a person of good moral character" and because he "failed to show that he did not advocate the overthrow of the Government of the United States or California by force [or] violence." At hearings before the Committee of Bar Examiners, Konigsberg had offered evidence to show his good moral character and to demonstrate that he did not advocate violent overthrow. (The record contained what the Court in a later case described as "some, though weak, independent evidence that [he] had once been connected with the Communist Party.") However, Konigsberg refused, on First Amendment grounds, to answer questions about his political associations and beliefs. Justice HARLAN's dissent, joined by Justice Clark, stated: "The Court decides the case as if the issue were whether the record contains evidence demonstrating [that] Konigsberg had a bad moral character. I do not think this is the issue. The question before us [is] whether it violates the [Constitution] for a state bar committee to decline to certify for admission to the bar an applicant who obstructs a proper investigation into his qualifications by deliberately, and without constitutional justification, refusing to answer questions relevant to his fitness under valid standards, and who is therefore deemed by the State [to] have failed to carry his burden of proof to establish that he is qualified." That approach prevailed when Konigsberg's case returned to the Court in 1961.

Security (1958), and Gellhorn, Individual Freedom and Governmental Restraints (1956).

Although the cases above stemmed from state security programs, the federal loyalty-security program was also vigorously enforced during the 1950s. There were several constitutional challenges to the federal program, but the Court usually avoided the constitutional issues by holding that the administrators had violated the applicable regulations or statutes. That pattern was set by Peters v. Hobby, 349 U.S. 331 (1955). Compare Joint Anti-Fascist Refugee Committee v. McGrath, 341 U.S. 123 (1951).

c. On remand of Konigsberg I, there was another hearing before the bar committee, and Konigsberg was once again denied admission to the bar. But this time, the state explicitly relied on his refusal to answer, and the Court sustained that action in a 5 to 4 decision in Konigsberg II in 1961. As Justice HARLAN's majority opinion described the second round of bar committee hearings, "Konigsberg introduced further evidence as to his good moral character (none of which was rebutted), reiterated unequivocally his disbelief in violent overthrow, and stated that he had never knowingly been a member of any organization which advocated such action. He persisted, however, in his refusals to answer any questions relating to his membership in the Communist Party. The Committee again declined to certify him, this time on the ground that his refusals to answer had obstructed a full investigation into his qualifications." Justice Harlan accepted that ground. He emphasized even more strongly than he had in his earlier, public employees opinions the distinction between exclusions or dismissals for refusals to answer relevant questions and substantive grounds for denials of employment or a license. The scope of inquiry, he reiterated, was broader than the scope of grounds for disqualification: the state could deny admission for refusing to answer relevant questions even if affirmative answers to the questions would not by themselves have justified exclusion. In short, he insisted that a state may deny admission to a bar applicant if he refuses to provide unprivileged answers to questions having substantial relevance to his qualifications. He dismissed as "untenable" the claim "that the questions as to Communist Party membership were made irrelevant [by] the fact that bare, innocent membership is not a ground for disqualification." He quoted the bar committee's response as the "entirely correct" answer to that contention: "You see, by failing to answer the initial question there certainly is no basis and no opportunity for us to investigate with respect to the other matters to which the initial question might very well be considered preliminary."[4]

Konigsberg's final claim was that "he was privileged not to respond to questions dealing with Communist Party membership because they unconstitutionally impinged upon rights of free speech and association." Rejecting that First Amendment argument, Justice Harlan stated: "[We] regard the State's interest in having lawyers who are devoted to the law in its broadest sense, including not only its substantive provisions, but also its procedures for orderly change, as clearly sufficient to outweigh the minimal effect upon free association occasioned by compulsory disclosure in the circumstances here presented. There is here no likelihood that deterrence of association may result from foreseeable private action [NAACP v. Alabama], for bar committee interrogations such as this are conducted in private. [Nor] is there the possibility that the State may be afforded the opportunity for imposing undetectable arbitrary consequences upon protected association [see Shelton v. Tucker, p. 1371 below], for a bar applicant's exclusion by reason of Communist Party membership is subject to judicial review."[5]

Justice BLACK's dissent, joined by Chief Justice Warren and Justice Douglas, insisted that the record showed, "beyond any shadow of a doubt, that the reason Konigsberg has been rejected is because the Committee suspects that he

---

4. Consider, in examining the later cases, whether the distinction between scope of inquiry and scope of disqualification—so heavily relied on by Justice Harlan in this group of cases— survives the decisions of the 1960s and 1970s below. See especially the 1971 Bar Admission Cases, p. 1381 below.

5. That passage evoked an extensive debate between Justices Harlan and Black on "abso-

lutes" and "balancing." Excerpts from that debate are printed with the introductory materials to chap. 11, above. See also their similar debate two years earlier, in the congressional investigations context, in Barenblatt v. United States, p. 1408 below.

was at one time a member of the Communist Party. [The] majority avoids the otherwise unavoidable necessity of reversing [on] that ground by simply refusing to look beyond the reason given by the Committee to justify Konigsberg's rejection." He argued, moreover, that the majority's result was indefensible even if its balancing approach were justifiable. He commented: "It seems plain to me that the inevitable effect of the majority's decision is to condone a practice that will have a substantial deterrent effect upon the associations entered into by anyone who may want to become a lawyer in California. [I]mportant constitutional rights have once again been 'balanced' away." (Justice BRENNAN also dissented.) [6]

DEMANDS FOR INFORMATION: THE IMPACT OF THE EXPANDED SELF–INCRIMINATION PRIVILEGE

In some of the cases of the 1950s (e.g., Lerner), one of the assumptions supporting the Court's position regarding the permissible scope of state inquiries affecting public employees was that the federal self-incrimination privilege did not apply to the states. The same premise surfaced in the context of the legal profession. In Cohen v. Hurley, 366 U.S. 117 (1961), the 5 to 4 decision sustained the disbarment of a lawyer who had refused to produce information relating to alleged "ambulance chasing" in a bar inquiry into his professional fitness. Justice Harlan's majority opinion noted that the federal self-incrimination privilege was unavailable in state proceedings and found that the state had drawn no "unfavorable inference" from petitioner's assertion of the privilege; rather, it had rested "solely upon his refusal to discharge obligations which, as a lawyer, he owed to the court." But in 1964, in Malloy v. Hogan, 378 U.S. 1, the Court found the Fifth Amendment privilege applicable to the states by "incorporating" it into the 14th Amendment. (Recall chap. 7 above.) That development soon affected the constitutionally accepted scope of inquiries. The impact of Malloy and the Fifth Amendment warrant notation here (before turning to the effect of modern evolutions in First Amendment doctrines on the constitutionally acceptable scope of inquiries, in sec. 6B below).

6. In a companion case to Konigsberg II, In re Anastaplo, 366 U.S. 82 (1961), the Court upheld Illinois' refusal to admit petitioner to the bar, largely on the authority of Konigsberg. Was the Anastaplo case so clearly governed by Konigsberg II? Did Anastaplo have a stronger case? Did the differences between his case and Konigsberg's warrant more careful treatment?

Justice Harlan's majority opinion in Anastaplo described the proceedings before the bar committee as "a wide-ranging exchange [in] which the Committee sought to explore Anastaplo's ability conscientiously to swear support of the Federal and State Constitutions [and] Anastaplo undertook to expound and defend, on historical and ideological premises, his abstract belief in the 'right of revolution,' and to resist, on grounds of asserted constitutional right and scruple, Committee questions which he deemed improper." Justice Harlan insisted that Konigsberg was not distinguishable merely because in that case "there was some, though weak, independent evidence that the applicant had once been connected with the Communist Party, while here there was no such evidence as to Anastaplo." [Did the California Committee thus have stronger "probable

cause" to question Konigsberg than Illinois could demonstrate in Anastaplo's case? On "probable cause" for inquiries in later cases, see Gibson, p. 1412 below.] Good faith belief in the need for inquiry was enough for Justice Harlan: "Where, as with membership in the bar, the State may withhold a privilege available only to those possessing the requisite qualifications, it is of no constitutional significance whether the state's interrogation of an applicant on matters relevant to these qualifications—in this case Communist Party membership—is prompted by information which it already has about him from other sources, or arises merely from a good faith belief in the need for exploratory or testing questioning of the applicant. Were it otherwise, a bar examining committee such as this, having no resources of its own for independent investigation, might be placed in the untenable position of having to certify an applicant without assurance as to the significant aspect of his qualifications which the applicant himself is best circumstanced to supply. The Constitution does not so unreasonably fetter the states." Justice Black again dissented, joined by Chief Justice Warren and Justices Douglas and Brennan.

Three years after the Malloy v. Hogan "incorporation" decision, Cohen v. Hurley was overruled in Spevack v. Klein, 385 U.S. 511 (1967). Justice Douglas' plurality opinion concluded that the self-incrimination privilege, now applicable in state proceedings, "should not be watered down by imposing the dishonor of disbarment and the deprivation of a livelihood as a price for asserting it." In a companion case, Garrity v. New Jersey, 385 U.S. 493 (1967), the Court held that evidence obtained from policemen in a state investigation after they had been warned that they would be discharged if they refused to answer could not be used against them in a criminal proceeding. And in Gardner v. Broderick, 392 U.S. 273 (1968), the Court held that a policeman could not be discharged for refusing to sign a waiver of immunity from prosecution after he was summoned before a grand jury investigating police misconduct. The Court emphasized that appellant was "discharged [not] for failure to answer relevant questions about his official duties, but for refusal to waive a constitutional right." It suggested, however, that a public employee *could* be discharged for refusal to answer questions relating to official duties *if* he were granted immunity from prosecution. That suggestion was elaborated in Lefkowitz v. Turley, 414 U.S. 70 (1973), invalidating New York laws providing that, if contractors refused to waive immunity when called to testify concerning their contracts, their contracts would be cancelled and they would be disqualified from state contracts for five years. As Justice White restated the modern view as it had evolved in Garrity and Gardner, "employees of the State do not forfeit their constitutional privilege," but "they may be compelled to respond to questions about the performance of their duties but only if their answers cannot be used against them in subsequent criminal prosecutions." [1]

2. THE CHANGES SINCE THE SIXTIES

Introduction. During the late 1950s, while First Amendment defenses to governmental demands for information in the subversion context were typically unsuccessful, the Court blocked a state effort to obtain access to the membership lists of a civil rights organization, in NAACP v. Alabama (1958; p. 1350 above). That case is of special importance in the evolution of the First Amendment approach to governmental inquiries that flourished in later decades. Unlike the 1950s decisions that rejected First Amendment claims, NAACP v. Alabama articulated the competing contentions with special care. In addition, it is an early and major example of the Court finding inadequate justification for a state demand for information although the information was conceded to be "relevant" to a legitimate state interest. Perhaps most important, the case articulated the need for strict scrutiny and compelling state interests in the First Amendment area in a manner that was to become commonplace in later years. The Court's sensitivity in NAACP v. Alabama to collateral impacts of disclosure on First Amendment interests as well as its critical examination of the asserted state justifications for the inquiry foreshadowed the more speech-protective approach reflected in the materials in this subsection.

Although the NAACP v. Alabama result was similar to the Warren Court's disposition of most challenges to disclosure and disqualification requirements during the 1960s, the Warren Court's methodology was typically quite different. Careful balancing was the hallmark of NAACP v. Alabama; but the far more frequent speech-protective results of the 1960s rarely rested on explicit

---

1. Lefkowitz v. Turley was distinguished when the Court upheld conditioning receipt of federal financial aid for college education on registration for the draft. See Selective Service v. Minn. Publ. Int. Res. Gp. (1984; p. 1374 below).

balancing. Instead, the Court in the last decade of the Warren era resorted to a range of other techniques, from "least restrictive means" and overbreadth analyses in Shelton v. Tucker, which follows, to vagueness and bill of attainder analyses in loyalty oath cases. (See p. 1373 below.) The techniques invoked as alternatives to balancing were often unclear about the contours of protected speech and association and were sometimes criticized as evasive and unprincipled. Yet those techniques had their advantages as well. They did achieve speech-protective results. They did so without exposing the Court to the charges of engaging in quasi-legislative behavior that are characteristic responses to overt balancing decisions.[1] Most important, the results achieved by these arguably evasive techniques enabled the majority to assert by the late 1960s that the governing principles for inquiries and disqualifications had substantially changed from the 1950s, albeit without the fuller explanation that a balancing approach would have required. By the late 1960s, and especially in the Keyishian case at p. 1377 below, it became clear that the grounds for disqualification from public employment and public "privileges" had shrunk considerably and had, in the subversion area, become essentially synonymous with the grounds for criminal punishment as developed in the Scales-Yates-Brandenburg line of cases in sec. 1 of chap. 11. Moreover, it had become clear that the scope of inquiry, which had been much broader than the scope of disqualifying criteria in the 1950s, no longer extended much beyond the scope of permissible grounds for disqualification. The Burger Court has adhered to the 1960s results that had been reached in often obscure ways; but the 1970s opinions have been far more ready than those of the 1960s to speak explicitly in balancing terms. See, e.g., the 1971 Bar Admission Cases, p. 1381 below.[2]

SHELTON v. TUCKER

364 U.S. 479, 81 S.Ct. 247, 5 L.Ed.2d 231 (1960).

[This case held unconstitutional an Arkansas statute—Act 10—which required every teacher, as a condition of employment in a state-supported school or college, to file "annually an affidavit listing without limitation every organization to which he has belonged or regularly contributed within the preceding five years." Shelton, who had taught in the Little Rock schools for 25 years, refused to file an affidavit pursuant to the Act for the 1959–60 school year, and his teaching contract was not renewed. In his lower federal court proceeding to challenge the Act, the evidence showed that he was not a member of any organization advocating the overthrow of the Government and that he was a member of the NAACP. The trial court upheld Act 10, finding that the information sought was "relevant."[1]]

Mr. Justice STEWART delivered the opinion of the [Court].

It is urged [that] Act 10 deprives teachers in Arkansas of their rights to personal, associational, and academic liberty. [I]n considering this contention, we deal with two basic postulates. *First.* There can be no doubt of the right of a state to investigate the competence and fitness of those whom it hires to teach in its schools. [Here], by contrast [to NAACP v. Alabama and Bates v. Little

---

1. Recall the comments on the Warren Court's aversion to balancing in the introductory notes on overbreadth and "least restrictive means" analyses, in sec. 1 of chap. 12 above.

2. There was at least one significant Warren Court decision which *did* speak explicitly in modern First Amendment, strict-scrutiny balancing terms in holding a governmental demand for information unconstitutional; but that case arose in the context of legislative investigations into allegedly subversive activities rather than of regulation of public employment and "privileges." See the Gibson case, p. 1412 below.

1. In the same proceeding, the lower court did hold unconstitutional a companion law barring NAACP members from public employment.

Rock], there can be no question of the relevance of a state's inquiry into the fitness and competence of its teachers.[2]

Second. It is not disputed that to compel a teacher to disclose his every associational tie is to impair that teacher's right of free association, a right closely allied to freedom of speech and a right which, like free speech, lies at the foundation of a free society. Such interference with personal freedom is conspicuously accented when the teacher serves at the absolute will of those to whom the disclosure must be made. [The] statute does not provide that the information it requires be kept confidential. [The] record contains evidence to indicate that fear of public disclosure is neither theoretical nor groundless.[3] Even if there were no disclosure to the general public, the pressure upon a teacher to avoid any ties which might displease those who control his professional destiny would be constant and heavy. [The] vigilant protection of constitutional freedoms is nowhere more vital than in the community of American [schools].

The question to be decided here is not whether the State of Arkansas can ask certain of its teachers about all their organizational relationships. It is not whether the State can ask all of its teachers about certain of their associational ties. It is not whether teachers can be asked how many organizations they belong to, or how much time they spend in organizational activity. The question is whether the State can ask every one of its teachers to disclose every single organization with which he has been associated over a five-year period. The scope of the inquiry required by Act 10 is completely unlimited. [The Act] requires a teacher [to] list, without number, every conceivable kind of associational tie—social, professional, political, avocational, or religious. Many such relationships could have no possible bearing upon the teacher's occupational competence or fitness. In a series of decisions this Court has held that, even though the governmental purpose be legitimate and substantial, that purpose cannot be pursued by means that broadly stifle fundamental personal liberties when the end can be more narrowly achieved.[4] The breadth of legislative abridgment must be viewed in the light of less drastic means for achieving the same basic purpose. [The] unlimited and indiscriminate sweep of the statute now before us brings it within the ban of our prior cases. The statute's comprehensive interference with associational freedom goes far beyond what might be justified in the exercise of the State's legitimate inquiry into the fitness and competency of its teachers.

Reversed.

Mr. Justice FRANKFURTER, [dissenting].[1]

Where state assertions of authority are attacked as impermissibly restrictive upon thought, expression, or association, the existence *vel non* of other possible less restrictive means of achieving the object which the State seeks is, of course,

---

2. The declared purpose of Act 10 is "to provide assistance in the administration and financing of the public schools." The declared justification for the emergency clause is "to assist in the solution" of problems raised by "the decisions of the United States Supreme Court in the school segregation cases." [But] neither the breadth and generality of the declared purpose nor the possible irrelevance of the emergency provision detract from the existence of an actual relevant state interest in the inquiry. [Footnote by Justice Stewart.]

3. In the state court proceedings a witness who was a member of the Capital Citizens Council testified that his group intended to gain access to some of the Act 10 affidavits with a view to

eliminating from the school system persons who supported organizations unpopular with the group. Among such organizations he named the American Civil Liberties Union, the Urban League, the American Association of University Professors, and the Women's Emergency Committee to Open Our Schools. [Footnote by Justice Stewart.]

4. [Cf.] Dean Milk Co. v. Madison, 340 U.S. 349 [state regulation of commerce—chap. 5, p. 270 above]. [Footnote by Justice Stewart.]

1. Justices Clark, Harlan, and Whittaker joined Justice Frankfurter's dissent. (Justice Harlan also submitted a separate dissent, joined by the other dissenters.)

a constitutionally relevant consideration. [But, though consideration] of alternatives may focus the precise exercise of state legislative authority which is tested in this Court by the standard of reasonableness, [it] does not alter or displace that standard. The issue remains whether, in light of the particular kind of restriction upon individual liberty which a regulation entails, it is reasonable for a legislature to choose that form of regulation rather than others less restrictive. [Here], the Court strikes down [a law] requiring that teachers disclose to school officials all of their organizational relationships, on the ground that "many such relationships could have no possible bearing upon the teacher's occupational competence or fitness." Granted that a given teacher's membership in the First Street Congregation is, standing alone, of little relevance to what may rightly be expected of a teacher, is that membership equally irrelevant when it is discovered that the teacher is in fact a member of the First Street Congregation *and* the Second Street Congregation *and* the Third Street Congregation *and* the 4–H Club *and* the 3–H Club *and* half a dozen other groups? Presumably, a teacher may have so many divers associations, so many divers commitments, that they consume his time and energy and interest at the expense of his work or even of his professional dedication. [A] school board is entitled to inquire whether any of its teachers has placed himself, or is placing himself, in a condition where his work may suffer. Of course, the State might ask: "To how many organizations do you belong?" or "How much time do you expend at organizational activity?" But the answer to such questions could reasonably be regarded by a state legislature as insufficient, both because the veracity of the answer is more difficult to test, [and] because an estimate of time presently spent in organizational activity reveals nothing as to the quality and nature of that activity, upon the basis of which, necessarily, judgment or prophesy of the extent of future involvement must be based. A teacher's answers to the questions which Arkansas asks, moreover, may serve the purpose of making known to school authorities persons who come into contact with the teacher in all of the phases of his activity in the community, and who can be questioned, if need be, concerning the teacher's conduct in matters which this Court can certainly not now say are lacking in any pertinence to professional fitness. It is difficult to understand how these particular ends could be achieved by asking "certain of [the State's] teachers about all their organizational relationships," or "all of its teachers about certain of their associational ties," or all of its teachers how many associations currently involve them or during how many hours; and difficult, therefore, to appreciate why the Court deems unreasonable and forbids what Arkansas [does ask].[2]

LOYALTY OATHS AND OTHER EMPLOYEE SECURITY PROGRAMS IN THE 1960s

Introduction. In the 1960s, the Warren Court struck down a series of state-imposed loyalty oaths. Typically, the Court rested on "void-for-vagueness" grounds;[1] most often, that approach shed little light on the contours of protected First Amendment activity. Moreover, that approach did not explicitly examine the competing demands of governmental interests and individual

---

2. Shelton v. Tucker, an early "less restrictive means" case, is characteristically silent in explaining what narrower means to achieve the State's proper objectives were available. Alexander Bickel, in The Least Dangerous Branch (1962), argued that a decision such as Shelton, in failing to spell out fully in what respect the means were too broad, "lacks intellectual coherence." Would greater clarity have been produced by resorting more explicitly to a balancing analysis? Note that overbreadth cases in later years of the decade managed to provide greater clarity and guidance regarding the means available to further state interests. See Keyishian, p. 1377 below.

1. Recall the discussion of "vagueness" objections in sec. 1 of chap. 12, above.

rights. Nevertheless, these loyalty oath cases were relied on by the Court in later years to announce new substantive First Amendment safeguards in the area of public employment and "privileges." This note summarizes some of the highlights of the vagueness rulings. It is followed by Elfbrandt v. Russell, p. 1375 below, which was a little more explicit about the evolving new rules, though with little explanation of precisely why the less speech-protective rules of the 1950s were no longer acceptable. Not until a year after Elfbrandt, in Keyishian, p. 1377 below, did the new rules emerge with greater clarity and somewhat fuller explanation.

1. *Loyalty oaths in the early 1960s.* Characteristic of the "vagueness" emphasis of the decisions invalidating loyalty oaths in the early 1960s is CRAMP v. BOARD OF PUBLIC INSTRUCTION, 368 U.S. 278 (1961). There, the Court invalidated a Florida law requiring public employees to swear that they had never "knowingly lent their aid, support, advice, counsel or influence to the Communist Party." Even though the state court had construed the law to include "the element of scienter," Justice STEWART emphasized its "extraordinary ambiguity" and found it "completely lacking [in] terms suscepti-ble of objective measurement." He added that the "vice of unconstitutional vagueness [was] further aggravated [because the law] operates to inhibit the exercise of individual freedoms affirmatively protected by the Constitution." [2]

2. See also Baggett v. Bullitt, 377 U.S. 360 (1964), where the Court, in partial reliance on Cramp, invalidated two state loyalty oath re-quirements, including one obligating state em-ployees to swear that they were not members of a "subversive organization." The majority found the requirements "invalid on their face because their language is unduly vague, uncertain and broad." Justice Clark's dissent complained that the decision had in effect overruled Gerende, one of the 1950s oath cases, p. 1364 above.

In the 1950s and 1960s, several Justices argued in separate opinions, that loyalty oaths should be struck down on the basis of the prohibition of bills of attainder, Art. I, §§ 9 and 10. [On post-Civil War rulings striking down, as bills of at-tainder, loyalty oaths directed at former support-ers of the Confederacy, see Cummings v. Missou-ri, 4 Wall. 277 (1867) and Ex parte Garland, 4 Wall. 333 (1867).] But the Court has relied on the bill of attainder ban in only one modern case, and since then that case has played no significant role in the consideration of employment and licensing barriers. The case was United States v. Brown, 381 U.S. 437 (1965), holding unconstitu-tional a federal law making it a crime for a member of the Communist Party to serve as an officer or an employee of a labor union. Chief Justice Warren's majority opinion emphasized that it was not necessary that a bill of attainder name the parties to be punished. He found a broader sweep to the prohibition, viewing it "as an implementation of the separation of powers, a general safeguard against legislative exercise of the judicial function, or more simply—trial by legislature." [For other references to the bill of attainder limitation, see Flemming v. Nestor, chap. 4, p. 215 above, and Nixon v. Adminis-trator of General Services, (1977; chap. 6 above)].

More recently, a bill of attainder claim was rejected in Selective Service v. Minnesota Publ.

Int. Res. Gp., 468 U.S. —— (1984), involving a challenge to a federal law denying financial aid to any college student who had failed to register for the draft. The claim, based in part on Garland and Cummings, argued that the statute "singled out nonregistrants and made them ineligible for aid based on their past conduct, i.e., failure to register." But the Court distinguished Cum-mings and Garland by noting that the statute here permitted late registration, and thus there was no action taken on the basis of any irreversi-ble act. Because any given individual could still register and escape the sanctions, the Act did not single out specific individuals. The Court also held that even if this specificity element had been satisfied, the withholding of financial aid did not constitute a punishment for purposes of the Bill of Attainder clause: "A statute that leaves open perpetually the possibility of qualifying for aid does not fall within the historical meaning of forbidden legislative punishment." Moreover, Chief Justice Burger's majority opinion found a lack of punitive intent, since the purpose of Congress was to encourage registration rather than to punish non-registrants. The Court re-jected as well the claim that the statute violated the Fifth Amendment by forcing late registrants to incriminate themselves in the process of regis-tration in order to qualify for aid. Justice Mar-shall, joined in part by Justice Brennan, dissent-ed, arguing that the statute constituted compulsory self-incrimination in violation of the Fifth Amendment and the Court's prior teach-ings in cases such as Lefkowitz v. Turley, as noted above. Justice Marshall also argued that the statute violated equal protection by imposing a distinction based on wealth, since only those in need of financial aid would be faced with these sanctions for failure to register.

2. *Loyalty oaths and employee security programs in the late 1960s.* Beginning with Elfbrandt, which follows, the Warren Court moved beyond vagueness concerns and began to treat loyalty oaths more directly as First Amendment problems, albeit on overbreadth grounds which tended to obscure the reasons *why* the governmental interests found sufficient in the 1950s were being rejected now. Elfbrandt, despite its obscurities, is arguably explainable as an implicit repudiation of the approach of the 1950s, as reflected in such cases as Lerner (p. 1366 above). Elfbrandt suggested the emergence of a new approach which did not become clear until Keyishian: the standards of criminal cases on subversion (sec. 1 of chap. 11) were incorporated into the government employees and licensees area; the bases for disqualification shrank; and the scope of inquiry became little more extensive than the bases for disqualification.

ELFBRANDT v. RUSSELL

384 U.S. 11, 86 S.Ct. 1238, 16 L.Ed.2d 321 (1966).

Mr. Justice DOUGLAS delivered the opinion of the Court.

This [case] involves questions concerning the constitutionality of an Arizona Act requiring an oath from state employees. [The] oath reads in conventional fashion [to require support of the Constitution].[1] The Legislature put a gloss on the oath by subjecting to a prosecution for perjury and for discharge from public office anyone who took the oath and who "knowingly and wilfully becomes or remains a member of the communist party of the United States or its successors or any of its subordinate organizations" or "any other organization" having for "one of its purposes" the overthrow of the government of Arizona or any of its political subdivisions where the employee had knowledge of the unlawful purpose. Petitioner, a teacher and a Quaker, decided she could not in good conscience take the oath, not knowing what it meant and not having any chance to get a hearing at which its precise scope and meaning could be determined. [She sued for declaratory relief].

We recognized in [Scales, p. 1030 above] [that] a "blanket prohibition of association with a group having both legal and illegal aims" would pose "a real danger that legitimate political expression or association would be impaired." Any lingering doubt that proscription of mere knowing membership, without any showing of "specific intent," would run afoul of the Constitution was set at rest by our decision in [Aptheker, p. 1034 above]. [The passport law there] covered membership which was not accompanied by a specific intent to further the unlawful aims of the organization, and we held it unconstitutional. The oath and accompanying statutory gloss challenged here suffer from an identical constitutional infirmity. One who subscribes to this Arizona oath and who is, or thereafter becomes, a knowing member of an organization which has as "one of its purposes" the violent overthrow of the government, is subject to immediate discharge and criminal penalties. Nothing in the oath, the statutory gloss, or the construction of the oath and statutes given by the Arizona Supreme Court purports to exclude association by one who does not subscribe to the organization's unlawful ends. Here as in [Baggett] the "hazard of being prosecuted for knowing but guiltless behavior" is a reality. People often label as "communist" ideas which they oppose; and they make up our juries. "[P]rosecutors too are

---

1. The "conventional" oath read as follows: "I, (type or print name) do solemnly swear (or affirm) that I will support the Constitution of the United States and the Constitution and laws of the State of Arizona; that I will bear true faith and allegiance to the same, and defend them against all enemies [whatever]; and that I will faithfully and impartially discharge the duties of the office of (name of office) according to the best of my ability, so help me God (or so I do affirm)."

human." [Cramp.] Would a teacher be safe and secure in going to a Pugwash Conference? Would it be legal to join a seminar group predominantly Communist and therefore subject to control by those who are said to believe in the overthrow of the government by force and violence? Juries might convict though the teacher did not subscribe to the wrongful aims of the organization. And there is apparently no machinery provided for getting clearance in advance.

Those who join an organization but do not share its unlawful purposes and who do not participate in its unlawful activities surely pose no threat, either as citizens or as public employees. Laws such as this which are not restricted in scope to those who join with the "specific intent" to further illegal action impose, in effect, a conclusive presumption that the member shares the unlawful aims of the organization. See [Aptheker]. [This] Act threatens the cherished freedom of association protected by the First Amendment. [A] statute touching those protected rights must be "narrowly drawn." [Legitimate] legislative goals "cannot be pursued by means that broadly stifle fundamental personal liberties when the end can be more narrowly achieved." [Shelton v. Tucker.] [A] law which applies to membership without the "specific intent" to further the illegal aims of the organization infringes unnecessarily on protected freedoms. It rests on the doctrine of "guilt by association" which has no place [here].

Reversed.

Mr. Justice WHITE, with whom Mr. Justice CLARK, Mr. Justice HARLAN and Mr. Justice STEWART concur, dissenting.

According to unequivocal prior holdings of this Court, a state is entitled to condition public employment upon its employees abstaining from knowing membership in the Communist Party and other organizations advocating the violent overthrow of the government which employs them; the state is constitutionally authorized to inquire into such affiliations and it may discharge those who refuse to affirm or deny them. [Gerende; Garner; Adler; Beilan; Lerner; Nelson; see also Wieman; Slochower—all in sec. 4A1 above.] The Court does not mention or purport to overrule these cases; nor does it expressly hold that a state must retain, even in its most sensitive positions, those who lend such support as knowing membership entails to those organizations, such as the Communist Party, whose purposes include the violent destruction of democratic government. Under existing constitutional law, then, Arizona is free to require its teachers to refrain from knowing membership in the designated organizations and to bar from employment all knowing members as well as those who refuse to establish their qualifications to teach by executing the oath [prescribed].

It would seem, therefore, that the Court's judgment is aimed at the criminal provisions of the Arizona law which expose an employee to a perjury prosecution if he swears falsely about membership when he signs the oath or if he later becomes a knowing member while remaining in public employment. But the State is entitled to condition employment on the absence of knowing membership; and if an employee obtains employment by falsifying his present qualifications, there is no sound constitutional reason for denying the State the power to treat such false swearing as perjury. By the same token, since knowing membership in specified organizations is a valid disqualification, Arizona cannot sensibly be forbidden to make it a crime for a person, while a state employee, to join an organization knowing of its dedication to the forceful overthrow of his employer and knowing that membership disqualifies him for state employment. The crime provided by the Arizona law is not just the act of becoming a member of an organization but it is that membership plus concurrent public employment. If a State may disqualify for knowing membership and impose criminal penalties for falsifying employment applications, it is likewise within its powers to move criminally against the employee who knowingly engages in disqualifying acts during his employment. If a government may remove from office [United Public Workers v. Mitchell, the Hatch Act case at p. 1391 below] and criminally punish its employees who engaged in certain political activities, it is unsound to hold that it may not, on pain of criminal penalties, prevent its employees from affiliating with the Communist Party or other organizations prepared to employ violent means to overthrow constitutional government. Our Constitution does not require this kind of protection for the secret proselyting of government employees into the Communist Party. [There] is nothing in [Scales, Noto, or Aptheker] dictating the result reached by the Court. [In] any event, [those cases] did not deal with the government employee who is a knowing member of the [Communist Party].[1]

KEYISHIAN v. BOARD OF REGENTS

385 U.S. 589, 87 S.Ct. 675, 17 L.Ed.2d 629 (1967).

Mr. Justice BRENNAN delivered the opinion of the Court.

As faculty members of the State University, [appellants'] continued employment was conditioned upon their compliance with a New York plan, formulated partly in statutes and partly in administrative regulations, which the State utilizes to prevent the appointment or retention of "subversive" persons in state employment. [Each appellant] refused to sign, as regulations then in effect required, [the "Feinberg Certificate"—] a certificate that he was not a Communist, and that if he had ever been a Communist, he had communicated that fact to the President of the State University of New York. Each was notified that his failure to sign the certificate would require his dismissal. [A lower federal court rejected appellants' constitutional challenges to the program.] We reverse.

We considered some aspects of the constitutionality of the New York plan 15 years ago in Adler [p. 1364 above], after New York passed the Feinberg Law which added § 3022 to the Education Law. The Feinberg Law was enacted to implement and enforce two earlier statutes. The first was a 1917 law, now § 3021 of the Education Law, under which "the utterance of any treasonable or seditious word or words or the doing of any treasonable or seditious act" is a ground for dismissal from the public school system. The second was a 1939 law [now § 105 of the Civil Service Law]. This law disqualifies from [employment] any person who advocates the overthrow of government by force, violence, or any unlawful means, or publishes material advocating such overthrow or organizes or joins any society or group of persons advocating such doctrine. The Feinberg Law charged the State Board of Regents with the duty of [making] a list, after notice and hearing, of "subversive" organizations. [Moreover], the Board was directed to provide in its rules and regulations that membership in any listed organization should constitute prima facie evidence of disqualification for appointment to or retention in any

---

1. In a forceful critique of the obscurity of the majority ruling in Elfbrandt, a commentator stated: "[O]pinions relying on the 'overbroadness' rule often provide no more indication of the Court's analysis than a conclusionary statement that a particular aspect of the statutory infringement on speech was overly broad as it applied to the particular interest that the state advanced in that case. [Elfbrandt] fits this pattern and, indeed, is more delinquent, since the Court failed in large part even to identify the state interest against which the legislation was balanced." Israel, "Elfbrandt v. Russell: The Demise of the Oath?" 1966 Sup.Ct.Rev. 193. Was that comment justified? Is it less applicable to Keyishian? Keyishian, though also an overbreadth case, was more articulate about the range of constitutionally protected activity and about the First Amendment limits on inquiries and grounds for disqualification. To what extent has the scope of inquiry become synonymous with the scope of disqualifying criteria? For the Burger Court's divided answer, see the 1971 Bar Admission Cases, noted after Keyishian, at p. 1381 below. For the Burger Court's treatment of loyalty oaths, see Cole v. Richardson, p. 1380 below.

office or position in the public schools of the State. [The Board thereupon issued implementing regulations.]

Adler [held], in effect, that there was no constitutional infirmity in [the predecessor to § 105] or in the Feinberg Law on their faces and that they were capable of constitutional application. But the contention urged in this case that both § 3021 and § 105 are unconstitutionally vague was not heard or decided. [T]hat question is not properly before us. [Moreover], to the extent that Adler sustained the provision of the Feinberg Law constituting membership in an organization advocating forceful overthrow of government a ground for disqualification, pertinent constitutional doctrines have since rejected the premises upon which that conclusion [rested].

Section 3021 requires removal for "treasonable or seditious" utterances or acts. The 1958 amendment to § 105 of the Civil Service Law, now subdivision 3 of that section, added such utterances or acts as a ground for removal under that law also. [The] difficulty centers upon the meaning of "seditious." Subdivision 3 equates the term "seditious" with "criminal anarchy" as defined in the Penal Law. [See Gitlow, p. 1002 above.] The teacher cannot know the extent, if any, to which a "seditious" utterance must transcend mere statement about abstract doctrine, the extent to which it must be intended to and tend to indoctrinate or incite to action in furtherance of the defined doctrine. The crucial consideration is that no teacher can know just where the line is drawn between "seditious" and nonseditious utterances and acts. Other provisions of § 105 also have the same defect of [vagueness]. We emphasize once again [that] "standards of permissible statutory vagueness are strict in the area of free expression. [Because] First Amendment freedoms need breathing space to survive, government may regulate in the area only with narrow specificity." [NAACP v. Button.] New York's complicated and intricate scheme plainly violates that standard. [The] danger of that chilling effect upon the exercise of vital First Amendment rights must be guarded against by sensitive tools which clearly inform teachers what is being proscribed. [The] regulatory maze [here] has the quality of "extraordinary ambiguity" found to be fatal to the oaths considered in Cramp and [Baggett]. Vagueness of wording is aggravated by prolixity and profusion of statutes, regulations, and administrative machinery, and by manifold cross-references to interrelated enactments and rules. We therefore hold that § 3021 of the Education Law and [several subdivisions] of § 105 of the Civil Service Law [are] unconstitutional.

Appellants have also challenged the constitutionality of the discrete provisions of subdivision (1)(c) of § 105 and subdivision 2 of the Feinberg Law, which make Communist Party membership, as such, prima facie evidence of disqualification. [Subsection] 2 of the Feinberg Law [was] before the Court in Adler and its constitutionality was sustained. But constitutional doctrine which has emerged since that decision has rejected its major premise. That premise was that public employment, including academic employment, may be conditioned upon the surrender of constitutional rights which could not be abridged by direct government action. [That] theory was expressly rejected in a series of decisions following Adler. [See, e.g., Wieman; Slochower; Cramp.] In Sherbert v. Verner [p. 1514 below], we said: "It is too late in the day to doubt that the liberties of religion and expression may be infringed by the denial of or placing of conditions upon a benefit or privilege." [1]

We proceed then to the question of the validity of the provisions of subdivision (c) of § 105 and subdivision 2 of § 3022, barring employment to members of listed organizations. Here again constitutional doctrine has devel-

---

1. See also the note on denial of government benefits other than employment, at p. 1402 below.

oped since Adler. Mere knowing membership without a specific intent to further the unlawful aims of an organization is not a constitutionally adequate basis for exclusion from such positions as those held by appellants. [After reviewing Elfbrandt and Aptheker, the Court continued:] [M]ere Party membership, even with knowledge of the Party's unlawful goals, can not suffice to justify criminal punishment, see [Scales, Noto, Yates]; nor may it warrant a finding of moral unfitness justifying disbarment. [Schware.] [Elfbrandt] and Aptheker state the governing standard: legislation which sanctions membership unaccompanied by specific intent to further the unlawful goals of the organization or which is not active membership violates constitutional limitations. Measured against this standard, both [provisions] sweep overbroadly into association which may not be proscribed. The presumption of disqualification arising from proof of mere membership may be rebutted, but only by (a) a denial of membership, (b) a denial that the organization advocates the overthrow of government by force, or (c) a denial that the teacher has knowledge of such advocacy. [Thus] proof of nonactive membership or a showing of the absence of intent to further unlawful aims will not rebut the presumption. [Thus, the provisions] suffer from impermissible "overbreadth." They seek to bar employment both for association which legitimately may be proscribed and for association which may not be proscribed consistently with First Amendment rights. Where statutes have an overbroad sweep, just as where they are vague, "the hazard of loss of substantial impairment of those precious rights may be critical," [since] those covered by the statute are bound to limit their behavior to that which is unquestionably safe. [Shelton v. Tucker.] We therefore hold that Civil Service Law § 105(1)(c) and Education Law § 3022(2) are invalid insofar as they proscribe mere knowing membership without any showing of specific intent to further the unlawful aims of the [Communist Party].

Reversed and remanded.

Mr. Justice CLARK, with whom Mr. Justice HARLAN, Mr. Justice STEWART and Mr. Justice WHITE join, [dissenting].

It is clear that the Feinberg Law, in which this Court found "no constitutional infirmity" in 1952, has been given its death blow today. [No] court has ever reached out so far to destroy so much with so little. [This] Court has again and again [approved] procedures either identical or at least similar to the ones [it] condemns today. [Justice Clark quoted from Garner, Adler, Beilan and Lerner.] Since that time the Adler line of cases has been cited again and again with approval [Shelton v. Tucker; Cramp; Konigsberg II; Anastaplo; cf. Baggett]. In view of this long list of decisions covering over 15 years of this Court's history, in which no opinion of this Court even questioned the validity of the Adler line of cases, it is strange to me that the Court now finds that "the constitutional doctrine which has emerged since [has] rejected [Adler's] major premise." With due respect, as I read them, our cases have done no such [thing]. The majority says that the Feinberg Law is bad because it has an "overbroad sweep." I regret to say [that] the majority has by its broadside swept away one of our most precious rights, namely, the right of self-preservation. [The] minds of our youth are developed [in our educational system] and the character of that development will determine the future of our land. [The] issue here is a very narrow one. It is not freedom of speech [or] of assembly, or of association, even in the Communist Party. It is simply this: May the State provide that one who, after a hearing with full judicial review, is found to have wilfully and deliberately advocated, advised, or taught that our Government should be overthrown by force or violence or other unlawful means; or to have wilfully and deliberately printed, published, etc., any book or paper that so advocated *and who personally* advocated such doctrine himself; or to have wilfully and deliberately become a member of an organization that advocates such doctrine, is prima facie disqualified from teaching in its university?   My answer, in keeping with all of our cases up until today, [is "Yes"!].

LOYALTY OATHS AND THE BURGER COURT

The Burger Court's major confrontation with the loyalty oath problem came in COLE v. RICHARDSON, 405 U.S. 676 (1972).   In a departure from the results typical in the Warren era, the Burger Court sustained the oath.   But Chief Justice Burger's recital of the governing constitutional principles (footnote 3 below) was remarkably similar to what had emerged during the prior decade, and the oath was sustained only after the majority had given it a narrow construction.   The 4 to 3 decision in Cole rejected an attack on a two-part loyalty oath required of all Massachusetts public employees.   The first part required a promise to "uphold and defend the federal and state constitutions"; the second, a promise to "oppose the overthrow of the [government] by force, violence or by any illegal or unconstitutional method."   The lower federal court had sustained the first part on the basis of prior decisions, but it found the second part unconstitutional.   The Court read the "oppose the overthrow" clause as imposing no significantly greater obligation than the "uphold and defend" provision and accordingly concluded that both parts of the oath were constitutional.

Chief Justice BURGER's opinion for the Court found the first, "uphold and defend" clause indistinguishable from the traditionally valid "support" oath—an oath "addressed to the future, promising constitutional support in broad terms."[1]   And the Chief Justice insisted that the lower court had been "rigidly literal" in finding in the second, "oppose" clause "the specter of vague, undefinable responsibilities actively to combat a potential overthrow of the government."   In the Court's view, the second clause did not "require specific action in some hypothetical or actual situation."   Instead, "it is a commitment not to use illegal and constitutionally unprotected force to change the constitutional system.   [It] does not expand the obligation of the first; it simply makes clear the application of the first clause to a particular issue.   [That] the second clause may be redundant is no ground to strike it down; we are not charged with correcting grammar but with enforcing a constitution."   So read, the oath was not void for vagueness.   It was punishable only by a perjury prosecution, and the requirement that there be "a knowing and willful falsehood" removed any fair notice problem.[2]

But the dissenters read the "oppose" clause more broadly and hence found it unconstitutional.   Justice DOUGLAS' dissent charged that the prevailing opinion had "emasculated" the word "oppose."   In his view, the "oppose" oath made advocacy of overthrow, protected by cases such as Brandenburg, "a possible offense": the oath required the employee to "oppose" what he has "an indisputable right to advocate."   Justice MARSHALL's dissent, joined by Justice Brennan, found the "oppose" clause "not only vague, but also overbroad."   He added: "Perhaps we have become so inundated with a variety of these oaths that we tend to ignore the difficult constitutional issues that they present."   Compare Chief Justice Burger's comment, in a footnote: "The time may come

---

1. The Court cited Knight v. Board of Regents, 269 F.Supp. 339, affirmed per curiam 390 U.S. 36 (1968), sustaining a New York requirement that teachers affirm that they "will support" the federal and state constitutions and that they "will faithfully discharge" their duties. Note the Burger Court's similar ruling in Connell v. Higginbotham, 403 U.S. 207 (1971), and see the further consideration and approval of "mere

support" oaths in Wadmond, one of the 1971 Bar Admission Cases, p. 1381 below.

2. In a concurring notation, Justice STEWART, joined by Justice White, commented: "[I]f 'uphold' and 'defend' are not words that suffer from vagueness and overbreadth, then surely neither does the word 'oppose' in the second part of the oath."

when the value of oaths in routine public employment will be thought not 'worth the candle' for all the division of opinion they engender."[3]

THE BURGER COURT ON SCOPE OF INQUIRY AND GROUNDS FOR DISQUALIFICATION: THE 1971 BAR ADMISSION CASES

Introduction. In three 5 to 4 decisions in 1971, the Court returned to the problem of cases such as Konigsberg, p. 1367 above: the scope of the state's power to inquire about subversion-related matters in the course of determining the moral fitness of applicants for admission to the bar. In two of the cases, Baird and Stolar, the petitioner prevailed; in the third, Wadmond, the constitutional challenge failed. What light do these cases throw on the continuing vitality of the Warren Court decisions culminating in Keyishian? Do they throw light on the problem of regulating government employment, not merely on bar admission issues? Are the bases of disqualification now coextensive with the standards for criminal liability as developed in cases such as Yates, Scales, and Brandenburg? Is the scope of inquiry now the same as the scope of disqualification criteria? Or may government continue to ask questions—as it was permitted to do in the 1950s—even though an affirmative answer would not be a ground for disqualification, on the ground that the questions are relevant steps in determining whether grounds for disqualification exist? Note especially the position of Justice Stewart in these cases.[1] He cast his vote in Baird and Stolar to *prohibit* questions seeking information about membership in "subversive" groups or a listing of all organizations to which the bar applicants belonged. But in Wadmond, his majority opinion *sustained* two-tiered questioning: applicants were asked about knowing membership in subversive groups and, if they answered in the affirmative, about their specific intent to further the groups' unlawful purposes.[2]

3. A passage in Chief Justice Burger's opinion is of special interest for its effort to summarize the principles established by the prior oath cases. He stated that government may not condition employment on taking oaths which "impinge" First Amendment rights, "as for example those relating to political beliefs." [Here, he cited the 1971 Bar Admission Cases, which follow.] "Nor may employment be conditioned on an oath that one has not engaged, or will not engage, in protected speech activities such as the following: criticizing institutions of government; discussing political doctrine that approves the overthrow of certain forms of government; and supporting candidates for political office. [Keyishian; Baggett v. Bullitt; Cramp.] Employment may not be conditioned on an oath denying past, or abjuring future, associational activities within constitutional protection; such protected activities include membership in organizations having illegal purposes unless one knows of the purpose and shares a specific intent to promote the illegal purpose. [E.g., Keyishian; Elfbrandt; Wieman.]" And there had been special concern with vagueness in the oath cases "because uncertainty as to an oath's meaning may deter individuals from engaging in constitutionally protected activity conceivably within the scope of the oath. An underlying, seldom articulated concern running throughout these cases is that the oaths under consideration often required individuals to

reach back into their pasts to recall minor, sometimes innocent, activities." Is that passage faithful to the spirit of the Warren Court employee oath cases? Did Chief Justice Burger apply those principles in that spirit in Cole v. Richardson?

1. Justice Stewart's votes were decisive: in all three cases, Justices Black, Douglas, Brennan and Marshall voted against the state; in all three cases, Chief Justice Burger and Justices Harlan, White and Blackmun voted for the state; Justice Stewart submitted concurring opinions in Baird and Stolar to join judgments sustaining the constitutional challenges and wrote the majority opinion in Wadmond sustaining the state's power.

2. What, if any, principles underlie Justice Stewart's view regarding the extent to which the scope of inquiry may extend beyond the scope of disqualification? Is it possible to rely simultaneously (as he does) on the Konigsberg and Anastaplo decisions, reflecting the view of the 1950s, and on decisions from the late 1960s, reflecting a quite different approach?

For a comprehensive and critical modern review of the theory and practice of moral character requirements for admission to the bar, see Rhode, "Moral Character as a Professional Credential," 94 Yale L.J. 491 (1985). Professor Rhode concludes: "As currently implemented,

1. *Baird.* In BAIRD v. STATE BAR OF ARIZONA, 401 U.S. 1 (1971), petitioner was denied admission to the bar because of her refusal to answer one of the questions on the Arizona Bar Committee's questionnaire. The question (No. 27) was whether she had ever been a member of the Communist Party or any organization "that advocates overthrow of the United States Government by force or violence." Justice BLACK's plurality opinion, joined by Justices Douglas, Brennan and Marshall, concluded that the First Amendment protected petitioner "from being subjected to a question potentially so hazardous to her liberty." He explained: "The [Amendment's] protection of association prohibits a State from excluding a person from a profession or punishing him solely because he is a member of a particular political organization or because he holds certain beliefs. [Robel; Keyishian.] Similarly, when a State attempts to make inquiries about a person's beliefs or associations, its power is limited by the First Amendment. Broad and sweeping state inquiries into these protected areas, as Arizona has engaged in here, discourage citizens from exercising rights protected by the Constitution. [Shelton v. Tucker; Gibson (p. 1412 below).] When a State seeks to inquire about an individual's beliefs and associations a heavy burden lies upon it to show that the inquiry is necessary to protect a legitimate state interest. [Gibson.] Of course Arizona has a legitimate interest in determining whether petitioner has the qualities of character and the professional competence requisite to the practice of law. But here petitioner has already supplied the Committee with extensive personal and professional information to assist its determination. By her answers to questions other than No. [27], and her listing of former employers, law school professors, and other references, she has made available to the Committee the information relevant to her fitness to practice law.[3] And whatever justification may be offered, a State may not inquire about a man's views or associations solely for the purpose of withholding a right or benefit because of what he believes."

Justice STEWART explained his decisive vote for concurring in the judgment very curtly: "The Court has held that under some circumstances simple inquiry into present or past Communist Party membership of an applicant for admission to the Bar is not as such unconstitutional. [Konigsberg; Anastaplo.] Question 27, however, goes further and asks applicants whether they have ever belonged to any organization 'that advocates overthrow of the United States Government by force or violence.' Our decisions have made clear that such inquiry must be confined to knowing membership to satisfy the [First Amendment]. See, e.g., [Robel; Wadmond, note 3 below]. It follows from these decisions that mere membership in an organization can never, by itself, be sufficient ground for a State's imposition of civil disabilities or criminal punishment. Such membership can be quite different from knowing membership in an organization advocating the overthrow of the Government by force or violence, on the part of one sharing the specific intent to further the organization's illegal goals. See [Scales; Wadmond]. There is a further constitutional infirmity in [the question]. The [State Bar's] explanation of its purpose in

the moral fitness requirement both subverts and trivializes the professional ideals it purports to sustain."

3. "Respondent has argued that even when an applicant has answered question 25, listing the organizations to which she has belonged since the age of 16 [as Ms. Baird had], question 27 still serves a useful and legitimate function. Respondent urges: 'Assume an answer including an organization by name such as "The Sons and Daughters of I Will Arise." This could truly be a Christian group with religious objectives. But it could also be an organization devoted to the objectives of Lenin, Stalin or any other deceased person whose teachings and objectives were not conducive to the continued security and welfare of our government and way of life.' The organizations petitioner listed in response to question 25 were: Church Choir; Girl Scouts; Girls Athletic Association; Young Republicans; Young Democrats; Stanford Law Association; Law School Civil Rights Research Council. Respondent does not state which of these organizations may threaten the security of the Republic." [Footnote by Justice Black.]

asking the question makes clear that the question must be treated as an inquiry into political beliefs. For [it] explicitly states that it would recommend denial of admission solely because of an applicant's beliefs that the respondent found objectionable. Cf. Wadmond. Yet the [First Amendment bars] a State from acting against any person merely because of his beliefs."

There were three dissenting opinions. All of the dissenters joined the first of these—an opinion by Justice Blackmun, joined by Chief Justice Burger and Justices Harlan and White. Justice BLACKMUN recalled at length the second Konigsberg decision and noted that petitioner had asserted that Konigsberg, "although perhaps distinguishable," warranted "delimiting, and perhaps even overruling in light of the trend since 1961." He added: "In my view, Mrs. Baird has now had striking success in her overruling endeavor despite the majority's seeming recognition of [the case] and the separate concurrence's definite bow in [its] direction." He commented that her refusal to answer Question 27 was "reminiscent of the obstructionist tactics condemned in Konigsberg." He added: "By her refusal to answer Question 27, she would place on [the State] the burden of determining which of the organizations she listed, if any, was an arm of the Communist Party or advocated forceful or violent overthrow of the Government. That, however, is not the task of the [State]. It is Sara Baird's task. [She] either knew the answer or she did not know it. If she knew, she coupled her knowledge with an attempt to conceal. If she did not know, she had only to state her lack of knowledge." Justice Blackmun insisted, moreover, that "a realistic reading of the question discloses that it is directed not at mere belief but at advocacy and at the call to violent action and force in pursuit of that advocacy. [I] find nothing in this record that indicates that Mrs. Baird automatically would have been denied admission to the Bar had she answered Question 27 in the affirmative." He concluded: "I doubt if this Court is the proper tribunal to judge the sufficiency of materials supplied for legal practice in Arizona. Of course there is a constitutional limit, but that limit is marked by the relevant, by the excesses of unreasonableness and of harassment, and by the otherwise constitutionally forbidden. It should not be marked at an arbitrary point where the applicant, for reasons of convenience or assumed self-protection or contrariness, decides that enough is enough." [4]

2. *Stolar.* The Justices viewed IN RE STOLAR, 401 U.S. 23 (1971), as raising issues closely akin to Baird and accordingly reversed Ohio's refusal of bar admission with an identical division on the Court. The applicant, a member of the New York bar, sought admission to practice in Ohio. He made available to Ohio all the information he had furnished New York a year earlier, including his answer to a question about his associational affiliations and his negative reply to a question about membership in any group seeking to effect changes in our form of government or to advance the interest of a foreign country. However, he refused to answer three of the questions on the Ohio application: Question 12(g), which asked about membership in "any organization which advocates the overthrow of the government of the United States by force"; Question 13,

---

4. Justice WHITE, in a separate dissent applicable to Stolar as well as Baird, stated: "[T]he Constitution does not require a State to admit to practice a lawyer who believes in violence and intends to implement that belief in his practice of law and advice to clients. [Moreover], the State may ask applicants preliminary questions which will permit further investigation and reasoned, articulated judgment as to whether the applicant will or will not advise lawless conduct as a practicing lawyer. Arizona has no intention of barring applicants based on belief alone." Justice HARLAN also submitted a separate opinion, applicable to all three cases. He insisted that the records showed "no more than a refusal to certify candidates who deliberately, albeit in good faith, refuse to assist the Bar Admission authorities in their 'fitness' investigation by declining fully to answer the questionnaires." The questionnaires were not unconstitutional means: "I do not consider that the 'less drastic means' test which has been applied in some First Amendment cases [see NAACP v. Alabama] suffices to justify this Court in assuming general oversight of state investigatory procedures relating to Bar admissions."

which asked for a list of all "organizations of which you are or have been a member"; and Question 7, which sought a list of all organizations "of which you are or have been a member since registering as a law student." He was denied admission to the bar because of his refusal to answer these questions.

The plurality opinion by Justice BLACK, joined by Justices Douglas, Brennan and Marshall, concluded that the refusals to answer here were, as in Baird, "protected by the First Amendment." Questions 13 and 7 were "impermissible in light of the First Amendment, as was made clear in [Shelton v. Tucker]. Law students who know they must survive this screening process before practicing their profession are encouraged to protect their future by shunning unpopular or controversial organizations. [T]he First Amendment prohibits Ohio from penalizing an applicant by denying him admission to the Bar solely because of his membership in an organization. [Baird; cf. Robel; Keyishian.] Nor may the State penalize petitioner solely because he personally, as the committee suggests, 'espouses illegal aims.' " Justice Black also noted that Stolar had supplied the State with extensive information "to enable it to make the necessary investigation and determination." "Moreover, even though irrelevant to his fitness to practice law, Stolar's answers to questions on the New York application provided Ohio with substantially the information it was seeking." Question 12(g) was found impermissible as well: since the First Amendment barred the State "from penalizing a man solely because he is a member of a particular organization," there was "no legitimate state interest which is served by a question which sweeps so broadly into areas of belief and association."

Justice STEWART was able to explain his decisive concurring vote in two sentences: "Ohio's Questions 7 and 13 are plainly unconstitutional under [Shelton v. Tucker]. In addition, Question 12(g) suffers from the same constitutional deficiency as does Arizona's Question 27 in [Baird]." Justice BLACKMUN again spoke for the dissenters. He explained: "I may assume, for present purposes, that the general and broadly phrased list-your-organizations inquiries, that is, Questions 13 and 7, are improper and impermissible under [Shelton v. Tucker], despite the presence of what seems to me to be a somewhat significant difference between nontenured school teachers and about-to-be-licensed attorneys. This assumption, however, does not terminate Stolar's case," and Question 12(g), the inquiry about membership in organizations advocating overthrow by force, was permissible in his view, in accordance with his Baird dissent. Justice Blackmun rejected the suggestion that Stolar's answers to New York should suffice for responses to Ohio: "Time passes and changes can take place even within a few months."

3. *Wadmond.* The challenge in LAW STUDENTS RESEARCH COUNCIL v. WADMOND, 401 U.S. 154 (1971), did not arise from a refusal to admit a particular bar applicant. Rather, it was "a broad attack, primarily on First Amendment vagueness and overbreadth grounds," on New York's bar admission screening system, brought by individuals and organizations (including the Law Students Civil Rights Research Council) representing a class of law students and graduates "seeking or planning to seek admission to practice law in New York." The "basic thrust" of the attack, as described by the Court, was that the screening system "by its very existence works a 'chilling effect' upon the free exercise of the rights of speech and association of students." Several items on the New York questionnaire were revised as a result of the trial court proceedings, but that court rejected the rest of the challenge. The Court agreed that the revised New York scheme was constitutional.

Justice STEWART, whose concurrences had been decisive in sustaining the constitutional challenges in Baird and Stolar, now joined the dissenters in those cases and wrote the opinion for a new majority rejecting the constitutional attack. The most difficult aspect of the case, as in Baird and Stolar, was the constitutionality of the specific questions under challenge. The disputed two-tier question was as follows:

"26. (a) Have you ever organized or helped to organize or become a member of any organization or group of persons which, during the period of your membership or association, you knew was advocating or teaching that the government of the United States or any state or any political subdivision thereof should be overthrown or overturned by force, violence, or any unlawful [means]?

"(b) If your answer to (a) is in the affirmative, did you, during the period of such membership or association, have the specific intent to further the aims of such organization or group of persons to overthrow or overturn the government of the United States or any state or any political subdivision thereof by force, violence or any unlawful means?"

Justice Stewart's disposition of this aspect of the case, joined by Chief Justice Burger and Justices Harlan, White and Blackmun, follows: [5]

"Question 26 is precisely tailored to conform to the relevant decisions of this Court. Our cases establish that inquiry into associations of the kind referred to is permissible under the limitations carefully observed here. We have held that knowing membership in an organization advocating the overthrow of the Government by force or violence, on the part of one sharing the specific intent to further the organization's illegal goals, may be made criminally punishable. [Scales.] It is also well settled that Bar examiners may ask about Communist affiliations as a preliminary to further inquiry into the nature of the association and may exclude an applicant for refusal to answer. [Konigsberg.] See also, e.g., [Robel; Keyishian; Elfbrandt; Beilan; Garner].[6] Surely a State is constitutionally entitled to make such an inquiry of an applicant for admission to a profession dedicated to the peaceful and reasoned settlement of disputes between men, and between a man and his government. The very Constitution that the appellants invoke stands as a living embodiment of that ideal."

In the concluding passage of his opinion, Justice Stewart turned to "a more fundamental claim" in the challenge: that, apart from the details, there inhered in New York's screening system "so constant a threat to applicants that constitutional deprivations will be inevitable." He commented: "The implication of this argument is that no screening would be constitutionally permissible beyond academic examination and extremely minimal checking for serious, concrete character deficiencies. The principal means of policing the Bar would then be the deterrent and punitive effects of such post-admission sanctions as contempt, disbarment, malpractice suits, and criminal prosecutions." That broad-gauged attack was rejected: "Such an approach might be wise policy, but decisions based on policy alone are not for us to make. [We] are not persuaded

---

5. Before turning to the central issue, Justice Stewart upheld New York's statutory "character and fitness" requirement because it had a "well defined" meaning from "long usage" and because the State had construed it narrowly as including no more than "dishonorable conduct relevant to the legal profession." Moreover, he found no flaw in Rule 9406, the Rule that was the basis for the challenged question designed to determine whether an applicant "believe[d] in the form of the government of the United States and [was] loyal to such government." The Rule was justified in part because it related to a "support the Constitution" oath required of applicants—an oath that was clearly valid. (See p. 1380 above.) And Rule 9406 was also valid as construed: no burden of proof was placed upon the applicant; and its general terms had been narrowly read—

e.g., "belief" and "loyalty" meant "no more than willingness to take the constitutional oath and ability to do so in good faith." Accordingly, there was "no showing of an intent to penalize political beliefs. [Konigsberg.]"

6. "Division of question 26 into two parts is wholly permissible under Konigsberg, which approved asking whether an applicant had ever been a member of the Communist Party without asking in the same question whether the applicant shared its illegal goals. Moreover, this division narrows the class of applicants as to whom the Committees are likely to find further investigation appropriate. For those who answer part (a) in the negative, that is the end of the matter." [Footnote by Justice Stewart.]

that careful administration of such a system as New York's need result in chilling effects upon the exercise of constitutional freedoms." [7]

Justice BLACK's dissent, joined by Justice Douglas, stated: "In my view, the First Amendment absolutely prohibits a State from penalizing a man because of his beliefs. Hence a State cannot require that an applicant's belief in our form of government be established before he can become a lawyer." Moreover, he found the specific questions here "flatly inconsistent with the First Amendment." He added: "I fail to see how the majority's approval of [Questions 26(a) and (b)] can be reconciled with [Baird] and [Stolar]." He explained: "In [Baird] and [Stolar], we hold today that States may not require an applicant to the Bar to answer the question 'have you been a member of any organization that advocates overthrow of the government by force?' Ohio recognized in Stolar that it could not exclude an applicant unless he had knowledge of the organization's aims at the time of his membership. However, it argued that its question was appropriate because it was merely a prelude to determining whether petitioner was a 'knowing' member. We rejected that argument and held that the First Amendment barred Ohio from demanding an answer to that question which required an applicant to supply information about political activities protected by the First Amendment. Here the majority seems to concede that New York could not possibly exclude an applicant unless he had been a member of an organization advocating forcible overthrow, he knew of these aims, and *he had a specific intent to help bring them about.* Since even on the majority's theory New York cannot exclude an applicant unless *all* these requirements are met, why is the State permitted to ask Question 26(a) which makes no reference to 'specific intent'? In Baird and Stolar five members of the Court agreed that questions asked by Bar admissions committees were invalid because they inquired about activities protected by the First Amendment. Why then is the same result not required here?"

Justice Black continued: "It may be argued, of course, that Question 26 is sufficiently specific under the majority's standard because parts (a) and (b) *taken together* do include a 'specific intent' requirement. But the Court's holding permits the knowledge and specific intent elements of Question 26 to be split into two parts. This allows the State to force an applicant to supply information about his associations, which, even under the majority's rationale, are protected by the First Amendment. But even if Questions 26(a) and 26(b) were combined into one question, this would not satisfy the standards set by the Court in [Robel] and [Brandenburg]. [For] their failure to meet the Brandenburg [incitement] requirements, the New York questions are overbroad. After our decision in Robel, it should make no difference that New York threatens to exclude people from their chosen livelihood rather than putting them in jail."

Justice MARSHALL joined by Justice Brennan, after agreeing with the wide range of other challenges to the New York screening program, stated his objections to Question 26 as follows: "Question 26(a) reveals itself as an indiscriminate and highly intrusive device designed to expose an applicant's political affiliations to the scrutiny of screening authorities. As such, it comes into conflict with principles that bar overreaching official inquiry undertaken with a view to predicating the denial of a public benefit on activity protected by

---

7. Note also Justice Stewart's reliance on— and restatement of—the distinctions he sought to develop in the Bar Admission Cases, in his separate opinion in Connell v. Higginbotham, 403 U.S. 207, a 1971 public employees' oath case. In Connell, in urging state clarification of an oath provision, Justice Stewart explained: "If the clause embraces the teacher's philosophical or political beliefs, I think it is constitutionally infirm. [Baird.] If on the other hand, the clause does no more than test whether the first clause of the oath [a "support" oath] can be taken 'without mental reservation or purpose of evasion,' I think it is constitutionally valid. [Wadmond.]"

the First Amendment.[8] Three particular difficulties may be mentioned. First, Question 26(a) is undeniably overbroad in that it covers the affiliations of those who do not adhere to teachings concerning unlawful political change, or are simply indifferent to this aspect of an association's activities. [Elfbrandt v. Russell; Aptheker.] Second, no attempt has been made to limit Question 26(a) to associational advocacy of concrete, specific, and imminent illegal acts, or to associational activity which creates a serious likelihood of harm through imminent illegal conduct. See [Brandenburg; Keyishian]. Third, would-be Bar applicants are left to wonder whether particular political acts amount to 'becoming a member' of a 'group of persons'—law students and others, when embarking on associational activities, must guess whether the association's teachings fall within the nebulous formula of Question 26(a), or more to the point, whether their own assessment of an association's teachings would coincide with that of screening officials. There are penalties for failing to 'state the facts' required by Question 26(a) when the time to make application comes. The indefinite scope of Question 26(a) expectedly operates to induce prospective applicants to resolve doubts by failing to exercise their First Amendment rights. See [e.g., Baggett]."

GOVERNMENT DEMANDS FOR INFORMATION AND THE BURGER COURT: COMPELLED DISCLOSURE OF POLITICAL CAMPAIGN CONTRIBUTIONS

[Sec. 4A concludes with selections from those portions of the opinions in BUCKLEY v. VALEO, 424 U.S. 1 (1976), that address the challenges to the *disclosure requirements* of the Federal Election Campaign Act.[1] No major information demands by government in the subversion context have come before the Burger Court since the 1971 Bar Admission Cases, above. But the more recent Buckley opinion illustrates the Burger Court's perception of governing constitutional principles when demands for information are challenged as impinging on First Amendment interests. Moreover, the Buckley excerpts raise the question of whether the Court, in applying First Amendment principles in the political campaign financing context, faithfully adhered to the precedents, or whether it exercised less than the strict scrutiny that evolved in such cases as NAACP v. Alabama and Keyishian, above. The Buckley majority stated its position in the following passages of its per curiam opinion:]

II. *Reporting and Disclosure Requirements*

Unlike the limitations on contributions and expenditures, [the] disclosure requirements of the Act are not challenged by appellants as per se unconstitutional restrictions on the exercise of First Amendment freedoms of speech and association. [The] particular requirements embodied in the Act are attacked as overbroad—both in their application to minor-party and independent candidates

---

8. "Part (a) of Question 26 is not rendered harmless by reason of the fact that part (b) limits somewhat the breadth of the question as a whole. [Overreaching] inquiries are not cured simply by adding narrower follow-up questions. Obviously a State cannot hope to justify the sort of informational demand condemned today in [Stolar] on the theory that the overintrusive inquiry is part of a series that culminates in a sufficiently narrow question. When the questioning is directed at the political activities and affiliations of applicants for a public benefit, the scope of questioning must be carefully limited in light of the permissible criteria for denying the benefit. [Shalton.] There is no justification for a requirement of overbroad disclosure that chills the exercise of First Amendment freedoms and is not tailored to serve valid governmental interests. See [Gibson, Bates, NAACP v. Alabama]." [Footnote by Justice Marshall.]

1. Recall the earlier excerpts from Buckley at p. 1301 above, pertaining to the constitutionality of the contributions and expenditures limits imposed by the Act.

and in their extension to contributions as small as $10 or $100. Appellants also challenge the provision for disclosure by those who make independent contributions and expenditures, § 434(e). [We reject the challenges based] on overbreadth and hold that § 434(e), if narrowly construed, also is within [constitutional bounds].

A. *General Principles.* We long have recognized that significant encroachments on First Amendment rights of the sort that compelled disclosure imposes cannot be justified by a mere showing of some legitimate governmental interest. Since [NAACP v. Alabama] we have required that the subordinating interests of the State must survive exacting scrutiny. We also have insisted that there be a "relevant correlation" [Bates v. Little Rock] or "substantial relation" [Gibson, p. 1412 below] between the governmental interest and the information required to be disclosed. This type of scrutiny is necessary even if any deterrent effect on the exercise of First Amendment rights arises, not through direct government action, but indirectly as an unintended but inevitable result of the government's conduct in requiring disclosure. [NAACP v. Alabama.]

Appellees argue that the disclosure requirements of the Act differ significantly from those at issue in Alabama and its progeny because the Act only requires disclosure of the names of contributors and does not compel political organizations to submit the names of their members. [T]he invasion of privacy of belief may be as great when the information sought concerns the giving and spending of money as when it concerns the joining of [organizations]. Our past decisions have not drawn fine lines between contributors and members but have treated them interchangeably. The strict test established by Alabama is necessary because compelled disclosure has the potential for substantially infringing the exercise of First Amendment rights. But we have acknowledged that there are governmental interests sufficiently important to outweigh the possibility of infringement, particularly when the "free functioning of our national institutions" is involved. Communist Party v. SACB [p. 1033 above].

The governmental interests sought to be vindicated by the disclosure requirements are of this magnitude. They fall into three categories. First, disclosure provides the electorate with information "as to where political campaign money comes from and how it is spent by the candidate" in order to aid the voters in evaluating those who seek Federal office. [Second], disclosure requirements deter actual corruption and avoid the appearance of corruption by exposing large contributions and expenditures to the light of publicity. [Third], and not least significant, recordkeeping, reporting and disclosure requirements are an essential means of gathering the data necessary to detect violations of the contribution limitations.

The disclosure requirements, as a general matter, directly serve substantial governmental interests. In determining whether these interests are sufficient to justify the requirements we must look to the extent of the burden they place on individual rights. It is undoubtedly true that public disclosure of contributions to candidates and political parties will deter some individuals who otherwise might contribute. In some instances, disclosure may even expose contributors to harassment or retaliation. These are not insignificant burdens on individual rights, and they must be weighed carefully against the interests which Congress has sought to promote by this legislation. In this process, we [agree] with appellants' concession that disclosure requirements—certainly in most applications—appear to be the least restrictive means of curbing the evils of campaign ignorance and corruption that Congress found to exist. Appellants argue, however, that the balance tips against disclosure when it is required of contributors to certain parties and candidates. We turn now to this contention.

B. *Application to Minor Parties and Independents.* Appellants contend that the Act's requirements are overbroad insofar as they apply to contributions to minor parties and independent candidates because the governmental interest in this information is minimal and the danger of significant infringement on First Amendment rights is greatly increased.

1. *Requisite Factual Showing.* [NAACP v. Alabama] is inapposite where, as here, any serious infringement on First Amendment rights brought about by the compelled disclosure of contributors is highly speculative. It is true that the governmental interest in disclosure is diminished when the contribution in question is made to a minor party with little chance of winning an election. [We] are not unmindful that the damage done by disclosure to the associational interests of the minor parties and their members and to supporters of independents could be significant. [In] some instances fears of reprisal may deter contributions to the point where the movement cannot survive. [There] could well be a case, similar to those before the Court in Alabama and Bates, where the threat to the exercise of First Amendment rights is so serious and the state interest furthered by disclosure so insubstantial that the Act's requirements cannot be constitutionally applied. But no appellant in this case has tendered record evidence of the sort proffered in Alabama. [On] this record, the substantial public interest in disclosure identified by the legislative history of this Act outweighs the harm generally alleged.

2. *Blanket Exemption.* Appellants [argue], however, that a blanket exemption for minor parties is necessary lest irreparable injury be done before the required evidence can be gathered. [We] recognize that unduly strict requirements of proof could impose a heavy burden, but it does not follow that a blanket exemption for minor parties is necessary. Minor parties must be allowed sufficient flexibility in the proof of injury to assure a fair consideration of their claim. The evidence offered need show only a reasonable probability that the compelled disclosure of a party's contributors' names will subject them to threats, harassment or reprisals from either government officials or private parties. The proof may include, for example, specific evidence of past or present harassment of members due to their associational ties, or of harassment directed against the organization itself. [Where] it exists the type of chill and harassment identified in Alabama can be shown. We cannot assume that courts will be insensitive to similar showings when made in future cases. We therefore conclude that a blanket exemption is not [required].[2]

C. *Section 434(e).* Section 434(e), [unlike] the other disclosure provisions, [does] not seek the contribution list of any association. Instead, it requires direct disclosure of what an individual or group contributes or spends. In considering this provision we must apply the same strict standard of scrutiny, for the right of associational privacy developed in Alabama derives from the rights of the organization's members to advocate their personal points of view in the

---

2. The possibility held out by Buckley—that certain minor parties might, on a proper showing, obtain exemptions from compelled disclosures—was realized in Brown v. Socialist Workers' 74 Campaign Committee (Ohio), 459 U.S. 87 (1982). In an opinion by Justice Marshall, the Court held, unanimously on this point, that the Party in Ohio had made a sufficient showing of a "reasonable probability of threats, harassment, or reprisals" so that it could not be constitutionally compelled to disclose information concerning campaign contributions. The Court also held, over the dissents of Justices O'Connor, Rehnquist, and Stevens, that the same showing also exempted the Party from compelled disclosure of campaign *disbursements.* The Court reasoned that many disbursements consist of "reimbursements, advances, or wages paid to party mem-

bers, campaign workers, and supporters, whose activities lie at the very core of the First Amendment." Other disbursements go to those who, whether supporters or not, might be deterred by disclosure from dealing with a party espousing unpopular views. The dissent, written by Justice O'Connor, argued that the balance between governmental interests and the First Amendment interests of the Party would be sufficiently different in the case of expenditures that there should be a "separately focused inquiry" into whether disclosure of expenditures, taken alone, would subject the Party or recipients of the disbursements to threats, harassment, or reprisals. The dissenters, although agreeing that such a possibility existed for contributors, believed that in this case it did not exist for recipients of expenditures.

most effective way. Appellants attack § 434(e) as a direct intrusion on privacy of belief, in violation of Talley v. California, 362 U.S. 60 (1960), and as imposing "very real, practical burdens [certain] to deter individuals from making expenditures for their independent political speech" analogous to those held to be impermissible in Thomas v. Collins, 323 U.S. 516 (1945). [Sec. 434(e)] [3] does not contain the infirmities of the regulations before the Court in Talley v. California and Thomas v. Collins. The ordinance found wanting in Talley forbade all distribution of handbills that did not contain the name of the printer, author, or manufacturer, and the name of the distributor. [Here], the disclosure requirement is narrowly limited to those situations where the information sought has a substantial connection with the governmental interests sought to be advanced. Thomas held unconstitutional a prior restraint in the form of a registration requirement for labor organizers. [The] burden imposed by § 434(e) is no prior restraint, but a reasonable and minimally restrictive method of furthering First Amendment values by opening the basic processes of our federal election system to public view.

D. *Thresholds.* Appellants' third contention, based on alleged overbreadth, is that the monetary thresholds in the record-keeping and reporting provisions lack a substantial nexus with the claimed governmental interests, for the amounts involved are too low even to attract the attention of the candidate, much less have a corrupting influence. The provisions contain two thresholds. Records are to be kept by political committees of the names and addresses of those who make contributions in excess of $10. [If] a person's contributions to a committee or candidate aggregate more than $100, his name and address, as well as his occupation and principal place of business, are to be included in reports filed by committees and candidates with the Commission and made available for [public inspection]. The $10 and $100 thresholds are indeed low. Contributors of relatively small amounts are likely to be especially sensitive to recording or disclosure of their political preferences. These strict requirements may well discourage participation by some citizens in the political process, a result that Congress hardly could have intended. Indeed, there is little in the legislative history to indicate that Congress focused carefully on the appropriate level at which to require recording and disclosure. Rather, it seems merely to have adopted the thresholds existing in similar disclosure laws since 1910. But we cannot require Congress to establish that it has chosen the highest reasonable threshold. The line is necessarily a judgmental decision, best left in the context of this complex legislation to congressional discretion. We cannot say, on this bare record, that the limits designated are wholly without [rationality].

[Chief Justice BURGER's separate opinion stated:]

Disclosure. [The] public right-to-know ought not be absolute when its exercise reveals private political convictions. Secrecy, like privacy, is not per se criminal. On the contrary, secrecy and privacy as to political preferences and convictions are fundamental in a free society. [E.g., NAACP v. Button.] [We] all seem to agree that whatever the legitimate public interests in this area, proper analysis requires us to scrutinize the precise means employed to implement that interest. [I] suggest the Court has failed to give the traditional standing to some of the First Amendment values at stake here. Specifically, it has failed to confine the particular exercise of governmental power within limits reasonably required. [Shelton v. Tucker.] [It] seems to me that the threshold

---

3. The Court noted that § 434(e), as it had been construed to avoid "serious problems of vagueness," "imposes independent reporting requirements on individuals and groups that are not candidates or political committees only in the following circumstances: (1) when they make contributions earmarked for political purposes or authorized or requested by a candidate or his agent, to some person other than a candidate or political committee, and (2) when they make an expenditure for a communication that expressly advocates the election or defeat of a clearly identified candidate."

limits fixed at $10 and $100 for anonymous contributions are constitutionally impermissible on their face. [Congress] gave little or no thought, one way or the other, to these limits, but rather lifted figures out of a 65-year-old statute. [To] argue that a 1976 contribution of $10 or $100 entails a risk of corruption or its appearance is simply too extravagant to be maintained. No public right-to-know justifies the compelled disclosure of such contributions, at the risk of discouraging them. There is, in short, no relation whatever between the means used and the legitimate goal of ventilating possible undue influence. Congress has used a shotgun to kill wrens as well as hawks.

In saying that the lines drawn by Congress are "not wholly without rationality," the Court plainly fails to apply the traditional test [of, e.g., NAACP v. Button]. The Court's abrupt departure [4] from traditional standards is wrong; surely a greater burden rests on Congress than merely to avoid "irrationality" when regulating in the core area of the First Amendment. Even taking the Court at its word, the particular dollar amounts fixed by Congress that must be reported to the Commission fall short of meeting the test of rationality when measured by the goals sought to be achieved.

Finally, no legitimate public interest has been shown in forcing the disclosure of modest contributions that are the prime support of new, unpopular or unfashionable political causes. There is no realistic possibility that such modest donations will have a corrupting influence, especially on parties that enjoy only "minor" status. Major parties would not notice them; minor parties need [them]. Flushing out the names of supporters of minority parties will plainly have a deterrent effect on potential [contributors].[5]

B. REGULATION OF PUBLIC EMPLOYEES OUTSIDE THE SUBVERSION AREA: THE MODERN CONTEXT OF STATE RESTRICTIONS

Introduction. Most of the modern Court's concern with government employees does not arise out of the fear-of-subversion context of earlier decades. Instead, the recent cases involve a range of First Amendment activities and political backgrounds of government employees. Two types of issues should be distinguished. The first is the extent to which an employee's First Amendment rights *as a citizen* may be restricted because of the government's interest in regulating public employment. The second concerns the public employee's free speech rights *as an employee.* The first type of issue is raised in the cases considered in the next two notes. The second issue is explored in the 1983 decision in Connick v. Myers, printed as a principal case below. (Note that Connick discusses prior decisions involving both types of issues, including those considered in the introductory notes that follow.)

1. *Prohibitions of political activities by public employees.* a. As long ago as 1947, in United Public Workers v. Mitchell, 330 U.S. 75, the Court sustained the constitutionality of § 9(a) of the Hatch Act of 1940 prohibiting federal employees in the executive branch from taking "any active part in political management or in political campaigns."[1] After the changes in First Amend-

---

4. Ironically, the Court seems to recognize this principle when dealing with the limitations on contributions. [Footnote by Chief Justice Burger. See the discussion of contributions in Buckley, at p. 1301 above.]

5. The record does not show systematic harassment of the sort in NAACP v. Alabama. But uncontradicted evidence was adduced with respect to actual experiences of minor parties

indicating a sensitivity on the part of potential contributors to the prospect of disclosure. This evidence suffices when the governmental interest in putting the spotlight on the sources of support for minor parties or splinter groups is so tenuous. [Footnote by Chief Justice Burger.]

1. The justiciability issues in Mitchell, pertaining to considerations of "ripeness," are considered in chap. 15 below, at p. 1581.

ment limits on regulations of public employees traced in this section, a second major challenge to the Act was brought in the 1970s. But it also failed: in CSC v. LETTER CARRIERS, 413 U.S. 548 (1973), the Court rejected an on-the-face, overbreadth attack on § 9(a) and "unhesitatingly reaffirm[ed]" Mitchell: "Neither the right to associate nor the right to participate in political activities is absolute. [P]lainly identifiable acts of political management and political campaigning may constitutionally be prohibited on the part of federal employees." Justice WHITE's majority opinion deferred to the congressional judgment that "partisan political activities by federal employees must be limited if the Government is to operate effectively and fairly, elections are to play their proper part in representative government, and employees themselves are to be sufficiently free from improper influences." He noted that the restrictions were "not aimed at particular parties, groups or points of view, but apply equally to all [covered] partisan activities. [Nor] do they seek to control political opinions or beliefs, or to interfere with or influence anyone's vote at the polls." [2]

b. In the Letter Carriers case, Justice White quoted and applied a balancing approach that had been set forth five years earlier in PICKERING v. BOARD OF EDUCATION, 391 U.S. 563 (1968). In Pickering, the employee's First Amendment claims were sustained. Pickering involved a teacher dismissed for writing a letter to a newspaper attacking a school board's handling of financing matters. Justice MARSHALL's majority opinion concluded: "In these circumstances, [the] interest of the school administration in limiting teachers' opportunities to contribute to public debate is not significantly greater than its interest in limiting a similar contribution by any member of the general public." Accordingly, absent satisfaction of the New York Times "malice" standard in libel cases (see chap. 11, above), the teacher could not be dismissed. The balancing approach of Pickering (as quoted in Letter Carriers) stated that "the government has an interest in regulating the conduct and 'the speech of its employees that differ[s] significantly from those it possesses in connection with regulation of the speech of the citizenry in general. The problem in any case is to arrive at a balance between the interests of the [employee], as a citizen, in commenting upon matters of public concern and the interest of the [government], as an employer, in promoting the efficiency of the public services it performs through its employees.'" In Pickering, Justice Marshall relied especially on Keyishian and cited Wieman as well as Shelton v. Tucker. Before enunciating his standard, Justice Marshall stated in Pickering: "To the extent that the [state court] opinion may be read to suggest that teachers may constitutionally be compelled to relinquish the First Amendment rights they would otherwise enjoy as citizens to comment on matters of public interest in connection with the operation of the public schools in which they work, it proceeds on a premise that has been unequivocally rejected in numerous prior decisions of this Court." [3]

2. *Patronage dismissals of public employees.* In two modern decisions, the Court has sharply curtailed governmental power to dismiss non-civil service employees on party allegiance grounds under traditional patronage systems.

---

2. Most of the opinion in Letter Carriers was devoted to rejecting the overbreadth attack in this and a companion case, Broadrick v. Oklahoma, which involved a state restriction on political activities by civil servants. Broadrick and the "substantial overbreadth" approach of these cases is discussed at length in sec. 1 of chap. 12, above.

3. In Pickering, Justice DOUGLAS joined by Justice Black, concurred in the judgment in a separate notation, and Justice WHITE submitted an opinion concurring in part and dissenting in part. Compare the unanimous decision in Givhan v. Western Line Consolidated School District, 439 U.S. 410 (1979), extending the Pickering principle to "private" as well as "public" speech. There, the teacher alleged that she was dismissed because of her statements in a series of private encounters with a school principal. See Schauer, " 'Private' Speech and the 'Private' Forum: Givhan v. Western Line School District," 1979 Sup.Ct.Rev. 217. (Recall also Board of Regents v. Roth and Perry v. Sindermann (1972; chap. 8, sec. 4, above).)

The process began with Elrod v. Burns, 427 U.S. 347 (1976), a 5 to 3 decision holding that a newly elected Democratic Sheriff could not discharge several Republican employees—three process servers and a juvenile court bailiff and security guard. The reach of that decision was unclear. Justice Brennan's plurality opinion, joined by Justices White and Marshall, relied on the First Amendment principles of such cases as Keyishian to conclude that patronage dismissals must be limited to "policymaking positions." Justice Stewart's concurrence, joined by Justice Blackmun, pursued a narrower analysis and concluded that "a nonpolicymaking, nonconfidential government employee [cannot be discharged] from a job that he is satisfactorily performing upon the sole ground of his political beliefs." [4] Four years later in BRANTI v. FINKEL, 445 U.S. 507 (1980), the Court reconsidered patronage systems, reexamined and expanded the immunity of non-civil service employees from patronage dismissals, but left the contours of the broadened constitutional protections somewhat unclear. The new governing rule in Branti invoked criteria differing from Elrod: "the ultimate inquiry is not whether the label 'policymaker' or 'confidential' fits a particular position; rather, the question is whether the hiring authority can demonstrate that party affiliation is an appropriate requirement for the effective performance of the public office involved." [5]

In Branti, two Republican assistant county public defenders successfully challenged their dismissal by the newly-named Democratic head of the public defender's office. Justice STEVENS' majority opinion concluded, under his newly formulated standard, that "it is manifest that the continued employment of an assistant public defender cannot properly be conditioned upon his allegiance to the political party in control of the county government." He noted that any policymaking in a public defender's office relates to the needs of individual clients, not to any partisan political interests, and that the assistant public defenders' access to confidential information arising out of attorney-client relationships had no bearing on party concerns. Accordingly, "it would undermine, rather than promote, the effective performance of an assistant public defender's office to make his tenure dependent on his allegiance to the dominant political party." He conceded that "party affiliation may be an acceptable requirement for some types of government employment," but insisted that the "policymaking or confidential position" criteria did not adequately delineate the proper use of party considerations. He explained: "Under some circumstances, a position may be appropriately considered political even though it is neither confidential nor policymaking in character." (He gave as an example the use of local election judges of different parties to supervise elections at the precinct level.) He added: "It is equally clear that party affiliation is not necessarily relevant to every policymaking or confidential position." (In illustrating that statement he noted that a "policymaking" football coach could not be discharged on party affiliation grounds, but that the position of a speechwriting assistant to a governor could properly involve party allegiance if it was to be performed "effectively.")

Justice POWELL, in the major dissent, objected both to the majority's new "vague, overbroad" standard and to its application of First Amendment principles. With respect to the former, he saw the "substantially expanded standard

---

4. Justice Powell wrote the main dissent, joined by Chief Justice Burger and Justice Rehnquist. Justice Stevens did not participate.

5. Justice Stevens, the author of the new standard, had not participated in Elrod. Justice STEWART, the author of the concurring opinion in Elrod, dissented in Branti on the ground that the positions involved in the 1980 case were not "nonconfidential" ones. But Justice BLACKMUN, who had joined Justice Stewart's concurrence in Elrod, was with the majority in 1980. Moreover, Chief Justice BURGER, among the dissenters in Elrod in 1976, also joined the majority in 1980. Justice Powell elaborated his dissenting views in Elrod in a strong dissent in Branti, joined by Justice Rehnquist and, in part, Justice Stewart.)

for determining which governmental employees may be retained or dismissed on the basis of political affiliation" as creating "vast uncertainty." [6] But he reserved most of his criticism for the majority's "more fundamental" error in applying the First Amendment, claiming that the ruling constituted "new law from inapplicable precedents." The precedents relied on, he noted, had neither discussed patronage nor involved positions that "traditionally had been regarded as patronage positions." [7] He insisted: "No constitutional violation exists if patronage practices further sufficiently important interests to justify tangential burdening of First Amendment rights." Constitutionality, in short, depended upon the "governmental interests served by patronage"; and the majority had inadequately identified and weighed them. Examining these interests, Justice Powell emphasized that patronage appointments "helped build stable political parties" and that "the importance of political parties was self-evident." Political parties served "a variety of substantial governmental interests." They helped candidates "to muster donations of time and money necessary to capture the attention of the electorate" and thus contribute to the democratic process; moreover, they "aid effective governance after election campaigns end." The majority's approach, he argued, imposed "unnecessary constraints upon the ability of responsible officials to govern effectively and to carry out new policies." [8] Moreover, the "breakdown of party discipline that handicaps elected officials also limits the ability of the electorate to choose wisely among candidates." He concluded: "In sum, the effect of the Court's decision will be to decrease the accountability and denigrate the role of our national political parties."

   3. *Restrictions on disclosure of confidential information by former government employees.* The question of government remedies against a former government employee who had agreed not to disclose confidential government information without authorization came before the Court in SNEPP v. UNITED STATES, 444 U.S. 507 (1980).[9] Snepp, a former CIA employee, had agreed not to divulge classified information without authorization and not to publish any information relating to the Agency without prepublication clearance. Without submitting his manuscript for clearance, he published a book about CIA activities in Viet Nam. (The Government did not claim that the book contained classified data.) The Court of Appeals held that Snepp could be subjected to punitive damages, but refused to impress a constructive trust on his profits from the book. The Supreme Court's per curiam reversal, without argument, held that punitive damages were an inappropriate and inadequate remedy and instead imposed a constructive trust on Snepp's profits. The

6. Justice Powell noted, e.g., that "it would be difficult to say [under the new standard] that 'partisan' concerns properly are relevant to the performance of the duties of a United States Attorney." The majority, by contrast, suggested that "an official such as a prosecutor" has "broader public responsibilities" than a public defender and accordingly expressed "no opinion as to whether the deputy of such an official could be dismissed on grounds of political party affiliation or loyalty."

7. He especially objected to the reliance on Keyishian and on Perry v. Sindermann (p. 571 above), both involving the dismissal of teachers from state educational institutions because of their political views. The plurality in Elrod and the majority in Branti had also referred to Barnette, the Flag Salute Case (p. 1510 below), which, as Justice Powell noted, did not involve public employment at all.

8. He elaborated: "[I]n view of the Court's new holding that some policymaking positions may not be filled on the basis of political affiliation, elected officials may find changes in public policy thwarted by policymaking employees protected from replacement by the Constitution. The official with a hostile or footdragging subordinate will now be in a difficult position. In order to replace such a subordinate, he must be prepared to prove that the subordinate's 'private political beliefs [will] interfere with the discharge of his public duties.'"

9. In earlier dicta, some Justices had indicated that the government may seek civil and criminal remedies against former employees who publish secret information. See especially the Pentagon Papers Case, New York Times Co. v. United States (1971; sec. 6, p. 1420 below).

majority's only mention of the First Amendment came in a footnote insisting that "this Court's cases make clear that—even in the absence of an express agreement—the CIA could have acted to protect substantial government interests by imposing reasonable restrictions on employee activities that in other contexts might be protected by the First Amendment. [The Court cited, inter alia, Letter Carriers, Greer v. Spock, and Cole v. Richardson.] The Government has a compelling interest in protecting both the secrecy of information important to our national security and the appearance of confidentiality so essential to the effective operation of our foreign intelligence service. The agreement that Snepp signed is a reasonable means for protecting this vital interest." A strong dissent by Justice STEVENS, joined by Justices Brennan and Marshall, objected not only to the Court's extraordinary procedure (deciding without argument an issue raised only in the Government's conditional cross-petition for certiorari, filed to bring the entire case up in the event the Court granted Snepp's certiorari petition) but also to the Court's fashioning of a "drastic new remedy [to] enforce a species of prior restraint on a citizen's right to criticize his government." [10]

CONNICK v. MYERS

461 U.S. 138, 103 S.Ct. 1684, 75 L.Ed.2d 708 (1983).

Justice WHITE delivered the opinion of the Court.

[Justice White began by quoting the balancing formulation in the Pickering decision in 1968 (p. 1392 above), noting that the ultimate question was, in the words of Pickering, arriving "at a balance between the interests of the [employee], as a citizen, in commenting upon matters of public concern and the interest of the State, as an employer, in promoting the efficiency of the public services it performs through its employees." He continued:] We return to this problem today and consider whether the [First Amendment prevents] the discharge of a state employee for circulating a questionnaire concerning internal office affairs.

I. The respondent, Sheila Myers, was employed as an Assistant District Attorney in New Orleans for five and a half years. She served at the pleasure of petitioner Harry Connick, the District Attorney for Orleans Parish. During this period Myers competently performed her responsibilities of trying criminal cases.

In [1980] Myers was informed that she would be transferred to prosecute cases in a different section of the criminal court. Myers was strongly opposed to the proposed transfer [1] and expressed her view to several of her supervisors, including Connick. Despite her objections, [Myers] was notified that she was being transferred. Myers again spoke with Dennis Waldron, one of the first

---

10. Justice Stevens elaborated on his prior restraint objection as follows: "Inherent in this prior restraint is the risk that the reviewing agency will misuse its authority to delay the publication of a crucial work or to persuade an author to modify the contents of his work beyond the demands of secrecy. The character of the covenant as a prior restraint on free speech surely imposes an especially heavy burden on the censor to justify the remedy it seeks. It would take more than the Court has written to persuade me that that burden has been met." He added in a footnote that the prepublication review requirement was a form of prior restraint "that would not be tolerated in other contexts. See, e.g., [Pentagon Papers; Nebraska Press (both in sec. 6

below)]. In view of the national interest in maintaining an effective intelligence service, I am not prepared to say that the restraint is necessarily intolerable in this context. I am, however, prepared to say that, certiorari having been granted, the issue surely should not be resolved in the absence of full briefing and argument."

1. Myers' opposition was at least partially attributable to her concern that a conflict of interest would have been created by the transfer because of her participation in a counseling program for convicted defendants released on probation in the section of the criminal court to which she was to be assigned. [Footnote by Justice White.]

assistant district attorneys, expressing her reluctance to accept the transfer. [Myers] later testified that, in response to Waldron's suggestion that her concerns were not shared by others in the office, she informed him that she would do some research on the matter.

That night Myers prepared a questionnaire soliciting the views of her fellow staff members concerning office transfer policy, office morale, the need for a grievance committee, the level of confidence in supervisors, and whether employees felt pressured to work in political campaigns. [Myers distributed] the questionnaire to 15 assistant district attorneys. Shortly after noon, Dennis Waldron learned that Myers was distributing the survey. He immediately phoned Connick and informed him that Myers was creating a "mini-insurrection" within the office. Connick returned to the office and told Myers that she was being terminated because of her refusal to accept the transfer. She was also told that her distribution of the questionnaire was considered an act of insubordination. Connick particularly objected to the question which inquired whether employees "had confidence in and would rely on the word" of various superiors in the office, and to a question concerning pressure to work in political campaigns which he felt would be damaging if discovered by the press.[2]

II. For at least 15 years, it has been settled that a state cannot condition public employment on a basis that infringes the employee's constitutionally protected interest in freedom of expression. [Keyishian v. Board of Regents; Pickering; Perry v. Sindermann; Branti.] [The lower courts misapplied the balancing approach of Pickering] and consequently [erred] in striking the balance for respondent.

A. The District Court got off on the wrong foot [by] initially finding that, "[t]aken as a whole, the issues presented in the questionnaire relate to the effective functioning of the District Attorney's Office and are matters of public importance and concern." Connick contends at the outset that no balancing of interests is required in this case because Myers' questionnaire concerned only internal office matters and that such speech is not upon a matter of "public concern," as the term was used in Pickering. Although we do not agree that Myers' communication in this case was wholly without First Amendment protection, there is much force to Connick's submission. The repeated emphasis in Pickering on the right of a public employee "as a citizen, in commenting upon matters of public concern," was not accidental. This language [reflects] both the historical evolvement of the rights of public employees, and the common sense realization that government offices could not function if every employment decision became a constitutional matter.

For most of this century, the unchallenged dogma was that a public employee had no right to object to conditions placed upon the terms of employment—including those which restricted the exercise of constitutional rights. The classic formulation of this position was that of Justice Holmes [in his 1892 state court decision in the McAuliffe case, quoted at p. 1361 above]. For many years, Holmes' epigram expressed this Court's law. [E.g., Adler; Garner; United Public Workers v. Mitchell.] The Court cast new light on the matter in a series of cases arising from the widespread efforts in the 1950s and early 1960s to require public employees, particularly teachers, to swear oaths of loyalty to the state and reveal the groups with which they associated. [E.g., Wiemann; Keyishian.] In [these precedents] in which Pickering is rooted, the

---

2. Myers filed a federal suit claiming that she had been discharged because she had exercised her constitutionally protected right of free speech. The District Court sustained her claim, finding that, despite Connick's assertion that she was fired because of her refusal to accept the transfer, the facts showed that her questionnaire

was the real reason for her termination. The District Court then proceeded to hold that Myers' questionnaire involved matters of public concern and that the state had not "clearly demonstrated" that the survey "substantially interfered" with the operations of the DA's office. The Court of Appeals affirmed that ruling.

invalidated statutes and actions sought to suppress the rights of public employees to participate in public affairs. The issue was whether government employees could be prevented or "chilled" by the fear of discharge from joining political parties and other associations that certain public officials might find "subversive." The explanation for the Constitution's special concern with threats to the right of citizens to participate in political affairs is no mystery. The First Amendment "was fashioned to assure unfettered interchange of ideas for the bringing about of political and social changes desired by the people." [Roth; New York Times v. Sullivan.] [Accordingly], the Court has frequently reaffirmed that speech on public issues occupies the "highest rung of the hierarchy of First Amendment values," and is entitled to special protection. [Claiborne Hardware; Carey v. Brown.]

[Pickering] followed from this understanding of the First Amendment. In Pickering, the Court held impermissible [the] dismissal of a high school teacher for openly criticizing the Board of Education on its allocation of school funds between athletics and education and its methods of informing taxpayers about the need for additional revenue. Pickering's subject was "a matter of legitimate public concern" upon which "free and open debate is vital to informed decision-making by the electorate." [See also, e.g., Perry v. Sindermann; Givhan.] Pickering, its antecedents and progeny, lead us to conclude that if Myers' questionnaire cannot be fairly characterized as constituting speech on a matter of public concern, it is unnecessary for us to scrutinize the reasons for her discharge. When employee expression cannot be fairly considered as relating to any matter of political, social, or other concern to the community, government officials should enjoy wide latitude in managing their offices, without intrusive oversight by the judiciary in the name of the [First Amendment].

We do not suggest, however, that Myers' speech, even if not touching upon a matter of public concern, is totally beyond the protection of the First Amendment. [We] in no sense suggest that speech on private matters falls into one of the narrow and well-defined classes of expression which carries so little social value, such as obscenity, that the state can prohibit and punish such expression by all persons in its jurisdiction. For example, an employee's false criticism of his employer on grounds not of public concern may be cause for his discharge but would be entitled to the same protection in a libel action accorded an identical statement made by a man on the street. We hold only that when a public employee speaks not as a citizen upon matters of public concern, but instead as an employee upon matters only of personal interest, absent the most unusual circumstances, a federal court is not the appropriate forum in which to review the wisdom of a personnel decision taken by a public agency allegedly in reaction to the employee's behavior. Our responsibility is to ensure that citizens are not deprived of fundamental rights by virtue of working for the government; this does not require a grant of immunity for employee grievances not afforded by the First Amendment to those who do not work for the state.

Whether an employee's speech addresses a matter of public concern must be determined by the content, form, and context of a given statement, as revealed by the whole record.[3] In this case, with but one exception, the questions posed by Myers to her coworkers do not fall under the rubric of matters of "public concern." We view the questions pertaining to the confidence and trust that Myers' coworkers possess in various supervisors, the level of office morale, and the need for a grievance committee as mere extensions of Myers' dispute over her transfer to another section of the criminal court. [Myers] did not seek to inform the public that the District Attorney's office was not discharging its governmental responsibilities in the investigation and prosecution of criminal

---

3. The inquiry into the protected status of speech is one of law, not fact. Thus, we [need not defer] to the views of the [District Court]. [Footnote by Justice White.]

cases. Nor did Myers seek to bring to light [wrongdoing] or breach of public trust on the part of Connick and others. Indeed, the questionnaire, if released to the public, would convey no information at all other than the fact that a single employee is upset with the status quo. While discipline and morale in the workplace are related to an agency's efficient performance of its duties, the focus of Myers' questions is not to evaluate the performance of the office but rather to gather ammunition for another round of controversy with her superiors. These questions reflect one employee's dissatisfaction with a transfer and an attempt to turn that displeasure into a cause celèbre. To presume that all matters which transpire within a government office are of public concern would mean that virtually every remark—and certainly every criticism directed at a public official—would plant the seed of a constitutional case. While as a matter of good judgment, public officials should be receptive to constructive criticism offered by their employees, the First Amendment does not require a public office to be run as a roundtable for employee complaints over internal office affairs.

One question in Myers' questionnaire, however, does touch upon a matter of public concern. Question 11 inquires if assistant district attorneys "ever feel pressured to work in political campaigns on behalf of office supported candidates." We have recently noted that official pressure upon employees to work for political candidates not of the worker's own choice constitutes a coercion of belief in violation of fundamental constitutional rights. Branti v. Finkel; Elrod v. Burns. In addition, there is a demonstrated interest in this country that government service should depend upon meritorious performance rather than political service. [E.g., Letter Carriers.] Given this history, we believe it apparent that the issue of whether assistant district attorneys are pressured to work in political campaigns is a matter of interest to the community upon which it is essential that public employees be able to speak out freely without fear of retaliatory dismissal.

B. Because one of the questions in Myers' survey touched upon a matter of public concern, and contributed to her discharge, we must determine whether Connick was justified in discharging Myers. Here the District Court again erred in imposing an unduly onerous burden on the state to justify Myers' discharge. The District Court viewed the issue of whether Myers' speech was upon a matter of "public concern" as a threshold inquiry, after which it became the government's burden to "clearly demonstrate" that the speech involved "substantially interfered" with official responsibilities. Yet Pickering unmistakably states [that] the state's burden in justifying a particular discharge varies depending upon the nature of the employee's expression. Although such particularized balancing is difficult, the courts must reach the most appropriate possible balance of the competing interests.

C. The Pickering balance requires full consideration of the government's interest in the effective and efficient fulfillment of its responsibilities to the public. [We] agree with the District Court that there is no demonstration here that the questionnaire impeded Myers' ability to perform her responsibilities. The District Court was also correct to recognize that "it is important to the efficient and successful operation of the District Attorney's office for Assistants to maintain close working relationships with their superiors." Connick's judgment [was] that Myers' questionnaire was an act of insubordination which interfered with working relationships. When close working relationships are essential to fulfilling public responsibilities, a wide degree of deference to the employer's judgment is appropriate. Furthermore, we do not see the necessity for an employer to allow events to unfold to the extent that the disruption of the office and the destruction of working relationships is manifest before taking action. We caution that a stronger showing may be necessary if the employee's speech more substantially involved matters of public concern.

[Also] relevant is the manner, time, and place in which the questionnaire was distributed. As noted in [Givhan], "Private expression [may] in some situations bring additional factors to the Pickering calculus. When a government employee personally confronts his immediate superior, the employing agency's institutional efficiency may be threatened not only by the content of the employee's message but also by the manner, time, and place in which it is delivered." Here the questionnaire was prepared, and distributed at the office; the manner of distribution required not only Myers to leave her work but for others to do the same in order that the questionnaire be completed. Although some latitude in when official work is performed is to be allowed when professional employees are involved, [the fact] that Myers, unlike Pickering, exercised her rights to speech at the office supports Connick's fears that the functioning of his office was endangered.

Finally, the context in which the dispute arose is also significant. This is not a case where an employee, out of purely academic interest, circulated a questionnaire so as to obtain useful research. Myers acknowledges that it is no coincidence that the questionnaire followed upon the heels of the transfer notice. When employee speech concerning office policy arises from an employment dispute concerning the very application of that policy to the speaker, additional weight must be given to the supervisor's view that the employee has threatened the authority of the employer to run the office. Although we accept the District Court's factual finding that Myers' reluctance to accede to the transfer order was not a sufficient cause in itself for her dismissal, [this] does not render irrelevant the fact that the questionnaire emerged after a persistent dispute between Myers and Connick and his deputies over office transfer policy.

III. Myers' questionnaire touched upon matters of public concern in only a most limited sense; her survey, in our view, is most accurately characterized as an employee grievance concerning internal office policy. The limited First Amendment interest involved here does not require that Connick tolerate action which he reasonably believed would disrupt the office, undermine his authority, and destroy close working relationships. Myers' discharge therefore did not offend the First Amendment. We reiterate, however, the caveat we expressed in Pickering: "Because of the enormous variety of fact situations in which critical statements [by] public employees may be thought by their superiors [to] furnish grounds for dismissal, we do not deem it either appropriate or feasible to lay down a general standard against which all such statements may be judged."

Our holding today is grounded in our long-standing recognition that the First Amendment's primary aim is the full protection of speech upon issues of public concern, as well as the practical realities involved in the administration of a government office. Although today the balance is struck for the government, this is no defeat for the First Amendment. For it would indeed be a Pyrrhic victory for the great principles of free expression if the Amendment's safeguarding of a public employee's right, as a citizen, to participate in discussions concerning public affairs were confused with the attempt to constitutionalize the employee grievance that we see presented here.

[Reversed.]

Justice BRENNAN, with whom Justice MARSHALL, Justice BLACKMUN, and Justice STEVENS join, dissenting.

[The] Court concludes that [Myers'] dismissal does not violate the First Amendment [because] the questionnaire addresses matters that [are] not of public concern. It is hornbook law, however, that speech about "the manner in which government is operated or should be operated" is an essential part of the communications necessary for self-governance the protection of which was a central purpose of the First Amendment. Because the questionnaire addressed such matters and its distribution did not adversely affect the operations of the District Attorney's Office or interfere with Myers' working relationship with her fellow employees, I dissent.

I. [The] balancing test articulated in Pickering comes into play only when a public employee's speech implicates the government's interests as an employer. When public employees engage in expression unrelated to their employment while away from the work place, their First Amendment rights are, of course, no different from those of the general public. Thus, whether a public employee's speech addresses a matter of public concern is relevant to the constitutional inquiry only when the statements at issue—by virtue of their content or the context in which they were made—may have an adverse impact on the government's ability to perform its duties efficiently.

The Court's decision today is flawed in three respects. First, the Court distorts the balancing analysis required under Pickering by suggesting that one factor, the context in which a statement is made, is to be weighed *twice* —first in determining whether an employee's speech addresses a matter of public concern and then in deciding whether the statement adversely affected the government's interest as an employer. Second, in concluding that the effect of respondent's personnel policies on employee morale and the work performance of the District Attorney's Office is not a matter of public concern, the Court impermissibly narrows the class of subjects on which public employees may speak out without fear of retaliatory dismissal. Third, the Court misapplies the Pickering balancing test in holding that Myers could constitutionally be dismissed for circulating a questionnaire addressed to at least one subject that *was* "a matter of interests to the community," in the absence of evidence that her conduct disrupted the efficient functioning of the District Attorney's Office.

II. [The] standard announced by the Court suggests that the manner and context in which a statement is made must be weighed on *both* sides of the Pickering balance. It is beyond dispute that how and where a public employee expresses his views are relevant in the second half of the Pickering inquiry— determining whether the employee's speech adversely affects the government's interests as an employer. [But] the fact that a public employee has chosen to express his views in private has nothing whatsoever to do with the first half of the Pickering calculus—whether those views relate to a matter of public concern. [The Court] suggests that there are two classes of speech of public concern: statements "of public import" because of their content, form and context, and statements that, by virtue of their subject matter, are "inherently of public concern." In my view, however, whether a particular statement by a public employee is addressed to a subject of public concern does not depend on where it was said or why. The First Amendment affords special protection to speech that may inform public debate about how our society is to be governed— regardless of whether it actually becomes the subject of a public controversy.

[We] have long recognized that one of the central purposes of the First Amendment's guarantee of freedom of expression is to protect the dissemination of information on the basis of which members of our society may make reasoned decisions about the government. [Unconstrained] discussion concerning the manner in which the government performs its duties is an essential element of the public discourse necessary to informed self-government. [The] constitutionally protected right to speak out on governmental affairs would be meaningless if it did not extend to statements expressing criticism of governmental officials. [In] Pickering we held that the First Amendment affords similar protection to critical statements by a public school teacher directed at the Board of Education for whom he worked. In so doing, we recognized that "free and open debate" about the operation of public schools "is vital to informed decision-making by the electorate."

[Applying] these principles, I would hold that Myers' questionnaire addressed matters of public concern because it discussed subjects that could reasonably be expected to be of interest to persons seeking to develop informed opinions about the manner in which [the] District Attorney, an elected official, discharges his responsibilities. The questionnaire sought primarily to obtain information about the impact of the recent transfers on morale in the District Attorney's Office. It is beyond doubt that personnel decisions that adversely affect discipline and morale may ultimately impair an agency's efficient performance of its duties. Because I believe the First Amendment protects the right of public employees to discuss such matters so that the public may be better informed about how their elected officials fulfill their responsibilities, I would affirm the District Court's conclusion that the questionnaire related to matters of public importance and concern.

The Court's adoption of a far narrower conception of what subjects are of public concern seems prompted by its fears that a broader view "would mean that [every] criticism directed at a public official [would] plant the seed of a constitutional case." Obviously, not every remark directed at a public official by a public employee is protected by the First Amendment.[1] But deciding whether a particular matter is of public concern is an inquiry that, by its very nature, is a sensitive one for judges charged with interpreting a constitutional provision intended to put "the decision as to what views shall be voiced largely into the hands of each of [us]." Cohen v. California. [The] Court's decision ignores these precepts. [The] Court implicitly determines that information concerning employee morale at an important government office will not inform public debate. [The] proper means to ensure that the courts are not swamped with routine employee grievances mischaracterized as First Amendment cases is not to restrict artificially the concept of "public concern," but to require that adequate weight be given to the public's important interests in the efficient performance of governmental functions and in preserving employee discipline and harmony sufficient to achieve that end.

III. Although the Court finds most of Myers' questionnaire unrelated to matters of public interest, it does hold that one question—asking whether Assistants felt pressured to work in political campaigns on behalf of office-supported candidates—addressed a matter of public importance and concern. The Court also recognizes that this determination of public interest must weigh heavily in the balancing of competing interests required by Pickering. Having gone that far however, the Court misapplies the Pickering test and holds—against our previous authorities—that a public employer's mere apprehension that speech will be disruptive justifies suppression of that speech when all the objective evidence suggests that those fears are essentially [unfounded]. Such extreme deference to the employer's judgment is not appropriate when public employees voice critical views concerning the operations of the agency for which they work. Although an employer's determination that an employee's statements have undermined essential working relationships must be carefully weighed in the Pickering balance, we must bear in mind that "the threat of dismissal from public employment [is] a potent means of inhibiting speech." Pickering. If the employer's judgment is to be controlling, public employees will not speak out when what they have to say is critical of their supervisors. In order to protect public employees' First Amendment right to voice critical views

1. Perhaps the simplest example of a statement by a public employee that would not be protected by the First Amendment would be answering "No" to a request that the employee perform a lawful task within the scope of his duties. Although such a refusal is "speech," which implicates First Amendment interests, it is also insubordination, and as such it may serve as the basis for a lawful dismissal. [Footnote by Justice Brennan.]

on issues of public importance, the courts must make their own appraisal of the effects of the speech [in question].

IV. The Court's decision today inevitably will deter public employees from making critical statements about the manner in which government agencies are operated for fear that doing so will provoke their dismissal. As a result, the public will be deprived of valuable information with which to evaluate the performance of elected officials. Because protecting the dissemination of such information is an essential function of the First Amendment, I dissent.

GOVERNMENTAL BENEFITS OTHER THAN EMPLOYMENT

The principle that governmental benefits may not be conditioned on relinquishing First Amendment rights has not been limited to employment. Thus, in Speiser v. Randall, 357 U.S. 513 (1958), the Court overturned a California requirement that property tax exemptions for veterans would be available only to those who would declare that they did not advocate the forcible overthrow of the government. Rejecting California's claim that it could condition the award of a "privilege" or "bounty," Justice Brennan's opinion for the Court noted that "to deny an exemption to claimants who engage in certain forms of speech is in effect to penalize them for such speech."

In REGAN v. TAXATION WITH REPRESENTATION OF WASHINGTON, 461 U.S. 540 (1983), a unanimous Court found Speiser clearly distinguishable in a challenge to the Internal Revenue Code's prohibition on lobbying for tax-exempt organizations. Under § 501(c)(3) of the Internal Revenue Code, tax-exempt status is limited to those organizations "no substantial part of the activities of which is carrying on propaganda, or otherwise attempting to influence legislation." Because it engaged in lobbying activities, the respondent (TWR) was denied tax-exempt status. The most important consequence of that action was that contributions to TWR would not be deductible by the contributors. TWR filed suit, claiming that § 501(c)(3) violated the First Amendment and the principles of Speiser by conditioning tax-exempt status on refraining from lobbying, an activity protected by the First Amendment.

Justice REHNQUIST's opinion for the Court noted that both tax exemptions and tax-deductibility "were a form of subsidy that is administered through the tax system." Implicit in the Court's decision rejecting TWR's challenge was an important distinction. In Speiser the exercise of First Amendment activity caused the loss of a benefit otherwise available, a benefit itself unrelated to the First Amendment activity. But here support for the First Amendment activity itself was the very benefit sought. Justice Rehnquist stated: "TWR is certainly correct when it states that we have held that the government may not deny a benefit to a person because he exercises a constitutional right. See Perry v. Sindermann. But TWR is just as certainly incorrect when it claims that this case fits the Speiser-Perry model. The Code does not deny TWR the right to receive deductible contributions to support its non-lobbying activity, nor does it deny TWR any independent benefit on account of its intention to lobby. Congress has merely refused to pay for the lobbying out of public monies. [This] aspect of the case is controlled by Cammarano v. United States, 358 U.S. 498 (1959), in which we upheld a Treasury Regulation that denied business expense deductions for lobbying activities. We held that Congress is not required by the First Amendment to subsidize lobbying. [Congress] has not infringed any First Amendment rights or regulated any First Amendment activity. Congress has simply chosen not to pay for TWR's lobbying. We again reject the 'notion that First Amendment rights are somehow not fully realized unless they are subsidized by the State.' " [1]

Justice BLACKMUN submitted a separate concurring opinion, joined by Justices Brennan and Marshall. He agreed that "the First Amendment does not require the Government to subsidize protected activity, and that this principle controls disposition of [TWR's claim]." But he wrote separately "to make clear that in my view the result under the First Amendment depends entirely on the Court's necessary assumption—which I share—about the manner in which the [IRS] administers § 501. If viewed in isolation, the lobbying restriction contained in § 501(c)(3) violates the principle, reaffirmed today, 'that the Government may not deny a benefit to a person because he exercises a Constitutional right.' Section 501(c)(3) does not merely deny a subsidy for lobbying activities; it deprives an otherwise eligible organization of its tax-exempt status and its eligibility to receive tax-deductible contributions for all its activities, whenever one of those activities is 'substantial lobbying.' Because lobbying is protected by the First Amendment, § 501(c)(3) therefore denies a significant benefit to organizations choosing to exercise their constitutional rights."

But here, the "constitutional defect that would inhere in § 501(c)(3) alone is avoided by § 501(c)(4). [TWR] may use its present § 501(c)(3) organization for its nonlobbying activities and may create a § 501(c)(4) affiliate to pursue its charitable goals through lobbying. The § 501(c)(4) affiliate would not be eligible to receive tax-deductible contributions. [It] must be remembered that § 501(c)(3) organizations retain their constitutional right to speak and to petition the Government. Should the IRS attempt to limit the control these organizations exercise over the lobbying of their § 501(c)(4) affiliates, the First Amendment problems would be insurmountable. [Similarly], an attempt to prevent § 501(c)(4) organizations from lobbying explicitly on behalf of their § 501(c)(3) affiliates would perpetuate § 501(c)(3) organizations' inability to make known their views on legislation without incurring the unconstitutional penalty. Such restrictions would extend far beyond Congress' mere refusal to subsidize lobbying [and] would render the statutory scheme unconstitutional." In short, Justice Blackmun found that the ability to create a § 501(c)(4) organization to engage in lobbying activities meant that a § 501(c)(3) organization did not have to relinquish its lobbying activities in order to qualify for the tax exemption: "A § 501(c)(3) organization's right to speak is not infringed, because it is free to make known its views on legislation through its § 501(c)(4) affiliate without losing tax benefits for its nonlobbying activities." But if this relationship had not existed, Justice Blackmun would have reached a different conclusion.

———————

1. TWR also presented an equal protection challenge, based on the fact that veterans' organizations are free to lobby without losing their tax-exempt status. TWR argued that strict scrutiny was appropriate because Congress chose to subsidize the speech of only certain organizations. The Court rejected this "content regulation" challenge as well: "The case would be different if Congress were to discriminate invidiously in its subsidies in such a way as to 'ai[m] at the suppression of dangerous ideas.' But the veterans' organizations [are] entitled to receive tax-deductible contributions regardless of the content of any speech they may use, including lobbying.

[The statute was not] intended to suppress any [ideas]."

Recall the comments on the relationship between the First Amendment's restrictions on content regulations and equal protection, in chap. 12, at p. 1164 above. Recall the questions raised there about whether it is more appropriate to rest claims such as TWR's on equal protection rather than the First Amendment. If a tax deduction were available to Republicans but not to Democrats, would this be a First Amendment or an equal protection violation? Does it matter which part of the Constitution is used?

SECTION 5. GOVERNMENT DEMANDS FOR INFORMATION THROUGH LEGISLATIVE INVESTIGATIONS

BACKGROUND AND EARLY CASES

Extensive Supreme Court litigation regarding the permissible scope of legislative investigations is a fairly recent phenomenon. But legislative committees have long conducted investigations. Congress authorized an investigation of a military disaster as early as 1792, for example. In the early years, congressional inquiries dealt mainly with the conduct of the executive department. By the 1820s, however, committees began to summon witnesses to aid in considering proposed legislation.[1] And ever since 1857, Congress has provided criminal penalties for witnesses who refuse to answer questions pertinent to a legislative investigation. Kilbourn v. Thompson, 103 U.S. 168 (1881), was the first important Supreme Court decision on congressional investigations. The Court invalidated the imprisonment of a recalcitrant witness at an inquiry into Jay Cooke's financial operations.[2] Justice Miller condemned investigations that were "judicial" in nature and stated that Congress cannot constitutionally inquire "into the private affairs of individuals" where the investigation "could result in no valid legislation on the subject to which the inquiry referred."[3] In the 1920s, attempts to punish recalcitrant witnesses fared better than in Kilbourn. In McGrain v. Daugherty, 273 U.S. 135 (1927), the Court, in a case arising out of an investigation of Attorney General Daugherty's conduct of the Justice Department, stated that "the power of inquiry" is "an essential and appropriate auxiliary to the legislative function." And, in order to obtain information needed to exercise the legislative function, Congress could "compel a private individual to appear before it or one of its committees." The McGrain Court noted that Kilbourn had not dealt with investigations in aid of "contemplated legislation." Two years later, in Sinclair v. United States, 279 U.S. 263 (1929), the Court reemphasized that it no longer subscribed to the Kilbourn attitude of hostility to congressional inquiries. In Sinclair, the witness in an investigation of federal oil leases refused to answer on the grounds that the questions related to his private affairs and that judicial proceedings were pending. After conceding that "Congress is without authority to compel disclosures for the purpose of aiding the prosecution of pending suits," the Court insisted that the authority "to require pertinent disclosures in aid of its own constitutional power is not abridged because the information sought to be elicited may also be of use in such suits." The Court noted, however, that a witness need not answer "where the bounds of the power are exceeded or where the questions asked are not pertinent to the matter under inquiry."

---

1. For a useful study, see Taylor, Grand Inquest—The Story of Congressional Investigations (1955).

2. Kilbourn had been imprisoned by an order of the House, for contempt of Congress. (Congress has the implied power to impose direct punishment upon persons in contempt of its authority, without resorting to the courts. See Anderson v. Dunn, 6 Wheat. 204 (1821), a case involving an attempted bribe of a Congressman.)

3. Compare Woodrow Wilson's famous statement, in Congressional Government (1885), 303: "The informing function of Congress should be preferred even to its legislative function." But see Justice Douglas' opinion in Russell v. United States, 369 U.S. 749 (1962): "Wilson was speaking not of a congressional inquiry roaming at large, but one that inquired into and discussed the functions and operations of government."

LEGISLATIVE INVESTIGATIONS IN THE 1950s

Introduction. Claims that congressional investigators were unconstitutionally engaging in "exposure for exposure's sake" and were violating First Amendment rights were frequently made in cases involving inquiries into subversion that came to the Court in the early 1950s. In the early cases, however, these challenges typically were joined with Fifth Amendment objections; the Court accordingly was able to decide the cases on the basis of broad interpretations of the protection against self-incrimination, without reaching other constitutional issues. See, e.g., Quinn v. United States, 349 U.S. 155 (1955). Two years later, however, in Watkins, no Fifth Amendment claim was raised, and the Court began to address other constitutional issues—albeit mainly in dictum at first. At the same time, state inquiries came under scrutiny, in Sweezy v. New Hampshire. In examining the congressional and state investigation cases below, note the parallels to the evolution of the Court's approach in the earlier materials pertaining to the subversion context.[1] Consider to what extent legislative inquiries raise distinctive questions.

1. WATKINS v. UNITED STATES, 354 U.S. 178 (1957): Watkins was a labor union official who had been called as a witness before the House Un-American Activities Committee. He testified freely about his own political activities, stating that he had never been a Communist Party member but that he had "cooperated" with the Party. Moreover, he was willing to identify Party members he had known, provided that he thought "they still were members." He refused to answer, however, when asked to tell whether he knew a number of persons to have been members of the Party: "I am not going to plead the fifth amendment, but I refuse to answer certain questions that I believe are outside the proper scope of your committee's activities"; he would not testify about persons "who to my best knowledge and belief have long since removed themselves from the Communist movement." He was convicted of "contempt of Congress," for refusing to answer questions "pertinent to the questions under inquiry."

The Court reversed. The specific basis for the holding was that Watkins was not "accorded a fair opportunity to determine whether he was within his rights in refusing to answer, and his conviction is necessarily invalid under [due process]." Chief Justice WARREN's opinion stated that a defendant under 2 U.S.C. § 192, the congressional contempt statute, must be accorded "every right which is guaranteed to defendants in all other criminal cases," including the right to have "knowledge of the subject to which the interrogation is deemed pertinent," "with the same degree of explicitness and clarity that [due process] requires in the expression of any element of a criminal offense." The Chief Justice's opinion went considerably beyond that due process, vagueness basis for reversal, however. He also spoke at length about "basic premises" pertaining to the history and constitutional status of legislative investigations. His opinion included the following passages:

"Clearly an investigation is subject to the command [of the First Amendment]. [It is] part of lawmaking. It is justified solely as an adjunct to the legislative process. The First Amendment may be invoked against infringement

---

1. Compare especially the changes in the approach from the 1950s to the 1960s in the context of criminal prosecutions of subversive speech, from Dennis through Yates and Scales to Brandenburg, in sec. 1 of chapter 11; and recall also the similar changes regarding limits on governmental inquiries directed to public employees and licensees, in the cases from Garner and Lerner in the 1950s to Keyishian in the 1960s and the Bar Admission Cases in the 1970s, in sec. 4 of this chapter. In examining the materials that follow, consider whether the standards of the criminal cases in the subversion area should define the scope of the legislative investigating power. Consider, moreover, whether the limits on legislative investigations should be the same as those on governmental inquiries into the fitness of employees and licensees.

of the protected freedoms by law or by lawmaking. [The] critical element [in accommodating 'the congressional need for particular information with the individual and personal interest in privacy'] is the existence of, and the weight to be ascribed to, the interest of the Congress in demanding disclosures from an unwilling witness. [To simply assume] that every congressional investigation is justified by a public need and overbalances any private rights affected [would be] to abdicate [the courts' constitutional responsibility] to ensure that the Congress does not unjustifiably encroach upon an individual's right to privacy nor abridge his liberty of speech, press, religion, or assembly. [T]here is no congressional power to expose for the sake of exposure. The public is, of course, entitled to be informed concerning the workings of its government. That cannot be inflated into a general power to expose where the predominant result can only be an invasion of the private rights of individuals. But a solution to our problem is not to be found in testing the motives of committee members for this purpose. [Their] motives alone would not vitiate an investigation which had been instituted by a House of Congress if that assembly's legislative purpose is being served. It is the responsibility of the Congress, in the first instance, to insure that compulsory process is used only in furtherance of a legislative purpose. That requires that the instructions to an investigating committee spell out that group's jurisdiction and purpose with sufficient particularity. [An] excessively broad charter, like that of the [Committee], places the courts in an untenable position if they are to strike a balance between the public need for a particular interrogation and the right of citizens to carry on their affairs free from unnecessary governmental interference. It is impossible in such a situation to ascertain whether any legislative purpose justifies the disclosures sought and, if so, the importance of that information to the Congress in furtherance of its legislative function." [2]

2. SWEEZY v. NEW HAMPSHIRE, 354 U.S. 234 (1957): This case, decided on the same day as Watkins, was the first of several Court encounters with state rather than congressional investigations. The Court held that a New Hampshire contempt conviction for refusal to answer violated due process. The state legislature had authorized the state Attorney General to act as a one-man investigation committee into subversive activities. Petitioner refused to answer questions about the Progressive Party and about a lecture he had delivered at the University of New Hampshire. He insisted that the questions "were not pertinent to the matter under inquiry" and that they "infringed upon an area protected [by] the First Amendment." At the request of the Attorney General, a lower state court then put the questions to the petitioner. When he persisted in his refusal, he was jailed for contempt.

As in Watkins, Chief Justice WARREN's plurality opinion [3] concluded with a relatively narrow holding after some broad introductory observations: "We do not now conceive of any circumstance wherein a state interest would justify infringement of rights in these fields. But we do not need to reach such

---

2. Justice FRANKFURTER's concurring opinion stated his understanding of the Court's holding: "[B]y making the federal judiciary the affirmative agency for enforcing the authority that underlies the congressional power to punish for contempt, Congress necessarily brings into play the specific provisions of the Constitution relating to the prosecution of offenses and those implied restrictions under which courts function. [T]he actual scope of the inquiry that the Committee was authorized to conduct and the relevance of the questions to that inquiry must be shown to have been luminous at the time when asked and not left, at best, in cloudiness. The circumstances of this case were wanting in these

essentials." Justice CLARK dissented, objecting to the "mischievous curbing of the informing function of Congress" and finding the Court's requirements for the operation of legislative inquiries "both unnecessary and unworkable."

3. In Sweezy, unlike Watkins, the Chief Justice did not speak for a majority: his opinion announcing the judgment of the Court was joined only by Justices Black, Douglas and Brennan. The votes necessary for reversal of the conviction came from Justice Frankfurter's concurring opinion, joined by Justice Harlan, noted below. Justice Clark, joined by Justice Burton, dissented.

fundamental questions of state power to decide this case." Although the highest state court had held that the questions were authorized by the legislature, Chief Justice Warren found that "it cannot be stated authoritatively that the legislature asked the Attorney General to gather the kind of facts comprised in the subjects upon which petitioner was interrogated." He concluded: "[I]f the Attorney General's interrogation of petitioner were in fact wholly unrelated to the object of the legislature in authorizing the inquiry, [due process] would preclude the endangering of constitutional liberties. We believe that an equivalent situation is presented in this case. The lack of any indications that the legislature wanted the information the Attorney General attempted to elicit from petitioner must be treated as the absence of authority. It follows that the use of the contempt power, notwithstanding the interference with constitutional rights, was not in accordance with [due process]."

Justice FRANKFURTER's concurrence, joined by Justice Harlan, rested squarely on a substantive "balancing" analysis in finding a violation of "liberty" under the 14th Amendment. He dissociated himself from the Chief Justice's rationale, insisting that this case was "very different" from Watkins and arguing that it "must be judged as though the whole body of the legislature had demanded the information of petitioner." Turning to the substantive claim, he stated: "For a citizen to be made to forego even a part of so basic a liberty as his political autonomy, the subordinating interest of the State must be compelling.[4] [The] inviolability of privacy belonging to a citizen's political loyalty has so overwhelming an importance to the well-being of our kind of society that it cannot be constitutionally encroached upon on the basis of so meagre a countervailing interest of the State as may be argumentatively found in the remote, shadowy threat to the security of New Hampshire allegedly presented [by Sweezy's relationship to the Progressive Party]. [Whatever may be] the justification for not regarding the Communist Party as a conventional political party, no such justification has been afforded in regard to the Progressive Party." Explicitly balancing, he concluded: "When weighed against the grave harm resulting from governmental intrusion into the intellectual life of a university,[5] [the] justification for compelling a witness to discuss the contents of his lecture appears grossly inadequate. Particularly is this so where the witness has sworn that neither in the lecture nor at any other time did he ever advocate overthrowing the Government by force and violence."[6]

---

4. Note the references in later cases to Justice Frankfurter's balancing approach in Sweezy— e.g., in NAACP v. Alabama, p. 1350 above. Note also the frequent use in later cases of his formulation that "the subordinating interests of the State must be compelling." (Recall also his early use of another term that was to become very popular in First Amendment opinions, the antecedent of the "chilling effects" metaphor, in his opinion in Wieman, p. 1364 above. Compare his widely criticized balancing opinion in Dennis, p. 1017 above; cf. Barenblatt, which follows).

5. Justice Frankfurter's comment on academic freedom was among the first to include that concept within the First Amendment. In addition to the passage in text, note his remark: "In the political realm, as in the academic, thought and action are presumptively immune from inquisition by political authority." His academic freedom references have been repeatedly relied upon in later cases, and not only in the First

Amendment area. See, e.g., Justice Powell's opinion in Bakke, p. 745 above.

6. The decisions in Watkins and Sweezy— together with several contemporaneous ones bearing on subversion, e.g., Yates, p. 1028 above, and Konigsberg I, p. 1367 above—provoked considerable criticism and were frequently mentioned in congressional debates on the 1958 proposals to curtail the Court's appellate jurisdiction. Recall chap. 1, sec. 3, above.

Compare Barenblatt and Uphaus, the federal and state investigation cases of 1959, which follow. Can those decisions be explained as responses to the hostile congressional reaction? Is there basis for the allegations that the 1959 decisions were inconsistent with—and marked a retreat from—Watkins and Sweezy, the 1957 cases? Cf. Murphy, Congress and the Court—A Case Study in the American Political Process (1962), and Pritchett, Congress Versus the Supreme Court, 1957–1960 (1961).

BARENBLATT v. UNITED STATES

360 U.S. 109, 79 S.Ct. 1081, 3 L.Ed.2d 1115 (1959).

Mr. Justice HARLAN delivered the opinion of the [Court].

Broad as it is, the [congressional investigating power] is not, however, without limitations. Since Congress may only investigate into those areas in which it may potentially legislate or appropriate, it cannot inquire into matters which are within the exclusive province of one of the other branches of the Government. [And] Congress, in common with all branches of the Government, must exercise its powers subject to the limitations placed by the Constitution on governmental action, more particularly in the context of this case the relevant limitations of the Bill of Rights. [In] the present case congressional efforts to learn the extent of a nation-wide, indeed world-wide, problem have brought one of its investigating committees into the field of education. Of course, broadly viewed, inquiries cannot be made into the teaching that is pursued in any of our educational institutions. When academic teaching-freedom and its corollary learning-freedom [are] claimed, this Court will always be on the alert against intrusion by Congress into this constitutionally protected domain. But this does not mean that the Congress is precluded from interrogating a witness merely because he is a teacher. An educational institution is not a constitutional sanctuary from inquiry into matters that may otherwise be within the constitutional legislative domain merely for the reason that inquiry is made of someone within its [walls].

We here review petitioner's conviction under 2 U.S.C. § 192 for contempt of Congress, arising from his refusal to answer certain questions put to him by a Subcommittee of the House Committee on Un-American Activities during the course of an inquiry concerning alleged Communist infiltration into the field of education. [Pursuant] to a subpoena, [petitioner] appeared as a witness before [the Subcommittee in June 1954]. After answering a few preliminary questions and testifying that he had been a graduate student and teaching fellow at the University of Michigan from 1947 to 1950 and an instructor in psychology at Vassar College from 1950 to shortly before his appearance before the Subcommittee, petitioner objected generally to the right of the Subcommittee to inquire into his "political" and "religious" beliefs or any "other personal and private affairs" or "associational activities," upon grounds set forth in a previously prepared memorandum [relying, inter alia, on the First, Ninth and Tenth Amendments and on separation of powers]. Thereafter petitioner specifically declined to answer [the following] questions: "Are you now a member of the Communist Party? "Have you ever been a member of the [Communist Party]? "Were you ever a member of the Haldane Club of the Communist Party while at the [University of Michigan]?" [Petitioner] expressly disclaimed reliance upon "the Fifth Amendment." [He was convicted and sentenced to six months' imprisonment.]

Undeniably, the First Amendment in some circumstances protects an individual from being compelled to disclose his associational relationships. However, the protections of the First Amendment, unlike a proper claim [under] the Fifth Amendment, do not afford a witness the right to resist inquiry in all circumstances. Where First Amendment rights are asserted to bar governmental interrogation resolution of the issue always involves a balancing by the courts of the competing private and public interests at stake in the particular circumstances shown. [The] first question is whether this investigation was related to a valid legislative purpose. [That Congress] has wide power to legislate in the field of Communist activity in this country, and to conduct appropriate investigations in aid thereof, is hardly debatable. [I]t is sufficient to say [that] Congress has enacted or considered in this field a wide range of legislative measures, not a few of which have stemmed from recommendations of the very Committee whose actions have been drawn in question here. In the last analysis this power rests on the right of self-preservation, "the ultimate value of any society" [Dennis]. Justification for its exercise in turn rests on the long and widely accepted view that the tenets of the Communist Party include the ultimate overthrow of the [Government] by force and violence, a view which has been given final expression by the Congress.

We think that investigatory power in this domain is not to be denied Congress solely because the field of education is involved. [Indeed] we do not understand petitioner here to suggest that Congress in no circumstances may inquire into Communist activity in the field of education. Rather, his position is in effect that this particular investigation was aimed not at the revolutionary aspects but at the theoretical classroom discussion of communism. [In] our opinion this position rests on a too constricted view of the nature of the investigatory process, and is not supported by a fair assessment of the record before us. An investigation of advocacy of or preparation for overthrow certainly embraces the right to identify a witness as a member of the [Party] and to inquire into the various manifestations of the Party's tenets. The strict requirements of a prosecution under the Smith Act, see [Dennis; Yates], are not the measure of the permissible scope of a congressional investigation into "overthrow," for of necessity the investigatory process must proceed step by step. Nor can it fairly be concluded that this investigation was directed at controlling what is being taught at our universities rather than at [overthrow].

Nor can we accept the further contention that this investigation should not be deemed to have been in furtherance of a legislative purpose because the true objective of the Committee and of the Congress was purely "exposure." So long as Congress acts in pursuance of its constitutional power, the judiciary lacks authority to intervene on the basis of the motives which spurred the exercise of that power. [Watkins.] Having scrutinized this record we cannot say that [the Court of Appeals was] wrong in concluding that "the primary purposes of the inquiry were in aid of legislative processes." [Finally], the record is barren of other factors which in themselves might sometimes lead to the conclusion that the individual interests at stake were not subordinate to those of the state. There is no indication in this record that the Subcommittee was attempting to pillory witnesses. Nor did petitioner's appearance as a witness follow from indiscriminate dragnet procedures, lacking in probable cause for belief that he possessed information which might be helpful to the Subcommittee. And the relevancy of the questions put to him by the Subcommittee is not open to doubt. We conclude that the balance between the individual and the governmental interests here at stake must be struck in favor of the latter, and that therefore the provisions of the First Amendment have not been [offended].

Affirmed.

Mr. Justice BLACK, with whom The Chief Justice [WARREN] and Mr. Justice DOUGLAS concur, [dissenting].

I do not agree that laws directly abridging First Amendment freedoms can be justified by a congressional or judicial balancing process. There are, of course, cases suggesting that a law which primarily regulates conduct but which might also indirectly affect speech can be upheld if the effect on speech is minor in relation to the need for control of the conduct. With these cases I agree. Typical of them are [Cantwell and Schneider, chap. 12 above]. Both of these involved the right of a city to control its streets. [But] even such laws governing conduct, we emphasize, must be tested, though only by a balancing process, if they indirectly affect ideas. [But those cases do not] even remotely suggest that a law directly aimed at curtailing speech and political persuasion could be saved through a balancing process.*

[But] even assuming what I cannot assume, that some balancing is proper in this case, I feel that the Court after stating the test ignores it completely. At most it balances the right of the Government to preserve itself, against Barenblatt's right to refrain from revealing Communist affiliations. Such a balance, however, mistakes the factors to be weighed. In the first place, it completely leaves out the real interest in Barenblatt's silence, the interest of the people as a whole in being able to join organizations, advocate causes and make political "mistakes" without later being subjected to governmental penalties for having dared to think for themselves. It is this right, the right to err politically, which keeps us strong as a Nation. [It] is these interests of society, rather than Barenblatt's own right to silence, which I think the Court should put on the balance. [Instead] they are not mentioned, while on the other side the demands of the Government are vastly overstated and called "self-preservation." [Such] a result reduces "balancing" to a mere play on words and is completely inconsistent with the rules this Court has previously given for applying a "balancing test," where it is proper.

Finally, I think Barenblatt's conviction violates the Constitution because the chief aim, purpose and practice of the House Un-American Activities Committee, as disclosed by its many reports, is to try witnesses and punish them because they are or have been Communists or because they refuse to admit or deny Communist affiliations. The punishment imposed is generally punishment by humiliation and public shame. [It] seems to me that the proof that the [Committee] is here undertaking a purely judicial function is [overwhelming]. [A separate dissent by Justice BRENNAN agreed with the last paragraph of Justice Black's dissent: "[N]o purpose for the investigation of Barenblatt is revealed by the record except exposure purely for the sake of exposure."]

————————

UPHAUS v. WYMAN: The Uphaus case, 360 U.S. 72 (1959), was decided on the same day as the congressional Barenblatt case.[1] Like Sweezy, the Uphaus case arose out of an investigation by the New Hampshire Attorney General, acting as a one-man legislative committee investigating subversion. Uphaus, Executive Director of World Fellowship, Inc., a corporation maintaining a summer camp in the state, was held in contempt for refusing to produce a list of all the guests at the camp during 1954 and 1955. Justice CLARK's majority opinion affirmed the civil contempt order and rejected the First Amendment claim. In contrast to Sweezy, the majority accepted the state court's finding that the Attorney General *was* authorized to demand the information and continued: "[T]he Attorney General had valid reason to believe that the speakers and guests at World Fellowship might be subversive persons within the meaning of the [state law]. Although the evidence as to the nexus between World Fellowship and subversive activities may not be conclusive, we believe it sufficiently relevant to support the Attorney General's action. [The] record reveals that [Uphaus] had participated in 'Communist front' activities and that '[n]ot less than nineteen speakers invited by Uphaus to talk at World Fellowship had either been members of the Communist Party or had

---

* Recall the renewal and elaboration of the debate about "balancing" between Justices Black and Harlan in Konigsberg II, the 1961 Bar Admission Case, p. 1367 above. Excerpts from that Konigsberg debate are printed in the introduction to the chap. 11, above.

1. Recall the parallel in 1957: Sweezy, the state investigation case, was decided on the same day as Watkins, the congressional inquiry decision. For the Court's third encounter with New Hampshire legislative investigations, see the DeGregory case, p. 1415 below. DeGregory was decided in 1966; by then, First Amendment limits on governmental inquiries had expanded considerably from the days of Sweezy and Uphaus.

connections or affiliations with it or with one or more of the organizations cited as subversive or Communist controlled in the United States Attorney General's list.' [Certainly] the investigatory power of the State need not be constricted until sufficient evidence of subversion is gathered to justify the institution of criminal proceedings. [We] recognize, of course, that compliance with the subpoena will result in exposing the fact that the persons therein named were guests at World Fellowship. But so long as a committee must report to its legislative parent, exposure—in the sense of disclosure—is an inescapable incident of an investigation into the presence of subversive persons within a State. And the governmental interest in self-preservation is sufficiently compelling to subordinate the interest in associational privacy of persons who, at least to the extent of the guest registration statute, made public at the inception the association they now wish to keep private."

Justice BRENNAN, joined by Chief Justice Warren, Justice Black and Justice Douglas, dissented: "[This record] not only fails to reveal any interest of the State sufficient to subordinate appellant's constitutionally protected rights, but affirmatively shows that the investigatory objective was the impermissible one of exposure for exposure's sake. [The] Court describes the inquiry we must make in this matter as a balancing of interests, [but] there has been no valid legislative interest of the State actually [shown] in the investigation as it operated, so that there is really nothing against which the appellant's rights of association and expression can be balanced. [The] evidence inquired about was simply an effort to get further details about an activity as to which there already were considerable details in the hands of the Attorney General. I can see no serious and substantial relationship between the furnishing of these further minutiae about what was going on at the [camp] and the process of legislation. [We] must demand some initial showing by the State sufficient to counterbalance the interest in privacy as it relates to freedom of speech and assembly. [The State] has not made such a showing here."

LEGISLATIVE INVESTIGATIONS IN THE 1960s

For a brief period after Barenblatt, the Court adhered to its deferential stance and refused to impose strict constitutional restraints on legislative inquiries.[1] But a changing mood was foreshadowed when, contemporaneously, the Court began to reverse contempt of Congress convictions on nonconstitutional grounds.[2] Soon after, the Court changed course regarding First Amendment limits on legislative inquiries. In the 1963 decision in Gibson, which follows, a state legislative inquiry into subversive influences in the NAACP came before the Court, and that decision indicated a significant shift from the Barenblatt approach.[3] Gibson illustrates a number of ingredients of the "strict scrutiny" of state impingements upon free expression elaborated by the Warren Court in the late 1960s.[4]

---

1. See, e.g., Wilkinson v. United States, 365 U.S. 399 (1961), and Braden v. United States, 365 U.S. 431 (1961).

2. See, e.g., Russell v. United States, 369 U.S. 749 (1962), where Justice Clark complained in dissent that "the Court has now upset 10 convictions under § 192" since Watkins.

3. Recall the contemporaneous shift in direction of First Amendment doctrine in the government employee and licensee cases (in sec. 4 above) and in the criminal cases directed against subversive speech (in sec. 1 of chap. 11).

4. Did Gibson manage to distinguish the 1950s decisions successfully? Note that Gibson was decided in the early 1960s, at a time when the Warren Court was unwilling to engage in explicit balancing in most areas. Yet Gibson is a balancing opinion; recall (and contrast) the opinions two years later by Justice Goldberg, the author of Gibson, in the Cox v. Louisiana cases, pp. 1225 and 1228 above.

Does the Gibson approach retain vitality on the Burger Court? No major legislative investigation cases have come before the Burger Court.

GIBSON v. FLORIDA LEGISLATIVE COMM.

372 U.S. 539, 83 S.Ct. 889, 9 L.Ed.2d 929 (1963).

Mr. Justice GOLDBERG delivered the opinion of the Court.

This case is the culmination of protracted litigation involving legislative investigating committees of the State of Florida and the Miami branch of the [NAACP]. [In 1957, an earlier legislative committee had sought the entire membership list of the local NAACP branch. Florida's highest court barred that request but stated that the committee could compel the custodian of the records to bring them to committee hearings and to refer to them to determine whether specific individuals, identified as or suspected of being Communists, were NAACP members. The respondent Committee here was established in 1959 to resume the investigation. Gibson, the President of the Miami branch, was ordered to bring the records pertaining to the identity of members of and contributors to the Miami and state NAACP organizations. The Committee announced that "the inquiry would be directed at Communists and Communist activities, including infiltration of Communists into organizations operating [in] described fields" such as race relations. Gibson, relying on the First Amendment, did not bring the records but told the Committee that he would answer questions concerning membership in the NAACP on the basis of his personal knowledge. He was given the names and shown photographs of 14 persons previously identified as being involved in Communist or Communist-front affairs. Gibson said that he could associate none of them with the NAACP. For his failure to produce the records, a state court found him in contempt and sentenced him to six months' imprisonment and a $1200 fine.]

[R]ights of association are within the ambit of the constitutional protections afforded by the [First Amendment]. [E.g., NAACP v. Alabama.] And it is equally clear that the guarantee encompasses protection of privacy of association in organizations such as [the NAACP]. At the same time, however, this Court's prior holdings demonstrate that there can be no question that the State has power adequately to inform itself—through legislative investigation, if it so desires—in order to act and protect its legitimate and vital interests. [Watkins; Barenblatt.] It is no less obvious, however, that the legislative power to investigate, broad as it may be, is not without limit. [Validation] of the broad subject matter under investigation does not necessarily carry with it automatic and wholesale validation of all individual questions, subpoenas, and [demands].

Significantly, the parties are in substantial agreement as to the proper test to be applied to reconcile the competing claims of government and individual and to determine the propriety of the Committee's demands. As declared by the respondent Committee in its brief to this Court, "Basically, this case hinges entirely on the question of whether the evidence before the Committee [was] sufficient to show probable cause or nexus between the NAACP Miami Branch, and Communist activities." We understand this to mean—regardless of the label applied, be it "nexus," "foundation," or whatever—that it is an essential prerequisite to the validity of an investigation which intrudes into the area of constitutionally protected rights of speech, press, association and petition that the State convincingly show a substantial relation between the information sought and a subject of overriding and compelling state interest. Absent such a relation between the NAACP and conduct in which the State may have a compelling regulatory concern, the Committee has not "demonstrated so cogent

Note, however, Branzburg v. Hayes, the 1972 decision rejecting a reporter's privilege claim in investigations by a grand jury rather than a legislative committee (noted in sec. 6, at p. 1431 below). In Branzburg, Justice Stewart's dissent tried to develop a journalists' privilege on the basis of the Gibson approach. Contrast the treatment of Gibson in Justice White's plurality opinion in Branzburg.

an interest in obtaining and making public" the membership information sought [as] to "justify the substantial abridgment of associational freedom which such disclosures will effect." [Bates v. Little Rock.]

Applying these principles [here], the respondent Committee contends that the prior decisions of this Court in [e.g., Uphaus and Barenblatt] compel a result here upholding the legislative right of inquiry. In [those cases], however, it was a refusal to answer a question or questions concerning the witness' *own* past or present membership *in the Communist Party* which supported his conviction. It is apparent that the necessary preponderating governmental interest and, in fact, the very result in those cases were founded on the holding that the Communist Party is not an ordinary or legitimate political party [and] that, because of its particular nature, membership therein is *itself* a permissible subject of regulation and legislative scrutiny. Assuming the correctness of the premises on which those cases were decided, no further demonstration of compelling governmental interest was deemed necessary, since the direct object of the challenged questions there was discovery of membership in [the Party]. Here, however, it is not alleged Communists [are] the witnesses before the Committee and it is not discovery of their membership in that party which is the object of the challenged inquiries. Rather, it is the NAACP itself which is the subject of the investigation, and it is its local president [who was] held in contempt. [There] is no suggestion that the Miami branch of the NAACP or the national organization with which it is affiliated was, or is, itself a subversive organization [or that their] activities or policies [were] either Communist dominated or influenced. In fact, this very record indicates that the association was and is against communism and has voluntarily taken steps to keep Communists from being [members].

[Compelling] such an organization, engaged in the exercise of [First Amendment] rights, to disclose its membership presents, under our cases, a question wholly different from compelling the Communist Party to disclose its own membership. Moreover, even to say, as in Barenblatt, that it is permissible to inquire into the subject of Communist infiltration of educational or other organizations does not mean that it is permissible to demand or require from such other groups disclosure of their membership by inquiry into their records when such disclosure will seriously inhibit or impair the exercise of constitutional rights and has not itself been demonstrated to bear a crucial relation to a proper governmental interest or to be essential to fulfillment of a proper governmental purpose. The prior holdings that governmental interest in controlling subversion and the particular character of the Communist Party and its objectives outweigh the right of individual Communists to conceal party membership or affiliations by no means require the wholly different conclusion that other groups—concededly legitimate—automatically forfeit their rights to privacy of association simply because the general subject matter of the legislative inquiry is Communist subversion or infiltration. The fact that [the] governmental interest was deemed compelling in Barenblatt [does] not resolve the issues here, where the challenged questions go to membership in an admittedly lawful organization. Respondent's reliance on [Uphaus is] similarly misplaced. There, [the] Court found that there was demonstrated a sufficient connection between subversive activity—held there to be a proper subject of governmental concern—and the World Fellowship itself to justify discovery of the guest list; no semblance of such a nexus between the NAACP and subversive *activities* has been shown here. [Finally], in Uphaus, the State was investigating whether subversive persons were within its boundaries and whether their presence constituted a threat to the State. No such purpose or need is evident here. The Florida Committee is not seeking to identify subversives by questioning the petitioner; apparently it is satisfied that it already knows who they are.

In the absence of directly determinative authority, we turn, then, to consideration of the facts now. before us. [W]e rest our result on the fact that the record in this case is insufficient to show a substantial connection between the Miami branch of the NAACP and Communist *activities* which the respondent Committee itself concedes is an essential prerequisite to demonstrating the immediate, substantial, and subordinating state interest necessary to sustain its right of inquiry into the membership lists. [The] evidence discloses the utter failure to demonstrate the existence of any substantial relationship between the NAACP and subversive or Communist activities. In essence, there is here merely indirect, less than unequivocal, and mostly hearsay testimony that in years past some 14 people who were asserted to be, or to have been, Communists or members of Communist front or "affiliated organizations" attended occasional meetings of the Miami branch of the NAACP "and/or" were members of that branch, which had a total membership of about 1,000. On the other hand, there was no claim made at the hearings, or since, that the NAACP or its Miami branch was engaged in any subversive activities or that its legitimate activities have been dominated or influenced by Communists. [W]ithout any showing of a meaningful relation between the NAACP Miami branch and subversives [we] are asked to find the compelling and subordinating state interest which must exist if essential freedoms are to be curtailed or inhibited. This we cannot do. The respondent Committee has laid no adequate foundation for its direct demands upon the officers and records of a wholly legitimate organization for disclosure of its membership. [The] strong associational interest in maintaining the privacy of membership lists of groups engaged in the constitutionally protected free trade in ideas and beliefs may not be substantially infringed upon such a slender showing as here made by the respondent. While, of course, all legitimate organizations are the beneficiaries of these protections, they are all the more essential here, where the challenged privacy is that of persons espousing beliefs already unpopular with their neighbors and the deterrent and "chilling" effect on the free exercise of constitutionally enshrined rights of free speech, expression, and association is consequently the more immediate and substantial. [Of] course, a legislative investigation—as any investigation—must proceed "step by step" [Barenblatt], but step by step or in totality, an adequate foundation for inquiry must be laid. [No] such foundation has been laid [here]. Nothing we say here impairs or denies the existence of the underlying legislative right to investigate or legislate with respect to subversive activities by Communists or anyone else; our decision today deals only with the manner in which such power may be exercised and we hold simply that groups which themselves are neither engaged in subversive or other illegal or improper activities nor demonstrated to have any substantial connections with such activities are to be protected in their rights of free and private [association].

Reversed.[1]

Mr. Justice HARLAN, whom Mr. Justice CLARK, Mr. Justice STEWART, and Mr. Justice WHITE join, [dissenting].

The Court's reasoning is difficult to grasp. I read its opinion as basically proceeding on the premise that the governmental interest in investigating Communist infiltration into admittedly nonsubversive organizations, as distinguished from investigating organizations themselves suspected of subversive activities, is not sufficient to overcome the countervailing right to freedom of association. On this basis "nexus" is seemingly found lacking. [But], until today, I had never supposed that any of our decisions relating [to] power to

1. Justices BLACK and DOUGLAS joined Justice Goldberg's opinion but added additional reasons for supporting the result.

investigate in the field of Communist subversion could possibly be taken as suggesting any difference in the degree [of] investigatory interest as between Communist infiltration *of* organizations and Communist activity *by* organizations. See, e.g., [Barenblatt] (infiltration into education); [Wilkinson] and [Braden] (infiltration into basic industries); Russell v. United States (infiltration of newspaper business). [Given] the unsoundness of the basic premise underlying the Court's holding as to the absence of "nexus," this decision surely falls of its own weight. For unless "nexus" requires an investigating agency to prove in advance the very things it is trying to find out, I do not understand how it can be said that the information preliminarily developed by the Committee's investigator was not sufficient to satisfy, under any reasonable test, the requirement of "nexus." Apart from this, the issue of "nexus" is surely laid at rest by the NAACP's own "Anti-Communism" resolution, first adopted in 1950, which petitioner had voluntarily furnished the Committee before the curtain came down on his examination.[2] It hardly meets the point at issue to suggest [that] the resolution only serves to show that the Miami Branch was in fact free of any Communist influences—unless self-investigation is deemed constitutionally to block official inquiry. I also find it difficult to see how this case really presents any serious question as to interference with freedom of association. Given the willingness of the petitioner to testify from recollection as to individual memberships in the local branch of the NAACP, the germaneness of the membership records to the subject matter of the Committee's investigation, and the limited purpose for which their use was sought—as an aid to refreshing the witness' recollection, involving their divulgence only to the petitioner himself—this case of course bears no resemblance whatever to [NAACP v. Alabama] or [Bates], [where] the State had sought general divulgence of local NAACP membership lists without any showing of a justifying state interest. In effect what we are asked to hold here is that the petitioner had a constitutional right to give only partial or inaccurate testimony, and that indeed seems to me the true effect of the Court's holding [today].[3]

DeGREGORY v. NEW HAMPSHIRE ATTORNEY GENERAL, 383 U.S. 825 (1966): The DeGregory case, like Sweezy and Uphaus, stemmed from a New Hampshire subversive activities investigation. Appellant was jailed for contempt for a 1964 refusal to answer, on First Amendment grounds, questions relating to Communist activities prior to 1957. The Court, applying the principles of Gibson and asserting distinctions from Uphaus, reversed in a 6 to 3 decision. Justice DOUGLAS' majority opinion concluded: "New Hampshire's interest [here] is too remote and conjectural to override the guarantee of the First Amendment that a person can speak or not, as he chooses, free of all governmental compulsion." He explained: "On the basis of our prior cases, appellant had every reason to anticipate that the details of his political associations to which he might testify would be reported in a pamphlet purporting to describe the nature of subversion in New Hampshire. (See [Uphaus], Brennan, J., dissenting.) [W]hatever justification may have supported such exposure in Uphaus is absent here; the staleness of both the basis for the investigation [1] and

2. The resolution's recitals included a statement that "there is a well-organized, nationwide conspiracy by Communists either to capture or split and wreck the NAACP" and a direction that the National Board of Directors "take the necessary action to eradicate such *infiltration.*"

3. In a separate dissent, Justice WHITE stated that it was difficult "to understand how under today's decision a Communist in the process of performing his assigned job could be required to

divulge not only his membership in the [Party], but his membership or activities in the target organization as well. [The] decision today represents a marked departure from the principles of [Barenblatt] and like cases."

1. To justify his renewed investigation of DeGregory, the Attorney General of New Hampshire had relied entirely on a 1955 report linking DeGregory to the Communist Party only until

its subject matter makes indefensible such exposure of one's associational and political past. [There] is no showing of 'overriding and compelling state interest' [Gibson] that would warrant intrusion into the realm of political and associational privacy protected by the First Amendment. The information being sought was historical, not current. Lawmaking at the investigatory stage may properly probe historic events for any light that may be thrown on present conditions and problems. But the First Amendment prevents [the Government from] using the power to investigate enforced by the contempt power to probe at will and without relation to existing need. [Watkins.] The present record is devoid of any evidence that there is any Communist movement in New Hampshire. [There] is no showing whatsoever of present danger of sedition against the State itself, the only area to which the authority of the State extends. There is thus absent that 'nexus' between petitioner and subversive activities in New Hampshire which the Court found to exist in [Uphaus]." [2]

SECTION 6. SPECIAL PROTECTION FOR THE PRESS UNDER THE FIRST AMENDMENT?

Scope Note. This section brings together a range of materials bearing on the constitutional protection of the press. A pervasive theme is whether the Constitution affords to the press protections more extensive than those generally available to disseminators of information and opinion. The opening note probes whether a special protection can rest on the text of the First Amendment, which specifically mentions "press" as well as "speech." The section then turns to three clusters of distinguishable functional problems that have given rise to recurrent litigation regarding the contours of press protections. In sec. 6A, government resorts to prior restraints to prevent the press from publishing information already in its hands, in furtherance of such interests as protecting national security and assuring fair trials. Sec. 6B involves problems also stemming from materials already in the hands of the press; but here, the government, instead of seeking a prior restraint on publication, resorts to sanctions designed to compel journalists to divulge information they possess, in aid of such state interests as criminal law enforcement. Sec. 6C moves beyond the problems of information already in the hands of journalists: it deals with claims of the press to a constitutional right of access to such places as jails and courtrooms in order to obtain additional newsworthy information. Sec. 6D, finally, considers whether the media enjoy a special immunity when tax or regulatory laws single out the "press" for special treatment, even where no hostile, discriminatory purpose is demonstrated.*

1953, over ten years before the investigation challenged here began.

2. Justice HARLAN, joined by Justices Stewart and White, dissented. The dissent argued that the state should be free to investigate "without first being asked to produce evidence of the very type to be sought in the course of the inquiry." He added: "I cannot say as a constitutional matter that inquiry into the current operations of the local Communist Party could not be advanced by knowledge of its operations a decade ago."

* In addition to the materials gathered in this section, note also the press-related problems that have surfaced earlier in this book. See, e.g., the discussion of First Amendment limit on state interference with the media's editorial judgment, considered in the context of state-supported private claims of access to newspapers or broadcasting facilities, noted in connection with the examination of the public forum problem in the preceding chapter. See, e.g., the Tornillo and Red Lion cases, pp. 1300 and 1295 above. Note also the unsuccessful attempts to penalize press comments allegedly interfering with the administration of justice, considered in sec. 2B of this chapter, and the early materials on prior restraints in sec. 2 of chap. 12.

THE PRESS CLAUSE AND THE SPEECH CLAUSE OF THE FIRST AMENDMENT

1. *Chief Justice Burger's dicta in the Bellotti case.* The First Amendment protects not only "the freedom of speech" but also freedom "of the press." Does that specific reference to the "press" entitle the media to special constitutional protection? Or are press claims more properly analyzed as an aspect of the general freedom of expression guaranteed by the "speech" clause? Those questions have seldom been directly confronted by the Court,[1] but they often surface in popular commentary and they point to significant undercurrents in the cases in this section. A rare explicit discussion of the problem appears in Chief Justice BURGER's concurring opinion in FIRST NATIONAL BANK OF BOSTON v. BELLOTTI, 435 U.S. 765 (1978).[2] The Chief Justice accurately noted: "The Court has not yet squarely resolved whether the Press Clause confers upon the 'institutional press' any freedom from government restraints not enjoyed by all others." After several pages of "tentative probings," he suggested that the Press Clause did *not* confer "a special status on a limited group." He concluded instead: "Because the First Amendment was meant to guarantee freedom to express and to communicate ideas, I can see no difference between the right of those who seek to disseminate ideas by way of a newspaper and those who give lectures or speeches that seek to enlarge the audience by publication and wide dissemination." He explained: "I perceive two fundamental difficulties with a narrow reading of the Press Clause. First although certainty on this point is not possible, the history of the Clause does not suggest that the authors contemplated a 'special' or 'institutional' privilege.[3] [Indeed] most pre-First Amendment commentators 'who employed the term "freedom of speech" with great frequency used it synonymously with freedom of the press.'[4] Those interpreting the Press Clause as extending protection only to, or creating a special role for, the 'institutional press' must either (a) assert such an intention on the part of the Framers for which no supporting evidence is available; (b) argue that events after 1791 somehow operated to 'constitutionalize' this interpretation; or (c) candidly acknowledging the absence of historical support, suggest that the intent of the Framers is not important today.

"To conclude that the Framers did not intend to limit the freedom of the press to one select group is not necessarily to suggest that the Press Clause is redundant. The Speech Clause standing alone may be viewed as a protection of the liberty to express ideas and beliefs, while the Press Clause focuses specifically on the liberty to disseminate expression broadly and 'comprehends every sort of publication which affords a vehicle of information and opinion.' Lovell v. Griffin. Yet there is no fundamental distinction between expression and dissemination. The liberty encompassed by the Press Clause, although complementary to and a natural extension of Speech Clause liberty, merited special mention simply because it had been more often the object of official restraints. Soon after the invention of the printing press, English and continental monarchs, fearful of the power implicit in its use and the threat to Establishment thought and order—political and religious—devised restraints, such as licensing, censors,

---

1. However, two of the Justices have made important extrajudicial comments on the Press clause. On Justice Stewart's Yale address, see footnote 6 below. On Justice Brennan's Rutgers address, see the discussion in his opinion in the Richmond Newspapers case, p. 1445 below. See also the Court's decision in the Minneapolis Star & Tribune case (1983; sec. 6D, p. 1453 below).

2. The Bellotti case, invalidating restrictions on corporate expenditures to influence votes in a state referendum campaign, is noted at p. 1316

above. The Chief Justice conceded that his remarks on the Press Clause were only tenuously related to the central issue in that case.

3. The Chief Justice cited Lange, "The Speech and Press Clauses," 23 U.C.L.A.L.Rev. 77 (1975). Compare Bezanson, "The New Free Press Guarantee," 63 Va.L.Rev. 731 (1977).

4. The Chief Justice was quoting from Levy, Legacy of Suppression: Freedom of Speech and Press in Early American History (1963).

indices of prohibited books, and prosecutions for seditious libel, which generally were unknown in the pre-printing press era. Official restrictions were the official response to the new, disquieting idea that this invention would provide a means for mass communication.

"The second fundamental difficulty with interpreting the Press Clause as conferring special status on a limited group is one of definition. The very task of including some entities within the 'institutional press' while excluding others, whether undertaken by legislature, court or administrative agency, is reminiscent of the abhorred licensing system of Tudor and Stuart England—a system the First Amendment was intended to ban from this country. Further, the officials undertaking that task would be required to distinguish the protected from the unprotected on the basis of such variables as content of expression, frequency or fervor of expression, or ownership of the technological means of dissemination. Yet nothing in this Court's opinions supports such a confining approach to the scope of Press Clause protection.[5] Indeed, the Court has plainly intimated the contrary view: [Branzburg v. Hayes, p. 1431 below, quoting Lovell v. Griffin]. [In short], the First Amendment does not 'belong' to any definable category of persons or entities: it belongs to all who exercise its freedoms."

2.   *The inattention to the Press Clause: What difference does it make? Is adequate protection of the press possible under the Speech Clause?* Chief Justice Burger's disinclination to rest media protections on the Press Clause has been the typical position of the Court. Most press claims have been adjudicated by analysis of the Speech Clause and of general principles of freedom of expression. In recent years, only Justice Stewart has emphasized the Press Clause: he is on record with an important lecture on the special role of the press. See Stewart, "Or of the Press," 26 Hast.L.J. 631 (1975).[6] Moreover, he submitted several dissenting opinions urging broader press rights than the majority was willing to recognize.[7] Yet Justice Stewart's voting pattern in press cases suggests that a Justice's readiness to place special emphasis on the Press Clause does not provide a litmus test of that Justice's readiness to support a particular press claim before the Court. A Justice who finds press protections under the Speech Clause may be more ready to endorse a particular press claim than one who puts special reliance on the Press Clause. Thus, despite Justice Stewart's Press Clause emphasis, he is not always receptive to media claims.[8] The limits of his

5. "Near v. Minnesota, which examined the meaning of freedom of the press, did not involve a traditional institutionalized newspaper but rather an occasional publication (nine issues) more nearly approximating the product of a pamphleteer than the traditional newspaper." [Footnote by Chief Justice Burger.]

6. Justice Stewart's essay—a speech given at Yale Law School—stated that "the Free Press guarantee is, in essence, a *structural* provision of the Constitution. [It] extends protection to an institution. The publishing business [is] the only organized private business that is given explicit constitutional protection. This basic understanding is essential [to] avoid an elementary error of constitutional law [—that the Press Clause really guarantees the same freedom of expression assured to all by the Speech Clause]. [If] the Free Press guarantee meant no more than freedom of expression, it would be a constitutional redundancy. [It] is also a mistake to suppose that the only purpose of the constitutional guarantee of a free press is to insure that a newspaper will serve as a neutral forum for debate, a 'market place for

ideas,' a kind of Hyde Park Corner for the community. A related theory sees the press as a neutral conduit of information between the people and their elected leaders. These theories, in my view, again give insufficient weight to the institutional autonomy of the press that it was the purpose of the Constitution to guarantee."

7. See especially his dissents in Branzburg v. Hayes (1972; p. 1431 below) and in Zurcher v. Stanford Daily (1978; p. 1438 below).

8. Note, e.g., that Chief Justice Burger was able to rely on Justice Stewart's Press Clause lecture, "Or of the Press," in rejecting a press claim of access to prisons in Houchins v. KQED, Inc. (1978; p. 1441 below). Relying on Justice Stewart's language, the Chief Justice stated: "The First Amendment is 'neither a Freedom of Information Act nor an Official Secrets Act.' The guarantee of 'freedom of speech' and 'of the press' only 'establishes the contest [for information], not its resolution.' " [But see the opinions of Justice Stewart and of the Chief Justice in the

support of the press are illustrated by the "right of access" cases in sec. 6C below—cases in which the press sought information not generally available to the public. Justice Stewart's usual position can be characterized as a "sporting theory": under his view of the Press Clause, the press cannot be penalized for publishing any information in its possession; but it is *not* entitled to special judicial help in getting newsworthy information it does not already have. As he put it in his concurrence in the Landmark case (1978; chap. 11, at p. 1027 above): "Though government may deny access to information and punish its theft, government may not prohibit or punish the publication of that information once it falls into the hands of the press, unless the need for secrecy is manifestly overwhelming."

By contrast, Justice Powell, who relies on the First Amendment generally rather than the Press Clause in particular, has been more receptive than Justice Stewart to some media "right of access" claims. See, e.g., the decisions involving unsuccessful attacks on regulations curtailing press access to prisoners: Justice Stewart was on the prevailing side; Justice Powell's dissent, relying on the First Amendment generally, exhibited special concern about restrictions on "the ability of the press to perform its constitutionally established function of informing the people on the conduct of their government. [In] seeking out the news the press [acts] as an agent of the public at large"; special press protection was therefore warranted not because of the Press Clause but because of the general First Amendment interest "in preserving free public discussion of governmental affairs." [9]

Thus, even special emphasis on the Press Clause may produce only limited press protection; and emphasis instead on the First Amendment generally rather than the Press Clause may produce quite broad and sometimes special press protection, by viewing the press as the instrument for implementing the general public's First Amendment interest in newsworthy matters. See Richmond Newspapers (1980; p. 1445 below). In short, the Court as a whole has frequently supported press claims to the extent that they reach no further than First Amendment claims that may be asserted by the public generally. Would it be preferable to rest any "special status" rights of the press on further elaboration of the Press Clause, or does the press receive adequate protection under the readings of the Speech Clause and the First Amendment generally?

A. PRIOR RESTRAINTS:
PREVENTING PUBLICATION OF MATERIALS ALREADY IN THE HANDS OF THE PRESS

Introduction. Prior restraints are especially disfavored under the First Amendment, and the press has often been the beneficiary of that principle. The first major Court articulation of the principle came in NEAR v. MINNESOTA, the 1931 decision printed in the introductory section on prior restraints (sec. 2 of chap. 12, at p. 1157 above). That section also raises questions about the traditional distinction between highly suspect prior restraints and less troublesome subsequent punishments, and those materials can usefully be reviewed at this point. This subsection examines the role of the judicial hostility to prior restraints in modern contexts. It begins with a group of cases where national

---

Richmond Newspapers case (1980; p. 1445 below).]

9. See Pell v. Procunier (1974; p. 1440 below) and Saxbe v. Washington Post Co. (1974; p. 1440 below); and see especially the later endorse- ment (by a 7 to 1 majority, with Justice Powell not participating) of a First Amendment access claim to criminal trials, in the Richmond Newspapers case (1980; p. 1445 below).

security interests are urged to justify prior restraints on the press and concludes with the decisions where the interest in a fair trial is alleged to justify restraints on publication.

NEW YORK TIMES CO. v. UNITED STATES
[THE PENTAGON PAPERS CASE]

403 U.S. 713, 91 S.Ct. 2140, 29 L.Ed.2d 822 (1971).

PER CURIAM.

We granted certiorari in these cases in which the United States seeks to enjoin the New York Times and the Washington Post from publishing the contents of a classified study entitled "History of U.S. Decision-Making Process on Viet Nam Policy." [1]

"Any system of prior restraints of expression comes to this Court bearing a heavy presumption against its constitutional validity." [Bantam Books, Inc. v. Sullivan (p. 1162 above); see also Near v. Minnesota.] The Government "thus carries a heavy burden of showing justification for the enforcement of such a restraint." Organization for a Better Austin v. Keefe [p. 1212 above]. The [District Court] in the New York Times case and the [District Court] and the [Court of Appeals] in the Washington Post case held that the Government had not met that burden. We agree. The judgment of the Court of Appeals for the District of Columbia Circuit is therefore affirmed. The order of the Court of Appeals for the Second Circuit is reversed and the case is remanded with directions to enter a judgment affirming the judgment of the District Court. [The] stays entered June 25, 1971, by the Court are vacated. The mandates shall issue forthwith.

So ordered.

Mr. Justice BLACK, with whom Mr. Justice DOUGLAS joins, concurring.

I adhere to the view that the Government's case against the Washington Post should have been dismissed and that the injunction against the New York Times should have been vacated without oral argument when the cases were first presented to this Court. I believe that every moment's continuance of the injunctions against these newspapers amounts to a flagrant, indefensible, and continuing violation of the First Amendment. Furthermore, after oral arguments, I agree completely [with] my Brothers Douglas and Brennan. In my view it is unfortunate that some of my Brethren are apparently willing to hold that the publication of news may sometimes be enjoined. Such a holding would make a shambles of the First Amendment. [The] press was protected [by the First Amendment] so that it could bare the secrets of government and inform the people. Only a free and unrestrained press can effectively expose deception in government. [To] find that the President has "inherent power" to halt the publication of news by resort to the courts would wipe out the First Amendment. [The] word "security" is a broad, vague generality whose contours should not be invoked to abrogate the fundamental law embodied in the [First Amendment].

---

1. Portions of that secret Defense Department study (popularly known as the "Pentagon Papers") were published by The New York Times (beginning June 13, 1971) and the Washington Post (on June 18, 1971). Government actions to restrain further publication made their way through two district courts and two courts of appeals between June 15 and June 23. On June 25, the Supreme Court granted certiorari in the Times and Post cases. The cases were argued on June 26 and the decision was issued on June 30, 1971. Restraining orders remained in effect while the decision was pending. (Four Justices—Black, Douglas, Brennan and Marshall—dissented from the grants of certiorari, urged summary action, and stated that they "would not continue the restraint" on the newspapers.)

Mr. Justice DOUGLAS, with whom Mr. Justice BLACK joins, [concurring].

[The First Amendment] leaves [no] room for governmental restraint on the press. There is, moreover, no statute barring the publication by the press of the material which the Times and Post seek to use. [18 U.S.C. § 793(e), prohibiting "communication" of information relating to the national defense that could be used to the injury of the United States, does not apply to publication.] [I]t is apparent that Congress was capable of and did distinguish between publishing and communication in the various sections of the Espionage Act.[2] So any power that the Government possesses must come from its "inherent power." The power to wage war is "the power to wage war successfully." But the war power stems from a declaration of war. The Constitution by Article I, § 8, gives Congress, not the President, power "to declare War." Nowhere are presidential wars authorized. We need not decide therefore what leveling effect the war power of Congress might have.

These disclosures[3] may have a serious impact. But that is no basis for sanctioning a previous restraint on the press. [Near.] [The] Government says that it has inherent powers to go into court and obtain an injunction to protect [national] security. [Near] repudiated that expansive doctrine in no uncertain terms. The dominant purpose of the First Amendment was to prohibit the widespread practice of governmental suppression of embarrassing information. [A] debate of large proportions goes on in the Nation over our posture in Vietnam. [Open] debate and discussion of public issues are vital to our national health. [The] stays in these cases that have been in effect for more than a week constitute a flouting of the principles of the First Amendment as interpreted in [Near].

Mr. Justice BRENNAN, [concurring].

The error that has pervaded these cases from the outset was the granting of any injunctive relief whatsoever, interim or otherwise. The entire thrust of the Government's claim throughout these cases has been that publication of the material sought to be enjoined "could," or "might," or "may" prejudice the national interest in various ways. But the First Amendment tolerates absolutely no prior judicial restraints of the press predicated upon surmise or conjecture that untoward consequences may result.[1] Our cases, it is true, have indicated that there is a single, extremely narrow class of cases in which the First Amendment's ban on prior judicial restraint may be overridden. Our cases have thus far indicated that such cases may arise only when the Nation "is at

2. Justice Douglas added: "The other evidence that § 793 does not apply to the press is a rejected version of § 793. That version read: 'During any national emergency, [the] President may [prohibit] the publishing or communicating of [any] information relating to the national defense which, in his judgment, is of such character that it is or might be useful to the enemy.' During the [1917] debates in the Senate the First Amendment was specifically cited and that provision was defeated."

3. There are numerous sets of this material in existence and they apparently are not under any controlled custody. Moreover, the President has sent a set to the Congress. We start then with a case where there already is rather wide distribution of the material that is destined for publicity, not secrecy. I have gone over the material listed in the in camera brief of the United States. It is all history, not future events. None of it is more recent than 1968. [Footnote by Justice Douglas.]

1. Freedman v. Maryland [p. 1160 above] and similar cases regarding temporary restraints of allegedly obscene materials are not in point. For those cases rest upon the proposition that "obscenity is not protected by the freedoms of speech and press." Here there is no question but that the material sought to be suppressed is within the protection of the First Amendment; the only question is whether, notwithstanding that fact, its publication may be enjoined for a time because of the presence of an overwhelming national interest. Similarly, copyright cases have no pertinence here: the Government is not asserting an interest in the particular form of words chosen in the documents, but is seeking to suppress the ideas expressed therein. And the copyright laws, of course, protect only the form of expression and not the ideas expressed. [Footnote by Justice Brennan.]

war" [Schenck], during which times "no one would question but that a government might prevent actual obstruction to its recruiting service or the publication of the sailing dates of transports or the number and location of troops." [Near.] Even if the present world situation were assumed to be tantamount to a time of war, or if the power of presently available armaments would justify even in peacetime the suppression of information that would set in motion a nuclear holocaust,[2] in neither of these actions has the Government presented or even alleged that publication of items from or based upon the material at issue would cause the happening of an event of that nature. "The chief purpose of [the First Amendment's] guarantee [is] to prevent previous restraints upon publication." [Near.] Thus, only governmental allegation and proof that publication must inevitably, directly and immediately cause the occurrence of an event kindred to imperiling the safety of a transport already at sea can support even the issuance of an interim restraining order. [Unless] and until the Government has clearly made out its case, the First Amendment commands that no injunction may issue.

Mr. Justice STEWART, with whom Mr. Justice WHITE joins, concurring.

[The] only effective restraint upon executive policy and power in the areas of national defense and international affairs may lie in an enlightened citizenry. [For] this reason, it is perhaps here that a press that is alert, aware, and free most vitally serves the basic purpose of the First Amendment. [Yet] it is elementary that the successful conduct of international diplomacy and the maintenance of an effective national defense require both confidentiality and secrecy. [I] think there can be but one answer to this dilemma, if dilemma it be. The responsibility must be where the power is. [The] Executive must have the largely unshared duty to determine and preserve the degree of internal security necessary to exercise [its] power successfully.* [It] is the constitutional duty of the Executive—as a matter of sovereign prerogative and not as a matter of law as the courts know law—through the promulgation and enforcement of executive regulations to protect the confidentiality necessary to carry out its responsibilities in the fields of international relations and national defense. This is not to say that Congress and the courts have no role to play. Undoubtedly Congress has the power to enact specific and appropriate criminal laws to protect government property and preserve government secrets. [But] in the cases before us we are asked neither to construe specific regulations nor to apply specific laws. We are asked, instead, to perform a function that the Constitution gave to the Executive, not the Judiciary. We are asked, quite simply, to prevent the publication by two newspapers of material that the Executive Branch insists should not, in the national interest, be published. I am convinced that the Executive is correct with respect to some of the documents involved. But I cannot say that disclosure of any of them will surely result in direct, immediate, and irreparable damage to our Nation or its people. That being so, there can under the First Amendment be but one judicial resolution of the issues before us. I join the judgments of the. Court.

Mr. Justice WHITE, with whom Mr. Justice STEWART joins, concurring.

I concur in today's judgments, but only because of the concededly extraordinary protection against prior restraints enjoyed by the press under our constitutional system. I do not say that in no circumstances would the First Amendment permit an injunction against publishing information about government plans or operations.[1] Nor, after examining the materials the Government characterizes

---

2. See the Progressive case, which follows.

* Recall Snepp v. United States (1980; sec. 4B, at p. 1394 above).

1. The Congress has authorized a strain of prior restraints against private parties in certain

[instances]. However, those enjoined under the statutes relating to the National Labor Relations Board and the Federal Trade Commission are private parties, not the press; and when the press is enjoined under the copyright laws the com-

as the most sensitive and destructive, can I deny that revelation of these documents will do substantial damage to public interests. Indeed, I am confident that their disclosure will have that result. But I nevertheless agree that the United States has not satisfied the very heavy burden which it must meet to warrant an injunction against publication in these cases, at least in the absence of express and appropriately limited congressional authorization for prior restraints in circumstances such as these.

The Government's position is simply stated: The responsibility of the Executive for the conduct of the foreign affairs and for the security of the Nation is so basic that the President is entitled to an injunction against publication of a newspaper story whenever he can convince a court that the information to be revealed threatens "grave and irreparable" injury to the public interest;[2] and the injunction should issue whether or not the material to be published is classified, whether or not publication would be lawful under relevant criminal statutes enacted by Congress and regardless of the circumstances by which the newspaper came into possession of the information. At least in the absence of legislation by Congress, based on its own investigations and findings, I am quite unable to agree that the inherent powers of the Executive and the courts reach so far as to authorize remedies having such sweeping potential for inhibiting publications by the press. [To] sustain the Government in these cases would start the courts down a long and hazardous road that I am not willing to travel, at least without congressional guidance and direction.

[Prior] restraints require an unusually heavy justification under the First Amendment; but failure by the Government to justify prior restraints does not measure its constitutional entitlement to a conviction for criminal publication. That the Government mistakenly chose to proceed by injunction does not mean that it could not successfully proceed in another way. [Justice White discussed a number of "potentially relevant" criminal provisions.] It is thus clear that Congress has addressed itself to the problems of protecting the security of the country and the national defense from unauthorized disclosure of potentially damaging information. Cf. [the Steel Seizure Case, chap. 6 above]. It has not, however, authorized the injunctive remedy against threatened publication. It has apparently been satisfied to rely on criminal sanctions and their deterrent effect on the responsible as well as the irresponsible press. I am not, of course, saying that either of these newspapers has yet committed a crime or that either would commit a crime if they published all the material now in their possession. That matter must await resolution in the context of a criminal proceeding if one is [instituted].[3]

plainant is a private copyright holder enforcing a private right. These situations are quite distinct from the Government's request for an injunction against publishing information about the affairs of government, a request admittedly not based on any statute. [Footnote by Justice White.]

2. The "grave and irreparable danger" standard is that asserted by the Government in this Court. In remanding to Judge Gurfein for further hearings in the Times litigation, five members of the Court of Appeals for the Second Circuit directed him to determine whether disclosure of certain items specified with particularity by the Government would "pose such grave and immediate danger to the security of the United States as to warrant their publication being enjoined." [Footnote by Justice White.]

3. On July 1, 1971—the day after the decision in this case—Attorney General Mitchell

commented that the Justice Department "will prosecute all those who have violated federal criminal laws in connection with this matter" and added: "A review of the Court's opinions indicates that there is nothing in them to affect the situation." Daniel Ellsberg and Anthony Russo were subsequently indicted by a grand jury in Los Angeles under provisions of federal espionage, theft and conspiracy laws. (Another federal grand jury, in Boston, investigated the involvement of newspapers and reporters.) On May 11, 1973, District Judge Byrne dismissed the Ellsberg-Russo indictment and granted a mistrial because the "totality of the circumstances" of improper government conduct "offends 'a sense of justice.'" [Note also the materials on the impeachment of President Nixon, chap. 6 above.]

Mr. Justice MARSHALL, [concurring].

[I] believe the ultimate issue in this case [is] whether this Court or the Congress has the power to make law. [I]n some situations it may be that under whatever inherent powers the [Executive may have], there is a basis for the invocation of the equity jurisdiction of this Court as an aid to prevent the publication of material damaging to "national security," however that term may be defined. It would, however, be utterly inconsistent with the concept of separation of powers for this Court to use its power of contempt to prevent behavior that Congress has specifically declined to prohibit. There would be a similar damage to the basic concept of these co-equal branches of Government if when the [executive] had adequate authority granted by Congress to protect "national security" it can choose instead to invoke the contempt power of a court to enjoin the threatened conduct. [In] these cases we are not faced with a situation where Congress has failed to provide the Executive with broad power to protect the Nation from disclosure of damaging state secrets. [See the power to "classify" secret materials in 18 U.S.C. Chap. 37, Espionage and Censorship.] [It] is plain that Congress has specifically refused to grant the authority the Government seeks from this Court. [It] is not for this Court to fling itself into every breach perceived by some Government [official].

Mr. Justice HARLAN, with whom The Chief Justice [BURGER] and Mr. Justice BLACKMUN join, dissenting.

[I] consider that the Court has been almost irresponsibly feverish in dealing with these cases. [The] frenzied train of events [see footnote 1 at p. 1420 above] took place in the name of the presumption against prior restraints created by the First Amendment. Due regard for the extraordinarily important and difficult questions involved in these litigations should have led the Court to shun [its] precipitate timetable. In order to decide the merits of these cases properly, some or all of the following questions should have been [faced].[1] These are difficult questions of fact, of law, and of judgment; the potential consequences of erroneous decision are enormous. The time which has been available to us, to the lower courts, and to the parties has been wholly inadequate for giving these cases the kind of consideration they deserve. It is a reflection on the stability of the judicial process that these great issues—as important as any that have arisen during my time on the Court—should have been decided under the pressures engendered by the torrent of publicity that has attended these litigations from their inception.

1. The questions posed by Justice Harlan were as follows:

1. Whether the Attorney General is authorized to bring these suits in the name of the United States. Compare [In re Debs, 158 U.S. 564 (1895)] with [the Steel Seizure Case]. This question involves as well the construction and validity of a singularly opaque statute—the Espionage Act, 18 U.S.C. § 793(e).

2. Whether the First Amendment permits the federal courts to enjoin publication of stories which would present a serious threat to national security. See [Near] (dictum).

3. Whether the threat to publish highly secret documents is of itself a sufficient implication of national security to justify an injunction on the theory that regardless of the contents of the documents harm enough results simply from the demonstration of such a breach of secrecy.

4. Whether the unauthorized disclosure of any of these particular documents would seriously impair the national security.

5. What weight should be given to the opinion of high officers in the Executive Branch of the Government with respect to questions 3 and 4.

6. Whether the newspapers are entitled to retain and use the documents notwithstanding the seemingly uncontested facts that the documents, or the originals of which they are duplicates, were purloined from the Government's possession and that the newspapers received them with knowledge that they had been feloniously acquired.

7. Whether the threatened harm to the national security or the Government's possessory interest in the documents justifies the issuance of an injunction against publication in light of—

a. The strong First Amendment policy against prior restraints on publication; b. The doctrine against enjoining conduct in violation of criminal statutes; and c. The extent to which the materials at issue have apparently already been otherwise disseminated.

Forced as I am to reach the merits of these cases, I dissent from the opinion and judgments of the Court. Within the severe limitations imposed by the time constraints under which I have been required to operate, I can only state my reasons in telescoped form. [It] is plain to me that the scope of the judicial function in passing upon the activities of the Executive Branch of the Government in the field of foreign affairs is very narrowly restricted. This view is, I think, dictated by the concept of separation of powers upon which our constitutional system rests. [I] agree that, in performance of its duty to protect the values of the First Amendment against political pressures, the judiciary must review the initial Executive determination to the point of satisfying itself that the subject matter of the dispute does lie within the proper compass of the President's foreign relations power. [Moreover], the judiciary may properly insist that the determination that disclosure of the subject matter would irreparably impair the national security be made by the head of the Executive Department concerned [after] actual personal consideration by that officer. [But] in my judgment the judiciary may not properly go beyond these two inquiries and redetermine for itself the probable impact of disclosure on the national security. "[T]he very nature of executive decisions as to foreign policy is political, not judicial. Such decisions are wholly confided by our Constitution to the political departments. [See chaps. 6 and 15.] They are delicate, complex, and involve large elements of prophecy. They are and should be undertaken only by those directly responsible to the people whose welfare they advance or imperil. They are decisions of a kind for which the Judiciary has neither aptitude, facilities nor responsibility and which has long been held to belong in the domain of political power not subject to judicial intrusion or inquiry." Chicago & Southern Air Lines v. Waterman Steamship Corp., 333 U.S. 103, 111 (1948) (Jackson, J.).

Even if there is some room for the judiciary to override the executive determination, it is plain that the scope of review must be exceedingly narrow. I can see no indication in the opinions of [the lower courts] in the Post litigation that the conclusions of the Executive were given even the deference owing to an administrative agency, much less that owing to a co-equal branch of the Government operating within the field of its constitutional prerogative. [Pending] further hearings in each case conducted under the appropriate ground rules, I would continue the restraints on publication. I cannot believe that the doctrine prohibiting prior restraints reaches to the point of preventing courts from maintaining the status quo long enough to act responsibly in matters of such national importance as those involved here.

Mr. Justice BLACKMUN.

I join Mr. Justice Harlan in his dissent. [The] First Amendment, after all, is only one part of an entire Constitution. [See, e.g., the Executive's power in Art. II.] First Amendment absolutism has never commanded a majority of this Court. [E.g., Near; Schenck.] What is needed here is a weighing, upon properly developed standards, of the broad right of the press to print and of the very narrow right of the Government to prevent. Such standards are not yet developed. The parties here are in disagreement as to what those standards should be. But even the newspapers concede that there are situations where restraint is in order and is constitutional. [I] therefore would remand these cases to be developed expeditiously, of course, but on a schedule permitting [orderly presentation of evidence]. [I] add one final comment. [Judge Wilkey], dissenting in the District of Columbia case, [concluded] that there were a number of examples of documents that, [if] published, "could clearly result in great harm to the nation," and he defined "harm" to mean "the death of soldiers, the destruction of alliances, the greatly increased difficulty of negotiation with our enemies, the inability of our diplomats to negotiate." [I] share his concern. I hope that damage has not already been done. If, however, damage has been done, and if, with the Court's action today, these newspapers proceed to publish the critical documents and there results therefrom "the death of soldiers, the destruction of alliances, the greatly increased difficulty of negotiation with our enemies, the inability of our diplomats to negotiate," to which list I might add the factors of prolongation of the war and of further delay in the freeing of United States prisoners, then the Nation's people will know where the responsibility for these sad consequences rests.*

PRIOR RESTRAINTS IN THE INTEREST OF NATIONAL SECURITY: THE PROGRESSIVE CASE

Were the principles of Near and the Pentagon Papers case properly applied in UNITED STATES v. PROGRESSIVE, INC., 467 F.Supp. 990 (W.D.Wis. 1979)? There, the District Court issued an order enjoining The Progressive, a monthly magazine, from publishing technical material on hydrogen bomb design in an article entitled "The H-Bomb Secret: How We Got It, Why We're Telling It." The author and publisher claimed that the article merely synthesized information available in public documents, insisting that the article would contribute to informed opinion about nuclear weapons and would benefit the nation by demonstrating that open debate was preferable to "an oppressive and ineffective system of secrecy and classification." In issuing the temporary injunction, the District Judge distinguished the Pentagon Papers case on three grounds: (1) the documents there had contained only "historical data"; (2) the Government there had not proved that publication affected the national security; and (3) the Government there had failed to establish a statutory basis for injunctive relief.[1]

Although the Government conceded that at least some of the information in the article had been declassified or was in the public domain, it argued that the interest in "national security" permitted it to bar publication of information "originating in the public domain, if when drawn together, synthesized and collated, such information acquires the character of presenting immediate, direct and irreparable harm to the interests of the United States." It submitted affidavits from Cabinet members asserting that publication would increase the risk of thermonuclear proliferation. The District Judge accepted the Government's key claims. He noted that the article "contains concepts that are not found in the public realm, concepts that are vital to the operation of the bomb." Moreover, despite the prior declassification of some of the materials in the article, he found that "the danger lies in the exposition of certain concepts never heretofore disclosed in conjunction with one another." Though the District Judge conceded that the article probably did not "provide a 'do-it-yourself' guide for the hydrogen bomb," he noted that the article "could possibly provide sufficient information to allow a medium size nation to move faster in developing a hydrogen weapon."

---

* Chief Justice BURGER's dissent stated that he agreed "generally" with Justices Harlan and Blackmun, but that he was "not prepared to reach the merits." He urged that the temporary restraining orders be extended pending a full trial on the merits. He commented that the cases had been "conducted in unseemly haste" and that "we literally, do not know what we are acting on."

1. For statutory support, the District Court relied primarily upon the Atomic Energy Act of 1954, which imposes sanctions on anyone who "communicates, transmits, or discloses [restricted data] with reason to believe such data will be utilized to injure the United States or to secure an advantage to any foreign nation." 42 U.S.C. § 2274(b). The Act also authorizes the Government to seek injunctive relief, 42 U.S.C. § 2280. The trial court ruled that the statute and its definition of "restricted data"—including "all data concerning design, manufacture, or utilization of atomic weapons"—were neither vague nor overbroad "[a]s applied to this case" and that the prohibition against one who "communicates" extended to publication in a magazine.

In justifying "the first instance of prior restraint against a publication in this fashion in the history of this country," the District Judge explained: "A mistake in ruling against The Progressive [will] curtail defendants' First Amendment rights in a drastic and substantial fashion. [But a] mistake in ruling against the United States could pave the way for thermonuclear annihilation for us all. In that event, our right to life is extinguished and the right to publish becomes moot." He concluded: "Because of this 'disparity of risk,' because the government has met its heavy burden of showing justification for the imposition of a prior restraint, [and] because the Court is unconvinced that suppression of the objected-to technical portions of the [article] would in any plausible fashion impede the defendants in their laudable crusade to stimulate public knowledge of nuclear armament and bring about enlightened debate on national policy questions, the Court finds that the objected-to portions of the article fall within the narrow area recognized by the Court in Near v. Minnesota in which a prior restraint on publication is appropriate." [2] He added: "In view of the showing of harm made by the United States, a preliminary injunction would be warranted even in the absence of statutory authorization because of the existence of the likelihood of direct, immediate and irreparable injury to our nation and its people. New York Times (Justice Stewart)." [3]

PRIOR RESTRAINTS ON PUBLICATION TO ASSURE FAIR TRIALS: "GAG ORDERS"

1. *The Nebraska Press decision.* In NEBRASKA PRESS ASS'N v. STUART, 427 U.S. 539 (1976), the Court for the first time considered the permissibility of a prior restraint on the press imposed in the interest of protecting a criminal defendant's right to a fair trial before an impartial jury. The Court reemphasized the high constitutional barriers to prior restraints and held the challenged pretrial restraint unconstitutional. There were several opinions in support of that judgment. Although the majority opinion by Chief Justice Burger was a narrow one limited to the facts of this case, the several concurring opinions indicated that most of the Justices were even more reluctant than the Chief Justice to sustain "gag orders" in the interest of fair trials.

The state court order, issued in anticipation of a trial in a widely publicized mass murder, prohibited publication or broadcasting of the accused's confessions or admissions, and of any other facts "strongly implicative" of the accused. In his majority opinion, Chief Justice BURGER found that "the showing before the state court" did not justify the order. Evidently anxious to avoid writing broadly, the Chief Justice emphasized that "[w]e cannot resolve all" of the issues raised by conflicts between the free press and fair trial guarantees: "[I]t is not the function of this Court to write a code. We look instead to this particular case." Yet even that narrow focus yielded some broad reiterations of the strong presumption against prior restraints. Though the Chief Justice rejected the plea to announce a priority, "applicable in all circumstances," of the

2. In arguing that the Near exception applied, the District Judge pointed to the "troop movements" reference there and added: "Times have changed significantly since 1931 when Near was decided. Now war by foot soldiers has been replaced in large part by war by machines and bombs. No longer need there be any advance warning or any preparation time before a nuclear war could be commenced. In light of these factors, this court concludes that publication of the technical information of the hydrogen bomb contained in the article is analogous to publica-

tion of troop movements or locations in time of war and falls within the extremely narrow exception to the rule against prior restraint."

3. The Government's proceedings against the "Progressive" were abandoned before full appellate proceedings and a hearing regarding a permanent injunction could be had, apparently because similar information pertaining to nuclear weapons was published by others while the litigation was under way.

"right to publish" over the "right of an accused," he found a common thread in the prior decisions such as Near and Pentagon Papers: "[P]rior restraints [are] the most serious and least tolerable infringement on First Amendment rights. A criminal penalty or [a defamation judgment] is subject to the whole panoply of protections afforded by deferring the impact of the judgment until all avenues of appellate review have been exhausted. [A] prior restraint [has] an immediate and irreversible sanction. If it can be said that a threat of criminal or civil sanctions after publication 'chills' speech, prior restraint 'freezes' it at least for the time." Moreover, "the protection against prior restraints should have particular force as applied to reporting of criminal proceedings." He cautioned that the First Amendment's "extraordinary protections" imposed special fiduciary duties on editors and publishers—duties "not always observed." Despite that admonition, however, he indicated that courts could do little to enforce that "fiduciary duty": "[T]he barriers to prior restraint remain high."

Turning to a scrutiny of the justifications for the "gag order," the Chief Justice drew on Learned Hand's formulation in the Dennis case (p. 1017 above). The Chief Justice stated: "We turn now to the record in this case to determine whether, as Learned Hand put it, 'the gravity of the "evil" discounted by its improbability, justified such invasion of free speech as is necessary to avoid the danger.' To do so, we must examine the evidence before the trial judge when the order was entered to determine (a) the nature and extent of pretrial news coverage; (b) whether other measures would be likely to mitigate the effects of unrestrained pretrial publicity; (c) how effectively a restraining order would operate to prevent the threatened danger. The precise terms of the restraining order are also important. We must then consider whether the record supports the entry of a prior restraint on publication, one of the most extraordinary remedies known to our jurisprudence." In executing that analysis, the Chief Justice noted that, though the trial judge could reasonably conclude, "based on common human experience, that publicity might impair" the defendant's rights, his conclusion about the impact of publicity on prospective jurors "was of necessity speculative." With respect to possible alternative measures to curb the impact of media publicity, he concluded that the record could not support a finding that alternatives would have been ineffective. He noted several possible alternatives: change of venue; postponement of the trial; careful questioning of jurors; jury instructions; sequestration of jurors; and curbing statements by the contending lawyers, the police, and witnesses. [See Sheppard v. Maxwell, 384 U.S. 333 (1966).] The Chief Justice also questioned the efficacy of any restraint of the media, in view, e.g., of the likelihood of rumors in a sensational case. Turning to the terms of the order, he especially objected to the ban on reporting "implicative" information as "too vague and too broad" in a First Amendment context. He concluded that, though there was no doubt about "the gravity of the evil pretrial publicity can work, [the] probability that it would do so here was not demonstrated with the degree of certainty our cases on prior restraint require."[1]

---

1. Justices POWELL and WHITE, while joining the majority opinion, submitted brief concurring statements of their own. Justice Powell emphasized "the unique burden" on a proponent of prior restraint on pretrial publicity, elaborating: "In my judgment, a prior restraint properly may issue only when it is shown to be necessary to prevent the dissemination of prejudicial publicity that otherwise poses a high likelihood of preventing, directly and irreparably, the impaneling of a jury meeting the Sixth Amendment's requirement of impartiality. This requires a showing that (i) there is a clear threat to the fairness of trial, (ii) such a threat is posed by the actual publicity to be restrained, and (iii) no less restrictive alternatives are available. Notwithstanding such a showing, restraint may not issue unless it also is shown that previous publicity or publicity from unrestrained sources will not render the restraint inefficacious." Justice White's statement indicated his "grave doubt [whether] orders with respect to the press such as were entered in this case would ever be justifiable."

In a lengthy opinion concurring only in the judgment, Justice BRENNAN, joined by Justices Stewart and Marshall, urged an absolute ban on prior restraints issued in the interest of a fair trial. He concluded: "I would hold [that] resort to prior restraints on the freedom of the press is a constitutionally impermissible method for enforcing [the right to a fair trial]; judges have at their disposal a broad spectrum of devices for ensuring that fundamental fairness is accorded the accused without necessitating so drastic an incursion on the equally fundamental and salutary constitutional mandate that discussion of public affairs in a free society cannot depend on the preliminary grade of judicial censors." He emphasized that "[c]ommentary and reporting on the criminal justice system is at the core of First Amendment values." Though he recognized pretrial publicity could "destroy the fairness of a criminal trial," he insisted that established law as to prior restraints on the press barred any prohibition regarding pending judicial proceedings, "no matter how shabby the means by which the information is obtained." He added in a footnote that this did "not necessarily immunize [the press] from civil liability for libel or invasion of privacy or from criminal liability for transgressions of general criminal laws during the course of obtaining that information."

Justice Brennan stressed that, under Near and its progeny, exceptions to the ban on prior restraints were confined to "exceptional cases." He insisted that the narrow national security exception recognized in dicta in Near and Pentagon Papers did not mean, as the highest state court had assumed in this case, "that prior restraints can be justified on an ad hoc balancing approach that concludes that the 'presumption' must be overcome in light of some perceived 'justification.'" Rather, "prior restraints even within a recognized exception to the rule against prior restraints will be extremely difficult to justify; but as an initial matter, the purpose for which a prior restraint is sought to be imposed 'must fit within one of the narrowly defined exceptions to the prohibition against prior restraints.'" And there was no justification here for creating "a new, potentially pervasive exception [for fair trial purposes] to this settled rule of virtually blanket prohibition of prior restraints." He added that "speculative deprivation of an accused's Sixth Amendment right to an impartial jury [is not] comparable to the damage to the Nation or its people that Near and New York Times would have found sufficient to justify a prior restraint on reporting. Damage to that Sixth Amendment right could never be considered so direct, immediate and irreparable, and based on such proof rather than speculation, that prior restraints on the press could be justified on this basis." Justice Brennan commented, moreover, that any "fair trial" exception would "inevitably interject judges [into] censorship roles that are simply inappropriate and impermissible under the First Amendment." To him, no real "choice" between First Amendment rights and fair trial guarantees was necessary, since "judges possess adequate tools short of injunctions against reporting for relieving [the] tension" between rights of the press and rights of criminal defendants. He recognized that "the press may be arrogant, tyrannical, abusive, and sensationalist, just as it may be incisive, probing, and informative. But at least in the context of prior restraints on publication, the decision of what, when, and how to publish is for editors, not judges." [2]

---

2. In another separate opinion concurring in the judgment, Justice STEVENS stated that he subscribed to "most" of the reasons "eloquently stated" by Justice Brennan, but pointed out some problems he was not yet ready to resolve: "Whether the same absolute protection would apply no matter how shabby or illegal the means by which the information is obtained, no matter how serious an intrusion on privacy might be involved, no matter how demonstrably false the information might be, no matter how prejudicial it might be to the interests of innocent persons, and no matter how perverse the motivation for publishing it, is a question I would not answer without further argument."

Note the reliance on Nebraska Press in Oklahoma Pub. Co. v. District Court, 430 U.S. 308 (1977), summarily setting aside a state court pretrial order enjoining the media from publish-

2. *Some comments: Does the emphasis on the unacceptability of prior restraints leave undue room for other types of restrictions on the press?* In striking down the "gag order" in Nebraska Press, the Chief Justice's opinion mentioned a number of other alternatives available to judges in assuring a fair trial, but he did not include the possibility of closing criminal proceedings to the press and the public as one of the alternatives. Instead, both the Burger and Brennan opinions noted in footnotes that the issue of closing proceedings was not before the Court. Three years later, a divided Court rejected constitutional attacks on an order closing pretrial hearings. (See the Gannett case, noted in sec. 6C at p. 1443 below.) Excluding the press and others from courtrooms avoids the "prior restraint" pejorative. But does that make closure orders truly more acceptable under the First Amendment?

Does the Court's special hostility to prior restraints, manifested in this group of materials, unduly focus on only one type of sanction that risks First Amendment impingements? Does that emphasis implicitly open the door to other sanctions, such as subsequent punishments and exclusion orders, that may threaten free speech and press to a similar degree?[3] Consider the extensive criticism of Nebraska Press in Barnett, "The Puzzle of Prior Restraint," 29 Stan. L.Rev. 539 (1977).[4] Barnett suggests that "single-minded application of the prior restraint doctrine" as in Nebraska Press "can warp the law by diminishing the protection afforded against restrictions on speech that do not carry the label 'prior restraint'—though they may be no less suppressive in fact—and by diminishing the force of other protective doctrines even in 'prior restraint' cases. More generally, it can confuse first amendment analysis by diverting attention from other doctrinal considerations that may be more apt, such as the substantive dimensions of protected speech."[5] He views Nebraska Press "as balancing the liberality of prior restraint doctrine with receptivity toward other ways of restricting pretrial reporting."[6]

3. *Protective orders as prior restraints.* In SEATTLE TIMES CO. v. RHINEHART, 467 U.S. ___ (1984), a Washington state trial court had, in the course of a civil action for libel, restricted the defendant from publishing materials obtained from the plaintiff in the course of discovery. The trial judge's protective order prohibited the newspaper from using the information (which included the identity of donors to a religious group) for any purpose other than the trial of the case. The Court upheld the protective order (issued pursuant to a state rule modeled on Rule 26(c) of the Federal Rules of Civil Procedure) against the newspaper's claim that it constituted an impermissible

---

ing the name or picture of a juvenile involved in a pending delinquency proceeding. (The media had obtained the information at an earlier detention hearing which could have been closed under state law, but had not been.) The Court also relied on the Cox Broadcasting case, p. 1064 above. (Recall also the conflicts between the First Amendment and contempt of court orders issued in the interest of the fair administration of justice, in the Bridges line of cases (including Wood v. Georgia, p. 1337 above).)

3. Recall the earlier critical comments on the Court's sharp distinction between prior restraints and subsequent punishments, in sec. 2 of chap. 12, above.

4. The article was part of a Symposium Issue of the Stanford Law Review on the Nebraska Press decision.

5. Barnett comments more generally: "What is special [about the prior restraint doctrine] is that, within the framework of the facts presented,

the doctrine focuses on the form or method of the restraint instead of the substance of the speech (or conduct). The doctrine thus has the attraction of producing narrow, technical, tentative holdings, decisions that focus on means rather than ends and that avoid, or at least subordinate, consideration of the substantive scope of protected speech. In this it strongly resembles other techniques of First Amendment adjudication, particularly the doctrine of 'overbreadth' or 'less restrictive alternatives.'" Is Barnett's criticism justified?

6. Nebraska Press deals with limits directly on the press in order to assure a fair trial. Would limitations on the out-of-court statements of the parties be permissible? What about restrictions imposed upon the attorneys? Jurors? See KPNX Broadcasting Co. v. Arizona Superior Court, 459 U.S. 1302 (1982) (Rehnquist, J., as Circuit Justice, denying stay).

prior restraint on its right to publish information lawfully obtained. In finding that the pre-trial protective order did not violate the First Amendment, Justice POWELL's opinion for the Court emphasized that the order did not prevent a party from disseminating identical information obtained by independent means. Restraints on the use of information discovered, but not yet admitted into evidence, did not restrict a "traditionally public source of information." In this context, the normally stringent standard applicable to prior restraints was inapplicable. Finding that Rule 26(c) furthered a substantial interest unrelated to the suppression of expression and that the limitation was no greater than necessary to protect the governmental interest, the Court concluded that the provision required, "in itself, no heightened First Amendment scrutiny." [7]

B. OTHER SANCTIONS AGAINST THE PRESS STEMMING FROM INFORMATION ALREADY IN ITS POSSESSION: GOVERNMENTAL DEMANDS FOR INFORMATION

Introduction. Restraints against publication are not the only sanctions that may confront the press because of information in its possession. The materials that follow arise from situations in which government, typically in the interest of law enforcement, demands that journalists disclose information they have obtained in the course of their newsgathering activities. Can the First Amendment be read to grant to journalists a special immunity from governmental inquiries? The Branzburg case raises that question in the context of grand jury investigations.* The Zurcher case involves a claimed press privilege against newsroom searches based on ex parte warrants.†

BRANZBURG v. HAYES

408 U.S. 665, 92 S.Ct. 2646, 33 L.Ed.2d 626 (1972).

Opinion of the Court [by Justice WHITE].

The issue in these cases is whether requiring newsmen to appear and testify before state or federal grand juries abridges the freedom of speech and press guaranteed by the First Amendment. We hold that it does not.

[The journalists] [1] press First Amendment claims that may be simply put: that to gather news it is often necessary to agree either not to identify the source

---

7. Justice BRENNAN's concurring opinion, joined by Justice Marshall, noted that the very application of the substantial interest and least restrictive alternative standard properly represented First Amendment scrutiny of the system of protective orders. The concurrence also seemed to suggest that First Amendment scrutiny of individual protective orders might be appropriate.

* In examining Branzburg, recall the series of cases of the 1950s and 1960s involving claimed First Amendment privileges against legislative rather than grand jury investigations. Recall especially the successful effort to assert a strong First Amendment defense in the Gibson case, sec. 5, at p. 1412 above. Note the references to Gibson in the plurality and dissenting opinions in Branzburg. Does the Branzburg ruling weaken the First Amendment protections announced in Gibson?

† In addition to the sanctions against the press considered in this subsection, recall the disposition of a law providing of mandatory access to newspapers in Miami Herald Publishing Co. v. Tornillo (1974; chap. 12, at p. 1300 above).

1. This decision rejected the claim of three journalists: Branzburg, Pappas, and Caldwell. Branzburg, a Louisville reporter, had written articles about drug activities he had observed. He refused to testify before a state grand jury, refusing to identify the persons he had seen possessing marijuana or making hashish. Pappas, a Massachusetts television reporter covering a "civil disorder," was allowed to remain in Black Panther headquarters for several hours on the condition that he disclose nothing. He

of information published or to publish only part of the facts revealed, or both; that if the reporter is nevertheless forced to reveal these confidences to a grand jury, the source so identified and other confidential sources of other reporters will be measurably deterred from furnishing publishable information, all to the detriment of the free flow of information protected by the First Amendment. Although [the journalists] do not claim an absolute privilege against official interrogation in all circumstances, they assert that the reporter should not be forced either to appear or to testify before a grand jury or at trial until and unless sufficient grounds are shown for believing that the reporter possesses information relevant to a crime the grand jury is investigating, that the information the reporter has is unavailable from other sources, and that the need for the information is sufficiently compelling to override the claimed invasion of First Amendment interests occasioned by the disclosure. Principally relied upon are [precedents] requiring that official action with adverse impact on First Amendment rights be justified by a public interest that is "compelling" or "paramount," and those precedents establishing the principle that justifiable governmental goals may not be achieved by unduly broad means having an unnecessary impact on protected rights of speech, press, or association. The heart of the claim is that the burden on news gathering from compelling reporters to disclose confidential information outweighs any public interest in obtaining the information.

[N]ews gathering [qualifies] for First Amendment protection; without some protection for seeking out the news, freedom of the press could be eviscerated. But this case involves no intrusions upon speech or assembly, [and] no penalty, civil or criminal, related to the content of published material, is at issue here. The use of confidential sources by the press is not forbidden or restricted. [No] attempt is made to require the press to publish its sources of information or indiscriminately to disclose them on request. The sole issue [is] the obligation of reporters to respond to grand jury subpoenas as other citizens do and to answer questions relevant to an investigation into the commission of crime. [The Constitution does not protect] the average citizen from disclosing to a grand jury information that he has received in confidence. The claim is, however, that reporters are [exempt].

[T]he First Amendment does not invalidate every incidental burdening of the press that may result from the enforcement of civil or criminal statutes of general applicability. [It] has generally been held that the First Amendment does not guarantee the press a constitutional right of special access to information not available to the public generally.[2] [Despite] the fact that news gathering may be hampered, the press is regularly excluded from grand jury proceedings, our own conferences, the meetings of other official bodies gathered in executive session, and the meetings of private organizations. Newsmen have no constitutional right of access to the scenes of crime or disaster when the general public is excluded, and they may be prohibited from attending or publishing information about trials if such restrictions are necessary to assure a defendant a fair trial before an impartial tribunal. [It] is thus not surprising that the great weight of authority is that newsmen are not exempt from the normal

broadcast no report and refused to tell a grand jury about what had taken place inside the headquarters. Caldwell was a New York Times reporter who had written articles about the Black Panthers after interviewing their leaders. He refused to appear before a federal grand jury investigating "possible violations of a number of criminal statutes" (including those protecting the President against assassination). The trial court issued a protective order stating that he was not required to reveal confidential information unless the government showed "a compelling national interest" in his testimony "which cannot be served by any alternative means." Caldwell thought that limited privilege inadequate, refused to appear, and was sentenced for contempt. Caldwell's conviction was set aside by the Court of Appeals. The Branzburg and Pappas convictions were affirmed by state courts.

2. But note the right of access claims considered in sec. 6C below.

duty of appearing before a grand jury and answering questions relevant to a criminal [investigation].

The prevailing constitutional view of the newsman's privilege is very much rooted in the ancient role of the grand jury. [I]ts investigative powers are necessarily broad. [The] longstanding principle that "the public has a right to every man's evidence," except for those persons protected by a constitutional, common law, or statutory privilege, is particularly applicable to grand jury proceedings. A [minority] of States have provided newsmen a statutory privilege of varying breadth; [none] has been provided by federal statute. [We] are asked to [interpret] the First Amendment to grant newsmen a testimonial privilege that other citizens do not enjoy. This we decline to do. [On] the records now before us, we perceive no basis for holding that the public interest in law enforcement and in ensuring effective grand jury proceedings is insufficient to override the consequential, but uncertain, burden on news gathering which is said to result from insisting that reporters, like other citizens, respond to relevant questions put to them in the course of a valid grand jury investigation or criminal trial. This conclusion [does not] threaten the vast bulk of confidential relationships between reporters and their sources. [Only] where news sources themselves are implicated in crime or possess information relevant to the grand jury's task need they or the reporter be concerned about grand jury subpoenas. Nothing before us indicates that a large number or percentage of *all* confidential news sources fall into either category and would in any way be deterred by our [holding].

There remain those situations where a source is not engaged in criminal conduct but has information suggesting illegal conduct by others. Newsmen frequently receive information from such sources pursuant to a tacit or express agreement to withhold the source's name and suppress any information that the source wishes not published. [The] argument that the flow of news will be diminished by compelling reporters to aid the grand jury in a criminal investigation is not irrational, nor are the records before us silent on the matter. But we remain unclear how often and to what extent informers are actually deterred from furnishing information when newsmen are forced to testify before a grand jury. The available data indicate that some newsmen rely a great deal on confidential sources and that some informants are particularly sensitive to the threat of exposure and may be silenced if it is held by this Court that, ordinarily, newsmen must testify pursuant to subpoenas, but the evidence fails to demonstrate that there would be a significant constriction of the flow of news to the public if this Court reaffirms the prior common-law and constitutional rule regarding the testimonial obligations of newsmen. Estimates of the inhibiting effect of such subpoenas on the willingness of informants to make disclosures to newsmen are widely divergent and to a great extent speculative. It would be difficult to canvass the views of the informants themselves; surveys of reporters on this topic are chiefly opinions of predicted informant behavior and must be viewed in the light of the professional self-interest of the interviewees.[3] [Accepting] the fact, however, that an undetermined number of informants not themselves implicated in crime will nevertheless, for whatever reason, refuse to talk to newsmen if they fear identification by a reporter in an official investigation, we cannot accept the argument that the public interest in possible future news about crime from undisclosed, unverified sources must take precedence over the public interest in pursuing and prosecuting those crimes reported to the press by informants and in thus deterring the commission of such crimes in the [future].

---

3. In his Press Subpoenas: An Empirical and Legal Analysis, Study Report of the Reporters' Committee on Freedom of the Press 6–12 (1971), Prof. Blasi discusses these methodological [problems]. [Footnote by Justice White.]

We are admonished that refusal to provide a First Amendment reporter's privilege will undermine the freedom of the press to collect and disseminate news. But this is not the lesson history teaches us. [From] the beginning of our country the press has operated without constitutional protection for press informants, and the press has flourished. [It] is said that currently press subpoenas have multiplied, that mutual distrust and tension between press and officialdom have increased, that reporting styles have changed, and that there is now more need for confidential sources, particularly where the press seeks news about minority cultural and political groups or dissident organizations suspicious of the law and public officials. These developments, even if true, are treacherous grounds for a far-reaching interpretation of the [First Amendment].

The argument for such a constitutional privilege rests heavily on those cases holding that the infringement of protected First Amendment rights must be no broader than necessary to achieve a permissible governmental purpose. We do not deal, however, with a governmental institution that has abused its proper function, as a legislative committee does when it "expose[s] for the sake of exposure." [Watkins.] [Nor] did the grand juries attempt to invade protected First Amendment rights by forcing wholesale disclosure of names and organizational affiliations for a purpose which was not germane to the determination of whether crime has been committed [cf., e.g., NAACP v. Alabama], and the characteristic secrecy of grand jury proceedings is a further protection against the undue invasion of such rights. [The] requirements of those cases [e.g., NAACP v. Alabama] which hold that a State's interest must be "compelling" or "paramount" to justify even an indirect burden on First Amendment rights, are also met here. As we have indicated, the investigation of crime by the grand jury implements a fundamental governmental role of securing the safety of the person and property of the [citizen]. If the test is that the government "convincingly show a substantial relation between the information sought and a subject of overriding and compelling state interest" [Gibson], it is quite apparent (1) that the State has the necessary interests in extirpating the traffic in illegal drugs, in forestalling assassination attempts on the President, and in preventing the community from being disrupted by violent disorders endangering both persons and property; and (2) that, based on the stories Branzburg and Caldwell wrote and Pappas' admitted conduct, the grand jury called these reporters as they would others—because it was likely that they could supply information to help the government determine whether illegal conduct had occurred and, if it had, whether there was sufficient evidence to return an indictment.

Similar considerations dispose of the reporters' claims that preliminary to requiring their grand jury appearance, the State must show that a crime has been committed and that they possess relevant information not available from other sources, for only the grand jury itself can make this determination. [We] see no reason to hold that these reporters, any more than other citizens, should be excused from furnishing information that may help the grand jury in arriving at its initial determinations. The privilege claimed here is conditional, not absolute; given the suggested preliminary showings and compelling need, the reporter would be required to testify. Presumably, such a rule would reduce the instances in which reporters could be required to appear, but predicting in advance when and in what circumstances they could be compelled to do so would be difficult. Such a rule would also have implications for the issuance of compulsory process to reporters at civil and criminal trials and at legislative hearings. If newsmen's confidential sources are as sensitive as they are claimed to be, the prospect of being unmasked whenever a judge determines the situation justifies it is hardly a satisfactory solution to the problem. For them, it would appear that only an absolute privilege would suffice.

We are unwilling to embark the judiciary on a long and difficult journey to such an uncertain destination. The administration of a constitutional newsman's privilege would present practical and conceptual difficulties of a high order. Sooner or later, it would be necessary to define those categories of newsmen who qualified for the privilege, a questionable procedure in light of the traditional doctrine that liberty of the press is the right of the lonely pamphleteer who uses carbon paper or a mimeograph just as much as of the large metropolitan publisher who utilizes the latest photocomposition methods. [The] informative function asserted by representatives of the organized press in the present cases is also performed by lecturers, political pollsters, novelists, academic researchers, and dramatists. Almost any author may quite accurately assert that he is contributing to the flow of information to the public, that he relies on confidential sources of information, and that these sources will be silenced if he is forced to make disclosures before a grand jury. [In] each instance where a reporter is subpoenaed to testify, the courts would also be embroiled in preliminary factual and legal determinations with respect to whether the proper predicate had been laid for the reporter's appearance. [In] the end, by considering whether enforcement of a particular law served a "compelling" governmental interest, the courts would be inextricably involved in distinguishing between the value of enforcing different criminal laws. [At] the federal level, Congress has freedom to determine whether a statutory newsman's privilege is necessary and desirable and to fashion standards and rules as narrow or broad as deemed necessary [and], equally important, to refashion those rules as experience from time to time may dictate. There is also merit in leaving state legislatures free, within First Amendment limits, to fashion their own standards. [In addition], there is much force in the pragmatic view that the press has at its disposal powerful mechanisms of communication and is far from helpless to protect itself from harassment or substantial [harm].

[Finally], news gathering is not without its First Amendment protections, and grand jury investigations, if instituted or conducted other than in good faith, would pose wholly different issues for resolution under the First Amendment. Official harassment of the press undertaken not for purposes of law enforcement but to disrupt a reporter's relationship with his news sources would have no justification. Grand juries are subject to judicial control and subpoenas to motions to quash. We do not expect courts will forget that grand juries must operate within the limits of the First Amendment as well as the Fifth.

So ordered.[4]

Mr. Justice POWELL, concurring in the opinion of the Court.

I add this brief statement to emphasize what seems to me to be the limited nature of the Court's holding. The Court does not hold that newsmen, subpoenaed to testify before a grand jury, are without constitutional rights with respect to the gathering of news or in safeguarding their sources. [As] indicated in the concluding portion of the opinion, the Court states that no harassment of newsmen will be tolerated. If a newsman believes that the grand jury investigation is not being conducted in good faith he is not without remedy. Indeed, if the newsman is called upon to give information bearing only a remote and tenuous relationship to the subject of the investigation, or if he has some other reason to believe that his testimony implicates confidential source relationships without a legitimate need of law enforcement, he will have access to the Court on a motion to quash and an appropriate protective order

---

4. The Court disposed of the three cases as follows: Caldwell had no constitutional privilege to refuse appearance before the grand jury; Branzburg was obligated to answer the questions about the criminal conduct he had observed; Pappas was required to appear before the grand jury "to answer the questions put to him, subject, of course, to the supervision of the presiding judge as to 'the propriety, purposes, and scope of the grand jury inquiry and the pertinence of the probable testimony.'"

may be entered. The asserted claim to privilege should be judged on its facts by the striking of a proper balance between freedom of the press and the obligation of all citizens to give relevant testimony with respect to criminal conduct. The balance of these vital constitutional and societal interests on a case-by-case basis accords with the tried and traditional way of adjudicating such questions.[1] In short, the courts will be available to newsmen under circumstances where legitimate First Amendment interests require protection.[2]

Mr. Justice STEWART, with whom Mr. Justice BRENNAN and Mr. Justice MARSHALL join, dissenting.

The Court's crabbed view of the First Amendment reflects a disturbing insensitivity to the critical role of an independent press in our society. The question whether a reporter has a constitutional right to a confidential relationship with his source is of first impression here, but the principles that should guide our decision are as basic as any to be found in the Constitution. While Mr. Justice Powell's enigmatic concurring opinion gives some hope of a more flexible view in the future, the Court in these cases holds that a newsman has no First Amendment right to protect his sources when called before a grand jury. The Court thus invites state and federal authorities to undermine the historic independence of the press by attempting to annex the journalistic profession as an investigative arm of government. Not only will this decision impair performance of the press' constitutionally protected functions, but it will, I am convinced, in the long run, harm rather than help the [administration of justice].

The reporter's constitutional right to a confidential relationship with his source stems from the broad societal interest in a full and free flow of information to the public. It is this basic concern that underlies the Constitution's protection of a free press. [As] private and public aggregations of power burgeon in size and the pressures for conformity necessarily mount, there is obviously a continuing need for an independent press to disseminate a robust variety of information and opinion through reportage, investigation and [criticism]. A corollary of the right to publish must be the right to gather news. [This right] implies, in turn, a right to a confidential relationship between a

1. It is to be remembered that Caldwell asserts a constitutional privilege not even to appear before the grand jury unless a court decides that the Government has made a showing that meets the three preconditions specified in the dissenting opinion of Mr. Justice Stewart. To be sure, this would require a "balancing" of interests by the court, but under circumstances and constraints significantly different from the balancing that will be appropriate under the Court's decision. The newsman witness, like all other witnesses, will have to appear; he will not be in a position to litigate at the threshold the State's very authority to subpoena him. Moreover, absent the constitutional preconditions that Caldwell and the dissenting opinion would impose as heavy burdens of proof to be carried by the State, the court—when called upon to protect a newsman from improper or prejudicial questioning—would be free to balance the competing interests on their merits in the particular case. The new constitutional rule endorsed by that dissenting opinion would, as a practical matter, defeat such a fair balancing and the essential societal interest in the detection and prosecution of crime would be heavily subordinated. [Footnote by Justice Powell.]

2. Compare Justice Powell's dissent two years later in Saxbe v. Washington Post Co.

(1974; p. 1440 below), supporting a press right of access to jails to interview prisoners on the basis of the First Amendment generally rather than the Press Clause specifically. (Justice Stewart, who emphasizes the Press Clause, was in the majority in Saxbe.) In Saxbe, Justice Powell distinguished the Branzburg ruling as reflecting "no more than a sensible disinclination to follow the right-of-access argument as far as dry logic might extend."

Justice Powell's concurrence in Branzburg, putting a more speech-protective gloss on the majority ruling, has contributed to the fact that, according to most studies, not nearly as many journalists have been compelled to give grand jury testimony in the wake of Branzburg as had been predicted at the time of the decision. Most lower court judges apparently have followed the tenor of the Powell rather than the White opinion in Branzburg. [Note the similar division of the Court six years later, in Zurcher (1978; p. 1438 below), where Justice Powell's decisive concurrence once again put a more speech-protective gloss on Justice White's majority opinion, in the context of challenges to ex parte warrants authorizing searches of newsrooms. Once again, such searches have been far more rare than was predicted in press commentary at the time of the decision.]

reporter and his source. [This] follows as a matter of simple logic once three factual predicates are recognized: (1) newsmen require informants to gather news; (2) confidentiality [is] essential to the creation and maintenance of a news-gathering relationship with informants; and (3) the existence of an unbridled subpoena power [will] either deter sources from divulging information or deter reporters from gathering and publishing information. After today's decision, the potential [source must] choose between risking exposure by giving information or avoiding the risk by remaining silent. The reporter must speculate about whether contact with a controversial source or publication of controversial material will lead to a [subpoena].

The impairment of the flow of news cannot, of course, be proved with scientific precision, as the Court seems to demand. [But] we have never before demanded that First Amendment rights rest on elaborate empirical studies demonstrating beyond any conceivable doubt that deterrent effects [exist]. Rather, on the basis of common sense and available information, we have asked, often implicitly, (1) whether there was a rational connection between the cause (the governmental action) and the effect (the deterrence or impairment of First Amendment activity) and (2) whether the effect would occur with some regularity, i.e., would not be de minimis. And in making this determination, we have shown a special solicitude towards the "indispensable liberties" protected by the First Amendment. [Once] this threshold inquiry has been satisfied, we have then examined the competing interests in determining whether there is an unconstitutional infringement of First Amendment freedoms. [E.g., NAACP v. Alabama.] Surely the analogous claim of deterrence here is as securely grounded in evidence and common sense as the claims in [earlier cases], although the Court calls the claim "speculative." [To] require any greater burden of proof is to shirk our duty to protect values securely embedded in the Constitution. [We] cannot escape the conclusion that when neither the reporter nor his source can rely on the shield of confidentiality against unrestrained use of the grand jury's subpoena power, valuable information will not be published and the public dialogue will inevitably be impoverished.

Posed against the First Amendment's protection of the newsman's confidential relationships in these cases is society's interest in the use of the grand jury to administer justice fairly and effectively. [Any] exemption from the duty to testify before the grand jury "presupposes a very real interest to be protected." Such an interest must surely be the First Amendment protection of a confidential relationship. [In] striking the proper balance, [we] must begin with the basic proposition [that] First Amendment rights require special safeguards. [Thus], when an investigation impinges on First Amendment rights, the government must not only show that the inquiry is of "compelling and overriding importance" but it must also "convincingly" demonstrate that the investigation is "substantially related" to the information sought. [Gibson; NAACP v. Button.] Governmental officials must, therefore, demonstrate that the information sought is *clearly* relevant to a *precisely* defined subject of governmental inquiry. [Watkins; Sweezy.] They must demonstrate that it is reasonable to think the witness in question has that information. [Sweezy; Gibson.] And they must show that there is not any means of obtaining the information less destructive of First Amendment liberties. [E.g., Shelton v. Tucker.] I believe [that] the safeguards developed in our decisions involving governmental investigations must apply to the grand jury inquiries in these cases. Surely the function of the grand jury [is] no more important than the function of the legislature. [T]he vices of vagueness and overbreadth which legislative investigations may manifest are also exhibited by grand jury inquiries, [since] standards of materiality and relevance are greatly [relaxed].

Accordingly, when a reporter is asked to appear before a grand jury and reveal confidences, I would hold that the government must (1) show that there is probable cause to believe that the newsman has information which is clearly relevant to a specific probable violation of law; (2) demonstrate that the information sought cannot be obtained by alternative means less destructive of First Amendment rights; and (3) demonstrate a compelling and overriding interest in the information.[1] [It] is obviously not true that the only persons about whom reporters will be forced to testify [under the Court's decision] will be those "confidential informants involved in actual criminal conduct" and those having "information suggesting illegal conduct by others." [Given] the grand jury's extraordinarily broad investigative powers and the weak standards of relevance and materiality that apply during such inquiries, reporters, if they have no testimonial privilege, will be called to give information about informants who have neither committed crimes nor have information about crime. It is to avoid deterrence of such sources and thus to prevent needless injury to First Amendment values that I think the government must be required to show [probable cause]. Both the "probable cause" and "alternative means" requirements [would] serve the vital function of mediating between the public interest in the administration of justice and the constitutional protection of the full flow of information. These requirements would avoid a direct conflict between these competing concerns, and they would generally provide adequate protection for newsmen.[2] No doubt the courts would be required to make some delicate judgments in working out this accommodation. But that, after all, is the function of courts of law. Better such judgments, however difficult, than the simplistic and stultifying absolutism adopted by the Court in denying any force to the First Amendment in these cases.[3]

SEARCHES OF NEWSROOMS PURSUANT TO EX PARTE WARRANTS

The Court once more rejected a press claim for special protection from law enforcement demands for information in ZURCHER v. STANFORD DAILY, 436 U.S. 547 (1978). The Court upheld an ex parte warrant authorizing a

1. Justice Stewart added at this point: "This is not to say that a grand jury could not issue a subpoena until such a showing were made, and it is not to say that a newsman would be in any way privileged to ignore any subpoena that was issued. Obviously, before the government's burden to make such a showing were triggered, the reporter would have to move to quash the subpoena, asserting the basis on which he considered the particular relationship a confidential one."

2. We need not, therefore, reach the question of whether government's interest in these cases is "overriding and compelling." I do not, however, believe, as the Court does, that *all* grand jury investigations automatically would override the newsman's testimonial privilege. [Footnote by Justice Stewart.]

3. Justice Stewart urged that the Branzburg and Pappas judgments be reversed and remanded. He also urged affirmance in Caldwell, even though the lower court had decided that Caldwell need not even appear before the grand jury. But Justice Stewart limited his endorsement of that immunity to "the particularized circumstances in the Caldwell case."

Justice DOUGLAS also dissented, taking a broader position. He concluded that "there is no 'compelling need' that can be shown which qualifies the reporter's immunity from appearing or testifying before a grand jury, unless the reporter himself is implicated in a crime. His immunity in my view [is] quite complete." He commented, moreover, that "the journalist's status as a reporter is less relevant than is his status as a student who affirmatively pursued empirical research to enlarge his own intellectual viewpoint."

→ In response to Branzburg, numerous bills to establish a journalists' privilege were introduced in state legislatures and in Congress. Typically, absolute immunity proposals did not fare well; qualified privilege proposals attracted more support. Progress of some of the proposals was retarded by divisions within the news community: some media representatives refused to support any proposals providing less than absolute immunity; other critics argued that "what Congress gives, Congress can take away" and accordingly opposed all "shield" legislation, preferring to "rely on the First Amendment and reasonable conduct by the courts."

search of a campus newspaper office for photographs of a violent demonstration.[1] Justice WHITE's majority opinion emphasized the Fourth Amendment rather than the First. His opinion in Zurcher was as skeptical as that in Branzburg about press allegations of chilling effects and risks to confidential sources. His reasoning contained only one sentence suggesting that First Amendment considerations be taken into account in applying Fourth Amendment search warrant criteria in the media context: "[Prior cases insist] that courts apply the warrant requirements with particular exactitude when First Amendment interests would be endangered by the search." As in Branzburg, Justice POWELL's concurrence built upon a passing remark in the prevailing opinion and elaborated the relevance of First Amendment concerns, stating: "This is not to say that a warrant which would be sufficient to support the search of an apartment or an automobile necessarily would be reasonable in supporting the search of a newspaper office. [While] there is no justification for the establishment of a separate Fourth Amendment procedure for the press, a magistrate asked to issue a warrant for the search of press offices can and should take cognizance of the independent values protected by the First Amendment—such as those highlighted by Mr. Justice Stewart—when he weighs such factors." And he added in a footnote that his separate opinion here, like that in Branzburg, could be read as supporting the view "that under the warrant requirement of the Fourth Amendment, the magistrate should consider the values of a free press as well as the societal interests in enforcing the criminal law." Justice STEWART's dissent argued that warrants to search newspaper offices should issue only when a magistrate finds probable cause to believe that it would be impractical to obtain the evidence by a subpoena. He emphasized that subpoena applications permit the press to obtain an adversary hearing prior to producing the information, by making a motion to quash; ex parte warrants, by contrast, provide "no opportunity to challenge the necessity for the search until after it has occurred and the constitutional protection of the newspaper has been irretrievably invaded."[2]

C. A PRESS RIGHT OF ACCESS TO NEWSWORTHY GOVERNMENTAL INFORMATION?

Introduction. In the preceding materials in this section, the press complained about government sanctions pertaining to information already in its possession.

1. The division on the Court was strikingly similar to that in Branzburg. Justice Powell once again supplied the critical vote for the majority with a separate concurrence putting a more speech-protective gloss on Justice White's opinion; Justice Stewart once again dissented on First Amendment grounds, this time joined only by Justice Marshall. (Justice Brennan did not participate in the case.) Justice Stevens, who had replaced Justice Douglas since Branzburg, submitted a separate dissent, based on the Fourth Amendment.

2. As a result of legislative efforts that began in the wake of the Stanford Daily decision, Congress adopted the Privacy Protection Act in 1980. 94 Stat. 1879. The Act requires state and federal law enforcement officers to use subpoena procedures to obtain documents from persons engaged in the communications industry. Search warrants are permitted only in exceptional circumstances, such as when there is a fear that the needed materials would be destroyed. Is it clear that Congress has the power to make these rules for state as well as federal proceedings? Recall the materials on the commerce power, chap. 3 above, and the questions regarding the scope of congressional enforcement power under the 14th Amendment, especially after Katzenbach v. Morgan (1966; chap. 10, at p. 946 above).

Recall the media protests against another decision soon after Stanford Daily, Herbert v. Lando (1979; p. 1058 above), rejecting a television producer's claim to a broad First Amendment privilege that would preclude a wide range of questions in pretrial discovery procedures in a suit by a "public figure" for defamation, a suit concededly subject to The New York Times "malice" standard (p. 1052 above). (For another unsuccessful First Amendment claim by the media, see New York Times Co. v. Jascalevich, 439 U.S. 1301 (1978).)

In the following materials, the press insists that the First Amendment entitles it to obtain information the government seeks to withhold. During the 1970s, claims of a special press right of access did not fare well. Recall that even Justice Stewart, the Justice most inclined to recognize the special status of the media under the Press Clause, stated bluntly that "government may deny access to information" (as well as punish its theft): to him, the Press Clause simply barred government from prohibiting or punishing the publication of information "once it falls into the hands of the press, unless the need for secrecy is manifestly overwhelming." [1] What support emerged on the Court for right of access claims during the 1970s came from those who, unlike Justice Stewart, relied on First Amendment principles generally rather than on the Press Clause.[2] In 1980, however, a 7 to 1 majority endorsed an access claim to criminal trials, in the Richmond Newspapers case (p. 1445 below). What is the proper scope of that newly recognized access right?

PRESS ACCESS TO JAILS

1. *Pell and Saxbe.* The Court first confronted press demands for access to jails in companion cases, PELL v. PROCUNIER, 417 U.S. 817 (1974) and SAXBE v. WASHINGTON POST CO., 417 U.S. 843 (1974). In Pell, the majority rejected an attack on a California rule providing that "press and other media interviews with specific individual inmates will not be permitted." And in Saxbe, the Court turned back a challenge to a Federal Bureau of Prisons prohibition of press interviews of individually designated prisoners in most federal prisons. Justice STEWART delivered the majority opinion in each case. He insisted that there was no violation of the First Amendment rights of the media because the regulations did not "deny the press access to sources of information available to members of the general public." He noted in Pell that the regulation had been adopted in 1971 "in response to a violent episode" that prison officials felt "was at least partially attributable to the former policy with respect to face-to-face prisoner-press interviews." And he emphasized that the new prohibition "did not impose a discrimination against press access, but merely eliminated a special privilege formerly given to representatives of the press vis-a-vis members of the public generally." Central to his rejection of the journalists' claim was his assertion that, although the First Amendment bars "government from interfering in any way with the free press," it does not "require government to accord the press special access to information not shared by members of the public generally." He explained: "It is one thing to say that a journalist is free to seek out sources of information not available to members of the general public, that he is entitled to some constitutional protection of the confidentiality of such sources, cf. [Branzburg], and that government cannot restrain the publication of news emanating from such sources. Cf. [Pentagon Papers]. It is quite another thing to suggest that the Constitution imposes upon government the affirmative duty to make available to journalists sources of information not available to members of the public generally."

Justice POWELL found that approach unduly simplistic. He concluded in Pell that an absolute ban on interviews "impermissibly restrains the ability of the press to perform its constitutionally established function of informing the people on the conduct of their government." Elaborating that position in Saxbe in a lengthy dissent joined by Justices Brennan and Marshall, he stated: "I cannot follow the Court in concluding that *any* governmental restriction on press access

---

1. See Justice Stewart's concurrence in the Landmark case (1978; p. 1341 above).

2. See, e.g., Justice Powell's dissents in Pell and Saxbe, which follow.

to information, so long as it is nondiscriminatory, falls outside the purview of First Amendment concern. [It] goes too far to suggest that the government must justify under the stringent standards of First Amendment review every regulation that might affect in some tangential way the availability of information to the news media. But to my mind it is equally impermissible to conclude that no governmental inhibition of press access to newsworthy information warrants constitutional scrutiny. At some point official restraints on access to news sources, even though not directed solely at the press, may so undermine the function of the First Amendment that it is both appropriate and necessary to require the Government to justify such regulations in terms more compelling than discretionary authority and administrative convenience." He argued that "this sweeping prohibition of prisoner-press interviews substantially impairs a core value of the First Amendment." He noted that freedom of speech protects two kinds of interests, individual and societal. Here, the "societal function" of "preserving free public discussion of governmental affairs" was critical. He explained: "For most citizens the prospect of personal familiarity with newsworthy events is hopelessly unrealistic. In seeking out the news the press therefore acts as an agent of the public at large. It is the means by which the people receive that free flow of information and ideas essential to intelligent self-government. [The] underlying right is the right of the public generally. The press is the necessary representative of the public's interest in this context and the instrumentality which effects the public's right." [1]

2. *The KQED case.* Press access claims similar to those rejected in Pell and Saxbe resurfaced four years later. But in HOUCHINS v. KQED, INC., 438 U.S. 1 (1978), the 7-person Court, in an unusual division, sustained a portion of the claim of access to jails. The Court divided 3 to 1 to 3: Chief Justice Burger's opinion, joined by Justices White and Rehnquist, found Pell controlling, reiterated its premise that the press has no broader access rights than the general public, and found no basis for judicial relief. Justice Stevens' dissent, joined by Justices Brennan and Powell, insisted that Pell was distinguishable. Although the dissenters accepted the premise that the press has no special access rights, they argued for broad relief for the media claimants because of the general First Amendment support for the public's right to be informed. The decisive vote assuring some relief for the press came from Justice Stewart's separate opinion: although he shared Chief Justice Burger's premises, he found in "equal access" notions a basis for providing some special treatment for the press.[1]

1. Exercising traditional First Amendment scrutiny, Justice Powell found in Saxbe that "the First Amendment requires the Bureau to abandon its absolute ban against press interviews." But he rejected the District Court's conclusion "that interview requests be evaluated on a case-by-case basis." "Ad hoc balancing of the competing interests involved in each request for an interview" was not necessary. Rather, "a press interview policy that substantially accommodates the public's legitimate interest in a free flow of information and ideas about federal prisons should survive constitutional review."

In a separate dissent, Justice DOUGLAS, joined by Justices Brennan and Marshall, similarly rested on the right "of the people": "the public's interest in being informed about prisons [is] paramount." Accordingly, the interview bans were "an unconstitutional infringement on the public's right to know protected by the free press guarantee of the First Amendment."

1. Justices Marshall and Blackmun did not participate in the case.

The case arose from the following circumstances: San Francisco public television station KQED brought a federal suit to gain access to Santa Rita jail in Alameda County, especially to investigate allegedly shocking conditions in the Greystone portion of the jail. After the suit was filed, Sheriff Houchins modified his "no-access" policy of barring the general public and the media from Santa Rita and launched a monthly tour program limited to groups of 25 persons. Those on the tour were not permitted to take photographs or interview inmates. The lower federal court awarded KQED preliminary relief, giving the news media access to Santa Rita, including Greystone, "at reasonable times and hours" and authorizing inmate interviews and the use of photographic and sound equipment. Chief Justice Burger's opinion found that preliminary injunction wholly unjustified; Justice Ste-

Chief Justice BURGER's opinion viewed the case as governed by Pell and Saxbe and found "no discernible basis for a constitutional duty to disclose, or for standards governing disclosure of or access to [governmental] information. [Until] the political branches decree otherwise, [the media have] no right of special access to the [jail] different from or greater than that accorded the public generally." Justice STEVENS' dissent insisted that Pell was distinguishable because in Pell there had been "substantial press and public access" to the jail: there, the rejected media claim asserted the additional right "to interview specifically designated inmates"; but the Pell ruling was no basis for upholding the general "no access" policy that prevailed at the jail at the time KQED brought suit. He asserted that "the Court has never intimated that a nondiscriminatory policy of excluding entirely both the public and the press from access to information about prison conditions would avoid constitutional scrutiny. Indeed, Pell itself strongly suggests the contrary." He stated that "the probable existence of a constitutional violation rested upon the special importance of allowing a democratic community access to knowledge about how its servants were treating [prisoners]." He added: "[E]ven though the Constitution provides the press with no greater right of access to information than that possessed by the public at large, a preliminary injunction is not invalid simply because it awards special relief to a successful litigant which is a representative of the press." In elaborating the constitutional premises for that decision, he put special emphasis on the belief that "information-gathering is entitled to some measure of constitutional protection. [Without] some protection for the acquisition of information about the operation of public institutions such as prisons by the public at large, the process of self-governance contemplated by the Framers would be stripped of its substance." That conclusion stemmed from both the First Amendment right to "receipt of information and ideas" and the "essential societal function" of the First Amendment in promoting self-government. KQED, accordingly, should prevail in his view not because of any special press privilege but as an advocate of "the public's right to be informed." [2]

Justice STEWART's decisive concurrence agreed with the Chief Justice's basic premises that the press had no special access rights, stating: "The Constitution does no more than assure the public and the press equal access once government has opened its doors." But he differed from the Chief Justice in applying those principles here: "Whereas [Chief Justice Burger] appears to view 'equal access' as meaning access that is identical in all respects, I believe that the concept of equal access must be accorded more flexibility in order to accommodate the practical distinctions between the press and the general public." That "practical accommodations" approach permitted him to find a basis for limited relief for KQED. Emphasizing the "critical role played by the press in American society," he explained: "[T]erms of access that are reasonably imposed on individual members of the public may, if they impede effective reporting without sufficient justification, be unreasonable as applied to journal-

vens' dissent supported the entire order; Justice Stewart's decisive "concurring" position found the order proper in part, as noted in the text.

2. Justice Stevens emphasized, however, that the access claim he recognized here did not apply to all governmental operations. The "right to be informed" about prison conditions, he suggested, was narrower than access claims pertaining to "the operation of most governmental activity. Such matters involve questions of policy which generally must be resolved by the political branches. [Moreover], there are unquestionably occasions when governmental activity may prop-

erly be carried on in complete secrecy. [In] such situations the reasons for withholding information from the public are both apparent and legitimate. In this case, however, [the claimants] 'do not assert a right to a forced disclosure of confidential information or to invade in any way the decisionmaking processes of governmental officials.' They simply seek an end to [the Sheriff's] policy of concealing prison conditions from the public. Those conditions are wholly without claim to confidentiality. [T]here is no legitimate, penological justification for concealing from citizens the conditions [in jails]."

ists who are there to convey to the general public what the visitors see."
Accordingly, the First Amendment "required the Sheriff to give members of the
press *effective* access" to all areas open to the public. Simply permitting reporters
to sign up for the monthly tours "on the same terms as the public" was
inadequate "as a matter of constitutional law." Accordingly, the trial court's
order permitting press access "on a more flexible and frequent basis than
scheduled monthly tours" was justified in order "to keep the public informed,"
as was the order permitting the media to bring cameras and recording equipment into the jail. (However, Justice Stewart found the preliminary injunction
overbroad in authorizing press access to the closed Greystone area and in
permitting interviews of randomly encountered inmates. Those aspects of the
injunction "gave the press access to areas and sources of information from which
persons on the public tours had been excluded, and thus enlarged the scope of
what [was] opened to public view.")[3]

ACCESS TO COURTROOM PROCEEDINGS: CLOSURE ORDERS

In GANNETT CO. v. DePASQUALE, 443 U.S. 368 (1979), a divided
Court rejected a newspaper publisher's attack on an order barring the public,
including the press, from a pretrial hearing on suppression of evidence in a
murder case. The prevailing opinion held that the press and the public had no
independent constitutional right to insist upon access to such pretrial proceedings when the accused, the prosecutor, and the trial judge all had agreed to
close the hearing in order to assure a fair trial. Although the Justices focused
primarily on the Sixth Amendment provision that, in "all criminal prosecutions,
the accused shall enjoy the right to [a] public trial," some comments on First
Amendment issues surfaced in most of the opinions. All of the Justices agreed
that the problem here was distinguishable from that in Nebraska Press (p. 1427
above), since the issue here was "not one of prior restraint on the press but,
[rather], one of *access* to a judicial proceeding." Although Justice Stewart spoke
for the majority, an understanding of the implications of the holding also
requires careful attention to the concurring opinions of Justices Powell and
Rehnquist, who placed their own, contrasting glosses on the majority opinion
that they joined.

Justice STEWART conceded that the Sixth Amendment's public trial guarantee reflected not only defendants' interests: there was also "an independent
public interest" in its enforcement. But he argued that "our adversary system
of criminal justice is premised upon the proposition that the public interest is
fully protected by the participants of the litigation," who had agreed to the
closure order here. He found nothing in the structure, text or history of the
Sixth Amendment to support "any correlative right in members of the public to
insist upon a public trial." Only after canvassing the Sixth Amendment
concerns at length did Justice Stewart turn briefly to the claim of a First
Amendment right of access. He found it unnecessary to decide whether there
was any First Amendment right to attend criminal trials: "[E]ven assuming,
arguendo, that the [First Amendment] may guarantee such access in some
situations, a question we do not decide, this putative right was given all
appropriate deference by the [trial judge] in the present case."[1]

---

3. Is Justice Stewart's position internally consistent? Does not access by the press "on a more
flexible and frequent basis than scheduled monthly tours," "at reasonable times and hours," provide the media *broader* access than that available
to the general public? Recall the consideration

of "equal access" vs. "assured minimum access"
claims in "public forum" contexts, in sec. 4 of
the preceding chapter.

1. In finding that "appropriate deference," he
noted that none of the spectators in the court-

Justice POWELL's concurring opinion considered the First Amendment issue more fully and concluded: "Because of the importance of the public's having accurate information concerning the operation of its criminal justice system, I would hold explicitly that petitioner's reporter had an interest protected by the [First Amendment] in being present at the pretrial suppression hearing." He relied on the approach of his dissent in Saxbe. He recognized, however, that the First Amendment right of access to courtroom proceedings was not absolute: "It is limited both by the constitutional right of defendants to a fair trial and by the needs of government to obtain just convictions and to preserve the confidentiality of sensitive information and the identity of informants." To assure adequate protection of First Amendment interests, he insisted, the Court should "identify for the guidance of trial courts the constitutional standard by which they are to judge whether closure is justified, and the minimal procedure by which this standard is to be applied." He thought a "strictly and inescapably necessary" standard for closure (see Justice Blackmun's dissent, below) too inflexible and too insensitive to the defendant's fair trial right. Instead, he argued for "a more flexible accommodation," recalling his concurrence in Branzburg. He accordingly concluded that the question for a trial court considering a closure motion at a pretrial suppression hearing "is whether a fair trial for the defendant is likely to be jeopardized by publicity." He added: "Although the strict standard of Nebraska Press is not applicable to decisions concerning closure of courtroom proceedings, much of the discussion in that case of the factors to be considered in making decisions with respect to 'gag orders' is relevant to closure decisions." [2] Justice REHNQUIST's concurring opinion took a far narrower view of the First Amendment. He stated: "Despite the Court's seeming reservation of the [question], it is clear that this Court repeatedly has held that there is no First Amendment right of access in the public or the press to judicial or other governmental proceedings." In his view, the Court had "emphatically" rejected Justice Powell's view "that the First Amendment is some sort of constitutional 'sunshine law' that requires notice, an opportunity to be heard and substantial reasons before a governmental proceeding may be closed to the public and press." [3]

Justice BLACKMUN's partial dissent, joined by Justices Brennan, White and Marshall, emphasized (as had Justice Stewart) the Sixth Amendment rather than the First. He derived a public right of access from the Sixth Amendment and lamented the majority's "unfortunate" decision: "The result is that the important interests of the public and the press (as a part of that public) in open judicial proceedings are rejected and cast aside as of little value or significance." He argued that states could not exclude the public "from a proceeding within the ambit of the Sixth Amendment's guarantee without affording full and fair consideration to the public's interest in maintaining an open proceeding." Emphasizing the "societal interest in the public trial that exists separately from,

---

room, including Gannett's reporter, had objected when the defendants made their closure motion; that counsel for Gannett was nevertheless given a later opportunity to object to closure; that the trial judge had acknowledged a First Amendment access interest, but had concluded that it was outweighed by the defendants' right to a fair trial in this case; and that denial of access here was in any event "not absolute but only temporary," since the lower court made available a transcript of the suppression hearing after the alleged danger of prejudice had dissipated.

2. Applying his standards, Justice Powell found that the First Amendment right of access had been "adequately respected" by the trial judge in this case.

3. Justice Rehnquist also sought to put his gloss on the Sixth Amendment aspects of the Gannett holding. He stated that, "since the Court holds that the public does not have *any* Sixth Amendment rights of access to such proceedings, it necessarily follows that if the parties agree on a closed proceeding, the trial court is not required by the Sixth Amendment to advance any reason whatsoever for declining to open a pretrial hearing or trial to the public." (But see a separate concurring notation by Chief Justice BURGER: he joined the majority with a special emphasis on the fact that this case involved "not a *trial*" but a "*pre*trial hearing.")

and at times in opposition to, the interests of the accused," he argued that a court may not give effect to "an accused's attempt to waive his public trial right" in all circumstances: "[The] public trial interest cannot adequately be protected by the prosecutor and judge in conjunction, or connivance, with the defendant." Justice Blackmun recognized, however, that "the publication of information learned in an open proceeding may harm irreparably, under certain circumstances, the ability of the defendant to obtain a fair trial." He proceeded to delineate guidelines under which trial judges would be permitted to make "limited exceptions to the principle of publicity where necessary to protect some other interest [e.g., fair trials]." [4]

THE NEWLY RECOGNIZED ACCESS RIGHT: HOW BROAD A RIGHT TO OBTAIN "NEWSWORTHY MATTER"?

1. *Richmond Newspapers.* A year after Gannett, the 7 to 1 decision in RICHMOND NEWSPAPERS, INC. v. VIRGINIA, 448 U.S. 555 (1980), held that, "[a]bsent an overriding interest articulated in findings, the trial of a criminal case must be open to the public." [1] Justice Stevens' separate opinion stated that this was the first square holding "that the acquisition of newsworthy matter is entitled to any constitutional protection whatsoever": "Today, [for] the first time, the Court unequivocally holds that an arbitrary interference with access to important information is an abridgment of the freedoms of speech and of the press protected by the First Amendment." Is Justice Stevens' description of the decision as a "watershed case" persuasive? How broad an access claim *does* the ruling support? To what extent should it extend beyond criminal trials to other governmental information and proceedings?

Chief Justice BURGER's opinion announcing the judgment (joined by Justices White and Stevens) stated that the "narrow question" was "whether the right of the public and press to attend criminal trials is guaranteed under [the] Constitution." In answering that question in the affirmative, he emphasized that Gannett had focused on the Sixth Amendment and had involved pretrial proceedings, so that this case was the first to raise the issue "whether a criminal trial itself may be closed to the public upon the unopposed request of a defendant, without any demonstration that closure is required to protect the defendant's superior right to a fair trial, or that some other overriding consideration requires closure." After reviewing the historical practice of having trials

---

4. Justice Blackmun, like Justice Stewart, paid little separate attention to the First Amendment. He merely noted that "this Court heretofore has not found and does not today find any First Amendment right of access to judicial or other governmental proceedings." And he saw no need to reach the First Amendment access issue here, since the media petitioner had ample support for its claim under the Sixth Amendment.

In the months after Gannett in 1979, an unusual number of Justices made public comments suggesting that, contrary to Justice Rehnquist's position, Gannett did *not* confer blanket authority to close all pretrial and trial proceedings where the participants to the litigation consented. Soon after, in Richmond Newspapers (1980), which follows in note 1—involving a criminal trial rather than pretrial hearings—the Court emphasized the First, not the Sixth, Amendment, in granting press access. And in a number of subsequent cases which follow in note 2 below,

the Court expanded the First Amendment right announced in Richmond Newspapers. But in Waller v. Georgia, 467 U.S. ___ (1984), the Court relied once again on the Sixth Amendment when it returned to the pretrial setting. Justice Powell's opinion for a unanimous Court held that the Sixth Amendment does indeed require opening of pretrial suppression hearings unless, as in Gannett, the defendant consents. Only in "rare" circumstances would closure be permitted in the face of a defendant's Sixth Amendment claim; and in determining when those "rare" circumstances existed, the standards set forth in Press-Enterprise (a First Amendment case in 1984, Note 2b below) should govern.

1. Each of the seven members of the majority submitted a separate statement of his views. Justice Rehnquist was the sole dissenter. Justice Powell, the author of the earlier "right of access" opinions in the jails and courtroom contexts, did not participate in the case.

"open to all who cared to observe," he concluded that, when the Constitution was adopted, "criminal trials both here and in England had long been presumptively open." He noted the "nexus between openness, fairness, and the perception of fairness" and commented: "To work effectively, it is important that society's criminal process 'satisfy the appearance of justice,' and the appearance of justice can best be provided by allowing people to observe it." Although attendance at trials "is no longer a wide-spread pastime," that merely validated "the media claim of functioning as surrogates for the public" in the modern context. The "unbroken, uncontradicted history" supported his conclusion that "a presumption of openness inheres in the very nature of a criminal trial under our system of justice."

Turning to the constitutional sources for an access claim not explicitly guaranteed, he concluded that "the right to attend criminal trials is implicit in the guarantees of the First Amendment."[2] In reaching that conclusion, he discussed the interrelationship of several provisions of the First Amendment, and the relevance of the Ninth Amendment as well. The First Amendment protections of speech, press, and the right to assemble "share a common core purpose of assuring freedom of communication on matters relating to the functioning of government. Plainly it would be difficult to single out any aspect of government of higher concern and importance to the people than the manner in which criminal trials are conducted." Accordingly, the First Amendment could be read "as protecting the right of everyone to attend trials so as to give meaning to those explicit guarantees"; thus, "the First Amendment guarantees of speech and press, standing alone, prohibit government from summarily closing courtroom doors." He added: "It is not crucial whether we describe this right to attend criminal trials to hear, see, and communicate observations concerning them as a 'right of access' [cf. Justice Powell in Gannett and in the Saxbe and Pell cases][3] or a 'right to gather information,' for we have recognized that 'without some protection for seeking out the news, freedom of the press could be eviscerated.' Branzburg v. Hayes. The explicit, guaranteed rights to speak and to publish concerning what takes place at a trial would lose much meaning if access to observe the trial could [be] foreclosed arbitrarily."

The Chief Justice noted that the First Amendment right of assembly, not only the guarantees of speech or the press, was also relevant to the "right of access to places traditionally open to the public, as criminal trials have long been." He noted that the right of assembly was in part "a catalyst to augment the free exercise of the other First Amendment rights" and that, "[s]ubject to the traditional time, place, and manner restrictions, streets, sidewalks, and parks are places traditionally open, where First Amendment rights may be exercised; a trial courtroom also is a public place where the people generally—and representatives of the media—have a right to be present, and where their presence historically has been thought to enhance the integrity and quality of what takes place." The Chief Justice conceded that, despite these relevant provisions, the Constitution did not spell out a "right of the public to attend trials." But he noted that this had not "precluded recognition of important rights not enumerated": "Notwithstanding the appropriate caution against reading into the Constitution rights not explicitly defined, the Court has acknowledged that certain unarticulated rights are implicit in enumerated guarantees. For example, the rights of association and of privacy [as well as] the

2. He added in a footnote: "Whether the public has a right to attend trials of civil cases is a question not raised by this case, but we note that historically both civil and criminal trials have been presumptively open."

3. In a footnote, the Chief Justice noted that the Pell and Saxbe cases were "distinguishable in

the sense that they were concerned with penal institutions which, by definition, are not 'open' or public places. Penal institutions do not share the long tradition of openness." He added: "See also Greer v. Spock [p. 1252 above] (military bases)."

right to travel appear nowhere in the Constitution or Bill of Rights. Yet these important but unarticulated rights have nonetheless been found to share constitutional protection in common with explicit guarantees." [He noted that the Ninth Amendment had been adopted "to allay the fears of those who were concerned that expressing certain guarantees could be read as excluding others."] In short, "fundamental rights, even though not expressly guaranteed, have been recognized by the Court as indispensable to the enjoyment of rights explicitly defined," and "the right to attend criminal trials" could accordingly be found "implicit in the guarantees of the First Amendment." [4]

Justice STEVENS, who joined the Chief Justice's opinion, also submitted a separate concurrence emphasizing the "watershed" nature of this case, as noted in the introductory paragraph above. He viewed the Court as recognizing a broad right of access to "newsworthy matter" and suggested that this was an adoption by the majority of the positions advanced by Justice Powell in Saxbe and by Justice Stevens in Houchins. He concluded that, for his reasons in the Houchins opinion "as well as those stated by The Chief Justice today, I agree that the First Amendment protects the public and the press from abridgment of their rights of access to information about the operation of their government, including the Judicial Branch; given the total absence of any record justification for the closure order entered in this case, that order violated the First Amendment." In a lengthy opinion concurring in the judgment, Justice BRENNAN, joined by Justice Marshall, stated: "Because I believe that the First Amendment [secures a] public right of access [to trial proceedings], I agree with those of my Brethren who hold that, without more, agreement of the trial judge and the parties cannot constitutionally close a trial to the public." He argued that the prior decisions had *not* "ruled out a public access component to the First Amendment in every circumstance," but had held only that "any privilege of access to governmental information is subject to a degree of restraint dictated by the nature of the information and countervailing interests in security or confidentiality."

In developing his First Amendment approach, Justice Brennan relied in part on his "Address," 32 Rutgers L.Rev. 173 (1979). He argued that "the First Amendment embodies more than a commitment to free expression and communicative interchange for their own sakes; it has a *structural* role to play in securing and fostering our republican system of self-government. Implicit in this structural role is not only 'the principle that debate on public issues should

---

4. The Chief Justice's evaluation of the facts of the case was very brief. The trial judge had closed the criminal trial—the defendant's fourth trial on a murder charge—relying on his broad discretion under Virginia law. The defendant had requested the closure; the prosecution had not objected. The trial judge made no findings to support closure, nor any inquiry "as to whether alternative solutions would have met the need to ensure fairness; there was no recognition of any right under the Constitution for the public or press to attend the trial." Various "tested alternatives" to assure fairness were available: e.g., any problems with witnesses could presumably have been dealt with by their exclusion from the courtroom or their sequestration during the trial. "All of the alternatives admittedly present difficulties for trial courts, but none of the factors relied on here was beyond the realm of the manageable." Thus, "[a]bsent an overriding interest articulated in findings," there was no justification for closing the criminal trial here. [The Chief Justice added in a footnote: "We have no

occasion here to define the circumstances in which all or parts of a criminal trial may be closed to the public, but our holding today does not mean that the First Amendment rights of the public and representatives of the press are absolute." A trial judge could impose "reasonable limitations on access to a trial" in the interests of the fair administration of justice. "It is far more important that trials be conducted in a quiet and orderly setting than it is to preserve that atmosphere on city streets. Moreover, since courtrooms have limited capacity, there may be occasions when not every person who wishes to attend can be accommodated. In such situations, reasonable restrictions on general access are traditionally imposed, including preferential seating for media representatives."] In a brief separate statement Justice WHITE, who joined the Chief Justice's opinion, noted that this decision would have been unnecessary if the majority had adopted the dissent's Sixth Amendment position in Gannett.

be uninhibited, robust, and wide open,' but the antecedent assumption that valuable public debate [must] be informed.[5] The structural model links the First Amendment to that process of communication necessary for a democracy to survive, and thus entails solicitude not only for communication itself, but for the indispensable conditions of meaningful communication." He added, however: "[B]ecause 'the stretch of this protection is theoretically endless,' it must be invoked with discrimination and temperance. [An] assertion of the prerogative to gather information must accordingly be assayed by considering the information sought and the opposing interests invaded. This judicial task is as much a matter of sensitivity to practical necessities as it is of abstract reasoning. But at least two helpful principles may be sketched. First, the case for a right of access has special force when drawn from an enduring and vital tradition of public entree to particular proceedings or information. [Second], the value of access must be measured in specifics. Analysis is not advanced by rhetorical statements that all information bears upon public issues; what is crucial in individual cases is whether access to a particular government process is important in terms of that very process. To resolve the case before us, therefore, we must consult historical and current practice with respect to open trials, and weigh the importance of public access to the trial process itself." [6]

Applying that approach, he found, perusing materials similar to those relied on by the Chief Justice, that, "[a]s a matter of law and virtually immemorial custom, public trials have been the essentially unwavering rule in ancestral England and in our own Nation." Moreover, publicity served several "particular purposes" of the judicial process. He noted, for example, that a trial "plays a pivotal role in the entire judicial process, and, by extension, in our form of government. Under our system, judges are not mere umpires, but, in their own sphere, lawmakers—a coordinate branch of *government*. [Thus], so far as the trial is the mechanism for judicial factfinding, as well as the initial forum for legal decisionmaking, it is a genuine governmental proceeding. It follows that the conduct of the trial is preeminently a matter of public interest. [Popular] attendance at trials, in sum, substantially furthers the particular public purposes of that critical judicial proceeding. In that sense, public access is an indispensable element of the trial process itself." He accordingly concluded: "[Our] ingrained tradition of public trials and the importance of public access to the broader purposes of the trial process, tip the balance strongly toward the rule that trials be open. What countervailing interest might be sufficiently compelling to reverse this presumption of openness need not concern us now,[7] for the statute at stake here authorizes trial closures at the unfettered discretion of the judge and parties."

A separate opinion by Justice STEWART concurring in the judgment emphasized that Gannett had left open the First Amendment issues reached here and concluded: "Whatever the ultimate answer to [the First Amendment] question may be with respect to pretrial suppression hearings in criminal cases, the [First Amendment] clearly give[s] the press and the public a right of access to trials themselves, civil as well as criminal. [With] us, a trial is by very definition a proceeding open to the press and to the public. In conspicuous

---

5. He noted that this idea had been foreshadowed in Justice Powell's dissent in Saxbe.

6. In a footnote, Justice Brennan noted: "A conceptually separate, yet related, question is whether the media should enjoy greater access rights than the general public. But no such contention is at stake here. Since the media's right of access is at least equal to that of the general public, this case is resolved by a decision that the state statute unconstitutionally restricts public access to trials. As a practical matter,

however, the institutional press is the likely, and fitting, chief beneficiary of a right of access because it serves as the 'agent' of interested citizens, and funnels information about trials to a large number of individuals."

7. Justice Brennan added in a footnote at this point: "For example, national security concerns about confidentiality may sometimes warrant closures during sensitive portions of trial proceedings, such as testimony about state secrets."

contrast to a military base, a jail, or a prison, a trial courtroom is a public place. Even more than city streets, sidewalks, and parks as areas of traditional First Amendment activity, a trial courtroom is a place where representatives of the press and of the public are not only free to be, but where their presence serves to assure the integrity of what goes on." [8] He added, however, that the access right was not "absolute": "Just as a legislature may impose reasonable time, place and manner [restrictions], so may a trial judge impose reasonable limitations upon the unrestricted occupation of a courtroom. [Much] more than a city street, a trial courtroom must be a quiet and orderly place. Moreover, every courtroom has a finite physical capacity, and there may be occasions when not all who wish to attend a trial may do so.[9] And while there exist many alternative ways to satisfy the constitutional demands of a fair trial, those demands may also sometimes justify limitations upon the unrestricted presence of spectators in the courtroom." Here, reversal was in order because "the trial judge appears to have given no recognition to the right of representatives of the press and members of the public to be present at [the] murder trial."

In still another opinion concurring in the judgment, Justice BLACKMUN reiterated his Sixth Amendment position in Gannett and went beyond: "[W]ith the Sixth Amendment set to one side in this case, I am driven to conclude, as a secondary position, that the First Amendment must provide some measure of protection for public access to the trial. [It] is clear and obvious to me, on the approach the Court has chosen to take, that, by closing this criminal trial, the trial judge abridged [the] First Amendment interests of the public." [10] Justice REHNQUIST, the sole dissenter, adhered to his position in Gannett and commented more generally: "[To] gradually rein in, as this Court has done over the past generation, all of the ultimate decisionmaking power over how justice shall be administered, not merely in the federal system but in each of 50 States, is a task that no Court consisting of nine persons, however gifted, is equal to. [However] high minded the impulses which originally spawned this trend may have been, [it] is basically unhealthy to have so much authority concentrated in a small group of lawyers who have been appointed to the Supreme Court and enjoy virtual life tenure." He found nothing in the First, Sixth, or Ninth Amendments, or in any other constitutional provision, to prohibit what the state trial judge had done in this case.

2. *The scope of Richmond Newspapers.* a. In GLOBE NEWSPAPER CO. v. SUPERIOR COURT, 457 U.S. 596 (1982), the Court explored the bases and implications of Richmond Newspapers. In Globe, unlike Richmond Newspapers, a majority of the Justices managed to agree on an opinion for the Court. The majority concluded that the First Amendment had been violated by a Massachusetts law which had been construed to *require* the exclusion of the press and the general public from the courtroom during the testimony of a minor who had allegedly been a victim of a sex offense. The case arose when the Boston Globe unsuccessfully sought access to a state court trial where the defendant had been charged with the rape of three girls who were minors. In upholding the State's mandatory closure rule, the highest state court had distinguished Rich-

---

8. Contrast Justice Stewart's opposition to an affirmative First Amendment access right in his opinions and extrajudicial comments during the 1970s, as noted earlier.

9. Justice Stewart added in a footnote: "In such situations representatives of the press must be assured access. Houchins (concurring opinion)."

10. Justice Blackmun expressed some reservations about the Chief Justice's "veritable potpourri" of constitutional sources. He thought the reliance on various clauses of the First

Amendment, the Ninth Amendment, and "a cluster of penumbral guarantees" "troublesome," noting that "uncertainty marks the nature—and strictness—of the standard of closure the Court adopts."

For comments on the implications of Richmond Newspapers, see, e.g., Cox, "Freedom of Expression in the Burger Court," 94 Harv.L.Rev. 1 (1980), and Lewis, "A Public Right to Know About Public Institutions: The First Amendment as Sword," 1980 Sup.Ct.Rev. 1.

mond Newspapers by emphasizing "at least one notable exception" to the tradition of "openness" in criminal trials: "cases involving sexual assault." The mandatory closure law accordingly operated "in an area of traditional sensitivity to the needs of victims."

Justice BRENNAN, writing for the majority, found the law invalid under the principles of Richmond Newspapers. In his view, Richmond Newspapers "firmly established for the first time that the press and general public have a constitutional right of access to criminal trials," even though no such right was "explicitly mentioned [in] the First Amendment." He added: "The First Amendment [is] broad enough to encompass those rights that, while not unambiguously enumerated in the very terms of the Amendment, are nonetheless necessary to the enjoyment of other First Amendment rights." Protecting "the free discussion of governmental affairs" was a major purpose of the Amendment; offering such protection served "to ensure that the individual citizen can effectively participate in and contribute to our republican system of self-government." A "right of access to *criminal trials*" was properly afforded by the First Amendment [11] because "the criminal trial historically has been open to the press and general public" and because "the right of access to criminal trials plays a particularly significant role in the functioning of the judicial process and the government as a whole." He noted that "the institutional value of the open criminal trial is recognized in both logic and experience." This constitutional right of access, though not "absolute," was entitled to protection unless the State showed "that the denial [of access] is necessitated by a compelling governmental interest, and is narrowly tailored to serve that interest." [12] Massachusetts' defense of its law could not survive that strict scrutiny.

Justice Brennan conceded that the first of the two interests put forth by the state—protecting the physical and psychological well-being of minor victims of sex crimes from further trauma and embarrassment—was "a compelling one." But the closure law was not "a narrowly tailored means of accommodating the State's asserted interest: That interest could be served just as well by requiring the trial court to determine on a case-by-case basis whether the State's legitimate concern for the well-being of the minor victim necessitates closure. Such an approach ensures that the constitutional right of the press and public to gain access to criminal trials will not be restricted except where necessary to protect the State's interest." [13] Nor could the closure law be sustained on the basis of the State's second asserted interest—"the encouragement of minor victims of sex crimes to come forward and provide accurate testimony." In rejecting that argument, Justice Brennan stated: "Not only is the claim speculative in empirical terms, but it is also open to serious question as a matter of logic and common sense. Although [the law] bars the press and general public from the court-

---

11. Justice Brennan devoted only a footnote to rejecting the argument advanced by the state court, that criminal trials have *not* traditionally been open during the testimony of minors who were sex victims: "Even if appellee is correct in this regard, the argument is unavailing. In Richmond Newspapers, the Court discerned a First Amendment right of access to *criminal trials* based in part on the recognition that as a general matter criminal trials have long been presumptively open. Whether the First Amendment right of access to criminal trials can be restricted in the context of any particular criminal trial, such as a murder trial (the setting for the dispute in Richmond Newspapers) or a rape trial, depends not on the historical openness of that type of criminal trial but rather on the state interests assertedly supporting the restriction."

12. "Of course, limitations on the right of access that resemble 'time, place, and manner' restrictions on protected speech would not be subjected to such strict scrutiny." [Footnote by Justice Brennan.]

13. Justice Brennan elaborated the required "case-by-case" approach only briefly: "Among the factors to be weighed [by a trial court seeking to determine whether closure is necessary to protect the welfare of a victim] are the minor victim's age, psychological maturity, and understanding, the nature of the crime, the desires of the victim, and the interests of parents and relatives."

room during the testimony of minor sex victims, the press is not denied access to the transcript, court personnel, or any other possible source that could provide an account of the minor victim's testimony. Thus, [the law] cannot prevent the press from publicizing the substance of a minor victim's testimony, as well as his or her identity. If [the State's] interest in encouraging minor victims to come forward depends on keeping such matters secret, [the law] hardly advances that interest in an effective manner. And even if [the law] effectively advanced the State's interest, it is doubtful that the interest would be sufficient to overcome the constitutional attack, for that same interest could be relied on to support an array of mandatory-closure rules designed to encourage victims to come forward: Surely it cannot be suggested that minor victims of sex crimes are the *only* crime victims who, because of publicity, [are] reluctant to come forward and testify. The State's argument based on this interest therefore proves too much, and runs contrary to the very foundation of the right of access recognized in Richmond Newspapers.'' [14]

Chief Justice BURGER, joined by Justice Rehnquist, were the only members of the Court to dissent on the merits.[15] The Chief Justice disagreed with the majority's ''expansive interpretation'' of Richmond Newspapers and ''its cavalier rejection of the serious interests supporting Massachusetts' mandatory closure rule.'' He thought the ruling ''advance[d] a disturbing paradox'': ''Although states are permitted, for example, to mandate the closure of all proceedings in order to protect a 17-year-old charged with rape, they are not permitted to require the closing of part of criminal proceedings in order to protect an innocent child who has been raped or otherwise sexually abused.'' He claimed that Richmond Newspapers had *not* established ''a First Amendment right of access to all aspects of all criminal trials under all circumstances.'' Although Richmond Newspapers had emphasized the traditional openness of criminal trials in general, there was ''clearly a long history of exclusion of the public from trials involving sexual assaults, particularly those against minors. [It] would misrepresent the historical record to state that there is an 'unbroken, uncontradicted history' of open proceedings in cases involving the sexual abuse of minors''; and such a specific ''history of openness'' was necessary to invoke Richmond Newspapers.

The Chief Justice also found the majority's ''wooden application'' of strict scrutiny ''inappropriate.'' He emphasized: ''Neither the purpose of the law nor its effect is primarily to deny the press or public access to information; the verbatim transcript is made available to the public and the media and may be used without limit. We therefore need only examine whether the restrictions imposed are reasonable and whether the interests of the [State] override the very limited incidental effects of the law on First Amendment rights.'' To him, it seemed ''beyond doubt, considering the minimal impact of the law on First Amendment rights and the overriding weight of the [State's] interest in

14. In a concluding footnote, Justice Brennan summarized the holding as follows: ''We emphasize that our holding is a narrow one: that a rule of mandatory closure respecting the testimony of minor sex victims is constitutionally infirm. In individual cases, and under appropriate circumstances, the First Amendment does not necessarily stand as a bar to the exclusion from the courtroom of the press and general public during the testimony of minor sex-offense victims. But a mandatory rule, requiring no particularized determinations in individual cases, is unconstitutional.''

Justice O'CONNOR concurred only in the judgment. She stated that she did not interpret Richmond Newspapers ''to shelter every right that is 'necessary to the enjoyment of other First Amendment rights.' Instead, Richmond Newspapers rests upon our long history of open criminal trials and the special value, for both public and accused, of that openness. [Thus] I interpret neither Richmond Newspapers nor [today's decision] to carry any implications outside the context of criminal trials.''

15. Justice STEVENS dissented on the ground that the case should have been dismissed for mootness. He charged the majority with rendering an ''advisory, hypothetical, and, at best, premature'' opinion.

protecting child rape victims, that the Massachusetts law is not unconstitutional. [The] law need not be precisely tailored so long as the state's interest overrides the law's impact on First Amendment rights and the restrictions imposed further that interest. Certainly this [law] rationally serves the [State's] overriding interest in protecting the child [from] severe—possibly permanent—psychological damage." Moreover, there was adequate justification for making the law mandatory rather than discretionary: "[V]ictims and their families are entitled to assurance [of] protection. The legislature did not act irrationally in deciding not to leave the closure determination to the idiosyncracies of individual judges subject to the pressures available to the media." He concluded: "Many will find it difficult to reconcile the concern so often expressed for the rights of the accused with the callous indifference exhibited today for children who, having suffered the trauma of rape or other sexual abuse, are denied the modest protection the Massachusetts legislature provided."

    b. In another broad interpretation of Richmond Newspapers, the Court in PRESS–ENTERPRISE CO. v. SUPERIOR COURT, 464 U.S. 501 (1984), held Richmond Newspapers applicable to voir dire examination of prospective jurors in a criminal trial—in this instance, a trial involving charges of rape and murder of a teenage girl. Chief Justice BURGER's opinion for the Court rejected a generalized interest in protecting the privacy of prospective jurors, relying extensively on history to show that public jury selection has long been an integral part of public trials. As in both Richmond Newspapers and Globe, however, the Court did not hold the right of public access to this facet of a trial to be absolute: "Closed proceedings, although not absolutely precluded, must be rare and only for cause shown that outweighs the value of openness." He elaborated: "The presumption of openness may be overcome only by an overriding interest based on findings that closure is essential to preserve higher values and is narrowly tailored to serve that interest. The interest is to be articulated along with findings specific enough that a reviewing court can determine whether the closure order was properly entered."

    The Chief Justice found this standard unmet in this case, especially in light of the trial court's failure to consider alternatives to closure to protect the privacy of prospective jurors. And he suggested a specific alternative: "The jury selection process may, in some circumstances, give rise to a compelling interest of a prospective juror when interrogation touches on deeply personal [matters]. For example a prospective juror might privately inform the judge that she, or a member of her family, had been raped but had declined to seek prosecution because of the embarrassment and emotional trauma from the very disclosure of the [episode]. By requiring the prospective juror to make an affirmative request, the trial judge can ensure that there is in fact a valid basis for a belief that disclosure infringes a significant interest in privacy." [16]

---

16. Justice BLACKMUN's concurring opinion expressed some reservations about the extent of the privacy right in jurors recognized by the majority. But Justice STEVENS, in another concurring opinion, expressed the view, consistent with many of his other First Amendment opinions, that inquiry into the content of the questions and answers was an entirely appropriate way of determining the extent of the right of access. Justice MARSHALL concurred only in the judgment, arguing that the majority opinion would still permit closure too readily. For him, only "the most extraordinary circumstances" should be allowed to interfere with scrutiny of voir dire examinations by the public and the press.

D. LAWS SINGLING OUT THE PRESS FOR SPECIAL TREATMENT

MINNEAPOLIS STAR v. MINNESOTA COMM'R OF REV.

460 U.S. 575, 103 S.Ct. 1365, 75 L.Ed.2d 295 (1983).

Justice O'CONNOR delivered the opinion of the Court.

This case presents the question of a State's power to impose a special tax on the press and, by enacting exemptions, to limit its effect to only a few newspapers.

I. Since 1967, Minnesota has imposed a sales tax on most sales of goods. In general, the tax applies only to retail sales. [As] part of this general system of taxation and in support of the sales tax, Minnesota also enacted a tax on the "privilege of using, storing or consuming in Minnesota tangible personal property." This use tax applies to any nonexempt tangible personal property unless the sales tax was paid on the sales price. Like the classic use tax, this use tax protects the State's sales tax by eliminating the residents' incentive to travel to States with lower sales taxes to buy goods rather than buying them in Minnesota.

The appellant, Minneapolis Star & Tribune Company, "Star Tribune," is the publisher of a morning [and] an evening newspaper (until 1982) in Minneapolis. From 1967 until 1971, it enjoyed an exemption from the sales and use tax provided by Minnesota for periodic publications. In 1971, however, while leaving the exemption from the sales tax in place, the legislature amended the scheme to impose a "use tax" on the cost of paper and ink products consumed in the production of a publication. Ink and paper used in publications became the only items subject to the use tax that were components of goods to be sold at retail. In 1974, the legislature again amended the statute, this time to exempt the first $100,000 worth of ink and paper consumed by a publication in any calendar year, in effect giving each publication an annual tax credit of $4,000. Publications remained exempt from the sales tax. After the enactment of the $100,000 exemption, 11 publishers, producing 14 of the 388 paid circulation newspapers in the State, incurred a tax liability in 1974. Star Tribune was one of the 11, and, of the $893,355 collected, it paid $608,634, or roughly two-thirds of the total revenue raised by the tax. In 1975, 13 publishers, producing 16 out of 374 paid circulation papers, paid a tax. That year, Star Tribune again bore roughly two-thirds of the total receipts from the use tax on ink and paper.

Star Tribune instituted this action to seek a refund of the use taxes it paid from January 1, 1974 to May 31, 1975. It challenged the imposition of the use tax on ink and paper used in publication as a violation of the guarantees of freedom of the press and [equal protection]. The Minnesota Supreme Court upheld the [tax].

II. Star Tribune argues that we must strike this tax on the authority of Grosjean v. American Press Co., 297 U.S. 233 (1936). Although there are similarities, [we] agree with the State that Grosjean is not controlling. In Grosjean, [Louisiana] imposed a license tax of 2% of the gross receipts from the sale of advertising on all newspapers with a weekly circulation above 20,000. Out of at least 124 publishers in the State, only 13 were subject to the tax. After noting that the tax was "single in kind" and that keying the tax to circulation curtailed the flow of information, this Court held the tax invalid as an abridgment of the freedom of the press. [The argument of the publishers] emphasized the events leading up to the tax and the contemporary political climate in Louisiana. All but one of the large papers subject to the tax had "ganged up" on Senator Huey Long, and a circular distributed by Long and the governor to each member of the state legislature described "lying newspapers" as conducting "a vicious campaign" and the tax as "a tax on lying." [Although] the Court's opinion did not describe this history, it stated, "[The tax] is bad because, in the light of its history and of its present setting, it is seen to be a deliberate and calculated device in the guise of a tax to limit the circulation of information," an explanation that suggests that the motivation of the legislature may have been significant.

Our subsequent cases have not been consistent in their reading of Grosjean on this point. Compare O'Brien (stating that legislative purpose was irrelevant in Grosjean) with [e.g.] Houchins v. KQED (plurality opinion) (suggesting that purpose was relevant in Grosjean). Commentators have generally viewed Grosjean as dependent on the improper censorial goals of the legislature. We think that the result in Grosjean may have been attributable in part to the perception on the part of the Court that the state imposed the tax with an intent to penalize a selected group of newspapers. In the case currently before us, however, there is no legislative history and no indication, apart from the structure of the tax itself, of any impermissible or censorial motive on the part of the legislature. We cannot resolve the case by simple citation to Grosjean. Instead, we must analyze the problem anew under the general principles of the First Amendment.

III. Clearly, the First Amendment does not prohibit all regulation of the press. It is beyond dispute that [government] can subject newspapers to generally applicable economic regulations without creating constitutional problems.[1] Minnesota, however, has not chosen to apply its general sales and use tax to newspapers. Instead, it has created a special tax that applies only to certain publications protected by the First Amendment. Although the State argues now that the tax on paper and ink is part of the general scheme of taxation, the use tax provision is facially discriminatory, singling out publications for treatment that [is] unique in Minnesota tax law.

Minnesota's treatment of publications differs from that of other enterprises in at least two important respects: it imposes a use tax that does not serve the function of protecting the sales tax, and it taxes an intermediate transaction rather than the ultimate retail sale. A use tax ordinarily serves to complement the sales tax by eliminating the incentive to make major purchases in States with lower sales taxes; it requires the resident who shops out-of-state to pay a use tax equal to the sales tax savings. [As] the regulations state, "The 'use tax' is a compensatory or complementary tax." Thus, in general, items exempt from the sales tax are not subject to the use tax, for, in the event of a sales tax exemption, there is no "complementary function" for a use tax to serve. But the use tax on ink and paper serves no such complementary function; it applies to all uses, whether or not the taxpayer purchased the ink and paper in-state, and it applies to items exempt from the sales tax. Further, the ordinary rule in Minnesota [is] to tax only the ultimate, or retail, sale rather than the use of components like ink and paper. [Publishers], however, are taxed on their purchase of components, even though they will eventually sell their publications at retail.

By creating this special use tax, which [is] without parallel in the State's tax scheme, Minnesota has singled out the press for special treatment. We then must determine whether the First Amendment permits such special taxation. A

---

1. Among the prior decisions Justice O'Connor cited as illustrations were Citizens Publishing Co. v. United States (1969; antitrust laws); Breard v. Alexandria (1951; prohibition of door-to-door solicitation); Oklahoma Press Publishing Co. v. Walling (1946; Fair Labor Standards Act); and Associated Press v. NLRB (1937; NLRA). She added, as a "see also" citation, Branzburg v. Hayes (1972; enforcement of subpoenas; p. 1431 above).

tax that burdens rights protected by the First Amendment cannot stand unless the burden is necessary to achieve an overriding governmental interest. Any tax that the press must pay, of course, imposes some "burden." [This] Court has long upheld economic regulation of the press. The cases approving such economic regulation, however, emphasized the general applicability of the challenged regulation to all businesses, suggesting that a regulation that singled out the press might place a heavier burden of justification on the State, and we now conclude that the special problems created by differential treatment do indeed impose such a burden.

There is substantial evidence that differential taxation of the press would have troubled the Framers of the First Amendment.[2] [When] the Constitution was proposed without an explicit guarantee of freedom of the press, the Antifederalists objected. Proponents of the [Constitution] responded that such a guarantee was unnecessary because the Constitution granted Congress no power to control the press. [The] concerns voiced by the Antifederalists led to the adoption of the Bill of Rights. The fears of the Antifederalists were well-founded. A power to tax differentially, as opposed to a power to tax generally, gives a government a powerful weapon against the taxpayer selected. When the State imposes a generally applicable tax, there is little cause for concern. We need not fear that a government will destroy a selected group of taxpayers by burdensome taxation if it must impose the same burden on the rest of its constituency. When the State singles out the press, though, the political constraints that prevent a legislature from passing crippling taxes of general applicability are weakened, and the threat of burdensome taxes becomes acute. That threat can operate as effectively as a censor to check critical comment by the press, undercutting the basic assumption of our political system that the press will often serve as an important restraint on government. "[A]n untrammeled press [is] a vital source of public information," Grosjean, and an informed public is the essence of working democracy. Further, differential treatment, unless justified by some special characteristic of the press, suggests that the goal of the regulation is not unrelated to suppression of expression, and such a goal is presumptively unconstitutional. See, e.g. [Mosley]; cf. Brown v. Hartlage. Differential taxation of the press, then, places such a burden on the interests protected by the First Amendment that we cannot countenance such treatment unless the State asserts a counterbalancing interest of compelling importance that it cannot achieve without differential taxation.[3]

IV. The main interest asserted by Minnesota in this case is the raising of revenue. [Standing alone], however, it cannot justify the special treatment of the press, for an alternative means of achieving the same interest without raising concerns under the First Amendment is clearly available: the State could raise

---

2. It is true that our opinions rarely speculate on precisely how the Framers would have analyzed a given regulation of expression. In general, though, we have only limited evidence of exactly how the Framers intended the First Amendment to apply. [Consequently], we ordinarily simply apply those general principles, requiring the government to justify any burdens on First Amendment rights by showing that they are necessary to achieve a legitimate overriding governmental interest. But when we do have evidence that a particular law would have offended the Framers, we have not hesitated to invalidate it on that ground alone. Prior restraints, for instance, clearly strike to the core of the Framers' concerns, leading this Court to treat them as particularly suspect. [Near; cf. Grosjean.] [Footnote by Justice O'Connor.]

3. Justice Rehnquist's dissent analyzes this case solely as a problem of equal protection, applying the familiar tiers of scrutiny. We, however, view the problem as one arising directly under the First Amendment, for [the] Framers perceived singling out the press for taxation as a means of abridging the freedom of the press. The appropriate method of analysis thus is to balance the burden implicit in singling out the press against the interest asserted by the State. Under a long line of precedent, the regulation can survive only if the governmental interest outweighs the burden and cannot be achieved by means that do not infringe First Amendment rights as significantly. [E.g., O'Brien; NAACP v. Alabama.] [Footnote by Justice O'Connor.]

the revenue by taxing businesses generally, avoiding the censorial threat implicit in a tax that singles out the press. Addressing the concern with differential treatment, Minnesota invites us to look beyond the form of the tax to its substance. The tax is, according to the State, merely a substitute for the sales tax, which, as a generally applicable tax, would be constitutional as applied to the press.[4] There are two fatal flaws in this reasoning. First, the State has offered no explanation of why it chose to use a substitute for the sales tax rather than the sales tax itself. The court below speculated that the State might have been concerned that collection of a tax on such small transactions would be impractical. That suggestion is unpersuasive, for sales of other low-priced goods are not exempt. If the real goal of this tax is to duplicate the sales tax, it is difficult to see why the State did not achieve that goal by the obvious and effective expedient of applying the sales tax.

Further, even assuming that the legislature did have valid reasons for substituting another tax for the sales tax, we are not persuaded that this tax does serve as a substitute. The State asserts that this scheme actually *favors* the press over other businesses, because the same rate of tax is applied, but, for the press, the rate applies to the cost of components rather than to the sales price. We would be hesitant to fashion a rule that automatically allowed the State to single out the press for a different method of taxation as long as the effective burden was no different from that on other taxpayers or the burden on the press was lighter than that on other businesses. One reason for this reluctance is that the very selection of the press for special treatment threatens the press not only with the current *differential* treatment, but with the possibility of subsequent differentially *more burdensome* treatment. Thus, even without actually imposing an extra burden on the press, the government might be able to achieve censorial effects, for "[t]he threat of sanctions may deter [the] exercise of [First Amendment] rights almost as potently as the actual application of sanctions." NAACP v. Button.[5]

A second reason to avoid the proposed rule is that courts as institutions are poorly equipped to evaluate with precision the relative burdens of various methods of taxation. The complexities of factual economic proof always present a certain potential for error, and courts have little familiarity with the process of evaluating the relative economic burden of taxes. In sum, the possibility of error inherent in the proposed rule poses too great a threat to concerns at the heart of the First Amendment, and we cannot tolerate that possibility.[6] Minne-

4. Star Tribune insists that the premise of the State's argument—that a generally applicable sales tax would be constitutional—is incorrect, citing [e.g., Murdock v. Pennsylvania, 319 U.S. 105 (1943)]. We think that Breard v. Alexandria [1951; p. 1213 above] is more relevant and rebuts Star Tribune's argument. There, we upheld an ordinance prohibiting door-to-door [sales] of subscriptions to magazines, an activity covered by the First Amendment. Although Martin v. Struthers [1943; p. 1213 above] had struck down a similar ordinance as applied to the distribution of free religious literature, the Breard Court explained that case as emphasizing that the information distributed was religious in nature and that the distribution was noncommercial. [Footnote by Justice O'Connor.]

5. Justice Rehnquist's dissent deprecates this concern, asserting that there is no threat, because this Court will invalidate any differentially more burdensome tax. That assertion would provide more security if we could be certain that courts will always prove able to identify differentially more burdensome taxes, a question we explore further, infra. [Footnote by Justice O'Connor.]

6. If a State employed the same *method* of taxation but applied a lower *rate* to the press, so that there could be no doubt that the legislature was not singling out the press to bear a more burdensome tax, we would, of course, be in a position to evaluate the relative burdens. And, given the clarity of the relative burdens, as well as the rule that differential methods of taxation are not automatically permissible if less burdensome, a lower tax rate for the press would not raise the threat that the legislature might later impose an extra burden that would escape detection by the courts. Thus, our decision does not, as the dissent suggests, require Minnesota to impose a greater tax burden on publications. [Footnote by Justice O'Connor.]

sota, therefore, has offered no adequate justification for the special treatment of newspapers.[7]

V.　Minnesota's ink and paper tax violates the First Amendment not only because it singles out the press, but also because it targets a small group of newspapers.　The effect of the $100,000 exemption enacted in 1974 is that only a handful of publishers pay any tax at all, and even fewer pay any significant amount of tax.　The State explains this exemption as part of a policy favoring an "equitable" tax system, although there are no comparable exemptions for small enterprises outside the press.　[Whatever] the motive of the legislature in this case, we think that recognizing a power in the State not only to single out the press but also to tailor the tax so that it singles out a few members of the press presents such a potential for abuse that no interest suggested by Minnesota can justify the scheme.　It has asserted no interest other than its desire to have an "equitable" tax system.　The current system, it explains, promotes equity because it places the burden on large publications that impose more social costs than do smaller publications and that are more likely to be able to bear the burden of the tax.　Even if we were willing to accept the premise that large businesses are more profitable and therefore better able to bear the burden of the tax, the State's commitment to this "equity" is questionable, for the concern has not led the State to grant benefits to small businesses in general.　And when the exemption selects such a narrowly defined group to bear the full burden of the tax, the tax begins to resemble more a penalty for a few of the largest newspapers than an attempt to favor struggling smaller enterprises.

VI.　We need not and do not impugn the motives of the Minnesota legislature in passing the ink and paper tax.　Illicit legislative intent is not the sine qua non of a violation of the First Amendment.　See NAACP v. Button; NAACP v. Alabama; Lovell v. Griffin.　We have long recognized that even regulations aimed at proper governmental concerns can restrict unduly the exercise of rights protected by the First Amendment.　E.g., Schneider v. State.　A tax that singles out the press, or that targets individual publications within the press, places a heavy burden on the State to justify its action.　Since Minnesota has offered no satisfactory justification for its tax on the use of ink and paper, the tax violates the First Amendment.

[Reversed.][8]

Justice WHITE, concurring in part and dissenting in part.

This case is not difficult.　The exemption for the first $100,000 of paper and ink limits the burden of the Minnesota tax to only a few papers.　This feature alone is sufficient reason to invalidate the Minnesota tax.　[Having] found fully sufficient grounds for decision, the Court need go no further.　The question whether [a] state may impose a use tax on paper and ink that is not targeted on a small group of newspapers could be left for another day.　The Court, however, undertakes the task today.　[The] Court concludes that the State has offered no satisfactory explanation for selecting a substitute for a sales tax.　If this is so, that could be the end of the matter, and the Minnesota tax would be invalid for a second reason.

The Court nevertheless moves on to opine that the State could not impose such a tax even if "the effective burden was no different from that on other

7.　Justice O'Connor suggested that some of Justice Rehnquist's economic calculations might, under different hypotheses, lead to a greater rather than lesser economic burden on newspapers.　She stated: "The dissent's calculations, [can] only be characterized as hypothetical. Taking the chance that [such calculations] are erroneous is a risk that the First Amendment forbids."

8.　Justice BLACKMUN joined the majority opinion "except footnote 12." Footnote 12, dealing with the Court's capacity to undertake economic analyses of the burdens of taxation in areas outside of the First Amendment context, is omitted here.

taxpayers or the burden on the press was lighter than that on other businesses." The fear is that the government might use the tax as a threatened sanction to achieve a censorial purpose. As Justice Rehnquist demonstrates, the proposition that the government threatens the First Amendment by favoring the press is most questionable, but for the sake of argument, I let it pass.

Despite having struck down the tax for three separate reasons, the Court is still not finished. "A second reason" to eschew inquiry into the relative burden of taxation is presented. The Court submits that "courts as institutions are poorly equipped to evaluate with precision the relative burdens of various methods of taxation." [Why] this is so is not made clear, and I do not agree that the courts are so incompetent to evaluate the burdens of taxation that we must decline the task in this case. [Justice White described other areas in which the Court evaluates relative tax burdens.] There may be cases, I recognize, where the Court cannot confidently ascertain whether a differential method of taxation imposes a greater burden upon the press than a generally applicable tax. In these circumstances, I too may be unwilling to entrust freedom of the press to uncertain economic proof. But, as Justice Rehnquist clearly shows, this is not such a case. Since it is plainly evident that Minneapolis Star is not disadvantaged and is almost certainly benefitted by a use tax vis-à-vis a sales tax, I cannot agree that the First Amendment forbids a state from choosing one method of taxation over another.

Justice REHNQUIST, dissenting.

Today we learn from the Court that a State runs afoul of the First Amendment [where] the State structures its taxing system to the advantage of newspapers. [While] the Court purports to rely on the intent of the "Framers of the First Amendment," I believe it safe to assume that in 1791 "abridge" meant the same thing it means today: to diminish or curtail. Not until the Court's decision in this case, nearly two centuries after adoption of the First Amendment, has it been read to prohibit activities which in no way diminish or curtail the freedoms it protects. [The Court recognizes that Minnesota] could avoid constitutional problems by imposing on newspapers the 4% sales tax that it imposes on other retailers. Rather than impose such a tax, however, the Minnesota legislature decided to provide newspapers with an exemption from the sales tax and impose a 4% use tax on ink and paper; thus, while both taxes are part of one [system], newspapers are classified differently within that system. The problem the Court finds too difficult to deal with is whether this difference in treatment results in a significant burden on newspapers.

[Had] a 4% sales tax been imposed, the Minneapolis Star & Tribune would have been liable for $1,859,950 in 1974. The same "complexities of factual economic proof" can be analyzed for 1975. [Had] the sales tax been imposed, as the Court agrees would have been permissible, the Minneapolis Star & Tribune's liability for 1974 and 1975 would have been $3,685,092. The record further indicates that the Minneapolis Star & Tribune paid $608,634 in use taxes in 1974 and $636,113 in 1975—a total liability of $1,244,747. We need no expert testimony from modern day Euclids or Einsteins to determine that the $1,224,747 paid in use taxes is significantly less burdensome than the $3,685,092 that could have been levied by a sales tax. A fortiori, the Minnesota taxing scheme which singles out newspapers for "different treatment" has benefited, not burdened, the "freedom of speech, [and] of the press."

Ignoring these calculations, the Court concludes that "differential treatment" alone in Minnesota's sales and use tax scheme requires that the statutes be found "presumptively unconstitutional" and declared invalid "unless the State asserts a counterbalancing interest of compelling importance that it cannot achieve without differential taxation." The "differential treatment" standard that the

Court has conjured up is unprecedented and unwarranted. To my knowledge this Court has never subjected governmental action to the most stringent constitutional review solely on the basis of "differential treatment" of particular groups. The case relied on by the Court [Mosley, p. 1164 above] certainly does not stand for this proposition. In Mosley, all picketing except "peaceful picketing" was prohibited within a particular public area. Thus, "differential treatment" was not the key to the Court's decision; rather, the essential fact was that unless a person was considered a "peaceful picketer" his speech through this form of expression would be totally abridged within the area.

Of course, all governmentally created classifications must have some "rational basis." The fact that they have been enacted by a presumptively rational legislature, however, arms them with a presumption of rationality. We have shown the greatest deference to state legislatures in devising their taxing schemes. [Where] the State devises classifications that infringe on the fundamental guaranties protected by the Constitution, the Court has demanded more of the State in justifying its action. But there is no *infringement,* and thus the Court has never required more, unless the State's classifications *significantly burden* these specially protected rights. [To] state it in terms of the freedoms at issue here, no First Amendment issue is raised unless First Amendment rights have been [infringed].

Today the Court departs from this rule, refusing to look at the record and determine whether the classifications in the Minnesota use and sales tax statutes significantly burden the First Amendment rights of petitioner and its fellow newspapers. The Court offers as an explanation for this failure the self-reproaching conclusion that "courts as institutions are poorly equipped to evaluate with precision the relative burdens of various methods of taxation." [Considering] the complexity of issues this Court resolves each Term, this admonition as a general rule is difficult to understand. Considering the specifics of this case, this confession of inability is incomprehensible.

Wisely not relying solely on its inability to weigh the burdens of the Minnesota tax scheme, the Court also says that even if the resultant burden on the press is lighter than on others: "[T]he very selection of the press for special treatment threatens the press [with] the possibility of subsequent differentially *more burdensome* treatment." [Surely] the Court does not mean what it seems to say. The Court should be well aware from its discussion of [Grosjean] that this Court is quite capable of dealing with changes in state taxing laws which are intended to penalize newspapers. [The] State is required to show that its taxing scheme is rational. But in this case that showing can be made easily. [In summary], so long as the State can find another way to collect revenue from the newspapers, imposing a sales tax on newspapers would be to no one's advantage; not the newspaper and its distributors who would have to collect the tax, not the State who would have to enforce collection, and not the consumer who would have to pay for the paper in odd amounts. The reasonable alternative Minnesota chose was to impose the use tax on ink and paper.

[The] Court finds in very summary fashion that the exemption newspapers receive for the first $100,000 of ink and paper used also violates the [First Amendment]. I cannot agree. [The] exemption is in effect a $4,000 credit which benefits all newspapers. Minneapolis Star & Tribune was benefited to the amount of $16,000 in the two years in question; $4,000 each year for its morning paper and $4,000 each year for its evening paper. Absent any improper motive on the part of the Minnesota legislature in drawing the limits of this exemption, it cannot be construed as violating the First Amendment. [There] is no reason to conclude that the State, in drafting the $4,000 credit, acted other than reasonably and rationally to fit its sales and use tax scheme to its own local needs and usages. To collect from newspapers their fair share of taxes under the sales and use tax scheme and at the same time avoid abridging the freedoms of speech and press, the Court holds today that Minnesota must subject newspapers to millions of additional dollars in sales tax liability. Certainly this is a hollow victory for the newspapers and I seriously doubt the Court's conclusion that this result would have been intended by the ["Framers of the First Amendment"].

SOME COMMENTS ON MINNEAPOLIS STAR

1. *Is the press special?* The Court in Minneapolis Star emphasizes the dangers involved in singling out "the press" for special regulatory treatment. Yet, as the preceding materials in this section illustrate, the Court typically has refused to recognize claims of the press to special protection beyond that available to anyone who exercises First Amendment rights by communicating information and opinion.[1] Is the Court's focus on "the press" in Minneapolis Star therefore superfluous or inconsistent with prior decisions? Or does this case suggest that in some areas the press *will* receive more protection than other claimants under the First Amendment?

If the latter reading is unwarranted and there remains nothing constitutionally special about the press, does Minneapolis Star suggest instead that certain subjects—e.g., criticism of government in a broad sense—will receive special protection? Assuming that the holding transcends the particular context of the press, what does it imply about other areas in which regulatory schemes contain categories involving activities encompassed by the First Amendment? Recall the comments about "format discrimination" earlier in these free expression chapters, especially at p. 1168 above.[2] Is there currently a constitutionally significant difference between an ordinance regulating parades, picketing, or demonstrations, as such, and one dealing more broadly with, e.g., traffic control or obstruction of sidewalks? Should it be permissible, for example, for zoning regulations to single out bookstores or billboards for special treatment?

2. *Slippery slopes.* Although couched in different terms, Justice Rehnquist's objections to the majority's creation of a prophylactic rule to safeguard the press against future abuses of the taxing power raise the perennial problem of the use and misuse of "slippery slope" arguments. The same argument appears in numerous guises, including the search for a "stopping point," the fear of "a foot in the door," the question of "Where do you draw the line?," and the wariness of abuse of power. Perhaps the most noteworthy characterization is Justice Stewart's use of an Arabian proverb in his dissent in Pittsburgh Press Co. v. Human Relations Commission (1973; p. 1129 above): "The camel's nose is in the tent." But regardless of how phrased, the point is the same—if we permit

---

1. For a post-Minneapolis Star decision in accord with the general pattern of not extending special protection to the media, see Calder v. Jones, 465 U.S. ___ (1984), a unanimous ruling that due process principles regulating the exercise of a state's personal jurisdiction would not be modified in actions for defamation media defendants. The Court rejected "the suggestion that First Amendment concerns enter into the jurisdictional analysis." As noted briefly in chap. 11, sec. 2, the Court stated that the "potential chill on protected First Amendment activity stemming from libel and defamation actions is already taken into account in the constitutional limitations on the substantive law governing such suits. To reintroduce those concerns at the jurisdictional stage would be a form of double counting." See also Keeton v. Hustler Magazine, Inc., 465 U.S. ___ (1984).

2. On this issue, consider whether Minneapolis Star suggests that laws singling out the press (even though they do not suppress or even burden the press) are so suspect as to warrant striking them down on prophylactic grounds. On that reading, Minneapolis Star makes the press an especially highly protected format of communication. Recall and contrast the less clearly protected formats considered in earlier chapters,—e.g., billboards and loudspeakers; but cf. the fate of laws on distribution of leaflets.

this seemingly innocuous exercise of a power, we are on a slippery slope leading inevitably to much more dangerous exercises of that same power.[3]

The contrast between the majority and Justice Rehnquist's dissent makes Minneapolis Star an appropriate vehicle for reconsidering under what circumstances, if any, a currently innocuous exercise of power should be precluded for fear that it will lead to a far less innocuous abuse. Is Court review of every abuse likely? Will such review be timely? If the Court cannot check every abuse, can lower courts serve that function? Can nonjudicial bodies be trusted to follow the spirit as well as the letter of constitutional decisions? But does eagerness to decide cases on the basis of where a currently innocuous policy might lead fly in the face of the Court's reluctance to decide anything other than the case before it? Is a slippery slope argument a variant of an advisory opinion, in the sense that the basis for the decision is a hypothetical scenario that has not yet occurred and indeed may never occur? Could we not prevent all abuses of power by granting no power whatsoever?

3. *The role of original intent.* Footnote 2 of Justice O'Connor's opinion suggests that specific evidence that the Framers would have been offended by a particular law commands that the Court invalidate that law. But is the Court's general reluctance to look at the Framer's intent in First Amendment cases solely a function of the "limited evidence of exactly how the Framers intended the First Amendment to apply"? If the specific views of the Framers, when known, must invalidate a law inconsistent with those views, can equally specific evidence defeat a First Amendment challenge to a law that would *not* have offended the Framers?

REGULATION OF THE BROADCAST MEDIA

To what extent are the constitutional restrictions regarding regulations of the print media applicable to the broadcast media? That issue has arisen repeatedly in materials in these three chapters on free speech. Recall, e.g., the Pacifica case (1978; chap. 11, p. 1114 above) justifying regulation on the ground of the intrusions into the home associated with broadcasting. Recall also the emphasis on the unique nature of broadcasting in decisions on rights of access to the broadcasting media, in cases such as Red Lion (chap. 12, p. 1295 above). In all those situations, the Court upheld restrictions upon broadcasters that would have been impermissible if imposed on those seeking to communicate by print or the non-broadcast spoken word.

The scope of permissible regulation of the broadcast media was before the Court in FCC v. LEAGUE OF WOMEN VOTERS OF CALIFORNIA, 468 U.S. ___ (1984). The case involved a challenge to 47 U.S.C. § 399, which prohibits "editorializing" by noncommercial educational broadcasting stations receiving funds from the Corporation for Public Broadcasting. In striking down the statute as an impermissible content regulation, the Court did not deny that special concerns dictated applying a standard lower than that of a "compelling interest" to content regulation of the broadcast media. But Justice BRENNAN's majority opinion refused to take spectrum scarcity and related concerns as justifying total deference to legislative regulation. Instead, regulation of the content of broadcasting would be upheld "only when we [are]

---

3. Reactions against the use or overuse of slippery slope arguments predate Justice Rehnquist's dissent. As far back as Martin v. Hunter's Lessee (1816; p. 29, chap. 1 above), Justice Story commented that it is "always a doubtful course, to argue against the use or existence of a power, from the possibility of its abuse." In Wil-

liams v. Florida, 399 U.S. 78 (1970), Justice White noted that one can get off a slippery slope before reaching the bottom, and in Walz v. Tax Commission (1969; chap. 14 below), Justice Harlan's concurrence pointed out that slippery slopes can have constitutional toeholds.

satisfied that the restriction is narrowly tailored to further a substantial governmental interest, such as ensuring adequate and balanced coverage of public issues."

Because the restriction on expression of editorial opinion was found to lie "at the heart of First Amendment protection," the Court applied its standard carefully and found the government's justifications insufficient to justify the restriction. One proffered justification was to prevent public broadcasting stations from being excessively influenced by government, in light of the source of some of their funding. But Justice Brennan found this admirable desire to preserve independence served in other ways not necessitating content regulation. And he was even more skeptical of the asserted interest "in preventing private groups from propagating their own views via public broadcasting." Because this regulation was limited to "the suppression of editorial speech by station management," the statute was too over- and underinclusive to satisfy the Court's standards.

Justice STEVENS' dissenting opinion distinguished this restriction from one that was based on the particular viewpoint espoused. In the absence of any explicit viewpoint discrimination, and in the absence of any indication that one point of view would be affected more than any other, he would have found sufficient "the overriding interest in forestalling the creation of propaganda organs for the Government." Justice REHNQUIST, joined by Chief Justice Burger and Justice White, also dissented. Justice Rehnquist relied on Regan v. Taxation With Representation of Washington (1983; p. 1402 above) to argue that the connection between federal funding and the restriction made the restriction permissible. (Justice Brennan's majority opinion distinguished Taxation With Representation because the law applied to all public broadcasting stations that receive federal funds, even if they received a very small amount of federal funding—and because there was no practical or legally permissible way to separate the activities supported by federal money from those supported by private funds.)

Chapter 14

THE CONSTITUTION AND RELIGION: "ESTABLISHMENT" AND "FREE EXERCISE"

Introduction. The First Amendment contains two references to religion: the "establishment clause" (prohibiting laws "respecting an establishment of religion"), and the "free exercise clause" (forbidding laws "prohibiting the free exercise thereof"). Sec. 1 of this chapter focuses on "establishment"; sec. 2, on "free exercise." But that organization should not obscure the fact that the two clauses are interrelated. The provisions protect overlapping values, but they often exert conflicting pressures.[1] Consider the common practice of exempting church property from taxation. Does the benefit conveyed by government to religion via that exemption constitute an "establishment"? Would the "free exercise" of religion be unduly burdened if church property were not exempted from taxation? Articulating satisfactory criteria to accommodate the sometimes conflicting emanations of the two religion clauses is a recurrent challenge in this chapter.

Sec. 1 focuses primarily on two establishment clause issues. These issues stem from two basic ways in which the separation of church and state may be threatened. Sec. 1A discusses the rendering of governmental aid to activities conducted by religious organizations. Sec. 1B considers the intrusion of religious matters into governmental activities. Most of the cases raising these issues have arisen in the educational context. Recently, however, the Court has considered an increasing number of establishment clause cases arising in contexts unrelated to education.

Sec. 2 examines cases in which "free exercise" claimants raised religious objections to the application of general regulations. Is the free exercise guarantee limited to the protection of religious *beliefs?* Does it also protect against interference with *conduct* based on religious convictions? The modern Court has found some religion-based activities protected by the First Amendment; the most difficult problems turn on the extent of that protection. For example, may the Amish claim constitutional exemption from compulsory education laws? Such claims raise one of the tensions arising from the coexistence of the two religion clauses: If a state *must* grant an exemption because of the "free exercise" command, is it not granting a preference to religion in violation of the "establishment" provision? Even if government is not compelled to exempt, *may* it, without running afoul of "establishment," afford special treatment because of individual religious scruples (as the conscientious objection exemption from the draft laws purported to do)?

Accommodating the religion clauses. Some commentators have suggested that the two religion clauses can be harmonized by recognizing that "establishment" and "free exercise" serve a single value—protecting the individual's freedom of religious belief and practices, with "free exercise" barring the curbing of that freedom through penalties and "establishment" barring inhibitions on individual choice that arise from governmental aids and rewards to religion. Yet viewing

---

1. For an argument that a court's ultimate characterization of an issue—i.e., as either an establishment clause question or a free exercise question—can determine the outcome of a case, see Johnson, "Concepts and Compromise in First Amendment Religious Doctrine," 72 Calif.L.Rev. 817 (1984).

the clauses as protecting that single goal does not eliminate the potential tensions. If either the anti-penalties or anti-rewards theme is taken as an absolute, the competing theme will be unduly denigrated: if all penalties are barred, undue benefit to religion may result; if all benefits are barred, undue burdens on religion may be the consequence. Identifying a single "freedom" value, then, does not eliminate the need for accommodation.

Moreover, the establishment clause may serve values beyond those of avoiding penalties and benefits that impinge upon individual religious freedom; [2] the "establishment" barrier applies even when individual liberties are not significantly affected. [3] Would "neutrality" be a better reconciling theme? Can the religion clauses be read as making the Constitution "religion-blind"? That was the suggestion of Professor Kurland: he proposed as the unifying principle that "the freedom and separation clauses should be read as a single precept that government cannot utilize religion as a standard for action or inaction because these clauses prohibit classification in terms of religion either to confer a benefit or to impose a burden." [4] Is the "neutrality" theme adequate for the problems raised in this chapter? Or is the search for all-encompassing principles futile? Does the range of religion problems require more complex criteria? If balancing is the most useful approach, what are the appropriate ingredients and weights for the balancing scale? [5]

---

2. Note, e.g., the effort, in a thoughtful essay, to identify the "three distinct sources" that originally supported the religion clauses, in Van Alstyne, "Trends in the Supreme Court: Mr. Jefferson's Crumbling Wall—A Comment on Lynch v. Donnelly," 1984 Duke L.J. 770. Van Alstyne suggests that the "diverse inputs were the concerns of voluntarism, separatism, and federalism. [Voluntarism] was derived largely from the moderate spirit of religious toleration associated with the Quaker tradition of Pennsylvania. [Separatism] was derived principally from the successful efforts of Madison and Jefferson in Virginia to disentangle the affairs of government from religious establishments, especially in respect to taxes and levies for religious assistance. The third, federalism, was derived from the preferences of other states that—in contrast with Virginia— maintained particular religious establishments, which they were concerned to keep free from the interference of the national government. It was quite consistent with all three concerns that they would converge in a single proposition: Congress should be disabled from legislating on religion." As Van Alstyne summarizes these strands: "Voluntarism [was] the principle of personal choice. Separatism was the principle of non-entanglement. Federalism was the principle of pure state autonomy [respecting] policies that affect religion." Van Alstyne notes that, with the abandonment in the 1830s of the last state-established religion and the adoption of the 14th Amendment, the original limits on Congress became applicable to the states as well. (On the controversy regarding this development, see p. 1470 below.) (For Van Alstyne's view that Lynch v. Donnelly, the crèche decision in 1984—at p. 1498 below—represents a "paradigmatic disregard of the establishment clause in virtually every dimension of its concerns," see p. 1508 below.)

3. Note, e.g., the "standing" aspects (cf. chap. 15) of the Schempp case (1963; p. 1488 below), where Bible reading in schools was challenged. The Court stated that "the requirements for standing to challenge state action under the Establishment Clause, unlike those relating to the free exercise clause, do not include proof that particular religious freedoms are infringed." Here, it was enough that the challengers, students and their parents, were "directly affected" by the practice. (See, also note 2 following Everson, at p. 1477 below.)

4. See Kurland, "Of Church and State and the Supreme Court," 29 U.Chi.L.Rev. 1 (1961). See also Katz, Religion and American Constitutions (1964). (For a critical comment on Kurland's position, see Pfeffer's book review, "Religion-Blind Government," 15 Stan.L.Rev. 389 (1963).)

5. These problems have generated much controversy and an extraordinary amount of writing. See, e.g.—in addition to the pieces cited in the preceding footnotes and later in this chapter— Pfeffer, Church, State and Freedom (1967); Oaks (ed.), The Wall Between Church and State (1963); Kauper, Religion and the Constitution (1964); Giannella, "Religious Liberty, Nonestablishment, and Doctrinal Development," 80 Harv. L.Rev. 1381 (1967) and 81 Harv.L.Rev. 513 (1968); Choper, "The Establishment Clause and Aid to Parochial Schools," 56 Calif.L.Rev. 260 (1968); Nowak, "The Supreme Court, the Religion Clauses and the Nationalization of Education," 70 Nw.U.L.Rev. 883 (1976); Cord, Separation of Church and State (1982); Choper, "The Religion Clauses of the First Amendment: Reconciling the Conflict," 41 U.Pitt.L.Rev. 673 (1980); Esbeck, "Establishment Clause Limits on Governmental Interference with Religious Organizations," 41 Wash. & Lee L.Rev. 347 (1984);

SECTION 1.　"ESTABLISHMENT": THE SEPARATION OF CHURCH AND STATE

A.　FINANCIAL AID TO RELIGIOUS INSTITUTIONS

An introductory overview.　The Court did not become fully engaged in deciding issues of financial assistance to religious institutions until the late 1940s.　Earlier encounters with the problem were inconclusive.　Thus, Bradfield v. Roberts, 175 U.S. 291 (1899)—the Court's first decision in the area— sustained a federal appropriation for the construction of a public ward to be administered as part of a hospital under control of sisters of the Roman Catholic church; but the Court in Bradfield did not reach the issue of whether aid to religious institutions is permissible, because it held that the hospital was not a religious body.　Nine years later, in Quick Bear v. Leupp, 210 U.S. 50 (1908), the Court upheld federal payments to parochial schools on behalf of members of the Sioux Indian tribe; but, once again, the Court did not fully address the issue of whether governmental aid to religious institutions is permissible, because it found that the transfer in this case was pursuant to a preexisting obligation on the part of the national government.

Several decades later, the issue of aid to religious institutions reached the Court once more and produced the Court's first full-scale examination of constitutional guidelines, in Everson v. Board of Education, 330 U.S. 1 (1947; p. 1466 below).　Two major factors explain why the Court heard so few aid cases before Everson.　First, the Court's decision in Frothingham v. Mellon (1923; chap. 15, at p. 1543 below) had adopted a restrictive notion of taxpayer standing, and that made litigants' challenges to federal aid to religious institutions nearly impossible for many years.[1]　Second, the Court's earliest suggestions that the religion clauses of the First Amendment applied to the states did not come until 1940 (in Cantwell v. Connecticut, p. 1204 above), and Everson, indeed, was the first case to examine in detail the establishment provision of the First Amendment.

In considering Everson, note the Court's recognition of the tension between anti-establishment and free exercise values.　Note also that the aid challenged in that case—provision of free school bus access to parochial school students—was aid directed to individuals (as distinguished from direct aid to the parochial institutions themselves).　Since Everson, the Court has often accorded great weight to the identity of the immediate recipient of aid in determining whether an aid program violates the establishment clause.　Finally, note the efforts by both the majority and the dissent to classify the aid program in Everson.　The majority likens the program to the provision of fire, police, and sanitation services to parochial schools.[2]　The dissent, on the other hand, rejects this

Note, "Rebuilding the Wall: The Case for a Return to the Strict Interpretation of the Establishment Clause," 81 Colum.L.Rev. 1463 (1981); Buchanan, "Accommodation of Religion in [Public Schools]," 28 U.C.L.A.L.Rev. 1000 (1981); and Merel, "The Protection of Individual Choice: A Consistent Understanding of Religion Under the First Amendment," 45 U.Chi.L.Rev. 805 (1978).

1.　The Court broadened the concept of litigants' standing in establishment clause cases in Flast v. Cohen (1968; p. 1544 below), but later narrowed that concept once again in Valley Forge College v. Americans United (1982; p.

1551 below).　These cases, and the concept of "standing to sue" generally, are discussed in chap. 15 below.

2.　For a recent commentary joining the opposition to the Everson majority position, see Buchanan, "Governmental Aid to Sectarian Schools: A Study in Corrosive Precedents," 15 Hous.L.Rev. 783 (1978).　According to Buchanan, invalidating the Everson aid program would not be inconsistent with continued provision of police, fire, and sanitation services to parochial schools.　He proposes the following test: An aid program is unconstitutional if "to receive the aid the recipient must be a school or a

comparison and instead analogizes the Everson aid program to the provision of "textbooks of school lunches, of athletic equipment, [and] of writing and other materials." Which attempts at classification are more persuasive? Is the effort to classify useful in cases such as this? Would some type of "bright line" rule be preferable in this area, or should the Court adopt a balancing test similar to the one developed in other First Amendment areas?

EVERSON v. BOARD OF EDUCATION

330 U.S. 1, 67 S.Ct. 504, 91 L.Ed. 711 (1947).

Mr. Justice BLACK delivered the opinion of the [Court].

[A New Jersey statute authorized school districts to make rules and contracts to transport children to and from school, "including the transportation of school children to and from school other than a public school, except such school as is operated for profit." Pursuant to that law, a local school board authorized reimbursement for money spent by parents to transport their children on public buses. A local taxpayer challenged those payments going to parents of Roman Catholic parochial school students.[1] The highest state court denied relief.]

The only contention here is that the state statute and the resolution, insofar as they authorized reimbursement to parents of children attending parochial schools, violate the Federal Constitution [in] two respects, which to some extent overlap. *First.* They authorize the State to take by taxation the private property of some and bestow it upon others, to be used for their own private purposes [in violation of due process]. *Second.* The statute and the resolution forced inhabitants to pay taxes to help support and maintain schools which are dedicated to, and which regularly teach, the Catholic Faith. This is alleged to be a use of state power to support church schools contrary to the prohibition of the First Amendment which the 14th Amendment made applicable to the states.

First. [It] is much too late to argue that legislation intended to facilitate the opportunity of children to get a secular education serves no public purpose. Cochran v. Louisiana State Board of Education, 281 U.S. 370.[2] [The] same thing is no less true of legislation to reimburse needy parents, or all parents, for payment of the fares of their children so that they can ride in public busses to and from schools rather than run the risk of traffic and other hazards incident to walking or [hitchhiking].

Second. The New Jersey statute is challenged as a "law respecting an establishment of religion." [Whether this law] is one respecting an "establishment of religion" requires an understanding of the meaning of that language, particularly with respect to the imposition of [taxes]. [After noting that the religion clauses "reflected in the minds of early Americans a vivid mental picture of conditions and practices which they fervently wished to stamp out in order to preserve liberty," Justice Black reviewed the history of religious

---

student who has incurred or will incur a school related expense" and if "sectarian schools [are] among the recipients of such aid." Because police, fire, and sanitation services are not in connection with school-related expenses, states may constitutionally provide them.

1. The dissenting opinions of Justices Jackson and Rutledge took a somewhat different view of the scope of the school board's reimbursement policy. They noted that the board resolution authorizing reimbursement mentioned only the public high schools and the "Catholic Schools." Justice Rutledge commented: "There is no show-

ing that there are no other private or religious schools in this populous district. I do not think it can be assumed there were none." He added, however, that "in the view I have taken, it is unnecessary to limit grounding to these matters."

2. In Cochran in 1930, the Court sustained the expenditure of state funds for the purchase of books for children attending private and parochial schools, against a "no public purpose" challenge. The Court said of the legislation: "Its interest is education, broadly; its method, comprehensive." There was no establishment clause challenge in the case.

persecution in Europe during the centuries "immediately before and contemporaneous with the colonization of America" and the transplanting of many of these practices to colonial America. In Europe, there had been "turmoil, civil strife, and persecutions, generated in large part by established sects determined to maintain their absolute political and religious supremacy." In this country, persons of faiths "who happened to be in a minority in a particular locality were persecuted because they steadfastly persisted in worshipping God only as their own consciences dictated and [these] dissenters were compelled to pay tithes and taxes to support government-sponsored churches whose ministers preached inflammatory sermons designed to strengthen and consolidate the established faith by generating a burning hatred against dissenters." The abhorrence of these practices by "freedom-loving colonials" "reached its dramatic climax in Virginia in 1785–86," in the protest against the renewal of Virginia's tax levy for the support of the established church. Madison wrote his "great Memorial and Remonstrance against the law," arguing that no person "should be taxed to support a religious institution of any kind." Soon after, the Virginia Assembly enacted the "Virginia Bill for Religious Liberty," drafted by Jefferson.[3] Justice Black added: "This Court has previously recognized that the provisions of the First Amendment, in the drafting and adoption of which Madison and Jefferson played such leading roles, had the same objective and were intended to provide the same protection against governmental intrusion on religious liberty as the Virginia statute. [The] interrelationship of [the religion clauses] was well summarized [in] Watson v. Jones, 13 Wall. 679 [1871]: 'The structure of our government has, for the preservation of civil liberty, rescued the temporal institutions from religious interference. On the other hand, it has secured religious liberty from the invasion of the civil authority.'"]

The "establishment of religion" clause of the First Amendment means at least this: Neither a state nor the Federal Government can set up a church. Neither can pass laws which aid one religion, aid all religions, or prefer one religion over another. Neither can force nor influence a person to go to or to remain away from church against his will or force him to profess a belief or disbelief in any religion. No person can be punished for entertaining or professing religious beliefs or disbeliefs, for church attendance or non-attendance. No tax in any amount, large or small, can be levied to support any religious activities or institutions, whatever they may be called, or whatever form they may adopt to teach or practice religion. Neither a state nor the Federal Government can, openly or secretly, participate in the affairs of any religious organizations or groups and vice versa. In the words of Jefferson, the clause against establishment of religion by law was intended to erect "a wall of separation between church and State."

We must [not strike down the New Jersey law] if it is within the State's constitutional power even though it approaches the verge of that power. New Jersey cannot consistently with the establishment clause of the First Amendment contribute tax-raised funds to the support of an institution which teaches the tenets and faith of any church. On the other hand, other language of the amendment commands that New Jersey cannot hamper its citizens in the free exercise of their own religion. Consequently, it cannot exclude individual Catholics, Lutherans, Mohammedans, Baptists, Jews, Methodists, Non-believers, Presbyterians, or the members of any other faith, *because of their faith, or lack of it,* from receiving the benefits of public welfare legislation. While we do not mean to intimate that a state could not provide transportation only to children attending public schools, we must be careful, in protecting the citizens of New

---

3. The Virginia law provided that "no man shall be compelled to frequent or support any religious worship, place, or ministry whatsoever, nor shall be enforced, restrained, molested, or burthened in his body or goods, nor shall otherwise suffer on account of his religious opinions or belief."

Jersey against state-established churches, to be sure that we do not inadvertently prohibit New Jersey from extending its general state law benefits to all its citizens without regard to their religious belief.

Measured by these standards, we cannot say that the First Amendment prohibits New Jersey from spending tax-raised funds to pay the bus fares of parochial school pupils as a part of a general program under which it pays the fares of pupils attending public and other schools. It is undoubtedly true that children are helped to get to church schools. There is even a possibility that some of the children might not be sent to the church schools if the parents were compelled to pay their children's bus fares out of their own pockets when transportation to a public school would have been paid for by the State. [Similarly], parents might be reluctant to permit their children to attend schools which the state had cut off from such general government services as ordinary police and fire protection, connections for sewage disposal, public highways and sidewalks. Of course, cutting off church schools from these services, so separate and so indisputably marked off from the religious function, would make it far more difficult for the schools to operate. But such is obviously not the purpose of the First Amendment. That Amendment requires the state to be a neutral in its relations with groups of religious believers and non-believers; it does not require the state to be their adversary. State power is no more to be used so as to handicap religions than it is to favor them.

This Court has said that parents may, in the discharge of their duty under state compulsory education laws, send their children to a religious rather than a public school if the school meets the secular educational requirements which the state has power to impose. See Pierce v. Society of Sisters (1925; chap. 8 above). It appears that these parochial schools meet New Jersey's requirements. The State contributes no money to the schools. It does not support them. Its legislation, as applied, does no more than provide a general program to help parents get their children, regardless of their religion, safely and expeditiously to and from accredited schools.

The First Amendment has erected a wall between church and state. That wall must be kept high and impregnable. We could not approve the slightest breach. New Jersey has not breached it here.

Affirmed.

Mr. Justice JACKSON [joined by Mr. Justice FRANKFURTER], [dissenting].

[The] Court's opinion marshals every argument in favor of state aid and puts the case in its most favorable light, but much of its reasoning confirms my conclusions that there are no good grounds upon which to support the present legislation. In fact, the undertones of the opinion, advocating complete and uncompromising separation of Church from State, seem utterly discordant with its conclusion yielding support to their commingling in educational matters. The case which irresistibly comes to mind as the most fitting precedent is that of Julia who, according to Byron's reports, ["whispering 'I will ne'er consent,'—consented"].

Mr. Justice RUTLEDGE, with whom Mr. Justice FRANKFURTER, Mr. Justice JACKSON and Mr. Justice BURTON agree, [dissenting].

The Amendment's purpose was [to] create a complete and permanent separation of the spheres of religious activity and civil authority by comprehensively forbidding every form of public aid or support for religion. [Justice Rutledge provided an extensive review of history.] Does New Jersey's action furnish support for religion by use of the taxing power? Certainly it does, if the test remains undiluted as Jefferson and Madison made it, that money taken by taxation from one is not to be used or given to support another's religious training or belief, or indeed one's own. [T]he prohibition is absolute. The funds used here [in] fact give aid and encouragement to religious instruction. [The reimbursement program] not only helps the children to get to school and the parents to send them. It aids them in a substantial way to get the very thing which they are sent to the particular school to secure, namely, religious training and teaching. [T]here is undeniably an admixture of religious with secular teaching in all such institutions. That is the very reason for their being. [Commingling] the religious with the secular teaching does not divest the whole of its religious permeation and emphasis. [Indeed], on any other view, the constitutional prohibition always could be brought to naught by adding a modicum of the secular. [T]ransportation where it is needed is as essential to education as any other element. Its cost is as much a part of the total expense, except at times in amount, as the cost of textbooks, of school lunches, of athletic equipment, of writing and other materials. [No] rational line can be drawn between payment for such larger, but not more necessary, items and payment for transportation. [Now], as in Madison's time, not the amount but the principle of assessment is wrong.

But we are told that the New Jersey statute is valid in its present application because the appropriation is for a public, not a private purpose, namely, the promotion of education, and the majority accept this idea in the conclusion that all we have here is "public welfare legislation." If that is true and the Amendment's force can be thus destroyed, what has been said becomes all the more pertinent. For then there could be no possible objection to more extensive support of religious education by New Jersey. [It] is not because religious teaching does not promote the public or the individual's welfare, but because neither is furthered when the state promotes religious education, that the Constitution forbids it to do so. [In] failure to observe [that distinction] lies the fallacy of the "public function"-"social legislation" argument, a fallacy facilitated by easy transference of the argument's basing from due process unrelated to any religious aspect to the First Amendment.

[Public] money devoted to payment of religious costs, education or other, brings request for more. It brings, too, the struggle of sect against sect for the larger share or for any. [That] is precisely the history of societies which have had an established religion and dissident groups. It is the very thing Jefferson and Madison [sought] to guard against, whether in its blunt or in its more screened forms. The end of such strife cannot be other than to destroy the cherished liberty. The dominating group will achieve the dominant benefit; or all will embroil the state in their dissensions.

[No] one conscious of religious values can be unsympathetic toward the burden which our constitutional separation puts on parents who desire religious instruction mixed with secular for their children. [Nor] can one happily see benefits denied to children which others receive. But if those feelings should prevail, there would be an end to our historic constitutional policy and command. No more unjust or discriminatory in fact is it to deny attendants at religious schools the cost of their transportation than it is to deny them tuitions, sustenance for their teachers, or any other educational expense which others receive at public cost. [D]iscrimination in the legal sense does not exist. The child attending the religious school has the same right as any other to attend public school. But he foregoes exercising it because the same guaranty which assures this freedom forbids [any state agency] to give or aid him in securing the religious instruction he seeks. [Nor] is the case comparable to one of furnishing fire or police protection, or access to public highways. These things are matters of common right, part of the general need for safety.[1] Certainly the fire department must not stand idly by while the church [burns].

---

1. The protections are of a nature which does not require appropriations specially made from the public treasury and earmarked, as is New Jersey's here, particularly for religious institu-

Two great drives are constantly in motion to abridge, in the name of education, the complete division of religion and civil authority which our forefathers made. One is to introduce religious education and observances into the public schools. The other, to obtain public funds for the aid and support of various private religious schools. [Both] avenues were closed by the Constitution. Neither should be opened by this [Court].

EVERSON, THE "WALL OF SEPARATION," AND THE "INCORPORATION" OF THE ESTABLISHMENT CLAUSE INTO THE 14TH AMENDMENT

1. *The "wall of separation."* The Everson majority invoked Jefferson's "wall of separation" metaphor as a means of delineating the constitutional relationship between church and state. Did the Court breach this wall in Everson? Is the metaphor itself an accurate reflection of the proper requirements of the religion clauses?[1]

In establishment clause cases in the years immediately following Everson, the Court repeatedly cited the "wall of separation" metaphor approvingly. The Burger Court, however, has been less enthusiastic about the metaphor than its predecessors had been. In his majority opinion in Lemon v. Kurtzman, 403 U.S. 602 (1971), for example, Chief Justice Burger commented: "[We] must recognize that the line of separation, far from being a 'wall,' is a blurred, indistinct, and variable barrier depending on all the circumstances of a particular relationship." Justice Stevens, on the other hand, has argued that the Court should "resurrect the 'high and impregnable' wall between church and state constructed by the Framers of the First Amendment." Committee for Public Education v. Regan, 444 U.S. 646 (1980) (Stevens, J., dissenting). Justice Stevens' effort to revive the vitality of the metaphor appears to have failed, however. In Lynch v. Donnelly (1984; p. 1498 below), Chief Justice Burger's opinion of the Court called the "wall of separation" metaphor "a useful figure of speech," but went on to say that "the metaphor itself is not a wholly accurate description of the practical aspects of the relationship that in fact exists between church and state." This pronouncement may dampen the force of the metaphor in the coming years.

2. *"Incorporating" the establishment guarantee into the 14th Amendment.* Both Cantwell and Everson assumed without much discussion that the establishment clause was incorporated into the 14th Amendment and was therefore applicable to the states. In neither case did the Court address the contention that the language of the 14th Amendment may present a textual barrier to incorporation of the establishment clause.[2] Note Justice Brennan's comments in his concur-

tions or uses. The First Amendment does not exclude religious property or activities from protection against disorder or the ordinary accidental incidents of community life. It forbids support, not protection from interference or [destruction]. [Footnote by Justice Rutledge.]

1. For an argument that the Court's post-Everson interpretations of the "wall of separation" metaphor ignored an important strain of thought—that of the evangelist, separationist Roger Williams—see Howe, The Garden and the Wilderness (1965).

2. The "incorporation" of the establishment clause in Everson took place without considering the textual difficulty of using the "liberty" of the 14th Amendment as the incorporation route.

Note further that the First Amendment's establishment clause may have been designed primarily as a federalistic limitation: established churches existed in the states when the Bill of Rights was adopted; the main purpose of "establishment" may have been to keep Congress out of that area. Yet incorporation made "establishment"—arguably a "special," non-"liberty" limitation on the national government—effective against the states. See Howe, "Religion and the Free Society: The Constitutional Question" (1960), suggesting that "some legislative enactments respecting an establishment of religion affect most remotely, if at all, the personal rights of religious liberty." [See Justice Brennan's response in Schempp, in the text.]

rence in Schempp (1963; p. 1488 below): "It [has] been suggested that the 'liberty' guaranteed by the 14th Amendment logically cannot absorb the Establishment Clause because that clause is not one of the provisions of the Bill of Rights which in terms protects a 'freedom' of the individual. The fallacy in this contention [is] that it underestimates the role of the Establishment Clause as a coguarantor, with the Free Exercise Clause, of religious liberty. The Framers did not entrust the liberty of religious beliefs to either clause alone." [3]

AID TO PAROCHIAL EDUCATION SINCE EVERSON

The Court was silent on the issue of aid to parochial education for two decades after Everson. But it returned to the issue in Board of Education v. Allen, 392 U.S. 236 (1968), holding that a state may lend books to parochial school students without violating the establishment clause. In the years between Everson and Allen, however, the Court considered establishment claims in several cases involving alleged religious intrusions into governmental activities. (These developments are examined in sec. 1B below.) In one of these cases, Abington School District v. Schempp, 374 U.S. 203 (1963), the Court enunciated a test for determining whether challenged programs violate the establishment clause. The Court stated that, to survive an establishment clause challenge, an activity must have "a secular legislative purpose and a primary effect that neither advances nor inhibits religion." In Allen, the Court relied on this test in the context of aid to parochial education. Soon after, in Walz v. Tax Commission, 397 U.S. 664 (1970), the Court upheld tax exemptions for religious organizations. In doing so, it added a new ingredient to the establishment clause test, stating that the challenged program must not foster "excessive government entanglement with religion." [1] The "entanglement" test was formally combined with the Schempp "purpose" and "effect" tests to articulate a three-pronged establishment clause standard in Lemon v. Kurtzman, 403 U.S. 602 (1971).[2] In several cases since Lemon, the Court has announced that the

3. Note also Justice Brennan's response in Schempp to other objections to "incorporating" the establishment clause: "It has been suggested, with some support in history, that absorption of the First Amendment's [establishment ban] is conceptually impossible because the Framers meant the Establishment Clause also to foreclose any attempt by Congress to disestablish the existing official state churches. [But] it is clear on the record of history that the last of the formal state establishments was dissolved more than three decades before the 14th Amendment was ratified, and thus the problem of protecting official state churches from federal encroachments could hardly have been any concern of those who framed the post-Civil War Amendments.

"[It has also been contended] that absorption of the Establishment Clause is precluded by the absence of any intention on the part of the Framers of the 14th Amendment to circumscribe the residual powers of the States to aid religious activities and institutions in ways which fell short of formal establishments. That argument relies in part upon the express terms of the abortive Blaine Amendment—proposed several years after the adoption of the 14th Amendment—which would have added to the First Amendment a provision that '[n]o state shall make any law respecting an establishment of religion.' Such a restriction would have been superfluous, it is said, if the 14th Amendment had already made the Establishment Clause binding upon the States. The argument proves too much, for the 14th Amendment's protection of the free exercise of religion can hardly be questioned; yet the Blaine Amendment would also have added an explicit protection against state laws [abridging that liberty]."

[Many state constitutions prohibit aid to religions. Some state provisions have been interpreted to bar practices sustained against First Amendment "establishment" attacks. See Antieau, Carroll & Burke, Religion under the State Constitutions (1965).]

1. The "entanglement" test has come under attack, both from members of the Court, see, e.g., Roemer v. Maryland Public Works Board, 426 U.S. 736 (1976) (White, J., concurring), and by legal scholars, see, e.g., Ripple, "The Entanglement Test of the Religion Clauses—A Ten Year Assessment," 27 U.C.L.A.L.Rev. 1195 (1980), and Schotten, "The Establishment Clause and Excessive Governmental-Religious Entanglement: The Constitutional Status of Aid to Nonpublic Elementary and Secondary Schools," 15 Wake Forest L.Rev. 207 (1979).

2. In Lemon, the Court also suggested the possibility of a "divisiveness" inquiry, stating: "Ordinarily political debate and division, howev-

Lemon approach is no more than a helpful signpost; but it has nonetheless applied the test in all but one of its post-Lemon cases.[3]

The Court's decisions involving aid to parochial education have been far from consistent. In Wolman v. Walter, 433 U.S. 229 (1977), for example, the Court held that states cannot constitutionally lend maps, magazines, transparencies, tape recorders, and other instructional materials to parochial school students, despite its holding in Allen that lending *books* to such students is permissible. Wolman also held that states cannot provide transportation for parochial school students to take field trips, despite its holding in Everson that states *can* provide such students with transportation to and from school. In Levitt v. Committee for Public Education, 413 U.S. 472 (1973), the Court held that states may not reimburse parochial schools for the cost of administering tests that are state-required but teacher-prepared. In Committee for Public Education v. Regan, 444 U.S. 646 (1980), however, the Court held that states *may* subsidize parochial schools for the expense of administering state-prepared examinations. And in Mueller v. Allen (1983; p. 1473 below), the Court upheld a form of financial aid to parents of parochial school students (tax deductions) despite its rejection of a similar type of aid (tuition rebates and tax deductions) in Committee for Public Education v. Nyquist, 413 U.S. 756 (1973).

In attempting to reconcile these decisions the Court has relied on a number of distinctions.[4] It has invoked two of these distinctions quite frequently. One distinction is based on the breadth of the statutory class of beneficiaries: the broader the class, the more likely the Court is to uphold the statute. Is a distinction on the basis of breadth of statutory class a tenable one? The Court has upheld statutes that provide aid to private school students, as opposed to *all* students, on several occasions, presumably because the public school students were already receiving the aid in question. If this reasoning is extended, however, does it not suggest that financial aid to parochial school students is permissible, so long as the statutory class includes all private school students? If this is the case, does the breadth-of-statutory-classification distinction require anything more than that parochial school students not receive benefits that students in other schools do not receive?

A second distinction upon which the Court has frequently relied is based upon the identity of the initial recipient of the aid. The Court has been far more receptive to programs that channel aid to parochial school students and their parents than it has been to programs that give aid directly to parochial schools. Is this distinction a helpful one? Does it not ignore the economic reality that parochial schools benefit whenever parents of parochial school students benefit? (Recall the debate in Everson.) When reading Mueller, which follows, note the Court's reliance upon the two distinctions just noted. Is

---

er vigorous or even partisan, are normal and healthy manifestations of our democratic system of government, but political division along religious lines was one of the principal evils against which the First Amendment was intended to protect." Several commentators have criticized reliance upon divisiveness inquiries, see, e.g., Choper, "The Religion Clauses of the [First Amendment]," 41 U.Pitt.L.Rev. 673 (1980); Gaffney, "Political Divisiveness Along Religious Lines: The Entanglement of the Court in Sloppy History and Bad Public Policy," 24 St. Louis U.L.J. 205 (1980). The Court itself now seems in doubt about the wisdom of divisiveness inquiries. In Lynch v. Donnelly, (1984; p. 1498 be-

low), Chief Justice Burger, who had articulated the divisiveness standard in the first place, stated that "this Court has not held that political divisiveness alone can serve to invalidate otherwise permissible conduct."

3. For an argument that the Court is moving toward renouncing the Lemon test generally and the "effect" part of that test in particular, see Note, "The Supreme Court, Effect Inquiry, and Aid to Parochial Education," 37 Stan.L.Rev. 219 (1985).

4. For an extended critical discussion of these distinctions, see the Note cited in the preceding footnote.

the Court's reasoning persuasive? Or is the dissent's claim that this case is indistinguishable from Nyquist closer to the mark?[5]

––––––

MUELLER v. ALLEN

463 U.S. 388, 103 S.Ct. 3062, 77 L.Ed.2d 721 (1983).

Justice REHNQUIST delivered the opinion of the Court.

Minnesota allows taxpayers, in computing their state income tax, to deduct certain expenses incurred in providing for the education of their children. The [Court of Appeals] held that the Establishment Clause [was] not offended by this arrangement. We now affirm.

Minnesota [provides] free elementary and secondary schooling. [820,000] students attended this school system in the most recent school year. During the same year, approximately 91,000 elementary and secondary students attended some 500 privately supported schools located in Minnesota, and about 95% of these students attended schools considering themselves to be sectarian. Minnesota, by a law originally enacted in 1955, [permits] state taxpayers to claim a deduction from gross income for certain expenses incurred in educating their children. The deduction is limited to actual expenses incurred for the "tuition, textbooks and transportation" of dependents attending elementary or secondary schools. A deduction may not exceed $500 per dependent in grades K through six and $700 per dependent in grades seven through twelve.

[Today's] case is no exception to our oft-repeated statement that the Establishment Clause presents especially difficult questions of interpretation and application. It is easy enough to quote the few words comprising that [Clause]. It is not at all easy, however, to apply this Court's various decisions construing the Clause to governmental programs of financial assistance to sectarian schools and the parents of children attending those schools. Indeed, in many of these decisions "we have expressly or implicitly acknowledged that 'we can only dimly perceive the lines of demarcation in this extraordinarily sensitive area of constitutional law.'" [Lemon, quoted with approval in Nyquist.] [One] fixed principle in this field is our consistent rejection of the argument that "any program which in some manner aids an institution with a religious affiliation" violates the Establishment Clause. For example, it is now well-established that a state may reimburse parents for expenses incurred in transporting their children to school [Everson], and that it may loan secular textbooks to all school-children within the state. [Allen.]

Notwithstanding the repeated approval given programs such as those in Allen and Everson, our decisions also have struck down arrangements resembling, in many respects, these forms of assistance. See, e.g., [Lemon; Levitt v. Committee for Public Education, 413 U.S. 472 (1973); Meek v. Pittenger, 421 U.S. 349 (1975); Wolman v. Walter, 433 U.S. 229 (1977)].[1] In this case we

––––––

5. By February 1985, eight cases involving establishment clause challenges—including challenges to financial aid to parochial education—were pending in the Court. The rulings in these cases—which may resolve some of the uncertainties noted in this chapter and may clarify the Burger Court's emerging tolerance of "accommodations" between church and state—will be reported in the 1985 Supplement to this edition of the book.

1. In [Lemon], the Court concluded that the state's reimbursement of non-public schools for the cost of teachers' salaries, textbooks, and instructional materials, and its payment of a salary supplement to teachers in nonpublic schools, resulted in excessive entanglement of church and state. In [Levitt], we struck down on Establishment Clause grounds a state program reimbursing nonpublic schools for the cost of teacher-prepared examinations. Finally, in [Meek and Wolman], we held unconstitutional a direct loan of instructional materials to nonpublic schools, while upholding the loan of textbooks to individual students. [Footnote by Justice Rehnquist.]

are asked to decide whether Minnesota's tax deduction bears greater resemblance to those types of assistance to parochial schools we have approved, or to those we have struck down. Petitioners place particular reliance on our decision in [Nyquist], where we held invalid a New York statute providing public funds for the maintenance and repair of the physical facilities of private schools and granting thinly disguised "tax benefits," actually amounting to tuition grants, to the parents of children attending private schools. [We] conclude that [the provision here] bears less resemblance to the arrangement struck down in Nyquist than it does to assistance programs upheld in our prior decisions and those discussed with approval in Nyquist.

The general nature of our inquiry in this area has been guided, since the decision in [Lemon], by the "three-part" test laid out in that case: "First, the statute must have a secular legislative purpose; second, its principal or primary effect must be one that neither advances nor inhibits [religion]; finally, the statute must not foster 'an excessive government entanglement with religion.' " While this principle is well settled, our cases have also emphasized that it provides 'no more than [a] helpful signpost' in dealing with establishment clause challenges. With this caveat in mind, we turn to the specific challenges raised [here] under the Lemon framework.

Little time need be spent on the question of whether the Minnesota tax deduction has a secular purpose. Under our prior decisions, governmental assistance programs have consistently survived this inquiry even when they have run afoul of other aspects of the Lemon framework. This reflects, at least in part, our reluctance to attribute unconstitutional motives to the states, particularly when a plausible secular purpose for the state's program may be discerned from the face of the statute. A state's decision to defray the cost of educational expenses incurred by parents—regardless of the type of schools their children attend—evidences a purpose that is both secular and understandable. An educated populace is essential to the political and economic health of any community, and a state's efforts to assist parents in meeting the rising cost of educational expenses plainly serves this secular purpose of ensuring that the state's citizenry is well-educated. Similarly, Minnesota, like other states, could conclude that there is a strong public interest in assuring the continued financial health of private schools, both sectarian and non-sectarian. By educating a substantial number of students such schools relieve public schools of a correspondingly great burden—to the benefit of all taxpayers. In addition, private schools may serve as a benchmark for [public schools]. All these justifications are [sufficient] to satisfy the secular purpose inquiry of Lemon.

We turn therefore to the more difficult but related question whether the Minnesota statute has "the primary effect of advancing the sectarian aims of the nonpublic schools." In concluding that it does not, we find several features of the Minnesota tax deduction particularly significant. First, an essential feature of Minnesota's arrangement is the fact that the provision is only one among many deductions—such as those for medical expenses and charitable contributions—available under the Minnesota tax laws. Our decisions consistently have recognized that traditionally "[l]egislatures have especially broad latitude in creating classifications and distinctions in tax statutes," Regan v. Taxation with Representation [1983; p. 1402 above], in part because the "familiarity with local conditions" enjoyed by legislators especially enables them to "achieve an equitable distribution of the tax burden." Under our prior decisions, the Minnesota legislature's judgment that a deduction for educational expenses fairly equalizes the tax burden of its citizens and encourages desirable expenditures for educational purposes is entitled to substantial deference.[2]

2. Our decision in Nyquist is not to the contrary on this point. We expressed considerable doubt there that the "tax benefits" provided by New York law properly could be regarded as

Other characteristics of [the provision] argue equally strongly for the provision's constitutionality. Most importantly, the deduction is available for educational expenses incurred by *all* parents, including those whose children attend public schools and those whose children attend non-sectarian private schools or sectarian private schools. Just as in [Widmar v. Vincent (1981; p. 1493 below)], where we concluded that the state's provision of a forum neutrally "open to a broad class of nonreligious as well as religious speakers" does not "confer any imprimatur of State approval," so here: "the provision of benefits to so broad a spectrum of groups is an important index of secular effect."

In this respect, as well as others, this case is vitally different from the scheme struck down in Nyquist. There, public assistance amounting to tuition grants was provided only to parents of children in *nonpublic* schools. This fact had considerable bearing on our decision striking down the New York statute at issue; we explicitly distinguished both Allen and Everson on the grounds that "In both cases the class of beneficiaries included *all* schoolchildren, those in public as well as those in private schools." Moreover, we intimated that "public assistance (e.g., scholarships) made available generally without regard to the sectarian-nonsectarian or public-nonpublic nature of the institution benefited" might not offend the Establishment Clause. We think the tax deduction adopted by Minnesota is more similar to this latter type of program than it is to the arrangement struck down in Nyquist. Unlike the assistance at issue in Nyquist, [the Minnesota law] permits *all* parents—whether their children attend public school or private—to deduct their childrens' educational expenses. As Widmar and our other decisions indicate, a program [that] neutrally provides state assistance to a broad spectrum of citizens is not readily subject to challenge under the Establishment Clause.

We also agree [that], by channeling whatever assistance it may provide to parochial schools through individual parents, Minnesota has reduced the Establishment Clause objections to which its action is subject. It is true, of course, that financial assistance provided to parents ultimately has an economic effect comparable to that of aid given directly to the schools attended by their children. It is also true, however, that under Minnesota's arrangement public funds become available only as a result of numerous, private choices of individual parents of school-age children. [It] is noteworthy that all but one of our recent cases [Nyquist] invalidating state aid to parochial schools have involved the direct transmission of assistance from the state to the schools themselves. [Where], as here, aid to parochial schools is available only as a result of decisions of individual parents no "imprimatur of State approval," Widmar, can be deemed to have been conferred on any particular religion, or on religion generally.

We find it useful [to] compare the attenuated financial benefits flowing to parochial schools from the [provision here] to the evils against which the Establishment Clause was designed to protect. These dangers are well-described by our statement that "what is at stake as a matter of policy [in establishment clause cases] is preventing that kind and degree of government involvement in religious life that, as history teaches us, is apt to lead to strife and frequently strain a political system to the breaking point." Nyquist, quoting [Walz]. It is important, however, to "keep these issues in perspective":

parts of a genuine system of tax laws. [Indeed], the question whether a program having the elements of a "genuine tax deduction" would be constitutionally acceptable was expressly reserved in Nyquist. While the economic consequences of the program in Nyquist and that in this case may be difficult to distinguish, we have recognized on other occasions that "the form of the [state's assistance to parochial schools must be examined] for the light that it casts on the substance." [Lemon.] The fact that the Minnesota plan embodies a "genuine tax deduction" is thus of some relevance, especially given the traditional rule of deference accorded legislative classifications in tax statutes. [Footnote by Justice Rehnquist.]

"At this point in the 20th century we are quite far removed from the dangers that prompted the Framers to [adopt the establishment clause]. The risk of significant religious or denominational control over our democratic processes— or even of deep political division along religious lines—is remote, and when viewed against the positive contributions of sectarian schools, [any] such risk seems entirely tolerable in light of the continuing oversight of this Court." Wolman [separate opinion by Powell, J.]. The Establishment Clause of course extends beyond prohibition of a state church or payment of state funds to one or more churches. We do not think, however, that its prohibition extends to the type of tax deduction established by Minnesota. The historic purposes of the clause simply do not encompass the sort of attenuated financial benefit, ultimately controlled by the private choices of individual parents, that eventually flows to parochial schools from the neutrally available tax benefit at issue in this case.

Petitioners argue that, notwithstanding [its facial neutrality], in application the statute primarily benefits religious institutions. Petitioners rely [on] a statistical analysis of the type of persons claiming the tax deduction. They contend that most parents of public school children incur no tuition expenses, and that other expenses deductible under [the provision] are negligible in value; moreover, they claim that 96% of the children in private schools in 1978–1979 attended religiously-affiliated institutions. Because of all this, they reason, the bulk of deductions taken [will] be claimed by parents of children in sectarian schools. Respondents reply that petitioners have failed to consider the impact of deductions for items such as transportation, summer school tuition, tuition paid by parents whose children attended schools outside the school districts in which they resided, rental or purchase costs for a variety of equipment, and tuition for certain types of instruction not ordinarily provided in public schools.

We need not consider these contentions in detail. We would be loath to adopt a rule grounding the constitutionality of a facially neutral law on annual reports reciting the extent to which various classes of private citizens claimed benefits under the law. Such an approach would scarcely provide the certainty that this field stands in need of, nor can we perceive principled standards by which such statistical evidence might be evaluated. Moreover, the fact that private persons fail in a particular year to claim the tax relief to which they are entitled—under a facially neutral statute—should be of little importance in determining the constitutionality of the statute permitting such relief.

Finally, private educational institutions, and parents paying for their children to attend these schools, make special contributions to the areas in which they operate. [If] parents of children in private schools choose to take especial advantage of the relief provided by [the law], it is no doubt due to the fact that they bear a particularly great financial burden in educating their children. More fundamentally, whatever unequal effect may be attributed to the statutory classification can fairly be regarded as a rough return for the benefits [provided] to the state and all taxpayers by parents sending their children to parochial schools. In the light of all this, we believe it wiser to decline to engage in the type of empirical inquiry into those persons benefited by state law which petitioners urge.[3] Thus, we hold that the Minnesota tax deduction for educa-

---

3. Our conclusion is unaffected by the fact that [the provision] permits deductions for amounts spent for textbooks and transportation as well as tuition. In [Everson], we approved a statute reimbursing parents of *all* schoolchildren for the costs of transporting their children to school. Doing so by means of a deduction rather than a direct grant, only serves to make the state's action less objectionable. Likewise, in [Allen], we approved state loans of textbooks to *all* schoolchildren; although we disapproved in

[Meek and Wolman] direct loans of instructional materials to sectarian schools, we do not find those cases controlling. First, they involved assistance provided to the schools themselves, rather than tax benefits directed to individual parents. Moreover, we think that state assistance for the rental of calculators, ice skates, tennis shoes, and the like, scarcely poses the type of dangers against which the Establishment Clause was intended to guard. [Footnote by Justice Rehnquist.]

tional expenses satisfies the primary effect inquiry of our Establishment Clause cases.

Turning to the third part of the Lemon inquiry, we have no difficulty in concluding that the Minnesota statute does not "excessively entangle" the state in religion. The only plausible source of the "comprehensive, discriminating, and continuing state surveillance" necessary to run afoul of this standard would lie in the fact that state officials must determine whether particular textbooks qualify for a deduction. In making this decision, state officials must disallow deductions taken from "instructional books and materials used in the teaching of religious tenets, doctrines or worship, the purpose of which is to inculcate such tenets, doctrines or worship." Making decisions such as this does not differ substantially from making the types of decisions approved in earlier opinions of this Court. [See, e.g., Allen.] [4]

[Affirmed.]

Justice MARSHALL, with whom Justice BRENNAN, Justice BLACKMUN and Justice STEVENS join, dissenting.

The Establishment Clause [prohibits] a State from subsidizing religious education, whether it does so directly or indirectly. In my view, this principle of neutrality forbids [any] tax benefit, including the tax deduction at issue here, which subsidizes tuition payments to sectarian schools. I also believe that the Establishment Clause prohibits the tax deductions that Minnesota authorizes for the cost of books and other instructional materials used for sectarian purposes.

I. The majority today does not question the continuing vitality of this Court's decision in Nyquist. That decision established that a State may not support religious education either through direct grants to parochial schools or through financial aid to parents of parochial school students. Nyquist also established that financial aid to parents of students attending parochial schools is no more permissible if it is provided in the form of a tax credit than if provided in the form of cash payments. Notwithstanding these accepted principles, the Court today upholds a statute that provides a tax deduction for the tuition charged by religious schools. The Court concludes that the Minnesota statute is "vitally different" from the New York statute at issue in Nyquist. As demonstrated below, there is no significant difference between the two schemes. The Minnesota tax statute violates the Establishment Clause for precisely the same reason as the statute struck down in Nyquist: it has a direct and immediate effect of advancing religion.

A. [Like] the law involved in Nyquist, the Minnesota law can be said to serve a secular purpose: promoting pluralism and diversity among the State's public and nonpublic schools. But the Establishment Clause requires more than that legislation have a secular purpose. [As] we recognized in Nyquist, direct government subsidization of parochial school tuition is impermissible because "the effect of the aid is unmistakably to provide desired financial support for nonpublic, sectarian institutions." "[A]id to the educational function of [parochial] schools [necessarily] results in aid to the sectarian enterprise as a whole" because "[t]he very purpose of those schools is to provide an integrated secular and religious education." [Meek.] For this reason, aid to sectarian schools

---

4. No party to this litigation has urged that the Minnesota plan is invalid because it runs afoul of the rather elusive inquiry, subsumed under the third part of the Lemon test, whether the Minnesota statute partakes of the "divisive political potential" condemned in Lemon. The argument is advanced, however, by [amicus]. The Court's language in [Lemon] respecting political divisiveness was made in the context of Pennsylvania and Rhode Island statutes which provided for either direct payments of, or reimbursement of, a proportion of teachers' salaries in parochial schools. We think, in the light of the treatment in [later] cases, the language must be regarded as confined to cases where direct financial subsidies are paid to parochial schools or to teachers in parochial schools. [Footnote by Justice Rehnquist.]

must be restricted to ensure that it may not be used to further the religious mission of those schools.

Indirect assistance in the form of financial aid to parents for tuition payments is [impermissible] because it is not "subject [to] restrictions" which " 'guarantee the separation between secular and religious educational functions [and] ensure that State financial aid supports only the former.' " [Nyquist, quoting Lemon.] By ensuring that parents will be reimbursed for tuition payments they make, the Minnesota statute requires that taxpayers in general pay for the cost of parochial education and extends a financial "incentive to parents to send their children to sectarian schools." Nyquist. [That] parents receive a reduction of their tax liability, rather than a direct reimbursement, is of no greater significance here than it was in Nyquist. "[F]or purposes of determining whether such aid has the effect of advancing religion," it makes no difference whether the qualifying "parent receives an actual cash payment [or] is allowed to reduce [the] sum he would otherwise be obliged to pay over to the State." [Nyquist.] It is equally irrelevant whether a reduction in taxes takes the form of a tax "credit," a tax "modification," or a tax "deduction." What is of controlling significance is not the form but the "substantive impact" of the [financial aid].

B. 1. [The] majority first attempts to distinguish Nyquist on the ground that Minnesota makes all parents eligible to deduct up to $500 or $700 for each dependent, whereas the New York law allowed a deduction only for parents whose children attended nonpublic schools. Although Minnesota taxpayers who send their children to local public schools may not deduct tuition expenses because they incur none, they may deduct other expenses, such as the cost of gym clothes, pencils, and notebooks, which are shared by all parents of school-age children. This, in the majority's view, distinguishes the Minnesota scheme from the law at issue in Nyquist. That the Minnesota statute makes some small benefit available to all parents cannot alter the fact that the most substantial benefit provided by the statute is available only to those parents who send their children to schools that charge tuition. It is simply undeniable that the single largest expense that may be deducted under the Minnesota statute is tuition. The statute is little more than a subsidy of tuition masquerading as a subsidy of general educational expenses. The other deductible expenses are de minimis in comparison to tuition expenses.

Contrary to the majority's suggestion, the bulk of the tax benefits afforded by the Minnesota scheme are enjoyed by parents of parochial school children not because parents of public school children fail to claim deductions to which they are entitled, but because the latter are simply *unable* to claim the largest tax deduction that Minnesota authorizes. Fewer than 100 of more than 900,000 school-age children in Minnesota attend public schools that charge a general tuition. Of the total number of taxpayers who are eligible for the tuition deduction, approximately 96% send their children to religious schools.[1] Parents who send their children to free public schools are simply ineligible to obtain the full benefit of the deduction except in the unlikely event that they buy $700 worth of pencils, notebooks, and bus rides for their school-age children. Yet parents who pay at least $700 in tuition to nonpublic, sectarian schools can claim the full deduction even if they incur no other educational expenses.

That this deduction has a primary effect of promoting religion can easily be determined without any resort to the type of "statistical evidence" that the majority fears would lead to constitutional uncertainty. [In] this case, it is

1. Indeed, in this respect the Minnesota statute has an even greater tendency to promote religious education than the New York statute struck down in Nyquist, since the percentage of private schools that are nonsectarian is far greater in New York than in Minnesota. [Footnote by Justice Marshall.]

undisputed that well over 90% of the children attending tuition-charging schools in Minnesota are enrolled in sectarian schools. History and experience likewise instruct us that any generally available financial assistance for elementary and secondary school tuition expenses mainly will further religious education because the majority of the schools which charge tuition are sectarian. Because Minnesota, like every other State, is committed to providing free public education, tax assistance for tuition payments inevitably redounds to the benefit of nonpublic, sectarian schools and parents who send their children to those schools.

2. The majority also asserts that the Minnesota statute is distinguishable from the statute struck down in Nyquist in another respect: the tax benefit available under Minnesota law is a "genuine tax deduction," whereas the New York law provided a benefit which, while nominally a deduction, also had features of a "tax credit." Under the Minnesota law, the amount of the tax benefit varies directly with the amount of the expenditure. Under the New York law, the amount of deduction was not dependent upon the amount actually paid for tuition but was a predetermined amount which depended on the tax bracket of each taxpayer. The deduction was designed to yield roughly the same amount of tax "forgiveness" for each taxpayer. This is a distinction without a difference. Our prior decisions have rejected the relevance of the majority's formalistic distinction between tax deductions and the tax benefit at issue in [Nyquist].[2]

C. The majority incorrectly asserts that Minnesota's tax deduction for tuition expenses "bears less resemblance to the arrangement struck down in Nyquist than it does to assistance programs upheld in our prior decisions and discussed with approval in Nyquist." One might as well say that a tangerine bears less resemblance to an orange than to an apple. The two cases relied on by the majority [Allen and Everson] are inapposite today for precisely the same reasons that they were inapposite in Nyquist.[3] [The] Minnesota tuition tax deduction is not available to *all* parents, but only to parents whose children attend schools that charge tuition, which are comprised almost entirely of sectarian schools. More importantly, the assistance that flows to parochial schools as a result of the tax benefit is not restricted, and cannot be restricted, to the secular functions of those [schools].

II. In my view, Minnesota's tax deduction for the cost of textbooks and other instructional materials is also constitutionally infirm. The majority is simply mistaken in concluding that a tax deduction, unlike a tax credit or a direct grant to parents, promotes religious education in a manner that is only "attenuated." A tax deduction has a primary effect that advances religion if it is provided to offset expenditures which are not restricted to the secular activities of parochial schools. The instructional materials which are subsidized by the Minnesota tax deduction plainly may be used to inculcate religious values and

---

2. [The] deduction at issue in this case does differ from the tax benefits in Nyquist and our other prior cases in one respect: by its very nature the deduction embodies an inherent limit on the extent to which a State may subsidize religious education. Unlike a tax credit, which may wholly subsidize the cost of religious education if the size of the credit is sufficiently large, or a tax deduction of an arbitrary sum, a deduction of tuition payments from adjusted gross income can never "provide a basis [for] *complete subsidization* [of] religious schools." Nyquist. Nyquist made clear, however, that absolutely no subsidization is permissible unless it is restricted to the purely secular functions of those schools. [Footnote by Justice Marshall.]

3. Justice Marshall noted that Allen and Everson had been distinguished in Nyquist and also in Sloan v. Lemon, 413 U.S. 825 (1973). Quoting from the opinion in Sloan, Justice Marshall stated: "Financial assistance for tuition payments has a consequence that 'is quite unlike the sort of "indirect" and "incidental" benefits that flowed to sectarian schools from programs aiding *all* parents by supplying bus transportation and secular text books for their children. *Such benefits were carefully restricted to the purely secular side of church-affiliated institutions* and provided no special aid for those who had chose to support religious schools. Yet such aid approached the "verge" of the constitutionally impermissible.' [Sloane] (emphasis added in part)."

belief. [Secular] textbooks, like other secular instructional materials, contribute to the religious mission of the parochial schools that use those books. Although this Court upheld the loan of secular textbooks to religious schools in [Allen], the Court believed at that time that it lacked sufficient experience to determine "based solely on judicial notice" that "the processes of secular and religious training are so intertwined that secular textbooks furnished to students by the public [will always be] instrumental in the teaching of religion." This basis for distinguishing secular instructional materials and secular textbooks is simply untenable, and is inconsistent with many of our more recent decisions concerning state aid to parochial schools. See [Wolman; Meek]. In any event, the Court's assumption in Allen that the textbooks at issue there might be used only for secular education was based on the fact that those very books had been chosen by the State for use in the public schools. In contrast, the Minnesota statute does not limit the tax deduction of those books which the State has approved for use in public schools. [Indeed], under the [Minnesota scheme], textbooks chosen by parochial schools but not used by public schools are likely to be precisely the ones purchased by parents for their children's [use].

    III. [In] focusing upon the contributions made by church-related schools, the majority has lost sight of the issue before us in this case. "The sole question is whether state aid to these schools can be squared with the dictates of the Religion Clauses. Under our system the choice has been made that government is to be entirely excluded from the area of religious instruction. [The] Constitution decrees that religion must be a private matter for the individual, the family, and the institutions of private choice, and that while some involvement and entanglement are inevitable, lines must be drawn." [Lemon.] In my view, the lines drawn in Nyquist were drawn on a reasoned basis with appropriate regard for the principles of neutrality embodied by the Establishment Clause. I do not believe that the same can be said of the lines drawn by the majority today. For the first time, the Court has upheld financial support for religious schools without any reason at all to assume that the support will be restricted to the secular functions of those schools and will not be used to support religious instruction. This result is flatly at odds with the fundamental principle that a State may provide no financial support whatsoever to promote religion. As the Court stated in Everson and has often repeated, see, e.g., [Meek; Nyquist], "No tax in any amount, large or small, can be levied to support any religious activities or institutions, whatever they may be called, or whatever form they may adopt to teach or practice religion." I dissent.

AID TO HIGHER EDUCATION

    The majority of the Court has typically found fewer establishment clause barriers to financial aid to colleges than to elementary and secondary schools. Although the Court has applied the three-part test developed in the pre-college context ("purpose," "effect," and "entanglement"), the Justices have found it more readily satisfied in higher education cases and have been less prone to find excessive "entanglement" in state supervision schemes. The distinction between the levels of education was first articulated in Chief Justice BURGER's plurality opinion in TILTON v. RICHARDSON, 403 U.S. 672 (1971): "There are generally significant differences between the religious aspects of church-related institutions of higher learning and parochial elementary and secondary schools. [C]ollege students are less impressionable and less susceptible to religious indoctrination. [Furthermore], by their very nature, college and postgraduate courses tend to limit the opportunities for sectarian influence by virtue of their own internal disciplines. [Since] religious indoctrination is not a substantial purpose [of] these church-related colleges, [there] is less likelihood than in primary and secondary schools that religion will permeate the area of secular education. This reduces the risk that government aid will in fact serve to support religious activities. Correspondingly the necessity for intensive government surveillance is diminished and the resulting entanglements between government and religion lessened. Such inspection as may be necessary to ascertain that the facilities are devoted to secular education is minimal."

Tilton upheld federal construction grants to church-related colleges. The funds had to be used for facilities devoted exclusively to secular educational purposes.[1] The pattern of Tilton was followed two years later in Hunt v. McNair, 413 U.S. 734 (1973), where a divided Court sustained a construction aid program using state-issued revenue bonds to permit colleges to borrow funds at low interest. In its most recent encounter with the problem at the college level, ROEMER v. MARYLAND PUBLIC WORKS BD., 426 U.S. 736 (1976), the majority went a step further: it approved annual noncategorical grants to eligible private colleges, including some church-related ones, subject only to the restriction that the funds not be used for "sectarian purposes." Justice BLACKMUN's plurality opinion conceded that the "entanglement" problem arising from the supervision needed to assure that funds were used only for secular purposes was more serious in the context of annual grants than with "one-time" aid. He nevertheless found the program permissible.[2]

OTHER FORMS OF AID TO RELIGION

As noted above, a vast majority of the Court's cases involving aid to religious institutions have been in the context of parochial education. An important recent exception, however, is LARKIN v. GRENDEL'S DEN, INC., 459 U.S. 116 (1982). The challenged Massachusetts law in Larkin gave churches and schools the power to veto the issuance of liquor licenses to applicants located within a five hundred foot radius of these churches and schools. A nearly unanimous Court balked at the notion that governmental authority could be conferred on religious organizations and invalidated the law.[1] Chief Justice BURGER's majority opinion stated:

1. Chief Justice BURGER's plurality opinion was joined by Justices Harlan, Stewart and Blackmun. Justice WHITE, who would impose fewer establishment clause restraints, joined in the judgment. Justices DOUGLAS, BLACK, MARSHALL and BRENNAN dissented.

The plurality opinion also noted that the risk of entanglement was reduced by the fact that, unlike the typical pre-college education grants, the government aid here was a "one-time, single-purpose construction grant." (But see Roemer, the 1976 case noted in text.) The Tilton majority struck down only one provision of the program: the 20-year time limit on the "secular purposes only" restriction on the use of buildings constructed with federal funds. The Court excised that time limit. The leading dissent, by Justice Douglas, was particularly troubled by the federal surveillance needed to assure that the facilities would not be put to sectarian uses.

2. Justice BLACKMUN's plurality opinion was joined only by Chief Justice Burger and Justice Powell. Justice WHITE's opinion concurring in the judgment (and joined by Justice Rehnquist) thought the "entanglement" criterion superfluous. The dissenting opinions were writ-ten by Justice BRENNAN, joined by Justice Marshall, and by Justice STEVENS.

Maryland's surveillance was accomplished mainly through monitoring annual college reports identifying the aided nonsectarian expenditures. Justice Blackmun noted that the "political divisiveness" potential of grants to higher education was less than at the pre-college level, emphasizing that the state aid was "extended to private colleges generally, more than two-thirds of which [had] no religious affiliation, [in] sharp contrast to Nyquist, for example, where 95% of the aided schools were Roman Catholic parochial schools."

1. The Larkin case is noted here because in one sense it involves the grant of a special power to a religious institution—the power to veto issuance of liquor licenses. In that sense, it is plausibly viewed as an aspect of governmental aid to religion. Yet, as the Court's analysis makes clear, in another sense, it is also a case of religious intrusion into governmental affairs, the theme of sec. 1B, which follows. As the Court notes in Larkin, one of the perceived problems was that a religious institution had been permit-ted excessive involvement in the exercise of the government's zoning power. Larkin accordingly

"Appellants contend that the State may, without impinging on the Establishment Clause of the First Amendment, enforce what it describes as a 'zoning' law in order to shield schools and places of divine worship from the presence nearby of liquor dispensing establishments. [Plainly] schools and churches have a valid interest in being insulated from certain kinds of commercial establishments, including those dispensing liquor. [The] zoning function is traditionally a governmental [task], and courts should properly 'refrain from reviewing the merits of [such] decisions, absent a showing of arbitrariness or irrationality.' [But the law here] is not simply a legislative exercise of zoning power. [It] delegates to private, nongovernmental entities power to veto certain liquor license applications. This is a power ordinarily vested in agencies of government. [We] need not decide whether, or upon what conditions, such power may ever be delegated to nongovernmental entities; here, of two class of institutions to which the legislature has delegated this important decisionmaking power, [one] is religious. Under these circumstances, the deference normally due a legislative zoning judgment is not merited.

"The purposes of the First Amendment guarantees relating to religion were twofold: to foreclose state interference with the practice of religious faiths, and to foreclose the establishment of a state religion familiar in other Eighteenth Century systems. Religion and government, each insulated from the other, could then coexist. Jefferson's idea of a 'wall' was a useful figurative illustration to emphasize the concept of separateness. Some limited and incidental entanglement between church and state authority is inevitable in a complex modern society, but the concept of a 'wall' of separation is a useful signpost. Here that 'wall' is substantially breached by vesting discretionary governmental powers in religious bodies."

After noting the three Lemon criteria and finding "valid secular legislative purposes," the Chief Justice insisted that "the statute can be seen as having a 'primary' and 'principal' effect of advancing religion." Noting that the state courts had construed the law "as conferring upon churches a veto power over governmental licensing authority," he commented: "The churches' power under the statute is standardless, calling for no reasons, findings, or reasoned conclusions. That power may therefore be used by churches to promote goals beyond insulating the church from undesirable neighbors; it could be employed for explicitly religious goals, for example, favoring liquor licenses for members of that congregation or adherents of that faith. [In addition], the mere appearance of a joint exercise of legislative authority by Church and State provides a significant symbolic benefit to religion in the minds of some by reasons of the power conferred."

Turning to the third prong of the Lemon standard, he noted that "we have not previously had occasion to consider the entanglement implications of a statute vesting significant governmental authority in churches. This statute enmeshes churches in the exercise of substantial governmental powers contrary to our consistent interpretation of the Establishment Clause. [As the] cases make clear, the core rationale underlying the Establishment Clause is preventing 'a fusion of governmental and religious functions.' The Framers did not set up a system of government in which important, discretionary governmental powers would be delegated to or shared with religious institutions. [The law] substitutes the unilateral and absolute power of a church for the reasoned decisionmaking of a public legislative body acting on evidence and guided by standards, on issues with significant economic and political implications. The challenged statute thus enmeshes churches in the processes of government and creates the danger of '[p]olitical fragmentation and divisiveness along religious lines.'

provides a useful bridge between the themes of
sec. 1A and sec. 1B.

[Lemon.] Ordinary human experience and a long line of cases teach that few entanglements could be more offensive to the spirit of the Constitution."

Justice REHNQUIST, the sole dissenter, argued that because the state could have banned all liquor establishments within a five hundred foot radius of any church or school, the establishment clause could not prevent the state from electing a less drastic alternative such as the one here. He insisted that the question was not whether a law granting actual legislative power to churches was prohibited by the establishment clause, but rather "whether [this law] is such a statute." He argued that it was not, noting that the law did not "sponsor or subsidize any religious group or activity," and did not "encourage, much less compel, anyone to participate in religious activities or to support religious institutions." He added that to claim that the law "advances" religion was "to strain at the meaning of that word": "The State does [not] 'advance' religion by making provision for those who wish to engage in religious activities, as well as those who wish to engage in educational activities, to be unmolested by activities at a neighboring bar or tavern that have historically been thought incompatible. [The] State can constitutionally protect churches from liquor for the same reasons it can protect them from fire, noise, and other harm. The heavy First Amendment artillery that the Court fires at this sensible and unobjectionable Massachusetts statute is both unnecessary and unavailing."

B. ALLEGED INTRUSION OF RELIGION INTO GOVERNMENTAL ACTIVITIES

There are several similarities between the aid to religion cases discussed in sec. 1A, above, and the cases involving alleged intrusion of religion into governmental activities that are the focus of this subsection. In terms of context, the bulk of both types of cases has arisen in the educational context. The former group of cases involved parochial schools; this group involves public schools. The Court has used a single test to decide both types of cases, although the test itself has changed and developed over time.[1] The final similarity between the two groups of problems is that each area is replete with cases that seem inconsistent with one another.

"RELEASED TIME" PROGRAMS IN PUBLIC SCHOOLS

The Court subjected itself to charges of inconsistency in its initial encounters with problems involving allegedly excessive intrusions of religious themes into governmental activities. In McCollum v. Board of Education, 333 U.S. 203 (1948), the Court struck down a school board's practice of permitting students to attend sectarian classes held in the public schools during school hours by parochial school instructors. Just four years later, however, the Court held in Zorach (which follows) that releasing children during school hours to attend sectarian classes *outside* the public school did *not* violate the establishment clause. In examining Zorach, consider especially the persuasiveness of the Court's insistence that the challenged program there was sufficiently unlike that in McCollum to warrant a different result.

---

1. The Court has failed to rely on the multi-prong establishment test derived from cases such as Lemon and Walz on only one occasion. That case—Marsh v. Chambers (1983, p. 1495 be- low)—was one involving alleged inclusion of religion into governmental activities. Cf. Larson v. Valente (1982; p. 1496 below).

ZORACH v. CLAUSON

343 U.S. 306, 72 S.Ct. 679, 96 L.Ed. 954 (1952).

Mr. Justice DOUGLAS delivered the opinion of the Court.

New York City has a program which permits its public schools to release students during the school day so that they may leave the school buildings and school grounds and go to religious centers for religious instruction or devotional exercises. A student is released on written request of his parents. Those not released stay in the classrooms. The churches make weekly reports to the schools, sending a list of children who have been released from public school but who have not reported for religious instruction. This "released time" program involves neither religious instruction in public school classrooms nor the expenditure of public funds. All costs, including the application blanks, are paid by the religious organizations. The case is therefore unlike [McCollum], which involved a "released time" program from Illinois. In that case the classrooms were turned over to religious instructors. We accordingly held that the program violated the First Amendment.

[Appellants, taxpayers and residents whose children attend public schools, challenge the law], contending it is in essence not different from the one involved in [McCollum]. Their [argument] reduces itself to this: the weight and influence of the school is put behind a program for religious instruction; public school teachers police it, keeping tab on students who are released; the classroom activities come to a halt while the students who are released for religious instruction are on leave; the school is a crutch on which the churches are leaning for support in their religious training; without the cooperation of the schools this "released time" program, like the one in [McCollum], would be futile and ineffective. [The highest state court sustained the law.]

It takes obtuse reasoning to inject any issue of the "free exercise" of religion into the present case. No one is forced to go to the religious classroom and no religious exercise or instruction is brought to the classrooms of the public schools. A student need not take religious instruction. He is left to his own desires as to the manner or time of his religious devotions, if any. There is a suggestion that the system involves the use of coercion to get public school students into religious classrooms. There is no evidence in the record before us that supports that conclusion. [If] in fact coercion were used, if it were established that any one or more teachers were using their office to persuade or force students to take the religious instruction, a wholly different case would be presented.[1] [Hence] we put aside that claim of coercion both as respects the "free exercise" of religion and "an establishment of religion."

Moreover, apart from that claim of coercion, we do not see how New York by this type of "released time" program has made a law respecting an establishment of [religion]. There cannot be the slightest doubt that the First Amendment reflects the philosophy that Church and State should be separated [and] within the scope of its coverage permits no exception; the prohibition is absolute. The First Amendment, however, does not say that in every and all respects there shall be a separation of Church and State. Rather, it studiously defines the manner, the specific ways, in which there shall be no concert or union or dependency one on the other. That is the common sense of the matter. Otherwise the state and religion would be aliens to each other—hostile,

---

1. Appellants contend that they should have been allowed to prove that the system is in fact administered in a coercive manner. The New York Court of Appeals declined to grant a trial on this issue, noting, inter alia, that appellants had not properly raised their claim in the manner required by state practice. [This] independent state ground for decision precludes appellants from raising the issue of maladministration in this [proceeding]. [Footnote by Justice Douglas.]

suspicious, and even unfriendly. Churches could not be required to pay even property taxes. Municipalities would not be permitted to render police or fire protection to religious groups. Policemen who helped parishioners into their places of worship would violate the Constitution. Prayers in our legislative halls; the appeals to the Almighty in the messages of the Chief Executive; the proclamations making Thanksgiving Day a holiday; "so help me God" in our courtroom oaths—these and all other references to the Almighty that run through our laws, our public rituals, our ceremonies would be flouting the First Amendment. A fastidious atheist or agnostic could even object to the supplication with which the Court opens each session: "God save the United States and this Honorable Court."

We would have to press the concept of separation of Church and State to these extremes to condemn the present law on constitutional grounds. The nullification of this law would have wide and profound effects. A Catholic student applies to his teacher for permission to leave the school during hours on a Holy Day of Obligation to attend a mass. A Jewish student asks his teacher for permission to be excused for Yom Kippur. A Protestant wants the afternoon off for a family baptismal ceremony. In each case the teacher requires parental consent in writing. In each case the teacher, in order to make sure the student is not a truant, goes further and requires a report from the priest, the rabbi, or the minister. The teacher in other words cooperates in a religious program to the extent of making it possible for her students to participate in it. Whether she does it occasionally for a few students, regularly for one, or pursuant to a systematized program designed to further the religious needs of all the students does not alter the character of the act.

We are a religious people whose institutions presuppose a Supreme Being. We guarantee the freedom to worship as one chooses. [We] sponsor an attitude on the part of government that shows no partiality to any one group and that lets each flourish according to the zeal of its adherents and the appeal of its dogma. When the state encourages religious instruction or cooperates with religious authorities by adjusting the schedule of public events to sectarian needs, it follows the best of our traditions. For it then respects the religious nature of our people and accommodates the public service to their spiritual needs. To hold that it may not would be to find in the Constitution a requirement that the government show a callous indifference to religious groups. That would be preferring those who believe in no religion over those who do believe. [Government] may not coerce anyone to attend church, to observe a religious holiday, or to take religious instruction. But it can close its doors or suspend its operations as to those who want to repair to their religious sanctuary for worship or instruction. No more than that is undertaken here. [The] constitutional standard is the separation of Church and State. The problem [is] one of degree.

In the McCollum case the classrooms were used for religious instruction and the force of the public school was used to promote that instruction. Here, [the] public schools do no more than accommodate their schedules to a program of outside religious instructions. We follow [McCollum]. But we cannot expand it to cover the present released time program unless separation of Church and State means that public institutions can make no adjustments of their schedules to accommodate the religious needs of the people. We cannot read into the Bill of Rights such a philosophy of hostility to religion.

Affirmed.

Mr. Justice BLACK, [dissenting].

In the New York program, as in that of Illinois [invalidated in McCollum], the school authorities release some of the children on the condition that they attend the religious classes, get reports on whether they attend, and hold the other children in the school building until the religious hour is over. As we attempted to make categorically clear, the McCollum decision would have been the same if the religious classes had not been held in the school buildings. [New York] is manipulating its compulsory education laws to help religious sects get pupils. This is not separation but combination of [Church and State].

Mr. Justice JACKSON, dissenting.

This released time program is founded upon a use of the State's power of coercion, which, for me, determines its unconstitutionality. Stripped to its essentials, the plan has two stages, first, that the State compel each student to yield a large part of his time for public secular education and, second, that some of it be "released" to him on condition that he devote it to sectarian religious purposes. [If] public education were taking so much of the pupils' time as to injure the public or the students' welfare by encroaching upon their religious opportunity, simply shortening everyone's school day would facilitate voluntary and optional attendance at Church classes. But that suggestion is rejected upon the ground that if they are made free many students will not go to the Church. Hence, they must be deprived of freedom for this period, with Church attendance put to them as one of the two permissible ways of using it.

The greater effectiveness of this system over voluntary attendance after school hours is due to the truant officer who, if the youngster fails to go to the Church school, dogs him back to the public schoolroom. Here schooling is more or less suspended during the "released time" so the nonreligious attendants will not forge ahead of the churchgoing absentees. But it serves as a temporary jail for a pupil who will not go to Church. It takes more subtlety of mind than I possess to deny that this is governmental constraint in support of religion. [I] challenge the Court's suggestion that opposition to this plan can only be antireligious, atheistic, or agnostic. My evangelistic brethren confuse an objection to compulsion with an objection to religion. It is possible to hold a faith with enough confidence to believe that what should be rendered to God does not need to be decided and collected by Caesar. [A] number of Justices just short of a majority of the majority that promulgates today's passionate dialectics [and "epithetical jurisprudence"] joined in answering them in [McCollum]. The distinction attempted between that case and this is trivial, almost to the point of cynicism. [The] wall which the Court was professing to erect between Church and State has become even more warped and twisted than I expected. Today's judgment will be more interesting to students of psychology and of the judicial processes than to students of constitutional law.[1]

"RELEASED TIME" PROGRAMS: ZORACH, McCOLLUM, AND "COERCION"

1. *A distinction between Zorach and McCollum?* In McCollum, Justice Black's majority opinion had found two major problems with the Illinois program. First, public school buildings were used for the purpose of providing religious education. Second, the program afforded "sectarian groups an invaluable aid in that it help[ed] to provide pupils for their religious classes through use of the state's compulsory public school machinery." Was Justice Douglas' effort to distinguish the Zorach program from the one in McCollum persuasive? Does not Justice Jackson's dissent demonstrate that at least with respect to the second

1. Justice FRANKFURTER, who agreed with Justice Jackson, also submitted a dissent, emphasizing that "the school system did not 'close its doors' "; instead, "formalized religious instruction [was] substituted for other activity which those who do not participate in the re-leased-time program are compelled to attend." [For a review of the relations among the Justices at the time of these early establishment cases, see Note, "[A] Study of Group Decisionmaking by the Supreme Court," 83 Yale L.J. 1202 (1974).]

flaw in the McCollum program, the Zorach program was indistinguishable? Did Zorach then implicitly overrule McCollum? Does Zorach indicate that the Court had moved to a position—explicitly endorsed in Justice Douglas' concurrence in Engel v. Vitale (1962), below—that the presence or absence of government financing should be the determinative criterion? [1]

2. *Permissible religious intrusions into school practices and "coercion."* Can a general standard be stated to govern the extent to which accommodations between religion and the schools are permissible? Consider the suggestion in Choper, "Religion in the Schools," 47 Minn.L.Rev. 329 (1963): "The proposed constitutional standard is that for problems concerning religious intrusion in the public schools, the establishment clause [is] violated when the state engages in what may be fairly characterized as *solely religious activity* that is likely to result in (1) *compromising* the student's religious or conscientious beliefs or (2) *influencing* the student's freedom of religious or conscientious choice." Is that approach justifiable? Why should it not be enough that the school practices are "solely religious"? Why should it also be necessary to demonstrate impact on student beliefs or choice? What is the relevant "impact" or "coercion" in the preceding cases and those that follow? Is "coercion" a question of judicial assessment of probable consequences of the challenged practice? Or is it a question of fact in each case, to be proved at trial? [2]

THE SCHOOL PRAYER CASES

1. So far, the Court has demonstrated none of the inconsistency that characterized the released time cases in the context of school prayers. Its unequivocal position has been that school prayers of any sort violate the establishment clause. The Court's first encounter with the problem came in ENGEL v. VITALE, 370 U.S. 421 (1962). There, the New York Board of Regents had prepared a "non-denominational" prayer for use in the public schools. A local school board directed that the prayer be recited daily by each class.[1] That practice was challenged by parents of a number of students who claimed that it was "contrary to the beliefs, religions, or religious practices of both themselves and their children." The highest state court upheld the practice, so long as the schools did not compel any student to join in the prayer over a parent's objection. Justice BLACK's majority opinion held the practice "wholly inconsistent with the Establishment Clause." The practice was clearly "a religious activity" and the establishment clause "must at least mean that [it] is no part of the business of government to compose official prayers for any group

---

1. Was there really significant "financing" in Engel? More than in Zorach? Compare Justice Brennan's insistence that Zorach had not overruled McCollum, in his concurrence in Schempp (1963; p. 1488 below). Justice Brennan argued that the distinction between McCollum and Zorach lay not in "the difference in expenditures involved," but rather a "deeper difference": "the McCollum program placed the religious instructor in the public school classroom in precisely the position of authority held by the regular teachers of secular subjects, while the Zorach program did not." Was Justice Brennan's effort to distinguish the cases more persuasive than Justice Douglas'?

2. Note Justice Clark's test in Schempp (p. 1488 below), emphasizing the "purpose" and the "primary effect" of the practice and insisting that

a showing of coercion is unnecessary to sustain an establishment claim. Compare Justice Stewart's dissent in Schempp, insisting that it must be shown that a particular school exercise is coercive in the particular case. Would a case-by-case determination of coerciveness produce inadequate guidance as to permissible state practices? Would it put an undue premium on finding plaintiffs who are both "coerced" enough and strong enough to bring law suits challenging the practice? Cf. Brown, "Quis Custodiet Ipsos Custodes?—The School Prayer Cases," 1963 Sup.Ct. Rev. 1.

1. The prayer read: "Almighty God, we acknowledge our dependence upon Thee, and we beg Thy blessings upon us, our parents, our teachers and our Country."

of the American people to recite as a part of a religious program carried on by government."

Justice Black noted that objections to "this very practice of establishing governmentally composed prayers" prompted many of the colonists to leave England. He added: "Neither the fact that the prayer may be denominationally neutral, nor the fact that its observance on the part of the students is voluntary, can serve to free it from the limitations of the Establishment Clause, as it might from the Free Exercise [Clause]. Although these two clauses may in certain instances overlap, they forbid two quite different kinds of governmental encroachment upon religious freedom. The Establishment Clause, unlike the Free Exercise Clause, does not depend upon any showing of direct governmental compulsion and is violated by the enactment of laws which establish an official religion whether those laws operate directly to coerce nonobserving individuals or not. This is not to say, of course, that laws officially prescribing a particular form of religious worship do not involve coercion of such individuals. When the power, prestige and financial support of government is placed behind a particular religious belief, the indirect coercive pressure upon religious minorities to conform to the prevailing officially approved religion is plain. But the purposes underlying the Establishment Clause go much further than that. [Its] most immediate purpose rested on the belief that a union of government and religion tends to destroy government and to degrade religion. [Another] purpose [rested upon] an awareness of the historical fact that governmentally established religions and religious persecutions go hand in hand."

Justice DOUGLAS' concurrence saw the central issue as "whether the Government can constitutionally finance a religious exercise." He added: "Our system at the federal and state levels is presently honeycombed with such financing. [I] think it is an unconstitutional undertaking whatever form it takes." [2] Justice STEWART's dissent quoted Justice Douglas' Zorach opinion ["We are a religious people whose institutions presuppose a Supreme Being"] and concluded that New York's practice merely recognized "the deeply entrenched and highly cherished spiritual traditions of our Nation"—and that the references to religion and to God in such practices as congressional prayers and official oaths was similarly justified.[3]

2. One year after Engel, the Court extended the principles of that case beyond state-composed prayers—and in the process put forth an important reformulation of establishment criteria. ABINGTON SCHOOL DIST. v. SCHEMPP, 374 U.S. 203 (1963), held that the establishment clause prohibits state laws and practices "requiring the selection and reading at the opening of the school day of verses from the Holy Bible and the recitation of the Lord's Prayer by the students in unison." The Pennsylvania law in Schempp provided: "At least ten verses from the Holy Bible shall be read, without comment, at the opening of each public school on each school day. Any child shall be excused

---

2. Justice Douglas acknowledged the tension between his vote here and the decision in Everson, which he had joined. He stated that he had concluded that, "in retrospect," Everson was "out of line with the First Amendment" and that Justice Rutledge's dissent there was correct. (Justices Frankfurter and White did not participate in Engel.)

3. The Engel ruling provoked widespread public criticism, with repercussions that have reverberated ever since. Congressional attempts to propose constitutional amendments authorizing school prayers failed in 1966 and again in 1971, although a simple majority of both houses approved the resolutions. The school prayer

campaign resurfaced in the spring of 1979, when the Senate amended a Supreme Court jurisdiction bill to include a provision removing all jurisdiction from the federal courts to hear challenges to voluntary school prayer programs. Senator Helms, the bill's sponsor, stated: "There simply is no liberty contained in the Establishment Clause to be 'incorporated' through the 14th Amendment." The Helms provision was not adopted by Congress. (Recall chap. 1, sec. 3, above.) But the efforts in Congress to modify or overturn the Court's school prayer rulings continued into the 1980s. The developments in recent years are traced in footnote 9 below.

from such Bible reading, or attending such Bible reading, upon the written request of his parent or guardian." The Schempp family, members of the Unitarian Church, successfully challenged high school opening exercises involving the recitation of the Lord's Prayer as well as the reading of the Bible verses.[4]

a. *The majority standard.* Justice CLARK's opinion for the Court stated: "The wholesome 'neutrality' of which this Court's cases speak [stems] from a recognition of the teachings of history that powerful sects or groups might bring about a fusion of governmental and religious functions or a concert or dependency of one upon the other to the end that official support of the State or Federal Government would be placed behind the tenets of one or of all orthodoxies. This the Establishment Clause prohibits. And a further reason for neutrality is found in the Free Exercise Clause, which recognizes the value of religious training, teaching and observance and, more particularly, the right of every person to freely choose his own course with reference thereto, free of any compulsion from the state. This the Free Exercise Clause guarantees. Thus, [the] two clauses may overlap. [The] test may be stated as follows: *what are the purpose and the primary effect of the enactment?* If either is the advancement or inhibition of religion then the enactment exceeds the scope of legislative power as circumscribed by the Constitution. That is to say that to withstand the strictures of the Establishment Clause *there must be a secular legislative purpose and a primary effect that neither advances nor inhibits religion.* [Everson; McGowan (1961; p. 1495 below).] The [purpose of the] Free Exercise Clause [is] to secure religious liberty in the individual by prohibiting any invasions thereof by civil authority. Hence it is necessary in a free exercise case for one to show the coercive effect of the enactment as it operates against him in the practice of his religion. The distinction between the two clauses is apparent—a violation of the Free Exercise Clause is predicated on coercion while the Establishment Clause violation need not be so attended."[5]

Applying those principles, Justice Clark concluded that "the laws require religious exercises and such exercises are being conducted in direct violation of the rights of the [challengers]." Permitting individual students to be excused from the exercises "furnishes no defense. [Engel.] Further, it is no defense to urge that the religious practices here may be relatively minor encroachments on the First Amendment. The breach of neutrality that is today a trickling stream may all too soon become a raging torrent." He rejected the argument that "unless these religious exercises are permitted a 'religion of secularism' is established in the schools." He added: "[W]e cannot accept that the concept of neutrality [collides] with the majority's right to free exercise of religion. While the Free Exercise Clause clearly prohibits the use of state action to deny the rights of free exercise to *anyone,* it has never meant that a majority could use the machinery of the State to practice its beliefs." He noted that the decision did not bar the "study of the Bible or of religion, when presented objectively as part of a secular program of education." But that was not the case here: these were "religious exercises,[6] required by the State in violation of the command of

4. In Murray v. Curlett, a Maryland case decided together with Schempp, Mrs. Murray and her son, "both professed atheists," challenged a Baltimore school rule providing for the holding of opening exercises consisting primarily of the "reading, without comment, of a chapter in the Holy Bible and/or the use of the Lord's Prayer." As in Schempp, the practice permitted children to be excused at the request of a parent.

5. Emphasis added. (The italicized passages mark the origin of two of the three prongs of the modern Court's establishment standard frequently applied in the cases in sec. 1A above.)

6. In Schempp, the Court relied on the trial court's finding that the practices constituted "religious exercises." There was no such finding in Murray, but the Court rejected the argument that the programs could be justified as efforts to promote such secular purposes as "the promotion of moral values." Justice Clark noted that the King James version of the Bible had been used, which demonstrated the religious character. He added: "But even if [the] purpose is not strictly religious, it is sought to be accomplished through readings [from] the Bible. Surely the place of

the First Amendment that the Government maintain strict neutrality, neither aiding nor opposing religion."

b. *The concurrences.* Three Justices who joined the opinion of the Court submitted separate statements as well. Justice DOUGLAS saw two different violations of the establishment clause: the practices were unconstitutional not only because they constituted state-conducted religious exercises in violation of the required "neutrality" but also because "public funds, though small in amount, are being used to promote a religious exercise." Justice GOLDBERG, joined by Justice Harlan, spoke of the "unavoidable accommodations necessary" to achieve the "fullest realization of true religious liberty" but concluded: "The practices [here] do not fall within any sensible or acceptable concept of compelled or permitted accommodation and involve the state so significantly and directly in the realm of the sectarian as to give rise to those very divisive influences and inhibitions of freedom which both religion clauses of the First Amendment preclude." Justice BRENNAN's concurrence was by far the most extensive. He explored at length the history and interpretations of the religion clauses to explain his conclusion that "not every involvement of religion in public life is unconstitutional." His discussion of "the line we must draw between the permissible and the impermissible" noted: "What the Framers meant to foreclose [are] those involvements of religious with secular institutions which (a) serve the essentially religious activities of religious institutions; (b) employ the organs of government for essentially religious purposes; or (c) use essentially religious means to serve governmental ends, where secular means would suffice. [On] the other hand, there may be myriad forms of involvements of government with religion which do not import such dangers and therefore should [not be] deemed to violate the Establishment Clause." [7]

c. *The Stewart dissent.* Justice STEWART, the sole dissenter, insisted that "religion and government must necessarily interact in countless ways" and that "there are areas in which a doctrinaire reading of the Establishment Clause leads to irreconcilable conflict with the Free Exercise Clause." He elaborated: "That the central value embodied in the First Amendment—and, more particularly, in the guarantee of 'liberty' contained in the 14th—is the safeguarding of an individual's right to free exercise of his religion has been consistently recognized. [This] makes the cases before us such difficult ones for me. For there is involved in these cases a substantial free exercise claim on the part of those who affirmatively desire to have their children's school day open with the reading of passages from the [Bible]. Our decisions make clear that there is no constitutional bar to the use of government property for religious purposes. On the contrary, this Court has consistently held that the discriminatory barring of religious groups from public property is itself a violation of [First Amendment] guarantees. [E.g., Niemotko v. Maryland, chap. 12 above.] [The] dangers both to government and to religion inherent in official support of instruction in the tenets of various religious sects [see McCollum] are absent in the present cases, which involve only a reading from the Bible unaccompanied by comments which might otherwise constitute instruction. [In] the absence of coercion

---

the Bible as an instrument of religion cannot be gainsaid."

7. Among the "involvements" Justice Brennan suggested as permissible were such "accommodations" between establishment and free exercise as providing chaplains for prisoners and soldiers and granting draft exemptions for ministers and conscientious objectors. He added: "I do not say the government *must* provide chaplains or draft exemptions." Moreover, he suggested that congressional prayers and chaplains

were permissible because legislators are "mature adults." And, relying on McGowan (below), he suggested that "the various patriotic exercises" in public schools that contain religious references might be permissible because, "whatever [their] origins, [they] no longer have a religious purpose or meaning. The reference to divinity in the revised pledge of allegiance, for example, may merely recognize the historical fact that our Nation was believed to have been founded 'under God.'"

upon those who do not wish to [participate], such provisions cannot [be] held to represent the type of support of religion barred by the [Establishment Clause].

"I have said that these provisions authorizing religious exercises are properly to be regarded as measures making possible the free exercise of religion. But it is important to stress [that] the question presented is not whether exercises such as those at issue here are constitutionally compelled, but rather whether they are constitutionally invalid. And that issue, in my view, turns on the question of coercion. [To] be specific, it seems to me clear that certain types of exercises would present situations in which no possibility of coercion on the part of secular officials could be claimed to exist. [But] a law which provided for religious exercises during the school day and which contained no excusal provision would obviously be unconstitutionally coercive upon those who did not wish to participate. And even under a law containing an excusal provision, if the exercises were held during the school day, and no equally desirable alternative were provided by the school authorities, the likelihood that children might be under at least some psychological compulsion to participate would be great. In a case such as the latter, however, I think we would err if we *assumed* such coercion in the absence of any evidence. Viewed in this light, it seems to be clear that the records in both of the cases before us are wholly inadequate to support an informed or responsible decision." He accordingly urged remand of the cases for additional evidence regarding coercion in the challenged programs.

Transitional note. Engel and Schempp seemed to resolve the school prayer issue, at least so far as the courts are concerned.[8] However, the school prayer issue continues to be a controversial political issue in Congress and throughout the Nation, as it has been almost continuously since Engel in 1962.[9] Note, moreover, that the Court has decided a number of other cases involving

8. However, state and local communities have continued efforts to find ways to permit opportunities for "voluntary" prayer or meditation in classroom contexts, and those efforts have produced recurrent litigation in state and lower federal courts. A case raising the issue of silent prayer opportunities in a modern context was pending in the Court in February 1985. For the Court's decision, and possible reexamination of the Engel-Schempp line of cases, see the 1985 Supplement to this book.

9. In Congress in the early 1980s, Senator Helms' efforts to deal with the school prayer issue through jurisdiction-curbing legislation (see footnote 3 above) continued. But that legislative approach seems to have lost some of its force, at least partly as a result of actions by the Reagan Administration. First, Attorney General Smith cast doubt on the constitutionality of curbing Court jurisdiction, as noted in chap. 1 above. Second, President Reagan, in May 1982, proposed a constitutional amendment providing that "[n]othing in this Constitution shall be construed to prohibit individual or group prayer in public schools or other public institutions. No person shall be required by the United States or any state to participate in prayer." Although nothing came of that proposal in 1982, there was extensive attention to it (and intensive lobbying about it) in the 98th Congress (1983–84). The opponents argued primarily that it was unwise to introduce any kind of prayer into the public schools, and that any prayer recitation approved

or led by school authorities carried with it strong if unspoken pressure to participate. At one point in the Committee consideration of the Amendment, Senator Hatch drafted a compromise provision stating that nothing in the Constitution prohibits "individual or group silent prayer or meditation" and banning any required participation in or government encouragement of "any particular form of prayer or meditation." Both President Reagan's proposal, as modified, and Senator Hatch's were sent to the Senate floor by the Senate Judiciary Committee. In two weeks of floor debates during March, 1984, it became clear that the President's proposal stood the best chance of adoption. The vote on that Amendment finally came on March 20, 1984, with 56 in favor and 44 against. Thus, the proposal fell 11 votes short of the required two-thirds majority in the Senate. President Reagan responded with a promise to continue the struggle, Senator Hatch has stated that he will try to revive the issue, and Senator Helms has pledged to renew pressure for his jurisdiction-stripping proposal.

How far would President Reagan's proposed constitutional amendment reach? Would it undercut Engel or Schempp? McCollum? Stone v. Graham (which follows)? For a comprehensive review of the proposal, see Ackerman, "Legal Analysis of President Reagan's Proposed Constitutional Amendment on School Prayer" (Congressional Research Service, The Library of Congress, June 2, 1982).

allegedly excessive religious influence in public schools, as the next group of notes illustrates.

OTHER ALLEGED INTRUSIONS OF RELIGION INTO PUBLIC EDUCATION

1. STONE v. GRAHAM, 449 U.S. 39 (1980): The Court held unconstitutional a Kentucky law that required the posting of a copy of the Ten Commandments, purchased with private contributions, in public school classrooms. In sustaining the law, the state trial court had emphasized that the law's "avowed purpose" was "secular and not religious." The Court, relying in part on its school prayer and Bible reading rulings, reversed summarily, without hearing argument on the merits. The majority's per curiam opinion concluded that the law had "no secular legislative purpose," even though it required that each display of the Ten Commandments have a notation in small print stating: "The secular application of the Ten Commandments is clearly seen in its adoption as the fundamental legal code of Western Civilization and the Common Law of the United States." The majority viewed the predominant purpose of the posting requirement as "plainly religious," since the Ten Commandments are "undeniably a sacred text in the Jewish and Christian faiths." Even though some of the Commandments address secular matters, "the first part of the Commandments concerns the religious duties of believers." The Court noted that this was not a case "in which the Ten Commandments are integrated into the school curriculum, where the Bible may constitutionally be used in an appropriate study of history, civilization, ethics, comparative religion, or the like. Posting of religious texts on the wall serves no such educational function." [1]

2. EPPERSON v. ARKANSAS, 393 U.S. 97 (1968): The Court invalidated the Arkansas version of the Tennessee "anti-evolution" law that gained national notoriety in the Scopes "monkey law" trial in 1927. The Court found the law to be in conflict with the establishment clause mandate of "neutrality." The Arkansas law prohibited teachers in state schools from teaching "the theory or doctrine that mankind ascended or descended from a lower order of animals." The highest state court had expressed "no opinion" on "whether the Act prohibits any explanation of the theory of evolution or merely prohibits teaching that the theory is true." On either interpretation, Justice FORTAS' majority opinion concluded, the law could not stand: "The overriding fact is that Arkansas' law selects from the body of knowledge a particular segment which it proscribes for the sole reason that it is deemed to conflict with a particular religious doctrine; that is, with a particular interpretation of the Book of Genesis by a particular religious group." The Court found it unnecessary to rely on broad academic freedom principles [2] because of the availability of the "narrower terms" of the First Amendment's religion provisions: "The State's

---

1. Justice REHNQUIST's dissent insisted that the Court's ruling was "without precedent in Establishment Clause jurisprudence." He noted: "The fact that the asserted secular purpose may overlap what some may see as a religious objective does not render [the law] unconstitutional." He added: "The Court's emphasis on the religious nature of the first part of the Ten Commandments is beside the point. The document as a whole has had significant secular impact, and the Constitution does not require that Kentucky students see only an expurgated or redacted version containing only the elements with directly traceable secular effects." Justice STEWART also dissented on the merits; Chief Justice BURGER and Justice BLACKMUN objected to the summary disposition, arguing that the case should have been given plenary consideration.

2. Recall the discussion of freedom of expression issues in the school context in the preceding chapter. Recall especially the consideration of problems of government speech and arguable limits on the state authority to prescribe curricula and school library books in Board of Education v. Pico (1982; p. 1323 above).

undoubted right to prescribe the curriculum for its public schools" did not include the right to bar "the teaching of a scientific theory or doctrine where that prohibition is based upon reasons that violate the First Amendment." Here, given the history of the 1928 Arkansas law, "fundamentalist sectarian conviction was and is the law's reason for existence." This plainly was not the required religious neutrality: "Arkansas did not seek to excise from the curricula of its schools and universities all discussion of the origin of man. The law's effort was confined to an attempt to blot out a particular theory because of its supposed conflict with the Biblical account, literally read."

In separate opinions, Justices BLACK and STEWART explained that they concurred solely on the ground of vagueness. Justice Black criticized the majority for reaching out to "troublesome" First Amendment questions. He noted, for example, that "a state law prohibiting all teaching of human development or biology is constitutionally quite different from a law that compels a teacher to teach as true only one theory of a given doctrine" and he stated that he was not ready to hold "that a person hired to teach schoolchildren takes with him into the classroom a constitutional right to teach sociological, economic, political, or religious subjects that the school's managers do not want discussed." He questioned, moreover, whether the majority's view achieved "religious neutrality": If some considered evolution anti-religious, was the state constitutionally bound to permit teaching of anti-religious doctrine? Did the Court's holding infringe "the religious freedom of those who consider evolution an anti-religious doctrine?" Since there was no indication that the "literal Biblical doctrine" of evolution was taught, could not the removal of the subject of evolution be justified as leaving the State "in a neutral position toward these supposedly competing religious and anti-religious doctrines?"[3]

3. WIDMAR v. VINCENT, 454 U.S. 263 (1981): This case (already noted earlier, for its free speech aspects, at p. 1265 above) arose in the context of a free speech challenge to a state university's ban on the use of its facilities for prayer and religious discussion by student groups. As noted in the earlier note on the case, the university, in its effort to defend its policy against the First Amendment challenge, contended that it had a "compelling interest" in promoting the separation of church and state mandated by the federal and state constitutions. A lower federal court agreed with the university's argument: it found the regulation not only justified, but required, by the establishment

---

3. Justice Black added: "It would be difficult to make a First Amendment case out of a state law eliminating the subject of higher mathematics, or astronomy, or biology from its curriculum. [I can imagine no reason] why a State is without power to withdraw from its curriculum any subject deemed too emotional and controversial for its public schools." He also objected to the majority's suggestion that the ruling rested on the improper "motives" of the law: "[I]t is simply too difficult to determine what [a legislature's] motives were."

But an inquiry into legislative motive did constitute a major part of the well-publicized litigation in McLean v. Arkansas Bd. of Education, 529 F.Supp. 1255 (E.D.Ark.1982). At issue was a 1981 Arkansas law requiring: "Public schools within this State shall give balanced treatment to creation-science and to evolution-science." After lengthy proceedings, Judge Overton enjoined enforcement of the law, finding it in violation of the establishment clause.

Applying the now-familiar three-part test, Judge Overton concluded that the law had a plainly religious purpose. "The State failed to produce any evidence which would warrant an inference or conclusion that at any point in the process anyone considered the legitimate educational value of the Act. It was simply and purely an effort to introduce the Biblical version of creation into the public school curricula. The only inference which can be drawn [is] that the Act was passed with the specific purpose [of] advancing religion." Additionally, the Act itself, regardless of the motivation for its introduction and passage, was found to be inescapably religious: "The idea of sudden creation from nothing [is] an inherently religious concept." Judge Overton supported this view by concluding that creation science "is simply not science." Because the teaching of creationism could have no effect other than a religious one, and because the discussion of "creation-science" in class would inevitably be a religious discussion, Judge Overton found that the law also failed the "effect" and "entanglement" parts of the establishment clause test.

clause. The Court, however, rejected the university's claim. The Court noted that the university had made its facilities generally available for the activities of student groups and had thereby created a public forum. The university's exclusionary policy thus violated "the fundamental principle that a state regulation of speech should be content-neutral"; and the university's claim that it was promoting establishment clause values could not justify its content-based exclusion.

In examining separation of church and state principles, Justice POWELL's majority opinion turned first to the impact of the Establishment Clause: "We agree that the interest of the University in complying with its constitutional obligations may be characterized as compelling. It does not follow, however, that an 'equal access' policy would be incompatible with this Court's Establishment Clause cases. Those cases hold that a policy will not offend the Establishment Clause if it can pass a three-pronged [test]." Here, two prongs of the test were clearly met: "an open-forum policy, including nondiscrimination against religious speech, would have [1] a secular purpose [4] and would [2] avoid entanglement with religion."

The university argued that an open-forum policy would nevertheless violate the third prong of the test, because it would have the "primary effect" of advancing religion. Justice Powell replied: "The University's argument misconceives the nature of this case. The question is not whether the creation of a religious forum would violate the Establishment Clause. [The] question is whether it can now exclude groups because of the content of their speech. In this context we are unpersuaded that the primary effect of the public forum, open to all forms of discourse, would be to advance religion." He conceded that religious groups would probably "benefit from access to University facilities," but emphasized that prior cases had explained that "a religious organization's enjoyment of merely 'incidental' benefits does not violate the prohibition against the 'primary advancement' of religion." He concluded: "We are satisfied that any religious benefits of an open forum at [the university] would be 'incidental' within the meaning of our cases. Two factors are especially relevant. First, an open forum in a public university does not confer any imprimatur of State approval on religious sects or practices. [Second], the forum is available to a broad class of non-religious as well as religious speakers; there are over 100 recognized student groups at [the university]. The provision of benefits to so broad a spectrum of groups is an important index of secular effect. [At] least in the absence of empirical evidence that religious groups will dominate [the university's] open forum, we [believe] that the advancement of religion would not be the forum's 'primary effect.'"[5]

---

4. In a footnote at this point, Justice Powell commented: "Because this case involves a forum already made generally available to student groups, it differs from those cases in which this Court has invalidated statutes permitting school facilities to be used for instruction by religious groups, but *not* by others. See, e.g., [McCollum]. In those cases the school may appear to sponsor the views of the speaker."

Justice STEVENS concurred only in the judgment. His separate opinion, emphasizing free speech analysis, is noted in chap. 12 above.

5. The university also sought to justify its policy on the ground that Missouri's constitutional provision prohibiting state aid to religion went further than the federal Establishment Clause. Justice Powell rejected that argument as

well. He noted that the challengers' "First Amendment rights are entitled to special constitutional solicitude" because "the most exacting scrutiny" is required when a state "undertakes to regulate speech on the basis of its content." He proceeded: "On the other hand, the State interest asserted here—in achieving greater separation of church and State than is already ensured under the Establishment Clause of the Federal Constitution—is limited by the Free Exercise Clause and in this case by the Free Speech Clause as well. In this constitutional context, we are unable to recognize the State's interest as sufficiently 'compelling' to justify content-based discrimination against [the challengers'] religious speech."

Justice WHITE, the sole dissenter, insisted that the university ban was permissible. Although he devoted most of his dissent to free speech and free exercise analyses (as noted earlier), he also commented on the Establishment Clause issue. He argued that the Establishment Clause only *limits* state action; "it does not establish what the State is *required* to do. I have long argued that Establishment Clause limits on state action which incidentally aids religion are not as strict as the Court has held. [In] my view, just as there is room under the Religion Clauses for state policies that may have some beneficial effect on religion, there is also room for state policies that may incidentally burden religion. In other words, I believe the states to be a good deal freer to formulate policies that affect religion in divergent ways than does the majority. The majority's position will inevitably lead to those contradictions and tensions between the Establishment and Free Exercise Clauses warned against by Justice Stewart in Sherbert v. Verner [p. 1514 below]."

OTHER CLAIMED VIOLATIONS OF THE ESTABLISHMENT CLAUSE

In the cases that follow, the Court considered claims that the separation of church and state had been violated in situations where government extended non-financial support to allegedly religious causes. In these cases, the Court has typically been less wary of establishment clause violations than in the contexts considered in the early portions of this section.

1. McGOWAN v. MARYLAND, 366 U.S. 420 (1961): McGowan was one of four companion cases in which the Court rejected claims that Sunday Closing Laws violated the religion clauses.[1] Chief Justice WARREN wrote the opinions for the Court. He noted in McGowan that there is "no dispute that the original laws which dealt with Sunday labor were motivated by religious forces." But he concluded: "In light of the evolution of our Sunday Closing Laws through the centuries, and of their more or less recent emphasis upon secular considerations, it is not difficult to discern that as presently written and administered, most of them, at least, are of a secular rather than of a religious character, and that presently they bear no relationship to establishment of religion as those words are used in the [Constitution]. The present purpose and effect of most of them is to provide a uniform day of rest for all citizens; the fact that this day is Sunday, a day of particular significance for the dominant Christian sects, does not bar the State from achieving its secular [goals]. Sunday is a day apart from all others. The cause is irrelevant; the fact exists."[2]

2. MARSH v. CHAMBERS, 463 U.S. 783 (1983): The Court upheld "the Nebraska Legislature's practice of opening each legislative day with a prayer by a chaplain paid by the State." Chief Justice BURGER's majority opinion relied largely on history to sustain the practice despite the fact that the position of chaplain had been held for 16 years by a Presbyterian, that the

---

1. In two of the cases (Two Guys from Harrison-Allentown, Inc. v. McGinley, 366 U.S. 582 (1961), as well as McGowan), the Court held that the establishment claim was the only religion issue that the challengers could raise. In McGowan, the Court pointed out that "appellants allege only economic injury to themselves; they do not allege any infringement of their own religious freedoms due to Sunday closing." In the two other cases (Braunfeld and Gallagher; noted at p. 1512 in sec. 2 below), the Court addressed the free exercise claim as well. (Recall also the rejection of an equal protection claim in McGowan, after extremely deferential scrutiny, as noted in chap. 9, sec. 1, above.)

2. Justice FRANKFURTER submitted an extensive separate opinion, joined by Justice Harlan, substantially agreeing with Chief Justice Warren in all four cases. Justice DOUGLAS dissented in all of the cases on establishment and free exercise grounds. (The views of Justices Brennan and Stewart, dissenting only on the free exercise issue, appear with Braunfeld, p. 1512 below.)

chaplain is paid at public expense, and that all of the prayers are "in the Judeo-Christian tradition." The majority did not rigidly apply the three-part test now familiar in establishment clause cases, but instead looked at the specific features of this practice in light of a long history of acceptance of legislative and other official prayers. The majority concluded: "Weighed against the historical background, [the allegedly vulnerable] factors do not serve to invalidate Nebraska's practice."

The Chief Justice viewed prayer in this context as "unique" in its historical roots: "The opening of legislative and other deliberative public bodies with prayer is deeply embedded in the history and tradition of this country. From colonial times through the founding of the Republic and ever since, the practice of legislative prayer has coexisted with the principles of disestablishment and religious freedom." He also noted the history of a paid chaplain in Congress as far back as the Continental Congress in 1774, the tradition of opening sessions of the Supreme Court and other courts with an invocation, and the long history of opening prayers and paid chaplains in most of the states. Especially in light of the actions of the First Congress, the Chief Justice saw the history as especially important here: "In this context, historical evidence sheds light not only on what the draftsmen intended the Establishment Clause to mean, but also on how they thought the Clause applied to the practice authorized by the First Congress—their actions reveal their intent. [This] unique history leads us to accept the interpretation of the First Amendment draftsmen who saw no real threat to the Establishment Clause arising from a practice of prayer similar to that now challenged. [In] light of the unambiguous and unbroken history of more than 200 years, there can be no doubt that the practice of opening legislative sessions with a prayer has become part of the fabric of our society. To invoke Divine guidance on a public body entrusted with making the laws is not, in these circumstances, an 'establishment' of religion or a step toward establishment; it is simply a tolerable acknowledgment of beliefs widely held among the people of this country."

Justice BRENNAN, joined by Justice Marshall, filed a lengthy dissent, one that is especially noteworthy because in Schempp (1963; p. 1488 above) he had come "very close to endorsing essentially the result reached by the Court today." In light of this, it is not surprising that Justice Brennan's dissent was quite restrained: "The Court today has written a narrow and, on the whole, careful opinion. [The] Court's [limited] rationale should pose little threat to the overall fate of the Establishment Clause. [The] Court makes no pretense of subjecting Nebraska's practice of legislative prayer to any of the formal 'tests' that have traditionally structured our inquiry under the Establishment Clause. That it fails to do so is, in a sense, a good thing, for it simply confirms that the Court is carving out an exception [rather] than reshaping Establishment Clause doctrine to accommodate legislative prayer. [But if] the Court were to judge legislative prayer through the unsentimental eye of our settled doctrine, it would have to strike it down as a clear violation of the [Clause]." [3]

3. LARSON v. VALENTE, 456 U.S. 228 (1982): Although the Court has generally been unreceptive to claims that government was providing nonfinancial support to particular religions, in Larson it demonstrated repugnance to what it viewed as a clear denominational preference. The Court invalidated portions of a Minnesota law regulating charitable solicitations. [4] The successful

3. Justice STEVENS also dissented, relying on the fact that the particular chaplain was presumably chosen "to reflect the faith of the majority of the lawmakers' constituents." Because the designation of the particular chaplain and the content of the prayers "constitutes the preference of one faith over another," he urged striking down the Nebraska practice on these grounds alone.

4. For the Court's consideration of other challenges to regulation on solicitation—challenges based on free speech grounds rather than on the religion clauses—recall chap. 12, sec. 4, above.

challenge was directed at provisions excepting some, but not all, religious organizations from the law's registration and reporting requirements. The Court found that the exception scheme violated the "clearest command of the Establishment Clause": "one religious denomination cannot be officially preferred over another." In its original form, the law, designed to prevent fraud, had exempted all "religious organizations." But in 1978 the exemption provision was modified to add a 50% rule—a rule providing that only those religious organizations receiving more than half of their total contributions from members could claim the exemption. The new scheme was challenged by the Unification Church (the "Moonies") on the ground that it preferred traditional religions, since the challenging group acquired most of its donations by soliciting contributions from nonmembers.

In invalidating the 50% rule, Justice BRENNAN's majority opinion applied strict scrutiny in an establishment clause case apparently for the first time. Justice Brennan stated that the rule "clearly grants denominational preferences of the sort consistently and firmly deprecated in our precedents." [5] Although the majority was willing to "assume arguendo" that the law furthered a "compelling" governmental interest, it was unconstitutional because the regulation was not "closely fitted to further the interest that it assertedly serves." [6] The majority's determination that the law could not survive "the means" prong of strict scrutiny was sufficient to support the result, but Justice Brennan went on to consider the typical three-part establishment clause test as well and concluded that the law violated the "entanglement" prong of the Lemon standard. After noting that this standard was "intended to apply to laws affording a uniform benefit to *all* religions, and not to provisions like [this] that discriminate *among* religions," he nevertheless proceeded to state that the Lemon test reflected "the same concerns that warranted the application of strict scrutiny [here]." He insisted that the law illustrated one of the dangers against which the "entanglement" barrier was designed to safeguard: "By their 'very nature,' the distinctions [here] 'engender a risk of politicizing religion'—a risk, indeed, that has already been substantially realized. [The rule effects] the *selective* legislative imposition of burdens and advantages upon particular denominations. The 'risk of politicizing religion' that inheres in such legislation is obvious, and indeed is confirmed by the provision's legislative history, [which] demonstrates that the provision was drafted with the explicit intention of including particular religious denominations and excluding others." [7] Justice Brennan found that the 50% rule's capacity "—indeed, its express design—to burden or favor selected

5. Justice Brennan rejected the argument that the law was merely one "based upon secular criteria which may not identically affect all religious organizations." He responded: "[The law] makes explicit and deliberate distinctions between different religious organizations. We agree with the Court of Appeals' observation that the provision effectively distinguishes between 'well-established churches' that have 'achieved strong but not total financial support from their members,' on the one hand, and 'churches which are new and lacking in a constituency, or which, as a matter of policy, may favor public solicitation over general reliance on financial support from members,' on the other hand."

6. Justice Brennan found "no substantial support [in] the record" for any of the "three distinct premises" inherent in the state's argument: "that members of a religious organization can and will exercise supervision and control over the organization's solicitation activities when membership contributions exceed [50%]; that membership control, assuming its existence, is an adequate safeguard against abusive solicitations; [and] that the need for public disclosure rises in proportion with the *percentage* [rather than the *"absolute amount"*] of nonmember contributions."

7. Justice Brennan noted, for example, that an earlier version of the 1978 amendment was eliminated when "the legislators perceived that [it] would bring a Roman Catholic Archdiocese within the Act." Moreover, there was evidence in the legislative record that some of the lawmakers were eager *not* to exempt other religious organizations from the law. Thus, a state senator, "who apparently had mixed feelings about the proposed [amendment], stated, 'I'm not sure why we're so hot to regulate the Moonies anyway.'"

religious denominations led the Minnesota Legislature to discuss the characteristics of various sects with a view towards 'religious gerrymandering.' " [8]

4. The most controversial ruling in this group of cases was the 5 to 4 decision in 1984 in Lynch v. Donnelly, which follows. In examining Lynch, consider the questions and comments in the note that follows the case.

LYNCH v. DONNELLY

465 U.S. ___, 104 S.Ct. 1355, 79 L.Ed.2d 604 (1984).

The Chief Justice [BURGER] delivered the opinion of the Court.

We granted certiorari to decide whether the Establishment Clause [prohibits] a municipality from including a crèche, or Nativity scene, in its annual Christmas display.

I. Each year, in cooperation with the downtown retail merchants' association, the City of Pawtucket, Rhode Island, erects a Christmas display as part of its observance of the Christmas holiday season. The display is situated in a park owned by a nonprofit organization and located in the heart of the shopping district. The display is essentially like those to be found in hundreds of towns or cities across the Nation—often on public grounds—during the Christmas season. The Pawtucket display comprises many of the figures and decorations traditionally associated with Christmas, including, among other things, a Santa Claus house, reindeer pulling Santa's sleigh, candy-striped poles, a Christmas tree, carolers, cutout figures representing such characters as a clown, an elephant, and a teddy bear, hundreds of colored lights, a large banner that reads "SEASONS GREETINGS," and the crèche at issue here. All components of this display are owned by the City. The crèche, which has been included in the display for 40 or more years, consists of the traditional figures, including the Infant Jesus, Mary and Joseph, angels, shepherds, kings, and animals, all ranging in height from 5" to 5'. In 1973, when the present crèche was acquired, it cost the City $1365; it now is valued at $200. The erection and dismantling of the crèche costs the City about $20 per year; nominal expenses are incurred in lighting the crèche. No money has been expended on its maintenance for the past 10 years. The District Court held that the City's inclusion of the crèche in the display violates the Establishment Clause. [A] divided panel of the [First] Circuit affirmed. [We] reverse.

II. A. [In] every Establishment Clause case, we must reconcile the inescapable tension between the objective of preventing unnecessary intrusion of either the church or the state upon the other, and the reality [that] total separation of the two is not possible. [The] concept of a "wall" of separation is a useful figure of speech probably deriving from views of Thomas Jefferson. The metaphor has served as a reminder that the Establishment Clause forbids an established church or anything approaching it. But the metaphor itself is not a wholly accurate description of the practical aspects of the relationship that in fact exists between church and state. No significant segment of our society and no institution within it can exist in a vacuum or in total or absolute isolation from

---

8. Justice STEVENS joined Justice Brennan's opinion in a separate notation.

Justice WHITE's dissent, joined by Justice Rehnquist, argued that the 50% rule was not an intentional preference of one denomination over another. He summarized his position as follows: "Without an adequate factual basis, the majority concludes that the provision in question deliberately prefers some religious denominations to others. Without an adequate factual basis, it

rejects the justifications offered by the State. It reaches its conclusions by applying a legal standard different from that considered by either of the courts below." (In another dissent, Justice REHNQUIST, joined by Chief Justice Burger and Justices White and O'Connor, insisted that the challengers lacked Article III standing and charged the majority with rendering "what is at best an advisory constitutional pronouncement.")

all the other parts, much less from government. "It has never been thought either possible or desirable to enforce a regime of total [separation]" [Nyquist]. Nor does the Constitution require complete separation of church and state; it affirmatively mandates accommodation, not merely tolerance, of all religions, and forbids hostility toward [any].

B. The Court's interpretation of the Establishment Clause has comported with what history reveals was the contemporaneous understanding of its guarantees. [The Chief Justice referred to the 1789 law providing for paid chaplains for the House and Senate. See Marsh v. Chambers, above.] [It] would be difficult to identify a more striking example of the accommodation of religious belief intended by the Framers.

C. There is an unbroken history of official acknowledgment by all three branches of government of the role of religion in American life from at least 1789. [Our] history is replete with official references to the value and invocation of Divine guidance in deliberations and pronouncements of the Founding Fathers and contemporary leaders. [Long] before Independence, a day of Thanksgiving was celebrated as a religious holiday to give thanks for the bounties of Nature as gifts from God. President Washington and his successors proclaimed Thanksgiving, with all its religious overtones, a day of national celebration and Congress made it a National Holiday more than a century ago. That holiday has not lost its theme of expressing thanks for Divine aid any more than has Christmas lost its religious significance. Executive Orders and other official announcements of Presidents and of the Congress have proclaimed both Christmas and Thanksgiving National Holidays in religious terms. And, by Acts of Congress, it has long been the practice that federal employees are released from duties on these National Holidays, while being paid from the same public revenues that provide the compensation of the Chaplains of the Senate and the House and the military services. Thus, it is clear that Government has long recognized—indeed it has subsidized—holidays with religious significance. Other examples of reference to our religious heritage are found in the statutorily prescribed national motto "In God We Trust," which Congress and the President mandated for our currency, and in the language "One nation under God," as part of the Pledge of Allegiance to the [American flag].

[Art galleries] supported by public revenues display religious paintings of the 15th and 16th centuries, predominantly inspired by one religious faith. The National Gallery in Washington, maintained with Government support, for example, has long exhibited masterpieces with religious messages, notably the Last Supper, and paintings depicting the Birth of Christ, the Crucifixion, and the Resurrection, among many others with explicit Christian themes and messages. The very chamber in which oral arguments on this case were heard is decorated with a notable and permanent—not seasonal—symbol of religion: Moses with Ten Commandments. Congress has long provided chapels in the Capitol for religious worship and meditation [and] has directed the President to proclaim a National Day of Prayer [each year]. Presidential Proclamations and messages have also [been issued] to commemorate Jewish Heritage Week and the Jewish High Holy Days. One cannot look at even this brief resume without finding that our history is pervaded by expressions of religious beliefs such as are found in Zorach. Equally pervasive is the evidence of accommodation of all faiths and all forms of religious expression, and hostility toward [none].

III. This history may help explain why the Court consistently has declined to take a rigid, absolutist view of the Establishment Clause. [In] our modern, complex society, whose traditions and constitutional underpinnings rest on and encourage diversity and pluralism in all areas, an absolutist approach in applying the Establishment Clause is simplistic and has been uniformly rejected by the Court. Rather than mechanically invalidating all governmental conduct or statutes that confer benefits or give special recognition to religion in general or to one faith—as an absolutist approach would dictate—the Court has scrutinized challenged legislation or official conduct to determine whether, in reality, it establishes a religion or religious faith, or tends to do so. In each case, the inquiry calls for line drawing; no fixed, per se rule can be framed. The Establishment Clause like the Due Process Clauses is not a precise, detailed provision in a legal code capable of ready application. The purpose of the Establishment Clause "was to state an objective, not to write a statute." [Walz.]

[In] the line-drawing process we have often found it useful to inquire whether the challenged law or conduct has a secular purpose, whether its principal or primary effect is to advance or inhibit religion, and whether it creates an excessive entanglement of government with religion. [Lemon.] But, we have repeatedly emphasized our unwillingness to be confined to any single test or criterion in this sensitive area. In two cases, the Court did not even apply the Lemon "test." We did not, for example, consider that analysis relevant in Marsh. Nor did we find Lemon useful in Larson, where there was substantial evidence of overt discrimination against a particular church.

In this case, the focus of our inquiry must be on the crèche in the context of the Christmas season. [The] Court has invalidated legislation or governmental action on the ground that a secular purpose was lacking, but only when it has concluded there was no question that the statute or activity was motivated wholly by religious considerations. See, e.g., [Stone; Epperson; Schempp; Engel]. Even where the benefits to religion were substantial, as in [Epperson; Allen; Walz; and Tilton], we saw a secular purpose and no conflict with the Establishment Clause.

The District Court inferred from the religious nature of the crèche that the City has no secular purpose for the display. In so doing, it rejected the City's claim that its reasons for including the crèche are essentially the same as its reasons for sponsoring the display as a whole. The District Court plainly erred by focusing almost exclusively on the crèche. When viewed in the proper context of the Christmas Holiday season, it is apparent that, on this record, there is insufficient evidence to establish that the inclusion of the crèche is a purposeful or surreptitious effort to express some kind of subtle governmental advocacy of a particular religious message. In a pluralistic society a variety of motives and purposes are implicated. The City, like the Congresses and Presidents, however, has principally taken note of a significant historical religious event long celebrated in the Western World. The crèche in the display depicts the historical origins of this traditional event long recognized as a National Holiday.

The narrow question is whether there is a secular purpose for Pawtucket's display of the crèche. The display is sponsored by the City to celebrate the Holiday and to depict the origins of that Holiday. These are legitimate secular purposes.[1] The District Court's inference, drawn from the religious nature of the crèche, that the City has no secular purpose was, on this record, clearly erroneous.

The District Court found that the primary effect of including the crèche is to confer a substantial and impermissible benefit on religion in general and on the Christian faith in particular. Comparisons of the relative benefits to religion of different forms of governmental support are elusive and difficult to make. But to conclude that the primary effect of including the crèche is to advance religion

---

1. The City contends that the purposes of the display are "exclusively secular." We hold only that Pawtucket has a secular purpose for its display, which is all that Lemon requires. Were the test that the government must have "exclu-sively secular" objectives, much of the conduct and legislation this Court has approved in the past would have been invalidated. [Footnote by Chief Justice Burger.]

in violation of the Establishment Clause would require that we view it as more beneficial to and more an endorsement of religion, for example, [than the financial benefits upheld in, e.g., Allen, Everson, Tilton, and Walz]. It would also require that we view it as more of an endorsement of religion than the [governmental activities upheld in McGowan, Zorach, and Marsh]. We are unable to discern a greater aid to religion deriving from inclusion of the crèche than from these benefits and endorsements previously held not violative of the Establishment Clause. What was said about the legislative prayers in Marsh and implied about the Sunday Closing Laws in McGowan is true of the City's inclusion of the crèche: its "reason or effect merely happens to coincide or harmonize with the tenets of [some] religions." See [McGowan]. Here, whatever benefit to one faith or religion or to all religions, is indirect, remote and incidental; display of the crèche is no more an advancement or endorsement of religion than the Congressional and Executive recognition of the origins of the Holiday itself as "Christ's Mass," or the exhibition of literally hundreds of religious paintings in governmentally supported [museums].[2]

IV. Justice Brennan describes the crèche as a "re-creation of an event that lies at the heart of Christian faith." The crèche, like a painting, is passive; admittedly it is a reminder of the origins of Christmas. [Of course] the crèche is identified with one religious faith but no more so than the examples we have set out from prior cases in which we found no conflict with the Establishment Clause. It would be ironic, however, if the inclusion of a single symbol of a particular historic religious event, as part of a celebration acknowledged in the Western World for 20 centuries, and in this country by the people, by the Executive Branch, by the Congress, and the courts for two centuries, would so "taint" the City's exhibit as to render it violative of the Establishment Clause. To forbid the use of this one passive symbol—the crèche—at the very time people are taking note of the season with Christmas hymns and carols in public schools and other public places, and while the Congress and Legislatures open sessions with prayers by paid chaplains, would be a stilted over-reaction contrary to our history and to our holdings. If the presence of the crèche in this display violates the Establishment Clause, a host of other forms of taking official note of Christmas, and of our religious heritage, are equally offensive to the Constitution.

The Court has acknowledged that the "fears and political problems" that gave rise to the Religion Clauses in the 18th century are of far less concern today. [Everson.] We are unable to perceive the Archbishop of Canterbury, the Vicar of Rome, or other powerful religious leaders behind every public acknowledgment of the religious heritage long officially recognized by the three constitutional branches of government. Any notion that these symbols pose a real danger of establishment of a state church is farfetched [indeed].

[Reversed.]

Justice O'CONNOR, concurring.

I concur in the opinion of the Court. I write separately to suggest a clarification of our Establishment Clause doctrine. The suggested approach leads to the same result in this case as that taken by the Court, and the Court's opinion, as I read it, is consistent with my analysis.

---

2. Chief Justice Burger agreed with the District Court that there had been "no administrative entanglement between religion and state" here. However, he disagreed with the District Court's conclusion that there was "excessive entanglement" stemming from the "political divisiveness" engendered by the litigation and the allegedly impermissible sectarian purpose and effect. He declined to hold that "political divisiveness alone can serve to invalidate otherwise permissible conduct." He noted that, "apart from this litigation, there is no evidence of political friction or divisiveness over the crèche in the 40-year history of Pawtucket's Christmas celebration." He added: "A litigant cannot, by the very act of commencing a lawsuit, [create] the appearance of divisiveness and then exploit it as evidence of entanglement."

I. The Establishment Clause prohibits government from making adherence to a religion relevant in any way to a person's standing in the political community. Government can run afoul of that prohibition in two principal ways. One is excessive entanglement with religious institutions, which may interfere with the independence of the institutions, give the institutions access to government or governmental powers not fully shared by nonadherents of the religion, and foster the creation of political constituencies defined along religious lines. [E.g., Larkin.] The second and more direct infringement is government endorsement or disapproval of religion. Endorsement sends a message to nonadherents that they are outsiders, not full members of the political community, and an accompanying message to adherents that they are insiders, favored members of the political community. Disapproval sends the opposite message. [Schempp.] Our prior cases have used the three-part test articulated in [Lemon] as a guide to detecting these two forms of unconstitutional government action. It has never been entirely clear, however, how the three parts of the test relate to the principles enshrined in the Establishment Clause. Focusing on institutional entanglement and on endorsement or disapproval of religion clarifies the Lemon test as an analytical device.

II. [In] my view, political divisiveness along religious lines should not be an independent test of constitutionality.

III. The central issue in this case is whether Pawtucket has endorsed Christianity by its display of the crèche. To answer that question, we must examine both what Pawtucket intended to communicate in displaying the crèche and what message the City's display actually conveyed. The purpose and effect prongs of the Lemon test represent these two aspects of the meaning of the City's action.

The meaning of a statement to its audience depends both on the intention of the speaker and on the "objective" meaning of the statement in the community. [The] purpose prong of the Lemon test asks whether government's actual purpose is to endorse or disapprove of religion. The effect prong asks whether, irrespective of government's actual purpose, the practice under review in fact conveys a message of endorsement or disapproval. An affirmative answer to either question should render the challenged practice invalid.

A. The purpose prong of the Lemon test requires that a government activity have a secular purpose. That requirement is not satisfied, however, by the mere existence of some secular purpose, however dominated by religious purposes. [The] proper inquiry under the purpose prong of Lemon I submit, is whether the government intends to convey a message of endorsement or disapproval of religion. Applying that formulation to this case, I would find that Pawtucket did not intend to convey any message of endorsement of Christianity or disapproval of nonChristian religions. The evident purpose of including the crèche in the larger display was not promotion of the religious content of the crèche but celebration of the public holiday through its traditional symbols. Celebration of public holidays, which have cultural significance even if they also have religious aspects, is a legitimate secular [purpose].

B. Focusing on the evil of government endorsement or disapproval of religion makes clear that the effect prong of the Lemon test is properly interpreted not to require invalidation of a government practice merely because it in fact causes, even as a primary effect, advancement or inhibition of religion. [What] is crucial is that a government practice not have the effect of communicating a message of government endorsement or disapproval of religion. It is only practices having that effect, whether intentionally or unintentionally, that make religion relevant, in reality or public perception, to status in the political community.

Pawtucket's display of its crèche, I believe, does not communicate a message that the government intends to endorse the Christian beliefs represented by the crèche. Although the religious and indeed sectarian significance of the crèche [is] not neutralized by the setting, the overall holiday setting changes what viewers may fairly understand to be the purpose of the display—as a typical museum setting, though not neutralizing the religious content of a religious painting, negates any message of endorsement of that content. The display celebrates a public holiday, and no one contends that declaration of that holiday is understood to be an endorsement of religion. The holiday itself has very strong secular components and traditions. Government celebration of the holiday, which is extremely common, generally is not understood to endorse the religious content of the holiday, just as government celebration of Thanksgiving is not so understood. The crèche is a traditional symbol of the holiday that is very commonly displayed along with purely secular symbols, as it was in Pawtucket.

These features combine to make the government's display of the crèche in this particular physical setting no more an endorsement of religion than such governmental "acknowledgments" of religion as legislative prayers of the type approved in [Marsh], government declaration of Thanksgiving as a public holiday, printing of "In God We Trust," and opening Court sessions with "God save the United States and this honorable court." Those government acknowledgments of religion serve, in the only ways reasonably possible in our culture, the legitimate secular purposes of solemnizing public occasions, expressing confidence in the future, and encouraging the recognition of what is worthy of appreciation in society. For that reason, and because of their history and ubiquity, those practices are not understood as conveying government approval of particular religious beliefs. The display of the crèche likewise [cannot] fairly be understood to convey a message of government endorsement of [religion].

IV. Every government practice must be judged in its unique circumstances to determine whether it constitutes an endorsement or disapproval of religion. In making that determination, courts must keep in mind both the fundamental place held by the Establishment Clause in our constitutional scheme and the myriad, subtle ways in which Establishment Clause values can be eroded. Government practices that purport to celebrate or acknowledge events with religious significance must be subjected to careful judicial scrutiny. [Giving] the challenged practice the careful scrutiny it deserves, I cannot say that the particular crèche display [here] was intended to endorse or had the effect of endorsing [Christianity].

Justice BRENNAN, with whom Justice MARSHALL, Justice BLACKMUN and Justice STEVENS join, dissenting.

[The Court's] decision implicitly leaves open questions concerning the constitutionality of the public display on public property of a crèche standing alone, or the public display of other distinctively religious symbols such as a cross. Despite the narrow contours of the Court's opinion, our precedents in my view compel the holding that Pawtucket's inclusion of a life-sized display depicting the biblical description of the birth of Christ as part of its annual Christmas celebration is unconstitutional. Nothing in the history of such practices or the setting in which the City's crèche is presented obscures or diminishes the plain fact that Pawtucket's action amounts to an impermissible governmental endorsement of a particular faith.

I. Last Term, I expressed the hope that the Court's decision in [Marsh] would prove to be only a single, aberrant departure from our settled method of analyzing Establishment Clause cases. That the Court today returns to the settled analysis of our prior cases gratifies that hope. At the same time, the Court's less than vigorous application of the Lemon test suggests that its commitment to those standards may only be superficial.[1] After reviewing the Court's opinion, I am convinced that this case appears hard not because the principles of decision are obscure, but because the Christmas holiday seems so familiar and agreeable. Although the Court's reluctance to disturb a community's chosen method of celebrating such an agreeable holiday is understandable, that cannot justify the Court's departure from controlling precedent. In my view, Pawtucket's maintenance and display at public expense of a symbol as distinctively sectarian as a crèche simply cannot be squared with our prior cases. And it is plainly contrary to the purposes and values of the Establishment Clause to pretend, as the Court does, that the otherwise secular setting of Pawtucket's nativity scene dilutes in some fashion the crèche's singular religiosity, or that the City's annual display reflects nothing more than an "acknowledgment" of our shared national heritage. Neither the character of the Christmas holiday itself, nor our heritage of religious expression, supports this [result].

A. Applying the three-part test to Pawtucket's crèche, I am persuaded that the City's inclusion of the crèche in its Christmas display simply does not reflect a "clearly secular purpose." [Two] compelling aspects of this case indicate that our generally prudent "reluctance to attribute unconstitutional motives" to a governmental body [Mueller] should be overcome. First, [all] of Pawtucket's "valid secular objectives can be readily accomplished by other means." [More] importantly, the nativity scene, unlike every other element of the Hodgson Park display, reflects a sectarian exclusivity that the avowed purposes of celebrating the holiday season and promoting retail commerce simply do not encompass. [The] inclusion of a distinctively religious element like the crèche [demonstrates] that a narrower sectarian purpose lay behind the decision to include a nativity scene. [The] "primary effect" of including a nativity scene in the City's display [is] to place the government's imprimatur of approval on the particular religious beliefs exemplified by the crèche. [The] effect on minority religious groups, as well as on those who may reject all religion, is to convey the message that their views are not similarly worthy of public recognition nor entitled to public support. [Finally], it is evident that Pawtucket's inclusion of a crèche [does] pose a significant threat of fostering "excessive entanglement."[2] [In sum], considering the District Court's careful findings of fact under the three-part analysis called for by our prior cases, I have no difficulty concluding that [this] display of the crèche is unconstitutional.

B. The Court advances two principal arguments to support its conclusion that the Pawtucket crèche satisfies the Lemon test. Neither is persuasive. *First.* The Court, by focusing on the holiday "context" in which the nativity scene appeared, seeks to explain away the clear religious import of the crèche and the findings of the District Court that most observers understood the crèche as both a symbol of Christian beliefs and a symbol of the City's support for those beliefs. [The] Court's struggle to ignore the clear religious effect of the crèche seems to be misguided for several reasons. [Most] importantly, even in the context of Pawtucket's seasonal celebration, the crèche retains a specifically Christian religious meaning. I refuse to accept the notion implicit in today's decision that

---

1. Although I agree with the Court that no single formula can ever fully capture the analysis that may be necessary to resolve difficult Establishment Clause problems, I fail to understand the Court's insistence upon referring to the settled test set forth in Lemon as simply one path that may be followed or not at the Court's option. [Despite] the Court's efforts to evade the point, the fact remains that [Marsh] is the only case in which the Court has not applied either the Lemon or a "strict scrutiny" analysis. I can only conclude that with today's unsupported as-

sertion, the Court hopes to provide a belated excuse for the failure in Marsh to address the analysis of the Lemon test. [Footnote by Justice Brennan.]

2. The suggestion in [Mueller, relied upon today,] that inquiry into potential political divisiveness is unnecessary absent direct subsidies to church-sponsored schools [derives] from a distorted reading of our prior [cases]. [Footnote by Justice Brennan, somewhat later in his opinion.]

non-Christians would find that the religious content of the crèche is eliminated by the fact that it appears as part of the City's otherwise secular celebration of the Christmas holiday. The nativity scene is clearly distinct in its purpose and effect from the rest of the Hodgson Park display for the simple reason that it is the only one rooted in a biblical account of Christ's birth. It is the chief symbol of the characteristically Christian belief that a divine Savior was brought into the world and that the purpose of this miraculous birth was to illuminate a path toward salvation and redemption. For Christians, that path is exclusive, precious and holy. But for those who do not share these beliefs, the symbolic re-enactment of the birth of a divine being who has been miraculously incarnated as a man stands as a dramatic reminder of their differences with Christian faith. [To] be so excluded on religious grounds by one's elected government is an insult and an injury that, until today, could not be countenanced by the Establishment Clause.

Second. The Court also attempts to justify the crèche by entertaining a beguilingly simple, yet faulty, syllogism. The Court begins by noting that government may recognize Christmas day as a public holiday; the Court then asserts that the crèche is nothing more than a traditional element of Christmas celebrations; and it concludes that the inclusion of a crèche as part of a government's annual Christmas celebration is constitutionally permissible. The Court apparently believes that once it finds that the designation of Christmas as a public holiday is constitutionally acceptable, it is then free to conclude that virtually every form of governmental association with the celebration of the holiday is also constitutional. The vice of this dangerously superficial argument is that it overlooks the fact that the Christmas holiday in our national culture contains both secular and sectarian elements. To say that government may recognize the holiday's traditional, secular elements of gift giving, public festivities and community spirit, does not mean that government may indiscriminately embrace the distinctively sectarian aspects of the holiday. Indeed, in its eagerness to approve the crèche, the Court has advanced a rationale so simplistic that it would appear to allow the Mayor of Pawtucket to participate in the celebration of a Christmas mass, since this would be just another unobjectionable way for the City to "celebrate the holiday." As is demonstrated below, the Court's logic is fundamentally flawed both because it obscures the reason why public designation of Christmas day as a holiday is constitutionally acceptable, and blurs the distinction between the secular aspects of Christmas and its distinctively religious character, as exemplified by the crèche.

When government decides to recognize Christmas day as a public holiday, it does no more than accommodate the calendar of public activities to the plain fact that many Americans will expect on that day to spend time visiting with their families, attending religious services, and perhaps enjoying some respite from pre-holiday activities. The Free Exercise Clause, of course, does not necessarily compel the government to provide this accommodation, but neither is the Establishment Clause offended by such a step. Cf. [Zorach]. Because it is clear that the celebration of Christmas has both secular and sectarian elements, it may well be that by taking note of the holiday, the government is simply seeking to serve the same kinds of wholly secular goals [that] were found to justify Sunday Closing laws in McGowan. If public officials go further and participate in the *secular* celebration of Christmas—by, for example, decorating public places with such secular images as wreaths, garlands or Santa Claus figures—they move closer to the limits of their constitutional power but nevertheless remain within the boundaries set by the Establishment Clause. But when those officials participate in or appear to endorse the distinctively religious elements of this otherwise secular event, they encroach upon First Amendment freedoms. For it is at that point that the government brings to the forefront the theological content of the holiday, and places the prestige, power and financial support of a civil authority in the service of a particular faith.

The inclusion of a crèche in Pawtucket's otherwise secular celebration of Christmas clearly violates these principles. Unlike such secular figures as Santa Claus, reindeer and carolers, a nativity scene represents far more than a mere "traditional" symbol of Christmas. The essence of the crèche's symbolic purpose and effect is to prompt the observer to experience a sense of simple awe and wonder appropriate to the contemplation of one of the central elements of Christian dogma—that God sent His son into the world to be a Messiah. Contrary to the Court's suggestion, the crèche is far from a mere representation of a "particular historic religious event." It is, instead, best understood as a mystical re-creation of an event that lies at the heart of Christian faith. To suggest, as the Court does, that such a symbol is merely "traditional" and therefore no different from Santa's house or reindeer is not only offensive to those for whom the crèche has profound significance, but insulting to those who insist for religious or personal reasons that the story of Christ is in no sense a part of "history" nor an unavoidable element of our national "heritage." For these reasons, the crèche in this context simply cannot be viewed as playing the same role that an ordinary museum display does. [The] fact that Pawtucket has gone to the trouble of making such an elaborate public celebration and of including a crèche in that otherwise secular setting inevitably serves to reinforce the sense that the City means to express solidarity with the Christian message of the crèche and to dismiss other faiths as unworthy of similar attention and support.

II. Although the Court's relaxed application of the Lemon test [is] regrettable, it is at least understandable and properly limited to the particular facts of this case. The Court's opinion, however, also sounds a broader and more troubling theme. [The] Court asserts [that] Pawtucket's inclusion of a crèche in its annual Christmas display poses no more of a threat to Establishment Clause values than [the] other official "acknowledgments" of religion [it discusses]. Intuition tells us that some official "acknowledgment" is inevitable in a religious society if government is not to adopt a stilted indifference to the religious life of the people. It is equally true, however, that if government is to remain scrupulously neutral in matters of religious conscience, as our Constitution requires, then it must avoid those overly broad acknowledgments of religious practices that may imply governmental favoritism toward one set of religious beliefs. This does not mean, of course, that public officials may not take account, when necessary, of the separate existence and significance of the religious institutions and practices in the society they govern. Should government choose to incorporate some arguably religious element into its public ceremonies, that acknowledgment must be impartial; it must not tend to promote one faith or handicap another; and it should not sponsor religion generally over non-religion. Thus, [we] have repeatedly held that any active form of public acknowledgment of religion indicating sponsorship or endorsement is forbidden. E.g., [Stone; Epperson; Schempp; Engel; McCollum].

Despite this body of case law, the Court has never comprehensively addressed the extent to which government may acknowledge religion by, for example, incorporating religious references into public ceremonies and proclamations, and I do not presume to offer a comprehensive approach. Nevertheless, it appears from our prior decisions that at least three principles—tracing the narrow channels which government acknowledgments must follow to satisfy the Establishment Clause—may be identified. First, although the government may not be compelled to do so by the Free Exercise Clause, it may, consistently with the Establishment Clause, act to accommodate to some extent the opportunities of individuals to practice their religion. That is the essential meaning, I submit, of [Zorach]. And for me that principle would justify government's decision to declare December 25th a public holiday. Second, our cases recognize that while a particular governmental practice may have derived from religious motivations and retain certain religious connotations, it is nonetheless permissible for the government to pursue the practice when it is continued today solely for secular reasons. [McGowan.] Thanksgiving Day, in my view, fits easily within this principle.

Finally, we have noted that government cannot be completely prohibited from recognizing in its public actions the religious beliefs and practices of the American people as an aspect of our national history and culture. While I remain uncertain about these questions, I would suggest that such practices as the designation of "In God We Trust" as our national motto [and] the references to God contained in the Pledge of Allegiance can best be understood [as] a form of "ceremonial deism," protected from Establishment Clause scrutiny chiefly because they have lost through rote repetition any significant religious content. Moreover, these references are uniquely suited to serve such wholly secular purposes as solemnizing public occasions, or inspiring commitment to meet some national challenge in a manner that simply could not be fully served in our culture if government were limited to purely non-religious phrases. The practices by which the government has long acknowledged religion are therefore probably necessary to serve certain secular functions, and that necessity, coupled with their long history, gives those practices an essentially secular meaning.

The crèche fits none of these categories. Inclusion of the crèche is not necessary to accommodate individual religious expression. [Nor] is the inclusion of the crèche necessary to serve wholly secular goals. And the crèche, because of its unique association with Christianity, is clearly more sectarian than those references to God that we accept in ceremonial phrases or in other contexts that assure neutrality. The religious works on display at the National Gallery, Presidential references to God during an Inaugural Address, or the national motto present no risk of establishing religion. To be sure, our understanding of these expressions may begin in contemplation of some religious element, but it does not end there. Their message is dominantly secular. In contrast, the message of the crèche begins and ends with reverence for a particular image of the divine. By insisting that such a distinctively sectarian message is merely an unobjectionable part of our "religious heritage," the Court takes a long step backwards to the days when Justice Brewer could arrogantly declare for the Court that "this is a Christian nation." Church of Holy Trinity v. United States, 143 U.S. 457 (1892). Those days, I had thought, were forever put behind us by the Court's decision in [Engel], in which we rejected a similar argument [in defense of the Regents' Prayer].

III. The American historical experience concerning the public celebration of Christmas, if carefully examined, provides no support for the Court's decision. [The] Court's approach suggests a fundamental misapprehension of the proper uses of history in constitutional interpretation. [Attention] to the details of history should not blind us to the cardinal purposes of the Establishment Clause, nor limit our central inquiry in these cases—whether the challenged practices "threaten those consequences which the Framers deeply feared." [The] Court has, until today, consistently limited its historical inquiry to the particular practice under review. [Yet today] the Court wholly fails to discuss the history of the public celebration of Christmas or the use of publicly-displayed nativity scenes.

[The] intent of the Framers with respect to the public display of nativity scenes is virtually impossible to discern primarily because the widespread celebration of Christmas did not emerge in its present form until well into the nineteenth century. [The] historical evidence with respect to public financing and support for governmental displays of nativity scenes is even more difficult to gauge. [In sum], there is no evidence whatsoever that the Framers would have expressly approved a Federal celebration of the Christmas holiday including public displays of a nativity scene; accordingly, the Court's repeated invocation of the decision in Marsh is not only baffling, it is utterly irrelevant. Nor is there any suggestion that publicly financed and supported displays of Christmas crèches are supported by a record of widespread, undeviating acceptance that extends throughout our history. Therefore, our prior decisions which relied upon concrete, specific historical evidence to support a particular practice simply have no bearing on the question presented in this case. Contrary to today's careless decision, those prior cases have all recognized that the "illumination" provided by history must always be focused on the particular practice at issue in a given case. Without that guiding principle and the intellectual discipline it imposes, the Court is at sea, free to select random elements of America's varied history solely to suit the views of five Members of this Court.

IV. [Pawtucket's] action should be recognized for what it is: a coercive, though perhaps small, step toward establishing the sectarian preferences of the majority at the expense of the minority, accomplished by placing public facilities and funds in support of the religious symbolism and theological tidings that the crèche conveys. [That] the Constitution sets [the religious] realm of thought and feeling apart from the pressures and antagonisms of government is one of its supreme achievements. Regrettably, the Court today tarnishes that [achievement].[3]

SOME THOUGHTS ABOUT LYNCH v. DONNELLY

In Lynch, both the majority and the dissenters purported to apply the three-pronged Lemon test: the majority found the Pawtucket practice constitutional under all three prongs; the dissent found it to violate all three prongs. Does this division cast doubt on the continued usefulness of the Lemon test? Compare Justice O'Connor's effort to articulate a somewhat different approach, and contrast the differing emphases in Justice Brennan's dissent. If the Court should decide that the Lemon approach is no longer appropriate, what analysis should it substitute?[1] The Lynch decision provoked widespread commentary, much of it

3. In a separate dissent, Justice BLACK-MUN, joined by Justice Stevens, noted that the majority had done "an injustice to the crèche and the message it manifests." Justice Blackmun noted: "The crèche has been relegated to the role of a neutral harbinger of the holiday season, useful for commercial purposes, but devoid of any inherent meaning and incapable of enhancing the religious tenor of a display of which it is an integral part. The city has its victory—but it is a Pyrrhic one indeed. The import of [the decision] is to encourage use of the crèche in a municipally sponsored display, a setting where Christians feel constrained in acknowledging its symbolic meaning and non-Christians feel alienated by its presence. Surely, this is a misuse of a sacred symbol. Because I cannot join the Court in denying either the force of our precedents or the sacred message that is at the core of the crèche, I dissent and join Justice Brennan's opinion."

1. Whether Lynch v. Donnelly signals an accelerated move by the majority away from the "wall of separation" metaphor toward greater accommodation of state and religion may be clarified by the end of the 1984–85 Term. As noted earlier, as of February 1985, several major cases involving establishment clause (as well as free exercise) claims were pending in the Court, with issues ranging from the constitutionality of a moment for silent prayer in public schools to government benefits to nonpublic schools. One of the issues is closely related to Lynch and is briefly anticipated in Justice Brennan's dissent. It arose from the action of a community with a large Jewish population (Scarsdale, N.Y.), as a result of a city decision eliminating the community's prior practice of displaying a nativity scene. That action was challenged on the ground that it violated free expression and free exercise rights. After Lynch, can it now be argued that the Constitution *requires* a city to display a nativity scene if it permits the communication of other messages? Recall Widmar v. Vincent (1981; noted at p. 1493 above). (The implications of Widmar will also be explored by the Court in another case in which the Court granted review

critical. For a particularly forceful criticism, see Van Alstyne, "Trends in the Supreme Court: Mr. Jefferson's Crumbling Wall—A Comment on Lynch v. Donnelly," 1984 Duke L.J. 770.[2]

SECTION 2. THE "FREE EXERCISE" OF RELIGION

Introduction. To some extent, freedom of expression claims and claims based on the freedom of religion overlap.[1] (Recall that, in many of the cases in chap. 12, free speech objections were raised by members of religious groups such as Jehovah's Witnesses.[2]) But the "free exercise" guarantee raises distinctive problems of its own. Two characteristic ones predominate. First, the "belief"-"action" distinction arises even more often in religion than in speech cases.[3] In the cases that follow, the "free exercise" claimant often argues that a govern-

in February 1985, but which it will probably not decide until the 1985–86 Term. It raises essentially the question whether Widmar applies to public high schools as well as to public universities. It involves a challenge to a Pennsylvania school board's rule denying the application of a student religious group, organized "to promote spiritual growth and positive attitudes in the lives of its members," to meet on the high school campus. A federal Court of Appeals supported the school's action, insisting that permission to allow the student group to meet would amount to an unconstitutional "establishment." The United States supported review because resolution of the issue would affect the constitutionality of a federal law adopted in July 1984, the Equal Access Act, which requires schools that provide a "limited open forum" for student activities generally to also permit religious groups to meet on school grounds.) (For the Court's disposition of all of the religion clause cases now pending before it, see the Supplements to this book, beginning with the 1985 Supplement.)

2. Van Alstyne views Lynch as "the clearest expression to date that acts affiliating government and religion may be deemed consistent with the First Amendment, at least if accomplished gradually, that is, incrementally." He sees Lynch as an illustration of "a larger drift that now appears to be winning acceptance in the Supreme Court," a trend that can be summed up as "a movement from one national epigram to another": "the movement from 'E Pluribus Unum' to 'In God We Trust.'" Under the new trend, even "the absorption of a dominant religion within government itself may be deemed altogether unexceptionable—as though it were but a part of natural history. It is thus symbiosis, not separation, that the first amendment may be interpreted to accommodate. At least I cannot understand Lynch v. Donnelly otherwise, although I think it very far removed from the interpretation of the first amendment originally agreed upon by all nine Justices [in Everson]." As Van Alstyne sees it, the dominant standard of the majority in Lynch is "an '*any more than*' test [—e.g.,] unless the court finds that the additional acts [the governmental acts challenged in the

case] are more egregious than other acts of government of a like kind—that is, unless the new acts advance this religion 'any more than' government has generally advanced a preferred religion—the court shall sustain the acts in question."

Van Alstyne argues that Lynch presented "a paradigmatic disregard of the Establishment Clause in virtually every dimension of its concerns." Under the Lynch facts, "the wall of separation [had] clearly been breached by a clear governmental, politicized, symbiotic embrace of one faith's preferred holy day." Van Alstyne suggests that in a variety of "marginal, gradual, ordinary ways, [virtually] from the beginning the nation has drifted, reidentified itself, and become, like so many others, accustomed to the political appropriation of religion for its own official uses. [Distinctly] religious practices, insofar as they serve the state, thus by definition have virtually succeeded in satisfying a secular purpose and promoting a secular interest. In this gradual absorptive fashion, then, satisfying the Court's current 'test' can scarcely ever be a problem." Note also Van Alstyne's final comment: "Lynch v. Donnelly was [not] a credit to an able and distinguished Court. Both the case and the tendency it represents are disappointing reminders that religious ethnocentrism, as well as religious insensitivity, are still with us. I do not know whether Mr. Jefferson would have been surprised, but I believe he would have been disappointed."

1. For an argument that the Court should treat free exercise as a subset of free speech, see Marshall, "Solving the Free Exercise Dilemma: Free Exercise as Expression," 67 Minn.L.Rev. 545 (1983).

2. E.g., Lovell v. Griffin, and Martin v. Struthers, both in chap. 12 above. In most such cases, the Court's discussion turned largely on freedom of expression.

3. Recall the occasional surfacing (and criticism) of the "speech"-"conduct" distinction in the three preceding chapters. See especially the critical comments on the Cox v. Louisiana cases, in chap. 12, above.

ment regulation—a general regulation resting on state interests not related to religion—either interferes with behavior allegedly dictated by religious belief or compels conduct forbidden by religious belief. Second, the establishment clause places special limits on exemptions for religious believers from general regulations: a state effort to accommodate religious believers by granting an exemption from general laws may be criticized as preferring religion in violation of the establishment guarantee; similarly, a Court effort to immunize religious believers from a general regulation on free exercise grounds may be attacked as a violation of establishment clause values.

FREE EXERCISE CHALLENGES
TO GOVERNMENTAL REGULATION

1. *The early view: The "belief"-"action" distinction.* The "belief"-"action" distinction originated in the first major "free exercise" case, REYNOLDS v. UNITED STATES, 98 U.S. 145 (1878), sustaining application of a federal law making bigamy a crime in the territories to a Mormon claiming polygamy was his religious duty. As Chief Justice WAITE read the First Amendment, "Congress was deprived of all legislative power over mere opinion, but was left free to reach actions which were in violation of social duties or subversive of good order." He added: "Suppose one believed that human sacrifices were a necessary part of religious worship, would it be seriously contended that the civil government [could] not interfere to prevent a sacrifice? Or if a wife religiously believed it was her duty to burn herself upon the funeral pyre of a dead husband, would it be beyond the power of the civil government to prevent her carrying her belief into practice?" After noting the traditional condemnation of polygamy, he concluded: "To permit [polygamy in the face of a bigamy law] would be to make the professed doctrines of religious beliefs superior to the law of the land, and in effect to permit every citizen to become a law unto himself. Government could exist only in name under such circumstances." CANTWELL v. CONNECTICUT, 310 U.S. 296 (1940), reiterated the "belief"-"action" distinction, but with a very different emphasis.[1] The Reynolds implication that conduct was wholly outside the First Amendment was abandoned; instead, Justice ROBERTS suggested that conduct, though subject to greater regulation than belief, may be protected under appropriate circumstances. He stated: "[Free exercise] embraces two concepts,—freedom to believe and freedom to act. The first is absolute, but in the nature of things, the second cannot be. [In] every case the power to regulate must be so exercised as not, in attaining a permissible end, unduly to infringe the protected freedom." (A more precise delineation of the extent to which religion-based conduct could claim exemption from general state regulation was left to the modern cases, below.)

The Court soon confronted religious objections once more in the Flag Salute Cases, where Jehovah's Witnesses attacked public school regulations requiring students to salute the flag. The challengers insisted that their participation in the exercises was "forbidden by command of scripture." In the first case, MINERSVILLE SCHOOL DIST. v. GOBITIS, 310 U.S. 586 (1940), the Court sustained the flag salute requirement; but the second case (only three years later) overruled Gobitis. BOARD OF EDUC. v. BARNETTE, 319 U.S. 624 (1943). Of special interest here are the relative emphases on the religion and

---

1. Cantwell was one of the Jehovah's Witnesses proselytizing cases. The reversal of the defendant's conviction was largely based on free speech grounds, as noted in chap. 12 above. In the portion of the opinion discussing the free exercise guarantee, the Court set aside a convic- tion for soliciting funds for a religious cause without a permit. Under the licensing statute, the administrator had to "determine whether such cause is a religious one or is a bona fide object of charity."

speech guarantees in the cases.[2] Justice FRANKFURTER's majority opinion in Gobitis rejected the free exercise claim with the comment: "The mere possession of religious convictions which contradict the relevant concerns of a political society does not relieve the citizen from the discharge of political responsibilities." He found no greater protection in free speech.[3] To Justice JACKSON in Barnette, the central issue was not freedom of religion but freedom of expression. He explained: "[The issue does not] turn on one's possession of particular religious views or the sincerity with which they are held. While religion supplies appellees' motive of enduring the discomforts of making the issue in this case, many citizens who do not share these religious views hold such a compulsory rite to infringe constitutional liberty of the individual. It is not necessary to inquire whether non-conformist beliefs will exempt from the duty to salute unless we first find power to make the salute a legal duty." And there is no such power, as Justice Jackson emphasized in a widely-quoted passage about a core theme of the First Amendment: [4] "The very purpose of the Bill of Rights was to withdraw certain subjects from the vicissitudes of political

2. The two cases also contained extensive general discussion of the Court's responsibilities in the protection of individual liberty. They were important in the evolution of the "double standard" in judicial review and its special protection of First Amendment rights.

3. Chief Justice STONE's dissent argued for "careful scrutiny" of efforts "to secure conformity of belief [by] a compulsory affirmation of the desired belief."

4. Recall the introduction to chap. 11. Note also the reliance on the Jackson opinion in Justice Harlan's opinion in Street v. New York (the 1969 flag mutilation case; chap. 12 above).

More recently, the majority relied heavily on Barnette in WOOLEY v. MAYNARD, 430 U.S. 705 (1977). The case involved a New Hampshire law requiring most autos to bear license plates carrying the state motto, "Live Free or Die." Challengers were a married couple, members of Jehovah's Witnesses, who found the motto repugnant to their moral, religious and political beliefs and who covered up the motto on their license plate, a misdemeanor. Chief Justice BURGER's majority opinion stated: "Here, as in Barnette, we are faced with a state measure which forces an individual [to] be an instrument for fostering public adherence to an ideological point of view he finds unacceptable. [The law] in effect requires that appellees use their private property as a 'mobile billboard' for the State's ideological message—or suffer a penalty," and that burden was not justified by any sufficiently weighty state interest. He emphasized that First Amendment freedom of thought "includes both the right to speak freely and the right to refrain from speaking at all"; both rights are "complementary components of a broader concept of 'individual freedom of mind.'"

But the Court distinguished Barnette and Wooley in rejecting a shopping center owner's First Amendment attack on a state court's decision granting access to the private property under the free speech and petition clauses of the state constitution. PruneYard Shopping Center v. Robins, 447 U.S. 74 (1980) (chap. 12, sec. 4, above). Justice Rehnquist's opinion for the Court found Wooley distinguishable on several grounds: the State had not dictated the message to be displayed on the owner's property; "the shopping center by choice of its owner is not limited to the personal use" of the owner; moreover, the owner could "expressly disavow any connection with the message by simply posting signs in the area where the speakers or handbillers stand." And Barnette was distinguishable because the challengers were not being compelled "to affirm their belief in any governmentally prescribed position or view."

In a separate opinion concurring in the result, Justice Powell, joined by Justice White, argued that the Court had read potential First Amendment defenses too narrowly. Asserting that some of the Court's language was "unnecessarily and perhaps confusingly broad," he insisted that "state action that transforms privately owned property into a forum for the expression of the public's views could raise serious First Amendment questions." He stated that, "even when no particular message is mandated by the State," "First Amendment interests are affected by state action that forces a property owner to admit third-party speakers. [For example] if a state law mandated public access to the bulletin board of a freestanding store [or] small shopping center, customers might well conclude that the messages reflect the view of the proprietor." Similarly, there might be valid First Amendment objections when speakers sought use of the premises "as a platform for views that [the owner] finds morally repugnant": "To require the owner to specify the particular ideas he finds objectionable enough to compel a response would force him to relinquish his 'freedom to maintain his own beliefs without public disclosure.' Thus, the right to control one's own speech may be burdened impermissibly even when listeners will not assume that the messages expressed on private property are those of the owner." Justice Powell accordingly concluded that, though he joined the Court's judgment, "I do not interpret our decision today as a blanket approval for state efforts to transform privately owned commercial property into public forums."

controversy, to place them beyond the reach of majorities and officials and to establish them as legal principles to be applied by the courts. [Much] of the vagueness of the due process clause disappears when the specific prohibitions of the First become its standard. [First Amendment rights] are susceptible of restriction only to prevent grave and immediate danger to interests which the State may lawfully protect. [Nor] does our duty [to apply the Bill of Rights] depend upon our possession of marked competence in the field where the invasion of rights occurs. [W]e act in these matters not by authority of our competence but by force of our commissions. [If] there is any fixed star in our constitutional constellation, it is that no official, high or petty, can prescribe what shall be orthodox in politics, nationalism, religion, or other matters of opinion or force citizens to confess by word or act their faith therein." [5]

Transitional Note. Many of the opinions above are skeptical about claims that religion-based conduct must be exempt from general regulatory laws. In the cases of the 1960s and 1970s, however, wide agreement developed that the religious objector can sometimes claim such exemption. These cases, which follow, focus on the most difficult modern problems of the free exercise guarantee: When is religion-based conduct constitutionally exempt from regulation? Do constitutionally compelled exemptions threaten establishment values? What burden of justification must the state meet to warrant regulation of religion-based conduct? Are the strict scrutiny criteria of the free speech cases—the emphases on "compelling" state interests and on resort to least restrictive alternatives—appropriate in this area? Is a distinction between "direct" and "indirect" burdens useful? [6] Are other analyses necessary to assure the proper accommodation between free exercise and establishment values? Even if an exemption is not constitutionally compelled, *may* the state exempt conduct based on religious belief without impinging upon the "neutrality" theme of the establishment cases?

THE EVOLUTION OF THE MODERN APPROACH: EXPANDING PROTECTION OF "FREE EXERCISE"; THREATS OF CONFLICT WITH "ESTABLISHMENT" PRINCIPLES

BRAUNFELD v. BROWN, 366 U.S. 599 (1961): Braunfeld was a companion case to McGowan v. Maryland (p. 1495 above). McGowan rejected Establishment Clause challenges to Sunday closing laws. Braunfeld was the principal case which examined free exercise challenges to such laws.[1] In Braunfeld, the majority rejected the free exercise challenge of orthodox Jewish

----

5. Justice BLACK, joined by Justice Douglas, submitted a "statement of reasons for our change of view" since Gobitis. Justice FRANKFURTER's lengthy dissent stated: "One who belongs to the most vilified and persecuted minority in history is not likely to be insensible to the freedoms guaranteed by our Constitution. [But] as a member of this Court I am not justified in writing my private notions of policy into the Constitution. [Of course] patriotism cannot be enforced by the flag salute. But neither can the liberal spirit be enforced by judicial invalidation of illiberal legislation." (Justices Roberts and Reed joined Justice Frankfurter in adhering to Gobitis.)

6. Note the reliance on a "direct"-"indirect" burden distinction in Chief Justice Warren's opinion in Braunfeld, the first of the 1960s cases,

which follows. Justice Brennan dissented from the Braunfeld holding that the free exercise clause does not compel an exemption for Orthodox Jews from Sunday closing laws. But two years later, in Sherbert (p. 1514 below), Justice Brennan was in the majority in holding that an exemption from a general statute was constitutionally compelled. See also the Yoder case (1972; p. 1521 below). Can those decisions be reconciled? Did they take adequate account of the tension between free exercise and establishment? See especially Justice Stewart's concurrence in Sherbert.

1. See also the companion free exercise case on Sunday closing laws, Gallagher v. Crown Kosher Market, 366 U.S. 617 (1961), which involved a challenge "similar" to Braunfeld, "although not as grave."

merchants who claimed that their ability "to earn a livelihood" would be impaired by Sunday closing because their religious beliefs barred work on Saturdays. Chief Justice WARREN's plurality opinion (joined by Justices Black, Clark and Whittaker) stated: "Compulsion by law of the acceptance of any creed or the practice of any form of worship is strictly forbidden. The freedom to hold religious beliefs and opinions is absolute. [Cantwell; Reynolds; Barnette.] [But] the freedom to act, even when the action is in accord with one's religious convictions, is not totally free from legislative restrictions. [Cantwell; Reynolds.] And, in Prince v. Massachusetts, 321 U.S. 158 [1944], this Court upheld a statute making it a crime for a girl [under 18] to sell any newspapers, periodicals or merchandise in public places despite the fact that a child of the Jehovah's Witnesses faith believed that it was her religious *duty* to perform this work. [In Reynolds and Prince], the religious practices themselves conflicted with the public interest. In such cases, to make accommodation between the religious action and an exercise of state authority is a particularly delicate task [because] resolution in favor of the State results in the choice to the individual of either abandoning his religious principle or facing criminal prosecution.

"But [the law here] does not make unlawful any religious practices of appellants; the Sunday law simply regulates a secular activity and, as applied to appellants, operates so as to make the practice of their religious beliefs more expensive. [Fully] recognizing that the alternatives open to appellants and others similarly situated [may] well result in some financial sacrifice in order to observe their religious beliefs, still the option is wholly different than when the legislation attempts to make a religious practice itself unlawful. To strike down, without the most critical scrutiny, legislation which imposes only an indirect burden on the exercise of religion, i.e., legislation which does not make unlawful the religious practice itself, would radically restrict the operating latitude of the [legislature]. Of course, to hold unassailable all legislation regulating conduct which imposes solely an indirect burden on the observance of religion would be a gross oversimplification. If the purpose or effect of a law is to impede the observance of one or all religions or is to discriminate invidiously between religions, that law is constitutionally invalid even though the burden may be characterized as being only indirect. But if the State regulates conduct by enacting a general law within its power, the purpose and effect of which is to advance the State's secular goals, the statute is valid despite its indirect burden on religious observance unless the State may accomplish its purpose by means which do not impose such a burden. See [Cantwell].

"As we pointed out in [McGowan], we cannot find a State without power to provide a weekly respite from all labor and, at the same time, to set one day of the week apart from the others as a day of rest, repose, recreation and tranquility. [Appellants] contend that the State should cut an exception from the Sunday labor proscription for those people who, because of religious conviction, observe a day of rest other than Sunday. [But] to permit the exemption might well undermine the State's goal of providing a day that, as best possible, eliminates the atmosphere of commercial noise and activity. [And] enforcement problems would be more difficult since there would be two or more days to police rather than one and it would be more difficult to observe whether violations were occurring. Additional problems might also be presented by a regulation of this sort. To allow only people who rest on a day other than Sunday to keep their businesses open on that day might well provide these people with an economic advantage over their competitors who must remain closed on that day. [And] there could well be the temptation for some, in order to keep their businesses open on Sunday, to assert that they have religious convictions which compel them to close their businesses on what had formerly been their least profitable day. This might make necessary a state-conducted inquiry into the sincerity of the individual's religious beliefs, a practice which a

State might believe would itself run afoul of the spirit of constitutionally protected religious guarantees. Finally, in order to keep the disruption of the day at a minimum, exempted employers would probably have to hire employees who themselves qualified for the exemption because of their own religious beliefs, a practice which a State might feel to be opposed to its general policy prohibiting religious discrimination in hiring." [2]

Justice BRENNAN's dissent insisted that the law violated the free exercise clause because it "put an individual to a choice between his business and his religion." He relied on Barnette for the appropriate standard of scrutiny and stated: "What, then, is the compelling state interest which impels [Pennsylvania] to impede appellants' freedom of worship? What overbalancing need is so weighty in the constitutional scale that it justifies this substantial, though indirect, limitation of appellants' freedom? It is not the desire to stamp out a practice deeply abhorred by society, such as polygamy, as in [Reynolds]. Nor is it the State's traditional protection of children, as in [Prince]. It is not even the interest in seeing that everyone rests one day a week, for appellants' religion requires that they take such a rest. It is the mere convenience of having everyone rest on the same day. It is to defend this interest that the Court holds that a State need not follow the alternative route of granting an exemption for those who in good faith observe a day of rest other than Sunday. It is true, I suppose, that the granting of such an exemption would make Sundays a little noisier, and the task of police and prosecutor a little more difficult. It is also true that a majority—21—of the 34 States which have general Sunday regulations have exemptions of this kind. We are not told that those States are significantly noisier, or that their police are significantly more burdened, than Pennsylvania's. [The Court] conjures up several difficulties with such a system which seem to me more fanciful than real. [E.g., we] are told that an official inquiry into the good faith with which religious beliefs are held might be itself unconstitutional. But this Court indicated otherwise in [Ballard, p. 1527 below]. In fine, the Court [has] exalted administrative convenience to a constitutional level high enough to justify making one religion economically disadvantageous." [3]

SHERBERT v. VERNER

374 U.S. 398, 83 S.Ct. 1790, 10 L.Ed.2d 965 (1963).

Mr. Justice BRENNAN delivered the opinion of the [Court].

[Appellant, a Seventh-day Adventist, was discharged by her employer "because she would not work on Saturday, the Sabbath Day of her faith." She was unable to obtain other employment because she would not take Saturday work. Her claim for South Carolina state unemployment compensation was denied because the state compensation law barred benefits to workers who failed, without good cause, to accept "suitable work when offered." The highest state court sustained the denial of benefits.]

[If the state decision is to stand] it must be either because her disqualification as a beneficiary represents no infringement by the State of her constitutional rights of free exercise; or because any incidental burden on the free exercise of appellant's religion may be justified by a "compelling state interest in the regulation of a subject within the State's constitutional power to regulate."

---

2. Justice FRANKFURTER, joined by Justice Harlan rejected the free exercise claim in a separate opinion.

was also a separate dissent by Justice DOUGLAS.

3. Justice STEWART also dissented, "substantially" agreeing with Justice Brennan. There

NAACP v. Button [p. 1353 above]. We turn first to the question whether the disqualification for benefits imposes any burden on the free exercise of appellant's religion. We think it is clear that it does. In a sense the consequences of such a disqualification to religious principles and practices may be only an indirect result of welfare legislation within the State's general competence to enact; it is true that no criminal sanctions directly compel appellant to work a six-day week. But this is only the beginning, not the end, of our inquiry. [The] ruling forces her to choose between following the precepts of her religion and forfeiting benefits, on the one hand, and abandoning one of the precepts of her religion in order to accept work, on the other hand. Governmental imposition of such a choice puts the same kind of burden upon the free exercise of religion as would a fine imposed against appellant for her Saturday worship. [Significantly] South Carolina expressly saves the Sunday worshipper from having to make the kind of choice which we here hold infringes the Sabbatarian's religious liberty. When in times of "national emergency" the textile plants are authorized by the [State] to operate on Sunday, "no employee shall be required to work on Sunday [who] is conscientiously opposed to Sunday work." [The] unconstitutionality of the disqualification of the Sabbatarian is thus compounded by the religious discrimination which South Carolina's general statutory scheme necessarily effects.

We must next consider whether some compelling state interest [justifies] the substantial infringement of appellant's First Amendment right. [The] appellees suggest no more than a possibility that the filing of fraudulent claims by unscrupulous claimants feigning religious objections to Saturday work might not only dilute the unemployment compensation fund but also hinder the scheduling by employers of necessary Saturday work. [But] no such objection appears to have been made before the [state courts, and] there is no proof whatever to warrant such fears of malingering or deceit. [Even] if consideration of such evidence is not foreclosed by the prohibition against judicial inquiry into the truth or falsity of religious beliefs, it is highly doubtful whether such evidence would be sufficient to warrant a substantial infringement of religious liberties. For even if [there were such risks], it would plainly be incumbent upon the appellees to demonstrate that no alternative forms of regulation would combat such abuses without infringing First Amendment rights. In these respects, then, the state interest asserted in the present case is wholly dissimilar to the interests which were found to justify the less direct burden upon religious practices in [Braunfeld]. [That statute was] saved by a countervailing factor which finds no equivalent in the instant case—a strong state interest in providing one uniform day of rest for all workers. That secular objective could be achieved, the Court found, only by declaring Sunday to be that day of rest. [Here] no such justifications underlie the determination of the state court that appellant's religion makes her ineligible to receive [benefits].

In holding as we do, plainly we are not fostering the "establishment" of the Seventh-day Adventist religion in South Carolina, for the extension of unemployment benefits to Sabbatarians in common with Sunday worshippers reflects nothing more than the governmental obligation of neutrality in the face of religious differences, and does not represent that involvement of religious with secular institutions which it is the object of the Establishment Clause to forestall. [Nor] do we, by our decision today, declare the existence of a constitutional right to unemployment benefits on the part of all persons whose religious convictions are the cause of their unemployment. This is not a case in which an employee's religious convictions serve to make him a nonproductive member of society. [Our] holding today is only that South Carolina may not constitutionally apply the eligibility provisions so as to constrain a worker to abandon his religious convictions respecting the [day of rest].

[Reversed and remanded.]

Mr. Justice STEWART, concurring in the result.

[I] cannot join the Court's opinion. This case presents a double-barreled dilemma, which in all candor I think the Court's opinion has not succeeded in papering over. The dilemma ought to be resolved. [After deploring the Court's "not only insensitive, but positively wooden," interpretations of the establishment clause in other cases, he continued:] But [the] decisions are on the books. And the result is that there are many situations where legitimate claims under the Free Exercise Clause will run into head-on collision with the Court's insensitive and sterile construction of the Establishment Clause. The controversy now before us is clearly such a case.

[The] Court says that South Carolina cannot under these circumstances declare her to be not "available for work" [because] to do so would violate her constitutional right to the free exercise of her religion. Yet what this Court has said about the Establishment Clause must inevitably lead to a diametrically opposite result. If the appellant's refusal to work on Saturdays were based on indolence, or on a compulsive desire to watch the Saturday television programs, no one would say that South Carolina could not hold that she was not "available for work" within the meaning of its statute. That being so, the Establishment Clause as construed by this Court not only *permits* but affirmatively *requires* South Carolina equally to deny the appellant's claim for unemployment compensation when her refusal to work on Saturdays is based upon her religious creed. To require South Carolina to so administer its laws as to pay public money to the appellant under the circumstances of this case is thus clearly to require the State to violate the Establishment Clause as construed by this Court. This poses no problem for me, because I think the Court's mechanistic concept of the Establishment Clause is historically unsound and constitutionally wrong. [And] I think that the guarantee of religious liberty embodied in the Free Exercise Clause affirmatively requires government to create an atmosphere of hospitality and accommodation to individual belief or disbelief.

South Carolina would deny unemployment benefits to a mother unavailable for work on Saturdays because she was unable to get a babysitter. Thus, we do not have before us a situation where a State provides unemployment compensation generally, and singles out for disqualification only those persons who are unavailable for work on religious grounds. This is not, in short, a scheme which operates so as to discriminate against religion as such. But the Court nevertheless holds that the State must prefer a religious over a secular ground for being unavailable for work.[1] Yet in cases decided under the Establishment Clause the Court has decreed otherwise. It has decreed that government must blind itself to the differing religious beliefs and traditions of the people. With all respect, I think it is the Court's duty to face up to the dilemma posed by the conflict between the [religion clauses]. [S]o long as the resounding but fallacious fundamentalist rhetoric of some of our Establishment Clause opinions remains on our books, to be disregarded at will as in the present case, or to be undiscriminatingly invoked as in [Schempp], so long will the possibility of consistent and perceptive decision in this most difficult and delicate area of constitutional law be impeded and impaired. And so long, I fear, will the guarantee of true religious freedom in our pluralistic society be uncertain and [insecure].

My second difference with the Court's opinion is that I cannot agree that today's decision can stand consistently with [Braunfeld]. The Court says that there was a "less direct burden upon religious practices" in that case than in this. With all respect, I think the Court is mistaken simply as a matter of fact.

---

1. See the discussion of this issue in Justice Harlan's dissent, below.

The Braunfeld case involved a *criminal* statute [and, as Justice Brennan's dissent there pointed out, involved a drastic impact on the challenger's business]. The impact upon the appellant's religious freedom in the present case is considerably less onerous [than in Braunfeld]. Even upon the unlikely assumption that the appellant could not find suitable non-Saturday employment, the appellant at the worst would be denied a maximum of 22 weeks of compensation payments. I agree with the Court that the possibility of that denial is enough to infringe upon the appellant's constitutional right to the free exercise of her religion. But it is clear to me that in order to reach this conclusion the Court must explicitly reject the reasoning of [Braunfeld]. I think the Braunfeld case was wrongly decided and should be overruled, and accordingly I concur in the result [here].[2]

Mr. Justice HARLAN, whom Mr. Justice WHITE joins, dissenting.

[The highest state court has] consistently held that one is not "available for work" if his unemployment has resulted not from the inability of industry to provide a job but rather from personal circumstances, no matter how compelling. [The] fact that these personal considerations sprang from her religious convictions was wholly without relevance to the state court's application of the law. Thus in no proper sense can it be said that the State discriminated against the appellant on the basis of her religious beliefs or that she was denied benefits *because* she was a Seventh-day Adventist. She was denied benefits just as any other claimant would be denied benefits who was not "available for work" for personal reasons.[1] With this background, this Court's decision comes into clearer focus. What the Court is holding is that if the State chooses to condition unemployment compensation on the applicant's availability for work, it is constitutionally compelled to *carve out an exception* —and to provide benefits—for those whose unavailability is due to their religious convictions.[2] Such a holding has particular significance in two respects.

First, despite the Court's protestations to the contrary, the decision necessarily overrules [Braunfeld]. Clearly, any differences between this case and Braunfeld cut against the present appellant. *Second,* the implications of the present decision are far more troublesome than its apparently narrow dimensions would indicate at first glance. [The meaning of the holding is that the

---

2. A concurring opinion by Justice DOUGLAS is omitted.

1. Note Justice Brennan's comment on this issue, in a footnote to his majority opinion: "It has been suggested that appellant is not within the class entitled to benefits under the South Carolina statute because her unemployment did not result from discharge or layoff due to lack of work. It is true that unavailability for work for some personal reasons not having to do with matters of conscience or religion has been held to be a basis of disqualification for benefits. [But] appellant claims that the Free Exercise Clause prevents the State from basing the denial of benefits upon the 'personal reason' she gives for not working on Saturday. Where the consequence of disqualification so directly affects First Amendment rights, surely we should not conclude that every 'personal reason' is a basis for disqualification in the absence of explicit language to that effect in the statute or decisions of the [state's highest court]."

Justice Harlan replied to this in a footnote of his own: "I am completely at a loss to understand [Justice Brennan's footnote]. Certainly the Court is not basing today's decision on the un-

supported supposition that *some* day, the [highest state court] may conclude that there is *some* personal reason for unemployment that may not disqualify a claimant for relief. In any event, I submit it is perfectly clear that South Carolina would not compensate persons who became unemployed for *any* personal reason, as distinguished from layoffs or lack of work, since the [state court's] decisions make it plain that such persons would not be regarded as 'available for work' within the manifest meaning of the eligibility requirements."

2. The Court does suggest, in a rather startling disclaimer, that its holding is limited in applicability to those whose religious convictions do not make them "nonproductive" members of society, noting that most of the Seventh-day Adventists in the Spartanburg area are employed. But surely [this cannot mean that the Court] will make a value judgment in each case as to whether a particular individual's religious convictions prevent him from being "productive." I can think of no more inappropriate function for this Court to perform. [Footnote by Justice Harlan. Cf. Yoder; 1972; below.]

State] must *single out* for financial assistance those whose behavior is religiously motivated, even though it denies such assistance to others whose identical behavior [is] not religiously motivated. It has been suggested that such singling out of religious conduct for special treatment may violate the constitutional limitations on state action.[3] My own view, however, is that at least under the circumstances of this case it would be a permissible accommodation of religion for the State, if it *chose* to do so, to create an exception to its eligibility requirements for persons like the appellant. The constitutional obligation of "neutrality" is not so narrow a channel that the slightest deviation from an absolutely straight course leads to condemnation. There are too many instances in which no such course can be charted, too many areas in which the pervasive activities of the State justify some special provision for religion to prevent it from being submerged by an all-embracing secularism. [But] I cannot subscribe to the conclusion that the State is constitutionally *compelled* to carve out an exception to its general rule of eligibility in the present case. Those situations in which the Constitution may require special treatment on account of religion are, in my view, few and far between. [Such] compulsion in the present case is particularly inappropriate in light of the indirect, remote, and insubstantial effect of the decision below on the exercise of appellant's religion and in light of the direct financial assistance to religion that today's decision [requires].

THOMAS v. REVIEW BD., IND. EMPL. SEC. DIV., 450 U.S. 707 (1981): The Court's 8 to 1 decision relied on Sherbert to invalidate Indiana's denial of unemployment compensation to a Jehovah's Witness who had left his job in a munitions factory because of his religious objections to war. The state had acted under a law barring benefits to "an individual who has voluntarily left his employment without good cause in connection with the work." [1] Chief Justice BURGER's majority opinion stated: "Here, as in Sherbert, the employee was put to a choice between fidelity to religious belief or cessation of work; the coercive impact on Thomas is indistinguishable from Sherbert. [Where] the state conditions receipt of an important benefit upon conduct proscribed by a religious faith, or where it denies such a benefit because of conduct mandated by religious belief, thereby putting substantial pressure on an adherent to modify his behavior and to violate his beliefs, a burden upon religion exists. While the compulsion may be indirect, the infringement upon free exercise is nonetheless substantial." He rejected the argument that Sherbert was inapposite because the employee there left her job because of her employer's action: "In both cases, the termination flowed from the fact that the employment, once acceptable, became religiously objectionable because of changed conditions."

Chief Justice Burger observed that the State could justify this burden on religion only "by showing that it is the least restrictive means of achieving some compelling state interest." Indiana relied on two interests: avoiding "the burden on the [unemployment] fund resulting if people were permitted to leave jobs for 'personal' reasons"; and preventing "a detailed probing by employers into job applicants' religious beliefs." The Chief Justice found that neither interest was "sufficiently compelling to justify the burden upon Thomas' religious liberty." Moreover, the majority summarily rejected the state court's argument that a grant of benefits to Thomas would violate the establishment clause. The Chief Justice conceded that there was, "in a sense, a 'benefit'" to Thomas deriving from his religious beliefs, but added that "this manifests no

---

3. See Kurland, "Of Church and State and the Supreme Court," 29 U.Chi.L.Rev. 1 (1961).

1. The highest state court held that quitting a job because of religion was not "good cause" objectively related to the work and suggested that in any event petitioner's views were more a matter of "personal philosophical choice" than of religious belief.

more than the tension between the two Religion Clauses which the Court resolved in Sherbert." [2]

Insisting that the decision "adds mud to the already muddied waters of First Amendment jurisprudence," Justice REHNQUIST, the sole dissenter, sharply criticized the majority's failure to resolve the "tension" between the free exercise and establishment clauses. The ruling simply left the tension "to be resolved on a case-by-case" basis. He insisted that the tension was "largely of this Court's making" and that it "would diminish almost to the vanishing point if the Clauses were properly interpreted." Objecting to the unduly broad reading of the free exercise clause, he urged acceptance of the Braunfeld approach and of Justice Harlan's dissent in Sherbert. With respect to the establishment clause, he supported Justice Stewart's dissent in Schempp. He claimed, moreover, that if the three-part test of Lemon were applied here, the grant of unemployment benefits to Thomas would "plainly" violate the Establishment Clause. He added: "It is unclear from the Court's opinion whether it has temporarily retreated from its expansive view of the Establishment Clause, or wholly abandoned it. I would welcome the latter." He concluded: "[M]y difficulty with today's decision is that it reads the Free Exercise Clause too broadly and it fails to squarely acknowledge that such a reading conflicts with many of our Establishment Clause cases. As such, the decision simply exacerbates the 'tension' between the two clauses." [3]

UNITED STATES v. LEE, 455 U.S. 252 (1982): Although Sherbert, Thomas, and Yoder clearly indicate that the free exercise clause requires exemptions from government regulations be accorded under certain circumstances, the Lee ruling indicates that the circumstances are not unlimited. Lee, a member of the Old Order Amish, employed several other Amish to work on his farm and in his carpentry shop. Relying on religious grounds, he objected to paying the Social Security tax imposed on employers. The Court found Yoder distinguishable. Chief Justice BURGER conceded that "there is a conflict between the Amish faith and the obligations imposed by the social security system" and accepted that strict scrutiny was appropriate. But the application of the tax law to Lee survived that scrutiny: "Congress and the courts have been sensitive to the needs flowing from the Free Exercise Clause, but every person cannot be shielded from all the burdens incident to exercising every aspect of the right to practice religious beliefs. When followers of a particular sect enter into commercial activity as a matter of choice, the limits they accept on their own conduct as a matter of conscience and faith are not to be superimposed on the statutory schemes which are binding on others in that activity." Here, strict scrutiny standards were satisfied because "the Government's interest in assuring mandatory and continuous participation in and contribution to the social security system is very high" and because "mandatory participation is indispensable to the fiscal vitality of the social security system." And denial of religious exemptions was necessary to protect the Social Security scheme. The Chief Justice added: "The tax system could not function if denominations were

---

2. A separate notation by Justice BLACKMUN stated that he joined the majority opinion only in its discussion of free exercise; with respect to establishment, he concurred only in the result.

3. Justice Rehnquist added in a footnote that, even if Sherbert was correctly decided, this ruling unjustifiably extended Sherbert. He argued that the Sherbert opinion seemed "to suggest by negative implication that where a State makes every 'personal reason' for leaving a job a basis for disqualification from unemployment benefits, the State need not grant an exemption to persons such as Sherbert who do quit for 'personal reasons.'" In Thomas, the highest state court had indeed construed the law "to make every personal subjective reason for leaving a job a basis for disqualification." That made Thomas' case distinguishable from Sherbert's: "Because Thomas left his job for a personal reason, the State of Indiana should not be prohibited from disqualifying him from receiving benefits."

allowed to challenge [it] because tax payments were spent in a manner that violates their religious belief." [1]

Justice STEVENS' concurring opinion thought a strict scrutiny standard inappropriate in exemption cases: "In my opinion, it is the objector who must shoulder the burden of demonstrating that there is a unique reason for allowing him a special exemption from a valid law of general applicability." He argued that there was "virtually no room for a 'constitutionally required exemption' on religious grounds from a valid tax law that is entirely neutral in its general application."[2] Moreover, he argued forcefully that the challenged law would *not* survive if the strict scrutiny the majority purported to exercise were truly applied, particularly "if we confine[d] the analysis to the Government's interest in rejecting the particular claim to an exemption at stake in this case." The majority's rejection of Lee's claim, he argued, rested ultimately on the "risk that a myriad of other claims would be too difficult to process." But the majority had overstated the magnitude of that risk, "because the Amish claim applies only to a small religious community with an established welfare system of its own."[3]

BOB JONES UNIVERSITY v. UNITED STATES, 461 U.S. 574 (1983): This case, like Lee, rejected a free exercise challenge to a federal law. At issue was the decision of the Internal Revenue Service to deny tax-exempt status to two educational institutions, Bob Jones University and Goldsboro Christian Schools. Both practiced racial discrimination, in keeping with the religious beliefs upon which they were founded.[1] The IRS, in denying tax-exempt status

1. Chief Justice Burger noted that the Social Security Act had provided some religious exemptions, but these did not apply to Lee because they were available only to self-employed Amish. He added: "We need not decide whether the Free Exercise Clause compelled an exemption [for the self-employed]; Congress' grant of the exemption was an effort toward accommodation. Nor do we need to decide whether, if Congress had [intended the exemption] to reach this case, conflicts with the Establishment Clause would arise."

2. In an important footnote at this point, Justice Stevens elaborated his approach as follows: "Today's holding is limited to a claim to a tax exemption. I believe, however, that a standard that places an almost insurmountable burden on any individual who objects to a valid and neutral law of general applicability on the ground that the law proscribes (or prescribes) conduct that his religion prescribes (or proscribes) better explains most of this Court's holdings than does the standard articulated by the Court today. See, e.g., Gillette v. United States (selective service laws); Braunfeld v. Brown (Sunday closing laws); Prince v. Massachusetts (child labor laws); Jacobson v. Massachusetts (compulsory vaccination laws); Reynolds v. United States (polygamy law). The principal exception is [Yoder, which follows]. The Court's attempt to distinguish Yoder is unconvincing because precisely the same religious interest is implicated in both cases and Wisconsin's interest in requiring its children to attend school until they reach the age of 16 is surely not inferior to the federal interest in collecting these social security taxes.

"There is also tension between this standard and the reasoning in [Thomas and Sherbert]. Arguably, however, laws intended to provide a

benefit to a limited class of otherwise disadvantaged persons should be judged by a different standard than that appropriate for the enforcement of neutral laws of general applicability. A tax exemption entails no cost to the claimant; if tax exemptions were dispensed on religious grounds, every citizen would have an economic motivation to join the favored sects. No comparable economic motivation could explain the conduct of the employees in Sherbert and Thomas. In both of those cases, changes in work requirements dictated by the employer forced the employees to surrender jobs that they would have preferred to retain rather than accept unemployment compensation. In each case the treatment of the religious objection to the new job requirements as though it were tantamount to a physical impairment that made it impossible for the employee to continue to work under changed circumstances could be viewed as a protection against unequal treatment rather than a grant of favored treatment for the members of the religious sect. In all events, the decision in Thomas was clearly compelled by Sherbert."

3. Justice Stevens added in a footnote: "In my opinion, the principal reason for adopting a strong presumption against such claims is not a matter of administrative convenience. It is the overriding interest in keeping the government [out] of the business of evaluating the relative merits of differing religious claims."

1. Bob Jones University, which had previously denied admission to non-whites, still maintained a policy against interracial marriage or dating by its students. Goldsboro Christian Schools had a racially discriminatory admissions policy that limited admissions to whites. (The cases produced a great deal of media attention, but relatively little new constitutional law.)

to both schools, argued that their racial discrimination practices were "contrary to settled public policy," disqualifying them as "charities." The bulk of Chief Justice BURGER's opinion for the Court focused on the issue of statutory interpretation and application. He found that the IRS policy was authorized by Congress and that the "public policy" limitation was applicable here.[2]

Having found that the denial of tax-exempt status was justified as a matter of statutory interpretation, the Court turned to the claim that the policy could not be applied here without violating the Free Exercise Clause. Part of the Court's reason for rejecting the Free Exercise claim was the impact of the compliance on the schools: "Denial of tax benefits will inevitably have a substantial impact on the operation of private religious schools, but will not prevent those schools from observing their religious tenets." But the most significant factor in the result was the Court's application of the Lee standard that "[t]he state may justify a limitation on religious liberty by showing that it is essential to accomplish an overriding governmental interest." The Court had little trouble finding that standard met in this case: "The governmental interest at stake here is compelling. [The] Government has a fundamental, overriding interest in eradicating racial discrimination in education. [That] governmental interest substantially outweighs whatever burden denial of tax benefits places on petitioners' exercise of their religious beliefs. The interests asserted by petitioners cannot be accommodated with that compelling governmental interest [Lee]; and no 'less restrictive means' [Thomas] are available to achieve the governmental interest."[3]

WISCONSIN v. YODER

406 U.S. 205, 92 S.Ct. 1526, 32 L.Ed.2d 15 (1972).

Mr. Chief Justice BURGER delivered the opinion of the Court.

[We] review a decision of the Wisconsin Supreme Court holding that respondents' convictions of violating the State's compulsory school-attendance law were invalid under the Free Exercise Clause. [We affirm.] Respondents Jonas Yoder and Wallace Miller are members of the Old Order Amish Religion, and respondent Adin Yutzy is a member of the Conservative Amish Mennonite Church. [Wisconsin's] compulsory school attendance law required them to cause their children to attend public or private school until reaching age 16 but the respondents declined to send their children, ages 14 and 15, to public school after they completed the eighth grade. [Respondents were convicted and fined $5 each.] Trial testimony showed that they believed that by sending their children to high school, they [would] endanger their own salvation and that of their children. The State stipulated that respondents' religious beliefs were [sincere].

[Amish] beliefs require members of the community to make their living by farming or closely related activities. [They object to formal education beyond the eighth grade because it] tends to emphasize intellectual and scientific

---

2. The Chief Justice stated: "[There] can no longer be any doubt that racial discrimination in education violates deeply and widely accepted views of elementary justice. [Whatever] may be the rationale for such private schools' policies, and however sincere the rationale may be, racial discrimination in education is contrary to public policy."

3. The Court also rejected the argument that denial of the tax-exempt status violated the establishment clause by preferring some religions over others. So long as the IRS policy had a secular and neutral basis, the clause was not violated "merely because [the regulation] 'happens to coincide or harmonize with the tenets of some or all religions.' [McGowan.]"

Justice POWELL's concurrence and Justice REHNQUIST's dissent focused on issues of statutory authority. Both, however, explicitly agreed with the majority regarding rejection of the free exercise claim.

accomplishments, self-distinction, competitiveness, worldly success, and social life with other students. Amish society emphasizes informal learning-through-doing; a life of "goodness," rather than a life of intellect; wisdom, rather than technical knowledge; community welfare, rather than competition; and separation from, rather than integration with, contemporary worldly society. [An expert] testified that compulsory high school attendance could not only result in great psychological harm to Amish children, because of the conflicts it would produce, but would [also] ultimately result in the destruction of the Old Order Amish church community. [Another expert testified] that the Amish succeeded in preparing their high school age children to be productive members of the Amish community. [The] evidence also showed that the Amish have an excellent record as law-abiding and generally self-sufficient members of society.

[A] State's interest in universal education, however highly we rank it, is not totally free from a balancing process when it impinges on fundamental rights and interests, such as those specifically protected by the Free Exercise Clause [and] the traditional interest of parents with respect to the religious upbringing of their children so long as [they] "prepare [them] for additional obligations." [Pierce v. Society of Sisters (1925; p. 502 above).] It follows that in order for Wisconsin to compel school attendance beyond the eighth grade against a claim that such attendance interferes with the practice of a legitimate religious belief, it must appear either that the State does not deny the free exercise of religious belief by its requirement, or that there is a state interest of sufficient magnitude to override the interest claiming protection under the Free Exercise Clause. [O]nly those interests of the highest order and those not otherwise served can overbalance legitimate claims to the free exercise of [religion].

[In evaluating respondents' claims], we must be careful to determine whether the Amish religious faith and their mode of life are, as they claim, inseparable and interdependent. A way of life, however virtuous and admirable, may not be interposed as a barrier to reasonable state regulation of education if it is based on purely secular considerations; to have the protection of the Religion Clauses, the claims must be rooted in religious belief. Although a determination of what is a "religious" belief or practice entitled to constitutional protection may present a most delicate question, the very concept of ordered liberty precludes allowing every person to make his own standards on matters of conduct in which society as a whole has important interests. Thus, if the Amish asserted their claims because of their subjective evaluation and rejection of the contemporary secular values accepted by the majority, much as Thoreau rejected the social values of his time and isolated himself at Walden Pond, their claim would not rest on a religious basis. Thoreau's choice was philosophical and personal rather than religious, and such belief does not rise to the demands of the Religion Clause.

Giving no weight to such secular considerations, however, we see that the record in this case abundantly supports the claim that the traditional way of life of the Amish is not merely a matter of personal preference, but one of deep religious conviction, shared by an organized group, and intimately related to daily living. [This] is shown by the fact that [the Amish life] is in response to their literal interpretation of the Biblical injunction from the Epistle of Paul to the Romans, "be not conformed to this world." [This] command is fundamental to the Amish faith. Moreover, for the Old Order Amish, religion is not simply a matter of theocratic belief. As the expert witnesses explained, [their] religion pervades and determines virtually their entire way of life, regulating it with the detail of the Talmudic diet through the strictly enforced rules of the [church community].

The impact of the compulsory-attendance law on respondents' practice of the Amish religion is not only severe, but inescapable, for the Wisconsin law affirmatively compels them, under threat of criminal sanction, to perform acts undeniably at odds with fundamental tenets of their religious beliefs. See [Braunfeld]. [It raises] a very real threat of undermining the Amish community and religious practice as they exist today; they must either abandon belief and be assimilated into society at large, or be forced to migrate to some other and more tolerant region. [In sum], enforcement of the State's requirement of compulsory formal education after the eighth grade would gravely endanger if not destroy the free exercise of respondents' religious beliefs. [The] Court must not ignore the danger that an exception from a general obligation of citizenship on religious grounds may run afoul of the Establishment Clause, but that danger cannot be allowed to prevent any exception no matter how vital it may be to the protection of values promoted by the right of [free exercise].

The State advances two primary arguments in support of its system of compulsory education. It notes [that] some degree of education is necessary to prepare citizens to participate effectively and intelligently in our open political system [and that] education prepares individuals to be self-reliant and self-sufficient participants in society. We accept these propositions. However, the evidence adduced by the Amish in this case is persuasively to the effect that an additional one or two years of formal high school for Amish children in place of their long-established program of informal vocational education would do little to serve those interests. [It] is one thing to say that compulsory education for a year or two beyond the eighth grade may be necessary when its goal is the preparation of the child for life in modern society as the majority live, but it is quite another if the goal of education be viewed as the preparation of the child for life in the separated agrarian community that is the keystone of the Amish faith.

The State attacks respondents' position as one fostering "ignorance" from which the child must be protected by the State. [But] this record strongly shows that the Amish community has been a highly successful social unit within our society, even if apart from the conventional "mainstream." Its members are productive and very law-abiding members of society; they reject public welfare in any of its usual modern views. The Congress itself recognized their self-sufficiency by authorizing exemption of such groups as the Amish from the obligation to pay social security taxes. A way of life that is odd or even erratic but interferes with no rights or interests of others is not to be condemned because it is different.

The State, however, supports its interest [because] of the possibility that some such children will choose to leave the Amish community, and that if this occurs they will be ill-equipped for life. [However], on this record, that argument is highly speculative. There is no specific evidence of the loss of Amish adherents by attrition, nor is there any showing that upon leaving the Amish community Amish children, with their practical agricultural training and habits of industry and self-reliance, would become burdens on society because of educational shortcomings. [In fact], not only do the Amish accept the necessity for formal schooling through the eighth grade level, but continue to provide [an] "ideal" vocational education for their children in the adolescent years. [Wisconsin's] interest in compelling attendance of Amish children to age 16 emerges as somewhat less substantial than requiring such attendance for children [generally]. Finally, the State, on authority of Prince v. Massachusetts, argues that a decision exempting Amish children from the State's requirement fails to recognize the subsequent right of the Amish child to a secondary education. [But] the Court was not confronted in Prince with a situation comparable to that of the Amish as revealed [here]. This case is not one in which any harm to the physical or mental health of the child or to the public safety, peace, order, or welfare has been demonstrated. [The] record is to the contrary.

[Contrary] to the suggestion [in Justice Douglas' dissent], our holding today in no degree depends on the assertion of the religious interest of the child as contrasted with that of the parents. It is the parents who are subject to prosecution here [and] it is their right of free exercise, not that of their children, that must determine Wisconsin's power to impose criminal penalties on the parent. The dissent argues that a child who expresses a desire to attend public high school in conflict with the wishes of his parents should not be prevented from doing so. There is no reason for the Court to consider that point since it is not an issue in the case. The children are not parties to this litigation. The State has at no point tried this case on the theory that respondents were preventing their children from attending school against their expressed desires, and indeed the record is to the [contrary].[1] Our holding in no way determines the proper resolution of possible competing interests of parents, children, and the State in an appropriate state court proceeding in which the power of the State is asserted on the theory that Amish parents are preventing their minor children from attending high school despite their expressed desires to the contrary. Recognition of the claim of the State in such a proceeding would, of course, call into question traditional concepts of parental control over the religious upbringing and education of their minor children recognized in this Court's past decisions.[2] It is clear that such an intrusion by a State into family decisions in the area of religious training would give rise to grave questions of religious freedom. [On] this record we neither reach nor decide those issues.[3]

[It] cannot be over-emphasized that we are not dealing with a way of life and mode of education by a group claiming to have recently discovered some "progressive" or more enlightened process for rearing children for modern life. [In light of the "convincing showing" by the Amish here], one that probably few other religious groups or sects could make, and weighing the minimal difference between what the State would require and what the Amish already accept, it was incumbent on the State to show with more particularity how its admittedly strong interest in compulsory education would be adversely affected by granting an exemption to the Amish. [Sherbert.]

Affirmed.[4]

1. The only relevant testimony in the record is to the effect that the wishes of the one child who testified corresponded with those of her parents. Testimony of Frieda Yoder, to the effect that her personal religious beliefs guided her decision to discontinue school attendance after the 8th grade. The other children were not called by either side. [Footnote by Chief Justice Burger.]

2. For later Court discussions of the rights of parents and of children (and other constitutional aspects of family law), under the aegis of substantive due process, recall chap. 8 above. (Note also the remarks on the rights of the Amish children in Justice Douglas' dissent, below.)

3. What we have said should meet the suggestion that the decision of the Wisconsin Supreme Court recognizing an exemption for the Amish from the State's system of compulsory education constituted an impermissible establishment of religion. [Accommodating] the religious beliefs of the Amish can hardly be characterized as sponsorship or active involvement. The purpose and effect of such an exemption are not to support, favor, advance, or assist the Amish, but to allow their centuries-old religious society, here long before the advent of any compulsory education, to survive free from the heavy impediment

of compliance with the Wisconsin compulsory-education law would impose. Such an accommodation "reflects nothing more than the governmental obligation of neutrality in the face of religious differences, and does not represent that involvement of religious with secular institutions which it is the object of the Establishment Clause to forestall." [Sherbert.]. [Footnote by Chief Justice Burger.]

4. Justices POWELL and REHNQUIST did not participate in the decision.

In a concurring notation, Justice WHITE, joined by Justices Brennan and Stewart, stated: "Decision in this case [will] inevitably involve the kind of close and perhaps repeated scrutiny of religious practices [which] the Court has heretofore been anxious to avoid. But such entanglement does not create a forbidden establishment of religion where it is essential to implement free exercise values threatened by an otherwise neutral program instituted to foster some permissible, nonreligious state objective. [Here], the State's valid interest in education has already been largely satisfied by the eight years the children have already spent in school." In another concurrence, Justice STEWART, joined by Justice Brennan, emphasized that this case did not involve the "interesting and important issue"

Mr. Justice DOUGLAS, [dissenting in part].

It is argued that the right of the Amish children to religious freedom is not presented by the facts of the case. [It] is essential to reach the question [because] no analysis of religious-liberty claims can take place in a vacuum. If the parents in this case are allowed a religious exemption, the inevitable effect is to impose the parents' notions of religious duty upon their children. Where the child is mature enough to express potentially conflicting desires, it would be an invasion of the child's rights to permit such an imposition without canvassing his views. [It] is an imposition resulting from this very litigation. As the child has no other effective forum, it is in this litigation that his rights should be considered. And, if an Amish child desires to attend high school, and is mature enough to have that desire respected, the State may well be able to override the parents' religiously motivated objections. [Crucial] are the views of the child whose parent is the subject of the suit. [Only Yoder's child has] testified that her own religious views are opposed to high-school education. I therefore join the judgment. [But that child's] views may not be those of [the two others]. I must dissent, therefore, as to [the two other respondents].

This issue has never been squarely presented before today. Our opinions are full of talk about the power of the parents over the child's education. Recent cases, however, have clearly held that the children themselves have constitutionally protectible interests. [E.g., Tinker, chap. 12 above.] While the parents, absent dissent, normally speak for the entire family, the education of the child is a matter on which the child will often have decided views. [It] is the student's judgment, not his parents', that is essential if we are to give full meaning to what we have said about [the] right of students to be masters of their own destiny. [The child] should be given an opportunity to be heard before the State gives the exemption which we honor [today].

I think the emphasis of the Court on the "law and order" record of this Amish group of people is quite irrelevant. A religion is a religion irrespective of what the misdemeanor or felony records of its members might be. I am not at all sure how the Catholics, Episcopalians, the Baptists, Jehovah's Witnesses, the Unitarians, and my own Presbyterians would make out if subjected to such a test. It is, of course, true that if a group or society was organized to perpetuate crime and if that is its motive, we would have rather startling problems akin to those that were raised when some years back a particular sect was challenged here as operating on a fraudulent basis. [Ballard, p. 1527 below.] But no such factors are present here, and the Amish, whether with a high or low criminal record,* certainly qualify by all historic standards as a religion within the meaning of the First Amendment.

The Court rightly rejects the notion that actions, even though religiously grounded, are always outside the protection of the Free Exercise Clause [and in so ruling] departs from the teaching of [Reynolds]. [What] we do today, at least in this respect, opens the way to give organized religion a broader base than it has ever enjoyed; and it even promises that in time Reynolds will be overruled. In another way, however, the Court retreats when in reference to

---

discussed in Justice Douglas' dissent—i.e., the rights of Amish children to attend school beyond the eighth grade if they wished to do so.

* The observation of Justice Heffernan, dissenting below, that the principal opinion in his Court portayed the Amish as leading a life of "idyllic agrarianism," is equally applicable to the majority opinion in this Court. So, too, is his observation that such a portrayal rests on a "mythological basis." [One of the expert witnesses relied on by the Court] has noted that,

"Drinking is common in all large Amish settlements." Moreover, "[i]t would appear that among the Amish the rate of suicide is just as high, if not higher, than for the nation." He also notes an unfortunate Amish "preoccupation with filthy stories," as well as significant "rowdyism and stress." These are not traits peculiar to the Amish, of course. The point is that the Amish are not people set apart and different. [Footnote by Justice Douglas.]

Henry Thoreau it says his "choice was philosophical and personal rather than religious, and such belief does not rise to the demands of the Religion Clause." That is contrary to what we held in [Seeger and Welsh, the conscientious objector cases at p. 1528 below].

PROBLEMS IN INTERPRETING "FREE EXERCISE"

1. *Reconciling "free exercise" and "establishment."* Do Yoder, Thomas, and Lee clarify the uncertainties left by the efforts to reconcile Braunfeld and Sherbert? Sherbert, Thomas, and Yoder at least indicate that religiously based conduct can sometimes claim constitutional exemption from regulatory statutes. Has a balancing analysis similar to the one used in the free speech area become the prevailing (and appropriate) one in this field as well? Is "strict scrutiny," requiring "compelling" state justifications and "least restrictive" means, now the norm in free exercise cases? Should it be?

Has the Court adequately addressed the additional religion clause problem presented by Sherbert, Thomas, Yoder, and Lee: the risk of impinging upon establishment clause values by finding a constitutionally mandated exemption for religiously based conduct? Do Sherbert, Thomas, and Yoder rule out Kurland's "neutrality" solution (p. 1464 above), barring any "classification in terms of religion either to confer a benefit or to impose a burden"?[1] If "neutrality" is inappropriate, is Justice Harlan's suggestion in Sherbert—that government may, but need not, carve out an exception in the face of religious scruples—preferable? Or does even that run counter to establishment clause values? Note that the Sherbert, Thomas, and Yoder results require even more "accommodation" than Justice Harlan would have supported. Do these decisions reinforce the view that the "wall of separation" metaphor—if it retains any significant force—is not taken very seriously by the modern Court?

2. *State regulation and religious scruples: Other examples.* Reexamine, in light of the criteria stated and applied in the recent cases, the earlier examples of conflicts of free exercise claims with state regulatory power—e.g., Barnette (flag salute), Reynolds (polygamy), and Prince v. Massachusetts (child labor).[2] Consider, too, other illustrations of claims to constitutional exemption from general

---

1. Can the course of decisions be reconciled with a "neutrality" principle by viewing "religion" as broadly as the Court has viewed it in interpreting statutory references to religion in the conscientious objector exemption to the draft laws? See, e.g., United States v. Seeger (1965; p. 1528 below).

2. Note also McDaniel v. Paty, 435 U.S. 618 (1978), invalidating a Tennessee provision disqualifying clergy from being legislators or constitutional convention delegates. Although the decision is of limited practical impact (Tennessee was the last state to retain the disqualification, once commonplace in state laws), the case is of interest because of the divided Court's difficulties in finding a rationale appropriate under the doctrines developed in this chapter. Chief Justice Burger's plurality opinion, joined by Justices Powell, Rehnquist and Stevens, found the absolute bar on interference with religious beliefs inapplicable, because the state barrier referred to "*status* [as] 'minister' or 'priest' " and ministerial status was "defined in terms of conduct and activity rather [than] belief." Instead, he applied the strict scrutiny approach developed in

Sherbert and Yoder and concluded that the State's "preventing-establishment-of-religion" rationale was inadequate to support the ban. Justice Brennan's concurrence (joined by Justice Marshall) found that the disqualification directly burdened religious belief and was accordingly absolutely prohibited rather than being subject to a balancing analysis. He found the appropriate precedent to be Torcaso v. Watkins, 367 U.S. 488 (1961), which had struck down a Maryland requirement that all holders of public office declare their belief in the existence of God; the Chief Justice, by contrast, found Torcaso distinguishable because it had focused on belief rather than conduct. Justice Brennan also concluded that the establishment clause had been violated: the state disqualification showed "hostility" toward religion; ordinarily, "government may not use religion as a basis of classification for the imposition of duties, penalties, privileges or benefits." Justice Stewart's concurrence substantially agreed with Justice Brennan. Justice White, finally, rested on the strict scrutiny equal protection approach to ballot access cases, chap. 9, sec. 4, above.

statutes on the basis of religious scruples: e.g., In re Jenison, 375 U.S. 14 (1963) (remanding for reconsideration in light of Sherbert a conviction of a woman who had refused jury duty for religious reasons; conviction reversed on remand); Jacobson v. Massachusetts, 197 U.S. 11 (1905) (compulsory smallpox vaccination); Application of Georgetown College, 331 F.2d 1000 (D.C.Cir.), cert. den., 377 U.S. 978 (1964) (compulsory blood transfusion); People v. Woody, 61 Cal.2d 716 (1964) (ban on the drug peyote unconstitutional as applied to use in bona fide religious practices by the Native American Church); and compare Lawson v. Commonwealth, 164 S.W.2d 972 (Ky.1942) (use of poisonous snakes in religious ceremonies).[3]

3. *Judicial determination of questions of religious doctrine and belief.* In the free exercise cases considered above, the Court questioned neither the accuracy of the belief alleged to conflict with the state regulation nor whether that belief in fact corresponded with the doctrine of the challenger's religion. The Court's most explicit statement of its typical refusal to inquire into the content and accuracy of beliefs came in UNITED STATES v. BALLARD, 322 U.S. 78 (1944), a ruling frequently cited in the modern cases. The defendants in Ballard were indicted under the federal mail fraud laws. They had solicited funds for the "I Am" movement. Among their representations were the claims that they had been selected as "divine messengers" to communicate the message of the "alleged divine entity, Saint Germain" and that they had, "by reason of supernatural attainments, the power to heal persons of ailments and diseases." Justice DOUGLAS' majority opinion stated that the First Amendment barred submission to the jury of "the truth or verity of respondents' religious doctrines or beliefs." He commented: "Men may believe what they cannot prove. They may not be put to the proof of their religious doctrines or beliefs. [The] miracles of the New Testament, the Divinity of Christ, life after death, the power of prayer are deep in the religious convictions of many. If one could be sent to jail because a jury in a hostile environment found those teachings false, little indeed would be left of religious freedom." Does that position bar submission to the jury of the question of the defendants' good faith? Could a jury find that defendants knew that their representations were false and that they therefore solicited funds fraudulently? Could such a finding be made without some evaluation of the nature of the defendants' representations?[4]

Although the Court is reluctant to inquire into the "truth" of religious beliefs, courts do occasionally adjudicate the "sincerity" of beliefs.[5] It is doubtful, however, that the "sincerity" can really be examined without treading on the supposedly forbidden area of the content of beliefs.[6]

---

3. See generally Marcus, "[Applying] Standards under the Free Exercise Clause," 1973 Duke L.J. 1217; Clark, "Guidelines for the Free Exercise Clause," 83 Harv.L.Rev. 327 (1969); Giannella, "The Religious Liberty Guarantee," 80 Harv.L.Rev. 1381 (1967); and Fernandez, "The Free Exercise of Religion," 36 S.Cal.L.Rev. 546 (1963).

4. Another source of controversy regarding judicial power to decide questions of religious doctrine has been the recurrent effort to draw courts into disputes arising from church schisms. The normal rule is that courts should try to stay out of internal church disputes. But "marginal judicial involvement" is permissible, so long as the courts do not decide church property disputes by "resolving underlying controversies [of] religious doctrine." The Court has said that courts may apply "[n]eutral principles of law,

developed for use in all property disputes," in adjudicating church property controversies, but that the religion clauses preclude determining matters "at the very core of a religion—the interpretation of particular church doctrines and the importance of those doctrines to religion." See Presbyterian Church v. Hull Church, 393 U.S. 440 (1969). The Court has been sharply divided over the application of these guidelines. See, e.g., Jones v. Wolf, 443 U.S. 595 (1979).

5. See, e.g., the conscientious objector draft exemption cases, in the next group of notes.

6. For example, can free exercise claims of exemption from general laws, on the ground that they intrude unduly into protected areas of belief and conduct, be evaluated without some examination of the content of religious doctrine? Re-

MILITARY SERVICE, THE CONSCIENTIOUS OBJECTOR, AND RELIGION

1. *The background.* Selective service laws have typically exempted from military service conscientious objectors opposed to "war in any form" on "religious" grounds. The Court has traditionally assumed that the exemption is a matter of legislative grace, is not compelled by the free exercise clause, and does not violate the establishment clause. Modern interpretations of the religion clauses may cast doubt on those assumptions. For the traditional view, see the sustaining of the World War I version of the conscientious objector exemption in the Selective Draft Law Cases, 245 U.S. 366 (1918), where the Court summarily rejected free exercise and establishment clause objections. See also Hamilton v. Regents, 293 U.S. 245 (1934), where a requirement that all male students take military science courses was sustained against a claim that it violated the religious beliefs of a conscientious objector.

2. *The scope of "religion" in modern draft laws.* Sec. 6(j) of the Universal Military Training and Service Act of 1948 exempted from combatant military service those persons who were conscientiously opposed to participation in war in any form by reason of their "religious training and belief." The quoted phrase was defined by the law as a "belief in a relation to a Supreme Being involving duties superior to those arising from any human relation, but [not including] essentially political, sociological, or philosophical views or a merely personal moral code."[1] The section was attacked under the establishment, free exercise, and due process clauses, on the grounds that it did not exempt nonreligious conscientious objectors and that it discriminated among different forms of religious expression. The Court did not reach these constitutional claims in three cases decided as UNITED STATES v. SEEGER, 380 U.S. 163 (1965); rather, Justice CLARK's opinion interpreted § 6(j) and its references to religion very broadly, so that all the petitioners proved entitled to the exemption: "We have concluded that Congress, in using the expression 'Supreme Being' rather than the designation 'God,' was merely clarifying the meaning of religious training and belief so as to embrace all religions and to exclude essentially political, sociological, or philosophical views. We believe that under this construction, the test of belief 'in a relation to a Supreme Being' is whether a given belief that is sincere and meaningful occupies a place in the life of its possessor parallel to that filled by the orthodox belief in God of one who clearly qualifies for the exemption. Where such beliefs have parallel positions in the lives of their respective holders we cannot say that one is 'in a relation to a Supreme Being' and the other is not."[2] In a concurring opinion, Justice DOUGLAS stated that he "would have difficulties" if he "read the statute differently" from the Court: "For then those who embraced one religious faith rather than another would be subject to penalties; and that kind of discrimination, as we held in [Sherbert], would violate the Free Exercise

call, e.g., the claims of the Orthodox Jew and the Amish parent in Braunfeld and Yoder, above.

1. A 1967 amendment deleted the statutory reference to a "belief in a relation to a Supreme Being."

2. In discussing the application of this standard, the Court emphasized "that in resolving these exemption problems one deals with the beliefs of different individuals who will articulate them in a multitude of ways. In such an intensely personal area, of course, the claim of the registrant that his belief is an essential part of a religious faith must be given great weight. [The] validity of what he believes cannot be questioned.

Some theologians, and indeed some examiners, might be tempted to question the existence of the registrant's 'Supreme Being' or the truth of his concepts. But these are inquiries foreclosed to Government. [Ballard.] Local boards and courts in this sense are not free to reject beliefs because they consider them 'incomprehensible.' Their task is to decide whether the beliefs professed by a registrant are sincerely held and whether they are, in his own scheme of things, religious. But we hasten to emphasize that while the 'truth' of a belief is not open to question, there remains the significant question whether it is 'truly held.'"

Clause [and] would also result in a denial of equal protection by preferring some religions over others." [3]

3. *The scope of "religion" and the draft law.* In WELSH v. UNITED STATES, 398 U.S. 333 (1970), the plurality opinion reversed petitioner's conviction with a statutory interpretation of § 6(j) that elaborated on Seeger. But in Welsh, several of the separate opinions reached constitutional issues.[4] Justice BLACK's plurality opinion found no adequate reason to distinguish Welsh from Seeger. Although Welsh had struck the word "religious" on his application, that did not bar the exemption: "[V]ery few registrants are fully aware of the broad scope of the word 'religious' as used in § 6(j)." Moreover, Welsh's claim was not barred by the exclusion in § 6(j) of those persons with "essentially political, sociological, or philosophical views or a merely personal moral code." That language, Justice Black concluded, should not be read "to exclude those who hold strong beliefs about our domestic and foreign affairs or even those whose conscientious objection to participation in all wars is founded to a substantial extent upon considerations of public policy. The two groups of registrants that obviously do fall within these exclusions from the exemption are those whose beliefs are not deeply held and those whose objection to war does not rest at all upon moral, ethical, or religious principle but instead rests solely upon considerations of policy, pragmatism, or expediency."

Justice HARLAN's opinion concurred in the result via a very different route. He found that the Seeger interpretation of § 6(j), which he had joined, exceeded the limits of permissible statutory interpretation; thought that § 6(j) must be read as limited to "those opposed to war in general because of theistic beliefs"; held that interpretation unconstitutional under the First Amendment; and concluded that the Court, rather than nullifying the exemption entirely, should extend its coverage to those who, like Welsh, had been unconstitutionally excluded. He stated that Congress "cannot draw the line between theistic or nontheistic religious beliefs on the one hand and secular beliefs on the other. Any such distinctions are not, in my view, compatible with the Establishment Clause." Justice WHITE's dissent concluded that, whether or not Seeger was an accurate reflection of legislative intent, he could not join a "construction of § 6(j) extending draft exemption to those who disclaim religious objections to war and whose views about war represent a purely personal code arising not from religious training and belief as the statute requires but from readings in philosophy, history, and sociology." And he would have found that the "religious training and belief" requirement did not constitute establishment even were it not required by the free exercise clause: "It is very likely that § 6(j) is a recognition by Congress of free exercise values. [That] judgment is entitled to respect." [5]

3. There has been extensive commentary on the problem of defining religion for purposes of both free exercise and establishment clause inquiries. For a representative sample, see Tribe, American Constitutional Law § 28–33 (1978) (advocating a double standard—a narrow definition for establishment clause issues and a broad definition for free exercise issues); Choper, "Defining 'Religion' in the First Amendment," 1982 U.Ill.L.Rev. 579 (confining the definition of religious belief to that necessarily involving fear of "extratemporal consequences"); and Greenawalt, "Religion as a Concept in Constitutional Law," 72 Cal.L.Rev. 753 (1984) (maintaining that one definition is satisfactory and that courts should proceed by analogy on a case-by-case basis).

4. Justice BLACK's plurality opinion was joined by Justices Douglas, Brennan and Mar-

shall. Justice HARLAN thought he had "made a mistake" in Seeger and adopted a narrower reading of the conscientious objector exemption; he nevertheless joined the judgment reversing the conviction because he found the narrowly construed statutory provision unconstitutional. Justice WHITE, joined by Chief Justice Burger and Justice Stewart, dissented. He did not think that petitioner qualified for an exemption under the Seeger interpretation; and he, like Justice Harlan, addressed the constitutional issue. (Justice Blackmun did not participate in the case.)

5. Justice White argued that it was surely "necessary and proper" in enacting laws for the raising of armies "to take account of the First Amendment and to avoid possible violations of the Free Exercise Clause. If this was the course Congress took, then just as in [Katzenbach v.

4. *Selective conscientious objection.* The 8 to 1 decision in GILLETTE v. UNITED STATES, 401 U.S. 437 (1971), held that the congressional refusal to exempt selective conscientious objectors from the draft was constitutional. The petitioners did not oppose all wars, but they did object to participation in the Vietnam conflict as an "unjust" war. One, for example, claimed that it was his duty as a faithful Catholic to discriminate between "just" and "unjust" wars, and to refuse participation in the latter. Justice MARSHALL's majority opinion rejected at the outset the argument that petitioners were entitled to statutory exemption under § 6(j) because they were "conscientiously opposed to participation in war in any form": "This language, on a straight-forward reading, can bear but one meaning: that conscientious scruples relating to war and military service must amount to conscientious opposition to participating personally in any war and all war." He found the exemption constitutional as so construed. He noted that, "despite free exercise overtones, the gist of the constitutional complaint is that § 6(j) impermissibly discriminates among types of religious belief and affiliation." He rejected that attack because he found "neutral, secular reasons to justify the line that Congress has drawn." The law did not discriminate among religions on its face; but that did not end the matter, "for the Establishment Clause forbids subtle departures from neutrality, 'religious gerrymanders,' as well as obvious abuses. [Still], a claimant alleging 'gerrymander' must be able to show the absence of a neutral, secular basis for the lines government has drawn." And that showing had not been made here: "We conclude not only that the affirmative purposes underlying § 6(j) are neutral and secular, but also that valid neutral reasons exist for limiting the exemption to objectors to all war, and that the section therefore cannot be said to reflect a religious preference." In examining the asserted justifications for limiting the exemption, he was most impressed by the Government's argument that "the interest in fairness would be jeopardized by expansion of § 6(j) to include conscientious objection to a particular war." He noted the "danger that as between two would-be objectors, [that] objector would succeed who is more articulate, better educated, or better counseled. There is even a danger of unintended religious discrimination—a danger that a claim's chances of success would be greater the more familiar or salient the claim's connection with conventional religiosity could be made to appear."

Justice Marshall recognized that the free exercise claim had "a reach of its own." He added, however: "Nonetheless, our analysis of § 6(j) for Establishment Clause purposes has revealed governmental interests of a kind and weight sufficient to justify under the Free Exercise Clause the impact of the conscription laws on those who object to particular wars." Even with neutral laws having secular aims, "the Free Exercise Clause may condemn certain applications clashing with imperatives of religion and conscience, when the burden on First Amendment values is not justifiable in terms of the Government's valid aims. [Sherbert.] However, the impact of conscription on objectors to particular wars is far from unjustified. [The laws] are not designed to interfere with any religious ritual or practice, and do not work a penalty against any theological position. The incidental burdens felt by persons in petitioners' position are strictly justified by substantial government interests that relate directly to the

Morgan, chap. 10, p. 946 above], where we accepted the judgment of Congress as to what legislation was appropriate to enforce [equal protection], here we should respect congressional judgment accommodating the Free Exercise Clause and the power to raise armies. This involves no surrender of the Court's function as ultimate arbiter in disputes over interpretation of the Constitution. But it was enough in Katzenbach 'to perceive a basis upon which the Congress might resolve the conflict as it did,' and plainly in the case before us there is an arguable basis for § 6(j) in the Free Exercise Clause."

very impacts questioned. And more broadly, of course, there is the Government's interest in procuring the manpower necessary for military purposes." [6]

5. *Denying veterans' benefits to conscientious objectors.* JOHNSON v. ROBISON, 415 U.S. 361 (1974), was a constitutional attack on the statutory scheme denying veterans' educational benefits to alternate service conscientious objectors while granting them to veterans of the armed forces. After disposing of an equal protection challenge (see chap. 9 above), Justice BRENNAN's majority opinion rejected the free exercise claim on the basis of an analysis closely tracking that of Gillette. He noted that members of the disadvantaged class were not required "to make any choice comparable to that required of the petitioners in Gillette. The withholding of educational benefits involves only an incidental burden upon appellee's free exercise of religion—if, indeed, any burden exists at all." [7] He found that "the Government's substantial interest in raising and supporting armies [is] of 'a kind and weight' clearly sufficient to sustain the challenged legislation." Justice DOUGLAS was once again the sole dissenter. He argued that the line of free exercise cases culminating in Sherbert and Yoder was applicable and insisted that government "may not place a penalty on anyone for asserting his religious scruples." He thought Gillette "irrelevant": the conscientious objector claim here was concededly valid; the classification was not neutral; and the burden on religious belief was not "incidental." He noted, moreover, that "the only governmental interest here is the financial one of [denying] educational benefits."

6. Justice Marshall added in a footnote: "We are not faced with the question whether the Free Exercise Clause itself would require exemption of any class other than objectors to particular wars. A free exercise claim on behalf of such objectors collides with the distinct governmental interests already discussed, and, at any rate, no other claim is presented. We note that the Court has previously suggested that relief for conscientious objectors is not mandated by the Constitution. See Hamilton v. Regents, 293 U.S. 245, 264 (1934)."

Justice DOUGLAS' dissent emphasized the "implied First Amendment right" of "conscience": "It is true that the First Amendment speaks of the free exercise of religion, not of the free exercise of conscience or belief. Yet conscience and belief are the main ingredients of First Amendment rights." And, he added, "[t]he constitutional infirmity in the present Act seems obvious once 'conscience' is the guide." He continued: "The law as written is a species of those which show an invidious discrimination in favor of religious persons and against others with like scruples."

7. Justice Brennan suggested in a footnote that "Congress' decision to grant educational benefits to military servicemen might arguably be viewed as an attempt to equalize the burdens of military service and alternate civilian service, rather than an effort by Congress to place a relative burden upon a conscientious objector's free exercise of religion."

Chapter 15

PROPER CONDITIONS FOR CONSTITUTIONAL ADJUDICATION: INTERESTED PARTIES; CONCRETE CONTROVERSIES; JUSTICIABLE ISSUES

AN INTRODUCTORY NOTE

This chapter returns to and elaborates themes introduced in chap. 1. That first chapter explored the legitimacy and framework of constitutional adjudication. This chapter examines some recurrent problems in the process of constitutional adjudication. What are the appropriate circumstances for constitutional adjudication? When may courts decide constitutional issues? At whose behest? At what stages of a dispute? As to what issues? The foundations of judicial authority in chap. 1 are essential but not adequate ingredients for an understanding of the institutional context of constitutional litigation. The "jurisdictional" and "procedural" materials which follow provide some amplifications.

The purpose of this chapter goes beyond the sharpening of professional skills in advancing constitutional claims for judicial consideration. The concern here is with court as well as with lawyer. What are the institutional limitations on constitutional adjudication? What are the justifications for those limits? These problems are not mere technicalities; they go to the heart of the Court's place in the governmental structure. This chapter seeks to provide a minimum of "federal jurisdiction" materials essential to an understanding of the role of the Court, which, according to Marbury v. Madison, only acts as an organ of constitutional elaboration because it is a *court,* a judicial body deciding cases. Who may go to court? When—at what stage in the evolution of a dispute? As to what constitutional issues? This chapter, then, explores the who, when and what of constitutional adjudication.[1]

The limits on adjudication: Sources and policies. Two related problems surface repeatedly with respect to each of the limits on constitutional adjudication considered in this chapter. *First, where does the limitation come from?* To what extent does each derive from the Constitution, especially Art. III? To what extent does it derive from congressional action with respect to jurisdiction and remedies? To what extent is the source simply the Court's own elaboration of rules and doctrines reflecting its view of the appropriate scope of judicial authority and the optimum conditions for its exercise? An effort to make sense of the cases dealing with these problems is worthwhile, if only because of the practical consequences. Thus, if a barrier to court access is derived from Art. III, Congress cannot readily remove it; but if a court's refusal to decide rests simply on a self-imposed limitation—a limit resting on judicial discretion rather than constitutional mandate—Congress can presumably remove the limitation and compel adjudication.

---

1. For a useful commentary on the "who" and "when," see Monaghan, "Constitutional Adjudication: The Who and When," 82 Yale L.J. 1363 (1973) (hereinafter cited as "The Who and When"). The themes of this chapter are more fully explored in federal jurisdiction courses. See generally Hart & Wechsler, Federal Courts (2d ed. 1973); Wright, Federal Courts (4th ed. 1983); Currie, Federal Courts (3d ed. 1982); and Tushnet & Fink, Federal Jurisdiction: Policy and Practice (1984).

Second, what are the policies that give rise to each of the limitations—and to what extent does each limitation truly serve to implement these policies? Consider especially the limits examined in the opening sections of this chapter, the limits going to the who and when of constitutional adjudication. The "who" question is especially raised by the cases on "standing" (sec. 2): How much of a personal stake must an individual have in the outcome of a controversy in order to obtain a court ruling? The "when" question is especially raised by the concept of "ripeness" (sec. 3): How far advanced must a dispute be, how fully developed must the issues be, to elicit a judicial resolution? To what extent do the answers to those questions turn on the Art. III limitation of the "judicial Power" to "Cases" and "Controversies"? What policy reasons support these limits? [2] To what extent are the limitations explainable by a desire to assure the best possible conditions for reasoned elaboration and thoughtful decision by courts—a desire "to assure that concrete adverseness which sharpens the presentation of issues upon which the court so largely depends for illumination of difficult questions," as the Court put it in Baker v. Carr (1962; p. 1617 below)? To what extent do the limitations reflect notions of judicial restraint and prudential judgments of institutional self-protection: notions of minimizing the occasions for and scope of judicial interventions; judgments designed to delay or avoid adjudications that are perceived as being unusually complex or controversial? To what extent do the limits reflect efforts to ration limited judicial resources? [3] To what extent do they reflect considerations of federalism: the interest in respecting state autonomy in its policymaking and judicial processes; the interest in avoiding federal-state friction? And to what extent do the various limitations flow from the justifications which underlie the legitimacy of judicial review?

The relevance of Marbury v. Madison. That last question invites reference back to Marbury v. Madison in chap. 1. In the materials in this chapter, the implications and ambiguities of the Marbury defense of constitutional adjudication play a central role. Recall the questions in chap. 1 about the nature of the judicial power Marshall defended in that case. A major thrust of Marshall's reasoning was that the power of constitutional adjudication was an incident of the Court's obligation to decide the particular "case" before it. That emphasis gives rise to a "private rights" model of constitutional adjudication: it looks to the kinds of "cases" ordinarily handled by courts, and it suggests that the kind of individual interest necessary to assure "standing" in a constitutional case is guided by the courts' ordinary rules as to private rights warranting judicial attention.

Yet there are some aspects of Marbury—including its emphasis on the importance of judicial enforcement of constitutional limitations—that view the Court as having a "special function" in interpreting constitutional norms. If constitutional adjudication is seen as the Court's primary function, and safeguarding constitutional values its special task, it is possible to argue that the "personal interests" that are a prerequisite to eliciting court decisions in private litigation are unduly confining limits for constitutional adjudication. In short, a broad view of Marbury reinforces arguments that courts can decide constitutional questions in proceedings which do not conform to the model of traditional private litigation and at the instance of litigants who have no special, personal

---

2. For a useful general discussion of the principles underlying the notions of ripeness, mootness and standing to sue, see Brilmayer, "The Jurisprudence of Article III: Perspectives on the 'Case or Controversy' Requirement," 93 Harv.L. Rev. 297 (1979). Brilmayer advances "three interrelated policies of Art. III: the smooth allocation of power among courts over time [the 'restraint' theme]; the unfairness of holding later litigants to an adverse judgment in which they

may not have been properly represented [the 'representation' theme]; and the importance of placing control over political processes in the hands of the people most closely involved [the 'self-determination' theme]."

3. See Scott, "Standing in the Supreme Court—A Functional Analysis," 86 Harv.L.Rev. 645 (1973).

stake in the outcome.[4]　That competition of views—between constitutional adjudication as an incidental byproduct and constitutional adjudication as a special function—may underlie a number of developments traced in the materials below.[5]

Rules, discretion, and the merits.　Most of the opinions below speak about a number of separate prerequisites to the exercise of the federal judicial function in constitutional cases: e.g., standing, ripeness, political questions.　But are these separately stated elements truly separable ones?　Or are these superficially separate requirements not truly separable at all, but rather merely illustrations of a single underlying institutional policy—e.g., the avoidance of constitutional questions unless absolutely necessary?　See especially secs. 1 and 4 below.　Is any such general policy compelled by the Constitution?　Is it a permissible position?　A principled one?　Or is it mainly a discretionary policy of institutional prudence, a policy of ad hoc judgments about the political propriety of judicial intervention—judgments resting, for example, on balancing the desirability of a decision against such institutional costs as hostile political reactions?[6] And to what extent are the concerns of this chapter really not institutional ones at all, but disguised judgments on the merits?[7]　The cases claim to worry about what courts are good for, and when.　But are they, at least occasionally, really concerned with how valuable the substantive claim is, and to whom?　To what extent do (and to what degree should) decisions about the availability of a judicial forum turn on the merits of the constitutional claim?

Scope Note.　Before turning to the major limits on constitutional adjudication, this chapter briefly considers, in sec. 1, the best-established outer boundary of judicial authority: the ban against "advisory opinions."　That section also explores some related themes, including overarching policy arguments that seek to tie the advisory opinion ban to other limits on constitutional adjudication. The remaining sections consider more specific ingredients of the limitations. Sec. 2 focuses on the requisite litigant interest—the ingredients of "standing" to sue.　Sec. 3 turns to problems of ripeness.　Sec. 4 considers additional, Court-developed restraints: the claim that the Court has discretion to refuse adjudication of cases, even cases within its remaining obligatory "appeal" jurisdiction; and restraints in the interest of federalism, reflected in doctrines about federal court abstention and about noninterference with controversies in the state courts.[8]　Sec. 5, finally turns to the most open-ended ingredients of the "political question" doctrine.[9]

4.　For a discussion of the "private rights" and "special function" models, see Monaghan, "The Who and When," 82 Yale L.J. 1363 (1973).

5.　Cf. Chayes, "The Role of the Judge in Public Law Litigation," 89 Harv.L.Rev. 1281 (1976).

6.　For disagreement on the question of whether these and related requirements must be as principled in their content as substantive constitutional doctrines themselves, or whether they are properly exercises of prudential judgment rather than delineations of principle, compare Bickel, The Least Dangerous Branch (1962), with Gunther, "The Subtle Vices of the 'Passive Virtues'—A Comment on Principle and Expediency in Judicial Review," 64 Colum.L.Rev. 1

(1964).　That dispute is more fully developed below, especially in sec. 4A, at p. 1590 below.

7.　See Berch, "Unchain the Courts: An Essay on the Role of the Federal Courts in the Vindication of Social Rights," 1976 Ariz.St.L.J. 437; cf. Tushnet, "The New Law of Standing: A Plea for Abandonment," 62 Cornell L.Rev. 663 (1977).

8.　Recall also the federalism-related limits on Court review reflected in the "adequate state grounds" barrier, considered in chap. 1 above.

9.　Sec. 5 also includes the Court's development of constitutional principles governing legislative reapportionment—issues that were, until the early 1960s, considered to be nonjusticiable "political questions."

SECTION 1. SOME PERVASIVE THEMES: ADVISORY OPINIONS, ART. III BARRIERS, AND DISCRETIONARY INSTITUTIONAL CONSIDERATIONS

1. *Advisory opinions: The 1793 refusal.*   In 1793, President Washington sought the advice of the Justices of the Court on some perplexing legal questions then confronting him.   The Justices declined to help.   Their refusal illustrates the most prominent, most continuously articulated boundary of justiciability: federal courts will not give "advisory opinions."   What justifies that limitation?   What are the objections to advisory opinions?   What distinguishes forbidden "advice" from permissible adjudication?

Washington's request to the Justices was understandable.   He genuinely needed legal assistance in dealing with a major national concern, America's neutrality toward the ongoing war between England and France.   Accordingly, on July 18, 1793, Secretary of State Jefferson, on behalf of the President, wrote to Chief Justice Jay and the Associate Justices as follows: "The war which has taken place among the powers of Europe produces frequent transactions within our ports and limits, on which questions arise of considerable difficulty, and of greater importance to the peace of the United States.   These questions depend for their solution on the construction of our treaties, on the laws of nature and nations, and on the laws of the land, and are often presented under circumstances *which do not give a cognizance of them to the tribunals of the country.*   Yet their decision is so little analogous to the ordinary functions of the executive, as to occasion much embarrassment and difficulty to them.   The President therefore would be much relieved if he found himself free to refer questions of this description to the opinions of the judges of the [Court], whose knowledge of the subject would secure us against errors dangerous to the peace of the United States, and their authority insure the respect of all parties.   He has therefore asked the attendance of such of the judges as could be collected in time for the occasion, to know, in the first place, their opinion, whether the public may, with propriety, be availed of their *advice on these questions?*   And if they may, to present, for their advice, the abstract questions which have already occurred, or may soon occur, from which they will themselves strike out such as any circumstances might, in their opinion, forbid them to pronounce on." [1]

A few weeks later, on August 8, 1793, the Justices replied to President Washington: "We have considered the previous question stated in [the letter above.   The] three departments of the government [being] in certain respects checks upon each other, and our being judges of a court in the last resort, are considerations which afford strong arguments against the propriety of our extrajudicially deciding the questions alluded to, especially as the power given by the Constitution to the President, of calling on the heads of departments for opinions, seems to have been *purposely* as well as expressly united to the *executive* departments. [See Art. II, § 2.]   We exceedingly regret every event that may cause embarrassment to your administration, but we derive consolation from the reflection that your judgment will discern what is right, and that your usual

---

1.   The Jefferson letter, some of the questions accompanying it, and the Justices' response are printed in Hart & Wechsler, Federal Courts (2d ed. 1973), 64–66.

Illustrative of the questions submitted to the Justices are: "Do the treaties between the United States and France give to France or her citizens a *right,* when at war with a power with whom the

United States are at peace, to fit out originally in and from the ports of the United States vessels armed for war, with or without commission?"   "If they give such a *right,* does it extend to all manner of armed vessels, or to particular kinds only?" and "May we, within our own ports, sell ships to both parties, prepared merely for merchandise?   May they be pierced for guns?"

prudence, decision, and firmness will surmount every obstacle to the preservation of the rights, peace, and dignity of the United States."

Most of President Washington's questions seemed "legal"; the need for answers was real; nevertheless, Chief Justice Jay and his colleagues refused. They relied in large part on separation of powers principles. Ever since, it has been accepted that federal courts cannot give advisory opinions. The desirability of early, authoritative resolution of constitutional doubts is often evident. For example, before the Court-packing crisis in 1937, President Roosevelt briefly considered a plan "for Congress to pass an act taking away from all lower courts the right to pass upon the constitutionality of statutes. This right would be given to the [Court] as a matter of original jurisdiction. The Court would be required to give advisory opinions. It would be expected to say in advance of the passing of a law whether it was unconstitutional." [2] Yet that plan was soon abandoned, partly because of its obvious unconstitutionality. (Note, however, that several state constitutions authorize state courts to issue advisory opinions at the request of the legislature or chief executive.) [3] What, then, are the reasons which make advisory opinions by federal courts impermissible?

2. *The arguments against advisory opinions.* a. *Constitutional text and Framers' intent.* Are advisory opinions clearly barred by the Art. III limitation of judicial power to "cases" and "controversies"? [4] Does a case inevitably require adverse parties, so that the Court may be informed by opposing arguments? Could "the difficulty of lack of adversary parties have been met [in 1793] if the Court gave notice to England and France to brief and argue the issues raised?" [5] Could the Justices in 1793 have found other ways to assure the presentation of all relevant facts in sufficiently concrete form? [6] Can more persuasive arguments against advisory opinions be derived from the Framers' intent? Recall the rejection of Madison's proposals that Justices sit on a Council of Revision, chap. 1 above. The proposed Council was rejected in part because of opposition to having Justices pass on "the policy of public measures." Does that provide compelling reasons against advisory opinions on questions of "law"? [7]

b. *Separation of powers and judicial finality.* Note that the Justices in 1793 referred to their "being judges of a court in the last resort." The view that it was essential to judicial decisions that they be final rather than tentative, and not subject to revision by the executive and legislative branches, had been voiced by the Justices a year before President Washington's request. In HAYBURN'S CASE, 2 Dall. 409 (1792), most of the Justices, sitting on circuit, had refused to certify eligible pension claimants to the Secretary of War because the statute authorizing such proceedings improperly assigned duties "not of a judicial

---

2. See The Secret Diary of Harold L. Ickes [Secretary of the Interior under Roosevelt]—The First Thousand Days, 1933–1936 (1953), 529.

3. See generally Field, "The Advisory Opinion—An Analysis," 24 Ind.L.J. 203 (1949); Note, "Advisory Opinions on the Constitutionality of Statutes," 69 Harv.L.Rev. 1302 (1956); and a classic article by Felix Frankfurter, "Advisory Opinion," in 1 Encyclopedia of the Social Sciences 475 (1930).

4. As the Court has several times explained, "the term 'controversies,' if distinguishable at all from 'cases,' is so in that it is less comprehensive than the latter, and includes only suits of a civil nature." See, e.g., Muskrat v. United States, 219 U.S. 346 (1911), which also states: "By cases and controversies are intended the claims of litigants brought before the courts for determination by such regular proceedings as are established by law or custom for the protection or enforcement

of rights, or the prevention, redress, or punishment of wrongs." (See also the discussion of mootness, p. 1578 below.)

5. Monaghan, "The Who and When," 82 Yale L.J. 1363, 1373 (1973).

6. Note that the Court has held that uncontested naturalization proceedings are cases or controversies within the judicial power—though the Court noted that the United States "is always a possible adverse party." Tutun v. United States, 270 U.S. 568 (1926). See Note, "Judicial Determinations in Nonadversary Proceedings," 72 Harv.L.Rev. 723 (1959).

7. Note, moreover, that a proposal to permit Congress or the President to obtain advisory opinions on "important questions of law" was before the Constitutional Convention and was not adopted.

nature" to the courts. Among the reasons given for the refusal to undertake the function assigned by statute to the judges was the fact that the judicial actions might be "revised and controuled by the legislature, and by an officer in the executive department. Such revision and controul we deemed radically inconsistent with the independence of that judicial power which is vested in the courts." [8]

    c. *Institutional considerations.* Does the refusal to give advisory opinions ultimately rest on institutional considerations? Because courts are less competent to give advice than to decide cases? Because courts would be too busy if they gave advice? Because courts would be more vulnerable to political attacks if they gave advice? To what extent does the avoidance of advisory opinions reflect a concern with assuring conditions that will maximize the prospects for informed and accurate decisionmaking by the courts? Do courts need a concrete factual context to develop law with adequate focus and understanding? Do courts need adversary presentations to assure adequately reasoned development of law? [9] To what extent do those needs vary with the substantive issues presented? Recall, e.g., the debate about "absolutes" and "balancing" in First Amendment adjudication, chap. 11 above. Would lack of a concrete record and lack of adversary argument present as much difficulty for a Justice reading the First Amendment "literally" and absolutely as for a Justice viewing the scope of freedom of expression as dependent upon circumstances and competing interests? (Note also the discussion of the Adler case, sec. 3 below.) Finally, is the ban on advisory opinions necessary to conserve the Court's strength? Would advisory opinions thrust courts into conflicts too early and too often? Is the ban on advisory opinions desirable because of the "value of having courts function as organs of the sober second thought of the community appraising action already taken, rather than as advisers at the front line of governmental action at the stage of initial decision"? Hart & Wechsler, Federal Courts (2d ed. 1973), 67.

    These questions about the justifications that may underlie the advisory opinions ban are not raised because the traditional barrier to advisory opinions is now vulnerable or likely to disappear. Rather, the questions are raised because the policies served by the ban on advisory opinions resemble some of the grounds for the "standing" and "ripeness" limits on constitutional adjudication, considered below. To a considerable degree, views as to the weight of these concerns will govern one's position as to the justifiability of barring access to courts through broadly read standing and ripeness limitations. In short, the

---

8. Note the modern reiteration of that principle in C. & S. Air Lines v. Waterman Corp., 333 U.S. 103 (1948), holding that courts could not pass on CAB awards of international air routes because such decisions were ultimately subject to modification by the President. The Court stated: "Judgments within the powers vested in courts by [Art. III] may not lawfully be revised, overturned or refused faith and credit by another Department of Government. To revise or review an administrative decision which has only the force of a recommendation to the President would be to render an advisory opinion in its most obnoxious form. [It] has been the firm and unvarying practice of Constitutional Courts to render no judgments not binding and conclusive on the parties and none that are subject to later review or alteration by administrative action." Are those arguments persuasive? Were all of the decisions examined in the preceding chapters truly immune from subsequent modification by the political branches?

9. Note the reflection of these institutional concerns in a passage in Flast v. Cohen (1968; p. 1544 below): "[T]he implicit policies embodied in Article III, and not history alone, impose the rule against advisory opinions. [The rule] implements the separation of powers [and] also recognizes that such suits often 'are not pressed before the Court with that clear concreteness provided when a question emerges precisely framed and necessary for decision from a clash of adversary argument exploring every aspect of a multifaceted situation embracing conflicting and demanding interests.' United States v. Fruehauf, 365 U.S. 146, 157 (1961). Consequently, the Article III prohibition against advisory opinions reflects the complementary constitutional considerations expressed by the justiciability doctrine: Federal judicial power is limited to those disputes which confine federal courts to a role consistent with a system of separated powers and which are traditionally thought to be capable of resolution through the judicial process."

varying doctrines about the "who" and "when" of constitutional adjudication are interrelated not only in some of their governing criteria but also in the institutional concerns underlying them. For example, the courts' concerns about optimum conditions for doing their job well and about protecting themselves from political controversy are pervasive; and to some degree, all of the strands of doctrine considered in the several sections of this chapter can be seen as manifestations of those concerns. (See also note 4 below.)

3. *Declaratory judgments.* Declaratory judgment actions are commonplace in modern litigation. Yet half a century ago, development of the declaratory judgment device was inhibited by fears that it might run afoul of the advisory opinions ban. Declaratory judgments were not among the characteristic remedies of courts at the time Art. III was drafted, and defining an Art. III "case" in terms of traditional common law practice might, it was feared, block acceptance of the new remedy.

a. That fear was reinforced by dicta in WILLING v. CHICAGO AUDITO-RIUM ASS'N, 277 U.S. 274 (1928). The facts in Willing were as follows: The Association held a long-term lease on land and had constructed an auditorium on it. It desired to tear down the building and erect a new one, but the lease did not explicitly authorize such action. During "an informal, friendly, private conversation" between Willing, one of the lessors, and an officer of the Association, Willing said that he did not think that the old building could be torn down without the consent of the lessors and the bondholders. The Association "never approached" most of the other lessors or the bondholders. A year after, it brought federal action against all the lessors and the trustee for the bondholders to establish its right to tear down the old building. Justice BRANDEIS' opinion for the Court concluded that "the proceeding does not present a case or controversy." He noted that there was "neither hostile act nor a threat. [What] the plaintiff seeks is simply a declaratory judgment. To grant that relief is beyond the power of the federal judiciary. [The] fact that the plaintiff's desires are thwarted by its own doubts, or by the fears of others, does not confer a cause of action. No defendant has wronged the plaintiff or has threatened to do so." Why was this not an Art. III controversy? Because the plans of the parties had not sufficiently jelled? Because there were too many contingencies on both sides—uncertainty as to precisely what the plaintiff would do, uncertainty as to what precisely the defendants would do? Apparently, this controversy lacked such concreteness, was so contingent, was so "unripe" as to lack the minimum ingredients of adverseness for an Art. III case. But was not Justice Brandeis' language too broad in asserting that granting declaratory relief was "beyond the power conferred upon the federal judiciary"? [10] Was that statement itself something of an advisory opinion?

b. Soon after Willing, however, the doubts about the permissibility of declaratory judgments evaporated. In NASHVILLE, C. & ST. L. RY. v. WALLACE, 288 U.S. 249 (1933), the Court reviewed a state court declaratory judgment after hearing argument on the question "whether a case or controversy is presented." The case involved a company threatened with an allegedly unconstitutional tax and seeking a declaratory judgment that the tax constituted an unconstitutional burden on interstate commerce. The Court emphasized that the controversy was clearly concrete enough to be adjudicable in a traditional injunction action. It noted, moreover, that the state courts authorized declaratory judgments only "when the complainant asserts rights which are challenged by

---

10. Contrast the "ripeness" cases in sec. 3, at p. 1580 below. In all of those cases, unlike Willing, the controversy was arguably concrete enough to meet minimum Art. III requirements; the Court refusals to adjudicate there arguably rested on discretionary "ripeness" considerations governing federal court remedies rather than on constitutional compulsion.

the defendant, and presents for decision an actual controversy to which he is a party, capable of final adjudication by the judgment [to] be rendered." In those circumstances, Justice STONE's opinion found no Art. III barrier to adjudication. Satisfying Art. III required concern "not with form, but with substance." Since the controversy would have been justiciable in the form of an injunction proceeding, it was no "less so because through a modified procedure appellant has been permitted to present it in the state courts, without praying for an injunction." He explained: "[T]he Constitution does not require that the case or controversy should be presented by traditional forms of procedure, invoking only traditional remedies. [Art. III] did not crystallize into changeless form the procedure of 1789 as the only possible means for presenting a case or controversy. [C]hanges merely in the form or method of procedure by which federal rights are brought to final adjudication in the state courts are not enough to preclude [Court review], so long as the case retains the essentials of an adversary proceeding, involving a real, not hypothetical, controversy, which is finally determined by the judgment below." [11]

4. *The relation of the advisory opinions ban to other limitations on constitutional adjudication: Policies of judicial restraint.* [A majority opinion by Justice Rutledge in RESCUE ARMY v. MUNICIPAL COURT OF LOS ANGELES, 331 U.S. 549 (1947), articulated some of the policy relationships between the advisory opinion ban and various other limitations on access to courts for constitutional adjudication. He emphasized the overarching theme of "strict necessity": the Court will not adjudicate constitutional issues unless such rulings are unavoidable. Though the application of these policies of restraint and avoidance in the Rescue Army case itself is questionable (see p. 1592 below), Justice RUTLEDGE's general survey of purposes and policies warrants attention here:]

From Hayburn's Case, [this] Court has followed a policy of strict necessity in disposing of constitutional issues. The earliest exemplifications [arose] in the Court's refusal to render advisory opinions. [The] policy [has] not been limited to jurisdictional determinations. For, in addition, "the Court [has] developed, for its own governance in the cases confessedly within its jurisdiction, a series of rules under which it has avoided passing upon a large part of all the constitutional questions pressed upon it for decision." [12] Thus, as those rules were listed in support of the statement quoted, constitutional issues affecting legislation will not be determined in friendly, nonadversary proceedings; in advance of the necessity of deciding them; in broader terms than are required by the precise facts to which the ruling is to be applied; if the record presents some

---

11. The decision in the Nashville case paved the way for the enactment of the federal Declaratory Judgment Act of 1934. That law authorizes federal declaratory judgments "[i]n a case of actual controversy" within federal jurisdiction. The Supreme Court sustained the constitutionality of the Act in Aetna Life Ins. Co. v. Haworth, 300 U.S. 227 (1937). In emphasizing that declaratory judgments were available only "to determine controversies which are such in the constitutional sense," Chief Justice Hughes explained in Aetna: "A justiciable controversy [is] distinguished from a difference or dispute of a hypothetical or abstract character; from one that is academic or moot. The controversy must be definite and concrete, touching the legal relations of parties having adverse legal interests. It must be a real and substantial controversy admitting of specific relief through a decree of a conclusive character, as distinguished from an opinion advising what the law would be upon a hypothetical state of facts. Where there is such a concrete case admitting of an immediate and definitive determination of the legal rights of the parties in an adversary proceeding upon the facts alleged, the judicial function may be appropriately exercised although the adjudication of the rights of the litigants may not require the award of process or the payment of damages."

12. The quotation is from a famous concurring opinion by Justice Brandeis in Ashwander v. Tennessee Valley Auth., (1936; p. 1591 below). For a further examination of the Brandeis rules in Ashwander—and for a criticism of the "neo-Brandeisian fallacy" of viewing those rules as legitimating discretionary dismissals of cases within the Court's obligatory appeal jurisdiction (a "fallacy" reflected in the disposition of the Rescue Army case itself)—see the materials on discretionary abstention in sec. 4A below.

other ground upon which the case may be disposed of; at the instance of one who fails to show that he is injured by the statute's operation, or who has availed himself of its benefits; or if a construction of the statute is fairly possible by which the question may be avoided.

Some, if not indeed all, of these rules have found "most varied applications." And every application has been an instance of reluctance, indeed, of refusal, to undertake the most important and the most delicate of the Court's functions, notwithstanding conceded jurisdiction, until necessity compels it in the performance of constitutional duty. Moreover the policy is neither merely procedural nor in its essence dependent for applicability upon the diversities of jurisdiction and procedure, whether of the state courts, the inferior federal courts, or this Court. Rather it is one of substance [13] grounded in considerations which transcend all such particular limitations. Like the case and controversy limitation itself and the policy against entertaining political questions, it is one of the rules basic to the federal system and this Court's appropriate place within that structure. Indeed in origin and in practical effects, though not in technical function, it is a corollary offshoot of the case and controversy rule. And often the line between applying the policy or the rule is very thin.[14]

[The] policy's ultimate foundations, some if not all of which also sustain the jurisdictional limitation, lie in all that goes to make up the unique place and character, in our scheme, of judicial review of governmental action for constitutionality. They are found in the delicacy of that function, particularly in view of possible consequences for others stemming also from constitutional roots; the comparative finality of those consequences; the consideration due to the judgment of other repositories of constitutional power concerning the scope of their authority; the necessity, if government is to function constitutionally, for each to keep within its power, including the courts; the inherent limitations of the judicial process, arising especially from its largely negative character and limited resources of enforcement; withal in the paramount importance of constitutional adjudication in our system.

[The execution of this policy] has involved a continuous choice between the obvious advantages it produces [and] the very real disadvantages, for the assurance of rights, which deferring decision very often entails. On the other hand it is not altogether speculative that a contrary policy, of accelerated decision, might do equal or greater harm for the security of private rights, without attaining any of the benefits of tolerance and harmony for the functioning of the various authorities in our scheme. For premature and relatively abstract decisions, which such a policy would be most likely to promote, have their part too in rendering rights uncertain and insecure. As with the case and controversy limitation, however, the choice has been made long since. Time and experience have given it sanction. They also have verified for both that the choice was wisely made. Any other indeed might have put an end to or seriously impaired the distinctively American institution of judicial review. And on the whole, in spite of inevitable exceptions, the policy has worked not only

---

13. "If there is one doctrine more deeply rooted than any other in the process of constitutional adjudication, it is that we ought not to pass on questions of constitutionality [unless] such adjudication is unavoidable." "It is not the habit of the Court to decide questions of a constitutional nature unless absolutely necessary to a decision of the case." [Footnote by Justice Rutledge.]

14. Indeed more than once the policy has been applied in order to avoid the necessity of deciding the "case or controversy" jurisdictional question, when constitutional issues were at stake on the merits, e.g., recently in declaratory judgment proceedings. [See] United Public Workers v. Mitchell [1947; p. 1581 below]. [Footnote by Justice Rutledge.]

for finding the appropriate place and function of the judicial institution in our governmental system, but also for the preservation of individual rights.[15]

SECTION 2.　STANDING TO LITIGATE:
THE REQUISITE PERSONAL INTEREST

Some introductory comments and questions. a. *The ingredients.* What is standing? How does it differ from ripeness (sec. 3) and other ingredients of justiciability considered in this chapter? Consider the suggestion that "clarity would be gained by viewing standing as involving problems of the nature and sufficiency of the litigant's concern with the subject matter of the litigation, as distinguished from problems of the justiciability—that is, the fitness for adjudication—of the legal questions which he tenders for decision. More precisely stated, the question of standing in this sense is the question whether the litigant has a sufficient personal interest in getting the relief he seeks, or is a sufficiently appropriate representative of other interested persons, to warrant giving him the relief, if he establishes the illegality alleged—and, by the same token, to warrant recognizing him as entitled to invoke the court's decision on the issue of illegality."[1]

What are the criteria for determining whether a litigant may obtain adjudication of an issue? In most cases, the question of the plaintiff's access to court presents no great difficulty: clearly, a plaintiff claiming physical injury in a tort action or economic damage in a contracts action has standing to sue. But in constitutional litigation such traditional bases for access to court are often lacking. For example, what of the plaintiff who claims that a law regulating protest demonstrations "chills" his or her First Amendment rights? What of the taxpayer who claims an unconstitutional expenditure of public funds? What of the citizen who is outraged by public officials' conduct allegedly violating separation of powers principles? Can and should there be access to court for plaintiffs claiming speculative or attenuated injuries? Is any injury in fact sufficient? Is injury in fact necessary? Must the plaintiff show some special injury singling the litigant out from the mass of citizens generally? Or should "public actions" also be permissible?[2]

---

15. Justice Rutledge's overview is printed here because of the light it throws on some of the reasons prompting the doctrines considered in the opening sections of this chapter. Some of the avoidance techniques he cites warrant further examination as to their scope and legitimacy. That examination is postponed, especially to sec. 4 below, on discretionary abstention.

1. Hart & Wechsler, Federal Courts (2d ed. 1973), 156. Note also the statement in the 1969 ruling in Flast v. Cohen, p. 1544 below: "The fundamental aspect of standing is that it focuses on the party [and] not on the issues he wishes to have adjudicated. [The question] is whether the person whose standing is challenged is a proper party to request an adjudication of a particular issue and not whether the issue itself is justiciable."

2. The central concerns of this section are these problems of plaintiffs' standing: the extent to which a plaintiff must show some traditional or special injury to achieve access to court. The rather different problem of defendants' standing is considered only briefly, at p. 1576 below. That problem is not one of *access* to court: the defendant has been brought into court by someone else—a private plaintiff or the government. Defendants' standing problems involve instead the question of what *issues* the defendant may raise. Is the defendant limited to issues that immediately affect him or her? Or, once the defendant is in court, may he or she assert the rights of others who may be subject to the statute under which the defendant is charged? Must the defendant be in some special relationship to the nonlitigant third party whose rights he or she seeks to assert? Aspects of that problem have occasionally surfaced earlier—recall, e.g., the consideration of the overbreadth doctrine in chap. 12, sec. 1, above.

Note, too, that this section emphasizes problems of plaintiffs' access to *federal* courts. State

b. *Who decides?* To what extent is standing an aspect of Art. III? To what extent is it a discretionary judgment regarding federal court remedies? To the extent the ingredients of standing are not dictated by Art. III, institutions other than the Court (e.g., Congress and the states) may claim a major voice in shaping standing. The cases in this section at times disclose a recognition of congressional authority to grant standing to plaintiffs to whom federal courts would not grant access in the absence of the congressionally created remedy.[3] (But see the Valley Forge College decision in 1982, at p. 1551 below.)

c. *How decided?* How does the Court determine whether a litigant has a sufficiently distinctive personal interest to warrant rendering the constitutional adjudication sought? As already noted under (a) above, that is the central question of this section. Is the existence of injury in fact enough? Or must there be an invasion of "legal rights"? What is a "legal" injury? Does standing depend in part on the nature of the substantive claim raised? Can courts dispense with the traditional requirement of a distinctive individualized injury so long as a person genuinely wishes to litigate a claim in a concrete factual setting—e.g., are "public actions" by "mere" citizens permissible? Consider the Court's own description of the purpose of standing rules in assuring the best conditions for informed adjudication: The "gist of the question of standing," the Court said in Baker v. Carr (1962; p. 1617 below), is whether the litigant alleges "such a personal stake in the outcome of the controversy as to assure that concrete adverseness which sharpens the presentation of issues upon which the court so largely depends for illumination of difficult constitutional questions." Is injury in fact truly necessary to "assure that concrete adverseness," to encourage the best possible "presentation of issues"? May not a concerned citizen's readiness to go to court provide adequate assurance of optimizing the conditions for informed adjudication? The "mere" citizen may not in fact present the arguments as well as possible. But is there truly greater assurance of optimum argument by insisting on a traditional "injured" plaintiff with a personalized injury—even though the "injury" may consist of no more than a small financial loss? Would opening of the doors to "citizens" or "private attorneys general" actions raise too many of the dangers of advisory opinions? To what extent should a decision on standing turn on the needs of the parties and the society at large, and to what extent on institutional values pertaining to the courts?

Questions such as these run through all of the materials that follow. During the 1960s, the Warren Court was quite lenient in recognizing standing. Increasingly, lower federal courts viewed that lenient approach as authorizing standing to raise constitutional issues by such nontraditional plaintiffs as taxpayers and citizens. Indeed, in Richardson (1974; p. 1547), the trial court had concluded that the concept of standing "has now been almost completely

courts have considerable autonomy to delineate their own standing rules. Those rules bear on federal litigation when Court review is sought in the case of a plaintiff who has obtained an adjudication in the state courts but who might not have been able to claim direct access to a lower federal court. The bearing of state standing rules on Court review is considered briefly at p. 1576 below.

3. This problem is pursued further in the materials on congressional control over standing, at p. 1573 below. It has long been recognized that granting remedies for the violation of federal rights is largely within the keeping of Congress (as illustrated by the materials on § 5 of the 14th Amendment, in chap. 10 above). The most common Art. III problem has been the extent to

which Congress can grant court access to new varieties of plaintiffs who do not show traditional injuries. But recent Court developments have brought to the fore a quite different aspect of Court-Congress relations in the delineation of remedies: What if Congress fails to grant explicit remedies for violations of constitutional rights? What if it fails to establish clear private remedies for the enforcement of new statutory rights? In some modern cases, the Court has gone quite far on its own to imply remedies directly from the Constitution, without specific congressional support. Moreover, it has repeatedly found private rights of action under statutes that have not clearly established private rights of action, as noted further below.

abandoned" by the Court. But, by finding the standing requirement unsatisfied in that case, the Burger Court signified that it was unwilling to abandon standing barriers entirely. Subsequent decisions confirmed that trend, as Warth v. Seldin (1975; p. 1559 below) and Valley Forge College (1982; p. 1551 below) illustrate. What explains the modern trend? Do the opinions adequately clarify the rules? Do they adequately articulate the underlying policies?[4] Are the modern resolutions of standing questions sound?

A. STANDING IN "PUBLIC ACTIONS": SUITS BY FEDERAL TAXPAYERS AND CITIZENS

---

1. FROTHINGHAM v. MELLON, 262 U.S. 447 (1923): Mrs. Frothingham brought suit as a federal taxpayer to enjoin the Secretary of the Treasury from making expenditures under the Maternity Act of 1921, which provided for conditional grants to state programs "to reduce maternal and infant mortality." She argued that the Act was "a usurpation of power not granted to [Congress]—an attempted exercise of the power of local self-government reserved to the States by the Tenth Amendment." She alleged that spending under the Act would increase her tax liability and that she would thereby be deprived of property without due process of law. A unanimous Court held that the suit "must be disposed of for want of jurisdiction" because the plaintiff "has no such interest in the subject-matter, nor is any such injury inflicted or threatened, as will enable her to sue." Was the decision based on Art. III? Or did the Court rely on its authority to fashion federal equitable remedies? Did the grounds of the decision preclude Congress from granting federal taxpayers standing to sue? Subsequent opinions and commentary divided on the question of whether the Frothingham decision rested on constitutional barriers. Consider Justice SUTHERLAND's reasoning in Frothingham:

"The interest of a taxpayer of a municipality in the application of its moneys is direct and immediate and the remedy by injunction to prevent their misuse is not inappropriate. [The] reasons which support the extension of the equitable remedy to a single taxpayer in such cases are based upon the peculiar relation of the corporate taxpayer to the corporation, which is not without some resemblance to that subsisting between stockholder and private corporation. But the relation of a taxpayer of the United States to the Federal Government is very different. His interest in the moneys of the Treasury [is] shared with millions of others; is comparatively minute and indeterminable; and the effect upon future taxation, of any payment out of the funds, so remote, fluctuating and uncertain, that no basis is afforded for an appeal to the preventive powers of a court of equity. [The] administration of any statute, likely to produce additional taxation to be imposed upon a vast number of taxpayers, the extent of whose several liability is indefinite and constantly changing, is essentially a matter of public and not of individual concern. If one taxpayer may champion and litigate such a cause, then every other taxpayer may do the same, not only in respect of the statute here under review but also in respect of every other appropriation act and statute whose administration requires the outlay of public money, and whose validity may be questioned. The bare suggestion of such a

---

4. Note the comment in Brown, "Quis Custodiet Ipsos Custodes?—The School-Prayer Cases," 1963 Sup.Ct.Rev. 1: "The fact, if it is a fact, that standards for standing may not be absolute does not mean that they do not exist. One can make some judgments, if only by history and analogy, of the occasions on which, and the facility with which, judicial power should be brought into action. One will, of course, be influenced if not guided by the extent to which one thinks of judges as specially appointed (or anointed) wardens and nurturers of our higher values and principles."

result, with its attendant inconveniences, goes far to sustain the conclusion which we have reached, that a suit of this character cannot be [maintained].

"The functions of government under our system are apportioned. [We] have no power per se to review and annul acts of Congress on the ground that they are unconstitutional. That question may be considered only when the justification for some direct injury suffered or threatened, presenting a justiciable issue, is made to rest upon such an act. The party who invokes [our "negative power to disregard an unconstitutional enactment"] must be able to show not only that the statute is invalid but that he has sustained or is immediately in danger of sustaining some direct injury as the result of its enforcement, and not merely that he suffers in some indefinite way in common with people generally. If a case for preventive relief be presented the court enjoins, in effect, not the execution of the statute, but the acts of the official, the statute notwithstanding. Here [the plaintiff has] no such case. Looking through forms of words to the substance of [the] complaint, it is merely that officials of the executive department of the government are executing and will execute an act of Congress asserted to be unconstitutional; and this we are asked to prevent. To do so would be not to decide a judicial controversy, but to assume a position of authority over the governmental acts of another and co-equal department, an authority which plainly we do not possess." [1]

2. FLAST v. COHEN, 392 U.S. 83 (1968): Federal taxpayers challenged aid to religious schools under the Elementary and Secondary Education Act of 1965. The lower court dismissed their complaint because of Frothingham. Chief Justice WARREN's majority opinion reversed, concluding that "the Frothingham barrier should be lowered when a taxpayer attacks a federal statute on the ground that it violates the Establishment and Free Exercise Clauses of the First Amendment." In reexamining the Frothingham limit on standing,[2] the Chief Justice stated: "Embodied in the words 'cases' and 'controversies' are two complementary but somewhat different limitations. In part those words limit the business of federal courts to questions presented in an adversary context and in a form historically viewed as capable of resolution through the judicial process. And in part those words define the role assigned to the judiciary in a tripartite allocation of power to assure that the federal courts will not intrude into areas committed to the other branches of government. Justiciability is the term of art employed to give expression to this dual limitation placed upon federal courts by the case-and-controversy doctrine. [T]he Government's posi-

---

1. On the recognition of taxpayers' standing in state courts and its impact on Court review authority, see Doremus (1952; p. 1576 below).

In a case decided in the same opinion as Mrs. Frothingham's, the State of Massachusetts proved no more successful in eliciting a constitutional ruling on the Maternity Act. Massachusetts v. Mellon, 262 U.S. 447 (1923). The Court held that the State "presents no justiciable controversy either in its own behalf or as the representative of its citizens." The complaint of invasion of states' rights was "political and not judicial in character." Nor could the State sue as representative of its citizens: "[The] citizens of Massachusetts are also citizens of the United States. It cannot be conceded that a State, as parens patriae, may institute judicial proceedings to protect citizens of the United States from the operation of the statutes thereof." For an extensive modern discussion of parens patriae standing, see Alfred L. Snapp & Son, Inc. v. Puerto Rico, 458 U.S. 592 (1982), holding that Puerto

Rico had a sufficient quasi-sovereign interest to sue Virginia apple growers on a claim that the Virginians had discriminated against Puerto Ricans in favor of foreign laborers. For cases where state interests *were* found sufficient for standing to challenge the constitutionality of federal laws, recall Missouri v. Holland (1920; chap. 4 above) (protection of migratory birds) and South Carolina v. Katzenbach (1966; chap. 10 above) (Voting Rights Act of 1965).

2. The Chief Justice noted that there had been "some confusion" as to "whether Frothingham establishes a constitutional bar to taxpayer suits or whether the Court was simply imposing a rule of self-restraint which was not constitutionally compelled." He commented that the Frothingham opinion "can be read to support either position," and that the "prevailing view of the commentators is that Frothingham announced only a nonconstitutional rule of self-restraint."

tion is that the constitutional scheme of separation of powers [presents] an absolute bar to taxpayer suits challenging the validity of federal spending programs. [An] analysis of the function served by standing limitations compels a rejection of the Government's [position].

"[W]hen standing is placed in issue in a case, the question is whether the person whose standing is challenged is a proper party to request an adjudication of a particular issue and not whether the issue itself is justiciable. [When] the emphasis in the standing problem is placed on whether the person invoking a federal court's jurisdiction is a proper party to maintain the action, the weakness of the Government's argument in this case becomes apparent. The question whether a particular person is a proper party to maintain the action does not, by its own force, raise separation of powers problems related to improper judicial interference in areas committed to other branches of the Federal Government. Such problems arise, if at all, only from the substantive issues the individual seeks to have adjudicated. Thus, in terms of [Art. III limits], the question of standing is related only to whether the dispute sought to be adjudicated will be presented in an adversary context and in a form historically viewed as capable of judicial resolution. It is for that reason that the emphasis in standing problems is on whether the party invoking federal court jurisdiction 'has a personal stake in the outcome of the controversy,' and whether the dispute touches upon 'the legal relations of parties having adverse legal interests.' A taxpayer may or may not have the requisite personal stake in the outcome, depending upon the circumstances of the particular case. Therefore, we find no absolute bar in Article III to suits by federal taxpayers challenging allegedly unconstitutional federal taxing and spending programs. There remains, however, the problem of determining the circumstances under which a federal taxpayer will be deemed to have the personal stake and interest that impart the necessary concrete adverseness to such litigation so that standing can be conferred on the taxpayer qua taxpayer consistent [with] Article III."

In examining that last question, Chief Justice Warren substituted for the simple Frothingham inquiry about the taxpayer's direct financial stake a more complex one involving a preliminary look at the substantive issues "to determine whether there is a logical nexus between the status asserted and the claim sought to be adjudicated." He elaborated: "The nexus demanded of federal taxpayers has two aspects to it. First, the taxpayer must establish a logical link between that status and the type of legislative enactment attacked. Thus, a taxpayer will be a proper party to allege the unconstitutionality only of exercises of congressional power under the taxing and spending clause of Art. I, § 8, of the Constitution. It will not be sufficient to allege an incidental expenditure of tax funds in the administration of an essentially regulatory [law]. Secondly, the taxpayer must establish a nexus between that status and the precise nature of the constitutional infringement alleged. Under this requirement, the taxpayer must show that the challenged enactment exceeds specific constitutional limitations imposed upon the exercise of the congressional taxing and spending power and not simply that the enactment is generally beyond the powers delegated to Congress by Art. I, § 8. When both nexuses are established, the litigant will have shown a taxpayer's stake in the outcome of the controversy and will be a proper and appropriate party to invoke a federal court's jurisdiction."

Under that double nexus approach, the Flast and Frothingham situations were distinguishable. In Flast, the Establishment Clause claim rested on a provision of the First Amendment which "operates as a specific constitutional limitation upon the exercise by Congress of the taxing and spending power conferred by Art. I, § 8." The "quite different" allegations in Frothingham failed to satisfy the second nexus: Mrs. Frothingham had not claimed that the Maternity Act violated a "specific limitation" on the taxing and spending power;

she had merely argued that Congress "had exceeded the general powers delegated to it by Art. I, § 8, and that Congress had thereby invaded the legislative province reserved to the States by the Tenth Amendment." To be sure, Mrs. Frothingham had relied on due process as well; but that clause "does not protect taxpayers against increases in tax liability." The Chief Justice concluded: "[W]e hold that a taxpayer will have standing consistent with Article III to invoke federal judicial power when he alleges that congressional action under the taxing and spending clause is in derogation of those constitutional provisions which operate to restrict the exercise of the taxing and spending power. The taxpayer's allegation in such cases would be that his tax money is being extracted and spent in violation of specific constitutional protections against such abuses of legislative power. Such an injury is appropriate for judicial redress, and the taxpayer has established the necessary nexus between his status and the nature of the allegedly unconstitutional action to support his claim of standing to secure judicial review. Under such circumstances, we feel confident that the questions will be framed with the necessary specificity, that the issues will be contested with the necessary adverseness and that the litigation will be pursued with the necessary vigor to assure that the constitutional challenge will be made in a form traditionally thought to be capable of judicial resolution. We lack that confidence in cases such as Frothingham where a taxpayer seeks to employ a federal court as a forum in which to air his generalized grievances about the conduct of government or the allocation of power in the Federal System." [3]

Justice HARLAN was the sole dissenter. His elaborate opinion insisted that the majority's criteria were "not in any sense a measurement of any plaintiff's interest in the outcome of any suit. [T]he Court's standard for the determination of standing and its criteria for the satisfaction of that standard are entirely unrelated." Excluding expenditures "incidental" to an "essentially regulatory program" had nothing to do with a plaintiff's interest in the outcome of a suit. Similarly, the "intensity of a plaintiff's interest in a suit is not measured, even obliquely, by the fact that the constitutional provision under which he claims is, or is not, a 'specific limitation' upon Congress' spending powers." He also questioned the argument that the establishment clause was "in some uncertain fashion a more 'specific' limitation upon Congress' powers than are the various other constitutional commands." The basic difficulty, as Justice Harlan saw it, was that the Court was trying to retain a theoretical "personal interest" requirement while in fact recognizing the rights of "private attorneys general" to sue. The interests and rights claimed by plaintiffs in cases such as Frothingham and Flast "are bereft of any personal or proprietary coloration. They are, as litigants, indistinguishable from any group selected at random from among the general population, taxpayers and nontaxpayers alike. These are and must

---

3. Justice DOUGLAS' concurrence stated: "While I have joined the opinion of the Court, I do not think that the test it lays down is a durable one for the reasons stated [in Justice Harlan's dissent]. I think, therefore, that it will suffer erosion and in time result in the demise of [Frothingham]. It would therefore be the part of wisdom, as I see the problem, to be rid of Frothingham here and now." He added that, unlike Justice Harlan, he would not "view with alarm" the elimination of all barriers to taxpayers. Frothingham "was in the heyday of substantive due process, [but] we no longer undertake to exercise that kind of power." He was convinced that taxpayers "can be vigilant private attorneys general" and concluded that he would not be "niggardly [in] giving private attorneys general standing to sue. I would certainly not wait for Congress to give its blessing to our deciding cases clearly within our Article III jurisdiction." There were also separate concurrences by Justices STEWART and FORTAS emphasizing that the Flast decision was limited to taxpayers' challenges to spending in violation of the Establishment Clause. Justice Stewart noted that since that Clause "plainly prohibits taxing and spending in aid of religion, every taxpayer can claim a personal constitutional right not to be taxed for the support of a religious institution."

be, to adopt Professor Jaffe's useful phrase, 'public actions' brought to vindicate public rights." [4]

Justice Harlan noted, however, that "private attorneys general" bringing "public actions" were *not* barred by Art. III. He thought it "clear that non-Hohfeldian plaintiffs as such are not *constitutionally* excluded from the federal courts. The problem ultimately presented [is] therefore to determine in what circumstances, consonant with the character and proper functioning of the federal courts, such suits should be permitted." His proposed solution was that the Court should not on its own grant access to taxpayers bringing "public actions," and that the permissibility of such suits should be left to Congress. He explained: "It seems to me clear that public actions [may] involve important hazards for the continued effectiveness of the federal judiciary. Although I believe such actions to be within the jurisdiction conferred upon the federal courts by [Art. III], there surely can be little doubt that they strain the judicial function and press to the limit judicial authority." Federal judicial authority should be "employed prudently." The majority evidently was aware of the hazards, but its limitations were "wholly untenable." A better resolution of the problem was available, one "that entirely satisfies the demands of the principle of separation of powers." Congress had authority to permit plaintiffs lacking economic or other personal interests to bring public actions, and the Court should wait for Congress to act: "Any hazards to the proper allocation of authority among the three branches of the Government would be substantially diminished if public actions had been pertinently authorized by Congress and the President." [5]

THE BURGER COURT'S RELUCTANCE TO ABANDON THE STANDING REQUIREMENT IN "PUBLIC ACTIONS"

1. *Taxpayers' standing.* In UNITED STATES v. RICHARDSON, 418 U.S. 166 (1974), Chief Justice BURGER's majority opinion held that a federal taxpayer did not have standing to claim that the Central Intelligence Agency Act of 1949, which provides that CIA expenditures not be made public, violates Art. I, § 9, cl. 7, of the Constitution—"a regular Statement of Account of the Receipts and Expenditures of all public Money shall be published from time to time." The Chief Justice concluded that Richardson did not meet the Flast standards for taxpayers' standing: "Respondent is seeking 'to employ a federal court as a forum in which to air his generalized grievances about the conduct of government.' Both Frothingham and Flast reject that basis for standing." He commented: "Respondent makes no claim that appropriated funds are being spent in violation of a 'specific constitutional limitation upon the [taxing and spending power].' Rather, he asks the courts to compel the Government to give him information on precisely how the CIA spends its funds. Thus there is no 'logical nexus' between the asserted status of taxpayer and the claimed failure of the Congress [to require more detailed reports of CIA expenditures]. [Richardson's] claim is that without detailed information on CIA expenditures,

---

4. The reference was to Jaffe, Judicial Control of Administrative Action (1965). Justice Harlan also referred to such plaintiffs as "non-Hohfeldian" plaintiffs. That was another phrase of Professor Jaffe's, derived from Hohfeld, Fundamental Legal Conceptions (1923). As Justice Harlan explained in a footnote: "I have here employed the phrases 'Hohfeldian' and 'non-Hohfeldian' plaintiffs to mark the distinction between the personal and proprietary interests of

the traditional plaintiff, and the representative and public interests of the plaintiff in a public action."

5. For the Burger Court's reexamination of Flast v. Cohen, and its narrow reading of that decision, see the 1982 ruling in Valley Forge College v. Americans United, printed as a principal case at p. 1551 below, after the early Burger Court decisions in the next group of notes.

[he] cannot intelligently follow the actions of Congress or the Executive, nor can he properly fulfill his obligations as a member of the electorate in voting for candidates seeking national office. [This] is surely the kind of a generalized grievance described in both Frothingham and Flast since the impact on him is plainly undifferentiated and 'common to all members of the public.' Ex parte Lévitt, 302 U.S. 633 (1937).[1] While we can hardly dispute that this respondent has a genuine interest in the use of funds and that his interest may be prompted by his status as a taxpayer, he has not alleged that, as a taxpayer, he is in danger of suffering any particular concrete injury as a result of the operation of this statute." The Chief Justice stated more generally: "It can be argued that if respondent is not permitted to litigate this issue, no one can do so. In a very real sense, the absence of any particular individual or class to litigate these claims gives support to the argument that the subject matter is committed to the surveillance of Congress, and ultimately to the political process." [2]

Justice POWELL, who joined the Chief Justice's opinion, submitted an extensive concurrence in part echoing Justice Harlan's dissent in Flast. He stated that he would not overrule Flast on its facts, but added that he would not "perpetuate the doctrinal confusion in the Flast two-part 'nexus' test" and would abandon it.[3] He added: "The ambiguities inherent in the Flast 'nexus' limitations on federal taxpayer standing are illustrated by this case. There can be little doubt about respondent's fervor in pursuing his case. [T]he intensity of his interest appears to bear no relationship to the fact that, literally speaking, he is not challenging directly a congressional exercise of the taxing and spending power. On the other hand, if the involvement of the taxing and spending power has some relevance, it requires no great leap in reasoning to conclude that the Statement and Account Clause, on which respondent relies, is inextricably linked to that power. And that clause might well be seen as a 'specific' limitation on congressional spending. Thus, although the Court's application of Flast to the instant case is probably literally correct, adherence to the Flast test in this instance suggests, as does Flast itself, that the test is not a sound or logical limitation on standing. The lack of real meaning and of principled content in the Flast 'nexus' test renders it likely that it will in time collapse of its own weight. [This] will present several options for the Court. It may either reaffirm pre-Flast prudential limitations on federal and citizen taxpayer standing; attempt new doctrinal departures in this area, as would Mr. Justice Stewart [below]; or simply drop standing barriers altogether, [as] would Mr. Justice Douglas. I believe the first option to be the appropriate course, for reasons which may be emphasized by noting the difficulties I see with the other two. And, while I do not disagree at this late date with the Baker v. Carr statement of the constitutional indicia of standing, I further believe that constitutional limitations are not the only pertinent considerations."

Justice Powell added more generally: "Relaxation of standing requirements is directly related to the expansion of judicial power. It seems to me inescapable that allowing unrestricted taxpayer or citizen standing would significant-

---

1. That case held that a litigant had no standing to challenge the appointment of a Justice of the Supreme Court under Art. I, § 6, cl. 2. (The suit was a challenge to Justice Black's appointment.)

2. The Chief Justice noted, however, that "Congress could grant standing to taxpayers or citizens, or both, limited, of course, by the 'cases' and 'controversies' provisions of Art. III."

3. In the course of elaborating his "several" difficulties with Flast, he noted that Flast had made the Baker v. Carr approach the "controlling definition of the irreducible Art. III case-or-

controversy requirements for standing." Under Baker v. Carr, as noted above, the "gist of the question of standing" is whether the party seeking relief has "alleged such a personal stake in the outcome of the controversy as to assure that concrete adverseness which sharpens the presentation of issues upon which the court so largely depends for illumination of difficult constitutional questions." Justice Powell added: "The test announced in Baker and reiterated in Flast reflects how far the Court has moved in recent years in relaxing standing restraints."

ly alter the allocation of power at the national level, with a shift away from a democratic form of government. I also believe that repeated and essentially head-on confrontations between the life-tenured branch and the representative branches of government will not, in the long run, be beneficial to either. To be sure standing barriers have been substantially lowered in the last three decades. [E.g., Sierra Club; SCRAP.] [4] [But the] revolution in standing doctrine that has occurred has not meant [that] standing barriers have disappeared altogether. [Despite] the diminution of standing requirements in the last decade, the Court has not broken with the traditional requirement that, in the absence of a specific statutory grant of the right of review, a plaintiff must allege some particularized injury that sets him apart from the man on the street. I recognize that the Court's allegiance to a requirement of particularized injury has on occasion required a reading of the concept that threatens to transform it beyond recognition. E.g., Baker v. Carr; Flast v. Cohen. But despite such occasional digressions, the requirement remains. [I] believe we should limit the expansion of federal taxpayer and citizen standing in the absence of specific statutory authorization to an outer boundary drawn by the *results* in Flast and Baker v. Carr. [We] should explicitly reaffirm traditional prudential barriers [against] public actions." [5]

Justice BRENNAN's dissent (applicable to Reservists, which follows, as well as to Richardson) stated: "The 'standing' of a plaintiff to be heard on a claim of invasion of his alleged legally protected right is established, in my view, by his good-faith allegation that ' "the challenged action has caused him injury in fact." ' Barlow v. Collins, 397 U.S. 159, 167 (1970) [separate opinion of Justice Brennan]. Richardson plainly alleged injury in fact [not] only in respect of his right as a citizen to know how Congress was spending the public fisc, but also in respect of his right as a voter to receive information to aid his decision how and for whom to vote. These claims may ultimately fail on the merits, but

4. Unlike many of the cases in the text, the Sierra Club and SCRAP cases, frequently cited by the Court in modern standing discussions, involved statutory rather than constitutional attacks on federal action and relied for standing on congressional grants of rights of action. In Sierra Club v. Morton, 405 U.S. 727 (1972), the majority imposed a limited restraint on the growing tendency of some lower federal courts to recognize the standing of organizations with special interests in such problems as environmental control and consumer protection. But a year later, United States v. SCRAP, 412 U.S. 669 (1973), demonstrated that the Sierra Club barrier was a minor, temporary, easily avoidable one. Both cases made clear that, at least where Congress has granted standing, noneconomic injuries, not merely economic ones, could be adequate to obtain access to court. In both cases, the plaintiffs relied on § 10 of the Administrative Procedure Act, authorizing judicial review by persons "adversely affected or aggrieved" or "suffering legal wrong."

5. "The doctrine of standing has always reflected prudential as well as constitutional limitations. Indeed, it might be said that the correct reading of the Flast nexus test is as a prudential limit, given the Baker v. Carr definition of the constitutional bare minima. [Whatever] may have been the Court's initial perception of the intent of the Framers [e.g., Frothingham], it is now settled that such rules of self-restraint are not required by Art. III but are 'judicially creat-

ed overlays that Congress may strip away . . . .' G. Gunther & N. Dowling, Cases and Materials on Constitutional Law 106 (8th ed. 1970). But where Congress does so, my objections to public actions are ameliorated by the congressional mandate. Specific statutory grants of standing in such cases alleviate the conditions that make 'judicial forbearance the part of wisdom.' [Flast] (Harlan, J., dissenting)." [Footnote by Justice Powell.]

Justice STEWART's dissent, joined by Justice Marshall, thought the Frothingham-Flast taxpayer standing issue need not be confronted here because a quite different analysis would justify standing. He explained that Richardson's claim was that "the Statement and Account Clause gives him a right to receive [the information], and burdens the Government with a correlative duty to supply it. [Courts] of law exist for the resolution of such right-duty disputes. When a party is seeking a judicial determination that a defendant owes him an affirmative duty, it seems clear to me that he has standing to litigate the issue of the existence vel non of this duty once he shows that the defendant has declined to honor his claim." There was no need to resort to the Flast nexus tests because "the duty itself" provided "fully adequate assurance that the plaintiff is not seeking to 'employ a federal court as a forum in which to air his generalized grievances.' " He added: "[S]tanding is not to be denied simply because many people suffer the same injury." Justice DOUGLAS also dissented.

Richardson has 'standing' to assert them. [I] would find that [Flast] supports the conclusion that these allegations of injury in fact are sufficient to give [Richardson] 'standing.' [After noting that Flast reiterated the Baker v. Carr statement that standing turns on a plaintiff's "personal stake in the outcome of the controversy," Justice Brennan continued:] The two-pronged test fashioned by Flast was not a qualification upon these general principles but was fashioned solely as a determinant of standing of plaintiffs alleging only injury as taxpayers who challenge alleged violations of the [religion clauses] of the First Amendment. The extension of that test to the very different challenges here only produces the confusion evidenced by the differing views of the Flast test expressed in the several opinions filed [today]. Outside its proper sphere, as my Brother Powell soundly observes, that test is not 'a reliable indicator of when a federal taxpayer has standing.' We avoid that confusion if, as I said in Barlow, we recognize that 'alleged injury in fact, reviewability, and the merits pose questions that are largely distinct from one another, each governed by its own considerations. To fail to isolate and treat each inquiry independently of the other two, so far as possible, is to risk obscuring what is at issue in a given case, and thus to risk uninformed, poorly reasoned decisions that may result in injustice.' "

2. *Citizens' standing.* The companion case to Richardson, SCHLESINGER v. RESERVISTS TO STOP THE WAR, 418 U.S. 208 (1974), reemphasized the majority's determination to maintain standing as a significant barrier to access to federal courts, despite the erosion of that concept in prior years. The plaintiffs in Reservists were an association of present and former members of the Reserves. They challenged the Reserve membership of certain Members of Congress as being in violation of the Incompatibility Clause—the clause in Art. I, § 6, cl. 2, stating that "no Person holding any Office under the United States, shall be a Member of either House during his continuance in Office." They alleged injury because members of Congress belonging to the Reserves were "subject to the possibility of undue influence by the Executive Branch" and subject to "possible inconsistent obligations which might cause them to violate their duty faithfully to perform as Reservists or as Members of Congress," thus depriving "plaintiffs and all other citizens and taxpayers of the United States of the faithful discharge by members of Congress who are members of the Reserves of their duties as members of Congress, to which all citizens and taxpayers are entitled."

Chief Justice BURGER's majority opinion concluded that the plaintiffs lacked standing either as taxpayers or as citizens. The taxpayer claim was disposed of readily: the Chief Justice simply noted that the plaintiffs had failed to satisfy the first nexus test of Flast, since they "did not challenge an enactment under Art. I, § 8, but rather the action of the Executive Branch in permitting Members of Congress to maintain their Reserve status." As to citizens' standing, the Chief Justice explained at length why a "generalized citizen interest" is not a sufficient basis for access to the federal courts. He stated that the claimed constitutional violation "would adversely affect only the generalized interest of all citizens in constitutional governance, and that is an abstract injury." In elaborating that barrier, he explained: "Concrete injury, whether actual or threatened, is that indispensable element of a dispute which serves in part to cast it in a form traditionally capable of judicial resolution. It adds the essential dimension of specificity to the dispute. [This] personal stake is what the Court has consistently held enables a complainant authoritatively to present to a court a complete perspective upon the adverse consequences flowing from the specific set of facts undergirding his grievance. [Only] concrete injury presents the factual context within which a court [is] capable of making decisions."

Moreover, the "concrete injury" requirement served the function of assuring that constitutional adjudication "does not take place unnecessarily." The fact that there was genuine adverseness between the parties, assuring able arguments, was not enough to justify recognition of standing: "[Plaintiffs'] motivation has indeed brought them sharply into conflict with [defendants, but] motivation is not a substitute for the actual injury needed by the courts and adversaries to focus litigation efforts and judicial decisionmaking." He added: "The proposition that all constitutional provisions are enforceable by any citizen simply because citizens are the ultimate beneficiaries of those provisions has no boundaries." And the fact that no one might be able to sue if plaintiffs could not was not determinative: "Our system of government leaves many crucial decisions to the political processes." [6]

VALLEY FORGE COLLEGE v. AMERICANS UNITED

454 U.S. 464, 102 S.Ct. 752, 70 L.Ed.2d 700 (1982).

Justice REHNQUIST delivered the opinion of the Court.

I. [Acting under the Property Clause of the Constitution, Art. IV, § 3, cl. 2, Congress adopted the Federal Property and Administrative Services Act of 1949 to provide for the disposal of surplus federal property. The Act, authorized the Secretary of HEW to dispose of surplus real property for educational purposes by selling or leasing it to nonprofit, tax-exempt educational institutions for consideration that took into account any benefit to the Government from the transferee's use of the property. Pursuant to that statutory authority, HEW conveyed certain property once used as a military hospital to the Valley Forge Christian College, a college operating under the supervision of a religious order. The purpose of the college is to train its students "for Christian service as either ministers or laymen." Although the appraised value of the land was over $500,000, the property was transferred without any financial payment because HEW allowed the college a 100% public benefit allowance.[1]] Because of the unusually broad and novel view of standing to litigate a substantive question in the federal courts adopted by the Court of Appeals, we granted certiorari and we now reverse.

II. [The] judicial power of the United States defined by Art. III is not an unconditioned authority to determine the constitutionality of legislative or executive acts. The power to declare the rights of individuals and to measure the authority of governments "[is] legitimate only in the last resort, and as a necessity in the determination of real, earnest and vital controversy." [As] an incident to the elaboration of this bedrock requirement, this Court has always required that a litigant have "standing" to challenge the action sought to be adjudicated in the lawsuit. The term "standing" subsumes a blend of constitutional requirements and prudential considerations, see Warth v. Seldin.[2] [I]t has not always been clear in the opinions of this Court whether particular

6. Justice STEWART submitted a concurring opinion. Justices DOUGLAS, BRENNAN and MARSHALL dissented.

1. This federal court challenge by Americans United for Separation of Church and State claimed that the property transfer violated the establishment clause. The District Court dismissed the case on the ground that the challengers lacked standing as taxpayers under Flast v. Cohen. The Court of Appeals agreed that the challengers could not sue as taxpayers, since this was a challenge to congressional action under the Property Clause, not the provisions involved in Flast—the taxing and spending powers of Art. I, § 8. Nevertheless, the majority of the Court of Appeals sustained standing on the ground that the challengers could sue as taxpayer plaintiffs claiming " 'injury in fact' to their shared individuated right to a government that 'shall make no law respecting the establishment of religion.' "

2. Warth v. Seldin is the next principal case. Most of the other cases cited by the Court appear elsewhere in this section.

features of the "standing" requirement have been required by Art. III ex proprio vigore, or whether they are requirements that the Court itself has erected and which were not compelled by the language of the Constitution. A recent line of decisions, however, has resolved that ambiguity, at least to the following extent: at an irreducible minimum, Art. III requires the party who invokes the court's authority to "show that he personally has suffered some actual or threatened injury as a result of the putatively illegal conduct of the defendant," Gladstone Realtors v. Bellwood, 441 U.S. 91 (1979), and that the injury "fairly can be traced to the challenged action" and "is likely to be redressed by a favorable decision."

The requirement of "actual injury redressable by the court" serves several of the "implicit policies embodied in Article III." It tends to assure that the legal questions presented to the court will be resolved, not in the rarified atmosphere of a debating society, but in a concrete factual context conducive to a realistic appreciation of the consequences of judicial action. The "standing" requirement serves other purposes. Because it assures an actual factual setting in which the litigant asserts a claim of injury in fact, a court may decide the case with some confidence that its decision will not pave the way for lawsuits which have some, but not all, of the facts of the case actually decided by the court. The Art. III aspect of standing also reflects a due regard for the autonomy of those persons likely to be most directly affected by a judicial order. The federal courts have abjured appeals to their authority which would convert the judicial process into "no more than a vehicle for the vindication of the value interests of concerned bystanders." Were the federal courts merely publicly funded forums for the ventilation of public grievances or the refinement of jurisprudential understanding, the concept of "standing" would be quite unnecessary. But the "cases and controversies" language of Art. III forecloses the conversion of courts of the United States into judicial versions of college debating forums. [The] exercise of judicial power [is] therefore restricted to litigants who can show "injury in fact" resulting from the action which they seek to have the Court adjudicate. The exercise of the judicial power also affects relationships between the coequal arms of the national government. [While] the exercise of that "ultimate and supreme function" is a formidable means of vindicating individual rights, when employed unwisely or unnecessarily it is also the ultimate threat to the continued effectiveness of the federal courts in performing that role. [Proper] regard for the complex nature of our constitutional structure requires neither that the judicial branch shrink from a confrontation with the other two coequal branches of the federal government, nor that it hospitably accept for adjudication claims of constitutional violation by other branches of government where the claimant has not suffered cognizable injury.

[Beyond] the constitutional requirements, the federal judiciary has also adhered to a set of prudential principles that bear on the question of standing. Thus, this Court has held that "the plaintiff generally must assert his own legal rights and interests, and cannot rest his claim to relief on the legal rights or interests of third parties." Warth v. Seldin. In addition, even when the plaintiff has alleged redressable injury sufficient to meet the requirements of Art. III, the Court has refrained from adjudicating "abstract questions of wide public significance" which amounted to "generalized grievances," pervasively shared and most appropriately addressed in the representative branches. Finally, the Court has required that the plaintiff's complaint fall within "the zone of interests to be protected or regulated by the statute or constitutional guarantee in question."

Merely to articulate these principles is to demonstrate their close relationship to the policies reflected in the Art. III requirement of actual or threatened injury amenable to judicial remedy. But neither the counsels of prudence nor the policies implicit in the "case or controversy" requirement should be mistaken for the rigorous Art. III requirements themselves. Satisfaction of the former cannot substitute for a demonstration of " 'distinct and palpable injury' [that] is likely to be redressed if the requested relief is granted." That requirement states a limitation on judicial power, not merely a factor to be balanced in the weighing of so-called "prudential" considerations. We need not mince words when we say that the concept of "Art. III standing" has not been defined with complete consistency in all of the various [cases], nor when we say that this very fact is probably proof that the concept cannot be reduced to a one-sentence or one-paragraph definition. But of one thing we may be sure: Those who do not possess Art. III standing may not litigate as suitors in the courts of the United States.[3] Art. III [is] not merely a troublesome hurdle to be overcome if possible so as to reach the "merits" of a lawsuit which a party desires to have adjudicated; it is a part of the basic charter promulgated by the [framers].

III. The injury alleged by respondents [is] the "depriv[ation] of the fair and constitutional use of [their] tax dollar." As a result, our discussion must begin with [Frothingham]. Following the decision in Frothingham, the Court confirmed that the expenditure of public funds in an allegedly unconstitutional manner is not an injury sufficient to confer standing, even though the plaintiff contributes to the public coffers as a taxpayer. [Doremus.] [The] Court again visited the problem of taxpayer standing in Flast v. Cohen. [The Flast Court] developed a two-part test to determine whether the plaintiffs had standing to sue. First, because a taxpayer alleges injury only by virtue of his liability for taxes, the Court held that "a taxpayer will be a proper party to allege the unconstitutionality only of exercises of congressional power under the taxing and spending clause of Art. I, § 8, of the Constitution." Second, the Court required the taxpayer to "show that the challenged enactment exceeds specific constitutional limitations upon the exercise of the taxing and spending power and not simply that the enactment is generally beyond the powers delegated to Congress by Art. I, § 8."

[Unlike] the plaintiffs in Flast, respondents fail the first prong of the test for taxpayer standing. Their claim is deficient in two respects. First, the source of their complaint is not a congressional action, but a decision by HEW to transfer a parcel of federal property.[4] Flast limited taxpayer standing to challenges directed "only [at] exercises of congressional power." Second, and perhaps redundantly, the property transfer about which respondents complain was not an exercise of authority conferred by the taxing and spending clause of Art. I, § 8. The authorizing legislation [was] an evident exercise of Congress' power under the Property Clause, Art. IV, § 3, cl. 2. [This] is decisive of any claim of taxpayer standing under the Flast precedent. Any doubt that once might have existed concerning the rigor with which the Flast exception to the Frothingham principle ought to be applied should have been erased by this Court's recent

---

3. The dissent takes us to task for "tend[ing] merely to obfuscate, rather than inform, our understanding of the meaning of rights under the law." Were this Court constituted to operate a national classroom on "the meaning of rights" for the benefit of interested litigants, this criticism would carry weight. The teaching of Art. III, however, is that constitutional adjudication is available only on terms prescribed by the Constitution, among which is the requirement of a plaintiff with standing to sue. The dissent asserts that this requirement "overrides no other provision of the Constitution," but just as surely the Art. III power of the federal courts does not

wax and wane in harmony with a litigant's desire for a "hospitable forum." Art. III obligates a federal court to act only when it is assured of the power to do so, that is, when it is called upon to resolve an actual case or controversy. Then, and only then, may it turn its attention to other constitutional provisions and presume to provide a forum for the adjudication of rights. [Footnote by Justice Rehnquist.]

4. Respondents do not challenge the constitutionality of the [Act] itself, but rather a particular Executive branch action arguably authorized by the Act. [Footnote by Justice Rehnquist.]

decisions in [Richardson and Reservists]. [Respondents], therefore, are plainly without standing to sue as taxpayers. [It] remains to be seen whether respondents have alleged any other basis for standing to bring this suit.

IV. Although the Court of Appeals properly doubted respondents' ability to establish standing solely on the basis of their taxpayer status, it considered their allegations of taxpayer injury to be "essentially an assumed role": "Plaintiffs have no reason to expect, nor perhaps do they care about, any personal tax saving that might result should they prevail. The crux of the interest at stake, the plaintiffs argue, is found in the Establishment Clause, not in the supposed loss of money as such. As a matter of primary identity, therefore, the plaintiffs are not so much taxpayers as separationists." In the court's view, respondents had established standing by virtue of an " 'injury in fact' to their shared individuated right to a government that 'shall make no law respecting the establishment of religion.' " The court distinguished this "injury" from "the question of 'citizen standing' as such." Although citizens generally could not establish standing simply by claiming an interest in governmental observance of the Constitution, respondents had "set forth instead a particular and concrete injury" to a "personal constitutional right."

In finding that respondents had alleged something more than "the generalized interest of all citizens in constitutional governance" [Reservists], the Court of Appeals relied on factual differences which we do not think amount to legal distinctions. The court decided that respondents' claim differed from those in [Reservists] and Richardson, which were predicated, respectively, on the Incompatibility and Accounts Clauses, because "it is at the very least arguable that the Establishment Clause creates in each citizen a 'personal constitutional right' to a government that does not establish religion." The court found it unnecessary to determine whether this "arguable" proposition was correct, since it judged the mere allegation of a legal right sufficient to confer standing.

This reasoning process merely disguises, we think with a rather thin veil, the inconsistency of the court's results with our decisions in [Reservists] and Richardson. The plaintiffs in those cases plainly asserted a "personal right" to have the government act in accordance with their views of the Constitution; indeed, we see no barrier to the *assertion* of such claims with respect to any constitutional provision. But assertion of a right to a particular kind of government conduct, which the government has violated by acting differently, cannot alone satisfy the requirements of Art. III without draining those requirements of meaning. Nor can Schlesinger and Richardson be distinguished on the ground that the Incompatibility and Accounts Clauses are in some way less "fundamental" than the Establishment Clause. Each establishes a norm of conduct which the federal government is bound to honor—to no greater or lesser extent than any other inscribed in the Constitution. To the extent the Court of Appeals relied on a view of standing under which the Art. III burdens diminish as the "importance" of the claim on the merits increases, we reject that notion. The requirement of standing "focuses on the party seeking to get his complaint before a federal court and not on the issues he wishes to have adjudicated." Flast. Moreover, we know of no principled basis on which to create a hierarchy of constitutional values or a complementary "sliding scale" of standing which might permit respondents to invoke the [judicial power].

[The] complaint in this case shares a common deficiency with those in [Reservists] and Richardson. Although they claim that the Constitution has been violated, they claim nothing else. They fail to identify any personal injury suffered by the plaintiffs *as a consequence* of the alleged constitutional error, other than the psychological consequence presumably produced by observation of conduct with which one disagrees. That is not an injury sufficient to confer standing under Art. III, even though the disagreement is phrased in constitutional terms. It is evident that respondents are firmly committed to the constitutional principle of separation of church and State, but standing is not measured by the intensity of the litigant's interest or the fervor of his advocacy. "[T]hat concrete adverseness which sharpens the presentation of issues," Baker v. Carr, is the anticipated consequence of proceedings commenced by one who has been injured in fact; it is not a permissible substitute for the showing of injury itself.

In reaching this conclusion, we do not retreat from our earlier holdings that standing may be predicated on noneconomic injury. See [e.g., SCRAP; Data Processing]. We simply cannot see that respondents have alleged an *injury of any kind,* economic or otherwise, sufficient to confer standing. Respondents complain of a transfer of property located in Chester County, Pennsylvania. The named plaintiffs reside in Maryland and Virginia; their organizational headquarters are located in Washington, D.C. They learned of the transfer through a news release. Their claim that the government has violated the Establishment Clause does not provide a special license to roam the country in search of governmental wrongdoing and to reveal their discoveries in federal court. The federal courts were simply not constituted as ombudsmen of the general welfare.

V. The Court of Appeals in this case ignored unambiguous limitations on taxpayer and citizen standing. It appears to have done so out of the conviction that enforcement of the Establishment Clause demands special exceptions from the requirement that a plaintiff allege " 'distinct and palpable injury to himself,' [that] is likely to be redressed if the requested relief is granted." [Warth v. Seldin.] The court derived precedential comfort from [Flast]: "The underlying justification for according standing in Flast it seems, was the implicit recognition that the Establishment Clause does create in every citizen a personal constitutional right, such that any citizen, including taxpayers, may contest under that clause the constitutionality of federal expenditures." The concurring opinion was even more direct. In its view, "statutes alleged to violate the Establishment Clause may not have an individual impact sufficient to confer standing in the traditional sense." To satisfy "the need for an available plaintiff," and thereby to assure a basis for judicial review, respondents should be granted standing because, "as a practical matter, no one is better suited to bring this lawsuit and thus vindicate the freedoms embodied in the Establishment Clause."

Implicit in the foregoing is the philosophy that the business of the federal courts is correcting constitutional errors, and that "cases and controversies" are at best merely convenient vehicles for doing so and at worst nuisances that may be dispensed with when they become obstacles to that transcendent endeavor. This philosophy has no place in our constitutional scheme. It does not become more palatable when the underlying merits concern the Establishment Clause. "[The] assumption that if respondents have no standing to sue, no one would have standing, is not a reason to find standing." [Schlesinger.] This view would convert standing into a requirement that must be observed only when satisfied. Moreover, we are unwilling to assume that injured parties are nonexistent simply because they have not joined respondent in their suit. The law of averages is not a substitute for standing. Were we to accept respondents' claim of standing in this case, there would be no principled basis for confining our exception to litigants relying on the Establishment Clause. Ultimately, that exception derives from the idea that the judicial power requires nothing more for its invocation than important issues and able litigants. The existence of injured parties who might not wish to bring suit becomes irrelevant. [W]e are unwilling to countenance such a departure from the limits on judicial power contained in [Art. III].

[Reversed.]

Justice BRENNAN, with whom Justice MARSHALL and Justice BLACK-MUN join, dissenting.

A plaintiff's standing is a jurisdictional matter for Article III courts, and thus a "threshold question" to be resolved before turning attention to more "substantive" issues. But in consequence there is an impulse to decide difficult questions of substantive law obliquely in the course of opinions purporting to do nothing more than determine what the Court labels "standing"; this accounts for the phenomenon of opinions, such as the one today, that tend merely to obfuscate, rather than inform, our understanding of the meaning of rights under the law. The serious by-product of that practice is that the Court disregards its constitutional responsibility when, by failing to acknowledge the protections afforded by the Constitution, it uses "standing to slam the courthouse door against plaintiffs who are entitled to full consideration of their claims on the merits."[1] The opinion of the Court is a stark example of this unfortunate trend of resolving cases at the "threshold" while obscuring the nature of the underlying rights and interests at stake. The Court waxes eloquent on the blend of prudential and constitutional considerations that combine to create our misguided "standing" jurisprudence. But not one word is said *about the Establishment Clause right that the plaintiff seeks to enforce.* And despite its pat recitation of our standing decisions, the opinion utterly fails, except by the sheerest form of ipse dixit, to explain why this case is unlike [Flast] and is controlled instead by [Frothingham].

I. There is now much in the way of settled doctrine in our understanding of the injury-in-fact requirement of Article III. At the core is the irreducible minimum [of the "personal stake" requirement of Baker v. Carr]. Cases of this Court have identified the two essential components of this "personal stake" requirement. Plaintiff must have suffered, or be threatened with, some "distinct and palpable injury," Warth v. Seldin. In addition, there must be some causal connection between plaintiff's asserted injury and defendant's challenged action. [Simon; Arlington Heights.] But the existence of Article III injury "often turns on the nature and source of the claim asserted." Warth v. Seldin. Neither "palpable injury" nor "causation" is a term of unvarying meaning. There is much in the way of "mutual understandings" and "common law traditions" that necessarily guides the definitional inquiry. *In addition,* the Constitution, and by legislation the Congress, may impart a new, and on occasion unique, meaning to the terms "injury" and "causation" in particular statutory or constitutional contexts. The Court makes a fundamental mistake when it determines that a plaintiff has failed to satisfy the two-pronged "injury-in-fact" test, or indeed any other test of "standing," without first determining whether the Constitution or a statute defines injury, and creates a cause of action for redress of that injury, in precisely the circumstance presented to the [Court].

The "case and controversy" limitation of Article III overrides no other provision of the Constitution.[2] To construe that Article to deny standing "to the class for whose sake [a] constitutional protection is given" simply turns the Constitution on its head. Article III was designed to provide a hospitable forum in which persons enjoying rights under the Constitution could assert those rights. How are we to discern whether a particular person is to be afforded a right of action in the courts? The Framers did not, of course, employ the modern vocabulary of standing. But this much is clear: The drafters of the Bill of Rights surely intended that the particular beneficiaries of their legacy should

1. Barlow v. Collins (Brennan, J., concurring in the result and dissenting). [Footnote by Justice Brennan.]

2. When the Constitution makes it clear that a particular person is to be protected from a particular form of government action, then that person has a "right" to be free of that action; when that right is infringed, then there is injury, and a personal stake, within the meaning of Article III. [Footnote by Justice Brennan.]

enjoy rights legally enforceable in courts of law. With these observations in mind, I turn to the problem of taxpayer standing in general, and this case in particular.

II. A. [Frothingham's] reasoning remains obscure.[3] The principal interpretive difficulty lies in the manner in which Frothingham chose to blend the language of policy with seemingly absolute statements about jurisdiction. [Frothingham] stressed the indirectness of the taxpayer's injury. But, *as a matter of Article III standing,* if the causal relationship is sufficiently certain, the length of the causal chain is irrelevant. [The] concept of taxpayer injury necessarily recognizes the continuing stake of the taxpayer in the disposition of the Treasury to which he has contributed his taxes, and his right to have those funds put to lawful uses. Until Frothingham there was nothing in our precedents to indicate that this concept [was] inconsistent with the framework of rights and remedies established by the Federal Constitution. The explanation for the limit on federal taxpayer "standing" imposed by Frothingham must be sought in more substantive realms. The Frothingham rule may be seen as founded solely on the prudential judgment by the Court that precipitate and unnecessary interference in the activities of a coequal branch of government should be avoided. Alternatively, Frothingham may be construed as resting upon an unarticulated, constitutionally established barrier between Congress' power to tax and its power to spend, which barrier makes it analytically impossible to mount an assault on the former through a challenge to the [latter].

Whatever its provenance, the general rule of Frothingham displays sound judgment: Courts must be circumspect in dealing with the taxing power in order to avoid unnecessary intrusion into the functions of the legislative and executive branches. Congress' *purpose* in taxing will not ordinarily affect the validity of the tax. Unless the tax *operates* unconstitutionally, the taxpayer may not object to the use of his funds. Mrs. Frothingham's argument, that the use of tax funds for purposes unauthorized by the Constitution amounted to a violation of due process, did not provide her with the required legal interest because [due process] does not protect taxpayers against increases in tax liability. Mrs. Frothingham's claim was thus reduced to an assertion of "the States' interest in their legislative prerogatives," a third-party claim that could properly be barred. But in Flast the Court faced a different sort of constitutional claim, and found itself compelled to retreat from the general assertion in Frothingham that taxpayers have *no* interest in the disposition of their tax payments. To understand why Frothingham's bar necessarily gave way in the face of an Establishment Clause claim, we must examine the right asserted by a taxpayer making such a claim.

B. In 1947, nine Justices of this Court recognized that the Establishment Clause does impose a very definite restriction on the power to tax. [Everson.] In determining whether the law challenged in Everson was one "respecting an establishment of religion," the Court [examined] the historic meaning of the constitutional [provision], "particularly with respect to the imposition of taxes." [It] is clear in the light [of] history [that] one of the primary purposes of the Establishment Clause was to prevent the use of tax monies for religious purposes. *The taxpayer was the direct and intended beneficiary of the prohibition on financial aid to religion.* [It] seems obvious that all the Justices who participated

---

3. The question apparently remains open whether Frothingham stated a prudential limitation or identified an Article III barrier. It was generally agreed at the time of Flast, and clearly the view of Justice Harlan in dissent, that the rule stated reflected prudential and policy considerations, not constitutional limitations. Perhaps the case is most usefully understood as a "sub-stantive" declaration of the legal rights of a taxpayer with respect to government spending, coupled with a prudential restriction on the taxpayer's ability to raise the claims of third parties. Under any construction, however, Frothingham must give way to a taxpayer's suit brought under the Establishment Clause. [Footnote by Justice Brennan.]

in Everson would have agreed with Justice Jackson's succinct statement of the question presented: "Is it constitutional to tax this complainant to pay the cost of carrying pupils to Church schools of one specified denomination?" Given this view of the issues, could it fairly be doubted that this taxpayer alleged injury in precisely the form that the Establishment Clause sought to make actionable?

C. [The] test of standing formulated by the Court in Flast sought to reconcile the developing doctrine of taxpayer "standing" with the Court's historical understanding that the Establishment Clause was intended to prohibit the federal government from using tax funds for the advancement of religion, and thus the constitutional imperative of taxpayer standing in certain cases brought pursuant to the Establishment Clause. The two-pronged "nexus" test offered by the Court, despite its general language, is best understood as "a determinant of standing of plaintiffs alleging only injury as taxpayers who challenge alleged violations of the Establishment and Free Exercise Clauses of the First Amendment," and not as a general statement of standing principles. The test explains what forms of governmental action may be attacked by someone alleging *only* taxpayer status, and, without ruling out the possibility that history might reveal another similarly founded provision, explains why an Establishment Clause claim is treated differently from any other assertion that the federal government has exceeded the bounds of the law in allocating its largesse. [The] nexus test that the Court "announced" sought to maintain necessary continuity with prior cases, and set forth principles to guide future cases involving taxpayer standing. But Flast did not depart from the principle that no judgment about standing should be made without a fundamental understanding of the rights at issue. The two-part Flast test did not supply the rationale for the Court's decision, but rather its exposition: That rationale was supplied by an understanding of the nature of the restrictions on government power imposed by the Constitution and the intended beneficiaries of those restrictions.

It may be that Congress can tax for almost any reason, or for no reason at all. There is, so far as I have been able to discern, but one constitutionally imposed limit on that authority. Congress cannot use tax money to support a church, or to encourage religion. That is *the* forbidden exaction." [The] history of the Establishment Clause [makes] this clear. History also makes it clear that the federal taxpayer is a singularly "proper and appropriate party to invoke a federal court's jurisdiction" to challenge a federal bestowal of largesse as a violation of the Establishment Clause. Each, and indeed every, federal taxpayer suffers precisely the injury that the Establishment Clause guards against when the federal government directs that funds be taken from the pocketbooks of the citizenry and placed into the coffers of the ministry. [Surely], a taxpayer must have standing at the time that he learns of the Government's alleged Establishment Clause violation to seek equitable relief in order to halt the continuing and intolerable burden on his pocketbook, his conscience, and his constitutional rights.

III. Blind to history, the Court attempts to distinguish this case from Flast by wrenching snippets of language from our opinions, and by perfunctorily applying that language under color of the first prong of Flast's two-part nexus test. The tortuous distinctions thus produced are specious, at best; at worst, they are pernicious to our constitutional heritage. First, the Court finds this case different from Flast because here the "source of [plaintiffs'] complaint is not *congressional* action, but a decision by HEW to transfer a parcel of federal property." This attempt at distinction cannot withstand scrutiny. [No] clear division can be drawn in this context between actions of the Legislative Branch and those of the Executive Branch. [The] First Amendment binds the Government as a [whole]. The Court's second purported distinction [is] equally unavailing. The majority finds it "decisive" that the [Act] "was an evident exercise of Congress' power under the Property Clause," while the Government action in Flast was taken under Art. I, § 8. The Court relies on [Richardson and Schlesinger] to support the distinction between the two [Clauses]. The standing defect in each case was *not,* however, the failure to allege a violation of the Spending Clause; rather, the taxpayers in those cases had not complained of the distribution of Government largesse, and thus failed to meet the essential requirement of taxpayer standing recognized in Doremus. It can make no constitutional difference in the case before us whether the donation to the [defendant] here was in the form of a cash grant to build a facility [or] in the nature of a gift of property including a facility already built. [Whether] undertaken pursuant to the Property Clause or the Spending Clause, the breach of the Establishment Clause, and the relationship of the taxpayer to that breach, is precisely the same.

IV. Plainly hostile to the Framers' understanding of the Establishment Clause, and Flast's enforcement of that understanding, the Court vents that hostility under the guise of standing, "to slam the courthouse door against plaintiffs who [as the Framers intended] are entitled to full consideration of their [Establishment Clause] claims on the merits." Therefore, I dissent.

Justice STEVENS, dissenting.

[For] the Court to hold that plaintiffs' standing depends on whether the Government's transfer was an exercise of its power to spend money, on the one hand, or its power to dispose of tangible property, on the other, is to trivialize the standing doctrine. [T]he plaintiffs' invocation of the Establishment Clause was of decisive importance in resolving the standing issue in [Flast]. [Today] the Court holds, in effect, that the Judiciary has no greater role in enforcing the Establishment Clause than in enforcing other "norm[s] of conduct which the federal government is bound to honor," such as the Accounts Clause [Richardson] and the Incompatibility Clause [Reservists]. Ironically, however, its decision rests on the premise that the difference between a disposition of funds pursuant to the Spending Clause and a disposition of realty pursuant to the Property Clause is of fundamental jurisprudential significance. With all due respect, I am persuaded that the essential holding of Flast v. Cohen attaches special importance to the Establishment Clause and does not permit the drawing of a tenuous distinction between the Spending Clause and [the Property Clause].

B. PLAINTIFFS IN TRADITIONAL PRIVATE (RATHER THAN "PUBLIC") ACTIONS: STANDING OUTSIDE THE TAXPAYERS AND CITIZENS CASES

WARTH v. SELDIN

422 U.S. 490, 95 S.Ct. 2197, 45 L.Ed.2d 343 (1975).

Mr. Justice POWELL delivered the opinion of the Court.

Petitioners, various organizations and individuals resident in the Rochester, N.Y., metropolitan area, brought this action [against] the town of Penfield, an incorporated municipality adjacent to Rochester, and against members of Penfield's Zoning, Planning, and Town Boards. Petitioners claimed that the town's zoning ordinance effectively excluded persons of low and moderate income from living in the town, in contravention of petitioners' [constitutional and statutory rights]. The [lower federal courts held] that none of the plaintiffs [had] standing. [W]e affirm.

I.   [In] sum, petitioners alleged that [the] town and its officials had made "practically and economically impossible the construction of sufficient numbers of low and moderate income [housing] in the Town of Penfield to satisfy the minimum housing requirements of both the [Penfield] and the metropolitan Rochester area." Petitioners alleged, moreover, that by precluding low- and moderate-cost housing, the town's zoning practices also had the effect of excluding persons of minority racial and ethnic groups, since most such persons have only low or moderate [incomes].

II.   [In] essence the question of standing is whether the litigant is entitled to have the court decide the merits of the dispute or of particular issues. This inquiry involves both constitutional limitations on federal court jurisdiction and prudential limitations on its exercise. E.g., Barrows v. Jackson [below]. In both dimensions it is founded in concern about the proper—and properly limited—role of the courts in a democratic society. In its constitutional dimension, standing imports justiciability: whether the plaintiff has made out a "case or controversy" between himself and the defendant within the meaning of Art. III. [The] Art. III judicial power exists only to redress or otherwise to protect against injury to the complaining party, even though the court's judgment may benefit others collaterally. A federal court's jurisdiction therefore can be invoked only when the plaintiff himself has suffered "some threatened or actual injury resulting from the putatively illegal action." [1] Linda R.S. v. Richard D.[2] Apart from this minimum constitutional mandate, this Court has recognized other limits on the class of persons who may invoke the courts' decisional and remedial powers. First, the Court has held that when the asserted harm is a "generalized grievance" shared in substantially equal measure by all or a large class of citizens, that harm alone normally does not warrant exercise of jurisdiction. [E.g., Reservists.] Second, even when the plaintiff has alleged injury sufficient to meet the "case or controversy" requirement, this Court has held that the plaintiff generally must assert his own legal rights and interests, and cannot rest his claim to relief on the legal rights or interests of third parties. [E.g., Tileston v. Ullman, below.] Without such limitations—closely related to Art. III concerns but essentially matters of judicial self-governance—the courts would be called upon to decide abstract questions of wide public significance even though other governmental institutions may be

1.   The standing question [bears] close affinity to questions of ripeness—whether the harm asserted has matured sufficiently to warrant judicial intervention—and of mootness—whether the occasion for judicial intervention persists. [Footnote by Justice Powell.]

2.   Linda R.S. v. Richard D., 410 U.S. 614 (1972), repeatedly cited in modern standing decisions, refused to find standing in a federal action by the mother of an illegitimate child who sought to compel the local prosecutor to enforce against the alleged father a Texas criminal law that punished parents who refused to provide for their children's support. (The state courts had construed that law to apply only to the parents of legitimate children, and the plaintiff claimed that that construction violated the equal protection clause.) Justice Marshall's majority opinion held that the mother lacked standing because she had "failed to allege a sufficient nexus between her injury and the government action which she attacks to justify judicial intervention. To be sure, [she] no doubt suffered an injury" because of the absence of support payments, but that "abstract injury" met only the first half of the standing requirement. Under Massachusetts v. Mellon, the plaintiff had also to show "some *direct* injury *as the result of* [a law's] enforcement." Here, the plaintiff had made no showing "that her failure to secure support payments [related to] the enforcement [of the law] as to her child's father." If she succeeded in obtaining relief, the child's father would be jailed; but the prospect that that would result in support payments in the future "can, at best, be termed only speculative."

Note the heavy reliance on that "nexus" emphasis of Linda R.S. in Warth v. Seldin. Was the standing barrier in Linda R.S. truly of constitutional dimensions? Can the specific ruling be explained as resting on the Court's reluctance to interfere with prosecutorial discretion? To what extent can Congress remove the "nexus" standing barrier? Note the additional invocations of Linda R.S. in the modern cases below.

more competent to address the questions and even though judicial intervention may be unnecessary to protect individual rights.

Although standing in no way depends on the merits of the plaintiff's contention that particular conduct is illegal, e.g., [Flast], it often turns on the nature and source of the claim asserted. The actual or threatened injury required by Art. III may exist solely by virtue of "statutes creating legal rights, the invasion of which creates standing." Moreover, the source of the plaintiff's claim to relief assumes critical importance with respect to the prudential rules of standing that, apart from Art. III's minimum requirements, serve to limit the role of the courts in resolving public disputes. Essentially, the standing question in such cases is whether the constitutional or statutory provision on which the claim rests properly can be understood as granting persons in the plaintiff's position a right to judicial relief.[3] In some circumstances, countervailing considerations may outweigh the concerns underlying the usual reluctance to exert judicial power when the plaintiff's claim to relief rests on the legal rights of third parties. In such instances, the Court has found, in effect, that the constitutional or statutory provision in question implies a right of action in the plaintiff. See Pierce v. Society of Sisters. Moreover, Congress may grant an express right of action to persons who otherwise would be barred by prudential standing rules. Of course, Art. III's requirement remains: the plaintiff still must allege a distinct and palpable injury to himself, even if it is an injury shared by a large class of other possible litigants. But so long as this requirement is satisfied, persons to whom Congress has granted a right of action, either expressly or by clear implication, may have standing to seek relief on the basis of the legal rights and interests of others, and, indeed, may invoke the general public interest in support of their [claim].

III. With these general considerations in mind, we turn first to the claims of petitioners Ortiz, Reyes, Sinkler, and Broadnax, each of whom asserts standing as a person of low or moderate income and, coincidentally, as a member of a minority racial or ethnic group. We must assume, taking the allegations of the complaint as true, that Penfield's zoning ordinance and the pattern of enforcement by respondent officials have had the purpose and effect of excluding persons of low and moderate income, many of whom are members of racial or ethnic minority groups. We also assume, for purposes here, that such intentional exclusionary practices, if proved in a proper case, would be adjudged violative of the constitutional and statutory rights of the persons excluded. But the fact that these petitioners share attributes common to persons who may have been excluded from residence in the town is an insufficient predicate for the conclusion that petitioners themselves have been excluded, or that the respondents' assertedly illegal actions have violated their rights. Petitioners must allege and show that they personally have been injured, not that injury has been suffered by other, unidentified members of the class to which they belong and which they purport to [represent].

In their complaint, petitioners Ortiz, Reyes, Sinkler, and Broadnax alleged in conclusory terms that they are among the persons excluded by respondents' actions. None of them has ever resided in Penfield; each claims at least implicitly that he desires, or has desired, to do so. Each asserts, moreover, that he made some effort, at some time, to locate housing in Penfield that was at once within his means and adequate for his family's needs. Each claims that his efforts proved fruitless. We may assume [that] respondents' actions have [contributed] to the cost of housing in Penfield. But there remains the

---

3. A similar standing issue arises when the litigant asserts the rights of third parties defensively, as a bar to judgment against him. E.g., Barrows v. Jackson. In such circumstances, there is no Art. III standing problem; but the prudential question is governed by considerations closely related to the question whether a person in the litigant's position would have a right of action on the claim. [Footnote by Justice Powell.]

question whether petitioners' inability to locate suitable housing in Penfield reasonably can be said to have resulted, in any concretely demonstrable way, from respondents' alleged constitutional and statutory infractions. Petitioners must allege facts from which it reasonably could be inferred that, absent the respondents' restrictive zoning practices, there is a substantial probability that they would have been able to purchase or lease in Penfield and that, if the court affords the relief requested, the asserted inability of petitioners will be removed. [Linda R.S.]

We find the record devoid of the necessary allegations. [N]one of these petitioners has a present interest in any Penfield property; none is himself subject to the ordinance's strictures; and none has ever been denied a variance or permit by respondent officials. Instead, petitioners claim that respondents' enforcement of the ordinance against third parties—developers, builders, and the like—has had the consequence of precluding the construction of housing suitable to their needs at prices they might be able to afford. The fact that the harm to petitioners may have resulted indirectly does not in itself preclude standing. When a governmental prohibition or restriction imposed on one party causes specific harm to a third party, harm that a constitutional provision or statute was intended to prevent, the indirectness of the injury does not necessarily deprive the person harmed of standing to vindicate his rights. E.g., Roe v. Wade. But it may make it substantially more difficult to meet the minimum requirement of Art. III: to establish that, in fact, the asserted injury was the consequence of the defendants' actions, or that prospective relief will remove the harm.

Here, by their own admission, realization of petitioners' desire to live in Penfield always has depended on the efforts and willingness of third parties to build low- and moderate-cost housing. The record specifically refers to only two such efforts: that of Penfield Better Homes Corp., in late 1969, to obtain the rezoning of certain land in Penfield to allow the construction of subsidized cooperative townhouses that could be purchased by persons of moderate income; and a similar effort by O'Brien Homes, Inc., in late 1971. But the record is devoid of any indication that these projects, or other like projects, would have satisfied petitioners' needs at prices they could afford, or that, were the court to remove the obstructions attributable to respondents, such relief would benefit petitioners. Indeed, petitioners' descriptions of their individual financial situations and housing needs suggest precisely the contrary—that their inability to reside in Penfield is the consequence of the economics of the area housing market, rather than of respondents' assertedly illegal acts. In short, the facts alleged fail to support an actionable causal relationship between Penfield's zoning practices and petitioners' asserted injury. [We] hold only that a plaintiff who seeks to challenge exclusionary zoning practices must allege specific, concrete facts demonstrating that the challenged practices harm *him,* and that he personally would benefit in a tangible way from the courts' intervention.[4] Absent the necessary allegations of demonstrable, particularized injury, there can be no confidence of "a real need to exercise the power of judicial review" or that relief can be framed "no broader than required by the precise facts to which the court's ruling would be applied." [Reservists.]

---

4. This is not to say that the plaintiff who challenges a zoning ordinance or zoning practices must have a present contractual interest in a particular project. A particularized personal interest may be shown in various ways, which we need not undertake to identify in the abstract. But usually the initial focus should be on a particular project. We also note that zoning laws and their provisions, long considered essential to effective urban planning, are peculiarly within the province of state and local legislative authorities. They are, of course, subject to judicial review in a proper case. But citizens dissatisfied with provisions of such laws need not overlook the availability of the normal democratic process. [Footnote by Justice Powell. Compare the finding of standing two years later in the Arlington Heights case, in the footnote at the end of this case.]

IV. The petitioners who assert standing on the basis of their status as taxpayers of the city of Rochester [claim] that Penfield's persistent refusal to allow or to facilitate construction of low- and moderate-cost housing forces the city of Rochester to provide more such housing than it otherwise would do; that to provide such housing, Rochester must allow certain tax abatements; and that as the amount of tax-abated property increases, Rochester taxpayers are forced to assume an increased tax burden in order to finance essential public services. [Apart] from the conjectural nature of [this] asserted injury, the line of causation between Penfield's actions and such injury is not apparent from the complaint. Whatever may occur in Penfield, the injury complained of— increases in taxation—results only from decisions made by the appropriate Rochester authorities who are not parties to this case. But even if we assume that the taxpayer-petitioners could establish that Penfield's zoning practices harm them, their complaint nonetheless was properly dismissed. Petitioners do not, even if they could, assert any personal right under the Constitution or any statute [but only] that Penfield's zoning ordinance and practices violate the constitutional and statutory rights of third parties, namely, persons of low and moderate income who are said to be excluded from Penfield. In short the claim of these petitioners falls squarely within the prudential standing rule that normally bars litigants from asserting the rights or legal interests of others in order to obtain relief from injury to [themselves].

V. We turn next to the standing problems presented by the petitioner associations. [There] is no question that an association may have standing in its own right to seek judicial relief from injury to itself and to vindicate whatever rights and immunities the association itself may enjoy. Moreover, in attempting to secure relief from injury to itself the association may assert the rights of its members, at least so long as the challenged infractions adversely affect its members' associational ties. E.g., NAACP v. Alabama. [Even] in the absence of injury to itself, an association may have standing solely as the representative of its members. The possibility of such representational standing, however, does not eliminate or attenuate the constitutional requirement of a case or controversy. The association must allege that its members, or any one of them, are suffering immediate or threatened injury as a result of the challenged action of the sort that would make out a justiciable case had the members themselves brought suit. So long as this can be established, and so long as the nature of the claim and of the relief sought does not make the individual participation of each injured party indispensable to proper resolution of the cause, the association may be an appropriate representative of its members, entitled to invoke the court's jurisdiction.

A. Petitioner Metro-Act's claims to standing on its own behalf as a Rochester taxpayer, and on behalf of its members who are Rochester taxpayers or persons of low or moderate income, are precluded by our holdings in Parts [III and IV]. Metro-Act [a civic action group] also alleges, however, that 9% of its membership is composed of present residents of Penfield. It claims that, as a result of the persistent pattern of exclusionary zoning, [its] members who are Penfield residents are deprived of the benefits of living in a racially and ethnically integrated community. [Metro-Act] does not assert on behalf of its members any right of action under the 1968 Civil Rights [Act]. In this, we think, lies the critical distinction between [Trafficante, below,] and the situation here. [Even] if we assume, arguendo, that apart from any statutorily created right the asserted harm to Metro-Act's Penfield members is sufficiently direct and personal to satisfy the case-or-controversy requirement of Art. III, prudential considerations strongly counsel against according them or Metro-Act standing to prosecute this action. We do not understand Metro-Act to argue that Penfield residents themselves have been denied any constitutional rights. [Instead], their complaint is that they have been harmed indirectly by the exclusion of others. This is an attempt to raise putative rights of third parties, and none of the exceptions that allow such claims is present [here].

B. Petitioner Home Builders [asserted] standing to represent its member firms engaged in the development and construction of residential housing in the Rochester area, including Penfield. Home Builders alleged that the Penfield zoning restrictions, together with refusals by the town officials to grant variances and permits for the construction of low- and moderate-cost housing, had deprived some of its members of "substantial business opportunities and profits." Home Builders claimed damages of $750,000 and also joined in the original plaintiffs' prayer for declaratory and injunctive relief. [Home Builders] alleges no monetary injury to itself, nor any assignment of the damages claims of its members. No award therefore can be made to the association as such. Moreover, in the circumstances of this case, the damages claims are not common to the entire membership, nor shared by all in equal degree. [Thus], to obtain relief in damages, each member of Home Builders who claims injury as a result of respondents' practices must be a party to the suit, and Home Builders has no standing to claim damages on his behalf. Home Builders' prayer for prospective relief fails for a different reason. It can have standing as the representative of its members only if it has alleged facts sufficient to make out a case or controversy had the members themselves brought suit. No such allegations were made. The complaint refers to no specific project of any of its members that is currently precluded either by the ordinance or by respondents' action in enforcing it. [In] short, insofar as the complaint seeks prospective relief, Home Builders has failed to show the existence of any injury to its members of sufficient immediacy and ripeness to warrant judicial intervention. See, e.g., United Public Workers v. Mitchell [sec. 3 below].

A like problem is presented with respect to petitioner Housing Council. [T]he Council includes in its membership "at least seventeen" groups that have been, are, or will be involved in the development of low- and moderate-cost housing. But, with one exception, the complaint does not suggest that any of these groups has focused its efforts on Penfield or has any specific plan to do so. [The] exception is the Penfield Better Homes Corp. [It] applied to respondents in late 1969 for a zoning variance to allow construction of a housing project designed for persons of moderate income. It is therefore possible that in 1969, or within a reasonable time thereafter, Better Homes itself and possibly Housing Council as its representative would have had standing to seek review of respondents' action. The complaint, however, does not allege that the Penfield Better Homes project remained viable in 1972 when this complaint was filed, or that respondents' actions continued to block a then-current construction project. In short, neither the complaint nor the record supplies any basis from which to infer that the controversy between respondents and Better Homes, however vigorous it may once have been, remained a live, concrete dispute when this complaint was filed.

VI. The rules of standing, whether as aspects of the Art. III case-or-controversy requirement or as reflections of prudential considerations defining and limiting the role of the courts, are threshold determinants of the propriety of judicial intervention. It is the responsibility of the complainant clearly to allege facts demonstrating that he is a proper party to invoke judicial resolution of the dispute and the exercise of the court's remedial powers. [N]one of the petitioners here has met this threshold requirement.

Affirmed.

Mr. Justice BRENNAN, with whom Mr. Justice WHITE and Mr. Justice MARSHALL, join, dissenting.

[The] opinion, which tosses out of court almost every conceivable kind of plaintiff who could be injured by the activity claimed to be unconstitutional, can be explained only by an indefensible hostility to the claim on the merits. I can appreciate the Court's reluctance to adjudicate the complex and difficult legal questions involved [and] I also understand that the merits of this case could involve grave sociological and political ramifications. But courts cannot refuse to hear a case on the merits merely because they would prefer not to, and it is quite clear, when the record is viewed with dispassion, that at least three of the groups of plaintiffs have made allegations, and supported them with affidavits and documentary evidence, sufficient to survive a motion to dismiss for lack of standing.

[O]ne glaring defect of the Court's opinion is that it views each set of plaintiffs as if it were prosecuting a separate lawsuit, refusing to recognize that the interests are intertwined. [For example], the Court says that the low-income minority plaintiffs have not alleged facts sufficient to show that but for the exclusionary practices claimed, they would be able to reside in Penfield. The Court then intimates that such a causal relationship could be shown only if "the initial focus [is] on a particular project." Later, the Court objects to the ability of the Housing Council to prosecute the suit on behalf of its member, Penfield Better Homes Corp., *despite* the fact that Better Homes *had* displayed an interest in a particular project, because that project was no longer live. Thus, we must suppose that even if the low-income plaintiffs had alleged a desire to live in the Better Homes project, that allegation would be insufficient because it appears that particular project might never be built. The rights of low-income minority plaintiffs who desire to live in a locality, then, seem to turn on the willingness of a third party to litigate the legality of preclusion of a particular project, despite the fact that the third party may have no economic incentive to incur the costs of litigation with regard to one project, and despite the fact that the low-income-minority plaintiffs' interest is *not* to live in a particular project but to live somewhere in the town in a dwelling they can afford. [In] effect, the Court tells the low-income minority and building company plaintiffs they will not be permitted to prove what they have alleged— that they could and would build and live in the town if changes were made in the zoning ordinance and its application—because they have not succeeded in breaching, before the suit was filed, the very barriers which are the subject of the suit.

Low-income and Minority Plaintiffs. [P]laintiffs Ortiz, Broadnax, Reyes, and Sinkler alleged that "as a result" of respondents' exclusionary practices, they were unable, despite attempts, to find the housing they desired in Penfield, and consequently have incurred high commuting expenses, received poorer municipal services, and, in some instances, have been relegated to live in substandard housing. [These] petitioners have alleged precisely what our cases require— that *because* of the exclusionary practices of petitioners they cannot live in Penfield and have suffered harm. [Here], the very fact [that] these petitioners' claim rests in part upon proving the intentions and capabilities of third parties to build in Penfield suitable housing which they can afford, coupled with the exclusionary character of the claim on the merits, makes it particularly inappropriate to assume that these petitioners' lack of specificity reflects a fatal weakness in their theory of causation. Obviously they cannot be expected, prior to discovery and trial, to know the future plans of building companies, the precise details of the housing market in Penfield, or everything which has transpired in 15 years of application of the Penfield zoning ordinance, including every housing plan suggested and refused. To require them to allege such facts is to require them to prove their case on paper in order to get into court at all, reverting to the form of fact pleading long abjured in the [federal courts].

Associations Including Building Concerns. [Again], the Court ignores the thrust of the complaints and asks petitioners to allege the impossible. According to the allegations, the building concerns' experience in the past with Penfield officials has shown any plans for low- and moderate-income housing to be futile for, again according to the allegations, the respondents are engaged in a purposeful, conscious scheme to exclude such housing. Particularly with regard to a low- or moderate-income project, the cost of litigating, with respect to any particular project, the legality of a refusal to approve it may well be prohibitive. And the merits of the exclusion of this or that project is not at the heart of the complaint; the claim is that respondents will not approve *any* project which will provide residences for low- and moderate-income people. When this sort of pattern-and-practice claim is at the heart of the controversy, allegations of past injury, which members of both of these organizations have clearly made, and of a future intent, if the barriers are cleared, again to develop suitable housing for Penfield, should be more than sufficient. The past experiences, if proved at trial, will give credibility and substance to the claim of interest in future building activity in Penfield. These parties, if their allegations are proved, certainly have the requisite personal stake in the outcome of *this* controversy, and the Court's conclusion otherwise is only a conclusion that *this* controversy may not be litigated in a [federal court].*

---

* Justice DOUGLAS also dissented.

Contrast, with the majority's refusal to find standing in Warth v. Seldin, the Court's recognition of standing in Arlington Heights v. Metropolitan Housing Corp. (1977; ruling on the merits in chap. 9, sec. 3 above)—a case which, like Warth, presented a racial discrimination claim in a zoning context. In Arlington Heights, the challenge was to a Chicago suburb's refusal to rezone a tract from a single-family to a multi-family classification. The prevailing opinion, as in Warth, was written by Justice Powell. The Court found that the developer had standing to challenge the allegedly discriminatory denial of rezoning, even though the developer's construction project was contingent not only on its ability to procure rezoning but also on its capacity to obtain financing and qualify for federal subsidies. Justice Powell noted that "all housing developments are subject to some extent to similar uncertainties. When a project is as detailed and specific as [this one], a court is not required to engage in undue speculation as a predicate for finding that the plaintiff has the requisite personal stake in the controversy."

The Court noted, moreover, that "economic injury is not the only kind of injury that can support a plaintiff's standing." The concern of the developer, a nonprofit corporation interested in providing low-cost housing, was "not mere abstract concern about a problem of general interest"; instead, its involvement in a specific project provided "that 'essential dimension of specificity' that informs judicial decision-making." The Court also found that an individual black plaintiff had standing to assert the racial discrimination claim. That plaintiff had alleged that he would qualify for the proposed housing and would probably move there if it were built, since it was closer to his job. Justice Powell

stated: "His is not a generalized grievance. Instead, as we suggested in Warth, it focuses on a particular project and is not dependent on speculation about the possible actions of third parties not before the court. Unlike the individual plaintiffs in Warth, [this plaintiff] has adequately averred an 'actionable causal relationship' between Arlington Heights' zoning practices and his asserted injury."

That injuries other than economic ones may confer standing was made especially clear in Heckler v. Mathews, 465 U.S. ___ (1984). The challenge was to a law that provided certain Social Security benefits in a way that allegedly discriminated on the basis of gender; but a severability provision provided that the relevant benefits would be denied to *everyone* in the event the challenged provision was struck down. Thus, there was no way that the plaintiff could in fact receive an increase in benefits even if he prevailed; the usual cure for gender-based classifications in a benefit scheme (expanding the eligible category to encompass the improperly excluded claimant's class) was unavailable here, because of the severability provision. The Court nevertheless found standing to sue. Because the right alleged was the right to receive benefits distributed without regard to gender, rather than the right to receive any particular amount of benefits, the plaintiff had alleged an injury that would be redressed by a favorable decision: "Although the severability clause would prevent a court from redressing this inequality by increasing the benefits payable to appellee, we have never suggested that the injuries caused by a constitutionally underinclusive scheme can be remedied only by extending the program's benefits to the excluded class." Thus, denial of benefits to everyone, not merely grant of benefits to all, would be a sufficient redress to satisfy the Warth requirement.

APPLYING AND ELABORATING THE WARTH v. SELDIN APPROACH TO STANDING

1. *Simon and the "injury in fact" requirement.* A year after Warth, the Court relied on it to reject another challenge by the poor to a governmental activity. SIMON v. EASTERN KY. WELFARE RIGHTS ORGANIZATION, 426 U.S. 26 (1976).[1] Justice POWELL's majority opinion emphasized—if anything, more strongly than in Warth—that there *were* minimal Art. III standing requirements beyond the control of Congress. The suit, brought by several indigents and organizations representing indigent interests, challenged an IRS Revenue Ruling granting favorable tax treatment to certain nonprofit hospitals which limited their aid to indigents to emergency room services. The plaintiffs sued the Secretary of the Treasury under § 10 of the Administrative Procedure Act, claiming that the new Revenue Ruling violated the IRC by reducing the amount of services hospitals had to render to indigents to qualify for favorable tax status as "charitable" corporations. (An earlier Ruling had required service to indigents to the extent of the hospitals' financial ability; under the new Ruling, emergency aid could be sufficient to qualify.) The plaintiffs alleged that the new Ruling "encourage[d]" hospitals to deny service to indigents.

Justice Powell concluded that the plaintiffs' allegations "failed to establish their standing to sue." Drawing on Warth, he stated: "[W]hen a plaintiff's standing is brought into issue, the relevant inquiry is whether, assuming justiciability of the claim, the plaintiff has shown an injury to himself that is likely to be redressed by a favorable decision." And that burden was not reduced by the fact that here, unlike Warth, the plaintiff relied on a congressional standing provision [2]—§ 10 of the APA, which gives a right to judicial review to any person "adversely affected or aggrieved by agency action." Though the "injury-in-fact" requirement in § 10 suits had been reduced over the years, it—and the showing of causal relationship between defendant's actions and plaintiff's injury—had not been eliminated: "The necessity that the plaintiff who seeks to invoke judicial power stand to profit in some personal interest remains an Art. III requirement." Justice Powell's examination of the complaint in light of those criteria quickly disposed of the organizational plaintiffs: as organizations, their concerns were merely "abstract" and could not "substitute for the concrete injury required by Art. III." Turning to the allegations of injury to indigent individuals, he recognized that they had "suffered injury" to their interest in access to hospital services "[i]n one sense." But this was "insufficient by itself to establish a case or controversy in the context of this suit, for no hospital is a defendant"; only Treasury Department officials had been sued. And Art. III required "that a federal court act only to redress injury that fairly [could] be traced to the challenged action of the defendant, and not injury that result[ed] from the independent action of some third party not before the court." Here, the allegation that the new Revenue Ruling had "encouraged" hospitals to deny services to indigents was inadequate: "It is purely speculative whether the denials of service specified in the complaint fairly can be traced to

1. Recall, however, the 1977 decision in Arlington Heights, in the preceding footnote.

2. Elsewhere in the opinion, Justice Powell recalled the reference in Linda R.S. v. Richard D. (p. 1560 above) to the "requirement that, *at least in the absence of a statute expressly conferring standing,* federal plaintiffs must allege some threatened or actual injury resulting from the putatively illegal action." (Emphasis added.) According to Justice Powell, that reference to "a statute expressly conferring standing" was "in recognition of Congress' power to create new interests the invasion of which will confer standing." But he added: "When Congress has so acted, the requirements of Art. III remain: 'the plaintiff still must allege a distinct and palpable injury to himself, even if it is an injury shared by a large class of other possible litigants.' [Warth v. Seldin.]" Note the reply to this emphasis on the limited congressional capacity to confer standing, in Justice Brennan's opinion below.

[IRS] 'encouragement' or instead result from decisions made by the hospitals without regard to the tax implications." [3]

Justice BRENNAN's opinion, joined by Justice Marshall, concurred in the result on the ground that there "simply [was] no ripe controversy" here (see sec. 3, below), but strongly disagreed with Justice Powell's opinion: he insisted that the Court had "abjure[d] analysis either of the Art. III policies heretofore assumed to inhere in the constitutional dimension of the standing doctrine, or of the relevant precedents of this Court." He argued that the majority had misapplied the injury-in-fact standing requirement. In his view, the plaintiffs' basic claim was that the IRC required the government to offer economic inducements to the relevant hospitals only under conditions which were likely to benefit the poor; and under that claim, the relevant injury was to the interest in the "opportunity and ability" to receive medical services. That injury adequately established the Art. III "personal stake" minimum. He added: "Nothing in the logic or policy of constitutionally required standing is added by the further injury-in-fact dimension required by the Court today—that [plaintiffs] allege that the hospitals affecting them would not have elected to forego the favorable tax treatment and that this would 'result in the availability to [plaintiffs] of' free or below cost medical services." Justice Brennan emphasized that the action had been brought under the judicial review provision of the APA and added: "Any prudential, nonconstitutional considerations that underlay the Court's disposition of the injury-in-fact standing requirement in cases such as [Linda R.S.] and [Warth] are simply inapposite when review is sought under a congressionally enacted statute conferring [standing]." The concluding part of his opinion is of special interest, for it challenged the majority's suggestions about Congress' limited capacity to confer standing. He stated: "[T]he most disturbing aspect of today's opinion is the Court's insistence on resting its decision regarding standing squarely on the irreducible Art. III minimum injury in fact, thereby effectively placing its holding beyond congressional power to rectify. Thus, any time Congress chooses to legislate in favor of certain interests by setting up a scheme of incentives for third parties, judicial review of administrative action that allegedly frustrates the congressionally intended objective will be denied, because any complainant will be required to make an almost impossible showing."

2. *Duke Power: A more generous view of standing? A principled view, consistent with the precedents?* Consider, in light of the modern decisions tightening (and constitutionalizing) standing criteria, the majority's finding of standing in DUKE POWER CO. v. CAROLINA ENV. STUDY GROUP, 438 U.S. 59 (1978). The central claim in Duke Power was that the Price-Anderson Act violated due process by limiting aggregate liability for a single nuclear power plant accident to $560 million. The argument was that the provision, in part designed to encourage the development of nuclear energy through federally licensed private companies, was unconstitutional because it did not assure

---

3. Justice Powell summarized his approach by concluding as follows: "The principle of Linda R.S. and Warth controls this case. As stated in Warth, that principle is that indirectness of injury, while not necessarily fatal to standing, 'may make it substantially more difficult to meet the minimum requirement of Art. III: to establish that, in fact, the asserted injury was the consequence of the defendants' actions, or that prospective relief will remove the harm.' [Plaintiffs] have failed to carry this burden. Speculative inferences are necessary to connect their injury to the challenged actions of [the defendants]. Moreover, the complaint suggests no

substantial likelihood that victory in this suit would result in [plaintiffs] receiving the hospital treatment they desire. A federal court, properly cognizant of the Art. III limitation upon its jurisdiction, must require more than [plaintiffs] have shown before proceeding to the merits."

A separate notation by Justice STEWART concurred in Justice Powell's opinion with the added comment "that I cannot now imagine a case, at least outside the First Amendment area, where a person whose own tax liability was not affected ever could have standing to litigate the federal tax liability of someone else."

adequate compensation to potential victims of nuclear power plant accidents.[4] The most difficult issue was whether the plaintiffs—40 individuals who lived near the planned power plants, an environmental group and a labor organization—had standing to seek a declaration that the Act was unconstitutional. The immediate injuries asserted pertained largely to environmental and aesthetic consequences stemming from the power plants. The majority nevertheless found standing to challenge the constitutionality of the limitation of liability provision.

Chief Justice BURGER's majority opinion stated that, as a result of "subsequent reformulation," the "personal stake in the outcome" requirement of Baker v. Carr had "come to be understood to require not only a 'distinct and palpable injury' to the plaintiff [Warth], but also a 'fairly traceable' causal connection between the claimed injury and the challenged conduct. [Arlington Heights; Simon; Linda R.S.]" The Chief Justice found these "constitutional standards" satisfied here. With respect to the plaintiffs' "injury," Chief Justice Burger stated: "It is enough that several of the 'immediate' adverse effects were found to harm appellees. Certainly the environmental and aesthetic consequences of the thermal pollution of the two lakes in the vicinity of the disputed power plants is the type of harmful effect which has been deemed adequate in prior cases to satisfy the 'injury in fact' standard. And the emission of non-natural radiation into appellees' environment would also seem a direct and present [injury]."

The Chief Justice continued: "The more difficult step in the standing inquiry is establishing that these injuries 'fairly can be traced to the challenged action of the defendant' [Simon], or put otherwise, that the exercise of the Court's remedial powers would redress the claimed injuries. The District Court discerned a 'but for' causal connection between the Price-Anderson Act 'and the construction of the nuclear plants which the [appellees] view as a threat to them.' [It] concluded that 'there is a substantial likelihood that Duke would not be able to complete the construction and maintain the operation of [the nuclear plants here] but for the protection provided by the Price-Anderson Act.'" After accepting these "but for" causal links, the Chief Justice added: "It is further contended that in addition to proof of injury and of a causal link between such injury and the challenged conduct, appellees must demonstrate a connection between the injuries they claim and the constitutional rights being asserted. This nexus requirement is said to find its origin in [Flast]. Since the environmental and health injuries claimed by appellees are not directly related to the constitutional attack on the Price-Anderson Act, such injuries, the argument continues, cannot supply a predicate for standing. We decline to accept this argument. The major difficulty with [it] is that it implicitly assumes that the nexus requirement formulated in the context of taxpayers suits has general applicability in suits of all other types brought in the federal courts. [We] cannot accept the contention that, outside the context of taxpayers suits, a litigant must demonstrate anything more than injury in fact and a substantial likelihood that the judicial relief requested will prevent or redress the claimed injury to satisfy the 'case and controversy' requirement of Art. III.

"Our prior cases have, however, acknowledged [other limits on standing], which derive from general prudential concerns. [Thus], we have declined to grant standing where the harm asserted amounts only to a generalized grievance shared by a large number of citizens in a substantially equal measure. See Richardson. We have also narrowly limited the circumstances in which one

---

4. Most of the Court's opinion was devoted to the jurisdictional issues. When it reached the merits, it rejected the constitutional attack after describing the liability limitation provision as a "classic example of an economic regulation" and applying deferential standards of economic due process review.

party will be given standing to assert the legal rights of another. Warth. This limitation on third party standing [see p. 1574 below] arguably suggests a connection between the claimed injury and the right asserted bearing some resemblance to the nexus requirement now urged upon us. There are good and sufficient reasons for this prudential limitation on standing when rights of third parties are implicated. [We] do not, however, find these reasons a satisfactory predicate for applying this limitation or a similar nexus requirement to all cases as a matter of course. Where a party champions his own rights, and where the injury alleged is a concrete and particularized one which will be prevented or redressed by the relief requested, the basic practical and prudential concerns underlying the standing doctrine are generally satisfied when the constitutional requisites are met. See, e.g., [Arlington Heights]. We conclude that appellees have [standing]." [5]

3. *The continuing vigor of the causation requirement.* Although Duke Power seemed to foreshadow a slightly less rigorous application of the causation requirement of Warth, failure to prove causation was central to the Court's denial of standing in ALLEN v. WRIGHT, 468 U.S. ___ (1984). The plaintiffs had claimed that the Internal Revenue Service had "not adopted sufficient standards and procedures to fulfill its obligation to deny tax-exempt status to racially discriminatory private schools," thus effectively providing subsidies to unlawful and unconstitutional segregation. Granting of such tax exemptions was alleged to violate various provisions of the Internal Revenue Code as well as the Constitution. The plaintiffs were parents of black public school children then attending school in districts that were in the process of being desegregated; allegedly racially discriminatory private schools receiving tax exemptions were located in there districts.

The parents alleged two different injuries as the basis for their claim of standing, but both were rejected in Justice O'CONNOR's opinion for the Court. The first was that they were, as blacks, stigmatized by the granting of tax exemptions to racially discriminatory schools. Although acknowledging that the stigma was undoubtedly real, Justice O'Connor refused to find an "abstract stigmatic injury" sufficient to overcome what she saw as still a general claim to have the government act in accordance with law. Relying on Valley Forge, Schlesinger, and Richardson, she noted that "the law of Art. III standing is built on a single basic idea—the idea of separation of powers." Separation of powers prevented the courts from enforcing generalized claims to have the government act in certain ways. The Court treated more seriously the plaintiffs' second claimed injury. Here the parents claimed a personal injury in terms of denial of their right to have their children attend a desegregated school. They claimed that the granting of tax-exempt status to racially discriminatory private schools helped to support those schools and to encourage parents to send their children to those schools. This in turn provided a subsidized alternative to desegregated public schools, and consequently made the task of desegregating the public schools more difficult.

The Court readily accepted as judicially cognizable the asserted injury of the plaintiffs' "children's diminished ability to receive an education in a racially

---

5. Justice STEWART's dissent argued that there was a lack of the "direct relationship between the plaintiff's federal claim and the injury" to warrant standing under cases such as Arlington Heights and Linda R.S. Justice STEVENS' opinion found the "string of contingencies" involved in the claim too "delicate" to satisfy the causation requirement. He noted: "The Court's [decision] will serve the national interest in removing doubts concerning the constitutionality of the [Act]." He argued that, although the Court's "statesmanship" in providing an advisory opinion might make sense as a matter of policy, "[we] are not statesmen; we are judges. [Whenever] we are persuaded by reasons of expediency to engage in the business of giving legal advice, we chip away a part of the foundation of our independence and our strength." Another separate opinion, by Justice REHNQUIST, joined by Justice Stevens, insisted that the Court lacked statutory jurisdiction as well.

integrated school." But this was found insufficient, "because the injury alleged is not fairly traceable to the Government conduct respondents challenge as unlawful." "The diminished ability of respondents' children to receive a desegregated education would be fairly traceable to unlawful IRS grants of tax exemptions only if there were enough racially discriminatory private schools receiving tax exemptions in respondents' communities for withdrawal of these exemptions to make an appreciable difference in public-school integration. Respondents have made no such allegation. It is, first, uncertain how many racially discriminatory private schools are in fact receiving tax exemptions. Moreover, it is entirely speculative [whether] withdrawal of a tax exemption from any particular school would lead the school to change its policies. It is just as speculative whether any given parent of a child attending such a private school would decide to transfer the child to public school as a result of any changes in educational or financial policy made by the private school once it was threatened with loss of tax-exempt status. It is also pure speculation whether, in a particular community, a large enough number of the numerous relevant school officials and parents would reach decisions that collectively would have a significant impact on the racial composition of the public schools." Thus, relying on Warth and Simon, and again referring to the principle of separation of powers, Justice O'Connor found that "the links in the chain of causation between the challenged Government conduct and the asserted injury [far] too weak for the chain as a whole to sustain respondents' standing."

Justice Marshall took no part in the decision of the case, but Justice BRENNAN dissented, as did Justice STEVENS, joined by Justice Blackmun. Both dissents angrily accused the majority of using the standing determination as a reflection of the Court's view of the merits. Justice Brennan noted that "the causation component of the Court's standing inquiry is no more than a poor disguise for the Court's view of the merits of the underlying claims." Justice Stevens, in addition to arguing that the chain of causation was considerably stronger than the majority concluded, questioned the utility of the majority's reliance on the concept of separation of powers: "That approach confuses the standing doctrine with the justiciability of the issues that [plaintiffs] seek to raise. The purpose of the standing inquiry is to measure the plaintiff's stake in the outcome, not whether a court has the authority to provide it with the outcome it [seeks]. The strength of the plaintiff's interest in the outcome has nothing to do with whether the relief it seeks would intrude upon the prerogatives of other branches of government; the possibility that the relief might be inappropriate does not lessen the plaintiff's stake in obtaining [that relief]. In short, I would deal with the questions of the legal limitations on the IRS' enforcement discretion on its merits, rather than by making the untenable assumption that the granting of preferential tax treatment to segregated schools does not make those schools more attractive to white students and hence does not inhibit the process of desegregation." [6]

---

6. In view of the focus in Warth on the relationship between the particular plaintiff and the type of relief sought, what type of inquiry is appropriate when a plaintiff claims several different forms of relief? In a case involving the victim of an allegedly unconstitutional police "chokehold," the Court indicated that separate inquiries must be conducted, and on that basis denied standing to claim injunctive relief although it was plain that there was standing to bring an action for damages. Los Angeles v. Lyons (1983; p. 1587 below).

C. THE INGREDIENTS OF STANDING: THE COURT'S ROLE, CONSTITUTIONAL CRITERIA, AND CONGRESSIONAL POWER

Introduction. Consider, in light of the preceding cases: To what extent are the standing barriers compelled by Art. III? To what extent are they judicially created, prudential overlays that Congress may strip away? Most of the cases above involved situations where Congress had not specifically sought to grant standing to the plaintiff. Are the Court's criteria governing access in that context coherent? Are they responsive to the policies that standing doctrines purport to promote? To what extent, if any, do these policies justify judicial invalidation of congressional acts granting access to courts in situations where the Court would not, on its own, find standing to sue?

1. *The Court's criteria.* The criteria most frequently reiterated by the modern Court—e.g., "injury in fact," "nexus," and "causation"—often purport to rest on the need to assure a sufficiently concrete record and sufficient adverseness, to aid informed decision of constitutional issues. Do the criteria truly promote these optimum conditions for constitutional adjudication? Are standing rules the proper vehicles for assuring adequate concreteness? Would the need for an adequate record be better met by emphasizing rules as to ripeness (sec. 3 below) rather than standing? To what extent do the modern standing criteria stem from a quite different consideration: Court concerns about excessive judicial involvement in governmental operations and about risks of confrontation with other branches? Are standing rules appropriate and legitimate expressions of *these* concerns? Or should these concerns more often be treated as "political question" problems of justiciability (see sec. 5 below)? In situations where Congress has not granted standing by statute, is the Court's control over remedies sufficiently comprehensive to justify denials of standing simply because of institutional fear of excessive engagement in substantive constitutional decisionmaking? Is there a similar breadth of judicial authority to deny standing (based on institutional considerations of self-restraint) even in the face of an explicit congressional grant of standing?

Should the Court be more generous than it has been in authorizing "public actions" by "private attorneys general," in citizens' and taxpayers' cases? Or would such grants of standing bring the Court too close to being the Council of Revision rejected at the Constitutional Convention? Is it realistic to speak of "personal" "injuries in fact" in cases such as Flast and SCRAP? Or are those decisions more realistically viewed as recognitions of "public actions"? Why should not a concerned citizen's or interest group's outrage at allegedly unconstitutional behavior qualify as injury sufficient for standing? Is it a less significant injury (in terms of the purposes the standing doctrines purport to serve with regard to assuring adequate records and adverseness) than the economic and noneconomic injuries the Court has already recognized as adequate for standing?[1]

---

1. See Jaffe, "Standing to Secure Judicial Review: Private Actions," 75 Harv.L.Rev. 255 (1961): "I find it difficult to accept the conclusion [that] an issue in every other respect apt for judicial determination should be nonjusticiable because there is no possibility of a conventional plaintiff—an issue in short in which everyone has a legitimate interest but only as a citizen." See also the same author's "The Citizen as Litigant in Public Actions: The Non-Hohfeldian or Ideological Plaintiff," 116 U.Pa.L.Rev. 1033 (1968), arguing that, "insofar as the argument for a traditional plaintiff runs in terms of the need for effective advocacy, the argument is not persuasive," since an ideological plaintiff willing to bear the costs of a lawsuit demonstrates "a quite exceptional kind of interest." But see Bickel, "Foreword: The Passive Virtues," 75 Harv.L. Rev. 40 (1961).

2. *Congress and standing rules.* Are there substantial Art. III barriers to congressional expansion of plaintiffs' access to federal courts? Recall that Justice Harlan in Flast and Justice Powell in Richardson, while urging the *Court* to be reluctant to grant standing as its own, advocated a generous stance toward *congressional* grants of remedies. Yet, later opinions—including Warth v. Seldin, Simon, and Valley Forge College—suggest an increased emphasis on the constitutional ingredients in standing rules and accordingly evidence a greater reluctance to permit Congress to expand access to courts. Is that reluctance justified? By the need for adverseness and an adequate record? By considerations of judicial self-restraint? Are judicial self-restraint considerations legitimate barriers to standing where Congress has asked the courts to resolve disputes? If Congress authorized "any taxpayer" or "any citizen" to bring suit against allegedly unconstitutional action, would that be tantamount to directing advisory opinions in violation of Art. III? [2]

What congressional power can justify congressional expansion of standing? Does the congressional power turn solely on any legislative control under Art. III over the law of remedies and the use of the federal courts? To what extent do sources outside of Art. III justify congressional lowerings of standing barriers? Consider especially Justice White's concurrence, joined by Justice Blackmun and Powell, in TRAFFICANTE v. METROPOLITAN LIFE INS. CO., 409 U.S. 205 (1972). In that case, the majority gave a "generous construction" to the standing requirements under the fair housing provisions of the Civil Rights Act of 1968. Justice DOUGLAS' opinion found that Congress had intended to define standing "as broadly as is permitted by Article III" and noted: "The role of 'private attorneys general' is not uncommon in modern legislative programs." But Justice WHITE's brief concurrence took a different route. If there were no statute, he explained, "I would have great difficulty in concluding that petitioners' complaint in this case presented a case or controversy" under Art. III. But the statute overcame his Art. III concerns: with the Civil Rights Act "purporting to give all those who are authorized to complain to the agency the right also to sue in court, I would sustain the statute insofar as it extends standing to those in the position of the petitioners." He added a significant citation: "Cf. Katzenbach v. Morgan; Oregon v. Mitchell." Is the controversial congressional power under the Katzenbach v. Morgan interpretation of § 5 of the 14th Amendment sufficient to overcome Art. III limitations? Recall the discussions of the Morgan problem in chap. 10, sec. 4, above. Rather than invoking Katzenbach v. Morgan, should the Trafficante issue more properly be viewed as one presenting no genuine Art. III difficulty? [3]

---

2. Compare a comment by Justice Stewart in his majority opinion in Sierra Club, p. 1549 above: "Congress may not confer jurisdiction on Art. III federal courts to render advisory opinions [or] to entertain 'friendly' suits [or] to resolve 'political questions' [because] suits of this character are inconsistent with the judicial function under Art. III. But where a dispute is otherwise justiciable, the question whether the litigant is a 'proper party to request an adjudication of a particular issue' is one within the power of Congress to determine." Have the more recent cases retreated from that broad view of congressional authority regarding standing?

3. For another source of tension between Court and Congress regarding the allocation of responsibility for creating rights of action, recall a number of modern cases in which a divided Court has implied private remedies without ex-

plicit congressional authorization, either under the Constitution directly or under federal laws. For an example of the former, note Davis v. Passman, 442 U.S. 228 (1979), where Justice Brennan's majority opinion implied a cause of action and a damage remedy directly from the Fifth Amendment for a sex discrimination suit by a former staff employee against her employer, a Congressman. In a strong dissent, Justice Powell, joined by Chief Justice Burger and Justice Rehnquist, argued that respect for other branches required a federal court "to stay its hand" rather than imply a right of action under the Constitution. The practice of implying remedies directly from the Constitution began with Bivens v. Six Unknown Named Agents, 403 U.S. 388 (1971) (Fourth Amendment violations). In Carlson v. Green, 446 U.S. 14 (1980), which implied a remedy from the Eighth Amendment, Justice

D. ADDITIONAL PROBLEMS: ASSERTING THE RIGHTS OF OTHERS; STATE STANDING RULES AND SUPREME COURT REVIEW; MOOTNESS

1. *Asserting the rights of third parties.* In the preceding materials, the recurrent problem is whether a potential litigant has a sufficiently individualized interest to justify access to court. This note deals with a quite different standing issue: here, the litigants' access to court to assert their own personal interests is clear; the question is whether the litigants may assert *the interests of others* as well as their own. The general rule, as frequently stated by the Court, is that "one may not claim standing [to] vindicate the constitutional rights of some third party"; but "the Court has created numerous exceptions which lack a coherent pattern and leave the significance of the rule in doubt." [1] In its numerous confrontations with the problem, the Court has identified three factors as important in justifying the wide-ranging exceptions to the barrier against raising the rights of third parties: "the presence of some substantial relationship between the claimant, and the third parties"; the impossibility of the third party rightholders "asserting their own constitutional rights"; and "the risk that the rights of third parties will be diluted" unless the party in court is allowed to assert their rights. Consider the role of those factors in the illustrative cases noted below. Consider as well the suggestion that the last of these factors should be the critical one—that emphasis on it would create more "coherent doctrine" out of the present "patchwork of exceptions." That suggestion

Brennan's majority opinion stated the general approach as follows: "Bivens established that the victims of a constitutional violation [have] a right to recover damages. [Such] a cause of action may be defeated [in] two situations. The first is when defendants demonstrate 'special factors counselling hesitation in the absence of affirmative action by Congress.' [The second is] when defendants show that Congress has provided an alternative remedy which it explicitly declared to be a *substitute* for recovery directly under the Constitution and viewed as equally effective."

In two modern cases, a unanimous Court found that "special factors counselling hesitation" were present and thus refused to imply private remedies directly from the Constitution. In Chappell v. Wallace, 462 U.S. 296 (1983), these factors consisted of the special nature of the military, and its distinct and parallel system of justice, causing the Court, in an opinion written by Chief Justice Burger, to refuse to allow military personnel to sue their superior officers for damages for alleged constitutional violations. And in Bush v. Lucas, 462 U.S. 367 (1983), Justice Stevens wrote for the Court in refusing to imply a damages remedy directly from the Constitution for a federal civil service employee who alleged that he had been demoted in retaliation for exercising his First Amendment rights. Relying heavily on the existence of the elaborate federal civil service system, Justice Stevens concluded that deference to Congress in light of this system once again counselled hesitation.

Even more commonly, there have been dissenting objections to majority implications of private

rights of action from congressional acts. See, e.g., Cannon v. University of Chicago, 441 U.S. 677 (1979), implying a private right of action for violation of Title IX of the Education Amendments of 1972. Title IX, which does not expressly authorize a private remedy, bars sex discrimination in federally funded programs. Justice Stevens' majority opinion relied on modern decisions congenial to implied private remedies for statutory rights. (See Cort v. Ash, 422 U.S. 66 (1975); note also Justice Stevens' opinion in Bakke, chap. 9 above.) Justice Powell's extensive dissent objected to the modern tendency to imply private rights of action, insisting that the Court's "mode of analysis" could not be "squared with the doctrine of the separation of powers." He added: "[We] should not condone the implication of any private action from a federal statute absent the most compelling evidence that Congress in fact intended such an action to exist." (For a recent revival of Justice Powell's separation of powers objections to the majority's modern tendency to imply private rights of action from congressional acts, see Merrill Lynch, Pierce, Fenner & Smith v. Curran, 456 U.S. 353 (1982).)

1. See Note, "Standing to Assert Constitutional Jus Tertii," 88 Harv.L.Rev. 423 (1974), an especially thoughtful effort to provide greater coherence in this area. The quoted passages in this paragraph are from that Note. (See also Sedler, "Standing to Assert Constitutional Jus Tertii in the Supreme Court," 71 Yale L.J. 599 (1962), and Hart & Wechsler, Federal Courts (2d ed. 1973), chap. 2, sec. 5.)

advocates a "practice of permitting claimants to assert *jus tertii* when the injury of which they complain also deprives third parties of constitutional rights."

In Pierce v. Society of Sisters, (1925; chap. 14 above), where a parochial school challenged the constitutionality of a statute requiring parents to send children to public schools, the school was permitted to assert the rights of the parents in defending its own property rights. And in NAACP v. Alabama (1958; chap. 13 above), the NAACP—in resisting a state order to disclose its membership lists—was permitted to assert the rights of its members. The Court stated that the Association "argues more appropriately the rights of its members [and] its nexus with them is sufficient to permit that it act as their representative before this Court." [2] Recall also Griswold v. Connecticut, 381 U.S. 479 (1965; chap. 8 above) where the appellants, who had given birth control information at a clinic (and were convicted as accessories to a violation of the contraceptives use ban) were permitted to raise the interests of users: "We think that appellants have standing to raise the constitutional rights of the married people with whom they had a professional relationship." [3]

Similarly, there are exceptions to the usual rule that one must be a member of the class discriminated against in order to have standing to attack a law as denying equal protection. Thus, Truax v. Raich, 239 U.S. 33 (1915), permitted an alien employee to enjoin the enforcement of a statute limiting the percentage of aliens on the employer's work force: the employee was permitted to raise the rights of the employer. And in BARROWS v. JACKSON (1953; chap. 10 above), a defendant in a state court damage suit for breach of a racially restrictive covenant was permitted to challenge the enforcement of the covenant although he was not a member of the class discriminated against. Justice MINTON's majority opinion in Barrows emphasized that the Art. III requirements at the core of the law of standing were encased in discretionary, prudential considerations: "The requirement of standing is often used to describe the constitutional limitation on the jurisdiction of this Court to 'cases' and 'controversies.' Apart from the jurisdictional requirement, this Court has developed a complementary rule of self-restraint for its own governance (not always clearly distinguished from the constitutional limitation) which ordinarily precludes a person from challenging the constitutionality of state action by invoking the rights of others. There are still other cases in which the Court has held that even though a party will suffer a direct, substantial injury from application of a statute, he cannot challenge its constitutionality unless he can show that he is within the class whose constitutional rights are allegedly infringed." That was "salutary" as a general rule, but in this case "it would be difficult if not impossible for the persons whose rights are asserted to present their grievance before any court." Under these "peculiar circumstances," accordingly, "we believe the reasons which underlie our rule denying standing to raise another's rights, which is only a rule of practice, are outweighed by the need to protect the fundamental rights which would be denied by permitting the damages actions to be maintained." [4]

---

2. But see Tileston v. Ullman (1943; p. 1577 below), where standing to assert the rights of others was denied. Note the questions raised about that decision below. See also McGowan v. Maryland (1961; chap. 14 above), where store employees prosecuted for violating a Sunday Closing Law were permitted to raise only "establishment" and not "free exercise" claims under the religion clauses of the First Amendment, since they did not allege any infringement of their own religious freedom.

3. Note also the refusal to find standing barriers in a subsequent challenge to contraception

laws, Eisenstadt v. Baird, 405 U.S. 438 (1972; chap. 8 above).

4. Justice Minton added: "The relation between the coercion exerted on respondent [the white seller who had sold property to a black buyer in violation of the covenant] and a possible pecuniary loss thereby is so close to the purpose of the restrictive covenant, to violate the constitutional rights of those discriminated against, that respondent is the only effective adversary of the unworthy covenant in its last stand."

The increasingly generous view of standing to assert the rights of others persists on the Burger Court.[5] An example is SINGLETON v. WULFF, 428 U.S. 106 (1976), one of the post-Roe v. Wade abortion cases. The Court endorsed the rights of physicians injured in fact by a statute to assert the rights of their patients as well. Justice BLACKMUN's plurality opinion approved standing to assert the rights of third parties in situations where (a) the plaintiff has a close relationship to those whose rights are sought to be asserted, and (b) where the third party confronts "some genuine obstacle" in asserting his or her own rights. Justice POWELL's partial dissent, joined by Chief Justice Burger and Justices Stewart and Rehnquist, thought the "some genuine obstacle" criterion too loose and feared that it might make the federal courts a "roving commission." He insisted that cases such as Barrows, NAACP, and Eisenstadt required more than "some obstacle" to the third party; he argued that a litigant could assert the rights of others only when litigation by the third parties was "in all practicable terms impossible." [Note also the modern cases in which vendors were permitted to assert the rights of their customers. See, e.g., Craig v. Boren (1976; chap. 9 above; sex discrimination in beer sales) and Carey v. Population Services Int'l (1977; chap. 10 above; restrictions on the distribution of contraceptives).][6]

2. *Standing to sue in state courts and Court review.* State courts are not merely authorized but compelled to adjudicate federal constitutional questions in appropriate cases. But states have considerable autonomy with respect to the operation of their judicial systems. Ordinarily, then, questions of standing to sue in state courts are questions of state law; and state rules regarding access to state courts may and frequently do differ from federal court standing rules. But what if Court review is sought in a case in which a plaintiff has gained access to state courts under more lenient standing rules than the federal ones? Do the federal standing rules considered in the preceding materials govern? May or must the Court refuse review in such a case? Or is the Court bound to adjudicate such a case?

As noted earlier, some states authorize their courts to issue advisory opinions. Presumably, the Court could not review such a case: it cannot exercise power beyond the limits of the Art. III case and controversy requirement. But consider a more common situation, presented in the Doremus case in 1952—a state court action by a state taxpayer challenging a state's funding program on establishment clause grounds, during the period before Flast v. Cohen, at a time when federal taxpayers lacked standing. During that period, the Court repeatedly decided the merits in municipal taxpayers' suits challenging local action without even discussing the standing issue. See, e.g., Everson (1947; chap. 14 above). But in DOREMUS v. BOARD OF EDUC., 342 U.S. 429 (1952), the Court dismissed an appeal from a state court decision which had rejected on the

---

5. Note, however, Chief Justice Burger's majority opinion in H.L. v. Matheson (1981; chap. 8 above), refusing to grant standing to a minor to raise an on-the-face overbreadth attack on a state law requiring physicians to notify parents before performing abortions on minors. The appellants sought to challenge the application of the law to *all* unmarried minors, including mature and emancipated ones, even though she was a dependent minor who did not claim that she was mature. (Recall also the discussion in the 1975 decision in Warth v. Seldin, p. 1559 above.)

6. Note also the somewhat related problem pertaining to the ability of a criminal defendant to attack the constitutionality of severable provisions of a criminal statute—provisions not being applied to the defendant. See United States v.

Raines, 362 U.S. 17 (1960), where Justice Brennan's majority opinion applied the general rule that "one to whom application of a statute is constitutional will not be heard to attack the statute on the ground that impliedly it might be taken as applying to other persons or other situations in which its application might be unconstitutional." He noted, however, that there were "exceptions" to that rule when nonseverable statutes were involved. For example, he indicated that the defendant might challenge the constitutionality of applications of the law to others where the application "would itself have an inhibitory effect on freedom of speech." (Recall the discussion of the Court's First Amendment "overbreadth" doctrine in chap. 12, sec. 1, above.)

merits an attack by taxpayers on the validity of Bible reading in the public schools. Justice JACKSON's majority opinion stated: "We do not undertake to say that a state court may not render an opinion on a federal constitutional question even under such circumstances that it can be regarded only as advisory. But, because our own jurisdiction is cast in terms of 'case or controversy,' we cannot accept as the basis for review, nor as the basis for conclusive disposition of an issue of federal law without review, any procedure which does not constitute such. The taxpayer's action can meet this test, but only when it is a good-faith pocketbook action. It is apparent that the grievance which it is sought to litigate here is not a direct dollars-and-cents injury but is a religious difference." Justice DOUGLAS, joined by Justices Reed and Burton, dissented: "If this were a suit to enjoin a federal law, it could not be maintained by reason of [Frothingham]. But New Jersey can fashion her own rules governing the institution of suits in her courts. If she wants to give these taxpayers the status to sue, [I] see nothing in the Constitution to prevent it. And where the clash of interests is as real and as strong as it is here, it is odd indeed to hold there is no case or controversy within the meaning of [Art. III]."

Were the majority's Art. III doubts justified? Was not Justice Douglas' response persuasive? And if there was no Art. III barrier, was there any justification for the Court's dismissal of a case within its obligatory appeal jurisdiction? Nevertheless, there have been frequent statements by Justices suggesting that state grants of standing may not be binding for review purposes, even where there is no statutory or constitutional barrier to Supreme Court review. Note Justice Frankfurter's comment in Coleman v. Miller (1939; p. 1610 below): "[T]he creation of a vast domain of legal interests is in the keeping of the states, and from time to time state courts and legislators give legal protection to new individual interests. [But] it by no means follows that a state court ruling on the adequacy of legal interest is binding here." Why not, if Art. III and the jurisdictional statute are satisfied? What if the state courts in Doremus had decided for the plaintiffs? Would the Court have adhered to its position on standing? Would it have entered orders dismissing the appeals— and left intact the state injunctions based on federal substantive law?[7]

Note the related problems raised by TILESTON v. ULLMAN, 318 U.S. 44 (1943), an early, unsuccessful effort to challenge the Connecticut ban on the use of contraceptives. Tileston was a state declaratory judgment action by a doctor alleging that the law would prevent his giving professional advice to three patients whose lives would be endangered by child-bearing. The state court reached the merits and held the law constitutional. The Court dismissed the appeal: "We are of the opinion that the proceedings in the state courts present no constitutional question which appellant has standing to assert. The sole constitutional attack upon the statutes under the 14th Amendment is confined to their deprivation of life—obviously not appellant's but his patients'. [The] patients are not parties to this proceeding and there is no basis on which we can say that he has standing to secure an adjudication of his patients' constitutional right to life, which they do not assert in their own behalf. No question is raised in the record with respect to the deprivation of appellant's liberty or property." The Court concluded "that appellant has no standing to litigate the constitution-

---

7. Should the question of standing to raise federal issues in state courts be considered one of federal law? Note Professor Freund's comment on Doremus, in Supreme Court and Supreme Law (Cahn ed., 1954), 35: "I think it is a needed change to make standing to raise a federal constitutional question itself a federal question, so that it will be decided uniformly throughout the country. I disagree with the Doremus case in so far as it lets the state judgment stand and merely declines to review it. It seems to me that the Court should have [vacated the state court decree] so that it would not be a precedent even in the state court." What, if any, constitutional justification is there for an approach such as that? (Recall in this connection the materials in chap. 1 above, on adequate state grounds and Court review.)

al question which the record presents"; and the Court therefore found it "unnecessary to consider whether the record shows the existence of a genuine case or controversy."[8] If there was no Art. III difficulty, what justified the Court's dismissal? Is there any source of Court discretion to decline adjudication in a case in which the state court decided the merits?[9] If the question of standing "is the question whether the litigant has a sufficient personal interest in getting the relief he seeks, or is a sufficiently appropriate representative of other interested persons," and if, "[s]o viewed, the question becomes inextricably bound up with the law of rights and remedies"—in short, if the Tileston variety of standing question is "one of remedy"[10]—why should not the Court bow to the state court's recognition of the physician's representative or fiduciary capacity to raise the interests of his patients?

3. *Mootness.* The mootness barrier to constitutional adjudication is related to the previously considered problems of standing and advisory opinions. The mootness cases involve litigants who clearly had standing to sue at the outset of the litigation. The problems arise from events occurring after the lawsuit has gotten under way—changes in the facts or in the law—which allegedly deprive the litigant of the necessary stake in the outcome. The mootness doctrine requires that "an actual controversy must be extant at all stages of review, not merely at the time the complaint is filed." The modern Court has repeatedly insisted that the mootness doctrine is an aspect of the Art. III case or controversy requirement. See, e.g., Liner v. Jafco, Inc., 375 U.S. 301 (1964). Yet, despite the supposed constitutional basis of the doctrine, the Court has frequently relaxed the mootness barrier, has found a number of exceptions to it, and has, in many observers' views, applied them erratically. To what extent do the exceptions rest on principled grounds? To what extent are they ad hoc invocations of prudential judgments? Note the attempt to summarize "the different kinds of harm which may prevent a case from being held moot: a continuing harm to the plaintiff;[11] the likelihood of future recurrence of past harm, either to the plaintiff personally or to the group he represents; and the probability that similar cases arising in the future will evade judicial review."[12] To what extent does and should the mootness doctrine serve as a discretionary avoidance device?[13]

For modern examples of erratic relaxations of mootness barriers, contrast the abortion decision, ROE v. WADE (1973; chap. 8 above) with the first preferential admissions case, DeFUNIS v. ODEGAARD (1974; chap. 9 above). In the abortion case, Ms. Roe's suit, brought in 1970, was not decided by the Court until January, 1973. She obviously was no longer pregnant by

---

8. Recall the previous note, on standing to raise the rights of third parties.

9. See also the materials on the Court's discretionary abstention from the exercise of jurisdiction, in sec. 4A below.

10. Hart & Wechsler, Federal Courts (1st ed. 1953), 156, 174.

11. For a common example of "continuing harm to the plaintiff" as barring a finding of mootness, note the growing reluctance to find appeals moot even though a convicted defendant has completed serving his sentence. The Court has reviewed such cases in recent years by finding a broad variety of "collateral consequences" to the conviction. See, e.g., Sibron v. New York, 392 U.S. 40 (1968), and North Carolina v. Rice, 404 U.S. 244 (1971). The Court has relied on "collateral consequences" which involved such disabilities as barriers to voting and to holding public office. Should adverse psychological or economic consequences be sufficient to bar a finding of mootness in such cases?

12. Note, "The Mootness Doctrine in the Supreme Court," 88 Harv.L.Rev. 373, 378 (1974). That Note observes that an appropriate mootness inquiry "should proceed sequentially, beginning with the interests of the plaintiff personally and proceeding to broader group interests."

13. See the Note cited in the preceding footnote, commenting: "The Court may be tempted in borderline cases to opt for holding the case moot when the substantive issues are particularly troublesome and avoidance is therefore especially welcome. [Cf. Justice Brennan's dissent in the DeFunis case, noted in the text.] So broad a consideration of the merits seems to be unwarranted, because it could deprive jurisdictional decisions of any principled content."

then, yet the Court refused to dismiss the case as moot. Justice BLACKMUN explained: "[W]hen, as here, pregnancy is a significant fact in the litigation, the normal 266-day human gestation period is so short that the pregnancy will come to term before the usual appellate process is complete. If that termination makes a case moot, pregnancy litigation seldom will survive much beyond the trial stage, and appellate review will be effectively denied. Our laws should not be that rigid. Pregnancy often comes more than once to the same woman, and in the general population, if man is to survive, it will always be with us. Pregnancy provides a classic justification for a conclusion of non-mootness. It truly could be 'capable of repetition, yet evading review.' " [14] However, the majority did find a mootness barrier in the DeFunis case. DeFunis had challenged a law school minority admissions program as racially discriminatory, but had attended the school while the case was in the courts. The per curiam decision took note of "DeFunis' recent registration for the last quarter of his final law school year, and the Law School's assurance that his registration is fully effective." DeFunis had not brought a class action and the Court did not find in his case the "exceptional situation" of an issue "capable of repetition, yet evading review": "If the admissions procedures of the Law School remain unchanged, there is no reason to suppose that a subsequent case attacking those procedures will not come with relative speed to this Court." Justice BRENNAN, joined by Justices Douglas, White and Marshall, insisted the case was not moot: "Any number of unexpected events—illness, economic necessity, even academic failure—might prevent his graduation at the end of the term." (The majority dismissed this argument as resting on "speculative contingencies.") Moreover, the dissenters thought the dismissal disserved the public interest, since the issues "must inevitably return to the federal courts and ultimately again to this Court."

The majority in DeFunis emphasized that the case had not been brought as a class action. How significant should that factor be? To be sure, mootness challenges have been rejected in a number of cases even though the plaintiff's controversy was no longer live, because the litigant had sued on behalf of a class. See, e.g., Dunn v. Blumstein (1972; chap. 9 above); Ramirez (1974; chap. 9 above). Yet the Court has sometimes accepted jurisdiction even though the interest of the plaintiff had expired and even though the suit had *not* been brought as a class action. Are the results in DeFunis and such voting rights cases as Ramirez nevertheless justifiable? Note the suggestion that in DeFunis "neither the issues of law nor the groups of interested persons were as well defined as in Ramirez." Apart from considering whether a decision on the merits will "obviate the necessity for future repetitious litigation," should the decision on mootness also turn on "whether the area of substantive law which [the Court] is asked to examine is one in which the legislature or the executive is currently [altering] its policy"? Should the Court be more ready to find mootness in situations where an adjudication "might unnecessarily restrict policymaking by the other branches"? [15] Are the usual considerations arguing against advisory opinions relevant to the typical mootness problem? Note that an arguably moot case usually has a concrete record. Does a decision in such a

---

14. The "capable of repetition, yet evading review" exception stems from Southern Pacific Terminal Co. v. ICC, 219 U.S. 498 (1911). But in Southern Pacific, it was the same plaintiff who might be harmed by future action of the defendant. As Roe illustrates, the rule "has come to have independent significance apart from the possible repetition of injury to the particular plaintiff." Note, 88 Harv.L.Rev. 373, 386 (1974).

For an elaboration of the Southern Pacific exception to the mootness doctrine, see Illinois State Bd. of Elections v. Socialist Workers Party, 440 U.S. 173 (1979), relying on Weinstein v. Bradford, 423 U.S. 147, 149 (1975), for the statement that a case is not moot when "(1) the challenged action was in its duration too short to be fully litigated prior to its cessation or expiration, and (2) there was a reasonable expectation that the same complaining party would be subjected to the same action again."

15. Note, 88 Harv.L.Rev. 373, 394, 395 (1974).

case nevertheless risk excessive judicial intervention in constitutional disputes? Is the lawsuit less likely to be marked by adversariness if the litigant will not be affected by the outcome? Does the growing practice of group litigation help to explain the erratic modern refusals to sustain mootness claims? [16]

SECTION 3. RIPENESS, CONTINGENCIES, AND ANTICIPATORY RELIEF

Introduction. When is a dispute sufficiently real, well developed, and specific to elicit adjudication? Concerns about concrete records and premature interventions have surfaced repeatedly in the preceding materials. Those concerns are central to the problem of "ripeness," the focus of this section. How ripe must a controversy be to present appropriate circumstances for the exercise of judicial power? At one extreme lies the much-reiterated premise that federal courts will not render "advisory opinions" on legal questions even though the litigants have intense curiosity about the answer. At the other end of the scale is the common situation of the defendant resisting enforcement of a criminal law against him: in that situation, typically, the relevant facts occurred in the past and are on the record; in that context, courts regularly adjudicate constitutional challenges. Most problems of ripeness arise from situations in between— between disputes not yet fully born or already dead and disputes as fully developed as they can be. How fully must a controversy have jelled to elicit a ruling? How eyeball-to-eyeball must the disputants' confrontation be? That problem arises most characteristically with requests for anticipatory relief— where plaintiffs, for example, seek a ruling on the legality of an action that they fear may be taken against them, rather than waiting to raise the issues as defendants in enforcement proceedings. It is in these actions for anticipatory relief that the problems of contingencies and uncertainties as to the facts are most prominent. In actions for declaratory or injunctive relief, courts may be most reluctant to intervene and may be most anxious to have the most clearly defined record to assure informed and narrow adjudication. The relationship between the parties is typically still in flux and developing. And the contingencies may affect both sides of the lawsuit. The plaintiffs may not yet be able to say specifically what actions they expect to take. Similarly, it may not yet be possible to say what specific actions the defendant will take against the plaintiffs. The record in such a case will typically consist in part of predictions about the

---

16. See the comment in Note, 88 Harv.L. Rev. 373, 396 (1974): "Recognition for jurisdictional purposes of harm to a group when there is no litigant with a stake in the outcome plainly represents a departure from traditional notions of a 'case or controversy.' The Court has been willing to continue the exercise of jurisdiction in such cases only when there are important justifications for refusing to find the case moot."

Note in this connection the considerable amount of modern litigation about the applications of mootness doctrines in class action contexts. See generally Comment, "A Search for Principles of Mootness in the Federal Courts: [Class] Actions," 54 Texas L.Rev. 1289 (1976); Comment, "Continuation and Representation of Class Actions Following Dismissal of the Class Representative," 1974 Duke L.J. 573. The Court divided sharply in examining issues in this area in United States Parole Comm'n v. Ger-

aghty, 445 U.S. 388 (1980), where the majority, referring to "the flexible character of the Art. III mootness doctrine," held that "an action brought on behalf of a class does not become moot upon expiration of the named plaintiff's substantive claim"; instead, the class representative may appeal the denial of a class certification motion even though the representative's personal claim has become moot.

[For an illustration of the rarely invoked ban on *collusive* suits, see United States v. Johnson, 319 U.S. 302 (1943), dismissing an action testing rent control because the nominal plaintiff, a tenant, had been procured by and at the expense of the defendant landlord. For a rare modern reliance on United States v. Johnson, see Justice Blackmun's dissent, joined by Justices Brennan and Marshall, in Nixon v. Fitzgerald (1982; chap. 6 above).]

probable conduct of both parties; the parties' behavior turns on contingencies and requires guesses about the future. And those uncertainties give rise to the ripeness problem.

As the preceding materials have already indicated, the Court frequently speaks of the need for a concrete controversy, for a sufficiently nonhypothetical, nonabstract, "ripe" dispute between truly "adverse" parties. What do those requirements mean? And what justifies the requirements? Are they all derived from the Art. III "case or controversy" requirement? Or are some of these limitations nonconstitutional in origin? Based on the federal courts' authority to help shape the law of remedies? Based on judicially developed policies responding to institutional self-defense perceptions—on prudential decisions to conserve the energies (and the political capital) of federal courts for a limited number of truly important constitutional cases?

CONCRETENESS AND THE PLAINTIFFS' PLANNED CONDUCT: THE MITCHELL AND ADLER CASES

The Mitchell and Adler cases both involved First Amendment challenges to restrictions on public employees. (Recall chap. 13, sec. 4, above). In Mitchell, the Court found most claims nonjusticiable; in Adler, by contrast, the Court reached the merits. Mitchell and Adler afford an initial opportunity to explore the nature and ingredients of ripeness: To what extent is ripeness derived from Art. III? What factors go into the determination of ripeness?

1. *Mitchell.* UNITED PUBLIC WORKERS v. MITCHELL, 330 U.S. 75 (1947), was an attack on § 9(a) of the Hatch Act of 1940, which prohibits federal employees in the executive branch from taking "any active part in political management or in political campaigns." Several employees and their union brought suit to restrain the Civil Service Commission from enforcing § 9(a) against them, and for a declaratory judgment that the section was unconstitutional. The lower court dismissed the suit on the merits. The Court affirmed the judgment, but on other grounds as to most of the plaintiffs. Justice REED's opinion contained the following passages:

"It is alleged that the individuals desire to engage in acts of political management and in political campaigns. [None of appellants, except one Poole, had violated the Act. Poole's situation is considered further below.][1] [At the threshold], we are called upon to decide whether the complaint states a controversy cognizable in this Court. The [employees other than Poole] have elaborated the grounds of their objection in individual affidavits for use in the hearing on the summary judgment. We select as an example one that contains the essential averments of all the others and print below the portions with significance in this suit.[2] The affidavits, it will be noticed, follow the generality

1. [The complaint stated:] "[T]he individual plaintiffs desire to engage in the following acts: write for publication letters and articles in support of candidates for office; be connected editorially with publications which are identified with the legislative program of UFWA [former name of the present union appellant] and candidates who support it; solicit votes, aid in getting out voters, act as accredited checker, watcher, or challenger; transport voters to and from the polls without compensation therefor; participate in and help in organizing political parades; initiate petitions, and canvass for the signatures of others on such petitions; serve as party ward committeeman or other party official; and perform any and all acts not prohibited by any provision of law other than [the Hatch Act]." [Footnote by Justice Reed.]

2. "[I] wish to engage in such activities on behalf of those candidates for public office who I believe will best serve the needs of this country and with the object of persuading others of the correctness of my judgments and of electing the candidates of my choice. This objective I wish to pursue by all proper means such as engaging in discussion, by speeches to conventions, rallies and other assemblages, by publicizing my views in letters and articles for publication in newspapers and other periodicals, by aiding in the campaign of candidates for political office, by posting banners and posters in public places, by distribut-

of purpose expressed by the complaint. [They] declare a desire to act contrary to the rule against political activity but not that the rule has been violated. In this respect, we think they differ from the type of threat adjudicated in Railway Mail Ass'n v. Corsi, 326 U.S. 88 [1944]. In that case, the refusal to admit an applicant to membership in a labor union on account of race was involved. Admission had been refused. [The] threats which menaced the affiants [in Mitchell] are closer to a general threat by officials to enforce those laws which they are charged to administer, than they are to the direct threat of punishment against a named organization for a completed act that made the [Corsi] case justiciable.

"[These] appellants seem clearly to seek advisory opinions upon broad claims of [constitutional rights. The] facts of their personal interest in their civil rights, of the general threat of possible interference with those rights by the [CSC] under its rules, if specified things are done by appellants, does not make a justiciable case or controversy. [Appellants'] generality of objection is really an attack on the political expediency of the Hatch Act, not the presentation of legal issues. It is beyond the competence of courts to render such a decision. [The] power of courts [to] pass upon the constitutionality of acts of Congress arises only when the interests of litigants require the use of this judicial authority for their protection against actual interference. A hypothetical threat is not enough. We can only speculate as to the kinds of political activity the appellants desire to engage in or as to the contents of their proposed public statements or the circumstances of their publication. It would not accord with judicial responsibility to adjudge, in a matter involving constitutionality, between the freedom of the individual and the requirements of public order except when definite rights appear upon the one side and definite prejudicial interferences upon the other. [Should] the courts seek to expand their power so as to bring under their jurisdiction ill-defined controversies over constitutional issues, they would become the organ of political theories. Such abuse of judicial power would properly meet rebuke and restriction from other branches. [No] threat of interference by the Commission with rights of these appellants appears beyond that implied by the existence of the law and the regulations. [These] reasons lead us to conclude that the determination of the trial court, that the individual appellants, other than Poole, could maintain this action, was erroneous.

"[The] appellant Poole does present by the complaint and affidavit matters appropriate for judicial determination. [Poole] has been charged by the Commission with political activity and a proposed order for his removal from his position adopted subject to his right under Commission procedure to reply to the charges and to present further evidence in refutation. We proceed to consider the controversy over constitutional power at issue between Poole and the Commission as defined by the charge and preliminary finding upon one side and the admissions of Poole's affidavit upon the other. Our determination is limited to those facts. This proceeding so limited meets the requirements of defined rights and a definite threat to interfere with a possessor of the menaced rights by a penalty for an act done in violation of the claimed restraint." [3]

ing leaflets, by 'ringing doorbells,' by addressing campaign literature, and by doing any and all acts of like character reasonably designed to assist in the election of candidates I favor. I desire to engage in these activities freely, openly, and without concealment. However, I understand that, [because of § 9(a)], if I engage in this activity, the Civil Service Commission [CSC] will order that I be dismissed from [federal employment]. I believe that Congress may not constitutionally abridge my right to engage in the politi-

cal activities mentioned above. However, unless the courts prevent the [CSC] from enforcing this unconstitutional law, I will be unable freely to exercise my rights as a [citizen]." [Footnote by Justice Reed.]

3. Poole's constitutional challenge was rejected on the merits. The Court reiterated its First Amendment position 26 years later, in Civil Service Comm'n v. Letter Carriers (1973; chap. 13, sec. 4 above). Contrast the plaintiffs' allega-

Justice RUTLEDGE dissented as to Poole and stated that he did not pass "upon the constitutional questions presented by the other appellants for the reason that he feels the controversy as to them is not yet appropriate for the discretionary exercise of declaratory judgment jurisdiction." Justice DOUGLAS dissented in part. As to justiciability, he said: "The requirement of an 'actual controversy' [seems] to me to be fully met here. What these appellants propose to do is plain enough. If they do what they propose to do, it is clear that they will be discharged from their positions. [Their] proposed conduct is sufficiently specific to show plainly that it will violate the Act. [To] require these employees first to suffer the hardship of a discharge is not only to make them incur a penalty; it makes inadequate, if not wholly illusory, any legal remedy which they may have. Men who must sacrifice their means of livelihood in order to test their rights to their jobs must either pursue prolonged and expensive litigation as unemployed persons or pull up their roots, change their life careers, and seek employment in other fields. Declaratory relief is the singular remedy available here to preserve the status quo while the constitutional rights of these appellants to make these utterances and to engage in these activities are determined. The threat against them is real not fanciful, immediate not remote. The case is therefore an actual not a hypothetical one." [4]

2. *Adler.* ADLER v. BOARD of EDUC., 342 U.S. 485 (1952), attacked New York's Feinberg Law of 1949, designed to eliminate "subversive persons from the public school system." The Act included provisions for the compilation of a list of subversive organizations by the school authorities; membership in any such organization constituted "prima facie evidence of disqualification" for any school position. The plaintiffs were taxpayers, parents of school children, and teachers. The state courts rejected their constitutional challenges on the merits. On appeal, the Supreme Court affirmed, without discussing justiciability. [See chap. 13, sec. 4, above.] Justice FRANKFURTER's dissent, however, argued that the justiciability issue in Adler was a substantial one, especially in light of Mitchell. He insisted that the case was not justiciable. With respect to the taxpayer and parent plaintiffs, he found lack of standing to sue. His discussion of the ripeness-Mitchell problem came in the course of his insistence that the teacher plaintiffs, too, had failed to present a claim that could be adjudicated at this time: "The allegations in the present action fall short of those found insufficient in [Mitchell]. These teachers do not allege that they have engaged in proscribed conduct or that they have any intention to do so. They do not suggest that they have been, or are, deterred from supporting causes or from joining organizations for fear of the Feinberg Law's interdict, except to say generally that the system complained of will have this effect on teachers as a group. They do not assert that they are threatened with action under the law, or that steps are imminent whereby they would incur the hazard of punishment for conduct innocent at the time, or under standards too vague to satisfy due process of law. They merely allege that the statutes and Rules permit such action against some teachers. Since we rightly refused in the

tions in the 1973 case with those found wanting in Mitchell. In Letter Carriers, one plaintiff, for example, simply alleged "that she desired to become a precinct Democratic Committeewoman"; another, "that he desired to, but did not, file as a candidate [for] Borough Councilman." Were those allegations more concrete than those in Mitchell? Did the specificity of the allegations differ so greatly as to justify failure to discuss the justiciability issue in the 1973 case? Note that the attack in Letter Carriers rested largely on overbreadth and vagueness grounds— arguments that had not yet become a significant

part of constitutional doctrine at the time of Mitchell. Recall especially that the particular facts of the case generally play a less significant role when overbreadth and vagueness attacks are made. Since the Court's primary concern in overbreadth analysis is the risk of application of the law to those not before the Court, concreteness and ripeness issues, like standing barriers, tend to be less important.

4. Justice FRANKFURTER concurred in a separate opinion; Justice BLACK submitted a dissent.

Mitchell case to hear government employees whose conduct was much more intimately affected by the law there attacked than are the claims of plaintiffs here, this suit is wanting in the necessary basis for our review." [5]

3. *Some questions about Mitchell and Adler.* a. *The Art. III and the Court review dimensions: Basis for reconciliation?* Mitchell and Adler raise questions on two levels—one involving the Art. III contours themselves, the other pertaining to the additional problems of Court review of state adjudications. As to Art. III: Does every dispute found not "ripe" fall short of being an Art. III "case"? Or may some disputes be concrete enough to fall within Art. III, yet not ripe enough to warrant grant of a discretionary federal remedy? As to Court review: If a state court adjudicates a dispute concrete enough to be an Art. III case, *must* not the Court decide the merits on appeal—even though, if the case had started in a federal court, declaratory or injunctive relief would have been denied on the basis of the discretionary, remedial aspect of the ripeness doctrine? Are Mitchell and Adler reconcilable?

There is good reason to criticize the majority's failure even to mention the justiciability issue in Adler. But the result—the decision to adjudicate—may have been justifiable: there were reasons to reach the merits in Adler that were lacking in Mitchell. To be sure, Mitchell and Adler do not seem reconcilable if only the Art. III and ripeness dimensions are considered: Mitchell seems hardly less ripe than Adler. But if the Court review dimension is also taken into account, Mitchell and Adler may be able to stand together: review of the Adler case may have been justified because it, unlike Mitchell, originated in the state courts—and was not so unripe as to fall short of being an Art. III case. If Mitchell is viewed as a discretionary denial of a federal declaratory judgments remedy, as Justice Rutledge's separate opinion suggested, can it truly be authority for dismissing a *state* court appeal such as Adler—even if the dispute in Adler was at least as unripe as that in Mitchell, as Justice Frankfurther claimed? In reviewing a state court decision falling within the obligatory appeal jurisdiction, must not the Court decide the merits unless Art. III is not satisfied? It is arguable, in short, that the Court has no discretion to abstain from decision in a case such as Adler—unlike the discretion it could properly exercise over a federal court remedy such as that sought in Mitchell. [6]

b. *Minimal concreteness: Art. III requirement or federal remedial discretion?* To what extent is ripeness an aspect of the "case or controversy" requirement of Art. III? To what extent is it a question of the law of remedies? A dispute may fall so far short of ripeness that it does not present a minimal Art. III "case." That may have been the flaw in Willing, sec. 1 above. Recall that Justice

---

5. Earlier in his dissent, Justice Frankfurter stated: "We are asked to adjudicate claims against its constitutionality before the scheme has been put into operation, before the limits that it imposes upon free inquiry and association, the scope of scrutiny that it sanctions, and the procedural safeguards that will be found to be implied for its enforcement have been authoritatively defined. I think we should adhere to the teaching of this Court's history to avoid constitutional adjudications on merely abstract or speculative issues and to base them on the concreteness afforded by an actual, present, defined controversy, appropriate for judicial judgment, between adversaries immediately affected by it."

Fifteen years after Adler, a renewed constitutional attack on the Feinberg Law proved successful. Recall Keyishian (1967; chap. 13 above). Note that First Amendment doctrine applicable to restrictions on public employees had changed drastically during the years between Adler and Keyishian. (On the bearing of views of the merits in the disposition of ripeness issues, see the additional comments below.)

6. Is it accurate to say, in other words, that discretionary considerations appropriate in federal court litigation have no place in Court review of state cases within the appeal jurisdiction? Or does the law of remedies become "federalized" in all cases of Court review? Because of the overriding institutional need of the Court to avoid premature and excessive interventions, and interventions based on inadequately developed records? Note the recurrent nature of these problems throughout this chapter. Recall, e.g., the comments on the Doremus case on state taxpayers' standing, sec. 2, p. 1576 above, and note the materials on discretionary abstention from the exercise of Court jurisdiction, sec. 4 below.

Brandeis noted the contingencies there in both the lessee's and lessor's plans, expressed fears about "advisory opinions," and commented: "No defendant has wronged the plaintiff or has threatened to do so." That case may have had so many contingencies on both sides that Art. III barred judicial resolution. However, a dispute may be sufficiently concrete to meet the minimum requirements of Art. III but nevertheless sufficiently contingent to warrant dismissal on ripeness grounds in the exercise of judicial discretion as to the federal declaratory judgments remedy. Arguably, Mitchell was such a case.

     c. *The premature, the concrete, and the underlying substantive issue.* In Adler, the state court thought some questions sufficiently "ripe" for adjudication. Was there not adequate ripeness to satisfy Art. III policies at least as to some issues in Adler? Obviously, the teachers in Adler could not complain of specific actions taken against them—that challenge would indeed have been premature. But could they not properly argue that there could be *no* constitutional applications of the Feinberg Law? And if the state courts chose to decide that claim, was not the Court compelled to review? But note that the importance of concrete, fully developed facts turns to some extent on the background of substantive law and on the plaintiff's legal theory—and on the Justices' views of the difficulties and proper analyses of the issues. Thus, a Justice who inclines toward case-by-case balancing is more likely to need a full record than one who tends to broad, near-absolute solutions. (All that the decision in Adler held was that the Feinberg Law was not in all possible situations unconstitutional—that it was constitutional in some conceivable applications. Litigants may be unwise to present so broad an issue to the courts; but if they are willing to do so, is there any justification for refusal to adjudicate? [7])

     4. *Some further questions on ripeness: Hardship to the parties and shape of the issues.* a. *Hardship to the parties.* In a number of cases involving review of administrative regulations, the Court's determinations of ripeness issues have explicitly turned on considerations of "hardship to the parties" and "fitness of the issues." [8] Does "hardship to the parties" play a significant, if less articulated, role in the constitutional adjudication cases as well? May the hardship of delaying relief to the litigant be so minimal as to make preenforcement adjudication inappropriate? Were the parties in Mitchell or Adler so unharmed by delay as to make immediate adjudication constitutionally improper? To what extent should "hardship to the parties" affect ripeness? [9] If ripeness is less of a

---

     7. Note also Times Film Corp. v. Chicago, 365 U.S. 43 (1961), an attack on a city censorship ordinance in which the challenger refused to submit a film to the censoring agency and sued to enjoin enforcement of the ordinance on the ground that *no* prior restraint mechanism could be constitutional. The Court rejected that claim. For a Justice viewing *all* prior restraints as unconstitutional (e.g., Justices Black and Douglas), the Times Film issue was easy, and no more concrete record was necessary. For Justices finding "balancing" more congenial than "absolutes," a fuller record—in obscenity cases, typically a view of the film itself—was desirable. But even "balancing" Justices should be able to reject the "absolute" urged by the claimant in Times Film. Does Justice Frankfurter's lone objection to the justiciability of Adler, then, mainly reflect the fact that he, especially, was inclined to "balance": that his preferred mode of constitutional adjudication turned heavily on the particular facts of the case?

     8. See, e.g., Abbott Laboratories v. Gardner, 387 U.S. 136 (1967), and its companion cases.

(The issues raised by judicial review of agency actions are more fully discussed in administrative law courses.)

     9. Note the Court's dismissal of the claim of one set of litigants in the abortion case, Roe v. Wade (1973; chap. 8 above). Though the Court adjudicated the complaint of Jane Roe (despite mootness questions, as noted in sec. 2), it dismissed the complaint of John and Mary Doe, a married childless couple seeking assurance that there could be an abortion if she became pregnant. Justice Blackmun's opinion commented that the Does claimed, "as their asserted immediate and present injury, only an alleged 'detrimental effect upon [their] marital happiness' because they are forced to [make] 'the choice of refraining from normal sexual relations or of endangering Mary Doe's health through a possible pregnancy.' Their claim is that sometime in the future Mrs. Doe [might] want an abortion." He stated: "This very phrasing of the Does' position reveals its speculative character. Their alleged injury rests on possible future contraceptive failure, possible future pregnancy, possible future

barrier when delay in adjudication constitutes a hardship to the plaintiff, what of hardship to the defendant (and to the public interest) from early adjudication? Should assessment of hardship vary with the nature of the legal claim?

b. *Shape of the issues.* In applying the "fitness of the issue" criterion in the administrative review cases (footnote 8 above), the Justices asked whether factual enforcement experience was necessary to decide the legal question. Does that need for facts itself depend upon what legal question is asked? On how the judge views the substantive law? Some legal standards *are* less dependent on factual variations than others. And some judges *are* more inclined than others to formulate legal standards as questions of degree. (Recall footnote 7 above.) Does the focus on the shape of the issues and on the hardship to the parties unduly deemphasize the Court's institutional values, especially in constitutional litigation? Should ripeness be primarily concerned with protecting the Court from premature opinions—opinions with some of the effects of advisory ones, in quality and in vulnerability? Or should assessment of the parties' (and society's) need for an adjudication be the major ingredient of the ripeness determination? [10]

CONCRETENESS, CONTINGENCIES, AND DEFENDANTS' BEHAVIOR

Concern about adequate development of the dispute—about adequate concreteness—goes to both sides of a lawsuit. Not only must plaintiffs seeking anticipatory relief ordinarily spell out their proposed conduct in some detail, but they must also demonstrate that some harm will befall them if they go through with their plans. Is it enough that there is a statute on the books which may subject the plaintiffs to criminal prosecution? [1] Or must the plaintiffs challenging a law show that government officials have in fact threatened to take action against them if the proposed course of conduct is undertaken? Consider the criteria announced in the modern cases below in which the Court requires that the existence of a genuine controversy be shown and that concrete injury be threatened. Are the criteria justifiable? Workable? What policies are they designed to serve? How effectively do they serve those policies?

1. O'SHEA v. LITTLETON, 414 U.S. 488 (1974): Justice WHITE's majority opinion found a federal court class action complaint inadequate "to satisfy the threshold requirement imposed by Art. III." The complaint grew out of years-long racial tension in Cairo, Illinois. It charged that the original defendants—a magistrate and a judge—were engaged in a continuing pattern of discriminatory bond, sentencing, and jury fee practices in criminal cases. Justice

---

unpreparedness for parenthood, and possible future impairment of health. Any one or more of these several possibilities may not take place and all may not combine. In the Does' estimation, these possibilities might have some real or imagined impact upon their marital happiness. But we are not prepared to say that the bare allegation of so indirect an injury is sufficient to present an actual case or controversy."

Since the Does did claim a present "impact upon their marital happiness," why was that impact not sufficient to warrant Court adjudication? Was the dismissal of the Does' suit based on discretionary considerations, partly influenced by the fact that Ms. Roe's claim *was* being adjudicated? Or is it really tenable to suggest that the Does' concern was so speculative as to take the controversy outside of Art. III limits?

10. See Goldwater v. Carter, 444 U.S. 996 (1979) (chap. 6 above), where the Court refused to decide whether the President may terminate a treaty without the participation of Congress. Most of the Justices who concluded that the complaint had to be dismissed relied on "political question" grounds, as noted in sec. 5 below. Justice Powell, who found the "political question" barrier inapplicable, relied instead on "[p]rudential considerations": he invoked the concept of ripeness, arguing that courts should not adjudicate presidential-congressional conflicts "until the political branches reach a constitutional impasse."

1. Recall the emphasis on the "chilling effect" of governmental action threatening First Amendment rights, in chaps. 11 to 13 above. Compare Laird v. Tatum, note 3 below.

White commented: "The nature of [plaintiffs'] activities is not described in detail and no specific threats are alleged to have been made against them. Accepting that they are deeply involved in a program to eliminate racial discrimination in Cairo and that tensions are high, we are nonetheless unable to conclude that the case or controversy requirement is satisfied by general assertions or inferences that in the course of their activities respondents will be prosecuted for violating valid criminal laws." He concluded that "the threat of injury from the alleged course of conduct they attack is simply too remote to satisfy the 'case or controversy' requirement." Justice DOUGLAS' dissent, joined by Justices Brennan and Marshall, insisted that the complaint alleged "a more pervasive scheme for suppression of Blacks and their civil rights than I have ever seen. It may not survive a trial. But if this case does not present a 'case or controversy' involving the named plaintiffs, then that concept has been so watered down as to be no longer recognizable." [2]

2. LOS ANGELES v. LYONS, 461 U.S. 95 (1983): The Court, relying on O'Shea v. Littleton and Rizzo v. Goode, denied standing in a case challenging the use of "chokeholds" by the Los Angeles Police Department. Justice WHITE's majority opinion concluded that Lyons lacked standing to seek injunctive relief against the police because "he was [un]likely to suffer future injury from the use of chokeholds by police officers." Lyons himself had in fact been the victim of the very type of chokehold, imposed during the course of a stop for a motor vehicle violation, that provided the basis for his claim. In short, there was no question but that Lyons had standing to bring an action for damages, in the course of which the constitutionality of the police practices could be adjudicated. But the Court decided that the "case or controversy" requirement of Art. III must be satisfied with respect to each separate claim for relief. The fact that Lyons' claim for damages satisfied the requirements of Art. III did not mean that all claims he brought could be adjudicated: "In order to establish an actual controversy [for the purposes of obtaining injunctive relief], Lyons would have had not only to allege that he would have another encounter with the police but also to make the incredible assertion either, (1) that *all* police officers in Los Angeles *always* choke any citizen with whom they happen to have an encounter whether for the purpose of arrest, issuing a citation or for questioning or, (2) that the City ordered or authorized police officers to act in

---

2. Note the majority's reliance on O'Shea v. Littleton in Rizzo v. Goode, 423 U.S. 362 (1976). Rizzo was a federal civil rights action against Philadelphia officials, charging unconstitutional mistreatment of individuals. The trial court had entered a broad decree directing the officials to draft a "comprehensive program for dealing adequately with civilian complaints." Justice Rehnquist's majority opinion held the trial court's action to be improper federal intervention in local law enforcement. He expressed "serious doubts" that the plaintiffs had demonstrated an Art. III controversy between themselves and the city officials. He insisted that the concerns expressed in O'Shea "apply here with even more force, for the [plaintiffs'] claim to 'real and immediate' injury rests not upon what the named [officials] might do to them in the future [but] upon what one of the small, unnamed minority of policemen might do to them [because] of that unknown policeman's perception of departmental disciplinary procedure. This hypothetical is even more attenuated than [the allegations found insufficient in O'Shea]"; accordingly, the plaintiffs lacked the requisite "personal stake in the outcome"—i.e., the order overhauling police disci-

plinary procedures. (In addition to these considerations "concerning the existence of a live controversy," Justice Rehnquist questioned the existence of "threshold statutory liability" under 42 U.S.C. § 1983 and the justification for federal equity relief in light of federalism principles.) Justice Blackmun, joined by Justices Brennan and Marshall, dissented, insisting that O'Shea was distinguishable on the facts.

See also Boyle v. Landry, 401 U.S. 77 (1971), where black residents of Chicago had obtained a federal injunction restraining local officials from enforcing an anti-"intimidation" law, claiming that it had been used to harass them and to deny them their First Amendment rights. Justice Black's opinion held that the issue should not have been decided: "Not a single one of the citizens who brought this action had ever been prosecuted, charged, or even arrested under the [law]. In fact, the complaint contains no mention of any specific threat by any [official to] arrest or prosecute any [of the plaintiffs]." (The case was a companion case to Younger v. Harris, sec. 4 below.)

such manner. Although Count V alleged that the City authorized the use of the control holds in situations where deadly force was not threatened, it did not indicate why Lyons might be realistically threatened by police officers who acted within the strictures of the City's policy."

The Court's decision to conduct separate Art. III standing inquiries for damage and equitable relief claims brought by the same plaintiff against the same defendant in the same action prompted a lengthy and vigorous dissent by Justice MARSHALL, joined by Justices Brennan, Blackmun and Stevens: "By fragmenting the standing inquiry and imposing a separate standing hurdle with respect to each form of relief sought, the decision today departs significantly from this Court's traditional conception of the standing requirement and of the remedial powers of the federal courts. We have never required more than that a plaintiff have standing to litigate a claim. Whether he will be entitled to obtain particular forms of relief should he prevail has never been understood to be an issue of standing. In determining whether a plaintiff has standing, we have always focused on his personal stake in the outcome of the controversy, not on the issues sought to be litigated [Flast] or the [precise nature of the relief sought]."

3. POE v. ULLMAN, 367 U.S. 497 (1961): This was one of a series of efforts to obtain a Court ruling on the constitutionality of Connecticut's ban on the use of contraceptives. In this controversial decision refusing to rule on the merits, Justice FRANKFURTER wrote the plurality opinion dismissing an appeal in a suit brought by two married couples and a physician. The couples claimed that they had sought contraceptive advice from the physician, who had not given it for fear of prosecution. Justice Frankfurter's opinion noted that the allegations did not "clearly" state that the prosecutor threatened to prosecute the challengers. Rather, they merely asserted "that, in the course of his public duty, he intends to prosecute any offenses against Connecticut law, and that he claims that use of and advice concerning contraceptives would constitute offenses." Justice Frankfurter commented: "The lack of immediacy of the threat described by these allegations might alone raise serious questions of non-justiciability. [Mitchell.] But even were we to read the allegations to convey a clear threat of imminent prosecutions, we are not bound to accept as true all that is alleged on the face of the complaint and admitted, technically, by demurrer. [Formal] agreement between parties that collides with plausibility is too fragile a foundation for indulging in constitutional adjudication." He noted that the Connecticut law had been on the books since 1879, that there had been only one reported prosecution, and that this and other circumstances showed the "unreality of these lawsuits." Contraceptives were commonly sold in Connecticut. "The undeviating policy of nullification by Connecticut of its anti-contraceptive [laws] bespeaks more than prosecutorial paralysis: '[T]raditional ways of carrying out state policy are often tougher and truer law than the dead words of the written text.'" He added: "If the prosecutor expressly agrees not to prosecute, a suit against him [is] not such an adversary case as will be reviewed here. [Eighty years of state practice] demonstrate a similar, albeit tacit agreement [here]. To find it necessary to pass on these statutes now, in order to protect appellants from the hazards of prosecution, would be to close our eyes to reality." Moreover, the "deterrent effect complained of was [not] grounded in a realistic fear of prosecution."

Justice DOUGLAS' dissent commented: "No lawyer, I think, would advise his clients to rely on that 'tacit agreement.' [What] are these people—doctor and patients—to do? Flout the law and go to prison? Violate the law surreptitiously and hope they will not get caught? [It] is not the choice they need have under the regime of declaratory judgment and our constitutional system." And in a lengthy dissent, Justice HARLAN commented that it was "pure conjecture, and indeed conjecture which to me seems contrary to realities, that an open violation of the statute by a doctor [would] not result in a substantial threat of prosecution." He added: "[The Court does not suggest] an estoppel against the State if it should attempt to prosecute appellants. [What] is meant is simply that the appellants are more or less free to act without fear of prosecution because the prosecuting authorities of the State, in their discretion and at their whim, are, as a matter of prediction, unlikely to decide to prosecute." [3]

4. LAIRD v. TATUM, 408 U.S. 1 (1972): This 5 to 4 decision found nonjusticiable respondents' First Amendment attack on the army's surveillance of "lawful and peaceful civilian activities." In the late 1960s, Army Intelligence had established a "data-gathering system" about "public activities" with a potential for "civil disorder." The lower federal court had held that the action was justiciable, since respondents contended that "the *present existence of this system* of gathering and distributing information, allegedly far beyond the mission requirements of the Army, constitutes an impermissible burden" on persons such as respondents and "exercises a *present inhibiting effect*" on their First Amendment rights: "under justiciability standards it is the operation of the system itself which is the breach of the Army's duty" and the case was "therefore ripe for adjudication." The basic claimed evil was overbreadth and there was "no indication that a better opportunity will later arise to test the constitutionality of the Army's action." Chief Justice BURGER's majority opinion reversed, quoting the Mitchell statement of hostility to advisory opinions and stating that "allegations of a subjective 'chill' are not an adequate substitute for a claim of specific present objective harm or a threat of specific future harm." He recognized that governmental action could be attacked "even though it has only an indirect effect" on First Amendment rights, but he insisted that an immediate risk of "direct injury" had to be shown. Here, by contrast, the essential claim was one of disagreement with executive use of Army data gathering, or a "perception of the system as inappropriate to the Army's role," or a belief "that it is inherently dangerous for the military to be concerned with activities in the civilian sector," or a fear resting on the "less generalized yet speculative apprehensiveness that the Army may at some future date misuse the information in some way that would cause direct harm to respondents." These concerns did not amount to "specific present objective harm" or "threat of specific future harm." [4]

---

3. The Court did not reach the merits of the issue it had avoided in Poe until Griswold v. Connecticut (1965; chap. 8, sec. 3, above). Justice Harlan, however, did reach the merits in Poe and found the law unconstitutional. His opinion in Poe is printed with Griswold, above, as an amplification of his concurrence in that case. (See the additional comments on Poe in sec. 4 below.)

Compare Doe v. Bolton (1973; chap. 8 above), the companion abortion case to Roe v. Wade. In Doe, the Georgia doctors' complaint was found sufficient when they alleged that the Georgia laws restricting abortions "chilled and deterred" them from practicing their profession, even though the record did not disclose "that any one of them has been prosecuted, or threatened with prosecution." Justice Blackmun explained: "The physician is the one against whom these criminal statutes directly operate in the event he procures an abortion that does not meet the statutory exceptions and conditions." Accordingly, the challengers were found to "assert a sufficiently direct threat of personal detriment. They should not be required to await and undergo a criminal prosecution as the sole means of seeking relief." But why were they not required to await a *specific* official *threat* to prosecute? Is Doe v. Bolton reconcilable with Poe v. Ullman?

4. Justice BRENNAN, joined by Justices Stewart and Marshall, dissented on the basis of the lower court's ruling on justiciability. Justice DOUGLAS, joined by Justice Marshall, also submitted a dissent.

SECTION 4. DISCRETION TO DECLINE THE EXERCISE OF JURISDICTION

A. SUPREME COURT REVIEW: DISCRETION AND THE OBLIGATORY APPEAL JURISDICTION

Introduction. The Court's appeal jurisdiction, unlike its certiorari jurisdiction, purports to be obligatory rather than discretionary. May the Court nevertheless assert a discretion to decline adjudication of a case apparently within its appeal jurisdiction, for reasons other than those grounded in the requirements of Art. III or the jurisdictional statute? At first glance, that question may seem a technical one of limited contemporary significance. As noted in chap. 1, at p. 54 above, proposals to eliminate most of the Court's obligatory "appeal" jurisdiction have been considered by Congress in recent years, and are likely to be enacted soon, so that the appeal-certiorari distinction is likely to have little practical importance in the future. Nevertheless, the Court's exercise of its appeal jurisdiction—and especially its occasional practice of avoiding decision on the merits in cases it is apparently obliged to decide—throws important light on the materials considered in the preceding sections. Repeatedly, nonconstitutional ingredients—ingredients of prudence rather than criteria drawn directly from Art. III—have influenced the Court's molding and application of such doctrines as standing and ripeness and mootness. Similar discretionary ingredients have played a role in the Court's exercise of its appeal jurisdiction, in the face of congressional mandates that the Court decide the cases. The inclination of the Justices to embroider constitutional and statutory norms with a judge-made discretionary gloss may be understandable in terms of institutional psychology; but, as these appeal jurisdiction materials illustrate with special sharpness, they also raise serious questions of legitimacy.

To what extent, then, do nonconstitutional ingredients of justiciability properly enter into the exercise of the appeal jurisdiction?[1] Consider, first, the contending positions summarized in the opening materials below. Are the statements by Chief Justice Marshall and by Justice Brandeis wholly inconsistent? Or can Marshall's emphasis on the duty to decide be reconciled with Brandeis' stress on avoidance of constitutional adjudication? Then, consider the sampling of modern dismissals of appeals. In cases such as Rescue Army, Naim v. Naim, and Poe v. Ullman, the Court declined to reach the merits in cases apparently within its obligatory review jurisdiction. Did the Court give adequate justification for not deciding those cases? Do the institutional reasons which underlie some of the doctrines considered in the preceding sections justify those avoidances of decision? Do the Court's concerns about excessive intervention and assured conditions for optimum decisionmaking legitimately carry over to the disposition of appeals?

MARSHALL AND BRANDEIS ON THE OBLIGATION TO DECIDE: CONFLICTING VIEWS?

1. *Marshall in Cohens.* Chief Justice Marshall in COHENS v. VIRGINIA, 6 Wheat. 264 (1821) (chap. 1 above): "It is most true that this Court will not take jurisdiction if it should not: but it is equally true, that it must take jurisdiction if it should. The judiciary cannot, as the legislature may, avoid a measure because it approaches the confines of the constitution. We cannot pass

---

1. That question, the central concern of this section, has arisen peripherally in some of the earlier materials. Recall, e.g., the dismissal of the appeal of the state taxpayers' suit in Doremus (sec. 2 above) and the ripeness discussion in the Adler case (sec. 3, above).

it by because it is doubtful. With whatever doubts, with whatever difficulties, a case may be attended, we must decide it, if it be brought before us. *We have no more right to decline the exercise of jurisdiction which is given, than to usurp that which is not given.* The one or the other would be treason to the constitution. Questions may occur which we would gladly avoid; but we cannot avoid them. All we can do is, to exercise our best judgment, and conscientiously to perform our duty." (Emphasis added.)

2. *Brandeis in Ashwander.* Justice Brandeis in ASHWANDER v. TVA, 297 U.S. 288, 346 (1936) (concurring opinion): "The Court developed, for its own governance in the cases confessedly within its jurisdiction, a series of rules under which *it has avoided passing upon a large part of all the constitutional questions pressed upon it for decision.* They are: [1.] The Court will not pass upon the constitutionality of legislation in a friendly, non-adversary, proceeding, declining because to decide such questions 'is legitimate only in the last resort, and as a necessity in the determination of real, earnest and vital controversy between individuals. It never was the thought that, by means of a friendly suit, a party beaten in the legislature could transfer to the courts an inquiry as to the constitutionality of the legislative act.' [2.] The Court will not 'anticipate a question of constitutional law in advance of the necessity of deciding it.' [3.] The Court will not 'formulate a rule of constitutional law broader than is required by the precise facts to which it is to be applied.' [4.] The Court will not pass upon a constitutional question although properly presented by the record, if there is also present some other ground upon which the case may be disposed of. This rule has found most varied application. Thus, if a case can be decided on either of two grounds, one involving a constitutional question, the other a question of statutory construction or general law, the Court will decide only the latter. [5.] The Court will not pass upon the validity of a statute upon complaint of one who fails to show that he is injured by its operation. [6.] The Court will not pass upon the constitutionality of a statute at the instance of one who has availed himself of its benefits. [7.] 'When the validity of an act of the Congress is drawn in question, and even if a serious doubt of constitutionality is raised, it is a cardinal principle that this Court will first ascertain whether a construction of the statute is fairly possible by which the question may be avoided.' " [Emphasis added.]

3. *Ashwander and the "Neo-Brandeisian Fallacy."* Note the comments on the content and uses of the Ashwander rules in Gunther, "The Subtle Vices of the 'Passive Virtues'—A Comment on Principle and Expediency in Judicial Review," 64 Colum.L.Rev. 1 (1964):[1] "[J]urisdiction under our system is rooted in Article III and congressional enactments; it is not a domain solely within the Court's keeping." The view that the Court has a general discretion not to adjudicate "frequently professes to find support in the Brandeis opinion in the Ashwander case. Brandeis' statement regarding "cases confessedly within [the Court's] jurisdiction" is "sound and of principled content; it is not an assertion of a vague Court discretion to deny a decision on the merits in a case within the statutory and constitutional bounds of jurisdiction. The Brandeis rules are a far cry from the neo-Brandeisian fallacy that there is a general 'Power To Decline the Exercise of Jurisdiction Which Is Given,' that there is a general discretion not to adjudicate though statute, Constitution, and remedial law present a 'case' for decision and confer no discretion. [The 'Power to Decline' quotation is from Bickel, The Least Dangerous Branch (1962), 127.]

"Of course the Court often may and should avoid 'passing upon a large part of all of the constitutional questions pressed upon it for decision.' Four of the

---

1. Reprinted with the permission of the publisher, © copyright 1964, The Directors of the Columbia Law Review Association, Inc.

seven Brandeis rules involve well-known instances of such avoidance—avoidance only of some or all of the constitutional questions argued, *not* avoidance of all decision on the merits of the case. [The] remaining rules given by Brandeis deal with situations in which there is no 'case' or 'controversy' in terms of the jurisdictional content of Article III—as with the 'non-adversary' proceeding of his first rule—or where there is a lack of what Bickel calls 'pure' standing in the constitutional sense, or where the state of the remedial law prevents a 'case' from arising. In these Brandeis categories, decision on the merits is precluded because the jurisdictional requirements of Article III are not met; in the earlier ones, the jurisdiction to decide the merits is in fact exercised and all that is avoided is decision on some or all of the constitutional issues presented.

"The only possible Brandeis contribution to the fallacy lies in his reference to all of the categories as 'cases confessedly within' the Court's jurisdiction. But that referred to the fact that all of the jurisdictional requirements added by the statute had been met; and adjudication on the merits did in fact result in all of his categories, except where a jurisdictional requirement originating in the Constitution had not been satisfied. There is a sad irony in the transformation of the Brandeis passage into a veritable carte blanche for Court discretion as to jurisdiction; and there is sad irony too in the invocation of Brandeis' principled concern with threshold questions by members and appraisers of the Court who would assert a virtually unlimited choice in deciding whether to decide. The neo-Brandeisian fallacy has fortunately not yet gained a firm, persistent foothold on the Court."[2]

SOME EXAMPLES OF DISCRETIONARY DISMISSALS OF APPEALS—AND SOME QUESTIONS

Introduction. Consider the following examples of Supreme Court refusals to adjudicate the merits of cases apparently within the Court's obligatory appeal jurisdiction. Was there any principled justification for any of these dismissals? Sometimes the Court purports to rely in part on Justice Brandeis' statement in Ashwander. Sometimes the Court merely states that the case is dismissed "for want of a properly presented federal question" or "because of the inadequacy of the record." Yet, in these cases, there was apparently nothing "improper" about the presentation of the federal question in the sense of compliance with governing statutes and Court rules. That variety of noncompliance would presumably have resulted in a simple dismissal for want of jurisdiction. What, if any, justification is there for the Court's exercise of discretion in these cases?

1. *The Rescue Army case.* In RESCUE ARMY v. MUNICIPAL COURT OF LOS ANGELES, 331 U.S. 549 (1947), the appeal concededly presented "substantial questions concerning the constitutional validity of [Los Angeles ordinances] governing the solicitation of contributions for charity." Moreover, the case was clearly within the appeal jurisdiction. Yet the majority disposed of the case without reaching the merits: "While [we] are unable to conclude that there is no jurisdiction in this cause, nevertheless compelling reasons exist for not exercising it." After making that statement, Justice Rutledge's majority opinion discussed at length the varied ingredients of the Court's "policy of strict necessity in disposing of constitutional issues." (See the excerpts in sec. 1

---

2. Chief Justice Warren discussed the Ashwander rules in his majority opinion in Flast v. Cohen, sec. 2 above. The Chief Justice pointed to them as illustrations of "not always clearly distinguished" strands of policy considerations and constitutional limitations. He elaborated: "Because the rules operate in 'cases confessedly within [the Court's] jurisdiction,' they find their source in policy, rather than purely constitutional, considerations. However, several of the cases cited by [Brandeis] articulated purely constitutional grounds for decision."

above.) Can that "policy of strict necessity" legitimately override the congressional mandate in the appeal statute?

The litigation arose as follows: Murdock, an officer of the Rescue Army, had been twice convicted in a local court of violations of the ordinances. Each conviction was reversed on evidentiary grounds. After the second reversal, Murdock and his organization filed an action in the highest state court seeking a writ of prohibition against further prosecution. The state supreme court denied the writ on the merits, in part relying on a parallel case, Gospel Army v. Los Angeles. In examining the Rescue Army appeal, the Court was troubled by the "interlacing relationships" between the various statutory provisions and the "difficult problems" as to the bearing of the state court's Gospel Army opinion on the Rescue Army litigation. Justice RUTLEDGE stated: "One aspect [of the application of the] 'policy of strict necessity' and avoidance of constitutional adjudication has been by virtue of the presence of other grounds for decision. But when such alternatives are absent, as in this case, application must rest upon considerations relative to the manner in which the constitutional issue itself is shaped and presented. These cannot be reduced to any precise formula or complete catalogue. But in general [they] are of the same nature as those which make the case and controversy limitation applicable, differing only in degree. To the more usual considerations of timeliness and maturity, of concreteness, definiteness, certainty, and of adversity of interests affected, are to be added in cases coming from state courts involving state legislation those arising when questions of construction, essentially matters of state law, remain unresolved or highly ambiguous. [Whether] decision of the constitutional issue will be made must depend upon the degree to which uncertainty exists. [F]or a variety of reasons the shape in which the underlying constitutional issues have reached this Court [in this case] presents, we think, insuperable obstacles to any exercise of jurisdiction to determine them. Those reasons comprise not only obstacles of prematurity and comparative abstractness arising from the nature of the proceeding in prohibition and the manner in which the parties have utilized it for presenting the constitutional questions. They also include related considerations growing out of uncertainties resulting from the volume of legislative provisions possibly involved [and] their intricate interlacing not only with each other on their face but also in the California Supreme Court's disposition of them. [C]onsistently with the ["strict necessity"] policy, jurisdiction here should be exerted only when the jurisdictional question presented by the proceeding in prohibition tenders the underlying constitutional issues in clean-cut and concrete form, unclouded by any serious problem of construction relating either to the terms of the questioned legislation or to its interpretation by the state courts. [The] appeal is dismissed." [1]

2. *Poe v. Ullman.* As already noted above, Justice Frankfurter's plurality opinion in POE v. ULLMAN, 367 U.S. 497 (1961), dismissed an appeal from a state decision upholding the Connecticut ban on the use of contraceptives, especially emphasizing ripeness considerations. But Justice FRANKFURTER's opinion also included more general comments, including reliance on Brandeis in Ashwander. He stated, for example:

---

1. Note also Mattiello v. Connecticut, 395 U.S. 209 (1969), applying the Rescue Army principle to dismiss an appeal of an appellant challenging a statute pursuant to which he had been placed in juvenile detention. Is that dismissal even more questionable than those in Poe (below) and Rescue Army, which were efforts to obtain anticipatory relief? Mattiello is noted in Hart & Wechsler, Federal Courts (2d ed. 1973), 660, with the comment: "Is there any justification for the Supreme Court declining an appeal in its 'discretion' when the result is to permit a state to act against a person who is asserting a federal constitutional defense against that action? If there is in such cases 'justice at the discretion of the Court,' what then is the significance of the Act of Congress creating appeal jurisdiction?" (Hart & Wechsler, at 656–62, provide additional illustrations of summary dismissals of appeals apparently within the obligatory jurisdiction.)

"The restriction of our jurisdiction to cases and controversies within the meaning of [Art. III is] not the sole limitation on the exercise of our appellate powers, especially in cases raising constitutional questions. The policy reflected in numerous cases and over a long period was thus summarized in [Brandeis' "avoidance" statement in Ashwander]. In part [the Ashwander rules] have derived from the historically defined, limited nature and function of courts and from the recognition that, within the framework of our adversary system, the adjudicatory process is most securely founded when it is exercised under the impact of a lively conflict between antagonistic demands, actively pressed, which make resolution of the controverted issue a practical necessity. [These] considerations press with special urgency in cases challenging legislative action or state judicial action as repugnant to the Constitution. [The] various doctrines of 'standing,' 'ripeness,' and 'mootness,' which this Court has evolved with particular, though not exclusive, reference to such cases are but several manifestations [of] the primary conception that federal judicial power is to be exercised to strike down legislation, whether state or federal, only at the instance of one who is himself immediately harmed, or immediately threatened with harm, by the challenged [action]. Justiciability is of course not a legal concept with a fixed content or susceptible of scientific verification. Its utilization is the resultant of many subtle pressures, including the appropriateness of the issues for decision by this Court and the actual hardship to the litigants of denying them the relief sought. Both these factors justify withholding adjudication of the constitutional issue raised under the circumstances and in the manner in which they are now before the Court."

Justice HARLAN's extensive dissent commented: "[T]hat justiciability is not precisely definable does not make it ineffable." He noted that Justice Frankfurter had referred to virtually every ingredient of justiciability and proceeded to reject most as "*not* involved in the present appeals." For example, the fact that the case was one seeking anticipatory relief clearly did not make the case premature. Nor was this a situation where lack of "ripeness" could be charged. And the lack of an actual prosecution was "not *alone* sufficient to make the case too remote, not ideally enough 'ripe' for adjudication, at the prior stage of anticipatory relief." Moreover, there was no lack of adversariness, nor lack of standing. There was simply the past history of failure to enforce the law; and that, as noted earlier, was no reason to refuse adjudication. Justice Harlan concluded: "I fear that the Court has indulged in a bit of sleight of hand to be rid of the case." Poe v. Ullman, like Rescue Army, was a refusal to adjudicate a state court case apparently within the Court's obligatory appeal jurisdiction. Was the Poe dismissal any more justifiable? [2]

3. *The Epperson case.* Compare with Poe v. Ullman the majority's summary disposition of the justiciability issue in EPPERSON v. ARKANSAS, 393 U.S. 97 (1968), a state court action challenging the constitutionality of a 1928 law

---

2. Note Gunther, "The Subtle Vices of the 'Passive Virtues'—A Comment on Principle and Expediency in Judicial Review," 64 Colum.L. Rev. 1, 18 (1964), commenting on Bickel, The Least Dangerous Branch (1962): "[Bickel states] that it was 'wise' and proper that the Court withheld decision [in Poe v. Ullman]. And nothing but a 'dictum in Cohens v. Virginia' stood in the way of the Court's refusal to adjudicate. Was that all that really stood in the way? John Marshall, in Cohens, uttered words which Bickel repeatedly undertakes to disparage, for they flatly contradict his notions of permissible Court abstention. 'We have no more right to decline the exercise of jurisdiction which is given,' Marshall said, 'than to usurp that which is not given.'

But the only way in which this can be viewed as insignificant dictum is to argue that there are no adequate reference points for determination of the jurisdiction assigned to the Court. But there are: there is the Constitution; there is the statute. Under Bickel's analysis as well as the Court's, Poe v. Ullman was a 'case' within Article III; moreover, it was one of that small group of cases Congress has made it the Court's duty to decide." See also Note, "The Discretionary Power of the Supreme Court to Dismiss Appeals from State Courts," 63 Colum.L.Rev. 688 (1963), and Note, "Threat of Enforcement—Prerequisite of a Justiciable Controversy," 62 Colum.L.Rev. 106 (1962).

barring the teaching of evolution. Before reaching the merits (see chap. 14 above), Justice FORTAS' majority opinion simply noted: "There is no record of any prosecutions in Arkansas under its statute. It is possible that the statute is presently more of a curiosity than a vital fact of life. Nevertheless, the present case was brought, the appeal as of right is properly here, and it is our duty to decide the issues presented." Only Justice BLACK dissented. Note the comment in Hart & Wechsler, Federal Courts (2d ed. 1973), 657: "Doesn't Epperson confirm what Justice Frankfurter's opinion [in Poe v. Ullman] clearly implies—that the Poe disposition was not compelled by the 'case or controversy' requirements of Article III? Isn't that also true of Rescue Army? What, then, justifies such refusals to adjudicate appeals?" [3]

4. *The Naim case.* a. *The litigation.* Mrs. Naim sued Mr. Naim for an annulment of their marriage "on the ground of their racial ineligibility to marry one another," in view of the Virginia miscegenation law. The parties had left Virginia in 1952 to be married in North Carolina, concededly "for the purpose of evading the Virginia law which forbade their marriage." After the marriage, they "immediately returned to Norfolk, Virginia, where they lived together as husband and wife." The state trial court found the marriage void and granted the annulment. The state appellate court affirmed. It considered the federal constitutional objections to the miscegenation law at length—and rejected them all. 87 S.E.2d 749 (1955). The case was brought to the Court by appeal. Its full opinion in NAIM v. NAIM, 350 U.S. 891 (1955), follows: "Per Curiam: The inadequacy of the record as to the relationship of the parties to [Virginia] at the time of the marriage in North Carolina and upon their return to Virginia, and the failure of the parties to bring here all questions relevant to the disposition of the case, prevents the constitutional issue of the validity of the Virginia statute on miscegenation tendered here being considered 'in clean-cut and concrete form, unclouded' by such problems. [Rescue Army.] The judgment is vacated and the case remanded [for] action not inconsistent with this opinion."

3. Recall that the Court disposes of many appeals summarily, in orders affirming lower federal court judgments or dismissing state cases for want of a substantial federal question. (See chap. 1, sec. 4, above.) Such summary dispositions (unlike cases of the Poe and Naim variety) are dispositions on the merits, though their summary nature may warrant less precedential value. In several modern cases, the Court has divided about the proper weight to be given summary dispositions. See, e.g., Hicks v. Miranda, 422 U.S. 332 (1975): "[T]he lower courts are bound by summary decisions by this Court 'until such time as the Court informs [them] that [they] are not'"; but compare Justice Brennan's dissent from the denial of certiorari in Colorado Springs Amusements, Ltd. v. Rizzo, 428 U.S. 913 (1976). For subsequent guidance from the Court, see Mandel v. Bradley, 432 U.S. 173 (1977) ("[summary actions] should not be understood as breaking new ground but as applying principles established by prior decisions to the particular facts involved"), and Illinois State Bd. of Elections v. Socialist Workers Party, 440 U.S. 173 (1979) ("summary affirmances have considerably less precedential value than an opinion on the merits").

In Anderson v. Celebrezze, 460 U.S. 780 (1983), the Court made one of its strongest re-

cent statements concerning "the limited precedential effect to be accorded summary dispositions." In his majority opinion, Justice Stevens went on to state that "[t]he Court of Appeals quite properly concluded that our summary affirmances [were] 'a rather slender reed' on which to rest its decision. We have often recognized that the precedential effect of a summary affirmance extends no further than 'the precise issues presented and necessarily decided by those actions.' A summary disposition affirms only the judgment of the court below, and no more may be read into our action than was necessary to sustain that judgment."

See generally Wright, Federal Courts (4th ed. 1983), 331 ("Since Hicks, [the] courts of appeals have held themselves bound to follow Supreme Court summary dispositions."). But the Court's position on the appropriate weight lower courts should give to summary dispositions continues to be inconsistent. Generally, Hicks is cited for the proposition that summary dispositions constitute strong authority; Edelman v. Jordan, 415 U.S. 651 (1974), for the proposition that "summary affirmances are obviously not of the same precedential value" as plenary dispositions.

On remand, the Virginia appellate court stated [90 S.E.2d 849 (1956)]: "[T]he material facts were not [in] dispute. The record showed that the complainant in the suit, a white woman, was an actual bona fide resident of, and domiciled in, Virginia, and had been for more than a year next preceding the commencement of the suit; that the defendant was a Chinese and a non-resident of Virginia at the time of the institution of the suit; that they had gone to North Carolina to be married for the purpose of evading the Virginia law which forbade their marriage, were married in North Carolina and immediately returned to and lived in Virginia as husband and wife. [The] record before the [trial court] was adequate for a decision of the issues presented to it. The record before this court was adequate for deciding the issues on review. The decision of the [trial court] adjudicated the issues presented to that court. The decision of this court adjudicated the issues presented to it. The decree of the trial court and the decree of this court affirming it have become final so far as these courts are concerned. We have no provision either under the rules of practice and procedure of this court or under [state statutes] by which this court may send the cause back to the [trial court] with directions to re-open the cause so decided, gather additional evidence and render a new decision. [We] therefore adhere to our decision of the [case]." The case was once again taken to the Court. That Court's per curiam opinion on the second appeal, 350 U.S. 985 (1956), follows in full: "The motion to recall the mandate and to set the case down for oral argument upon the merits, or, in the alternative, to recall and amend the mandate, is denied. The decision of the Supreme Court of Appeals of Virginia of January 18, 1956, in response to our order of November 14, 1955, 350 U.S. 891, leaves the case devoid of a properly presented federal question."

    b. *The justification.* Was there any justification for the Court's disposition of the Naim case? In law? In policy? Do you agree with the comment that the dismissal of the appeal rested "on procedural grounds [that] are wholly without basis in the law"? Wechsler, "Toward Neutral Principles of Constitutional Law," 73 Harv.L.Rev. 1, 34 (1959). Note also the Bickel-Gunther differences on this issue reflected in Gunther, "The Subtle Vices of the ['Passive Virtues']," 64 Colum.L.Rev. 1, 11–12 (1964): "[The] cavalier amalgamation of certiorari and appeal [in Bickel, The Least Dangerous Branch (1962)] is a vast if not mischievous overstatement, in fact and in law. [Bickel states:] 'Thus a decision on the validity of anti-miscegenation statutes was avoided through the dismissal of an appeal, which is to be explained in terms of the discretionary considerations that go to determine the lack of ripeness.' [In] an earlier chapter, Bickel praised that dismissal as an example of the operation of 'techniques that allow leeway to expediency without abandoning principle'; 'the Court found no insuperable difficulty,' he notes with admiration, 'in leaving open the question of the constitutionality of anti-miscegenation statutes, though it would surely seem to be governed by the principle of the Segregation Cases' decided two years earlier. I will withhold comment for the moment on Bickel's judgment that this achievement was possible without 'abandoning principle'; the immediate question is Bickel's reliance on this dismissal for descriptive and normative purposes in handling appeals generally. Where [is] the legal basis for the discretion Bickel would condone and indeed advocate in this and similar cases within the appeal jurisdiction? No doubt there were strong considerations of expediency against considering the constitutionality of anti-miscegenation statutes in 1956. But does not the appeal jurisdiction, too, have a 'content of its own'? The content of this 'passive virtue' device is of course more than minimal: it derives from congressional regulation of the [Court's] appellate jurisdiction. [The] Court, to be sure, has sometimes honored the appeal statute in the breach: the miscegenation case is on the books, and there are a very few dismissals similarly indefensible in law. But these are still only aberrations, and surely more can be expected of Bickel than to exaggerate them to the level of the commonplace and to elevate them to the level of the desirable and the acceptable." [4]

INTERPRETING STATUTES TO AVOID CONSTITUTIONAL QUESTIONS

The policy and its risks. a. *The principle.* "[I]t is a cardinal principle that this Court will first ascertain whether a construction of the statute is fairly possible by which the [constitutional] question may be avoided." So ended the last of Justice Brandeis' seven rules in Ashwander; and that statement echoes a principle enunciated by the Court from the beginning. Indeed, Marshall, in Cohen v. Virginia, the case juxtaposed with the Brandeis rules above, decided the merits on the basis of statutory interpretation: where such a basis is available, he said, "it will be unnecessary, and consequently improper, to pursue any inquiries, which would then be merely speculative, respecting the power of Congress in the case."

b. *The risks.* The principle has obvious limitations, however. See Chief Justice Vinson's warning in Shapiro v. United States, 335 U.S. 1, 31 (1948): "The canon of avoidance of constitutional doubts must, like the 'plain meaning' rule [in the interpretation of stautes], give way where its application would produce a futile result, or an unreasonable result 'plainly at variance with the policy of the legislation as a whole.'" This avoidance technique risks not only indefensible statutory interpretation but also irresponsible constitutional adjudication. There may be temptation to strain for a meaning in the statute beyond that "fairly possible" in order to avoid constitutional interpretation. Yet constitutional interpretation may not be wholly avoided: tentative interpretations may be ventured in the very process of stating *what* constitutional issues are being avoided; there may be temptation to launch constitutional trial balloons and indulge in free-floating constitutional dicta without the restraints of fashioning constitutional law dispositive of the case. Is the "constitutional trial balloon" risk illustrated by the disposition in KENT v. DULLES, 357 U.S. 116 (1958)? In Kent, the challenger had been denied a passport for failing to submit an affidavit as to whether he was or had ever been a Communist, as required by a State Department regulation. The Court's holding was simply that the applicable statutes did not "delegate to the [Secretary of State] the kind of authority exercised here." Justice DOUGLAS' majority opinion insisted that "we do not reach the question of constitutionality"; yet he wrote several passages elaborating the constitutional "right to travel" underlying the statutory

---

4. For a similar critical comment on Bickel's position, see Hart & Wechsler, Federal Courts (2d ed. 1973), 661. [Recall that, 15 years after Naim, the Court held the Virginia miscegenation law unconstitutional in Loving v. Virginia (1971; chap. 9 above).]

For another controversial, arguably "lawless" and "irresponsible," summary disposition of an appeal, see Doe v. Commonwealth's Attorney (1976) (rejecting a challenge by homosexuals to Virginia's sodomy law, as noted in chap. 8 above).

Note also the divided Court's dismissal of an appeal in Doe v. Delaware, 450 U.S. 382 (1981). The case raised important and controversial questions regarding the constitutionally mandated standards regarding burdens of proof in state proceedings for termination of parental rights.

After hearing argument, the majority summarily dismissed the appeal "for want of a properly presented federal question." Justice Brennan's dissent, joined by Justice White, called that disposition "unprecedented and inexplicable." He stated: "The appellate jurisdiction of this Court is not discretionary. Having raised the federal constitutional challenge, [and] having received a final judgment from the highest court of the State upholding the statute, appellants have a *right* to appellate review." He insisted that Naim v. Naim was distinguishable, claiming that the Court's dismissal of that appeal in 1956 "for want of a properly presented federal question" was "best understood [as] attributable to 'the failure of the parties to bring here all questions relevant to the disposition of the case.'"

interpretation. Though no prior decision had squarely said so, the Court announced (and explained) that the "right to travel is a part of the 'liberty' of which the citizen cannot be deprived without the due process of law of the Fifth Amendment." [1] A few years later, the Court relied squarely on that "right" (announced in a purportedly nonconstitutional decision) in holding unconstitutional a passport restriction in the Aptheker case (1964; chap. 11 above). Compare Haig v. Agee (1981; chap. 11 above), where three Justices viewed the majority opinion as abandoning the statutory interpretation approach of Kent v. Dulles. Haig v. Agee, like Kent, challenged the State Department's authority to revoke passports in certain cases. But in Agee, in contrast to Kent, the majority found that the challenged regulation was justified by the broad regulatory authority granted to the State Department in the Passport Act of 1926. [2]

B. RESTRAINING THE EXERCISE OF JURISDICTION IN THE INTEREST OF FEDERALISM: DISTRICT COURT ABSTENTION; NONINTERFERENCE WITH STATE COURT PROCEEDINGS

DISTRICT COURT ABSTENTION

Introduction. The Court is not the only tribunal that occasionally declines to adjudicate even though jurisdiction is granted by the Constitution and the statutes. The federal district courts, too, exercise a discretion to abstain—more frequently than the Court. The Court has often encouraged district courts to abstain; but the evolution of abstention standards in the Court has been fitful and often unclear. When should federal courts abstain so that state courts may decide? Is district court abstention more justifiable than the Court's failures to exercise its obligatory jurisdiction?

The abstention doctrine is a response to the problems caused by the existence of two sets of courts, state and federal, with authority to adjudicate questions of state and federal law. Federal district court abstention has been especially important and controversial in suits challenging state action on federal grounds—suits spurred by the nationalizing impacts of the post-Civil War Amendments, the enactment of civil rights laws, and the 1908 decision in Ex parte Young (note 1). Congress was asked to curtail the exercise of that jurisdiction, but the legislative restrictions imposed were of limited scope. Beginning in 1940, Court-developed doctrines have created significant additional restraints on the exercise of federal jurisdiction; and those doctrines have produced much confusion and delay. The abstention doctrine is often invoked

---

1. Were the constitutional statements in Kent akin to an advisory opinion? Is advice acceptable in this context because it is only tentative—because it serves to make Congress sensitive to constitutional issues, yet leaves to Congress the opportunity to change the scope of the law? Was the Court exercising a "remanding" function—sending the issue back to Congress for "a second reading" of a statutory problem "the implications of which Congress failed to see"? See Bickel and Wellington, "Legislative Purpose and the Judicial [Process]," 71 Harv.L.Rev. 1 (1957).

2. Justice Brennan's dissent, joined by Justice Marshall, charged the majority had departed

from the approach set forth in Kent "for determining whether Congress has delegated to the Executive Branch the authority to deny a passport." Justice Blackmun, in a concurring notation, acknowledged that the Court was "cutting back somewhat" on Kent and later cases. He added: "I would have preferred to have the Court disavow forthrightly the aspects of [those cases] that may suggest that evidence of a longstanding Executive policy or construction in this area is not probative of the issue of congressional authorization. Nonetheless, believing this is what the Court in effect has done, I join its opinion."

to avoid decisions on constitutional issues, in cases where construction of "unclear" state law may make a ruling on the federal question "unnecessary." (See note 2.) Though abstention is more fully considered in courses on federal jurisdiction, the following materials briefly trace the major developments. In examining them, consider whether such reasons as minimizing federal-state conflicts and avoiding unnecessary decision of federal constitutional issues are sufficiently compelling to justify the tortured course of decisions traced below. Are such reasons in any event sufficient to justify judge-made restraints on the exercise of congressionally mandated jurisdiction? Do the materials below provide rules of adequate clarity?

1. *Ex parte Young and statutory restrictions.* EX PARTE YOUNG, 209 U.S. 123 (1908), made possible the broad and frequently invoked application of federal jurisdiction to state official action. A federal district court had ordered Young, a state attorney general, to cease enforcing a law regulating railroad rates, on the ground that it violated the 14th Amendment. The Supreme Court held that the 11th Amendment assurance of state immunity from federal court suits did not bar the suit against the state official: "If the Act which the state Attorney General seeks to enforce be a violation of the Federal Constitution, the officer in proceeding under such enactment comes into conflict with the superior authority of that Constitution, and he is in that case stripped of his official or representative character and is subjected in his person to the consequences of his individual conduct." [1] Pleas that Congress close the doors opened by Ex parte Young met only limited success: in 1910, a statute was enacted requiring that there be three-judge federal courts in most cases challenging state action; [2] the Johnson Act of 1934 prohibited most federal injunctions against state rate orders where "a plain, speedy and efficient remedy" in state courts was available; and a 1937 law similarly barred federal injunctions against state taxes. But Congress left many doors to the federal courts open. Thereafter, the Court undertook to close some of the doors Congress had not seen fit to shut. How adequate were the justifications?

2. *The Pullman Case.* RAILROAD COMM'N v. PULLMAN CO., 312 U.S. 496 (1941), launched the modern history of judicially-developed doctrines encouraging district court abstention. There, a state agency's order was challenged as violating state law as well as the federal Constitution. Justice FRANKFURTER's opinion for a unanimous Court directed the District Court to "stay its hand": "to retain the bill pending a determination of proceedings, to be brought with reasonable promptness, in the state court." Adjudication of the unclear state law issue might make decision on the constitutional question unnecessary. A lower federal court's decision of the state issue "cannot escape being a forecast rather than a determination"; the "resources of equity are equal to an adjustment that will avoid the waste of a tentative decision as well as the friction of a premature constitutional adjudication." And this judge-made doctrine was found appropriate even though it went beyond the limitations Congress had seen fit to impose: "This use of equitable powers is a contribution of the courts in furthering the harmonious relation between state and federal authority without the need of rigorous congressional restriction of those powers." [3]

---

1. Two years later, the Court found that such "individual conduct"—not entitled to the 11th Amendment immunity of states—nevertheless constituted "state action" within the reach of the 14th Amendment. Home Telephone and Telegraph Co. v. Los Angeles, 227 U.S. 278 (1913).

2. Recall chap. 1 above, on the recent sharp curtailment of the availability of three-judge district courts (including the repeal, in 1976, of the

1910 law requiring such courts in suits to enjoin the enforcement of state laws on constitutional grounds).

3. The occasion for abstention under the Pullman doctrine often arose because of the Court's decision in Siler v. Louisville & Nashville Railroad Co., 213 U.S. 175 (1909). That case held that, in federal court actions seeking to enjoin state laws as violating federal law, the

3. *The consequences of abstention.* The Court has repeatedly insisted, as in Harrison v. NAACP, 360 U.S. 167 (1959), that absention does not "involve the abdication of federal jurisdiction but only the postponement of its exercise." Yet the federal as well as the state issues were often presented to the state court after the federal trial court abstained, and the state court's decision was often reviewable in the Court. Thus the case might never return to the federal trial court. Indeed, the Court has occasionally insisted that the federal as well as the state issue must be submitted to the state court. See Government Employees v. Windsor, 353 U.S. 364 (1957). But see the "clarification" in England v. Louisiana Medical Examiners, 375 U.S. 411 (1964): "The [Windsor] case does not mean that a party must litigate his federal claims in the state courts, but only that he must inform those courts what his federal claims are, so that the state statute may be construed 'in light of' those claims." What if the state courts then proceed to adjudicate the federal claim they have been "informed" about? [4]

4. *Abstention and the Burger Court: Some examples.* The Court divided over the propriety of abstention in WISCONSIN v. CONSTANTINEAU, 400 U.S. 433 (1971). Justice DOUGLAS' majority opinion rejected the claim that a challenge to the Wisconsin "posting" law should have been presented first to the state courts.[5] He found no unresolved question of state law with respect to the thrust of the federal constitutional challenge, the absence of notice and hearing, and concluded: "Where there is no ambiguity in the state statute, the federal court should not abstain but proceed to decide the federal constitutional

federal court should first decide if the challenged action violated state law before turning to the federal issue. But the Siler approach was in large part abandoned in Pennhurst State School v. Halderman, 451 U.S. 1 (1981), holding that injunctive relief based on state law in such cases is barred by the 11th Amendment. Under Pennhurst, federal courts must limit injunctive relief to claims based on federal law. The result of Pennhurst is that the Pullman doctrine has been made obsolete when the only unresolved state law issue is whether the challenged official activity violates state law. (The Pullman doctrine is still relevant, however, when the constitutionality of a challenged state law turns on the meaning of that law.) For a general discussion of the Pullman doctrine prior to the Pennhurst ruling, see Field, "Abstention in Constitutional Cases: The Scope of the Pullman Abstention Doctrine," 122 U.Pa.L.Rev. 1071 (1974).

4. Note the American Law Institute's suggestions for clarifying the groundrules for abstention, in its draft of a revised Title 28 of the United States Code. See ALI, Study of the Division of Jurisdiction within State and Federal Courts (1969). The core ALI provision, § 1371(c), states: "A district court may stay an action [on] the ground that the action presents issues of State law that ought to be determined in a State proceeding, if the court finds: (1) that the issues of State law cannot be satisfactorily determined in the light of the State authorities; and (2) that abstention from the exercise of federal jurisdiction is warranted either by the likelihood that the necessity for deciding a substantial question of federal constitutional law may thereby be avoided, or by a serious danger of embarrassing the effectuation of State policies by a decision of State law at variance with the view that may be

ultimately taken by the State court, or by other circumstances of like character; and (3) that a plain, speedy, and efficient remedy may be had in the courts of such State; and (4) that the parties' claims of federal right, if any, including any issues of fact material thereto, can be adequately protected by review of the State court decision by the Supreme Court of the United States."

Other provisions of the ALI proposals worth special note are the following: § 1371(f) bars abstention beyond the circumstances set forth above; it prohibits additional "judge-made notions of abstention." Subsection (d) clarifies the consequences of abstention: abstention produces a stay, not a dismissal; but ordinarily litigation through the state court route (with the possibility of Supreme Court review) ends the case. And subsection (g) excepts certain actions from the abstention authorization including some civil rights actions—on the ground that "there is an especially strong national interest in a federal forum for such cases." (The ALI decided against a broader authorization of abstention "merely to avoid a federal constitutional question.")

5. The "posting law" permitted various local officials or a man's wife to designate—and thereby forbid selling liquor to—any person who, because of "excessive drinking," exposed his family to want or was dangerous to the peace. There had been no construction of the statute by the state courts; the law did not provide a hearing on its face; and the challenger's name had been posted without a hearing. The lower court refused to abstain and held the lack of notice unconstitutional on procedural due process grounds.

claim." Chief Justice BURGER's dissent conceded that there was "no absolute duty to abstain," but argued that "a three-judge district court would be well advised in cases such as this, involving no urgency or question of large import, to decline to act." Some lower federal courts, purporting to draw on hints in early Burger Court decisions, sought to discourage resort to federal courts in challenging state legislation and tried to channel more litigation into the state courts. That tendency was curtailed by the Court's disposition of LAKE CARRIERS' ASS'N v. MacMULLAN, 406 U.S. 498 (1972). This was an attack by Great Lakes shipowners on a Michigan pollution control law apparently prohibiting the discharge of sewage and requiring the installation of on-board sewage storage devices. The lower court dismissed the suit, but Justice BRENNAN's majority opinion found that "abstention was not proper on the majority of grounds given by the District Court." For example, "the availability of declaratory relief in Michigan courts" was held to be "wholly beside the point," in view of the federal courts' obligation to give "due respect to a suitor's choice of a federal forum." (The only justification for abstention found applicable by the Supreme Court was the possibility that the state courts might resolve "ambiguities in the Michigan law" in such a way as to "avoid or significantly modify the federal questions appellants raise.") More generally, Justice Brennan reemphasized that abstention is appropriate "only in narrowly limited 'special circumstances' justifying 'the delay and expense to which application of the abstention doctrine inevitably gives rise.' " [6]

LIMITS ON FEDERAL JUDICIAL INTERVENTION IN STATE COURT PROCEEDINGS: THE BACKGROUND AND IMPACT OF YOUNGER v. HARRIS

Introduction. The abstention doctrines considered above limit the exercise of federal jurisdiction not only because of federalism concerns but also, and often predominantly, because of the federal judiciary's interest in avoiding unnecessary constitutional decisions. Another doctrine—one that has produced considerable controversy in recent years—rests more heavily on federalism concerns. In a variety of settings, the Court has enforced a policy of noninterference in state judicial proceedings. While the partial abstention theories noted above merely mean (at least in theory and form) *postponement* of the exercise of federal jurisdiction, the Younger nonintervention doctrine produces *total* abstention—a total barrier to District Court adjudication.

6. Compare Harris County Commissioners Court v. Moore, 420 U.S. 77 (1975), an 8 to 1 decision ordering abstention because of uncertain questions of state law underlying the federal constitutional claims.

For a careful modern survey and criticism of abstention doctrines—both those considered under the principles discussed in this group of notes, and those drawn from Younger v. Harris, in the next group of notes—see Redish, "Abstention, Separation of Powers, and the Limits of the Judicial Function," 94 Yale L.J. 71 (1984). Redish argues that "neither total nor partial judge-made abstention is acceptable as a matter of legal process and separation of powers, wholly apart from the practical advisability of either form of the doctrine. Moreover, [the] high transaction costs imposed by most forms of these abstention doctrines are not justified by their supposed benefits, and [their] total abolition would not seriously undermine the efficient working of judicial federalism. [The] interests of federalism would be sufficiently protected by existing statutorily-dictated abstention [see note 1 above], by long established equitable limitations, and by the contours and limits of the substantive federal rights being enforced. Thus, little would be lost and much gained by simple judicial adherence to the valid legislative commands of existing federal substantive and jurisdictional enactments." Redish adds: "It may well be that, if Congress were to consider the matter today, it would choose to structure abstention much as the federal courts have. But the comparative arguments for and against such forms of abstention are by no means so one-sided as to make that conclusion inescapable. In a constitutional democracy, in any event, such decisions are most appropriately rendered by the legislature, not the judiciary."

Like abstention, the nonintervention policy rests in part on statutory grounds but even more heavily on judge-made doctrines. Thus, a federal statute, 28 U.S.C. § 2283, bars federal court injunctions "to stay proceedings in a State court except as expressly authorized by Act of Congress, or where necessary in aid of its jurisdiction, or to protect or effectuate its judgments." But that law, after a period of uncertainty, was held inapplicable to federal actions under the federal civil rights laws, including the wide-ranging 42 U.S.C. § 1983.[1] (See p. 859 above.) Since the bulk of modern constitutional litigation rests on the civil rights jurisdictional provision, the anti-injunction statute is of little force with respect to most constitutional litigation. Hence it is the judicially developed nonintervention doctrines that provide the major barrier to access to federal courts by those challenging the enforcement of state legislation. In DOMBROWSKI v. PFISTER, 380 U.S. 479 (1965), the Court seemed to open the federal doors wide to a variety of civil liberties claims, and that decision was read very broadly by many lower courts. However, ever since Younger v. Harris (note 1 below), the Court has imposed significant restraints on the Dombrowski development. The impact of these cases has been particularly great on First Amendment litigation and on the availability of overbreadth and vagueness attacks. The review of Younger v. Harris and its progeny, below, is designed to convey a sense of recent developments.

In Dombrowski, the challengers claimed that state criminal laws were about to be invoked against them in bad faith, as well as that those statutes were "overly broad and vague regulations of expression." Justice BRENNAN's majority opinion, emphasizing the "chilling effect" of such laws, concluded that in such a case "abstention and the denial of injunctive relief may well result in the denial of any effective safeguards against the loss of protected freedoms of expression, and cannot be justified." In the wake of Dombrowski, constitutional challenges to state criminal statutes in federal courts proliferated. The Younger v. Harris group of cases in 1971 curbed that trend. Dombrowski itself had sustained federal relief against *future* state prosecutions. In most of the 1971 cases, the lower courts had gone beyond Dombrowski to grant injunctive or declaratory relief against state criminal prosecutions already under way. The Court's specific holdings in 1971 were addressed to the latter situation, found federal relief against *pending* state proceedings justified only in exceptional circumstances, and concluded that the lower court interventions challenged here had all been improper. Justice Black's opinion in Younger was, however, written very broadly and was read by many as having an importance going beyond the specific situations before the Court. There were passages that appeared significant not only in cases of federal relief against *pending* state prosecutions but also in Dombrowski-like suits to block *future* prosecutions. Moreover, Younger raised the question whether its restraint vis-à-vis criminal cases might carry over to civil proceedings as well. The following materials survey the content and expanding scope of the Younger approach.[2]

1. *Younger v. Harris.* YOUNGER v. HARRIS, 401 U.S. 37 (1971), was a federal action originally brought by Harris to hold a California criminal syndicalism law unconstitutional on its face under the First Amendment.[3]

1. Mitchum v. Foster, 407 U.S. 225 (1972), held 42 U.S.C. § 1983 to be an "expressly authorized" exception to § 2283. Cf. Fair Assessment in Real Estate Assn. v. McNary (1981, note 5 below).

2. Other passages in Younger suggested changing attitudes regarding the receptiveness of federal courts to "on the face" overbreadth attacks on legislation—a litigation technique that had gained significant added impetus as a result of Dombrowski. (Although later overbreadth

opinions have not curtailed that technique as much as some of the dicta in Younger suggested, Younger did prove to be the beginning of a trend of limiting the availability of overbreadth attacks. Recall the materials on the new "substantial overbreadth" emphasis, in chap. 12, sec. 1, above.)

3. The act had been held constitutional in Whitney v. California (1927; chap. 11 above); Whitney was overruled by Brandenburg v. Ohio (1969; chap. 11 above).

Harris had been indicted under the act and sued to enjoin prosecution. The District Court found the law unconstitutional and enjoined "further prosecution of the currently pending action" against Harris. Justice BLACK's opinion [4] concluded that the lower court should not have adjudicated Harris' claim because of "the settled doctrines that have always confined very narrowly the availability of injunctive relief against state criminal prosecutions." Justice Black reviewed the Court's repeated insistence "that the normal thing to do when federal courts are asked to enjoin pending proceedings in state courts is not to issue such injunctions." [5]

Justice Black articulated the underlying reasons for the "long standing public policy against federal court interference with state court proceedings" as follows: "One is the basic doctrine of equity jurisprudence that courts of equity should not act, and particularly should not act to restrain a criminal prosecution, when the moving party has an adequate remedy at law and will not suffer irreparable injury if denied equitable relief. [The policy of] restraining courts of equity from interfering with criminal prosecutions is reinforced by an even more vital consideration, the notion of 'comity,' that is, a proper respect for state functions, a recognition of the fact that the entire country is made up of a Union of separate state governments, and a continuance of the belief that the National Government will fare best if the States and their institutions are left free to perform their separate functions in their separate ways. This, perhaps for lack of a better and clearer way to describe it, is referred to by many as 'Our Federalism.' [What] the concept [represents] is a system in which there is sensitivity to the legitimate interests of both State and National Governments, and in which the National Government, anxious though it may be to vindicate and protect federal rights and federal interests, always endeavors to do so in ways that will not unduly interfere with the legitimate activities of the States."

Justice Black then turned to the impact of Dombrowski on this settled doctrine—and, contrary to the District Court, found none.[6] He stated: "The district court [thought] that the Dombrowski decision substantially broadened the availability of injunctions against state criminal prosecutions and that under that decision the federal courts may give equitable relief, without regard to any showing of bad faith or harassment, whenever a state statute is found 'on its face' to be vague or overly broad, in violation of the First Amendment. We recognize that there are some statements in the Dombrowski opinion that would seem to support this argument. [But] such statements were unnecessary to the decision of that case, because the Court found that the plaintiffs had alleged a basis for equitable relief under the long-established standards. In addition, we

---

4. Justice Black wrote an opinion joined by Chief Justice Burger and Justices Harlan, Stewart and Blackmun. But Justice Stewart, joined by Justice Harlan, also filed a concurring opinion— and the narrowness of that concurring opinion suggested that some of the passages in Justice Black's "opinion of the Court" represented only a plurality view. Justice Brennan, joined by Justices White and Marshall, filed a separate opinion concurring only in the result. Justice Douglas was the only dissenter in the case. [The statute challenged by Harris was subsequently held unconstitutional by a state court. In re Harris, 97 Cal.Rptr. 844 (1971).]

5. Justice Black relied on Fenner v. Boykin, 271 U.S. 240 (1926), where the Court had made clear "that such a suit, even with respect to state criminal proceedings not yet formally instituted, could be proper only under very special circumstances." The Fenner case had spoken of "extra-

ordinary circumstances where the danger of irreparable loss is both great and immediate." Justice Black emphasized in Younger that, because of "the fundamental policy against federal interference," it was necessary to show more than "irreparable injury, the traditional prerequisite to obtaining an injunction": "even irreparable injury is insufficient unless it is 'both great and immediate.'" Accordingly, an injunction was improper here: Harris had an opportunity to raise his constitutional claims in the pending prosecution against him; there was "no suggestion that this single prosecution against Harris is brought in bad faith or is only one of a series of repeated prosecutions to which he will be subjected."

6. Some of his comments on Dombrowski, especially his criticism of the overbreadth technique, are quoted more fully above, in chap. 12, sec. 1.

do not regard the reasons adduced to support this position as sufficient to justify such a substantial departure from the established doctrines regarding the availability of injunctive relief. [T]he existence of a 'chilling effect,' even in the area of First Amendment rights, has never been considered a sufficient basis, in and of itself, for prohibiting state action. [T]he chilling effect that admittedly can result from the very existence of certain laws on the statute books does not in itself justify prohibiting the State from carrying out the important and necessary task of enforcing these laws against socially harmful conduct that the State believes in good faith to be punishable under its laws and the Constitution.

"Beyond all this is another, more basic consideration. Procedures for testing the constitutionality of a statute 'on its face' in the manner apparently contemplated by Dombrowski, and for then enjoining all action to enforce the statute until the State can obtain court approval for a modified version, are fundamentally at odds with the function of the federal courts in our constitutional plan. The power and duty of the judiciary to declare laws unconstitutional is in the final analysis derived from its responsibility for resolving concrete disputes brought before the courts for decision. [Marbury v. Madison.] But this vital responsibility, broad as it is, does not amount to an unlimited power to survey the statute books and pass judgment on laws before the courts are called upon to enforce them. [T]he task of analyzing a proposed statute, pinpointing its deficiencies, and requiring correction of these deficiencies before the statute is put into effect, is rarely if ever an appropriate task for the judiciary. The combination of the relative remoteness of the controversy, the impact on the legislative process of the relief sought, and above all the speculative and amorphous nature of the required line-by-line analysis of detailed statutes [ordinarily] results in a kind of case that is wholly unsatisfactory for deciding constitutional questions, whichever way they might be decided. In light of this fundamental conception of the Framers as to the proper place of the federal courts in the governmental processes of passing and enforcing laws, it can seldom be appropriate for these courts to exercise any such power of prior approval or veto over the legislative process.

"For these reasons, fundamental not only to our federal system but also to the basic functions of the [Judicial Branch], we hold that the Dombrowski decision should not be regarded as having upset the settled doctrines that have always confined very narrowly the availability of injunctive relief against state criminal prosecutions. [There] may, of course, be extraordinary circumstances in which the necessary irreparable injury can be shown even in the absence of the usual prerequisites of bad faith and harassment. For example, as long ago as [Watson v. Buck, 313 U.S. 599 (1942)], we indicated: 'It is of course conceivable that a statute might be flagrantly and patently violative of express constitutional prohibitions in every clause, sentence and paragraph, and in whatever manner and against whomever an effort might be made to apply it.' Other unusual situations calling for federal intervention might also arise, but there is no point in our attempting now to specify what they might be. It is sufficient [here to hold] that the possible unconstitutionality of a statute 'on its face' does not in itself justify an injunction against good faith attempts to enforce it." [7]

2. *Samuels v. Mackell.* One of the companion cases to Younger, SAMUELS v. MACKELL, 401 U.S. 66 (1971), provided Justice Black with the occasion to discuss an issue not reached in his Younger opinion—the question of *declaratory* rather than injunctive relief against *pending* state prosecutions. The appellants had been indicted under New York's criminal anarchy law. They sought

---

7. For an elaboration of the "extraordinary circumstances" exception to the Younger barrier, see Kugler v. Helfant, 421 U.S. 117 (1975).

injunctive or declaratory relief in the federal court. Justice BLACK's opinion concluded that "under ordinary circumstances the same considerations that require the withholding of injunctive relief will make declaratory relief equally inappropriate." He explained his view that "the propriety of declaratory and injunctive relief should be judged by essentially the same standards" as follows: "In both situations deeply rooted and long-settled principles of equity have narrowly restricted the scope for federal intervention, and ordinarily a declaratory judgment will result in precisely the same interference with and disruption of state proceedings that the long-standing policy limiting injunctions was designed to avoid. This is true for at least two reasons. In the first place, [under the statutes] a declaratory judgment issued while state proceedings are pending might serve as the basis for a subsequent injunction against those proceedings to 'protect or effectuate' the declaratory judgment and thus result in a clearly improper interference with the state proceedings. Secondly, even if the declaratory judgment is not used as a basis for actually issuing an injunction, the declaratory relief alone has virtually the same practical impact as a formal injunction would. [We] therefore hold that, in cases where the state criminal prosecution was begun prior to the federal suit, the same equitable principles relevant to the propriety of an injunction must be taken into consideration by federal district courts [and] that where an injunction would be impermissible under these principles, declaratory relief should ordinarily be denied as well." [8]

3. *Federal relief against threatened (rather than pending) state prosecutions.* Younger and Samuels were explicitly limited to interference in *pending* prosecutions, despite some broader overtones in Justice Black's opinion. Three years later, the Court made it clear that the principles would *not* extend to interference in *threatened* state prosecutions. In STEFFEL v. THOMPSON, 416 U.S. 452 (1974), Justice Brennan had the opportunity in a majority opinion to adopt for the Court the views he had expressed in his separate opinion in one of the companion cases to Younger, Perez v. Ledesma, 401 U.S. 82, 93 (1971). Petitioners in Steffel had stopped distributing antiwar leaflets at a shopping center because of threats of prosecution under a state criminal trespass law. They sued for declaratory relief that the law was unconstitutional. The lower court had concluded that the bad faith harassment prerequisite for federal relief against *pending* state prosecutions, established in Younger and Samuels, should be carried over to actions for *declaratory* relief against *threatened* state prosecutions as well. Justice BRENNAN's opinion for a unanimous Court in Steffel rejected that view and concluded instead that declaratory relief against a threatened rather than pending state prosecution is permissible without a showing of bad faith harassment. The Court concluded that "federal declaratory relief is not precluded when no state prosecution is pending and a federal plaintiff demonstrates a genuine threat of enforcement of a disputed state criminal statute, whether an attack is made on the constitutionality of the statute on its face or as applied." (Steffel authorized *declaratory* relief against threatened state criminal proceedings. Several subsequent cases indicate that, despite Justice Black's tenor in the 1971 cases, *injunctive* relief against threatened prosecution is also available in some circumstances.[9])

8. Note also Justice White's majority opinion in the 5 to 4 decision in Hicks v. Miranda, 422 U.S. 332 (1975), holding that "where state criminal proceedings are begun against the federal plaintiffs after the federal complaint is filed but before any proceedings of substance on the merits have taken place in the federal court, the principles of [Younger] should apply in full force."

9. See, e.g., Doran v. Salem Inn, Inc., 422 U.S. 922 (1975), holding that where a plaintiff is properly in a federal court seeking declaratory relief under Steffel, the federal court may also grant preliminary injunctive relief "without regard to Younger's restrictions." That development was extended two years later in Wooley v. Maynard (1977; chap. 12 above), where Chief Justice Burger's majority opinion authorized a permanent injunction, not merely a preliminary one, against further state prosecutions.

4. *The extension of Younger principles to pending state civil proceedings.* At the time of Younger, it was unclear whether its approach would apply to federal court intervention in pending state *civil* proceedings. In Younger itself, Justice Stewart's concurrence noted that, in the civil rather than criminal context, "the balance might be struck differently." But a year later, Justice White's dissent in Lynch v. Household Finance Corp., 405 U.S. 538 (1972), argued that the "relevant considerations [are] equally applicable where state civil litigation is in progress." That dispute was resolved in a series of subsequent cases: the Court has steadily expanded the application of Younger principles to the civil action context. The sequence began with HUFFMAN v. PURSUE, LTD., 420 U.S. 592 (1975). That case involved a state proceeding to close a theater for showing obscene movies, under an Ohio "public nuisance" law. The appellee had obtained a federal injunction on overbreadth grounds. Justice REHNQUIST's majority opinion held that the injunction should not have been granted: "[W]hatever may be the [standard] in civil litigation with private parties, we deal here with a state proceeding which in important respects is more akin to a criminal prosecution than most civil cases"; accordingly, the Younger principles applied.[10] Huffman was a small first step; others soon followed. In JUIDICE v. VAIL, 430 U.S. 327 (1977), debtors under delinquent state judgments were held in contempt for failing to respond in New York proceedings for discovery of their assets. They challenged the state procedures on constitutional grounds and obtained federal injunctive relief. Justice REHNQUIST's majority opinion reversed, insisting that the Younger principles applied: "A State's interest in the contempt process [is] surely an important interest. [We] think it is of sufficiently great import to require application of the principles of [Younger and Huffman]. [Whether] disobedience of a court-sanctioned subpoena, and the resulting process leading to a finding of contempt of court, is labeled civil, quasi-criminal, or criminal in nature, we think the salient fact is that federal-court interference with the State's contempt process is 'an offense to the State's interest [likely] to be every bit as great as it would be were this a criminal proceeding,' Huffman." [11]

Two months after Judice, the majority continued on its path of extending the Younger principles to civil litigation in TRAINOR v. HERNANDEZ, 431 U.S. 434 (1977). Although Justice WHITE's majority opinion insisted that "we have no occasion to decide whether Younger principles apply to all civil litigation," most of the dissenters in this 5 to 4 ruling feared that the majority had gone a long way in that direction. In Trainor, Illinois officials had sued the appellees to recover welfare payments allegedly fraudulently obtained. As ancillary to that suit, the officials began attachment proceedings against appellees' savings. The appellees then obtained a federal injunction on the ground that the attachment law violated due process. The majority decision reversing that injunction emphasized "that the State was a party to the suit in its role of administering its public assistance programs." Justice White added that the State suit and its attachment proceedings "were brought to vindicate important state policies such as safeguarding the fiscal integrity of those programs. The State authorities also have the option of vindicating these policies through criminal prosecutions. [The] principles of Younger and Huffman are broad enough to apply to interference by a federal court with an ongoing civil enforcement action such as this, brought by the State in its sovereign capacity."

10. Justice BRENNAN's dissent, joined by Justices Douglas and Marshall, feared that the decision was "obviously only the first step toward extending [the Younger principles] to state *civil* proceedings generally."

11. A dissent by Justice BRENNAN, joined by Justice Marshall, characterized the decisions in Huffman and Juidice as "only covers for the ultimate goal of denying § 1983 plaintiffs the federal forum in any case, civil or criminal, when a pending state proceeding may hear the federal plaintiff's federal claims." Justice STEWART also dissented. Justice STEVENS concurred only in the result.

Justice BRENNAN, joined by Justice Marshall, submitted a strong dissent, echoing many of his criticisms in Juidice. In another strong dissent, Justice STEVENS accused the majority of adding a number of "new complexities to a doctrine that has bewildered other federal courts for several years." He insisted that "a principled application of [Younger principles] forecloses abstention in cases in which the federal challenge is to the constitutionality of the state procedure itself." Justice STEWART's dissent stated that he "substantially agree[d]" with the Brennan and Stevens positions.[12]

5. *"Comity" as a barrier to federal court actions for damages.* In FAIR ASSESSMENT IN REAL ESTATE v. McNARY, 454 U.S. 100 (1981), a sharply divided Court, drawing in part on Younger principles, held that "taxpayers are barred by the principle of comity from asserting § 1983 actions against the validity of state tax systems in federal courts." The case involved a § 1983 action for damages brought by taxpayers challenging the allegedly unconstitutional administration of a state property tax system. Justice REHNQUIST's majority opinion perceived two "conflicting lines of authority" bearing on the case. On the one hand, the Tax Injunction Act of 1937 and antecedent decisions of the Court reflected "the fundamental principle of comity between federal courts and state governments that is essential to 'Our Federalism,' particularly in the area of state taxation." That line of authority barred at least federal injunctive and declaratory judgment challenges to state tax laws. On the other hand, federal cases since Monroe v. Pape in 1961 indicated that "comity does not apply where § 1983 is involved." Both lines of authority "cannot govern this case," Justice Rehnquist noted. He chose to go in the direction of federal restraint: in cases such as this, "the principle of comity controls." He explained that "comity" had been relied upon in several modern cases outside the state tax area: "Its fullest articulation was given in the now familiar language of [Younger]. [The] principles of federalism recognized in Younger have not been limited to federal court interference in state criminal proceedings, but have been extended to some state civil actions. Although these modern expressions of comity have been limited in their application to federal cases which seek to enjoin state judicial proceedings, a limitation which we do not abandon here, they illustrate the principles that bar petitioners' suit under § 1983. [P]etitioners' § 1983 action would be no less disruptive of Missouri's

---

12. See also the 5 to 4 decision in Moore v. Sims, 442 U.S. 415 (1979), where Justice Rehnquist's majority opinion held that abstention was proper under Younger principles, with the dissent by Justice Stevens, joined by Justices Brennan, Stewart and Marshall, charging that the Court had applied "the Younger doctrine where it simply does not belong." The suit arose out of parents' efforts to regain custody of their child from the State after alleged instances of child abuse. Turning to the federal courts, they launched a broad constitutional challenge to the Texas Family Code's definition of the contours of the parent-child relationship and the permissible areas and modes of state intervention. The majority held that, in view of the pending state court custody proceedings, the federal trial court should not have exercised jurisdiction.

By 1982, when Middlesex Cty. Ethics Comm. v. Garden St. Bar Assn., 457 U.S. 423, was decided, the prevailing opinion was able to make the general statement: "The policies underlying Younger are fully applicable to noncriminal judicial proceedings when important state interests are involved. Moore v. Sims; [Huffman]." In

Middlesex, the Court held that "a federal court should abstain from considering a challenge to the constitutionality of disciplinary rules [regarding unethical conduct by attorneys] that are the subject of a pending state disciplinary proceeding within the jurisdiction of the New Jersey Supreme Court." Chief Justice Burger's opinion for the Court stated that such proceedings "implicate important state interests," and that there was "an adequate opportunity in the state proceedings to raise [the federal] constitutional challenges." Justice Brennan, concurring in the judgment, noted that he continued "to adhere to [his] view [that] Younger v. Harris is in general inapplicable to civil proceedings." He supported the result here because the "traditional and primary responsibility of state courts for establishing and enforcing standards for members of their bars and the quasi-criminal nature of bar disciplinary proceedings call for exceptional deference by the courts." (Justice Marshall, joined by Justices Brennan, Blackmun and Stevens, also submitted a brief statement concurring in the judgment.)

tax system than would the historic equitable efforts to enjoin the collection of taxes, efforts which were early held barred by considerations of comity." [13]

A lengthy opinion by Justice BRENNAN, joined by Justices Marshall, Stevens and O'Connor, strongly disagreed with the majority's approach, even though the dissenters supported the result (but solely on the ground that the petitioners had failed to exhaust state administrative remedies). Justice Brennan emphasized: "I cannot agree that this case, and the jurisdiction of the federal courts over an action for damages brought pursuant to express congressional authority, is to be governed by applying a 'principle of comity' grounded solely on this Court's notion of an appropriate division of responsibility between the federal and state judicial systems. Subject only to constitutional constraints, it is exclusively Congress' responsibility to determine the jurisdiction of the federal courts. Federal courts have historically acted within their assigned jurisdiction in accordance with established principles respecting the prudent exercise of equitable power. But this practice lends no credence to the authority which the Court asserts today to renounce jurisdiction over an entire class of damages actions brought pursuant to [§ 1983]. Where Congress has granted the federal courts jurisdiction, we are not free to repudiate that authority. [The] power to control the jurisdiction of the lower federal courts is assigned by the Constitution to Congress, not to this Court. In its haste to rid the federal courts of a class of cases that it thinks unfit for federal scrutiny, the Court today departs from this fundamental precept. [T]here is absolutely no support, in either the cases of this Court or in Congress' action, for total abdication of federal power in this field."

SECTION 5. NONJUSTICIABLE "POLITICAL QUESTIONS," "JUDICIALLY DISCOVERABLE AND MANAGEABLE STANDARDS," AND REAPPORTIONMENT LITIGATION

Introduction. This section pursues the consideration of the "political question" doctrine begun in the concluding portions of chap. 6, at p. 397 above. Those materials should be reexamined at this point. As noted there, the concept that some constitutional issues are nonjusticiable because they are "political" is well established; but what the ingredients of that concept are has produced considerable controversy. There are at least three strands to the "political question" doctrine. The first, most confined, most clearly legitimate one is the "constitutional commitment" strand. That variety of political question reflects separation of powers principles and rests on the position that the Constitution commits the final determination of some constitutional questions to agencies other than courts. But the Court's political question decisions cannot all be explained on that "constitutional commitment" ground. As noted in chap. 6: "Some decisions on political questions nonjusticiability emphasize the nature of the question and its aptness for judicial resolution in view of judicial competence: that strand of the political questions doctrine finds some issues nonjusticiable because they cannot be resolved by 'judicially manageable standards,' or on the basis of data available to the courts. Still another, even more open-ended strand of the doctrine, suggests that the political questions notion is essentially a problem of judicial discretion, of prudential judgments that some

---

13. Contrast the majority's approach in Mc-Nary with a decision a few months later in Patsy v. Florida Board of Regents, 457 U.S. 496 (1982). In Patsy, the majority adhered to prior decisions by holding that exhaustion of state administrative remedies is not required as a prerequisite to bringing a § 1983 action.

issues ought not to be decided by the courts because they are too controversial or could produce enforcement problems or other institutional difficulties."

The political questions materials in chap. 6 emphasized the first, most clearly "constitutional interpretation" strand of the doctrine. It dealt with the arguable commitment of some issues to other branches for final decision, in such contexts as the reviewability of convictions upon impeachment and the Powell v. McCormack case. This section focuses on the more amorphous "judicially discoverable and manageable" strand of the doctrine. The third, broadly prudential, ingredient of political questions notions has already surfaced in chap. 6 and underlies some of the materials in this section as well. After sampling some varieties of political question contentions, this section explores at greater length one area once thought to be nonjusticiable and "political" and now a fertile source of constitutional litigation: the area of legislative districting. Baker v. Carr, Reynolds v. Sims, and their progeny provide the best modern examples of an area in which the "judicially manageable standards" obstacle proved a formidable but not insuperable one.

In examining the materials that follow, recall again the Court's effort to summarize the ingredients of the political questions doctrine, in the passage from Baker v. Carr, 369 U.S. 186 (1962), quoted in chap. 6 and worth reiterating here: "It is apparent that several formulations which vary slightly according to the settings in which the questions arise may describe a political question, although each has one or more elements which identify it as essentially a function of the separation of powers. Prominent on the surface of any case held to involve a political question is found a textually demonstrable constitutional commitment of the issue to a coordinate political department; or a lack of judicially discoverable and manageable standards for resolving it; or the impossibility of deciding without an initial policy determination of a kind clearly for nonjudicial discretion; or the impossibility of a court's undertaking independent resolution without expressing lack of the respect due coordinate branches of government; or an unusual need for unquestioning adherence to a political decision already made; or the potentiality of embarrassment from multifarious pronouncements by various departments on one question."

The "textually demonstrable constitutional commitment" branch of the doctrine has already been examined, in chap. 6. To what extent are the other ingredients also "essentially a function of the separation of powers"? The "judicially discoverable and manageable standards" facet is a major concern below. Does the final group of factors listed in Baker v. Carr comprise essentially prudential considerations? Do the concerns about "lack of the respect due coordinate branches" and "embarrassment from multifarious pronouncements" retain vitality, in view of the Court's handling of such concerns in Powell v. McCormack and United States v. Nixon, in chap. 6? To the extent that prudential considerations remain an articulated part of the doctrine, do they represent a broad reservoir of discretion not to adjudicate? Is that a justifiable discretion? Is it consistent with the view of the bases of the Court's authority at the time of Marbury v. Madison? Is it an outgrowth of the view that has gained considerable acceptance since Marbury, that the Court has a "special function" in constitutional interpretation, and that that special function justifies broad discretion as to the occasion for the exercises of the Court's powers? Is that discretion legitimate? Recall the related questions raised in sec. 4A above.

"LACK OF JUDICIALLY DISCOVERABLE AND MANAGEABLE STANDARDS" AND PRUDENTIAL CONSIDERATIONS: SOME EXAMPLES

1. *Lack of decisional criteria and relevant data: The Coleman v. Miller formulation.* a. *Chief Justice Hughes' opinion.* The passage below illustrates the "lack of judicially discoverable and manageable standards" strand of the political questions doctrine. To what extent is that lack an independent, justifiable ground of nonjusticiability? The passage below is from Chief Justice HUGHES' opinion in COLEMAN v. MILLER, 307 U.S. 433 (1939). Chief Justice Hughes sought to explain why courts could not decide whether the Child Labor Amendment, proposed by Congress in 1924, had lost its vitality through lapse of time and accordingly could not be ratified by a state legislature in 1937. The proposed Amendment was designed to overturn the Court invalidations of congressional efforts to prohibit child labor.[1] In Coleman, members of the Kansas legislature who had voted against ratification sued to enjoin state officials from certifying the legislature's 1937 ratification resolution. One of the grounds of their suit was that "by reason [of] the failure of ratification within a reasonable time the proposed amendment had lost its vitality." The Court affirmed the state court's denial of relief. In explaining why the "reasonable time" issue was not justiciable, Chief Justice Hughes stated:[2]

"*Where are to be found the criteria for such a judicial determination?* None are to be found in Constitution or statute. [Petitioners] have suggested that at least two years should be allowed; that six years would not seem to be unreasonably long; that seven years had been used by the Congress as a reasonable period; that one year, six months and thirteen days was the average time used in passing upon amendments which have been ratified since the first ten amendments; that three years, six months and twenty-five days has been the longest time used in ratifying. To this list of variables, [petitioners] add that 'the nature and extent of publicity and the activity of the public and of the legislatures of the several States in relation to any particular proposal should be taken into consideration.' That statement is pertinent, but there are additional matters to be examined and weighed. When a proposed amendment springs from a conception of economic needs, it would be necessary, in determining whether a reasonable time had elapsed since its submission, to consider the economic conditions prevailing in the country, whether these had so far changed since the submission as to make the proposal no longer responsive to the conception which inspired it or whether conditions were such as to intensify the feeling of need and the appropriateness of the proposed remedial action. *In short, the question of a reasonable time in many cases would involve, as in this case it does involve, an appraisal of a great variety of relevant conditions, political, social and economic, which can hardly be said to be within the appropriate range of evidence receivable in a court of justice and as to which it would be an extravagant extension of judicial authority to assert judicial notice as the basis of deciding a controversy with respect to the validity of an amendment actually ratified.* On the other hand, these conditions are appropriate for the consideration of the political departments of the Government. The questions they involve are essentially political and not justiciable. They can be decided by the Congress with the full knowledge and appreciation ascribed to the national

---

1. Recall Hammer v. Dagenhart, chap. 3 above, and the Child Labor Tax Case, chap. 4 above.

2. Chief Justice Hughes' opinion was joined by only two other members of the seven-man majority. Several of the other Justices who joined in the result emphasized the legislators' lack of standing and the argument that problems of the amendment process were examples of issues wholly committed by the Constitution for final decision to a coordinate political department—to Congress. (The latter argument reflects the "constitutional interpretation" strand of the political questions doctrine considered in chap. 6 above.)

legislature of the political, social and economic conditions which have prevailed during the period since the submission of the amendment." (Emphasis added.) [3]

b. *The adequacy of the formulation.* Does Chief Justice Hughes' formulation provide persuasive reasons for a finding of nonjusticiability? What were the critical reasons? The need for "appraisal of a great variety of relevant conditions, political, social and economic," not "within the appropriate range of evidence receivable" in the courts? Recall the variety of data relied on by the Court in constitutional decisions in the preceding chapters under such provisions as due process and equal protection and the First Amendment. For example, did Brown v. Board of Education (chap. 9) involve a narrower range of "relevant conditions"? Did Dennis (chap. 11) involve greater difficulties in gathering relevant data?

Instead of the "range of evidence" concern, was the central difficulty in Coleman that of formulating manageable judicial standards—the concern expressed in Chief Justice Hughes' opening question: "Where are to be found the criteria for such a judicial determination?" Selecting a particular time period as the "reasonable time" is awkward for courts, to be sure. But would it have been improper for the Court to select a period such as seven years? (Many amendments submitted by Congress in recent years have carried such a seven-year time limitation.) Was it more difficult to formulate a seven-year limit in Coleman than, e.g., to devise the "one person-one vote" rule in Reynolds v. Sims, below? Did Coleman ultimately rest on broader, prudential considerations? Note Scharpf's comment that the Court's invalidations of congressional efforts to curb child labor were "difficult enough to square [with] democratic principle" and that "it would seem to be quite a different matter" if the Court, by imposing restrictions on the amendment process, had barred use of the amendment route to overturn the Court decisions. Though there might be constitutional flaws in the process of adopting a particular amendment, "this seems to be one instance in which the Court cannot assume responsibility for saying 'what the law is' without, at the same time, undermining the legitimacy of its power to do so." [4]

3. Are the constitutional amendment provisions in Art. V "textually demonstrable commitments" to another branch? Note the concurring opinion by Justice BLACK in Coleman, for four of the Justices, objecting that the Court had not made it clear enough that the Constitution "grants Congress exclusive power to control submission of constitutional amendments." The Court has, however, passed on amendment process issues in some contexts. See, e.g., Leser v. Garnett, 258 U.S. 130 (1922), finding the 19th Amendment validly adopted despite alleged procedural irregularities in the legislatures of two states. Moreover, Dillon v. Gloss, 256 U.S. 368 (1921), sustained the power of Congress to fix a time limit on ratification. (See also the earlier materials on the amendment process, in sec. 3 of chap. 4.)

4. Scharpf, "Judicial Review and the Political Question: A Functional Analysis," 75 Yale L.J. 517 (1966). Note also Scharpf's more general effort to formulate the ingredients of the political questions barrier: "[The Court may find a political question] when its access to relevant information is insufficient to assure the correct determination of particular issues, when the Court would have to question the position taken by the government in an international dispute, or when an independent determination by the Court would interfere with the specific responsibilities of another department for dealing with a wider context which itself would be beyond the Court's reach. But even though one or more of these factors may be present, the Court will not usually apply the doctrine to the constitutional guarantees of individual rights and to conflicts of competence among the departments of the federal government and between the federal government and the states."

Compare Henkin's suggestion that "there may be no doctrine requiring abstention from judicial review of 'political questions.' The cases which are supposed to have established the political question doctrine required no such extra-ordinary abstention from judicial review; they called only for the ordinary respect by the courts for the political domain. Having reviewed, the Court refused to invalidate the challenged actions because they were within the constitutional authority of President or Congress. In no case did the Court have to use the phrase 'political question.'" Henkin, "Is There a 'Political Question' Doctrine?" 85 Yale L.J. 597 (1976).

    c. *Complexity, justiciability, and the merits.* Does the mere complexity of the question justify finding it nonjusticiable? Is that what Chief Justice Hughes suggested by his reference to "a great variety of relevant conditions"? Were the questions in Coleman truly more complex than those in many of the cases considered in the preceding chapters—or in Baker v. Carr and Reynolds v. Sims, below? To what extent does the concern over complexity more properly go to the merits rather than to the issue of justiciability? Compare Justice Frankfurter's exploration of multiple variables in Baker v. Carr with the simple "one person-one vote" rule ultimately adopted by the majority in Reynolds v. Sims. Was the majority's view on the merits the critical ingredient that turned the reapportionment issue once considered nonjusticiable into one the Court did undertake to decide: in short, was ultimate agreement on the "one person-one vote" rule critical to the surmounting of the "lack of manageable criteria" hurdle? Once so simple a rule was found justifiable on the merits, the difficulty as to the manageability of judicial criteria largely disappeared. Even if a simple "one person-one vote" rule is constitutionally unjustifiable, and even if the Justices who saw reapportionment issues as more complex were correct, was a finding of nonjusticiability defensible? Compare Justice Frankfurter's view in Baker v. Carr with that of Justice Harlan in Reynolds v. Sims: What justification was there for finding Baker nonjusticiable, rather than holding on the merits that the challenged action was not unconstitutional?

    2. *Lack of standards and criteria: Foreign affairs.* a. *The Brennan summary.* Some, but not all, questions in the foreign affairs area have been found nonjusticiable. What explains the nonjusticiability of some foreign relations issues? To what extent are they issues which are constitutionally "committed to another branch" for final decision? To what extent do the nonjusticiability rulings rest on prudential judgments? To what extent do they involve difficulties of access to relevant data or of lack of manageable criteria? Consider the Court's effort at summary in the passage below, from Justice Brennan's majority opinion in Baker v. Carr: "There are sweeping statements to the effect that all questions touching on foreign relations are political questions. Not only does resolution of such issues frequently turn on standards that defy judicial application, or involve the exercise of a discretion demonstrably committed to the executive or legislature; but many such questions uniquely demand single-voiced statement of the Government's views. Yet it is error to support that every [case] which touches foreign relations lies beyond judicial cognizance. Our cases in this field seem invariably to show a discriminating analysis of the particular question posed, in terms of the history of its management by the political branches, of its susceptibility to judicial handling in the light of its nature and posture in the specific case, and of the possible consequences of judicial action. For example, though a court will not ordinarily inquire whether a treaty has been terminated, [if] there has been no conclusive 'governmental action' then a court can construe a treaty and may find it provides the answer."

    b. *Congressional participation in the termination of treaties.* In GOLDWATER v. CARTER, 444 U.S. 996 (1979) (chap. 6 above), the Court refused to decide whether the President could terminate a treaty without the participation of Congress; but the majority could not agree on the reasons why the issue was nonjusticiable. The largest bloc—Justice Rehnquist, joined by Chief Justice Burger and Justices Stewart and Stevens—found that the case presented a nonjusticiable "political question"; Justice Powell strongly disagreed. Justice REHNQUIST claimed the issue was "political" because "it involves the authority of the President in the conduct of our country's foreign relations." He argued that the controversy "should be left for resolution by the Executive and Legislative Branches," since the Constitution "is silent as to [the Senate's] participation in the abrogation of a Treaty." He stated that the question "must surely be controlled by political standards" and noted that this was "a dispute between coequal branches of our government, each of which has resources available to protect and assert its interests, resources not available to private litigants outside the judicial forum." Justice POWELL, by contrast, insisted that the issue was not "political" under the Baker v. Carr criteria. There was no "textually demonstrable constitutional commitment" of the treaty termination power to the President. Nor was there any "lack of judicially discoverable and manageable standards": "Resolution of the question may not be easy, but it only requires us to apply normal principles of interpretation to the constitutional provisions at issue. [The case] involves neither review of the President's activities as Commander-in-Chief nor impermissible interference in the field of foreign affairs. [This] case 'touches' foreign relations, but the [question] concerns only the constitutional division of power between Congress and the President." He added: "Finally, the political-question doctrine rests in part on prudential concerns," such as avoiding "the potentiality of embarrassment [that would result] from multifarious pronouncements by various departments on one question." But those prudential inhibitions were not appropriate here: "Interpretation of the Constitution does not imply lack of respect for a coordinate branch. If the President and the Congress had reached irreconcilable positions, final disposition of the question presented by this case would eliminate, rather than create, multiple constitutional interpretations. The spectre of [the] Government brought to a halt because of the mutual intransigence of the President and the Congress would require this Court to provide a resolution pursuant to our duty 'to say what the law is.' [U.S. v. Nixon, quoting Marbury v. Madison.]" But this dispute, in Justice Powell's view, was not ripe for decision.

3. *Prudential considerations.* a. *The Vietnam controversy.* Alexander Bickel contended that the political questions doctrine does not involve "constitutional interpretation" at all, insisting: "There is something different about it, in kind, not in degree, from the general 'interpretive process'; something greatly more flexible, something of prudence, not construction and principle."[5] To what extent do the materials considered in this section ultimately rest on prudential considerations? Were those considerations determinative, for example, in the Court's repeated refusals to consider the constitutionality of American military involvement in Vietnam? Recall the examples cited in chap. 6, especially Justice Stewart's dissent from the denial of certiorari in Mora v. McNamara (1967; p. 370 above): "These are large and deeply troubling questions. Whether the Court would ultimately reach them depends, of course, upon the resolution of serious preliminary issues of justiciability." What issues of justiciability did those cases involve? Commitment of the issues to other branches? Judicial difficulties in formulating manageable criteria or getting access to relevant data? Or merely prudential avoidance?

b. *Political party conventions.* Were prudential considerations predominant in the Court's refusal to intervene in a party convention dispute in O'BRIEN v. BROWN, 409 U.S. 1 (1972)? That litigation reached the Court three days before the Democratic National Convention of 1972. The Convention's Credentials Committee had recommended seating groups of California and Illinois delegates. The excluded delegations challenged the Committee's actions in the federal courts. The California claimants, pledged to Senator Humphrey, at-

---

5. Note also Bickel's comment, in The Least Dangerous Branch (1962), that the political questions doctrine rests on "the Court's sense of lack of capacity, compounded in unequal parts of (a) the strangeness of the issue and its intractability to principled resolution; (b) the sheer momentousness of it, which tends to unbalance judicial judgment; (c) the anxiety, not so much that the judicial judgment will be ignored, as that perhaps it should be but will not be; (d) finally, [the] inner vulnerability, the self-doubt of an institution which is electorally irresponsible and has no earth to draw strength from." Did the Vietnam war and the party convention dispute, below, present such "momentous" issues? More momentous than the reapportionment and school segregation disputes? Was Luther v. Borden, below, a case that fits Bickel's description? Do the criteria he lists justify Court refusals to adjudicate?

tacked a winner-take-all primary election scheme. The excluded Illinois delegation, led by Mayor Daley, had been excluded because it was not adequately representative, and the Illinois plaintiffs claimed, inter alia, that the Credentials Committee had established minority quotas in violation of equal protection. The District Court dismissed the actions as nonjusticiable, but the Court of Appeals reached the merits, holding for the California claimants and against those from Illinois. The Supreme Court's 6 to 3 per curiam ruling stayed the Court of Appeals decision: "In light of the availability of the convention as a forum to review the recommendations of the Credentials Committee, in which process the complaining parties might obtain the relief they have sought from the federal courts, the lack of precedent to support the extraordinary relief granted by the Court of Appeals, and the large public interest in allowing the political process to function free from judicial supervision, we conclude the judgment of the Court of Appeals must be stayed." In the course of its brief opinion, the majority cited Luther v. Borden (below) and stated: "No case is cited to us in which any federal court has undertaken to interject itself into the deliberative processes of a national political convention." [6]

4. *The Guarantee Clause.* a. The Court has long asserted—and reiterated in Baker v. Carr, below—that the opening provision of Art. IV, § 4, is nonjusticiable. That provision states: "The United States shall guarantee to every State in this Union a Republican Form of Government." Note, e.g., PACIFIC STATES TELEPHONE & TELEGRAPH CO. v. OREGON, 223 U.S. 118 (1912), refusing to adjudicate a claim that a law enacted via Oregon's initiative lawmaking procedure violated the Guarantee Clause. The Court's opinion emphasized "the inconceivable expansion of the judicial power and the ruinous destruction of legislative authority in matters purely political which would necessarily be occasioned by giving sanction to the doctrine which underlies and would be necessarily involved in sustaining the propositions contended for." Chief Justice WHITE stated that adjudication of such an issue would mean examination of contentions "as to the illegal existence of a State" and, "if such contention be thought well founded, to disregard the existence in fact of the State [and] of its recognition by all of the departments of the Federal Government." Courts would have to build new state governments on "the ruins of the previously established" ones, and would have to "control the [Congress] in the recognition of such new government and the admission of representatives therefrom." Would justiciability of the Guarantee Clause inevitably involve such cataclysmic consequences? Is this an example of "too momentous" an issue for the courts? The majority in Baker v. Carr explained the decision on the ground that the clause "is not a repository of judicially manageable standards." Was Baker v. Carr nevertheless really "a Guarantee Clause claim masquerading under a different label," as Justice Frankfurter's dissent argued? Should the Clause be found justiciable, at least in some contexts? [7]

---

6. Justices DOUGLAS, WHITE and MARSHALL dissented. Justice Marshall's dissent, joined by Justice Douglas, insisted that any claim of "political question" nonjusticiability was misconceived since that doctrine dealt with the "very different problem" of avoiding conflict with the coordinate branches of government. (Three days later, the Convention seated the California McGovern slate but refused to seat the Illinois Daley delegation.)

Cf. Cousins v. Wigoda, 419 U.S. 477 (1975), holding that a state court could not interfere with the selection of delegates to a national party convention. The Court stated that a national party and its supporters "enjoy a constitutionally

protected right of political association" and that a state's interest in the integrity of its electoral process is not a "compelling" justification for interference in the selection of delegates.

7. See Bonfield, "Baker v. Carr: New Light on the Constitutional Guarantee of Republican Government," 50 Calif.L.Rev. 245 (1962): "The clause is neither textually committed to the exclusive enforcement of another department, nor bare of judicially discoverable or manageable standards." See also Bonfield, "The Guarantee Clause of Article IV, Section 4: A Study in Constitutional Desuetude," 46 Minn.L.Rev. 513 (1962).

b. The best known Guarantee Clause case is LUTHER v. BORDEN, 7 How. 1 (1849). In summarizing political questions decisions in Baker v. Carr, Justice Brennan described the case as follows: "Luther v. Borden, though in form simply an action for damages for trespass was, as Daniel Webster said in opening the argument for the defense, 'an unusual case.' The defendants, admitting an otherwise tortious breaking and entering, sought to justify their action on the ground that they were agents of the established lawful government of Rhode Island, which State was then under martial law to defend itself from active insurrection; that the plaintiff was engaged in that insurrection; and that they entered under orders to arrest the plaintiff. The case arose 'out of the unfortunate political differences which agitated the people of Rhode Island in 1841 and 1842,' and which had resulted in a situation wherein two groups laid competing claims to recognition as the lawful government. The plaintiff's right to recover depended on which of the two groups was entitled to such recognition; but the lower court's refusal to receive evidence or hear argument on that issue, its charge to the jury that the earlier established or 'charter' government was lawful, and the verdict for the defendants, were affirmed upon appeal to this Court. [Clearly], several factors were thought by the Court in Luther to make the question there 'political': the commitment to the other branches of the decision as to which is the lawful state government; the unambiguous action by the President, in recognizing the charter government as the lawful authority; the need for finality in the executive's decision; and the lack of criteria by which a court could determine which form of government was republican."

But Chief Justice TANEY's opinion in Luther v. Borden also expressed concerns similar to those of Chief Justice White in the Pacific Tel. & Tel. case, above. He stated that if the Court were to enter the controversy and decide "that the charter government had no legal existence during the period of time above mentioned, [then] the laws passed by the legislature during that time were nullities; its taxes wrongfully collected; its salaries and compensation to its officers illegally paid; its public account improperly settled; and the [judgments of its courts] null and void." Does Justice Brennan's summary of the case adequately reflect that "momentousness" concern? Would that concern be present in every case in which a Guarantee Clause claim might be raised? [8]

LEGISLATIVE APPORTIONMENT: THE FORMULATION AND ELABORATION OF JUDICIALLY MANAGEABLE STANDARDS

Introduction. Before 1962, legislative districting controversies were thought to be nonjusticiable. But in that year, in Baker v. Carr, the divided Court rejected the claim that equal protection challenges to legislative apportionments were nonjusticiable. Instead, the Court expressed confidence that judicially manageable standards could be formulated. The formulation of standards began two years later, with the "one person-one vote" decision in Reynolds v.

---

8. For the political background of Luther v. Borden, see generally Gettleman, The Dorr Rebellion (1973), and Wiecek, The Guarantee Clause of the U.S. Constitution (1972).

Note a footnote in Justice Douglas' separate opinion in Baker v. Carr, insisting: "The statement in [Luther v. Borden] that this guaranty is enforceable only by Congress or the Chief Executive is not maintainable. [T]he abdication of all judicial functions respecting voting rights, however justified by the peculiarities of the charter form of government in Rhode Island at the time

of Dorr's Rebellion, states no general principle. It indeed is contrary [to] the modern decisions of the Court that give the full panoply of judicial protection to voting rights. [Recall chap. 9, sec. 4.] Moreover, the Court's refusal to examine the legality of the regime of martial law which had been laid upon Rhode Island is indefensible." Note also Justice Douglas' further comment, in another footnote in Baker v. Carr: "The category of the 'political' question is, in my view, narrower than the decided cases indicate."

Sims. Since then, the Court has had frequent occasion to elaborate and administer the equal protection approach of Reynolds. In examining the predecessors and progeny of Reynolds, consider the implications for the "judicially discoverable and manageable standards" strand of the political questions doctrine. Did the judgment in Baker that manageable standards could be fashioned imply a preliminary judgment on the merits? Did it take the simple-sounding Reynolds "one person-one vote" principle to lay to rest the doubts about the manageability of reapportionment standards? Are Reynolds and its progeny adequately responsive to the values regarding representation that the Court has found in the equal protection clause? What are those values? (Recall the earlier voting rights materials, in chap. 9, sec. 4, above.)

    The situation before Baker v. Carr. The pre-Baker attitude as to the justiciability of districting disputes is reflected in Justice Frankfurter's opinion in COLEGROVE v. GREEN, 328 U.S. 549 (1946). There, the majority refused to reach the merits of a federal court challenge to the congressional districting scheme in Illinois. The challengers contended that the Illinois law prescribing congressional districts was unconstitutional because the districts were not approximately equal in population. Only seven Justices participated in the decision. Justice FRANKFURTER announced the judgment of the Court affirming the dismissal of the complaint, but his opinion was joined only by Justices Reed and Burton. He stated: "[T]he petitioners ask of this Court what is beyond its competence to grant. This is one of those demands on judicial power which cannot be met by verbal fencing about 'jurisdiction.' [E]ffective working of our government revealed this issue to be of a peculiarly political nature and therefore not meet for judicial determination. [T]his controversy concerns matters that bring courts into immediate and active relations with party contests. From the determination of such issues this Court has traditionally remained aloof. It is hostile to a democratic system to involve the judiciary in the politics of the people. [D]ue regard for the Constitution as a viable system precludes judicial correction. Authority for dealing with such problems resides elsewhere. [Art. I, § 4.] The short of it is that the Constitution has conferred upon Congress exclusive authority to secure fair representation by the States in the popular [House]. Courts ought not to enter this political thicket." The deciding vote was cast by Justice RUTLEDGE, who concurred in the result. He thought the issue was justiciable, but concluded that the complaint should be dismissed for want of equity: "I think the case is of so delicate a character [that] the jurisdiction should be exercised only in the most compelling circumstances. [The] right here is not absolute. And the cure sought may be worse than the disease. I think, therefore, the case is one in which the Court may properly, and should, decline to exercise its jurisdiction." Justice BLACK, joined by Justices Douglas and Murphy, dissented, insisting that "the complaint presented a justiciable case and controversy." [1]

---

1. See also South v. Peters, 339 U.S. 276 (1950), challenging Georgia's county unit system in state elections. The Supreme Court affirmed the lower court's dismissal of the suit: "Federal courts consistently refuse to exercise their equity powers in cases posing political issues arising from a state's geographical distribution of electoral strength among its political subdivisions." (The county unit system was held unconstitution-

al after Baker v. Carr, in Gray v. Sanders, 372 U.S. 368 (1963).)

Compare Gomillion v. Lightfoot (1960; chap. 9, sec. 3, above), where Justice Frankfurter wrote for the Court in holding a redrawing of the city boundaries of Tuskegee, Alabama, unconstitutional as a device to disenfranchise blacks, in violation of the 15th Amendment.

BAKER v. CARR

369 U.S. 186, 82 S.Ct. 691, 7 L.Ed.2d 663 (1962).

Mr. Justice BRENNAN delivered the opinion of the [Court].

[The appellants claimed that the apportionment of the Tennessee General Assembly violated their equal protection rights "by virtue of the debasement of their votes." They alleged that, although the state constitution allocated representation on a population basis, the Assembly had not been reapportioned since 1901, even though there had been substantial growth and redistribution of the population since then. They also argued that, because of the malapportioned legislature, redress through changes in state law was difficult or impossible. They sought an injunction against further elections under the 1901 system and asked the federal trial court either to direct elections at large or to decree a reapportionment "by mathematical application of the Tennessee constitutional formulae to the most recent Federal Census figures." The lower court denied relief.]

[W]e hold today only (a) that the court possessed jurisdiction of the subject matter; (b) that a justiciable cause of action is stated upon which appellants would be entitled to appropriate relief; and (c) [that] the appellants have standing to challenge the Tennessee apportionment statutes. Beyond noting that we have no cause at this stage to doubt the District Court will be able to fashion relief if violations of constitutional rights are found, it is improper now to consider what remedy would be most appropriate if appellants prevail at the [trial].

In holding that the subject matter of this suit was not justiciable, the District Court relied on [cases such as Colegrove v. Green]. [The District Court read those cases] as compelling the conclusion that since the appellants sought to have a legislative apportionment held unconstitutional, their suit presented a "political question" and was therefore nonjusticiable. We hold that this challenge to an apportionment presents no nonjusticiable "political question." [Of course] the mere fact that the suit seeks protection of a political right does not mean it presents a political question. Such an objection "is little more than a play upon words." Rather, it is argued that apportionment cases, whatever the actual wording of the complaint, can involve no federal constitutional right except one resting on the guaranty of a republican form of government, and that complaints based on that clause have been held to present political questions which are nonjusticiable. We hold that the claim pleaded here neither rests upon nor implicates the Guaranty Clause and that its justiciability is therefore not foreclosed by our decisions of cases involving that clause. [But] because there appears to be some uncertainty as to why those cases did present political questions, and specifically as to whether this apportionment case is like those cases, we deem it necessary first to consider the contours of the "political question" doctrine. [Our] review reveals that in the Guaranty Clause cases and in the other "political question" cases, it is the relationship between the judiciary and the coordinate branches of the Federal Government, and not the federal judiciary's relationship to the States, which gives rise to the ["political question" barrier].

It is apparent that several formulations which vary slightly according to the settings in which the questions arise may describe a political question, although each has one or more elements which identifies it as essentially a function of the separation of powers. Prominent on the surface of any case held to involve a political question is found a textually demonstrable constitutional commitment of the issue to a coordinate political department; or a lack of judicially discoverable and manageable standards for resolving it; or the impossibility of deciding without an initial policy determination of a kind clearly for nonjudicial discretion; or the impossibility of a court's undertaking independent resolution without expressing lack of the respect due coordinate branches of government; or an unusual need for unquestioning adherence to a political decision already made; or the potentiality of embarrassment from multifarious pronouncements by various departments on one question.

Unless one of these formulations is inextricable from the case at bar, there should be no dismissal for nonjusticiability on the ground of a political question's presence. [But] it is argued that this case shares the characteristics of [cases] concerning the [Guaranty Clause]. [We] shall discover that Guaranty Clause claims involve those elements which define a "political question," and for that reason and no other, they are nonjusticiable. In particular, we shall discover that the nonjusticiability of such claims has nothing to do with their touching upon matters of state governmental organization. [T]he only significance that [Luther v. Borden] could have for our immediate purposes is in its holding that the Guaranty Clause is not a repository of judicially manageable standards which a court could utilize independently in order to identify a State's lawful government. The Court has since refused to resort to the Guaranty Clause—which alone had been invoked for the purpose—as the source of a constitutional standard for invalidating state [action].

We come, finally to the ultimate inquiry whether our precedents as to what constitutes a nonjusticiable "political question" bring the case before us under the umbrella of that doctrine. A natural beginning is to note whether any of the common characteristics which we have been able to identify and label descriptively are present. We find none: The question here is the consistency of state action with the [Constitution]. We have no question decided, or to be decided, by a political branch of government co-equal with this Court. Nor do we risk embarrassment of our government abroad, or grave disturbance at home if we take issue with Tennessee as to the constitutionality of her action here challenged. Nor need the appellants, in order to succeed in this action, ask the Court to enter upon policy determinations for which judicially manageable standards are lacking. Judicial standards under [equal protection] are well developed and familiar, and it has been open to courts since the enactment of the 14th Amendment to determine [that] a discrimination reflects *no* policy, but simply arbitrary and capricious action. This case does, in one sense, involve the allocation of political power within a State, and the appellants might conceivably have added a claim under the Guaranty Clause. Of course, as we have seen, any reliance on that clause would be futile. But because any reliance on the Guaranty Clause could not have succeeded it does not follow that appellants may not be heard on the equal protection claim which in fact they tender. [We] conclude that the complaint's allegations of a denial of equal protection present a justiciable constitutional cause of action upon which appellants are entitled to a trial and a decision. The right asserted is within the reach of judicial protection under the [14th Amendment].

Reversed and remanded.[1]

Mr. Justice CLARK, [concurring].

[Try] as one may, Tennessee's apportionment just cannot be made to fit the pattern cut by its Constitution. An examination of Table I accompanying this opinion [omitted here] conclusively reveals that the apportionment picture in Tennessee is a topsy-turvical of gigantic proportions. This is not to say that some of the disparity cannot be explained, but when the entire Table is

---

1. A concurring opinion by Justice DOUG-LAS is omitted. (Justice Whittaker did not participate in the decision of the case.)

examined—comparing the voting strength of counties of like population as well as contrasting that of the smaller with the larger counties—it leaves but one conclusion, namely that Tennessee's apportionment is a crazy quilt without [rational basis]. Although I find the Tennessee apportionment statute offends [equal protection], I would not consider intervention by this Court into so delicate a field if there were any other relief available to the people of Tennessee. But the majority of the people of Tennessee have no "practical opportunities for exerting their political weight at the polls" to correct the existing "invidious discrimination." Tennessee has no initiative and referendum. [T]he legislative policy has riveted the present seats in the Assembly to their respective constituencies, and by the votes of their incumbents a reapportionment of any kind is prevented. [We must] conclude that the people of Tennessee are stymied and without judicial intervention will be saddled with the present discrimination in the affairs of their [state government].

Mr. Justice STEWART, [concurring].

Contrary to the suggestion of my brother Harlan, the Court does not say or imply that "state legislatures must be so structured as to reflect with approximate equality the voice of every voter." [The] Court does not say or imply that there is anything in the Federal Constitution "to prevent a State, acting not irrationally, from choosing any electoral legislative structure it thinks best suited to the interests, temper, and customs of its people." [T]he Court today decides only: (1) that the District Court possessed jurisdiction of the subject matter; (2) that the complaint presents a justiciable controversy; (3) that the appellants have standing. [The] merits of this case are not before us [now].

Mr. Justice FRANKFURTER, whom Mr. Justice HARLAN joins, [dissenting].

A hypothetical claim resting on abstract assumptions is now for the first time made the basis for affording illusory relief for a particular evil even though it foreshadows deeper and more pervasive difficulties in consequence. The claim is hypothetical and the assumptions are abstract because the Court does not vouchsafe the lower courts—state and federal—guidelines for formulating specific, definite, wholly unprecedented remedies for the inevitable litigations that today's umbrageous disposition is bound to stimulate in connection with politically motivated reapportionments in so many States. In such a setting, to promulgate jurisdiction in the abstract is meaningless. It is as devoid of reality as "a brooding omnipresence in the sky" for it conveys no intimation what relief, if any, a District Court is capable of affording that would not invite legislatures to play ducks and drakes with the judiciary. [Even] assuming the indispensable intellectual disinterestedness on the part of judges in such matters, they do not have accepted legal standards or criteria or even reliable analogies to draw upon for making judicial [judgments].

Considering the gross inequality among legislative electoral units within almost every State, the Court naturally shrinks from asserting that in districting at least substantial equality is a constitutional requirement enforceable by courts. Room continues to be allowed for weighting. This of course implies that geography, economics, urban-rural conflict, and all the other non-legal factors which have throughout our history entered into political districting are to some extent not to be ruled out in the undefined vista now opened up by review in the federal courts of state reapportionments. To some extent—aye, there's the rub. In effect, today's decision empowers the courts of the country to devise what should constitute the proper composition of the legislatures of the fifty States. [T]here is not under our Constitution a judicial remedy for every [political mischief].

The [Colegrove v. Green] doctrine [was] not an innovation. It represents long judicial thought and experience. From its earliest opinions this Court has consistently recognized a class of controversies which do not lend themselves to judicial standards and judicial remedies. [From some of the cases] emerge unifying considerations that are compelling. [The] influence of these converging considerations—the caution not to undertake decision where standards meet for judicial judgment are lacking, the reluctance to interfere with matters of state government in the absence of an unquestionable and effectively enforceable mandate, the unwillingness to make courts arbiters of the broad issues of political organization historically committed to other institutions and for whose adjustment the judicial process is ill-adapted—has been decisive of the settled line of cases [holding] that Art. IV, § 4, [is] not enforceable through the [courts]. The present case involves all of the elements that have made the Guarantee Clause cases non-justiciable. It is, in effect, a Guarantee Clause claim masquerading under a different label. But it cannot make the case more fit for judicial action that appellants invoke the 14th Amendment rather than Art. IV, § 4, where, in fact, the gist of their complaint is the same—unless it can be found that the 14th Amendment speaks with greater particularity to their situation. [Art. IV, § 4] is not committed by express constitutional terms to Congress. It is the nature of the controversies arising under it, nothing else, which has made it judicially [unenforceable].

What, then, is this question of legislative apportionment? Appellants invoke the right to vote and to have their votes counted. But they are permitted to vote and their votes are counted. They go to the polls, they cast their ballots, they send their representatives to the state councils. Their complaint is simply that the representatives are not sufficiently numerous or powerful—in short, that Tennessee has adopted a basis of representation with which they are dissatisfied. Talk of "debasement" or "dilution" is circular talk. One cannot speak of "debasement" or "dilution" of the value of a vote until there is first defined a standard of reference as to what a vote should be worth. What is actually asked of the Court in this case is to choose among competing bases of representation—ultimately, really, among competing theories of political philosophy—in order to establish an appropriate frame of government for the [states].

[Apportionment], by its character, is a subject of extraordinary complexity, involving—even after the fundamental theoretical issues concerning what is to be represented in a representative legislature have been fought out or compromised—considerations of geography, demography, electoral convenience, economic and social cohesions or divergencies among particular local groups, communications, the practical effects of political institutions like the lobby and the city machine, ancient traditions and ties of settled usage, respect for proven incumbents of long experience and senior status, mathematical mechanics, censuses compiling relevant data, and a host of others. [The] practical significance of apportionment is that the next election results may differ because of it. Apportionment battles are overwhelmingly party or intra-party contests. It will add a virulent source of friction and tension in federal-state relations to embroil the federal judiciary in [them].

Dissenting opinion of Mr. Justice HARLAN, whom Mr. Justice FRANK-FURTER [joins].

Once one cuts through the thicket of discussion devoted to "jurisdiction," "standing," "justiciability," and "political question," there emerges a straightforward issue which [is] determinative of this case. Does the complaint disclose a violation of a federal constitutional [right]? The majority opinion [seems] to decide it "sub silentio." However, in my opinion, appellants' allegations, accepting all of them as true, do not, parsed down or as a whole, show an infringement by Tennessee of any rights assured by the 14th Amendment. Accordingly, I believe the complaint should have been dismissed for "failure to state a claim upon which relief can be granted." [Until] it is first decided [whether] what Tennessee has done or failed to do in this instance runs afoul of any [constitutional] limitation, we need not reach the issues of "justiciability" or "political question."

The suggestion of my Brother Frankfurter that courts lack standards by which to decide such cases as this is relevant not only to the question of "justiciability," but also, and perhaps more fundamentally, to the determination whether any cognizable constitutional claim has been asserted in this case. Courts are unable to decide when it is that an apportionment originally valid becomes void because the factors entering into such a decision are basically matters appropriate only for legislative judgment. And so long as there exists a possible rational legislative policy for retaining an existing apportionment, such a legislative decision cannot be said to breach the bulwark against arbitrariness and caprice that the 14th Amendment affords. [Those] observers of the Court who see it primarily as the last refuge for the correction of all inequality or injustice, no matter what its nature or source, will no doubt applaud this decision and its break with the past. Those who consider that continuing national respect for the Court's authority depends in large measure upon its wise exercise of self-restraint and discipline in constitutional adjudication, will view the decision with deep concern.[1]

REYNOLDS v. SIMS

377 U.S. 533, 84 S.Ct. 1362, 12 L.Ed.2d 506 (1964).

[Within a year of Baker v. Carr, suits challenging state legislative apportionment schemes were instituted in over 30 states. The major decision answering some of the questions left open by Baker came two years later, in Reynolds v. Sims. That case was a challenge to the malapportionment of the Alabama legislature. The challengers claimed discrimination against voters in counties whose populations had grown proportionately far more than others since the 1900 census. The complainants noted that the existing districting scheme was based on the 1900 census, even though the state constitution required legislative representation based on population and decennial reapportionment. The lower federal court found the old apportionment as well as two new ones devised by the legislature violative of equal protection. It ordered temporary reapportionment by combining features of the two plans newly devised by the legislature. Both sides in the lawsuit appealed.]

Mr. Chief Justice WARREN delivered the opinion of the [Court].

1. For a sampling of the extensive commentary on Baker v. Carr, see Neal, "Baker v. Carr: Politics in Search of Law," 1962 Sup.Ct.Rev. 252; McCloskey, "Foreword: The Reapportionment Case," 76 Harv.L.Rev. 54 (1962); and McKay, "Political Thickets and Crazy Quilts: Reapportionment and Equal Protection," 61 Mich.L.Rev. 645 (1963).

Between Baker v. Carr in 1962, and Reynolds v. Sims in 1964 (which follows), the Court decided two important cases discussed in the majority opinion in Reynolds v. Sims, which follows. Gray v. Sanders, 372 U.S. 368 (1963), struck down Georgia's county unit system in primary elections of state-wide officers. The Court purported not to reach most of the questions left open by Baker v. Carr. The majority insisted that this was "only a voting case" and empha-

sized that the case had nothing to do "with the composition of the state or federal legislature."

In the second major case, Wesberry v. Sanders, 376 U.S. 1 (1964), the Court held—without reaching the 14th Amendment claims—"that, construed in its historical context, the command of Art. I, § 2, that Representatives be chosen 'by the People of the several States' means that as nearly as practicable one man's vote in a congressional election is to be worth as much as another's." The Court accordingly struck down Georgia's congressional districting statute. Note the use made of these decisions in Reynolds v. Sims. (On the Court's use—or misuse—of historical materials in Wesberry, see, e.g., Kelly, "Clio and the Court: An Illicit Love Affair," 1965 Sup.Ct. Rev. 119.)

[Gray v. Sanders and Wesberry v. Sanders] are of course not dispositive of or directly controlling [in] these cases involving state legislative apportionment controversies. [But] neither are they wholly inapposite. [Gray] established the basic principle of equality among voters within a State, and held that voters cannot be classified, constitutionally, on the basis of where they live, at least with respect to voting in statewide elections. [And] Wesberry clearly established that the fundamental principle of representative government in this country is one of equal representation for equal numbers of people, without regard to race, sex, economic status, or place of residence within a State. Our problem, then, is to ascertain, in the instant cases, whether there are any constitutionally cognizable principles which would justify departures from the basic standard of equality among voters in the apportionment of seats in state legislatures. [A] predominant consideration in determining whether a State's legislative apportionment scheme constitutes an invidious discrimination violative of rights asserted under [equal protection] is that the rights allegedly impaired are individual and personal in nature. [Undoubtedly], the right of suffrage is a fundamental matter in a free and democratic society. Especially since the right to exercise the franchise in a free and unimpaired manner is preservative of other basic civil and political rights, any alleged infringement of the right of citizens to vote must be carefully and meticulously [scrutinized].

Legislators represent people, not trees or acres. Legislators are elected by voters, not farms or cities or economic interests. As long as ours is a representative form of government, [the] right to elect legislators in a free and unimpaired fashion is a bedrock of our political system. It could hardly be gainsaid that a constitutional claim had been asserted by an allegation that certain otherwise qualified voters had been entirely prohibited from voting for members of their state legislature. And, if a State should provide that the votes of citizens in one part of the State should be given two times, or five times, or 10 times the weight of votes of citizens in another part of the State, it could hardly be contended that the right to vote of those residing in the disfavored areas had not been effectively diluted. [Of] course, the effect of state legislative districting schemes which give the same number of representatives to unequal numbers of constituents is [identical]. Weighting the votes of citizens differently, by any method or means, merely because of where they happen to reside, hardly seems [justifiable].

Logically, in a society ostensibly grounded on representative government, it would seem reasonable that a majority of the people of a State could elect a majority of that State's legislators. [To] sanction minority control of state legislative bodies would appear to deny majority rights in a way that far surpasses any possible denial of minority rights that might otherwise be thought to result. [And] the concept of equal protection has been traditionally viewed as requiring the uniform treatment of persons standing in the same relation to the governmental action questioned or challenged. With respect to the allocation of legislative representation, all voters, as citizens of a State, stand in the same relation regardless of where they live. Any suggested criteria for the differentiation of citizens are insufficient to justify any discrimination, as to the weight of their votes, unless relevant to the permissible purposes of legislative apportionment. Since the achieving of fair and effective representation for all citizens is concededly the basic aim of legislative apportionment, we conclude that [equal protection] guarantees the opportunity for equal participation by all voters in the election of state legislators. Diluting the weight of votes because of place of residence impairs basic constitutional rights under the 14th Amendment just as much as invidious discriminations based upon factors such as race [or] economic status. Our constitutional system amply provides for the protection of minorities by means other than giving them majority control of state legislatures.

[We] are told that the matter of apportioning representation in a state legislature is a complex and many-faceted one. We are advised that States can rationally consider factors other than population. [We] are admonished not to restrict the power of the States to impose differing views as to political philosophy on their citizens. We are cautioned about the dangers of entering into political thickets and mathematical quagmires. Our answer is this: a denial of constitutionally protected rights demands judicial protection; our oath and our office require no less of us. [To] the extent that a citizen's right to vote is debased, he is that much less a citizen. [T]he weight of a citizen's vote cannot be made to depend on where he lives. Population is, of necessity, the starting point for consideration and the controlling criterion for judgment in legislative apportionment controversies. A citizen, a qualified voter, is no more nor no less so because he lives in the city or on the farm. This is the clear and strong command of [equal protection]. This is an essential part of the concept of a government of laws and not men. This is at the heart of Lincoln's vision of "government of the people, by the people, [and] for the people." [We] hold that, as a basic constitutional standard, [equal protection] requires that the seats in both houses of a bicameral state legislature must be apportioned on a population basis. Simply stated, an individual's right to vote for state legislators is unconstitutionally impaired when its weight is in a substantial fashion diluted when compared with votes of citizens living in other parts of the [State].

[We] find the federal analogy inapposite and irrelevant to state legislative districting schemes. Attempted reliance on the federal analogy appears often to be little more than an after-the-fact rationalization offered in defense of malad-justed state apportionment arrangements. [The] system of representation in the two Houses [of Congress] is one conceived out of compromise and concession indispensable to the establishment of our federal republic [and] is based on the consideration that in establishing our type of federalism a group of formerly independent States bound themselves together under one national government. [Political] subdivisions of States—counties, cities, or whatever—never were and never have been considered as sovereign entities. Rather, they have been traditionally regarded as subordinate governmental instrumentalities created by the [State].

[The] right of a citizen to equal representation and to have his vote weighted equally with those of all other citizens in the election of members of one house of a bicameral state legislature would amount to little if States could effectively submerge the equal-population principle in the apportionment of seats in the other [house]. Deadlock between the two bodies might result in compromise and concession on some issues. But in all too many cases the more probable result would be frustration of the majority will through minority veto in the house not apportioned on a population basis. [We] do not believe that the concept of bicameralism is rendered anachronistic and meaningless when the predominant basis of representation in the two state legislative bodies is required to be the same—population. A prime reason for bicameralism, modernly considered, is to insure mature and deliberate consideration of, and to prevent precipitate action on, proposed legislative measures. Simply because the controlling criterion for apportioning representation is required to be the same in both houses does not mean that there will be no differences in the composition and complexion of the two [bodies].

[Equal protection] requires that a State make an honest and good faith effort to construct districts, in both houses of its legislature, as nearly of equal population as is practicable. We realize that it is a practical impossibility to arrange legislative districts so that each one has an identical number of residents, or citizens, or voters. Mathematical exactness or precision is hardly a workable constitutional requirement. [So] long as the divergences from a strict population standard are based on legitimate considerations incident to the effectuation of a rational state policy, some deviations from the equal-population principle are constitutionally permissible, [but] neither history alone, nor economic or other sorts of group interests, are permissible factors in attempting to justify disparities from population-based representation. Citizens, not history or economic interests, cast votes. Considerations of area alone provide an insufficient justification for deviations from the equal-population principle. Again, people, not land or trees or pastures, vote. Modern developments and improvements in transportation and communications make rather hollow, in the mid-1960's, most claims [for] allowing such deviations in order to insure effective representation for sparsely settled areas and to prevent legislative districts from becoming so large that the availability of access of citizens to their representatives is impaired. [A] consideration that appears to be of more substance in justifying some deviations from population-based representation in state legislatures is that of insuring some voice to political subdivisions, as political subdivisions. [In] many States much of the legislature's activity involves the enactment of so-called local legislation, directed only to the concerns of particular political subdivisions. And a State may legitimately desire to construct districts along political subdivision lines to deter the possibilities of gerrymandering. [But] if, even as a result of a clearly rational state policy of according some legislative representation to political subdivisions, population is submerged as the controlling consideration, [the] right of all of the State's citizens to cast an effective and adequately weighted vote would be unconstitutionally [impaired].

[Affirmed and remanded.]

[In five companion cases to Reynolds v. Sims, the Court relied on its principles to invalidate apportionment schemes in Colorado, New York, Maryland, Virginia, and Delaware.[1] The Colorado case, LUCAS v. FORTY-FOURTH GEN. ASSEMBLY, 377 U.S. 713, warrants special mention, because the defenders of the districting there argued that it should be sustained because it had been approved by the voters of the state. The Colorado scheme—relying on the federal analogy in apportioning only one of the two houses on the basis of population—had been approved in 1962 by a statewide referendum. Moreover, the voters had rejected a plan to apportion both houses on the basis of population. Chief Justice WARREN's opinion concluded that that background did not justify deviation from the Reynolds requirement. He stated: "An individual's constitutionally protected right to cast an equally weighted vote cannot be denied even by a vote of a majority of a State's electorate, if the apportionment scheme adopted by the voters fails to measure up to the requirements of [equal protection]. Manifestly, the fact that an apportionment plan is adopted in a popular referendum is insufficient to sustain its constitutionality or to induce a court of equity to refuse to act. [A] citizen's constitutional rights can hardly be infringed simply because a majority of the people choose that it be. We hold that the fact that a challenged legislative apportionment plan was approved by the electorate is without federal constitutional significance, if the scheme adopted fails to satisfy the basic requirements of [equal protection], as delineated [in Reynolds]."]

Mr. Justice HARLAN, dissenting [in all six cases].[2]

The Court's constitutional discussion [is] remarkable [for] its failure to address itself at all to the 14th Amendment as a whole or to the legislative

1. The Colorado case was Lucas v. Forty-Fourth Gen. Assembly, 377 U.S. 713 (1964); the New York case was WMCA, Inc. v. Lomenzo, 377 U.S. 633 (1964). The others: Maryland Committee for Fair Representation v. Tawes, 377 U.S. 656 (1964); Davis v. Mann, 377 U.S. 678 (1964) (Virginia); and Roman v. Sincock, 377 U.S. 695 (1964) (Delaware).

2. Justice Frankfurter was no longer on the Court at the time of this decision. He had retired in 1962, soon after Baker and well before Reynolds. He died a year after Reynolds.

history of the Amendment pertinent to the matter at hand. Stripped of aphorisms, the Court's argument boils down to the assertion that petitioners' right to vote has been invidiously "debased" or "diluted" by systems of apportionment which entitle them to vote for fewer legislators than other voters, an assertion which is tied to [equal protection] only by the constitutionally frail tautology that "equal" means "equal." [The] history of the adoption of the 14th Amendment provides conclusive evidence that neither those who proposed nor those who ratified the Amendment believed that [equal protection] limited the power of the States to apportion their legislatures as they saw fit. Moreover, the history demonstrates that the intention to leave this power undisturbed was deliberate and was widely believed to be essential to the adoption of the Amendment. [See also § 2 of the 14th Amendment. An extensive review of the history is omitted.]

Although [the Court] provides only generalities in elaboration of its main thesis, its opinion nevertheless fully demonstrates how far removed these problems are from fields of judicial competence. Recognizing that "indiscriminate districting" is an invitation to "partisan gerrymandering," [the] Court nevertheless excludes virtually every basis for the formation of electoral districts other than "indiscriminate districting." In one or another of today's opinions, the Court declares it unconstitutional for a State to give consideration to any of the following in establishing legislative districts: (1) history; (2) "economic or other sorts of group interests"; (3) area; (4) geographical considerations; (5) a desire "to insure effective representation for sparsely settled areas"; (6) "availability of access of citizens to their representatives"; (7) theories of bicameralism (except those approved by the Court); (8) occupation; (9) "an attempt to balance urban and rural power"; (10) the preference of a majority of voters in the State. So far as presently appears, the *only* factor which a state may consider, apart from numbers, is political subdivisions. But even "a clearly rational state policy" recognizing this factor is unconstitutional if "population is submerged as the controlling consideration." [I] know of no principle of logic or practical or theoretical politics, still less any constitutional principle, which establishes all or any of these exclusions. [The Court] says only that "legislators represent people, not trees or acres." [This] may be conceded. But it is surely equally obvious, and, in the context of elections, more meaningful to note that people are not ciphers and that legislators can represent their electors only by speaking for their interests—economic, social, political—many of which do reflect the place where the electors live. The Court does not establish, or indeed even attempt to make a case for the proposition that conflicting interests within a State can only be adjusted by disregarding them when voters are grouped for purposes of [representation].[3]

Mr. Justice STEWART, whom Mr. Justice CLARK joins, dissenting [in the Colorado and New York cases].[4]

[My] own understanding of the various theories of representative government is that no one theory has ever commanded unanimous assent. [But] even if it were thought that the rule announced today by the Court is, as a matter of political theory, the most desirable general rule which can be devised, [I] could not join in the fabrication of a constitutional mandate which imports and forever

3. Justice CLARK concurred in the results in all of the cases except those from Colorado and New York. In his concurrence in Reynolds, he argued that the majority had gone "much beyond the necessities of this case in laying down a new 'equal population' principle," suggesting: "It seems to me that all that the Court need say in this case is that each plan considered by the trial court is 'a crazy quilt,' clearly revealing invidious discrimination in each house of the Legislature."

4. Justice Stewart concurred in the results in the Alabama, Delaware, and Virginia cases, finding those apportionment schemes "completely lacking in rationality." In addition to the dissent printed here, he also submitted a brief dissent in the Maryland case.

freezes one theory of political thought into our Constitution, and forever denies to every State any opportunity for enlightened and progressive innovation in the design of its democratic institutions, so as to accommodate within a system of representative government the interests and aspirations of diverse groups of people, without subjecting any group or class to absolute domination by a geographically concentrated or highly organized majority. Representative government is a process of accommodating group interests through democratic institutional arrangements. [Appropriate] legislative apportionment, therefore, should ideally be designed to insure effective representation in the State's legislature, in cooperation with other organs for political power, of the various groups and interests making up the electorate. In practice, of course, this ideal is approximated in the particular apportionment system of any State by a realistic accommodation of the diverse and often conflicting political forces operating within the [State].

The fact is, of course, that population factors must often to some degree be subordinated in devising a legislative apportionment plan which is to achieve the important goal of ensuring a fair, effective, and balanced representation of the regional, social, and economic interests within a State. And the further fact is that throughout our history the apportionments of State Legislatures have reflected the strongly felt American tradition that the public interest is composed of many diverse interests, and that in the long run it can better be expressed by a medley of component voices than by the majority's monolithic command. What constitutes a rational plan reasonably designed to achieve this objective will vary from State to State, [but] so long as a State's apportionment plan reasonably achieves, in the light of the State's own characteristics, effective and balanced representation of all substantial interests, without sacrificing the principle of effective majority rule, that plan cannot be considered irrational.

[I] think that [equal protection] demands but two basic attributes of any plan of state legislative apportionment. First, it demands that, in the light of the State's own characteristics and needs, the plan must be a rational one. Secondly, it demands that the plan must be such as not to permit the systematic frustration of the will of a majority of the electorate of the State. I think it is apparent that any plan of legislative apportionment which could be shown to reflect no policy, but simply arbitrary and capricious action or inaction, and that any plan which could be shown systematically to prevent ultimate effective majority rule, would be invalid under accepted [equal protection] standards. But, beyond this, I think there is nothing in the [Constitution] to prevent a State from choosing any electoral legislative structure it thinks best suited to the interests, temper, and customs of its people. In the light of these standards, I turn to the Colorado and New York plans of legislative apportionment.

COLORADO. [In] the Colorado House, the majority unquestionably rules supreme, with the population factor untempered by other considerations. In the Senate rural minorities do not have effective control, and therefore do not have even a veto power over the will of the urban majorities. It is true that, as a matter of theoretical arithmetic, a minority of 36% of the voters could elect a majority of the Senate, but this percentage has no real meaning in terms of the legislative process.[5] [No] possible combination of Colorado senators from rural

---

5. The theoretical figure is arrived at by placing the legislative districts for each house in rank order of population, and by counting down the smallest population end of the list a sufficient distance to accumulate the minimum population which could elect a majority of the house in question. It is a meaningless abstraction as applied to a multimembered body because the factors of political party alignment and interest representation make such theoretical bloc voting a practical impossibility. For example, 31,000,000 people in the 26 least populous States representing only 17% of United States population have 52% of the Senators in the United States Senate. But no one contends that this bloc controls the Senate's legislative process. [Footnote by Justice Stewart.]

districts, even assuming arguendo that they would vote as a bloc, could control the Senate. To arrive at the 36% figure, one must include with the rural districts a substantial number of urban districts, districts with substantially dissimilar interests. [If] per capita representation were the rule in both houses of the Colorado Legislature, counties having small populations would have to be merged with larger counties having totally dissimilar interests. Their representatives would not only be unfamiliar with the problems of the smaller county, but the interests of the smaller counties might well be totally submerged by the interests of the larger counties with which they are joined. Since representatives representing conflicting interests might well pay greater attention to the views of the majority, the minority interest could be denied any effective representation at all. Its votes would not be merely "diluted," [but] rendered totally nugatory. [The] present apportionment, adopted overwhelmingly by the people in a 1962 popular referendum, [is] entirely rational. [The] majority has consciously chosen to protect the minority's interests, and under the liberal initiative provisions of the Colorado Constitution, it retains the power to reverse its decision to do so. Therefore, there can be no question of frustration of the basic principle of majority rule.

NEW YORK. [The apportionment is] not a crazy quilt; it is rational, it is applied systematically, and it is kept reasonably current. The formula provides that each county shall have at least one representative in the Assembly, that the smaller counties shall have somewhat greater representation in the legislature than representation based solely on numbers would accord, and that some limits be placed on the representation of the largest counties in order to prevent one megalopolis from completely dominating the legislature. [A] policy guaranteeing minimum representation to each county is certainly rational, particularly in a State like New York. [The formula] is clearly designed to protect against overcentralization of power. To understand fully the practical importance of this consideration in New York, one must look to its unique characteristics. New York is one of the few States in which the central cities can elect a majority of representatives to the legislature. [The] 10 most populous counties in the State control both houses of the legislature under the existing apportionment system. Each of these counties is heavily urban; each is in a metropolitan [area]. Obviously, [the] existing system of apportionment clearly guarantees effective majority representation and control in the State Legislature. But this is not the whole story. New York City [has], by virtue of its concentration of population, homogeneity of interest, and political cohesiveness, acquired an institutional power and political influence of its own hardly measurable simply by counting the number of its representatives in the legislature. [Surely] it is not irrational for the State [to] be justifiably concerned about balancing such a concentration of political power, and certainly there is nothing in our [Constitution] which prevents a State from reasonably translating such a concern into its [apportionment formula].[6]

---

6. In the wake of Reynolds, an intense but ultimately unsuccessful drive was launched to overturn it by constitutional amendment. The most widely supported proposal would have permitted one house of a state legislature to be apportioned on a basis other than population, if a majority of the state's voters approved the plan. (Recall Lucas, the Colorado apportionment case, above.) But all efforts failed, and the implementation of the "one person-one vote" principle proceeded with remarkable rapidity. By the end of the decade most state legislatures were reapportioned in accordance with the equal population standard. See McKay, "Reapportionment: Success Story of the Warren Court," 67 Mich.L. Rev. 223 (1968). Observers have been divided about the impact of reapportionment on politics and governmental policy. See, e.g., Polsby, ed., Reapportionment in the 1970s (1971). Chief Justice Warren thought Reynolds the most important decision of his tenure. For a skeptical view about its contribution, see Bickel, The Supreme Court and the Idea of Progress (1970).

THE PROGENY OF REYNOLDS v. SIMS:
SOME ELABORATIONS OF THE
"ONE PERSON–ONE VOTE" THEME

Introduction. Did Reynolds provide a "judicially manageable standard"? Was that standard a justifiable inference from equal protection? Do the "distorting" effects of party cohesion on the equality principle justify or require the Court to limit gerrymandering? (See note 3 below.) Would Justice Stewart's emphasis on "systematic frustration of the majority" have been a preferable, more realistic focus for judicial inquiry? Would it have been a "judicially manageable" standard? Do the emphases on voter equality and majority rule make supermajority requirements impermissible? (See note 4 below.) Do the Reynolds principles permit excluding some voters from special purpose elections? Questions such as these are suggested by the following sampling of some of the progeny of Reynolds. Although compliance in most states was rapid, the widespread reapportionment of the state legislatures has not ended the Court's task of elaborating the principles of Reynolds. In recent years, for example, the Court has divided about the applicability of the principles to units of government other than state legislatures and has permitted some deviations from mathematical equality. The materials that follow illustrate some of the difficulties in implementing Reynolds in the more than two decades since that decision.

1. *Application of Reynolds v. Sims to local government.* AVERY v. MIDLAND COUNTY, 390 U.S. 474 (1968), was the first decision to apply the equal representation requirement to a unit of local government. The case involved a Texas county Commissioners Court—an agency with "general governmental powers." The county had been divided into four districts for purposes of representation on the Commissioners Court. The city of Midland located in the county constituted one district, with over 67,000 people; the rural area was divided into three districts, with less than 1,000 people each. Justice WHITE's majority opinion rejected the argument that the Commissioners Court was an administrative rather than a legislative body and concluded "that the Constitution permits no substantial variation from equal population in drawing districts for units of local government having general governmental powers over the entire geographic area served by the body." Whether state power was exercised through the legislature or through local elected officials, equal protection required assurance "that those qualified to vote have the right to an equally effective voice in the election process." [1] (Justices HARLAN, FORTAS and STEWART submitted separate dissents.)

A divided Court extended the principles of Avery to a case involving the election of trustees of a junior college district in HADLEY v. JUNIOR COLLEGE DIST., 397 U.S. 50 (1970). The junior college district comprised eight local school districts; the Court found it impermissible to give a district with more than half of the junior college district population the right to elect only half of the trustees. The majority stated the "general rule" as follows: "[W]henever a state or local government decides to select persons by popular election to perform governmental functions, [equal protection] requires that

---

1. Justice White left open the possibility that deviations from equal population districting might be permissible for special purpose units of government. And he insisted that the Court would be sensitive to "the greatly varying problems" of local government, pointing to earlier decisions in Sailors v. Board of Education, 387 U.S. 105 (1967) ("administrative" school board), and Dusch v. Davis, 387 U.S. 112 (1967).

In recent years, the Court has sustained several deviations from the "one person-one vote" rule in the context of "property owners only" elections for directors of special purpose governmental units such as water districts. The cases are reviewed in sec. 4 of chap. 9, at p. 813 above. For the most recent example, see Ball v. James (1981; p. 814 above).

each qualified voter must be given an equal opportunity to participate in that election, and when members of an elected body are chosen from separate districts, each district must be established on a basis which will insure, as far as is practicable, that equal numbers of voters can vote for proportionally equal numbers of officials. It is of course possible that there might be some case in which a State elects certain functionaries whose duties are so far removed from normal governmental activities and so disproportionately affect different groups that a popular election in compliance with [Reynolds] might not be required."

2. *Mathematical inequalities: Permissible deviations from "one person-one vote."* In the years since Reynolds and Wesberry v. Sanders, the Court has adhered rigidly to the maximum possible mathematical equality in districting for congressional elections. But the Court has gradually permitted somewhat greater deviations from equality in state districting, over the dissents of some Justices claiming that the Reynolds principles were being undercut.

a. *Congressional districting.* KIRKPATRICK v. PREISLER, 394 U.S. 526 (1969), drew from the congressional districting principles of Wesberry v. Sanders the requirement "that as nearly as is practicable, one man's vote in a congressional election is to be worth as much as another's." Kirkpatrick rejected a Missouri plan which varied from the "absolute population equality" ideal within a range of 2.8% below and 3.1% above. Justice BRENNAN's majority opinion insisted that variations from absolute equality could not be justified on de minimis grounds, nor by a desire to avoid fragmenting political subdivisions or even to deter political gerrymandering. Instead, states were required to "make a good-faith effort to achieve precise mathematical equality." In 1973, WHITE v. WEISER, 412 U.S. 783, adhered to the "precise equality" approach for congressional districting, even while the Court drifted away from that strictness in a group of state legislative reapportionment cases noted below. The majority insisted that even "small" population variances were impermissible in congressional districting. In a concurring opinion, Justice POWELL, joined by Chief Justice Burger and Justice Rehnquist, argued that the state redistricting cases, below, "strengthen the case against attempting to hold any reapportionment scheme—state or congressional—to slide-rule precision." But since Kirkpatrick was "virtually indistinguishable," he agreed to follow it "unless and until the Court decides to reconsider that decision."

In KARCHER v. DAGGETT, 462 U.S. 725 (1983), a 5 to 4 majority continued to adhere to Kirkpatrick and White in requiring that states, in congressional districting, "come as nearly as practicable to population equality." In the context of a New Jersey apportionment with a maximum variance of approximately 0.7%, the Court, with Justice BRENNAN writing for the majority, maintained its refusal to acknowledge a de minimis exception as long as the state was unable to show why more precise results could not be achieved "using the best available census data." The Court did, however, indicate that certain "consistently applied legislative policies might justify some variance, including, for instance, making districts compact, respecting municipal boundaries, preserving the cores of prior districts, and avoiding contests between incumbent Representatives. [The] State must, however, show with some specificity that a particular objective required the specific deviations in its plan, rather than simply relying on general assertions." Because New Jersey could not make such a showing, even its relatively minor variations were deemed fatal. Justice WHITE, joined by Chief Justice Burger and Justices Powell and Rehnquist, dissented, concluding that if Kirkpatrick and White required overturning an apportionment with so little variance, then it was time that those cases be reconsidered.

b. *State districting.* After rejecting a state's redistricting plan involving substantial variations from population equality in Swann v. Adams, 385 U.S.

440 (1967), the Court in the 1970s began to manifest considerable tolerance toward smaller deviations from the equality ideal. The new trend began in ABATE v. MUNDT, 403 U.S. 182 (1971), where the Court found justification for an 11.9% total deviation from population equality in the apportionment of a county legislature—a larger deviation than those found impermissible in a few earlier cases. Justice MARSHALL's majority opinion insisted that deviations "must be justified by legitimate state considerations," but found adequate justifications here—including the fact that the local body reflected a "long history of, and perceived need for, close cooperation between the county and its constituent towns." Justice BRENNAN, joined by Justice Douglas, thought the majority had diluted the Reynolds standard.

Even greater tolerance was manifested in a leading modern case, a case involving a state legislature—MAHAN v. HOWELL, 410 U.S. 315 (1973). That decision made it clear that the new majority was more receptive to claimed justifications for deviations from equality. (And other decisions, soon after, indicated that the Court would not even demand justification for "minor"— apparently, up to 10%—deviations.) Mahan approved a redistricting of the lower house of the Virginia legislature with a maximum variance of 16.4% from population equality. Justice REHNQUIST's majority opinion stated that "more flexibility was constitutionally permissible with respect to state legislative reapportionment than in congressional redistricting," because of the interest in "the normal functioning of state and local governments." Here, the deviations from the equality ideal were justified by "the State's policy of maintaining the integrity of political subdivision lines." But even rational state justifications, he insisted, could not "be permitted to emasculate the goal of substantial equality." The deviation in Virginia "may well approach tolerable limits," but "we do not believe it exceeds them." [2]

The loosening of Court reins on state reapportionment plans became even more manifest a few months later, in two decisions which not only reaffirmed the Mahan receptiveness to a broader range of state justifications, but also found a new category of "minor" deviations in population equality requiring no justifications at all. The cases involved the Connecticut and Texas legislatures. In the Connecticut case, GAFFNEY v. CUMMINGS, 412 U.S. 735 (1973), there was a maximum variation among districts of about 8% and an average deviation of about 2% from the ideal. In the Texas case, WHITE v. REGESTER, 412 U.S. 755 (1973), there was a maximum deviation of 9.9% and an average deviation of less than 2%. Justice WHITE's majority opinion found these to be "relatively minor" population deviations, insufficient to meet the "threshold requirement of proving a prima facie case of invidious discrimination" and accordingly requiring no justifications from the States. He distinguished these cases from the "enormous," unjustifiable variations struck down in the "early cases beginning with Reynolds" and from cases such as Mahan,

---

2. Justice BRENNAN's dissent, joined by Justices Douglas and Marshall, thought the state plan demonstrated "a systematic pattern of substantial deviation from the constitutional ideal." And he objected to the notion of "different constitutional *standards*" as to state and congressional districting. A state might have a broader range of interests to submit as justifications for deviations, but the state burden of proof or the applicable standard should not be any lighter.

Contrast with Mahan the Court's rejection of a *court-ordered* redistricting plan for the Mississippi legislature, because of excessive and unexplained deviations from the goal of population equality among districts. Connor v. Finch, 431

U.S. 407 (1977). The maximum population deviations in the Mississippi plan were 16.5% in the Senate districts and 19.3% in the House districts—comparable to the maximum deviation approved in the Virginia plan involved in Mahan v. Howell. Justice Stewart's majority opinion pointed out that a court-ordered plan must be examined more critically than one adopted by a state legislature. Here, unlike Mahan, the Court was not persuaded that the substantial deviations from the "one person-one vote" rule were justified by the interest in protecting "the integrity of political subdivisions or historical boundary lines."

involving deviations "sufficiently large to require justification" but nonetheless justifiable. "It is now time to recognize," he added, "that minor deviations from mathematical equality among state legislative districts are insufficient to make out a prima facie case [so] as to require justification by the State." Attainment of the "worthy goal" of Reynolds "does not in any commonsense way depend upon eliminating the insignificant population variation" here. He added: "That the Court was not deterred by the hazards of the political thicket when it undertook to adjudicate the reapportionment cases does not mean that it should become bogged down in a vast, intractable apportionment slough, particularly when there is little, if anything, to be accomplished by doing so." When "only minor population variations" are shown, judicial involvement "should never begin." [3]

The Court continued its more relaxed scrutiny of state legislative apportionment in BROWN v. THOMSON, 463 U.S. 835 (1983). Under the general Wyoming reapportionment formula, Niobrara County would have been entitled to no representatives; but, pursuant to a provision of the state constitution, it was allowed one representative, even though the result, in the case of this county, was a disparity of 60% below the mean. Despite this disparity, however, the Court, with Justice POWELL writing for the majority, upheld the apportionment. Relying on Abate and Mahan, Justice Powell determined that the historical adherence to county boundaries in Wyoming justified a disparity of even this magnitude. Moreover, the Court evaluated the disparity marginally, in terms of how the statewide apportionment would be affected if this one county's representative was taken away. Because the grant of a representative to this county was not in itself "a significant cause of the population deviations" that existed in Wyoming apportionment, the Court refused to overturn the apportionment. Justice BRENNAN, joined by Justices White, Marshall, and Blackmun, dissented, finding the 60% deviation for this county and the 89% maximum deviation for the state as a whole in excess of constitutionally tolerable limits.

3. *The unwillingness to scrutinize political gerrymanders.* The challengers in the 1973 Connecticut case above, GAFFNEY v. CUMMINGS (in note 2), raised a claim going beyond that of population equality: they also argued "that even if acceptable population-wise, the [plan] was invidiously discriminatory because a 'political fairness principle' was followed." The plan was admittedly drawn to create districting "that would achieve a rough approximation of the statewide political strengths of the Democratic and Republic Parties," and the challengers characterized the plan "as nothing less than a gigantic political gerrymander, invidiously discriminatory under the 14th Amendment." In the course of rejecting that claim, Justice WHITE's majority opinion chilled most hopes that political gerrymanders might be subjected to careful judicial scrutiny. He stated that "compactness or attractiveness have never been held to constitute an independent federal constitutional requirement of state legislative districts." And the "political fairness" principle was permissible: "Politics and political considerations are inseparable from districting and apportionment. [It] is not only obvious, but absolutely unavoidable, that the location and shape of districts may well determine the political complexion of the area. [The] reality is that districting inevitably has and is intended to have substantial political conse-

3. Justice BRENNAN, joined by Justices Douglas and Marshall, dissented. He commented that "one can reasonably surmise," in view of the fact that justification had been required for an 11.9% deviation in Abate v. Mundt in 1971, "that a line has been drawn at 10%—deviations in excess of that amount are apparently acceptable only on a showing of justification by the State; deviations less than that amount require no justification whatsoever." He insisted that the plans now sustained involved "substantial inequalities" and thought that the majority approach "effects a substantial and very unfortunate retreat from the principles established in our earlier cases."

quences. It may be suggested that those who redistrict and reapportion should work with census, not political, data, and achieve population equality without regard for political impact. But this politically mindless approach may produce, whether intended or not, the most grossly gerrymandered results, and, in any event, it is most unlikely that the political impact of such a plan would remain undiscovered by the time it was proposed or adopted, in which event the results would be both known and, if not changed, intended." He added: "It is much more plausible to assume that those who redistrict and reapportion work with both political and census data. Within the limits of the population equality standards of [equal protection], they seek, through compromise or otherwise, to achieve the political or other ends of the State, its constituents, and its office-holders. What is done in so arranging for elections, or to achieve political ends or allocate political power, is not wholly exempt from judicial scrutiny under the 14th Amendment. [F]or example, multimember districts may be vulnerable, if racial or political groups have been fenced out of the political process and their voting strength invidiously minimized.[4] Beyond this, we have not ventured far or attempted the impossible task of extirpating politics from what are the essentially political processes of the sovereign States. Even more plainly, judicial interest should be at its lowest ebb when a State purports fairly to allocate political power to the parties in accordance with their voting strength. [N]either we nor the district courts have a constitutional warrant to invalidate a state plan, otherwise within tolerable population limits, because it undertakes, not to minimize or eliminate the political strength of any group or party, but to recognize it and, through districting, provide a rough sort of proportional representation in the legislative halls of the State."[5]

4. *Supermajorities.* West Virginia requires that political subdivisions may not incur bonded indebtedness or exceed constitutional tax rates without the approval of 60% of the voters in a referendum election. A county school bond proposal received only slightly more than 50% of the vote and was therefore defeated. The highest state court found that the 60% requirement violated equal protection because "the votes of those who favored the issuance of the bonds had a proportionately smaller impact on the outcome of the election than the votes of those who opposed issuance of the bonds." The Court reversed. GORDON v. LANCE, 403 U.S. 1 (1971). Chief Justice BURGER called the state court's reliance on voting rights cases such as Cipriano v. Houma (chap. 9, sec. 4, above) "misplaced." He explained: "The defect this Court found in those cases lay in the denial or dilution of voting power because of group

---

4. Attacks on multimember districts as tools of racial discrimination have been a prolific source of litigation on the modern Court. The problem has been considered earlier (in chap. 9, above) and is accordingly not developed here, beyond a brief review. In one of the earliest post-Reynolds v. Sims cases, Burns v. Richardson, 384 U.S. 73 (1966), the Court held that, although multimember rather than single-member districts were permissible, they could be attacked if they were "designed to or would operate to minimize or cancel out the voting strength of racial or political elements of the voting population." See also Fortson v. Dorsey, 379 U.S. 433 (1965). In the early 1970s, the Court began to undertake the task of scrutinizing the purpose and impact of multimember districts. Whitcomb v. Chavis, 403 U.S. 124 (1971), rejected a claim that a multimember district underrepresented minorities, but articulated standards that laid the groundwork for future challenges. These guidelines bore fruit soon after: in White v. Regester,

412 U.S. 755 (1973), the Court for the first time sustained such a claim. (Cf. Connor v. Finch, 431 U.S. 407 (1977), on alleged dilution of black voting strength in single-member districts under a court-ordered redistricting plan.) The most important examinations of constitutional "purposeful discrimination" standards in this area came in Mobile v. Bolden (1980) and Rogers v. Lodge (1982). These cases are considered more fully in chap. 9 above. [On the impact of the Voting Rights Act (including its "effect" rather than "purpose" standards and its easier burdens of proof), see Rome v. United States (1980; chap. 10, sec. 4, above).]

5. In very recent years, however, several Justices have written lengthy opinions urging that purely political gerrymandering should be considered violative of equal protection. See, e.g., Justice Stevens' concurrence and Justice Powell's dissent in Karcher v. Daggett (1983; note 2a above).

characteristics—geographic location and property ownership—that bore no valid relation to the interest of those groups in the subject matter of the election; moreover, the dilution or denial was imposed irrespective of how members of those groups actually voted." He stated more generally: "Certainly any departure from strict majority rule gives disproportionate power to the minority. But there is nothing in the language of the Constitution, our history or our cases that requires that a majority always prevail on every issue. [The] Constitution itself provides that a simple majority vote is insufficient on some issues. [The] constitutions of many States prohibit or severely limit the power of the legislature to levy new taxes or to create or increase bonded indebtedness, thereby insulating entire areas from majority control. [We] conclude that so long as such provisions do not discriminate against or authorize discrimination against any identifiable class they do not violate [equal protection]." In a footnote, he added: "We intimate no view on the constitutionality of a provision requiring unanimity or giving a veto power to a very small group. Nor do we decide whether a State may, consistent with the Constitution, require extraordinary majorities for the election of public officers." [6]

Can Gordon v. Lance be reconciled with Reynolds and its emphasis on political equality? Were not the apportionment plans invalidated in Reynolds attempts to protect minorities? Why were those attempts invalid, while the West Virginia supermajority requirement was valid? Is there adequate explanation in Chief Justice Burger's comment in Gordon v. Lance that, "[u]nlike the restrictions in our previous cases, the West Virginia Constitution singles out no 'discrete and insular minority' for special treatment. The three-fifths requirement applies equally to all bond issues for any purpose, whether for schools, sewers, or highways"?

---

6. Note also the sustaining, in Lockport v. Citizens for Community Action, 430 U.S. 259 (1977), of a concurrent majority requirement for referenda on new county charters. Under New York law, a new county charter must be approved by two separate majorities in the county—the urban voters and the rural voters. In rejecting a "one person-one vote" attack on that scheme, Justice Stewart's opinion emphasized:

"The equal protection principles applicable in gauging the fairness of an election involving the choice of legislative representatives are of limited relevance [in] analyzing the propriety of recognizing distinctive voter interests in a 'single-shot' referendum." In his view, "the differing interests of city and noncity voters in the adoption of a new county charter" were sufficient to justify the scheme.

*

APPENDIX A

THE CONSTITUTION
OF THE UNITED STATES OF AMERICA

We the People of the United States, in Order to form a more perfect Union, establish Justice, insure domestic Tranquility, provide for the common defence, promote the general Welfare, and secure the Blessings of Liberty to ourselves and our Posterity, do ordain and establish this Constitution for the United States of America.

ARTICLE I.

SECTION 1. All legislative Powers herein granted shall be vested in a Congress of the United States, which shall consist of a Senate and House of Representatives.

SECTION 2. The House of Representatives shall be composed of Members chosen every second Year by the People of the several States, and the Electors in each State shall have the Qualifications requisite for Electors of the most numerous Branch of the State Legislature.

No Person shall be a Representative who shall not have attained to the Age of twenty five Years, and been seven Years a Citizen of the United States, and who shall not, when elected, be an Inhabitant of that State in which he shall be chosen.

Representatives and direct Taxes shall be apportioned among the several States which may be included within this Union, according to their respective Numbers, which shall be determined by adding to the whole Number of free Persons, including those bound to Service for a Term of Years, and excluding Indians not taxed, three fifths of all other Persons. The actual Enumeration shall be made within three Years after the first Meeting of the Congress of the United States, and within every subsequent Term of ten Years, in such Manner as they shall by Law direct. The Number of Representatives shall not exceed one for every thirty Thousand, but each State shall have at Least one Representative; and until such enumeration shall be made, the State of New Hampshire shall be entitled to chuse three, Massachusetts eight, Rhode Island and Providence Plantations one, Connecticut five, New-York six, New Jersey four, Pennsylvania eight, Delaware one, Maryland six, Virginia ten, North Carolina five, South Carolina five, and Georgia three.

When vacancies happen in the Representation from any State, the Executive Authority thereof shall issue Writs of Election to fill such Vacancies.

The House of Representatives shall chuse their Speaker and other Officers; and shall have the sole Power of Impeachment.

SECTION 3. The Senate of the United States shall be composed of two Senators from each State, chosen by the Legislature thereof, for six Years; and each Senator shall have one Vote.

Immediately after they shall be assembled in Consequence of the first Election, they shall be divided as equally as may be into three Classes. The Seats of the Senators of the first Class shall be vacated at the Expiration of the second Year, of the second Class at the Expiration of the fourth Year, and of the third Class at the Expiration of the sixth Year, so that one third may be chosen every second Year; and if Vacancies happen by Resignation, or otherwise, during the Recess of the Legislature of any State, the Executive thereof may make temporary Appointments until the next Meeting of the Legislature, which shall then fill such Vacancies.

No Person shall be a Senator who shall not have attained to the Age of thirty Years, and been nine Years a Citizen of the United States, and who shall not, when elected, be an Inhabitant of that State for which he shall be chosen.

The Vice President of the United States shall be President of the Senate, but shall have no Vote, unless they be equally divided.

The Senate shall chuse their other Officers, and also a President pro tempore, in the Absence of the Vice President, or when he shall exercise the Office of President of the United States.

The Senate shall have the sole Power to try all Impeachments. When sitting for that Purpose, they shall be on Oath or Affirmation. When the President of the United States is tried the Chief Justice shall preside: And no Person shall be convicted without the Concurrence of two thirds of the Members present.

Judgment in Cases of Impeachment shall not extend further than to removal from Office, and disqualification to hold and enjoy any Office of honor, Trust or Profit under the United States: but the Party convicted shall nevertheless be liable and subject to Indictment, Trial, Judgment and Punishment, according to Law.

SECTION 4. The Times, Places and Manner of holding Elections for Senators and Representatives, shall be prescribed in each State by the Legislature thereof; but the Congress may at any time by Law make or alter such Regulations, except as to the Places of chusing Senators.

The Congress shall assemble at least once in every Year, and such Meeting shall be on the first Monday in December, unless they shall by Law appoint a different Day.

SECTION 5. Each House shall be the Judge of the Elections, Returns and Qualifications of its own Members, and a Majority of each shall constitute a Quorum to do Business; but a smaller Number may adjourn from day to day, and may be authorized to compel the Attendance of absent Members, in such Manner, and under such Penalties as each House may provide.

Each House may determine the Rules of its Proceedings, punish its Members for disorderly Behaviour, and, with the Concurrence of two thirds, expel a Member.

Each House shall keep a Journal of its Proceedings, and from time to time publish the same, excepting such Parts as may in their Judgment require Secrecy; and the Yeas and Nays of the Members of either House on any question shall, at the Desire of one fifth of those Present, be entered on the Journal.

Neither House, during the Session of Congress, shall, without the Consent of the other, adjourn for more than three days, nor to any other Place than that in which the two Houses shall be sitting.

SECTION 6. The Senators and Representatives shall receive a Compensation for their Services, to be ascertained by Law, and paid out of the Treasury of the United States. They shall in all Cases, except Treason, Felony and Breach of the Peace, be privileged from Arrest during their Attendance at the Session of their respective Houses, and in going to and returning from the same; and for any Speech or Debate in either House, they shall not be questioned in any other Place.

No Senator or Representative shall, during the Time for which he was elected, be appointed to any civil Office under the Authority of the United

States, which shall have been created, or the Emoluments whereof shall have been encreased during such time; and no Person holding any Office under the United States, shall be a Member of either House during his Continuance in Office.

SECTION 7. All Bills for raising Revenue shall originate in the House of Representatives; but the Senate may propose or concur with amendments as on other Bills.

Every Bill which shall have passed the House of Representatives and the Senate, shall, before it become a Law, be presented to the President of the United States; If he approve he shall sign it, but if not he shall return it, with his Objections to that House in which it shall have originated, who shall enter the Objections at large on their Journal, and proceed to reconsider it. If after such Reconsideration two thirds of that House shall agree to pass the Bill, it shall be sent, together with the Objections, to the other House, by which it shall likewise be reconsidered, and if approved by two thirds of that House, it shall become a Law. But in all such Cases the Votes of both Houses shall be determined by Yeas and Nays, and the Names of the Persons voting for and against the Bill shall be entered on the Journal of each House respectively. If any Bill shall not be returned by the President within ten Days (Sunday excepted) after it shall have been presented to him, the Same shall be a Law, in like Manner as if he had signed it, unless the Congress by their Adjournment prevent its Return, in which Case it shall not be a Law.

Every Order, Resolution, or Vote to which the Concurrence of the Senate and House of Representatives may be necessary (except on a question of Adjournment) shall be presented to the President of the United States; and before the Same shall take Effect, shall be approved by him, or being disapproved by him, shall be repassed by two thirds of the Senate and House of Representatives, according to the Rules and Limitations prescribed in the Case of a Bill.

SECTION 8. The Congress shall have Power To lay and collect Taxes, Duties, Imposts and Excises, to pay the Debts and provide for the common Defence and general Welfare of the United States; but all Duties, Imposts and Excises shall be uniform throughout the United States;

To borrow Money on the credit of the United States;

To regulate Commerce with foreign Nations, and among the several States, and with the Indian Tribes;

To establish an uniform Rule of Naturalization, and uniform Laws on the subject of Bankruptcies throughout the United States;

To coin Money, regulate the Value thereof, and of foreign Coin, and fix the Standard of Weights and Measures;

To provide for the Punishment of counterfeiting the Securities and current Coin of the United States;

To establish Post Offices and post Roads;

To promote the Progress of Science and useful Arts, by securing for limited Times to Authors and Inventors the exclusive Right to their respective Writings and Discoveries;

To constitute Tribunals inferior to the supreme Court;

To define and punish Piracies and Felonies committed on the high Seas, and Offences against the Law of Nations;

To declare War, grant Letters of Marque and Reprisal, and make Rules concerning Captures on Land and Water;

To raise and support Armies, but no Appropriation of Money to that Use shall be for a longer Term than two Years;

To provide and maintain a Navy;

To make Rules for the Government and Regulation of the land and naval Forces;

To provide for calling forth the Militia to execute the Laws of the Union, suppress Insurrections and repel Invasions;

To provide for organizing, arming, and disciplining, the Militia, and for governing such Part of them as may be employed in the Service of the United States, reserving to the States respectively, the Appointment of the Officers, and the Authority of training the Militia according to the discipline prescribed by Congress;

To exercise exclusive Legislation in all Cases whatsoever, over such District (not exceeding ten Miles square) as may, by Cession of particular States, and the Acceptance of Congress, become the Seat of the Government of the United States, and to exercise like Authority over all Places purchased by the Consent of the Legislature of the State in which the Same shall be, for the Erection of Forts, Magazines, Arsenals, dock-Yards, and other needful Buildings;—And

To make all Laws which shall be necessary and proper for carrying into Execution the foregoing Powers, and all other Powers vested by this Constitution in the Government of the United States, or in any Department or Officer thereof.

SECTION 9.   The Migration or Importation of such Persons as any of the States now existing shall think proper to admit, shall not be prohibited by the Congress prior to the Year one thousand eight hundred and eight, but a Tax or duty may be imposed on such Importation, not exceeding ten dollars for each Person.

The Privilege of the Writ of Habeas Corpus shall not be suspended, unless when in Cases of Rebellion or Invasion the public Safety may require it.

No Bill of Attainder or ex post facto Law shall be passed.

No Capitation, or other direct, Tax shall be laid, unless in Proportion to the Census or Enumeration herein before directed to be taken.

No Tax or Duty shall be laid on Articles exported from any State.

No Preference shall be given by any Regulation of Commerce or Revenue to the Ports of one State over those of another; nor shall Vessels bound to, or from, one State, be obliged to enter, clear or pay Duties in another.

No Money shall be drawn from the Treasury, but in Consequence of Appropriations made by Law; and a regular Statement and Account of the Receipts and Expenditures of all public Money shall be published from time to time.

No Title of Nobility shall be granted by the United States: And no Person holding any Office of Profit or Trust under them, shall, without the Consent of the Congress, accept of any present, Emolument, Office, or Title, of any kind whatever, from any King, Prince or foreign State.

SECTION 10.   No State shall enter into any Treaty, Alliance, or Confederation; grant Letters of Marque and Reprisal; coin Money; emit Bills of Credit; make any Thing but gold and silver Coin a Tender in Payment of Debts; pass any Bill of Attainder, ex post facto Law, or Law impairing the Obligation of Contracts, or grant any Title of Nobility.

No State shall, without the Consent of the Congress, lay any Imposts or Duties on Imports or Exports, except what may be absolutely necessary for executing its inspection Laws: and the net Produce of all Duties and Imposts, laid by any State on Imports or Exports, shall be for the Use of the Treasury of the United States; and all such Laws shall be subject to the Revision and Controul of the Congress.

No State shall, without the Consent of Congress, lay any Duty of Tonnage, keep Troops, or Ships of War in time of Peace, enter into any Agreement or Compact with another State, or with a foreign Power, or engage in War, unless actually invaded, or in such imminent Danger as will not admit of delay.

ARTICLE II.

SECTION 1. The executive Power shall be vested in a President of the United States of America. He shall hold his Office during the Term of four Years, and, together with the Vice President, chosen for the same Term, be elected, as follows

Each State shall appoint, in such Manner as the Legislature thereof may direct, a Number of Electors, equal to the whole Number of Senators and Representatives to which the State may be entitled in the Congress: but no Senator or Representative, or Person holding an Office of Trust or Profit under the United States, shall be appointed an Elector.

The Electors shall meet in their respective States, and vote by Ballot for two Persons, of whom one at least shall not be an Inhabitant of the same State with themselves. And they shall make a List of all the Persons voted for, and of the Number of Votes for each; which List they shall sign and certify, and transmit sealed to the Seat of the Government of the United States, directed to the President of the Senate. The President of the Senate shall, in the Presence of the Senate and House of Representatives, open all the Certificates, and the Votes shall then be counted. The Person having the greatest Number of Votes shall be the President, if such Number be a Majority of the whole Number of Electors appointed; and if there be more than one who have such Majority, and have an equal Number of Votes, then the House of Representatives shall immediately chuse by Ballot one of them for President; and if no Person have a Majority, then from the five highest on the List the said House shall in like Manner chuse the President. But in chusing the President, the Votes shall be taken by States, the Representation from each State having one Vote; a quorum for this Purpose shall consist of a Member or Members from two thirds of the States, and a Majority of all the States shall be necessary to a Choice. In every Case, after the Choice of the President, the Person having the greatest Number of Votes of the Electors shall be the Vice President. But if there should remain two or more who have equal Votes, the Senate shall chuse from them by Ballot the Vice President.

The Congress may determine the Time of chusing the Electors, and the Day on which they shall give their Votes; which Day shall be the same throughout the United States.

No Person except a natural born Citizen, or a Citizen of the United States, at the time of the Adoption of this Constitution, shall be eligible to the Office of President; neither shall any Person be eligible to that Office who shall not have attained to the Age of thirty five Years, and been fourteen Years a Resident within the United States.

In Case of the Removal of the President from Office, or of his Death, Resignation, or Inability to discharge the Powers and Duties of the said Office, the Same shall devolve on the Vice President, and the Congress may by Law provide for the Case of Removal, Death, Resignation or Inability, both of the President and Vice President, declaring what Officer shall then act as President, and such Officer shall act accordingly, until the Disability be removed, or a President shall be elected.

The President shall, at stated Times, receive for his Services, a Compensation, which shall neither be encreased nor diminished during the Period for which he shall have been elected, and he shall not receive within that Period any other Emolument from the United States, or any of them.

Before he enter on the Execution of his Office, he shall take the following Oath or Affirmation:—"I do solemnly swear (or affirm) that I will faithfully execute the Office of President of the United States, and will to the best of my Ability, preserve, protect and defend the Constitution of the United States."

SECTION 2. The President shall be Commander in Chief of the Army and Navy of the United States, and of the Militia of the several States, when called into the actual Service of the United States; he may require the Opinion, in writing, of the principal Officer in each of the executive Departments, upon any Subject relating to the Duties of their respective Offices, and he shall have Power to grant Reprieves and Pardons for Offences against the United States, except in Cases of Impeachment.

He shall have Power, by and with the Advice and Consent of the Senate, to make Treaties, provided two thirds of the Senators present concur; and he shall nominate, and by and with the Advice and Consent of the Senate, shall appoint Ambassadors, other public Ministers and Consuls, Judges of the supreme Court, and all other Officers of the United States, whose Appointments are not herein otherwise provided for, and which shall be established by Law: but the Congress may by Law vest the Appointment of such inferior Officers, as they think proper, in the President alone, in the Courts of Law, or in the Heads of Departments.

The President shall have Power to fill up all Vacancies that may happen during the Recess of the Senate, by granting Commissions which shall expire at the End of their next Session.

SECTION 3. He shall from time to time give to the Congress Information of the State of the Union, and recommend to their Consideration such Measures as he shall judge necessary and expedient; he may, on extraordinary Occasions, convene both Houses, or either of them, and in Case of Disagreement between them, with Respect to the Time of Adjournment, he may adjourn them to such Time as he shall think proper; he shall receive Ambassadors and other public Ministers; he shall take Care that the Laws be faithfully executed, and shall Commission all the Officers of the United States.

SECTION 4. The President, Vice President and all Civil Officers of the United States, shall be removed from Office on Impeachment for, and Conviction of, Treason, Bribery, or other high Crimes and Misdemeanors.

ARTICLE III.

SECTION 1. The judicial Power of the United States, shall be vested in one supreme Court, and in such inferior Courts as the Congress may from time to time ordain and establish. The Judges, both of the supreme and inferior Courts, shall hold their Offices during good Behaviour, and shall, at stated Times, receive for their Services, a Compensation, which shall not be diminished during their Continuance in Office.

SECTION 2. The judicial Power shall extend to all Cases, in Law and Equity, arising under this Constitution, the Laws of the United States, and Treaties made, or which shall be made, under their Authority;—to all Cases affecting Ambassadors, other public Ministers and Consuls;—to all Cases of admiralty and maritime Jurisdiction;—to Controversies to which the United

States shall be a Party;—to Controversies between two or more States;—between a State and Citizens of another State;—between Citizens of different States;—between Citizens of the same State claiming Lands under Grants of different States, and between a State, or the Citizens thereof, and foreign States, Citizens or Subjects.

In all Cases affecting Ambassadors, other public Ministers and Consuls, and those in which a State shall be Party, the Supreme Court shall have original Jurisdiction. In all the other Cases before mentioned, the supreme Court shall have appellate Jurisdiction, both as to Law and Fact, with such Exceptions, and under such Regulations as the Congress shall make.

The Trial of all Crimes, except in Cases of Impeachment, shall be by Jury; and such Trial shall be held in the State where the said Crimes shall have been committed; but when not committed within any State, the Trial shall be at such Place or Places as the Congress may by Law have directed.

SECTION 3. Treason against the United States, shall consist only in levying War against them, or in adhering to their Enemies, giving them Aid and Comfort. No Person shall be convicted of Treason unless on the Testimony of two Witnesses to the same overt Act, or on Confession in open Court.

The Congress shall have Power to declare the Punishment of Treason, but no Attainder of Treason shall work Corruption of Blood, or Forfeiture except during the Life of the Person attainted.

ARTICLE IV.

SECTION 1. Full Faith and Credit shall be given in each State to the public Acts, Records, and judicial Proceedings of every other State. And the Congress may by general Laws prescribe the Manner in which such Acts, Records and Proceedings shall be proved, and the Effect thereof.

SECTION 2. The Citizens of each State shall be entitled to all Privileges and Immunities of Citizens in the several States.

A Person charged in any State with Treason, Felony, or other Crime, who shall flee from Justice, and be found in another State, shall on Demand of the executive Authority of the State from which he fled, be delivered up, to be removed to the State having Jurisdiction of the Crime.

No Person held to Service or Labour in one State, under the Laws thereof, escaping into another, shall, in Consequence of any Law or Regulation therein, be discharged from such Service or Labour, but shall be delivered up on Claim of the Party to whom such Service or Labour may be due.

SECTION 3. New States may be admitted by the Congress into this Union; but no new State shall be formed or erected within the Jurisdiction of any other State; nor any State be formed by the Junction of two or more States, or Parts of States, without the Consent of the Legislatures of the States concerned as well as of the Congress.

The Congress shall have Power to dispose of and make all needful Rules and Regulations respecting the Territory or other Property belonging to the United States; and nothing in this Constitution shall be so construed as to Prejudice any Claims of the United States, or of any particular State.

SECTION 4. The United States shall guarantee to every State in this Union a Republican Form of Government, and shall protect each of them against Invasion; and on Application of the Legislature, or of the Executive (when the Legislature cannot be convened) against domestic Violence.

ARTICLE V.

The Congress, whenever two thirds of both Houses shall deem it necessary, shall propose Amendments to this Constitution, or, on the Application of the Legislatures of two thirds of the several States, shall call a Convention for proposing Amendments, which, in either Case, shall be valid to all Intents and Purposes, as Part of this Constitution, when ratified by the Legislatures of three fourths of the several States, or by Conventions in three fourths thereof, as the one or the other Mode of Ratification may be proposed by the Congress; Provided that no Amendment which may be made prior to the Year One thousand eight hundred and eight shall in any Manner affect the first and fourth Clauses in the Ninth Section of the first Article; and that no State, without its Consent, shall be deprived of its equal Suffrage in the Senate.

ARTICLE VI.

All Debts contracted and Engagements entered into, before the Adoption of this Constitution, shall be as valid against the United States under this Constitution, as under the Confederation.

This Constitution, and the Laws of the United States which shall be made in Pursuance thereof, and all Treaties made, or which shall be made, under the Authority of the United States, shall be the supreme Law of the Land; and the Judges in every State shall be bound thereby, any Thing in the Constitution or Laws of any State to the Contrary notwithstanding.

The Senators and Representatives before mentioned, and the Members of the several State Legislatures, and all executive and judicial Officers, both of the United States and of the several States, shall be bound by Oath or Affirmation, to support this Constitution; but no religious Test shall ever be required as a Qualification to any Office or public Trust under the United States.

ARTICLE VII.

The Ratification of the Conventions of nine States, shall be sufficient for the Establishment of this Constitution between the States so ratifying the Same.

* * *

ARTICLES IN ADDITION TO, AND AMENDMENT OF, THE CONSTITUTION OF THE UNITED STATES OF AMERICA, PROPOSED BY CONGRESS, AND RATIFIED BY THE SEVERAL STATES, PURSUANT TO THE FIFTH ARTICLE OF THE ORIGINAL CONSTITUTION.

AMENDMENT I [1791].

Congress shall make no law respecting an establishment of religion, or prohibiting the free exercise thereof; or abridging the freedom of speech, or of the press; or the right of the people peaceably to assemble, and to petition the Government for a redress of grievances.

AMENDMENT II [1791].

A well regulated Militia, being necessary to the security of a free State, the right of the people to keep and bear Arms, shall not be infringed.

AMENDMENT III [1791].

No Soldier shall, in time of peace be quartered in any house, without the consent of the Owner, nor in time of war, but in a manner to be prescribed by law.

AMENDMENT IV [1791].

The right of the people to be secure in their persons, houses, papers, and effects, against unreasonable searches and seizures, shall not be violated, and no Warrants shall issue, but upon probable cause, supported by Oath or affirmation, and particularly describing the place to be searched, and the persons or things to be seized.

AMENDMENT V [1791].

No person shall be held to answer for a capital, or otherwise infamous crime, unless on a presentment or indictment of a Grand Jury, except in cases arising in the land or naval forces, or in the Militia, when in actual service in time of War or public danger; nor shall any person be subject for the same offence to be twice put in jeopardy of life or limb; nor shall be compelled in any criminal case to be a witness against himself, nor be deprived of life, liberty, or property, without due process of law; nor shall private property be taken for public use, without just compensation.

AMENDMENT VI [1791].

In all criminal prosecutions, the accused shall enjoy the right to a speedy and public trial, by an impartial jury of the State and district wherein the crime shall have been committed, which district shall have been previously ascertained by law, and to be informed of the nature and cause of the accusation; to be confronted with the witnesses against him; to have compulsory process for obtaining Witnesses in his favor, and to have the Assistance of Counsel for his defence.

AMENDMENT VII [1791].

In Suits at common law, where the value in controversy shall exceed twenty dollars, the right of trial by jury shall be preserved, and no fact tried by a jury, shall be otherwise re-examined in any Court of the United States, than according to the rules of the common law.

AMENDMENT VIII [1791].

Excessive bail shall not be required, nor excessive fines imposed, nor cruel and unusual punishments inflicted.

AMENDMENT IX [1791].

The enumeration in the Constitution, of certain rights, shall not be construed to deny or disparage others retained by the people.

AMENDMENT X [1791].

The powers not delegated to the United States by the Constitution, nor prohibited by it to the States, are reserved to the States respectively, or to the people.

AMENDMENT XI [1798].

The Judicial power of the United States shall not be construed to extend to any suit in law or equity, commenced or prosecuted against one of the United States by Citizens of another State, or by Citizens or Subjects of any Foreign State.

AMENDMENT XII [1804].

The Electors shall meet in their respective states and vote by ballot for President and Vice-President, one of whom, at least, shall not be an inhabitant of the same state with themselves; they shall name in their ballots the person voted for as President, and in distinct ballots the person voted for as Vice-President, and they shall make distinct lists of all persons voted for as President, and of all persons voted for as Vice-President, and of the number of votes for each, which lists they shall sign and certify, and transmit sealed to the seat of the government of the United States, directed to the President of the Senate;—The President of the Senate shall, in the presence of the Senate and House of Representatives, open all the certificates and the votes shall then be counted;—The person having the greatest number of votes for President, shall be the President, if such number be a majority of the whole number of Electors appointed; and if no person have such majority, then from the persons having the highest numbers not exceeding three on the list of those voted for as President, the House of Representatives shall choose immediately, by ballot, the President. But in choosing the President, the votes shall be taken by states, the representation from each state having one vote; a quorum for this purpose shall consist of a member or members from two-thirds of the states, and a majority of all the states shall be necessary to a choice. And if the House of Representatives shall not choose a President whenever the right of choice shall devolve upon them, before the fourth day of March next following, then the Vice-President shall act as President, as in the case of the death or other constitutional disability of the President—The person having the greatest number of votes as Vice-President, shall be the Vice-President, if such number be a majority of the whole number of Electors appointed, and if no person have a majority, then from the two highest numbers on the list, the Senate shall choose the Vice-President; a quorum for the purpose shall consist of two-thirds of the whole number of Senators, and a majority of the whole number shall be necessary to a choice. But no person constitutionally ineligible to the office of President shall be eligible to that of Vice-President of the United States.

AMENDMENT XIII [1865].

SECTION 1. Neither slavery nor involuntary servitude, except as a punishment for crime whereof the party shall have been duly convicted, shall exist within the United States, or any place subject to their jurisdiction.

SECTION 2. Congress shall have power to enforce this article by appropriate legislation.

AMENDMENT XIV [1868].

SECTION 1. All persons born or naturalized in the United States and subject to the jurisdiction thereof, are citizens of the United States and of the State wherein they reside. No State shall make or enforce any law which shall abridge the privileges or immunities of citizens of the United States; nor shall any State deprive any person of life, liberty, or property, without due process of law; nor deny to any person within its jurisdiction the equal protection of the laws.

SECTION 2. Representatives shall be apportioned among the several States according to their respective numbers, counting the whole number of persons in each State, excluding Indians not taxed. But when the right to vote at any election for the choice of electors for President and Vice President of the United States, Representatives in Congress, the Executive and Judicial officers of a State, or the members of the Legislature thereof, is denied to any of the male inhabitants of such State, being twenty-one years of age, and citizens of the United States, or in any way abridged, except for participation in rebellion, or other crime, the basis of representation therein shall be reduced in the proportion which the number of such male citizens shall bear to the whole number of male citizens twenty-one years of age in such State.

SECTION 3. No person shall be a Senator or Representative in Congress, or elector of President and Vice President, or hold any office, civil or military, under the United States, or under any State, who, having previously taken an oath, as a member of Congress, or as an officer of the United States, or as a member of any State legislature, or as an executive or judicial officer of any State, to support the Constitution of the United States, shall have engaged in insurrection or rebellion against the same, or given aid or comfort to the enemies thereof. But Congress may by a vote of two-thirds of each House, remove such disability.

SECTION 4. The validity of the public debt of the United States, authorized by law, including debts incurred for payment of pensions and bounties for services in suppressing insurrection or rebellion, shall not be questioned. But neither the United States nor any State shall assume or pay any debt or obligation incurred in aid of insurrection or rebellion against the United States, or any claim for the loss of emancipation of any slave; but all such debts, obligations and claims shall be held illegal and void.

SECTION 5. The Congress shall have power to enforce, by appropriate legislation, the provisions of this article.

AMENDMENT XV [1870].

SECTION 1. The right of citizens of the United States to vote shall not be denied or abridged by the United States or by any State on account of race, color, or previous condition of servitude.

SECTION 2. The Congress shall have power to enforce this article by appropriate legislation.

AMENDMENT XVI [1913].

The Congress shall have power to lay and collect taxes on incomes, from whatever source derived, without apportionment among the several States, and without regard to any census or enumeration.

AMENDMENT XVII [1913].

The Senate of the United States shall be composed of two Senators from each State, elected by the people thereof, for six years; and each Senator shall have one vote. The electors in each State shall have the qualifications requisite for electors of the most numerous branch of the State legislatures.

When vacancies happen in the representation of any State in the Senate, the executive authority of such State shall issue writs of election to fill such vacancies: *Provided,* That the legislature of any State may empower the executive thereof to make temporary appointments until the people fill the vacancies by election as the legislature may direct.

This amendment shall not be so construed as to affect the election or term of any Senator chosen before it becomes valid as part of the Constitution.

AMENDMENT XVIII [1919].

SECTION 1.   After one year from the ratification of this article the manufacture, sale, or transportation of intoxicating liquors within, the importation thereof into, or the exportation thereof from the United States and all territory subject to the jurisdiction thereof for beverage purposes is hereby prohibited.

SECTION 2.   The Congress and the several States shall have concurrent power to enforce this article by appropriate legislation.

SECTION 3.   This article shall be inoperative unless it shall have been ratified as an amendment to the Constitution by the legislatures of the several States, as provided in the Constitution, within seven years from the date of the submission hereof to the States by the Congress.

AMENDMENT XIX [1920].

The right of citizens of the United States to vote shall not be denied or abridged by the United States or by any State on account of sex.

Congress shall have power to enforce this article by appropriate legislation.

AMENDMENT XX [1933].

SECTION 1.   The terms of the President and Vice President shall end at noon on the 20th day of January, and the terms of Senators and Representatives at noon on the 3d day of January, of the years in which such terms would have ended if this article had not been ratified; and the terms of their successors shall then begin.

SECTION 2.   The Congress shall assemble at least once in every year, and such meeting shall begin at noon on the 3d day of January, unless they shall by law appoint a different day.

SECTION 3.   If, at the time fixed for the beginning of the term of the President, the President elect shall have died, the Vice President elect shall become President. If a President shall not have been chosen before the time fixed for the beginning of his term, or if the President elect shall have failed to qualify, then the Vice President elect shall act as President until a President shall have qualified; and the Congress may by law provide for the case wherein neither a President elect nor a Vice President elect shall have qualified, declaring who shall then act as President, or the manner in which one who is to act shall be selected, and such person shall act accordingly until a President or Vice President shall have qualified.

SECTION 4.   The Congress may by law provide for the case of the death of any of the persons from whom the House of Representatives may choose a President whenever the right of choice shall have devolved upon them, and for the case of the death of any of the persons from whom the Senate may choose a Vice President whenever the right of choice shall have devolved upon them.

SECTION 5.   Sections 1 and 2 shall take effect on the 15th day of October following the ratification of this article.

SECTION 6.   This article shall be inoperative unless it shall have been ratified as an amendment to the Constitution by the legislatures of three-fourths of the several States within seven years from the date of its submission.

AMENDMENT XXI [1933].

SECTION 1.   The eighteenth article of amendment to the Constitution of the United States is hereby repealed.

SECTION 2. The transportation or importation into any State, Territory, or possession of the United States for delivery or use therein of intoxicating liquors, in violation of the laws thereof, is hereby prohibited.

SECTION 3. This article shall be inoperative unless it shall have been ratified as an amendment to the Constitution by conventions in the several States, as provided in the Constitution, within seven years from the date of the submission hereof to the States by the Congress.

AMENDMENT XXII [1951].

SECTION 1. No person shall be elected to the office of the President more than twice, and no person who has held the office of President, or acted as President, for more than two years of a term to which some other person was elected President shall be elected to the office of the President more than once. But this Article shall not apply to any person holding the office of President when this Article was proposed by the Congress, and shall not prevent any person who may be holding the office of President, or acting as President, during the term within which this Article becomes operative from holding the office of President or acting as President during the remainder of such term.

SECTION 2. This article shall be inoperative unless it shall have been ratified as an amendment to the Constitution by the legislatures of three-fourths of the several States within seven years from the date of its submission to the States by the Congress.

AMENDMENT XXIII [1961].

SECTION 1. The District constituting the seat of Government of the United States shall appoint in such manner as the Congress may direct:

A number of electors of President and Vice President equal to the whole number of Senators and Representatives in Congress to which the District would be entitled if it were a State, but in no event more than the least populous State; they shall be in addition to those appointed by the States, but they shall be considered, for the purposes of the election of President and Vice President, to be electors appointed by a State; and they shall meet in the District and perform such duties as provided by the twelfth article of amendment.

SECTION 2. The Congress shall have power to enforce this article by appropriate legislation.

AMENDMENT XXIV [1964].

SECTION 1. The right of citizens of the United States to vote in any primary or other election for President or Vice President, for electors for President or Vice President, or for Senator or Representative in Congress, shall not be denied or abridged by the United States or any State by reason of failure to pay any poll tax or other tax.

SECTION 2. The Congress shall have power to enforce this article by appropriate legislation.

AMENDMENT XXV [1967].

SECTION 1. In case of the removal of the President from office or of his death or resignation, the Vice President shall become President.

SECTION 2. Whenever there is a vacancy in the office of the Vice President, the President shall nominate a Vice President who shall take office upon confirmation by a majority vote of both Houses of Congress.

SECTION 3. Whenever the President transmits to the President pro tempore of the Senate and the Speaker of the House of Representatives his written declaration that he is unable to discharge the powers and duties of his office, and until he transmits to them a written declaration to the contrary, such powers and duties shall be discharged by the Vice President as Acting President.

SECTION 4. Whenever the Vice President and a majority of either the principal officers of the executive departments or of such other body as Congress may by law provide, transmit to the President pro tempore of the Senate and the Speaker of the House of Representatives their written declaration that the President is unable to discharge the powers and duties of his office, the Vice President shall immediately assume the powers and duties of the office as Acting President.

Thereafter, when the President transmits to the President pro tempore of the Senate and the Speaker of the House of Representatives his written declaration that no inability exists, he shall resume the powers and duties of his office unless the Vice President and a majority of either the principal officers of the executive department or of such other body as Congress may by law provide, transmit within four days to the President pro tempore of the Senate and the Speaker of the House of Representatives their written declaration that the President is unable to discharge the powers and duties of his office. Thereupon Congress shall decide the issue, assembling within forty-eight hours for that purpose if not in session. If the Congress, within twenty-one days after receipt of the latter written declaration, or, if Congress is not in session, within twenty-one days after Congress is required to assemble, determines by two-thirds vote of both Houses that the President is unable to discharge the powers and duties of his office, the Vice President shall continue to discharge the same as Acting President; otherwise, the President shall resume the powers and duties of his office.

AMENDMENT XXVI [1971].*

SECTION 1. The right of citizens of the United States, who are eighteen years of age or older, to vote shall not be denied or abridged by the United States or by any State on account of age.

SECTION 2. The Congress shall have power to enforce this article by appropriate legislation.

* The 26th Amendment was submitted to the States on March 23, 1971—three months after the Supreme Court decision holding unconstitutional the provisions of the Voting Rights Act Amendments of 1970 which had sought to authorize 18-year-olds to vote in state elections. See Oregon v. Mitchell, 400 U.S. 112 (1970) (chap. 10, sec. 4, above). Three months later, on June 30, 1971, the ratification process was completed.

APPENDIX B

TABLE OF JUSTICES

Two sets of dates are given for each Justice, indicating his entire life as well as his years on the Supreme Court; but only the term of office is indicated for each President. The Presidents who made no appointments to the Supreme Court are not included in the table. They were Presidents William H. Harrison (Mar.–Apr. 1841), Zachary Taylor (1849–50), Andrew Johnson (1865–1869), and Jimmy Carter (1977–1981).

The symbol * and the figure (1) designate the Chief Justices. The other figures trace lines of succession in filling vacancies among the Associate Justices. For example, by following the figure (2) it can be seen that Justice Rutledge was succeeded by Justice Thomas Johnson, he by Justice Paterson, he in turn by Justice Livingston, etc.[1]

Appointed by President Washington, Federalist from Virginia
(1789–1797)

* (1) Jay, John (1745–1829). Fed. from N.Y. (1789–1795). Resigned.
  (2) Rutledge, John (1739–1800). Fed. from S.C. (1789–1791). Resigned without ever sitting.
  (3) Cushing, William (1732–1810). Fed. from Mass. (1789–1810). Died.
  (4) Wilson, James (1724–1798). Fed. from Pa. (1789–1798). Died.
  (5) Blair, John (1732–1800). Fed. from Va. (1789–1796). Resigned.
  (6) Iredell, James (1750–1799). Fed. from N.C. (1790–1799). Died.
  (2) Johnson, Thomas (1732–1819). Fed. from Md. (1791–1793). Resigned.
  (2) Paterson, William (1745–1806). Fed. from N.J. (1793–1806). Died.
* (1) Rutledge, John (1739–1800). Fed. from S.C. (1795). [Unconfirmed recess appointment.]
  (5) Chase, Samuel (1741–1811). Fed. from Md. (1796–1811). Died.
* (1) Ellsworth, Oliver (1745–1807). Fed. from Conn. (1796–1800). Resigned.

Appointed by President John Adams, Federalist from Massachusetts
(1797–1801)

  (4) Washington, Bushrod (1762–1829). Fed. from Pa. and Va. (1798–1829). Died.
  (6) Moore, Alfred (1755–1810). Fed. from N.C. (1799–1804). Resigned.
* (1) Marshall, John (1755–1835). Fed. from Va. (1801–1835). Died.

Appointed by President Jefferson, Republican from Virginia
(1801–1809)

  (6) Johnson, William (1771–1834). Rep. from S.C. (1804–1834). Died.

---

1. This table was originally prepared by Professor Margaret Spahr, Hunter College of the City University of New York. [For biographical sketches of each of the Justices, see the four-volume collection, The Justices of the United States Supreme Court 1789–1969: Their Lives and Major Opinions (Friedman & Israel, eds., 1969).]

(2) Livingston, [Henry] Brockholst (1757–1823). Rep. from N.Y. (1806–1823). Died.

(7) Todd, Thomas (1765–1826). Rep. from Ky. (1807–1826). Died.

Appointed by President Madison, Republican from Virginia
(1809–1817)

(5) Duvall, Gabriel (1752–1844). Rep. from Md. (1811–1835). Resigned.

(3) Story, Joseph (1779–1845). Rep. from Mass. (1811–1845). Died.

Appointed by President Monroe, Republican from Virginia
(1817–1825)

(2) Thompson, Smith (1768–1843). Rep. from N.Y. (1823–1843). Died.

Appointed by President John Quincy Adams, Republican from Massachusetts
(1825–1829)

(7) Trimble, Robert (1777–1828). Rep. from Ky. (1826–1828). Died.

Appointed by President Jackson, Democrat from Tennessee
(1829–1837)

(7) McLean, John (1785–1861). Dem. (later Rep.) from Ohio (1829–1861). Died.

(4) Baldwin, Henry (1780–1844). Dem. from Pa. (1830–1844). Died.

(6) Wayne, James M. (1790–1867). Dem. from Ga. (1835–1867). Died.

* (1) Taney, Roger B. (1777–1864). Dem. from Md. (1836–1864). Died.

(5) Barbour, Philip P. (1783–1841). Dem. from Va. (1836–1841). Died.

Appointed by President Van Buren, Democrat from New York
(1837–1841)

(8) Catron, John (1778–1865). Dem. from Tenn. (1837–1865). Died.

(9) McKinley, John (1780–1852). Dem. from Ky. (1837–1852). Died.

(5) Daniel, Peter V. (1784–1860). Dem. from Va. (1841–1860). Died.

Appointed by President Tyler, Whig from Virginia
(1841–1845)

(2) Nelson, Samuel (1792–1873). Dem. from N.Y. (1845–1872). Resigned.

Appointed by President Polk, Democrat from Tennessee
(1845–1849)

(3) Woodbury, Levi (1789–1851). Dem. from N.H. (1845–1851). Died.

(4) Grier, Robert C. (1794–1870). Dem. from Pa. (1846–1870). Resigned.

Appointed by President Fillmore, Whig from New York
(1850–1853)

(3) Curtis, Benjamin R. (1809–1874). Whig from Mass. (1851–1857). Resigned.

APPENDIX B

Appointed by President Pierce, Democrat from New Hampshire
(1853–1857)

(9) Campbell, John A. (1811–1889). Dem. from Ala. (1853–1861). Resigned.

Appointed by President Buchanan, Democrat from Pennsylvania
(1857–1861)

(3) Clifford, Nathan (1803–1881). Dem. from Me. (1858–1881). Died.

Appointed by President Lincoln, Republican from Illinois
(1861–1865)

(7) Swayne, Noah H. (1804–1884). Rep. from Ohio (1862–1881). Resigned.

(5) Miller, Samuel F. (1816–1890). Rep. from Iowa (1862–1890). Died.

(9) Davis, David (1815–1886). Rep. (later Dem.) from Ill. (1862–1877). Resigned.

(10) Field, Stephen J. (1816–1899). Dem. from Cal. (1863–1897). Resigned.

* (1) Chase, Salmon P. (1808–1873). Rep. from Ohio (1864–1873). Died.

Appointed by President Grant, Republican from Illinois
(1869–1877)

(4) Strong, William (1808–1895). Rep. from Pa. (1870–1880). Resigned.

(6) Bradley, Joseph P. (1803–1892). Rep. from N.J. (1870–1892). Died.

(2) Hunt, Ward (1810–1886). Rep. from N.Y. (1872–1882). Resigned.

* (1) Waite, Morrison (1816–1888). Rep. from Ohio (1874–1888). Died.

Appointed by President Hayes, Republican from Ohio
(1877–1881)

(9) Harlan, John Marshall (1833–1911). Rep. from Ky. (1877–1911). Died.

(4) Woods, William B. (1824–1887). Rep. from Ga. (1880–1887). Died.

Appointed by President Garfield, Republican from Ohio
(Mar.–Sept. 1881)

(7) Matthews, Stanley (1824–1889). Rep. from Ohio (1881–1889). Died.

Appointed by President Arthur, Republican from New York
(1881–1885)

(3) Gray, Horace (1828–1902). Rep. from Mass. (1881–1902). Died.

(2) Blatchford, Samuel (1820–1893). Rep. from N.Y. (1882–1893). Died.

Appointed by President Cleveland, Democrat from New York
(1885–1889)

(4) Lamar, Lucius Q.C. (1825–1893). Dem. from Miss. (1888–1893). Died.

* (1) Fuller, Melville W. (1833–1910). Dem. from Ill. (1888–1910). Died.

Appointed by President Harrison, Republican from Indiana
(1889–1893)

(7) Brewer, David J. (1837–1910). Rep. from Kansas (1889–1910). Died.

(5) Brown, Henry B. (1836–1913). Rep. from Mich. (1890–1906). Resigned.

(6) Shiras, George (1832–1924). Rep. from Pa. (1892–1903). Resigned.

(4) Jackson, Howell E. (1832–1895). Dem. from Tenn. (1893–1895). Died.

Appointed by President Cleveland, Democrat from New York
(1893–1897)

(2) White, Edward D. (1845–1921). Dem. from La. (1894–1910). Promoted to chief justiceship.

(4) Peckham, Rufus W. (1838–1909). Dem. from N.Y. (1895–1909). Died.

Appointed by President McKinley, Republican from Ohio
(1897–1901)

(10) or (8)
McKenna, Joseph (1843–1926). Rep. from Cal. (1898–1925). Resigned.

Appointed by President Theodore Roosevelt, Republican from New York
(1901–1909)

(3) Holmes, Oliver Wendell (1841–1935). Rep. from Mass. (1902–1932). Resigned.

(6) Day, William R. (1849–1923). Rep. from Ohio (1903–1922). Resigned.

(5) Moody, William H. (1853–1917). Rep. from Mass. (1906–1910). Resigned.

Appointed by President Taft, Republican from Ohio
(1909–1913)

(4) Lurton, Horace H. (1844–1914). Dem. from Tenn. (1909–1914). Died.

(7) Hughes, Charles E. (1862–1948). Rep. from N.Y. (1910–1916). Resigned.

* (1) White, Edward D. (1845–1921). Promoted from associate justiceship. (1910–1921). Died.

(2) Van Devanter, Willis (1859–1941). Rep. from Wyo. (1910–1937). Retired.

(5) Lamar, Joseph R. (1857–1916). Dem. from Ga. (1910–1916). Died.

(9) Pitney, Mahlon (1858–1924). Rep. from N.J. (1912–1922). Retired.

Appointed by President Wilson, Democrat from New Jersey
(1913–1921)

(4) McReynolds, James C. (1862–1946). Dem. from Tenn. (1914–1941). Retired.

(5) Brandeis, Louis D. (1856–1941). Dem. from Mass. (1916–1939). Retired.

(7) Clarke, John H. (1857–1945). Dem. from Ohio (1916–1922). Resigned.

Appointed by President Harding, Republican from Ohio
(1921–1923)

* (1) Taft, William H. (1857–1930). Rep. from Conn. (1921–1930). Resigned.

(7) Sutherland, George (1862–1942). Rep. from Utah (1922–1938). Retired.

(6) Butler, Pierce (1866–1939). Dem. from Minn. (1922–1939). Died.

(9) Sanford, Edward T. (1865–1930). Rep. from Tenn. (1923–1930). Died.

Appointed by President Coolidge, Republican from Massachusetts
(1923–1929)

(8) Stone, Harlan F. (1872–1946). Rep. from N.Y. (1925–1941). Promoted to chief justiceship.

Appointed by President Hoover, Republican from California
(1929–1933)

* (1) Hughes, Charles E. (1862–1948). Rep. from N.Y. (1930–1941). Retired.

(9) Roberts, Owen J. (1875–1955). Rep. from Pa. (1930–1945). Resigned.

(3) Cardozo, Benjamin N. (1870–1938). Dem. from N.Y. (1932–1938). Died.

Appointed by President Franklin D. Roosevelt, Democrat from New York
(1933–1945)

(2) Black, Hugo, L. (1886–1971). Dem. from Ala. (1937–1971). Retired.

(7) Reed, Stanley F. (1884–1980). Dem. from Ky. (1938–1957). Retired.

(3) Frankfurter, Felix (1882–1965). Ind. from Mass. (1939–1962). Retired.

(5) Douglas, William O. (1898–1980). Dem. from Conn. and Wash. (1939–1975). Retired.

(6) Murphy, Frank (1893–1949). Dem. from Mich. (1940–1949). Died.

(4) Byrnes, James F. (1879–1972). Dem. from S.C. (1941–1942). Resigned.

* (1) Stone, Harlan F. (1872–1946). Promoted from associate justiceship (1941–1946). Died.

(8) Jackson, Robert H. (1892–1954). Dem. from N.Y. (1941–1954). Died.

(4) Rutledge, Wiley B. (1894–1949). Dem. from Ia. (1943–1949). Died.

Appointed by President Truman, Democrat from Missouri
(1945–1953)

(9) Burton, Harold H. (1888–1964). Rep. from Ohio (1945–1958). Retired.

* (1) Vinson, Fred M. (1890–1953). Dem. from Kentucky (1946–1953). Died.
 (6) Clark, Tom C. (1899–1977). Dem. from Texas (1949–1967). Retired.
 (4) Minton, Sherman (1890–1965). Dem. from Indiana (1949–1956). Retired.

Appointed by President Eisenhower, Republican from New York
(1953–1961)

* (1) Warren, Earl (1891–1974). Rep. from Cal. (1953–1969). Retired.
 (8) Harlan, John Marshall (1899–1971). Rep. from New York (1955–1971). Retired.
 (4) Brennan, William J., Jr., (1906–____). Dem. from New Jersey (1956–____).
 (7) Whittaker, Charles E. (1901–1973). Rep. from Missouri (1957–1962). Retired.
 (9) Stewart, Potter (1915–____). Rep. from Ohio (1958–1981). Retired.

Appointed by President Kennedy, Democrat from Massachusetts
(1961–1963)

 (7) White, Byron R. (1917–____). Dem. from Colorado (1962–____).
 (3) Goldberg, Arthur J. (1908–____). Dem. from Illinois (1962–1965). Resigned.

Appointed by President Lyndon B. Johnson, Democrat from Texas
(1963–1969)

 (3) Fortas, Abe (1910–____). Dem. from Tenn. (1965–1969). Resigned.
 (6) Marshall, Thurgood (1908–____). Dem. from N.Y. (1967–____).

Appointed by President Nixon, Republican from California
(1969–1974)

* (1) Burger, Warren E. (1907–____). Rep. from Va. and Minn. (1969–____).
 (3) Blackmun, Harry A. (1908–____). Rep. from Minn. (1970–____).
 (2) Powell, Lewis F., Jr., (1907–____). Dem. from Va. (1972–____).
 (8) Rehnquist, William H. (1924–____). Rep. from Ariz. (1972–____).

Appointed by President Ford, Republican from Michigan
(1974–1977)

 (5) Stevens, John Paul (1920–____). Rep. from Ill. (1975–____).

Appointed by President Reagan, Republican from California
(1981–____)

 (9) O'Connor, Sandra Day (1930–____). Rep. from Ariz. (1981–____).

INDEX

References are to Pages

†